D1096183

Please accept my sincere thanks for your friendship and support. I am grateful.

God bless you

Jerry Falwell

THE

TREASURY OF DAVID:

CONTAINING

AN ORIGINAL EXPOSITION OF THE BOOK OF PSALMS;

A COLLECTION OF ILLUSTRATIVE EXTRACTS FROM THE WHOLE
RANGE OF LITERATURE;

A SERIES OF HOMILETICAL HINTS UPON ALMOST EVERY VERSE;

AND LISTS OF WRITERS UPON EACH PSALM.

IN TWO VOLUMES

BY

C. H. SPURGEON.

VOLUME I

PSALM I to LXXXVII

THE OLD-TIME GOSPEL HOUR
Lynchburg, Virginia

ISBN 52256

Published in Nashville, Tennessee, by Thomas Nelson, Inc., Publishers
and distributed in Canada by Lawson Falle, Ltd.,
Cambridge, Ontario.
Manufactured in the United States of America.

1 2 3 4 5 6 7 8 9 10 – 85 84

C. H. SPURGEON IN HIS PULPIT.

Specially drawn for "The Treasury of David" by E. H. Fitchew.

PREFACE.

My Preface shall at least possess the virtue of brevity, as I find it difficult to impart to it any other.

The delightful study of the Psalms has yielded me boundless profit and ever-growing pleasure ; common gratitude constrains me to communicate to others a portion of the benefit, with the prayer that it may induce them to search further for themselves. That I have nothing better of my own to offer upon this peerless book is to me matter of deepest regret ; that I have anything whatever to present is subject for devout gratitude to the Lord of grace. I have done my best, but, conscious of many defects, I heartily wish I could have done far better.

The Exposition here given is my own. I consulted a few authors before penning it, to aid me in interpretation and arouse my thoughts ; but, still I can claim originality for my comments, at least so I honestly think. Whether they are better or worse for that, I know not ; at least I know I have sought heavenly guidance while writing them, and therefore I look for a blessing on the printing of them.

The collection of quotations was an after-thought. In fact, matter grew upon me which I thought too good to throw away. It seemed to me that it might prove serviceable to others, if I reserved portions of my reading upon the various Psalms ; those reserves soon acquired considerable bulk, so much so that even in this volume only specimens are given and not the bulk.

One thing the reader will please clearly to understand, and I beg him to bear it in mind : *I am far from endorsing all I have quoted.* I am neither responsible for the scholarship or orthodoxy of the writers. The names are given that each author may bear his own burden ; and a variety of writers have been quoted that the thoughts of many minds might be before the reader. Still I trust nothing evil has been admitted ; if it be so it is an oversight.

The research expended on this volume would have occupied far too much of my time, had not my friend and amanuensis, Mr. John L. Keys, most diligently aided me in investigations at the British Museum, Dr. Williams's Library, and other treasuries of theological lore. With his help I have ransacked books by the hundred, often without finding a memorable line as a reward, but at other times with the most satisfactory result. Readers little know how great labour the finding of but one pertinent extract may involve ; labour certainly I have not spared : my earnest prayer is that some measure of good may come of it to my brethren in the ministry and to the church at large.

The Hints to Preachers are very simple, and an apology is due to my ministerial readers for inserting them, but I humbly hope they may render assistance to those for whom alone they are designed, viz., lay preachers whose time is much occupied, and whose attainments are slender.

Should this first volume meet with the approbation of the judicious, I shall hope by God's grace to continue the work as rapidly as I can consistently with the research demanded and my incessant pastoral duties. Another volume will follow in all probability in twelve months' time, if life be spared and strength be given.

It may be added, that although the comments were the work of my health, the rest of the volume is the product of my sickness. When protracted illness and weakness laid me aside from daily preaching, I resorted to my pen as an available means of doing good. I would have preached had I been able, but as my Master denied me the privilege of thus serving him, I gladly availed myself of the other method of bearing testimony for his name. O that he may give me fruit in this field also, and his shall be all the praise.

C. H. Spurgeon

INDEX

OF AUTHORS QUOTED OR REFERRED TO.

EXPOSITIONS OF THE PSALMS.

PSALM I.

TITLE.—*This Psalm may be regarded as* THE PREFACE PSALM, *having in it a notification of the contents of the entire Book. It is the psalmist's desire to teach us the way to blessedness, and to warn us of the sure destruction of sinners. This then, is the matter of the first Psalm, which may be looked upon, in some respects, as the text upon which the whole of the Psalms make up a divine sermon.*

DIVISION.—*This Psalm consists of two parts : in the first (from verse 1 to the end of the 3rd) David sets out wherein the felicity and blessedness of a godly man consisteth, what his exercises are, and what blessings he shall receive from the Lord. In the second part (from verse 4 to the end) he contrasts the state and character of the ungodly, reveals the future, and describes, in telling language, his ultimate doom.*

EXPOSITION.

BLESSED *is* the man that walketh not in the counsel of the ungodly, nor standeth in the way of sinners, nor sitteth in the seat of the scornful.

2 But his delight *is* in the law of the LORD ; and in his law doth he meditate day and night.

" BLESSED "—see how this Book of Psalms opens with a benediction, even as did the famous Sermon of our Lord upon the Mount ! The word translated " blessed " is a very expressive one. The original word is plural, and it is a controverted matter whether it is an adjective or a substantive. Hence we may learn the multiplicity of the blessings which shall rest upon the man whom God hath justified, and the perfection and greatness of the blessedness he shall enjoy. We might read it, " Oh, the blessednesses ! " and we may well regard it (as Ainsworth does) as a joyful acclamation of the gracious man's felicity. May the like benediction rest on us !

Here the gracious man is described both negatively (verse 1) and positively (verse 2). He is a man *who does not walk in the counsel of the ungodly.* He takes wiser counsel, and walks in the commandments of the Lord his God. To him the ways of piety are paths of peace and pleasantness. His footsteps are ordered by the Word of God, and not by the cunning and wicked devices of carnal men. It is a rich sign of inward grace when the outward walk is changed, and when ungodliness is put far from our actions. Note next, *he standeth not in the way of sinners.* His company is of a choicer sort than it was. Although a sinner himself, he is now a blood-washed sinner, quickened by the Holy Spirit, and renewed in heart. Standing by the rich grace of God in the congregation of the righteous, he dares not herd with the multitude that do evil. Again it is said, " *nor sitteth in the seat of the scornful.*" He finds no rest in the atheist's scoffings. Let others make a mock of sin, of eternity, of hell and heaven, and of the Eternal God ; this man has learned better philosophy than that of the infidel, and has too much sense of God's presence to endure to hear his name blasphemed. The seat of the scorner may be very lofty, but it is very near to the gate of hell ; let us flee from it, for it shall soon be empty, and destruction shall swallow up the man who sits therein. Mark the gradation in the first verse :

He walketh not in the counsel of the ungodly,
Nor *standeth* in the *way* of *sinners.*
Nor SITTETH in the SEAT of SCORNFUL.

When men are living in sin they go from bad to worse. At first they merely *walk* in the counsel of the careless and *ungodly,* who forget God—the evil is rather practical than habitual—but after that, they become habituated to evil, and they *stand* in the way of open *sinners* who wilfully violate God's commandments ; and if let alone, they go one step further, and become themselves pestilent teachers and tempters of others, and thus they *sit in the seat of the scornful*. They have taken their degree in vice, and as true Doctors of Damnation they are installed, and are looked up to by others as Masters in Belial. But the blessed man, the man to whom all the blessings of God belong, can hold no communion with such characters as these. He keeps himself pure from these lepers ; he puts away evil things from him as garments spotted by the flesh ; he comes out from among the wicked, and goes without the camp, bearing the reproach of Christ. O for grace to be thus separate from sinners.

And now mark his positive character. " *His delight is in the law of the Lord.*" He is not *under* the law as a curse and condemnation, but he is *in* it, and he delights to be in it as his rule of life ; he delights, moreover, to *meditate* in it, to read it *by day*, and think upon it *by night*. He takes a text and carries it with him all day long ; and in the night-watches, when sleep forsakes his eyelids, he museth upon the Word of God. In the *day* of his prosperity he sings *psalms* out of the Word of God, and in the *night* of his affliction he comforts himself with *promises* out of the same book. " The law of the Lord " is the daily bread of the true believer. And yet, in David's day, how small was the volume of inspiration, for they had scarcely anything save the first five books of Moses ! How much more, then, should we prize the whole written Word which it is our privilege to have in all our houses ! But, alas, what ill-treatment is given to this angel from heaven ! We are not all Berean searchers of the Scriptures. How few among us can lay claim to the benediction of the text ! Perhaps some of you can claim a sort of negative purity, because you do not walk in the way of the ungodly ; but let me ask you— Is your delight in the law of God ? Do you study God's Word ? Do you make it the man of your right hand—your best companion and hourly guide ? If not, this blessing belongeth not to you.

3 And he shall be like a tree planted by the rivers of water, that bringeth forth his fruit in his season ; his leaf also shall not wither ; and whatsoever he doeth shall prosper.

" *And he shall be like a tree planted ;* " not a wild tree, but " a tree *planted*," chosen, considered as property, cultivated and secured from the last terrible up-rooting, for " every plant, which my heavenly Father hath not planted, shall be rooted up:" Matthew xv. 13. " *By the rivers of water ;* " so that even if one river should fail, he hath another. The rivers of pardon and the rivers of grace, the rivers of the promise and the rivers of the communion with Christ, are never-failing sources of supply. He is " like a tree planted by the rivers of water, *that bringeth forth his fruit in his season ;* " not unseasonable graces, like untimely figs, which are never full-flavoured. But the man who delights in God's Word, being taught by it, bringeth forth patience in the time of suffering, faith in the day of trial, and holy joy in the hour of prosperity. Fruitfulness is an essential quality of a gracious man, and that fruitfulness should be seasonable. " *His leaf also shall not wither ;* " his faintest word shall be everlasting ; his little deeds of love shall be had in remembrance. Not simply shall his fruit be preserved, but *his leaf* also. He shall neither lose his beauty nor his fruitfulness. " *And whatsoever he doeth shall prosper.*" Blessed is the man who hath such a promise as this. But we must not always estimate the fulfilment of a promise by our own eye-sight. How often, my brethren, if we judge by feeble sense, may we come to the mournful conclusion of Jacob, " All these things are against me ! " For though we know our interest in the promise, yet are we so tried and troubled, that sight sees the very reverse of what that promise foretells. But to the eye of faith this word is sure, and by it we perceive that our works are prospered, even when everything seems to go against us. It is not outward prosperity which the Christian most desires and values ; it is soul prosperity which he longs for. We often, like Jehoshaphat, make ships to go to Tarshish for gold, but they are broken at Ezion-geber ; but even here there is a true prospering, for it is often for the soul's health that we should be poor, bereaved, and persecuted. Our worst things are often our best things. As there is a curse wrapped up in the wicked man's mercies, so there is a blessing concealed in the righteous man's crosses, losses, and sorrows. The trials of the saint are a divine husbandry, by which he grows and brings forth abundant fruit.

4 The ungodly *are* not so : but *are* like the chaff which the wind driveth away.

We have now come to the second head of the Psalm.   In this verse the contrast of the ill estate of the wicked is employed to heighten the colouring of that fair and pleasant picture which precedes it.   The more forcible translation of the Vulgate and of the Septuagint version is—" *Not so the ungodly, not so.*"   And we are hereby to understand that whatever good thing is said of the righteous is not true in the case of the ungodly.   Oh ! how terrible is it to have a double negative put upon the promises ! and yet this is just the condition of the ungodly.   Mark the use of the term " *ungodly,*" for, as we have seen in the opening of the Psalm, these are the beginners in evil, and are the least offensive of sinners.   Oh ! if such is the sad state of those who quietly continue in their morality, and neglect their God, what must be the condition of open sinners and shameless infidels ?   The first sentence is a negative description of the ungodly, and the second is the positive picture. Here is their *character*—" *they are like chaff,*" intrinsically worthless, dead, un-serviceable, without substance, and easily carried away.   Here, also, mark their *doom*—" *the wind driveth away ;* " death shall hurry them with its terrible blast into the fire in which they shall be utterly consumed.

5 Therefore the ungodly shall not stand in the judgment, nor sinners in the congregation of the righteous.

They shall stand there to be judged, but not to be acquitted.   Fear shall lay hold upon them there ; they shall not stand their ground ; they shall flee away ; they shall not stand in their own defence ; for they shall blush and be covered with eternal contempt.

Well may the saints long for heaven, for no evil men shall dwell there, " *nor sinners in the congregation of the righteous.*"   All our congregations upon earth are mixed.   Every Church has one devil in it.   The tares grow in the same furrows as the wheat.   There is no floor which is as yet thoroughly purged from chaff.   Sinners mix with saints, as dross mingles with gold.   God's precious diamonds still lie in the same field with pebbles.   Righteous Lots are this side heaven continually vexed by the men of Sodom.   Let us rejoice then, that in " the general assembly and church of the firstborn " above, there shall by no means be admitted a single unrenewed soul.   Sinners cannot live in heaven.   They would be out of their element. Sooner could a fish live upon a tree than the wicked in Paradise.   Heaven would be an intolerable hell to an impenitent man, even if he could be allowed to enter ; but such a privilege shall never be granted to the man who perseveres in his iniquities.. May. God grant that we may have a name and a place in his courts above!

6 For the LORD knoweth the way of the righteous : but the way of the ungodly shall perish.

Or, as the Hebrew hath it yet more fully, " The Lord is *knowing* the way of the righteous."   He is constantly looking on their way, and though it may be often in mist and darkness, yet the Lord knoweth it.   If it be in the clouds and tempest of affliction, he understandeth it.   He numbereth the hairs of our head ; he will not suffer any evil to befall us.   " He knoweth the way that I take : when he hath tried me, I shall come forth as gold."   (Job xxiii. 10.)   " *But the way of the ungodly shall perish.*"   Not only shall *they* perish themselves, but *their way* shall perish too. The righteous carves his name upon the rock, but the wicked writes his remembrance in the sand.   The righteous man ploughs the furrows of earth, and sows a harvest here, which shall never be fully reaped till he enters the enjoyments of eternity ; but as for the wicked, he ploughs the sea, and though there may seem to be a shining trail behind his keel, yet the waves shall pass over it, and the place that knew him shall know him no more for ever.   The very " way " of the ungodly shall perish. If it exist in remembrance, it shall be in the remembrance of the bad ; for the Lord will cause the name of the wicked to rot, to become a stench in the nostrils of the good, and to be only known to the wicked themselves by its putridity.

May the Lord cleanse our hearts and our ways, that we may escape the doom of the ungodly, and enjoy the blessedness of the righteous !

EXPLANATORY NOTES AND QUAINT SAYINGS.

Whole Psalm.—As the book of the Canticles is called the Song of Songs by a Hebraism, it being the most excellent, so this Psalm may not unfitly be entitled, the Psalm of Psalms, for it contains in it the very pith and quintessence of Christianity. What Jerome saith on St. Paul's epistles, the same may I say of this Psalm; it is short as to the composure, but full of length and strength as to the matter. This Psalm carries blessedness in the frontispiece; it begins where we all hope to end: it may well be called a Christian's Guide, for it discovers the quicksands where the wicked sink down in perdition, and the firm ground on which the saints tread to glory.—*Thomas Watson's Saints' Spiritual Delight,* 1660.

This whole Psalm offers itself to be drawn into these two opposite propositions : a godly man is blessed, a wicked man is miserable; which seem to stand as two challenges, made by the prophet: one, that he will maintain a godly man against all comers, to be the only Jason for winning the golden fleece of blessedness; the other, that albeit make a show in the world of being happy, yet they of all men are most miserable.—*Sir Richard Baker,* 1640.

I have been induced to embrace the opinion of some among the ancient interpreters (Augustine, Jerome, etc.), who conceive that the first Psalm is intended to be descriptive of the character and reward of the Just One, *i.e.* the Lord Jesus. —*John Fry, B.A.,* 1842.

Verse 1.—The psalmist saith more to the point about true happiness in this short Psalm than any one of the philosophers, or all of them put together; they did but beat the bush, God hath here put the bird into our hand.—*John Trapp,* 1660.

Verse 1.—Where the word *blessed* is hung out as a sign, we may be sure that we shall find a godly man within.—*Sir Richard Baker.*

Verse 1.—The seat of the drunkard is the seat of the scornful.—*Matthew Henry,* 1662—1714.

Verse 1.—" *Walketh* NOT . . . . . NOR *standeth* . . . . . NOR *sitteth,*" etc. Negative precepts are in some cases more absolute and peremptory than affirmatives; for to say, " that hath walked in the counsel of the godly," might not be sufficient; for, he might walk in the counsel of the godly, and yet walk in the counsel of the ungodly too; not both indeed at once, but both at several times; where now, this negative clears him at all times.—*Sir Richard Baker.*

Verse 1.—The word אישׁ *haish* is emphatic, *that man*; that one among a *thousand* who lives for the accomplishment of the end for which God created him.—*Adam Clarke,* 1844.

Verse 1.—" *That walketh not in the counsel of the ungodly.*" Mark certain circumstances of their differing characters and conduct. I. The *ungodly man* has his *counsel.* II. The *sinner* has his *way;* and III. The *scorner* has his *seat.* The *ungodly man* is unconcerned about religion; he is neither zealous for his own salvation nor for that of others; and he *counsels* and *advises* those with whom he converses to adopt his plan, and not trouble themselves about praying, reading, repentance, etc., etc.; " there is no need for such things; live an honest life, make no fuss about religion, and you will fare well enough at last." Now, " blessed is the man who walks not in this man's counsel," who does not come into his measures, nor act according to his plan.

The *sinner* has his particular *way* of transgressing; one is a *drunkard,* another *dishonest,* another *unclean.* Few are given to every species of vice. There are many *covetous* men who abhor *drunkenness,* many *drunkards* who abhor *covetousness* and so of others. *Each has his easily besetting sin;* therefore, says the prophet, " *Let the wicked* forsake HIS WAY." Now, *blessed is he who stands not in such a man's* WAY.

The *scorner* has brought, in reference to himself, all religion and moral feeling to an end. He has *sat down*—is utterly confirmed in impiety, and makes a mock at sin. His conscience is seared, and he is a believer in all unbelief. Now, *blessed is the man who sits not down in his* SEAT.—*Adam Clarke.*

Verse 1.—In the Hebrew, the word " blessed " is a plural noun, *ashrey (blessednesses),* that is, all blessednesses are the portion of that man who has not gone away, etc.; as though it were said, " All things are well with that man who," etc. Why do you hold any dispute? Why draw vain conclusions? If a man has found that pearl of great price, to love the law of God and to be separate from the ungodly, all blessednesses belong to that man; but, if he does not find this jewel, he will seek for all blessednesses but will never find one! For as all things are pure unto the pure, so all things are lovely unto the loving, all things good unto the good; and, universally, such as thou art thyself, such is God himself unto thee, though he is not a creature. He is perverse unto the perverse, and holy unto the holy. Hence nothing can be good or saving unto him who is evil; nothing sweet unto him unto whom the law of God is not sweet. The word " counsel " is without doubt here to be received as signifying decrees and doctrines, seeing that no society of men exists without being formed and preserved by decrees and laws. David, however, by this term strikes at the pride and reprobate temerity of the ungodly. First, because they will not humble themselves so far as to walk in the law of the Lord, but rule themselves by their own counsel. And then he calls it their " counsel," because it is their prudence, and the way that seems to them to be without error. For this is the destruction of the ungodly—their being prudent in their own eyes and in their own esteem, and clothing their errors in the garb of prudence and of the right way. For if they came to men in the open garb of error, it would not be so distinguishing a mark of blessedness not to walk with them. But David does not here say, " in the folly of the ungodly," or " in the error of the ungodly; " and therefore he admonishes us to guard with all diligence against the appearance of what is right, that the devil transformed into an angel of light do not seduce us by his craftiness. And he contrasts the counsel of the wicked with the law of the Lord, that we may learn to beware of wolves in sheep's clothing, who are always ready to give counsel to all, to teach all, and to offer assistance unto all, when they are of all men the least qualified to do so. The term " stood " descriptively represents their obstinacy, and stiff-neckedness, wherein they harden themselves and make their excuses in words of malice, having become incorrigible in their ungodliness. For " to stand," in the figurative manner of Scripture expression, signifies to be firm and fixed: as in Rom, xiv. 4, " To his own master he standeth or falleth: yea, he shall be holden up, for God is able to make him stand." Hence the word " column " is by the Hebrew derived from their verb " to stand," as is the word statue among the Latins. For this is the very self-excuse and self-hardening of the ungodly—their appearing to themselves to live rightly, and to shine in the eternal show of works above all others. With respect to the term " seat," to sit in the seat, is to teach, to act the instructor and teacher; as in Matt. xxiii. 2, " The scribes sit in Moses' chair." They sit in the seat of pestilence, who fill the church with the opinions of philosophers, with the traditions of men, and with the counsels of their own brain, and oppress miserable consciences, setting aside, all the while, the word of God, by which alone the soul is fed, lives, and is preserved.—*Martin Luther*, 1536—1546.

Verse 1.—" *The scornful.*" *Peccator cum in profundum venerit contemnet*— when a wicked man comes to the depth and worst of sin, he despiseth. Then the Hebrew will despise Moses (Exodus ii. 14), " Who made thee a prince and a judge over us ? " Then Ahab will quarrel with Micaiah (1 Kings xxii. 18), because he doth not prophesy good unto him. Every child in Bethel will mock Elisha (2 Kings ii. 23), and be bold to call him " bald pate." Here is an original drop of venom swollen to a main ocean of poison: as one drop of some serpents' poison, lighting on the hand, gets into the veins, and so spreads itself over all the body till it hath stifled the vital spirits. God shall " laugh you to scorn," (Psalm ii. 4), for laughing him to scorn; and at last despise you that have despised him in us. That which a man spits against heaven, shall fall back on his own face. Your indignities done to your spiritual physicians shall sleep in the dust with your ashes, but stand up against your souls in judgment.—*Thomas Adams*, 1614.

Verse 2.—" *But his will is in the law of the Lord.*" The " will," which is here signified, is that delight of heart, and that certain pleasure, in the law, which does not look at what the law promises, nor at what it threatens, but at this only; that " the law is holy, and just, and good." Hence it is not only a love of the law, but that loving delight in the law which no prosperity, nor adversity, nor the world, nor the prince of it, can either take away or destroy; for it victoriously bursts its way through poverty, evil report, the cross, death, and hell, and in the midst of adversities, shines the brightest.—*Martin Luther*.

Verse 2.—" *His delight is in the law of the Lord.*"—This *delight* which the prophet here speaks of is the only delight that neither blushes nor looks pale ; the only delight that gives a repast without an after reckoning ; the only delight that stands in construction with all tenses ; and like Æneas Anchyses, carries his parents upon his back.—*Sir Richard Baker.*

Verse 2.—" In his law doth he meditate." In the plainest text there is a world of holiness and spirituality ; and if we in prayer and dependence upon God did sit down and study it, we should behold much more than appears to us. It may be, at once reading or looking, we see little or nothing ; as Elijah's servant went once, and saw nothing ; therefore he was commanded to look seven times. What now ? says the prophet, " I see a cloud rising, like a man's hand ; " and by-and-by, the whole surface of the heavens was covered with clouds. So you may look lightly upon a Scripture and see nothing ; *meditate often upon it*, and there you shall see a light, like the light of the sun."—*Joseph Caryl*, 1647.

Verse 2.—" In his law doth he meditate day and night."—The good man doth *meditate on the law of God day and night.* The pontificians beat off the common people from this common treasury, by objecting this supposed difficulty. Oh, the Scriptures are hard to be understood, do not you trouble your heads about them ; we will tell you the meaning of them. They might as well say, heaven is a blessed place, but it is a hard way to it ; do not trouble yourselves, we will go thither for you. Thus in the great day of trial, when they should be saved by their book, alas ! they have no book to save them. Instead of the Scriptures they can present images ; these are the laymen's books ; as if they were to be tried by a jury of carvers and painters, and not by the twelve apostles. Be not you so cheated ; but study the gospel as you look for comfort by the gospel. He that hopes for the inheritance, will make much of the conveyance.—*Thomas Adams.*

*Verse 2.—*To *" meditate,"* as it is generally understood, signifies to discuss, to dispute ; and its meaning is always confined to a being employed in words, as in Psalm xxxii. 30, " The mouth of the righteous shall meditate wisdom." Hence Augustine has, in his translation, " chatter " ; and a beautiful metaphor it is—as chattering is the employment of birds, so a continual conversing in the law of the Lord (for talking is peculiar to man), ought to be the employment of man. But I cannot worthily and fully set forth the gracious meaning and force of this word ; for this " meditating " consists first in an intent observing of the words of the law, and then in a comparing of the different Scriptures ; which is a certain delightful hunting, nay, rather a playing with stags in a forest, where the Lord furnishes us with the stags, and opens to us their secret coverts. And from this kind of employment, there comes forth at length a man well instructed in the law of the Lord to speak unto the people.—*Martin Luther.*

Verse 2.—" In his law doth he meditate day and night." The godly man will read the Word by *day*, that men, seeing his good works, may glorify his Father who is in heaven ; he will do it in the *night*, that he may not be seen of men : by *day*, to show that he is not one of those who dread the light ; by *night*, to show that he is one who can shine in the shade : by *day*, for that is the time for working—work whilst it is day ; by *night*, lest his Master should come as a thief, and find him idle. —*Sir Richard Baker.*

*Verse 2.—*I have no rest, but in a nook, with *the book.—Thomas à Kempis*, 1380—1471.

Verse 2.—" Meditate." Meditation doth discriminate and characterise a man ; by this he may take a measure of his heart, whether it be good or bad ; let me allude to that ; " For as he thinketh in his heart, so is he." Prov. xxiii. 7. As the meditation is, such is the man. Meditation is the touchstone of a Christian ; it shows what metal he is made of. It is a spiritual index ; the index shows what is in the book, so meditation shows what is in the heart.—*Thomas Watson's Saints' Spiritual Delight.*

Meditation chews the cud, and gets the sweetness and nutritive virtue of the Word into the heart and life : this is the way the godly bring forth much fruit. —*Bartholomew Ashwood's Heavenly Trade*, 1688.

The naturalists observe that to uphold and accommodate bodily life, there are divers sorts of faculties communicated, and these among the rest : 1. An attractive faculty, to assume and draw in the food ; 2. A retentive faculty, to retain it when taken in ; 3. An assimilating faculty, to concoct the nourishment ; 4. An augmenting faculty, for drawing to perfection. Meditation is all these. It helps judgment, wisdom, and faith to ponder, discern, and credit the things which reading and hearing supply and furnish. It assists the memory to lock up the jewels of divine truth in her sure treasury. It has a digesting power, and turns special truth into spiritual nourishment ; and lastly, it helps the renewed heart to grow upward and increase its power to know the things which are freely given to us of God.—*Condensed from Nathaniel Ranew, 1670.*

Verse 3.—" *A tree.*"—There is one tree, only to be found in the valley of the Jordan, but too beautiful to be entirely passed over ; the oleander, with its bright blossoms and dark green leaves, giving the aspect of a rich garden to any spot where it grows. It is rarely if ever alluded to in the Scriptures. But it may be the tree planted by the streams of water which bringeth forth his fruit in due season, and " whose leaf shall not wither."—*A. P. Stanley, D.D., in " Sinai and Palestine."*

Verse 3.—" *A tree planted by the rivers of water.*"—This is an allusion to the Eastern method of cultivation, by which rivulets of water are made to flow between the rows of trees, and thus, by artificial means, the trees receive a constant supply of moisture.

Verse 3.—" *His fruit in his season.*"—In such a case expectation is never disappointed. Fruit is expected, fruit is borne, and it comes also in the time in which it should come. A godly education, under the influences of the divine Spirit, which can never be withheld where they are earnestly sought, is sure to produce the fruits of righteousness ; and he who reads, prays, and meditates, will ever *see* the *work* which God has given him to do ; the *power* by which he is to perform it ; and the *times, places,* and *opportunities* for doing those things by which God can obtain most glory, his own soul most good, and his neighbour most edification.—*Adam Clarke.*

Verse 3.—" *In his season.*" The Lord reckons the times which pass over us, and puts them to our account : let us, therefore, improve them, and, with the impotent persons at the pool of Bethesda, step in when the angel stirs the water. Now the church is afflicted, it is a season of prayer and learning ; now the church is enlarged, it is a season of praise ; I am now at a sermon, I will hear what God will say ; now in the company of a learned and wise man, I will draw some knowledge and counsel from him ; I am under a temptation, now is a fit time to lean on the name of the Lord ; I am in a place of dignity and power, let me consider what it is that God requireth of me in such a time as this. And thus as the tree of life bringeth fruit every month, so a wise Christian, as a wise husbandman, hath his distinct employments for every month, bringing forth his fruit in his season.—*John Spencer's Things New and Old, 1658.*

Verse 3.—" *In his season.*" Oh, golden and admirable word ! by which is asserted the liberty of Christian righteousness. The ungodly have their stated days, stated times, certain works, and certain places ; to which they stick so closely, that if their neighbours were perishing with hunger, they could not be torn from them. But this blessed man, being free at all times, in all places, for every work, and to every person, will serve you whenever an opportunity is offered him ; whatsoever comes into his hands to do, he does it. He is neither a Jew, nor a Gentile, nor a Greek, nor a barbarian, nor of any other particular person. He gives his fruit in his season, so often as either God or man requires his work. Therefore his fruits have no name, and his times have no name.—*Martin Luther.*

Verse 3.—" *His leaf also shall not wither.*" He describes the fruit before he does the leaf. The Holy Spirit himself always teaches every faithful preacher in the church to know that the kingdom of God does not stand in word but in power. 1 Cor. iv. 20. Again, " Jesus began both to do and to teach." Acts i. 1. And again, " Which was a prophet mighty in deed and word." Luke xxiv. 19. And thus, let him who professes the word of doctrine, first put forth the fruits of life, if he would not have his fruit to wither, for Christ cursed the fig tree which bore no fruit. And as Gregory saith, that man whose life is despised is condemned by his doctrine, for he preaches to others, and is himself reprobated.—*Martin Luther.*

Verse 3.—" *His leaf also shall not wither.*" The Lord's trees are all evergreens. No winter's cold can destroy their verdure ; and yet, unlike evergreens in our country, they are all fruit bearers.—*C. H. S.*

Verse 3.—" *And whatsoever he doeth,* [or, *maketh or taketh in hand*] *shall prosper.*" And with regard to this " prospering," take heed that thou understandest not a carnal prosperity. This prosperity is hidden prosperity, and lies entirely secret in spirit ; and therefore if thou hast not this prosperity that is by faith, thou shouldst rather judge thy prosperity to be the greatest adversity. For as the devil bitterly hates this leaf and the word of God, so does he also those who teach and hear it, and he persecutes such, aided by all the powers of the world. Therefore thou hearest of a miracle the greatest of all miracles, when thou hearest that all things prosper which a blessed man doeth.—*Martin Luther*.

Verse 3.—A critical journal has shown that instead of " *Whatsoever it doeth shall prosper,*" the rendering might be, " *Whatsoever it produceth shall come to maturity.*" This makes the figure entire, and is sanctioned by some MSS. and ancient versions.

Verse 3 (last clause).—Outward prosperity, if it follow close walking with God, is very sweet ; as the cipher, when it follows a figure, adds to the number, though it be nothing in itself.—*John Trapp*.

Verse 4.—" *Chaff.*" Here by the way, we may let the wicked know they have a thanks to give they little think of ; that they may thank the godly for all the good days they live upon the earth, seeing it is for their sakes and not for their own that they enjoy them. For as the chaff while it is united and keeps close to the wheat, enjoys some privileges for the wheat's sake, and is laid up carefully in the barn ; but as soon as it is divided, and parted from the wheat, it is cast out and scattered by the wind ; so the wicked, whilst the godly are in company and live amongst them, partake for their sake of some blessedness promised to the godly ; but if the godly forsake them or be taken from them, then either a deluge of water comes suddenly upon them, as it did upon the old world when Noah left it ; or a deluge of fire, as it did upon Sodom, when Lot left it, and went out of the city.—*Sir Richard Baker*.

Verse 4.—" *Driveth away,*" or tosseth away ; the Chaldee translateth for " wind," " whirlwind."—*Henry Ainsworth*, 1639.

This shows the vehement tempest of death, which sweeps away the soul of the ungodly.

Verse 5.—" *Therefore the ungodly shall not stand in the judgment,*" etc. And may not a reason also be conceived thus, why the ungodly can never come to be of the congregation of the righteous : the righteous go a way that God knows, and the wicked go a way that God destroys ; and seeing that these ways can never meet, how should the men meet that go these ways ? And to make sure work that they shall never meet indeed, the prophet expresseth the way of the righteous by the first link of the chain of God's goodness, which is his *knowledge ;* but expresseth the way of the wicked by the last link of God's justice, which is his *destroying ;* and though God's justice and his mercy do often meet, and are contiguous one to another, yet the first link of his mercy and the last link of his justice can never meet, for it never comes to destroying till God be heard to say *Nescio vos,* " *I know you not,*" and *nescio vos* in God, and God's knowledge, can certainly never possibly meet together.—*Sir Richard Baker*.

Verse 5.—The Irish air will sooner brook a toad, or a snake, than heaven a sinner.—*John Trapp.*

Verse 6.—" *For the Lord knoweth the way of the righteous : but the way of the ungodly shall perish.*" Behold how David here terrifies us away from all prosperous appearances, and commends to us various temptations and adversities. For this " way " of the righteous all men utterly reprobate ; thinking also, that God knoweth nothing about any such way. But this is the wisdom of the cross. Therefore, it is God alone that knoweth the way of the righteous, so hidden is to it the righteous themselves. For his right hand leads them on in a wonderful manner, seeing that it is a way, not of sense, nor of reason, but of faith only ; even of that faith that sees in darkness, and beholds things that are invisible.—*Martin Luther*.

Verse 6.—" *The righteous.*" They that endeavour righteous living in themselves and have Christ's righteousness imputed to them.—*Thomas Wilcocks*, 1586.

HINTS TO PREACHERS.

Verse 1.—May furnish an excellent text upon " Progress in Sin," of " The Purity of the Christian," or " The Blessedness of the Righteous." Upon the last subject speak of the believer as BLESSED—1. By God ; 2. In Christ ; 3. With all blessings ; 4. In all circumstances ; 5. Through time and eternity ; 6. To the highest degree.

Verse 1.—Teaches a godly man to beware, (1) of the opinions, (2) of the practical life, and (3) of the company and association of sinful men. Show how meditation upon the Word will assist us in keeping aloof from these three evils.

The insinuating and progressive nature of sin.—*J. Morison.*

Verse 1, *in connection with the whole Psalm.* The wide difference between the righteous and the wicked.

Verse 2.—THE WORD OF GOD. 1. The believer's delight in it. 2. The believer's acquaintance with it. We long to be in the company of those we love.

Verse 2.—I. What is meant by " the law of the Lord." II. What there is in it for the believer to delight in. III. How he shows his delight, thinks of it, reads much, speaks of it, obeys it, does not delight in evil.

Verse 2 (*last clause*).—The benefits, helps, and hindrances of meditation.

Verse 3.—" *The fruitful tree.*" I. Where it grows. II. How it came there. III. What it yields. IV. How to be like it.

Verse 3.—" *Planted by the rivers of water.*" I. The origination of Christian life, " *planted.*" II. The streams which support it. III. The fruit expected from it.

Verse 3.—Influence of religion upon prosperity.—*Blair.*

The nature, causes, signs, and results of true prosperity.

" *Fruit in his season ;* " virtues to be exhibited at certain seasons—patience in affliction ; gratitude in prosperity ; zeal in opportunity, etc.

" *His leaf also shall not wither ;* " the blessing of retaining an unwithered profession.

Verses 3, 4.—See No. 280 of " Spurgeon's Sermons."—" The Chaff Driven Away."

Sin puts a negative on every blessing.

Verse 5.—The sinner's double doom. 1. Condemned at the judgment-bar. 2. Separated from the saints. Reasonableness of these penalties, " therefore," and the way to escape them.

" *The congregation of the righteous* " viewed as the church of the first-born above. This may furnish a noble topic.

Verse 6 (*first sentence*).—A sweet encouragement to the tried people of God. The knowledge here meant. 1. *Its character.*—It is a knowledge of observation and approbation. 2. *Its source.*—It is caused by omniscience and infinite love. 3. *Its results.*—Support, deliverance, acceptance, and glory at last.

Verse 6 (*last clause*).—His way of pleasure, of pride, of unbelief, of profanity, of persecution, of procrastinating, of self-deception, etc. ; all these shall come to an end.

PSALM II.

TITLE.—*We shall not greatly err in our summary of this sublime Psalm if we call it* THE PSALM OF MESSIAH THE PRINCE ; *for it sets forth as in a wondrous vision the tumult of the people against the Lord's anointed, the determinate purpose of God to exalt his own Son, and the ultimate reign of that Son over all his enemies. Let us read it with the eye of faith, beholding, as in a glass, the final triumph of our Lord Jesus Christ over all his enemies. Lowth has the following remarks upon this Psalm : " The establishment of David upon his throne, notwithstanding the opposition made to it by his enemies, is the subject of the Psalm. David sustains in it a twofold character, literal and allegorical. If we read over the Psalm, first with an eye to the literal David, the meaning is obvious, and put beyond all dispute by the sacred history. There is indeed an uncommon glow in the expression and sublimity in the figures, and the diction is now and then exaggerated, as it were on purpose to intimate, and lead us to the con-templation of higher and more important matters concealed within. In compliance with this admonition, if we take another survey of the Psalm as relative to the person and concerns of the spiritual David, a noble series of events immediately rises to view, and the meaning becomes more evident, as well as more exalted. The colouring which may perhaps seem too bold and glaring for the king of Israel, will no longer appear so when laid upon his great Antitype. After we have thus attentively considered the subjects apart, let us look at them together, and we shall behold the full beauty and majesty of this most charming poem. We shall perceive the two senses very distinct from each other, yet conspiring in perfect harmony, and bearing a wonderful resemblance in every feature and lineament, while the analogy between them is so exactly preserved, that either may pass for the original from whence the other was copied. New light is continually cast upon the phraseology, fresh weight and dignity are added to the sentiments, till, gradually ascending from things below to things above, from human affairs to those that are Divine, they bear the great important theme upwards with them, and at length place it in the height and brightness of heaven."*

DIVISION.—*This Psalm will be best understood if it be viewed as a four-fold picture. (In verses 1, 2, 3) the Nations are raging ; (4 to 6) the Lord in heaven derides them ; (7 to 9) the Son proclaims the decree ; and (from 10 to end) advice is given to the kings to yield obedience to the Lord's anointed. This division is not only suggested by the sense, but is warranted by the poetic form of the Psalm, which naturally falls into four stanzas of three verses each.*

EXPOSITION.

WHY do the heathen rage, and the people imagine a vain thing ?

2 The kings of the earth set themselves, and the rulers take counsel together, against the LORD, and against his anointed, *saying,*

3 Let us break their bands asunder, and cast away their cords from us.

We have, in these first three verses, a description of the hatred of human nature against the Christ of God. No better comment is needed upon it than the apostolic song in Acts iv. 27, 28 : " For of a truth against thy holy child Jesus, whom thou hast anointed, both Herod, and Pontius Pilate, with the Gentiles, and the people of Israel, were gathered together, for to do whatsoever thy hand and thy counsel determined before to be done." The Psalm begins abruptly with an angry interrogation ; and well it may : it is surely but little to be wondered at, that the sight of creatures in arms against their God should amaze the psalmist's mind. We see the *heathen raging,* roaring like the sea, tossed to and fro with restless waves, as the ocean in a storm ; and then we mark the people in their hearts *imagining a vain thing* against God. Where there is much rage there is generally some folly, and in this case there is an excess of it. Note, that the commotion is not caused by the people only, but their leaders foment the rebellion. " *The kings of the earth set themselves.*" In determined malice they arrayed themselves in opposition against God. It was not temporary rage, but deep-seated hate, for they *set them-selves* resolutely to withstand the Prince of Peace. " *And the rulers take counsel together.*" They go about their warfare craftly, not with foolish haste, but deliberately. They use all the skill which art can give. Like Pharaoh, they cry, " Let us deal wisely with them." O that men were half as careful in God's service to serve him wisely, as his enemies are to attack his kingdom craftily. Sinners have their wits about them, and yet saints are dull. But what say they? what is the meaning of this commotion? *" Let us break their bands asunder."* " Let us be free to commit all manner of abominations. Let us be our own gods. Let us rid ourselves of all restraint." Gathering impudence by the traitorous proposition of rebellion, they add—*" let us cast away;"* as if it were an easy matter,—" let us fling off ' *their cords from us.'* " What! O ye kings, do ye think yourselves Samsons? and are the bands of Omnipotence but as green withs before you? Do you dream that you shall snap to pieces and destroy the mandates of God—the decrees of the Most High—as if they were but tow? And do ye say, " Let us cast away their cords from us?" Yes! There are monarchs who have spoken thus, and there are still rebels upon thrones. However mad the resolution to revolt from God, it is one in which man has persevered ever since his creation, and he continues in it to this very day. The glorious reign of Jesus in the latter day will not be consummated, until a terrible struggle has convulsed the nations. His coming will be as a refiner's fire, and like fuller's soap, and the day thereof shall burn as an oven. Earth loves not her rightful monarch, but clings to the usurper's sway : the terrible conflicts of the last days will illustrate both the world's love of sin and Jehovah's power to give the kingdom to his only Begotten. To a graceless neck the yoke of Christ is intolerable, but to the saved sinner it is easy and light. We may judge ourselves by this, do we love that yoke, or do we wish to cast it from us?

4 He that sitteth in the heavens shall laugh : the Lord shall have them in derision.

Let us now turn our eyes from the wicked council-chamber and raging tumult of man, to the secret place of the majesty of the Most High. What doth God say? What will the King do unto the men who reject his only-begotten Son, the Heir of all things?

Mark the quiet dignity of the Omnipotent One, and the contempt which he pours upon the princes and their raging people. He has not taken the trouble to rise up and do battle with them—he despises them, he knows how absurd, how irrational, how futile are their attempts against him—he therefore *laughs* at them.

5 Then shall he speak unto them in his wrath, and vex them in his sore displeasure.

6 Yet have I set my king upon my holy hill of Zion.

After he has laughed he shall *speak;* he needs not smite ; the breath of his lips is enough. At the moment when their power is at its height, and their fury most violent, *then* shall his Word go forth against them. And what is it that he says?—it is a very galling sentence—" *Yet,*" says he, " despite your malice, despite your tumultuous gatherings, despite the wisdom of your counsels, despite the craft of your lawgivers, ' *yet have I set my king upon my holy hill of Zion.'* " Is not that a grand exclamation! He has already done that which the enemy seeks to prevent. While they are proposing, he has disposed the matter. Jehovah's will is done, and man's will frets and raves in vain. God's Anointed is appointed, and shall not be disappointed. Look back through all the ages of infidelity, hearken to the high and hard things which men have spoken against the Majesty of heaven, listen to the rolling thunder of earth's volleys against the Majesty of heaven, and then think that God is saying all the while, " Yet have I set my king upon my holy hill of Zion." Yet Jesus reigns, yet he sees of the travail of his soul, and " his unsuffering kingdom yet shall come " when he shall take unto himself his great power, and reign from the river unto the ends of the earth. Even now he reigns in Zion, and our glad lips sound forth the praises of the Prince of Peace. Greater conflicts may here be foretold, but we may be confident that victory will be given to our Lord and King. Glorious triumphs are yet to come ; hasten them, we pray thee, O Lord! It is Zion's glory and joy that her King is in her, guarding her from foes, and filling her with good things. Jesus sits upon the throne of grace, and the throne of power in the midst of his church. In him is Zion's best safeguard; let her citizens be glad in him.

> "Thy walls are strength, and at thy gates
> A guard of heavenly warriors waits;
> Nor shall thy deep foundations move,
> Fixed on his counsels and his love.
>
> Thy foes in vain designs engage;
> Against his throne in vain they rage,
> Like rising waves, with angry roar,
> That dash and die upon the shore."

7 I will declare the decree: the LORD hath said unto me, Thou *art* my son; this day have I begotten thee.

8 Ask of me, and I shall give *thee* the heathen *for* thine inheritance, and the uttermost parts of the earth *for* thy possession.

9 Thou shalt break them with a rod of iron; thou shalt dash them in pieces like a potter's vessel.

This Psalm wears something of a dramatic form, for now another person is introduced as speaking. We have looked into the counsel-chamber of the wicked, and to the throne of God, and now we behold the Anointed declaring his rights of sovereignty, and warning the traitors of their doom.

God has laughed at the counsel and ravings of the wicked, and now Christ the Anointed himself comes forward, as the Risen Redeemer, " declared to be the Son of God with power, according to the spirit of holiness, by the resurrection from the dead." Rom. i. 4. Looking into the angry faces of the rebellious kings, the Anointed One seems to say, " If this sufficeth not to make you silent, ' *I will declare the decree.*' " Now this decree is directly in conflict with the device of man, for its tenour is the establishment of the very dominion against which the nations are raving. " *Thou art my Son.*" Here is a noble proof of the glorious Divinity of our Immanuel. " For unto which of the angels said he at any time, Thou art my Son, this day have I begotten thee?" What a mercy to have a Divine Redeemer in whom to rest our confidence! " *This day have I begotten thee.*" If this refers to the Godhead of our Lord, let us not attempt to fathom it, for it is a great truth, a truth reverently to be received, but not irreverently to be scanned. It may be added, that if this relates to the Begotten One in his human nature, we must here also rejoice in the mystery, but not attempt to violate its sanctity by intrusive prying into the secrets of the Eternal God. The things which are revealed are enough, without venturing into vain speculations. In attempting to define the Trinity, or unveil the essence of Divinity, many men have lost themselves: here great ships have foundered. What have we to do in such a sea with our frail skiffs?

" *Ask of me.*" It was a custom among great kings to give to favoured ones whatever they might ask. (See Esther v. 6; Matt. xiv. 7.) So Jesus hath but to ask and have. Here he declares that his very enemies are his inheritance. To their face he declares this decree, and " Lo! here," cries the Anointed One, as he holds aloft in that once pierced hand the sceptre of his power, " He hath given me this, not only the right to be a king, but the power to conquer." Yes! Jehovah hath given to his Anointed a rod of iron with which he shall break rebellious nations in pieces, and, despite their imperial strength, they shall be but as potters' vessels, easily dashed into shivers, when the rod of iron is in the hand of the omnipotent Son of God. Those who will not bend must break. Potters' vessels are not to be restored if dashed in pieces, and the ruin of sinners will be hopeless if Jesus shall smite them.

> " Ye sinners seek his grace,
> Whose wrath ye cannot bear;
> Fly to the shelter of his cross,
> And find salvation there."

10 Be wise now therefore, O ye kings: be instructed, ye judges of the earth.

11 Serve the LORD with fear, and rejoice with trembling.

12 Kiss the Son, lest he be angry, and ye perish *from* the way, when his wrath is kindled but a little. Blessed *are* all they that put their trust in him.

The scene again changes, and counsel is given to those who have taken counsel to rebel. They are exhorted to obey, and give the kiss of homage and affection to him whom they have hated.
" *Be wise.*"—It is always wise to be willing to be instructed, especially when such instruction tends to the salvation of the soul. " Be wise *now, therefore ;* " delay no longer, but let good reason weigh with you. Your warfare cannot succeed, therefore desist and yield cheerfully to him who will make you bow if you refuse his yoke. O how wise, how infinitely wise is obedience to Jesus, and how dreadful is the folly of those who continue to be his enemies ! " *Serve the Lord with fear ;* " let reverence and humility be mingled with your service. He is a great God, and ye are but puny creatures ; bend ye, therefore, in lowly worship, and let a filial fear mingle with all your obedience to the great Father of the Ages. " *Rejoice with trembling.*"—There must ever be a holy fear mixed with the Christian's joy. This is a sacred compound, yielding a sweet smell, and we must see to it that we burn no other upon the altar. Fear, without joy, is torment ; and joy, without holy fear, would be presumption. Mark the solemn argument for reconciliation and obedience. It is an awful thing to *perish* in the midst of sin, in the very *way* of rebellion ; and yet how easily could *his wrath* destroy us suddenly. It needs not that his anger should be heated seven times hotter ; let the fuel kindle *but a little*, and we are consumed. O sinner ! Take heed of the terrors of the Lord ; for " our God is a consuming fire." Note the benediction with which the Psalm closes :—" *Blessed are all they that put their trust in him.*" Have we a share in this blessedness ? Do we trust in *him ?* Our faith my be slender as a spider's thread ; but if it be real, we are in our measure blessed. The more we trust, the more fully shall we know this blessedness. We may therefore close the Psalm with the prayer of the apostles :— " Lord, increase our faith."
The first Psalm was a contrast between the righteous man and the sinner; the second Psalm is a contrast between the tumultuous disobedience of the ungodly world and the sure exaltation of the righteous Son of God. In the first Psalm, we saw the wicked driven away like chaff ; in the second Psalm, we see them broken in pieces like a potter's vessel. In the first Psalm, we beheld the righteous like a tree planted by the rivers of water ; and here, we contemplate Christ, the Covenant Head of the righteous, made better than a tree planted by the rivers of water, for *he* is made king of all the islands, and all the heathen bow before him and kiss the dust ; while he himself gives a blessing to all those who put their trust in him. The two Psalms are worthy of the very deepest attention ; they are, in fact, the preface in the entire Book of Psalms, and were by some of the ancients, joined into one. They are, however, two Psalms ; for Paul speaks of this as the second Psalm. (Acts xiii. 33.) The first shows us the character and lot of the righteous ; and the next teaches us that the Psalms are Messianic, and speak of Christ the Messiah—the Prince who shall reign from the river even unto the ends of the earth. That they have both a far-reaching prophetic outlook we are well assured, but we do not feel competent to open up that matter, and must leave it to abler hands.

EXPLANATORY NOTES AND QUAINT SAYINGS.

Verse 1.—" *Why do nations make a noise,*" tumultuate or rage ? The Hebrew verb is not expressive of an internal feeling, but of the ourward agitation which denotes it. There may be an allusion to the rolling and roaring of the sea, often used as an emblem of popular commotion, both in the Scriptures and the classics. The past tense of this verb (*why have they raged ?*) refers to the commotion as already begun, while the future in the next clause expresses its continuance.—*J. A. Alexander,* D.D., 1850.
Verse 1.—" *Rage.*" The word with which Paul renders this in the Greek denotes rage, pride, and restiveness, as of horses that neigh, and rush into the battle.

Ἐφρύαξαν, from Φρυάσσω, to snort or neigh, properly applied to a high-mettled horse. See Acts iv. 25.

Verse 1.—" *A vain thing.*" A medal was struck by Diocletian, which still remains bearing the inscription, " The name of Christians being extinguished." And in Spain, two monumental pillars were raised, on which were written :— I. " Diocletian Jovian Maximian Herculeus Cæsares Augusti, for having extended the Roman Empire in the east and the west, and for having extinguished the name of Christians, who brought the Republic to ruin." II. " Diocletian Jovian Maximian Herculeus Cæsares Augusti, for having adopted Galerius in the east, for having everywhere abolished the superstition of Christ, for having extended the worship of the gods." As a modern writer has elegantly observed : " We have here a monument raised by Paganism, over the grave of its vanquished foe. But in this, ' the people imagined a vain thing ;' so far from being deceased, Christianity was on the eve of its final and permanent triumph, and the stone guarded a sepulchre empty as the urn which Electra washed with her tears. Neither in Spain, nor elsewhere, can be pointed out the burial place of Christianity ; it is not, for the living have no tomb."

Verses 1—4.—Herod, the fox, plotted against Christ, to hinder the course of his ministry and mediatorship, but he could not perform his enterprise ; 'tis so all along, therefore it is said, " *Why do the heathen imagine a vain thing ?* " A vain thing, because a thing successless, their hands could not perform it. It was vain, not only because there was no true ground of reason why they should imagine or do such a thing, but vain also because they laboured in vain, they could not do it, and therefore it follows, " *He that sitteth in the heavens shall laugh : the Lord shall have them in derision.*" The Lord see what fools they are, and men (yea, themselves) shall see it. The prophet gives us an elegant description to this purpose. Isaiah lix. 5, 6. " *They weave the spider's web . . . . . Their webs shall not become garments, neither shall they cover themselves with their works.*" As if he had said, they have been devising and setting things in a goodly frame to catch flies ; they have been spinning a fine thread out of their brains, as the spider doth out of her bowels ; such is their web, but when they have their web they cannot cut it out, or make it up into a garment. They shall go naked and cold, notwithstanding all their spinning and weaving, all their plotting and devising. The next broom that comes will sweep away all their webs and the spiders too, except they creep apace. God loves and delights to cross worldly proverbs and worldly craft.—*Joseph Caryl*, 1647.

Verse 2.—The *many* had done their part, and now the *mighty* show themselves. —*John Trapp.*

Verse 2.—" *They banded themselves against the Lord, and against his Anointed.*" But why did they band themselves against the Lord, or against his Anointed ? What was their desire of him ? To have his goods ? No, he had none for himself ; but they were richer than he. To have his liberty ? Nay, that would not suffice them, for they had bound him before. To bring the people into dislike of him ? Nay, that would not serve them, for they had done so already, until even his disciples were fled from him. What would they have then ? his blood ? Yea, " they took counsel," saith Matthew, " to put him to death." They had the devil's mind, which is not satisfied but with death. And how do they contrive it ? He saith, " they took counsel about it."—*Henry Smith*, 1578.

Verse 2.—" *Against Jehovah and against his Anointed.*" What an honour it was to David to be thus publicly associated with Jehovah ! And, because he was HIS anointed, to be an object of hatred and scorn to the ungodly world ! If this very circumstance fearfully augmented the guilt, and sealed the doom of these infatuated heathen, surely it was that which above everything else would preserve the mind of David calm and serene, yea, peaceful and joyful notwithstanding the proud and boastful vauntiness of his enemies . . . . . . When writing this Psalm David was like a man in a storm, who hears only the roaring of the tempest, or sees nothing but the raging billows threatening destruction on every side of him. And yet his faith enabled him to say, " *The people imagine a vain thing.*" They cannot succeed. They canot defeat the counsels of heaven. They cannot injure the Lord's Anointed.—*David Pitcairn*, 1851.

Verse 3.—Resolved they were to run riot as lawless, and aweless, and therefore they slander the sweet laws of Christ's kingdom as bonds and thick cords, which are signs of slavery. Jer. xxvii. 2, 6, 7. But what saith our Saviour ? " My yoke is easy, and my burden is light." It is no more burden to a regenerate man than wings to a bird. The law of Christ is no more as bands and cords, but as girdles and garters which gird up his loins and expedite his course.—*John Trapp*.

Verse 4.—"*He that sitteth in the heavens.*" Hereby it is clearly intimated, (1) that the Lord is far above all their malice and power, (2) that he seeth all their plots, looking down on all; (3) that he is of omnipotent power, and so can do with his enemies as he lists. "Our God is in the heavens : he hath done whatsoever he pleased." Psalm cxv. 3.—*Arthur Jackson*, 1643.

Verse 4.—"*He that sitteth in the heavens shall laugh,*" etc. Sinners' follies are the just sport of God's infinite wisdom and power ; and those attempts of the kingdom of Satan, which in our eyes are formidable, in his are despicable.—*Mathew Henry.*

Verse 4.—"*He that sitteth in the heavens shall laugh.*" They scoff at us, God laughs at them. Laugh ? This seems a hard word at the first view : are the injuries of his saints, the cruelties of their enemies, the derision, the persecution of all that are round about us, no more but matter of laughter ? Severe Cato thought that laughter did not become the gravity of Roman consuls ; that it is a diminution of states, as another told princes ; and is it attributed to the Majesty of heaven ? According to our capacities, the prophet describes God, as ourselves would be in a merry disposition, deriding vain attempts. He laughs, but it is in scorn ; he scorns, but it is with vengeance. Pharaoh imagined that by drowning the Israelite males, he had found a way to root their name from the earth ; but when at the same time, his own daughter, in his own court, gave princely education to Moses, their deliverer, did not God laugh ?

Short is the joy of the wicked. Is Dagon put up to his place again ? God's smile shall take off his head and his hands, and leave him neither wit to guide nor power to subsist . . . . . We may not judge of God's works until the fifth act : the case, deplorable and desperate in outward appearance, may with one smile from heaven find a blessed issue. He permitted his temple to be sacked and rifled, the holy vessels to be profaned and caroused in ; but did not God's smile make Belshazzar to tremble at the handwriting on the wall ? Oh, what are his frowns, if his smiles be so terrible !—*Thomas Adams.*

Verse 4.—The expression, "*He that sitteth in the heavens,*" at once fixes our thoughts on a being infinitely exalted above man, who is of the earth, earthly. And when it is said, "HE shall *laugh*," this word is designed to convey to our minds the idea, that the greatest confederacies amongst kings and peoples, and their most extensive and vigorous preparations, to defeat HIS purposes or to injure HIS servants, are in HIS sight altogether insignificant and worthless. HE looks upon their poor and puny efforts, not only without uneasiness or fear, but HE laughs at their folly ; HE treats their impotency with derision. He knows how HE can crush them like a moth when HE pleases, or consume them in a moment with the breath of HIS mouth. How profitable it is for us to be reminded of truths such as these ! Ah ! it is indeed "*a vain thing*" for the potsherds of the earth to strive with the glorious Majesty of Heaven.—*David Pitcairn.*

Verse 4.—"*The Lord,*" in Hebrew, Adonai, mystically signifieth my stays, or my sustainers—my pillars. Our English word "Lord" hath much the same force, being contracted of the old Saxon word "Llaford," or "Hlafford," which cometh from "Laef," to sustain, refresh, cherish.—*Henry Ainsworth.*

Verse 4.—"*He that sitteth in the heavens shall laugh at them : the Lord shall have them in derision.*" This tautology or repetition of the same thing, which is frequent in the Scriptures, is a sign of the thing being established : according to the authority of the patriarch Joseph (Gen. xli. 32), where, having interpreted the dreams of Pharaoh he said, "And for that the dream was doubled unto Pharaoh twice ; it is because the thing is established by God, and God will shortly bring it to pass." And therefore, here also, "*shall laugh at them,*" and "*shall have them in derision,*" is a repetition to show that there is not a doubt to be entertained that all these things will most surely come to pass. And the gracious Spirit does all this for our comfort and consolation, that we may not faint under temptation, but lift up our heads with the most certain hope ; because "he that shall come will come, and will not tarry." Hebrews x. 37.—*Martin Luther.*

Verse 5.—"*Vex them ;*" either by horror of conscience, or corporal plagues ; one way or the other he will have his pennyworths of them, as he always has had of the persecutors of his people.—*John Trapp.*

Verses 5, 9.—It is easy for God to destroy his foes . . . . . Behold Pharaoh, his wise men, his hosts, and his horses plouting and plunging, and sinking like lead in the Red sea.   Here is the end of one of the greatest plots ever formed against God's chosen.   Of thirty Roman emperors, governors of provinces, and others high in office, who distinguished themselves by their zeal and bitterness in persecuting the early Christians, one became speedily deranged after some atrocious cruelty, one was slain by his own son, one became blind, the eyes of one started out of his head, one was drowned, one was strangled, one died in a miserable captivity, one fell dead in a manner that will not bear recital, one died of so loathsome a disease that several of his physicians were put to death because they could not abide the stench that filled his room, two committed suicide, a third attempted it, but had to call for help to finish the work, five were assassinated by their own people or servants, five others died the most miserable and excruciating deaths, several of them having an untold complication of diseases, and eight were killed in battle, or after being taken prisoners.   Among these was Julian the apostate.   In the days of his prosperity he is said to have pointed his dagger to heaven defying the Son of God, whom he commonly called the Galilean.   But when he was wounded in battle, he saw that all was over with him, and he gathered up his clotted blood, and threw it into the air, exclaiming, " Thou hast conquered, O thou Galilean."   Voltaire has told us of the agonies of Charles IX. of France, which drove the blood through the pores of the skin of that miserable monarch, after his cruelties and treachery to the Huguenots.—*William S. Plummer, D.D., LL.D.,* 1867.

Verse 6.—" *Yet have I set my King.*"   Notice—1. The royal office and character of our glorious Redeemer : he is a King, " This name he hath on his vesture and on his thigh." Rev. xix. 16.   2. The authority by which he reigns ; he is " *my King,*" says God the Father, and I have set him up from everlasting : " The Father judgeth no man ; but hath committed all judgment unto the Son."   The world disowns his authority, but I own it ; I have set him, I have " given him to be head over all things to the church."   3. His particular kingdom over which he rules ; it is over " *my holy hill of Zion* "—an eminent type of the gospel church.   The temple was built upon Mount Zion and therefore called a *holy hill.*   Christ's throne is in his church, it is his head-quarters, and the place of his peculiar residence.   Notice the firmness of the divine purpose with respect unto this matter.   " *Yet have I set* " him " *King ;* " *i.e.,* whatever be the plots of hell and earth to the contrary, he reigns by his Father's ordination.—*Stephen Charnock,* 1628—1680.

Verse 6.—" *Yet have I set my* King," etc.—Jesus Christ is a threefold King. *First,* his enemies' King ; *secondly,* his saints' King ; *thirdly,* his Father's King.

First.   Christ is his enemies' King, that is, he is King over his enemies.   Christ is a King above all kings.   What are all the mighty men, the great, the honourable men of the earth to Jesus Christ ?   They are but like a little bubble in the water ; for if all the nations, in comparison to God, be but as the drop of the bucket, or the dust of the balance, as the prophet speaks in Isaiah xl. 15, how little then must be the kings of the earth !   Nay, beloved, Christ Jesus is not only higher than kings, but he is higher than the angels ; yea, he is the head of angels ; and, therefore, all the angels in heaven are commanded to worship him.   Col. ii. 12 Heb. i. 6 . . . . . He is King over all kingdoms, over all nations, over all governments, over all powers, over all people Dan. vii. 14 . . . . . The very heathen are given to Christ, and the uttermost parts of the earth for his possession.   Psalm ii. 8.

Secondly.   Jesus Christ is his saints' King.   He is King of the bad, and of the good ; but as for the wicked, he rules over them by his power and might ; but the saints, he rules in them by his Spirit and graces.   Oh ! this is Christ's spiritual kingdom, and here he rules in the hearts of his people, here he rules over their consciences, over their wills, over their affections, over their judgments and understandings, and nobody hath anything to do here but Christ.   Christ is not only the King of nations, but the King of saints ; the one he rules over, the other he rules in.

Thirdly.   Jesus Christ is his Father's King too, and so his Father calls him : " *I have set my King upon my holy hill of Zion.*"   Well may he be our King, when he is God's King.   But you may say, how is Christ the Father's King ?   Because he rules for his Father.   There is a twofold kingdom of God committed to Jesus Christ ; *first,* a spiritual kingdom, by which he rules in the hearts of his people, and so is King of saints ; and, *secondly,* a providential kingdom, by which he rules the affairs of this world, and so he is King of nations.—*Condensed from William Dyer's Christ's Famous Titles*, 1665.

Verse 6.—" *Zion.*" The *name* " Zion " signifies a " distant view " (*speculam.*) And the church is called " a distant view " (*specula*), not only because it views God and heavenly things by faith (that is, afar off), being wise unto the things that are above, not unto those that are on the earth : but also, because there are within her true viewers, or seers, and watchmen in the spirit, whose office it is to take charge of the people under them, and to watch against the snares of enemies and sins ; and such are called in the Greek bishops ('επίσκοποι), that is, spyers or seers ; and you may for the same reason give them, from the Hebrew, the appellation of Zionians of Zioners.—*Martin Luther.*

Verse 7.—The dispute concerning the eternal filiation of our Lord betrays more of presumptuous curiosity than of reverent faith. It is an attempt to explain where it is far better to adore. We could give rival expositions of this verse, but we forbear. The controversy is one of the most unprofitable which ever engaged the pens of theologians.—*C. H. S.*

Verse 8.—" *Ask of me.*" The priesthood doth not appear to be settled upon Christ by any other expression than this, " Ask of me." The Psalm speaks of his investiture in his kingly office ; the apostle refers this to his priesthood, his commission, for both took date at the same time ; both bestowed, both confirmed by the same authority. The office of asking is grounded upon the same authority as the honour of king. Ruling belonged to his royal office, asking to his priestly. After his resurrection, the Father gives him a power and command of asking.—*Stephen Charnock.*

Verse 8.—As the limner looks on the person whose picture he would take, and draws his lines to answer him with the nearest similitude that he can, so God looks on Christ as the archetype to which he will conform the saint, in suffering, in grace, in glory ; yet so that Christ hath the pre-eminence in all. Every saint must suffer, because Christ suffered : Christ must not have a delicate body under a crucified head ; yet never any suffered, or could, what he endured. Christ is holy, and therefore so shall every saint be, but in an inferior degree ; an image cut in clay cannot be so exact as that engraved on gold. Now, our conformity to Christ appears, that as the promises made to him were performed upon his prayers to his Father, his promises made to his saints are given to them in the same way of prayer : " *Ask of me,*" saith God to his Son, " *and I shall give thee.*" And the apostle tells us, " Ye have not, because ye ask not." God hath promised support to Christ in all his conflicts. Isaiah xlii. 1. " Behold my servant, whom I uphold ; " yet he prayed " with strong cries and tears," when his feet stood within the shadow of death. A seed is promised to him, and victory over his enemies, yet for both these he prays. Christ towards us acts as a king, but towards his Father as a priest. All he speaks to God is by prayer and intercession. So the saints, the promise makes them kings over their lusts, conquerors over their enemies ; but it makes them priests towards God, by prayer humbly to sue out those great things given in the promise.—*William Gurnall,* 1617—1679.

Verse 8.—It will be observed in our Bible that two words of verse eight are in italics, intimating that they are not translations of the Hebrew, but additions made for the purpose of elucidating the meaning. Now if the " *thee* " and the " *for* " are left out, the verse will read thus, " Ask of me, and I shall give the heathen, thine inheritance, and thy possession, the uttermost parts of the earth." And this reading is decidedly preferable to the other. It implies that by some previous arrangement on the part of God, he had already assigned an inheritance of the heathen, and the possession of the earth, to the person of whom he says, " Thou art my Son." And when God says, " I will give," etc., he reveals to his Anointed, not so much in what the inheritance consisted, and what was the extent of possession destined for him, as the promise of his readiness to bestow it. The heathen were already " the inheritance," and the ends of the earth " the possession," which God had *purposed* to give to his Anointed. Now he says to him, " Ask of me," and he *promises* to fulfil his purpose. This is the idea involved in the words of the text, and the importance of it will become more apparent, when we consider its application to the *spiritual* David, to the true Son of God, " whom he hath appointed the heir of all things."

Verse 9.—The "*rod*" has a variety of meanings in Scripture. It might be of different materials, as it was employed for different purposes. At an early period, a wooden rod came into use as one of the insignia of royalty, under the name of sceptre. By degrees the sceptre grew in importance, and was regarded as characteristic of an empire, or of the reign of some particular king. A golden sceptre denoted wealth and pomp. The right, or straight sceptre of which we read in Psalm xlv. 6, is expressive of the justice and uprightness, the truth and equity, which shall distinguish Messiah's reign, after his kingdom on earth has been established. But when it is said in Rev. xix. 15, that he, " whose name is called the Word of God," will smite the nations, and " rule them with a rod of iron," if the rod signifies " his sceptre," then the " iron " of which it is made must be designed to express the severity of the judgments which this omnipotent " King of kings " will inflict on all who resist his authority. But to me it appears doubtful whether the " rod of iron " symbolizes the royal sceptre of the Son of God at his second advent. It is mentioned in connection with " a sharp sword," which leads me to prefer the opinion that it also ought to be regarded as a weapon of war ; at all events, the " rod of iron " mentioned in the Psalm we are endeavouring to explain, is evidently not the emblem of sovereign power, although represented as in the hands of a king, but an instrument of correction and punishment. In this sense the word " rod " is often used . . . . When the correcting rod, which usually was a wand or cane, is represented, as in the second Psalm, to be of " iron " it only indicates how weighty, how severe, how effectual the threatened chastisement will be—it will not merely bruise, but it will break. " *Thou shalt break them with a rod of iron.*"

Now it is just such a complete breaking as would not readily be effected excepting by *an iron rod*, that is more fully expressed in the following clause of the verse, " Thou shalt dash them in pieces like a potter's vessel." The completeness of the destruction, however, depends on two things. Even an iron rod if gently used, or used against a hard and firm substance, might cause little injury ; but, in the case before us, it is supposed to be applied with great force, " Thou shalt *dash* them ; " and it is applied to what will prove as brittle and frangible as " *a potter's vessel* "— " Thou shalt dash them *in pieces.*" . . . . . Here, as is other respects, we must feel that the predictions and promises of this Psalm were but very partially fulfilled in the history of the literal David. Their real accomplishment, their awful completion, abides the day when the spiritual David shall come in glory and in majesty as Zion's King, with a rod of iron to dash in pieces the great antichristian confederacy of kings and peoples, and to take possession of his long-promised and dearly-purchased inheritance. And the signs of the times seem to indicate that the coming of the Lord draws nigh.—*David Pitcairn.*

Verse 10.—" *Be wise now, therefore, O ye kings,*" etc. As Jesus is King of kings and Judge of judges, so the gospel is the teacher of the greatest and wisest. If any are so great as to spurn its admonitions, God will make little of them ; and if they are so wise as to despise its teachings, their fancied wisdom shall make fools of them. The gospel takes a high tone before the rulers of the earth, and they who preach it should, like Knox and Melville, magnify their office by bold rebukes and manly utterances even in the royal presence. A clerical sycophant is only fit to be a scullion in the devil's kitchen.—*C. H. S.*

Verse 11.—" *Serve the Lord with fear.*" This fear of God qualifies our joy. If you abstract fear from joy, joy will become light and wanton ; and if you abstract joy from fear, fear then will become slavish.—*William Bates, D.D., 1625—1699.*

Verse 11.—" *Serve the Lord with fear, and rejoice with trembling.*" There are two kinds of serving and rejoicing in God. First, a serving in security, and a rejoicing in the Lord without fear ; these are peculiar to hypocrites, who are secure, who please themselves, and who appear to themselves to be not unuseful servants, and to have great merit on their side, concerning whom it is said (Psalm x. 5), " Thy judgments are far above out of his sight ; " and also afterwards (Psalm xxxvi. 1), " There is no fear of God before his eyes." These do righteousness without judgment at all times ; and permit not Christ to be the Judge to be feared by all, in whose sight no man living is justified. Secondly, a serving with fear and a rejoicing with trembling ; these are peculiar to the righteous who do righteousness at all times, and always rightly attemper both ; never being without judgments, on the one hand, by which they are terrified and brought to despair of themselves and of all their own works ; nor without that righteousness, on the other, on which they rest, and in which they rejoice in the mercy of God. It is the work of the whole lives of these characters to accuse themselves in all things, and in all things to justify and praise God. And thus they fulfil that word of Proverbs, " Blessed is the man that feareth alway " (xxviii. 14) ; and also that of Philip. iv. 4, " Rejoice in the Lord alway." Thus, between the upper and nether mill-stone (Deut. xxiv. 6), they are broken in pieces and humbled, and the husks thus being bruised off, they come forth the all-pure wheat of Christ.—*Martin Luther.*

Verse 11.—The fear of God promotes spiritual joy ; it is the morning star which ushers in the sunlight of comfort. " Walking in the fear of God, and in the comfort of the Holy Ghost." God mingles joy with fear, that fear may not be slavish. —*Thomas Watson*, 1660.

Verse 12.—" *Kiss*," a sign of love among equals : Gen. xxxiii. 4 ; 1 Sam. xx. 41 ; Rom. xvi. 16 ; 1 Cor. xvi. 20. Of subjection in inferiors : 1 Sam. x. 1. Of religious adoration in worshippers : 1 Kings xix. 18 ; Job xxxi. 27.—*John Richardson, Bishop of Ardagh*, 1655.

Verse 12.— " *Kiss the Son, lest he be angry.*" From the Person, *the Son*, we shall pass to the act (*Osculamini, kiss the Son*) ; in which we shall see, that since this is an act which licentious men have depraved (carnal men do it, and treacherous men do it—*Judas* betrayed his Master by a kiss), and yet God commands this, and expresses love in this ; everything that hath, or may be abused, must not therefore be abandoned ; the turning of a thing out of the way, is not a taking of that thing away, but good things deflected to ill uses by some, may be by others reduced to their first goodness. Then let us consider and magnify the goodness of God, that hath brought us into this distance, that we may *kiss the Son*, that the expressing of this love lies in our hands, and that, whereas the love of the church, in the Old Testament, even in the Canticle, went no farther but to the *Osculatur me* (*O that he would kiss me with the kisses of his mouth !* Cant. i. 1), now, in the Christian church, and in the visitation of a Christian soul, he hath invited us, enabled us to kiss him, for he is presentially amongst us. This leads us to give an earnest persuasion and exhortation *to kiss the Son*, with all those affections, which we shall there find to be expressed in the Scriptures, in that testimony of true love, *a holy kiss*. But then lest that persuasion by love should not be effectual and powerful enough to us, we shall descend from that duty, to the danger, from love, to fear, " *lest he be angry;*" and therein see first, that God, who is love, can be angry ; and then, that this God who is angry here, is the Son of God, he that hath done so much for us, and therefore in justice may be angry ; he that is our Judge, and therefore in reason we are to fear his anger : and then, in a third branch, we shall see how easily this anger departs—a kiss removes it.

Verse 12.—" *Kiss the Son.*" That is, embrace him, depend upon him all these ways : as thy kinsman, as thy sovereign ; at thy going, at thy coming ; at thy reconciliation, in the truth of religion in thyself, in a peaceable unity with the church, in a reverent estimation of those men, and those means whom he sends. Kiss him, and be not ashamed of kissing him ; it is that which the spouse desired, " *I would kiss thee, and not be despised.*" Cant. vii. 1. If thou be despised for loving Christ in his gospel, remember that when David was thought base, for dancing before the ark, his way was to be more base. If thou be thought frivolous for thrusting in at service, in the forenoon, be more frivolous, aud come again in the afternoon : " *Tanto major requies, quanto ab amore Jesu nulla requies;*" * " The more thou troublest thyself, or art troubled by others for Christ, the more peace thou hast in Christ." . . . . . " *Lest he be angry.*" Anger, as it is a passion that troubles, and disorders, and discomposes a man, so it is not in God ; but anger, as it is a sensible discerning of foes from friends, and of things that conduce, or disconduce to his glory, so it is in God. In a word, Hilary hath expressed it well : " *Pœna patientis, ira decernentis;*" " Man's suffering is God's anger." When God inflicts such punishments as a king justly incensed would do, then God is thus angry. Now here, our case is heavier ; it is not this great, and almighty, and majestical God, that may be angry—that is like enough ; but even the *Son*, whom we must *kiss*, may be *angry ;* it is not a person whom we consider merely as God, but as man ; nay, not as man neither, but *a worm, and no man*, and he may be angry, and angry

---

* Gregory.

to our ruin ..... "*Kiss the Son,*" and he will not *be angry;* if he be, kiss the rod, and he will be angry no longer—love him lest he be ; fear him when he is angry : the preservative is easy, and so is the restorative too : the balsamum of this kiss is all, to suck spiritual milk out of the left breast, as well as out of the right, to find mercy in his judgments, reparation in his ruins, feasts in his lents, joy in his anger.—*From Sermons of John Donne, D.D., Dean of St. Paul's,* 1621—1631.

Verse 12.—"*Kiss the Son.*" To make peace with the Father, kiss the Son. "Let him kiss me," was the church's prayer. Cant. i. 2. Let us kiss him—that be our endeavour. Indeed, the Son must first kiss us by his mercy, before we can kiss him by our piety. Lord, grant in these mutual kisses and interchangeable embraces now, that we may come to the plenary wedding supper hereafter ; when the choir of heaven, even the voices of angels, shall sing epithalamiums, nuptial songs, at the bridal of the spouse of the Lamb.—*Thomas Adams.*

Verse 12.—"*If his wrath be kindled but a little ;*" the Hebrew is, if his nose or nostril be kindled but a little ; the nostril, being an organ of the body in which wrath shows itself, is put for wrath itself. Paleness and snuffling of the nose are symptoms of anger. In our proverbials, to take a thing in snuff, is to take it in anger.—*Joseph Caryl.*

Verse 12.—"*His wrath.*" Unspeakable must the wrath of God be when it is kindled fully, since perdition may come upon the *kindling of it but a little.*—*John Newton.*

HINTS TO PREACHERS.

Whole Psalm.—Shows us the nature of sin, and the terrible results of it if it could reign.

Verse 1.—*Nothing is more irrational than irreligion.* A weighty theme.

The reasons why sinners rebel against God, stated, refuted, lamented, and repented of.

The crowning display of human sin in man's hatred of the Mediator.

Verses 1 *and* 2.—Opposition to the gospel, unreasonable and ineffectual.—*Two sermons by John Newton.*

Verses 1 *and* 2.—These verses show that all trust in man in the service of God is vain. Inasmuch as men oppose Christ, it is not good to hang our trust upon *the multitude* for their number, *the earnest* for their zeal, *the mighty* for their countenance, or *the wise* for their counsel, since all these are far oftener against Christ than for him.

Verse 2.—"Spurgeon's Sermons," No. 495, "The Greatest Trial on Record."

Verse 3.—The true reason of the opposition of sinners to Christ's truth, viz. : their hatred of the restraints of godliness.

Verse 4.—God's derision of the rebellious, both now and hereafter.

Verse 5.—*The voice of wrath.* One of a series of sermons upon the voices of the divine attributes.

Verse 6.—*Christ's sovereignty.* 1. The opposition to it : "yet." 2. The certainty of its existence : "*Yet have I set.*" 3. The power which maintains it : "*have I set.*" 4. The place of its manifestation : "*my holy hill of Zion.*" 5. The blessings flowing from it.

Verse 7.—The divine decree concerning Christ, in connection with the decrees of election and providence. The Sonship of Jesus.

This verse teacheth us faithfully to declare, and humbly to claim, the gifts and calling that God hath bestowed upon us.—*Thomas Wilcocks.*

Verse 8.—Christ's inheritance.—*William Jay.*

Prayer indispensable.—*Jesus must ask.*

Verse 9.—*The ruin of the wicked.* Certain, irresistible, terrible, complete, irretrievable, "like a potter's vessel."

The destruction of systems of error and oppression to be expected. The gospel an iron rod quite able to break mere pots of man's making.

Verse 10.—True wisdom, fit for kings and judges, lies in obeying Christ.

The gospel, a school for those who would learn how to rule and judge well. They may consider its principles, its exemplar, its spirit, etc.

Verse 11.—*Mingled experience.* See the case of the women returning from the sepulchre. Matt. xxviii. 8. This may be rendered a very comforting subject, if the Holy Spirit direct the mind of the preacher.

True religion, a compound of many virtues and emotions.

Verse 12.—*An earnest invitation.* 1. *The command.* 2. *The argument.* 3. *The benediction* upon the obedient.—" Spurgeon's Sermons," No. 260.

Last clause.—Nature, object, and blessedness of saving faith.

PSALM III.

TITLE.—" A Psalm of David when he fled from Absalom his Son." *You will remember the sad story of David's flight from his own palace, when, in the dead of the night, he forded the brook Kedron, and went with a few faithful followers to hide himself for awhile from the fury of his rebellious son. Remember that David in this was a type of the Lord Jesus Christ. He, too, fled ; he, too, passed over the brook Kedron when his own people were in rebellion against him, and with a feeble band of followers he went to the garden of Gethsemane. He, too, drank of the brook by the way, and therefore doth he lift up the head. By very many expositors this is entitled* THE MORNING HYMN. *May we ever wake with holy confidence in our hearts, and a song upon our lips !*

DIVISION.—*This Psalm may be divided into four parts of two verses each. Indeed, many of the Psalms cannot be well understood unless we attentively regard the parts into which they are to be divided. They are not continuous descriptions of one scene, but a set of pictures of many kindred subjects. As in our modern sermons, we divide our discourse into different heads, so it is in these Psalms. There is always unity, but it is the unity of a bundle of arrows, and not of a single solitary shaft. Let us now look at the Psalm before us. In the first two verses you have David making a complaint to God concerning his enemies ; he then declares his confidence in the Lord* (3, 4), *sings of his safety in sleep* (5, 6), *and strengthens himself for future conflict* (7. 8).

EXPOSITION.

LORD, how are they increased that trouble me ! many *are* they that rise up against me.

2 Many *there be* which say of my soul, *There is* no help for him in God. Selah.

The poor broken-hearted father complains of the multitude of his enemies, and if you turn to 2 Samuel xv. 12, you will find it written that " the conspiracy was strong ; for the people increased continually with Absalom," while the troops of David constantly diminished ! " *Lord how are they increased that trouble me !* " Here is a note of exclamation to express the wonder of woe which amazed and perplexed the fugitive father. Alas ! I see no limit to my misery, for my troubles are enlarged ! There was enough at first to sink me very low ; but lo ! my enemies multiply. When Absalom, my darling, is in rebellion against me, it is enough to break my heart ; but lo ! Ahithophel hath forsaken me, my faithful counsellors have turned their backs on me ; lo ! my generals and soldiers have deserted my standard. " How are they increased that trouble me ! " Troubles always come in flocks. Sorrow hath a numerous family.

" *Many are they that rise up against me.*" Their hosts are far superior to mine ! Their numbers are too great for my reckoning !

Let us here recall to our memory the innumerable hosts which beset our Divine Redeemer. The legions of our sins, the armies of fiends, the crowd of bodily pains, the host of spiritual sorrows, and all the allies of death and hell, set themselves in battle against the Son of Man. O how precious to know and believe that he has routed their hosts, and trodden them down in his anger ! They who would have troubled us he has removed into captivity, and those who would have risen up against us he has laid low. The dragon lost his sting when he dashed it into the soul of Jesus.

David complains before his loving God of the worst weapon of his enemies' attacks, and the bitterest drop of his distresses. " Oh ! " saith David, " *many there be that say of my soul, There is no help for him in God.*" Some of his distrustful friends said this sorrowfully, but his enemies exultingly boasted of it, and longed to see their words proved by his total destruction. This was the unkindest cut of all, when they declared that his God had forsaken him. Yet David knew in his own conscience that he had given them some ground for this exclamation, for he had committed sin against God in the very light of day. Then they flung his crime with Bathsheba into his face, and they said, " Go up, thou bloody man ; God hath forsaken thee and left thee." Shimei cursed him and swore at him to his very face, for he was bold because of his backers, since multitudes of the men of Belial thought of David in like fashion. Doubtless, David felt this infernal suggestion to be staggering to his faith. If all the trials which come from heaven, all the temptations which ascend from hell, and all the crosses which arise from earth, could be mixed and pressed together, they would not make a trial so terrible as that which is contained in this verse. It is the most bitter of all afflictions to be led to fear that there is no help for us in God. And yet remember our most blessed Saviour had to endure this in the deepest degree when he cried, " My God, my God, why hast thou forsaken me ? " He knew full well what it was to walk in darkness and to see no light. This was the curse of the curse. This was the wormwood mingled with the gall. To be deserted of his Father was worse than to be the despised of men. Surely we should love him who suffered this bitterest of temptations and trials for our sake. It will be a delightful and instructive exercise for the loving heart to mark the Lord in his agonies as here portrayed, for there is here, and in very many other Psalms, far more of David's Lord than of David himself.

" Selah." This is a musical pause ; the precise meaning of which is not known. Some think it simply a rest, a pause in the music ; others say it means, " Lift up the strain—sing more loudly—pitch the tune upon a higher key—there is nobler matter to come, therefore retune your harps." Harp-strings soon get out of order and need to be screwed up again to their proper tightness, and certainly our heart-strings are evermore getting out of tune. Let " Selah " teach us to pray

> " O may my heart in tune be found
> Like David's harp of solemn sound."

At least, we may learn that wherever we see " Selah," we should look upon it as a note of observation. Let us read the passage which precedes and succeeds it with greater earnestness, for surely there is always something excellent where we are required to rest and pause and meditate, or when we are required to lift up our hearts in grateful song. " SELAH."

3 But thou, O LORD, *art* a shield for me ; my glory, and the lifter up of mine head.

4 I cried unto the LORD with my voice, and he heard me out of his holy hill. Selah.

Here David avows his confidence in God. " *Thou, O Lord, art a shield for me.*" The word in the original signifies more than a shield ; it means a buckler round about, a protection which shall surround a man entirely, a shield above, beneath, around, without and within. Oh ! what a shield is God for his people ! He wards off the fiery darts of Satan from beneath, and the storms of trials from above, while, at the same instant, he speaks peace to the tempest within the breast. Thou art " *my glory.*" David knew that though he was driven from his capital in contempt and scorn, he should yet return in triumph, and by faith he looks upon God as honouring and glorifying him. O for grace to see our future glory amid present shame ! Indeed, there is a present glory in our afflictions, if we could but discern it ; for it is no mean thing to have fellowship with Christ in his sufferings. David was honoured when he made the ascent of Olivet, weeping, with his head covered ; for he was in all this made like unto his Lord. May we learn, in this respect, to glory in tribulations also ! " *And the lifter up of mine head*"—thou shalt yet exalt me. Though I hang my head in sorrow, I shall very soon lift it up in joy and thanksgiving. What a divine trio of mercies is contained in this verse !—defence for the defenceless, glory for the despised, and joy for the comfortless. Verily we may well say, " There is none like the God of Jeshurun."

" *I cried unto the Lord with my voice.*" Why doth he say, " with my voice ? " Surely, silent prayers are heard. Yes, but good men often find that, even in secret, they pray better aloud than they do when they utter no vocal sound. Perhaps, moreover, David would think thus :—" My cruel enemies clamour against me ; *they* lift up their voices, and, behold, *I* lift up mine, and my cry outsoars them all. They clamour, but the cry of my voice in great distress pierces the very skies, and is louder and stronger than all their tumult ; for there is one in the sanctuary who hearkens to me from the seventh heaven, and he hath ' *heard me out of his holy hill.*' '' Answers to prayers are sweet cordials for the soul. We need not fear a frowning world while we rejoice in a prayer-hearing God.

Here stands another *Selah.* Rest awhile, O tried believer, and change the strain to a softer air.

5 I laid me down and slept; I awaked; for the LORD sustained me.

6 I will not be afraid of ten thousands of people, that have set *themselves* against me round about.

David's faith enabled him to *lie down;* anxiety would certainly have kept him on tiptoe, watching for an enemy. Yea, he was able to sleep, *to sleep* in the midst of trouble, surrounded by foes. " So he giveth his beloved sleep." There is a sleep of presumption; God deliver us from it! There is a sleep of holy confidence; God help us so to close our eyes! But David says he *awaked* also. Some sleep the sleep of death; but he, though exposed to many enemies, reclined his head on the bosom of his God, slept happily beneath the wing of Providence in sweet security, and then awoke in safety. " *For the Lord sustained me.*" The sweet influence of the Pleiades of promise shone upon the sleeper, and he awoke conscious that the Lord had preserved him. An excellent divine has well remarked—" This quietude of a man's heart by faith in God, is a higher sort of work than the natural resolution of manly courage, for it is the gracious operation of God's Holy Spirit upholding a man above nature, and therefore the Lord must have all the glory of it."

Buckling on his harness for the day's battle, our hero sings, " *I will not be afraid of ten thousands of people, that have set themselves against me round about.*" Observe that he does not attempt to under-estimate the number or wisdom of his enemies. He reckons them at tens of thousands, and he views them as cunning huntsmen chasing him with cruel skill. Yet he trembles not, but looking his foeman in the face he is ready for the battle. There may be no way of escape; they may hem me in as the deer are surrounded by a circle of hunters; they may surround me on every side, but in the name of God I will dash through them; or, if I remain in the midst of them, yet shall they not hurt me; I shall be free in my very prison.

But David is too wise to venture to the battle without prayer; he therefore betakes himself to his knees, and cries aloud to Jehovah.

7 Arise, O LORD; save me, O my God: for thou hast smitten all mine enemies *upon* the cheek bone; thou hast broken the teeth of the ungodly.

His only hope is in his God, but that is so strong a confidence, that he feels the Lord hath but to *arise* and he is saved. It is enough for the Lord to stand up, and all is well. He compares his enemies to wild beasts, and he declares that God hath broken their jaws, so that they could not injure him; " *Thou hast broken the teeth of the ungodly.*" Or else he alludes to the peculiar temptations to which he was then exposed. They had spoken against him; God, therefore, has smitten them upon the cheek bone. They seemed as if they would devour him with their mouths; God hath broken their teeth, and let them say what they will, their toothless jaws shall not be able to devour him. Rejoice, O believer, thou hast to do with a dragon whose head is broken, and with enemies whose teeth are dashed from their jaws!

8 Salvation *belongeth* unto the LORD: thy blessing *is* upon thy people. Selah.

This verse contains the sum and substance of Calvinistic doctrine. Search Scripture through, and you must, if you read it with a candid mind, be persuaded that the doctrine of salvation by grace alone is the great doctrine of the word of God: " *Salvation belongeth unto the Lord.*" This is a point concerning which we are daily fighting. Our opponents say, " Salvation belongeth to the free will of man; if not to man's merit, yet at least to man's will;" but we hold and teach that salvation from first to last, in every iota of it, belongs to the Most High God. It is God that chooses his people. *He* calls them by his grace; *he* quickens them by his Spirit, and keeps them by his power. It is not of man, neither by man; " not of him that willeth, nor of him that runneth, but of God that showeth mercy." May we all learn this truth experimentally, for our proud flesh and blood will never permit us to learn it in any other way. In the last sentence the peculiarity and

speciality of salvation are plainly stated : " *Thy blessing is upon thy people.*"
Neither upon Egypt, nor upon Tyre, nor upon Nineveh ; thy blessing is upon thy
chosen, thy blood-bought, thine everlastingly-beloved people. " *Selah :* " lift up
your hearts, and pause, and meditate upon this doctrine. " Thy blessing is upon
thy people." Divine, discriminating, distinguishing, eternal, infinite, immutable
love, is a subject for constant adoration. Pause my soul, at this *Selah*, and consider
thine own interest in the salvation of God ; and if by humble faith thou art enabled
to see Jesus as thine by his own free gift of himself to thee, if this greatest of all
blessings be upon thee, rise up and sing—

> " Rise, my soul ! adore and wonder !
> Ask, ' O why such love to me ? '
> Grace hath put me in the number
> Of the Saviour's family :
> Hallelujah !
> Thanks, eternal thanks to thee."

EXPLANATORY NOTES AND QUAINT SAYINGS.

Title.—With regard to the authority of the Titles, it becomes us to speak with
diffidence, considering the very opposite opinions which have been offered upon
this subject by scholars of equal excellence. In the present day, it is too much the
custom to slight or omit them altogether, as though added, nobody knows when or
by whom, and as, in many instances, inconsistent with the subject-matter of the
Psalm itself : while Augustine, Theodoret, and various other early writers of the
Christian church, regard them as a part of the inspired text ; and the Jews still
continue to make them a part of their chant, and their rabbins to comment upon
them.

It is certainly unknown who invented or placed them where they are : but
it is unquestionable that they have been so placed from time immemorial ; they
occur in the Septuagint, which contains also in a few instances titles to Psalms that
are without any in the Hebrew ; and they have been copied after the Septuagint by
Jerome. So far as the present writer has been able to penetrate the obscurity that
occasionally hangs over them, they are a direct and most valuable key to the general
history or subject of the Psalms to which they are prefixed ; and, excepting where
they have been evidently misunderstood or misinterpreted, he has never met with a
single instance in which the drift of the title and its respective Psalm do not exactly
coincide. Many of them were, doubtless, composed by Ezra at the time of editing
his own collection, at which period some critics suppose the whole to have been
written ; but the rest appear rather to be coeval, or nearly so, with the respective
Psalms themselves, and to have been written about the period of their production.
—*John Mason Good, M.D., F.R.S.,* 1854.

See title. Here we have the first use of the word *Psalm.* In Hebrew, *Mizmor*,
which hath the signification of pruning, or cutting off superfluous twigs, and is
applied to songs made of short sentences, where many superfluous words are put
away.—*Henry Ainsworth.*

Upon this note an old writer remarks, " Let us learn from this, that in times of
sore trouble men will not fetch a compass and use fine words in prayer, but will offer
a prayer which is pruned of all luxuriance of wordy speeches."

Whole Psalm.—Thus you may plainly see how God hath wrought in his church
in old time, and therefore should not discourage yourselves for any sudden change ;
but with David, acknowledge your sins to God, declare unto him how many there
be that vex you and rise up against you, naming you Huguenots, Lutherans, Heretics,
Puritans, and the children of Belial, as they named David. Let the wicked idolators
brag that they will prevail against you and overcome you, and that God hath given
you over, and will be no more your God. Let them put their trust in Absalom, with
his large golden locks : and in the wisdom of Ahithophel, the wise counsellor ; yet

say you, with David, " *Thou, O Lord, art my defender, and the lifter up of my head.*"
Persuade yourselves, with David, that the Lord is your defender, who hath compassed you round about, and is, as it were, a " *shield* " that doth cover you on every
side.   It is he only that may and will compass you about with glory and honour.
It is he that will thrust down those proud hypocrites from their seat, and exalt the
lowly and meek.   It is he which will " *smite* " your " *enemies on the cheek bone,*"
and burst all their teeth in sunder.   He will hang up Absalom by his own long hairs ;
and Ahithophel through desperation shall hang himself.   The bands shall be broken
and you delivered ; for this belongeth unto the Lord, to save his from their enemies,
and to bless his people, that they may safely proceed in their pilgrimage to heaven
without fear.—*Thomas Tymme's " Silver Watch Bell,"* 1634.

Verse 1.—Absalom's faction, like a snowball, strangely gathered in its motion.
David speaks of it as one amazed ; and well he might, that a people he had so many
ways obliged, should almost generally revolt from him, and rebel against him, and
choose for their head such a silly, giddy young fellow as Absalom was.   How slippery
and deceitful are the many !   And how little fidelity and constancy is to be found
among men !   David had had the hearts of his subjects as much as ever any king
had, and yet now of a sudden he had lost them !   As people must not trust too much
to princes (Psalm cxlvi. 3), so princes must not build too much upon their interest
in the people.   Christ the Son of David had many enemies, when a great multitude
came to seize him, when the crowd cried, " Crucify him, crucify him," how were
they then increased that troubled him !   Even good people must not think it
strange if the stream be against them, and the powers that threaten them grow
more and more formidable.—*Matthew Henry.*

Verse 2.—When the believer questions the power of God, or his interest in
it, his joy gusheth out as blood out of a broken vein.   This verse is a sore stab
indeed.—*William Gurnall.*

Verse 2.—A child of God startles at the very thought of despairing of help in
God ; you cannot vex him with anything so much as if you offer to persuade him,
" *There is no help for him in God.*"   David comes to God, and tells him what his
enemies said of him, as Hezekiah spread Rabshakeh's blasphemous letter before
the Lord ; they say, " *There is no help for me in thee ;* " but, Lord, if it be so, I am
undone.   They say to my soul, " *There is no salvation* " (for so the word is) " *for
him in God ;* " but, Lord, do thou say unto my soul, " *I am thy salvation* " (Psalm
xxxv. 3), and that shall satisfy me, and in due time silence them.—*Matthew Henry.*

Verses 2, 4, 8.—" *Selah* צֶ֫לָה.   Much has been written on this word, and still
its meaning does not appear to be wholly determined.   It is rendered in the Targum
or Chaldee paraphrase, לְעָלְמִין, *lealmin, for ever*, or *to eternity.*   In the Latin Vulgate,
it is omitted, as if it were no part of the text.   In the Septuagint it is rendered Διάψαλμα,
supposed to refer to some variation or modulation of the voice in singing.
Schleusner, *Lex.*   The word occurs seventy-three times in the Psalms, and three
times in the book of Habakkuk (iii. 3, 9, 13).   It is never translated in our version,
but in all these places the original word *Selah* is retained.   It occurs only in poetry,
and is supposed to have had some reference to the singing or cantillation of poetry,
and to be probably a musical term.   In general, also, it indicates a pause in the
sense, as well as in the musical performance.   Gesenius (*Lex.*) supposes that the
most probable meaning of this musical term or note is *silence* or *pause*, and that
its use was, in chanting the words of the Psalm, to direct the singer *to be silent, to
pause a little*, while the instruments played an interlude or harmony.   Perhaps
this is all that can now be known of the meaning of the word, and this is enough to
satisfy every reasonable enquiry.   It is probable, if this was the use of the term,
that it would commonly correspond with the sense of the passage, and be inserted
where the sense made a pause suitable ; and this will doubtless be found usually
to be the fact.   But any one acquainted at all with the character of musical notation
will perceive at once that we are not to suppose that this would be invariably or
necessarily the fact, for the musical pauses by no means always correspond with
pauses in the sense.   This word, therefore, can furnish very little assistance in deter-
mining the meaning of the passages where it is found.   Ewald supposes, differing
from this view, that it rather indicates that in the places where it occurs the voice
is to be raised, and that it is synonymous with *up, higher, loud*, or *distinct*, from סֹל,

sal, ללס salal, *to ascend.* Those who are disposed to enquire further respecting its meaning, and the uses of musical pauses in general, may be referred to Ugolin, " Thesau. Antiq. Sacr.," tom. xxii.—*Albert Barnes,* 1868.

Verses 2, 4, 8.—*Selah,* סלה, is found seventy-three times in the Psalms, generally at the end of a sentence or paragraph ; but in Psalm lv. 19 and lvii. 3, it stands in the middle of the verse. While most authors have agreed in considering this word as somehow relating to the *music,* their conjectures about its precise meaning have varied greatly. But at present these two opinions chiefly obtain. Some, including Herder, De Wette, Ewald (*Poet Bücher,* i. 179), and Delitzsch, derive it from סלה, or ללס, *to raise* and understand an *elevation* of the voice or music; others, after Gesenius, in *Thesaurus,* derive it from סלה, *to be still* or *silent,* and understand a pause in the singing. So Rosenmüller, Hengstenberg, and Tholuck. Probably *selah* was used to direct the singer to be silent, or to pause a little, while the instruments played an interlude (so Sept., διάψαλμα) or symphony. In Psalm ix. 16, it occurs in the expression *higgaion selah,* which Gesenius, with much probability, renders *instrumental, pause ; i.e.,* let the instruments strike up a symphony, and let the singer pause. By Tholuck and Hengstenberg, however, the two words are rendered *meditation, pause ; i.e.,* let the singer meditate while the music stops.—*Benjamin Davis, Ph.D., LL.D., article Psalms, in Kitto's Cyclopædia of Biblical Literature.*

Verse 3.—*" Lifter up of my head."* God will have the body partake with the soul—as in matters of grief, so in matters of joy ; the lanthorn shines in the light of the candle within.—*Richard Sibbs,* 1639.

There is a lifting up of the head by elevation to office, as with Pharaoh's butler ; this we trace to the divine appointment. There is a lifting up in honour after shame, in health after sickness, in gladness after sorrow, in restoration after a fall, in victory after a temporary defeat ; in all these respects the Lord is the lifter up of our head.—*C. H. S.*

Verse 4.—When prayer leads the van, in due time deliverance brings up the rear.—*Thomas Watson.*

Verse 4.—*" He heard me."* I have often heard persons say in prayer, " Thou art a prayer-hearing and a prayer-answering God," but the expression contains a superfluity, since for God to hear is, according to Scripture, the same thing as to answer.—*C. H. S.*

Verse 5.—*" I laid me down and slept ; I awaked : for the Lord sustained me."* The title of the Psalm tells us when David had this sweet night's rest ; not when he lay on his bed of down in his stately palace at Jerusalem, but when he fled for his life from his unnatural son Absalom, and possibly was forced to lie in the open field under the canopy of heaven. Truly it must be a soft pillow indeed that could make him forget his danger, who then had such a disloyal army at his back hunting of him ; yea, so transcendent is the influence of this peace, that it can make the creature lie down as cheerfully to sleep in the grave, as on the softest bed. You will say that child is willing that calls to be put to bed ; some of the saints have desired God to lay them at rest in their beds of dust, and that not in a pet and discontent with their present trouble, as Job did, but from a sweet sense of this peace in their bosoms. " Now let thy servant depart in peace, for mine eyes have seen thy salvation," was the swan-like song of old Simeon. He speaks like a merchant that had got all his goods on ship-board, and now desires the master of the ship to hoist sail, and be gone homewards. Indeed, what should a Christian, that is but a foreigner here, desire to stay any longer for in the world, but to get his full lading in for heaven ? And when hath he that, if not when he is assured of his peace with God ? This peace of the gospel, and sense of the love of God in the soul, doth so admirably conduce to the enabling of a person in all difficulties, and temptations, and troubles, that ordinarily, before he calls his saints to any hard service, or hot work, he gives them a draught of this cordial wine next their hearts, to cheer them up and embolden them in the conflict.—*William Gurnall.*

Verse 5.—Gurnall, who wrote when there were houses on old London Bridge, has quaintly said, " Do you not think that they sleep as soundly who dwell on London Bridge as they who live at Whitehall or Cheapside ? for they know that the waves which rush under them cannot hurt them. Even so may the saints rest quietly over the floods or trouble or death, and fear no ill."

Verse 5.—Xerxes, the Persian, when he destroyed all the temples in Greece, caused the temple of Diana to be preserved for its beautiful structure : that soul which hath the beauty or holiness shining in it, shall be preserved for the glory of the structure ; God will not suffer his own temple to be destroyed.   Would you be secured in evil times ?   Get grace and fortify this garrison ; a good conscience is a Christian's fort-royal.   David's enemies lay round about him ; yet saith he, " *I laid me down and slept.*"   A good conscience can sleep in the mouth of a cannon ; grace is a Christian's coat of mail, which fears not the arrow or bullet.   True grace may be shot at, but can never be shot through ; grace puts the soul into Christ, and there it is safe, as the bee in the hive, as the dove in the ark.   " There is no condemnation to them which are in Christ Jesus." Rom. viii. 1.—*Thomas Watson.*

Verse 5.—" *The Lord sustained me.*"   It would not be unprofitable to consider the sustaining power manifested in us while we lie asleep.   In the flowing of the blood, heaving of the lung, etc., in the body and the continuance of mental faculties while the image of death is upon us.—*C. H. S.*

Verse 6.—" *I will not be afraid of ten thousands of people, that have set themselves against me round about.*"   The psalmist will trust, *despite appearances.*   He will not be afraid though ten thousands of people have set themselves against him round about.   Let us here limit our thoughts to this one idea, " despite appearances." What could look worse to human sight than this array of ten thousands of people ? Ruin seemed to stare him in the face ; wherever he looked an enemy was to be seen.   What was one against ten thousand ?   It often happens that God's people come into circumstances like this ; they say, " All these things are against me ;" they seem scarce able to count their troubles ; they cannot see a loophole through which to escape ; things look very black indeed ; it is great faith and trust which says under these circumstances " I will not be afraid."

These were the circumstances under which Luther was placed, as he journeyed towards Worms.   His friend Spalatin heard it said, by the enemies of the Reformation, that the safe conduct of a heretic ought not to be respected, and became alarmed for the reformer.   " At the moment when the latter was approaching the city, a messenger appeared before him with this advice from the chaplin, ' Do not enter Worms !'   And this from his best friend, the elector's confidant, from Spalatin himself ! . . . . . But Luther, undismayed, turned his eyes upon the messenger, and replied, ' Go and tell your master, that even should there be as many devils in Worms as tiles upon the housetops, still I would enter it.'   The messenger returned to Worms, with this astounding answer : ' I was then undaunted,' said Luther, a few days before his death, ' I feared nothing.' "

At such seasons as these, the reasonable men of the world, those who walk by sight and not by faith, will think it reasonable enough that the Christian should be afraid ; they themselves would be very low if they were in such a predicament. Weak believers are now ready to make excuses for us, and we are only too ready to make them for ourselves ; instead of rising above the weakness of the flesh, we take refuge under it, and use it as an excuse.   But let us think prayerfully for a little while, and we shall see that it should not be thus with us.   To trust only when appearances are favourable, is to sail only with the wind and tide, to believe only when we can see.   Oh ! let us follow the example of the psalmist, and seek that unreservedness of faith which will enable us to trust God, come what will, and to say as he said, " *I will not be afraid of ten thousands of people, that have set themselves against me round about.*"—*Philip Bennett Power's ' I wills' of the Psalms,* 1862.

Verse 6.—" *I will not be afraid,*" etc.   It makes no matter what our enemies be, though for number, legions ; for power, principalities ; for subtilty, serpents ; for cruelty, dragons ; for vantage of place, a prince of the air ; for maliciousness, spiritual wickedness ; stronger is he that is in us, than they who are against us ; nothing is able to separate us from the love of God.   In Christ Jesus our Lord, we shall be more than conquerors.—*William Cowper,* 1612.

Verse 7.—" *Arise, O Lord,*" Jehovah !   This is a common scriptural mode of calling upon God to manifest his presence and his power, either in wrath or favour. By a natural anthropomorphism, it describes the intervals of such manifestation as periods of inaction or of slumber, out of which he is besought to rouse himself. " *Save me,*" even me, of whom they say there is no help for him in God.   " *Save me, O my God,*" mine by covenant and mutual engagement, to whom I therefore have a right to look for deliverance and protection. This confidence is warranted, moreover, by experience. " *For thou hast*," in former exigencies, " *smitten all mine enemies*," without exception " (*on the*) *cheek* " or *jaw*, an act at once violent and insulting. —*J. A. Alexander, D.D.*

Verse 7.—" *Upon the cheek bone*."—The language seems to be taken from a comparison of his enemies with wild beasts. The cheek bone denotes the bone in which the teeth are placed, and to break that is to disarm the animal.—*Albert Barnes, in loc.*

Verse 7.—When God takes vengeance upon the ungodly, he will smite in such a manner as to make them feel his almightiness in every stroke. All his power shall be exercised in punishing and none in pitying. O that every obstinate sinner would think of this, and consider his unmeasurable boldness in thinking himself able to grapple with Omnipotence !—*Stephen Charnock.*

Verse 8.—" *Salvation belongeth unto the Lord :* " parallel passage in Jonah ii. 9, " *Salvation is of the Lord*." The mariners might have written upon their ship, instead of Castor and Pollux, or the like device, *Salvation is the Lord's ;* the Ninevites might have written upon their gates, *Salvation is the Lord's ;* and whole mankind, whose cause is pitied and pleaded by God against the hardness of Jonah's heart, in the last, might have written on the palms of their hands, *Salvation is the Lord's.* It is the argument of both the Testaments, the staff and supportation of heaven and earth. They would both sink, and all their joints be severed, if the salvation of the Lord were not. The birds in the air sing no other notes, the beasts in the field give no other voice, than *Salus Jehovæ*, Salvation is the Lord's. The walls and fortresses to our country's gates, to our cities and towns, bars to our houses, a surer cover to our heads than a helmet of steel, a better receipt to our bodies than the confection of apothecaries, a better receipt to our souls than the pardons of Rome, is *Salus Jehovæ*, the salvation of the Lord. *The Salvation of the Lord* blesseth, preserveth, upholdeth all that we have ; our basket and our store, the oil in our cruses, our presses, the sheep in our fold, our stalls, the children in the womb, at our tables, the corn in our field, our stores, our garners ; it is not the virtue of the stars, nor nature of all things themselves, that giveth being and continuance to any of these blessings. And, " What shall I more say ? " as the apostle asked (Heb. xi.), when he had spoken much, and there was much more behind, but time failed him. Rather, what should I not say ? for the world is my theatre at this time, and I neither think nor can feign to myself anything that hath not dependence upon this acclamation, *Salvation is the Lord's.* Plutarch writeth, that the Amphictions in Greece, a famous council assembled of twelve sundry people, wrote upon the temple of Apollo Pythius, instead of the Iliads of Homer, or songs of Pindarus (large and tiring discourses), short sentences and memoratives, as, *Know thyself, Use moderation, Beware of suretyship*, and the like ; and doubtless though every creature in the world, whereof we have use, be a treatise and narration unto us of the goodness of God, and we might weary our flesh, and spend our days in writing books of that inexplicable subject, yet this short apothegm of Jonah comprehendeth all the rest, and standeth at the end of the song, as the altars and stones that the patriarch set up at the parting of the ways, to give knowledge to the after-world by what means he was delivered. I would it were daily preached in our temples, sung in our streets, written upon our door-posts, painted upon our walls, or rather cut with an adamant claw upon the tables of our hearts, that we might never forget salvation to be the Lord's. We have need of such remembrances to keep us in practice of revolving the mercies of God. For nothing decayeth sooner than love : *nihil facilius quam amor putrescit.* And of all the powers of the soul, memory is most delicate, tender, and brittle, and first waxeth old, *memoria delicata, tenera, fragilis, in quam primum senectus incurrit ;* and of all the apprehensions of memory, first benefit *primum senescit beneficium.*—*John King's Commentary on Jonah,* 1594.

Verse 8.—" *Thy blessing is upon thy people*." The saints are not only blessed when they are comprehensors, but while they are viators. They are blessed before they are crowned. This seems a paradox to flesh and blood : what, reproached and maligned, yet blessed ! A man that looks upon the children of God with a carnal eye, and sees how they are afflicted, and like the ship in the gospel, which was covered with waves (Matt. viii. 24), would think they were far from blessedness. Paul brings a catalogue of his sufferings (2 Cor. xi. 24—26), " Thrice was I beaten with rods, once was I stoned, thrice I suffered shipwreck," etc. And those Christians

of the first magnitude, of whom the world was not worthy, " Had trails of cruel
mockings and scourgings, they were sawn asunder, they were slain with the sword."
Heb. xi. 36, 37. What ! and were all these during the time of their sufferings
blessed ? A carnal man would think, if this be to be blessed, God deliver him from
it. But, however sense would give their vote, our Saviour Christ pronounceth the
godly man blessed ; though a mourner, though a martyr, yet blessed. Job on the
dunghill was blessed Job. The saints are blessed when they are cursed. Shimei
did curse David (2 Samuel xvi. 5), " He came forth and cursed him ; " yet when he
was cursed David he was blessed David. The saints though they are bruised, yet
they are blessed. Not only they shall be blessed, but they are so. Psalm cxix. 1.
" Blessed are the undefiled." Psalm iii. 8. " *Thy blessing is upon thy people.*"
—*Thomas Watson.*

---

*As a curious instance of Luther's dogmatical interpretations, we give very considerable
extracts from his rendering of this Psalm without in any degree endorsing them.
—C. H. S.*

Whole Psalm.—That the meaning of this Psalm is not historical, is manifest
from many particulars, which militate against its being so understood. And first
of all, there is this which the blessed Augustine has remarked ; that the words,
" I laid me down to sleep and took my rest," seem to be the words of Christ rising
from the dead. And then that there is at the end the blessing of God pronounced
upon the people, which manifestly belongs to the whole church. Hence, the blessed
Augustine interprets the Psalm in a threefold way : first, concerning Christ the
head ; secondly concerning the whole of Christ, that is, Christ and his church, the
head and the body ; and thirdly, figuratively, concerning any private Christian.
Let each have his own interpretation. I, in the meantime, will interpret it concerning Christ ; being moved so to do by the same argument that moved Augustine
—that the fifth verse does not seem appropriately to apply to any other but Christ.
First, because, " lying down " and " sleeping," signify in this place altogether a
natural death, not a natural sleep. Which may be collected from this—because
it then follows, " and rose again." Whereas if David had spoken concerning the
sleep of the body, he would have said, " and awoke ; " though this does not make
so forcibly for the interpretation of which we are speaking, if the Hebrew word be
closely examined. But again, what new thing would he advance by declaring that
he laid him down and slept ? Why did he not say also that he walked, ate, drank,
laboured, or was in necessity, or mention particularly some other work of the body ?
And moreover, it seems an absurdity under so great a tribulation, to boast of nothing
else but the sleep of the body ; for that tribulation would rather force him to a
privation from sleep, and to be in peril and distress ; especially since those two
expressions, " I laid me down," and " I slept," signify the quiet repose of one lying
down in his place, which is not the state of one who falls asleep from exhausture
through sorrow. But this consideration makes the more forcibly for us—that he
therefore glories in his rising up again because it was the Lord that sustained him,
who raised him up while sleeping, and did not leave him in sleep. How can such a
glorying agree, and what new kind of religion can make it agree, with any particular
sleep of the body ? (for in that case, would it not apply to the daily sleep also ?) and
especially, when this sustaining of God indicates at the same time an utterly forsaken
state in the person sleeping, which is not the case in corporal sleep ; for there the
person sleeping may be protected even by men being his guards ; but this sustaining
being altogether of God, implies, not a sleep, but a heavy conflict. And lastly, the
word HEKIZOTHI itself favours such an interpretation ; which, being here put
absolutely and transitively, signifies, " I caused to arise or awake." As if he had
said, " I caused myself to awake, I roused myself." Which certainly more aptly
agrees with the resurrection of Christ than with the sleep of the body ; both because
those who are asleep are accustomed to be roused and awaked, and because it is
no wonderful matter, nor a matter worthy of so important a declaration, for any
one to awake of himself, seeing that it is what takes place every day. But this
matter being introduced by the Spirit as a something new and singular, is certainly
different from all that which attends common sleeping and waking.

Verse 2.—" *There is no help for him in his God.*" In the Hebrew the expression is simply, " in God," without the pronoun " *his,*" which seems to me to give clearness and force to the expression. As if he had said, They say of me that I am not only deserted and oppressed by all creatures, but that even God, who is present with all things, and preserves all things, and protects all things, forsakes me as the only thing out of the whole universe that he does not preserve. Which kind of temptation Job seems also to have tasted where he says, " Why hast thou set me as a mark against thee ? " vii. 20. For there is no temptation, no, not of the whole world together, nor of all hell combined in one, equal unto that wherein God stands contrary to a man, which temptation Jeremiah prays against (xvii. 17), " Be not a terror unto me ; thou art my hope in the day of evil ; " and concerning which also the sixth Psalm following saith, " O Lord, rebuke me not in thine anger ; " and we find the same petitions throughout the psaltery. This temptation is wholly unsupportable, and is truly hell itself ; as it is said in the same sixth Psalm, " for in death there is no remembrance of thee," etc. In a word, if you have never experienced it, you can never form any idea of it whatever.

Verse 3.—" *For thou, O Lord, art my helper, my glory, and the lifter up of my head.*" David here contrasts three things with three ; helper, with many troubling ; glory, with many rising up ; and the lifter up of the head, with the blaspheming and insulting. Therefore, the person here represented is indeed alone in the estimation of man, and even according to his own feelings also ; but in the sight of God, and in a spiritual view, he is by no means alone ; but protected with the greatest abundance of help ; as Christ saith (John xvi. 32), " Behold, the hour cometh when ye shall leave me alone ; and yet I am not alone, because the Father is with me." .... The words contained in this verse are not the words of nature, but of grace ; not of free-will, but of the spirit of strong faith ; which, even though seeing God, as in the darkness of the storm of death and hell, a deserting God, acknowledges him a sustaining God ; when seeing him as a persecuting God, acknowledges him a helping God ; when seeing him as a condemner, acknowledges him a Saviour. Thus this faith does not judge of things according as they seem to be, or are felt, like a horse or mule which have no understanding ; but it understands things which are not seen, for " hope that is seen is not hope : for what a man seeth, why doth he yet hope for ? " Romans viii. 24.

Verse 4.—" *I cried unto the Lord with my voice, and he heard me out of his holy hill.*" In the Hebrew, the verb is in the future, and is, as Hieronymus translates it, " I will cry," and, " he shall hear ; " and this pleases me better than the perfect tense ; for they are the words of one triumphing in, and praising and glorifying God, and giving thanks unto him who sustained, preserved, and lifted him up, according as he had hoped in the preceding verse. For it is usual with those that triumph and rejoice, to speak of those things which they have done and suffered, and to sing a song of praise unto their helper and deliverer ; as in Psalm lxvi. 16, " Come, then, all ye that fear God, and I will declare what he hath done for my soul. I cried unto him with my mouth, and he was extolled with my tongue." And also Psalm lxxxi. 1, " Sing aloud unto God our strength." And so again, Exodus xv. 1, " Let us sing unto the Lord, for he hath triumphed gloriously." And so here, being filled with an overflowing sense of gratitude and joy, he sings of his being dead, of his having slept and rose up again, of his enemies being smitten, and of the teeth of the ungodly being broken. This it is which causes the change ; for he who hitherto had been addressing God in the second person, changes on a sudden his address to others concerning God, in the third person, saying, " *and he heard me,*" not " and thou heardest me ; " and also, " *I cried unto the Lord,*" not " I cried unto thee," for he wants to make all know what benefits God has heaped upon him ; which is peculiar to a grateful mind.

Verse 5.—" *I laid me down and slept ; I awaked ; for the Lord sustained me.*" Christ, by the words of this verse signifies his death and burial .... For it is not to be supposed that he would have spoken so importantly concerning mere natural rest and sleep ; especially since that which precedes, and that which follows, compel us to understand him as speaking of a deep conflict and a glorious victory over his enemies. By all which things he stirs us up and animates us to faith in God, and commends unto us the power and grace of God ; that he is able to raise us up from the dead ; an example of which he sets before us, and proclaims it unto us as wrought in himself . . . . And this is shown also farther in his using gentle words, and such as tend wonderfully to lessen the terror of death. " *I laid me down* (saith he), *and slept.*" He does not say, I died and was buried ; for death and the tomb had lost both their name and their power. And now death is not death, but a sleep ; and the tomb not a tomb, but a bed and resting place ; which was the reason why the words of this prophecy were put somewhat obscurely and doubtfully, that it might by that means render death most lovely in our eyes (or rather most contemptible), as being that state from which, as from the sweet rest of sleep, an undoubted arising and awaking are promised. For who is not most sure of an awaking and arising, who lies down to rest in a sweet sleep (where death does not prevent) ? This person, however, does not say that he died, but that he laid him down to sleep, and that therefore he awaked. And moreover, as sleep is useful and necessary for a better renewal of the powers of the body (as Ambrosius says in his hymn), and as sleep relieves the weary limbs, so is death also equally useful, and ordained for the arriving at a better life. And this is what David says in the following Psalm, " I will lay me down in peace, and take my rest, for thou, Lord, in a singular manner hast formed me in hope." Therefore, in considering death, we are not so much to consider death itself, as that most certain life and resurrection which are sure to those who are in Christ ; that those words (John viii. 51) might be fulfilled, " If a man keep my saying, he shall never see death." But how is it that he shall never see it ? Shall he not feel it ? Shall he not die ? No ! he shall only see sleep, for, having the eyes of his faith fixed upon the resurrection, he so glides through death, that he does not even see death ; for death, as I have said, is to him no death at all. And hence, there is that also of John xi. 25, " He that believeth in me, though he were dead, yet shall he live."

Verse 7.—" *For thou hast smitten all mine enemies upon the cheek bone ; thou hast broken the teeth of the ungodly.*" Hieronymus uses this metaphor of " *cheek bones,*" and " *teeth,*" to represent cutting words, detractions, calumnies, and other injuries of the same kind, by which the innocent are oppressed : according to that of Proverbs xxx. 14, " There is a generation whose teeth are as swords, and their jaw-teeth as knives, to devour the poor from off the earth, and the needy from among men." It was by these that Christ was devoured, when, before Pilate he was condemned to the cross by the voices and accusations of his enemies. And hence it is that the apostle saith (Gal. v. 15), " But if ye bite and devour one another, take heed that ye be not consumed one of another."

Verse 8.—" *Salvation is of the Lord, and thy blessing is upon thy people.*" A most beautiful conclusion this, and, as it were, the sum of all the feelings spoken of. The sense is, it is the Lord alone that saves and blesses : and even though the whole mass of all evils should be gathered together in one against a man, still, it is the Lord who saves : salvation and blessing are in his hands. What then shall I fear ? What shall I not promise myself ? When I know that no one can be destroyed, no one reviled, without the permission of God, even though all should rise up to curse and to destroy ; and that no one of them can be blessed and saved without the permission of God, how much soever they may bless and strive to save themselves. And as Gregory Nazianzen says, " Where God gives, envy can avail nothing ; and where God does not give labour can avail nothing." And in the same way also Paul saith (Rom. viii. 31), " If God be for us, who can be against us ? " And so, on the contrary, if God be against them, who can be for them ? And why ? Because " *salvation is of the Lord,*" and not of them, nor of us, for " vain is the help of man."—*Martin Luther.*

HINTS TO PREACHERS.

Verse 1.—" *The saint telling his griefs to his God.* (1) His right to do so. (2) The proper manner of telling them. (3) The fair results of such holy communications with the Lord.

When may we expect increased troubles ? Why are they sent ? What is our wisdom in reference to them ?

Verse 2.—The lie against the saint and the libel upon his God.

Verse 3.—The threefold blessing which God affords to his suffering ones— Defence, Honour, Joy. Show how all these may be enjoyed by faith, even in our worst estate.

Verse 4.—(1) In dangers we should pray. (2) God will graciously hear. (3) We should record his answers of grace. (4) We may strengthen ourselves for the future by remembering the deliverances of the past.

Verse 5.—(1) Describe sweet sleeping. (2) Describe happy waking. (3) Show how both are to be enjoyed, *" for the Lord sustained me."*

Verse 6.—Faith surrounded by enemies and yet triumphant.

Verse 7.—(1) Describe the Lord's past dealing with his enemies ; " thou hast." (2) Show that the Lord should be our constant resort, " O Lord," " O my God." (3) Enlarge upon the fact that the Lord is to be stirred up : " Arise." (4) Urge believers to use the Lord's past victories as an argument with which to prevail with him.

Verse 7 (last clause).—Our enemies vanquished foes, toothless lions.

Verse 8 (first clause).—Salvation of God from first to last. (See the exposition).

Verse 8 (last clause).—They were blessed *in* Christ, *through* Christ, and shall be blessed *with* Christ. The blessing rests upon their persons, comforts, trials, labours, families, etc. It flows from grace, is enjoyed by faith, and is insured by oath, etc.
—*James Smith's Portions,* 1802—1862.

PSALM IV.

TITLE.—*This Psalm is apparently intended to accompany the third, and make a pair with it. If the last may be entitled* THE MORNING PSALM, *this from its matter is equally deserving of the title of* THE EVENING HYMN. *May the choice words of the 8th verse be our sweet song of rest as we retire to our repose!*

> " Thus with my thoughts composed to peace,
>   I'll give mine eyes to sleep ;
>   Thy hand in safety keeps my days,
>   And will my slumbers keep."

The Inspired title runs thus : " To the chief Musician on Neginoth, a Psalm of David." *The chief musician was the master or director of the sacred music of the sanctuary. Concerning this person carefully read* 1 Chron. vi. 31, 32 ; xv. 16—22 ; xxv. 1, 7. *In these passages will be found much that is interesting to the lover of sacred song, and very much that will throw a light upon the mode of praising God in the temple. Some of the titles of the Psalms are, we doubt not, derived from the names of certain renowned singers, who composed the music to which they were set.*

On Neginoth, *that is, on stringed instruments, or* hand *instruments, which were played on with the hand alone, as harps and cymbals. The joy of the Jewish church was so great that they needed music to set forth the delightful feelings of their souls, our holy mirth is none the less overflowing because we prefer to express it in a more spiritual manner, as becometh a more spiritual dispensation. In allusion to these instruments to be played on with the hand, Nazianzen says. "Lord I am an instrument for thee to touch." Let us lay ourselves open to the Spirit's touch, so shall we make melody. May we be full of faith and love, and we shall be living instruments of music.*

Hawker says " The Septuagint read the word which we have rendered in our translation chief musician Lamenetz, *instead of* Lamenetzoth, *the meaning of which is* unto the end." *From whence the Greek and Latin fathers imagined, that all psalms which bear this inscription refer to the Messiah the great end. If so, this Psalm is addressed to Christ ; and well it may, for it is all of Christ, and spoken by Christ, and hath respect only to his people as being one with Christ. The Lord the Spirit give the reader to see this, and he will find it most blessed.*

DIVISION.—*In the first verse David pleads with God for help. In the second he expostulates with his enemies, and continues to address them to the end of verse 5. Then from verse 6 to the close he delightfully contrasts his own satisfaction and safety with the disquietude of the ungodly in their best estate. The Psalm was most probably written upon the same occasion as the preceding, and is another choice flower from the garden of affliction. Happy is it for us that David was tried. or probably we should never have heard these sweet sonnets of faith.*

EXPOSITION.

HEAR me when I call, O God of my righteousness : thou hast enlarged me *when I was* in distress ; have mercy upon me, and hear my prayer.

This is another instance of David's common habit of pleading past mercies as a ground for present favour. Here he reviews his Ebenezers and takes comfort from them. It is not to be imagined that he who has helped us in six troubles will leave us in the seventh. God does nothing by halves, and he will never cease to help us until we cease to need. The manna shall fall every morning until we cross the Jordan.

Observe, that David speaks first to God and then to men. Surely we should all speak the more boldly to men if we had more constant converse with God. He who dares to face his Maker will not tremble before the sons of men.

The name by which the Lord is here addressed, " *God of my righteousness,*" deserves notice, since it is not used in any other part of Scripture. It means, Thou art the author, the witness, the maintainer, the judge, and the rewarder of my righteousness ; to thee I appeal from the calumnies and harsh judgments of men. Herein is wisdom, let us imitate it and always take our suit, not to the petty courts of human opinion. but into the superior court, the King's Bench of heaven.

" *Thou hast enlarged me when I was in distress.*" A figure taken from an army enclosed in a defile, and hardly pressed by the surrounding enemy. God hath dashed down the rocks and given me room ; he hath broken the barriers and set me in a large place. Or, we may understand it thus :—" God hath enlarged my heart with joy and comfort when I was like a man imprisoned by grief and sorrow." God is a never-failing comforter.

" *Have mercy upon me.*" Though thou mayest justly permit my enemies to destroy me, on account of my many and great sins, yet I flee to thy mercy, and I beseech thee *hear my prayer*, and bring thy servant out of his troubles. The best of men need mercy as truly as the worst of men. All the deliverances of saints, as well as the pardons of sinners, are the free gifts of heavenly grace.

2 O ye sons of men, how long *will ye turn* my glory into shame ? *how long* will ye love vanity, *and* seek after leasing ? Selah.

In this second division of the Psalm, we are led from the closet of prayer into the field of conflict. Remark the undaunted courage of the man of God. He allows that his enemies are great men (for such is the import of the Hebrew words translated —*sons of men*), but still he believes them to be foolish men, and therefore chides them, as though they were but children. He tells them that they *love vanity, and seek after leasing*, that is, lying, empty fancies, vain conceits, wicked fabrications. He asks them *how long* they mean to make his honour a jest, and his fame a mockery ? A little of such mirth is too much, why need they continue to indulge in it ? Had they not been long enough upon the watch for his halting ? Had not repeated disappointments convinced them that the Lord's anointed was not to be overcome by all their calumnies ? Did they mean to jest their souls into hell, and go on with their laughter until swift vengeance should turn their merriment into howling ? In the contemplation of their perverse continuance in their vain and lying pursuits, the Psalmist solemnly pauses and inserts a *Selah*. Surely we too may stop awhile, and meditate upon the deep-seated folly of the wicked, their continuance in evil, and their sure destruction ; and we may learn to admire that grace which has made us to differ, and taught us to *love* truth, and *seek* after *righteousness*.

3 But know that the LORD hath set apart him that is godly for himself : the LORD will hear when I call unto him.

" *But know.*" Fools will not learn, and therefore they must again and again be told the same thing, especially when it is such a bitter truth which is to be taught them, viz :—the fact that the godly are the chosen of God, and are, by distinguishing grace, set apart and separated from among men. Election is a doctrine which un- renewed men cannot endure, but nevertheless, it is a glorious and well-attested truth, and one which should comfort the tempted believer. Election is the guarantee of complete salvation, and an argument for success at the throne of grace. HE who chose us for himself will surely hear our prayers. The Lord's elect shall not be con- demned, nor shall their cry be unheard. David was king by divine decree, and we are the Lord's people in the same manner ; let us tell our enemies to their faces, that they fight against God and destiny, when they strive to overthrow our souls. O beloved, when you are on your knees, the fact of your being *set apart* as God's own peculiar treasure, should give you courage and inspire you with fervency and faith. " Shall not God avenge his own elect, which cry day and night unto him ? " Since he chose to love us he cannot but chose to hear us.

4 Stand in awe, and sin not : commune with your own heart upon your bed, and be still. Selah.

" *Tremble and sin not.*" How many reverse this counsel and sin but tremble not. O that men would take the advice of this verse and *commune with their own hearts*. Surely a want of thought must be one reason why men are so mad as to despise Christ and hate their own mercies. O that for once their passions would be quiet and let them *be still*, that so in solemn silence they might review the past, and meditate upon their inevitable doom. Surely a thinking man might have enough sense to discover the vanity of sin and the worthlessness of the world. Stay, rash sinner, stay ere thou take the last leap. Go to *thy bed* and think upon thy ways.

Ask counsel of thy pillow, and let the quietude of night instruct thee ! Throw not away thy soul for nought ! Let reason speak ! Let the clamorous world be still awhile, and let thy poor soul plead with thee to bethink thyself before thou seal its fate, and ruin it for ever ! *Selah.* O sinner ! pause while I question thee awhile in the words of a sacred poet,—

> " Sinner, is thy heart at rest ?
>   Is thy bosom void of fear ?
> Art thou not by guilt oppress'd ?
>   Speaks not conscience in thine ear ?
>
> Can this world afford thee bliss ?
>   Can it chase away thy gloom ?
> Flattering, false, and vain it is ;
>   Tremble at the worldling's doom !
>
> Think, O sinner, on thy end,
>   See the judgment-day appear,
> Thither must thy spirit wend,
>   There thy righteous sentence hear.
>
> Wretched, ruin'd, helpless soul,
>   To a Saviour's blood apply ;
> He alone can make thee whole,
>   Fly to Jesus, sinner, fly ! "

5 Offer the sacrifices of righteousness, and put your trust in the LORD.

Provided that the rebels had obeyed the voice of the last verse, they would now be crying,—" What shall we do to be saved ? " And in the present verse, they are pointed to the *sacrifice*, and exhorted to *trust in the Lord.* When the Jew offered sacrifice righteously, that is, in a spiritual manner, he thereby set forth the Redeemer, the great sin-atoning Lamb ; there is, therefore, the full gospel in this exhortation of the Psalmist. O sinners, flee ye to the sacrifices of Calvary, and there put your whole confidence and *trust*, for he who died for men is the LORD JEHOVAH.

6 *There be* many that say, Who will shew us *any* good ? LORD, lift thou up the light of thy countenance upon us.

We have now entered upon the third division of the Psalm, in which the faith of the afflicted one finds utterance in sweet expressions of contentment and peace. There were many, even among David's own followers, who wanted to *see* rather than to believe. Alas ! this is the tendency of us all ! Even the regenerate sometimes groan after the sense and sight of prosperity, and are sad when darkness covers all good from view. As for worldlings, this is their unceasing cry. " *Who will shew us any good ?* " Never satisfied, their gaping mouths are turned in every direction, their empty hearts are ready to drink in any fine delusion which impostors may invent ; and when these fail, they soon yield to despair, and declare that there is no good thing in either heaven or earth. The true believer is a man of a very different mould. His face is not downward like the beasts', but upward like the angels'. He drinks not from the muddy pools of Mammon, but from the fountain of life above. The light of God's countenance is enough for him. This is his riches, his honour, his health, his ambition, his ease. Give him this, and he will ask no more. This is joy unspeakable, and full of glory. Oh, for more of the indwelling of the Holy Spirit, that our fellowship with the Father and with his Son Jesus Christ may be constant and abiding !

7 Thou hast put gladness in my heart, more than in the time *that* their corn and their wine increased.

" It is better," said one, " to feel God's favour one hour in our repenting souls, than to sit whole ages under the warmest sunshine that this world affordeth." Christ in the heart is better than corn in the barn, or wine in the vat. Corn and wine are but fruits of the world, but the light of God's countenance is the ripe fruit of heaven. " Thou art with me," is a far more blessed cry than " Harvest home." Let my granary be empty, I am yet full of blessings if Jesus Christ smiles upon me ; but if I have all the world, I am poor without Him.

We should not fail to remark that this verse is the *saying* of the righteous man, in opposition to the saying of the many. How quickly doth the tongue betray the character! " *Speak*, that I may see thee!" said Socrates to a fair boy. The metal of a bell is best known by its sound. Birds reveal their nature by their song. Owls cannot sing the carol of the lark, nor can the nightingale hoot like the owl. Let us, then, weigh and watch our words, lest our speech should prove us to be foreigners, and aliens from the commonwealth of Israel.

8 I will both lay me down in peace, and sleep: for thou, LORD, only makest me dwell in safety.

Sweet Evening Hymn! I shall not sit up to watch through fear, but I will *lie down ;* and then I will not lie awake listening to every rustling sound, but I will lie down *in peace and sleep*, for I have nought to fear. He that hath the wings of God above him needs no other curtain. Better than bolts or bars is the protection of the Lord. Armed men kept the bed of Solomon, but we do not believe that he slept more soundly than his father, whose bed was the hard ground, and who was haunted by blood-thirsty foes. Note the word " *only*," which means that God alone was his keeper, and that though alone, without man's help, he was even then in good keeping, for he was " alone with God." A quiet conscience is a good bedfellow. How many of our sleepless hours might be traced to our untrusting and disordered minds. They slumber sweetly whom faith rocks to sleep. No pillow so soft as a promise ; no coverlet so warm as an assured interest in Christ.

O Lord, give us this calm repose on thee, that like David we may lie down in peace, and sleep each night while we live ; and joyfully may we lie down in the appointed season, to sleep in death, to rest in God!

Dr. Hawker's reflection upon this Psalm is worthy to be prayed over and fed upon with sacred delight. We cannot help transcribing it.

" Reader! let us never lose sight of the Lord Jesus while reading this psalm. He is the Lord our righteousness ; and therefore, in all our approaches to the mercy seat, let us go there in a language corresponding to this which calls Jesus the Lord our righteousness. While men of the world, from the world are seeking their chief good, let us desire his favour which infinitely transcends corn and wine, and all the good things which perish in the using. Yes, Lord, *thy favour is better than life itself.* Thou causest them that love thee to inherit substance, and fillest all their treasure.

Oh! thou gracious God and Father, hast thou in such a wonderful manner set apart one in our nature for thyself? Hast thou indeed chosen one out of the people? Hast thou beheld him in the purity of his nature,—as one in every point godly? Hast thou given him as the covenant of the people? And hast thou declared thyself well pleased in him? Oh! then, well may my soul be well pleased in him also. Now do I know that my God and Father will hear me when I call upon him in Jesus' name, and when I look up to him for acceptance for Jesus' sake? Yes, my heart is fixed, O Lord, my heart is fixed ; Jesus is my hope and righteousness, the Lord will hear me when I call. And henceforth will I both lay me down in peace and sleep securely in Jesus, accepted in the Beloved ; for *this is the rest wherewith the Lord causeth the weary to rest, and this is the refreshing.*

EXPLANATORY NOTES AND QUAINT SAYINGS.

Verse 1.—" *Hear me when I call*," etc. Faith is a good orator and a noble dis-puter in a strait ; it can reason from God's readiness to hear : " *Hear me when I call, O God.*" And from the everlasting righteousness given to the man in the justi-fication of his person : " *O God of my righteousness.*" And from God's constant justice in defending the righteousness of his servant's cause : " *O God of my righteous-ness.*" And from both present distresses and those that are by-past, wherein he hath been, and from by-gone mercies received : " *Thou hast enlarged me when I was in distress.*" And from God's grace, which is able to answer all objections from the man's unworthiness or ill-deserving : " *Have mercy upon me, and hear my prayer.*"—*David Dickson*, 1653.

Verse 1.—" *Hear me.*" The great Author of nature and of all things does nothing in vain. He instituted not this law, and, if I may so express it, art of praying, as a vain and insufficient thing, but endows it with wonderful efficacy for producing the greatest and happiest consequences. He would have it to be the key by which all the treasures of heaven should be opened. He has constructed it as a powerful machine, by which we may, with easy and pleasant labour, remove from us the most dire and unhappy machinations of our enemy, and may with equal ease draw to ourselves what is most propitious and advantageous. Heaven and earth, and all the elements, obey and minister to the hands which are often lifted up to heaven in earnest prayer. Yea, all works, and, which is yet more and greater, all the words of God obey it. Well known in the sacred Scriptures are the examples of Moses and Joshua, and that which James (v. 17) particularly mentions of Elijah, whom he expressly calls ὁμοιοπαθὴς, *a man subject to like infirmities* with ourselves, that he might illustrate the admirable force of prayer, by the common and human weakness of the person by whom it was offered. And that Christian legion under Antoninus is well known and justly celebrated, which, for the singular ardour and efficacy of its prayers, obtained the name of κεραυνοβόλος, *the thundering legion.—Robert Leighton, D.D., Archbishop of Glasgow*, 1611—1684.

Verse 2.—" *O ye sons of men, how long will ye turn my glory into shame? how long will ye love vanity, and seek after leasing? Selah.*" Prayer soars above the violence and impiety of men, and with a swift wing commits itself to heaven, with happy omen, if I may allude to what the learned tell us of the augury of the ancients, which I shall not minutely discuss. Fervent prayers stretch forth a strong, wide-extended wing, and while the birds of night hover beneath, they mount aloft, and point out, as it were, the proper seats to which we should aspire. For certainly there is nothing that cuts the air so swiftly, nothing that takes so sublime, so happy, and so auspicious a flight as prayer, which bears the soul on its pinions, and leaves far behind all the dangers, and even the delights of this low world of ours. Behold this holy man, who just before was crying to God in the midst of distress, and with urgent importunity entreating that he might be heard, now, as if he were already possessed of all he had asked, taking upon him boldly to rebuke his enemies, how highly soever they were exalted, and how potent soever they might be even in the royal palace.—*Robert Leighton, D.D.*

Verse 2.—" *O ye sons of men, how long will ye turn my glory into shame?*" etc. We might imagine every syllable of this precious Psalm used by our Master some evening, when about to leave the temple for the day, and retiring to his wonted rest at Bethany (verse 8), after another fruitless expostulation with the men of Israel. And we may read it still as the very utterance of his heart, longing over man, and delighting in God. But further, not only is this the utterance of the Head, it is also the language of one of his members in full sympathy with him in holy feeling. This is a Psalm with which the righteous may make their dwellings resound, morning and evening, as they cast a sad look over a world that rejects God's grace. They may sing it while they cling more and more every day to Jehovah, as their all-sufficient heritage, now and in the age to come. They may sing it, too, in the happy confidence of faith and hope, when the evening of the world's day is coming, and may then fall asleep in the certainty of what shall greet their eyes on the resurrection morning—

> " Sleeping embosomed in his grace,
> Till morning-shadows flee."

Andrew A. Bonar, 1859.

Verse 2.—" *Love Vanity.*" They that love sin, love *vanity ;* they chase a bubble, they lean upon a reed, their hope is as a spider's web.

" *Leasing.*" This is an old Saxon word signifying falsehood.

Verse 2.—" *How long will ye love vanity, and seek after leasing?*" "Vanity of vanities, and all is vanity." This our first parents found, and therefore named their second son Abel, or vanity. Solomon, that had tried these things, and could best tell the vanity of them, he preacheth this sermon over again and again, " Vanity of vanities, and all is vanity." It is sad to think how many thousands there be that can say with the preacher, " Vanity of vanities, all is vanity;" nay, swear it, and yet follow after these things as if there were no other glory, nor felicity, but what is to be found in these things they call vanity. Such men will sell Christ, heaven, and their souls, for a trifle, that call these things vanity, but do not cordially believe them to be vanity, but set their hearts upon them as if they were their crown, the top of all their royalty and glory. Oh! let your souls dwell upon the vanity of all things here below, till your hearts be so thoroughly convinced and persuaded of the vanity of them, as to trample upon them, and make them a footstool for Christ to get up, and ride in a holy triumph in your hearts.

Gilemex, king of Vandals, led in triumph by Belisarius, cried out, "Vanity of vanities, all is vanity." The fancy of Lucian, who placeth Charon on the top of a high hill, viewing all the affairs of men living, and looking on their greatest cities as little birds' nests, is very pleasant. Oh, the imperfection, the ingratitude, the levity, the inconstancy, the perfidiousness of those creatures we most servilely affect! Ah, did we but weigh man's pain with his payment, his crosses with his mercies, his miseries with his pleasures, we should then see that there is nothing got by the bargain, and conclude, "Vanity of vanities, all is vanity." Chrysostom said once, "That if he were the fittest in the world to preach a sermon to the whole world, gathered together in one congregation, and had some high mountain for his pulpit, from whence he might have a prospect of all the world in his view, and were furnished with a voice of brass, a voice as loud as the trumpets of the archangel, that all the world might hear him, he would choose to preach upon no other text than that in the Psalms, O mortal men, ' How long will ye love vanity, and follow after leasing?'"—*Thomas Brooks*, 1608—1680.

Verse 2.—" *Love Vanity*." Men's affections are according to their principles; and every one loves that most *without him* which is most suitable to somewhat *within him : liking* is founded in *likeness*, and has therefore that word put upon it. It is so in whatsoever we can imagine ; whether in temporals or spirituals, as to the things of this life, or of a better. Men's love is according to some working and impression upon their own spirits. And so it is here in the point of vanity ; those which are vain persons, they delight in vain things ; as children, they love such matters as are most agreeable to their childish dispositions, and as do suit them in that particular. Out of the heart comes all kind of evil.—*Thomas Horton*, 1675.

Verse 3.—" *The Lord hath set apart him that is godly for himself.*" When God chooseth a man, he chooseth him for himself ; for himself to converse with, to communicate himself unto him as a friend, a companion, and his delight. Now, it is holiness that makes us fit to live with the holy God for ever, since without it we cannot see him (Heb. xii. 14), which is God's main aim, and more than our being his children ; as one must be supposed a man, one of mankind, having a soul reasonable, ere we can suppose him capable of adoption, or to be another man's heir. As therefore it was the main first design in God's eye, before the consideration of our happiness, let it be so in ours.—*Thomas Goodwin*, 1600—1679.

Verse 3.—What rare persons the godly are : " The righteous is more excellent than his neighbour." Prov. xii. 26. As the flower of the sun, as the wine of Lebanon, as the sparkling upon Aaron's breastplate, such is the orient splendour of a person embellished with godliness . . . . . The godly are precious, therefore they are set apart for God, " *Know that the Lord hath set apart him that is godly for himself.*" We set apart things that are precious ; the godly are set apart as God's peculiar treasure (Psalm cxxxv. 4) ; as his garden of delight (Cant. iv. 12) ; as his royal diadem (Isaiah xliii. 3) ; the godly are the excellent of the earth (Psalm xvi. 3) ; comparable to fine gold (Lam. iv. 2) ; double refined. Zech. xiii. 9. They are the glory of the creation. Isaiah xlvi. 13. Origen compares the saints to sapphires and crystals : God calls them jewels. Mal. iii. 17.—*Thomas Watson*.

Verse 3.—" *The Lord will hear when I call unto him.*" Let us remember that the experience of one of the saints concerning the verity of God's promises, and of the certainty of the written privileges of the Lord's people, is a sufficient proof of the right which all his children have to the same mercies, and a ground of hope that they also shall partake of them in their times of need.—*David Dickson*, 1653.

Verse 4.—" *Stand in awe, and sin not.*" Jehovah is a name of great power and efficacy, a name that hath in it five vowels, without which no language can be expressed ; a name that hath in it also three syllables, to signify the Trinity of persons, the eternity of God, One in Three and Three in One ; a name of such dread and reverence amongst the Jews, that they tremble to name it, and therefore they use the name *Adonai* (*Lord*) in all their devotions. And thus ought every one to " *stand in awe, and sin not,*" by taking the name of God in vain ; but to sing praise, and honour, to remember, to declare, to exalt, to praise and bless it ; for holy and reverend, only worthy and excellent is his name.—*Rayment*, 1630.

Verse 4.—" *Commune with your own heart.*" The language is similar to that which we use when we say, " Consult your better judgment," or, " Take counsel of your own good sense."—*Albert Barnes, in loc.*

Verse 4.—If thou wouldst exercise thyself to godliness in solitude, accustom thyself to soliloquies, I mean to conference with thyself. He needs never be idle that hath so much business to do with his own soul. It was a famous answer which Antisthenes gave when he was asked what fruit he reaped by all his studies. By them, saith he, I have learned both to live and talk with myself. Soliloquies are the best disputes ; every good man is best company for himself of all the creatures. Holy David enjoineth this to others, " *Commune with your own hearts upon your bed, and be still.*" " *Commune with your own hearts ;*" when ye have none to speak with, talk to yourselves. Ask yourselves for what end ye were made, what lives ye have led, what times ye have lost, what love ye have abused, what wrath ye have deserved. Call yourselves to a reckoning, how ye have improved your talents, how true or false ye have been to your trust, what provision ye have laid in for an hour of death, what preparation ye have made for a great day of account. " *Upon your beds.*" Secrecy is the best opportunity for this duty. The silent night is a good time for this speech. When we have no outward objects to disturb us, and to call our eyes, as the fool's eyes are always, to the ends of the earth ; then our eyes, as the eyes of the wise, may be in our heads ; and then our minds, like the windows in Solomon's temple, may be broad inwards. The most successful searches have been made in the night season ; the soul is then wholly shut up in the earthly house of the body, and hath no visits from strangers to disquiet its thoughts. Physicians have judged dreams a probable sign whereby they might find out the distempers of the body. Surely, then, the bed is no bad place to examine and search into the state of the soul. " *And be still.*" Self-communion will much help to curb your headstrong, ungodly passions. Serious consideration, like the casting up of earth amongst bees, will allay inordinate affections when they are full of fury, and make such a hideous noise. Though sensual appetites and unruly desires are, as the people of Ephesus, in an uproar, pleading for their former privilege, and expecting their wonted provision, as in the days of their predominancy, if conscience use its authority, commanding them in God's name, whose officer it is, to keep the king's peace, and argue it with them, as the town-clerk of Ephesus, " We are in danger to be called in question for this days's uproar, there being no cause whereby we may give an account of this day's concourse ; " all is frequently by this means hushed, and the tumult appeased without any further mischief.—*George Swinnock*, 1627—1673.

Verse 4.—" *Commune with your own heart upon your bed, and be still.*" When we are most retired from the world, then we are most fit to have, and usually have, most communion with God. If a man would but abridge himself of sleep, and wake with holy thoughts, when deep sleep falleth upon sorrowful labouring men, he might be entertained with visions from God, though not such visions as Eliphaz and others of the saints have had, yet visions he might have. Every time God communicates himself to the soul, there is a vision of love, or mercy, or power, somewhat of God in his nature, or in his will, is showed unto us. David shows us divine work when we go to rest. The bed is not all for sleep : " *Commune with your own heart upon your bed, and be still.*" Be still or quiet, and then commune with your hearts ; and if *you* will commune with your hearts, God will come and commune with your hearts too, his Spirit will give you a loving visit and visions of his love.—*Joseph Caryl.*

Verse 4.—" *Stand in awe.*"

> With sacred *awe* pronounce his name,
> Whom words nor thoughts can reach.
>   *John Needham*, 1768.

Verse 6.—Where Christ reveals himself there is satisfaction in the slenderest portion, and without Christ there is emptiness in the greatest fulness.—*Alexander Grosse, on enjoying Christ*, 1632.

Verse 6.—" *Many*," said David, " *ask who will shew us any good ?* " meaning riches, and honour, and pleasure, which are not good. But when he came to godliness itself, he leaves out " *many*," and prayeth in his own person, " *Lord, lift thou up the light of thy countenance upon us ;* " as if none would join with him.—*Henry Smith.*

Verse 6.—" *Who will shew us any good ?* " This is not a fair translation. The word *any* is not in the text, nor anything equivalent to it ; and not a few have quoted *it*, and preached upon the text, placing the principal emphasis upon this illegitimate. The place is sufficiently emphatic. There are *multitudes who say, Who will shew us good ?* Man wants *good ;* he hates *evil* as evil, because he has *pain, suffering*, and *death* through it ; and he wishes to find that *supreme good* which will content his heart, and save him from evil. But men mistake this good. They look for a good that is to gratify their *passions ;* they have no notion of any happiness that does not come to them through the *medium of their senses.* Therefore they reject *spiritual good*, and they reject the supreme God, by whom alone all the powers of the soul of man can be gratified.—*Adam Clarke.*

Verse 6.—" *Lift thou up*," etc. This was the blessing of the high priest and is the heritage of all the saints. It includes reconciliation, assurance, communion, benediction, in a word, the fulness of God. Oh, to be filled therewith !—*C. H. S.*

Verses 6, 7.—Lest riches should be accounted evil in themselves, God sometimes gives them to the righteous; and lest they should be considered as the *chief good*, he frequently bestows them on the wicked. But they are more generally the portion of his enemies than his friends. Alas ! what is it to receive and not to be received ? to have none other dews of blessing than such as shall be followed by showers of brimstone ? We may compass ourselves with sparks of security, and afterwards be secured in eternal misery. This world is a floating island, and so sure as we cast anchor *upon* it, we shall be carried away *by* it. God, and all that he has made, is not more than God without anything that he has made. He can never want treasure who has such a golden mine. *He* is enough without the creature, but the *creature* is not anything without him. It is, therefore, better to enjoy him without anything else, than to enjoy everything else without him. It is better to be a wooden vessel filled with wine, than a golden one filled with water. *William Secker's Nonsuch Professor,* 1660.

Verse 7.— What madness and folly is it that the favourites of heaven should envy the men of the world, who at best do but feed upon the scraps that come from God's table ! Temporals are the bones ; spirituals are the marrow. Is it below a man to envy the dogs, because of the bones ? And is it not much more below a Christian to envy others for temporals, when himself enjoys spirituals ? *Thomas Brooks.*

Verse 7.—" *Thou hast put gladness in my heart.*" The comforts which God reserves for his mourners are filling comforts (Rom. xv. 13) ; " The God of hope fill you with joy " (John xvi. 24) ; " Ask that your joy may be full." When God pours in the joys of heaven they fill the heart, and make it run over (2 Cor. vii. 4); " I am exceeding joyful ; " the Greek is, I overflow with joy, as a cup that is filled with wine till it runs over. Outward comforts can no more fill the heart than a triangle can fill a circle. Spiritual joys are satisfying (Psalm lxiii. 5) ; " My heart shall be satisfied as with marrow and fatness ; and my mouth shall praise thee with joyful lips ; " " *Thou hast put gladness in my heart.*" Worldly joys do put gladness into the face, but the spirit of God puts gladness into the heart; divine joys are heart joys (Zech. x. 7 ; John xvi. 22) ; " Your heart shall rejoice " (Luke i. 47) ; " My spirit rejoiced in God." And to show how filling these comforts are, which are of a heavenly extraction, the Psalmist says they create greater joy than when " *corn and wine increase.*" Wine and oil may delight but not satisfy ; they have their vacuity and indigence. We may say, as Zech. x. 2, " They comfort in vain ; " outward comforts do sooner cloy than cheer, and sooner weary than fill. Xerxes offered great rewards to him that could find out a new pleasure ; but the comforts of the Spirit are satisfactory, they recruit the heart (Psalm xciv. 19), " Thy comforts delight my soul." There is as much difference between heavenly comforts and earthly, as between a banquet that is eaten, and one that is painted on the wall.—*Thomas Watson.*

Verse 8.—It is said of the husbandman, that having cast his seed into the ground, he sleeps and riseth day and night, and the seed springs and grows he knoweth not how. Mark iv. 26, 27. So a good man having by faith and prayer cast his care upon God, he resteth night and day, and is very easy, leaving it to his God to perform all things for him according to his holy will.—*Matthew Henry.*

Verse 8.—When you have walked with God from morning until night, it remaineth that you *conclude* the day well, when you would give yourself to rest at night. Wherefore, first look back and take a strict view of your whole carriage that *day past.* Reform what you find amiss ; and rejoice, or be grieved, as you find you have done well or ill, as you have advanced or declined in grace that day. Secondly, since you cannot sleep in safety if God, who is your *keeper* (Psalm cxi. 4, 5), do not *wake and watch for you* (Psalm cxxvii, 1) ; and though you have God to watch when you sleep, you cannot be safe, if he that watcheth be your *enemy.* Wherefore it is very convenient that at night you renew and confirm your peace with God by faith and prayer, commending and committing yourself to God's tuition by prayer (Psalm iii. 4, 5 ; Psalm xcii. 2), with thanksgiving before you go to bed. Then shall you lie *down in safety.* Psalm iv. 8. All this being done, yet while you are *putting off* your apparel, when you are *lying down,* and when you are *in bed,* before you sleep, it is good that *you commune with* your *own heart.* Psalm iv. 4. If possibly you can fall asleep with *some heavenly meditation,* then will your sleep be *more sweet* (Prov. iii. 21, 24, 25) ; and *more secure* (Prov. vi. 21, 22) ; your *dreams* fewer, or more *comfortable ;* your head will be fuller of good thoughts (Prov. vi. 22), and your heart will be in a *better frame* when you *awake,* whether in the night or in the morning.—*Condensed from Henry Scudder's Daily Walk,* 1633.

Verse 8.—" *I will both,*" etc. We have now to retire for a moment from the strife of tongues and the open hostility of foes, into the stillness and privacy of the chamber of sleep. Here, also, we find the " I will" of trust. " *I will both lay me down in peace, and sleep ; for thou, Lord, only makest me dwell in safety.*" God is here revealed to us as exercising *personal care in the still chamber.* And there is something here which should be inexpressibly sweet to the believer, for this shows the minuteness of God's care, the individuality of his love ; how it condescends and stoops, and acts, not only in great, but also in little spheres ; not only where glory might be procured from great results, but where nought is to be had save the gratitude and love of a poor feeble creature, whose life has been protected and preserved, in a period of helplessness and sleep. How blessed would it be if we made a larger recognition of God in the still chamber ; if we thought of him as being there in all hours of illness, of weariness, and pain ; if we believed that his interest and care are as much concentrated upon the feeble believer there as upon his people when in the wider battle field of the strife of tongues. There is something inexpressibly touching in this " laying down " of the Psalmist. In thus lying down he voluntarily gave up guardianship of himself ; he resigned himself into the hands of another ; he did so completely, for in the absence of all care he slept ; there was here a perfect trust. Many a believer lies down, but it is not to sleep. Perhaps he feels safe enough so far as his body is concerned, but cares and anxieties invade the privacy of his chamber ; they come to try his faith and trust ; they threaten, they frighten, and alas! prove too strong for trust. Many a poor believer might say, " I will lay me down, but not to sleep." The author met with a touching instance of this, in the case of an aged minister whom he visited in severe illness. This worthy man's circumstances were narrow, and his family trials were great ; he said, " The doctor wants me to sleep, but how can I sleep with care sitting on my pillow ? " It is the experience of some of the Lord's people, that although equal to an emergency or a continued pressure, a reaction sets in afterwards ; and when they come to be alone their spirits sink, and they do not realise that strength from God, or feel that confidence in him which they felt while the pressure was exerting its force...... There is a trial in stillness ; and oftentimes the still chamber makes a larger demand upon loving trust than the battle field. O that we could trust God more and more with personal things ! O that he were the God of our chamber, as well as of our temples and houses ! O that we could bring him more and more into the minutiæ of daily life ! If we did thus, we should experience a measure of rest to which we are, perhaps, strangers now ; we should have less dread of the sick chamber ; we should have that unharassed mind which conduces most to repose, in body and soul ; we should be able to say, " I will lie down and sleep, *and leave to-morrow with God !* " Ridley's brother offered to remain with him during the night preceding his martyrdom, but the bishop declined, saying, that " he meant to go to bed, and sleep as quietly as ever he did in his life."—*Philip Bennett Power's ' I Wills' of the Psalms.*

Verse 8.—Due observation of Providence will both beget and secure inward tranquility in your minds amidst the vicissitudes and revolutions of things in this unstable vain world. " *I will both lay me down in peace, and sleep ; for the Lord only maketh me dwell in safety.*" He resolves that sinful fears of events shall not rob him of his inward quiet, nor torture his thoughts with anxious presages : he will commit all his concerns into that faithful fatherly hand that had hitherto wrought all things for him ; and he means not to lose the comfort of one night's rest, nor bring the evil of to-morrow upon the day ; but knowing in whose hand he was, wisely enjoys the sweet felicity of a resigned will. Now this tranquility of our minds is as much begotten and preserved by a due consideration of providence as by anything whatsoever.—*John Flavel*, 1627—1691.

Verse 8.—Happy is the Christian, who having nightly with this verse, committed himself to his bed as to his grave, shall at last, with the same words, resign himself to his grave as to his bed, from which he expects in due time to arise, and sing a morning hymn with the children of the resurrection.—*George Horne, D.D.*, 1776.

Verse 9.—" *Sleep.*"

> " How blessed was that *sleep*
> The sinless Saviour knew !
> In vain the storm-winds blew,
> Till he awoke to others' woes,
> And hushed the billows to repose.
>
> How beautiful is *sleep*—
> The *sleep* that Christians know !
> Ye mourners ! cease your woe,
> While soft upon his Saviour's breast,
> The righteous sinks to endless rest."
>
> Mrs. *M'Cartree.*

HINTS TO PREACHERS.

Verse 1.—Is full of matter for a sermon upon, *past mercies a plea for present help.* The first sentence shows that believers desire, expect, and believe in a God that heareth prayer. The title—*God of my righteousness*, may furnish a text (see exposition), and the last sentence may suggest a sermon upon, " The best of saints must still appeal to God's mercy and sovereign grace."

Verse 2.—*Depravity of man* as evinced (1) by continuance in despising Christ, (2) loving vanity in his heart, and (3) seeking lies in his daily life.

Verse 2.—The length of the sinner's sin. " How long ? " May be bounded by repentance, shall be by death, and yet shall continue in eternity.

Verse 3.—*Election.*—Its aspects towards God, our enemies, and ourselves.

Verse 3.—" *The Lord will hear when I call unto him.*" Answers to prayer certain to special persons. Mark out those who can claim the favour.

Verse 3.—*The gracious Separatist.* Who is he ? Who separated him ? With what end ? How to make men know it ?

Verse 4.—The sinner directed to review himself, that he may be convinced of sin.—*Andrew Fuller*, 1754—1815.

Verse 4.—" *Be still.*" Advice—good, practical, but hard to follow. Times when seasonable. Graces needed to enable one to be still. Results of quietness. Persons who most need the advice. Instances of its practice. Here is much material for a sermon.

Verse 5.—The nature of those sacrifices of righteousness which the Lord's people are expected to offer.—*William Ford Vance*, 1827.

Verse 6.—The cry of the world and the church contrasted. *Vox populi* not always *Vox Dei.*

Verse 6.—The cravings of the soul all satisfied in God.

Verses 6, 7.—An assurance of the Saviour's love, the source of unrivalled joy.

Verse 7.—The believer's joys. (1) Their source, " *Thou ;* " (2) their season—

even now—" *Thou hast;* " (3) their position, " *in my heart;* " (4) their excellence, " *more than in the time that their corn and their wine increased.*"

Another excellent theme suggests itself—" The superiority of the joys of grace to the joys of earth;" or, " Two sort of prosperity—which is to be the more desired?"

Verse 8.—The peace and safety of the good man.—*Joseph Lathrop, D.D.*, 1805.

Verse 8.—A bedchamber for believers, a vesper song to sing in it, and a guard to keep the door.

Verse 8.—The Christian's good-night.

Verses 2 to 8.—The means which a believer should use to win the ungodly to Christ. (1). Expostulation, verse 2. (2.) Instruction, verse 3. (3.) Exhortation, verses 4, 5. (4.) Testimony to the blessedness of true religion, as in verses 6, 7. (5.) Exemplification of that testimony by the peace of faith, verse 8.

PSALM V.

TITLE.—" To the Chief Musician upon Nehiloth, a Psalm of David."   *The Hebrew word Nehiloth is taken from another word, signifying " to perforate," " to bore through," whence it comes to mean a pipe or a flute ; so that this song was probably intended to be sung with an accompaniment of wind instruments, such as the horn, the trumpet, flute, or cornet.   However, it is proper to remark that we are not sure of the interpretation of these ancient titles, for the Septuagint translates it, " For him who shall obtain inheritance," and Aben Ezra thinks it denotes some old and well-known melody to which this Psalm was to be played.   The best scholars confess that great darkness hangs over the precise interpretation of the titles ; nor is this much to be regretted, for it furnishes an internal evidence of the great antiquity of the Book.   Throughout the first, second, third, and fourth Psalms, you will have noticed that the subject is a contrast between the position, the character, and the prospects of the righteous and of the wicked.   In this Psalm you will note the same.   The Psalmist carries out a contrast between himself made righteous by God's grace, and the wicked who opposed him.   To the devout mind there is here presented a precious view of the Lord Jesus, of whom it is said that in the days of his flesh, he offered up prayers and supplication with strong crying and tears.*

DIVISION.—*The Psalm should be divided into two parts, from the first to the seventh verse, and then from the eight to the twelfth.   In the first part of the Psalm David most vehemently beseeches the Lord to hearken to his prayer, and in the second part he retraces the same ground.*

EXPOSITION.

G IVE ear to my words, O LORD, consider my meditation.

There are two sorts of prayers—those expressed in words, and the unuttered longings which abide as silent meditations.   Words are not the essence but the garments of prayer.   Moses at the Red Sea cried to God, though he said nothing. Yet the use of language may prevent distraction of mind, may assist the powers of the soul, and may excite devotion.   David, we observe, uses both modes of prayer, and craves for the one a hearing, and for the other a *consideration.*   What an expressive word!   *" Consider my meditation."*   If I have asked that which is right, give it to me; if I have omitted to ask that which I most needed, fill up the vacancy in my prayer.   " Consider my meditation."   Let thy holy soul *consider* it as presented through my all-glorious Mediator :   then regard thou it in thy wisdom, weigh it in the scales, judge thou of my sincerity, and of the true state of my necessities, and answer me in due time for thy mercy's sake !   There may be prevailing intercession where there are no words ;   and alas !   there may be words where there is no true supplication.   Let us cultivate the *spirit* of prayer which is even better than the *habit* of prayer.   There may be seeming prayer where there is little devotion.   We should begin to pray before we kneel down, and we should not cease when we rise up.

2 Hearken unto the voice of my cry, my King, and my God : for unto thee will I pray.

" The voice of my cry."   In another Psalm we find the expression, " The voice of my weeping."   Weeping has a voice—a melting, plaintive tone, an ear-piercing shrillness, which reaches the very heart of God : and *crying* hath a voice—a soul-moving eloquence ;   coming from *our* heart it reaches *God's* heart.   Ah ! my brothers and sisters, sometimes we cannot put our prayers into words: they are nothing but a *cry :*   but the Lord can comprehend the meaning, for he hears a voice in our cry.   To a loving father his children's cries are music, and they have a magic influence which his heart cannot resist.   *" My King and my God."*   Observe carefully these little pronouns, " *my* King, and *my* God."   They are the pith and marrow of the plea.   Here is a grand argument why God should answer prayer—because he is *our* King and *our* God.   We are not aliens to him : he is the King of our

country. Kings are expected to hear the appeals of their own people. We are not strangers to him ; we are his worshippers, and he is our God : ours by covenant, by promise, by oath, by blood."

"*For unto thee will I pray.*" Here David expresses his declaration that he will seek to God, and to God alone. God is to be the only object of worship : the only resource of our soul in times of need. Leave broken cisterns to the godless, and let the godly drink from the Divine fountain alone. "Unto thee *will I* pray." He makes a resolution, that as long as he lived he would pray. He would never cease to supplicate, even though the answer should not come.

3 My voice shalt thou hear in the morning, O Lord ; in the morning will I direct *my prayer* unto thee, and will look up.

Observe, this is not so much a prayer as a resolution, "'*My voice shalt thou hear,*' I will not be dumb, I will not be silent, I will not withhold my speech, I *will* cry to thee, for the fire that dwells within compels me to pray." We can sooner die than live without prayer. None of God's children are possessed with a dumb devil.

"*In the morning.*" This is the fittest time for intercourse with God. An hour in the morning is worth two in the evening. While the dew is on the grass, let grace drop upon the soul. Let us give to God the mornings of our days and the morning of our lives. Prayer should be the key of the day and the lock of the night. Devotion should be both the morning star and the evening star.

If we merely read our English version, and want an explanation of these two sentences, we find it in the figure of an archer, "*I will direct my prayer unto thee,*" I will put my prayer upon the bow, I will direct it towards heaven, and then when I have shot up my arrow, *I will look up* to see where it has gone. But the Hebrew has a still fuller meaning than this—"I will *direct* my prayer." It is the word that is used for the laying in order of the wood and the pieces of the victim upon the altar, and it is used also for the putting of the shewbread upon the table. It means just this : "I will arrange my prayer before thee ;" I will lay it out upon the altar in the morning, just as the priest lays out the morning sacrifice. I will *arrange* my prayer ; or, as old Master Trapp has it, "I will marshal up my prayers," I will put them in order, call up all my powers, and bid them stand in their proper places, that I may pray with all my might, and pray acceptably.

"*And will look up,*" or, as the Hebrew might better be translated, "'I will look out,' I will look out for the answer ; after I have prayed, I will expect that the blessing shall come." It is a word that is used in another place where we read of those who watched for the morning. So will I watch for thine answer, O my Lord ! I will spread out my prayer like the victim on the altar, and I will look up, and expect to receive the answer by fire from heaven to consume the sacrifice.

Two questions are suggested by the last part of this verse. Do we not miss very much of the sweetness and efficacy of prayer by a want of careful meditation before it, and of hopeful expectation after it ? We too often rush into the presence of God without forethought or humility. We are live men who present themselves before a king without a petition, and what wonder is it that we often miss the end of prayer ? We should be careful to keep the stream of meditation always running ; for this is the water to drive the mill of prayer. It is idle to pull up the flood-gates of a dry brook, and then hope to see the wheel revolve. Prayer without fervency is like hunting with a dead dog, and prayer without preparation is hawking with a blind falcon. Prayer is the work of the Holy Spirit, but he works by means. God made man, but he used the dust of the earth as a material : the Holy Ghost is the author of prayer, but he employs the thoughts of a fervent soul as the gold with which to fashion the vessel. Let not our prayers and praises be the flashes of a hot and hasty brain, but the steady burning of a well-kindled fire.

But, furthermore, do we not forget to watch the result of our supplications ? We are like the ostrich, which lays her eggs and looks not for her young. We sow the seed, and are too idle to seek a harvest. How can we expect the Lord to open the windows of his grace, and pour us out a blessing, if we will not open the windows of expectation and look up for the promised favour ? Let holy preparation link hands with patient expectation, and we shall have far larger answers to our prayers.

4 For thou *art* not a God that hath pleasure in wickedness : neither shall evil dwell with thee.

5 The foolish shall not stand in thy sight : thou hatest all workers of iniquity.

6 Thou shalt destroy them that speak leasing : the LORD will abhor the bloody and deceitful man.

And now the Psalmist having thus expressed his resolution to pray, you hear him putting up his prayer. He is pleading against his cruel and wicked enemies. He uses a most mighty argument. He begs of God to put them away from him, because they were displeasing to God himself. "*For thou art not a God that hath pleasure in wickedness : neither shall evil dwell with thee.*" "When I pray against my tempters," says David, "I pray against the very things which thou thyself abhorrest." *Thou* hatest evil : Lord, I beseech thee, deliver *me* from it ! Let us learn here the solemn truth of the hatred which a righteous God must bear towards sin. *He has no pleasure in wickedness,* however wittily, grandly, and proudly it may array itself. Its glitter has no charm for him. Men may bow before the successful villainy, and forget the wickedness of the battle in the gaudiness of the triumph, but the Lord of Holiness is not such-an-one as we are. "*Neither shall evil dwell with thee.*" He will not afford it the meanest shelter. Neither on earth nor in heaven shall evil share the mansion of God. Oh, how foolish are we if we attempt to entertain two guests so hostile to one another as Christ Jesus and the devil ! Rest assured, Christ will not live in the parlour of our hearts if we entertain the devil in the cellar of our thoughts. "*The foolish shall not stand in thy sight.*" Sinners are fools written large. A little sin is a great folly, and the greatest of all folly is great sin. Such sinful fools as these must be banished from the court of heaven. Earthly kings were wont to have fools in their trains, but the only wise God will have no fools in his palace above. "*Thou hatest all workers of iniquity.*" It is not a little dislike, but a thorough hatred which God bears to workers of iniquity. To be hated of God is an awful thing. O let us be very faithful in warning the wicked around us, for it will be a terrible thing for them to fall into the hands of an angry God ! Observe, that evil speakers must be punished as well as evil workers, for "*thou shalt destroy them that speak leasing.*" All liars shall have their portion in the lake which burneth with fire and brimstone. A man may lie without danger of the law of man, but he will not escape the law of God. Liars have short wings, their flight shall soon be over, and they shall fall into the fiery floods of destruction. "*The Lord will abhor the bloody and deceitful man.*" Bloody men shall be made drunk with their own blood, and they who began by deceiving others shall end with being deceived themselves. Our old proverb saith, "Bloody and deceitful men dig their own graves." The voice of the people is in this instance the voice of God. How forcible is the word *abhor !* Does it not show us how powerful and deep-seated is the hatred of the Lord against the workers of iniquity ?

7 But as for me, I will come *into* thy house in the multitude of thy mercy : *and* in thy fear will I worship toward thy holy temple.

With this verse the first part of the Psalm ends. The Psalmist has bent his knee in prayer : he has described before God, as an argument for his deliverance, the character and the fate of the wicked ; and now he contrasts this with the condition of the righteous. "*But as for me, I will come into thy house.*" I will not stand at a distance, I will come into thy sanctuary, just as a child comes into his father's house. But I will not come there by my own merits ; no, I have a multitude of sins, and therefore I will come *in the multitude of thy mercy.* I will approach thee with confidence because of thy immeasurable grace. God's judgments are all numbered, but his mercies are innumerable ; he gives his wrath by weight, but without weight his mercy. "*And in thy fear will I worship toward thy holy temple,*"—towards the temple of thy holiness. The temple was not built on earth at that time ; it was but a tabernacle ; but David was wont to turn his eyes spiritually to that temple of God's holiness where between the wings of the Cherubim Jehovah dwells in light ineffable. Daniel opened his window towards Jerusalem, but we open our hearts towards heaven.

8 Lead me, O LORD, in thy righteousness because of mine enemies ; make thy way straight before my face.

Now we come to the second part, in which the Psalmist repeats his arguments, and goes over the same ground again.

"*Lead me, O Lord*," as a little child is led by its father, as a blind man is guided by his friend. It is safe and pleasant walking when God leads the way. "*In thy righteousness*," not in *my* righteousness, for that is imperfect, but in *thine*, for thou art righteousness itself. "*Make thy way*," not *my* way, "*straight before my face*." Brethren, when we have learned to give up our own way, and long to walk in God's way, it is a happy sign of grace ; and it is no small mercy to see the way of God with clear vision straight before our face. Errors about duty may lead us into a sea of sins, before we know where we are.

9 For *there is* no faithfulness in their mouth ; their inward part *is* very wickedness ; their throat *is* an open sepulchre ; they flatter with their tongue.

This description of depraved man has been copied by the Apostle Paul, and, together with some other quotations, he has placed it in the second chapter of Romans, as being an accurate description of the whole human race, not of David's enemies only, but of all men by nature. Note that remarkable figure, "*Their throat is an open sepulchre*," a *sepulchre* full of loathsomeness, of miasma, of pestilence and death. But, worse than that, it is an *open* sepulchre, with all its evil gases issuing forth, to spread death and destruction all around. So, with the throat of the wicked, it would be a great mercy if it could always be closed. If we could seal in continual silence the mouth of the wicked it would be like a sepulchre shut up, and would not produce much mischief. But "their throat is an *open* sepulchre," consequently all the wickedness of their heart exhales, and comes forth. How dangerous is an open sepulchre ; men in their journeys might easily stumble therein, and find themselves among the dead. Ah ! take heed of the wicked man, for there is nothing that he will not say to ruin you ; he will long to destroy your character, and bury you in the hideous sepulchre of his own wicked throat. One sweet thought here, however. At the resurrection there will be a resurrection not only of bodies, but characters. This should be a great comfort to a man who has been abused and slandered. "Then shall the righteous shine forth as the sun." The world may think you vile, and bury your character ; but if you have been upright, in the day when the graves shall give up their dead, this open sepulchre of the sinner's throat shall be compelled to give up your heavenly character, and you shall come forth and be honoured in the sight of men. "*They flatter with their tongue.* Or, as we might read it, "They have an oily tongue, a smooth tongue." A smooth tongue is a great evil ; many have been bewitched by it. There be many human ant-eaters that with their long tongues covered with oily words entice and entrap the unwary and make their gain thereby. When the wolf licks the lamb, he is preparing to wet his teeth in its blood.

10 Destroy thou them, O God ; let them fall by their own counsels ; cast them out in the multitude of their transgressions ; for they have rebelled against thee.

"*Against thee :*" not against *me*. If they were *my* enemies I would forgive them, but I cannot forgive *thine*. We are to forgive *our* enemies, but God's enemies it is not in our power to forgive. These expressions have often been noticed by men of over refinement as being harsh, and grating on the ear. "Oh !" say they, "they are vindictive and revengeful." Let us remember that they might be translated as prophecies, not as wishes ; but we do not care to avail ourselves of this method of escape. We have never heard of a reader of the Bible who, after perusing these passages, was made revengeful by reading them, and it is but fair to test the nature of a writing by its effects. When we hear a judge condemning a murderer, however severe his sentence, we do not feel that we should be justified in condemning others for any private injury done to us. The Psalmist here speaks as a judge, *ex officio ;* he speaks as God's mouth, and in condemning the wicked he gives us no excuse whatever for uttering anything in the way of malediction upon those who have caused us personal offence. The most shameful way of cursing another is by pretending to bless him. We were all somewhat amused by noticing the toothless malice of that wretched old priest of Rome when he foolishly cursed the Emperor of France with his blessing. He was blessing him in form and cursing him in reality. Now, in direct contrast we put this healthy commination of David, which is intended to be a blessing by warning the sinner of the impending curse. O impenitent man, be it known unto thee that all thy godly friends will give their solemn assent to the awful sentence of the Lord, which he shall pronounce upon thee in the day of doom! Our verdict shall applaud the condemning curse which the Judge of all the earth shall thunder against the godless.

In the following verse we once more find the contrast which has marked the preceding Psalms.

11 But let all those that put their trust in thee rejoice : let them ever shout for joy, because thou defendest them : let them also that love thy name be joyful in thee.

Joy is the privilege of the believer. When sinners are destroyed our rejoicing shall be full. They laugh first and weep ever after ; we weep now, but shall rejoice eternally. When they howl we shall *shout*, and as they must groan for ever, so shall we *ever shout* for joy. This holy bliss of ours has a firm foundation, for O Lord, we are *joyful in thee*. The eternal God is the well-spring of our bliss. We love God, and therefore we delight in him. Our heart is at ease in our God. We fare sumptuously every day because we feed on him. We have music in the house, music in the heart, and music in heaven, for the Lord Jehovah is our strength and our song ; he also is become our salvation.

12 For thou, LORD, wilt bless the righteous ; with favour wilt thou compass him as *with* a shield.

Jehovah has ordained his people the heirs of blessedness, and nothing shall rob them of their inheritance. With all the fulness of his power he will bless them, and all his attributes shall unite to satiate them with divine contentment. Nor is this merely for the present, but the blessing reaches into the long and unknown future. " *Thou Lord, wilt bless the righteous.*" This is a promise of infinite length, of unbounded breadth, and of unutterable preciousness.

As for the defence which the believer needs in this land of battles, it is here promised to him in the fullest measure. There were vast shields used by the ancients as extensive as a man's whole person, which would surround him entirely. So says David, " *With favour wilt thou compass him as with a shield.*" According to Ainsworth there is here also the idea of being crowned, so that we wear a royal helmet, which is at once our glory and defence. O Lord, ever give to us this gracious coronation !

EXPLANATORY NOTES AND QUAINT SAYINGS.

Verse 1.—" *Give ear to my words, O Lord, consider my meditation.*" It is certain that the greater part of men, as they babble out vain, languid, and inefficacious prayers, most unworthy the ear of the blessed God, so they seem in some degree to set a just estimate upon them, neither hoping for any success from them, nor indeed seeming to be at all solicitous about it, but committing them to the mind as vain words, which in truth they are. But far be it from a wise and pious man, that he should so foolishly and coldly trifle in so serious an affair ; his prayer has a certain tendency and scope, at which he aims with assiduous and repeated desires, and doth not only pray that he may pray, but that he may obtain an answer ; and as he firmly believes that it may be obtained, so he firmly, and constantly, and eagerly urges his petition, that he may not flatter himself with an empty hope. *Robert Leighton, D.D.*

Verses 1, 2.—Observe the order and force of the words, " *my cry,*" " *the voice of my prayer ;*" and also, " *give ear,*" " *consider,*" " *hearken.*" These expressions all evince the urgency and energy of David's feelings and petitions. First, we

have, " *give ear ;* " that is, hear me. But it is of little service for the words to
be heard, unless the " *cry,*" or the roaring, or the meditation, be *considered.* As
if he had said, in a common way of expression, I speak with deep anxiety and
concern, but with a failing utterance ; and I cannot express myself, nor make
myself understood as I wish. Do thou, therefore, understand from my feelings
more than I am able to express in words. And, therefore, I add my " *cry ;* " that
what I cannot express in words for thee to hear, I may by my " *cry*" signify to
thine understanding. And when thou hast understood me, then, O Lord " *Hearken
unto the voice of my prayer,*" and despise not what thou hast thus heard and understood. We are not, however, to understand that hearing, understanding, and
hearkening, are all different acts in God, in the same way as they are in us ; but
that our feelings towards God are to be thus varied and increased ; that is, that
we are first to desire to be heard, and then, that our prayers which are heard may
be understood ; and then, that being understood, they may be hearkened unto,
that is, not disregarded.—*Martin Luther.*

Verse 1.—" *Meditation* " fits the soul for supplication ; meditation fills the soul
with good liquor, and then prayer broaches it, and sets it a-running. David first
mused, and then spake with his tongue, " Lord, make me to know mine end."
Psalm xxxix. 3, 4. Nay, to assure us that meditation was the mother which bred
and brought forth prayer, he calls the child by its parent's name, " *Give ear to my
words, O Lord, consider my meditation.*" Meditation is like the charging of a piece,
and prayer the discharging of it. " Isaac went into the field to meditate."
Genesis xxiv. 63. The Septuagint, the Geneva translation, and Tremellius,
in his marginal notes on it, read it to " pray ; " and the Hebrew word שׂיח used
there signifieth both to *pray* and *meditate ;* whereby we may learn they are very
near akin ; like twins, they be in the same womb, in the same word. Meditation
is the best beginning of prayer, and prayer is the best conclusion of meditation.
When the Christian, like Daniel, hath first opened the windows of his soul by contemplation, then he may kneel down to prayer.—*George Swinnock.*

Verse 3.—" *My voice shalt thou hear in the morning, O Lord.*"

> When first thy eyes unveil, give thy soul leave
>   To do the like ; our bodies but forerun
> The spirit's duty ; true hearts spread and heave
>   Unto their God, as flowers do to the sun :
> Give him thy first thoughts, then, so shalt thou keep
> Him company all day, and in him sleep.
>
> Yet never sleep the sun up ; prayer should
>   Dawn with the day, there are set awful hours
> 'Twixt heaven and us ; the manna was not good
>   After sun-rising, for day sullies flowers.
> Rise to prevent the sun ; sleep doth sins glut,
> And heaven's gate opens when the world's is shut.
>
> Walk with thy fellow creatures ; note the hush
>   And whisperings amongst them. Not a spring
> Or leaf but hath his *morning* hymn ; each bush
>   And oak doth know I AM—canst thou not sing ?
> O leave thy cares and follies ! Go this way,
> And thou art sure to prosper all the day.
>
> *Henry Vaughan, 1621—1695.*

Verse 3.—" *My voice shalt thou hear in the morning.*" " *In the morning shall
my prayer prevent thee,*" said Heman. That is the fittest time for devotion, you
being then fresh in your spirits, and freest from distractions. Which opportunity
for holy duties may fitly be called *the wings of the morning.*—*Edward Reyner, 1658.*

Verse 3.—" *In the morning.*" " In the days of our fathers," says Bishop Burnet,
" when a person came early to the door of his neighbour, and desired to speak with
the master of the house, it was as common a thing for the servants to tell him with
freedom—' My master is at prayer,' as it now is to say, ' My master is not up.' "

Verse 3.—" *In the morning I will direct my prayer unto thee, and will look up,*"
or *I will marshal my prayer,* I will bring up petition after petition, pleading after
pleading, even till I become like Jacob, a prince with God, till I have won the field
and got the day. Thus the word is applied by a metaphor both to disputations

with men and supplications to God. Further, we may take the meaning plainly without any strain of rhetoric, *Set thy words in order before me.* Method is good in everything, either an express or covert method. Sometimes it is the best of art to cover it ; in speaking there is a special use of method, for though, as one said very well (speaking of those who are more curious about method than serious about matter), " *Method never converted any man ;* " yet method and the ordering of words is very useful. Our speeches should not be heaps of words, but words bound up; not a throng of words, but words set in array, or, as it were, in rank and file.—*Joseph Caryl.*

Verse 3.—" *I will direct my prayer unto thee, and will look up.*" In the words you may observe two things : first, David's posture in prayer ; secondly, his practice after prayer. First, his posture in prayer, " *I will direct my prayer unto thee.*" Secondly, his practice after prayer, " *And I will look up.*" The prophet in these words, makes use of two military words. First, he would not only pray, but marshal up his prayers, he would put them in battle array ; so much the Hebrew word עָרַךְ imports. Secondly, when he had done this, then he would be as a spy upon his watch-tower, to see whether he prevailed, whether he got the day or no ; and so much the Hebrew word צָפָה imports. When David had set his prayers, his petitions, in rank and file, in good array, then he was resolved he would look abroad, he would look about him to see at what door God would send in an answer of prayer. He is either a fool or a madman, he is either very weak or very wicked, that prays and prays, but never looks after his prayers ; that shoots many an arrow towards heaven, but never minds where his arrows alight.—*Thomas Brooks.*

Verse 3.—David would *direct his prayer to God and look up;* not down to the world, down to corruption, but up to God what he would speak. Psalm lxxxv. 8. " I will hear what God the Lord will speak." Let the resolution of the prophet be thine, " I will look unto the Lord ; I will wait for the God of my salvation : my God will hear me." Micah vii. 7.—*William Greenhill, 1650.*

Verse 3.—" *I will direct my prayer to thee, and will look up,*" that is, I will trade, I will send out my spiritual commodities, and expect a gainful return ; I will make my prayers, and not give them for lost, but look up for an answer. God will bring man home by a way contrary to that by which he wandered from him. Man fell from God by distrust, by having God in suspicion ; God will bring him back by trust, by having good thoughts of him. Oh, how richly laden might the vessel which thou sendest out come home, wouldst thou but long and look for its return ! —*George Swinnock.*

Verse 3.—Faith hath a supporting art after prayer : it supports the soul to expect a gracious answer : " *I will direct my prayer unto thee, and will look up,*" or I will look ; for what, but for a return ? An unbelieving heart shoots at random, and never minds where his arrow lights, or what comes of his praying ; but faith fills the soul with expectation. As a merchant, when he casts up his estate, he counts what he hath sent beyond sea, as well as what he hath in hand ; so doth faith reckon upon what he hath sent to heaven in prayer and not received, as well as those mercies which he hath received, and are in hand at present. Now this expectation which faith raiseth in the soul after prayer, appears in the power that it hath to quiet and compose the soul in the interim between the sending forth, as I may say, the ship of prayer, and its return home with its rich lading it goes for, and it is more or less, according as faith's strength is. Sometimes faith comes from prayer in triumph, and cries, *Victoria.* It gives such a being and existence to the mercy prayed for in the Christian's soul before any likelihood of it appears to sense and reason, that the Christian can silence all his troubled thoughts with the expectation of its coming. Yea, it will make the Christian disburse his praises for the mercy long before it is received...... For want of looking up many a prayer is lost. If you do not believe, why do you pray ? And if you believe, why do you not expect ? By praying you seem to depend on God ; by not expecting, you again renounce your confidence. What is this, but to take his name in vain ? O Christian, stand to your prayer in a holy expectation of what you have begged upon the credit of the promise. . . . Mordecai, no doubt, had put up many prayers for Esther, and therefore he waits at the king's gate, looking what answer God would in his providence give thereunto. Do thou likewise.—*William Gurnall.*

Verse 4.—" *Thou art not a God that hath pleasure in wickedness.*" As a man that cutteth with a dull knife is the cause of cutting, but not of the ill-cutting and hacking of the knife—the knife is the cause of that ; or if a man strike upon an instrument that is out of tune, he is the cause of the sound, but not of the jarring sound—that is the fault of the untuned strings ; or, as a man riding upon a lame horse, stirs him—the man is the cause of the motion, but the horse himself of the halting motion : thus God is the author of every action, but not of the evil of that action—that is from man. He that makes instruments and tools of iron or other metal, he maketh not the rust and canker which corrupteth them, that is from another cause ; nor doth that heavenly workman, God Almighty, bring in sin and iniquity ; nor can he be justly blamed if his creatures do soil and besmear themselves with the foulness of sin, for he made them good.—*Spencer's Things New and Old.*

Verses 4—6.—Here the Lord's alienation from the wicked is set forth gradually, and seems to rise by six steps. First, *he hath no pleasure in them;* secondly, *they shall not dwell with them ;* thirdly, he casteth them forth, *they shall not stand in his sight ;* fourthly, his heart turns from them, *thou hatest all the workers of iniquity ;* fifthly, his hand is turned upon them, *thou shalt destroy them that speak leasing ;* sixthly, his spirit riseth against them, and is alienated from them, *the Lord will abhor the bloody man.* This estrangement is indeed a *strange* (yet a certain) *punishment* to " *the workers of iniquity.*" These words, " *the workers of iniquity,*" may be considered two ways. First, as intending (not all degrees of sinners, or sinners of every degree, but) the highest degree of sinners, great, and gross sinners, resolved and wilful sinners. Such as sin industriously, and, as it were, artificially, with skill and care to get themselves a name, as if they had an ambition to be accounted *workmen* that need not be ashamed in doing that whereof all ought to be ashamed ; these, in strictness of Scripture sense, are " *workers of iniquity.*" Hence note, *notorious sinners made sin their business, or their trade.* Though every sin be *a work of iniquity,* yet only some sinners are " *workers of iniquity ;* " and they who are called so, make it their calling to sin. We read of some *who love and make a lie.* Rev. xxii. 15. A lie may be told by those who neither love nor make it ; but there are lie-makers, and they, sure enough, are lovers of a lie. Such craftsmen in sinning are also described in Psalm lviii. 2.—" Yea, in heart ye work wickedness ; ye weigh the violence of your hands in the earth." The psalmist doth not say, they had wickedness in their heart, but they did work it there ; *the heart is a shop within, an underground shop ;* there they did closely contrive, forge, and hammer out their wicked purposes, and fit them into actions.—*Joseph Caryl.*

Verse 5.—What an astonishing thing is sin, which maketh the God of love and Father of mercies an enemy to his creatures, and which could only be purged by the blood of the Son of God ! Though all must believe this who believe the Bible, yet the exceeding sinfulness of sin is but weakly apprehended by those who have the deepest sense of it, and will never be fully known in this world.—*Thomas Adam's Private Thoughts,* 1701—1784.

Verse 5 (*last clause*).—" *Thou hatest all workers of iniquity.*" For what God thinks of sin, see Deut. vii. 22 ; Prov. vi. 16 ; Rev. ii. 6, 15 ; where he expresseth his detestation and hatred of it, from which hatred proceeds all those direful plagues and judgments thundered from the fiery mouth of his most holy law against it ; nay, not only the work, but *worker* also of iniquity becomes the object of his hatred. *William Gurnall.*

· Verse 5 (*last clause*).—" *Thou hatest all workers of iniquity.*" If God's hatred be against the workers of iniquity, how great is it against iniquity itself ! If a man hate a poisonous creature, he hates poison much more. The strength of God's hatred is against sin, and so should we hate sin, and hate it with strength ; it is an abomination unto God, let it be so unto us. Prov. vi. 16—19, " These six things doth the Lord hate ; yea, seven are an abomination unto him ; a proud look, a lying tongue, and hands that shed innocent blood, an heart that deviseth wicked imaginations, feet that be swift in running to mischief, a false witness that speaketh lies, and he that soweth discord among brethren."—*William Greenhill.*

Verse 5 (*last clause*).—Those whom the Lord hates must perish. But he hates impenitent sinners, " *Thou hatest all workers of iniquity.*" Now, who are so properly workers of iniquity as those who are so eager at it that they will not leave this work, though they be in danger to perish for it ? Christ puts it out of doubt. The workers of iniquity must perish. Luke xiii. 27. Those whom the Lord will tear in his wrath must perish with a witness ; but those whom he hates, he tears, &c.

Job xvi. 8. What more due to such impenitent sinners than hatred ! What more proper than wrath, since they treasure up wrath ? Rom. ii. Will he entertain those in the bosom of love whom his soul hates ? No ; destruction is their portion. Prov. xxi. 15. If all the curses of the law, all the threatenings of the gospel, all judgments in earth or in hell, will be the ruin of him, he must perish. If the Lord's arm be strong enough to wound him dead, he must die. Psalm lxviii. 21. . . . . . Avoid all that Christ hates. If you love, approve, entertain that which is hateful to Christ, how can he love you ? What is that which Christ hates ? The psalmist (Psalm xlv. 7) tells us, making it one of Christ's attributes, to hate wickedness. . . . As Christ hates iniquity, so the " workers of iniquity." You must not love them, so as to be intimate with them, delight in the company of evil doers, openly profane, scorners of godliness, obstructors of the power of it. 2 Cor. vi. 14—18. If you love so near relations to wicked men, Christ will have no relation to you. If you would have communion with Christ in sweet acts of love, you must have no fellowship with the unfruitful works of darkness, nor those that act them.—*David Clarkson, B.D.*, 1621—1686.

Verse 6.—" *Thou shalt destroy them that speak leasing,*" whether in jest or earnest· Those that lie in jest will (without repentance) go to hell in earnest.—*John Trapp.*

Verse 6.—" *Thou shalt destroy them that speak leasing,*" etc. In the same field wherein Absalom raised battle against his father, stood the oak that was his gibbet. The mule whereon he rode was his hangman, for the mule carried him to the tree, and the hair wherein he gloried served for a rope to hang. Little know the wicked how everything which now they have, shall be a snare to trap them when God begins to punish them.—*William Cowper,* 1612.

Verse 7.—" *In thy fear will I worship.*" As natural fear makes the spirits retire from the outward parts of the body to the heart, so a holy fear of miscarrying, in so solemn a duty, would be a means to call thy thoughts from all exterior carnal objects, and fix them upon the duty in hand. As the sculpture is on the seal, so will the print on the wax be ; if the fear of God be deeply engraven on thy heart, there is no doubt but it will make a suitable impression on the duty thou performest. *William Gurnall.*

Verse 7.—David saith, " *In thy fear will I worship toward thy holy temple.*" The temple did shadow forth the body of our Lord Christ, the Mediator, in whom only our prayers and services are accepted with the Father which Solomon respected in looking towards the temple.—*Thomas Manton, D.D.*, 1620—1677.

Verse 7.—" *But as for me,*" etc. A blessed verse this ! a blessed saying ! The words and the sense itself, carry with them a powerful contrast. For there are two things with which this life is exercised, HOPE and FEAR, which are, as it were, those two springs of Judges i. 15, the one from above, the other from beneath. *Fear* comes from beholding the threats and fearful judgments of God ; as being a God in whose sight no one is clean, every one is a sinner, every one is damnable. But *hope* comes from beholding the promises, and the all-sweet mercies of God ; as it is written (Psalm xxv. 6), " Remember, O Lord, thy lovingkindnesses, and thy tender mercies which have been ever of old." Between these two, as between the upper and nether millstone, we must always be ground and kept, that we never turn either to the right hand or to the left. For this turning is the state peculiar to hypocrites, who are exercised with the two contrary things, security and presumption. *Martin Luther.*

Verse 9.—If the whole soul be infected with such a desperate disease, what a great and difficult work is it to regenerate, to restore men again to spiritual life and vigour, when every part of them is seized by such a mortal distemper ! How great a cure doth the Spirit of God effect in restoring a soul by sanctifying it ! To heal but the lungs or the liver, if corrupted, is counted a great cure, though performed but upon one part of thee ; but all thy inward parts are very rottenness. " *For there is no faithfulness in their mouth ; their inward part is very wickedness : their throat is an open sepulchre ; they flatter with their tongue.*" How great a cure is it then to heal thee ! Such as is only in the skill and power of God to do.—*Thomas Goodwin.*

Verse 9.—" *Their throat is an open sepulchre.*" This figure graphically portrays the filthy conversation of the wicked. Nothing can be more abominable to the senses than an open sepulchre, when a dead body beginning to putrefy steams forth its tainted exhalations. What proceeds out of their mouth is infected and putrid; and as the exhalation from a sepulchre proves the corruption within, so it is with the corrupt conversation of sinners.—*Robert Haldane's "Expositions of the Epistle to the Romans,"* 1835.

Verse 9.—*" Their throat is an open sepulchre."* This doth admonish us, (1) that the speeches of natural unregenerate men are unsavoury, rotten, and hurtful to others; for, as a sepulchre doth send out noisome savours and filthy smells, so evil men do utter rotten and filthy words. (2) As a sepulchre doth consume and devour bodies cast into it, so wicked men do with their cruel words destroy others; they are like a gulf to destroy others. (3) As a sepulchre, having devoured many corpses, is still ready to consume more, being never satisfied, so wicked men, having overthrown many with their words, do proceed in their outrage, seeking whom they may devour.—*Thomas Wilson*, 1653.

Verse 9.—*" Their inward part,"* etc. Their hearts are storehouses for the devil.—*John Trapp.*

Verse 10.—All those portions where we find apparently prayers that breathe revenge, are never to be thought of as anything else than the *breathed assent of righteous souls* to the justice of their God, who taketh vengeance on sin. When taken as the words of Christ himself, they are no other than an echo of the Intercessor's acquiescence at last in the sentence on the barren fig-tree. It is as if he cried aloud, " Hew it down now, I will intercede no longer, the doom is righteous, *destroy them, O God; cast them out in* (or, for) *the multitude of their transgressions, for they have rebelled against thee."* And in the same moment he may be supposed to invite his saints to sympathise in his decision; just as in Rev. xviii. 20, " Rejoice over her, thou heaven, and ye holy apostles and prophets." In like manner, when one of Christ's members, in entire sympathy with his Head, views the barren fig-tree from the same point of observation, and sees the glory of God concerned in inflicting the blow, he too can cry, " Let the axe smite! " Had Abraham stood beside the angel who destroyed Sodom, and seen how Jehovah's name required the ruin of these impenitent rebels, he would have cried out, " Let the shower descend; let the fire and brimstone come down! " not in any spirit of revenge; not from want of tender love to souls, but from intense earnestness of concern for the glory of his God. We consider this explanation to be the real key that opens all the difficult passages in this book, where curses seem to be called for on the head of the ungodly. They are no more than a carrying out of Deut. xxvii. 15—26, " Let all the people say, Amen," and an entering into the Lord's holy abhorrence of sin, and delight in acts of justice expressed in the " Amen hallelujah," of Rev. xix. 3.—*Andrew A. Bonar*, 1859.

Verse 10.—*(Or imprecatory passages generally).* Lord, when in my daily service I read David's Psalms, give me to alter the accent of my soul according to their several subjects. In such Psalms wherein he confesseth his sins, or requesteth thy pardon, or praiseth for former, or prayeth for future favours, in all these give me to raise my soul to as high a pitch as may be. But when I come to such Psalms wherein he curseth his enemies, O there let me bring my soul down to a lower note. For those words were made only to fit David's mouth. I have the like breath, but not the same spirit to pronounce them. Nor let me flatter myself, that it is lawful for me, with David, to curse thine enemies, lest my deceitful heart entitle mine enemies to be thine, and so what was religion in David, prove malice in me, whilst I act revenge under the pretence of piety.—*Thomas Fuller, D.D.*, 1608—1661.

Verse 12.—When the strong man armed comes against us, when he darts his fiery darts, what can hurt us, if God compass us about with *his lovingkindness as with a shield?* He can disarm the tempter and restrain his malice, and tread him under our feet. If God be not with us, if he do not give us sufficient grace, so subtle, so powerful, so politic an enemy, will be too hard for us. How surely are we foiled, and get the worse, when we pretend to grapple with him in our own strength! How many falls, and how many bruises by those falls have we got, by relying too much on our own skill? How often have we had the help of God when we have humbly asked it! And how sure are we to get the victory, *if Christ pray for us that we do not fail!* Luke xxii. 31. Where can we go for shelter but unto God our Maker! When this lion of the forest does begin to roar, how will he terrify and vex us, till he that permits him for awhile to trouble us, be pleased to chain him up again!—*Timothy Rogers*, 1691.

Verse 12.—" *As with a shield.*" Luther, when making his way into the presence of Cardinal Cajetan, who had summoned him to answer for his heretical opinions at Augsburg, was asked by one of the Cardinal's minions, where he should find a shelter, if his patron, the Elector of Saxony, should desert him? " Under the shelter of heaven ! " was the reply. The silenced minion turned round and went his way.

Verse 12.—" *With favour wilt thou compass him as with a shield.*" The shield is not for the defence of any particular part of the body, as almost all the other pieces are : helmet, fitted for the head ; plate designed for the breast ; and so others, they have their several parts, which they are fastened to ; but the shield is a piece that is intended for the defence of the whole body. It was used therefore to be made very large ; for its broadness, called a gate or door, because so long and large, as in a manner to cover the whole body. And if the shield were not large enough at once to cover every part, yet being a movable piece of armour, the skilful soldier might turn it this way or that way, to catch the blow or arrow from lighting on any part they were directed to. And this indeed doth excellently well set forth the universal use that faith is of to the Christian. It defends the whole man : every part of the Christian by it is preserved . . . . . The shield doth not only defend the whole body, but it is a defence to the soldier's armour also ; it keeps the arrow from the helmet as well as head, from the breast and breastplate also. Thus faith, it is armour upon armour, a grace that preserves all the other graces.—*William Gurnall.*

HINTS TO PREACHERS.

Verses 1, 2.—Prayer in its threefold form. " *Words, meditation, cry.*" Showing how utterance is of no avail without heart, but that fervent longings and silent desires are accepted, even when unexpressed.

Verse 3.—The excellence of morning devotion.

Verse 3 (*last two clauses*).—1. Prayer directed. 2. Answers expected.

Verse 4.—God's hatred of sin an example to his people.

Verse 5.—" *The foolish.*" Show why sinners are justly called fools.

Verse 7.—" *Multitude of thy mercy.*" Dwell upon the varied grace and goodness of God.

Verse 7.— The devout resolution.

Verse 7.—I. Observe the *singularity* of the resolution. II. Mark the *object* of the resolution. It regards the service of God in the sanctuary. " I will come into thine *house* . . . . . in thy fear will I *worship* towards thy *holy temple.*" III. The *manner* in which he would accomplish the resolution. (1) Impressed with a sense of the divine goodness : " I will come into thy house in *the multitude of thy mercy.*" (2) Filled with holy veneration : " And *in thy fear* will I worship."—*William Jay,* 1842.

Verse 8.—God's guidance needed always, and especially when enemies are watching us.

Verse 10.—Viewed as a threatening. The sentence, " Cast them out in the multitude of their transgressions," is specially fitted to be the groundwork of a very solemn discourse.

Verse 11.—I. The character of the righteous : *faith and love.* II. The privileges of the righteous. (1) *Joy*—great, pure, satisfying, triumphant (*shout*), constant (*ever*). (2) *Defence*—by power, providence, angels, grace, etc.

Verse 11.—Joy in the Lord both a duty and a privilege.

Verse 12 (*first clause*).—*The divine blessing upon the righteous.* It is ancient, effectual, constant, extensive, irreversible, surpassing, eternal, infinite.

Verse 12 (*second clause*).—A sense of divine favour a defence to the soul.

PSALM VI.

TITLE.—*This Psalm is commonly known as the first of* THE PENITENTIAL PSALMS,* *and certainly its language well becomes the lip of a penitent, for it expresses at once the sorrow (verses 3, 6, 7), the humiliation (verses 2 and 4), and the hatred of sin (verse 8), which are the unfailing marks of the contrite spirit when it turns to God. O Holy Spirit, beget in us the true repentance which needeth not to be repented of. The title of this Psalm is,* " To the chief Musician on Neginoth upon Sheminith,‡ A Psalm of David," *that is, to the chief musician with stringed instruments, upon the eight, probably the octave. Some think it refers to the bass or tenor key, which would certainly be well adapted to this mournful ode. But we are not able to understand these old musical terms, and even the term* " Selah," *still remains untranslated. This, however, should be no difficulty in our way. We probably lose but very little by our ignorance, and it may serve to confirm our faith. It is a proof of the high antiquity of these Psalms that they contain words, the meaning of which is lost even to the best scholars of the Hebrew language. Surely these are but incidental (accidental I might almost say, if I did not believe them to be designed by God), proofs of their being, what they profess to be, the ancient writings of King David of olden times.*

DIVISION.— *You will observe that the Psalm is readily divided into two parts. First, there is the Psalmist's plea in his great distress, reaching from the first to the end of the seventh verse. Then you have, from the eighth to the end, quite a different theme. The Psalmist has changed his note. He leaves the minor key, and betakes himself to sublime strains. He tunes his note to the high key of confidence, and declares that God hath heard his prayer, and hath delivered him out of all his troubles.*

EXPOSITION.

O LORD, rebuke me not in thine anger, neither chasten me in thy hot displeasure.

2 Have mercy upon me, O LORD; for I *am* weak: O LORD, heal me; for my bones are vexed.

3 My soul is also sore vexed: but thou, O LORD, how long?

4 Return, O LORD, deliver my soul: oh save me for thy mercies' sake.

5 For in death *there is* no remembrance of thee: in the grave who shall give thee thanks?

6 I am weary with my groaning; all the night make I my bed to swim; I water my couch with my tears.

7 Mine eye is consumed because of grief; it waxeth old because of all mine enemies.

Having read through the first division, in order to see it as a whole, we will now look at it verse by verse. " *O Lord, rebuke me not in thine anger.*" The Psalmist is very conscious that he deserves to be rebuked, and he feels, moreover, that the rebuke in some form or other must come upon him, if not for condemnation, yet for conviction and sanctification. " Corn is cleaned with wind, and the soul with chastenings." It were folly to pray against the golden hand which enriches us by its blows. He does not ask that the rebuke may be totally withheld, for he might thus lose a blessing in disguise; but, " Lord, rebuke me not in *thine anger.*" If thou remindest me of my sin, it is good; but, oh, remind me not of it as one incensed against me, lest thy servant's heart should sink in despair. Thus saith Jeremiah, " O Lord, correct me, but with judgment; not in thine anger, lest thou bring me to nothing." I know that I must be chastened, and though I shrink from the rod yet do I feel that it will be for my ben·fit; but, oh, my God, " *chasten me not in thy hot displeasure,*" lest the rod become a sword, and lest in smiting, thou shouldest also kill. So may we pray that the chastisements of our gracious God, if they may not

---

* The other six are, xxxii., xxxviii., li., cii., cxxx., cxliii.   ‡ 1 Chron. xv. 21.

be entirely removed, may at least be sweetened by the consciousness that they are " not in anger, but in his dear covenant love."

2, 3. " *Have mercy upon me, O Lord ; for I am weak.*" Though I deserve destruction, yet let thy mercy pity my frailty. This is the right way to plead with God if we would prevail. Urge not your goodness or your greatness, but plead your sin and your littleness. Cry, " *I am weak,*" therefore O Lord, give me strength and crush me not. Send not forth the fury of thy tempest against so weak a vessel. Temper the wind to the shorn lamb. Be tender and pitiful to a poor withering flower, and break it not from its stem. Surely this is the plea that a sick man would urge to move the pity of his fellow if he were striving with him, " Deal gently with me, ' for I am weak.' " A sense of sin had so spoiled the Psalmist's pride, so taken away his vaunted strength, that he found himself weak to obey the law, weak through the sorrow that was in him, too weak, perhaps, to lay hold on the promise. " *I am weak.*" The original may be read, " I am one who droops," or withered like a blighted plant. Ah ! beloved, we know what this means, for we, too, have seen our glory stained, and our beauty like a faded flower.

" *O Lord heal me ; for my bones are vexed.*" Here he prays for *healing*, not merely the mitigation of the ills he endured, but their entire removal, and the curing of the wounds which had arisen therefrom. His bones were " *shaken,*' as the Hebrew has it. His terror had become so great that his very bones shook ; not only did his flesh quiver, but the bones, the solid pillars of the house of manhood, were made to tremble. " My bones are shaken." Ah, when the soul has a sense of sin, it is enough to make the bones shake ; it is enough to make a man's hair stand up on end to see the flames of hell beneath him, an angry God above him, and danger and doubt surrounding him. Well might he say, " My bones are shaken." Lest, however, we should imagine that it was merely bodily sickness—although bodily sickness might be the outward sign—the Psalmist goes on to say, " *My soul is also sore vexed.*" Soul-trouble is the very soul of trouble. It matters not that the bones shake if the soul be firm, but when the soul itself is also sore vexed this is agony indeed. " *But thou, O Lord, how long ?*" This sentence ends abruptly, for words failed, and grief drowned the little comfort which dawned upon him. The Psalmist had still, however, some hope ; but that hope was only in his God. He therefore cries, " O Lord, how long ? " The coming of Christ into the soul in his priestly robes of grace is the grand hope of the penitent soul ; and, indeed, in some form or other, Christ's appearance is, and ever·has been, the hope of the saints.

Calvin's favourite exclamation was " Domine usque quo "—" *O Lord, how long ?*" Nor could his sharpest pains, during a life of anguish, force from him any other word. Surely this is the cry of the saints under the altar, " O Lord, how long ? " And this should be the cry of the saints waiting for the millennial glories, " Why are his chariots so long in coming ; Lord, how long ? " Those of us who have passed through conviction of sin knew what it was to count our minutes hours, and our hours years, while mercy delayed its coming. We watched for the dawn of grace, as they that watch for the morning. Earnestly did our anxious spirits ask, " O Lord, how long ? "

4 " *Return, O Lord ; deliver my soul.*" As God's absence was the main cause of his misery, so his return would be enough to deliver him from his trouble. " *Oh save me for thy mercies' sake.*" He knows where to look, and what arm to lay hold upon. He does not lay hold on God's left hand of justice, but on his right hand of mercy. He knew his iniquity too well to think of merit, or appeal to anything but the grace of God.

" *For thy mercies' sake.*" What a plea that is ! How prevalent it is with God ! If we turn to justice, what plea can we urge ? but if we turn to mercy we may still cry, notwithstanding the greatness of our guilt, " Save me for thy mercies' sake."

Observe how frequently David here pleads the name of Jehovah, which is always intended where the word LORD is given in capitals. Five times in four verses we here meet with it. Is not this a proof that the glorious name is full of consolation to the tempted saint ? Eternity, Infinity, Immutability, Self-existence, are all in the name Jehovah, and all are full of comfort.

5. And now David was in great fear of death—death temporal, and perhaps death eternal. Read the passage as you will, the following verse is full of power. " *For in death there is no remembrance of thee ; in the grave who shall give thee thanks?*" Churchyards are silent places ; the vaults of the sepulchre echo not with songs. Damp earth covers dumb mouths. " O Lord ? " said he, " if thou wilt spare me I

will praise thee. If I die, then must my mortal praise at least be suspended ; and if I perish in hell, then thou wilt never have any thanksgiving from me. Songs of gratitude cannot rise from the flaming pit of hell. True, thou wilt doubtless be glorified, even in my eternal condemnation, but then, O Lord, I cannot glorify thee voluntarily ; and among the sons of men, there will be one heart the less to bless thee." Ah ! poor trembling sinners, may the Lord help you to use this forcible argument. It is for God's glory that a sinner should be saved. When we seek pardon, we are not asking God to do that which will stain his banner, or put a blot on his escutcheon. He delighteth in mercy. It is his peculiar, darling attribute. Mercy honours God. Do not we ourselves say, " Mercy blesseth him that gives, and him that takes ? " And surely, in some diviner sense, this is true of God, who, when he gives mercy, glorifies himself.

6, 7.—The Psalmist gives a fearful description of his long agony : " *I am weary with my groaning.*" He had groaned till his throat was hoarse ; he had cried for mercy till prayer became a labour. God's people may groan, but they may not grumble. Yea, they must groan, being burdened, or they will never shout in the day of deliverance. The next sentence, we think, is not accurately translated. It should be, " *I shall make my bed to swim every night,*" (when nature needs rest, and when I am most alone with my God). That is to say, my grief is fearful even now, but if God do not soon save me, it will not stay of itself, but will increase, until my tears will be so many, that my bed itself shall swim. A description rather of what he feared would be, than of what had actually taken place. May not our forebodings of future woe become arguments which faith may urge when seeking present mercy ? " *I water my couch with my tears. Mine eye is consumed because of grief ; it waxeth old because of all mine enemies.*" As an old man's eye grows dim with years, so says David, my eye is grown red and feeble through weeping. Conviction sometimes has such an effect upon the body, that even the outward organs are made to suffer. May not this explain some of the convulsions and hysterical attacks which have been experienced under convictions in the revivals in Ireland ? Is it surprising that some should be smitten to the earth, and begin to cry aloud ; when we find that David himself made his bed to swim, and grew old while he was under the heavy hand of God ? Ah ! brethren, it is no light matter to feel one's self a sinner, condemned at the bar of God. The language of this Psalm is not strained and forced, but perfectly natural to one in so sad a plight.

8 Depart from me, all ye workers of iniquity ; for the LORD hath heard the voice of my weeping.

9 The LORD hath heard my supplication ; the LORD will receive my prayer.

10 Let all mine enemies be ashamed and sore vexed : let them return *and* be ashamed suddenly.

8. Hitherto, all has been mournful and disconsolate, but now—

> " Your harps, ye trembling saints,
> Down from the willows take."

Ye must have your times of weeping, but let them be short. Get ye up, get ye up, from your dunghills ! Cast aside your sackcloth and ashes ! Weeping may endure for a night, but joy cometh in the morning.

David has found peace, and rising from his knees he begins to sweep his house of the wicked. " *Depart from me, all ye workers of iniquity.*" The best remedy for us against an evil man is a long space between us both. " Get ye gone ; I can have no fellowship with you." Repentance is a practical thing. It is not enough to bemoan the desecration of the temple of the heart, we must scourge out the buyers and sellers, and overturn the tables of the money changers. A pardoned sinner *will hate the sins* which cost the Saviour his blood. Grace and sin are quarrelsome neighbours, and one or the other must go to the wall.

" *For the Lord hath heard the voice of my weeping.*" What a fine Hebraism, and what grand poetry it is in English ! " He hath heard the voice of my weeping." Is there a voice in weeping ? Does weeping speak ? In what language doth it utter its meaning ? Why, in that universal tongue which is known and understood in all the earth, and even in heaven above. When a man weeps, whether he be a Jew or Gentile, Barbarian, Scythian, bond or free, it has the same meaning in it. Weeping is the eloquence of sorrow. It is an unstammering orator, needing no interpreter, but understood of all. Is it not sweet to believe that our tears are understood even when words fail ! Let us learn to think of tears as liquid prayers, and of weeping as a constant dropping of importunate intercession which will wear its way right surely into the very heart of mercy, despite the stony difficulties which obstruct the way. My God, I will " weep " when I cannot plead, for thou hearest the voice of my weeping.

9. " *The Lord hath heard my supplication.*" The Holy Spirit had wrought into the Psalmist's mind the confidence that his prayer was heard. This is frequently the privilege of the saints. Praying the prayer of faith, they are often infallibly assured that they have prevailed with God. We read of Luther that, having on one occasion wrestled hard with God in prayer, he came leaping out of his closet crying, " *Vicimus, vicimus;*" that is, "We have conquered, we have prevailed with God." Assured confidence is no idle dream, for when the Holy Ghost bestows it upon us, we know its reality, and could not doubt it, even though all men should deride our boldness. " *The Lord will receive my prayer.*" Here is past experience used for future encouragement. *He hath, he will.* Note this, O believer, and imitate its reasoning.

10. " *Let all mine enemies be ashamed and sore vexed.*" This is rather a prophecy than an imprecation, it may be read in the future. " All my enemies shall be ashamed and sore vexed." *They shall return and be ashamed instantaneously,*—in a moment ;—their doom shall come upon them suddenly. Death's day is doom's day, and both are sure and may be sudden. The Romans were wont to say, " The feet of the avenging Deity are shod with wool." With noiseless footsteps vengeance nears its victim, and sudden and overwhelming shall be its destroying stroke. If this were an imprecation, we must remember that the language of the old dispensation is not that of the new. We pray *for* our enemies, not *against* them. God have mercy on them, and bring them into the right way.

Thus the Psalm, like those which precede it, shows the different estates of the godly and the wicked. O Lord, let us be numbered *with* thy people, both now and for ever !

EXPLANATORY NOTES AND QUAINT SAYINGS.

Whole Psalm.—David was a man that was often exercised with sickness and troubles from enemies, and in all the instances almost that we meet with in the Psalms of these his afflictions, we may observe the outward occasions of trouble brought him under the suspicion of God's wrath and his own iniquity ; so that he was seldom sick, or persecuted, but this called on the disquiet of conscience, and brought his sin to remembrance ; as in this Psalm, which was made on the occasion of his sickness, as appears from verse eight, wherein he expresseth the vexation of his soul under the apprehension of God's anger ; all his other griefs running into this channel, as little brooks, losing themselves in a great river, change their name and nature. He that was at first only concerned for his sickness, is now wholly concerned with sorrow and smart under the fear and hazard of his soul's condition ; the like we may see in Psalm xxxviii, and many places more.—*Richard Gilpin*, 1677.

Verse 1.—" *Rebuke me not.*" God hath two means by which he reduceth his children to obedience ; his word, by which he rebukes them ; and his rod, by which he chastiseth them. The word precedes, admonishing them by his servants whom he hath sent in all ages to call sinners to repentance : of the which David himself saith, " Let the righteous rebuke me ; " and as a father doth first rebuke his disordered child, so doth the Lord speak to them. But when men neglect the warnings of his word, then God as a good father, takes up the rod and beats them. Our Saviour wakened the three disciples in the garden three times, but seeing that served not, he told them that Judas and his band were coming to awaken them whom his own voice could not waken.—*A. Symson*, 1638.

Verse 1.—" *Jehovah, rebuke me not in thine anger,*" etc. He does not altogether refuse punishment, for that would be unreasonable ; and to be without it, he judged would be more hurtful than beneficial to him ; but what he is afraid of is the wrath of God, which threatens sinners with ruin and perdition. To anger and indignation David tacitly opposes fatherly and gentle chastisement, and this last he was willing to bear.—*John Calvin, 1509—1564.*

Verse 1.—" *O Lord, rebuke me not in thine anger.*"

> The anger of the Lord ? Oh, dreadful thought !
> How can a creature frail as man endure
> The tempest of his wrath ? Ah, whither flee
> To 'scape the punishment he well deserves ?
> Flee to the cross ! the great atonement there
> Will shield the sinner, if he supplicate
> For pardon with repentance true and deep,
> And faith that questions not. Then will the frown
> Of anger pass off the face of God,
> Like a black tempest cloud that hides the sun.   *Anon.*

Verse 1.—" *Lord, rebuke me not in thine anger,*" etc. ; that is, do not lay upon me that thou hast threatened in thy law ; where anger is not put for the decree, nor the execution, but for the denouncing. So (Matt. iii. 11, and so Hos. xi. 9), " I will not execute the fierceness of mine anger," that is, I will not execute my wrath as I have declared it. Again, it is said, he executes punishment on the wicked ; he declares it not only, but executeth it, so anger is put for the execution of anger.—*Richard Stock, 1641.*

Verse 1.—" *Neither chasten me in thine hot displeasure.*"

> O keep up life and peace within,
> If I must feel thy chastening rod !
> Yet kill not me, but kill my sin,
> And let me know thou art my God.
> O give my soul some sweet foretaste
> Of that which I shall shortly see !
> Let faith and love cry to the last,
> " Come, Lord, I trust myself with thee ! "
>
>   *Richard Baxter, 1615—1691.*

Verse 2.—" *Have mercy upon me, O Lord.*" To fly and escape the anger of God, David sees no means in heaven or in earth, and therefore retires himself to God, even to him who wounded him that he might heal him. He flies not with Adam to the bush, nor with Saul to the witch, nor with Jonah to Tarshish ; but he appeals from an angry and just God to a merciful God, and from himself to himself. The woman who was condemned by King Philip, appealed from Philip being drunken to Philip being sober. But David appeals from one virtue, justice, to another, mercy. There may be appellation from the tribunal of man to the justice-seat of God ; but when thou art indicted before God's justice-seat, whither or to whom wilt thou go but to himself and his mercy-seat, which is the highest and last place of appellation ? " I have none in heaven but thee, nor in earth besides thee." . . . . David, under the name of *mercy*, includeth all things, according to that of Jacob to his brother Esau, " I have gotten mercy, and therefore I have gotten all things." Desirest thou any thing at God's hands ? Cry for *mercy*, out of which fountain all good things will spring to thee.—*Archibald Symson.*

Verse 2.—" *For I am weak.*" Behold, what rhetoric he useth to move God to cure him, " *I am weak*," an argument taken from his weakness, which indeed were a weak argument to move any man to show his favour, but is a strong argument to prevail with God. If a diseased person would come to a physician, and only lament the heaviness of his sickness, he would say, God help thee ; or an oppressed person come to a lawyer, and show him the estate of his action and ask his advice, that is a golden question ; or to a merchant to crave raiment, he will either have present money or a surety ; or a courtier favour, you must have your reward ready in your hand. But coming before God the most forcible argument that ye can use is your necessity, poverty, tears, misery, unworthiness, and confessing them to him, it shall be an open door to furnish you with all things that he hath. . . . . The tears of our misery are forcible arrows to pierce the heart of our heavenly Father, to deliver us and pity our hard case. The beggars lay open their sores to the view of the world, that the more they may move men to pity them. So let us deplore our miseries to God, that he, with the pitiful Samaritan, at the sight of our wounds, may help us in due time.—*Archibald Symson.*

Verse 2.—"*Heal me*," etc. David comes not to take physic upon wantonness, but because the disease is violent, because the accidents are vehement ; so vehement, so violent, as that it hath pierced *ad ossa*, and *ad animam*, "*My bones are vexed, and my soul is sore troubled*," therefore "*heal me ;*" which is the reason upon which he grounds this second petition, "*Heal me, because my bones are vexed*," etc.—*John Donne.*

Verse 2.—"*My bones are vexed.*" The Lord can make the strongest and most insensible part of man's body sensible of his wrath when he pleaseth to touch him, for here David's bones are vexed.—*David Dickson.*

Verse 2.—The term "*bones*" frequently occurs in the psalms, and if we examine we shall find it used in three different senses. (1.) It is sometimes applied literally to our blessed Lord's human body, to the body which hung upon the cross, as, "They pierced my hands and my feet ; I may tell all my bones." (2.) It has sometimes also a further reference to his mystical body the church. And then it denotes all the members of Christ's body that stand firm in the faith, that cannot be moved by persecutions, or temptations, however severe, as, "All my bones shall say, Lord, who is like unto thee ? " (3.) In some passages the term bones is applied to the soul, and not to the body, to the inner man of the individual Christian. Then it implies the strength and fortitude of the soul, the determined courage which faith in God gives to the righteous. This is the sense in which it is used in the second verse of Psalm vi., "*O Lord, heal me ; for my bones are vexed.*"—*Augustine, Ambrose, and Chrysostom ; quoted by F. H. Dunwell, B.A., in "Parochial Lectures on the Psalms,"* 1855.

Verse 3.—"*My soul.*" Yokefellows in sin are yokefellows in pain ; the soul is punished for informing, the body for performing, and as both the informer and performer, the cause and the instrument, so shall the stirrer up of sin and the executer of it be punished.—*John Donne.*

Verse 3.—"*O Lord, how long ?*" Out of this we have three things to observe ; first, that there is an appointed time which God hath measured for the crosses of all his children, before which time they shall not be delivered, and for which they must patiently attend, not thinking to prescribe time to God for their delivery, or limit the Holy One of Israel. The Israelites remained in Egypt till the complete number of four hundred and thirty years were accomplished. Joseph was three years and more in the prison till the appointed time of his delivery came. The Jews remained seventy years in Babylon. So that as the physician appointeth certain times to the patient, both wherein he must fast, and be dieted, and wherein he must take recreation, so God knoweth the convenient times both of our humiliation and exaltation. Next, see the impatiency of our nature in our miseries, our flesh still rebelling against the Spirit, which oftentimes forgetteth itself so far, that it will enter into reasoning with God, and quarrelling with him as we may read of Job, Jonas, etc., and here also of David. Thirdly, albeit the Lord delay his coming to relieve his saints, yet hath he great cause if we could ponder it ; for when we were in the heat of our sins, many times he cried by the mouth of his prophets and servants, "O fools, how long will you continue in your folly ? " And we would not hear ; and therefore when we are in the heat of our pains, thinking long, yea, every day a year till we be delivered, no wonder it is if God will not hear ; let us consider with ourselves the just dealing of God with us ; that as he cried and we would not hear, so now we cry, and he will not hear.—*A. Symson.*

Verse 3.—"*O Lord, how long?*" As the saints in heaven have their *usque quo,* how long, Lord, holy and true, before thou begin to execute judgment ? So, the saints on earth have their *usque quo.* How long, Lord, before thou take off the execution of this judgment upon us ? For, our deprecatory prayers are not mandatory, they are not directory, they appoint not God his ways, or his times ; but as our postulatory prayers are, they also are submitted to the will of God, and have all in them that ingredient, that herb of grace, which Christ put into his own prayer, that *veruntamen, yet not my will, but thy will be fulfilled ;* and they have that ingredient which Christ put into our prayer, *fiat voluntas, thy will be done in earth as it is in heaven ;* in heaven there is no resisting of his will ; yet in heaven there is a soliciting, a hastening, an accelerating of the judgment, and the glory of the resurrection ; so though we resist not his corrections here upon earth, we may humbly present to God the sense which we have of his displeasure, for this sense and apprehension of his corrections is one of the principal reasons why he sends them; he corrects us therefore that we might be sensible of his corrections; that when we, being humbled under his hand, have said with his prophet, "*I will bear the wrath of the Lord because I have sinned against him*" (Mic. vii. 9), he may be pleased to say to his correcting angel, as he did to his destroying angel, *This is enough*, and so burn his rod now, as he put up his sword then.—*John Donne.*

Verse 4.—"*Return, O Lord, deliver my soul*," etc. In this his besieging of God, he brings up his works from afar off, closer; he begins in this Psalm, at a deprecatory prayer; he asks nothing, but that God would do nothing, that he would forbear him—*rebuke me not, correct me not.* Now, it costs the king less to give a pardon than to give a pension, and less to give a reprieve than to give a pardon, and less to connive, not to call in question, than either reprieve, pardon, or pension; to forbear is not much. But then as the mathematician said, that he could make an engine, a screw, that should move the whole frame of the world, if he could have a place assigned him to fix that engine, that screw upon, so that it might work upon the world; so prayer, when one petition hath taken hold upon God, works upon God, moves God, prevails with God, entirely for all. David then having got this ground, this footing in God, he brings his works closer; he comes from the deprecatory to a postulatory prayer; not only that God would do nothing against him, but that he would do something for him. God hath suffered man to see *Arcana imperii*, the secrets of his state, how he governs—he governs by precedent; by precedents of his predecessors, he cannot, he hath none; by precedents of other gods he cannot, there are none; and yet he proceeds by precedents, by his own precedents, he does as he did before, *habenti dat*, to him that hath received he gives more, and is willing to be wrought and prevailed upon, and pressed with his own example. And, as though his doing good were but to learn how to do good better, still he writes after his own copy, and *nulla dies sine linea*. He writes something to us, that is, he doth something for us every day. And then, that which is not often seen in other masters, his copies are better than the originals; his latter mercies larger than his former; and in this postulatory prayer, larger than the deprecatory, enters our text, "*Return, O Lord; deliver my soul: O save me*," etc.—*John Donne.*

Verse 5.—"*For in death there is no remembrance of thee, in the grave who will give thee thanks?*" Lord, be thou pacified and reconciled to me . . . for shouldst thou now proceed to take away my life, as it were a most direful condition for me to die before I have propitiated thee, so I may well demand what increase of glory or honour will it bring unto thee? Will it not be infinitely more glorious for thee to spare me, till by true contrition I may regain thy favour?—and then I may live to praise and magnify thy mercy and thy grace: thy mercy in pardoning so great a sinner, and then confess thee by vital actions of all holy obedience for the future, and so demonstrate the power of thy grace which hath wrought this change in me; neither of which will be done by destroying me, but only thy just judgments manifested in thy vengeance on sinners.—*Henry Hammond, D.D.,* 1659.

Verse 6.—"*I fainted in my mourning.*" It may seem a marvellous change in David, being a man of such magnitude of mind, to be thus dejected and cast down. Prevailed he not against Goliath, against the lion and the bear, through fortitude and magnanimity? But now he is sobbing, sighing, and weeping as a child! The answer is easy; the diverse persons with whom he hath to do occasioneth the same. When men and beasts are his opposites, then he is more than a conqueror; but when he hath to do with God against whom he sinned, then he is less than nothing.

Verse 6.—"*I caused my bed to swim.*" . . . . . Showers be better than dews, yet it is sufficient if God at least hath bedewed our hearts, and hath given us some sign of a penitent heart. If we have not rivers of waters to pour forth with David, neither fountains flowing with Mary Magdalen, nor as Jeremy, desire to have a fountain in our head to weep day and night, nor with Peter weep bitterly; yet if we lament that we cannot lament, and mourn that we cannot mourn: yea, if we have the smallest sobs of sorrow and tears of compunction, if they be true and not counterfeit, they will make us acceptable to God; for as the woman with the bloody issue that touched the hem of Christ's garment, was no less welcome to Christ than Thomas, who put his fingers in the print of the nails; so, God looketh not at the quantity, but the sincerity of our repentance.

Verse 6.—"*My bed.*" The place of his sin is the place of his repentance, and so it should be ; yea, when we behold the place where we have offended, we should be pricked in the heart, and there again crave him pardon. As Adam sinned in the garden, and Christ sweat bloody tears in the garden. " Examine your hearts upon your beds, and convert unto the Lord ; " and whereas ye have stretched forth yourselves upon your bed to devise evil things, repent there and make them sanctuaries to God. Sanctify by your tears every place which ye have polluted by sin. And let us seek Christ Jesus on our own bed, with the spouse in the Canticles, who saith, " By night on my bed I sought him whom my soul loveth."—*Archibald Symson.*

Verse 6.—" *I water my couch with tears.*" Not only I *wash*, but also I *water*. The faithful sheep of the great Shepherd go up from the *washing* place, every one bringeth forth twins, and none barren among them. Cant. iv. 2. For so Jacob's sheep, having conceived at the watering troughs, brought forth strong and party-coloured lambs. David likewise, who before had erred and strayed like a lost sheep, making here his bed a washing place, by so much the less is barren in obedience, by how much the more he is fruitful in repentance. In Solomon's temple stood the caldrons of brass, to wash the flesh of those beasts which where to be sacrificed on the altar. Solomon's father maketh a water of his tears, a caldron of his bed, an altar of his heart, a sacrifice, not of the flesh of unreasonable beasts, but of his own body, a living sacrifice, which is his reasonable serving of God. Now the Hebrew word here used signifies properly, to cause to swim, which is more than simply to wash. And thus the Geneva translation readeth it, I cause my bed every night to swim. So that as the priests used to swim in the molten sea, that they might be pure and clean, against they performed the holy rites and services of the temple, in like manner the princely prophet washeth his bed, yea, he swimmeth in his bed, or rather he causeth his bed to swim in tears, as in a sea of grief and penitent sorrow for his sin.—*Thomas Playfere*, 1604.

Verse 6.—" *I water my couch with my tears.*" Let us water our bed every night with our tears. Do not only blow upon it with intermissive blasts, for then like fire, it will resurge and flame the more. Sin is like a stinking candle newly put out, it is soon lighted again. It may receive a wound, but like a dog it will easily lick itself whole ; a little forbearance multiplies it like Hydra's heads. Therefore, whatsoever aspersion the sin of the day has brought upon us, let the tears of the *night* wash away.—*Thomas Adams.*

Verses 6, 7.—Soul-trouble is attended usually with great pain of body too, and so a man is wounded and distressed in every part. There is no soundness in my flesh, because of thine anger, says David. " The arrows of the Almighty are within me, the poison whereof drinketh up my spirit." Job vi. 4. Sorrow of heart contracts the natural spirits, making all their motions slow and feeble ; and the poor afflicted body does usually decline and waste away ; and, therefore, saith Heman, " My soul is full of troubles, and my life draweth nigh unto the grave." In this inward distress we find our strength decay and melt, even as wax before the fire, for sorrow darkeneth the spirits, obscures the judgment, blinds the memory as to all pleasant things, and beclouds the lucid part of the mind, causing the lamp of life to burn weakly. In this troubled condition the person cannot be without a countenance that is pale, and wan, and dejected, like one that is seized with strong fear and consternation ; all his motions are sluggish, and no sprightliness nor activity remains. A merry heart doth good, like a medicine ; but a broken spirit drieth the bones. Hence come those frequent complaints in Scripture : My moisture is turned into the drought of the summer : I am like a bottle in the smoke ; my soul cleaveth unto the dust : my face is foul with weeping, and on my eyelid is the shadow of death. Job xvi. 16, xxx. 17, 18—19. My bones are pierced in me, in the night season, and my sinews take no rest ; by the great force of my disease is my garment changed. He hath cast me into the mire, and I am become like dust and ashes. Many times indeed the trouble of the soul does begin from the weakness and indisposition of the body. Long affliction, without any prospect of remedy, does, in process of time, begin to distress the soul itself. David was a man often exercised with sickness and the rage of enemies ; and in all the instances almost that we meet with in the Psalms, we may observe that the outward occasions of trouble brought him under an apprehension of the wrath of God for his sin. (Psalm vi. 1, 2 ; and the reasons given, verses 5 and 6.) All his griefs running into this most terrible thought, that God was his enemy. As little brooks lose themselves in a great river, and change their name and nature, it most frequently happens, that when our pain is long and sharp, and helpless and unavoidable, we begin to question the sincerity of our estate towards God, though at its first assault we had few doubts or fears about it. Long weakness of body makes the soul more susceptible of trouble, and uneasy thoughts.—*Timothy Rogers on Trouble of Mind.*

Verse 7.—*" Mine eye is consumed."* Many make those eyes which God hath given them, as it were two lighted candles to let them see to go to hell ; and for this God in justice requiteth them, that seeing their minds are blinded by the lust of the eyes, the lust of the flesh, and the pride of life, God I say, sendeth sickness to debilitate their eyes which were so sharp-sighted in the devil's service, and their lust now causeth them to want the necessary sight of their body.

Verse 7.—*" Mine enemies."* The pirates seeing an empty bark, pass by it ; but if she be loaded with precious wares, then they will assault her. So, if a man have no grace within him, Satan passeth by him, as not a convenient prey for him, but being loaded with graces, as the love of God, his fear, and such other spiritual virtues, let him be persuaded that according as he knows what stuff is in him, so will he not fail to rob him of them, if in any case he may.—*Archibald Symson.*

Verse 7.—That eye of his that had looked and lusted after his neighbour's wife is now dimmed and darkened with grief and indignation. He had wept himself almost blind.—*John Trapp.*

Verse 8.—*" Depart from me,"* etc., *i.e.*, you may now go your way ; for that which you look for, namely, my death, you shall not have at this present ; *for the Lord hath heard the voice of my weeping, i.e.*, has graciously granted me that which with tears I asked of him.—*Thomas Wilcocks.*

Verse 8.—*" Depart from me, all ye workers of iniquity."* May not too much familiarity with profane wretches be justly charged upon church members ? I know man is a sociable creature, but that will not excuse saints as to their carelessness of the choice of their company. The very fowls of the air, and beasts of the field, love not heterogeneous company. " Birds of a feather flock together." I have been afraid that many who would be thought eminent, of a high stature in grace and godliness, yet see not the vast difference there is between nature and regeneration, sin and grace, the old and the new man, seeing all company is alike unto them.—*Lewis Stuckley's " Gospel Glass,"* 1667.

Verse 8.—*" The voice of my weeping."* Weeping hath a voice, and as music upon the water sounds farther and more harmoniously than upon the land, so prayers, joined with tears, cry louder in God's ears, and make sweeter music than when tears are absent. When Antipater had written a large letter against Alexander's mother unto Alexander, the king answered him, " One tear from my mother will wash away all her faults." So it is with God. A penitent tear is an undeniable ambassador, and never returns from the throne of grace unsatisfied. *Spencer's Things New and Old.*

Verse 8.—The wicked are called *" workers of iniquity,* because they are free and ready to sin, they have a strong tide and bent of spirit to do evil, and they do it not to halves but throughly ; they do not only begin or nibble at the bait a little (as a good man often doth), but greedily swallow it down, hook and all ; they are fully in it, and do it fully ; they make a work of it, and so are *" workers of iniquity."*—*Joseph Caryl.*

Verse 8.—Some may say, " My constitution is such that I cannot weep ; I may as well go to squeeze a rock, as think to get a tear." But if thou canst not weep for sin, canst thou grieve ? Intellectual mourning is best ; there may be sorrow where there are no tears, the vessel may be full though it wants vent ; it is not so much the weeping eye God respects as the broken heart ; yet I would be loath to stop their tears who can weep. God stood looking on Hezekiah's tears (Isaiah xxxviii. 5), " I have seen thy tears." David's tears made music in God's ears, *" The Lord hath heard the voice of my weeping."* It is a sight fit for angels to behold, tears as pearls dropping from a penitent eye.—*T. Watson.*

Verse 8.—*" The Lord hath heard the voice of my weeping."* God hears the voice of our looks, God hears the voice of our tears sometimes better than the voice of our words ; for it is the Spirit itself that makes intercession for us. Rom. viii. 26. *Gemitibus inenarrabilibus,* in those *groans,* and so in those *tears,* which we *cannot utter ; ineloquacibus,* as Tertullian reads that place, devout, and simple tears, which cannot speak, speak aloud in the ears of God ; nay, tears which we cannot utter ; not only not utter the force of the tears, but not utter the very tears themselves. As God sees the water in the spring in the veins of the earth before it bubble upon the face of the earth, so God sees tears in the heart of a man before they blubber his face ; God hears the tears of that sorrowful soul, which for sorrow cannot shed tears. From this casting up of the eyes, and pouring out the sorrow of the heart at the eyes, at least opening God a window through which he may see a wet heart through a dry eye ; from these overtures of repentance, which are as those imperfect sounds of words, which parents delight in, in their children, before they speak plain, a penitent sinner comes to a verbal and a more express prayer. To these prayers, these vocal and verbal prayers from David, God had given ear, and from this hearing of those prayers was David come to this thankful confidence, " *The Lord hath heard, the Lord will hear.*"—*John Donne.*

Verse 8.—What a strange change is here all on a sudden ! Well might Luther say, " Prayer is the leech of the soul, that sucks out the venom and swelling thereof." " Prayer," said another, " is an exorcist with God, and an exorcist against sin and misery." Bernard saith, " How oft hath prayer found me despairing almost, but left me triumphing, and well assured of pardon ! " The same in effect saith David here, " Depart from me, all ye workers of iniquity ; for the Lord hath heard the voice of my weeping." What a word is that to his insulting enemies ! Avaunt ! come out ! vanish ! These be words used to devils and dogs, but good enough for a Doeg or a Shimei. And the Son of David shall say the same to his enemies when he comes to judgment.—*John Trapp.*

Verse 9.—" *The Lord hath heard my supplication,*" etc. The Psalmist three times expresses his confidence of his prayers being heard and received, which may be either in reference to his having prayed so many times for help, as the apostle Paul did (2 Cor. xii. 8) ; and as Christ his antitype did (Matt. xxvi. 39, 42, 44) ; or to express the certainty of it, the strength of his faith in it, and the exuberance of his joy on account of it.—*John Gill, D.D.*, 1697—1771.

Verse 10.—" *Let all mine enemies be ashamed,*" etc. If this were an impreca- tion, a malediction, yet it was medicinal, and had *rationem boni*, a charitable tincture and nature in it ; he wished the men no harm as men. But it is rather *prædictorium*, a prophetical vehemence, that if they will take no knowledge of God's declaring himself in the protection of his servants, if they would not consider that God had heard, and would hear, had rescued, and would rescue his children, but would continue their opposition against him, heavy judgments would certainly fall upon them ; their punishment should be certain, but the effect should be un- certain ; for God only knows whether his correction shall work upon his enemies to their mollifying, or to their obduration. . . . In the second word, " *Let them be sore vexed,*" he wishes his enemies no worse than himself had been, for he had used the same word of himself before, *Ossa turbata, My bones are vexed;* and, *Anima turbata, My soul is vexed ;* and considering that David had found this vexation to be his way to God, it was no malicious imprecation to wish that enemy the same physic that he had taken, who was more sick of the same disease than he was. For this is like a troubled sea after a tempest ; the danger is past, but yet the billow is great still; the danger was in the calm, in the security, or in the tempest, by mis- interpreting God's corrections to our obduration, and to a remorseless stupefaction; but when a man is come to his holy vexation, to be troubled, to be shaken with the sense of the indignation of God, the storm is past, and the indignation of God is blown over. The soul is in a fair and near way of being restored to a calmness, and to reposed security of conscience that is come to this holy vexation.— *John Donne.*

Verse 10.—" *Let all mine enemies* [or *all mine enemies shall*] *be ashamed, and sore vexed,*" etc. Many of the mournful Psalms end in this manner, to instruct the believer that he is continually to look forward, and solace himself with be- holding that day, when his warfare shall be accomplished ; when sin and sorrow shall be no more ; when sudden and everlasting confusion shall cover the enemies of righteousness ; when the sackcloth of the penitent shall be exchanged for a robe of glory, and every tear become a sparkling gem in his crown ; when to sighs and groans shall succeed the songs of heaven, set to angelic harps, and faith shall be resolved into the vision of the Almighty.—*George Horne.*

HINTS TO PREACHERS.

Verse 1.—A Sermon for afflicted souls. I. God's twofold dealings. (1) *Rebuke* by a telling sermon, a judgment on another, a slight trial in our own person, or a solemn monition in our conscience by the Spirit. (2) *Chastening.* This follows the other when the first is disregarded. Pain, losses, bereavements, melancholy, and other trials. II. The evils in them to be most dreaded, anger and hot displeasure. III. The means to avert these ills. Humiliation, confession, amendment, faith in the Lord, etc.

Verse 1.—The believer's greatest dread, the anger of God. What this fact reveals in the heart ? Why it is so ? What removes the fear ?

Verse 2.—The *argumentum ad misericordiam.*

Verse 2.—First sentence—Divine healing. 1. What precedes it, *my bones are vexed.* 2. How it is wrought. 3. What succeeds it.

Verse 3.—The impatience of sorrow ; its sins, mischief, and cure.

Verse 3.—A fruitful topic may be found in considering the question, How long will God continue afflictions to the righteous ?

Verse 4.—" Return, O Lord." A prayer suggested by a sense of the Lord's absence, excited by grace, attended with heart searching and repentance, backed by pressing danger, guaranteed as to its answer, and containing a request for all mercies.

Verse 4.—The prayer of the deserted saint. 1. *His state :* his soul is evidently in bondage and danger: 2. *His hope :* it is in the Lord's *return.* 3. *His plea :* mercy only.

Verse 5.—The final suspension of earthly service considered in various practical aspects.

Verse 5.—The duty of praising God while we live.

Verse 6.—Saints' tears in quality, abundance, influence, assuagement, and final end.

Verse 7.—The voice of weeping. What it is.

Verse 8.—The pardoned sinner forsaking his bad companions.

Verse 9.—Past answers the ground of present confidence. He *hath,* he *will.*

Verse 10.—The shame reserved for the wicked.

PSALM VII.

TITLE.—" Shiggaion of David, which he sang unto the Lord, concerning the words of Cush the Benjamite."—" *Shiggaion of David.*" *As far as we can gather from the observations of learned men, and from a comparison of this Psalm with the only other Shiggaion in the Word of God (Hab. iii.), this title seems to mean "variable songs," with which also the idea of solace and pleasure is associated. Truly our life-psalm is composed of variable verses ; one stanza rolls along with the sublime metre of triumph, but another limps with the broken rhythm of complaint. There is much bass in the saint's music here below. Our experience is as variable as the weather in England.*

From the title we learn the occasion of the composition of this song. It appears probable that Cush the Benjamite had accused David to Saul of treasonable conspiracy against his royal authority. This the king would be ready enough to credit, both from his jealousy of David, and from the relation which most probably existed between himself, the son of Kish, and this Cush, or Kish, the Benjamite. He who is near the throne can do more injury to a subject than an ordinary slanderer.

This may be called the SONG OF THE SLANDERED SAINT. *Even this sorest of evils may furnish occasion for a Psalm. What a blessing would it be if we could turn even the most disastrous event into a theme for song, and so turn the tables upon our great enemy. Let us learn a lesson from Luther, who once said, " David made Psalms ; we also will make Psalms, and sing them as well as we can to the honour of our Lord, and to spite and mock the devil."*

DIVISION.—*In the first and second verses the danger is stated, and prayer offered. Then the Psalmist most solemnly avows his innocence (3, 4, 5). The Lord is pleaded with to arise to judgment (6, 7). The Lord, sitting upon his throne, hears the renewed appeal of the Slandered Supplicant (8, 9). The Lord clears his servant, and threatens the wicked (10, 11, 12, 13). The slanderer is seen in vision bringing a curse upon his own head (14, 15, 16) while David retires from trial singing a hymn of praise to his righteous God. We have here a noble sermon upon that text : " No weapon that is formed against thee shall prosper, and every tongue that riseth against thee in judgment thou shalt condemn."*

EXPOSITION.

O LORD my God, in thee do I put my trust : save me from all them that persecute me, and deliver me :

2 Lest he tear my soul like a lion, rending *it* in pieces, while *there is* none to deliver.

David appears before God to plead with him against the Accuser, who had charged him with treason and treachery. The case is here opened with an avowal of confidence in God. Whatever may be the emergency of our condition we shall never find it amiss to retain our reliance upon our God. " *O Lord my God,*" mine by a special covenant, sealed by Jesus' blood, and ratified in my own soul by a sense of union to thee ; " *in thee,*" and in thee only, " *do I put my trust,*" even now in my sore distress. I shake, but my rock moves not. It is never right to distrust God, and never vain to trust him. And now, with both divine relationship and holy trust to strengthen him, David utters the burden of his desire— " *save me from all them that persecute me.*" His pursuers were very many, and any one of them cruel enough to devour him ; he cries, therefore, for salvation from them *all.* We should never think our prayers complete until we *ask for* preservation from *all* sin, and all enemies. " *And deliver me,*" extricate me from their snares, acquit me of their accusations, give a true and just deliverance in this trial of my injured character. See how clearly his case is stated ; let us see to it, that we know what we would have when we are come to the throne of mercy. Pause a little while before you pray, that you may not offer the sacrifice of fools. Get a distinct idea of your need, and then you can pray with the more fluency of fervency.

" *Lest he tear my soul.*" Here is the plea of fear co-working with the plea of faith. There was one among David's foes mightier than the rest, who had both dignity, strength, and ferocity, and was, therefore, " *like a lion.*" From this foe he urgently seeks deliverance. Perhaps this was Saul, his royal enemy ; but in our own case there is one who goes about like a lion, seeking whom he may devour, concerning whom we should ever cry, " Deliver us from the Evil One." Notice the vigour of the description—" *rending it in pieces, while there is none to deliver.*" It is a picture from the shepherd-life of David. When the fierce lion had pounced upon the defenceless lamb, and had made it his prey, he would rend the victim in pieces, break all the bones, and devour all, because no shepherd was near to protect the lamb or rescue it from the ravenous beast. This is a soul-moving portrait of a saint delivered over to the will of Satan. This will make the bowels of Jehovah yearn. A father cannot be silent when a child is in such peril. No, he will not endure the thought of his darling in the jaws of a lion, he will arise and deliver his persecuted one. Our God is very pitiful, and he will surely rescue his people from so desperate a destruction. It will be well for us here to remember that this is a description of the danger to which the Psalmist was exposed from slanderous tongues. Verily this is not an overdrawn picture, for the wounds of a sword will heal, but the wounds of the tongue cut deeper than the flesh, and are not soon cured. Slander leaves a slur, even if it be wholly disproved. Common fame, although notoriously a common liar, has very many believers. Once let an ill word get into men's mouths, and it is not easy to get it fully out again. The Italians say that good repute is like the cypress, once cut, it never puts forth leaf again ; this is not true if our character be cut by a stranger's hand, but even then it will not soon regain its former verdure. Oh, 'tis a meanness most detestable to stab a good man in his reputation, but diabolical hatred observes no nobility in its mode of warfare. We must be ready for this trial, for it will surely come upon us. If God was slandered in Eden, we shall surely be maligned in this land of sinners. Gird up your loins, ye children of the resurrection, for this fiery trial awaits you all.

3 O LORD my God, if I have done this ; if there be iniquity in my hands ;

4 If I have rewarded evil unto him that was at peace with me ; (yea, I have delivered him that without cause is mine enemy :)

5 Let the enemy persecute my soul, and take *it ;* yea, let him tread down my life upon the earth, and lay mine honour in the dust. Selah.

The second part of this wandering hymn contains a protestation of innocence, and an invocation of wrath upon his own head, if he were not clear from the evil imputed to him. So far from hiding treasonable intentions in his hands, or un-gratefully requiting the peaceful deeds of a friend, he had even suffered his enemy to escape when he had him completely in his power. Twice had he spared Saul's life ; once in the cave of Adullam, and again when he found him sleeping in the midst of his slumbering camp ; he could, therefore, with a clear conscience, make his appeal to heaven. He needs not fear the curse whose soul is clear of guilt. Yet is the imprecation a most solemn one, and only justifiable through the extremity of the occasion, and the nature of the dispensation under which the Psalmist lived. *We* are commanded by our Lord Jesus to let our yea be yea, and our nay, nay ; " for whatsoever is more than this cometh of evil." If we cannot be believed on our word, we are surely not to be trusted on our oath ; for to a true Christian his simple word is as binding as another man's oath. Especially beware, O un-converted men ! of trifling with solemn imprecations. Remember the woman at Devizes, who wished she might die if she had not paid her share in a joint purchase, and who fell dead there and then with the money in her hand.

Selah. David enhances the solemnity of this appeal to the dread tribunal of God by the use of the usual pause.

From these verses we may learn that no innocence can shield a man from the calumnies of the wicked. David had been scrupulously careful to avoid any appearance of rebellion against Saul, whom he constantly styled "the Lord's anointed ;" but all this could not protect him from lying tongues. As the shadow follows the substance, so envy pursues goodness. It is only at the tree laden with fruit that men throw stones. If we would live without being slandered we must wait till we get to heaven. Let us be very heedful not to believe the flying rumours which are always harassing gracious men. If there are no believers in lies there will be but a dull market in falsehood, and good men's characters will be safe. Ill-will never spoke well. Sinners have an ill-will to saints, and therefore, be sure they will not speak well of them.

6 Arise, O LORD, in thine anger, lift up thyself because of the rage of mine enemies : and awake for me *to* the judgment *that* thou hast commanded.

7 So shall the congregation of the people compass thee about : for their sakes therefore return thou on high.

We now listen to a fresh prayer, based upon the avowal which he has just made. We cannot pray too often, and when our heart is true, we shall turn to God in prayer as naturally as the needle to its pole.

" *Arise, O Lord, in thine anger.*" His sorrow makes him view the Lord as a judge who had left the judgment-seat and retired into his rest. Faith would move the Lord to avenge the quarrel of his saints. " *Lift up thyself because of the rage of mine enemies* "—a still stronger figure to express his anxiety that the Lord would assume his authority and mount the throne. Stand up, O God, rise thou above them all, and let thy justice tower above their villainies. "*Awake for me to the judgment that thou hast commanded.*" This is a bolder utterance still, for it implies sleep as well as inactivity, and can only be applied to God in a very limited sense. He never slumbers, yet doth he often seem to do so ; for the wicked prevail, and the saints are trodden in the dust. God's silence is the patience of longsuffering, and if wearisome to the saints, they should bear it cheerfully in the hope that sinners may thereby be led to repentance.

" *So shall the congregation of the people compass thee about.*" Thy saints shall crowd to thy tribunal with their complaints, or shall surround it with their solemn homage : " *for their sakes therefore return thou on high.*" As when a judge travels at the assizes, all men take their cases to his court that they may be heard, so will the righteous gather to their Lord. Here he fortifies himself in prayer by pleading that if the Lord will mount the throne of judgment, multitudes of the saints would be blessed as well as himself. If I be too base to be remembered, yet "*for their sakes,*" for the love thou bearest to thy chosen people, come forth from thy secret pavilion, and sit in the gate dispensing justice among the people. When my suit includes the desires of all the righteous it shall surely speed, for " shall not God avenge his own elect ? "

8 The LORD shall judge the people : judge me, O LORD, according to my righteousness, and according to mine integrity *that* is in me.

9 Oh let the wickedness of the wicked come to an end ; but establish the just : for the righteous God trieth the hearts and reins.

If I am not mistaken, David has now seen in the eye of his mind the Lord ascending to his judgment-seat, and beholding him seated there in royal state, he draws near to him to urge his suit anew. In the last two verses he besought Jehovah to arise, and now that he is arisen, he prepares to mingle with " the congregation of the people " who compass the Lord about. The royal heralds proclaim the opening of the court with the solemn words, " *The Lord shall judge the people.*" Our petitioner rises at once, and cries with earnestness and humility, " *Judge me, O Lord, according to my righteousness, and according to mine integrity that is in me.*" His hand is on an honest heart, and his cry is to a righteous Judge. He sees a smile of complacency upon the face of the King, and in the name of all the assembled congregation he cries aloud, " *Oh let the wickedness of the wicked come to an end ; but establish the just.*" Is not this the universal longing of the whole company of the elect ? When shall we be delivered from the filthy conversation of these men of Sodom ? When shall we escape from the filthiness of Mesech and the blackness of the tents of Kedar ?

What a solemn and weighty truth is contained in the last sentence of the ninth verse ! How deep is the divine knowledge !—" *he trieth.*" How strict, how accurate, how intimate his search !—" *he trieth the hearts,*" the secret thoughts, " *and reins,*" the inward affections. " All things are naked and opened to the eyes of him with whom we have to do."

10 My defence *is* of God, which saveth the upright in heart.

11 God judgeth the righteous, and God is angry *with the wicked* every day.

12 If he turn not, he will whet his sword; he hath bent his bow, and made it ready.

13 He hath also prepared for him the instruments of death; he ordaineth his arrows against the persecutors.

The judge has heard the cause, has cleared the guiltless, and uttered his voice against the persecutors. Let us draw near, and learn the results of the great assize. Yonder is the slandered one with his harp in hand, hymning the justice of his Lord, and rejoicing aloud in his own deliverance. *" My defence is of God, which saveth the upright heart."* Oh, how good to have a true and *upright* heart. Crooked sinners, with all their craftiness, are foiled by the upright in heart. God defends the right. Filth will not long abide on the pure white garments of the saints, but shall be brushed off by divine providence, to the vexation of the men by whose base hands it was thrown upon the godly. When God shall try our cause, our sun has risen, and the sun of the wicked is set for ever. Truth, like oil, is ever above, no power of our enemies can drown it ; we shall refute their slanders in the day when the trumpet wakes the dead, and we shall shine in honour when lying lips are put to silence. O believer, fear not all that thy foes can do or say against thee, for the tree which God plants no winds can hurt. *" God judgeth the righteous,"* he hath not given thee up to be condemned by the lips of persecutors. Thine enemies cannot sit on God's throne, nor blot thy name out of his book. Let them alone, then, for God will find time for his revenges.

" God is angry with the wicked every day." He not only detests sin, but is angry with those who continue to indulge in it. We have no insensible and stolid God to deal with ; he can be angry, nay, he is angry to-day and every day with you, ye ungodly and impenitent sinners. The best day that ever dawns on a sinner brings a curse with it. Sinners may have many feast days, but no safe days. From the beginning of the year even to its ending, there is not an hour in which God's oven is not hot, and burning in readiness for the wicked, who shall be as stubble.

" If he turn not, he will whet his sword." What blows are those which will be dealt by that long uplifted arm ! God's sword has been sharpening upon the revolving stone of our daily wickedness, and if we will not repent, it will speedily cut us in pieces. Turn or burn is the sinner's only alternative. *" He hath bent his bow and made it ready."* Even now the thirsty arrow longs to wet itself with the blood of the *persecutor*. The bow is bent, the aim is taken, the arrow is fitted to the string, and what, O sinner, if the arrow should be let fly at thee even now ! Remember, God's arrows never miss the mark, and are, every one of them, " instruments of death." Judgment may tarry, but it will not come too late. The Greek proverb saith, " The mill of God grinds late, but grinds to powder."

14 Behold, he travaileth with iniquity, and hath conceived mischief, and brought forth falsehood.

15 He made a pit, and digged it, and is fallen into the ditch *which* he made.

16 His mischief shall return upon his own head, and his violent dealing shall come down upon his own pate.

In three graphic pictures we see the slanderer's history. A woman in travail furnishes the first metaphor. *" He travaileth with iniquity."* He is full of it, pained until he can carry it out, he longs to work his will, he is full of pangs until his evil intent is executed. *" He hath conceived mischief."* This is the original of his base design. The devil has had doings with him, and the virus of evil is in him. And now behold the progeny of this unhallowed conception. The child is worthy of its father, his name of old was " the father of lies," and the birth doth not belie the parent, for *he brought forth falsehood*. Thus, one figure is carried out to perfection ; the Psalmist now illustrates his meaning by another taken from the stratagems of the hunter. *" He made a pit and digged it."* He was cunning in his plans, and industrious in his labours. He stooped to the dirty work of digging. He did not fear to soil his own hands, he was willing to work in *a ditch* if others might fall therein. What mean things men will do to wreak revenge on the godly. They hunt for good men, as if they were brute beasts ; nay, they will not give them the fair chase afforded to the hare or the fox, but must secretly entrap them, because they can neither run them down nor shoot them down. Our enemies will not meet us to the face, for they fear us as much as they pretend to despise us. But let us look on to the end of the scene. The verse says, he " *is fallen into the ditch which he made.*" Ah! there he is, let us laugh at his disappointment. Lo! he is himself the beast, he has hunted his own soul, and the chase has brought him a goodly victim. Aha, aha, so should it ever be. Come hither and make merry with this entrapped hunter, this biter who has bitten himself. Give him no pity, for it will be wasted on such a wretch. He is but rightly and richly rewarded by being paid in his own coin. He cast forth evil from his mouth, and it has fallen into his bosom. He has set his own house on fire with the torch which he lit to burn a neighbour. He sent forth a foul bird, and it has come back to its nest. The rod which he lifted on high, has smitten his own back. He shot an arrow upward, and it has "*returned upon his own head.*" He hurled a stone at another, and it has "*come down upon his own pate.*" Curses are like young chickens, they always come home to roost. Ashes always fly back in the face of him that throws them. "As he loved cursing, so let it come unto him" (Ps. cix. 17.) How often has this been the case in the histories of both ancient and modern times. Men have burned their own fingers when they were hoping to brand their neighbour. And if this does not happen now, it will hereafter. The Lord has caused dogs to lick the blood of Ahab in the midst of the vineyard of Naboth. Sooner or later the evil deeds of persecutors have always leaped back into their arms. So will it be in the last great day, when Satan's fiery darts shall all be quivered in his own heart, and all his followers shall reap the harvest which they themselves have sown.

17 I will praise the LORD according to his righteousness : and will sing praise to the name of the LORD most high.

We conclude with the joyful contrast. In this all these Psalms are agreed ; they all exhibit the blessedness of the righteous, and make its colours the more glowing by contrast with the miseries of the wicked. The bright jewel sparkles in a black foil. *Praise* is the occupation of the godly, their eternal work, and their present pleasure. *Singing* is the fitting embodiment for praise, and therefore do the saints make melody before the Lord Most High. The slandered one is now a singer : his harp was unstrung for a very little season, and now we leave him sweeping its harmonious chords, and flying on their music to the third heaven of adoring praise.

EXPLANATORY NOTES AND QUAINT SAYINGS.

Title.—" Shiggaion," though some have attempted to fix on it a reference to the moral aspect of the world as depicted in this Psalm, is in all probability to be taken as expressing the *nature of the composition.* It conveys the idea of something *erratic* (שׁגה, to wander) in the style ; something not so calm as other Psalms ; and hence *Ewald* suggests that it might be rendered, " a confused ode," a Dithyramb. This characteristic of excitement in the style, and a kind of disorder in the sense, suits Habakkuk iii. 1, the only other place where the word occurs.—*Andrew A. Bonar.*

Whole Psalm.—Whatever might be the occasion of the Psalm, the real subject seems to be the Messiah's appeal to God against the false accusations of his enemies ; and the predictions which it contains of the final conversion of the whole world, and of the future judgment, are clear and explicit.—*Samuel Horsley, LL.D.,* 1733—1806.

Verse 1.—" *O Lord, my God, in thee do I put my trust.*" This is the first instance in the Psalms where David addresses the Almighty by the united names Jehovah and my God. No more suitable words can be placed at the beginning of any act of prayer or praise. These names show the ground of the confidence afterwards expressed. They " denote at once supreme reverence and the most endearing confidence. They convey a recognition of God's infinite perfections, and of his covenanted and gracious relations."—*William S. Plumer.*

Verse 2.—"*Lest he tear my soul like a lion,*" etc. It is reported of tigers, that they enter into a rage upon the scent of fragrant spices ; so do ungodly men at the blessed savour of godliness. I have read of some barbarous nations, who, when the sun shines hot upon them, they shoot up their arrows against it ; so do wicked men at the light and heat of godliness. There is a natural antipathy between the spirits of godly men and the wicked. Genesis iii. 15. "I will put enmity between thy seed and her seed."—*Jeremiah Burroughs*, 1660.

Verse 3.—"*O Lord, my God, if I have done this, if there be iniquity in my hands.*" In the primitive times the people of God were then a people under great reproach. What strange things does Tertullian tell us they reproached them withal ; as that in their meetings they made Thyestes suppers, who invited his brother to a supper, and presented him with a dish of his own flesh. They charged them with uncleanness because they met in the night (for they durst not meet in the day), and said, they blew out the candles when they were together, and committed filthiness. They reproached them for ignorance, saying, they were all unlearned ; and therefore the heathens in Tertullian's time used to paint the God of the Christians with an ass's head, and a book in his hand, to signify that though they pretended learning, yet they were an unlearned, silly people, rude and ignorant. Bishop Jewel in his sermon upon Luke xi. 5, cites this out of Tertullian, and applies it to his time :— "Do not our adversaries do the like," saith he, "at this day, against all those that profess the gospel of Christ ? Oh, say they, who are they that favour this way ? they are none but shoemakers, tailors, weavers, and such as were never at the university ; " they are the bishop's own words. He cites likewise Tertullian a little after, saying, that the Christians were accounted the public enemies of the State. And Josephus tells us of Apollinaris, speaking concerning the Jews and Christians, that they are more foolish than any barbarian. And Paulus Fagius reports a story of an Egyptian, concerning the Christians, who said, "They were a gathering together of a most fifthy, lecherous people ; " and for the keeping of the Sabbath, he says, "they had a disease that was upon them, and they were fain to rest the seventh day because of that disease." And so in Augustine's time, he hath this expression, "Any one that begins to be godly, presently he must prepare to suffer reproach from the tongues of adversaries ; " and this was their usual manner of reproach, "What shall we have of you, an Elias ? a Jeremy ? " And Nazianzen in one of his orations says, "It is ordinary to reproach, that I cannot think to go free myself." And so Athanasius, they called him Sathanasius, because he was a special instrument against the Arians. And Cyprian, they called him Coprian, one that gathers up dung, as if all the excellent things that he had gathered in his works were but dung.—*Jeremiah Burroughs*.

Verse 3.—"*If I have done this ; if there be iniquity in my hands.*" I deny not but you may, and ought to be sensible of the wrong done to your name, for as "a good name is a precious ointment" (Cant. i. 3), so to have an evil name is a great judgment ; and therefore you ought not to be insensible of the wrong done to your name by slanders and reproaches, saying, "Let men speak of me what they please, I care not, so long as I know mine own innocency," for though the testimony of your own innocency be a ground of comfort unto you, yet your care must be not only to approve yourselves unto God, but also unto men, to be as careful of your good names as possibly ye can ; but yet you are not to manifest any distemper or passion upon the reproachful speeches of others against you.—*Thomas Gouge*, 1660.

Verse 3.—It is a sign that there is some good in thee if a wicked world abuse thee. "*Quid mali feci ?*" said Socrates, what evil have I done that this bad man commends me ? The applause of the wicked usually denotes some evil, and their censure imports some good.—*Thomas Watson*.

Verse 3.—"*If there be iniquity in my hands.*" Injustice is ascribed to the *hand*, not because injustice is always, though usually it be, done by the hand. With the hand men take away, and with that men detain the right of others. David speaks thus (1 Chron. xii. 17), "Seeing there is no wrong in mine hands ; " that is, I have done no wrong.—*Joseph Caryl*.

Verses 3, 4.—A good conscience is a flowing spring of assurance. "For our rejoicing is this, the testimony of our conscience, that in simplicity and godly sincerity, not with fleshly wisdom, but by the grace of God, we have had our conversation in the world, and more abundantly to you-ward." 2 Cor. i. 12. "Beloved, if our heart condemn us not, then have we confidence towards God." 1 John iii. 21. A good conscience has sure confidence. He who has it sits in the midst of all combustions and distractions, Noah-like, all sincerity and serenity, uprightness and boldness. What the probationer disciple said to our Saviour, " Master, I will follow thee whithersover thou goest," that a good conscience says to the believing soul ; I will stand by thee ; I will strengthen thee ; I will uphold thee ; I will be a comfort to thee in life, and a friend to thee in death. " Though all should leave thee, yet will I never forsake thee."—*Thomas Brooks.*

Verse 4.—" *Yea, I have delivered him that without cause is mine enemy.*" Meaning Saul, whose life he twice preserved, once in Engedi, and again when he slept on the plain.—*John Gill.*

Verse 4.—" *If I have rewarded evil unto him that was at peace with me.*" To do evil for good, is human corruption ; to do good for good, is civil retribution ; but to do good for evil, is Christian perfection. Though this be not the grace of nature, yet it is the nature of grace.—*William Secker.*

Verse 4.—Then is grace victorious, and then hath a man a noble and brave spirit, not when he is overcome by evil (for that argueth weakness), but when he can overcome evil. And it is God's way to shame the party that did the wrong, and to overcome him too ; it is the best way to get the victory over him. When David had Saul at an advantage in the cave, and cut off the lap of his garment, and did forbear any act of revenge against him, Saul was melted, and said to David, " Thou art more righteous than I." 1 Sam. xxiv. 17. Though he had such a hostile mind against him, and chased and pursued him up and down, yet when David forbore revenge when it was in his power it overcame him, and he falls a–weeping.—*Thomas Manton.*

Verse 5.—" *Let him tread down my life upon the earth.*" The allusion here is to the manner in which the vanquished were often treated in battle, when they were rode over by horses, or trampled by men in the dust. The idea of David is, that if he was guilty he would be willing that his enemy should triumph over him, should subdue him, should treat him with the utmost indignity and scorn.—*Albert Barnes, in loc.*

Verse 5.—" *Mine honour in the dust.*" When Achilles dragged the body of Hector in the dust around the walls of Troy, he did but carry out the usual manners of those barbarous ages. David dares in his conscious innocence to imprecate such an ignominious fate upon himself if indeed the accusation of the black Benjamite be true. He had need have a golden character who dares to challenge such an ordeal.—*C. H. S.*

Verse 6.—" *The judgment which thou hast ordained.*" In the end of the verse he shows that he asks nothing but what is according to the appointment of God. And this is the rule which ought to be observed by us in our prayers ; we should in everything conform our requests to the divine will, as John also instructs us. 1 John iv. 14. And, indeed, we can never pray in faith unless we attend, in the first place, to what God commands, that our minds may not rashly and at random start aside in desiring more than we are permitted to desire and pray for. David, therefore, in order to pray aright, reposes himself on the word and promise of God ; and the import of his exercise is this : Lord, I am not led by ambition, or foolish head-strong passion, or depraved desire, inconsiderately to ask from thee whatever is pleasing to my flesh ; but it is the clear light of thy word which directs me, and upon it I securely depend.—*John Calvin.*

Verse 7.—" *The congregation of the people :*" either, 1. A great number of all sorts of people, who shall observe thy justice, and holiness, and goodness in pleading my righteous cause against my cruel and implacable oppressor. Or rather, 2. The whole body of thy people Israel, by whom both these Hebrew words are commonly ascribed in Holy Scripture. " *Compass thee about ;*" they will, and I, as their king and ruler in thy stead, will take care that they shall come from all parts and meet together to worship thee, which in Saul's time they have grossly neglected, and been permitted to neglect, and to offer to thee praises and sacrifices for thy favour to me, and for the manifold benefits which they shall enjoy by my means, and under my government. " *For their sakes ;*" or, *for its sake, i.e.,* for the sake of thy congregation, which now is woefully dissipated and oppressed, and has in a great measure lost all administration of justice, and exercise of religion. *" Return thou on high,"* or, *return to thy high place, i.e.* to thy tribunal, to sit there and judge my cause. An allusion to earthly tribunals, which generally are set up on high above the people. 1 Kings x. 19.—*Matthew Pool,* 1624—1679.

Verse 8.—Believers! let not the terror of that day dispirit you when you meditate upon it; let those who have slighted the Judge, and continue enemies to him and the way of holiness, droop and hang down their heads when they think of his coming; but lift ye up your heads with joy, for the last day will be your best day. The Judge is your Head and Husband, your Redeemer and your Advocate. Ye must appear before the judgment-seat; but ye shall not come into condemnation. His coming will not be against you, but for you. It is otherwise with unbelievers, *a neglected Saviour* will be a *severe Judge.*—*Thomas Boston,* 1676—1732.

Verse 9.—*" The righteous God trieth the hearts and reins."* As common experience shows that the workings of the mind, particularly the passions of joy, grief, and fear, have a very remarkable effect on the *reins* or *kidneys* (see Prov. xxiii. 16; Psalm lxxiii. 21), so from their retired situation in the body, and their being hid in fat, they are often used to denote the most secret workings and affections of the soul. And to " see or examine the *reins,*" is to see or examine those most secret thoughts or desires of the soul.—*John Parkhurst,* 1762.

Verse 9 (last clause).—*" The righteous God trieth the hearts and reins."*

> " I that alone am infinite, can try
> How deep within itself thine heart doth lie.
> Thy seamen's plummet can but reach the ground,
> I find that which thine heart itself ne'er found."

Francis Quarles, 1592—1644.

Verse 9.—*" The heart"* may signify the cogitations, and the *" reins "* the affections.—*Henry Ainsworth.*

Verse 10.—*" My defence is of God."* Literally, *" My shield is upon God,"* like Psalm lxii. 8, " My salvation is *upon* God." The idea may be taken from the armour-bearer, ever ready at hand to give the needed weapon to the warrior.—*Andrew A. Bonar.*

Verse 11.—*" God judgeth the righteous,"* etc. Many learned disputes have arisen as to the meaning of this verse; and it must be confessed that its real import is by no means easily determined: without the words written in italics, which are not in the orginal, it will read thus, " God judgeth the righteous, and God is angry every day." The question still will be, is this a good rendering? To this question it may be replied, that there is strong evidence for a contrary one. AINSWORTH translates it, " God *is* a just judge; and God angrily threateneth every day." With this corresponds the reading of COVERDALE's Bible, " God is a righteous judge, and God is ever threatening." In King Edward's Bible, of 1549, the reading is the same. But there is another class of critics who adopt quite a different view of the text, and apparently with much colour of argument. BISHOP HORSLEY reads the verse, " God is a righteous judge, although he is not angry every day." In this rendering he seems to have followed most of the ancient versions. The VULGATE reads it, " God is a judge, righteous, strong, and patient; will he be angry every day?" The SEPTUAGINT reads it, " God is a righteous judge, strong, and longsuffering; not bringing forth his anger every day." The SYRIAC has it, " God is the judge of righteousness; he is not angry every day." In this view of the text Dr. A. Clarke agrees, and expresses it as his opinion that the text was first corrupted by the CHALDEE. This learned divine proposes to restore the text thus, "אל, *el,* with the vowel point *tseri,* signifies God; אל, *al,* the same letters, with the point *pathach,* signifies *not."* There is by this view of the original no repetition of the divine name in the verse, so that it will simply read, as thus restored, " God is a righteous judge, and is NOT angry every day." The text at large, as is intimated in the VULGATE, SEPTUAGINT, and some other ancient versions, conveys a strong intimation of the longsuffering of God, whose hatred of sin is unchangeable, but whose anger against transgressors is marked by infinite patience, and does not burst forth in vengeance every day.—*John Morison, in " An Exposition of the Book of Psalms,"* 1829.

Verse 11.—" *God is angry.*" The original expression here is very forcible. The true idea of it appears to be, to *froth* or *foam at the mouth* with indignation.—*Richard Mant, D.D.*, 1824.

Verses 11, 12.—God hath set up his royal standard in defiance of all the sons and daughters of apostate Adam, who from his own mouth are proclaimed rebels and traitors to his crown and dignity ; and as against such he hath taken the field, as with fire and sword, to be avenged on them. Yea, he gives the world sufficient testimony of his incensed wrath, by that of it which is revealed from heaven daily in the judgments executed upon sinners, and those many but of a span long, before they can show what nature they have by actual sin, yet crushed to death by God's righteous foot, only for the viperous kind of which they come. At every door where sin sets its foot, there the wrath of God meets us. Every faculty of soul, and member of body, are used as a weapon of unrighteousness against God ; so every one hath its portion of wrath, even to the tip of the tongue. As man is sinful all over, so is he cursed all over. Inside and outside, soul and body, is written all with woes and curses, so close and full, that there is not room for another to interline, or add to what God hath written.—*William Gurnall.*

Verses 11—13.—The idea of God's righteousness must have possessed great vigour to render such a representation possible. There are some excellent remarks upon the ground of it in Luther, who, however, too much overlooks the fact, that the Psalmist presents before his eyes this form of an angry and avenging God, primarily with the view of strengthening by its consideration his own hope, and pays too little regard to the distinction between the Psalmist, who only indirectly teaches what he described as part of his own inward experience, and the prophet : " The prophet takes a lesson from a coarse human similitude, in order that he might inspire terror unto the ungodly. For he speaks against stupid and hardened people, who would not apprehend the reality of a divine judgment of which he had just spoken ; but they might possibly be brought to consider this by greater earnestness on the part of man. Now, the prophet is not satisfied with thinking of the sword, but he adds thereto the bow ; even this does not satisfy him, but he describes how it is already stretched, and aim is taken, and the arrows are applied to it as here follows. So hard, stiff-necked, and unabashed are the ungodly, that however many threatenings may be urged against them, they will still remain unmoved. But in these words he forcibly describes how God's anger presses hard upon the ungodly, though they will never understand this until they actually experience it. It is also to be remarked here, that we have had so frightful a threatening and indignation against the ungodly in no Psalm before this ; neither has the Spirit of God attacked them with so many words. Then in the following verses, he also recounts their plans and purposes, shows how these shall not be in vain, but shall return again upon their own head. So that it clearly and manifestly appears to all those who suffer wrong and reproach, as a matter of consolation, that God hates such revilers and slanderers above all other characters."—*E. W. Hengstenberg, in loc.*, 1845.

Verse 12.—" *If he turn not,*" etc. How few do believe what a quarrel God hath with wicked men ? And that not only with the loose, but the formal and hypocritical also ? If we did we would tremble as much as to be among them as to be in a house that is falling ; we would endeavour to " save " ourselves " from this untoward generation." The apostle would not so have abjured them, so charged, so entreated them, had he not known the danger of wicked company. " *God is angry with the wicked every day ;*" his *bow is bent, the arrows are on the string ;* the instruments for their ruin are all prepared. And is it safe to be there where the arrows of God are ready to fly about our ears ? How was the apostle afraid to be in the bath with Cerinthus ! " Depart," saith God by Moses, " from the tents of Korah, Dathan, and Abiram, lest ye be consumed in all their sins." How have the baskets of good figs suffered with the bad ! Is it not prejudicial to the gold to be with the dross ? Lot had been ruined by his neighbourhood to the Sodomites if God had not wrought wonderfully for his deliverance. Will you put God to work miracles to save you from your ungodly company ? It is dangerous being in the road with thieves whilst God's hue and cry of vengeance is at their backs. " A companion of fools shall be destroyed." The very beasts may instruct you to consult better for your security : the very deer are afraid of a wounded chased deer, and therefore for their preservation thrust him out of their company.—*Lewis Stuckley.*

Verse 12.—" *If he turn not, he will whet his sword,*" etc. The whetting of the sword is but to give a keener edge that it may cut the deeper. God is silent as long as the sinner will let him ; but when the sword is whet, it is to cut ; and when the bow is bent, it is to kill ; and woe be to that man who is the butt.—*William Secker.*

Verse 13.—"*He hath also prepared for him the instruments of death ; he ordaineth his arrows against the persecutors.*" It is said that God hath ordained his arrows against the persecutors ; the word signifies such as burn in anger and malice against the godly ; and the word translated *ordained*, signifies God hath wrought his arrows ; he doth not shoot them at random, but he works them against the wicked. Illiricus hath a story which may well be a commentary upon this text in both the parts of it. One Felix, Earl of Wartenberg, one of the captains of the Emperor Charles V., swore in the presence of divers at supper, that before he died he would ride up to the spurs in the blood of the Lutherans. Here was one that burned in malice, but behold how God works his arrows against him : that very night the hand of God so struck him, that he was strangled and choked in his own blood ; so he rode not, but bathed himself, not up to the spurs, but up to the throat, not in the blood of the Lutherans, but in his own blood before he died.—*Jeremiah Burroughs.*

Verse 13.—"*He ordaineth his arrows.*" This might more exactly be rendered, " He maketh his arrows burning." This image would seem to be deduced from the use of fiery arrows.—*John Kitto*, 1804—1854.

Verse 14.—"*Behold, he travaileth with iniquity,*" etc. The words express the *conception, birth, carriage,* and *miscarriage,* of a *plot* against David. In which you may consider :—(1.) What his *enemies* did. (2.) What *God* did. (3.) What *we all* should do : his enemies' *intention,* God's *prevention,* and our *duty ;* his enemies' intention, *he travaileth with iniquity, and conceiveth mischief ;* God's prevention, *he brought forth a lie ;* our duty, *Behold* . . . . . Observe the aggravation of the sin, *he conceiveth.* He was not put upon it, or forced into it ; it was voluntary. The more liberty we have not to sin, makes our sin the greater. He did not this in passion, but in cold blood. The less will, less sin.—*Richard Sibbs.*

Verse 14.—"*He travaileth with iniquity, and hath conceived mischief.*" All note that conceiving is before travailing, but here travailing, as a woman in labour, goeth first ; the reason whereof is, that the wicked are so hotly set upon the evil which they maliciously intend, that they would be immediately acting of it if they could tell how, even before they have conceived by what means ; but in fine they bring forth but a lie, that is, they find that their own hearts lied to them, when they promised good success, but they had evil. For their haste to perpetrate mischief is intimated in the word rendered " *persecutors* " (verse 13), which properly signifieth *ardentes,* burning ; that is, with a desire to do mischief—and this admits of no delay. A notable common-place, both setting forth the evil case of the wicked, especially attempting anything against the righteous, to move them to repentance—for thou hast God for thine enemy warring against thee, whose force thou canst not resist— and the greedy desire of the wicked to be evil, but their conception shall all prove abortive.—*J. Mayer, in loc.*

Verse 14.—"*And hath brought forth falsehood.*" Every sin is a lie.—*Augustine.*

Verse 14.—

> " Earth's entertainments are like those of Jael,
> Her left hand brings me milk, her right, a nail."
>
> *Thomas Fuller.*

Verses 14, 15.—"*They have digged a pit for us*"—and that low, unto hell—" *and are fallen into it themselves.*"

> " No juster law can be devised or made,
> Than that sin's agents fall by their own trade."

The order of hell proceeds with the same degrees ; though it give a greater portion, yet still a just proportion, of torment. These wretched guests were too busy with the waters of sin ; behold, now they are in the depth of a pit, " where no water is." Dives, that wasted so many tuns of wine, cannot now procure water, not a pot of water, not a handful of water, not a drop of water, to cool his tongue. *Desideravit guttam, qui non dedit micam.** A just recompense ! He would not give a crumb ; he shall not have a drop. Bread hath no smaller fragment than a crumb, water

---

* Aug. Hom. 7.

no less fraction than a drop. As he denied the least comfort to Lazarus living, so Lazarus shall not bring him the least comfort dead. Thus the pain for sin answers the pleasure of sin . . . . . Thus damnable sins shall have semblable punishments ; and as Augustine of the tongue, so we may say of any member . . . . . If it will not serve God in action, it shall serve him in passion.—*Thomas Adams.*

Verse 15.—"*He made a pit and digged it.*" The practice of making pitfalls was anciently not only employed for ensnaring wild beasts, but was also a stratagem used against men by the enemy, in time of war. The idea, therefore, refers to a man who, having made such a pit, whether for man or beast, and covered it over so as completely to disguise the danger, did himself inadvertently tread on his own trap, and fall into the pit he had prepared for another.—*Pictorial Bible.*

Verse 16.—That most witty of commentators, Old Master Trapp, tells the following notable anecdote, in illustration of this verse :—That was a very remarkable instance of Dr. Story, who, escaping out of prison in Queen Elizabeth's days, got to Antwerp, and there thinking himself out of the reach of God's rod, he got commission under the Duke of Alva to search all ships coming thither for English books. But one Parker, an English merchant, trading to Antwerp, laid his snare fair (saith our chronicler), to catch this foul bird, causing secret notice to be given to Story, that in his ship were stores of heretical books, with other intelligence that might stand him in stead. The Canonist conceiving that all was quite sure, hasted to the ship, where, with looks very big upon the poor mariners, each cabin, chest, and corner above-board were searched, and some things found to draw him futher on : so that the hatches must be opened, which seemed to be unwillingly done, and great signs of fear were showed by their faces. This drew on the Doctor to descend into the hold, where now in the trap the mouse might well gnaw, but could not get out, for the hatches were down, and the sails hoisted up, which, with a merry gale were blown into England, where ere long he was arraigned, and condemned of high treason, and accordingly executed at Tyburn, as he had well deserven.

Verse 16.—The story of Phalaris's bull, invented for the torment of others, and serving afterwards for himself, is notorious in heathen story . . . . It was a voluntary judgment which Archbishop Cranmer inflicted on himself when he thrust that very hand into the fire, and burnt it, with which he had signed to the popish articles, crying out, " *Oh, my unworthy right hand !* " but who will deny that the hand of the Almighty was also concerned in it ?—*William Turner in " Divine Judgments by way of Retaliation,"* 1697.

Verse 17.—To bless God for mercies is the way to increase them; to bless him for miseries is the way to remove them : no good lives so long as that which is thankfully improved ; no evil dies so soon as that which is patiently endured.—*William Dyer.*

HINTS TO PREACHERS.

Verse 1.—The necessity of faith when we address ourselves to God. Show the worthlessness of prayer without trust in the Lord.

Verses 1, 2.—Viewed as a prayer for deliverance from all enemies, especially Satan the lion.

Verse 3.—Self-vindication before men. When possible, judicious, or serviceable. With remarks upon the spirit in which it should be attempted.

Verse 4.—" *The best revenge.*" Evil for good is devil-like, evil for evil is beast-like, good for good is man-like, good for evil is God-like.

Verse 6.—How and in what sense divine anger may become the hope of the righteous.

Fire fought by fire, or man's anger overcome by God's anger.

Verse 7.—" *The congregation of the people.*" 1. Who they are. 2. Why they congregate together with one another. 3. Where they congregate. 4. Why they choose such a person to be the centre of their congregation.

Verse 7.—The gathering of the saints around the Lord Jesus.

Verse 7 (*last clause*).—The coming of Christ to judgment for the good of his saints.

Verse 8.—The character of the Judge before whom we all must stand.

Verse 9 (*first clause*).—(1) By changing their hearts ; or (2) by restraining their wills, (3) or depriving them of power, (4) or removing them.   Show the times when, the reasons why, such a prayer should be offered, and how, in the first sense, we may labour for its accomplishment.

Verse 9.—This verse contains two grand prayers, and a noble proof that the Lord can grant them.

Verse 9.—The period of sin, and the perpetuity of the righteous :—*Matthew Henry.*

Verse 9.—"*Establish the just."*   By what means and in what sense the just are established, or, the true established church.

Verse 9 (*last clause*).—God's trial of men's hearts.

Verse 10.—"*Upright in heart."*   Explain the character.

Verse 10.—The believer's trust in God, and God's care over him.   Show the action of faith in procuring defence and protection, and of that defence upon our faith by strengthening it, etc.

Verse 11.—The Judge, and the two persons upon their trial.

Verse 11 (*second clause*).—God's present, daily, constant, and vehement anger, against the wicked.

Verse 12.—See "Spurgeon's Sermons," No. 106.   "Turn or Burn."

Verses 14, 15, 16.—Illustrate by three figures the devices and defeat of persecutors.

Verse 17.—The excellent duty of praise.

Verse 17.—View the verse in connection with the subject of the Psalm, and show how the deliverance of the righteous, and the destruction of the wicked are themes for song.

PSALM VIII.

TITLE.—" To the Chief Musician upon Gittith, a Psalm of David." *We are not clear upon the meaning of the word Gittith. Some think it refers to Gath, and may refer to a tune commonly sung there, or an instrument of music there invented, or a song of Obededom the Gittite, in whose house the ark rested, or, better still, a song sung over Goliath of Gath. Others, tracing the Hebrew to its root, conceive it to mean a song for the winepress, a joyful hymn for the treaders of grapes. The term Gittith is applied to two other Psalms (lxxxi. and lxxxiv.), both of which, being of a joyous character, it may be concluded, that where we find that word in the title, we may look for a hymn of delight.*

We may style this Psalm the song of the Astronomer : let us go abroad and sing it beneath the starry heavens at eventide, for it is very probable that in such a position, it first occurred to the poet's mind. Dr. Chalmers says, " There is much in the scenery of a nocturnal sky, to lift the soul to pious contemplation. That moon, and these stars, what are they ? They are detached from the world, and they lift us above it. We feel withdrawn from the earth, and rise in lofty abstraction from this little theatre of human passions and human anxieties. The mind abandons itself to reverie, and is transferred in the ecstasy of its thought to distant and unexplored regions. It sees nature in the simplicity of her great elements, and it sees the God of nature invested with the high attributes of wisdom and majesty."

DIVISION.—*The first and last verses are a sweet song of admiration, in which the excellence of the name of God is extolled. The intermediate verses are made up of holy wonder at the Lord's greatness in creation, and at his condescension towards man. Poole, in his annotation, has well said, " It is a great question among interpreters, whether this Psalm speaks of man in general, and of the honour which God puts upon him in his creation ; or only of the man Christ Jesus. Possibly both may be reconciled and put together, and the controversy, if rightly stated, may be ended, for the scope and business of this Psalm seems plainly to be this : to display and celebrate the great love and kindness of God to mankind, not only in his creation, but especially in his redemption by Jesus Christ, whom, as he was man, he advanced to the honour and dominion here mentioned, that he might carry on his great and glorious work. So Christ is the principal subject of this Psalm, and it is interpreted of him, both by our Lord himself (Matt. xxi. 16), and by his holy apostle (1 Cor. xv. 27 ; Heb. ii. 6, 7).*

EXPOSITION.

O LORD our Lord, how excellent *is* thy name in all the earth ! who hast set thy glory above the heavens.

Unable to express the glory of God, the Psalmist utters a note of exclamation. O Jehovah our Lord ! We need not wonder at this, for no heart can measure, no tongue can utter, the half of the greatness of Jehovah. The whole creation is full of his glory and radiant with the excellency of his power ; his goodness and his wisdom are manifested on every hand. The countless myriads of terrestrial beings, from man the head, to the creeping worm at the foot, are all supported and nourished by the Divine bounty. The solid fabric of the universe leans upon his eternal arm. Universally is he present, and everywhere is his name excellent. God worketh ever and everywhere. There is no *place* where God is not. The miracles of his power await us on all sides. Traverse the silent valleys where the rocks enclose you on either side, rising like the battlements of heaven till you can see but a strip of the blue sky far overhead ; you may be the only traveller who has passed through that glen ; the bird may start up affrighted, and the moss may tremble beneath the first tread of human foot ; but God is there in a thousand wonders, upholding yon rocky barriers, filling the flowercups with their perfume, and refreshing the lonely pines with the breath of his mouth. Descend, if you will, into the lowest depths of the ocean, where undisturbed the water sleeps, and the very sand is motionless in unbroken quiet, but the glory of the Lord is there, revealing its excellence in the silent palace of the sea. Borrow the wings of the morning and fly to the uttermost parts of the sea, but God is there. Mount to the highest heaven, or dive into the deepest hell, and God is in both hymned in everlasting song, or justified in terrible vengeance. Everywhere, and in every place, God dwells and is manifestly at work. Nor on earth alone is Jehovah extolled, for his brightness shines forth in the firmament above the earth. His glory exceeds the glory of the starry heavens ; above the region of the stars he hath set fast his everlasting throne, and there he dwells in light ineffable. Let us adore him "who alone spreadeth out the heavens, and treadeth upon the waves of the sea ; who maketh Arcturus, Orion, and Pleiades, and the chambers of the south." (Job ix. 8, 9.) We can scarcely find more fitting words than those of Nehemiah, " Thou even thou, art Lord alone ; thou hast made heaven, the heaven of heavens, with all their hosts, the earth, and all things that are therein, the seas, and all that is therein, and thou preservest them all ; and the host of heaven worshippeth thee." Returning to the text we are led to observe that this Psalm is addressed to God, because none but the Lord himself can fully know his own glory. The believing heart is ravished with what it sees, but God only knows the glory of God. What a sweetness lies in the little word *our*, how much is God's glory endeared to us when we consider our interest in him as our Lord. *How excellent is thy name !* no words can express that excellency ; and therefore it is left as a note of exclamation. The very *name* of Jehovah is excellent, what must his person be. Note the fact that even the heavens cannot contain his glory, it is set *above the heavens*, since it is and ever must be too great for the creature to express. When wandering amid the Alps, we felt that the Lord was infinitely greater than all his grandest works, and under that feeling we roughly wrote these few lines :—

> Yet in all these how great soe'er they be,
> We see not Him. The glass is all too dense
> And dark, or else our earthborn eyes too dim.
>
> Yon Alps, that lift their heads above the clouds
> And hold familiar converse with the stars,
> Are dust, at which the balance trembleth not,
> Compared with His divine immensity.
> The snow-crown'd summits fail to set Him forth,
> Who dwelleth in Eternity, and bears
> Alone, the name of High and Lofty One.
> Depths unfathomed are too shallow to express
> The wisdom and the knowledge of the Lord,
> The mirror of the creatures has no space
> To bear the image of the Infinite.
> 'Tis true the Lord hath fairly writ His name,
> And set His seal upon creation's brow.
> But as the skilful potter much excels
> The vessel which he fashions on the wheel,
> E'en so, but in proportion greater far,
> Jehovah's self transcends His noblest works.
> Earth's ponderous wheels would break, her axles snap,
> If freighted with the load of Deity.
> Space is too narrow for the Eternal's rest,
> And time too short a footstool for His throne.
> E'en avalanche and thunder lack a voice,
> To utter the full volume of His praise.
> How then can I declare Him ! Where are words
> With which my glowing tongue may speak His name !
> Silent I bow, and humbly I adore.

2 Out of the mouth of babes and sucklings hast thou ordained strength because of thine enemies, that thou mightest still the enemy and the avenger.

Nor only in the heavens above is the Lord seen, but the earth beneath is telling forth his majesty. In the sky, the massive orbs, rolling in their stupendous grandeur, are witnesses of his power in great things, while here below, the lisping utterances of babes are the manifestations of his strength in little ones. How often will children tell us of a God whom we have forgotten ! How doth their simple prattle refute those learned fools who deny the being of God ! Many men have been made to hold their tongues, while sucklings have borne witness to the glory of the God of heaven. It is singular how clearly the history of the church expounds this verse. Did not the children cry " Hosannah ! " in the temple, when proud Pharisees were silent and contemptuous ? and did not the Saviour quote these very words as a justification of their infantile cries ? Early church history records many amazing instances of the testimony of children for the truth of God, but perhaps more modern instances will be most interesting. Foxe tells us, in the Book of Martyrs, that when Mr. Lawrence was burnt in Colchester, he was carried to the fire in a chair, because, through the cruelty of the Papists, he could not stand upright, several young children came about the fire and cried, as well as they could speak, " Lord, strengthen thy servant, and keep thy promise." God answered their prayer, for Mr. Lawrence died as firmly and calmly as any one could wish to breathe his last. When one of the Popish chaplains told Mr. Wishart, the great Scotch martyr, that he had a devil in him, a child that stood by cried out, " A devil cannot speak such words as yonder man speaketh." One more instance is still nearer to our time. In a postcript to one of his letters, in which he details his persecution when first preaching in Moorfields, Whitfield says, " I cannot help adding that several little boys and girls, who were fond of sitting round me on the pulpit while I preached, and handed to me people's notes—though they were often pelted with eggs, dirt, &c., thrown at me— never once gave way ; but, on the contrary, every time I was struck, turned up their little weeping eyes, and seemed to wish they could receive the blows for me. God make them, in their growing years, great and living martyrs for him who, out of the mouth of babes and sucklings, perfects praise ! " He who delights in the songs of angels is pleased to honour himself in the eyes of his enemies by the praises of little children. What a contrast between the glory above the heavens, and the mouths of babes and sucklings ! yet by both the name of God is made excellent.

3 When I consider thy heavens, the work of thy fingers, the moon and the stars, which thou hast ordained ;

4 What is man, that thou art mindful of him ? and the son of man, that thou visitest him ?

At the close of that excellent little manual entitled " The Solar System," written by Dr. Dick, we find an eloquent passage which beautifully expounds the text :— A survey of the solar system has a tendency to moderate the pride of man and to promote humility. Pride is one of the distinguishing characteristics of puny man, and has been one of the chief causes of all the contentions, wars, devastations, systems of slavery, and ambitious projects which have desolated and demoralized our sinful world. Yet there is no disposition more incongruous to the character and circumstance of man. Perhaps there are no rational beings throughout the universe among whom pride would appear more unseemly or incompatible than in man, considering the situation in which he is placed. He is exposed to numerous degradations and calamities, to the rage of storms and tempests, the devastations of earthquakes and volcanoes, the fury of whirlwinds, and the tempestuous billows of the ocean, to the ravages of the sword, famine, pestilence, and numerous diseases ; and at length he must sink into the grave, and his body must become the companion of worms ! The most dignified and haughty of the sons of men are liable to these and similar degradations as well as the meanest of the human family. Yet, in such circumstances, man—that puny worm of the dust, whose knowledge is so limited, and whose follies are so numerous and glaring—has the effrontery to strut in all the haughtiness of pride, and to glory in his shame.

When other arguments and motives produce little effect on certain minds, no considerations seem likely to have a more powerful tendency to counteract this deplorable propensity in human beings, than those which are borrowed from the objects connected with astronomy. They show us what an insignificant being— what a mere atom, indeed, man appears amidst the immensity of creation ! Though he is an object of the paternal care and mercy of the Most High, yet he is but as a grain of sand to the whole earth, when compared to the countless myriads of beings that people the amplitudes of creation. What is the whole of this globe on which we dwell compared with the solar system, which contains a mass of matter ten thousand times greater ? What is it in comparison of the hundred millions of suns and worlds which by the telescope have been described throughout the starry regions ? What, then, is a kingdom, a province, or a baronial territory, of which we are as proud as if we were the lords of the universe and for which we engage in so much devastation and carnage ? What are they, when set in competition with the glories of the sky ? Could we take our station on the lofty pinnacles of heaven, and look down on this scarcely distinguishable speck of earth, we should be ready to exclaim with Seneca, " Is it to this little spot that the great designs and vast desires of men are confined ? Is it for this there is so much disturbance of nations, so much carnage, and so many ruinous wars ? Oh, the folly of deceived men, to imagine great kingdoms in the compass of an atom, to raise armies to decide a point of earth with the sword ! " Dr. Chalmers, in his Astronomical Discourses, very truthfully says, " We gave you but a feeble image of our comparative insignificance, when we said that the glories of an extended forest would suffer no more from the fall of a single leaf, than the glories of this extended universe would suffer though the globe we tread upon, ' and all that it inherits, should dissolve.' "

5 For thou hast made him a little lower than the angels, and hast crowned him with glory and honour.

6 Thou madest him to have dominion over the works of thy hands ; thou hast put all *things* under his feet :

7 All sheep and oxen, yea, and the beasts of the field ;

8 The fowl of the air, and the fish of the sea, *and whatsoever* passeth through the paths of the sea.

These verses may set forth man's position among the creatures before he fell ; but as they are, by the apostle Paul, appropriated to man as represented by the Lord Jesus, it is best to give most weight to that meaning. In order of dignity, man stood next to the angels, and a little lower than they ; in the Lord Jesus this was accomplished, for he was made a little lower than the angels by the suffering of death. Man in Eden had the full command of all creatures, and they came before him to receive their names as an act of homage to him as the vicegerent of God to them. Jesus in his glory, is now Lord, not only of all living, but of all created things, and, with the exception of him who put all things under him, Jesus is Lord of all, and his elect, in him, are raised to a dominion wider than that of the first Adam, as shall be more clearly seen at his coming. Well might the Psalmist wonder at the singular exaltation of man in the scale of being, when he marked his utter nothingness in comparison with the starry universe.

Thou madest him a little lower than the angels—a little lower in nature, since they are immortal, and but a little, because time is short ; and when that is over, saints are no longer lower than the angels. The margin reads it, " A little while inferior to." *Thou crownest him.* The dominion that God has bestowed on man is a great *glory and honour* to him ; for all dominion is honour, and the highest is that which wears the crown. A full list is given of the subjugated creatures, to show that all the dominion lost by sin is restored in Christ Jesus. Let none of us permit the possession of any earthly creature to be a snare to us, but let us remember that we are to reign over them, and not to allow them to reign over us. Under our feet we must keep the world, and we must shun that base spirit which is content to let worldly cares and pleasures sway the empire of the immortal soul.

9 O Lord our Lord, how excellent is thy name in all the earth !

Here, like a good composer, the poet returns to his key-note, falling back, as it were, into his first state of wondering adoration. What he started with as a proposition in the first verse, he closes with as a well proven conclusion, with a sort of *quod erat demonstrandum.* O for grace to walk worthy of that excellent name which has been named upon us, and which we are pledged to magnify !

EXPLANATORY NOTES AND QUAINT SAYINGS.

Title.—" *Gittith,*" was probably a musical instrument used at their rejoicings after the vintage. The vintage closed the civil year of the Jews, and this Psalm directs us to the latter-day glory, when the Lord shall be King over all the earth, having subdued all his enemies. It is very evident that the vintage was adopted as a figurative representation of the final destruction of all God's enemies. Isaiah lxiii. 1—6 ; Rev. xix. 18—20. The ancient Jewish interpreters so understood this Psalm, and apply it to the mystic vintage. We may then consider this interesting composition as a prophetic anticipation of the kingdom of Christ, to be established in glory and honour in the "world to come," the habitable world. Heb. ii. 5. We see not yet all things put under his feet, but we are sure that the Word of God shall be fulfilled, and every enemy, Satan, death, and hell, shall be for ever subdued and destroyed, and creation itself delivered from the bondage of corruption into the glorious liberty of the children of God. Rom. viii. 17—23. In the use of this Psalm, then, we anticipate that victory, and in the praise we thus celebrate, we go on from strength to strength till, with him who is our glorious Head, we appear in Zion before God.—*W. Wilson, D.D., in loc.*

Whole Psalm.—Now, consider but the scope of the Psalm, as the apostle quoteth it to prove the world to come. Heb. ii. Any one that reads the Psalm would think that the Psalmist doth but set forth old Adam in his kingdom, in his paradise, made a little lower than the angels—for we have spirits wrapped up in flesh and blood, whereas they are spirits simply—a degree lower, as if they were dukes, and we marquises ; one would think, I say, that this were all his meaning, and that it is applied to Christ but by way of allusion. But the truth is, the apostle bringeth it in to prove and to convince these Hebrews, to whom he wrote, that that Psalm was meant of Christ, of that man whom they expected to be the Messiah, the Man Christ Jesus. And that he doth it, I prove by the sixth verse—it is the observation that Beza hath—" One in a certain place," quoting David, διεμαρτύρατο, hath testified ; so we may translate it, hath testified it, *etiam atque etiam*, testified most expressly ; he bringeth an express proof for it that it was meant of the Man Christ Jesus ; therefore it is not an allusion. And indeed it was Beza that did first begin that interpretation that I read of, and himself therefore doth excuse it and make an apology for it, that he diverteth out of the common road, though since many others have followed him.

Now the scope of the Psalm is plainly this : in Rom. v. 14, you read that Adam was a type of him that was to come. Now in Psalm viii. you find there Adam's world, the type of a world to come ; he was the first Adam, and had a world, so the second Adam hath a world also appointed for him ; there are his oxen and his sheep, and the fowls of the air, whereby are meant other things, devils perhaps, and wicked men, the prince of the air ; as by the heavens there, the angels, or the apostles rather—" the heavens declare the glory of God ; " that is applied to the apostles, that were preachers of the gospel.

To make this plain to you, that that Psalm where the phrase is used, "All things under his feet," and quoted by the apostle in Eph. i. 22—therefore it is proper— was not meant of man in innocency, but of the Messiah, the Lord Jesus Christ ; and therefore, answerably, that the world there is not this world, but a world on purpose made for this Messiah, as the other was for Adam.

First, it was not meant of man in innocency properly and principally. Why ? Because in the second verse he saith, " Out of the mouth of babes and sucklings hast thou ordained strength." There were no babes in the time of Adam's innocency, he fell before there were any. Secondly, he addeth, " That thou mightest still the enemy and the avenger ; " the devil that is, for he showed himself the enemy there, to be a manslayer from the beginning. God would use man to still him ; alas ! he overcame Adam presently. It must be meant of another therefore, one that is able to still this enemy and avenger.

Then he saith, " How excellent is thy name in all the earth ! who hast set thy glory above the heavens." Adam had but paradise, he never propagated God's name over all the earth ; he did not continue so long before he fell as to beget sons ; much less did he found it in the heavens.

Again, verse 4, " What is man, and the son of man ? " Adam, though he was man, yet he was not the son of man ; he is called indeed, " the son of God " (Luke iii. 38), but he was not *filius hominis*. I remember Ribera urgeth that.

But take an argument the apostle himself useth to prove it. This man, saith he, must have all subject to him ; all but God, saith he ; he must have the angels subject to him, for he hath put all principalities and powers under his feet, saith he. This could not be Adam, it could not be the man that had this world in a state of innocency ; much less had Adam all under his feet. No, my brethren, it was too great a vassalage for Adam to have the creatures thus bow to him. But they are thus to Jesus Christ, angels and all ; they are all under his feet, he is far above them.

Secondly, it is not meant of man fallen, that is as plain ; the apostle himself saith so. "We see not," saith he, "all things subject unto him." Some think that it is meant as an objection that the apostle answereth ; but it is indeed to prove that man fallen cannot be meant in Psalm viii. Why ? Because, saith he, we do not see anything, all things at least, subject unto him ; you have not any one man, or the whole race of man, to whom all things have been subject ; the creatures are sometimes injurious to him. We do not see him, saith he ; that is, the nature of man in general considered. Take all the monarchs in the world, they never conquered the whole world ; there was never any one man that was a sinner that had all subject to him. "But we see," saith he—mark the opposition—"but we see Jesus," that Man, "crowned with glory and honour ; " therefore, it is this Man, and no man else ; the opposition implieth it." . . . So now it remaineth then, that it is only Christ, God-man, that is meant in Psalm viii. And indeed, and in truth, Christ himself interpreteth the Psalm of himself ; you have two witnesses to confirm it, Christ himself and the apostle. Matt. xxi. 16. When they cried hosanna to Christ, or "save now," and made him the Saviour of the world, the Pharisees were angry, our Saviour confuteth them by this very Psalm : "Have ye not read," saith he, "out of the mouths of babes and sucklings thou hast perfected praise ?" He quoteth this very Psalm which speaks of himself ; and Paul, by his warrant, and perhaps from that hint, doth thus argue out of it, and convince the Jews by it.—*Thomas Goodwin.*

Verse 1.—"*How excellent is thy name in all the earth !* " How illustrious is the name of Jesus throughout the world ! His incarnation, birth, humble, and obscure life, preaching, miracles, passion, death, resurrection, and ascension, are celebrated through the whole world. His religion, the gifts and graces of his Spirit, his people—Christians, his gospel, and the preachers of it, are everywhere spoken of. No name is so universal, no power and influence so generally felt, as those of the Saviour of mankind. Amen.—*Adam Clarke.*

Verse 1.—"*Above the heavens ;*" not in the heavens, but "*above the heavens ;*" even greater, beyond, and higher than they ; "angels, principalities, and powers, being made subject unto him." As Paul says, he hath "ascended up far above all heavens." And with this his glory above the heaven is connected, his sending forth his name upon earth through his Holy Spirit. As the apostle adds in this passage, "He hath ascended up far above all heavens ; and he gave some apostles." And thus here : "Thy name excellent in all the world ; " "Thy glory above the heavens."—*Isaac Williams.*

Verse 2.—"*Out of the mouth of babes and sucklings hast thou ordained strength,*" etc. In a prophetic manner, speaking of that which was to be done by children many hundreds of years after, for the asserting of his infinite mercy in sending his Son Jesus Christ into the world to save us from our sins. For so the Lord applieth their crying, "Hosannah to the Son of David " in the temple. And thus both Basil and other ancients, and some new writers also understand it. But Calvin will have it meant of God's wonderful providing for them, by turning their mothers' blood into milk, and giving them the faculty to suck, thus nourishing and preserving them, which sufficiently convinceth all gainsayers of God's wonderful providence towards the weakest and most shiftless of all creatures.—*John Mayer,* 1653.

Verse 2.—Who are these "*babes and sucklings ?* " 1. Man in general, who springeth from so weak and poor a beginning as that of babes and sucklings, yet is at length advanced to such power as to grapple with, and overcome the enemy and the avenger. 2. David in particular, who being but a ruddy youth, God used him as an instrument to discomfit Goliath of Gath. 3. More especially our Lord Jesus Christ, who assuming our nature and all the sinless infirmities of it, and submitting to the weakness of an infant, and after dying is gone in the same nature to reign in heaven, till he hath brought all his enemies under his feet. Psalm cx. 1, and 1 Cor. xv. 27. Then was our human nature exalted above all other creatures, when the Son of God was made of a woman, carried in the womb. 4. The apostles, who to outward appearance were despicable, in a manner children and sucklings in comparison of the great ones of the world; poor despised creatures, yet principal instruments of God's service and glory. Therefore 'tis notable, that when Christ glorifieth his Father for the wise and free dispensation of his saving grace (Matt. xi. 25), he saith, " I thank thee, O Father, Lord of heaven and earth, because thou hast hid these things from the wise and prudent, and hast revealed them unto babes," so called from the meanness of their condition. . . . And you shall see it was spoken when the disciples were sent abroad, and had power given them over unclean spirits. " In that hour Jesus rejoiced in spirit, and said, I thank thee, O Father, Lord of heaven and earth, that thou hast hid these things from the wise and prudent, and hast revealed them unto babes." This he acknowledged to be an act of infinite condescension in God. 5. Those children that cried *Hosanna* to Christ, make up part of the sense, for Christ defendeth their practice by this Scripture. . . . 6. Not only the apostles, but all those that fight under Christ's banner, and are listed into his confederacy, may be called babes and sucklings ; first, because of their condition ; secondly, their disposition. . . . . 1. Because of their condition. . . . God in the government of the world is pleased to subdue the enemies of his kingdom by weak and despised instruments. 2. Because of their disposition : they are most humble spirited. We are told (Matt. xviii. 3), " Except ye be converted, and become as little children," etc. As if he had said, you strive for pre-eminence and worldly greatness in my kingdom ; I tell you my kingdom is a kingdom of babes and containeth none but the humble, and such as are little in their own eyes, and are contented to be small and despised in the eyes of others, and so do not seek after great matters in the world. A young child knoweth not what striving or state meaneth, and therefore by an emblem and visible representation of a child set in the midst of them, Christ would take them off from the expectation of a carnal kingdom.—*Thomas Manton, 1620—1677.*

Verse 2.—" That thou mightest still the enemy and the avenger." This very confusion and revenge upon Satan, who was the cause of man's fall, was aimed at by God at first ; therefore is the first promise and preaching of the gospel to Adam brought in rather in sentencing him than in speaking to Adam, that the seed of the woman should break the serpent's head, it being in God's aim as much to confound him as to save poor man.—*Thomas Goodwin.*

Verse 2.—The work that is done in love loses half its tedium and difficulty. It is as with a stone, which in the air and on the dry ground we strain at but cannot stir. Flood the field where it lies, bury the block beneath the rising water ; and now, when its head is submerged, bend to the work. Put your strength to it. Ah ! it moves, rises from its bed, rolls on before your arm. So, when under the heavenly influences of grace the tide of love rises, and goes swelling over our duties and difficulties, a child can do a man's work, and a man can do a giant's. Let love be present in the heart, and *" out of the mouth of babes and sucklings* God ordaineth strength."—*Thomas Guthrie, D.D.*

Verse 2.—" Out of the mouth of babes and sucklings," etc. That poor martyr, Alice Driver, in the presence of many hundreds, did so silence Popish bishops, that she and all blessed God that the proudest of them could not resist the spirit in a silly woman; so I say to thee, *"Out of the mouth of babes and sucklings"* God will be honoured. Even thou, silly worm, shalt honour him, when it shall appear what God hath done for thee, what lusts he hath mortified, and what graces he hath granted thee. The Lord can yet do greater things for thee if thou wilt trust him. He can carry thee upon eagles' wings, enable thee to bear and suffer strong affliction for him, to persevere to the end, to live by faith, and to finish thy course with joy. Oh ! in that he hath made thee low in heart, thy other lowness shall be so much the more honour to thee. Do not all as much and more wonder at God's rare workmanship in the ant, the poorest bug that creeps, as in the biggest elephant? That so many parts and limbs should be united in such a little space ; that so poor a creature should provide in the summer-time her winter food. Who sees not as much of God in a bee as in a greater creature ? Alas ! in a great body we look for great abilities and wonder not. Therefore, to conclude, seeing God hath clothed thy uncomely parts with the more honour, bless God, and bear thy baseness more equally ; thy greatest glory is yet to come, that when the wise of the world have rejected the counsel of God, thou hast (with those poor publicans and soldiers), magnified the ministry of the gospel. Surely the Lord will also be admired in thee (1 Thess. i.), a poor silly creature, that even thou wert made wise to salvation and believest in that day. Be still poor in thine own eyes, and the Lord will make thy proudest scornful enemies to worship at thy feet, to confess God hath done much for thee, and wish thy portion when God shall visit them.—*Daniel Rogers, 1642.*

Verse 3.—" When I consider." Meditation fits for humiliation. When David had been contemplating the works of creation, their splendour, harmony, motion, influence, he lets the plumes of pride fall, and begins to have self-abasing thoughts. *" When I consider thy heavens, the work of thy fingers, the moon and the stars which thou hast ordained, what is man that thou art mindful of him ? "—Thomas Watson.*

Verse 3.—" When I consider thy heavens," etc. David surveying the firmament, broke forth into this consideration : *" When I consider thy heavens, the work of thy fingers, the moon and the stars, which thou hast created, what is man ? "* etc. How cometh he to mention the moon and stars, and omit the sun ? the other being but his pensioners, shining with that exhibition of light which the bounty of the sun allots them. It is answered, this was David's night meditation, when the sun, departing to the other world, left the lesser lights only visible in heaven ; and as the sky is best beheld by day in the glory thereof, so too it is best surveyed by night in the variety of the same. Night was made for man to rest in. But when I cannot sleep, may I, with the Psalmist, entertain my waking with good thoughts. Not to use them as opium, to invite my corrupt nature to slumber, but to bolt out bad thoughts, which otherwise would possess my soul.—*Thomas Fuller, 1608—1661.*

Verse 3.—" Thy heavens." The carnal mind sees God in nothing, not even in spiritual things, his word and ordinances. The spiritual mind sees him in everything, even in natural things, in looking on the heavens and the earth and all the creatures—" Thy *heavens ;* " sees all in that notion, in their relation to God as his work, and in them his glory appearing ; stands in awe, fearing to abuse his creatures and his favours to his dishonour. *" The day is thine, and the night also is thine ; "* therefore ought not I to forget thee through the day, nor in the night.—*Robert Leighton, D.D.*

Verse 3.—" The stars." I cannot say that it is chiefly the contemplation of their infinitude, and the immeasurable space they occupy, that enraptures me in the stars. These conditions rather tend to confuse the mind ; and in this view of countless numbers and unlimited space there lies, moreover, much that belongs rather to a temporary and human than to an eternally abiding consideration. Still less do I regard them absolutely with reference to the life after this. But the mere thought that they are so far beyond and above everything terrestrial—the feeling, that before them everything earthly so utterly vanishes to nothing—that the single man is so infinitely insignificant in the comparison with these worlds strewn over all space—that his destinies, his enjoyments, and sacrifices, to which he attaches such a minute importance—how all these fade like nothing before such immense objects ; then, that the constellations bind together all the races of man, and all the eras of the earth, that they have beheld all that has passed since the beginning of time, and will see all that passes until its end ; in thoughts like these I can always lose myself with a silent delight in the view of the starry firmament. It is, in very truth, a spectacle of the highest solemnity, when, in the stillness of night, in a heaven quite clear, the stars, like a choir of worlds, arise and descend, while existence, as it were, falls asunder into two separate parts ; the one, belonging to earth, grows dumb in the utter silence of night, and thereupon the other mounts upward in all its elevation, splendour, and majesty. And, when contemplated from this point of view, the starry heavens have truly a moral influence on the mind.—*Alexander Von Humboldt, 1850.*

Verse 3.—" When I consider thy heavens," etc. Could we transport ourselves above the moon, could we reach the highest star above our heads, we should instantly discover new skies, new stars, new suns, new systems, and perhaps more magnificently adorned. But even there, the vast dominions of our great Creator would not terminate ; we should then find, to our astonishment, that we had only arrived at the borders of the works of God. It is but little that we can know of his works, but that little should teach us to be humble, and to admire the divine power and goodness. How great must that Being be who produced these immense globes out of nothing, who regulates their courses, and whose mighty hand directs and supports them all. What is the clod of earth which we inhabit, with all the magnificent scenes it presents to us, in comparison of those innumerable worlds ? Were this earth annihilated, its absence would no more be observed than that of a grain of sand from the sea shore. What then are provinces and kingdoms when compared with those worlds ? They are but atoms dancing in the air, which are discovered to us by the sunbeams. What then am I, when reckoned among the infinite number of God's creatures ? I am lost in mine own nothingness ! But little as I appear in this respect, I find myself great in others. There is great beauty in this starry firmament which God has chosen for his throne! How admirable are those celestial bodies! I am dazzled with their splendour, and enchanted with their beauty! But nothwithstanding this, however beautiful, and however richly adorned, yet this sky is void of intelligence. It is a stranger to its own beauty, while I, who am mere clay, moulded by a divine hand, am endowed with sense and reason. I can contemplate the beauty of these shining worlds; nay, more, I am already, to a certain degree, acquainted with their sublime Author; and by faith I see some small rays of his divine glory. O may I be more and more acquainted with his works, and make the study of them my employ, till by a glorious change I rise to dwell with him above the starry regions.—*Christopher Christian Sturm's " Reflections," 1750—1786.*

Verse 3.—" *Work of God's fingers."* That is most elaborate and accurate: a metaphor from embroiderers, or from them that make tapestry.—*John Trapp.*

Verse 3.—" *When I consider thy heavens,"* etc. It is truly a most Christian exercise to extract a sentiment of piety from the works and the appearances of nature. It has the authority of the sacred writers upon its side, and even our Saviour himself gives it the weight and the solemnity of his example. " Behold the lilies of the field; they toil not, neither do they spin, yet your heavenly Father careth for them." He expatiates on the beauty of a single flower, and draws from it the delightful argument of confidence in God. He gives us to see that taste may be combined with piety, and that the same heart may be occupied with all that is serious in the contemplations of religion, and be at the same time alive to the charms and the loveliness of nature. The Psalmist takes a still loftier flight. He leaves the world, and lifts his imagination to that mighty expanse which spreads above it and around it. He wings his way through space, and wanders in thought over its immeasurable regions. Instead of a dark and unpeopled solitude, he sees it crowded with splendour, and filled with the energy of the divine presence. Creation rises in its immensity before him, and the world, with all which it inherits, shrinks into littleness at a contemplation so vast and so overpowering. He wonders that he is not overlooked amid the grandeur and the variety which are on every side of him; and, passing upward from the majesty of nature to the majesty of nature's Architect, he exclaims, " What is man, that thou art mindful of him, or the son of man that thou shouldest deign to visit him ? " It is not for us to say whether inspiration revealed to the psalmist the wonders of the modern astronomy. But, even though the mind be a perfect stranger to the science of these enlightened times, the heavens present a great and an elevating spectacle, an immense concave reposing upon the circular boundary of the world, and the innumerable lights which are suspended from on high, moving with solemn regularity along its surface. It seems to have been at night that the piety of the Psalmist was awakened by this contemplation; when the moon and the stars were visible, and not when the sun had risen in his strength and thrown a splendour around him, which bore down and eclipsed all the lesser glories of the firmament.—*Thomas Chalmers, D.D., 1817.*

Verse 3.—" *Thy heavens" :—*

> This prospect vast, what is it ?—weigh'd aright.
> 'Tis nature's system of divinity,
> And every student of the night inspires.
> 'Tis elder Scripture, writ by God's own hand:
> Scripture authentic! uncorrupt by man.
>
> *Edward Young.*

Verse 3.—" *The stars."* When I gazed into these stars, have they not looked down on me as if with pity from their serene spaces, like eyes glistening with heavenly tears over the little lot of man !—*Thomas Carlyle.*

Verses 3, 4.—" *When I consider thy heavens,"* etc. Draw spiritual inferences from occasional objects. David did but wisely consider the heavens, and he breaks out into self-abasement and humble admirations of God. Glean matter of instruction to yourselves, and praise to your Maker from everything you see; it will be a degree of restoration to a state of innocency, since this was Adam's task in paradise. Dwell not upon any created object only as a *virtuoso,* to gratify your rational curiosity, but as a Christian, call religion to the feast, and make a spiritual improvement. No creature can meet our eyes but affords us lessons worthy of our thoughts, besides the general notices of the power and wisdom of the Creator. Thus may the sheep read us a lesson of patience, the dove of innocence, the ant and bee raise blushes in us for our sluggishness, and the stupid ox and dull ass correct and shame our ungrateful ignorance. . . . . He whose eyes are open cannot want an instructor, unless he wants a heart.—*Stephen Charnock.*

Verse 4.—"*What is man, that thou art mindful of him?*" etc.   My readers must be careful to mark the design of the Psalmist, which is to enhance, by this comparison, the infinite goodness of God ; for it is, indeed, a wonderful thing that the Creator of heaven, whose glory is so surpassingly great as to ravish us with the highest admiration, condescends so far as graciously to take upon him the care of the human race.   That the Psalmist makes this contrast may be inferred from the Hebrew word אֱנוֹשׁ, *enosh*, which we have rendered *man*, and which expresses the frailty of man rather than any strength or power which he possesses. . . . . . Almost all interpreters render פָּקַד, *pakad*, the last word of this verse, *to visit ;* and I am unwilling to differ from them, since this sense suits the passage very well. But as it sometimes signifies *to remember,* and as we will often find in the Psalms the repetition of the same thought in different words, it may here be very properly translated *to remember ;* as if David had said, " This is a marvellous thing, that God thinks upon men, and remembers them continually."—*John Calvin,* 1509—1564.

Verse 4.—"*What is man?*"   But, O God, what a little lord hast thou made over this great world !   The least corn of sand is not so small to the whole earth, as man is to the heaven.   When I see the heavens, the sun, the moon, and stars, O God, what is man ?   Who would think thou shouldst make all these creatures for one, and that one well-near the least of all ?   Yet none but he can see what thou hast done ; none but he can admire and adore thee in what he seeth : how had he need to do nothing but this, since he alone must do it !   Certainly the price and value of things consist not in the quantity ; one diamond is worth more than many quarries of stone ; one loadstone hath more virtue than mountains of earth. It is lawful for us to praise thee in ourselves.   All thy creation hath not more wonder in it than one of us : other creatures thou madest by a simple command ; Man, not without a divine consultation : others at once ; man thou didst form, then inspire : others in several shapes, like to none but themselves ; man, after thine own image : others with qualities fit for service ; man, for dominion.   Man had his name from thee ; they had their names from man.   How should we be consecrated to thee above all others, since thou hast bestowed more cost on us than other !— *Joseph Hall, D.D., Bishop of Norwich,* 1574—1656.

Verse 4.—"*What is man, that thou art mindful of him? or the son of man, that thou shouldst visit him?*"   And (Job vii. 17, 18) " What is man, that thou shouldst magnify him ? and that thou shouldst set thy heart upon him ? and that thou shouldst visit him every morning ? "   Man, in the pride of his heart, seeth no such great matter in it ; but a humble soul is filled with astonishment.   " Thus saith the high and lofty One that inhabiteth eternity, whose name is Holy ; I dwell in the high and holy place, with him also that is of a contrite and humble spirit, to revive the spirit of the humble, and to revive the heart of the contrite ones." Isaiah lvii. 15.   Oh, saith the humble soul, will the Lord have respect unto such a vile worm as I am ?   Will the Lord acquaint himself with such a sinful wretch as I am ?   Will the Lord open his arms, his bosom, his heart to me ?   Shall such a loathsome creature as I find favour in his eyes ?   In Ezek. xvi. 1—5, we have a relation of the wonderful condescension of God to man, who is there resembled to a wretched infant cast out in the day of its birth, in its blood and filthiness, no eye pitying it ; such loathsome creatures are we before God ; and yet when he passed by, and saw us polluted in our blood, he said unto us, " Live."   It is doubled because of the strength of its nature ; it was " the time of love " (verse 8).   This was love indeed, that God should take a filthy, wretched thing, and spread his skirts over it, and cover its nakedness, and swear unto it, and enter into a covenant with it, and make it his ; that is, that he should espouse this loathsome thing to himself, that he would be a husband to it ; this love unfathomable, love inconceivable, self-principle love ; this is the love of God to man, for God is love.   Oh, the depth of the riches of the bounty and goodness of God !   How is his love wonderful, and his grace past finding out ! How do you find and feel your hearts affected upon the report of these things ? Do you not see matter of admiration and cause of wonder ?   Are you not as it were launched forth into an ocean of goodness, where you can see no shore, nor feel no bottom ?   Ye may make a judgment of yourselves by the motions and affections that ye feel in yourselves at the mention of this.   For thus Christ judged of the faith of the centurion that said unto him, " Lord, I am not worthy that thou shouldst come under my roof. When Jesus heard this, he marvelled, and said to them that followed him, I say unto you, I have not found so great faith, no, not in Israel." Matthew viii. 8–10. If, then, you feel not your souls mightily affected with the condescension of God, say thus unto your souls, What aileth thee, O my soul, that thou art no more affected with the goodness of God ? Art thou dead, that thou canst not feel ? Or art thou blind that thou canst not see thyself compassed about with astonishing goodness ? Behold the King of glory descending from the habitation of his majesty, and coming to visit thee ! Hearest not thou his voice, saying, " Open to me, my sister: behold, I stand at the door and knock. Lift up yourselves, O ye gates, and be ye lifted up, ye everlasting doors, that the King of glory may come in ? " Behold, O my soul, how he waits still while thou hast refused to open to him ! Oh, the wonder of his goodness ! Oh, the condescension of his love, to visit me, to sue unto me, to wait upon me, to be acquainted with me ! Thus work up your souls into an astonishment at the condescension of God.—*James Janeway*, 1674.

Verse 4.—*Man*, in Hebrew—infirm or miserable man—by which it is apparent that he speaks of man not according to the state of his creation, but as fallen into a state of sin, and misery, and mortality. *Art mindful of him*, *i.e.*, carest for him, and conferrest such high favours upon him. *The son of man*, Heb., *the son of Adam* that great apostate from and rebel against God ; the sinful son of a sinful father— his son by likeness of disposition and manners, no less than by procreation ; all which tends to magnify the divine mercy. *That thou visitest him*—not in anger, as that word is sometimes used, but with thy grace and mercy, as it is taken in Gen. xxi. 1 ; Ex. iv. 31 ; Psalm lxv. 9 ; cvi. 4 ; cxliv. 3.

Verse 4.—" *What is man ?* " The Scripture gives many answers to this question. Ask the prophet Isaiah, " *What is man ?* " and he answers (xl. 6), man is " grass "—" All flesh is grass, and all the goodliness thereof is as the flower of the field." Ask David, " *What is man ?* " He answers (Psalm lxii. 9), man is " *a lie*," not a liar only, or a deceiver, but " *a lie*," and a deceit. All the answers the Holy Ghost gives concerning man, are to humble man : man is ready to flatter himself, and one man to flatter another, but God tells us plainly what we are. . . . . It is a wonder that God should vouchsafe a gracious look upon such a creature as man ; it is wonderful, considering the distance between God and man, as man is a creature and God the creator. " *What is man*," that God should take notice of him ? Is he not a clod of earth, a piece of clay ? But consider him as a sinful and an unclean creature, and we may wonder to amazement : what is an unclean creature that God should magnify him ? Will the Lord indeed put value upon filthiness, and fix his approving eye upon an impure thing ? One step further ; what is rebellious man, man an enemy to God, that God should magnify him ! what admiration can answer this question ? Will God prefer his enemies, and magnify those who would cast him down ? Will a prince exalt a traitor, or give him honour who attempts to take away his life ? The sinful nature of man is an enemy to the nature of God, and would pull God out of heaven ; yet God even at that time is raising man to heaven : sin would lessen the great God, and yet God greatens sinful man.—*Joseph Caryl.*

Verse 4.—" *What is man ?* " Oh, the grandeur and littleness, the excellence and the corruption, the majesty and meanness of man !—*Pascal*, 1623—1662.

Verse 4.—" *Thou visitest him.*" To visit is, first, to afflict, to chasten, yea, to punish ; the highest judgments in Scripture come under the notions of visitations. " Visiting the iniquity of the fathers upon the children " (Ex. xxxiv. 7), that is, punishing them. . . . And it is a common speech with us when a house hath the plague, which is one of the highest strokes of temporal affliction, we use to say, " Such a house is visited." Observe then, afflictions are visitations. . . . Secondly, to visit, in a good sense, signifies to show mercy, and to refresh, to deliver and to bless ; " Naomi heard how that the Lord had visited his people in giving them bread." Ruth i. 6. " The Lord visited Sarah," etc. Gen xxi. 1, 2. That greatest mercy and deliverance that ever the children of men had, is thus expressed, " The Lord hath visited and redeemed his people." Luke i. 68. Mercies are visitations ; when God comes in kindness and love to do us good, he visiteth us. And these mercies are called visitations in two respects: 1. Because *God comes near to us* when he doth us good ; mercy is a drawing near to a soul, a drawing near to a place. As when God sends a judgment, or afflicts, he is said to depart and go away from that place ; so when he doth us good, he comes near, and as it were applies himself in favour to our persons and habitations. 2. They are called a visitation because of *the freeness of them.* A visit is one of the freest things in the world ; there is no obligation but that of love to make a visit ; because such a man is my friend and I love him, therefore I visit him. Hence, that greatest act of free grace in redeeming the world is called a visitation, because it was as freely done as ever any friend made a visit to see his friend, and with infinite more freedom. There was no obligation on man's side at all, many unkindnesses and neglects there were ; God in love came to redeem man. Thirdly, to visit imports an act of care and inspection, of tutorage and direction. The pastor's office over the flock is expressed by this act (Zech. x. 3 ; Acts xv. 36) ; and the care we ought to have of the fatherless and widows is expressed by visiting them. " Pure religion," saith the apostle James, " is this, To visit the fatherless and widows in their affliction " (chap. i. 27) ; and in Matt. xxv. 34, Christ pronounceth the blessing on them who, when he was in prison, visited him, which was not a bare seeing, or asking ' how do you,' but it was care of Christ in his imprisonment, and helpfulness and provision for him in his afflicted members. That sense also agrees well with this place, Job vii. 17, 18, " *What is man, that thou shouldst visit him ?* "—*Joseph Caryl.*

Verse 4.—" *What is man, that thou art mindful of him ? or the son of man, that thou visitest him ?* "

Lord, what is man that thou
So mindful art of him ? Or what's the son
Of man, that thou the highest heaven didst bow,
And to his aide didst runne ?

Man's but a piece of clay
That's animated by thy heavenly breath,
And when that breath thou tak'st away,
He's clay again by death.
He is not worthy of the least
Of all thy mercies at the best.

Baser than clay is he,
For sin hath made him like the beasts that perish,
Though next the angels he was in degree ;
Yet this beast thou dost cherish.
He is not worthy of the least,
Of all thy mercies, he's a beast.

Worse than a beast is man,
Who after thine own image made at first,
Became the divel's sonne by sin. And can
A thing be more accurst ?
Yet thou thy greatest mercy hast
On this accursed creature cast.

Thou didst thyself abase,
And put off all thy robes of majesty,
Taking his nature to give him thy grace,
To save his life didst dye.
He is not worthy of the least
Of all thy mercies ; one's a feast.

Lo ! man is made now even
With the blest angels, yea, superior farre.
Since Christ sat down at God's right hand in heaven,
And God and man are one.
Thus all thy mercies man inherits
Though not the least of them he merits.

Thomas Washbourne. D.D., 1654.

Verse 4.—" *What is man ?* "—

How poor, how rich, how abject, how august,
How complicate, how wonderful is man !
How passing wonder HE who made him such !
Who centred in our make such strange extremes !
From different natures marvellously mix'd,
Connexion exquisite of distant worlds !
Distinguish'd link in being's endless chain !

Midway from nothing to the Deity !
A beam ethereal, sullied and absorb'd,
Though sullied and dishonour'd, still divine !
Dim miniature of greatness absolute !
An heir of glory ! a frail child of dust !
Helpless, immortal ! insect *infinite !*
A worm ! a god ! I tremble at myself,
And in myself am lost.

Edward Young, 1681—1775.

Verses 4—8.—" What is man," etc.

——Man is ev'ry thing,
And more : he is a tree, yet bears no fruit ;
A beast, yet is, or should be more :
Reason and speech we onely bring.
Parrats may thank us, if they are not mute,
They go upon the score.

Man is all symmetrie,
Full of proportions, one limbe to another,
And all to all the world besides :
Each part may call the farthest, brother.
For head with foot hath private amitie,
And both with moons and tides.

Nothing hath got so farre,
But man hath caught and kept it, as his prey.
His eyes dismount the highest starre :
He is in little all the sphere.
Herbs gladly cure our flesh, because that they
Finde their acquaintance there.

For us the windes do blow ;
The earth doth rest, heav'n move, and fountains flow.
Nothing we see, but means our good,
As our *delight*, or as our *treasure* :
The whole is, either our cupboard of *food*,
Or cabinet of *pleasure*.

The starres have us to bed ;
Night draws the curtain, which the sun withdraws :
Musick and light attend our head.
All things unto our *flesh* are kinde
In their *descent* and *being ;* to our *minde*
In their *ascent* and *cause*.

Each thing is full of dutie :
Waters united are our navigation ;
Distinguished, our habitation ;
Below, our drink ; above, our meat :
Both are our cleanlinesse. Hath one such beautie ?
Then how are all things neat !

More servants wait on man,
Than he'l notice of : in ev'ry path
He treads down that which doth befriend him,
When sicknesse makes him pale and wan,
Oh, mightie love ! Man is one world, and hath
Another to attend him.

George Herbert, 1593.

Verse 5.—" Thou hast made him a little lower than the angels." Perhaps it was not so much in nature as in position that man, as first formed, was inferior to the angels. At all events, we can be sure that nothing higher could be affirmed of the angels, than that they were made in the image of God. If, then, they had originally superiority over man, it must have been in the degree of resemblance. The angel was made immortal, intellectual, holy, powerful, glorious, and in these properties lay their likeness to the Creator. But were not these properties given also to man ? Was not man made immortal, intellectual, holy, powerful, glorious ? And if the angel excelled the man, it was not, we may believe, in the possession of properties which had no counterpart in the man ; both bore God's image, and both therefore had lineaments of the attributes which centre in Deity. Whether or not these lineaments were more strongly marked in the angel than in the man, it were presumptuous to attempt to decide ; but it is sufficient for our present purposes that the same properties must have been common to both, since both were modelled after the same divine image ; and whatever originally the relative positions of the angel and the man, we cannot question that since the fall man has been fearfully inferior to the angels.   The effect of transgression has been to debase all his powers, and so bring him down from his high rank in the scale of creation ; but, however degraded and sunken, he still retains the capacities of his original formation, and since these capacities could have differed in nothing but degree from the capacities of the angel, it must be clear that they may be so purged and enlarged as to produce, if we may not say to restore, the equality . . . . . Oh ! it may be, we again say, that an erroneous estimate is formed, when we separate by an immense space the angel and the man, and bring down the human race to a low station in the scale of creation.   If I search through the records of science, I may indeed find that, for the furtherance of magnificent purposes, God hath made man " a little lower than the angels ; " and I cannot close my eyes to the melancholy fact, that as a consequence upon apostasy there has been a weakening and a rifling of those splendid endowments which Adam might have transmitted unimpaired to his children.   And yet the Bible teems with notices, that so far from being by nature higher than men, angels even now possess not an importance which belongs to our race.   It is a mysterious thing, and one to which we scarcely dare allude, that there has arisen a Redeemer of fallen men, but not of fallen angels.   We would build no theory on so awful and inscrutable a truth ; but is it too much to say, that the interference on the behalf of man and the non-interference on the behalf of angels, gives ground for the persuasion, that men occupy at least not a lower place than angels in the love and the solicitude of their Maker ?   Besides, are not angels represented as " ministering spirits, sent forth to minister to the heirs of salvation ? "   And what is the idea coveyed by such a representation, if it be not that believers, being attended and waited on by angels, are as children of God marching forwards to a splendid throne, and so elevated amongst creatures, that those who have the wind in their wings, and are brilliant as a flame of fire, delight to do them honour ?   And, moreover, does not the repentance of a single sinner minister gladness to a whole throng of angels ?   And who shall say that this sending of a new wave of rapture throughout the hierarchy of heaven does not betoken such immense sympathy with men as goes far towards proving him the occupant of an immense space in the scale of existence ?   We may add also, that angels learn of men ; inasmuch as Paul declares to the Ephesians, that " now unto the principalities and powers in heavenly places is made known by the church, the manifold wisdom of God."   And when we further remember, that in one of those august visions with which the Evangelist John was favoured, he beheld the representatives of the church placed immediately before the eternal throne, whilst angels, standing at a greater distance, thronged the outer circle, we seem to have accumulated proof that men are not to be considered as naturally inferior to angels—that however they may have cast themselves down from eminence, and sullied the lustre and sapped the strength of their first estate, they are still capable of the very loftiest elevation, and require nothing but the being restored to their forfeited position, and the obtaining room for the development of their powers, in order to their shining forth as the illustrious ones of the creation, the breathing, burning images of the Godhead . . . . . The Redeemer is represented as submitting to be humbled—" made a little lower than the angels," for the sake or with a view to the glory that was to be the recompense of his sufferings.   This is a very important representation—one that thould be most attentively considered ; and from it may be drawn, we think, a strong and clear argument for the divinity of Christ.

We could never see how it could be humility in any creature, whatever the dignity of his condition, to assume the office of a Mediator and to work out our reconciliation. We do not forget to how extreme degradation a Mediator must consent to be reduced, and through what suffering and ignominy he could alone achieve our redemption ; but neither do we forget the unmeasured exaltation which was to be the Mediator's reward, and which, if Scripture be true, was to make him far higher than the highest of principalities and powers ; and we know not where would have been the amazing humility, where the unparalleled condescension, had any mere creature consented to take the office on the prospect of such a recompense.   A being who knew that he should be immeasurably elevated if he did a certain thing, can hardly be commended for the greatness of his humility in doing that thing. The nobleman who should become a slave, knowing that in consequence he should be made a king, does not seem to us to afford any pattern of condescension. He must be the king already, incapable of obtaining any accession to his greatness, ere his entering the state of slavery can furnish an example of humility. And, in like manner, we can never perceive that any being but a divine Being can justly be said to have given a model of condescension in becoming our Redeemer . . . . . If he could not lay aside the perfections, he could lay aside the glories of Deity; without ceasing to be God he could appear to be man; and herein we believe was the humiliation—herein that self-emptying which Scripture identifies with our Lord's having been "made a little lower than the angels." In place of manifesting himself in the form of God, and thereby centering on himself the delighted and reverential regards of all unfallen orders of intelligences, he must conceal himself in the form of a servant, and no longer gathering that rich tribute of homage, which had flowed from every quarter of his unlimited empire, produced by his power, sustained by his providence, he had the same essential glory, the same real dignity, which he had ever had. These belonged necessarily to his nature, and could no more be parted with, even for a time, than could that nature itself. But every outward mark of majesty and of greatness might be laid aside; and Deity, in place of coming down with such dazzling manifestations of supremacy as would have compelled the world he visited to fall prostrate and adore, might so veil his splendours, and so hide himself in an ignoble form, that when men saw him there should be no "beauty that they should desire him." And this was what Christ did, in consenting to be "made a little lower than the angels;" and in doing this he emptied himself, or "made himself of no reputation." The very being who in the form of God had given its light and magnificence to heaven, appeared upon earth in the form of a servant; and not merely so—for every creature is God's servant, and therefore the form of a servant would have been assumed, had he appeared as an angel or an archangel—but in the form of the lowest of these servants, being "made in the likeness of men"—of men the degraded, the apostate, the perishing.—*Henry Melvill, B.D.,* 1854.

Verses 5, 6.—God magnifies man in the work of creation. The third verse shows us what it was that raised the Psalmist to this admiration of the goodness of God to man: " *When I consider thy heavens, the work of thy fingers, the moon and the stars, which thou hast ordained; Lord, what is man?*" God in the work of creation made all these things serviceable and instrumental for the good of man. What is man, that he should have a sun, moon, and stars, planted in the firmament for him? What creature is this? When great preparations are made in any place, much provisions laid in, and the house adorned with richest furnitures, we say, " *What is this man that comes to such a house?*" When such a goodly fabric was raised up, the goodly house of the world adorned and furnished, we have reason admiringly to say, What is this man that must be the tenant or inhabitant of his house? There is yet a higher exaltation of man in the creation; man was magnified with the stamp of God's image, one part whereof the Psalmist describes in the sixth verse, " *Thou madest him to have dominion over the works of thy hands; thou hast put all things under his feet,*" etc. Thus man was magnified in creation. What was man that he should have the rule of the world given him? That he should be lord over the fish of the sea, and over the beasts of the field, and over the fowls of the air? Again, man was magnified in creation, in that God set him in the next degree to the angels; " *Thou hast made him a little lower than the angels;*" there is the first part of the answer to this question, man was magnified in being made so excellent a creature, and in having so many excellent creatures made for him. All which may be understood of man as created in God's image; but since the transgression it is peculiar to Christ, as the apostle applies it (Heb. ii. 6), and if those who have their blood and dignity restored by the work of redemption, which is the next part of man's exaltation.—*Joseph Caryl.*

Verses 5—8.—Augustine having allegorised much about the wine-presses in the title of this Psalm, upon these words, " What is man, or the son of man," the one being called אֱנוֹשׁ, from *misery*, the other בְּן־אָדָם, the *Son of Adam*, or *man*, saith, that by the first is meant man in the state of sin and corruption, by the other, man regenerated by grace, yet called the son of man because made more excellent by the change of his mind and life, from old corruption to newness, and from an old to a new man; whereas he that is still carnal is miserable; and then ascending from the body to the head, Christ, he extols his glory as being set over all things, even the angels and heavens, and the whole world as is elsewhere showed that he is. Eph. i. 21. And then leaving the highest things he descended to " *sheep and oxen ;* " whereby we may understand *sanctified men* and *preachers,* for to *sheep* are the *faithful* often compared, and *preachers* to *oxen.* 1 Cor. ix. " Thou shalt not muzzle the mouth of the ox that treadeth out the corn." " *The beasts of the field* " set forth the *voluptuous* that live at large, going in the broad way : *the fowls of the air,* the *lifted up by pride :* " *the fishes of the sea,*" such as through a covetous desire of riches pierce into the lower parts of the earth, as the fishes dive to the bottom of the sea. And because men pass the seas again and again for riches, he addeth, " *that passeth through the way of the sea,*" and to that of diving to the bottom of the waters may be applied (1 Tim. vi. 9), " They that will be rich, fall into many noisome lusts, that drown the soul in perdition." And hereby seem to be set forth the three things of the world of which it is said, " they that love them, the love of the Father is not in them." " The lust of the heart " being sensuality ; " the lust of the eyes," covetousness ; to which is added, " the pride of life." Above all these Christ was set, because without all sin ; neither could any of the devil's three temptations, which may be referred hereunto, prevail with him. And all these, as well as " sheep and oxen," are in the church, for which it is said, that into the ark came all manner of beasts, both clean and unclean, and fowls ; and all manner of fishes, good and bad, came into the net, as it is in the parable. All which I have set down, as of which good use may be made by the discreet reader.—*John Mayer.*

Verse 6.—" *Thou hast put all things under his feet.*" Hermodius, a nobleman born, upbraided the valiant captain Iphicrates for that he was but a shoemaker's son. " My blood," saith Iphicrates, " taketh beginning at me ; and thy blood, at thee now taketh her farewell ; " intimating that he, not honouring his house with the glory of his virtues, as the house had honoured him with the title of nobility, was but as a wooden knife put into an empty sheath to fill up the place ; but for himself, he, by his valorous achievements was now beginning to be the raiser of his family. Thus, in the matter of spirituality, he is the best gentleman that is the best Christian. The men of Berea, who received the word with all readiness, were more noble than those of Thessalonica. The burgesses of God's city be not of base lineage, but truly noble ; they boast not of their generations, but their regeneration, which is far better ; for, by their second birth they are the sons of God, and the church is their mother, and Christ their elder brother, the Holy Ghost their tutor, angels their attendants, and all other creatures their subjects, the whole world their inn, and heaven their home.—*John Spencer's " Things New and Old."*

Verse 6.—" *Thou madest him to have dominion over the works of thy hands,*" etc. For thy help against wandering thoughts in prayer . . . . . labour to keep thy distance to the world, and that sovereignty which God hath given thee over it in its profits and pleasures, or whatever else may prove a snare to thee. While the father and master know their place, and keep their distance, so long children and servants will keep theirs by being dutiful and officious ; but when they forget this, the father grows fond of the one, and the master too familiar with the other, then they begin to lose their authority, and the others to grow saucy and under no command ; bid them go, and it may be they will not stir ; set them a task, and they will bid you do it yourself. Truly, thus it fares with the Christian ; all the creatures are his servants, and so long as he keeps his heart at a holy distance from them, and maintains his lordship over them, not laying them in his bosom, which God hath put " *under his feet,*" all is well ; he marches to the duties of God's worship in a goodly order. He can be private with God, and these not be bold to crowd in to disturb him.— *William Gurnall.*

Verses 7, 8.—He who rules over the material world, is Lord also of the intellectual or spiritual creation represented thereby. The souls of the faithful, lowly and harmless are the sheep of his pasture ; those who, like oxen, are strong to labour in the church, and who, by expounding the Word of Life, tread out the corn for the nourishment of the people, own him for their kind and beneficent Master ; nay, tempers fierce and untractable as the beasts of the desert, are yet subject to his will ; spirits of the angelic kind, that, like the birds of the air, traverse freely the superior region, move at his command ; and those evil ones whose habitation is in the deep abyss, even to the great leviathan himself, all are put under the feet of King Messiah.—*George Horne, D.D.*

Verse 8.—Every dish of fish and fowl that comes to our table, is an instance of this dominion man has over the works of God's hands, and it is a reason of our subjection to God our chief Lord, and to his dominion over us.

HINTS TO PREACHERS.

Verse 1.—"*O Lord, our Lord.*"—Personal appropriation of the Lord as ours. The privilege of holding such a portion.

"*How excellent,*" etc. The excellence of the name and nature of God in all places, and under all circumstances.

Sermon or lecture upon the glory of God in creation and providence.

"*In all the earth.*" The universal revelation of God in nature and its excellency.

"*Thy glory above the heavens.*" The incomprehensible and infinite glory of God.

"*Above the heavens.*" The glory of God outsoaring the intellect of angels, and the splendour of heaven.

Verse 2.—Infant piety, its possibility, potency, "strength," and influence, "that thou mightest still," etc.

The strength of the gospel not the result of eloquence or wisdom in the speaker.

Great results from small causes when the Lord ordains to work.

Great things which can be said and claimed by babes in grace.

The stilling of the powers of evil by the testimony of feeble believers.

The stilling of the Great Enemy by the conquests of grace.

Verse 4.—Man's insignificance. God's mindfulness of man. Divine visits. The question, "What is man?" Each of these themes may suffice for a discourse, or they may be handled in one sermon.

Verse 5.— Man's relation to the angels.

The position which Jesus assumed for our sakes.

Manhood's crown—the glory of our nature in the person of the Lord Jesus.

Verses 5, 6, 7, 8.—The universal providential dominion of our Lord Jesus.

Verse 6.—Man's rights and responsibilities towards the lower animals.

Verse 6.—Man's dominion over the lower animals, and how he should exercise it.

Verse 6 (second clause).—The proper place for all worldly things, "*under his feet.*"

Verse 9.—The wanderer in many climes enjoying the sweetness of his Lord's name in every condition.

PSALM IX.

TITLE.—"To the Chief Musician upon Muth-labben, a Psalm of David." *The meaning of this title is very doubtful. It may refer to the tune to which the Psalm was to be sung, so Wilcocks and others think ; or it may refer to a musical instrument now unknown, but common in those days ; or it may have a reference to Ben, who is mentioned in 1 Chron. xv. 18, as one of the Levitical singers. If either of these conjectures should be correct, the title of Muth-labben has no teaching for us, except it is meant to show us how careful David was that in the worship of God all things should be done according to due order. From a considerable company of learned witnesses we gather that the title will bear a meaning far more instructive, without being fancifully forced : it signifies a Psalm concerning the death of the Son. The Chaldee has, " concerning the death of the Champion who went out between the camps," referring to Goliath of Gath, or some other Philistine, on account of whose death many suppose this Psalm to have been written in after years by David. Believing that out of a thousand guesses this is at least as consistent with the sense of the Psalm as any other, we prefer it ; and the more especially so because it enables us to refer it mystically to the victory of the Son of God over the champion of evil, even the enemy of souls (verse 6). We have here before us most evidently a triumphal hymn ; may it strengthen the faith of the militant believer, and stimulate the courage of the timid saint, as he sees here* THE CONQUEROR, *on whose vesture and thigh is the name written, King of kings and Lord of lords.*

ORDER.—*Bonar remarks, " The position of the Psalms in their relations to each other is often remarkable. It is questioned whether the present arrangement of them was the order in which they were given forth to Israel, or whether some later compiler, perhaps Ezra, was inspired to attend to this matter, as well as to other points connected with the canon. Without attempting to decide this point, it is enough to remark that we have proof that the order of the Psalms is as ancient as the completing of the canon, and if so, it seems obvious that the Holy Spirit wished this book to come down to us in its present order. We make these remarks, in order to invite attention to the fact, that as the eight caught up the last line of the seventh, this ninth Psalm opens with an apparent reference to the eighth :—*

> "I will praise thee, O Lord, with my whole heart ;
> I will shew forth all thy marvellous works.
> I will be glad and rejoice in thee. (Comp. Song i. 4 ; Rev. xix. 7.)
> I will sing to THY NAME, O thou Most High." Verses 1, 2.

As if " The Name," so highly praised in the former Psalm, were still ringing in the ear of the sweet singer of Israel. And in verse 10, he returns to it, celebrating their confidence who " know " that " name " as if its fragrance still breathed in the atmosphere around."

DIVISION.—*The strain so continually changes, that it is difficult to give an outline of it methodically arranged : we give the best we can make. From verses 1 to 6 is a song of jubilant thanksgiving ; from 7 to 12, there is a continual declaration of faith as to the future. Prayer closes the first great division of the Psalm in verses 13 and 14. The second portion of this triumphal ode, although much shorter, is parallel in all its parts to the first portion, and is a sort of rehearsal of it. Observe the song for past judgments, verses 15, 16 ; the declaration of trust in future justice, 17, 18 ; and the closing prayer, 19, 20. Let us celebrate the conquests of the Redeemer as we read this Psalm, and it cannot but be a delightful task if the Holy Ghost be with us.*

EXPOSITION.

I WILL praise *thee*, O LORD, with my whole heart ; I will shew forth all thy marvellous works.

2 I will be glad and rejoice in thee : I will sing praise to thy name, O thou most High.

3 When mine enemies are turned back, they shall fall and perish at thy presence.

4 For thou hast maintained my right and my cause; thou satest in the throne judging right.

5 Thou hast rebuked the heathen, thou hast destroyed the wicked, thou hast put out their name for ever and ever.

6 O thou enemy, destructions are come to a perpetual end: and thou hast destroyed cities; their memorial is perished with them.

1. With a holy resolution the songster begins his hymn; *I will praise thee, O Lord.* It sometimes needs all our determination to face the foe and bless the Lord in the teeth of his enemies; vowing that whoever else may be silent *we* will bless his name; here, however, the overthrow of the foe is viewed as complete, and the song flows with sacred fulness of delight. It is our duty to praise the Lord; let us perform it as a privilege. Observe that David's praise is all given to the Lord. Praise is to be offered to God alone; we may be grateful to the intermediate agent, but our thanks must have long wings and mount aloft to heaven. *With my whole heart.* Half heart is no heart. *I will show forth.* There is true praise in the thankful telling forth to others of our heavenly Father's dealings with us; this is one of the themes upon which the godly should speak often to one another, and it will not be casting pearls before swine if we make even the ungodly hear of the loving-kindness of the Lord to us. *All thy marvellous works.* Gratitude for one mercy refreshes the memory as to thousands of others. One silver link in the chain draws up a long series of tender remembrances. Here is eternal work for us, for there can be no end to the showing forth of *all* his deeds of love. If we consider our own sinfulness and nothingness, we must feel that every work of preservation, forgiveness, conversion, deliverance, sanctification, &c., which the Lord has wrought for us, or in us is a *marvellous* work. Even in heaven, divine loving-kindness will doubtless be as much a theme of surprise as of rapture.

2. Gladness and joy are the appropriate spirit in which to praise the goodness of the Lord. Birds extol the Creator in notes of overflowing joy, the cattle low forth his praise with tumult of happiness, and the fish leap up in his worship with excess of delight. Moloch may be worshipped with shrieks of pain, and Juggernaut may be honoured by dying groans and inhuman yells, but he whose name is Love is best pleased with the holy mirth, and sanctified gladness of his people. Daily rejoicing is an ornament to the Christian character, and a suitable robe for God's choristers to wear. God loveth a *cheerful* giver, whether it be the gold of his purse or the gold of his mouth which he presents upon his altar. *I will sing praise to thy name, O thou most High.* Songs are the fitting expressions of inward thankfulness, and it were well if we indulged ourselves and honoured our Lord with more of them. Mr. B. P. Power has well said, " The sailors give a cheery cry as they weigh anchor, the ploughman whistles in the morning as he drives his team; the milkmaid sings her rustic song as she sets about her early task; when soldiers are leaving friends behind them, they do not march out to the tune of the Dead March in 'Saul,' but to the quick notes of some lively air. A praising spirit would do for us all that their songs and music do for them; and if only we could determine to praise the Lord, we should surmount many a difficulty which our low spirits never would have been equal to, and we should do double the work which can be done if the heart be languid in its beating, if we be crushed and trodden down in soul. As the evil spirit in Saul yielded in the olden time to the influence of the harp of the son of Jesse, so would the spirit of melancholy often take flight from us, if only we would take up the song of praise."

3. God's presence is evermore sufficient to work the defeat of our most furious foes, and their ruin is so complete when the Lord takes them in hand, that even flight cannot save them, they fall to rise no more when he pursues them. We must be careful, like David, to give all the glory to him whose presence gives the victory. If we have here the exultings of our conquering Captain, let us make the triumphs of the Redeemer the triumphs of the redeemed, and rejoice with him at the total discomfiture of all his foes.

4. One of our nobility has for his motto, " I will maintain it;" but the Christian has a better and more humble one, " Thou hast maintained it." " God and my right," are united by my faith: while God lives my right shall never be taken from me. If we seek to maintain the cause and honour of our Lord we may suffer reproach and misrepresentation, but it is a rich comfort to remember that he who

sits in the throne knows our hearts, and will not leave us to the ignorant and ungenerous judgment of erring man.

5. God rebukes before he destroys, but when he once comes to blows with the wicked he ceases not until he has dashed them in pieces so small that their very name is forgotten, and like a noisome snuff their remembrance is put out for ever and ever. How often the word " thou " occurs in this and the former verse, to show us that the grateful strain mounts up directly to the Lord as doth the smoke from the altar when the air is still. My soul send up all the music of all thy powers to him who has been and is thy sure deliverance.

6. Here the Psalmist exults over the fallen foe. He bends as it were, over his prostrate form, and insults his once vaunted strength. He plucks the boaster's song out of his mouth, and sings it for him in derision. After this fashion doth our Glorious Redeemer ask of death, " Where is thy sting ? " and of the grave, " Where is thy victory ? " The spoiler is spoiled, and he who made captive is led into captivity himself. Let the daughters of Jerusalem go forth to meet their King, and praise him with timbrel and harp.

7 But the LORD shall endure for ever : he hath prepared his throne for judgment.

8 And he shall judge the world in righteousness, he shall minister judgment to the people in uprightness.

9 The LORD also will be a refuge for the oppressed, a refuge in times of trouble.

10 And they that know thy name will put their trust in thee : for thou LORD, hast not forsaken them that seek thee.

11 Sing praises to the LORD, which dwelleth in Zion : declare among the people his doings.

12 When he maketh inquisition for blood, he remembereth them : he forgetteth not the cry of the humble.

In the light of the past the future is not doubtful. Since the same Almighty God fills the throne of power, we can with unhesitating confidence, exult in our security for all time to come.

7. The enduring existence and unchanging dominion of our Jehovah, are the firm foundations of our joy. The enemy and his destructions shall come to a perpetual end, but God and his throne *endure for ever*. The eternity of divine sovereignty yields unfailing consolation. By the throne being *prepared for judgment*, are we not to understand the swiftness of divine justice. In heaven's court suitors are not worn out with long delays. Term-time lasts all the year round in the court of King's Bench above. Thousands may come at once to the throne of the Judge of all the earth, but neither plaintiff nor defendant shall have to complain that he is not prepared to give their cause a fair hearing.

8. Whatever earthly courts may do, heaven's throne ministers judgment in uprightness. Partiality and respect of persons are things unknown in the dealings of the Holy One of Israel. How the prospect of appearing before the impartial tribunal of the Great King should act as a check to us when tempted to sin, and as a comfort when we are slandered or oppressed.

9. He who gives no quarter to the wicked in the day of judgment, is the defence and refuge of his saints in the day of trouble. There are many forms of oppression ; both from man and from Satan oppression come to us ; and for all its forms, a refuge is provided in the Lord Jehovah. There were cities of refuge under the law, God is our refuge-city under the gospel. As the ships when vexed with tempest make for harbour, so do the oppressed hasten to the wings of a just and gracious God. He is a high tower so impregnable, that the hosts of hell cannot carry it by storm, and from its lofty heights faith looks down with scorn upon her enemies.

10. Ignorance is worst when it amounts to ignorance of God, and knowledge is best when it exercises itself upon *the name* of God. This most excellent knowledge leads to the most excellent grace of faith. O, to learn more of the attributes and character of God. Unbelief, that hooting nightbird, cannot live in the light of divine knowledge, it flies before the sun of God's great and gracious name. If we read this verse literally, there is, no doubt, a glorious fulness of assurance in the

names of God. We have recounted them in the "Hints for Preachers," and would direct the reader's attention to them. By knowing his name is also meant an experimental acquaintance with the attributes of God, which are everyone of them anchors to hold the soul from drifting in seasons of peril. The Lord may hide his face for a season from his people, but he never has utterly, finally, really, or angrily, *forsaken them that seek him.* Let the poor seekers draw comfort from this fact, and let the finders rejoice yet more exceedingly, for what must be the Lord's faithfulness to those who find if he is so gracious to those who seek.

> " O hope of every contrite heart,
>   O joy of all the meek,
> To those who fall how kind thou art,
>   How good to those who seek.

> " But what to those who find, ah, this
>   Nor tongue nor pen can show
> The love of Jesus what it is,
>   None but his loved ones know."

11. Being full of gratitude himself, our inspired author is eager to excite others to join the strain, and praise God in the same manner as he had himself vowed to do in the first and second verses. The heavenly spirit of praise is gloriously contagious, and he that hath it is never content unless he can excite all who surround him to unite in his sweet employ. Singing and preaching, as means of glorifying God, are here joined together, and it is remarkable that, connected with all revivals of gospel ministry, there has been a sudden outburst of the spirit of song. Luther's Psalms and Hymns were in all men's mouths, and in the modern revival under Wesley and Whitfield, the strains of Charles Wesley, Cennick, Berridge, Toplady, Hart, Newton, and many others, were the outgrowth of restored piety. The singing of the birds of praise fitly accompanies the return of the gracious spring of divine visitation through the proclamation of the truth. Sing on brethren, and preach on, and these shall both be a token that the Lord still dwelleth in Zion. It will be well for us when coming up to Zion, to remember that the Lord dwells among his saints, and is to be had in peculiar reverence of all those that are about him.

When an inquest is held concerning the blood of the oppressed, the martyred saints will have the first remembrance ; he will avenge his own elect. Those saints who are living shall also be heard ; they shall be exonerated from blame, and kept from destruction, even when the Lord's most terrible work is going on ; the man with the inkhorn by his side shall mark them all for safety, before the slaughtermen are permitted to smite the Lord's enemies. The humble cry of the poorest saints shall neither be drowned by the voice of thundering justice nor by the shrieks of the condemned.

13 Have mercy upon me, O LORD ; consider my trouble *which I suffer* of them that hate me, thou that liftest me up from the gates of death :

14 That I may shew forth all thy praise in the gates of the daughter of Zion : I will rejoice in thy salvation.

Memories of the past and confidences concerning the future conducted the man of God to the mercy seat to plead for the needs of the present. Between praising and praying he divided all his time. How could he have spent it more profitably ? His first prayer is one suitable for all persons and occasions, it breathes a humble spirit, indicates self knowledge, appeals to the proper attributes, and to the fitting person. *Have mercy upon me, O Lord.* Just as Luther used to call some texts little Bibles, so we may call this sentence a little prayer-book ; for it has in it the soul and marrow of prayer. It is multum in parvo, and like the angelic sword turns every way. The ladder looks to be short, but it reaches from earth to heaven.

What a noble title is here given to the Most High. *Thou that liftest me up from the gates of death!* What a glorious lift ! In sickness, in sin, in despair, in temptation, we have been brought very low, and the gloomy portal has seemed as if it would open to imprison us, but, underneath us were the everlasting arms, and, therefore, we have been uplifted even to the gates of heaven. Trapp quaintly says, " He commonly reserveth his hand for a dead lift, and rescueth those who were even talking of their graves." We must not overlook David's object in desiring mercy, it is God's glory : *" that I may show forth all thy praise."* Saints are not so selfish as to look only to self ; they desire mercy's diamond that they may let others see it flash and sparkle, and may admire Him who gives such priceless gems to his beloved. The contrast between the gates of death and the gates of the New Jerusalem is very striking ; let our songs be excited to the highest and most rapturous pitch by the double consideration of whence we are taken, and to what we have been advanced, and let our prayers for mercy be made more energetic and agonizing by a sense of the grace which such a salvation implies. When David speaks of his showing forth *all* God's praise, he means that, in his deliverance grace in all its heights and depths would be magnified. Just as our hymn puts it :—

> " O the length and breadth of love !
> Jesus, Saviour, can it be ?
> All thy mercy's height I prove,
> All the depth is seen in me."

Here ends the first part of this instructive psalm, and in pausing awhile we feel bound to confess that our exposition has only flitted over its surface, and has not digged into the depths. The verses are singularly full of teaching, and if the Holy Spirit shall bless the reader, he may go over this Psalm, as the writer has done scores of times, and see on each occasion fresh beauties.

15 The heathen are sunk down in the pit *that* they made : in the net which they hid is their own foot taken.

16 The LORD is known *by* the judgment *which* he executeth : the wicked is snared in the work of his own hands. Higgaion. Selah.

In considering this terrible picture of the Lord's overwhelming judgments of his enemies, we are called upon to ponder and meditate upon it with deep seriousness by the two untranslated words, Higgaion, Selah. Meditate, pause. Consider, and tune your instrument. Bethink yourselves and solemnly adjust your hearts to the solemnity which is so well becoming the subject. Let us in a humble spirit approach these verses, and notice, first, that the character of God requires the punishment of sin. *Jehovah is known by the judgment which he executeth ;* his holiness and abhorrence of sin are thus displayed. A ruler who winked at evil would soon be known by all his subjects to be evil himself, and he, on the other hand, who is severely just in judgment reveals his own nature thereby. So long as our God is God, he will not, he cannot spare the guilty ; except through that one glorious way in which he is just, and yet the justifier of him that believeth in Jesus. We must notice, secondly, that the manner of his judgment is singularly wise, and indisputably just. He makes the wicked become their own executioners. " The heathen are sunk down in the pit that they made, &c." Like cunning hunters they prepared a pitfall for the godly and fell into it themselves : the foot of the victim escaped their crafty snares, but the toils surrounded themselves : the cruel snare was laboriously manufactured, and it proved its efficacy by snaring its own maker. Persecutors and oppressors are often ruined by their own malicious projects. " Drunkards kill themselves ; prodigals beggar themselves ; " the contentious are involved in ruinous costs ; the vicious are devoured with fierce diseases ; the envious eat their own hearts ; and blasphemers curse their own souls. Thus, men may read their sin in their punishment. They sowed the seed of sin, and the ripe fruit of damnation is the natural result.

17 The wicked shall be turned into hell, *and* all the nations that forget God.

18 For the needy shall not alway be forgotten : the expectation of the poor shall *not* perish for ever.

17. The justice which has punished the wicked, and preserved the righteous, remains the same, and therefore in days to come, retribution will surely be meted out. How solemn is the seventeenth verse, especially in its warning to forgetters of God. The moral who are not devout, the honest who are not prayerful, the benevolent who are not believing, the amiable who are not converted, these must all have their portion with the openly wicked in the hell which is prepared for the

devil and his angels. There are whole nations of such ; the forgetters of God are far more numerous than the profane or profligate, and according to the very forceful expression of the Hebrew, the nethermost hell will be the place into which all of them shall be hurled headlong. Forgetfulness seems a small sin, but it brings eternal wrath upon the man who lives and dies in it.

18. Mercy is as ready to her work as ever justice can be. Needy souls fear that they are forgotten ; well, if it be so, let them rejoice that they *shall not alway* be so. Satan tells poor tremblers that their hope shall perish, but they have here divine assurance that *their expectation shall not perish for ever*. " The Lord's people are a humbled people, afflicted, emptied, sensible of need, driven to a daily attendance on God, daily begging of him, and living upon the hope of what is promised ; " such persons may have to wait, but they shall find that they do not wait in vain.

19 Arise, O LORD ; let not man prevail : let the heathen be judged in thy sight.

20 Put them in fear, O LORD, *that* the nations may know themselves *to be but* men. Selah.

19. Prayers are the believer's weapons of war. When the battle is too hard for us, we call in our great ally, who, as it were, lies in ambush until faith gives the signal by crying out, " Arise, O Lord." Although our cause be all but lost, it shall be soon won again if the Almighty doth but bestir himself. He will not suffer man to prevail over God, but with swift judgments will confound their gloryings. In the very sight of God the wicked will be punished, and he who is now all tenderness will have no bowels of compassion for them, since they had no tears of repentance while their day of grace endured.

20. One would think that men would not grow so vain as to deny themselves to be but men, but it appears to be a lesson which only a divine schoolmaster can teach to some proud spirits. Crowns leave their wearers *but men*, degrees of eminent learning make their owners not more than *men*, valour and conquest cannot elevate beyond the dead level of " *but men ;* " and all the wealth of Crœsus, the wisdom of Solon, the power of Alexander, the eloquence of Demosthenes, if added together, would leave the possessor but a man. May we ever remember this, lest like those in the text, we should be *put in fear*.

Before leaving this Psalm, it will be very profitable if the student will peruse it again as the triumphal hymn of the Redeemer, as he devoutly brings the glory of his victories and lays it down at his Father's feet. Let us joy in his joy, and our joy shall be full.

EXPLANATORY NOTES AND QUAINT SAYINGS.

Whole Psalm.—We are to consider this song of praise, as I conceive, to be the language of our great Advocate and Mediator, " in the midst of the church giving thanks unto God," and teaching us to anticipate by faith his great and final victory over all the adversaries of our peace temporal and spiritual, with especial reference to his assertion of his royal dignity on Zion, his holy mountain. The victory over the enemy, we find by the fourth verse, is again ascribed to the decision of divine justice, and the award of a righteous judge, who has at length resumed his tribunal. This renders it certain, that the claim preferred to the throne of the Almighty, could proceed from the lips of none but our MELCHIZEDEC.—*John Fry, B.A.*, 1842.

Verse 1.—" *I will praise thee, O Lord, with my whole heart.*" As a vessel by the scent thereof tells what liquor is in it, so should our mouths smell continually of that mercy wherewith our hearts have been refreshed : for we are called vessels of mercy.—*William Cowper*, 1612.

Verse 1.—" *I will praise the Lord with my whole heart, I will shew forth all thy marvellous works.*" The words, " *With my whole heart,*" serve at once to show the greatness of the deliverances wrought for the psalmist, and to distinguish him from the hypocrites—the coarser, who praise the Lord for his goodness merely with the lips ; and the more refined, who praise him with just half their heart, while they secretly ascribe the deliverance more to themselves than to him. "*All thy wonders,*" the marvellous token of thy grace. The Psalmist shows by this term, that he recognised them in all their greatness. Where this is done, there the Lord is also praised with the whole heart. *Half-heartedness,* and the depreciation of divine grace, go hand in hand. The ? is the ? *instrum.* The heart is the instrument of praise, the mouth only its organ.—*E. W. Hengstenberg.*

Verse 1 (second clause).—When we have received any special good thing from the Lord, it is well, according as we have opportunities, to tell others of it. When the woman who had lost one of her ten pieces of silver, found the missing portion of her money, she gathered her neighbours and her friends together, saying, " Rejoice with me, for I have found the piece which I had lost." We may do the same ; we may tell friends and relations that we have received such-and-such a blessing, and that we trace it directly to the hand of God. Why have we not already done this ? Is there a lurking unbelief as to whether it really came from God ; or are we ashamed to own it before those who are perhaps accustomed to laugh at such things ? Who knows so much of the marvellous works of God as his own people ; if they be silent, how can we expect the world to see what he has done ? Let us not be ashamed to glorify God, by telling what we know and feel he has done ; let us watch our opportunity to bring out distinctly the fact of his acting ; let us feel delighted at having an opportunity, from our own experience, of telling what must turn to his praise ; and them that honour God, God will honour in turn ; if we be willing to talk of his deeds, he will give us enough to talk about.—*P.B. Power, in ' I Wills' of the Psalms.*

Verses 1, 2.—" *I will confess unto thee, O Lord, with my whole heart,*" etc. Behold, with what a flood of the most sweet affections he says that he "*will confess,*" "*show forth,*" "*rejoice,*" "*be glad,*" and "*sing,*" being filled with ecstasy ! He does not simply say, "*I will confess,*" but, "*with my heart,*" and "*with my whole heart.*" Nor does he propose to speak simply of "*works,*" but of the "*marvellous works*" of God, and of "*all*" those "*works.*" Thus his spirit (like John in the womb) exults and rejoices in God his Saviour, who has done great things for him, and those marvellous things which follow. In which words are opened the subject of this Psalm : that is, that he therein sings the marvellous works of God. And these works are wonderful, because he converts, by those who are nothing, those who have all things, and, by the ALMUTH who live in hidden faith, and are dead to the world, he humbles those who flourish in glory, and are looked upon in the world. Thus accomplishing such mighty things without force, without arms, without labour, by the cross only and blood. But how will his saying, that he will show forth "*all*" his marvellous works, agree with that of Job. ix. 10, " which doeth great things past finding out ; yea, and wonders without number " ? For who can show forth all the marvellous works of God ? We may say, therefore, that these things are spoken in that excess of feeling in which he said (Psalm vi. 6), " I will water my couch with my tears." That is, he hath such an ardent desire to speak of the wonderful works of God, that, as far as his wishes are concerned, he *would* set them "*all*" forth, though he *could* not do it, for love has neither bounds nor end : and as Paul saith (1 Cor. xiii. 7), " Love beareth all things, believeth all things, hopeth all things ; " hence it can do all things, and does do all things, for God looketh at the heart and spirit.—*Martin Luther.*

Verse 3.—" *When mine enemies are turned back,*" etc. *Were turned back,* repulsed, and put to flight. To render this in the present time, as our translators did, is certainly improper ; it destroys the coherence, and introduces obscurity. Ainsworth saw this, and rendered in the past, " When mine enemies turned backward." "*At thy presence.*" That is, by thine anger. For as God's presence or face denotes his favour to such as fear and serve him, so it denotes his anger towards the wicked. " The face of Jehovah is against them that do evil."—*B. Boothroyd, 1824.*

Verse 3.—" *They shall fall and perish.*" It refers to those that either faint in a march, or are wounded in a battle, or especially that in flight meet with galling haps in their way, and so are galled and lamed, rendered unable to go forward, and so fall, and become liable to all the chances of pursuits, and as here, are overtaken and perish in the fall.—*Henry Hammond, D.D.*

Verse 5.—" *Thou hast rebuked the heathen,*" etc.—Augustine applieth all this mystically, as is intimated (verse 1) that it should be applied for, " I will speak," said he, " of all thy wonderful works ; " and what so wonderful as the turning of the spiritual enemy backward, whether the devil, as when he said, " Get thee behind me, Satan ; " or the old man, which is turned backward when he is put off, and the new man put on ?—*John Mayer.*

Verse 8.—" *He shall judge the world in righteousness.*" In this judgment tears will not prevail, prayers will not be heard, promises will not be admitted, repentance will be too late ; and as for riches, honourable titles, sceptres, and diadems, these will profit much less ; and the inquisition shall be so curious and diligent, that not one light thought nor one idle word (not repented of in the life past), shall be forgotten. For truth itself hath said, not in jest, but in earnest, " Of every idle word which men have spoken, they shall give an account in the day of judgment." Oh, how many which now sin with great delight, yea, even with greediness (as if we served a god of wood or of stone, which seeth nothing, or can do nothing), will be then astonished, ashamed, and silent ! Then shall the days of thy mirth be ended, and thou shalt be overwhelmed with everlasting darkness ; and instead of thy pleasures, thou shalt have everlasting torments.—*Thomas Tymme.*

Verse 8.—" *He shall judge the world in righteousness.*" Even Paul, in his great address on Mars' Hill, a thousand years after, could find no better words in which to teach the Athenians the doctrine of the judgment-day than the Septuagint rendering of this clause.—*William S. Plumer.*

Verse 8.—The guilty conscience cannot abide this day. The silly sheep, when she is taken, will not bleat, but you may carry her and do what you will with her, and she will be subject ; but the swine, if she be once taken, she will roar and cry, and thinks she is never taken but to be slain. So of all things the guilty conscience cannot abide to hear of this day, for they know that when they hear of it, they hear of their own condemnation. I think if there were a general collection made through the whole world that there might be no judgment-day, then God would be so rich that the world would go a-begging and be a waste wilderness. Then the covetous judge would bring forth his bribes ; then the crafty lawyer would fetch out his bags ; the usurer would give his gain, and a double thereof. But all the money in the world will not serve for our sin, but the judge must answer his bribes, he that hath money must answer how he came by it, and just condemnation must come upon every soul of them ; then shall the sinner be ever dying and never dead, like the salamander, that is ever in the fire and never consumed.—*Henry Smith.*

Verse 9.—It is reported of the Egyptians that, living in the fens, and being vexed with gnats, they used to sleep in high towers, whereby, those creatures not being able to soar so high, they are delivered from the biting of them : so would it be with us when bitten with cares and fear, did we but run to God for refuge, and rest confident of his help.—*John Trapp.*

Verse 10.—" *They that know thy name will put their trust in thee.*" Faith is an intelligent grace ; though there can be knowledge without faith, yet there can be no faith without knowledge. One calls it quicksighted faith. Knowledge must carry the torch before faith. 2 Tim. i. 12. " For I know whom I have believed." As in Paul's conversion a light from heaven " shined round about him " (Acts ix. 3), so before faith be wrought, God shines in with a light upon the understanding. A blind faith is as bad as a dead faith : that eye may as well be said to be a good eye which is without sight, as that faith is good without knowledge. Devout ignorance damns ; which condemns the church of Rome, that think it a piece of their religion to be kept in ignorance ; these set up an altar to an unknown God. They say ignorance is the mother of devotion ; but sure where the sun is set in the understanding, it must needs be night in the affections. So necessary is knowledge to the being of faith, that the Scriptures do sometimes baptise faith with the name of knowledge. Isa. liii. 11. " By his knowledge shall my righteous servant justify many." Knowledge is put there for faith.—*Thomas Watson.*

Verse 10.—" *They that know thy name will put their trust in thee : for thou, Lord, hast not forsaken them that seek thee.*" The mother of unbelief is ignorance of God, his faithfulness, mercy, and power. *They that know thee, will trust in thee.* This confirmed Paul, Abraham, Sarah, in the faith. " I know whom I have believed, and am persuaded that he is able to keep that which I have committed unto him

against that day." 2 Tim. i. 12. " He is faithful that promised," and " able also
to perform." Heb. x. 23, and xi. 11 ; Rom. iv. 21. The free promises of the Lord
are all certain, his commandments right and good, the recompense of reward in-
estimably to be valued above thousands of gold and silver ; trust therefore in the
Lord, O my soul, and follow hard after him. Thou hast his free promise, who never
failed, who hath promised more than possibly thou couldst ask or think, who hath
done more for thee than ever he promised, who is good and bountiful to the wicked
and ungodly ; thou doest his work, who is able and assuredly will bear thee out.
There is a crown of glory proposed unto thee above all conceit of merit ; stick fast
unto his word, and suffer nothing to divide thee from it. Rest upon his promises
though he seem to kill thee ; cleave unto his statutes though the flesh lust, the world
allure, the devil tempt by flatteries or threatenings to the contrary.—*John Ball*,
1632.

Verse 10.—" *They that know thy name will put their trust in thee.*" They can do
no otherwise who savingly know God's sweet attributes, and noble acts for his
people. We never trust a man till we know him, and bad men are better known than
trusted. Not so the Lord ; for where his name is ointment poured forth, the virgins
love him, fear him, and rejoice in him, and repose upon him.—*John Trapp.*

Verse 12.—" *When he maketh inquisition for blood he remembereth them.*" There
is a time when God will make inquisition for innocent blood. The Hebrew word
doresh, from *darash*, that is here rendered *inquisition*, signifies not barely to seek,
to search, but to seek, search, and enquire with all diligence and care imaginable.
Oh, there is a time a-coming when the Lord will make a very diligent and careful
search and enquiry after all the innocent blood of his afflicted and persecuted people,
which persecutors and tyrants have spilt as water upon the ground ; and woe to
persecutors when God shall make a more strict, critical, and careful enquiry after
the blood of his people than ever was made in the inquisition of Spain, where all
things are carried with the greatest diligence, subtlety, secrecy, and severity.
O persecutors, there is a time a-coming, when God will make a strict enquiry after
the blood of Hooper, Bradford, Latimer, Taylor, Ridley, etc. There is a time
a-coming, wherein God will enquire who silenced and suspended such-and-such
ministers, and who stopped the mouths of such-and-such, and who imprisoned,
confined, and banished such-and-such, who were once burning and shining lights,
and who were willing to spend and be spent that sinners might be saved, and that
Christ might be glorified. There is a time when the Lord will make a very narrow
enquiry into all the actions and practices of ecclesiastical courts, high commissions,
committees, assizes, etc., and deal with persecutors as they have dealt with his
people.—*Thomas Brooks.*

Verse 12.—" *When he maketh inquisition for blood, he remembereth them.*" There
is *vox sanguinis*, a voice of blood ; and " he that planted the ear, shall he not hear ? "
It covered the old world with waters. The earth is filled with cruelty ; it was
vox sanguinis that cried, and the heavens heard the earth, and the windows of heaven
opened to let fall judgment and vengeance upon it.—*Edward Marbury*, 1649.

Verse 12.—" *When he maketh inquisition for blood,*" etc. Though God may
seem to wink for a time at the cruelty of violent men, yet will call them at last to a
strict account for all the innocent blood they have shed, and for their unjust and unmerciful usuage of meek and humble persons ; whose cry he never forgets (though
he doth not presently answer it), but takes a fit time to be avenged of their
oppressors.—*Symon Patrick, D.D.*, 1626—1707.

Verse 12.—" *He maketh inquisition for blood.*" He is so stirred at this sin, that
he will up, search out the authors, contrivers, and commissioners of this scarlet
sin, he will avenge for blood.—*William Greenhill.*

Verse 12.—" *He forgetteth not the cry of the humble.*" Prayer is a haven to the
shipwrecked man, an anchor to them that are sinking in the waves, a staff to the
limbs that totter, a mine of jewels to the poor, a healer of diseases, and a guardian
of health. Prayer at once secures the continuance of our blessings, and dissipates
the clouds of our calamities. O blessed prayer ! thou art the unwearied conqueror
of human woes, the firm foundation of human happiness, the source of ever-enduring
joy, the mother of philosophy. The man who can pray truly, though languishing
in extremest indigence, is richer than all beside, whilst the wretch who never bowed
the knee, though proudly sitting as monarch of all nations, is of all men most
destitute.—*Chrysostom.*

Verse 14.—" *That I may show forth all thy praise,*" etc. To show forth *all* God's praise is to enter largely into the work. An occasional " *God, I thank thee,*" is no fit return for a perpetual stream of rich benefits.—*William S. Plumer.*

Verse 15.—" *The heathen are sunk down in the pit that they made,*" etc. Whilst they are digging pits for others, there is a pit a-digging and a grave a-making for themselves. They have a measure to make up, and a treasure to fill, which at length will be broken open, which, methinks, should take off them which are set upon mischief from pleasing themselves in their plots. Alas! they are but plotting their own ruin, and building a Babel which will fall upon their own heads. If there were any commendation in plotting, then that great plotter of plotters, that great engineer, Satan, would go beyond us all and take all the credit from us. But let us not envy Satan and his in their glory. They had need of something to comfort them. Let them please themselves with their trade. The day is coming wherein the daughter of Sion shall laugh them to scorn. There will be a time wherein it shall be said, " Arise, Sion, and thresh." Micah iv. 13. And usually the delivery of God's children is joined with the destruction of his enemies; Saul's death, and David's deliverance; the Israelites' deliverance, and the Egyptians' drowning. The church and her opposites are like the scales of a balance; when one goes up, the other goes down.—*Richard Sibbs.*

Verses 15—17. It will much increase the torment of the damned, in that their torments will be as large and strong as their understandings and affections, which will cause those violent passions to be still working. Were their loss never so great, and their sense of it never so passionate, yet if they could but lose the use of their memory, those passions would die, and that loss being forgotten, would little trouble them. But as they cannot lay by their life and being, though then they would account annihilation of singular mercy, so neither can they lay aside any part of their being. Understanding, conscience, affections, memory, must all live to torment them, which should have helped to their happiness. And as by these they should have fed upon the love of God, and drawn forth perpetually the joys of his presence, so by these must they now feed upon the wrath of God, and draw forth continually the dolours of his absence. Therefore, never think, that when I say the hardness of their hearts, and their blindness, dulness, and forgetfulness shall be removed, that therefore they are more holy and happy than before: no, but morally more vile, and hereby far more miserable. Oh, how many times did God by his messengers here call upon them, " Sinners, consider whither you are going. Do but make a stand awhile, and think where your way will end, what is the offered glory that you so carelessly reject: will not this be bitterness in the end?" And yet these men would never be brought to consider, But in the latter days, saith the Lord, they shall perfectly consider it, when they are *ensnared in the work of their own hands,* when God hath arrested them, and judgment is passed upon them, and vengeance is poured out upon them to the full, then they cannot choose but consider it, whether they will or no. Now they have no leisure to consider, nor any room in their memories for the things of another life. Ah! but then they shall have leisure enough, they shall be where they shall have nothing else to do but consider it: their memories shall have no other employment to hinder them; it shall even be engraven upon the tables of their hearts. God would have the doctrine of their eternal state to have been written on the posts of their doors, on their houses, on their hands, and on their hearts: he would have had them mind it and mention it, as they rise and lie down, and as they walk abroad, that so it might have gone well with them at their latter end. And seeing they rejected this counsel of the Lord, therefore shall it be written always before them in the place of their thraldom, that which way soever they look they may still behold it.—*Richard Baxter.*

Verse 16.—" *The Lord is known by the judgment which he executeth.*" Now if the Lord be known by the judgment which he executeth; then, the judgment which he executeth must be known; it must be an open judgment; and such are very many of the judgments of God, they are acted as upon a stage. And I may give you an account in three particulars why the Lord will sometimes do justice in the place of beholders, or in the open sight of others. First, that there may be witnesses enough of what he doth, and so a record of it be kept, at least in the minds and memories of faithful men for the generations to come. Secondly, the Lord doth it not only that he may have witnesses of his justice, but also that his justice and the proceedings of it, may have effect and a fruit upon those who did not feel it, nor fall under it. This was the reason why the Lord threatened to punish Jerusalem in the sight of the nations. Ezek. v. 6, 7, 8, 14, 15. . . . . God would execute judgment in Jerusalem, a city placed in the midst of the nations that as the nations had taken notice of the extraordinary favours, benefits, deliverances, and salvations which God wrought for Jerusalem, so they might also take notice of his judgments and sore displeasure against them. Jerusalem was not seated in some nook, corner, or by-place of the world, but in the midst of the nations, that both the goodness and severity of God towards them might be conspicuous . . . . . God lets some sinners suffer, or punisheth them openly, both because he would have all others take notice that he dislikes what they have done, as also because he would not have others do the like, lest they be made like them, both in the matter and manner of their sufferings. 'Tis a favour as well as our duty, to be taught by other men's harms, and to be instructed by their strokes to prevent our own . . . . . Thirdly, God strikes some wicked men in open view, or in the place of beholders for the comfort of his own people, and for their encouragement. Psalm lviii. 10, 11. "The righteous shall rejoice when he seeth the vengeance ; " not that he shall be glad of the vengeance, purely as it is a hurt or a suffering to the creature ; but the righteous shall be glad when he seeth the vengeance of God as it is a fulfilling of the threatening of God against the sin of man, and an evidence of his own holiness . . . . . It is said (Exod. xiv. 30, 31), that God having overwhelmed the Egyptians in the Red Sea, the Israelites saw the Egyptians dead upon the sea shore : God did not suffer the carcases of the Egyptians to sink to the bottom of the sea, but caused them to lie upon the shore, that the Israelites might see them ; and when Israel saw that dreadful stroke of the Lord upon the Egyptians, it is said, " The people feared the Lord, and believed the Lord, and his servant Moses." Thus they were confirmed in their faith by God's open judgments upon the Egyptians. They were smitten in the place of beholders, or in the open sight of others.—*Condensed from Joseph Caryl.*

Verse 16.—" *The Lord is known by the judgments which he executeth* ; " when he lays his hand upon sinners, saints tremble, consider his power, majesty, greatness, the nature of his judgments, and so judge themselves, and remove out of the way whatever may provoke . . . . As fire begets a splendour round about where it is, so do the judgments of God set out to the world his glory, justice, holiness.—*William Greenhill.*

Verse 16.—" *Snared in the work of his own hands.*" The wages that sin bargains with the sinner are life, pleasure and profit ; but the wages it pays him with are death, torment, and destruction. He that would understand the falsehood and deceit of sin, must compare its promises and its payments together.—*Robert South, D.D.*, 1633—1716.

Verse 16.—" *Higgaion, Selah,*" that is, as Ainsworth renders it, " Meditation, Selah : " showing this ought to be seriously considered of. The word " *Higgaion* " is again had (Psalm xcii. 3) ; being mentioned among other musical instruments, whereby we may gather it to be one of them ; for there is psaltery, nable, higgaion, and harp.—*John Mayer.*

Verse 16.—" *The wicked is snared in the works of his own hands.*" Not only do we read it in the word of God, but all history, all experience, records the same righteous justice of God, in snaring the wicked in the work of their own hands. Perhaps the most striking instance on record, next to Haman on his own gallows, is one connected with the horrors of the French Revolution, in which we are told that, " within nine months of the death of the queen Marie Antoinette by the guillotine, every one implicated in her untimely end, her accusers, the judges, the jury, the prosecutors, the witnesses, all, every one at least whose fate is known, perished by the same instrument as their innocent victim." " In the net which they had laid for her was their own foot taken—into the pit which they digged for her did they themselves fall."—*Barton Bouchier,* 1855.

Verse 17.—The ungodly at death must undergo God's fury and indignation. " *The wicked shall be turned into hell.*" I have read of a loadstone in Ethiopia which hath two corners, with one it draws the iron to it, with the other it puts the iron from it ; so God hath two hands, of mercy and justice ; with the one he will draw the godly to heaven, with the other he will thrust the sinner to hell ; and oh, how dreadful is that place ! It is called a fiery lake (Rev. xx. 15) ; a lake, to denote the plenty of torments in hell ; a fiery lake to show the fierceness of them : fire is the most torturing element. Strabo in his geography mentions a lake in Galilee of such a pestiferous nature that it scaldeth off the skin of whatsoever is cast into it ; but, alas ! that lake is cool compared with this fiery lake into which the damned are thrown. To demonstrate this fire terrible, there are two most pernicious qualities in it. 1. It is sulphureous, it is mixed with brimstone (Rev. xxi. 8), which is unsavoury and suffocating. 2. It is inextinguishable ; though the wicked shall be choked in the flames, yet not consumed (Rev. xx. 10) ; " And the devil was cast into the lake of fire and brimstone, where the beast and the false prophet are, and shall be tormented day and night for ever and ever." Behold the deplorable condition of all ungodly ones in the other world, they shall have a life that always dies, and a death that always lives : may not this affright men out of their sins, and make them become godly ? unless they are resolved to try how hot the hell-fire is.—*Thomas Watson.*

Verse 17.—" *The wicked shall be turned into hell,*" etc. By " *the wicked* " man we must understand unregenerate persons, whoever they are that are in a state of unregeneracy . . . . . . That person is here spoken of us a " *wicked* " man that " *forgets God,*" who does not think of him frequently, and with affection, with fear and delight, and those affections that are suitable to serious thoughts of God . . . . . . To forget God and to be a wicked person is all one. And these two things will abundantly evince the truth of this assertion : namely, that this forgetfulness of God excludes the prime and main essentials of religion, and also includes in it the highest and most heinous pieces of wickedness, and therefore must needs denominate the subject, a wicked person. . . . . . Forgetfulness of God excludes the principal and essential parts of religion. It implies that a man doth neither esteem nor value the all-sufficiency and holiness of God, as his happiness and portion, as his strength and support ; nor doth he fear him, nor live in subjection to his laws and commands, as his rule ; nor doth he aim at the glory of God as his end : therefore every one who thus forgets God must certainly be a wicked person . . . . To exclude God out of our thoughts and not to let him have a place there, not to mind, nor think upon God, is the greatest wickedness of the thoughts that can be. And, therefore, though you cannot say of such a one, he will be drunk, or he will swear, cozen, or oppress ; yet if you can say he will forget God, or that he lives all his days never minding nor thinking upon God, you say enough to speak him under wrath, and to turn him into hell without remedy.—*John Howe,* 1630—1705.

Verse 17.—" The wicked shall be turned into hell." לשאולה, *Lisholah—headlong into hell, down into hell.* The original is very emphatic.—*Adam Clarke.*

Verse 17.—All wickedness came originally with the wicked one from hell ; thither it will be again remitted, and they who hold on its side must accompany it on its return to that place of torment, there to be shut up for ever. The true state both of " nations," and the individuals of which they are composed, is to be estimated from one single circumstance ; namely, whether in their doings they remember, or " forget God." Remembrance of him is the well-spring of virtue ; forgetfulness of him, the fountain of vice.—*George Horne, D.D.*

Verse 17.—

> Hell, their fit habitation, fraught with fire
> Unquenchable, the house of woe and pain.
>
> *John Milton,* 1608—1674.

Verse 17.—

> Will without power, the element of *hell,*
> Abortive all its acts returning still
> Upon itself ; . . . . . Oh, anguish terrible !
> Meet guerdon of self-love, its proper ill !
> Malice would scowl upon the foe he fears ;
> And he with lip of scorn would seek to kill ;
> But neither sees the other, neither hears—
> For darkness each in his own dungeon bars,
> Lust pines for dearth, and grief drinks its own tears—
> Each in its solitude apart. Hate wars
> Against himself, and feeds upon his chain,
> Whose iron penetrates the soul it scars,
> A dreadful solitude each mind insane,
> Each its own place, its prison all alone,
> And finds no sympathy to soften pain.
>
> *J. A. Heraud.*

Verse 18.—" *For the needy shall not alway be forgotten,*" etc. This is a sweet promise for a thousand occasions, and when pleaded before the throne in his name who comprehends in himself every promise, and is indeed himself the great promise of the Bible, it would be found like all others, yea and amen.—*Robert Hawker, D.D.,* 1820.

Verse 18.—" *The expectation of the poor shall not perish.*" A heathen could say, when a bird, scared by a hawk, flew into his bosom, I will not betray thee unto thy enemy, seeing thou comest for sanctuary unto me. How much less will God yield up a soul unto its enemy, when it takes sanctuary in his name, saying, Lord I am haunted with such a temptation, dogged with such a lust ; either thou must pardon it, or I am damned ; mortify it, or I shall be a slave to it ; take me into the bosom of thy love for Christ's sake ; castle me in the arms of thy everlasting strength ; it is in thy power to save me from, or give me up into the hands of my enemy ; I have no confidence in myself or any other : into thy hands I commit my cause myself, and rely on thee. This dependence of a soul undoubtedly will awaken the almighty power of God for such a one's defence. He hath sworn the greatest oath that can come out of his blessed lips, even by himself, that such as thus fly for refuge to hope in him, shall have strong consolation. Heb. vi. 17. This indeed may give the saint the greater boldness of faith to expect kind entertainment when he repairs to God for refuge, because he cannot come before he is looked for ; God having set up his name and promises as a strong tower, both calls his people into these chambers and expects they should betake themselves thither.—*William Gurnall.*

Verse 18.—As sometimes God is said to hear us in not hearing, us, so we may say he should sometimes deny us if he did not delay us. It is (saith Chrysostom) like money, which lying long in the bank, comes home at last with a duck in its mouth, with use upon use ; when money is out a great time, it makes a great return : we can stay thus upon men, and cannot we, shall not we, stay upon the Lord, and for the Lord, for a large return. God causeth us by delay to make the more prayers ; and the more we pray, the longer we stay, the more comfort we shall have, and the more sure we are that we shall have it in the latter end. Distinguish between denying and delaying. . . . . In God *our Father* are all dimensions of love, and that in an infinite degree ; infinitely infinite : what if he defer us ? so do we our children, albeit we mean no other but to give them their own asking, yet we love to see them wait, that so they may have from us the best things when they are at the best, in the best time, and in the best manner : if a mother should forget her only boy, yet God hath an infinite memory, he nor can, nor will forget ; the expectation of the *waiter* shall not fail *for ever,* that is, *never.*—*Richard Capel.*

Verse 19.—" *Arise, O Lord,*" etc. What does this mean ? Are we to consider the Psalmist as praying for the destruction of his enemies, as pronouncing a malediction, a curse upon them ? No ; these are not the words of one who is wishing that mischief may happen to his enemies ; they are the words of a prophet, of one who is foretelling, in Scripture language, the evil that must befall them on account of their sins.—*Augustine.*

Verse 20.—" *Put them in fear, O Lord,*" etc. We should otherwise think ourselves gods. We are so inclined to sin that we need strong restraints, and so swelled with a natural pride against God, that we need thorns in the flesh to let out the corrupt matter. The constant hanging the rod over us makes us lick the dust, and acknowledge ourselves to be altogether at the Lord's mercy. Though God hath pardoned us, he will make us wear the halter about our necks to humble us.—*Stephen Charnock.*

Verse 20.—" *That the nations may know themselves to be but men.*" The original word is אֱנוֹשׁ, *enosh ;* and therefore it is a prayer that they may know themselves to be but miserable, frail, and dying men. The word is in the singular number, but it is used collectively.—*John Calvin.*

HINTS TO PREACHERS.

Verse 1.—I. The only object of our praise—" thee, O Lord." II. The abundant themes of praise—" all thy marvellous works." III. The proper nature of praise—" with my whole heart."—*B. Davies.*

Verse 1.—" *I will show forth."* Endless employment and enjoyment.

Verse 1.—" *Thy marvellous works."* Creation, Providence, Redemption, are all marvellous, as exhibiting the attributes of God in such a degree as to excite the wonder of all God's universe. A very suggestive topic.

Verse 2.—Sacred song : its connection with holy gladness.

The duty, excellence, and grounds of holy cheerfulness.

Verse 4.—(1) The rights of the righteous are sure to be assailed, (2) but equally sure to be defended.

Verse 6.—I. The great enemy. II. The destructions he has caused. III. The means of his overthrow. IV. The rest which shall ensue.

Verse 7 (*first clause*).—The eternity of God—the comfort of saints, the terror of sinners.

Verse 8.—The justice of God's moral government, especially in relation to the last great day.

Verse 9.—Needy people, needy times, all-sufficient provision.

Verse 10.—I. All-important knowledge—" know thy name." II. Blessed result—" will put their trust in thee." III. Sufficient reason—" for thou, Lord, hast not forsaken them that seek thee."—*T. W. Medhurst.*

Knowledge, Faith, Experience, the connection of the three.

Verse 10.—The names of God inspire trust. JEHOVAH *Jireh, Tsidkenu, Rophi, Shammah, Shalom, Nissi,* ELOHIM, SHADDAI, ADONAI, etc.

Verse 11.—I. Zion, what is it ? II. Her glorious inhabitant, what doth he ? III. The twofold occupation of her sons—" sing praises," " declare among the people his doings." IV. Arguments from the first part of the subject to encourage us in the double duty.

Verse 12.—I. God on awful business. II. Remembers his people ; to spare, honour, bless, and avenge them. III. Fulfils their cries, in their own salvation, and overthrow of enemies. A consolatory sermon for times of war or pestilence.

Verse 13.—" *Have mercy upon me, O Lord."* The publican's prayer expounded, commended, presented, and fulfilled.

Verse 13.—" *Thou liftest me up from the gates of death."* Deep distresses. Great deliverances. Glorious exaltations.

Verse 14.—" *I will rejoice in thy salvation."* Especially because it is *thine,* O God, and therefore honours thee. In its freeness, fulness, suitability, certainty, everlastingness. Who can rejoice in this ? Reasons why they should always do so.

Verse 15.—*Lex talionis.* Memorable instances.

Verse 16.—Awful knowledge ; a tremendous alternative as compared with verse 10.

Verse 17.—A warning to forgetters of God.

Verse 18.—Delays in deliverance. I. Unbelief's estimate of them—" forgotten," " perish." II. God's promise—" not always." III. Faith's duty—wait.

Verse 19.—" *Let not man prevail."* A powerful plea. Cases when employed in Scripture. The reason of its power. Times for its use.

Verse 20.—A needful lesson, and how it is taught.

PSALM X.

Since this Psalm has no title of its own, it is supposed by some to be a fragment of Psalm ix. We prefer, however, since it is complete in itself, to consider it as a separate composition. We have had instances already of Psalms which seem meant to form a pair (Ps. i. and ii., Ps. iii. and iv.), and this, with the ninth, is another specimen of the double Psalm.

The prevailing theme seems to be the oppression and persecution of the wicked; we will, therefore, for our own guidance, entitle it, The Cry of the Oppressed.

Division.—*The first verse, in an exclamation of surprise, explains the intent of the Psalm, viz., to invoke the interposition of God for the deliverance of his poor and persecuted people. From verse 2 to 11, the character of the oppressor is described in powerful language. In verse 12, the cry of the first verse bursts forth again, but with a clearer utterance. In the next place (verses 13—15), God's eye is clearly beheld as regarding all the cruel deeds of the wicked ; and as a consequence of divine omniscience the ultimate judgment of the oppressed is joyously anticipated (verses 16—18). To the Church of God during times of persecution, and to individual saints who are smarting under the hand of the proud sinner, this Psalm furnishes suitable language both for prayer and praise.*

EXPOSITION.

WHY standest thou afar off, O Lord ? *why* hidest thou *thyself* in times of trouble ?

To the tearful eye of the sufferer the Lord seemed to *stand* still, as if he calmly looked on, and did not sympathize with his afflicted one. Nay, more, the Lord appeared to be *afar off*, no longer " a very present help in trouble," but an inaccessible mountain, into which no man would be able to climb. The presence of God is the joy of his people, but any suspicion of his absence is distracting beyond measure. Let us, then, ever remember that the Lord is nigh us. The refiner is never far from the mouth of the furnace when his gold is in the fire, and the Son of God is always walking in the midst of the flames when his holy children are cast into them. Yet he that knows the frailty of man will little wonder that when we are sharply exercised, we find it hard to bear the apparent neglect of the Lord when he forbears to work our deliverance.

" *Why hidest thou thyself in times of trouble ?* " It is not the trouble, but the hiding of our Father's face, which cuts us to the quick. When trial and desertion come together, we are in as perilous a plight as Paul, when his ship fell into a place where two seas met (Acts xxvii. 41). It is but little wonder if we are like the vessel which ran aground, and the fore-part stuck fast, and remained unmovable, while the hinder part was broken by the violence of the waves. When our sun is eclipsed, it is dark indeed. If we need an answer to the question, " Why hidest thou thyself ? " it is to be found in the fact that there is a " needs-be," not only for trial, but for heaviness of heart under trial (1 Pet. i. 6) ; but how could this be the case, if the Lord should shine upon us while he is afflicting us ? Should the parent comfort his child while he is correcting him, where would be the use of the chastening ? A smiling face and a rod are not fit companions. God bares the back that the blow may be felt ; for it is only *felt* affliction which can become *blest* affliction. If we are carried in the arms of God over every stream, where would be the trial, and where the experience, which trouble is meant to teach us ?

2 The wicked in *his* pride doth persecute the poor : let them be taken in the devices that they have imagined.

3 For the wicked boasteth of his heart's desire, and blesseth the covetous, *whom* the Lord abhorreth.

4 The wicked, through the pride of his countenance, will not seek *after* God : God *is* not in all his thoughts.

5 His ways are always grievous ; thy judgments *are* far above out of his sight : *as for* all his enemies, he puffeth at them.

6 He hath said in his heart, I shall not be moved : for *I shall* never *be* in adversity.

7 His mouth is full of cursing and deceit and fraud : under his tongue *is* mischief and vanity.

8 He sitteth in the lurking places of the villages : in the secret places doth he murder the innocent : his eyes are privily set against the poor.

9 He lieth in wait secretly as a lion in his den : he lieth in wait to catch the poor : he doth catch the poor, when he draweth him into his net.

10 He croucheth, *and* humbleth himself, that the poor may fall by his strong ones.

11 He hath said in his heart, God hath forgotten : he hideth his face ; he will never see *it*.

2. The second verse contains the formal indictment against the wicked : " *The wicked in his pride doth persecute the poor.*" The accusation divides itself into two distinct charges,—pride and tyranny ; the one the root and cause of the other. The second sentence is the humble petition of the oppressed : " *Let them be taken in the devices that they have imagined.*" The prayer is reasonable, just, and natural. Even our enemies themselves being judges, it is but right that men should be done by as they wished to do to others. We only weigh you in your own scales, and measure your corn with your own bushel. Terrible shall be the day, O persecuting Babylon ! when thou shalt be made to drink of the winecup which thou thyself hast filled to the brim with the blood of saints. There are none who will dispute the justice of God, when he shall hang every Haman on his own gallows, and cast all the enemies of his Daniels into their own den of lions.

3. The indictment being read, and the petition presented, the evidence is now heard upon the first count. The evidence is very full and conclusive upon the matter of *pride*, and no jury could hesitate to give a verdict against the prisoner at the bar. Let us, however, hear the witnesses one by one. The first testifies that he is a boaster. " *For the wicked boasteth of his heart's desire.*" He is a very silly boaster, for he glories in a mere desire : a very brazen-faced boaster, for that desire is villainy ; and a most abandoned sinner, to boast of that which is his shame. Bragging sinners are the worst and most contemptible of men, especially when their filthy desires,—too filthy to be carried into act—become the theme of their boastings. When Mr. Hate-Good and Mr. Heady are joined in partnership, they drive a brisk trade in the devil's wares. This one proof is enough to condemn the prisoner at the bar. Take him away, jailor ! But stay, another witness desires to be sworn and heard. This time, the impudence of the proud rebel is even more apparent ; for he " *blesseth the covetous, whom the Lord abhorreth.*" This is insolence, which is pride unmasked. He is haughty enough to differ from the Judge of all the earth, and bless the men whom God hath cursed. So did the sinful generation in the days of Malachi, who called the proud happy, and set up those that worked wickedness (Mal. iii. 15). These base pretenders would dispute with their Maker ; they would—

> " Snatch from his hand the balance and the rod,
> Rejudge his justice, be the god of God."

How often have we heard the wicked man speaking in terms of honour of the covetous, the grinder of the poor, and the sharp dealer ! Our old proverb hath it—

> " I wot well how the world wags ;
> He is most loved that hath most bags."

Pride meets covetousness, and compliments it as wise, thrifty, and prudent. We say it with sorrow, there are many professors of religion who esteem a rich man, and flatter him, even though they know that he has fattened himself upon the flesh and blood of the poor. The only sinners who are received as respectable are covetous men. If a man is a fornicator, or a drunkard, we put him out of the church ; but who ever read of church discipline against that idolatrous wretch,—

the covetous man ? Let us tremble, lest we be found to be partakers of this atrocious sin of pride, " blessing the covetous, whom Jehovah abhorreth."

4. The proud boastings and lewd blessing of the wicked have been received in evidence against him, and now his own face confirms the accusation, and his empty closet cries aloud against him. " *The wicked, through the pride of his countenance, will not seek after God.*" Proud hearts breed proud looks and stiff knees. It is an admirable arrangement that the heart is often written on the countenance, just as the motion of the wheels of a clock find their record on its face. A brazen face and a broken heart never go together. We are not quite sure that the Athenians were wise when they ordained that men should be tried in the dark lest their countenances should weigh with the judges ; for there is much more to be learned from the motions of the muscles of the face than from the words of the lips. Honesty shines in the face, but villainy peeps out at the eyes.

See the effect of pride ; it kept the man from seeking God. It is hard to pray with a stiff neck and an unbending knee. " *God is not in all his thoughts :*" he thought much, but he had no thoughts for God. Amid heaps of chaff there was not a grain of wheat. The only place where God is not is in the thoughts of the wicked. This is a damning accusation ; for where the God of heaven is not, the Lord of hell is reigning and raging ; and if God be not in our thoughts, our thoughts will bring us to perdition.

5. " *His ways are always grievous.*" To himself they are hard. Men go a rough road when they go to hell. God has hedged-up the way of sin : O what folly to leap these hedges and fall among the thorns ! To others, also, his ways cause much sorrow and vexation ; but what cares he ? He sits like the idol god upon his monstrous car, utterly regardless of the crowds who are crushed as he rolls along. " *Thy judgments are far above out of his sight :*" he looks high, but not high enough. As God is forgotten, so are his judgments. He is not able to comprehend the things of God ; a swine may sooner look through a telescope at the stars than this man study the Word of God to understand the righteousness of the Lord. " *As for all his enemies, he puffeth at them.*" He defies and domineers ; and when men resist his injurious behaviour, he sneers at them, and threatens to annihilate them with a puff. In most languages there is a word of contempt borrowed from the action of puffing with the lips, and in English we should express the idea by saying, " He cries ' Pooh ! Pooh !' at his enemies." Ah ! there is one enemy who will not thus be puffed at. Death will puff at the candle of his life and blow it out, and the wicked boaster will find it grim work to brag in the tomb.

6. The testimony of the sixth verse concludes the evidence against the prisoner upon the first charge of pride, and certainly it is conclusive in the highest degree. The present witness has been prying into the secret chambers of the heart, and has come to tell us what he has heard. " *He hath said in his heart, I shall not be moved : for I shall never be in adversity.*" O impertinence run to seed ! The man thinks himself immutable, and omnipotent too, for *he, he* is never to be in adversity. He counts himself a privileged man. He sits alone, and shall see no sorrow. His nest is in the stars, and he dreams not of a hand that shall pluck him thence. But let us remember that this man's house is built upon the sand, upon a foundation no more substantial than the rolling waves of the sea. He that is too secure is never safe. Boastings are not buttresses, and self-confidence is a sorry bulwark. This is the ruin of fools, that when they succeed they become too big, and swell with self-conceit, as if their summer would last for ever, and their flowers bloom on eternally. Be humble, O man ! for thou art mortal, and thy lot is mutable.

The second crime is now to be proved. The fact that the man is proud and arrogant may go a long way to prove that he is vindictive and cruel. Haman's pride was the father of a cruel design to murder all the Jews. Nebuchadnezzar builds an idol ; in pride he commands all men to bow before it ; and then cruelty stands ready to heat the furnace seven times hotter for those who will not yield to his imperious will. Every proud thought is twin brother to a cruel thought. He who exalts himself will despise others, and one step further will make him a tyrant.

7. Let us now hear the witnesses in court. Let the wretch speak for himself, for out of his own mouth he will be condemned. " *His mouth is full of cursing and deceit and fraud.*" There is not only a little evil there, but his mouth is full of it. A three-headed serpent hath stowed away its coils and venom within the den of his black mouth. There is *cursing* which he spits against both God and men, *deceit* with which he entraps the unwary, and *fraud* by which, even in his

common dealings, he robs his neighbours. Beware of such a man : have no sort
of dealing with him : none but the silliest of geese would go to the fox's sermon,
and none but the most foolish will put themselves into the society of knaves. But
we must proceed. Let us look under this man's tongue as well as in his mouth ;
" *under his tongue is mischief and vanity.*" Deep in his throat are the unborn words
which shall come forth as mischief and iniquity.

8. Despite the bragging of this base wretch, it seems that he is as cowardly
as he is cruel. "*He sitteth in the lurking places of the villages : in the secret places
doth he murder the innocent : his eyes are privily set against the poor.*" He acts the
part of the highwayman, who springs upon the unsuspecting traveller in some
desolate part of the road. There are always bad men lying in wait for the saints.
This is a land of robbers and thieves ; let us travel well armed, for every bush
conceals an enemy. Everywhere there are traps laid for us, and foes thirsting
for our blood. There are enemies at our table as well as across the sea. We are
never safe, save when the Lord is with us.

9. The picture becomes blacker, for here is the cunning of the lion, and of the
huntsman, as well as the stealthiness of the robber. Surely there are some men
who come up to the very letter of this description. With watching, perversion,
slander, whispering, and false swearing, they ruin the character of the righteous,
and murder the innocent ; or, with legal quibbles, mortgages, bonds, writs, and
the like, they catch the poor, and draw them into a net. Chrysostom was peculiarly severe upon this last phase of cruelty, but assuredly not more so than was
richly merited. Take care, brethren, for there are other traps besides these.
Hungry lions are crouching in every den, and fowlers spread their nets in every
field.

Quarles well pictures our danger in those memorable lines,—

> " The close pursuers' busy hands do plant
> Snares in thy substance ; snares attend thy want ;
> Snares in thy credit ; snares in thy disgrace ;
> Snares in thy high estate ; snares in thy base ;
> Snares tuck thy bed ; and snares surround thy board ;
> Snares watch thy thoughts ; and snares attack thy word ;
>
> Snares in thy quiet ; snares in thy commotion ;
> Snares in thy diet ; snares in thy devotion :
> Snares lurk in thy resolves ; snares in thy doubt ;
> Snares lie within thy heart, and snares without ;
> Snares are above thy head, and snares beneath ;
> Snares in thy sickness ; snares are in thy death."

O Lord ! keep thy servants, and defend us from all our enemies !

10. "*He croucheth and humbleth himself, that the poor may fall by his strong
ones.*" Seeming humility is often armour-bearer to malice. The lion crouches
that he may leap with the greater force, and bring down his strong limbs upon
his prey. When a wolf was old and had tasted human blood, the old Saxon cried,
"Ware, wolf !" and we may cry, "Ware, fox !'" They who crouch to our feet
are longing to make us fall. Be very careful of fawners ; for friendship and flattery
are deadly enemies.

11. As upon the former count, so upon this one ; a witness in forthcoming,
who has been listening at the keyhole of the heart. Speak up, friend, and let us
hear your story. "*He hath said in his heart, God hath forgotten : he hideth his face ;
he will never see it.*" This cruel man comforts himself with the idea that God is
blind, or, at least, forgetful : a fond and foolish fancy, indeed. Men doubt
Omniscience when they persecute the saints. If we had a sense of God's presence
with us, it would be impossible for us to ill-treat his children. In fact, there can
scarcely be a greater preservation from sin than the constant thought of " thou,
God, seest me."

Thus has the trial proceeded. The case has been fully stated ; and now it is
but little wonder that the oppressed petitioner lifts up the cry for judgment, which
we find in the following verse :—

12 Arise, O LORD ; O God, lift up thine hand ; forget not the humble

With what bold language will faith address its God ! and yet what unbelief
is mingled with our strongest confidence. Fearlessly the Lord is stirred up to

arise and lift up his hand, yet timidly is he begged not to forget the humble ; as if Jehovah could ever be forgetful of his saints. This verse is the incessant cry of the Church, and she will never refrain therefrom until her Lord shall come in his glory to avenge her of all her adversaries.

13 Wherefore doth the wicked contemn God ? he hath said in his heart, Thou wilt not require *it*.

14 Thou hast seen *it ;* for thou beholdest mischief and spite, to requite *it* with thy hand : the poor committeth himself unto thee ; thou art the helper of the fatherless.

15 Break thou the arm of the wicked and the evil *man :* seek out his wickedness *till* thou find none.

In these verses the description of the wicked is condensed, and the evil of his character traced to its source, viz., atheistical ideas with regard to the government of the world. We may at once perceive that this is intended to be another urgent plea with the Lord to show his power, and reveal his justice. When the wicked call God's righteousness in question, we may well beg him to teach them terrible things in righteousness. In verse 13, the hope of the infidel and his heart-wishes are laid bare. He despises the Lord, because he will not believe that sin will meet with punishment : *" he hath said in his heart, Thou wilt not require it."* If there were no hell for other men, there ought to be one for those who question the justice of it. This vile suggestion receives its answer in verse 14. *" Thou hast seen it ; for thou beholdest mischief and spite, to requite it with thy hand."* God is all-eye to see, and all-hand to punish his enemies. From Divine oversight there is no hiding, and from Divine justice there is no fleeing. Wanton mischief shall meet with woeful misery, and those who harbour spite shall inherit sorrow. Verily there is a God which judgeth in the earth. Nor is this the only instance of the presence of God in the world ; for while he chastises the oppressor, he befriends the oppressed. *" The poor committeth himself unto thee."* They give themselves up entirely into the Lord's hands. Resigning their judgment to his enlightenment, and their wills to his supremacy, they rest assured that he will order all things for the best. Nor does he deceive their hope. He preserves them in times of need, and causes them to rejoice in his goodness. *" Thou art the helper of the fatherless."* God is the parent of all orphans. When the earthly father sleeps beneath the sod, a heavenly Father smiles from above. By some means or other, orphan children are fed, and well they may when they have such a Father.

15. In this verse we hear again the burden of the Psalmist's prayer: *" Break thou the arm of the wicked and the evil man."* Let the sinner lose his power to sin ; stop the tyrant, arrest the oppressor, weaken the loins of the mighty, and dash in pieces the terrible. They deny thy justice : let them feel it to the full. Indeed, they shall feel it ; for God shall hunt the sinner for ever : so long as there is a grain of sin in him it shall be sought out and punished. It is not a little worthy of note, that very few great persecutors have ever died in their beds : the curse has manifestly pursued them, and their fearful sufferings have made them own *that* divine justice at which they could at one time launch defiance. God permits tyrants to arise as thorn-hedges to protect his church from the intrusion of hypocrites, and that he may teach his backsliding children by them, as Gideon did the men of Succoth with the briers of the wilderness ; but he soon cuts up these Herods, like the thorns, and casts them into the fire. Thales, the Milesian, one of the wise men of Greece, being asked what he thought to be the greatest rarity in the world, replied, " To see a tyrant live to be an old man." See how the Lord breaks, not only the arm, but the neck of proud oppressors ! To the men who had neither justice nor mercy for the saints, there shall be rendered justice to the full, but not a grain of mercy.

16 The LORD *is* King for ever and ever : the heathen are perished out of his land.

17 LORD, thou hast heard the desire of the humble : thou wilt prepare their heart, thou wilt cause thine ear to hear :

18 To judge the fatherless and the oppressed, that the man of the earth may no more oppress.

The Psalm ends with a song of thanksgiving to the great and everlasting King, because he has granted the desire of his humble and oppressed people, has defended the fatherless, and punished the heathen who trampled upon his poor and afflicted children. Let us learn that we are sure to speed well, if we carry our complaint to the King of kings. Rights will be vindicated, and wrongs redressed, at his throne. His government neglects not the interests of the needy, nor does it tolerate oppression in the mighty. Great God, we leave ourselves in thine hand ; to thee we commit thy church afresh. Arise, O God, and let the man of the earth—the creature of a day—be broken before the majesty of thy power. Come, Lord Jesus, and glorify thy people. Amen and Amen.

EXPLANATORY NOTES AND QUAINT SAYINGS.

Whole Psalm.—There is not, in my judgment, a Psalm which describes the mind, the manners, the works, the words, the feelings, and the fate of the ungodly with so much propriety, fulness, and light, as this Psalm. So that, if in any respect there has not been enough said heretofore, or if there shall be anything wanting in the Psalms that shall follow, we may here find a perfect image and representation of iniquity. This Psalm, therefore, is a type, form, and description of that man, who, though he may be in the sight of himself and of men more excellent than Peter himself, is detestable in the eyes of God ; and this it was that moved Augustine, and those who followed him, to understand the Psalm of ANTICHRIST. But as the Psalm is without a title, let us embrace the most general and common understanding of it (as I said), and let us look at the picture of ungodliness which it sets before us. Not that we would deny the propriety of the acceptation in which others receive it, nay, we will, in our general acceptation of the Psalm, include also its reference to ANTICHRIST. And, indeed, it will not be at all absurd if we join this Psalm with the preceding, in its order thus. That David, in the preceding spoke of the ungodly converted, and prayed for those who were to be converted. But that here he is speaking of the ungodly that are still left so, and in power prevailing over the weak ALMUTH, concerning whom he has no hope, or is in a great uncertainty of mind, whether they ever will be converted or not.—*Martin Luther.*

Verse 1.—" *Why hidest thou thyself in times of trouble ?* " The answer to this is not far to seek, for if the Lord did not hide himself it would not be a time of trouble at all. As well ask why the sun does not shine at night, when for certain there could be no night if he did. It is essential to our thorough chastisement that the Father should withdraw his smile : there is a needs be not only for manifold temptations, but that we be in heaviness through them. The design of the rod is only answered by making us smart. If there be no pain, there will be no profit. If there be no hiding of God, there will be no bitterness, and consequently no purging efficacy in his chastisements.—*C. H. S.*

Verse 1 (last clause).—" *Times of trouble* " should be times of confidence ; fixedness of heart on God would prevent fears of heart. Psalm cxii. 7. " He shall not be afraid of evil tidings : his heart is fixed." How ? " Trusting in the Lord. His heart is established, he shall not be afraid." Otherwise without it we shall be as light as a weather-cock, moved with every blast of evil tidings, our hopes will swim or sink according to the news we hear. Providence would seem to sleep unless faith and prayer awaken it. The disciples had but little faith in their Master's account, yet that little faith awakened him in a storm, and he relieved them. Unbelief doth only discourage God from showing his power in taking our parts.— *Stephen Charnock.*

Verse 2.—" *The wicked in his pride doth persecute the poor.*" THE OPPRESSOR'S PLEA. I seek but what is my own by law ; it was his own free act and deed—the execution lies for goods and body ; and goods or body I will have, or else my money. What if his beggarly children pine, or his proud wife perish ? they perish at their own charge, not mine ; and what is that to me ? I must be paid, or he lie by it until I have my utmost farthing, or his bones. The law is just and good ; and, being ruled by that, how can my fair proceedings be unjust ? What is thirty in the hundred to a man of trade ? Are we born to thrum caps or pick straws ? and sell our livelihood for a few tears, and a whining face ? I thank God they move me not so much as a howling dog at midnight. I'll give no day if heaven itself would be security. I must have present money, or his bones. . . . . Fifteen shillings in the pound composition ! I'll hang first. Come, tell me not of a good conscience : a good conscience is no parcel of my trade ; it hath made more bankrupts than all the loose wives in the universal city. My conscience is no fool : it tells me my own is my own, and that a well crammed bag is no deceitful friend, but will stick close to me when all my friends forsake me. If to gain a good estate out of nothing, and to regain a desperate debt which is as good as nothing, be the fruits and sign of a bad conscience, God help the good. Come, tell me not of griping and oppression. The world is hard, and he that hopes to thrive must gripe as hard. What I give I give, and what I lend I lend. If the way to heaven be to turn beggar upon earth, let them take it that like it. I know not what you call oppression, the law is my direction ; but of the two, it is more profitable to oppress than to be oppressed. If debtors would be honest and discharge, our hands were bound ; but when their failing offends my bags, they touch the apple of my eye, and I must right them.— *Francis Quarles.*

Verse 2.—That famous persecutor, Domitian, like others of the Roman emperors, assumed divine honours, and heated the furnace seven times hotter against Christians because they refused to worship his image. In like manner, when the popes of Rome became decorated with the blasphemous titles of *Masters of the World,* and *Universal Fathers,* they let loose their blood-hounds upon the faithful. Pride is the egg of persecution.—*C. H. S.*

Verse 2.—" *Pride,*" is a vice which cleaveth so fast unto the hearts of men, that if we were to strip ourselves of all faults one by one, we should undoubtedly find it the very last and hardest to put off.—*Richard Hooker, 1554—1600.*

Verse 3.—" *The wicked boasteth,*" etc. He braggeth of his evil life, whereof he maketh open profession ; or he boasteth that he will accomplish his wicked designs ; or glorieth that he hath already accomplished them. Or it may be understood that he commendeth others who are according to the desires of his own soul ; that is, he respecteth or honoureth none but such as are like him, and them only he esteemeth. Psalm xxxvi. 4, and xlix. 18 ; Rom. i. 32.—*John Diodati, 1648.*

Verse 3.—" *The wicked . . . blesseth the covetous.*" Like will to like, as the common proverb is. Such as altogether neglect the Lord's commandments not only commit divers gross sins, but commend those who in sinning are like themselves. For in their affections they allow them, in their speeches they flatter and extol them, and in their deeds they join with them and maintain them.—*Peter Muffet, 1594.*

Verse 3.—" *The covetous.*" Covetousness is the desire of possessing that which we have not, and attaining unto great riches and worldly possessions. And whether this be not the character of trade and merchandise and traffic of every kind, the great source of those evils of over-trading which are everywhere complained of, I refer to the judgment of the men around me, who are engaged in the commerce and business of life. Compared with the regular and quiet diligence of our fathers, and their contentment with small but sure returns, the wild and widespread speculation for great gains, the rash and hasty adventures which are daily made, and the desperate gamester-like risks which are run, do reveal fully surely that a spirit of covetousness hath been poured out upon men within the last thirty or forty years. And the providence of God corresponding thereto, by wonderful and unexpected revolutions, by numerous inventions for manufacturing the productions of the earth, in order to lead men into temptation, hath impressed upon the whole face of human affairs, a stamp of earnest worldliness not known to our fathers : insomuch that our youth do enter life no longer with the ambition of providing things honest in the sight of men, keeping their credit, bringing up their family, and realising a competency, if the Lord prosper them, but with the ambition of making a fortune, retiring to their ease, and enjoying the luxuries of the present life. Against which crying sin of covetousness, dearly beloved brethren, I do most earnestly call upon you to wage a good warfare. This place is its seat, its stronghold, even this metropolitan city of Christian Britain ; and ye who are called by the grace of God out of the great thoroughfare of Mammon, are so elected for the express purpose of testifying against this and all other the backslidings of the church planted here; and especially against this, as being in my opinion, one of the most evident and the most common of them all. For who hath not been snared in the snare of covetousness ?—*Edward Irving*, 1828.

Verse 3.—" *The covetous, whom the Lord abhorreth.*" Christ knew what he spake when he said, " No man can serve two masters." Matt. vi. 24. Meaning God and the world, because each would have all. As the angel and the devil strove for the body of Moses (Jude 9), not who should have a part, but who should have the whole, so they strive still for our souls, who shall have all. Therefore, the apostle saith, " The love of this world is enmity to God (James iv. 4), signifying such emulation between these two, that God cannot abide the world should have a part, and the world cannot abide that God should have a part. Therefore, the love of the world must needs be enmity to God, and therefore the lovers of the world must needs be enemies to God, and so no covetous man is God's servant, but God's enemy. For this cause covetousness is called idolatry (Eph. v. 5), which is the most contrary sin to God, because as treason sets up another king in the king's place, so idolatry sets up another god in God's place.—*Henry Smith.*

Verse 4.—" *The wicked, through the pride of his countenance, will not seek after God.*" He is judged a proud man (without a jury sitting on him), who when condemned will not submit, will not stoop so low as to accept of a pardon. I must indeed correct myself, men are willing to be justified, but they would have their duties to purchase their peace and the favour of God. Thousands will die and be damned rather than they will have a pardon upon the sole account of Christ's merits and obedience. Oh, the cursed pride of the heart! When will men cease to be wiser than God? To limit God? When will men be contented with God's way of saving them by the blood of the everlasting covenant? How dare men thus to prescribe to the infinitely wise God? Is it not enough for thee that thy destruction is of thyself? But must thy salvation be of thyself too? Is it not enough that thou hast wounded thyself, but wilt thou die for ever, rather than be beholden to a plaister of free grace? Wilt be damned unless thou mayest be thine own Saviour? God is willing (" God so loved the world that he gave his only Son "), art thou so proud as that thou wilt not be beholden to God? Thou wilt deserve, or have nothing. What shall I say? Poor thou art, and yet proud; thou hast nothing but wretchedness and misery, and yet thou art talking of a purchase. This is a provocation. " God resisteth the proud," especially the spiritually proud. He that is proud of his clothes and parentage, is not so contemptible in God's eyes as he that is proud of his abilities, and so scorns to submit to God's methods for his salvation by Christ, and by his righteousness alone.—*Lewis Stuckley.*

Verse 4.—" *The wicked, through the pride of his countenance, will not seek after God.*" The pride of the wicked is the principal reason why they will not seek after the knowledge of God. This knowledge it prevents them from seeking in various ways. In the first place, it renders God a disagreeable object of contemplation to the wicked, and a knowledge of him as undesirable. Pride consists in an unduly exalted opinion of one's self. It is, therefore, impatient of a rival, hates a superior, and cannot endure a master. In proportion as it prevails in the heart, it makes us wish to see nothing above us, to acknowledge no law but our own wills, to follow no rule but our own inclinations. Thus it led Satan to rebel against his Creator, and our first parents to desire to be as gods. Since such are the effects of pride, it is evident that nothing can be more painful to a proud heart than the thoughts of such a being as God; one who is infinitely powerful, just and holy; who can neither be resisted, deceived, nor deluded; who disposes, according to his own sovereign pleasure, of all creatures and events; and who, in an especial manner, hates pride, and is determined to abase and punish it. Such a being pride can contemplate only with feelings of dread, aversion, and abhorrence. It must look upon him as its natural enemy, the great enemy, whom it has to fear. But the knowledge of God directly tends to bring this infinite, irristible, irreconcilable enemy full to the view of the proud man. It teaches him that he has a superior, a master, from whose authority he cannot escape, whose power he cannot resist, and whose will he must obey, or be crushed before him, and be rendered miserable for ever. It shows him what he hates to see, that, in despite of his opposition, God's counsel shall stand, that he will do all his pleasure, and that in all things wherein men deal proudly, God is above them. These truths torture the proud unhumbled hearts of the wicked, and hence they hate that knowledge of God which teaches these truths, and will not seek it. On the contrary, they wish to remain ignorant of such a being, and to banish all thoughts of him from their minds. With this view, they neglect, pervert, or explain away those passages of revelation which describe God's true character, and endeavour to believe that he is altogether such a one as themselves.

How foolish, how absurd, how ruinous, how blindly destructive of its own object, does pride appear! By attempting to soar, it only plunges itself in the mire; and while endeavouring to erect for itself a throne, it undermines the ground on which it stands, and digs its own grave. It plunged Satan from heaven into hell; it banished our first parents from paradise; and it will, in a similar manner, ruin all who indulge in it. It keeps us in ignorance of God, shuts us out from his favour, prevents us from resembling him, deprives us in this world of all the honour and happiness which communion with him would confer; and in the next, unless previously hated, repented of, and renounced, will bar for ever against us the door of heaven, and close upon us the gates of hell. O then, my friends, beware, above all things, beware of pride! Beware, lest you indulge it imperceptibly, for it is perhaps, of all sins, the most secret, subtle, and insinuating.—*Edward Payson, D.D.,* 1783—1827.

Verse 4.—David speaks in Psalm x. of great and potent oppressors and politicians, who see none on earth greater than themselves, none higher than they, and think therefore that they may *impunè* prey upon the smaller, as beasts use to do; and in the fourth verse this is made the root and ground of all, that God is not in all his thoughts. "*The wicked, through the pride of his countenance, will not seek after God: God is not in all his thoughts.*" The words are diversely read, and all make for this sense. Some read it, "No God in all his crafty presumptuous purposes;" others, "All his thoughts are, there is no God." The meaning whereof is not only that among the swarm and crowd of thoughts that fill his mind, the thought of God is seldom to be found, and comes not in among the rest, which yet is enough for the purpose in hand; but further, that in all his projects and plots, and consultations of his heart (the first reading of the words intends), whereby he contrives and lays the plot, form, and draught of all his actions, he never takes God or his will into consideration or consultation, to square and frame all accordingly, but proceeds and goes on in all, and carries on all as if there were no God to be consulted with. He takes not him along with him, no more than if he were no God; the thoughts of him and his will sway him not. As you use to say, when a combination of men leave out some one they should advise with, that such a one is not of their counsel, is not in the plot; so nor is God in their purposes and advisings, they do all without him. But this is not all the meaning, but farther, all their thought is, that there is no God. This is there made the bottom, the foundation, the groundwork and reason of all their wicked plots and injurious projects, and deceitful carriages and proceedings, that seeing there is no God or power above them to take notice of it, to regard or requite them, therefore they may be bold to go on.—*Thomas Goodwin.*

Verse 4.—"*Of his countenance.*" Which pride he carrieth engraven in his very countenance and forehead, and makes it known in all his carriages and gestures. "*Will not seek,*" namely, he contemneth all divine and human laws, he feareth not, respecteth not God's judgments; he careth for nothing, so he may fulfil his desires; enquires after, nor examines nothing; all things are indifferent to him.—*John Diodati.*

Verse 4.—"*All his thoughts are,* there is *no God;*" thus some read the passage. Seneca says, there are no atheists, though there would be some; if any say there is no God, they lie; though they say it in the day time, yet in the night when they are alone they deny it; howsoever some desperately harden themselves, yet if God doth but show himself terrible to them, they confess him. Many of the heathens and others, have denied that there is a God, yet when they were in distress, they did fall down and confess him, as Diagoras, that grand atheist, when he was troubled with the strangullion, acknowledged a deity which he had denied. These kind of atheists I leave to the tender mercies of God, of which I doubt it whether there be any for them.—*Richard Stock.*

Verse 4.—"*God is not in all his thoughts.*" It is the black work of an ungodly man or an atheist, that God is not in all his thoughts. What comfort can be had in the being of God without thinking of him with reverence and delight? A God forgotten is as good as no God to us.—*Stephen Charnock.*

Verse 4.—Trifles possess us, but "*God is not in all our thoughts,*" seldom the sole object of them. We have durable thoughts of transitory things, and flitting thoughts of a durable and eternal good. The covenant of grace engageth the whole heart to God, and bars anything else from engrossing it ; but what strangers are God and the souls of most men ! Though we have the knowledge of him by creation, yet he is for the most part an unknown God in the relations wherein he stands to us, because a God undelighted in. Hence it is, as one observes, that because we observe not the ways of God's wisdom, conceive not of him in his vast perfections, nor are stricken with an admiration of his goodness, that we have fewer good sacred poems than of any other kind. The wits of men hang the wing when they come to exercise their reasons and fancies about God. Parts and strength are given us, as well as corn and wine to the Israelites, for the service of God, but those are consecrated to some cursed Baal, Hosea ii. 8. Like Venus in the poet, we forsake heaven to follow some Adonis.—*Stephen Charnock.*

Verses 4, 5.—The world hath a spiritual fascination and witchcraft, by which, where it hath once prevailed, men are enchanted to an utter forgetfulness of themselves and God, and being drunk with pleasures, they are easily engaged to a madness and height of folly. Some, like foolish children, are made to keep a great stir in the world for very trifles, for a vain show ; they think themselves great, honourable, excellent, and for this make a great bustle, when the world hath not added one cubit to their stature of real worth. Others are by this Circe transformed into savage creatures, and act the part of lions and tigers. Others, like swine, wallow in the lusts of uncleanness. Others are unmanned, putting off all natural affections, care not who they ride over, so they may rule over or be made great. Others are taken with ridiculous frenzies, so that a man that stands in the cool shade of a sedate composure would judge them out of their wits. It would make a man admire to read of the frisks of Caius Caligula, Xerxes, Alexander, and many others, who because they were above many men, thought themselves above human nature. They forgot they were born and must die, and did such things as would have made them, but that their greatness overawed it, a laughing-stock and common scorn to children. Neither must we think that these were but some few or rare instances of worldly intoxication, when the Scripture notes it as a general distemper of all that bow down to worship this idol. They live " without God in the world," saith the apostle, that is, they so carry it as if there were no God to take notice of them to check them for their madness. " *God is not in all his thoughts.*" Verse 4. " *The judgments of God are far above out of his sight ;* " he puffs at his enemies (ver. 5), and saith in his heart, he " *shall never be moved.*" Verse 6. The whole Psalm describes the worldling as a man that hath lost all his understanding, and is acting the part of a frantic bedlam. What then can be a more fit engine for the devil to work with than the pleasures of the world ?—*Richard Gilpin.*

Verse 5.—" *Grievous,*" or troublesome ; that is, all his endeavours and actions aim at nothing but at hurting others. " *Are far above,*" for he is altogther carnal, he hath not any disposition nor correspondence with the justice of thy law, which is altogether spiritual ; and therefore cannot lively represent unto himself thy judgments, and the issue of the wicked according to the said law. Rom. vii. 14 ; 1 Cor. ii. 14. " *He puffeth ;* " he doth most arrogantly despise them, and is confident he can overthrow them with a puff.—*John Diodati.*

Verse 5.—" *Thy judgments are far above out of his sight.*" Because God does not immediately visit every sin with punishment, ungodly men do not see that in due time he judges all the earth. Human tribunals must of necessity, by promptness and publicity, commend themselves to the common judgment, but the Lord's modes of dealing with sin are sublimer and apparently more tardy, hence the bat's eyes of godless men cannot see them, and the grovelling wits of men cannot comprehend them. If God sat in the gate of every village and held his court there, even fools might discern his righteousness, but they are not capable of perceiving that for a matter to be settled in the highest court, even in heaven itself, is a far more solemn matter. Let believers take heed lest they fall in a degree into the same error, and begin to criticise the actions of The Great Supreme, when they are too elevated for human reason to comprehend them.—*C. H. S.*

Verse 5.—" *The judgments of God are far above out of his sight.*" Out of his sight, as an eagle at her highest towering so lessens herself to view, that he sees not the talons, nor fears the grip. Thus man presumes till he hath sinned, and then despairs as fast afterwards. At first, " Tush, doth God see it ? " At last, " Alas ! will God forgive it ? "   But if a man will not know his sins, his sins will know him ; the eyes which presumption shuts, commonly despair opens.—*Thomas Adams.*

Verse 5.—"*As for all his enemies, he puffeth at them.*" David describeth a *proud* man, *puffing at his enemies :* he is puffed up and swelled with high conceits of himself, as if he had some great matter in him, and he puffs at others as if he could do some great matter against them, forgetting that himself is but, as to his being in this world, a puff of wind which passeth away.—*Joseph Caryl.*

Verse 5.—"*As for all his enemies he puffeth at them ;* " literally, " *He whistles at them.*" He is given over to the dominion of gloomy indifference, and he cares as little for others as for himself. Whosoever may be imagined by him to be an enemy he cares not. Contempt and ridicule are his only weapons ; and he has forgotten how to use others of a more sacred character. His mental habits are marked by scorn ; and he treats with contempt the judgments, opinions, and practices of the wisest of men.—*John Morison.*

Verse 6.—"*He hath said in his heart, I shall not be moved : for I shall never be in adversity.*" Carnal security opens the door for all impiety to enter into the soul. Pompey, when he had in vain assaulted a city, and could not take it by force, devised this stratagem in way of agreement ; he told them he would leave the siege and make peace with them, upon condition that they would let in a few weak, sick, and wounded soldiers among them to be cured. They let in the soldiers, and when the city was secure, the soldiers let in Pompey's army. A carnal settled security will let in a whole army of lusts into the soul.—*Thomas Brooks.*

Verse 6.—"*He hath said in his heart, I shall not be moved : for I shall never be in adversity.*" To consider religion always on the comfortable side ; to congratulate one's self for having obtained the end before we have made use of the means ; to stretch the hands to receive the crown of righteousness before they have been employed to fight the battle ; to be content with a false peace, and to use no efforts to obtain the graces to which true consolation is annexed: this is a dreadful calm, like that which some voyagers describe, and which is a very singular forerunner of a very terrible event. All on a sudden, in the wide ocean, the sea becomes calm, the surface of the water clear as a crystal, smooth as glass—the air serene ; the un-skilled passenger becomes tranquil and happy, but the old mariner trembles. In an instant the waves froth, the winds murmur, the heavens kindle, a thousand gulfs open, a frightful light inflames the air, and every wave threatens sudden death. This is an image of many men's assurance of salvation.—*James Saurin, 1677—1730.*

Verse 7.—"*Under his tongue is mischief and vanity.*" The striking allusion of this expression is to certain venomous reptiles, which are said to carry bags of poison under their teeth, and with great subtlety to inflict the most deadly injuries upon those who come within their reach. How affectingly does this represent the sad havoc which minds tainted with infidelity inflict on the community ! By their perversions of truth, and by their immoral sentiments and practices, they are as injurious to the mind as the deadliest poison can be to the body.—*John Morison.*

Verse 7.—Cursing men are cursed men.—*John Trapp.*

Verses 7—9. In Anne Askew's account of her examination by Bishop Bonner, we have an instance of the cruel craft of persecutors : " On the morrow after, my lord of London sent for me at one of the clock, his hour being appointed at three. And as I came before him, he said he was very sorry of my trouble, and desired to know my opinion in such matters as were laid against me. He required me also boldly in any wise to utter the secrets of my heart ; bidding me not to fear in any point, for whatsoever I did say within his house no man should hurt me for it. I answered, ' For so much as your lordship hath appointed three of the clock, and my friends shall not come till that hour, I desire you to pardon me of giving answer till they come ' " Upon this Bale remarks : " In this preventing of the hour may the diligent perceive the greediness of this Babylon bishop, or bloodthirsty wolf, con-cerning his prey. ' Swift are their feet,' saith David, ' in the effusion of innocent blood, which have fraud in their tongues, venom in their lips, and most cruel ven-geance in their mouths.' David much marvelleth in the spirit that, taking upon them the spiritual governance of the people, they can fall into such frenzy or for-getfulness of themselves, as to believe it lawful thus to oppress the faithful, and to devour them with as little compassion as he that greedily devoureth a piece of bread. If such have read anything of God, they have little minded their true duty therein.

'More swift,' saith Jeremy, 'are our cruel persecutors than the eagles of the air. They follow upon us over the mountains, and lay privy wait for us in the wilderness.' He that will know the crafty hawking of bishops to bring in their prey, let him learn it here. Judas, I think, had never the tenth part of their cunning workmanship.'" *John Bale, D.D., Bishop of Ossory,* 1495—1563, *in " Examination of Anne Askew." Parker Society's Publications.*

Verse 8.—" *He sitteth in the lurking places of the villages,*" etc. The Arab robber lurks like a wolf among these sand-heaps, and often springs out suddenly upon the solitary traveller, robs him in a trice, and then plunges again into the wilderness of sand-hills and reedy downs, where pursuit is fruitless. Our friends are careful not to allow us to straggle about, or lag behind, and yet it seems absurd to fear a surprise here—Kaifa before, Acre in the rear, and travellers in sight on both sides. Robberies, however, do often occur, just where we now are. Strange country ! and it has always been so. There are a hundred allusions to just such things in the history, the Psalms, and the prophets of Israel. A whole class of imagery is based upon them. Thus, in Psalm x. 8—10, " He sits in the lurking places of the villages : in the secret places doth he murder the innocent : he lieth in wait secretly as a lion in his den : he lieth in wait to catch the poor : he doth catch the poor, when he draweth him into his net ; he croucheth and humbleth himself, that the poor may fall by his strong ones." And a thousand rascals, the living originals of this picture, are this day crouching and lying in wait all over the country to catch poor helpless travellers. You observe that all these people we meet or pass are armed ; nor would they venture to go from Acre to Kaifa without their musket, although the cannon of the castles seem to command every foot of the way. Strange, most strange land ! but it tallies wonderfully with its ancient story.—*W. M. Thomson, D.D., in " The Land and the Book,"* 1859.

Verse 8.—My companions asked me if I knew the danger I had escaped. " No," I replied ; " What danger ? " They then told me that, just after they started, they saw a wild Arab skulking after me, crouching to the ground, with a musket in his hand ; and that, as soon as he had reached within what appeared to them musket-shot of me, he raised his gun ; but, looking wildly around him, as a man will do who is about to perpetrate some desperate act, he caught sight of them and disappeared. Jeremiah knew something of the ways of these Arabs when he wrote, (chap. iii. 2) " In the ways hast thou sat for them, as the Arabian in the wilderness ; " and the simile is used in Psalm x. 9, 10, for the Arabs wait and watch for their prey with the greatest eagerness and perseverance.—*John Gadsby, in " My Wanderings,"* 1860.

Verse 8.—" *He sitteth in the lurking places of the villages : in the secret places doth he murder the innocent : his eyes are privily set against the poor."* All this strength of metaphor and imagery is intended to mark the assiduity, the cunning, the low artifice, to which the enemies of truth and righteousness will often resort in order to accomplish their corrupt and vicious designs. The extirpation of true religion is their great object ; and there is nothing to which they will not stoop in order to effect that object. The great powers which have oppressed the church of Christ, in different ages, have answered to this description. Both heathen and papistical authorities have thus condescended to infamy. They have sat, as it were, in ambush for the poor of Christ's flock ; they have adopted every stratagem that infernal skill could invent ; they have associated themselves with princes in their palaces, and with beggars on their dunghill ; they have resorted to the villages, and they have mingled in the gay and populous city ; and all for the vain purpose of attempting to blot out a " name which shall endure for ever, and which shall be continued as long as the sun."—*John Morison.*

Verse 9.—" *He doth catch the poor."* The poor man is the beast they hunt, who must rise early, rest late, eat the bread of sorrow, sit with many a hungry meal, perhaps his children crying for food, while all the fruit of his pains is served into Nimrod's table. Complain of this while you will, yet, as the orator said of Verres, *pecuniosus nescit damnari.* Indeed, a money-man may not be damnified, but he may be damned. For this is a crying sin, and the wakened ears of the Lord will hear it, neither shall his provoked hands forbear it. *Si tacuerint pauperes loquentur lapides.* If the poor should hold their peace, the very stones would speak. The fines, rackings, enclosures, oppressions, vexations, will cry to God for vengeance.

" The stone will cry out of the wall, and the beam out of the timber shall answer it. Hab. ii. 11. You see the beasts they hunt. Not foxes, nor wolves, nor boars, bulls, nor tigers.   It is a certain observation, no beast hunts its own kind to devour it. Now, if these should prosecute wolves, foxes, &c., they should then hunt their own kind ; for they are these themselves, or rather worse than these, because here *homo homini lupus.*   But though they are men they hunt, and by nature of the same kind, they are not so by quality, for they are lambs they persecute.   In them there is blood, and flesh, and fleece to be had ; and therefore on these do they gorge themselves.   In them there is weak armour of defence against their cruelties ; therefore over these they may domineer.   I will speak it boldly : there is not a mighty Nimrod in this land that dares hunt his equal ; but over his inferior lamb he insults like a young Nero.   Let him be graced by high ones, and he must not be saluted under twelve score off.   In the country he proves a termagant ; his very scowl is a prodigy, and breeds an earthquake.   He would be a Cæsar, and tax all.   It is well if he prove not a cannibal !   Only Macro salutes Sejanus so long as he is in Tiberius's favour ; cast him from that pinnacle, and the dog is ready to devour him.—*Thomas Adams.*

Verse 9.—" *He draweth him into his net.*"   " They hunt with a net."   Micah vii. 2.   They have their politic gins to catch men ; gaudy wares and dark shops (and would you have them love the light that live by darkness, as many shopkeepers ?) draw and tole customers in, where the crafty leeches can soon feel their pulses ; if they must buy, they shall pay for their necessity.   And though they plead, We compel none to buy our ware, *caveat emptor ;* yet with fine voluble phrases, damnable protestations, they will cast a mist of error before an eye of simple truth, and with cunning devices hunt them in.   So some among us have feathered their nests, not by open violence, but politic circumvention.   They have sought the golden fleece, not by Jason's merit, but by Medea's subtlety, by Medea's sorcery.   If I should intend to discover these hunters' plots, and to deal punctually with them, I should afford you more matter than you would afford me time.   But I limit myself, and answer all their plans with Augustine.   Their tricks may hold *in jure fori,* but not *in jure poli*—in the common-pleas of earth, not before the king's bench in heaven. *Thomas Adams.*

Verse 9.—Oppression turns princes into roaring lions, and judges into evening wolves.   It is an unnatural sin, against the light of nature.   No creatures do oppress them of their own kind.   Look upon the birds of prey, as upon eagles, vultures, hawks, and you shall never find them preying upon their own kind.   Look upon the beasts of the forest, as upon the lion, the tiger, the wolf, the bear, and you shall ever find them favourable to their own kind ; and yet men unnaturally prey upon one another, like the fish in the sea, the great swallowing up the small.—*Thomas Brooks.*

Verse 10.—" *He croucheth, and humbleth himself,*" etc.   There is nothing too mean or servile for them, in the attempt to achieve their sinister ends.   You shall see his holiness the Pope washing the pilgrims' feet, if such a stratagem be necessary to act on the minds of the deluded multitude ; or you shall see him sitting on a throne of purple, if he wishes to awe and control the kings of the earth.—*John Morison.*

Verse 10.—If you take a wolf in a lambskin, hang him up ; for he is the worst of the generation.—*Thomas Adams.*

Verse 11.—" *He hath said in his heart, God hath forgotten.*"   Is it not a senseless thing to be careless of sins committed long ago ?   The old sins forgotten by men, stick fast in an infinite understanding.   Time cannot raze out that which hath been known from eternity.   Why should they be forgotten many years after they were acted, since they were foreknown in an eternity before they were committed, or the criminal capable to practise them ?   Amalek must pay their arrears of their ancient unkindness to Israel in the time of Saul, though the generation that committed them were rotten in their graves.   1 Sam. xv. 2.   Old sins are written in a book, which lies always before God ; and not only our own sins, but the sins of our fathers to be requited upon their posterity.   " Behold it is written." Isa. lxv. 6. What a vanity is it then to be regardless of the sins of an age that went before us ; because they are in some measure out of our knowledge, are they therefore blotted out of God's remembrance ?   Sins are bound up with him, as men do bonds, till they resolve to sue for the debt.   " The iniquity of Ephraim is bound up." Hosea

xiii. 12. As his foreknowledge extends to all acts that shall be done, so his remembrance extends to all acts that have been done. We may as well say, God foreknows nothing that shall be done to the end of the world, as that he forgets anything that hath been done from the beginning of the world.—*Stephen Charnock.*

Verse 11.—" *He hath said in his heart, God hath forgotten : he hideth his face ; he will never see it.*" Many say in their hearts, " God seeth them not," while with their tongues they confess he is an all-seeing God. The heart hath a tongue in it as well as the head, and these two tongues seldom speak the same language. While the head-tongue saith, " We cannot hide ourselves from the sight of God," the heart-tongue of wicked men will say, " God will hide himself from us, he will not see." But if their heart speak not thus, then as the prophet saith (Isa. xxix. 15), " They dig deep to hide their counsel from the Lord ; " surely they have a hope to hide their counsels, else they would not dig deep to hide them. Their digging is nor proper, but tropical ; as men dig deep to hide what they would not have in the earth, so they by their wits, plots, and devices, do their best to hide their counsels from God, and they say, " Who seeth, who knoweth ? We, surely, are not seen either by God or man."—*Joseph Caryl.*

Verse 11.—The Scripture everywhere places sin upon this root. " *God hath forgotten : he hideth his face ; he will never see it.*" He hath turned his back upon the world. This was the ground of the oppression of the poor by the wicked, which he mentions, verses 9, 10. There is no sin but receives both its birth and nourishment from this bitter root. Let the notion of providence be once thrown out, or the belief of it faint, how will ambition, covetousness, neglect of God, distrust, impatience, and all other bitter gourds, grow up in a night ! It is from this topic all iniquity will draw arguments to encourage itself ; for nothing so much discountenances those rising corruptions, and puts them out of heart, as an actuated belief that God takes care of human affairs.—*Stephen Charnock.*

Verse 11.—" *He hath said in his heart,*" etc. " Because sentence against an evil work is not executed speedily, therefore the heart of the sons of men is fully set in them to do evil." Eccl. viii. 11. God forbears punishing, therefore men forbear repenting. He doth not smite upon their back by correction, therefore they do not smite upon their thigh by humiliation. Jer. xxxi. 19. The sinner thinks thus : " God hath spared me all this while, he hath eked out patience into longsuffering ; surely he will not punish." " *He hath said in his heart, God hath forgotten.*" God sometimes in infinite patience adjourns his judgments and puts off the sessions a while longer ; he is not willing to punish. 2 Peter iii. 9. The bee naturally gives honey, but stings only when it is angered. The Lord would have men make their peace with him. Isa. xxvii. 5. God is not like a hasty creditor that requires the debt, and will give no time for the payment ; he is not only gracious, but " waits to be gracious." (Isa. xxx. 18) ; but God by his patience would bribe sinners to repentance ; but alas ! how is this patience abused. God's longsuffering hardens : because God stops the vials of his wrath, sinners stop the conduit of tears.—*Thomas Watson.*

Verse 11.—" *He hath said in his heart, God hath forgotten : he hideth his face ; he will never see it.*" Because the Lord continues to spare them, therefore they go on to provoke him. As he adds to their lives, so they add to their lusts. What is this, but as if a man should break all his bones because there is a surgeon who is able to set them again ? . . . . . Because justice seems to *wink*, men suppose her *blind ;* because she delays punishment, they imagine she denies to punish them ; because she does not always reprove them for their sins, they suppose she always approves of their sins. But let such know, that the silent arrow can destroy as well as the roaring cannon. Though the patience of God be *lasting*, yet it is not *everlasting.* —*William Secher.*

Verses 11, 12, 13.—The atheist denies God's ordering of sublunary matters. " Tush, doth the Lord see, or is there knowledge in the Most High ? " making him a maimed Deity, without an eye of providence, or an arm of power, and at most restraining him only to matters above the clouds. But he that dares to confine the King to heaven, will soon after endeavour to depose him and fall at last flatly to deny him.—*Thomas Fuller.*

Verse 13.—" *He hath said in his heart, Thou wilt not require it.*"—As when the desperate pirate, ransacking and rifling a bottom, was told by the master, that though no law could touch him for the present, he should answer it at the day of judgment, replied, " If I may stay so long ere I come to it, I will take thee and thy vessel too." A conceit wherewith too many land-thieves and oppressors flatter themselves in their hearts, though they dare not utter it with their lips.—*Thomas Adams.*

Verses 13, 14.—What, do you think that God doth not remember our sins which we do not regard? for while we sin the score runs on, and the Judge setteth down in that table of remembrance, and his scroll reacheth up to heaven. Item, for lending to usury ; item, for racking of rents ; item, for starching thy ruffs ; item, for curling thy hair ; item, for painting thy face ; item, for selling of benefices ; item, for starving of souls ; item, for playing at cards ; item, for sleeping in the church ; item, for profaning the Sabbath-day, with a number more hath God to call to account, for every one must answer for himself. The fornicator, for taking of filthy pleasure ; the careless prelate, for murthering so many thousand souls ; the landlord, for getting money from his poor tenants by racking of his rents ; see the rest, all they shall come like very sheep when the trumpet shall sound, and the heaven and earth shall come to judgment against them ; when the heavens shall vanish like a scroll, and the earth shall consume like fire, and all the creatures standing against them ; the rocks shall cleave asunder and the mountains shake and the foundation of the earth shall tremble, and they shall say to the mountain, Cover us, fall upon us, and hide us from the presence of his anger and wrath, whom we have not cared to offend. But they shall not be covered and hid ; but then shall they go the back way, to the snakes and serpents, to be tormented of devils for ever.—*Henry Smith.*

Verse 14.—" *Thou hast seen it ; for thou beholdest mischief and spite, to requite it with thy hands,*" etc. This should be a terror to the wicked, to think that whatsoever they do, they do it in the *sight* of him that shall *judge* them, and call them to a strict account for every thought conceived against his majesty ; and therefore, it should make them afraid to sin ; because that when they burn with lust, and toil with hatred, when they scorn the just and wrong the innocent, they do all this, not only *in conspectu Dei*, within the compass of God's sight, but also in *sinu divinitatis*, in the bosom of that Deity, who, though he suffered them for a time to run on, like " a wild ass used to the wilderness," yet he will find them out at the last, and then cut them off and destroy them. And as this is terror unto the wicked, so it may be a comfort unto the godly to think that he who should hear their prayers and send them help, is so near unto them ; and it should move them to rely still upon him, because we are sure of his presence wherever we are.—*G. Williams*, 1636.

Verse 14.—" *The poor committeth himself unto thee.*" The awkwardness of our hearts to suffer comes much from distrust. An unbelieving soul treads upon the promise as a man upon ice ; at first going upon it he is full of fears and tumultuous thoughts lest it should crack. Now, daily resignation of thy heart, as it will give thee an occasion of conversing more with the thoughts of God's power, faithfulness, and other of his attributes (for want of familiarity with which, jealousies arise in our hearts when put to any great plunge), so also it will furnish thee with many experiences of the reality both of his attributes and promises ; which, though they need not any testimony from sense, to gain them credit with us, yet so much are we made of sense, so childish and weak is our faith, that we find our hearts much helped by those experiences we have had, to rely on him for the future. Look, therefore, carefully to this ; every morning leave thyself and ways in God's hand, as the phrase is. Psalm x. 14. And at night look again how well God hath looked to his trust, and sleep not till thou hast affected thy heart with his faithfulness, and laid a stronger charge on thy heart to trust itself again in God's keeping in the night. And when any breach is made, and seeming loss befalls thee in any enjoyment, which thou hast by faith insured of thy God, observe how God fills up that breach, and makes up that loss to thee ; and rest not till thou hast fully vindicated the good name of God to thy own heart. Be sure thou lettest no discontent or dissatisfaction lie upon thy spirit at God's dealings ; but chide thy heart for it, as David did his. Psalm xlii. And thus doing, with God's blessing, thou shalt keep thy faith in breath for a longer race, when called to run it.—*W. Gurnall.*

Verse 14.—" *Thou art the helper of the fatherless.*" God doth exercise a more special providence over men, as clothed with miserable circumstances ; and therefore among his other titles this is one, to be a " *helper of the fatherless.*" It is the argument the church used to express her return to God ; Hosea xiv. 3, " For in thee the fatherless find mercy." Now what greater comfort is there than this, that there is one presides in the world who is so wise he cannot be mistaken, so faithful he cannot deceive, so pitiful he cannot neglect his people, and so powerful that he can make stones even to be turned into bread if he please ! . . . . . God doth not govern the world only by his will as an absolute monarch, but by his wisdom and goodness as a tender father. It is not his greatest pleasure to show his sovereign power, or his inconceivable wisdom, but his immense goodness, to which he makes the other attributes subservient.—*Stephen Charnock.*

Verse 14.—" *Thou hast seen it,*" etc. If God did not see our ways, we might sin and go unpunished ; but forasmuch as he seeth them with purer eyes than to behold iniquity and approve it, he is engaged both in justice and honour to punish all that iniquity of our ways which he seeth or beholdeth. David makes this the very design of God's superintendency over the ways of men : " *Thou hast seen it : for thou beholdest mischief and spite to requite it with thy hand : the poor committeth himself unto thee ; thou art the helper of the fatherless.*" Thus the Psalmist represents the Lord as having taken a view or survey of the ways of men. " *Thou hast seen.*" What hath God seen ? Even all that wickedness and oppression of the poor spoken of in the former part of the Psalm, as also the blasphemy of the wicked against himself (verse 13), " *Wherefore doth the wicked contemn God ? he hath said in his heart, Thou wilt not require it.*" What saith the Psalmist concerning God, to this vain, confident man ? " *Thou,*" saith he, " *beholdest mischief and spite ;* " but to what purpose ? the next words tell us that—" *to requite it with thy hand.*" As thou hast seen what mischief they have done spitefully, so in due time thou wilt requite it righteously. The Lord is not a bare spectator, he is both a rewarder and an avenger. Therefore, from the ground of this truth, that the Lord seeth all our ways, and counteth all our steps, we, as the prophet exhorts (Isaiah iii. 10, 11), may " say to the righteous, that it shall be well with him : for they shall eat the fruit of their doings." We may also say, " Woe unto the wicked ! it shall be ill with him : for the reward of his hands shall be given him." Only idols which have eyes and see not, have hands and strike not.—*Joseph Caryl.*

Verse 14.—" *Thou hast seen it ; for thou beholdest mischief and spite, to requite it with thy hand : the poor committeth himself unto thee ; thou art the helper of the fatherless.*" Let the poor know that their God doth take care of them, to visit their sins with rods who spoil them, seeing they have forgotten that we are members one of another, and have invaded the goods of their brethren ; God will arm them against themselves, and beat them with their own staves ; either their own compassing and over-reaching wits shall consume their store, or their unthrifty posterity shall put wings upon their riches to make them fly ; or God shall not give them the blessing to take use of their wealth, but they shall leave to such as shall be merciful to the poor. Therefore let them follow the wise man's counsel (Eccles. x. 20), " Curse not the rich, no, not in thy bedchamber ; " let no railing and unchristian bitterness wrong a good cause ; let it be comfort enough to them that God is both their supporter and avenger. Is it not sufficient to lay all the storms of discontent against their oppressors, that God sees their affliction, and cometh down to deliver and avenge them ?—*Edward Marbury.*

Verse 14.—" *Thou hast seen it ; for thou beholdest mischief and spite, to requite it with thy hand,*" etc. God considers all your works and ways, and will not you consider the works, the ways of God ? Of this be sure, whether you consider the ways of God, his word-ways, or work-ways, of this be sure, God will consider your ways, certainly he will ; those ways of yours which in themselves are not worth the considering or looking upon, your sinful ways, though they are so vile, so abominable, that if yourselves did but look upon them and consider them, you would be utterly ashamed of them ; yea, though they are an abomination to God while he beholds them, yet he will behold and consider them. The Lord who is of purer eyes than to behold any the least iniquity, to approve it, will yet behold the greatest of your iniquities, and your impurest ways to consider them. " *Thou,*" said David, " *beholdest mischief and spite, to requite it :* " God beholdeth the foulest, dirtiest ways of men, their ways of oppression and unrighteousness, their ways of intemperance and lasciviousness, their ways of wrath and maliciousness, at once to detest, detect, and requite them. If God thus considereth the ways of men, even those filthy and crooked ways of men, should not men consider the holy, just and righteous ways of God ?—*Joseph Caryl.*

Verses 14—18.—" *God delights to help the poor.*" He loves to take part with the best, though the weakest side. Contrary to the course of most, who when a controversy arises use to stand in a kind of indifferency or neutrality, till they see which part is strongest, not which is justest. Now if there be any consideration (besides the cause) that draws or engages God, it is the weakness of the side. He joins with many, because they are weak, not with any, because they are strong; therefore he is called *the helper of the friendless, and with him the fatherless* (the orphans) *find mercy.* By fatherless we are not to understand such only whose parents are dead, but any one that is in distress; as Christ promiseth his disciples; "*I will not leave you orphans*," that is, helpless, and (as we translate) *comfortless;* though ye are as children without a father, yet I will be a father to you. Men are often like those clouds which dissolve into the sea; they send presents to the rich, and assist the strong; but God sends his rain upon the dry land, and lends his strength to those who are weak. . . . . . The prophet makes this report to God of himself (Isaiah xxv. 4): "*Thou hast been a strength to the poor,* a strength to the needy in his distress, a refuge from the storm," etc.—*Joseph Caryl.*

Verse 16.—"*The Lord is King for ever and ever: the heathen are perished out of his land.*" Such confidence and faith must appear to the world strange and unaccountable. It is like what his fellow citizens may be supposed to have felt (if the story be true) toward that man of whom it is recorded, that his powers of vision were so extraordinary, that he could distinctly see the fleet of the Carthaginians entering the harbour of Carthage, while he stood himself at Lilybœum, in Sicily. A man seeing across an ocean, and able to tell of objects so far off! he could feast his vision on what others saw not. Even thus does faith now stand at its Lilybœum, and see the long tossed fleet entering safely the desired haven, enjoying the bliss of that still distant day, as if it was already come.—*Andrew A. Bonar.*

Verse 17.—There is a humbling act of faith put forth in prayer. Others style it praying in humility; give me leave to style it praying in faith. In faith which sets the soul in the presence of that mighty God, and by the sight of him, which faith gives us, it is that we see our own vileness, sinfulness, and abhor ourselves, and profess ourselves unworthy of any, much less of those mercies we are to seek for. Thus the sight of God had wrought in the prophet (Isaiah vi. 5), "Then said I, Woe is me! for I am undone; because I am a man of unclean lips: for mine eyes have seen the King, the Lord of hosts." And holy Job speaks thus (Job xlii. 5, 6), "Now mine eye seeth thee: wherefore I abhor myself, and repent in dust and ashes." This is as great a requisite to prayer as any other act; I may say of it alone, as the apostle (James i. 7), that without it we shall receive nothing at the hands of God! God loves to fill empty vessels, he looks to broken hearts. In the Psalms how often do we read that God hears the prayers of the humble; which always involves and includes faith in it. Psalm ix. 12, "He forgetteth not the cry of the humble," and Psalm x. 17, "*Lord thou hast heard the desire of the humble: thou wilt prepare their heart, thou wilt cause thine ear to hear.*" To be deeply humbled is to have the heart prepared and fitted for God to hear the prayer; and therefore you find the Psalmist pleading *sub forma pauperis*, often repeating, "I am poor and needy." And this prevents our thinking much if God do not grant the particular thing we do desire. Thus also Christ himself in his great distress (Psalm xxii), doth treat God (verse 2), "O my God, I cry in the day-time, but thou hearest not; and in the night season am not silent. Our fathers trusted in thee. They cried unto thee, and were delivered. But I am a worm, and no man; reproached of men, and despised of the people; (verse 6) "and he was "heard" in the end "in what he feared." And these deep humblings of ourselves, being joined with vehement implorations upon the mercy of God to obtain, is reckoned into the account of praying by faith, both by God and Christ. Matt. viii.—*Thomas Goodwin.*

Verse 17.—"*Lord, thou hast heard the desire of the humble.*" A spiritual prayer is a *humble* prayer. Prayer is the asking of an alms, which requires humility. "The publican, standing afar off, would not lift up so much as his eyes unto heaven, but smote upon his breast, saying, God be merciful to me a sinner." Luke xviii. 13. God's incomprehensible glory may even amaze us and strike a holy consternation into us when we approach nigh unto him: "O my God, I am ashamed and blush to lift up my face to thee." Ezra ix. 6. It is comely to see a poor nothing lie prostrate at the feet of its Maker. "Behold now, I have taken upon me to speak unto the Lord, which am but dust and ashes." Gen. xviii. 27. The lower the heart descends, the higher the prayer ascends.—*Thomas Watson.*

Verse 17.—" *Lord, thou hast heard the desire of the humble,*" etc. How pleasant is it, that these benefits, which are of so great a value both on their own account, and that of the divine benignity from whence they come, should be delivered into our hands, marked, as it were, with this grateful inscription, *that they have been obtained by prayer !*—*Robert Leighton.*

Verse 17.—" *The desire of the humble.*" Prayer is the offering up of our desires to God in the name of Christ, for such things as are agreeable to his will. It is an offering of our *desires.* Desires are the soul and life of prayer ; words are but the body ; now as the body without the soul is dead, so are prayers unless they are animated with our desires : " *Lord, thou hast heard the desire of the humble.*" God heareth not words, but *desires.*—*Thomas Watson.*

Verse 17.—God's choice acquaintances are humble men.—*Robert Leighton.*

Verse 17.—He that sits nearest the dust, sits nearest heaven.—*Andrew Gray, of Glasgow,* 1616.

Verse 17.—There is a kind of omnipotency in prayer, as having an interest and prevalency with God's omnipotency. It hath loosed iron chains (Acts xvi. 25, 26) ; it hath opened iron gates (Acts xii. 5—10) ; it hath unlocked the windows of heaven (1 Kings xviii. 41) ; it hath broken the bars of death (John xi. 40, 43). Satan hath three titles given in the Scriptures, setting forth his malignity against the church of God : a dragon, to note his malice ; a serpent, to note his subtlety ; and a lion, to note his strength. But none of all these can stand before prayer. The greatest malice of Haman sinks under the prayer of Esther ; the deepest policy, the counsel of Ahithophel, withers before the prayer of David ; the largest army, a host of a thousand Ethiopians, run away like cowards before the prayer of Asa.— *Edward Reynolds,* 1599—1676.

Verse 18.—" *To judge the fatherless and the oppressed,*" etc. The tears of the poor fall down upon their cheeks, *et ascendunt ad cœlum,* and go up to heaven and cry for vengeance before God, the judge of widows, the father of widows and orphans. Poor people be oppressed even by laws. Woe worth to them that make evil laws against the poor, what shall be to them that hinder and mar good laws ? What will ye do in the day of great vengeance when God shall visit you ? he saith he will hear the tears of the poor woman, when he goeth on visitation. For their sake he will hurt the judge, be he never so high, he will for widows' sakes change realms, bring them into temptation, pluck his judges' skins over their heads. Cambyses was a great emperor, such another as our master is, he had many lord deputies, lord presidents, and lieutenants under him. It is a great while ago since I read the history. It chanced he had under him in one of his dominions a briber, a gift-taker, a gratifier of rich men ; he followed gifts as fast as he that followed the pudding ; a handmaker in his office, to make his son a great man, as the old saying is " Happy is the child whose father goeth to the devil." The cry of the poor widow came to the emperor's ear, and caused him to slay the judge quick, and laid his skin in his chair of judgment, that all judges that should give judgment afterward, should sit in the same skin. Surely it was a goodly sign, a goodly monument, the sign of the judge's skin. I pray God we may once see the sign of the skin in England. Ye will say, peradventure, that this is cruelly and uncharitably spoken. No, no ; I do it charitably, for a love I bear to my country. God saith, " I will visit." God hath two visitations ; the first is when he revealeth his word by preachers ; and where the first is accepted, the second cometh not. The second visitation is vengeance. He went to visitation when he brought the judge's skin over his ears. If this word be despised, he cometh with the second visitation with vengeance.—*Hugh Latimer,* 1480—1555.

Verse 18.—" *Man of the earth,*" etc. In the eighth Psalm (which is a circular Psalm ending as it did begin, " O Lord our God, how excellent is thy name in all the world ! " That whithersoever we turn our eyes, upwards or downwards, we may see ourselves beset with his glory round about), how doth the prophet base and discountenance the nature and whole race of man ; as may appear by his disdainful and derogatory interrogation, "What is man that thou art mindful of him ; and the Son of Man, that thou regardest him ? " In the ninth Psalm, " Rise, Lord ; let not man have the upper hand ; let the nations be judged in thy sight. Put them in fear, O Lord, that the heathen may know themselves to be but men." Further, in the tenth Psalm, " Thou judgest the fatherless and the poor, that the man of the earth do no more violence."

The Psalms, as they go in order, so, methinks they grow in strength, and each hath a weightier force to throw down our presumption. 1. We are "men," and the "sons of men," to show our descent and propagation. 2. "Men in our own knowledge," to show that conscience and experience of infirmity doth convict us. 3. "Men of the earth," to show our orginal matter whereof we are framed. In the twenty-second Psalm, he addeth more disgrace; for either in his own name, regarding the misery and contempt wherein he was held, or in the person of Christ, whose figure he was, as if it were a robbery for him to take upon him the nature of man, he falleth to a lower style, *at ego sum vermis et non vir ;* but I am a worm, and no man. For as corruption is the father of all flesh, so are the worms his brethren and sisters, according to the old verse—

> "First man, next worms, then stench and loathsomeness,
> Thus man to no man alters by changes."

Abraham, the father of the faithful (Genesis xviii.), sifteth himself into the coarsest man that can be, and resolveth his nature into the elements whereof it first rose. "Behold I have begun to speak to my Lord, being dust and ashes." And if any of the children of Abraham, who succeed him in the faith, or any of the children of Adam, who succeed him in the flesh, thinketh otherwise, let him know that there is a threefold cord twisted by the finger of God, that shall tie him to his first original, though he contend till his heart break. "O earth, earth, earth, hear the word of the Lord" (Jer. xxii); that is, earth by creation, earth by continuance, earth by resolution. Thou camest earth, thou remainest earth, and to earth thou must return.—*John King.*

Verse 18.—"*The man of the earth.*" Man dwelling in the earth, and made of earth.—*Thomas Wilcocks.*

HINTS TO PREACHERS.

Verse 1.—The answer to these questions furnishes a noble topic for an experimental sermon. Let me suggest that the question is not to be answered in the same manner in all cases. Past sin, trials of graces, strengthening of faith, discovery of depravity, instruction, etc., etc., are varied reasons for the hiding of our Father's face.

Verse 2.—Religious persecution in all its phases based on pride.

Verse 3.—God's hatred of covetousness : show its justice.

Verse 4.—Pride the barrier in the way of conversion.

Verse 4 (last clause).—Thoughts in which God is not, weighed and condemned.

Verse 5.—"*Thy judgments are far above out of his sight.*" Moral inability of men to appreciate the character and acts of God.

Verse 6.—The vain confidence of sinners.

Verse 8.—Dangers of godly men, or the snares in the way of believers.

Verse 9.—The ferocity, craftiness, strength, and activity of Satan.

Verse 9 (last clause).—The Satanic fisherman, his art, diligence, success, etc.

Verse 10.—Designing humility unmasked.

Verse 11.—Divine omniscience and the astounding presumption of sinners.

Verse 12.—"*Arise, O Lord.*" A prayer needful, allowable, seasonable, etc.

Verse 13 (first clause).—An astounding fact, and a reasonable enquiry.

Verse 13.—Future retribution : doubts concerning it. 1. By whom indulged : "*the wicked.*" II. Where fostered : "*in his heart.*" III. For what purpose : *quieting of conscience,* etc. IV. With what practical tendency : "*contemn God.*" He who disbelieves hell distrusts heaven.

Verses 13, 14.—Divine government in the world. I. Who doubt it ? and why ? II. Who believe it ? and what does this faith cause them to do ?

Verse 14 (last clause).—A plea for orphans.

Verse 16.—The Eternal Kingship of Jehovah.

Verse 17 (first clause).—I. The Christian's character—"*humble.*" II. An attribute of the Christian's whole life—"*desire :*" he desires more holiness, communion, knowledge, grace, and usefulness ; and then he desires glory. III. The Christian's great blessedness—"*Lord, thou hast heard the desire of the humble.*"

Verse 17 (whole verse).—I. Consider the nature of gracious desires. II. Their *origin.* III. Their *result.* The three sentences readily suggest these divisions, and the subject may be very profitable.

PSALM XI.

SUBJECT.—*Charles Simeon gives an excellent summary of this Psalm in the following sentences :—" The Psalms are a rich repository of experimental knowledge. David, at the different periods of his life, was placed in almost every situation in which a believer, whether rich or poor, can be placed ; and in these heavenly compositions he delineates all the workings of the heart. He introduces, too, the sentiments and conduct of the various persons who were accessory either to his troubles or his joys ; and thus sets before us a compendium of all that is passing in the hearts of men throughout the world. When he penned this Psalm he was under persecution from Saul, who sought his life, and hunted him ' as a partridge upon the mountains.' His timid friends were alarmed for his safety, and recommended him to flee to some mountain where he had a hiding-place, and thus to conceal himself from the rage of Saul. But David, being strong in faith, spurned the idea of resorting to any such pusillanimous expedients, and determined confidently to repose his trust in God."*

To assist us to remember this short, but sweet Psalm, we will give it the name of " THE SONG OF THE STEDFAST."

DIVISION. *From 1 to 3, David describes the temptation with which he was assailed, and from 4 to 7, the arguments by which his courage was sustained.*

EXPOSITION.

IN the LORD put I my trust : how say ye to my soul, Flee *as* a bird to your mountain ?

2 For, lo, the wicked bend *their* bow, they make ready their arrow upon the string, that they may privily shoot at the upright in heart.

3 If the foundations be destroyed, what can the righteous do ?

These verses contain an account of a temptation to distrust God, with which David was, upon some unmentioned occasion, greatly exercised. It may be, that in the days when he was in Saul's court, he was advised to flee at a time when this flight would have been charged against him as a breach of duty to the king, or a proof of personal cowardice. His case was like that of Nehemiah, when his enemies, under the garb of friendship, hoped to entrap him by advising him to escape for his life. Had he done so, they could then have found a ground of accusation. Nehemiah bravely replied, " Shall such a man as I flee ? " and David, in a like spirit, refuses to retreat, exclaiming, " *In the Lord put I my trust : how say ye to my soul, Flee as a bird to your mountain ?* " When Satan cannot overthrow us by presumption, how craftily will he seek to ruin us by distrust ! He will employ our dearest friends to argue us out of our confidence, and he will use such plausible logic, that unless we once for all assert our immovable trust in Jehovah, he will make us like the timid bird which flies to the mountain whenever danger presents itself. How forcibly the case is put ! The bow is bent, the arrow is fitted to the string : " Flee, flee, thou defenceless bird, thy safety lies in flight ; begone, for thine enemies will send their shafts into thy heart ; haste, haste, for soon wilt thou be destroyed ! " David seems to have felt the force of the advice, for it came home *to his soul ;* but yet he would not yield, but would rather dare the danger than exhibit a distrust in the Lord his God. Doubtless, the perils which encompassed David were great and imminent ; it was quite true that his enemies were *ready* to *shoot privily* at him ; it was equally correct that the very *foundations* of law and justice were *destroyed* under Saul's unrighteous government : but what were all these things to the man whose trust was in God alone ? He could brave the dangers, could escape the enemies, and defy the injustice which surrounded him. His answer to the question, " What can the righteous do ? " would be the counter-question, " What cannot they do ? " When prayer engages God on our side, and when faith secures the fulfilment of the promise, what cause can there be for flight, however cruel and mighty our enemies ? With a sling and a stone, David had smitten a giant before whom the whole hosts of Israel were trembling, and the Lord, who delivered him from the uncircumcised Philistine, could surely deliver him from King Saul and his myrmidons. There is no such word as "impossibility" in the language of faith; that martial grace knows how to fight and conquer, but she knows not how to flee.

4 The LORD *is* in his holy temple, the LORD's throne *is* in heaven : his eyes behold, his eyelids try, the children of men.

5 The LORD trieth the righteous : but the wicked and him that loveth violence his soul hateth.

6 Upon the wicked he shall rain snares, fire and brimstone, and an horrible tempest : *this shall be* the portion of their cup.

7 For the righteous LORD loveth righteousness ; his countenance doth behold the upright.

David here declares the great source of his unflinching courage. He borrows his light from heaven—from the great central orb of deity. The God of the believer is never far from him ; he is not merely the God of the mountain fastnesses, but of the dangerous valleys and battle plains.

"*Jehovah is in his holy temple.*" The heavens are above our heads in all regions of the earth, and so is the Lord ever near to us in every state and condition. This is a very strong reason why we should not adopt the vile suggestions of distrust. There is one who pleads his precious blood in our behalf in the temple above, and there is one upon the throne who is never deaf to the intercession of his Son. Why, then, should we fear? What plots can men devise which Jesus will not discover? Satan has doubtless desired to have us, that he may sift us as wheat, but Jesus is in the temple praying for us, and how can our faith fail? What attempts can the wicked make which Jehovah shall not behold? And since he is in his holy temple, delighting in the sacrifice of his Son, will he not defeat every device, and send us a sure deliverance?

"*Jehovah's throne is in the heavens ;*" he reigns supreme. Nothing can be done in heaven, or earth, or hell, which he doth not ordain and over-rule. He is the world's great Emperor. Wherefore, then, should we flee? If we trust this King of kings, is not this enough? Cannot he deliver us without our cowardly retreat? Yes, blessed be the Lord our God, we can salute him as Jehovah-nissi ; in his name we set up our banners, and, instead of flight, we once more raise the shout of war.

"*His eyes behold.*" The eternal Watcher never slumbers ; his eyes never know a sleep. "*His eyelids try the children of men :*" he narrowly inspects their actions, words and thoughts. As men, when intently and narrowly inspecting some very minute object, almost close their eyelids to exclude every other object, so will the Lord look all men through and through. God sees each man as much and as perfectly as if there were no other creature in the universe. He sees us always ; he never removes his eye from us ; he sees us entirely, reading the recesses of the soul as readily as the glancing of the eye. Is not this a sufficient ground of confidence, and an abundant answer to the solicitations of despondency? My danger is not hid from him ; he knows my extremity, and I may rest assured that he will not suffer me to perish while I rely alone on him. Wherefore, then, should I take the wings of the timid bird, and flee from the dangers which beset me.

"*The Lord trieth the righteous :*" he doth not hate them, but only tries them. They are precious to him, and therefore he refines them with afflictions. None of the Lord's children may hope to escape from trial, nor, indeed, in our right minds, would any of us desire to do so, for trial is the channel of many blessings.

> "'Tis my happiness below
> Not to live without the cross ;
> But the Saviour's power to know,
> Sanctifying every loss.
>
> * * * * *
>
> Trials make the promise sweet ;
> Trials give new life to prayer ;
> Trials bring me to his feet—
> Lay me low, and keep me there.

> Did I meet no trials here—
> No chastisement by the way—
> Might I not, with reason, fear
> I should prove a cast-away!
>
> Bastards may escape the rod,
> Sunk in earthly vain delight;
> But the true-born child of God
> Must not—would not, if he might."
>
> *William Cowper.*

Is not this a very cogent reason why we should not distrustfully endeavour to shun a trial ?—for in so doing we are seeking to avoid a blessing.

"*But the wicked and him that loveth violence his soul hateth :*" why, then, shall I flee from these wicked men ? If God hateth them, I will not fear them. Haman was very great in the palace until he lost favour, but when the king abhorred him, how bold were the meanest attendants to suggest the gallows for the man at whom they had often trembled ! Look at the black mark upon the faces of our persecutors, and we shall not run away from them. If God is in the quarrel as well as ourselves, it would be foolish to question the result, or avoid the conflict. Sodom and Gomorrah perished by a fiery hail, and by a brimstone shower from heaven ; so shall all the ungodly. They may gather together like Gog and Magog to battle, but the Lord will rain upon them " an overflowing rain, and great hailstones, fire, and brimstone :" Ezek. xxxviii. 22. Some expositors think that in the term "horrible tempest," there is in the Hebrew an allusion to that burning, suffocating wind, which blows across the Arabian deserts, and is known by the name of Simoom. "A burning storm," Lowth calls it, while another great commentator reads it " wrathwind ;" in either version the language is full of terrors. What a tempest will that be which shall overwhelm the despisers of God ! Oh ! what a shower will that be which shall pour out itself for ever upon the defenceless heads of impenitent sinners in hell ! Repent, ye rebels, or this fiery deluge shall soon surround you. Hell's horrors shall be your inheritance, your entailed estate, " the portion of your cup." The dregs of that cup you shall wring out, and drink for ever. A drop of hell is terrible, but what must a full cup of torment be ? Think of it— a cup of misery, but not a drop of mercy. O people of God, how foolish is it to fear the faces of men who shall soon be faggots in the fire of hell ! Think of their end, their fearful end, and all fear of them must be changed into contempt of their threatenings and pity for their miserable estate.

The delightful contrast of the last verse is well worthy of our observation, and it affords another overwhelming reason why we should be stedfast, unmovable, not carried away with fear, or led to adopt carnal expedients in order to avoid trial. "*For the righteous Lord loveth righteousness.*" It is not only his office to defend it, but his nature to love it. He would deny himself if he did not defend the just. It is essential to the very being of God that he should be just ; fear not, then, the end of all your trials, but " be just, and fear not." God approves, and, if men oppose, what matters it ? "*His countenance doth behold the upright.*" We need never be out of countenance, for God countenances us. He observes, he approves, he delights in the upright. He sees his own image in them, an image of his own fashioning, and therefore with complacency he regards them. Shall we dare to put forth our hand unto iniquity in order to escape affliction ? Let us have done with by-ways and short turnings, and let us keep to that fair path of right along which Jehovah's smile shall light us. Are we tempted to put our light under a bushel, to conceal our religion from our neighbours ? Is it suggested to us that there are ways of avoiding the cross, and shunning the reproach of Christ ? Let us not hearken to the voice of the charmer, but seek an increase of faith, that we may wrestle with principalities and powers, and follow the Lord, fully going without the camp, bearing his reproach. Mammon, the flesh, the devil, will all whisper in our ear, " Flee as a bird to your mountain ;" but let us come forth and defy them all. " Resist the devil, and he will flee from you." There is no room or reason for retreat. Advance ! Let the vanguard push on ! To the front ! all ye powers and passions of our soul. On ! on ! in God's name, on ! for " the Lord of hosts is with us ; the God of Jacob is our refuge."

EXPLANATORY NOTES AND QUAINT SAYINGS.

Whole Psalm.—The most probable account of the occasion of this Psalm is that given by Amyraldus. He thinks it was composed by David while he was in the court of Saul, at a time when the hostility of the king was beginning to show itself, and before it had broken out into open persecution. David's friends, or those professing to be so, advised him to flee to his native mountains for a time, and remain in retirement, till the king should show himself more favourable. David does not at that time accept the counsel, though afterwards he seems to have followed it. This Psalm applies itself to the establishment of the church against the calumnies of the world and the compromising counsel of man, in that confidence which is to be placed in God the Judge of all.—*W. Wilson, D.D., in loc.,* 1860.

Whole Psalm.—If one may offer to make a modest conjecture, it is not improbable this Psalm might be composed on the sad murder of the priests by Saul (1 Sam. xxii. 19), when after the slaughter of Abimelech, the high priest, Doeg, the Edomite, by command from Saul, " slew in one day fourscore and five persons which wore a linen ephod." I am not so carnal as to build the spiritual church of the Jews on the material walls of the priests' city at Nob (which then by Doeg was smitten with the edge of the sword), but this is most true, that " knowledge must preserve the people ; " and (Mal. ii. 7), "The priests' lips shall preserve knowledge;" and then it is easy to conclude, what an earthquake this massacre might make in the *foundations of religion.—Thomas Fuller.*

Whole Psalm.—Notice how remarkably the whole Psalm corresponds with the deliverance of Lot from Sodom. This verse, with the angel's exhortation, " Escape to the mountains, lest thou be consumed," and Lot's reply, " I cannot escape to the mountains, lest some evil take me and I die." Genesis xix. 17—19. And again, " *The Lord's seat is in heaven,* and *upon the ungodly he shall rain snares, fire, brimstone, storm and tempest,*" with " Then the Lord rained upon Sodom and Gomorrah brimstone and fire out of heaven : " and again, " *His countenance will behold the thing that is just,*" with " Delivered just Lot . . . . for that righteous man vexed his righteous soul with their ungodly deeds." 2 Peter ii. 7, 8.—*Cassiodorus* (A.D., 560) *in John Mason Neale's " Commentary on the Psalms, from Primitive and Mediæval Writers,"* 1860.

Whole Psalm.—The combatants at the Lake Thrasymene are said to have been so engrossed with the conflict, that neither party perceived the convulsions of nature that shook the ground—

> " An earthquake reeled unheedingly away,
> None felt stern nature rocking at his feet."

From a nobler cause, it is thus with the soldiers of the Lamb. They believe, and, therefore, make no haste ; nay, they can scarcely be said to feel earth's convulsions as other men, because their eager hope presses forward to the issue at the advent of the Lord.—*Andrew A. Bonar.*

Verse 1.—"*I trust in the Lord : how do ye say to my soul, Swerve on to your mountain like a bird ?*" (others, " *O thou bird.*") Saul and his adherents mocked and jeered David with such taunting speeches, as conceiving that he knew no other shift or refuge, but so betaking himself unto wandering and lurking on the mountains ; hopping, as it were, from one place to another like a silly bird ; but they thought to ensnare and take him well enough for all that, not considering God who was David's comfort, rest and refuge.—*Theodore Haak's " Translation of the Dutch Annotations, as ordered by the Synod of Dort, in 1618."* London, 1657.

Verse 1.—" *With Jehovah I have taken shelter ; how say ye to my soul, Flee, sparrows, to your hill ?* " " *Your hill,*" that hill from which you say your help cometh : a sneer. Repair to that boasted hill, which may indeed give you the help which it gives the sparrow : a shelter against the inclemencies of a stormy sky, no defence against our power.—*Samuel Horsley, in loc.*

Verse 1.—" *In the Lord put I my trust : how say ye to my soul, Flee as a bird to your mountain ?* " The holy confidence of the saints in the hour of great trial is beautifully illustrated by the following ballad which Anne Askew, who was burned at Smithfield in 1546, made and sang when she was in Newgate :—

Like as the armèd knight,
Appointed to the field,
With this world will I fight,
And Christ shall be my shield.

Faith is that weapon strong,
Which will not fail at need :
My foes, therefore, among
Therewith will I proceed.

As it is had in strength
And force of Christe's way,
It will prevail at length,
Though all the devils say nay.

Faith in the fathers old
Obtained righteousness ;
Which make me very bold
To fear no world's distress.

I now rejoice in heart,
And hope bids me do so ;
For Christ will take my part,
And ease me of my woe.

Thou say'st Lord, whoso knock,
To them wilt thou attend :
Undo therefore the lock,
And thy strong power send.

More enemies now I have
Than hairs upon my head :
Let them not me deprave,
But fight thou in my stead.

On thee my care I cast,
For all their cruel spite :
I set not by their haste ;
For thou art my delight.

I am not she that list
My anchor to let fall
For every drizzling mist,
My ship substantial.

Not oft use I to write,
In prose, nor yet in rhyme ;
Yet will I shew one sight
That I saw in my time.

I saw a royal throne,
Where justice should have sit,
But in her stead was one
Of moody, cruel wit.

Absorbed was righteousness.
As of the raging flood :
Satan, in his excess,
Sucked up the guiltless blood.

Then thought I, Jesus Lord,
When thou shall judge us all,
Hard it is to record
On these men what will fall.

Yet, Lord, I thee desire,
For that they do to me,
Let them not taste the hire
Of their iniquity.

Verse 1.—" *How say ye to my soul, Flee as a bird to your mountain ?* " We may observe, that David is much pleased with the metaphor in frequently comparing himself to a bird, and that of several sorts : first, to an eagle (Psalm ciii. 5), " My youth is renewed like the eagle's ; " sometimes to an owl (Psalm cii. 6), " I am like an owl in the desert ; " sometimes to a pelican, in the same verse, " Like a pelican in the wilderness ; " sometimes to a sparrow (Psalm cii. 7), " I watch, and am as a sparrow ; " sometimes to a partridge, " As when one doth hunt a partridge." I cannot say that he doth compare himself to a dove, but he would compare himself (Psalm lv. 6), " O that I had the wings of a dove, for then I would flee away, and be at rest." Some will say, How is it possible that birds of so different a feather should all so fly together as to meet in the character of David ? To whom we answer, That no two men can more differ one from another, than the same servant of God at several times differeth from himself. David in prosperity, when commanding, was like an *eagle ;* in adversity, when contemned, like an *owl ;* in devotion, when retired, like a *pelican ;* in solitariness, when having no company, like a *sparrow ;* in persecution, when fearing too much company (of *Saul*), like a *partridge.* This general metaphor of a *bird,* which David so often used on himself, his enemies in the first verse of this Psalm used on him, though not particularising the kind thereof : " *Flee as a bird to your mountain ;* " that is, speedily betake thyself to thy God, in whom thou hopest for succour and security.

Seeing this counsel was both good in itself, and good at this time, why doth David seem so angry and displeased thereat ? Those his words, " *Why say you to my soul, Flee as a bird to your mountain ?* " import some passion, at leastwise, a disgust of the advice. It is answered, David was not offended with the counsel, but with the manner of the propounding thereof. His enemies did it ironically in a gibing, jeering way, as if his flying thither were to no purpose, and he unlikely to find there the safety he sought for. However, David was not hereby put out of conceit with the counsel, beginning this Psalm with this his firm resolution, " *In the Lord put I my trust : how say ye then to my soul,*" etc. Learn we from hence, when men give us good counsel in a jeering way, let us take the counsel, and practise it ; and leave them the jeer to be punished for it. Indeed, corporal cordials may be envenomed by being wrapped up in poisoned papers ; not so good spiritual advice where the good matter receives no infection from the ill manner of the delivery thereof. Thus, when the chief priests mocked our Saviour (Matt. xxvii. 43), " He trusteth in God, let him deliver him now if he will have him." Christ trusted in God never a whit the less for the fleere and flout which their profaneness was pleased to bestow upon him. Otherwise, if men's mocks should make us to undervalue good counsel, we might in this age be mocked out of our God, and Christ, and Scripture, and heaven ; the apostle Jude, verse 18, having foretold that in the last times there should be mockers, walking after their own lusts.—*Thomas Fuller.*

Verse 1.—It is as great an offence to make a new, as to deny the true God. *" In the Lord put I my trust ; "* how then *" say ye unto my soul "* (ye seducers of souls), *" that she should fly unto the mountains as a bird ; "* to seek unnecessary and foreign helps, as if the Lord alone were not sufficient ?   " The Lord is my rock, and my fortress, and he that delivereth me, my God, and my strength ; in him will I trust : my shield, the horn of my salvation, and my refuge. I will call upon the Lord, who is worthy to be praised, so shall I be safe from mine enemies."   " Whom have I in heaven but thee," amongst those thousands of angels and saints, what Michael or Gabriel, what Moses or Samuel, what Peter, what Paul ? " and there is none in earth that I desire in comparison of thee."—*John King,* 1608.

Verse 1.—In temptations of inward trouble and terror, it is not convenient to dispute the matter with Satan. David in Psalm xlii. 11, seems to correct himself for his mistake ; his soul was cast down within him, and for the cure of that temptation, he had prepared himself by arguments for a dispute ; but perceiving himself in a wrong course, he calls off his soul from disquiet to an immediate application to God and the promises, " Trust still in God, for I shall yet praise him ; " but here he is more aforehand with his work ; for while his enemies were acted by Satan to discourage him, he rejects the temptation at first, before it settled upon his thoughts, and chaseth it away as a thing that he would not give ear to. *" In the Lord put I my trust : how say ye to my soul, Flee as a bird to your mountain ? "* And there are weighty reasons that should dissuade us from entering the lists with Satan in temptation of inward trouble.—*Richard Gilpin.*

Verse 1.—The shadow will not cool except in it. What good to have the shadow though of a mighty rock, when we sit in the open sun ? To have almighty power engaged for us, and we to throw ourselves out of it, by bold sallies in the mouth of temptation ! The saints' falls have been when they have run out of their trench and stronghold ; for, like the conies, they are a weak people in themselves, and their strength lies in the rock of God's almightiness, which is their habitation.— *William Gurnall.*

Verse 1.—The saints of old would not accept deliverances on base terms. They scorned to fly away for the enjoyment of rest except it were with the wings of a dove, covered with silver innocence. As willing were many of the martyrs to die, as to dine. The tormentors were tired in torturing Blandina. " We are ashamed, O Emperor ! The Christians laugh at your cruelty, and grow the more resolute," said one of Julian's nobles. This the heathen counted obstinacy ; but they knew not the power of the Spirit, nor the secret armour of proof which saints wear about their hearts.—*John Trapp.*

Verse 2.—*" For, lo, the wicked bend their bow,"* etc. This verse presents an unequal combat betwixt *armed power, advantaged with policy,* on the one side ; and *naked innocence* on the other. First, *armed power :* " *They bend their bows, and make ready their arrows,*" being all the artillery of that age ; secondly, *advantaged with policy :* " *that they may privily shoot,*" to surprise them with an ambush unawares, probably pretending amity and friendship unto them ; thirdly, *naked innocence :* if innocence may be termed naked, which is its own armour ; *" at the upright in heart."*—*Thomas Fuller.*

Verse 2.—*" For, lo, the ungodly bend their bow, and make ready their arrows within the quiver : that they may privily shoot at them which are true of heart."* The plottings of the chief priests and Pharisees that they might take Jesus by subtlety and kill him. They bent their bow, when they hired Judas Iscariot for the betrayal of his Master ; they made ready their arrows within the quiver when they sought " false witnesses against Jesus to put him to death." Matt. xxvi. 59. *" Them which are true of heart."* Not alone the Lord himself, the only true and righteous, but his apostles, and the long line of those who should faithfully cleave to him from that time to this. And as with the Master, so with the servants : witness the calumnies and the revilings that from the time of Joseph's accusation by his mistress till the present day, have been the lot of God's people.—*Michael Ayguan, 1416, in J. M. Neale's Commentary.*

Verse 2.—"*That they may secretly shoot at them which are upright in heart.*" They bear not their bows and arrows as scarecrows in a garden of cucumbers, to fray, but *to shoot*, not at stakes, but men ; their arrows are *jacula mortifera* (Psalm vii.), deadly arrows, and lest they should fail to hit, they take advantage of the dark, of privacy and secrecy ; they shoot *privily.* Now this is the covenant of hell itself. For what created power in the earth is able to dissolve that work which *cruelty* and *subtlety*, like Simeon and Levi, brothers in evil, are combined and confederate to bring to pass ? Where subtlety is ingenious, insidious to invent, cruelty barbarous to execute, subtlety giveth counsel, cruelty giveth the stroke. Subtlety ordereth the time, the place, the means, accommodateth, concinnateth circumstances ; cruelty undertaketh the act : subtlety hideth the knife, cruelty cutteth the throat : subtlety with a cunning head layeth the ambush, plotteth the train, the stratagem ; and cruelty with as savage a heart, sticketh not at the dreadfullest, direfullest objects, ready to wade up to the ankles, the neck, in a whole red sea of human, yea, country blood : how fearful is their plight that are thus assaulted !—*John King.*

Verse 3.—"*If the foundations be destroyed, what can the righteous do ?*" But now we are met with a giant objection, which with Goliath must be removed, or else it will obstruct our present proceedings. Is it possible that the *foundations of religion* should be destroyed ? Can God be in so long a sleep, yea, so long a lethargy, as patiently to permit the ruins thereof ? If he looks on, and yet doth not see these *foundations* when destroyed, where then is his *omnisciency* ? If he seeth it, and cannot help it, where then is his *omnipotency* ? If he seeth it, can help it, and will not, where then is his *goodness* and *mercy* ? Martha said to Jesus (John xi. 21), " Lord, if thou hadst been here, my brother had not died. " But many will say, Were God effectually present in the world with his aforesaid attributes, surely the *foundations* had not *died*, had not been *destroyed.* We answer negatively, that it is impossible that the *foundations* of religion should ever be *totally* and *finally destroyed*, either in relation to the church in general, or in reference to every true and lively member thereof. For the first, we have an express promise of Christ. Matt. xvi. 18. "The gates of hell shall not prevail against it." *Fundamenta tamen stant inconcussa Sionis.* And as for every particular Christian (2 Tim. ii. 19), " Nevertheless, the foundation of God standeth sure, having this seal, the Lord knoweth them that are his." However, though for the reasons aforementioned in the objections (the inconsistency thereof with the attributes of God's omnipotency, omnisciency, and goodness), the *foundations* can never totally and finally, yet may they partially be destroyed, *quoad gradum*, in a fourfold degree, as followeth. First, *in the desires and utmost endeavours of wicked men.*

They bring their
$\begin{cases} 1. \textit{ Hoc velle,} \\ 2. \textit{ Hoc agere,} \\ 3. \textit{ Totum posse.} \end{cases}$

If they *destroy* not the foundations, it is no thanks to them, seeing all the world will bear them witness they have done *their best* (that is, *their worst*), what their might and malice could perform. Secondly, *in their own vainglorious imaginations :* they may not only vainly boast, but also verily believe that they have *destroyed the foundations.* Applicable to this purpose, is that high rant of the Roman emperor (Luke ii. 1) : " And it came to pass in those days, that there went out a decree from Cæsar Augustus, that all the world should be taxed." All the world ! whereas he had, though much, not all in Europe, little in Asia, less in Africa, none in America, which was so far from being conquered, it was not so much as known to the Romans. But *hyperbole* is not a figure, but the ordinary language of pride ; because indeed Augustus had very much, he proclaimeth himself to have all the world. . . . Thirdly, *the foundations may be destroyed* as to all outward visible illustrious apparition. The church in persecution is like unto a ship in a tempest ; down go all their masts, yea, sometimes for the more speed they are forced to cut them down : not a piece of canvas to play with the winds, no sails to be seen; they lie close knotted to the very keel, that the tempest may have the less power upon them, though when the storm is over, they can hoist up their sails as high, and spread their canvas as broad as ever before. So the church in the time of persecution *feared,* but especially *felt,* loseth all gayness and gallantry which may attract and allure the eyes of beholders, and contenteth itself with its own secrecy. In a word, on the work-days of affliction she weareth her worst clothes, whilst her best are laid up in her wardobe, in sure and certain hope that God will give her a *holy* and *happy day,* when with joy she shall wear her best garments. Lastly they may be *destroyed* in the *jealous apprehensions* of the best saints and servants of God, especially in their melancholy fits. I will instance in no puny, but in a star of the first magnitude and greatest eminency, even Elijah himself complaining (1 Kings xix. 10) : " And I, even I only, am left ; and they seek my life, to take it away."—*Thomas Fuller.*

Verse 3.—" If." It is the only word of comfort in the text, that what is said is not *positive, but suppositive ;* not thetical, but hypothetical. And yet this comfort which is but a spark (at which we would willingly kindle our hopes), is quickly sadded with a double consideration. First, impossible suppositions produce impossible consequences, "As is the mother, so is the daughter." Therefore, surely God's Holy Spirit would not suppose such a thing but what was feasible and possible, but what either had, did, or might come to pass. Secondly, the Hebrew word is not the conditional *im, si, si forte,* but *chi, quia, quoniam,* because, and (although here it be favourably rendered *if*), seemeth to import, more therein, that the sad case had already happened in David's days. I see, therefore, that this *if,* our only hope in the text, is likely to prove with Job's friends, but a miserable comforter. Well, it is good to know the worst of things, that we may provide ourselves accordingly ; and therefore let us behold this doleful case, not as doubtful, but as done ; not as feared, but felt ; not as suspected, but at this time really come to pass.—*Thomas Fuller.*

Verse 3.—" If the foundations," etc. My text is an answer to a tacit objection which some may raise ; namely, that the righteous are wanting to themselves, and by their own easiness and inactivity (not daring and doing so much as they might and ought), betray themselves to that bad condition. In whose defence David shows, that if God in his wise will and pleasure seeth it fitting, for reasons best known to himself to suffer religion to be reduced to terms of extremity, it is not placed in the power of the best man alive to remedy and redress the same. *" If the foundations be destroyed, what can the righteous do ? "* My text is hung about with *mourning,* as for a funeral sermon, and contains: First, a sad case supposed, *" If the foundations be destroyed."* Secondly, a sad question propounded, *" What can the righteous do ? "* Thirdly, a sad answer implied, namely, that they can do just nothing, as to the point of re-establishing the destroyed foundation.—*Thomas Fuller.*

Verse 3.—" If the foundations be destroyed," etc. The civil foundation of a nation or people, is their laws and constitutions. The order and power that's among them, that's the foundation of a people ; and when once this foundation is destroyed, *" What can the righteous do ? "* What can the best, the wisest in the world, do in such a case ? What can any man do, if there be not a foundation of government left among men ? There is no help nor answer in such a case but that which follows in the fourth verse of the Psalm, *" The Lord is in his holy temple, the Lord's throne is in heaven : his eyes behold, his eyelids try, the children of men ; "* as if he had said, in the midst of these confusions, when as it is said (Psalm lxxxii. 5), " All the foundations of the earth are out of course ; " yet God keeps his course still, he is where he was and as he was, without variableness or shadow of turning.—*Joseph Caryl.*

Verse 3.—" The righteous." The righteous indefinitely, equivalent to the righteous universally ; not only the righteous as a single arrow, but in the whole sheaf ; not only the righteous in their personal, but in their diffusive capacity. Were they all collected into one body, were all the righteous living in the same age wherein the *foundations are destroyed,* summoned up and modelled into one corporation, all their joint endeavours would prove ineffectual to the re-establishing of the fallen *foundations,* as not being man's work, but only God's work to perform.—*Thomas Fuller.*

Verse 3.—" The foundations." Positions, the things formerly fixed, placed, and settled. It is not said, if the roof be ruinous, or if the side walls be shattered, but if the *foundations.*

Verse 3.—" Foundations be destroyed." In the plural. Here I will not warrant my skill in architecture, but conceive this may pass for an undoubted truth : it is possible that a building settled on several entire *foundations* (suppose them *pillars*) close one to another, if one of them fall, yet the structure may still stand, or rather hang (at the least for a short time) by virtue of the *complicative*, which it receiveth from such foundations which still stand secure. But in case there be a total rout, and an utter ruin of all the *foundations*, none can fancy to themselves a possibility of that building's subsistence.—*Thomas Fuller.*

Verse 3.—" *What* CAN *the righteous ?* " The *can* of the righteous is a limited *can*, confined to the rule of God's word ; they *can* do nothing but what they *can* lawfully do. 2 Cor. xiii. 8. " For we *can* do nothing against the truth, but for the truth : " *Illud possumus, quod jure possumus.* Wicked men can do anything ; their conscience, which is so wide that it is none at all, will bear them out to act anything how unlawful soever, to stab, poison, massacre, by any means, at any time, in any place, whosoever standeth betwixt them and the effecting their desires. Not so the righteous ; they have a rule whereby to walk, which they will not, they must not, they dare not, cross. If therefore a righteous man were assured, that by the breach of one of God's commandments he might restore decayed religion, and re-settle it *statu quo prius*, his hands, head, and heart are tied up, he *can* do nothing, because *their damnation is just who say* (Rom. iii. 8), " *Let us do evil that good may come thereof.*"

Verse 3.—" *Do.*" It is not said, *What can they think ?* It is a great blessing which God hath allowed injured people, that though otherwise oppressed and straitened, they may freely enlarge themselves in their thoughts.—*Thomas Fuller.*

Verse 3.—Sinning times have ever been the saints' praying times : this sent Ezra with a heavy heart to confess the sin of his people, and to bewail their abominations before the Lord. Ezra ix. And Jeremiah tells the wicked of his degenerate age, that " his soul should weep in secret places for their pride." Jer. xiii. 17. Indeed, sometimes sin comes to such a height, that this is almost all the godly can do, to get into a corner, and bewail the general pollutions of the age. " *If the foundations be destroyed, what can the righteous do ?* " Such dismal days of national confusion our eyes have seen, when foundations of government were destroyed, and all hurled into military confusion. When it is thus with a people, " *What can the righteous do ?* " Yes, this they may, and should do, " fast and pray." There is yet a God in heaven to be sought to, when a people's deliverance is thrown beyond the help of human policy or power. Now is the fit time to make their appeal to God, as the words following hint : " *The Lord is in his holy temple, the Lord's throne is in heaven ;* " in which words God is presented sitting in heaven as a temple, for their encouragement, I conceive, in such a desperate state of affairs, to direct their prayers thither for deliverance. And certainly this hath been the engine that hath been instrumental, above any, to restore this poor nation again, and set it upon the foundation of that lawful government from which it had so dangerously departed.—*William Gurnall.*

Verse 4.—The infinite understanding of God doth exactly know the sins of men ; he knows so as to consider. He doth not only know them, but intently behold them : " *His eyelids try the children of men,*" a metaphor taken from men, that contract the eyelids when they would wistly and accurately behold a thing : it is not a transient and careless look.—*Stephen Charnock.*

Verse 4.—" *His eyes behold,*" etc. God searcheth not as man searcheth, by enquiring into that which before was hid from him ; his searching is no more but his beholding ; he seeth the heart, he beholdeth the reins ; God's very sight is searching. Heb. iv. 13. " All things are naked and opened unto his eyes," τετραχηλισμένα, *dissected or anatomised.* He hath at once as exact a view of the most hidden things, the very entrails of the soul, as if they had been with never so great curiosity anatomised before him.—*Richard Alleine*, 1611—1681.

Verse 4.—" *His eyes behold,*" etc. Consider that God not only sees into all you do, but he sees it to that very end that he may examine and search into it. He doth not only behold you with a common and indifferent look, but with a searching, watchful, and inquisitive eye : he pries into the reasons, the motives, the ends of all your actions. " *The Lord's throne is in heaven : his eyes behold, his eyelids try, the children of men.*" Rev. i. 14, where Christ is described, it is said, *his eyes are as a flame of fire :* you know the property of fire is to search and make trial of those things which are exposed unto it, and to separate the dross from the pure metal : so, God's eye is like fire, to try and examine the actions of men : he knows and discerns how much your very purest duties have in them of mixture, and base ends of formality, hypocrisy, distractedness, and deadness : he sees through all your specious pretences, that which you cast as a mist before the eyes of men when yet thou art but a juggler in religion : all your tricks and sleights of outward profession, all those things that you use to cozen and delude men withal, cannot possibly impose upon him : he is a God that can look through all those fig-leaves of outward profession, and discern the nakedness of your duties through them.—*Ezekiel Hopkins, D.D.*

Verse 4.—" *His eyes behold,*" etc.   Take God into thy counsel.   Heaven over-looks hell.   God at any time can tell thee what plots are hatching there against thee.—*William Gurnall.*

Verse 4.—" *His eyes behold, his eyelids try, the children of men.*"   When an offender, or one accused for any offence, is brought before a judge, and stands at the bar to be arraigned, the judge looks upon him, eyes him, sets his eye upon him, and he bids the offender look up in his face ; " Look upon me," saith the judge, " and speak up : " guiltiness usually clouds the forehead and clothes the brow ; the weight of guilt holds down the head ! *the evil doer hath an ill look*, or dares not look up ; how glad is he if the judge looks off him.   We have such an expression here, speaking of the Lord, the great Judge of heaven and earth : " *His eyelids try the children of men,*" as a judge tries a guilty person with his eye and reads the characters of his wickedness printed in his face.   Hence we have a common speech in our language, such a one *looks suspiciously*, or, *he hath a guilty look*.   At that great gaol-delivery described in Rev. vi. 16, All the prisoners cry out *to be hid from the face of him that sat upon the throne.*   They could not look upon Christ, and they could not endure Christ should look on them ; the eyelids of Christ try the children of men. . . .   Wickedness cannot endure to be under the observation of any eye, much less of the eye of justice.   Hence the actors of it say, " *Who seeth us ?* "   It is very hard not to show the guilt of the heart in the face, and it is as hard to have it seen there.—*Joseph Caryl.*

Verse 5.—" *The Lord trieth the righteous.*"   Except our sins, there is not such plenty of anything in all the world as there is of troubles which come from sin, as one heavy messenger came to Job after another.   Since we are not in para-dise, but in the wilderness, we must look for one trouble after another.   As a bear came to David after a lion, and a giant after a bear, and a king after a giant, and Philistines after a king, so, when believers have fought with poverty, they shall fight with envy ; when they have fought with envy, they shall fight with infamy ; when they have fought with infamy, they shall fight with sickness ; they shall be like a labourer who is never out of work.—*Henry Smith.*

Verse 5.—" *The Lord trieth the righteous.*"—Times of affliction and persecution will distinguish the precious from the vile, it will difference the counterfeit professor from the true.   Persecution is a Christian's touchstone, it is a *lapis lydius* that will try what metal men are made of, whether they be silver or tin, gold or dross, wheat or chaff, shadow or substance, carnal or spiritual, sincere or hypocritical. Nothing speaks out more soundness and uprightness than a pursuing after holiness, even then when holiness is most afflicted, pursued, and persecuted in the world : to stand fast in fiery trials argues much integrity within.—*Thomas Brooks.*

Verse 5.—Note the singular opposition of the two sentences.   God hates the wicked, and therefore in contrast he loves the righteous ; but it is here said that he tries them : therefore it follows that to try and to love are with God the same thing.—*C. H. S.*

Verse 6.—" *Upon the wicked he shall rain snares.*"   Snares to hold them ; then if they be not delivered, follow fire and brimstone, and they cannot escape.   This is the case of a sinner if he repent not ; if God pardon not, he is in the snare of Satan's temptation, he is in the snare of divine vengeance ; let him therefore cry aloud for his deliverance, that he may have his feet in a large room.   The wicked lay snares for the righteous, but God either preventeth them that their souls ever escape them, or else he subventeth them : " The snares are broken, and we are delivered."   No snares hold us so fast as those of our own sins ; they keep down our heads, and stoop us that we cannot look up : a very little ease they are to him that hath not a seared conscience.—*Samuel Page*, 1646.

Verse 6.—" *He shall rain snares.*"   As in hunting with the lasso, the huntsman casts a snare from above upon his prey to entangle its head or feet, so shall the Lord from above with many twistings of the line of terror, surround, bind, and take captive the haters of his law.—*C. H. S.*

Verse 6.—" *He shall rain snares,*" etc. He shall rain upon them when they least think of it even in the midst of their jollity, as rain falls on a fair day. Or, he shall rain down the vengeance when he sees good, for it rains not always. Though he defers it, yet will it rain.—*William Nicholson, Bishop of Gloucester, in "David's Harp Strung and Tuned,"* 1662.

Verse 6.—" *Upon the wicked he shall rain snares, fire and brimstone, and an horrible tempest.*" The strange dispensation of affairs in this world is an argument which doth convincingly prove that there shall be such a day wherein all the *involucra* and entanglements of providence shall be clearly unfolded. Then shall the riddle be dissolved, why God hath given this and that profane wretch so much wealth, and so much power to do mischief: is it not *that they might be destroyed for ever?* Then shall they be called to a strict account for all that plenty and prosperity for which they are now envied; and the more they have abused, the more dreadful will their condemnation be. Then it will be seen that God gave them not as mercies, but as " *snares.*" It is said that God " *will rain on the wicked snares, fire and brimstone, and an horrible tempest:*" when he scatters abroad the desirable things of this world, riches, honours, pleasures, etc., then he rains " *snares*" upon them; and when he shall call them to an account for these things, then he will rain upon them " *fire and brimstone, and an horrible tempest*" of his wrath and fury. Dives, who caroused on earth, yet, in hell could not obtain so much as one poor drop of water to cool his scorched and flaming tongue: had not his excess and intemperance been so great in his life, his fiery thirst had not been so tormenting after death; and therefore, in that sad item that Abraham gives him (Luke xvi. 25), he bids him " *remember, that thou, in thy lifetime, receivedst thy good things, and likewise Lazarus evil things; but now he is comforted, and thou art tormented.*" I look upon this as a most bitter and a most deserved sarcasm; upbraiding him for his gross folly, in making the trifles of this life his good things. Thou hast received thy good things, but now thou art tormented. Oh, never call Dives's purple and delicious fare *good things,* if they thus end in torments! Was it good for him to be wrapped in purple who is now wrapped in flames? Was it good for him to fare deliciously who was only thereby fatted up against the day of slaughter?—*Ezekiel Hopkins.*

Verse 6.—" *Snares, fire and brimstone, storm and tempest: this shall be the portion of their cup.*" After the judgment follows the condemnation: pre-figured as we have seen, by the overthrow of Sodom and Gomorrah. " *Snares:*" because the allurements of Satan in this life will be their worst punishments in the next; the fire of anger, the brimstone of impurity, the tempest of pride, the lust of the flesh, the lust of the eyes, and the pride of life. " *This shall be their portion;*" compare it with the Psalmist's own saying, " The Lord himself is the portion of my inheritance and my cup." Psalm xvi. 5.—*Cassiodorus, in J. M. Neale's Commentary.*

Verse 6.—" *The portion of their cup.*" Heb., the allotment of their cup. The expression has reference to the custom of distributing to each guest his mess of meat.—*William French and George Skinner,* 1842.

Verse 7.—That God may give grace without glory is intelligible; but to admit a man to communion with him in glory without grace, is not intelligible. It is not agreeable to God's holiness to make any inhabitant of heaven, and converse freely with him in a way of intimate love, without such a qualification of grace: " *The righteous Lord loveth righteousness; his countenance doth behold the upright;*" he looks upon him with a smiling eye, and therefore he cannot favourably look upon an unrighteous person; so that this necessity is not founded only in the command of God that we should be renewed, but in the very nature of the thing, because God, in regard of his holiness, cannot converse with an impure creature. God must change his nature, or the sinner's nature must be changed. There can be no friendly communion between two of different natures without the change of one of them into the likeness of the other. Wolves and sheep, darkness and light, can never agree. God cannot love a sinner as a sinner, because he hates impurity by a necessity of nature as well as a choice of will. It is as impossible for him to love it as to cease to be holy.—*Stephen Charnock.*

HINTS TO PREACHERS.

Verse 1.—Faith's bold avowal, and brave refusal.

Verse 1.—Teacheth us to trust in God, how great soever our dangers be ; also that we shall be many times assaulted to make us put far from us this trust, but yet that we must cleave unto it, as the anchor of our souls, sure and steadfast. —*Thomas Wilcocks.*

Verse 1.—The advice of cowardice, and the jeer of insolence, both answered by faith. Lesson—Attempt no other answer.

Verse 2.—The craftiness of our spiritual enemies.

Verse 3.—This may furnish a double discourse. I. *If God's oath and promise could remove*, what could we do ? Here the answer is easy. II. *If all earthly things fail*, and the very State fall to pieces, what can we do ? We can suffer joyfully, hope cheerfully, wait patiently, pray earnestly, believe confidently, and triumph finally.

Verse 3.—Necessity of holding and preaching foundation truths.

Verse 4.—The elevation, mystery, supremacy, purity, everlastingness, invisibility, etc., of the throne of God.

Verses 4, 5.—In these verses mark the fact that the children of men, as well as the righteous, are tried ; work out the contrast between the two trials in their design and result, etc.

Verse 5.—" *The Lord trieth the righteous.*" I. Who are tried ? II. What in them is tried ?—Faith, love, etc. III. In what manner ?—Trials of every sort. IV. How long ? V. For what purposes ?

Verse 5.—" *His soul hateth.*" The thoroughness of God's hatred of sin. Illustrate by providential judgments, threatenings, sufferings of the Surety, and the terrors of hell.

Verse 5.—The trying of the gold, and the sweeping out of the refuse.

Verse 6. " *He shall rain.*" Gracious rain and destroying rain.

Verse 6.—The portion of the impenitent.

Verse 7.—The Lord possesses righteousness as a personal attribute, loves it in the abstract, and blesses those who practise it.

PSALM XII.

TITLE. *This Psalm is headed, " To the Chief Musician upon Sheminith, a Psalm of David," which title is identical with that of the sixth Psalm, except that Neginoth is here omitted. We have nothing new to add, and therefore refer the reader to our remarks on the dedication of Psalm VI. As Sheminith signifies the eight, the Arabic version says it is concerning the end of the world, which shall be the eighth day, and refers it to the coming of the Messiah : without accepting so fanciful an interpretation, we may read this song of complaining faith in the light of His coming who shall break in pieces the oppressor. The subject will be the better before the mind's eye if we entitle this Psalm : " GOOD THOUGHTS IN BAD TIMES." It is supposed to have been written while Saul was persecuting David, and those who favoured his cause.*

DIVISION.—*In the first and second verses David spreads his plaint before the Lord concerning the treachery of his age ; verses 3 and 4 denounce judgments upon proud traitors ; in verse 5, Jehovah himself thunders out his wrath against oppressors ; hearing this, the Chief Musician sings sweetly of the faithfulness of God and his care of his people, in verses 6 and 7 ; but closes on the old key of lament in verse 8, as he observes the abounding wickedness of his times. Those holy souls who dwell in Mesech, and sojourn in the tents of Kedar, may read and sing these sacred stanzas with hearts in full accord with their mingled melody of lowly mourning and lofty confidence.*

EXPOSITION.

HELP, LORD ; for the godly man ceaseth ; for the faithful fail from among the children of men.

2 They speak vanity every one with his neighbour : *with* flattering lips *and* with a double heart do they speak.

" *Help, Lord.*" A short, but sweet, suggestive, seasonable, and serviceable prayer ; a kind of angel's sword, to be turned every way, and to be used on all occasions. Ainsworth says the word rendered " help," is largely used for all manner of saving, helping, delivering, preserving, etc. Thus it seems that the prayer is very full and instructive. The Psalmist sees the extreme danger of his position, for a man had better be among lions than among liars ; he feels his own inability to deal with such sons of Belial, for " he who shall touch them must be fenced with iron ; " he therefore turns himself to his all-sufficient Helper, the Lord, whose help is never denied to his servants, and whose aid is enough for all their needs. " *Help, Lord,*" is a very useful ejaculation which we may dart up to heaven on occasions of emergency, whether in labour, learning, suffering, fighting, living, or dying. As small ships can sail into harbours which larger vessels, drawing more water, cannot enter, so our brief cries and short petitions may trade with heaven when our soul is wind-bound, and business-bound, as to longer exercises of devotion, and when the stream of grace seems at too low an ebb to float a more laborious supplication. " *For the godly man ceaseth ;* " the death, departure, or decline of godly men should be a trumpet-call for more prayer. They say that fish smell first at the head, and when godly men decay, the whole commonwealth will soon go rotten. We must not, however, be rash in our judgment on this point, for Elijah erred in counting himself the only servant of God alive, when there were thousands whom the Lord held in reserve. The present times always appear to be peculiarly dangerous, because they are nearest to our anxious gaze, and whatever evils are rife are sure to be observed, while the faults of past ages are further off, and are more easily overlooked. Yet we expect that in the latter days, " because iniquity shall abound, the love of many shall wax cold," and then we must the more thoroughly turn from man, and address ourselves to the Churches' Lord, by whose help the gates of hell shall be kept from prevailing against us. " *The faithful fail from among the children of men ;* " when godliness goes, faithfulness inevitably follows ; without fear of God, men have no love of truth. Common honesty is no longer common, when common irreligion leads to universal godlessness. David had his eyes on Doeg, and the men of Ziph and Keilah, and perhaps remembered the murdered priests of Nob, and the many banished ones who consorted with him in the cave of Adullam, and wondered where the state would drift without the anchors of its godly and faithful men. David, amid the general misrule, did not betake himself to seditious plottings, but to solemn petitionings ; nor did he join with the multitude to do evil, but took up the arms of prayer to withstand their attacks upon virtue.

"*They speak vanity every one with his neighbour.*" They utter that which is vain *to hear*, because of its frivolous, foolish, want of worth ; vain to *believe*, because it was false and lying ; vain to *trust to*, since it was deceitful and flattering ; vain to *regard*, for it lifted up the hearer, filling him with proud conceit of himself. It is a sad thing when it is the fashion to talk vanity. "Ca' me, and I'll ca' thee," is the old Scotch proverb ; give me a high-sounding character, and I will give you one. Compliments and fawning congratulations are hateful to honest men ; they know that if they take they must give them, and they scorn to do either. These accommodation-bills are most admired by those who are bankrupt in character. Bad are the times when every man thus cajoles and cozens his neighbour. "*With flattering lips and with a double heart do they speak.*" He who puffs up another's heart, has nothing better than wind in his own. If a man extols me to my face, he only shows me one side of his heart, and the other is black with contempt for me, or foul with intent to cheat me. Flattery is the sign of the tavern where duplicity is the host. The Chinese consider a man of two hearts to be a very base man, and we shall be safe in reckoning all flatterers to be such.

3 The LORD shall cut off all flattering lips, *and* the tongue that speaketh proud things :

4 Who have said, With our tongue will we prevail ; our lips *are* our own : who *is* lord over us ?

Total destruction shall overwhelm the lovers of flattery and pride, but meanwhile how they hector and fume ! Well did the apostle call them "raging waves of the sea, foaming out their own shame." Free-thinkers are generally very free-talkers, and they are never more at ease than when railing at God's dominion, and arrogating to themselves unbounded license. Strange is it that the easy yoke of the Lord should so gall the shoulders of the proud, while the iron bands of Satan they bind about themselves as chains of honour : they boastfully cry unto God, "Who is lord over us ?" and hear not the hollow voice of the evil one, who cries from the infernal lake, "I am your lord, and right faithfully do ye serve me." Alas, poor fools, their pride and glory shall be cut off like a fading flower ! May God grant that our soul may not be gathered with them. It is worthy of observation that flattering lips, and tongues speaking proud things, are classed together : the fitness of this is clear, for they are guilty of the same vice, the first flatters another, and the second flatters himself, in both cases a lie is in their right hands. One generally imagines that flatterers are such mean parasites, so cringing and fawning, that they cannot be proud ; but the wise man will tell you that while all pride is truly meanness, there is in the very lowest meanness no small degree of pride. Cæsar's horse is even more proud of carrying Cæsar, than Cæsar is of riding him. The mat on which the emperor wiped his shoes, boasts vaingloriously, crying out, "I cleaned the imperial boots." None are so detestably domineering as the little creatures who creep into office by cringing to the great ; those are bad times, indeed, in which these obnoxious beings are numerous and powerful. No wonder that the justice of God in cutting off such injurious persons is matter for a Psalm, for both earth and heaven are weary of such provoking offenders, whose presence is a very plague to the people afflicted thereby. Men cannot tame the tongues of such boastful flatterers ; but the Lord's remedy if sharp is sure, and is an unanswerable answer to their swelling words of vanity.

5 For the oppression of the poor, for the sighing of the needy, now will I arise, saith the LORD ; I will set *him* in safety *from him that* puffeth at him.

In due season the Lord will hear his elect ones, who cry day and night unto him, and though he bear long with their oppressors, yet will he avenge them speedily. Observe that the mere oppression of saints, however silently they bear it, is in itself a cry to God: Moses was heard at the Red Sea, though he said nothing; and Hagar's affliction was heard despite her silence. Jesus feels with his people, and their smarts are mighty orators with him. By-and-by, however, *they* begin to sigh and express their misery, and then relief comes post-haste. Nothing moves a father like the cries of his children; he bestirs himself, wakes up his manhood, overthrows the enemy, and sets his beloved in safety. A *puff* is too much for the child to bear, and the foe is so haughty, that he laughs the little one to scorn; but the Father comes, and then it is the child's turn to laugh, when he is set above the rage of his tormentor. What virtue is there in a poor man's sighs, that they should move the Almighty God to arise from his throne. The needy did not dare to speak, and could only sigh in secret, but the Lord heard, and could rest no longer, but girded on his sword for the battle. It is a fair day when our soul brings God into her quarrel, for when his bare arm is seen, Philistia shall rue the day. The darkest hours of the Church's night are those which precede the break of day. Man's extremity is God's opportunity. Jesus will come to deliver just when his needy ones shall sigh, as if all hope had gone for ever. O Lord, set thy *now* near at hand, and rise up speedily to our help. Should the afflicted reader be able to lay hold upon the promise of this verse, let him gratefully fetch a fulness of comfort from it. Gurnal says, "As one may draw out the wine of a whole hogshead at one tap, so may a poor soul derive the comfort of the whole covenant to himself through one promise, if he be able to apply it." He who promises to set us in safety, means thereby preservation on earth, and eternal salvation in heaven.

6 The words of the LORD *are* pure words: *as* silver tried in a furnace of earth, purified seven times.

7 Thou shalt keep them, O LORD, thou shalt preserve them from this generation for ever.

Verse 6.—What a contrast between the vain words of man, and the pure words of Jehovah. Man's words are yea and nay, but the Lord's promises are yea and amen. For truth, certainty, holiness, faithfulness, the words of the Lord are pure as well-refined silver. In the original there is an allusion to the most severely-purifying process known to the ancients, through which silver was passed when the greatest possible purity was desired; the dross was all consumed, and only the bright and precious metal remained; so clear and free from all alloy of error or unfaithfulness is the book of the words of the Lord. The Bible has passed through the furnace of persecution, literary criticism, philosophic doubt, and scientific discovery, and has lost nothing but those human interpretations which clung to it as alloy to precious ore. The experience of saints has tried it in every conceivable manner, but not a single doctrine or promise has been consumed in the most excessive heat. What God's words are, the words of his children should be. If we would be Godlike in conversation, we must watch our language, and maintain the strictest purity of integrity and holiness in all our communications.

7. To fall into the hands of an evil generation, so as to be baited by their cruelty, or polluted by their influence, is an evil to be dreaded beyond measure; but it is an evil foreseen and provided for in the text. In life many a saint has lived a hundred years before his age, as though he had darted his soul into the brighter future, and escaped the mists of the beclouded present: he has gone to his grave unreverenced and misunderstood, and lo! as generations come and go, upon a sudden the hero is unearthed, and lives in the admiration and love of the excellent of the earth; preserved for ever from the generation which stigmatised him as a sower of sedition, or burned him as a heretic. It should be our daily prayer that we may rise above our age as the mountain-tops above the clouds, and may stand out as heaven-pointing pinnacle high above the mists of ignorance and sin which roll around us. O Eternal Spirit, fulfil in us the faithful saying of this verse! Our faith believes those two assuring words, and cries, " Thou shalt," " thou shalt."

8 The wicked walk on every side, when the vilest men are exalted.

8. Here we return to the fount of bitterness, which first made the Psalmist run to the wells of salvation, namely, the prevalence of wickedness. When those in power are vile, their underlings will be no better. As a warm sun brings out noxious flies, so does a sinner in honour foster vice everywhere. Our turf would not so swarm with abominables if those who are styled honourables did not give their

countenance to the craft. Would to God that the glory and triumph of our Lord Jesus would encourage us to walk and work on every side ; as like acts upon like, since an exalted sinner encourages sinners, our exalted Redeemer must surely excite, cheer, and stimulate his saints. Nerved by a sight of his reigning power we shall meet the evils of the times in the spirit of holy resolution, and shall the more hopefully pray, " Help, Lord."

EXPLANATORY NOTES AND QUAINT SAYINGS.

Verse 1.—" *Help, Lord.*" 'Twas high time to call to heaven for help, when Saul cried, " Go, kill me up the priests of Jehovah " (the occasion as it is thought of making this Psalm), and therein committed the sin against the Holy, as some grave divines are of opinion. 1 Sam. xxii. 17. David, after many sad thoughts about that slaughter, and the occasion of it, Doeg's malicious information, together with the paucity of his fast friends, and the multitude of his sworn enemies at court, breaks forth abruptly into these words, " *Help Lord,*" help at a dead lift. The Arabic version hath it, *Deliver me by main force,* as with weapons of war, for " the Lord is a man of war." Ex. xv. 3.—*John Trapp.*

Verse 1.—" *The faithful.*" " *A faithful man,*" as a parent, a reprover, an adviser, one " without guile," " *who can find ?* " Prov. xx. 6. Look close. View thyself in the glass of the word. Does thy neighbour or thy friend, find thee *faithful* to him ? What does our daily intercourse witness ? Is not the attempt to speak what is agreeable oft made at the expense of truth ? Are not professions of regard sometimes utterly inconsistent with our real feelings ? In common life, where gross violations are restrained, a thousand petty offences are allowed, that break down the wall between sin and duty, and, judged by the divine standard, are indeed guilty steps upon forbidden ground.—*Charles Bridges,* 1850.

Verse 1.—A " *faithful* " man must be, first of all, faithful to himself ; then, he must be faithful to God ; and then, he must be faithful to others, particularly the church of God. And this, as it regards ministers, is of peculiar importance. *Joseph Irons,* 1840.

Verse 1.—Even as a careful mother, seeing her child in the way when a company of unruly horses run through the streets in full career, presently whips up her child in her arms and taketh him home ; or as the hen, seeing the ravenous kite over her head, clucks and gathers her chickens under her wings ; even so when God hath a purpose to bring a heavy calamity upon a land, it hath been usual with him to call and cull out to himself, such as are his dearly beloved. He takes his choice servants from the evil to come. Thus was Augustine removed a little before Hippo (wherein he dwelt) was taken ; Parœus died before Heidelburg was sacked ; and Luther was taken off before Germany was overrun with war and bloodshed.—*Ed. Dunsterville in a Sermon at the Funeral of Sir Sim. Harcourt,* 1642.

Verse 1.—" *Help, Lord ; for the godly man ceaseth,*" etc. :—

> Back then, complainer, loathe thy life no more,
> Nor deem thyself upon a desert shore,
>   Because the rocks the nearer prospect close.
> Yet in fallen Israel are there hearts and eyes,
> That day by day in prayer like thine arise ;
>   Thou knowest them not, but their Creator known.
> Go, to the world return, nor fear to cast
> Thy bread upon the waters, sure at last
>   In joy to find it after many days.
>
> *John Keble,* 1792—1866.

Verses 1, 2, 4.—Consider our markets, our fairs, our private contracts and bargains, our shops, our cellars, our weights, our measures, our promises, our protestations, our politic tricks and villanous Machiavelism, our enhancing of the prices of all commodities, and tell, whether the twelfth Psalm may not as fitly be applied to our times as to the days of the man of God ; in which the feigning, and lying, and facing, and guile, and subtlety of men provoked the psalmist to cry out,

" *Help, Lord ; for there is not a godly man left : for the faithful are failed from among the children of men : they speak deceitfully every one with his neighbour, flattering with their lips, and speak with a double heart, which have said, With our tongue we will prevail ; our lips are our own : who is Lord over us ? "—R. Wolcombe. 1612.*

Verse 2.—" *They speak vanity every one with his neighbour : with flattering lips and with a double heart do they speak.*" The feigned zeal is just like a water-man, that looks one way and rows another way ; for this man *pretends* one thing and *intends* another thing ; as Jehu pretended the zeal of God's glory, but his aim was at his master's kingdom ; and his zeal to God's service was but to bring him to the sceptre of the kingdom. So Demetrius professed great love unto Diana, but his drift was to maintain the honour of his profession ; and so we have too many that make great show of holiness, and yet their hearts aim at other ends ; but they may be sure, though they can deceive the world and destroy themselves, yet not God, who knoweth the secrets of all hearts.—*Gr. Williams*, 1636.

Verse 2.—" *They speak vanity.*"—

Faithless is earth, and faithless are the skies !
Justice is fled, and truth is now no more !
Virgil's Æneid, IV. 373.

Verse 2.—" *With a double heart.*" Man is nothing but insincerity, falsehood, and hypocrisy, both in regard to himself and in regard to others. He does not wish that he should be told the truth, he shuns saying it to others ; and all these moods, so inconsistent with justice and reason, have their roots in his heart.—*Blaise Pascal.*

Verse 2.—" *With flattering lips and with a double heart do they speak.*" There is no such stuff to make a cloak of as religion ; nothing so fashionable, nothing so profitable : it is a livery wherein a wise man may serve two masters, God and the world, and make a gainful service by either. I serve both, and in both myself, by prevaricating with both. Before man none serves his God with more severe devotion : for which, among the best of men, I work my own ends, and serve myself. In private, I serve the world ; not with so strict devotion, but with more delight ; where fulfilling of her servants' lusts, I work my end and serve myself. The house of prayer who more frequents than I ? In all Christian duties who more forward than I ? I fast with those that fast, that I may eat with those that eat. I mourn with those that mourn. No hand more open to the cause than mine, and in their families none prays longer and with louder zeal. Thus when the opinion of a holy life hath cried the goodness of my conscience up, my trade can lack no custom, my wares can want no price, my words can need no credit, my actions can lack no praise. If I am covetous it is interpreted providence ; if miserable, it is counted temperance ; if melancholy, it is construed godly sorrow ; if merry, it is voted spiritual joy ; if I be rich, it is thought the blessing of a godly life ; if poor, supposed the fruit of conscionable dealing ; if I be well spoken of, it is the merit of holy conversation ; if ill, it is the malice of malignants. Thus I sail with every wind, and have my end in all conditions. This cloak in summer keeps me cool, in winter warm, and hides the nasty bag of all my secret lusts. Under this cloak I walk in public fairly with applause, and in private sin securely without offence, and officiate wisely without discovery. I compass sea and land to make a proselyte ; and no sooner made, but he makes me. At a fast I cry Geneva, and at a feast I cry Rome If I be poor, I counterfeit abundance to save my credit ; if rich, I dissemble poverty to save charges. I most frequent schismatical lectures, which I find most profitable ; from thence learning to divulge and maintain new doctrines ; they maintain me in suppers thrice a week. I use the help of a lie sometimes, as a new stratagem to uphold the gospel ; and I colour oppression with God's judgments executed upon the wicked. Charity I hold an extraordinary duty, therefore not ordinarily to be performed. What I openly reprove abroad, for my own profit, that I secretly act at home, for my own pleasure. But stay, I see a handwriting in my heart which damps my soul. It is charactered in these said words, " Woe be to you, hypocrites." Matt. xxiii. 13.—*Francis Quarles' " Hypocrite's Soliloquy."*

Verse 2.—" *With flattering lips,*" etc. The world indeed says that society could not exist if there were perfect truthfulness and candour between man and man ; and that the world's propriety would be as much disturbed if every man said what he pleased, as it was in those days of Israelitish history, when every man did that which was right in his own eyes. The world is assuredly the best judge of its own condition and mode of government, and therefore I will not say what a libel does such a remark contain, but oh, what a picture does it present of the social edifice, that its walls can be cemented and kept together only by flattery and falsehood.—*Barton Bouchier.*

Verse 2.—"*Flattering lips.*" The philosopher Bion being asked what animal he thought the most hurtful, replied, "That of wild creatures a tyrant, and of tame ones a flatterer." The flatterer is the most dangerous enemy we can have. Raleigh, himself a courtier, and therefore initiated into the whole art of flattery, who discovered in his own career and fate its dangerous and deceptive power, its deep artifice and deeper falsehood, says, "A flatterer is said to be a beast that biteth smiling. But it is hard to know them from friends—they are so obsequious and full of protestations ; for, as a wolf resembles a dog, so doth a flatterer a friend."—*The Book of Symbols*, 1844.

Verse 2.—"*They speak with a double heart.*" The original is, "A heart and a heart : " one for the church, another for the change ; one for Sundays, another for working-days ; one for the king, another for the pope. A man without a heart is a wonder, but a man with two hearts is a monster. It is said of Judas " There were many hearts in one man ; " and we read of the saints, "There was one heart in many men." Acts. iv. 32. *Dabo illis cor unum ;* a special blessing.—*Thomas Adams.*

Verse 2.—When men cease to be faithful to their God, he who expects to find them so to each other will be much disappointed. The primitive sincerity will accompany the primitive piety in her flight from the earth ; and then interest will succeed conscience in the regulation of human conduct, till one man cannot trust another farther than he holds him by that tie. Hence, by the way, it is, that though many are infidels themselves, yet few choose to have their families and dependants such ; as judging, and rightly judging, that true Christians are the only persons to be depended on for the exact discharge of social duties.—*George Horne.*

Verse 3.—"*The Lord shall cut off all flattering lips,*" etc. They who take pleasure in deceiving others, will at the last find themselves most of all deceived, when the Sun of truth, by the brightness of his rising, shall at once detect and consume hypocrisy.—*George Horne.*

Verse 3.—"*Cut off lips and tongues.*" May there not be here an allusion to those terrible but suggestive punishments which Oriental monarchs were wont to execute on criminals ? Lips were cut off and tongues torn out when offenders were convicted of lying or treason. So terrible and infinitely more so are the punishments of sin.—*C. H. S.*

Verses 3, 4.—It need not now seem strange to tell you that the Lord is the owner of our bodies, that he has so much propriety therein that they are more his than ours. The apostle tells us as much. 1 Cor. vi. 20. " Glorify God in your bodies which are his." Our bodies and every member thereof, are his : for if the whole be so, no part is exempted. And therefore they spake proud things, and presumptuously usurped the propriety of God, who said, " Our lips are our own ; " as though their lips had not been his who is Lord and Owner of all, but they had been lords thereof, and might have used them as they list. This provoked God to show what right he had to dispose of such lips and tongues, by *cutting them off.*—*David Clarkson.*

Verse 4.—" *Who have said, With our tongues will we prevail ; who is Lord over us ?* " So it was : twelve poor and unlearned men on the one side, all the eloquence of Greece and Rome arrayed on the other. From the time of Tertullus to that of Julian the apostate, every species of oratory, learning, wit, was lavished against the church of God ; and the result, like the well-known story of that dispute between the Christian peasant and the heathen philosopher, when the latter, having challenged the assembled fathers of a synod to silence him, was put to shame by the simple faith of the former " In the name of our Lord Jesus Christ, I command thee to be dumb." *Who is Lord over us ?* " Who is the Lord, that I should obey his voice to let Israel go ? " Ex. v. 2. " What is the Almighty, that we should serve him ? " Job. xxi. 15. " Who is that God that shall deliver you ? " Dan. iii. 15.—*Michael Ayguan, in J. M. Neale's Commentary.*

Verse 4.—" *Our lips are our own.*" If we have to do with God, we must quit claim to ourselves and look on God as our owner ; but this is fixed in the hearts of men, We will be our own ; we will not consent to the claim which God makes to us : " *Our lips are our own.*" Wicked men might as well say the same thing of their whole selves ; our bodies, strength, time, parts, etc., are our own, and who is Lord over us ?—*John Howe.*

Verse 4.—From the faults of the wicked we must learn three contrary lessons ; to wit : 1. That nothing which we have is our own. But, 2. Whatsoever is given to us of God is for service to be done to him. 3. That whatsoever we do or say, we have a Lord over us to whom we must be answerable when he calleth us to account.—*David Dickson.*

Verse 5.—" *For the oppression of the poor,*" etc. When oppressors and persecutors do snuff and puff at the people of God, when they defy them, and scorn them, and think that they can with a blast of their breath blow them away, then God will arise to judgment, as the Chaldee has it ; at that very nick of time when all seems to be lost, and when the poor, oppressed, and afflicted people of God can do nothing but sigh and weep, and weep and sigh, then the Lord will arise and ease them of their oppressions, and make their day of extremity a glorious opportunity to work for his own glory and his people's good. Matt. xxii. 6, 7. " And the remnant took his servants, and entreated them spitefully, and slew them. But when the king heard thereof, he was wroth : and he sent forth his armies and destroyed those murderers, and burned up their city."—*Thomas Brooks.*

Verse 5.—Fear ye, whosoever ye be, that do wrong the poor ; you have power and wealth, and the favour of the judges, but they have the strongest weapons of all, sighings and groanings, which fetch help from heaven for them. These weapons dig down houses, throw up foundations, overthrow whole nations.—*Chrysostom.*

Verse 5.—" *For the sighing of the needy, now will I arise, saith the Lord.*" God is pleased to take notice of *every grace,* even the least and lowest, and every gracious inclination in any of his servants. *To fear his name* is no great matter, yet these have a promise. *To think on his name* less, yet set down in a " book of remembrance." God sets down how many good *thoughts* a poor soul hath had. As evil thoughts in wicked men are taken notice of—they are the first fruits of the evil heart (Matt. xv. 19)—so good thoughts are they which lie uppermost, and best discover a good heart. *A desire* is a small matter, especially of the poor man, yet God regards the desire of the poor, and calls a good desire the greatest kindness ; " The desire of a man is his kindness." A *tear* makes no great noise, yet hath a voice, " God hath heard the voice of my weeping." It is no pleasant water, yet God bottles it up. A *groan* is a poor thing, yet is the best part of a prayer sometimes (Rom. viii. 26) ; *a sigh* is less, yet *God is awakened and raised up by it.* Psalm xii. 5. *A look* is less than all these, yet this is regarded (Jonah ii. 4) ; *breathing* is less, yet (Lam. iii. 56), the church could speak of no more ; *panting* is less than breathing, when one is spent for lack of breath, yet this is all the godly can sometimes boast of. Psalm xlii. 1. The description of a godly man is ofttimes made from his least *quod sic.* Blessed are the *poor,* the *meek,* they that *mourn,* and they who *hunger* and *thirst.* Never did Hannah pray better than when she could get out never a word, but cried, " Hard, hard heart." Nor did the publican, than when he smote his breast and cried, " Lord, be merciful to me a sinner." Nor Mary Magdalene, than when she came behind Christ, sat down, wept, but kept silence. How sweet is music upon the *waters !* How fruitful are the lowest valleys ! Mourning hearts are most musical, lowest most fruitful. The good shepherd ever takes most care of his weak lambs and feeble sheep. The father makes most of the least, and the mother looks most after the sick child. How comfortable is that of our Saviour, " It is not the will of your Father which is in heaven that one of these little ones should perish ! " And that heaven is not to be entered but by such as are like the little child.—*John Sheffield,* 1654.

Verse 5.—" *The oppression of the poor.*" Insolent and cruel oppressing of the poor is a sin that brings desolating and destroying judgments upon a people. God sent ten wasting judgments one after another upon Pharaoh, his people, and land, to revenge the cruel oppression of his poor people. " Rob not the poor, because he is poor : neither oppress the afflicted in the gate : for the Lord will plead their cause." Prov. xxii. 22, 23. To rob and oppress the rich is a great sin ; but to rob and oppress the poor is a greater ; but to rob and oppress the poor because he is poor, and wants money to buy justice, is the top of all inhumanity and impiety. To oppress any one is sin ; but to oppress the oppressed is the height of sin. Poverty, and want, and misery, should be motives to pity ; but oppressors make them the whetstones of their cruelty and severity, and therefore the Lord will plead the cause of his poor oppressed people against their oppressors without fee or fear ; yea, he will plead their cause with pestilence, blood, and fire. Gog was a great oppressor of the poor (Ezekiel xxxviii. 8—14), and God pleads against him with pestilence, blood, and fire (verse 22) ; " and I will plead against him, with pestilence and with blood ; and I will rain upon him, and upon his bands, and upon the many people that are with him, an overflowing rain, and great hailstones, fire and brimstone."—*Thomas Brooks.*

Verse 6.—" *The words of the Lord are pure words,*" etc. How beautifully is this verse introduced, by way of contrast to what was said before concerning ! Do sinners talk of vanity ? let saints then speak of Jesus and his gospel. Do they talk impure words ? then let the faithful use the pure words of God, which like silver, the more used, the more melted in the fire, the more precious will they be. It is true, indeed, despisers will esteem both God and his word as trifling ; but oh, what an unknown treasure doth the word, the promises, the covenant relation of the divine things of Jesus contain ! They are more to be desired than gold, yea, than pure gold ; sweeter also than honey and the honeycomb.—*Robert Hawker.*

Verse 6.—" *The words of the Lord are pure words,*" etc. They that purify silver to the purpose, use to put it in the fire again and again, that it may be thoroughly tried. So is the truth of God ; there is scarce any truth but hath been tried over and over again, and still if any dross happen to mingle with it, then God calls it in question again. If in former times there have been Scriptures alleged that have not been pertinent to prove it, that truth shall into the fire again, that what is dross may be burnt up ; the Holy Ghost is so curious, so delicate, so exact, he cannot bear that falsehood should be mingled with the truths of the gospel. That is the reason, therefore, why that God doth still, age after age, call former things in question, because that there is still some dross one way or other mingled with them ; either in the stating the opinions themselves, or else in the Scriptures that are brought and alleged for them, that have passed for current, for he will never leave till he have purified them. The doctrine of God's free grace hath been tried over, and over, and over again. Pelagius begins, and he mingles his dross with it : he saith, grace is nothing but nature in man. Well, his doctrine was purified, and a great deal of dross purged out. Then come the semi-Pelagians, and they part stakes ; they say, nature can do nothing without grace, but they make nature to concur with grace, and to have an influence as well as grace ; and the dross of that was burnt up. The Papists, they take up the same quarrel, but will neither be Pelagians nor semi-Pelagians, yet still mingle dross. The Arminians, they come, and they refine popery in that point anew ; still they mingle dross. God will have this truth tried seven times in the fire, till he hath brought it forth as pure as pure may be. And I say it is because that truth is thus precious.—*Thomas Goodwin.*

Verse 6.—The Scripture is the sun ; the church is the clock. The sun we know to be sure, and regularly constant in his motions ; the clock, as it may fall out, may go too fast or too slow. As then. we should condemn him of folly that should profess to trust the clock rather than the sun, so we cannot but justly tax the credulity of those who would rather trust to the church than to the Scripture.—*Bishop Hall.*

Verse 6.—" *The words of the Lord are pure words.*" Men may inspect detached portions of the Book, and please themselves with some things, which, at first view, have the semblance of conniving at what is wrong. But let them read it, let them read the whole of it ; let them carry along in their minds the character of the persons to which the different portions of it were addressed ; the age of the world, and the circumstances under which the different parts of it were written, and the particular objects which even those portions of it have in view, which to an infidel mind appear the most exceptionable ; and they may be rationally convinced that, instead of originating in the bosom of an impostor, it owes its origin to men who wrote " as they were moved by the Holy Ghost." Let them scrutinise it with as much severity as they please ; only let their scrutiny be well informed, wisely directed, and with a fair and ingenuous mind, and we have no fears for the issue.   There are portions of it on which ignorance and folly have put constructions that are forced and unnatural, and which impure minds have viewed in shadows reflected from their own impurity.   Montesquieu said of Voltaire, *Lorsque Voltaire lit un livre, il le fait, puis il écrit contre ce qu'il a fait :* " When Voltaire reads a book, he makes it what he pleases, and then writes against what he has made."   It is no difficult matter to besmear and blot its pages, and then impute the foul stains that men of corrupt minds have cast upon it, to its stainless Author.   But if we honestly look at it as it is, we shall find that like its Author, it is without blemish and without spot.—*Gardiner Spring, D.D.*

Verse 6.—" *The words of the Lord are pure words : as silver tried in a furnace of earth, purified seven times.*"   The expression may import two things : first, the infallible certainty of the word ;   and, secondly, the exact purity.   First, the infallible certainty of the word, as gold endureth in the fire when the dross is consumed.   Vain conceits comfort us not in a time of trouble ;   but the word of God, the more it is tried, the more you will find the excellency of it—the promise is tried, as well as we are tried, in deep afflictions ;   but, when it is so, it will be found to be most pure,   " The word of the Lord is tried ;   he is a buckler to all those that trust in him " (Prov. xxx. 5) ;   as pure gold suffers no loss by the fire, so the promises suffer no loss when they are tried, but stand to us in our greatest troubles.   Secondly, it notes the exact perfection of the word :   there is no dross in silver and gold that hath been often refined ;   so there is no defect in the word of God.—*Thomas Manton.*

Verse 6.—Fry thus translates this verse :—

> The words of Jehovah are pure words—
> Silver refined in the crucible—
> Gold, seven times washed from the earth.

מְזֻקָּק though sometimes applied to express the purity of silver, is more strictly an epithet of gold, from the peculiar method made use of in separating it from the soil by repeated washings and decantations.—*John Fry, in loc.*

Verse 6.—" *Seven times.*"   I cannot but admit that there may be a mystic meaning in the expression " *seven times,*" in allusion to the seven periods of the church, or to that perfection, implied in the figure seven, to which it is to be brought at the revelation of Jesus Christ.   This will be more readily allowed by those who admit of the prophetic interpretation of the seven epistles of the Book of Revelation. *W. Wilson, D.D., in loc.*

Verse 8.—" *When the vilest men are exalted :*" Heb., *vilities,* οὐτίδανοι, the abstract for the concrete, *quisquiliæ,* οὐτίδανοι.   Oft, empty vessels swim aloft, rotten posts are gilt with adulterate gold, the worst weeds spring up bravest.   Chaff will get to the top of the fan, when good corn, as it lieth at the bottom of the heap, so it falls low at the feet of the fanner.   The reason why wicked men " *walk* " on every side, are so brisk, so busy (and who but they ?) is given to be this, because losels and rioters were exalted.   See Prov. xxviii. 12, 18, and xxix. 2.   As rheums and catarrhs fall from the head to the lungs and cause a consumption of the whole body, so it is in the body politic.   As a fish putrefies first in the head and then in all the parts, so here.   Some render the text thus, " *When they* (that is, the wicked) *are exalted,*" it is a " *shame* for the sons of men," that other men who better deserve preferment, are not only slighted, but vilely handled by such worthless ambitionists, who yet the higher they climb, as apes, the more they discover their deformities."— *John Trapp.*

Verse 8.—Good thus translates this verse :—

> Should the wicked advance on every side ;
> Should the dregs of the earth be uppermost ?

The original is given literally, זֻלּוּת means " fœces, fœculences, dregs." כְּרֻם is here an adverb, and imports *uppermost*, rather than *exalted.*—*J. Mason Good, in loc.*

HINTS TO PREACHERS.

Verse 1.—" *Help, Lord.*" I. The Prayer itself, short, suggestive, seasonable, rightly directed, vehement. II. Occasions for its use. III. Modes of its answer. IV. Reasons for expecting gracious reply.

First two clauses.—Text for funeral of an eminent believer.

Whole verse.—I. *The fact bewailed*—describe godly and faithful, and show how they fail. II. *The feeling excited.* Mourning the loss, fears for church, personal need of such companions, appeal to God. III. *The forebodings aroused.* Failure of the cause, judgments impending, etc. IV. *The faith remaining :* " Help, Lord."

Verse 1.—Intimate connection between yielding honour to God and honesty to man, since they decline together.

Verse 2 (first clause).—A discourse upon the prevalence and perniciousness of vain talk.

The whole verse.—Connection between flattery and treachery.

" A double heart." Right and wrong kinds of hearts, and the disease of duplicity.

Verse 3.—God's hatred of those twin sins of the lips—Flattery and Pride (which is self flattery). Why he hates them. How he shows his hatred. In whom he hates them most. How to be cleansed from them.

Verse 3, 4.—I. *The revolt of the tongue.* Its claim of power, self-possession, and liberty. Contrast between this and the believer's confession, " we are not our own." II. *The method of its rebellion*—" flattery, and speaking proud things." III. *The end of its treason*—" cut off."

Verse 5.—The Lord aroused—How ! Why ! What to do ! When !

Last clause.—Peculiar danger of believers from those who despise them and their special safety. Good practical topic.

Verse 6.—The purity, trial, and permanency of the words of the Lord.

Seven crucibles in which believers try the word. A little thought will suggest these.

Verse 7.—Preservation from one's generation in life and for ever. A very suggestive theme.

Verse 8.—*Sin in high places specially infectious.* Call to the rich and prominent to remember their responsibility. Thankfulness for honourable rulers. Discrimination to be used in choice of our representatives, or civic magistrates.

PSALM XIII.

OCCASION.—*The Psalm cannot be referred to any especial event or period in David's history. All attempts to find it a birthplace are but guesses. It was, doubtless, more than once the language of that much tried man of God, and is intended to express the feelings of the people of God in those ever-returning trials which beset them. If the reader has never yet found occasion to use the language of this brief ode, he will do so ere long, if he be a man after the Lord's own heart. We have been wont to call this the "How Long Psalm." We had almost said the Howling Psalm, from the incessant repetition of the cry "how long?"*

DIVISION.—*This Psalm is very readily to be divided into three parts :—the question of anxiety, 1, 2 ; the cry of prayer, 3, 4 ; the song of faith, 5, 6.*

EXPOSITION.

HOW long wilt thou forget me, O Lord ? for ever ? how long wilt thou hide thy face from me ?

2 How long shall I take counsel in my soul, *having* sorrow in my heart daily ? how long shall mine enemy be exalted over me ?

" *How long ?* "—This question is repeated no less than four times. It betokens very intense desire for deliverance, and great anguish of heart. And what if there be some impatience mingled therewith ; is not this the more true a portrait of our own experience ? It is not easy to prevent desire from degenerating into impatience. O for grace that, while we wait on God, we may be kept from indulging a murmuring spirit ! " *How long ?* " Does not the oft-repeated cry become a very HOWLING ? And what if grief should find no other means of utterance ? Even then, God is not far from the voice of our roaring ; for he does not regard the music of our prayers, but his own Spirit's work in them in exciting desire and inflaming the affections.

" *How long ?* " Ah ! how long do our days appear when our soul is cast down within us !

> " How wearily the moments seem to glide
> O'er sadness ! How the time
> Delights to linger in its flight ! "

Time flies with full-fledged wing in our summer days, but in our winters he flutters painfully. A week within prison-walls is longer than a month at liberty. Long sorrow seems to argue abounding corruption ; for the gold which is long in the fire must have had much dross to be consumed, hence the question " how long ? " may suggest deep searching of heart. " *How long wilt thou forget me ?* " Ah, David ! how like a fool thou talkest ! Can God *forget ?* Can Omniscience fail in memory ? Above all, can Jehovah's heart forget his own beloved child ? Ah ! brethren, let us drive away the thought, and hear the voice of our covenant God by the mouth of the prophet, " But Zion said, The Lord hath forsaken me, and my Lord hath forgotten me. Can a woman forget her sucking child, that she should not have compassion on the son of her womb ? yea, they may forget, yet will I not forget thee. Behold, I have graven thee upon the palms of my hands ; thy walls are continually before me." " *For ever ?* " Oh, dark thought ! It was surely bad enough to suspect a temporary forgetfulness, but shall we ask the ungracious question, and imagine that the Lord will for ever cast away his people ? No, his anger may endure for a night, but his love shall abide eternally. " *How long wilt thou hide thy face from me ?* " This is a far more rational question, for God may hide his face, and yet he may remember still. A hidden face is no sign of a forgetful heart. It is in love that his face is turned away ; yet to a real child of God, this hiding of his Father's face is terrible, and he will never be at ease until once more he hath his Father's smile. " *How long shall I take counsel in my soul, having sorrow in my heart daily ?* " There is in the original the idea of " laying up " counsels in his heart, as if his devices had become innumerable but unavailing. Herein we have often been like David, for we have considered and reconsidered day after day, but have not discovered the happy device by which to escape from our trouble.

Such store is a sad sore. Ruminating upon trouble is bitter work. Children fill their mouths with bitterness when they rebelliously chew the pill which they ought obediently to have taken at once. *"How long shall mine enemy be exalted over me ? "* This is like wormwood in the gall, to see the wicked enemy exulting while our soul is bowed down within us. The laughter of a foe grates horribly upon the ears of grief. For the devil to make mirth of our misery is the last ounce of our complaint, and quite breaks down our patience ; therefore let us make it one chief argument in our plea with mercy.

Thus the careful reader will remark that the question " how long ? " is put in four shapes. The writer's grief is viewed, as it seems to be, as it is, as it affects himself within, and his foes without. We are all prone to play most on the worst string. We set up monumental stones over the graves of our joys, but who thinks of erecting monuments of praise for mercies received ? We write four books of Lamentations and only one of Canticles, and are far more at home in wailing out a *Miserere* than in chanting a *Te Deum.*

3 Consider *and* hear me, O Lord my God   lighten mine eyes, lest I sleep the *sleep* of death ;

4 Lest mine enemy say, I have prevailed against him ; *and* those that trouble me rejoice when I am moved.

But now prayer lifteth up her voice, like the watchman who proclaims the day-break. Now will the tide turn, and the weeper shall dry his eyes. The mercy-seat is the life of hope and the death of despair. The gloomy thought of God's having forsaken him is still upon the Psalmist's soul, and he therefore cries, " *Consider and hear me.*" He remembers at once the root of his woe, and cries aloud that it may be removed. The final absence of God is Tophet's fire, and his temporary absence brings his people into the very suburbs of hell. God is here entreated to *see* and *hear,* that so he may be doubly moved to pity. What should we do if we had no God to turn to in the hour of wretchedness ?

Note the cry of faith, " *O Lord* MY *God !* " Is it not a very glorious fact that our interest in our God is not destroyed by all our trials and sorrows ? We may lose our gourds, but not our God. The title-deed of heaven is not written in the sand, but in eternal brass.

" *Lighten mine eyes :* " that is, let the eye of my faith be clear, that I may see my God in the dark ; let my eye of watchfulness be wide open, lest I be entrapped, and let the eye of my understanding be illuminated to see the right way. Perhaps, too, here is an allusion to that cheering of the spirits so frequently called the en-lightening of the eyes because it causes the face to brighten, and the eyes to sparkle. Well may we use the prayer, " Lighten our darkness, we beseech thee, O Lord ! " for in many respects we need the Holy Spirit's illuminating rays. " *Lest I sleep the sleep of death.*" Darkness engenders sleep, and despondency is not slow in making the eyes heavy. From this faintness and dimness of vision, caused by despair, there is but a step to the iron sleep of death. David feared that his trials would end his life, and he rightly uses his fear as an argument with God in prayer ; for deep distress has in it a kind of claim upon compassion, not a claim of right, but a plea which has power with grace. Under the pressure of heart sorrow, the Psalmist does not look forward to the sleep of death with hope and joy, as assured believers do, but he shrinks from it with dread, from which we gather that bondage from fear of death is no new thing.

Another plea is urged in the fourth verse, and it is one which the tried believer may handle well when on his knees. We make use of our arch-enemy for once, and compel him, like Samson, to grind in our mill while we use his cruel arrogance as an argument in prayer. It is not the Lord's will that the great enemy of our souls should overcome his children. This would dishonour God, and cause the evil one to boast. It is well for us that our salvation and God's honour are so intimately connected, that they stand or fall together.

Our covenant God will complete the confusion of all our enemies, and if for awhile we become their scoff and jest, the day is coming when the shame will change sides, and the contempt shall be poured on those to whom it is due.

5 But I have trusted in thy mercy ; my heart shall rejoice in thy salvation.

6 I will sing unto the Lord, because he hath dealt bountifully with me.

What a change is here! Lo, the rain is over and gone, and the time of the singing of birds is come. The mercy-seat has so refreshed the poor weeper, that he clears his throat for a song. If we have mourned with him, let us now dance with him. David's heart was more often out of tune than his harp. He begins many of his Psalms sighing, and ends them singing; and others he begins in joy and ends in sorrow; "so that one would think," says Peter Moulin, "that those Psalms had been composed by two men of a contrary humour." It is worthy to be observed that the joy is all the greater because of the previous sorrow, as calm is all the more delightful in recollection of the preceding tempest.

> "Sorrows remembered sweeten present joy."

Here is his avowal of his confidence: "*But I have trusted in thy mercy.*" For many a year it had been his wont to make the Lord his castle and tower of defence, and he smiles from behind the same bulwark still. He is sure of his faith, and his faith makes him sure; had he doubted the reality of his trust in God, he would have blocked up one of the windows through which the sun of heaven delights to shine. Faith is now in exercise, and consequently is readily discovered; there is never a doubt in our heart about the existence of faith while it is in action; when the hare or partridge is quiet we see it not, but let the same be in motion and we soon perceive it. All the powers of his enemies had not driven the Psalmist from his stronghold. As the shipwrecked mariner clings to the mast, so did David cling to his faith; he neither could nor would give up his confidence in the Lord his God. O that we may profit by his example, and hold by our faith as by our very life!

Now hearken to the music which faith makes in the soul. The bells of the mind are all ringing, "*My heart shall rejoice in thy salvation.*" There is joy and feasting within doors, for a glorious guest has come, and the fatted calf is killed. Sweet is the music which sounds from the strings of the heart. But this is not all; *the voice* joins itself in the blessed work, and the tongue keeps tune with the soul, while the writer declares, "*I will sing unto the Lord.*"

> "I will praise thee every day,
> Now thine anger's turned away;
> Comfortable thoughts arise
> From the bleeding sacrifice."

The Psalm closes with a sentence which is a refutation of the charge of forget-fulness which David had uttered in the first verse, "*He hath dealt bountifully with me.*" So shall it be with us if we wait awhile. The complaint which in our haste we utter shall be joyfully retracted, and we shall witness that the Lord hath dealt bountifully with us.

EXPLANATORY NOTES AND QUAINT SAYINGS.

Verse 1.—"*How long wilt thou forget me, O Lord?*" etc. The departures of God from true believers are never final; they may be tedious, but they are temporary. As the evil spirit is said to depart from Christ for a season (Luke iv. 13; though he quitted that temptation, he did not quit his design, so as to tempt no more), so the good Spirit withdraws from those that are Christ's for a season only, 'tis with a purpose of coming again. When he hath most evidently forsaken, 'tis as unquestionable that sooner or later he will return; and the happiness of his return will richly recompense for the sadness of his desertion; Isa. liv. 7, "For a small moment have I forsaken thee; but with great mercies will I gather thee;" here is not only a gathering after a forsaking, but "*great mercies*" to make amends for "*a small moment.*" He who hath engaged to be our God for ever, cannot depart for ever.—*Timothy Cruso, 1696.*

Verse 1.—"*How long wilt thou forget me, O Lord?*" Whatever be the pressing need of Christ's followers in troubles, and their constant cleaving to duty for all that; and whatever be Christ's purpose of love towards them, yet he seeth it fit ofttimes not to come to them at first, but will let the trial go on till it come to a height, and be a trial indeed, and put them seriously to it; for before he came he lets them row " about five and twenty or thirty furlongs " (the last of which make near four miles, eight furlongs going to a mile) ; and (Mark vi. 48) he came not till the fourth watch of the night, which is the morning watch. We are indeed very sparing of ourselves in trouble, and do soon begin to think that we are low and tried enough, and therefore would be delivered ; but our wise Lord seeth that we need more.—*George Hutcheson*, 1657.

Verse 1.—" *How long,*" etc. Enquire into the cause of God's anger. He is never angry but when there is very great reason, when we force him to be so. What is that accursed thing in our hearts, or in our lives, for which God hides his face, and frowns upon us ? What particular disobedience to his commands is it for which he has taken up the rod ? Job x. 2 ; " I will say unto God, Do not condemn me ; shew me wherefore thou contendest with me ;" as if he should say, Lord, my troubles and my sorrows are very well known. . . . We must not cease to be solicitous to know what are the particular sins that have made him to tear us up by the roots, to throw us down as with a whirlwind ; what is it that has made him so long angry with us, and so long to delay his help, that if any evil be undiscovered in our souls, we may lament it with a seasonable grief, and get a pardon for it. It is not the common course of God's providence to cover his servants with so thick a darkness as this is, which our troubled souls labour under in the day, or rather in the night of his displeasure ; and, therefore, we may with humility desire to know why he proceeds with us in a way that is so singular ; for it is some way delightful to the understanding to pierce into the reasons and causes of things.—*Timothy Rogers.*

Verse 1.—" *How long wilt thou forget me,*" etc. For God *to forget* David, not to mind him, or look after him, is much ! If his eye be never so little once off us, the spiritual adversary is ready presently to seize on us, as the kite on the chick if the hen look not carefully after it. . . . As a father will sometimes cross his son to try the child's disposition, to see how he will take it, whether he will mutter and grumble at it, and grow humorous and wayward, neglect his duty to his father because his father seemeth to neglect him, or make offer to run away and withdraw himself from his father's obedience because he seemeth to carry himself harshly and roughly towards him, and to provoke him thereunto ; so doth God likewise ofttimes cross his children and seemeth to neglect them, so to try their disposition, what metal they are made of, how they stand affected towards him : whether they will neglect God because God seemeth to neglect them, forbear to serve him because he seemeth to forget them, cease to depend upon him because he seemeth not to look after them, to provide for them, or to protect them. Like Joram's prophane pursuivant, " This evil," saith he, " is of the Lord ; what should I wait for the Lord any longer ? " Or whether they will still constantly cleave to him, though he seem not to regard them, nor to have any care of them ; and say with Isaiah, " Yet will I wait upon God, though he have hid his face from us, and I will look for him though he look not on us ; " for, " They are blessed that wait on him ; and he will not fail in due time to show mercy unto all them that do so constantly wait on him." Isa. viii. 17 ; xxx. 18. As Samuel dealt with Saul ; he kept away till the last hour, to see what Saul would do when Samuel seemed not to keep touch with him. So doth God with his saints, and with those that be in league with him ; he withdraweth himself oft, and keeps aloof oft for a long time together to try what they will do, and what courses they will take when God seemeth to break with them and to leave them in the suds, as we say ; amidst many difficulties much perplexed, as it was with David at this time.—*Thomas Gataker*, 1637.

Verse 1.—1. For desertions. I think them like lying fallow of lean and weak land for some years, while it gathers sap for a better crop. It is possible to gather gold, where it may be had, with moonlight. Oh, if I could but creep one foot, or half a foot, nearer in to Jesus, in such a dismal night as that when he is away, I should think it a happy absence ! 2. If I knew that the Beloved were only gone away for trial, and further humiliation, and not smoked out of the house with new provocations, I would forgive desertions and hold my peace at his absence. But Christ's bought absence (that I bought with my sin), is two running boils at once, one upon each side ; and what side then can I lie on ? 3. I know that, as night and shadows are good for flowers, and moonlight and dews are better than a continual sun, so is Christ's absence of special use, and that it hath some nourishing virtue in it, and giveth sap to humility, and putteth an edge on hunger, and furnisheth a fair field to faith to put forth itself, and to exercise its fingers in gripping it seeth not what.—*Samuel Rutherford*, 1600—1661.

Verses 1, 2.—That which the French proverb hath of sickness is true of all evils, that they come on horseback and go away on foot ; we have often seen that a sudden fall, or one meal's surfeit, has stuck by many to their graves ; whereas pleasures come like oxen, slow and heavily, and go away like post-horses, upon the spur. Sorrows, because they are lingering guests, I will entertain but moderately, knowing that the more they are made of the longer they will continue : and for pleasures, because they stay not, and do but call to drink at my door, I will use them as passengers with slight respect. He is his own best friend that makes the least of both of them.—*Joseph Hall.*

Verses 1, 2.—" *How* LONG *wilt thou forget me ? How* LONG *wilt thou hide thy face from me ? How* LONG *shall I take counsel in my soul ? "* The intenseness of the affliction renders it trying to our fortitude ; but it is by the continuance of it that patience is put to the test. It is not under the sharpest, but the longest trials, that we are most in danger of fainting. In the first case, the soul collects all its strength, and feels in earnest to call in help from above ; but, in the last, the mind relaxes, and sinks into despondency. When Job was accosted with evil tidings, in quick succession, he bore it with becoming fortitude ; but when he could see no end to his troubles, he sunk under them.—*Andrew Fuller.*

Verses 1—4.—Everything is strangely changed ; all its comeliness, and beauty, and glory, vanishes when the *life* is gone : life is the pleasant thing ; 'tis sweet and comfortable ; but death with its pale attendants, raises a horror and aversion to it everywhere. The saints of God dread the removal of his favour, and the hiding of his face ; and when it is hid, a faintness and a cold amazement and fear seizes upon every part, and they feel strange bitterness, and anguish, and tribulation, which makes their joints to tremble, and is to them as the very pangs of death.— *Timothy Rogers.*

Verses 1, 5, 6.—Prayer helps towards the increase and growth of grace, by drawing the habits of grace into exercise. Now, as exercise brings benefit to the body, so does prayer to the soul. Exercise doth help to digest or breathe forth those humours that clog the spirits. One that stirs little we see grow pursy, and is soon choked up with phlegm, which exercise clears the body of. Prayer is the saint's exercise-field, where his graces are breathed ; it is as the wind to the air, it brightens the soul ; as bellows to the fire, which clears the coal of those ashes that smother them. The Christian, while in this world, lives in an unwholesome climate ; one while, the delights of it deaden and dull his love of Christ ; another while, the trouble he meets in it damps his faith on the promise. How now should the Christian get out of these distempers, had he not a throne of grace to resort to, where if once his soul be in a melting frame, he (like one laid in a kindly sweat), soon breathes out the malignity of his disease, and comes ino his right temper again ? How often do we find the holy prophet, when he first kneels down to pray, full of fears and doubts, who, before he and the duty part, grows into a sweet familiarity with God, and repose in his own spirit ! (Psalm xiii. 1) He begins his prayer as if he thought God would never give him a kind look more : " *How long wilt thou forget me, O Lord ? for ever ? "* But by that time he had exercised himself a little in duty, his distemper wears off, the mists scatter, and his faith breaks out as the sun in its strength, verses 5, 6 : " *I have trusted in thy mercy ; my heart shall rejoice in thy salvation. I will sing unto the Lord."* Thus his faith lays the cloth, expecting a feast ere long to be set on : he that now questioned whether he should ever hear good news from heaven, is so strong in faith as to make himself merry with the hopes of that mercy which will come at last. Abraham began with fifty, but his faith got ground on God every step till he brought down the price of their lives to ten.—*William Gurnall.*

Verses 1, 6.—Whatever discouragements thou meetest with in thine attendance on God in ordinances, be like the English jet, fired by water, and not like our ordinary fires, quenched by it ; let them add to, not diminish, thy resolution and courage ; let not one repulse beat thee off ; be violent, give a second storm to the kingdom of heaven. Parents sometimes hide themselves to make their children continue seeking. He that would not at first open his mouth, nor vouchsafe the woman of Canaan a word, doth, upon her continued and fervent petitions, at last open his hand and give her whatsoever she asks: "O woman, be it unto thee as thou wilt." Continued importunity is undeniable oratory. And truly, if after all thy pains thou findest Jesus Christ, will it not make amends for thy long patience ? Men that venture often at a lottery, though they take blanks twenty times, if afterwards they get a golden bason and ewer, it will make them abundant satisfaction. Suppose thou shouldst continue knocking twenty, nay, forty years, yet if at last, though but one hour before thou diest thy heart be opened to Christ, and he be received into thy soul, and when thou diest heaven be opened to thee, and thy soul received into it, will it not infinitely requite thee for all thy labour? Oh, think of it, and resolve never to be dumb while God is deaf, never to leave off prayer till God return a gracious answer. And for thy comfort, know that he who began his Psalm with, " *How long wilt thou forget me, O Lord? for ever? how long wilt thou hide thy face from me?* " comes to conclude it with, " *I will sing unto the Lord, because he hath dealt bountifully with me.*"—*George Swinnock.*

Verse 2.—" *How long?* " There are many situations of the believer in this life in which the words of this Psalm may be a consolation, and help to revive sinking faith. A certain man lay at the pool of Bethesda, who had an infirmity thirty and eight years. John v. 5. A woman had a spirit of infirmity eighteen years, before she was "loosed." Luke xiii. 11. Lazarus all his life long laboured under disease and poverty, till he was released by death and transferred to Abraham's bosom. Luke xvi. 20—22. Let every one, then, who may be tempted to use the complaints of this Psalm, assure his heart that God does not forget his people, help will come at last, and, in the meantime, all things shall work together for good to them that love him.—*W. Wilson, D.D.*

Verse 2.—" *How long shall I take counsel in my soul, having sorrow in my heart daily?* " There is such a thing as to pore on our guilt and wretchedness, to the overlooking of our highest mercies. Though it be proper to know our own hearts, for the purposes of conviction, yet, if we expect consolation from this quarter, we shall find ourselves sadly disappointed. Such, for a time, appears to have been the case of David. He seems to have been in great distress; and as is common in such cases, his thoughts turned inward, casting in his mind what he should do, and what would be the end of things. While thus exercised, he had *sorrow in his heart daily*: but, betaking himself to God for relief, he succeeded, *trusting in his mercy, his heart rejoiced in his salvation.* There are many persons, who, when in trouble, imitate David in the former part of this experience: I wish we may imitate him in the latter.—*Andrew Fuller.*

Verses 2, 4.—" *How shall mine enemy be exalted over me?* " 'Tis a great relief to the miserable and afflicted, to be pitied by others. It is some relief when others, though they cannot help us, yet seem to be truly concerned for the sadness of our case; when by the kindness of their words and of their actions they do a little smooth the wounds they cannot heal; but 'tis an unspeakable addition to the cross, when a man is brought low under the sense of God's displeasure, to have men to mock at his calamity, or to revile him, or to speak roughly; this does inflame and exasperate the wound that was big enough before; and it is a hard thing when one has a dreadful sound in his ears to have every friend to become a son of thunder. It is a small matter for people that are at ease, to deal severely with such as are afflicted, but they little know how their severe speeches and their angry words pierce them to the very soul. 'Tis easy to blame others for complaining, but if such had felt but for a little while what it is to be under the fear of God's anger, they would find that they could not but complain. It cannot but make any person restless and uneasy when he apprehends that God is his enemy. It is no wonder if he makes every one that he sees, and every place that he is in, a witness of his grief; but now it is a comfort in our temptations and in our fears, that we have so compassionate a friend as Christ is to whom we may repair, " For we have not an high priest which cannot be touched with the feeling of our infirmities; but was in all points tempted like as we are, yet without sin." Heb. iv. 15.—*Timothy Rogers.*

Verse 3.—" *Lighten mine eyes, lest I sleep the sleep of death.*" In time of sickness and grief, the " eyes " are dull and heavy; and they grow more and more so as death approaches, which closes them in darkness. On the other hand, health and joy render the organs of vision bright and sparkling, seeming, as it were, to impart " light " to them from within. The words, therefore, may be fitly applied to a recovery of the body natural, and thence, of the body politic, from their respective maladies. Nor do they less significantly describe the restoration of the soul to a state of spiritual health and holy joy, which will manifest themselves in like manner, by " the eyes of the understanding being enlightened ; " and in this case, the soul is saved from the sleep of sin, as the body is in the other, from the sleep of death.— *George Horne.*

Verse 3.—Why dost *thou hide thy face ?* happily thou wilt say, None can see thy face and live. Ah, Lord, let me die, that I may see thee ; let me see thee, that I may die : I would not live, but die ; that I may see Christ, I desire death ; that I may live with Christ, I despise life.—*Augustine.*

Verse 3.—" *How long wilt thou hide thy face from me ?* " Oh, excellent hiding, which is become my perfection ! My God, thou hidest thy treasure to kindle my desire ! Thou hidest thy pearl, to inflame the seeker ; thou delayest to give, that thou mayest teach me to importune ; seemest not to hear, to make me persevere.— *John Anselm,* 1034—1109.

Verse 4.—

> Ah ! can you bear contempt ; the venom'd tongue
> Of those whom ruin pleases, the keen sneer,
> The lewd reproaches of the rascal herd ;
> Who for the selfsame actions, if successful,
> Would be as grossly lavish in your praise ?
> To sum up all in one—can you support
> The scornful glances, the malignant joy,
> Or more detested pity of a rival—
> Of a triumphant rival ?
>
> *James Thomson,* 1700—1748.

Verse 4.—" *And those that trouble me rejoice when I am moved* "—compose comedies out of my tragedies.—*John Trapp.*

Verse 5.—" *I have trusted in thy mercy ; my heart shall rejoice in thy salvation.*" Faith rejoiceth in tribulations, and triumpheth before the victory. The patient is glad when he feels his physic to work, though it make him sick for the time because he hopes it will procure health. We rejoice in afflictions, not that they are joyous for the present, but because they shall work for our good. As faith rejoiceth, so it triumpheth in assurance of good success ; for it seeth not according to outward appearance, but when all means fail, it keepeth God in sight, and beholdeth him present for our succour.—*John Ball.*

Verse 5.—" *I have trusted in thy mercy ; my heart shall rejoice in thy salvation.*" Though passion possess our bodies, let " patience possess our souls." The law of our profession binds us to a warfare ; *patiendo vincimus,* our troubles shall end, our victory is eternal. Here David's triumph (Psalm xviii. 38—40), " I have wounded them, that they were not able to rise ; they are fallen under my feet. Thou hast subdued under me those that rose up against me. Thou hast also given me the neck of mine enemies," etc. They have wounds for their wounds ; and the treaders down of the poor are trodden down by the poor. The Lord will subdue those to us that would have subdued us to themselves ; and though for a short time they rode over our heads, yet now at last we shall everlastingly tread upon their necks. Lo, then, the reward of humble patience and confident hope. *Speramus et superamus.* Deut. xxxii. 31. " Our God is not as their God, even our enemies being judges." Psalm xx. 7. " Some put their trust in chariots, and some in horses." But no chariot hath strength to oppose, nor horse swiftness to escape, when God pursues. Verse 8. " They are brought down and fallen ; we are risen and stand upright." Their trust hath deceived them ; down they fall, and never to rise. Our God hath helped us ; we are risen, not for a breathing space, but to stand upright for ever.—*Thomas Adams.*

Verse 5.—None live so easily, so pleasantly, as those that live by faith.—*Matthew Henry.*

Verse 5.—Wherefore I say again, " Live by faith ; " again I say, always live by it, rejoice through faith in the Lord. I dare boldly say it is thy fault and neglect of its exercise if thou suffer either thy own melancholy humour or Satan to interrupt thy mirth and spiritual alacrity, and to detain thee in dumps and pensiveness at any time. What if thou beest of a sad constitution ? of a dark complexion ? Is not faith able to rectify nature ? Is it not stronger than any hellebore ? Doth not an experienced divine and physician worthily prefer one dram of it before all the drugs in the apothecary's shop for this effect ? Hath it not sovereign virtue in it, to excerebrate all cares, expectorate all fears and griefs, evacuate the mind

of all ill thoughts and passions, to exhilarate the whole man ?   But what good
doth it to any to have a cordial by him if he use it not ?   To wear a sword, soldier-
like, by his side, and not to draw it forth in an assault ?   When a dump overtakes
thee, if thou wouldst say to thy soul in a word or two, " Soul, why art thou disquieted ? know and consider in whom thou believest," would it not presently
return to its rest again ?   Would not the Master rebuke the winds and storms,
and calm thy troubled mind presently ?   Hath not every man something or other
he useth to put away dumps, to drive away the evil spirit, as David with his harp ?
Some with merry company, some with a cup of sack, most with a pipe of tobacco,
without which they cannot ride or go.   If they miss it a day together they are
troubled with rheums, dulness of spirits.   They that live in fens and ill airs dare
not stir out without a morning draught of some strong liquor.   Poor, silly, smoky
helps, in comparison with the least taste (but for dishonouring faith I would say
whiff) or draught of faith.—*Samuel Ward*, 1577—1653.

   Verse 6.—" *I will sing unto the Lord, because he hath dealt bountifully with me.*"
Faith keeps the soul from sinking under heavy trials, by bringing in former experiences of the power, mercy, and faithfulness of God to the afflicted soul.   Hereby
was the Psalmist supported in distress.   Oh, saith faith, remember what God hath
done both for thy outward and inward man : he hath not only delivered thy body
when in trouble, but he hath done great things for thy soul; he hath brought thee
out of a state of black nature, entered into a covenant relation with thee, made
his goodness pass before thee ; he hath helped thee to pray, and many times hath
heard thy prayers and thy tears.   Hath he not formerly brought thee out of the
horrible pit, and out of the miry clay, and put a new song in thy mouth, and made
thee to resolve never to give way to such unbelieving thoughts and fears again?
and how unbecoming is it for thee now to sink in trouble ?—*John Willison*,
1680—1750.
   Verse 6.—" *I will sing unto the Lord.*"   Mr. John Philpot having lain for some
time in the bishop of London's coal-house, the bishop sent for him, and amongst
other questions, asked him why they were so merry in prison ? singing (as the
prophet speaks) *Exultantes in rebus pessimis*, rejoicing in your naughtiness, whereas
you should rather lament and be sorry.   Mr. Philpot answered, " My lord, the
mirth which we make is but in singing certain Psalms, as we are commanded by
Paul to rejoice in the Lord, singing together hymns and Psalms, for we are in a
dark, comfortless place, and therefore, we thus solace ourselves.   I trust, therefore,
your lordship will not be angry, seeing the apostle saith, ' If any be of an upright
heart, let him sing Psalms ; ' and we, to declare that we are of an upright mind to
God, though we are in misery, yet refresh ourselves with such singing."   After
some other discourse, saith he, " I was carried back to my lord's coal-house, where I,
with my six fellow prisoners, do rouze together in the straw, as cheerfully (I thank
God) as others do in their beds of down."   And in a letter to a friend, he thus writes :
" Commend me to Mr. Elsing and his wife, and thank them for providing me some
ease in my prison ; and tell them that though my lord's coal-house be very black,
yet it is more to be desired of the faithful than the Queen's palace.   The world
wonders how we can be so merry under such extreme miseries ; but our God is
omnipotent, who turns misery into felicity.   Believe me, there is no such joy in
the world, as the people of God have under the cross of Christ : I speak by experience,
and therefore believe me, and fear nothing that the world can do unto you, for when
they imprison our bodies, they set our souls at liberty to converse with God ; when
they cast us down, they lift us up ; when they kill us, then do they send us to everlasting life.   What greater glory can there be than to be made conformable to our
Head, Christ ?   And this is done by affliction.   O good God, what am I, upon whom
thou shouldst bestow so great a mercy ?   This is the day which the Lord hath
made ; let us rejoice and be glad in it.   This is the way, though it be narrow,
which is full of the peace of God, and leadeth to eternal bliss.   Oh, how my heart
leapeth for joy that I am so near the apprehension thereof!   God forgive me my
unthankfulness and unworthiness of so great glory.   I have so much joy, that though
I be in a place of darkness and mourning, yet I cannot lament ; but both night and
day am so full of joy, as I never was so merry before ; the Lord's name be praised
for ever.   Our enemies do fret, fume, and gnash their teeth at it.   O pray instantly
that this joy may never be taken from us ; for it passeth all the delights in this
world.   This is the peace of God that passeth all understanding.   This peace, the

more his chosen be afflicted, the more they feel it, and therefore cannot faint neither for fire nor water."—*Samuel Clarke's " Mirrour," 1671.*

Verse 6.—*" I will sing unto the Lord."* How far different is the end of this Psalm from the beginning !—*John Trapp.*

Verse 6.—*" I will sing unto the Lord,"* etc. I never knew what it was for God to stand by me at all turns, and at every offer of Satan to afflict me, etc., as I have found him since I came in hither ; for look how fears have presented themselves, so have supports and encouragements ; yet, when I have started, even as it were at nothing else but my shadow, yet God, as being very tender of me, hath not suffered me to be molested, but would with one Scripture or another, strengthen me against all ; insomuch that I have often said, *Were it lawful, I could pray for greater trouble, for the greater comfort's sake.* Eccles. vii. 14 ; 2 Cor. i. 5.—*John Bunyan, 1628—1688.*

HINTS TO PREACHERS.

Verse 1.—The apparent length of sorrow, only apparent. Contrast with days of joy, with eternal misery and eternal joy. Impatience, and other evil passions, cause the seeming length. Means of shortening, by refusing to forestall, or to repine afterwards.

Verse 1 (second clause).—Hiding of the divine face. Why at all ? Why from me ? Why so long ?

Verse 2.—Advice to the dejected, or the soul directed to look out of itself for consolation.—*A. Fuller.*

Verse 2 (first clause).—*Self-torture*, its cause, curse, crime, and cure.

Verse 2.—*" Having sorrow in my heart daily."* I. The cause of daily sorrow. Great enemy, unbelief, sin, trial, loss of Jesus' presence, sympathy with others, mourning for human ruin. II. The necessity of daily sorrow. Purge corruptions, excite graces, raise desires heavenward. III. The cure of daily sorrow. Good food from God's table, old wine of promises, walks with Jesus, exercise in good works, avoidance of everything unhealthy.—*B. Davis.*

Verse 2.—*(second clause).*—Time anticipated when defeat shall be turned into victory.

Verse 3.—By accommodating the text to the believer. I. True character of Satan, "enemy." II. Remarkable fact that his enemy is exalted over us. III. Pressing enquiry, "How long ?"—*B. Davis.*

Verse 3.—*" Lighten mine eyes."* A prayer fit for (1) Every benighted sinner. (2) Every seeker of salvation. (3) Every learner in Christ's school. (4) Every tried believer. (5) Every dying saint.—*B. Davis.*

Verse 4.—Noteth the nature of the wicked two ways ; namely, the more they prevail the more insolent they are ; they wonderfully exult over those that are afflicted.—*T. Wilcocks.*

Verse 5.—Experience and perseverance. " I have," " my heart shall."

Verse 6.—The bountiful giver and the hearty singer.

The whole Psalm would make a good subject, showing the stages from mourning to rejoicing, dwelling especially upon the turning point, prayer. There are two verses for each, mourning, praying, rejoicing.—*A. G. Brown.*

PSALM XIV.

TITLE.—*This admirable ode is simply headed, " To the Chief Musician by David." The dedication to the Chief Musician stands at the head of fifty-three of the Psalms, and clearly indicates that such Psalms were intended, not merely for the private use of believers, but to be sung in the great assemblies by the appointed choir at whose head was the overseer, or superintendent, called in our version, " the Chief Musician," and by Ainsworth, " the master of the Music." Several of these Psalms have little or no praise in them, and were not addressed directly to the Most High, and yet were to be sung in public worship ; which is a clear indication that the theory of Augustine lately revived by certain hymn-book makers, that nothing but praise should be sung, is far more plausible than Scriptural. Not only did the ancient Church chant hallowed doctrine and offer prayer amid her spiritual songs, but even the wailing notes of complaint were put into her mouth by the sweet singer of Israel who was inspired of God. Some persons grasp at any nicety which has a gloss of apparent correctness upon it, and are pleased with being more fancifully precise than others ; nevertheless it will ever be the way of plain men, not only to magnify the Lord in sacred canticles, but also, according to Paul's precept, to teach and admonish one another in Psalms and hymns and spiritual songs, singing with grace in their hearts unto the Lord.*

As no distinguishing title is given to this Psalm, we would suggest as an assistance to the memory, the heading—CONCERNING PRATICAL ATHEISM. *The many conjectures as to the occasion upon which it was written are so completely without foundation, that it would be a waste of time to mention them at length. The apostle Paul, in Romans iii., has shown incidentally that the drift of the inspired writer is to show that both Jews and Gentiles are all under sin ; there was, therefore, no reason for fixing upon any particular historical occasion, when all history reeks with terrible evidence of human corruption. With instructive alterations, David has given us in Psalm liii. a second edition of this humiliating psalm, being moved of the Holy Ghost thus doubly to declare a truth which is ever distasteful to carnal minds.*

DIVISION.—*The world's foolish creed (verse 1); its practical influence in corrupting morals, 1, 2, 3. The persecuting tendencies of sinners, 4 ; their alarms, 5 ; their ridicule of the godly, 6 ; and a prayer for the manifestation of the Lord to his people's joy.*

EXPOSITION.

THE fool hath said in his heart, *There is* no God. They are corrupt, they have done abominable works, *there is* none that doeth good.

" *The fool.*" The Atheist is *the* fool pre-eminently, and *a* fool universally. He would not deny God if he were not a fool by nature, and having denied God it is no marvel that he becomes a fool in practice. Sin is always folly, and as it is the height of sin to attack the very existence of the Most High, so is it also the greatest imaginable folly. To say there is no God is to belie the plainest evidence, which is obstinacy ; to oppose the common consent of mankind, which is stupidity ; to stifle consciousness, which is madness. If the sinner could by his atheism destroy the God whom he hates there were some sense, although much wickedness, in his infidelity ; but as denying the existence of fire does not prevent its burning a man who is in it, so doubting the existence of God will not stop the Judge of all the earth from destroying the rebel who breaks his laws ; nay, this atheism is a crime which much provokes heaven, and will bring down terrible vengeance on the fool who indulges it. The proverb says, "A fool's tongue cuts his own throat," and in this instance it kills both soul and body for ever : would to God the mischief stopped even there, but alas ! one fool makes hundreds, and a noisy blasphemer spreads his horrible doctrines as lepers spread the plague. Ainsworth, in his " Annotations," tells us that the word here used is *Nabal*, which has the signification of fading, dying, or falling away, as a withered leaf or flower ; it is a title given to the foolish man as having lost the juice and sap of wisdom, reason, honesty, and godliness. Trapp hits the mark when he calls him " that sapless fellow, that carcase of a man, that walking sepulchre of himself, in whom all religion and right reason is withered and wasted, dried up and decayed." Some translate it *the apostate*, and others *the wretch*. With what earnestness should we shun the appearance of doubt as to the presence, activity, power and love of God, for all such mistrust is of the nature of folly, and who among us would wish to be ranked with the fool in the text? Yet let us never forget that all unregenerate men are more or less such fools.

The fool *" hath said in his heart."* May a man with his mouth profess to believe, and yet in heart say the reverse? Had he hardly become audacious enough to utter his folly with his tongue? Did the Lord look upon his thoughts as being in the nature of words to him though not to man? Is this where man first becomes an unbeliever?—in his heart, not in his head? And when he talks atheistically, is it a foolish heart speaking and endeavouring to clamour down the voice of conscience? We think so. If the affections were set upon truth and righteousness, the understanding would have no difficulty in settling the question of a present personal Deity, but as the heart dislikes the good and the right, it is no wonder that it desires to be rid of that Elohim, who is the great moral Governor, the Patron of rectitude and the Punisher of iniquity. While men's hearts remain what they are, we must not be surprised at the prevalence of scepticism; a corrupt tree will bring forth corrupt fruit. "Every man," says Dickson, "so long as he lieth unrenewed and unreconciled to God is nothing in effect but a madman." What wonder then if he raves? Such fools as those we are now dealing with are common to all time, and all countries; they grow without watering, and are found all the world over. The spread of mere intellectual enlightenment will not diminish their number, for since it is an affair of the heart, this folly and great learning will often dwell together. To answer sceptical cavilings will be labour lost until grace enters to make the mind willing to believe; fools can raise more objections in an hour than wise men can answer in seven years, indeed it is their mirth to set stools for wise men to stumble over. Let the preacher aim at the heart, and preach the all-conquering love of Jesus, and he will by God's grace win more doubters to the faith of the gospel than any hundred of the best reasoners who only direct their arguments to the head.

" The fool hath said in his heart, There is no God," or *" no God."* So monstrous is the assertation, that the man hardly dared to put it as a positive statement, but went very near to doing so. Calvin seems to regard this saying "no God," as hardly amounting to a syllogism, scarcely reaching to a positive, dogmatical declaration; but Dr. Alexander clearly shows that it does. It is not merely the wish of the sinner's corrupt nature, and the hope of his rebellious heart, but he manages after a fashion to bring himself to assert it, and at certain seasons he thinks that he believes it. It is a solemn reflection that some who worship God with their lips may in their hearts be saying, "no God." It is worthy of observation that he does not say there is no Jehovah, but there is no Elohim; Deity in the abstract is not so much the object of attack, as the covenant, personal, ruling and governing presence of God in the world. God as ruler, lawgiver, worker, Saviour, is the butt at which the arrows of human wrath are shot. How impotent the malice! How mad the rage which raves and foams against him in whom we live and move and have our being! How horrible the insanity which leads a man who owes his all to God to cry out, *" No God"!* How terrible the depravity which makes the whole race adopt this as their hearts' desire, *" no God"!*

" They are corrupt." This refers to all men, and we have the warrant of the Holy Ghost for so saying; see the third chapter of the Epistle to the Romans. Where there is enmity to God, there is deep, inward depravity of mind. The words are rendered by eminent critics in an active sense, "they have done corruptly:" this may serve to remind us that sin is not only in our nature passively as the source of evil, but we ourselves actively fan the flame and corrupt ourselves, making that blacker still which was black as darkness itself already. We rivet our own chains by habit and continuance.

" They have done abominable works." When men begin with renouncing the Most High God, who shall tell where they will end? When the Master's eyes are put out, what will not the servants do? Observe the state of the world before the flood, as pourtrayed in Genesis vi. 12, and remember that human nature is unchanged. He who would see a terrible photograph of the world without God must read that most painful of all inspired Scriptures, the first chapter of the epistle to the Romans. Learned Hindoos have confessed that the description is literally correct in Hindostan at the present moment; and were it not for the restraining grace of God, it would be so in England. Alas! it is even here but too correct a

picture of things which are done of men in secret. Things loathsome to God and man are sweet to some palates.

"*There is none that doeth good.*" Sins of omission must abound where transgressions are rife. Those who do the things which they ought not to have done, are sure to leave undone those things which they ought to have done. What a picture of our race is this! Save only where grace reigns, there is none that doeth good; humanity, fallen and debased, is a desert without an oasis, a night without a star, a dunghill without a jewel, a hell without a bottom.

2 The LORD looked down from heaven upon the children of men, to see if there were any that did understand, *and* seek God.

3 They are all gone aside, they are *all* together become filthy: *there is* none that doeth good, no, not one

"*The Lord looked down from heaven upon the children of men.*" As from a watch-tower, or other elevated place of observation, the Lord is represented as gazing intently upon men. He will not punish blindly, nor like a tyrant command an indiscriminate massacre because a rumour of rebellion has come up to his ears. What condescending interest and impartial justice are here imagined! The case of Sodom, visited before it was overthrown, illustrates the careful manner in which Divine Justice beholds the sin before it avenges it, and searches out the righteous that they perish not with the guilty. Behold then the eyes of Omniscience ransacking the globe, and prying among every people and nation, "*to see if there were any that did understand and seek God.*" He who is looking down knows the good, is quick to discern it, would be delighted to find it ; but as he views all the unregenerate children of men his search is fruitless, for of all the race of Adam, no unrenewed soul is other than an enemy to God and goodness. The objects of the Lord's search are not wealthy men, great men, or learned men ; these, with all they can offer, cannot meet the demands of the great Governor : at the same time, he is not looking for superlative eminence in virtue, he seeks for *any that understand* themselves, their state, their duty, their destiny, their happiness ; he looks for any that *seek God*, who, if there be a God, are willing and anxious to find him out. Surely this is not too great a matter to expect ; for if men have not yet known God, if they have any right understanding, they will seek him. Alas! even this low degree of good is not to be found even by him who sees all things ; but men love the hideous negation of "No God," and with their backs to their Creator, who is the sun of their life, they journey into the dreary region of unbelief and alienation, which is a land of darkness as darkness itself, and of the shadow of death without any order and where the light is as darkness.

"*They are all gone aside.*" Without exception, all men have apostatized from the Lord their Maker, from his laws, and from the eternal principles of right. Like stubborn heifers they have sturdily refused to receive the yoke, like errant sheep they have found a gap and left the right field. The original speaks of the race as a whole, as a totality ; and humanity as a whole has become depraved in heart and defiled in life. "*They have altogether become filthy ;*" as a whole they are spoiled and soured like corrupt leaven, or, as some put it, they have become putrid and even stinking. The only reason why we do not more clearly see this foulness is because we are accustomed to it, just as those who work daily among offensive odours at last cease to smell them. The miller does not observe the noise of his own mill, and we are slow to discover our own ruin and depravity. But are there no special cases, are all men sinful? "Yes," says the Psalmist, in a manner not to be mistaken, "they are." He has put it positively, he repeats it negatively, "*There is none that doeth good, no, not one.*" The Hebrew phrase is an utter denial concerning any mere man that he of himself doeth good. What can be more sweeping? This is the verdict of the all-seeing Jehovah, who cannot exaggerate or mistake. As if no hope of finding a solitary specimen of a good man among the unrenewed human family might be harboured for an instant. The Holy Spirit *is not* content with saying all and altogether, but adds the crushing threefold negative, "*none, no, not one.*" What say the opponents to the doctrine of natural depravity to this? Rather what do we *feel* concerning it? Do we not confess that we by nature are corrupt, and do we not bless the sovereign grace which has renewed us in the spirit of our minds, that sin may no more have dominion over us, but that grace may rule and reign?

4 Have all the workers of iniquity no knowledge ? who eat up my people *as* they eat bread, and call not upon the LORD.

Hatred of God and corruptness of life are the motive forces which produce persecution. Men who having no saving knowledge of divine things, enslave themselves to become workers of iniquity, have no heart to cry to the Lord for deliverance, but seek to amuse themselves with devouring the poor and despised people of God. It is hard bondage to be a "*worker of iniquity ;*" a worker at the galleys, or in the mines of Siberia, is not more truly degraded and wretched ; the toil is hard and the reward dreadful ; those who have no knowledge choose such slavery, but those who are taught of God cry to be rescued from it. The same ignorance which keeps men bondsmen to evil, makes them hate the freeborn sons of God ; hence they seek to eat them up "*as they eat bread,*"—daily, ravenously, as though it were an ordinary, usual, every-day matter to oppress the saints of God. As pikes in a pond eat up little fish, as eagles prey on smaller birds, as wolves rend the sheep of the pasture, so sinners naturally and as a matter of course persecute, malign, and mock the followers of the Lord Jesus. While thus preying, they forswear all praying, and in this act consistently, for how could they hope to be heard while their hands are full of blood ?

5 There **were** they in great fear : for God *is* in the generation of the righteous.

Oppressors have it not all their own way, they have their fits of trembling and their appointed seasons of overthrow. *There*—where they denied God and hectored against his people ; *there*—where they thought of peace and safety, they were made to quail. "*There were they*"—these very loud-mouthed, iron-handed, proud-hearted Nimrods and Herods, these heady, high-minded sinners—"*there were they in great fear.*" A panic terror seized them : "they feared a fear," as the Hebrew puts it ; an undefinable, horrible, mysterious dread crept over them. The most hardened of men have their periods when conscience casts them into a cold sweat of alarm. As cowards are cruel, so all cruel men are at heart cowards. The ghost of past sin is a terrible spectre to haunt any man, and though unbelievers may boast as loudly as they will, a sound is in their ears which makes them ill at ease.

"*For God is in the generation of the righteous.*" This makes the company of godly men so irksome to the wicked because they perceive that God is with them. Shut their eyes as they may, they cannot but perceive the image of God in the character of his truly gracious people, nor can they fail to see that he works for their deliverance. Like Haman, they instinctively feel a trembling when they see God's Mordecais. Even though the saint may be in a mean position, mourning at the gate where the persecutor rejoices in state, the sinner feels the influence of the believer's true nobility and quails before it, for God is there. Let scoffers beware, for they persecute the Lord Jesus when they molest his people ; the union is very close between God and his people, it amounts to a mysterious indwelling, for God is in the generation of the righteous.

6 Ye have shamed the counsel of the poor, because the LORD *is* his refuge.

Notwithstanding their real cowardice, the wicked put on the lion's skin and lord it over the Lord's poor ones. Though fools themselves, they mock at the truly wise as if the folly were on their side ; but this is what might be expected, for how should brutish minds appreciate excellence, and how can those who have owl's eyes admire the sun ? The special point and butt of their jest seems to be the confidence of the godly in their Lord. What can your God do for you now ? Who is that God who can deliver out of our hand ? Where is the reward of all your praying and beseeching ? Taunting questions of this sort they thrust into the faces of weak but gracious souls, and tempt them to feel ashamed of their refuge. Let us not be laughed out of our confidence by them, let us scorn their scorning and defy their jeers ; we shall need to wait but a little, and then the Lord our refuge will avenge his own elect and ease himself of his adversaries, who once made so light of him and of his people.

7 Oh that the salvation of Israel *were come* out of Zion ! when the LORD bringeth back the captivity of his people, Jacob shall rejoice, *and* Israel shall be glad.

Natural enough is this closing prayer, for what would so effectually convince atheists, overthrow persecutors, stay sin, and secure the godly, as the manifest appearance of Israel's great Salvation ? The coming of Messiah was the desire of the godly in all ages, and though he has already come with a sin-offering to purge away iniquity, we look for him to come a second time, to come without a sin-offering unto salvation. O that these weary years would have an end ! Why tarries he so long ? He knows that sin abounds and that his people are down-trodden ; why comes he not to the rescue ? His glorious advent will restore his ancient people from literal captivity, and his spiritual seed from spiritual sorrow. Wrestling Jacob and prevailing Israel shall alike rejoice before him when he is revealed as their salvation. O that he were come ! What happy, holy, halcyon, heavenly days should we then see ! But let us not count him slack, for behold, he comes, he comes quickly ! Blessed are all they that wait for him.

EXPLANATORY NOTES AND QUAINT SAYINGS.

Whole Psalm.—There is a peculiar mark upon this Psalm, in that it is twice in the Book of Psalms. The fourteenth Psalm and the fifty-third Psalm are the same with the alteration of one or two expressions at most. And there is another mark put upon it, that the apostle transcribes a great part of it.—Rom. iii. 10—12.

It contains a description of a most deplorable state of things in the world— ay, in Israel ; a most deplorable state, by reason of the general corruption that was befallen all sorts of men, in their principles, and in their practices, and in their opinions.

First, it was a time when there was a mighty prevalent *principle* of atheism got into the world, got among the great men of the world. Saith he, " That is their principle, they say in their hearts, ' There is no God.' " It is true, they did not absolutely profess it ; but it was the principle whereby all their actings were regulated and which they conformed unto. " *The fool,*" saith he, " *hath said in his heart, There is no God.*" Not this or that particular man, but the fool—that is, those foolish men ; for in the next word he tells you " *They are corrupt ;* " and verse 3, " *They are all gone aside.*" " The fool " is taken indefinitely for the great company and society of foolish men, to intimate that whatsoever they were divided about else, they were all agreed in this. " They are all a company of atheists," saith he, " practical atheists."

Secondly, their *affections* were suitable to this principle, as all men's affections and actions are suitable to their principles. What are you to expect from men whose principle is, that there is no God ? Why, saith he, for their affections, " They are corrupt ; " which he expresseth again (verse 3), " They are all gone aside, they are all together become filthy." " All gone aside." The word in the original is, " They are all grown sour ; " as drink, that hath been formerly of some use, but when grown vapid—lost all its spirits and life—it is an insipid thing, good for nothing. And, saith he, "*They are altogether become filthy* "—" become stinking," as the margin hath it. They have corrupt affections, that have left them no life, no savour ; but stinking, corrupt lusts prevail in them universally. They say, " There is no God ; " and they are filled with stinking, corrupt lusts.

Thirdly, if this be their principle and these their affections, let us look after their *actions,* to see if they be any better. But consider their actions. They be of two sorts :—1. How they act in the world, 2. How they act towards the people of God.

1. How do they act in the world ? Why, consider that, as to their duties which they omit, and as to the wickednesses which they perform. What good do they do ? Nay, saith he, " *None of them doeth good.*" Yea, some of them. " *No, not one.*" Saith he, verses 1, 3, " There is none that doeth good, no, not one." If there was any one among them that did attend to what was really good and useful in the world, there was some hope. " No," saith he, " their principle is atheism, their affections are corrupt ; and for good, there is not one of them doeth any good— they omit all duties."

What do they do for evil? Why saith he, " *They have done abominable works* " —" works." saith he, " not to be named, not to be spoken of—works which God abhors, which all good men abhor." "Abominable works," saith he, "such as the very light of nature would abhor ; " and give me leave to use the expression of the Psalmist—"Stinking, filthy works." So he doth describe the state and condition of things under the reign of Saul, when he wrote this Psalm.

2. " If thus it be with them, and if thus it be with their own ways, yet they let the people of God alone ; they will not add that to the rest of their sins." Nay, it is quite otherwise, saith he, " *They eat up my people as they eat bread.*" " Those workers of iniquity have no knowledge, who eat up my people as they eat bread, and call not upon the LORD." What is the reason why he brings it in in that manner ? Why could he not say, " They have no knowledge that do such abominable things ; " but brings it in thus, " They have no knowledge who eat up my people as they eat bread " ? " It is strange, that after all my dealings with them and declaration of my will, they should be so brutish as not to know this would be their ruin. Don't they know this will devour them, destroy them, and be called over again in a particular manner ? " In the midst of all the sins, and greatest and highest provocations that are in the world, God lays a special weight upon the eating of his people. They may feed upon their own lusts what they will ; but, " Have they no knowledge, that they eat up my people as they eat bread ? "

There are very many things that might be observed from all this ; but I aim to give but a few hints from the Psalm.

Well, what is the state of things now ? You see what it was with them. How was it with the providence of God in reference unto them ? Which is strange, and a man would scarce believe it in such a course as this is, he tells you (verse 5), notwithstanding all this, they were in great fear. " *There were they in great fear,*" saith he. May be so, for they saw some evil coming upon them. No, there was nothing but the hand of God in it ; for in Psalm liii. 5, where these words are repeated, it is, " There were they in great fear, where no fear was "—no visible cause of fear ; yet they were in great fear.

God by his providence seldom gives an absolute, universal security unto men in their height of sin, and oppression, and sensuality, and lusts ; but he will secretly put them in fear where no fear is : and though there be nothing seen that should cause them to have any fear, they shall act like men at their wits' end with fear.

But whence should this fear arise ? Saith he, it ariseth from hence, " *For God is in the generation of the righteous.*" Plainly they see their work doth not go on ; their meat doth not digest with them ; their bread doth not go well down. " They were eating and devouring my people, and when they came to devour them, they found God was among them (they could not digest their bread) ; and this put them in fear ; quite surprised them." They came, and thought to have found them a sweet morsel : when engaged, God was there filling their mouth and teeth with gravel ; and he began to break out the jawbone of the terrible ones when they came to feed upon them. Saith he, " God was there." (Verse 5.)

The Holy Ghost gives an account of the state of things that was between those two sorts of people he had described—between the fool and the people of God—them that were devouring, and them that had been utterly devoured, had not God been among them. Both were in fear—they that were to be devoured, and those that did devour. And they took several ways for their relief ; and he showeth what those ways were, and what judgment they made upon the ways of one another. Saith he, " *Ye have shamed the counsel of the poor, because the Lord is his refuge.*"

There are the persons spoken of—they are " the poor ; " and that is those who are described in the verses foregoing, the people that were ready to be eaten up and devoured.

And there is the hope and refuge that these poor had in such a time as this, when all things were in fear ; and that was " the LORD." The poor maketh the Lord his refuge.

And you may observe here, that as he did describe all the wicked as one man, " the fool," so he describes all his own people as one man, " the poor "—that is, the poor man : " Because the LORD is his refuge." He keeps it in the singular number. Whatsoever the people of God may differ in, they are all as one man in this business.

And there is the way whereby these poor make God their refuge. They do it by " counsel," saith he. It is not a thing they do by chance, but they look upon it as their wisdom. They do it upon consideration, upon advice. It is a thing of great wisdom.

Well, what thoughts have the others concerning this acting of theirs? The poor make God their refuge; and they do it by counsel. What judgment, now, doth the world make of this counsel of theirs? Why, they "shame it;" that is, they cast shame upon it, contemn it as a very foolish thing, to make the Lord their refuge. "Truly, if they could make this or that great man their refuge, it were something; but to make the Lord their refuge, this is the foolishest thing in the world," say they. To shame men's counsel, to despise their counsel as foolish, is as great contempt as they can lay upon them.

Here you see the state of things as they are represented in this Psalm, and spread before the Lord; which being laid down, the Psalmist showeth what our duty is upon such a state of things—what is the duty of the people of God, things being thus stated. Saith he, "Their way is to go to prayer:" verse 7, "*O that the salvation of Israel were come out of Zion! when the Lord bringeth back the captivity of his people, Jacob shall rejoice, and Israel shall be glad.*" If things are thus stated, then cry, then pray, "O that the salvation of Israel were come out of Zion," etc. There shall a revenue of praise come to God out of Zion, to the rejoicing of his people.—*John Owen.*

Verse 1.—"*The fool.*" That sapless fellow, that carcase of a man, that walking sepulchre of himself, in whom all religion and right reason is withered and wasted, dried up and decayed. That apostate in whom natural principles are extinct, and from whom God is departed, as when the prince is departed, hangings are taken down. That mere animal that hath no more than a reasonable soul, and for little other purpose than as salt, to keep his body from putrefying. That wicked man hereafter described, that studieth atheism.—*John Trapp.*

Verse 1.—"*The fool,*" etc. The world we live in is a world of fools. The far greater part of mankind act a part entirely irrational. So great is their infatuation, that they prefer time to eternity, momentary enjoyments to those that shall never have an end, and listen to the testimony of Satan in preference to that of God. Of all folly, that is the greatest, which relates to eternal objects, because it is the most fatal and when persisted in through life, entirely remediless. A mistake in the management of temporal concerns may be afterwards rectified. At any rate, it is comparatively of little importance. But an error in spiritual and eternal matters, as it is in itself of the greatest moment, if carried through life, can never be remedied; because after death there is no redemption. The greatest folly that any creature is capable of, is that of denying or entertaining unjust apprehensions of the being and perfections of the great Creator. Therefore, in a way of eminence, the appellation of *fool* is given by the Spirit of God, to him who is chargeable with this guilt. "*The fool hath said in his heart, There is no God.*"—*John Jamieson, M.A.,* 1789.

Verse 1.—"*The fool,*" a term in Scripture signifying a wicked man, used also by the heathen philosophers to signify a vicious person, נָבָל as coming from נָבֵל signifies the extinction of life in men, animals, and plants; so the word נָבֵל is taken, Isaiah xl. 7, צִיץ נָבֵל "the flower fadeth" (Isaiah xxviii. 1), a plant that hath lost all that juice that made it lovely and useful. So a fool is one that hath lost his wisdom and right notion of God and divine things, which were communicated to man by creation; one dead in sin, yet one not so much void of rational faculties, as of grace in those faculties; not one that wants reason, but abuses his reason.—*Stephen Charnock.*

Verse 1.—"*The fool hath said,*" etc. This folly is bound up in every heart. It is bound, but it is not tongue-tied; it speaks blasphemous things against God, *it says* there is "*no God.*" There is a difference indeed in the language: gross sins speak this louder, there are crying sins; but though less sins speak it not so loud they whisper it. But the Lord can hear the language of the heart, the whisperings of its motions, as plainly as we hear one another in our ordinary discourse. Oh, how heinous is the least sin, which is so injurious to the very being of the great God! *David Clarkson.*

Verse 1.—"*The fool hath said in his heart, There is no God.*" If you will turn over some few leaves as far as the fifty-third Psalm, you shall not only find my text, but this whole Psalm, without any alteration, save only in the fifth verse, and that not at all in the sense neither. What shall we say? Took the Holy Spirit of God such especial particular notice of the sayings and deeds of a *fool*, that one expression of them would not serve the turn? Or, does the babbling and madness of a fool so much concern us, as that we need to have them urged upon us once and again, and a third time in the third of the Romans ? Surely not any one of us present here, is this fool ! Nay, if any one of us could but tell where to find such a fool as this, that would offer to say, though in his heart, *" There is no God,"* he should not rest in quiet, he should soon perceive we were not of his faction, We that are able to tell David an article or two of faith more than ever he was acquainted with ! Nay, more ; can we with any imaginable ground of reason be supposed liable to any suspicion of atheism, that are able to read to David a lecture out of his own Psalms, and explain the meaning of his own prophecies much clearer than himself which held the pen to the Holy Spirit of God ? Though we cannot deny but that in other things there may be found some spice of folly and imperfection in us, but it cannot be imagined that we, who are almost cloyed with the heavenly manna of God's word, that can instruct our teachers, and are able to maintain opinions and tenets, the scruples whereof not both the universities in this land, nor the whole clergy are able to resolve, that it should be possible for us ever to come to that perfection and excellency of folly and madness, as to entertain thought that *there is no God :* nay, we are not so uncharitable as to charge a Turk or an infidel with such a horrible imputation as this.

Beloved Christians, be not wise in your own conceits : if you will seriously examine the third of Romans (which I mentioned before), you shall find that Paul, out of this Psalm, and the like words of Isaiah, doth conclude the whole posterity of Adam (Christ only excepted), under sin and the curse of God ; which inference of his were weak and inconcluding, unless every man of his own nature were such a one as the prophet here describes ; and the same apostle in another place expresses, *" Even altogether without God in the world,"* i.e., not maintaining it as an opinion which they would undertake by force of argument to confirm, That there is no God : for we read not of above three or four among the heathens that were of any fashion, which went thus far ; but such as though in their discourse and serious thoughts they do not question a deity, but would abhor any man that would not liberally allow unto God all his glorious attributes, yet in their hearts and affections they deny him ; they live as if there was no God, having no respect at all to him in all their projects and therefore, indeed and in God's esteem, become formally, and in strict propriety of speech very atheists.—*William Chillingworth,* 1602—1643.

Verse 1.—" The fool hath said in his heart, There is no God." Why do men resist God's authority, against which they cannot dispute ? and disobey his commands, unto which they cannot devise to frame an exception ? What but the spirit of enmity, can make them regret " so easy a yoke," reject so " light a burden," shun and fly off from so peaceful and pleasant paths ? yea, and take ways that so manifestly " take hold of hell, and lead down to the chambers of death," rather choosing to perish than obey ? Is not this the very height of enmity ? What further proof would we seek of a disaffected and implacable heart ? Yet to all this we may cast in that fearful addition, their saying in their heart, " No God ; " as much as to say, " O that there were none ! " This is enmity not only to the highest pitch of *wickedness,* to wish their common parent extinct, the author of their being, but even unto *madness* itself. For in the forgetful heat of this transport, it is not thought on that they wish the most absolute impossibility; and that, if it were possible, they wish, with his, the extinction of their own and of all being ; and that the sense of their hearts, put into words, would amount to no less than a direful and most horrid execration and curse upon God and the whole creation of God at once ! As if, by the blasphemy of their poisonous breath, they would wither all nature, blast the whole universe of being, and make it fade, languish, and droop into nothing. This is to set their mouth against heaven and earth, themselves, and all things at once, as if they thought their feeble breath should overpower the omnipotent Word, shake and shiver the adamantine pillars of heaven and earth, and the Almighty *fiat* be defeated by their *nay,* striking at the root of all ! So fitly is it said " The *fool* hath in his heart " muttered thus. Nor are there few such fools ; but this is plainly given us as the common character of apostate man, the whole revolted race, of whom it is said in very general terms, " They are all gone back, there is none that doeth good." This is their sense, one and all, that is, comparatively ; and the true state of the case being laid before them, it is more their temper and sense to say, " No God," than to repent, " and turn to him." What mad enmity is this ! Nor can we devise into what else to resolve it.—*John Howe.*

Verse 1.—" The fool hath said in his heart, there is no God." He that shall deny there is a God, sins with a very high hand against the light of nature ; for every creature, yea, the least gnat and fly, and the meanest worm that crawls upon the ground will confute and confound that man that disputes whether there be a God or no. The name of God is written in such full, fair and shining characters upon the whole creation, that all men may run and read that there is a God. The notion of a deity is so strongly and deeply impressed upon the tables of all men's hearts, that to deny a God is to quench the very principles of common nature ; yea, it is formally *deicidium*, a killing of God, as much as in the creature lies. There are none of these atheists in hell, for the devils believe and tremble. James ii. 19. The Greek word φρισσουσι, that is here used, signifies properly the roaring of the sea ; it implies such an extreme fear, as causeth not only trembling, but also a roaring and screeching out. Mark vi. 49 ; Acts xvi. 29. The devils believe and acknowledge four articles of our faith. Matt. viii. 29. (1.) They acknowledge God ; (2.) Christ ; (3) The day of judgment ; (4.) That they shall be tormented then ; so that he that doth not believe that there is a God, is more vile than a devil. To deny there is a God, is a sort of atheism that is not to be found in hell.

> "On earth are atheists many,
> In hell there is not any."

Augustine, speaking of atheists saith, " That albeit there be some who think, or would persuade themselves, that there is no God, yet the most vile and desperate wretch that ever lived would not say, there was no God." Seneca hath a remarkable speech, *Mentiuntur qui dicunt se non sentire Deum esse : nam etsi tibi affirmant interdiù noctu tamen dubitant.* They lie, saith he, who say they perceive not there is a God ; for although they affirm it to thee in the daytime, yet by night they doubt of it. Further, saith the same author, I have heard of some that deny that there was a God ; yet never knew the man, but when he was sick he would seek unto God for help ; therefore they do but lie that say there is no God ; they sin against the light of their own consciences ; they who most studiously go about to deny God, yet cannot do it but some check of conscience will fly in their faces. Tully would say that there was never any nation under heaven so barbarous as to deny that there was a God.—*T. Brooks.*

Verse 1.—" *The fool hath said in his heart, There is no God.*" Popery has not won to itself so great wits as atheism ; it is the superfluity of wit that makes atheists. These will not be beaten down with impertinent arguments ; disordered hail-shot of Scriptures will never scare them ; they must be convinced and beaten by their own weapons. " Hast thou appealed to Cæsar ? To Cæsar thou shalt go." Have they appealed to reason ? Let us bring reason to them, that we may bring them to reason. We need not fear the want of weapons in that armoury, but our own ignorance and want of skill to use them. There is enough even in philosophy to convince atheism, and make them confess, " We are foiled with our own weapons ;" for with all their wit atheists are fools.—*Thomas Adams.*

Verse 1.—As there is no wound more mortal than that which plucketh forth man's heart or soul ; so, likewise, is there no person or pestilence of greater force suddenly in men to kill all faith, hope, and charity, with the fear of God, and consequently to cast them headlong into the pit of hell, than to deny the principle and foundation of all religion—namely, that there is a God.—*Robert Cawdray's* " *Treasury or Storehouse of Similes,*" 1609.

Verse 1.—" *The fool hath said in his heart, There is no God.*"—Who in the world is a verier fool, a more ignorant, wretched person, than he that is an atheist ? A man may better believe there is no such man as himself, and that he is not in being, than that there is no God ; for himself can cease to be, and once was not, and shall be changed from what he is, and in very many periods of his life knows not that he is ; and so it is every night with him when he sleeps ; but none of these can happen to God ; and if he knows it not, he is a fool. Can anything in this world be more foolish than to think that all this rare fabric of heaven and earth can come by chance, when all the skill of art is not able to make an oyster ? To see rare effects, and no cause ; an excellent government and no prince ; a motion without an immovable ; a circle without a centre ; a time without eternity ; a second without a first ; a thing that begins not from itself, and therefore, not to perceive there is something from whence it does not begin, which must be without beginning ; these things are so against philosophy and natural reason, that he must needs be a beast in his understanding that does not assent to them ; this is the atheist : " *The fool hath said in his heart, There is no God."* That is his character ; the thing framed, says that nothing framed it ; the tongue never made itself to speak, and yet talks against him that did ; saying, that which is made, is, and that which made it, is not. But this folly is as infinite as hell, as much without light or bound, as the chaos of the primitive nothing.—*Jeremy Taylor*, 1613—1667.

Verse 1.—*" The fool hath said in his heart, There is no God."* A wise man, that lives up to the principles of reason and virtue, if one considers him in his solitude as taking in the system of the universe, observing the mutual dependence and harmony by which the whole frame of it hangs together, beating down his passions, or swelling his thoughts with magnificent ideas of providence, makes a nobler figure in the eye of an intelligent being, than the greatest conqueror amidst the pomps and solemnities of a triumph. On the contrary, there is not a more ridiculous animal than an atheist in his retirement. His mind is incapable of rapture or elevation : he can only consider himself as an insignificant figure in a landscape, and wandering up and down in a field or a meadow, under the same terms as the meanest animals about him, and as subject to as total a mortality as they, with this aggravation, that he is the only one amongst them who lies under the apprehension of it. In distresses he must be of all creatures the most helpless and forlorn ; he feels the whole pressure of a present calamity, without being relieved by the memory of anything that is past, or the prospect of anything that is to come. Annihilation is the greatest blessing that he proposes to himself, and a halter or a pistol the only refuge he can fly to. But if you would behold one of these gloomy miscreants in his poorest figure, you must consider them under the terrors or at the approach of death. About thirty years ago, I was a shipboard with one of these vermin, when there arose a brisk gale, which could frighten nobody but himself. Upon the rolling of the ship he fell upon his knees, and confessed to the chaplain, that he had been a vile atheist and had denied a Supreme Being ever since he came to his estate. The good man was astonished, and a report immediately ran through the ship, that there was an atheist upon the upper deck. Several of the common seamen, who had never heard the word before, thought it had been some strange fish ; but they were more surprised when they saw it was a man, and heard out of his own mouth, " That he never believed till that day that there was a God." As he lay in the agonies of confession, one of the honest tars whispered to the boatswain, " That it would be a good deed to heave him overboard." But we were now within sight of port, when of a sudden the wind fell, and the penitent relapsed, begging all of us that were present, as we were gentlemen, not to say anything of what had passed. He had not been ashore above two days, when one of the company began to rally him upon his devotion on shipboard, which the other denied in so high terms, that it produced the lie on both sides, and ended in a duel. The atheist was run through the body, and after some loss of blood, became as good a Christian as he was at sea, till he found that his wound was not mortal. He is at present one of the free-thinkers of the age, and now writing a pamphlet against several received opinions concerning the existence of fairies.—*Joseph Addison* (1671—1719), *in " The Tattler."*

Verse 1.—

" ' There is no God,' the fool in secret said :
' There is no God that rules or earth or sky.'
Tear off the band that binds the wretch's head,
That God may burst upon his faithless eye !
Is there no God ?—The stars in myriads spread,
If he look up, the blasphemy deny ;
While his own features, in the mirror read,
Reflect the image of Divinity.
Is there no God ?—The stream that silver flows,
The air he breathes, the ground he treads, the trees,
The flowers, the grass, the sands, each wind that blows,
All speak of God ; throughout, one voice agrees,
And, eloquent, his dread existence shows :
Blind to thyself, ah, see him, fool, in these ! "   *Giovanni Cotta.*

Verse 1.—

" The owlet, *Atheism*,
Sailing on obscene wings across the noon,
Drops his blue-fringed lids, and shuts them close,
And, hooting at the glorious sun in heaven,
Cries out, ' Where is it ? ' "

Samuel Taylor Coleridge, 1772—1834.

Verse 1.—" *They are corrupt, they have done abominable works."* Sin pleaseth the flesh. *Omne simile nutrit simile.* Corruption inherent is nourished by the accession of corrupt actions. Judas's covetousness is sweetened with unjust gain. Joab is heartened and hardened with blood. 1 Kings ii. 5. Theft is fitted to and fatted in the thievish heart with obvious booties. Pride is fed with the officious compliments of observant grooms. Extortion battens in the usurer's affections by the trolling in of his moneys. Sacrilege thrives in the church-robber by the pleasing distinctions of those sycophant priests, and helped with their not laborious profit. Nature is led, is fed with sense. And when the citadel of the heart is once won, the turret of the understanding will not long hold out. As the suffumigations of the oppressed stomach surge up and cause the headache, or as the thick spumy mists, which vapour up from the dark and foggy earth, do often suffocate the brighter air, and to us more than eclipse the sun, the black and corrupt affections, which ascend out of the nether part of the soul, do no less darken and choke the understanding. Neither can the fire of grace be kept alive at God's altar (man's heart), when the clouds of lust shall rain down such showers of impiety on it. *Perit omne judicium, cum res transit ad affectum.* Farewell the perspicuity of judgment, when the matter is put to the partiality of affection.—*Thomas Adams.*

Verse 1.—" *They are corrupt, they have done abominable things : there is none that doeth good."* " Men," says Bernard, " because they are *corrupt* in their minds, become *abominable* in their doings : *corrupt* before God, *abominable* before men. There are three sorts of men of which none doeth good. There are those who neither understand nor seek God, and they are the dead : there are others who understand him, but seek him not, and they are the wicked. There are others that seek him but understand him not, and they are the fools." " O God," cries a writer of the middle ages, " how many are here at this day who, under the name of Christianity, worship idols, and are abominable both to thee and to men ! For every man worships that which he most loves. The proud man bows down before the idol of worldly power ; the covetous man before the idol of money ; the adulterer before the idol of beauty ; and so of the rest." And of such, saith the apostle, " They profess that they know God, but in works deny him, being *abominable* and disobedient, and unto every good work reprobate." Titus i. 16. " *There is none that doeth good."* Notice how Paul avails himself of this testimony of the epistle to the Romans, where he is proving concerning " both Jews and Gentiles, that they are all under sin." Rom. iii. 9.—*John Mason Neale, in loc.*

Verse 1.—The argument of my text is the atheist's divinity, the brief of his belief couched all in one article, and that negative too, clean contrary to the fashion of all creeds, " *There is no God."* The article but one ; but so many absurdities tied to the train of it, and itself so irreligious, so prodigiously profane, that he dares not speak it out, but saith it softly to himself, in secret, " *in his heart."* So the text yields these three points ; Who is he ? A " *fool."* What he saith, " *no God."* How he speaks it, " *in his heart."* A fool, his bolt, and his draught. I will speak of them severally . . . . . There is a child in years, and there is a child in manners, *ætate et moribus,* saith Aristotle. So there is a fool ; for fools and children both are called νηπιοι. There is a fool in wit, and there is a fool in life; *stultus in scientia, et stultus in conscientia,* a witless and a graceless fool. The latter is worthy of the title as the first ; both void of reason ; not of the faculty but of the use. Yea, the latter fool is indeed the more kindly of the twain ; for the sot would use his reason if he could ; the sinner will not though he may. It is not the natural, but the moral fool that David means, the wicked and ungracious person, for so is the sense of the original term . . . . . It is time we leave the person, and come unto the act. What hath this fool done ? Surely nothing ; he hath only *said.* What hath he *said* ? Nay, nothing either ; he hath only *thought :* for to *say in heart,* is but to *think.* There are two sorts of saying in the Scripture, one meant indeed so properly, the other but in hope ; one by word of mouth, the other by thought of heart. You see the Psalmist means here the second sort. The bolt the fool here shoots is atheism : he makes no noise at the loss of it, as bowmen use ; he draws and delivers closely, and stilly, out of sight, and without sound : he saith, " *God is not,"* but " *in heart."* The heart hath a mouth ; *intus est os cordis,* saith Augustine. God, saith Cyprian, is *cordis auditor,* he hears the heart ; then belike it hath some speech. When God said to Moses, *quare clamas ?* why criest thou ? we find no words he uttered : *silens auditur,* saith Gregory, he is heard through saying nothing. There is a silent speech (Psalm iv. 4), " Commune with your own heart," saith David, " and be still." Speech is not the heart's action, no more than meditation is the mouth's. But sometimes the heart and mouth exchange offices ; *lingua mea meditabitur,* saith David. Psalm xxxv. 28. There is *lingua meditans,* a musing tongue ; here is *cor loquens,* a speaking heart. And to say the truth, the philosopher saith well, it is the heart doth all things, *mens videt, mens audit, mens loquitur.* It is the heart that speaks, the tongue is but the instrument to give the sound. It is but the heart's echo to repeat the words after it. Except when the tongue doth run before the wit, the heart doth dictate to the mouth ; it suggests what it shall say. The heart is the soul's herald : look what she will have proclaimed, the heart reads it, and the mouth cries it. The tongue saith nought but what the heart saith first. Nay, in very deed, the truest and kindest speech is the heart's. The tongue and lips are Jesuits, they lease, and lie, and use equivocations : flattery, or fear, or other by-respect, other wry respect adulterate their words. But the heart speaks as it means, worth twenty mouths, if it could speak audibly.—*Richard Clerke. D.D., 1634 (one of the translators of our English Bible).*

Verses 1, 4.—The Scripture give this as a cause of the notorious courses of wicked men, that " God is not in all their thoughts." Psalm x. 4. They forget there is a God of vengeance and a day of reckoning. " *The fool* " would needs enforce upon his heart, that " *there is no God,*" and what follows : " *Corrupt they are, there is none doeth good : they eat up my people as bread,*" etc. They make no more bones of devouring men and their estates, than they make conscience of eating a piece of bread. What a wretched condition hath sin brought man unto, that the great God who " filleth heaven and earth " (Jer. xxiii. 24) should yet have no place in the heart which he hath especially made for himself ! The sun is not so clear as this truth, that God is, for all things in the world are because God is. If he were not, nothing could be. It is from him that wicked men have that strength they have to commit sin, therefore sin proceeds from atheism, especially these plotting sins ; for if God were more thought on, he would take off the soul from sinful contrivings, and fix it upon himself.—*Richard Sibbes.*

Verse 2.—" *To see if there were any that did understand . . seek God.*" None seek him aright, and as he ought to be sought, nor can do while they live in sin ; for men in seeking God fail in many things : as, First, men seek him not for himself. Secondly, they seek him not alone, but other things with him. Thirdly, they seek other things before him, as worldlings do. Fourthly, they seek him coldly or carelessly. Fifthly, they seek him inconstantly ; example of Judas and Demas. Sixthly, they seek him not in his word, as heretics do. Seventhly, they seek him not in all his word, as hypocrites do. Lastly, they seek him not seasonably and timely, as profane, impenitent sinners do ; have no care to depend upon God's word, but follow their own lusts and fashions of this world.—*Thomas Wilson,* 1653.

Verses 2, 3.—What was the issue of God's so looking upon men ? " *They are all gone aside,*" that is, from him and his ways ; " *They are altogether become filthy ;* " their practices are such as make them stink ; " *There is none that doeth good, no, not one ;* " of so many millions of men as are upon the earth, there is not one doeth good. There were men of excellent parts then in the world, men of soul, but not one of them did know God, or seek after God : Paul therefore hath laid it down for a universal maxim, that the animal, natural, or intellectual man, receives not the things of the Spirit of God for they are foolishness unto him, and so are rejected by him.—*William Greenhill.*

Verse 3.—The ungodly are " vile " persons (Nah. i. 14). " I will make thy grave ; for thou art vile." Sin makes men base, it blots their name, it taints their blood : " *They are altogether become filthy ;* " in the Hebrew it is, they are become stinking. Call wicked men ever so bad, you cannot call them out of their name ; they are " swine " (Matt. vii. 6) ; " vipers " (Matt. iii. 7) ; " devils " (John vi. 70). The wicked are the dross and refuse (Psa. cxix. 119) ; and heaven is too pure to have any dross mingle with it.—*Thomas Watson.*

Verse 3.—" *Altogether become filthy.*" Thus the Roman satirist describes his own age :

> " Nothing is left, nothing, for future times
> To add to the full catalogue of crimes ;
> The baffled sons must feel the same desires,
> And act the same mad follies as their sires,
> Vice has attained its zenith."
> *Juvenal, Sat. 1.*

Verse 3.—" *There is none that doeth good, no not one.*"   Origen maketh a question how it could be said that there was none, neither among the Jews nor Gentiles, that did any good; seeing there were many among them which did clothe the naked, feed the hungry, and did other good things :   he hereunto maketh this answer :— That like as one that layeth a foundation, and buildeth upon it a wall or two, yet cannot be said to have built a house till he have finished it ;   so although those might do some good things, yet they attained not unto perfect goodness, which was only to be found in Christ.   But this is not the apostle's meaning only to exclude men from the perfection of justice ;   for even the faithful and believers were short of that perfection which is required ;   he therefore showeth what men are by nature, all under sin and in the same state of damnation, without grace and faith in Christ :   if any perform any good work, either it is of grace, and so not of themselves, or if they did it by the light of nature, they did it not as they ought, and so it was far from a good work indeed.—*Andrew Willet* (1562—1621), *on Romans* iii, 10.

Verse 4.—" *Have the workers of iniquity no knowledge ?*"   Men's ignorance is the reason why they fear not what they should fear.   Why is it that the ungodly fear not sin ?   Oh, it's because they know it not.   " *Have the workers of iniquity no knowledge ?*"   Sure enough they have none, for " *they eat up my people as they eat bread ;* " such morsels would scald their mouths, they would not dare to be such persecutors and destroyers of the people of God ;   they would be afraid to touch them if they did but know what they did.—*Richard Alleine.*

Verse 4.—" *Who eat up my people as they eat bread.*"—That is, *quotidiè,* daily, saith Austin ;   as duly as they eat bread ;   or, with the same eagerness and voracity. These man-eaters, these Λαοβόροι, cruel cannibals, make no more conscience to undo a poor man, than to eat a good meal when they are hungry.   Like pickerels in a pond, or sharks in the sea, they devour the poorer, as those do the lesser fishes ;   and that many times with a plausible, invisible consumption ;   as the usurer, who, like the ostrich, can digest any metal ;   but especially money.—*John Trapp.*

Verse 4.—" *Who eat up my people as they eat bread.*"   Oh, how few consult and believe the Scriptures setting forth the enmity of wicked men against God's people ! The Scripture tells us " *they eat up God's people as bread,*" which implies a strange inclination in them to devour the saints, and that they take as great delight therein as a hungry man in eating, and that it is natural to them to molest them.   The Scripture compares them, for their hateful qualities, to the lions and bears, to foxes for subtlety, to wild bulls, to greedy swine, to scorpions, to briers and thorns (grievous and vexing things).   The Scripture represents them as industrious and unwearied in their bloody enterprises, they cannot sleep without doing mischief. Herodias had rather have the blood of a saint than half a kingdom.   Haman would pay a great fine to the king that the scattered Jews (who keep not the king's laws) may be cut off.   Wicked men will run the hazard of damning their own souls, rather than not fling a dagger at the apple of God's eye.   Though they know what one word—aha !—cost, yet they will break through all natural, civil, and moral obligations, to ruin God's people.   The Holy Ghost calls them " implacable " men, fierce and headstrong ;   they are like the hot oven for fury, like the sea for boundless rage ;   yet " who hath believed " this Scripture " report " ?   Did we believe what enemies all wicked men are unto all saints, we should not lean to our own prudence and discretion to secure us from any danger by these men ;   we would get an ark to secure us from the deluge of their wrath ;   if at any time we be cast among them and delivered, we would bless God with the three children, that the hot fiery oven did not consume us ;   we would not wonder when we hear of any of their barbarous cruelty, but rather wonder at God's restraining them every day ;   we would be suspicious of receiving hurt when cast among light and frothy companions ; we would shun their company as we do lions and scorpions ;   we would never commit any trust or secret into their hands ;   we would not be light-hearted whilst in their society ;   we would not rely on their promises any more than we would on the promise of the devil, their father ;   we would long for heaven, to be delivered from " the tents of Kedar ; " we would not count any of the saints secured from danger, though related to any great wicked man ;   we would not twist ourselves with them by matching ourselves or children to these sons and daughters of Belial ;   neither would we make choice of devils to be our servants.—*Lewis Stuckley.*

Verse 4.—This is an evil world.   It hates the people of God.   " Because ye are not of the world, therefore the world hateth you." John xv. 19. Haman's hatred was against the whole seed of the Jews. When you can find a serpent without a sting, or a leopard without spots, then may you expect to find a wicked world without hatred to the saints. Piety is the target which is aimed at. "They are mine adversaries because I follow the thing that good is." Psalm xxxviii. 20. The world pretends to hate the godly for something else, but the ground of the quarrel is holiness. The world's hatred is implacable : anger may be reconciled, hatred cannot. You may as soon reconcile heaven and hell as the two seeds. If the world hated Christ, no wonder that it hates us. "The world hated me before it hated you." John xv. 18. Why should any hate Christ? This blessed Dove had no gall, this rose of Sharon did send forth a most sweet perfume ; but this shows the world's baseness, it is a Christ-hating and a *saint-eating* world.—*Thomas Watson.*

Verse 5.—"*There were they in great fear.*" That we may not mistake the meaning of the point, we must understand that this faintheartedness and cowardliness doth not always come upon presumptuous sinners when they behold imminent dangers, for though none of them have true courage and fortitude, yet many of them have a kind of desperate stoutness and resolution when they do, as it were, see death present before their faces ; which proceedeth from a kind of deadness that is upon their hearts, and a brawniness that hath overgrown their conscience to their greater condemnation. But when it pleaseth the Lord to waken them out of the dead slumber, and to set the worm of conscience awork within them, then this doctrine holdeth true without any exception, that the boldest sinners prove at length the basest cowards : and they that have been most audacious in adventuring upon the most mischievous evils, do become of all others most timorous when God's revenging hand seizeth upon them for the same.—*John Dod*, 1547—1645.

Verse 5.—"*God is in the generation of the righteous ;*" that is, he favours that generation or sort of men ; God is in all generations, but such he delights in most : the wicked have cause enough to fear those in whom God delights.—*Joseph Caryl.*

Verse 5.—The King of Glory cannot come into the heart (as he is is said to come into the hearts of his people as such ; Psalm xxiv. 9, 10), but some glory of himself will appear ; and as God doth accompany the word with majesty because it is his word, so he doth accompany his own children, and their ways, with majesty, yea, even in their greatest debasements. As when Stephen was brought before the council as a prisoner at the bar for his life, then God manifested his presence to him, for it is said, "his face shone as the face of an angel of God." (Acts vi. 15) ; in a proportionable manner it is ordinarily true what Solomon says of all righteous men, "A man's wisdom makes his face to shine." Eccles. viii. 1. Thus Peter also speaks (1 Peter iv. 14) : "If you be reproached for the name of Christ, happy are you, for the Spirit," not only of God, or of grace, but "of glory, resteth upon you." And so in the martyrs ; their innocency and carriage, and godly behaviour, what majesty had it with it ! What an amiableness in the sight of the people, which daunted, dashed and confounded their most wretched oppressors ; so that although the wicked persecutors "*did eat up God's people as bread*" (verse 4), yet it is added that they were in great fear upon this very account, that "*God is in the generation of the just.*" Verse 5. God stands, as it were, astonished at their dealings : "*Have the workers of iniquity no knowledge,*" (so in the words afore) "*that eat up my people as bread,*" and make no more ado of it than a man doth that heartily eats of his meat ? They seem to do thus, they would carry it and bear it out ; but for all that they are in great fear whilst they do thus, and God strikes their hearts with terror then when they most insult. Why ? For, "*God is in the generation of, or dwelleth in the just,*" and God gives often some glimmerings, hints, and warnings to the wicked (such as Pilate had concerning Christ), that his people are righteous. And this you may see in Phil. i. 28 : "And in nothing terrified by your adversaries, which is to them an evident token of perdition, but to you of salvation, and that of God." In that latter passage, I observe that an assurance of salvation, and a spirit of terror, and that of God, is given to either. In the Old Testament it is recorded of David (1 Sam. xviii. 12), that although Saul hated him (verse 9), and sought to destroy him (verses 10, 11), "yet Saul was afraid of David, because the Lord was with him, and was departed from Saul ;" which is the reason in hand. God manifested his presence in David, and struck Saul's conscience with his godly and wise carriage, and that made him afraid.—*Thomas Goodwin.*

Verse 6.—"*Ye have shamed the counsel of the poor, because the Lord is his refuge.*"

In the fifty-third Psalm it is, "Thou hast put them to shame, because God hath despised them." Of course, the allusion is totally different in each ; in this Psalm it is the indignant remonstrance of the Psalmist with "the workers of iniquity" for undervaluing and putting God's poor to shame ; the other affirms the final shame and confusion of the ungodly, and the contempt in which the Lord holds them. In either case it sweetly illustrates God's care of his poor, not merely the poor in spirit, but literally the poor and lowly ones, the oppressed and the injured. It is this character of God which is so conspicuously delineated in his word. We may look through all the Shasters and Vedas of the Hindoo, the Koran of the Mahometan, the legislation of the Greek, and the code of the Roman, aye, and the Talmud of the Jew, the bitterest of all; and not in one single line or page shall we find a vestige or trace of that tenderness, compassion, or sympathy for the wrongs, and oppressions, and trials, and sorrows of God's poor, which the Christian's Bible evidences in almost every page.—*Barton Bouchier.*

Verse 6.—" *Ye have shamed.*" Every fool that saith in his heart there is no God, hath out of the same quiver a bolt to shoot at goodness. Barren Michal hath too many sons, who, like their mother, jeer at holy David.—*John Trapp.*

Verse 6.—"*Ye have shamed,*" saith he, "*the counsel of the poor.*" There is nothing that wicked men do so despise as the making God a refuge—nothing which they scorn in their hearts like it. "They shame it," saith he, "It is a thing to be cast out of all consideration. The wise man trusts in his wisdom, the strong man in his strength, the rich man in his riches ; but this trusting in God is the foolishest thing in the world." The reasons of it are—1. They know not God ; and it is a foolish thing to trust one knows not whom. 2. They are enemies to God, and God is their enemy ; and they account it a foolish thing to trust their enemy. 3. They know not the way of God's assistance and help. And—4. They seek for such help, such assistance, such supplies as God will not give ; to be delivered, to serve their lusts ; to be preserved, to execute their rage, filthiness, and folly. They have no other design or end of these things ; and God will give none of them. And it is a foolish thing in any man to trust God to be preserved in sin. It is true their folly is their wisdom, considering their state and condition. It is a folly to trust in God to live in sin, and despise the counsel of the poor.—*John Owen.*

Verse 6.—" *Ye have made a mock of the counsel of the poor :* " and why ? " *because the Lord is his trust.*" This is the very true cause, whatsoever other pretences there be. Whence observe this doctrine ; that true godliness is that which breeds the quarrel between God's children and the wicked. Ungodly men may say what they list, as, namely, that they hate and dislike them for that they are proud and saucy in meddling with their betters ; for that they are so scornful and disdainful towards their neighbours ; for that they are malcontent, and turbulent, and I know not what ; but the true reason is yielded by the Lord in this place, to wit, because they make him their stay and their confidence, and will not depend upon lying vanities as the men of the world do.—*John Dod.*

Verse 6.—" *The Lord is his refuge.*"—Be persuaded actually to hide yourselves with Jesus Christ. To have a hiding-place and not to use it, is as bad as to want one ; fly to Christ ; run into the holes of this Rock.—*Ralph Robinson,* 1656.

Verse 7.—" *O that the salvation,*" etc. Like as when we be in quiet, we do pray either nothing at all, or very coldly unto God ; so in adversity and trouble, our spirit is stirred up and enkindled to prayer, whereof we do find examples everywhere in the Psalms of David : so that affliction is as it were the sauce of prayer, as hunger is unto meat. Truly their prayer is usually unsavoury who are without afflictions, and many of them do not pray truly, but do rather counterfeit a prayer, or pray for custom.—*Wolfgang Musculus,* 1497—1563.

Verse 7.—" *Out of Zion.*" Zion the church is no Saviour, neither dare we trust in her ministers or ordinances, and yet salvation comes to men through her. The hungry multitudes are fed by the hands of the disciples, who delight to act as the servitors of the gospel feast. Zion becomes the site of the fountain of healing waters which shall flow east and west till all nations drink thereat. What a reason for maintaining in the utmost purity and energy all the works of the church of the living God!—*C. H. S.*

Verse 7.—" *When the Lord turneth the captivity of his people : then shall Jacob rejoice and Israel shall be glad.*"—Notice that by Israel we are to understand those other sheep which the Lord has that are not of this fold, but which he must also bring, that they may hear his voice. For it is Israel, not Judah ; Sion, not Jerusalem. *" When the Lord turneth the captivity of his people." " Then,"* as it is in the parallel passage, *" were we like unto them that dream."* A glorious dream indeed, in which, fancy what we may, the half of the beauty, the half of the splendour, will not be reached by our imagination. *" The captivity "* of our souls to the law of concupiscence, of our bodies to the law of death ; the captivity of our senses to fear ; the captivity, the conclusion of which is so beautifully expressed by one of our greatest poets :—namely, *Giles Fletcher* (1588—1623), *in his " Christ's Triumph over Death."*

> " No sorrow now hangs clouding on their brow ;
> No bloodless malady impales their face ;
> No age drops on their hairs his silver snow ;
> No nakedness their bodies doth embrace ;
> No poverty themselves and theirs disgrace ;
> No fear of death the joy of life devours ;
> No unchaste sleep their precious time deflowers ;
> No loss, no grief, no change, wait on their winged hours."

John Mason Neale, in loc.

HINTS TO PREACHERS.

Verse 1 *(first clause).*—The folly of atheism.

Verse 1.—Atheism of the heart.—*Jamieson's Sermons on the Heart.*

Verse 1 *(whole verse).*—Describe : I. The creed of the fool. II. The fool who holds the creed : or thus, Atheism. I. Its source : *" the heart."* II. Its creed : *" no God."* III. Its fruits : *" corrupt,"* etc.

Verse 1.—I. The great source of sin—alienation from God. II. Its place of dominion—the heart. III. Its effect upon the intellect—makes man a fool. IV. Its manifestations in the life—acts of commission and omission.

Verse 1 *(last clause).*—The lantern of Diogenes. Hold it up upon all classes, and denounce their sins.

Verse 2.—I. Condescending search. II. Favoured subjects. III. Generous intentions.

Verse 2.—What God looks for, and what we should look for. Men usually are quick to see things congruous to their own character.

Verses 2, 3.—God's search for a naturally good man ; the results ; lessons to be learned therefrom.

Verse 3.—Total depravity of the race.

Verse 4.—*" Have all the workers of iniquity no knowledge ? "* If men rightly knew God, his law, the evil of sin, the torment of hell, and other great truths, would they sin as they do ? Or if they know these and yet continue in their iniquities, how guilty and foolish they are ! Answer the question both positively and negatively, and it supplies material for a searching discourse.

Verse 4.—*(first clause).*—The crying sin of transgressing against light and knowledge.

Verse 4 *(last clause).*—Absence of prayer, a sure mark of a graceless state.

Verse 5.—The foolish fears of those who have no fear of God.

Verse 5.—The Lord's nearness to the righteous, its consequences to the persecutor, and its encouragement to saints.

Verse 6.—The wisdom of making the Lord our refuge.—*John Owen.*

Verse 6.—Describe I. The poor man here intended. II. His counsel. III. His reproach. IV. His refuge.

Verse 6.—Trust in God, a theme for mockery to fools only. Show its wisdom.

Verse 7.—Longings for the Advent.

Verse 7.—*" Out of Zion."* The church, the channel of blessings to men.

Verse 7.—Discourse to promote revival. I. Frequent condition of the church, " captivity." II. Means of revival—the Lord's coming in grace. III. Consequences, " rejoice," " be glad."

Verse 7.—Captivity of soul. What it is. How provided for. How accomplished. With what results.

PSALM XV.

SUBJECT, &c.—*This Psalm of David bears no dedicatory title at all indicative of the occasion upon which it was written, but it is exceedingly probable that, together with the twenty-fourth Psalm, to which it bears a striking resemblance, its composition was in some way connected with the removal of the ark to the holy hill of Zion. Who should attend upon the ark was a matter of no small consequence, for because unauthorised persons had intruded into the office, David was unable on the first occasion to complete his purpose of bringing the ark to Zion. On the second attempt he is more careful, not only to allot the work of carrying the ark to the divinely appointed Levites (1 Chron. xv. 2), but also to leave it in charge of the man whose house the Lord had blessed, even Obededom, who, with his many sons, ministered in the house of the Lord. (1 Chron. xxvi. 8, 12.) Spiritually we have here a description of the man who is a child at home in the Church of God on earth, and who will dwell in the house of the Lord for ever above. He is primarily Jesus, the perfect man, and in him all who through grace are conformed to his image.*

DIVISION.—*The first verse asks the question ; the rest of the verses answer it. We will call the Psalm* THE QUESTION AND ANSWER.

EXPOSITION.

LORD, who shall abide in thy tabernacle ? who shall dwell in thy holy hill ?

1.—THE QUESTION. *Jehovah.* Thou high and holy One, who shall be permitted to have fellowship with thee ? The heavens are not pure in thy sight, and thou chargedst thine angels with folly, who then of mortal mould shall dwell with thee, thou dread consuming fire ? A sense of the glory of the Lord and of the holiness which becomes his house, his service, and his attendants, excites the humble mind to ask the solemn question before us. Where angels bow with veiled faces, how shall man be able to worship at all ? The unthinking many imagine it to be a very easy matter to approach the Most High, and when professedly engaged in his worship they have no questionings of heart as to their fitness for it ; but truly humbled souls often shrink under a sense of utter unworthiness, and would not dare to approach the throne of the God of holiness if it were not for him, our Lord, our Advocate, who can abide in the heavenly temple, because his righteousness endureth for ever. " *Who shall abide in thy tabernacle ?* " Who shall be admitted to be one of the household of God, to sojourn under his roof and enjoy communion with himself ? " *Who shall dwell in thy holy hill ?* " Who shall be a citizen of Zion, and an inhabitant of the heavenly Jerusalem ? The question is raised, because it is a question. All men have not this privilege, nay, even among professors there are aliens from the commonwealth, who have no secret intercourse with God. On the grounds of law no mere man can dwell with God, for there is not one upon earth who answers to the just requirements mentioned in the succeeding verses. The questions in the text are asked of the *Lord,* as if none but the Infinite Mind could answer them so as to satisfy the unquiet conscience. We must know from the Lord of the tabernacle what are the qualifications for his service, and when we have been taught of him, we shall clearly see that only our spotless Lord Jesus, and those who are conformed unto his image, can ever stand with acceptance before the Majesty on high.

Impertinent curiosity frequently desires to know who and how many shall be saved ; if those who thus ask the question, " Who shall dwell in thy holy hill ? " would make it a soul-searching enquiry in reference to themselves they would act much more wisely. Members of the visible church, which is God's tabernacle of worship, and hill of eminence, should diligently see to it, that they have the preparation of heart which fits them to be inmates of the house of God. Without the wedding-dress of righteousness in Christ Jesus, we have no right to sit at the banquet of communion. Without uprightness of walk we are not fit for the imperfect church on earth, and certainly we must not hope to enter the perfect church above.

2 He that walketh uprightly, and worketh righteousness, and speaketh the truth in his heart.

3 *He that* backbiteth not with his tongue, nor doeth evil to his neighbour, nor taketh up a reproach against his neighbour.

4 In whose eyes a vile person is contemned ; but he honoureth them that fear the LORD. *He that* sweareth to *his own* hurt, and changeth not.

5 *He that* putteth not out his money to usury, nor taketh reward against the innocent. He that doeth these *things* shall never be moved.

2.—THE ANSWER. The Lord in answer to the question informs us by his Holy Spirit of the character of the man who alone can dwell in his holy hill. In perfection this holiness is found only in the Man of Sorrows, but in a measure it is wrought in all his people by the Holy Ghost. Faith and the graces of the Spirit are not mentioned, because this is a description of outward character, and where fruits are found the root may not be seen, but it is surely there. Observe the accepted man's *walk, work and word.* "*He that walketh uprightly,*" he keeps himself erect as those do who traverse high ropes ; if they lean on one side over they must go, or as those who carry precious but fragile ware in baskets on their heads, who lose all if they lose their perpendicular. True belivers do not cringe as flatterers, wriggle as serpents, bend double as earth-grubbers, or crook on one side as those who have sinister aims ; they have the strong backbone of the vital principle of grace within, and being themselves upright, they are able to walk uprightly. Walking is of far more importance than talking. He only is right who is upright in walk and downright in honesty. "*And worketh righteousness.*" His faith shows itself by good works, and therefore is no dead faith. God's house is a hive for workers, not a nest for drones. Those that rejoice that everything is done for them by another, even the Lord Jesus, and therefore hate legality, are the best doers in the world upon gospel principles. If we are not positively serving the Lord, and doing his holy will to the best of our power, we may seriously debate our interest in divine things, for trees which bear no fruit must be hewn down and cast into the fire. "*And speaketh the truth in his heart.*" The fool in the last Psalm spoke falsely in his heart ; observe both here and elsewhere in the two Psalms, the striking contrast. Saints not only desire to love and speak truth with their lips, but they seek to be true within ; they will not lie even in the closet of their hearts, for God is there to listen ; they scorn double meanings, evasions, equivocations, white lies, flatteries, and deceptions. Though truths, like roses, have thorns about them, good men wear them in their bosoms. Our heart must be the sanctuary and refuge of truth, should it be banished from all the world beside, and hunted from among men ; at all risk we must entertain the angel of truth, for truth is God's daughter. We must be careful that the heart is really fixed and settled in principle, for tenderness of conscience towards truthfulness, like the bloom on a peach, needs gentle handling, and once lost it were hard to regain it. Jesus was the mirror of sincerity and holiness. Oh, to be more and more fashioned after his similitude !

3. After the positive comes the negative. "*He that backbiteth not with his tongue.*" There is a sinful way of backbiting with the heart when we think too hardly of a neighbour, but it is the tongue which does the mischief. Some men's tongues bite more than their teeth. The tongue is not steel, but it cuts, and its wounds are very hard to heal ; its worst wounds are not with its edge to our face, but with its back when our head is turned. Under the law, a night hawk was an unclean bird, and its human image is abominable everywhere. All slanderers are the devil's bellows to blow up contention, but those are the worst which blow at the back of the fire. "*Nor doeth evil to his neighbour.*" He who bridles his tongue will not give a licence to his hand. Loving our neighbour as ourselves will make us jealous of his good name, careful not to injure his estate, or by ill example to corrupt his character. "*Nor taketh up a reproach against his neighbour.*" He is a fool if not a knave who picks up stolen goods and harbours them ; in slander as well as robbery, the receiver is as bad as the thief. If there were no gratified hearers of ill reports, there would be an end of the trade of spreading them. Trapp says, that " the tale-bearer carrieth the devil in his tongue, and the tale-hearer carries the devil in his ear." The original may be translated, " endureth ; " implying that it is a sin to endure or tolerate tale-bearers. " Show that man out ! " we should say of a drunkard, yet it is very questionable if his unmannerly behaviour will do us so much mischief

as the tale-bearer's insinuating story. "Call for a policeman!" we say if we see a thief at his business; ought we to feel no indignation when we hear a gossip at her work? Mad dog! Mad dog!! is a terrible hue and cry, but there are few curs whose bite is so dangerous as a busybody's tongue. Fire! fire!! is an alarming note, but the tale-bearer's tongue is set on fire of hell, and those who indulge it had better mend their manners, or they may find that there is fire in hell for un-bridled tongues. Our Lord spake evil of no man, but breathed a prayer for his foes; we must be like him, or we shall never be with him.

4. "*In whose eyes a vile person is contemned; but he honoureth them that fear the Lord.*" We must be as honest in paying respect as in paying our bills. Honour to whom honour is due. To all good men we owe a debt of honour, and we have no right to hand over what is their due to vile persons who happen to be in high places. When bad men are in office, it is our duty to respect the office, but we cannot so violate our consciences as to do otherwise than contemn the men; and on the other hand, when true saints are in poverty and distress, we must sumpathize with their afflictions and honour the men none the less. We may honour the roughest cabinet for the sake of the jewels, but we must not prize false gems because of their setting. A sinner in a gold chain and silken robes is no more to be compared with a saint in rags than a rushlight in a silver candlestick with the sun behind a cloud. The proverb says, that "ugly women, finely dressed, are the uglier for it," and so mean men in high estate are the more mean because of it. "*He that sweareth to his own hurt, and changeth not.*" Scriptural saints under the New Testament rule "swear not at all," but their word is as good as an oath: those men of God who think it right to swear, are careful and prayerful lest they should even seem to overshoot the mark. When engagements have been entered into which turn out to be unprofitable, "the saints are men of honour still." Our blessed Surety swore to his own hurt, but how gloriously he stood to his suretiship! what a comfort to us that he changeth not, and what an example to us to be scrupulously and precisely exact in fulfilling our covenants with others! The most far-seeing trader may enter into engagements which turn out to be serious losses, but whatever else he loses, if he keeps his honour, his losses will be bearable; if that be lost all is lost.

5 "*He that putteth not out his money to usury.*" Usury was and is hateful both to God and man. That a lender should share with the borrower in gains made by his money is most fitting and proper; but that the man of property should eat up the poor wretch who unfortunately obtained a loan of him is abominable. Those who grind poor tradesmen, needy widows, and such like, by charging them interest at intolerable rates, will find that their gold and their silver are cankered. The man who shall ascend into the hill of the Lord must shake off this sin as Paul shook the viper into the fire. "*Nor taketh reward against the innocent.*" Bribery is a sin both in the giver and the receiver. It was frequently practised in Eastern courts of justice; that form of it is now under our excellent judges almost an unheard-of thing; yet the sin survives in various forms, which the reader needs not that we should mention; and under every shape it is loathsome to the true man of God. He remembers that Jesus instead of taking reward against the innocent died for the guilty.

5 "*He that doeth these things shall never be moved.*" No storm shall tear him from his foundations, drag him from his anchorage, or uproot him from his place. Like the Lord Jesus, whose dominion is everlasting, the true Christian shall never lose his crown. He shall not only be *on* Zion, but *like* Zion, fixed and firm. He shall dwell in the tabernacle of the Most High, and neither death nor judgment shall remove him from his place of privilege and blessedness.

Let us betake ourselves to prayer and self-examination, for this Psalm is as fire for the gold, and as a furnace for silver. Can we endure its testing power?

EXPLANATORY NOTES AND QUAINT SAYINGS.

Verse 1.—"*Lord, who shall abide in thy tabernacle?*"—In that the church of Christ upon earth is a "*tabernacle,*" we may note, that neither the church itself nor the members of it, have any fixed or firm seat of habitation in this world: "Arise, depart, for this is not your rest." Micah ii. 10. "Here have we no continuing city, but we seek one to come." Heb. xiii. 14. God's tabernacle, being a movable temple, wandered up and down, sometimes in the desert, sometimes in Shiloh, sometimes among the Philistines, sometimes in Kirjathjearim, and never found any settled place till it was translated into the mountain of God : even so the church of God wandereth as a straggler and a stranger in the wilderness of this world, being destitute, tormented, and afflicted on every side, persecuted from this city to that, and never enjoying any constant habitation of sound and sure rest until it be translated unto " *God's holy hill.*" The verb גּוּר *gur* (as the learned in Hebrew note) signifying to dwell as a stranger, or a sojourner, imports that a citizen of heaven is a pilgrim on earth . . . . In that the church is a *tabernacle*, we may see that it is not a fort, compassed about with any strong walls, armed with any human forces ; and yet such as keep within her are defended from heat of sun, and hurt of storms. Her strength is not here, but from above, for Christ her Head is in all her troubles a present help, a refuge against the tempest, a shadow against the heat. Isa. xxv. 4. The church on earth is indeed a *tabernacle*, but it is *God's* tabernacle, wherein he dwelleth as in his house ; " Lord, who shall abide in *thy* tabernacle ? " for to this end the Lord commanded the tabernacle to be made, that he might dwell among them ; and again, whereas he promised by Moses to set his tabernacle among them the blessed apostle construeth it of his dwelling among them. 2 Cor. vi. 16. " You are," saith he, " the temple of the living God, as God hath said, I will dwell in them, and walk in them." To the same purpose, God is said elsewhere to dwell in Sion, and to walk in the midst of the seven golden candlesticks, that is, in the midst of the seven churches in the midst of his city (Psa. xlvi. 5), in the midst of his people. Isa. xii. 6.—*John Boys, D.D., Dean of Canterbury, 1571—1625.*

Verse 1.—" *Lord, who shall abide,*" etc. If David, a man endued with an excellent and divine spirit, one in whom singular wisdom, rare knowledge, and deep understanding of hidden secrets appeared, who being taught of God in heavenly things, far surpassed and exceeded in wisdom all his teachers and counsellors, did notwithstanding desire to know the sheep from the goats, the good from the bad, the saints from the hypocrites, the true worshippers of God from dissemblers, the true inhabitants of the holy tabernacle from the intruders of the wicked, lest therein he should be deceived ; how great cause have we, in whom neither the like spirit, neither such wisdom, nor equal knowledge, nor comparable understanding, by many degrees appeareth to fear our own weakness, to doubt of our own judgments, to confess our own infirmity, and to suspect the subtle sleights and coloured pretences of men : and for further knowledge in hidden, deep, and secret things, with David to demand and ask this question, " Lord, who shall abide in thy tabernacle ? who shall dwell in thy holy hill ? " . . . . . . Where David saith, " Who shall abide in thy holy hill ? " he giveth us to understand that there is no true and sound rest but in the *holy hill of the Lord,* which is the church. Then the wicked and ungodly which are not of God's house, of his *holy hill,* of the church, have no quiet, rest, nor sound peace ; but they are in continual perplexity, continual torment, continual disquietness of their minds.—*Richard Turnbull,* 1606.

Verse 1.—" *Abide in thy tabernacle,*" etc.—The worshippers in the outer court only will get their eternal abode without among the dogs, sorcerers, etc.; but they that shall be inhabitants of heaven, come further in, even unto the tabernacle itself : their souls are fed at his table, they find the smell of his garments as of myrrh, aloes, and cassia ; and if they miss it at any time, it is the grief of their souls, and they are never at rest till they recover it again.—*Thomas Boston.*

Verse 1.—" *Who shall dwell,*" etc.

> " Now, who is he ? Say, if ye can,
> Who *so* shall gain the firm abode ?
> Pilate shall say, ' Behold the Man ! '
> And John, ' Behold the Lamb of God ! ' "
>
> *John Barclay, quoted by A. A. Bonar, in loc.*

Verse 1.—"*Holy Hill.*"—Heaven is aptly compared to a hill, hell to a hole. Now who shall ascend unto this holy mount ? None but those whom this mount comes down unto, that have sweet communion with God in this life present, whose conversation is in heaven, though their commoration be for awhile upon earth, who do here eat, and drink, and sleep, eternal life.—*John Trapp.*

Verses 1, 2.—The disguising and counterfeiting of hypocrites in all ages, occasioned haply this query : for, as Paul speaks, " all are not Israel that are of Israel," a great many living in the church are not of the church, according to that of the doctors upon this place, *multi sunt corpore qui non sunt fide, multi nomine qui non sunt nomine.* Wherefore David, here perceiving that sundry people were shuffled into God's tabernacle like goats among the sheep, and tares among the corn, being Jews outwardly, but not inwardly, deceiving others often, and sometimes themselves also, with a bare profession of religion, and false opinion of true piety, cometh unto God (as to the searcher and trier of the hearts of men, acquainted with all secrets, and best understanding who are his own), saying unto him, O Lord, forsomuch as there is so much unsoundness and hypocrisy reigning among those that dwell in thy tabernacle, professing thy word, and frequenting the places of thy worship ; I beseech thee most humbly, to declare to thy people some tokens and cognizances by which a true subject of thy kingdom may be discerned from the children of this world. Here then, observe, that an external profession of faith, and outward communion with the church of God, is not sufficient unto salvation, unless we lead an incorrupt life correspondent to the same, doing the thing which is right, and speaking the truth in our heart. And, therefore, the silly Papist is exceedingly deceived in relying so much upon the church's outside, to wit upon the succession of Roman bishops, upon the multitudes of Roman Catholics, upon the power and pomp of the Roman synagogue, crying as the Jews in old time, " The temple of the Lord, the temple of the Lord," our church is the temple of the Lord. The carnal and careless gospeller is deceived also, placing all his religion in the formal observation of outward service, for a mere verbal Christian is a real atheist, according to that of Paul (Titus i. 16), " In word they profess that they know God, but in their works they deny him ; " and so many who seem to sojourn in God's tabernacle for a time, shall never rest upon his " *holy hill ;* " and this assertion is expressly confirmed by Christ himself : " Not every one (saith he) that saith unto me, Lord, Lord, shall enter into the kingdom of heaven ; but he that doeth the will of my Father which is in heaven. Many will say to me in that day, Lord, Lord, have we not prophesied in thy name ? and in thy name have cast out devils ? and in thy name have done many wonderful works ? And then will I profess unto them, I never knew you : depart from me ye that work iniquity." Matt. vii. 21—23. Consider this, all ye which are Christians in lip only, but not in life, making a mask of religion, or rather a very vizard, with eyes, and mouth, and nose, fairly painted and proportioned to all pretences and purposes. O think on this, all ye that forget God, he that dwelleth on high, and beholds the things here below, suffers none *to rest upon the mountain of his holiness* but such as *walk uprightly, doing that which is just, and speaking that which is true.—John Boys.*

Verse 2.—"He that walketh uprightly," etc.—If neither the golden reason of excellency can move us, nor the silver reason of profit allure us, then must the iron reason of necessity enforce us to *integrity* and *uprightness of heart.* For first, such is the necessity thereof, that without integrity the best graces we seem to have are counterfeit, and, therefore, but glorious sins ; the best worship we can perform is but hypocrisy, and therefore abominable in God's sight. For uprightness is the soundness of all grace and virtues, as also of all religion and worship of God, without which they are unsound and nothing worth. And first, as touching graces, if they be not joined with uprightness of heart, they are sins under the masks or vizards of virtue, yea, as it may seem, double sins : for as Augustine saith, *Simulata æquitas est duplex iniquitas, quia et iniquitas est, et simulatio :* Feigned equity is double iniquity, both because it is iniquity, and because it is feigning.—*George Downame, D.D.,* 1604.

Verse 2.—" He that walketh uprightly."—Here two questions are moved : First. Why David describes a sound member of the church, and inheritor of heaven, by works rather than by faith, seeing the kingdom of heaven is promised unto faith, and the profession thereof also maketh one a member of the visible church ? Secondly. Why, among all the fruits of faith, almost innumerable, he makes choice of those duties especially which concern our neighbours ? To the first, answer may be, that in this, and in all other places of Holy Scripture, where good works are commanded or commended in any, faith is ever presupposed, according to that apostolical maxim, " Whatsoever is not of faith is sin ; " " Without me," saith our blessed Saviour, " ye can do nothing " (John xv. 5) ; and without faith in him it is impossible to please God (Heb. xi. 6) ; *fides est operum fomes,* as Paulinus wittily : " *Faith* (as our church speaks), *is the nest of good works ;* albeit our birds be never so fair, though haply we *do that which is right, and speak that which is true,* yet all these will be lost, except it be brought forth in a true belief." Aristides was so just in his government that he would not tread awry for any respect to friend or despite of foe. Pomponius is said to have been so true, that he never made lie himself, nor suffered a lie in other. Curtius at Rome, Menæceus at Thebes, Codrus at Athens, exposed themselves unto voluntary death, for the good of their neighbours and country : yet, because they wanted the rest of true faith in the world's Saviour where to lay their young, we cannot (if we speak with our prophet here from God's oracle), say that they shall ever rest upon his holy hill. Another answer may be, that faith is an inward and hidden grace, and many deceive themselves and others with a feigned profession thereof, and therefore the Holy Spirit will have every man's faith to be tried and known by their fruits, and howsoever eternal life be promised to faith, and eternal damnation be threatened against infidelity, yet the sentence of salvation and condemnation shall be pronounced according to works, as the clearest evidence of both. It is truly said, out of Bernard, that although our good works are not *causa regnandi,* yet they be *via regni,* the causeway wherein, albeit not the cause wherefore, we must ascend God's holy hill. To the second demand, why the duties immediately belonging to God, are not mentioned here, but only such as concern our brother ? Answer is made, that this question is propounded of such as, living in the visible church, openly profess the faith, and would seem to be devout, hearing the word of God, and calling upon his name ; for of such as are profane atheists, and do not so much as make a semblance of holiness, there is no question to be made, for, without all doubt, there can be no resting place for such in the kingdom of heaven. Now that we may discern aright which of those that profess religion are sound, and which unsound ; the marks are not to be taken from an outward hearing of the word, or receiving of the sacraments, and much less from a formal observation of human traditions in God's tabernacle (for all these things hypocrites usually perform), but from the duties of righteousness, giving every man his due, because the touchstone of piety towards God is charity towards our brother. "Herein," saith John, "are the children of God known, and the children of the devil : whosoever doth not righteousness is not of God, neither he that loveth not his brother."—*John Boys.*

Verse 2.—There is no ascertaining the quality of a tree but by its fruits. When the wheels of a clock move within, the hands on the dial will move without. When the heart of a man is sound in conversion, then the life will be fair in profession. When the conduit is walled in, how shall we judge of the spring but by the waters which run through the pipes ?—*William Secker.*

Verse 2.—" *And worketh righteousness.*" A man must first be righteous before he can work righteousness of life. "He that doeth righteousness is righteous, even as he is righteous." 1 John iii. 7. The tree makes the fruit, not the fruit the tree ; and therefore the tree must be good before the fruit can be good. Matt. vii. 18. A righteous man may make a righteous work, but no work of an unrighteous man can make him righteous. Now, we become righteous only by faith, through the righteousness of Christ imputed to us. Rom. v. 1. . . . . . Wherefore let men work as they will, if they be not true believers in Christ, they are not workers of righteousness ; and, consequently they will not be dwellers in heaven. Ye must then close with Christ in the first place, and by faith receive the gift of imputed righteousness, or ye will never truly bear this character of a citizen of Zion. A man shall as soon force fruit out of a branch broken off from the tree and withered, as work righteousness without believing in, and uniting with Christ. These are two things by which those that hear the gospel are ruined.—*Thomas Boston.*

Verse 2.—" *Worketh righteousness.*" Jacob's ladder had stairs, upon which he saw none standing still, but all either ascending, or else descending by it. Ascend you likewise to the top of the ladder, to heaven, and there you shall hear one say, " My Father doth now work, and I work also." Whereupon Basil noteth that King David having first said, " *Lord, who shall dwell in thy tabernacle ?* " adds then, not he that hath wrought righteousness heretofore, but *he that doth now work righteousness,* even as Christ saith, " My Father doth now work, and I work also."—*Thomas Playfere.*

Verse 2.—But here observe David saith, " that *worketh* righteousness ; " not that talks about, thinks about, or hears of, righteousness ; because, " not the hearers of the law, but the doers of the law, shall be justified." What then do we owe unto others ? That which Christ saith (Matt. vii.), " Whatsoever ye would that men should do unto you, do ye also unto them," even unto your enemies : that is, to injure no one, to succour those that suffer injury, and to do good unto all men. But these things, I say, are spoken especially unto those who have respect of persons ; as if he had said, It is not because thou art a priest, nor because thou art of a religious order, nor because thou prayest much, nor because thou dost miracles, nor because thou teachest excellently, nor because thou art dignified with the title of father, nor because thou art the doer of any work (except righteousness), that thou shalt rest in the holy hill of the Lord ; for if thou be destitute of the work of righteousness, neither all thy good works, nor thy indulgences, nor thy votes and suffrages, nor thy intercessions, shall avail thee anything. Therefore, the truth is firm ; that it is the walker without spot, and the doer of righteousness, that shall rest in the taber- nacle of the Lord. Yet how many are there, who build, increase and adorn churches, monasteries, altars, vessels, garments, etc., who, all the while never so much as think of the works of righteousness ; nay, who tread righteousness under foot that they may work these their own works, and because of them hope to gain the pardon of their unrighteousness, while thousands are deceived by these means ! Hence, in the last day, Christ will say, " I was an hungered, I was thirsty, I was naked, I was in prison, I was a stranger." He will not say one word about those works which are done and admired at this day. And on the other hand, it is of no account against thee that thou art a layman, or poor, or sick or contemptible, or how vile soever thou art, if thou workest righteousness, thou shalt be saved. The only work that we must hope will be considered and accounted of, is the work of righteous- ness : all other works that either urge or allure us on under a show of godliness, are a thing of nought.—*Martin Luther.*

Verse 2.—*"And speaketh the truth in his heart."* Anatomists have observed that the tongue in man is tied with a double string to the heart. And so in *truth spoken* there is necessary a double agreement of our words. 1. With our heart. That is, to the speaking of truth, it is necessary our words agree with our mind and thoughts about the thing. We must speak as we think, and our tongues must be faithful interpreters of our mind ; otherwise we lie, not speaking as we think. So what is truth in itself may be spoken by a man, and yet he be a liar ; namely, if he does not think as he speaks. 2. With the thing as it is in itself. Though we think a thing to be so, which is not so, we lie, when we affirm it ; because it is not as we say, though we really think it is so. For our mistaken notions of things can never stamp lies to pass current for truths. 2 Thess ii. 11.—*Thomas Boston.*

Verse 2.—I this day heard a sermon from Psalm xv. 2, " *And speaketh the truth in his heart."* . . . . . . O my soul, receive the admonition that has been given thee ! Study truth in the inward parts ; let integrity and truth always accompany thee, and preserve thee : speak the truth in thy heart. I am thankful for any conviction and sense I have of the evil of lying ; Lord, increase my abhorrence of it : as a further assistance and help against this mean, sordid, pernicious vice, I would endeavour, and resolve, in pursuit of the directions laid before us in the sermon, to mortify those passions and corruptions from whence this sin of lying more ordinarily flows, and which are the chief occasion of it, as " out of the heart proceed evil thoughts " (Matt. xv. 19) ; so, from the same fountain proceed evil words. And I would, with the greatest zeal, set myself against such corruptions as upon observation I find more commonly betray me into this iniquity : pride often indites our speech, and coins many a lie ; so envy, covetousness, malice, etc. I would endeavour to cleanse myself from all this filthiness : there never will be a mortified tongue while there is an unmortified heart. If I love the world inordinately, it is a thousand to one I shall be often stretching a point to promote a worldly interest ; and if I hate my brother, it is the same odds I shall reproach him. Lord, help me to purge the foun- tain, and then the streams will be pure. When the spring of a clock, and all the movements are right, the hand will go right ; and so it is here. The tongue follows the inward inclination. I would resolve to do nothing that may need a lie. If Gehazi's covetousness had not shamed him, he had not wanted a lie to excuse him, " He that walks uprightly, walks surely " and safely in this, as well as other respects. Prov. x. 9. May I do nothing that is dishonourable and mean, nothing that cannot bear the light, and then I shall have little temptation to lying. I would endeavour for a lively sense of the eye of God upon me, acting and speaking in his presence. Lord, I desire to set thee always before me ; thou understandest my thoughts as perfectly as others do my words. I would consider before I speak, and not speak much or rashly. Prov. xxix. 20. I would often think of the severity of a future judgment, when every secret shall be made manifest, and the hypocrite and liar exposed before angels and men. Lastly, I would frequently beg divine assistance herein. Psalm cxix. 29 ; Prov. xxx. 8. O my God, help me in my future conduct, remove from me the way of lying ; may the law of kindness and truth be in my tongue ; may I take heed to my ways, that I sin not with my tongue. I bewail my past miscarriages in this respect, and flee to thy mercy through the blood of Christ ; bless to me the instructions that have been this day given me ; let no iniquity prevail against me ; "Keep back thy servant from presumptuous sins, and cleanse me from secret faults." I commit my thoughts, desires, and tongue, to thy conduct and government ; may I think and act in thy fear, and always speak the truth in my heart.—*Benjamin Bennet's "Christian Oratory,"* 1728.

Verses 2, 5.—As the eagle casteth off her beak, and so reneweth her youth, and the snake strippeth off her old skin, and so maketh herself smooth : even so he that will enter into the joys of God, and rest upon his holy mountain, must, as the Scripture speaks, put off the old man and put on the new, which, after God, is created in righteousness and true holiness, repenting truly, speedily, steadily.—*Robert Cawdray.*

Verse 3.—" *He that backbiteth not with his tongue, nor doeth evil to his neighbour.*" Lamentation for the gross neglect of this duty, or the frequent commission of this sin. What tears are sufficient to bewail it ? How thick do censures and reproaches fly in all places, at all tables, in all conventions ! And this were the more tolerable, if it were only the fault of ungodly men, of strangers and enemies to religion ; for so saith the proverb, " Wickedness proceedeth from the wicked." When a man's heart is full of hell, it is not unreasonable to expect that his tongue should be set on fire of hell ; and it is no wonder to hear such persons reproach good men, yea, even for their goodness. But alas ! the disease doth not rest here, this plague is not only among the Egyptians but Israelites too. It is very doleful to consider how professors sharpen their tongues like swords against professors ; and one good man censures and reproaches another, and one minister traduceth another ; and who can say, " I am clean from this sin " ? O that I could move your pity in this case ! For the Lord's sake pity yourselves, and do not pollute and wound your consciences with this crime. Pity your brethren ; let it suffice that godly ministers and Christians are loaded with reproaches by wicked men—there is no need that you should combine with them in this diabolical work. You should support and strengthen their hands against the reproaches of the ungodly world, and not add affliction to the afflicted. O pity the world, and pity the church which Christ hath purchased with his own blood, which methinks bespeaks you in the words, " Have pity upon me, have pity upon me, O ye my friends ; for the hand of God hath touched me." Job. xix. 21. Pity the mad and miserable world, and help it against this sin ; stop the bloody issue ; restrain this wicked practice amongst men as much as possibly you can, and lament it before God, and for what you cannot do yourselves, give God no rest until he shall please to work a cure.—*Matthew Poole,* 1624—1679.

Verse 3.—" *He that backbiteth not,*" etc. Detraction or slander is not lightly to be passed over, because we do so easily fail in this point. For the good name of a man, as saith Solomon, is a precious thing to every one, and to be preferred before much treasure, insomuch that it is no less grievous to hurt a man with the tongue than with a sword : nay, ofttimes the stroke of a tongue is grievouser than the wound of a spear, as it is in the French proverb. And therefore the tongue must be bridled, that we hurt not in any wise the good name of our neighbour ; but preserve it unto him safe and sound as much as in us shall lie. That which he addeth touching evil or injury not to be done to our neighbour, is like unto that which we have seen already concerning the working or exercising of righteousness. He would have us therefore so to exercise all upright dealing, that we might be far from doing any damage or wrong to our neighbours. And by the name of neighbour, is meant every man and woman, as it is plain and evident. For we are all created of God, and placed in this world that we might live uprightly and sincerely together. And therefore he breaketh the law of human society (for we are all tied and bound by this law of nature) that doth hurt or injury to another. The third member of this verse is, *nor that reproacheth another,* or, that maintaineth not a false report given one against another ; which latter particle seemeth to be the better, since he had spoken before expressly, touching the good name of another, not to be hurt or wronged with our tongue. To the which fault this is next in degree, wherewith we are too much encumbered, and which we scarce acknowledge to be a fault, when we further and maintain the slanders devised and given out by another against a man, either by hearing them or by telling them forth to others, as we heard them. For why? It seemeth for the most part to be enough for us if we can say, that we feign not this or that, nor make it of our own heads, but only tell it forth as we heard it of others, without adding anything of our own brain. But as oft as we do this we fail in our duty doing, in not providing for our neighbour's credit, as were requisite for the things, which being uttered by others ought to be passed over in silence and to lie dead, we gather up, and by telling them forth, disperse them abroad, which whether it be a sin or no, when as we ought by all means possible to wish and do well unto our neighbour, all men do see. And therefore thou that travellest towards eternal life, must not only not devise false reports and slanders against other men, but also not so much as have them in thy mouth being devised by others, neither by any means assist or maintain them in slandering; but by all honest and lawful means, provide for the credit and estimation of thy neighbour, so much as in thee lieth.—*Peter Baro, D.D., 1560.*

Verse 3.—*" He that backbiteth not with his tongue."* The Hebrew word רָגַל signifieth to play the spy, and by a metaphor to *backbite* or *slander,* for *backbiters* and whisperers, after the manner of spies, go up and down dissembling their malice, that they may espy the faults and defects of others, whereof they may make a malicious relation to such as will give ear to their slanders. So that *backbiting* is a malicious defamation of a man behind his back . . . . . . And that the citizen of heaven doth and ought to abhor from *backbiting,* the horrible wickedness of this sin doth evince. For first, Lev. xix. 16, where it is straightly forbidden, the " *tale-bearer* " is compared to a pedlar: "Thou shalt not walk about with tales and slanders, as it were a pedlar among thy people." So much רָכִיל signifieth. For as the pedlar having bought his wares of some one or more goeth about from house to house that he may sell the same to others; so *backbiters* and *tale-bearers,* gathering together tales and rumours, as it were wares, go from one to another, that such wares as either themselves have invented, or have gathered by report, they may utter in the absence of their neighbour to his infamy and disgrace. Likewise Psalm l. 20, it is condemned as a notable crime, which God will not suffer to go unpunished; Ezek. xxii. 9, it is reckoned among the abominations of Jerusalem, for which destruction is denounced against it; and Rom. i. 29, 30, among the crimes of the heathen, given over unto a reprobate sense, this is placed: they were " *whisperers and backbiters."*—*George Downame.*

Verse 3.—*" He that backbiteth not."* He that is guilty of backbiting, that speaks evil of another behind his back, if that which he speaks be false, is guilty of lying, which is prejudicial to salvation. If that which he speaks be true, yet he is void of charity in seeking to defame another. For as Solomon observes, " Love covereth all sins." Prov. x. 12. Where there is love and charity, there will be a covering and concealing of men's sins as much as may be. Now, where charity is wanting, their salvation is not to be expected. 1 Cor. xiii. 1, etc.; 1 John iii. 14, 15.—*Christopher Cartwright,* 1602—1658.

Verse 3.—*" Backbiteth not."* This crime is a conjugation of evils, and is productive of infinite mischiefs; it undermines peace, and saps the foundation of friendship; it destroys families, and rends in pieces the very heart and vitals of charity; it makes an evil man party, and witness, and judge, and executioner of the innocent. *Bishop Taylor.*

Verse 3.—*" Backbiteth."* The scorpion hurteth none but such as he toucheth with the tip of his tail; and the crocodile and basilisk slay none but such as either the force of their sight, or strength of their breath reacheth. The viper woundeth none but such as it biteth; the venomous herbs or roots kill none but such as taste, or handle, or smell them, and so come near unto them; but the poison of slanderous tongues is much more rank and deadly; for that hurteth and slayeth, woundeth and killeth, not only near, but afar off; not only at hand, but by distance of place removed; not only at home, but abroad, not only in our own nation but in foreign countries; and spareth neither quick nor dead.—*Richard Turnbull.*

Verse 3.—*" Backbiteth."* The word here used comes from a root signifying *foot,* and denotes a person who goes about from house to house, speaking things he should not (1 Tim. v. 13); and a word from this root signifies *spies;* and the phrase here may point at persons who creep into houses, pry into the secrets of families, divulge them, and oftentimes represent them in a false light. Such are ranked among the worst of men, and are very unfit to be in the society of saints, or in a church of Christ. See Rom. i. 30.—*John Gill.*

Verse 3.—" *Nor taketh up a reproach against his neighbour.*" The saints of God must not be too light of hearing, much less of believing all tales, rumours, and reports of their brethren ; and charity requireth that we do not only stop and stay them, but that we examine them before we believe them. Saul, the king, too light of belief in this point, believed the slanderous and false reports of David's enemies, who put into Saul's head that David imagined evil against him. Yea, David himself showed his great infirmity in that, that without due examination and proof of the matter, he believed the false report of Ziba against Mephibosheth, the son of Jonathan ; of whom to David the king, persecuted by Absalom his son, Ziba reported falsely, that he should say, " This day shall the house of Israel restore unto me the kingdom of my father." The example of whose infirmity in Scripture reproved, must not we follow ; but let us rather embrace the truth of that heavenly doctrine which, through God's Spirit, here he preacheth, that we believe not false reports against our neighbours.—*Richard Turnbull.*

Verse 3.—Despise not thy neighbour, but think thyself as bad a sinner, and that the like defects may befall thee. If thou canst not excuse his doing, excuse his, intent which may be good ; or if the deed be evil, think it was done of ignorance ; if thou canst no way excuse him, think some great temptation befell him, and that thou shouldst be worse if the like temptation befell thee ; and give God thanks that the like as yet hath not befallen thee. Despise not a man being a sinner, for though he be evil to-day, he may turn to-morrow.—*Williams Perkins,* 1558—1602.

Verses 3, 4, 5.—They that cry down moral honesty, cry down that which is a great part of religion, my duty towards God, and my duty towards man. What care I to see a man run after a sermon, if he cozens and cheats as soon as he comes home ? On the other side, morality must not be without religion, for it so, it may change as I see convenience. Religion must govern it. He that has not religion to govern his morality, is not a dram better than my mastiff-dog ; so long as you stroke him, and please him, and do not pinch him, he will play with you as finely as may be, he is a very good moral mastiff ; but if you hurt him, he will fly in your face, and tear out your throat.—*John Seldon,* 1584—1654.

Verse 4.—" *In whose eyes a vile person is contemned,*" etc. When wicked Jehoram, king of Israel, came to Eliseus, the prophet, to ask counsel of the Lord, and to entreat for waters, having in company Jehoshaphat, the king of Judah, being virtuous ; the prophet showeth his contempt to the one being wicked, and his reverence to the other, being godly, faithful and virtuous, said, " As the Lord of hosts liveth, before whom I stand, were it not that I regard the presence of Jehoshaphat, the king of Judah, I would not look toward thee, nor see thee." 2 Kings iii. 14. Thus was the wicked *vile* in his sight ; thus did he not flatter the ungodly. In like manner godly Mordecai, the Jew, having Haman the ambitious and proud Agagite in contempt, would in no wise bow the knee unto him in sign of honour, as the rest of the people did ; for which cause he was extremely hated, menaced and molested of proud and wicked Haman. To wink at their wickedness, to uphold them in their iniquity, to fawn upon them and flatter them, to praise them when they deserve just reproof, is, as it were, an honouring of them ; to which, as to a most grievous sin, the prophet denounceth a most bitter curse : " Woe unto them that call evil good, and good evil ; that put darkness for light, and light for darkness ; that put bitter for sweet, and sweet for bitter ! " Isaiah v. 20.—*Richard Turnbull.*

Verse 4.—" *In whose eyes a vile person is contemned.*" To *contemn* the wicked and honour the godly, are opposite the one to the other. But the former may seem not to be sufficiently beseeming to a godly man. For why should he contemn or despise others, who is commanded by all means to care for the credit of others, as we heard even now ? Nay, a godly man, letting others go, ought to search into himself, and to accuse himself, but not to judge of others. But this saying of the prophet is to be understood rather of the faults than of the person. As every man therefore is to be loved, so are the faults of every man to be hated of the godly. For so is God himself, whom we desire to be like unto, that we might dwell with him, affected and disposed. For why ? he hateth no man, nay, he hateth nothing at all in this whole universal world, but only sin. For he is the author and preserver of all things that be ; and therefore doth good and wisheth well to all ; only of sin he is not the author, but the free and unconstrained will of man and

Satan. Notwithstanding God doth so greatly hate sin, that by reason thereof he doth sometimes neglect and forsake men, yea, and have them in contempt. So then a godly man hateth no man, nor contemneth any; but yet notwithstanding he disliketh sin in sinful men, and that he sticketh not to let them perceive either by reproving them, or shunning their company, or by doing of some other thing, whereby they may know they are misliked of good men for their enormities, and see themselves to be contemned of others for their wicked and ungodly life. A good man therefore must not flatter the ungodly in their ungracious attempts, but must freely declare that he disalloweth their course and conversation.—*Peter Baro.*

Verse 4.—" *In whose eyes a vile person is contemned.*" Augustine, as Posidonius writeth, showing what hatred he had to tale-bearers and false reporters of others, had two verses written over his table; by translation these:—

> " He that doth love with bitter speech the absent to defame,
>   Must surely know that at this board no place is for the same."

Richard Turnbull.

Verse 4.—" *In whose eyes a vile person is contemned.*" The burgess of the New Jerusalem, *reprobos reprobat, et probos probat;* he cannot flatter any man, nor fancy such as in whom he findeth not *aliquid Christi,* something of the image of God. A golden Colosse stuffed with rubbish, he cannot stoop to, " *But he honoureth them that fear the Lord,*" as the only earthly angels, though never so mean and despicable in the world's eye. Mr. Fox, being asked whether he remembered not such a poor servant of God who had received succour from him in time of trouble? answered " I remember him well; I tell you, I forget the lords and ladies, to remember such."—*John Trapp.*

Verse 4.—" *He honoureth them that fear the Lord.*" Though the godly some way or other be injurious unto us, we ought nevertheless to honour and not to despise them. So Joseph did Mary, though he supposed her to have dealt injuriously with him; and she had done so, indeed, if it had been with her as he imagined. Calvin's resolution concerning Luther was very admirable in this respect. They differed much about the presence of Christ in the sacrament; and Luther being of a vehement spirit, wrote bitterly against those that did hold otherwise in that point than himself did. This enforced some, who were more nearly concerned in the business, to prepare to answer Luther; which Calvin understanding, and fearing lest they, being provoked by Luther's tartness, should deal with him in the like kind, he wrote unto Bullinger, a prime man among them, persuading and exhorting him to carry the business so as to show all due respect unto Luther, considering what worth and excellency there was in him, however he had demeaned himself in that particular. And he adds, that he often used to say, that although Luther should call him devil, yet he would do him that honour to acknowledge him a choice servant of God. —*Christopher Cartwright.*

Verse 4.—" *He honoureth them that fear the Lord.*" I have read of one that said, If he should meet a preacher and an angel together, he would first salute the preacher and then the angel.—*Charles Bradbury's "Cabinet of Jewels," 1785.*

Verse 4.—" *He that sweareth to his own hurt, and changeth not.*"

> " His words are bonds, his oaths are oracles;
>   His love sincere, his thoughts immaculate;
>   His tears pure messengers, sent from his heart;
>   His heart as far from fraud as heaven from earth."

William Shakespere.

Verse 5.—The Puritanic divines are almost all of them against the taking of any interest upon money, and go the length of saying that one penny per cent. per annum will shut a man out of heaven if persisted in. It appeared to me to be useless to quote opinions in which I cannot agree, especially as this would occupy space better employed. The demanding of excessive and grinding interest is a sin to be detested; the taking of the usual and current interest in a commercial country is not contrary to the law of love. The Jews were not engaged in commerce, and to lend money even at the lowest interest to their fellow farmers in times of poverty would have been usurious; but they might lend to strangers, who would usually be occupied in commerce, because in the commercial world, money is a fruitful thing, and the lender has a right to a part of its products; a loan to enable a non-trader to live over a season of want is quite another matter.—*C. H. S.*

Verse 5.—"*He that putteth not out his money to usury.*" By usury is generally understood the gain of anything above the principal, or that which was lent, exacted only in consideration of the loan, whether it be in money, corn, wares, or the like. It is most commonly taken for an unlawful profit which a person makes of his money or goods. The Hebrew word for usury signifies biting. The law of God prohibits rigorous imposing conditions of gain for the loan of money or goods, and exacting them without respect to the condition of the borrower, whether he gain or lose ; whether poverty occasioned his borrowing, or a visible prospect of gain by employing the borrowed goods. It is said in Exod. xxii. 25, 26, " If thou lend money to any of my people that is poor by thee, thou shalt not be to him as an *usurer*, neither shalt thou lay upon him *usury*," etc. And in Lev. xxv. 35, 36, 37, " If thy brother be waxen poor, and fallen into decay with thee, then thou shalt relieve him ; yea, though he be a stranger, or a sojourner, that he may live with thee : take thou no *usury* of him," etc. This law forbids the taking *usury* from a brother that was poor, an Israelite reduced to poverty, or from a proselyte ; but in Deut. xxiii. 20, God seems to tolerate *usury* towards strangers ; " Unto a stranger thou mayest lend upon *usury.*" By *strangers*, in this passage, some understand the Gentiles in general, or all such as were not Jews, excepting proselytes. Others think that by *strangers* are meant the Canaanites, and the other people that were devoted to slavery and subjection ; of these the Hebrews were permitted to exact *usury*, but not of such *strangers* with whom they had no quarrel, and against whom the Lord had not denounced his judgments. The Hebrews were plainly commanded in Exod. xxii. 25, etc., not to receive *usury* for money from any that borrowed from necessity, as in that case in Neh. v. 5, 7. And such provision the law made for the preserving of estates to their families by the year of jubilee ; for a people that had little concern in trade, could not be supposed to borrow money but out of necessity : but they were allowed to lend upon *usury* to strangers, whom yet they must not oppress. This law, therefore, in the strictness of it, seems to have been peculiar to the Jewish state ; but in the equity of it, it obligeth us to show mercy to those we have advantage against, and to be content to share with those we lend to in loss, as well as profit, if Providence cross them. And upon this condition, a valuable commentator says, " It seems as lawful for me to receive interest for money, which another takes pains with, improves, but runs the hazard of in trade, as it is to receive rent for my land, which another takes pains with, improves, but runs the hazard of in husbandry."—*Alexander Cruden,* 1701—1770.

Verse 5.—"*He that putteth not out his money to usury.*" " *If thou lend money to any of my people that is poor by thee.*" Exod. xxii. 25. Rather, according to the letter of the original, " If thou lend money to my people, even to a poor man with thee." The Israelites were a people but little engaged in commerce, and therefore could not in general be supposed to borrow money but from sheer necessity ; and of that necessity the lender was not to take advantage by usurious exactions. The law is not to be understood as a prohibition of interest at any rate whatever, but of excessive interest or usury. The clause, " Thou shalt not be to him as an usurer," is equivalent to saying, " Thou shalt not domineer and lord it over him rigorously and cruelly." That this class of men were peculiarly prone to be extortionate and oppressive in their dealings with debtors would seem to be implied by the etymology of the original term for usury (נֶשֶׁךְ *neshek*), which comes from a root signifying *to bite ;* and in Neh. v. 2—5, we have a remarkable case of the bitter and grinding effects resulting from the exercise of the creditor's rights over the debtor. A large portion of the people had not only mortgaged their lands, vineyards and houses, but had actually sold their sons and daughters into bondage, to satisfy the claims of their grasping creditors. In this emergency Nehemiah espoused the cause of the poor, and compelled the rich, against whom he called the people together, to remit the whole of their dues ; and, moreover, exacted from them an oath that they would never afterwards oppress their poor brethren for the payment of those debts. This was not because every part of those proceedings had been contrary to the letter of the Mosaic law, but because it was a flagrant breach of equity under the circumstances. It was taking a cruel and barbarous advantage of the necessities of their brethren, at which God was highly indignant, and which his servants properly rebuked. From this law the Hebrew canonists have gathered a general rule, that " Whoso exacteth of a poor man, and knoweth that he hath not aught to pay with, he transgresseth against this prohibition, Thou shalt not be to him as an exacting creditor." (*Maimonides, in Ainsworth.*) We nowhere learn from the institutes delivered by Moses that the simple taking of interest, especially from the neighbouring nations (Deut. xxiii. 19, 20), was forbidden to the Israelites ; but the divine law would give no countenance to the griping and extortionate practices to which miserly money-lenders are always prone. The deserving and industrious poor might sometimes be reduced to such straits, that pecuniary accommodations might be very desirable to them ; and towards such God would inculcate a mild, kind, and forbearing spirit, and the precept is enforced by the relation which they sustained to him : *q.d.*, " Remember that you are lending to *my* people, *my* poor ; and therefore take no advantage of their necessities. Trust me against the fear of loss, and treat them kindly and generously."—*George Bush, in " Notes on the Book of Exodus," 1856.*

Verse 5.—" *He that putteth not out his money to usury.*" With respect to the first clause, as David seems to condemn all kinds of usury in general, and without exception, the very name has been everywhere held in detestation. But crafty men have invented specious names under which to conceal the vice ; and thinking by this artifice to escape, they have plundered with greater excess than if they had lent on usury avowedly and openly. God, however, will not be dealt with and imposed upon by sophistry and false pretences. He looks upon the thing as it really is. There is no worse species of usury than an unjust way of making bargains, where equity is disregarded on both sides. Let us, then, remember that all bargains, in which the one party unrighteously strives to make gain by the loss of the other party, whatever name may be given to them, are here condemned. It may be asked, whether all kinds of usury are to be put into this denunciation, and regarded as alike unlawful ? If we condemn all without distinction, there is a danger lest many, seeing themselves brought into such a strait as to find that sin must be incurred, in whatever way they can turn themselves, may be rendered bolder by despair, and may rush headlong into all kinds of usury without choice or discrimination. On the other hand, whenever we concede that something may be lawfully done in this way, many will give themselves loose reins, thinking that a liberty to exercise usury, without control or moderation, has been granted them. In the first place, therefore, I would, above all things, counsel my readers to beware of ingeniously contriving deceitful pretexts by which to take advantage of their fellow men, and let them not imagine that anything can be lawful to them which is grievous and hurtful to others. . . . . It is not without cause that God has in Lev. xxv. 35, 36, forbidden usury, adding this reason : "And if thy brother be waxen poor, and fallen in decay with thee ; then thou shalt relieve him : yea, though he be a stranger, or a sojourner ; that he may live with thee. Take thou no usury of him, or increase." We see that the end for which the law was framed was that man should not cruelly oppress the poor, who ought rather to receive sympathy and compassion. This was, indeed, a part of the judicial law which God appointed for the Jews in particular ; but it is a common principle of justice, which extends to all nations, and to all ages, that we should keep ourselves from plundering and devouring the poor who are in distress and want. Whence it follows, that the gain which he who lends his money upon interest acquires, without doing injury to any one, is not to be included under the head of unlawful usury. The Hebrew word נֶשֶׁךְ *neshek*, which David employs, being derived from another word which signifies *to bite*, sufficiently shows that usuries are condemned in so far as they involve in them, or lead to, a license of robbing or plundering our fellow men. Ezekiel, indeed (chapters xviii. 17, and xxii. 12), seems to condemn the taking of any interest whatever upon money lent ; but he, doubtless, has an eye to the unjust and crafty arts of gaining by which the rich devoured the poor people. In short, provided we had engraven on our hearts the rule of equity which Christ prescribes in Matt. vii. 12, " Therefore, all things whatsoever ye would that men should do to you, do ye even so to them," it would not be necessary to enter into lengthened disputes concerning usury.—*John Calvin, in loc.*

Verse 5 (first clause).—The Mosaic law forbids the lending of money for interest to an Israelite. Exod. xxii. 25 ; Lev. xxv. 37 ; Deut. xxiii. 19 ; Prov. xxviii. 8 ; Ezek. xviii. 8. In several of the passages referred to, it is expressly supposed that money is lent only to the poor, a supposition which has its ground in the simple relations of the Mosaic times, in which lending, for the purpose of speculation and gain, had no existence. Such lending ought only to be a work of brotherly love ; and it is a great violation of that if any one, instead of helping his neighbour, takes advantage of his need to bring him into still greater straits. The Mosaic regulation in question has, accordingly, its import also for New Testament times. With the interest-lending of capitalists, who borrow for speculation, it has nothing to do. This belongs to a quite different matter, as is implied even by the name יֶשֶׁך, *a mordendo*, according to which only such usury can be meant as plagues and impoverishes a neighbour. By unseasonable comparison with our modes of speech, many would expound, " His money he puts not to interest."—*E. W. Hengstenberg.*

Verse 5 (*first clause*).—The worm called in Latin *teredo*, whereof Pliny hath reported something in his story, breeding in wood, to the touch is soft, yet it hath such teeth as endeavoureth and consumeth the hard timber. So the usurer is a soft beast at first to handle, but in continuance of time the hardness of his teeth will eat thee up, both flesh and bone, if thou beware not. He pleadeth love, but not for thy sake, but for his own ; for as the ivy colleth and claspeth the oak as a lover, but thereby it groweth up and overtoppeth the oak, and sucketh out the juice and sap thereof, that it cannot thrive nor prosper ; so the usurer colleth, embraceth, and claspeth in arms the borrower, that thereby himself may grow richer, and suck all wealth, goods, and riches from him, that he never thriveth or prospereth after. The pleasure the usurer showeth is like the playing of the cat with the silly mouse : the cat playeth with the mouse, but the play of the cat is the death of the mouse. The usurer pleasureth the borrower ; but the pleasure of the usurer is the undoing of the borrower. The fox through craft slideth and tumbleth, and maketh much pastime till he come to the prey, then he devoureth : the usurer maketh many fair speeches, giveth out many fair promises, pretendeth very great kindness, until he have got thee within his compass, then he crusheth and cruciateth thee. The usurer preyeth upon the poor, he waxeth rich of the penury of his brother, he clotheth himself with the coat of the naked, he gathereth riches of the indigency and want of his neighbour ; he feedeth himself of the bread of the hungry, and devoureth his poor brother, as the great beasts do the smaller ; than which, saith Ambrose, there is no greater inhumanity and cruelty, no greater wretchedness and iniquity, as Chrysostom in many places, and Basil upon this Psalm, have well observed.—*Richard Turnbull.*

Verse 5.—The rich make the poor to fill them ; for *usurers* feed upon the poor, even as great fishes devour the small. Therefore, he which said, Let there not be a beggar in Israel (Deut. xv. 4), said too, Let there not be an usurer in Israel. For if there be usurers in Israel there will be beggars in Israel ; for usurers make beggars, even as lawyers make quarrellers. . . . It is a miserable occupation to live by sin, and a great comfort to a man when he looketh upon his gold and silver, and his heart telleth him, All this is well gotten ; and when he lieth upon his death-bed, and must leave all to his children, he can say unto them, I leave you mine own ; but the usurer cannot say, I leave you mine own, but I leave you other men's ; therefore the usurer can never die in peace, because if he die before he maketh restitution, he dieth in his sin.—*Henry Smith.*

Verse 5.—Biting *usurers* were so abhorred in the primitive church, that as they condemned the usurer himself, so they made the scribes, who wrote the bonds, and also the witnesses, incapable of any benefit ; and that no testament or latter will, written by such should be valid. The house of the usurer was called *domus Satanæ*, the house of the devil ; and they ordained that no man should eat or drink with such usurers, nor fetch fire from them ; and after they were dead that they should not be buried in Christian burial. The conclusion of this is (Ezek. xviii. 13), this sin is matched with theft ; and verse 11, with adultery ; and verse 12, with violence ; it is the daughter of oppression and sister to idolatry, and he that doth these things shall not *dwell in God's holy hill*. Albeit, these worldings think themselves more honest than thieves and adulterers, yet the Lord maketh their case all alike.—*John Weemse*, 1636.

Verse 5.—" *Taketh reward against the innocent*."—I am sure this is *scala inferni*, the right way to hell, to be covetous, to take bribes, and pervert justice. If a judge should ask me the way to hell, I should show him this way : First, let him be a covetous man ; let his heart be poisoned with covetousness. Then let him go a little further and take bribes ; and, lastly, pervert judgments. Lo, here is the mother, and the daughter, and the daughter's daughter. Avarice is the mother ; she brings forth bribe-taking, and bribe-taking perverting of judgment. There lacks a fourth thing to make up the mess, which, so help me God, if I were judge, should be *hangum tuum*, a Tyburn tippet to take with him ; an it were the judge of the King's Bench, my Lord Judge of England, yea, an it were my Lord Chancellor himself, to Tyburn with him.—*Hugh Latimer.*

Verse 5.—" *Taketh reward against the innocent.*" I come to corrupt lawyers and advocates, who so often *take rewards against the innocent*, as they do take upon them the defence of such causes as they in their own conscience are persuaded to be evil and unjust. Which being so common a fault among lawyers, as that very few which plead causes, either in civil or ecclesiastical courts, do seem to make any conscience thereof, to whom all is fish that cometh to their nets ; therefore all lawyers are to be exhorted to apply this note unto themselves.—*George Downame.*

Verse 5.—" *He that doeth.*" 'Tis not said he that *professes* this or that, or he that *believes* thus and thus, or he that is of such or such an *opinion* or *way of worship*, or he that sets up *new lights*, and pretends the *Spirit* for his immediate guide ; 'tis not he that *hears* much or *talks* much of religion ; no, nor he that *preaches* and *prays* much, nor he that *thinks* much of these things, and *means well ;* but 'tis he that "*doeth these things*"—that is actually employed about them—that is the religious and truly godly man. 'Tis not, I say, a formal *professor*, a confidant *solifidian*, a wild *opinionist*, a high flown *perfectist ;* it is not a constant *hearer*, or a mighty *talker*, or a laborious *teacher*, or a *gifted brother*, or a simple *well-wisher* must pass ; but 'tis the honest and sincere *doer* of these things, that will abide the test and stand the trial ; when all other flashy pretences shall, in those searching flames, be burnt and consumed like " hay and stubble," as the apostle expresses it. To wear Christ's livery and to do him no service is but to mock a gracious Master ; to own him in our *profession* and deny him in our *practice*, is, with Judas, to betray him with a kiss of homage ; with the rude soldiers to bow the knee before him, and, in the meantime, to beat his sacred head with his reeden sceptre, and with Pilate to crown him with thorns, to crucify the Lord and write over his head, " King of the Jews : " in a word, to grieve him with our honours, and wound him with our acknowledgments. A Christian profession without a life answerable, will be so far from saving any one, that 'twill highly aggravate his condemnation ; when a dissembled friendship at the great day of discoveries shall be looked upon as the worst of enmities. A mere outside formality of worship, is at best but Prometheus' sacrifice, a skeleton of bones and a religious cheat. . . . The harmless humour of *meaning well* is not enough to approve a man's spiritual state, to acquit obligations, or to ascertain his expectations. For he that bids us " eschew evil" does immediately subjoin, that we must " follow " and " hold fast that which is good." It will be no good account not to have done evil, unless we make it appear that we have been doing good too ; since the non-commission of great sins will not excuse our omission of great duties. In the busy commonwealth of bees, the drone without a sting, as she has no weapon for mischief, so, wanting a tool for employ, is deservedly cashiered the hive.—*Condensed from Adam Littleton, D.D.*, 1627—1694.

Verse 5.—" *He that doeth these things, shall never be moved.*" Mark how the prophet saith not, he that readeth these things, or he that heareth these things, but he that *doth* them, shall never be removed. For were it enough to read or hear these precepts, then should an infinite number of vain and wicked persons enter into, and continue in the church, which notwithstanding have no place therein ; for there are very few, or none at all which have not read, or at least have not heard these things, yet they will not do them. Neither doth he say, he that talketh of these things, but he that *doth* them ; for many now in these days can talk gloriously of uprightness, justice, truth, in whom notwithstanding, there is neither upright dealings, nor sound righteousness, nor unfeigned truth to be found. Many can say that slander is sin, injury is iniquity, to receive false reports is uncharitable, that it becometh not the saints to flatter the wicked, that to break promise and falsify their oaths is unseemly, to give upon usury is oppression, to receive bribes against the innocent is extreme cruelty ; yet themselves backbite and hurt their neighbour, they themselves believe every tale that is brought them, they flatter and fawn upon the wicked for advantage, they swear and forswear for commodity, they oppress through usury, and receive gifts of bribery against the innocent ; and so in word they speak of these things, but *do them not* indeed. . . . . Neither doth David say he that preacheth these, "*shall never be removed*," for then not only many other wicked persons, which can speak of, yea many ungodly men which can also preach of virtue, should have the place in the Lord's tabernacle, and rest upon his holy hill ; but also among others, even Balaam the covetous prophet, should have a sure place in God's tabernacle ; for he could say,

' If Balak would give me his house full of silver and gold, I cannot go beyond the word of the Lord my God, to do less or more " (Num. xxii. 18) ; yet he took rewards ; yet he was carried away with covetousness, as much as in him lay, to work the destruction of Israel, the innocent people of the Lord.—*Richard Turnbull.*

Verse 5.—" *Shall never be moved.*" Moved he may be for a time, but not removed for ever. His soul is bound up in the bundle of life, near unto the throne of glory ; when the souls of the wicked are restless as a stone in the midst of a sling, saith the Targum in 1 Sam. xxv.—*John Trapp.*

Verse 5 (last clause).—The holy soul is the love of God, the joy of angels ; her eyes dare look upon the glorious Judge whom she knows to be her Saviour. Her heart is courageous ; she dares stand the thunder ; and when guilty minds creep into corners, she is confident in him that he will defend her. She challengeth the whole world to accuse her of injustice, and fears not the subornation of false witnesses, because she knows the testimony of her own conscience. Her language is free and bold, without the guiltiness of broken stops. Her forehead is clear and smooth, as the brow of heaven. Her knees are ever bent to the throne of grace ; her feet travelling towards Jerusalem ; her hands weaving the web of righteousness. Good men bless her ; good angels guard her ; the Son of God doth kiss her ; and when all the world shall be turned to a burning pile, she shall be brought safe to the mountain of joy, and set in a throne of blessedness for ever.—*Thomas Adams.*

HINTS TO PREACHERS.

Verse 1.—Qualifications for church membership on earth and in heaven. A subject for self-examination.

Verse 1.—I. *Comparison of the church to the tabernacle.* God's presence manifested, sacrifice offered, and vessels of grace preserved in it ; mean externally, glorious within. II. *Comparison of its double position to that of the tabernacle.* Moving in the wilderness, and fixed on the hill. III. Enquire into qualifications for admittance into church and tabernacle. Parallel with the priests, etc.

Verse 1.—The great question. Asked by idle curiosity, despair, godly fear, earnest enquirer, soul troubled by falls of others, holy faith. Give answer to each.

Verse 1.—The citizen of Zion described.—*Thomas Boston's Sermons.*

Verse 1.—Anxiety to know the true saints, how far lawful and profitable.

Verse 1.—God the only infallible discerner of true saints.

Verse 2.—" *He that walketh uprightly.*" I. What he must be. He must be upright in heart. A man himself bent double cannot walk uprightly. II. How he must act. Neither from impulse, ambition, gain, fear, or flattery. He must not be warped in any direction, but stand perpendicularly. III. What he must expect. Snares, etc. to trip him. IV. Where he must walk. Path of duty, the only one in which he can walk uprightly. V. Where he must look. Up, right-up, and then he will be upright.

Verse 2.—" *Speaketh the truth in his heart.*" Subject :—Heart falsehood and heart truth.

Verse 2 (first clause).—The citizen of Zion an upright walker.

Verse 2 (middle clause).—The citizen of Zion, a worker of righteousness.

Verse 2 (last clause).—The citizen of Zion, a speaker of truth.—*Four Sermons in Thomas Boston's Works.*

Verse 3.—The evils of detraction. It affects three persons here mentioned : the backbiter, the suffering neighbour, and the taker-up of the reproach.

Verse 3.—" *Nor taketh up a reproach.*" The sin of being too ready to believe ill reports. Common, cruel, foolish, injurious, wicked.

Verse 4.—The duty of practically honouring those who fear the Lord. Commendation, deference, assistance, imitation, etc.

Verse 4.—The sin of estimating persons other than by their practical characters.

Verse 4 (last clause).—The Lord Jesus as our unchanging Surety, his oath and his hurt.

Verse 5.—The evidences and privileges of godly men.

Verse 5 (last clause).—The fixedness and safety of the godly.

PSALM XVI.

TITLE.—MICHTAM OF DAVID. *This is usually understood to mean* THE GOLDEN PSALM, *and such a title is most appropriate, for the matter is as the most fine gold. Ainsworth calls it " David's jewel, or notable song."* Dr. Hawker, *who is always alive to passages full of savour, devoutly cries, " Some have rendered it* precious, *others* golden, *and others,* precious jewel ; *and as the Holy Ghost, by the apostles Peter and Paul, hath shown us that it is all about the Lord Jesus Christ, what is here said of him is precious, is golden, is a jewel indeed ! " We have not met with the term* Michtam *before, but if spared to write upon Psalms lvi., lvii., lviii., lix. and lx., we shall see it again, and shall observe that like the present these Psalms, although they begin with prayer, and imply trouble, abound in holy confidence and close with songs of assurance as to ultimate safety and joy.* Dr. Alexander, *whose notes are peculiarly valuable, thinks that the word is most probably a simple derivative of a word signifying* to hide, *and signifies a secret or mystery, and indicates the depth of doctrinal and spiritual import in these sacred compositions. If this be the true interpretation it well accords with the other, and when the two are put together, they make up a name which every reader will remember, and which will bring the precious subject at once to mind.* THE PSALM OF THE PRECIOUS SECRET.

SUBJECT.—*We are not left to human interpreters for the key to this golden mystery, for, speaking by the Holy Ghost,* Peter *tells us, " David speaketh concerning* HIM." *(Acts ii. 25). Further on in his memorable sermon he said, " Men and brethren, let me freely speak unto you of the patriarch David, that he is both dead and buried, and his sepulchre is with us unto this day. Therefore being a prophet, and knowing that God had sworn with an oath to him, that of the fruit of his loins, according to the flesh, he would raise up Christ to sit on his throne ; he seeing this before spake of the resurrection of Christ, that his soul was not left in hell, neither his flesh did see corruption." (Acts ii. 29—31.) Nor is this our only guide, for the apostle Paul, led by the same infallible inspiration, quotes from this Psalm, and testifies that David wrote of the man through whom is preached unto us the forgiveness of sins. (Acts xiii. 35—8.) It has been the usual plan of commentators to apply the Psalm both to David, to the saints, and to the Lord Jesus, but we will venture to believe that in it " Christ is all ; " since in the ninth and tenth verses, like the apostles on the mount, we can see " no man but Jesus only."*

DIVISION.—*The whole is so compact that it is difficult to draw sharp lines of division. It may suffice to note our Lord's prayer of faith, verse 1, avowal of faith in Jehovah alone, 2, 3, 4, 5, the contentment of his faith in the present, 6, 7, and the joyous confidence of his faith for the future (8, 11.)*

EXPOSITION.

PRESERVE me, O God : for in thee do I put my trust.

" *Preserve me,*" *keep, or save me,* or as Horsley thinks, " *guard me,*" even as bodyguards surround their monarch, or as shepherds protect their flocks. Tempted in all points like as we are, the manhood of Jesus needed to be preserved from the power of evil ; and though in itself pure, the Lord Jesus did not confide in that purity of nature, but as an example to his followers, looked to the Lord, his God, for preservation. One of the great names of God is " the Preserver of men," (Job vii. 20), and this gracious office the Father exercised towards our Mediator and Representative. It had been promised to the Lord Jesus in express words, that he should be preserved, Isa. xlix. 7, 8. " Thus saith the Lord, the Redeemer of Israel and his Holy One, to him whom man despiseth, to him whom the nation abhorreth, I will preserve thee, and give thee for a covenant of the people." This promise was to the letter fulfilled, both by providential deliverance and sustaining power, in the case of our Lord. Being preserved himself, he is able to restore the preserved of Israel, for we are " preserved in Christ Jesus and called." As one with him, the elect were preserved in his preservation, and we may view this mediatorial supplication as the petition of the Great High Priest for all those who are in him. The intercession recorded in John xvii. is but an amplification of this cry, " Holy Father, keep through thine own name those whom thou hast given me, that they may be one, as we *are*." When he says " preserve me," he means his members, his mystical body, himself, and all in him. But while we rejoice in the fact that the Lord Jesus used this prayer for his members, we must not forget that he employed it most surely for himself ; he had so emptied himself, and so truly taken upon him the form of a servant, that as man he needed divine keeping even as we do, and often cried unto the strong for strength. Frequently on the mountain-top he breathed forth this desire, and on one occasion in almost the same words, he publicly prayed, " Father, save me from this hour." (John xii. 27.) If Jesus looked out of himself for protection, how much more must we, his erring followers, do so !

" *O God.*" The word for God here used in EL אל, by which name the Lord Jesus, when under a sense of great weakness, as for instance when upon the cross, was wont to address the Mighty God, the Omnipotent Helper of his people. We, too, may turn to *El*, the Omnipotent One, in all hours of peril, with the confidence that he who heard the strong cryings and tears of our faithful High Priest, is both able and willing to bless us in him. It is well to study the name and character of God, so that in our straits we may know how and by what title to address our Father who is in heaven.

" *For in thee do I put my trust,*" or, *I have taken shelter in thee.* As chickens run beneath the hen, so do I betake myself to thee. Thou art my great overshadowing Protector, and I have taken refuge beneath thy strength. This is a potent argument in pleading, and our Lord knew not only how to *use* it with God, but how to yield to its power when wielded by others upon himself. " According to thy faith be it done unto thee," is a great rule of heaven in dispensing favour, and when we can sincerely declare that we exercise faith in the Mighty God with regard to the mercy which we seek, we may rest assured that our plea will prevail. Faith, like the sword of Saul, never returns empty ; it overcomes heaven when held in the hand of prayer. As the Saviour prayed, so let us pray, and as he became more than a conqueror, so shall we also through him ; let us when buffeted by storms right bravely cry to the Lord as he did, " in thee do I put my trust."

2 *O my soul,* thou hast said unto the LORD, Thou *art* my Lord : my goodness *extendeth* not to thee :

3 *But* to the saints that *are* in the earth, and *to* the excellent, in whom *is* all my delight.

4 Their sorrows shall be multiplied *that* hasten *after* another *god :* their drink offerings of blood will I not offer, nor take up their names into my lips.

5 The LORD *is* the portion of mine inheritance and of my cup : thou maintainest my lot.

" *O my soul, thou hast said unto the Lord, Thou art my Lord.*" In his inmost heart the Lord Jesus bowed himself to do service to his Heavenly Father, and before the throne of Jehovah his soul vowed allegiance to the Lord for our sakes. We are like him when our soul, truly and constantly in the presence of the heart-searching God, declares her full consent to the rule and government of the Infinite Jehovah, saying, " Thou art my Lord." To avow this with the lip is little, but for *the* soul to say it, especially in times of trial, is a gracious evidence of spiritual health ; to profess it before men is a small matter, but to declare it before Jehovah himself is of far more consequence. This sentence may also be viewed as the utterance of appropriating faith, laying hold upon the Lord by personal covenant and enjoyment ; in this sense may it be our daily song in the house of our pilgrimage.

" *My goodness extendeth not to thee.*" The work of our Lord Jesus was not needful on account of any necessity in the Divine Being. Jehovah would have been inconceivably glorious had the human race perished, and had no atonement been offered. Although the life-work and death-agony of the Son did reflect unparalleled lustre upon every attribute of God, yet the Most Blessed and Infinitely Happy God stood in no need of the obedience and death of his Son ; it was for our sakes that the work of redemption was undertaken, and not because of any lack or want on the part of the Most High. How modestly does the Saviour here estimate his

own goodness ! What overwhelming reasons have we for imitating his humility !
" If thou be righteous, what givest thou him ? or what receiveth he of thine hand ? "
(Job xxxv. 7.)

"*But to the saints that are in the earth.*" These sanctified ones, although still
upon the earth, partake of the results of Jesus' mediatorial work, and by his goodness are made what they are. The peculiar people, zealous for good works, and
hallowed to sacred service, are arrayed in the Saviour's righteousness and washed
in his blood, and so receive of the goodness treasured up in him; these are the persons
who are profited by the work of the man Christ Jesus ; but that work added nothing
to the nature, virtue, or happiness of God, who is blessed for evermore. How much
more forcibly is this true of us, poor unworthy servants, not fit to be mentioned
in comparison with the faithful Son of God ! Our hope must ever be that haply
some poor child of God may be served by us, for the Great Father can never need
our aid. Well may we sing the verses of Dr. Watts :

> " Oft have my heart and tongue confess'd
>   How empty and how poor I am ;
> My praise can never make thee blest,
>   Nor add new glories to thy name.
> Yet, Lord, thy saints on earth may reap
>   Some profit by the good we do ;
> These are the company I keep,
>   These are the choicest friends I know."

Poor believers are God's receivers, and have a warrant from the Crown to receive
the revenue of our offerings in the King's name. Saints departed we cannot bless ;
even prayer for them is of no service ; but while they are here we should practically
prove our love to them, even as our Master did, for they are *the excellent of the earth.*
Despite their infirmities, their Lord thinks highly of them, and reckons them to
be as nobles among men. The title of " His Excellency " more properly belongs
to the meanest saint than to the greatest governor. The true aristocracy are
believers in Jesus. They are the only Right Honourables. Stars and garters are
poor distinctions compared with the graces of the Spirit. He who knows them
best says of them, " *in whom is all my delight.*" They are his Hephzibah and his
land Beulah, and before all worlds his delights were with these chosen sons of men.
Their own opinion of themselves is far other than their Beloved's opinion of them ;
they count themselves to be less that nothing, yet he makes much of them, and
sets his heart towards them. What wonders the eyes of Divine Love can see w ere
the hands of Infinite Power have been graciously at work. It was this quicksighted
affection which led Jesus to see in us a recompense for all his agony, and susta ned
him under all his sufferings by the joy of redeeming us from going down into the pit.

The same loving heart which opens towards the chosen people is fast closed
against those who continue in their rebellion against God. Jesus hates all
wickedness, and especially the high crime of idolatry. The text while it shows
our Lord's abhorrence of sin, shows also the sinner's greediness after it. Professed
believers are often slow towards the true Lord, but sinners " *hasten after another god.*"
They run like madmen where we creep like snails. Let their zeal rebuke our
tardiness. Yet theirs is a case in which the more they haste the worse they speed,
for *their sorrows are multiplied* by their diligence in multiplying their sins. Matthew
Henry pithily says, " They that multiply gods multiply griefs to themselves ; for
whosoever thinks one god too little, will find two too many, and yet hundreds not
enough." The cruelties and hardships which men endure for their false gods is
wonderful to contemplate ; our missionary reports are a noteworthy comment
on this passage ; but perhaps our own experience is an equally vivid exposition ;
for when we have given our heart to idols, sooner or later we have had to smart
for it. Near the roots of our self-love all our sorrows lie, and when that idol is
overthrown, the sting is gone from grief. Moses broke the golden calf and ground
it to powder, and cast it into the water of which he made Israel to drink, and so
shall our cherished idols become bitter portions for us, unless we at once forsake
them. Our Lord had no selfishness ; he served but one Lord, and served him only.
As for those who turn aside from Jehovah, he was separate from them, bearing their
reproach without the camp. Sin and the Saviour had no communion. He came
to destroy, not to patronize or be allied with the works of the devil. Hence he
refused the testimony of unclean spirits as to his divinity, for in nothing would he
have fellowship with darkness. We should be careful above measure not to connect

ourselves in the remotest degree with falsehood in religion ; even the most solemn of Popish rites we must abhor. "*Their drink offerings of blood will I not offer.*" The old proverb says, " It is not safe to eat at the devil's mess, though the spoon be never so long." The mere mentioning of ill names it were well to avoid,—" *nor take up their names into my lips.*" If we allow poison upon the lip, it may ere long penetrate to the inwards, and it is well to keep out of the mouth that which we would shut out from the heart. If the Church would enjoy union with Christ, she must break all the bonds of impiety, and keep herself pure from all the pollutions of carnal will-worship, which now pollute the service of God. Some professors are guilty of great sin in remaining in the communion of Popish churches, where God is as much dishonoured as in Rome herself, only in a more crafty manner.

" *The Lord is the portion of mine inheritance and of my cup.*" With what confidence and bounding joy does Jesus turn to Jehovah, whom his soul possessed and delighted in ! Content beyond measure with his portion in the Lord his God, he had not a single desire with which to hunt after other gods ; his cup was full, and his heart was full too ; even in his sorest sorrows he still laid hold with both his hands upon his Father, crying, " My God, my God ; " he had not so much as a thought of falling down to worship the prince of this world, although tempted with an " all these will I give thee." We, too, can make our boast in the Lord ; he is the meat and the drink of our souls. He is our portion, supplying all our necessities, and our cup yielding royal luxuries ; our cup in this life, and our inheritance in the life to come. As children of the Father who is in heaven, we inherit, by virtue of our joint heirship with Jesus, all the riches of the covenant of grace ; and the portion which falls to us sets upon our table the bread of heaven and the new wine of the kingdom. Who would not be satisfied with such dainty diet ? Our shallow cup of sorrow we may well drain with resignation, since the deep cup of love stands side by side with it, and will never be empty. " *Thou maintainest my lot.*" Some tenants have a covenant in their leases that they themselves shall maintain and uphold, but in our case Jehovah himself maintains our lot. Our Lord Jesus delighted in this truth, that the Father was on his side, and would maintain his right against all the wrongs of men. He knew that his elect would be reserved for him, and that almighty power would preserve them as his lot and reward for ever. Let us also be glad, because the Judge of all the earth will vindicate our righteous cause.

6 The lines are fallen unto me in pleasant *places ;* yea, I have a goodly heritage.

7 I will bless the LORD, who hath given me counsel : my reins also instruct me in the night seasons.

Jesus found the way of obedience to lead into " *pleasant places.*" Notwithstanding all the sorrows which marred his countenance, he exclaimed, " Lo, I come ; in the volume of the book it is written of me, I delight to do thy will, O my God : yea, thy law is within my heart." It may seem strange, but while no other man was ever so thoroughly acquainted with grief, it is our belief that no other man ever experienced so much joy and delight in service, for no other served so faithfully and with such great results in view as his recompense of reward. The joy which was set before him must have sent some of its beams of splendour a-down the rugged places where he endured the cross, despising the shame, and must have made them in some respects pleasant places to the generous heart of the Redeemer. At any rate, we know that Jesus was well content with the blood-bought portion which the lines of electing love marked off as his spoil with the strong and his portion with the great. Therein he solaced himself on earth, and delights himself in heaven ; and he asks no more " GOODLY HERITAGE " than that his own beloved may be with him where he is and behold his glory. All the saints can use the language of this verse, and the more thoroughly they can enter into its contented, grateful, joyful spirit the better for themselves, and the more glorious to their God. Our Lord was poorer than we are, for he had not where to lay his head, and yet when he mentioned his poverty he never used a word of murmuring ; discontented spirits are as unlike Jesus as the croaking raven is unlike the cooing dove. Martyrs have been happy in dungeons. " From the delectable orchard of the Leonine prison the Italian martyr dated his letter, and the presence of God made the gridiron of Laurence pleasant to him." Mr. Greenham was bold enough to say, " They never felt God's love, or tasted forgiveness of sins, who are discontented." Some divines think that discontent was the first sin, the rock which wrecked our race in paradise; certainly there can be no paradise where this evil spirit has power, its slime will poison all the flowers of the garden.

"*I will bless the Lord, who hath given me counsel.*" Praise as well as prayer was presented to the Father by our Lord Jesus, and we are not truly his followers unless our resolve be, " I will bless the Lord." Jesus is called Wonderful, Counsellor, but as man he spake not of himself, but as his Father had taught him. Read in confirmation of this, John vii. 16; viii. 28; and xii. 49, 50; and the prophecy concerning him in Isaiah xi. 2, 3. It was our Redeemer's wont to repair to his Father for direction, and having received it, he blessed him for giving him counsel. It would be well for us if we would follow his example of lowliness, cease from trusting in our own understanding, and seek to be guided by the Spirit of God. "*My reins also instruct me in the night seasons.*" By the reins understand the inner man, the affections and feelings. The communion of the soul with God brings to it an inner spiritual wisdom which in still seasons is revealed to itself. Our Redeemer spent many nights alone upon the mountain, and we may readily conceive that together with his fellowship with heaven, he carried on a profitable commerce with himself; reviewing his experience, forecasting his work, and considering his position. Great generals fight their battles in their own mind long before the trumpet sounds, and so did our Lord win our battle on his knees before he gained it on the cross. It is a gracious habit after taking counsel from above to take counsel within. Wise men see more with their eyes shut by night than fools can see by day with their eyes open. He who learns from God and so gets the seed, will soon find wisdom within himself growing in the garden of his soul ; " Thine ears shall hear a voice behind thee, saying, This is the way, walk ye in it, when ye turn to the right hand and when ye turn to the left." The night season which the sinner chooses for his sins is the hallowed hour of quiet when believers hear the soft still voices of heaven, and of the heavenly life within themselves.

8 I have set the LORD always before me : because *he is* at my right hand, I shall not be moved.

9 Therefore my heart is glad, and my glory rejoiceth : my flesh also shall rest in hope.

10 For thou wilt not leave my soul in hell ; neither wilt thou suffer thine Holy One to see corruption.

11 Thou wilt shew me the path of life : in thy presence *is* fulness of joy ; at thy right hand *there are* pleasures for evermore.

The fear of death at one time cast its dark shadow over the soul of the Redeemer, and we read that " he was heard in that he feared." There appeared unto him an angel, strengthening him; perhaps the heavenly messenger reassured him of his glorious resurrection as his people's surety,—and of the eternal joy into which he should admit the flock redeemed by blood. Then hope shone full upon our Lord's soul, and, as recorded in these verses, he surveyed the future with holy confidence because he had a continued eye to Jehovah, and enjoyed his perpetual presence. He felt that thus sustained, he could never be driven from his life's grand design ; nor was he, for he stayed not his hand till he could say, " It is finished." What an infinite mercy was this for us ! In this immoveableness, caused by simple faith in the divine help, Jesus is to be viewed as our exemplar ; to recognize the presence of the Lord is the duty of every believer ; " *I have set the Lord always before me ;* " and to *trust* the Lord as our champion and guard is the privilege of every saint ; " *because he is at my right hand, I shall not be moved.*" The apostle translates this passage, " I foresaw the Lord always before my face ;" Acts ii. 25; the eye of Jesus' faith could discern beforehand the continuance of divine support to his suffering Son, in such a degree that he should never be moved from the accomplishment of his purpose of redeeming his people. By the power of God at his right hand he foresaw that he should smite through all who rose up against him, and on that power he placed the firmest reliance. He clearly foresaw that he must die, for he speaks of his flesh resting, and of his soul in the abode of separate spirits ; death was full before his face, or he would not have mentioned corruption ; but such was his devout reliance upon his God, that he sang over the tomb, and rejoiced in vision of the sepulchre. He knew that the visit of his soul to Sheol, or the invisible world of disembodied spirits, would be a very short one, and that his body in a very brief space would leave the grave, uninjured by its sojourn there ; all this made him say, " *my heart is glad*," and moved his tongue, the *glory* of his frame, to *rejoice* in God, the strength of his salvation. Oh for such holy faith in the prospect of trial and of death ! It is the work of faith, not merely to create a peace which passeth all understanding, but to fill the heart full of gladness until the tongue, which, as the organ of an intelligent creature, is our glory, bursts forth in notes of harmonious praise. Faith gives us living joy, and bestows dying rest. "*My flesh also shall rest in hope.*"

Our Lord Jesus was not disappointed in his hope. He declared his Father's faithfulness in the words, " *thou wilt not leave my soul in hell*," and that faithfulness was proven on the resurrection morning. Among the departed and disembodied Jesus was not left ; he had believed in the resurrection, and he received it on the third day, when his body rose in glorious life, according as he had said in joyous confidence, " *neither wilt thou suffer thine Holy One to see corruption.*" Into the outer prison of the grave his body might go, but into the inner prison of corruption he could not enter. He who in soul and body was pre-eminently God's " Holy One," was loosed from the pains of death, because it was not possible that he should be holden of it. This is noble encouragement to all the saints ; die they must, but rise they shall, and though in their case they shall see corruption, yet they shall rise to everlasting life. Christ's resurrection is the cause, the earnest, the guarantee, and the emblem of the rising of all his people. Let them, therefore, go to their graves as to their beds, resting their flesh among the clods as they now do upon their couches.

> " Since Jesus is mine, I'll not fear undressing,
>   But gladly put off these garments of clay ;
> To die in the Lord is a covenant blessing,
>   Since Jesus to glory through death led the way."

Wretched will that man be who, when the Philistines of death invade his soul, shall find that, like Saul, he is forsaken of God ; but blessed is he who has the Lord at his right hand, for he shall fear no ill, but shall look forward to an eternity of bliss.

11.—" *Thou wilt shew me the path of life.*" To Jesus first this way was shown, for he is the first-begotten from the dead, the first-born of every creature. He himself opened up the way through his own flesh, and then trod it as the forerunner of his own redeemed. The thought of being made the path of life to his people, gladdened the soul of Jesus. " *In thy presence is fulness of joy.*" Christ being raised from the dead ascended into glory, to dwell in constant nearness to God, where joy is at its full for ever : the foresight of this urged him onward in his glorious but grievous toil. To bring his chosen to eternal happiness was the high ambition which inspired him, and made him wade through a sea of blood. O God, when the worldling's mirth has all expired, for ever with Jesus may we dwell " *at thy right hand*," where " *there are pleasures for evermore ;* " and meanwhile, may we have an earnest by tasting thy love below. Trapp's note on the heavenly verse which closes the Psalm is a sweet morsel, which may serve for a contemplation, and yield a foretaste of our inheritance. He writes, " Here is as much said as can be, but words are too weak to utter it. For *quality* there is in heaven joy and pleasures ; for *quantity*, a fulness, a torrent whereat they drink without let or loathing ; for *constancy*, it is at God's right hand, who is stronger than all, neither can any take us out of his hand ; it is a constant happiness without intermission : and for *perpetuity* it is for evermore. Heaven's joys are without measure, mixture, or end."

EXPLANATORY NOTES AND QUAINT SAYINGS.

Title.—There is a diversity of opinion as to the meaning of the title of this Psalm. It is called " *Michtam of David*," but *Michtam* is the Hebrew word untranslated— the Hebrew word in English letters—and its signification is involved in obscurity. According to some, it is derived from a verb which means *to hide*, and denotes a mystery or secret. Those who adopt this view, regard the title as indicating a depth of doctrinal and spiritual import in the Psalm, which neither the writer nor any of his contemporaries had fathomed. According to others, it is derived from a verb which means *to cut, to grave, to write,* and denotes simply a writing of David. With this view agree the Chaldee and Septuagint versions, the former translating it, " a straight sculpture of David ; " and the latter, " an inscription upon a pillar to David." Others again, look upon " *Michtam,*" as being derived from a noun which means gold, and they understand it as denoting a golden Psalm—a Psalm of surpassing excellence, and worthy of being written in letters of gold. This was the opinion of our translators, and hence they have rendered it on the margin— "*A golden Psalm of David.*" The works of the most excellent Arabian poets were called golden, because they were written in letters of gold ; and this golden song may have been written and hung up in some conspicuous part of the Temple. Many other interpretations have been given of this term, but at this distance of time, we can only regard it as representing some unassignable peculiarity of the composition.— *James Frame,* 1858.

Title.—Such are the riches of this Psalm, that some have been led to think the obscure title, "*Michtam,*" has been prefixed to it on account of its *golden stores.* For כֶּתֶם is used of the " gold of Ophir " (*e.g.,* Psalm xlv. 9), and מִכְתָּם might be a derivative from that root. But as there is a group of five other Psalms (namely, lvi., lvii., lviii., lix., lx.), that bear this title, whose subject-matter is various, but which all end in a *tone of triumph, it* has been suggested that the Septuagint may be nearly right in their Στηλογραφία, as if " A Psalm to be hung up or inscribed on a pillar to commemorate victory." It is, however, more likely still that the term "*Michtam*" (like "*Maschil* "), is a musical term, whose real meaning and use we have lost, and may recover only when the ransomed house of Israel return home with songs. Meanwhile, the subject-matter of this Psalm itself is very clearly this—*the righteous one's satisfaction with his lot.*—*Andrew A. Bonar.*

Whole Psalm.—Allow that in verse ten it is clear that our Lord is in this Psalm, yet the application of every verse to Jesus *in Gethsemane* appears to be far-fetched, and inaccurate. How verse nine could suit the agony and bloody sweat, it is hard to conceive, and equally so is it with regard to verse six. The " cup " of verse five is so direct a contrast to that cup concerning which Jesus prayed in anguish of spirit, that it cannot be a reference to it. Yet we think it right to add, that Mr. James Frame has written a very valuable work on this Psalm, entitled, " Christ in Gethsemane," and he has supported his theory by the opinion of many of the ancients. He says, " All the distinguished interpreters of ancient days, such as Eusebius, Jerome, and Augustine, explain the Psalm as referring to the Messiah, in his passion and his victory over death and the grave, including his subsequent exaltation to the right hand of God ; " and in a foot note he gives the following quotations : *Jerome.*—" The Psalm pertains to Christ, who speaks in it. . . . . It is the voice of our King, which he utters in the human nature that he had assumed, but without detracting from his divine nature. . . . The Psalm pertains to his passion." *Augustine.*—" Our King speaks in this Psalm in the person of the human nature that he assumed, at the time of his passion, the royal title inscribed will show itself conspicuous."—*C. H. S.*

Whole Psalm.—The present Psalm is connected in thought and language with the foregoing, and linked on to the following Psalm by catchwords. It is entitled in the Syriac and Arabic versions, a Psalm on the Election of the Church, and on the Resurrection of Christ."—*Christopher Wordsworth, D.D.,* 1868.

Verse 1.—" *Preserve me, O God.*" Here David desireth not deliverance from any special trouble, but generally prayeth to be fenced and defended continually by the providence of God, wishing that the Lord would continue his mercy towards him unto the end, and in the end ; whereby he foresaw it was as needful for him to be safe guarded by God, his protection in the end, as at the time present ; as also how he made no less account of it in his prosperity than in adversity. So that the man of God still feared his infirmity, and therefore acknowledgeth himself ever to stand in need of God his help. And here is a sure and undoubted mark of the child of God, when a man shall have as great a care to continue and grow in well-doing, as to begin ; and this paying for the gift of final perseverance is a special note of the child of God. This holy jealousy of the man of God made him so to desire to be preserved at all times, in all estates, both in soul and body.—*Richard Greenham,* 1531—1591.

Verse 1.—" *For in thee do I put my trust.*" Here the prophet setteth down the cause why he prayeth to God : whereby he declareth, that none can truly call upon God unless they believe. Rom. x. 14. " How shall they call on him in whom they have not believed ? " In regard whereof, as he prayeth to God to be his Saviour, so he is fully assured that God will be his Saviour. If, then, without faith we cannot truly call upon God, the men of this world rather prate like parrots than pray like Christians, at what time they utter these words ; for that they trust not in God they declare both by neglecting the lawful means, and also in using unlawful means. Some we see trust in friends ; some shoulder out, as they think, the cross with their goods ; some fence themselves with authority ; others bathe and baste themselves in pleasure to put the evil day far from them ; others make flesh their arm ; and others make the wedge of gold their confidence ; and these men when they seek for help at the Lord, mean in their hearts to find it in their friends, good authority and pleasure, howsoever for fear, they dare not say this outwardly. Again, here we are to observe under what shelter we may harbour ourselves in the showers of adversity, even under the protection of the Almighty. And why ? " Whoso dwelleth in the secret of the Most High, shall abide in the shadow of the Almighty." And here in effect is showed, that whosoever putteth his trust in God shall be preserved ; otherwise the prophet's reason here had not been good. Besides, we see he pleadeth not by merit, but sueth by faith, teaching us that if we come with like faith, we may obtain the like deliverance.—*Richard Greenham.*

Verse 2.—" *O my soul, thou hast said unto the Lord, Thou art my Lord.*" I wish I could have heard what you said to yourself when these words were first mentioned. I believe I could guess the language of some of you. When you heard me repeat these words, " *O my soul, thou hast said unto the Lord, Thou art my Lord,*" you thought, " I have never said anything to the Lord, unless when I cried out, Depart from me, for I desire not the knowledge of thy ways." Has not something like this passed in your minds ? I will try again. When I first mentioned the text, " Let me consider," you secretly said, " I believe that I did once say to the Lord, Thou art my Lord ; but it was so long ago, that I had almost forgotten it ; but I suppose that it must have been at such a time when I was in trouble. I had met with disappointments in the world ; and then, perhaps, I cried, Thou art my portion, O Lord. Or, perhaps, when I was under serious impressions, in the hurry of my spirits, I might look up to God and say, Thou art my Lord. But, whatever I could or did formerly say, I am certain that I cannot say it at present." Have none of you thought in this manner ? I will hazard one conjecture more ; and I doubt not but in this case I shall guess rightly. When I repeated these words, " O my soul, thou hast said unto the Lord, Thou art my Lord;" "So have I," thought one ; " So have I," thought another ; I have said it often, but I said it with peculiar solemnity and pleasure, when, in an act of humble devotion, I lately threw my ransomed, rescued, grateful soul at his feet, and cried, " O Lord, truly I am thy servant ; I am thy servant ; thou hast loosed my bonds." The very recollection of it is pleasant ; and I shall now have an opportunity of renewing my vows, and hope to recover something of the divine serenity and joy which I at that time experienced."—*Samuel Lavington's Sermons,* 1810.

Verse 2.—" *Thou art my Lord.*" He acknowledgeth the Lord Jehovah ; but he seeth him not as it were then afar off, but drawing near unto him, he sweetly embraceth him ; which thing is proper unto faith, and to that particular applying which we say to be in faith.—*Robert Rollock,* 1600.

Verse 2.—" *My goodness extendeth not to thee.*" I think the words should be understood of what the Messiah was doing for men. My goodness, טובָתִי *tobhathi,* " my bounty " is not to thee. What I am doing can add nothing to thy divinity ; thou art not providing this astonishing sacrifice because thou canst derive any excellence from it ; but this bounty extends *to the saints*—to all the spirits of just men made perfect, whose bodies are still in the earth ; and to the excellent, אַדִּירֵי *addirey,* " the noble or super-eminent ones," those who through faith and patience inherit the promises. The saints and illustrious ones not only taste of my goodness, but enjoy my salvation. Perhaps *angels* themselves may be intended ; they are not uninterested in the incarnation, passion, death, and resurrection of our Lord. They *desire to look into these* things ; and the victories of the cross in the conversion of sinners cause joy among the angels of God.—*Adam Clarke.*

Verse 2.—" *My goodness extendeth not to thee ;* " " My well-doing extendeth not to thee." Oh, what shall I render unto thee, my God, for all thy benefits towards me ? what shall I repay ? Alas ! I can do thee no good, for mine imperfect goodness cannot pleasure thee who art most perfect and goodness itself ; my well-doing can do thee no good, my wickedness can do thee no harm. I receive all good from thee, but no good can I return to thee ; wherefore I acknowledge thee to be most rich, and myself to be most beggarly ; so far off is it that thou standest in any need of me. Wherefore I will join myself to thy people, that whatsoever I have they may profit by it ; and whatsoever they have I may profit by it, seeing the things that I have received must be put out to loan, to gain some comfort to others. Whatsoever others have, they have not for their own private use, but that by them, as by pipes and conduits, they liberally should be conveyed unto me also. Wherefore in this strain we are taught, that if we be the children of God, we must join ourselves in a holy league to his people, and by mutual participation of the gifts of God, we must testify each to other, that we be of the number and communion of saints ; and this is an undoubted badge and cognizance of him that loveth God, if he also loveth them that are begotten of God. Wherefore, if we so profess ourselves to be of God and to worship him, then we must join ourselves to the church of God which with us doth worship God. And this must we do of necessity, for it is a branch of our belief that there is a communion of saints in the church ; and if we believe that there is a God, we must also believe that there is a remnant of people, unto whom God revealeth himself, and communicateth his mercies, in whom we must have all our delight, to whom we must communicate according to the measure of grace unto every one of us.—*Richard Greenham.*

Verse 2.—" *My goodness extendeth not to thee.*" Oh, how great is God's goodness to you ! He calls upon others for the same things, and conscience stands as Pharaoh's taskmasters, requiring the tale of bricks but not allowing straw ; it impels and presseth, but gives no enlargement of heart, and buffets and wounds them for neglect : as the hard creditor that, taking the poor debtor by the throat, saith, " Pay me that thou owest me," but yields him no power to do it ; thus God might deal with you also, for *he oweth not assistance to us ;* but *we owe obedience* to him. Remember, we had power, and it is just to demand what we cannot do, because the weakness that is in us is of ourselves : we have impoverished ourselves. Therefore, when in much mercy he puts forth his hand into the work with thee, be very thankful. If the work be not done, he is no loser ; if done, and well done, he is no gainer. Job xxii. 2 ; xxxv. 6—8. But the gain is all to thee ; all the good that comes by it is to thyself.—*Joseph Symonds,* 1639.

Verse 2 (last clause).—It is a greater glory to us that we are allowed to serve God, than it is to him that we offer him that service. He is not rendered happy by us ; but we are made happy by him. He can do without such earthly servants ; but we cannot do without such a heavenly Master.—*William Secker.*

Verse 2 (last clause).—There is nothing added to God : he is so perfect, that no sin can hurt him ; and so righteous, that no righteousness can benefit him. *O Lord, my righteousness extendeth not to thee ! thou hast no need of my righteousness.* Acts xvii. 24, 25. God hath no need of anything.—*Richard Stock,* 1641.

Verse 2.—As Christ is the head of man, so is God the head of Christ (1 Cor. xi. 3) ; and as man is subject unto Christ, so is Christ subject to God ; not in regard of the divine nature, wherein there is an equality, and consequently no dominion of jurisdiction ; nor only in his human nature, but in the economy of a Redeemer, considered as one designed, and consenting to be incarnate, and take our flesh ; so that after this agreement God had a sovereign right to dispose of him according to the articles consented to. In regard of his undertaking and the advantage he was to bring to the elect of God upon earth, he calls God by the solemn title of " his Lord." " O my soul, thou hast said unto the Lord, Thou art my Lord : my goodness extendeth not to thee ; but to the saints that are in the earth." It seems to be the speech of Christ in heaven, mentioning the saints on earth as at a distance from him. I can add nothing to the glory of thy majesty, but the whole fruit of my meditation and suffering will redound to the saints on earth.—*Stephen Charnock.*

Verses 2, 3.—" *My goodness extendeth not to thee ; but to the saints.*" God's goodness to us should make us merciful to others. It were strange indeed a soul should come out of his tender bosom with a hard uncharitable heart. Some children do not indeed take after their earthly parents, as Cicero's son, who had nothing of his father but his name ; but God's children all partake of their heavenly Father's nature. Philosophy tells us, that there is no reaction from the earth to the heavens ; they indeed shed their influences upon the lower world, which quicken and fructify it, but the earth returns none back to make the sun shine the better. David knew that *his goodness extendeth not unto God*, but this made him reach it forth to his brethren. Indeed, God hath left his poor saints to receive the rents we owe unto him for his mercies. An ingenuous guest, though his friend will take nothing for his entertainment, yet, to show his thankfulness, will give something to his servants. *William Gurnall.*

Verse 3.—" *But to the saints that are in the earth, and to the excellent, in whom is all my delight.*"—My brethren, look upon saintship as the greatest excellency to love it. So did Christ. His eye was " upon the excellent ones in the earth ; " that is, upon the saints, who were excellent to him ; yea, also even when not saints, because God loved them. Isaiah xliii. 4. It is strange to hear how men by their speeches will undervalue a saint as such, if without some other outward excellency. For whilst they acknowledge a man a saint, yet in other respects, they will contemn him ; " He is a holy man," they will say, " but he is weak," etc. But is he a saint ? And can there be any such other imperfection or weakness found as shall lay him low in thy thoughts in comparison of other carnal men more excellent ? Hath not Christ loved him, bought him, redeemed him ?—*Thomas Goodwin.*

Verse 3.—" *But to the saints.*" I understand that a man then evinces affection towards God, and towards those who love God, when his soul yearns after them— when he obliges himself to love them by practically serving and benefiting them— acting towards them as he would act towards God himself were he to see him in need of his service, as David says he did.—*Juan de Valdes,* 1550.

Verse 3.—" *The saints.*" The Papists could abide no saints but those which are in heaven ; which argueth that they live in a kingdom of darkness, and err, not knowing the Scriptures, nor the power of God ; for if they were but meanly conversant in the Scriptures, in the holy epistles, they should find almost in every epistle mention made of the saints who are thereunto called in Jesus Christ, through whom they are sanctified by the Holy Ghost. And mark, he calleth them " *excellent.*" Some think rich men to be excellent, some think learned men to be excellent, some count men in authority so to be, but here we are taught that those men are *excellent* who are sanctified by God's graces.—*Richard Greenham.*

Verse 3.—By David's language, there were many singular saints in his day : " *To the saints that are in the earth, and to the excellent, in whom is all my delight.*" Was it so then, and should it not be so now ? We know the New Testament outshines the Old as much as the sun outshines the moon. If we then live in a more glorious dispensation, should we not maintain a more glorious conversation ? . . . . . " *The excellent.*" Were the sun to give no more delight than a star, you could not believe he was the regent of the day ; were he to transmit no more heat than a glow-worm, you would question his being the source of elementary heat. Were God to do no more than a creature, where would his Godhead be ? Were a man to do no more than a brute, where would his manhood be ? Were not a saint to *excel* a sinner, where would his sanctity be ?—*William Secker.*

Verse 3.—Ingo, an ancient king of the Draves, who making a stately feast, appointed his nobles, at that time Pagans, to sit in the hall below, and commanded certain poor Christians to be brought up into his presence-chamber, to sit with him at his table, to eat and drink of his kingly cheer, at which many wondering, he said, he accounted Christians, though never so poor, a greater ornament to his table, and more worthy of his company than the greatest peers unconverted to the Christian faith ; for when these might be thrust down to hell, those might be his comforts and fellow princes in heaven. Although you see the stars sometimes by their reflections in a puddle, in the bottom of a well, or in a stinking ditch, yet the stars have their situation in heaven. So, although you see a godly man in a poor, miserable, low, despised condition, for the things of this world, yet he is fixed in heaven, in the region of heaven : " Who hath raised us up," saith the apostle, " and made us sit together in heavenly places in Christ Jesus."—*Charles Bradbury's* " *Cabinet of Jewels,*" 1785.

Verse 3.—To sum up all, we must know that we neither do nor can love the godly so well as we should do ; but all is well if we would love them better, and do like ourselves the less because we do love them no more, and that this is common or usual with me, then I am right : so that we are to love the godly first because God commands it, because they are good ; and in these cases our faith doth work by our love to good men. Next, when I am at the worst, like a sick sheep, I care not for the company of other sheep, but do mope in a corner by myself ; but yet I do not delight in the society of goats or dogs, it proves that I have some good blood left in me ; it is because for the present I take little or no delight in myself or in my God, that I delight no better in the godly : yet as I love myself for all that, so I may be said to love them for all this.   Man indeed is a sociable creature, a company-keeper by nature when he is himself ; and if we do not associate ourselves with the ungodly, though for the present, and care not much to show ourselves amongst the godly, the matter is not much, it is a sin of infirmity, not a fruit of iniquity.   The disciples went from Christ, but they turned not to the other side as Judas did, who did forsake his Master and joined himself to his Master's enemies, but they got together. Some say Demas did repent (which I think to be the truth), and then he did " embrace this present world," but for the present fit : put case he did forsake Paul ; so did better men than he.   Indeed as long as a man hath his delights about him, he will embrace the delights of this present world, or the delights which belong to the world to come ; join with Paul, or cleave to the world.   In this temptation our stay is, first, that we care not for the company of goats ; next, that as we should, so we would, and desire that we may take delight in the company of sheep, to count them the only *excellent* men in the world, *in whom is all our delight.*   The conclusion is, that to love the saints as saints, is a sound proof of faith ; the reason is, for that we cannot master our affections by love, but first we must master our understandings by faith.—*Richard Capel,* 1586—1656.

Verse 4.—" *Drink offerings of blood.*"   The Gentiles used to offer, and sometimes to drink part of the blood of their sacrifices, whether of beasts or of men, as either of them were sacrificed.—*Matthew Poole.*

Verse 4.—" *Drink offerings of blood.*"   It is uncertain whether this expression is to be understood literally to be blood, which the heathen actually mixed in their libations when they bound themselves to the commission of some dreadful deed, or whether their libations are figuratively called offerings of blood to denote the horror with which the writer regarded them.—*George R. Noyes, in loc,* 1846.

Verse 4 (last clause).—A sin rolled under the tongue becomes soft and supple, and the throat is so short and slippery a passage, that insensibly it may slide down from the mouth into the stomach ; and contemplative wantonness quickly turns into practical uncleanness.—*Thomas Fuller.*

Verse 5.—" *The Lord is the portion of mine inheritance.*"   If the Lord be thy portion, then thou mayst conclude omnipotency is my portion, immensity, all-sufficiency, etc.   Say not, If so, then I should be omnipotent, etc.   There is a vast difference betwixt identity and interest, betwixt conveying of a title and trans-mutation of nature.   A friend gives thee an invaluable treasure, and all the securities of it that thou canst desire ; wilt thou deny it is thine because thou art not changed into its nature ?   The attributes are thine, as thy inheritance, as thy lands are thine ; not because thou art changed into their nature, but because the title is conveyed to thee, it is given thee, and improved for thy benefit.   If another manage it, who can do it with greater advantage to thee than thou to thyself, it is no infringement of thy title . . . . . .   The Lord is our *portion,* and this is incomparably more than if we had heaven and earth ; for all the earth is but as a point compared with the vastness of the heavens, and the heavens themselves are but a point compared with God. What a large possession have we then !   There is no confiscation of it, no banishment from it.   Our portion fills heaven and earth, and is infinitely above heaven and below earth, and beyond both.   Poor men boast and pride themselves of a kingdom, but we have more than all the kingdoms of the world and the glory thereof.   Christ has given us more than the devil could offer him.—*David Clarkson.*

Verse 5.—" *Portion of mine inheritance and of my cup,*" may contain an allusion to the daily supply of food, and also to the inheritance of Levi.   Deut. xviii. 1, 2. " *Critical and Explanatory Pocket Bible.*"   By *A. R. Fausset and B. M. Smith,* 1867.

Verses 5, 6.—" *The Lord is the portion of mine inheritance : the lines are fallen unto me in pleasant places ; yea, I have a goodly heritage.*"   "Blessed are the people that are in such a case ; yea, blessed are the people whose God is the Lord."   No greater mercy can be bestowed upon any people, family, or person, than this, for God to dwell among them.   If we value this mercy according to the excellency and worth of that which is bestowed, it is the greatest ; if we value it according to the good will of him that gives it, it will appear likewise to be the greatest favour. The greatness of the good will of God in giving himself to be our acquaintance, is evident in the nature of the gift. A man may give his estate to them to whom his love is not very large, but he never gives himself but upon strong affection. God gives abundantly to all the works of his hands ; he causeth the sun to shine upon the evil and upon the good, and the rain to descend upon the just and the unjust ; but it cannot be conceived that he should give himself to be a portion, a friend, father, husband, but in abundance of love. Whosoever therefore shall refuse acquaintance with God, slighteth the greatest favour that ever God did bestow upon man. Now, consider what a high charge this is ; to abuse such a kindness from God is an act of the greatest vileness. David was never so provoked as when the king of Ammon abused his kindness, in his ambassadors, after his father's death. And God is highly provoked when his greatest mercies, bestowed in the greatest love, are rejected and cast away. What could God give more and better than himself ? . . . . . Ask David what he thinks of God ; he was well acquainted with him, he dwelt in his house, and by his good will would never be out of his more immediate presence and company : enquire, I pray, what he found amiss in him. That you may know his mind the better, he hath left it upon record in more than one or two places, what a friend he hath had of God. *"The lines are fallen unto me in pleasant places ; yea, I have a goodly heritage."* Why, what is that you boast of so much, O David ? Have not others had kingdoms as well as you ? No, that's not the thing ; a crown is one of the least jewels in my cabinet : *"The Lord is the portion of mine inheritance and of my cup."—James Janeway.*

*Verses 5, 6.—*Take notice not only of the mercies of God, but of God in the mercies. Mercies are never so savoury as when they savour of a Saviour.—*Ralph Venning, 1620—1673.*

Verse 6.—" The lines are fallen unto me in pleasant places ; yea, I have a goodly heritage." Bitter herbs will go down very well, when a man has such delicious " meats which the world knows not of." The sense of our Father's love is like honey at the end of every rod ; it turns stones into bread, and water into wine, and the valley of trouble into a door of hope ; it makes the biggest evils seem as if they were none, or better than none ; for it makes our deserts like the garden of the Lord, and when we are upon the cross for Christ, as if we were in paradise with Christ. Who would quit his duty for the sake of suffering, that hath such relief under it ? Who would not rather walk in truth, when he hath such a cordial to support him, than by the conduct of fleshly wisdom, to take any indirect or irregular method for his own deliverance ?—*Timothy Cruso.*

Verse 6.—" The lines." Probably alluding to the division of the land by lot, and the measuring of it off by ropes and lines. David believed in an overruling destiny which fixed the bounds of his abode, and his possessions ; he did more, he was satisfied with all the appointment of the predestinating God.—*C. H. S.*

Verse 7.—"I will bless the Lord, who hath given me counsel." The Holy Ghost is a spirit of counsel, powerfully instructing and convincingly teaching how to act and walk, for he directs us to set right steps, and to walk with a right foot, and thereby prevents us of many a sin, by seasonable instruction set on upon our hearts with a strong hand ; as Isaiah viii. 11. For, as the same prophet says (Isaiah xi. 2), he is the spirit of counsel and of might. Of counsel to direct ; of might, to strengthen the inner man. Such he was to Christ the Head, of whom it is there spoken. For instance, in that agony (on the determination of which our salvation depended), and conflict in the garden, when he prayed, " Let this cup pass," it was this good Spirit that counselled him to die ; and he blesseth God for it. " I bless the Lord that hath given me counsel." It was that counsel that in that case caused his heart to say, " Not my will, but thine."—*Thomas Goodwin.*

Verse 7.—" My reins." Common experience shows that the workings of the mind, particularly the passions of joy, grief, and fear, have a very remarkable effect on the reins or kidneys, and from their retired situation in the body, and their being hid in fat, they are often used in Scripture to denote the most secret working of the soul and affections.—*John Parkhurst.*

Verse 7.—" My reins also instruct me in the night seasons." This shows that God, who, he says, was always present to him, had given him some admonition in his dreams, or at least his waking thoughts by night, from whence he gathered a certain assurance of his recovery; possibly he might be directed to some remedy. Antonine thanks the gods for directing him in his sleep to remedies.—*Z. Mudge, in loc*, 1744.

Verse 7.—"*My reins also instruct me in the night seasons.*" We have a saying among ourselves that "the pillow is the best counsellor;" and there is much truth in the saying, especially if we have first committed ourselves in prayer to God, and taken a prayerful spirit with us to our bed. In the quiet of its silent hours, undisturbed by the passions, and unharassed by the conflicts of the world, we can commune with our own heart, and be instructed and guarded as to our future course even "*in the night season.*" David especially seems to have made these seasons sources of great profit as well as delight. Sometimes he loved to meditate upon God as he lay upon his bed; and it was no doubt as he meditated on the Lord's goodness and on the way by which he had led him, that he was, as it were, constrained, even at midnight, to arise and pray. While, therefore, we acknowledge the pillow to be a good counsellor, let us with David here acknowledge also that it is the Lord who gives the counsel, and sends the instruction in the night season.—*Barton Bouchier.*

Verse 8.—"*I have set the Lord always before me.*" David did not by fits and starts set the Lord before him; but he "*always*" set the Lord before him in his course; he had his eye upon the Lord, and so much the Hebrew word imports: I have equally set the Lord before me; that is the force of the original word, that is, I have set the Lord before me, at one time as well as another, without any irregular affections or passions, etc. In every place, in every condition, in every company, in every employment, and in every enjoyment, I have set the Lord equally before me; and this raised him, and this will raise any Christian, by degrees, to a very great height of holiness.—*Thomas Brooks.*

Verse 8.—"*I have set the Lord always before me.*" Hebrew, I have *equally set*, or proposed. The apostle translateth it, " I foresaw the Lord always before my face." Acts ii. 25. I set the eye of my faith full upon him, and suffer it not to take to other things; I look him in the face, *oculo irretorto*, as the eagle looketh upon the sun; and *oculo adamantino*, with an eye of adamant, which turns only to one point: so here *I have equally set the Lord before me*, without irregular affections and passions. And this was one of those lessons that his *reins had taught* him, that the Holy Spirit had dictated unto him.—*John Trapp.*

Verse 8.—"*I have set the Lord* ALWAYS *before me.*" Like as the gnomon doth ever behold the north star, whether it be closed and shut up in a coffer of gold, silver, or wood, never losing its nature; so a faithful Christian man, whether he abound in wealth or be pinched with poverty, whether he be of high or low degree in this world, ought continually to have his faith and hope surely built and grounded upon Christ, and to have his heart and mind fast fixed and settled in him, and to follow him through thick and thin, through fire and water, through wars and peace, through hunger and cold, through friends and foes, through a thousand perils and dangers, through the surges and waves of envy, malice, hatred, evil speeches, railing sentences, contempt of the world, flesh, and devil, and even in death itself, be it never so bitter, cruel, and tyrannical, yet never to lose sight and view of Christ, never to give over faith, hope, and trust in him.—*Robert Cawdray.*

Verse 8.—"*I have set the Lord always before me.*" By often thinking of God, the heart will be enticed into desires after him. Isaiah xxvi. 8. "The desire of our soul is to thy name, and to the remembrance of thee;" and see what follows, verse 9: "With my soul have I desired thee in the night; yea, with my spirit within me will I seek thee early." Love sets the soul on musing, and from musing to praying. Meditation is prayer in bullion, prayer in the ore—soon melted and run into holy desires. The laden cloud soon drops into rain; the piece charged soon goes off when fire is put to it. A meditating soul is in *proxima potentia* to praying.—*William Gurnall.*

Verse 8.—"*I have set the Lord always before me,*" etc. He that by faith eyes God continually as his protector in trouble "*shall not be moved*" with any evil that he suffers, and he that eyes God by faith as his pattern in holiness, shall not be moved from doing that which is good. This thought—*the Lord is at our right hand*—keeps us from turning either to the right hand or to the left. It is said of Enoch, that " he walked with God" (Genesis v. 22), and though the history of his life be very short, yet 'tis said of him a second time (verse 24), that " he walked with God."

He walked so much with God that he walked as God : he did not " *walk* " (which kind of walking the apostle reproves, 1 Cor. iii. 3), " *as men.*" He walked so little like the world that his stay was little in the world. " He was not," saith the text, " for God took him." He took him from the world to himself, or, as the author to the Hebrews reports it, " he was translated that he should not see death, for he had this testimony, that he pleased God."—*Joseph Caryl.*

Verse 8.—" *Because he is at my right hand,*" etc. Of ourselves we stand not at any time, by his power we may overcome at all times. And when we are sorest asaulted he is ever ready *at our right hand* to support and stay us that we shall not fall. He hath well begun, and shall happily go forward in his work, who hath in truth begun. For true grace well planted in the heart, how weak, soever, shall hold out for ever. All total decays come from this—that the heart was never truly mollified, nor grace deeply and kindly rooted therein.—*John Ball.*

Verse 8.—" *He is at my right hand.*" This phrase of speech is borrowed from those who, when they take upon them the patronage, defence, or tuition of any, will set them on their right hand, as in place of most safeguard. Experience confirmeth this in children, who in any imminent danger shroud and shelter themselves under their father's arms or hands, as under a sufficient buckler. Such was the estate of the man of God, as here appeareth, who was hemmed and edged in with the power of God, both against present evils, and dangers to come.—*Richard Greenham*

Verse 8.—Even as a column or pillar is sometimes on thy right hand, and sometimes on thy left hand, because thou dost change thy standing, sitting, or walking, for it is unmovable and keepeth one place ; so God is sometimes favourable and bountiful unto thee, and sometimes seemeth to be wroth and angry with thee, because thou dost fall from virtue to vice, from obedience and humility to pride and presumption ; for in the Lord there is no change, no, not so much as any shadow of change. He is immutable, always one and everlasting. If thou wilt bend thyself to obedience, and to a virtuous and godly life, thou shalt ever have him a strong rock, whereupon thou mayst boldly build a castle and tower of defence. He will be unto thee a mighty pillar, bearing up heaven and earth, whereto thou mayst lean and not be deceived, wherein thou mayst trust and not be disappointed. He will ever be at thy right hand, that thou shalt not fall. He will take thy part, and will mightily defend thee against all enemies of thy body and of thy soul; but if thou wilt shake hands with virtue, and bid it adieu, and farewell, and, forsaking the ways of God, wilt live as thou list, and follow thy own corruption, and make no conscience of aught thou doest, defiling and blemishing thyself with all manner of sin and iniquity, then be sure the Lord will appear unto thee in his fury and indignation. From his justice and judgments none shall ever be able to deliver thee.—*Robert Cawdray.*

Verse 9.—" *My heart is glad.*" Men may for a time be hearers of the gospel, men may for order's sake pray, sing, receive the sacraments ; but if it be without joy, will not that hyprocrisy in time break out ? Will they not begin to be weary ? Nay will they not be as ready to hear any other doctrine ? Good things cannot long find entertainment in our corruptions, unless the Holy Ghost hath changed us from our old delights to conceive pleasure in these things.—*Richard Greenham.*

Verse 9.—" *My heart is glad, and my glory rejoiceth.*" His inward joy was not able to contain itself. We testify our pleasure on lower occasions, even at the gratification of our senses ; when our ear is filled with harmonious melody, when our eye is fixed upon admirable and beauteous objects, when our smell is recreated with agreeable odours, and our taste also by the delicacy and rareness of provisions ; and much more will our soul show its delight, when its faculties, that are of a more exquisite constitution, meet with things that are in all respects agreeable and pleasant to them ; and in God they meet with all those : with his light our understanding is refreshed, and so is our will with his goodness and his love.—*Timothy Rogers.*

Verse 9.—" *Therefore my heart is glad,*" etc. That is, I am all over in very good plight, as well as heart can wish, or require ; I do over-abound exceedingly with joy ; " God forgive me mine unthankfulness and unworthiness of so great glory " (as that martyr said) : " In all the days of my life I was never so merry as now I am in this dark dungeon," etc. Wicked men rejoice in appearance, and not in heart (2 Cor. v. 12) ; their joy is but skin deep, their mirth frothy and flashy, such as wetteth the mouth, but warmeth not the heart. But David is *totus totus, quantus quantus exultabundus ;* his *heart, glory, flesh,* (answerable, as some think to that of the apostle, 1 Thess. v. 23 ; *spirit, soul, and body*) were all overjoyed.—*John Trapp.*

Verse 9.—" *My flesh shall rest in hope.*" If a Jew pawned his bed-clothes, God provided mercifully that it should be restored before night : " For," saith he, " that is his covering : wherein shall he sleep ? " Exodus xxii. 27. Truly, hope is the saint's covering, wherein he wraps himself, when he lays his body down to sleep in the grave : " *My flesh,*" saith David, " *shall rest in hope.*" O Christian, bestir thyself to redeem thy hope before this sun of thy temporal life goes down upon thee, or else thou art sure to lie down in sorrow. A sad going to the bed of the grave he hath who hath no hope of a resurrection to life.—*William Gurnall.*

Verse 9.—" *My flesh shall rest in hope.*" That hope which is grounded on the word, gives rest to the soul ; 'tis an anchor to keep it steady. Heb. vi. 13. Which shows the unmovableness of that which our anchor is fastened to. The promise sustains our faith, and our faith is that which supports us. He that hopes in the Word as David did (Psalm cxix. 81), lays a mighty stress upon it ; as Samson did when he leaned upon the pillars of the house, so as to pull it down upon the Philistines. A believer throws the whole weight of all his affairs and concernments, temporal, spiritual, and eternal, upon the promises of God, like a man resolved to stand or fall with them. He ventures himself, and all that belongs to him, entirely upon this bottom, which is in effect to say, if they will not bear me up, I am content to sink ; I know that there shall be a performance of those things which have been told me from the Lord, and therefore I will incessantly look for it.—*Timothy Cruso.*

Verse 10.—" *For thou wilt not leave my soul in hell,*" etc. The title of this golden text may be—*The embalming of the dead saints :* the force whereof is to free the souls from dereliction in the state of death, and to secure the bodies of God's saints from corruption in the grave. It is the art which I desire to learn, and at this time, teach upon this sad occasion,* even the preparing of this confection against our burials.—*George Hughes,* 1642.

Verse 10.—Many of the elder Reformers held that our Lord in soul actually descended into hell, according to some of them to suffer there as our surety, and according to others to make a public triumph over death and hell. This idea was almost universally, and, as we believe, most properly repudiated by the Puritans. To prove this fact, it may be well to quote from Corbet's witty itinerary of,

> " Foure clerkes of Oxford, doctors two, and two
>   That would be docters."

He laments the secularisation of church appurtenances at Banbury, by the Puritans whom he describes as,

> ———————— " They which tell
> That Christ hath nere descended into hell,
> But to the grave."

C. H. S. *The quotation is from Richard Corbet's Poems,* 1632.

Verse 10.—" *My soul in hell.*" Christ in soul descended into hell, when as our surety he submitted himself to bear those hellish sorrows (or equivalent to them), which we were bound by our sins to suffer for ever. His descension is his projection of himself into the sea of God's wrath conceived for our sins, and his ingression into most unspeakable straits and torments in his soul, which we should else have suffered for ever in hell. This way of Christ's descending into hell is expressly uttered in the person of David, as the type of Christ. Psalm lxxxvi. 13 ; cxvi. 3 ; lxix. 1–3. Thus the prophet Isaiah saith, " His soul was made an offering." Isaiah liii. 10. And this I take it David means, when he said of Christ, " *Thou wilt not leave my soul in hell.*" Psalm xvi ; Acts ii. And thus Christ descended into hell when he was alive, not when he was dead. Thus his soul was in hell when in the garden he did sweat blood, and on the cross when he cried so lamentably, " My God, my God, why hast thou forsaken me ? " Matt. xxvi. 38.—*Nicholas Byfield's "Exposition of the Creed,"* 1676.

Verse 10.—" *In hell.*" Sheol here, as *hades* in the New Testament, signifies the state of the dead, the separate state of souls after death, the invisible world of souls, where Christ's soul was, though it did not remain there, but on the third day returned

———————————————————————————————————
* A Funeral Sermon.

to its body again. It seems best of all to interpret this word of the grave as it is rendered ; Gen. xlii. 38 ; Isaiah xxxviii. 18.—*John Gill.*

Verse 10.—" *Thine Holy. One.*" *Holiness* preserves the soul from dereliction, in the state of death, and the body of the saint from corruption in the grave. If it be desired by any that doubt of it, to see the clear issue of this from the text, I shall guide them to read this text with a great accent upon that term, " *Thine Holy One,*" that they may take special notice of it, even the quality of that man exempted from these evils. In this the Spirit of God puts an emphasis upon *holiness*, as counter-working and prevailing over death and the grave. It is this and nothing but this, that thus keeps the man, dead and buried, from desertion in death, and corruption in the grave.—*George Hughes.*

Verse 10.—The great promise to Christ is, that though he took a corruptible body upon him, yet he should " *not see corruption,*" that is, *partake of corruption*, corruption should have no communion with, much less power over him.—*Joseph Caryl.*

Verse 10.—Quoted by the apostle Peter (Acts ii. 27); on which Hackett (*Com. in loc.*) observes :—" The sense then may be expressed thus : Thou wilt not give me up as a prey to death ; he shall not have power over me, to dissolve the body and cause it to return to dust."

Verse 11.—In this verse are four things observable :—1. *A Guide*, Thou. 2. *A Traveller*, Me. 3. *A Way*, the Path. 4. *The End*, Life, described after. For that which follows is but the description of this life.

This verse is a proper subject for a *meditation.* For, all three are solitary. *The guide* is but one ; the *traveller*, one ; the *way*, one ; and the *life*, the only one. To meditate well on this is to bring all together ; and at last make them all but *one.* Which that we may do, let us first seek our *Guide.*

The Guide. Him we find named in the first verse—Jehovah. Here we may begin, as we ought in all holy exercises, with *adoration.* For, " unto him all knees shall bow ; " nay, unto his *name.* For holy is his name. Glory be to thee, O God ! He is *Deus*, therefore *holy ;* he is *Deus fortis*, therefore *able.* " For the strength of the hills is his ; " and if there be a *way* on earth, he can " *show* " it ; for in his hands are all the corners of the earth. But is he *willing* to " *show* " ? Yes, though he be *Deus*, *holy* (which is a word terrible to poor flesh and blood), yet he is *Deus meus*, my holiness. That takes away servile fear. He is *meus*, we have a property in him ; and he is willing : " *Thou wilt show*," etc. And that you may know *he will guide*, David shows a little above how diligently he will guide. First, he will *go before*, he will lead the way himself : if I can but follow, I shall be sure to go right. And he that hath a *guide* before him, and will not follow, is worthy to be left behind. But say, I am willing, I do desire to go, and I do follow : what if, through faintness in the long way, I fall often ? or, for want of care step out of the way, shall I not then be left behind ? Fear not ; for " He is at my right hand, so that I shall not slip." Verse 8. This is some comfort indeed. But we are so soon weary in this way, and do fall and err so often, that it would weary the patience of a good *guide* to lead us but one day. Will he bear with us, and continue to the end ? Yes, always ; or this text deceives us ; for all this is found in the eighth verse. We must have *him* or none ; for he is one, and the only one. So confessed Asaph : " Whom have I on earth but thee ? " Seek this *good Guide*, he is easy to be found : " Seek, and ye shall find." You shall find that he is first *holy ;* secondly, *able ;* thirdly, *willing ;* fourthly, *diligent ;* and fifthly, *constant.* O my soul ! to follow him, and he will make thee both *able* to follow to the end ; and *holy* in the end.

The traveller. Having found the *Guide*, we shall not long seek for one that wants him ; for, see, here is a *man out of his way.* And that will soon appear if we consider his condition. For, he is a *stranger* (" *Thou wilt show me* ") ; and what am I ? " I am a stranger, and a sojourner, as all my fathers were," says he, in another place. But this was in the old time under the law ; what, are we, their sons, in the gospel, any other ? Peter tells us no : that we are strangers and pilgrims too ; that is, travellers. We travel, as being *out of our country ;* and we are strangers to those we converse with. For neither the natives be our friends, nor anything we possess truly our own. It is time we had *animum revertendi ;* and surely so we have if we could but pray on the *way.* *Converte nos Domine.* But it is so long since we came hither, we have forgot the way home : *obliti sunt montis mei.* Yet still we are travelling ; and, we think, homewards. For all hope well : *oculi omnium sperant in te.* But *right*, like pilgrims, or rather, wanderers. For we scarce know if we go right; and, which is worse, have little care to enquire.

"*Me.*" David still keeps the singular number. As there is but *one* guide, so he speaks in the person but of *one traveller*. There is somewhat, peradventure, in that. It is to show his *confidence*. The Lord's prayer is in the plural, but the creed in the singular. We may pray that God would guide *all*; but we can be confident for none but ourselves. "*Thou wilt show*," or thou dost, or hast, as some translate: all is but to show particular confidence. "*Thou wilt show me*;" *me*, not *us*, a number indefinite wherein I *may be* one; but *me* in particular that am out of the way; that am myself *alone*; that must walk in "*the path*" *alone*. Either I must follow, or go before others; I must work for myself alone; believe for myself alone; and be saved by one alone. *The way* in this text that I must walk is but one; nay, it is but a "*path*" where but one can go: this is no highway, but a *way* of sufferance by favour: it is none of ours. It is no *road*; you cannot hurry here, or gallop by troops: it is but *semita*, a small *footpath* for one to go alone in. Nay, as it is a *way* for *one* alone, so it is *a lonely way: preparate vias ejus in solitudine*, saith John, and he knew which way God went, who is our *Guide in solitudine*: there is the sweetness of solitariness, the comforts of meditation. For God is never more familiar with man than when man is *in solitudine, alone*, in his *path* by himself. Christ himself came thus, all *lonely*; without troop, or noise, and ever avoided the tumultuous multitude, though they would have made him a king. And he never spake to them but in parables; but to *his* that sought him, *in solitudine*, in private, he spake plain; and so doth he still love to do to the soul, in private and particular. Therefore well said David, "*Thou wilt show me*," in particular, and in the singular number. But how shall I know that I, in particular, shall be taught and *showed* this *way*? This prophet, that had experience, will tell us: *mites docebit*, the *humble he will teach*. Psalm xxv. 9. If thou canst humble thyself, thou mayst be sure to see thy *guide*; Christ hath crowned this virtue with a blessing: "Blessed are the meek;" for them he will call to him and teach. But thou must be humble then. For heaven is built like our churches, high-roofed within, but with a strait low gate; they then that enter there must stoop, ere they can see God. Humility is the mark at every cross, whereby thou shalt know if thou be in the way: if any be otherwise minded, God also shall reveal it unto you, for, "*Thou wilt show*."

"*The path.*" But let us now see *what* he will *show* us: "*the path*." We must know, that as men have *many paths* out of their highway—the world—but they all end in destruction; so God hath *many paths* out of his highway, the word, but they all end in salvation. Let us oppose ours to his (as indeed they are opposite), and see how they agree. *Ours* are not worth *marking*, *his marked* with an *attendite*, to begin withal; *ours* bloody, *his* unpolluted; *ours* crooked, *his* straight; *ours* lead to hell, *his* to heaven. Have not we strayed then? We had need to turn and take another path, and that quickly: we may well say, *semitas nostras, à viâ tuâ.* Well, here is *the Book*, and here are the *ways* before you; and he will *show* you. Here is *semita mandatorum*, in the one hundred-and-nineteenth Psalm, verse thirty-five; here is *semita pacifica* (Prov. iii. 17); here is *semita æquitatis* (Prov. iv. 11); here is *semita justitiæ* (Psalm xxiii. 3); here is *semita judicii* (Prov. xvii. 23); and many others. These are, every one of them, *God's ways*; but these are somewhat too many and too far off: we must seek the *way* where all these meet, and that will bring us into "*the path*;" these are many, but I will show you yet "a more excellent way," saith Paul. 1 Cor. xii. 31.

We must begin to enter at *via mandatorum*; for till then we are in the dark and can distinguish no *ways*, whether they be good or bad. But there we shall meet with a *lantern* and a *light* in it. Thy commandment is a lantern, and the law a light. Prov. vi. 23. Carry this with thee (as a good man should, *lex Dei in corde ejus*); and it will bring thee into the *way*. And see how careful our *Guide* is; for lest the wind should blow out this light, he hath put it into a lantern to preserve it. For the fear, or sanction, of the "commandments," preserves the memory of the law in our hearts, as a lantern doth a light burning within it. The law is the light, and the commandment the lantern. So that neither flattering Zephyrus, nor blustering Boreas shall be able to blow it out, so long as the fear of the sanction keeps it in. This is *lucerna pedibus* (Psalm cxix. 105); and will not only *show* thee where thou shalt tread, but what pace thou shalt keep. When thou hast this light, take Jeremy's counsel; enquire for *semita antiqua*, before thou goest any further. "Stand (saith he) in the ways and behold and ask for the old way ; which is the good way, and walk therein, and ye shall find rest for your souls." This will bring you some whither where you may *rest* awhile. And whither is that ? Trace this *path*, and you shall find this " old way " to run quite through all the Old Testament till it end in the New, the gospel of peace, and there is *rest.* And that this is so Paul affirms. For the law, which is the " old way," is but the pedagogue to the gospel. This then is " a more excellent way " than the law, the ceremonies whereof in respect of this were called " beggarly rudiments." When we come there, we shall find the way pleasant and very *light,* so that we shall plainly see before us that *very path,* that *only path,* " the path of life " (*semita vitæ*), in which the gospel ends, as the law ends in the gospel. Now what is *semita vitæ* that we seek for ? "All the ways of God are *truth,*" saith David. Psalm cxix. 151. He doth not say they are *veræ,* or *veritates,* but *veritas ;* all one truth. So, all the *ways* of God end in one truth. *Semita vitæ,* then, is *truth.* And so sure a *way* to life is *truth,* that John says, he had " no greater joy " than to hear that his sons " walked in truth." 3 John i. 3. " No greater joy : " for it brings them certainly to a joy, than which there is none greater. *Via veritatis* is " the gospel of truth." but *semita vitæ* is the truth itself. Of these, Esay prophesied, *et erit ibi semita et via,* etc. " There shall be a path, and a way ; " and the way shall be called *holy,* the proper epithet of the gospel : " *the holy gospel,*" that is *the way.* But the *path* is the epitome of this *way* (called in our text, by way of excellence, " *the path,*" in the singular); than which there is no other. " The gospel of your salvation," saith Paul, is " the word of truth ; " and " thy word is truth," saith our Saviour to his Father. *Truth,* then, is " *the path of life,*" for it is the epitome of the gospel, which is the *way.* This is that truth which Pilate (unhappy man) asked after, but never stayed to be resolved of. He himself is the word ; the word is the truth ; and the truth is " *the path of life,*" trodden by all the patriarchs, prophets, apostles, martyrs and confessors, that ever went to heaven before us. The abstract of the gospel, the gate of heaven, *semita vitæ,* " *the path of life,*" even Jesus Christ the righteous, who hath beaten the way for us, gone himself before us, and left us the prints of his footsteps for us to follow, where he himself sits ready to receive us. So, the law is the light, the gospel is the way, and Christ is " *the path of life.*"—*William Austin,* 1637.

Verse 11.—It is Christ's triumphing in the consideration of his exaltation, and taking pleasure in the fruits of his sufferings : " *Thou wilt show me the paths of life.*" God hath now opened the way to paradise, which was stopped up by a flaming sword, and made the path plain by admitting into heaven the head of the believing world. This is part of the joy of the soul of Christ ; he hath now a fulness of joy, a satisfying delight instead of an overwhelming sorrow; a "fulness of joy," not only some sparks and drops as he had now and then in his debased condition ; and that in the presence of his Father. His soul is fed and nourished with a perpetual vision of God, in whose face he beholds no more frowns, no more designs of treating him as a servant, but such smiles that shall give a perpetual succession of joy to him, and fill his soul with fresh and pure flames. Pleasures they are, pleasantness in comparison whereof the greatest joys in this life are anguish and horrors. His soul hath joys without mixture, pleasures without number, a fulness without want, a constancy without interruption, and a perpetuity without end.—*Stephen Charnock.*

Verse 11.—" *In thy presence,*" etc. To the blessed soul resting in Abraham's bosom, there shall be given an immortal, impassible, resplendent, perfect, and glorious body. Oh, what a happy meeting will this be, what a sweet greeting between the soul and body, the nearest and dearest acquaintance that ever were ! What a welcome will that soul give to her beloved body ! Blessed be thou (will she say), for thou hast aided me to the glory I have enjoyed since I parted with thee ; blessed art thou that sufferedst thyself to be mortified, giving " thy members as weapons of righteousness unto God." Rom. vi. 13. Cheer up thyself, for now the time of labour is past, and the time of rest is come. Thou wast sown and buried in the dust of earth with ignominy, but now raised in glory ; sown in weakness, but raised in power ; sown a natural body, but raised a spiritual body ; sown in corruption, but raised in incorruption. 1 Cor. xv. 43. O my dear companion and familiar, we took sweet counsel together, we two have walked together as friends in God's house (Psalm lv. 14), for when I prayed inwardly, thou didst attend my devotions with bowed knees and lifted-up hands outwardly. We two have been fellow labourers in the works of the Lord, we two have suffered together, and now we two shall ever reign together ; I will enter again into thee, and so both of us together will enter into our Master's joy, where we shall have *pleasures at his right hand for evermore.*

The saints, entered as it were into the chamber of God's presence, shall have joy to their ears in hearing their own commendating and praise, " Well done, good and faithful servant " (Matt. xxv. 21) ; and in hearing the divine language of heavenly Canaan ; for our bodies shall be *vera et viva,* perfect like Christ's glorious body, who did both hear other and speak himself after his resurrection, as it is apparent in the gospels' history. Now, then, if the words of the wise spoken in due places be like " apples of gold with pictures of silver " (Prov. xxv. 11), if the mellifluous speech of Origen, the silver trumpet of Hillary, the golden mouth of Chrysostom, bewitched as it were their auditory with exceeding great delight ; if the gracious eloquence of heathen orators, whose tongues were never touched with a coal from God's altar, could steal away the hearts of their hearers, and carry them up and down whither they would, what a " *fulness of joy* " will it be to hear not only the sanctified, but also the glorified tongues of saints and angels in the kingdom of glory ? . . . . . . Bonaventure fondly reports at all adventure, that St. Francis hearing an angel a little while playing on a harp, was so moved with extraordinary delight, that he thought himself in another world. Oh ! what a " *fulness of joy* " will it be to hear more than twelve legions of angels, accompanied with a number of happy saints which no man is able to number, all at once sing together, " Hallelujah, holy, holy, holy, Lord God Almighty, which was, and is, and is to come." "And every creature which is in heaven, and on earth, and under the earth, and such as are in the sea, and all that are in them, heard I saying, Blessing, and honour, and glory, and power, be unto him that sitteth upon the throne, and unto the Lamb for ever and ever." Rev. iv. 8 ; v. 13. If the voices of mortal men, and the sound of cornet, trumpet, harp, sackbut, psaltery, dulcimer, and other well-tuned instruments of music, passing through our dull ears in this world be so powerful, that all our affections are diversely transported according to the divers kinds of harmony, then how shall we be ravished in God's presence when we shall hear heavenly airs with heavenly ears !

Concerning " *fulness of joy* " to the rest of the senses I find a very little or nothing in holy Scriptures, and therefore seeing God's Spirit will not have a pen to write, I may not have a tongue to speak. Divines in general affirm, that the smelling, and taste, and feeling, shall have joy proportionable to their blessed estate, for this corruptible must put on incorruption, and this mortal immortality ; the body which is sown in weakness is to be raised in power ; it is sown a natural body, but it is raised a spiritual body, buried in dishonour, raised in glory ; that is, capable of good, and, as being impassible, no way subject to suffer evil, insomuch that it cannot be hurt if it should be cast into hell fire, no more than Shadrach, Meshech, and Abednego, were hurt in the burning oven. In one word, God is not only to the souls, but also to the bodies of the saints, *all in all things;* a glass to their sight, honey to their taste, music to their hearing, balm to their smelling.—*John Boys.*

Verse 11.—" *In thy presence is fulness of joy.*" The saints on earth are all but *viatores,* wayfaring men, wandering pilgrims far from home ; but the saints in heaven are *comprehensores,* safely arrived at the end of their journey. All we here present for the present, are but mere strangers in the midst of danger, we are losing ourselves and losing our lives in the land of the dying. But ere long, we may find our lives and ourselves again in heaven with the Lord of life, being found of him in the land of the living. If when we die, we be in the Lord of life, our souls are sure to be bound up in the bundle of life, that so when we live again we may be sure to find them in the life of the Lord. Now we have but a dram, but a scruple, but a grain of happiness, to an ounce, to a pound, to a thousand weight of heaviness ; now we have but a drop of joy to an ocean of sorrow ; but a moment of ease to an age of pain ; but then (as St. Austin very sweetly in his *Soliloquies*), we shall have endless ease without any pain, true happiness without any heaviness, the greatest measure of felicity without the least of misery, the fullest measure of joy that may be, without any mixture of grief. Here therefore (as St. Gregory the divine adviseth us), let us ease our heaviest loads of sufferings, and sweeten our bitterest cups of sorrows with the continual meditation and constant expectation of *the fulness of joy in the presence of God, and of the pleasure at his right hand for evermore.*

" *In thy presence,* is," etc., *there it is,* not there it was, nor there it may be, nor there it will be, but *there it is,* there it *is* without cessation or intercision, there it always hath been, and is, and must be. It is an assertion *æternæ veritatis,* that is always true, it may at any time be said that there it *is*. " In thy presence *is* the fulness of joy;" and herein consists the consummation of felicity; for what does any man here present wish for more than joy? And what measure of joy can any man wish for more than fulness of joy? And what kind of fulness would any man wish for rather than this fulness, the fulness κατ' ἐξοχὴν? And where would any man wish to enjoy this fulness of joy rather than in the presence of God, which is the ever-flowing and the over-flowing fountain of joy? And when would any man wish for this enjoyment of the fulness of joy in the very fountain of joy rather than presently, constantly, and incessantly? Now all these desirables are encircled within the compass of the first remarkable, to make up the consummation of true felicity. " *In thy presence is fulness of joy.*"—" *The Consummation of Felicity," by Edward Willan,* 1645.

Verse 11.—The human nature of Christ in heaven hath a double capacity of glory, happiness and delight; one on that mere fellowship and communion with his Father and the other persons, through his personal union with the Godhead. Which joy of his in this fellowship, Christ himself speaks of as to be enjoyed by him: " *In thy presence is fulness of joy, and at thy right hand are pleasures for evermore.*" And this is a constant and settled fulness of pleasure, such as admits not any addition or diminution, but is always one and the same, and absolute and entire in itself; and of itself alone sufficient for the Son of God, and heir of all things to live upon, though he should have had no other comings in of joy and delight from any creature. And this is his natural inheritance.—*Thomas Goodwin.*

Verse 11.—" *In thy presence is* FULNESS *of joy.*" In heaven they are free from want; they can want nothing there unless it be want itself. They may find the want of evil, but never find the evil of want. Evil is but the want of good, and the want of evil is but the absence of want. God is good, and no want of good can be in God. What want then can be endured in the presence of God, where no evil is, but all good that the fulness of joy may be enjoyed? Here some men eat their meat without any hunger, whilst others hunger without any meat to eat, and some men drink extremely without any thirst, whilst others thirst extremely without any drink. But in the glorious presence of God, not any one can be pampered with too much, nor any one be pined with too little. They that gather much of the heavenly manna, " have nothing over;" and " they that gather little have no lack. They that are once possessed of that presence of God, are so possessed with it that they can never feel the misery of thirst or hunger.—*Edward Willan.*

Verse 11.—" *Fulness.*" Every soul shall there enjoy an infinite happiness, because it shall enjoy infinite goodness. And it shall be for ever enjoyed, without disliking of it, or losing of it, or lacking any of it. Every soul shall enjoy as much good in that presence, by the presence of that good, as it shall be able to receive, or to desire to receive. As much as shall make it fully happy. Every one shall be filled so proportionately full; and every desire in any soul shall be fulfilled so perfectly in that presence of glory, with the glory of that presence, that no one shall ever wish for any more, or ever be weary of that it has, or be willing to change it for any other.—*Edward Willan.*

Verse 11.—" *Fulness of joy.*" When a man comes to the sea, he doth not complain that he wants his cistern of water: though thou didst suck comfort from thy relations; yet when thou comest to the ocean, and art with Christ, thou shalt never complain that thou hast left thy cistern behind. There will be nothing to breed sorrow in heaven; there shall be *joy, and nothing but joy*, heaven is set out by that phrase, " Enter thou into the joy of thy Lord." Here joy enters into us, there we enter into joy; the joys we have here are from heaven; the joys that we shall have with Christ are without measure and without mixture. " *In thy presence is fulness of joy.*"—*Thomas Watson.*

Verse 11.—" *In thy presence is fulness of joy.*" In this life our joy is mixed with sorrow like a prick under the rose. Jacob had joy when his sons returned home from Egypt with the sacks full of corn, but much sorrow when he perceived the silver in the sack's mouth. David had much joy in bringing up the ark of God, but at the same time great sorrow for the breach made upon Uzza. This is the Lord's great wisdom to temper and moderate our joy. As men of a weak constitution must have their wine qualified with water for fear of distemper, so must we in this life (such is our weakness), have our joy mixed with sorrow, lest we turn giddy and insolent. Here our joy is mixed with fear (Psalm ii.), " Rejoice with trembling;" the women departed from the sepulchre of our Lord " with fear and great joy." Matthew xxviii. 8. In our regenerate estate, though we have joy from Christ that is "formed in us," yet the impression of the terrors of God before the time of our new birth remains in us ; as in a commotion of the sea by a great tempest after a stormy wind hath ceased, yet the impression of the storm remains and makes an agitation. The tender mother recovering her young child from danger of a fall hath joy from the recovery; but with much fear with the impression of the danger : so after we are recovered here from our dangerous falls by the rich and tender mercies of our God, sometime preventing us, sometime restoring us, though we rejoice in his mercy, and in our own recovery out of the snares of Satan, yet in the midst of our joy the remembrance of former guiltiness and danger do humble our hearts with much sorrow, and some trepidation of heart. As our joy here is mixed with fears, so with sorrow also. Sound believers do look up to Christ crucified, and do rejoice in his incomparable love, that such a person should have died such a death for such as were enemies to God by sinful inclinations and wicked works ; they look down also upon their own sins that have wounded and crucified the Lord of glory, and this breaketh the heart, as a widow should mourn, who by her froward and lewd behaviour hath burst the heart of a kind and loving husband.

The sound believers look to their small beginnings of grace, and they rejoice in the work of God's hands ; but when they compare it with that original and primitive righteousness, they mourn bitterly, as the elders of Israel did at the rebuilding of the temple (Ezra iii. 12); "They who had seen the first house wept." But in heaven our joy will be full, without mixture of sorrow (John xvi. 20); "Your sorrow," saith our Lord, "shall be turned into joy." Then will there be no sorrow for a present trouble, nor present fear of future troubles. Then their eye will deeply affect their heart : the sight and knowledge of God the supreme and infinite good will ravish, and take up all their heart with joy and delight. Peter in the Mount (Matthew xvii.), was so affected with that glorious sight, that he forgot both the delights and troubles that were below ; "It is good to be here," said he. How much more will all worldly troubles and delights be forgot at that soul-satisfying sight in heaven, which is as far above that of Peter in the Mount, as the third heaven is above that Mount, and as the uncreated is above the created glory !—*William Colvill's "Refreshing Streams," 1655.*

Verse 11.—"*In thy presence is fulness of joy ; at thy right hand there are pleasures for evermore.*" Mark, for quality, there are *pleasures ;* for quantity, *fulness ;* for dignity, *at God's right hand ;* for eternity, *for evermore.* And millions of years multiplied by millions, make not up one minute to this eternity of joy that the saints shall have in heaven. In heaven there shall be no sin to take away your joy, nor no devil to take away your joy ; nor no man to take away your joy. "Your joy no man taketh from you." John xvi. 22. The joy of the saints in heaven is never ebbing, but always flowing to all contentment. The joys of heaven never fade, never wither, never die, nor never are lessened nor interrupted. The joy of the saints in heaven is a constant joy, an everlasting joy, in the root and in the cause, and in the matter of it and in the objects of it. "Their joy lasts for ever whose objects remain for ever"—*Thomas Brooks.*

Verse 11.—"*Pleasures for evermore.*" The soul that is once landed at the heavenly shore is past all storms. The glorified soul shall be for ever bathing itself in the *rivers of pleasure.* This is that which makes heaven to be heaven, "We shall be ever with the Lord." 1 Thess. iv. 17. Austin saith, "Lord, I am content to suffer any pains and torments in this world, if I might see thy face one day ; but alas ! were it only a day, then to be ejected heaven, it would rather be an aggravation of misery ;" but this word, "*ever with the Lord,*" is very accumulative, and makes up the garland of glory : a state of eternity is a state of security.—*Thomas Watson.*

Verse 11.—This then may serve for a ground of comfort to every soul distressed with the tedious bitterness of this life ; for short sorrow here, we shall have eternal joy ; for a little hunger, an eternal banquet ; for light sickness and affliction, everlasting health and salvation ; for a little imprisonment, endless liberty ; for disgrace, glory. Instead of the wicked who oppress and afflict them, they shall have the angels and saints to comfort and solace them, instead of Satan to torment and tempt them, they shall have Jesus to ravish and affect them. Joseph's prison shall be turned into a palace ; Daniel's lions' den into the presence of the Lion of the Tribe of Judah ; the three children's hot fiery furnace, into the New Jerusalem of pure gold ; David's Gath, into the tabernacle of the living God.—*John Cragge's "Cabinet of Spirituall Jewells," 1657.*

Verse 11.—This heavenly feast will not have an end, as Ahasuerus's feast had, though it lasted many days ; but " *At thy right hand are pleasures for evermore.*" *William Colvill.*

HINTS TO PREACHERS.

Michtam of David.—Under the title of " The Golden Psalm," Mr. Canon Dale has published a small volume, which is valuable as a series of good simple discourses, but ought hardly to have been styled " an exposition." We have thought it right to give the headings of the chapters into which his volume is divided, for there is much showiness, and may be some solidity in the suggestions.

Verse 1.—*The seeking of the gold.* The believer conscious of danger, trusting in God only for deliverance.

Verses 2, 3.—*The possessing of the gold.* The believer looking for justification to the righteousness of God alone, while maintaining personal holiness by companionship with the saints.

Verses 4, 5.—*The testing of the gold.* The believer finding his present portion, and expecting his eternal inheritance in the Lord.

Verse 6.—*The prizing or valuing of the gold.* The believer congratulating himself on the pleasantness of his dwelling and the goodness of his heritage.

Verses 7, 8.—*The occupying of the gold.* The believer seeking instruction from the counsels of the Lord by night, and realising his promise by day.

Verses 9, 10.—*The summing or reckoning of the gold.* The believer rejoicing and praising God for the promise of a rest in hope and resurrection into glory.

Verse 11.—*The perfecting of the gold.* The believer realising at God's right hand the fulness of joy and the pleasures for evermore.

Upon this suggestive Psalm we offer the following few hints out of many—

Verse 1.—The prayer and the plea. The preserver and the truster. The dangers of the saints and the place of their confidence.

Verse 2.—" *Thou art my Lord.*" The soul's appropriation, allegiance, assurance and avowal.

Verses 2, 3.—The influence and sphere of goodness. No profit to God, or departed saints or sinners, but to *living men.* Need of promptness, etc.

Verses 2, 3.—Evidence of true faith. I. Allegiance to divine authority. II. Rejection of self-righteousness. III. Doing good to the saints. IV. Appreciation of saintly excellence. V. delight in their society.

Verse 3.—*Excellent of the earth.* May be translated noble, wonderful, magnificent. They are so in their new birth, nature, clothing, attendance, heritage, etc., etc.

Verse 3.—" *In whom is all my delight.*" Why Christians should be objects of our delight. Why we do not delight in them more. Why they do not delight in us. How to make our fellowship more delightful.

Verse 3.—Collection sermon for poor believers. I. Saints. II. Saints on the earth. III. These are excellent. IV. We must delight in them. V. We must extend our goodness to them.—*Matthew Henry.*

Verse 4.—Sorrows of idolatry illustrated in heathens and ourselves.

Second clause.—The duty of complete separation from sinners in life and lip.

Verse 5.—Future inheritance and present cup found in God. (See Exposition).

Last clause.—What our " lot " is. What danger it is in. Who defends it.

Verse 6.—" *Pleasant places.*" Bethlehem, Calvary, Olivet, Tabor, Zion, Paradise, etc. II. *Pleasant purposes,* which made these lines fall to me. III. *Pleasant praises.* By service, sacrifice, and song.

Verse 6 (second clause).—I. A heritage. II. A goodly heritage. III. I have it. IV. Yea, or the Spirit's witness.

Verse 6.—" *A goodly heritage.*" That which makes our portion good is—I. The favour of God with it. II. That it is from a Father's hand. III. That it comes through the covenant of grace. IV. That it is the purchase of Christ's blood. V. That it is an answer to prayer, and a blessing from above upon honest endeavours.

Verse 6.—We may put this acknowledgment into the mouth of—I. *An indulged child of providence.* II. *An inhabitant of this favoured country.* III. *A Christian with regard to his spiritual condition.*—*William Jay.*

Verse 7.—*Taking counsel's opinion.* Of whom ? Upon what ? Why ? When ? How ? What then ?

Verse 7.—Upward and inward, or two schools of instruction.

Verse 8.—Set the Lord always before you as—I. Your *protector.* II. Your *leader.* III. *Your example.* IV. Your *observer.*—*William Jay.*

Verses 8, 9.—A sense of the divine presence our best support. It yields. I. Good confidence concerning things without. " *I shall not be moved.*" II. Good cheer within. " *My heart is glad.*" III. Good music for the living tongue. " *My glory rejoiceth.*" IV. Good hope for the dying body. " *My flesh also,*" etc.

Verse 9 (last clause).—I. The saint's Sabbath (*rest*). II. His sarcophagus (*in hope*). III. His salvation (for which he *hopes*).

Verses 9, 10.—Jesus cheered in prospect of death by the safety of his soul and body ; our consolation in him as to the same.

Verse 10.—Jesus dead, the place of his soul and his body. A difficult but interesting topic.

Verses 10, 11.—Because he lives we shall live also. The believer, therefore, can also say, " Thou wilt show *me* the path of life." This life means the blessedness reserved in heaven for the people of God after the resurrection. It has three characters. The first regards its *source*—it flows from " *his presence.*" The second regards its plenitude—it is " *fulness*" of joy. The third regards its *permanency*—the pleasures are " *for evermore.*"—*William Jay.*

Verse 11.—A sweet picture of heaven. (See Exposition.)

PSALM XVII.

TITLE AND SUBJECT.—A Prayer of David. *David would not have been a man after God's own heart, if he had not been a man of prayer. He was a master in the sacred art of supplication. He flies to prayer in all times of need, as a pilot speeds to the harbour in the stress of tempest. So frequent were David's prayers that they could not all be dated and entitled ; and hence this simply bears the author's name, and nothing more. The smell of the furnace is upon the present Psalm, but there is evidence in the last verse that he who wrote it came unharmed out of the flame. We have in the present plaintive song,* AN APPEAL TO HEAVEN *from the persecutions of earth. A spiritual eye may see Jesus here.*

DIVISIONS.—*There are no very clear lines of demarcation between the parts ; but we prefer the divisions adopted by that precious old commentator, David Dickson. In verses 1—4, David craves justice in the controversy between him and his oppressors. In verses 5 and 6, he requests of the Lord grace to act rightly while under the trial. From verse 7—12, he seeks protection from his foes, whom he graphically describes ; and in verses 13 and 14, pleads that they may be disappointed ; closing the whole in the most comfortable confidence that all would certainly be well with himself at the last.*

EXPOSITION.

HEAR the right, O LORD, attend unto my cry, give ear unto my prayer, *that goeth* not out of feigned lips.

2 Let my sentence come forth from thy presence ; let thine eyes behold the things that are equal.

3 Thou hast proved mine heart ; thou hast visited *me* in the night ; thou hast tried me, *and* shalt find nothing ; I am purposed *that* my mouth shall not transgress.

4 Concerning the works of men, by the word of thy lips I have kept *me from* the paths of the destroyer.

1. *"Hear the right, O Lord."* He that has the worst cause makes the most noise ; hence the oppressed soul is apprehensive that its voice may be drowned, and therefore pleads in this one verse for a hearing no less than three times. The troubled heart craves for the ear of the great Judge, persuaded that with him to hear is to redress. If our God could not or would not hear us, our state would be deplorable indeed ; and yet some professors set such small store by the mercy-seat, that God does not hear them for the simple reason that they neglect to plead. As well have no house if we persist like gipsies in living in the lanes and commons ; as well have no mercy-seat as be always defending our own cause and never going to God. There is more fear that *we* will not hear the Lord than that the Lord will not hear us. *"Hear the right ;"* it is well if our case is good in itself and can be urged as a right one, for right shall never be wronged by our righteous Judge ; but if our suit be marred by our infirmities, it is a great privilege that we may make mention of the righteousness of our Lord Jesus, which is ever prevalent on high. *Right* has a voice which Jehovah always hears ; and if my wrongs clamour against me with great force and fury, I will pray the Lord to hear that still louder and mightier voice of the right, and the rights of his dear Son. *"Hear, O God, the just One ;" i.e.,* "hear the Messiah," is a rendering adopted by Jerome, and admired by Bishop Horsley, whether correct or not as a translation, it is proper enough as a plea. Let the reader plead it at the throne of the righteous God, even when all other arguments are unavailing.

"Attend unto my cry." This shows the vehemence and earnestness of the petitioner ; he is no mere talker, he weeps and laments. Who can resist a cry ? A real hearty, bitter, piteous cry, might almost melt a rock, there can be no fear of its prevalence with our heavenly Father. A cry is our earliest utterance, and in many ways the most natural of human sounds ; if our prayer should like the

infant's cry be more natural than intelligent, and more earnest than elegant, it will be none the less eloquent with God. There is a mighty power in a child's cry to prevail with a parent's heart. " *Give ear unto my prayer.*" Some repetitions are not vain. The reduplication here used is neither superstition nor tautology, but is like the repeated blow of a hammer hitting the same nail on the head to fix it the more effectually, or the continued knocking of a beggar at the gate who cannot be denied an alms. " *That goeth not out of feigned lips.*" Sincerity is a *sine quâ non* in prayer. Lips of deceit are detestable to man and much more to God. In intercourse so hallowed as that of prayer, hypocrisy even in the remotest degree is as fatal as it is foolish. Hypocritical piety is double iniquity. He who would feign and flatter had better try his craft with a fool like himself, for to deceive the all-seeing One is as impossible as to take the moon in a net, or to lead the sun into a snare. He who would deceive God is himself already most grossly deceived. Our sincerity in prayer has no merit in it, any more than the earnestness of a mendicant in the street ; but at the same time the Lord has regard to it, through Jesus, and will not long refuse his ear to an honest and fervent petitioner.

2. " *Let my sentence come forth from thy presence.*" The Psalmist has now grown bold by the strengthening influence of prayer, and he now entreats the Judge of all the earth to give sentence upon his case. He had been libelled, basely and maliciously libelled ; and having brought his action before the highest court, he, like an innocent man, has no desire to escape the enquiry, but even invites and sues for judgment. He does not ask for secrecy, but would have the result come forth to the world. He would have sentence pronounced and executed forthwith. In some matters we may venture to be as bold as this ; but except we can plead something better than our own supposed innocence, it were terrible presumption thus to challenge the judgment of a sin-hating God. With Jesus as our complete and all-glorious righteousness we need not fear, though the day of judgment should commence at once, and hell open her mouth at our feet, but might joyfully prove the truth of our hymn writer's holy boast—

> " Bold shall I stand in that great day ;
> For who ought to my charge shall lay ?
> While, through thy blood, absolved I am
> From sin's tremendous curse and shame."

" *Let thine eyes behold the things that are equal.*" Believers do not desire any other judge than God, or to be excused from judgment, or even to be judged on principles of partiality. No ; our hope does not lie in the prospect of favouritism from God, and the consequent suspension of his law ; we expect to be judged on the same principles as other men, and through the blood and righteousness of our Redeemer we shall pass the ordeal unscathed. The Lord will weigh us in the scales of justice fairly and justly ; he will not use false weights to permit us to escape, but with the sternest equity those balances will be used upon us as well as upon others ; and with our blessed Lord Jesus as our all in all we tremble not, for we shall not be found wanting. In David's case, he felt his cause to be so right that he simply desired the Divine eyes to rest upon the matter, and he was confident that equity would give him all that he needed.

3. " *Thou hast proved mine heart.*" Like Peter, David uses the argument, " Thou knowest all things, thou knowest that I love thee." It is a most assuring thing to be able to appeal at once to the Lord, and call upon our Judge to be a witness for our defence. " Beloved, if our heart condemn us not, then have we confidence towards God." " *Thou hast visited me in the night.*" As if he had said, " Lord, thou hast entered my house at all hours ; and thou hast seen me when no one else was nigh ; thou hast come upon me unawares and marked my unrestrained actions, and thou knowest whether or no I am guilty of the crimes laid at my door." Happy man who can thus remember the omniscient eye, and the omnipresent visitor, and find comfort in the remembrance. We hope we have had our midnight visits from our Lord, and truly they are sweet ; so sweet that the recollection of them sets us longing for more of such condescending communings. Lord, if, indeed, we had been hypocrites, should we have had such fellowship, or feel such hungerings after a renewal of it ? " *Thou hast tried me, and shalt find nothing.*" Surely the Psalmist means nothing hypocritical or wicked in the sense in which his slanderers accused him ; for if the Lord should put the best of his people into the crucible, the dross would be a fearful sight, and would make penitence

open her sluices wide. Assayers very soon detect the presence of alloy, and when the chief of all assayers shall, at the last, say of us that he has found nothing, it will be a glorious hour indeed—" They are without fault before the throne of God." Even here, as viewed in our covenant Head, the Lord sees no sin in Jacob, nor perverseness in Israel; even the all-detecting glance of Omniscience can see no flaw where the great Substitute covers all with beauty and perfection. *" I am purposed that my mouth shall not transgress."* Oh those sad lips of ours! we had need purpose to purpose if we would keep them from exceeding their bounds. The number of diseases of the tongue is as many as the diseases of all the rest of the man put together, and they are more inveterate. Hands and feet one may bind, but who can fetter the lips? iron bands may hold a madman, but what chains can restrain the tongue? It needs more than a purpose to keep this nimble offender within its proper range. Lion-taming and serpent-charming are not to be mentioned in the same day as tongue-taming, for the tongue can no man tame. Those who have to smart from the falsehoods of others should be the more jealous over themselves; perhaps this led the Psalmist to register this holy resolution; and, moreover, he intended thereby to aver that if he had said too much in his own defence, it was not intentional, for he desired in all respects to tune his lips to the sweet and simple music of truth. Nothwithstanding all this David was slandered, as if to show us that the purest innocence will be bemired by malice. There is no sunshine without a shadow, no ripe fruit unpecked by the birds.

4. *" Concerning the works of men."* While we are in the midst of men we shall have their works thrust under our notice, and we shall be compelled to keep a corner in our diary headed " concerning the works of men." To be quite clear from the dead works of carnal humanity is the devout desire of souls who are quickened by the Holy Spirit. *" By the word of thy lips I have kept me from the paths of the destroyer."* He had kept the highway of Scripture, and not chosen the bye-paths of malice. We should soon imitate the example of the worst of men if the grace of God did not use the Word of God as the great preservative from evil. The paths of the destroyer have often tempted us; we have been prompted to become destroyers too, when we have been sorely provoked, and resentment has grown warm; but we have remembered the example of our Lord, who would not call fire from heaven upon his enemies, but meekly prayed, " Father, forgive them." All the ways of sin are the paths of Satan,—the Apollyon or Abaddon, both of which words signify the destroyer. Foolish indeed are those who give their hearts to the old murderer, because for the time he panders to their evil desires. That heavenly Book which lies neglected on many a shelf is the only guide for those who would avoid the enticing and entangling mazes of sin; and it is the best means of preserving the youthful pilgrim from ever treading those dangerous ways. We must follow the one or the other; the Book of Life, or the way of death; the word of the Holy Spirit, or the suggestion of the Evil Spirit. David could urge as the proof of his sincerity that he had no part or lot with the ungodly in their ruinous ways. How can we venture to plead our cause with God, unless we also can wash our hands clean of all connection with the enemies of the Great King?

5 Hold up my goings in thy paths, *that* my footsteps slip not.
6 I have called upon thee, for thou wilt hear me, O God : incline thine ear unto me, *and hear* my speech.

5. Under trial it is not easy to behave ourselves aright; a candle is not easily kept alight when many envious mouths are puffing at it. In evil times prayer is peculiarly needful, and wise men resort to it at once. Plato said to one of his disciples, " When men speak ill of thee, live so that no one will believe them; " good enough advice, but he did not tell us how to carry it out. We have a precept here incorporated in an example; if we would be preserved, we must cry to the Preserver, and enlist divine support upon our side. *" Hold up my goings "*—as a careful driver holds up his horse when going down hill. We have all sorts of paces, both fast and slow, and the road is never long of one sort, but with God to hold up our goings, nothing in the pace or in the road can cast down. He who has been down once and cut his knees sadly, even to the bone, had need redouble his zeal when using this prayer; and all of us, since we are so weak on our legs through Adam's fall, had need use it every hour of the day. If a perfect father fell, how shall an imperfect son dare to boast? *" In thy paths."* Forsaking Satan's paths,

he prayed to be upheld in God's paths. We cannot keep *from* evil without keeping *to* good. If the bushel be not full of wheat, it may soon be once more full of chaff. In all the appointed ordinances and duties of our most holy faith, may the Lord enable us to run through his upholding grace! " *That my footsteps slip not.*" What! slip in God's ways? Yes, the road is good, but our feet are evil, and therefore slip, even on the King's highway. Who wonders if carnal men slide and fall in ways of their own choosing, which, like the vale of Siddim, are full of deadly slime-pits? One may trip over an ordinance as well as over a temptation. Jesus Christ himself is a stumbling-block to some, and the doctrines of grace have been the occasion of offence to many. Grace alone can hold up our goings in the paths of truth.

6. " *I have called upon thee, for thou wilt hear me, O God.*" Thou hast always heard me, O my Lord, and therefore I have the utmost confidence in again approaching thine altar. Experience is a blessed teacher. He who has tried the faithfulness of God in hours of need, has great boldness in laying his case before the throne. The well of Bethlehem, from which we drew such cooling draughts in years gone by, our souls long for still; nor will we leave it for the broken cisterns of earth. " *Incline thine ear unto me, and hear my speech.*" Stoop out of heaven and put thine ear to my mouth; give me thine ear all to myself, as men do when they lean over to catch every word from their friend. The Psalmist here comes back to his first prayer, and thus sets us an example of pressing our suit again and again, until we have a full assurance that we have succeeded.

7 Shew thy marvellous lovingkindness, O thou that savest by thy right hand them which put their trust *in thee* from those that rise up *against them.*

8 Keep me as the apple of the eye, hide me under the shadow of thy wings.

9 From the wicked that oppress me, *from* my deadly enemies, *who* compass me about.

10 They are inclosed in their own fat : with their mouth they speak proudly.

11 They have now compassed us in our steps : they have set their eyes bowing down to the earth ;

12 Like as a lion *that* is greedy of his prey, and as it were a young lion lurking in secret places.

7. " *Shew thy marvellous lovingkindness.*" Marvellous in its antiquity, its distinguishing character, its faithfulness, its immutability, and above all, marvellous in the wonders which it works. That marvellous grace which has redeemed us with the precious blood of God's only begotten, is here invoked to come to the rescue. That grace is sometimes hidden; the text says, " Shew it." Present enjoyments of divine love are matchless cordials to support fainting hearts. Believer, what a prayer is this! Consider it well. O Lord, shew thy marvellous lovingkindness; shew it to my intellect, and remove my ignorance; shew it to my heart, and revive my gratitude; shew it to my faith, and renew my confidence; shew it to my experience, and deliver me from all my fears. The original word here used is the same which in Psalm iv. 3 is rendered *set apart*, and it has the force of, Distinguish thy mercies, set them out, and set apart the choicest to be bestowed upon me in this hour of my severest affliction. " *O thou that savest by thy right hand them which put their trust in thee from those that rise up against them.*" The title here given to our gracious God is eminently consolatory. He is the God of salvation; it is his present and perpetual habit to save believers; he puts forth his best and most glorious strength, using his right hand of wisdom and might, to save all those, of whatsoever rank or class, who trust themselves with him. Happy faith thus to secure the omnipotent protection of heaven! Blessed God, to be thus gracious to unworthy mortals, when they have but grace to rely upon thee! The right hand of God is interposed between the saints and all harm; God is never at a loss for means; his own bare hand is enough. He works without tools as well as with them.

8. " *Keep me as the apple of the eye.*" No part of the body more precious, more tender, and more carefully guarded than the eye; and of the eye, no portion more peculiarly to be protected than the central apple, the pupil, or, as the Hebrew calls it, " the daughter of the eye." The all-wise Creator has placed the eye in a well-protected position; it stands surrounded by projecting bones like Jerusalem

encircled by mountains. Moreover, its great Author has surrounded it with many tunics of inward covering, besides the hedge of the eyebrows, the curtain of the eyelids, and the fence of the eyelashes ; and, in addition to this, he has given to every man so high a value for his eyes, and so quick an apprehension of danger, that no member of the body is more faithfully cared for than the organ of sight. Thus, Lord, keep thou me, for I trust I am one with Jesus, and so a member of his mystical body. *" Hide me under the shadow of thy wings."* Even as the parent bird completely shields her brood from evil, and meanwhile cherishes them with the warmth of her own heart, by covering them with her wings, so do thou with me, most condescending God, for I am thine offspring, and thou hast a parent's love in perfection. This last clause is in the Hebrew in the future tense, as if to show that what the writer had asked for but a moment before he was now sure would be granted to him. Confident expectation should keep pace with earnest supplication.

9. *" From the wicked that oppress me, from my deadly enemies, who compass me about."* The foes from whom David sought to be rescued were *wicked* men. It is hopeful for us when our enemies are God's enemies. They were *deadly enemies,* whom nothing but his death would satisfy. The foes of a believer's soul are mortal foes most emphatically, for they who war against our faith aim at the very life of our life. Deadly sins are deadly enemies, and what sin is there which hath not death in its bowels ? These foes *oppressed* David, they laid his spirit waste, as invading armies ravage a country, or as wild beasts desolate a land. He likens himself to a besieged city, and complains that his foes *compass him about.* It may well quicken our business upward, when all around us, every road, is blockaded by deadly foes. This is our daily position, for all around us dangers and sins are lurking. O God, do thou protect us from them all.

10. *" They are inclosed in their own fat."* Luxury and gluttony beget vainglorious fatness of heart, which shuts up its gates against all compassionate emotions and reasonable judgments. The old proverb says that full bellies make empty skulls, and it is yet more true that they frequently make empty hearts. The rankest weeds grow out of the fattest soil. Riches and self-indulgence are the fuel upon which some sins feed their flames. Pride and fulness of bread were Sodom's twin sins. (Ezek. xvi. 49.) Fed hawks forget their masters ; and the moon at its fullest is furthest from the sun. Eglon was a notable instance that a well-fed corporation is no security to life, when a sharp message comes from God, addressed to the inward vitals of the body. *" With their mouth they speak proudly."* He who adores himself will have no heart to adore the Lord. Full of selfish pleasure within his heart, the wicked man fills his mouth with boastful and arrogant expressions. Prosperity and vanity often lodge together. Woe to the fed ox when it bellows at its owner, the poleaxe is not far off.

11. *" They have now compassed us in our steps."* The fury of the ungodly is aimed not at one believer alone, but at all the band ; they have compassed *us.* All the race of the Jews were but a morsel for Haman's hungry revenge, and all because of one Mordecai. The prince of darkness hates all the saints for their Master's sake. The Lord Jesus is one of the *us,* and herein is our hope. He is the Breaker, and will clear a way for us through the hosts which environ us. The hatred of the powers of evil is continuous and energetic, for they watch every *step,* hoping that the time may come when they shall catch us by surprise. If our spiritual adversaries thus compass every step, how anxiously should we guard all our movements, lest by any means we should be betrayed into evil ! *"They have set their eyes bowing down to the earth."* Trapp wittily explains this metaphor by an allusion to a bull when about to run at his victim ; he lowers his head, looks downward, and then concentrates all his force in the dash which he makes. It most probably denotes the malicious jealousy with which the enemy watches the steps of the righteous ; as if they studied the ground on which they trod, and searched after some wrong footmark to accuse them for the past, or some stumbling-stone to cast in their future path to trip them in days to come.

12. Lions are not more greedy, nor their ways more cunning than are Satan and his helpers when engaged against the children of God. The blood of souls the adversary thirsts after, and all his strength and craft are exercised to the utmost to satisfy his detestable appetite. We are weak and foolish like sheep ; but we have a shepherd wise and strong, who knows the old lion's wiles, and is more than a match for his force ; therefore will we not fear, but rest in safety in the fold. Let

us beware, however, of our lurking foe ; and in those parts of the road were we feel most secure, let us look about us lest, peradventure, our foe should leap upon us.

13 Arise, O LORD, disappoint him, cast him down : deliver my soul from the wicked, *which is* thy sword :

14 From men *which are* thy hand, O LORD, from men of the world, *which have* their portion in *this* life, and whose belly thou fillest with thy hid *treasure :* they are full of children, and leave the rest of their *substance* to their babes.

13. *"Arise, O Lord."* The more furious the attack, the more fervent the Psalmist's prayer. His eye rests singly upon the Almighty, and he feels that God has but to rise from the seat of his patience and the work will be performed at once. Let the lion spring upon us, if Jehovah steps between we need no better defence. When God meets our foe face to face in battle, the conflict will soon be over. *"Disappoint him."* Be beforehand with him, outwit and outrun him. Appoint it otherwise than he has appointed, and so disappoint him. *"Cast him down."* Prostrate him. Make him sink upon his knees. Make him bow as the conquered bows before the conqueror. What a glorious sight will it be to behold Satan prostrate beneath the foot of our glorious Lord ! Haste, glorious day ! *"Deliver my soul from the wicked, which is thy sword."* He recognizes the most profane and oppressive as being under the providential rule of the King of kings, and used as a sword in the divine hand. What can a sword do unless it be wielded by a hand ? No more could the wicked annoy us, unless the Lord permitted them so to do. Most translators are, however, agreed that this is not the correct reading, but that it should be as Calvin puts it, " Deliver my soul from the ungodly man by thy sword." Thus David contrasts the sword of the Lord with human aids and reliefs, and rests assured that he is safe enough under the patronage of heaven.

14. Almost every word of this verse has furnished matter for discussion to scholars, for it is very obscure. We will, therefore, rest content with the common version, rather than distract the reader with divers translations. " *From men which are thy hand."* Having styled the ungodly a sword in his Father's hand, he now likens them to that hand itself, to set forth his conviction that God could as easily remove their violence as a man moves his own hand. He will never slay his child with his own hand. " *From men of the world,"* mere earthworms ; not men of the world to come, but mere dwellers in this narrow sphere of mortality ; having no hopes or wishes beyond the ground on which they tread. " *Which have their portion in this life."* Like the prodigal, they have their portion, and are not content to wait their Father's time. Like Passion in the " Pilgrim's Progress," they have their best things first, and revel during their little hour. Luther was always afraid lest he should have his portion here, and therefore frequently gave away sums of money which had been presented to him. We cannot have earth and heaven too for our choice and portion ; wise men choose that which will last the longest. " *Whose belly thou fillest with thy hid treasure."* Their sensual appetite gets the gain which it craved for. God gives to these swine the husks which they hunger for. A generous man does not deny dogs their bones ; and our generous God gives even his enemies enough to fill them, if they were not so unreasonable as never to be content. Gold and silver which are locked up in the dark treasuries of the earth are given to the wicked liberally, and they therefore roll in all manner of carnal delights. Every dog has his day, and they have theirs, and a bright summer's day it seems ; but ah ! how soon it ends in night ! " *They are full of children."* This was their fondest hope, that a race from their loins would prolong their names far down the page of history, and God has granted them this also ; so that they have all that heart can wish. What enviable creatures they seem, but it is only seeming ! " *They are full of children, and leave the rest of their substance to their babes."* They were fat housekeepers, and yet leave no lean wills. Living and dying they lacked for nothing but grace, and alas ! that lack spoils everything. They had a fair portion within the little circle of time, but eternity entered not into their calculations. They were penny wise, but pound foolish ; they remembered the present, and forgot the future ; they fought for the shell, and lost the kernel. How fine a description have we here of many a successful merchant, or popular statesman ; and it is, at first sight, very showy and tempting, but in contrast with the glories of the world to come, what are these paltry molehill

joys. Self, self, self, all these joys begin and end in basest selfishness; but oh, our God, how rich are those who begin and end in thee! From all the contamination and injury which association with wordly men is sure to bring us, deliver thou us, O God!

15 As for me, I will behold thy face in righteousness: I shall be satisfied, when I awake, with thy likeness.

15. *"As for me."* " I neither envy nor covet these men's happiness, but partly have and partly hope for a far better." To behold God's face and to be changed by that vision into his image, so as to partake in his righteousness, this is my noble ambition; and in the prospect of this I cheerfully waive all my present enjoyments. My satisfaction is to come; I do not look for it as yet. I shall sleep awhile, but I shall wake at the sound of the trumpet; wake to everlasting joy, because I arise in thy likeness, O my God and King! Glimpses of glory good men have here below to stay their sacred hunger, but the full feast awaits them in the upper skies. Compared with this deep, ineffable, eternal fulness of delight, the joys of the worldling are as a glowworm to the sun, or the drop of a bucket to the ocean.

EXPLANATORY NOTES AND QUAINT SAYINGS.

Title.—" *A prayer of David.*" Since many of the Psalms consist of *prayers*, the question may be asked why such an inscription more especially belongs to this. But though the others contain divers prayers mixed with other matters, this is a supplication through its whole course.—*The Venerable Bede*, 672—735.

Verse 1.—" *Hear . . . attend . . . give ear.*" This petition repeated thrice, indicates a great power of feeling and many tears; because the craft of the ungodly, in truth, grieves and afflicts the spiritual man more than their power and violence, for we can get a knowledge of open force and violence, and, when we see the danger, can in some way guard against it.—*Martin Luther.*

Verse 1.—" *That goeth not out of feigned lips.*"—There are such things as " *feigned lips;* " a contradiction between the heart and the tongue, a clamour in the voice and scoffing in the soul, a crying to God, " Thou art my father, the guide of my youth; " and yet speaking and doing evil to the utmost of our power (Jer. iii. 4, 5), as if God could be imposed upon by fawning pretences, and, like old Isaac, take Jacob for Esau, and be cozened by the smell of his garments; as if he could not discern the negro heart under an angel's garb. . . . This is an unworthy conceit of God, to fancy that we can satisfy for inward sins, and avert approaching judgments by external offerings, by a loud voice, with a false heart, as if God (like children), would be pleased with the glittering of an empty shell, or the rattling of stones, the chinking of money, a mere voice, and crying without inward frames and intentions of service.—*Stephen Charnock.*

Verse 1.—" *Not out of feigned lips.*" It is observable, that the eagle soareth on high, little intending to fly to heaven, but to gain her prey; and so it is that many do carry a great deal of seeming devotion in lifting up their eyes towards heaven; but they do it only to accomplish with more ease, safety, and applause their wicked and damnable designs here on earth; such as without are Catos, within Neros; hear them, no man better; search and try them, no man worse; they have Jacob's voice, but Esau's hands; they profess like saints, but practise little Satans; they have their long prayers, but short prayings; they are like apothecaries' gallipots—having without the title of some excellent preservative, but within they are full of deadly poison; counterfeit holiness is their cloak for all manner of villanies, and the midwife to bring forth all their devilish designs. —*Peter Bales, in Spencer's " Things New and Old."*

Verse 1.—" *Not out of feigned lips.*" Not only a righteous cause, but a righteous prayer are urged as motives why God should hear. Calvin remarks on the importance of joining prayer to the testimony of a good conscience, lest we defraud God of his honour by not committing all judgment to him.—*J. J. Stewart Perowne.*

Verse 1.—Though thy prayers be never so well framed in regard of words, and reverently performed as to thy external gestures ; yet all is nothing, *if thy heart be not in the duty.* For prayer is not a work of the head, or hand, or eyes only, but chiefly a work of the heart, and therefore called in Scripture, the " pouring out of the soul " (1 Sam. i. 15) ; and the " pouring out of the heart." Psalm lxii. 8. And, indeed, the very soul of prayer lieth in the pouring out of the soul before the Lord. Whensoever, therefore, thou drawest near unto God in prayer, let it be with thine heart and soul, otherwise thou canst have no assurance of audience, and acceptance ; for as Cyprian speaketh, *Quomodo te audiri a Deo postulas,* etc. How canst thou expect the Lord should hear thee, when thou hearest not thyself ? or that he should regard thy prayers, when thou regardest not what thou prayest ? Certainly that prayer reacheth not the heart of God, which reacheth not our own.—*Thomas Gouge,* 1605—1681.

Verse 2.—David appeals unto God to judge the righteousness of his heart to-wards Saul—"*Let my sentence come forth from thy presence.*" From Saul and his courtiers there comes a hard sentence ; they call me traitor, they call me rebel ; but, Lord, leave me not unto their sentence, "*Let my sentence come from thy presence ;* " that I know will be another sentence than what cometh from them, for thou hast proved me, and tried me, and findest nothing in me.—*Jeremiah Burroughs.*

Verse 3.—" *Thou hast proved mine heart :* "—

What ! take it at adventure, and not try
What metal it is made of ? No, not I.
  Should I now lightly let it pass,
Take sullen lead for silver, sounding brass,
  Instead of solid gold, alas !
What would become of it in the great day
Of making jewels, 'twould be cast away.

The heart thou giv'st me must be such a one,
As is the same throughout. I will have none
  But that which will abide the fire.
'Tis not a glitt'ring outside I desire,
  Whose seeming shows do soon expire :
But real worth within, which neither dross,
Nor base alloys, make subject unto loss.

If, in the composition of thine heart,
A stubborn, steely wilfulness have part,
  That will not bow and bend to me,
Save only in a mere formality
  Of tinsel-trimm'd hypocrisy,
I care not for it, though it show as fair
As the first blush of the sun-gilded air.

The heart that in my furnace will not melt,
When it the glowing heat thereof hath felt,
  Turn liquid, and dissolve in tears
Of true repentance for its faults, that hears
  My threat'ning voice, and never fears,
Is not an heart worth having. If it be
An heart of stone, 'tis not an heart for me.

The heart, that, cast into my furnace, spits
And sparkles in my face, falls into fits
  Of discontented grudging, whines
When it is broken of its will, repines
  At the least suffering, declines
My fatherly correction, is an heart
On which I care not to bestow mine art.

   *   *   *   *   *

The heart that vapours out itself in smoke.
And with these cloudy shadows thinks to cloke
  Its empty nakedness, how much
Soever thou esteemest, it is such
  As never will endure my touch.

I'll bring it to my furnace, and there see
What it will prove, what it is like to be.
If it be gold, it will be sure
The hottest fire that can be to endure.
And I shall draw it out more pure.
Affliction may refine, but cannot waste
That heart wherein my love is fixed fast.

Francis Quarles.

Verse 3.—" *Thou hast visited me in the night,*" etc. In the night the soul is free from business with the world, and therefore freest for business with God; and then did God prove and visit David, that is, examine and sift him, by calling to his mind all his ways and works in former passages; and the issue of this trial was *he found nothing;* not that his soul was empty of good things, or that there was nothing evil in him; but God, upon examination, found nothing of that evil in him which some men suspected him of; namely, either any ill will or evil design against Saul, in reference to whom he called his cause a righteous cause, or " *the right*" (verse 1); " Hear the right, O Lord."—*Joseph Caryl.*

Verse 3 (third clause, New Translation).—" *Thou hast smelted me, and found in me no dross.*" A metaphor taken from the smelting of metals to purify them from extraneous matter.—*Geddes.*

Verse 3.—" *Proved . . . visited in the night . . . tried.*" Tribulation, whereby, when examined, I was found righteous, is called not only night, in that it is wont to disturb with fear, but fire in that it actually burns.—*Augustine.*

Verse 3.—" *I am purposed that my mouth shall not transgress.*"—Wherefore, if thou be upon a mountain, look not backward again unto Sodom as Lot's wife did; if thou be within the ark, fly not out again into the world as Noah's crow did; if thou be well washed, return not again to the mire as the hog doth; if thou be clean, run not again to thy filth, as the dog doth; if thou be going towards the land of Canaan, think not on the flesh-pots of Egypt; if thou be marching against the host of Midian, drink not of the waters of Harod; if thou be upon the housetop, come not down; if thou have set thy hand to the plough, look not behind thee; remember not those vices which are behind thee.—*Thomas Playfere.*

Verses 3, 4, 5.—Where there is true grace, there is hatred of all sin, for hatred is πρὸς τὸ γένος. Can a man be resolved to commit what he hates? No, for his inward aversion would secure him more against it than all outward obstacles. As this inward purpose of a good man is against all sin, so more particularly against that which doth so easily beset him. David seems in several places to be naturally inclined to lying, but he takes up a particular resolution against it: (verse 3), " *I am purposed that my mouth shall not transgress;*" זמתי—I have contrived to waylay and intercept the sin of lying when it hath an occasion to approach me. A good man hath not only purposes, but he endeavours to fasten and strengthen those purposes by prayer; so David (verse 5), " *Hold up my goings in thy paths, that my footsteps slip not.*" He strengthens himself by stirring up a liveliness in duty, and by avoiding occasions of sin; (verse 4), " *I have kept me from the paths of the destroyer;* " whereas, a wicked man neither steps out of the way of temptation, nor steps up to God for strength against it.—*Stephen Charnock.*

Verse 4.—" *Concerning the works of men, by the word of thy lips I have kept me from the paths of the destroyer:* " as if he had said, Would you know how it comes to pass that I escape those ungodly works and practices which men ordinarily take liberty to do? I must ascribe it to the good word of God; it is this I consult with, and by it I am kept from those foul ways whereinto others, that make no use of the word for their defence, are carried by Satan the destroyer. Can we go against sin and Satan with a better weapon than Christ used to vanquish the tempter with? And, certainly, Christ did it to set us an example how we should come armed into the field against them; for Christ could with one beam shot from his Deity (if he had pleased to exert it), have as easily laid the bold fiend at his foot, as afterward he did them that came to attack him; but he chose rather to conceal the majesty of his Divinity, and let Satan come up closer to him, that so he might confound him with the word, and thereby give him a proof of that sword of his saints, which he was to leave them for their defence against the same enemy. The devil is set out by the leviathan (Isaiah xxvii. 1), him God threatens to punish with his strong sword; alluding to that great fish, the whale, which fears no fish like the sword-fish, by whom this great devourer of all other fish is so often killed; for, receiving one prick from his sword, he hasteneth to the shore, and beats himself against it till he dies. Thus the devil, the great devourer of souls, who sports himself in the sea of this world, as the leviathan in the waters, and swallows the greatest part of mankind without any power to make resistance against him, is himself vanquished by the word. When he has to do with a saint armed with this sword, and instructed how to use this weapon, he then, and not till then, meets his match.—*William Gurnall.*

Verse 4.—"*By the word of thy lips,*" etc. It is a great relief against temptations to have the word ready. The word is called, "The sword of the Spirit," Eph. vi. 17. In spiritual conflicts there is none like to that. Those that ride abroad in time of danger, will not be without a sword. We are in danger, and had need handle the sword of the Spirit. The more ready the Scripture is with us, the greater advantage in our conflicts and temptations. When the devil came to assault Christ, he had Scripture ready for him, whereby he overcame the tempter. The door is barred upon Satan, and he cannot find such easy entrance when the word is hid in our hearts, and made use of pertinently. "I write unto you, young men, because ye are strong." Where lies their strength? "And the word of God abideth in you, and ye have overcome the wicked one." 1 John ii. 14. Oh, it is a great advantage when we have the word not only by us, but in us, engrafted in the heart; when it is present with us, we are more able to resist the assaults of Satan. Either a man forgets the word, or hath lost his affection to it, before he can be drawn to sin.—*Thomas Manton.*

Verse 5.—"*Hold up my goings in thy paths, that my footsteps slip not.*" Lord, whatsoever the wrath of Saul be against me, yet let neither that, nor any other thing put me out of thy way, but keep my heart close unto thee, and keep my paths in thy way; let not my footsteps so much as slide from thee, for, Lord, they watch for my halting; if they can find but the least slip from me, they take advantage of it to the utmost; and I am a poor and a weak creature, therefore Lord help me, that my footsteps may not slide.—*Jeremiah Burroughs.*

Verse 5.—"*Hold up my goings in thy paths, that my footsteps slip not.*" As a stone cast up into the air cannot go any higher, neither yet there abide when the power of the hurler ceaseth to drive it; even so, seeing our corrupt nature can go downward only, and the devil, the world, and the flesh, driveth to the same way; how can we proceed further in virtue, or stand therein, when we are tempted, if our merciful and good God do not by his Holy Spirit, from time to time, guide and govern us?—*Robert Cawdray.*

Verse 5.—"*Hold up my goings in thy paths, that my footsteps slip not.*" Lord, hold me up, that I may hold out. Thou hast set the crown at the end of the race; let me run the race, that I may wear the crown. It was Beza's prayer, and let it be ours, "Lord, perfect what thou hast begun in me, that I may not suffer shipwreck when I am almost at the haven."—*Thomas Watson.*

Verse 5.—In fierce assaults and strong temptations, when Satan layeth siege to the soul, shooting his fiery darts, and using stratagems of policy, joining his endeavours with our corruptions, as wind with tide, then we have cause to pray as David, "*Hold up my goings in thy paths, that my footsteps slip not.*" The apostle also found he had need of help from heaven when he was assaulted, and therefore he prayed "*thrice,*" that the thing that he feared might depart from him. 2 Cor. xii. Christ hath taught us to pray daily, "Lead us not into temptation," for it is dangerous; and then temptations are most dangerous, when, 1. *Most suitable*—when Satan joins with our disposition or constitution; 2. *Continual;* 3. When *opportunity* and power is greatest.—*Joseph Symonds.*

Verse 6.—"*I have called upon thee, for thou wilt hear me.*" I have cried, says the Psalmist, because thou hast heard me. One would think he should have said contrariwise: thou hast heard me because I have cried; yet, he says, I have cried because thou hast heard me; to show that crying doth not always go before hearing with God, as it doth with us; but that God will not only hear our cry, but also hear us before we cry, and will help us.—*T. Playfere.*

Verse 6.—"*I have called upon thee,*" etc. Prayer is the best remedy in a calamity. This is indeed a true *catholicon*, a general remedy for every malady. Not like the empiric's *catholicon*, which sometimes may work, but for the most part fails, but that which upon assured evidence and constant experience hath its *probatum est ;* being that which the most wise, learned, honest, and skilful Physician that ever was, or can be, hath prescribed, even he that teacheth us how to bear what is to be borne, or how to heal and help what hath been borne.—*William Gouge,* 1575—1653.

Verse 6.—I have called upon thee formerly, therefore, Lord, hear me now. It will be a great comfort to us if trouble, when it comes, finds the wheels of prayer a-going, for then may we come with the more boldness to the throne of grace. Tradesmen are willing to oblige those that have been long their customers.—*Matthew Henry.*

Verse 8.—" *Keep me as the apple of the eye."* He prays for deliverance (verse 7), " *Show thy marvellous lovingkindness* " to me ; Lord, my straits they are marvellous, I know not what to do, whither to turn me, but my eyes are towards thee ; as straits are marvellous, so let the lovingkindness of God be marvellous towards me, and *"Keep me as the apple of thy eye."* O Lord, unto them I am but a dog, a vile creature in the eyes of Saul and those about him : but blessed be thy name, I can look up to thee, and know that I am dear unto thee *as the apple of thy eye.* All the saints of God are dear to God at all times, but the persecuted saints, they are the apple of God's eye ; if at any time they are dear to God, then especially when they are most persecuted ; now they are *the apple of his eye,* and *the apple of an eye* is weak, and little able to resist any hurt, but so much the more is the man tender of the apple of his eye. The saints are weak and shiftless for themselves, but the Lord is so much the more tender over them.—*Jeremiah Burroughs.*

Verse 8.—Does it not appear to thee to be a work of providence, that considering the weakness of the eye, he has protected it with eyelids, as with doors, which whenever there is occasion to use it are opened, and are again closed in sleep? And that it may not receive injury from the winds, he has planted on it eyelashes like a strainer ; and over the eyes has disposed the eyebrows like a penthouse, so that the sweat from the head may do no mischief.—*Socrates, in Xenophon.*

Verse 9.—" *From the wicked :* " as though he had said, They are equally enemies to thee and me ; not more opposite to me by their cruelty, than by their wickedness they are to thee. Vindicate then, at once, thyself, and deliver me."—*John Howe.*

Verse 10.—" *They are inclosed in their own fat,"* or *their fat has inclosed them ;* either their eyes, that they can hardly see out of them, or their hearts, so that they are stupid and senseless, and devoid of the fear of God ; the phrase is expressive of the multitude of their wealth, and increase of power, by which they were swelled with pride and vanity, and neither feared God nor regarded man ; so the Targum paraphrases it, " their riches are multiplied, their fat covers them."—*John Gill.*

Verse 10.—" *They are inclosed in their own fat."* Their worldly prosperity puffeth them up, and makes them insensible and obdurate against all reason and just fear ; and the Scripture doth use this term of a fattened heart in this sense, because that the fat of man hath no feeling in it, and those that are very fat are less subject to the passion of fear.—*John Diodati.*

Verse 10.—" *They are inclosed in their own fat."* To say a man is fat, often means he is very proud. Of one who speaks pompously it is said, " What can we do ? *tassi kullap ināl,"* that is, " from the fat of his flesh he declares himself." " Oh, the fat of his mouth ! how largely he talks ! " " Take care, fellow ! or I will restrain the fat of thy mouth."—*J. Roberts, in " Oriental Illustrations :* " 1844.

Verse 11.—" *They have now compassed us in our steps : they have set their eyes bowing down to the earth.* A man who has people watching him to find out a cause for accusation against him to the king, or to great men, says, " Yes, they are around my legs and my feet ; their eyes are always open ; they are ever watching my " *suvadu,"* " steps ; " that is, they are looking for the impress or footsteps in the earth. For this purpose the eyes of the enemies of David were " *bowing down to the earth."*—*Joseph Roberts.*

Verse 11.—" *They have now compassed us in our steps."* Like those who destroy game by battue, and so make a ring around their prey from which their victims cannot escape.—*C. H. S.*

Verse 11.—" *They have set their eyes bowing down to the earth."* The allusion

probably is to the huntsman tracing the footmarks of the animal he pursues.—
Religious Tract Society's Commentary.

Verse 11.—" *They have set their eyes bowing to the earth.*" It is an allusion, as
I conceive, to hunters, who go poring upon the ground to prick the hare, or to find
the print of the hare's claw, when the hounds are at a loss, and can make nothing of
it by the scent.—*Joseph Caryl.*

Verse 12.—" *Like a lion,*" etc. In " *Paradise Lost,*" we have a fine poetical
conception of the arch enemy prowling around our first parents when he first beheld
their happiness, and resolved to ruin them.

> ———— About them round
> A lion now, he stalks with fiery glare ;
> Then, as a tiger, who by chance hath spied
> In some purlieu, two gentle fawns at play,
> Straight crouches close, then rising, changes oft
> His couchant watch, as one who chose his ground,
> Whence rushing he might surest seize them both,
> Grip'd in each paw.
>
> > *John Milton.*

Verse 12.—We were consulting as to the best means of getting at a rhinoceros
cow which we saw standing at some distance under a tree, when a troop of impalas
came charging down, with a fine old lioness after them. We went and saw her
lying down, but so flat to the ground, head and all, that no man could shoot with
any certainty ; and she never for a moment took her eyes from us. When we
got up to her, she was lying down flat as a plate to the ground ; but her head might
have been on a pivot, as her watchful eye glared on us all round, without appearing
to move her body, as we decreased the circle, in the hopes she would stand up and
give us a fair chance of a shot behind the shoulder. . . . I looked for a tree to climb
up, near enough to make tolerably sure of my shot, and was just getting up one,
when the lioness made off.—*William Charles Baldwin, F.R.G.S., in " African
Hunting,"* 1863.

Verse 13.—" *The wicked, which is thy sword.*"—The devil and his instruments
both are God's instruments, therefore " *the wicked* " are called his " *sword,*" his
" *axe* " (Psalm xvii. 13 ; Isaiah x. 15) ; now let God alone to wield the one, and
handle the other. He is but a bungler that hurts and hackles his own legs with
his own axe ; which God should do if his children should be the worse for Satan's
temptations. Let the devil choose his way, God is a match for him at every weapon.
If he will try it by force of arms, and assaults the saints by persecution, as the " Lord
of hosts " he will oppose him. If by policy and subtlety, he is ready there also.
The devil and his whole council are but fools to God ; nay, their wisdom foolishness.—
William Gurnall.

Verses 13, 14.—" *Thy sword. . . . thy hand.*" Thou canst as easily command
and manage them, as a man may wield his sword, or move his hand. Wilt thou
suffer thine own sword, thine own hand, to destroy thine own servant ?—*J. Howe.*

Verse 14 (*first clause*).—How wonderful are the dispensations of the providence
of God, who can use even the wicked to promote the present happiness and the
final salvation of his saints !—*J. Edwards, M.A.,* 1856.

Verse 14.—" *Men of the world, which have their portion in this life.*" Time and
this lower world, bound all their hopes and fears. They have no serious believing
apprehensions of anything beyond this present life ; therefore, have nothing to
withhold them from the most injurious violence, if thou withhold them not ; men
that believe not another world, are the ready actors of any imaginable mischiefs
and tragedies in this.—*John Howe.*

Verse 14.—" *Men which are thy hand,*" etc. What shall we say then ? Because
God maketh use of thy sins, art thou excused ? Is not thine evil evil, because he
picketh good out of it ? Deceive not thyself therein. When thou hast done such
service to thy Master and Maker, though seven and seven years, as Jacob did service
to Laban, thou shalt lose thy wages and thy thanks too. Oh, well were thou if
thou didst but lose, for thou shalt also gain a sorrowful advantage. It is unprofitable,
nay, miserable service which thou hast thus bestowed. Babylon shall be the hammer
of the Lord a long time to bruise the nations, himself afterwards bruised ; Asshur

his rod to scourge his people, but Asshur shall be more scourged. These hammers, rods, axes, saws, other instruments, when they have done their offices, which they never meant, shall be thrown themselves into the fire, and burnt to ashes. Satan did service to God, it cannot be denied, in the afflicting of Job, winnowing of Peter, buffeting of Paul, executing of Judas, and God did a work in all these, either to prove patience, or to confirm faith, or to try strength, or to commend justice; yet is Satan "reserved in chains, under darkness, to the retribution of the great day." Judas did service to God, in getting honour to his blessed name for the redemption of mankind, whilst the world endureth, yet was his wages an alder-tree to hang himself upon, and which is worse, he hangeth in hell for eternal generations. He had his wages, and lost his wages. That which the priest gave him, he lost, and lost his apostleship, but gained the recompense of everlasting unhappiness, and lies in the lowest lake, for the worm and death to gnaw upon without ceasing. *John King.*

Verse 14.—" *Thy hand.*" The hand of God, his correcting or cherishing hand, sometimes is an immediate, and sometimes a mediate hand. Sometimes it is immediate, when God by himself doth chasten, or punish, or afflict, when no second cause doth appear or intervene. So it may seem Satan means, when he saith (Job i. 11), " *Put forth thy hand,*" that is, do it thine own self, let no other have the handling of Job but thyself. God doth send such immediate afflictions; a man is afflicted in his body, in his estate, and many other ways, and he cannot find anything in the creature whence it should come; it is an immediate stroke of God, he cannot see how, or which way, or at what door this evil came in upon him; therefore it is called a creating of evil. Isaiah xlv. 7. " I make peace, and create evil." Now creation is out of nothing, there is nothing out of which it is wrought. So many times God bringeth evil upon a people or person when there is no appearance of second causes, no matter out of which it is made, but it comes as a creature, formed by the only hand of God. Sometimes likewise it is called God's hand, when it is the hand of a creature; it is God's hand in a creature's hand; God's hand when it is the hand of wicked men, God's hand when it is Satan's hand. So that place is translated (Psalm xvii. 13, 14), " *Deliver my soul from the wicked, which is thy sword: from men which are thy hand:*" so that " *thy hand*" may be understood of an instrument; Satan himself is God's hand to punish in that sense, as wicked men here are said to be God's hand: " *from men which are thy hand,*" though there be other readings of that place; some read it, *deliver me from men by thy hand;* and others, *deliver me from men of thy hand;* but our translation may very well carry the sense of the original in it, " *from men which are thy hand;*" as Nebuchadrezzar, that wicked king, is called *God's servant* (Jer. xliii. 10), " I will send and take Nebuchadrezzar my servant:" God speaks of him as his servant, or as his *hand* in the thing.—*Joseph Caryl.*

Verse 14.—" *Men of the world, which have their portion in this life.*" The large portion of the wicked in the things of this world, may tell the righteous of how little value this is, in the account of God; in that these things are often given to his enemies plentifully, when denied in such a measure to his children. Now this cannot be because he loves or favours his enemies most; but because these lower things, given them in what degree soever, are so mean in his account, as that his chosen may learn by his distribution of them, to regard them as he does; namely, as no part of their felicity, but as common favours to all his creatures, good or bad, enemies or friends.—*Daniel Wilcox.*

Verse 14.—" *Men which have their portion in this life.*" God gives wicked men a portion here to show unto them what little good there is in all these things, and to show the world what little good there is in all the things that are here below in the world. Certainly if they were much good they should never have them: it is an argument there is no great excellency in the strength of body, for an ox hath it more than you; an argument there is no great excellency in agility of body, for a dog hath it more than you; an argument no great excellency in gay clothes, for a peacock hath them more than you; an argument there is not any great excellency in gold and silver, for the Indians that know not God have them more than you; and if these things had any great worth in them, certainly God would never give them to wicked men—a certain argument. As it is an argument there is no great evil in affliction in this world, because that the saints are so much afflicted; so no great argument there is any great good in this world, for the wicked they enjoy so much of it. Luther hath such an expression as this in his comment upon Genesis, saith he, " The Turkish empire, as great as it is, is but a crumb, that the Master of the family, that God, casts to dogs : " the whole Turkish empire, such an esteem had Luther of it ; and indeed it is no more. All the things of the world, God in giving of them to Turks and wicked ones, his enemies, shows there is not much excellency and good in them : God therefore will cast them promiscuously up and down in the world, because he looks upon them as worthless things ; God doth not so much regard whether men be prepared to give him the glory of them, yea or no, they shall have them; however he is content to venture them. Indeed, when God comes unto his choice mercies in Christ, there he looks to have glory from them, and he doth never give them to any, but first he prepares them, that they may give him the glory of those mercies. But it is otherwise with others ; us, suppose you see a man gathering of crabs, although swine be under the tree, he cares not much to drive them away ; they are but crabs, let them have them ; but if he were gathering any choice and precious fruit, if any swine should come under, he drives them away. As for outward things, crabs, the Lord suffers the swine of the world to come grunting and take them up ; but when he comes to his choice mercies in his Christ, there he makes a distinction. Oh, this is precious fruit ! A blacksmith that is working upon iron, though a great many cinders and little bits of iron fly up and down, he regards them not ; but a goldsmith that is working upon gold, he preserves every rag, and every dust of gold ; and a lapidary that is working upon precious stones, every little bit he will be sure to preserve ; a carpenter that is only hewing of timber, he regards it not much if chips fly up and down ; but it is not so with a lapidary. So these outward things are but as the chips and cinders, and such kind of things as those are, and therefore God ever gives a portion to wicked men out of them.—*Jeremiah Burroughs.*

Verse 14.—" *Men which have their portion in this life.*" I have read of Gregory, that being advanced to preferment, professed that there was no Scripture that went so to his heart, that struck such a trembling into his spirit, that daunted him so much, as this Scripture did :—" Here you have your reward, son ; in your life-time you have had your pleasure." Oh, this was a dreadful Scripture that sounded in his ears continually, as Hierom speaks of that Scripture, " Arise, ye dead, and come to judgment : " night and day he thought that Scripture sounded in his ears ; so Gregory :—" Here you have your reward ; in this life you have had your pleasure." This was the Scripture that night and day sounded in his ears. O that it might please God to assist so far, to speak out of this Scripture to you, that I might make this Scripture ring in your ears even when you lie upon your beds, after the sermon is done ; that yet you may think this Scripture rings in your ears : "*Men of this world, who have their portion in this life.*"—*Jeremiah Burroughs.*

Verse 14.—" *Which have their portion in this life.*" The earth and the commodities thereof God distributeth without respect of persons, even to them that are his children by creation only, and not by adoption. But yet there is a difference between the prosperity of the one and the other ; for the one is but with anxiety of heart (even in laughter their heart is heavy) ; the others' is with cheerfulness and joy in the Spirit ; the one's is a pledge of the greater preferment in the world to come, the others' is their *whole* portion, and as if God should say, " Let them take *that* and look for no more." The one's is with the blessing of the people, who wish they had more ; the others' with their curse and hatred, who are grieved that they have so much."—*Miles Smith.*

Verse 14.—" *Their portion in this life.*" The good man's *best*, and the bad man's worst, lie in *shall be's* (Isaiah iii. 10, 11), in reversion. Here Dives had nothing but his " good things," but hereafter he had no good thing. Here Lazarus had his " evil things," but afterwards no evil thing. The good man when he dies, takes his leave of, and departs from, all evil ; and the evil man when he dies, takes his leave of, and departs from, all his goods, which was all the good he had. " Now he is comforted, but thou art tormented." Luke xvi. 25. Oh ! 'tis a sad thing to have one's *portion of good* only in this life.—*Ralph Venning's* " *Helps to Piety,*" 1620—1673.

Verse 14.—" *This life.*" There is yet another thing to be seen far more monstrous in this creature ; that whereas he is endued with reason and counsel, and knoweth that this life is like unto a shadow, to a dream, to a tale that is told, to a watch in the night, to smoke, to chaff which the wind scattereth, to a water-bubble, and such-like fading things ; and that life to come shall never have end ; he yet neverthe-less setteth his whole mind most carefully upon this present life, which is to-day, and to-morrow is not ; but of the life which is everlasting he doth not so much as think. If this be not a monster, I know not what may be called monstrous.— *Thomas Tymme.*

Verse 14.—What wicked men possess of this world is all that ever they can hope for : why should we grudge them filled bags, or swelling titles ! it is their whole portion ; they now receive their good things. Hast thou food and clothing ? that is children's fare ; envy not ungodly men, who flaunt it in the gallantry of the world : they have more than you ; but it is all they are like to have ; the Psalmist gives us an account of their estate. They are *the men of* this *world, which have their portion in this life, and whose bellies God filleth with his hid treasure.* Whereas thou, O Christian, who possessest nothing, art heir-apparent of heaven, co-heir with Jesus Christ, who is the heir of all things, and hast an infinite mass of riches laid up for thee ; so great and infinite, that all the stars of heaven are too few to account it by : you have no reason to complain of being kept short ; for all that God hath is yours, whether prosperity or adversity, life or death, all is yours. What God gives is for your comfort ; what he denies or takes away is for your trial : it is for the increase of those graces which are far more gracious than any temporal enjoyment. If, by seeing wicked and ungodly men flow in wealth and ease, when thou art forced to struggle against the inconveniences and difficulties of a poor estate, thou hast learnt a holy contempt and disdain of the world, believe it, God hath herein given thee more than if he had given thee the world itself.—*Ezekiel Hopkins.*

Verse 14.—To show that wicked men have often the greatest *portion in this world,* I need not speak much ; the experience of all ages since the beginning of the world confirms it, your own observation, I believe, can seal to it ; however, Scripture abundantly evinces it. The first *murderer* that ever was, carries possession in his very name : *Cain* signifies so much. Gen. iv. 8. Go on in the whole series of Scripture, and you shall find Joseph persecuted by his brethren ; Esau (as Rivet observes on Gen. xxxii.), advanced in the world for a time far above Jacob ; go on, and you find the Israelites, God's peculiar, in captivity, and Pharaoh upon the throne ; Saul ruling, and David in a cave, or in a wilderness ; Job upon the dunghill ; Jeremy in the dungeon ; Daniel in the den, and the children in the furnace, and Nebuchadnezzar on the throne. In the New Testament you have Felix on the bench, Paul at the bar ; Dives in the palace, Lazarus at his gate (Luke xvi. 19) ; he clothed in purple, Lazarus in rags and overspread with sores ; he banqueted and fared deliciously every day, the other desired but the crumbs from the table, and could not have them ; Dives beset with his rich and stately attendance, Lazarus hath no other society but the dogs which came to lick his sores ; all which Austin and Tertullian against Marcion (lib. 4), conceive to be a true history of what was really acted, though others think it parabolical. Job tells us that " the tabernacles of robbers " sometimes " prosper " (Job xii. 6), which prosperity he at large describes (chap. xxi. from verses 7 to 14) ; exalted in " *power,*" verse 7 ; multiplied in their *posterity,* verses 8, 11 ; *safe at home,* verse 9 ; *increased abroad,* verse 10 ; have their fill of *pleasure,* verse 12, and *wealth* at will, verse 13. David speaks his own experience of this. Psalm xxxvii. 35 ; lxxiii. 7. So in the text, they enjoy not only common favours, as air to breathe in, earth to walk on ; their bellies are filled with his " *hid treasure,*" and that not for themselves only, but for their posterity too ; they " *leave the rest of their substance to their babes ;* " in a word, " *they have their portion in this life.*"—*John Frost,* 1657.

Verse 14.—A master or lord pays his *servant* his present wages, while he cuts his *son* short in his allowance during his nonage, that he may learn to depend upon his father for the inheritance. Thus doth God, the great Lord of all, deal with his *slaves,* who serve him for the hire of some temporal advantage ; he gives them their present reward and wages ; but though his goodness hath determined a better *portion* to be a reward to the piety and obedience of his *children,* yet he gives it them in reversion, little in hand, that they may learn to live upon the promise, and by faith to depend upon the goodness and faithfulness of their Father for their heavenly inheritance; that they, walking not by sight but faith (which is a Christian's work and condition here), may "not look at the things which are seen," etc. 2 Cor iv. 18. . . . This discovers that rotten foundation upon which many men build their hopes of heaven. Surely (are many ready to argue) if God did not love me he would not give me such a portion in the world. Deceive not thyself in a matter of so great concernment. Thou mayest as well say God loved Judas, because he had the bags, or Dives, because he fared deliciously, who are now roaring in hell.—*John Frost.*

Verse 14.—The word which denotes the "*belly*" may have been fixed, by the divine Spirit, to indicate the fact, that a very great proportion of the sin of worldly and depraved characters is connected with the indulgence of base and degrading lusts ; and that they abuse the very bounty of heaven, in riveting the chain of sense upon their unhappy souls. But let them remember, that their sensual idolatries will, at last, be followed up by the most fearful visitations of divine wrath.—*John Morison.*

Verse 14.—"*Whose belly thou fillest with thy hid treasure.*" Wicked men may abound in earthly things. They may have the earth and the fulness of it, the earth, and all that is earthly ; their bellies are filled by God himself with hidden treasure. Precious things are usually hidden, and all that's named treasure, though it be but earthly, hath a preciousness in it. Hidden treasures of earth fill their bellies who slight the treasures of heaven, and whose souls shall never have so much as a taste of heavenly treasures : riches and honour are the lots of their inheritance who have no inheritance among those whose lot is glory. They have the earth in their hands (Job ix. 24), who have nothing of heaven in their hearts ; they bear sway in the world who are slaves to the world ; they govern and order others at their will who are led captive by Satan at his will. Be not offended and troubled to see the reins of government in their hands who know not how to govern themselves, or to see them rule the world who are unworthy to live in the world.—*Joseph Caryl.*

Verse 14.—"*Whose belly thou fillest with thy hid treasure.*" The hearts of saints only are filled with the "*hidden manna,*" but the bellies of the wicked are often filled with *hidden treasure ;* that is, with those dainties and good things which are virtually hidden in, and formally spring out of, the belly and bowels of the earth. The Lord easily grants them their wish in such things, and gives them "*their portion,*" which is all their portion, "*in this life.*" For as they are but common professors, so these are but common mercies, such as many of his enemies receive, who are but fatted as oxen for the slaughter, and fitted for destruction. True happiness is not to be judged by lands or houses, by gold or silver. The world is a narrow bound : unless we get beyond the creature, and set our hopes above this world, we cannot be happy. As hypocrites desire, so they attain much of the world, but they shall attain no more, how much soever they seem to desire it.—*Joseph Caryl.*

Verse 14.—"*Whose belly thou fillest.*" That is, their sensual appetite, as oftentimes that term is used (Rom. xvi. 18 ; Phil. iii. 19), "*with thy hid treasures ;*" namely the riches which either God is wont to hide in the bowels of the earth, or lock up in the repository of providence, dispensing them at his own pleasure.—*John Howe.*

Verse 14.—"*Whose belly thou fillest,*" etc. :—

> Thou from thy hidden store,
> Their bellies, Lord, hast fill'd ;
> Their sons are gorg'd, and what is o'er,
> To their sons' sons they yield.
>
> *Richard Mant.*

Verse 14.—"*They are full of children.*" So it appears by that which follows, it ought to be read, and not according to that gross, but easy (υἴων for υἱῶν), mistake of some transcribers of the seventy. As if in all this he pleaded thus : "Lord, thou hast abundantly indulged those men already, what need they more ? They have themselves, from thy unregarded bounty, their own vast swollen desires sufficiently filled, enough for their own time ; and when they can live no longer in their persons, they may in their posterity, and leave not strangers, but their numerous offspring, their heirs. Is it not enough that their avarice be gratified, except their malice be also ? that they have whatsoever they can conceive desirable for themselves, unless they may also infer whatever they can think mischievous on me ?" To this description of his enemies, he *ex opposito*, subjoins some account of himself in this his closure of the Psalm. "*As for me,*" here he is at his statique point ; and, after some appearing discomposure, his spirit returns to a consistency, in consideration of his own more happy state, which he opposes and prefers to theirs, in the following respects. That *they* were wicked, *he* righteous. "I will behold thy face in righteousness." That *their* happiness was worldly, terrene, such only as did spring from the earth ; *his* heavenly and divine, such as should result from the face and image of God. *Theirs* present, temporary, compassed within this life; *his* future, everlasting, to be enjoyed when he should awake. *Theirs* partial, defective, such as would but gratify their bestial part, fill their bellies; *his* adequate, complete (the εὐδαιμονία τοῦ συνετοῦ, *a happiness of proportion*), such as should satisfy the man. " I shall be *satisfied*," etc.—*John Howe*.

Verse 14.—" *They are full of children.*" Margin, *their children are full.* The margin probably expresses the sense of the Hebrew better than the text. The literal rendering would be, " satisfied are their sons; " that is, they have enough to satisfy the wants of their children. The expression, " they are full of children," is harsh and unnatural, and is not demanded by the original, or by the main thought in the passage. The obvious signification is, that they have enough for themselves and for their children.—*Albert Barnes*.

Verse 15.—" *I will behold thy face.*" I look upon the face of a stranger and it moves me not; but upon a friend, and his face presently transforms mine into a lively, cheerful aspect. " As iron sharpeneth iron, so doth the face of a man his friend " (Prov. xxvii. 17), puts a sharpness and a quickness into his looks. The soul that loves God, opens itself to him, admits his influences and impressions, is easily moulded and wrought to his will, yields to the transforming power of his appearing glory. There is no resistant principle remaining when the love of God is perfected in it; and so overcoming is the first sight of his glory upon the awaking soul, that it perfects it, and so his likeness, both at once.—*John Howe*.

Verse 15.—" *I will behold,*" etc. In the words we have, 1. The time of his complete and consummate happiness—" *When I awake.*" 2. The matter of his happiness, and the manner of enjoying it; the matter and object—" *God's face, or likeness;* " the manner of enjoying—" *I will behold thy face.*" 3. His perfect disposition and condition in the state of happiness—" *I shall behold in righteousness,*" having my heart perfectly conformed to the will of God, the perfect and adequate rule of righteousness. 4. The measure of his happiness—" *I shall be satisfied;* " my happiness will be full in the measure, without want of anything that can make me happy; all my desires shall be satisfied, and my happiness in respect of duration shall be eternal, without a shadow or fear of a change.—*William Colvill*.

Verse 15.—He doth profess his resolution, yet notwithstanding all the danger he was in, to go on in the ways of God, and expects a gracious issue; *but I,* saith he, " *will behold thy face in righteousness;* " indeed, I cannot behold the face of the king without danger to me; there are a great many that run to kill me, and they desire his face; but though I cannot see his face, yet, Lord, I shall behold *thy* face; " *I will behold thy face,*" and it shall be " *in righteousness;* " I will still keep on in the ways of righteousness, and " *when I awake* "—for I believe that these troubles will not hold long—I shall not sleep in perpetual sleep, but *I shall awake* and be delivered, and then " *I shall be satisfied with thy likeness:* " there shall be the manifestation of thy glory to me, that shall satisfy me for all the trouble that I have endured for thy name's sake, that my soul shall say, I have enough.—*Jeremiah Burroughs*.

Verse 15.—" *I shall be satisfied,*" etc. The fulness of the felicity of heaven may appear if we *compare it with the joys and comforts of the Holy Spirit.* Such they are, as that the Scripture styles them *strong consolations* (Heb. vi. 17); *full joys* (John xv. 11); *joy unspeakable and full of glory* (1 Pet. i. 8); *abounding consolations.* 2 Cor. i. 5. And yet all the joy and peace that believers are partakers of in this life is but as a drop to the ocean, as a single cluster to the whole vintage, as the thyme or honey upon the thigh of a bee to the whole hive fully fraught with it, or as the break and peep of day to the bright noontide. But yet these tastes of the water, wine, and honey of this celestial Canaan, with which the Holy Spirit makes glad the hearts of believers, are both far more desirable and satisfactory than the overflowing streams of all earthly felicities. And there are none who have once tasted of them, but say as the Samaritan woman did, " Lord, give me that water, that I thirst not, neither come hither to draw." John iv. 15. So also the first and early dawnings of the heavenly light fill the soul with more serenity, and ravish it with more pure joy, than the brightest sunshine of all worldly splendour can ever do. I have read of a devout person who but dreaming of heaven, the signatures and impression it made upon his fancy were so strong, as that when he awake he knew not his cell, could not distinguish the night from the day, nor difference by his taste, oil from wine; still he was calling for his vision and saying, *Redde mihi campos floridos, columnam auream, comitem Hieronymum, assistentes angelos:* give me my fresh and fragrant fields again, my golden pillar of light, Jerome my companion, angels my assistants. If heaven in a dream produce such ecstacies as drown and overwhelm the exercises of the senses to inferior objects, what trances and complacencies must the fruition of it work in those who have their whole rational appetite filled, and their body beautified with its endless glory?— *William Spurstow,* 1656.

Verse 15.—" I shall be satisfied." Have you never seen how when they were finishing the interior of buildings they kept the scaffolding up? The old Pope, when he had Michael Angelo employed in decorating the interior of that magnificent structure, the Sistine Chapel, demanded that the scaffolding should be taken down so that he could see the glowing colours that with matchless skill were being laid on. Patiently and assiduously did that noble artist labour, toiling by day, and almost by night, bringing out his prophets and sibyls and pictures wondrous for their beauty and significance, until the work was done. The day before it was done, if you had gone into that chapel and looked up, what would you have seen? Posts, planks, ropes, lime, mortar, slop, dirt. But when all was finished, the workmen came, and the scaffolding was removed. And then, although the floor was yet covered with rubbish and litter, when you looked up, it was as if heaven itself had been opened, and you looked into the courts of God and angels. Now, the scaffolding is kept around men long after the fresco is commenced to be painted; and wondrous disclosures will be made when God shall take down this scaffolding body, and reveal what you have been doing. By sorrow and by joy; by joys which are but bright colours, and by sorrows which are but shadows of bright colours; by prayer; by the influences of the sanctuary; by your pleasures; by your business; by reverses; by successes and by failures; by what strengthened your confidence, and by what broke it down; by the things that you rejoiced in, and by the things that you mourned over—by all that God is working in you. And you are to be perfected, not according to the things that you plan, but according to the divine pattern. Your portrait and mine are being painted, and God by wondrous strokes and influences is working us up to his own ideal. Over and above what you are doing for yourself, God is working to make you like him. And the wondrous declaration is, that when you stand before God, and see what has been done for you, you shall be *" satisfied."* Oh, word that has been wandering solitary and without a habitation ever since the world began, and the morning stars sang together for joy! Has there ever been a human creature that could stand on earth while clothed in the flesh, and say, " I am satisfied"? What is the meaning of the word? Sufficiently filled; filled full; filled up in every part. And when God's work is complete, we shall stand before him, and, with the bright ideal and glorified conception of heavenly aspiration upon us, looking up to God, and back on ourselves, we shall say, " I am satisfied;" for we shall be like him. Amen. Why should we not be satisfied?—*Henry Ward Beecher, in " Royal Truths,"* 1862.

Verse 15.—" When I awake, I shall be satisfied with thy likeness." He speaks here of the resurrection; he calls it an awaking, for you know death is called a sleep. " Those that are asleep in the Lord shall rise first." He had spoken before of those that had put their happiness in the comforts of this life, suitable to their bodies, to the animal state of their bodies; that is clear by the fourteenth verse, " Deliver me from the men that are thine hand, O Lord, who have their portion in this life, whose belly thou fillest with thy treasure: they are full of children, and leave to them outward things," bodily things. " But as for me," said he, " I will behold thy face in thy righteousness " (there is the vision of God which is his happiness in his soul): " and I shall be satisfied when I awake " (when I rise again), " with thine image." It is not the image of God only upon himself that he means here. Why? Because that doth not satisfy a holy heart, but it is that image of the invisible God which the human nature of Jesus Christ is, who, in opposition to all these outward pleasures, will be all in all to us; he is a spiritual creature, his human nature is spiritualised, made glorious, and our bodies shall be made spiritual likewise. " The body is made for the Lord, and the Lord for the body," and this when they are both raised up; Christ is raised up already, and because he hath ordained the one to be serviceable to the other, he will also raise up our bodies; and when he doth raise me up, saith David, though other men have their bellies full here, and have animal pleasures they delight in; yet when I shall awake at latter day, and shall see this image of thine, shall see thy Son, I shall be satisfied: "When I awake, I shall be satisfied with thine image."—*Thomas Goodwin.*

Verse 15.—" I shall be satisfied, when I awake, with thy likeness." In this Psalm holy David's afflictions are neither few nor small; his *innocency* that is wounded by malicious slanderers, his *life* that is in jeopardy by deadly enemies that compass him about; his *present condition* that is embittered unto him by the pressing wants of a barren wilderness, while his foes live deliciously in Saul's court. And yet under the weight and combination of so many sore evils, David carries himself as one that is neither hopeless nor forsaken, yea, lays his estate in the balance against theirs, and in this low ebb of his, vies with them for happiness; and at last shutting up the Psalm with a triumphant *epiphonema*, concludes himself to be by far the better man. "*As for me, I will behold thy face in righteousness: I shall be satisfied, when I awake, with thy likeness.*" They, 'tis true, enjoy the face of their king, whose favour is as a cloud of latter rain promising a fruitful harvest of many blessings, "*but I,*" saith he, "*shall behold the face of God* in righteousness," whose loving-kindness is better than life, clothed with all its royalties. They have their bellies filled with hidden treasure, having more than a common hand of bounty opened unto them; but I have more gladness put into my heart, more than in the time that their corn and wine increased. They have their portion in hand, and as being men of this world; but I have mine laid up in the other: "*I shall be satisfied, when I awake, with thy likeness.*" In these words we have his and every believer's eternal happiness in the other life, set forth in three particulars as a most effectual antidote against present troubles and temptations that arise from the malice of wicked men against them.—*William Spurstow.*

Verse 15.—" I shall be satisfied, when I awake, with thy likeness." The saints in heaven have not yet awaked in God's likeness. The bodies of the righteous still sleep, but they are to be satisfied on the resurrection morn, when they awake. When a Roman conqueror had been at war, and won great victories, he would return to Rome with his soldiers, enter privately into his house, and enjoy himself till the next day, when he would go out of the city to re-enter it publicly in triumph. Now, the saints, as it were, enter privately into heaven without their bodies; but on the last day, when their bodies wake up, they will enter into their triumphal chariots. Methinks I see that grand procession, when Jesus Christ first of all, with many crowns on his head, with his bright, glorious, immortal body, shall lead the way. Behind him come the saints, each of them clapping their hands, or pouring sweet melody from their golden harps; all entering in triumph. And when they come to heaven's gates, and the doors are opened wide to let the King of glory in, how will the angels crowd at the windows and on the housetops, like the inhabitants in the Roman triumphs, to watch the pompous procession, and scatter heaven's roses and lilies upon them, crying, "Hallelujah! hallelujah! hallelujah! the Lord God Omnipotent reigneth." "I shall be satisfied" in that glorious day when all the angels of God shall come to see the triumphs of Jesus, and when his people shall be victorious with him.—*Spurgeon's Sermons.*

Verse 15.—" I shall be satisfied . . . with thy likeness." Let a man who is thirsty be brought to an ocean of pure water, and he has enough. If there be enough in God to satisfy the angels, then sure there is enough to satisfy us. The soul is but finite, but God is infinite. Though God be a good that satisfies, yet he does not surfeit. Fresh joys spring continually from his face; and he is as much to be desired after millions of years by glorified souls as at the first moment. There is a fulness in God that satisfies, and yet so much sweetness that the soul still desires. God is a *delicious* good. That which is the chief good must ravish the soul with pleasure; there must be in it rapturous delight and quintessence of joy. *In Deo quadam dulcedine delectatur anima immo rapitur:* the love of God drops such infinite suavity into the soul as is unspeakable and full of glory. If there be so much delight in God, when we see him only by faith (1 Peter i. 8), what will the joy of vision be, when we shall see him face to face! If the saints have found so much delight in God while they were suffering, oh, what joy and delight will they have when they are being crowned! If flames are beds of roses, what will it be to lean on the bosom of Jesus! What a bed of roses that will be! God is a *superlative* good. He is better than anything you can put in competition with him; he is better than health, riches, honour. Other things maintain life, he gives life. Who would put anything in balance with the Deity? Who would weigh a feather against a mountain of gold ? God excels all other things more infinitely than the sun the light of a taper. God is an *eternal* good. He is the Ancient of days, yet never decays, nor waxes old. Daniel vii. 9. The joy he gives is eternal, the crown fadeth not away. 1 Peter v. 4. The glorified soul shall be ever solacing itself in God, feasting on his love, and sunning itself in the light of his countenance. We read of the river of pleasure at God's right hand ; but will not this in time be dried up? No. There is a fountain at the bottom which feeds it. Psalm xxxvi. 9. " With the Lord is a fountain of life." Thus God is the chief good, and the enjoyment of God for ever is the highest felicity of which the soul is capable.—*Thomas Watson.*

Verse 15.—" *When I awake,*" etc. The sincere Christian is progressive, never at his journey's end till he gets to heaven ; this keeps him always in motion, advancing in his desires and endeavours forward : he is thankful for little grace, but not content with great measures of grace. " *When I awake,*" saith David, "*I shall be satisfied with thy likeness.*" He had many a sweet entertainment at the house of God in his ordinances. The Spirit of God was the messenger that brought him many a covered dish from God's table, inward consolations which the world knew not of. Yet David has not enough, it is heaven alone that can give him his full draught. They say the Gauls, when they first tasted of the wines of Italy, were so taken with their lusciousness and sweetness, that they could not be content to trade thither for this wine, but resolved they would conquer the land where they grew. Thus the sincere soul thinks it not enough to receive a little now and then of grace and comfort from heaven, by trading and holding commerce at a distance with God in his ordinances here below, but projects and meditates a conquest of that holy land and blessed place from which such rich commodities come, that he may drink the wine of that kingdom in that kingdom.—*William Gurnall.*

Verse 15.—" *When I awake.*" How apt and obvious is the analogy between our awaking out of natural sleep, and the holy soul's rising up out of the darkness and torpor of its present state into the enlivening light of God's presence ? It is truly said so to *awake* at its first quitting these darksome regions, when it lays aside its cumbersome night-veil. It doth so more perfectly in the joyful morning of the resurrection-day when mortality is swallowed up in life, and all the yet hovering shadows of it are vanished and fled away. And how known and usual an application this is of the metaphorical terms of sleeping and awaking in Holy Writ, I need not tell them who have read the Bible. Nor doth this interpretation less fitly accord to the other contents of this verse ; for to what state do the sight of God's face, and satisfaction with his likeness, so fully agree, as to that of future blessedness in the other world ? But then the contexture of discourse in this and the foregoing verse together, seems plainly to determine us to this sense : for what can be more conspicuous in them, than a purposed comparison, an opposition of two states of felicity mutually to each other ? That of the wicked whom he calls *men of time* (as the words מְמְתִים מֵחֶלֶד are rendered by Pagninus—*Homines de tempore*—and do literally signify) and whose portion, he tells us, is in this life : and the righteous man's, his own ; which he expected not to be till he should awake, that is, not till after his life.—*John Howe.*

Verse 15.—There is a sleep of deadness of spirit, out of which the shining of God's loving countenance doth awake a believer and revive the spirit of the contrite ones ; and there is a sleep of death bodily, out of which the lovingkindness of the Lord shall awake all his own in the day of the resurrection, when he shall so change them into the similitude of his own holiness and glorious felicity that they shall be fully contented for ever : and this first and second delivery out of all trouble may every believer expect and promise to himself. " I shall be satisfied when I awake with thy likeness."—*David Dickson.*

Verse 15.—There is a threefold meaning in this verse, inasmuch as it is in Christ alone, the firstborn from the dead, the express image of Jehovah's glory, that the saints will rise immortal, incorruptible, and be like the angels in heaven. 1. They will greatly delight in the glorious state in which they will rise. 2. They will greatly delight in Jesus, in whom, and by whom, resurrection and immortality are brought to light ; and 3. They will delight greatly in beholding the blessed and reconciled countenance of Jehovah, the Father, whom no eye of flesh can see. This is the difference between the appearance of God to Israel on Mount Sinai, and the happy state in which the saints will behold him in the resurrection. Glorious as the scene on Sinai was, yet the Lord said to Israel, " You have seen no תְּמוּנָה (Temunah), no manner of similitude," or likeness, or countenance ; but David speaks of the spiritual glory of the triumphant saints in the resurrection, when they shall see Jehovah as he is, and rejoice in his beatific presence for ever and ever.—*Benjamin Weiss, in loc*, 1858.

Verse 15.—Everlasting life and salvation in heaven, is not a truth revealed only by the gospel, but was well known, clearly revealed, and firmly believed, by the saints of old. They had assurance of this, that they should live with God for ever in glory. *" When I awake, with thy likeness."* Psalm xvii. 15. *" Thou wilt receive me to glory."* Psalm lxxiii. 24. *" In thy presence is fulness of joy ; at thy right hand there are pleasures for evermore."* Psalm xvi. 11. They looked for another country, whereof Canaan was but a type and shadow, as the apostle shows in the epistle to the Hebrews, chap. xi. 16. They knew there was an eternal state of happiness for the saints, as well as an eternal state of misery for the wicked ; they did believe this in those days.—*Samuel Mather on the " Types,"* 1705.

HINTS TO PREACHERS.

Verse 1.—The voice of Jesus—our Righteousness, and our own voice. Work out the thought of both coming up to the ear of heaven, noting the qualities of our prayer as indicated by the psalmist's language, such as earnestness, perseverance, sincerity, etc.

Verse 2.—*" Let my sentence come forth from thy presence."* I. When it will come. II. Who dare meet it *now*. III. How to be among them.

Verse 3.—*" Thou hast proved mine heart."* The metal, the furnace, the refiner, etc.

Verse 3.—*" Thou hast visited me in the night."* I. Glorious visitor. II. Favoured individual. III. Peculiar season. IV. Refreshing remembrance. V. Practical result.

Verse 3 (last sentence).—Transgressions of the lip, and how to avoid them.

Verse 4.—The highway and the by-paths. *The world and sin.* *" The paths of the destroyer"*—a significant name for transgression.

Verse 5.—*" Hold up."* I. Who ? God. II. What ? *" My goings."* III. When ? Present tense. IV. Where ? *" In thy paths."* V. Why ? *" That my footsteps slip not."*

Verse 5.—Let me observe David and learn to pray as he prayed, "Hold up my goings in thy paths, that my footsteps slip not." I. See his *course*. He speaks of his " goings." Religion does not allow a man to sit still. He speaks of his goings " in God's paths." These are threefold. (1). The path of his *commands*. (2). The path of his *ordinances*. (3). The path of his *dispensations*. II. His *concern* respecting this course. It is the language of—(1) *conviction ;* (2) *of apprehension ;* (3) of *weakness ;* (4) of *confidence.*—*William Jay.*

Verse 6.—*Two words*, both great, though little, " call " and " hear." *Two persons*, one little and the other great, " I," " Thee, O God." *Two tenses :* past, " I have ; " future, " Thou wilt." *Two wonders*, that we do not call more, and that God hears such unworthy prayers.

Verse 7 (first sentence).—See Exposition. A view of divine lovingkindness desired.

Verse 7.—*" O thou,"* etc. God, the Saviour of believers.

Verse 8.—Two most suggestive emblems of tenderness and care. Involving in the one case *living unity*, as the eye with the body, and in the other, *loving relationship*, as the bird and its young.

Verse 14.—*"Men of the world, which have their portion in this life."* Who they are ? What they have ? Where they have it ? What next ?

Verse 14.—*" Men which are thy hand."* Providential control and use of wicked men.

Verse 15.—This is the language (1) of a man whose mind is made up ; who has decided for himself ; who does not suspend his conduct upon the resolution of others. (2) Of a man rising in life, and with great prospects before him. (3) It is the language of a Jew.

Verse 15.—*The beholding of God's face* signifies two things. I. The enjoyment of his favour. II. Intimate communion with him.—*William Jay.*

Verse 15.—See " Spurgeon's Sermons," No. 25. Title, " The Hope of Future Bliss." Divisions. I. The Spirit of this utterance. II. The matter of it. III. The contrast implied in it.

Verse 15.—To see God and to be like him, the believer's desire.—*J. Fawcett.*

PSALM XVIII.

TITLE.—" To the chief Musician, *a Psalm* of David, the servant of the Lord, who spake unto the Lord the words of this song in the day *that* the Lord delivered him from the hand of all his enemies, and from the hand of Saul." *We have another form of this Psalm with significant variations* (2 Sam. xxii), *and this suggests the idea that it was sung by David at different times when he reviewed his own remarkable history, and observed the gracious hand of God in it all. Like Addison's hymn beginning, " When all thy mercies, O my God," this Psalm is the song of a grateful heart over-whelmed with a retrospect of the manifold and marvellous mercies of God. We will call it* THE GRATEFUL RETROSPECT. *The title deserves attention. David, although at this time a king, calls himself " the servant of Jehovah," but makes no mention of his royalty ; hence we gather that he counted it a higher honour to be the Lord's servant than to be Judah's king. Right wisely did he judge. Being possessed of poetic genius, he served the Lord by composing this Psalm for the use of the Lord's house ; and it is no mean work to conduct or to improve that delightful part of divine worship, the singing of the Lord's praises. Would that more musical and poetical ability were consecrated, and that our* chief *musicians were fit to be trusted with devout and spiritual psalmody. It should be observed that the words of this song were not composed with the view of gratifying the taste of men, but were spoken unto Jehovah. It were well if we had a more single eye to the honour of the Lord in our singing, and in all other hallowed exercises. That praise is little worth which is not directed solely and heartily to the Lord. David might well be thus direct in his gratitude, for he owed all to his God, and in the day of his deliverance he had none to thank but the Lord whose right hand had preserved him. We too should feel that to God and God alone we owe the greatest debt of honour and thanksgiving.*

If it be remembered that the second and the forty-ninth verses are both quoted in the New Testament (Heb. ii. 13 ; Rom. xv. 9) *as the words of the Lord Jesus, it will be clear that a greater than David is here. Reader, you will not need our aid in this respect : if you know Jesus you will readily find him in his sorrows, deliverance, and triumphs all through this wonderful Psalm.*

DIVISION.—*The first three verses are the proem or preface in which the resolve to bless God is declared. Delivering mercy is most poetically extolled from verse 4 to verse 19 ; and then the happy songster, from verse 20 to 28, protests that God had acted righteously in thus favouring him. Filled with grateful joy he again pictures his deliverance, and anticipates future victories from verse 29—45 ; and in closing speaks with evident prophetic foresight of the glorious triumphs of the Messiah, David's seed and the Lord's anointed.*

EXPOSITION.

I WILL love thee, O LORD, my strength.

2 The LORD *is* my rock, and my fortress, and my deliverer ; my God, my strength, in whom I will trust ; my buckler, and the horn of my salvation, *and* my high tower.

3 I will call upon the LORD, *who is worthy* to be praised : so shall I be saved from mine enemies.

1. "*I will love thee, O Lord.*" With strong, hearty affection will I cling to thee ; as a child to its parent, or a spouse to her husband. The word is intensely forcible, the love is of the deepest kind. " I will love heartily, with my inmost bowels." Here is a fixed resolution to abide in the nearest and most intimate union with the Most High. Our triune God deserves the warmest love of all our hearts. Father, Son and Spirit have each a claim upon our love. The solemn purpose never to cease loving naturally springs from present fervour of affection, It is wrong to make rash resolutions, but this when made in the strength of God is most wise and fitting. "*My strength.*" Our God is the strength of our life, our graces, our works, our hopes, our conflicts, our victories. This verse is not found in 1 Sam. xxii., and is a most precious addition, placed above all and after all to form the pinnacle of the temple, the apex of the pyramid. Love is still the crowning grace.

2. "*The Lord is my rock and my fortress.*" Dwelling among the crags and mountain fastnesses of Judea, David had escaped the malice of Saul, and here he compares his God to such a place of concealment and security. Believers are often hidden in their God from the strife of tongues and the fury of the storm of trouble. The clefts of the Rock of Ages are safe abodes. "*My deliverer*," interposing in my hour of peril. When almost captured the Lord's people are rescued from the hand of the mighty by him who is mightier still. This title of "*deliverer*" has many sermons in it, and is well worthy of the study of all experienced saints. "*My God;*" this is all good things in one. There is a boundless wealth in this expression; it means, my perpetual, unchanging, infinite, eternal good. He who can say truly "my God," may well add, "my heaven, my all." "*My strength;*" this word is really "*my rock,*" in the sense of strength and immobility. My sure, unchanging, eternal confidence and support. Thus the word rock occurs twice, but it is no tautology, for the first time it is a rock for concealment, but here a rock for firmness and immutability. "*In whom I will trust.*" Faith must be exercised, or the preciousness of God is not truly known; and God must be the object of faith, or faith is mere presumption. "*My buckler,*" warding off the blows of my enemy, shielding me from arrow or sword. The Lord furnishes his warriors with weapons both offensive and defensive. Our armoury is completely stored so that none need go to battle unarmed. "*The horn of my salvation,*" enabling me to push down my foes, and to triumph over them with holy exultation. "*My high tower,*" a citadel high planted on a rocky eminence beyond the reach of my enemies, from the heights of which I look down upon their fury without alarm, and survey a wide landscape of mercy reaching even unto the goodly land beyond Jordan. Here are many words, but none too many; we might profitably examine each one of them had we leisure, but summing up the whole, we may conclude with Calvin, that David here equips the faithful from head to foot.

3. In this verse the happy poet resolves to invoke the Lord in joyful song, believing that in all future conflicts his God would deal as well with him as in the past. It is well to pray to God as to one who deserves to be praised, for then we plead in a happy and confident manner. If I feel that I can and do bless the Lord for all his past goodness, I am bold to ask great things of him. That word *So* has much in it. To be saved singing is to be saved indeed. Many are saved mourning and doubting; but David had such faith that he could fight singing, and win the battle with a song still upon his lips. How happy a thing to receive fresh mercy with a heart already sensible of mercy enjoyed, and to anticipate new trials with a confidence based upon past experiences of divine love!

> "No fearing or doubting with Christ on our side,
> We hope to die shouting, 'The Lord will provide.'"

4 The sorrows of death compassed me, and the floods of ungodly men made me afraid.

5 The sorrows of hell compassed me about : the snares of death prevented me.

6 In my distress I called upon the LORD, and cried unto my God : he heard my voice out of his temple, and my cry came before him, *even* into his ears.

7 Then the earth shook and trembled; the foundations also of the hills moved and were shaken, because he was wroth.

8 There went up a smoke out of his nostrils, and fire out of his mouth devoured : coals were kindled by it.

9 He bowed the heavens also, and came down : and darkness *was* under his feet.

10 And he rode upon a cherub, and did fly : yea, he did fly upon the wings of the wind.

11 He made darkness his secret place ; his pavilion round about him *were* dark waters *and* thick clouds of the skies.

12 At the brightness *that was* before him his thick clouds passed, hail stones and coals of fire.

13 The LORD also thundered in the heavens, and the Highest gave his voice ; hail *stones* and coals of fire.

14 Yea, he sent out his arrows, and scattered them ; and he shot out lightnings, and discomfited them.

15 Then the channels of waters were seen, and the foundations of the world were discovered at thy rebuke, O LORD, at the blast of the breath of thy nostrils.

16 He sent from above, he took me, he drew me out of many waters.

17 He delivered me from my strong enemy, and from them which hated me : for they were too strong for me.

18 They prevented me in the day of my calamity : but the LORD was my stay.

19 He brought me forth also into a large place ; he delivered me, because he delighted in me.

In most poetical language the Psalmist now describes his experience of Jehovah's delivering power. Poesy has in all her treasures no gem more lustrous than the sonnet of the following verses ; the sorrow, the cry, the descent of the Divine One, and the rescue of the afflicted, are here set to a music worthy of the golden harps. The Messiah our Saviour is evidently, over and beyond David or any other believer, the main and chief subject of this song ; and while studying it we have grown more and more sure that every line here has its deepest and profoundest fulfilment in Him ; but as we are desirous not to extend our comment beyond moderate bounds, we must leave it with the devout reader to make the very easy application of the passage to our once distressed but now triumphant Lord.

4. " *The sorrows of death compassed me.*" Death like a cruel conqueror seemed to twist round about him the cords of pain. He was environed and hemmed in with threatening deaths of the most appalling sort. He was like a mariner broken by the storm and driven upon the rocks by dreadful breakers, white as the teeth of death. Sad plight for the man after God's own heart, but thus it is that Jehovah dealeth with his sons. " *The floods of ungodly men made me afraid.*" Torrents of ungodliness threatened to swamp all religion, and to hurry away the godly man's hope as a thing to be scorned and despised ; so far was this threat fulfilled, that even the hero who slew Goliath began to be afraid. The most seaworthy bark is sometimes hard put to it when the storm fiend is abroad. The most courageous man, who as a rule hopes for the best, may sometimes fear the worst. Beloved reader, he who pens these lines has known better than most men what this verse means, and feels inclined to weep, and yet to sing, while he writes upon a text so descriptive of his own experience. On the night of the lamentable accident at the Surrey Music Hall, the floods of Belial were let loose, and the subsequent remarks of a large portion of the press were exceedingly malicious and wicked ; our soul was afraid as we stood encompassed with the sorrows of death and the blasphemies of the cruel. But oh, what mercy was there in it all, and what honey of goodness was extracted by our Lord out of this lion of affliction ! Surely God hath heard me ! Art thou in an ill plight ? Dear friend, learn thou from our experience to trust in the Lord Jehovah, who forsaketh not his chosen.

5. " *The sorrows of hell compassed me about.*" From all sides the hell-hounds barked furiously. A cordon of devils hemmed in the hunted man of God ; every way of escape was closed up. Satan knows how to blockade our coasts with the iron war-ships of sorrow, but, blessed be God, the port of all prayer is still open, and grace can run the blockade bearing messages from earth to heaven, and blessings in return from heaven to earth. " *The snares of death prevented me.*" The old enemy hunts for his prey, not only with the dogs of the infernal kennel, but also with the snares of deadly craft. The nets were drawn closer and closer until the contracted circle completely prevented the escape of the captive :—

' About me cords of hell were wound,
And snares of death my footsteps bound."

Thus hopeless was the case of this good man, as hopeless as a case could be, so utterly desperate that none but an almighty arm could be of any service. According to the four metaphors which he employs, he was bound like a malefactor for execution; overwhelmed like a shipwrecked mariner; surrounded and standing at bay like a hunted stag; and captured in a net like a trembling bird. What more of terror and distress could meet upon one poor defenceless head?

6. "*In my distress I called upon the Lord, and cried unto my God.*" Prayer is that postern gate which is left open even when the city is straitly besieged by the enemy; it is that way upward from the pit of despair to which the spiritual miner flies at once when the floods from beneath break forth upon him. Observe that he *calls*, and then *cries;* prayer grows in vehemence as it proceeds. Note also that he first invokes his God under the name of Jehovah, and then advances to a more familiar name, "*my God;*" thus faith increases by exercise, and he whom we at first viewed as Lord is soon seen to be our God in covenant. It is never an ill time to pray; no distress should prevent us from using the divine remedy of supplication. Above the noise of the raging billows of death, or the barking dogs of hell, the feeblest cry of a true believer will be heard in heaven. "*He heard my voice out of his temple, and my cry came before him, even into his ears.*" Far up within the bejewelled walls, and through the gates of pearl, the cry of the suffering suppliant was heard. Music of angels and harmony of seraphs availed not to drown or even to impair the voice of that humble call. The king heard it in his palace of light unsufferable, and lent a willing ear to the cry of his own beloved child. O honoured prayer, to be able thus through Jesus' blood to penetrate the very ears and heart of Deity. The voice and the cry are themselves heard directly by the Lord, and not made to pass through the medium of saints and intercessors; "*My cry came before Him;*" the operation of prayer with God is immediate and personal. We may cry with confident and familiar importunity, while our Father himself listens.

7. There was no great space between the cry and its answer. The Lord is not slack concerning his promise, but is swift to rescue his afflicted. David has in his mind's eye the glorious manifestations of God in Egypt, at Sinai, and on different occasions to Joshua and the judges; and he considers that his own case exhibits the same glory of power and goodness, and that, therefore, he may accommodate the descriptions of former displays of the divine majesty into his hymn of praise. "*Then the earth shook and trembled.*" Observe how the most solid and immovable things feel the force of supplication. Prayer has shaken houses, opened prison doors, and made stout hearts to quail. Prayer rings the alarm bell, and the Master of the house arises to the rescue, shaking all things beneath his tread. "*The foundations also of the hills moved and were shaken, because of his wrath.*" He who fixed the world's pillars can make them rock in their sockets, and can upheave the cornerstones of creation. The huge roots of the towering mountains are torn up when the Lord bestirs himself in anger to smite the enemies of his people. How shall puny man be able to face it out with God when the very mountains quake with fear? Let not the boaster dream that his present false confidence will support him in the dread day of wrath.

8. "*There went up a smoke out of his nostrils.*" A violent oriental method of expressing fierce wrath. Since the breath from the nostrils is heated by strong emotion, the figure portrays the Almighty Deliverer as pouring forth smoke in the heat of his wrath and the impetuousness of his zeal. Nothing makes God so angry as an injury done to his children. He that toucheth you toucheth the apple of mine eye. God is not subject to the passions which govern his creatures, but acting as he does with all the energy and speed of one who is angry, he is here aptly set forth in poetic imagery suitable to human understandings. The opening of his lips is sufficient to destroy his enemies; "*and fire out of his mouth devoured.*" This fire was no temporary one but steady and lasting; "*Coals were kindled by it.*" The whole passage is intended to depict God's descent to the help of his child, attended by earthquake and tempest: at the majesty of his appearing the earth rocks, the clouds gather like smoke, and the lightning as flaming fire devours, setting the world on a blaze. What grandeur of description is here! Bishop Mant very admirably rhymes the verse thus:—

"Smoke from his heated nostrils came,
And from his mouth devouring flame;
Hot burning coals announced his ire,
And flashes of careering fire."

9. Amid the terror of the storm Jehovah the Avenger descended, bending beneath his foot the arch of heaven. " *He bowed the heavens also, and came down.*" He came in haste, and spurned everything which impeded his rapidity. The thickest gloom concealed his splendour, " *and darkness was under his feet ;* " he fought within the dense vapours, as a warrior in clouds of smoke and dust, and found out the hearts of his enemies with the sharp falchion of his vengeance. Darkness is no impediment to God ; its densest gloom he makes his tent and secret pavilion. See how prayer moves earth and heaven, and raises storms to overthrow in a moment the foes of God's Israel. Things were bad for David before he prayed, but they were much worse for his foes so soon as the petition had gone up to heaven. A trustful heart, by enlisting the divine aid, turns the tables on its enemies. If I must have an enemy let him not be a man of prayer, or he will soon get the better of me by calling in his God into the quarrel.

10. There is inimitable grandeur in this verse. Under the Mosaic system the cherubim are frequently represented as the chariot of God ; hence Milton, in " Paradise Lost," writes of the Great Father,—

> " He on the wings of cherubim
> Uplifted, in paternal glory rode
> Far into chaos."

Without speculating upon the mysterious and much-disputed subject of the cherubim, it may be enough to remark that angels are doubtless our guards and ministering friends, and all their powers are enlisted to expedite the rescue of the afflicted. " *He rode upon a cherub, and did fly.*" Nature also yields all her agents to be our helpers, and even the powers of the air are subservient : " *yea, he did fly upon the wings of the wind.*" The Lord comes flying when mercy is his errand, but he lingers long when sinners are being wooed to repent. The flight here pictured is as majestic as it is swift ; " flying all abroad " is Sternhold's word, and he is not far from correct. As the eagle soars in easy grandeur with wings outspread, without violent flapping and exertion, so comes the Lord with majesty of omnipotence to aid his own.

11. The storm thickened, and the clouds pouring forth torrents of rain combined to form the secret chamber of the invisible but wonder-working God. " Pavilioned in impervious shade " faith saw him, but no other eye could gaze through the " *thick clouds of the skies.*" Blessed is the darkness which encurtains my God ; if I may not see him, it is sweet to know that he is working in secret for my eternal good. Even fools can believe that God is abroad in the sunshine and the calm, but faith is wise, and discerns him in the terrible darkness and threatening storm.

12. Suddenly the terrible artillery of heaven was discharged ; the *brightness* of lightning lit up the clouds as with a glory proceeding from him who was concealed within the cloudy pavilion ; and volleys of hailstones and coals of fire were hurled forth upon the enemy. The lightnings seemed to cleave the clouds and kindle them into a blaze, and then hailstones and flakes of fire with flashes of terrific grandeur terrified the sons of men.

13. Over all this splendour of tempest pealed the dread thunder. "*The Lord also thundered in the heavens, and the Highest gave his voice.*" Fit accompaniment for the flames of vengeance. How will men bear to hear it at the last when addressed to them in proclamation of their doom, for even now their hearts are in their mouths if they do but hear it muttering from afar ? In all this terror David found a theme for song, and thus every believer finds even in the terrors of God a subject for holy praise. " *Hailstones and coals of fire* " are twice mentioned to show how certainly they are in the divine hand, and are the weapons of Heaven's vengeance. Horne remarks that " every thunderstorm should remind us of that exhibition of power and vengeance, which is hereafter to accompany the general resurrection ; " may it not also assure us of the real power of him who is our Father and our friend, and tend to assure us of our safety while he fights our battles for us. The prince of the power of the air is soon dislodged when the cherubic chariot is driven through his dominions ; therefore let not the legions of hell cause us dismay. He who is with us is greater than all they that be against us.

14. The lightnings were darted forth as forked arrows upon the hosts of the foe, and speedily " *scattered them.*" Boastful sinners prove to be great cowards when Jehovah enters the lists with them. They despise his words, and are very

tongue-valiant, but when it comes to blows they fly apace. The glittering flames, and the fierce bolts of fire *"discomfited them."* God is never at a loss for weapons. Woe be unto him that contendeth with his Maker ! God's arrows never miss their aim ; they are feathered with lightning, and barbed with everlasting death. Fly, O sinner, to the rock of refuge before these arrows stick fast in thy soul.

15. So tremendous was the shock of God's assault in arms that the order of nature was changed, and the bottoms of rivers and seas were laid bare. *" The channels of waters were seen ; "* and the deep cavernous bowels of the earth were upheaved till *" the foundations of the world were discovered."* What will not Jehovah's *" rebuke "* do ? If *" the blast of the breath of thy nostrils,"* O Lord, be so terrible, what must thine arm be ? Vain are the attempts of men to conceal anything from him whose word unbars the deep, and lifts the doors of earth from their hinges ! Vain are all hopes of resistance, for a whisper of his voice makes the whole earth quail in abject terror.

16. Now comes the rescue. The Author is divine, *" He sent ; "* the work is heavenly, *" from above ; "* the deliverance is marvellous, *" He drew me out of many waters."* Here David was like another Moses, drawn from the water ; and thus are all believers like their Lord, whose baptism in many waters of agony and in his own blood has redeemed us from the wrath to come. Torrents of evil shall not drown the man whose God sitteth upon the floods to restrain their fury.

17. When we have been rescued, we must take care to ascribe all the glory to God by confessing our own weakness, and remembering the powers of the conquered enemy. God's power derives honour from all the incidents of the conflict. Our great spiritual adversary is a *" strong enemy "* indeed, much too strong for poor, weak creatures like ourselves, but we have been delivered hitherto and shall be even to the end. Our weakness is a reason for divine help ; mark the force of the *" for "* in the text.

18. It was an ill day, a day of *calamity,* of which evil foes took cruel advantage while they used crafty means utterly to ruin him, yet David could say, *" but the Lord is my stay."* What a blessed *but* which cuts the Gordian knot, and slays the hundred-headed hydra ! There is no fear of deliverance when our stay is in Jehovah.

19. *" He brought me forth also into a large place."* After pining awhile in the prison-house Joseph reached the palace, and from the cave of Adullam David mounted to the throne. Sweet is pleasure after pain. Enlargement is the more delightful after a season of pinching poverty and sorrowful confinement. Besieged souls delight in the broad fields of the promise when God drives off the enemy and sets open the gates of the environed city. The Lord does not leave his work half done, for having routed the foe he leads out the captive into liberty. Large indeed is the possession and place of the believer in Jesus, there need be no limit to his peace, for there is no bound to his privilege. *" He delivered me, because he delighted in me."* Free grace lies at the foundation. Rest assured, if we go deep enough, sovereign grace is the truth which lies at the bottom of every well of mercy. Deep sea fisheries in the ocean of divine bounty always bring the pearls of electing, discriminating love to light. Why Jehovah should delight in us is an answerless question, and a mystery which angels cannot solve ; but that he does delight in his beloved is certain, and is the fruitful root of favours as numerous as they are precious. Believer, sit down, and inwardly digest the instructive sentence now before us, and learn to view the uncaused love of God as the cause of all the loving-kindness of which we are the partakers.

20 The LORD rewarded me according to my righteousness ; according to the cleanness of my hands hath he recompensed me.

21 For I have kept the ways of the LORD, and have not wickedly departed from my God.

22 For all his judgments *were* before me, and I did not put away his statutes from me.

23 I was also upright before him, and I kept myself from mine iniquity.

24 Therefore hath the LORD recompensed me according to my righteousness, according to the cleanness of my hands in his eyesight.

25 With the merciful thou wilt shew thyself merciful ; with an upright man thou wilt shew thyself upright ;

26 With the pure thou wilt shew thyself pure ; and with the froward thou wilt shew thyself froward.

27 For thou wilt save the afflicted people ; but wilt bring down high looks.

28 For thou wilt light my candle : the LORD my God will enlighten my darkness.

20. "*The Lord rewarded me according to my righteousness.*" Viewing this Psalm as prophetical of the Messiah, these strongly-expressed claims to righteousness are readily understood, for his garments were white as snow ; but considered as the language of David they have perplexed many. Yet the case is clear, and if the words be not strained beyond their original intention, no difficulty need occur. Albeit that the dispensations of divine grace are to the fullest degree sovereign and irrespective of human merit, yet in the dealings of Providence there is often discernible a rule of justice by which the injured are at length avenged, and the righteous ultimately delivered. David's early troubles arose from the wicked malice of envious Saul, who no doubt prosecuted his persecutions under cover of charges brought against the character of "the man after God's own heart." These charges David declares to have been utterly false, and asserts that he possessed a grace-given righteousness which the Lord had graciously rewarded in defiance of all his calumniators. Before God the man after God's own heart was a humble sinner, but before his slanderers he could with unblushing face speak of the "*cleanness of his hands*" and the righteousness of his life. He knows little of the sanctifying power of divine grace who is not at the bar of human equity able to plead innocence. There is no self-righteousness in an honest man knowing that he is honest, nor even in his believing that God rewards him in providence because of his honesty, for such is often a most evident matter of fact ; but it would be self-righteousness indeed if we transferred such thoughts from the region of providential government into the spiritual kingdom, for there grace reigns not only supreme but sole in the distribution of divine favours. It is not at all an opposition to the doctrine of salvation by grace, and no sort of evidence of a Pharisaic spirit, when a gracious man, having been slandered, stoutly maintains his integrity, and vigorously defends his character. A godly man has a clear conscience, and knows himself to be upright ; is he to deny his own consciousness, and to despise the work of the Holy Ghost, by hypocritically making himself out to be worse than he is ? A godly man prizes his integrity very highly, or else he would not be a godly man at all ; is he to be called proud because he will not readily lose the jewel of a reputable character ? A godly man can see that in divine providence uprightness and truth are in the long run sure to bring their own reward ; may he not, when he sees that reward bestowed in his own case, praise the Lord for it ? Yea rather, must he not show forth the faithfulness and goodness of his God ? Read the cluster of expressions in this and the following verses as the song of a good conscience, after having safely outridden a storm of obloquy, persecution, and abuse, and there will be no fear of our upbraiding the writer as one who set too high a price upon his own moral character.

21. Here the assertion of purity is repeated, both in a positive and a negative form. There is "*I have*" and "*I have not*," both of which must be blended in a truly sanctified life ; constraining and restraining grace must each take its share. The words of this verse refer to the saint as a traveller carefully keeping to "*the ways of the Lord*," and "*not wickedly*," that is, designedly, wilfully, persistently, defiantly forsaking the ordained pathway in which God favours the pilgrim with his presence. Observe how it is implied in the expression "*and have not wickedly departed from my God*," that David lived habitually in communion with God, and knew him to be his own God, whom he might speak of as "*my God.*" God never departs from his people, let them take heed of departing from him.

22. "*For all his judgments were before me.*" The word, the character, and the actions of God should be evermore before our eyes ; we should learn, consider, and reverence them. Men forget what they do not wish to remember, but the excellent attributes of the Most High are objects of the believer's affectionate and delighted admiration. We should keep the image of God so constantly before us that we become in our measure conformed unto it. This inner love to the right must be the main spring of Christian integrity in our public walk. The fountain must be filled with love to holiness, and then the streams which issue from it will

be pure and gracious. *" I did not put away his statutes from me."* To put away the Scriptures from the mind's study is the certain way to prevent their influencing the outward conversation. Backsliders begin with dusty Bibles, and go on to filthy garments.

23. *" I was also upright before him."* Sincerity is here claimed; sincerity, such as would be accounted genuine before the bar of God. Whatever evil men might think of Him, David felt that he had the good opinion of his God. Moreover, freedom from his one great besetting sin he ventures also to plead, *" I kept myself from mine iniquity."* It is a very gracious sign when the most violent parts of our nature have been well guarded. If the weakest link in the chain is not broken, the stronger links will be safe enough. David's impetuous temper might have led him to slay Saul when he had him in his power, but grace enabled him to keep his hands clean of the blood of his enemy; but what a wonder it was, and how well worthy of such a grateful record as these verses afford! It will be a sweet cordial to us one of these days to remember our self-denials, and to bless God that we were able to exhibit them.

24. God first gives us holiness, and then rewards us for it. We are his workmanship; vessels made unto honour; and when made, the honour is not withheld from the vessel; though, in fact, it all belongs to the Potter upon whose wheel the vessel was fashioned. The prize is awarded to the flower at the show, but the gardener reared it; the child wins the prize from the schoolmaster, but the real honour of his schooling lies with his master, although instead of receiving he gives the reward.

25. The dealings of the Lord in his own case, cause the grateful singer to remember the usual rule of God's moral government; he is just in his dealings with the sons of men, and metes out to each man according to his measure. *"With the merciful thou wilt shew thyself merciful; with an upright man thou wilt shew thyself upright."* Every man shall have his meat weighed in his own scales, his corn meted in his own bushel, and his land measured with his own rod. No rule can be more fair, to ungodly men more terrible, or to the generous more honourable. How would men throw away their light weights, and break their short yards, if they could but believe that they themselves are sure to be in the end the losers by their knavish tricks? Note that even the merciful need mercy; no amount of generosity to the poor, or forgiveness to enemies, can set us beyond the need of mercy. Lord, have mercy upon me, a sinner.

26. *" With the pure thou wilt shew thyself pure; and with the froward thou wilt shew thyself froward."* The sinner's frowardness is sinful and rebellious, and the only sense in which the term can be applied to the Most Holy God is that of judicial opposition and sternness, in which the Judge of all the earth will act at cross-purposes with the offender, and let him see that all things are not to be made subservient to wicked whims and wilful fancies. Calvin very forcibly says, "This brutish and monstrous stupidity in men compels God to invent new modes of expression, and as it were to clothe himself with a different character. There is a similar sentence in Leviticus xxvi. 21—24, where God says, " and if ye walk contrary unto (or perversely with) me, then will I also walk contrary unto (or perversely, or roughly, or at random with) you." As if he had said that their obstinacy and stubbornness would make him on his part forget his accustomed forbearance and gentleness, and cast himself recklessly or at random against them. We see then what the stubborn at length gain by their obduracy; it is this, that God hardens himself still more to break them in pieces, and if they are of stone, he causes them to feel that he has the hardness of iron. The Jewish tradition was that the manna tasted according to each man's mouth; certainly God shows himself to each individual according to his character.

27. *" For thou wilt save the afflicted people."* This is a comforting assurance for the poor in spirit whose spiritual griefs admit of no sufficient solace from any other than a divine hand. They cannot save themselves nor can others do it, but God will save them. *" But wilt bring down high looks."* Those who look down on others with scorn shall be looked down upon with contempt ere long. The Lord abhors a proud look. What a reason for repentance and humiliation! How much better to be humble than to provoke God to humble us in his wrath! A considerable number of clauses occur in this passage in the future tense; how forcibly are we thus brought to remember that our present joy or sorrow is not to have so much weight with us as the great and eternal future!

28. "*For thou wilt light my candle.*" Evén the children of the day sometimes need candle-light. In the darkest hour light will arise ; a candle shall be lit, it will be comfort such as we may fittingly use without dishonesty—it will be our own candle ; yet God himself will find the holy fire with which the candle shall burn ; our evidences are our own, but their comfortable light is from above. Candles which are lit by God the devil cannot blow out. All candles are not shining, and so there are some graces which yield no present comfort ; but it is well to have candles which may by and by be lit, and it is well to possess graces which may yet afford us cheering evidences. The metaphor of the whole verse is founded upon the dolorous nature of darkness and the delightfulness of light ; " truly the light is sweet, and a pleasant thing it is for the eyes to behold the sun ; " and even so the presence of the Lord removes all the gloom of sorrow, and enables the believer to rejoice with exceeding great joy. The lighting of the lamp is a cheerful moment in the winter's evening, but the lifting up of the light of God's countenance is happier far. It is said that the poor in Egypt will stint themselves of bread to buy oil for the lamp, so that they may not sit in darkness; we could well afford to part with all earthly comforts if the light of God's love could but constantly gladden our souls.

29 For by thee I have run through a troop ; and by my God have I leaped over a wall.

30 *As for* God, his way *is* perfect : the word of the Lord is tried : he *is* a buckler to all those that trust in him.

31 For who *is* God save the Lord ? or who *is* a rock save our God ?

32 *It is* God that girdeth me with strength, and maketh my way perfect.

33 He maketh my feet like hinds' *feet,* and setteth me upon my high places.

34 He teacheth my hands to war, so that a bow of steel is broken by mine arms.

35 Thou hast also given me the shield of thy salvation : and thy right hand hath holden me up, and thy gentleness hath made me great.

36 Thou hast enlarged my steps under me, that my feet did not slip.

37 I have pursued mine enemies, and overtaken them : neither did I turn again till they were consumed.

38 I have wounded them that they were not able to rise : they are fallen under my feet.

39 For thou hast girded me with strength unto the battle : thou hast subdued under me those that rose up against me.

40 Thou hast also given me the necks of mine enemies ; that I might destroy them that hate me.

41 They cried, but *there was* none to save *them : even* unto the Lord, but he answered them not.

42 Then did I beat them small as the dust before the wind : I did cast them out as the dirt in the streets.

43 Thou hast delivered me from the strivings of the people ; *and* thou hast made me the head of the heathen : a people *whom* I have not known shall serve me.

44 As soon as they hear of me, they shall obey me : the strangers shall submit themselves unto me.

45 The strangers shall fade away, and be afraid out of their close places.

Some repetitions are not vain repetitions. Second thoughts upon God's mercy should be and often are the best. Like wines on the lees our gratitude grows stronger and sweeter as we meditate upon divine goodness. The verses which we have now to consider are the ripe fruit of a thankful spirit ; they are apples of gold as to matter, and they are placed in baskets of silver as to their language. They describe the believer's victorious career and his enemies' confusion.

29. " *For by thee I have run through a troop ; and by my God have I leaped over*

a wall." Whether we meet the foe in the open field or leap upon them while they lurk behind the battlements of a city, we shall by God's grace defeat them in either case ; if they hem us in with living legions, or environ us with stone walls, we shall with equal certainty obtain our liberty. Such feats we have already performed, hewing our way at a run through hosts of difficulties, and scaling impossibilities at a leap. God's warriors may expect to have a taste of every form of fighting, and must by the power of faith determine to quit themselves like men ; but it behoves them to be very careful to lay all their laurels at Jehovah's feet, each one of them saying, "*by my God*" have I wrought this valiant deed. Our *spolia optima*, the trophies of our conflicts, we hereby dedicate to the God of Battles, and ascribe to him all glory and strength.

30. "*As for God, his way is perfect.*" Far past all fault and error are God's dealings with his people ; all his actions are resplendent with justice, truth, tenderness, mercy, and holiness. Every way of God is complete in itself, and all his ways put together are matchless in harmony and goodness. Is it not very consolatory to believe that he who has begun to bless us will perfect his work, for all his ways are "*perfect*?" Nor must the divine "*word*" be without its song of praise. "*The word of the Lord is tried,*" like silver refined in the furnace. The doctrines are glorious, the precepts are pure, the promises are faithful, and the whole revelation is superlatively full of grace and truth. David had tried it, thousands have tried it, we have tried it, and it has never failed. It was meet that when way and word had been extolled, the Lord himself should be magnified ; hence it is added, "*He is a buckler to all those that trust in him.*" No armour of proof or shield of brass so well secures the warrior as the covenant God of Israel protects his warring people. He himself is the buckler of trustful ones ; what a thought is this ! What peace may every trusting soul enjoy !

31. Having mentioned his God, the Psalmist's heart burns, and his words sparkle ; he challenges heaven and earth to find another being worthy of adoration or trust in comparison with Jehovah. His God, as Matthew Henry says, is a None-such. The idols of the heathen he scorns to mention, snuffing them all out as mere nothings when Deity is spoken of. "*Who is God save the Lord?*" Who else creates, sustains, foresees, and overrules ? Who but he is perfect in every attribute, and glorious in every act ? To whom but Jehovah should creatures bow ? Who else can claim their service and their love ? "*Who is a rock save our God?*" Where can lasting hopes be fixed ? Where can the soul find rest ? Where is stability to be found ? Where is strength to be discovered ? Surely in the Lord Jehovah alone can we find rest and refuge.

32. Surveying all the armour in which he fought and conquered, the joyful victor praises the Lord for every part of the panoply. The girdle of his loins earns the first stanza : "*It is God that girdeth me with strength, and maketh my way perfect.*" Girt about the loins with power from heaven, the warrior was filled with vigour, far above all created might ; and, whereas, without this wonderous belt he would have been feeble and effeminate, with relaxed energies and scattered forces, he felt himself, when braced with the girdle of truth, to be compact in purpose, courageous in daring, and concentrated in power ; so that his course was a complete success, so undisturbed by disastrous defeat as to be called "perfect." Have we been made more than conquerors over sin, and has our life hitherto been such as becometh the gospel ? Then let us ascribe all the glory to him who girt us with his own inexhaustible strength, that we might be unconquered in battle and unwearied in pilgrimage.

33. The conqueror's feet had been shod by a divine hand, and the next note must, therefore, refer to them. "*He maketh my feet like hinds' feet, and setteth me upon my high p'aces.*" Pursuing his foes the warrior had been swift of foot as a young roe, but, instead of taking pleasure in the legs of a man, he ascribes the boon of swiftness to the Lord alone. When our thoughts are nimble, and our spirits rapid, like the chariots of Amminadib, let us not forget that our best Beloved's hand has given us the choice favour. Climbing into impregnable fortresses, David had been preserved from slipping, and made to stand where scarce the wild goat can find a footing ; herein was preserving mercy manifested. We, too, have had our *high places* of honour, service, temptation, and danger, but hitherto we have been kept from falling. Bring hither the harp, and let us emulate the Psalmist's joyful thanksgiving ; had we fallen, our wailings must have been terrible ; since we have stood, let our gratitude be fervent.

34. "*He teacheth my hands to war.*" Martial prowess and skill in the use of weapons are gratefully acknowledged to be the result of divine teaching ; no sacrifice is offered at the shrine of self in praise of natural dexterity, or acquired skilfulness ; but, regarding all warlike prowess as a gift of heavenly favour, thankfulness is presented to the Giver. The Holy Spirit is the great Drill-master of heavenly soldiers. "*So that a bow of steel is broken by mine arms.*" A bow of brass is probably meant, and these bows could scarcely be bent by the arms alone, the archer had to gain the assistance of his foot ; it was, therefore, a great feat of strength to bend the bow, so far as even to snap it in halves. This was meant of the enemies' bow, which he not only snatched from his grasp, but rendered useless by breaking it in pieces. Jesus not only destroyed the fiery suggestions of Satan, but he broke his arguments with which he shot them, by using Holy Scripture against him ; by the same means we may win a like triumph, breaking the bow and cutting the spear in sunder by the sharp edge of revealed truth. Probably David had by nature a vigorous bodily frame ; but it is even more likely that, like Samson, he was at times clothed with more than common strength ; at any rate, he ascribes the honour of his feats entirely to his God. Let us never wickedly rob the Lord of his due, but faithfully give unto him the glory which is due unto his name.

35. "*Thou hast also given me the shield of thy salvation.*" Above all we must take the shield of faith, for nothing else can quench Satan's fiery darts ; this shield is of celestial workmanship, and is in all cases a direct gift from God himself ; it is the channel, the sign, the guarantee, and the earnest of perfect salvation. "*Thy right hand hath holden me up.*" Secret support is administered to us by the preserving grace of God, and at the same time Providence kindly yields us manifest aid. We are such babes that we cannot stand alone ; but when the Lord's right hand upholds us, we are like brazen pillars which cannot be moved. "*Thy gentleness hath made me great.*" There are several readings of this sentence. The word is capable of being translated, "thy *goodness* hath made me great." David saw much of benevolence in God's action towards him, and he gratefully ascribed all his greatness not to his own goodness, but to the goodness of God. "*Thy providence*" is another reading, which is indeed nothing more than goodness in action. Goodness is the bud of which providence is the flower ; or goodness is the seed of which providence is the harvest. Some render it, "thy *help*," which is but another word for providence ; providence being the firm ally of the saints, aiding them in the service of their Lord. Certain learned annotators tell us that the text means, "thy *humility* hath made me great." "Thy *condescension*" may, perhaps, serve as a comprehensive reading, combining the ideas which he have already mentioned, as well as that of humility. It is God's making himself little which is the cause of our being made great. We are so little that if God should manifest his greatness without condescension, we should be trampled under his feet ; but God, who must stoop to view the skies and bow to see what angels do, looks to the lowly and contrite, and makes them great. While these are the translations which have been given to the adopted text of the original, we find that there are other readings altogether; as for instance, the Septuagint, which reads, "thy discipline"—thy fatherly correction— "hath made me great ;" while the Chaldee paraphrase reads, "thy word hath increased me." Still the idea is the same. David ascribes all his own greatness to the condescending goodness and graciousness of his Father in heaven. Let us all feel this sentiment in our own hearts, and confess that whatever of goodness or greatness God may have put upon us, we must cast our crowns at his feet, and cry, "*thy gentleness hath made me great.*"

36. "*Thou hast enlarged my steps.*" A smooth pathway leading to spacious possessions and camping-grounds had been opened up for him. Instead of threading the narrow mountain paths, and hiding in the cracks and corners of caverns, he was able to traverse the plains and dwell under his own vine and fig tree. It is no small mercy to be brought into full Christian liberty and enlargement, but it is a greater favour still to be enabled to walk worthily in such liberty, not being permitted to slip with our feet. To stand upon the rocks of affliction is the result of gracious upholding, but that aid is quite as much needed in the luxurious plains of prosperity.

37. The preservation of the saints bodes ill for their adversaries. The Amalekites thought themselves clear away with their booty, but when David's God guided him in the pursuit, they were soon overtaken and cut in pieces. When God is with us sins and sorrows flee, and all forms of evil are "*consumed*" before the power

of grace. What a noble picture this and the following verses present to us of the victories of our glorious Lord Jesus!

38. The destruction of our spiritual enemies is complete. We may exult over sin, death and hell, as disarmed and disabled *for* us by our conquering Lord; may he graciously give them a like defeat *within* us.

39 and 40. It is impossible to be too frequent in the duty of ascribing all our victories to the God of our salvation. It is true that we have to wrestle with our spiritual antagonists, but the triumph is far more the Lord's than ours. We must not boast like the ambitious votaries of vainglory, but we may exult as the willing and believing instruments in the Lord's hands of accomplishing his great designs.

41. *" They cried, but there was none to save them ; even unto the Lord, but he answered them not."* Prayer is so notable a weapon that even the wicked will take to it in their fits of desperation. Bad men have appealed to God against God's own servants, but all in vain ; the kingdom of heaven is not divided, and God never succours his foes at the expense of his friends. There are prayers to God which are no better than blasphemy, which bring no comfortable reply, but rather provoke the Lord to greater wrath. Shall I ask a man to wound or slay his own child to gratify my malice ? Would he not resent the insult against his humanity ? How much less will Jehovah regard the cruel desires of the enemies of the church, who dare to offer their prayers for its destruction calling its existence schism, and its doctrine heresy !

42. The defeat of the nations who fought with King David was so utter and complete that they were like powders pounded in a mortar ; their power was broken into fragments and they became as weak as dust before the wind, and as mean as the mire of the roads. Thus powerless and base are the enemies of God now become through the victory of the Son of David upon the cross. Arise, O my soul, and meet thine enemies, for they have sustained a deadly blow, and will fall before thy bold advance.

> " Hell and my sins resist my course,
> But hell and sin are vanquish'd foes ;
> My Jesus nail'd them to his cross,
> And sung the triumph when he rose."

43. *" Thou hast delivered me from the strivings of the people."* Internal strife is very hard to deal with. A civil war is war in its most miserable form ; it is a subject for warmest gratitude when concord rules within. Our poet praises Jehovah for the union and peace which smiled in his dominions, and if we have peace in the three kingdoms of our spirit, soul, and body, we are in duty bound to give Jehovah a song. Unity in a church should assuredly excite like gratitude. *" Thou hast made me the head of the heathen ; a people whom I have not known shall serve me."* The neighbouring nations yielded to the sway of Judah's prince. Oh when shall all lands adore King Jesus, and serve him with holy joy ? Surely there is far more of Jesus than of David here. Missionaries may derive rich encouragement from the positive declaration that heathen lands shall own the Headship of the Crucified.

44. *" As soon as they hear of me, they shall obey me."* Thus readily did the once struggling captain become a far-renowned victor, and thus easy shall be our triumphs. We prefer, however, to speak of Jesus. In many cases the gospel is speedily received by hearts apparently unprepared for it. Those who have never heard the gospel before, have been charmed by its first message, and yielded obedience to it ; while others, alas ! who are accustomed to its joyful sound, are rather hardened than softened by its teachings. The grace of God sometimes runs like fire among the stubble, and a nation is born in a day. " Love at first sight " is no uncommon thing when Jesus is the wooer. He can write Cæsar's message without boasting, *Veni, vidi, vici* ; his gospel is in some cases no sooner heard than believed. What inducements to spread abroad the doctrine of the cross !

45. *" The strangers shall fade away."* Like sear leaves or blasted trees our foes and Christ's foes shall find no sap and stamina remaining in them. Those who are strangers to Jesus are strangers to all lasting happiness ; those must soon fade who refuse to be watered from the river of life. *"And be afraid out of their close places."* Out of their mountain fastnesses the heathen crept in fear to own allegiance to Israel's king, and even so, from the castles of self-confidence and the dens of carnal security, poor sinners come bending before the Saviour, Christ the Lord. Our sins which have entrenched themselves in our flesh and blood as in impregnable forts, shall yet be

driven forth by the sanctifying energy of the Holy Spirit, and we shall serve the Lord in singleness of heart.

Thus with remembrances of conquests in the past, and with glad anticipations of victories yet to come the sweet singer closes the description, and returns to exercise of more direct adoration of his gracious God.

46 The LORD liveth ; and blessed *be* my rock ; and let the God of my salvation be exalted.

47 *It is* God that avengeth me, and subdueth the people under me.

48 He delivereth me from mine enemies : yea, thou liftest me up above those that rise up against me : thou hast delivered me from the violent man.

49 Therefore will I give thanks unto thee, O LORD, among the heathen, and sing praises unto thy name.

50 Great deliverance giveth he to his king ; and sheweth mercy to his anointed, to David, and to his seed for evermore.

46. "*The Lord liveth.*" Possessing underived, essential, independent and eternal life. We serve no inanimate, imaginary, or dying God. He only hath immortality. Like loyal subjects let us cry, Live on, O God. Long live the King of kings. By thine immortality do we dedicate ourselves afresh to thee. As the Lord our God liveth so would we live to him. "*And blessed be my rock.*" He is the ground of our hope, and let him be the subject of our praise. Our hearts bless the Lord, with holy love extolling him.

> Jehovah lives, my rock be blest !
> Praised be the God who gives me rest !

"*Let the God of my salvation be exalted.*" As our Saviour, the Lord should more than ever be glorified. We should publish abroad the story of the covenant and the cross, the Father's election, the Son's redemption, and the Spirit's regeneration. He who rescues us from deserved ruin should be very dear to us. In heaven they sing, "Unto him that loved us and washed us in his blood;" the like music should be common in the assemblies of the saints below.

47. "*It is God that avengeth me, and subdueth the people under me.*" To rejoice in personal revenge is unhallowed and evil, but David viewed himself as the instrument of vengeance upon the enemies of God and his people, and had he not rejoiced in the success accorded to him he would have been worthy of censure. That sinners perish is in itself a painful consideration, but that the Lord's law is avenged upon those who break it is to the devout mind a theme for thankfulness. We must, however, always remember that vengeance is never ours, vegeance belongeth unto the Lord, and he is so just and withal so long-suffering in the excercise of it, that we may safely leave its administration in his hands.

48. From all enemies, and especially from one who was pre-eminent in violence, the Lord's anointed was preserved, and at the last over the head of Saul and all other adversaries he reigned in honour. The like end awaits every saint, because Jesus who stooped to be lightly esteemed among men is now made to sit far above all principalities and powers.

49. Paul cites this verse (Rom. xv. 9) : "And that the Gentiles might glorify God for his mercy ; as it is written, For this cause I will confess to thee among the Gentiles, and sing unto thy name." This is clear evidence that David's Lord is here, but David is here too, and is to be viewed as an example of a holy soul making its boast in God even in the presence of ungodly men. Who are the despisers of God that we should stop our mouths for them ? We will sing to our God whether they like it or no, and force upon them the knowledge of his goodness. Too much politeness to traitors may be treason to our King.

50. This is the winding-up verse into which the writer throws a fulness of expression, indicating the most rapturous delight of gratitude. "*Great deliverance.*" The word "*deliverance*" is plural, to show the variety and completeness of the salvation ; the adjective "*great*" is well placed if we consider from what, to what, and how we are saved. All this mercy is given to us in our King, the Lord's Anointed, and those are blessed indeed who as his seed may expect mercy to be built up for evermore. The Lord was faithful to the literal David, and he will not break his

covenant with the spiritual David, for that would far more involve the honour of his crown and character.

The Psalm concludes in the same loving spirit which shone upon its commencement ; happy are they who can sing on from love to love, even as the pilgrims marched from strength to strength.

EXPLANATORY NOTES AND QUAINT SAYINGS.

Whole Psalm.—The general argument of the Psalm may be thus stated : it is a magnificent eucharistic ode. It begins with a celebration of the glorious perfections of the Divinity, whose assistance the speaker had so often experienced. He describes, or rather, he delineates, his perils, the power of his enemies, his sudden deliverance from them, and the indignation and power of his divine deliverer manifested in their overthrow. He paints these in so lively colours, that while we read we seem to see the lightning, to hear the thunders, to feel the earthquake. He afterwards describes his victories, so that we seem to be eye-witnesses of them, and take part in them. He predicts a wide-extended empire, and concludes with a lofty expression of grateful adoration of Jehovah, the Author of all his deliverances and triumphs. The style is highly oratorical and poetical, sublime, and full of uncommon figures of speech. It is the natural language of a person of the highest mental endowments, under a divine inspiration, deeply affected by remarkable divine benefits, and filled with the most lofty conceptions of the divine character and dispensations.—*John Brown, D.D.*, 1853.

Whole Psalm.—Kitto, in " The Pictorial Bible," has the following note upon 2 Samuel xxii. :—" This is the same as the eighteenth Psalm . . . . The Rabbins reckon up seventy-four differences between the two copies, most of them very minute. They probably arose from the fact that the poem was, as they conjecture, composed by David in his youth, and revised in his later days when he sent it to the chief musician. The present is, of course, supposed to be the earlier copy."

Whole Psalm.—The eighteenth Psalm is called by Michaelis more artificial, and less truly terrible than the Mosaic odes. In structure it may be so, but surely not in spirit. It appears to many besides us, one of the most magnificent lyrical raptures in the Scriptures. As if the poet had dipped his pen in " the brightness of that light which was before his eye," so he describes the descending God. Perhaps it may be objected that the *nodus* is hardly worthy of the *vindex*—to deliver David from his enemies, could Deity ever be imagined to come down ? But the objector knows not the character of the ancient Hebrew mind. God in its view had not to descend from heaven ; he was nigh—a cloud like a man's hand might conceal—a cry, a look might bring him down. And why should not David's fancy clothe him, as he came, in a panoply befitting his dignity, in clouds spangled with coals of fire ? If he was to descend, why not in state ? The proof of the grandeur of this Psalm is in the fact, that it has borne the test of almost every translation, and made doggerel erect itself, and become divine. Even Sternhold and Hopkins its fiery whirlwind lifts up, purifies, touches into true power, and then throws down, helpless and panting, upon their ancient common. Perhaps the great charm of the eighteenth, apart from the poetry of the descent, is the exquisite and subtle alternation of the *I* and the *Thou*. We have spoken of parallelism, as the key to the mechanism of Hebrew song. We find this as existing between David and God—the delivered and the deliverer—beautifully pursued throughout the whole of this Psalm. "I will love thee, O Lord, my strength." " I will call upon the Lord, who is worthy to be praised." "He sent from above ; he took me ; he drew me out of many waters." " Thou wilt light my candle." " Thou hast given me the shield of thy salvation." " Thou hast girded me with strength unto battle." " Thou hast given me the necks of mine enemies." " Thou hast made me the head of the heathen." It has been ingeniously argued, that the existence of the *I* suggests, inevitably as a polar opposite, the thought of the *Thou*, that the personality of man proves thus the personality of God ; but, be this as it may, David's perception of that personality is nowhere so intense as here. He seems not only to see, but to feel and touch, the object of his gratitude and worship.—*George Gi fillan, in " The Bards of the Bible," 1852.*

Whole Psalm.—He that would be wise, let him read the Proverbs ; he that would be holy, let him read the Psalms. Every line in this book breathes peculiar sanctity. This Psalm, though placed among the first, was penned among the last, as the preface assures us, and is left as the epitome of the general history of David's life. It is twice recorded in the Scripture (2 Sam. xxii., and in this book of Psalms), for the excellency and sweetness thereof ; surely that we should take double notice of it. Holy David, being near the shore, here looks on his former dangers and deliverances with a thankful heart, and writes this Psalm to bless the Lord : as if each of you that are grown into years should review your lives and observe the wonderful goodness and providence of God towards you ; and then sit down and write a modest memorial of his most remarkable mercies, for the comfort of your- selves and posterity ; an excellent practice. What a comfort would it be for you to read how good your God was to your father or grandfather, that are dead and gone! So would your children rejoice in the Lord upon the reading of his goodness to you ; and you cannot have a better pattern for this than holy David, who wrote this Psalm when he was threescore and seven years old ; when he had outlived most of his troubles, and almost ready for his journey to his Father in heaven, he resolves to leave this good report of him upon earth. And I pray mark how he begins : he sets not up trophies to himself, but triumphs in his God—" *I will love thee, O Lord, my strength.*" As the *love of God* is the beginning of all our mercies, so *love to God* should be the end and effect of them all. As the stream leads us to the spring, so all the gifts of God must lead us to the giver of them. Lord, thou hast saved me from sickness, " *I will love thee ;* " from death and hell, " *I will love thee ;* " on me thou hast bestowed grace and comfort, " *I will love thee, O Lord, my strength.*" And after he had heaped on God all the sweet names he could devise (verse 2), as the true saint thinks he can never speak too well of God, or too ill of himself, then he begins his narative. 1. Of his *dangers* (verse 4) ; " *Snares of death,*" " *Floods of ungodly men,*" " *Sorrows of hell.*" Hell and earth are combined against each holy man, and will trouble sufficiently in this world, if they cannot keep him out of a better. 2. Of his *retreat,* and that was, earnest prayer to God (verse 6), " *I called upon the Lord, and cried unto my God.*" When our prayers are cries ardent and importunate, then they speed : " *My cry came before him, even into his ears.*" The mother trifles while the child whimpers, but when he raises his note—strains every nerve and cries every vein—then she throws all aside, and gives him his desire. While our prayers are only whispers, our God can take his rest ; but when we fall to crying, " Now will I arise, saith the Lord." 3. Of his *rescue* (verses 7 to 20), by the powerful and terrible arm of the Lord, who is in a lofty strain brought in to his servant's help, as if he would mingle heaven and earth together, rather than leave his child in the lion's paws. 4. Of the *reason* of this gracious dealing of God with him (verse 20, etc.) He was a righteous person, and he had a righteous cause. And thereupon he turns to God, saying, Thou hast dealt with me just as thou art wont to do, for " *with the merciful thou wilt show thyself merciful ; with an upright man thou wilt show thyself upright.*"—*Richard Steele's " Plain Discourse upon Uprightness," 1670.*

Whole Psalm.—Sometimes the Lord cheers and comforts the hearts of his people with smiling and reviving providences, both public and personal. There are times of lifting up, as well as casting down by the hand of providence. The scene changes, the aspects of providence are very cheerful and encouraging ; their winter seems to be over ; they put off their garments of mourning ; and then, ah, what sweet returns are made to heavenly gracious souls ! Doth God lift them up by prosperity ? they also will lift up their God by praises. See title, and verses 1—3 of Psalm xviii. So Moses, and the people with him (Exodus xv.), when God had delivered them from Pharaoh, how do they exalt him in a song of thanksgiving, which for the elegancy and spirituality of it, is made an emblem of the doxologies given to God in glory by the saints. Rev. xv. 1.—*John Flavel.*

Title.—" *The servant of the Lord ;* "—the name given to Moses (Josh. i. 1, 13, 15, and in nine other places of that book) and to Joshua (Josh. xxiv. 29 ; Judg. ii. 8) ; but to none other except David (here, and in the title to Ps. xxxvi.). Cp. Acts xiii. 36, ὑπηρετήσας. This is significant ; reminding us of the place occupied by David in the history of Israel. He was the appointed successor of Moses and Joshua,

who extended the power of Israel over the whole region allotted to them by Divine promise.—*W. Kay,* 1871.

Title.—This Psalm, which is entitled a *shirah* (or song), is David's hymn of praise to God for his deliverance from all his enemies (see the title, and above, 2 Sam. xxii), and has an appropriate place in the present group of Psalms, which speak of resurrection after suffering. It is entitled a Psalm of David, "*the servant of the Lord,*" and thus is coupled with another Psalm of deliverance, Ps. xxxvi.—*Christopher Wordsworth.*

Verse 1.—"*I will love thee, O Lord.*"—The word whereby the Psalmist expresseth his entire affection, in the noun signifieth a womb, and importeth such an affection as cometh from the innermost part of man (םֶחֶר matrix), from his bowels, from the bottom of his heart, as we speak. It is, therefore, oft put for such pity and compassion as moveth the bowels. Some, therefore, thus translate that phrase, " From my innermost bowels will I love thee, O Lord." To give evidence of his entire and ardent love of God, he oft professeth his wonderful great love to God's commandments, whereof he saith with admiration, " Oh, how I love thy law ! I love thy commandments above gold ; yea, above fine gold. I love them exceedingly " (Psalm cxix. 97, 127, 167) ; therefore, he saith to God, " Consider how I love thy precepts " (verse 159).—*William Gouge,* 1575—1653.

Verse 1.—" *I will love thee.*" Intimately as a mother loves the child that comes out of her womb.—*Westminster Assembly's Annotations,* 1651.

Verses 1, 2.—God hath, as it were, made himself over to believers. David doth not say, God will give or bestow salvation upon me ; but he saith, " He is the horn of my salvation." It is God himself who is the salvation and the portion of his people. They would not care much for salvation if God were not their salvation. It more pleaseth the saints that they enjoy God, than that they enjoy salvation. False and carnal spirits will express a great deal of desire after salvation, for they like salvation, heaven, and glory well ; but they never express any longing desire after God and Jesus Christ. They love salvation, but they care not for a Saviour. Now that which faith pitcheth most upon is God himself ; he shall be my salvation, let me have him, and that is salvation enough ; he is my life, he is my comfort, he is my riches, he is my honour, and he is my all. Thus David's heart acted immediately upon God, "*I will love thee, O Lord, my strength. The Lord is my rock, and my fortress, and my deliverer ; my God, my strength, in whom I will trust ; my buckler, and the horn of my salvation, and my high tower.*" It pleased holy David more that God was his strength, than that God gave him strength ; that God was his deliverer, than that he was delivered ; that God was his fortress, his buckler, his horn, his high tower, than that he gave him the effect of all these. It pleased David, and it pleases all the saints more that God is their salvation, whether temporal or eternal, than that he saves them : the saints look more at God than at all that is God's.—*Joseph Caryl.*

Verses 1, 2.—David speaks like one in love with God, for he doth adorn him with confession of praise, and his mouth is filled with the praise of the Lord, which he expresseth in this exuberancy and redundancy of holy oratory.—*Edward Marbury.*

Verse 2.—" *The Lord is my rock.*" As the rocks that are hard to be clambered unto are good refuges to fly unto from the face of pursuers, so God is the safety of all such as in distress do fly to him for succour.—*Robert Cawdray.*

Verse 2.—" *My deliverer.*" He who betook himself to one of these inaccessible retreats, was sometimes obliged by famine to surrender to his enemy, who lay in wait for him beneath ; but Jehovah gives him not only security but liberty ; not only preserves him, as it were, in an inaccessible retreat, but at the same time enables him to go forth in safety.—*Jarchi.*

Verse 2.—" *The horn of my salvation.*" The allusion here is doubtful. Some have supposed the reference to be to the horns of animals, by which they defend themselves and attack their enemies. " God is to me, does for me, what their horns do for them." Others consider it as referring to the well-established fact, that warriors were accustomed to place horns, or ornaments like horns, on their helmets. The horn stands for the helmet ; and " the helmet of salvation " is an expression equivalent to " a saving, a protecting helmet." Others consider the reference as to the corners or handles of the altar in the court of the tabernacle or temple, which are called its horns. Others suppose the reference to be to the highest point of a lofty and precipitous mountain, which we are accustomed to call its peak. No doubt, in the Hebrew language, horn is used for mountain as in Isaiah v. 1. A very fertile mountain is called a horn of oil. The sense is substantially the same, whichever of these views we take ; though, from the connection with " shield " or " buckler," I am induced to consider the second of these views as the most probable. It seems the same idea as that expressed, Psalm cxl. 7, "Thou hast covered," and thou wilt cover " my head in the day of battle."—*John Brown.*

Verse 2.—" *The horn of my salvation.*" Horns are the well-known emblems of strength and power, both in the sacred and profane writers ; by a metaphor taken from horned animals, which are frequently made subjects of comparison by poetical writers, and the strength of which, whether for offence or defence, consists principally in their horns. Bruce speaks of a remarkable head-dress worn by the governors of provinces in Abyssinia, consisting of a large broad fillet, bound upon their foreheads and tied behind their heads, and having in the middle of it a horn, or a conical piece of silver, gilt, about four inches long, much in the shape of our common candle extinguishers. It is called *kirn* or horn, and is only worn on reviews or parades after victory. He supposes this, like other Abyssinian usages, to be taken from the Hebrews, and is of opinion that there are many allusions to the practice in Scripture, in the expressions, "lifting up the horn," "exalting the horn," and the like.—*Richard Mant.*

Verse 2.—" *The Lord is my high tower.*" If a man do run to a tower, yet if that be a weak and an insufficient tower, without men and munition, and a ruinous shaken tower ; or if a man do make choice of a tower, a strong sufficient tower, yet if in his danger he betake not himself to that tower, but he sit still; or if he sit not still, yet he but only go and walk on easily towards it, he may well be met withal, and a danger may arrest him, surprise him, and cut him off before he get the tower over his head. But the man that will be safe, as he must choose a strong tower, so he must go to, nay, *run* into that tower. Running will not secure a man unless the tower be strong . . . . . David was got unto his *tower*, and in that *tower* there was thundering ordnance, and David put fire to them by prayer, verse 6, " In my distress I called upon the Lord, and cried unto my God : he heard my voice out of his temple, and my cry came before him, even into his ears." Here David prays and gives fire to the cannon, and what followed ? See verses 7, 8, 13, 14. " Then the earth shook and trembled," etc. " There went up a smoke out of his nostrils," etc. " The Lord also thundered in the heavens, and the Highest gave his voice ; hail stones and coals of fire. Yea, he sent out his arrows, and scattered them ; and he shot out lightnings, and discomfited them." There were no guns nor ordnance invented and in use in David's time, and yet David's prayers being in this tower, did him as good service against his enemies as all the ordnance and cannons in the world have done. David had thundering ordnance, and with them discomfited his enemies long before powder and guns were invented. It is a memorable and well known story of that Christian legion that was in Marcus Aurelius's army : the enemy being in great straits, those Christian soldiers did by their prayers not only procure rain, by which his languishing army was refreshed, but also obtained hail mixed with thunderbolts against his enemies, upon which he honoured them with the name of *Legio fulminatrix*, the Thundering Legion. They used David's cannon against the enemy, and discharged that thundering ordnance by their prayers, and that to the confusion of their enemies.—*Jeremiah Dyke's* " *Righteous Man's Tower,*" 1639.

Verse 2.—" *My high tower.*" Even as the fowls of the air, that they may escape the nets and snares of the fowlers, are wont to fly up on high ; so we, to avoid the infinite snares of innumerable temptations, must fly to God ; and lift up ourselves from the corruptions, lying vanities, and deceitful sleights of the world.—*Robert Cawdray.*

Verse 3.—" *I will call upon the Lord, who is worthy to be praised.*" Prayer and invocation of God should always be joined with praises and thanksgivings, and used as a means whereby faith shall extract the good which it knoweth is in God, and of which he hath made promise.—*David Dickson.*

Verse 3.—" *So shall I be saved from mine enemies.*" Whoso comes to God as he should will not call in vain. The right kind of prayer is the most potent instrumentality known on earth.—*William S. Plumer.*

Verse 4.—" *Sorrows of death.*" It is heaven's peculiar to be the land of the living ; all this life is at most but the *shadow* of death, the *gate* of death, the *sorrows* of death, the *snares* of death, the *terrors* of death, the *chambers* of death, the *sentence* of death, the *savour* of death, the *ministration* of death, the *way* of death. *Matthew Griffith*. 1634.

Verse 4.—" *The bands or cords of death encompassed me.*" It is not very easy to fix the precise meaning of the phrase, " bands " or " cords " of death. It may either be considered as equivalent to " the bands by which the dead are bound," in which case, to be encircled with the bands of death is just a figurative expression for being dead; or it may be considered as equivalent to the bands in which a person is bound in the prospect of a violent death, and by which his violent death is secured, he being prevented from escaping. It has been supposed by some, that the allusion is to the ancient mode of hunting wild animals. A considerable tract of country was surrounded with strong ropes. The circle was gradually contracted, till the object of pursuit was so confined as to become an easy prey to the hunter. These cords were the cords of death, securing the death of the animal. The phrase is applicable to our Lord in both senses; but as " the floods " of wickedness, or the wicked, are represented as making him afraid subsequently to his being encircled with the cords of death, I am disposed to understand it in the latter of these two senses.—*John Brown.*

Verse 4.—" *The floods.*" There is no metaphor of more frequent occurrence with the sacred poets, than that which represents dreadful and unexpected calamities under the images of overwhelming waters. This image seems to have been especially familiar with the Hebrews, inasmuch as it was derived from the peculiar habit and nature of their own country. They had continually before their eyes the river Jordan, annually overflowing its banks, when at the approach of summer the snows of Libanus and the neighbouring mountains melted, and, suddenly pouring down in torrents, swelled the current of the river. Besides, the whole country of Palestine, although it was not watered by many perennial streams, was, from the mountainous character of the greater part of it, liable to numerous torrents, which precipitated themselves through the narrow valleys after the periodical rainy seasons. This image, therefore, however known, and adopted by other poets, may be considered as particularly familar and, as it were, domestic with the Hebrews; who accordingly introduce it with greater frequency and freedom.—*Robert Lowth (Bishop)*, 1710—1787.

Verse 5.—" *The snares of death prevented me.*" The word " snares," signifies such traps or gins as are laid for birds and wild beasts. The English word " prevent " has changed its meaning in some measure since our authorised translation of the Bible was made. Its original meaning is to " come before."—*John Brown.*

Verse 6.—" *In my distress.*" If you listen even to David's harp, you shall hear as many hearse-like airs as carols; and the pencil of the Holy Spirit hath laboured more in describing the afflictions of Job than the felicities of Solomon. Prosperity is not without many fears and distastes; and adversity is not without comforts and hopes. We see, in needleworks and embroideries, it is more pleasing to have a lively work upon a sad and solemn ground, than to have a dark and melancholy work upon a lightsome ground; judge, therefore, of the pleasures of the heart by the pleasures of the eye. Certainly virtue is like precious odours—most fragrant when they are crushed; for prosperity doth best discover vice, but adversity doth best discover virtue.—*Francis Bacon, Baron of Verulam, etc.*, 1561—1626.

Verse 6.—" *I called upon the Lord and cried.*" Prayer is not eloquence but earnestness; not the definition of helplessness, but the feeling of it; it is the cry of faith to the ear of mercy.—*Hannah Moore*, 1745—1833.

Verse 6.—" *He heard my voice out of his temple,*" etc. The Ædiles or chamberlains among the Romans, had ever their doors standing open for all who had occasion of request or complaint to have free access to them. " God's mercy-doors are wide open to the prayers of his faithful people." The Persian kings held it a piece of their silly glory to deny an easy access to their greatest subjects. It was death to solicit them uncalled. Esther herself was afraid. But the king of heaven manifesteth himself to his people, he calls to his spouse, with, " Let me see thy face, let me hear thy voice," etc., and assigneth her negligence herein as the cause of her soul-sickness. The door of the tabernacle was not of any hard or debarring matter, but a veil, which is easily penetrable. And whereas in the temple none came near to worship, but only the high priest, others stood without in the outer court. God's people are now a kingdom of priests, and are said to worship in the temple, and at the altar. Rev. xi. 1. " Let us therefore draw near with a true heart in full assurance of faith : " " let us come boldly to the throne of grace, that we may obtain mercy, and find grace to help in time of need." Heb. x. 22 ; iv. 16.—*Charles Bradbury's " Cabinet of Jewels," 1785.*

Verse 6.—Oh ! how true is that saying, that " Faith is safe when in danger, and in danger when secure ; and prayer is fervent in straits, but in joyful and prosperous circumstances, if not quite cold and dead, at least lukewarm." Oh, happy straits, if they hinder the mind from flowing forth upon earthly objects, and mingling itself with the mire ; if they favour our correspondence with heaven, and quicken our love to celestial objects, without which, what we call life, may more properly deserve the name of death !—*Robert Leighton, D.D.*

Verses 6, 7.—The prayer of a single saint is sometimes followed with wonderful effects ; " *In my distress I called upon the Lord, and cried unto my God : he heard my voice out of his temple, and my cry came before him, even into his ears. Then the earth shook and trembled ; the foundations also of the hills moved and were shaken, because he was wroth :* " what then can a thundering legion of such praying souls do ? It was said of Luther, *iste vir potuit cum Deo quicquid voluit*, That man could have of God what he would ; his enemies felt the weight of his prayers ; and the church of God reaped the benefits thereof. The Queen of Scots professed she was more afraid of the prayers of Mr. Knox, than of an army of ten thousand men. These were mighty wrestlers with God, howsoever contemned and vilified among their enemies. There will a time come when God will hear the prayers of his people who are continually crying in his ears, " How long, Lord, how long ? "—*John Flavel.*

Verse 7.—" *Then the earth shook and trembled.*" The word וגﬠ signifies, to move or shake violently : it is employed, also, to denote the reeling and staggering of a drunken man. Jer. xxv. 16.—*John Morison, in loc.*

Verse 7.—Let no appearing impossibilities make you question God's accomplishment of any of his gracious words. Though you cannot see how the thing can be done, 'tis enough if God hath said that he will do it. There can be no obstructions to promised salvation which we need to fear. He who is the God of this salvation and the Author of the promise will prepare his own way for the doing of his own work, so that " every valley shall be filled, and every mountain and hill shall be brought low." Luke iii. 5. Though the valleys be so deep that we cannot see the bottom, and the mountains so high that we cannot see the tops of them, yet God knows how to raise the one and level the other. Isaiah lxiii. 1. " I that speak in righteousness (or faithfulness) am mighty to save." If anything would keep back the kingdom of Christ, it would be our infidelity ; but he will come though he should find no faith on the earth. See Rom. iii. 3. Cast not away your confidence because he defers his performances. Though providences run cross, though they move backwards and forwards, you have a sure and faithful word to rely upon. Promises, though they be for a time seemingly delayed, cannot be finally frustrated. Dare not to harbour such a thought within yourselves as Psalm lxxvii. 8 ; " Doth his promise fail for evermore ? " The being of God may as well fail as the promise of God. That which does not come in your time, will be hastened in his time, which is always the more convenient season. Accuse him not of slowness who hath said, " I come quickly," that is, he comes as soon as all things are ready and ripe for his appearance. 'Tis as true that " the Lord is not slack concerning his promise " (2 Peter iii. 9), as that he is never guilty of breaking his promise. Wait, therefore, how long soever he tarry ; do not give over expecting : the heart of God is not turned though his face be hid ; and prayers are not flung back, though they be not instantly answered.—*Timothy Cruso.*

Verses 7, 8.—The volcanic phenomena of Palestine open a question of which the data are, in a scientific point of view, too imperfect to be discussed ; but there is enough in the history and literature of the people to show that there was an agency of this kind at work. The valley of the Jordan, both in its desolation and vegetation, was one continued portent ; and from its crevices ramified even into the interior of Judæa the startling appearances, if not of the volcano, at least of the earthquake. Their historical effect in the special theatres of their operation will appear as we proceed ; but their traces on the permanent feeling of the nation must be noticed here. The writings of the psalmists and prophets abound with indications which escape the eye of a superficial reader. Like the soil of their country, they actually heave and labour with the fiery convulsions which glow beneath their surface.— *Arthur Penrhyn Stanley.*

Verses 7—9.—While Jesus hung on the cross a preternatural " darkness covered all the land ; " and no sooner had he yielded up his spirit, than " the vail of the temple was rent in twain from the top even to the bottom, and the earth did quake, and the rocks rent, and the graves were opened ; and many bodies of the saints that slept arose, and came out of the graves, after his resurrection, and went into the holy city, and appeared unto many."—*John Brown.*

Verses 7—9.—In the night in which the Idumæans lay before Jerusalem, there arose a prodigious tempest and fierce winds, with most vehement rains, frequent lightnings, and terrible thunderings, and great roarings of the shaken earth ; and it was manifest that the state of the universe was disordered at the slaughter of men ; so that one might guess that these were signs of no small calamity . . . . . At the day of Pentecost, when the priests, by night, went into the inner temple, according to their custom, to execute their office, they said they perceived, first of all, a shake and a noise, and after that a sudden voice, " Let us go hence." . . . . . A few days after the feast of unleavened bread, a strange and almost incredible sight was seen, which would, I suppose, be taken for a mere fable, were it not related by such as saw it, and did not the miseries which followed appear answerable to the signs ; for, before the sun set, were seen on high, in the air, all over the country, chariots and armed regiments moving swiftly in the clouds, and encompassing the city.—*Flavius Josephus,* 37—103.

Verse 8.—" *There went up a smoke out of his nostrils,*" עָלָה עָשָׁן בְּאַפּוֹ. Or there *ascended into his nose,* as the words, literally rendered, signify. The ancients placed the seat of anger in the nose, or nostrils ; because when it grows warm and violent, it discovers itself, as it were, by a heated vehement breath, that proceeds from them.—*Samuel Chandler, D.D., F.R. and A.S.S.,* 1766.

Verses 8—19.—David calls the full force of poetical imagery to aid, to describe in a becoming manner the marvels of his deliverances. He means to say that they were as manifest as the signs of heaven and earth, as sudden and powerful as the phenomena in the kingdom of nature surprise terrified mortals. *Deliverance* being his theme, he might have taken the figure from the *peaceable* phenomena of the heavens. But since man heeds heaven more in *anger* than in *blessing,* and regards God more when he descends on earth in the *storm* than in the *rainbow,* David describes the blessed condescension of God by the figure of a tempest. In order to thoroughly appreciate the beauty and truthfulness of this figure, we should endeavour to realise the full power of an Oriental storm, as it is described in Psalm xxix. Solitary lightning precedes the discharge—this is meant by the *coals* in verse 8: the clouds approach the mountain summits—*the heavens bow,* as verse 9 has it ; the storm shakes its pinions ; enwrapped in thick clouds as in a tent, God descends to the earth; hail (not unfrequently attending Eastern storms) and lightning issue from the black clouds, through the dissolving layers of which is seen the fiery splendour which hides the Lord of nature. He speaks, and thunder is his voice ; he shoots, and flashes of lightning are his arrows. At his rebuke, and at the blast of his breath the earth recedes—the sea foams up, and its beds are seen—the land bursts, and the foundations of the world are discovered. And lo ! an arm of deliverance issues forth from the black clouds, and the destructive fire grasps the wretched one who had cried out from the depths, pulls him forth, and delivers him from all his enemies ! Yes, the hand of the Lord has done marvellous things in the life of David. But the *eye of faith* alone could perceive in them all the hand of God. Thousands whose experiences of the delivering hand of God are not less signal than those of David, stop short at the powers of nature, and instead of bending the knee before the All-merciful God, content themselves to express with cold hearts their admiration of the changes of the destiny of man.—*Augustus F. Tholuck, D.D., Ph.D.* 1856.

Verse 9.—" *He bowed the heavens also, and came down.*" As in a tempest the clouds come nearer to the earth, and from the mountains to the valleys, so the Psalmist adopts this figure peculiar to such occasions as described God's near approach to judgment (Psalm cxliv. 5, etc. ; Heb. iii. 6); "*and darkness was under his feet.*" We have here the increase of the horrors of the tempest, and its still nearer approach, but God is not yet revealed, it is darkness under his feet. Thick darkness was the

accompaniment of God's descent on Mount Sinai (Exod. xx. 21 ; Deut. iv. 11) ;
and it invests his throne, to veil from us the overwhelming majesty of deity.
Psalm xcvii. 2.   But this darkness, while it hides his coming judgment, bespeaks
sorrow and anguish to the objects of his wrath.   Luke xxi. 25, 26.—*W. Wilson,
in loc.*

Verses 9—11 :—

> " He also bowed the heavens,
> And thence he did descend ;
> And thickest clouds of darkness did
> Under his feet attend.
>
> And he upon a cherub rode,
> And thereon he did fly ;
> Yea, on the swift wings of the wind,
> His flight was from on high.
>
> He darkness made his secret place ;
> About him for his tent
> Dark waters were, and thickest clouds
> Of the airy firmament."

Scotch Version, 1649.

Verses 9—12 :—

> " In his descent, bow'd heaven with earth did meet,
> And gloomy darkness roll'd beneath his feet ;
> A golden winged cherub he bestrid,
> And on the swiftly-flying tempest rid.
>
> He darkness made his secret cabinet ;
> Thick fogs and dropping clouds about him set ;
> The beams of his bright presence these expel,
> Whence showers of burning coals and hailstones fell."

George Sandys, 1577—1643.

Verse 10.—" *Cherub.*"   The Hebrew name hath affinity with *Rechub,* a chariot,
used in Psalm civ. 3, almost in like sense as " *cherub* " is here ; and the *cherubims* are
called a chariot, 1 Chron. xxviii. 18 ; and God's angels are his chariots, Psalm
lxviii. 18, and they seem to be meant in this place ; for as the angels are said to fly,
Dan. ix. 21 ; so the *cherubims* had wings, Exod. xxv. 20, and are by the apostle
called " cherubims of glory," Heb. ix. 5.   In Psalm lxxx. 2, God is said " to sit
on the cherubims," as here, to ride ; and " *a cherub* " may be put for many, or all
the *cherubims,* as chariot for chariots, Psalm lxviii. 18.—*Henry Ainsworth.*

Verse 10.—" *Cherubs.*"   The " *cherub* " with the countenances of man, the lion,
the bull, and the eagle (combining in itself, as it were, the intelligence, majesty,
strength, and life of nature), was a symbol of the powers of nature.   When powerful
elements, as in a storm, are serving God, he is said to " *ride on a cherub.*"—*Augustus
F. Tholuck.*

Verse 10.—" *Cherub.*"—

> " He on the wings of *cherub* rode sublime
> On the crystalline sky."

John Milton.

Verse 10.—When God comes to punish his foes and rescue his people, nothing
has ever surprised his friends or foes more than the admirable swiftness with which
he moves and acts : *He flies " upon the wings of the wind."*—*William S. Plumer.*

Verse 10.—Every circumstance that can add to the splendour of Jehovah's
descent upon his enemies is thrown into the narrative by the inspired poet.   It
is not enough that the heavens should bend beneath him, and that clouds of darkness
should be seen rolling, in terrible majesty, under his feet ; cherubic legions also
are the willing supporters of his throne, and, swift as air, he flies " *upon the wings
of the wind.*"   Into this amazing scene the awful appendages of the mercy-seat are
introduced ; on the bending heavens, the cloudy chariot rides sublime, and the
winds of heaven bear it majestically along.—*J. Morison.*

Verse 12.—" *Coals of fire.*"   The word signifies, living, *burning coals.*   Where
the lightning fell, it devoured all before it, and burned whatever it touched into
burning embers.—*Samuel Chandler.*

Verse 14.—"*Yea, he sent out his arrows, and scattered them,*" etc. O that you who are now strangers to God would but consider these things ! O that you would but think what this battle may be, where the combatants are so unequal ! Stand still, O sun, in the valley of Ajalon, till the Lord have avenged him of his enemies ! Muster yourselves, O ye stars, and fight in your courses against those miserable sinners that have waged war against their Maker ; plant your mighty cannons, shoot down huge hailstones, arrows of fire, and hot thunderbolts ! Oh, how do the wounded fall ! How many are the slain of the Lord, multitudes in the Valley of Decision, for the day of the Lord is terrible. Behold, God's enemies falling by thousands, behold the garments rolling in blood, hear the prancing of his terrible ones, the mountains are covered with horses and chariots of fire. God's soldiers run from one place to another with their flaming swords in their hands, armed with the justice of God, jealousy, power, and indignation ! Oh, the dreadful slaughter that is made ! Millions, millions fall ; they are not able to stand ; not one of them can lift up his hand ; their hearts fail them ; paleness and trembling hath seized upon the stoutest of them all. The bow of the Lord is strong ; from the blood of the slain, from the fat of the mighty, the bow of the Lord turneth not back, the sword of the Almighty returns not empty. How do the mighty ones fall in this battle! A hot battle indeed, in which none escape ! Who is he that cometh from Edom, with dyed garments from Bozrah ? He that is glorious in his apparel, and thy garments like him that treadeth the wine fat ? I have trodden the wine-press alone, and of the people there was none with me. For I will tread them in mine anger and trample them in my fury ; and I will bring down their strength to the earth : the hand of the Lord shall be known, the power of the mighty Jehovah shall be felt, and his indignation towards his enemies. For behold he will come with fire and with chariots like a whirlwind, to render his anger with fury, and his rebuke with flames of fire ; for by fire and by his sword will he plead with all flesh ; and the slain of the Lord shall be many, and the saints shall go forth and look upon the carcases of the men that have transgressed against me. For their worm shall not die, neither shall their fire be quenched, and they shall be an abhorring unto all flesh. Upon the wicked he shall rain snares, fire, and brimstone, and a horrible tempest. This shall be the portion of their cup ! This it is to fight against God ! This it is to defy the Lord of Hosts !—*James Janeway.*

Verse 14.—"*He shot out his lightnings.*" בְּרָקִים רָב. LXX ἀστραπὰς ἐπλήθυνε. *Fulgura multiplicavit ;* Vulg. and so all the versions. He multiplied his thunder-bolts ; or, shot them out thick one after another ; as the word properly signifies.

וַיְהֻמֵּם. *And discomfited them,* as we render the word ; or rather, as I think it should be translated, *and melted them ;* namely, the heavens.—*Samuel Chandler.*

Verse 14 (last clause).—It is written, "*destroyed them,*" because the Holy Ghost would not so much as name, by the mouth of his prophet, the evil spirits to whom he refers.—*Euthymius Zigabenus* (1125) *quoted by J. M. Neale.*

Verse 15.—"*The foundations of the world were discovered ; i.e.,* such large and deep chasms, or apertures, were made by the violence of the earthquake, as one might almost see the very foundations, or as Jonah calls them, *the bottoms,* or rather, *the extremities of the mountains,* in the bottom of the sea. Jonah ii. 6.—*Samuel Chandler.*

Verse 15.—The Lord interposed with the same notoriety of his presence, as when the waters of the sea were driven back by a strong east wind, and the deep turned into dry ground (Ex. xiv. 21, 22), to give the Israelites a safe passage out of their thraldom, and to drown the Egyptians.—*Henry Hammond.*

Verse 16.—"*He sent from above,*" etc. He "*sent*" angels, or assistance otherwise.—*Matthew Poole.*

Verse 16.—"*He took.*" God's grasp cannot be broken. None can pluck his chosen out of his hand.—*William S. Plumer.*

Verse 16.—"*Drew me out of many waters.*" This hath reference to Moses' case, who was " drawn out of the water," and thereupon called *Mosheh* (Ex. ii. 10) ; that word *Mashah* is used here by David, and nowhere else in Scripture. "*Waters,*" signify *troubles,* and sometimes multitudes of *people.*—*H. Ainsworth.*

Verse 18.—"*They prevented me in the day of my calamity ;*" *i.e.,* came on me suddenly unawares, when I was unprovided and helpless, and must have destroyed me had not God upheld and supported me when I was in danger of perishing. God was to the Psalmist לְמִשְׁעָן, *for a staff* to support him. What the staff is to one that is ready to fall, the means of recovering and preserving him; that was God to David in the time of his extremity. For he several times preserved him from Saul, when he, David, thought his destruction by him almost unavoidable. See 1 Sam. xxiii. 26, 27.—*Samuel Chandler.*

Verse 18.—" *They prevented me in the day of my calamity : but the Lord was my stay.*" When Henry the Eighth had spoken and written bitterly against Luther; saith Luther, Tell the Henries, the bishops, the Turks, and the devil himself, do what they can, we are the children of the kingdom, worshipping of the true God, whom they, and such as they, spit upon and crucified. And of the same spirit were many martyrs. Basil affirms of the primitive saints, that they had so much courage and confidence in their sufferings, that many of the heathens seeing their heroic zeal and constancy, turned Christians.—*Charles Bradbury.*

Verse 20.—" *The Lord rewarded me according to my righteousness ; according to the cleanness of my hands hath he recompensed me.*" We must stand our ground, and be stiff for ourselves against all misjudgings. It is good to be zealously affected always in a good matter, whether it respects the glory of God immediately and alone, or whether it respects the credit of our brethren or our own. To desire to be famous in the world, and as those giants in the old world (Gen. vi. 4), men of renown, or, as the original text hath it, men of name, is a very great vanity ; but to protect and preserve our good name is a great and necessary duty.—*Joseph Caryl.*

Verse 21.—" *I have not wickedly departed from my God ;* " that is, with a purpose and resolution of heart to continue in a way of sinning ; and that is the property of sincerity. A man indeed may be overtaken and surprised by a temptation, but it is not with a resolution to forsake God and to cleave unto the sin, or rest in it. He will not sleep in it, spare it, or favour it ; that is, to do wickedly against God, to have a double heart and a double eye ; to look upon two objects, partly at God and partly at sin ; so to keep God, as to keep some sin also, as it is with all false-hearted men in the world. They look not upon God alone, let them pretend to religion never so much, yet they look not unto God alone, but upon something else together with God ; as Herod regarded John, but regarded his Herodias more ; and the young man in the gospel, comes to Christ, yet he looks after his estate ; and Judas followed in Christ, yet looks after the bag ; this is *to depart wickedly from God.*—*William Strong,* 1650.

Verse 21 (last clause).—Although a godly man may break a particular command-ment again and again against knowledge, yet his knowledge never suffers him to go so far as to venture knowingly to break the covenant of grace with God, and to depart from him ; when he hath gone on so far in a sin as he comes to apprehend he must break with God, and lose him if he goes on any further, this apprehension stays him, stops and brings him back again ; he may presumptuously venture (though seldom ; and always to his cost) to commit an act of sin against knowledge, because he may withal think, that by one act the covenant is not broken, nor all friendship and love hazarded between God and him, nor his interest in the state of grace, nor God, quite lost by it, though he may well think he would be displeased with him ; but if he should begin to allow himself in it, and to continue to go on again and again in it, then he knows the covenant would be broken, it cannot stand with grace ; and when this apprehension comes, and comes in strongly, he cannot sin against it, for this were to cast away the Lord, and to depart wickedly from him, now so he doth not. So David, though he sinned highly and presumptuously, yet says he, " *I have not departed wickedly from my God ;* " that is, I have not so far departed from him as though I apprehended I should utterly lose my interest in him, yet I would go on. No ; for he is my God, there lies the consideration that kept him from departing from him. So Psalm xliv. 17, " We have not dealt falsely in thy covenant," says the church there. Many acts of displeasing him may pass and be ventured, but if the holy soul thinks that the covenant lay at stake, that he and God must utterly part and break off, thus far he will never go.—*Thomas Goodwin.*

Verses 22, 23.—An unsound soul will not take notice of such a precept as opposeth his special sin ; such a precept must go for a blank, which the soul throws by, and will not think of, but as conscience now and then puts him in mind of it, whether he will or no. But it is not so with a man in whom sincerity is : that precept which doth most oppose that sin to which he is most inclined, he labours to obey as well as any other. An unsound soul sets so many of God's statutes before him, as rulers to walk by, as suits with himself and the times, and no more. Such precepts as oppose his special corruptions, or displease the times, and so expose him to suffering, these he baulks and puts away, as David here saith, and calls them as the rotten Scribes and Pharisees were wont to do, "least commandments," small things not to be regarded ; which rottenness Christ took up roundly in those ironical words, "Whosoever shall break one of these least commandments, shall be called the least in the kingdom of God." Godly sincerity makes no difference of greatest and least between the precepts of God, but sets all before a man as a rule to walk by, and makes the soul laborious to observe all. " Then shall I not be ashamed, when I have respect unto all thy commandments." Psalm cxix. 6.—*Nicholas Lockyer*, 1649.

Verse 23.—" *I was also upright before him, and I kept myself from mine iniquity.*" He who says, " Lo, I come : in the volume of the book it is written of me, I delight to do thy will, O my God ; yea, thy law is within my heart ; " and who by the apostle, in the tenth chapter of the epistle to the Hebrews, is identified with Jesus Christ, says also (verse 12), " innumerable evils have compassed me about ; mine iniquities have taken hold upon me, so that I am not able to look up : they are more than the hairs of mine head ; therefore mine heart faileth me ; " and in the forty-first Psalm, "He whose familiar friend, to whom he had committed a trust, who ate of his bread, lifted up his heel against him," whom our Lord in the thirteenth chapter of the gospel of John identifies with himself, says (verse 4), "Lord, be merciful to me : heal my soul for I have sinned ; " I am guilty " before thee." The difficulty is removed by the undoubtedly true principle—the principle which, above all others, gives Christianity its peculiar character—" He who knew no sin, was made sin ; " " On his righteous servant, Jehovah made to fall the iniquities of us all." In this sense, " innumerable iniquities compassed him," the inquities made to fall on him made " his " as to their liabilities—by divine appointment laid hold of him. In the sense of *culpa*—blame-worthiness—he had no sin. In the sense of *reatus*— liability to the penal effects of sin—never had any one so much sin to bear as he—" He bore the sins of many."—*John Brown.*

Verse 23.—" *I was upright before him.*" Hence observe :—first, that a godly man may have his heart upright and perfect even in the imperfection of his ways. Secondly, a man that is sincere is in God's account a perfect man : sincerity is the truth of all grace, the highest pitch that is to be attained here. Thirdly, sincerity of heart gives a man boldness even in the presence of God, notwithstanding many failings. The Lord doth " charge his angels with folly," how much more man that " dwells in a house of clay " ? Job. iv. David, whose faith failed, and who had said, " I shall one day perish by the hand of Saul," and whose tongue had faltered also to Abimelech, the priest ; three or four several lies he had told ; yet David can say to God, that he was *perfect* with him for all that. It is a strange boldness that the saints have in the presence of God by virtue of the new covenant. All their sins shall be laid open at the last day as a cancelled bond, that they wonder how they shall look upon them and not blush ; but the same spirit of sonship that shall give them perfect boldness then, doth give them boldness in a great measure even now in this life ; that they shall be able to say, "Neither height nor depth," etc., nothing " shall separate us from the love of Christ."—*William Strong.*

Verse 23.—" *I was upright,*" etc. An upright Christian will not allow himself in any known sin ; he dares not touch the forbidden fruit. Gen xxxix. 9. " How then can I do this great wickedness, and sin against God ? " Though it be a com-plexion-sin, he disinherits it. There is no man but doth propend and incline more to one sin than another ; as in the body there is one humour predominant, or as in the hive there is one master-bee ; so in the heart there is one master-sin ; there is one sin which is not only near to a man as the garment, but dear to him as the right eye. This is Satan's fort-royal, all his strength lies here ; and though we beat down his out-works, gross sin, yet if we let him hold this fort of complexion-sin, it is as much as he desires. The devil can hold a man as fast by this one link, as by a whole chain of vices. The fowler hath the bird fast enough by one wing. Now, an uprigh. Christian will not indulge himself in this complexion-sin : " *I was upright before him, and kept myself from mine iniquity.*" An upright Christian takes the sacrificing knife of mortification, and runs it through his dearest sin. Herod did many things, but there was one sin so dear to him, that he would sooner behead the prophet, than behead that sin. Herod would have a gap for his incest. An upright heart is not only angry with sin (which may admit of reconciliation), but hates sin ; and if he sees this serpent creeping into his bosom, the nearer it is the more he hates it.—*Thomas Watson.*

Verse 23.—" *I kept myself.*" Kept himself! Who made man his own keeper? It's the Lord that is his keeper : he is the keeper of Israel, and the preserver of man. If a man cannot keep himself from sorrow, how is he able to keep himself from sin ? God indeed in our first conversion works upon us as he did upon the earth, or Adam's body in paradise, before he breathed a soul into it, and made it a living creature ; such a power as Christ put forth on Lazarus in his grave, for we are " dead in trespasses and sins ;" but yet being living he must walk and act of himself, the Lord will have us to co-operate together with him, for we are built upon Christ, not as dead, but as " living stones." 1 Pet. ii. 5. The grace whereby we are made alive is his, and the power is his ; he it is that works in us both to will and to do, when we perform anything ; and yet by his grace we do it also ; *ille facit ut nos faciamus, quæ præcepit* (*Augustine*).—*William Strong.*

Verse 23.—" *I kept myself from mine iniquity.*" It is possible to keep ourselves from such sins as David did, who professes here of himself great sincerity, that he had *kept* himself from that *iniquity* to which he was strongly tempted, and which he was prone to fall into. The method which holy David made use of gives us the first and best direction ; and that is, by constant and fervent prayer to implore the divine aid and the continual assistance of his Holy Spirit, that God would not only keep us from falling into them, but even turn our hearts from inclining to them, and help us to see our folly and our danger. For alas ! we are not able of ourselves to help ourselves, not so much as to think a good thought, much less to resist an evil inclination, or a strong temptation ; but " our sufficiency is of God : " " It is God (says the Psalmist here), that girdeth me with strength, and maketh my way perfect : " verse 32. . . . . . Next, that we take care to avoid such things and decline such occasions as are most likely to snare us and gain upon us, lest one thing hook in another, and we be caught in the gin before we suspect the danger.—*Henry Dove,* 1690.

Verse 23.—" *Mine iniquity.*" A man's darling sin may change with the change of a man's condition, and some occasion that may present itself. What was Saul's and Jehu's sin before they came unto the crown we know not ; but surely it was that wherein their lust did afterwards run out—the establishing a kingdom upon their posterity. Wantonness may be the darling of a man's youth, and worldliness the darling of his age ; and a man's being raised unto honour, and having the opportunities that he had not in times past, the lust may run in another channel, he having now such an opportunity as before he never expected.—*William Strong.*

Verse 23.—" *Mine iniquity.*" There is some particular sin to which one is more prone than to another, of which he may say by way of emphasis, 'tis " *mine iniquity,*" at which he may point with his finger, and say, " That's it." . . . . There are more temptations to some sins than others, from the different professions or courses of life men take upon themselves. If they follow the court I need not tell you what temptations and snares there are to divers sins, and what danger there is of falling into them, unless your vows for virtue, and a tender regard to the honour which cometh of God only, keep you upright. If they be listed in the camp, that tempts them to rapine and violence, neglect of God's worship, and profaneness. If they exercise trading and merchandise, they meet with greater enticements to lying and cozening, over-reaching and unjust dealing ; and the mystery of some trades, as bad men manage them, is a downright " mystery of iniquity." If husbandry, to anxiety about the things of the world, a distrust of God's providence, or murmuring against it. Nay, I could wish in the most sacred profession of all there might be an exception made in this particular ; but Paul tells us that even in his days " some preached Christ even of envy and strife," some for filthy lucre only, as well as " some of good will." Phil. i. 15.—*Henry Dove.*

Verse 23.—" *Mine iniquity.*" The actual reign of sin is commonly of some particular master-lust, which is as the viceroy over all the rest of the sins in the soul, and commands them all as lord paramount, and makes them all subservient and subordinate unto it ; and this is according to custom, calling, constitution, abilities, relations, and according to the different administrations of the Spirit of God ; for though God be not the author of sin, yet he is the orderer of sin. So that

It is that way of sin and death that a man chooseth to himself, he having looked abroad upon all the contentments of the world, his own corrupt inclination doth choose unto himself to follow with greatest sweetness and contentment and delight as that wherein the happiness of his life consists ; that as in the body there is in every one some predominant humour, so there is in the body of sin also ; that as in the natural man, though there be all the faculties, yet some faculties are in some more lively and vigorous than in others, some are more witty, some are more strong, some quick of sight, some have a ready ear, and others a nimble tongue, etc. So it is in the old man also ; there is all the power of sin in an unregenerate man, but in some more dexterous one way than another ; as men in the choice of calling, some have a greater inclination to one thing than to another, so it is in the choice of contentments also : as in the appetite for food, so it is in lust, being nothing else but the appetite of the creature corrupted to some sinful object.—*William Strong.*

Verse 23.—Growth in mortification . . . . . Men may deceive themselves when they estimate their progress herein by having overcome such lusts as their natures are not so prone unto. The surest way is to take a judgment of it from the decay of a man's bosom-sin, even as David did estimate his uprightness by his " *keeping himself from his iniquity ;* " so a man of his growth in uprightness, When physicians would judge of a consumption of the whole, they do it not by the falling away of any part whatever, as of the flesh in the face alone, or any the like ; such a particular abatement of flesh in some one part may come from some other cause ; but they use to judge by the falling away of the brawn of the hands, or arms and thighs, etc., for these are the more solid parts. The like judgments do physicians make upon other diseases, and of the abatement of them from the decrease in such symptoms as are pathognomical, and proper, and peculiar to them. In like manner also the estimate of the progress of the victories of a conqueror in an enemy's kingdom is not taken from the taking or burning of a few villages or dorps, but by taking the forts and strongest holds, and by what ground he hath won upon the chief strength, and by what forces he hath cut off the main army. Do the like in the decrease of, and victory over, your lusts.—*Thomas Goodwin.*

Verse 23.—We must always remember that though the grace of God prevents us, that we may have a good will, and works in us when we have it, that so we may find success ; yet in vain do we expect the continuance of his help without diligent endeavours. Whilst he assists our weakness, he does not intend to encourage our laziness, and therefore we are also " to labour, and strive according to his working, which worketh in us mightily," as the apostle expresses it, Col. i. 29.—*Henry Dove.*

Verses 24—26.—As you may see a proportion between sins and punishments which are the rewards of them, that you can say, Such a sin brought forth this affliction, it is so like the father ; so you might see the like proportion between your prayers and your walking with God, and God's answers to you, and his dealings with you. So did David ; " *According to the cleanness of my hands hath he recompensed me,*" etc. His speech notes some similitude or likeness ; as, for example, the more by-ends or carnal desires you had in praying, and the more you mingled of these with your holy desires, and the more want of zeal, fervency, etc., were found in your prayers, the more you shall, it may be, find of bitterness mingled with the mercy, when it is granted, and so much imperfection, and want of comfort in it. So says David in this same Psalm (verses 25, 26), " *With the pure thou wilt show thyself pure.*" Pure prayers have pure blessings ; *et è contra,* " *With the froward thou wilt show thyself froward.*" And again, as you in praying sometimes slackened and grew cold, so you might see the business in like manner to cool, and cast backward ; as, " When Moses' hands were down, Amalek prevailed ; but when they were lifted up, Israel had the better." Exod. xvii. 12. God let him see a proportion, which argued his prayer was the means of prevailing. A man finds in praying that his suit sometimes sticks, and goes not on as he expected ; this is because he gives not so good a fee as he was wont, and doth not ply God and solicit him ; but on the contrary, when he was stirred up to pray, then still he found things to go well. By this a man may clearly see that it was the prayer which God did hear and regarded. Thus, likewise, when a man see hills and dales in a business, fair hopes often and then all dashed again, and the thing in the end brought to pass, let him look back upon his prayers. Didst not thou in like manner just deal with God ? when thou hadst prayed earnestly, and thought thou hadst even carried it, then dash all again by interposing some sin, and thus again and again ? Herein God would have you observe a proportion, and it may help you to discern how and when they are answered and obtained by prayer, because God deals thus with you therein in such a proportion to your prayers.—*Thomas Goodwin.*

Verses 24—27.—Even as the sun, which, unto eyes being sound and without disease, is very pleasant and wholesome, but unto the same eyes, when they are feeble, sore and weak, is very troublesome and hurtful, yet the sun is ever all one and the selfsame that was before; so God, who hath ever shown himself benign and bountiful to those who are kind and tender-hearted towards his saints, and are merciful to those who show mercy. But unto the same men, when they fall into wickedness and grow to be full of beastly cruelty, the Lord showeth himself to be very wrathful and angry, and yet is one and the same immutable God from everlasting to everlasting.—*Robert Cawdray.*

Verse 25.—" *With the merciful thou wilt show thyself merciful ; with an upright man thou wilt shew thyself upright.*" " *An upright* "—the same word is oft translated " perfect," he is good throughout, though not thoroughly ; not one that personates religion, but that is a religious person. He is perfect, because he would be so. So Noah is termed (Gen. vi. 9) ; " Noah was a just man and perfect (*i.e.,* upright) in his generation : " he was a good man in a bad age. He was like a glowing spark of fire in a sea of water, which is perfect goodness ; and therefore the Holy Ghost doth so hang upon his name, as if he could not give over—it is an excellent preacher's observation—verse 8, " But Noah was a just man and perfect in his generation, and Noah walked with God. And Noah found grace in the eyes of the Lord. These are the generations of Noah : Noah begat three sons." Noah, Noah, Noah, I love the sound of thy name ; and so are all your names precious to God, though hated by men, if the name of God be dear and sweet to you. 'Tis also sometimes translated " plain." Gen. xxv. 27. Jacob was םּ שׁיא, " a plain," that is, an upright man, " dwelling in tents." Esau was " *a cunning* hunter," but Jacob was a plain man without welt or gard ; you might well know his heart by his tongue, save once when Rebekah put a cunning trick into his head, otherwise he was a most " *upright,*" downright man. And the plain meaning of it is, a simple, cordial, unfeigned, and exact man : this is the man we are looking for.

" *Man.*" This substantive the Hebrews use to drown in the adjective, but here the Holy Ghost exhibits a word, and a choice one too, signifying *a strong, valiant man ;* the same word (Psalm xlv. 3), " O mighty man ! " that's meant of our Lord Christ, who was a most strong and valiant man, that could meet the wrath of God, the malice of the devil, and the sin of man, in the face. and come off with triumph. And so the Dutch translate this clause in 2 Sam. xxii. : " With the right valiant person, thou behavest thyself upright." In short, if the words were literally translated, they run thus :—*a man of uprightness:* that is every way you behold him, an upright man : like an even die, cast him which way you will he will be found square and right ; a stiff and strong man to tread down both lusts within and temptations without ; an *Athanasius contra mundum,* a *Luther contra Romam ;* this is a man of an excellent spirit, and such is our upright man. " *Thou wilt show thyself upright,*" or, " wilt be upright with him ; " for one word in the Hebrew makes all these six, " Thou wilt *upright* it with him." If men will deal plainly with God, he will deal plainly with them. He that is upright in performing his duty shall find God upright in performing his promises. It is God's way to carry to men as they carry to him. If thou hast a design to please him, he will have a design to please thee ; if thou wilt echo to him when he calls, he'll echo to thee when thou callest. On the other side ; if a man will wrestle with God, he will wrestle with him ; if thou wilt be fast and loose with him, and walk *frowardly* towards him, thou shalt have as good as thou bringest ; if thou wilt provoke him with never-ending sins, he will pursue thee with never-ending torments ; if thou wilt sin in *tuo eterno,* thou must suffer in *suo eterno,* and every man shall find like for like . . . . . An upright heart is *single without division.* Unto an hypocrite there be " gods many and lords many," and he must have an heart for each ; but to the *upright* there is but one God the Father, and one Lord Jesus Christ, and one heart will serve them both. He that fixes his heart upon the creatures, for every creature he must have an heart, and the dividing of his heart destroys him. Hos. x. 2. Worldly profits knock at the door, he must have an heart for them ; carnal pleasures present themselves, he must have an heart for them also ; sinful preferments appear, they must have an heart too—*Necessariorum numerus parvus, opinionum nullus ;* of necessary objects the number is few, of needless vanities the number is endless. The *upright* man hath made choice of God and hath enough.—*Richard Steele.*

Verse 25.—"*With the merciful,*" etc. In Jupiter's hall-floor there are set two barrels of gifts, the one of good gifts or blessings, the other of evil gifts or plagues. Thus spake Homer falsely of Jupiter ; it may be truly spoken of the true God, Jehovah ; that he hath in his hand two cups, the one of comforts, the other of crosses, which he poureth out indifferently for the good and for the bad ; "*with the kind* (or merciful) he will shew himself kind, and with the froward, froward.*" Now this is not to make God the author of evil, but of justice, which is good ; *quorum deus non est author eorum est justus ultor,* saith Augustine; "God is not the author of sin, but he punisheth the sinner justly."—*Miles Smith (Bishop),* 1632.

Verse 26.—"*With the pure thou wilt shew thyself pure,*" etc. But doth the Lord take colour from every one he meets, or change his temper as the company changes ? That's the weakness of sinful man : he cannot do so with whom there is no variableness nor shadow of changing. God is pure, and upright with the unclean and hypocritical, as well as with the pure and upright, and his actions show him to be so. God shows himself froward with the froward when he deals with him as he hath said he will deal with the froward—deny them and reject them. God shows himself pure with the pure, when he deals with them as he hath said he will—hear them and accept them. Though there be nothing in purity and sincerity which deserveth mercy, yet we cannot expect mercy without them. Our comforts are not grounded upon our graces, but our comforts are the fruits or consequents of our graces.— *Joseph Caryl.*

Verse 26.—"*The froward one.*" Here, as in the first promise, the two combatants stand contrasted—the seed of the woman and the serpent—the benignantly bountiful, perfect, pure One, and the froward one, whose works he came to destroy, and who made it his great business to circumvent him whom he feared. The literal meaning of the word is "tortuous," or "crooked," and both the ideas of perversity and cunning which the figure naturally suggests, are very applicable to "that old serpent the devil." From the concluding part of the sentence, I think there is no doubt that it is the latter idea that is intended to be conveyed. God cannot deal perversely with any one ; but he outwits the wise, and takes the cunning in their own craftiness.—*John Brown.*

Verse 26.—"*With the froward thou wilt shew thyself froward.*" The Hebrew word in the root signifieth to wrest or writhe a thing, or to wrest or turn a thing, as wrestlers do their bodies. Hence by a trope, it is translated often to wrestle, because a cunning man in wrestling, turneth and windeth his body, and works himself in and out every way, to get an advantage of his adversary any way ; therefore your cunning-headed men, your crafty men, are fitly presented under this word ; they are like wrestlers who turn and wind themselves in and out, and lie for all advantages ; or as we speak, they "lie at catch." A man knows not where to have them, or what they mean when they speak plainest, or swear solemnest ; when we think we see their faces, we see but their vizards ; all their promises and performances too are under a disguise . . . . . And this word is applied to the Lord himself, "*With the froward thou wilt shew thyself froward ;*" that is, if men will be winding and turning, and thinking to catch others or over-reach the Lord himself with tricks and turnings of wit, the Lord will meet and answer them in their own kind ; he can turn as fast as they, he can put himself into such intricate labyrinths of infinite wisdom and sacred craft, as shall entangle and ensnare the most cunning wrestler or tumbler of them all. He will Cretize the Cretians, supplant the supplanters of his people.—*Joseph Caryl.*

Verse 26.—"*Wilt shew thyself froward.*" It is a similitude taken from wrestlers, and noteth a writhing of one's self against an adversary. Compare herewith Deut. xxxii. 5. "They are a perverse and crooked generation," the same two words that are here in this text ; the latter importeth that they wriggled and writhed after the manner of wrestlers that wave up and down, and wind the other way, when one thinks to have him here or there. But all will not serve their turn to save them from punishment. God will be sure to meet with them, his Word will lay hold on them, and their sin shall find them out.—*John Trapp.*

Verse 27.—"*The afflicted people.*" The word rendered "*afflicted,*" properly signifies "poor" or "needy." The persons spoken of are obviously afflicted ones, for they need to be saved or delivered ; but it is not their affliction, so much as their poverty, that is indicated by the epithet here given them ; and, from the poor being contrasted, not with the wealthy, but with the proud—for that is the meaning of the figurative expression, " the man of high looks "—it seems plain that, though the great body of the class referred to have always been found among the comparatively " poor in this world," the reference is to those poor ones whom our Lord represents as " poor in spirit."—*John Brown.*

Verse 27.—" *High looks :* " namely, *the proud ;* the raising up of the eyebrows being a natural sign of that vice. Psalm ci. 5 ; Prov. vi. 17.—*John Diodati.*

Verse 28.—" *For thou wilt light my candle,*" etc. The Psalmist speaks in this place of artificial light ; " *a candle,*" or " lamp ; " which has been supposed to be illustrated by the custom prevailing in Egypt of never suffering their houses to be without lights, but burning lamps even through the night, so that the poorest people would rather retrench part of their food than neglect it. Supposing this to have been the ancient custom, not only in Egypt, but in the neighbouring countries of Arabia and Judæa, " the lighting of the lamp " in this passage may have had a special allusion. In the parallel passage, 2 Sam. xxii. 29, Jehovah is figuratively styled the " lamp " of the Psalmist, as above.—*Richard Mant.*

Verse 28 (*first clause*).—" *Thou also shalt* "—when none else can. And notice too, how here, and often elsewhere, the Psalmist begins with speaking *of* God, and ends with speaking *to* him. So the bride in the Canticles, " Let him kiss me with the kisses of *his* mouth, for *thy* love is better than wine."—*Dionysius the Carthusian* (1471), *quoted by J. M. Neale.*

Verse 29.—" *By thee I have run through a troop,*" etc. David ascribes his victories to God, declaring that, under his conduct, he *had broken through the wedges or phalanxes* of his enemies, and had taken by storm their fortified cities. Thus we see that, although he was a valiant warrior, and skilled in arms, he arrogates nothing to himself.—*John Calvin.*

Verse 29.—" *By my God have I leaped over a wall ;* " or, " taken a fort."—*Henry Hammond.*

Verse 29.—" *Leaped over a wall.*" This probably refers to his having taken some remarkable town by scaling the ramparts.—*John Kitto, in " The Pictorial Bible."*

Verse 31.—" *For who is God save the Lord ?* " Here first in the Psalms, occurs the name *Eloah,* rendered *God.* It occurs more than *fifty* times in the Scriptures, but only *four* times in the Psalms. It is the singular of Elohim. Many have supposed that this name specially refers to God as an object of religious worship. That idea may well be prominent in this place.—*William S. Plumer.*

Verse 32.—" *It is God that girdeth me with strength.*" One of the few articles of Eastern dress which I wore in the East, was the *girdle,* which was of great use as a support to the body in the long and weary camel-rides through the Desert. The support and *strengthening* I received in this way, gave me a clearer idea than I had before the meaning of the Psalmist.—*John Anderson, in " Bible from Bible Lands,"* 1856.

Verse 33.—" *He maketh my feet like hinds' feet, and setteth me upon my high places :* " that is, he doth give swiftness and speed to his church ; as Augustine interpreteth it, *transcendendo spinosa, et umbrosa implicamenta hujus sæculi,* passing lightly through the thorny and shady incumbrances of this world. " He will make me walk upon my high places." David saith, " He setteth me upon high places." For, consider David, as he then was, when he composed this Psalm, it was at the time when God had delivered him from the hand of all his enemies, and from the hand of Saul. For then God set his feet on high places, settling his kingdom, and establishing him in the place of Saul.—*Edward Marbury.*

Verse 33.—" *He maketh my feet like hinds' feet :* " רַגְלַי כָּאַיָּלוֹת מְשַׁוֶּה. Celerity of motion was considered as one of the qualities of an ancient hero. Achilles is celebrated for being πόδας ὠκύς. Virgil's Nisus is hyperbolically described, " *Et ventis et fulminis ocior alis ;* " and the men of God, who came to David, " Men of might, and men of war fit for the battle, that could handle shield and buckler," are said to have had " faces like the faces of lions," and to have been " as swift as the roes upon the mountains.") 1 Chron. xii. 8. Asahel is described as "light of foot as a wild roe" (2 Sam. ii. 18); and Saul seems called the *roe* (in the English translation, " the beauty) of Israel." 2 Sam. i. 19. It has been said that the legs of the hind are straighter than those of the buck, and that *she* is swifter than *he* is ; but there is no sufficient proof of this. Gataker gives the true account of it when he says, " The female formula is often used for the species." This is not uncommon in Hebrew. The female ass obviously stands for the ass species. Gen. xii. 16 ; Job. i. 3 ; xlii. 12. Some (at the head of whom is Bochart, *Hierozoicon*, P. i. L. ii. c. 17), have supposed the reference to be to the peculiar hardness of the hoof of the roe, which enables it to walk firmly, without danger of falling, on the roughest and rockiest places. Virgil calls the hind "*æri-pedem*," brass-footed. Others suppose the reference to be to its agility and celerity. There is nothing to prevent our supposing that there is a reference to both these distinguishing qualities of the hind's feet. *John Brown.*

Verse 33.—" *He maketh my feet like hinds' feet*," etc. *He maketh me able to stand on the sides of mountains and rocks,* which were anciently used as fastnesses in time of war. The feet of the sheep, the goat, and the hart are particularly adapted to standing in such places. Mr. Merrick has here very appositely cited the following passage from Xenophon ; *Lib. de Venatione :* Επισκοπεῖν δεῖ ἔχοντα τὰς κύνας τὰς μὲν ἐν ὄρεσι ἑστώσας 'Λαφους. See also Psalm civ. 18, where the same property of standing on the rocks and steep cliffs is attributed to the wild goat.—*Stephen Street, M.A., in loc., 1790.*

Verse 34.—" *He teacheth my hands to war,*" etc. To him I owe all that military skill, or strength, or courage, which I have. My strength is sufficient, not only to bend " a *bow of steel,*" but to break it.—*Matthew Poole.*

Verse 34.—" *Steel.*" The word so rendered in the authorised version, properly means " copper " (נחשה). It is doubtful if the Hebrews were acquainted with the process of hardening iron into steel, for though the " northern iron " of Jer. xv. 12, has been supposed by some to be steel, this is by no means certain ; it may have only been a superior sort of iron.—*William Lindsay Alexander, in " Kitto's Cyclopædia."*

Verse 34.—The drawing of a mighty bow was a mark of great slaughter and skill.

" So the great master drew the mighty bow,
And drew with ease. One hand aloft display'd,
The bending horns, and one the string essay'd."
Alexander Pope, 1688—1744. [Translation of Homer.

Verses 37, 38 :—

Oh, I have seen the day,
When with a single word,
God helping me to say,
" My trust is in the Lord ; "
My soul has quelled a thousand foes,
Fearless of all that could oppose.
William Cowper, 1731—1800.

Verse 38.—" *I have wounded them,*" etc. Greater is he that is in us than he that is against us, and God shall bruise Satan under our feet shortly. Rom. xv. 20. *W. Wilson.*

Verses 38—40.—Though passion possess our bodies, let " patience possess our souls." The law of our profession binds us to a warfare ; *patiendo vincimus,* our troubles shall end, our victory is eternal. Hear David's triumph, " *I have wounded them that they were not able to rise : they are fallen under my feet. Thou hast subdued under me those that rose up against me. Thou hast given me the necks of mine enemies,*" etc. They have wounds for their wounds ; and the treaders down of the poor are trodden down by the poor. The Lord will subdue those to us that would have subdued us to themselves ; and though for a short time they rode over our heads, yet now at last we shall everlastingly tread upon their necks. Lo, then, the reward of humble patience and confident hope !—*Thomas Adams.*

Verse 39.—To be well girt was to be well armed in the Greek and Latin idioms, as well as in the Hebrew.—*Alexander Geddes, LL.D., 1737—1802.*

Verse 41.—" *They shall cry, but there shall be none to help them,"* etc. Sad examples enough there are of the truth of this prophecy. Of Esau it is written that he " found no place of repentance, though he sought it carefully with tears." Heb. xii. 17. Of Antiochus, though he vowed in his last illness, " that also he would become a Jew himself, and go through all the world that was inhabited, and declare the power of God, yet," continues the historian, "for all this his pains would not cease, for the just judgment of God was come upon him." 2 Macc. ix. 17, 18. But most appropriately to this passage, it is written of Saul, " When he enquired of the Lord, the Lord answered him not, neither by dreams nor by Urim, nor by prophets." 1 Sam. xxviii. 6. And therefore, the prophet warns us : " Give glory to the Lord your God, before he cause darkness, and before your feet stumble upon the dark mountains (Jer. xiii. 16) : as Saul's feet, indeed, stumbled on the dark mountains of Gilboa. " *Even unto the Lord shall they cry :* " but not, as it has been well remarked, by a Mediator : and so, crying to him in their own name, and by their own merits, they cry in vain.—*John Lorinus* (1569—1634), *and Remigius* (900), *quoted by J. M. Neale.*

Verse 41.—" *Even unto the Lord.*" As nature prompteth men in an extremity to look up for help ; but because it is but the prayer of the flesh for ease, and not of the Spirit for grace, and a good use of calamities, and not but in extreme despair of help elsewhere, therefore God hears them not. In Samuel it is, " They looked, but there was none to save them," *q.d.*, If they could have made any other shift, God should never have heard of them.—*John Trapp.*

Verse 42.—" *I did cast them out as the dirt in the streets,"* or rather " of the streets." In the East, all household refuse and filth is cast forth into the streets, where all of it that is at all edible is soon cleared away by birds and dogs, and all that is not is speedily dried up by the sun. To cast forth any one, therefore, as the dirt of the streets, is a strong image of contempt and rejection.—*John Kitto.*

Verses 43, 44.—If these words can be explained literally of David, they apply much more naturally to Jesus Christ, who has been delivered from the strivings of the Jewish people ; when, after the terrible opposition he met with on their part, to the establishment of the gospel, he was made the head of the Gentiles who were a strange people, and whom he had not formerly acknowledged as his, but who nevertheless obeyed him with astonishing readiness as soon as they heard his voice. *Louis Isaac le Maistre de Stacy,* 1613—1684.

Verse 45.—The first clause is comparatively easy. " *The strangers shall fade away* "—" shall gradually wither and disappear ; " but the second clause is very difficult, " *They shall be afraid out of their close places.*" One Jewish scholar interprets it, " They shall fear for the prisons in which I will throw them and keep them confined."* Another, " They shall tremble in their castles to which they have betaken themselves for fear of me." Another,† " They shall surrender themselves from their fortresses." The general meaning is plain enough. The class referred to are represented as reduced to a state of complete helpless subjugation. As to the event referred to, if we keep to the rendering of our translators the meaning may be, " The Pagans, retired now generally to villages and remote places, shall gradually dwindle away, and fearfully anticipate the complete extinction of their religion." This exactly accords with history. If with some interpreters we read, " The strangers shall fade away, and be afraid because of their prisons," then the meaning may be, " that they who only feigned submission, when persecution for the word should arise should openly apostatise." This, too, would be found consonant with fact. The first of these interpretations seems the more probable.—*John Brown.*

Verse 46.—" *The Lord liveth : and blessed be my rock ; and let the God of my salvation be exalted.*"—Let us unite our hearts in this song for a close of our praises. Honours *die,* pleasures *die,* the world *dies ;* but " *The Lord liveth.*" My flesh is as *sand ;* my fleshly life, strength, glory, is as *a word written on sand ;* but *blessed be my* Rock." Those are for a moment ; this stands for ever. The curse shall devour those ; everlasting blessings on the head of this. Let outward salvations vanish ; let the saved be crucified ; let the " *God* " of our salvations " *be exalted.*" This Lord is *my rock ;* this God is *my salvation.*—*Peter Sterry,* 1649.

---

* Jarchi. † Abenezra.

Verse 46.—*"The Lord liveth."* Why do you not oppose one God to all the armies of evils that beset you round ? why do you not take the more content in God when you have the less of the creature to take content in ? why do you not boast in your God ? and bear up yourselves big with your hopes in God and expectations from him ? Do you not see young heirs to great estates act and spend accordingly ? And, why shall you, being the King of heaven's son, be lean and ragged from day to day, as though you were not worth a groat ? O sirs, live upon your portion, chide yourselves for living besides what you have. There are great and precious promises, rich, enriching mercies ; you may make use of God's all-sufficiency ; you can blame none but yourselves if you be defective or discouraged. A woman, truly godly for the main, having buried a child, and sitting alone in sadness, did yet bear up her heart with the expression, "God lives " ; and having parted with another, still she redoubled, "Comforts die, but God lives." At last her dear husband dies, and she sat oppressed and most overwhelmed with sorrow. A little child she had yet surviving, having observed what before she spoke to comfort herself, comes to her and saith, " Is God dead, mother ? is God dead ? " This reached her heart, and by God's blessing recovered her former confidence in her God, who is a *living* God. Thus do you chide yourselves ; ask your fainting spirits under pressing outward sorrows, is not God alive ? and why then doth not thy soul revive ? why doth thy heart die within thee when comforts die ! Cannot a living God support thy dying hopes ? Thus, Christians, argue down your discouraged and disquieted spirits as David did.—*Oliver Heywood's " Sure Mercies of David." 1672.*

Verse 47.—*" It is God."* Sir, this is none other than the hand of God ; and to him alone belongs the glory, wherein none are to share with him. The General served you with all faithfulness and honour ; and the best commendation I can give him is that I dare say he attributes all to God, and would rather perish than assume to himself."—*Written to the Speaker of the House of Commons, after the battle of Naseby, June* 14, 1645, *by* OLIVER CROMWELL.

Verse 49.—I admire King David a great deal more when I see him in the quire than when I see him in the camp ; when I see him singing as the sweet singer of Israel, than when I see him fighting as the worthy warrior of Israel. For fighting with others he did overcome all others ; but singing, and delighting himself, he did overcome himself.—*Thomas Playfere.*

HINTS TO PREACHERS.

Verse 1.—Love's resolve, love's logic, love's trials, love's victories.
James Hervey has two sermons upon " Love to God " from this text.
Verse 2.—The many excellences of Jehovah to his people.
Verse 2.—God the all-sufficient portion of his people.—*C. Simeon's Works*, Vol. v., p. 85.
Verse 3.—Prayer resolved upon ; praise rendered ; result anticipated.
Verses 4—6.—Graphic picture of a distressed soul, and its resorts in the hour of extremity.
Verse 5 *(first clause)*.—The condition of a soul convinced of sin.
Verse 5 *(second clause)*.—The way in which snares and temptations are, by Satanic craft, arranged so as to forestall or prevent us.
Verse 6.—The time, the manner, the hearing, and the answering of prayer.
Verse 7.—The quaking of all things in the presence of an angry God.
Verse 10.—Celestial and terrestrial agencies subservient to the divine purposes.
Verse 11.—The darkness in which Jehovah hides. Why ? When ? What then ? etc.
Verse 13.—*" Hailstones and coals of fire."* The terrific in its relation to Jehovah.
Verse 16.—The Christian, like Moses, " one taken out of the water." The whole verse a noble subject ; may be illustrated by life of Moses.
Verse 17.—The saint's pæan of victory over Satan, and all other foes.
Verse 17 *(last clause)*.—Singular but sound reason for expecting divine help.

Verse 18.—The enemy's "craft," "*They prevented me in the day of my calamity.*" The enemy chained. "*But the Lord was my stay.*"

Verse 19.—The reason of grace, and the position in which it places its chosen ones.

Verse 21.—Intregrity of life, its measure, source, benefit, and dangers.

Verse 22.—The need of considering sacred things, and the wickedness of carelessly neglecting them.

Verse 23.—The upright heart and its darling sin.—*W. Strong's Sermons.*

Verse 23.—*Peccata in deliciis;* a discourse of bosom sins.—*P. Newcome.*

Verse 23.—The sure trial of uprightness.—*Dr. Bates.*

Verse 26.—Echoes, in providence, grace, and judgment.

Verse 25.—Equity of the divine procedure.—*C. Simeon.*

Verse 27.—Consolation for the humble, and desolation for the proud.

Verse 27 (*second clause*).—The bringing down of high looks. In a way of grace and justice. Among saints and sinners, etc. A wide theme.

Verse 28.—A comfortable hope for an uncomfortable state.

Verse 29.—Believing exploits recounted. Variety, difficulty in themselves, ease in performance, completeness, impunity, and dependence upon divine working.

Verse 30.—God's way, word, and warfare.

Verse 31.—A challenge. I. To the *gods*. World, pleasure, etc. Which among these deserve the name? II. To the *rocks*, self-confidence, superstition, etc. On which can we trust?

Verses 32—34.—Trying positions, gracious adaptations, graceful accomplishments, secure abidings, grateful acknowledgement.

Verse 35.—"*The shield of thy salvation.*" What it is? Faith. Whence it comes? "Thou hast given." What it secures? "Salvation." Who have received it?

Verse 35.—See "Spurgeon's Sermons," No. 683. "Divine Gentleness Acknowledged."

Verse 36.—Divine benevolence in the arranging of our lot.

Verse 39.—The Red Cross Knight armed for the fray.

Verse 41.—Unavailing prayers—on earth and in hell.

Verse 42.—The sure overthrow, final shame, and ruin of evil.

Verse 43 (*last clause*).—Our natural and sinful distance from Christ, no bar to grace.

Verse 44.—Rapid advance of the gospel in some places, slow progress in others. Solemn considerations.

Verse 46.—The living God, and how to bless and exalt him.

Verse 50.—The greatness of salvation, "*great deliverance;*" its channel, *the King;*" and its perpetuity, "*for evermore.*"

PSALM XIX.

SUBJECT.—*It would be idle to enquire into the particular period when this delightful poem was composed, for there is nothing in its title or subject to assist us in the enquiry. The heading, " To the chief Musician, a Psalm of David," informs us that David wrote it, and that it was committed to the Master of the service of song in the sanctuary for the use of the assembled worshippers. In his earliest days the Psalmist, while keeping his father's flock, had devoted himself to the study of God's two great books—nature and Scripture ; and he had so thoroughly entered into the spirit of these two only volumes in his library, that he was able with a devout criticism to compare and contrast them, magnifying the excellency of the Author as seen in both. How foolish and wicked are those who instead of accepting the two sacred tomes, and delighting to behold the same divine hand in each, spend all their wits in endeavouring to find discrepancies and contradictions. We may rest assured that the true " Vestiges of Creation " will never contradict Genesis, nor will a correct " Cosmos" be found at variance with the narrative of Moses. He is wisest who reads both the world-book and the Word-book as two volumes of the same work, and feels concerning them, " My Father wrote them both."*

DIVISION.—*This song very distinctly divides itself into three parts, very well described by the translators in the ordinary heading of our version. The creatures show God's glory, 1—6. The word showeth his grace, 7—11. David prayeth for grace, 12—14. Thus praise and prayer are mingled, and he who here sings the work of God in the world without, pleads for a work of grace in himself within.*

EXPOSITION.

THE heavens declare the glory of God ; and the firmament sheweth his handywork.

2 Day unto day uttereth speech, and night unto night sheweth knowledge.

3 *There is* no speech nor language, *where* their voice is not heard.

4 Their line is gone out through all the earth, and their words to the end of the world. In them hath he set a tabernacle for the sun,

5 Which *is* as a bridegroom coming out of his chamber, *and* rejoiceth as a strong man to run a race.

6 His going forth *is* from the end of the heaven, and his circuit unto the ends of it : and there is nothing hid from the heat thereof.

1. " *The heavens declare the glory of God.*" The book of nature has three leaves, heaven, earth, and sea, of which heaven is the first and the most glorious, and by its aid we are able to see the beauties of the other two. Any book without its first page would be sadly imperfect, and especially the great Natural Bible, since its first pages, the sun, moon, and stars, supply light to the rest of the volume, and are thus the keys, without which the writing which follows would be dark and undiscerned. Man walking erect was evidently made to scan the skies, and he who begins to read creation by studying the stars begins the book at the right place. The *heavens* are plural for their variety, comprising the watery heavens with their clouds of countless forms, the aerial heavens with their calms and tempests, the solar heavens with all the glories of the day, and the starry heavens with all the marvels of the night ; what the Heaven of heavens must be hath not entered into the heart of man, but there in chief all things are telling the glory of God. Any part of creation has more instruction in it than human mind will ever exhaust, but the celestial realm is peculiarly rich in spiritual lore. The heavens *declare*, or are *declaring*, for the continuance of their testimony is intended by the participles employed ; every moment God's existence, power, wisdom, and goodness, are being sounded abroad by the heavenly heralds which shine upon us from above. He who would guess at divine sublimity should gaze upward into the starry vault ; he who would imagine infinity must peer into the boundless expanse ; he who desires

to see divine wisdom should consider the balancing of the orbs ; he who would know divine fidelity must mark the regularity of the planetary motions ; and he who would attain some conceptions of divine power, greatness, and majesty, must estimate the forces of attraction, the magnitude of the fixed stars, and the brightness of the whole celestial train.   It is not merely glory that the heavens declare, but the " glory of God," for they deliver to us such unanswerable arguments for a conscious, intelligent, planning, controlling, and presiding Creator, that no unprejudiced person can remain unconvinced by them.   The testimony given by the heavens is no mere hint, but a plain, unmistakeable declaration ; and it is a declaration of the most constant and abiding kind.   Yet for all this, to what avail is the loudest declaration to a deaf man, or the clearest showing to one spiritually blind ?   God the Holy Ghost must illuminate us, or all the suns in the milky way never will.

" *The firmament sheweth his handy-work ;* " not *handy,* in the vulgar use of that term, but hand-work.   The expanse is full of the works of the Lord's skilful, creating hands ; hands being attributed to the great creating Spirit to set forth his care and workmanlike action, and to meet the poor comprehension of mortals.   It is humbling to find that even when the most devout and elevated minds are desirous to express their loftiest thoughts of God, they must use words and metaphors drawn from the earth.   We are children, and must each confess, " I think as a child, I speak as a child."   In the expanse above us God flies, as it were, his starry flag to show that the King is at home, and hangs out his escutcheon that atheists may see how he despises their denunciations of him.   He who looks up to the firmament and then writes himself down an atheist, brands himself at the same moment as an idiot or a liar.   Strange is it that some who love God are yet afraid to study the God-declaring book of nature ; the mock-spirituality of some believers, who are too heavenly to consider the heavens, has given colour to the vaunts of infidels that nature contradicts revelation.   The wisest of men are those who with pious eagerness trace the goings forth of Jehovah as well in creation as in grace ; only the foolish have any fears lest the honest study of the one should injure our faith in the other.   Dr. M'Cosh has well said, " We have often mourned over the attempts made to set the works of God against the Word of God, and thereby excite, propagate, and perpetuate jealousies fitted to separate parties that ought to live in closest union.   In particular, we have always regretted that endeavours should have been made to depreciate nature with a view of exalting revelation ; it has always appeared to us to be nothing else than the degrading of one part of God's works in the hope thereby of exalting and recommending another.   Let not science and religion be reckoned as opposing citadels, frowning defiance upon each other, and their troops brandishing their armour in hostile attitude.   They have too many common foes, if they would but think of it, in ignorance and prejudice, in passion and vice, under all their forms, to admit of their lawfully wasting their strength in a useless warfare with each other.   Science has a foundation, and so has religion ; let them unite their foundations, and the basis will be broader, and they will be two compartments of one great fabric reared to the glory of God.   Let the one be the outer and the other the inner court.   In the one, let all look, and admire and adore ; and in the other, let those who have faith kneel, and pray, and praise.   Let the one be the sanctuary where human learning may present its richest incense as an offering to God, and the other the holiest of all, separated from it by a veil now rent in twain, and in which, on a blood-sprinkled mercy-seat, we pour out the love of a reconciled heart, and hear the oracles of the living God."

2. " *Day unto day uttereth speech, and night unto night sheweth knowledge.*"   As if one day took up the story where the other left it, and each night passed over the wondrous tale to the next.   The original has in it the thought of pouring out, or welling over, with speech ; as though days and nights were but a fountain flowing evermore with Jehovah's praise.   Oh to drink often at the celestial well, and learn to utter the glory of God !   The witnesses above cannot be slain or silenced ; from their elevated seats they constantly preach the knowledge of God, unawed and unbiassed by the judgments of men.   Even the changes of alternating night and day are mutely eloquent, and light and shade equally reveal the Invisible One ; let the vicissitudes of our circumstances do the same, and while we bless the God of our days of joy, let us also extol him who giveth " songs in the night."

The lesson of day and night is one which it were well if all men learned.   It should be among our day-thoughts and night-thoughts to remember the flight of time, the changeful character of earthly things, the brevity both of joy and sorrow, the preciousness of life, our utter powerlessness to recall the hours once flown, and the irresistible approach of eternity. Day bids us labour, night reminds us to prepare for our last home ; day bids us work for God, and night invites us to rest in him ; day bids us look for endless day, and night warns us to escape from everlasting night.

3. *" There is no speech nor language, where their voice is not heard."* Every man may hear the voices of the stars. Many are the languages of terrestrials, to celestials there is but one, and that one may be understood by every willing mind. The lowest heathen are without excuse, if they do not discover the invisible things of God in the works which he has made. Sun, moon, and stars are God's travelling preachers ; they are apostles upon their journey confirming those who regard the Lord, and judges on circuit condemning those who worship idols.

The margin gives us another rendering, which is more literal, and involves less repetition ; *" no speech, no words, their voice is not heard ; "* that is to say, their teaching is not addressed to the ear, and is not uttered in articulate sounds ; it is pictorial, and directed to the eye and heart ; it touches not the sense by which faith comes, for faith cometh by hearing. Jesus Christ is called the Word, for he is a far more distinct display of Godhead than all the heavens can afford ; they are, after all, but dumb instructors ; neither star nor sun can arrive at a word, but Jesus is the express image of Jehovah's person, and his name is the Word of God.

4. *" Their line is gone out through all the earth, and their words to the end of the world."* Although the heavenly bodies move in solemn silence, yet in reason's ear they utter precious teachings. They give forth no literal *words*, but yet their instruction is clear enough to be so described. Horne says that the phrase employed indicates a language of signs, and thus we are told that the heavens speak by their significant actions and operations. Nature's words are like those of the deaf and dumb, but grace tells us plainly of the Father. By their line is probably meant the *measure* of their domain which, together with their testimony, has gone out to the utmost end of the habitable earth. No man living beneath the copes of heaven dwells beyond the bounds of the diocese of God's Court-preachers ; it is easy to escape from the light of ministers, who are as stars in the right hand of the Son of Man ; but even then men, with a conscience yet unseared, will find a Nathan to accuse them, a Jonah to warn them, and an Elijah to threaten them in the silent stars of night. To gracious souls the voices of the heavens are more influential far, they feel the sweet influences of the Pleiades, and are drawn towards their Father God by the bright bands of Orion.

" In them hath he set a tabernacle for the sun." In the midst of the heavens the sun encamps, and marches like a mighty monarch on his glorious way. He has no fixed abode, but as a traveller pitches and removes his tent, a tent which will soon be taken down and rolled together as a scroll. As the royal pavilion stood in the centre of the host, so the sun in his place appears like a king in the midst of attendant stars.

5. *" Which is as a bridegroom coming out of his chamber."* A bridegroom comes forth sumptuously apparelled, his face beaming with a joy which he imparts to all around ; such, but with a mighty emphasis, is the rising Sun. *" And rejoiceth as a strong man to run a race."* As a champion girt for running cheerfully addresses himself to the race, so does the sun speed onward with matchless regularity and unwearying swiftness in his appointed orbit. It is but mere play to him ; there are no signs of effort, flagging or exhaustion. No other creature yields such joy to the earth as her bridegroom the sun ; and none, whether they be horse or eagle, can for an instant compare in swiftness with that heavenly champion. But all his glory is but the glory of God ; even the sun shines in light borrowed from the Great Father of Lights.

> " Thou sun, of this great world both eye and soul,
> Acknowledge Him thy greater ; sound His praise
> Both when thou climb'st, and when high noon hast gained,
> And when thou fall'st."

6. *" His going forth is from the end of the heaven, and his circuit unto the ends of it."* He bears his light to the boundaries of the solar heavens, traversing the zodiac with steady motion, denying his light to none who dwell within his range. *" And there is nothing hid from the heat thereof."* Above, beneath, around, the heat of the sun exercises an influence. The bowels of the earth are stored with the ancient produce of the solar rays, and even yet earth's inmost caverns feel

their power. Where light is shut out, yet heat and other more subtle influences find their way.

There is no doubt a parallel intended to be drawn between the heaven of grace and the heaven of nature. God's way of grace is sublime and broad, and full of his glory ; in all its displays it is to be admired and studied with diligence ; both its lights and its shades are instructive ; it has been proclaimed, in a measure, to every people, and in due time shall be yet more completely published to the ends of the earth. Jesus, like a sun, dwells in the midst of revelation, tabernacling among men in all his brightness ; rejoicing, as the Bridegroom of his church, to reveal himself to men ; and, like a champion, to win unto himself renown. *He* makes a circuit of mercy, blessing the remotest corners of the earth ; and there are no seeking souls, however degraded and depraved, who shall be denied the comfortable warmth and benediction of his love—even death shall feel the power of his presence, and resign the bodies of the saints, and this fallen earth shall be restored to its pristine glory.

7 The law of the Lord *is* perfect, converting the soul : the testimony of the Lord *is* sure, making wise the simple.

8 The statutes of the Lord *are* right, rejoicing the heart : the command-ment of the *Lord is* pure, enlightening the eyes.

9 The fear of the Lord *is* clean, enduring for ever : the judgments of the Lord *are* true *and* righteous altogether.

10 More to be desired *are they* than gold, yea, than much fine gold : sweeter also than honey and the honeycomb.

11 Moreover by them is thy servant warned : *and* in keeping of them *there is* great reward.

In the three following verses we have a brief but instructive hexapla containing six descriptive titles of the word, six characteristic qualities mentioned, and six divine effects declared. Names, nature, and effect are well set forth.

7. " *The law of the Lord is perfect ;* " by which he means not merely the law of Moses but the doctrine of God, the whole run and rule of sacred Writ. The doctrine revealed by God he declares to be perfect, and yet David had but a very small part of the Scriptures, and if a fragment, and that the darkest and most historical portion, be perfect, what must the entire volume be ? How more than perfect is the book which contains the clearest possible display of divine love, and gives us an open vision of redeeming grace. The gospel is a complete scheme or law of gracious salvation, presenting to the needy sinner everything that his terrible necessities can possibly demand. There are no redundancies and no omissions in the Word of God, and in the plan of grace ; why then do men try to paint this lily and gild this refined gold ? The gospel is perfect in all its parts, and perfect as a whole : it is a crime to add to it, treason to alter it, and felony to take from it.

" *Converting the soul.*"—Making the man to be returned or restored to the place from which sin had cast him. The practical effect of the Word of God is to turn the man to himself, to his God, and to holiness ; and the turn or conversion is not outward alone, " *the soul* " is moved and renewed. The great means of the conversion of sinners is the Word of God, and the more closely we keep to it in our ministry the more likely are we to be successful. It is God's Word rather than man's comment on God's Word which is made mighty with souls. When the law drives and the gospel draws, the action is different but the end is one, for by God's Spirit the soul is made to yield, and cries, " Turn me, and I shall be turned." Try men's depraved nature with philosophy and reasoning, and it laughs your efforts to scorn, but the Word of God soon works a transformation.

" *The testimony of the Lord is sure.*" God bears his testimony against sin, and on behalf of righteousness ; he testifies of our fall and of our restoration ; this testimony is plain, decided, and infallible, and is to be accepted as sure. God's witness in his Word is so sure that we may draw solid comfort from it both for time and eternity, and so sure that no attacks made upon it, however fierce or subtle, can ever weaken its force. What a blessing that in a world of uncertainties we have something sure to rest upon ! We hasten from the quicksands of human speculations to the *terra firma* of Divine Revelation.

"*Making wise the simple.*" Humble, candid, teachable minds receive the word, and are made wise unto salvation. Things hidden from the wise and prudent are revealed unto babes. The persuadable grow wise, but the cavillers continue fools. As a law or plan the Word of God converts, and then as a testimony it instructs; it is not enough for us to be converts, we must continue to be disciples; and if we have felt the power of truth, we must go on to prove its certainty by experience. The perfection of the gospel converts, but its sureness edifies; if we would be edified it becomes us not to stagger at the promise through unbelief, for a doubted gospel cannot make us wise, but truth of which we are assured will be our establishment.

8. "*The statutes of the Lord are right.*" His precepts and decrees are founded in righteousness, and are such as are right or fitted to the right reason of man. As a physician gives the right medicine, and a counsellor the right advice, so does the Book of God. "*Rejoicing the heart.*" Mark the progress; he who was converted was next made wise and is now made happy; that truth which makes the heart right then gives joy to the right heart. Free grace brings heart-joy. Earthborn mirth dwells on the lip, and flushes the bodily powers; but heavenly delights satisfy the inner nature, and fill the mental faculties to the brim. There is no cordial of comfort like that which is poured from the bottle of Scripture.

> "Retire and read thy Bible to be gay."

"*The commandment of the Lord is pure.*" No mixture of error defiles it, no stain of sin pollutes it; it is the unadulterated milk, the undiluted wine. "*Enlightening the eyes,*" purging away by its own purity the earthly grossness which mars the intellectual discernment: whether the eye be dim with sorrow or with sin, the Scripture is a skilful oculist, and makes the eye clear and bright. Look at the sun and it puts out your eyes, look at the more than sunlight of Revelation and it enlightens them; the purity of snow causes snow-blindness to the Alpine traveller, but the purity of God's truth has the contrary effect, and cures the natural blindness of the soul. It is well again to observe the gradation; the convert became a disciple and next a rejoicing soul, he now obtains a discerning eye, and as a spiritual man discerneth all things, though he himself is discerned of no man.

9. "*The fear of the Lord is clean.*" The doctrine of truth is here described by its spiritual effect, viz., inward piety, or the fear of the Lord; this is clean in itself, and cleanses out the love of sin, sanctifying the heart in which it reigns. Mr. Godly-fear is never satisfied till every street, lane, and alley, yea, and every house and every corner of the town of Mansoul is clean rid of the Diabolonians who lurk therein. "*Enduring for ever.*" Filth brings decay, but cleanness is the great foe of corruption. The grace of God in the heart being a pure principle is also an abiding and incorruptible principle, which may be crushed for a time, but cannot be utterly destroyed. Both in the Word and in the heart, when the Lord writes, he says with Pilate, "What I have written, I have written;" he will make no erasures himself, much less suffer others to do so. The revealed will of God is never changed; even Jesus came not to destroy but to fulfil, and even the ceremonial law was only changed as to its shadow, the substance intended by it is eternal. When the governments of nations are shaken with revolution, and ancient constitutions are being repealed, it is comforting to know that the throne of God is unshaken, and his law unaltered.

"*The judgments of the Lord are true and righteous altogether;*"—jointly and severally the words of the Lord are true; that which is good in detail is excellent in the mass; no exception may be taken to a single clause separately, or to the book as a whole. God's judgments, all of them together, or each of them apart, are manifestly just, and need no laborious excuses to justify them. The judicial decisions of Jehovah, as revealed in the law, or illustrated in the history of his providence, are truth itself, and commend themselves to every truthful mind; not only is their power invincible, but their justice is unimpeachable.

10. "*More to be desired are they than gold, yea, than much fine gold.*" Bible truth is enriching to the soul in the highest degree; the metaphor is one which gathers force as it is brought out;—gold—fine gold—much fine gold; it is good, better, best, and therefore it is not only to be desired with a miser's avidity, but with more than that. As spiritual treasure is more noble than mere material wealth, so should it be desired and sought after with greater eagerness. Men speak of solid gold, but what is so solid as solid truth? For love of gold pleasure is forsworn, ease renounced, and life endangered; shall we not be ready to do as much for love

of truth ?   " *Sweeter also than honey and the honeycomb.*"   Trapp says, " Old people
are all for profit, the young for pleasure ;   here's gold for the one, yea, the finest
gold in great quantity ;   here's honey for the other, yea, live honey dropping from
the comb."   The pleasures arising from a right understanding of the divine testimonies are of the most delightful order ;   earthly enjoyments are utterly contemptible,
if compared with them.   The sweetest joys, yea, the sweetest of the sweetest falls
to his portion who has God's truth to be his heritage.

11. " *Moreover by them is thy servant warned.*"   We are warned by the Word
both of our duty, our danger, and our remedy.   On the sea of life there would
be many more wrecks, if it were not for the divine storm-signals which give to the
watchful a timely warning.   The Bible should be our Mentor, our Monitor, our
Memento Mori, our Remembrancer, and the Keeper of our Conscience.   Alas,
that so few men will take the warning so graciously given ;   none but servants
of God will do so, for they alone regard their Master's will.   Servants of God not
only find his service delightful in itself, but they receive good recompense ;   "*In
keeping of them there is great reward.*"   There is a wage, and a great one ; though
we earn no wages of debt, we win great wages of grace.   Saints may be losers for
a time, but they shall be glorious gainers in the long run, and even now a quiet
conscience is in itself no slender reward for obedience.   He who wears the herb
called heart's-ease in his bosom is truly blessed.   However, the main reward is
yet to come, and the word here used hints as much, for it signifies *the heel*, as if
the reward would come to us at the end of life when the work was done ;—not while
the labour was in the hand, but when it was gone and we could see the heel of it.
Oh, the glory yet to be revealed !   It is enough to make a man faint for joy at
the prospect of it.   Our light affliction, which is but for a moment, is not worthy
to be compared with the glory which shall be revealed in us.   Then shall we know
the value of the Scriptures when we swim in that sea of unutterable delight to
which their streams will bear us, if we commit ourselves to them.

12 Who can understand *his* errors ? cleanse thou me from secret *faults*.

13 Keep back thy servant also from presumptuous *sins ;* let them not
have dominion over me : then shall I be upright, and I shall be innocent from
the great transgression.

14 Let the words of my mouth, and the meditation of my heart, be
acceptable in thy sight, O LORD, my strength, and my redeemer.

12. " *Who can understand his errors ?* "   A question which is its own answer.   It
rather requires a note of exclamation than of interrogation.   By the law is the
knowledge of sin, and in the presence of divine truth, the Psalmist marvels at the
number and heinousness of his sins.   He best knows himself who best knows the
Word, but even such an one will be in a maze of wonder as to what he does not
know, rather than on the mount of congratulation as to what he does know.   We
have heard of a comedy of errors, but to a good man this is more like a tragedy.
Many books have a few lines of errata at the end, but our errata might be as
large as the volume if we could but have sense enough to see them.   Augustine
wrote in his older days a series of Retractations ;   ours might make a library if we
had enough grace to be convinced of our mistakes and to confess them.   " *Cleanse
thou me from secret faults.*"   Thou canst mark in me faults entirely hidden from
myself.   It were hopeless to expect to see all my spots ;   therefore, O Lord, wash
away in the atoning blood even those sins which my conscience has been unable to
detect.   Secret sins, like private conspirators, must be hunted out, or they may
do deadly mischief ;   it is well to be much in prayer concerning them.   In the Lateran
Council of the Church of Rome, a decree was passed that every true believer must
confess his sins, all of them, once in a year to the priest, and they affixed to it this
declaration, that there is no hope of pardon but in complying with that decree.
What can equal the absurdity of such a decree as that ?   Do they suppose that
they can tell their sins as easily as they can count their fingers ?   Why, if we could
receive pardon for all our sins by telling every sin we have committed in one hour,
there is not one of us who would be able to enter heaven, since, besides the sins
that are known to us and that we may be able to confess, there are a vast mass of
sins, which are as truly sins as those which we lament, but which are secret, and
come not beneath our eyes.   If we had eyes like those of God, we should think very
differently of ourselves.   The transgressions which we see and confess are but

like the farmer's small samples which he brings to market, when he has left his granary full at home. We have but a very few sins which we can observe and detect, compared with those which are hidden from ourselves and unseen by our fellow-creatures.

13. *"Keep back thy servant also from presumptuous sins; let them not have dominion over me."*—This earnest and humble prayer teaches us that saints may fall into the worst of sins unless restrained by grace, and that therefore they must watch and pray lest they enter into temptation. There is a natural proneness to sin in the best of men, and they must be held back as a horse is held back by the bit or they will run into it. Presumptuous sins are peculiarly dangerous. All sins are great sins, but yet some sins are greater than others. Every sin has in it the very venom of rebellion, and is full of the essential marrow of traitorous rejection of God; but there be some sins which have in them a greater development of the essential mischief of rebellion, and which wear upon their faces more of the brazen pride which defies the Most High. It is wrong to suppose that because all sins will condemn us, that therefore one sin is not greater than another. The fact is, that while all transgression is a greatly grievous and sinful thing, yet there are some transgressions which have a deeper shade of blackness, and a more double scarlet-dyed hue of criminality than others. The presumptuous sins of our text are the chief and worst of all sins; they rank head and foremost in the list of iniquities. It is remarkable that though an atonement was provided under the Jewish law for every kind of sin, there was this one exception: "But the soul that sinneth presumptuously shall have no atonement; it shall be cut off from the midst of my people." And now under the Christian dispensation, although in the sacrifice of our blessed Lord there is a great and precious atonement for presumptuous sins, whereby sinners who have erred in this manner are made clean, yet without doubt, presumptuous sinners, dying without pardon, must expect to receive a double portion of the wrath of God, and a more terrible portion of eternal punishment in the pit that is digged for the wicked. For this reason is David so anxious that he may never come under the reigning power of these giant evils. *"Then shall I be upright, and I shall be innocent from the great transgression."* He shudders at the thought of the unpardonable sin. Secret sin is a stepping-stone to presumptuous sin, and that is the vestibule of "the sin which is unto death." He who is not wilful in his sin, will be in a fair way to be innocent so far as poor sinful man can be; but he who tempts the devil to tempt him is in a path which will lead him from bad to worse, and from the worse to the worst.

14. *"Let the words of my mouth, and the meditation of my heart, be acceptable in thy sight, O Lord, my strength, and my Redeemer."* A sweet prayer, and so spiritual that it is almost as commonly used in Christian worship as the apostolic benediction. *Words of the mouth* are mockery if the heart does not *meditate;* the shell is nothing without the kernel; but both together are useless unless *accepted;* and even if accepted by man, it is all vanity if not acceptable in *the sight of God.* We must in prayer view Jehovah as our *strength* enabling, and our *Redeemer* saving, or we shall not pray aright, and it is well to feel our personal interest so as to use the word *my,* or our prayers will be hindered. Our near Kinsman's name, our Goel or Redeemer, makes a blessed ending to the Psalm; it began with the heavens, but it ends with him whose glory fills heaven and earth. Blessed Kinsman, give us now to meditate acceptably upon thy most sweet love and tenderness.

EXPLANATORY NOTES AND QUAINT SAYINGS.

Whole Psalm.—The magnificent scenery to which the poem alludes is derived entirely from a contemplation of nature, in a state of pastoral seclusion; and a contemplation indulged in, at noontide or in the morning, when the sun was travelling over the horizon, and eclipsing all the other heavenly bodies by his glory. On which account it forms a perfect contrast with the eighth Psalm, evidently composed in the evening, and should be read in connection with it, as it was probably written nearly at the same time: and as both are songs of praise derived from natural phenomena, and therefore peculiarly appropriate to rural or pastoral life.—*John Mason Good.*

Whole Psalm.—The world resembleth a divinity-school, saith Plutarch, and Christ, as the Scripture telleth, is our doctor, instructing us by his works, and by his words. For as Aristotle had two sorts of writings, one called *exoterical*, for his common auditors, another acroamatical, for his private scholars and familiar acquaintance : so God hath two sorts of books, as David intimates in this Psalm ; namely, the book of his creatures, as a common-place book for all men in the world : " *The heavens declare the glory of God,*" verses 1—6 ; the book of his Scriptures as a statute-book for his domestical auditory, the church : " *The law of the Lord is an undefiled law,*" verses 7, 8. The great book of the creatures in folio, may be termed aptly *the shepherd's kalendar,* and the *ploughman's alphabet,* in which even the most ignorant may run (as the prophet speaks) and read. It is a letter patent, or open epistle for all, as David, in our text, *Their sound is gone out into all lands, and their words unto the ends of the world ; there is neither speech nor language but have heard of their preaching.* For albeit, heaven, and the sun in heaven, and the light in the sun are mute, yet *their voices* are well understood, catechising plainly the first elements of religion, as, namely, that there is a God, and that this God is but one God, and that this one God excelleth all other things infinitely both in might and majesty. *Universus mundus* (as one pithily) *nihil aliud est quàm Deus explicatus :* the whole world is nothing else but God expressed. So St. Paul, Rom. i. 20 : God's *invisible things,* as his eternal power and Godhead, " are clearly seen " by the creation of the world, " being understood by the things that are made." The heavens declare this, and the firmament showeth this, and the day telleth this, and the night certifieth this, the sound of the thunder proclaimeth, as it were, this in all lands, and the words of the whistling wind unto the ends of the world. More principally *the sun, which as a bridegroom cometh out of his chamber, and rejoiceth as a giant to run his course.* The body thereof (as mathematicians have confidently delivered) is one hundred and sixty-six times bigger than the whole earth, and yet it is every day carried by the finger of God so great a journey, so long a course, that if it were to be taken on the land, it should run every several hour of the day two hundred and twenty-five German miles. It is true that God is incapable to sense, yet he makes himself, as it were, visible in his works ; as the divine poet (Du Bartas) sweetly :—

> " Therein our fingers feel, our nostrils smell,
> Our palates taste his virtues that excel,
> He shows him to our eyes, talks to our ears,
> In the ordered motions of the spangled spheres."

So " *the heavens declare,*" that is, they make men declare the glory of God, by their admirable structure, motions, and influence. Now, the preaching of *the heavens* is wonderful in three respects. 1. As preaching all the night and all the day without intermission : verse 2. *One day telleth another, and one night certifieth another.* 2. As preaching in every kind of language : verse 3, *There is neither speech, nor language, but their voices are heard among them.* 3. As preaching in every part of the world, and in every parish of every part, and in every place of every parish : verse 4, *Their sound is gone into all lands, and their words unto the ends of the world.* They be diligent pastors, as preaching at all times ; and learned pastors, as preaching in all tongues ; and catholic pastors, as preaching in all towns. Let us not then in this University (where the voices of so many great doctors are heard), be like to truants in other schools, who gaze so much upon the babies*, and gilded cover, and painted margent of their book, that they neglect the text and lesson itself. This is *God's primer,* as it were, for all sorts of people ; but he hath another book proper only for his domestical auditory the church : " He sheweth his word unto Jacob, his statutes and his judgments unto Israel. He hath not dealt so with any nation, neither have the heathen knowledge of his laws." Psa. cxlvii. 19, 20. Heathen men read in his primer, but Christian men are well acquainted with his Bible. The primer is a good book, but it is imperfect ; for after a man hath learned it he must learn more ; but " *the law of the Lord,*" that is, the body of the Holy Scriptures, is a most absolute canon of all doctrines appertaining either to faith or good manners ; it is a *perfect law, converting the soul, giving wisdom to the simple, sure, pure, righteous, and rejoicing the heart,*" etc.—*John Boys.*

Whole Psalm. Saint Chrysostom conjectures that the main intention of the greatest part of this Psalm consists in the discovery of divine providence, which

---

* The pictures or illustrations of a book.

manifests itself in the motions and courses of the heavenly bodies, concerning, which the Psalmist speaketh much, from verse 1 to verse 7. Saint Austin upon the place, is of a quite different opinion, who conjectures that Christ is the whole subject of this Psalm; whose person is compared to the sun for excellency and beauty, and the course of whose doctrine was dispersed round about the world by his apostles, to which Saint Paul alludes (Rom. x. 18); "Have they not heard? Yes, verily, their sound went into all the earth," etc., and the efficacy of whose gospel is like the heat of the sun, which pierceth into the very heart of the earth, so that into the secrets of the soul. I confess this allegorical exposition is not altogether impertinent, neither is that literal exposition of Saint Chrysostom to be blamed, for it hath its weight. But to omit all variety of conjectures, this Psalm contains in it:

1. A double kind of *the knowledge of God*, of which one is *by the book of the creature* ; and this divines call a natural knowledge : there is not any one creature, but it is a leaf written all over with the description of God ; his eternal power and Godhead may be understood by the things that are seen, saith the apostle. Rom. i. 20. And, as every creature, so especially *" the heavens "* do lead us to the knowledge of a God : so verse 1 of this Psalm : *" The heavens declare the glory of God, and the firmament sheweth his handywork ; "* they are the theatres, as it were, of his wisdom, and power, and glory. Another is *by the book of Scripture ;* and this knowledge is far more distinct and explicit : with the other even the heathens do grope after a deity, but with this Christians do behold God, as it were, with open face. The characters here are now fresh, spiritual, complete, and lively. The word of God is the singular means to know God aright. Look, as the light which comes from the sun, so that word of God, which is light, is the clearest way to know God who is light itself. Hence it is that the Psalmist stands much upon this from verse 7 to verse 12, where he sets open the word in its several encomiums and operations ; namely, in its perfection, its certainties and firmness ; its righteousness, and purity, and truth ; and then in its efficacy—that it is a converting word, an enlightening word, an instructing word, a rejoicing word, a desirable word, a warning word, and a rewarding word.

2. *A singular and experimental knowledge of himself.*—So it seemeth, that that word which David did so much commend, he did commend it from an experimental efficacy ; he had found it to be a righteous, and holy, and pure, and discovering word, laying open, not only visible and gross transgressions, but also, like the light of the sun, those otherwise unobserved and secret atoms of senses flying within the house ; I mean in the secret chambers of the soul.—*Obadiah Sedgwick*, 1660.

Verse 1.—*" The heavens declare the glory of God,"* etc.—The eminent saints of ancient times were watchful observers of the objects and operations of nature. In every event they saw the agency of God ; and, therefore, they took delight in its examination. For they could not but receive pleasure from witnessing the manifestations of his wisdom and beneficence, whom they adored and loved. They had not learned, as we have in modern times, to interpose unbending laws between the Creator and his works ; and then, by giving inherent power to these laws, virtually to remove God away from his creation into an ethereal extramundane sphere of repose and happiness. I do not say that this is the universal feeling of the present day. But it prevails extensively in the church, and still more in the world. The ablest philosophers of modern times do, indeed, maintain that a natural law is nothing more than the uniform mode in which God acts ; and that, after all, it is not the efficiency of the law, but God's own energy, that keeps all nature in motion; that he operates immediately and directly, not remotely and indirectly, in bringing about every event, and that every natural change is as really the work of God as if the eye of sense could see his hand turning round the wheels of nature. But, although the ablest philosophy of modern times has reached this conclusion, the great mass of the community, and even of Christians, are still groping in the darkness of that mechanical system which ascribes the operations of the natural world to nature's laws instead of nature's God. By a sort of figure, indeed, it is proper, as the advocates of this system admit, to speak of God as the author of natural events, because he originally ordained the laws of nature. But they have no idea that he exerts any direct and immediate agency in bringing them about ; and, therefore, when they look upon these events they feel no impression of the presence and active agency of Jehovah.

But how different, as already remarked, were the feelings of ancient saints. The Psalmist could not look up to heaven without exclaiming, " *The heavens declare the glory of God ; and the firmament sheweth his handywork. Day unto day uttereth speech, and night unto night sheweth knowledge. There is no speech nor language where their voice is not heard."* When he cast his eyes abroad upon the earth, his full heart cried out, " O Lord, how manifold are thy works ! In wisdom hast thou made them all ; the earth is full of thy riches." In his eye everything was full of God. It was God who " sent springs into the valleys, which run among the hills." When the thunder-storm passed before him, it was " God's voice in the heavens, and his lightnings that lighted the world." When he heard the bellowings, and saw the smoke of the volcano, it was " God who looketh on the earth, and it trembleth ; he toucheth the hills, and they smoke."—*Edward Hitchcock, D.D., LL.D.,* 1867.

Verse 1.—" *The heavens declare,"* etc. Man has been endued by his Creator with mental powers capable of cultivation. He has employed them in the study of the wonderful works of God which the universe displays. His own habitation has provided a base which has served him to measure the heavens. He compares his own stature with the magnitude of the earth on which he dwells ; the earth, with the system in which it is placed ; the extent of the system, with the distance of the nearest fixed stars ; and that distance again serves as a unit of measurement for other distances which observation points out. Still no approach is made to any limit. How extended these wonderful works of the Almighty may be no man can presume to say. The sphere of creation appears to extend around us indefinitely on all sides ; " to have its centre everywhere, its circumference nowhere." These are considerations which from their extent almost bewilder our minds. But how should they raise our ideas toward their great Creator, when we consider that all these were created from nothing, by a word, by a mere volition of the Deity. " Let them be," said God, and they were. " By the word of the Lord were the heavens made, and all the host of them by the breath of his mouth." " For he spake, and it was done. He commanded, and it stood fast." Psalm xxxiii. 6, 9. What must be that power which so formed worlds on worlds ; worlds in comparison of which this earth which we inhabit sinks into utter nothingness ! Surely when we thus lift up our thoughts to the heavens, the moon and the stars which he hath ordained, we must feel, if we can ever feel, how stupendous and incomprehensible is that Being who formed them all ; that " *the heavens "* do indeed " *declare the glory of God ; and the firmament sheweth his handywork."*—*Temple Chevallier, in " The Hulsean Lectures for* 1827."

Verse 1.—I have often been charmed and awed at the sight of the nocturnal heavens, even before I knew how to consider them in their proper circumstances of majesty and beauty. Something like magic has struck my mind, on transient and unthinking survey of the æthereal vault, tinged throughout with the purest azure, and decorated with innumerable starry lamps. I have felt, I know not what, powerful and aggrandising impulse, which seemed to snatch me from the low entanglements of vanity, and prompted an ardent sigh for sublimer objects. Methought I heard, even from the silent spheres, a commanding call to spurn the abject earth, and pant after unseen delights. Henceforth I hope to imbibe more copiously this moral emanation of the skies, when, in some such manner as the preceding, they are rationally seen, and the sight is duly improved. The stars, I trust, will teach as well as shine, and help to dispel both nature's gloom and my intellectual darkness. To some people they discharge no better a service than that of holding a flambeau to their feet, and softening the horrors of their night. To me and my friends may they act as ministers of a superior order, as counsellors of wisdom, and guides to happiness ! Nor will they fail to execute this nobler office, if they gently light our way into the knowledge of their adored Maker— if they point out with their silver rays our path to his beatific presence.—*James Hervey, A.M.,* 1713—1758.

Verse 1.—Should a man live underground, and there converse with the works of art and mechanism, and should afterwards be brought up into the open day, and see the several glories of the heaven and earth, he would immediately pronounce them the works of such a Being as we define God to be.—*Aristotle.*

Verse 1.—When we behold " *the heavens,"* when we contemplate the celestial bodies, can we fail of conviction ? Must we not acknowledge that there is a Divinity, a perfect Being, a ruling intelligence, which governs ; a God who is everywhere and directs all by his power ? Anybody who doubts this may as well deny there is a sun that lights us. Time destroys all false opinions, but it confirms those which are formed by nature. For this reason, with us as well as with other nations, the worship of the gods and the holy exercises of religion, increase in purity and extent every day.—*Cicero.*

Verse 1.—" *The heavens declare the glory of God,*" etc. They discover his *wisdom*, his *power*, his *goodness ;* and so there is not any one creature, though never so little, but we are to admire the Creator in it. As a chamber hung round about with looking-glasses represents the face upon every turn, thus all the world doth the mercy and the bounty of God ; though that be visible, yet it discovers an invisible God and his invisible properties.—*Anthony Burgess,* 1656.

Verse 1.—None of the elect are in that respect so unwise as to refuse to hear and consider the works and words of God as not appertaining unto him. God forbid. No man in the world doth with more fervency consider the works of God, none more readily lift up their ears to hear God speak than even they who have the inward revelation of the Holy Spirit.—*Wolfgang Musculus.*

Verse 1.—During the French revolution Jean Bon St. André, the Vendean revolutionist, said to a peasant, " I will have all your steeples pulled down, that you may no longer have any object by which you may be reminded of your old superstitions." "But," replied the peasant, "*you cannot help leaving us the stars.*"— *John Bate's " Cyclopædia of Moral and Religious Truths,"* 1865.

Verse 1.—" *The heavens declare the glory of God* "—

> How beautiful this dome of sky,
> And the vast hills in fluctuation fixed
> At thy command, how awful ! Shall the soul,
> Human and rational, report of thee
> Even less than these ? Be mute who will, who can,
> Yet I will praise thee with impassioned voice.
> My lips, that may forget thee in the crowd,
> Cannot forget thee here, where thou hast built
> For thine own glory, in the wilderness !

William Wordsworth, 1770—1850.

Verse 1.—" *The firmament sheweth his handywork* "—

> The glittering stars
> By the deep ear of meditation heard,
> Still in their midnight watches sing of him.
> He nods a calm. The tempest blows his wrath :
> The thunder is his voice ; and the red flash
> His speedy sword of justice. At his touch
> The mountains flame. He shakes the solid earth,
> And rocks the nations. Nor in these alone—
> In ev'ry common instance God is seen.

James Thomson.

Verse 1.—

> These are thy glorious works, Parent of good,
> Almighty ! Thine this universal frame,
> Thus wondrous fair. Thyself how wondrous, then
> Unspeakable, who sitt'st above these heavens
> To us invisible, or dimly seen
> In these thy lowest works ; yet these declare
> Thy goodness beyond thought, and power divine.

John Milton.

Verses 1, 2.—In order more fully to illustrate the expressive richness of the Hebrew, I would direct the attention of my reader to the beautiful phraseology of the XIX. Psalm. The literal reading of the first and second verses may be thus given :—

> " The heavens are *telling* the glory of God,
> The firmament *displaying* the work of his hands ;
> Day unto day *welleth forth* speech,
> Night unto night *breatheth out* knowledge."

Thus the four distinct terms in the original are preserved in the translation ; and the overflowing fulness with which day unto day pours forth divine instruction, and the gentle whisperings of the silent night, are contrasted as in the Hebrew.— *Henry Craik,* 1860.

Verses 1—4.—Though all preachers on earth should grow silent, and every human mouth cease from publishing the glory of God, the heavens above will never cease to declare and proclaim his majesty and glory. They are for ever preaching; for, like an unbroken chain, their message is delivered from day to day and from night to night. At the silence of one herald another takes up his speech. One day, like the other, discloses the same spectacles of his glory, and one night, like the other, the same wonders of his majesty. Though nature be *hushed* and *quiet* when the sun in his glory has reached the zenith on the azure sky—though the world keep her *silent* festival when the stars shine brightest at night—yet, says the Psalmist, *they speak;* ay, holy silence itself is a speech, provided there be the ear to hear it.—*Augustus T. Tholuck.*

Verses 1—4.—" *The heavens declare the glory of God, and the firmament showeth his handywork.*" If the heavens declare the glory of God, we should observe what that glory is which they declare. The heavens preach to us every day. . . . . " *Their line is gone out through all the earth, and their words to the end of the world.*" Sun, moon, and stars are preachers; they are universal, they are natural apostles. The world is their charge; " *their words,*" saith the Psalm, " *go to the end of the world.*" We may have good doctrine from them, especially this doctrine in the text, of the wisdom and power of God. And it is very observable that the apostle alludes to this text in the Psalm for a proof of gospel preaching to the whole world. Rom. x. 18. The gospel, like the sun, casts his beams over, and sheds his light into all the world. David in the Psalm saith, " *Their line is gone out,*" etc. By which word he shows that the heavens, being so curious a fabric, made, as it were, by a line and level, do clearly, though silently, preach the skill and perfections of God. Or, that we may read divine truths in them as a line formed by a pen into words and sentences (the original signifies both a measuring line and a written line), letters and words in writing being nothing but lines drawn into several forms or figures. But the Septuagint, whose translation the apostle citeth, for *Kavam, their line,* read *Kolam, their sound;* either misreading the word or studiously mollifying the sense into a nearer compliance with the latter clause of the verse, " *And their words to the end of the world.*"—*Joseph Caryl.*

Verses 1—4.—Like as the sun with his light beneficially comforteth all the world, so Christ, the Son of God, reacheth his benefits unto all men, so that they will receive them thankfully, and not refuse them disobediently.—*Robert Cawdray.*

Verse 2.—" *Day unto day,*" etc. But what is the meaning of the next word —*One day telleth another, and one night certifieth another?* Literally, *dies diem dicit,* is nothing else but *dies diem docet.* One day telleth another, is one day teacheth another. The day past is instructed by the day present: every new day doth afford new doctrine. The day is a most apt time to learn by reading and conference; the night a most fit time for invention and meditation. Now that which thou canst not understand this day thou mayest haply learn the next, and that which is not found out in one night may be gotten in another. Mystically (saith Heirom), Christ is this " *day,*" who saith of himself, " I am the light of the world," and his twelve apostles are the twelve hours of the day; for Christ's Spirit revealed by the mouths of his apostles the mysteries of our salvation, in other ages not so fully known unto the sons of men. *One day telleth another,* that is, the spiritual utter this unto the spiritual; and *one night certifieth another,* that is, Judas insinuates as much unto the Jews in the night of ignorance, saying, " Whomsoever I shall kiss, that is he, lay hold on him." Matt. xxvi. 28. Or, the Old Testament only shadowing Christ is *the night,* and the New Testament plainly showing Christ, is *the day.*—*John Boys.*

Verse 2.—" *Day unto day,*" or day after day; the vicissitude or continual succession of day and night speaketh much divine knowledge. The assiduity and constancy without any intermission by the heavens preaching is hereby expressed.—*John Richardson.*

Verse 2.—" *Uttereth,*" poureth forth abundantly; " *sheweth,*" demonstrates clearly and effectively, without ambiguity. Job xxxvi. 2. Many in the full light of gospel day, hear not that speech, who yet in the night of affliction and trouble, or in the conviction of their natural darkness, have that knowledge communicated to them which enables them to realise the joy that cometh in the morning.—*W. Wilson.*

Verse 2.—" *Sheweth knowledge.*" We may illustrate the differing measures in which natural objects convey knowledge to men of differing mental and spiritual capacity by the story of our great English artist. He is said to have been engaged upon one of his immortal works, and a lady of rank looking on remarked, " But, Mr. Turner, I do not see in nature all that you describe there." " Ah, Madam," answered the painter, " do you not wish you could ? "—*C. H. S.*

Verse 3.—" *There is no speech,*" etc. The sunset was one of the most glorious I ever beheld, and the whole earth seemed so still that *the voice of neither God nor man was heard.* There was not a ripple upon the waters, not the leaf of a tree nor even of a blade of grass moving, and the rocks upon the opposite shore reflected the sun's " after-glow," and were again themselves reflected from or in the river during the brief twilight, in a way I do not remember ever to have beheld before. No ! I will not say *the voice of God* was not heard ; it spoke in the very stillness as loud as in roaring thunder, in the placid scene as in rocks and cliffs impassable, and louder still in *the heavens and in the firmament,* and in the magnificent prospect around me. His wondrous works declared him to be near, and I felt as if the very ground upon which I was treading was holy.—*John Gadsby.*

Verse 4.—" *Their line is gone out,*" etc. " Their *sound* went," etc. Rom. x. 18. The relations which the gospel of Christ Jesus hath to the Psalms of David I find to be more than to all the Bible besides, that seldom anything is written in the New Testament, but we are sent to fetch our proofs from these. The margin here sends me to the Psalm, and the Psalm sends me back to this again ; showing that they both speak one thing. How comes it then that it is not one, for " *line* " and " *sound* " are not one thing ? Is there not some mistake here ? Answer—To fetch a proof from a place is one thing, an allusion is another. Sometimes the evangelists are enforced to bring their proofs for what they write out of the Old Testament, else we should never believe them, and then they must be very sure of the terms, when they say, " This was done that it might be fulfilled which was spoken," etc. But the apostle was not now upon that account ; only showing to the Romans the marvellous spreading of the gospel, alluding to this passage of David discoursing of " *the heavens,*" to which the prophet compared the publication of the word ; the sun and moon and stars not only shining through, but round all the earth. The same subject Paul was now upon, and for this purpose makes use of a term fitter to express the preaching of the gospel, by the word " *sound,*" than that other word expressing the limitations of the law, by the word " *line :* " both of these agreeing that there is no fitter comparison to be fetched from anything in nature than from " *the heavens,*" their motions, revolutions, influences upon sublunary bodies ; also in their eclipses, when one text seems to darken another, as if it were put out altogether by crossing and opposing, which is but seemingly so to the ignorant, they agree sweetly enough in themselves ; no bridegroom can agree better with his bride, nor rejoice more to run his course. So they both conclude in this, that the sun never saw that nation yet where the world of truth, in one degree or other (all the world, you must think, cannot be right under the meridian) hath not shined.—*William Streat, in " The Dividing of the Hoof,*" 1654.

Verse 4.—" *Unto the end of the world.*" Venantius Fortunatus eleven hundred years ago witnesses to the peregrinations of Paul the apostle.

> He passed the ocean's curled wave,
> As far as islands harbours have ;
> As far as Brittain yields a bay,
> Or Iceland's frozen shore a stay.

John Cragge, 1557.

Verse 4.—" *Their line is gone out through all the earth,*" etc. The molten sea did stand upon twelve oxen, that is, as Paul doth interpret it, upon twelve apostles (1 Cor. ix. 10) ; which in that they looked four ways, east, west, north, and south, they did teach all nations. And in that they looked three and three together, they did represent the blessed Trinity. Not only teaching all nations, but also in that sea of water, baptising them in the name of the Father, and of the Son, and of the Holy Ghost. Wherefore, though the two kine which carried the ark wherein were the tables of the law, went straight and kept one path, turning neither to the right hand nor to the left ; yet these twelve oxen which carried the molten sea, signifying the doctrine of the gospel, went not straight, neither kept one path, but turned into the way of the Gentiles ; yea, they looked all manner of ways, east, west, north, and south. And those two kine stood still and lowed no more when they came to the field of Joshua, dwelling in Bethshemesh, that is, the house of the sun. To note, that all the kine, and calves, and sacrifices, and ceremonies of the old law were to cease and stand still when they came to Jesus, who is the true Joshua, dwelling in heaven, which is the true Bethshemesh. But these twelve oxen were so far from leaving off, either to go, or to low, when they came to Christ, that even then they went much faster and lowed much louder ; so that now *" their sound is gone out into all lands, and their words to the end of the world ; "* and *" in them hath God set "* Bethshemesh, that is, a house or *" tabernacle for the sun."* Therefore, as the material sun, through the twelve signs of the Zodiac, goeth forth from the utter-most parts of the heaven, and runneth about to the end of it again : in like sort, the spiritual *Sun of Righteousness,* by the twelve apostles, as by twelve signs, hath been borne round about the world, that he might be not only " the glory of his people Israel," but also " a light to lighten the Gentiles ; " and that all, *" all* the ends of the earth might see the salvation of our God."—*Thomas Playfere.*

Verses 4—6.—It appears to me very likely that the Holy Ghost in these ex-pressions, which he most immediately uses about the rising of the sun, has an eye to the rising of the Sun of Righteousness from the grave, and that the expressions that the Holy Ghost here uses are conformed to such a view. The times of the Old Testament are times of night in comparison of the gospel day, and are so repre-sented in Scripture, and therefore the approach of the day of the New Testament dispensation in the birth of Christ, is called the day-spring from on high visiting the earth (Luke i. 78), " Through the tender mercy of our God ; whereby the day-spring from on high hath visited us ; " and the commencing of the gospel dispensation as it was introduced by Christ, is called the Sun of Righteousness rising. Mal. iv. 2. But this gospel dispensation commences with the resurrection of Christ. Therein the Sun of Righteousness rises from under the earth, as the sun appears to do in the morning, and comes forth as a bridegroom. He rose as the joyful, glorious bridegroom of his church ; for Christ, especially as risen again, is the proper bride-groom, or husband, of his church, as the apostle teaches (Rom. vii. 4), " Wherefore, my brethren, ye also are become dead to the law by the body of Christ ; that ye should be married to another, even to him who is raised from the dead, that we should bring forth fruit unto God." He that was covered with contempt, and overwhelmed in a deluge of sorrow, has purchased and won his spouse, for he loved the church, and gave himself for it, that he might present it to himself ; now he comes forth as a bridegroom to bring home his purchased spouse to him in spiritual marriage, as he soon after did in the conversion of such multitudes, making his people willing in the day of his power, and hath also done many times since, and will do in a yet more glorious degree. And as the sun when it rises comes forth like a bridegroom gloriously adorned, so Christ in his resurrection entered on his state of glory. After his state of sufferings, he rose to shine forth in ineffable glory as the King of heaven and earth, that he might be a glorious bridegroom, in whom his church might be unspeakably happy. Here the Psalmist says that God *has placed a tabernacle for the sun in the heavens :* so God the Father had prepared an abode in heaven for Jesus Christ ; he had set a throne for him there, to which he ascended after he rose. The sun after it is risen ascends up to the midst of heaven, and then at that end of its race descends again to the earth ; so Christ when he rose from the grave ascended up to the height of heaven, and far above all heavens, but at the end of the gospel day will descend again to the earth. It is here said that the risen sun " rejoiceth as a strong man to run a race." So Christ, when he rose, rose as a man of war, as the Lord strong and mighty, the Lord mighty in battle ; he rose to conquer his enemies, and to show forth his glorious power in subduing all things to himself, during that race which he had to run, which is from his resurrection to the end of the world, when he will return to the earth again. . . . . That the Holy Ghost here has a mystical meaning, and has respect to the light of the Sun of Righteousness, and not merely the light of the natural sun, is confirmed by the verses that follow in which the Psalmist himself seems to apply them to the word of God, which is the light of that Sun, even of Jesus Christ, who himself revealed the word of God : see the very next words, " The law of the Lord is perfect," etc.—*Jonathan Edwards,* 1703—1758.

Verse 5.—" *Which is as a bridegroom,*" etc. The sun is described like a bridegroom coming out of his chamber, dressed and prepared, and as a giant rejoicing to run his race ; but though the sun be thus prepared, and dressed, and ready, yet if the Lord send a writ and a prohibition to the sun to keep within his chamber, he cannot come forth, his journey is stopped. Thus also he stops man in his nearest preparations for any action. If the Lord will work, who shall let it ? Isaiah xliii. 13. That is, there is no power in heaven or earth which can hinder him. But if the Lord will let, who shall work ? Neither sun, nor stars, nor men, nor devils, can work, if he forbids them. The point is full of comfort.—*Joseph Caryl.*

Verse 5.—" *Which is as a bridegroom,*" etc. The Sun of Righteousness appeared in three signs especially ; *Leo, Virgo, Libra.* 1. In *Leo,* roaring as a lion, in the law ; so that the people could not endure his voice. 2. In *Virgo,* born of a pure virgin in the gospel. 3. In *Libra,* weighing our works in his balance at the day of judgment. Or as Bernard distinguisheth his threefold coming aptly—*venit ad homines, venit in homines, venit contra homines :* in the time past he came *unto* men as upon this day * ; in the time present, he comes by his spirit *into* men every day ; in the time future, he shall come *against* men at the last day. The coming here mentioned is his coming in the flesh—for so the fathers usually gloss the text— he came forth of the virgin's womb, " *as a bridegroom out of his chamber.*" As a *bridegroom,* for the King of heaven at this holy time made a great wedding for his Son. Matt. xxii. 1. Christ is the *bridegroom,* man's nature the bride, the con- junction and blessed union of both in one person is his marriage. The best way to reconcile two disagreeing families is to make some marriage between them : even so, the Word became flesh, and dwelt among us in the world that he might hereby make our peace, reconciling God to man and man to God. By this happy match the Son of God is become the Son of Man, even flesh of our flesh, and bone of our bones ; and the sons of men are made the sons of God, " of his flesh and of his bones," as Paul saith, Eph. v. 30. So that now the church being Christ's own spouse, saith, " I am my Beloved's, and my Beloved is mine." Cant. vi. 3. My sin is his sin, and his righteousness is my righteousness. He who knew no sin, for my sake was made sin ; and I, contrariwise, having no good thing, am made the righteousness of God in him : I which am *brown* by persecution, and *black* by nature (Cant. i. 5), so foul as the sow that walloweth in the mire, through his favour am comely, without spot or wrinkle, so white as the snow, like a lily among thorns, even the fairest among women. Cant. ii. 2. This happy *marriage* is not a *mar age,* but it makes a *merry age,* being " the consolation of Israel," and comfort of Jerusalem's heart. Indeed, Christ our husband doth absent himself from us in his body for a time ; but when he did ascend into heaven he took with him our pawn, namely his flesh ; and he gave us his pawn, namely, his Spirit, assuring us that we shall one day, when the world is ended, enter with him into the wedding chamber, and there feast with him, and enjoy his blessed company for evermore.—*John Boys.*

Verse 6.—" *There is nothing hid from the heat thereof.*"—This is literally the case. The earth receives its heat from the sun, and by conduction, a part of it enters the crust of our globe. By convection, another portion is carried to the atmosphere, which it warms. Another portion is radiated into space, according to laws yet imperfectly understood, but which are evidently connected with the colour, chemical composition, and mechanical structure of parts of the earth's surface. At the same time the ordinary state of the air, consisting of gases and vapour, modifies the heat rays and prevents scorching. Thus, the solar heat is equalised by the air. Nothing on earth or in air is hid from the heat of the sun. . . . Even the colour of some bodies is changed by heat. . . . Heat also is in bodies in a state which is not sensible, and is therefore called latent heat, or heat of fluidity, because it is regarded as the cause of fluidity in ponderable substances. It can fuse every substance it does not decompose below the melting point, as in the case of wood. Every gas may be regarded as consisting of heat, and some basis of ponderable matter, whose cohesion it overcomes, imparting a tendency to great expansion, when no external obstacle prevents, and this expansive tendency is their elasticity or tension. Certain gases have been liquefied under great pressure, and extreme cold. Heat, also, at certain temperatures, causes the elasticity of vapours to overcome the atmospheric pressure which can no longer restrain them. An example of this is the boiling point of water ; and, indeed, in every case the

---

* The Nineteenth Psalm is one " appointed to be read" on *Christmas Day.*

true instance is the boiling point. Philosophers are agreed that the affinity of heat for any ponderable substance is superior to all other forces acting upon it. No ponderable matters can combine without disengagement of heat. . . . And the same occurs from every mechanical pressure and condensation of a body. In all these cases, and many more, there are like evidences of the presence and influences of heat ; but the facts now advanced are sufficient to show us the force of the expression, that in terrestrial things nothing is hid from, or can by any possibility escape the agency of heat.—*Edwin Sidney, A.M., in " Conversations on the Bible and Science,"* 1866.

Verse 6 (*last clause*).—*" There is nothing hid from the heat,"* nothing from the light of Christ. It is not solely on the mountain top that he shines, as in the days before he was fully risen, when his rays, although unseen by the rest of the world, formed a glory round the heads of his prophets, who saw him while to the chief part of mankind he was still lying below the horizon. Now, however, that he is risen, he pours his light through the valley, as well as over the mountain ; nor is there any one, at least in these countries, who does not catch some gleams of that light, except those who burrow and hide themselves in the dark caverns of sin. But it is not light alone that Christ sheds from his heavenly tabernacle. As nothing is hid from his light, neither is anything hid from his heat. He not only enlightens the understanding, so that it shall see and know the truth ; he also softens, and melts, and warms the heart, so that it shall love the truth, and calls forth fruit from it, and ripens the fruit he has called forth ; and that too on the lowliest plant which creeps along the ground, as well as the loftiest tree. . . .

Though while he was on earth, he had fullest power of bestowing every earthly gift, yet, in order that he should be able to bestow heavenly gifts with the same all-healing power, it was necessary that he should go up into heaven. When he had done so, when he had ascended into *his tabernacle in the heavens,* then, he promises his disciples, he would send down the Holy Spirit of God, who should bring them heavenly gifts, yea, who should enter into their hearts, and make them bring forth all the fruits of the Spirit in abundance ; should make them abound in love, in peace, in longsuffering, in gentleness, in goodness, in faith, in meekness, in temperance. These are the bright heavenly rays, which, as it were, make up the pure light of Christ ; *and from this heat nothing is hid.* Even the hardest heart may be melted by it ; even the foulest may be purified.—*Julius Charles Hare, M.A.,* 1841.

Verse 7.—*" The law of the Lord is perfect, converting the soul."* To man fallen, the law only convinceth of sin, and bindeth over to death, it is nothing but a killing letter ; but the gospel, accompanied by the power of the Spirit, bringeth life. Again, it is said, " *The law of the Lord is perfect, converting the soul ;* " therefore it seems the law may also be a word of salvation to the creature. I answer ; by the law there, is not meant only that part of the word which we call the covenant of works, but there it is put for the whole word, for the whole doctrine of the covenant of life and salvation ; as Psalm i. 2 : " His delight is in the law of the Lord ; and in his law doth he meditate day and night." And if you take it in that stricter sense, then it converteth the soul but by accident, as it is joined with the gospel, which is the ministry of life and righteousness, but in itself it is the law of sin and death. Look, as a thing taken simply, would be poison and deadly in itself, yet mixed with other wholesome medicines, it is of great use, is an excellent physical ingredient ; so the law is of great use as joined with the gospel, to awaken and startle the sinner, to show him his duty, to convince him of sin and judgment ; but it is the gospel properly that pulls in the heart.—*Thomas Manton.*

Verse 7.—*The law,* or doctrine, an orderly manner of instruction, an institution or disposition, called in Hebrew *torah,* which implies both doctrine and an orderly disposition of the same. Therefore where one prophet, relating David's words, saith *the law* of man (2 Sam. vii. 19), another saith, *the orderly estate,* or, *course* of man. 1 Cor. xvii. 17. The Holy Ghost, in Greek, calls it *Nomos,* a law (Heb. viii. 10), from Jer. xxxi. 33. This name is most commonly ascribed to the precepts given by Moses at Mount Sinai (Deut. xxxii. 4 ; Mal. iv. 4 ; John i. 17, and vii. 19) ; it is also largely used for all his writings. For the history of Genesis is called *law* (Gal. iv. 21), from Gen. xvi. And though sometimes the law be distinguished from the Psalms and Prophets (Luke xvi. 16, and xxiv. 24), yet the other prophets' books are called *law* (1 Cor. xiv. 21), from Isa. xxviii. 11 ; the Psalms are also thus named (John x. 24 and xv. 25), from Psalm lxxxii. 6 and xxxv. 19. Yea, one Psalm is called a *law* (Psalm lxxviii. 1) ; and the many branches of Moses' doctrine as the *law* of the sin-offering, etc., Lev. vi. 25. And generally it is used for any *doctrine*, as the *law* of works, the *law* of faith, etc. Rom. iii. 27.—*Henry Ainsworth.*

Verse 7.—" *Converting the soul.*" This version conveys a sense good and true in itself, but is not in accordance with the design of the Psalmist which is, to express the divine law on the feelings and affections of good men. The Hebrew terms properly mean, " bringing back the spirit," when it is depressed by adversity, by refreshing and consoling it : like food, it restores the faint, and communicates vigour to the disconsolate.—*William Walford*, 1837.

Verse 7.—" *Converting the soul.*" The heart of man is the most free and hard of anything to work upon, and to make an impression and stamp upon this hard heart, this heart that is so stony, adamantine, " harder than the nether millstones," as the Scripture teacheth. To compel this free-will, this *Domina sui actus*, the queen in the soul, the empress, it cannot be without a divine power, without a hand that is omnipotent ; but the ministers do this by the Word—they mollify, and wound, and break this heart, they incline, and bow, and draw this free-will whither the spirit listeth. And Clemens Alexandrinus is not afraid to say, that if the fables of Orpheus and Amphion were true—that they drew birds, beasts, and stones, with their ravishing melody—yet the harmony of the Word is greater, which translates men from Helicon to Zion, which softens the hard heart of man obdurate against the truth, that "raises up children to Abraham of stones," that is (as he interprets), of unbelievers, which he calls stocks and stones, that put their trust in stones and stocks ; which metamorphoses men that are beastlike, wild birds for their lightness and vanity, serpents for their craft and subtlety, lions for their wrath and cruelty, swine for voluptuousness and luxury, etc. ; and charms them so that of wild beasts they become tame men ; that makes living *stones* (as he did others) come of their own accord to the building of the walls of Jerusalem (as he of Thebes), to the building of a living temple to the everliving God. This must needs be a truly persuasive charm, as he speaks.—*John Stoughton's " Choice Sermons,"* 1640.

Verse 7.—" *Making wise the simple.*" The apostle Paul in Eph. i. 8, expresseth conversion, and the whole work inherently wrought in us, by the making of a man wise. It is usual in the Scriptures, and you may ofttimes meet with it : " *converting the soul,*" " *making wise the simple.*" The beginning of conversion, and so all along, the increase of all grace to the end, is expressed by wisdom entering into a man's heart. " If wisdom enter into thy heart," and so goes on to do more and more ; not unto thy head only—a man may have all that, and be a fool in the end, but when it entereth into the heart, and draws all the affections after it, and along with it, " when knowledge is pleasant to thy soul," then a man is converted ; when God breaks open a man's heart, and makes wisdom fall in, enter in, and make a man wise.—*Thomas Goodwin.*

Verse 7.—This verse, and the two next following, which treat of God's law, are in Hebrew, written each of them with ten words, according to the number of the ten commandments, which are called the ten words. Exodus xxxiv. 28.— *Henry Ainsworth.*

Verses 7, 8.—" *The testimony of the Lord is pure, enlightening the eyes,*" revealing the object, ennobling the organ.—*Richard Stock.*

Verses 7—11.—All of us are by nature the children of wrath ; our souls are like the *porches* of Bethesda (John v.), in which are lodged a great many " sick folk, blind, halt, withered ; " and the Scriptures are like the *pool* of Bethesda, into which whosoever entereth, after God's Holy Spirit hath a little stirred the water, is " made whole of whatsoever disease he hath." He that hath anger's frenzy, being as furious as a lion, by stepping into this pool shall in good time become as gentle as a lamb ; he that hath the blindness of intemperance, by washing in this pool shall easily see his folly ; he that hath envy's rust, avarice's leprosy, luxury's palsy, shall have means and medicines here for the curing of his maladies. *The word of God* is like the drug *catholicon*, that is instead of all purges ; and like the herb *panaces*, that is good for all diseases. Is any man heavy ? *the statutes of the Lord rejoice the heart :* is any man in want ? *the judgments of the Lord are more to be desired than gold, yea, than much fine gold, and by keeping of them there is great reward :* is any man ignorant ? *the testimonies of the Lord give wisdom to the simple,* that is, to little ones, both in standing and understanding. In standing, as unto little Daniel, little John the evangelist, little Timothy : to little ones in understanding ; for the great philosophers who were the wizards of the world, because they were not acquainted with God's law became fools while they professed themselves wise. Rom. i. 22. But our prophet saith, " I have more understanding than all my teachers, because thy testimonies are my meditation," and my study. Psalm cxix. 99. To conclude, whatsoever we are by corruption of nature, God's law *converteth* us, and maketh us to speak with new tongues, and to sing new songs unto the Lord, and to become new men and new creatures in Christ. 2 Cor. v. 17.— *J. Boys.*

Verse 8.—" *The statutes.*" Many divines and critics, and Castalio in particular, have endeavoured to attach a distinct shade of meaning to the words, *law, testimony, the statutes, commandments, fear, judgments*, occurring in this context. תּוֹרָה, *the law*, has been considered to denote the preceptive part of revelation. עֵדוּת, *the testimony*, has been restricted to the doctrinal part. פִּקּוּדִים, *the statutes*, has been regarded as relating to such things as have been given in charge. מִצְוָה, *the commandment*, has been taken to express the general body of the divine law and doctrine. יִרְאָה, *religious fear*. מִשְׁפָּטִים, *the judgments*, the civil statutes of the Mosaic law, more particularly the penal sanctions.—*John Morison.*

Verse 8.—" *The statutes of the Lord are right, rejoicing the heart.*" How odious is the profaneness of those Christians who neglect the Holy Scriptures, and give themselves to reading other books ! How many precious hours do many spend, and that not only on work days, but holy days, in foolish romances, fabulous histories, lascivious poems ! And why this, but that they may be cheered and delighted, when as full joy is only to be had in these holy books. Alas ! the joy you find in those writings is perhaps pernicious, such as tickleth your lust, and promoteth contemplative wickedness. At the best it is but vain, such as only pleaseth the fancy and affecteth the wit ; whereas these holy writings (to use David's expression), are " *right, rejoicing the heart.*" Again, are there not many who more set by Plutarch's morals, Seneca's epistles, and such like books, than they do by the Holy Scriptures ? It is true, Beloved, there are excellent truths in those moral writings of the heathen, but yet they are far short of these sacred books. Those may comfort against outward trouble, but not against inward fears ; they may rejoice the mind, but cannot quiet the conscience ; they may kindle some flashy sparkles of joy, but they cannot warm the soul with a lasting fire of solid consolations. And truly, brethren, if ever God give you a spiritual ear to judge of things aright, you will then acknowledge there are no bells like to those of Aaron's, no harp like to that of David's, no trumpet like to that of Isaiah's, no pipes like to those of the apostle's ; and, you will confess with Petrus Damianus, that those writings of heathen orators, philosophers, poets, which formerly were so pleasing, are now dull and harsh in comparison of the comfort of the Scriptures.—*Nathanael Hardy, D.D.,* 1618—1670.

Verse 10.—" *Sweeter than honey and the honeycomb.*" Love the word written. Psa. cxix. 97. " Oh, how love I thy law ! " " Lord," said Augustine, " let the holy Scriptures be my chaste delight." Chrysostom compares the Scripture to a garden, every truth is a fragrant flower, which we should wear, not on our bosom, but in our heart. David counted the word " *sweeter than honey and the honeycomb.*" There is that in Scripture which may breed delight. It shows us the way to riches : Deut. xxviii. 5, Prov. iii. 10 ; to long life : Psa. xxxiv. 12 ; to a kingdom : Heb. xii. 28. Well, then, may we count those the *sweetest hours* which are spent in reading the holy Scriptures ; well may we say with the prophet (Jer. xv. 16), " Thy words were found and I did eat them ; and they were the joy and rejoicing of my heart."— *Thomas Watson.*

Verse 10.—" *Sweeter than honey and the honeycomb.*" There is no difference made amongst us between the delicacy of honey in the comb and that which is separated from it. From the information of Dr. Halle, concerning the diet of the Moors of Barbary, we learn that they esteem honey a very wholesome breakfast, " and the most delicious that which is in the comb with the young bees in it, before they come out of their cases, whilst they still look milk-white." (*Miscellanea Curiosa*, vol. iii. p. 382.) The distinction made by the Psalmist is then perfectly just and conformable to custom and practice, at least of more modern, and probably, equally so of ancient times.—*Samuel Burder, A.M., in " Oriental Customs,"* 1812.

Verse 11.—"*Moreover by them is thy servant warned.*" A certain Jew had formed a design to poison Luther, but was disappointed by a faithful friend, who sent Luther a portrait of the man, with a warning against him. By this, Luther knew the murderer and escaped his hands. Thus the word of God, O Christian, shows thee the face of those lusts which Satan employs to destroy thy comforts and poison thy soul.—*G. S. Bowes, B.A., in " Illustrative Gatherings for Preachers and Teachers,"* 1860.

Verse 11.—"*In keeping of them there is great reward.*" This " keeping of them " implies great carefulness to know, to remember, and to observe ; and the " reward " (lit. " the end "), *i.e.*, the recompense, is far beyond anticipation.—*W. Wilson.*

Verse 11.—"*In keeping of them there is great reward.*" Not only for keeping, but in keeping of them, there is great reward. The joy, the rest, the refreshing, the comforts, the contents, the smiles, the incomes that saints now enjoy, in the ways of God, are so precious and glorious in their eyes, that they would not exchange them for ten thousands worlds. Oh ! if the vails,* be thus sweet and glorious before pay-day comes, what will be that glory that Christ will crown his saints with for cleaving to his service in the face of all difficulties, when he shall say to his Father, " Lo, here am I, and the children which thou hast given me." Isa. viii. 18. If there be so much to be had in the wilderness, what then shall be had in paradise !—*Thomas Brooks.*

Verse 11.—"*In keeping of them there is great reward.*" Not only *for keeping* but *in keeping* of them. As every flower hath its sweet smell, so every good action hath its sweet reflection upon the soul : and as Cardan saith, that every precious stone hath some egregious virtue ; so here, righteousness is its own reward, though few men think so, and act accordingly. Howbeit, the chief reward is not till the last cast, till we come to heaven. The word here rendered " *reward*," signifieth *the heel*, and by a metaphor, the *end* of a work, and the *reward* of it, which is not till the end.—*John Trapp.*

Verse 11.—"*Reward.*" Though we should not serve God for a reward, yet we shall have a reward for our service. The time is coming when ungodliness shall be as much prosecuted by justice, as in times past godliness had been persecuted by injustice. Though our reward be not for our good works, yet we shall have our good works rewarded, and have a good reward for our works. Though the best of men (they being at the best but unprofitable servants) deserve nothing at the hands of God, yet they may deserve much at the hands of men ; and if they have not the recompense they deserve, yet it is a kind of recompense to have deserved. As he said, and nobly, " I had rather it should be said, Why doth not Cato's image stand here ? than that it should be said, Why doth it stand here ? "—*Ralph Venning.* 1620—1673.

Verse 12.—"*Who can understand his errors ?*" After this survey of the works and word of God, he comes at last to peruse the third book, his *conscience ;* a book which though wicked men may keep shut up, and naturally do not love to look in to it, yet will one day be laid open before the great tribunal in the view of the whole world, to the justifying of God when he judges, and to impenitent sinners' eternal confusion. And what finds he here ? A foul, blurred copy that he is puzzled how to read ; " *who*," says he, " *can understand his errors ?* " Those notions which God had with his own hand imprinted upon conscience in legible characters, are partly defaced and slurred with scribble and interlinings of " *secret faults ;* " partly obliterated and quite razed out with capital crimes, "presumptuous sins." And yet this *manuscript* cannot be so abused, but it will still give in evidence for God; there being no argument in the world that can with more force extort an acknowledgment of God from any man's conscience than the conviction of guilt itself labours under. For the sinner cannot but know he has transgressed a law, and he finds within him, if he is not past all sense, such apprehensions that though at present he "walk in the ways of his heart and in the sight of his eyes " (as the wise man ironically advises the young man to do, Ecc. xi. 9), yet he knows (as the same wise man there from his own experience tells him) that " for all these things God will bring him into judgment." The *conscience* being thus convicted of sin, where there is any sense of true piety the soul will, with David, here address itself to God for pardon, that it may be " *cleansed from secret faults ;* " and for grace, that by its restraints, and

---

* Gratuities, presents.

preventions, and assistances, it may be *" kept back from presumptuous sins,"* and if unhappily engaged, that it may be freed at least from the *" dominion "* of them— *" Keep back thy servant also from presumptuous sins ; let them not have dominion over me,"* etc.—*Adam Littleton.*

Verse 12.—The prophet saith, *" Who can understand his own faults ? "* No man can, but God can ; therefore reason after this manner, as Saint Bernard saith : I know and am known ; I know but in part, but God knows me and knows me wholly ; but what I know, I know but in part. So the apostle reasons ; " I know nothing of myself, yet am I not hereby justified."

Admit that thou keepest thyself so free, and renewest thy repentance so daily that thou knowest nothing by thyself, yet mark what the apostle adds farther ; " Notwithstanding, I do not judge myself I am not hereby justified, but he that judgeth me is the Lord." This is the condition of all men ; he that is infinite knows them ; therefore they should not dare to judge themselves, but with the prophet David, in Psalm xix., entreat the Lord that he would cleanse them from their secret sins.—*Richard Stock.*

Verse 12.—*" Who can understand his own errors ? "* None can to the depth and bottom. In this question there are two considerables :—1. A concession ; 2. A confession. He makes a grant that *our life is full of errors ;* and the Scriptures say the same, while they affirm that " All we like sheep have gone astray " (Isa. liii. 6) ; " I have gone astray like a lost sheep " (Psa. cxix. 176) ; that the " house of Israel " hath " lost sheep," Matt. x. 6. I need not reckon up the particulars, as the errors of our senses, understandings, consciences, judgments, wills, affections, desires, actions, and occurrences. The whole man *in nature* is like a tree nipped at root, which brings forth worm-eaten fruits. The whole man *in life* is like an instrument out of tune, which jars at every stroke. If we cannot understand them, certainly they are very many.—*Robert Abbot,* 1646.

Verse 12.—*" Who can understand his errors ? "* If a man repent not until he have made confession of all his sins in the ear of his ghostly father, if a man cannot have absolution of his sins until his sins be told by tale and number in the priest's ear ; in that, as David saith, *none* can understand, much less, then, utter all his sins : *Delicta quis intelligat ? " Who can understand his sins ? "* In that David of himself complaineth elsewhere how that his " sins are overflowed his head, and as a heavy burden do depress him " (Psa. xxxviii. 4) ; alas ! shall not a man by this doctrine be utterly driven from repentance ? Though they have gone about something to make plasters for their sores, of confession or attrition to assuage their pain, bidding a man to hope well of his contrition, though it be not so full as is required, and of his confession, though he have not numbered all his sins, if so be that he do so much as in him lieth ; dearly beloved, in that there is none but that herein he is guilty (for who doth as much as he may ?) trow ye that this plaster is not like salt for sore eyes ? Yes, undoubtedly, when they have done all they can for the appeasing of consciences in these points, this is the sum, that we yet should hope well, but yet so hope that we must stand in a mammering* and doubting whether our sins be forgiven. For to believe *remissionem peccatorum,* that is to be certain of " forgiveness of sins," as our creed teacheth us, they count it a presumption. Oh, abomination ! and that not only herein, but in all their penance as they paint it.—*John Bradford (Martyr)* 1510—1555.

Verse 12.—*" Who can understand his errors ? "* By *" errors "* he means his unwitting and inconsiderate mistakes. There are sins, some of which are committed when the sun shines—*i.e.*, with light and knowledge ; and then, as it is with colours when the sun shines, you may see them ; so these, a man can see, and know, and confess them particularly to be transgressions. There are other sins which are committed either in the times of ignorance, or else (if there be knowledge), yet with unobservance. Either of these may be so heaped up in the particular number of them, that as a man did when he did commit them, take no notice of them ; so now, after the commission, if he should take the brightest candle to search all the records of his soul, yet many of them would escape his notice. And, indeed, this is a great part of our misery, that we cannot understand all our debts. We can easily see too many, yet many more lie, as it were, dead and out of sight. To sin is one great misery, and then to forget our sins is a misery too. If in repentance we could set the battle in array, point to every individual sin in the true and

---

* Hesitating.

particular times of acting and re-acting, oh, how would our hearts be more broken with shame and sorrow, and how would we adore the richness of the treasure of mercy which must have a multitude in it to pardon the multitude of our infinite errors and sins. But this is the comfort; though we cannot understand every particular sin, or time of sinning, yet if we be not idle to search and cast over the books, and if we be heartily grieved for these sins which we have found out, and can by true repentance turn from them unto God, and by faith unto the blood of Jesus Christ, I say that God, who knows our sins better than we can know them, and who understands the true intentions and dispositions of the heart—that if it did see the unknown sins it would be answerably carried against them—he will for his own mercy sake forgive them, and he, too, will not remember them. Nevertheless, though David saith, " *Who can understand his errors ?* " as the prophet Jeremiah spake also, " The heart of man is desperately wicked, who can know it ? " yet must we bestir ourselves at heaven to get more and more heavenly light, to find out more and more of our sinnings. So the Lord can search the heart; and, though we shall never be able to find out all our sins which we have committed, yet it is proper and beneficial for us to find out yet more sins than yet we do know. And you shall find these in your own experience ; that as soon as ever grace entered your hearts, you saw sin in another way than you ever saw it before ; yea, and the more grace hath traversed and increased in the soul the more full discoveries hath it made of sins. It hath shown new sins as it were ; new sins, not for their being, not as if they were not in the heart and life before, but for their evidence and our apprehension. We do now see such wages and such inclinations to be sinful which we did not think to be so before. As physic brings those humours which had their residence before now more to the sense of the patient, or as the sun makes open the motes of dust which were in the room before, so doth the light of the word discover more corruption.—*Obadiah Sedgwick.*

Verse 12.—" *Who can understand his errors ?* " Who can tell how oft he offendeth ? No man. The hairs of a man's head may be told, the stars appear in multitudes, yet some have undertaken to reckon them ; but no arithmetic can number our sins. Before we can recount a thousand we shall commit ten thousand more ; and so rather multiply by addition than divide by subtraction ; there is no possibility of numeration. Like Hydra's head, while we are cutting off twenty by repentance, we find a hundred more grown up. It is just, then, that infinite sorrows shall follow infinite sins.—*Thomas Adams.*

Verse 12.—" *Cleanse thou me from secret faults.*" It is the desire of a holy person to be cleansed, not only from public, but also from *private and secret sins.* Rom. vii. 24. " O wretched man (saith Paul), who shall deliver me ? " Why, O blessed apostle ! what is it that holds thee ? What is it that molests thee ? Thy life, thou sayest, was unblamable before thy conversion, and since thy conversion. Phil. iii. Thou hast exercised thyself to have always a conscience void of offence toward God and toward men. Acts xxiv. 16. And yet thou criest out, " O wretched man," and yet thou complainest, " Who shall deliver me ? " Verily, brethren, it was not sin abroad, but at home : it was not sin without, but at this time sin within ; it was not Paul's sinning with man, but Paul's sinning within Paul : oh ! that " law of his members warring (secretly within him) against the law of his mind ; " this, this made that holy man so to cry out, so to complain. As Rebekah was weary of her life, not as we read for any foreign disquietments, but because of domestic troubles : " The daughters of Heth " within the house made her " weary of her life ; " so the private and secret birth of corruption within Paul—the workings of that—that was the cause of his trouble, that was the ground of his exclamation and desires, " Who shall deliver me ? " I remember that the same Paul adviseth the Ephesians as " to put off the former conversation " so " to put on the renewed spirit of the mind " (Eph. iv. 22, 23) ; intimating that there are sins lurking within as well as sins walking without ; and that true Christians must not only sweep the door, but wash the chamber ; my meaning is, not only come off from sins which lie open in the conversation, but also labour to be cleansed from sins and sinning which remain secret and hidden in the spirit and inward disposition.—*Obadiah Sedgwick.*

Verse 12.—" *Cleanse thou me from secret faults.*" Learn to see thy spots. Many have unknown sins, as a man may have a mole on his back and himself never know it. Lord, cleanse me from my secret faults. But have we not spots whereof we are not ignorant ? In diseases sometimes nature is strong enough to put forth spots, and there she cries to us by these outward declarations that we are sick. Sometimes she cannot do it but by the force of cordials. Sometimes conscience of herself shows us our sins ; sometimes she cannot but by medicines, arguments that convince us out of the holy word. Some can see, and will not, as Balaam ; some would see, and cannot, as the eunuch ; some neither will nor can, as Pharaoh ; some both can and will, as David. . . . We have many spots which God does not hear from us, because we see them not in ourselves. Who will acknowledge that error, whereof he does not know himself guilty ? The sight of sins is a great happiness, for it causeth an ingenuous confession.—*Thomas Adams.*

Verse 12.—*" Cleanse thou me from secret faults."*—The law of the Lord is so holy that forgiveness must be prayed for, even for hidden sins. (*Note*—This was a principal text of the Reformers against the auricular confession of the Roman Catholics.)—*T. C. Barth's " Bible Manual,"* 1865.

Verse 12.—*" Secret faults."* Sins may be termed *" secret "* either, 1. *When they are coloured and disguised*—though they do fly abroad, yet not under that name, but apparelled with some semblance of virtues. Cyprian complains of such tricks in his second epistle, which is to Donatus. 2. *When they are kept off from the stage of the world ;* they are like fire in the chimney ; though you do not see it, yet it burns. So many a person, like those in Ezekiel, " commit abominations in secret "—that is, so as the public eye is not upon them. He is sinful, and acts it with the greatest vileness ; all the difference betwixt another sinner and him is this—that he is, and the other saith he is, a sinner. Just as 'twixt a book shut and a book opened ; that which is shut hath the same lines and words, but the other being opened every man may see and read them. 3. *When they are kept, not only from the public eye, but from any mortal eye ;* that is, the carnal eye of him who commits the sins sees them not : he doth, indeed, see them with the eye of conscience, but not with an eye of natural sense. Even those persons with whom he doth converse, and who highly commend the frame of his ways, cannot yet see the secret discoursings and actings of sin in his mind and heart. For, brethren, all the actings of sin are not without, they are not visible ; but there are some, yea, the most dangerous actings within the soul, where corruption lies as a fountain and root. The heart of man is a scheme of wickedness ; nay, a man saith that in his heart which he dares not speak with his tongue, and his thought will do that which his hands dare not to execute. Well, then, sin may be called *" secret "* when it is sin, and acted as sin, even there, where none but God and conscience can see. Methinks sin is like a candle in a lantern, where the shining is first within and then bursting out at the windows ; or like evils and ulcerous humours, which are scabs and scurvy stuff, first within the skin, and afterwards they break out to the view on the outside. So it is with sin ; it is a malignant humour and a fretting leprosy, diffusing itself into several secret acts and workings within the mind, and then it breaks abroad and dares adventure the practice of itself to the eye of the world ; and be it that it may never see the light, that it may be like a child born and buried in the womb, yet as that child is a man, a true man there closeted in that hidden frame of nature, so sin is truly sin, though it never gets out beyond the womb which did conceive and enliven it.—*Obadiah Sedgwick.*

Verse 12.—*" Secret faults."* *" Secret sins "* are more dangerous to the person in some respects than open sins. For *a man doth, by his art of sinning, deprive himself of the help of his sinfulness.* Like him who will carry his wound covered, or who bleeds inwardly, help comes not in because the danger is not descried nor known. If a man's sin breaks out there is a minister at hand, a friend near, and others to reprove, to warn, to direct ; but when he is the artificer of his lusts, he bars himself of all public remedy, and takes great order and care to damn his soul, by covering his *" secret sins "* with some plausible varnish which may beget a good opinion in others of his ways. *A man does by his secrecy give the reins unto corruption :* the mind is fed all the day long either with sinful contemplations or projectings, so that the very strength of the soul is wasted and corrupted. Nay, *secret actings do but heat and inflame natural corruption.* As in shouldering in a crowd, when one hath got out of the door, two or three are ready to fall out after ; so when a man hath given his heart leave to act a secret sin, this begets a present, and quick, and strong flame in corruption to repeat and multiply and throng out the acts. Sinful acts are not only fruits of sin, but helps and strengths, all sinning being more sinful by more sinning, not only in the effects but in the cause : the spring and cause of sin will grow mad and insolent hereby, and more corrupt ; this being a truth, that if the heart gives way for one sin, it will be ready for the next ; if it will yield to bring forth once at the devil's pleasure, it will bring it forth twice by its own motion. A man by "*secret sins*" *doth but polish and square the hypocrisy of his heart* : he doth strive to be an exact hypocrite ; and the more cunning he is in the palliating of his sinnings, the more perfect he is in his hypocrisy.—*Obadiah Sedgwick.*

Verse 12.—"*Secret faults.*" Beware of committing acts which it will be necessary to conceal. There is a singular poem by Hood, called "The Dream of Eugene Aram "—a most remarkable piece it is indeed, illustrating the point on which we are now dwelling. Aram had murdered a man, and cast his body into the river— "a sluggish water, black as ink, the depth was so extreme." The next morning he visited the scene of his guilt—

> "And sought the black accursed pool,
> With a wild misgiving eye ;
> And he saw the dead in the river bed,
> For the faithless stream was dry."

Next he covered the corpse with heaps of leaves, but a mighty wind swept through the wood and left the secret bare before the sun—

> "Then down I cast me on my face,
> And first began to weep,
> For I knew my secret then was one
> That earth refused to keep ;
> On land or sea though it should be
> Ten thousand fathoms deep."

In plaintive notes he prophesies his own discovery. He buried his victim in a cave, and trod him down with stones, but when years had run their weary round, the foul deed was discovered and the murderer put to death.

Guilt is a "grim chamberlain," even when his fingers are not bloody red. Secret sins bring fevered eyes and sleepless nights, until men burn out their consciences, and become in very deed ripe for the pit. Hypocrisy is a hard game to play at, for it is one deceiver against many observers ; and for certain it is a miserable trade, which will earn at last, as its certain climax, a tremendous bankruptcy. Ah ! ye who have sinned without discovery, "Be sure your sin will find you out ; " and bethink you, it may find you out ere long. Sin, like murder, will come out ; men will even tell tales about themselves in their dreams. God has made men to be so wretched in their consciences that they have been obliged to stand forth and confess the truth. Secret sinner ! if thou wantest the foretaste of damnation upon earth, continue in thy secret sins ; for no man is more miserable than he who sinneth secretly, and yet trieth to preserve a character. Yon stag, followed by the hungry hounds, with open mouths, is far more happy than the man who is pursued by his sins. Yon bird, taken in the fowler's net, and labouring to escape, is far more happy than he who hath weaved around himself a web of deception, and labours to escape from it, day by day making the toils more thick and the web more strong. Oh the misery of secret sins ! One may well pray, "Cleanse thou me from secret faults."—*Spurgeon's Sermon* (No. 116), on "Secret Sins."

Verse 12.—The sin through ignorance (שְׁגָגָה) is the same that David prays against in Psalm xix. 12, "Who can understand his *errors* (שְׁגִיאוֹת) ? cleanse thou me from secret things ! " These are not sins of omission, but acts committed by a person, when at the time, he did not suppose that what he did was sin. Although he did the thing deliberately, yet he did not perceive the sin of it. So deceitful is sin, we may be committing that abominable thing which cast angels into an immediate and an eternal hell, and yet at the moment be totally unaware ! Want of knowledge of the truth, and too little tenderness of conscience to hide it from us. Hardness of heart and a corrupt nature cause us to sin unperceived. But here again the form of the Son of Man appears ! Jehovah, God of Israel, institutes sacrifice for *sins of ignorance*, and thereby discovers the same compassionate and considerate heart that appears in our High Priest, "who can have compassion on *the ignorant !* " Heb. v. 2. Amidst the types of this tabernacle, we recognise the presence of Jesus—it is his voice that shakes the curtains, and speaks in the ear of Moses, "If a soul shall sin through ignorance !" The same yesterday, to-day, and for ever !—*Andrew A. Bonar, in "Commentary on Leviticus,"* ch. iv. v. 2.

Verse 12 (*last clause*).—This is a singular difference between pharisaical and real sanctity : that is curious to look abroad, but seeth nothing at home : so that Pharisee condemned the Publican, and saw nothing in himself worthy of blame ; but this careful to look at home, and searcheth into the secret corners, the very spirit of the mind. So did good David when he prayed, " *Cleanse thou me from secret faults.*"— *Nathanael Hardy.*

Verse 12.—Our corruptions have made us such combustible matter, that there is scarce a dart thrown at us in vain : when Satan tempts us, it is but like the casting of fire into tinder, that presently catcheth : our hearts kindle upon the least spark that falls ; as a vessel that is brimful of water, upon the least jog, runs over. Were we but true to ourselves, though the devil might knock by his temptations, yet he could never burst open the everlasting doors of our hearts by force or violence : but, alas ! we ourselves are not all of one heart and one mind : Satan hath got a strong party within us, that, as soon as he knocks, opens to him, and entertains him. And hence it is, that many times, small temptations and very petty occasions draw forth great corruptions ; as a vessel, that is full of new liquor, upon the least vent given, works over into foam and froth ; so truly, our hearts, almost upon every slight and trivial temptation, make that inbred corruption that lodgeth there, swell and boil, and run over into abundance of scum and filth in our lives and conversations.—*Ezekiel Hopkins.*

Verse 12.—Sins are many times hid from the godly man's eye, though he commits them, because he is not diligent and accurate in making a search of himself, and in an impartial studying of his own ways. If any sin be hid, as Saul was behind the stuff, or as Rahab had hid the spies, unless a man be very careful to search, he shall think no sin is there where it is. Hence it is that the Scripture doth so often command that duty of *searching* and *trying*, of examining and communing with our hearts. Now what need were there of this duty, but that it is supposed many secrets and subtle lusts lie lurking in our hearts, which we take no notice of ? If then the godly would find out their hidden lusts, know the sins they not yet know, they must more impartially judge themselves ; they must take time to survey and examine themselves ; they must not in an overly and slight manner, but really and industriously look up and down as they would search for thieves ; and they must again and again look into this dark corner, and that dark corner of their hearts, as the woman sought for the lost groat. This self-scrutiny and self-judging, this winnowing and sifting of ourselves, is the only way to see what is chaff and what is wheat, what is mere refuse and what is enduring.—*Anthony Burgess.*

Verse 12.—Sin is of a growing and advancing nature. From weakness to wilfulness, from ignorance to presumption, is its ordinary course and progress. The cloud that Elijah's man saw, was at first no bigger than a hand's-breadth, and it threatened no such thing as a general tempest ; but yet, at last, it overspread the face of the whole heavens ; so truly, a sin that at first ariseth in the soul but as a small mist, and is scarcely discernible ; yet, if it be not scattered by the breath of prayer, it will at length overspread the whole life, and become most tempestuous and raging. And therefore, David, as one experienced in the deceitfulness of sin, doth thus digest and methodise his prayer : first against secret and lesser sins ; and then against the more gross and notorious ; as knowing the one proceeds and issues from the other : Lord, *cleanse me from my secret faults ;* and this will be a most effectual means to preserve and *keep thy servant from presumptuous sins.*— *Ezekiel Hopkins.*

Verses 12, 13.—That there is a difference betwixt *infirmities* and *presumptuous sins* is not to be denied ; it is expressly in the Holy Scripture. Papists say that the man who doth a mortal sin is not in the state of grace ; but for venials, a man may commit (in their divinity) who can tell how many of them, and yet be in Christ for all that ! I hope there is no such meaning in any of our divines as to tie up men's consciences, to hang on such a distinction of sins ; since it is beyond the wit of man to set down a distinct point between mortal and venial sins. Now when it is an impossible matter punctually to set down to the understanding of man which is, and which is not a venial sin, they must pardon me for giving the least way to such divinity as must needs leave the conscience of a man in a maze and labyrinth. I find that the nature of infirmities doth so depend upon circumstances, that that is an infirmity in one man which is a gross sin in another ; and some men plead for themselves that the things they do are but infirmities. He that *will* sin, and when he hath done will say—not to comfort his soul against Satan, but—

to flatter himself in his sin, that it is but an infirmity ; for aught I know, he may go to hell for his infirmities. Besides, if that be good divinity, that a man who is in the state of grace may do infirmities, but not commit gross sins, then I would I could see a man that would undertake to find us out some rule out of the word, by which a sinner may find by his sin, when he is in Christ and when out of Christ ; at what degrees of sinning—where lies the mathematical point and stop—that a man may say, " Thus far may I go and yet be in grace ; but if I step a step farther, then I am none of Christ's." We all know that sins have their latitude ; and for a man to hang his conscience on such a distinction as hath no rule to define where the difference lies, is not safe divinity. The conscience on the rack will not be laid and said with forms and quiddities. The best and nearest way to quiet the heart of man is to say, that be the sin a sin of *infirmity* when we strive and strive but yield at last ; or, of *precipitancy*, when we be taken in haste, as he was who said in his haste, " All men are liars ; " or, a mere *gross* sin in the matter : ay, say it be a *presumptuous* sin, yet if we allow it not, it hinders not but we are in Christ, though we do with reluctancy act and commit it. And I say that we do resist it if we do not allow it. For let us not go about to deny that a godly man during his being a godly man may possibly commit *gross* and *presumptuous sins ;* and for infirmities, if we allow them and like them that we know to be sins, then we do not resist them ; and such a man who allows himself in one is guilty of all, and is none of Christ's as yet. Be the sin what it will, James makes no distinction ; and, where the law distinguisheth not, we must not distinguish. I speak not of *doing* a sin, but *allowing ;* for a man may do it, and yet allow it not ; as in Paul (Rom. vii. 15, 16), " That which I would not, that I do ; " and he that allows not sin doth resist it. Therefore, a man may resist it, hate it, and yet do it. All the difference that I know is this : 1. That a man may live after his conversion all his days, and yet never fall into a gross sin. By gross here I mean *presumptuous* sins also. So David saith not " *cleanse,*" but KEEP BACK *thy servant from presumptuous sins.*" We may, then, be *kept* from them. I speak not that all are, but some be ; and, there-fore, in itself all might be. 2. For lesser sins, " *secret faults,*" we cannot live without them—they are of daily and almost hourly incursions ; but yet we must be *cleansed* from them, as David speaks. Daily get your pardon ; there is a pardon, of course, for them ; they do not usually distract and plague the conscience, but yet we must not see them and allow them ; if we do our case is to be pitied, we are none of Christ's as yet. 3. Great staring sins a man cannot usually and commonly practise them, but he shall allow them. So Psalm xix. 13, " *Keep back thy servant from presumptuous sins ; let them not have dominion over me,*" implying that except we be kept back from them they will *have dominion over us.* It follows, " *then shall I be upright ; "* so that the man in whom *gross or presumptuous sin or sins* have no *dominion,* he is an *upright man.—Richard Capel.*

Verses 12, 13.—The Psalmist was sensible of sin's force and power ; he was weary of sin's dominion ; he cries unto God to deliver him from the reign of all the sins he knew ; and those sins which were secret and concealed from his view, he begs that he might be convinced of them, and throughly cleansed from them. The Lord can turn the heart perfectly to hate the sin that was most of all beloved ; and the strength of sin is gone when once 'tis hated ; and as the hatred grows stronger and stronger, sin becomes weaker and weaker daily.—*Nathaniel Vincent,* 1695.

Verse 13.—" *Keep back thy servant also from all presumptuous sins.*" He doth desire absolutely to be kept from " *presumptuous sins ; "* but then, he adds by way of supposition and reserve, that if he could not by reason of his naughty heart be kept from them, yet that they might not have full power and dominion over him.—*Thomas Manton.*

Verse 13.—" *Keep back thy servant.*" It is an evil man's cross to be restrained, and a good man's joy to be *kept back* from sin. When sin puts forth itself, the evil man is putting forth his hand to the sin ; but when sin puts forth itself, the good man is putting forth his hand to heaven ; if he finds his heart yielding, out he cries, O *keep back thy servant.* An evil man is *kept back* from sin, as a friend from a friend, as a lover from his lover, with knit affections and projects of meeting ; but a good man is *kept back* from sin, as a man from his deadly enemy, whose presence he hates, and with desires of his ruin and destruction. It is the good man's misery that he hath yet a heart to be more tamed and mastered ; it is an evil man's vexation and discontent, that still, or at any time, he is held in by cord or bridle. And thus you see what David aims at in desiring to be *kept back from presumptuous sins*, namely, not a mere suspension, but a mortification, not a not acting only, but a subduing of the inclination ; not for a time, but for ever.—*Obadiah Sedgwick*.

Verse 13.—" *Keep back thy servant,*" etc. Even all the people of God, were they not kept by God's grace and power, they would every moment be undone both in soul and body. It is not our grace, our prayer, our watchfulness keeps us, but it is the power of God, his right arm, supports us ; we may see David praying to God that he would " *keep* " him in both these respects from temporal dangers (Psalm xvii. 8, 9 ; " *keep me,*") etc. ; where he doth not only pray to be kept, but he doth insinuate how carefully God keeps his people, and in what precious account their safety is, even as " the apple of the eye," and for spiritual preservation he often begs it. Though David be God's " *servant* " yet he will, like a wild horse, run violently, and that into " *presumptuous sins,*" if God " *keep* " him not " *back,*" yea, he prayeth that God would " *keep*" the particular parts of his body that they sin not : " keep the door of my lips " (Psalm cxli. 3) ; he entreateth God to " *keep* " his lips and to set a watch about his mouth, as if he were not able to set guard sure enough : thus much more are we to pray that God would " *keep* " our hearts, our minds, our wills, our affections, for they are more masterful.—*Anthony Burgess*.

Verse 13.—" *Keep back thy servant.*" God *keeps back* his servants from sin 1. *By preventing grace*, which is, by infusing such a nature as is like a bias into a bowl, drawing it aside another way ; 2. *By assisting grace*, which is a further strength superadded to that first-implanted nature of holiness ; like a hand upon a child holding him in ; 3. *By quickening grace*, which is, when God doth enliven our graces to manifest themselves in actual opposition ; so that the soul shall not yield, but keep off from entertaining the sin ; 4. *By directing grace*, which is, when God confers that effectual wisdom to the mind, tenderness to the conscience, watchfulness to the heart, that his servants become greatly solicitous of his honour, scrupulously jealous of their own strength, and justly regardful of the honour of their holy profession ; 5. *By doing grace*, which is, when God effectually inclines the hearts of his servants to the places and ways of their refuge, safeties, and preservation from sin, by enlarging the spirit of supplication, and framing the heart to the reverent and affectionate use of his ordinances.—*Condensed from Obadiah Sedgwick*.

Verse 13.—" *Thy servant :* " as if he had said, " O God, thou art my Lord, I have chosen thee, to whom I will give obedience ; thou art he whom I will follow ; I bestow all that I am on thee. Now a Lord will help his servant against an enemy, who for the Lord's service is the servant's enemy. O my Lord, help me ! I am not able by my own strength to uphold myself, but thou art All-sufficiency "—" *Keep back thy servant from presumptuous sins.*" . . . Beloved, it is a great thing to stand in near relations to God ; and then it is a good thing to plead by them with God, forsomuch as nearer relations have strongest force with all. The servant can do more than a stranger, and the child than a servant, and the wife than a child. . . . . There be many reasons against sinning. . . . Now this also may come in, namely, the speciality of our relation to God, that we are his children, and he is our Father ; we are his servants, and he is our Lord : though the common obligations are many and sufficient, yet the special relations are also a further tie : the more near a person come to God, the more careful he should be not to sin against God.—*Obadiah Sedgwick*.

Verse 13.—" *Presumptuous sins.*" The Rabbins distinguish all sins unto those committed בִּשׁוֹגֵג *ignorantly*, and בְּיָד *presumptuously*.—*Benjamin Kennicott, D.D.*, 1718—1783.

Verse 13.—" *Presumptuous sins.*" When sin grows up from act to delight, from delight to new acts, from repetition of sinful acts to vicious indulgence, to habit and custom and a second nature, so that anything that toucheth upon it is grievous and strikes to the man's heart ; when it is got into God's place, and requires to be loved with the whole strength, makes grace strike sail, and other vices do it homage, demands all his concerns to be sacrificed to it and to be served with his reputation, his fortunes, his parts, his body and soul, to the irreparable loss of his time and eternity both—this is the height of its *dominion*—then sin becomes " exceeding sinful," and must needs make strange and sad alterations in the state of saints themselves, and be great hindrances to them in their way to Heaven, having brought them so near to Hell.—*Adam Littleton*.

Verse 13.—" *Presumptuous sins.*" The distribution of sins into sins of *ignorance*, of *infirmity*, and of *presumption*, is very usual and very useful, and complete enough without the addition (which some make) of a fourth sort, to wit, sins of *negligence* or *inadvertency*, all such sins being easily reducible to some of the former three. The ground of the distinction is laid in the soul of man, where there are three distinct prime faculties, from which all our actions flow—the understanding, the will, and the sensual appetite or affections. . . . The enquiry must be, when a sin is done, where the fault lay most ; and thence it must have the right denomination. 1. If the *understanding* be most in fault, not apprehending that good it should, or not aright, the sin is so done, though possibly it may have in it somewhat both of infirmity and presumption withal, is yet properly a sin of *ignorance*. 2. If the main fault be in the *affections*, through some sudden passion or perturbation of mind, blinding, or corrupting, or but outrunning the judgment—as of fear, anger, desire, joy, or any of the rest—the sin thence arising, though perhaps joined with some ignorance or presumption withal, is yet properly a sin of *infirmity*. But if the understanding be competently informed with knowledge, and not much blinded or transported with the incursion of any sudden, or violence of any vehement perturbation, so as the greatest blame must remain upon the untowardness of the *will*, resolvedly bent upon the evil, the sin arising from such *wilfulness*, though probably not free from all mixture of ignorance and infirmity withal, is yet properly *a wilful presumption*, such a *presumptuous sin* as we are now in treaty of. Rules are soonest learned and best remembered when illustrated with fit examples ; and of such the rich storehouse of the Scripture affordeth us in each kind variety and choice enough, whence it shall suffice us to propose but one eminent of each sort. *The men*, all of them for their holiness, of singular and worthy renown : David, St. Peter, and St. Paul. *The sins*, all of them for their matter, of the greatest magnitude : murdering of the innocent, abnegation of Christ, persecution of the church : Paul's persecution a grievous sin, yet a sin of *ignorance ;* Peter's denial a grievous sin, yet a sin of *infirmity ;* David's murder, a far more grievous sin than either of both, because a sin of *presumption*. St. Paul, before his conversion, whilst he was Saul, persecuted and wasted the church of God to the utmost of his power, making havoc of the professors of Christ, entering into their very houses, and haling thence to prison, both men and women ; and posting abroad with letters into remote quarters, to do all the mischief he could, everywhere with great fury, as if he had been mad, breathing out, wherever he came, nothing but threatenings and slaughter against the disciples of the Lord. His *affections* were not set against them through any personal provocations, but merely out of zeal to the law ; and surely his zeal had been good had it not been blind. Nor did his *will* run cross to his judgment, but was led by it, for he " verily thought in himself that he ought to do many things contrary to the name of Jesus ; " and verily his will had been good had it not been misled. But the error was in his *understanding*, his judgment being not yet actually convinced of the truth of the Christian religion. He was yet fully persuaded that Jesus was an impostor, and Christianity a pestilent sect, raised by Satan, to the disgrace and prejudice of Moses and the law. If these things had indeed been so, as he apprehended them, his *affections* and *will*, in seeking to root out such a sect, had been not only blameless, but commendable. It was his erroneous judgment that poisoned all, and made that which otherwise had been zeal, to become persecution. But, however, the first discernible obliquity therein being in the *understanding*, that persecution of his was therefore *a sin of ignorance*, so called, and under that name condemned by himself. 1 Tim. i. 13. But such was not Peter's denial of his Master. He *knew* well enough who he was, having conversed so long with him, and having, long before, so amply confessed him. And he *knew* also that he ought not, for anything in the world, to have denied him. That made him so confident before that he *would not* do it, because he was abundantly satisfied that he *should not* do it. Evident it is, then, that Peter wanted no *knowledge*, either of the Master's person, or of his own duty ; and so no plea left him of *ignorance*, either *facti* or *juris*. Nor was the fault so much in his *will* as to make it a sin properly of *presumption*. For albeit *de facto* he did deny him when he was put to it, and that with fearful oaths and imprecations, yet was it not done with any prepensed apostasy, or out of design, yea, he came rather with a *contrary resolution*, and he still honoured his Master *in his heart*, even then when he denied him with his tongue ; and as soon as ever the watchword was given him by the second cock, to prefer to his consideration what he had done, it grieved him sore that he had so done, and he wept bitterly for it. We find no circumstance, in the whole relation, that argueth any deep obstinacy in his *will*. But in his *affections*, then ! Alas ! there was the fail ! A sudden qualm of fear surprising his soul when he saw his Master so despitefully used before his face (which made him apprehensive of what hard usage himself might fall under if he should there and then have owned him) took from him for that time the benefit and use of his reason, and so drew all his thoughts to this one point—how to decline the present danger—that he had never a thought at so much liberty as to consult his judgment, whether it were a sin or no. And this, proceeding from such a sudden distemper of passion, Peter's denial was a sin properly of *infirmity.* But David's sin, in contriving the death of Uriah, was of a yet higher pitch, and of a deeper dye than either of these. He was no such stranger in the law of God as not to know that the wilful murder of an innocent party, such as he also knew Uriah to be, was a most loud crying sin ; and therefore nothing surer than that it was not merely a sin of *ignorance.* Neither yet was it a sin properly of *infirmity,* and so capable of that extenuating circumstance of being done in the heat of anger, as his uncleanness with Bathsheba was in the heat of lust, although that extenuation will not be allowed to pass there, unless *in tanto* only, and as it standeth in comparison with this fouler crime. But having time and leisure enough to bethink himself what he was about, he doth it *in cool blood,* and with much advised *deliberation,* plotting and contriving this way and that way to perfect his design. He was *resolved,* whatsoever should become of it, to have it done ; in regard of which *settled resolution of his will,* this sin of David was therefore a high presumptuous sin.—*Robert Sanderson (Bishop of Lincoln),* 1587—1662-3.

Verse 13.—"*Presumptuous sins.*" David prays that God would keep him back from "*presumptuous sins,*" from known and evident sins, such as proceed from the choice of the perverse will against the enlightened mind, which are committed with deliberation, with design, resolution, and eagerness, against the checks of conscience, and the motions of God's spirit : such sins are direct rebellion against God, a despising of his command, and they provoke his pure eyes.—*Alexander Cruden.*

Verse 13.—"*Then shall I be innocent from the great transgression.*" It is in the motions of a tempted soul to sin, as in the motions of a stone falling from the brow of a hill ; it is easily stopped at first, but when once it is set a-going, who shall stay it ? And therefore it is the greatest wisdom in the world to observe the first motions of the heart, to check and stop it there.—*G. H. Salter.*

Verse 13.—"*The great transgression.*" Watch very diligently against all sin ; but above all, take special heed of those sins that come near to the sin against the Holy Ghost ; and these are, hypocrisy, taking only the outward profession of religion, and so dissembling and mocking of God ; sinning wilfully against conviction of conscience, and against great light and knowledge, sinning presumptuously, with a high hand. These sins, though none of them are the direct sin against the Holy Ghost, yet they will come very near to it : therefore take special heed of them, lest they, in time, should bring you to the committing of that unpardonable sin.— *Robert Russel,* 1705.

Verse 13.—"*Let them not have dominion over me.*" Any small sin may get the upper-hand of the sinner and bring him under in time, and after that is once habituated by long custom so as he cannot easily shake off the yoke, neither redeem himself from under the tyranny thereof. We see the experiment of it but too often and too evidently in our common swearers and drunkards. Yet do such kind of sins, for the most part, grow on by little and little, steal into the throne insensibly, and do not *exercise dominion* over the enslaved soul till they have got strength *by many and multiplied acts.* But a *presumptuous sin* worketh a great alteration in the state of the soul *at once,* and by one single act advanceth marvellously, weakening the spirit, and giving a mighty advantage to the flesh, even to the hazard of *a complete conquest.—Robert Sanderson.*

Verse 13.—To sin presumptuously is the highest step. So in David's account ; for first he prays, " *Lord keep me from secret sins,*" which he maketh sins of ignorance, and then next he prays against " *presumptuous sins,*" which, as the opposition shows, are sins against knowledge ; for says he, " if they get dominion over me, I shall not be free from that great offence," that is, that unpardonable sin which shall never be forgiven : so as these are nearest it of any other, yet not so as that every one that falls into such a sin commits it, but he is nigh to it, at the next step to it. For to commit that sin, but two things are required—light in the mind, and malice in the heart ; not malice alone, unless there be light, for then that apostle had sinned it, so as knowledge is the parent of it, it is " after receiving the knowledge of the truth." Heb. x. 27, 28.—*Thomas Goodwin.*

Verse 13.—Happy souls, who, under a sense of peace through the blood of Jesus, are daily praying to be kept by the grace of the Spirit. Such truly know themselves, see their danger of falling, will not, dare not palliate or lesson the odious nature, and hateful deformity of their sin. They will not give a softer name to sin than it deserves, lest they depreciate the infinite value of that precious blood which Jesus shed to atone its guilt. Far will they be from flattering themselves into a deceitful notion that they are perfect, and have no sin in them. The spirit of truth delivers them from such errors ; he teacheth them as poor sinners to look to the Saviour, and to beseech him to " *keep back* " the headstrong passions, the unruly lusts, and evil concupiscences which dwell in their sinful natures. Alas ! the most exalted saint, the most established believer, if left to himself, how soon might the blackest crimes, the most " *presumptuous sins*," get the " *dominion* " over him ! David had woeful experience of this for a season. He prays from a heartfelt sense of past misery, and the dread of future danger, and he found the blessing of that covenant-promise : " Sin shall not have dominion over you ; for ye are not under the law, but under grace." Rom. vi. 14.—*William Mason, 1719—1791, in " A Spiritual Treasury for the Children of God."*

Verse 14.—" *Let the words of my mouth, and the meditation of my heart, be acceptable in thy sight, O Lord,*" was David's prayer. David could not bear it, that a word or a thought of his should miss acceptation with God. It did not satisfy him that his actions were well witnessed unto men on earth, unless his very thoughts were witnessed to by the Lord in heaven.—*Joseph Caryl.*

Verse 14.—" *Let the words of my mouth,*" etc. The best of men have their failing, and an honest Christian may be a weak one ; but weak as he may be, the goodness and sincerity of his heart will entitle him to put the petition of this verse, which no hypocrite or cunning deceiver can ever make use of.—*Thomas Sherlock (Bishop),* 1676—1761.

Verse 14.—" *Let the words of my mouth, and the meditation of my heart be acceptable in thy sight, O Lord, my strength, and my Redeemer.*" Fast and pray ; Lord, I do fast, and I would pray ; for to what end do I withhold sustenance from my body if it be not the more to cheer up my soul ? my hungry, my thirsty soul ? But the bread, the water of life, both which I find nowhere but in thy word, I partake not but by exercising my soul therein. This I begin to do, and fain would do it well, but in vain shall I attempt except thou do bless : bless me then, O Lord ; bless either part of me, both are thine, and I would withhold neither part from thee. Not my body ; I would set my tongue on work to speak of thee ; not my soul, I would exercise my heart in thinking on thee ; I would join them in devotion which thou hast joined in creation. Yea, Lord, as they have conspired to sin against thee, so do they now consort to do their duty to thee ; my tongue is ready, my heart is ready ; I would think, I would speak ; think upon thee, speak to thee. But, Lord, what are my *words* ? what are my *thoughts* ? Thou knowest the thoughts of men, that they are altogether vanity, and our words are but the blast of such thoughts ; both are vile. It were well it were no more ; both are wicked, my heart a corrupt fountain, and my tongue an unclean stream ; and shall I bring such a sacrifice to God ? The halt, the lame, the blind, though otherwise the beasts be clean, yet are they sacrifices abominable to God : how much more if we offer those beasts which are unclean ? And yet, Lord, my sacrifice is no better, faltering words, wandering thoughts, are neither of them presentable to thee ; how much less evil thoughts and idle words ? Yet such are the best of mine. What remedy ? If any, it is in thee, O Lord, that I must find it, and for it now do I seek unto thee. Thou only, O Lord, canst hallow my tongue, and hallow my heart that my tongue may speak, and my heart think that which may " *be acceptable unto thee,*" yea, that which may be thy delight. Do not I lavish ? Were it not enough that God should bear with, that he should not punish, the defects of my words, of my thoughts ? May I presume that God shall accept of me ? nay, delight in me ? Forget I who the Lord is ? Of what majesty ? Of what felicity ? Can it stand with his Majesty to vouchsafe acceptance ? with his felicity to take content in the words of a worm ? in the thoughts of a wretch ? And, Lord, I am too proud that vilify myself so little, and magnify thee no more. But see whither the desire of thy servant doth carry him ; how, willing to please, I consider not how hard it is for dust and ashes to please God, to do that wherein God should take content. But Lord, here is my comfort, that I may set God to give content unto God ; God is *mine*, and I cannot want

access unto God, if God may approach himself.   Let me be weak, yet God is strong ;
O Lord, thou are " *my strength.*"   Let me be a slave to sin, God is a *Saviour ;* O
Lord, thou art *my Saviour ;* thou hast *redeemed* me from all that woful state whereunto Adam cast me, yea, thou hast built me upon a rock, strong and sure, that the
gates of hell might never prevail against me.   These two things hast thou done
for me, O Lord, and what may not he presume of for whom thou hast done these
things !   I fear not to come before thee.   I presume my devotion shall content
thee ; be thine eyes never such all-seeing eyes, I will be bold to present my inward,
my outward man before thee ; be thy eyes never so holy eyes, I will not fly with
Adam to hide my nakedness from thee, for I am able to keep my ground ; seeing I
am supported by *my Lord*, I doubt not but to prove a true Israelite, and to prevail
with God.   For all my woe, for all my sin, I will not shrink, nay, I will approach,
approach to thee, for thou art " *My Redeemer.*"   The nearer I come to thee, the
freer shall I be both from sin and woe.   Oh, blessed state of man who is so weak, so
strong ; so wretched, and so happy ; weak in himself, strong in God ; most happy
in God, though in himself a sinful wretch.   And now, my soul, thou wouldst be
devout ; thou mayst be what thou wouldst : sacrifice to God thy words, sacrifice
to God thy thoughts, make thyself a holocaust, doubt not but thou shalt be accepted,
thou shalt content even the most glorious the most holy eyes of God.   Only presume
not of thyself, presume on him ; build thy words, build thy thoughts upon thy
Rock, they shall not be shaken ; free thy words, free thy thoughts (thoughts and
words enthralled to sin), by thy Saviour, and thy sacrifice shall be accepted.   So
let me build on thee, so let me be enlarged by thee, in soul, in body, that " *The
words of my mouth, and the meditation of my heart, be acceptable in thy sight, O Lord.
my strength and my Redeemer.*"—*Arthur Lake (Bishop), in " Divine Meditations," 1629,*

HINTS TO PREACHERS.

Verse 1.—" Chalmers' Astronomical Discourses " will suggest to the preacher
many ways of handling this theme.   The power, wisdom, goodness, punctuality,
faithfulness, greatness, and glory of God are very visible in the heavens.

Verses 1—5.—Parallel between the heavens and the revelation of Scripture,
dwelling upon Christ as the central Sun of Scripture.

Verse 1.—" *The heavens declare the glory of God.*"   Work in which we may unite,
the nobility, pleasure, usefulness, and duty of such service.

Verse 2.—Voices of the day and of the night.   Day and night thoughts.

Verse 3.—The marginal reading, coupled with verse four, suggests the eloquence
of an unobtrusive life—silent yet heard.

Verse 4.—In what sense God is revealed to all men.

Verses 4, 5, 6.—The Sun of righteousness.   I. His tabernacle.   II. His appearance as a Bridegroom.   III. His joy as a champion.   IV. His circuit and his
influence.

Verse 5.—" *Rejoiceth as a strong man,*" etc.   The joy of strength, the joy of
holy labour, the joy of the anticipated reward.

Verse 6.—The permeating power of the gospel.

Verse 7 (first clause).—Holy Scripture.   I. What it is—" law."   II. Whose
it is—" of the Lord."   III. What is its character—"perfect."   IV. What its result
—" converting the soul."

Verse 7 (second clause).—I. Scholars.   II. Class-book.   III. Teacher.
IV. Progress.

Verses 7, 8, 9.—The Hexapla.   *See Notes.*

Verse 7 (last clause).—The wisdom of a simple faith.

Verse 8 (first clause). The heart-cheering power of the Word.   I. Founded in
its righteousness.   II. Real in its quality.   III. Constant in its operation.

Verse 8 (second clause).—Golden ointment for the eyes.

Verse 9.—The purity and permanence of true religion, and the truth and justice
of the principles upon which it is founded.

Verse 10.—Two arguments for loving God's statutes—Profit and Pleasure.

Verse 10.—The inexpressible delights of meditation on Scripture.

Verse 11 (*first clause*).—I. What ? "Warned." II. How ? "By them."
III. Who ? "Thy servant." IV. When ? "Is"—present.

Verse 11 (*second clause*).—Evangelical rewards—"*In,*" not *for* keeping.

Verse 12.—See "Spurgeon's Sermons," No 116. "Secret Sins."

Verses 12, 13.—The three grades of sin—secret, presumptuous, unpardonable.

Verse 13.—See "Spurgeon's Sermons," No. 135. "Presumptuous Sins."

Verse 13 (*last clause*).—"*The great transgression.*" What it is not, may be, involves, and suggests.

Verse 14.—A prayer concerning our holy things.

Verse 14.—All wish to please. Some please *themselves.* Some please *men.* Some seek to please *God.* Such was David. I. The prayer shows his *humility.* II. The prayer shows his *affection.* III. The prayer shows a *consciousness of duty.* IV. The prayer shows a *regard to self-interest.—William Jay.*

Verse 14.—The harmony of heart and lips needful for acceptance.

PSALM XX.

SUBJECT.—*We have before us a* National Anthem, *fitted to be sung at the outbreak of war, when the monarch was girding on his sword for the fight. If David had not been vexed with wars, we might never have been favoured with such Psalms as this. There is a needs be for the trials of one saint, that he may yield consolation to others. A happy people here plead for a beloved sovereign, and with loving hearts cry to Jehovah, "God save the King." We gather that this song was intended to be sung in public, not only from the matter of the song, but also from its dedication "To the Chief Musician." We know its author to have been Israel's sweet singer, from the short title, "A Psalm of David." The particular occasion which suggested it, it would be mere folly to conjecture, for Israel was almost always at war in David's day. His sword may have been hacked, but it was never rusted. Kimchi reads the title, concerning David, or, for David, and it is clear that the King is the subject as well as the composer of the song. It needs but a moment's reflection to perceive that this hymn of prayer is prophetical of our Lord Jesus, and is the cry of the ancient church on behalf of her Lord, as she sees him in vision enduring a great fight of afflictions on her behalf. The militant people of God, with the great Captain of salvation at their head, may still in earnest plead that the pleasure of the Lord may prosper in his hand. We shall endeavour to keep to this view of the subject in our brief exposition, but we cannot entirely restrict our remarks to it.*

DIVISION.—*The first four verses are a prayer for the success of the king. Verses 5, 6, and 7 express unwavering confidence in God and his Anointed; verse 8 declares the defeat of the foe, and verse 9 is a concluding appeal to Jehovah.*

EXPOSITION.

THE LORD hear thee in the day of trouble; the name of the God of Jacob defend thee;

2 Send thee help from the sanctuary, and strengthen thee out of Zion;

3 Remember all thy offerings, and accept thy burnt sacrifice; Selah.

4 Grant thee according to thine own heart, and fulfil all thy counsel.

1. "*The Lord hear thee in the day of trouble.*" All loyal subjects pray for their king, and most certainly citizens of Zion have good cause to pray for the Prince of Peace. In times of conflict loving subjects redouble their pleas, and surely in the sorrows of our Lord his church could not but be in earnest. All the Saviour's days were days of trouble, and he also made them days of prayer; the church joins her intercession with her Lord's, and pleads that he may be heard in his cries and tears. The agony in the garden was especially a gloomy hour, but he was heard in that he feared. He knew that his Father heard him always, yet in that troublous hour no reply came until thrice he had fallen on his face in the garden; then sufficient strength was given in answer to prayer, and he rose a victor from the conflict. On the cross also his prayer was not unheard, for in the twenty-second Psalm he tells us, "thou hast heard me from the horns of the unicorns." The church in this verse implies that her Lord would be himself much given to prayer; in this he is our example, teaching us that if we are to receive any advantage from the prayers of others, we must first pray for ourselves. What a mercy that we *may* pray in the day of trouble, and what a still more blessed privilege that no trouble can prevent the Lord from hearing us! Troubles roar like thunder, but the believer's voice will be heard above the storm. O Jesus, when thou pleadest for us in our hour of trouble, the Lord Jehovah will hear thee. This is a most refreshing confidence, and it may be indulged in without fear.

"*The name of the God of Jacob defend thee;*" or, as some read it, "set thee in a high place." By "the name" is meant the revealed character and Word of God; we are not to worship "the unknown God," but we should seek to know the covenant God of Jacob, who has been pleased to reveal his name and attributes to his people. There may be much in a royal name, or a learned name, or a venerable name, but it will be a theme for heavenly scholarship to discover all that is contained in the divine name. The glorious power of God defended and preserved the Lord Jesus through the battle of his life and death, and exalted him above all his enemies. His warfare is now accomplished in his own proper person, but in his mystical body, the church, he is still beset with dangers, and only the eternal arm of our God in covenant can defend the soldiers of the cross, and set them on high out of the reach of their foes. The day of trouble is not over, the pleading Saviour is not silent, and the name of the God of Israel is still the defence of the faithful. The name, " *God of Jacob*," is suggestive ; Jacob had his day of trouble, he wrestled, was heard, was defended, and in due time was set on high, and his God is our God still, the same God to all his wrestling Jacobs. The whole verse is a very fitting benediction to be pronounced by a gracious heart over a child, a friend, or a minister, in prospect of trial ; it includes both temporal and spiritual protection, and directs the mind to the great Source of all good. How delightful to believe that our heavenly Father has pronounced it upon our favoured heads !

2. " *Send thee help from the sanctuary.*" Out of heaven's sanctuary came the angel to strengthen our Lord, and from the precious remembrance of God's doings in his sanctuary our Lord refreshed himself when on the tree. There is no help like that which is of God's sending, and no deliverance like that which comes out of his sanctuary. The sanctuary to us is the person of our blessed Lord, who was typified by the temple, and is the true sanctuary which God has pitched, and not man: let us fly to the cross for shelter in all times of need, and help will be sent to us. Men of the world despise sanctuary help, but our hearts have learned to prize it beyond all material aid. They seek help out of the armoury, or the treasury, or the buttery, but we turn to the sanctuary. " *And strengthen thee out of Zion.*" Out of the assemblies of the pleading saints who had for ages prayed for their Lord, help might well result to the despised sufferer, for praying breath is never spent in vain. To the Lord's mystical body the richest good comes in answer to the pleadings of his saints assembled for holy worship as his Zion. Certain advertisers recommend a strengthening plaster, but nothing can give such strength to the loins of a saint as waiting upon God in the assemblies of his people. This verse is a benediction befitting a Sabbath morning, and may be the salutation either of a pastor to his people, or of a church to its minister. God in the sanctuary of his dear Son's person, and in the city of his chosen church is the proper object of his people's prayers, and under such a character may they confidently look to him for his promised aid.

3. " *Remember all thy offerings, and accept thy burnt sacrifice. Selah.*" Before war kings offered sacrifice, upon the acceptance of which they depended for success ; our blessed Lord presented himself as a victim, and was a sweet savour unto the Most High, and then he met and routed the embattled legions of hell. Still does his burnt sacrifice perfume the courts of heaven, and through him the offerings of his people are received as *his* sacrifices and oblations. We ought in our spiritual conflicts to have an eye to the sacrifice of Jesus, and never venture to war until first the Lord has given us a token for good at the altar of the cross, where faith beholds her bleeding Lord. " *Selah.*" It is well to pause at the cross before we march onward to battle, and with the Psalmist cry " Selah." We are too much in a hurry to make good haste. A little pausing might greatly help our speed. Stay, good man, there is a haste which hinders ; rest awhile, meditate on the burnt sacrifice, and put thy heart right for the stern work which lieth before thee.

4. " *Grant thee according to thine own heart, and fulfil all thy counsel.*" Christ's desire and counsel were both set upon the salvation of his people ; the church of old desired for him good speed in his design, and the church in these latter days, with all her heart desires the complete fulfilment of his purpose. In Christ Jesus sanctified souls may appropriate this verse as a promise ; they shall have their desire, and their plans to glorify their Master shall succeed. We may have our own will when our will is God's will. This was always the case with our Lord, and yet he said, " not as I will, but as thou wilt." What need for submission in our case ; if it was necessary to him, how much more for us !

5 We will rejoice in thy salvation, and in the name of our God we will set up *our* banners : the LORD fulfil all thy petitions.

6 Now know I that the LORD saveth his anointed ; he will hear him from his holy heaven with the saving strength of his right hand.

7 Some *trust* in chariots, and some in horses : but we will remember the name of the LORD our God.

5. " *We will rejoice in thy salvation.*" In Jesus there is salvation ; it is his own, and hence it is called thy *salvation ;* but it is ours to receive and ours to rejoice in. We should fixedly resolve that come what may, we will rejoice in the saving arm of the Lord Jesus. The people in this Psalm, before their king went to battle, felt sure of victory, and therefore began to rejoice beforehand ; how much more ought we to do this who have seen the victory completely won ! Unbelief begins weeping for the funeral before the man is dead ; why should not faith commence piping before the dance of victory begins ? Buds are beautiful, and promises not yet ful- filled are worthy to be admired. If joy were more general among the Lord's people, God would be more glorified among men ; the happiness of the subjects is the honour of the sovereign. "*And in the name of our God we will set up our banners.*" We lift the standard of defiance in the face of the foe, and wave the flag of victory over the fallen adversary. Some proclaim war in the name of one king and some of another but the faithful go to war in Jesu's name, the name of the incarnate God, Immanuel, God with us. The times are evil at present, but so long as Jesus lives and reigns in his church we need not furl our banners in fear, but advance them with sacred courage.

> " Jesu's tremendous name
> Puts all our foes to flight ;
> Jesus, the meek, the angry Lamb
> A lion is in fight."

The church cannot forget that Jesus is her advocate before the throne, and there- fore she sums up the desires already expressed in the short sentence, " *The Lord fulfil all thy petitions.*" Be it never forgotten that among those petitions is that choice one, " Father, I will that they also whom thou hast given me be with me where I am."

6. " *Now know I that the Lord saveth his anointed.*" We live and learn, and what we learn we are not ashamed to acknowledge. He who thinks he knows every- thing will miss the joy of finding out new truth ; he will never be able to cry, " now know I," for he is so wise in his own conceit that he knows all that can be revealed and more. Souls conscious of ignorance shall be taught of the Lord, and rejoice as they learn. Earnest prayer frequently leads to assured confidence. The church pleaded that the Lord Jesus might win the victory in his great struggle, and now by faith she sees him saved by the omnipotent arm. She evidently finds a sweet relish in the fragrant title of " anointed ; " she thinks of him as ordained before all worlds to his great work, and then endowed with the needful qualifications by being anointed of the Spirit of the Lord ; and this is evermore the choicest solace of the believer, that Jehovah himself hath anointed Jesus to be a Prince and a Saviour, and that our shield is thus the Lord's own anointed. " *He will hear him from his holy heaven with the saving strength of his right hand.*" It is here asserted confidently that God's holiness and power would both come to the rescue of the Saviour in his conflict, and surely these two glorious attributes found congenial work in answering the sufferer's cries. Since Jesus was heard, we shall be ; God is in heaven, but our prayers can scale those glorious heights ; those heavens are holy, but Jesus purifies our prayers, and so they gain admittance ; our need is great, but the divine arm is strong, and all its strength is " saving strength ; " that strength, moreover, is in the hand which is most used and which is used most readily—the right hand. What encouragements are these for pleading saints !

7. Contrasts frequently bring out the truth vividly, and here the church sets forth the creature-confidences of carnal men in contrast with her reliance upon the Prince Immanuel and the invisible Jehovah. " *Some trust in chariots, and some in horses.*" Chariots and horses make an imposing show, and with their rattling, and dust, and fine caparisons, make so great a figure that vain man is much taken with them ; yet the discerning eye of faith sees more in an invisible God than in all these. The most dreaded war-engine of David's day was the war-chariot, armed with scythes, which mowed down men like grass : this was the boast and glory of the neighbouring nations ; but the saints considered the name of Jehovah to be a far better defence. As the Israelites might not keep horses, it was natural for them to regard the enemy's cavalry with more than usual dread. It is, therefore, all the greater evidence of faith that the bold songster can here disdain even the horse of

Egypt in comparison with the Lord of hosts. Alas, how many in our day who profess to be the Lord's are as abjectly dependent upon their fellow-men or upon an arm of flesh in some shape or other, as if they had never known the name of Jehovah at all. Jesus, be thou alone our rock and refuge, and never may we mar the simplicity of our faith. " *We will remember the name of the Lord our God.*" " Our God " in covenant, who has chosen us and whom we have chosen ; this God is our God. The name of our God is JEHOVAH, and this should never be forgotten ; the self-existent, independent, immutable, ever-present, all-filling I AM. Let us adore that matchless name, and never dishonour it by distrust or creature-confidence. Reader, you must *know* it before you can *remember* it. May the blessed Spirit reveal it graciously to your soul !

8 They are brought down and fallen : but we are risen, and stand upright.

9 Save, LORD : let the king hear us when we call.

8. How different the end of those whose trusts are different ! The enemies of God are uppermost at first, but they ere long are brought down by force, or else fall of their own accord. Their foundation is rotten, and therefore when the time comes it gives way under them ; their chariots are burned in the fire, and their horses die of pestilence, and where is their boasted strength ? As for those who rest on Jehovah, they are often cast down at the first onset, but an Almighty arm uplifts them, and they joyfully stand upright. The victory of Jesus is the inheritance of his people. The world, death, Satan and sin, shall all be trampled beneath the feet of the champions of faith ; while those who rely upon an arm of flesh shall be ashamed and confounded for ever.

9. The Psalm is here recapitulated. That Jesus might himself be delivered, and might then, as our King, hear us, is the two-fold desire of the Psalm. The first request is granted, and the second is sure to all the seed ; and therefore we may close the Psalm with the hearty shout " God save the King." " God save King Jesus, and may he soon come to reign."

EXPLANATORY NOTES AND QUAINT SAYINGS.

Whole Psalm.—This Psalm is the prayer which the church might be supposed offering up, had all the redeemed stood by the cross, or in Gethsemane, in full consciousness of what was doing there. Messiah, in reading these words, would know that he had elsewhere the sympathy he longed for, when he said to the three disciples, " Tarry ye here, and watch with me." Matt. xxvi. 38. It is thus a pleasant song, of the sacred singer of Israel, to set forth the feelings of the redeemed in their Head, whether in his sufferings or in the glory that was to follow.—*Andrew A. Bonar.*

Whole Psalm.—There are traces of liturgical arrangement in many of the Psalms. There is frequently an adaptation to the circumstances of public worship. Thus, when the Jewish church wished to celebrate the great act of Messiah the High Priest making a sacrifice for the people on the day of atonement, as represented in the twenty-second Psalm, a subject so solemn, grand, and affecting, was not commenced suddenly and unpreparedly, but first a suitable occasion was sought, proper characters were introduced, and a scene in some degree appropriate to the great event was fitted for its reception. The priests and Levites endeavour to excite in the minds of the worshippers an exalted tone of reverential faith. The majesty and power of God, all the attributes which elevate the thoughts, are called in to fill the souls of the worshippers with the most intense emotion ; and when the feelings are strung to the highest pitch, an awful, astounding impression succeeds, when the words are slowly chanted, " My God, my God, why hast thou forsaken me ? " We are to suppose, then, that the series of Psalms, from the twentieth to the twenty-fourth inclusive, was used as a service or office in the public worship of the Jewish church.* *R. H. Ryland, M.A., in " The Psalms Restored to Messiah," 1853.*

Whole Psalm.—Really good wishes are good things, and should be expressed in words and deeds. The whole Psalm thus teaches. Christian sympathy is a great

---

* This is a purely gratuitous statement, but is less unlikely than many other assertions of annotators who have a cause to plead.—C. H. S.

branch of Christian duty. There may be a great deal of obliging kindness in that which costs us little.—*William S. Plumer.*

Verse 1.—" *The Lord hear thee in the day of trouble.*" All the days of Christ were *days of trouble.* He was a brother born for adversity, a man of sorrows and acquainted with griefs. . . . . But more particularly it was a " *day of trouble* " with him when he was in the garden, heavy and sore amazed, and his sweat was, as it were, droops of blood falling on the ground, and his soul was exceeding sorrowful, even unto death ; but more especially this was his case when he hung upon the cross . . . . . when he bore all the sins of his people, endured the wrath of his Father, and was forsaken by him. Now, in this " *day of trouble,*" both when in the garden and on the cross, he prayed unto his Father, as he had been used to do in other cases, and at other times ; and the church here prays that God would hear and answer him, as he did.—*Condensed from John Gill.*

Verse 1.—" *The name.*" Whereas they say, " *The name of the God of Jacob,*" thereby they mean God himself ; but they thus speak of God because all the knowledge that we have of God ariseth from the knowledge of his name, and as to that end he hath given himself in the Scriptures sundry names, that thereby we might know not only what he is in himself, so far as it is meet for us to know, but especially what he is to us, so by them, and them principally, we know him to be, as he is, not only in himself, but unto us. . . . . From this knowledge of the name of God ariseth confidence in prayer ! as when they know him, and here call him " *the God of Jacob,*" that is, he that hath made a covenant of mercy with him and with his posterity, that he will be their God and they shall be his people, that they may be bold to flee to him for succour, and confidently call upon him in the day of their trouble to hear them, and to help them, as they do. And the more that they know of his name, that is, of his goodness, mercy, truth, power, wisdom, justice, etc., so may they the more boldly pray unto him, not doubting but that he will be answerable unto his name. . . . For as among men, according to the good name that they have for liberality and pity, so will men be ready to come unto them in their need, and the poor will say, " I will go to such an house for they have a good name, and are counted good to the poor, and merciful, all men speak well of them for their liberality ; " and this name of theirs giveth the encouragement to come boldly and often. So when we know God thus by his name, it will make us bold to come unto him in prayer. . . . . Or, if a man be never so merciful, and others know it not, and so they are ignorant of his good name that he hath, and that he is worthy of, they cannot, with any good hope, come unto him, for they know not what he is ; they have heard nothing of him at all. So when, by unbelief, we hardly conceive of God and of his goodness, or for want of knowledge are ignorant of his good name, even of all his mercy, and of his truth, pity and compassion that is in him, and so know not his great and glorious name, we can have little or no heart at all to come unto him in trouble, and seek unto him for help by prayer, as these did here ; and this maketh some so forward unto prayer, they are so well acquainted with *the name of God,* that they doubt not of speeding, and others again are so backward unto it, they are so wholly ignorant of his name.—*Nicholas Bownd,* 1604.

Verse 1.—" *The name of the God of Jacob defend thee.*" This is a beautiful allusion to the history of the patriarch Jacob. Jehovah had appeared for him, when he fled from his brother Esau, at Bethel, and Jacob said to his household, " Let us arise, and go up to Bethel ; and I will make there an altar unto God, *who answered m* in *the day of my distress,* and was with me in the way which I went." Gen. xxxv. 3.—*John Morison.*

)*Verse 1.*—" *The name of the God of Jacob defend thee.*" Hebrew, " *set thee in an high place,*" such as God's name is. Prov. xviii. 10. " The righteous runneth into it and is safe," as in a tower of brass, or town of war. By *the name of God* is meant, *Deus nominatissimus,* the most renowned God, saith Junius, and " worthy to be praised," as Psalm xviii. 3 ; and he is called the God of Jacob here, saith another, first, because Jacob was once in the like distress (Gen. xxxii. 6, 7) ; secondly, because he prayed to the like purpose (Gen. xxxv. 3); thirdly, because he prevailed with God as a prince ; " and there God spake with us " (Hosea xii. 4) ; fourthly, because *God of Jacob* is the same with " God of Israel," and so the covenant is pleaded.—*John Trapp.*

Verse 1.—" *The name of the God of Jacob defend thee.*"—There is an assurance of thy protection, of thy safety, in the midst of ten thousand foes, and of thy perseverance to the end. But you will say, how will the name of the God of Jacob defend me? Try it. I have, over and over again; therefore I speak what I do know and testify what I have seen. " The name of the God of Jacob defend thee." I was once goaded by a poor silly Irish papist to try it, who told me, in his consummate ignorance and bigotry, that if a priest would but give him a drop of holy water, and make a circle with it around a field full of wild beasts, they would not hurt him. I retired in disgust at the abominable trickery of such villains, reflecting, what a fool I am that I cannot put such trust in my God as this poor deluded man puts in his priest and a drop of holy water! And I resolved to try what " the name of the God of Jacob " would do, having the Father's fixed decrees, the Son's unalterable responsibility, and the Spirit's invincible grace and operation around me. I tried it and felt my confidence brighten. O brethren, get encircled with covenant engagements, and covenant blood, and covenant grace, and covenant promises, and covenant securities: then will " the Lord hear you in the time of trouble, and the name of the God of Jacob will defend you."—Joseph Irons.

Verse 1.—A sweeter wish, or a more consolatory prayer for a child of sorrow was never uttered by man, " The Lord hear thee in the day of trouble; the name of the God of Jacob defend thee." And who is there of the sons of men to whom a " day of trouble " does not come, whose path is not darkened at times, or with whom is it unclouded sunshine from the cradle to the grave? " Few plants," says old Jacomb, " have both the morning and the evening sun;" and one far older than he said, " Man is born to trouble." A " day of trouble," then, is the heritage of every child of Adam. How sweet, as I have said, how sweet the wish, " The Lord hear thee in the day of trouble." It is the prayer of another in behalf of some troubled one, and yet it implies that the troubled one himself had also prayed, " The Lord hear thee "— hear and answer thine own prayer!—Barton Bouchier.

Verses 1, 2.—The scene presented in this place to the eye of faith is deeply affecting. Here is the Messiah pouring out his heart in prayer in the day of his trouble; his spouse overhears his agonising groans; she is moved with the tenderest sympathy towards him; she mingles her prayers with his; she entreats that he may be supported and defended. . . . . It may now, perhaps, be said, he is out of the reach of trouble, he is highly exalted, he does not want our sympathies or our prayers. True; yet still we may pray for him—see Matthew xxv. 40—" Inasmuch as ye have done it unto one of the least of these my brethren, ye have done it unto me." We can pray for him in his members. And thus is fulfilled what is written in Psalm lxxii. 15, " And he shall live, and to him shall be given of the gold of Sheba: prayer also shall be made for him continually (that is, in his suffering members): and daily shall he be praised " (that is, in his own admirable person).—Hamilton Verschoyle, 1843.

Verses 1—5.—These are the words of the people, which they spake unto God in the behalf of their king; and so they did as David desired them, namely, pray for him. If they did thus pray for him, being desired thereunto, and it was their bound duty so to do, and they knew it to be so, and therefore did make conscience of it, and it had been a great fault for them to have failed in it; then by consequence it followeth of necessity, that whensoever any of our brethren or sisters in Christ shall desire this duty at our hands, we must be careful to perform it; and it were a fault not to be excused in us, both against God and them, to fail in it. Therefore we must not think that when godly men and women at their parting or otherwise, desire our prayers, and say, " I pray you pray for me," or, " remember me in your prayers," that these are words of course (though I do not deny, but that many do so use them, and so doing they take the name of God in vain); but we should be persuaded, that out of the abundance of their feeling of their own wants they speak unto us, and so be willing by our prayers to help to supply them. And especially we should do it when they shall make known their estate unto us, as here David did to the people, giving them to understand that he should or might be in great danger of his enemies, and so it was " a time of trouble " unto him, as he called it. . . . Most of all this duty of prayer ought to be carefully performed when we have promised it unto any upon such notice of their estate. For as all promises ought to be kept, yea, though it be to our own hindrance, so those most of all that so nearly concern them. And as if when any should desire us to speak to some great man for them, and we promise to do it, and they trust to it, hoping that we will be as good as our words; it were a great deceit in us to fail them, and so to frustrate their expectation; so when any have desired us to speak to God for them, and upon our promise they would comfort themselves over it, if we should by negligence deceive them, it were a great fault in us, and that which the Lord would require at our hands, though they should never know of it.   Therefore, as we ought daily to pray one for another unasked, as our Saviour Christ hath taught us, " O our Father which art in heaven," etc., so more specially and by name should we do it for them that have desired it of us.   And so parents especially should not forget their children in their prayers, which daily ask their blessing, and hope to be blessed of God by their prayers. Secondarily, if we should neglect to pray for them that have desired it at our hands, how could we have any hope that others whom we have desired to pray for us should perform that duty unto us ?   Nay, might not we justly fear that they would altogether neglect it, seeing we do neglect them ? and should it not be just with God so to punish us ? according to the saying of our Saviour Christ, " With what measure ye mete, it shall be measured to you again."   Matt. vii. 2.   And I remember that this was the saying of a reverend father in the church, who is now fallen asleep in the Lord, when any desired him to pray for them (as many did, and more than any that I have known), he would say unto them, " I pray you pray for me, and pray that I may remember you, and then I hope I shall not forget you."   Therefore if we would have others pray for us, let us pray for them.—*Nicholas Bownd.*

Verses 1, 5.—In the first verse the Psalmist says, " *The Lord hear thee in the day of trouble ;* " and in the fifth he says, "*The Lord perform all thy petitions.*" Does he in both these cases refer to one and the same time ?   The prayers mentioned in the first verse are offered in " *the day of trouble,*" in the days of his flesh ; are the petitions to which he refers in the fourth verse also offered in the days of his flesh ? Many think not.   Before our blessed Saviour departed out of this world, he prayed to the Father for those whom he had given him, that he would keep them from the evil of the world, that they might be one, even as he was one with the Father. He prayed too for his murderers.   After his ascension into heaven, he sat down at the right hand of the Father, where he " maketh intercession for us."   " If any man sin, we have an advocate with the Father, Jesus Christ, the righteous."   It is to this, as many think, that the prophet refers when he says, " *The Lord perform all thy petitions ;* " to the intercession which he is continually making for us.—*F. H. Dunwell.*

Verse 2.—" *Send thee help from the sanctuary.*"   Here we see the nature of true faith, that it causeth us to see *help* in *heaven*, and so to pray for it when there is none to be seen in the earth.   And this is the difference between faith and unbelief ; that the very unbelievers can by reason conceive of help, so long as they have any means to help them ; but if they fail they can see none at all ; so they are like unto those that are purblind, who can see nothing but near at hand.   But faith seeth afar off, even into heaven, so that it is " the evidence of things that are not seen ; " for it looketh unto the power of God, who hath all means in his hand, or can work without them, who made all of nothing, and " calleth the things that be not, as though they were."   So that as the holy martyr Stephen, when his enemies were ready to burst for anger and gnash at him with their teeth, looked steadfastly into heaven, and saw Christ standing at the right hand of God ready to defend him ; so faith in the promises of the word doth see help in heaven ready for us, when there are no means in earth.—*Nicholas Bownd.*

Verse 2.—" *Send thee help from the sanctuary.*"   Why " *from the sanctuary,*" but because the Lord presented himself there as upon the mercy-seat !   The sanctuary was in Zion, the mercy-seat was in the sanctuary, the Lord was in the mercy-seat ; he would have himself set forth as residing there.   Herein they pray, and pray in faith for help and strength.—*David Clarkson.*

Verse 2.—" *Strengthen thee out of Zion.*"   That is, out of the assemblies of the saints, where they are praying hard for thy welfare.—*John Trapp.*

Verse 3.—" *Remember all thy offerings, and accept thy burnt sacrifice.*"   " *All thy offerings :* " the humiliation that brought him from heaven to earth ; the patient tabernacling in the womb of the holy Virgin; the poor nativity ; the hard manger; ox and ass for courtiers ; the weary flight into Egypt ; the poor cottage in Nazareth ; the doing all good, and bearing all evil ; the miracles, the sermons, the teachings ; the being called a man gluttonous and a wine-bibber, the friend of publicans and sinners ; the attribution of his wondrous deeds to Beelzebub.   " *And accept thy burnt sacrifice.*"   As every part of the victim was consumed in a burnt sacrifice, so what limb, what sense of our dear Lord did not agonise in his passion ?   The thorny crown on his head : the nails in his hands and feet ; the reproaches that filled his ears ; the gloating multitude on whom his dying gaze rested ; the vinegar and the gall ; the evil odours of the hill of death and corruption. The ploughers ploughed upon his back, and made long furrows ; his most sacred face was smitten with the palm of the hand, his head with the reed. What could have been done more for the vineyard than he did not do in it ? Isa. v. 4. So, what more could have been borne by the vine, that this dear Vine did not bear ? " *Remember* " them now, O Father, call to mind for us sinners, for us miserable sinners, and for our salvation, " *all* " these " *offerings* ; " " *accept*," instead of our eternal punishment, who are guilty, his " *burnt sacrifice*," who did no sin, neither was guile found in his mouth !—*Dionysius, and Gerhohus* (1093—1169), *quoted by J. M. Neale.*

Verse 3.—" *Accept :* " Hebrew, " *turn to ashes*," by fire from heaven, in token of his acceptance as was usual.—*Matthew Poole.*

Verse 3.—" *That thy burnt offering may be fat.*" That is, abundant, fruitful, and full. But here we must understand this burnt offering, as we did the sacrifice, in a spiritual sense, as we have before observed. Thus Christ offered up himself wholly upon the cross to be consumed by the fire of love. And here, instead of " all thy sacrifice," it might be rendered " the whole of thy sacrifice." Even as burnt sacrifice (*holocaustum*) signifies the whole of it being burnt with fire. By which groaning of the Spirit, he shows and teaches the righteous, that they should pray and hope that none of their sufferings shall be vain, but that all shall be well-pleasing, remembered, and fully acceptable.—*Martin Luther.*

Verse 3.—" *Selah.*"*—This word, in the judgment of the learned, is sometime *vox optantis,* the voice of one that wisheth, equivalent to *amen ;* or *vox admirantis,* the voice of one admiring, showing some special matter ; or *vox affirmantis,* of one affirming, avouching what is said ; or *vox meditantis,* of one meditating, requiring consideration of what is said. But withal, it is a rest in music. Jerome saith it is *commutatio metri,* or *vicissitudo canendi.*—*Edward Marbury.*

Verse 4.—" *Grant thee according to thine own heart, and fulfil all thy counsel.*" Let us here call to mind the zealous and earnest desire of the Redeemer to accomplish his work, " I have a baptism to be baptised with ; and how am I straitened till it be accomplished." Luke xii. 50. " With desire I have desired to eat this passover with you before I suffer " (Luke xxii. 15) ; that he might leave a memorial of his sufferings and death, for the strengthening and refreshing of their souls. These earnest desires and anticipations did the Father satisfy, as of one with whom he was well pleased.—*W. Wilson.*

Verse 4.—" *Fulfil all thy counsel ;* " whatever was agreed upon in the counsel and covenant of peace between him and his Father, relating to his own glory, and the salvation of his people.—*John Gill.*

Verse 4.—" *Fulfil all thy counsel.*" Answer thee, *ad cardinem desiderii,* as a father, Augustine, expresseth it ; let it be unto thee even as thou wilt. Sometimes God doth not only grant a man's prayer, but fulfilleth his counsel ; that is, in that very way, by that very means, which his judgment pitched upon in his thoughts.—*John Trapp.*

Verse 5 (first clause).—Whosoever do partake with Christ's subjects in trouble, shall share with them also in the joy of their deliverance ; therefore it is said, " *We will rejoice in thy salvation.*"—*David Dickson.*

Verse 5.—" *In the name of our God.*" As those cried out, Judges vii. 20, " The sword of the Lord and of Gideon ; " and as we have it in Joshua vi. 20, " And the people shouted, and the walls of Jericho fell down ; " and king Abiah, crying out with his men in the same, killed five hundred thousand of the children of Israel ; and so now also, according to the military custom in our day, the soldiers boast in the name and glory of their general, in order to encourage themselves against their enemies. And it is just this custom that the present verse is now teaching, only in a godly and religious manner.—*Martin Luther.*

Verse 5.—" *In the name of our God we will set up our banners.*" The banners formerly so much used were a part of military equipage, borne in times of war to assemble, direct, distinguish, and encourage the troops. They might possibly be used for other purposes also. Occasions of joy, splendid processions, and especially

---

* See pages 23, 26, 27, 35, 318.

a royal habitation, might severally be distinguished in this way. The words of the Psalmist may perhaps be wholly figurative: but if they should be literally understood, the allusion of erecting a banner in the name of the Lord, acknowledging his glory, and imploring his favour, might be justified from an existing practice. Certain it is that we find this custom prevalent on this very principle in other places, into which it might originally have been introduced from Judea. Thus Mr. Turner (*Embassy to Thibet*, p. 31), says, " I was told that it was a custom with the Soobah to ascend the hill every month, when he sets up a white flag, and performs some religious ceremonies, to conciliate the favour of a dewta, or invisible being, the genius of the place, who is said to hover about the summit, dispensing at his will, good and evil to every thing around him."—*Samuel Burder's " Oriental Customs,"* 1812.

Verse 5.—" *In the name of our God we will set up our banners.*" In all religious as well as warlike processions the people carry banners. Hence, on the pinnacles of their sacred cars, on the domes or gateways of their temples, and on the roof of a new house, may be seen the banner of the caste or sect, floating in the air. Siva the Supreme, also, is described as having a banner in the celestial world.—*Joseph Roberts' " Oriental Illustrations."*

Verse 5.—" *In the name of our God we will set up our banners.*" 1. We will wage war in his name, we will see that our cause be good, and make his glory our end in every expedition; we will ask counsel at his mouth, and take him along with us; we will follow his conduct, implore his aid, and depend upon it, and refer the issue to him. David went against Goliath in the name of the Lord of hosts. 1 Sam. xvii. 45. 2. We will celebrate our victories in his name. When " *we lift up our banners*" in triumph, and set up our trophies, it shall be " *in the name of our God*," he shall have all the glory of our success, and no instrument shall have any part of the honour that is due to him.—*Matthew Henry.*

Verse 5.—" *We will set up our banners.*"—Confession of Christ, as the only name whereby we can be saved, is the " *banner* " which distinguishes his faithful people. O that this confession were more distinct, more pure, more zealous, in those who seem to be his followers, then would they be more united, more bold, in the profession of their religion, more successful in the cause of Christ, terrible as an army with " *banners.*" Cant. vi. 4.—*W. Wilson.*

Verse 5.—" *Our banners.*" Will you know the staff, the colours, and the flag or streamer of this ensign? Why, the staff is his cross, the colours are blood and water, and the streamer the gospel, or preaching of them to the world. The staff that carried the colours was of old time fashioned like a cross, a cross bar near the top there was, from which the flag or streamer hung; so as it were prefiguring, that all the hosts and armies of the nations were one day to be gathered under the *banner of the cross*, to which soldiers should daily flow out of all the nations and kingdoms of the earth.—*Mark Frank,* 1613—1664.

Verse 5.—" *The Lord fulfil all thy petitions,*" for thyself and for others, now that thou sittest on the right hand of the Father, pleading for us and showing thy side and thy wounds.—*Dionysius, quoted by Isaac Williams.*

Verse 6.—" *Now know I.*" A sudden change of number, speaking in the person of one, thereby to note the unity and consent of the people to this prayer, as though they had been all one, and uttered it all with one mouth. " *The Lord will help his anointed ;* " that is, his king, whom he hath established. See Psalm ii. 2; xviii. 50. " *And will hear him* (see verse 1), *from his sanctuary.*" One readeth it thus—" from the heavens of his holiness ; " meaning, from heaven where his holiness dwelleth. *Thomas Wilcocks.*

Verse 6.—" *He will hear him.*" I would be glad of the prayers of all the churches of Christ; O that there were not a saint on earth but that I were by name in his morning and evening prayer (whosoever thou art that readest, I beseech thee pray for me); but above all, let me have a property in those prayers and intercessions that are proper only to *Christ;* I am sure then I should never miscarry: Christ's prayers are heavenly, glorious, and very effectual.—*Isaac Ambrose,* 1592—1674.

Verse 6.—" *His anointed.*" As priests, and sometimes kings and prophets, were among the Jews *anointed* to their offices, so our Saviour was anointed as a Prophet, to preach glad tidings to the meek; as a Priest, to bind up the broken-hearted; and as a King to deliver the captives. As the unction means designation and ordination, it is properly applied to the divine person of the Mediator: he is spoken of as God, who was "anointed with the oil of gladness above his fellows." Heb. i. 8, 9. As the anointing with the Holy Spirit signifies the *gifts* and *aids* of the Holy Spirit, it terminates upon his human nature only, and not his divine person, which has all the perfections in itself, and cannot properly, in the sense last mentioned be said to be anointed with the Holy Spirit. But yet as the human nature is taken into a subsistence in his divine person, the anointed may properly enough be predicated and affirmed of his Person. The unction of our Redeemer has a great *stress* laid upon it in Scripture. And therefore we read, "Whosoever believeth that Jesus is the Christ, is born of God." "Who is a liar but he that denieth that Jesus is the Christ ?" 1 John v. 1 ; ii. 22. Our Saviour's enemies were sensible of this, when they made an order, that if "any man did confess that he was Christ, he should be put out of the synagogue." John ix. 22. Our Saviour's anointing was *superior* to that of any other, and more excellent as to the work to which he was consecrated. The apostles and others, who are called his followers, had the Spirit *by measure*, but Christ *without measure*. He is "fairer than the sons of men" (Psalm xlv. 2) ; and had a glory as the "only begotten of the Father, full of grace and truth" (John i. 14, 16) ; and of his fulness the apostles and all others receive. Christ's anointing answers to that of Aaron his type ; the precious ointment which was "poured upon his head, ran down to the skirts of his garments." Psalm cxxxiii. 2.

Our Saviour was so anointed, as to "fill all in all." Eph. i. 23. He filleth all his members, and all their faculties, with all those measures of the Spirit, which they ever receive.—*Condensed from John Hurrion*, 1675—1731.

Verse 7.—"*Some trust in chariots, and some in horses : but we will remember the name of the Lord our God.*"—About Michaelmas I was in the utmost extremity, and having gone out in very fine weather, I contemplated the azure heavens, and my heart was so strengthened in faith (which I do not ascribe to my own powers, but solely to the grace of God), that I thought within myself, "What an excellent thing it is when we have nothing, and can rely upon nothing, but yet are acquainted with the living God, who made heaven and earth, and place our confidence alone in him, which enables us to be so tranquil even in necessity ! " Although I was well aware that I required something that very day, yet my heart was so strong in faith that I was cheerful, and of good courage. On coming home I was immediately waited upon by the overseer of the workmen and masons, who, as it was Saturday, required money to pay their wages. He expected the money to be ready, which he wished to go and pay, but enquired, however, whether I had received anything. "Has anything arrived ? " asked he. I answered, "No, but I have faith in God." Scarcely had I uttered the words when a student was announced, who brought me thirty dollars from some one, whom he would not name. I then went into the room again, and asked the other "how much he required this time for the workmen's wages ? " He answered, "Thirty dollars." "Here they are," said I, and enquired at the same time, "if he needed any more ? " He said, "No," which very much strengthened the faith of both of us, since we so visibly saw the miraculous hand of God, who sent it at the very moment when it was needed.—*Augustus Herman Franke*, 1663—1727.

Verse 7.—"*Some trust in chariots*," etc.—Vain is the confidence of all wickedness. In war, chariots, horses, navies, numbers, discipline, former successes, are relied on ; but the battle is not to the strong. "Providence favours the strong battalions" may sound well in a worldling's ear, but neither Providence nor the Bible so teaches. In peace, riches, friends, ships, farms, stocks, are relied upon, yet they can neither help nor save. Let him that glorieth glory in the Lord.—*William S. Plumer.*

Verse 7.—"*We will remember the name of the Lord our God.*" By *the name of God* is generally understood, in Holy Writ, the various properties and attributes of God : these properties and attributes make up and constitute the *name* of God. As when Solomon says, "The name of the Lord is a strong tower ; the righteous runneth into it and is safe." And, by remembering, considering, meditating upon this name of God, the Psalmist represents himself as comforted or strengthened, whatever might be the duties to which he was called, or the dangers to which he was exposed. Others were for looking to other sources of safety and strength, "some trusting in chariots, and some in horses;" but the Psalmist always set himself to the "remembering the name of the Lord our God :" and always, as it would seem, with satisfaction and success. And here is the peculiarity of the passage on which we wish to dwell, and from which we hope to draw important lessons and truths—the Psalmist "remembers the name of the Lord his God;" not any one property or attribute to God; but the whole combination of divine perfections. And he "*remembers*" this "name;" the expression implying, not a transient thought, but meditation—consideration; and yet the result of the recollection is gladness and confidence.—*Henry Melvill.*

Verse 7.—It is easy to persuade papists to lean on priests and saints, on old rags and painted pictures—on any idol; but it is hard to get a Protestant to trust in the living God.—*William Arnot, 1858.*

Verse 7.—Weak man cannot choose but have some confidence without himself in case of apparent difficulties, and natural men do look first to some earthly thing wherein they confide. "*Some trust in chariots, and some in horses,*" some in one creature, some in another. The believer must quit his confidence in these things, whether he have them or want them, and must rely on what God hath promised in his word to do unto us. "*But we will remember the name of the Lord our God,*" *David Dickson.*

Verse 7.—They that "*trust in chariots and horses,*" will have no king but Cæsar; but the "armies in heaven" which follow thee have themselves no arms, and no strength but in following thee.—*Isaac Williams.*

Verse 7.—Numa being told that his enemies were coming upon him, as he was offering sacrifices, thought it was sufficient for his safety that he could say, I am about the service of my God. When Jehoshaphat had once established a preaching ministry in all the cities of Judah, then, and not till then, the fear of the Lord fell on the neighbouring nations, and they made no war; albeit, he had before that placed forces in all the fenced cities.—*Charles Bradbury.*

Verse 7 :—

> "Some their warrior horses boast,
> Some their chariots marshall'd host;
> But our trust will we proclaim
> In our God Jehovah's name."

Richard Mant.

Verse 8.—"*They are brought down*" from their horses and chariots in which they trusted. Hebrew: *they bowed down,* as being unable to stand longer because of their mortal wounds. Compare Judges v. 27. "*Stand upright.*" Standing firmly upon our legs, and keeping the field, as conquerors use to do.—*Matthew Poole.*

HINTS TO PREACHERS.

This Psalm has been much used for coronation, thanksgiving, and fast sermons, and no end of nonsense and sickening flattery has been tacked thereto by the trencher-chaplains of the world's church. If kings had been devils, some of these gentry would have praised their horns and hoofs; for although some of their royal highnesses have been very obedient servants of the prince of darkness, these false prophets have dubbed them "most gracious sovereigns," and have been as much dazzled in their presence as if they had beheld the beatific vision.—*C. H. S.*

Whole Psalm.—A loyal song and prayer for subjects of King Jesus.

Verse 1.—Two great mercies in great trouble—hearing at the throne, and defence from the throne.

Verses 1, 2.—I. The Lord's trouble in its nature and its cause. II. How the Lord exercised himself in his trouble. III. We ought not to be unmoved spectators of the trouble of Jesus.—*Hamilton Verschoyle.*

Verses 1—3.—A model of good wishes for our friends. I. *They include personal piety.* The person who is spoken of prays, goes to the sanctuary, and offers sacrifice. We must wish our friends grace. II. *They point upward.* The blessings are distinctly recognised as divine. III. *They do not exclude trouble.* IV. *They are eminently spiritual.* Acceptance, etc.

Verse 2.—Sanctuary help—a suggestive topic.

Verse 3.—God's ceaseless respect to the sacrifice of Jesus.

Verses 3, 4.—The great privilege of this fourfold acceptance in the Beloved.

Verse 5.—Joy in salvation, to be resolved on and practised.

Verse 5.—*Setting up the banner.* Open avowal of allegiance, declaration of war, index of perseverance, claim of possession, signal of triumph.

Verse 5 (*last clause*).—The prevalence of our Lord's intercession, and the acceptance of our prayers through him.

Verse 6.—" *His anointed.*" Our Lord as the Anointed. When? With what unction? How? For what offices? etc.

Verse 6.—" *He will hear him.*" The ever-prevalent Intercessor.

Verse 6.—God's " *saving strength;*" the strength of his most used and most skilful hand.

Verse 6 (*first clause*).—" *Now know I.*" The moment when faith in Jesus fills the soul. The time when assurance is given. The period when a truth gleams into the soul, etc.

Verse 7.—*Creature confidence.* Apparently mighty, well adapted, showy, noisy, etc. *Faithful trust.* Silent, spiritual, divine, etc.

Verse 7.—" *The name of the Lord our God.*"—Comfortable reflections from the name and character of the true God.

Verse 8.—*Tables turned.*

Verse 9.—" *Save, Lord.*" One of the shortest and most pithy prayers in the Bible.

Verse 9 (*last clause*).—I. To whom we come, and what then. " *To a king.*" II. How we come, and what it means. " *We call.*" III. What we want, and what it implies. " *Hear us.*"

PSALM XXI.

SUBJECT.—*The title gives us but little information; it is simply*, To the chief Musician, a Psalm of David. *Probably written by David, sung by David, relating to David, and intended by David to refer in its fullest reach of meaning to David's Lord. It is evidently the fit companion of Psalm Twenty, and is in its proper position next to it. Psalm Twenty anticipates what this regards as realized. If we pray to-day for a benefit and receive it, we must, ere the sun goes down, praise God for that mercy, or we deserve to be denied the next time. It has been called David's triumphant song, and we may remember it as* The Royal Triumphal Ode. *" The king " is most prominent throughout, and we shall read it to true profit if our meditation of him shall be sweet while perusing it. We must crown him with the glory of our salvation ; singing of his love, and praising his power. The next Psalm will take us to the foot of the cross, this introduces us to the steps of the throne.*

DIVISION.—*The division of the translators will answer every purpose. A thanksgiving for victory, verses 1 to 6. Confidence of further success, verses 7 to 13.*

EXPOSITION.

THE king shall joy in thy strength, O Lord ; and in thy salvation how greatly shall he rejoice !

2 Thou hast given him his heart's desire, and hast not withholden the request of his lips. Selah.

3 For thou preventest him with the blessings of goodness : thou settest a crown of pure gold on his head.

4 He asked life of thee, *and* thou gavest *it* him, *even* length of days for ever and ever.

5 His glory *is* great in thy salvation : honour and majesty hast thou laid upon him.

6 For thou hast made him most blessed for ever : thou hast made him exceeding glad with thy countenance.

1. *" The king shall joy in thy strength, O Lord."* Jesus is a Royal Personage. The question, " Art thou a King then ? " received a full answer from the Saviour's lips : " Thou sayest that I am a King. To this end was I born, and for this prupose came I into this world, that I might bear witness unto the truth." He is not merely *a* King, but *the* King ; King over minds and hearts, reigning with a dominion of love, before which all other rule is but mere brute force. He was proclaimed King even on the cross, for there, indeed, to the eye of faith, he reigned as on a throne, blessing with more than imperial munificence the needy sons of earth. Jesus has wrought out the salvation of his people, but as a man he found his strength in Jehovah his God, to whom he addressed himself in prayer upon the lonely mountain's side, and in the garden's solitary gloom. That strength so abundantly given is here gratefully acknowledged, and made the subject of joy. The Man of Sorrows is now anointed with the oil of gladness above his fellows. Returned in triumph from the overthrow of all his foes, he offers his own rapturous *Te Deum* in the temple above, and joys in the power of the Lord. Herein let every subject of King Jesus imitate the King ; let us lean upon Jehovah's strength, let us joy in it by unstaggering faith, let us exult in it in our thankful songs. Jesus not only has thus rejoiced, but he *shall* do so as he sees the power of divine grace bringing out from their sinful hiding-places the purchase of his soul's travail ; we also shall rejoice more and more as we learn by experience more and more fully the strength of the arm of our covenant God Our weakness unstrings our harps, but his strength tunes them anew. If we cannot sing a note in honour of our own strength, we can at any rate rejoice in our omnipotent God.

" And in thy salvation how greatly shall he rejoice ! " Everything is ascribed

to God ; the source is *thy strength* and the stream is *thy salvation*. Jehovah planned and ordained it, works it and crowns it, and therefore it is his salvation. The joy here spoken of is described by a note of exclamation and a word of wonder : " *how greatly !* " The rejoicing of our risen Lord must, like his agony, be unutterable. If the mountains of his joy rise in proportion to the depth of the valleys of his grief, then his sacred bliss is high as the seventh heaven. For the joy which was set before him he endured the cross, despising the shame, and now that joy daily grows, for he rests in his love and rejoices over his redeemed with singing, as in due order they are brought to find their salvation in his blood. Let us with our Lord rejoice in salvation, as coming from God, as coming to us, as extending itself to others, and as soon to encompass all lands. We need not be afraid of too much rejoicing in this respect ; this solid foundation will well sustain the loftiest edifice of joy. The shoutings of the early Methodists in the excitement of the joy were far more pardonable than our own lukewarmness. Our joy should have some sort of inexpressibleness in it.

2. " *Thou hast given him his heart's desire.*" That desire he ardently pursued when he was on earth, both by his prayer, his actions, and his suffering ; he manifested that his heart longed to redeem his people, and now in heaven he has his desire granted him, for he sees his beloved coming to be with him where he is. The desires of the Lord Jesus were from his heart, and the Lord heard them ; if our hearts are right with God, he will in our case also " fulfil the desire of them that fear him."

" *And hast not withholden the request of his lips.*" What is in the well of the heart is sure to come up in the bucket of the lips, and those are the only true prayers where the heart's desire is first, and the lip's request follows after. Jesus prayed vocally as well as mentally ; speech is a great assistance to thought. Some of us feel that even when alone we find it easier to collect our thoughts when we can pray aloud. The requests of the Saviour were not withheld. He was and still is a prevailing Pleader. Our Advocate on high returns not empty from the throne of grace. He asked for his elect in the eternal council-chamber, he asked for blessings for them here, he asked for glory for them hereafter, and his requests have speeded. He is ready to ask for us at the mercy-seat. Have we not at this hour some desire to send up to his Father by him ? Let us not be slack to use our willing, loving, allprevailing Intercessor.

" *Selah.*" Here a pause is very properly inserted, that we may admire the blessed success of the king's prayers, and that we may prepare our own requests which may be presented through him. If we had a few more quiet rests, a few more Selahs in our public worship, it might be profitable.

3. " *For thou preventest him with the blessings of goodness.*" The word *prevent* formerly signified to precede or go before, and assuredly Jehovah preceded his Son with blessings. Before he died saints were saved by the anticipated merit of his death, before he came believers saw his day and were glad, and he himself had his delights with the sons of men. The Father is so willing to give blessings through his Son, that instead of his being constrained to bestow his grace, he outstrips the Mediatorial march of mercy. " I say not that I will pray the Father for you, for the Father himself loveth you." Before Jesus calls the Father answers, and while he is yet speaking he hears. Mercies may be bought with blood, but they are also freely given. The love of Jehovah is not caused by the Redeemer's sacrifice, but that love, with its blessings of goodness, preceded the great atonement, and provided it for our salvation. Reader, it will be a happy thing for thee if, like thy Lord, thou canst see both providence and grace preceding thee, forestalling thy needs, and preparing thy path. Mercy, in the case of many of us, ran before our desires and prayers, and it ever outruns our endeavours and expectancies, and even our hopes are left to lag behind. Prevenient grace deserves a song ; we may make one out of this sentence, let us try. All our mercies are to be viewed as " *blessings ;*" gifts of a blessed God, meant to make us blessed ; they are " *blessings of goodness,*" not of merit, but of free favour ; and they come to us in a *preventing way*, a way of prudent foresight, such as only preventing love could have arranged. In this light the verse is itself a sonnet !

" *Thou settest a crown of pure gold on his head.*" Jesus wore the thorn-crown, but now wears the glory-crown. It is a " *crown,*" indicating royal nature, imperial power, deserved honour, glorious conquest, and divine government. The crown is of the richest, rarest, most resplendent, and most lasting order—" *gold,*" and that gold of the most refined and valuable sort, " *pure gold,*" to indicate the excellence of his dominion. This crown is set upon his head most firmly, and whereas other monarchs find their diadems fitting loosely, his is fixed so that no power can move it, for Jehovah himself has set it upon his brow. Napoleon crowned himself, but Jehovah crowned the Lord Jesus ; the empire of the one melted in an hour, but the other has an abiding dominion. Some versions read," a crown of precious stones ;" this may remind us of those beloved ones who shall be as jewels in his crown, of whom he has said, " They shall be mine in the day when I make up my jewels." May we be set in the golden circlet of the Redeemer's glory, and adorn his head for ever !

4. " *He asked life of thee, and thou gavest it him, even length of days for ever and ever.*" The first words may suit King David, but the length of days for ever and ever can only refer to the King Messiah. Jesus, as man, prayed for resurrection and he received it, and now possesses it in immortality. He died once, but being raised from the dead he dieth no more. " Because I live, ye shall live also," is the delightful intimation which the Saviour gives us, that we are partakers of his eternal life. We had never found this jewel, if he had not rolled away the stone which covered it.

5. " *His glory is great in thy salvation.*" Immanuel bears the palm ; he once bore the cross. The Father has glorified his Son, so that there is no glory like unto that which surroundeth him. See his person as it is described by John in the Revelation ; see his dominion as it stretches from sea to sea ; see his splendour as he is revealed in flaming fire. Lord, who is like unto thee ? Solomon in all his glory could not be compared with thee, thou once despised Man of Nazareth ! Mark, reader : salvation is ascribed to God ; and thus the Son, as our Saviour, magnifies his Father ; but the Son's glory is also greatly seen, for the Father glorifies his Son.

" *Honour and majesty hast thou laid upon him.*" Parkhurst reads, " splendour and beauty." These are put upon Jesus, as chains of gold, and stars and tokens of honour are placed upon princes and great men. As the wood of the tabernacle was overlaid with pure gold, so is Jesus covered with glory and honour. If there be a far more exceeding and eternal weight of glory for his humble followers, what must there be for our Lord himself ? The whole weight of sin was laid upon him ; it is but meet that the full measure of the glory of bearing it away should be laid upon the same beloved person. A glory commensurate with his shame he must and will receive, for well has he earned it. It is not possible for us to honour Jesus too much ; what our God delights to do, we may certainly do to our utmost. Oh for new crowns for the lofty brow which once was marred with thorns !

> " Let him be crowned with majesty
>   Who bowed his head to death,
> And be his honours sounded high
>   By all thing that have breath."

6. " *For thou hast made him most blessed for ever.*" He is most blessed in himself, for he is God over all, blessed for ever ; but this relates to him as our Mediator, in which capacity blessedness is given to him as a reward. The margin has it, *thou hast set him to be blessings ;* he is an overflowing wellspring of blessings to others, a sun filling the universe with light. According as the Lord sware unto Abraham, the promised seed is an everlasting source of blessings to all the nations of the earth. He is set for this, ordained appointed, made incarnate with this very design, that he may bless the sons of men. Oh that sinners had sense enough to use the Saviour for that end to which he is ordained, viz., to be a Saviour to lost and guilty souls.

" *Thou hast made him exceeding glad with thy countenance.*" He who is a blessing to others cannot but be glad himself ; the unbounded good-doing of Jesus ensures him unlimited joy. The loving favour of his Father, the countenance of God, gives Jesus exceeding joy. This is the purest stream to drink of, and Jesus chooses no other. His joy is full. Its source is divine. Its continuance eternal. Its degree exceeding all bounds. The countenance of God makes the Prince of Heaven glad ; how ought we to seek it, and how careful should we be lest we should provoke him by our sins to hide his face from us ! Our anticipations may cheerfully fly forward to the hour when the joy of our Lord shall be shed abroad on all the saints, and the countenance of Jehovah shall shine upon all the blood-bought. So shall we " enter into the joy of our Lord."

So far all has been " the shout of them that triumph, the song of them that feast." Let us shout and sing with them, for Jesus is our King, and in his triumphs we share a part.

7 For the king trusteth in the LORD, and through the mercy of the most High he shall not be moved.

8 Thine hand shall find out all thine enemies : thy right hand shall find out those that hate thee.

9 Thou shalt make them as a fiery oven in the time of thine anger : the LORD shall swallow them up in his wrath, and the fire shall devour them.

10 Their fruit shalt thou destroy from the earth, and their seed from among the children of men.

11 For they intended evil against thee : they imagined a mischievous device, *which* they are not able *to perform*.

12 Therefore shalt thou make them turn their back, *when* thou shalt make ready *thine arrows* upon thy strings against the face of them.

13 Be thou exalted, LORD, in thine own strength : *so* will we sing and praise thy power.

7. *" For the king trusteth in the Lord."* Our Lord, like a true King and leader, was a master in the use of the weapons, and could handle well the shield of faith, for he has set us a brilliant example of unwavering confidence in God. He felt himself safe in his Father's care until his hour was come, he knew that he was always heard in heaven ; he committed his cause to him that judgeth right, and in his last moments he committed his spirit into the same hands. The joy expressed in the former verses was the joy of faith, and the victory achieved was due to the same precious grace. A holy confidence in Jehovah is the true mother of victories. This Psalm of triumph was composed long before our Lord's conflict began, but faith overleaps the boundaries of time, and chants her " Io triumphe," while yet she sings her battle song.

" Through the mercy of the Most High he shall not be moved." Eternal mercy secures the mediatorial throne of Jesus. He who is Most High in every sense, engages all his infinite perfections to maintain the throne of grace upon which our King in Zion reigns. He was not moved *from* his purpose, nor *in* his sufferings, nor *by* his enemies, nor shall he be moved *from* the completion of his designs. He is the same yesterday, to-day, and for ever. Other empires are dissolved by the lapse of years, but eternal mercy maintains his growing dominion evermore ; other kings fail because they rest upon an arm of flesh, but our monarch reigns on in splendour because he trusteth in Jehovah. It is a great display of divine mercy to men that the throne of King Jesus is still among them : nothing but divine mercy could sustain it, for human malice would overturn it to-morrow if it could. We ought to trust in God for the promotion of the Redeemer's kingdom, for in Jehovah the King himself trusts : all unbelieving methods of action, and especially all reliance upon mere human ability, should be for ever discarded from a kingdom where the monarch sets the example of walking by faith in God.

8. *" Thine hand shall find out all thine enemies : thy right hand shall find out those that hate thee."* The destruction of the wicked is a fitting subject for joy to the friends of righteousness ; hence here, and in most scriptural songs, it is noted with calm thanksgiving. " Thou hast put down the mighty from their seats," is a note of the same song which sings, " and hast exalted them of low degree." We pity the lost for they are men, but we cannot pity them as enemies of Christ. None can escape from the wrath of the victorious King, nor is it desirable that they should. Without looking for his flying foes he will find them with his hand, for his presence is about and around them. In vain shall any hope for escape, he will find out all, and be able to punish all, and that too with the ease and rapidity which belong to the warrior's right hand. The finding out relates, we think, not only to the discovery of the hiding-places of the haters of God, but to the touching of them in their tenderest parts, so as to cause the severest suffering. When he appears to judge the world hard hearts will be subdued into terror, and proud spirits humbled into shame. He who has the key of human nature can touch all its springs at his will, and find out the means of bringing the utmost confusion and terror upon those who aforetime boastfully expressed their hatred of him.

9. "*Thou shalt make them as a fiery oven in the time of thine anger.*" They themselves shall be an oven to themselves, and so their own tormentors. Those who burned with anger against thee shall be burned by thine anger. The fire of sin will be followed by the fire of wrath. Even as the smoke of Sodom and Gomorrah went up to heaven, so shall the enemies of the Lord Jesus be utterly and terribly consumed. Some read it, "thou shalt put them as it were into a furnace of fire." Like faggots cast into an oven they shall burn furiously beneath the anger of the Lord; "they shall be cast into a furnace of fire, there shall be weeping and gnashing of teeth." These are terrible words, and those teachers do not well who endeavour by their sophistical reasonings to weaken their force. Reader, never tolerate slight thoughts of hell, or you will soon have low thoughts of sin. The hell of sinners must be fearful beyond all conception, or such language as the present would not be used. Who would have the Son of God to be his enemy when such an overthrow awaits his foes? The expression, "the time of thine anger," reminds us that as now is the time of his grace, so there will be a set time for his wrath. The judge goes upon assize at an appointed time. There is a day of vengeance of our God; let those who despise the day of grace remember this day of wrath.

"*The Lord shall swallow them up in his wrath, and the fire shall devour them.*" Jehovah will himself visit with his anger the enemies of his Son. The Lord Jesus will, as it were, judge by commission from God, whose solemn assent and co-operation shall be with him in his sentences upon impenitent sinners. An utter destruction of soul and body, so that both shall be swallowed up with misery, and be devoured with anguish, is here intended. Oh, the wrath to come! The wrath to come! Who can endure it? Lord, save us from it, for Jesu's sake.

10. "*Their fruit shalt thou destroy from the earth.*" Their life's work shall be a failure, and the result of their toil shall be disappointment. That in which they prided themselves shall be forgotten; their very names shall be wiped out as abominable, "*and their seed from among the children of men.*" Their posterity following in their footsteps shall meet with a similar overthrow, till at last the race shall come to an end. Doubtless the blessing of God is often handed down by the righteous to their sons, as almost a heirloom in the family, while the dying sinner bequeaths a curse to his descendants. If men will hate the Son of God, they must not wonder if their own sons meet with no favour.

11. "*For they intended evil against thee.*" God takes notice of intentions. He who would, but could not, is as guilty as he who did. Christ's church and cause are not only attacked by those who do not understand it, but there are many who have the light and yet hate it. Intentional evil has a virus in it which is not found in sins of ignorance; now as ungodly men with malice aforethought attack the gospel of Christ, their crime is great, and their punishment will be proportionate. The words "*against thee*" show us that he who intends evil against the poorest believer means ill to the King himself: let persecutors beware.

"*They imagined a mischievous device, which they are not able to perform.*" Want of power is the clog on the foot of the haters of the Lord Jesus. They have the wickedness to *imagine*, and the cunning to *devise*, and the malice to *plot* mischief, but blessed be God, they fail in ability; yet they shall be judged as to their hearts, and the will shall be taken for the deed in the great day of account. When we read the boastful threatenings of the enemies of the gospel at the present day, we may close our reading by cheerfully repeating, "*which they are not able to perform.*" The serpent may hiss, but his head is broken; the lion may worry, but he cannot devour; the tempest may thunder, but cannot strike. Old Giant Pope bites his nails at the pilgrims, but he cannot pick their bones as aforetime. Growling forth a hideous "non possumus," the devil and all his allies retire in dismay from the walls of Zion, for the Lord is there.

12. "*Therefore shalt thou make them turn their back, when thou shalt make ready thine arrows upon thy strings against the face of them.*" For a time the foes of God may make bold advances, and threaten to overthrow everything, but a few ticks of the clock will alter the face of their affairs. At first they advance impudently enough, but Jehovah meets them to their teeth, and a taste of the sharp judgments of God speedily makes them flee in dismay. The original has in it the thought of the wicked being set as a butt for God to shoot at, a target for his wrath to aim at. What a dreadful situation! As an illustration upon a large scale, remember Jerusalem during the siege; and for a specimen in an individual, read the story

of the death-bed of Francis Spira. God takes sure aim; who would be his target? His arrows are sharp and transfix the heart; who would wish to be wounded by them? Ah, ye enemies of God, your boastings will soon be over when once the shafts begin to fly!

13. "*Be thou exalted, Lord, in thine own strength.*" A sweet concluding verse. Our hearts shall join in it. It is always right to praise the Lord when we call to remembrance his goodness to his Son, and the overthrow of his foes. The exaltation of the name of God should be the business of every Christian; but since such poor things as we fail to honour him as he deserves, we may invoke his own power to aid us. Be high, O God, but do thou maintain thy loftiness by thine own almightiness, for no other power can worthily do it.

"*So will we sing and praise thy power.*" For a time the saints may mourn, but the glorious appearance of their divine Helper awakens their joy. Joy should always flow in the channel of praise. All the attributes of God are fitting subjects to be celebrated by the music of our hearts and voices, and when we observe a display of his *power*, we must extol it. He wrought our deliverance alone, and he alone shall have the praise.

EXPLANATORY NOTES AND QUAINT SAYINGS.

Whole Psalm.—The last Psalm was a litany before the king went forth to battle This is apparently a *Te Deum* on his return.—*J. J. Stewart Perowne, B.D., in the " Book of Psalms : a New Translation, with Introductions and Notes,"* 1864.

Whole Psalm.—The prayer which the church offers up at the conclusion of the preceding Psalm now issues in a hymn of praise, the result of a believing view of the glory which is to follow, when Messiah's sufferings are ended. This is one of the beautiful songs of which we find many in Scripture, prepared by the Holy Spirit to awaken and enliven the hopes and expectations of the church while she waits for the Lord, and to give utterance to her joy at the time of his arrival. The theme is Messiah's exaltation and glory, and the time chosen for its delivery is just the moment when darkness covered the earth, and all nature seemed about to die with its expiring Lord. Scripture deals largely in contrasts. It seems to be suitable to the human mind to turn from one extreme to another. Man can endure any change, however violent and contradictory, but a long continuance, a sameness either of joy or sorrow, has a debilitating and depressing effect.—*R. H. Ryland.*

Whole Psalm.—" After this I looked . . . and behold a throne was set in heaven, and one sat on the throne." Rev. iv. 1, 2. Such may be considered as the description of this Psalm, after the foregoing prayer. "He who in the preceding Psalm," says St. Jerome, " was prayed for as having taking the form of a servant, in this is King of kings, and Lord of lords."—*Isaac Williams.*

Whole Psalm.—I am persuaded that there is not one who consents to the application of the preceding Psalm to Christ in his trouble, who will fail to recognise in this, Christ in his triumph. There he was in the dark valley—the valley of Achor; now he is on the mount of Zion; there he was enduring sorrow and travail; now he remembers no more the anguish, for joy that a spiritual seed is born into the world; there he was beset with deadly enemies, who encompassed him on every side; but here he has entered upon that which is written in Psalm lxxviii. 65, 66, " Then the Lord awaked as one out of sleep, and like a mighty man that shouteth by reason of wine. And he smote his enemies in the hinder parts: he put them to a perpetual reproach."—*Hamilton Verschoyle.*

Whole Psalm.—As you have already observed in the heading of this Psalm, it is said to have been composed by David. He wrote of himself in the third person, and as " *the king.*" He penned the Psalm, not so much for his own use, as for his people's. It is, in fact, a national anthem, celebrating the majesty and glory of David, but ascribing both to God—expressing confidence in David's future, but building that confidence upon God alone.—*Samuel Martin, in " Westminster Chapel Pulpit,"* 1860.

Verse 1.—" *Thy strength . . . thy salvation.*" So you have two words, " *virtus* and *salus*," strength and salvation. Note them well ; for not *virtus* without *salus*, nor *salus* without *virtus*, neither without the other is full, nor both without *Tua Domine*. In *virtute* is well, so it have in *salute* after it. For not in strength alone is there matter of joy, every way considered. No, not in *God's strength*, if it have not *salvation* behind it. Strength, not to smite us down, but strength to deliver ; this is the joyful side. Now turn it the other way. As strength, if it end in salvation, is just cause for joy, so salvation, if it go with strength, makes joy yet more joyful ; for it becomes a strong salvation, a mighty deliverance.—*Launcelot Andrews* (*Bishop*), 1555—1626, in " *Conspiracie of the Gowries.*"

Verse 1.—" *In thy salvation how greatly shall he rejoice.*" Oh, it is good rejoicing in the strength of that arm which shall never wither, and in the shadow of those wings which shall never cast their feathers ! in him that is not there yesterday and here to-day, but the same yesterday, to-day, and for ever ! For as he is, so shall the joy be.—*Launcelot Andrews.*

Verse 2.—" *Thou hast given him the desire of his soul.*" He desired to eat the passover, and to lay down his life when he would and again when he would to take it ; and thou hast given it to him. " *And hast not deprived him of the good pleasure of his lips.*" " My peace," saith he, " I leave with you ; " and it was done.—*Augustine, in loc.*

Verse 2 (first clause).—Good men are sure to have out their prayers either in money, or in money's worth, as they say—in that very thing, or a better.—*John Trapp.*

Verse 2.—" *Selah.*" See pp. 23, 26, 27, 35, 307.

Verse 3.—" *For thou preventest him with the blessings of goodness : thou settest a crown of pure gold on his head.*" The Son of God could not be more ready to ask for the blessings of the divine goodness, than the Father was to give them ; and his disposition is the same towards all his adopted sons. Christ, as King and Priest, weareth a crown of glory, represented by the purest and most resplendent of metals—gold. He is pleased to esteem his saints, excelling in different virtues, as the rubies, the sapphires, and the emeralds, which grace and adorn that crown. Who would not be ambitious of obtaining a place therein ?—*George Horne.*

Verse 3.—" *Thou hast prevented him with the blessings of goodness.*" As if he should say, " Lord, I never asked a kingdom, I never thought of a kingdom, but thou hast prevented me with the blessings of thy goodness." . . . . From whence I take up this note or doctrine, that it is a sweet thing and worthy of all our thankful acknowledgments, to be prevented with the blessings of God's goodness, or God's good blessings. . . . It is no new thing for God to walk in a way of preventing love and mercy with the children of men. Thus he hath always dealt, doth deal, and will deal ; thus he hath always dealt with the world, with the nations of the world, with great towns and places, with families, and with particular souls. . . . As for particular souls, you know how it was with Matthew the publican, sitting at the receipt of custom. " Come and follow me," says Christ ; preventing of him. And you know how it was with Paul : " I was a blasphemer, and I was a persecutor, but I obtained mercy." How so ? Did he seek it first ? ' No,' says he, ' I went breathing out threatenings against the people of God, and God met me, and un-horsed me ; God prevented me with his grace and mercy.' Thus Paul. And pray tell me what do you think of that whole chapter of Luke—the fifteenth ? There are three parables : the parable of the lost groat, of the lost sheep, and of the lost son. The woman lost her groat, and swept to find it, but did the groat make first towards the woman, or the woman make after the groat first ? The shepherd lost his sheep, but did the sheep make first after the shepherd, or the shepherd after the sheep ? Indeed, it is said concerning the lost son, that he first takes up a resolution, " I will return home to my father," but when his father saw him afar off, he ran and met him, and embraced him, and welcomed him home. Why ? But to show that the work of grace and mercy shall be all along carried on in a way of preventing love.—*Condensed from William Bridge*, 1600—1670.

Verse 3.—" *For thou hast prevented him with the blessings of sweetness.*" Because he had first quaffed the blessing of thy sweetness, the gall of our sins did not hurt him.—*Augustine.*

Verse 3.—" *Thou preventest him.*" The word " *prevent* " is now generally used to represent the idea of hindrance. " *Thou preventest him*," would mean commonly, " Thou hinderest him." But here the word " prevent " means *to go before*. Thou goest before him with the blessings of thy goodness as a pioneer, to make crooked ways straight, and rough places smooth ; or, as one who strews flowers in the path of another, to render the way beautiful to the eye and pleasant to the tread.— *Samuel Martin.*

Verse 3 (first clause).—The text is an acknowledgment of God's goodness. God had anticipated David's wants ; and he writes. " *Thou preventest*—thou goest before him—*with goodness*." The words " *blessings of goodness* " suggest that God's gifts are God's love embodied and expressed. And this greatly enhances the value of our blessings—that they are cups as full of God and of God's kindness as of happiness and blessedness.—*Samuel Martin.*

Verse 3 (first clause).—A large portion of our blessing is given us before our asking or seeking. Existence, reason, intellect, a birth in a Christian land, the calling of our nation to the knowledge of Christ, and Christ himself, with many other things, are unsought bestowed on men, as was David's right to the throne on him. No one ever asked for a Saviour till God of his own motion promised " the seed of the woman."—*William S. Plumer.*

Verse 3.—" *Thou settest a crown of pure gold on his head.*" Christ may be said to have a fourfold glory, or crown. 1. As God co-essential with the Father ; "the brightness of the Father's glory, and the express image of his person." Heb. i. 2, 3. 2. He hath a crown and glory as Mediator, in respect of the power, authority, and glory wherewith he is invested as God's great deputy, and anointed upon the hill of Zion, having power, and a rod of iron, even in reference to enemies. 3. He hath a crown and glory in respect of the manifestation of his glory in the executing of his offices, when he makes his mediatory power and glory apparent in particular steps : thus sometimes he is said *to take his power to him* (Rev. xi. 17) ; and is said *to be crowned* when the white horse of the gospel rides in triumph. Rev. vi. 2. The last step of this glory will be in the day of judgment ; in short, this consists in his exercising his former power committed to him as Mediator. 4. There is a crown and glory which is in a manner put on him by particular believers, when he is glorified by them, not by adding anything to his infinite glory, but by their acknowledging of him to be so.—*James Durham, 1622—1658.*

Verse 3.—The " *crown of pure gold* " has respect to his exaltation at the right hand of God, where he is crowned with glory and honour, and this " *crown* " being of " *pure gold*," denotes the purity, glory, solidity, and perpetuity of his kingdom.— *John Gill.*

Verse 4.—" *He asked life of thee, and thou gavest it him, even length of days for ever and ever.*" The glory of God is concerned in Christ's living for ever. 1. The glory of his *faithfulness :* for eternal life and blessedness were pledged to Immanuel in covenant as the reward of his work (Psalm cx. 1—4 ; Isaiah ix. 6, 7, etc.) ; and it was in the anticipation and confident hope of this, that he " endured the cross, despising the shame." Heb. xii. 2 ; Psalm xvi. 8—11. 2. The glory of his *justice*. The justice of God was honoured and fully satisfied in all its righteous demands by the death of Christ. His subsequent life is the expression on the part of God of that satisfaction. His perpetual life is a permanent declaration that in him and his finished work the everlasting righteousness of Jehovah rests for ever satisfied. Death can " never more have dominion over him : " for to inflict the penalty again would be a violation of justice. 3. The glory of his *grace*. The glory of this grace he now lives actively to promote. John xvii. 2. By living " *ever* " at God's right hand, he appears as an eternal memorial of God's love in making him our Mediator and Substitute—our Saviour from sin and wrath ; and his permanent appearance there will keep all heaven perpetually in mind that " by the grace of God they are what they are," owing all to the sovereign mercy of God through Jesus Christ. He shall appear as the blessed medium through which all the gifts and joys of salvation shall flow to the guilty for evermore. Thus the power of God and all his moral attributes secure the perpetuity of the life of the risen and exalted Saviour.—*Ralph Wardlaw, D.D.*

Verse 4.—" *He asked life of thee, and thou gavest it him.*" He asked a resurrection saying " Father, glorify thy Son ;" and thou gavest it him, " *Length of days for ever and ever.*" The prolonged ages of this world which the church was to have, and after them an eternity, world without end.—*Augustine.*

Verse 4.—" *He asked life of thee,*" etc. Thus God is better to his people than their prayers ; and when they ask but one blessing, he answereth them as Naaman did Gehazi, with Nay, take two. Hezekiah asked but one life, and God gave him fifteen years, which we reckon at two lives and more. He giveth liberally and like himself ; as great Alexander did when he gave the poor beggar a city ; and when he sent his schoolmaster a ship full of frankincense, and bade him sacrifice freely.—*John Trapp.*

Verses 4—8.—If David had before been without the symbol of his royal dignity, namely, the diadem, he was the more justified in praising the goodness of God, which had now transferred it from the head of an enemy to his own.—*Augustus F. Tholuck.*

Verse 5.—" *His glory is great in thy salvation.*"—I remember one dying and hearing some discourses of Jesus Christ ; " Oh," said she, " speak more of this— let me hear more of this—be not weary of telling his praise ; I long to see him, how should I but long to hear of him ? " Surely I cannot say too much of Jesus Christ. On this blessed subject no man can possibly hyperbolise. Had I the tongues of men and angels, I could never fully set forth Christ. It involves an eternal contradiction, that the creature can see to the bottom of the Creator. Suppose all the sands on the sea-shore, all the flowers, herbs, leaves, twigs of trees in woods and forests, all the stars of heaven, were all rational creatures ; and had they that wisdom, and tongues of angels to speak of the loveliness, beauty, glory, and excellency of Christ, as gone to heaven, and sitting at the right hand of his Father, they would, in all their expressions, stay millions of miles on this side Jesus Christ. Oh, the loveliness, beauty, and glory of his countenance ! Can I speak, or you hear of such a Christ ? And are we not all in a burning love, in a seraphical love, or at least in a conjugal love ? O my heart, how is it thou art not love sick ? How is it thou dost not charge the daughters of Jerusalem as the spouse did : " I charge you, O daughters of Jerusalem if ye find my beloved, that ye shall tell him, that I *am* sick of love." Cant. v. 8.—*Isaac Ambrose.*

Verse 5.—" *Honour and majesty hast thou laid upon him.*" If it be demanded whether Christ were exalted unto his glory and dignity, according to both his natures, both his Godhead and his manhood, I answer, according to both. According to his Godhead, not as it is considered in itself, but inasmuch as his Godhead, which from his birth unto his death did little show itself, after his resurrection was made manifest in his manhood ; for, as the apostle saith (Rom. i. 4), " He was declared mightily to be the Son of God by the resurrection from the dead," even by the resurrection, and after his resurrection from the dead, he which was thought only to be man, was most plainly manifested likewise to be God. Now, as touching his manhood, he was therein exalted unto highest majesty in the heavenly places, not only shaking off all infirmities of man's nature, but also being beautified and adorned with all qualities of glory, both in his soul and in his body, yet so that he still retaineth the properties of a true body, for even as he was man, he was set at the right hand of the Father, to rule and reign over all, till all his enemies be destroyed, and put under his feet. To knit up all in a word, Christ, God, and man, after his resurrection, was crowned with glory and honour, even such as plainly showed him to be God, and was set on the throne of God, there to rule and reign as sovereign Lord and King, till he come in the clouds to judge both quick and dead. Here, then, is both matter of comfort and consolation unto the godly, and likewise of fear and astonishment unto the wicked and ungodly.—*Henry Airay*, 1560—1616.

Verse 5 (*last clause.*)—Christ was " a man of sorrows " on earth, but he is full of joy in heaven. He that " wipes away all tears from the eyes of his people," surely has none of his own. There was a *joy set before him* before he suffered, and doubtless it was given him when he sat down at God's right hand. We may take the latter to be an actual donation of the former ; the joy he had in prospect when he suffered he had in possession when he came to his throne. This is the time of his receiving the Father's public approbation, and the tokens of his love, before the whole heavenly assembly, which must be matter of great joy to him who so much valued and delighted in his Father's love.—*John Hurrion*, 1675—1731.

Verse 5.—Happy he who hath a bone, or an arm, to put the crown upon the head of our highest King, whose chariot is paved with love. Were there ten thousand millions of heavens created above these highest heavens, and again as many above them, and as many above them, till angels were wearied with counting, it were but too low a seat to fix the princely throne of that Lord Jesus (whose ye are) above them all.—*Samuel Rutherford.*

Verse 6.—" *Thou hast made him exceeding glad :* " literally, " brightened him," possibly in allusion to the brightness of Moses' face.—*Dalman Hapstone, M.A., in " The Ancient Psalms . . . . A Literal Translation and Notes,"* etc , 1867.

Verse 6.—" *Thou hast made him exceeding glad with thy countenance.*" Though this be metaphorically used for *favour*, yet is the speech not all metaphor, and that well-experienced Christians will tell you.—*Zachary Bogan, in " The Mirth of a Christian Life,"* 1653.

Verse 6 (first clause).—Literally, as in the Bible marginal translation, " Thou hast set him *to be* blessings for ever." Most truly said of the King in whom all the nations of the earth were to be blessed.—*Richard Mant.*

Verse 8.—" *Thine hand shall find out all thine enemies : thy right hand shall find out those that hate thee.*" By a kind of climax in the form of expression, " hand," is followed by " *right hand,*" a still more emphatic sign of active strength. To " *find,*" in this connection, includes the ideas of detecting and reaching. Compare 1 Sam. xxiii. 17 ; Isaiah x. 10 ; in the latter of which places the verb is construed with a preposition (ל), as it is in the first clause of the verse before us, whereas in the other clause it governs the noun directly. If any difference of meaning was intended, it is probably not greater than that between *find* and *find out* in English. *Joseph Addison Alexander.*

Verse 8.—" *Thine hand shall find out all thine enemies : thy right hand shall find out those that hate thee.*" Saul killed himself, for fear of falling into the hands of his enemies, and thought death less terrible than the shame that he would have endured in seeing himself in their power. What will it be then " to fall into the hands of the living God " (Heb. x. 31), of an offended God ? of God unchangeably determined to be avenged ? " Who can stand before his indignation ? " says the prophet Nahum (chap. i. 6). Who will dare look on him ? Who will dare show himself ? " *Who may abide the day of his coming* " (Mal. iii. 2) without shuddering and fainting for fear ? If Joseph's brethren were so terrified that they " could not answer him," when he said, " I am Joseph your brother," how will it be with sinners, when they shall hear the voice of the Son of God, when he shall triumph over them in his wrath, and say unto them, " I am he " whom ye despised ; " I am he " whom ye have offended ; " I am he " whom ye have crucified ? If these words, " I am he," over- threw the soldiers in the garden of Olives (John xviii. 6), though spoken with extreme gentleness, how will it be when his indignation bursts forth, when it falls upon his enemies like a thunderbolt, and reduces them into dust ? Then will they cry out in terror and say to the mountains, " *Fall on us, and hide us from the face of him that sitteth on the throne, and from the wrath of the Lamb.*" Rev. vi. 16.—*James Nouet.*

Verse 8.—" *Thine hand shall find out,*" etc. It is not meant only of a discovery of a person (though it be a truth, that the Lord will discover all that are his enemies), but *thine hand shall find them out*, is, it shall take hold of them, grasp them, and arrest them. "Thine hand shall find out " *all* " thine enemies," though close, though covert enemies ; not only thy above-ground enemies, but thy under-ground enemies ; as well those that undermine thee, as those that assault thee.—*Joseph Caryl.*

Verse 9.—" *Thou shalt make them as a fiery oven in the time of thine anger : the Lord shall swallow them up in his wrath, and the fire shall devour them.*" How then shall it fare with sinners, when, after all, shall come that general fire so often foretold, which shall either fall from heaven, or ascend out of hell, or (according to Albertus Magnus), proceed from both, and shall devour and consume all it meets with ? Whither shall the miserable fly, when that river of flames, or (to say better), that inundation and deluge of fire shall so encompass them, as no place of surety shall be left where nothing can avail but a holy life ; when all besides shall perish, in that universal ruin of the whole world ? What lamentations were in Rome, when it burnt for seven days together ! What shrieks were heard in Troy, when it was wholly consumed with flames ! What howling and astonishment in Pentapolis, when those cities were destoyed with fire from heaven ! What weeping was there in Jerusalem, when they beheld the house of God, the glory of their kingdom, the wonder of the world, involved in fire and smoke ! Imagine what these people felt; they saw their houses and goods on fire, and no possibility of saving them; when the husband heard the shrieks and cries of his dying wife; the father, of his little children; and, unawares, perceived himself so encompassed with flames, that he could neither relieve them, nor free himself. What shall it then profit the worldlings, to have rich vessels of gold and silver, curious embroideries, precious tapestries, pleasant gardens, sumptuous palaces, and all what the world now esteems, when they shall with their own eyes, behold their costly palaces burnt, their rich and curious pieces of gold melted, and their flourishing and pleasant orchards consumed, without power to preserve them or themselves? All shall burn, and with it the world, and all the memory and fame of it shall die; and that which mortals thought to be immortal, shall then end and perish.—*Jeremy Taylor.*

Verse 9.—" *Thou shalt make them as a fiery oven in the time of thine anger.*" They shall not only be cast into a furnace of fire (Matt. xiii. 42), but he shall make them themselves as a fiery oven or furnace, they shall be their own tormentors, the reflections and terrors of their own consciences will be their hell. Those that might have had Christ to rule and save them, but rejected him, and fought against him, even the remembrance of that will be enough to make them to eternity a fiery oven to themselves.—*Matthew Henry.*

Verse 9.—" *Thou shalt make them as a fiery oven :*" thou shalt make them on fire within, by the consciousness of their ungodliness: " *In the time of thy countenance ;*" in the time of thy manifestation.—*Augustine.*

Verse 9.—"*As a fiery oven,*" where the burning is extremely hot, the heat striking upon what is in it from all sides, above, below, and about, on all hands, and the door closed from going out, or from suffering any cool refreshment to come in.—*David Dickson.*

Verse 9.—"*As a fiery oven.*" Shall make them like a vault of fire, literally, " *an oven,*" as in our translation, or " furnace of fire." Bishop Horsley remarks, " It describes the smoke of the Messiah's enemies perishing by fire, ascending like the smoke of a furnace. ' The smoke of their torments shall ascend for ever and ever.' " How awfully grand is that description of the ruins of the cities of the plain, as the prospect struck on Abraham's eye on the fatal morning of their destruction! " And he looked toward Sodom and Gomorrah, and toward all the land of the plain, and beheld, and, lo, the smoke of the country went up as the smoke of a furnace." Milton puts it—

> " Overhead the dismal hiss
> Of fiery darts in flaming volleys flew,
> And flying vaulted either host with fire."

Richard Mant.

Verse 9.—The Chaldee reads :—" The fire of Gehenna, or hell."—*John Morison.*

Verse 9.—" *The time of thine anger.*" If God be willing to pour out his heavy displeasure upon those that displease him, what can hinder his mighty arm from performing? Creatures indeed may be angry, but oftentimes, like drones without stings, cannot hurt; as cannons charged with powder without shot only make a roaring; like the Pope's Bulls, threaten many, hurt none but those whose consciences are enslaved. Saul may be angry at David, but cannot find him out; but from God's all-piercing eye none can hide himself. Satan may desire to kill Job, Jonah may be angry till death for Nineveh's preservation; yet God puts a bit in both their mouths, who, if he be angry, nothing can be holden out of his reach. Princes, if they take captives, may have them rescued from them again, as Lot was from the King of Sodom; bought with a price, as Joseph of the Ishmaelites. But no power can rescue us from God's anger, no ransom but Christ's blood redeem us. God's will being set afoot, all his attributes follow; if his will say, Be angry, his eye seeks out the object of his anger, and finds it; his wisdom tempers the cup, his hand whets the sword, his arm strikes the blow. Thus you see there is a time of God's anger for sin, because he will have it so.—*John Cragge.*

Verse 9.—" *The fire shall devour them.*" Being troubled by the vengeance of the Lord, after the accusation of their conscience, they shall be given up to eternal fire to be devoured.—*Augustine.*

Verse 9.—I have read that a frown of Queen Elizabeth killed Sir Christopher Hatton, the Lord Chancellor of England. What then shall the frowns of the King of nations do? If the rocks rend, the mountains melt, and the foundations of the earth tremble under his wrath; how will the ungodly sinner appear when he comes in all his royal glory to take vengeance on all that knew him not, and that obeyed not his glorious gospel.—*Charles Bradbury.*

Verse 10.—" *Their fruit shalt thou destroy from the earth, and their seed from among the children of men.*" A day is coming when all the " *fruits* " of sin, brought forth by sinners in their words, their writings, and their actions shall be " *destroyed ;* " yea, the tree itself, which had produced them, shall be rooted up, and cast into the fire. The " *seed* " and posterity of the wicked, if they continue in the way of their forefathers, will be punished like them. Let parents consider, that upon their principles and practices may depend the salvation or destruction of multitudes after them. The case of the Jews, daily before their eyes, should make them tremble.—*George Horne.*

Verse 11.—" *They intended,*" or warped. Hebrew, *hvae bent or stretched.* A similitude taken from weavers, who warp their yarn before they weave : or from archers, who, when they have bent their bow and put in their arrow, do take their aim.—*John Diodati.*

Verse 12.—" *Therefore shalt thou make them turn their back,*" or, *thou shalt set them as a butt,* "*when thou shalt make ready thine arrows upon thy strings against the face of them.*" The judgments of God are called his " *arrows,*" being sharp, swift, sure, and deadly. What a dreadful situation, to be set as a mark and " *butt* " at which these arrows are directed ! View Jerusalem encompassed by the Roman armies without, and torn to pieces by the animosity of desperate and bloody factions within ! No farther commentary is requisite upon this verse.—*George Horne.*

HINTS TO PREACHERS.

Verse 1.—The joy of Jesus and of his people in the strength and salvation of God.

Verses 1, 2.—The doctrine of the resurrection of Jesus Christ contained in the text, may be considered under three heads :—I. *As an answer to prayer.* II. *His joy therein—even in the resurrection.* III. As a necessary appendage to this— *our own individual concern in his glory and in his joy.*—*Hamilton Verschoyle.*

Verse 2.—The successful Advocate.

Verse 3 (first clause).—Preventing mercies.

Verse 3 (first clause).—GOD GOING BEFORE US, or, God's anticipation of our necessities by his merciful dispensations. God prevents us with the blessings of his goodness :—I. When we come into the world. II. When we become personal transgressors. III. When we enter upon the duties and upon the cares of mature life. IV. When, in the general course of life, we enter upon new paths. V. In the dark " valley of the shadow of death." VI. By giving us many mercies without our asking for them ; and thus creating occasion, not for prayer, but for praise only. VII. By opening to us the gate of heaven, and by storing heaven with every provision for our blessedness.—*Samuel Martin.*

Verse 3 (second clause).—Jesus crowned. I. His previous labours. II. The dominion bestowed. III. The character of the crown. IV. The divine coronant.

Verse 4.—Jesus ever living.

Verse 5.—The glory of the Mediator.

Verse 6.—The blessedness of Jesus.

Verse 7.—Jesus, an example of faith and of its results.

Verse 8.—The secret sinner unearthed, and deprived of all hope of concealment.

Verses 8, 9.—The certainty and terror of the punishment of the wicked.

Verses 11, 12.—The guilt and punishment of evil intentions.

Verse 12.—The retreat of the grand army of hell.

Verse 13.—*A devout Doxology.* I. God exalted. II. God alone exalted. III. God exalted by his own strength. IV. His people singing his praise.

PSALM XXII.

TITLE.—" To the chief Musician upon Aijeleth Shahar. A Psalm of David."
*This ode of singular excellence was committed to the most excellent of the temple
songsters : the chief among ten thousand is worthy to be extolled by the chief Musician ;
no meaner singer must have charge of such a strain ; we must see to it that we call up
our best abilities when Jesus is the theme of praise.* The words Aijeleth Shahar *are
enigmatical, and their meaning is uncertain ; some refer them to a musical instrument
used upon mournful occasions, but the majority adhere to the translation of our margin,
" Concerning the hind of the morning." This last interpretation is the subject of much
enquiry and conjecture. Calmet believes that the Psalm was addressed to the music
master who presided over the band called the " Morning Hind," and Adam Clarke
thinks this to be the most likely of all the conjectural interpretations, although he himself
inclines to the belief that no interpretation should be attempted, and believes that it is a
merely arbitrary and unmeaning title, such as Orientals have always been in the habit
of appending to their songs. Our Lord Jesus is so often compared to a hind, and
his cruel huntings are so pathetically described in this most affecting psalm, that we
cannot but believe that the title indicates the Lord Jesus under a well-known poetical
metaphor ; at any rate, Jesus is that Hind of the morning concerning whom David
here sings.*

SUBJECT.—*This is beyond all others* THE PSALM OF THE CROSS. *It may have been
actually repeated word by word by our Lord when hanging on the tree ; it would be
too bold to say that it was so, but even a casual reader may see that it might have been.
It begins with, " My God, my God, why hast thou forsaken me ? " and ends, according
to some, in the original with " It is finished." For plaintive expressions uprising
from unutterable depths of woe we may say of this Psalm, " there is none like it." It
is the photograph of our Lord's saddest hours, the record of his dying words, the lachrymatory of his last tears, the memorial of his expiring joys. David and his afflictions
may be here in a very modified sense, but, as the star is concealed by the light of the
sun, he who sees Jesus will probably neither see nor care to see David. Before us we
have a description both of the darkness and of the glory of the cross, the sufferings of
Christ and the glory which shall follow. Oh for grace to draw near and see this great
sight ! We should read reverently, putting off our shoes from off our feet, as Moses
did at the burning bush, for if there be holy ground anywhere in Scripture it is in this
Psalm.*

DIVISION.—*From the commencement to the twenty-first verse is a most pitiful cry
for help, and from verse 21 to 31 is a most precious foretaste of deliverance. The first
division may be sub-divided at the tenth verse, from verse 1 to 10 being an appeal based
upon covenant relationship ; and from verse 10 to 21 being an equally earnest plea
derived from the imminence of his peril.*

EXPOSITION.

MY God, my God, why hast thou forsaken me ? *why art thou so* far from
helping me, *and from* the words of my roaring ?

2 O my God, I cry in the daytime, but thou hearest not ; and in the night
season, and am not silent.

3 But thou *art* holy, *O thou* that inhabitest the praises of Israel.

4 Our fathers trusted in thee : they trusted, and thou didst deliver them.

5 They cried unto thee, and were delivered : they trusted in thee, and
were not confounded.

6 But I *am* a worm, and no man ; a reproach of men, and despised of
the people.

7 All they that see me laugh me to scorn : they shoot out the lip, they
shake the head, *saying,*

8 He trusted on the LORD *that* he would deliver him : let him deliver him, seeing he delighted in him.

9 But thou *art* he that took me out of the womb : thou didst make me hope *when I was* upon my mother's breasts.

10 I was cast upon thee from the womb : thou *art* my God from my mother's belly.

1. "*My God, my God, why hast thou forsaken me?*" This was the startling cry of Golgotha : Eloi, Eloi, lama sabacthani. The Jews mocked, but the angels adored when Jesus cried this exceeding bitter cry. Nailed to the tree we behold our great Redeemer in extremities, and what see we? Having ears to hear let us hear, and having eyes to see let us see! Let us gaze with holy wonder, and and mark the flashes of light amid the awful darkness of that midday-midnight. First, our Lord's faith beams forth and deserves our reverent imitation ; he keeps his hold upon his God with both hands and cries twice, "*My God, my God!*" The spirit of adoption was strong within the suffering Son of Man, and he felt no doubt about his interest in his God. Oh that we could imitate this cleaving to an afflicting God! Nor does the sufferer distrust the power of God to sustain him, for the title used—"*El*"—signifies *strength*, and is the name of the Mighty God. He knows the Lord to be the all-sufficient support and succour of his spirit, and therefore appeals to him in the agony of grief, but not in the misery of doubt. He would fain know why he is left, he raises that question and repeats it, but neither the power nor the faithfulness of God does he mistrust. What an enquiry is this before us! "*Why hast thou forsaken me?*" We must lay the emphasis on every word of this saddest of all utterances. "*Why?*" what is the great cause of such a strange fact as for God to leave his own Son at such a time and in such a plight? There was no cause in him, why then was he deserted? "*Hast:*" it is done, and the Saviour is feeling its dread effect as he asks the question ; it is surely true, but how mysterious! It was no threatening of forsaking which made the great Surety cry aloud, he endured that forsaking in very deed. "*Thou:*" I can understand why traitorous Judas and timid Peter should be gone, but *thou*, my God, my faithful friend, how canst thou leave me? This is worst of all, yea worse than all put together. Hell itself has for its fiercest flame the separation of the soul from God. "*Forsaken:*" if thou hadst chastened I might bear it, for they face would shine ; but to forsake me utterly, ah! why is this? "*Me:*" thine innocent, obedient, suffering Son, why leavest thou *me to* perish? A sight of self seen by penitence, and of Jesus on the cross seen by faith will best expound this question. Jesus is forsaken because our sins had separated between us and our God.

"*Why art thou so far from helping me, and from the words of my roaring?*" The Man of Sorrows had prayed until his speech failed him, and he could only utter moanings and groanings as men do in severe sicknesses, like the roarings of a wounded animal. To what extremity of grief was our Master driven! What strong crying and tears were those which made him too hoarse for speech! What must have been his anguish to find his own beloved and trusted Father standing afar off, and neither granting help nor apparently hearing prayer. This was good cause to make him "roar." Yet there was a reason for all this which those who rest in Jesus as their Substitute well know.

2. "*O my God, I cry in the daytime, but thou hearest not.*" For our prayers to appear to be unheard is no new trial, Jesus felt it before us, and it is observable that he still held fast his believing hold on God, and cried still, "*My God.*" On the other hand his faith did not render him less importunate, for amid the hurry and horror of that dismal day he ceased not his cry, even as in Gethsemane he had agonized all through the gloomy night. Our Lord continued to pray even though no comfortable answer came, and in this he set us an example of obedience to his own words, "men ought always to pray, and not to faint." No daylight is too glaring, and no midnight too dark to pray in ; and no delay or apparent denial, however grievous, should tempt us to forbear from importunate pleading.

3. "*But thou art holy, O thou that inhabitest the praises of Israel.*" However ill things may look, there is no ill in thee, O God! We are very apt to think and speak hardly of God when we are under his afflicting hand, but not so the obedient Son. He knows too well his Father's goodness to let outward circumstances libel his character. There is no unrighteousness with the God of Jacob, he deserves

no censures ; let him do what he will, he is to be praised, and to reign enthroned amid the songs of his chosen people. If prayer be unanswered it is not because God is unfaithful, but for some other good and weighty reason. If we cannot perceive any ground for the delay, we must leave the riddle unsolved, but we must not fly in God's face in order to invent an answer. While the holiness of God is in the highest degree acknowledged and adored, the afflicted speaker in this verse seems to marvel how the holy God could forsake him, and be silent to his cries. The argument is, thou art holy, oh ! why is it that thou dost disregard thy holy One in his hour of sharpest anguish ? We may not question the holiness of God, but we may argue from it, and use it as a plea in our petitions.

4. "*Our fathers trusted in thee : they trusted, and thou didst deliver them.*" This is the rule of life with all the chosen family. Three times over is it mentioned, they *trusted,* and *trusted,* and *trusted,* and never left off trusting, for it was their very life ; and they fared well too, for *thou didst deliver them.* Out of all their straits, difficulties, and miseries faith brought them by calling their God to the rescue ; but in the case of our Lord it appeared as if faith would bring no assistance from heaven, he alone of all the trusting ones was to remain without deliverance. The experience of other saints may be a great consolation to us when in deep waters if faith can be sure that their deliverance will be ours ; but when we feel ourselves sinking, it is poor comfort to know that others are swimming. Our Lord here pleads the past dealings of God with his people as a reason why he should not be left alone ; here again he is an example to us in the skilful use of the weapon of all prayer. The use of the plural pronoun "*our*" shows how one with his people Jesus was even on the cross. We say, "Our Father which art in heaven," and he calls those "our fathers" through whom we came into the world, although he was without father as to the flesh.

5. "*They cried unto thee, and were delivered : they trusted in thee, and were not confounded.*" As if he had said, "How is it that I am now left without succour in my overwhelming griefs, while all others have been helped?" We may remind the Lord of his former lovingkindnesses to his people, and beseech him to be still the same. This is true wrestling ; let us learn the art. Observe, that ancient saints *cried* and *trusted,* and that in trouble we must do the same ; and the invariable result was that they were not ashamed of their hope, for deliverance came in due time ; this same happy portion shall be ours. The prayer of faith can do the deed when nothing else can. Let us wonder when we see Jesus using the same pleas as ourselves, and immersed in griefs far deeper than our own.

6. "*But I am a worm, and no man.*" This verse is a miracle in language. How could the Lord of glory be brought to such abasement as to be not only lower than the angels, but even lower than men. What a contrast between "I AM" and "*I am a worm*" ! yet such a double nature was found in the person of our Lord Jesus when bleeding on the tree. He felt himself to be comparable to a helpless, powerless, down-trodden worm, passive while crushed, and unnoticed and despised by those who trod upon him. He selects the weakest of creatures, which is all flesh ; and becomes, when trodden upon, writhing, quivering flesh, utterly devoid of any might except strength to suffer. This was a true likeness of himself when his body and soul had become a mass of misery—the very essence of agony—in the dying pangs of crucifixion. Man by nature is but a worm ; but our Lord puts himself even beneath man, on account of the scorn which was heaped upon him and the weakness which he felt, and therefore he adds, "*and no man.*" The privileges and blessings which belonged to the fathers he could not obtain while deserted by God, and common acts of humanity were not allowed him, for he was rejected of men ; he was outlawed from the society of earth, and shut out from the smile of heaven. How utterly did the Saviour empty himself of all glory, and become of no reputation for our sakes ! "*A reproach of men*"—their common butt and jest ; a byword and a proverb unto them : the sport of the rabble, and the scorn of the rulers. Oh the caustic power of reproach, to those who endure it with patience, yet smart under it most painfully ! "*And despised of the people.*" The *vox populi* was against him. The very people who would once have crowned him then contemned him, and they who were benefited by his cures sneered at him in his woes. Sin is worthy of all reproach and contempt, and for this reason Jesus, the Sinbearer, was given up to be thus unworthily and shamefully entreated.

7, 8. "*All they that see me laugh me to scorn.*" Read the evangelistic narrative of the ridicule endured by the Crucified One, and then consider, in the light of this expression, how it grieved him. The iron entered into his soul. Mockery has for its distinctive description " cruel mockings ; " those endured by our Lord were of the most cruel kind. The scornful ridicule of our Lord was universal ; all sorts of men were unanimous in the derisive laughter, and vied with each other in insulting him. Priest and people, Jews and Gentiles, soldiers and civilians, all united in the general scoff, and that at the time when he was prostrate in weakness and ready to die. Which shall we wonder at the most, the cruelty of man or the love of the bleeding Saviour ? How can we ever complain of ridicule after this ?

" *They shoot out the lip, they shake the head.*" These were gestures of contempt. Panting, grinning, shaking of the head, thrusting out of the tongue, and other modes of derision were endured by our patient Lord ; men made faces at him before whom angels vail their faces and adore. The basest signs of disgrace which disdain could devise were maliciously cast at him. They punned upon his prayers, they made matter for laughter of his sufferings, and set him utterly at nought. Herbert sings of our Lord as saying,—

> "Shame tears my soul, my body many a wound ;
> Sharp nails pierce this, but sharper that confound ;
> Reproaches which are free, while I am bound.
> Was ever grief like mine ? "

" *Saying, He trusted on the Lord that he would deliver him : let him deliver him, seeing he delighted in him.*" Here the taunt is cruelly aimed at the sufferer's faith in God, which is the tenderest point in a good man's soul, the very apple of his eye. They must have learned the diabolical art from Satan himself, for they made rare proficiency in it. According to Matthew xxvii. 39—44, there were five forms of taunt hurled at the Lord Jesus ; this special piece of mockery is probably mentioned in this psalm because it is the most bitter of the whole ; it has a biting, sarcastic irony in it, which gives it a peculiar venom ; it must have stung the Man of Sorrows to the quick. When we are tormented in the same manner, let us remember him who endured such contradiction of sinners against himself, and we shall be comforted. On reading these verses one is ready, with Trapp, to ask, Is this a prophecy or a history ? for the description is so accurate. We must not lose sight of the truth which was unwittingly uttered by the Jewish scoffers. They themselves are witnesses that Jesus of Nazareth trusted in God : why then was he permitted to perish ? Jehovah had aforetime delivered those who rolled their burdens upon him : why was this man deserted ? Oh that they had understood the answer ! Note further, that their ironical jest, " *seeing he delighted in him,*" was true. The Lord did delight in his dear Son, and when he was found in fashion as a man, and became obedient unto death, he still was well pleased in him. Strange mixture ! Jehovah delights in him, and yet bruises him ; is well pleased, and yet slays him.

9. " *But thou art he that took me out of the womb.*" Kindly providence attends with the surgery of tenderness at every human birth ; but the Son of Man, who was marvellously begotten of the Holy Ghost, was in an especial manner watched over by the Lord when brought forth by Mary. The destitute state of Joseph and Mary, far away from friends and home, led them to see the cherishing hand of God in the safe delivery of the mother, and the happy birth of the child ; that Child now fighting the great battle of his life, uses the mercy of his nativity as an argument with God. Faith finds weapons everywhere. He who wills to believe shall never lack reasons for believing. " *Thou didst make me hope when I was upon my mother's breasts.*" Was our Lord so early a believer ? Was he one of those babes and sucklings out of whose mouths strength is ordained ? So it would seem ; and if so, what a plea for help ! Early piety gives peculiar comfort in our after trials, for surely he who loved us when we were children is too faithful to cast us off in our riper years. Some give the text the sense of " gave me cause to trust, by keeping me safely," and assuredly there was a special providence which preserved our Lord's infant days from the fury of Herod, the dangers of travelling, and the ills of poverty.

10. " *I was cast upon thee from the womb.*" Into the Almighty arms he was first received, as into those of a loving parent. This is a sweet thought. God begins his care over us from the earliest hour. We are dandled upon the knee of mercy, and cherished in the lap of goodness ; our cradle is canopied by divine love, and our first totterings are guided by his care. " *Thou art my God from my mother's belly.*" The psalm begins with " *My God, my God,*" and here, not only is the claim repeated, but its early date is urged. Oh noble perseverance of faith, thus to con-

tinue pleading with holy ingenuity of argument ! Our birth was our weakest and most perilous period of existence ; if we were then secured by Omnipotent tenderness surely we have no cause to suspect that divine goodness will fail us now. He who was our God when we left our mother will be with us till we return to mother earth, and will keep us from perishing in the belly of hell.

11 Be not far from me ; for trouble *is* near ; for *there is* none to help

12 Many bulls have compassed me : strong *bulls* of Bashan have beset me round.

13 They gaped upon me *with* their mouths, *as* a ravening and a roaring lion.

14 I am poured out like water, and all my bones are out of joint, my heart is like wax ; it is melted in the midst of my bowels.

15 My strength is dried up like a potsherd ; and my tongue cleaveth to my jaws ; and thou hast brought me into the dust of death.

16 For dogs have compassed me : the assembly of the wicked have inclosed me : they pierced my hands and my feet.

17 I may tell all my bones : they look *and* stare upon me.

18 They part my garments among them, and cast lots upon my vesture.

19 But be not thou far from me, O LORD : O my strength, haste thee to help me.

20 Deliver my soul from the sword ; my darling from the power of the dog.

21 Save me from the lion's mouth : for thou hast heard me from the horns of the unicorns.

The crucified Son of David continues to pour out his complaint and prayer. We need much grace that while reading we may have fellowship with his sufferings. May the blessed Spirit conduct us into a most clear and affecting sight of our Redeemer's woes.

11. *" Be not far from me."* This is the petition for which he has been using such varied and powerful pleas. His great woe was that God had forsaken him, his great prayer is that he would be near him. A lively sense of the divine presence is a mighty stay to the heart in times of distress. *" For trouble is near ; for there is none to help."* There are two " fors," as though faith gave a double knock at mercy's gate ; that is a powerful prayer which is full of holy reasons and thoughtful arguments. The nearness of trouble is a weighty motive for divine help ; this moves our heavenly Father's heart, and brings down his helping hand. It is his glory to be our very present help in trouble. Our Substitute had trouble in his inmost heart, for he said, "the waters have come in, even unto my soul ; " well might he cry, *" be not far from me."* The absence of all other helpers is another telling plea. In our Lord's case none either could or would help him, it was needful that he should tread the winepress alone ; yet was it a sore aggravation to find that all his disciples had forsaken him, and lover and friend were put far from him. There is an awfulness about absolute friendlessness which is crushing to the human mind, for man was not made to be alone, and is like a dismembered limb when he has to endure heart-loneliness.

12. *" Many bulls have compassed me : strong bulls of Bashan have beset me round."* The mighty ones in the crowd are here marked by the tearful eye of their victim. The priests, elders, scribes, Pharisees, rulers, and captains bellowed round the cross like wild cattle, fed in the fat and solitary pastures of Bashan, full of strength and fury ; they stamped and foamed around the innocent One, and longed to gore him to death with their cruelties. Conceive of the Lord Jesus as a helpless, unarmed, naked man, cast into the midst of a herd of infuriated wild bulls. They were brutal as bulls, many, and strong, and the Rejected One was all alone, and bound naked to the tree. His position throws great force into the earnest entreaty, " Be not far from me."

13. *" They gaped upon me with their mouths, as a ravening and a roaring lion."* Like hungry cannibals they opened their blasphemous mouths as if they were about to swallow the man whom they abhorred. They could not vomit forth their anger fast enough through the ordinary aperture of their mouths, and therefore set the

doors of their lips wide open like those who gape. Like roaring lions they howled out their fury, and longed to tear the Saviour in pieces, as wild beasts raven over their prey. Our Lord's faith must have passed through a most severe conflict while he found himself abandoned to the tender mercies of the wicked, but he came off victorious by prayer ; the very dangers to which he was exposed being used to add prevalence to his entreaties.

14. Turning from his enemies, our Lord describes his own personal condition in language which should bring the tears into every loving eye. " *I am poured out like water.*" He was utterly spent, like water poured upon the earth ; his heart failed him, and had no more firmness in it than running water, and his whole being was made a sacrifice, like a libation poured out before the Lord. He had long been a fountain of tears ; in Gethsemane his heart welled over in sweat, and on the cross he gushed forth with blood ; he poured out his strength and spirit, so that he was reduced to the most feeble and exhausted state. " *All my bones are out of joint,*" as if distended upon a rack. Is it not most probable that the fastening of the hands and feet, and the jar occasioned by fixing the cross in the earth, may have dislocated the bones of the Crucified One ? If this is not intended, we must refer the expression to that extreme weakness which would occasion relaxation of the muscles and a general sense of parting asunder thoroughout the whole system. " *My heart is like wax ; it is melted in the midst of my bowels.*" Excessive debility and intense pain made his inmost life to feel like wax melted in the heat. The Greek liturgy uses the expression, " thine unknown sufferings," and well it may. The fire of Almighty wrath would have consumed our souls for ever in hell ; it was no light work to bear as a substitute the heat of an anger so justly terrible. Dr. Gill wisely observes, "if the heart of Christ, the Lion of the tribe of Judah, melted at it, what heart can endure or hands be strong, when God deals with them in his wrath ? "

15. " *My strength is dried up like a potsherd.*" Most complete debility is here portrayed ; Jesus likens himself to a broken piece of earthenware, or an earthen pot, baked in the fire till the last particle of moisture is driven out of the clay. No doubt a high degree of feverish burning afflicted the body of our Lord. All his strength was dried up in the tremendous flames of avenging justice, even as the paschal lamb was roasted in the fire. " *My tongue cleaveth to my jaws ;* " thirst and fever fastened his tongue to his jaws. Dryness and a horrible clamminess tormented his mouth, so that he could scarcely speak. " *Thou hast brought me into the dust of death ;* " so tormented in every single part as to feel dissolved into separate atoms, and each atom full of misery ; the full price of our redemption was paid, and no part of the Surety's body or soul escaped its share of agony. The words may set forth Jesus as having wrestled with Death until he rolled into the dust with his antagonist. Behold the humiliation of the Son of God ! The Lord of Glory stoops to the dust of death. Amid the mouldering relics of mortality Jesus condescends to lodge !

Bishop Mant's version of the two preceding verses is forcible and accurate :—

> " Pour'd forth like water is my frame ;
>   My bones asunder start ;
> As wax that feels the searching flame,
>   Within me melts my heart.
> My wither'd sinews shrink unstrung
>   Like potsherd dried and dead :
> Cleaves to my jaws my burning tongue
>   The dust of death my bed."

16. We are to understand every item of this sad description as being urged by the Lord Jesus as a plea for divine help ; and this will give us a high idea of his perseverance in prayer. " *For dogs have compassed me.*" Here he marks the more ignoble crowd, who, while less strong than their brutal leaders, were not less ferocious, for there they were howling and barking like unclean and hungry dogs. Hunters frequently surround their game with a circle, and gradually encompass them within an ever-narrowing ring of dogs and men. Such a picture is before us. In the centre stands, not a panting stag, but a bleeding, fainting man, and around him are the enraged and unpitying wretches who have hounded him to his doom. Here we have the " hind of the morning " of whom the psalm so plaintively sings, hunted by bloodhounds, all thirsting to devour him. *The assembly of the wicked have inclosed me :* thus the Jewish people were unchurched, and that which called itself an

assembly of the righteous is justly for its sins marked upon the forehead as an assembly of the wicked. This is not the only occasion when professed churches of God have become synagogues of Satan, and have persecuted the Holy One and the Just. *They pierced my hands and my feet.* This can by no means refer to David, or to any one but Jesus of Nazareth, the once crucified but now exalted Son of God. Pause, dear reader, and view the wounds of thy Redeemer.

17. So emaciated was Jesus by his fastings and sufferings that he says, " *I may tell all my bones."* He could count and re-count them. The posture of the body on the cross, Bishop Horne thinks, would so distend the flesh and skin as to make the bones visible, so that they might be numbered. The zeal of his Father's house had eaten him up ; like a good soldier he had endured hardness. Oh that we cared less for the body's enjoyment and ease and more for our Father's business ! It were better to count the bones of an emaciated body than to bring leanness into our souls.

" They look and stare upon me." Unholy eyes gazed insultingly upon the Saviour's nakedness, and shocked the sacred delicacy of his holy soul. The sight of the agonizing body ought to have ensured sympathy from the throng, but it only increased their savage mirth, as they gloated their cruel eyes upon his miseries. Let us blush for human nature and mourn in sympathy with our Redeemer's shame. The first Adam made us all naked, and therefore the second Adam became naked that he might clothe our naked souls.

18. *" They part my garments among them, and cast lots upon my vesture."* The garments of the executed were the perquisites of the executioners in most cases, but it was not often that they cast lots at the division of the spoil ; this incident shows how clearly David in vision saw the day of Christ, and how surely the Man of Nazareth is he of whom the prophets spake: " these things, *therefore,* the soldiers did." He who gave his blood to cleanse us gave his garments to clothe us. As Ness says, " this precious Lamb of God gave up his golden fleece for us." How every incident of Jesus' griefs is here stored up in the treasury of inspiration, and embalmed in the amber of sacred song ; we must learn hence to be very mindful of all that concerns our Beloved, and to think much of everything which has a connection with him. It may be noted that the habit of gambling is of all others the most hardening, for men could practise it even at the cross-foot while besprinkled with the blood of the Crucified. No Christian will endure the rattle of the dice when he thinks of this.

19. *" But be not thou far from me, O Lord."* Invincible faith returns to the charge, and uses the same means, viz., importunate prayer. He repeats the petition so piteously offered before. He wants nothing but his God, even in his lowest state. He does not ask for the most comfortable or nearest presence of God, he will be content if he is not far from him ; humble requests speed at the throne. *" O my strength, haste thee to help me."* Hard cases need timely aid: when necessity justifies it we may be urgent with God as to time and cry, " make haste ; " but we must not do this out of wilfulness. Mark how in the last degree of personal weakness he calls the Lord " *my strength ;* " after this fashion the believer can sing, " when I am weak, then am I strong."

20. *" Deliver my soul from the sword."* By the sword is probably meant entire destruction, which as a man he dreaded ; or perhaps he sought deliverance from the enemies around him, who were like a sharp and deadly sword to him. The Lord had said, " Awake, O sword," and now from the terror of that sword the Shepherd would fain be delivered as soon as justice should see fit. *" My darling from the power of the dog."* Meaning his soul, his life, which is most dear to every man. The original is, " my only one," and therefore is our soul dear, because it is our only soul. Would that all men made their souls their darlings, but many treat them as if they were not worth so much as the mire of the streets. *The dog* may mean Satan that infernal Cerberus, that cursed and cursing cur ; or else the whole company of Christ's foes, who though many in number were as unanimous as if there were but one, and with one consent sought to rend him in pieces. If Jesus cried for help against the dog of hell, much more may we. *Cave canem,* beware of the dog, for his power is great, and only God can deliver us from him. When he fawns upon us, we must not put ourselves in his power ; and when he howls at us, we may remember that God holds him with a chain.

21. *" Save me from the lion's mouth : for thou hast heard me from the horns of the unicorns."* Having experienced deliverance in the past from great enemies, who

were strong as the unicorns, the Redeemer utters his last cry for rescue from death, which is fierce and mighty as the lion. This prayer was heard, and the gloom of the cross departed. Thus faith, though sorely beaten, and even cast beneath the feet of her enemy, ultimately wins the victory. Is was so in our Head, it shall be so in all the members. We have overcome the unicorn, we shall conquer the lion, and from both lion and unicorn we shall take the crown.

22 I will declare thy name unto my brethren : in the midst of the congregation will I praise thee.

23 Ye that fear the LORD, praise him ; all ye the seed of Jacob, glorify him ; and fear him, all ye the seed of Israel.

24 For he hath not despised nor abhorred the affliction of the afflicted ; neither hath he hid his face from him ; but when he cried unto him, he heard.

25 My praise *shall be* of thee in the great congregation : I will pay my vows before them that fear him.

26 The meek shall eat and be satisfied : they shall praise the LORD that seek him : your heart shall live for ever.

27 All the ends of the world shall remember and turn unto the LORD : and all the kindreds of the nations shall worship before thee.

28 For the kingdom *is* the LORD'S : and he *is* the governor among the nations.

29 All *they that be* fat upon earth shall eat and worship : all they that go down to the dust shall bow before him : and none can keep alive his own soul.

30 A seed shall serve him ; it shall be accounted to the Lord for a generation.

31 They shall come, and shall declare his righteousness unto a people that shall be born, that he hath done *this*.

The transition is very marked ; from a horrible tempest all is changed into calm. The darkness of Calvary at length passed away from the face of nature, and from the soul of the Redeemer, and beholding the light of his triumph and its future results the Saviour smiled. We have followed him through the gloom, let us attend him in the returning light. It will be well still to regard the words as a part of our Lord's soliloquy upon the cross, uttered in his mind during the last few moments before his death.

22. " *I will declare thy name unto my brethren.*" The delights of Jesus are always with his church, and hence his thoughts, after much distraction, return at the first moment of relief to their usual channel ; he forms fresh designs for the benefit of his beloved ones. He is not ashamed to call them brethren, " Saying, I will declare thy name unto my brethren, in the midst of the church will I sing praise unto thee." Among his first resurrection words were these, " Go to my brethren." In the verse before us, Jesus anticipates happiness in having communication with his people ; he purposes to be their teacher and minister, and fixes his mind upon the subject of his discourse. The *name, i.e.*, the character and conduct of God are by Jesus Christ's gospel proclaimed to all the holy brotherhood ; they behold the fulness of the Godhead dwelling bodily in him, and rejoice greatly to see all the infinite perfections manifested in one who is bone of their bone and flesh of their flesh. What a precious subject is the name of our God ! It is the only one worthy of the only Begotten, whose meat and drink it was to do the Father's will. We may learn from this resolution of our Lord, that one of the most excellent methods of showing our thankfulness for deliverances is to tell to our brethren what the Lord has done for us. We mention our sorrows readily enough ; why are we so slow in declaring our deliverances ? " *In the midst of the congregation will I praise thee.*" Not in a little household gathering merely does our Lord resolve to proclaim his Father's love, but in the great assemblies of his saints, and in the general assembly and church of the first-born. This the Lord Jesus is always doing by his representatives, who are the heralds of salvation, and labour to praise God. In the great universal church Jesus is the One authoritative teacher, and all others, so far as they are worthy to be called

teachers, are nothing but echoes of his voice. Jesus, in this second sentence, reveals his object in declaring the divine name, it is that God may be praised ; the church continually magnifies Jehovah for manifesting himself in the person of Jesus, and Jesus himself leads the song, and is both precentor and preacher in his church. Delightful are the seasons when Jesus communes with our hearts concerning divine truth ; joyful praise is the sure result.

23. *" Ye that fear the Lord praise him."* The reader must imagine the Saviour as addressing the congregation of the saints. He exhorts the faithful to unite with him in thanksgiving. The description of " fearing the Lord " is very frequent and very instructive ; it is the beginning of wisdom, and is an essential sign of grace. " I am a Hebrew and I fear God " was Jonah's confession of faith. Humble awe of God is so necessary a preparation for praising him that none are fit to sing to his honour, but such as reverence his word ; but this fear is consistent with the highest joy, and is not to be confounded with legal bondage, which is a fear which perfect love casteth out. Holy fear should always keep the key of the singing pew. Where Jesus leads the tune none but holy lips may dare to sing. *" All ye the seed of Jacob glorify him."* The genius of the gospel is praise. Jew and Gentile saved by sovereign grace should be eager in the blessed work of magnifying the God of our salvation. *All* saints should unite in the song ; no tongue may be silent, no heart may be cold. Christ calls us to glorify God, and can we refuse ? *" And fear him all ye the seed of Israel."* The spiritual Israel all do this, and we hope the day will come when Israel after the flesh will be brought to the same mind. The more we praise God the more reverently shall we fear him, and the deeper our reverence the sweeter our songs. So much does Jesus value praise that we have it here under his dying hand and seal that all the saints must glorify the Lord.

24. *" For he hath not despised nor abhorred the affliction of the afflicted."* Here is good matter and motive for praise. The experience of our covenant Head and Representative should encourage all of us to bless the God of grace. Never was man so afflicted as our Saviour in body and soul from friends and foes, by heaven and hell, in life and death ; he was the foremost in the ranks of the afflicted, but all those afflictions were sent in love, and not because his Father despised and abhorred him. 'Tis true that justice demanded that Christ should bear the burden which as a substitute he undertook to carry, but Jehovah always loved him, and in love laid that load upon him with a view to his ultimate glory and to the accomplishment of the dearest wish of his heart. Under all his woes our Lord was honourable in the Father's sight, the matchless jewel of Jehovah's heart. *" Neither hath he hid his face from him."* That is to say, the hiding was but temporary, and was soon removed ; it was not final and eternal. *" But when he cried unto him, he heard."* Jesus was heard in that he feared. He cried *in extremis* and *de profundis*, and was speedily answered ; he therefore bids his people join him in singing a *Gloria in excelsis.*

Every child of God should seek refreshment for his faith in this testimony of the Man of Sorrows. What Jesus here witnesses is as true to-day as when it was first written. It shall never be said that any man's affliction or poverty prevented his being an accepted suppliant at Jehovah's throne of grace. The meanest applicant is welcome at mercy's door :—

> " None that approach his throne shall find
> A God unfaithful or unkind."

25. *" My praise shall be of thee in the great congregation."* The one subject of our Master's song is the Lord alone. The Lord and the Lord only is the theme which the believer handleth when he gives himself to imitate Jesus in praise. The word in the original is " from thee,"—true praise is of celestial origin. The rarest harmonies of music are nothing unless they are sincerely consecrated to God by hearts sanctified by the Spirit. The clerk says, " Let us sing to the praise and glory of God ; " but the choir often sing to the praise and glory of themselves. Oh when shall our service of song be a pure offering ? Observe in this verse how Jesus loves the public praises of the saints, and thinks with pleasure of the great congregation. It would be wicked on our part to despise the twos and threes ; but, on the other hand, let not the little companies snarl at the greater assemblies as though they were necessarily less pure and less approved, for Jesus loves the praise of the great congregation. *" I will pay my vows before them that fear him."* Jesus dedicates himself anew to the carrying out of the divine purpose in fulfilment of his vows

made in anguish. Did our Lord when he ascended to the skies proclaim amid the redeemed in glory the goodness of Jehovah? And was that the vow here meant? Undoubtedly the publication of the gospel is the constant fulfilment of covenant engagements made by our Surety in the councils of eternity. Messiah vowed to build up a spiritual temple for the Lord, and he will surely keep his word.

26. " *The meek shall eat and be satisfied.*" Mark how the dying Lover of our souls solaces himself with the result of his death. The spiritually poor find a feast in Jesus, they feed upon him to the satisfaction of their hearts; they were famished until he gave himself for them, but now they are filled with royal dainties. The thought of the joy of his people gave comfort to our expiring Lord. Note the characters who partake of the benefit of his passion; "*the meek,*" the humble, and lowly. Lord make us so. Note also the certainty that gospel provisions shall not be wasted, "*they shall eat;*" and the sure result of such eating, "*and be satisfied.*" " *They shall praise the Lord that seek him.*" For a while they may keep a fast, but their thanksgiving days must and shall come. "*Your heart shall live for ever.*" Your spirits shall not fail through trial, you shall not die of grief, immortal joys shall be your portion. Thus Jesus speaks even from the cross to the troubled seeker. If his dying words are so assuring, what consolation may we not find in the truth that he ever liveth to make intercession for us! They who eat at Jesus' table receive the fulfilment of the promise, " Whosoever eateth of this bread shall live for ever."

27. In reading this verse one is struck with the Messiah's missionary spirit. It is evidently his grand consolation that Jehovah will be known thoughout all places of his dominion. " *All the ends of the world shall remember and turn unto the Lord.*" Out from the inner circle of the present church the blessing is to spread in growing power until the remotest parts of the earth shall be ashamed of their idols, mindful of the true God, penitent for their offences, and unanimously earnest for reconcilation with Jehovah. Then shall false worship cease, " *and all the kindreds of the nations shall worship before thee,*" O thou only living and true God. This hope which was the reward of Jesus is a stimulus to those who fight his battles.

It is well to mark the order of conversion as here set forth; they shall " remember " —this is reflection, like the prodigal who came unto himself; " *and turn unto Jehovah* —this is repentance, like Manasseh who left his idols and " *worship* "—this is holy service, as Paul adored the Christ whom once he abhorred.

28. " *For the kingdom is the Lord's.*" As an obedient Son the dying Redeemer rejoiced to know that his Father's interests would prosper through his pains. " The Lord reigneth " was *his* song as it is ours. He who by his own power reigns supreme in the domains of creation and providence, has set up a kingdom of grace, and by the conquering power of the cross that kingdom will grow until all people shall own its sway and proclaim that " *he is the governor among the nations.*" Amid the tumults and disasters of the present the Lord reigneth; but in the halcyon days of peace the rich fruit of his dominion will be apparent to every eye. Great Shepherd, let thy glorious kingdom come.

29. " *All they that be fat upon earth,*" the rich and great are not shut out, Grace now finds the most of its jewels among the poor, but in the latter days the mighty of the earth " *shall eat,*" shall taste of redeeming grace and dying love, and shall " *worship* " with all their hearts the God who deals so bountifully with us in Christ Jesus. Those who are spiritually fat with inward prosperity shall be filled with the marrow of communion, and shall worship the Lord with peculiar fervour. In the covenant of grace Jesus has provided good cheer for our high estate, and he has taken equal care to console us in our humiliation, for the next sentence is, "*all they that go down to the dust shall bow before him.*" There is relief and comfort in bowing before God when our case is at its worst; even amid the dust of death prayer kindles the lamp of hope.

While all who come to God by Jesus Christ are thus blessed, whether they be rich or poor, none of those who despise him may hope for a blessing. " *None can keep alive his own soul.*" This is the stern counterpart of the gospel message of " look and live." There is no salvation out of Christ. We must hold life, and have life as Christ's gift, or we shall die eternally. This is very solid evangelical doctrine, and should be proclaimed in every corner of the earth, that like a great hammer it may break in pieces all self-confidence.

30. " *A seed shall serve him.*" Posterity shall perpetuate the worship of the Most High. The kingdom of truth on earth shall never fail. As one generation

is called to its rest, another will arise in its stead. We need have no fear for the true apostolic succession ; that is safe enough. "*It shall be accounted to the Lord for a generation.*" He will reckon the ages by the succession of the saints, and set his accounts according to the families of the faithful. Generations of sinners come not into the genealogy of the skies. God's family register is not for strangers, but for the children only.

31. "*They shall come.*" Sovereign grace shall bring out from among men the bloodbought ones. Nothing shall thwart the divine purpose. The chosen shall come to life, to faith, to pardon, to heaven. In this the dying Saviour finds a sacred satisfaction. Toiling servant of God, be glad at the thought that the eternal purpose of God shall suffer neither let nor hindrance. "*And shall declare his righteousness unto a people that shall be born.*" None of the people who shall be brought to God by the irresistible attractions of the cross shall be dumb, they shall be able to tell forth the righteousness of the Lord, so that future generations shall know the truth. Fathers shall teach their sons, who shall hand it down to their children ; the burden of the story always being "*that he hath done this,*" or, that "It is finished." Salvation's glorious work is done, there is peace on earth, and glory in the highest. "It is finished," these were the expiring words of the Lord Jesus, as they are the last words of this Psalm. May we by living faith be enabled to see our salvation finished by the death of Jesus !

EXPLANATORY NOTES AND QUAINT SAYINGS.

Title.—Aijeleth Shahar. The title of the twenty-second Psalm is Aijeleth Shahar —*the morning hart.* The whole Psalm refers to Christ, containing much that cannot be applied to another : parting his garments, casting lots for his vesture, etc. He is described as a kindly, meek and beautiful hart, started by the huntsmen at the dawn of the day. Herod began hunting him down as soon as he appeared. Poverty, the hatred of men, and the temptation of Satan, joined in the pursuit. There always was some "dog," or "bull," or "unicorn," ready to attack him. After his first sermon the huntsmen gathered about him, but he was too fleet of foot, and escaped. The church had long seen the Messiah "like a roe, or a young hart, upon the mountains," had "heard the voice of her Beloved," and had cried out, "Behold, he cometh, leaping upon the mountains, skipping upon the hills ; " sometimes he was even seen with the dawn of the day, in the neighbourhood of the temple, and beside the enclosures of the vineyards. The church requested to see him " on the mountains of Bether," and upon " the mountains of spices." The former probably signifying the place of his sufferings, and the latter the sublime acclivities of light, glory, and honour, where the "hart" shall be hunted no more. But in the afternoon, the huntsmen who had been following the "young roe" from early day-break, had succeeded in driving him to the mountains of Bether. Christ found Calvary a craggy, jagged, and fearful hill—"a mountain of division." Here he was driven by the huntsmen to the edges of the awful precipices yawning destruction from below, while he was surrounded and held at bay by all the beasts of prey and monsters of the infernal forest. The "unicorn," and the "bulls of Bashan," gored him with their horns ; the great "lion" roared at him ; and the "dog" fastened himself upon him. But he foiled them all. In his own time he bowed his head and gave up the ghost. He was buried in a new grave ; and his assailants reckoned upon complete victory. They had not considered that he was a "morning hart." Surely enough, at the appointed time, did he escape from the hunter's net, and stand forth on the mountains of Israel ALIVE, and *never*, NEVER to die again. Now he is with Mary in the garden, giving evidence of his own resurrection ; in a moment he is at Emmaus, encouraging the too timid and bewildered disciples. Nor does it cost him any trouble to go thence to Galilee to his friends, and again to the Mount of Olives, "on the mountains of spices," *carrying with him the day-dawn*, robed in life and beauty for evermore.—*Christmas Evans, 1766—1838.*

Title.—It will be very readily admitted that the *hind* is a very appropriate emblem of the suffering and persecuted righteous man who meets us in this Psalm. . . . That the *hind* may be a figurative expression significant of suffering innocence, is put beyond a doubt by the fact, that the wicked and the persecutors in this Psalm, *whose peculiar physiognomy is marked by emblems drawn from the brute creation,* are designed by the terms *dogs, lions, bulls,* etc.—*E. W. Hengstenberg.*

Title.—" *The hind.*" Much extraordinary symbolism has by old authors been conjured up and clustered around the hind. According to their curious natural history, there exists a deadly enmity between the deer and the serpent, and the deer by its warm breath draws serpents out of their holes in order to devour them. The old grammarians derived *Elaphas,* or hart, from *elaunein tous opheis,* that is, of driving away serpents. Even the burning a portion of the deer's horns was said to drive away all snakes. If a snake had escaped the hart after being drawn out by the hart by its breath, it was said to be more vehemently poisonous than before. The timidity of the deer was ascribed to the great size of its heart, in which they thought was a bone shaped like a cross.—*Condensed from Wood's " Bible Animals," by C. H. S.*

Whole Psalm,—This is a kind of gem among the Psalms, and is peculiarly excellent and remarkable. It contains those deep, sublime, and heavy sufferings of Christ, when agonizing in the midst of the terrors and pangs of divine wrath and death which surpass all human thought and comprehension. I know not whether any Psalm throughout the whole book contains matter more weighty, or from which the hearts of the godly can so truly perceive those sighs and groans, inexpressible by man, which their Lord and Head, Jesus Christ, uttered when conflicting for us in the midst of death, and in the midst of the pains and terrors of hell. Wherefore this Psalm ought to be most highly prized by all who have any acquaintance with temptations of faith and spiritual conflicts.—*Martin Luther.*

Whole Psalm.—This Psalm, as it sets out the sufferings of Christ to the full, so also his three great offices. His sufferings are copiously described from the beginning of the Psalm to verse 22. The prophetical office of Christ, from verse 22 to verse 25. That which is foretold about his vows (verse 25), hath respect to his priestly function. In the rest of the Psalm the kingly office of Christ is set forth. *William Gouge, D.D* (1575—1653), *in " A Commentary on the whole Epistle to the Hebrews."**

Whole Psalm.—This Psalm seems to be less a prophecy than a history. *Cassiodorus.*

Whole Psalm.—This Psalm must be expounded, word for word, entire and in every respect, of Christ only ; without any allegory, trope, or *anagoge.*—*Bakius,* quoted by *F. Delitzsch, D.D., on Hebrews,* ii. 12.

Whole Psalm.—A prophecy of the passion of Christ, and of the vocation of the *Gentiles.*—*Eusebius of Cæsarea.*

Verse 1.—" *My God, my God, why hast thou forsaken me ?* " We contrast this with John xvi. 32, " *I am not alone, because the Father is with me.*" That these words in David were not withstanding the words of Christ, there is no true believer ignorant ; yet how cross our Lord's words in John ! Answer :—It is one thing to speak out of present sense of misery, another thing to be confident of a never-separated Deity. The condition of Christ in respect of his human state (not the divine), is in all outward appearances, like ours ; we conceive the saints' condition very lamentable at times, as if God were for ever gone. And Christ (to teach us to cry after God the Father, like children after the mother, whose very stepping but at the door, ofttimes makes the babe believe, and so saith that his father is gone for ever), presents in his own sufferings how much he is sensible of ours in that case. As for his divine nature, he and his Father can never sunder in that, and so at no time is he alone, but the Father is always with him.—*William Streat, in " The Dividing of the Hoof,"* 1654.

Verse 1.—" *My God, my God,*" etc. There is a tradition that our Lord, hanging on the cross, began, as we know from the gospel, this Psalm ; and repeating it and those that follow gave up his most blessed spirit when he came to the fifth verse of the thirty-first Psalm. However that may be, by taking these first words on his lips he stamped the Psalm as belonging to himself.—*Ludolph, the Carthusian (ci. ca.* 1350), *in J. M. Neale's Commentary.*

Verse 1.—" *My God, my God,*" etc. It was so sharp, so heavy an affliction to Christ's soul, that it caused him who was meek under all other sufferings as a lamb,

---

* Reprinted in Nichol's Series of Commentaries.

to roar under this like a lion. For so much those words of Christ signify, " *My God, my God, why hast thou forsaken me ? why art thou so far from helping me, and from the words of my roaring ?* " It comes from a root that signifies to howl or roar as a lion, and rather signifies the noise made by a wild beast than the voice of a man. And it is as much as if Christ had said, O my God, no words can express my anguish, I will not speak, but roar, howl out my complaints. Pour it out in volleys of groans. I roar as a lion. It's no small matter will make that majestic creature to roar. And sure so great a spirit as Christ's would not have roared under a slight burden.

Did God really forsake Jesus Christ upon the cross ? then from the desertion of Christ singular consolation springs up to the people of God ; yea, manifold consolation. Principally it's a support in these two respects, as it is *preventive* of your final desertion and a comfortable *pattern* to you in your present sad desertions. 1. Christ's desertion is *preventive* of your final desertion. Because he was forsaken for a time you shall not be forsaken for ever. For he was forsaken for you. It is every way as much for the dear Son of God, the darling delight of his soul, to be forsaken of God for a time, as if such a poor inconsiderable thing as thou art shouldst be cast off to eternity. Now, this being equivalent and borne in thy room, must needs give thee the highest security in the world that God will never finally withdraw from thee. 2. Moreover, this sad desertion of Christ becomes a comfortable *pattern* to poor deserted souls in divers respects ; and the proper business of such souls, at such times, is to eye it believingly. Though God deserted Christ, yet at the same time he powerfully supported him. His omnipotent arms were under him, though his pleased face was hid from him. He had not indeed his smiles, but he had his supportations. So, Christian, just so shall it be with thee. Thy God may turn away his face, he will not pluck away his arm. When one asked of holy Mr. Baines how the case stood with his soul, he answered, " Supports I have, though suavities I want." Our Father in this deals with us as we ourselves sometimes do with a child that is stubborn and rebellious. We turn him out of doors and bid him begone out of our sight, and there he sighs and weeps ; but however for the humbling of him, we will not presently take him into house and favour ; yet we order, at least permit the servants to carry him meat and drink : here is fatherly care and support, though no former smiles or manifested delights . . . . . Though God forsook Christ, yet at that time he could justify God. So you read, " O my God (saith he), I cry in the day time ; but thou hearest not, and in the night season, and am not silent ; but thou art holy." Is not thy spirit according to thy measure, framed like Christ's in this ; canst thou not, say even when he writes bitter things against thee, he is a holy, faithful and good God for all this ! I am deserted but not wronged. There is not one drop of injustice in all the sea of my sorrows. Though he condemned me I must and will justify him : this also is Christ-like.—*John Flavel.*

Verse 1.—" *My God, my God.*" The repetition is expressive of fervent desire— " *My God,*" in an especial sense, as in his words after the resurrection to Mary Magdalene, " I ascend unto my God, and your God ; " " My God," not as the Son of God only, but in that nature which he hath assumed, as the beloved Son in whom the Father is well pleased ; who is loved of the Father and who loveth the Father more than the whole universe. It is observed that this expression, " My God," is three times repeated.—*Dionysius, quoted by Isaac Williams.*

Verse 1.—" *My God.*" It was possible for Christ by *faith* to know that he was beloved of God, and he did know that he was beloved of God, when yet as to *sense* and *feeling* he tasted of God's *wrath.* Faith and the want of sense are not inconsistent ; there may be no present sense of God's love, nay, there may be a present sense of his wrath, and yet there may be faith at the same time.—*John Row's* " Emmanuel," 1680.

Verse 1.—This word, " *My God,*" takes in more than all the philosophers in the world could draw out of it.—*Alexander Wedderburn,* 1701.

Verse 1.—That there is something of a singular force, meaning, and feeling in these words is manifest from this—the evangelists have studiously given us this verse in the very words of the Hebrew, in order to show their emphatic force. And moreover I do not remember any one other place in the Scriptures where we have this repetition, ELI, ELI.—*Martin Luther.*

Verse 1.—" *Why ?*" Not the " *why* " of impatience or despair, not the sinful questioning of one whose heart rebels against his chastening, but rather the cry of a lost child who cannot understand why his father has left him, and who longs to see his father's face again.—*J. J. Stewart Perowne.*

Verse 1.—"*My roaring.*" שַׁאֲגָתִי seems primarily to denote the roaring of a lion; but, as applied to intelligent beings, it is generally expressive of profound mental anguish poured forth in audible and even vehement strains. Psalm xxxviii. 9; xxxiii. 3; Job iii. 24. Thus did the suffering Messiah pour forth strong crying and tears, to him that was able to save him from death. Heb. v. 7.—*John Morison.*

Verse 1.—When Christ complains of having been forsaken by God, we are not to understand that he was forsaken by the First Person, or that there was a dissolution of the hypostatic union, or that he lost the favour and friendship of the Father; but he signifies to us that God permitted his human nature to undergo those dreadful torments, and to suffer an ignominious death, from which he could, if he chose, most easily deliver him. Nor did such complaints proceed either from impatience or ignorance, as if Christ were ignorant of the cause of his suffering, or was not most willing to bear such abandonment in his suffering; such complaints were only a declaration of his most bitter sufferings. And whereas, through the whole course of his passion, with such patience did our Lord suffer, as not to let a single groan or sigh escape from him, so now, lest the bystanders may readily believe that he was rendered impassible by some superior power; therefore, when his last moments were nigh, he protests that he is true man, truly passible : forsaken by his Father in his sufferings, the bitterness and acuteness of which he then intimately felt. *Robert Bellarmine (Cardinal)*, 1542—1621.

Verse 1.—Divines are wont commonly to say, that Christ, from the moment of his conception, had the sight of God, his human soul being immediately united to the Deity, Christ from the very moment of his conception had the sight of God. Now for our Saviour, who had known experimentally how sweet the comfort of his Father's face had been, and had lived all his days under the warm beams and influences of the Divinity, and had had his soul all along refreshed with the sense of the Divine presence, for him to be left in that horror and darkness, as to have no taste of comfort, no glimpse of the Divinity breaking in upon his human soul, how great an affliction must that needs be unto him !—*John Row.*

Verse 1.—Desertion is in itself no sin; for Christ endured its bitterness, ay, he was so deep in it, that when he died, he said, "*Why hast thou forsaken me ?*" A total, a final desertion ours is not; partial the best have had and have. God turns away his face, David himself is troubled : "*The just shall live by faith,*" and not by feeling.—*Richard Capel.*

Verse 1.—Oh ! how will our very hearts melt with love, when we remember that as we have been distressed for our sins against him; so he was in greater agonies for us ? We have had gall and wormwood, but he tasted a more bitter cup. The anger of God has dried up our spirits, but he was scorched with a more flaming wrath. He was under violent pain in the garden, and on the cross; ineffable was the sorrow that he felt, being forsaken of his Father, deserted by his disciples, affronted and reproached by his enemies, and under a curse for us. This Sun was under a doleful eclipse, this living Lord was pleased to die, and in his death was under the frowns of an angry God. The face was then hid from him that had always smiled before; and his soul felt that horror and that darkness which it had never felt before. So that there was no separation between the divine and human nature, yet he suffered pains equal to those which we had deserved to suffer in hell for ever. God so suspended the efficacies of his grace that it displayed in that hour none of its force and virtue on him. He had no comfort from heaven, none from his angels, none from his friends, even in that sorrowful hour when he needed comfort most. Like a lion that is hurt in the forest, so he roared and cried out, though there was no despair in him; and when he was forsaken, yet there was trust and hope in these words, "*My God, my God.*"—*Timothy Rogers.*

Verse 1.—Here is comfort to *deserted souls ;* Christ himself was deserted; therefore, if thou be deserted, God dealeth no otherwise with thee than he did with Christ. Thou mayst be beloved of God and not feel it; Christ was so, he was beloved of the Father, and yet had no present sense and feeling of his love. This may be a great comfort to holy souls under the suspension of those comforts and manifestations which sometimes they have felt; Christ himself underwent such a suspension, therefore such a suspension of divine comfort may consist with God's love. Thou mayst conclude possibly, " I am a hypocrite, and therefore God hath forsaken me ; " this is the complaint of some doubting Christians, " I am a hypocrite, and therefore God hath forsaken me ; " but thou hast no reason so to conclude : there was no failure in Christ's obedience, and yet Christ was forsaken in point of comfort; therefore desertion, in point of comfort, may consist with truth of grace, yea, with the highest measure of grace ; so it did in our Saviour.—*John Row.*

Verse 1.—Lord, thou knowest what it is for a soul to be forsaken, it was sometime thine own case when thou complainedst, " *My God, why hast thou forsaken me ?* " not, O my Lord ! but that thou hadst a divine supportment, but thou hadst not (it seemeth) that inward joy which at other times did fill thee ; now thou art in thy glory, pity *a worm* in misery, that mourns and desires more after thee than all things : Lord, thou paidst dear for my good, let good come unto me.—*Joseph Symonds,* 1658.

Verse 1.—The first verse expresses a species of suffering that never at any other time was felt in this world, and never will be again—the vengeance of the Almighty upon his child—" My God, why hast thou forsaken me ? "—*R. H. Ryland.*

Verse 2.—" *O my God, I cry in the daytime, but thou hearest not,*" etc. How like is this expostulation to that of a human child with its earthly parent ! It is based on the ground of relationship—" I am thine ; I cry day and night, yet I am not heard. Thou art my God, yet nothing is done to silence me. In the daytime of my life I cried ; in this night season of my death I intreat. In the garden of Gethsemane I occupied the night with prayers ; with continual ejaculations have I passed through this eventful morning. O my God, thou hast not yet heard me, therefore am I not yet silent; I cannot cease till thou answerest." Here Christ urges his suit in a manner which none but filial hearts adopt. The child knows that the parent yearns over him. His importunity is strengthened by confidence in paternal love. He keeps not silence, he gives him no rest because he confides in his power and willingness to grant the desired relief. This is natural. It is the argument of the heart, an appeal to the inward yearnings of our nature. It is also scriptural, and is thus stated, " If ye then being evil, know how to give good gifts unto your children, how much more shall your heavenly Father give the Holy Spirit to them that ask him ? " Luke xi. 13. *John Stevenson, in " Christ on the Cross,"* 1842.

Verse 2.—The princely prophet says, " *Lord, I cry unto thee in the daytime, but thou hearest not, also in the night time, and yet this is not to be thought folly to me.*"* Some perhaps would think it a great point of folly for a man to cry and call unto him who stops his ears, and seems not to hear. Nevertheless, this folly of the faithful is wiser than all the wisdom of the world. For we know well enough, that howsoever God seem at the first not to hear, yet the Lord is a sure refuge *in due time— in affliction.* Psalm ix. 9.—*Thomas Playfere.*

Verses 2, 3.—Well, what hears God from him, now he hears nothing from God, as to the deliverance prayed for ? No murmuring at God's proceedings ; nay, he hears quite the contrary, for he justifies and praises God : " *But thou art holy, O thou that inhabitest the praises of Israel.*" Observe whether thou canst not gather something from the manner of God's denying the thing prayed for, which may sweeten it to thee ! Haply thou shalt find he denies thee, but it is with a smiling countenance, and ushers it in with some expressions of grace and favour, that may assure thee his denial proceeds not from displeasure. As you would do with a dear friend, who, may be, comes to borrow a sum of money of you ; lend it you dare not, because you see plainly it is not for his good ; but in giving him the denial, lest he should misinterpret it, as proceeding from want of love and respect, you preface it with some kind of language of your hearty affection to him, as that you love him, and therefore deny him, and shall be ready to do for him more than that comes to. Thus God sometimes wraps up his denials in such sweet intimations of love, as prevents all jealousies arising in the hearts of his people.—*William Gurnall.*

Verses 2, 3.—They that have conduit-water come into their houses, if no water come they do not conclude the spring to be dry, but the pipes to be stopped or broken. If prayer speed not, we must be sure that the fault is not in God, but in ourselves ; were we but ripe for mercy, he is ready to extend it to us, and even waits for the purpose.—*John Trapp.*

Verse 3.—" *But thou art holy.*" Here is the triumph of faith—the Saviour stood like a rock in the wide ocean of temptation. High as the billows rose, so did his faith, like the coral rock, wax greater and stronger till it became an island of salvation to our shipwrecked souls. It is as if he had said, " It matters not what I endure.

---

* Septuagint version.

Storms may howl upon me ; men depise ; devils tempt ; circumstances over-power ; and God himself forsake me, still God is holy ; there is no unrighteousness in him."—*John Stevenson.*

Verse 3.—*" But thou art holy."*   Does it seem strange that the heart in its darkness and sorrow should find comfort in this attribute of God ?   No, for God's holiness is but another aspect of his faithfulness and mercy.   And in that remarkable name, " the Holy One *of Israel*," we are taught that he who is the *" holy "* God is also the God who has made a covenant with his chosen.   It would be impossible for an Israelite to think of God's holiness without thinking also of that covenant rela-tionship.   " Be ye holy ; for I, the Lord your God am holy," were the words in which Israel was reminded of their relation to God.   See especially Lev. xix. 1. We see something of this feeling in such passages as Psalm lxxxix, 16—19 ; xcix. 5—9 ; Hosea xi. 8, 9 ; Isaiah xli. 14 ; xlvii. 4.—*J. J. Stewart Perowne.*

Verse 3.—Were temptations never so black, faith will not hearken to an ill word spoken against God, but will justify God always.—*David Dickson.*

Verses 4, 5.—Those who look upon this Psalm as having a primary reference to the King of Israel, attribute great beauty to these words, from the very pleasing conjecture that David was, at the time of composing them, sojourning at Mahanaim, where Jacob, in his distress, wrestled with the angel, and obtained such signal blessings.   That, in a place so greatly hallowed by associations of the past, he should make his appeal to the God of his fathers, was alike the dictate of patriarchal feeling and religion.—*John Morison, D.D., in " Morning Meditations."*

Verse 5.—*" Thou didst deliver them,"* but thou wilt not deliver me ; nay, rather thou didst deliver them because thou wilt not deliver me.—*Gerhohus.*

Verse 6.—*" But I am a worm, and no man."*   A fisherman, when he casts his angle into the river, doth not throw the hook in bare, naked, and uncovered, for then he knows the fish will never bite, and therefore he hides the hook within a worm, or some other bait, and so, the fish, biting at the worm, is catched by the hook.   Thus Christ, speaking of himself, saith, *" Ego vermis et non homo."*   He, coming to perform the great work of our redemption, did cover and hide his God-head within the worm of his human nature.   The grand water-serpent, Leviathan, the devil, thinking to swallow the worm of his humanity, was caught upon the hook of his divinity.   This hook stuck in his jaws, and tore him very sore.   By thinking to destroy Christ, he destroyed his own kingdom, and lost his own power for ever.—*Lancelot Andrews.*

Verse 6.—*"I am a worm."*   Christ calls himself *" a worm "* . . . . on account of the opinion that men of the world had of him. . . . . The Jews esteemed Christ as a worm, and treated him as such ; he was loathsome to them and hated by them ; every one trampled upon him, and trod him under foot as men do worms. . . . . The Chaldee paraphrase renders it here *a weak worm ;* and though Christ is the mighty God, and is also the Son of man, whom God made strong for himself ; yet there was a weakness in his human nature, and he was crucified through it, 2 Cor. xiii. 4 : and it has been observed by some, that the word נבליה there used signifies the scarlet worm, or the worm that is in the grain or berry with which scarlet is dyed ; and like this scarlet worm did our Lord look, when by way of mockery he was clothed with a scarlet robe ; and especially when he appeared in his dyed garments, and was red in his apparel, as one that treadeth in the wine fat ; when his body was covered with blood when he hung upon the cross, which was shed to make crimson and scarlet sins as white as snow.—*John Gill.*

Verse 6.—*"I am a worm."*   An humble soul is emptied of all swelling thoughts of himself.   Bernard calls humility a self-annihilation.   Job xxii. 29.   " Thou wilt save the humble ; " in the Hebrew it is, " Him that is of low eyes."   An humble man hath lower thoughts of himself than others can have of him ; David, though a king, yet looked upon himself as *" a worm : " " I am a worm, and no man."*   Bradford a martyr, yet subscribes himself " a sinner."   Job x. 15.   "If I be righteous, yet will I not lift up my head : " like the violet, a sweet flower, but hangs down the head.—*Thomas Watson.*

Verse 6.—*"A worm."*   So trodden under foot, trampled on, maltreated, buffeted and spit upon, mocked and tormented, as to seem more like a worm than a man. Behold what great contempt hath the Lord of Majesty endured, that his confusion may be our glory ; his punishment our heavenly bliss ! Without ceasing impress this spectacle, O Christian, on thy soul !—*Dionysius, quoted by Isaac Williams.*

Verse 6.—" *I am a worm.*" Among the Hindoos, when a man complains and abhors himself, he asks : " What am I ? A worm ! a worm ! " " Ah, the proud man ! he regarded me as a worm, well should I like to say to him, ' We are all worms.' " " Worm, crawl out of my presence."—*Joseph Roberts.*

Verse 7.—"*All they that see me laugh me to scorn,*" etc. Imagine this dreadful scene. Behold this motley multitude of rich and poor, of Jews and Gentiles ! Some stand in groups and gaze. Some recline at ease and stare. Others move about in restless gratification at the event. There is a look of satisfaction on every countenance. None are silent. The velocity of speech seems tardy. The theme is far too great for one member to utter. Every lip, and head, and finger, is now a tongue. The rough soldiers, too, are busied in their coarse way. The work of blood is over. Refreshment has become necessary. Their usual beverage of vinegar and water is supplied to them. As they severally are satisfied, they approach the cross, hold some forth to the Saviour, and bid him drink as they withdraw it. Luke xxiii. 36. They know he must be suffering an intense thirst, they therefore aggravate it with the mockery of refreshment. Cruel Romans ! and ye, O regicidal Jews ! Was not death enough ? Must mockery and scorn be added ? On this sad day Christ made you *one* indeed ! Dreadful unity—which constituted you the joint mockers and murderers of the Lord of glory !—*John Stevenson.*

Verse 7.—"*All they that see me laugh me to scorn,*" etc. There have been persons in our own days, whose crimes have excited such detestation that the populace would probably have torn them in pieces, before, and even after their trial, if they could have had them in their power. Yet when these very obnoxious persons have been executed according to their sentence, if, perhaps, there was not one spectator who wished them to escape, yet neither was one found so lost to sensibility as to insult them in their dying moments. But when Jesus suffers, *all that see him laugh* him *to scorn ; they shoot out the lip, they shake the head ;* they insult his character and his hope.—*John Newton.*

Verse 7.—" *They shoot out the lip.*" To protrude the lower lip is, in the East, considered a very strong indication of contempt. Its employment is chiefly confined to the lower orders.—*Illustrated Commentary.*

Verses 7, 8.—It was after his crucifixion, and during the hours that he hung upon the cross, that his sufferings in this way—the torment of beholding and hearing the scorn and mockery which was made of the truth of his person and doctrine—exceedingly abounded, and in such and so many kinds of mockery and insult that some consider this to have been the chiefest pain and sorrow which he endured in his most sacred passion. For as, generally, those things are considered the most painful to endure of which we are most sensible, so it seems to these persons, that sufferings of this kind contain in them more cause for feeling than any other sufferings. And, therefore, although all the torments of the Lord were very great, so that each one appears the greatest, and no comparison can be made between them ; yet, nevertheless, this kind of suffering appears to be the most painful. Because in other troubles, not only the pain and suffering of them, but the troubles themselves, in themselves, may be desired by us, and such as we suffer for love's sake, in order by them to evince that love. Wherefore, the stripes, the crown of thorns, the buffetings, the cross, the gall, the vinegar, and other bodily torments, besides that they torment the body, are often a means for promoting the divine honour, which it holds in esteem above all else. But to blaspheme God, to give the lie to eternal truths, to deface the supreme demonstrations of the divinity and majesty of the Son of God (although God knoweth how to extract from these things the good which he intends), nevertheless are, in their nature, things, which, from their so greatly affecting the divine honour, although they may be, for just considerations, endured, can never be desired by any one, but must be abhorrent to all. Our Lord then, being, of all, the most zealous for the divine honour, for which he also died, found in this kind of suffering, more than in all other, much to abhor and nothing to desire. Therefore with good reason it may be held to be the greatest of all, and that in which, more than in all other, he exhibited the greatest suffering and patience. *Fra Thomé de Jesu, in " The Sufferings of Jesus,"* 1869.

Verses 7—9.—All that see me made but a laughynge stocke on me, they mocked me wyth their lyppes, and wagged theyr heades at me. Sayenge, thys vyllayne referred all thynges to the Lord, let him now delyver hym yf he wyll, for he loveth hym well. But yet thou arte he whyche leddest me oute of my mother's wombe myne one refuge, even from my mother's teates. As sone as I came into this worlde, I was layde in thy lappe, thou art my God even from my mother's wombe.—*From "The Psalter of David in English, truly translated out of Latyn," in "Devout Psalms," etc., by E. Whitchurche,* 1547.

Verse 8.—Here are recorded some of those very words, by which the persecutors of our Lord expressed their mockery and scorn. How remarkable to find them in a Psalm written so many hundred years before!—*John Stevenson.*

Verses 9, 10.—Faith is much strengthened by constant evidences of God's favour. Herewith did he support his faith that said to God, "*Thou art he that took me out of the womb : thou didst make me hope when I was upon my mother's breasts. I was cast upon thee from the womb : thou art my God from my mother's belly.*" "Thou art my trust from my youth. By thee have I been holden up from the womb : thou art he that took me out of my mother's bowels." Psalm lxxi. 5, 6. It was not only the disposition of Obadiah towards God, but also the evidence that thereby he had of God's affection towards him, that made him with confidence say to Elijah, "I fear the Lord from my youth." 1 Kings xviii. 12. By long continuance of ancient favour, many demonstrations are given of a fast, fixed and unremovable affection. So as if, by reason of temptations, one or more evidences should be questioned, yet others would remain to uphold faith, and to keep it from an utter languishing, and a total falling away. As when a house is supported by many pillars, though some be taken away, yet by the support of them which remain, the house will stand.—*William Gouge.*

Verses 9, 10.—David acknowledges ancient mercies, those mercies which had been cast upon him long ago, these were still fresh and new in his memory, and this is one affection and disposition of a thankful heart—to remember those mercies which another would have quite forgotten, or never thought of. Thus does David here ; the mercies of his *infancy,* and his *childhood,* and his *younger years,* which one would have imagined, that now in his age had been quite out of his mind ; yet these does he here stir up himself to remember and bring to his thoughts. "*Took me out of the womb :*" when was that ? It may have been threescore years ago when David penned the Psalms. He thinks of those mercies which God vouchsafed him *when he was not capable of thinking,* nor considering what was bestowed upon him ; and so are we taught hence to do, in an imitation of his holy example which is here set before us : those mercies which God hath bestowed in our minority we are to call to mind and acknowledge in our riper years.—*Thomas Horton.*

Verses 9, 10.—Here the tribulation begins to grow lighter, and hope inclines towards victory ; a support, though small, and sought out with deep anxiety, is now found. For after he had felt that he had suffered without any parallel or example, so that the wonderful works of God as displayed toward the fathers afforded him no help, he comes to the wonderful works of God toward himself, and in these he finds the goodwill of God turned towards him, and which was displayed towards him alone in so singular a way.—*Martin Luther.*

Verses 9, 10.—The bitter severity of the several taunts with which his enemies assailed our Lord, had no other effect than to lead the Saviour to make a direct appeal to his Father. . . . . That appeal is set before us in these two verses. It is of an unusual and remarkable nature. The argument on which it is founded is most forcible and conclusive. At the same time, it is the most seasonable and appropriate that can be urged. We may thus paraphrase it, " I am now brought as a man to my extremity. It is said that God disowns me ; but it cannot be so. My first moment of existence he tenderly cared for. When I could not even ask for, or think of his kindness, he bestowed it upon me. If, of his mere good pleasure he brought me into life at first, he will surely not forsake me when I am departing out of it. In opposition, therefore, to all their taunts, I can and I will appeal to himself. Mine enemies declare, O God, that thou hast cast me off—*but thou art he that took me out of the womb.* They affirm that I do not, and need not trust in thee ; but *thou didst make me hope* (or, *keptest me in safety,* margin) *when I was upon my mother's breasts.* They insinuate that thou wilt not acknowledge me as thy Son ; but *I was cast upon thee from the womb ; thou art my God from my mother's belly.*"— *John Stevenson.*

Verse 10.—" *I was cast upon thee from the womb : thou art my God from my mother's belly.*" There is a noble passage in Eusebius, in which he shows the connection between our Lord's incarnation and his passion : that he might well comfort himself while hanging on the cross by the remembrance that the very same body that " marred more than any man, and his form more than the sons of men " (Isaiah liii. 14), was that which had been glorified by the Father with such singular honour, when the Holy Ghost came upon Mary, and the power of the Highest overshadowed her. That this body, therefore, though now so torn and so mangled, as it had once been the wonder, so it would for ever be the joy, of the angels ; and having put on immortality, would be the support of his faithful people to the end of time—*J. M. Neale, in loc.*

Verse 10.—I was like one forsaken by his parent, and wholly cast upon Providence. I had no father upon earth, and my mother was poor and helpless.—*Matthew Poole.*

Verse 11.—" *Be not far from me ; for trouble is near ; "* and so it is high time for thee to put forth a helping hand. *Hominibus profanis mirabilis videtur hæc ratio,* to profane persons, this seemeth to be a strange reason, saith an interpreter ; but it is a very good one, as this prophet knew, who therefore makes it his plea.— *John Trapp.*

Verse 12.—"*Strong bulls of Bashan have beset me round.*" These animals are remarkable for the proud, fierce, and sullen manner in which they exercise their great strength. Such were the persecutors who now beset our Lord. These were first, human, and secondly, spiritual foes ; and both were alike distinguished by the proud, fierce, and sullen manner in which they assaulted him.—*John Stevenson.*

Verses 12, 13.—"*Bashan*" was a fertile country (Numb. xxxii. 4), and the cattle there fed were fat and "strong." Deut. xxxii. 14. Like them, the Jews in that good land " waxed fat and kicked," grew proud and rebelled ; forsook God " that made them, and lightly esteemed the rock of their salvation."—*George Horne.*

Verse 13.—A helpless infant, or a harmless lamb, surrounded by furious bulls and hungry lions, aptly represented the Saviour encompassed by his insulting and bloody persecutors.—*Thomas Scott,* 1747—1881.

Verse 14.—" *I am poured out like water, and all my bones are out of joint : my heart is like wax ; it is melted in the midst of my bowels.*" He was faint. *Such* a feeling of languor and faintness supervened that language fails to express it, and the emblem of " water poured out " is employed to represent it. As the water falls from the vessel to the earth, see how its particles separate farther and farther from each other. Its velocity increases as it falls. It has no power to stay itself midway, much less to return to its place. It is the very picture of utter weakness. So did our Lord feel himself to be when hanging on the cross. He was faint with weakness. The sensations experienced when about to faint away are very over-powering. We appear to our own consciousness to be nothing but weakness, as water poured out. All our bones feel relaxed and out of joint ; we seem as though we had none. The strength of bone is gone, the knitting of the joints is loosened, and the muscular vigour fled. A sickly giddiness overcomes us. We have no power to bear up. All heart is lost. Our strength disappears like that of wax, of melting wax, which drops upon surrounding objects, and is lost. Daniel thus describes his sensations on beholding the great vision, " There remained no strength in me : for my vigour was turned into corruption, and I retained no strength." Dan. x. 8. In regard, however, to the faintness which our Lord experienced, we ought to notice this additional and remarkable circumstance, that he did not alto-gether faint away. The relief of insensibility he refused to take. When consciousness ceases, all perception of pain is necessarily and instantly terminated. But our Lord retained his full consciousness throughout this awful scene ; and patiently endured for a considerable period, those, to us, insupportable sensations which precede the actual swoon.—*John Stevenson.*

Verse 14.—" *I am poured out like water : "* that is, in the thought of my enemies I am utterly destroyed. " For we must needs die, and are as water spilt on the ground, which cannot be gathered up again." 2 Sam. xiv. 14. " What marvel," asks St. Bernard, " that the name of the Bridegroom should be as ointment poured forth, when he himself, for the greatness of his love, was poured forth like water ! "— *J. M. Neale.*

Verse 14.—"*I am poured out like water,*" *i.e.*, I am almost past all recovery, as water spilt upon the ground.—*John Trapp.*

Verse 14.—"*All my bones are out of joint.*" The *rack* is devised as a most exquisite pain, even for terror. And the *cross* is a *rack*, whereon he was stretched till, saith the Psalm, "*all his bones were out of joint.*" But even to *stand*, as he *hung*, three long hours together, holding up but the arms at length, I have heard it avowed of some that have felt it, to be a pain scarce credible. But the hands and the feet being so cruelly *nailed* (part, of all other, most sensible, by reason of the texture of sinews there in them most) it could not but make his pain out of measure painful. It was not for nothing, that *dolores acerrimi dicuntur cruciatus* (saith the heathen man), that the most sharp and bitter pains of all other have their name from hence, and are called *cruciatus*—pains like those of the *cross*. It had a meaning, that *they gave him,* that he had (for his *welcome* to the cross) a cup mixed with gall or myrrh ; and (for his *farewell*) *a sponge of vinegar ;* to show by the one the *bitterness,* and by the other the *sharpness* of the pains of this painful death.—*Lancelot Andrewes.*

Verse 14.—"*All my bones are out of joint.*" We know that the greatest and most intolerable pain that the body can endure, is that arising from a bone out of its place, or dislocated joint. Now when the Lord was raised up upon the cross, and his sacred body hung in the air from the nails, all the joints began to give, so that the bones were parted the one from the other so visibly that, in very truth (as David had prophesied) *they might tell all his bones,* and thus, throughout his whole body, he endured acute torture. Whilst our Lord suffered these torments, his enemies, who had so earnestly desired to see him crucified, far from pitying him, were filled with delight, as though celebrating a victory.—*Fra Thomè de Jesu.*

Verse 15.—"*My strength is dried up,*" etc. Inflammation must have commenced early and violently in the wounded parts—then been quickly imparted to those that were strained, and have terminated in a *high degree of feverish burning over the whole body.* The animal juices would be thus dried up, and the watery particles of the blood absorbed. The skin parched by the scorching sun till midday would be unable to supply or to imbibe any moisture. The loss of blood at the hands and feet would hasten the desiccation. Hence our Lord says, "My strength is dried up like a potsherd, and my tongue cleaveth to my jaws." The fever would devour his small remaining strength. And THIRST, that most intolerable of all bodily privations, must have been overpowering. His body appeared to his feeling like a potsherd that had been charred in the potter's kiln. It seemed to have neither strength nor substance left in it. So feeble had he become, so parched and dried up that CLAMMINESS OF THE MOUTH, one of the forerunners of immediate dissolution, had already seized him ; "My tongue cleaveth to my jaws, and thou hast brought me into the dust of death."—*John Stevenson.*

Verse 15.—"*My strength is dried up ;*" not as in the trial of gold and silver, but "*like a potsherd,*" as the earthen vessel dried up by the heat, spoken in humiliation.—*Isaac Williams, in loc.*

Verse 15.—"*A potsherd.*" חרשׂ, rendered *potsherd,* is a word which denotes a piece of earthenware, frequently in a broken state. As employed in the verse under consideration, it seems to derive considerable illustration from the corresponding word in ARABIC, which expresses roughness of skin, and might well convey to the mind an idea of the bodily appearance of one in whom the moisture of the fluids had been dried up by the excess of grief.—*John Morison.*

Verse 15.—That hour what his feelings were it is dangerous to define : we know them not ; we may be too bold to determine of them. To very good purpose it was that the ancient Fathers of the Greek church in their liturgy, after they had recounted all the particular pains, as they are set down in his passion, and by all and by everyone of them called for mercy, do, after all, shut up with this Δι αγνωστων κοπῶν κὶ βασάνων ελέησον κὶ σῶσον ἡμᾶς. By thine unknown sorrows and sufferings, felt by thee, but not distinctly known by us, have mercy upon us and save us.— *Lancelot Andrewes.*

Verse 16.—"*Dogs have compassed me.*" So great and varied was the malignity exhibited by the enemies of our Lord, that the combined characteristics of two species of ferocious animals were not adequate to its representation. Another emblematical figure is therefore introduced. The assembly of the wicked is compared to that of "dogs" who haunt about the cities, prowl in every corner snarl over the carrion, and devour it all with greediness—like " dogs," with their wild cry in full pursuit, with unfailing scent tracking their victim, with vigilant eye on all its movements, and with a determination which nothing can falter, they run it on to death. The Oriental mode of hunting, both in ancient and modern times, is murderous and merciless in the extreme. A circle of several miles in circumference is beat round ; and the men, driving all before them, and narrowing as they advance, inclose the prey on every side. Having thus made them prisoners, the cruel hunters proceed to slaughter at their own convenience. So did the enemies of our Lord : long before his crucifixion it is recorded that they used the most treacherous plans to get him into their power.—*John Stevenson.*

Verse 16.—*" Dogs have compassed me."* At the hunting of the lion, a whole district is summoned to appear, who, forming themselves first into a circle, enclose a space of four or five miles in compass, according to the number of the people and the quality of the ground which is pitched upon for the scene of action. The footmen advance first, rushing into the thickets with their dogs and spears, to put up the game ; while the horsemen, keeping a little behind, are always ready to charge upon the first sally of the wild beast. In this manner they proceed, still contracting their circle, till they all at last close in togther, or meet with some other game to divert them.—*Dr. Shaw's Travels, quoted in Paxton's " Illustrations of Scripture."*

Verse 16.—*" They pierced my hands and my feet ; "* namely, when they nailed Christ to the cross. Matt. xxvii. 35 ; John xx. 25. Where let me simulate, saith a learned man, the orator's gradation, *Facinus vincire civem Romanum,* etc. It was much for the Son of God to be bound, more to be beaten, most of all to be slain ; *Quid dicam in crucem tolle ?* but what shall I say to this, that he was crucified ? That was the most vile and ignominious ; it was also a cruel and cursed kind of death, which yet he refused not ; and here we have a clear testimony for his cross. *John Trapp.*

Verse 16.—*" They pierced my hands and my feet."* Of all sanguinary punishments, that of crucifixion is one of the most dreadful—no vital part is immediately affected by it. The hands and feet which are furnished with the most numerous and sensitive organs, are perforated with nails, which must necessarily be of some size to suit their intended purpose. The tearing asunder of the tender fibres of the hands and feet, the lacerating of so many nerves, and bursting so many bloodvessels, must be productive of intense agony. The nerves of the hand and foot are intimately connected, through the arm and leg, with the nerves of the whole body ; their laceration therefore must be felt over the entire frame. Witness the melancholy result of even a needle's puncture in even one of the remotest nerves. A spasm is not unfrequently produced by it in the muscles of the face, which locks the jaws inseparably. When, therefore the hands and feet of our blessed Lord were transfixed with nails, he must have felt the sharpest pangs shoot through every part of his body. Supported only by his lacerated limbs, and suspended from his pierced hands, our Lord had nearly six hours' torment to endure.—*John Stevenson.*

Verse 16.—*" They pierced my hands and my feet."* That evangelical prophet testifies it, " Behold I have graven thee upon the palms of my hands." Isaiah xlix. 16. Were we not engraven there when his hands were pierced for us ? " They digged my hands and my feet." And they digged them so deep, that the very prints remained after his resurrection, and their fingers were thrust into them for evidence sake. Some have thought that those scars remain still in his glorious body, to be showed at his second appearing : " They shall see him whom they have pierced." That is improbable, but this is certain ; there remains still an impression upon Christ's hands and his heart, the sealing and wearing of the elect there, as precious jewels.—*Thomas Adams.*

Verse 17.—*" I may tell all my bones : they look and stare upon me."* The skin and flesh were distended by the posture of the body on the cross, that the bones, as through a thin veil, became visible, and might be counted.—*George Horne.*

Verse 17.—*" I may tell all my bones."* For, as the first Adam by his fall, lost the robe of innocence, and thence forth needed other garments, so the second Adam vouchsafed to be stripped of his earthly vestments, to the end it might hereafter be said to us, " Bring forth the first robe, and put it on him." Luke xv. 22.—*Gerhohus, quoted by J. M. Neale.*

Verse 17.—*" They look and stare upon me."* Sensitively conscious of his condition upon the cross, the delicate feelings of the holy Saviour were sorely pained by the gaze of the multitude. With impudent face they looked upon him. To view him better they halted as they walked. With deliberate insolence they collected in groups, and made their remarks to each other on his conduct and appearance. Mocking his naked, emaciated, and quivering body, they " looked and stared upon him."—*John Stevenson.*

Verse 17.—" *They look and stare upon me.*" Oh, how different is that look which the awakened sinner directs to Calvary, when faith lifts up her eye to him who agonised, and bled, and died, for the guilty! And what gratitude should perishing men feel, that from him that hangs upon the accursed tree there is heard proceeding the inviting sound, " Look unto me, and be ye saved, all ye ends of the earth, for I am God, and besides me there is none else."—*John Morison.*

Verse 18.—" *They part my garments,*" etc. Perfectly naked did the cruciarii hang upon the cross, and the executioners received their clothes. There is nothing to show that there was a cloth even round the loins. The clothes became the property of the soldiers, after Roman usage. The outer garment was divided probably into four, by ripping up the seams. Four soldiers were counted off as a guard, by the Roman code. The under garment could not be divided, being woven ; and this led the soldiers to the dice-throwing.—*J. P. Lange, D.D., on Matthew* xxvii. 35.

Verse 18.—" *They part my garments,*" etc. Instruments will not be wanting to crucify Christ, if it were but for his old clothes, and those but little worth ; for these soldiers crucify him, though they got but his garments for their reward. Christ did submit to suffer naked, hereby to teach us :—1. That all flesh are really naked before God by reason of sin (Exodus xxxii. 25 ; 2 Chron. xxviii. 19), and therefore our Surety behoved to suffer naked. 2. That he offered himself a real captive in his sufferings, that so he might fully satisfy justice by being under the power of his enemies, till he redeemed himself by the strong hand, having fully paid the price ; for therefore did he submit to be stripped naked, as conquerors use to do with prisoners. 3. That by thus suffering naked he would expiate our abuse of apparel, and purchase to us a liberty to make use of suitable raiment, and such as becometh us in our station. 4. That by this suffering naked he would purchase unto them who flee to him to be covered with righteousness and glory, and to walk with him in white for ever, and would point out the nakedness of those who, not being found clothed with his righteousness, shall not be clothed upon with immortality and glory. 2 Cor. v. 2, 3. 5. He would also by this, teach all his followers to resolve on nakedness in their following of him, as a part of their conformity with their Head (1 John iv. 17 ; Rom. viii. 35; Heb. xi. 37), and that therefore they should not dote much on their apparel when they have it.—*George Hutcheson,* 1657.

Verse 18.—"*And cast lots upon my vesture.*" Trifling as this act of casting the lot for our Lord's vesture may appear, it is most significant. It contains a double lesson. It teaches us how greatly that seamless shirt was valued ; how little he had to whom it belonged. It seemed to say, this garment is more valuable than its owner. As it was said of the thirty pieces of silver, "A goodly price at which I was prized at of them ; " so may we say regarding the casting of the lot, " How cheaply Christ was held ! "—*John Stevenson.*

Verse 20.—"*My darling* " had better be rendered " my lonely, or solitary one." For he wishes to say that his soul was lonely and forsaken by all, and that there was no one who sought after him as a friend, or cared for him, or comforted him : as we have it, Psalm cxlii. 4, " Refuge failed me ; no one cared for my soul ; I looked on my right hand, but there was no one who would know me ; " that is, solitude is of itself a certain cross, and especially so in such great torments, in which it is most grievous to be immersed without an example and without a companion. And yet, in such a state, everyone of us must be, in some suffering or other, and especially in that of death ; and we must be brought to cry out with Psalm xxv. 16, " Turn thee unto me, and have mercy upon me, for I am desolate and afflicted."—*Martin Luther.*

Verse 20.—" *The dog.*" It is scarcely possible for a European to form an idea of the intolerable nuisance occasioned in the villages and cities of the East, by the multitude of dogs that infest the streets. The natives, accustomed from their earliest years to the annoyance, come to be regardless of it ; but to a stranger, these creatures are the greatest plague to which he is subjected ; for as they are never allowed to enter a house, and do not constitute the property of any particular owner, they display none of those habits of which the domesticated species among us are found susceptible, and are destitute of all those social qualities which often render the dog the trusty and attached friend of man. . . . . The race seems wholly to degenerate in the warm regions of the East, and to approximate to the character of beasts of prey, as in disposition they are ferocious, cunning, bloodthirsty, and possessed of the most insatiable voracity : and even in their very form there is something repulsive ; their sharp and savage features ; their wolf-like eyes ; their long hanging ears ; their straight and pointed tails ; their lank and emaciated forms, almost entirely without a belly, give them an appearance of wretchedness and degradation, that stands in sad contrast with the general condition and qualities of the breed in Europe. . . . . These hideous creatures, dreaded by the people for their ferocity, or avoided by them as useless and unclean, are obliged to prowl about everywhere in search of a precarious existence. . . . . They generally run in bands, and their natural ferocity, inflamed by hunger, and the consciousness of strength, makes them the most troublesome and dangerous visitors to the stranger who unexpectedly finds himself in their neighbourhood, as they will not scruple to seize whatever he may have about him, and even, in the event of his falling, and being otherwise defenceless, to attack and devour him. . . . These animals, driven by hunger, greedily devour everything that comes in their way ; they glut themselves with the most putrid and loathsome substances that are thrown about the cities, and of nothing are they so fond as of human flesh, a repast, with which the barbarity of the despotic countries of Asia frequently supplies them, as the bodies of criminals slain for murder, treason, or violence, are seldom buried, and lie exposed till the mangled fragments are carried off by the dogs.—*From "Illustrations of Scripture, by the late Professor George Paxton, D.D., revised and enlarged by Robert Jamieson," 1843.*

Verse 21.—" *Save me from the lion's mouth.*" Satan is called a lion, and that fitly ; for he hath all the properties of the lion : as bold as a lion, as strong as a lion, as furious as a lion, as terrible as the roaring of a lion. Yea, worse : the lion wants subtlety and suspicion ; herein the devil is beyond the lion. The lion will spare the prostrate, the devil spares none. The lion is full and forbears, the devil is full and devours. He seeks all ; let not the simple say, He will take no notice of me ; nor the subtle, He cannot overreach me ; nor the noble say, He will not presume to meddle with me ; nor the rich, He dares not contest with me ; for he seeks to devour all. He is our common adversary, therefore let us cease all quarrels amongst ourselves, and fight with him.—*Thomas Adams.*

Verse 21.—" *Save me . . . from the horns of the unicorns.*" Those who are in great trouble from the power or cruelty of others, often cry out to their gods, " Ah ! save me from the tusk of the elephant from the mouth of the tiger and the tusks of the boar, deliver me, deliver me ! " " Who will save me from the horn of the *Kándam ?* " This animal is now extinct in these regions, and it is not easy to determine what it was ; the word in the Sathur—*Agaráthe*—is rendered " jungle cow."—*Joseph Roberts.*

Verse 21.—" *The horns of the unicorns.*" On turning to the Jewish Bible we find that the word רְאֵם is translated as buffalo, and there is no doubt that this rendering is nearly the correct one, and at the present day naturalists are nearly agreed that the reëm of the Old Testament must have been now the extinct urus. . . . . The presence of these horns affords a remarkable confirmation to a well-known passage in Julius Cæsar's familar " Commentaries." " The uri are little inferior to elephants in size " (" *magnitudine paulo infra elephantos ;*") " but are bulls in their nature, colour, and figure. Great is their strength, and great their swiftness ; nor do they spare man or beast when they have caught sight of them."—*J. G. Wood, M.A., F.L.S., in "Bible Animals," 1869.*

Verse 22.—" *I will declare thy name unto my brethren.*" Having thus obtained relief from the oppressive darkness, and regained conscious possession of the joy and light of his Father's countenance, the thoughts and desires of the Redeemer flow into their accustomed channel. The glory of God in the salvation of his church.—*John Stevenson.*

Verse 22.—" *My brethren.*" This gives evidence of the low condescension of the Son of God, and also of the high exaltation of sons of men ; for the Son of God to be a brother to sons of men is a great degree of humiliation, and for sons of men to be made brethren with the Son of God is a high degree of exaltation ; for Christ's brethren are in that respect sons of God, heirs of heaven, or kings, not earthly, but heavenly ; not temporary, but everlasting kings . . . . . This respect of Christ to his brethren is a great encouragement and comfort to such as are despised and scorned by men of this world for Christ's professing of them.—*William Gouge.*

Verse 24.—*" For he hath not despised nor abhorred the prayer of the poor, neither hath he hid his face from me ; but when I cried unto him, he heard me."* Let him, therefore, that desires to be of the seed of Israel, and to rejoice in the grace of the gospel, become poor, for this is a fixed truth, our God is one that has respect unto the poor ! And observe the fulness and diligence of the prophet. He was not content with having said " will not despise," but adds, " and will not abhor ; " and again, " will not turn away his face ; " and again, " will hear." And then he adds himself as an example, saying " When I cried," as our translation has it. As if he had said, " Behold ye, and learn by my example, who have been made the most vile of all men, and numbered among the wicked ; when I was despised, cast out, rejected, behold ! I was held in the highest esteem, and taken up, and heard. Let not this state of things, therefore, after this, my encouraging example, frighten you ; the gospel requires a man to be such a character before it will save him." These things, I say, because our weakness requires so much exhortation, that it might not dread being humbled, nor despair when humbled, and thus might, after the bearing of the cross, receive the salvation.—*Martin Luther.*

Verse 25.—*" My praise shall be of thee in the great congregation,"* etc. The joy and gratitude of our adorable Lord rise to such a height at this great deliverance, his heart so overflows with fresh and blessed consciousness of his heavenly Father's nearness, that he again pours forth the expression of his praise. By its repetition, he teaches us that this is not a temporary burst of gratitude, but an abiding determination, a full and settled resolution.—*John Stevenson.*

Verse 25.—*" In the great congregation."* Saints are fittest witnesses of sacred duties. That which, in Psa. cxvi. 14, is implied under this particle of restraint, " his," in " the presence of all his people," is in Psa. xxii. 25, more expressly noted by a more apparent description, thus : *" I will pay my vows before them that fear him."* None but true saints do truly fear God. 1. This property of God's people, that they fear the Lord, showeth that they will make the best use of such sacred, solemn duties performed in their presence. They will glorify God for this your zeal ; they will join their spirits with your spirit in this open performance of duty ; they will become followers of you, and learn of you to vow and pay unto the Lord, and that openly, publicly. 2. As for others, they are no better than such hogs and dogs as are not meet to have such precious pearls and holy things cast before them, lest they trample them under their feet.—*William Gouge.*

Verse 26.—*" The meek shall eat and be satisfied : they shall praise the Lord that seek him ; your heart shall live for ever."* A spiritual banquet is prepared in the church for the " *meek* " and lowly in heart. The death of Christ was the sacrifice for sin ; his flesh is meat indeed, and his blood is drink indeed. The poor in spirit feed on this provision, in their hearts by faith, and are *satisfied*, and thus, whilst they " *seek* " the *Lord*, they " *praise* " him also, and their " *hearts* " (or souls), are preserved unto eternal life.—*" Practical Illustrations of the Book of Psalms,"* 1836.

Verse 26.—*" The meek."* Bonaventure engraved this sweet saying of our Lord, " Learn of me, for I am meek and lowly in heart," in his study. O that this saying was engraved upon all your foreheads, and upon all your hearts !—*Charles Bradbury.*

Verse 26.—*" They shall praise the Lord that seek him ; your heart shall live for ever."* Now, I would fain know the man that ever went about to form such laws as should bind the *hearts* of men, or prepare such rewards as should reach the souls and consciences of men ! Truly, if any mortal man should make a law that his subjects should love him with all their hearts and souls, and not dare, upon peril of his greatest indignation, to entertain a traitorous thought against his royal person, but presently confess it to him, or else he would be avenged on him, he would deserve to be more laughed at for his pride and folly, than Xerxes for casting his fetters into the Hellespont, to chain the waves into his obedience ; or Caligula, that threatened the air, if it durst rain when he was at his pastimes, who durst not himself so much as look into the air when it thundered. Certainly a madhouse would be more fit for such a person than a throne, who should so far forfeit his reason, as to think that the thoughts and hearts of men were within his jurisdiction.—*William Gurnall.*

Verse 26.—" *Your heart,*" that is, not your outward man, but the hidden man of the heart (Ezek. xxxvi. 26) ; the new man which is created after the image of God in righteousness and true holiness, " *shall live for ever.*" The life which animates it is the life of the Spirit of God.—*John Stevenson.*

Verse 27.—" *All the ends of the world shall remember and turn unto the Lord ; and all the kindreds of the nations shall worship before him.*" This passage is a prediction of the conversion of the Gentiles. It furnishes us with two interesting ideas ; the nature of true conversion—and the extent of it under the reign of the Messiah. 1. The NATURE of true conversion :—It is to " *remember* "—to " *turn to the Lord* " —and to " *worship before him.*" This is a plain and simple process. Perhaps the first religious exercise of mind of which we are conscious is reflection. A state of unregeneracy is a state of forgetfulness. God is forgotten. Sinners have lost all just sense of his glory, authority, mercy, and judgment ; living as if there were no God, or as if they thought there was none. But if ever we are brought to be the subjects of true conversion, we shall be brought to remember these things. This divine change is fitly expressed by the case of the prodigal, who is said to have *come to himself,* or to his right mind. But further, true conversion consists not only in remembering but in " *turning to the Lord.*" This part of the passage is expressive of a cordial relinquishment of our idols, whatever they have been, and an acquiescence in the gospel way of salvation by Christ alone. Once more, true conversion to Christ will be accompanied with the " *worship* " of him. Worship, as a religious exercise, is the homage of the heart, presented to God according to his revealed will . . . . 2. The EXTENT of conversion under the kingdom or reign of the Messiah : " *All the ends of the world shall remember and turn unto the Lord ; and all the kindreds of the nations shall worship before him.*" It was fit that the accession of the Gentiles should be reserved for the gospel day, that it might grace the triumph of Christ over his enemies, and appear to be what it is, " the travail of his soul." This great and good work, begun in the apostles' days, *must* go on, and " must increase," till " *All the ends of the world shall remember and turn,*" and " *all the kindreds of the nations shall worship before him.*" Conversion work has been *individual ;* God has gathered sinners one by one. Thus it is at present with us ; but it will not be thus always. People will flock to Zion as doves to their windows. Further, conversion work has hitherto been circumscribed within certain parts of the world. But the time will come when " all the kindreds of the earth " shall worship. These hopes are not the flight of an ardent imagination ; they are founded on the true sayings of God. Finally, while we are concerned for the world, let us not forget our own souls. So the whole world be saved and we lost, what will it avail us ?—*Condensed from Andrew Fuller.*

Verse 27.—"*All the ends of the world shall* REMEMBER "—this is a remarkable expression. It implies that man has forgotten God. It represents all the successive generations of the world as but *one,* and then it exhibits that one generation, as if it had been once in paradise, suddenly remembering the Lord whom it had known there, but had long forgotten . . . . . The converted nations, we learn by this verse, will not only obtain remembrance of their past loss, but will also be filled with the knowledge of present duty.—*John Stevenson.*

Verse 27.—" *All the nations of the world* " (וְזָכְרוּ *jizkeru,* the same Hebrew root with אֶזְכִּיר *azkir*) " *shall remember ;*" why ? what is that ? or what shall they remember ? Even this : they shall turn to the Lord, and worship him, in his name, in his ordinances ; as is explained in the words following of the verse : " *And all the families of the nations* " (וְיִשְׁתַּחֲווּ *jishtachavu,* " shall bow " down themselves, or) " *worship before thee,*" etc. And so in Psalm lxxxvi. 9, " All nations whom thou hast made shall come " (וְיִשְׁתַּחֲווּ *vejishtachavu*) " and they shall worship before thee ; " and how shall they do so ? Even by recording, remembering, and making mention of the glory of thy name ; as in the words following (וִיכַבְּדוּ לִשְׁמֶךָ *vicabbedu lishmecha,*) " and shall glorify thy name."—*William Strong's " Saints' Communion with God,*" 1656.

Verses 27, 28.—The one undeviating object of the Son all through was, the glory of the Father : he came to do his will, and he fulfilled it with all the unvarying intensity of the most heavenly affection. What, then, will not be the exuberant joy of his heart, when in his glorious kingdom, he shall see the Father beyond all measure glorified ? . . . The praise and honour and blessing which will be yielded to the Father in that day through him, so that God shall be all in all, will make him feel he underwent not a sorrow too much for such a precious consummation. . . . Every note of thanksgiving which ascends to the Father, whether from the fowls of the air, or the beasts of the field, or the fishes of the sea, or the hills, or the mountains, or the trees of the forest, or the rivers of the valleys—all shall gladden his heart, as sweet in the ears of God, for the sake of him who redeemed even them from the curse, and restored to them a harmony more musical than burst from them on the birthday of their creation. And man! renewed and regenerated man! for whose soul the blood was spilt, and for the redemption of whose body death was overcome, how shall the chorus of his thanksgiving, in its intelligent and articulate hallelujahs, be the incense which that Saviour shall still love to present unto the Father, a sweet-smelling savour through himself, who, that he might sanctify his people by his own blood, suffered without the camp. How are the channels choked up or impaired in this evil world, wherein the praises and glory of our God should flow as a river! How will Christ then witness, to the delight of his soul, all cleared and restored! No chill upon the heart, no stammering in the tongue, in his Father's praises! No understanding dull, or eye feeble, in the apprehension of his glory! No hand unready, or foot stumbling, in the fulfilling of his commandments. God, the glory of his creatures: his glory their service and their love; and *all* this the reward to Jesus of once suffering himself.—*C. J. Goodhart, M.A., in " Bloomsbury Lent Lectures," 1848.*

Verse 29.—"*And they shall bow that go down into the dust; their soul liveth not:*" that is, *whose soul liveth not,* by an Hebraism; it being meant, that he who is of most desperate condition, being without hope of life and salvation, his sins are so notorious, shall " eat " also of this feast, and be turned to God to " worship " and serve him; being thus plucked out of the jaws of death and everlasting destruction, as it were, being before this very hour ready to seize upon him. The new translation, " *None can keep alive his own soul,*" as it agreeth not with the Hebrew, so it makes the sense more perplexed. By " *him that goeth down to the dust, whose soul liveth not,*" some understand the most miserably poor, who have nothing to feed upon, whereby their life may be preserved, yet shall feed also of this feast as well as the rich, and praise God. Ainsworth is for either spiritually poor and miserable, because most wicked, or worldly poor; and there is an exposition of Basil's, understanding by the rich, the rich in faith and grace, touching which, or the rich properly so called, he is indifferent. But because it is said, " *The fat of the earth,*" I prefer the former, and that the close of the verse may best answer to the first part; the latter by " *those that are going to the dust,*" understand the miserably poor. So that there is a commonplace of comfort for all, both richest, and poorest, if they be subjects of God's kingdom of grace: their souls shall be alike fed by him and saved.—*John Mayer.*

Verse 29.—" *All they that go down to the dust;* " either those who stand quivering on the brink of the grave, or those who occupy the humble, sequestered walks of life. As the great and opulent of the earth are intended in the first clause, it is not by any means unnatural to suppose that the image of going " *down to the dust,*" is designed to represent the poor and mean of mankind, who are unable to support themselves, and to provide for their multiplied necessities. If the grave be alluded to, as is thought by many eminent divines, the beautiful sentiment of the verse will be, that multitudes of dying sinners shall be brought to worship Jehovah, and that those who cannot save or deliver themselves shall seek that shelter which none can find but those who approach the mercy-seat. " Rich and poor," as Bishop Horne, observes, " are invited "—that is, to " worship God; " " and the hour is coming when all the race of Adam, as many as sleep in the ' dust ' of the earth, unable to raise themselves from thence, quickened and called forth by the voice of the Son of Man, must bow the knee to King Messiah."—*John Morison.*

Verse 29.—To be brought to the dust, is, first, a circumlocution or description of death: " *Shall the dust praise thee, shall it declare thy truth?* " Psalm xxx. 9. That is shall I praise thee when I am among the dead? " *What profit is there in my blood, when I go down to the pit?* " Not that profit, sure, I cannot bring thee in the tribute of praise when my life's gone out. Secondly, to be brought to the dust is a description of any low and poor condition. " *All they that be fat upon earth* (that is, the great and mighty), " *shall eat and worship* " " *all they that go down to the dust* " (that is, the mean and base), " *shall bow before him.*" As if he had said, rich and poor, high and low, the king and the beggar, have alike need of salvation by Jesus Christ, and must submit unto him, that they may be saved, for, as it there follows, "*none can keep alive his own soul.*" The capitivity of the Jews in Babylon is expressed under those notions of *death,* and of *dwelling in the dust* (Isaiah xxvi. 19); to show how low, that no power but his who can raise the dead, could work their deliverance.—*Joseph Caryl.*

Verse 29.—"*None can keep alive his own soul.*" And yet we look back to our conversion, and its agonies of earnestness, its feelings of deep, helpless dependence— of Christ's being absolutely our daily, hourly need—supplier—as a *past* something—a stage of spiritual life which is *over.* And we are satisfied to have it so. The Spirit of God moved over our deadness, and breathed into us the breath of life. My soul became *a living soul.* But was this enough? God's word says, No. "None can *keep alive* his own soul." My heart says, No. Truth must ever answer to truth. I cannot (ah! have I not tried, and failed?) I cannot *keep alive* my own soul. We cannot live upon ourselves. Our physical life is kept up by supply from without— air, food, warmth. So must the spiritual life. Jesus gives, Jesus feeds us day by day, else must the life fade out and die. "None can *keep alive* his own soul." It is not enough to be made alive. I must be fed, and guided, and taught, and kept in life. Mother, who hast brought a living babe into the world, is your work done? Will you not nurse it, and feed it, and care for it, that it may be *kept alive?* Lord, I am this babe. I live indeed, for I can crave and cry. Leave me not, O my Saviour. Forsake not the work of thine own hands. In thee I live. Hold me, carry me, feed me, let me abide in thee. "For the kingdom is the Lord's: and he is the governor among the nations. All they that be fat upon earth shall eat and worship: all they that go down to the dust shall bow before him: and none can keep alive his own soul." In our work for God, we need to remember this. Is not the conversion, the arousing of sinners, the great, and with many, the sole aim in working for God? Should it be so? Let us think of this other work. Let us help to *keep alive.* Perhaps it is less distinguished, as it may be less distinguished to feed a starving child than to rescue a drowning man. But let us walk less by sight, more by faith. Let us not indeed neglect to call to life those who are spiritually dead. But oh! let us watch for the more hidden needs of the living—the fading, starving, fainting souls, which yet can walk and speak, and cover their want and sorrow. Let us be fellow-workers with God in *all* his work. And with a deep heart-feeling of the need of *constant* life supplies from above, let us try how often, how freely, we may be made the channels of those streams of the "water of life,"—for "none can keep alive his own soul."—*Mary B. M. Duncan, in "Bible Hours,"* 1866.

Verse 29.—Having considered the vastness and glory of the prospect, our Lord next contemplates the reality and minuteness of its accomplishment. He sets before his mind individual cases and particular facts. He appears to look upon this picture of the future as we do upon a grand historical painting of the past. It seems natural to gaze with silent admiration on the picture as a whole, then to fix the attention on particular groups, and testify our sense of the general excellence, by expatiating on the truth and beauty of the several parts.—*John Stevenson.*

Verse 30.—"*A seed shall serve him.*" This figurative expression signifies Christ and his people, who yield true obedience to God—they are called by this name in a spiritual and figurative, but most appropriate sense. The idea is taken from the operations of the husbandman who carefully reserves every year a portion of his grain for seed. Though it be small, compared with all the produce of his harvest, yet he prizes it very highly and estimates it by the value of that crop which it may yield in the succeeding autumn. Nor does he look only to the quantity, he pays particular regard to the quality of the seed. He reserves only the best, nay, he will put away his own if spoiled, that he may procure better. The very smallest quantity of really good seed, is, to him, an object of great desire, and if by grievous failure of crops, he should not be able to procure more than a single grain, yet would he accept it thankfully, preserve it carefully, and plant it in the most favourable soil. Such is the source from which the metaphor is taken.—*John Stevenson.*

Verse 31.—"*And shall declare his righteousness.*" The occupation of the seed is to "*declare,*" to testify from their own experience, from their own knowledge and convictions, that grand subject, theme, or lesson, which they have learned . . . . . . They will declare the righteousness of God the Holy Ghost in his convictions of sin, in his reproofs of conscience, in his forsaking of the impenitent, and in his abiding with the believer. And in a special manner, they will declare the righteousness of God the Son, during his human life, in his sufferings, and death, as man's surety, by which he "magnified the law, and made it honourable" (Isa. xlii. 21), and on account of which they are able to address him by this name, "The Lord our Righteousness." (Jer. xxiii. 6.)—*John Stevenson.*

Verse 31.—"*A people that shall be born.*" What is this? What people is there that is not born? According to my apprehensions I think this is said for this reason —because the people of other kings are formed by laws, by customs, and by manners; by which, however, you can never move a man to true righteousness: it is only a fable of righteousness, and a mere theatrical scene or representation. For even the law of Moses could form the people of the Jews unto nothing but unto hypocrisy. But the people of this King are not formed by laws to make up an external appearance, but they are begotten by water and by the Spirit unto a new creature of truth.— *Martin Luther.*

HINTS TO PREACHERS.

Whole Psalm.—The volume entitled "Christ on the Cross," by Rev. J. Stevenson, has a sermon upon every verse. We give the headings, they are suggestive. *Verse* 1. The Cry. 2. The Complaint. 3. The Acknowledgment. 4—6. The Contrast. 6. The Reproach. 7. The Mockery. 8. The Taunt. 9, 10. The Appeal. 11. The Entreaty. 12, 13. The Assault. 14. The Faintness. 15. The Exhaustion. 16. The Piercing. 17. The Emaciation. 17. The Insulting Gaze. 18. The Partition of the Garments and Casting Lots. 19—21. The Importunity. 21. The Deliverance. 22. The Gratitude. 23. The Invitation. 24. The Testimony. 25. The Vow. 26. The Satisfaction of the Meek; the Seekers of the Lord praising Him; the Eternal Life. 27. The Conversion of the World. 28. The Enthronement. 29. The Author of the Faith. 30. The Seed. 31. The Everlasting Theme and Occupation. The Finish of the Faith.

Verse 1.—The Saviour's dying cry.

Verse 2.—*Unanswered prayer.* Enquire the reasons for it; encourage our hope concerning it; urge to continuance in importunity.

Verse 3.—Whatever God may do, we must settle it in our minds that he is holy and to be praised.

Verse 4.—God's faithfulness in past ages a plea for the present.

Verses 4, 5.—Ancient saints. I. Their life. "*They trusted.*" II. Their practice. "*They cried.*" III. Their experience. "*Were not confounded.*" IV. Their voice to us.

Verses 6—18.—Full of striking sentences upon our Lord's sufferings.

Verse 11.—A saint's troubles, his arguments in prayer.

Verse 20.—"*My darling.*" A man's soul to be very dear to him.

Verse 21 (first clause).—"*Lion's mouth.*" Men of cruelty. The devil. Sin. Death. Hell.

Verse 22.—Christ as a brother, a preacher, and a precentor.

Verse 22.—A sweet subject, a glorious preacher, a loving relationship, a heavenly exercise.

Verse 23.—*A threefold duty,* "praise him," "glorify him;" "fear him;" *towards one object,* "the Lord;" *for three characters,* "ye that fear him, seed of Jacob, seed of Israel," *which are but one person.*

Verse 23.—Glory to God the fruit of the tree on which Jesus died.

Verse 24.—A consoling fact in history attested by universal experience.

Verse 24 (first clause).—A common fear dispelled.

Verse 25.—Public praise. I. A delightful exercise—"praise." II. A personal participation—"My praise." III. A fitting object—"of thee." IV. A special source—"from thee." V. An appropriate place—"in the great congregation."

Verse 25 (second clause).—*Vows.* What vows to make, when and how to make them, and the importance of paying them.

Verse 26.—*Spiritual feasting.* The guests, the food, the host, and the satisfaction.

Verse 26 (*second clause*).—*Seekers who shall be singers.* Who they are? What they shall do? When? and what is the reason for expecting that they shall?

Verse 27 (*last clause*).—*Life ev rlasting.* What lives? Source of life. Manner of life. Why for ever? What occupation? What comfort to be derived from it?

Verse.—Nature of true conversion, and extent of it under the reign of the Messiah.—*Andrew Fuller.*

Verse 27.—The universal triumph of Christianity certain.

Verse 27.—The order of conversion. See the Exposition.

Verse 28.—The empire of the Kings of kings as it is, and as it shall be.

Verse 29.—Grace for the rich, grace for the poor, but all lost without it.

Verse 29 (*last clause*).—A weighty text upon the vanity of self-confidence.

Verse 30.—The perpetuity of the church.

Verse 30 (*last clause*).—Church history, the marrow of all history.

Verse 31.—Future prospects for the church. I. Conversions certain. II. Preachers promised. III. Succeeding generations blest. IV. Gospel published. V. Christ exalted.

PSALM XXIII.

There is no inspired title to this Psalm, and none is needed, for it records no special events, and needs no other key than that which every Christian may find in his own bosom. It is David's Heavenly Pastoral; a surpassing ode, which none of the daughters of music can excel. The clarion of war here gives place to the pipe of peace, and he who so lately bewailed the woes of the Shepherd tunefully rehearses the joys of the flock. Sitting under a spreading tree, with his flock around him, like Bunyan's shepherd-boy in the Valley of Humiliation, we picture David singing this unrivalled pastoral with a heart as full of gladness as it could hold; or, if the Psalm be the product of his after years, we are sure that his soul returned in contemplation to the lonely water-brooks which rippled among the pastures of the wilderness, where in early days he had been wont to dwell. This is the pearl of Psalms whose soft and pure radiance delights every eye; a pearl of which Helicon need not be ashamed, though Jordan claims it. Of this delightful song it may be affirmed that its piety and its poetry are equal, its sweetness and its spirituality are unsurpassed.

The position of this Psalm is worthy of notice. It follows the twenty-second, which is peculiarly the Psalm of the Cross. There are no green pastures, no still waters on the other side of the twenty-second Psalm. It is only after we have read, "My God, my God, why hast thou forsaken me!" that we come to "The Lord is my Shepherd." We must by experience know the value of the blood-shedding, and see the sword awakened against the Shepherd, before we shall be able truly to know the sweetness of the good Shepherd's care.

It has been said that what the nightingale is among birds, that is this divine ode among the Psalms, for it has sung sweetly in the ear of many a mourner in his night of weeping, and has bidden him hope for a morning of joy. I will venture to compare it also to the lark, which sings as it mounts, and mounts as it sings, until it is out of sight, and even then is not out of hearing. Note the last words of the Psalm—"I will dwell in the house of the Lord for ever;" these are celestial notes, more fitted for the eternal mansions than for these dwelling places below the clouds. Oh that we may enter into the spirit of the Psalm as we read it, and then we shall experience the days of heaven upon the earth!

EXPOSITION.

THE Lord *is* my shepherd; I shall not want.

2 He maketh me to lie down in green pastures : he leadeth me beside the still waters.

3 He restoreth my soul : he leadeth me in the paths of righteousness for his name's sake.

4 Yea, though I walk through the valley of the shadow of death, I will fear no evil : for thou *art* with me ; thy rod and thy staff they comfort me.

5 Thou preparest a table before me in the presence of mine enemies : thou anointest my head with oil ; my cup runneth over.

6 Surely goodness and mercy shall follow me all the days of my life : and I will dwell in the house of the Lord for ever.

1. "*The Lord is my shepherd.*" What condescension is this, that the Infinite Lord assumes towards his people the office and character of a Shepherd ! It should be the subject of grateful admiration that the great God allows himself to be compared to anything which will set forth his great love and care for his own people. David had himself been a keeper of sheep, and understood both the needs of the sheep and the many cares of a shepherd. He compares himself to a creature weak, defenceless, and foolish, and he takes God to be his Provider, Preserver, Director, and, indeed, his everything. No man has a right to consider himself the Lord's sheep unless his nature has been renewed, for the scriptural description of unconverted men does not picture them as sheep, but as wolves or goats. A sheep is an object

of property, not a wild animal ; its owner sets great store by it, and frequently it is bought with a great price. It is well to know, as certainly as David did, that we belong to the Lord. There is a noble tone of confidence about this sentence. There is no " if " nor " but," nor even " I hope so ; " but he says, " The Lord *is* my shepherd." We must cultivate the spirit of assured dependence upon our heavenly Father. The sweetest word of the whole is that monosyllable, "*My.*" He does not say, " The Lord is the shepherd of the world at large, and leadeth forth the multitude as his flock," but " The Lord is *my* shepherd ; " if he be a Shepherd to no one else, he is a Shepherd to *me ;* he cares for *me,* watches over *me,* and preserves *me.* The words are in the present tense. Whatever be the believer's position, he is even now under the pastoral care of Jehovah.

The next words are a sort of inference from the first statement—they are sententious and positive—"*I shall not want.*" I might want otherwise, but when the Lord is my Shepherd he is able to supply my needs, and he is certainly willing to do so, for his heart is full of love, and therefore "*I shall not want.*" I shall not lack for *temporal things.* Does he not feed the ravens, and cause the lilies to grow ? How, then, can he leave his children to starve ? I shall not want *for spirituals,* I know that his grace will be sufficient for me. Resting in him he will say to me, " As thy day so shall thy strength be." I may not possess all that I wish for, but " I shall not *want.*" Others, far wealthier and wiser than I, may want, but *I shall not.*" " The young lions *do* lack, and suffer hunger : but they that seek the Lord shall not want any good thing." It is not only " I do not want," but "*I shall not* want." Come what may, if famine should devastate the land, or calamity destroy the city, "*I shall not want.*" Old age with its feebleness shall not bring me any lack, and even death with its gloom shall not find me destitute. I have all things and abound ; not because I have a good store of money in the bank, not because I have skill and wit with which to win my bread, but because " *The Lord is my Shepherd.*" The wicked always want, but the righteous never ; a sinner's heart is far from satisfaction, but a gracious spirit dwells in the palace of content.

2. " *He maketh me to lie down in green pastures : he leadeth me beside the still waters.*" The Christian life has two elements in it, the contemplative and the active, and both of these are richly provided for. First, the contemplative, "*He maketh me to lie down in green pastures.*" What are these " *green pastures* " but the Scriptures of truth—always fresh, always rich, and never exhausted ? There is no fear of biting the bare ground where the grass is long enough for the flock to lie down in it. Sweet and full are the doctrines of the gospel ; fit food for souls, as tender grass is natural nutriment for sheep. When by faith we are enabled to find rest in the promises, we are like the sheep that lie down in the midst of the pasture ; we find at the same moment both provender and peace, rest and refreshment, serenity and satisfaction. But observe : " He *maketh* me to lie down." It is the Lord who graciously enables us to perceive the preciousness of his truth, and to feed upon it. How grateful ought we to be for the power to appropriate the promises ! There are some distracted souls who would give worlds if they could but do this. They know the blessedness of it, but they cannot say that this blessedness is theirs. They know the " *green pastures,*" but they are not made to " *lie down* " in them. Those believers who have for years enjoyed a " full assurance of faith " should greatly bless their gracious God.

The second part of a vigorous Christian's life consists in gracious activity. We not only think, but we act. We are not always lying down to feed, but are journeying onward toward perfection ; hence we read, " he *leadeth me beside the still waters.*" What are these " *still waters* " but the influences and graces of his blessed Spirit ? His Spirit attends us in various operations, like waters—in the plural—to cleanse, to refresh, to fertilise, to cherish. They are " *still* waters," for the Holy Ghost loves peace, and sounds no trumpet of ostentation in his operations. He may flow into our soul, but not into our neighbour's, and therefore our neighbour may not perceive the divine presence ; and though the blessed Spirit may be pouring his floods into one heart, yet he that sitteth next to the favoured one may know nothing of it.

> "In sacred silence of the mind
> My heaven, and there my God I find."

Still waters run deep. Nothing more noisy than an empty drum. That silence is golden indeed in which the Holy Spirit meets with the souls of his saints. Not to raging waves of strife, but to peaceful streams of holy love does the Spirit of God conduct the chosen sheep. He is a dove, not an eagle ; the dew, not the hurricane. Our Lord leads us beside these " *still waters ;* " we could not go there of ourselves, we need his guidance, therefore is it said, " *he leadeth me.*" He does not drive us. Moses drives us by the law, but Jesus leads us by his example, and the gentle drawings of his love.

3. " *He restoreth my soul.*" When the soul grows sorrowful he revives it ; when it is sinful he sanctifies it ; when it is weak he strengthens it. " *He* " does it. His ministers could not do it if he did not. His Word would not avail by itself. "*He restoreth* my soul." Are any of us low in grace ? Do we feel that our spirituality is at its lowest ebb ? He who turns the ebb into the flood can soon restore our soul. Pray to him, then, for the blessing—" Restore thou me, thou Shepherd of my soul ! "

" *He leadeth me in the paths of righteousness for his name's sake.*" The Christian delights to be obedient, but it is the obedience of love, to which he is constrained by the example of his Master. " *He leadeth* me." The Christian is not obedient to some commandments and neglectful of others ; he does not pick and choose, but yields to all. Observe, that the plural is used—" the *paths* of righteousness." Whatever God may give us to do we would do it, led by his love. Some Christians overlook the blessing of sanctification, and yet to a thoroughly renewed heart this is one of the sweetest gifts of the covenant. If we could be saved from wrath, and yet remain unregenerate, impenitent sinners, we should not be saved as we desire, for we mainly and chiefly pant to be saved *from* sin and led in the way of holiness. All this is done out of pure free grace ; " *for his name's sake.*" It is to the honour of our great Shepherd that we should be a holy people, walking in the narrow way of righteousness. If we be so led and guided we must not fail to adore our heavenly Shepherd's care.

4. " *Yea, though I walk through the valley of the shadow of death, I will fear no evil : for thou art with me ; thy rod and thy staff they comfort me.*" This unspeakably delightful verse has been sung on many a dying bed, and has helped to make the dark valley bright times out of mind. Every word in it has a wealth of meaning. " Yea, though I *walk*," as if the believer did not quicken his pace when he came to die, but still calmly *walked* with God. To walk indicates the steady advance of a soul which knows its road, knows its end, resolves to follow the path, feels quite safe, and is therefore perfectly calm and composed. The dying saint is not in a flurry, he does not run as though he were alarmed, nor stand still as though he would go no further, he is not confounded nor ashamed, and therefore keeps to his old pace. Observe that it is not walking *in* the valley, but *through* the valley. We go through the dark tunnel of death and emerge into the light of immortality. We do not die, we do but sleep to wake in glory. Death is not the house but the porch, not the goal but the passage to it. The dying article is called a *valley*. The storm breaks on the mountain, but the valley is the place of quietude, and thus full often the last days of the Christian are the most peaceful in his whole career ; the mountain is bleak and bare, but the valley is rich with golden sheaves, and many a saint has reaped more joy and knowledge when he came to die than he ever knew while he lived. And, then, it is not " the valley of death," but " the valley *of the shadow* of death," for death in its substance has been removed, and only the shadow of it remains. Some one has said that when there is a shadow there must be light somewhere, and so there is. Death stands by the side of the highway in which we have to travel, and the light of heaven shining upon him throws a shadow across our path ; let us then rejoice that there is a light beyond. Nobody is afraid of a shadow, for a shadow cannot stop a man's pathway even for a moment. The shadow of a dog cannot bite ; the shadow of a sword cannot kill ; the shadow of death cannot destroy us. Let us not, therefore, be afraid. " *I will fear no evil.*" He does not say there shall not be any evil ; he had got beyond even that high assurance, and knew that Jesus had put all evil away ; but " I will *fear* no evil ; " as if even his fears, those shadows of evil, were gone for ever. The worst evils of life are those which do not exist except in our imagination. If we had no troubles but real troubles, we should not have a tenth part of our present sorrows. We feel a thousand deaths in fearing one, but the Psalmist was cured of the disease of fearing. " I will fear *no evil*," not even the Evil One himself ; I will not dread the last enemy, I will look upon him as a conquered foe, an enemy to be destroyed, " *For thou art with me.*" This is the joy of the Christian ! " *Thou* art with me." The little child out at sea in the storm

is not frightened like all the other passengers on board the vessel, it is asleep in its mother's bosom ; it is enough for it that its mother is with it ; and it should be enough for the believer to know that Christ is with him. " *Thou* art with me ; I have in having thee, all that I can crave : I have perfect comfort and absolute security, for *thou* art with me." " *Thy rod and thy staff*," by which thou governest and rulest thy flock, the ensigns of thy sovereignty and of thy gracious care—" *they comfort me.*" I will believe that thou reignest still. The rod of Jesse shall still be over me as the sovereign succour of my soul.

Many persons profess to receive much comfort from the hope that they shall not die. Certainly there will be some who will be " alive and remain " at the coming of the Lord, but is there so very much of advantage in such an escape from death as to make it the object of Christian desire ? A wise man might prefer of the two to die, for those who shall not die, but who " shall be caught up together with the Lord in the air," will be losers rather than gainers. They will lose that actual fellowship with Christ in the tomb which dying saints will have, and we are expressly told they shall have no preference beyond those who are asleep. Let us be of Paul's mind when he said that " To die is gain," and think of " departing to be with Christ, which is far better." This twenty-third Psalm is not worn out, and it is as sweet in a believer's ear now as it was in David's time, let novelty-hunters say what they will.

5. " *Thou preparest a table before me in the presence of mine enemies.*" The good man has his enemies. He would not be like his Lord if he had not. If we were without enemies we might fear that we were not the friends of God, for the friendship of the world is enmity to God. Yet see the quietude of the godly man in spite of, and in the sight of, his enemies. How refreshing is his calm bravery ! " *Thou preparest a table before me.*" When a soldier is in the presence of his enemies, if he eats at all he snatches a hasty meal, and away he hastens to the fight. But observe : " Thou *preparest* a table," just as a servant does when she unfolds the damask cloth and displays the ornaments of the feast on an ordinary peaceful occasion. Nothing is hurried, there is no confusion, no disturbance, the enemy is at the door and yet God prepares a table, and the Christian sits down and eats as if everything were in perfect peace. Oh ! the peace which Jehovah gives to his people, even in the midst of the most trying circumstances !

> " Let earth be all in arms abroad,
> They dwell in perfect peace."

" *Thou anointest my head with oil.*" May we live in the daily enjoyment of this blessing, receiving a fresh anointing for every day's duties. Every Christian is a priest, but he cannot execute the priestly office without unction, and hence we must go day by day to God the Holy Ghost, that we may have our heads anointed with oil. A priest without oil misses the chief qualification for his office, and the Christian priest lacks his chief fitness for service when he is devoid of new grace from on high. " *My cup runneth over.*" He had not only enough, a cup full, but more than enough, a cup which overflowed. A poor man may say this as well as those in higher circumstances. " What, all this, and Jesus Christ too ? " said a poor cottager as she broke a piece of bread and filled a glass with cold water. Whereas a man may be ever so wealthy, but if he be discontented his cup cannot run over ; it is cracked and leaks. Content is the philosopher's stone which turns all it touches into gold ; happy is he who has found it. Content is more than a kingdom, it is another word for happiness.

6. " *Surely goodness and mercy shall follow me all the days of my life.*" This is a fact as indisputable as it is encouraging, and therefore a heavenly *verily*, or " *surely* " is set as a seal upon it. This sentence may be read, " *only* goodness and mercy," for there shall be unmingled mercy in our history. These twin guardian angels will always be with me at my back and my beck. Just as when great princes go abroad they must not go unattended, so it is with the believer. Goodness and mercy follow him always—" *all the days of his life* "—the black days as well as the bright days, the days of fasting as well as the days of feasting, the dreary days of winter as well as the bright days of summer. Goodness supplies our needs, and mercy blots out our sins. " *And I will dwell in the house of the Lord for ever.*" "A servant abideth not in the house for ever, but the son abideth ever." While I am here I will be a child at home with my God ; the whole world shall be his house to me ; and when I ascend into the upper chamber I shall not change my company, nor

even change the house ; I shall only go to dwell in the upper storey of the house of the Lord for ever.

May God grant us grace to dwell in the serene atmosphere of this most blessed Psalm !

EXPLANATORY NOTES AND QUAINT SAYINGS.

Whole Psalm.—David has left no sweeter Psalm than the short twenty-third. It is but a moment's opening of his soul ; but, as when one, walking the winter street, sees the door opened for some one to enter, and the red light streams a moment forth, and the forms of gay children are running to greet the comer, and genial music sounds, though the door shuts and leaves the night black, yet it cannot shut back again all that the eyes, the ear, the heart, and the imagination have seen—so in this Psalm, though it is but a moment's opening of the soul, are emitted truths of peace and consolation that will never be absent from the world. The twenty-third Psalm is the nightingale of the Psalms. It is small, of a homely feather, singing shyly out of obscurity ; but, oh ! it has filled the air of the whole world with melodious joy, greater than the heart can conceive. Blessed be the day on which that Psalm was born ! What would you say of a pilgrim commissioned of God to travel up and down the earth singing a strange melody, which, when one heard, caused him to forget whatever sorrow he had ? And so the singing angel goes on his way through all lands, singing in the language of every nation, driving away trouble by the pulses of the air which his tongue moves with divine power. Behold just such an one ! This pilgrim God has sent to speak in every language on the globe. It has charmed more griefs to rest than all the philosophy of the world. It has remanded to their dungeon more felon thoughts, more black doubts, more thieving sorrows, than there are sands on the sea-shore. It has comforted the noble host of the poor. It has sung courage to the army of the disappointed. It has poured balm and consolation into the heart of the sick, of captives in dungeons, of widows in their pinching griefs, of orphans in their loneliness. Dying soldiers have died easier as it was read to them ; ghastly hospitals have been illuminated ; it has visited the prisoner, and broken his chains, and, like Peter's angel, led him forth in imagination, and sung him back to his home again. It has made the dying Christian slave freer than his master, and consoled those whom, dying, he left behind mourning, not so much that he was gone, as because they were left behind, and could not go too. Nor is its work done. It will go singing to your children and my children, and to their children, through all the generations of time ; nor will it fold its wings till the last pilgrim is safe, and time ended ; and then it shall fly back to the bosom of God, whence it issued, and sound on, mingled with all those sounds of celestial joy which make heaven musical for ever.—*Henry Ward Beecher, in* "*Life Thoughts.*"

Whole Psalm.—This Psalm may well be called David's *bucolicon,* or pastoral, so daintily hath he struck upon the whole string, through the whole hymn. *Est Psalmus honorabilis,* saith Aben-Ezra ; it is a noble Psalm, written and sung by David, not when he fled into the forest of Hareth (1 Sam. xxii. 5), as some Hebrews will have it ; but when as having overcome all his enemies, and settled his kingdom, he enjoyed great peace and quiet, and had one foot, as it were, upon the battlements of heaven. The Jews at this day use for most part to repeat this Psalm after they are sat down to meat.—*John Trapp.*

Whole Psalm.—Augustine is said to have beheld, in a dream, the one hundred and nineteenth Psalm rising before him as a tree of life in the midst of the paradise of God. This twenty-third may be compared to the fairest flowers that grew around it. The former has even been likened to the sun amidst the stars—surely this is like the richest of the constellations, even the Pleiades themselves !—*John Stoughton, in* "*The Songs of Christ's Flock,*" 1860.

Whole Psalm.—Some pious souls are troubled because they cannot at all times, or often, use, in its joyous import, the language of this Psalm. Such should remember that David, though he lived long, never wrote but one twenty-third Psalm. Some of his odes do indeed express as lively a faith as this, and faith can walk in darkness. But where else do we find a whole Psalm expressive of personal confidence, joy, and triumph, from beginning to end ?   God's people have their seasons of darkness and their times of rejoicing.—*William S. Plumer.*

Verse 1.—" *The Lord is my shepherd ; I shall not want.*"   Let them say that will, " My lands shall keep me, I shall have no want, my merchandise shall be my help, I shall have no want ; " let the soldier trust unto his weapons, and the husbandman unto his labour ; let the artificer say unto his art, and the tradesman unto his trade, and the scholar unto his books, " These shall maintain me, I shall not want."   Let *us* say with the church, as we both say and sing, " The Lord is my keeper, I shall not want."   He that can truly say so, contemns the rest, and he that desires more than God, cannot truly say, the Lord is his, the Lord is this shepherd, governor and commander, and therefore I shall not want.—*John Hull, B.D., in " Lectures on Lamentations,"* 1617.

Verse 1.—" *The Lord is my shepherd ; I want nothing :* " thus it may be equally well rendered, though in our version it is in the future tense.—*J. R. Macduff, D.D., in " The Shepherd and his Flock,"* 1866.

Verse 1.—" *The Lord is my shepherd.*"   We may learn in general from the metaphor, that it is the property of a gracious heart to draw some spiritual use or other from his former condition.   David himself having sometimes been a shepherd, as himself confesseth when he saith, " he took David from the sheepfold from following the sheep," etc., himself having been a shepherd, he beholds the Lord the same to him.   Whatsoever David was to his flock—watchful over them, careful to defend them from the lion and the bear, and whatsoever thing else might annoy them, careful of their pasturage and watering, etc., the same and much more he beholds the Lord to himself.   So Paul : " I was a persecutor, and an oppressor : but the Lord had mercy on me."   This we may see in good old Jacob : " With this staff," saith he, " I passed over Jordan ; " and that now God had blessed him and multiplied him exceedingly.   The doctrine is plain ; the reasons are, first, because true grace makes no object amiss to gather some gracious instruction : it skills not what the object be, so that the heart be gracious ; for that never wants matter to work upon. And, secondly, it must needs be so, for such are guided by God's Spirit, and therefore are directed to a spiritual use of all things.—*Samuel Smith's " Chiefe Shepheard,"* 1625.

Verse 1.—" *Shepherd.*"   May this sweet title persuade Japhet to dwell in the tents of Shem : my meaning is, that those who as yet never knew what it was to be enfolded in the bosom of Jesus, who as yet were never lambs nor ewes in Christ's fold, consider the sweetness of this Shepherd, and come in to him.   Satan deals seemingly sweet, that he may draw you into sin, but in the end he will be really bitter to you.   Christ, indeed, is seemingly bitter to keep you from sin, hedging up your way with thorns.   But he will be really sweet if you come into his flock, even notwithstanding your sins.   Thou lookest into Christ's fold, and thou seest it hedged and fenced all about to keep you in from sin, and this keeps thee from entering ; but oh ! let it not.   Christ, indeed, is unwilling that any of his should wander, and if they be unwilling too, it's well.   And if they wander he'll fetch them in, it may be with his shepherd's *dog* (some affliction) ; but he'll not be, as we say, *dogged* himself. No, he is and will be sweet.   It may be, now Satan smiles, and is pleasant to you while you sin ; but know, he'll be bitter in the end.   He that sings syren-like now, will devour lion-like at last.   He'll torment you and vex you, and be burning and bitterness to you.   O come in therefore to Jesus Christ ; let him be now the shepherd of thy soul.   And know then, he'll be sweet in endeavouring to keep thee from sin before thou commit it ; and he'll be sweet in delivering thee from sin after thou hast committed it.   O that this thought—that Jesus Christ is sweet in his carriage unto all his members, unto all his flock, especially the sinning ones, might persuade the hearts of some sinners to come in unto his fold.—*John Durant,* 1652.

Verse 1 (*first clause*).—*Feedeth me,* or, is *my feeder, my pastor.*   The word comprehendeth all duties of a good herd, as together feeding, guiding, governing, and defending his flock.—*Henry Ainsworth.*

Verse 1.—" *The Lord is my shepherd.*"   Now the reasons of this resemblance I take to be these :—First, one property of a good shepherd is, skill to know and judge aright of his sheep, and hence is it that it is a usual thing to set mark upon sheep, to the end that if they go astray (as of all creatures they are must subject to wander), the shepherd may seek them up and bring them home again.   The same thing is affirmed of Christ, or rather indeed Christ affirmeth the same thing of himself,

" I know them, and they follow me." John x. 27. Yea, doubtless, he that hath numbered the stars, and calleth them all by their names, yea, the very hairs of our head, taketh special notice of his own children, " the sheep of his pasture," that they may be provided for and protected from all danger. Secondly, a good shepherd must have skill in the pasturing of his sheep, and in bringing them into such fruitful ground, as they may battle and thrive upon : a good shepherd will not suffer his sheep to feed upon rotten soil, but in wholesome pastures. . . . . Thirdly, a good shepherd, knowing the straying nature of his sheep, is so much the more diligent to watch over them, and if at any time they go astray, he brings them back again. This is the Lord's merciful dealing towards poor wandering souls. . . . Fourthly, a good shepherd must have will to feed his sheep according to his skill : the Lord of all others is most willing to provide for his sheep. How earnest is Christ with Peter, to " feed his sheep," urging him unto it three several times ! Fifthly, a good shepherd is provided to defend his flock. . . . The Lord is every way provided for the safety and defence of his sheep, as David confesseth in this Psalm (verse 4), " *Thy rod and thy staff they comfort me.*" And again, " I took unto me two staves " (saith the Lord), " the one I called Beauty, and the other I called Bands ; and I fed the flock." Zech. xi. 7. Sixthly, it is the property of a good shepherd, that if any of his sheep be weak and feeble, or his lambs young, for their safety and recovery he will bear them in his arms. The Lord is not wanting to us herein. Isa. xl. 11. And lastly, it is the property of a good shepherd to rejoice when the strayed sheep is brought home. The Lord doth thus rejoice at the conversion of a sinner. Luke xv. 7.—*Samuel Smith.*

Verse 1.—" *The Lord is my shepherd.*" I notice that some of the flock keep near the shepherd, and follow whithersoever he goes without the least hesitation, while others stray about on either side, or loiter far behind ; and he often turns round and scolds them in a sharp, stern cry, or sends a stone after them. I saw him lame one just now. Not altogether unlike the good Shepherd. Indeed, I never ride over these hills, clothed with flocks, without meditating upon this delightful theme. Our Saviour says that the good shepherd, when he putteth forth his own sheep, goeth before them, and they follow. John x. 4. This is true to the letter. They are so tame and so trained that they *follow* their keeper with the utmost docility. He leads them forth from the fold, or from their houses in the villages, just where he pleases. As there are many flocks in such a place as this, each one takes a different path, and it is his business to find pasture for them. It is necessary, therefore, that they should be taught to follow, and not to stray away into the unfenced fields of corn which lie so temptingly on either side. Any one that thus wanders is sure to get into trouble. The shepherd calls sharply from time to time to remind them of his presence. They know his voice, and follow on ; but, if a stranger call, they stop short, lift up their heads in alarm, and, if it is repeated, they turn and flee, because they know not the voice of a stranger. This is not the fanciful costume of a parable, it is simple fact. I have made the experiment repeatedly. The shepherd goes before, not merely to point out the way, but to see if it is practicable and safe. He is armed in order to defend his charge, and in this he is very courageous. Many adventures with wild beasts occur, not unlike that recounted by David (1 Sam. xvii. 34—36), and in these very mountains ; for though there are now no lions here, there are wolves in abundance ; and leopards and panthers, exceeding fierce, prowl about the wild wadies. They not unfrequently attack the flock in the very presence of the shepherd, and he must be ready to do battle at a moment's warning. I have listened with intense interest to their graphic descriptions of downright and desperate fights with these savage beasts. And when the thief and the robber come (and come they do), the faithful shepherd has often to put his life in his hand to defend his flock. I have known more than one case in which he had literally to lay it down in the contest. A poor faithful fellow last spring, between Tiberias and Tabor, instead of fleeing, actually fought three Bedawîn robbers until he was hacked to pieces with their khanjars, and died among the sheep he was defending. Some sheep always keep near the shepherd, and are his special favourites. Each of them has a name, to which it answers joyfully, and the kind shepherd is ever distributing to such, choice portions which he gathers for that purpose. These are the contented and happy ones. They are in no danger of getting lost or into mischief, nor do wild beasts or thieves come near them. The great body, however, are mere worldlings, intent upon their mere pleasures or selfish interests. They run from bush to bush, searching for variety or delicacies, and only now and then lift their heads to see where the shepherd is, or, rather, where the general flock is, lest they get so far away as to occasion a remark in their little community, or rebuke from their keeper. Others, again, are restless and discontented, jumping into everybody's field, climbing into bushes, and even into leaning trees, whence they often fall and break their limbs. These cost the good shepherd incessant trouble.—*W. M. Thomson, D.D., in " The Land and the Book."*

Verse 1.—" Shepherd." As we sat, the silent hillsides around us were in a moment filled with life and sound. The shepherds led their flocks forth from the gates of the city. They were in full view, and we watched them and listened to them with no little interest. Thousands of sheep and goats were there, grouped in dense, confused masses. The shepherds stood together until all came out. Then they separated, each shepherd taking a different path, and uttering as he advanced a shrill peculiar call. The sheep heard them. At first the masses swayed and moved, as if shaken by some internal convulsion ; then points struck out in the direction taken by the shepherds ; these became longer and longer until the confused masses were resolved into long, living streams, flowing after their leaders. Such a sight was not new to me, still it had lost none of its interest. It was perhaps one of the most vivid illustrations which human eyes could witness of that beautiful discourse of our Lord recorded by John, " And the sheep hear the shepherd's voice : and he calleth his own sheep by name, and leadeth them out. And when he putteth forth his own sheep, he goeth before them, and the sheep follow him : for they know his voice. And a stranger will they not follow, but will flee from him : for they know not the voice of strangers," chap. x. 3—5. The shepherds themselves had none of that peaceful and placid aspect which is generally associated with pastoral life and habits. They looked more like warriors marching to the battle-field—a long gun slung from the shoulder, a dagger and heavy pistols in the belt, a light battle-axe or ironheaded club in the hand. Such were the equipments ; and their fierce flashing eyes and scowling countenances showed but too plainly that they were prepared to use their weapons at any moment.—*J. L. Porter, A.M., in " The Giant Cities of Bashan,"* 1867.

Verse 1.—"I shall not want." You must distinguish 'twixt *absence*, and 'twixt *indigence*. *Absence* is when some thing is not present; *indigence* or *want*, is when a needful good is not present. If a man were to walk, and had not a staff, here were something absent. If a man were to walk, and had but one leg, here were something whereof he were indigent. It is confessed that there are many good things which are absent from a good person, but no good thing which he wants or is indigent of. If the good be absent and I need it not, this is no want; he that walks without his cloak, walks well enough, for he needs it not. As long as I can walk carefully and cheerfully in my general or particular calling, though I have not such a load of accessories as other men have, yet I *want* nothing, for my little is enough and serves the turn. . . . . Our corruptions are still craving, and they are always inordinate, they can find more wants than God needs to supply. As they say of fools, they can propose more questions than twenty wise men need to answer. They in James iv. 3, did *ask*, but *received not ;* and he gives two reasons for it :—1. This *asking* was but a *lusting :* " ye lust and have not " (verse 4) : another, they did ask *to consume it upon their lusts* (verse 3). God will see that his people shall not want ; but withal, he will never engage himself to the satisfying of their corruptions, though he doth to the supply of their conditions. It is one thing what the sick man wants, another what his disease wants. Your ignorance, your discontents, your pride, your unthankful hearts, may make you to believe that you dwell in a barren land, far from mercies (as melancholy makes a person to imagine that he is drowning, or killing, etc.) ; whereas if God did open your eyes as he did Hagar's, you might see fountains and streams, mercies and blessings sufficient ; though not many, yet enough, though not so rich, yet proper, and every way convenient for your good and comfort ; and thus you have the genuine sense, so far as I can judge of David's assertion, " I shall not want."—*Obadiah Sedgwick.*

Verse 1.—" I shall not want." Only he that can want does not want ; and he that cannot does. You tell me that a godly man wants these and these things, which the wicked man hath ; but I tell you he can no more be said to " *want* " them than a butcher may be said to want Homer, or such another thing, because his disposition is such, that he makes no use of those things which you usually mean. 'Tis but only necessary things that he cares for, and those are not many. But *one* thing is necessary, and that he hath chosen, namely, *the better part.*

And therefore if he have nothing at all of all other things, he does not *want*, neither is there anything *wanting* which might make him rich enough, or by absence whereof his riches should be said to be deficient. A body is not *maimed* unless it have lost a principal part : only *privative* defects discommend a thing, and not those that are *negative.* When we say, there is nothing *wanting* to such-and-such a creature or thing that a man hath made, we mean that it hath all that belongs necessarily to it. We speak not of such things as may be added for compliments or ornaments or the like, such as are those things usually wherein wicked men excel the godly. Even so it is when we say that a godly man *wanteth nothing.* For though in regard of unnecessary goods he be " as having nothing ; " yet in regard of others he is as if he possessed all things. He wants nothing that is necessary either for his glorifying of God (being able to do that best in and by his afflictions), or for God's glorifying of him, and making him happy, having God himself for his portion and supply of his wants, who is abundantly sufficient at all times, for all persons, in all conditions. *Zachary Bogan.*

Verse 1.—"*I shall not want.*" To be raised above the fear of want by committing ourselves to the care of the Good Shepherd, or by placing our confidence in worldly property, are two distinct and very opposite things. The confidence in the former case, appears to the natural man to be hard and difficult, if not unreasonable and impossible : in the latter it appears to be natural, easy, and consistent. It requires, however, no lengthened argument to prove that he who relies on the promise of God for the supply of his temporal wants, possesses an infinitely greater security than the individual who confides in his accumulated wealth. The ablest financiers admit that there must be appended to their most choice investments, this felt or expressed proviso—" So far as human affairs can be secure." . . . . . Since then no absolute security against want can be found on earth, it necessarily follows, that he who trusts in God is the most wise and prudent man. Who dare deny that the promise of the living God is an absolute security ?—*John Stevenson.*

Verse 1.—" *I shall not want.*" The sheep of Christ may change their pasture, but they shall never want a pasture. " Is not the life more than meat, and the body than raiment ? " Matt vi. 25. If he grant unto us great things, shall we distrust him for small things ? He who has given us heavenly beings will also give us earthly blessings. The great Husbandman never overstocked his own commons. *William Secker.*

Verse 1.—" *I shall not want.*" Ever since I heard of your illness, and the Lord's mercy in sustaining and restoring, I have been intending to write, to bless the Lord with my very dear sister, and ask for some words to strengthen my faith, in detail of your cup having run over in the hour of need. Is it not, indeed, the bleating of Messiah's sheep, " *I shall not want* " ? " shall not want," because the Lord is our Shepherd ! Our Shepherd the All-sufficient ! nothing can unite itself to him ; nothing mingle with him ; nothing add to his satisfying nature ; nothing diminish from his fulness. There is a peace and fulness of expression in this little sentence, known only to the sheep. The remainder of the Psalm is a drawing out of this, " *I shall not want.*" In the unfolding we find repose, refreshment, restoring mercies, guidance, peace in death, triumph, an overflowing of blessings ; future confidence, eternal security in life or death, spiritual or temporal, prosperity or adversity, for time or eternity. May we not say, " *The Lord is my Shepherd*"? for we stand on the sure foundation of the twenty-third Psalm. How can we want, when united to him ! we have a right to use all his riches. Our wealth is his riches and glory. With him nothing can be withheld. Eternal life *is* ours, with the promise that *all* shall be added ; all *he* knows we want. Our Shepherd has learned the wants of his sheep by experience, for he was himself " led as a sheep to the slaughter." Does not this expression, dictated by the Spirit, imply a promise, and a full promise, when connected with his own words, " *I know my sheep,*" by what painful discipline he was instructed in this knowledge, subjected himself to the wants of every sheep, every lamb of his fold, that he might be able to be touched with a feeling of their infirmities ? The timid sheep has nothing to fear ; fear not want, fear not affliction, fear not pain ; " *fear not ;* " according to your want shall be your supply, " The Lord is my portion, saith my soul ; *therefore* will I trust in him."—*Theodosia A. Howard, Viscountess Powerscourt* (1830), *in* "*Letters,*" *etc., edited by Robert Daly, D.D.,* 1861.

Verse 1.—" *I shall not want.*" One of the poor members of the flock of Christ was reduced to circumstances of the greatest poverty in his old age, and yet he never murmured. "You must be badly off," said a kind-hearted neighbour to him one day as they met upon the road, " you must be badly off ; and I don't know how an old man like you can maintain yourself and your wife ; yet you are always cheerful !" "Oh, no !" he replied, "we are not badly off, I have a rich Father, and he does not suffer me to want." "What ! your father not dead yet ? he must be very old indeed !" "Oh !" said he, "my Father never dies, and he always takes care of me !" This aged Christian was a daily pensioner on the providence of his God. His struggles and his poverty were known to all ; but his own declaration was, that he never wanted what was absolutely necessary. The days of his greatest straits were the days of his most signal and timely deliverances. When old age benumbed the hand of his industry, the Lord extended to him the hand of charity. And often has he gone forth from his scanty breakfast, not knowing from what earthly source his next meal was to be obtained. But yet with David he could rely on his Shepherd's care, and say, " I shall not want ; " and as certainly as he trusted in God, so surely, in some unexpected manner was his necessity supplied. *John Stevenson.*

Verse 1.—In the tenth chapter of John's gospel, you will find six marks of Christ sheep :—1. They *know their Shepherd ;* 2. They *know his voice* ; 3. They *hear him* calling them each by name ; 4. They *love* him ; 5. They *trust* him ; 6. They *follow him.—In " The Shepherd King," by the Authoress of " The folded Lamb "* [*Mrs. Rogers*], 1856.

Verses 1—4.—Come down to the river ; there is something going forward worth seeing. Yon shepherd is about to lead his flock across ; and as our Lord says of the good shepherd—you observe that he goes before, and the sheep follow. Not all in the same manner, however. Some enter boldly, and come straight across. These are the loved ones of the flock, who keep hard by the footsteps of the shepherd, whether sauntering through green meadows by the still waters, feeding upon the mountains, or resting at noon beneath the shadow of great rocks. And now others enter, but in doubt and alarm. Far from their guide, they miss the ford, and are carried down the river, some more, some less ; and yet, one by one, they all struggle over and make good their landing. Notice those little lambs. They refuse to enter, and must be driven into the stream by the shepherd's dog, mentioned by Job in his " parable." Poor things ! how they leap, and plunge, and bleat in terror ! That weak one yonder will be swept quite away, and perish in the sea. But no ; the shepherd himself leaps into the stream, lifts it into his bosom, and bears it trembling to the shore. All safely over, how happy they appear ! The lambs frisk and gambol about in high spirits, while the older ones gather round their faithful guide, and look up to him in subdued but expressive thankfulness. Now, can you watch such a scene, and not think of that Shepherd who leadeth Joseph like a flock ; and of another river, which all his sheep must cross ? He, too, goes before, and, as in the case of this flock, they who keep near him " fear no evil." They hear his sweet voice saying, " When thou passest through the waters, I will be with thee ; and through the rivers they shall not overflow thee." Isaiah xliii. 2. With eye fastened on him, they scarcely see the stream, or feel its cold and threatening waves. *W. M. Thomson.*

Verse 2.—" *He maketh me to lie down in green pastures,*" etc. Not only he hath " *green pastures* " to lead me into, which shows his ability, but he *leads me into them,* which shows his goodness. He leads me not into pastures that are withered and dry, that would distaste me before I taste them ; but he leads me into " *green pastures,*" as well to please my eye with the verdure as my stomach with the herbage ; and inviting me, as it were, to eat by setting out the meat in the best colour. A meat though never so good, yet if it look not handsomely, it dulls the appetite ; but when besides the goodness it hath also a good look, this gives the appetite another edge, and makes a joy before enjoying. But yet the goodness is not altogether in the greenness. Alas ! green is but a colour, and colours are but deceitful things ; they might be green leaves, or they might be green flags or rushes ; and what good were to me in such a greenness ? No, my soul : the goodness is in being " green *pastures,*" for now they perform as much as they promise ; and as in being *green* they were a comfort to me as soon as I saw them, so in being green " *pastures* " they are a refreshing to me now as soon as I taste them. As they are pleasant to look on, so they are wholesome to feed on : as they are sweet to be tasted, so they are easy to be digested ; that I am now, methinks, in a kind of paradise and seem not to want anything unless perhaps a little water with which now and then to wash my mouth, at most to take sometimes a sip : for though sheep be no great drinkers, and though their pastures being green, and full of sap, make drink the less needful ; yet some drink they must have besides. And now see the great goodness of this Shepherd, and what just cause there is to depend upon his providence; for he lets not his sheep want this neither, but " *he leadeth them besides still waters,*" not waters that roar and make a noise, enough to fright a fearful sheep, but waters "*still*" and quiet; that though they drink but little, yet they may drink that little without fear. And may I not justly say now, " *The Lord is my Shepherd; I shall not want*"? And yet perhaps there will be *want* for all this; for is it enough that he lead them into green pastures and beside still waters ? May he not lead them in, and presently take them out again before their bellies be half full ; and so instead of making them happy, make them more miserable ? set them in a longing with the sight, and then frustrate them of their expectation ? No, my soul ; the measure of this Shepherd's goodness is more than so. He not only leadeth them into green pastures, but " *he makes them to lie down* " *in them*—he leads them not in to post over their meat as if they were to eat a passover, and to take it *in transitu*, as dogs drink Nylus ; but, " *he makes them to lie down in green pastures,*" that they may eat their fill and feed at leisure ; and when they have done, " *lie down* " and take their case, that their after reckoning may be as pleasing as their repast.—*Sir Richard Baker.*

Verse 2.—" *He leadeth me.*" Our guiding must be mild and gentle, else it is not *duxisti*, but *traxisti*—drawing and driving, and no *leading*. *Leni spiritu non dur? manu*—rather by an inward sweet influence to be *led*, than by an outward extreme violence to be forced forward. . . . Touching what kind of cattle, to very good purpose, Jacob, a skilful shepherd, answereth Esau (who would have had Jacob and his flocks have kept company with him in his *hunting* pace), Nay, not so, sir, said Jacob, it is a tender cattle that is under my hands, and must be softly driven, as they may endure : if one " should over drive them but one day," they would all die or be laid up for many days after. Gen xxxiii. 13.—*Lancelot Andrewes.*

Verse 2.—" *He leadeth me,*" etc. In ordinary circumstances the shepherd does not *feed* his flock, except by leading and guiding them where they may gather for themselves ; but there are times when it is otherwise. Late in autumn, when the pastures are dried up, and in winter, in places covered with snow, he must furnish them food or they die. In the vast oak woods along the eastern sides of Lebanon, between Baalbek and the cedars, there are there gathered innumerable flocks, and the shepherds are all day long in the bushy trees, cutting down the branches, upon whose green leaves and tender twigs the sheep and goats are entirely supported. The same is true in all mountain districts, and large forests are preserved on purpose.—*W. M. Thomson.*

Verse 2.—" *Lie down* "—" *leadeth.*" Sitting Mary and stirring Martha are emblems of contemplation and action, and as they dwell in one house, so must these in one heart.—*Nathanael Hardy.*

Verse 2.—This short but touching epitaph is frequently seen in the catacombs at Rome, "*In Christo, in pace* "—(In Christ, in peace). Realise the constant presence of the Shepherd of peace. " HE maketh me to lie down ! " " HE leadeth me."—*J. R. Macduff, D.D.*

Verse 2 (*last clause*).—" *Easily leadeth,*" or " *comfortably guideth me :* " it noteth a soft and gentle leading, with sustaining of infirmity.—*H. Ainsworth.*

Verse 2.—" *Green pastures.*" Here are many pastures, and every pasture rich so that it can never be eaten bare ; here are many streams, and every stream so deep and wide that it can never be drawn dry. The sheep have been eating in these pastures ever since Christ had a church on earth, and yet they are as full of grass as ever. The sheep have been drinking at these streams ever since Adam, and yet they are brim full to this very day, and they will so continue till the sheep are above the use of them in heaven !—*Ralph Robinson*, 1656.

Verse 2.—" *Green pastures . . . . . beside the still waters.*" From the top of the mound [of Arban on the Khabour] the eye ranged over a level country bright with flowers, and spotted with black tents, and innumerable flocks of sheep and camels. During our stay at Arban, the colour of these great plains was undergoing a continual change. After being for some days of a golden yellow, a new family of flowers would spring up, and it would turn almost in a night to a bright scarlet, which would again as suddenly give way to the deepest blue. Then the meadows would be mottled with various hues, or would put on the emerald green of the most luxuriant of pastures. The glowing descriptions I had so frequently received from the Bedouins, of the beauty and fertility of the banks of the Khabour were more than realised. The Arabs boast that its meadows bear three distinct crops of grass during the year, and the wandering tribes look upon its wooded banks and constant green sward as a paradise during the summer months, where man can enjoy a cool shade, and beast can find fresh and tender herbs, whilst all around is yellow, parched, and sapless. *Austin H. Layard*, 1853.

Verse 2.—With guidance to " *green pastures*," the Psalmist has, with good reason, associated guardianship beside " *still waters ;* " for as we can only appropriate the word through the Spirit, so we shall ordinarily receive the Spirit through the word ; not indeed only by hearing it, not only by reading it, not only by reflecting upon it.   The Spirit of God, who is a most free agent, and who is himself the source of liberty, will come into the heart of the believer when he will, and how he will, and as he will. But the effect of his coming will ever be the realisation of some promise, the recognition of some principle, the attainment of some grace, the understanding of some mystery, which is already in the word, and which we shall thus find, with a deeper impression, and with a fuller development, brought home with power to the heart.—*Thomas Dale, M.A., in " The Good Shepherd,"* 1847.

Verse 2 —" *Still waters ;* " which are opposed to great rivers, which both affright the sheep with their noise, and expose them to the danger of being carried away by their swift and violent streams, whilst they are drinking at them.—*Matthew Poole.*

Verse 2.—" *Still waters ;* " Hebrew, " Waters of rests," *ex quibus diligunt oves bibere*, saith Kimchi, such as sheep love to drink of, because void of danger, and yielding a refreshing air. Popish clergymen are called the " inhabitants of the sea," Rev. xii. 12, because they set abroach gross, troubled, brackish, and sourish doctrine, which rather bringeth barrenness to their hearts, and gnaweth their entrails than quencheth their thirst, or cooleth their heat. The doctrine of the gospel, like the waters of Siloe (Isa. viii. 8), run gently, but taste pleasantly.—*John Trapp.*

Verse 3.—" *He restoreth my soul,*" etc. The subjects experimentally treated in this verse are, first, the believer's liability to fall, or deviate even within the fold of the church, else wherefore should he need to be " *restored ?* "   Next, the promptitude of the Good Shepherd to interpose for his rescue. " *He restoreth my soul.*" Then, Christ's subsequent care " *to lead him in the paths of righteousness ;* " and, lastly, the reason assigned wherefore he will do this—resolving all into the spontaneousness, the supremacy, the omnipotence of grace. He will do all, " *for his own name's sake.*"—*Thomas Dale.*

Verse 3.—" *He restoreth my soul.*"   The same hand which first rescued us from ruin, reclaims us from all our subsequent aberrations. Chastisement itself is blended with tenderness ; and the voice which speaks reproof, saying, " They have perverted their way, and they have forsaken the Lord their God," utters the kindest invitation, " Return, ye backsliding children, and I will heal your backslidings." Nor is the voice unheard, and the call unanswered or unfelt. " Behold, we come unto thee ; for thou art the Lord our God." Jer. iii. 22. " When thou saidst, Seek my face ; my heart said unto thee, Thy face, Lord, will I seek."—*J. Thornton's " Shepherd of Israel,"* 1826.

Verse 3.—" *He restoreth my soul.*"   He restores it to its original purity, that was now grown foul and black with sin ; for also, what good were it to have " *green* " pastures and a *black* soul ! He " *restores* " it to its natural temper in affections, that was grown distempered with violence of passions ; for alas ! what good were it to have " *still* " waters and *turbulent* spirits ! He " *restores* " it indeed to life, that was grown before in a manner quite dead ; and who could " *restore my soul* " to life, but he only that is the Good Shepherd and gave his life for his sheep ?—*Sir Richard Baker.*

Verse 3.—" *He shall convert my soul ;* " turn me not only from sin and ignorance, but from every false confidence, and every deceitful refuge. " *He shall bring me forth in paths of righteousness ;* " in those paths of imputed righteousness which are always adorned with the trees of holiness, are always watered with the fountains of consolation, and always terminate in everlasting rest. Some, perhaps, may ask, why I give this sense to the passage ? Why may it not signify the paths of duty, and the way of our own obedience ?   Because such effects are here mentioned as never have resulted, and never can result, from any duties of our own.   These are not " *green pastures,*" but a parched and blasted heath.   These are not " *still waters,*" but a troubled and disorderly stream.   Neither can these speak peace or administer comfort when we pass through the valley and shadow of death.   To yield these blessings, is the exalted office of Christ, and the sole prerogative of his obedience. *James Hervey.*

Verse 3.—" *He restoreth my soul :* "   Hebrew   He bringeth it back ; " either, 1. From its errors or wandering ;   or, 2. Into the body, out of which it was even departing and fainting away.   He reviveth or comforteth me.—*Matthew Poole.*

Verse 3.—" *Paths of righteousness.*"   Alas !   O Lord, these " *paths of righteousness* " have a long time so little been frequented, that prints of a *path* are almost clean worn out ;   that it is a hard matter now, but to find where the *paths* lie, and if we can find them, yet they are so narrow and so full of ruts, that without special assistance it is an impossible thing not to fall or go astray.   Even so angels, and those no mean ones, were not able to go right in these " *paths of righteousness,*" but for want of leading, went away and perished.   O, therefore, thou the Great Shepherd of my soul, as thou art pleased of thy grace to lead me *into* them, so vouchsafe with thy grace to lead me *in* them ;   for though in themselves they be " paths of *righteousness,*" yet to me they will be but paths of *error* if thou vouchsafe not, as well to lead me *in* them, as *into* them.—*Sir Richard Baker.*

Verse 3.—" *Paths.*"   In the wilderness and in the desert there are no raised paths, the paths being merely tracks ;   and sometimes there are six or eight paths running unevenly alongside each other.   No doubt this is what is figuratively referred to in Psalm xxiii. 3, " *He leadeth me in the paths of righteousness,*" all leading to one point.—*John Gadsby.*

Verse 3.—" *For his name's sake.*"   Seeing he hath taken upon him the *name* of a " *Good Shepherd,*" he will discharge his part, whatever his sheep be.   It is not their being *bad sheep* that can make him leave being a " *Good Shepherd,*" but he will be " *good,*" and maintain the credit of " his name" in spite of all their badness; and though no benefit come to them of it, yet there shall glory accrue to him by it, and " *his name* " shall nevertheless be magnified and extolled.—*Sir Richard Baker.*

Verse 4.—" *Yea, though I walk through the valley of the shadow of death, I will fear no evil.*"   To " fear no evil," then, " in the valley of the shadow of death," is a blessed privilege open to every true believer !   For death shall be to him no death at all, but a very deliverance from death, from all pains, cares, and sorrows, miseries and wretchedness of this world, and the very entry into rest, and a beginning of everlasting joy :   a tasting of heavenly pleasures, so great, that neither tongue is able to express, neither eye to see, nor ear to hear them, no, nor any earthly man's heart to conceive them. . . . And to comfort all Christian persons herein, holy Scripture calleth this bodily death a sleep, wherein man's senses be, as it were, taken from him for a season, and yet, when he awaketh, he is more fresh than when he went to bed ! . . . . Thus is this bodily death a door or entering into life, and therefore not so much dreadful, if it be rightly considered, as it is comfortable ;   not a mischief, but a remedy for all mischief ; no enemy, but a friend ;   not a cruel tyrant, but a gentle guide :   leading us not to mortality, but to immortality   not to sorrow and pain, but to joy and pleasure, and that to endure for ever !—*Homily against the Fear of Death,* 1547.

Verse 4.—" *Yea, though I walk through the valley of the shadow of death, I will fear no evil.*"   Though I were called to such a sight as Ezekiel's vision, a valley full of dead men's bones ;   though the king of terrors should ride in awful pomp through the streets, slaying heaps upon heaps, and thousands should fall at my side, and ten thousands at my right hand, I will fear no evil.   Though he should level his fatal arrows at the little circle of my associates, and put lover and friend far from me, and mine acquaintance into darkness, I will fear no evil.   Yea, though I myself should feel his arrow sticking fast in me, the poison drinking up my spirits ; though I should in consequence of that fatal seizure, sicken and languish, and have all the symptoms of approaching dissolution, still I will fear no evil.   Nature, indeed, may start back and tremble, but I trust that he who knows the flesh to be weak, will pity and pardon these struggles.   However I may be afraid of the agonies of dying, I will fear no evil in death.   The venom of his sting is taken away.   The point of his arrow is blunted so that it can pierce no deeper than the body.   My soul is invulnerable. I can smile at the shaking of his spear ; look unmoved on the ravages which the unrelenting destroyer is making on my tabernacle ; and long for the happy period when he shall have made a breach wide enough for my heaven-aspiring spirit to fly away and be at rest.—*Samuel Lavington.*

Verse 4.—" *Yea, though I walk through the valley of the shadow of death, I will fear no evil.*" " I want to talk to you about heaven," said a dying parent* to a member of his family. " We may not be spared to each other long. May we meet around the throne of glory, one family in heaven !" Overpowered at the thought, his beloved daughter exclaimed, " Surely you do not think there is any danger ? " Calmly and beautifully he replied, " Danger, my darling ! Oh, do not use that word ! There can be no danger to the Christian, whatever may happen ! All is right ! All is well ! God is love ! All is well ! Everlastingly well ! Everlastingly well ! "—*John Stevenson.*

Verse 4.—" *Though I walk through the valley of the shadow of death, I will fear no evil.*" What not fear then ? Why, what friend is it that keeps up your spirits, that bears you company in that black and dismal region ? He will soon tell you God was with him, and in those slippery ways he leaned upon his staff, and these were the cordials that kept his heart from fainting. I challenge all the gallants in the world, out of all their merry, jovial clubs, to find such a company of merry cheerful creatures as the friends of God are. It is not the company of God, but the want of it, that makes sad. Alas ! you know not what their comforts be, and strangers intermeddle not with their joy. You think they cannot be merry when their countenance is so grave ; but they are sure you cannot be truly merry when you smile with a curse upon your souls. They know that he spoke that sentence which could not be mistaken, " Even in laughter the heart is sorrowful ; and the end of that mirth is heaviness." Prov. xiv. 13. Then call your roaring, and your singing, and laughter, mirth ; but the Spirit of God calls it madness. Eccl. ii. 2. When a carnal man's heart is ready to die within him, and with Nabal, to become like a stone, how cheerfully then can those look that have God for their friend ! Which of the valiant ones of the world can outface death, look joyfully into eternity ? Which of them can hug a fagot, embrace the flames ? This the saint can do, and more too ; for he can look infinite justice in the face with a cheerful heart ; he can hear of hell with joy and thankfulness ; he can think of the day of judgment with great delight and comfort. I again challenge all the world to produce one out of all their merry companies, one that can do all this. Come, muster up all your jovial blades together ; call for your harps and viols ; add what you will to make the concert complete ; bring in your richest wines ; come, lay your heads together, and study what may still add to your comfort. Well, is it done ? Now, come away, sinner, this night thy soul must appear before God. Well now, what say you, man ? What ! doth your courage fail you ? Now call for your merry companions, and let them cheer thy heart. Now call for a cup, a whore ; never be daunted, man. Shall one of thy courage quail, that could make a mock at the threatenings of the Almighty God ? What so boon and jolly but now, and now down in the mouth ! Here's a sudden change indeed ! Where are thy merry companions, I say again ? All fled ? Where are thy darling pleasures ? Have all forsaken thee ? Why shouldst thou be dejected ; there's a poor man in rags that's smiling ? What ! art thou quite bereft of all comfort ? What's the matter, man ? What's the matter ? There's a question with all my heart, to ask a man that must appear before God to-morrow morning. Well, then, it seems your heart misgives you. What then did you mean to talk of joys and pleasures ? Are they all come to this ? Why, there stands one that now hath his heart as full of comfort as ever it can hold, and the very thoughts of eternity, which do so daunt your soul, raise his ! And would you know the reason ? He knows he is going to his Friend ; nay, his Friend bears him company through that dirty lane. Behold how good and how pleasant a thing it is for God and the soul to dwell together in unity ! This it is to have God for a friend. " Oh blessed is the soul that is in such a case ; yea, blessed is the soul whose God is the Lord." Psa. cxliv. 15.—*James Janeway.*

Verse 4.—" *Though I walk through the valley of the shadow of death.*" Any darkness is evil, but *darkness and the shadow of death* is the utmost of evils. David put the worst of his case and the best of his faith when he said, " *Though I walk in the valley of the shadow of death, I will fear no evil ;* " that is, in the greatest evil I will fear no

---

* The late Rev. Hugh Stowell, Rector of Ballaugh, Isle of Man.

evil. . . . . . Again, to be under the shadow of a thing, is to be under the power of a thing. . . . . . Thus, to be under the shadow of death, is to be so under the power or reach of death, that death may take a man and seize upon him when it pleaseth. *" Though I walk in the valley of the shadow of death,"* that is, though I be so near death, that it seems to others death may catch me every moment, though I be under so many appearances and probabilities of extreme danger, that there appears an impossibility, in sense, to escape death, *" yet I will not fear."* *Joseph Caryl.*

Verse 4.—*" Valley of the shadow of death."* A valley is a low place, with mountains on either side. Enemies may be posted on those mountains to shoot their arrows at the traveller, as ever was the case in the East ; but he *must* pass through it. The Psalmist, however, said he would fear no evil, not even the fiery darts of Satan, for the Lord was with him. The figure is not *primarily,* as is sometimes supposed, our dying moments, though it will beautifully bear that explanation ; but it is the valley beset with enemies, posted on the hills. David was not only protected in that valley, but even in the presence of those enemies, his table was bountifully spread (verse 5). The Bedouin, at the present day often post themselves on the hills to harass travellers, as they pass along the valleys.—*John Gadsby.*

Verse 4.—*" I will fear no evil."* It hath been an ancient proverb, when a man had done some great matter, he was said to have " plucked a lion by the beard ; " when a lion is dead, even to little children it hath been an easy matter. As boys, when they see a bear, a lion, or a wolf dead in the streets, they will pull off their hair, insult over them, and deal with them as they please ; they will trample upon their bodies, and do that unto them being *dead,* which they durst not in the least measure venture upon whilst they are *alive.* Such a thing is *death,* a furious beast, a ramping lion, a devouring wolf, the *helluo generis humani* (eater up of mankind), yet Christ hath laid him at his length, hath been the *death of death,* so that *God's children* triumph over him, such as those refined ones in the ore of the church, those martyrs of the primitive times, who cheerfully offered themselves to the fire, and to the sword, and to all the violence of this hungry beast ; and have played upon him, scorned and derided him, by the faith that they had in the life of Christ, who hath subdued him to himself. 1 Cor. xv.—*Martin Day,* 1660.

Verse 4.—*" Thou art with me."* Do you know the sweetness, the security, the strength of *" Thou art with me"* ? When anticipating the solemn hour of death, when the soul is ready to halt and ask, How shall it then be? can you turn in soul-affection to your God and say, " There is nothing in death to harm me, while thy love is left to me " ? Can you say, " O death, where is thy sting " ? It is said, when a bee has left its sting in any one, it has no more power to hurt. Death has left its sting in the humanity of Christ, and has no more power to harm his child. Christ's victory over the grave is his people's. " At that moment I am with you," whispers Christ ; " the same arm you have proved strong and faithful all the way up through the wilderness, which has never failed, though you have been often forced to lean on it all your weakness." " On this arm," answers the believer, " *I feel at home ;* with soul-confidence, I repose on my Beloved ; for he has supported through so many difficulties, from the contemplation of which I shuddered. He has carried over so many depths, that I know his arm to be the arm of love." How can that be dark, in which God's child is to have the accomplishment of the longing desire of his life ? How can it be dark to come in contact with the light of life ? It is *" his rod,"* *" his staff ;"* therefore they *" comfort."* Prove him—prove him now, believer! it is your privilege to do so. It will be precious to him to support your weakness ; prove that when weak, then are you strong ; that you may be secure, his strength shall be perfected in your perfect weakness. Omnipotent love must fail before one of his sheep can perish ; for, says Christ, " none shall pluck my sheep out of my hand." " I and my Father are one ; " therefore we may boldly say, " *Yea, though I walk through the valley of the shadow of death, I will fear no evil ; for thou art with me."*—*Viscountess Powerscourt.*

Verse 4.—*" Thy rod."* Of the *virga pastoralis* there are three uses :—1. Nu*merare oves*—to reckon up or count the sheep ; and in this sense they are said " to pass under the rod " (Lev. xxvii. 32), the shepherd tells them one by one. And even so are the people of God called the rod of his inheritance (Jer. x. 16), such as he takes special notice or account of. And take the words in this sense—*" Thy rod doth comfort me "*—it holds well ; *q.d.* " Though I am in such eminent dangers by reason of evil men, yet this is my comfort—I am not neglected of thee ; thou dost not suffer me to perish ; thou takest notice of me ; thou dost take and make an account of me ; thy special care looks after me." 2. *Provocare oves :* when the sheep are negligent and remiss in following or driving, the shepherd doth, with his rod, put them on, quicken their pace. And in this sense also David saith well, " *Thy rod doth comfort me ; "* for it is a work which doth breed much joy and comfort in the hearts of God's people, when God doth put them out of a lazy, cold, formal walking, and doth, some way or other, cause them to mend their pace, to grow more active and fervent in his service and worship. 3. *Revocare oves :* the sheep sometimes are *petulante divagantes,* idly and inconsiderably straying from the flock, grazing alone, and wandering after other pastures, not considering the dangers which attend them by such a separation and wandering ; and, therefore, the shepherd doth with his rod strike and fetch them in again, and so preserve them. In this sense also David might well say, " *Thy rod doth comfort me ; "* for it is a great comfort that the Lord will not leave his sheep to the ways of discomfort, but brings them off from sinful errings and wanderings, which always do expose them to their greatest dangers and troubles. So that the words do intimate a singular part of God's gubernation or careful providence of his flock.—*Obadiah Sedgwick.*

Verse 4.—" *Rod and staff."* The shepherd invariably carries a staff or rod with him when he goes forth to feed his flock. It is often bent or hooked at one end, which gave rise to the shepherd's crook in the hand of the Christian bishop. With this staff he rules and guides the flock to their green pastures, and defends them from their enemies. With it also he corrects them when disobedient, and brings them back when wandering. This staff is associated as inseparably with the shepherd as the goad is with the ploughman.—*W. M. Thomson.*

Verse 4.—The Psalmist will trust, *even though all be unknown.* We find him doing this in Psalm xxiii. 4 : " *Yea, though I walk through the valley of the shadow of death, I will fear no evil."* Here, surely there is trust the most complete. We dread the unknown far above anything that we can see ; a little noise in the dark will terrify, when even great dangers which are visible do not affright : the unknown, with its mystery and uncertainty often fills the heart with anxiety, if not with foreboding and gloom. Here, the Psalmist takes the highest form of the unknown, the aspect which is most terrible to man, and says, that even in the midst of it he will trust. What could be so wholly beyond the reach of human experience or speculation, or even imagination, as " *the valley of the shadow of death,"* with all that belonged to it ? but the Psalmist makes no reservation against it ; he will trust where he cannot see. How often are we terrified at the unknown ; even as the disciples were, "who feared as they entered the cloud ;" how often is the uncertainty of the future a harder trial to our faith than the pressure of some present ill ! Many dear children of God can trust him in all *known* evils ; but why those fears and forebodings and sinkings of heart, if they trust him equally for the *unknown ?* How much, alas ! do we fall short of the true character of the children of God, in this matter of the unknown ! A child practically acts upon the declaration of Christ that " sufficient unto the day is the evil thereof," we, in this respect far less wise than he, people the unknown with phantoms and speculations, and too often forget our simple trust in God.—*Philip Bennett Power.*

Verse 4.—" *For thou art with me ; thy rod and thy staff comfort me. Thou shalt prepare a table before me, against them that trouble me. Thou hast anointed my head with oil, and my cup shall be full."* Seeing thou art with me, at whose power and will all troubles go and come, I doubt not but to have the victory and upper hand of them, how many and dangerous soever they are ; for thy rod chasteneth me when I go astray, and thy staff stayeth me when I should fall—two things most necessary for me, good Lord ; the one to call me from my fault and error, and the other to keep me in thy truth and verity. What can be more blessed than to be sustained and kept from falling by the staff and strength of the Most High ? And what can be more profitable than to be beaten with his merciful rod when we go astray ? For he chasteneth as many as he loveth, and beateth as many as he receiveth into his holy profession. Notwithstanding, while we are here in this life, he feeds us with the sweet pastures of the wholesome herbs of his holy word, until we come to eternal life ; and when we put off these bodies, and come into heaven, and know the blessed fruition and riches of his kingdom, then shall we not only be his sheep, but also the guests of his everlasting banquet ; which, Lord, thou settest before all them that love thee in this world, and dost so anoint and make glad our minds with thine Holy Spirit, that no adversities nor troubles can make us sorry. In this sixth part, the prophet declares the old saying amongst wise men, " It is no less mastery to keep the thing that is won, than it was to win it." King David perceives right well the same ; and therefore, as before in the Psalm he said, the Lord turned his soul, and led him into the pleasant pastures, where virtue and justice reigned, *for his name's sake*, and not for any righteousness of his own ; so saith he now, that being brought into the pastures of truth, and into the favour of the Almighty, and accounted and taken for one of his sheep, it is only God that keeps and maintains him, in the same state, condition, and grace. For he could not pass through the troubles and shadow of death, as he and all God's elect people must do, but only by the assistance of God, and, therefore, he saith, he passes through all peril because he was with him. *John Hooper (martyr)*, 1495—1555.

Verse 4.—By the way, I note that David amidst his green pastures, where he wanted nothing, and in his greatest ease and highest excellency, recordeth the valley of misery and shade of death which might ensue, if God so would ; and therewithal reckoneth of his safest harbour and firm repose, even in God alone. And this is true wisdom indeed, in fair weather to provide for a tempest ; in health to think of sickness ; in prosperity, peace and quietness, to forecast the worst, and with the wise emmet, in summer to lay up for the winter following. The state of man is full of trouble, the condition of the godly man more. Sinners must be corrected, and sons chastised, there is no question. The ark was framed for the waters, the ship for the sea ; and happy is the mariner that knoweth where to cast anchor ; but oh ! blessed is the man that can take a right sanctuary, and knoweth whereupon to rely, and in whom to trust in the day of his need. *" I will not fear, for thou art with me."* In this Psalm, I take it, is rather vouched not what the prophet always performed, but what in duty must be performed, and what David's purpose was to endeavour unto for the time to come. For after so many pledges of God's infinite goodness, and by the guidance of his rod and stay of his sheep-hook, God willing, he would not fear, and this is the groundwork of his affiance. Peter in the gospel by our Saviour, in consideration of infirmity through fear denying his Master, is willed after his conversion by that favourable aspect of our Saviour, to confirm his brethren, and to train them in constancy ; for verily God requireth settled minds, resolute men, and confirmed brethren. So upon occasions past, David found it true that he should not have been heretofore at any time, and therefore professeth, that for the time to come he would be no marigold-servant of the Lord, to open with the sun and shut with the dew—to serve him in calmer times only, and at a need, to shoot neck out of collar, fearfully and faithlessly to slip aside or shrink away. Good people, in all heartless imperfections, mark, I pray you, that they who fear every mist that ariseth or cloud that appeareth—who are like the mulberry tree, that never shooteth forth or showeth itself, till all hard weather be past—who, like standers-by and lookers-on, neuters and internimists—who, like Metius Suffetius, dare not venture upon, nor enter into, nor endeavour any good action of greatest duty to God, prince, or country, till all be sure in one side—are utterly reproved by this ensample.—*John Prime*, 1588.

Verse 4.—The death of those that are under sin, is like a malefactor's execution : when he is panelled and justly convicted, one pulleth the hat doggedly from him, another his band, a third bindeth his hands behind his back ; and the poor man, overcome with grief and fear, is dead before he die. But I look for the death of the righteous, and a peaceable end, that it shall be as a going to bed of an honest man : his servants with respect take off his clothes and lay them down in order ; a good conscience then playing the page ordereth all, so that it confirmeth and increaseth his peace; it biddeth good night to Faith, Hope, and such other attending graces and gifts in the way—when we are come home to heaven there is no use of them—but it directeth Love, Peace, Joy, and other *home graces*, that as they conveyed us in the way, so they attend at death, and enter into the heavens with us. *William Struther.*

Verse 4.—The Lord willeth us in the day of our troubles to call upon him, adding this promise—that he will deliver us. Whereunto the prophet David did so trust, feeling the comfortable truth thereof at sundry times in many and dangerous perils, that he persuaded himself (all fear set apart), to undergo one painful danger, or other whatsoever; yea, if it were to *" walk in the valley of the shadow of death,"* that he should not have cause to fear ; comforting himself with his saying (which was God's promise made unto all), " For thou art with me ; thy rod and thy staff they comfort me." Is God's " staff " waxen so weak, that we dare not now lean too much thereon, lest it should break? or is he now such a changeling, that he will not be with us in our trouble according to his promise? Will he not give us his "*staff*" to stay us by, and reach us his hand to hold us up, as he hath been wont to do? No doubt but that he will be most ready in all extremity to help, according to his promise. The Lord that created thee, O Jacob, and he that formed thee, O Israel, saith thus; Fear not, for I will defend thee," etc. Isaiah xliii.—*Thomas Tymme.*

Verse 4.—Not long before he died, he blessed God for the assurance of his love, and said, He could now as easily die as shut his eyes; and added, Here am I longing to be silent in the dust, and enjoying Christ in glory. I long to be in the arms of Jesus. It is not worth while to weep for me. Then, remembering how busy the devil had been about him, he was exceedingly thankful to God for his goodness in rebuking him.—*Memoir of James Janeway.*

Verse 4.—When Mrs. Hervey, the wife of a missionary in Bombay, was dying, a friend said to her, that he hoped the Saviour would be with her as she walked through the dark valley of the shadow of death. "If this," said she, "is the dark valley, it has not a dark spot in it; all is light." She had, during most of her sickness, bright views of the perfections of God. "His awful holiness," she said, "appeared the most lovely of all his attributes." At one time she said she wanted words to express her views of the glory and majesty of Christ. "It seems," said she, "that if all other glory were annihilated and nothing left but his bare self, it would be enough; it would be a universe of glory!"

Verse 4, 5.—A readiness of spirit to suffer gives the Christian the true enjoyment of life. . . . The Christian, that hath this preparation of heart, never tastes more sweetness in the enjoyments of this life, than when he dips these morsels in the meditation of death and eternity. It is no more grief to his heart to think of the remove of these, which makes way for those far sweeter enjoyments, than it would be to one at a feast, to have the first course taken off, when he hath fed well on it, that the second course of all rare sweetmeats and banqueting stuff may come on, which it cannot till the other be gone. Holy David, in this place, brings in, as it were, a death's head with his feast. In the same breath almost, he speaks of his dying (verse 4), and of the rich feast he at present sat at through the bounty of God (verse 5), to which he was not so tied by the teeth, but if God, that gave him this cheer, should call him from it, to look death in the face, he could do it, and *fear no evil* when *in the valley of the shadow of it.* And what think you of the blessed apostle Peter? Had not he, think you, the true enjoyment of his life, when he could sleep so sweetly in a prison (no desirable place), fast bound between two soldiers (no comfortable posture), and this the very night before Herod would have brought him forth, in all probability, to his execution? no likely time, one would think, to get any rest; yet we find him, even there, thus, and then, so sound asleep, that the angel, who was sent to give him his gaol deliverance, smote him on the side to awake him. Acts xii. 6, 7. I question whether Herod himself slept so well that night, as this his prisoner did. And what was the potion that brought this holy man so quietly to rest? No doubt this preparation of the gospel of peace—*he was ready to die,* and that made him able to sleep. Why should that break his rest in this world, which if it had been effected, would have brought him to his eternal rest in the other?—*William Gurnall.*

Verses 4, 6.—The Psalmist expresseth an exceeding confidence in the midst of most inexpressible troubles and pressures. He supposes himself "*walking through the valley of the shadow of death.*" As "*death*" is the worst of evils, and comprehensive of them all, so the "*shadow*" of death is the most dismal and dark representation of those evils to the soul, and the "*valley*" of that shadow the most dreadful bottom and depth of that representation. This, then, the prophet supposed that he might be brought into. A condition wherein he may be overwhelmed with sad apprehensions of the coming of a confluence of all manner of evils upon him—and that not for a short season, but he may be necessitated to "*walk*" in them, which denotes a state of some continuance, a conflicting with most dismal evils, and in their own nature tending to death—is in the supposal. What, then, would he do if he should be brought into this estate? Saith he, "Even in that condition, in such distress, wherein I am, to my own and the eyes of others, hopeless, helpless, gone, and lost, 'I will fear no evil.'" A noble resolution, if there be a sufficient bottom and foundation for it, that it may not be accounted rashness and groundless confidence, but true spiritual courage and holy resolution. Saith he, "It is because the Lord is with me." But, alas! what if the Lord should now forsake thee in this condition, and give thee up to the power of thine enemies, and suffer thee, by the strength of thy temptations, wherewith thou art beset, to fall utterly from him? Surely then thou wouldst be swallowed up for ever; the waters would go over thy soul, and thou must for ever lie down in the shades of death. "Yea," saith he, "but I have an assurance to the contrary; '*Goodness and mercy shall follow me all the days of my life.*'"—*John Owen.*

Verse 5.—"*Thou preparest a table before me in the presence of mine enemies.*" God doth not at all depend upon wicked men in the benediction of his servants; they concur not with him, neither *per modum principii,* for he alone is the cause; nor *per modum auxilii,* for he without them can bless his all: their malicious renitency of spirit, or attempt against God's blessing of his people, is too impotent to frustrate God's intention and pleasure. An effectual impediment must not only have contrariety in it, but superiority: a drop of water cannot put out the fire, for though it hath a contrary nature, yet it hath not greater power. Now the malice and contrivances of evil men are too short and weak for the divine intention of blessing, which is accompanied with an almighty arm. Evil men are but men, and God is a God; and being but men, they can do no more than men. The Lord will clear it to all the world, that he rules the earth, and that "his counsel shall stand;" and where he blesseth, that man shall be blessed; and whom he curseth, that man shall be cursed; that the creatures can do neither good nor evil; that his people are the generation of his care and love, though living in the midst of deadly enemies.—*Condensed from Obadiah Sedgwick.*

Verse 5.—"*In the presence of mine enemies:*" they seeing and envying and fretting at it, but not being able to hinder it.—*Matthew Poole.*

Verse 5.—"*Thou anointest my head with oil; my cup runneth over.*" In the East the people frequently anoint their visitors with some very fragrant perfume; and give them a cup or glass of some choice wine, which they are careful to fill till it runs over. The first was designed to show their love and respect; the latter to imply that while they remained there, they should have an abundance of everything. To something of this kind the Psalmist probably alludes in this passage.—*Samuel Burder.*

Verse 5.—"*Thou anointest my head with oil.*" Anointing the head with oil is a great refreshment. There are three qualities of oil—*lævor, nitor, odor,* a smoothness to the touch, brightness to the sight, fragrancy to the smell, and so, gratifying the senses, it must needs cause delight to those anointed with it. To this Solomon alludes when persuading to a cheerful life, he saith, "Let thy head lack no ointment." How fully doth this represent the Spirit's unction which alone rejoices and exhilarates the soul! It is called the "oil of gladness," and the "joy of the Holy Ghost."—*Nathanael Hardy.*

Verse 5.—"*Thou anointest my head with oil.*" It is an act of great respect to pour perfumed oil on the head of a distinguished guest; the woman in the gospel thus manifested her respect for the Saviour by pouring "precious ointment" on his head. An English lady went on board an Arabian ship which touched at Trincomalee, for the purpose of seeing the equipment of the vessel, and to make some little purchases. After she had been seated some time in the cabin, an Arabian female came and poured perfumed oil on her head.—*Joseph Roberts.*

Verse 5.—"*Thou anointest my head with oil.*" In the East no entertainment could be without this, and it served, as elsewhere a bath does, for (bodily) refreshment. Here, however, it is naturally to be understood of the spiritual oil of gladness.—*T. C. Barth.*

Verse 5.—"*Thou anointest my head with oil.*" Thou hast not confined thy bounty merely to the necessaries of life, but thou hast supplied me also with its luxuries.—*In "A plain Explanation of Difficult Passages in the Psalms,"* 1831.

Verse 5.—"*Thou anointest my head with oil.*" The unguents of Egypt may preserve our bodies from corruption, ensuring them a long duration in the dreary shades of the sepulchre, but, O Lord, the precious perfumed oil of thy grace which thou dost mysteriously pour upon our souls, purifies them, adorns them, strengthens them, sows in them the germs of immortality, and thus it not only secures them from a transitory corruption, but uplifts them from this house of bondage into eternal blessedness in thy bosom.—*Jean Baptiste Massillon,* 1663—1742.

Verse 5.—"*My cup runneth over.*" He had not only a fulness of *abundance,* but of *redundance*. Those that have this happiness must carry their cup upright, and see that it overflow into their poor brethren's emptier vessels.—*John Trapp.*

Verse 5.—" *My cup runneth over.*" Wherefore doth the Lord make your cup run over, but that other men's lips might taste the liquor ? The showers that fall upon the highest mountains, should glide into the lowest valleys. " Give, and it shall be given you," is a maxim little believed. Luke vi. 38.—*William Secker.*

Verse 5.—" *My cup runneth over.*" Or as it is in the Vulgate : *And my inebriating chalice, how excellent it is !* With this cup were the martyrs inebriated, when, going forth to their passion, they recognised not those that belonged to them ; not their weeping wife, not their children, not their relations ; while they gave thanks and said, " I will take the cup of salvation ! "—*Augustine.*

Verse 6.—" *I will dwell in the house of the Lord for ever.*" A wicked man, it may be, will turn into God's house, and say a prayer, etc., but the prophet would (and so all godly men must) *dwell* there *for ever ;* his soul lieth always at the throne of grace, begging for grace. A wicked man prayeth as the cock croweth ; the cock crows and ceaseth, and crows again, and ceaseth again, and thinks not of crowing till he crows again : so a wicked man prays and ceaseth, prays and ceaseth again ; his mind is never busied to think whether his prayers speed or no ; he thinks it is good religion for him to pray, and therefore he takes for granted that his prayers speed, though in very deed God never hears his prayers, nor no more respects them than he respects the lowing of oxen, or the gruntling of hogs.—*William Fenner, B.D. (1600—1640), in " The Sacrifice of the Faithful."*

Verse 6.—" *I will dwell in the house of the Lord for ever.*" This should be at once the crown of all our hopes for the future, and the one great lesson taught us by all the vicissitudes of life. The sorrows and the joys, the journeying and the rest, the temporary repose and the frequent struggles, all these should make us sure that there is an end which will interpret them all, to which they all point, for which they all prepare. We get the table in the wilderness here. It is as when the son of some great king comes back from foreign soil to his father's dominions, and is welcomed at every stage in his journey to the capital with pomp of festival and messengers from the throne, until at last he enters his palace home, where the travel-stained robe is laid aside, and he sits down with his father at his table.—*Alexander Maclaren,* 1863.

Verse 6.—Mark David's resolute persuasion, and consider how he came unto it, namely, by experience of God's favour at sundry times, and after sundry manners. For before he set down this resolution, he numbered up divers benefits received of the Lord ; *that he fed him in green pastures, and led him by the refreshing waters* of God's word ; that he *restores him and leads him in the paths of righteousness ;* that he strengthened him in great dangers, even of death, and preserveth him ; that in despite of his enemies, he enricheth him with many benefits. By means of all these mercies of God bestowed on him, he came to be persuaded of the continuance of the favour of God towards him.—*William Perkins.*

HINTS TO PREACHERS.

Verse 1.—Work out the similitude of a shepherd and his sheep. He rules, guides, feeds, and protects them ; and they follow, obey, love, and trust him. Examine as to whether we are sheep ; show the lot of the goats who feed side by side with the sheep.

Verse 1 (second clause). The man who is beyond the reach of want for time and eternity.

Verse 2 (first clause).—Believing rest. I. Comes from God—" *He maketh.*" II. Is deep and profound—" *lie down.*" III. Has solid sustenance—" *in green pastures.*" IV. Is subject for constant praise.

Verse 2.—The contemplative and the active element provided for.

Verse 2.—The freshness and richness of Holy Scripture.

Verse 2 (second clause).—Onward. The Leader, the way, the comforts of the road, and the traveller in it.

Verse 3.—Gracious restoration, holy guidance, and divine motives.

Verse 4.—The soft silence of the Spirit's work.

Verse 4.—God's presence the only sure support in death.

Verse 4.—Life in death and light in darkness.

Verse 4 (second clause).—The calm and quiet of the good man's end.

Verse 4 (last clause).—The tokens of divine government—the consolation of the obedient.

Verse 5.—The warrior feasted, the priest anointed, the guest satisfied.

Verse 5 (last clause). The means and uses of the continued anointings of the Holy Spirit.

Verse 5.—Providential super-aboundings, and what is our duty concerning them.

Verse 6 (first clause).—The blessedness of content.

Verse 6.—On the road and at home, or heavenly attendants and heavenly mansions.

PSALM XXIV.

TITLE.—A Psalm of David. *From the title we learn nothing but the authorship ; but this is interesting, and leads us to observe the wondrous operations of the Spirit upon the mind of Israel's sweet singer, enabling him to touch the mournful string in Psalm twenty-two, to pour forth gentle notes of peace in Psalm twenty-three, and here to utter majestic and triumphant strains. We can do or sing all things when the Lord strengtheneth us.*

This sacred hymn was probably written to be sung when the ark of the covenant was taken up from the house of Obed-edom, to remain within curtains upon the hill of Zion. The words are not unsuitable for the sacred dance of joy in which David led the way upon that joyful occasion. The eye of the Psalmist looked, however, beyond the typical upgoing of the ark to the sublime ascension of the King of glory. We will call it The Song of the Ascension.

DIVISION.—*The Psalm makes a pair with the fifteenth Psalm. It consists of three parts. The first glorifies* the true God, *and sings of his universal dominion ; the second describes* the true Israel, *who are able to commune with him ; and the third pictures the ascent of* the true Redeemer, *who has opened heaven's gates for the entrance of his elect.*

EXPOSITION.

THE earth *is* the LORD's, and the fulness thereof ; the world, and they that dwell therein.

2 For he hath founded it upon the seas, and established it upon the floods.

1. How very different is this from the ignorant Jewish notion of God which prevailed in our Saviour's day. The Jews said, " The holy land is God's, and the seed of Abraham are his only people ; " but their great Monarch had long before instructed them,—" *The earth is the Lord's, and the fulness thereof.*" The whole round world is claimed for Jehovah, " *and they that dwell therein* " are declared to be his subjects. When we consider the bigotry of the Jewish people at the time of Christ, and how angry they were with our Lord for saying that many widows were in Israel, but unto none of them was the prophet sent, save only to the widow of Sarepta, and that there were many lepers in Israel, but none of them was healed except Naaman the Syrian,—when we recollect, too, how angry they were at the mention of Paul's being sent to the Gentiles, we are amazed that they should have remained in such blindness, and yet have sung this Psalm, which shows so clearly that God is not the God of the Jews only, but of the Gentiles also. What a rebuke is this to those wiseacres who speak of the negro and other despised races as though they were not cared for by the God of heaven ! If a man be but a man the Lord claims him, and who dares to brand him as a mere piece of merchandise ! The meanest of men is a dweller in the world, and therefore belongs to Jehovah. Jesus Christ has made an end of the exclusiveness of nationalities. There is neither barbarian, Scythian, bond nor free ; but we all are one in Christ Jesus.

Man lives upon " *the earth,*" and parcels out its soil among his mimic kings and autocrats ; but the earth is not man's. He is but a tenant at will, a lease-holder upon most precarious tenure, liable to instantaneous ejectment. The great Landowner and true Proprietor holds his court above the clouds and laughs at the title-deeds of worms of the dust. The fee-simple is not with the lord of the manor nor the freeholder, but with the Creator. The " *fulness* " of the earth may mean its harvests, its wealth, its life, or its worship ; in all these senses the Most High God is Possessor of all. The earth is full of God ; he made it full and he keeps it full, notwithstanding all the demands which living creatures make upon its stores. The sea is full, despite all the clouds which rise from it ; the air is full, notwithstanding all the lives which breathe it ; the soil is full, though millions of plants derive their nourishment from it. Under man's tutored hand the world is coming to a greater fulness than ever, but it is all the Lord's ; the field and the fruit, the earth and all earth's wonders are Jehovah's. We look also for a sublimer fulness when the true ideal of a world for God shall have been reached in millennial glories, and then most clearly the earth will be the Lord's, and the fulness thereof. These words are now upon London's Royal Exchange, they shall one day be written in letters of light across the sky.

The term " *world* " indicates the habitable regions, wherein Jehovah is especially to be acknowledged as Sovereign. He who rules the fish of the sea and the fowl of the air should not be disobeyed by man, his noblest creature. Jehovah is the Universal King, all nations are beneath his sway : true Autocrat of all the nations, emperors and czars are but his slaves. Men are not their own, nor may they call their lips, their hearts, or their substance their own ; they are Jehovah's rightful servants. This claim especially applies to us who are born from heaven. We do not belong to the world or to Satan, but by creation and redemption we are the peculiar portion of the Lord.

Paul uses this verse twice, to show that no food is unclean, and that nothing is really the property of false gods. All things are God's ; no ban is on the face of nature, nothing is common or unclean. The world is all God's world, and the food which is sold in the shambles is sanctified by being my Father's, and I need not scruple to eat thereof.

2. In the second verse we have the reason why the world belongs to God, namely, because he has created it, which is a title beyond all dispute. " *For he hath founded it upon the seas.*" It is God who lifts up the earth from out of the sea, so that the dry land, which otherwise might in a moment be submerged, as in the days of Noah, is kept from the floods. The hungry jaws of ocean would devour the dry land if a constant fiat of Omnipotence did not protect it. " *He hath established it upon the floods.*" The world is Jehovah's, because from generation to generation he preserves and upholds it, having settled its foundations. Providence and Creation are the two legal seals upon the title-deeds of the great Owner of all things. He who built the house and bears up its foundation has surely a first claim upon it. Let it be noted, however, upon what insecure foundations all terrestrial things are founded. Founded on the seas ! Established on the floods ! Blessed be God the Christian has another world to look forward to, and rests his hopes upon a more stable foundation than this poor world affords. They who trust in worldly things build upon the sea ; but we have laid our hopes, by God's grace, upon the Rock of Ages ; we are resting upon the promise of an immutable God, we are depending upon the constancy of a faithful Redeemer. Oh ! ye worldlings, who have built your castles of confidence, your palaces of wealth, and your bowers of pleasure upon the seas, and established them upon the floods ; how soon will your baseless fabrics melt, like foam upon the waters ! Sand is treacherous enough, but what shall be said of the yet more unstable seas ?

3 Who shall ascend into the hill of the LORD ? or who shall stand in his holy place ?

4 He that hath clean hands, and a pure heart ; who hath not lifted up his soul unto vanity, nor sworn deceitfully.

5 He shall receive the blessing from the LORD, and righteousness from the God of his salvation.

6 This *is* the generation of them that seek him, that seek thy face, O Jacob. Selah.

Here we have the true Israel described. The men who shall stand as courtiers in the palace of the living God are not distinguished by race, but by character ; they are not Jews only, nor Gentiles only, nor any one branch of mankind peculiarly, but a people purified and made meet to dwell in the holy hill of the Lord.

3. " *Who shall ascend into the hill of the Lord ?* " It is uphill work for the creature to reach the Creator. Where is the mighty climber who can scale the towering heights ? Nor is it height alone ; it is glory too. Whose eye shall see the King in his beauty and dwell in his palace ? In heaven he reigns most gloriously, who shall be permitted to enter into his royal presence ? God has made all, but he will not save all ; there is a chosen company who shall have the singular honour of dwelling with him in his high abode. These choice spirits desire to commune with God, and their wish shall be granted them. The solemn enquiry of the text is repeated in another form. Who shall be able to " *stand* " or continue there ?

He casteth away the wicked, who then can abide in his house? Who is he that can gaze upon the Holy One, and can abide in the blaze of his glory? Certainly none may venture to commune with God upon the footing of the law, but grace can make us meet to behold the vision of the divine presence. The question before us is one which all should ask for themselves, and none should be at ease till they receive an answer of peace. With careful self-examination let us enquire, " Lord, is it I?"

4. " *He that hath clean hands.*" Outward, practical holiness is a very precious mark of grace. To wash in water with Pilate is nothing, but to wash in innocency is all-important. It is to be feared that many professors have perverted the doctrine of justification by faith in such a way as to treat good works with contempt; if so, they will receive everlasting contempt at the last great day. It is vain to prate of inward experience unless the daily life is free from impurity, dishonesty, violence, and oppression. Those who draw near to God must have " *clean hands.*" What monarch would have servants with filthy hands to wait at his table? They who were ceremonially unclean could not enter into the Lord's house which was made with hands, much less shall the morally defiled be allowed to enjoy spiritual fellowship with a holy God. If our hands are now unclean, let us wash them in Jesu's precious blood, and so let us pray unto God, lifting up pure hands. But " *clean hands*" would not suffice, unless they were connected with " *a pure heart.*" True religion is heart-work. We may wash the outside of the cup and the platter as long as we please, but if the inward parts be filthy, we are filthy altogether in the sight of God, for our hearts are more truly ourselves than our hands are. We may lose our hands and yet live, but we could not lose our heart and still live; the very life of our being lies in the inner nature, and hence the imperative need of purity within. There must be a work of grace in the core of the heart as well as in the palm of the hand, or our religion is a delusion. May God grant that our inward powers may be cleansed by the sanctifying Spirit, so that we may love holiness and abhor all sin. The pure in heart shall see God, all others are but blind bats; stone-blindness in the eyes arises from stone in the heart. Dirt in the heart throws dust in the eyes.

The soul must be delivered from delighting in the grovelling toys of earth; the man who is born for heaven " *hath not lifted up his soul unto vanity.*" All men have their joys, by which their souls are lifted up; the worldling lifts up his soul in carnal delights, which are mere empty vanities; but the saint loves more substantial things; like Jehoshaphat, he is lifted up in the ways of the Lord. He who is content with the husks will be reckoned with the swine. If we suck our consolation from the breasts of the world, we prove ourselves to be its home-born children. Does the world satisfy thee? Then thou hast thy reward and thy portion in this life; make much of it, for thou shalt know no other joy.

" *Nor sworn deceitfully.*" The saints are men of honour still. The Christian man's word is his only oath; but that is as good as twenty oaths of other men. False speaking will shut any man out of heaven, for a liar shall not enter into God's house, whatever may be his professions or doings. God will have nothing to do with liars, except to cast them into the lake of fire. Every liar is a child of the devil, and will be sent home to his father. A false declaration, a fraudulent statement, a cooked account, a slander, a lie—all these may suit the assembly of the ungodly, but are detested among true saints: how could they have fellowship with the God of truth, if they did not hate every false way?

5. It must not be supposed that the persons who are thus described by their inward and outward holiness are saved by the merit of their works; but their works are the evidences by which they are known. The present verse shows that in the saints grace reigns and grace alone. Such men wear the holy livery of the Great King because he has of his own free love clothed them therewith. The true saint wears the wedding garment, but he owns that the Lord of the feast provided it for him, without money and without price. " *He shall receive the blessing from the Lord, and righteousness from the God of his salvation.*" So that the saints need salvation; they receive righteousness, and " *the blessing*" is a boon from God their Saviour. They do not ascend the hill of the Lord as givers but as receivers, and they do not wear their own merits, but a righteousness which they have received. Holy living ensures a blessing as its reward from the thrice Holy God, but it is itself a blessing of the New Covenant and a delightful fruit of the Spirit. God first gives us good works, and then rewards us for them. Grace is not obscured by God's

demand for holiness, but is highly exalted as we see it decking the saint with jewels, and clothing him in fair white linen ; all this sumptuous array being a free gift of mercy.

6. " *This is the generation of them that seek him, that seek thy face, O Jacob.*" These are the regeneration, these are in the line of grace ; these are the legitimate seed. Yet they are only seekers ; hence learn that true seekers are very dear in God's esteem, and are entered upon his register. Even *seeking* has a sanctifying influence ; what a consecrating power must lie in finding and enjoying the Lord's face and favour ! To desire communion with God is a purifying thing. Oh to hunger and thirst more and more after a clear vision of the face of God ; this will lead us to purge ourselves from all filthiness, and to walk with heavenly circumspection. He who longs to see his friend when he passes takes care to clear the mist from the window, lest by any means his friend should go by unobserved. Really awakened souls seek the Lord above everything, and as this is not the usual desire of mankind, they constitute a generation by themselves ; a people despised of men but beloved of God. The expression " *O Jacob* " is a very difficult one, unless it be indeed true that the God of Jacob here condescends to be called Jacob, and takes upon himself the name of his chosen people.

The preceding verses correct the inordinate boastings of those Jews who vaunted themselves as the favourites of heaven ; they are told that their God is the God of all the earth, and that he is holy, and will admit none but holy ones into his presence. Let the mere professor as he reads these verses listen to the voice which saith, " without holiness no man shall see the Lord."

" *Selah.*" Lift up the harp and voice, for a nobler song is coming ; a song of our Well-beloved.

7 Lift up your heads, O ye gates ; and be ye lift up, ye everlasting doors ; and the King of glory shall come in.

8 Who *is* this King of glory ? The LORD is strong and mighty, the LORD mighty in battle.

9 Lift up your heads, O ye gates ; even lift *them* up, ye everlasting doors ; and the King of glory shall come in.

10 Who is this King of glory ? The LORD of hosts, he *is* the King of glory. Selah.

7. These last verses reveal to us the great representative man, who answered to the full character laid down, and therefore by his own right ascended the holy hill of Zion. Our Lord Jesus Christ could ascend into the hill of the Lord because his hands were clean and his heart was pure, and if we by faith in him are conformed to his image we shall enter too. We have here a picture of our Lord's glorious ascent. We see him rising from amidst the little group upon Olivet, and as the cloud receives him, angels reverently escort him to the gates of heaven.

The ancient gates of the eternal temple are personified and addressed in song by the attending cohort of rejoicing spirits.

> " Lo his triumphal chariot waits,
> And angels chant the solemn lay,
> ' Lift up your heads, ye heavenly gates ;
> Ye everlasting doors, give way.' "

They are called upon " *to lift up their heads,*" as though with all their glory they were not great enough for the Allglorious King. Let all things do their utmost to honour so great a Prince ; let the highest heaven put on unusual loftiness in honour of " *the King of Glory.*" He who, fresh from the cross and the tomb, now rides through the gates of the New Jerusalem is higher than the heavens ; great and everlasting as they are, those gates of pearl are all unworthy of him before whom the heavens are not pure, and who chargeth his angels with folly. " *Lift up your heads, O ye gates.*"

8. The watchers at the gate hearing the song look over the battlements and ask, " *Who is this King of glory ?* " A question full of meaning and worthy of the meditations of eternity. Who is he in person, nature, character, office and work ? What is his pedigree ? What his rank and what his race ? The answer given in a mighty wave of music is, " *The Lord strong and mighty, the Lord mighty*

in battle." We know the might of Jesus by the battles whch he has fought, the victories which he has won over sin, and death, and hell, and we clap our hands as we see him leading captivity captive in the majesty of his strength. Oh for a heart to sing his praises! Mighty hero, be thou crowned for ever King of kings and Lord of lords.

9. *" Lift up your heads, O ye gates ; even lift them up, ye everlasting doors ; and the King of glory shall come in."* The words are repeated with a pleasing variation. There are times of deep earnest feeling when repetitions are not vain but full of force. Doors were often taken from their hinges when Easterns would show welcome to a guest, and some doors were drawn up and down like a portcullis, and may possibly have protruded from the top ; thus literally lifting up their heads. The picture is highly poetical, and shows how wide heaven's gate is set by the ascension of our Lord. Blessed be God, the gates have never been shut since. The opened gates of heaven invite the weakest believer to enter.

Dear reader, it is possible that you are saying, " I shall never enter into the heaven of God, for I have neither clean hands nor a pure heart." Look then to Christ, who has already climbed the holy hill. He has entered as the forerunner of those who trust him. Follow in his footsteps, and repose upon his merit. He rides triumphantly into heaven, and you shall ride there too if you trust him. " But how can I get the character described ? " say you. The Spirit of God will give you that. He will create in you a new heart and a right spirit. Faith in Jesus is the work of the Holy Spirit, and has all virtues wrapped up in it. Faith stands by the fountain filled with blood, and as she washes therein, clean hands and a pure heart, a holy soul and a truthful tongue are given to her.

10. The closing note is inexpressibly grand. Jehovah of hosts, Lord of men and angels, Lord of the universe, Lord of the worlds, is the King of glory. All true glory is concentrated upon the true God, for all other glory is but a passing pageant, the painted pomp of an hour. The ascended Saviour is here declared to be the Head and Crown of the universe, the King of Glory. Our Immanuel is hymned in sublimest strains. Jesus of Nazareth is Jehovah Sabaoth.

EXPLANATORY NOTES AND QUAINT SAYINGS.

Whole Psalm.—It will be seen that this Psalm was written to be chanted in responsive parts, with two choruses. To comprehend it fully, it should be understood that Jerusalem, as the city of God, was by the Jews regarded as a type of heaven. It so occurs in the Apocalypse, whence we have adopted it in our poetical and devotional aspirations. The court of the tabernacle was the scene of the Lord's more immediate residence—the tabernacle his palace, and the ark his throne. With this leading idea in his mind, the most cursory reader— if there be cursory readers of the Bible—cannot fail to be struck with the beauty and sublimity of this composition, and its exquisite suitableness to the occasion. The chief musician, who was probably in this case the king himself, appears to have begun the sacred lay with a solemn and sonorous recital of these sentences :—

> " The earth is the Lord's, and the fulness thereof ;
> The world, and they that dwell therein.
> For he hath founded it upon the seas,
> And established it upon the floods."

The chorus of vocal music appears to have then taken up the song, and sung the same words in a more tuneful and elaborate harmony ; and the instruments and the whole chorus of the people fell in with them, raising the mighty declaration to heaven. There is much reason to think that the people, or a large body of them, were qualified or instructed to take their part in this great ceremonial. The historical text says, " David, and *all the house of Israel played before the Lord* upon all manner of instruments," etc. We may presume that the chorus then divided, each singing in their turns, and both joining at the close—

> " For he hath founded it upon the seas,
> And established it upon the floods."

This part of the music may be supposed to have lasted until the procession reached the foot of Zion, or came in view of it, which, from the nature of the enclosed site, cannot be till one comes quite near to it. Then the king must be supposed to have stepped forth, and begun again, in a solemn and earnest tone—

> "Who shall ascend into the hill of the Lord?
> Or who shall stand in his holy place?"

To which the first chorus responds—

> "He that hath clean hands, and a pure heart;
> Who hath not lifted up his soul unto vanity, nor sworn deceitfully."

And then the second chorus—

> "He shall receive the blessing from the Lord,
> And righteousness from the God of his salvation."

This part of the sacred song may, in like manner, be supposed to have lasted till they reached the gate of the city, when the king began again in this grand and exalted strain:—

> "Lift up your heads, O ye gates;
> And be ye lift up, ye everlasting doors,
> And the King of glory shall come in!"

repeated then, in the same way as before, by the general chorus.
The persons having charge of the gates on this high occasion ask—

> "Who is the King of glory?"

To which the first chorus answers—

> "It is Jehovah, strong and mighty—
> Jehovah mighty in battle."

which the second chorus then repeats in like manner as before, closing it with the grand universal chorus,

> "He is the King of glory! He is the King of glory!"

We must now suppose the instruments to take up the same notes, and continue them to the entrance to the court of the tabernacle. There the king again begins—

> "Lift up your heads, O ye gates;
> And be ye lift, up, ye everlasting doors;
> And the King of glory shall come in."

This is followed and answered as before—all closing, the instruments sounding, the chorus singing, the people shouting—

> "He is the King of Glory!"
> *John Kitto's " Daily Bible Illustrations."*

Whole Psalm.—The coming of the Lord of glory, the high demands upon his people proceeding from this, the absolute necessity to prepare worthily for his arrival, form the subject-matter of this Psalm.—*E. W. Hengstenberg.*

Whole Psalm.—We learn from the rabbins, that this was one of certain Psalms which were sung in the performance of Jewish worship on each day in the week:—

The 24th Psalm on the 1st, the Lord's-day, our Sunday.

48th	,,	2nd	,,
82nd	,,	3rd	,,
94th	,,	4th	,,
81st	,,	5th	,,
93rd	,,	6th	,,
92	,,	7th, the Jewish Sabbath.

This Psalm, then, appropriated to the Lord's-day, our Sunday, was intended to celebrate the resurrection of Messiah, and his ascension into heaven, there to sit as a priest upon God's throne, and from thence to come down bringing blessings and mercies to his people.—*R. H. Ryland.*

Whole Psalm.—Anthem of praise, performed when the heads of the gates of Jerusalem were lifted up to receive the ark ; and those of the Israelites who were ceremoniously clean, were alone permitted to accompany it into the court of the tabernacle.   A Psalm of David.   Verses 1, 2, chorus.   3. First voice.   4, 5. Second voice.   6. Chorus.   7. Semi-chorus accompanying the ark.   8. Voice from within the gates.   8. Chorus of priests accompanying the ark.   9. Chorus of priests and people with the ark.   10. Voice within the gates.   10. Grand chorus.—*From " The Psalms, with Prefatory Titles, etc., from the Port Royal Avthors," by Mary Anne Schimmelpenninck,* 1825.

Whole Psalm.   How others may think upon this point, I cannot say, nor pretend to describe, but for my own part, I have no notion of hearing, or of any man's ever having seen or heard, anything so great, so solemn, so celestial, on this side the gates of heaven.—*Patrick Delany, D.D.,* 1686—1768.

Verse 1.—" *The earth is the Lord's,*" that is, Christ's, who is the " Lord of lords " (Rev. xix. 16) ; for the whole world and all the things therein are his by a twofold title.   First, by donation of God his Father, having " all power given unto him in heaven and in earth " (Matt. xxviii. 18), even whatsoever things the Father hath are his (John xvi. 15) ; and so consequently " made heir of all things."   Heb. i. 2. Secondly, the earth is Christ's and all that therein is, by right of creation, for " *he founded it,*" saith our prophet, and that after a wonderful manner, " *upon the seas and floods.*" . . . All things then are Christ's, in respect of *creation,* " by whom all things were made " (John i. 3) ; in respect of *sustentation,* as upholding all things by his mighty word (Heb. i. 3) ; in respect of *administration,* as reaching from one end to another, and ordering all things sweetly (Wis. viii. 1) ; in one word— " Of him, and through him, and to him, are all things."   Rom. xi. 36.   From hence we may learn   (1), That Christ is " the King of glory," " Lord of Hosts," even Almighty God.   For he that made all, is " Lord over all ; " he that is the Creator of heaven and earth is Almighty (saith our Creed) ; able to do whatsoever he will, and more than he will too—more by his absolute power, than he will by his actual—" able to raise up children unto Abraham " out of the very stones of the street, though he doth not actually produce such a generation.   His almightiness evidently proves him to be God, and his *founding of the world* his almightiness ; for " The gods that have not made the heaven and earth shall perish from the earth, and from under these heavens."   Jer. x. 11.   (2). Seeing the compass of the world and all they that dwell therein are the Lord's, it is plain that the church is not confined within the limits of one region, or glued, as it were, to one seat only. The Donatists in old time, would tie the church only to Cartenna in Africa, the Papists in our time to Rome in Italy ; but the Scriptures plainly affirm that the golden candlesticks are removed from one place to another, and that the kingdom of God is taken away from one nation and given unto another country that brings forth the fruit thereof ; in every region he that feareth God and worketh righteousness is accepted of him.   Acts x. 35.—*John Boys.*

Verse 1.—" *The earth is Jehovah's.*"—The object of the beginning of the Psalm is to show that the Jews had nothing of themselves which could entitle them to approach nearer or more familiarly to God than the Gentiles.   As God by his providence preserves the world, the power of his government is alike extended to all, so that he ought to be worshipped by all, even as he also shows to all men, without exception, the fatherly care he has about them.—*J. Calvin.*

Verse 1.—" *The earth is the Lord's.*"   It is Christ's by creation (verse 2 ; John i. 1, 2), and it is his by resurrection (Matt. xxviii. 18), and by his glorious ascension into heaven, where he is enthroned King of the world in his human nature.   This Psalm takes up the language of the first Ascension Psalm (Psalm viii.)—*Christopher Wordsworth, D.D. in loc.*

Verse 1.—St. Chrysostom, suffering under the Empress Eudoxia, tells his friend Cyriacus how he armed himself beforehand :   εἰ μέν βούλεται ἡ βασίλισσα ἐ ξορίσαι μέ, etc. " I thought, will she banish me?   ' *The earth is the Lord's, and the fulness thereof.*' Take away my goods ?   ' *Naked came I into the world, and naked must I return.*' Will she stone me ?   I remembered Stephen.   Behead me ?   John Baptist came into my mind," etc.   Thus it should be with every one that intends to live and die comfortably : they must, as we say, lay up something for a rainy day ; they must stock themselves with graces, store up promises, and furnish themselves with experiences of God's lovingkindness to others and themselves too, that so, when the evil day comes, they may have much good coming thereby.—*John Spencer.*

Verse 1.—" *The earth is the Lord's.*" As David, in his youthful days, was tending his flocks on Bethlehem's fertile plains, the spirit of the Lord descended upon him, and his senses were opened, and his understanding enlightened, so that he could understand the songs of the night. The heavens proclaimed the glory of God, the glittering stars formed the general chorus, their harmonious melody resounded upon earth, and the sweet fulness of their voices vibrated to its utmost bounds.

" *Light* is the countenance of the Eternal," sung the setting sun : " I am the hem of his garment," responded the soft and rosy twilight. The clouds gathered themselves together and said, " We are his nocturnal tent." And the waters in the clouds, and the hollow voices of the thunders, joined in the lofty chorus, " The voice of the Eternal is upon the waters, the God of glory thundereth in the heavens, the Lord is upon many waters."

" He flieth upon my wings," whispered the winds, and the gentle air added, " I am the breath of God, the aspirations of his benign presence." " We hear the songs of praise," said the parched earth ; " all around is praise ; I alone am sad and silent." Then the falling dew replied, " I will nourish thee, so that thou shalt be refreshed and rejoice, and thy infants shall bloom like the young rose." " Joyfully we bloom," sang the refreshed meads ; the full ears of corn waved as they sang, " We are the blessing of God, the hosts of God against famine."

" We bless thee from above," said the gentle moon ; " We, too, bless thee," responded the stars ; and the lightsome grasshopper chirped, " Me, too, he blesses in the pearly dew-drop." " He quenched my thirst," said the roe ; " And refreshed me," continued the stag ; " And grants us our food," said the beasts of the forest ; " And clothes my lambs," gratefully added the sheep.

" He heard me," croaked the raven, " when I was forsaken and alone ; " " He heard me," said the wild goat of the rocks, " when my time came, and I brought forth." And the turtle-dove cooed, and the swallow and other birds joined the song, " We have found our nests, our houses, we dwell upon the altar of the Lord, and sleep under the shadow of his wing in tranquillity and peace." "And peace," replied the night, and echo prolonged the sound, when chanticleer awoke the dawn, and crowed with joy, " Open the portals, set wide the gates of the world ! The King of glory approaches. Awake ! Arise, ye sons of men, give praises and thanks unto the Lord, for the King of glory approaches."

The sun arose, and David awoke from his melodious rapture. But as long as he lived the strains of creation's harmony remained in his soul, and daily he recalled them from the strings of his harp.—*From the " Legend of the Songs of the Night," in the Talmud, quoted in " Biblical Antiquities." By F. A. Cox, D.D., LL.D.,* 1852.

Verse 1.—The pious mind views all things in God, and God in all things.—*Ingram Cobbin,* 1839.

Verse 2.—" *He hath founded it upon the seas, and established it upon the floods.*" This *founding the land upon the seas,* and preparing it *upon the floods,* is so wonderfully wonderful, that Almighty God asked his servant Job, " Whereupon are the foundations thereof fastened ? " Job xxxviii. 6. Xerxes commanded his soldiers to fetter the waters of Hellispontus ; and so God bindeth, as it were, the floods in fetters, as St. Basil plainly, *Ligatum est mare præcepto Creatoris quasi compedibus ;* he saith unto the sea, " Hitherto shalt thou come, but no further, there shall it stay thy proud waves." " He gathereth the waters of the sea together as an heap ; he layeth up the depth in storehouses " (Job xxxviii. 11 ; Psalm xxxiii. 7) ; so that without his leave not so much as one drop can overflow the land.—*John Boys.*

Verse 2.—(*New translation.*) " *For he hath founded it upon the seas, and upon streams doth he make it fast.*" The reference is no doubt to the account of the Creation, in Genesis, the dry land having emerged from the water, and seeming to rest upon it. (Comp. cxxxvi. 6 ; Prov. viii. 29.) It would, however, be quite out of place to suppose that in such language we have the expression of any theory, whether popular or scientific, as to the structure of the earth's surface : Job says (xxvi. 7), " He hangeth the earth upon nothing." Such expressions are manifestly poetical. See Job xxxviii. 6.—*J. J. Stewart Perowne.*

Verse 2.—" *Upon the seas :* " that is, upon the great abyss of waters which is under the earth, enclosed in great hollow places, whence the heads of rivers do spring, and other waters bubble out upon the earth.—*John Diodati.*

Verse 2.—"*Above the floods he hath established it.*" Both the words בל (Al) in the two clauses of this verse mean either " above " as we have rendered it, and refer to Gen. i. 9, 10, denoting that Jehovah hath called forth dry land from the midst of the seas, and established it above the floods, and hath set a boundary to the latter never to turn and overflow it (see Job xxxviii. 8 ; Psalm civ. chronologically Psalm vii. 9) ; or " by, or at," as they often denote, and refer to the same subject of the omnipotence of God in relation to the same quoted passages, *i.e.*, that though our globe is situated at or by the floods—is surrounded with mighty waters whose single wave could bury it for ever, still the Lord has so established it that this never can happen. This is a mighty reason why the earth and all its fulness and inhabitants belong to Jehovah.—*Benjamin Weiss.*

Verse 2.—Hereby is mystically meant, that he hath set his church above the waters of adversities, so that how high soever they arise, it is kept still above them in safety, and so shall be for evermore ; or it may agree thus—he will take in all nations to be his in grace, because all be his creatures ; he made them so admirable an habitation at the first, and upholds it still, showing hereby how much he regards them ; therefore he will now extend his favour further towards them, by taking them in to be his people.—*Augustine, quoted by Mayer.*

Verse 3.—" *Who shall ascend ?* " Indeed, if none must ascend but he that is clean and pure, and without vanity and deceit, the question is quickly answered, None shall, for there is none *so :* dust is our matter, so not clean ; defiled is our nature, so not pure ; lighter, the heaviest of us, than vanity, and deceitful upon the balance the best of us ; so no ascending so high for any of us. Yet there is One we hear of, or might have heard of to-day, that rose and ascended up on high, was thus qualified as the Psalmist speaks of, all clean and pure, no chaff at all, no guile found in his mouth. 1 Pet. ii. 22. Yea, but it was but One that was so ; what's that to all the rest? Yes, somewhat 'tis. *He* was our *Head,* and if the Head be once risen and ascended, the members will all follow after in their time.—*Mark Frank.*

Verse 3.—" *The hill of the Lord,*" can be no other than a hill of glory. His holy place is no less than the very place and seat of glory. And being such, you cannot imagine it but *hard to come by,* the very petty glories of the world are so. This is a *hill* of glory, hard to climb, difficult to ascend, craggy to pass up, steep to clamber, no plain campagnia to it, the broad easy way leads some whither else (Matt. vii. 13) ; the way to this is narrow (verse 14) ; 'tis rough and troublesome. To be of the number of Christ's true faithful servants is no slight work ; 'tis a fight, 'tis a race, 'tis a continual warfare ; fastings and watchings, and cold and nakedness, and hunger and thirst, bonds, imprisonments, dangers and distresses, ignominy and reproach, afflictions and persecutions, the world's hatred and our friends' neglect, all that we call hard or difficult is to be found in the way we are to go. A man cannot leave a lust, shake off bad company, quit a course of sin, enter upon a way of virtue, profess his religion or stand to it, cannot ascend the spiritual *hill,* but he will meet some or other of these to contest and strive with. But not only to ascend, but to *stand* there, as the word signifies ; to continue at so high a pitch, to be constant in truth and piety, that will be hard indeed, and bring more difficulties to contest with.—*Mark Frank.*

Verses 3, 4.—The Psalm begins with a solicitous enquiry, subjoins a satisfactory answer, and closes with a most pertinent but rapturous apostrophe. This is the enquiry, " *Who shall ascend into the hill of the Lord ? or who shall stand in his holy place ?* " This is the answer, "*He that hath clean hands, and a pure heart ;* " " *he shall receive the blessing*" of plenary remission " *from the Lord, and righteousness also from the God of his salvation :* " even that perfect righteousness which is not acquired by man, but bestowed by Jehovah ; which is not performed by the saint, but received by the sinner ; which is the only solid basis to support our hopes of happiness, the only valid plea for an admission into the mansions of joy. Then follows the apostrophe : the prophet foresees the ascension of Christ and his saints into the kingdom of heaven. He sees his Lord marching at the head of the redeemed world, and conducting them into regions of honour and joy. Suitably to such a view, and in a most beautiful strain of poetry, he addresses himself to the heavenly portals. " *Lift up your heads, O ye gates ; and be ye lift up, ye everlasting doors ; and the King of glory,*" with all the heirs of his grace and righteousness, shall make their triumphant entry ; " *shall enter in,*" and go out no more.—*James Hervey.*

Verses 3, 4.—It is not he who sings so well or so many Psalms, nor he who fasts or watches so many days, nor he who divides his own among the poor, nor he who preaches to others, nor he who lives quietly, kindly and friendly ; nor, in fine, is it he who knows all sciences and languages, nor he who works all virtuous and all good works that ever any man spoke or read of, but it is he alone, who is pure within and without.—*Martin Luther.*

Verse 4.—" *He that hath clean hands, and a pure heart.*" Shall I tell you, then, who is a moral man in the sight of God ? It is he that bows to the divine law as the supreme rule of right ; he that is influenced by a governing regard to God in all his actions ; he that obeys other commands spontaneously, because he has obeyed the first and great command, " Give me thy *heart.*" His conduct is not conformed to custom or expediency, but to one consistent, immutable standard of duty. Take this man into a court of justice, and call on him to testify, and he will not bear false witness. Give him the charge of untold treasures, he will not steal. Trust him with the dearest interests of yourself or family, you are safe, because he has a living principle of truth and integrity in his bosom. He is as worthy of confidence in the dark as at noonday ; for he is a moral man, not because reputation or interest demands it, not because the eye of public observation is fixed upon him, but because the love and fear of God have predominant ascendancy in his heart.—*Ebenezer Porter, D.D.,* 1834.

Verse 4.—Conditions that suit none but Christ. [Bellarmine.] " *He that hath clean hands ;*" " the clean of hands," Marg. :—those hands from which went forth virtue and healing ; hands ever lifted up in prayer to God, or in blessing to man ; hands stretched forth on the cross for the cleansing of the whole world.—*Isaac Williams, in loc.*

Verse 4.—" *Who hath not lifted up his soul unto vanity,*" is read by Arius Montanus, " He that hath not received his soul in vain." Oh ! how many receive their souls in vain, making no more use of them than the swine, of whom the philosopher observes, *cujus anima pro sale,* their souls are only for salt to keep their bodies from stinking. Who would not grieve to think that so choice a piece should be employed about so vain a use !—*George Swinnock.*

Verse 4.—" *Nor sworn deceitfully ;*" or inured his tongue to any other kind of the language of hell's rotten communication, to the dishonouring of God, or deceiving of others. Perjury is here instanced for the rest, as one of the most heinous. But Peraldus reckoneth up four-and-twenty several sins of the tongue, all which every burgess of the New Jerusalem is careful to avoid, as the devil's drivel, no way becoming his pure lip.—*John Trapp.*

Verse 4.—Now we come to the four conditions requisite to render such an ascent possible. 1. Abstinence from evil doing : " *He that hath clean hands.*" 2. Abstinence from evil thought : " *and a pure heart.*" 3. Who does that duty which he is sent into the world to do : " *That hath not lift up his mind unto vanity ;*" or, as it is in the Vulgate, " *Who hath not received his soul in vain.*" And, 4. Remembers the vows by which he is bound to God : " *nor sworn to deceive.*" And in the fullest sense, there was but One in whom all these things were fulfilled ; so that in reply to the question, " Who shall ascend into the hill of the Lord ? " he might well answer, " No man hath ascended up to heaven, but he that came down from heaven, even the Son of man which is in heaven." John iii. 13. " Therefore it is well written," says St. Bernard, " that such an High Priest became us, because he knows the difficulty of that ascent to the celestial mountain, he knows the weakness of us that have to ascend."—*Lorinus and Bernard, quoted by J. M. Neale.*

Verse 4.—Heaven is not won with good words and a fair profession. The doing Christian is the man that shall stand, when the empty boaster of his faith shall fall. The great talkers of religion are often the least doers. His religion is in vain whose profession brings not letters testimonial from a holy life.—*William Gurnall.*

Verse 5.—" *He shall receive the blessing ;*" as before, " Thou shalt set him to be a blessing." Psalm xxi. 6. His name is never without blessing. In him shall all the nations of the earth be blessed. On the mount of his beatitudes, on the heavenly Mount Sion, crowned as " the Son of the blessed." " *From the Lord ;*" even the " God and Father of our Lord Jesus Christ." Eph. i. 3.—*Isaac Williams.*

Verse 5.—" *He shall receive . . . . righteousness.*" As for our own righteousness which we have without him, Esay telleth us, " it is a defiled cloth ; " and St. Paul, that it is but " dung." Two very homely comparisons, but they be the Holy Ghost's own ; yet nothing so homely as in the original, where they be so odious, as what manner of defiled cloth, or what kind of dung we have not dared to translate. Our own then being no better, we are driven to seek for it elsewhere. " *He shall receive his righteousness,*" saith the prophet ; and " *the gift of righteousness,*" saith the apostle. Phil. iii. 8, 9 ; Rom. v. 17. It is then another, to be *given us,* and to be *received* by us, which we must seek for. And whither shall we go for it ? Job alone dispatcheth this point (chap. xv. 15 ; iv. 18 ; xxv. 5.) Not to *the heavens* or *stars,* they are *unclean in his sight.* Not to the *saints,* for in them *he found folly.* Not to the *angels,* for neither in them found he *steadfastness.* Now, if none of these will serve, we see a necessary reason why Jehovah must be a part of this name, " the LORD our righteousness." Jer. xxiii. 6.—*Lancelot Andrewes.*

Verse 6.—" *This is the generation of them that seek him, that seek thy face.*" Christians must be seekers. This is *the generation of seekers.* All mankind, if ever they will come to heaven, they must be a generation of seekers. Heaven is a generation of finders, of possessors, of enjoyers, seekers of God. But here we are a generation of seekers. We want somewhat that we must seek. When we are at best, we want the accomplishment of our happiness. It is a state of seeking here, because it is a state of want ; we want something alway. But to come more particularly to this *seeking the face of God,* or the presence of God. . . . . The presence of God meant here is, that presence that he shows *in the time of need, and in his ordinances.* He shows a presence in need and necessity, that is, a gracious presence to his children, a gracious face. As in want of direction, he shows his presence of light to direct them ; in weakness he shows his strength ; in trouble and perplexity he will show his gracious and comfortable presence to comfort them. In perplexity he shows his presence to set the heart at large, answerable to the necessity. So in need God is present with his children, to direct them, to comfort them, to strengthen them, if they need that.—*Richard Sibbes.*

Verse 6.—" *This is the generation.*" By the demonstrative pronoun " *this,*" the Psalmist erases from the catalogue of the servants of God all counterfeit Israelites, who, trusting only to their circumcision and the sacrifice of beasts, have no concern about offering themselves to God ; and yet, at the same time, they rashly thrust themselves into the church.—*John Calvin.*

Verse 6 —" *That seek thy face, O Jacob.*" In Prov. vii. 15, and xxix. 26, we have " *seeking the face of* " in the sense of seeking the favour of, or showing delight in. Their delight is not in Esau, who got " the fatness of earth " (Gen xxvii 39) as his portion. And those writers may be right who consider Jacob as a name for Messiah, to whom belong the true birthright and blessing.—*Andrew A. Bonar.*

Verse 6.—" *That seek thy face, O Jacob.*" He is " the seed of Jacob ; " he is " the Holy One of Israel ; " " the face of thine Anointed " is the face of him who is both God and man ; for " we shall see him as he is."—*Isaac Williams.*

Verse 6.—" *O Jacob,*" or, O God of Jacob. As the church is called *Christ* (1 Cor. xii. 12), so God is here called " *Jacob ;* " such a near union there is betwixt him and his people. Or, *this is* Jacob. So the true *seekers* are fitly called, first, because Israelites indeed (John i. 47 ; Rom. ix. 6) ; secondly, because they see God face to face, as Jacob did at Peniel (Gen. xxxii. 24—30) ; thirdly, because they also, as he, do bear away a blessing (Hos. xii. 4), even " righteousness from the God of their salvation," as in the verse aforegoing.—*John Trapp.*

Verse 7.—" *Lift up your heads, O ye gates.*" The gates of the temple were indeed as described, very lofty and magnificent, in proportion to the gigantic dimensions of that extraordinary edifice. But the phrase, " *Lift up your heads,*" refers not so much to their loftiness, as to the upper part being formed so as to be lifted up ; while the under portion opened in folding doors.—*Robert Jamieson, in Paxton's "Illustrations of Scripture."*

Verse 7.—" *Lift up your heads, O ye gates.*" At the castle of Banias, in Syria, are the remains of an ancient gate which was drawn up, like a blind, the gate fitting in grooves. This will fully explain the term.—*John Gadsby.*

Verse 7.—" *Lift up.*" A phrase or term taken from triumphal arches or great porticoes, set up, or beautified and adorned for the coming in of great, victorious, and triumphant captains.—*John Diodati.*

Verse 7.—" Be ye lift up, ye everlasting doors ; and the King of glory shall come in." Some interpret this of the doors of our heart, according to that (Rev. iii. 20), "Behold, I stand at the door, and knock : if any man hear my voice, and open the door, I will come in to him," etc. In the gospel history, we find that Christ had a fourfold entertainment among men. Some received him into house, not into heart, as Simon the Pharisee (Luke vii. 44), who gave him no kiss nor water to his feet ; some into heart, but not into house, as the faithful centurion (Matt. viii. 8), esteeming himself unworthy that Christ should come under his roof ; some neither into house nor heart, as the graceless Gergesites (Matt. viii. 34) ; some both into house and heart, as Lazarus, Mary, Martha. John iii. 15 ; Luke x. 38. Now that Christ may dwell in our hearts by faith, and that our bodies may be temples of his Holy Spirit, we must as our prophet exhorts here, *lift up our souls,* that is, in the words of St. Paul (Col. iii. 2), our affections must be set on things which are above, and not on things which are on earth : if we desire to lift up our hearts unto Christ's verity, we may not lift them up unto the world's vanity ; that is, we must not fasten our love too much upon the things of this life, but on those pleasures at God's right hand which are evermore ; that as we have borne the image of the first Adam, who was earthly, so we should bear the image of the second Adam, which is heavenly. 1 Cor. xv. 49. The prophane worldling sings a *Nunc dimittis* unto Christ, and saith as the devils, " Ah ! what have we to do with thee, thou Jesus of Narazeth ? " (Mark i. 24) ; and as Job reports his words, " Depart from us, for we desire not the knowledge of thy ways." Job xxi. 14. On the contrary, the religious soul, enjoying the possession of the Saviour, chanteth a merry *Magnificat,* and a pleasant *Te Deum :* she saith unto Christ, as Ruth unto Naomi (Ruth i. 16), " Intreat me not to leave thee, or to return from following after thee." Nay, death itself shall not part us, for when I am loosed out of my body's prison, I hope to be with Christ ; as Ittai then unto David, I say unto Jesus, " As the Lord liveth, and as my Lord the king liveth, surely in what place the lord my king shall be, whether in death, or life, even there also will thy servant be." 2 Sam. xv, 21. O Lord, which art the God of my salvation, I lift my heart to thee, desirous to seek thee, both in the right *ubi*—where thou mayst be found, and in the right *quando*—while thou mayst be found. Psalm xviii. 47 ; xxv. 1. Open my dull ears and hard heart, that thy Son my Saviour may come in and dwell with me. Grant me grace that I may still hear while he calleth, open while he knocketh, and hold him also when I have him ; that I may both *ascend thine hill,* and *stand in thine holy places ;* that I may not only sojourn in thy tabernacle, but also rest and dwell upon the mountain of thine holiness.—*John Boys.*

Verse 7.—"Everlasting doors." Heaven's gates are called *"everlasting,"* because they shall endure for ever, or because they be the doors unto the life which is everlasting.—*John Boys.*

Verse 7.—Whatever we may think of these things, David thought it high time for him to bid such a messenger welcome, and to open his heart for the receiving his God. Hear what he saith to his own heart and others : " *Lift up your heads, O ye gates ; and be ye lift up, ye everlasting doors ; and the King of glory shall come in.*" And because the door of men's hearts is locked, and barred and bolted, and men are in a deep sleep, and will not hear the knocking that is at the gate, though it be loud, though it be a king ; therefore David knocks again, " *Lift up, ye everlasting doors.*" Why, what haste, saith the sinner ? What haste ? Why, here's the King at your gates ; and that not an ordinary king neither ; he is a glorious King, that will honour you so far, if you open quickly, as to lodge within, to take up his abode in your house, to dwell with you. But the soul for all this doth not yet open, but stands still questioning, as if it were an enemy rather than a friend that stood there, and asks, " *Who is this King of glory ?*" Who ? He answers again, " *It is the Lord of Hosts ;*" he, that if you will not open quickly and thankfully too, can easily pull your house down about your ears ; he is the Lord of hosts, that King who hath a mighty army always at his command, who stand ready for their commission, and then you should know who it is you might have had for your friend ; " Lift up, therefore, your heads, O ye gates." Open quickly, ye that had rather have God for your friend than for your enemy. Oh, why should not the soul of every sinner cry out, Lord, the door is locked, and thou hast the key ; I have been trying what I can do, but the wards are so rusty that I cannot possibly turn the key ? But, Lord, throw the door off the hinges, anything in the world so thou wilt but come in and dwell here. Come, O mighty God, break through doors of iron, and bars of brass, and make way for thyself by thy love and power. Come, Lord, and make thyself welcome ; all that I have is at thy service ; O fit my soul to entertain thee !—*James Janeway.*

Verse 7.—He hath left with us the earnest of the Spirit, and taken from us the earnest of our flesh, which he hath carried into heaven as a pledge that the whole shall follow after.—*Tertullian.*

Verse 7.—Christ is gone to heaven as a victor ; leading sin, Satan, death, hell, and all his enemies in triumph at his chariot wheels. He has not only overcome his enemies for himself, but for all his people, whom he will make conquerors, yea, " more than conquerors." As he has overcome, so shall they also overcome ; and as he is gone to heaven a victor, they shall follow in triumph. He is in heaven as a Saviour. When he came from heaven it was in the character of a Saviour ; when on earth he obtained eternal salvation ; in heaven he lives as a Saviour ; when he comes again from heaven he will come as a Saviour ; and when he will return, he will return as a Saviour. He is also gone to heaven as the rightful heir. He is not gone to heaven as a sojourner, but as " the heir of all things." He is the heir of heavenly glory and happiness, and believers are " heirs of God, and joint heirs with Christ." *Henry Pendlebury, 1626—1695.*

Verse 7.—" O clap your hands together, all ye people ; sing unto God with the voice of melody. God is gone up with a merry noise, and the Lord with the sound of the trump." Psalm xlvii. 1, 5. This Ark, which has saved the world from destruction, after floating on a deluge of blood, rests at length on the mountain. This innocent Joseph, whose virtue had been oppressed by the synagogue, is brought out of the dungeon to receive a crown. This invincible Samson has carried away the gates of hell, and goes in triumph to the everlasting hills. This victorious Joshua has passed over Jordan with the ark of the covenant, and takes possession of the land of the living. This Sun of righteousness, which had gone down ten degrees, returns backward to the place which it had left. He who was " a worm " at his birth, a Lamb in his passion, and a Lion in his resurrection, now ascends as an Eagle to heaven, and encourages us to follow him thither. This day heaven learns to endure man's presence, and men to walk above the stars ; the heavenly Jerusalem receives its rightful King, the church its High Priest, the house of God its Heritor, the whole world its Ruler. " O sing praises, sing praises unto our God : O sing praises, sing praises unto our King." Psalm xlvii. 6—8. " God reigneth over the heathen, God sitteth upon his holy seat." " The princes of the people are joined unto " him ; " he is very highly exalted " above them.—*From " The Life of Jesus Christ in Glory," translated from the French of James Nouet.*

Verses 7, 8.—Christ being now arrived at heaven's doors, those heavenly spirits that accompanied him began to say, " *Lift up your heads, O ye gates ; and be ye lift up, ye everlasting doors ; and the King of glory shall come in !* " to whom some of the angels that were within, not ignorant of his person, but admiring his majesty and glory, said again, " *Who is the King of glory ?* " and then they answered, " *The Lord strong and mighty, the Lord mighty in battle ;* " and thereupon those twelve gates of the holy city, of new Jerusalem, opened of their own accord, and Jesus Christ with all his ministering spirits entered in. O my soul, how should this heighten thy joy and enlarge thy comforts, in that Christ is now received up into glory ? Every sight of Christ is glorious, and in every sight thou shouldst wait on the Lord Jesus Christ for some glorious manifestations of himself. Come, live up to the rate of this great mystery ; view Christ as entering into glory, and thou wilt find the same sparkles of glory on thy heart. Oh ! this sight is a transforming sight : " We all, with open face beholding as in a glass the glory of the Lord, are changed into the same image from glory to glory, even as by the Spirit of the Lord." 2 Cor. iii. 18. *Isaac Ambrose.*

Verses 7, 8.—Ye that are thus the living temples of the Lord, and have already entertained his sanctifying Spirit into you, do you lift up your hearts in the use of holy ordinances through faith, in joyful desires and assured expectation of him ; yea, be you abundantly lift up by faith in the use of holy means, who are the everlasting habitation of an everlasting God, with a joyful and assured welcome of him ; for so shall you invite and undoubtedly entertain the high and mighty Potentate, the Lord Christ into your souls, with the glorious manifestation and ravishing operation of his love, benefits, and graces. And know, O all ye faithful and obedient ones, for your courage and comfort, who, and of what quality this glorious King, the Lord Jesus is, whom the world despises but you honour. Why, he is the Almighty God, of power all-sufficient to preserve and defend his people and church, that in trust of him do love and serve him, against all the strength and power of men and devils that do or shall malign or oppose themselves against them, and to put them to the foil, as we his Israel in the letter have found by experience for your instruction and corroboration that are his people in spirit.—*George Abbot, in "Brief Notes upon the whole Book of Psalms,"* 1651.

Verses 7—10.—Oh, what tongue of the highest archangel of heaven can express the welcome of thee, the King of glory, into these blessed regions of immortality? Surely the empyreal heaven never resounded with so much joy: God ascended with jubilation, and the Lord with the sound of the trumpet. It is not for us, weak and finite creatures, to wish to conceive those incomprehensible, spiritual, divine gratulations, that the glorious Trinity gave to the victorious and now glorified human nature. Certainly, if, when he brought his only-begotten Son into the world, he said, " Let all the angels worship him;" much more now that he " ascends on high, and hath led captivity captive, hath he given him a name above all names, that at the name of Jesus all knees should bow." And if the holy angels did so carol at his birth, in the very entrance into that state of humiliation and infirmity with what triumph did they receive him now returning from the perfect achievement of man's redemption? and if, when his type had vanished Goliath, and carried his head into Jerusalem, the damsels came forth to meet him with dances and timbrels, how shall we think those angelical spirits triumphed in meeting of the great Conqueror of hell and death? How did they sing, *" Lift up your heads, ye gates! and be lifted up, ye everlasting doors; and the King of glory shall come in."* Surely as he shall come, so he went; and, " Behold, he shall come with thousands of his holy ones; thousand thousands ministered unto him, and ten thousand thousands stood before him; " from all whom, methinks I hear that blessed applause, " Worthy is the Lamb that was killed, to receive power, and riches, and wisdom, and strength, and honour, and glory, and praise: praise and honour, and glory, and power, be to him that sitteth upon the throne, and to the Lamb for evermore." And why dost not thou, O my soul, help to bear thy part with that happy choir of heaven? Why art not thou rapt out of my bosom, with an ecstacy of joy, to see this human nature of ours exalted above all the powers of heaven adored of angels, archangels, cherubim, seraphim, and all those mighty and glorious spirits, and sitting there crowned with infinite glory and majesty?—*Joseph Hall.*

Verses 7—10—In the twenty-fourth Psalm, we have an account of the actual entrance of Christ into heaven. When the King of England wishes to enter the city of London, through the Temple Bar, the gate being closed against him, the herald demands entrance. " Open the gate." From within a voice is heard, " Who is there?" The herald answers, " The King of England!" The gate is at once opened, and the king passes, amidst the joyful acclamations of his people. This is an ancient custom, and the allusion is to it in this Psalm. " The Lord ascended with a shout; " he approached the heavenly portal—the herald in his escort demanded an entrance, *" Lift up your heads, O ye gates; and be ye lift up, ye everlasting doors; and the King of glory shall come in."* The celestial watchers within ask, *" Who is the King of glory?"* The heralds answer, *" The Lord strong and mighty, the Lord mighty in battle."* The question and answer being repeated once more, the gates lift up their heads, and the everlasting doors are lifted up. The Prince enters his Father's palace, greeted with the acclamations of heaven, all whose inhabitants unite in one shout of joy ineffable: *" The Lord of Hosts, he is the King of glory! "*—*Christmas Evans.*

Verses 7—10.—If we follow our Redeemer in his ascension and session at the right hand of God, where he is constituted Lord of all, angels, principalities, and powers being made subject to him, and where he sits till his enemies are made his footstool, we shall observe the tide of celestial blessedness rise higher and higher still. The return of a great and beloved prince, who should by only hazarding his life, have saved his country, would fill a nation with ecstasy. Their conversation in every company would turn upon him, and all their thoughts and joys concentrate in him. See then the King of kings, after having by death abolished death, and brought life and immortality to light; after spoiling the powers of darkness, and ruining all their schemes; see him return in triumph! There was something like triumph when he entered into Jerusalem. All the city was moved, saying, " Who is this? " And the multitude answered, It is Jesus, the prophet of Nazareth; and the very children sung, Hosannah to the Son of David: blessed be he that cometh in the name of the Lord; hosannah in the highest! How much greater then must be the triumph of his entry into the heavenly Jerusalem ! Would not all the city be " moved " in this case, saying " Who is this ? " See thousands of angels attending him, and ten thousand times ten thousand come forth to meet him ! The entrance of the ark into the city of David was but a shadow of this, and the responsive strains which were sung on that occasion would on this be much more applicable.—*Andrew Fuller.*

Verses 7—10.—Why is the song repeated ? Why are the everlasting gates invited to lift up their heads a second time ? We may not pretend here, or in any place, to know all the meaning of the divine Psalms. But what if the repetition of this verse was meant to put us in mind that our Saviour's ascension will be repeated also ? He will not indeed die any more ; death can no more have any dominion over him ; " there remaineth no more sacrifice for sin." Neither of course can he rise again any more. But as he will come again at the end of the world, to judge the quick and the dead, so after that descent he will have to ascend again. And I say, this second ascension may be signified by the Psalmist calling on the everlasting doors to lift up their heads a second time, and make way for the King of glory. Now observe the answer made this second time, " *Who is the King of glory ? The Lord strong and mighty, the Lord mighty in battle. Lift up your heads, O ye gates ; even lift them up, ye everlasting doors ; and the King of glory shall come in. Who is this King of glory ? The Lord of hosts, he is the King of glory.*" Before, it was " *the Lord strong and mighty, the Lord mighty in battle;*" now it is " *The Lord of Hosts.*" Christ ascending the first time, to intercede for us at his Father's right hand, is called " *The Lord mighty in battle.*" But Christ, ascending the second time, after the world hath been judged, and the good and bad separated for ever. is called " *the Lord of hosts.*" Why this difference in his divine titles ? We may reverently take it, that it signifies to us the difference between his first and second coming down to earth, his first and second ascension into heaven. As in other respects his first coming was in great humility, so in this, that he came, in all appearance, alone. The angels were indeed waiting round him, but not visibly, not in glory. " He trode the winepress alone, and of the people there was none with him." He wrestled with death, hell and Satan, alone. Alone he rose from the dead : alone, as far as man could see, he went up to heaven. Thus he showed himself " the Lord mighty in battle," mighty in that single combat which he, as our champion, our David, victoriously maintained against our great enemy. But when he shall come down and go up the second time, he will show himself " the Lord of hosts." Instead of coming down alone in mysterious silence, as in his wonderful incarnation, he will be followed by all the armies of heaven. " The Lord my God will come, and all his saints with him." " The Lord cometh with ten thousand of his saints." " The Son of Man will come in the glory of his Father, and all the holy angels with him." " Thousand thousands will stand around him, and ten thousand times ten thousand will minister unto him." Instead of the silence of that quiet chamber at Nazareth, and of the holy Virgin's womb, there will be the voice of the archangel, and the trump of God accompanying him. Thus he will come down as the Lord of hosts, and as the Lord of hosts he will ascend again to his Father. After the judgment, he will pass again through the everlasting doors, with a greater company than before ; for he will lead along with him, into the heavenly habitation, all those who shall have been raised from their graves and found worthy. Hear how the awful sight is described by one who will doubtless have a high place in that day near the Judge. The great apostle and prophet, St. Paul, says, " The Lord himself shall descend from heaven with a shout ; and the dead in Christ shall rise first: then we which are alive and remain shall be caught up together with them in the clouds, to meet the Lord in the air, and so shall we ever be with the Lord."—*John Keble, M.A.*

Verses 7—10.—

In his blessed life
I see the path, and in his death the price,
And in his great ascent the proof supreme
Of immortality. And did he rise ?
Hear, O ye nations ! hear it, O ye dead !
He rose ! He rose ! He burst the bars of
　death.
Lift up your heads, ye everlasting gates !
And give the King of glory to come in.
Who is the King of glory ? He who left
His throne of glory for the pangs of death.

Lift up your heads, ye everlasting gates !
And give the King of glory to come in.
Who is the King of glory ? He who slew
The ravenous foe that gorged all human
　race.
The King of glory, he whose glory filled
Heaven with amazement at his love to
　man.
And with divine complacency beheld
Powers most illumined 'wildered in the
　theme.

Edward Young.

Verses 7—10.—

> Lift up your heads, ye gates, and, O prepare,
> Ye living orbs, your everlasting doors,
> The King of glory comes!
> What King of glory? He whose puissant might
> Subdued Abaddon, and the infernal powers
> Of darkness bound in adamantine chains:
> Who, wrapp'd in glory, with the Father reigns,
> Omnipotent, immortal, infinite!
>
> *James Scott.*

Verse 8.—" Who is the King of glory?" Christ in two respects is *" the King of glory."* 1. For that all honour and glory belong properly to him—his is " the kingdom, the power, and the glory " (Matt. vi. 13), called in this regard, " The Lord of glory." 1 Cor. ii. 8. 2. For that Christ maketh us partakers of his glory, termed in this respect our glorious Lord Jesus. James ii. 1. If the Lord of hosts, strong and mighty in battle, be the King of glory, then Christ, (having conquered all his enemies, and made them his footstool, triumphing over death, and the devil which is the founder of death, and sin which is the sting of death, and the grave which is the prison of death, and hell itself which is the proper dominion of the devil and death) is doubtless in himself, *" the King of glory."* And for as much as he died for our sins, and is risen again for our justification, and is ascended on high to give gifts unto men—in this life grace, in the next glory—what is he less than a *" King of glory "* towards us, of whom and through whom alone we that fight his battles are delivered from the hands of all that hate us, and so made victors (1 Cor. xv. 57), yea, " more than conquerors." Rom. viii. 37.—*John Boys.*

Verse 8.—" The Lord strong and mighty." *" Strong and mighty,"* in subduing all adversaries; and overcoming death and the devil who had the power of death. *Ludolphus, quoted by Isaac Williams.*

Verse 10.—" Jehovah of hosts," or, as the Hebrew is, *Jehovah Tsebaoth,* for so the word is used by the apostles, untranslated in the Greek, *Sabaoth.* Rom. ix. 29. It signifieth *hosts* or *armies* standing ready in martial order, and in battle array, and comprehendeth all creatures in heaven and in earth, which are pressed to do the will of God.—*Henry Ainsworth.*

HINTS TO PREACHERS.

Verse 1.—The great Proprietor, his estates and his servants, his rights and wrongs.

Verse 1.—" The earth is the Lord's." I. *Mention other claimants*—idols: pope, man, devil, etc. II. *Try the suit.* III. *Carry out the verdict.* Use our substance, preach everywhere, claim all things for God. IV. *See how glorious the earth looks when she bears her Master's name.*

Verse 1 (last clause).—All men belong to God. His sons or his subjects, his servants or his serfs, his sheep or his goats, etc.

Verse 2.—Divine purposes accomplished by singular means.

Verse 2.—Founded on the seas. Instability of terrestrial things.

Verse 3.—The all-important question.

Verse 4 (first clause).—Connection between outward morality and inward purity.

Verse 4 (second clause).—Men judged by their delights.

Verse 4.—" Clean hands." 1. How to get them clean. II. How to keep them clean. III. How to defile them. IV. How to get them clean again.

Verses 4, 5.—Character manifested and favour received.

Verse 5 (second clause).—The good man receiving righteousness and needing salvation, or the evangelical meaning of apparently legal passages.

Verse 6.—Those who truly seek fellowship with God.

Verse 7.—Accommodate the text to the entrance of Jesus Christ into our hearts.

I. There are obstacles, "*gates*," "*doors*." II. We must will to remove them: "*lift up*." III. Grace must enable us: "*be ye lift up*." IV. Our Lord will enter. V. He enters as "*King*," and "*King of glory*."

Verse 7.—The ascension and its teachings.

Verses 7—10.—I: His title—the Lord of hosts. II. His victories, implied in the expression, The Lord strong and mighty in battle. III. His mediatorial title, The King of glory. IV. His authoritative entrance into the holy place.—*John Newton's " Messiah."*

Verse 8.—The mighty Hero. His pedigree, his power, his battles, his victories.

Verse 10.—The sovereignty and glory of God in Christ.

PSALM XXV.

TITLE.—*A Psalm of David. David is pictured in this Psalm as in a faithful miniature. His holy trust, his many conflicts, his great transgressions, his bitter repentance, and his deep distresses are all here; so that we see the very heart of " the man after God's own heart." It is evidently a composition of David's later days, for he mentions the sins of his youth, and from its painful references to the craft and cruelty of his many foes, it will not be too speculative a theory to refer it to the period when Absalom was heading the great rebellion against him. This has been styled the second of the seven Penitential Psalms. It is the mark of a true saint that his sorrows remind him of his sins, and his sorrow for sin drives him to his God.*

SUBJECT AND DIVISION.—*The twenty-two verses of this Psalm begin in the original with the letters of the Hebrew alphabet in their proper order. It is the first instance we have of an inspired acrostic or alphabetical song. This method may have been adopted by the writer to assist the memory; and the Holy Spirit may have employed it to show us that the graces of style and the arts of poetry may lawfully be used in his service. Why should not all the wit and ingenuity of man be sanctified to noblest ends by being laid upon the altar of God? From the singularity of the structure of the Psalm, it is not easy to discover any marked divisions; there are great changes of thought, but there is no variation of subject; the moods of the writer's mind are twofold—prayer and meditation; and as these appear in turns, we shall thus divide the verses. Prayer from verses 1 to 7; meditation, verses 8, 9, 10; prayer, verse 11; meditation, verses 12—15; prayer, verses 16 to end.*

EXPOSITION.

UNTO thee, O LORD, do I lift up my soul.

2 O my God, I trust in thee: let me not be ashamed, let not mine enemies triumph over me.

3 Yea, let none that wait on thee be ashamed: let them be ashamed which transgress without cause.

4 Shew me thy ways, O LORD; teach me thy paths.

5 Lead me in thy truth, and teach me: for thou *art* the God of my salvation; on thee do I wait all the day.

6 Remember, O LORD, thy tender mercies and thy lovingkindnesses; for they *have been* ever of old.

7 Remember not the sins of my youth, nor my transgressions: according to thy mercy remember thou me for thy goodness' sake, O LORD.

1. *" Unto thee, O Lord."*—See how the holy soul flies to its God like a dove to its cote. When the storm-winds are out, the Lord's vessels put about and make for their well-remembered harbour of refuge. What a mercy that the Lord will condescend to hear our cries in time of trouble, although we may have almost forgotten him in our hours of fancied prosperity. *" Unto thee, O Jehovah, do I lift up my soul."* It is but mockery to uplift the hands and the eyes unless we also bring our souls into our devotions. True prayer may be described as the soul rising from earth to have fellowship with heaven; it is taking a journey upon Jacob's ladder, leaving our cares and fears at the foot, and meeting with a covenant God at the top. Very often the soul cannot rise, she has lost her wings, and is heavy and earth-bound; more like a burrowing mole than a soaring eagle. At such dull seasons we must not give over prayer, but must, by God's assistance, exert all our power to lift up our hearts. Let faith be the lever and grace be the arm, and the dead lump will yet be stirred. But what a lift it has sometimes proved! With all our tugging and straining we have been utterly defeated, until the heavenly loadstone of our Saviour's love has displayed its omnipotent attractions, and then our hearts have gone up to our Beloved like mounting flames of fire.

2. *" O my God."* This title is more dear and near than the name Jehovah,

which is used in the first sentence. Already the sweet singer has drawn nearer to his heavenly helper, for he makes bold to grasp him with the hand of assured possession, calling him, my God. Oh the more than celestial music of that word— " *my God!* " It is to be observed that the Psalmist does not deny expression to those gracious feelings with which God had favoured him ; he does not fall into loathsome mock modesty, but finding in his soul a desire to seek the Lord he avows it ; believing that he had a rightful interest in Jehovah he declares it, and knowing that he had confidence in his God he professes it ; " *O my God, I trust in thee.* " Faith is the cable which binds our boat to the shore, and by pulling at it we draw ourselves to the land ; faith unites us to God, and then draws us near to him. As long as the anchor of faith holds there is no fear in the worst tempest ; if that should fail us there would be no hope left. We must see to it that our faith is sound and strong, for otherwise prayer cannot prevail with God. Woe to the warrior who throws away his shield ; what defence can be found for him who finds no defence in God ? " *Let me not be ashamed* " Let not my disappointed hopes makes me feel ashamed of my former testimonies to thy faithfulness. Many were on the watch for this. The best of men have their enemies, and should pray against them that they may not see their wicked desires accomplished. " *Let not mine enemies triumph over me.* " Suffer no wicked mouth to make blasphemous mirth out of my distresses by asking " Where is thy God ? " There is a great jealousy in believers for the honour of God, and they cannot endure that unbelievers should taunt them with the failure of their expectations from the God of their salvation. All other trusts will end in disappointment and eternal shame, but our confidences shall never be confounded.

3. " *Yea, let none that wait on thee be ashamed.* " Suffering enlarges the heart by creating the power to sympathize. If we pray eagerly for ourselves, we shall not long be able to forget our fellow-sufferers. None pity the poor like those who have been or are still poor, none have such tenderness for the sick as those who have been long in ill health themselves. We ought to be grateful for occasional griefs if they preserve us from chronic hard-heartedness ; for of all afflictions, an unkind heart is the worst, it is a plague to its possessor, and a torment to those around him. Prayer when it is of the Holy Ghost's teaching is never selfish ; the believer does not sue for monopolies for himself, but would have all in like case to partake of divine mercy with him. The prayer may be viewed as a promise ; our Heavenly Father will never let his trustful children find him untrue or unkind. He will ever be mindful of his covenant. " *Let them be ashamed which transgress without cause.* " David had given his enemies no provocation ; their hatred was wanton. Sinners have no justifiable reason or valid excuse for transgressing ; they benefit no one, not even themselves by their sins ; the law against which they transgress is not harsh or unjust ; God is not a tyrannical ruler, providence is not a bondage : men sin because they will sin, not because it is either profitable or reasonable to do so. Hence shame is their fitting reward. May they blush with penitential shame now, or else they will not be able to escape the everlasting contempt and the bitter shame which is the promotion of fools in the world to come.

4. " *Shew me thy ways, O Lord.* " Unsanctified natures clamour for their own way, but gracious spirits cry, " Not my will, but thine be done." We cannot at all times discern the path of duty, and at such times it is our wisdom to apply to the Lord himself. Frequently the dealings of God with us are mysterious, and then also we may appeal to him as his own interpreter, and in due time he will make all things plain. Moral, providential and mental forms of guidance are all precious gifts of a gracious God to a teachable people. The second petition, " *teach me thy paths,* " appears to mean more than the first, and may be illustrated by the case of a little child who should say to his father, " Father, first tell me which is the way, and then teach my little trembling feet to walk in it." What weak dependent creatures we are ! How constantly we cry to the Strong for strength !

5. " *Lead me in thy truth, and teach me.* " The same request as in the last verse. The little child having begun to walk, asks to be still led onward by its parent's helping hand, and to be further instructed in the alphabet of truth. Experimental teaching is the burden of this prayer. Lead me according to thy truth, and prove thyself faithful ; lead me into truth that I may know its preciousness, lead me by the way of truth that I may manifest its spirit. David knew much, but he felt his ignorance and desired to be still in the Lord's school ; four times over in these two verses he applies for a scholarship in the college of grace. It were well for many professors

if instead of following their own devices, and cutting out new paths of thought for themselves, they would enquire for the good old ways of God's own truth, and beseech the Holy Ghost to give them sanctified understandings and teachable spirits. "*For thou art the God of my salvation.*" The Three-One Jehovah is the Author and Perfector of salvation to his people. Reader, is he the God of *your* salvation? Do you find in the Father's election, in the Son's atonement, and in the Spirit's quickening all the grounds of your eternal hopes? If so, you may use this as an argument for obtaining further blessings; if the Lord has ordained to save you, surely he will not refuse to instruct you in his ways. It is a happy thing when we can address the Lord with the confidence which David here manifests, it gives us great power in prayer, and comfort in trial. "*On thee do I wait all the day.*" Patience is the fair handmaid and daughter of faith; we cheerfully wait when we are certain that we shall not wait in vain. It is our duty and our privilege to wait upon the Lord in service, in worship, in expectancy, in trust all the days of our life. Our faith will be tried faith, and if it be of the true kind, it will bear continued trial without yielding. We shall not grow weary of waiting upon God if we remember how long and how graciously he once waited for us.

6. "*Remember, O Lord, thy tender mercies and thy loving-kindnesses.*" We are usually tempted in seasons of affliction to fear that our God has forgotten us, or forgotten his usual kindness towards us; hence the soul doth as it were put the Lord in remembrance, and beseech him to recollect those deeds of love which once he wrought towards it. There is a holy boldness which ventures thus to deal with the Most High, let us cultivate it; but there is also an unholy unbelief which suggests our fears, let us strive against it with all our might. What gems are those two expressions, "*tender mercies and loving-kindnesses*"! They are the virgin honey of language; for sweetness no words can excel them; but as for the gracious favours which are intended by them, language fails to describe them.

> "When all thy mercies, O my God,
> My rising soul surveys,
> Transported with the view, I'm lost
> In wonder, love and praise."

If the Lord will only do unto us in the future as in the past, we shall be well content. We seek no change in the divine action, we only crave that the river of grace may never cease to flow.

"*For they have been ever of old.*" A more correct translation would be "from eternity." David was a sound believer in the doctrine of God's eternal love. The Lord's loving-kindnesses are no novelties. When we plead with him to bestow them upon us, we can urge use and custom of the most ancient kind. In courts of law men make much of precedents, and we may plead them at the throne of grace. "Faith," saith Dickson, "must make use of experiences and read them over unto God out of the register of a sanctified memory, as a recorder to him who cannot forget" With an unchangeable God it is a most effectual argument to remind him of his ancient mercies and his eternal love By tracing all that we enjoy to the fountain-head of everlasting love we shall greatly cheer our hearts, and those do us but sorry service who try to dissuade us from meditating upon election and its kindred topics.

7 "*Remember not the sins of my youth.*" Sin is *the* stumbling-block. This is the thing to be removed. Lord, pass an act of oblivion for all my sins, and especially for the hot-blooded wanton follies of my younger years. Those offences which we remember with repentance God forgets, but if we forget them, justice will bring them forth to punishment. The world winks at the sins of young men, and yet they are not so little after all; the bones of our youthful feastings at Satan's table will stick painfully in our throats when we are old men. He who presumes upon his youth is poisoning his old age. How large a tear may wet this page as some of us reflect upon the past! "*Nor my transgressions.*" Another word for the same evils. Sincere penitents cannot get through their confessions at a gallop; they are constrained to use many bemoanings, for their swarming sins smite them with so innumerable griefs. A painful sense of any one sin provokes the believer to repentance for the whole mass of his iniquities. Nothing but the fullest and clearest pardon will satisfy a thoroughly awakened conscience. David would have his sins not only forgiven, but forgotten.

"*According to thy mercy remember thou me for thy goodness' sake, O Lord.*" David and the dying thief breathe the same prayer, and doubtless they grounded it upon the same plea, viz., the free grace and unmerited goodness of Jehovah. We dare not ask to have our portion measured from the balances of justice, but we pray to be dealt with by the hand of mercy.

8 Good and upright *is* the LORD : therefore will he teach sinners in the way.

9 The meek will he guide in judgment : and the meek will he teach his way.

10 All the paths of the LORD *are* mercy and truth unto such as keep his covenant and his testimonies.

These three verses are a meditation upon the attributes and acts of the Lord. He who toils in the harvest field of prayer should occasionally pause awhile and refresh himself with a meal of meditation.

8. "*Good and upright is the Lord : therefore will he teach sinners in the way.*" Here the goodness and the rectitude of the divine character are beheld in friendly union ; he who would see them thus united in bonds of perfect amity must stand at the foot of the cross and view them blended in the sacrifice of the Lord Jesus. It is no less true than wonderful that through the atonement the justice of God pleads as strongly as his grace for the salvation of the sinners whom Jesus died to save. Moreover, as a good man naturally endeavours to make others like himself, so will the Lord our God in his compassion bring sinners into the way of holiness and conform them to his own image ; thus the goodness of our God leads us to expect the reclaiming of sinful men. We may not conclude from God's goodness that he will save those sinners who continue to wander in their own ways, but we may be assured that he will renew transgressors' hearts and guide them into the way of holiness. Let those who desire to be delivered from sin take comfort from this. God himself will condescend to be the teacher of sinners. What a ragged school is this for God to teach in ! God's teaching is practical ; he teaches sinners not only the doctrine, but *the way*.

9. "*The meek will he guide in judgment.*" Meek spirits are in high favour with the Father of the meek and lowly Jesus, for he sees in them the image of his only-begotten Son. They know their need of guidance, and are willing to submit their own understandings to divine will, and therefore the Lord condescends to be their guide. Humble spirits are in this verse endowed with a rich inheritance ; let them be of good cheer. Trouble puts gentle spirits to their wits' ends, and drives them to act without discretion, but grace comes to the rescue, enlightens their mind to follow that which is just, and helps them to discern the way in which the Lord would have them to go. Proud of their own wisdom fools will not learn, and therefore miss their road to heaven, but lowly hearts sit at Jesu's feet, and find the gate of glory, for " *the meek will he teach his way*." Blessed teacher ! Favoured scholar ! Divine lesson ! My soul, be thou familiar with the whole.

10. This is a rule without an exception. God is good to those that be good. Mercy and faithfulness shall abound towards those who through mercy are made faithful. Whatever outward appearances may threaten we should settle it steadfastly in our minds that while grace enables us to obey the Lord's will we need not fear that Providence will cause us any real loss. There shall be mercy in every unsavoury morsel, and faithfulness in every bitter drop ; let not our hearts be troubled, but let us rest by faith in the immutable covenant of Jehovah, which is ordered in all things and sure. Yet this is not a general truth to be trampled upon by swine, it is a pearl for a child's neck. Gracious souls, by faith resting upon the finished work of the Lord Jesus, *keep* the *covenant* of the Lord, and, being sanctified by the Holy Spirit, they walk in *his testimonies ;* these will find all things co-working for their good, but to the sinner there is no such promise. Keepers of the covenant shall be kept by the covenant ; those who follow the Lord's commands shall find the Lord's mercy following them.

11 For thy name's sake, O LORD, pardon mine iniquity ; for it *is* great.

This sentence of prayer would seem out of place were it not that prayer is always in its place, whether in season or out of season. Meditation having refreshed the Psalmist, he falls to his weighty work again, and wrestles with God for the remission of his sin. *" For thy name's sake, O Lord."* Here is a blessed, never-failing plea. Not for our sakes or our merits' sake, but to glorify thy mercy, and to show forth the glory of thy divine attributes. *" Pardon mine iniquity."* It is confessed, it is abhorred, it is consuming my heart with grief ; Lord forgive it ; let thine own lips pronounce my absolution. *" For it is great."* It weighs so heavily upon me that I pray thee remove it. Its greatness is no difficulty with thee, for thou art a great God, but the misery which it causes to me is my argument with thee for speedy pardon. Lord, the patient is sore sick, therefore, heal him. To pardon a great sinner will bring thee great glory, therefore for thy name's sake pardon me. Observe how this verse illustrates the logic of faith, which is clean contrary to that of a legal spirit ; faith looks not for merit in the creature, but hath regard to the goodness of the Creator ; and instead of being staggered by the demerits of sin it looks to the precious blood, and pleads all the more vigorously because of the urgency of the case.

12 What man *is* he that feareth the LORD ? him shall he teach in the way *that* he shall choose.

13 His soul shall dwell at ease ; and his seed shall inherit the earth.

14 The secret of the LORD *is* with them that fear him ; and he will shew them his covenant.

15 Mine eyes *are* ever toward the LORD ; for he shall pluck my feet out of the net.

12. *" What man is he that feareth the Lord ?"* Let the question provoke self-examination. Gospel privileges are not for every pretender. Art thou of the seed royal or no ? *" Him shall he teach in the way that he shall choose."* Those whose hearts are right shall not err for want of heavenly direction. Where God sanctifies the heart he enlightens the head. We all wish to choose our way ; but what a mercy is it when the Lord directs that choice, and makes free-will to be good-will ! If we make our will God's will, God will let us have our will. God does not violate our will, but leaves much to our choice ; nevertheless, he instructs our wills, and so we choose that which is well-pleasing in his sight. The will should be subject to law ; there is a way which we should choose, but so ignorant are we that we need to be taught, and so wilful that none but God himself can teach us effectually.

13. He who fears God has nothing else to fear. *" His soul shall dwell at ease."* He shall lodge in the chamber of content. One may sleep as soundly in the little bed in the corner as in the Great Bed of Ware ; it is not abundance but content that gives true ease. Even here, having learned by grace both to abound and to be empty, the believer dwells at ease ; but how profound will be the ease of his soul for ever ! There he will enjoy the *" otium cum dignitate ; "* ease and glory shall go together. Like a warrior whose battles are over, or a husbandman whose barns are full, his soul shall take its ease, and be merry for ever. *" His seed shall inherit the earth."* God remembers, Isaac for the sake of Abraham, and Jacob for the sake of Isaac. Good men's sons have a goodly portion to begin the world with, but many of them, alas ! turn a father's blessing into a curse. The promise is not broken because in some instances men wilfully refuse to receive it ; moreover, it is in its spiritual meaning that it now holds good ; our spiritual seed do inherit all that was meant by *" the earth,"* or Canaan ; they receive the blessing of the new covenant. May the Lord make us the joyful parents of many spiritual children, and we shall have no fears about their maintenance, for the Lord will make each one of them princes in all the earth.

14. *" The secret of the Lord is with them that fear him."* Some read it " the friendship : " it signifies familiar intercourse, confidential intimacy, and select fellowship. This is a great secret. Carnal minds cannot guess what is intended by it, and even believers cannot explain it in words, for it must be felt to be known. The higher spiritual life is necessarily a path which the eagle's eye hath not known, and which the lion's whelp has not travelled ; neither natural wisdom nor strength can force a door into this inner chamber. Saints have the key of heaven's hierogly-phics ; they can unriddle celestial enigmas. They are initiated into the fellowship of the skies ; they have heard words which it is not possible for them to repeat to their fellows. *" And he will shew them his covenant."* Its antiquity, security, righteousness, fulness, graciousness and excellence shall be revealed to their hearts

and understandings, and above all, their own part in it shall be sealed to their souls by the witness of the Holy Spirit. The designs of love which the Lord has to his people in the covenant of grace, he has been pleased to show to believers in the Book of Inspiration, and by his Spirit he leads us into the mystery, even the hidden mystery of redemption. He who does not know the meaning of this verse, will never learn it from a commentary ; let him look to the cross for the secret lies there.

15. "*Mine eyes are ever toward the Lord.*" The writer claims to be fixed in his trust, and constant in his expectation ; he looks in confidence and waits in hope. We may add to this look of faith and hope the obedient look of service, the humble look of reverence, the admiring look of wonder, the studious look of meditation and the tender look of affection. Happy are those whose eyes are never removed from their God. "The eye," says Solomon, " is never satisfied with seeing," but this sight is the most satisfying in the world. "*For he shall pluck my feet out of the net.*" Observe the conflicting condition in which a gracious soul may be placed, his eyes are in heaven and yet his feet are sometimes in a net ; his nobler nature ceases not to behold the glories of God, while his baser parts are enduring the miseries of the world. A net is the common metaphor for temptation. The Lord often keeps his people from falling into it, and if they have fallen he rescues them. The word "*pluck*" is a rough word, and saints who have fallen into sin find that the means of their restoration are not always easy to the flesh ; the Lord plucks at us sharply to let us feel that sin is an exceeding bitter thing. But what a mercy is here ! Believer, be very grateful for it. The Lord will deliver us from the cunning devices of our cruel enemy, and even if through infirmity we have fallen into sin, he will not leave us to be utterly destroyed but will pluck us out of our dangerous state ; though our feet are in the net, if our eyes are up unto God, mercy certainly will interpose.

16 Turn thee unto me, and have mercy upon me ; for I *am* desolate and afflicted.

17 The troubles of my heart are enlarged : O bring thou me out of my distresses.

18 Look upon mine affliction and my pain ; and forgive all my sins.

19 Consider mine enemies ; for they are many ; and they hate me with cruel hatred.

20 O keep my soul, and deliver me : let me not be ashamed ; for I put my trust in thee.

21 Let integrity and uprightness preserve me ; for I wait on thee.

22 Redeem Israel, O God, out of all his troubles.

16. His own eyes were fixed upon God, but he feared that the Lord had averted his face from him in anger. Oftentimes unbelief suggests that God has turned his back upon us. If we know that we turn to God we need not fear that he will turn from us, but may boldly cry, "*Turn thee unto me.*" The ground of quarrel is always in ourselves, and when that is removed there is nothing to prevent our full enjoyment of communion with God. "*Have mercy upon me.*" Saints still must stand upon the footing of mercy ; notwithstanding all their experience they cannot get beyond the publican's prayer, "Have mercy upon me." "*For I am desolate and afflicted.*" He was lonely and bowed down. Jesus was in the days of his flesh in just such a condition ; none could enter into the secret depths of his sorrows, he trod the winepress alone, and hence he is able to succour in the fullest sense those who tread the solitary path.

> "Christ leads me through no darker rooms
> Than he went through before ;
> He that into God's kingdom comes,
> Must enter by this door."

17. "*The troubles of my heart are enlarged.*" When trouble penetrates the heart it is trouble indeed. In the case before us, the heart was swollen with grief like a lake surcharged with water by enormous floods ; this is used as an argument for deliverance, and it is a potent one. When the darkest hour of the night arrives we may expect the dawn ; when the sea is at its lowest ebb the tide must surely turn ; and when our troubles are enlarged to the greatest degree, then may we hopefully pray, "*O bring thou me out of my distresses.*"

18. " *Look upon mine affliction and my pain.*" Note the many trials of the saints ; here we have no less than six words all descriptive of woe. " Desolate, and afflicted, troubles enlarged, distresses, affliction, and pain." But note yet more the submissive and believing spirit of a true saint ; all he asks for is, " Lord, look upon my evil plight ; " he does not dictate or even express a complaint ; a look from God will content him, and that being granted he asks no more. Even more noteworthy is the way in which the believer under affliction discovers the true source of all the mischief, and lays the axe at the root of it. " *Forgive all my sins,*" is the cry of a soul that is more sick of sin than of pain, and would sooner be forgiven than healed. Blessed is the man to whom sin is more unbearable than disease, he shall not be long before the Lord shall both forgive his iniquity and heal his diseases. Men are slow to see the intimate connection between sin and sorrow, a grace-taught heart alone feels it.

19. " *Consider mine enemies.*" Watch them, weigh them, check them, defeat them. " *For they are many.*" They need the eyes of Argus to watch them, and the arms of Hercules to match them, but the Lord is more than sufficient to defeat them. The devils of hell and the evils of earth are all vanquished when the Lord makes bare his arm. " *They hate me with cruel hatred.*" It is the breath of the serpent's seed to hate ; their progenitor was a hater, and they themselves must needs imitate him. No hate so cruel as that which is unreasonable and unjust. A man can forgive one who has injured him, but one whom he has injured he hates implacably. " Behold I send you forth as sheep in the midst of wolves," is still our Master's word to us.

20. " *O keep my soul* " out of evil, " *and deliver me* " when I fall into it. This is another version of the prayer, " Lead us not into temptation, but deliver us from evil."

" *Let me not be ashamed.*" This is the one fear which like a ghost haunted the Psalmist's mind. He trembled lest his faith should become the subject of ridicule through the extremity of his affliction. Noble hearts can brook anything but shame. David was of such a chivalrous spirit, that he could endure any torment rather than to be put to dishonour. " *For I put my trust in thee.*" And therefore the name of God would be compromised if his servants were deserted ; this the believing heart can by no means endure.

21. " *Let integrity and uprightness preserve me.*" What better practical safeguards can a man require ? If we do not prosper with these as our guides, it is better for us to suffer adversity. Even the ungodly world admits that " honesty is the best policy." The heir of heaven makes assurance doubly sure, for apart from the rectitude of his public life, he enlists the guardian care of heaven in secret prayer : " *for I wait on thee.*" To pretend to wait on God without holiness of life is religious hypocrisy, and to trust to our own integrity without calling upon God is presumptuous atheism. Perhaps the integrity and uprightness referred to are those righteous attributes of God, which faith rests upon as a guarantee that the Lord will not forfeit his word.

22. " *Redeem Israel, O God, out of all his troubles.*" This is a very comprehensive prayer, including all the faithful and all their trials. Sorrow had taught the Psalmist sympathy, and given him communion with the tried people of God ; he therefore remembers them in his prayers. *Israel*, the tried, the wrestling, the conquering hero, fit representative of all the saints. Israel in Egypt, in the wilderness, in wars with Canaanites, in captivity, fit type of the church militant on earth. Jesus is the Redeemer from trouble as well as sin, he is a complete Redeemer, and from every evil he will rescue every saint. Redemption by blood is finished : O God, send us redemption by power. Amen and Amen.

EXPLANATORY NOTES AND QUAINT SAYINGS.

Whole Psalm —This is the first of the seven alphabetical Psalms, the others being the 34th, 37th, 111th, 112th, 119th, and 145th. They are specimens of that acrostic mode of writing which seems to have been once so fashionable among the Jews, as is testified by numerous instances of such composition, which are to be met with in their works. Other poetic artifices were likewise adopted. We find many instances of poems being so constructed, that a prayer name, or some particular sentiment, would be not unfrequently expressed by the initial letters of the verses. See Bartolocci's " Bibliotheca Rabbinica," vol. ii. p. 260, where examples of such artifices are cited.—*George .Phillips, B.D., in " The Psalms in Hebrew with a Commentary,"* 1846.

Whole Psalm.—This is the first fully *alphabetic* Psalm . . . . . The only lesson which the use of the *alphabetic* form may teach is this :—that the Holy Spirit was willing to throw his words into all the moulds of human thought and speech ; and whatever ingenuity man may exhibit in intellectual efforts, he should consecrate these to his Lord, making him the *"Alpha and Omega"* of his pursuits.—*Andrew A. Bonar.*

Whole Psalm.—Saving grace is a secret that no man knows but the elect and the elect cannot know it neither without special illumination :—1. Special showing—*" Shew me thy ways, O Lord,"* saith David. 2. Barely showing will not serve the turn, but there must be a special teaching—*" Teach me thy paths,"* ver. 4. 3. Bare teaching will not avail neither, but there must be a special inculcative teaching—*" Teach me in thy ways,"* to ver. 8. 4. Inculcative teaching will not do the deed neither, but there must be a special directive teaching—*" Guide in judgment and teach,"* ver. 9. 5. Directive teaching will not be sufficient neither, but there must be a special manu-ductive teaching—*" Lead me forth in thy truth, and teach me,"* ver. 5. 6. Manu-ductive teaching will not be effectual, but there must ye also a special, choice teaching, a determination of the very will, an elective teaching—*" Him shall he teach in the way that he shall choose,"* verse 12. And what secret is this ? not common grace, for that is not the secret of the elect, but special and peculiar. grace. 1. The special grace of prayer—*" Unto thee, O Lord, do I lift up my soul,"* verse 1. 2. A special grace of faith—*" My God, I trust in thee,"* ver. 2. 3. A special grace of repentance—*" Remember not the sins of my youth,"* etc., verse 7. 4. A special grace of hope—*" My hope is in thee,"* verse 21. 5. A special grace of continual living in God's sight, and dependence upon God—*" Mine eyes are ever toward the Lord,"* verse 15. 6. Which is the root of all God's special and eternal favour and mercy—*" Remember, O Lord thy tender mercies and thy lovingkindnesses ; for they have been ever of old,"* verse 6 ; even God's special mercy to him in particular, verse 11.— *William Fenner, in " Hidden Manna,"* 1626.

Whole Psalm.—In these four Psalms which immediately follow one another we may find the soul of David presented in all the several postures of piety—*lying, standing, sitting, kneeling.* In the twenty-second Psalm, he is lying all along, falling flat on his face, low grovelling on the ground, even almost entering into a degree of despair. Speaking of himself in the history of Christ in the mystery, " My God. why hast thou forsaken me ? " In the twenty-third Psalm, he is *standing,* and through God's favour, in despite of his foes, trampling and triumphing over all opposition ; " The Lord is my shepherd, therefore shall I lack nothing." In the twenty-fourth Psalm he is *sitting,* like a doctor in his chair, or a professor in his place, reading a lecture of divinity, and describing the character of that man—how he must be accomplished—" who shall ascend into the holy hill," and hereafter be partaker of happiness. In this twenty-fifth Psalm, he is *kneeling,* with hands and voice lifted up to God, and on these two hinges the whole Psalm turneth ; the one is a hearty beseeching of God's mercy, the other a humble bemoaning of his own misery.— *Thomas Fuller.*

Verse 1.—*" Unto thee, O Lord, do I lift up my soul."* *The lifting up of the heart* presupposeth a former dejection of his soul. The soul of man is pressed down with sin and with the cares of this world, which, as lead doth the net, draweth it so down, that it cannot mount above till God send spiritual prayers, as cork to the net, to exalt it ; which arise out of faith, as the flame doth out of the fire, and which must be free of secular cares, and all things pressing down, which showeth unto us that worldlings can no more pray than a mole is able to fly. But Christians are as eagles which mount upward. Seeing then the heart of man by nature is fixed to the earth, and of itself is no more able to rise therefrom than a stone which is fixed in the ground, till God raises it by his power, word, and workmen ; it should be our principal petition to the Lord, that it would please him to draw us, that we might run after him ; that he would exalt and lift up our hearts to heaven, that they may not lie still in the puddle of this earth.—*Archibald Symson.*

Verse 1.—*" Unto thee, O Lord, do I lift up my soul."* A godly man prays as a builder builds. Now a builder first layeth a foundation, and because he cannot finish in one day, he comes the second day, and finds the frame standing that he made the first day, and then he adds a second day's work ; and then he comes a third day and finds his two former days' work standing ; then he proceeds to a third day's work, and makes walls to it, and so he goes on till his building be finished. So prayer is the building of the soul till it reach up to heaven ; therefore a godly heart prays, and reacheth higher and higher in prayer, till at last his prayers reach up to God.—*William Fenner.*

Verse 1.—" *Unto thee, O Lord, do I lift up my soul :* " *unto thee* in the fulness of thy merits, *unto thee* in the riches of thy grace ; *unto thee* in the embraces of thy love and comforts of thy Spirit ; *unto thee*, that thy thorns may be my crown, thy blood my balsam, thy curse my blessing, thy death my life, thy cross my triumph. Thus is my " life hid with Christ in God ; " and if so, then where should be my soul, but where is my life ? And, therefore, " *unto thee, O Lord, do I lift up my soul.*" . . . . . O make good thy name of Lord unto me ; as Lord, rebuke Satan and restrain all earthly and carnal affections, that they do not once dare to whisper a temptation to my soul, a distraction to my thoughts, whilst I am in communion with thee, in prayer at thy holy ordinance. Do thou as Lord, rule me by thy grace, govern me by thy Spirit, defend me by thy power, and crown me with thy salvation. Thou Lord, the preserver of heaven and earth, " thou openest thy hand, and satisfiest the desire of every living thing." Psalm cxlv. 16. O open now thine hand, thy bosom, thy bounty, thy love, and satisfy the desires of my longing soul, which I here " *lift up unto thee.*"—*Robert Mossom,* 1657.

Verse 1.—" *Unto thee, O Lord, do I lift up my soul.*" Cyprian saith, that in the primitive times the minister was wont to prepare the people's minds to pray, by prefacing, *Sursum corda,* lift up your hearts. The Jews at this day write upon the walls of their synagogues these words, *Tephillah belo cavannah ceguph belo neshamah ;* that is, A prayer without the intention of the affection is like a body without a soul. And yet their devotion is a mere outside, saith one—a brainless head and a soulless body : " This people draweth nigh to me with their lips, but their heart is far from me." Isaiah xxix. 13. A carnal man can as little *lift up his heart* in prayer, as a mole can fly. A David finds it a hard task ; since the best heart is lumpish, and naturally beareth downwards, as the poise of a clock, as the lead of a net. Let us therefore " lay aside every weight, and the sin that doth so easily beset us ; " and pray to God to draw us up to himself, as the loadstone doth the iron. *John Trapp.*

Verse 1.—" *Unto thee* I lift up my *soul.*" This follows by a natural consequence after the sublime appeal in the foregoing Psalm to the gates of heaven to *lift up* their heads to receive Christ, the Lord of hosts and the King of glory, ascending into heaven. As the Collect for Ascension-day expresses it, " Grant, O Lord, that like as we do believe thy only-begotten Son, our Lord Jesus Christ, to have ascended into the heavens, so we may also in *heart* and *mind* thither *ascend ;*" and for the Sunday after Ascension, " O God, who hast *exalted* thine only Son with great triumph to thy kingdom in heaven, send thy Holy Ghost to comfort us, and *exalt us* to the same place, whither our Saviour Christ is gone before."—*Christopher Wordsworth, in loc.*

Verse 1.—" *I lift up my soul,* alluding to the sacrifices, which were wont to be *lifted up.* Hence prayers not answered, not accepted, are said to be stopped from ascending. Lam. iii. 44. When you met with such expressions in the Old Testament concerning prayer, you must still understand them to be allusions to the sacrifices, because the sacrifices were *lifted up* and did ascend.—*Joseph Caryl.*

Verse 1.—" *My soul.* But how shall I call it mine, seeing it is thine, thine by purchase, thine having bought it with thy blood ? Yea, is it not thy spouse whom thou hast wedded to thyself by thy Spirit through faith ? And is not this holy sacrament the marriage feast ? If so, sure then, my Jesus, I was lost in myself, till found in thee ; and therefore my soul is now, and not till now, truly mine, in being wholly thine ; so that I can say with confidence, " *I lift up my soul unto thee.*" *Robert Mossom.*

Verse 2, 3.—When David had prayed, " *O my God, I trust in thee ; let me not be ashamed !* " In the next verse, as if conscious to himself that his prayers were too restrictive, narrow, and niggardly, he enlargeth the bounds thereof, and builds them on a broader bottom, " *Yea, let none that wait on thee be ashamed.* Thus it is that charity in the midst of our religious devotions must have *rehoboth* (room enough to expatiate in). Our petitions must not be pent or confined to our own private good, but extended to the benefit of all God's servants, in what condition soever.—*Thomas Fuller.*

Verse 3.—" *Yea, let none that wait on thee be ashamed.*" To wit, neither by their own disappointments, nor mine. For this last some add, because if he should fail of his hopes, he knew this would be a great discouragement of others.—*Arthur Jackson, M.A., 1593—1666.*

Verse 3.—" *Let them be ashamed which transgress without cause.*" All persons who transgress, do it, in some sense, without cause ; since they cannot excuse or justify their conduct. God is so amiable and excellent in every part of his great name, that he deserves our constant reverence and love. His law is so holy, just, and good, and all his precepts concerning all things so righteous and calculated to make us happy, that the mouth of every transgressor must be stopped. Hence we all must be covered with shame, if dealt with according to our deserts, for all have sinned. But since God has promised to be merciful to those who truly repent, and unfeignedly believe his holy gospel, shame will be the portion of those only who wilfully persist in their wickedness, and refuse to return to God by Jesus Christ. These then are the persons whom the Psalmist speaks of as transgressing without cause, and doubtless these have no cloak for their sin.—*William Richardson, 1825.*

Verse 3.—" *Let them be ashamed which transgress without cause.*" Let shame be sent to the right owner, even to those that deal disloyally, unprovoked on my part. And so it was ; for Achitophel hanged himself Absalom was trussed up by the hand of God, and dispatched by Joab ; the people that conspired with him, partly perished by the sword, and partly fled home, much ashamed of their enterprise. Oh, the power of prayer ! what may not the saints have for asking ?—*John Trapp.*

Verse 4.—" *Shew me thy ways, O Lord,*" etc. There are the " *ways* " of men, and the " *ways* " of God ; the " *paths* " of sin, and the " *paths* " of righteousness : there are " *thy ways,*" and there are *my* ways ; *thine* the ways of truth, *mine* the ways of error ; *thine* which are good in thine eyes, and *mine* which are good in mine eyes ; *thine* which lead to heaven, *mine* which lead to hell. Wherefore, " *Shew me thy ways, O Lord ; teach me thy paths,*" lest I mistake mine own ways for thine ; yea, lead me in the truth, and teach me, lest I turn out of thy ways into mine own : " *shew me thy ways,*" by the ministry of thy word ; " *teach me thy paths,*" in the guidance of thy Spirit, " *lead me in thy truth,*" by the assistance of thy grace.—*Robert Mossom.*

Verses 4, 5, 9.—Do what you know, and God will teach you what to do. Do what you know to be your *present* duty, and God will acquaint you with your *future* duty as it comes to be *present.* Make it your business to avoid *known* omissions, and God will keep you from feared commissions. This rule is of great moment, and therefore I will charge it upon you by express Scripture. " *Shew me thy ways, O Lord,*" i.e., those way wherein I cannot err. " *Teach me thy paths,*" i.e., that narrow path which is too commonly unknown, those commands that are most strict and difficult, verse 5. " *Lead me in thy truth, and teach me,*" i.e., teach me evidently, that I may not be deceived ; so teach me, that I may not only know thy will, but do it. Here's his prayer, but what grounds hath he to expect audience ? " *For thou art the God of my salvation,*" q.d., thou Lord, wilt save me, and therefore do not refuse to teach me. " *On thee do I wait all the day,*" i.e., the whole day, and every day. Other arguments are couched in the following verses, but *what* answer ? verse 9, " *The meek will he guide in judgment : and the meek will he teach his way,*" i.e., those that submit their neck to his yoke, those that are not conceited that they can guide themselves ; in necessary, great, and weighty matters they shall not err.—*Samuel Annesley, D.D., (1620—1696), in " Morning Exercises at Cripplegate."*

Verse 5.—" *Lead me in thy truth, and teach me.*" The soul that is unsatiable in prayer, he proceeds, he gets near to God, he gains something, he winds up his heart higher. As a child that seeth the mother have an apple in her hand, and it would fain have it, it will come and pull at the mother's hand for it : now she lets go one finger, and yet she holds it, and then he pulls again ; and then she lets go another finger, and yet she keeps it, and then the child pulls again, and will never leave pulling and crying till it hath got it from its mother. So a child of God, seeing all graces to be in God, he draws near to the throne of grace begging for it, and by his earnest and faithful prayers he opens the hands of God to him ; God dealing as parents to their children, holds them off for awhile ; not that he is unwilling to give, but to make them more earnest with God, to draw them the nearer to himself.—*William Fenner.*

Verse 5.—"*On thee do I wait all the day.*" We must "*wait all the day.*" 1. Though it be a *long* day, though we be kept waiting a great while, quite beyond our own reckoning ; though when we have waited long, we are still put to wait longer, and are bid, with the prophet's servant, to go yet seven times (1 Kings xviii. 43), before we perceive the least sign of mercy coming . . . . . . 2. Though it be a *dark* day, yet let us wait upon God "*all the day.*" Though while we are kept waiting for what God will do, we are kept in the dark concerning what he is doing, and what is best for us to do, yet let us be content to wait in the dark. Though we see not our signs, though there is none to tell us how long, yet let us resolve to wait, how long soever it may be ; for though what God doth we know not now, yet we shall know hereafter when the mystery of God shall be finished . . . . . 3. Though it be a *stormy* day, yet we must wait upon God "*all the day.*" Though we are not only becalmed, and do not get forward, but though the wind be contrary, and drive us back ; nay, though it be boisterous, and the church be tossed with tempests, and ready to sink, yet we must hope the best, yet we must wait, and weather the storm by patience. It is some comfort that Christ is in the ship ; the church's cause is Christ's own cause, he has espoused it, and he will own it ; he is embarked in the same bottom with his people, and therefore why are you fearful ? . . . . *To wait on God,* is—1. To live a life of desire towards God ; to wait on him as the beggar waits on his benefactor, with earnest desires to receive supplies from him, as the sick and sore at Bethesda's pool waited for the stirring of the water, and attended in the porches with desire to be helped in and healed. . . . . 2. It is to live a life of delight in God, as the lover waits on his beloved. Desire is love in motion, as a bird upon the wing ; delight is love at rest, as a bird upon the rest ; now, though our desire must still be so towards God, as that we must be wishing for more of God, yet our delight must be so in God, as that we must never wish for more than God. . . . . . 3. It is to live a life of dependence on God, as the child waits on his father, whom he has confidence in, and on whom he casts all his care. To wait on God is to expect all good to come to us from him, as the worker of all good for us and in us, the giver of all good to us, and the protector of us from all evil. Thus David explains himself (Psalm lxii. 5), "My soul, wait thou only upon God," and continue still to do so, for "my expectation is from him." . . . . 4. It is to live a life of devotedness to God, as the servant waits on his master, ready to observe his will, and to do his work, and in everything to consult his honour and interest. To wait on God is entirely and unreservedly to refer ourselves to his wise and holy directions and disposals, and cheerfully to acquiesce in them, and comply with them. The servant that waits on his master, chooseth not his own way, but follows his master step by step. Thus must we wait on God, as those that have no will of our own but what is wholly resolved into his, and must therefore study to accommodate ourselves to his.— *Condensed from Matthew Henry, on " Communion with God."*

Verse 5.—"*On thee do I wait all the day.*" "*On thee,*" whose hand of bounty, whose bosom of love, yea, whose bowels of mercy are not only opened, but enlarged to all humble penitents. "*On thee do I wait,*" *wait* to hear the secret voice of thy Spirit, speaking peace unto my conscience, *wait* to feel the reviving vigour of thy grace, quickening mine obedience ; *wait* to see the subduing power of thy Holy Spirit quelling my rebellious sin ; *wait* to feel the cheering virtue of thy heavenly comforts, refreshing my fainting soul ; for all these thy blessings, "*O thou God of my salvation, on thee do I wait all the day.*" "*All the day :* " being never satisfied with thy goodness, as not more eagerly to long after thy heavenly fulness ; wherefore now refresh my faintings, quench not my desires ; but the more freely thou givest, let me the more eagerly covet ; the more sweet is thy mercy, let be the more eager my longings, that so my whole life on earth may be a continual breathing after that eternal fellowship and communion with thee in heaven ; thus, thus, *let me wait,* even all my life, *all the day.—Robert Mossom.*

Verse 6.—"*Thy tender mercies.*" Oh, how does one deep call upon another ! The depth of my multiplied miseries, calls, loudly calls, upon the depth of thy manifold mercies ; even *that mercy* whereby thou dost pardon my sin and help mine infirmities ; *that mercy* whereby thou dost sanctify me by thy grace, and comfort me by thy Spirit; *that mercy* whereby thou dost deliver me from hell, and possess me of heaven. "*Remember, O Lord,*" all those thy mercies, *thy tender mercies*, which have been "*of old*" unto thy saints.—*Robert Mossom.*

Verse 6.—"*Thy tender mercies and thy lovingkindnesses . . . . have been ever of old.*" Let the ancientness of divine love draw up our hearts to a very dear and honourable esteem of it. Pieces of antiquity, though of base metal, and otherwise of little use or value, how venerable are they with learned men! and ancient charters, how careful are men to preserve them; although they contain but temporary privileges, and sometimes but of trivial moment! How then should the great charter of heaven, so much older than the world, be had in everlasting remembrance, and the thoughts thereof be very precious to us; lying down, rising up, and all the day long accompanying of us! . . . That which is from everlasting shall be to everlasting; if the root be eternal, so are the branches. . . . Divine love is an eternal fountain that never leaves running while a vessel is empty or capable of holding more; and it stands open to all comers: therefore, come; and if ye have not sufficient of your own, go and borrow vessels, empty vessels, not a few; "pay your debts out of it, and live on the rest" (2 Kings iv. 7), to eternity.—*Elisha Coles on "God's Sovereignty,"* 1678.

Verse 7.—"*Remember not the sins of my youth, nor my transgressions.*" In the first place, considering that he had not begun only of late to commit sin, but that he had for a long time heaped up sin upon sin, he bows himself, if we may so speak, under the accumulated load; and, in the second place, he intimates, that if God should deal with him according to the rigour of the law, not only the sins of yesterday, or of a few days, would come into judgment against him, but all the instances in which he had offended, even from his infancy, might now with justice be laid to his charge. As often, therefore, as God terrifies us by his judgments and the tokens of his wrath, let us call to our remembrance, not only the sins which we have lately committed, but also all the transgressions of our past life, proving to us the ground of renewed shame and renewed lamentation.—*John Calvin.*

Verse 7.—"*Remember not the sins of my youth.*" This may seem but a superfluous prayer of David; for whereas in charity it may and must be presumed that David long since had begged pardon for his youthful sins, that upon his begging God had granted it, that upon his granting God never revoked it. What need now had David to prefer this petition for pardon of antiquated sin, time out of mind committed by him, time out of mind remitted by God? To this objection I shape a fourfold answer. *First*, though David no doubt long since had been truly sorrowful for his youthful sins, yet he was sensible in himself, that if God would be extreme to mark what was done amiss, though he had repented of those sins, yet he had sinned in that his repentance. *Secondly*, though God had forgiven David's sins so far forth as to pardon him eternal damnation, yet he had not remitted unto him temporal afflictions which perchance pressing upon him at this present, he prayeth in this Psalm for the removing or mitigating of them. So then the sense of his words sounds thus, "*Remember not, Lord, the sins of my youth,*" that is, Lord, lighten and lessen the afflictions which lie upon me in this mine old age, justly inflicted on me for my youthful sins. *Thirdly*, God's pardon for sins past, is ever granted with this condition, that the party so pardoned is bound to his good behaviour for the time to come, which if he breaks, he deserves in the strictness of justice to forfeit the benefit of his pardon. Now David was guilty afterward in that grand transgression of Bathsheba and Uriah, which might in the extremity of justice have made all his youthful sins to be punished afresh upon him. *Lastly*, grant David certainly assured of the pardon of his youthful sins, yet God's servants may pray for those blessings they have in possession, not for the obtaining of that they have—that is needless—but for the keeping of what they have obtained, that is necessary. Yea, God is well pleased with such prayers of his saints, and interprets them to be praises unto him, and then these words, "*Remember not the sins of my youth,*" amount to this effect: blessed be thy gracious goodness, who hast forgiven me the sins of my youth.—*Thomas Fuller.*

Verse 7.—"*Remember not the sins of my youth.*" David, after he was called by the power of the word, cries out, "*Lord, remember not,*" etc.; that gravelled and galled his conscience, the *sins of his youth* before his call. O beloved, the sins of your youth, though you should be Jobs converted, yet they will bring great disquietness and great horror when you come to age. The lusts of youth, and the vanities of youth, and the sensual pleasures of your youthful days, they will lay a foundation of sorrow when you come to grey hairs to be near your graves. So Job. xx. 11.—*Christopher Love*, 1654.

Verse 7.—" *Remember not the sins of my youth ;* " let them not move thee to punish or be avenged on me for them ; as men, when they remember injuries, seek to be avenged on those who have done them.—*William Greenhill*.

Verse 7.—" *Remember not the sins of my youth.*" It is not safe to be at odds with the " Ancient of days."—*John Trapp*.

Verse 7.—" *The sins of my youth.*" Before we come to the principal point we must first clear the text from the incumbrance of a double objection. The first is this:—It may seem (may some say) very improbable that David should have any sins of his youth, if we consider the principals whereupon his youth was past. The first was *poverty*. We read that his father Jesse passed for an *old* man, we read not that he passed for a *rich* man ; and probably his seven sons were the principal part of his wealth. Secondly, *painfulness*. David, though the youngest, was not made a darling, but a drudge ; sent by his father to follow the ewes big with young ; where he may seem to have learned innocence and simplicity from the sheep he kept. Thirdly, *piety* (Psalm lxxi. 5), " For thou art my hope, O Lord God ; thou art my trust from my youth." And again in the seventeenth verse of the same Psalm, " O God, thou hast taught me from my youth : " David began to be good betimes, *a young saint*, and yet crossed that pestilent proverb, was no *old devil*. And what is more still, he was constantly in the furnace of affliction. Psalm lxxxviii. 15. " Even from my youth up, thy terrors have I suffered with a troubled mind." The question then will be this, How could that water be corrupted which was daily clarified ? How could that steel gather rust which was daily filed ? How could David's soul in his *youth* be sooty with sin, which was constantly scoured with suffering ? But the answer is easy ; for though David for the main were a man after God's own heart (the best transcript of the best copy), yet he, especially in his youth, had his faults and infirmities, yea, his sins and transgressions. Though the Scripture maketh mention of no eminent sin in his youth, the business with Bathsheba being justly to be referred to David's reduced and elder age. I will not conclude that David was of a wanton constitution because of a reddy complexion. It is as injurious an inference to conclude all bad which are beautiful, as it is a false and flattering consequence to say all are honest who are deformed. Rather we may collect David's youth guilty of wantonness from his having so many wives and concubines. But what go I about to do ? Expect not that I should tell you the particular sins, when he could not tell his own. Psalm xix. " Who can tell how oft he offendeth ? " Or how can David's sins be known to me, which he confesseth were unknown to himself, which made him say, " O Lord, cleanse me from secret sins " ? But to silence our curiosity, that our conscience may speak :—If David's youth, which was poor, painful, and pious, was guilty of sins, what shall we say, of such whose education hath been wealthy, wanton, and wicked ? And I report the rest to be acted with shame, sorrow, and silence in every man's conscience.—*Thomas Fuller*.

Verse 7.—" *The sins of my youth.*" Two aged disciples, one eighty-seven years old, one day met. " Well," enquired the younger of his fellow pilgrim, " how long have you been interested in religion ? " " Fifty years," was the old man's reply. " Well, have you ever regretted that you began when young to devote yourself to religion ? " " Oh, no ! " said he, and the tears trickled down his furrowed cheeks ; " I weep when I think of the sins of my youth ; it is this which makes me weep now."—*From K. Arvine's " Cyclopædia of Moral and Religious Anecdotes,*" 1859.

Verse 7.—" *According to* THY *mercy,*" *not mine ;* for I have forsaken those *mercies* thou madest *mine own* (Jonah ii. 8 ; Psalm lix. 10, 17), in being cruel to myself by my sin, through distrust of thy promise, and upon presumption in thy mercy ; yea, let it be, " *for* THY *goodness' sake,*" not *mine*, for in me, that is, in my flesh, dwelleth no manner of thing that is good. Let thy goodness, then, be the motive, thy mercy the rule of all that grace, and of all those blessings thou vouchsafest unto my soul.—*Robert Mossom*.

Verse 7.—"*According to thy mercy.*" Moses was the first that brought up this happy expression, "*According to thy mercy*" (I know not where is is used by any other man), that is, according to the infinite mercy that is in thy heart and nature. David did next use it (Psalm xxv.), and in the great case of his sin and adultery

(Psalm li. 1), " that he would be merciful to him, according to the multitude of his mercies," And as he needed all the mercies in God, so he confessed the sin of his nature, and hath recourse to the mercies in God's nature. But it is Psalm xxv. 7, I pitch on ; there he doth not content himself only with this expression, "*According to thy mercy*," but he adds another phrase, " For thy mercy's sake," and " *goodness' sake.*" Muis observes in this coherence, " *Good and upright is the Lord* " (verse 8), that he centres in his nature. Thou hast a merciful nature ; deal with me according to that, and for the sake of that, " according to thy mercy," " for thy goodness' sake." The meditation of that attribute was the foundation of his faith and prayer herein. When he hath done, he referreth himself to Moses, verse 11, " *For thy name's sake, O Lord, pardon mine iniquity ; for it is great.*" He refers to that name proclaimed before Moses. Exodus xxxiv. 6, 7. But you will say, How do these expressions, " for thy name's sake," " for thy goodness' sake," " for thy mercy's sake," imply the same as " for himself," " for his own sake " ? how do they involve the Godhead ? Look to Isaiah xliii. 25, " I, even I, am he that blotteth out thy transgressions for mine own sake," that is, for myself. Isaiah xlviii. 11. " For mine own sake, even for mine own sake, will I do it." You have it twice in one verse ; and that which is " for mercy's sake " in one place, is " for mine own sake " in another, and behold it is I, I am he, as I am God, who doth it. What is this, but " Jehovah, Jehovah, God merciful " ?—*Thomas Goodwin.*

Verse 8.—" *Good and upright is the Lord : therefore will he teach sinners in the way.*" As election is the effect of God's sovereignty, our pardon the fruit of his mercy, our knowledge a stream from his wisdom, our strength an impression of his power ; so our purity is a beam from his holiness. As the rectitude of the creature at the first creation was the effect of his holiness, so the purity of the creature by a new creation, is a draught of the same perfection. He is called the Holy One of Israel more in Isaiah, that evangelical prophet, in erecting Zion, and forming a people for himself, than in the whole Scripture besides.—*Stephen Charnock.*

Verse 8.—" *Good and upright is the Lord : therefore will he teach sinners in the way.*" Will not the Lord, who is good, be as gracious to his enemies as he requires us to be to ours ? It is his own law, " If thou meet thine enemy's ox or his ass going astray, thou shalt surely bring it back to him again." Exodus xxiii. 4. Now God meets us sinners, and all sinners as such are his enemies ; he meets us straying like the beast without understanding ; and what ? will he not bring us again unto himself, the sole proprietary, by that first right of creation, and that more firm right of redemption ?—*Robert Mossom.*

Verse 9.—" *The meek will he guide in judgment ;* " or, *the poor* (namely, in spirit), will he make to tread in judgment, to foot it aright, to walk judiciously, to behave themselves wisely, as David did (1 Sam. xxiv.), so that Saul feared him. Natural conscience cannot but stoop to the image of God, shining in the hearts and lives of the really religious.—*John Trapp.*

Verse 9.—" *The meek will he guide in judgment.*" They have been made meek, *i.e.*, desirous of being taught, and praying to be so ; but, being now sensible of unworthiness, they are afraid that God will not teach them. This may be done to other sinners but not to them. Therefore they are told who may expect teaching, even they who desire and pray for teaching.—*John Berridge, 1716—1793.*

Verse 9.—" *He will guide the poor in judgment.*" Never will this docility be found in any man, until the heart, which is naturally elated and filled with pride, has been humbled and subdued. As the Hebrew word denotes the *poor* or *afflicted*, and is employed in a metaphorical sense, to denote *the meek and humble*, it is probable that David, under this term, includes the afflictions which serve to restrain and subdue the frowardness of the flesh, as well as the grace of humility itself ; as if he had said, When God has first humbled them, then he kindly stretches forth his hand to them, and leads and guides them throughout the whole course of their life.—*John Calvin.*

Verse 9.—" *The meek*," etc. Pride and anger have no place in the school of Christ. The Master himself is " meek and lowly of heart ; " much more, surely, ought the scholars to be so. He who hath no sense of his ignorance, can have no desire, or capability of knowledge, human or divine.—*George Horne.*

Verse 9 (last clause).—The Lord will teach the humble his secrets, he will not teach proud scholars.—*Thomas Goodwin.*

Verse 9 (*last clause*).—Such as lie at his feet and say, " Speak, Lord, for thy servant heareth," such whose hearts are *supple* and *soluble*, tractable, and teachable, so that a *little child* may *lead them.* (Isaiah xi. 6.) Austin was such an one. Saith he, " I am here an old man ready to learn of a young man, my coadjutor in the ministry, who hath scarce been one year in the service."—*John Trapp.*

Verse 10.—*"All the paths of the Lord,"* אָרְחוֹת *orchoth* signifies the tracks or ruts made by the wheels of wagons by often passing over the same ground. Mercy and truth are the paths in which God constantly walks in reference to the children of men ; and so frequently does he show them mercy, and so frequently does he fulfil his truth, that his paths are easily discerned. How frequent, how deeply indented, and how multiplied are those tracks to every family and individual ! Wherever we go, we see that God's mercy and truth have been there by the deep tracks they have left behind them. But he is more abundantly merciful to those who keep his covenant and his testimonies ; *i.e.,* those who are conformed, not only to the letter, but to the spirit of his pure religion.—*Adam Clarke.*

Verse 10.—*"All the paths of the Lord are mercy and truth."*—As his *nature* is *love and truth,* so all his *ways* are *mercy and truth.* They are " *mercy* " in respect of aiming at our good, and " *truth* " in respect of fulfilling his promises and faithful carriage to us ; therefore whatsoever befalls thee, though it be clean contrary to thy expectation, interpret it in love. Many actions of men are such as a good interpretation cannot be put upon them, nor a good construction made of them ; therefore interpreters restrain those sayings of love, that it believes all, etc. ; that is, *credibilia,* all things believable, otherwise to put all upon charity, will eat out charity. But none of God's ways are such, but love and faith may pick a good meaning out of these. *A bono Deo nil nisi bonum,* from a good God there comes nothing but what is good ; and therefore says Job, " Though he kill me, I will trust in him." Endeavour to spy out some end of his for good at the present, and if none ariseth to thy conjecture, resolve it into faith, and make the best of it.—*Thomas Goodwin.*

Verse 10.—" *Unto such as keep,*" etc. : he is never out of the road of mercy unto them.—*Thomas Goodwin.*

Verse 11.—" *For thy name's sake, O Lord, pardon mine iniquity ; for it is great.*" I cannot do better than quote one of those beautiful passages of the great Vieyra, which gave him the character of the first preacher of his age :—" I confess, my God, that it is so ; that we are all sinners in the highest degree." He is preaching on a fast on occasion of the threatened destruction of the Portuguese dominion in Brazil by the Dutch. " But so far am I from considering this any reason why I should cease from my petition, that I behold in it a new and convincing argument which may influence thy goodness. All that I have said before is based on no other foundation than the glory and honour of thy most holy Name. *Propter nomen tuum.* And what motive can I offer more glorious to that same Name, than that our sins are many and great ? *For thy name's sake, O Lord, be merciful unto my sin, for it is great.* I ask thee, saith David, to pardon, not every-day sins, but numerous sins, but great sins : *multum est enim.* O motive worthy of the breast of God ! Oh, consequence which can have force only when it bears on supreme goodness ! So that in order to obtain remission of his sins, the sinner alleges to God that they are many and great. Verily so ; and that not for love of the sinner nor for the love of sin, but for the love of the honour and glory of God ; which glory, by how much the sins he forgives are greater and more numerous, by so much the more ennobles and exalts itself. The same David distinguishes in the mercy of God greatness and multitude : greatness, *secundum magnam misericordiam tuam ;* multitude, *et secundum multitudinem miserationum tuarum.* And as the greatness of the divine mercy is immense, and the multitude of his lovingkindnesses infinite ; and forasmuch as the immense cannot be measured, nor the infinite counted, in order that the one and the other may in a certain manner have a proportionate material of glory, it is necessary to the very greatness of mercy that the sins to be pardoned should be great and necessary to the very multitude of lovingkindnesses that they should be many. *Multum est enim.* Reason have I then, O Lord, not to be dismayed because our sins are many and great. Reason have I also to demand the reason from thee, why thou dost not make haste to pardon them ? "—*Vieyra, quoted by J. M. Neale.*

Verse 11.—" *For thy name's sake, O Lord, pardon mine iniquity.*" It is a very usual notion by "*name*" to understand honour and glory. When God saith to David, " I have made thee a name like the name of men that are in the earth ; " when the church saith to God, "Thou didst get thee a name as it is this day ; " it is manifest that by name glory is intended. Suitable to this it is that famous men are called by the Hebrews, םֵשַּׁה יֵשְׁנַא (Gen. vi. 4), and by the Latins, *viri nominum*, men of name, in which sense the poet adorneth it with these epithets—

"Magnum et memorabile nomen,"

or great and memorable. Thus, when God forgiveth sin, he doth it *for his name's sake*, that is, for his own honour and glory. Indeed, God's own glory is the ultimate end of all his actions. As he is the first, so he is the last, the efficient, and the final cause ; nor is there anything done by him which is not for him. The end of our actions must be his glory, because both our being and working are from him ; but the end of his work is his own glory, because his being and acting are of and from himself. Among all divine works, there is none which more setteth forth his glory than this of remission. Sin, by committing it, brings God a great deal of dishonour, and yet, by forgiving it, God raiseth to himself a great deal of honour. " It is the glory of a man," and much more of God, " to pass by an offence ; " as acts of power, so acts of grace, are exceeding honourable. The attributes of God's grace, mercy, goodness, clemency, shine forth in nothing so much as in pardoning sins. Paul speaks of riches of goodness which attend God's forbearance ; how much greater riches must there needs be in forgiveness ? Nay, indeed, God hath so ordered the way of pardon, that not only the glory of his mercy, but justice, yea, of his wisdom in the wonderful contemporation of both these, is very illustrious. *Nomen quasi notamen, quia notificat*, the name is that which maketh one known ; and by remission of sins, God maketh known his choice and glorious attributes ; and for this end it is that he vouchsafeth it. It is a consideration that may be our consolation. Since God forgiveth sins *for his name's sake*, he will be ready to forgive many sins as well as few, great as small ; indeed, the more and greater our sins are, the greater is the forgiveness, and, consequently, the greater is God's glory ; and therefore David, upon this consideration of God's name and glory, maketh the *greatness of his iniquity* a motive of forgiveness. Indeed, to run into gross sins, that God may glorify himself by forgiving them, is an odious presumption, but to hope that those gross sins we have run into may, and will, be forgiven by God to us, being truly penitent, *for his name's sake*, is a well grounded expectation, and such as may support our spirits against the strongest temptations to despair.—*Nathanael Hardy.*

Verse 11.—"*Pardon mine iniquity ; for it is great.*" He pleads the greatness of his sin, and not the smallness of it : he enforces his prayer with this consideration, that his sins are very heinous. But how could he make this a plea for pardon ? I answer, Because the greater his iniquity was, the more *need* he had of pardon. It is as much as if he had said, Pardon mine iniquity, for it is so great that I cannot bear the punishment ; my sin is so great that I am in necessity of pardon ; my case will be exceedingly miserable, unless thou be pleased to pardon me. He makes use of the greatness of his sin, to enforce his plea for pardon, as a man would make use of the greatness of calamity in begging for relief. When a beggar begs for bread, he will plead the greatness of his poverty and necessity. When a man in distress cries for pity, what more suitable plea can be urged than the extremity of his case ? And God allows such a plea as this : for he is moved to mercy towards us by nothing in us, but the miserableness of our case. He doth not pity sinners because they are worthy, but because they need his pity. . . . Herein doth the *glory of grace* by the redemption of Christ much consist ; namely, in its sufficiency for the pardon of the *greatest* sinners. The whole contrivance of the way of salvation is for this end, to glorify the free grace of God. God had it on his heart from all eternity to glorify this attribute ; and therefore it is, that the device of saving sinners by Christ was conceived. The greatness of divine grace appears very much in this, that God by Christ saves the *greatest* offenders. The *greater* the guilt of any sinner is, the more glorious and wonderful is the grace manifested in his pardon. Rom. v. 20. " Where sin abounded, grace did much more abound." The apostle, when telling how great a sinner he had been, takes notice of the abounding of grace in his pardon, of which his great guilt was the occasion. 1 Tim. i. 13, 14. " Who was before a blasphemer, and a persecutor, and injurious : but I obtained mercy, because I did it ignorantly in unbelief. And the grace of our Lord was exceeding abundant with faith and love which is in Christ Jesus." The Redeemer is glorified, in that he proves sufficient to redeem those who are exceeding sinful, in that his blood proves sufficient to wash away the greatest guilt, in that he is able to save men to the uttermost, and in that he redeems even from the greatest misery. It is the honour of Christ to save the greatest sinners, when they come to him, as it is the honour of a physician that he cures the most desperate diseases or wounds. Therefore, no doubt, Christ will be willing to save the greatest sinners, if they come to him ; for he will not be backward to glorify himself, and to commend the value and virtue of his own blood. Seeing he hath so laid out himself to redeem sinners, he will not be unwilling to show that he is able to redeem to the uttermost.—*Jonathan Edwards.*

Verse 11.—" *Pardon mine iniquity ; for it is great.*" Is any man miserable, are his miseries great, are they spiritual, are they temporal ? Undoubtedly, if he be humbled in the sense of them, and see himself unworthy of any mercy, he may still be assured of mercy. Though there be spiritual evils, yet if a man see himself wretched, and miserable, the more heavy he finds his iniquity to be, the more hope of mercy there is for him : the Lord's mercy is over all his works, therefore is he much more merciful to such. If a man hath a feeling of his miseries and unworthiness then he may use this argument for mercy, *my miseries are great :* even as David did, " *O Lord, be merciful to me, and pardon my iniquity, for it is great.*" And the more miserable men are in their own sense, the fitter objects they are for God to show mercy unto. Thus it was with the publican, and so with the prodigal ; therefore never doubt, though thy iniquities be never so great, there is a sea of mercy in God. Bernard well observes the difference between justice and mercy ; justice requires that there should be desert, but mercy looks upon them that are miserable ; and, saith the father, true mercy doth affect misery ; mercy doth not stand upon inquisition, but it is glad to find occasion of exercising itself.—*Richard Stock.*

Verse 11.—" *Mine iniquity . . . is great.*" Such who come to God to have their sins pardoned, they look upon them as great sins. " *Pardon mine iniquity, for it is great.*" The original word as well signifies *many* as *great*—" My sins are great and many," many great sins lie upon me, pardon, oh ! pardon them, O Lord, &c. . . . . . In the opening of this point, I would show *why* such as come in a right way for pardon do look upon their sins as *great* sins. 1. Sinners that come to God for pardon and find it, do look upon their sins as *great sins, because* against a *great God,* great in power, great in justice, great in holiness. I am *a worm,* and yet sin, and that boldly against a God so *great ;* for a worm to lift up himself against a great and infinite God ; oh ! this makes every little sin *great,* and calls for *great* vengeance from so *great* a God. 2. Because *they have sinned against great patience,* despising the goodness, forbearance, and longsuffering of God, which is called, " treasuring up wrath." Rom. ii. 4, 5. . . . 3. Sins do appear *great* because *against great mercies.* Oh ! against how many mercies and kindnesses do sinners sin, and turn all the mercies of God into sin ! . . . . 4. That which *greatens* sin in the eyes of poor sinners that cry for pardon, is, that *they have sinned against great light*—light in the conscience ; this heightens sin exceedingly, especially to such as are under gospel means ; and is indeed the sin of all in this nation ; there's nothing more abaseth a soul than this, nothing makes it more difficult to believe pardon, when humbled for it. . . . . . . 5. *Continuance in sin* much *greatens* sin to a poor soul that is after pardon ; especially such as are not very early converted. Psalm lxviii. 21. Oh ! I added sin unto sin, saith a poor soul, spending the choice time of my youth in sin, when I might have been getting the knowledge of Jesus Christ and honouring of God. This lay close upon David's spirit, as appears from the seventh verse : " Oh ! remember not the sins of my youth." Yet we do not find that David's youth was notoriously sinful ; but inasmuch as he spent not his youth to get knowledge, and to serve the Lord fully, 'twas his burden and complaint before the Lord ; much more such whose youth was spent in nothing but vanity, profaneness, lying, swearing, profaning of the Sabbath, sports, pastimes, excess of riot, and the like, when God lays it in upon their consciences, must be grievous and abominable to their souls. . . . . . . 6. *Multitudes of sins* do make sin appear great ; this made David cry out for " multitude of mercies." Psalm li., and xl. 12. . . . . 7. Another thing that *greatens* sin is, that it was *against purposes and resolutions of forsaking such and such sins ;* and yet all broken, sometimes against solemn vows, against prayers. . . . . 8. Sin appears *great* when seen by a poor soul, because it was *reigning* sin. Rom. v. 6. " Sin reigned unto death," etc. Oh ! saith a poor humbled sinner, I did not only *commit* sin, but I was the *servant* and *slave* of sin. . . . . 9. Sin *in the fountain makes it great.* As it may be said, there is more water in the fountain than in the pools and streams it makes. . . . . So in the nature, in the heart, is there, as in the fountain, and therefore 'tis more there than in the breakings forth of it in the outward man. . . . . 10. A sinner drawing nigh to God for pardon sees his sin as *great*, because thereby he was *led captive by the devil* at his will. . . . 11. Sin appears *great*, because *great is the wrath of God against sin.* Rom. ii. 12. The way of any sinner's deliverance from such wrath shows sin to be exceeding great *in the price and ransom that is paid for the salvation of him from his sins*—the price of the blood of the eternal Son of God. . . . . 13. Lastly, this consideration also *greatens* sin, inasmuch as a poor creature *hath drawn and tempted others* to sin with him, especially such as have lived more vainly and loosely, and it lies hard upon many a poor soul after thorough conviction.—*Anthony Palmer* (——1678), *in* "*The Gospel New-creature.*"

Verse 11.—I plead not, Lord, my merits, who am less than the least of thy mercies and as I look not upon my merit, so nor do thou look upon my demerit ; as I do not view my worthiness, so nor do thou view my unworthiness ; but thou who art called *the God of mercy*, be unto me what thou art called ; make good the glory of thine own name in being merciful unto my sin, of which I cannot say as Lot of Zoar, "Is it not a little one ? " No, it is *great*, for that it is against thee so great a God and so good to me : *great*, for that my place, my calling, my office, is great. The sun, the higher it is, the less it seems ; but my sins, the higher I am the greater they are, even in thine and others' eyes.—*Robert Mossom.*

Verse 11.—Plead we the greatness of our sins not to keep us from mercy, but to prevail for it : "*Pardon mine iniquity ;*" why so ? "*for it is great.*" "Heal my soul for I have sinned against thee." Psalm xli. 4. 'Do thou it for thy name's sake : for our backslidings are many ; we have sinned against thee." Jer. xiv. 7. This is a strong plea, when sincerely urged by an humble and contrite spirit. It glorifieth God as one that is abundant in goodness, rich in mercy, and one with whom are forgivenesses and plenteous redemption ; and it honoureth Christ as infinite in mercy. Hence also the Lord himself, when he would stir up himself to choice acts of mercy to his poor people, he first aggravateth their sin against him to the highest, and then he expresseth his royal act of grace to them. So Isaiah xliii. 22—25. "Thou hast not called upon me, O Jacob, but thou hast been weary of me, O Israel ; thou hast not honoured me with thy sacrifices, but thou hast wearied me with thine iniquities. I, even I, am he that blotteth out thy transgressions for mine own sake, and will not remember thy sins."—*Thomas Cobbet*, 1608—1686.

Verse 11.—"Oh," says Pharaoh, "take away these filthy frogs, this dreadful thunder ! " But what says holy David ? "Lord, take away the iniquity of thy servant ! " The one would be freed from punishment, the effect of sin ; the other from sin, the cause of punishment. And it is most true that a true Christian man is more troubled at sin than at frogs and thunder ; he sees more filthiness in sin than in frogs and toads, more horror than in thunder and lightning.—*Jeremiah Dyke's* "*Worthy Communicant,*" 1645.

Verse 11.—Pharaoh more lamented the hard strokes that were upon him, than the hard heart which was within him. Esau mourned not because he sold the birthright, which was his sin, but because he lost the blessing, which was his punishment. This is like weeping with an onion ; the eye sheds tears because it smarts. A mariner casts overboard that cargo in a tempest, which he courts the return of when the winds are silenced. Many complain more of the sorrows to which they are born, than of the sins with which they were born : they tremble more at the vengeance of sin, than at the venom of sin ; one delights them, the other affrights them.—*William Secker.*

Verse 12.—"*What man is he that feareth the Lord ?*" Blessed shall he be— 1. In the sacred knowledge of Christ's will ; "*Him shall he teach in the way that he shall choose.*" 2. Blessed shall he be in the quiet peace of a good conscience ; "*His soul shall dwell at ease.*" 3. Blessed he shall be in the present comfort of a hopeful progeny ; "*His seed shall inherit the earth.*"—*Robert Mossom.*

Verse 12.—"*What man is he that feareth the Lord ?*" There is nothing so effectual to obtain grace, to retain grace, as always to be found before God not over wise, but *to fear :* happy art thou, if thy heart be replenished with three fears ; a fear for received grace, a greater fear for lost grace, a greatest fear to recover grace.—*Bernard.*

Verse 12.—" *He that feareth the Lord.*" Present fear begetteth eternal security : fear God, which is above all, and no need to fear man at all.—*Augustine.*

Verse 12.—" *Him shall he teach in the way that he shall choose,*" *i.e.,* that the good man shall pitch upon. God will direct him in all dealings to make a good choice, and will give good success. This is not in a man's own power to do. Jer. x. 23.—*John Trapp.*

Verse 13.—" *His soul shall dwell at ease ; and his seed shall inherit the earth.*" The holy fear of God shall destroy all sinful fears of men, even as Moses' serpent devoured all those serpents of the magicians. The fear of God hath this good effect that it makes other things not to be feared ; so that the soul of him who feareth the Lord doth dwell, as *in rest,* so in goodness ; as *in peace,* so in patience, till this moment of time be swallowed up in the fulness of eternity, and he change his earthly dwelling for an heavenly mansion, and his spiritual peace for an everlasting blessedness.—*Robert Mossom.*

Verse 13.—" *His soul shall dwell at ease.*" Shall tarry in good things, as it is in the Vulgate. Unlike the soul of Adam, who, being put into possession of the delights of paradise, tarried there but a few days or hours.—*Gerhohus, quoted by J. M. Neale.*

Verse 13.—" *His soul shall dwell at ease.*" He expresses with great sweetness spiritual delectation, when he says, " *His soul shall tarry in good things.*" For whatever is carnally sweet yields without doubt a delectation for the time to such as enjoy it, but cannot tarry long with them ; because, while by its taste it provokes appetite, by its transit it cheats desire. But spiritual delights, which neither pass away as they are tasted, nor decrease while they refresh, nor cloy while they satiate, can tarry for ever with their possessors.—*Hugo Victorinus* (1130), *quoted by J. M. Neale.*

Verse 13 *(first clause).*—In the reception of the gifts of God, they do not devour them without feeling a sense of their sweetness, but really relish them, so that the smallest competency is of more avail to satisfy them that the greatest abundance is to satisfy the ungodly. Thus, according as every man is contented with his condition, and cheerfully cherishes a spirit of patience and tranquility, his soul is said *to dwell in good.*—*John Calvin.*

Verse 13.—" *The earth,*" or *the land,* to wit, Canaan ; which was promised and given, as an earnest of the whole covenant of grace, and all its promises, and therefore it is synecdochically put for all of them. The sense is, his seed shall be blessed.—*Matthew Pool.*

Verse 14.—" *The secret of the Lord is with them that fear him,*" etc. It is the righteous that is God's friend, it is to him that God is joined in a loving familiarity, it is to him that God revealeth his secret, telling him what misery and torments he hath reserved for them who by wickedness flourish in this world. And indeed the Lord doth not more hate the wicked than he loves the godly : if he keeps far from the froward, as being an abomination unto him, his very secret shall be with the righteous, as with his dearest friend. It is an honour to him to whom a secret is committed by another, a greater honour to him to whom the king shall commit his own secret ; but how is he honoured to whom God committeth his secret ? for where the secret of God is, there is his heart and there is himself. Thus was his secret with St. John, of whom St. Bernard saith, by occasion of the beginning of his gospel, " Doth he not seem unto thee to have dived into the bowels of the divine Word, and from the secrets of his breast, to have drawn a sacred pith of concealed wisdom ? " Thus was his secret with St. Paul, who saith, " We speak the wisdom of God in a mystery, even the hidden wisdom, which none of the princes of this world knew." 1 Cor. ii. 7, 8. St. Gregory reads, for the secret of God, as the Vulgar Latin doth *sermocinatio Dei,* the communication of God is with the righteous ; but then addeth, *Dei sermocinari est per illustrationem suæ præsentiæ humanis mentibus arcana revelare,* God's communication is, by the illustration of his presence, to reveal secrets to the minds of men. But to consider the words somewhat more generally. There is no less a secret of godliness, than there is of any other trade or profession. Many profess an art or a trade, but thrive not by it, because they have not the secret and mystery of it ; and many profess godliness, but are little the better for it, because they have not the true secret of it : he hath that, with whom God is in secret in his heart ; and he that is righteous in secret, where no man sees him, he is the righteous man with whom the secret of the Lord is.—*Michael Jermin, D.D.,* 1591—1659.

Verse 14.—" *The secret of the Lord is with them that fear him,*" etc.   There is a vital sense in which " the natural man discerneth not the things of the Spirit of God;" and in which all the realities of Christian experience are utterly hid from his perceptions.   To speak to him of communion with God, of the sense of pardon, of the lively expectation of heaven, of the witness of the Holy Ghost, of the struggles of the spiritual life, would be like reasoning with a blind man about colours, or with one deaf about musical harmony.—*John Morison.*

Verse 14.—" *The secret of the Lord is with them that fear him,*" etc.   Albeit the Lord's covenant with the visible church be open, and plain in itself to all men in all the articles thereof, yet it is a mystery to know the inward sweet fellowship which a soul may have with God by virtue of this covenant ; and a man fearing God shall know this mystery, when such as are covenanters only in the letter do remain ignorant thereof ; for to *the fearers of God* only is this promise made—that to *them* the Lord *will show his covenant.*—*David Dickson.*

Verse 14.—" *The secret of the Lord is with them that fear him.*"   The gospel, though published to all the world, yet it is entitled a mystery, and a mystery hid, for none know it but the saints, who are taught of God, and are his scholars.   John vi. 45.   That place shows that there must be a secret teaching by God, and a secret learning.   " If they have heard, and been taught of God."   Now God teacheth none but saints, for all that are so taught come unto him : " Every one who hath heard, and learned of the Father, cometh unto me."   Ay, but you will say, Do not many carnal men know the gospel, and discourse of things in it, through strength of learning, etc. ?   I answer out of the text (Col. i. 26, 27), that though they may know the things which the gospel reveals, yet not the riches and glory of them, that same rich knowledge spoken of in the word, they want, and therefore know them not ; as a child and a jeweller looking upon a pearl, both look upon it, and call it by the same name ; but the child yet knows it not as a pearl in the worth and riches of it as the jeweller doth, and therefore cannot be said to know it.   Now in Matt. xiii. 45, a Christian only is likened to a merchantman, that finds a pearl of great price, that is, discovered to be so, and sells all he hath for it, for he knows the worth of it.   But you will say, Do not carnal men know the worth of the things in the gospel, and can they not discourse of the rich grace of Christ, and of his worth ?   I answer, yes, as a man who hath gotten an inventory by heart, and the prices also, and so may know it ; yet never was he led into the exchequer and treasury, to see all the jewels themselves, the wardrobe of grace, and Christ's righteousness, to see the glory of them ; for these are all " spiritually discerned," as the apostle says expressly, 1 Cor. ii. 14.—*Thomas Goodwin.*

Verse 14.—" *The secret of the Lord is with them that fear him.*"   The truth and sincerity of God to his people appears in the openness and plainness of his heart to them.   A friend that is close and reserved, deservedly comes under a cloud in the thoughts of his friend ; but he who carries, as it were, a window of crystal in his breast, through which his friend may read what thoughts are writ in his very heart, delivers himself from the least suspicion of unfaithfulness.   Truly, thus open-hearted is God to his saints : " *The secret of the Lord is with them that fear him.*" He gives us his key, that will let us into his very heart, and acquaint us what his thoughts are, yea, were, towards us, before a stone was laid in the world's foundation; and this is no other than his Spirit (1 Cor. ii. 10, 11), " One who knows the deep things of God ;" for he was at the council-table in heaven, where all was transacted. This, his Spirit, he employed to put forth and publish in the Scriptures, indited by him, the substance of those counsels of love which had passed between the Trinity of Persons for our salvation ; and that nothing may be wanting for our satisfaction, he hath appointed the same Holy Spirit to abide in his saints, that as Christ in heaven presents our desires to him, so he may interpret his mind out of his word to us ; which word answers the heart of God, as face answers face in the glass.—*William Gurnall.*

Verse 14.—" *The secret of the Lord.*"   This " *secret* " is called a *secret* three ways. 1. *Secret* to the eye of sole nature, and thus it is not meant ; for so the grace of Christ is a *secret* only to heathens and such as are blind as they, for common Christians know it—the rind of it.   2. *Secret* to the eye of taught nature, nor thus is it meant ; for so the grace of Christ is a *secret* only to the ignorant sort of Christians ; many carnal gospellers that sit under a good ministry know it and the bark of it.   3. *Secret* to the eye of enlightened nature, and thus it is meant ; for so the grace of Christ is a *secret* to all unsanctified professors, whether learned or unlearned, namely, the pith of it ; for though great doctors and profound clerks, and deep studied divines unconverted, know the doctrine of grace, and the truth of grace ; though they can dispute of grace and talk of the glory of grace, yea, and taste a little the good word of grace, yea, and understand it generally, it may be as well as St. Paul and St. Peter, as Judas did, yet the special and the spiritual knowledge thereof, for all their dogmatical illumination, is a *secret* unto them.—*William Fenner.*

Verse 14.—" *The secret.*" Arminius and his company ransack all God's *secrets*, divulge and communicate them to the seed of the woman, and of the serpent all alike ; they make God's eternal love of election no *secret*, but a vulgar idea ; they make the mystery of Christ, and him crucified, no *secret*, but like an apothecary's drug, catholical ; they make the especial grace of God no *secret*, but a common quality ; faith no *secret*, but a general virtue ; repentance and the new creature no *secret*, but an universal gift ; no *secret* favour to St. Peter, but make God a party *unto*, not to love St. Peter more than Judas; no *secret* intent to any one person more than another ; but that Christ might have died for all him, and never a man saved ; no *secret* working of the Lord in any more than other ; but for anything that either God the Father hath done by creating, God the Son by redeeming, or God the Holy Ghost by sanctifying, all the world were left to their scrambling—take it if you will, if you will not, refuse. They say God would have men to be saved, but that he will not work it for his own part, rather for this man of that man determinatively that he be saved.—*William Fenner.*

Verse 14.—" *He will shew them his covenant,*" or, *and he will make them to know* (for the infinitive is here thought to be put for the future tense of the indicative, as it is Eccles. iii. 14, 15, 18 ; Hos. ix. 13 ; xii. 3), *his covenant, i.e.,* he will make them clearly to understand it, both its duties or conditions, and its blessings or privileges ; neither of which ungodly men rightly understand. Or, he will make them to know it by experience, or by God's making it good to them ; as, on the contrary, God threatens to make ungodly men to *know his breach of promise.* Numb. xiv. 34. Or, as it is in the margins of our Bibles, *and his covenant* (is, *i.e.,* he hath engaged himself by his promise or covenant) *to make them know* it, to wit his secret, *i.e.,* that he will manifest either his word or his favour to them.—*Matthew Pool.*

Verse 14.—It is neither learning nor labour that can give insight into God's secrets, those *Arcana imperii,* " The mysteries of the kingdom of heaven." Matt. xiii. 11. " The mind of Christ." 1 Cor. ii. 16. These things come by revelation rather than by discourse of reason, and must therefore be obtained by prayer. Those that diligently seek him shall be of his *Cabinet Council,* shall know his soul secrets, and be admitted into a gracious familiarity and friendship. " Henceforth I call you not servants ; for the servant knoweth not what his lord doeth : but I have called you friends ; for all things that I have heard of my Father I have made known unto you." John xv. 15.—*John Trapp.*

Verse 14.—Walking with God is the best way to know the mind of God ; friends who walk together impart their secrets one to another : " *The secret of the Lord is with them that fear him.*" Noah walked with God, and the Lord revealed a great *secret* to him, of destroying the old world, and having him in the ark. Abraham walked with God, and God made him one of his privy council : " Shall I hide from Abraham that thing which I do ? " Gen. xxiv. 40, and xviii. 17. God doth sometimes sweetly unbosom himself to the soul in prayer, and in the holy supper, as Christ made himself known to the disciples in the breaking of bread. Luke xxiv. 35.—*Thomas Watson.*

Verse 15.—" *Mine eyes are ever toward the Lord.*" Though we cannot see him by reasons of our present distance and darkness, yet we must look towards him, towards the place where his honour dwells, as those that desire the knowledge of him and his will, and direct all to his honour as the mark we aim at, labouring in this, that " whether present or absent, we may be accepted of him."—*Matthew Henry.*

Verse 15.—" *Mine eyes.*" As the sense of sight is very quick, and exercises an entire influence over the whole frame, it is no uncommon thing to find all the affections denoted by the term " *eyes.*"—*John Calvin.*

Verse 15.—" *He shall pluck my feet out of the net.*" An unfortunate dove, whose feet are taken in the snare of the fowler, is a fine emblem of the soul, entangled in the cares or pleasures of the world ; from which she desires, through the power of grace, to fly away, and to be at rest, with her glorified Redeemer.—*George Horne.*

Verse 17.—" *The troubles of my heart are enlarged."* Let no good man be surprised that his affliction is great, and to him of an unaccountable character. It has always been so with God's people. The road to heaven is soaked with the tears and blood of the saints.—*William S. Plumer.*

Verse 17.—" *O bring thou me out of my distresses."* We may not complain of God, but we may complain to God. With submission to his holy will we may earnestly cry for help and deliverance.—*William S. Plumer.*

Verse 18.—" *Look upon mine affliction and my pain ; and forgive all my sins."* We may observe here, that *sickness and weakness of the body come from sin, and is a fruit of sin.* Some are weak, and some are sick, " for this cause." I shall not need to be long in the proof of that, which you have whole chapters for, as Deut. xxviii. 27, *seq.* ; and many Psalms, cvii., and others. It is for the sickness of the soul that God visits with the sickness of the body. He aims at the cure of the soul in the touch of the body. And therefore in this case, when God visits with sickness, we should think our work is more in heaven with God than with men or physic. Begin first with the soul. So David (Psa. xxxii. 5), till he dealt roundly with God, without all kind of guile and confessed his sins, he roared ; his moisture was turned into the thought of summer. But when he dealt directly and plainly with God, and confessed nis sins, then God forgave him them, and healed his body too. And therefore the best method, when God visits us in this kind, is to think that we are to deal with God. Begin the cure there with the soul. When he visits the body, it is for the soul's sake : " Many are weak and sickly among you."—*Richard Sibbes.*

Verse 18.—" *Look upon mine affliction and my pain."* In sickness of body trust to Jesus, he is as powerful and as willing to help us now as he was to help others in the days of his flesh. All things are possible to us if we believe. It is but a word for him to rebuke all storms and tempests whatsoever. Let us not do like Asa, trust only in the physician, or in subordinate means, but know that all physic is but dead means without him. 2 Chron. xvi. 12. Therefore, with the means, run to Christ, that he may work with them, and know that virtue and strength comes from him to bless or curse all sort of means.—*Richard Sibbes.*

Verse 19.—" *Consider mine enemies,"* etc. Or *look* upon them ; but with another kind of look ; so as he looked through the pillar of fire upon the Egyptians, and troubled them (Exod. xiv. 24), with a look of wrath and vengeance. The arguments he uses are taken both from the quantity and quality of his enemies, their number and their nature, " *For they are many ;* " the hearts of the people of Israel, in general, being after Absalom (2 Sam. xv. 12, 13) ; and so the spiritual enemies of the Lord's people are many ; their sins and corruptions, Satan, and his principalities and powers, and the men of this world. " *And they hate me with cruel hatred ;* " like that of Simeon and Levi (Gen. xliv. 7) ; their hatred broke out in a cruel manner, in acts of force and cruelty ; and it was the more cruel, inasmuch as it was without cause ; and such is the hatred of Satan and his emissaries against the followers of Christ ; who breathe out cruelty, thirst after their blood, and make themselves drunk with it ; even their tender mercies are cruel, and much more their hatred.—*John Gill.*

Verse 19.—" *Consider mine enemies."* God needeth not hound out many creatures to punish man, he doeth that on himself. There is no kind of creature so hurtful to itself as he. Some hurt other kinds and spare their own, but mankind in all sorts of injuries destroyeth itself. Man to man is more crafty than a fox, more cruel than the tiger, and more fierce than a lion, and in a word, if he be left to himself man unto man is a devil.—*William Struther's " Christian Observations,"* 1629.

Verses 19, 20.—" *Consider mine enemies. . . . . O keep my soul and deliver me."* We may say of original concupiscence, strengthened and heightened by customary transgressions, its name is legion, for it is many. Hydra-like, it is a body with many heads ; and when we cut off one head, one enormous impiety, there presently sprouts up another of like monstrous nature, like venomous guilt. From the womb then it is of original sin and sinful custom, as from the belly of the Trojan horse, there does issue forth a whole army of unclean lusts, to surround the soul in all its faculties, and the body too in all its members.—*Robert Mossom.*

Verse 20.—" *Let me be not ashamed ; for I put my trust in thee."* When David reaches verse 20, we are reminded of Coriolanus betaking himself to the hall of

Attius Tullus, and sitting as a helpless stranger there, claiming the king's hospitality, though aware of his having deserved to die at his hands. The Psalmist throws himself on the compassions of an injured God with similar feelings ; " *I trust in thee !* "—*Andrew A. Bonar.*

Verse 21.—" *For I trust in, or wait on thee.*" As preservation is a continued creation, so is *waiting* a continued trusting ; for, what trust believes by faith, it *waits for* by hope ; and thus is trust a compound of both.—*Robert Mossom.*

Verse 22.—" *Redeem Israel, O God, out of all his troubles.*" If thou wilt not pity and help me, yet spare thy people, who suffer for my sake, and in my sufferings.—*Matthew Pool.*

Verse 22.—" *Redeem Israel,*" etc. *In vita vel post mortem meam,** either whiles I live, or after my death. This is every good man's care and prayer. None is in case to pray for the church, that hath not first made his own peace with God.—*John Trapp.*

Verse 22.—This most beautiful of " Psalms and hymns and spiritual songs " closes with a sweet petition—such an one, as every one of the true Israel of God would wish to depart with on his lips, " *Redeem Israel, O God, out of all his troubles.*" It breathes the same holy aspiration as the aged Simeon's, " Lord ! now lettest thy servant depart in peace, for mine eyes have seen thy salvation."—*Barton Bouchier.*

HINTS TO PREACHERS.

Verse 1.—Heavenly machinery for uplifting an earthbound soul.

Verse 1.—Genuine devotion described and commended.

Verse 2.—The soul at anchor, and the two rocks from which it would be delivered.

Verse 3.—Shame out of place and in place.

Verse 4.—Practical divinity the best study ; God the best teacher ; Prayer the mode of entrance into the school.

Verses 4, 5. " *Shew.*" " *Teach.*" " *Lead.*" Three classes in the school of grace.

Verse 5.—I. Sanctification desired. II. Knowledge sought. III. Assurance enjoyed. IV. Patience exercised.

Verse 5.—" *Thou art the God of my salvation.*" A rich and overflowing text.

Verse 5 (last clause).—How to spend the day with God.—*Matthew Henry.*

Verse 6.—The antiquity of mercy.

Verses 6, 7.—The three Remembers.

Verse 7 (first clause).—The best Act of Oblivion.—*Thomas Fuller.*

Verse 7.—Oblivion desired and remembrance entreated. Note " *my,*" and " *thy.*"

Verse 8.—Opposing attributes co-working. God teaching sinners—a great wonder.

Verse 9.—" *The meek.*" Who they are ? What are their privileges ? How to be like them ?

Verse 9 (first clause).—Moral purity needful to a well-balanced judgment.

Verse 10.—God's mercy and faithfulness in providence, and the persons who may derive comfort therefrom.

Verse 11.—A model prayer. Confession, argument, entreaty, etc.

Verse 11.—Great guilt no obstacle to the pardon of the returning sinner.—*Jonathan Edwards.*

Verse 12.—Holiness the best security for a well ordered life. Free-will at school, questioned and instructed.

Verse 13.—A man at ease for time and eternity.

Verse 14.—I. A secret, and who know it. II. A wonder, and who see it.

---

* Rabbi David

Verse 15. I. What we are like. A silly bird. II. What is our danger? "Net." III. Who is our friend? "The Lord." IV. What is our wisdom? "Mine eyes," etc.

Verse 16.—A desolate soul seeking heavenly company, and an afflicted spirit crying for divine mercy. Our God the balm of all our wounds.

Verses 16—18.—David is a petitioner as well as a sufferer; and those sorrows will never injure us that bring us near to God. Three things he prays for:— I. *Deliverance.* This we are called to desire, consistently with resignation to the divine will. II. *Notice.* A kind look from God is desirable at any time, in any circumstances; but in affliction and pain, it is like life from the dead. III. *Pardon.* Trials are apt to revive a sense of guilt.—*William Jay.*

Verse 17.—Special seasons of trouble and special resort to prayer for special deliverance.

Verse 18.—Two things are here taught us:—I. That a kind look from God is very desirable in affliction. II. That the sweetest cordial under trouble would be an assurance of divine forgiveness. I. That a kind look, etc. (subdivisions), 1. It is a look of special observation. 2. It is a look of tender compassion. 3. It is a look of support and assistance (with God, power and compassion go together). II. That the sweetest cordial, etc. (subdivisions), 1. Because trouble is very apt to bring our sins to remembrance. 2. Because a sense of pardon will in great measure remove all distressing fears of death and judgment. *Improvement.* 1. Let us adore the goodness of God, that one so great and glorious should bestow a favourable look upon any of our sinful race. 2. Let the benefit we have received from the Lord's looking upon us in *former* afflictions, engage us to *pray*, and encourage us to *hope*, that he will now look upon us again. 3. If a kind look from God be so comfortable, what must *heaven* be!—*Samuel Lavington.*

Verse 18.—I. It is well when our sorrows remind us of our sins. II. When we are as earnest to be forgiven as to be delivered. III. When we bring both to the right place in prayer. IV. When we are submissive about our sorrows— "*Look*," etc.—but very explicit about our sins—"*Forgive*," etc.

Verse 19.—The spiritual enemies of the saint. Their number, malice, craft, power, etc.

Verse 20.—Soul preservation. I. Its twofold character, "Keep," and "deliver." II. Its dreadful alternative, "Let me not be ashamed." III. Its effectual guarantee, "I put my trust in thee."

Verse 20.—A superhuman keeping, a natural fear, a spiritual trust.

Verse 21.—The open way of safety in action, and the secret way of safety in devotion.

Verse 22.—Jacob's life, as typical of ours, may illustrate this prayer.

Verse 22.—A prayer for the church militant.

PSALM XXVI.

TITLE.—*A Psalm of David. The sweet singer of Israel appears before us in this Psalm as one enduring reproach; in this he was the type of the great Son of David, and is an encouraging example to us to carry the burden of slander to the throne of grace. It is an ingenious surmise that this appeal to heaven was written by David at the time of the assassination of Ish-bosheth, by Baanah and Rechab, to protest his innocence of all participation in that treacherous murder; the tenor of the Psalm certainly agrees with the supposed occasion, but it is not possible with such a slender clue to go beyond conjecture.*

DIVISION.—*Unity of subject is so distinctly maintained, that there are no sharp divisions. David Dickson has given an admirable summary in these words:—" He appealeth to God, the supreme Judge, in the testimony of a good conscience, bearing him witness; first, of his endeavour to walk uprightly as a believer, verses 1, 2, 3; secondly, of his keeping himself from the contagion of the evil counsel, sinful courses, and example of the wicked, verses 4, 5; thirdly, of his purpose still to behave himself holily and righteously, out of love to the partaker of the public privileges of the Lord's people in the congregation, verses 6, 7, 8. Whereupon he prayeth to be free of the judgment coming upon the wicked, verses 9, 10, according as he had purposed to eschew their sins, verse 11; and he closeth his prayer with comfort and assurance of being heard, verse 12.*

EXPOSITION.

JUDGE me, O LORD; for I have walked in mine integrity: I have trusted
   also in the LORD; *therefore* I shall not slide.

2 Examine me, O LORD, and prove me; try my reins and my heart.

3 For thy lovingkindness *is* before mine eyes: and I have walked in thy
truth.

1. "*Judge me, O Jehovah.*"—A solemn appeal to the just tribunal of the heart-searching God, warranted by the circumstances of the writer, so far as regarded the particular offences with which he was wrongly charged. Worried and worn out by the injustice of men, the innocent spirit flies from its false accusers to the throne of Eternal Right. He had need have a clear case who dares to carry his suit into the King's Bench of heaven. Such an appeal as this is not to be rashly made on any occasion; and as to the whole of our walk and conversation, it should never be made at all, except as we are justified in Christ Jesus: a far more fitting prayer for a sinful mortal is the petition, " Enter not into judgment with thy servant." "*For I have walked in mine integrity.*" He held integrity as his principle, and walked in it as his practice. David had not used any traitorous or unrighteous means to gain the crown, or to keep it; he was conscious of having been guided by the noblest principles of honour in all his actions with regard to Saul and his family. What a comfort it is to have the approbation of one's own conscience! If there be peace within the soul, the blustering storms of slander which howl around us are of little consideration. When the little bird in my bosom sings a merry song, it is no matter to me if a thousand owls hoot at me from without. "*I have trusted also in the Lord.*" Faith is the root and sap of integrity. He who leans upon the Lord is sure to walk in righteousness. David knew that God's covenant had given him the crown, and therefore he took no indirect or unlawful means to secure it; he would not slay his enemy in the cave, nor suffer his men-at-arms to smite him when he slept unguarded on the plain. Faith will work hard for the Lord, and in the Lord's way, but she refuses so much as to lift a finger to fulfil the devices of unrighteous cunning. Rebecca acted out a great falsehood in order to fulfil the Lord's decree in favour of Jacob—this was unbelief; but Abraham left the Lord to fulfil his own purposes, and took the knife to slay his son—this was faith. Faith trusts God to accomplish his own decrees. Why should I steal when God has promised to supply my need? Why should I avenge myself when I know that the Lord has espoused my cause? Confidence in God

is a most effectual security against sin. *" Therefore I shall not slide."* Slippery as the way is, so that I walk like a man upon ice, yet faith keeps my heels from tripping, and will continue to do so. The doubtful ways of policy are sure sooner or later to give a fall to those who run therein, but the ways of honesty, though often rough, are always safe. We cannot trust in God if we walk crookedly; but straight paths and simple faith bring the pilgrim happily to his journey's end.

2. There are three modes of trial here challenged, which are said in the original to refer to trial by touch, trial by smell, and trial by fire. The Psalmist was so clear from the charge laid against him, that he submitted himself unconditionally to any form of examination which the Lord might see fit to employ. *" Examine me, O Lord."* Look me through and through; make a minute survey; put me to the question, cross-examine my evidence. *" And prove me."* Put me again to trial; and see if I would follow such wicked designs as my enemies impute to me. *" Try my reins and my heart."* Assay me as metals are assayed in the furnace, and do this to my most secret parts, where my affections hold their court; see, O God, whether or no I love murder, and treason, and deceit. All this is a very bold appeal, and made by a man like David, who feared the Lord exceedingly, it manifests a most solemn and complete conviction of innocence. The expressions here used should teach us the thoroughness of the divine judgment, and the necessity of being in all things profoundly sincere, lest we be found wanting at the last. Our enemies are severe with us with the severity of spite, and this a brave man endures without a fear; but God's severity is that of unswerving right, who shall stand against such a trial? The sweet singer asks " Who can stand before his cold ? " and we may well enquire, " Who can stand before the heat of his justice ? "

3. *" For thy lovingkindness is before mine eyes."*—An object of memory and a ground of hope. A sense of mercy received sets a fair prospect before the faithful mind in its gloomiest condition, for it yields visions of mercies yet to come, visions not visionary but real. Dwell, dear reader, upon that celestial word *loving-kindness.* It has a heavenly savour. Is it not an unmatchable word, unexcelled, unrivalled? The goodness of the Lord to us should be before our eyes as a motive actuating our conduct; we are not under the bondage of the law, but we are under the sweet constraints of grace, which are far more mighty, although far more gentle. Men sin with the law before their eyes, but divine love when clearly seen, sanctifies the conversation. If we were not so forgetful of the way of mercy in which God walks towards us, we should be more careful to walk in the ways of obedience towards him. *" And I have walked in thy truth."* The Psalmist was preserved from sin by his assurance of the truthfulness of God's promise, which truth he endeavoured to imitate as well as to believe. Observe from this verse, that an experience of divine love will show itself in a practical following of divine truth; those who neglect either the doctrinal or practical parts of truth must not wonder if they lose the experimental enjoyment of it. Some *talk of* truth, it is better to *walk in* it. Some vow to do well in future, but their resolutions come to nothing; only the regenerate man can say *" I have walked in thy truth."*

4 I have not sat with vain persons, neither will I go in with dissemblers.

5 I have hated the congregation of evil doers; and will not sit with the wicked.

So far from being himself an open offender against the laws of God, the Psalmist had not even associated with the lovers of evil. He had kept aloof from the men of Belial. A man is known by his company, and if we have kept ourselves apart from the wicked, it will always be evidence in our favour should our character be impugned. He who was never in the parish is not likely to have stolen the corn. He who never went to sea is clearly not the man who scuttled the ship.

4. *" I have not sat with vain persons."*—True citizens have no dealings with traitors. David had no seat in the parliament of triflers. They were not his boon companions at feasts, nor his advisers in council, nor his associates in conversation. We must needs see, and speak, and trade, with men of the world, but we must on no account take our rest and solace in their empty society. Not only the profane, but the vain are to be shunned by us. All those who live for this life only are vain, chaffy, frothy men, quite unworthy of a Christian's friendship. Moreover, as this vanity is often allied with falsehood, it is well to save ourselves altogether from this untoward generation, lest we should be led from bad

to worse, and from tolerating the vain, should come to admire the wicked.
"*Neither will I go in with dissemblers.*" Since I know that hypocritical piety is
double iniquity, I will cease all acquaintance with pretenders. If I must needs
walk the same street, I will not enter the same door and spend my time in their
society. The congregation of the hypocrites is not one with which we should
cultivate communion ; their ultimate rendezvous will be the lowest pit of hell,
let us drop their acquaintance now ! for we shall not desire it soon. They hang
their beads around their necks, and carry the devil in their hearts. This clause
is in the future tense, to indicate that the writer felt no desire to begin an
acquaintance with characters whom up till then he had shunned. We must maintain the separated path with more and more circumspection as we see the great
redemption day approaching. Those who would be transfigured with Jesus, must
not be disfigured by conformity to the world. The resolution of the Psalmist
suggests, that even among professed followers of truth we must make distinctions,
for as there are vain persons out of the church, so there are dissemblers in it, and
both are to be shunned with scrupulous decision.

5. "*I have hated the congregation of evil doers.*"—A severe sentence, but not
too severe. A man who does not hate evil terribly, does not love good heartily.
Men, as men, we must always love, for they are our neighbours, and therefore to
be loved as ourselves ; but evil doers, as such, are traitors to the Great King, and
no loyal subject can love traitors. What God hates we must hate. The congregation
or assembly of evil doers, signifies violent men in alliance and conclave for the
overthrow of the innocent ; such synagogues of Satan are to be held in abhorrence.
What a sad reflection it is that there should be a congregation of evil doers as well
as a congregation of the upright, a church of Satan as well as a church of God ;
a seed of the serpent as well as a seed of the woman ; an old Babylon as well as a
new Jerusalem ; a great whore sitting upon many waters, to be judged in wrath,
as well as a chaste bride of the Lamb to be crowned at his coming. "*And will
not sit with the wicked.*" Saints have a seat at another table, and will never leave
the King's dainties for the husks of the swine-trough. Better to sit with the blind,
and the halt, and the lame, at the table of mercy, than with the wicked in their
feasts of ungodliness, yea, better to sit on Job's dunghill than on Pharaoh's throne.
Let each reader see well to his company, for such as we keep in this world, we are
likely to keep in the next.

6 I will wash mine hands in innocency so will I compass thine altar,
O LORD :

7 That I may publish with the voice of thanksgiving, and tell of all thy
wondrous works.

8 LORD, I have loved the habitation of thy house, and the place where
thine honour dwelleth.

6. "*I will wash mine hands in innocency.*"—He would publicly avow himself
to be altogether clear of the accusations laid against him, and if any fault in other
matters could be truthfully alleged against him, he would for the future abstain
from it. The washing of the hands is a significant action to set forth our having
no connection with a deed, as we still say, " I wash my hands of the whole business."
As to perfect innocence, David does not here claim it, but he avows his innocence
of the crimes whereof he was slanderously accused ; there is, however, a sense in
which we may be washed in absolute innocence, for the atoning blood makes us
clean every whit. We ought never to rest satisfied short of a full persuasion of
our complete cleansing by Jesus' precious blood. " *So will I compass thine altar,
O Lord.*" Priests unto God must take great care to be personally cleansed ; the
brazen laver was as needful as the golden altar ; God's worship requires us to be
holy in life. He who is unjust to man cannot be acceptably religious towards God.
We must not bring our thankofferings with hands defiled with guilt. To love
justice and purity is far more acceptable to God than ten thousands of the fat of
fed beasts. We see from this verse that holy minds delight in the worship of the
Lord, and find their sweetest solace at his altar ; and that it is their deepest concern
never to enter upon any course of action which would unfit them for the most sacred
communion with God. Our eye must be upon the altar which sanctifieth both the
giver and the gift, yet we must never draw from the atoning sacrifice an excuse
for sin, but rather find in it a most convincing argument for holiness.

7. "*That I may publish with the voice of thanksgiving.*" David was so far instructed that he does not mention the typical offering, but discerns the spiritual offering which was intended thereby, not the groans of bullocks, but songs of gratitude the spiritual worshipper presents. To sound abroad the worthy praises of the God of all grace should be the every-day business of a pardoned sinner. Let men slander us as they will, let us not defraud the Lord of his praises ; let dogs bark, but let us like the moon shine on. "*And tell of all thy wondrous works.*" God's people should not be tongue-tied. The wonders of divine grace are enough to make the tongue of the dumb sing. God's works of love are wondrous if we consider the unworthiness of their objects, the costliness of their method, and the glory of their result. And as men find great pleasure in discoursing upon things remarkable and astonishing, so the saints rejoice to tell of the great things which the Lord hath done for them.

8. "*Lord, I have loved the habitation of thy house.*" Into the abodes of sin he would not enter, but the house of God he had long loved, and loved it still. We were sad children if we did not love our Father's dwelling-place. Though we own no sacred buildings, yet the church of the living God is the house of God, and true Christians delight in her ordinances, services, and assemblies. O that all our days were Sabbaths ! "*And the place where thine honour dwelleth.*" In his church where God is had in honour at all times, where he reveals himself in the glory of his grace, and is proclaimed by his people as the Lord of all. We come not together as the Lord's people to honour the preacher, but to give glory to God ; such an occupation is most pleasant to the saints of the Most High. What are those gatherings where God is not honoured, are they not an offence to his pure and holy eyes, and are they not a sad stumbling-block to the people of God ? It brings the scalding-tear upon our cheek to hear sermons in which the honour of God is so far from being the preacher's object, that one might almost imagine that the preacher worshipped the dignity of manhood, and thought more of it than of the Infinite Majesty of God.

9 Gather not my soul with sinners, nor my life with bloody men :
10 In whose hand *is* mischief, and their right hand is full of bribes.

9. "*Gather not my soul with sinners.*"—Lord, when, like fruit, I must be gathered, put me not in the same basket with the best of sinners, much less with the worst of them. The company of sinners is so distasteful to us here, that we cannot endure the thought of being bound up in the same bundle with them to all eternity. Our comfort is, that the Great Husbandman discerns the tares from the wheat, and will find a separate place for distinct characters. In the former verses we see that the Psalmist kept himself clear of profane persons, and this is to be understood as a reason why he should not be thrust into their company at the last. Let us think of the doom of the wicked, and the prayer of the text will forcibly rise to our lips ; meanwhile, as we see the rule of judgment by which like is gathered to its like, we who have passed from death unto life have nothing to fear. "*Nor my life with bloody men.*" Our soul sickens to hear them speak ; their cruel dispatches, in which they treat the shooting of their fellow-men as rare sport, are horrifying to us ; Lord, let us not be shut up in the same prison with them ; nay, the same paradise with such men would be a hell, if they remained as they now are.

10. "*In whose hands is mischief.*"—They have both hands full of it, plotting it and carrying it out. "*And their right hand,*" with which they are most dexterous, "*is full of bribes ;*" like thieves who would steal with impunity, they carry a sop for the dogs of justice. He who gives bribes is every way as guilty as the man who takes them, and in the matter of our parliamentary elections the rich villain who gives the bribe is by far the worse. Bribery, in any form or shape, should be as detestable to a Christian as carrion to a dove, or garbage to a lamb. Let those whose dirty hands are fond of bribes remember that neither death nor the devil can be bribed to let them escape their well-earned doom.

11 But as for me, I will walk in mine integrity : redeem me, and be merciful unto me.

Here is the lover of godliness entering his personal protest against unrighteous gain. He is a Nonconformist, and is ready to stand alone in his Nonconformity.

Like a live fish, he swims against the stream. Trusting in God, the Psalmist resolves that the plain way of righteousness shall be his choice, and those who will, may prefer the tortuous paths of violence and deceit. Yet he is by no means a boaster, or a self-righteous vaunter of his own strength, for he cries for redemption and pleads for mercy. Our integrity is not absolute nor inherent, it is a work of grace in us, and is marred by human infirmity; we must, therefore, resort to the redeeming blood and the throne of mercy, confessing that though we are saints among men, we must still bow as sinners before God.

12 My foot standeth in an even place : in the congregations will I bless the LORD.

The song began in the minor, but it has now reached the major key. Saints often sing themselves into happiness. The *even place* upon which our foot stands is the sure, covenant faithfulness, eternal promise and immutable oath of the Lord of Hosts ; there is no fear of falling from this solid basis, or of its being removed from under us. Established in Christ Jesus, by being vitally united to him, we have nothing left to occupy our thoughts but the praises of our God. Let us not forsake the assembling of ourselves together, and when assembled, let us not be slow to contribute our portion of thanksgiving. Each saint is a witness to divine faithfulness, and should be ready with his testimony. As for the slanderers, let them howl outside the door while the children sing within.

EXPLANATORY NOTES AND QUAINT SAYINGS.

Whole Psalm.—This Psalm is coupled on to the foregoing by thoughts and words. At the close of the foregoing the Psalmist had prayed for *integrity* (verse 1). Unless this Psalm is regarded as a sequel to the preceding one, it will seem vainglorious ; but being combined with the penitential acknowledgments of sin, and with the earnest supplications for pardon and grace, and with the earnest profession of faith that God has heard his prayer, which breathe forth in the foregoing Psalm, it will be seen that the declarations which the Psalmist now makes of integrity, are not assertions of human merit, but acknowledgments of divine mercy. As Augustine says, " *Non merita mea, sed misericordia tua, ante oculos meos est.*"—*Christopher Wordsworth.*

Verse 1.—" *Judge me, O Lord ; for I have walked in mine integrity.*"—A good cause, a good conscience, and a good deportment, are good grounds of appeal to God.—*Ingram Cobbin.*

Verse 1.—" *Judge me, O Lord.*" Nothing is so pleasing to him that is upright as to know that God knoweth he is so. As it is a small matter with those who are sincere to be condemned by men, so it is not much with them to be commended or approved by them ; for indeed neither " he that commendeth himself," as the apostle speaks (2 Cor. x. 18), nor he that is commended by others, " is approved, but whom the Lord commendeth." The testimony, or letters commendatory of all the men in the world will do us no good, unless God give us his also.—*Joseph Caryl.*

Verse 1.—" *Judge me, O Lord.*" As an instance of appeal to heaven, we quote that mighty preacher of the Word, George Whitfield. " However some may account me a mountebank and an enthusiast, one that is only going to make you methodically mad ; they may breathe out their invectives against me, yet Christ knows all ; he takes notice of it, and I shall leave it to him to plead my cause, for he is a gracious Master. I have already found him so, and am sure he will continue so. Vengeance is his, and he will repay it."—*George Whitfield, 1714–1770.*

Verse 1.—" *Integrity.*" םֹת, or תֻּמִּים is used of whatever is uninjured, or is free from any spot or blemish ; and hence we find the term applied to an unblemished animal offered in sacrifice. Lev. i. 3 ; iii. 9.—*George Phillips.*

Verse 1.—" *Mine integrity.*" There is a force in the possessive pronoun " my," which must be attended to. The Psalmist intimates that he had proceeded in one uniform course, notwithstanding all the devices of his enemies.—*W. Wilson, D.D.*

Verse 1.—" *I have trusted in the Lord.*" Trust in God is the *fountain* of "integrity." Whoever places his hope in God need not seek to advance his worldly interests by violating his duty towards his neighbour : he waits for everything *from above*, and is, at the same time, always determined that he will not be deprived of the favour of his heavenly Father through violating his commandments. —*E. W. Hengstenberg.*

Verse 1.—" *I shall not slide.*" It is a striking word, as fully expressive of the completeness of God's protection and the security of his upholding hand as the Psalmist's language of the integrity of his walk and trust in God. It is not, as in our Prayer-book version, " I shall not fall," but it is, " *I shall not even slide ;* " not even make a false step or stumble.—*Barton Bouchier.*

Verse 2.—The Psalmist uses three words, " *examine,*" " *prove,*" " *try.*" These words are designed to include all the modes in which the reality of anything is tested ; and they imply together that he wished the most *thorough* investigation to be made ; he did not shrink from any test.—*Albert Barnes.*

Verse 2.—" *Examine* "—" *prove* "—" *try.*" As gold, by fire, is severed and parted from dross, so singleness of heart and true Christian simplicity is best seen and made most evident in troubles and afflictions. In prosperity every man will seem godly, but afflictions do draw out of the heart whatsoever is there, whether it be good or bad.—*Robert Cawdray.*

Verse 2.—" *Prove me.*" The work of conscience within us doth *prove* us. God hath set up a light within us, and when this is enlightened by the Word, then it makes a man's breast full of light. Now a faithful godly man loveth that this should be tender, active, speaking out of God's Word for every duty, and against every sin. You see the quickness of it in David, when it is said, " His heart smote him ; " and 1 John iii., " If thy heart condemn thee, God is greater than thy heart." Alas ! if thou within thy own self judgest thyself to sin thus and thus, God doth much more. Try thy integrity ; art thou willing to have a tender conscience, and an informed conscience ? Dost thou love to hear what that speaks out of God's Word ? whether peace or duty ? this is comfortable. But on the other side, if thou art a man that rebellest against the light of it, wouldst fain put out the sting of it, wouldst be glad to feel no such living thing in thy breast, then thou hast cause to suspect thyself. Oh, it is to be feared that there are many that give themselves to lusts, and carnal pleasures, that so they may put a foggy mist between their conscience and themselves. Others dig into the world, labouring to become senseless, that so there may be an eclipse of this light by the interposition of the earth. Others run to damnable heresies, denying Scriptures, God, heaven, hell ; pleading for an universal salvation of all. What are these but refuges of guilty consciences ? We must distinguish between our carnal concupiscence, and conscience ; between deluded imaginations, and conscience ; between an erroneous and scrupulous conscience, and a well-grounded and truly informed conscience ; and when we have done so, we must follow conscience as far as that follows the Word.—*Anthony Burgess.*

Verse 2.—" *Reins . . . . . heart.*"—The " *reins,*" as the seat of the lower animal passions ; the " *heart,*" as comprising not only the higher affections, but also the will and the conscience. He thus desires to keep nothing back ; he will submit himself to the searching flame of the Great Refiner, that all dross of self-deception may be purged away.—*J. J. Stewart Perowne.*

Verse 3.—The practical effect of divine goodness is seen in this text. As the chief thing communicated from God is the divine nature, whereby we are made to resemble him, so the promises of God set home upon the soul are the means of communication ; they are the milk and honey of the Scripture, which do not cherish the old man, but support the new ; they are not pillows for sinful sloth, but spurs to holy diligence. The promises of grace animate the soul to duty ; and when we thus see the goodness of the Lord, it encourages our subjection to his government.—*Timothy Cruso.*

Verses 3, 4.—" *I have walked in thy truth, I have not sat with vain persons.*" Be as careful as thou canst, that the persons thou choosest for thy companions be such as fear God. The man in the gospel was possessed with the devil, who dwelt amongst the tombs, and conversed with graves and carcases. Thou art far from walking after the good Spirit, if thou choosest to converse with open sepulchres, and such as are dead in sins and trespasses. God will not shake the wicked by the hand, as the Vulgate reads (Job viii. 20), neither must the godly man. David proves the sincerity of his course, by his care to avoid such society: *"I have walked in thy truth; I have not sat with vain persons."* There is a twofold *" truth."* 1. Truth of doctrine. Thy law is the truth, free from all dross of corruption and falsehood of error. 2. Truth of affection, or of the inward parts. This may be called *" thy truth,"* or God's truth, though man be the subject of it, partly because it proceedeth from him, partly because it is so pleasant to him; in which respect a broken heart is called the *" sacrifice of God."* Psalm li. 6. As if he had said, I could not have walked in the power of religion, and in integrity, if I had associated with vile and vain company; I could never have walked in thy precepts if I had *" sat with vain persons."* Observe the phrase, *"I have not sat with vain persons."* 1. Sitting is a posture of choice. It is at a man's liberty, whether he will sit or stand. 2. Sitting is a posture of pleasure. Men sit for their ease, and with delight; therefore, the glorified are said to *" sit in heavenly places."* Eph. ii. 6. 3. Sitting is a posture of staying or abiding. 2 Kings v. 3. Standing is a posture of going, but sitting of staying. The blessed, who shall for ever be with the Lord and his chosen, are mentioned *" to sit down with Abraham, Isaac, and Jacob, in the kingdom of heaven."* Matt. viii. 11. David in neither of these senses durst *sit with vain persons.* He might, as his occasions required, use their company, but durst not knowingly choose such company. They could not be the object of his election who were not the object of his affection. *"I hate the congregation of evil doers,"* saith he. As sitting is a posture of pleasure, he did not sit with vain persons. He was sometimes amongst them to his sorrow, but not to his solace. They were to him, as the Canaanites to the Israelites, pricks in his eyes, and thorns in his sides. *"* Woe is *me,* that I sojourn in Mesech, that I dwell in the tents of Kedar!*"* Psalm cxx. 5. It caused grief, not gladness, that he was forced to be amongst the profane.—*George Swinnock.*

Verse 4.—*"I have not sat with vain persons."* There is a necessary commerce with men in buying and selling, or as the apostle says, " We must needs go out of the world," but do not voluntarily choose the company of the wicked. 1 Cor. v. 10. " I have written unto you not to keep company," etc. 1 Cor. v. 11. Do not be too familiar with them. What do Christ's doves among birds of prey? What do virgins among harlots? The company of the wicked is very defiling, it is like going among them that have the plague. " They were mingled among the heathen and learned their works." If you mingle bright armour with rusty, the bright armour will not brighten the rusty, but the rusty armour will spoil the bright. Pharaoh taught Joseph to swear, but Joseph did not teach Pharaoh to pray.— *Thomas Watson.*

Verse 4.—*"Neither will I go in with dissemblers."* Chaldee: " I will not go in with those that hide themselves to do evil." Wickedness is uncandid, and loves concealment, while truth and righteousness are open, and seek scrutiny. Job xxiv. 13–17; John iii. 20, 21. None will deny that the candid man has far fewer troubles with his own conduct than the tortuous and deceitful. The righteous shun the wicked both for the *sin* and for the misery that are in their ways.— *William S. Plumer.*

Verse 4.—*" Dissemblers."* The hypocrite has much angel without, more devil within. He fries in words, freezes in works; speaks by ells, doth good by inches. He is a stinking dunghill, covered over with snow; a loose-hung mill that keeps great clacking, but grinds no grist; a lying hen that cackles when she hath not laid.—*Thomas Adams.*

Verse 4.—*" Dissemblers."* Perhaps when the bright sunbeams of an early spring have robed all nature in a smiling garb, you have taken your little baskets, and gone in quest of a bank of sweet-smelling modest violets, and you may have found flowers so like them, in form and colour, that you have been deceived, and eagerly grasped your prize; but alas! the sweet odour which should have scented the gale, was found wanting, and betrayed the dog violet. An apt emblem this of those, who, " having the form of godliness, deny the power thereof." 2 Tim. iii. 5. —*Mrs. Rogers, in " The Shepherd King."*

Verses 4, 5.—As rotten apples corrupt those sound ones that do touch them and lie close to them, even so the evil manners and bad conditions of the ungodly do infect those that keep them company.—*Robert Cawdray.*

Verses 4, 5.—" It is difficult (saith a late ingenious writer) even to a miracle to keep God's commandments and evil company too." How suddenly after your soul-refreshments in your closet communion have you lost all your heats and spiritual fervencies, which you had in secret, and have instantly cooled by going forth into cold and corrupt air ! When a saint hath been in private ravished with the love of God and the joys of heaven, and afterwards meets with company, which neither doth nor can speak one word of such matters, what a damp is it to him ! What a quenching, as it were, of the Spirit of God in him ! Nay, is not that true which one saith, that " the people of God do generally lose more by worldly men, that are of a blameless conversation before men, than they lose by wicked and profane men " ?—*Lewis Stuckley.*

Verses 4, 5, 9.—He that would not be found amongst sinners in the other world, must take heed that he do not frequent their company in this. Those whom the constable finds wandering with vagrants, may be sent with them to the house of correction. " Lord," said a good woman, on her death bed, when in some doubt of her salvation, " send me not to hell amongst wicked men, for thou knowest I never loved their company all my life long." David deprecates their future doom upon the like ground, and argueth it as a sign of his sincerity : " *I have not sat with vain persons, neither will I go in with dissemblers. I have hated the congregation of evil doers ; and will not sit with the wicked. . . . O gather not my soul with sinners.*" Lord, I have not loved the wicked so well as to sit with them for a little time, and shall I live with them for ever ? I have not lain amongst them rotting on the earth ; and wilt thou gather my soul with those sticks for the unquenchable fire of hell ? Lord, I have been so far from liking, that thou knowest I have loathed the congregation of evil doers. Do not I hate them that hate thee ? Yea, I hate them with perfect hatred ; and shall thy friends fare as thy foes ? I appeal to thy Majesty, that my great comfort is in thy chosen. I rejoice only to be amongst thy children here, and shall I be excluded their company hereafter ? " *O do not gather my soul with sinners,*" for the wine-press of thine eternal anger ! Marcion, the heretic, seeing Polycarp, wondered that he would not own him. Do you not know me, Polycarp ? Yea, saith Polycarp, " *Scio te esse primogenitum diaboli ;* " " I know thee to be the firstborn of the devil," and so despised him.—*George Swinnock.*

Verse 5.—" *I have hated the congregation of evil doers,*" etc. The hatred of God's enemies, *quà* his enemies—" yea, I hate them right sore " so entirely opposed to the indifferentism of the present day, has always been one distinguishing mark of his ancient servants. Witness Phinehas (Psalm cvi. 31) ; "And that was counted unto him for righteousness unto all generations for evermore ; " Samuel with Agag ; Elias with the priests of Baal. And notice the commendation of the angel of Ephesus, " Thou canst not bear them that are evil." Rev. ii. 2.—*J. M. Neale.*

Verse 5.—" *I have hated the congregation of evil doers.*" We consider them as God's enemies, so we hate them ; not their persons, but their vices ; for that, as Augustine defineth, it is *odium perfectum,* a perfect hatred. And indeed it is the hatred that God beareth to his enemies ; for " the wrath of God is revealed from heaven against all ungodliness and unrighteousness of men " (Rom. i. 18) ; not against their persons—they are his workmanship, and carry his image in some sort, though much disfigured ; but against the unrighteousness and ungodliness of men, by which their persons do stand obnoxious to his displeasure. And thus I find the saints of God have triumphed over the wicked, as Israel over Pharaoh, and the Gileadites over the children of Ammon ; not rejoicing in the destruction of God's creatures, but of God's enemies ; and wishing with Deborah and Barak, " So let all thine enemies perish, O Lord." This is no more but an applauding of the judgment of God, and a celebration of his justice.—*Edward Marbury.*

Verse 5.—" *I have hated,*" etc. Consider that there can be no true friendship betwixt a godly and a wicked person ; therefore it concerneth thee to be the more wary in thy choice. He that in factions hath an eye to power, in friendship will have an eye to virtue. Friendship, according to the philosopher, is one soul in two bodies. But how can they ever be of one soul that are as different as air and earth, and as contrary as fire and water ? All true love is, *motus animi ad fruendum Deo propter ipsum ; se et proximo propter Deum*—a motion of the soul towards the enjoyment of God for himself, and his neighbours for God's sake; so that he can never truly love man who doth not love his Maker. God is the only foundation upon which we can build friendship; therefore such as live without him, cannot love us in him. That building which is loose, without this foundation can never stand long. A wicked man may call that profession he maketh to his brother by the name of love, but heathens can tell us that virtue alone is the hand which can twist the cords of love; that other combinations are but a confederacy, and all other but conjunctions in hypocrisy.—*George Swinnock.*

Verse 5.—Wheresoever we perceive any people to worship God truly after his word, there we may be certain the church of Christ to be, unto the which we ought to associate ourselves, and to desire, with the prophet David, to praise God in the midst of this church. But if we behold, through the iniquity of time, congregations to be made with counterfeit religion, otherwise than the word of God doth teach, we ought then, if we be required to be companions thereof, to say again with David, "*I have hated the synagogue of the malignant, and will not sit with the wicked.*" In the Apocalypse, the church of Ephesus is highly commended, because she tried such as said they were apostles and were not in deed, and therefore would not abide the company of them. Further, God commanded his people that they should not seek Bethel, neither enter into Galgala, where idolatry was used, by the mouth of his prophet Amos.—*John Philpot (Martyr). Burnt at Smithfield, 1555.*

Verse 5.—How few consider how they harden wicked men by an intimacy with them, whereas withdrawment from them might be a means to make them ashamed! Whilst we are merry and jovial with them, we make them believe their condition is not deplorable, their danger is not great; whereas if we shunned them, as we would a bowed wall, whilst they remain enemies to the Lord, this might do them good, for the startling of them, and rousing of them out of their unhappy security and strong delusions wherein they are held.—*Lewis Stuckley.*

Verse 6.— '*I will wash mine hands in innocency.*" There are two eminent lavers in the gospel; the first, Christ's bath, a hot bath, *lavacrum sanguinis,* the laver of Christ's blood; the second, our bath, a cold bath, *lavacrum lachrimarum,* the laver of repentance. These two mixed together will prove a sovereign composition, wrought first by Christ himself when he sweat water and blood. The first is as that pool of Bethesda into which whosoever enters with *faith,* is healed; the blood of Christ is the true laver of regeneration, a fountain set open for Judah and Jerusalem to wash in. "The blood of Christ purgeth us from all sins." 1 John i. 7. We account it charity in mothers to feed their children with their own milk: how dear is the love of Christ, that both washeth and feeds us with his own blood! No sooner are we born in Christ, but just as our mother's, so Christ's blood is turned into milk, nourishing us to everlasting salvation. What is *calamus benjamini,* or storax, or a thousand rivers of oil, to make us clean, except the Lord purge and cleanse us? No; 'tis his blood "that speaks better things than the blood of Abel." "Unto him, therefore, that loved us, and washed us from our sins in his own blood, and hath made us kings and priests to God and his Father: to him be glory and dominion for ever." Rev. i. 5, 6. But yet 'tis the second bath, the laver of repentance, that must apply and make the first operative. This bath of Mary Magdalene's repentance, it is a kind of rebaptisation, giving strength and effect to the first washing. And it implies a threefold act: first, to bruise our hearts by *contrition:* secondly, to lay our wounds open by *confession* to God; thirdly, to *wash our hands in innocency,* by *satisfaction* to men. . . . . Wash now and wash all; from the crown of the head to the sole of the foot there is nothing in us but wounds and sores; yet above all there is something here in it that David washeth his "*hands.*" Indeed it is not enough to come with wet eyes, if we come with foul hands, to offer with unwashen hands; the Gentiles would not do it. Contrition and confession to God make not up complete repentance without satisfaction to men. *Non remittitur peccatum nisi restituatur ablatum :** it is as true as old, and in old father Latimer's English it is, "Either there must be restitution, open or secret, or else hell." Whoever repairs not the wrong, rejoiceth in the sin. Prov. ii. 14. Where there is no satisfaction, *Non agitur sed fingitur pænitentia,*" saith St. Augustine; and those who restore not all, wash not their whole hands, they dip only the tips of their fingers. Extortion,

---

* Augustine.

rapine, bribery, these are the sins of the hands (sins so proper to the Jews, that they may well conceive as they do that the devil lies all night on their hands, and that is it makes them so diligent in washing) ; but as for us Christians, unless these vipers be shaken off our hands, though ye cover the altar of the Lord with tears, with weeping, and with crying out, yet if you continue in your pollutions, God regards not your offering any more, nor will he receive it with good will at your hands. Matt. ii. 13.—*Isaac Bargrave's Sermon before the House of Commons,* 1623.

Verse 6.—" I will wash my hands in innocency : so will I compass thine altar, O Lord." If *greatness* might have privileged this person from impurity, David was a king ; if the *grace of his soul* might have freed him from the soil of sin, he was " a man after God's own heart." But let not great men put too much trust in their greatness ; the longer the robe is, the more soil it contracts : great power may prove the mother of great damnation. And as for purity, there is a generation that say there's no sin in them, but they deceive themselves ; there is no truth in them. Whatever Rome's φυσιόλογοι pretend for the power of nature, and of free will, we wretched sinners are taught to conceive more truly of our own infirmity. Christ's own apostle, stout Thomas, failed in the faith of his resurrection ; Peter (whose chair is now the pretended seat of infallibility) denied his Master ; David, " a man after God's own heart," hath need of *washing ;* and who can say, I am pure in the sight of the Lord ? Certainly, O Lord, no flesh is righteous in thy sight. No ; this is the best ground of Christian felicity, if with David we fall to a sight of our own sins ; if with the Publican we strike our own breasts, and not with the Pharisee, cast our eye so much upon other men's faults. Why should we, like tailors, measure all men but ourselves ? as if the best of us had not sin enough of his own to think on. See how David calls himself to account for his own sins ; " O Lord, I know mine iniquity, and my sin is ever before me." Oh, the powerful effect of Christian devotion, when by the reflective act of the understanding, science is turned into conscience, and our knowledge is but the glass of our own imperfection, the glass wherein the sight of our sins sends us presently to God, as it did David here, who makes this account only betwixt God and his own soul, *"I, O Lord."* First, he takes his rise from humility and the sight of his own sins, and he soars up by the wings of faith to the throne of God's mercy : *" I, O Lord."* He sees with his own eyes, and not only with the church, or the priest's spectacles ; he is his own penitentiary and confessor ; here's no intercession by saints, no masses, merits, indulgencies, trentals, dirges : all's done betwixt God and him : *"I, O Lord."* With the eye of *humility* he looks to himself and his own misery ; then with the eye of *faith* to God and his mercy, and from both these results a third virtue of *repentance* in the act of preparation, washing the soil of sin in the bath of sorrow : *"I will wash mine hands,"* etc.—*Isaac Bargrave.*

Verse 6.—" I will wash my hands in purity." Referring in these words, to the ordinary use of the sacrifices, he makes a distinction between himself and those who professed to offer the same divine worship, and thrust themselves forward in the services of the sanctuary, as if they alone had the sole right to perform them. As David, therefore, and these hypocrites were one in this respect, that they entered the sanctuary, and surrounded the sacred altar together, he proceeds to show that he was a true worshipper, declaring that he not only diligently attended to the external rites, but came to worship God with unfeigned devotion. It is obvious that he alludes to the solemn rite of washing which was practised under the law. He, accordingly, reproves the gross superstition of hypocrites, who, in seeking only the purification of water, neglected true purification ; whereas it was God's design, in the appointment of the outward sign, to put men in mind of their inward pollution, and thus to encourage them to repentance. The outward washing alone, instead of profiting hypocrites, kept them at a greater distance from God. When the Psalmist, therefore, says, *" I will wash my hands in innocence,"* he intimates that they only gather more pollution and filth by their washings. The Hebrew word, נִקָּיוֹן *nikkayon,* signifies the cleanness of anything, and is figuratively used for *innocence.* We thus see, that as hypocrites derive no moral purity whatever from their washings, David mocks at the labour with which they vainly toil and torment themselves in such rites.—*John Calvin.*

Verse 6.—" I will wash mine hands," etc. David willing to express his coming with a pure heart to pray to God, doth it by this similitude of a priest ; that as a priest *washes his hands,* and *then offers oblation,* so had he constantly joined *purity* and *devotion* together.—*Henry Hammond.*

Verse 6.—" *In innocency.*" The very ἀκμή and crown of all our preparation, the purest water we can wash in, is *innocency;* and *innocency* is a virtue of the heart as well as of the hand. " Cleanse your hands, ye sinners ; and purify your hearts, ye double minded." James iv. 8. I could wish our washing might be like Cyprian's baptising, *ad tincturam,* even till we were dyed in repentance and the blood of Christ. Let the quantity of thy sins be the measure of thy repentance. First offer thine *innocency,* then thy *sacrifice.* It is not enough that you come this day by order, you must come with *innocency.* God requires the duty of the second table, as well as of the first ; he abhors the outward act of piety where he finds no conscience and practice of *innocency.*—*Isaac Bargrave.*

Verse 6 (first clause).—One morning, as Gotthold was pouring water into a basin, he recollected the words of Scripture : " *I will wash my hands in innocency,*" a text which shows how diligently the royal prophet had endeavoured to lead a blameless life, and walk habitually in the fear of God. Upon this he mused, and said, Henceforth, my God, every time I pour out water to wash with, I will call to mind that it is my duty to cleanse my hands from wicked actions, my mouth from wicked words, and my heart from wicked lusts and desires, that so I may be enabled to lift holy hands unto thee, and with unspotted lips and heart worship thee, to the best of my ability. What will it profit me to strive after outward purity, if my heart is filthy and abominable in thy sight ? Can the food nourish me which I have earned with polluted hands, or seized with violence and injustice, or eaten with insensibility and ingratitude ? Ah ! no, my God ; far from me be food like this. My first care shall be to maintain a blameless walk ; my next, when I have thoughtlessly defiled myself, to cleanse and wash away the stain, and remove mine iniquity from thine eyes. " *Purge me, O my God, and I shall be clean : wash me, and I shall be whiter than snow.*" Psalm li. 7.—*Christian Scriver* (1629–1693), in " *Gotthold's Emblems.*"

Verse 6.—" *I will compass thine altar, O Lord.*" On the next day after this feast [the Feast of Tabernacles], the people compassed the altar seven times, with palm boughs in their hands, in the remembrance of the overthrow of Jericho. . . . Not only the boughs, but the days of this whole Feast of Tabernacles, were termed *Hosannoth,* from the usual acclamation of the people whilst they carried the boughs up and down.—*Thomas Godwyn, B.D.* (1587—1643), in " *Moses and Aaron.*"

Verse 6.—By the phrase *compassing the altar,* either he alludes to some Levitical custom of going about the altar, as the priests did in the oblation of their sacrifices ; and the people, especially those of them who were more devout and zealous, who possibly moved from place to place, but still within their own court, that they might discern what was done on the several sides of the altar, and so be the more affected with it ; or rather he implies that he would offer many sacrifices together, which would employ the priests round about the altar.—*Matthew Pool.*

Verse 8.—" *Lord, I have loved the habitation of thy house,*" etc. " I have in my congregation," said a venerable minister of the gospel, " a worthy, aged woman, who has for many years been so deaf as not to distinguish the loudest sound, and yet she is always one of the first in the meeting. On asking the reason of her constant attendance (as it was impossible for her to hear my voice), she answered, ' Though I cannot hear you, I come to God's house because I love it, and would be found in his ways ; and he gives me many a sweet thought upon the text when it is pointed out to me : another reason is, because there I am in the best company, in the more immediate presence of God, and among his saints, the honourable of the earth. I am not satisfied with serving God in private ; it is my duty and privilege to honour him regularly in public." What a reproof this is to those who have their hearing, and yet always come to a place of worship late, or not at all !—*K. Arvine.*

Verse 9.—" *Gather not my soul with sinners.*" Now is the time that people should be in care and concern, that their souls be not gathered with sinners in the other world. In discoursing from this doctrine we shall—1. Consider some things implied in it. 2. Show who are the sinners, that we are to have a horror of our souls being gathered with in the other world. 3. What it is for one's soul to be gathered with sinners in the other world. 4. Consider this care and concern, or show what is implied in this earnest request, " Gather not my soul with sinners."

5. Give the reasons why we should be in such care and concern. 6. Make application.

Death is the gathering time, which the Psalmist has in view in the text. Ye have a time here that ye call the gathering time, about the term when the servants are going away, wherein ye gather your strayed sheep, that every one may get their own again. Death is God's gathering time wherein he gets the souls belonging to him, and the devil those belonging to him. They did go long together, but then they are parted ; and saints are taken home to the congregation of saints, and sinners to the congregation of sinners. And it concerns us to say, " Gather not my soul with sinners." Whoever be our people here, God's people or the devil's, death will gather our souls to them.

It is a horrible thing to be gathered with sinners in the other world. To think of our souls being gathered with them there, may make the hair of one's head stand up. Many now like no gathering like the gathering with sinners ; it is the very delight of their hearts, it makes a brave jovial life in their eyes. And it is a pain to them to be gathered with saints, to be detained before the Lord on a Sabbath-day. But to be gathered with them in the other world, is a horror to all sorts. 1. The saints have a horror of it, as in the text. To think to be staked down in their company in the other world would be a hell of itself to the godly. David never had such a horror of the society of the diseased, the persecuted, etc., as of sinners. He is content to be gathered with saints of whatever condition ; but, " Lord," says he, " Gather not my soul with sinners." 2. The wicked themselves have a horror of it. Numb. xxiii. 10. " Let me die the death of the righteous," said the wicked Balaam, " and let my last end be like his." Though they would be content to live with them, or be with them in life, their consciences bear witness that they have a horror of being with them in death. They would live with sinners, but they would die with saints. A poor, unreasonable, self-condemning thought.—*Thomas Boston.*

Verse 9.—" *Gather not my soul with sinners.*" Bind me not up in the same bundle with them, like the tares for the fire. Matt. xiii. 30. The contrast to this is seen in the following Psalm (verse 10), " When my father and my mother forsake me, then the Lord will take me up ; " literally, will *gather me* to his fold.— *Christopher Wordsworth.*

Verse 9.—" *Gather not my soul with sinners.*" The Lord hath a harvest and a gleaning time also, set for cutting down and binding together, in the fellowship of judgments, God's enemies, who have followed the same course of sinning : for here we are given to understand that God will " *gather their souls*," and so will let none escape.—*David Dickson.*

Verse 9.—" *Gather not my soul with sinners.*" After all, it may be objected that this concern seems to be common to saints and sinners. Even a wicked Balaam said, " Let me die the death of the righteous, and let my last end be like his." Numb. xxiii. 10. Take a few differences between them in this matter. 1. It is separation from Christ that makes the saints to have a horror at being gathered with sinners hereafter. Separation from Christ is the main ground of the believer's horror : but if other things were to be right with the sinner in the other world, he would be easy under separation from Christ. 2. The believer has a horror at being gathered with sinners on account of their filthiness ; but the thing that makes the sinner concerned is the prospect of punishment. No doubt, a principle of self-preservation must make punishment frightful to all ; but abstracted from that, the saints have a concern not to be gathered with sinners in the other world, upon account of their unholiness and filthiness. " He who is filthy, let him be filthy still," is enough to make a saint abhor the lot of sinners in the life to come. 3. The concern of the saints has a mighty influence upon them, to make them study holiness here ; but sinners live unholy for all their concern. " And every man that hath this hope in him purifieth himself, even as he is pure." 1 John iii. 3. What hope ? The hope of seeing Christ as he is, and of being perfectly like him, of being separated from sinners. 4. Lastly, the concern of the saints is such, that they do with purpose of heart come out from among sinners more and more in this world ; but sinners are not concerned to be separated from sinners here. Balaam wished to die the death of the righteous ; but he had no concern to live the life of the righteous, and to be separated from sinners here.— *James Scot,* 1773.

Verses 9—12.—David prays that God would not " gather his soul with sinners, whose right hand is full of bribes ; " such as, for advantage, would be bribed to sin, to which wicked gang he opposeth himself, verse 11 : " *But as for me, I will walk in mine integrity ;* " where he tells us what kept him from being corrupted and enticed, as they were, from God—it was his *integrity.* A soul walking in its integrity will take bribes neither from men, nor sin itself ; and therefore he saith (verse 12), " His foot stood in an even place ; " or, as some read it, " My foot standeth in righteousness."—*William Gurnall.*

Verse 10.—" *Their right hand is full of bribes.*" If the great men in Turkey should use their religion of Mahomet to sell, as our patrons commonly sell benefices here (the office of preaching, the office of salvation), it should be taken as an intolerable thing ; the Turk would not suffer it in his commonwealth. Patrons be charged to see the office done, and not to seek a lucre and a gain by their patronship. There was a patron in England that had a benefice fallen into his hand, and a good brother of mine came unto him, and brought him thirty apples in a dish, and gave them to his man to carry them to his master. It is like he gave one to his man for his labour, to make up the gain, and so there was thirty-one. This man cometh to his master, and presented him with the dish of apples, saying, " Sir, such a man hath sent you a dish of fruit, and desireth you to be good unto him for such a benefice." " Tush, tush," quoth he, " this is no apple matter, I will none of his apples, I have as good as these (or any he hath) in mine own orchard." The man came to the priest again, and told him what his master said. " Then," quoth the priest, " desire him yet to prove one of them for my sake, he shall find them much better than they look for." He cut one of them, and found ten pieces of gold in it. " Marry," quoth he, " this is a good apple." The priest standing not far off, hearing what the gentleman said, cried out and answered, " they are all one apples, I warrant you, sir ; they grew all on one tree, and have all one taste." " Well, he is a good fellow, let him have it," quoth the patron, etc. Get you a graft of this same tree, and I warrant you it shall stand you in better stead than all St. Paul's learning.—*Hugh Latimer.*

Verse 10.—" *Bribes.*" They that see furthest into the law, and most clearly discern the cause of justice, if they suffer the dust of bribes to be thrown into their sight, their eyes will water and twinkle, and fall at last to blind connivance. It is a wretched thing when justice is made a hackney that may be backed for money, and put on with golden spurs, even to the desired journey's end of injury and iniquity. Far be from our souls this wickedness, that the ear which should be open to complaints should be stopped with the earwax of partiality. Alas ! poor truth, that she must now be put to the charges of a golden earpick, or she cannot be heard !—*Thomas Adams.*

Verse 10.—

> What makes all doctrines plain and clear ?
> About two hundred pounds a-year,
> And that which was proved true before
> Proved false again ? Two hundred more.

Samuel Butler (1600—1680), *in* " *Hudibras.*" Part III. Canto I.

Verse 12 (first clause).—The upright man's " *foot,*" is said to " *stand in an even place ;* " he walks not haltingly and uncomely, as those who go in unequal ways, which are hobbling, and up and down, or those whose feet and legs are not even (as Solomon saith), " The legs of the lame are not equal," and so cannot *stand in an even place*, because one is long and the other short ; the sincere man's feet are *even*, and legs of a length, as I may say ; his care alike conscientious to the whole will of God. The hypocrite, like the badger, hath one foot shorter than another ; or, like a foundered horse, he doth not stand, as we say, right of all four ; one foot at least you shall perceive he favours, loth to put it down.—*William Gurnall.*

Verse 12.—" *On an even place.*" As a man whose feet are firmly fixed upon even ground is apprehensive of no fall, so the pious worshippers of Jehovah feel no dread lest their adversaries should finally triumph over them.—*William Walford.*

HINTS TO PREACHERS.

Verse 1.—I. *Two inseparable companions*—faith and holiness. II. *The blessedness of the man who possesses them.* He needs not fear the judgment, nor the danger of the way. III. *The only means of procuring them.*

Verse 1 (*last sentence*).—The upholding power of trust in God.

Verse 2.—*Divine examinations.* Their variety, severity, searching nature, accuracy, certainty: when to be desired, and when to be dreaded.

Verse 3.—Delight for the eyes and safety for the feet; or the good man's sweet contemplation and holy practice; or the heavenly compound of godliness—motive, and motion, enjoying and acting, love and truth, free grace and good works.

Verse 3.—" *Thy lovingkindness is before mine eyes.*" It might be well to follow David and to keep the lovingkindness of God before *our* eyes. This should be done in four ways:—I. As a subject of contemplation. II. As the source of encouragement. III. As an incitement to praise. IV. As an example for imitation.—*William Jay.*

Verse 4.—" *Vain persons.*" Who they are. Why they are to be avoided. What will become of them. " *Dissemblers.*" Describe this numerous family. Show what their objects are. The mischief done to believers by their craftiness. The need of shunning them, and their fearful end.

Verse 5.—*Bad company.* Cases of its evil results, excuses for it answered, warnings given, motives urged for relinquishing.

Verse 6.—The necessity of personal holiness in order to acceptable worship.

Verse 7.—I. The believer's calling—a publisher. II. The author selected, and the quality of his works. " *Thy wondrous works.*" III. The mode of advertising—" *voice of thanksgiving,*" " *tell,*" etc.

Verse 8.—God's house. Why we love it. What we love in it. How we show our love. How our love will be rewarded.

Verse 9.—See " Spurgeon's Sermons," No. 524. " The Saints' Horror at the Sinners' Hell."

Verse 11.—The best men needing redemption and mercy; or the outward walk before men, and the secret walk with God.

Verse 12.—Secure standing, honoured position, grateful praise.

Verse 12 (*last clause*).—Congregational Psalmody, and our personal share in it.

THE BIRTHPLACE OF C. H. SPURGEON, AT KELVEDON.

Specially drawn for "The Treasury of David" by E. H. Fitchew.

THE METROPOLITAN TABERNACLE: The Scene of C. H. Spurgeon's famous Ministry.

Specially drawn for "The Treasury of David" by E. H. Fitchew.

THE
TREASURY OF DAVID

PREFACE.

GREATLY encouraged by the generous reception awarded to my first volume, I have laboured on with diligence, and am now able to present the reader with the second instalment of my work. Whether life and health shall be given me to complete my task, which will probably extend to six volumes, remains with the gracious Preserver of men ; but with his aid and allowance, my face is set towards that design, and I pray that my purpose may be achieved, if it be for the divine glory, and for the good of his church.

In this volume, which contains thirty-one sacred odes, we have several of the more memorable and precious of Zion's songs. In commenting upon some of them, I have been overwhelmed with awe, and said with Jacob, " How dreadful is this place, it is none other than the house of God." Especially was this case with the fifty-first ; I postponed expounding it week after week, feeling more and more my inability for the work. Often I sat down to it, and rose up again without having penned a line. It is a bush burning with fire yet not consumed, and out of it a voice seemed to cry to me, " Draw not nigh hither, put off thy shoes from off thy feet." The Psalm is very human, its cries and sobs are of one born of woman ; but it is freighted with an inspiration all divine, as if the Great Father were putting words into his child's mouth. Such a Psalm may be wept over, absorbed into the soul, and exhaled again in devotion ; but, commented on—ah ! where is he who having attempted it can do other than blush at his defeat ?

I have followed the same plan as in the former volume, not only because I am committed to it by the law of uniformity, but also because it is on the whole advantageous. Some have suggested alterations, but many more have commended the very features which would have been improved away, and therefore I have continued in the selfsame method.

Greater use has, in this volume, been made of the Latin writers. Extracts have been made not only from those which are condensed in Pool's Synopsis ; but from many others. These works are a mine of exposition far too little known. If the index shall serve to introduce fresh expositions to my ministerial readers, I shall not have laboured in vain.

The acknowledgments of obligation made in Volume I. might very justly be repeated as concerning Volume II. ; the reader will consider them as again recorded. It may also be needful to repeat the statement that as I give the name of each Author quoted, each authority is personally responsible for his own sentiments ; and I do not wish it to be supposed that I endorse all that is inserted. It is often useful to us to know what has been said by authors whose views we could by no means accept.

More and more is the conviction forced upon my heart that every man must traverse the territory of the Psalms himself if he would know what a goodly land they are. They flow with milk and honey, but not to strangers; they are only fertile to lovers of their hills and vales. None but the Holy Spirit can give a man the key to the Treasury of David; and even he gives it rather to experience than to study. Happy he who for himself knows the secret of the Psalms.

If permitted by the Great Master whom I serve, I shall now proceed with another portion of this TREASURY OF DAVID; but the labour and research are exceedingly great, and my other occupations are very pressing, and therefore I must crave the patience of the Christian public.

C. H. Spurgeon.

INDEX

OF AUTHORS QUOTED OR REFERRED TO.

PSALM XXVII.

TITLE AND SUBJECT.—*Nothing whatever can be drawn from the title as to the time when this Psalm was written, for the heading, " A Psalm of David," is common to so many of the Psalms ; but if one may judge from the matter of the song, the writer was pursued by enemies, verses 2 and 3, was shut out from the house of the Lord, verse 4, was just parting from father and mother, verse 10, and was subject to slander, verse 12 ; do not all these meet in the time when Doeg, the Edomite, spake against him to Saul ? It is a song of cheerful hope, well fitted for those in trial who have learned to lean upon the Almighty arm. The Psalm may with profit be read in a threefold way, as the language of David, of the Church, and of the Lord Jesus. The plenitude of Scripture will thus appear the more wonderful.*

DIVISION.—*The poet first sounds forth his sure confidence in his God, 1—3, and his love of communion with him, 4—6. He then betakes himself to prayer, 7—12, and concludes with an acknowledgment of the sustaining power of faith in his own case, and an exhortation to others to follow his example.*

EXPOSITION.

THE LORD *is* my light and my salvation ; whom shall I fear ? the LORD *is* the strength of my life ; of whom shall I be afraid ?

2 When the wicked, *even* mine enemies and my foes, came upon me to eat up my flesh they stumbled and fell.

3 Though an host should encamp against me, my heart shall not fear : though war should rise against me, in this *will* I *be* confident.

1. " *The Lord is my light and my salvation.*"—Here is personal interest, " *my light,*" " *my salvation ;* " the soul is assured of it, and therefore, declaring it boldly. " *My light*"—into the soul at the new birth divine light is poured as the precursor of salvation ; where there is not enough light to see our own darkness and to long for the Lord Jesus, there is no evidence of salvation. Salvation finds us in the dark, but it does not leave us there ; it gives light to those who sit in the valley of the shadow of death. After conversion our God is our joy, comfort, guide, teacher, and in every sense our light ; he is light within, light around, light reflected from us, and light to be revealed to us. Note, it is not said merely that the Lord gives light, but that he " *is* " light ; nor that he gives salvation, but that he is salvation ; he, then, who by faith has laid hold upon God has all covenant blessings in his possession. Every light is not the sun, but the sun is the father of all lights. This being made sure as a fact, the argument drawn from it is put in the form of a question, " *Whom shall I fear ?* " A question which is its own answer. The powers of darkness are not to be feared, for the Lord, our light, destroys them ; and the damnation of hell is not to be dreaded by us, for the Lord is our salvation. This is a very different challenge from that of boastful Goliath, for it is based upon a very different foundation ; it rests not upon the conceited vigour of an arm of flesh, but upon the real power of the omnipotent I AM. " *The Lord is the strength of my life.*" Here is a third glowing epithet, to show that the writer's hope was fastened with a threefold cord which could not be broken. We may well accumulate terms of praise where the Lord lavishes deeds of grace. Our life derives all its strength from him who is the author of it ; and if he deigns to make us strong we cannot be weakened by all the machinations of the adversary. " *Of whom shall I be afraid ?* " The bold question looks into the future as well as the present. " If God be for us," who can be against us, either now or in time to come ?

2. This verse records a past deliverance, and is an instance of the way in which experience should be employed to reassure our faith in times of trial. Each word is instructive. " *When the wicked.*" It is a hopeful sign for us when the wicked hate us ; if our foes were godly men it would be a sore sorrow, but as for the wicked their hatred is better than their love. " *Even mine enemies and my foes.*"

There were many of them, they were of different sorts, but they were unanimous in mischief and hearty in hatred. "*Came upon me*"—advanced to the attack, leaping upon the victim like a lion upon its prey. "*To eat up my flesh*," like cannibals they would make a full end of the man, tear him limb from limb, and make a feast for their malice. The enemies of our souls are not deficient in ferocity, they yield no quarter, and ought to have none in return. See in what danger David was; in the grip and grasp of numerous, powerful, and cruel enemies, and yet observe his perfect safety and their utter discomfiture! "*They stumbled and fell.*" God's breath blew them off their legs. There were stones in the way which they never reckoned upon, and over these they made an ignominious tumble. This was literally true in the case of our Lord in Gethsemane, when those who came to take him went backward and fell to the ground; and herein he was a prophetic representative of all wrestling believers who, rising from their knees shall, by the power of faith, throw their foes upon their faces.

3. "*Though an host should encamp against me, my heart shall not fear.*" Before the actual conflict, while as yet the battle is untried, the warrior's heart, being held in suspense, is very liable to become fluttered. The encamping host often inspires greater dread than the same host in actual affray. Young tells us of some—

> "Who feel a thousand deaths in fearing one."

Doubtless the shadow of anticipated trouble is, to timorous minds, a more prolific source of sorrow than the trouble itself, but faith puts a strengthening plaister to the back of courage, and throws out of the window the dregs of the cup of trembling. "*Though war should rise against me, in this will I be confident.*" When it actually comes to push of pike, faith's shield will ward off the blow; and if the first brush should be but the beginning of a war, yet faith's banners will wave in spite of the foe. Though battle should succeed battle, and one campaign should be followed by another, the believer will not be dismayed at the length of the conflict. Reader, this third verse is the comfortable and logical inference from the second, confidence is the child of experience. Have you been delivered out of great perils? then set up your ensign, wait at your watch-fire, and let the enemy do his worst.

4 One *thing* have I desired of the LORD, that will I seek after; that I may dwell in the house of the LORD all the days of my life to behold the beauty of the LORD, and to enquire in his temple.

5 For in the time of trouble he shall hide me in his pavilion: in the secret of his tabernacle shall he hide me; he shall set me up upon a rock.

6 And now shall mine head be lifted up above mine enemies round about me: therefore will I offer in his tabernacle sacrifices of joy; I will sing, yea, I will sing praises unto the LORD.

4. "*One thing.*" Divided aims tend to distraction, weakness, disappointment. The man of one book is eminent, the man of one pursuit is successful. Let all our affection be bound up in one affection, and that affection set upon heavenly things. "*Have I desired*"—what we cannot at once attain, it is well to desire. God judges us very much by the desire of our hearts. He who rides a lame horse is not blamed by his master for want of speed, if he makes all the haste he can, and would make more if he could; God takes the will for the deed with his children. "*Of the Lord.*" This is the right target for desires, this is the well into which to dip our buckets, this is the door to knock at, the bank to draw upon; desire of men, and lie on the dunghill with Lazarus: desire of the Lord, and be carried of angels into Abraham's bosom. Our desires of the Lord should be sanctified, humble, constant, submissive, fervent, and it is well if, as with the Psalmist, they are all molten into one mass. Under David's painful circumstances we might have expected him to desire repose, safety, and a thousand other good things, but no, he has set his heart on the pearl, and leaves the rest. "*That will I seek after.*" Holy desires must lead to resolute action. The old proverb says, "Wishers and woulders are never good housekeepers," and "wishing never fills a sack." Desires are seeds which must be sown in the good soil of activity for they will yield no harvest. We shall find our desires to be like clouds without

rain, unless followed up by practical endeavours. *"That I may dwell in the house of the Lord all the days of my life."* For the sake of communion with the King, David longed to dwell always in the palace; so far from being wearied with the services of the Tabernacle, he longed to be constantly engaged in them, as his life-long pleasure. He desired above all things to be one of the household of God, a home-born child, living at home with his Father. This is our dearest wish, only we extend it to those days of our immortal life which have not yet dawned. We pine for our Father's house above, the home of our souls; if we may but dwell there for ever, we care but little for the goods or ills of this poor life. "Jerusalem the golden" is the one and only goal of our heart's longings. *"To behold the beauty of the Lord."* An exercise both for earthly and heavenly worshippers. We must not enter the assemblies of the saints in order to see and be seen, or merely to hear the minister; we must repair to the gatherings of the righteous, intent upon the gracious object of learning more of the loving Father, more of the glorified Jesus, more of the mysterious Spirit, in order that we may the more lovingly admire, and the more reverently adore our glorious God. What a word is that, " *the beauty of the Lord !* " Think of it, dear reader! Better far—behold it by faith! What a sight will that be when every faithful follower of Jesus shall behold "the King in his beauty!" Oh, for that infinitely blessed vision! *"And to enquire in his temple."* We should make our visits to the Lord's house enquirers' meetings. Not seeking sinners alone, but assured saints should be enquirers. We must enquire as to the will of God and how we may do it; as to our interest in the heavenly city, and how we may be more assured of it. We shall not need to make enquiries in heaven, for there we shall know even as we are known; but meanwhile we should sit at Jesus' feet, and awaken all our faculties to learn of him.

5. This verse gives an excellent reason for the Psalmist's desire after communion with God, namely, that he was thus secured in the hour of peril. *"For in the time of trouble,"* that needy time, that time when others forsake me, *"he shall hide me in his pavilion:"* he shall give me the best of shelter in the worst of danger. The royal pavilion was erected in the centre of the army, and around it all the mighty men kept guard at all hours; thus in that divine sovereignty which almighty power is sworn to maintain, the believer peacefully is hidden, hidden not by himself furtively, but by the king, who hospitably entertains him. *"In the secret of his tabernacle shall he hide me."* Sacrifice aids sovereignty in screening the elect from harm. No one of old dared to enter the most holy place on pain of death; and if the Lord has hidden his people there, what foe shall venture to molest them? *"He shall set me up upon a rock."* Immutability, eternity, and infinite power here come to the aid of sovereignty and sacrifice. How blessed is the standing of the man whom God himself sets on high above his foes, upon an impregnable rock which never can be stormed! Well may we desire to dwell with the Lord who so effectually protects his people.

6. *"And now shall mine head be lifted up above mine enemies round about me."*— He is quite sure of it. Godly men of old prayed in faith, nothing wavering, and spoke of the answer to their prayers as a certainty. David was by faith so sure of a glorious victory over all those who beset him, that he arranged in his own heart what he would do when his foes lay all prostrate before him; that arrangement was such as gratitude suggested. *"Therefore will I offer in his tabernacles sacrifices of joy."* That place for which he longed in his conflict, should see his thankful joy in his triumphant return. He does not speak of jubilations to be offered in his palace, and feastings in his banqueting halls, but holy mirth he selects as most fitting for so divine a deliverance. *"I will sing."* This is the most natural mode of expressing thankfulness. *"Yea, I will sing praises unto the Lord."* The vow is confirmed by repetition, and explained by addition, which addition vows all the praise unto Jehovah. Let who will be silent, the believer when his prayer is heard, must and will make his praise to be heard also; and let who will sing unto the vanities of the world, the believer reserves his music for the Lord alone.

7 Hear, O LORD, *when* I cry with my voice: have mercy also upon me, and answer me.

8 *When thou saidst,* Seek ye my face; my heart said unto thee, Thy face, LORD, will I seek.

9 Hide not thy face *far* from me; put not thy servant away in anger:

thou hast been my help; leave me not, neither forsake me, O God of my salvation.

10 When my father and my mother forsake me, then the LORD will take me up.

11 Teach me thy way, O LORD, and lead me in a plain path, because of mine enemies.

12 Deliver me not over unto the will of mine enemies: for false witnesses are risen up against me, and such as breathe out cruelty.

7. "*Hear, O Lord, when I cry with my voice.*"—The pendulum of spirituality swings from prayer to praise. The voice which in the last verse was tuned to music is here turned to crying. As a good soldier, David knew how to handle his weapons, and found himself much at home with the weapon of "all prayer." Note his anxiety to be heard. Pharisees care not a fig for the Lord's hearing them, so long as they are heard of men, or charm their own pride with their sounding devotions; but with a genuine man, the Lord's ear is everything. The *voice* may be profitably used even in private prayer; for though it is unnecessary, it is often helpful, and aids in preventing distractions. "*Have mercy also upon me.*" Mercy is the hope of sinners and the refuge of saints. All acceptable petitioners dwell much upon this attribute. "*And answer me.*" We may expect answers to prayer, and should not be easy without them any more than we should be if we had written a letter to a friend upon important business, and had received no reply.

8. In this verse we are taught that if we would have the Lord hear our voice, we must be careful to respond to *his* voice. The true heart should echo the will of God as the rocks among the Alps repeat in sweetest music the notes of the peasant's horn. Observe, that the command was in the plural, to all the saints, "*Seek ye;*" but the man of God turned it into the singular by a personal application, "*Thy face, Lord, will I seek.*" The voice of the Lord is very effectual where all other voices fail, "*When thou saidst,*" then my "*heart,*" my inmost nature was moved to an obedient reply. Note the promptness of the response—no sooner said than done; as soon as God said "*seek,*" the heart said, "*I will seek.*" Oh, for more of this holy readiness! Would to God that we were more plastic to the divine hand, more sensitive of the touch of God's Spirit.

9. "*Hide not thy face far from me.*" The word "*far*" is not in the original, and is a very superfluous addition of the translators, since even the least hiding of the Lord's face is a great affliction to a believer. The command to seek the Lord's face would be a painful one if the Lord, by withdrawing himself, rendered it impossible for the seeker to meet with him. A smile from the Lord is the greatest of comforts, his frown the worst of ills. "*Put not thy servant away in anger.*" Other servants had been put away when they proved unfaithful, as for instance, his predecessor Saul; and this made David, while conscious of many faults, most anxious that divine long-suffering should continue him in favour. This is a most appropriate prayer for us under a similar sense of unworthiness. "*Thou hast been my help.*" How truly can we join in this declaration; for many years, in circumstances of varied trial, we have been upheld by our God, and must and will confess our obligation. "Ingratitude," it is said, "is natural to fallen man," but to spiritual men it is unnatural and detestable. "*Leave me not, neither forsake me.*" A prayer for the future, and an inference from the past. If the Lord had meant to leave us, why did he begin with us? Past help is but a waste of effort if the soul now be deserted. The first petition, "*leave me not,*" may refer to temporary desertions, and the second word to the final withdrawal of grace, both are to be prayed against; and concerning the second, we have immutable promises to urge. "*O God of my salvation.*" A sweet title worthy of much meditation.

10. "*When my father and my mother forsake me.*" These dear relations will be the last to desert me, but if the milk of human kindness should dry up even from their breasts, there is a Father who never forgets. Some of the greatest of the saints have been cast out by their families, and persecuted for righteousness' sake. "*Then the Lord will take me up.*" Will espouse my cause, will uplift me from my woes, will carry me in his arms, will elevate me above my enemies, will at last receive me to his eternal dwelling place.

11. "*Teach me thy way, O Lord.*" He does not pray to be indulged with his own way, but to be informed as to the path in which the righteous Jehovah would

have him walk. This prayer evinces an humble sense of personal ignorance, great teachableness of spirit, and cheerful obedience of heart. "*Lead me in a plain path.*" Help is here sought as well as direction; we not only need a map of the way, but a guide to assist us in the journey. A path is here desired which shall be open, honest, straightforward, in opposition to the way of cunning, which is intricate, tortuous, dangerous. Good men seldom succeed in fine speculations and doubtful courses; plain simplicity is the best spirit for an heir of heaven: let us leave shifty tricks and political expediences to the citizens of the world—the New Jerusalem owns plain men for its citizens. Esau was a cunning hunter, Jacob was a plain man, dwelling in tents. "*Because of mine enemies.*" These will catch us if they can, but the way of manifest, simple honesty is safe from their rage. It is wonderful to observe how honest simplicity baffles and outwits the craftiness of wickedness. Truth is wisdom. "Honesty is the best policy."

12. "*Deliver me not over unto the will of mine enemies;*" or I should be like a victim cast to the lions, to be rent to pieces and utterly devoured. God be thanked that our foes cannot have their way with us, or Smithfield would soon be on a blaze again. "*For false witnesses are risen up against me.*" Slander is an old-fashioned weapon out of the armoury of hell, and is still in plentiful use; and no matter how holy a man may be, there will be some who will defame him. "Give a dog an ill name, and hang him;" but glory be to God, the Lord's people are not dogs, and their ill names do not injure them. "*And such as breathe out cruelty.*" It is their vital breath to hate the good; they cannot speak without cursing them; such was Paul before conversion. They who breathe out cruelty may well expect to be sent to breathe their native air in hell; let persecutors beware!

13 *I had fainted*, unless I had believed to see the goodness of the LORD in the land of the living.

13. Faintness of heart is a common infirmity; even he who slew Goliath was subject to its attacks. Faith puts its bottle of cordial to the lip of the soul, and so prevents fainting. Hope is heaven's balm for present sorrow. In this land of the dying, it is our blessedness to be looking and longing for our fair portion in the land of the living, whence the goodness of God has banished the wickedness of man, and where holy spirits charm with their society those persecuted saints who were vilified and despised among men. We must believe to see, not see to believe; we must wait the appointed time, and stay our soul's hunger with fore-tastes of the Lord's eternal goodness which shall soon be our feast and our song.

14 Wait on the LORD : be of good courage, and he shall strengthen thine heart : wait, I say, on the LORD.

14. "*Wait on the Lord.*" Wait at his door with prayer; wait at his foot with humility; wait at his table with service; wait at his window with expectancy. Suitors often win nothing but the cold shoulder from earthly patrons after long and obsequious waiting; he speeds best whose patron is in the skies. "*Be of good courage.*" A soldier's motto. Be it mine. Courage we shall need, and for the exercise of it we have as much reason as necessity, if we are soldiers of King Jesus. "*And he shall strengthen thine heart.*" He can lay the plaister right upon the weak place. Let the heart be strengthened, and the whole machine of humanity is filled with power; a strong heart makes a strong arm. What strength is this which God himself gives to the heart? Read the "Book of Martyrs," and see its glorious deeds of prowess; go to God rather, and get such power thyself. "*Wait, I say, on the Lord.*" David, in the words "*I say*," sets his own private seal to the word which, as an inspired man, he had been moved to write. It is *his* testimony as well as the command of God, and indeed he who writes these scanty notes has himself found it so sweet, so reviving, so profitable to draw near to God, that on his own account he also feels bound to write, "*Wait, I say, on the Lord.*"

EXPLANATORY NOTES AND QUAINT SAYINGS.

Verse 1.—" *The Lord is my light and my salvation ; whom shall I fear ?* "
Alice Driver, martyr, at her examination, put all the doctors to silence, so that
they had not a word to say, but one looked upon another ; then she said, " Have
you no more to say ? God be honoured, you be not able to resist the Spirit of
God, in me, a poor woman.   I was an honest poor man's daughter, never brought
up at the University as you have been ; but I have driven the plough many a time
before my father, I thank God ; yet, notwithstanding, in the defence of God's
truth, and in the cause of my Master, Christ, by his grace I will set my foot against
the foot of any of you all, in the maintenance and defence of the same ; and if I
had a thousand lives they should go for payment thereof." So the Chancellor
condemned her, and she returned to the prison joyful.—*Charles Bradbury.*

Verse 1.—" *The Lord is my light,*" etc. St. John tells us, that " in Christ was
life ; and the life was the light of men ; " but he adds that " the light shineth in
darkness ; and the darkness comprehended it not."   John i. 4, 5.   There is a
great difference between the *light*, and the eye that sees it.   A blind man may know
a great deal about the shining of the sun, but it does not shine for him—it gives
him no light.   So, to know that " God is light," is one thing (1 John i. 5), and
to be able to say, " The Lord is *my* light," is quite another thing.   The Lord must
be the light by which the way of life is made plain to us—the light by which we
may see to walk in that way—the light that exposes the darkness of sin—the light by
which we can discover the hidden sins of our own hearts. When he is thus *our
light*, then he is *our salvation* also.   He is pledged to guide us right ; not only to
show us sin, but to save us from it.   Not only to make us see God's hatred of sin,
and his curse upon it, but also to draw us unto God's love, and to take away the
curse.   With the Lord lighting us along the road of salvation, who, or what need
we fear ?   Our life is hid with Christ in God. Col. iii. 3.   We are weak, very weak,
but his " strength is made perfect in weakness." 2 Cor. xii. 9.   With the Lord
himself pledged to be the strength of our life, of whom need we be afraid ?—*From
Sacramental Meditations on the Twenty-seventh Psalm,* 1843.

Verse 1.—" *The Lord is my light.*"   " *Light*" which makes all things visible,
was the first made of all visible things ; and whether God did it for our example,
or no, I know not ; but ever since, in imitation of this manner of God's proceeding,
the first thing we do when we intend to do anything, is to get us " *light.*"—
Sir Richard Baker.

Verse 1.—" *The Lord is my light.*"   Adorable Sun, cried St. Bernard, I cannot
walk without thee : enlighten my steps, and furnish this barren and ignorant mind
with thoughts worthy of thee.   Adorable fulness of light and heat, be thou the true
noonday of my soul ; exterminate its darkness, disperse its clouds ; burn, dry up,
and consume all its filth and impurities.   Divine Sun, rise upon my mind, and
never set.—*Jean Baptiste Elias Avrillon,* 1652—1729.

Verse 1.—" *Whom shall I fear ?* "   Neither spiritual nor military heroes do
exploits through cowardice.   Courage is a necessary virtue.   In Jehovah is the
best possible foundation for unflinching intrepidity.—*William S. Plumer.*

Verse 1.—"*Of whom shall I be afraid ?* "   I have no notion of a timid, disingenuous
profession of Christ.   Such preachers and professors are like a rat playing at
hide-and-seek behind a wainscot, who puts his head through a hole to see if the
coast is clear, and ventures out if nobody is in the way ; but slinks back again if
danger appears.   We cannot be honest to Christ except we are bold for him.   He
is either worth *all* we can lose for him, or he is worth *nothing.*—*H. G. Salter, A.M.,
in " The Book of Illustrations,*" 1840.

Verse 2.—" *When the wicked, even mine enemies and my foes, came upon me to
eat up my flesh, they stumbled and fell.*"   There is no such dainty dish to a malicious
stomach, as the flesh of an enemy ; it goes down without chewing, and they swallow
it up whole like cormorants.   But though malice have a ravenous stomach, yet she
hath but slow digestion ; though her teeth be sharp, yet her feet are lame, at least
apt to stumble ; and this made well for David, for when his enemies came upon
him to eat up his flesh, because they came upon the feet of malice, " *they stumbled
and fell.*"   A man may *stumble* and yet not *fall ;* but to stumble and fall withal,
is the proper stumbling of " *the wicked,*" and especially of the maliciously wicked ;

and such, it seems, was the stumbling of David's enemies, because the enemies were such ; and such I doubt not shall be the stumbling of mine enemies, because mine are such ; and of what then, of whom now, should I be afraid ?—*Sir Richard Baker*.

Verse 2.—" *When the wicked, even mine enemies and my foes, came upon me to eat up my flesh, they stumbled and fell.*" He describes his enemies by their malice, and by their ruin. 1. His enemies were *cruel enemies*, blood-suckers, eaters of flesh. We call them cannibals. As indeed men that have not grace, if they have greatness, and be opposed, their greatness is inaccessible, one man is a devil to another. The Scripture calls them " wolves, that leave nothing till morning." Zeph. iii. 3. As the great fishes eat up the little ones, so great men they make no more conscience of eating up other men, than of eating bread ; they make no more bones of overthrowing men and undoing them, than of eating bread. " They eat up my people as they eat bread." Psalm xiv. 4. 2. But notwithstanding their cruelty, *they were overthrown.* Saith David, " *When my foes came upon me to eat up my flesh, they stumbled and fell.*" For, indeed, God's children, when they are delivered, it is usually with the confusion of their enemies. God doth two things at once, because the special grievance of God's children it is from inward and outward enemies. He seldom or never delivers them but with the confusion of their enemies. This will be most apparent at the day of judgment, when Satan, and all that are led by his spirit, all the malignant church, shall be sent to their own place, and the church shall be for ever free from all kind of enemies. When the church is most free, then the enemies of the church are nearest to destruction ; like a pair of balances, when they are up at the one end, they are down at the other. So when it is up with the church, down go the enemies.—*Richard Sibbes*.

Verse 2.—" *The wicked, mine enemies.*" The wicked hate the godly ; there is enmity between the seed of the woman and the serpent. Gen. iii. 15. As in nature there is an antipathy between the vine and the bay-tree, the elephant and the dragon. Vultures have an antipathy against sweet smells : so in the wicked there is an antipathy against the people of God ; they hate the sweet perfumes of their graces. It is true the saints have their infirmities ; but the wicked do not hate them for these, but for their holiness ; and from this hatred ariseth open violence : the thief hates the light, therefore would blow it out.—*Thomas Watson*.

Verse 2.—There was great wisdom in the prayer of John Wesley : " Lord, if I must contend, let it not be with thy people." When we have for foes and enemies those who hate good men, we have at least this consolation, that God is not on their side, and therefore it is essentially weak.—*William S. Plumer*.

Verse 3.—" *Though an host should encamp against me,*" etc. He puts the case of the greatest danger that can be. Though an host should encompass me, " *my heart shall not fear : though war should rise against me, in this I will be confident.*" Here is great *courage* for the time to come. *Experience breeds hope and confidence.* David was not so courageous a man of himself ; but upon experience of God's former comfort and assistance, his faith brake as fire out of the smoke, or as the sun out of a cloud. Though I was in such-and-such perplexities, yet for the time to come, I have such confidence and experience of God's goodness, that I will not fear. He that seeth God by a spirit of faith in his greatness and power, he sees all other things below as nothing. Therefore, he saith here, he cares not for the time to come for any opposition ; no, not of an army. " If God be with us, who can be against us ? " Rom. viii. 31. He saw God in his power ; and then, looking from God to the creature, alas ! who was he ? As Micah, when he had seen God sitting upon his throne ; what was Ahab to him, when he had seen God once ? So when the prophet David had seen God once, then " *though an host should encamp against me, my heart shall not fear,*" etc.—*Richard Sibbes*.

Verse 3.—" *Though an host should encamp against me,*" etc. If I love my God, and I love him with a noble-spirited love, all my enemies will fight against me in vain ; I shall never fear them, and the whole world cannot harm me. Charity cannot be offended, because she takes offence at nothing. Enemies, enviers, slanderers, persecutors, I defy you ; if I love, I shall triumph over your attacks. Ye can take away my goods ; but if my love has a generous spirit, I shall be always rich enough, and ye cannot take away my love, which alone makes all my riches and treasures. Ye may blacken my reputation ; but as I hold you cheaply quit of all homage of praise and applause, I, with all my heart, give you a free leave to blame and to defame. Happily for me, ye cannot blacken me before my God, and his esteem alone makes amends to me, and rewards me, for all your contempt. Ye can persecute my body, but there I even will help you on by my penances ; the sooner it shall perish, the sooner shall I be delivered from this domestic enemy, which is a burden to me. What harm, then, can ye do me ? If I am resolved to suffer all and if I think I deserve all the outrages ye can do me, ye will only give more loftiness of spirit to my love, more brilliancy to my crown.—*Jean Baptiste Elias Avrillon.*

Verse 3.—Those who are willing to be combatants *for* God, shall also be more than conquerors *through* God. None are so truly courageous as those who are truly religious. If a Christian live, he knows by whose might he stands ; and if he die, he knows for whose sake he falls. Where there is no confidence *in* God, there will be no continuance *with* God. When the wind of faith ceases to fill the sails, the ship of obedience ceases to plough the seas. The taunts of Ishmael shall never make an Isaac disesteem his inheritance.—*William Secker.*

Verses 3, 4.—The favourite grows great by the many favours, gifts, jewels, offices, the prince bestows on him. The Christian grows rich in *experiences*, which he wears as bracelets, and keeps as his richest jewels. He calls one *Ebenezer*—" hitherto God hath helped ; " another *Naphtali*—" I have wrestled with God and prevailed ; " another *Gershom*—" I was a stranger ; " another *Joseph*—" God will yet add more ; " and another, *Peniel*—" I have seen the face of God." 1 Sam. vii. 12 ; Gen. xxx. 8 ; Ex. ii. 22 ; Gen. xxx. 24, and xxxii. 30. I have been delivered from the *lion,* therefore shall be from the *bear ;* from lion and bear, therefore from the *Philistines ;* from the Philistine, therefore from *Saul ;* from Saul, therefore God will deliver me from every evil work, and preserve me blameless to his heavenly kingdom.—*John Sheffield.*

Verse 4.—" *One thing have I desired of the Lord, that will I seek after ; that I may dwell in the house of the Lord all the days of my life, to behold the beauty of the Lord, and to enquire in his temple.*" Some interpreters vary concerning what the Psalmist aims at ; I understand thus much in a generality, which is clear, that he means a communion and fellowship with God, which is that *one thing*, which if a Christian had, he needs desire no more : that we should all desire and desire again and be in love with, and that is enough even to satisfy us, the fruition of God, and the beholding of him in his ordinances, in his temple, to have correspondency and fellowship and communion with him there. O God, vouchsafe us that ! Now this is so infinitely sweet, that it was the Psalmist's only desire, and the sum of all his desires here, and therefore much more in the tabernacle of heaven which doth make up the consummation and completeness of all our happiness.—*John Stoughton.*

Verse 4.—" *One thing have I desired of the Lord,*" etc. Seeing David would make but *one* request to God, why would he not make a greater ? for, alas ! what a poor request is this—to desire *to dwell in God's house ?* and what to do ? but only *to see ?* and to see what ? but only a *beauty*, a fading thing, at most but *to enquire ;* and what is enquiring ? but only to hear news ; a vain fancy. And what cause in any of these why David should make it his request to God ? But mark, O my soul, what goes with it ! Take altogether—" *to behold the beauty of the Lord, and to enquire in his temple.*" And now tell me, if there be, if there can be, any greater request to be made ? any greater cause to be earnest about it ? For though worldly beauty be a fading thing, yet " *the beauty of the Lord,*" shall continue when the world shall fade away ; and though enquiring after news be a vain fancy, yet *to enquire in God's Temple* is the way to learn there is no new thing under the sun, and there it was that Solomon learned that " all is vanity." Indeed, this " *one thing*," that David desires, is in effect that *unum necessarium* that Christ speaks of in the gospel ; which Mary makes choice of there, as David doth here.—*Sir Richard Baker.*

Verse 4.—" *One thing,*" etc. A heavenly mind gathers itself up into one wish and no more. " *One thing have I desired of the Lord, which I will require.*" Grant me thyself, O Lord, and I will ask no more. The new creature asks nothing of God, but to enjoy God : give me this, O Lord, and for the rest, let Ziba take all. I will part with all to buy that one pearl, the riches of heavenly grace.—*Jeremy Taylor.*

Verse 4.—" *One thing.*" The first thing, then, is David's choice, summarily described in the word, " *one thing.*" So Christ confirmeth the prophet's word while he called Mary's choice, " *one thing.*" Luke x. 42. And that for these three reasons : First, because it is not a common but a *chief* good. If there be any good above it, it is not the chief good ; and if there be any good equal unto it, it is not alone. Next, because it is the *last end* which we mind eternally to enjoy ; if there be any end beyond it, it is not the last, but amids, and a degree to it. All mids and ends are used for it, but it is sought for itself, and, therefore, must be but one. Thirdly, it is a *centre* whereunto all reasonable spirits draw. As all lines from a circle meet in the centre, so every one that seeketh happiness aright meeteth in the chief good, as the only thing which they intend, and, therefore, must be *one*. *William Struther, in " True Happiness, or King David's Choice,"* 1633.

Verse 4.—" *One thing.*" Changes, great changes, and many bereavements there have been in my life. I have been emptied from vessel to vessel. But one thing has never failed—one thing makes me feel that my life has been *one* ; it has calmed my joys, it has soothed my sorrows, it has guided me in difficulty, it has strengthened me in weakness. It is the *presence* of God—a faithful and loving God. Yes, brethren, the presence of God is not only *light*, it is *unity*. It gives *unity* to the heart that believes it—*unity* to the life that is conformed to it. It was the presence of God in David's soul that enabled him to say, " *One* thing have I desired of the Lord ; " and in St. Paul's that enabled him to say, " This one thing I do."—*George Wagner, in the " Wanderings of the Children of Israel,"* 1862.

Verse 4.—" *One thing.*"—

One master passion in the breast.
Like Aaron s serpent, swallows up the rest.

Alexander Pope.

Verse 4.—" *That I may dwell in the house of the Lord all the days of my life.*" To approach continually unto the temple, and thither continually to repair was the *dwelling*, no doubt, here meant ; to *dwell*, to reside continually there, not to come for a spurt or a fit. . . . And thus dwelt Hannah, the daughter of Phanuel, who is said, in the second of Luke, for the space of four score and four years not to have gone out of the temple. Not that she was there always, but often, saith Lyra ; and venerable Bede to the same purpose. Not that she was never absent, no, not an hour ; but for that she was often in the temple. And the same St. Luke, speaking of our Saviour's disciples, after they had seen him ascended into heaven—" They returned," saith he, " to Jerusalem with great joy : and were continually in the temple, praising and blessing God," chapter xxiv. 52, 53. Thus, St. Austin's mother, in her time too, might be said to *dwell* in God's house, whereunto she came so duly and truly twice a day, " That she, in thy Scriptures," saith St. Austin, " might hear, O God, what thou saidst to her, and thou, in her prayers, what she said to thee." In a word, such were the Christians the same St. Austin speaks of in another place, whom he calleth *the emmets of God*. " Behold the emmet of God," saith he, " it riseth early every day, it runneth to God's church, it there prayeth, it heareth the lesson read, it singeth a Psalm, it ruminateth what it heareth, it meditateth thereupon, and hoardeth up within itself the precious corn gathered from that barn-floor." *John Day's " David's Desire to go to Church,"* 1609.

Verse 4.—" *That I may dwell in the house of the Lord all the days of my life.*" In the beginning of the Psalm, David keeps an audit of his soul's accounts, reckoning up the large incomes and lasting treasures of God's bounty, grace, and mercy ; the sum whereof is this : The Lord is my light and my life, my strength and my salvation. And now, where shall David design his presence, but where is his light ? Where shall he desire his person, but where is his strength ? Where shall he wish his soul, but where is his life ? and where shall he fix his habitation, but where is his salvation ? even in communion with his God ; and this, especially, in the holy worship of his sanctuary. No wonder, then, if above all things he desires and seeks after this " one thing," " to dwell in the house of the Lord," etc.—*Robert Mossom.*

Verse 4.—" *The house of the Lord.*" It [the tabernacle, the sanctuary] is called the house of God because he is present there, as a man delights to be present in his house. It is the place where God will be met withal. As a man will be found in his house, and there he will have suitors come to him, where he reveals his secrets. A man rests, he lies, and lodgeth in his house. Where is a man so familiar as in his house ? and what other place hath he such care to protect and provide for as his house ? and he lays up his treasures and his jewels in his house. So God lays up all the treasures of grace and comfort in the visible church. In the church he is to be spoken with as a man in his house. There he gives us sweet meetings ; there are mutual, spiritual kisses. " Let him kiss me with the kisses of his mouth." Cant. i. 2. A man's house is his castle, as we say, that he will protect and provide for.

God will be sure to protect and provide for his church. Therefore he calls the church of God, that is, the tabernacle (that was the church at that time), *the house of God.* If we apply it to our times, that that answers the tabernacle now, is particular visible churches under particular pastors, where the means of salvation are set up. Particular visible churches now are God's tabernacle. The church of the Jews was a national church. There was but one church, but one place, and one tabernacle ; but now God hath erected particular tabernacles. Every particular church and congregation under one pastor, their meeting is the church of God, a several church independent. *Richard Sibbes.*

Verse 4.—" *To behold the beauty of the Lord.*" That was one end of his desire, to dwell in the house of God ; not to feed his eyes with speculations and goodly sights (as indeed there were in the tabernacle goodly things to be seen). No ; he had a more spiritual sight than that. He saw the inward spiritual beauty of those spiritual things. The other were but outward things, as the apostle calls them. I desire to dwell in the house of the Lord, " *to behold the beauty of the Lord,*" the inward beauty of the Lord especially.—*Richard Sibbes.*

Verse 4.—" *The beauty of the Lord.*" In connection with these words, we would try to show that the character of God is attractive, and fitted to inspire us with love for him, and to make us, as it were, run after him. The discussion of our subject may be arranged under three heads. I. Some of the elements of the beauty of the Lord. II. Where the beauty of the Lord may be seen. III. Peculiar traits of the beauty of the Lord. I. Some of the elements of the beauty of the Lord. God is a Spirit. Hence his beauty is spiritual, and its elements must be sought for in spiritual perfection. 1. One of the elements of this beauty is holiness. 2. But the elements of the divine beauty on which we intend at this time to dwell, are those which are included under the general description of God's mercy and grace. The attractiveness of these is more easily perceived, and their influence is sooner felt by persons in our fallen condition. It is mainly through the instrumentality of these that sinners are won over from their enmity against God, and that the Holy Ghost sheds abroad the love of God in our hearts. 3. Another thing, which we may call an element of beauty in God, is the combination of his various attributes in one harmonious whole. The colours of the rainbow are beautiful, when taken one by one : but there is a beauty in the rainbow, which arises not from any single tint ; there is a beauty in it which would not exist if the several hues were assumed in succession—a beauty which is the result of their assemblage and collocation, and consists in their blended radiance. In like manner do the several perfections, which co-exist and unite in the nature of God, produce a glorious beauty. Holiness is beautiful ; mercy is beautiful ; truth is beautiful. But, over and above, there is a beauty which belongs to such combinations and harmonies as the Psalmist describes, when he tells us, " Mercy and truth are met together ; righteousness and peace have kissed each other." " Thy mercy, O Lord, is in the heavens ; and thy faithfulness reacheth unto the clouds. Thy righteousness is like the great mountains ; thy judgments are a great deep," etc. II. We are next to enquire where the beauty of the Lord may be seen. It may so far be seen in the *natural world.* The throne of nature, although in some respects clouds and darkness are round about it, is not without its rainbow of beauty, any more than the throne of grace. The beauty of the Lord may be seen in the *moral law.* In the law ! Even so. In the unbending law, with its terrible anathema, his beauty and amiableness shine forth. The law is full of love. The duties of the law are duties of love. Love is the fulfilling of the law. The curse of the law is designed and employed for the maintenance of love. Obedience to the law, and the reign of love, are but different aspects of the same state of things. And one of the sublimest lessons of the law is the fact, that God is love. Again, the beauty of the Lord may be seen in the *gospel.* We see it, as it were, by reflection, in the law ; in the gospel, we see it directly. The law shows us the hearts of men, as God would have them to be ; the gospel shows us God's own heart. Again, the beauty of the Lord is seen in *Christ.* It is seen in Christ, for he is the brightness of the Father's glory, and the express image of his person ; and he that hath seen Christ, hath seen the Father. The beauty of the Lord is seen in Christ, when we consider him as the Father's gift, and when we look to his offices and to his character. The character of Christ was the finest spectacle of moral beauty which men or angels ever set their eyes on. III. We conclude by noticing some traits of the beauty of the Lord. 1. It never deceives. 2. It never fades. 3. It never loses its power. 4. It never disappoints.—*Condensed from Andrew Gray* (1805—1861), *in " Gospel Contrasts and Parallels."*

Verse 4.—*" The beauty of the Lord."* The Lord's *beauty,* to be seen in his house, is not the beauty of his essence, for so no man can see God and live (Exod. xxxiii. 18, 20) ; before this glorious beauty the angels cover their faces with their wings (Isa. vi. 1, 2) ; but it is the beauty of his ordinances, wherein God doth reveal to the eyes of men's minds, enlightened by his Spirit, the pleasant beauty of his goodness, justice, love, and mercy in Jesus Christ.—*Thomas Pierson, M.A.,* 1570—1633.

Verse 4.—*" The beauty of the Lord."*—*" Beauty "* is too particular a word to express the fulness of the Holy Ghost, the pleasantness or the delight of God. Take the word in a general sense, in your apprehensions. It may be the object of all senses, inward and outward. Delight is most transcendent for pleasantness ; for indeed God in his ordinances, is not only " beauty " to the eye of the soul, but is ointment to the smell, and sweetness to the taste, and all in all to all the powers of the soul. God in Christ, therefore, he is delightful and sweet. . . . *" The beauty of the Lord "* is especially the amiable things of God, which is his mercy and love, that makes all other things beautiful that is in the church.—*Richard Sibbes.*

Verse 4.—*" To enquire in his temple."* The more grace the more business ye will find ye have to do with God in his ordinances ; little grace hath little to do, and much grace hath much to do ; he hath always business with God, special earnest business. *" To behold the beauty of the Lord, and to enquire in his temple."* Oh, I have somewhat to enquire after ; I am to do something by this duty, and therefore cannot trifle. He that comes to visit his friend in a compliment, he talks, he walks, he trifles, and goes home again ; but he that comes upon business, he is full of it : he is like Abraham's honest and faithful servant. Gen. xxiv. 33. "And there was set meat before him to eat : but he said, I will not eat, until I have told my errand." I have great business with the Lord, about the church, and about my soul, and I will not eat, nor talk, nor think, nor dally about anything, till I have told mine errand, or heard my Maker's errand unto me. And for this end it's a rare thing to carry somewhat always on the spirit, to spread before God, a heart pregnant with some needful request or matter whereof to treat with God. Psalm xlv. 1.—*Richard Steele's "Antidote against Distractions,"* 1673.

Verse 4.—It was David's earnest prayer, *" One thing have I desired of the Lord, that will I seek after ; that I may dwell in the house of the Lord all the days of my life, to behold the beauty of the Lord, and to enquire in his temple."* There are many that pray David's words, but not with David's heart. *Unum petii,* one thing have I desired, *de præterito,* for the time past ; *et hoc requiram,* this I will still seek after, *de futuro,* for the time to come : I have required it long, and this suit I will urge till I have obtained it. What ? To dwell in some of the houses of God all the days of my life, and to leave them to my children after me ; not to serve him there with devotion, but to make the place mine own possession ? These love the house of God too well ; they love it to have and to hold : but because the conveyance is made by the lawyer, and not by the minister, their title will be found nought in the end ; and if there be not a *nisi prius* to prevent them, yet at that great day of universal audit, the Judge of all the world shall condemn them. By this way, the nearer to the church, the further from God. The Lord's temple is ordained to gain us to him, not for us to gain it from him. If we love the Lord, we " will love the habitation of his house, and the place where his honour dwelleth ; " that so by being humble frequenters of his temple below, we may be made noble saints of his house above, the glorious kingdom of Jesus Christ.—*Thomas Adams.*

Verse 4.—David being in this safe condition, what doth he now think upon or look at, as his main scope ? Not as Pyrrhus, king of Epirus, to sit still and be merry, when he had overcome the Romans and all his enemies, as he sometime said to Cyneas, the philosopher, but to improve his rest to perpetual piety, in going from day to day to God's house, as Hannah is said afterwards to have done. Luke ii. And this, first, for the solace of his soul, in seeing the beauty of his sanctuary. Secondly, that he might still be directed aright and be safe. Thirdly, that he might yet be more highly exalted in kingly glory. Fourthly, for all this, as he should have abundant cause, sacrificing and singing Psalms to God without ceasing: see verses 5, 6.—*John Mayer.*

Verse 4.—O my soul, what sights have I seen in the house of God! what provisions have I tasted ! what entertainments have I had ! what enlargements in prayer and answers thereto ! what impressions under his word, what entertainment at his table, as he has sometimes brought me into his banqueting-house, and his banner over me has been love! And though I cannot, it may be, say so much of this as some others ; yet what I have found, I cannot but remember with thankfulness, and desire more ; and as this was *in the house of God, here* would I still desire to dwell.—*Daniel Wilcox,* 1676—1733.

Verse 5.—" *The time of trouble.*" Though God does not always deliver his people out of trouble, yet he delivers them from the evil of trouble, the despair of trouble, by supporting the spirit ; nay, he delivers by trouble, for he sanctifies the trouble to cure the souls, and by less troubles delivers from greater.—*From a Broad Sheet in the British Museum, dated, " London : printed for D.M.,* 1678."

Verse 5.—" *He shall hide me.*" The word here used means to hide, to secrete, and then, to defend or protect. It would properly be applied to one who had fled from oppression, or from any impending evil, and who should be *secreted* in a house or cavern, and thus rendered safe from pursuers, or from the threatening evil.—*Albert Barnes.*

Verse 5.—" *Pavilion* " comes from *papilio,* a *butterfly.* It signifies a *tent* made of cloth stretched out on poles, which in form resembles in some measure the insect above named.—*Adam Clarke.*

Verse 5.—" *In the secret of his tabernacle shall he hide me.*" He alludes to the ancient custom of offenders, who used to flee to the tabernacle or altar, where they esteemed themselves safe. 1 Kings ii. 28.—*Matthew Pool.*

Verse 5.—" *In the secret of his tabernacle.*" Were there no other place, he would put me in the *holy of holies,* so that an enemy would not dare to approach me.—*Adam Clarke.*

Verse 6.—" *Now shall mine head be lifted up above mine enemies round about me.*" A man cannot drown so long as his head is above water. Now, it is the proper office of hope to do this for the Christian in times of any danger. Luke xxi. 28. " When these things begin to come to pass, then look up, and lift up your heads : for your redemption draweth nigh." A strange time, one would think, for Christ then to bid his disciples *lift up their heads* in, when they see other men's hearts failing them for fear, and for looking after those things which are coming on the earth (verse 26) ; yet now is the time of the rising of their sun, when others' is setting, and the blackness of darkness is overtaking others ; because now the Christian's feast is coming, for which hope hath saved its stomach so long. " Your redemption draweth nigh." Two things make the head hang down—fear and shame ; hope easeth the Christian's heart of both these, and so forbids him to give any sign of a desponding mind by a dejected countenance.—*William Gurnall.*

Verse 6.—" *Therefore will I offer in his tabernacle sacrifices of joy.*" " Surely." some may say, " he could have called on God beyond the precincts of the temple, Wherever he wandered as an exile, he carried with him the precious promise of God, so that he needed not to put so great a value upon the sight of the external edifice. He appears, by some gross imagination or other, to suppose that God could be enclosed by wood and stones." But if we examine the words more carefully, it will be easy to see, that his object was altogether different from a mere sight of the noble building and its ornaments, however costly. He speaks, indeed, of the temple, but he places that beauty not so much in the goodliness that was to be seen by the eye, as in its being the celestial pattern which was shown to Moses, as it is written in Exod. xxv. 40 : " And look that thou make them after their pattern, which was showed thee in the mount." As the fashion of the temple was not framed according to the wisdom of man, but was an image of spiritual things, the prophet directed his eyes and all his affections to this object. Their madness is, therefore, truly detestable who wrest this place in favour of pictures and images, which, instead of deserving to be numbered among temple ornaments, are rather like dung and filth, defiling all the purity of holy things.—*John Calvin.*

Verse 8.—" *When thou saidst, Seek ye my face ; my heart said unto thee, Thy face, Lord, will I seek.*" In the former verse, David begins a prayer to God, " Hear, O Lord ; have mercy upon me, and answer me." This verse is a ground of that prayer, " Seek ye my face," saith God. The heart answers again, " *Thy face, Lord, will I seek ;*" therefore I am encouraged to pray to thee. In the words are contained God's command and David's obedience. God's warrant and David's work answerable, the voice and the echo: the voice, "*Seek my face;*" the rebound back again of a gracious heart, "*Thy face, Lord, will I seek.*" "*When thou saidst.*" It is not in the original. It only makes way to the sense. Passionate speeches are usually abrupt: "*Seek my face:*" "*Thy face, Lord, will I seek.*" . . . *God is willing to be known.* He is willing to open and discover himself; God delights not to hide himself. God stands not upon state, as some emperors do that think their presence diminisheth respect. God is no such God, but he may be searched into. Man, if any weakness be discovered, we can soon search into the depth of his excellency; but with God it is clean otherwise. The more we know of him, the more we shall admire him. None admire him more than the blessed angels, that see most of him, and the blessed spirits that have communion with him. Therefore he hides not himself, nay, he desires to be known; and all those that have his Spirit desire to make him known. Those that suppress the knowledge of God in his will, what he performs for men, and what he requires of them, they are enemies to God and of God's people. They suppress the opening of God, clean contrary to God's meaning; "*Seek my face;*" I desire to be made known, and lay open myself to you. Therefore we may observe by the way, that when we are in any dark condition, that a Christian finds not the beams of God shining on him, let him not lay the blame upon God, as if God were a God that delighted to hide himself. Oh, no! it is not his delight. He loves not strangeness to his poor creatures. It is not a point of his policy. He is too great to affect* such poor things. No; the fault is altogether in us. We walk not worthy of such a presence; we want humility and preparation. If there be any darkness in the creature, that he finds God doth not so shine on him as in former times, undoubtedly the cause is in himself; for God saith, "*Seek my face.*" He desires to reveal himself.— *Richard Sibbes.*

Verse 8.—"*When thou saidst, Seek ye my face,*" etc. All the Spirit's motions are seasonable, and therefore not to be put off; for delay is a kind of denial, and savours of such ungrateful contempt, as must needs be very displeasing to him. "*When thou saidst, Seek ye my face; my heart said unto thee, Thy face, Lord, will I seek.*" God does not only expect such an answer, but expects it immediately upon his call. Whenever he blows with his wind, he looks that we should spread our sails. If we refuse his offered help, we may deservedly want it when desired. As Christ withdrew himself from the spouse because she let him stand knocking so long at the door of her heart, and she still deferred to open, and tired out his loving forbearance with vain and frivolous excuses. Sol. Song, v. 2, etc. But as we must not omit the present performance of any duty which he excites unto, we must not check his influences by being weary of the duties which he assists us in: if we do not improve extraordinary aids by holding out the longer, we provoke him to depart.—*Timothy Cruso.*

Verse 8.—"*When thou saidst, Seek ye my face,*" etc. We see here thus much, that God must *begin* with us, before we can *close with him;* God must seek us, before we can seek him; God must first desire that we should draw near to him, before we for our particulars are able to draw near unto God. Thou saidst, Seek my face; and then, and not till then my heart said, Thy face, Lord, will I seek.—*Thomas Horton.*

Verse 8.—"*When thou saidst,*" etc. Now God then speaks to the heart to pray when not only he puts upon the duty by saying to the conscience, This thou oughtest to do; but God's speaking to pray is such as his speech at first was, when he made the world, when he said, "Let there be light, and there was light:" so he says, let there be a prayer, and there is a prayer; that is, he pours upon a man a spirit of grace and supplication, a praying disposition; he puts in motives, suggests arguments and pleas to God; all which you shall find come in readily, and of themselves, and that likewise with a quickening heat and enlargement of affection, and with a lingering, and longing, and restlessness of spirit to be alone, to pour out the soul to God, and to vent and form those motions and suggestions into a prayer, till you have laid them together, and made a prayer of them. And this is a speaking to the heart. Observe such times when God doth thus, and neglect them not, then to strike whilst the iron is hot; thou hast then his ear; it is a special opportunity for that business, such a one as thou mayst never have the like. Suitors at court observe *molissima fandi tempora*, their times of begging when they have

---

* Choose=love.

kings in a good mood, which they will be sure to take the advantage of ; but especially if they should find that the king himself should begin of himself to speak of the business which they would have of him : and thus that phrase of Psalm x. 17, that God prepares the heart, is understood by some, that God prepares the heart, and causeth the ear to hear ; that is, he fashions it and composeth it into a praying frame. And sure it is a great sign that God means to hear us when himself shall thus indite the petition.—*Thomas Goodwin.*

Verse 8.—" *When thou saidst,*" etc. And well may this be pleaded, in that God useth not so to stir up and strengthen us to seek him, but when he intendeth to be found of us. Psalm x. 17. " Thou hast heard the desire of the humble : thou wilt prepare their heart, thou wilt cause thine ear to hear." Jer. xxix. 13. " And ye shall seek me, and find me, when ye shall search for me with all your heart." And God maketh it an argument to himself, that if he say to any inwardly as well as outwardly, " *Seek my face,*" he that speaketh righteousness cannot speak thus to them, and frustrate their prayers, and so bid them seek his face in vain. Isaiah xlv. 19, " I said not unto the seed of Jacob, Seek ye me in vain ; I the Lord speak right things." If Ahasuerus bid his spouse to ask, surely he will not fail to grant her petition (Esther vii. 2) ; so here. And as when Christ called the blind man to come to him to tell him his grievance, it was truly said to him by them, " Be of good comfort, rise, for he calleth thee." Mark x. 49. So it is in this case.—*Thomas Cobbett.*

Verse 8.—" *My heart said unto thee.*" The heart is between God and our obedience, as it were, an ambassador. It understands from God what God would have done, and then it lays a command upon the whole man. The heart and conscience of man is partly divine, partly human. It hath some divinity in it, especially if the man be a holy man. God speaks, and the heart speaks. God speaks to the heart, and the heart speaks to us. And ofttimes when we hear conscience speaking to us, we neglect it ; and as St. Augustine said of himself, " God spake often to me, and I was ignorant of it." When there is no command in the word that the heart directly thinks of (as indeed many profane careless men scarce have a Bible in their houses), God speaks to them thus ; conscience speaks to them some broken command, that they learn against their wills. They heed it not, but David did not so. God said, " Seek ye my face ; " his *heart* answers, " Thy face, Lord, will I seek." The heart looks upward to God, and then to itself, " *My heart said.*" It said to thee, and then to itself. First, his heart said to God, " Lord, I have encourage-ment from thee. Thou hast commanded that I should seek thy face." So his heart looked to God, and then it speaks to itself, " Thy face, Lord, will I seek." It looks first to God, and then to all things that come from itself.—*Richard Sibbes.*

Verse 8.—There are divers things considerable of us in this *answer* and *compliance* of David's with God's *command* or *invitation* to him. First, it was *seasonable, and in due time ;* presently does David make this return : " Thy face, Lord, will I seek." This is the property and disposition of every wise and prudent Christian, to close with the very first opportunities of God's invitation. Secondly, this answer, as it was seasonable and present, so it was also *full and complete ;* the performance was proportionable to the injunction. Ye shall have some kind of people in the world that God bids them do one thing and they will be sure to do the quite contrary ; or, at least, not do as much as they should do, but do it by halves. But, now, here David makes return to God in the full extent and proportion of obedience. God said, " Seek my face," and he answered, " Thy face, Lord, will I seek." Thirdly, it was *real and entire, and sincere ;* " My heart said." It is one thing to say it with the *mouth,* and it is another thing to say it with the *heart.* With the *mouth* it is both easy and ordinary, and nothing more usual. Lord, thy face will we seek, especially in any trouble or calamity, which is incident unto us ; but for the heart to say it, that is not so frequent. Fourthly, it was *settled, and peremptory,* " Thy face will I seek ; " there is nothing shall hinder me of it, or keep me from it, but I will do it against all opposition. Lastly, this protestation of David was *absolute and indefinite and unlimited ;* " I will seek thy face ; " without prescription of time, or place, or condition ; not only now, but hereafter ; not only for a time, but for ever, in all seasons, in all estates, in all circumstances, still I shall keep me to this—to hold my communion with thee. Then are we Christians, indeed, when we are so immutably and irreversibly and independently upon the opinions or practices of any other person.—*Condensed from Thomas Horton.*

Verse 8.—God hath promised his favour, and, therefore, his people may seek his favour. Nay, he hath commanded his people to seek his favour, and therefore they should seek it. It is an unadvised folly, during the suspension of God's favour, to unson ourselves, and unpeople ourselves, *i.e.*, by denying the grace and spiritual relation which exist between us and God. That is not the way to gain favour; for when we have undone our relation of children we exclude ourselves from the expectation of favour. No, the wisest and surest way is to seek the renewing of God's loving countenance, and not to be driven away from God by our unbelief.— *Obadiah Sedgwick, in " The Doubting Believer," 1653.*

Verse 9.—" *Hide not thy face far from me.*" When I seek thy face, vouchsafe, O God, not to hide thy face from me ; for to what purpose should I seek it if I cannot find it ? and what hope of finding it if thou be bent to hide it ?—*Sir Richard Baker.*

Verse 9.—" *Put not thy servant away in anger.*" God puts away many in anger for their supposed goodness, but not any at all for their confessed badness.—*John Trapp.*

Verse 9.—" *Thy servant.*" It is a blessed and happy thing to be God's true " *servant.*" Consider what the Queen of Sheba said of Solomon's servants (1 Kings x. 8) : " Happy are these thy servants," etc. Now Christ Jesus is greater than Solomon (Matt. xii. 42), and so a better Master. Good earthly masters will honour good servants, as Prov. xxvii. 18, " He that waiteth on his master shall be honoured ; " chap. xvii. 2, " A wise servant shall have a portion, or inheritance, among the brethren." But however some earthly masters may be Nabals and Labans, yet God will not be so : John xii. 26 : " Where I am, there shall also my servant be." " If any man serve me, him will my Father honour," see Luke xii. 37. The watchful servants are blessed ; their master will make them to sit down to meat, and will come forth and serve them, as Matt. xxv. 21, 23 : " Well done, thou good and faithful servant : thou hast been faithful over a few things, I will make thee ruler over many things : enter thou into the joy of thy Lord."—*Thomas Pierson.*

Verse 9.—" *Thou hast been my help ; leave me not,*" etc. One act of mercy engages God to another. Men argue thus : I have showed you kindness already, therefore trouble me no more ; but because God has shown mercy he is more ready still to show mercy ; his mercy in election makes him justify, adopt, glorify.—*Thomas Watson.*

Verse 9.—" *Leave me not ;* " rather, " dismiss me not ; " " let not go thy hold of me." This is the proper sense of the Hebrew verb שׁטׁנ, to set a thing loose, to let it go, to abandon it.—*Samuel Horsley.*

Verse 10.—" *When my father and my mother forsake me.*" As there seems to be some difficulty in supposing the Psalmist's parents to have " deserted " him, they might perhaps be said to have " *forsaken* " him (as Muis conjectures), that is, to have left him behind them, as being dead.—*James Merrick, M.A., 1720—1769.*

Verse 10.—" *When my father and my mother forsake me.*" It is indeed the nature of all living creatures, though never so tender of their young ones, yet when they are grown to a ripeness of age and strength, to turn them off to shift for themselves ; and even a father and a mother, as tender as they are, have yet somewhat of this common nature in them ; for while their children are young they lead them by the hand, but when they are grown up they leave them to their own legs, and if they chance to fall let them rise as they can. But God even then takes his children up, for he knows of what they are made ; he knows their strength must be as well supported as their weakness is assisted ; he knows they must as well be taken up when they fall, as be held up when they stand.—*Sir Richard Baker.*

Verse 10.—" *Father and Mother.*" First, who are they ? Properly and chiefly our natural parents, of whom we were begotten and born ; to whom (under God) we owe our being and breeding. Yet here, not they only ; but by *synecdoche* all other kinsfolks, neighbours, friends, acquaintances, or, indeed, more generally yet, all worldly comforts, stays, and helps whatsoever. 2. But, then, why these named the rathest, and the rest to be included in these ? Because we promise to ourselves more help from them than from any of the other. We have a nearer relation to, and a greater interest in them than any other ; and they of all other are the unlikeliest to forsake us. The very brute creatures forsake not their young ones. A hen will not desert her chickens, nor a bear endure to be robbed of her whelps. 3. But, then, thirdly, why *both* named—*father* and *mother* too ? Partly because it can hardly be imagined that both of them should forsake their child, though one should hap to be unkind. Partly because the *father's love* being commonly with more *providence*, the *mother's* with more *tenderness;* both together do better express than alone either would do, the abundant love of God towards us, who is infinitely dear over us, beyond the care of the most provident father, beyond the affection of the tenderest mother. 4. But, then, fourthly, when may they be said to *forsake* us? When at any time they leave us destitute of such help as we stand in need of; whether it be out of *choice*, when they list not to help us, though they might if they would; or out of *necessity*, when they cannot help us, though they would if they could.—*Robert Sanderson.*

Verse 10.—" *Then the Lord will take me up."* But *dictum factum :* these are but *words :* Are there producible any *deeds* to make it good? Verily, there are, and that to the very letter. When Ishmael's mother, despairing of his life, had *forsaken* him, and laid him down gasping (his last, for ought she knew or could do to help it), in the wilderness, the Lord *took him up ;* he opened a new spring of water, and opened her eyes to see it, and so the child was preserved. Genesis xxi. When Moses' parents had also *forsaken* him (for they durst not stand by him any longer), and laid him down among the rushy flags, the Lord *took him up* too. He provided him of a saviour, the king's own daughter, and of a nurse the child's own mother—and so he was preserved too. Exodus ii. 6—9. Take but two examples more, out of either Testament one. David and St. Paul, both *forsaken* of men, both *taken up* of God. How was David forsaken, in Psalm cxlii. 4, when he had looked upon his right hand, and saw no man that would know him ; he had no place to fly unto, and no man cared for his soul. But all the while *Dominus ad dextris*, there was one at his right hand (though at first he was not aware of him), ready to *take him up ;* as it there followeth, verse 5, " I cried unto thee, O Lord ; I said, Thou art my refuge and my portion in the land of the living." And how St. Paul was forsaken ; take it from himself, 2 Timothy iv. 16, " At my first answer no man stood with me, but all men forsook me : " a heavy case, and had been heavier had there not been one ready to take his part, at the next verse, " Nevertheless the Lord stood with me, and strengthened me," etc. What need we any more witnesses? *In ore duorum*—in the mouth of two such witnesses the point is sufficiently established. But you will yet say, these two might testify what they had already found *post factum.* But David, in the text, pronounceth it *de futuro*, beforehand, and that somewhat confidently : " *The Lord will take me up."* As he doth also elsewhere : " Sure I am that the Lord will avenge the poor, and maintain the cause of the helpless." Psalm cxl. But is there any ground for that? Doubtless there is ; a *double* ground ; one in the *nature*, another in the *promise* of God. In his *nature* four *qualities* there are (we take leave so to speak, suitably to our own low apprehensions, for in the Godhead there are properly no *qualities*) ; but call them *qualities* or *attributes*, or what else you will ; there are *four perfections* in God, opposite to those *defects* which in our *earthly parents* we have found to be the chief causes why they do so oft *forsake* us ; which give us full assurance that he will *take us up* when all other succours fail us. Those are his *love*, his *wisdom*, his *power*, his *eternity*, and all in his nature. To which *four*, add his *promise*, and you have the fulness of all the assurance that can be desired.—*Robert Sanderson.*

Verse 10.—" *The Lord will take me up :* " Hebrew, *will gather me*, that is, take me into his care and keeping. In the civil law we find provision made for outcasts and friendless persons ; some hospitals to entertain them, some liberties to comfort and compensate their trouble. 'Tis sure, that in God the forlorn and fatherless find mercy.—*John Trapp.*

Verse 11.—" *Teach me thy way, O Lord."* Having compared himself to an exposed, deserted infant, adopted by God, he anon fairly asks to be shown how to walk. He asks the grace of being able to observe all his holy commandments, which he never loses sight of through the whole one hundred-and-fifty Psalms. What else could he do? when it was the only path to that heavenly house of God, which he had just declared to be the only wish and desire of his heart.—*Robert Bellarmine (Cardinal), 1542—1621.*

Verse 11.—" *Lead me in a plain path, because of mine enemies."* If a man, travelling in the King's highway, be robbed between sun and sun, satisfaction is recoverable upon the county where the robbery was made ; but if he takes his journey in the night, being an unseasonable time, then it is at his own peril, he must take what falls. So, if a man keep in *God's ways*, he shall be sure of God's protection; but if he stray out of them, he exposeth himself to danger.—*Robert Skinner (Bishop)*, 1636.

Verse 11.—" *Because of mine enemies.*" If once a man commence a professor, the eyes of all are upon him ; and well they may, for his profession *in* the world is a separation *from* the world. Believers condemn those by their lives who condemn them by their lips. Righteous David saw many who were waiting to triumph in his mistakes. Hence the more they watched, the more he prayed : " Teach me thy way, O Lord, and lead me in a plain path, because of mine enemies." It may be rendered, *because of mine observers.* Christian, if you dwell in the open tent of licentiousness, the wicked will not walk backward, like modest Shem and Japheth, to cover your shame : but they will walk forward, like cursed Ham, to publish it. Thus they make use of your weakness as a plea for their wickedness. Men are merciless in their censures of Christians ; they have no sympathy for their infirmity : while God weighs them in more equal scales, and says, " The spirit is willing, but the flesh is weak." While a saint is a *dove* in the eyes of God, he is only a *raven* in the estimation of sinners.—*William Secker.*

Verse 13.—" *I had fainted,*" etc. Study much the all-sufficiency, the power, the goodness, the unchangeableness of God. 1. The all-sufficiency of God. What fulness there is in him to make up all you can lose for him ; what refreshments there are in him to sweeten all you can suffer for him. What fulness ! You may as well doubt that all the waters of the ocean cannot fill a spoon, as that the divine fulness cannot be enough to you, if you should have nothing left in this world ; for all the waters that cover the sea are not so much as a spoonful, compared with the boundless and infinite fulness of all-sufficiency. What refreshments in him ! One drop of divine sweetness is enough to make one in the very agony of the cruellest death to cry out with joy, " The bitterness of death is past." Now in him there are not only drops, but rivers ; not a scanty sprinkling, but an infinite fulness. 2. Eye much the power of God, how it can support under the cross, what it can bring to pass for you by the cross. No cross so sharp and grievous, but he can make it sweet and comfortable. No cross so heavy and intolerable, but he can make light and easy. No cross so ignominious and reproachful, but he can turn it to your honour. No cross so fastened to you, but he can easily remove it. 3. His *goodness*. His all-sufficiency and power make him able, his *goodness* makes him willing to do for his people under the cross what his all-sufficiency and almighty power can afford. His *goodness* sets his mighty power a-work for his suffering saints. His *goodness* sets his all-sufficiency, his fulness, abroach for them, so that it runs freely upon them ; and never more freely than when they are under the cross. " *I had fainted unless I had believed to see the goodness of the Lord,*" &c. What is it that makes you ready to *faint* under the cross, or thoughts and foresight of it ? Look to the *goodness of God*, there is support.—*Condensed from David Clarkson.*

Verse 13.—" *I had fainted.*" The words in italics are supplied by our translators ; but, far from being necessary, they injure the sense. Throw out the words *I had fainted,* and leave a *break* after the verse, and the elegant figure of the Psalmist will be preserved : " Unless I had believed to see the goodness of the Lord in the land of the living "——what ! what, alas ! should have become of me !—*Adam Clarke.*

Verse 13.—" *Unless I had believed to see the goodness of the Lord in the land of the living.*" In the Hebrew this verse is elliptical, as Calvin here translates it. In the French version he supplies the ellipsis, by adding to the end of the verse the words, " C'estoit fait de moy," " I had perished." In our English version, the words, " I had fainted," are introduced as a supplement in the beginning of the verse. Both the supplement of Calvin, and that of our English version, which are substantially the same, doubtless explain the meaning of the passage ; but they destroy the elegant abrupt form of the expression employed by the Psalmist, who breaks off in the middle of his discourse without completing the sentence, although what he meant to say is very evident.—*Editorial Note to Calvin, in loc.*

Verse 13.—Under sore trouble and distress, labour to exercise a strong and lively faith. It was a noble and heroic resolution in that holy man Job, under his singular trials (Job xiii. 15) : " Though he slay me, yet will I trust in him ; " as if he had said, Let my strokes be never so sore and heavy, yet I will not let go my grips of his word and promises, I will not raze these foundations of my hope.

It was the way the Psalmist kept himself from sinking under his heavy burdens : " *I had fainted, unless I had believed to see the goodness of the Lord in the land of the living.*" . . . . Faith brings new strength and auxiliary supplies of grace from heaven, when the former supply is exhausted and spent ; whereof David had the sweet experience here. As God doth plant and actuate grace in the soul, so he is pleased to come in with seasonable supplies and reinforcements to the weak and decayed graces of his people, answerable to their present exigences and pressures; and thus he doth from time to time feed the believer's lamp with fresh oil, give in more faith, more love, more hope, and more desires ; and hereby he gives power to the faint, and strengthens the things which remain when ready to die.—*John Willison.*

Verse 13.—" *Unless I had believed to see the goodness of the Lord in the land of the living :* " a cordial made up of three sovereign ingredients—a hope *to see ;* and to see *the goodness of God ;* and the goodness of God *in the land of the living.*—*Sir Richard Baker.*

Verse 13.—" *The land of the living.*" Alas ! what a *land of the living* is this, in which there are more dead than living, more under ground than above it ; where the earth is fuller of graves than houses ; where life lies trembling under the hand of death ; and where death hath power to tyrannise over life ! No, my soul, *there* only is the *land of the living* where there are none but the living ; where there is a church, not militant, but triumphant ; a church indeed, but no church-yard, because none dead, nor none that can die ; where life is not passive, nor death active ; where life sits crowned, and where death is swallowed up in victory.—*Sir Richard Baker.*

Verse 14.—" *Wait on the Lord, be of good courage.*" Be comfortable, hold fast (as the Greek hath), *be manly,* or, *quit thee as a man ;* which word the apostle useth. 1 Cor. xvi. 13. These are the words of encouragement against remissness, fear, faintness of heart, or other infirmities.—*Henry Ainsworth.*

Verse 14.—" *Wait on the Lord, be of good courage.*"

> Stand but your ground, your ghostly foes will fly—
> Hell trembles at a heaven-directed eye ;
> Choose rather to defend than to assail—
> Self-confidence will in the conflict fail :
> When you are challenged you may dangers meet—
> True *courage* is a fixed, not sudden heat ;
> Is always humble, lives in self-distrust,
> And will itself into no danger thrust.
> Devote yourself to God, and you will find
> God fights the battles of a will resigned.
> Love Jesus ! love will no base fear endure—
> Love Jesus ! and of conquest rest secure.

Thomas Ken (Bishop), 1637—1710—**11.**

Verse 14.—Think not the government is out of Christ's hand, when men are doing many sad things, and giving many heavy blows to the work of God. No, no ; men are but his hand ; and it is the hand of God that justly and righteously is lying heavy upon his people. Look above men, then ; you have not to do with them : there is a turn of matters, just as he is pleased to turn his hand.—*Ralph Erskine,* 1685—1752.

HINTS TO PREACHERS.

Verse 1 *(first clause).*—The relation of illumination to salvation, or the need of light if men would be saved.

Verse 1.—The Christian hero, and the secret springs of his courage.

Verse 1.—The believer's fearless challenge.

Verse 2.—The character, number, power, and cruelty of the enemies of the church, and the mysterious way in which they have been defeated.

Verse 3.—Christian peace. I. Exhibited in the calm foresight of trouble.

II. Displayed in the confident endurance of affliction. III. Sustained by divine help and past experience (*verses* 1, 2). IV. Producing the richest results, glory to God, etc.

Verse 4.—Model Christian life. I. Unity of desire. II. Earnestness of action. III. Nearness of communion. IV. Heavenliness of contemplation. V. Progress in divine education.

Verse 4.—The affection of moral esteem towards God.—*Thomas Chalmers.*

Verse 4.—A breathing after God.—*R. Sibbes's Sermon.*

Verse 4 (*last clause*).—Sabbath occupations and heavenly delights.

Verse 4 (*final clause*).—Matters for enquiry in the Temple of old opened up in the light of the New Testament.

Verse 5.—The threefold shelter. See Exposition.

Verse 6.—The saint's present triumph over his spiritual foes, his practical gratitude, and his vocal praises.

Verse 7.—Prayer. To whom addressed? How? "*Cry*," etc. When? *Left indefinite.* On what it is based? "*Mercy.*" What it needs? "*Hear,*" "*answer.*"

Verse 8.—The heart in tune with its God. Note, the promptness, heartiness, personality, unreservedness, accuracy, and resolution of the response to the precept.

Verse 8.—The successful seeker.—*R. Sibbes's Sermon.*

Verse 8.—The echo. See Spurgeon's Sermons. No. 767.

Verse 9.—I. Desertion deprecated in all its forms. II. Experience pleaded. III. Divine aid implored.

Verse 9.—The horror of saints at the hell of sinners.—*James Scot.*

Verse 10.—The portion of the orphan, the comfort of the persecuted, the paradise of the departing.

Verse 11.—The plain man's pathway desired, described, divinely approved, "*thy way,*" "*a plain way,*" and divinely taught, "*teach me, O Lord,*" "*lead me.*"

Verse 13.—Faith, its precedence of sight, its objects, its sustaining power.

Verse 13.—Believing to see. See Spurgeon's Sermons. No. 766.

Verse 11.—The believer's position, "*wait;*" his condition, "*good courage;*" his support, "*he shall,*" etc.; his perseverance, "*wait*" repeated a second time; his reward.

PSALM XXVIII.

TITLE AND SUBJECT.—*Again, the title, " A Psalm of David," is too general to give us any clue to the occasion upon which it was written. Its position, as following the twenty-seventh, seems to have been designed, for it is a most suitable pendant and sequel to it. It is another of those " songs in the night " of which the pen of David was so prolific. The thorn at the breast of the nightingale was said by the old naturalists to make it sing : David's griefs made him eloquent in holy psalmody. The main pleading of this Psalm is that the suppliant may not be confounded with the workers of iniquity for whom he expresses the utmost abhorrence ; it may suit any slandered saint who, being misunderstood by men, and treated by them as an unworthy character, is anxious to stand aright before the bar of God. The Lord Jesus may be seen here pleading as the representative of his people.*

DIVISION.—*The first and second verses earnestly entreat audience of the Lord in a time of dire emergency. From verses 2—5, the portion of the wicked is described and deprecated. In verses 6, 7, and 8, praise is given for the Lord's mercy in hearing prayer, and the Psalm concludes with a general petition for the whole host of militant believers.*

EXPOSITION.

UNTO thee will I cry, O LORD my rock ; be not silent to me, lest, *if* thou be silent to me, I become like them that go down into the pit.

2 Hear the voice of my supplications, when I cry unto thee, when I lift up my hands toward thy holy oracle.

1. " *Unto thee will I cry, O Lord my rock.*"—A cry is the natural expression of sorrow, and is a suitable utterance when all other modes of appeal fail us ; but the cry must be alone directed to the Lord, for to cry to man is to waste our entreaties upon the air. When we consider the readiness of the Lord to hear, and his ability to aid, we shall see good reason for directing all our appeals at once to the God of our salvation, and shall use language of firm resolve like that in the text, " I will cry." The immutable Jehovah is our *rock*, the immovable foundation of all our hopes and our refuge in time of trouble : we are fixed in our determination to flee to him as our stronghold in every hour of danger. It will be in vain to call to the rocks in the day of judgment, but our rock attends to our cries. " *Be not silent to me.*" Mere formalists may be content without answers to their prayers, but genuine suppliants cannot ; they are not satisfied with the results of prayer itself in calming the mind and subduing the will—they must go further and obtain actual replies from heaven, or they cannot rest ; and those replies they long to receive at once, if possible ; they dread even a little of God's silence. God's voice is often so terrible that it shakes the wilderness ; but his silence is equally full of awe to an eager suppliant. When God seems to close his ear, we must not therefore close our mouths, but rather cry with more earnestness ; for when our note grows shrill with eagerness and grief, he will not long deny us a hearing. What a dreadful case should we be in if the Lord should become for ever silent to our prayers ! This thought suggested itself to David, and he turned it into a plea, thus teaching us to argue and reason with God in our prayers. " *Lest, if thou be silent to me, I become like them that go down into the pit.*" Deprived of the God who answers prayer, we should be in a more pitiable plight than the dead in the grave, and should soon sink to the same level as the lost in hell. We *must* have answers to prayer : ours is an urgent case of dire necessity ; surely the Lord will speak peace to our agitated minds, for he never can find it in his heart to permit his own elect to perish.

2. This is much to the same effect as the first verse, only that it refers to future as well as present pleadings. Hear me ! Hear me ! " *Hear the voice of my supplications !*" This is the burden of both verses. We cannot be put off with a refusal when we are in the spirit of prayer ; we labour, use importunity, and agonise in supplications until a hearing is granted us. The word " supplications," in the plural, shows the number, continuance, and variety of a good man's prayers,

while the expression, " hear *the voice*," seems to hint that there is an inner meaning, or heart-voice, about which spiritual men are far more concerned than for their outward and audible utterances. A silent prayer may have a louder voice than the cries of those priests who sought to awaken Baal with their shouts. *" When I lift up my hands toward thy holy oracle : "* which holy place was the type of our Lord Jesus ; and if we would gain acceptance, we must turn ourselves evermore to the blood-besprinkled mercy seat of his atonement. Uplifted hands have ever been a form of devout posture, and are intended to signify a reaching upward towards God, a readiness, an eagerness to receive the blessing sought after. We stretch out empty hands, for we are beggars ; we lift them up, for we seek heavenly supplies ; we lift them towards the mercy seat of Jesus, for there our expectation dwells. O that whenever we use devout gestures, we may possess contrite hearts, and so speed well with God.

3 Draw me not away with the wicked, and with the workers of iniquity, which speak peace to their neighbours, but mischief *is* in their hearts.

4 Give them according to their deeds, and according to the wickedness of their endeavours : give them after the work of their hands ; render to them their desert.

5 Because they regard not the works of the LORD, nor the operation of his hands, he shall destroy them, and not build them up.

3. *" Draw me not away with the wicked."*—They shall be dragged off to hell like felons of old drawn on a hurdle to Tyburn, like logs drawn to the fire, like fagots to the oven. David fears lest he should be bound up in their bundle, drawn to their doom ; and the fear is an appropriate one for every godly man. The best of the wicked are dangerous company in time, and would make terrible companions for eternity ; we must avoid them in their pleasures, if we would not be confounded with them in their miseries. *" And with the workers of iniquity."* These are overtly sinful, and their judgment will be sure ; Lord, do not make us to drink of their cup. Activity is found with the wicked even if it be lacking to the righteous. Oh ! to be " workers " for the Lord. *" Which speak peace to their neighbours, but mischief is in their hearts."* They have learned the manners of the place to which they are going : the doom of liars is their portion for ever, and lying is their conversation on the road. Soft words, oily with pretended love, are the deceitful meshes of the infernal net in which Satan catches the precious life ; many of his children are learned in his abominable craft, and fish with their father's nets, almost as cunningly as he himself could do it. It is a sure sign of baseness when the tongue and the heart do not ring to the same note. Deceitful men are more to be dreaded than wild beasts : it were better to be shut up in a pit with serpents than to be compelled to live with liars. He who cries " peace " too loudly, means to sell it if he can get his price. " Good wine needs no bush : " if he were so very peaceful he would not need to say so ; he means mischief, make sure of that.

4. When we view the wicked simply as such, and not as our fellow-men, our indignation against sin leads us entirely to coincide with the acts of divine justice which punish evil, and to wish that justice might use her power to restrain by her terrors the cruel and unjust ; but still the desires of the present verse, as our version renders it, are not readily made consistent with the spirit of the Christian dispensation, which seeks rather the reformation than the punishment of sinners. If we view the words before us as prophetic, or as in the future tense, declaring a fact, we are probably nearer to the true meaning than that given in our version. Ungodly reader, what will be your lot when the Lord deals with you according to your desert, and weighs out to you his wrath, not only in proportion to what you have actually done, but according to what you would have done if you could ? Our *" endeavours "* are taken as facts ; God takes the will for the deed, and punishes or rewards accordingly. Not in this life, but certainly in the next, God will repay his enemies to their faces, and give them the wages of their sins. Not according to their fawning words, but after the measure of their mischievous deeds, will the Lord mete out vengeance to them that know him not.

5. *" Because they regard not the works of the Lord, nor the operation of his hands."* God works in creation—nature teems with proofs of his wisdom and goodness, yet purblind atheists refuse to see him : he works in providence, ruling and overruling,

and his hand is very manifest in human history, yet the infidel will not discern him : he works in grace—remarkable conversions are still met with on all hands, yet the ungodly refuse to see the operations of the Lord. Where angels wonder, carnal men despise. God condescends to teach, and man refuses to learn. "*He shall destroy them :* " he will make them "behold, and wonder, and perish." If they would not see the hand of judgment upon others, they shall feel it upon themselves. Both soul and body shall be overwhelmed with utter destruction for ever and ever. "*And not build them up.*" God's curse is positive and negative ; his sword has two edges, and cuts right and left. Their heritage of evil shall prevent the ungodly receiving any good ; the ephah shall be too full of wrath to contain a grain of hope. They have become like old, rotten, decayed houses of timber, useless to the owner, and harbouring all manner of evil, and, therefore, the Great Builder will demolish them utterly. Incorrigible offenders may expect speedy destruction : they who will not mend, shall be thrown away as worthless. Let us be very attentive to all the lessons of God's word and work, lest being found disobedient to the divine will, we be made to suffer the divine wrath.

6 Blessed *be* the LORD, because he hath heard the voice of my supplications.

7 The LORD *is* my strength and my shield ; my heart trusted in him, and I am helped : therefore my heart greatly rejoiceth ; and with my song will I praise him.

8 The LORD *is* their strength, and he is the saving strength of his anointed.

6. "*Blessed be the Lord.*" Saints are full of benedictions ; they are a blessed people, and a blessing people ; but they give their best blessings, the fat of their sacrifices, to their glorious Lord. Our Psalm was prayer up to this point, and now it turns to praise. They who pray well, will soon praise well : prayer and praise are the two lips of the soul ; two bells to ring out sweet and acceptable music in the ears of God ; two angels to climb Jacob's ladder ; two altars smoking with incense ; two of Solomon's lilies dropping sweet-smelling myrrh ; they are two young roes that are twins, feeding upon the mountain of myrrh and the hill of frankincense. "*Because he hath heard the voice of my supplications.*" Real praise is established upon sufficient and constraining reasons ; it is not irrational emotion, but rises, like a pure spring, from the deeps of experience. Answered prayers should be acknowledged. Do we not often fail in this duty ? Would it not greatly encourage others, and strengthen ourselves, if we faithfully recorded divine goodness, and made a point of extolling it with our tongue ? God's mercy is not such an inconsiderable thing that we may safely venture to receive it without so much as thanks. We should shun ingratitude, and live daily in the heavenly atmosphere of thankful love.

7. Here is David's declaration and confession of faith, coupled with a testimony from his experience. "*The Lord is my strength.*" The Lord employs his power on our behalf, and moreover, infuses strength into us in our hour of weakness. The Psalmist, by an act of appropriating faith, takes the omnipotence of Jehovah to be his own. Dependence upon the invisible God gives great independence of spirit, inspiring us with confidence more than human. "*And my shield.*" Thus David found both sword and shield in his God. The Lord preserves his people from unnumbered ills ; and the Christian warrior, sheltered behind his God, is far more safe than the hero when covered with his shield of brass or triple steel. "*My heart trusted in him, and I am helped.*" Heart work is sure work ; heart trust is never disappointed. Faith must come before help, but help will never be long behind-hand. Every day the believer may say, "I am helped," for the divine assistance is vouchsafed us every moment, or we should go back unto perdition ; when more manifest help is needed, we have but to put faith into exercise, and it will be given us. "*Therefore my heart greatly rejoiceth ; and with my song will I praise him.*" The heart is mentioned twice to show the truth of his faith and his joy. Observe the adverb "*greatly,*" we need not be afraid of being too full of rejoicing at the remembrance of grace received. We serve a great God, let us greatly rejoice in him. A song is the soul's fittest method of giving vent to its happiness, it were well if we were more like the singing lark, and less like the croaking raven. When the heart is glowing, the lips should not be silent. When God blesses us, we should bless him with all our heart.

8. "*The Lord is their strength.*"—The heavenly experience of one believer is a pattern of the life of all. To all the militant church, without exception, Jehovah is the same as he was to his servant David, "the least of them shall be as David." They need the same aid and they shall have it, for they are loved with the same love, written in the same book of life, and one with the same anointed Head. "*And he is the saving strength of his anointed.*" Here behold king David as the type of our Lord Jesus, our covenant Head, our anointed Prince, through whom all blessings come to us. He has achieved full salvation for us, and we desire saving strength from him, and as we share in the unction which is so largely shed upon him, we expect to partake in his salvation. Glory be unto the God and Father of our Lord Jesus Christ, who has magnified the power of his grace in his only begotten Son, whom he has anointed to be a Prince and a Saviour unto his people.

9 Save thy people, and bless thine inheritance : feed them also, and lift them up for ever.

9. This is a prayer for the church militant, written in short words, but full of weighty meaning. We must pray for the whole church, and not for ourselves alone. "*Save thy people.*" Deliver them from their enemies, preserve them from their sins, succour them under their troubles, rescue them from their temptations, and ward off from them every ill. There is a plea hidden in the expression, "*thy people ;*" for it may be safely concluded that God's interest in the church, as his own portion, will lead him to guard it from destruction. "*Bless thine inheritance.*" Grant positive blessings, peace, plenty, prosperity, happiness ; make all thy dearly-purchased and precious heritage to be comforted by thy Spirit. Revive, refresh, enlarge and sanctify thy church. "*Feed them also.*" Be a shepherd to thy flock, let their bodily and spiritual wants be plentifully supplied. By thy word, and ordinances, direct, rule, sustain, and satisfy those who are the sheep of thy hand. "*And lift them up for ever.*" Carry them in thine arms on earth, and then lift them into thy bosom in heaven. Elevate their minds and thoughts, spiritualise their affections, make them heavenly, Christlike, and full of God. O Lord, answer this our petition, for Jesus' sake.

EXPLANATORY NOTES AND QUAINT SAYINGS.

Verse 1.—"*Unto thee do I cry.*" It is of the utmost importance that we should have a *definite object* on which to fix our thoughts. Man, at the best of times, has but little power for realising abstractions ; but least of all in his time of sorrow. Then he is helpless ; then he needs every possible aid ; and if his mind wander in vacancy, it will soon weary, and sink down exhausted. God has graciously taken care that this need not be done. He has so manifested himself to man in his word, that the afflicted one can fix his mind's eye on him, as the definite object of his faith, and hope, and prayer. "Call unto *me*, and *I* will answer thee, and show thee great and mighty things, which thou knowest not." Jer. xxxiii. 3. This was what the Psalmist did ; and the definiteness of God, as the object of his trust in prayer, is very clearly marked. And specially great is the privilege of the *Christian* in this matter. He can fix his eye on Jesus ; he, without any very great stretch of imagination, can picture that Holy One looking down upon him ; listening to him ; feeling for him ; preparing to answer him. Dear reader, in the time of your trouble, do not roam ; do not send out your sighs into vacancy ; do not let your thoughts wander, as though they were looking for some one on whom to fix ; for some one to whom you could tell the story of your heart's need and desolation. Fix your heart as the Psalmist did, and say, "Unto *thee* will I cry." . . . Oh ! how happy is that man, who feels and knows that when trouble comes, he cannot be bewildered and confused by the stroke, no matter how heavy it may be. Sorrow-stricken he will be, but he has his resource, and he *knows* it, and will avail himself of it. His is no vague theory of the general sympathy of God for man ; his is a knowledge of God, as a personal and feeling God ; he says with the Psalmist, "Unto *thee* will I cry."—*Philip Bennett Power.*

Verse 1.—"*My rock.*" One day a female friend called on the Rev. William

Evans, a pious minister in England, and asked how he felt himself. " I am weakness itself," he replied ; " but I am on the *Rock*. I do not experience those transports which some have expressed in the view of death ; but my dependence is on the mercy of God in Christ. Here my religion began, and here it must end."

Verse 1.—" *My rock.*" The Rev. John Rees, of Crown Street, Soho, London, was visited on his death-bed by the Rev. John Leifchild, who very seriously asked him to describe the state of his mind. This appeal to the honour of his religion roused him, and so freshened his dying lamp, that raising himself up in his bed, he looked his friend in the face, and with great deliberation, energy, and dignity, uttered the following words :—" Christ in his person, Christ in the love of his heart, and Christ in the power of his arm, is the Rock on which I rest ; and now " (reclining his head gently on the pillow), " Death, strike ! "—*K. Arvine.*

Verse 1.—" *Be not silent to me.*" Let us next observe *what the heart desires from God.* It is that he would speak. " *Be not silent to me.*" Under these circumstances, when we make our prayer, we desire that God would let us know that he hears us, and that he would appear for us, and that he would say, he is our Father. And what do we desire God to say ? We want him to let us know that he hears us ; we want to hear him speak as distinctly to us, as we feel that we have spoken to him. We want to *know, not only by faith* that we have been heard, but *by God's having spoken to us on the very subject whereupon we have spoken to him.* When we feel thus assured that God has heard us, we can with the deepest confidence leave the whole matter about which we have been praying, in his hands. Perhaps an answer cannot come for a long time ; perhaps things, meanwhile, seem working in a contrary way ; it may be, that there is no direct appearance at all of God upon the scene ; still faith will hold up and be strong ; and there will be comfort in the heart, from the felt consciousness that God has heard our cry about the matter, and that he has told us so. We shall say to ourselves, " God knows all about it ; God has in point of fact told me so ; therefore I am in peace." And let it be enough for us that God tells us this, when he will perhaps tell us no more ; let us not want to try and induce him to speak much, when it is his will to speak but little : the best answer we can have at certain times is simply the statement that " he hears ; " by this answer to our prayer he at once encourages and exercises our faith. " It is said," said Rutherford, speaking of the Saviour's delay in responding to the request of the Syrophenician woman, " ' *he answered* not a 'vord,' but it is not said, he *heard* not a word. These two differ much. Christ often heareth when he doth not answer—his *not* answering *is an answer*, and speaks thus —' pray on, go on and cry, for the Lord holdeth his door fast bolted, not to keep you out, but that you may knock, and knock, and it shall be opened.' "—*Philip Bennett Power.*

Verse 1.—" *Lest . . . I become like them that go down into the pit.*" Thou seest, great God, my sad situation. Nothing to me is great or desirable upon this earth but the felicity of serving thee, and yet the misery of my destiny, and the duties of my state, bring me into connection with men who regard all godliness as a thing to be censured and derided. With secret horror I daily hear them blaspheming the ineffable gifts of thy grace, and ridiculing the faith and fervour of the godly as mere imbecility of mind. Exposed to such impiety, all my consolation, O my God, is to make my cries of distress ascend to the foot of thy throne. Although for the present, these sacrilegious blasphemies only awaken in my soul emotions of horror and pity, yet I fear that at last they may enfeeble me and seduce me into a crooked course of policy, unworthy of thy glory, and of the gratitude which I owe to thee. I fear that insensibly I may become such a coward as to blush at thy name, such a sinner as to resist the impulses of thy grace, such a traitor as to withhold my testimony against sin, such a self-deceiver as to disguise my criminal timidity by the name of prudence. Already I feel that this poison is insinuating itself into my heart, for while I would not have my conduct resemble that of the wicked who surround me, yet I am too much biassed by the fear of giving them offence. I dare not imitate them, but I am almost as much afraid of irritating them. I know that it is impossible both to please a corrupt world and a holy God, and yet I so far lose sight of this truth, that instead of sustaining me in decision, it only serves to render my vacillation the more inexcusable. What remains for me but to implore thy help ! Strengthen me, O Lord, against these declensions so injurious to thy glory, so fatal to the fidelity which is due to thee. Cause me to hear thy strengthening and encouraging voice. If the voice of thy grace be not lifted up in my spirit, reanimating my feeble faith, I feel that there is but a step between me and despair. I am on the brink of the precipice, I am ready to fall into a criminal complicity with those who would fain drag me down with them into the pit.—*Jean Baptiste Massillon*, 1663—1742, *freely translated by C. H. S.*

Verse 2.—"*I lift up my hands toward thy holy oracle.*" Called דְּבִיר, *debhir*, because there-hence God spake and gave answer. Toward this (a type of Christ, the Word essential), David lifteth up his hands, that it might be as a ladder, whereby his prayer might get up to heaven.—*John Trapp.*

Verse 3.—"*Draw me not away with the wicked . . . . which speak peace to their neighbours, but mischief is in their hearts.*" The godly man abhors dissimulation towards men ; his heart goes along with his tongue, he cannot flatter and hate, commend and censure. "Let love be without dissimulation." Romans xii. 9. Dissembled love is worse than hatred ; counterfeiting of friendship is no better than a lie (Psalm lxxviii. 36), for there is a pretence of that which is not. Many are like Joab : "He took Amasa by the beard to kiss him, and smote him with his sword in the fifth rib, that he died." There is a river in Spain, where the fish seem to be of a golden colour, but take them out of the water, and they are like other fish. All is not gold that glitters ; there are some pretend much kindness, but they are like great veins which have little blood ; if you lean upon them they are as a leg out of joint. For my part, I much question his truth towards God, that will flatter and lie to his friend. "He that hideth hatred with lying lips, and he that uttereth a slander is a fool." Proverbs x. 18.—*Thomas Watson.*

Verse 3.—"*Draw me not out with.*" An allusion, I conceive, to a shepherd selecting out a certain portion of his flock. "*Reckon me not among.*"—*Professor Lee.*

Verse 3.—"*Draw me not away.*" אַל־תִּמְשְׁכֵנִי from מָשַׁךְ ; that signifies, both to draw and apprehend, will be best rendered here, *seize not on me*, as he that *seizeth* on any to *carry* or *drag* him to *execution.*—*Henry Hammond.*

Verse 4.—"*Give them according to their deeds,*" etc. Here, again, occurs the difficult question about praying for vengeance, which, however, I shall despatch in a few words. In the first place, then, it is unquestionable, that if the flesh move us to seek revenge, the desire is wicked in the sight of God. He not only forbids us to imprecate evil upon our enemies in revenge for private injuries, but it cannot be otherwise than that all those desires which spring from hatred must be disordered. David's example, therefore, must not be alleged by those who are driven by their own intemperate passion to seek vengeance. The holy prophet is not inflamed here by his own private sorrow to devote his enemies to destruction ; but laying aside the desire of the flesh, he gives judgment concerning the matter itself. Before a man can, therefore, denounce vengeance against the wicked, he must first shake himself free from all improper feelings in his own mind. In the second place prudence must be exercised, that the heinousness of the evils which offend us drive us not to intemperate zeal, which happened even to Christ's disciples, when they desired that fire might be brought from heaven to consume those who refused to entertain their Master. Luke ix. 54. They pretended, it is true, to act according to the example of Elias, but Christ severely rebuked them, and told them that they knew not by what spirit they were actuated. In particular, we must observe this general rule, that we cordially desire and labour for the welfare of the whole human race. Thus it will come to pass, that we shall not only give way to the exercise of God's mercy, but shall also wish the conversion of those who seem obstinately to rush upon their own destruction. In short, David, being free from every evil passion, and likewise endued with the spirit of discretion and judgment, pleads here not so much his own cause as the cause of God. And by this prayer, he further reminds both himself and the faithful, that although the wicked may give themselves loose reins in the commission of every species of vice with impunity for a time, they must at length stand before the judgment-seat of God.—*John Calvin.*

Verse 4.—"*Give them according to their deeds, and according to the wickedness of their endeavours.*" Yes, great God, since thou hast from the beginning been only occupied in saving men, thou wilt surely strike with an eternal malediction these children of iniquity who appear to have been born only to be lost themselves, and to destroy others. Thy very benevolence towards mankind solicits thy thunders against these corrupters of society. The more thou hast done for our race, the more surely will the severity of thy justice reveal itself in destroying the wretches whose only study is to counteract thy goodness towards mankind. They labour incessantly to put men far away from thee, O my God, and in return thou wilt put them far away from thee for ever. They count it great gain to make their fellows thine enemies, and they shall have the desperate consolation of being such themselves to all eternity. What more fitting punishment for the wretches who desire to make all hearts rebel against thine adorable Majesty, than to lie through the baseness of their nature, under the eternal and frightful necessity of hating thee for ever.—*Jean Baptiste Massillon, rendered very freely by C. H. S.*

Verse 4.—"*Give them according to their deeds.*" The *Egyptians* killed the Hebrew male children, and God smote the firstborn of Egypt. *Sisera,* who thought to destroy Israel with his iron chariots, was himself killed with an iron nail, stuck through his temples. *Adoni-bezek,* Judges i. 5—7. *Gideon* slew forty elders of Succoth, and his sons were murdered by Abimelech. *Abimelech* slew seventy sons of Gideon upon one stone, and his own head was broken by a piece of millstone thrown by a woman. *Samson* fell by the "lust of the eye," and before death the Phillistines put out his eyes. *Agag,* 1 Sam. xx. 33. *Saul* slew the Gibeonites, and seven of his sons were hung up before the Lord. 2 Sam. xxi. 1—9. *Ahab,* after coveting Naboth's vineyard, 1 Kings xxi. 19, fulfilled 2 Kings ix. 24—26. *Jeroboam,* the same hand that was stretched forth against the altar was withered, 1 Kings xiii. 1—6. *Joab* having killed Abner, Amasa, and Absalom, was put to death by Solomon. *Daniel's accusers* thrown into the lions' den meant for Daniel. *Haman* hung upon the gallows designed for Mordecai. *Judas* purchased the field of blood, and then went and hanged himself. So in the history of *later days,* Bajazet was carried about by Tamerlane in an iron cage, as he intended to have carried Tamerlane. *Mazentius* built a bridge to entrap Constantine, and was over-thrown himself on that very spot. *Alexander VI.* was poisoned by the wine he had prepared for another. *Charles IX.* made the streets of Paris to stream with Protestant blood, and soon after blood streamed from all parts of his body in a bloody sweat. *Cardinal Beaton* condemned George Wishart to death, and presently died a violent death himself; he was murdered in bed, and his body was laid out in the same window from which he had looked upon Wishart's execution.—*G. S. Bowes, in "Illustrative Gatherings."*

Verse 4.—"*Render to them their desert.*" Meditate on God's righteousness, that it is not only his will, but his nature to punish sin; sin must damn thee without Christ, there is not only a possibility or probability that sin may ruin, but without an interest in Christ it must do so; whet much upon thy heart that *must;* God cannot but hate sin, because he is holy; and he cannot but punish sin, because he is righteous. God must not forego his own nature to gratify our humours. —*Christopher Fowler, in "Morning Exercises,"* 1676.

Verse 4.—He prayeth against his enemies, not out of any private revenge, but being led by the infallible spirit of prophecy, looking through these men to the enemies of Christ, and his people in all ages.—*David Dickson.*

Verses 4, 5.—In these verses, as indeed in most of the imprecatory passages, the imperative and the future are used promiscuously: "*Give them——render them——he shall destroy them.*" If therefore, the verbs, in all such passages, were uniformly rendered in the "future," every objection against the Scripture impre-cations would vanish at once, and they would appear clearly to be what they are, namely, prophecies of the divine judgments, which have been since executed against the Jews, and which will be executed against all the enemies of Jehovah, and his Christ; whom neither the "works" of creation, nor those of redemption, can lead to repentance.—*George Horne.*

Verse 6.—"*He hath heard.*" Prayer is the best remedy in a calamity. This is indeed a true *catholicum,* a general remedy for every malady. Not like the empiric's *catholicum,* which sometimes may work, but for the most part fails: but that which upon assured evidence and constant experience hath its *probatum est;* being that which the most wise, learned, honest, and skilful Physician that ever was, or can be, hath prescribed—even he that teacheth us how to bear what is to be borne, or how to heal and help what hath been borne.—*William Gouge.*

Verse 7.—" *The Lord is my strength."* Oh, sweet consolation ! If a man have a burthen upon him, yet if he have *strength* added to him, if the burthen be doubled, yet if his *strength* be trebled, the burden will not be heavier, but lighter than it was before to his natural strength ; so if our afflictions be heavy, and we cry out, Oh, we cannot bear them ! yet if we cannot bear them with our own strength, why may we not bear them with the strength of Jesus Christ ? Do we think that Christ could not bear them ? or if we dare not think but that Christ could bear them, why may not we come to bear them ? Some may question, can we have the strength of Christ ? Yes ; that very strength is made over to us by faith, for so the Scripture saith frequently, *The Lord is our strength ; God is our strength ; The Lord Jehovah is our strength ; Christ is our strength* (Psalm xxviii. 7 ; xliii. 2 ; cxviii. 14 ; Isaiah xii. 2 ; Hab. iii. 19 ; Col. i. 11) ; and, therefore, is Christ's strength ours, made over unto us, that we may be able to bear whatsoever lies upon us.—*Isaac Ambrose.*

Verse 7.—" *The Lord is my strength"* inwardly, " *and my shield"* outwardly. Faith finds both these in Jehovah, and the one not without the other, for what is a shield without strength, or strength without a shield ? " *My heart trusted in him, and I am helped : "* the idea of the former sentence is here carried out, that outward help was granted to inward confidence.—*W. Wilson, D.D.*

Verse 7.—" *My heart trusted in him, and I am helped."* Faith substantiateth things not yet seen ; it altereth the tenses, saith one, and putteth the future into the present tense as here.—*John Trapp.*

Verse 8.—" *The Lord is their strength : "* not mine only, but the strength of every believer. Note—the saints rejoice in their friends' comforts as well as their own ; for as we have not the less benefit by the light of the sun, so neither by the light of God's countenance, for others sharing therein ; for we are sure there is enough for all, and enough for each. This is our communion with all saints, that God is their strength and ours ; Christ their Lord and ours. 1 Cor. i. 2. He is their strength, the strength of all Israel, because he is the saving strength of " *his anointed,"* i.e., 1. Of David in the type : God in strengthening him that was their king and fought their battles, strengthened the whole kingdom. He calls himself God's anointed, because it was the unction he had received that exposed him to the envy of his enemies, and therefore entitled him to the divine protection. 2. Of Christ, his Anointed, his Messiah, in the antitype. God was his " *saving strength,"* qualified him for his undertaking, and carried him through it.—*Matthew Henry.*

Verse 9.—" *Lift them up."* The word here used may mean *sustain* them, or *support* them ; but it more properly means *bear*, and would be best expressed by a reference to the fact, that the shepherd carries the feeble, the young, and the sickly of his flock in his arms, or that he lifts them up when unable themselves to rise.—*Albert Barnes.*

HINTS TO PREACHERS.

Verse 1 (first clause).—A sinner's wise resolution in the hour of despondency.

Verse 1.—The saint's fear of becoming like the ungodly.

Verse 1.—God's silence—what terror may lie in it.

Verse 1 (last clause).—How low a soul may sink when God hides his face.

Verses 1, 2.—Prayer. I. *Its nature*—a " *cry."* 1. The utterance of life. 2. The expression of pain. 3. The pleading of need. 4. The voice of deep earnestness. II. *Its object*—" *O Lord, my rock."* God is our Foundation, Refuge, and immutable Friend. III. *Its aim*—" *Hear," " Be not silent."* We expect an answer, a clear and manifest answer, a speedy answer, a suitable answer, an effectual answer. IV. *Its medium*—" *Toward thy holy oracle.*" Our Lord Jesus, the true mercy seat, etc.

Verse 3.—The characters to be avoided, the doom to be dreaded, the grace to keep us from both.

Verse 4.—Measure for measure, or punishment proportioned to desert.

Verse 4.—Endeavour the measure of sin rather than mere result. Hence some are guilty of sins which they were unable to commit.

Verse 5.—Culpable negligence constantly persisted in, losing much blessing, and involving terrible condemnation.

Verse 6.—Answered prayers, a retrospect and song.

Verse 7.—The heart's possessions, confidence, experience, joy, and music.

Verse 7.—Adoring God for his mercies. I. What God is to the believer. II. What should be the disposition of our hearts towards him ?—*C. Simeon.*

Verse 8.—All power given to believers because of their union with Jesus.

Verse 9.—" A prayer for the church militant." See Exposition and Spurgeon's Sermons, No. 768.

PSALM XXIX.

TITLE.—A Psalm of David. *The title affords us no information beyond the fact that David is the author of this sublime song.*

SUBJECT.—*It seems to be the general opinion of modern annotators, that this Psalm is meant to express the glory of God as heard in the pealing thunder, and seen in an equinoctial tornado. Just as the eighth Psalm is to be read by moonlight, when the stars are bright, as the nineteenth needs the rays of the rising sun to bring out its beauty, so this can be best rehearsed beneath the black wing of tempest, by the glare of the lightning, or amid that dubious dusk which heralds the war of elements. The verses march to the tune of thunderbolts. God is everywhere conspicuous, and all the earth is hushed by the majesty of his presence. The word of God in the law and gospel is here also depicted in its majesty of power. True ministers are sons of thunder, and the voice of God in Christ Jesus is full of majesty. Thus we have God's works and God's word joined together : let no man put them asunder by a false idea that theology and science can by any possibility oppose each other. We may, perhaps, by a prophetic glance, behold in this Psalm the dread tempests of the latter days, and the security of the elect people.*

DIVISION.—*The first two verses are a call to adoration. From 3 to 10 the path of the tempest is traced, the attributes of God's word are rehearsed, and God magnified in all the terrible grandeur of his power ; and the last verse sweetly closes the scene with the assurance that the omnipotent Jehovah will give both strength and peace to his people. Let heaven and earth pass away, the Lord will surely bless his people.*

EXPOSITION.

GIVE unto the LORD, O ye mighty, give unto the LORD glory and strength.

2 Give unto the LORD the glory due unto his name ; worship the LORD in the beauty of holiness.

1. *" Give,"* i.e., ascribe. Neither men nor angels can confer anything upon Jehovah, but they should recognise his glory and might, and ascribe it to him in their songs and in their hearts. *" Unto the Lord,"* and unto him alone, must honour be given. Natural causes, as men call them, are God in action, and we must not ascribe power to them, but to the infinite Invisible who is the true source of all. *" O ye mighty."* Ye great ones of earth and of heaven, kings and angels, join in rendering worship to the blessed and only Potentate ; ye lords among men need thus to be reminded, for ye often fail where humbler men are ardent ; but fail no longer, bow your heads at once, and loyally do homage to the King of kings. How frequently do grandees and potentates think it beneath them to fear the Lord ; but, when they have been led to extol Jehovah, their piety has been the greatest jewel in their crowns. *" Give unto the Lord glory and strength,"* both of which men are too apt to claim for themselves, although they are the exclusive prerogatives of the self-existent God. Let crowns and swords acknowledge their dependence upon God. Not to your arms, O kings, give ye the glory, nor look for strength to your host of warriors, for all your pomp is but as a fading flower, and your might is as a shadow which declineth. When shall the day arrive when kings and princes shall count it their delight to glorify their God ? *" All worship be to God only,"* let this be emblazoned on every coat of arms.

2. *" Give unto the Lord the glory due unto his name."* A third time the admonition is given, for men are backward in glorifying God, and especially great men, who are often too much swollen with their own glory to spare time to give God his rightful praise, although nothing more is asked of them than is most just and right. Surely men should not need so much pressing to give what is due, especially when the payment is so pleasant. Unbelief and distrust, complaining and murmuring, rob God of his honour ; in this respect, even the saints fail to give due glory to their King. *" Worship the Lord,"* bow before him with devout homage and sacred awe, and let your worship be such as he appoints. Of old, worship was cumbered with ceremonial, and men gathered around one dedicated building, whose solemn

pomp was emblematic of " *the beauty of holiness ;* " but now our worship is spiritual, and the architecture of the house and the garments of the worshippers are matters of no importance ; the spiritual beauty of inward purity and outward holiness being far more precious in the eyes of our thrice holy God. O for grace ever to worship with holy motives and in a holy manner, as becometh saints ! The call to worship in these two verses chimes in with the loud pealing thunder, which is the church bell of the universe ringing kings and angels, and all the sons of earth to their devotions.

3 The voice of the LORD *is* upon the waters : the God of glory thundereth : the Lord *is* upon many waters.

4 The voice of the LORD *is* powerful ; the voice of the LORD *is* full of majesty.

5 The voice of the LORD breaketh the cedars ; yea, the LORD breaketh the cedars of Lebanon.

6 He maketh them also to skip like a calf, Lebanon and Sirion like a young unicorn.

7 The voice of the LORD divideth the flames of fire.

8 The voice of the LORD shaketh the wilderness ; the LORD shaketh the wilderness of Kadesh.

9 The voice of the LORD maketh the hinds to calve, and discovereth the forests : and in his temple doth every one speak of *his* glory.

10 The LORD sitteth upon the flood ; yea, the LORD sitteth King for ever.

3. " *The voice of the Lord is upon the waters.*" The thunder is not only poetically but instructively called " the voice of God," since it peals from on high ; it surpasses all other sounds, it inspires awe, it is entirely independent of man, and has been used on some occasions as the grand accompaniment of God's speech to Adam's sons. There is peculiar terror in a tempest at sea, when deep calleth unto deep, and the raging sea echoes to the angry sky. No sight more alarming than the flash of lightning around the mast of the ship ; and no sound more calculated to inspire a reverent awe than the roar of the storm. The children of heaven have often enjoyed the tumult with humble joy peculiar to the saints, and even those who know not God have been forced into unwilling reverence while the storm has lasted. " *The God of glory thundereth.*" Thunder is in truth no mere electric phenomenon, but is caused by the interposition of God himself. Even the old heathen spake of Jupiter Tonans ; but our modern wise men will have us believe in laws and forces, and anything or nothing so that they may be rid of God. Electricity of itself can do nothing, it must be called and sent upon its errand ; and until the almighty Lord commissions it, its bolt of fire is inert and powerless. As well might a rock of granite, or a bar of iron fly in the midst of heaven, as the lightning go without being sent by the great First Cause. " *The Lord is upon many waters.*" Still the Psalmist's ear hears no voice but that of Jehovah, resounding from the multitudinous and dark waters of the upper ocean of clouds, and echoing from the innumerable billows of the storm-tossed sea below. The waters above and beneath the firmament are astonished at the eternal voice. When the holy Spirit makes the divine promise to be heard above the many waters of our soul's trouble, then is God as glorious in the spiritual world as in the universe of matter. Above us and beneath us all is the peace of God when he gives us quiet.

4. " *The voice of the Lord is powerful.*" An irresistible power attends the lightning of which the thunder is the report. In an instant, when the Lord wills it, the force of electricity produces amazing results. A writer upon this subject, speaks of these results as including a light of the intensity of the sun in his strength, a heat capable of fusing the compactest metals, a force in a moment paralysing the muscles of the most powerful animals ; a power suspending the all-pervading gravity of the earth, and an energy capable of decomposing and recomposing the closest affinities of the most intimate combinations. Well does Thompson speak of " the unconquerable lightning," for it is the chief of the ways of God in physical forces, and none can measure its power.

As the voice of God in nature is so powerful, so is it in grace ; the reader will do well to draw a parallel, and he will find much in the gospel, which may be illustrated by the thunder of the Lord in the tempest. His voice, whether in nature or revelation, shakes both earth and heaven ; see that ye refuse not him that speaketh. If his voice be thus mighty, what must his hand be ! beware lest ye provoke a blow. *" The voice of the Lord is powerful ; the voice of the Lord is full of majesty."* The King of kings speaks like a king. As when a lion roareth, all the beasts of the forest are still, so is the earth hushed and mute while Jehovah thundereth marvellously.

> " 'Tis listening fear and dumb amazement all."

As for the written word of God, its majesty is apparent both in its style, its matter, and its power over the human mind ; blessed be God, it is the majesty of mercy wielding a silver sceptre ; of such majesty the word of our salvation is *full* to overflowing.

5. *" The voice of the Lord breaketh the cedars."*

> " Black from the stroke above, the smouldering pine
> Stands a sad shatter'd trunk."

Noble trees fall prostrate beneath the mysterious bolt, or stand in desolation as mementoes of its power. Lebanon itself is not secure, high as it stands, and ancient as are its venerable woods : *" Yea, the Lord breaketh the cedars of Lebanon."* The greatest and most venerable of trees or men, may not reckon upon immunity when the Lord is abroad in his wrath. The gospel of Jesus has a like dominion over the most inaccessible of mortals ; and when the Lord sends the word, it breaks hearts far stouter than the cedars.

6. *" He maketh them also to skip like a calf ; Lebanon and Sirion like a young unicorn."* Not only the trees, but the mountains themselves move as though they frisked and leaped like young bulls or antelopes. As our own poets would mention hills and valleys known to them, so the Psalmist hears the crash and roar among the ranges of Libanus, and depicts the tumult in graphic terms. Thus sings one of our own countrymen :—

> " Amid Carnarvon's mountains rages loud
> The repercussive roar : with mighty crash
> Into the flashing deep, from the rude rocks
> Of Penmaen Mawr, heap'd hideous to the sky.
> Tumble the smitten cliffs ; and Snowdon's peak,
> Dissolving, instant yields his wintry load.
> Far seen, the heights of heathy Cheviot blaze,
> And Thulè bellows through her utmost isles."

The glorious gospel of the blessed God has more than equal power over the rocky obduracy and mountainous pride of man. The voice of our dying Lord rent the rocks and opened the graves : his living voice still works the like wonders. Glory be to his name, the hills of our sins leap into his grave, and are buried in the red sea of his blood, when the voice of his intercession is heard.

7. *" The voice of the Lord divideth the flames of fire."* As when sparks fly from the anvil by blows of a ponderous hammer, so the lightning attends the thundering strokes of Jehovah.

> " At first heard solemn o'er the verge of heaven,
> The tempest growls ; but as it nearer comes,
> And rolls its awful burden on the wind,
> The lightnings flash a larger curve, and more
> The noise astounds : till overhead a sheet
> Of livid flame discloses wide ; then shuts
> And opens wider ; shuts and opens still
> Expansive, wrapping ether in a blaze."

The thunder seems to divide one flash from another, interposing its deepening roar between the flash which precedes it and the next. That the flashes are truly flames of fire is witnessed by their frequently falling upon houses, churches. etc., and wrapping them in a blaze. How easily could the Lord destroy his rebellious creatures with his hot thunderbolts ! how gracious is the hand which spares such great offenders, when to crush them would be so easy !

Flames of fire attend the voice of God in the gospel, illuminating and melting the hearts of men ; by these he consumes our lusts and kindles in us a holy flame of ever-inspiring love and holiness. Pentecost is a suggestive commentary upon this verse.

8. As the storm travelled, it burst over the desert. " *The voice of the Lord shaketh the wilderness ; the Lord shaketh the wilderness of Kadesh.*" God courts not the applause of men—his grandest deeds are wrought where man's inquisitive glance is all unknown. Where no sound of man was heard, the voice of God was terribly distinct. The vast and silent plains trembled with affright. Silence did homage to the Almighty voice. Low lying plains must hear the voice of God as well as lofty mountains ; the poor as well as the mighty must acknowledge the glory of the Lord. Solitary and barren places are to be gladdened by the gospel's heavenly sound. What a shaking and overturning power there is in the word of God ! even the conservative desert quivers into progress when God decrees it.

9. " *The voice of the Lord maketh the hinds to calve,*" those timid creatures, in deadly fear of the tempest, drop their burdens in an untimely manner. Perhaps a better reading is, " the oaks to tremble," especially as this agrees with the next sentence, *and " discovereth the forests.*" The dense shades of the forest are lit up with the lurid glare of the lightning, and even the darkest recesses are for a moment laid bare.

> " The gloomy woods
> Start at the flash, and from their deep recess
> Wide-flaming out, their trembling inmates shake."

Our first parents sought a refuge among the trees, but the voice of the Lord soon found them out, and made their hearts to tremble. There is no concealment from the fire-glance of the Almighty—one flash of his angry eye turns midnight into noon. The gospel has a like revealing power in dark hearts, in a moment it lights up every dark recess of the heart's ungodliness, and bids the soul tremble before the Lord.

" *In his temple doth every one speak of his glory.*" Those who were worshipping in the temple, were led to speak of the greatness of Jehovah as they heard the repeated thunder-claps. The whole world is also a temple for God, and when he rides abroad upon the wings of the wind, all things are vocal in his praise. We too, the redeemed of the Lord, who are living temples for his Spirit, as we see the wonders of his power in creation, and feel them in grace, unite to magnify his name. No tongue may be dumb in God's temple when his glory is the theme. The original appears to have the force of " every one crieth Glory," as though all things were moved by a sense of God's majesty to shout in ecstasy, " Glory, glory." Here is a good precedent for our Methodist friends and for the Gogoniants of the zealous Welsh.

10. " *The Lord sitteth upon the flood.*" Flood follows tempest, but Jehovah is ready for the emergency. No deluge can undermine the foundation of his throne. He is calm and unmoved, however much the deep may roar and be troubled : his government rules the most unstable and boisterous of created things. Far out on the wild waste of waters, Jehovah " plants his footsteps in the sea, and rides upon the storm," " *Yea, the Lord sitteth King for ever.*" Jesus has the government upon his shoulders eternally : our interests in the most stormy times are safe in his hands. Satan is not king, but Jehovah Jesus is ; therefore let us worship him, and rejoice evermore.

11 The Lord will give strength unto his people ; the Lord will bless his people with peace.

Power was displayed in the hurricane whose course this Psalm so grandly pictures ; and now, in the cool calm after the storm, that power is promised to be the strength of the chosen. He who wings the unerring bolt, will give to his redeemed the wings of eagles ; he who shakes the earth with his voice, will terrify the enemies of his saints, and give his children peace. Why are we weak when we have divine strength to flee to ? Why are we troubled when the Lord's own peace is ours ? Jesus the mighty God is our peace—what a blessing is this to-day ! What a blessing it will be to us in that day of the Lord which will be in darkness and not light to the ungodly !

Dear reader, is not this a noble Psalm to be sung in stormy weather ? Can you sing amid the thunder ? Will you be able to sing when the last thunders are let loose, and Jesus judges quick and dead ? If you are a believer, the last verse is your heritage, and surely that will set you singing.

EXPLANATORY NOTES AND QUAINT SAYINGS.

Whole Psalm.—In this Psalm, the strength of Jehovah is celebrated ; and the exemplification of it is evidently taken from a thunder-storm in Lebanon. The Psalm seems to be addressed to the angels. See Psalm lxxxix. 7. It thus begins :—

> " Render unto Jehovah, ye sons of the mighty,
> Render unto Jehovah glory and strength ;
> Render to Jehovah the glory of his name ;
> Bow down to Jehovah in the majesty of holiness ! "

Immediately follows the description of the thunder-storm, in which it does not seem fanciful to observe the historical progression which is usual on such occasions. The first lines seem to describe only the noise of the thunder, the description growing more intense as the rumbling draws nearer.

> " The voice of Jehovah is above the waters ;
> The God of glory thundereth
> Jehovah is louder than many waters,
> The voice of Jehovah in strength,
> The voice of Jehovah in majesty ! "

But now the effects become visible ; the storm has descended on the mountains and forests :—

> " The voice of Jehovah shivers the cedars,
> Even shivers Jehovah the cedars of Lebanon ;
> And makes them to skip, like a calf ;
> Lebanon and Sirion, like a young buffalo,
> The voice of Jehovah forketh the lightning's flash ! "

From the mountains the storm sweeps down into the plains, where, however, its effects are not so fearful as on the mountains—

> " The voice of Jehovah causeth the desert to tremble—
> The voice of Jehovah causeth to tremble the desert of Kadesh—
> The voice of Jehovah causeth the oaks to tremble,
> And lays bare the forests !
> Therefore, in his temple every one speaks of his glory."

The description of the swollen torrents closes the scene—

> " Jehovah upon the rain-torrent sitteth.
> Yea, sitteth Jehovah a king for ever."

And the moral or application of the whole is—

> " Jehovah to his people will give strength.
> Jehovah will bless his people with peace."
>   *Robert Murray M'Cheyne,* 1813—1843.

Whole Psalm.—There is no phenomenon in nature so awful as a thunder-storm, and almost every poet from Homer and Virgil down to Dante and Milton, or rather down to Grahame and Pollok, has described it. In the Bible, too, we have a thunder-storm, the twenty-ninth Psalm—the description of a tempest, which, rising from the Mediterranean, and travelling by Lebanon and along the inland mountains, reaches Jerusalem, and sends the people into the temple-porticoes for refuge ; and, besides those touches of terror in which the geographical progress of the tornado is described, it derives a sacred vitality and power from the presence of Jehovah in each successive peal.—*James Hamilton, D.D., in " The Literary Attractions of the Bible,"* 1849.

Whole Psalm.—A glorious Psalm of praise sung during a tempest, the majesty of which shakes universal nature, so much so that the greatness of the power of the Lord is felt by all in heaven and on earth. This Lord is the God of his people, who blesses them with strength and peace. To rightly appreciate the feelings of the bard, one ought to realise an Oriental storm, especially in the mountainous regions of Palestine, which, accompanied by the terrific echoes of the encircling mountains, by torrents of rain-like waterspouts, often scatters terror on man and beast, destruction on cities and fields. Wilson, the traveller, describes such a tempest in the neighbourhood of Baalbek : " I was overtaken by a storm, as if the floodgates of heaven had burst ; it came on in a moment, and raged with a power which suggested the end of the world. Solemn darkness covered the earth : the rain descended in torrents, and sweeping down the mountain side, became by the fearful power of the storm transmuted into thick clouds of fog." Compare also our Lord's parable, taken from life, in Matt. vii. 27.—*Augustus F. Tholuck, in loc.*

Verse 1.—" *Give unto the Lord.*" *Give, give, give.* This showeth how unwilling such are usually to give God his right, or to suffer a word of exhortation to this purpose.—*John Trapp.*

Verse 1.—" *O ye mighty.*" The Septuagint renders it, *O ye sons of rams !* These bell-wethers should not cast their noses into the air, and carry their crest the higher, because the shepherd hath bestowed a bell upon them, more than upon the rest of the flock.—*John Trapp.*

Verses 1, 2.—There are three *gives* in these two verses :—" *Give unto the Lord, give unto the Lord, give unto the Lord the glory that is due unto his name.*" Glory is God's right, and he stands upon his right ; and this the sincere Christian knows, and therefore he gives him his right, he gives him the honour and the glory that is due unto his name. But pray do not mistake me. I do not say that such as are really sincere do actually eye the glory of Christ in all their actions. Oh, no ! This is a happiness desirable on earth, but shall never be attained till we come to heaven. Bye and base ends and aims will be still ready to creep into the best hearts, but all sincere hearts sigh and groan under them. They complain to God of them, and they cry out for justice, justice upon them ; and it is the earnest desire and daily endeavours of their souls to be rid of them ; and therefore they shall not be imputed to them, nor keep good things from them. But now take a sincere Christian in his ordinary, usual, and habitual course, and you shall find that his aims and ends in all his actions and undertakings are to glorify God, to exalt God, and to lift up God in the world. If the hypocrite did in good earnest aim at the glory of God in what he does, then the glory of God would swallow up his bye-aims and carnal ends, as Aaron's rod swallowed up the magicians' rods. Exod. vii. 10—12. Look, as the sun puts out the light of the fire, so the glory of God, where it is aimed at, will put out and consume all bye and base ends. This is most certain, that which is a man's great end, that will work out all other ends. He that sets up the glory of God as his chief end, will find that his chief end will by degrees eat out all low and base ends. Look, as Pharaoh's lean kine ate up the fat (Gen. xli. 4), so the glory of God will eat up all those fat and worldly ends that crowd in upon the soul in religious work. Where the glory of God is kept up as a man's greatest end, there all bye and base ends will be kept at an under.—*Thomas Brooks.*

Verse 2.—" *Give unto the Lord the glory due unto his name.*" Which yet you cannot do, for his name is above all praise (Psalm cxlviii. 13) ; but you must aim at it. The Rabbins observe that God's holy name is mentioned eighteen several times in this Psalm ; that great men especially may give him the honour of his name, that they may stand in awe and not sin, that they may bring presents to him who ought to be feared, and those also the very best of the best, since he is a great king, and standeth much upon his seniority. Mal. i. 14.—*John Trapp.*

Verse 2.—" *Worship the Lord.*" If any should ask, Why is the Lord to be worshipped ? Why must he have such high honours from those that are high ? What doth he in the world that calls for such adoration ? David answereth meteorologically as well as theologically, he answers from the clouds (verses 3, 4), " The voice of the Lord is upon the waters : the God of glory thundereth : the Lord is upon many waters. The voice of the Lord is powerful ; the voice of the Lord is full of majesty ; " as if he had said, Although the Lord Jesus Christ will not set up an outward, pompous, political kingdom, such as that of Cyrus, Alexander, etc., yet by the ministry of the gospel he will erect a spiritual kingdom, and gather to himself a church that shall abide for ever, out of all the nations of the earth ; for the gospel shall be carried and preached, to not only the people of Israel, the Jews, but to the Gentiles, all the world over, that the minds of men may be enlightened, awakened, and moved with that unheard of doctrine of salvation by Christ, which had been hid from ages and generations.—*Joseph Caryl.*

Verse 3.—" *The voice of the Lord is upon the waters : the God of glory thundereth : the Lord is upon many waters.''* Yes, great God, these torrents of tears which flow down from my eyes announce thy divine presence in my soul. This heart hitherto so dry, so arid, so hard ; this rock which thou hast struck a second time, will not resist thee any longer, for out of it there now gushes healthful waters in abundance. The selfsame voice of God which overturns the mountains, thunders, lightens, and divides the heaven above the sinner, now commands the clouds to pour forth showers of blessings, changing the desert of his soul into a field producing a hundredfold ; that voice I hear.—*J. B. Massillon.*

Verses 3—10.—" *The Lord,''* etc. All things which we commonly say are the effects of the natural powers of matter and laws of motion, are, indeed (if we will speak strictly and properly), the effects of God's acting upon matter continually and at every moment, either immediately by himself, or mediately by some created intelligent being. Consequently there is no such thing as the cause of nature, or the power of nature.—*Samuel Clarke,** 1675—1729.

Verses 3—10.—

> The voice of the Lord on the ocean is known,
> The God of eternity thundereth abroad ;
> The voice of the Lord from the depth of his throne
> Is terror and power ;—all nature is awed.
>
> The voice of the Lord through the calm of the wood
> Awakens its echoes, strikes light through its caves,
> The Lord sitteth King on the turbulent flood,
> The winds are his servants, his servants the waves.

James Montgomery, 1771—1854.

Verses 3—11.—

> Messiah's voice is in the cloud,
> The God of glory thunders loud.
> Messiah rides along the floods,
> He treads upon the flying clouds.
> Messiah's voice is full of power,
> His lightnings play when tempests lower.
> Messiah's voice the cedars breaks,
> While Lebanon's foundation quakes.
> Messiah's voice removes the hills,
> And all the plains with rivers fills.
> The voice of their expiring God,
> Shall make the rocks to start abroad ;
> Mount Zion and Mount Sirion,
> Shall bound along with Lebanon :
> The flames of fire shall round him wreathe,
> When he shall on the ether breathe.
> Messiah's voice shall shake the earth,
> And, lo ! the graves shall groan in birth,
> Ten thousand thousand living sons
> Shall be the issue of their groans.
> The peace of God, the gospel sounds ;
> The peace of God, the earth rebounds ;
> The gospel everlasting shines
> A light from God that ne'er declines.
> This is the light Jehovah sends,
> To bless the world's remotest ends.

Barclay's Paraphrase.

Verse 4.—" *The voice of the Lord.''* These vehement repetitions resemble a series of thunder-claps ; one seems to hear the dread artillery of heaven firing volley after volley, while peal on peal the echo follows the sound.—*C. H. S.*

Verse 4.—" *The voice of the Lord is powerful.''* I would render unto God the glory due unto his name, for the admirable change which he has wrought in my heart. There was nothing to be found in me but an impious hardness and inveterate disorder. From this helpless state he changed me into a new man and made resplendent the glory of his name and the power of his grace. He alone can work such prodigies. Unbelievers who refuse to acknowledge the hand of God in creation must surely in this case admit, that " this is the finger of God." Yes, great God,

---

* " The friend and disciple of Newton."

chaos knows not how to resist thee, it hears thy voice obediently, but the obdurate heart repels thee, and thy mighty voice too often calls to it in vain. Thou art not so great and wonderful in creating worlds out of nothing as thou art when thou dost command a rebel heart to arise from its abyss of sin, and to run in the ways of thy commandments. To disperse a chaos of crime and ignorance by the majesty of thy word, to shed light on the direst darkness, and by the Holy Ghost to establish harmonious order where all was confusion, manifests in far greater measure thine omnipotence than the calling forth of heavenly laws and celestial suns from the first chaos.—*J. B. Massillon.*

Verse 4.—O may the evangelical " Boanerges " so cause the glorious sound of the gospel to be heard under the whole heaven, that the world may again be made sensible thereof ; before that voice of the Son of Man, which hath so often called sinners to repentance, shall call them to judgment.—*George Horne.*

Verse 4.—Where the word of a king is, there is power, but what imperial voice shall be likened unto the majestic thunder of the Lord ?—*C. H. S.*

Verse 5.—" *The voice of Jehovah.*" Philosophers think not that they have reasoned skilfully enough about inferior causes, unless they separate God very far from his works. It is a diabolical science, however, which fixes our contemplations on the works of nature, and turns them away from God. If any one who wished to know a man, should take no notice of his face, but should fix his eyes only on the points of his nails, his folly might justly be derided. But far greater is the folly of those philosophers, who, out of mediate and proximate causes, weave themselves vails lest they should be compelled to acknowledge the hand of God, which manifestly displays itself in his works.—*John Calvin.*

Verse 5.—" *The voice of the Lord breaketh the cedars,*" etc. Like as tempests when they arise, and lightning, quickly and in a trice, hurl down and overturn mountains and the highest trees ; even so doth the Lord bring down with a breakneck fall, the proud, haughty, arrogant, and insolent, who set themselves against God, and seek the spoil of those that be quiet and godly.—*Robert Cawdray.*

Verse 5.—" *The voice of the Lord breaketh the cedars.*" The ancient expositors remind us that the *breaking* of the *cedar trees* by the wind, is a figure of the laying low of the lofty and proud things of this world, by the rushing mighty wind of the Holy Spirit, given on that day. *Confringit cedros Deus, hoc est humiliat superbos.* (S. Jerome, and so S. Basil.)—*Christopher Wordsworth.*

Verse 5.—" *The Lord breaketh the cedars of Lebanon.*"—What a shame is it then that our hard hearts break not, yield not, though thunder-struck with the dreadful menaces of God's mouth !—*John Trapp.*

Verse 5.—" *Breaketh the cedars of Lebanon :* "—

> When high in air the pine ascends,
> To every ruder blast it bends.
> The palace falls with heavier weight,
> When tumbling from its airy height ;
> And when from heaven the lightning flies.
> It blasts the hills that proudest rise.

> *Horace, translated by Philip Francis, D.D.,* 1765.

Verse 5.—" *The cedars of Lebanon.*" These mighty trees of God, which for ages have stood the force of the tempest, rearing their ever-green colossal boughs in the region of everlasting snow, are the first objects of the fury of the lightning, which is well known to visit first the highest objects.—*Robert Murray M'Cheyne.*

Verse 6.—" *He maketh them also to skip like a calf ; Lebanon and Sirion like a young unicorn ;* " that is, the Lord by his thundering, powerful voice, first, will make them skip, as frighted with fear ; and secondly, as revived with joy. Yet more (verse 7), " *The voice of the Lord divideth the flames of fire ;* " that is, will send and divide to every one as they need (1 Cor. xii. 11), the Holy Spirit, who is compared to and called *fire* (Matt. iii. 11), and who came as with a thunder-storm *of a rushing mighty wind,* and with the appearance of *cloven tongues, like as of fire,* and sat upon each one of the apostles. Acts ii. 2, 3. Nor did this voice of thunder, accompanied with divided flames of fire reach Jerusalem only ; for, as it follows (verse 8), " *The voice of the Lord shaketh the wilderness ; the Lord shaketh the wilderness of Kadesh ;* " that is, the Lord by the voice of the gospel shall go forth with power to those Gentiles, who are like a wilderness, barren of goodness, and unmanured in spirituals, though they dwell in well-governed cities, and are well furnished with morals. It shall go forth also to those Gentiles who inhabit waste wildernesses, and are not so much as reduced to civility. These wildernesses, the thundering voice of the Lord hath shaken heretofore, and doth shake at this day, and will yet further shake, that the fulness of the Gentiles may come in. Many of these wildernesses hath the Lord turned into fruitful fields, and pleasant lands, by the voice of the gospel sounding among them. For in these wildernesses (as it followeth, verse 9), " *The voice of the Lord maketh the hinds to calve ;* " that is, they that were as wild, as untaught, and untamed as the *hind*, or any beast in the forest, he brings to the sorrows of their new birth, to repentance and gospel humiliation, and in doing this, " *he* (as the Psalmist goes on), *discovereth the forests ;* " that is, opens the hearts of men, which are as thick set and full grown with vanity, pride, hypocrisy, self-love, and self-sufficiency, as also with wantonness and sensuality, as any forest is overgrown with thickets of trees and bushes, which deny all passage through, till cleared away with burning down or cutting up. Such an opening, such a discovery, doth the Lord make in the forests of men's hearts, by the sword and fire, that is, by the word and spirit of the gospel ; and when all this is done, the forest becomes a *temple*, and as that verse concludes, " *In his temple doth every one speak of his glory.*" And if the *floods* of ungodliness rise up against this people, whom the thunder and lightning of the gospel have subdued to Christ, and framed into a holy temple, then the Psalmist assureth us (verse 10), " *The Lord sitteth upon the flood,*" that is, 'tis under his power, he ruleth and overruleth it ; " *Yea, the Lord sitteth King for ever ;*" and (verse 11), " *The Lord will give strength unto his people ; the Lord will bless his people with peace.*" Thus, the Lord " thundereth marvellously " (Job xxxvii. 5), and these are glorious marvels which he thundereth ; he converts sinners.

Thus, though I like not their way who are given to allegorise the Scriptures, yet I doubt not but we may make a profitable use of this and many other Scriptures by way of allegory. This being an undeniable truth, which is the ground of it—that the Lord puts forth, as it were, the power of thunder and lightning in the preaching of his Word ; these two things are to be marked.—*Joseph Caryl.*

Verse 6.—" *He maketh them also to skip like a calf.*" That is to say, he hath made the splinters and broken pieces of trees that have been struck with lightning, to fly up into the air, or when they have been shaken by the wind, storms, or by earthquakes.—*John Diodati.*

Verse 6.—The original is—

> " And makes them skip like a calf,
> Lebanon and Sirion, like a young buffalo."

At first sight it might appear that the cedars were still meant, and that Lebanon and Sirion were used by metonymy for the cedars which grew upon them. But, 1. We never hear of cedars growing upon Sirion, or Shenir, or Hermon, for it has all these names ; and, 2. There is a parallel passage where this interpretation will hardly answer in Psalm cxiv. Describing the exodus of Israel, it says—

> "The mountains skipped like rams,
> And the little hills like lambs."

The same verb occurs here, the verb which means " to skip, to dance," used in Nahum iii. 2, to signify the jolting of chariots, and also in Joel ii. 5. In both these instances, rough motion, accompanied with noise, seems intended. Now, though this may very well be understood as a highly figurative description, as it undoubtedly is, of the usual effects of a thunder-storm ; yet it is interesting to compare it with the following passage of Volney, which describes certain phenomena as frequent in Mount Lebanon, which may give a new meaning to the " *skipping of the mountains :* "—

" When the traveller," says he, " penetrates the interior of these mountains, the ruggedness of the roads, the steepness of the declivities, the depth of the precipices, have at first a terrific effect ; but the sagacity of the mules which bear him soon inspires him with confidence, and enables him to examine at his ease the picturesque scenes which succeed one another, so as almost to bewilder him. There, as in the Alps, he sometimes travels whole days to arrive at a spot which was in sight when he set out. He turns, he descends, he winds round, he climbs; and under the perpetual change of position, one is ready to think that a magical power is varying at every step the beauties of the landscapes. Sometimes villages are seen, ready as it were to slide down the deep declivities, and so disposed that the roofs of the one row of houses serve as a street to the row above. At another time, you see a convent seated on an isolated cone, like Marshaia in the valley of Tigré. Here a rock is pierced by a torrent, forming a natural cascade as at *Nahr-el-Leban;* there another rock assumes the appearance of a natural wall! Often on the sides, ledges of stones, washed down and left by the waters, resemble ruins disposed by art. In some places, the waters meeting with inclined beds, have undermined the intermediate earth, and have formed caverns, as at Nahr-el-Kelb, near Antoura. In other places, they have worn for themselves subterranean channels, through which flow little rivulets during part of the year, as at Mar Hama. Sometimes these picturesque circumstances have become tragical ones. Rocks loosened or thrown off their equilibrium by thaw or earthquake, have been known to precipitate themselves on the adjacent dwellings, and crush the inhabitants. An accident of this kind, about twenty years ago, buried a whole village near Mar Djordos, so as to leave no trace of its existence. More recently, and near the same spot, the soil of a hill planted with mulberry trees and vines detached itself by a sudden thaw, and, sliding over the surface of the rock which it had covered, like a vessel launched from the stocks, established itself entire in the valley below."—*Robert Murray M'Cheyne.*

Verse 7.—" *The voice of the Lord divideth the flames of fire."* By the power of God, the " *flames of fire* " are " *divided* " and sent abroad from the clouds upon the earth, in the terrible form of lightning, that sharp and glittering sword of the Almighty, which no substance can withstand. The same power of God goeth forth by his word, " quick and powerful, and sharper than any two-edged sword," penetrating, melting, enlightening, and inflaming the hearts of men. Acts ii. 3, Heb. iv. 12.—*George Horne.*

Verse 7.—" *The voice of the Lord divideth the flames of fire."* The voice of the Lord is here said to *divide the flames;* literally, *to hew out flames,* λατομεῖν φλόγας. The *Sept.* has διακόπτει φλόγα πυρός. In the words of Gesenius, " The voice of Jehovah *cutteth out flames* of fire, *i.e.,* " sendeth out divided flames of fire." This is (as Theodoret has observed) very descriptive of the divine action at Pentecost, sending forth *divided flames,* like " *tela trisulca,*" in the tongues of fire which were divided off from one heavenly source or fountain of flame, and sat upon the heads of the apostles, and which filled them with the fire of holy zeal and love.—*Christopher Wordsworth.*

Verse 7.—" *Divideth the flames of fire."* Marg., *cutteth out.* The Hebrew word אצב *khatzab* means properly *to cut, to hew, to hew out;* as for example, stones. The allusion here is undoubtedly to lightning; and the image is either that it seems to be cut out, or cut into tongues and streaks—or, more probably, that the *clouds* seem to be cut or hewed, so as to make openings or paths for the lightning. The eye is evidently fixed on the clouds, and on the sudden flash of lightning, as if the clouds had been *cleaved* or *opened* for the passage of it. The idea of the Psalmist is, that the " *voice of the Lord,*" or the thunder, seems to cleave or open the clouds for the flames of fire to play amidst the tempest.—*Albert Barnes.*

Verse 8.—" *The Lord shaketh the wilderness of Kadesh."* That Kadesh-Naphtali is meant, the geographical position of Lebanon would make us believe, though this is not necessary. And, although Syria is much exposed to earthquakes—as, for example, that of Aleppo, in 1822, which was sensibly felt at Damascus—yet it does not seem necessary to imagine anything farther than the usual effects of a thunder-storm. The *oaks and forests* of verse 9, suit well with the description given of the lower limbs of Lebanon, which abound in " thickets of myrtle, woods of fir, walnut trees, carob tres, and Turkish oaks." And the *rain-torrent* of verse 10 is admirably descriptive of the sudden swell of the thousand streams which flow from Lebanon. According to modern travellers, the number of water-courses descending from Lebanon is immense; and the suddenness of the rise of these streams may be gathered from the contradictions in their accounts. The Nahr-el-Sazib is described by one as " a rivulet, though crossed by a bridge of six arches;" by another it is called " a large river." The Damour (the ancient

Tamyras), which flows immediately from Lebanon, is "a river," says Mandrell, "apt to swell much upon sudden rains; in which case, precipitating itself from the mountains with great rapidity, it has been fatal to many a passenger." He mentions a French gentleman, M. Spon, who, a few years before, in attempting to ford it, was hurried down by the stream, and perished in the sea. This is one instance of very many in the mountains of Lebanon, where the brook, which is usually nearly dry, becomes all at once an impassable torrrent. When Volney looked upon the rivers of Syria in summer, he doubted whether they could be called rivers. But had he ventured to cross them aftr a thunder-storm, his scepticism would no longer have had room or time to exercise itself, and he would have felt the propriety of the Psalmist's painting, where he says—

> "Jehovah sitteth on the rain-torrents,
> Jehovah sitteth a King for ever."

Robert Murray M'Cheyne.

Verse 8.—"*The voice of the Lord shaketh the wilderness.*" Great God, I have laboured to escape thee! I sought refuge for my remorse in a retreat where nothing might recall me to my God. Far away from the succours of religion, remote from all the channels which bring to me the waters of grace, apart from all whose reproving witness might restrain me from iniquity; yet even there, Great God, where I believed that I had found an asylum inaccessible to thine eternal mercy, wherein I could sin with impunity, even there, in that wilderness, thy voice arrested me and laid me at thy feet.—*J. B. Massillon.*

Verse 9.—"*The voice of the Lord maketh the hinds to calve.*" With respect to the sense conveyed by the common reading, it may be observed, that hinds bring forth their young with great difficulty and pain, "bowing themselves, bruising their young ones, and casting out their sorrows" (Job xxxix. 4, 6); and it therefore heightens the description given of the terrific character of the thunder-storm, when the thunder which is here called "the voice of God" is represented as causing, through the terror which it inspires, the hinds in their pregnant state prematurely to drop their young; although, according to our ideas of poetical imagery, this may not accord so well with the other images in the passage, nor appear so beautiful and sublime as the image of the oaks trembling at the voice of Jehovah.—*John Calvin.*

Verses 9.—"*The voice of the Lord maketh the hinds to calve.*" The care and tenderness of God towards beasts turns to his praise, as well as the care which he hath of, and the tenderness which he shows to believers. As it doth exceedingly advance the glory of God, that he takes care of wild beasts, so it may exceedingly strengthen the faith of man that he will take care of him. Doth the Lord take care of *hinds?* then certainly he takes care of those that particularly belong to him. There is a special providence of God towards these and such like creaures for the production of their young. He—if I may so speak with reverence—shows his midwifery in helping these savage beasts when their pains come upon them. As the Lord takes man, in an eminent manner, "out of the womb" (Psalm xxii. 9), so in a manner he takes beasts out of the womb too. "The voice of the Lord shaketh the wilderness; the Lord shaketh the wilderness of Kadesh;" so we translate it; but the word which we render "*shaketh*" is the same with that in Job xxxix. 2, which signifieth *to bring forth;* and hence, some very learned in the Hebrew tongue do not render as we, "The voice of the Lord shaketh the wilderness," but "The voice of the Lord maketh the wilderness *to bring forth;* the Lord maketh the wilderness of Kadesh *to bring forth;*" which is not to be understood of the vegetative creatures (that's a truth, the Lord makes the trees of the forest to bring forth both leaves and fruit), but it is meant of animals or living creatures there. And then when he saith, "The voice of the Lord maketh the wilderness to bring forth," the meaning is, the Lord makes the wild beast of the wilderness to bring forth; which seems to be the clear sense of the place by that which followeth; for the Psalmist having said this in general at the eight verse, "*The voice of the Lord maketh the wilderness to bring forth,*" he in the ninth verse gives the special instance of the *hind*: "*The voice of the Lord maketh the hinds to calve.*"—*Joseph Caryl.*

Verse 9.—"*The voice of the Lord maketh the hinds to calve.*" It is with great propriety, says one of the ancients, that Jehovah demands, "The birth of the hinds dost thou guard?" (Job xxxix. 1), for since this animal is always in flight, and with fear and terror always leaping and skipping about, she could never bring her young to maturity without such a special protection. The providence of God, therefore, is equally conspicuous in the preservation of the mother and the fawn; both are the objects of his compassion and tender care; and, consequently, that afflicted man has no reason to charge his Maker with unkindness, who condescends to watch over the goats and the hinds. It seems to be generally admitted, that the hind brings forth her young with great difficulty; and so much appears to be suggested in the verse, " They bow themselves, they bring forth their young ones, they cast out their sorrows." But if Pliny, and other naturalists are worthy of credit, divine providence has been graciously pleased to provide certain herbs, which greatly facilitate the birth; and by instinct, he directs the hind to feed upon them, when the time of gestation draws towards a close. Whatever truth there may be in this assertion, we know from higher authority, that providence promotes the parturition of the hind, by awakening her fears, and agitating her frame by the rolling thunder :—" *The voice of Jehovah* (a common Hebrew phrase, denoting thunder) *maketh the hinds to calve.*" Nor ought we to wonder, that so timorous a creature as the hind, should be so much affected by that awful atmospheric convulsion, when some of the proudest men that ever existed, have have been known to tremble. Augustus, the Roman Emperor, according to Suetonius, was so terrified when it thundered, that he wrapped a seal-skin round his body, with the view of defending it from the lightning, and concealed himself in some secret corner till the tempest ceased. The tyrant Caligula, who sometimes affected to threaten Jupiter himself, covered his head, or hid himself under a bed; and Horace confesses he was reclaimed from atheism by the terror of thunder and lightning, the effects of which he describes with his usual felicity. (Odes, b. i. 34.)— *George Paxton's " Illustrations of Scripture."*

Verse 9.—" *The voice of the Lord maketh the hinds to calve."* " *Cervi sunt predicatores,*" says S. Jerome, who bring forth souls to Christ by the gospel which is God's *voice;* and the stripping of the leaves of the forest by the voice of the Lord, represents their work in humbling the strong oaks and lofty cedars of the world by the power of the gospel, and in stripping the souls of the worldly-minded of their manifold disguises (S. Basil). Others apply it to the act of the preachers of God's word, disclosing the dark thickets of divine mysteries in the holy Scriptures by evangelical light set forth by the Holy Ghost (S. Jerome).—*Christopher Wordsworth.*

Verse 9 (first clause).—" *The voice of Jehovah makes havoc of the oaks, and strippeth bare the forests."—Samuel Horsley.*

Verse 9.—" *In his temple."*—Some conceive that this Psalm was appointed by David to be sung in the temple in time of thunder, which is not unlikely. There are writers who make God to be the nominative case to the verb speaketh; and render it thus, *in his temple doth he utter all his glory.* As much as to say, much of his glory God uttereth in his thunder, but all in his temple, for whatsoever there he speaketh with his mouth he fulfilleth it with his hand.—*John Trapp.*

Verse 9 (last clause).—David speaking in the former part of the Psalm of the effects of natural thunder only, towards the close of the Psalm applieth it to the Word of God, while he saith, " *And in his temple doth every one speak of his glory;* " that is, the word and ordinances of God, ministered in his church or temple, will put every one to acknowledge and speak of the glorious power of God, even much more than the mighty thunder which soundeth in our ears, or the subtle lightning which flasheth in our eyes. There is far more royal power in the thunder of the Word, than in the word of thunder. This terrifieth only to conviction, but that terrifieth to salvation; for after God speaks terror there in his threatenings, he speaks comfort in the promises; and when he hath affrighted us with a sense of our sins and of his wrath due to us for our sins, as with an horrible tempest, he presently refresheth us with the gentle gales of revealed grace, and with the pleasant amiable sunshine of his favour by Jesus Christ.—*Joseph Caryl.*

Verse 11.—" *The Lord will give strength unto his people; the Lord will bless his people with peace;*" *i.e.*, he is in war their strength, and their felicity in peace; in war he is the Author of all that power wherewith they are enabled to oppose and overcome potent enemies; and in peace, he is their truly felicitating good, and makes them, by his own vouchsafed presence, a truly blessed people.—*John Howe.*

Verse 11.—" *The Lord will bless his people with peace.*" Though some precious souls that have closed with Christ, and embraced the gospel, be not at present brought to rest in their own consciences, but continue for awhile under some dissatisfaction and trouble in their own spirits, yet even then they have *peace* of conscience in a threefold respect ; *in pretio, in promisso, in semine.* First, every true believer hath peace of conscience *in pretio ;* the gospel puts that price into his hand, which will assuredly purchase it, and that is the blood of Christ. We say that is gold which is worth gold, which we may anywhere exchange for gold ; such is the blood of Christ ; it is peace of conscience, because the soul that hath this may exchange it for this. God himself cannot deny the poor creature that prays on these terms : Lord, give me peace of conscience ; here is Christ's blood, the price of it. That which could pay the debt, surely can procure the receipt. Peace of conscience is but a discharge under God's hand, that the debt due to divine justice is fully paid. The blood of Christ hath done that the greater for the believer, it shall therefore do this the less. If there were such a rare potion that did infallibly procure health to every one that takes it, we might safely say, as soon as the sick man hath drunk it down, that he hath drunk his health, it is in him, though at present he doth not feel himself to have it : in time it will appear. Secondly, *In promisso.* Every true believer hath peace of conscience in the promise, and that we count as good as ready money in the purse, which we have sure bond for. " *The Lord will bless his people with peace.*" He is resolved on it, and then who shall hinder it ? It is worth your reading the whole Psalm, to see what weight the Lord gives to this sweet promise, for the encouragement of our faith in expecting the performance thereof. Nothing more hard to enter into the heart of a poor creature (when all is in an uproar in his bosom, and his conscience threatening nothing but fire and sword, wrath, vengeance, from God for his sins), than thoughts or hopes of peace and comfort. Now the Psalm is spent in showing what great things God can do, and that with no more trouble to himself than a word speaking, " *The voice of the Lord is full of majesty* " (verse 4), " It breaks the cedars, it divides the flames, it shakes the wilderness, it makes the hinds to calve." This God that doth all this, promiseth *to bless his people with peace,* outward and inward ; for without this inward peace, though he might give them peace, yet could he never bless them with peace as he there undertakes. A sad peace, were it not, to have quiet streets, but cutting of throats in our houses ? yet infinitely more sad to have peace both in our streets and houses, but war and blood in our guilty consciences. What peace can a poor creature taste or relish, while the sword of God's wrath lies at the throat of conscience ? not peace with God himself. Therefore Christ purchased peace of pardon, to obtain peace of conscience for his pardoned ones, and accordingly hath bequeathed it in the promise to them, " Peace I leave with you, my peace I give unto you." John xiv. 27. Where you see he is both the testator to leave, and the executor of his own will, to give out with his own hands what his love hath left believers ; so that there is no fear but his will shall be performed to the full, seeing himself lives to see it done. Thirdly, *In semine.* Every believer hath this inward peace in the seed. " Light is sown for the righteous, and gladness for the upright in heart." Psalm xcvii. 11. Where sown, but in the believer's own bosom, when principles of grace and holiness were cast into it by the Spirit of God ? Hence it is called " the peaceable fruit of righteousness." Heb. xii. 11. It shoots as naturally from holiness, as any fruit in its kind doth from the seed proper to it. It is, indeed, most true, that the seed runs and ripens into this fruit sooner in some than it doth in others. This spiritual harvest comes not alike soon to all, no more than the other that is outward doth ; but here is the comfort—whoever hath a seed-time of grace pass over his soul, shall have his harvest-time also of joy.— *William Gurnall.*

Verse 11.—" *Peace.*" There is a threefold " peace," *externa, interna, æterna ;* temporal, spiritual, celestial peace. There is outward peace, the *blessing ;* inward peace, the *grace ;* and everlasting peace, of *glory.* And as in a stately palace there is a lodge or court that leads into the inmost goodly rooms, so external peace is the entrance or introduction to the inward lodgings of the sweet peace of conscience and of that eternal rest in which our peace in heaven shall be happy, inasmuch as external peace affords us many accommodations and helps to the gaining and obtaining both the one and the other.—*Ephraim Udall,* 1642.

HINTS TO PREACHERS.

Verse 1.—The duty of ascribing our strength and the honour of it to God ; the penalty of neglecting to do so ; the pleasure of so doing.

Verse 1.—National glorying should be in the Lord.

Verse 2 (first clause).—Royal dues, the royal treasury, loyal subjects paying their dues, the king receiving them. Smugglers and preventive men.

Verse 2 (second clause).—Inspired ritualism. What to do ? " *Worship.* " Whom ? " *The Lord.* " How ? " *In the beauty of holiness.* " Absence of all allusions to place, time, order, words, form, vestments, etc.

Verse 3.—God's voice heard in trouble and above trouble, or in great personal and national calamities.

Verse 4.—Power and majesty of the gospel. Illustrated by succeeding verses.

Verse 4 (last clause).—" The majestic voice." See Spurgeon's Sermons, No. 87.

Verse 5.—The breaking power of the gospel.

Verse 6.—The unsettling power of the gospel.

Verse 7.—The fire which goes with the word. This is a wide subject.

Verse 8.—The arousing and alarming of godless places by the preaching of the word.

Verse 9.—The revealing power of the word of God in the secrets of man's heart, and its regenerating force.

Verse 9 (last clause).—I. Matchless temple. II. Unanimous worship. III. Forcible motive. IV. General enthusiasm, " *glory.* " See Comment.

Verse 10.—The ever-present and undisturbed government of God.

Verse 11.—The twin blessings from the same source ; their connection, and their consummation.

Verse 11.—The two wills, the two blessings, the one people, the one Lord.

PSALM XXX.

TITLE.—**A Psalm and Song at the Dedication of the House of David**; *or rather,* A Psalm; a Song of Dedication for the House. By David. *A song of faith since the house of Jehovah, here intended, David never lived to see. A Psalm of praise, since a sore judgment had been stayed, and a great sin forgiven. From our English version it would appear that this Psalm was intended to be sung at the building of that house of cedar which David erected for himself, when he no longer had to hide himself in the Cave of Adullam, but had become a great king. If this had been the meaning, it would have been well to observe that it is right for the believer when removing, to dedicate his new abode to God. We should call together our Christian friends, and show that where we dwell, God dwells, and where we have a tent, God has an altar. But as the song refers to the temple, for which it was David's joy to lay by in store, and for the site of which he purchased in his later days the floor of Ornan, we must content ourselves with remarking the holy faith which foresaw the fulfilment of the promise made to him concerning Solomon. Faith can sing—*

> " Glory to thee for all the grace
> I have not tasted yet."

Throughout this Psalm there are indications that David had been greatly afflicted both personally and relatively, after having, in his presumption, fancied himself secure. When God's children prosper one way, they are generally tried another, for few of us can bear unmingled prosperity. Even the joys of hope need to be mixed with the pains of experience, and the more surely so when comfort breeds carnal security and self-confidence. Nevertheless, pardon soon followed repentance, and God's mercy was glorified. The Psalm is a song, and not a complaint. Let it be read in the light of the last days of David, when he had numbered the people, and God had chastened him, and then in mercy had bidden the angel sheathe his sword. On the floor of Ornan, the poet received the inspiration which glows in this delightful ode. It is the Psalm of the numbering of the people, and of the dedication temple which commemorated the staying of the plague.

DIVISION.—*In verses 1, 2, and 3, David extols the Lord for delivering him. Verses 4 and 5 he invites the saints to unite with him in celebrating divine compassion. In 6 and 7 he confesses the fault for which he was chastened, 8—10 repeats the supplication which he offered, and concludes with commemorating his deliverance and vowing eternal praise.*

EXPOSITION.

I WILL extol thee, O LORD; for thou hast lifted me up, and hast not made my foes to rejoice over me.

2 O LORD my God, I cried unto thee, and thou hast healed me.

3 O LORD, thou hast brought up my soul from the grave: thou hast kept me alive that I should not go down to the pit.

1. " *I will extol thee.*" I will have high and honourable conceptions of thee, and give them utterance in my best music. Others may forget thee, murmur at thee, despise thee, blaspheme thee, but " I will extol thee," for I have been favoured above all others. I will extol thy name, thy character, thine attributes, thy mercy to me, thy great forbearance to my people; but, especially will I speak well of thyself; " I will extol thee," O Jehovah, this shall be my cheerful and constant employ. " *For thou hast lifted me up.*" Here is an antithesis, " I will exalt thee, for thou hast exalted me." I would render according to the benefit received. The Psalmist's praise was reasonable. He had a reason to give for the praise that was in his heart. He had been drawn up like a prisoner from a dungeon, like Joseph out of the pit, and therefore he loved his deliverer. Grace has uplifted us from the pit of hell, from the ditch of sin, from the Slough of Despond, from the bed of sickness, from the bondage of doubts and fears: have we no song to offer for all this? How high has our Lord lifted us? Lifted us up into the children's place, to be adopted into the family; lifted us up into union with Christ, " to sit together

with him in heavenly places." Lift high the name of our God, for he has lifted us above the stars. "*And hast not made my foes to rejoice over me.*" This was the judgment which David most feared out of the three evils ; he said, let me fall into the hand of the Lord, and not into the hand of man. Terrible indeed were our lot if we were delivered over to the will of our enemies. Blessed be the Lord, we have been preserved from so dire a fate. The devil and all our spiritual enemies have not been permitted to rejoice over us ; for we have been saved from the fowler's snare. Our evil companions, who prophesied that we should go back to our old sins, are disappointed. Those who watched for our halting, and would fain say, "Aha ! Aha ! So would we have it ! " have watched in vain until now. O happy they whom the Lord keeps so consistent in character that the lynx eyes of the world can see no real fault in them. Is this our case ? let us ascribe all the glory to him who has sustained us in our integrity.

2. "*O Lord my God, I cried unto thee, and thou hast healed me.*" David sent up prayers for himself and for his people when visited with the pestilence. He went at once to head-quarters, and not roundabout to fallible means. God is the best physician, even for our bodily infirmities. We do very wickedly and foolishly when we forget God. It was a sin in Asa that he trusted to physicians and not to God. If we must have a physician, let it be so, but still let us go to our God first of all ; and, above all, remember that there can be no power to heal in medicine of itself ; the healing energy must flow from the divine hand. If our watch is out of order, we take it to the watchmaker ; if body or soul be in an evil plight, let us resort to him who created them, and has unfailing skill to put them in right condition. As for our spiritual diseases, nothing can heal these evils but the touch of the Lord Christ : if we do but touch the hem of his garment, we shall be made whole, while if we embrace all other physicians in our arms, they can do us no service. "*O Lord my God.*" Observe the covenant name which faith uses—"*my God.*" Thrice happy is he who can claim the Lord himself to be his portion. Note how David's faith ascends the scale ; he sang "O Lord " in the first verse, but it is "O Lord my God,"; in the second. Heavenly heart-music is an ascending thing, like the pillars of smoke which rose from the altar of incense. "*I cried unto thee.*" I could hardly pray, but I cried ; I poured out my soul as a little child pours out its desires. I cried to my God : I knew to whom to cry ; I did not cry to my friends, or to any arm of flesh. Hence the sure and satisfactory result—"*Thou hast healed me.*" I know it. I am sure of it. I have the evidence of spiritual health within me now : glory be to thy name ! Every humble suppliant with God who seeks release from the disease of sin, shall speed as well as the Psalmist did, but those who will not so much as seek a cure, need not wonder if their wounds putrefy and their soul dies.

3. "*O Lord, thou hast brought up my soul from the grave.*" Mark, it is not, "I hope so ; " but it is, "*Thou hast ; thou hast ; thou hast*"—three times over. David is quite sure, beyond a doubt, that God has done great things for him, whereof he is exceeding glad. He had descended to the brink of the sepulchre, and yet was restored to tell of the forbearance of God ; nor was this all, he owned that nothing but grace had kept him from the lowest hell, and this made him doubly thankful. To be spared from the grave is much ; to be delivered from the pit is more ; hence there is growing cause for praise, since both deliverances are alone traceable to the glorious right hand of the Lord, who is the only preserver of life, and the only Redeemer of our souls from hell.

4 Sing unto the Lord, O ye saints of his, and give thanks at the remembrance of his holiness.

5 For his anger *endureth* but a moment ; in his favour is life ; weeping may endure for a night, but joy *cometh* in the morning.

4. "*Sing unto the Lord, O ye saints of his.*" "Join my song ; assist me to express my gratitude." He felt that he could not praise God enough himself, and therefore he would enlist the hearts of others. "*Sing unto the Lord, O ye saints of his.*" David would not fill his choir with reprobates, but with sanctified persons, who could sing from their hearts. He calls to you, ye people of God, because ye are *saints :* and if sinners are wickedly silent, let your holiness constrain *you* to sing. You are *his* saints—chosen, blood-bought, called, and set apart for God ; sanctified on purpose that you should offer the daily sacrifice of praise. Abound

ye in this heavenly duty. " *Sing unto the Lord.*" It is a pleasing exercise; it is a profitable engagement. Do not need to be stirred up so often to so pleasant a service. " *And give thanks.*" Let your songs be grateful songs, in which the Lord's mercies shall live again in joyful remembrance. The very remembrance of the past should tune our harps, even if present joys be lacking. " *At the remembrance of his holiness.*" Holiness is an attribute which inspires the deepest awe, and demands a reverent mind; but still give thanks at the remembrance of it. "Holy, holy, holy!" is the song of seraphim and cherubim; let us join it not dolefully, as though we trembled at the holiness of God, but cheerfully, as humbly rejoicing in it.

5. "*For his anger endureth but a moment.*" David here alludes to those dispensations of God's providence which are the chastisement ordered in his paternal government towards his erring children, such as the plague which fell upon Jerusalem for David's sins; these are but short judgments, and they are removed as soon as real penitence sues for pardon and presents the great and acceptable sacrifice. What a mercy is this, for if the Lord's wrath smoked for a long season, flesh would utterly fail before him. God puts up his rod with great readiness as soon as its work is done; he is slow *to* anger and swift to end it. If his temporary and fatherly anger be so severe that it had need be short, what must be the terror of eternal wrath exercised by the Judge towards his adversaries? " *In his favour is life.*" As soon as the Lord looked favourably upon David, the city lived, and the king's heart lived too. We die like withered flowers when the Lord frowns, but his sweet smile revives us as the dews refresh the fields. His favour not only sweetens and cheers life, but it is life itself, the very essence of life. Who would know life, let him seek the favour of the Lord. " *Weeping may endure for a night;*" but nights are not for ever. Even in the dreary winter the day-star lights his lamp. It seems fit that in our nights the dews of grief should fall. When the Bridegroom's absence makes it dark within, it is meet that the widowed soul should pine for a renewed sight of the Well-beloved. " *But joy cometh in the morning.*" When the Sun of Righteousness comes, we wipe our eyes, and joy chases out intruding sorrow. Who would not be joyful that knows Jesus? The first beams of the morning bring us comfort when Jesus is the day-dawn, and all believers know it to be so. Mourning only lasts till morning: when the night is gone the gloom shall vanish. This is adduced as a reason for saintly singing, and forcible reason it is; short nights and merry days call for the psaltery and harp.

6 And in my prosperity I said, I shall never be moved.

7 Lord, by thy favour thou hast made my mountain to stand strong: thou didst hide thy face, *and* I was troubled.

6. "*In my prosperity.*" When all his foes were quiet, and his rebellious son dead and buried, then was the time of peril. Many a vessel founders in a calm. No temptation is so bad as tranquility. " *I said, I shall never be moved.*" Ah! David, you said more than was wise to say, or even to think, for God has founded the world upon the floods, to show us what a poor, mutable, movable, inconstant world it is. Unhappy he who builds upon it! He builds himself a dungeon for his hopes. Instead of conceiving that we shall never be moved, we ought to remember that we shall very soon be moved altogether. Nothing is abiding beneath the moon. Because I happen to be prosperous to-day, I must not fancy that I shall be in my high estate to-morrow. As in a wheel, the uppermost spokes descend to the bottom in due course, so is it with mortal conditions. There is a constant revolution; many who are in the dust to-day shall be highly elevated to-morrow; while those who are now aloft shall soon grind the earth. Prosperity had evidently turned the Psalmist's head, or he would not have been so self-confident. He stood by grace, and yet forgot himself, and so met with a fall. Reader, is there not much of the same proud stuff in all our hearts? let us beware lest the fumes of intoxicating success get into our brains and make fools of us also.

7. "*Lord, by thy favour thou hast made my mountain to stand strong.*" He ascribed his prosperity to the Lord's favour—so far good, it is well to own the hand of the Lord in all our stability and wealth. But observe that the good in a good man is not unmingled good, for this was alloyed with carnal security. His state he compares to a mountain, a molehill would have been nearer—we never think

too little of ourselves. He boasted that his mountain stood strong, and yet he had before, in Psalm xxix., spoken of Sirion and Lebanon as moving like young unicorns. Was David's state more firm than Lebanon? Ah, vain conceit, too common to us all! How soon the bubble bursts when God's people get conceit into their heads, and fancy that they are to enjoy immutability beneath the stars, and constancy upon this whirling orb. How touchingly and teachingly God corrected his servant's mistake: *"Thou didst hide thy face, and I was troubled."* There was no need to come to blows, a hidden face was enough. This proves, first, that David was a genuine saint, for no hiding of God's face on earth would trouble a sinner; and, secondly, that the joy of the saint is dependent upon the presence of his Lord. No mountain, however firm, can yield us rest when our communion with God is broken, and his face is concealed. However, in such a case, it is well to be troubled. The next best thing to basking in the light of God's countenance, is to be thoroughly unhappy when that bliss is denied us.

> " Lord, let me weep for nought but sin !
> And after none but thee !
> And then I would—O that I might,
> A constant weeper be ! "

8 I cried to thee, O LORD; and unto the LORD I made supplication.

9 What profit *is there* in my blood, when I go down to the pit? Shall the dust praise thee? shall it declare thy truth?

10 Hear, O LORD, and have mercy upon me: LORD, be thou my helper.

8. *" I cried to thee, O Lord."* Prayer is the unfailing resource of God's people. If they are driven to their wits' end, they may still go to the mercy-seat. When an earthquake makes our mountain tremble, the throne of grace still stands firm, and we may come to it. Let us never forget to pray, and let us never doubt the success of prayer. The hand which wounds can heal: let us turn to him who smites us, and he will be entreated of us. Prayer is better solace than Cain's building a city, or Saul's seeking for music. Mirth and carnal amusements are a sorry prescription for a mind distracted and despairing: prayer will succeed where all else fails.

9. In this verse we learn the form and method of David's prayer. It was an argument with God, an urging of reasons, a pleading of his cause. It was not a statement of doctrinal opinions, nor a narration of experience, much less a sly hit at other people under pretence of praying to God, although all these things and worse have been substituted for holy supplication at certain prayer-meetings. He wrestled with the angel of the covenant with vehement pleadings, and therefore he prevailed. Head and heart, judgment and affections, memory and intellect were all at work to spread the case aright before the Lord of love. *" What profit is there in my blood, when I go down to the pit?"* Wilt thou not lose a songster from thy choir, and one who loves to magnify thee? *" Shall the dust praise thee? shall it declare thy truth?"* Will there not be one witness the less to thy faithfulness and veracity? Spare, then, thy poor unworthy one for thine own name sake!

10. *" Hear, O Lord, and have mercy upon me."* A short and comprehensive petition, available at all seasons, let us use it full often. It is the publican's prayer; be it ours. If God hears prayer, it is a great act of mercy; our petitions do not merit a reply. *" Lord, be thou my helper."* Another compact, expressive, ever fitting prayer. It is suitable to hundreds of the cases of the Lord's people; it is well becoming in the minister when he is going to preach, to the sufferer upon the bed of pain, to the toiler in the field of service, to the believer under temptation, to the man of God under adversity; when God helps, difficulties vanish. He is the help of his people, a very present help in trouble. The two brief petitions of this verse are commended as ejaculations to believers full of business, denied to those longer seasons of devotion which are the rare privilege of those whose days are spent in retirement.

11 Thou hast turned for me my mourning into dancing: thou hast put off my sackcloth, and girded me with gladness.

12 To the end that *my* glory may sing praise to thee, and not be silent. O LORD my God, I will give thanks unto thee for ever.

11. Observe the contrast, God takes away the mourning of his people; and what does he give them instead of it? Quiet and peace? Ay, and a great deal more than that. "*Thou hast turned for me my mourning into dancing.*" He makes their hearts to dance at the sound of his name. He takes off their sackcloth. That is good. What a delight to be rid of the habiliments of woe! But what then? He clothes us. And how? With some common dress? Nay, but with that royal vestment which is the array of glorified spirits in heaven. "*Thou hast girded me with gladness.*" This is better than to wear garments of silk or cloth of gold, bedight with embroidery and bespangled with gems. Many a poor man wears this heavenly apparel wrapped around his heart, though fustian and corduroy are his only outward garb; and such a man needs not envy the emperor in all his pomp. Glory be to thee, O God, if, by a sense of full forgiveness and present justification, thou hast enriched my spiritual nature, and filled me with all the fulness of God.

12. "*To the end*"—namely, with this view and intent—"*that my glory*"—that is, my tongue or my soul—"*may sing praise to thee, and not be silent.*" It would be a shameful crime, if, after receiving God's mercies, we should forget to praise him. God would not have our tongues lie idle while so many themes for gratitude are spread on every hand. He would have no dumb children in the house. They are all to sing in heaven, and therefore they should all sing on earth. Let us sing with the poet :—

> "I would begin the music here,
> And so my soul should rise:
> Oh for some heavenly notes to bear
> My passions to the skies."

"*O Lord my God, I will give thanks unto thee for ever.*"

> "I'll praise him in life; I'll praise him in death;
> I'll praise him as long as he lendeth me breath;
> And say when the death-dew lies cold on my brow.
> If ever I loved thee, my Jesus, 'tis now."

EXPLANATORY NOTES AND QUAINT SAYINGS.

Title.—"*A Psalm and Song,*" etc. It is thought that when these two words of *Psalm and Song* are both put in the title of a Psalm, it is meant that the sound of instruments was to be joined with the voice when they were sung in the Temple, and that the voice went *before* when it is said *Song and Psalm*, and did come *after* when it is said *Psalm and Song.—John Diodati.*

Title.—At the dedication of it. חֲנֻכַּת הַבַּיִת. The original word חָנַן signifies *initiari*, ἐγκαινίζειν, *rei novæ primam usurpationem.* So Cocceius, to initiate, or the first use that is made of anything. It was common, when any person had finished a house and entered into it, to celebrate it with great rejoicing, and keep a festival, to which his friends were invited, and to perform some religious ceremonies, to secure the protection of heaven. Thus, when the second temple was finished, the Priests and Levites, and the rest of the captivity, kept the dedication of the house of God with joy, and offered numerous sacrifices. Ezra vi. 16. We read in the New Testament (John x. 22), of *the feast of the dedication* appointed by Judas Maccabæus, in memory of the purification and restoration of the temple of Jerusalem, after it had been defiled and almost laid in ruins by Antiochus Epiphanes; and celebrated annually, to the time of its destruction by Titus, by solemn sacrifices, music, songs, and hymns, to the praises of God, and feasts, and everything that could give the people pleasure, for eight days successively. Josephus Ant. i. xii. § 7. Judas ordained, that "the days of the dedication should be kept in their season, from year to year, with mirth and gladness." 1 Mac. iv. 59. And that this was customary, even amongst private persons, to keep a kind of religious festival, upon their first entrance into a new house, appears from the order of God (Deut. xx. 5), that no person who had built a new house should be forced into the army, "if he had not dedicated the house," *i.e.*, taken possession of it according to the usual ceremonies practised on such occasions ; a custom this that hath more or less prevailed amongst all nations. Thus the Romans dedicated their temples, their theatres, their statues, and their palaces and houses. Suet. Octav. c. xliii. § 13 ; c. xxxi. § 9.—*Samuel Chandler.*

Title.—The present Psalm is the only one that is called a *shir*, or song, in the first book of the Psalms, *i.e.*, Psalms i.—xli. The word שיר *shir* is found in the titles of Psalms xlv., xlvi., xlviii., lxv.—lxviii., lxxv., lxxxiii., lxxxvii., lxxxviii., xcii., cviii., cxx.—cxxxiv. Psalm xviii. is entitled, " *a shirah* (or *song*) of deliverance from his enemies," and the present *shir* may be coupled with it.—*Christopher Wordsworth.*

Title.—As by offering the first fruits to God they acknowledged that they received the increase of the whole year from him, in like manner, by consecrating their houses to God, they declared that they were God's tenants, confessing that they were strangers, and that it was he who lodged, and gave them a habitation there. If a levy for war, therefore, took place, this was a just cause of exemption, when any one alleged that he had not yet dedicated his house. Besides, they were at the same time admonished by this ceremony, that every one enjoyed his house aright and regularly, only when he so regulated it that it was as it were a sanctuary of God, and that true piety and the pure worship of God reigned in it. The types of the law have now ceased, but we must still keep to the doctrine of Paul, that whatsoever things God appoints for our use are still " sanctified by the word of God and prayer." 1 Tim. iv. 4, 5.—*John Calvin.*

Whole Psalm.—Calmet supposes it to have been made by David on the dedication of the place which he built on the threshing-floor of Araunah, after the grievous *plague* which had so nearly desolated the kingdom. 2 Sam. xxiv. 25 ; 1 Chron. xxi. 26. All the parts of the Psalm agree to this : and they agree to this so well, and to no other hypothesis, that I feel myself justified in modelling the comment on this principle alone.—*Adam Clarke.*

Whole Psalm.—In the following verses I have endeavoured to give the spirit of the Psalm, and to preserve the frequent antitheses.

> I will exalt thee, Lord of hosts,
> 　For thou'st exalted me ;
> Since thou hast silenced Satan's boasts,
> 　I'll therefore boast in thee.
>
> My sins had brought me near the grave,
> 　The grave of black despair ;
> I look'd but there was none to save,
> 　Till I look'd up in prayer.
>
> In answer to my piteous cries,
> 　From hell's dark brink I'm brought :
> My Jesus saw me from the skies,
> 　And swift salvation wrought.
>
> All through the night I wept full sore,
> 　But morning brought relief ;
> That hand, which broke my bones before,
> 　Then broke my bonds of grief.
>
> My mourning he to dancing turns,
> 　For sackcloth joy he gives,
> A moment, Lord, thine anger burns,
> 　But long thy favour lives.
>
> Sing with me then, ye favoured men,
> 　Who long have known his grace ;
> With thanks recall the seasons when
> 　Ye also sought his face.

　　　　　　　　　　　　　　　　　　　　C. H. S.

Verse 1.—" *I will extol thee, O Lord ; for thou hast lifted me up.*" I will lift thee up, for thou hast lifted me up.—*Adam Clarke.*

Verse 1.—" *Thou hast lifted me up.*" דִּלִּיתַנִי. The verb is used, in its original meaning, to denote the *reciprocating motion of the buckets of a well*, one descending as the other rises, and *vice versa ;* and is here applied with admirable propriety, to point out the various reciprocations and changes of David's fortunes, as described in this Psalm, as to prosperity and adversity ; and particularly that gracious reverse of his afflicted condition which he now celebrates, God having raised him up to great honour and prosperity ; for having built his palace, he " perceived that the Lord had established him king over Israel, and that he had exalted his kingdom for his people Israel's sake."—2 Sam. v. 12.—*Samuel Chandler.*

Verse 2.—" *Thou hast healed me.*" תִּרְפָּאֵנִי. The verb is used, either for the healing of bodily disorders (Psalm ciii. 3), or to denote the happy alteration of any person's affairs, either in private or public life, by the removal of any kind of distress, personal or national. Psalm cvii. 20 ; Isaiah xix. 22. So in the place before us : " *Thou hast healed me,*" means, Thou hast brought me out of my distresses, hast restored my health, and rendered me safe and prosperous. Under Saul, he was frequently in the most imminent danger of his life, out of which God wonderfully brought him, which he strongly expresses by saying, " *Thou hast brought up my soul from* Hades : *thou hast kept me alive, that I should not go down to the pit.*" I thought myself lost, and that nothing could prevent my destruction, and can scarce help looking on the deliverance thou hast vouchsafed me otherwise than as a kind of restoration from the dead : *Thou hast revived me,* or recovered me to life, *from amongst those who go down to the pit ;* according to the literal rendering ot the latter clause.—*Samuel Chandler.*

Verse 4.—" *Sing unto the Lord, O ye saints of his.*" If it were to sing of another thing, I should require the whole quire of God's creatures to join in the singing ; but now that it is to sing of God's " holiness," what should profane voices do in the concert ? None but " saints " are fit to sing of " holiness," and specially of God's holiness ; but most specially with songs of holiness.—*Sir Richard Baker.*

Verse 4.—" *Sing unto the Lord, O ye saints of his.*" As God requires outward and inward worship, so a spiritual frame for inward worship may be forwarded by the outward composure. Gazing drowsiness hinders the activity of the soul, but the contrary temper furthers and helps it. Singing calls up the soul into such a posture, and doth, as it were, awaken it : it is a lively rousing up of the heart. Singing God's praise is a work of the most meditation of any we perform in public. It keeps the heart longest upon the thing spoken. Prayer and hearing pass quick from one sentence to another ; this sticks long upon it. Meditation must follow after hearing the word, and praying with the minister—for new sentences, still succeeding, give not liberty, in the instant, well to muse and consider upon what is spoken : but in this you pray and meditate. God hath so ordered this duty, that, while we are employed in it, we feed and chew the cud together. " Higgaion," or " Meditation," is set upon some passages of the Psalms, as Psalm ix. 16. The same may be writ up the whole duty, and all parts of it ; namely, " Meditation." Set before you one in the posture to sing to the best advantage : eyes lifted to heaven, denote his desire that his heart may be there too ; he hath before him a line or verse of prayer, mourning, praise, mention of God's works ; how fairly now may his heart spread itself in meditation on the thing, while he is singing it over ! Our singing is measured in deliberate time not more for music than meditation. He that seeks not, finds not, this advantage in singing Psalms—hath not yet learned what it means.—*John Lightfoot,* 1602—1675.

Verse 5.—" *His anger.*" Seeing God is often angry with his own servants, what cause have those of you who fear him, to bless him that he is not angry with you, and that you do not feel his displeasure ! He sets up others as his mark against which he shoots his arrows ; you hear others groaning for his departure, and yet your hearts are not saddened as theirs are ; your eyes can look up towards heaven with hope, whilst theirs are clouded with a veil of sorrow ; he speaks roughly to them, but comfortable words to you ; he seems to set himself against them as his enemies, whilst he deals with you as a loving friend ; you see a reviving smile in his face and they can discern nothing there but one continued and dreadful frown. O admire, and for ever wonder at the sovereign, distinguishing grace of God. Are you that are at ease better than many of his people that are now thrown into a fiery furnace? Have you less dross than they? Have they sinned, think you, at a higher rate than you have ever done? He is angry with them for their lukewarmness, for their backsliding; and have your hearts always burned with love? Have your feet always kept his way and not declined? Have you never wandered? Have you never turned aside to the right hand or to the left? Surely you have; and therefore, what a mercy is it, that he is not angry with you as well as with them. . . . . . Do not presume for all this; for though he is not angry yet with you, he may be so. This was the fault of David: " *In my prosperity I said, I shall never be moved;* " but it immediately follows, " *Thou didst hide thy face, and I was troubled.* " The sun shines now upon you, the candle of the Lord does refresh your tabernacle; but you may meet with many storms, and clouds, and darkness before you come to your journey's end. The disciples were once greatly pleased with the glory of the transfiguration; and during the delightful interview between Christ, and Moses, and Elias, they thought themselves as in heaven; but a cloud came and obscured the preceding glory, and then the poor men were afraid. It is true the anger of God *endureth but for a moment;* but even that moment is very sad, and terrible beyond expression. Weeping endureth for " *a night;* " but it may be a very bitter and doleful night for all this. It is a night like that of the Egyptians: when they arose they saw all their first-born slain, and there was a hideous, universal cry and mourning throughout all the land. So this night of the anger of the Lord may destroy all our comforts, and make the first-born of our strength, the confidence and pleasure of our hopes to give up the ghost.—*Timothy Rogers.*

Verse 5.—" *In his favour is life.* "—Let us see wherein the weight of the blessing and cursing of sheep and goats doth lie. It is not the gift of eternal life that is our happiness in heaven; but as David saith, " *in his favour is life.* " If a damned soul should be admitted to the fruition of all the pleasures of eternal life without the favour of God, heaven would be hell to him. It is not the dark and horrid house of woe that maketh a soul miserable in hell, but God's displeasure, *ite maledicti.* If an elect soul should be cast thither, and retain the favour of God, hell would be an heaven to him, and his joy could not all the devils of hell take from him; his night would be turned into day.—*Edward Marbury.*

Verse 5.—As an apprentice holds out in hard labour and (it may be) bad usage for seven years together or more, and in all that time is serviceable to his master without any murmuring or repining, because he sees that the time wears away, and that his bondage will not last always, but he shall be set at large and made a freeman in the conclusion: thus should everyone that groaneth under the burthen of any cross or affliction whatsoever, bridle his affections, possess his soul in patience, and cease from all murmuring and repining whatsoever, considering well with himself, that the rod of the wicked shall not always rest upon the lot of the righteous; that *weeping may abide at evening, but joy cometh in the morning;* and that troubles will have an end, and not continue for ever.—*John Spencer.*

Verse 5.—How often have we experienced the literal truth of that verse, " *Weeping may endure for a night, but joy cometh in the morning!* " How heavily does any trouble weigh on us *at night!* Our wearied nerve and brain seem unable to bear up under the pressure. Our pulse throbs, and the fevered restless body refuses to help in the work of endurance. Miserable and helpless we feel; and passionately weep under the force of the unresisted attack. At last sleep comes. Trouble, temptation, whatever it be that strives to overcome us, takes the one step too far which overleaps its mark, and by sheer force drives our poor humanity beyond the present reach of further trial. After such a night of struggle, and the heavy sleep of exhaustion, we awake with a vague sense of trouble. Our thoughts gather, and we *wonder* over our own violence, as the memory of it returns upon us. What was it that seemed so hopeless—so dark? Why were we so helpless and despairing? Things do not look so *now*—sad indeed still, but endurable—hard, but no longer impossible—bad enough perhaps, but we despair no more. " *Weeping may endure for a night, but joy cometh in the morning.* " And so, when life with its struggles and toils and sins, bringing us perpetual conflict, ends at last in the fierce struggle of *death*, then God " giveth his beloved sleep." They sleep in Jesus, and awake to the joy of a morning which shall know no wane—the morning of joy. The Sun of Righteousness is beaming on them. Light is now on all their ways. And they can only wonder when they recall the despair and darkness, and toil, and violence of their earthly life, and say, as they have often said on earth, " Weeping has endured only for *the night*, and now it is morning, and joy has come!" And our sorrows, our doubts, our difficulties, our long looks forward, with despair of enduring strength for so long a night of trial—Where are they? Shall we not feel as is so beautifully described in the words of one of our hymns—

> "When in our Father's happy land
> We meet our own once more,
> Then we shall scarcely understand
> Why we have wept before."
>
> *Mary B. M. Duncan, 1825—1865.*

Verse 5.—"*Weeping may endure for a night, but joy cometh in the morning.*" Their mourning shall last but till morning. God will turn their winter's night into a summer's day, their sighing into singing, their grief into gladness, their mourning into music, their bitter into sweet, their wilderness into a paradise. The life of a Christian is filled up with interchanges of sickness and health, weakness and strength, want and wealth, disgrace and honour, crosses, and comforts, miseries and mercies, joys and sorrows, mirth and mourning; all honey would harm us, all wormwood would undo us; a composition of both is the best way in the world to keep our souls in a healthy constitution. It is best and most for the health of the soul that the south wind of mercy, and the north wind of adversity, do both blow upon it; and though every wind that blows shall blow good to the saints, yet certainly their sins die most, and their graces thrive best, when they are under the drying, nipping north wind of calamity, as well as under the warm, cherishing south wind of mercy and prosperity.—*Thomas Brooks.*

Verse 5.—"*Joy cometh in the morning.*" The godly man's joy "*cometh in the morning,*" when the wicked man's goeth; for to him "the morning is even as the shadow of death." Job xxiv. 17. He is not only afraid of reproof and punishment, but he grieves and suffers sufficiently, though nobody should know of his actions, for the impair and loss, and misspence of his strength and his time and his money.—*Zachary Bogan.*

Verse 5.—In the second half of the verse, "*weeping*" is personified, and represented by the figure of a wanderer, who leaves in the morning the lodging, into which he had entered the preceding evening. After him another guest arrives, namely, "*joy.*"—*E. W. Hengstenberg.*

Verse 5.—The princely prophet says plainly, "*heaviness may endure for a night, but joy cometh in the morning.*" As the two angels that came to Lot lodged with him for a night, and when they had despatched their errand, went away in the morning; so afflictions, which are the angels or the messengers of God. God sendeth afflictions to do an errand unto us; to tell us we forget God, we forget ourselves, we are too proud, too self-conceited, and such like; and when they have said as they were bid, then presently they are gone.—*Thomas Playfere.*

Verses 5—10.—When a man's heart is set upon the creatures, there being thorns in them all, therefore if he will grasp too much of them, or too hard, he shall find it. God's children are trained up so to it, that God will not let them go away with a sin; if they be too adulterously affected, they shall find a cross in such a thing. You may observe this in the thirtieth Psalm; there you may see the circle God goes in with his children. David has many afflictions, as appeareth by the fifth verse: I cried, and then God returned to me, and joy came. What did David then? "I said, I shall never be moved:" his heart grew wanton, but God would not let him go away so: "God turned away his face, and I was troubled." At the seventh verse he is, you see, in trouble again: well, David cries again, at the eighth and tenth verses, and then God turned his mourning into joy again. And this to be his dealing you shall find in all the Scriptures; but because we find this his dealing set so close together in this Psalm, therefore I name it.—*John Preston, D.D.* (1587—1628), *in "The Golden Scepter held forth to the Humble."*

Verse 6.—"*In my prosperity I said, I shall never be moved.*" Our entering upon a special service for God, or receiving a special favour from God, are two solemn seasons which Satan makes use of for temptation. . . . . We are apt to get proud, careless, and cofident, after or upon such employments and favours; even as men are apt to sleep or surfeit upon a full meal, or to forget themselves when they are advanced to honour. Job's great peace and plenty made him, as he confesseth, so confident, that he concluded he should "die in his nest."

Chap. xxix. 18. David enjoying the favour of God in a more than ordinary measure, though he was more acquainted with vicissitudes and changes than most of men, grows secure in his apprehension that he "*should never be moved;*" but he acknowledgeth his mistake, and leaves it upon record as an experience necessary for others to take warning by, that when he became warm under the beams of God's countenance, then he was apt to fall into security; and this it seems was usual with him in all such cases—when he was most secure he was nearest some trouble or disquiet. "*Thou didst hide thy face*"—and then to be sure the devil will show him his—"*and I was troubled.*" Enjoyments beget confidence; confidence brings forth carelessness; carelessness makes God withdraw, and gives opportunity to Satan to work unseen. And thus, as armies after victory growing secure, are oft surprised; so are we oft after our spiritual advancements thrown down.—*Richard Gilpin.*

Verse 6.—"*In my prosperity.*" בְּשַׁלְוִי The word denotes *peace and tranquility, arising from an affluent, prosperous condition.* When God had settled him quietly on the throne, he thought all his troubles were over, and that he should enjoy uninterrupted happiness; and that God "*had made his mountain so strong, as that it should never be moved;*" i.e., placed him as secure from all danger as though he had taken refuge upon an inaccessible mountain; or made his prosperity firm, and subject to no more alteration, than a mountain is liable to be removed out of its place; or, raised him to an eminent degree of honour and prosperity; a mountain, by its height, being a very natural representation of a very superior condition, remarkable for power, affluence, and dignity. He had taken the fortress of Mount Sion, which was properly *his mountain*, as he had fixed on it for his dwelling. It was strong by nature, and rendered almost impregnable by the fortifications he had added to it. This he regarded as the effect of God's favour to him, and promised himself that his peace and happiness for the future should be as undisturbed and unshaken as Mount Sion itself.—*Samuel Chandler.*

Verse 6.—"*In my prosperity.*" Prosperity is more pleasant than profitable to us. Though in show it look like a fair summer, yet it is indeed a wasting winter, and spendeth all the fruit we have reaped in the harvest of sanctified affliction. We are never in greater danger than in the sunshine of prosperity. To be always indulged of God, and never to taste of trouble, is rather a token of God's neglect than of his tender love.—*William Struther.*

Verse 7.—It is rare to receive much of this world, and not as the prodigal to go afar off; 'tis hard to keep close to God in prosperity, when we have much of this world to live upon and content ourselves with; to live upon God, and make him our content and stay, as if we had no other life nor livelihood but in him; we are very apt in such a case to contract a carnal frame, let go our hold of God, discustom ourselves to the exercise of faith, abate and estrange our affections from God. See how it was with David: "*I said, I shall never be moved, thou hast made my mountain so strong.*" I solaced myself on these outward accommodations, as if I needed no other support, strength, or content, and there were no fear of a change; no care now to make God my constant joy and stay, and reckon upon God only for my portion, and that I must follow him with a cross, and be conformed to my Saviour, in being crucified to the world. What comes of this? "*Thou didst hide thy face, and I was troubled;*" namely, because he had too much indulged a life of sense. Children that are held up by their nurses' hand, and mind not to feel their feet and ground when the nurses let them go, they fall, as if they had no feet or ground to stand upon. Or thus: we are like children, who, playing in the golden sunshine, and following their sport, stray so far from their father's house, that night coming upon them ere they are aware, they are as it were lost, and full of fears, not knowing how to recover home. The world steals away our hearts from God, gives so few opportunities for the exercise of the life of faith, and such advantages to a life of sense, wears off the sense of our dependence on God, and need thereof, so that when we are put to it by affliction, we are ready to miscarry ere we can recover our weapon or hold. Faith is our cordial (Psalm xxvii. 13); now if it be not at hand (as in health, when we have no need of it, it use to be) we may faint ere we recover the use of it.—*Elias Pledger's Sermon in* "*The Morning Exercises,*" 1677.

Verse 7.—"*Thou didst hide thy face, and I was troubled.*" What soul can be deserted and not be afflicted? Certainly his absence cannot but be lamented with greatest grief, whose presence the soul prizeth above all earthly joy ; when the evidence of salvation is obscured, the light of God's countenance darkened, the comforts of the Spirit detained, then the heavens appear not so clear, the promises taste not so sweet, the ordinances prove not so lively, yea, the clouds which hang over the soul gather blackness, doubts arise, fears overflow, terrors increase, troubles enlarge, and the soul becomes languishingly afflicted, even with all variety of disquietments.—*Robert Mossom.*

Verse 7.—" *Thou didst hide thy face, and I was troubled.*" A believer puts on the sackcloth of contrition, for having put off the garment of perfection. As the sugar-loaf is dissolved, and weeps itself way, when dipped in wine ; so do our hearts melt under a sense of divine love.—*William Secker.*

Verse 7 (*last clause*).—No verse can more plainly teach us that glorious and comforting truth on which the mediæval writers especially love to dwell, that it is the looking, or not looking, of God upon his creature, that forms the happiness or the misery of that creature ; that those secret springs of joy which sometimes seem to rise up of themselves, and with which a stranger intermeddleth not, are nothing but God's direct and immediate looking on us ; while the sorrow for which we cannot assign any especial cause—call it melancholy, or low spirits, or by whatever other name—is nothing but his turning away his face from us.—*John Mason Neale.*

Verse 7 (*last clause*).—Is spiritual desertion and the hiding of God's face matter of affliction, and casting down to believers ? Yes, yes ; it quails their hearts, nothing can comfort them. " *Thou didst hide thy face, and I was troubled.*" Outward afflictions do but break the skin, this touches the quick ; they like rain fall only upon the tiles, this soaks into the house ; but Christ brings to believers substantial matter of consolation against the troubles of desertion : he himself was deserted of God for a time, that they might not be deserted for ever.—*John Flavel.*

Verse 7 (*last clause*).—If God be thy portion, then there is no loss in all the world that lies so hard and so heavy upon thee as the loss of thy God. There is no loss under heaven that doth so affect and afflict a man that hath God for his portion, as the loss of his God. David met with many a loss, but no loss made so sad and so great a breach upon his spirit as the loss of the face of God, the loss of the favour of God : " *In my prosperity I said, I shall never be moved. Lord, by thy favour thou hast made my mountain to stand strong : thou didst hide thy face, and I was troubled.*" The Hebrew word בהל *bahal* signifies to be greatly troubled, to be sorely terrified, as you may see in that 1 Sam. xxviii. 21, " And the woman came unto Saul, and saw that he was sore troubled." Here is the same Hebrew word *bahal*. Saul was so terrified, affrighted, and disanimated with the dreadful news that the devil in Samuel's likeness told him, that his very vital spirits so failed him, that he fell into a deadly swoon. And it was even so with David upon God's hiding of his face. David was like a withered flower that had lost all its sap, life, and vigour, when God had wrapped himself up in a cloud. The life of some creatures lieth in the light and warmth of the sun ; and so doth the life of the saints lie in the light and warmth of God's countenance. And, as in an eclipse of the sun, there is a drooping in the whole frame of nature, so when God hides his face, gracious souls cannot but droop and languish, and bow down themselves before him. Many insensible creatures, some by opening and shutting, as marigolds and tulips, others by bowing and inclining the head, as the solsequy* and mallow-flowers, are so sensible of the presence and absence of the sun, that there seems to be such a sympathy between the sun and them, that if the sun be gone or clouded, they wrap up themselves or hang down their heads, as being unwilling to be seen by any eye but his that fills them : and just thus it was with David when God had hid his face in a cloud.—*Thomas Brooks.*

Verse 8.—" *I cried to thee, O Lord ; and unto the Lord I made supplication.*" Bernard, under a fiction, proposeth a fable well worthy our beholding : therein the kings of Babylon and Jerusalem, signifying the state of the world and the church, always warring together ; in which encounter, at length it fell out, that one of the soldiers of Jerusalem was fled to the castle of Justice. Siege laid to the castle, and a multitude of enemies entrenched round about it, Fear gave over

---

* The early name of the "*sun*-flower." The *solsequium* of Linnæus.

all hope, but Prudence ministered her comfort. "Dost thou not know," saith she, "that our king is the King of glory; the Lord strong and mighty, even the Lord mighty in battle? Let us therefore despatch a messenger that may inform him of our necessities." Fear replieth, "But who is able to break through? Darkness is upon the face of the earth, and our walls are begirt with a watchful troop of armed men, and we, utterly inexpert of the way into so far a country." Whereupon Justice is consulted. "Be of good cheer," saith Justice, "I have a messenger of especial trust, well known to the king and his court, Prayer by name, who knoweth to address herself by ways unknown in the stillest silence of the night, till she cometh to the secrets and chamber of the King himself." Forthwith she goeth, and findeth the gates shut, knocketh amain, "Open, ye gates of righteousness, and be ye opened, ye everlasting doors, that I may come in and tell the King of Jerusalem how our case standeth." Doubtless the trustiest and effectuallest messenger we have to send is Prayer. If we send up merits, the stars in heaven will disdain it, that we which dwell at the footstool of God dare to presume so far, when the purest creatures in heaven are impure in his sight. If we send up fear and distrustfulness, the length of the way will tire them out. They are as heavy and lumpish as gads of iron; they will sink to the ground before they come halfway to the throne of salvation. If we send up blasphemies and curses, all the creatures betwixt heaven and earth will band themselves against us. The sun and the moon will rain down blood; the fire, hot burning coals; the air, thunderbolts upon our heads. Prayer, I say again, is the surest ambassador; which neither the tediousness of the way, nor difficulties of the passage, can hinder from her purpose; quick of speed, faithful for trustiness, happy for success, able to mount above the eagles of the sky, into the heaven of heavens, and as a chariot of fire bearing us aloft into the presence of God to seek his assistance.—*John King.*

Verse 9.—"*What profit is there in my blood, when I go down to the pit?*" Implying that he would willingly die, if he could thereby do any real service to God, or his country. Phil. ii. 17. But he saw not what good could be done by his dying in the bed of sickness, as might be if he had died in the bed of honour. Lord, saith he, wilt thou sell one of "thine own people for nought, and not increase thy wealth by the price?" Psalm xliv. 12.—*Matthew Henry.*

Verse 9.—"*What profit is there in my blood,*" etc. The little gain that the Lord would have by denying his people in the mercies they request, may also be used as a plea in prayer. David beggeth his own life of God, using this plea, "*What profit is there in my blood?*" So did the captive church plead (Psalm xliv. 12); "Thou sellest thy people for nought, and dost not increase thy wealth by their price." So then, poor saints of God when they come and tell the Lord in their prayers that indeed he may condemn, or confound, or cut or cast them off; he may continue to frown upon them; he may deny such-and-such requests of theirs, for such-and-such just causes in them; but what will he gain thereby? He may gain many praises, etc., by hearing them, and helping them; but what good will it do him to see them oppressed by the enemies of their souls? or what delight would it be to him to see them sighing and sinking, and fainting under sad pressures, etc.? this is an allowed and a very successful kind of pleading.—*Thomas Cobbet.*

Verse 9.—"*Shall the dust praise thee?*" Can any number be sufficient to praise thee? Can there ever be mouths enough to declare thy truth? And may not I make one—a sinful one I know—but yet one in the number, if thou be pleased to spare me from descending into the pit?—*Sir Richard Baker.*

Verse 9.—Prayer that is likely to prevail with God must be argumentative. God loves to have us plead with him and overcome him with arguments in prayer.—*Thomas Watson.*

Verse 11.—"*Thou hast turned for me my mourning into dancing: thou hast put off my sackcloth, and girded me with gladness.*" This might be true of David, delivered from his calamity; it was true of Christ, arising from the tomb, to die no more; it is true of the penitent, exchanging his sackcloth for the garments of salvation; and it will be verified in us all, at the last day, when we shall put off the dishonours of the grave, to shine in glory everlasting.—*George Horne.*

Verse 11.—"*Thou hast turned.*" I do so like the ups and downs in the Psalms. —*Adelaide Newton.*

Verse 11.—"*Thou hast put off my sackcloth, and girded me with gladness.*"

I say with the apostle, " Overcome evil with good," sorrow with joy. Joy is the true remedy for sorrow. It never had, never could have any other. We must always give the soul that weeps reason to rejoice ; all other consolation is utterly useless.—*Alexander Rodolph Vinet, D.D.*, 1797—1847.

Verse 11.—"*Thou hast girded me with gladness.*" My "sackcloth" was but a loose garment about me, which might easily be put off at pleasure, but my "*gladness*" is *girt* about me, to be fast and sure, and cannot leave me though it would ; at least none shall be able to take it from me.—*Sir Richard Baker.*

Verse 12.—Even as the Chaldeans formerly measured their natural day differently from the Israelites ; they put the day first and the night after ; but the Israelites, on the contrary, according to the order that was observed in the creation ; for in the beginning darkness was upon the face of the deep, and of every one of the six days it is said, " The evening and the morning were the first day," etc. So the times of the world and of the church are differently disposed ; for the world begins hers by the day of temporal prosperity, and finishes it by a night of darkness and anguish that is eternal ; but the church, on the contrary, begins hers by the night of adversity, which she suffers for awhile, and ends them by a day of consolation which she shall have for ever. The prophet in this Psalm begins with the *anger* of God, but ends with his *favour :* as of old, when they entered into the tabernacle they did at first see unpleasant things, as the knives of the sacrifices, the blood of victims, the fire that burned upon the altar, which consumed the offerings ; but when they passed a little farther there was the holy place, the candlestick of gold, the shew-bread, and the altar of gold on which they offered perfumes ; and in fine, there was the holy of holies, and the ark of the covenant, and the mercy-seat and the cherubims, which was called the face of God.—*Timothy Rogers.*

Verse 12.—"*I will give thanks.*" What is praise ? The rent we owe to God ; and the larger the farm the greater the rent should be.—*G. S. Bowes*, 1863.

HINTS TO PREACHERS.

Title.—House dedication, and how to arrange it.

Whole Psalm.—In this ode we may see the workings of David's mind before, and under, and after, the affliction. I. *Before* the affliction : 6. II. *Under* the affliction : 7—10. III. *After* the affliction : 11, 12.—*William Jay.*

Verse 1 (first clause).—God and his people exalting each other.

Verse 1 (second clause).—The happiness of being preserved so as not to be the scorn of our enemies.

Verse 1.—The disappointments of the devil.

Verse 2.—The sick man, the physician, the night-bell, the medicine, and the cure ; or, a covenant God. a sick saint. a crying heart. a healing hand.

Verse 3.—*Upbringing and preservation*, two choice mercies ; made the more illustrious by two terrible evils, " *grave*," and " *pit* " ; traced immediately to the Lord, " *thou hast.*"

Verse 4.—*Song*, a sacred service ; " *saints* " especially called to it ; *divine holiness*, a choice subject for it ; *Memory*, an admirable aid in it.

Verse 5.—The anger of God in relation to his people.

Verse 5.—*The night of weeping, and the morning of joy.*

Verse 5.—" *Life* " in God's " *favour.*"

Verse 5.—The transient nature of the believer's trouble, and the permanence of his joy.

Verse 6.—The peculiar dangers of " *prosperity.*"

Verses 6—12.—David's prosperity had lulled him into a state of undue security : God sent him this affliction to rouse him from it. The successive frames of his mind are here clearly marked ; and must successively be considered as they are here presented to our view. I. His carnal security. II. His spiritual dereliction.

III. His fervent prayers. IV. His speedy recovery. V. His grateful acknowledgments.—*Charles Simeon.*

Verse 7 (first clause).—Carnal security ; its causes, dangers, and cures.

Verse 7 (last clause).—The gracious bemoanings of a soul in spiritual darkness.

Verse 8, in connection with verse 3, *prayer the universal remedy.*

Verse 9 (first clause).—Arguments with God for continued life and renewed favour.

Verse 9 (last clause).—The resurrection, a time in which the " *dust* " shall " *praise* " God, and " *declare* " his " *truth.*"

Verse 10.—Two gems of prayer ; short, but full and needful.

Verse 10.—" *Lord, be thou my helper.*" I see many fall ; I shall fall too except thou hold me up. I am weak ; I am exposed to temptation. My heart is deceitful. My enemies are strong. I cannot trust in man ; I dare not trust in myself. The grace I have received will not keep me without thee. " *Lord, be thou my helper.*" In every duty ; in every conflict ; in every trial ; in every effort to promote the Lord's cause ; in every season of prosperity ; in every hour we live, this short and inspired prayer is suitable. May it flow from our hearts, be often on our lips, and be answered in our experience. For if the Lord help us, there is no duty which we cannot perform ; there is no foe which we cannot overcome ; there is no difficulty which we cannot surmount.—*James Smith's Daily Remembrancer.*

Verse 11.—*Transformations.* Sudden ; complete ; divine, " *thou* ; " personal, " *for me* ; " gracious.

Verse 11.—*Holy dancing :* open up the metaphor.

Verse 11.—The believer's change of raiment : illustrate by life of Mordecai or Joseph ; mention all the garbs the believer is made to wear, as a mourner, a beggar, a criminal, etc.

Verse 12.—Our " *glory,*" and its relation to God's glory.

Verse 12.—The end of gracious dispensations.

Verse 12.—Silence—when sinful.

Verse 12 (last clause).—The believer's vow, and the time for making it. See the whole Psalm.

PSALM XXXI.

Title.—To the chief Musician—a Psalm of David. *The dedication to the chief musician proves that this song of mingled measures and alternate strains of grief and woe was intended for public singing, and thus a deathblow is given to the notion that nothing but praise should be sung. Perhaps the Psalms, thus marked, might have been set aside as too mournful for temple worship, if special care had not been taken by the Holy Spirit to indicate them as being designed for the public edification of the Lord's people. May there not also be in Psalms thus designated a peculiarly distinct reference to the Lord Jesus ? He certainly manifests himself very clearly in the twenty-second, which bears this title ; and in the one before us we plainly hear his dying voice in the fifth verse. Jesus is chief everywhere, and in all the holy songs of his saints he is the chief musician. The surmises that Jeremiah penned this Psalm need no other answer than the fact that it is " a Psalm of David."*

Subject.—*The Psalmist in dire affliction appeals to his God for help with much confidence and holy importunity, and ere long finds his mind so strengthened that he magnifies the Lord for his great goodness. Some have thought that the occasion in his troubled life which led to this Psalm, was the treachery of the men of Keilah, and we have felt much inclined to this conjecture ; but after reflection it seems to us that its very mournful tone, and its allusion to his iniquity demand a later date, and it may be more satisfactory to illustrate it by the period when Absalom had rebelled, and his courtiers were fled from him, while lying lips spread a thousand malicious rumours against him. It is perhaps quite as well that we have no settled season mentioned, or we might have been so busy in applying it to David's case as to forget its suitability to our own.*

Division.—*There are no great lines of demarcation ; throughout the strain undulates, falling into valleys of mourning, and rising with hills of confidence. However, we may for convenience arrange it thus : David testifying his confidence in God pleads for help, 1—6 ; expresses gratitude for mercies received, 7, 8 ; particularly describes his case, 9—13 ; vehemently pleads for deliverance, 14—18 ; confidently and thankfully expects a blessing, 19—22 ; and closes by showing the bearing of his case upon all the people of God.*

EXPOSITION.

IN thee, O Lord do I put my trust ; let me never be ashamed : deliver me in thy righteousness.

2 Bow down thine ear to me ; deliver me speedily ; be thou my strong rock, for an house of defence to save me.

3 For thou *art* my rock and my fortress ; therefore for thy name's sake lead me, and guide me.

4 Pull me out of the net that they have laid privily for me : for thou *art* my strength.

5 Into thine hand I commit my spirit : thou hast redeemed me, O Lord God of truth.

6 I have hated them that regard lying vanities ; but I trust in the Lord.

1. " *In thee, O Lord, do I put my trust.*" Nowhere else do I fly for shelter, let the tempest howl as it may. The Psalmist has one refuge, and that the best one. He casts out the great sheet anchor of his faith in the time of storm. Let other things be doubtful, yet the fact that he relies upon Jehovah, David lays down most positively ; and he begins with it, lest by stress of trial he should afterwards forget it. This avowal of faith is the fulcrum by means of which he labours to uplift and remove his trouble ; he dwells upon it as a comfort to himself and a plea with God. No mention is made of merit, but faith relies upon divine favour and faithfulness, and upon that alone. " *Let me never be ashamed.*" How can the

Lord permit the man to be ultimately put to shame who depends alone upon him ? This would not be dealing like a God of truth and grace. It would bring dishonour upon God himself if faith were not in the end rewarded. It will be an ill day indeed for religion when trust in God brings no consolation and no assistance. " *Deliver me in thy righteousness.*" Thou art not unjust to desert a trustful soul, or to break thy promises ; thou wilt vindicate the righteousness of thy mysterious providence, and give me joyful deliverance. Faith dares to look even to the sword of justice for protection : while God is righteous, faith will not be left to be proved futile and fanatical. How sweetly the declaration of faith in this first verse sounds, if we read it at the foot of the cross, beholding the promise of the Father as yea and amen through the Son ; viewing God with faith's eye as he stands revealed in Jesus crucified.

2. " *Bow down thine ear to me.*" Condescend to my low estate ; listen to me attentively as one who would hear every word. Heaven with its transcendent glories of harmony might well engross the divine ear, but yet the Lord has an hourly regard to the weakest moanings of his poorest people. " *Deliver me speedily.*" We must not set times and seasons, yet in submission we may ask for swift as well as sure mercy. God's mercies are often enhanced in value by the timely haste which he uses in their bestowal ; if they came late they might be too late—but he rides upon a cherub, and flies upon the wings of the wind when he intends the good of his beloved. " *Be thou my strong rock.*" Be my Engedi, my Adullam ; my immutable, immovable, impregnable, sublime, resort. " *For an house of defence to save me,*" wherein I may *dwell* in safety, not merely running to thee for temporary shelter, but abiding in thee for eternal salvation. How very simply does the good man pray, and yet with what weight of meaning ! he uses no ornamental flourishes, he is too deeply in earnest to be otherwise than plain : it were well if all who engage in public prayer would observe the same rule.

3. " *For thou art my rock and my fortress.*" Here the tried soul avows yet again its full confidence in God. Faith's repetitions are not vain. The avowal of our reliance upon God in times of adversity is a principal method of glorifying him. Active service is good, but the passive confidence of faith is not one jot less esteemed in the sight of God. The words before us appear to embrace and fasten upon the Lord with a fiducial grip which is not to be relaxed. The two personal pronouns, like sure nails, lay hold upon the faithfulness of the Lord. O for grace to have our heart fixed in firm unstaggering belief in God ! The figure of a rock and a fortress may be illustrated to us in these times by the vast fortress of Gibraltar, often besieged by our enemies, but never wrested from us : ancient strongholds, though far from impregnable by our modes of warfare, were equally important in those remoter ages—when in the mountain fastnesses, feeble bands felt themselves to be secure. Note the singular fact that David asked the Lord to be his rock (verse 2) because he was his rock ; and learn from it that we may pray to enjoy in experience what we grasp by faith. Faith is the foundation of prayer. " *Therefore for thy name's sake lead me, and guide me.*" The Psalmist argues like a logician with his fors and therefores. Since I do sincerely trust thee, saith he, O my God, be my director. To lead and to guide are two things very like each other, but patient thought will detect different shades of meaning, especially as the last may mean *provide for me*. The double word indicates an urgent need—we require double direction, for we are fools, and the way is rough. Lead me as a soldier, guide me as a traveller ! lead me as a babe, guide me as a man ; lead me when thou art with me, but guide me even if thou be absent ; lead me by thy hand, guide me by thy word. The argument used is one which is fetched from the armoury of free grace : not for my own sake, but *for thy name's sake* guide me. Our appeal is not to any fancied virtue in our own names, but to the glorious goodness and graciousness which shine resplendent in the character of Israel's God. It is not possible that the Lord should suffer his own honour to be tarnished, but this would certainly be the case if those who trusted him should perish. This was Moses' plea, " What wilt thou do unto thy great name ? "

4. " *Pull me out of the net that they have laid privily for me.*" The enemies of David were cunning as well as mighty ; if they could not conquer him by power, they would capture him by craft. Our own spiritual foes are of the same order— they are of the serpent's brood, and seek to ensnare us by their guile. The prayer before us supposes the possibility of the believer being caught like a bird ; and, indeed, we are so foolish that this often happens. So deftly does the fowler do his

work that simple ones are soon surrounded by it. The text asks that even out of the meshes of the net the captive one may be delivered; and this is a proper petition, and one which can be granted; from between the jaws of the lion and out of the belly of hell can eternal love rescue the saint. It may need a sharp *pull* to save a soul from the net of temptation, and a mighty pull to extricate a man from the snares of malicious cunning, but the Lord is equal to every emergency, and the most skilfully placed nets of the hunter shall never be able to hold his chosen ones. Woe unto those who are so clever at net laying: they who tempt others shall be destroyed themselves. Villains who lay traps in secret shall be punished in public. "*For thou art my strength.*" What an inexpressible sweetness is to be found in these few words! How joyfully may we enter upon labours, and how cheerfully may we endure sufferings when we can lay hold upon celestial power. Divine power will rend asunder all the toils of the foe, confound their politics and frustrate their knavish tricks; he is a happy man who has such matchless might engaged upon his side. Our own strength would be of little service when embarrassed in the nets of base cunning, but the Lord's strength is ever available; we have but to invoke it, and we shall find it near at hand. If by faith we are depending alone upon the strength of the strong God of Israel, we may use our holy reliance as a plea in supplication.

5. "*Into thine hand I commit my spirit.*" These living words of David were our Lord's dying words, and have been frequently used by holy men in their hour of departure. Be assured that they are good, choice, wise, and solemn words; we may use them now and in the last tremendous hour. Observe, the object of the good man's solicitude in life and death is not his body or his estate, but his spirit; this is his jewel, his secret treasure; if this be safe, all is well. See what he does with his pearl! He commits it to the hand of his God: it came from him, it is his own, he has aforetime sustained it, he is able to keep it, and it is most fit that he should receive it. All things are safe in Jehovah's hands; what we entrust to the Lord will be secure, both now and in that day of days towards which we are hastening. Without reservation the good man yields himself to his heavenly Father's hand; it is enough for him to be there; it is peaceful living and glorious dying to repose in the care of heaven. At all times we should commit and continue to commit our all to Jesus' sacred care, then, though life may hang on a thread, and adversities may multiply as the sands of the sea, our soul shall dwell at ease, and delight itself in quiet resting places. "*Thou hast redeemed me, O Lord God of truth.*" Redemption is a solid basis for confidence. David had not known Calvary as we have done, but temporal redemption cheered him; and shall not eternal redemption yet more sweetly console us? Past deliverances are strong pleas for present assistance. What the Lord has done he will do again, for he changes not. He is a God of veracity, faithful to his promises, and gracious to his saints; he will not turn away from his people.

6. "*I have hated them that regard lying vanities.*" Those who will not lean upon the true arm of strength, are sure to make to themselves vain confidences. Man must have a god, and if he will not adore the only living and true God, he makes a fool of himself, and pays superstitious regard to a lie, and waits with anxious hope upon a base delusion. Those who did this were none of David's friends; he had a constant dislike to them: the verb includes the present as well as the past tense. He hated them for hating God; he would not endure the presence of idolaters; his heart was set against them for their stupidity and wickedness. He had no patience with their superstitious observances, and calls their idols vanities of emptiness, nothings of nonentity. Small courtesy is more than Romanists and Puseyites deserve for their fooleries. Men who make gods of their riches, their persons, their wits, or anything else, are to be shunned by those whose faith rests upon God in Christ Jesus; and so far from being envied, they are to be pitied as depending upon utter vanities. "*But I trust in the Lord.*" This might be very unfashionable, but the Psalmist dared to be singular. Bad example should not make us less decided for the truth, but the rather in the midst of general defection we should grow the more bold. This adherence to his trust in Jehovah is the great plea employed all along: the troubled one flies into the arms of his God, and ventures everything upon the divine faithfulness.

7 I will be glad and rejoice in thy mercy: for thou hast considered my trouble; thou hast known my soul in adversities;

8 And hast not shut me up into the hand of the enemy : thou hast set my feet in a large room.

7. "*I will be glad and rejoice in thy mercy.*" For mercy past he is grateful, and for mercy future, which he believingly anticipates, he is joyful. In our most importunate intercessions, we must find breathing time to bless the Lord : praise is never a hindrance to prayer, but rather a lively refreshment therein. It is delightful at intervals to hear the notes of the high-sounding cymbals when the dolorous sackbut rules the hour. Those two words, *glad* and *rejoice,* are an instructive reduplication, we need not stint ourselves in our holy triumph ; this wine we may drink in bowls without fear of excess. "*For thou hast considered my trouble.*" Thou hast seen it, weighed it, directed it, fixed a bound to it, and in all ways made it a matter of tender consideration. A man's consideration means the full exercise of his mind ; what must God's consideration be ? "*Thou hast known my soul in adversities.*" God owns his saints when others are ashamed to acknowledge them ; he never refuses to know his friends. He thinks not the worse of them for their rags and tatters. He does not misjudge them and cast them off when their faces are lean with sickness, or their hearts heavy with despondency. Moreover, the Lord Jesus knows us in our pangs in a peculiar sense, by having a deep sympathy towards us in them all ; when no others can enter into our griefs, from want of understanding them experimentally, Jesus dives into the lowest depths with us, comprehending the direst of our woes, because he has felt the same. Jesus is a physician who knows every case ; nothing is new to him. When we are so bewildered as not to know our own state, he knows us altogether. He has known us and will know us : O for grace to know more of him ! "Man, know thyself," is a good philosophic precept, but "Man, thou art known of God," is a superlative consolation. *Adversities* in the plural—"Many are the afflictions of the righteous."

8. "*And hast not shut me up into the hand of the enemy.*" To be shut up in one's hand is to be delivered over absolutely to his power ; now, the believer is not in the hand of death or the devil, much less is he in the power of man. The enemy may get a temporary advantage over us, but we are like men in prison with the door open ; God will not let us be shut up, he always provides a way of escape. "*Thou hast set my feet in a large room.*" Blessed be God for liberty : civil liberty is valuable, religious liberty is precious, spiritual liberty is priceless. In all troubles we may praise God if these are left. Many saints have had their greatest enlargements of soul when their affairs have been in the greatest straits. Their souls have been in a large room when their bodies have been lying in Bonner's coalhole, or in some other narrow dungeon. Grace has been equal to every emergency ; and more than this, it has made the emergency an opportunity for displaying itself.

9 Have mercy upon me, O LORD, for I am in trouble : mine eye is consumed with grief, *yea,* my soul and my belly.

10 For my life is spent with grief, and my years with sighing : my strength faileth because of mine iniquity, and my bones are consumed.

11 I was a reproach among all mine enemies, but especially among my neighbours, and a fear to mine acquaintance : they that did see me without fled from me.

12 I am forgotten as a dead man out of mind : I am like a broken vessel.

13 For I have heard the slander of many : fear *was* on every side : while they took counsel together against me, they devised to take away my life.

9. "*Have mercy upon me, O Lord, for I am in trouble.*" Now, the man of God comes to a particular and minute description of his sorrowful case. He unbosoms his heart, lays bare his wounds, and expresses his inward desolation. This first sentence pithily comprehends all that follows, it is the text for his lamenting discourse. Misery moves mercy—no more reasoning is needed. "Have mercy" is the prayer ; the argument is as prevalent as it is plain and personal, "I am in trouble." "*Mine eye is consumed with grief.*" Dim and sunken eyes are plain indicators of failing health. Tears draw their salt from our strength, and floods of them are very apt to consume the source from which they spring. God would have us tell him the symptoms of our disease, not for his information, but to show

our sense of need. " *Yea, my soul and my belly* [*or body*]." Soul and body are so intimately united, that one cannot decline without the other feeling it. We, in these days, are not strangers to the double sinking which David describes ; we have been faint with physical suffering, and distracted with mental distress : when two such seas meet, it is well for us that the Pilot at the helm is at home in the midst of the waterfloods, and makes storms to become the triumph of his art.

10. " *For my life is spent with grief, and my years with sighing.*" It had become his daily occupation to mourn ; he spent all his days in the dungeon of distress. The sap and essence of his existence was being consumed, as a candle is wasted while it burns. His adversities were shortening his days, and digging for him an early grave. Grief is a sad market to spend all our wealth of life in, but a far more profitable trade may be driven there than in Vanity Fair ; it is better to go to the house of mourning than the house of feasting. Black is good wear. The salt of tears is a healthy medicine. Better spend our years in sighing than in sinning. The two members of the sentence before us convey the same idea ; but there are no idle words in Scripture, the reduplication is the fitting expression of fervency and importunity. " *My strength faileth because of mine iniquity.*" David sees to the bottom of his sorrow, and detects sin lurking there. It is profitable trouble which leads us to trouble ourselves about our iniquity. Was this the Psalmist's foulest crime which now gnawed at his heart, and devoured his strength ? Very probably it was so. Sinful morsels, though sweet in the mouth, turn out to be poison in the bowels : if we wantonly give a portion of our strength to sin, it will by-and-by take the remainder from us. We lose both physical, mental, moral, and spiritual vigour by iniquity. " *And my bones are consumed.*" Weakness penetrated the innermost parts of his system, the firmest parts of his frame felt the general decrepitude. A man is in a piteous plight when he comes to this.

11. " *I was a reproach among all mine enemies.*" They were pleased to have something to throw at me : my mournful estate was music to them, because they maliciously interpreted it to be a judgment from heaven upon me. Reproach is little thought of by those who are not called to endure it, but he who passes under its lash knows how deep it wounds. The best of men may have the bitterest foes, and be subjected to the most cruel taunts. " *But especially among my neighbours.*" Those who are nearest can stab the sharpest. We feel most the slights of those who should have shown us sympathy. Perhaps David's friends feared to be identified with his declining fortunes, and therefore turned against him in order to win the mercy if not the favour of his opponents. Self interest rules the most of men : ties the most sacred are soon snapped by its influence, and actions of the utmost meanness are perpetrated without scruple. " *And a fear to mine acquaintance.*" The more intimate before, the more distant did they become. Our Lord was denied by Peter, betrayed by Judas, and forsaken by all in the hour of his utmost need. All the herd turn against a wounded deer. The milk of human kindness curdles when a despised believer is the victim of slanderous accusations. " *They that did see me without fled from me.*" Afraid to be seen in the company of a man so thoroughly despised, those who once courted his society hastened from him as though he had been infected with the plague. How villainous a thing is slander which can thus make an eminent saint, once the admiration of his people, to become the general butt, the universal aversion of mankind ! To what extremities of dishonour may innocence be reduced !

12. " *I am forgotten as a dead man out of mind.*" All David's youthful prowess was now gone from remembrance : he had been the saviour of his country, but his services were buried in oblivion. Men soon forget the deepest obligations ; popularity is evanescent to the last degree : he who is in every one's mouth to-day may be forgotten by all to-morrow. A man had better be dead than be smothered in slander. Of the dead we say nothing but good, but in the Psalmist's case they said nothing but evil. We must not look for the reward of philanthropy this side of heaven, for men pay their best servants but sorry wages, and turn them out of doors when no more is to be got out of them. " *I am like a broken vessel,*" a thing useless, done for, worthless, cast aside, forgotten. Sad condition for a king ! Let us see herein the portrait of the King of kings in his humiliation, when he made himself of no reputation, and took upon him the form of a servant.

13. " *For I have heard the slander of many.*" One slanderous viper is death to all comfort—what must be the venom of a whole brood ? What the ear does not hear the heart does not rue ; but in David's case the accusing voices were loud

enough to break in upon his quiet—foul mouths had grown so bold, that they poured forth their falsehoods in the presence of their victim. Shimei was but one of a class, and his cry of " Go up, thou bloody man," was but the common speech of thousands of the sons of Belial. All Beelzebub's pack of hounds may be in full cry against a man, and yet he may be the Lord's anointed. " *Fear was on every side.*" He was encircled with fearful suggestions, threatenings, remembrances, and forebodings ; no quarter was clear from incessant attack. " *While they took counsel together against me, they devised to take away my life.*" The ungodly act in concert in their onslaughts upon the excellent of the earth : it is to be wondered at that sinners should often be better agreed than saints, and generally set about their wicked work with much more care and foresight than the righteous exhibit in holy enterprises. Observe the cruelty of a good man's foes ! they will be content with nothing less than his blood—for this they plot and scheme. Better fall into the power of a lion than under the will of malicious persecutors, for the beast may spare its prey if it be fed to the full, but malice is unrelenting and cruel as a wolf. Of all fiends the most cruel is envy. How sorely was the Psalmist bestead when the poisoned arrows of a thousand bows were all aimed at his life ! Yet in all this his faith did not fail him, nor did his God forsake him. Here is encouragement for us.

14 But I trusted in thee, O LORD : I said, Thou *art* my God.

15 My times *are* in thy hand : deliver me from the hand of mine enemies, and from them that persecute me.

16 Make thy face to shine upon thy servant : save me for thy mercies' sake.

17 Let me not be ashamed, O LORD ; for I have called upon thee : let the wicked be ashamed, *and* let them be silent in the grave.

18 Let the lying lips be put to silence ; which speak grievous things proudly and contemptuously against the righteous.

In this section of the Psalm he renews his prayers, urging the same pleas as at first : earnest wrestlers attempt over and over again the same means of gaining their point.

14. " *But I trusted in thee, O Lord.*" Notwithstanding all afflicting circumstances, David's faith maintained its hold, and was not turned aside from its object. What a blessed saving clause is this ! So long as our faith, which is our shield, is safe, the battle may go hard, but its ultimate result is no matter of question ; if that could be torn from us, we should be as surely slain as were Saul and Jonathan upon the high places of the field. " *I said, Thou art my God.*" He proclaimed aloud his determined allegiance to Jehovah. He was no fair-weather believer, he could hold to his faith in a sharp frost, and wrap it about him as a garment fitted to keep out all the ills of time. He who can say what David did need not envy Cicero his eloquence : " Thou art my God," has more sweetness in it than any other utterance which human speech can frame. Note that this adhesive faith is here mentioned as an argument with God to honour his own promise by sending a speedy deliverance.

15. " *My times are in thy hand.*" The sovereign arbiter of destiny holds in his own power all the issues of our life ; we are not waifs and strays upon the ocean of fate, but are steered by infinite wisdom towards our desired haven. Providence is a soft pillow for anxious heads, an anodyne for care, a grave for despair. " *Deliver me from the hand of mine enemies, and from them that persecute me.*" It is lawful to desire escape from persecution if it be the Lord's will ; and when this may not be granted us in the form which we desire, sustaining grace will give us deliverance in another form, by enabling us to laugh to scorn all the fury of the foe.

16. " *Make thy face to shine upon thy servant.*" Give me the sunshine of heaven in my soul, and I will defy the tempests of earth. Permit me to enjoy a sense of thy favour, O Lord, and a consciousness that thou art pleased with my manner of life, and all men may frown and slander as they will. It is always enough for a servant if he pleases his master ; others may be dissatisfied, but he is not their servant, they do not pay him his wages, and their opinions have no weight with him. " *Save me for thy mercies' sake.*" The good man knows no plea but mercy ; whoever might urge legal pleas, David never dreamed of it.

17. " *Let me not be ashamed, O Lord ; for I have called upon thee.*" Put not my

prayers to the blush! Do not fill profane mouths with jeers at my confidence in my God. "*Let the wicked be ashamed, and let them be silent in the grave.*" Cause them to their amazement to see my wrongs righted and their own pride horribly confounded. A milder spirit rules our prayers under the gentle reign of the Prince of Peace, and, therefore, we can only use such words as these in their prophetic sense, knowing as we do full well, that shame and the silence of death are the best portion that ungodly sinners can expect. That which they desired for despised believers shall come upon themselves by a decree of retributive justice, at which they cannot cavil "As he loved mischief, so let it come upon him."

18. "*Let the lying lips be put to silence.*" A right good and Christian prayer; who but a bad man would give liars more license than need be? May God silence them either by leading them to repentance, by putting them to thorough shame, or by placing them in positions where what they may say will stand for nothing. "*Which speak grievous things proudly and contemptuously against the righteous.*" The sin of slanderers lies partly in the matter of their speech; "they speak grievous things;" things cutting deep into the feelings of good men, and wounding them sorely in that tender place—their reputations. The sin is further enhanced by the manner of their speech; they speak proudly and contemptuously; they talk as if they themselves were the cream of society, and the righteous the mere scum of vulgarity. Proud thoughts of self are generally attended by debasing estimates of others. The more room we take up ourselves, the less we can afford our neighbours. What wickedness it is that unworthy characters should always be the loudest in railing at good men! They have no power to appreciate moral worth of which they are utterly destitute, and yet they have the effrontery to mount the judgment seat, and judge the men compared with whom they are as so much draff. Holy indignation may well prompt us to desire anything which may rid the world of such unbearable impertinence and detestable arrogance.

19 *Oh* how great *is* thy goodness, which thou hast laid up for them that fear thee; *which* thou hast wrought for them that trust in thee before the sons of men!

20 Thou shalt hide them in the secret of thy presence from the pride of man: thou shalt keep them secretly in a pavilion from the strife of tongues.

21 Blessed *be* the LORD: for he hath shewed me his marvellous kindness in a strong city.

22 For I said in my haste, I am cut off from before thine eyes: nevertheless thou heardest the voice of my supplications when I cried unto thee.

Being full of faith, the Psalmist gives glory to God for the mercy which he is assured will be his position.

19. "*Oh how great is thy goodness.*" Is it not singular to find such a joyful sentence in connection with so much sorrow? Truly the life of faith is a miracle. When faith led David to his God, she set him singing at once. He does not tell us how great was God's goodness, for he could not; there are no measures which can set forth the immeasurable goodness of Jehovah, who is goodness itself. Holy amazement uses interjections where adjectives utterly fail. Notes of exclamation suit us when words of explanation are of no avail. If we cannot measure we can marvel; and though we may not calculate with accuracy, we can adore with fervency. "*Which thou hast laid up for them that fear thee.*" The Psalmist in contemplation divides goodness into two parts, that which is in store and that which is wrought out. The Lord has laid up in reserve for his people supplies beyond all count. In the treasury of the covenant, in the field of redemption, in the caskets of the promises, in the granaries of providence, the Lord has provided for all the needs which can possibly occur to his chosen. We ought often to consider the laid-up goodness of God which has not yet been distributed to the chosen, but is already provided for them: if we are much in such contemplations, we shall be led to feel devout gratitude, such as glowed in the heart of David. "*Which thou hast wrought for them that trust in thee before the sons of men.*" Heavenly mercy is not all hidden in the storehouse; in a thousand ways it has already revealed itself on behalf of those who are bold to avow their confidence in God; before their fellow men this goodness of the Lord has been displayed, that a faithless generation might stand rebuked. Overwhelming are the proofs of the Lord's

favour to believers, history teems with amazing instances, and our own lives are full of prodigies of grace. We serve a good Master. Faith receives a large reward even now, but looks for her full inheritance in the future. Who would not desire to take his lot with the servants of a Master whose boundless love fills all holy minds with astonishment ?

20. "*Thou shalt hide them in the secret of thy presence from the pride of man.*" Pride is a barbed weapon : the proud man's contumely is iron which entereth into the soul ; but those who trust in God, are safely housed in the Holy of holies, the innermost court, into which no man may dare intrude ; here in the secret dwelling place of God the mind of the saint rests in peace, which the foot of pride cannot disturb. Dwellers at the foot of the cross of Christ grow callous to the sneers of the haughty. The wounds of Jesus distil a balsam which heals all the scars which the jagged weapons of contempt can inflict upon us ; in fact, when armed with the same mind which was in Christ Jesus, the heart is invulnerable to all the darts of pride. "*Thou shalt keep them secretly in a pavilion from the strife of tongues.*" Tongues are more to be dreaded than beasts of prey—and when they strive, it is as though a whole pack of wolves were let loose ; but the believer is secure even in this peril, for the royal pavilion of the King of kings shall afford him quiet shelter and serene security. The secret tabernacle of sacrifice, and the royal pavilion of sovereignty afford a double security to the Lord's people in their worst distresses. Observe the immediate action of God, " *Thou* shalt hide," " *Thou* shalt keep," the Lord himself is personally present for the rescue of his afflicted.

21. "*Blessed be the Lord.*" When the Lord blesses us we cannot do less than bless him in return. "*For he hath showed me his marvellous kindness in a strong city.*" Was this in Mahanaim, where the Lord gave him victory over the hosts of Absalom ? Or did he refer to Rabbath of Ammon, where he gained signal triumphs ? Or, best of all, was Jerusalem the strong city where he most experienced the astonishing kindness of his God ? Gratitude is never short of subjects : her Ebenezers stand so close together as to wall up her path to heaven on both sides. Whether in cities or in hamlets our blessed Lord has revealed himself to us, we shall never forget the hallowed spots : the lonely mount of Hermon, or the village of Emmaus, or the rock of Patmos, or the wilderness of Horeb, are all alike renowned when God manifests himself to us in robes of love.

22. Confession of faults is always proper ; and when we reflect upon the goodness of God, we ought to be reminded of our own errors and offences. "*For I said in my haste.*" We generally speak amiss when we are in a hurry. Hasty words are but for a moment on the tongue, but they often lie for years on the conscience. "*I am cut off from before thine eyes.*" This was an unworthy speech ; but unbelief will have a corner in the heart of the firmest believer, and out of that corner it will vent many spiteful things against the Lord if the course of providence be not quite so smooth as nature might desire. No saint ever was, or ever could be, cut off from before the eyes of God, and yet no doubt many have thought so, and more than one have said so. For ever be such dark suspicions banished from our minds. "*Nevertheless thou heardest the voice of my supplications when I cried unto thee.*" What a mercy that if *we* believe not, yet God abideth faithful, hearing prayer even when we are labouring under doubts which dishonour his name. If we consider the hindrances in the way of our prayers, and the poor way in which we present them, it is a wonder of wonders that they ever prevail with heaven.

23 O love the LORD, all ye his saints : *for* the LORD preserveth the faithful, and plentifully rewardeth the proud doer.

24 Be of good courage, and he shall strengthen your heart, all ye that hope in the LORD.

23. "*O love the Lord, all ye his saints.*" A most affecting exhortation, showing clearly the deep love of the writer to his God : there is the more beauty in the expression, because it reveals love towards a smiting God, love which many waters could not quench. To bless him who gives is easy, but to cling to him who takes away is a work of grace. All the saints are benefited by the sanctified miseries of one, if they are led by earnest exhortations to love their Lord the better. If saints do not love the Lord, who will ? Love is the universal debt of all the saved family : who would wish to be exonerated from its payment ? Reasons for love are given, for believing love is not blind. "*For the Lord preserveth the faithful.*"

They have to bide their time, but the recompense comes at last, and meanwhile all the cruel malice of their enemies cannot destroy them. "*And plentifully rewardeth the proud doer.*" This also is cause for gratitude: pride is so detestable in its acts that he who shall mete out to it its righteous due, deserves the love of all holy minds.

24. "*Be of good courage.*" Keep up your spirit, let no craven thoughts blanch your cheek. Fear weakens, courage strengthens. Victory waits upon the banners of the brave. "*And he shall strengthen your heart.*" Power from on high shall be given in the most effectual manner by administering force to the fountain of vitality. So far from leaving us, the Lord will draw very near to us in our adversity, and put his own power into us. "*All ye that hope in the Lord.*" Every one of you, lift up your heads and sing for joy of heart. God is faithful, and does not fail even his little children who do but *hope*, wherefore then should we be afraid?

EXPLANATORY NOTES AND QUAINT SAYINGS.

Verse 1.—" *In thee, O Lord, do I put my trust.*" Let us therefore shun mistrust; doubt is death, trust alone is life. Let us make sure that we trust the Lord, and never take our trust on trust. " *Let me never be ashamed.*" If David prays against being ashamed, let us strive against it. Lovers of Jesus should be ashamed of being ashamed.—*C. H. S.*

Verse 1.—" *Deliver me in thy righteousness.*" For supporting thy faith, mark well whereon it may safely rest; even upon God's *righteousness*, as well as upon his mercy. On this ground did the apostle in faith expect the crown of righteousness (2 Tim. iv. 7, 8), because the Lord from whom he expected it is a righteous judge; and the Psalmist is bold to appeal to the righteousness of God. Ps. xxxv. 24. For we may be well assured that what God's goodness, grace, and mercy moved him to promise, his truth, his faithfulness, and righteousness will move him to perform.—*William Gouge.*

Verses 1, 2, 3 :—

> Shadows are faithless, and the rocks are false;
> No trust in brass, no trust in marble walls;
> Poor cots are e'en as safe as princes' halls.
>
> Great God! there is no safety here below;
> Thou art my fortress, thou that seem'st my foe,
> 'Tis thou, that strik'st the stroke, must guard the blow.
>
> Thou art my God, by thee I fall or stand;
> Thy grace hath giv'n me courage to withstand
> All tortures, but my conscience and thy hand.
>
> I know thy justice is thyself; I know,
> Just God, thy very self is mercy too;
> If not to thee, where, whither shall I go?
>
> *Francis Quarles.*

Verse 2.—" *Bow down thine ear.*" Listen to my complaint. Put thy ear to my lips, that thou mayest hear all that my *feebleness* is capable of uttering. We generally put our ear near to the lips of the sick and dying that we may hear what they say. To this the text appears to allude.—*Adam Clarke.*

Verse 2.—" *Deliver me speedily.*" In praying that he may be delivered *speedily* there is shown the greatness of his danger, as if he had said, All will soon be over with my life, unless God make haste to help me.—*John Calvin.*

Verses 2, 3.—" *Be thou my strong rock,*" etc. What the Lord is engaged to be unto us by covenant, we may pray and expect to find him in effect. " *Be thou my strong rock,*" saith he, " *for thou art my rock.*"—*David Dickson.*

Verse 3.—" *For thy name's sake.*" If merely a creature's honour, the credit of ministers or the glory of angels were involved, man's salvation would indeed be uncertain. But every step involves the honour of God. We plead for *his name's sake*. If God should begin and not continue, or if he should carry on but not complete the work, all would admit that it was for some reason that must bring reproach on the Almighty. This can never be. God was self-moved to undertake man's salvation. His glorious name makes it certain the top-stone shall be laid in glory.—*William S. Plumer.*

Verse 3.—" *For thy name's sake.*" On account of the fame of thy power, thy goodness, thy truth, etc. " *Lead me.*" As a shepherd an erring sheep, as a leader military bands, or as one leads another ignorant of the way. See Gen. xxiv. 27 ; Neh. ix. 12, 13 ; Ps. xxiii. 3 ; lxxiii. 24. Govern my counsels, my affections, and my thoughts.—*Martin Geier, 1614—1681.*

Verse 4.—" *Pull me out of the net :* " that *noted net,* as the Hebrew hath it.— *John Trapp.*

Verse 4.—" *Pull me out of the net that they have laid privily for me.*" By these words, he intimateth that his enemies did not only by open force come against him, but by cunning and policy attempted to circumvent him, as when they put him on, as Saul instructed them, to be the king's son-in-law, and to this end set him on to get two hundred foreskins of the Philistines for a dowry, under a pretence of good-will, seeking his ruin ; and when wait also was laid for him to kill him in his house. But he trusted in God, and prayed to be delivered, if there should be any the like enterprise against him hereafter.—*John Mayer.*

Verse 4.—" *For thou art my strength.*" Omnipotence cuts the net which policy weaves. When we poor puny things are in the net, God is not. In the old fable the mouse set free the lion, here the lion liberates the mouse.—*C. H. S.*

Verse 5.—" *Into thine hand I commit my spirit.*" These were the last words of Polycarp, of Bernard, of Huss, of Jerome of Prague, of Luther, Melancthon, and many others. " Blessed are they," says Luther, " who die not only *for* the Lord, as martyrs, not only *in* the Lord, as all believers, but likewise *with* the Lord, as breathing forth their lives in these words, ' Into thine hand I commit my spirit.' " *J. J. Stewart Perowne.*

Verse 5.—" *Into thine hand I commit my spirit.*" These words, as they stand in the *Vulgate,* were in the highest credit among our ancestors ; by whom they were used in all dangers, difficulties, and in the article of death. *In manus tuas, Domine, commendo spiritum meum,* was used by the sick when about to expire, if they were sensible ; and if not, the priest said it in their behalf. In *forms of prayer* for sick and dying persons, these words were frequently inserted in Latin, though all the rest of the prayer was English ; for it was supposed there was something sovereign in the *language* itself. But let not the abuse of such words hinder their usefulness. For an ejaculation nothing can be better ; and when the pious or the tempted with confidence use them, nothing can exceed their effect.—*Adam Clarke.*

Verse 5.—" *Into thine hand I commit my spirit,*" etc. For what are the saints to commit their spirits into the hands of God by Jesus Christ ?

1. That they may be safe ; *i.e.,* preserved in their passage to heaven, from all the enemies and dangers that may stand in the way. When saints die, the powers of darkness would, doubtless, if possible, hinder the ascending of their souls to God. As they are cast out of heaven, they are filled with rage to see any out of our world going thither. One thing, therefore, which the saint means in committing his spirit into the hands of God, is, that the precious *depositum* may be kept from all that wish or would attempt its ruin. And they are sure that almighty power belongs to God : and if this is engaged for their preservation, none can pluck them out of his hand. The Redeemer hath spoiled principalities and powers, and proved it by his triumphant ascension to glory ; and hath all his and the believer's enemies in a chain, so that they shall be more than conquerors in and through him. Angels, for order's sake, are sent forth to minister to them and be their guard, who will faithfully attend them their charge, till they are brought to the presence of the common Lord of both. " I know," saith the apostle, " whom I have believed ; and I am persuaded that he is able to keep that which I have committed unto him against that day."

2. They commit their soul into the hands of God, that they may be admitted to dwell with him, even in that presence of his where there is fulness of joy, and

where there are pleasures for evermore : where all evil is excluded, and all good present, to fill their desires, and find them matter of praise to all eternity.

3. They commit their departing spirits into the hands of God, that their bodies may be at length raised and reunited to them, and that so they may enter at last into the blessedness prepared for them that love him. . . .

The grounds on which they may do this with comfort, *i.e.*, with lively hopes of being happy for ever, are many. To mention only two :—

1. God's interest in them, and upon the most endearing foundation, that of redemption. "*Into thine hand I commit my spirit : for thou hast redeemed me.*" *Redeemed me* from hell and the wrath to come, by giving thy Son to die for me. Lord, I am not only thy creature, but thy redeemed creature, bought with a price, saith the saint.

Redeemed me from the power of my inward corruption, and from love to it, and delight in it ; and with my consent hast drawn me to be thine, and thine for ever. *Lord, I am thine,* save me unchangeably.

2. His known faithfulness. "*Into thine hand I commit my spirit, O Lord God of truth.*" Into thine hand I commit my spirit, who hast been *a God of truth,* in performing thy promises to all thy people that are gone before me out of this world ; and hast been so to me hitherto, and, I cannot doubt, wilt continue so to the end.— *Daniel Wilcox.*

Verse 5.—"*Into thine hand.*" When those hands fail me, then am I indeed abandoned and miserable ! When they sustain and keep me, then am I safe, exalted, strong, and filled with good.

Receive me, then, O Eternal Father, for the sake of our Lord's merits and words ; for he, by his obedience and his death, hath now merited from thee everything which I do not merit of myself. Into thy hands, my Father and my God, I commend my spirit, my soul, my body, my powers, my desires. I offer up to thy hands, all ; to them I commit all that I have hitherto been, that thou mayest forgive and restore all ; my wounds, that thou mayest heal them ; my blindness, that thou mayest enlighten it ; my coldness, that thou mayest inflame it ; my wicked and erring ways, that thou mayest set me forth in the right path ; and all my evils, that thou mayest uproot them all from my soul. I commend and offer up into thy most sacred hands, O my God, what I am, which thou knowest far better than I can know, weak, wretched, wounded, fickle, blind, deaf, dumb, poor, bare of every good, nothing, yea, less than nothing, on account of my many sins, and more miserable than I can either know or express. Do thou, Lord God, receive me and make me to become what he, the divine Lamb, would have me to be. I commend, I offer up, I deliver over into thy divine hands, all my affairs, my cares, my affections, my success, my comforts, my labours, and everything which thou knowest to be coming upon me. Direct all to thy honour and glory; teach me in all to do thy will, and in all to recognise the work of thy divine hands ; to seek nothing else, and with this reflection alone to find rest and comfort in everything.

O hands of the Eternal God, who made and still preserve the heavens and earth for my sake, and who made me for yourselves, suffer me not ever to stray from you. In those hands I possess my Lamb, and all I love ; in them therefore must I be also, together with him. Together with him, in these loving hands I shall sleep and rest in peace, since he in dying left me hope in them and in their infinite mercies, placed me within them, as my only and my special refuge. Since by these hands I live and am what I am, make me continually to live through them, and in them to die ; in them to live in the love of our Lord, and from them only to desire and look for every good ; that from them I may at last, together with the Lord, receive the crown.—*Fra Thomé de Jesu.*

Verse 5.—"*Into thine hand I commit my spirit.*" No shadowy form of a dark destiny stands before him at the end of his career, although he must die on the cross, the countenance of his Father shines before him. He does not behold his life melting away into the gloomy floods of mortality. He commends it into the hands of his Father. It is not alone in the general spirit of humanity, that he will continue to live. He will live on in the definite personality of his own spirit, embraced by the special protection and faithfulness of his Father. Thus he does not surrender his life despondingly to death for destruction, but with triumphant consciousness to the Father for resurrection. It was the very centre of his testament ; assurance of life ; surrender of his life into the hand of a living Father.

With loud voice he exclaimed it to the world, which will for ever and ever sink into the heathenish consciousness of death, of the fear of death, of despair of immortality and resurrection, because it for ever and ever allows the consciousness of the personality of God, and of personal union with him, to be obscured and shaken. With the heart of a lion, the dying Christ once more testified of life with an expression which was connected with the word of the Old Testament Psalm, and testified that the Spirit of eternal life was already operative, in prophetic anticipation, in the old covenant. Thus living as ever, he surrendered his life, through death, to the eternally living One. His death was the last and highest fact, the crown of his holy life.—*J. P. Lange, D.D., in "The Life of the Lord Jesus Christ,"* 1864.

Verse 5.—" *Into thine hand I commit my spirit.*" David committed his spirit to God that he might not die, but Christ and all Christians after him, commit their spirit to God, that they may live for ever by death, and after death. This Psalm is thus connected with the twenty-second Psalm. Both of these Psalms were used by Christ on the cross. From the twenty-second he derived those bitter words of anguish, " Eloi, Eloi, lama sabachthani ? " From the present Psalm he derived those last words of love and trust which he uttered just before his death. The Psalter was the hymn-book and prayer-book of Christ.—*Christopher Wordsworth.*

Verse 6.—" *I have hated.*" Holy men have strong passions, and are not so mincing and charitable towards evil doers as smooth-tongued latitudinarians would have them. He who does not hate evil does not love good. There is such a thing as a good hater.—*C. H. S.*

Verse 6.—" *They that regard lying vanities.*" The Romanists feign miracles of the saints to make them, as they suppose, the more glorious. They say that the house wherein the Virgin Mary was when the angel Gabriel came unto her was, many hundred years after, translated, first, out of Galilee into Dalmatia, above 2,000 miles, and thence over the sea into Italy, where also it removed from one place to another, till at length it found a place where to abide, and many most miraculous cures, they say, were wrought by it, and that the very trees when it came, did bow unto it. Infinite stories they have of this nature, especially in the Legend of Saints, which they call " The Golden Legend," a book so full of gross stuff that Ludovicus Vives, a Papist, but learned and ingenuous, with great indignation cried out, " What can be more abominable than that book ? " and he wondered why they should call it "golden," when as he that wrote it was a man " of an iron mouth and of a leaden heart." And Melchior Canus, a Romish bishop, passed the same censure upon that book, and complains (as Vives also had done before him), that Laertius wrote the lives of philosophers, and Suetonius the lives of the Cæsars, more sincerely than some did the lives of the saints and martyrs. They are most vain and superstitious in the honour which they give to the relics of the saints ; as their dead bodies, or some parts of them ; their bones, flesh, hair ; yea, their clothes that they wore, or the like. " You may now, everywhere," saith Erasmus, " see held out for gain, Mary's milk, which they honour almost as much as Christ's consecrated body ; prodigious oil ; so many pieces of the cross, that if these were all gathered together a great ship would scarce carry them. Here Francis's hood set forth to view ; there the innermost garment of the Virgin Mary ; in one place, Anna's comb ; in another place, Joseph's stocking ; in another place, Thomas of Canterbury's shoe ; in another place, Christ's foreskin, which, though it be a thing uncertain, they worship more religiously than Christ's whole person. Neither do they bring forth these things as things that may be tolerated, and to please the common people, but all religion almost is placed in them."*—Christopher Cartwright.*

Verse 6.—The sense lies thus, that heathen men, when any danger or difficulty approacheth them, are solemnly wont to apply themselves to auguries and divinations, and so to false gods, to receive advice and direction from them : but doing so and observing their responses most superstitiously, they yet gain nothing at all by it. These David detests, and keeps close to God, hoping for no aid but from him.—*H. Hammond, D.D.*

Verse 7.—" *I will be glad and rejoice in thy mercy.*"—In the midst of trouble faith will furnish matter of joy, and promise to itself gladness, especially from

---

* Erasmus, on Matthew xxiii. 5.

the memory of by-past experiences of God's mercy; as here, "*I will be glad and rejoice in thy mercy.*" . . . The ground of our gladness, when we have found a proof of God's kindness to us should not be in the benefit so much as in the fountain of the benefit; for this giveth us hope to drink again of the like experience from the fountain which did send forth that benefit. Therefore David says, "*I will be glad and rejoice in thy mercy.*"—*David Dickson.*

Verse 7.—"*Thou hast considered my trouble:*"

> Man's plea to man, is, that he never more
> Will beg, and that he never begg'd before:
> Man's plea to God, is, that he did obtain
> A former suit, and, therefore sues again.
> How good a God we serve; that when we sue,
> Makes his old gifts the examples of his new!
>
> *Francis Quarles.*

Verse 7.—"*Thou hast known my soul in adversities.*" One day a person who, by the calamities of war, sickness, and other affliction, had been reduced from a state of affluence to penury, came to Gotthold in great distress. He complained that he had just met one of his former acquaintances, who was even not distantly related to him, but that he had not condescended to bow, far less to speak to him, and had turned his eyes away, and passed him as if he had been a stranger. O sir, he exclaimed with a sigh, how it pained me! I felt as if a dagger had pierced my heart! Gotthold replied, Don't think it strange at all. It is the way of the world to look high, and to pass unnoticed that which is humble and lowly. I know, however, of *One* who, though he dwelleth on high, humbleth himself to behold the things that are in heaven and in the earth (Ps. cxiii. 5, 6), and of whom the royal prophet testifies: "*Thou hast known my soul in adversities.*" Yes; though we have lost our rich attire, and come to him in rags; though our forms be wasted because of grief, and waxed old (Ps. vi. 7, Luth. Ver.); though sickness and sorrow have consumed our beauty like a moth (Ps. xxxix. 11); though blushes, and tears, and dust, overspread our face (Ps. lxix. 7), he still recognises, and is not ashamed to own us. Comfort yourself with this, for what harm will it do you at last, though men disown, if God the Lord have not forgotten you?—*Christian Scriver.*

Verse 8.—He openeth and no man shutteth. Let us bless the Lord for an open door which neither men nor devils can close. We are not in man's hands yet, because we are in the hands of God: else had our feet been in the stocks and not in the large room of liberty. Our enemies, if they were as able as they are willing, would long ago have treated us as fowlers do the little birds when they enclose them in their hand.—*C. H. S.*

Verse 9.—"*Mine eye is consumed with grief.*" This expression seems to suggest that the eye really suffers under the influence of grief. There was an old idea, which still prevails amongst the uninstructed, that the eye, under extreme grief, and with a constant profuse flow of tears, might sink away and perish under the ordeal. There is no solid foundation for this idea, but there is a very serious form of disease of the eyes, well known to oculists by the title of Glaucoma, which seems to be very much influenced by mental emotions of a depressing nature. I have known many striking instances of cases in which there has been a constitutional proneness to Glaucoma, and in which some sudden grief has brought on a violent access of the disease and induced blindness of an incurable nature. In such instances the explanation seems to be somewhat as follows. It is essential to the healthy performance of the functions of the eye, that it should possess a given amount of elasticity, which again results from an exact balance between the amount of fluid within the eye, and the external fibrous case or bag that contains or encloses it. If this is disturbed, if the fluid increases unduly in quantity, and the eye becomes too hard, pain and inflammation may be suddenly induced in the interior of the eye, and sight may become rapidly extinguished. There are a special set of nerves that preside over this peculiar physical condition, and keep the eye in a proper state of elasticity; and it is a remarkable fact, that through a long life, as a rule, we find that the eye preserves this elastic state. If, however, the function of these nerves is impaired, as it may readily be under the influence of extreme grief, or any depressing agent, the eye may become suddenly hard. Until a comparatively recent date, acute Glaucoma, or sudden hardening of the eye, attended with intense pain and inflammation, caused complete and hopeless blindness ; but in the present day it is capable of relief by means of an operation. The effect of grief in causing this form of blindness seems to be an explanation of the text, " *Mine eye is consumed with grief.*"*

Verses 9, 10 :—

> If thou wouldst learn, not knowing how to pray,
> Add but a faith, and say as beggars say :
> *Master, I'm poor, and blind, in great distress,*
> *Hungry, and lame, and cold, and comfortless ;*
> *O succour him that's gravell'd on the shelf*
> *Of pain, and want, and cannot help himself ;*
> *Cast down thine eye upon a wretch, and take*
> *Some pity on me, for sweet Jesus' sake :*
> But hold ! take heed this clause be not put in,
> *I never begged before, nor will again.*

Francis Quarles.

Verse 10.—" *Mine iniquity :* " Italian version, " *my pains ;* " because that death and all miseries are come into the world by reason of sin, the Scripture doth often confound the names of the cause and of the effects.—*John Diodati.*

Verse 10.—I find that when the saints are under trial and well humbled, little sins raise great cries in the conscience ; but in prosperity, conscience is a pope that gives dispensations and great latitude to our hearts. The cross is therefore as needful as the crown is glorious.—*Samuel Rutherford.*

Verse 11.—" *I was a reproach among all mine enemies.*" If anyone strives after patience and humility, he is a hypocrite. If he allows himself in the pleasures of this world, he is a glutton. If he seeks justice, he is impatient ; if he seeks it not, he is a fool. If he would be prudent, he is stingy ; if he would make others happy, he is dissolute. If he gives himself up to prayer, he is vainglorious. And this is the great loss of the church, that by means like these many are held back from goodness ! which the Psalmist lamenting says, " *I became a reproof among all mine enemies.*"—*Chrysostom, quoted by J. M. Neale.*

Verse 11.—" *They that did see me without fled from me.*" I once heard the following relation from an old man of the world, and it occurs to me, as illustrative of what we are now considering. He was at a public assembly, and saw there an individual withdrawing herself from the crowd, and going into a corner of the room. He went up to her, she was an old and intimate friend of his ; he addressed himself to her—she, with a sigh, said, " Oh, I have seen many days of trouble since we last met." What does the man of the world do ? Immediately he withdrew himself from his sorrow-stricken friend and hid himself in the crowd. Such is the sympathy of the world with Christ or his servants.—*Hamilton Verschoyle.*

Verse 12.—" *I am forgotten as a dead man out of mind.*" A striking instance of how the greatest princes are forgotten in death is found in the deathbed of Louis XIV. " The Louis that was, lies forsaken, a mass of abhorred clay ; abandoned ' to some poor persons, and priests of the *Chapelle Ardente,* ' who make haste to put him ' in two lead coffins, pouring in abundant spirits of wine.' The new Louis with his court is rolling towards Choisy, through the summer afternoon : the royal tears still flow ; but a word mispronounced by Monseigneur d'Artois sets them all laughing, and they weep no more."—*Thomas Carlyle in " The French Revolution."*

Verse 12.—" *I am forgotten,*" etc. As a dying man with curtains drawn, whom friends have no hope of, and therefore look off from ; or rather like a dead man laid aside out of sight and out of mind altogether, and buried more in oblivion than in his grave ; when the news is, " she is dead, trouble not the Master." Luke viii. 49. —*Anthony Tuckney, D.D., 1599—1670.*

Verse 12.—" *I am like a broken vessel.*" As a vessel, how profitable soever it hath been to the owner, and how necessary for his turn, yet, when it is broken is thrown away, and regarded no longer : even so such is the state of a man forsaken

---

* On application for information to the Royal London Ophthalmic Hospital, as to the effect of grief upon the eye, we received the above, with much other valuable information, from GEORGE CRITCHETT, ESQ., the senior medical officer. The courtesy of this gentleman, and of the secretary of that noble institution, deserves especial mention.

of those whose friend he hath been so long as he was able to stand them in stead, to be of advantage to them.—*Robert Cawdray.*

Verses 12—15 :—

> Forgot as those who in the grave abide,
> And as a broken vessel past repair,
> Slandered by many, fear on every side,
> Who counsel take and would my life ensnare
>
> But, Lord, my hopes on thee are fixed : I said,
> Thou art my God, my days are in thy hand ;
> Against my furious foes oppose thy aid.
> And those who persecute my soul withstand.
>
> *George Sandys.*

Verse 13.—" *I have heard the slander of many."* From my very childhood, when I was first sensible of the concernments of men's souls, I was possessed with some admiration to find that everywhere the religious, godly sort of people, who did but exercise a serious care of their own and other men's salvation, were made the wonder and obloquy of the world, especially of the most vicious and flagitious men ; so that they that professed the same articles of faith, the same commandments of God to be their law, and the same petitions of the Lord's prayer to be their desire, and so professed the same religion, did everywhere revile those that endeavoured to live in good earnest in what they said. I thought this was impudent hypocrisy in the ungodly, worldly sort of men—to take those for the most intolerable persons in the land who are but serious in their own religion, and do but endeavour to perform what all their enemies also vow and promise. If religion be bad, and our faith be not true, why do these men profess it ? If it be true and good, why do they hate and revile them that would live in the serious practice of it, if they will not practise it themselves ? But we must not expect reason when sin and sensuality have made men unreasonable.

But I must profess that since I observed the course of the world, and the concord of the word and providence of God, I took it for a notable proof of man's fall, and of the truth of the Scripture, and of the supernatural original of true sanctification, to find such a universal enmity between the holy and the serpentine seed, and to find Cain and Abel's case so ordinarily exemplified, and he that is born after the flesh persecuting him that is born after the Spirit. And methinks to this day it is a great and visible help for the confirmation of our Christian faith.—*Richard Baxter.*

Verse 13.—" *Slander."* Be thou as chaste as ice, as pure as snow, thou shalt not escape calumny.—*William Shakespeare.*

Verse 13.—" *They took counsel together against me,"* etc. While they mangled his reputation, they did it in such a manner as that they covered their wickedness under the appearance of grave and considerate procedure, in consulting among themselves to destroy him as a man who no longer ought to be tolerated on the earth. It is not to be wondered at, therefore, that his mind was wounded by so many and so sharp temptations.—*John Calvin.*

Verse 14.—" *But I trusted in thee, O Lord."* The rendering properly is, *And I have trusted in thee,* but the Hebrew copulative particle ו, *vau, and,* is used here instead of the adversitive particle *yet,* or *nevertheless.* David, setting the steadfastness of his faith in opposition to the assaults of the temptations of which he has made mention, denies that he had ever fainted, but rather maintains, on the contrary, that he stood firm in his hope of deliverance from God. Nor does this imply that he boasted of being so magnanimous and courageous that he could not be overthrown through the infirmity of the flesh. However contrary to one another they appear, yet these things are often joined together, as they ought to be, in the same person, namely, that while he pines away with grief, and is deprived of all strength, he is nevertheless supported by so strong a hope that he ceases not to call upon God. David, therefore, was not so overwhelmed in deep sorrow, and other direful sufferings, as that the hidden light of faith could not shine inwardly in his heart ; nor did he groan so much under the weighty load of his temptations, as to be prevented from arousing himself to call upon God. He struggled through many obstacles to be able to make the confession which he here makes. He next defines the manner of his faith, namely, that he reflected with himself thus—-that God would never fail him nor forsake him. Let us mark his manner of speech: *I have said, Thou art my God.* In these words he intimates that he was so entirely persuaded of this truth, that God was his God, that he would not admit even a suggestion to the contrary. And until this persuasion prevails so as to take possession of our minds, we shall always waver in uncertainty. It is, however, to be observed, that this declaration is not only inward and secret—made rather in the heart than with the tongue—but that it is directed to God himself, as to him who is the alone witness of it. Nothing is more difficult, when we see our faith derided by the whole world, than to direct our speech to God only, and to rest satisfied with this testimony which our conscience gives us, *that he is our God.* And certainly it is an undoubted proof of genuine faith, when, however fierce the waves are which beat against us, and however sore the assaults by which we are shaken, we hold fast this as a fixed principle, that we are constantly under the protection of God, and can say to him freely, *Thou art our God.—John Calvin.*

Verse 14.—" Thou art my God." How much it is more worth than ten thousand mines of gold, to be able to say, God is mine ! God's servant is apprehensive of it, and he seeth no defect, but this may be complete happiness to him, and therefore he delights in it, and comforts himself with it. As he did sometime who was a great courtier in King Cyrus's court, and one in favour with him ; he was to bestow his daughter in marriage to a very great man, and of himself he had no great means ; and therefore one said to him, O Sir, where will you have means to bestow a dowry upon your daughter proportionable to her degree ? Where are your riches ? He answered, What need I care, ὅπου Κυρος μοι φιλος, Cyrus is my friend. But may not we say much more, ὅπου Κυριος μοι φιλος, where the Lord is our friend, that hath those excellent and glorious attributes that cannot come short in any wants, or to make us happy, especially we being capable of it, and made proportionable.—*John Stoughton's " Righteous Man's Plea to True Happinesse," 1640.*

Verse 15.—" My times are in thy hand." It is observable that when, of late years, men grew weary of the long and tedious compass in their voyages to the East Indies, and would needs try a more compendious way by the North-West passage, it ever proved unsuccessful. Thus it is that we must not use any compendious way ; we may not neglect our body, nor shipwreck our health, nor anything to hasten death, because we shall gain by it. He that maketh haste (even this way) to be rich shall not be innocent ; for our times are in God's hands, and therefore to his holy providence we must leave them. We have a great deal of work to do, and must not, therefore, be so greedy of our Sabbath-day, our rest, as not to be contented with our working-day, our labour. Hence it is that a composed frame of heart, like that of the apostle's (Phil. i. 21), wherein either to stay and work, or to go and rest, is the best temper of all.—*Edward Reynolds, in J. Spencer's " Things New and Old."*

Verse 15.—" My times." He does not use the plural number, in my opinion, without reason ; but rather to mark the variety of casualties by which the life of man is usually harassed.—*John Calvin.*

Verse 15.—" In thy hand." The watch hangs ticking against the wall, when every tick of the watch is a sigh, and a consciousness, alas ! Poor watch ! I called once to see a friend, the physician and the secretary of one of the most noble and admirable of the asylums for the insane in this country. A poor creature, with a clear, bright intelligence, only that some of its chords had become unstrung, who had usually occupied itself innocently by making or unmaking watches, had just before I called, exhibited some new, alarming symptoms, dashing one and then another upon the stone floor, and shivering them. Removed into a more safe room, I visited him with the secretary. " How came you to destroy your favourite watches, so much as you loved them, and so quiet as you are ? " said my friend ; and the poor patient replied, in a tone of piercing agony, " I could not bear the tick, tick, ticking, and so I dashed it on the pavement." But when the watch is able to surrender itself to the maker, to the hand holding the watch, and measuring out the moments, it becomes a sight affecting indeed, but very beautiful, very sublime. We transfer our thought from the watch to *the hand* that holds the watch. " *My times,*" " *Thy hand ;* " the watch and the hour have a purpose, and are not in vain. God gives man permission to behold two things. Man can see the whole work, the plan's completeness, also the minutest work, the first step towards the plan's completeness. Nothing is more certain, nothing are men more indisposed to perceive than this. We have to

> " *Wait* for some transcendent life,
> Reserved by God to follow this." *

To this end God's real way is made up of all the ways of our life. His hand holds all our times. " *My times ;* " " *Thy hand.*" Some lives greatly differ from others. This we know ; but see, some lives fulfil life's course, gain life's crown—life in their degree. This, on the contrary, others quite miss. Yet, for even human strength there must be a love meted out to rule it. It is said, there is a moon to control the tides of every sea ; is there not a master power for souls ? It may not always be so, apparently, in the more earthly lives, but it is so in the heavenly : not more surely does the moon sway tides than God sways souls. It does seem sometimes as if man found no adequate external power, and stands forth ordained to be a law to his own sphere ; but even then his times are in the hands of God, as the pathway of a star is in the limitations of its system—as the movements of a satellite are in the forces of its planet. But while I would not pause on morbid words or views of life, so neither do I desire you to receive or charge me with giving only a moody, morbid view of the world, and an imperfect theology ; but far other. " *My times are in thy hand* "—*the hand of my Saviour.*

> " I report as a man may of God's work—all's love, but all's law.
> In the Godhead I seek and I find it, and so it shall be
> A face like my face that receives thee, a Man like to me
> Thou shalt love and be loved by for ever, a hand like this hand
> Shall throw open the gates of new life to thee : *See the Christ stand !* "*

And now he is " the restorer of paths to dwell in." The hand of Jesus is the hand which rules our times. He regulates our life-clock. Christ for and Christ in us. *My* times in *his* hand. My life can be no more in vain than was my Saviour's life in vain.—*E. Paxton Hood, in " Dark Sayings on a Harp,"* 1865.

Verse 15.—When David had Saul at his mercy in the cave, those about him said, *This is the time* in which God will deliver thee. 1 Sam. xxiv. 4. No, saith David, the time is not come for my deliverance till it can be wrought without sin, and I will wait for that time ; for it is God's time, and that is the best time.—*Matthew Henry.*

Verse 16.—" *Make thy face to shine upon thy servant.*" When the cloud of trouble hideth the Lord's favour, faith knoweth it may shine again, and therefore prayeth through the cloud for the dissolving of it. " *Make thy face to shine upon thy servant.*"—*David Dickson.*

Verse 18.—" *Lying lips . . . . which speak grievous things proudly and contemptuously against the righteous.*" The primitive persecutors slighted the Christians for a company of bad, illiterate fellows, and therefore they used to paint the God of the Christians with an ass's head and a book in his hand, saith Tertullian ; to signify, that though they pretended learning, yet they were silly and ignorant people. Bishop Jewel, in his sermon upon Luke xi. 15, cites this out of Tertullian and applies it to his times. Do not our adversaries the like, saith he, against all that profess the gospel ? Oh ! say they, who are those that favour this way ? None but shoemakers, tailors, weavers, and such as never were at the University. These are the bishop's own words. Bishop White said in open court, that the Puritans were all a company of blockheads.—*Charles Bradbury.*

Verse 18.—" *Lying lips . . . . which speak grievous things proudly and contemptuously against the righteous.*" In that venerable and original monument of the Vaudois Church, entitled " The Golden Lesson," of the date 1100, we meet with a verse, which has been thus translated :—

> " If there be any one who loves and fears Jesus Christ,
> Who will not curse, nor swear, nor lie,
> Nor be unchaste, nor kill, nor take what is another's,
> Nor take vengeance on his enemies ;
> They say that he is a Vaudès, and worthy of punishment."

Antoine Monastier, in " A History of Vaudois Church," 1859.

---

* Robert Browning.

Verse 19.—" *Oh how great is thy goodness, which thou hast laid up for them that fear thee.*" As a provident man will regulate his liberality towards all men in such a manner as not to defraud his children or family, nor impoverish his own house. by spending his substance prodigally on others ; so God, in like manner, in exercising his beneficence to aliens from his family, knows well how to reserve for his own children that which belongs to them, as it were by hereditary right ; that is to say, because of their adoption.—*John Calvin.*

Verse 19.—" *Oh how great is thy goodness, which thou hast laid up for them that fear thee.*"—Mark the phrase, " Laid up for them ; " his mercy and goodness it is intended for them, as a father that lays by such a sum of money, and writes on the bag, " This is a portion for such a child." But how comes the Christian to have this right to God, and all that vast and untold treasure of happiness which is in him ? This indeed is greatly to be heeded ; it is faith that gives him a good title to all this. That which maketh him a child, makes him an heir. Now, faith makes him a child of God. John i. 12, " But as many as received him, to them gave he power to become the sons of God, even to them that believe on his name." As therefore, if you would not call your birthright into question, and bring your interest in Christ and those glorious privileges that come along with him, under a sad dispute in your soul, look to your faith.—*William Gurnall.*

Verse 19.—" *How great is thy goodness, which thou hast laid up for them that fear thee.*" When I reflect upon the words of thy prophet, it seems to me that he means to depict God as a father who, no doubt, keeps his children under discipline, and subjects them to the rod ; but who, with all his labour and pains, still aims at nothing but to lay up for them a store which may contribute to their comfort when they have grown to maturity, and learned the prudent use of it. My Father, in this world thou hidest from thy children thy great goodness, as if it did not pertain to them. But being thy children, we may be well assured that the celestial treasure will be bestowed upon none else. For this reason, I will bear my lot with patience. But, oh ! from time to time, waft to me a breath of air from the heavenly land, to refresh my sorrowful heart ; I will then wait more calmly for its full fruition.—*Christian Scriver.*

Verse 19.—" *Oh how great is thy goodness.*" Let me, to set the crown on the head of the *duty of meditation,* add one thing over and above—let meditation be *carried up to admiration :* not only should we be affected, but transported, rapt up and ravished with the beauties and transcendencies of heavenly things ; act meditation to admiration, endeavour the highest pitch, coming the nearest to the highest patterns, the patterns of saints and angels in heaven, whose actings are the purest, highest ecstacies and admirations. Thus were these so excellent artists in meditation, David, an high actor of admiration in meditation, as often we see it in the Psalms ; so in Psalm viii. 1, 9 ; Psalm xxxi. 19 ; " *Oh how great is thy goodness,*" etc. ; Psalm civ. 24 ; " O Lord, how manifold are thy works," etc. ; and in other places David's meditation and admiration were as his harp, well tuned, and excellently played on, in rarest airs and highest strains ; as the precious gold, and the curious burnishing ; or the richest stone, and the exquisitest polishing and setting of it. So blessed Paul, who was a great artist in musing, acted high in admiration, his soul was very warm and flaming up in it : it was as a bird with a strong and long wing that soars and towers up aloft, and gets out of sight.—*Nathaniel Ranew.*

Verse 19.—" *Before the sons of men,*" i.e., *openly.* The Psalmist here perhaps refers to temporal blessings conferred on the pious, and evident to all. Some, however, have supposed the reference to be to the reward of the righteous, bestowed with the utmost publicity on the day of judgment ; which better agrees with our interpretation of the former part of the verse.—*Daniel Cresswell, D.D., F.R.S.* (1776–1844), *in loc.*

Verse 19.—Believe it, Sirs, you cannot conceive what a friend you shall have of God, would you but be persuaded to enter into covenant with him, to be his, wholly his. I tell you, many that sometimes thought and did as you do now, that is, set light by Christ and hate God, and see no loveliness in him, are now quite of another mind ; they would not for ten thousand worlds quit their interest in him. Oh, who dare say that he is a hard Master ? Who that knows him will say that he is an unkind friend ? Oh, what do poor creatures all, that they do entertain such harsh, sour thoughts of God ? What, do they think that there is nothing in that scripture, " *Oh how great is thy goodness, which thou hast laid up for them that fear thee!"* Doth the Psalmist speak too largely? Doth he say more than he and others could prove? Ask him, and he will tell you in verse 21, that he blesseth God. These were things he could speak to, from his own personal experience; and many thousands as well as he, to whom the Lord had showed his marvellous kindness, and therefore he doth very passionately plead with the people of God to love him, and more highly to express their sense of his goodness, that the world might be encouraged also to have good thoughts of him.—*James Janeway.*

Verse 19.—Very observable is that expression of the Psalmist, *" Oh how great is thy goodness, which thou hast laid up for them that fear thee; which thou hast wrought before the sons of men for them that trust in thee."* In the former clause, God's goodness is said to be *laid up*; in the latter, to be *wrought.* Goodness is laid up in the promise, wrought in the performance; and that goodness which is laid up is wrought for them that trust in God; and thus, as God's faithfulness engageth us to believe, so our faith, as it were, engageth God's faithfulness to perform the promise.—*Nathanael Hardy.*

Verse 20.—*" Thou shalt keep them secretly in a pavilion from the strife of tongues."* This our beloved God does secretly, so that no human eyes may or can see, and the ungodly do not know that a believer is, in God, and in the presence of God, so well protected, that no reproach or contempt, and no quarrelsome tongues can do him harm.—*Arndt, quoted by W. Wilson, D.D.*

Verse 22.—*" I said in my haste, I am cut off from before thine eyes: nevertheless thou heardest the voice of my supplications."* Who would have thought those prayers should ever have had any prevalency in God's ears which were mixed with so much infidelity in the petitioner's heart!—*William Secker.*

Verse 22.—*" I said in my haste, I am cut off from before thine eyes."*—No, no, Christian; a prayer sent up in faith, according to the will of God, cannot be lost, though it be delayed. We may say of it, as David said of Saul's sword and Jonathan's bow, that they never return empty. So David adds, *" Nevertheless thou heardest the voice of my supplications when I cried unto thee."*—*John Flavel.*

Verse 22.—*" I said in my haste, I am cut off from before thine eyes,"* etc. Let us with whom it was once night, improve that morning joy that now shines upon us. Let us be continual admirers of God's grace and mercy to us. He has prevented us with his goodness, when he saw nothing in us but impatience and unbelief, when we were like Jonas in the belly of hell, his bowels yearned over us, and his power brought us safe to land. What did we to hasten his deliverance, or to obtain his mercy? If he had never come to our relief till he saw something in us to invite him, we had not yet been relieved. No more did we contribute to our restoration than we do to the rising of the sun, or the approach of day. We were like dry bones without motion, and without strength. Ezek. xxxvii. 1—11. And we also said, that ' we were cut off for our parts, and our hope was gone, and he caused breath to enter into us, and we live.' Who is a God like to our God that pardoneth iniquity, transgression, and sin? that retains not his anger for ever? that is slow to wrath and delights in mercy? that has been displeased with us for a moment, but gives us hope of his everlasting kindness? Oh! what love is due from us to Christ, that has pleaded for us when we ourselves had nothing to say! That has brought us out of a den of lions, and from the jaws of the roaring lion! To say, as Mrs. Sarah Wright did, " I have obtained mercy, that thought my time of mercy past for ever; I have hope of heaven, that thought I was already damned by unbelief; I said many a time, there is no hope in mine end, and I thought I saw it; I was so desperate, I cared not what became of me. Oft was I at the very brink of death and hell, even at the very gates of both, and then Christ shut them. I was as Daniel in the lion's den, and he stopped the mouth of those lions, and delivered me. The goodness of God is unsearchable; how great is the excellency of his majesty, that yet he would look upon such a one as I; that he has given me peace that was full of terror, and walked continually, as amidst fire and brimstone."—*Timothy Rogers.*

Verse 22.—*" I said in my haste, I am cut off from before thine eyes:"*—i.e., Thou has quite forsaken me, and I must not expect to be looked upon or regarded by thee any more. I shall perish one day by the hand of Saul, and so be cut off before thine eyes, be ruined while thou lookest on (1 Sam. xxvii. 1). This he said in his flight (so some read it), which notes the distress of his affairs : Saul was just at his back, and ready to seize him, which made the temptation strong ; *in his haste* (so we read it), which notes the disturbance and discomposure of his mind, which made the temptation surprising, so that it found him off his guard. Note, it is a common thing to speak amiss, when we speak in haste and without consideration ; but what we speak amiss in haste, we must repent of at leisure, particularly that which we have spoken distrustfully of God.—*Matthew Henry.*

Verse 22.—"*I said in my haste.*"—Sometimes a sudden passion arises, and out it goes in angry and froward words, setting all in an uproar and combustion : by-and-by our hearts recur upon us, and then we wish, " O that I had bit my tongue, and not given it such an unbridled liberty." Sometimes we break out into rash censures of those that it may be are better than ourselves, whereupon when we reflect, we are ashamed that the fools' bolt was so soon shot, and wish we had been judging ourselves when we were censuring our brethren.—*Richard Alleine.*

Verse 22.—" *Nevertheless thou heardest the voice of my supplications when I cried unto thee.*" As if he had said, when I prayed with so little faith, that I, as it were, unprayed my own prayer, by concluding my case in a manner desperate ; yet God pardoned my hasty spirit, and gave me that mercy which I had hardly any faith to expect ; and what use doth he make of this experience, but to raise every saint's hope in a time of need ? " *Be of good courage, and he shall strengthen your heart, all ye that hope in the Lord.*"—*William Gurnall.*

Verse 22.—He confesseth the great distress he was in, and how weak his faith was under the temptation ; this he doth to his own shame acknowledge also, that he may give the greater glory to God. Whence learn, 1.—The faith of the godly may be slackened, and the strongest faith may sometimes show its infirmity. " *I said in my haste, I am cut off from before thine eyes.*" 2.—Though faith be shaken, yet it is fixed in the root, as a tree beaten by the wind keeping strong grips of good ground. Though faith seem to yield, yet it faileth not, and even when it is at the weakest, it is uttering itself in some act, as a wrestler, for here the expression of David's infirmity in faith, is directed to God, and his earnest prayer joined with it, " *I am cut off from before thine eyes : nevertheless thou heardest the voice of my supplications.*" 3.—Praying faith, how weak soever, shall not be misregarded of God ; for " *nevertheless,*" saith he, " *thou heardest the voice of my supplications.*" 4.—There may be in a soul at one time, both grief oppressing, and hope upholding ; both darkness of trouble, and the light of faith ; both desperately doubting, and strong gripping of God's truth and goodness ; both a fainting and a fighting ; a seeming yielding in the fight, and yet a striving of faith against all opposition ; both a foolish haste, and a settled stayedness of faith ; as here, " *I said in my haste,*" etc.—*David Dickson.*

Verse 22.—David vents his astonishment at the Lord's condescension in hearing his prayer. How do we wonder at the goodness of a petty man in granting our desires ! How much more should we at the humility and goodness of the most sovereign Majesty of heaven and earth !—*Stephen Charnock.*

Verse 23.—" *O love the Lord, all ye his saints.*" The holy Psalmist in the words does, with all the warmth of an affectionate zeal, incite us to the love of God, which is the incomparably noblest passion of a reasonable mind, its brightest glory and most exquisite felicity ; and it is, as appears evident from the nature of the thing, and the whole train of divine revelation, the comprehensive sum of that duty which we owe to our Maker, and the very soul which animates a religious life, that we " love the Lord with all our heart, and strength, and mind."—*William Dunlop, A.M.,* 1692—1720.

Verse 23.—" *O love the Lord, all ye his saints,*" etc. Some few words are to be attended in the clearing of the sense. " *Saints* " here in the text is or may be read, *ye that feel mercies.* " *Faithful,*" the word is sometimes taken for *persons,* sometimes *things ;* and so the Lord is said to preserve true men, and truths, faithful men, and faithfulnesses. " *He plenteously rewardeth the proud doer ;* " or, the Lord rewardeth plenteously ; *the Lord,* who doth wonderful things. *Plenteously* is either *in cumulum, abunde,* or *in nepotes,* as some would have it ; but I would rather *commend,* than go about to *amend* translations : though I could wish some of my learned brethren's quarrelling hours were spent rather upon clearing the originals, and so conveying over pure Scripture to posterity, than in scratching others with their sharpened pens, and making cock-pits of pulpits.—*Hugh*

Peters' " Sermon preached before both Houses of Parliament, the Lord Mayor and Aldermen of the City of London, and the Assembly of Divines, at the last Thanksgiving Day, April 2. For the recovering of the West, and disbanding 5,000 of the King's Horse, etc., 1645."

23. *" And plentifully rewardeth the proud doer."* The next query is, *how God rewardeth the proud doer?* in which, though the Lord's proceedings be diverse, and many times his paths in the clouds, and his judgments in the deep, and the uttermost farthing shall be paid the proud doer at the great day ; yet so much of his mind he hath left unto us, that even in this life he given out something to the proud which he calls " the day of recompense," which he commonly manifests in these particulars :—1. By way of *retaliation*—for *Adoni-bezek* that would be cutting off thumbs, had his thumbs cut off. Judges i. 7. So the poor Jews that cried so loud, " Crucify him, crucify him," were so many of them crucified, that if you believe Josephus, there was not wood enough to make crosses, nor in the usual place room enough to set up the crosses when they were made. Snares are made and pits are digged by the proud for *themselves* commonly, to which the Scripture throughout gives abundant testimony. 2. By shameful *disappointments*, seldom reaping what they sow, nor eating what they catch in hunting, which is most clear in the Jewish State when Christ was amongst them. *Judas* betrays him to get money, and hardly lived long enough to spend it. *Pilate*, to please Cæsar, withstands all counsels against it, and gives way to that murder, by which he ruined both himself and Cæsar. The Jewish priests, to maintain that domination and honour (which they thought the son of Joseph and Mary stole from them) cried aloud for his death, which proved a sepulchre to them and their glory. And the poor people that crucified him (through fear of the *Romans* taking their city) by his death had their gates opened to the *Romans*—yea, *Cæsar* himself, fearing a great change in his government by Christ living near him (which to-day sets all the kingcraft in the world to work) met such a change that shortly he had neither crown nor sceptre to boast of, if you read the story of Titus and Vespasian, all which dealings of God with the proud is most elegantly set forth unto us by the Psalmist. " Behold, he travaileth with iniquity, and hath conceived mischief, and brought forth falsehood. He made a pit, and digged it, and is fallen into the ditch which he made.—*Hugh Peters.*

24. *" Be of good courage."* Christian courage may thus be described. It is the undaunted audacity of a sanctified heart in adventuring upon difficulties and undergoing hardships for a good cause upon the call of God. The *genus*, the common nature of it is an undaunted audacity. This animosity, as some phrase it, is common both unto men and to some brutes. The lion is said to be the strongest among beasts, that turneth not away from any. Prov. xxx. 30. And there is an elegant description of the war horse in regard of boldness. Job xxxix. 19, etc. And this boldness that is in brutes is spoken of as a piece of this same *courage* that God is pleased to give to men. Ezek. iii. 9. This is the Lord's promise—" As an adamant harder than flint have I made thy forehead." The word " harder " is the same in the Hebrew that is here in my text—*fortiorem petra*—the rock that is not afraid of any weather, summer or winter, sun and showers, heat and cold, frost and snow ; it blusheth not, shrinketh not, it changeth not its complexion, it is still the same. Such a like thing is *courage*, in the common nature of it. Secondly, consider the subject, it is *the heart*, the castle where courage commands and exerciseth military discipline ; (shall I so say) it's within the bosom, it is the soul of a valiant soldier. Some conceive our English word *courage* to be derived from *cordis actio*, the very acting of the heart. A valiant man is described (2 Sam. xvii. 10) for to be a man whose heart is as the heart of a lion. And sometimes the original translated *courageous*, as Amos ii. 16, may most properly be rendered *a man of heart*. Beloved, valour doth not consist in a piercing eye, in a terrible look, in big words ; but it consists in the mettle, the vigour that is within the bosom. Sometimes a coward may dwell at the sign of a roaring voice and of a stern countenance ; whereas true fortitude may be found within his breast whose outward deportment promises little or nothing in that kind. Thirdly, note the qualification of this same subject ; I said a sanctified heart ; for I am not now speaking of fortitude as a moral virtue, whereof heathens that have not God are capable, and for which many among them that are not Christians, have been worthily commended. But I am now discoursing of courage as a virtue theological, as a gracious qualification, put upon the people of God by special covenant. And

there are three things that do characterise it, and which do distinguish it from the moral virtue of fortitude. (1) The *root*, whence it ariseth ; (2) the *rule*, whereby it is directed ; (3) the *end*, to which it is referred. The *root*, whence it ariseth, is *love to God :* all the saints of God that love the Lord be of good courage. The love of Christ constraineth me to make these bold and brave adventures, saith the apostle. 2 Cor. v. 14. The *rule*, whereby it is directed, is the *word of God*—what the Lord hath pleased to leave on record for a Christian's guidance in holy pages. 1 Chron. xxii. 12, 13. "Only the Lord give thee wisdom and understanding, and give thee charge concerning Israel, that thou mayest keep the law of the Lord thy God. Then shalt thou prosper, if thou takest heed to fulfil the statutes and judgments which the Lord charged Moses with concerning Israel : be strong, and of good courage : dread not, nor be dismayed." Be a man of mettle, but let thy mettle be according to my mind, according to this rule. And the *end*, to which it refers, is *God*. For every sanctified man being a self-denying and a God-advancing man, his God is his centre, wherein his actings, his undertakings rest ; and his soul is not, yea, it cannot be satisfied but in God.—*Simeon Ash's " Sermon preached before the Commanders of the Military Forces of the renowned Citie of London, 1642."*

Verse 24. " Be of good courage."—Shall I hint some of the weighty services that are charged upon all our consciences ? The work of mortification, to pick out our eyes, to chop off our hands, to cut off our feet ; do you think that a milksop, a man that is not a man of a stout spirit, will do this ? Now to massacre fleshly lusts, is (as it were) for a man to mangle and dismember his own body ; it is a work painful and grievous, as for a man to cut off his own feet, to chop off his own hands, and to pick out his own eyes, as Christ and the apostle Paul do express it. Besides this, there are in Christians' bosoms strongholds to be battered, fortifications to be demolished ; there are high hills and mountains that must be levelled with the ground ; there are trenches to be made, valleys to be filled. O beloved, I may not mention the hills that lie before us in heaven way, which we must climb up, and craggy rocks that we must get over ; and without courage certainly the work put upon our hands will not be discharged. There are also the walls of Jerusalem to be repaired, and the temple to be re-edified. If Nehemiah had not been a man of a brave spirit he would never have gone through stitch with that church work, those weighty services which he did undertake. How this is applicable to us fo: the present time, the time of our begun reformation, I speak not, but rather do refer it to your considerations. I beseech you to read Neh. iv. 17, 18, " They which builded on the wall, and they that bare burdens, with those that laded, every one with one of his hands wrought in the work, and with the other hand held a weapon. For the builders, every one had his sword girded by his side, and so builded, and he that sounded the trumpet was by me." While they were at work, they were all ready for war.—*Simeon Ash.*

Verse 24.—" *And he shall strengthen thy heart.*" Put thou thyself forth in a way of bold adventure for him, and his providence shall be sweetly exercised for thy good. A worthy commander, how careful is he of a brave blade, a man that will fight at a cannon's mouth ! Doth he hear from him that a bone is broken ? Send for the bone-setter. Is he like to bleed to death ? Call for the surgeon ; let him post away to prevent that peril. Doth he grow weaker and weaker ? Is there anything in the camp that may restore his spirit ? withhold nothing ; nothing is too good, too costly ; would he eat gold he should have it. Thus it is with God. Oh, what letters of commendation doth he give in manifestation of his own love to them in Pergamos upon this very ground. " Thou, saith the Lord, thou hast held forth my name, and not denied it, even in those days wherein Antipas was my faithful martyr, who was slain among you, where Satan dwelleth ! " thou didst fight for Christ in the cave where the devil commanded ; thou didst stand and appear for him when other men did lose heart and courage. Here is a man that God will own ; such a one shall have God's heart and hand to do him honour, to yield him comfort. And therefore I appeal to your consciences, is not this courage worth the having ? worth the seeking ?—*Simeon Ash.*

HINTS TO PREACHERS.

Verse 1.—Faith expressed, confusion deprecated, deliverance sought.

Verse 1 (*first clause*).—*Open avowal of faith.* 1. Duties which precede it, self-examination, etc. 2. Modes of making the confession. 3. Conduct incumbent on those who have made the profession.

Verse 1 (*last clause*).—How far the righteousness of God is involved in the salvation of a believer.

Verse 2 (*first clause*).—God's hearing prayer a great condescension.

Verse 2 (*second clause*).—How far we may be urgent with God as to time.

Verses 2, 3 (*last and first clauses*).—That which we have we may yet seek for.

Verse 3.—Work out the metaphor of God as a rocky fastness of the soul.

Verse 3 (*last clause*).—1. A blessing needed, " *lead me.*" 2. A blessing obtainable. 3. An argument for its being granted, " *for thy name's sake.*"

Verse 4.—*The rescue of the ensnared.* 1. The fowlers. 2. The laying of the net. 3. The capture of the bird. 4. The cry of the captive. 5. The rescue.

Verse 4 (*last clause*).—The weak one girt with omnipotence.

Verses 5.—I. Dying, in a saint's account, is a difficult work. II. The children of God, when considering themselves as dying, are chiefly concerned for their departing immortal spirits. III. Such having chosen God for their God, have abundant encouragement when dying, to commit their departing spirits into his hand, with hopes of their being safe and happy for ever with him.—*Daniel Wilcox.*

Verse 5.—The believer's requiem.

Redemption the foundation of our repose in God.

I. What we do—*commit ourselves to God.* II. What God has done—*redeemed us.*

Verse 6.—Holy detestation, as a virtue discriminated from bigotry : or, the good hater.

Verse 7.—I. An endearing attribute rejoiced in. II. An interesting experience related. III. A directly personal favour from God delighted in.

Verse 7 (*centre clause*).—*Consider* the measure, the effects, the time, the tempering, the ending, and the recompense.

Verse 7 (*last clause*).—The Lord's familiarity with his afflicted.

Verse 8.—Christian liberty, a theme for gladness.

Verse 9.—The mourner's lament.

Verse 9 (*last clauses*).—Excessive sorrow, its injurious effects on the body, the understanding, and the spiritual nature. Sin of it, cure of it.

Verses 9, 10.—The sick man's moan, a reminder to those who enjoy good health.

Verse 10.—*My strength faileth because of mine iniquity.* The weakening influence of sin.

Verse 11.—The good man evil spoken of.

Verse 12.—The world's treatment of its best friends.

Verse 14.—Faith peculiarly glorious in seasons of great trial.

The casting forth of the sheet anchor, in the storm.

Verse 15.—The believer the peculiar care of providence.

Verse 15 (*first clause*).—I. The character of the earthly experience of the saints, " My times," that is, the changes I shall pass through, etc. II. The advantage of this variety. 1. Changes reveal the various aspects of the Christian character. 2. Changes strengthen the Christian character. 3. Changes lead us to admire an unchanging God. III. Comfort for all seasons. 1. This implies that changes of life are subject to the divine control. 2. That God will support his people under them. 3. And, consequently, they shall result in our being abundantly profited. IV. The deportment which should characterise us. Courageous devotion to God in times of persecution ; resignation and contentment in times of poverty and suffering ; zeal and hope in times of labour.—*From Stems and Twigs, or Sermon Framework.*

Verse 16.—A sense of divine favour. 1. Its value. 2. How to lose it. 3. How to obtain a renewal of it. 4. How to retain it.

The heavenly servant's best reward.

Verse 16 (*last clause*).—A prayer for saints in all stages. Note its object, " *save me ;* " and its plea, " *thy mercies' sake.*" Suitable to the penitent, the sick, the doubting, the tried, the advanced believer, the dying saint.

Verse 17.—The shame and silence of the wicked in eternity.

The silence of the grave, its grave eloquence.

Verse 19.—See "Spurgeon's Sermons," No. 773. "David's Holy Wonder at the Lord's Great Goodness."

Verse 20.—The believer preserved from the sneers of arrogance by a sense of the divine presence, and kept from the bitterness of slander by the glory of the King whom he serves.

Verse 21.—*Marvellous kindness.* Marvellous that it should come to me in such a way, at such a time, in such a measure, for so long.

Verse 21.—Memorable events in life to be observed, recorded, meditated on, repeated, made the subject of gratitude, and the ground of confidence.

Verse 22.—Unbelief confessed and faithfulness adored.

The mischief of hasty speeches.

Verse 23.—An exhortation to love the Lord. 1. The matter of it, "*love the Lord.*" 2. To whom addressed, "*all ye his saints.*" 3. By whom spoken. 4. With what arguments supported, "*for the Lord preserveth,*" etc.

Verse 24.—Holy courage. Its excellences, difficulties, encouragements, and triumphs.

PSALM XXXII.

TITLE.—A Psalm of David, Maschil. *That David wrote this gloriously evangelic Psalm is proved not only by this heading, but by the words of the apostle Paul, in Romans iv. 6, 7, 8. "Even as David also describeth the blessedness of the man unto whom God imputeth righteousness without works," etc. Probably his deep repentance over his great sin was followed by such blissful peace, that he was led to pour out his spirit in the soft music of this choice song. In the order of history it seems to follow the fifty-first. Maschil is a new title to us, and indicates that this is an instructive or didactic Psalm. The experience of one believer affords rich instruction to others, it reveals the footsteps of the flock, and so comforts and directs the weak. Perhaps it was important in this case to prefix the word, that doubting saints might not imagine the Psalm to be the peculiar utterance of a singular individual, but might appropriate it to themselves as a lesson from the Spirit of God. David promised in the fifty-first Psalm to teach transgressors the Lord's ways, and here he does it most effectually. Grotius thinks that this Psalm was meant to be sung on the annual day of the Jewish expiation, when a general confession of their sins was made.*

DIVISION.—*In our reading we have found it convenient to note the benediction of the pardoned, verses 1, 2; David's personal confession, 3, 4, 5; and the application of the case to others, 6, 7. The voice of God is heard by the forgiven one in 8, 9; and the Psalm then concludes with a portion for each of the two great classes of men, 10, 11.*

EXPOSITION.

BLESSED *is he whose* transgression *is* forgiven, *whose* sin *is* covered.
2 Blessed *is* the man unto whom the LORD imputeth not iniquity and in whose spirit *there is* no guile.

1. "*Blessed.*" Like the sermon on the mount, this Psalm begins with beatitudes. This is the second Psalm of benediction. The first Psalm describes the result of holy blessedness, the thirty-second details the cause of it. The first pictures the tree in full growth, this depicts it in its first planting and watering. He who in the first Psalm is a reader of God's book, is here a suppliant at God's throne accepted and heard. "*Blessed is he whose transgression is forgiven.*" He is now blessed, and ever shall be. Be he ever so poor, or sick, or sorrowful, he is blessed in very deed. Pardoning mercy is of all things in the world most to be prized, for it is the only and sure way to happiness. To hear from God's own Spirit the words, "*absolvo te*" is joy unspeakable. Blessedness is not in this case ascribed to the man who has been a diligent lawkeeper, for then it would never come to us, but rather to a lawbreaker, who by grace most rich and free has been forgiven. Self-righteous Pharisees have no portion in this blessedness. Over the returning prodigal, the word of welcome is here pronounced, and the music and dancing begin. A full, instantaneous, irreversible pardon of transgression turns the poor sinner's hell into heaven, and makes the heir of wrath a partaker in blessing. The word rendered forgiven is in the original *taken off*, or *taken away*, as a burden is lifted or a barrier removed. What a lift is here   It cost our Saviour a sweat of blood to bear our load, yea, it cost him his life to bear it quite away. Samson carried the gates of Gaza, but what was that to the weight which Jesus bore on our behalf? "*Whose sin is covered.*" Covered by God, as the ark was covered by the mercy-seat, as Noah was covered from the flood, as the Egyptians were covered by the depths of the sea. What a cover must that be which hides away for ever from the sight of the all-seeing God all the filthiness of the flesh and of the spirit! He who has once seen sin in its horrible deformity, will appreciate the happiness of seeing it no more for ever. Christ's atonement is the propitiation, the covering, the making an end of sin; where this is seen and trusted in, the soul knows itself to be now accepted in the Beloved, and therefore enjoys a conscious blessedness which is the antepast of heaven. It is clear from the text that a man may *know* that he is pardoned: where would be the blessedness of an unknown forgiveness? Clearly it is a matter of knowledge, for it is the ground of comfort.

2. *"Blessed is the man unto whom the Lord imputeth not iniquity."* The word blessed is in the plural, *oh, the blessednesses!* the double joys, the bundles of happiness, the mountains of delight! Note the three words so often used to denote our disobedience : transgression, sin, and iniquity, are the three-headed dog at the gates of hell, but our glorious Lord has silenced its barkings for ever against his own believing ones. The trinity of sin is overcome by the Trinity of heaven. Non-imputation is of the very essence of pardon : the believer sins, but his sin is not reckoned, not accounted to him. Certain divines froth at the mouth with rage against imputed righteousness, be it ours to see our sin not imputed, and to us may there be as Paul words it, "Righteousness imputed without works." He is blessed indeed who has a substitute to stand for him to whose account all his debts may be set down. *"And in whose spirit there is no guile."* He who is pardoned, has in every case been taught to deal honestly with himself, his sin, and his God. Forgiveness is no sham, and the peace which it brings is not caused by playing tricks with conscience. Self-deception and hypocrisy bring no blessedness, they may drug the soul into hell with pleasant dreams, but into the heaven of true peace they cannot conduct their victim. Free from guilt, free from guile. Those who are justified from fault are sanctified from falsehood. A liar is not a forgiven soul. Treachery, double-dealing, chicanery, dissimulation, are lineaments of the devil's children, but he who is washed from sin is truthful, honest, simple, and childlike. There can be no blessedness to tricksters with their plans, and tricks, and shuffling, and pretending : they are too much afraid of discovery to be at ease ; their house is built on the volcano's brink, and eternal destruction must be their portion. Observe the three words to describe sin, and the three words to represent pardon, weigh them well, and note their meanings. (See note at the end.)

3 When I kept silence, my bones waxed old through my roaring all the day long.

4 For day and night thy hand was heavy upon me : my moisture is turned into the drought of summer. Selah.

5 I acknowledge my sin unto thee, and mine iniquity have I not hid. I said, I will confess my transgressions unto the LORD ; and thou forgavest the iniquity of my sin. Selah.

David now gives us his own experience : no instructor is so efficient as one who testifies to what he has personally known and felt. He writes well who like the spider spins his matter out of his own bowels.

3. *"When I kept silence."* When through neglect I failed to confess, or through despair dared not to do so, " *my bones,*" those solid pillars of my frame, the strongest portions of my bodily constitution, " *waxed old,*" began to decay with weakness, for my grief was so intense as to sap my health and destroy my vital energy. What a killing thing is sin ! It is a pestilent disease ! A fire in the bones ! While we smother our sin it rages within, and like a gathering wound swells horribly and torments terribly. *"Through my roaring all the day long."* He was silent as to confession, but not as to sorrow. Horror at his great guilt, drove David to incessant laments, until his voice was no longer like the articulate speech of man, but so full of sighing and groaning, that it resembled the hoarse roaring of a wounded beast. None know the pangs of conviction but those who have endured them. The rack, the wheel, the flaming fagot are ease compared with the Tophet which a guilty conscience kindles within the breast : better suffer all the diseases which flesh is heir to, than lie under the crushing sense of the wrath of almighty God. The Spanish inquisition with all its tortures was nothing to the inquest which conscience holds within the heart.

4. *"For day and night thy hand was heavy upon me."* God's finger can crush us —what must his hand be, and that pressing heavily and continuously! Under terrors of conscience, men have little rest by night, for the grim thoughts of the day dog them to their chambers and haunt their dreams, or else they lie awake in a cold sweat of dread. God's hand is very helpful when it uplifts, but it is awful when it presses down : better a world on the shoulder, like Atlas, than God's hand on the heart, like David. *"My moisture is turned into the drought of summer."* The sap of his soul was dried, and the body through sympathy appeared to be bereft of its needful fluids. The oil was almost gone from the lamp of life, and the flame flickered as though it would soon expire. Unconfessed transgression, like a fierce poison, dried up the fountain of the man's strength, and made him like a tree blasted by the lightning, or a plant withered by the scorching heat of a tropical sun. Alas ! for a poor soul when it has learned its sin but forgets its Saviour, it goes hard with it indeed. "Selah." It was time to change the tune, for the notes are very low in the scale, and with such hard usage, the strings of the harp are out of order : the next verse will surely be set to another key, or will rehearse a more joyful subject.

5. "*I acknowledged my sin unto thee.*" After long lingering, the broken heart bethought itself of what it ought to have done at the first, and laid bare its bosom before the Lord. The lancet must be let into the gathering ulcer before relief can be afforded. The least thing we can do, if we would be pardoned, is to acknowledge our fault ; if we are too proud for this we doubly deserve punishment. "*And mine iniquity have I not hid.*" We must confess the guilt as well as the fact of sin. It is useless to conceal it, for it is well known to God ; it is beneficial to us to own it, for a full confession softens and humbles the heart. We must as far as possible unveil the secrets of the soul, dig up the hidden treasure of Achan, and by weight and measure bring out our sins. "*I said.*" This was his fixed resolution. "*I will confess my transgressions unto the Lord.*" Not to my fellow men or to the high priest, but unto Jehovah ; even in those days of symbol the faithful looked to God alone for deliverance from sin's intolerable load, much more now, when types and shadows have vanished at the appearance of the dawn. When the soul determines to lay low and plead guilty, absolution is near at hand ; hence we read, "*And thou forgavest the iniquity of my sin.*" Not only was the sin itself pardoned, but the iniquity of it ; the virus of its guilt was put away, and that at once, so soon as the acknowledgment was made. God's pardons are deep and thorough : the knife of mercy cuts at the roots of the ill weed of sin. "*Selah.*" Another pause is needed, for the matter is not such as may be hurried over.

"Pause, my soul, adore and wonder,
Ask, O why such love to me ?
Grace has put me in the number
Of the Saviour's family.
Hallelujah !
Thanks, eternal thanks, to thee."

6 For this shall every one that is godly pray unto thee in a time when thou mayest be found : surely in the floods of great waters they shall not come nigh unto him.

7 Thou *art* my hiding place ; thou shalt preserve me from trouble ; thou shalt compass me about with songs of deliverance. Selah.

6. "*For this shall every one that is godly pray unto thee in a time when thou mayest be found.*" If the Psalmist means that *on account of* God's mercy others would become hopeful, his witness is true. Remarkable answers to prayer very much quicken the prayerfulness of other godly persons. Where one man finds a golden nugget others feel inclined to dig. The benefit of our experience to others should reconcile us to it. No doubt the case of David has led thousands to seek the Lord with hopeful courage who, without such an instance to cheer them, might have died in despair. Perhaps the Psalmist meant *for* this favour or the like all godly souls would seek, and here, again, we can confirm his testimony, for all will draw near to God in the same manner as he did when godliness rules their heart. The mercy seat is the way to heaven for all who shall ever come there. There is, however, a set time for prayer, beyond which it will be unavailing ; between the time of sin and the day of punishment mercy rules the hour, and God may be found, but when once the sentence has gone forth pleading will be useless, for the Lord will not be found by the condemned soul. O dear reader, slight not the accepted time, waste not the day of salvation. The godly pray while the Lord has promised to answer: the ungodly postpone their petitions till the Master of the house has risen up and shut to the door, and then their knocking is too late. What a blessing to be led to seek the Lord before the great devouring floods leap forth from their lairs, for then when they do appear we shall be safe. "*Surely in the floods of great waters they shall not come nigh unto him.*" The floods shall come, and the waves shall rage, and toss themselves like Atlantic billows ; whirlpools and waterspouts

shall be on every hand, but the praying man shall be at a safe distance, most surely secured from every ill. David was probably most familiar with those great land-floods which fill up, with rushing torrents, the beds of rivers which at other times are almost dry : these overflowing waters often did great damage, and, as in the case of the Kishon, were sufficient to sweep away whole armies. From sudden and overwhelming disasters thus set forth in metaphor the true suppliant will certainly be held secure. He who is saved from sin has no need to fear anything else.

7. *" Thou art my hiding place."* Terse, short sentences make up this verse, but they contain a world of meaning. Personal claims upon our God are the joy of spiritual life. To lay our hand upon the Lord with the clasp of a personal " my " is delight at its full. Observe that the same man who in the fourth verse was oppressed by the presence of God, here finds a shelter in him. See what honest confession and full forgiveness will do ! The gospel of substitution makes him to be our refuge who otherwise would have been our judge. *" Thou shalt preserve me from trouble."* Trouble shall do me no real harm when the Lord is with me, rather it shall bring me much benefit, like the file which clears away the rust, but does not destroy the metal. Observe the three tenses, we have noticed the sorrowful past, the last sentence was a joyful present, this is a cheerful future. *" Thou shalt compass me about with songs of deliverance."* What a golden sentence ! The man is encircled in song, surrounded by dancing mercies, all of them proclaiming the triumphs of grace. There is no breach in the circle, it completely rings him round ; on all sides he hears music. Before him hope sounds the cymbals, and behind him gratitude beats the timbrel. Right and left, above and beneath, the air resounds with joy, and all this for the very man who, a few weeks ago, was roaring all the day long. How great a change ! What wonders grace has done and still can do ! *" Selah."* There was need of a pause, for love so amazing needs to be pondered, and joy so great demands quiet contemplation, since language fails to express it.

8 I will instruct thee and teach thee in the way which thou shalt go ; I will guide thee with mine eye.

9 Be ye not as the horse, *or* as the mule, *which* have no understanding : whose mouth must be held in with bit and bridle, lest they come near unto thee.

8. *" I will instruct thee and teach thee in the way which thou shalt go."* Here the Lord is the speaker, and gives the Psalmist an answer to his prayer. Our Saviour is our instructor. The Lord himself deigns to teach his children to walk in the way of integrity, his holy word and the monitions of the Holy Spirit are the directors of the believer's daily conversation. We are not pardoned that we may henceforth live after our own lusts, but that we may be educated in holiness and trained for perfection. A heavenly training is one of the covenant blessings which adoption seals to us : " All thy children shall be taught by the Lord." Practical teaching is the very best of instruction, and they are thrice happy who, although they never sat at the feet of Gamaliel, and are ignorant of Aristotle, and the ethics of the schools, have nevertheless learned to follow the Lamb whithersoever he goeth. *" I will guide thee with mine eye."* As servants take their cue from the master's eye, and a nod or a wink is all that they require, so should we obey the slightest hints of our Master, not needing thunderbolts to startle our incorrigible sluggishness, but being controlled by whispers and love-touches. The Lord is the great overseer, whose eye in providence overlooks everything. It is well for us to be the sheep of his pasture, following the guidance of his wisdom.

9. *" Be ye not as the horse, or as the mule, which have no understanding."* Under-standing separates man from a brute—let us not act as if we were devoid of it. Men should take counsel and advice, and be ready to run where wisdom points them the way. Alas ! we need to be cautioned against stupidity of heart, for we are very apt to fall into it. We who ought to be as the angels, readily become as the beasts. *" Whose mouth must be held in with bit and bridle, lest they come near unto thee."* It is much to be deplored that we so often need to be severely chastened before we will obey. We ought to be as a feather in the wind, wafted readily in the breath of the Holy Spirit, but alas ! we lie like motionless logs, and stir not with heaven itself in view. Those cutting bits of affliction show how hard-mouthed we are, those bridles of infirmity manifest our headstrong and wilful manners.

We should not be treated like mules if there were not so much of the ass about us. If we will be fractious, we must expect to be kept in with tight rein. Oh for grace to obey the Lord willingly, lest like the wilful servant, we are beaten with many stripes. Calvin renders the last words, " Lest they kick against thee," a version more probable and more natural, but the passage is confessedly obscure—not, however, in its general sense.

10 Many sorrows *shall be* to the wicked : but he that trusteth in the LORD, mercy shall compass him about.

11 Be glad in the LORD, and rejoice, ye righteous : and shout for joy, all *ye that are* upright in heart.

10. " *Many sorrows shall be to the wicked.*" Like refractory horses and mules, they have many cuts and bruises. Here and hereafter the portion of the wicked is undesirable. Their joys are evanescent, their sorrows are multiplying and ripening. He who sows sin will reap sorrow in heavy sheaves. Sorrows of conscience, of disappointment, of terror, are the sinner's sure heritage in time, and then for ever sorrows of remorse and despair. Let those who boast of present sinful joys, remember the *shall be* of the future, and take warning. " *But he that trusteth in the Lord, mercy shall compass him about.*" Faith is here placed as the opposite of wickedness, since it is the source of virtue. Faith in God is the great charmer of life's cares, and he who possesses it, dwells in an atmosphere of grace, surrounded with a body-guard of mercies. May it be given to us of the Lord at all times to believe in the mercy of God, even when we cannot see traces of its working, for to the believer, mercy is as all-surrounding as omniscience, and every thought and act of God is perfumed with it. The wicked have a hive of wasps around them, *many sorrows ;* but we have a swarm of bees storing honey for us.

11. " *Be glad.*" Happiness is not only our privilege, but our duty. Truly we serve a generous God, since he makes it a part of our obedience to be joyful. How sinful are our rebellious murmurings ! How natural does it seem that a man blest with forgiveness should be glad ! We read of one who died at the foot of the scaffold of overjoy at the receipt of his monarch's pardon ; and shall we receive the free pardon of the King of kings and yet pine in inexcusable sorrow ? " *In the Lord.*" Here is the directory by which gladness is preserved from levity. We are not to be glad in sin, or to find comfort in corn, and wine, and oil, but in our God is to be the garden of our soul's delight. That there is a God and such a God, and that he is ours, ours for ever, our Father and our reconciled Lord, is matter enough for a never-ending Psalm of rapturous joy. " *And rejoice, ye righteous,*" redouble your rejoicing, peal upon peal. Since God has clothed his choristers in the white garments of holiness, let them not restrain their joyful voices, but sing aloud and shout as those who find great spoil. " *And shout for joy, all ye that are upright in heart.*" Our happiness should be demonstrative ; chill penury of love often represses the noble flame of joy, and men whisper their praises decorously where a hearty outburst of song would be far more natural. It is to be feared that the church of the present day, through a craving for excessive propriety, is growing too artificial ; so that enquirers' cries and believers' shouts would be silenced if they were heard in our assemblies. This may be better than boisterous fanaticism, but there is as much danger in the one direction as the other. For our part, we are touched to the heart by a little sacred excess, and when godly men in their joy overleap the narrow bounds of decorum, we do not, like Michal, Saul's daughter, eye them with a sneering heart. Note how the pardoned are represented as upright, righteous, and without guile ; a man may have many faults and yet be saved, but a false heart is everywhere the damning mark. A man of twisting, shifty ways, of a crooked, crafty nature, is not saved, and in all probability never will be ; for the ground which brings forth a harvest when grace is sown in it, may be weedy and waste, but our Lord tells us it is *honest* and good ground. Our observation has been that men of double tongues and tricky ways are the least likely of all men to be saved : certainly where grace comes it restores man's mind to its perpendicular, and delivers him from being doubled up with vice, twisted with craft, or bent with dishonesty.

Reader, what a delightful Psalm ! Have you, in perusing it, been able to claim a lot in the goodly land ? If so, publish to others the way of salvation.

EXPLANATORY NOTES AND QUAINT SAYINGS.

Title.—The term *Maschil* is prefixed to thirteen Psalms. Our translators have not ventured to do more, in the *text*, than simply print the word in English characters; in the *margin* however they render it, as the Geneva version had done before them, "to give instruction." It would be going too far to affirm that this interpretation is subject to no doubt. Some good Hebraists take exception to it; so that, perhaps, our venerable translators did well to leave it untranslated. Still, the interpretation they have set down in the margin, as it is the most ancient, so it is sustained by the great preponderance of authority. It agrees remarkably with the contents of the thirty-second Psalm, which affords the earliest instance of its use, for that Psalm is pre-eminently didactic. Its scope is to instruct the convicted soul how to obtain peace with God, and be compassed about with songs of deliverance.—*William Binnie, D.D., in "The Psalms: their History, Teachings, and Use," 1870.*

Whole Psalm.—This is a Didascalic Psalm, wherein David teacheth sinners to repent by his doctrine, who taught them to sin by his example. This science is universal and pertaineth to all men, and which necessarily we must all learn; princes, priests, people, men, women, children, tradesmen; all, I say, must be put to this school, without which lesson all others are unprofitable. But to the point. This is a mark of a true penitent, when he hath been a stumbling block to others, to be as careful to raise them up by his repentance as he was hurtful to them by his sin; and I never think that man truly penitent who is ashamed to teach sinners repentance, by his own particular proof. The Samaritan woman, when she was converted, left her bucket at the well, entered the city, and said, "Come forth, yonder is a man who hath told me all that I have done." And our Saviour saith to St. Peter, "When thou art converted, strengthen thy brethren." John iv. 29; Luke xxii. 32. St. Paul also, after his conversion is not ashamed to call himself chiefest of all sinners, and to teach others to repent of their sins by repenting for his own. Happy, and thrice happy, is the man who can build so much as he hath cast down.—*Archibald Symson.*

Whole Psalm.—It is told of Luther that one day being asked which of all the Psalms were the best, he made answer, "*Psalmi Paulini*," and when his friends pressed to know which these might be, he said, "The 32nd, the 51st, the 130th, and 143rd. For they all teach that the forgiveness of our sins comes, without the law and without works, to the man who believes, and therefore I call them Pauline Psalms; and David sings, 'There is forgiveness with thee, that thou mayest be feared,' this is just what Paul says, 'God hath concluded them all in unbelief, that he might have mercy upon all.' Rom. xi. 32. Thus no man may boast of his own righteousness. That word, 'That thou mayest be feared,' dusts away all merit, and teaches us to uncover our heads before God, and confess *gratia est, non meritum: remissio, non satisfactio*; it is mere forgiveness, not merit at all."—*Luther's Table Talk.*

Whole Psalm.—Some assert that this Psalm used to be sung on the day of expiation.—*Robert Leighton.*

The Penitential Psalms.—When Galileo was imprisoned by the Inquisition at Rome, for asserting the Copernican System, he was enjoined, as a penance, to repeat the Seven Penitential Psalms every week for three years. This must have been intended as extorting a sort of confession from him of his guilt, and acknowledgment of the justice of his sentence; and in which there certainly was some cleverness and, indeed, humour, however adding to the iniquity (or foolishness) of the proceeding. Otherwise it is not easy to understand what idea of painfulness or punishment the good fathers could attach to a devotional exercise such as this, which, in whatever way, could only have been agreeable and consoling to their prisoner.—*M. Montague, in The Seven Penitential Psalms in Verse . . . . with an Appendix and Notes," 1844.*

Verse 1.—"*Blessed.*" Or, O blessed man; or, Oh, the felicities of that man! to denote the most supreme and perfect blessedness. As the elephant, to denote its vast bulk, is spoken of in the plural number, *Behemoth.*—*Robert Leighton.*

Verse 1.—Notice, this is the first Psalm, except the first of all, which begins with Blessedness. In the first Psalm we have the blessing of innocence, or rather, of him who only was innocent : here we have the blessing of repentance, as the next happiest state to that of sinlessness.—*Lorinus, in Neale's Commentary.*

Verse 1.—" *Blessed is the man,*" saith David, " *whose sins are pardoned,*" where he maketh remission of sins to be true felicity. Now there is no true felicity but that which is enjoyed, and felicity cannot be enjoyed unless it be felt ; and it cannot be felt unless a man know himself to be in possession of it ; and a man cannot know himself to be in possession of it, if he doubt whether he hath it or not ; and therefore this doubting of the remission of sins is contrary to true felicity, and is nothing else but a torment of the conscience. For a man cannot doubt whether his sins be pardoned or not, but straightway, if his conscience be not seared with a hot iron, the very thought of his sin will strike a great fear into him ; for the fear of eternal death, and the horror of God's judgment will come to his remembrance, the consideration of which is most terrible. —*William Perkins.*

Verse 1.—" *Blessed is he whose transgression is forgiven, whose sin is covered.*" Get your sins hid. There is a covering of sin which proves *a curse.* Prov. xxviii. 13. " He that covereth his sins shall not prosper ; " there is a *covering* it, by not confessing it, or which is worse, by denying it—Gehazi's covering—a covering of sin by a lie ; and there is also a covering of sin by justifying ourselves in it. I have not done this thing ; or, I did no evil in it. All these are evil coverings : he that thus covereth his sin shall not prosper. But there is a *blessed* covering of sin : forgiveness of sin is the hiding it out of sight, and that is the blessedness.—*Richard Alleine.*

Verse 1.—" *Whose transgression is forgiven.*" We may lull the soul asleep with carnal delights, but the virtue of that opium will be soon spent. All those joys are but stolen waters, and bread eaten in secret—a poor sorry peace that dares not come to the light and endure the trial ; a sorry peace that is soon disturbed by a few serious and sober thoughts of God and the world to come ; but when once sin is pardoned, then you have true joy indeed. " Be of good cheer ; thy sins be forgiven thee." Matt. ix. 2.—*Thomas Manton.*

Verse 1.—" *Forgiven.*" Holy David, in the front of this Psalm shows us wherein true happiness consists ; not in beauty, honour, riches (the world's trinity), but in the forgiveness of sin. The Hebrew word to *forgive,* signifies to carry out of sight ; which well agrees with that Jer. l. 20, " In those days, saith the Lord, the iniquity of Israel shall be sought for, and there shall be none ; and the sins of Judah, and they shall not be found." This is an incomprehensible blessing, and such as lays a foundation for all other mercies. I shall but glance at it, and lay down these five assertions about it. 1. Forgiveness is an act of God's free grace. The Greek word *to forgive,* deciphers the original of pardon ; it ariseth not from anything inherent in us, but is the pure result of free grace. Isa. xliii. 25 : " I, even I, am he that blotteth out thy transgressions for mine own sake." When a creditor forgives a debtor, he doeth it freely. Paul cries out, " I obtained mercy." 1 Tim. i. 13. The Greek signifies, " I was be-mercied ; " he who is pardoned, is all bestrewed with mercy. When the Lord pardons a sinner, he doth not pay a debt, but give a legacy. 2. God in forgiving sin, remits the guilt and penalty. Guilt cries for justice : no sooner had Adam eaten the apple, but he saw the flaming sword, and heard the curse ; but in remission God doth indulge the sinner ; he seems to say thus to him : Though thou art fallen into the hands of my justice, and deservest to die, yet I will absolve thee, and whatever is charged upon thee shall be discharged. 3. Forgiveness of sin is through the blood of Christ. Free grace is the impulsive cause ; Christ's blood is the meritorious. " Without shedding of blood is no remission." Heb. ix. 22. Justice would be revenged either on the sinner or the surety. Every pardon is the price of blood. 4. Before sin is forgiven it must be repented of. Therefore repentance and remission are linked together. " That repentance and remission of sins should be preached in his name." Luke xxiv. 47. Not that repentance doth in a Popish sense merit forgiveness ; Christ's blood must wash our tears ; but repentance is a qualification, though not a cause. He who is humbled for sin will the more value pardoning mercy. 5. God having forgiven sin, he will call it no more into remembrance. Jer. xxxi. 34. The Lord will make an act of indemnity, he will not upbraid us with former unkindnesses, or sue us with a cancelled bond. " He will cast all our sins into the depths of the sea." Mic. vii. 19. Sin shall not be cast in as a cork which riseth up again, but as lead which sinks to the bottom. How should we all labour for this covenant blessing !—*Thomas Watson.*

Verse 1.—*" Sin is covered."* Every man that must be happy, must have something to hide and cover his sins from God's eyes ; and nothing in the world can do it, but Christ and his righteousness, typified in the ark of the covenant, whose cover was of gold, and called a propitiatory, that as it covered the tables that were within the ark, so God covers our sins against those tables. So the cloud covering the Israelites in the wilderness, signified God's covering us from the danger of our sins. —*Thomas Taylor's " David's Learning : or the Way to True Happinesse,"* 1617.

Verse 1.—*" Sin covered."* This *covering* hath relation to some nakedness and filthiness which should be covered, even sin, which defileth us and maketh us naked. Why, saith Moses to Aaron, hast thou made the people naked ? Ex. xxxii. 25. The garments of our merits are too short and cannot cover us, we have need therefore to borrow of Christ Jesus his merits and the mantle of his righteousness, that it may be unto us as a garment, and as those breeches of leather which God made unto Adam and Eve after their fall. Garments are ordained to cover our nakedness, defend us from the injury of the weather, and to adorn us. So the mediation of our Saviour serveth to cover our nakedness, that the wrath of God seize not upon us—he is that " white raiment " wherewith we should be clothed, that our filthy nakedness may not appear—to defend us against Satan—he is " mighty to save," etc.—and to be an ornament to decorate us, for he is that " *wedding garment :* " " Put ye on the Lord Jesus Christ." Rev. iii. 18 ; Isa. lxiii. 1 ; Matt. xxii. 11 ; Rom. xiii. 14.—*Archibald Symson.*

Verse 1.—The object of pardon—about which it is conversant, is set forth under divers expressions—*iniquity, transgression,* and *sin.* As in law, many words of like import and signification are heaped up and put together, to make the deed and legal instrument more comprehensive and effectual. I observe it the rather, because when God proclaims his name the same words are used, Exod. xxxiv. 7, " Taking away iniquity, transgression, and sin." Well, we have seen the meaning of the expression. Why doth the holy man of God use such vigour and vehemency of inculcation, *" Blessed is the man ! "* and again, *" Blessed is the man ! "* Partly with respect to his own case. David knew how sweet it was to have sin pardoned ; he had felt the bitterness of sin in his own soul, to the drying up of his blood, and therefore he doth express his sense of pardon in the most lively terms. And then, partly, too, with respect to those for whose use this instruction was written, that they might not look upon it as a light and trivial thing, but be thoroughly apprehensive of the worth of so great a privilege. Blessed, happy, thrice happy they who have obtained pardon of their sins, and justification by Jesus Christ.—*Thomas Manton.*

Verses 1, 2.—In these verses *four* evils are mentioned : 1. *Transgression,* פשע *pesha.* 2. *Sin,* חטאה *chataah.* 3. *Iniquity,* עון *avon.* 4. *Guile,* רמיה *remiyah.* The *first* signifies the *passing over a boundary, doing what is prohibited.* The *second* signifies the *missing of a mark,* not doing what was commanded ; but it is often taken to express *sinfulness,* or sin in the nature, producing transgression in the life. The *third* signifies *what is turned out of its proper course or situation ;* anything *morally distorted* or perverted. *Iniquity,* what is contrary to *equity* or *justice.* The *fourth* signifies *fraud, deceit, guile, etc.* To remove these evils, *three* acts are mentioned : *forgiving, covering,* and not *imputing.* 1. TRANSGRESSION, פשע *pesha,* must be *forgiven,* נשוי *nesui,* borne away, *i.e.,* by a vicarious sacrifice ; for *bearing sin,* or *bearing away sin,* always implies this. 2. SIN, חטאה *chataah,* must be *covered,* כסוי *kesui,* hidden from the sight. It is odious and abominable, and must be put out of sight. 3. INIQUITY, עון *avon,* what is *perverse* or *distorted,* must not be imputed, לא יחשב *lo yachshobh,* must *not be reckoned to his account.* 4. GUILE, רמיה *remiyah,* must be annihilated from the soul. *In whose spirit there is no* GUILE. The man whose *transgression* is forgiven ; whose *sin* is hidden, God having cast it as a millstone into the depths of the sea ; whose iniquity and perversion is not reckoned to his account ; and whose *guile,* the deceitful and desperately wicked heart, is annihilated, being emptied of sin, and filled with righteousness, is necessarily a happy man.—*Adam Clarke.*

Verses 1, 2.—*Transgression.* Prevarication. Some understand by it sins of omission and commission.

Sin. Some understand those inward inclinations, lusts, and motions, whereby the soul swerves from the law of God, and which are the immediate cause of external sins.

Iniquity. Notes original sin, the root of all.

Levatus, forgiven, eased, signifies to take away, to bear, to carry away. Two words in Scripture are chiefly used to denote remission, to expiate, to bear or carry away : the one signifies the manner whereby it is done, namely, atonement, the other the effect of this expiation, carrying away ; one notes the meritorious cause, the other the consequent.

Covered. Alluding to the covering of the Egyptians in the Red Sea. Menochius thinks it alludes to the manner of writing among the Hebrews, which he thinks to be the same with that of the Romans ; as writing with a pencil upon wax spread upon tables, which when they would blot out they made the wax plain, and drawing it over the writing, covered the former letters. And so it is equivalent with that expression of " blotting out sin," as in the other allusion it is with " casting sin into the depths of the sea."

Impute. Not charging upon account. As sin is a defection from the law, so it is forgiven ; as it is offensive to God's holiness, so it is covered ; as it is a debt involving man in a debt of punishment, so it is not imputed ; they all note the certainty, and extent, and perfection of pardon ; the three words expressing sin here, being the same that are used by God in the declaration of his name.—*Stephen Charnock.*

Verses 1, 2, 6, 7.—Who is blessed ? Not he who cloaks, conceals, confesses not his sin. As long as David was in this state he was miserable. There was guile in his spirit (2), misery in his heart, his very bones waxed old, his moisture was dried up as the drought in summer (3, 4). Who is blessed ? He that is without sin, he who sins not, he who grieves no more by his sin the bosom on which he reclines. This is superlative blessedness, its highest element, the happiness of heaven. To be like God, to yield implicit, ready, full, perfect obedience, the obedience of the heart, of our entire being ; this is to be blessed above all blessedness. But among those who live in a world of sin, who are surrounded by sin, who are themselves sinners, who is blessed ? *"He whose transgression is forgiven, whose sin is covered, to whom the Lord imputeth not iniquity ;"* and especially does he feel it to be so, who can, in some degree, enter into the previous state of David's soul (3, 4). Ah, in what a wretched state was the Psalmist previously to this blessedness ! How must sin have darkened and deadened his spiritual faculties, to have guile in the spirit of one who could elsewhere exclaim, " Search me, O God, and know my heart : try me, and know my thoughts : and see if there be any wicked way in me," any way of pain or grief, any way of sin which most surely leads to these. Ps. cxxxix. 23, 34. What a mournful condition of soul was his, who while he roared all the day long, yet kept silence before God, had no heart to open his heart unto God, was dumb before him, not in submission to his will, not in accepting the punishment of his iniquity (Lev. xxvi. 46), not in real confession, and honest, upright, and sincere acknowledgment of his iniquity to him against whom he had committed it. *" I kept silence,"* not merely I was silent, *" I kept* silence," resolutely, perseveringly ; I kept it notwithstanding all the remembrance of my past mercies, notwithstanding my reproaches of conscience, and my anguish of heart. I kept it notwithstanding *" thy hand was heavy upon me day and night,"* notwithstanding *" my moisture,"* all that was spiritual in me, my vital spirit, all that was indicative of spiritual life in my soul, seemed dried up and gone. Yes, Lord, notwithstanding all this, I *kept* it. But Nathan came, thou didst send him. He was to me a messenger full of reproof, full of faithfulness, but full of love. He came with thy word, and with the word of a King there was power. I acknowledged my sin unto him, and my iniquity did I not hide, but this was little. Against thee, thee only, did I sin, and to thee was my confession made. I acknowledged my sin unto thee, O Lord. I solemnly said that I would do so, and I did it. I confessed my transgression unto the Lord, *" and thou forgavest the iniquity of my sin."*

" Blessed is he whose transgression is forgiven." Behold the man who is blessed ; blessed in the state of his mind, his guileless spirit, his contrite heart, the fruit of the spirit of grace ; blessed in the forgiveness of a forgiving God ; a forgiveness, perfect, entire, lacking nothing, signified by sin " covered," " iniquity not imputed " of the Lord ; blessed in the blessings which followed it. *" Thou art my hiding place ; thou shalt preserve me from trouble ; thou shalt compass me about with songs of deliverance."* Beneath the hollow of that hand which was once

so heavy upon me, I can now repose. Thou art my hiding place, I dread thee no more ; nay, I dwell in thee as my habitation, and my high tower, my covert, my safety, my house. Safe in thy love, whatever trouble may be my portion, and by the mouth of Nathan thy servant thou hast declared that trouble shall be my portion, I shall yet be preserved ; yea, more, so fully wilt thou deliver me that I believe thou wilt encompass me so with the arms of thy mercy, as to call forth songs of grateful praise for thy gracious interposition.

Behold the blessedness of him whom God forgives ! No wonder, then, that the Psalmist adds, " *for this shall every one that is godly pray unto thee in a time when thou mayest be found : surely in the floods of great waters they shall not come nigh unto him.*" As much as if he said, Surely after this thy gracious conduct towards *me*, all that truly love and fear thee, " *every one that is godly,*" when he hears of thy dealings with *me*, " *will pray unto thee.*" Encouraged by my example, he will not keep silence as I foolishly and sinfully did, but will confess and supplicate before thee, since thou art to be " *found,*" and hast so wondrously shown that thou art, of all that truly seek thee, since there is *the place* of finding, as I lay my hand upon the victim, and look through that victim to him the promised Seed ; since there is *the time* of finding, declared in thy word, and manifested by the secret drawing of my heart to thee by thy grace : since the unwillingness is not in thee, but in thy sinning creature to come to thee ; " *for this shall every one that is godly pray unto thee,*" then, however deep the waterfloods may be, however fierce the torrent, and headlong the stream, they shall not even come nigh unto him, much less shall they overwhelm him.—*James Harrington Evans, M.A.*, 1785—1849.

Verse 2.—" *Unto whom the Lord imputeth not iniquity.*" Aben-Ezra paraphrases it, *of whose sins God does not think*, does not regard them, so as to bring them into judgment, reckoning them as if they were not ; οὐ μὴ λογιζεται *does not count or calculate them ;* does not require for them the debt of punishment. To us the remission is entirely free, our Sponsor having taken upon him the whole business of paying the ransom. His suffering is our impunity, his bond our freedom, and his chastisement our peace ; and therefore the prophet says, " The chastisement of our peace was upon him, and by his stripes we are healed."—*Robert Leighton.*

Verse 2.—" *In whose spirit there is no guile.*" In the saint's trouble, conscience is full of Scripture sometimes, on which it grounds its verdict, but very ill interpreted. Oh, saith the poor soul, this place is against me ! " *Blessed is the man unto whom the Lord imputeth not iniquity, and in whose spirit there is no guile.*" Here, saith he, is a description of a sincere soul, to be one in whose spirit there is no guile ; but I find much guile in me, therefore I am not the sincere one. Now this is a very weak yea, false inference. By a spirit without guile, is not meant a person that hath not the least deceitfulness and hypocrisy remaining in his heart. To be without sin, and to be without guile, in this strict sense are the same—a prerogative here on earth peculiar to the Lord Christ (1 Pet. ii. 22), " Who did no sin, neither was guile found in his mouth." And therefore when we meet with the same phrase attributed to the saints, as to Levi, Mal. ii. 6 : " Iniquity was not found in his lips ; " and to Nathanael, John i. 47 : " Behold an Israelite indeed, in whom is no guile ! " we must sense it in an inferior way, that may suit with their imperfect state here below, and not put that which was only Christ's crown on earth, and is the glorified saint's robe in heaven, on the weak Christian while militant here on earth, not only with a devil without, but with a body of sin within him. Wipe thine eyes again, poor soul, and then if thou readest such places, wherein the Spirit of God speaks so highly and hyperbolically of his saints' grace, thou shalt find he doth not assert the perfection of their grace, free from all mixture of sin, but rather to comfort poor drooping souls, and cross their misgiving hearts, which, from the presence of hypocrisy, are ready to overlook their sincerity as none at all, he expresseth his high esteem of their little grace, by speaking of it as if it were perfect, and their hypocrisy none at all.—*William Gurnall.*

Verse 2. " *In whose spirit there is no guile.*" When once pardon is realised the believer has courage to be truthful before God : he can afford to have done with " *guile* " in the spirit. Who would not declare all his debts when they are certain to be discharged by another ? Who would not declare his malady when he was sure of a cure ? True faith knows not only that " *guile* " before God is impossible, but also that it is no longer necessary. The believer has nothing to conceal : he sees himself as before God, stripped, and laid open, and bare ; and if he has learned to see himself as he is, so also has he learned to see God as he reveals himself. There is no guile in the spirit of one who is justified by faith ; because in the act of justification truth has been established in his inward parts. There is no guile in the spirit of him who sees the truth of himself in the light of the truth of God. For the truth of God shows him at once that in Christ he is perfectly righteous before God, and in himself he is the chief of sinners. Such a one knows he is not his own, for he is bought with a price, and therefore he is to glorify God. There is no guile in the spirit of him whose real object is to glorify Christ and not himself. But when a man is not quite true to Christ, and has not quite ceased to magnify self, there may be guile, for he will be more occupied with thoughts about himself than with the honour of Christ. But if the truth, and honour, and glory of Christ be his supreme care, he may leave himself out of the question, and, like Christ, " commit himself to him that judgeth righteously."—*J. W. Reeve, M.A., in " Lectures on the Thirty-second Psalm,"* 1860.

Verse 2.—"No guile." Sincerity is that property to which pardoning mercy is annexed. True, indeed, it is that Christ covers all our sins and failings ; but it is only the sincere soul over which he will cast his skirt. *" Blessed is he whose sin is covered. Blessed is the man unto whom the Lord imputeth not iniquity."* None will doubt this ; but which is the man ? The next words tell us his name ; *" And in whose spirit there is no guile."* Christ's rightousness is the garment which covers the nakedness and shame of our unrighteousness ; faith the grace that puts this garment on ; but what faith ? None but the faith unfeigned, as Paul calls it. 2 Tim. i. 5. " Here is water," said the eunuch, " what doth hinder me to be baptized ? " Acts viii. 36. Now mark Philip's answer, ver. 37 : "If thou believest with all thine heart, thou mayest ; " as if he had said, Nothing but an hypocritical heart can hinder thee. It is the false heart only that finds the door of mercy shut.—*William Gurnall.*

Verse 2.—"Guile." The guile of the spirit is an inward corruption in the soul of man, whereby he dealeth deceitfully with himself before God in the matter of salvation.—*Thomas Taylor.*

Verse 3.—" My bones waxed old." God sporteth not at the sins of his elect, but outwardly doth deal with them more hardly, and chastise them more rigorously than he doth the reprobate. David's troubles and pains were partly external, partly internal : external I call those that were cast on his body ; internal upon his conscience. And in the body there were torments and vexations, seizing sometimes on his flesh—which was less painful—sometimes on his bones, which was more grievous, yea, almost intolerable, as experience teacheth. And this is God's just recompence ; when we bestow our strength on sin, God abateth it, and so weakeneth us. Samson spent his strength on Delilah, but to what weakness was he brought! Let us, therefore, learn, that God hath given us bones and the strength thereof for another use, that is, to serve him, and not waste or be prodigal of them in the devil's service.—*Archibald Symson.*

Verse 3.—" My bones waxed old." By bones, the strength of the body, the inward strength and vigour of the soul is meant. The conscience of sin, and the terror of judgment doth break the heart of a true penitent, so long as he beholdeth his sin deserving death, his judge ready to pronounce the sentence of it, hell open to receive him for it, and the evil angels, God's executioners, at hand to hurry him to it.—*Samuel Page, in " David's Broken Heart,"* 1646.

Verse 3.—" My bones waxed old through my roaring all the day long." David here not only mourns for sin as a man, but he roars, as it were, like a pained beast. He seems fitter for a wilderness to cry out, than for a secret chamber to weep in ; at other times he can " water his couch " in the night, now he " *roars* " all the day long ; at other times " his *moisture* is dried," now his " *bones*," the pillars of his house, shake and wax old.—*Alexander Carmichael,* 1677.

Verse 4.—" Thy hand." A *correcting* hand, whereby God scourgeth and buffeteth his own children. Now the sense of God's power punishing or correcting, is called God's hand, as 1 Sam. v. 11. The hand of God was sore at Ekron, because of the ark ; and a *heavy* hand in resemblance, because when men smite they lay their hand heavier than ordinary. Hence, we may note three points of doctrine : first, that all afflictions are God's hand ; secondly, that God lays his hand heavily often upon his dear children ; thirdly, that God often continues his heavy hand night and day on them.—*Thomas Taylor.*

Verse 4.—"*My moisture is turned into the drought of summer.*" Another meaning may be attributed to these words. We may suppose the Psalmist to be referring to *spiritual drought.*—*Charles H. Bingham, B.A., in " Lectures on the Thirty-second Psalm,"* 1836.

Verse 4.—"*My moisture is turned into the drought of summer.*" The summer is from the middle of August to the middle of November. The intensity of the heat is great, and almost intolerable. . . Up to the beginning or middle of September there are no showers, rain being as scarce in summer as snow. . . . The dry grass of the fields sometimes takes fire, and produces desolating conflagrations, and the parched earth is cleft and broken into chasms.—*John Eadie, D.D., LL.D., in Biblical Cyclopædia,* 1868.

Verse 4.—"*The drought of summer.*" Dr. Russell, in his account of the weather at Aleppo, which very much resembles that of Judæa, says that the verdure of the spring fades before the middle of May, and before the end of that month the whole country puts on so parched and barren an aspect that one would scarce think it capable of producing anything, there being but very few plants that have vigour enough to resist the extreme heat.—*Thomas Harmer's " Observations,"* 1775.

Verse 4.—"*The drought of summer.*" During the twelve years from 1846 to 1859 only two slight showers fell in Jerusalem between the months of May and October. One fell in July, 1858, another in June, 1859.—*Dr. Whitty's " Water Supply of Jerusalem," quoted in Kitto's Cyclopædia.*

Verse 4.—If God striketh those so sore whom he favoureth, how sharply and sore will he strike them whom he favoureth not.—*Gregory.*

Verses 4, 5.—If our offences have been not gnats, but camels, our sorrow must be not a drop, but an ocean. Scarlet sins call for bloody tears ; and if Peter sin heinously he must weep bitterly. If, then, thy former life hath been a cord of iniquity, twisted with many threads, a writing full of great blots, a course spotted with various and grievous sins, multiply thy confessions and enlarge thy humiliation ; double thy fastings and treble thy prayers ; pour out thy tears, and fetch deep sighs ; in a word, iterate and aggravate thy acknowledgments, though yet, as the apostle saith in another case, I say in this, " Grieve not as without hope," that upon thy sincere and suitable repentance divine goodness will forgive thee thy sins.—*Nathanael Hardy.*

Verse 5.—" *Selah.*" See Vol. I., pp. 22, 23, 25, 27, 29.

Verse 5.—" *I acknowledged my sin unto thee, and mine iniquity have I not hid.*" The godly man is ingenuous in laying open his sins. The hypocrite doth vail and smother his sin ; he doth not *abscindere peccatum*, but *abscondere ;* like a patient that hath some loathsome disease in his body, he will rather die than confess his disease ; but a godly man's sincerity is seen in this—he will confess and shame himself for sin. " Lo, I have sinned, and I have done wickedly." 2 Sam. xxiv. 17. Nay a child of God will confess sin in particular ; an unsound Christian will confess sin by wholesale ; he will acknowledge he is a sinner in general, whereas David doth, as it were, point with his finger to the sore : " I have done this evil " (Psalm li. 4) ; he doth not say I have done evil, but this evil. He points at his blood-guiltiness.—*Thomas Watson.*

Verse 5.—" *I said, I will confess my transgressions unto the Lord ; and thou forgavest the iniquity of my sin.*" Be thine own accuser in the free confession of thy sins. *Peccavi pater* (as the prodigal child), " Father, I have sinned against heaven, and in thy sight." For it fares not in the court of heaven as it doth in our earthly tribunals. With men a free confession makes way for a condemnation ; but with God, the more a sinner bemoans his offence the more be extenuates the anger of his Judge. Sin cannot but call for justice, as it is an offence against God ; yet, when once 'tis a wound to the soul it moveth him to mercy and clemency. Wherefore, as David having but resolved to confess his sins, was accosted eftsoon with an absolution : so, *Tu agnosce, et Dominus ignoscet.** Be thou unfeigned in confessing, and God will be faithful in forgiving. 1 John i. 9. Only let *confessio peccati* be *professio desinendi* †—the acknowledgment of thy sin an obligation to leave it ; and then thou mayest build upon it. " He that confesseth and forsaketh shall have mercy." Prov. xxviii. 13.—*Isaac Craven's Sermon at Paul's Cross,* 1630.

Verse 5.—" *I said, I will confess,*" etc. Justified persons, who have their sins

---

* Augustine.   † Hilary.

forgiven, are yet bound to confess sin to God. . . . . There are many queries to be despatched in the handling of this point. The first query, is, what are the reasons why persons justified and pardoned are yet bound to make confession of sin unto God in private ? The reasons are six. First, they are to confess sin unto God because holy confession gives a great deal of ease and holy quiet unto the mind of a sinner : conceal edand indulged guilt constracts horror and dread on the conscience. Secondly, because God loves to hear the complaints and the confessions of his own people. Lying on the face is the best gesture, and the mourning weed the best garment that God is well pleased with. A third reason is, because confession of sin doth help to quicken the heart to strong and earnest supplication to God (see verse 6). Confession is to the soul as the whetstone is to the knife, that sharpens it and puts an edge on it ; so doth confession of sin. Confessing thy evils to God doth sharpen and put an edge on thy supplication ; that man will pray but faintly that doth confess sin but slightly. A fourth reason is, because confession of sin will work a holy contrition and a godly sorrow in the heart. (Psalm xxxviii. 18). Declaration doth work compunction. Confession of sin is but the causing of sin to recoil on the conscience, which causeth blushing and shame of face, and grief of heart. A fifth reason is, because secret confession of sin doth give a great deal of glory to God. It gives glory to God's justice. I do confess sin, and do confess God in justice may damn me for my sin. It gives glory to God's mercy. I confess sin, yet mercy may save me. It gives glory to God's omnisciency. In confessing sin I do acknowledge that God knoweth my sin. A sixth reason why justified persons must confess sin unto God is, because holy confession of sin will embitter sin, and endear Christ to them, when a man shall let sin recoil on his conscience by a confession.—*Condensed from Christopher Love's " Soul's Cordiall,"* 1683.

Verse 5.—*" I said I will confess . . . . and thou forgavest."* It remaineth as a truth, remission is undoubtedly annexed to confession. *Tantum valent tres syllabæ* PEC-CA-VI, saith St. Austin, of so great force are those three syllables in the Latin, three words in the English, when uttered with a contrite heart, *" I have sinned."—Nathanael Hardy.*

Verse 5.—*" Thou forgavest the iniquity of my sin."* This sin seems very probably to have been his adultery with Bathsheba, and murder of Uriah. Now David to make the pardoning mercy of God more illustrious, saith he did not only forgive his *sin*, but the *iniquity* of his sin ; and what was that ? Surely the worst that can be said of that, his complicated sin, is that there was so much hypocrisy in it, he woefully juggled with God and man in it ; this, I do not doubt to say, was *the iniquity* of his sin, and put a colour deeper on it than the blood which he shed. And the rather—I lay the accent there—because God himself, when he would set out the heinousness of this sin, seems to do it rather from the hypocrisy in the fact than the fact itself, as appears by the testimony given this holy man (1 Kings xv. 5): " David did that which was right in the eyes of the Lord, and turned not aside from anything that he commanded him all the days of his life, save only in the matter of Uriah the Hittite." Were there not other false steps which David took besides this ? Doth the Spirit of God, by excepting this, declare his approbation of all that else he ever did ? No, sure the Spirit of God records other sins that escaped this eminent servant of the Lord ; but all those are drowned here, and this mentioned as the only stain of his life. But why ? Surely because there appeared less sincerity, yea, more hypocrisy in this one sin than in all his others put together ; though David in them was wrong as to the matter of his actions, yet his heart was more right in the manner of committing them. But here his sincerity was sadly wounded, though not to the total destruction of the habit, yet to lay it in a long swoon, as to any actings thereof. And truly the wound went very deep when that grace was stabbed in which did run the life blood of all the rest. We see, then, God hath reason, though his mercy prompted him, yea, his covenant obliged him, not to let his child die of this wound, yet so to heal it that a scar might remain upon the place, a mark upon the sin, whereby others might know how odious hypocrisy is to God.—*William Gurnall.*

Verse 5.—*" Thou forgavest the iniquity of my sin."* We must observe the *matter forgiven,* and the *manner of forgiving.* The matter forgiven is the *iniquity of his sin.* It is disputed what is meant here by *iniquity,* whether *culpa* or *pœna.* Some under-stand *pœnam,* and think that an allusion is made in this word unto the message of Nathan, wherein God doth remit the heaviest stroke of his wrath, but yet retains some part in punishing the child, and permitting Absalom to rebel and abuse king

David's concubines: so Theodoret, *Deus non condigna pœna Davidem punivit.*
Some understand *culpam,* and will have this phrase to be an amplification of that,
as if *superbia defendens,* or *taciturnitas celans,* or *impietas contra Deum assurgens,* or
some such great guilt were meant by this phrase. But as I do not censure these
opinions, which may well stand, so I think the phrase looks back unto that word
which was in the *confession.* The sin confessed was עֶשַׁע, and this is but an analysis
of this word; for עֲוֹן חַטָּאתִי, what is it, word for word, but the *perverseness of my
aberration?* חַטָּאָה is an aberration from the scope or mark whereat we aim; all
men aim at felicity, but most men stray from it, because they are not led by the
law that guides unto it, the violating whereof is called חַטָּאָה. But some do stray out
of mere ignorance, and they only break the law; some out of stubbornness, which
will not submit themselves to the Lawgiver; these men's sin is called *perverseness,*
which God is said here to forgive. So that David did not confess more against
himself than God includes in his pardon. Well may God exceed our desire; he
never doth come short thereof if it do concern our spiritual, our eternal good. As
he doth exclude no sinner that doth confess, so doth he except against no sin that is
confessed.—*Arthur Lake.*

Verse 6.—" *For this shall every one that is godly pray unto thee in a time when thou
mayest be found,*" etc. Seeing he is such a God, who should refuse or delay his
return! Surely every rational and pious mind will, without delay, invoke so gentle
and mild a Lord; *will pray to him while he is exorable,* or, as the Hebrew expresses it,
in a time of finding. For he who promises pardon, does not promise to-morrow.
There are *tempora fandi*—certain times in which he may be spoken with, and a
certain appointed day of pardon and of grace, which if a man by stupid perverseness
despise, or by sloth neglect, surely he is justly overwhelmed with eternal might and
misery, and must necessarily perish by the deluge of divine wrath; since he has
contemned and derided that Ark of salvation which was prepared and in which
whoever enters into it shall be safe, while the world is perishing.—*Robert Leighton.*

Verse 6.—" *For this shall every one that is godly pray to thee,*" said David. " *For
this!*" What? Because of his sins. And who? Not the wickedest, but the
" *godly,*" in this respect, have cause to pray. And for what should he pray?
Surely, for renewed pardon, for increase of grace, and for the perfection of glory.
We cannot say we have no sin. Oh then, let us pray with David, "Enter not into
judgment with thy servant, O Lord!" Where there is a double emphasis observable
it is not *ab hoste,* but *a servo.* Though God's servant, yet he would not have God
to enter into judgment with him. And again, *ne intres,* it is the very entrance
into judgment that he dreads and prayeth against; not only do not *proceed,* but
not so much as enter.—*Nathanael Hardy.*

Verse 6.—" *For this shall every one that is godly.*" We are here furnished with a
fact which does not appear in the history of David. It is commonly supposed
that after his grievous fall, till Nathan reproved him, he had been careless and
stupefied; and this has often been adduced as a proof of the hardening nature of
sin. But the thing was far otherwise. He was all the while tortured in his mind
yet unwilling to humble himself before God, and condemn himself before men,
as he ought to have done. He kept silence, and endeavoured to pass off the distress
by time, palliation, and excuse. But the repression and concealment of his anguish
preyed not only upon his peace, but his health, and endangered life itself. At
length he was reduced to the deepest penitence, and threw himself, by an unqualified
confession, on the compassion of God. " *For this shall every one that is godly pray
unto thee.*" Here we see not only that all the godly pray, but every one of them
prays for pardon. This is the very thing which our Saviour teaches his disciples:
" When ye pray, say, Forgive us our trespasses." And this praying does not only
regard the manifestation of forgiving mercy, as some would have it but the exercise
of it.—*William Jay.*

Verse 6.—" *Godly.*" A godly man is like God, he hath the same judgment
with God! he thinks of things as God doth; he hath a God-like disposition; he
partakes of the divine nature. 2. Peter i. 4. A godly man doth bear God's name
and image: godliness is Godlikeness.—*Thomas Watson.*

Verse 6.—" *A time.*" There be seasons, which, if taken, sweeten actions, and
open the door for their better entertainment: Prov. xxv. 11, " A word fitly spoken
is like apples of gold in pictures of silver;" the Hebrew is, A word spoken upon
its wheels: fit times and seasons are wheels to carry words with great advantage.

And so for actions ; when things are done in due time they are beautiful, acceptable. When God gives rain to a land in season, how acceptable is it ! when a tree bears fruit in its season, it is grateful : so when angels or men do things seasonably, it is pleasing to the Lord Christ : there are fit times, which, if we miss, actions are unlovely, and miss of their aims. *" For this shall every one that is godly pray unto thee in a time when thou mayest be found."* There are times, if we have the wisdom to discern them, when prayer will be seasonable, acceptable, effectual.—*William Greenhill.*

Verse 6.—*" Surely in the floods of great waters they shall not come nigh unto him."* The effects of prayer heretofore have been wonderful. Prayer hath sent down hailstones from heaven to overcome five kings with their armies. Prayer hath shut up the windows of heaven that it should not rain, and again hath opened them that the earth might give her increase. Prayer hath stayed the swift course of the sun and caused it to go backward fifteen degrees. Prayer hath held God's hands that he could not strike when he was ready to plague his people. Prayer without any other help or means hath thrown down the strong walls of Jericho. Prayer hath divided the sea that the floods thereof could not come near the Israelites. In this place it delivereth the faithful man from all the dangers of this world. *" Surely in the floods of many waters they shall not come nigh unto him."* The sum is this, That no calamity of this world, no troubles of this life, no terrors of death, no guiltiness of sin, can be so great, but that a *" godly "* man by means of his faith and felicity in Christ shall wade out of them well enough. For howsoever other things go, still he shall have such a solace in his soul, such a comfort in his conscience, such a heaven in his heart, knowing himself reconciled to God and justified by faith, that *" Surely in the floods of many waters they shall not come nigh unto him."* Which, that it may better appear, I shall desire you to observe two things, the danger, the deliverance. The danger is in these words, *" In the floods of many waters ; "* where the tribulations that the godly man is subject to in this life are likened, first, to *waters ;* then, to *many* waters ; thirdly, to a *flood* of many waters. The deliverance is in these words, *" Surely they shall not come near him ; "* where the deliverance of the godly man hath three degrees also. First, *" they shall not come near ; "* secondly, *him,* *" they shall not come near him ; "* then, *surely*—*" surely they shall not come near him."*—*Thomas Playfere.*

Verse 6.—*" The floods of great waters."* The afflictions of the faithful are likened to *waters.* Fire and water have no mercy, we say. But of the two water is the worst. For any fire may be quenched with water ; but the force of water, if it begins to be violent, cannot by any power of man be resisted. But these our tribulations which are *" waters,"* are *" many* waters." Our common proverb is, *"* Seldom comes sorrow alone : " but as waters come rolling and waving many together, so the miseries of this life.—*Thomas Playfere.*

Verse 6.—*" Floods of great waters."*—Unfamiliar with the sudden flooding of thirsty water-courses, we seldom comprehend the full force of some of the most striking images in the Old and New Testaments.—*W. J. Conybeare, and J. S. Howson, in " Life and Epistles of St. Paul."*

Verse 6.—*" In the floods,"* etc.—Washed he may be, as Paul was in the shipwreck, but not drowned with those floods of great waters : be they never so great they are bounded.—*Joseph Trapp.*

Verse 6.—*" Him."* This word must in no case be omitted ; it helpeth us to answer a very strong objection. For it may be said, Many holy men have lost their goods, have suffered great torments in their body, have been troubled also in mind ; how then did not the *"* floods of many waters " come near them ? The word *" him "* helps us to answer. The very philosophers themselves reckoned their goods pertained no more to them, than, be it spoken with reverence and regard, the parings of their nails. Zenon hearing news he had lost all he had by sea, said only thus, Thou hast done very well, Fortune, to leave me nothing but my cloak. Another, called Anaxarchus, when as Nicocreon the tyrant commanded he should be beaten to death in a mortar, spake thus to the executioner, Beat and bray as long as thou wilt Anaxarchus his bag or satchel (so he called his own body), but Anaxarchus thou canst not touch. Yet these, making so small reckoning of their goods and body, set their mind notwithstanding at a high rate. The mind of a man is himself, say they. Hence it is that Julius Cæsar, when Amyclas the pilot was greatly afraid of the tempest, spake to him thus : What meanest thou to fear, base fellow ? dost thou not know thou carriest Cæsar with thee ? As if he should say,

Cæsar's body may well be drowned, as any other man's may ; but his mind, his magnanimity, his valour, his fortitude, can never be drowned. Thus far went philosophy ; but divinity goeth a degree further. For philosophy defineth *him,* that is, a man, by his reason, and the moral virtues of the mind ; but divinity defineth a Christian man by his faith, and his conjunction thereby with Christ. Excellently saith Saint Austin : Whence comes it that the soul dieth ? Because faith is not in it. Whence that the body dieth ? Because a soul is not in it. Therefore the soul of thy soul is faith. So that if we would know what is a faithful man, we must define him, not by his natural soul, as he is reasonable, but by the soul of his soul, which is his faith. And then we easily answer the objection, that a flood may come near a faithful man's goods, near his body, near his reasonable soul ; but to his faith, that is, to HIM, it can never come near.—*Thomas Playfere.*

Verse 6.—Few verses in the Psalms are harder to be understood than this : and none has given rise to more varied expositions among the commentators. " *For this.*" Some will have it : encouraged by this example, that after so foul a fall God so readily forgave. Others again : " *for this,*" namely, warned by this example, they who are holy shall make their prayers that they may not be permitted to fall as David did. Whichever be the sense, they well argue from this passage, that the state of absolute and enduring perfection is impossible to a Christian in this life.—*Lorinus, and Cajetan* (1469—1534), *quoted by Neale.*

Verse 7.—" *Thou art my hiding place.*" David does not say, " Thou art a hiding-place " merely as one among many ; or *the* " hiding-place," as the only one ; but, " Thou art *my* hiding-place." *There* lies all the excellency of the text. " He is *mine ;* I have embraced the offer of his salvation," says David ; " I have applied to him in my own person : I have, as a sinner, taken shelter in his love and compassion ; I have placed myself under his wings ; I have covered myself with the robe of his righteousness ; and now, therefore, I am safe." " Blessed is the man whose transgression is forgiven, whose sin is covered." This is having a part and a lot in the matter, having the personal and individual benefit of the Saviour's work of atonement. How different is an *appropriating* from a *speculative* faith ! Men tell us that they believe the doctrine, that they acknowledge the truth, that they .assent to our creed ; and they say, that to declare to them the character of Christ, as the sinner's only help and safety, is merely putting before them what they already know. Now, follow up the idea suggested by the figure in our text, and see the folly and danger of acting thus. Suppose a traveller upon a bleak and exposed heath to be alarmed by the approach of a storm. He looks out for shelter. But if his eye discern a place to hide him from the storm, does he stand still and say, " I see there *is* a shelter, and therefore I may remain where I am " ? Does he not betake himself to it ? Does he not run, in order to escape the stormy wind and tempest ? It was a " hiding-place " before ; but it was *his* hiding-place only when he ran into it, and was safe. Had he not gone into it, though it might have been a protection to a thousand other travellers who resorted there, to him it would have been as if no such place existed. Who does not see at once, from this simple illustration, that the blessings of the gospel are such only in their being *appropriated to* the soul ? The physician can cure only by being *applied to ;* the medicine can heal them by being *taken ;* money can enrich only by being *possessed ;* and the merchantman in the parable would have been none the wealthier for discovering that there was a " pearl of great price," had he not made it *his.* So with the salvation of the gospel : if Christ is the " Balm in Gilead," *apply* the remedy ; if he is the " Physician there," *go* to him ; if he is the " pearl of great price," sell all that you have and buy it ; and if he is the " hiding-place," *run into* it and be safe ; there will be no solid joy and peace in the mind until he is *your* " hiding-place."—*Fountain Elwin,* 1842.

Verse 7.—" *Thou art my hiding-place.*"—An allusion, probably, to the *city of refuge.*—*Adam Clarke.*

Verse 7.—" *Hiding place.*" Kirke White has a beautiful hymn upon this word, beginning, " Awake, sweet harp of Judah, wake." We have no room to quote it, but it will be found in " Our Own Hymn Book," No. 381.

Verse 7.—" *Thou shalt preserve me from trouble.*" If we content ourselves with that word which our translators have chosen here, " *trouble,*" we must rest in one of these two senses ; either that God shall arm, and indue those that are his with such a constancy, as those things that trouble others shall not trouble them ; but,

" As the sufferings of Christ abound in them, so their consolation also aboundeth by Christ:" "As unknown, and yet well known ; as dying, and behold we live ; as sorrowful, yet always rejoicing ; as poor, yet making many rich ; as having nothing, and yet possessing all things " (2 Cor. i. 5 ; vi. 9) ; for God uses both these ways in the behalf of his servants—sometimes to suspend the working of that that should work their torment, as he suspended the rage of the lions for Daniel, and the heat of the fire in the furnace for the others ; sometimes by imprinting a holy stupefaction and insensibleness in the person that suffers ; so St. Laurence was not only patient, but merry and facetious when he lay broiling upon the fire, and so we read of many other martyrs that have been less moved, less affected with their torments than their executioners or their persecutors have been. That which troubled others never troubled them ; or else the phrase must have this sense, that though they be troubled with their troubles, though God submit them so far to the common condition of men, that they be sensible of them, yet he shall preserve them from that trouble so as that it shall never overthrow them, never sink them into a dejection of spirit, or diffidence in his mercy ! they shall find storms, but a stout and strong ship under foot ; they shall feel thunder and lightning, but garlands of triumphant bays shall preserve them ; they shall be trodden into earth with scorns and contempts, but yet as seed is buried, to multiply to more. So far this word of our translators assists our devotion, " *Thou shalt preserve me from trouble,*" thou shalt make me insensible of it, or thou shalt make me victorious in it.—*John Donne.*

Verse 7.—" *Thou shalt compass me about with songs of deliverance.*" In these words the prophet David riseth up by a gradation, and goeth beyond that which he had formerly said concerning his confidence in God. First, he had said that God was his *hiding-place ;* secondly, that he would *preserve him in trouble ;* and now, thirdly, that the Lord would make him *joyful,* and to triumph over his troubles and enemies, by compassing him, instead of troubles, with mercies. . . . . Learn to acknowledge God's goodness to thyself with particular application, as David saith here, " Thou shalt compass *me* about with songs of deliverance." Not only confess his goodness to others, as to Abraham, Isaac, Jacob ; nor only his deliverance of Noah, Daniel, Lot ; but also his mercies to and deliverance of thyself, as Paul did : " Christ gave himself for *me,* and died for *me.*" Gal. ii. 20. This will exceedingly whet up thankfulness ; whereas only to acknowledge God good in himself, or to others, and not to thyself, will make thee murmur and repine.—*Thomas Taylor.*

Verse 7.—" *Thou shalt compass me about.*" This word importeth that as we are besieged on every side with troubles, so we are compassed with as many comforts and deliverances ; as our crosses grow daily, so our consolations are augmented day by day. We are on every side offended and on every side defended ; therefore we ought on every side to sound God's praise, as David saith, " Bless the Lord, O my soul ; and all that is within me." Ps. ciii. 1.—*Archibald Symson.*

Verse 7.—" *Songs of deliverance.*" In that he will not be content only with thanks, but also will have them conjoined with " *songs,*" he letteth us see how high all the strings of his heart are bended that he cannot contain himself for the mercies of God to his church, and for his manifold deliverances for the same. Many sing praises to God with an half-open mouth ; and, albeit, they can sing aloud any filthy ballad in their house, they make the mean, I warrant you, in the church, that scarce can they hear the sound of their own voice. I think they be ashamed to proclaim and show forth God's praises, or they fear to deafen God by their loud singing ; but David bended all his forces within and without to praise his God. *Archibald Symson.*

Verse 8.—" *I will instruct thee and teach thee in the way which thou shalt go.*" No other than God himself can undertake so much as is promised in the text. For here is faith, a rectifying of the understanding, " *I will instruct thee,*" and in the original there is somewhat more than our translation reaches to ; it is there, *Intelligere faciam te, I will make thee understand.* Man can instruct, God only can make us understand. And then it is *Faciam te,* I will make thee, *thee,* understand ; the work is the Lord's, the understanding is the man's : for God does not work in man as the devil did in idols and *in pythonissis,* and *in ventriloquis,* in possessed persons, who had no voluntary concurrence with the action of the devil, but were merely passive ; God works so in man as that he makes man work too, *faciam te,* I will make thee understand ; that that shall be done shall be done by me, but in thee ; the power that rectifies the act is God's, the act is man's ; *Faciam te,* says God, I

will make thee, *thee*, every particular person (for that arises out of this singular
and distributive word, *thee*, which threatens no exception, no exclusion), I will
make every person to whom I present instruction, capable of that instruction ;
and if he receive it not, it is only his, and not my fault.   And so this first part is an
instruction *de credendis*, of such things, as by God's rectifying of our understanding
we are bound to believe.   And then, in a second part, there follows a more particular
instructing, *Docebo*, " *I will teach thee*," and that *in via*, " *in the way ;* " it is not
only *de via*, to teach thee which is the way, that thou mayst find it, but *in via*, how
to keep the way when thou art in it ; he will teach thee, not only *ut gradiaris*, that
thou mayst walk in it, but *quomodo gradieris*, that thou mayst walk in
it and not stray ; and so this second part is an institution *de agendis*, of those things
which thine understanding being formerly rectified, and deduced into a belief,
thou art bound to do.   And then in the last words of the text, " *I will guide thee
with mine eye*," there is a third part, an establishment, a confirmation, by an
incessant watchfulness in God ; he will consider, consult upon us (for so much the
original word imports) he will not leave us to contingencies, to fortune ; no, nor
to his own general providence, by which all creatures are universally in his protection
and administration, but he will ponder us, consider us, study us ; and that with
his eye, which is the sharpest and most sensible organ and instrument, soonest
feels if anything be amiss, and so inclines him quickly to rectify us ; and so this
third part is an instruction *de sperandis*, it hath evermore a relation to the future.
to the constancy and perseverance of God's goodness towards us ; to the end, and
in the end he will guide us with his eye : except the eye of God can be put out we
cannot be put out of his sight and his care.   So that, both our freight which we are
to take in, that is, what we are to believe concerning God ; and the voyage which we
are to make, how we are to steer and govern our course, that is, our behaviour and
conversation in the household of the faithful ; and then the haven to which we
must go, that is, our assurance of arriving at the heavenly Jerusalem, are expressed
in this chart, in this map, in this instruction, in this text.—*John Donne.*

   Verse 8.—This threefold repetition, " *I will instruct thee*," " *I will teach thee*,"
" *I will guide thee*," teaches us three properties of a good teacher.   First, to make
the people understand the way of salvation ; secondly, to go before them; thirdly,
to watch over them and their ways.—*Archibald Symson.*

   Verse 8.—" *The way.*"   If we compare this way with all other ways, it will whet
our care to enter into and continue in it ; for, first, this is the *King's highway*, in
which we have promise of protection. Ps. xci. 11.   Secondly, God's ways are the
cleanest of all. 2 Sam. xxii. 31.   Thirdly, God's ways are the *rightest* ways ; and,
being rightest, they be also the *shortest* ways.   Hosea xiv. 9.   Fourthly, God's ways
are most *lightsome* and *cheerful*.   Prov. iii. 17.   Therefore, God's ways being the
safest, cleanest, rightest, shortest, and lightsomest ways, we must be careful to
walk in them.—*Condensed from Thomas Taylor.*

   Verse 8.—" *I will guide thee with mine eye.*"   We read in natural story[*] of some
creatures, *Qui solo oculorum aspectu fovent ova*,[†] which hatch their eggs only by
looking upon them.   What cannot the eye of God produce and hatch in us ?   *Plus
est quod probatur aspectu, quam quod sermone.*[‡]   A man may seem to commend
in words, and yet his countenance shall dispraise.   His word infuses good purposes
into us ; but if God continue his eye upon us it is a further approbation, for he is a
God of pure eyes, and will not look upon the wicked. " This land doth the Lord
thy God care for, and the eyes of the Lord are always upon it from the beginning of
the year, even to the end thereof."   Deut. xi. 12.   What a cheerful spring, what a
fruitful autumn hath that soul, that hath the eye of the Lord always upon her !
The eye of the Lord upon me makes midnight noon ; it makes Capricorn Cancer,
and the winter's the summer's solstice ; the eye of the Lord sanctifies, nay, more
than sanctifies, glorifies all the eclipses of dishonour, makes melancholy cheerfulness,
diffidence assurance, and turns the jealousy of the sad soul into infallibility. . . . This
guiding us with his eye manifests itself in these two great effects ; conversion to
him, and union with him.   First, his eye works upon ours ; his eye turns ours to
look upon him.   Still it is so expressed with an *Ecce ;* " Behold the eye of the Lord is

---

[*] A reviewer remarks upon the bad natural history which we quote.   We reply that to alter
it would be to spoil the allusions, and we are making a book for men, not for babes.   No person
in his senses is likely at this day to believe the fables which in former ages passed current for
facts.

[†] Pliny.   [‡] Ambrose.

upon all them that fear him ; " his eye calls ours to behold that ; and then our eye calls upon his, to observe our cheerful readiness. . . . When, as a well made picture doth always look upon him that looks upon it, this image of God in our soul is turned to him, by his turning to it, it is impossible we should do any foul, any uncomely thing in his presence. . . . The other great effect of his guiding us with his eye, is, that it unites us to himself ; when he fixes his eye upon us, and accepts the return of ours to him, then he " keeps " us as the " apple " of his " eye." Zech. ii. 8. . . . These are the two great effects of his guiding us by his eye, that first, his eye turns us to himself, and then turns us into himself ; first, his eye turns ours to him, and then, that makes us all one with himself, so as that our afflictions shall be put upon his patience, and our dishonours shall be injurious to him ; we cannot be safer than by being his ; but thus we are not only his, but he—to every persecutor, in every one of our behalf, he shall say, *Cur me ?* Why persecutest thou me ? And as he is all power, and can defend us, so here he makes himself all eye, which is the most tender part, and most sensible of our pressures.—*Condensed from John Donne.*

Verse 8.—" *I will guide thee with mine eye.*" Marg., *I will counsel thee, mine eye shall be upon thee.* The margin expresses the sense of the Hebrew. The literal *meaning* is, " I will counsel thee ; mine eye shall be upon thee." De Wette : " my eye shall be directed towards thee." The *idea* is that of one who is telling another what way he is to take in order that he may reach a certain place ; and he says he will watch him, or will keep an eye upon him ; he will not let him go wrong.— *Albert Barnes.*

Verse 8.—" *Mine eye.*" We may consider mercies as the beamings of the Almighty's eye when the light of his countenance is lifted up upon us ; and that man as guided by the eye, whom mercies attract and attach to his Maker. But oh ! let us refuse to be guided by the eye, and it will become needful that we be curbed with the hand. If we abuse our mercies, if we forget their Author, and yield him not gratefully the homage of our affections, we do but oblige him, by his love for our souls, to apportion us disaster and trouble. Complain not, then, that there is so much of sorrow in your lot ; but consider rather how much of it you may have wilfully brought upon yourselves. Listen to the voice of God. " *I will instruct thee and teach thee in the way which thou shalt go : I will guide thee with mine eye* "— mine eye, whose glance gilds all that is beautiful, whose light disperses all darkness prevents all danger, diffuses all happiness. And why, then, is it that ye are sorely disquieted ? why is it that " fear and the pit " are so often upon you ; that one blessing after another disappears from your circle ; and that God seems to deal with you as with the wayward and unruly, on whom any thing of gentleness would be altogether lost ? Ah ! if you would account for many mercies that have departed, if you would insure permanence to those that are yet left, examine how deficient you may hitherto have been, and strive to be more diligent for the future, in obeying an admonition which implies that we should be guided by the soft lustres of the eye, if our obduracy did not render indispensible the harsh constraints of the rein. *Henry Melvill.*

Verse 9.—" *Be ye not as the horse, or as the mule,*" etc. How many run mad of this cause, inordinate and furious lusts ! The prophet Jeremiah, chap. ii. 24, compareth Israel to " a swift dromedary, traversing her ways," and to a " wild ass used to the wilderness, that snuffeth up the wind at her pleasure." " *Be ye not,*" saith the Psalmographer, " as the horse, or as the mule, which have no under- standing : whose mouth must be held in with bit and bridle." Men have under- standing, not beasts ; yet when the frenzy of lust overwhelmeth their senses, we may take up the word of the prophet and pour it on them : " Every man is a beast by his own knowledge." And therefore " man that is in honour and understandeth not, is like unto beasts that perish " (Ps. xlix. 20). Did not the bridle of God's overruling providence restrain their madness, they would cast off the saddle of reason, and kick nature itself in the face.—*Thomas Adams.*

Verse 9.—" *Be ye not as the horse, or as the mule,*" etc. According to the several natures of these two beasts, the fathers and other expositors have made several interpretations ; at least, several allusions. They consider the horse and the mule to admit any rider, any burden, without discretion or difference, without debatement or consideration ;   they never ask whether their rider be noble or base, nor whether their load be gold for the treasure, or roots for the market. And those **expositors** find the same indifference in an habitual sinner to any kind of sin; whether he sin for pleasure, or sin for profit, or sin but for company, still he sins. They consider in the mule, that one of his parents being more ignoble than the other, he is likest the worst, he hath more of the ass than of the horse in him; and they find in us, that all our actions and thoughts taste more of the ignobler part of earth than of heaven. St. Hierome thinks fierceness and rashness to be presented in the horse, and sloth in the mule. And St. Augustine carries these two qualities far; he thinks that in this fierceness of the horse the Gentiles are represented, which ran far from the knowledge of Christianity; and by the laziness of the mule the Jews, who came nothing so fast, as they were invited by their former helps to the embracing thereof. They have gone far in these allusions and applications; and they might have gone as far further as it had pleased them; they have sea-room enough, that will compare a beast and a sinner together; and they shall find many times, in the way, the beast the better man.—*John Donne.*

Verse 9.—"*Be ye not as the horse, or as the mule,*" etc. Consider the causes why a broken leg is incurable in a horse, and easily curable in a man. The horse is incapable of counsel to submit himself to the farrier; and therefore in case his leg be set he flings, flounces, and flies out, unjointing it again by his misemployed mettle, counting all binding to be shackles and fetters unto him: whereas a man willingly resigns himself to be ordered by the *surgeon*, preferring rather to be a prisoner for some days, than a cripple all his life. "*Be ye not as the horse, or as the mule, which have no understanding;*" but "let patience have its perfect work in thee." James i. 4.—*Thomas Fuller.*

Verse 9.—"*Bit and bridle.*" מֶתֶג־וָרֶסֶן. The LXX render the first of these two words by χαλινῷ, the second by κημῷ. The word χαλινός signifies the iron of the common bridle, which is put into the horse's mouth, the bit, or curb. But κημός was something like a muzzle, which was put upon mischievous horses or mules to hinder them from biting. Xenophon says, that it allowed them to breathe, but kept the mouth shut, so that they could not bite. Not knowing the term of art for this contrivance, I call it a muzzle. The verb קרב is a military term, and signifies to advance, as an enemy, to attack. The "coming near," therefore, intended here, is a coming near to do mischief. The admonition given by the Psalmist to his companions, is to submit to the instruction and guidance graciously promised from heaven, and not to resemble, in a refractory disposition, those ill-conditioned colts which are not to be governed by a simple bridle; but, unless their jaws are confined by a muzzle, will attack the rider as he attempts to mount, or the groom as he leads them to the pasture and the stable.—*Samuel Horsley.*

Verse 9.—"*Lest they come near unto thee.*" The common version of this clause would be suitable enough in speaking of a wild beast, but in reference to a mule or a horse the words can only mean, because they will not follow or obey thee of their own accord; they must be constantly coerced, in the way both of compulsion and restraint.—*J. A. Alexander.*

Verse 9.—"Be ye not like a horse or mule, which have no understanding, and whose ornament is a bridle and bit, to hold them: they do not come unto thee *of themselves.*"—*Charles Carter, in "The Book of Psalms."* 1869. [*A new Translation.*]

Verse 10.—"*He that trusteth in the Lord, mercy shall compass him about.*" Even as in the midst of the sphere is the centre, from which all lines being drawn do tend towards their circumference: so a good Christian man hath God for his circumference; for whatever he thinketh, speaketh, or doth, it tendeth to Christ, of whom he is compassed round about.—*Robert Cawdray.*

Verse 10.—"*Mercy shall compass him about.*" He shall be *surrounded* with mercy—as one is surrounded by the air, or by the sunlight. He shall find mercy and favour everywhere—at home, abroad; by day, by night; in society, in solitude; in sickness, in health; in life, in death; in time, in eternity. He shall walk amidst mercies; he shall die amidst mercies; he shall live in a better world in the midst of eternal mercies.—*Albert Barnes.*

Verse 10.—"Mark that text," said Richard Adkins to his grandson Abel, who was reading to him the thirty-second Psalm. "Mark that text, 'He that trusteth in the Lord, mercy shall compass him about.' I read it in my youth and believed it; and now I read it in my old age, thank God, I know it to be true. Oh! it is a blessed thing in the midst of the joys and sorrows of the world, Abel, to trust in the Lord."—*The Christian Treasury,* 1848.

Verse 11.—"*Be glad in the Lord, and rejoice, ye righteous : and shout for joy, all ye that are upright in heart.*" This exhortation containeth three parts. First, what he doth exhort unto, *to rejoice.* Secondly, whom, the *righteous,* and *upright men.* Thirdly, the limitation, "*in the Lord.*" He exhorteth them three times—be glad, rejoice, and be joyful ; and as he made mention of a threefold blessing, so doth he of a threefold joy. Wherein we have two things necessary to be observed. First, the dulness of our natures, who as slow horses need many spurs and provocations to spiritual things, whereas we are naturally overmuch bent to carnal things, that we need no incitations thereunto. But by the contrary in spiritual things, we are cast into a deep sleep, who cannot be awakened at the first cry ; but as men after drink have need to be roused often, that they may behold the light ; so men drunken with the pleasures of sin, as Nazianzen saith, must be wakened by divers exhortations ; as this same prophet in the subsequent Psalm redoubleth his exhortations for the same effect. And the apostle to Philippians saith : "Rejoice in the Lord alway : and again I say, Rejoice" (chap. iv. 4). Next, perceive that this exhortation grows ; for the word *be glad,* properly in the original signifieth an inward and hearty joy, by the presence or hope at least of a thing desirable or good. The word *rejoice,* to express our joy by some outward gesture, sometimes used for dancing, as, "The hills skip for gladness." Ps. lxv. 12. The word *be joyful,* to cry for gladness, as the dumb man's tongue shall sing. This gradation teacheth us, that this is the nature of spiritual joy—that it still increaseth in us by certain degrees, until it come to the perfection of all joy, which is signified by the last word, importing, as it were, a triumph and shouting after victory. So that they are truly penitent who have overcome sin and Satan in their spiritual combat, and have triumphed over them as vanquished enemies.—*Archibald Symson.*

Verse 11.—"*Be glad in the Lord, and rejoice, ye righteous.*" There is never a joyful man alive but a believer. Will you say that men take pleasure in their sins ? Why, that is the *Devil's* joy ; or that they rejoice in full barns and bags ? That is the *fool's* joy ; or that they rejoice in wine, that is, all dainties that gratify the palate ? That is a *Bedlam* joy. Read and believe Eccl. ii. 3 ; indeed, from the first verse to the eleventh, the whole book, but especially that chapter, is the divinest philosophy that ever was or will be.—*Christopher Fowler* (1610—1678), *in "Morning Exercises."*

Verse 11.—"*Shout for joy, all ye that are upright in heart.*" When the poet Carpani enquired of his friend Haydn, how it happened that his church music was so cheerful, the great composer made a most beautiful reply. "I cannot," he said, "make it otherwise, I write according to the thoughts I feel : when I think upon God, my heart is so full of joy that the notes dance and leap, as it were, from my pen : and, since God has given me a cheerful heart, it will be pardoned me that I serve him with a cheerful spirit.—*John Whitecross's Anecdotes.*

Verse 11.—Here the sensual man, that haply would catch hold when it is said, "*Rejoice,*" by-and-by, when it is added, "*in the Lord,*" will let his hold go. But they that, by reason of the billows and waves of the troublesome sea of this world, cannot brook the speech when it is said, "*Rejoice,*" are to lay sure hold fast upon it when it is added, "*Rejoice in the Lord.*"—*Henry Airay.*

Verse 11.

O sing unto this glittering, glorious King ;
O praise his name, let every living thing ;
Let heart and voice, like bells of silver ring
The comfort that this day doth bring.

Kinwellmersh, quoted by A. Moody Stuart.

Verse 11.—It is storied by the famous Tully concerning Syracuse, that there is no day throughout the whole year so stormy and tempestuous in which the inhabitants have not some glimpse and sight of the sun. The like observation may be truly made on all those Psalms of David in which his complaints are most multiplied, his fears and pressures most insisted on ; that there is not any of them so totally overcast with the black darkness of despair, but that we may easily discern them to be here and there intervened and streaked with some comfortable expressions of his faith and hope in God. If in the beginning of a Psalm we find him restless in his motions, like Noah's dove upon the overspreading waters ; yet in the close we shall see him like the same dove returning with an olive branch in its mouth, and fixing upon the ark. If we find him in another Psalm staggering in the midst of his distresses, through the prevalency of carnal fears, we may also in it behold him recovering himself again, by fetching arguments from faith, whose topics are of a higher elevation than to be shaken by the timorous suggestions that arise from the flesh. If at another time we behold him like to a boat on drift, that is, tossed and beaten by the inconstant winds and fierce waves; yet we shall still find all his rollings and agitations to be such as carry him towards the standing shore, where he rides at last both in peace and safety.—*William Spurstowe.*

HINTS TO PREACHERS.

Verse 1.—Gospel benedictions. Take the first Psalm with thirty-second, show the doctrinal and practical harmoniously blended. Or, take the first, the thirty-second, and the forty-first, and show how we go from reading the word, to feeling its power, and thence to living charitably towards men.

Verse 1.—*Evangelical Blessedness.* I. The original condition of its possessor. II. The nature of the benefit received. III. The channel by which it came. IV. The means by which it may be obtained by us.

Verses 1, 2.—The nature of sin and the modes of pardon.

Verse 2.—Non-imputation, a remarkable doctrine. Prove, explain, and improve it.

Verse 2.—" *No guile.*" The honesty of heart of the pardoned man.

Verse 3.—*Retention of our griefs to ourselves.* Natural tendency of timidity and despair; danger of it; means of divulging grief; encouragements to do so; the blessed person who is ready to hear confession.

The silent mourner the greatest sufferer.

Verses 3, 4.—" Terrible Convictions and Gentle Drawings." See " Spurgeon's Sermons," No. 313.

Verse 4.—The sorrows of a convinced soul. Daily, nightly, from God, heavy, weakening, destroying.

Verse 4 (last clause).—Spiritual drought.

Verse 5.—The gracious results of a full confession; or, confession and absolution scripturally explained.

Verse 6.—The *godly* man's picture, drawn with a Scripture pencil.—*Thomas Watson.*

Verse 6.—The experience of one, the encouragement of all.

Verse 6 (first clause).—The day of grace, how to improve it.

Verse 6 (whole verse).—Pardon of sin the guarantee that other mercies shall be given.

Verse 6 (last clause).—Imminent troubles, eminent deliverances.

Verse 6 (last clause).—The felicity of the faithful.—*Thomas Playfere.*

Verse 7.—Danger felt, refuge known, possession claimed, joy experienced.

Verse 7 (first sentence).—Christ, a hiding-place from sin, Satan, and sorrow, in death, and at judgment.

Verse 7 (second sentence).—Troubles from which saints shall be preserved.

Verse 7 (last sentence).—The circle of song—who draws the circle, what is the circumference, who is in the centre.

Verse 7.—" *Songs of deliverance.*" From guilt, hell, death, enemies, doubts, temptations, accidents, plots, etc.

The divine schoolmaster, his pupils, their lessons, their chastisements and their rewards.

Verse 8.—The power of the eye.—*Henry Melvill.* In which he vainly tries to prove infant baptism and episcopacy, which he admits are not expressly taught in Scripture, but declares them to be hinted at as with the divine eye.

Verse 9.—God's bits and bridles, the mules who need them, and reasons why we ought not to be of the number.

Verse 9.—How far in our actions we are better, and how far worse than horses and mules.

Verse 10.—The many sorrows which result from sin. The encompassing mercy of the believer's life even in his most troublous times.

The portion of the wicked, and the lot of the faithful.

Verse 11.—A believer's gladness. *Its spring*, " in the Lord ; " *its vivacity*, " shout ; " *its propriety*, it is commanded ; *its beneficial results and its abundant reasons*.

Verse 11.—" *Upright in heart*," an instructive description. Not horizontal or grovelling, nor bent, nor inclined, but vertical in heart.

PSALM XXXIII.

TITLE.—*This song of praise bears no title or indication of authorship ; to teach us, says Dickson, " to look upon holy Scripture as altogether inspired of God, and not put price upon it for the writers thereof."*

SUBJECT AND DIVISIONS.—*The praise of Jehovah is the subject of this sacred song. The righteous are exhorted to praise him, verses* 1—3 ; *because of the excellency of his character,* 4, 5 ; *and his majesty in creation,* 6, 7. *Men are bidden to fear before Jehovah becauses his purposes are accomplished in providence,* 8—11. *His people are proclaimed blessed,* 12. *The omniscience and omnipotence of God, and his care of his people are celebrated, in opposition to the weakness of an arm of flesh,* 13—19 ; *and the Psalm concludes with a fervent expression of confidence,* 20, 21, *and an earnest prayer,* 22.

EXPOSITION.

REJOICE in the LORD, O ye righteous : *for* praise is comely for the upright.

2 Praise the LORD with harp : sing unto him with the psaltery *and* an instrument of ten strings.

3 Sing unto him a new song ; play skilfully with a loud noise.

1. *" Rejoice in the Lord."* Joy is the soul of praise. To delight ourselves in God is most truly to extol him, even if we let no notes of song proceed from our lips. That God is, and that he is such a God, and our God, ours for ever and ever, should wake within us an unceasing and overflowing joy. To rejoice in temporal comforts is dangerous, to rejoice in self is foolish, to rejoice in sin is fatal, but to rejoice in God is heavenly. He who would have a double heaven must begin below to rejoice like those above. *" O ye righteous."* This is peculiarly your duty, your obligations are greater, and your spiritual nature more adapted to the work, be ye then first in the glad service. Even the righteous are not always glad, and have need to be stirred up to enjoy their privileges. *" For praise is comely for the upright."* God has an eye to things which are becoming. When saints wear their choral robes, they look fair in the Lord's sight. A harp suits a blood-washed hand. No jewel more ornamental to a holy face than sacred praise. Praise is not comely from unpardoned professional singers ; it is like a jewel of gold in a swine's snout. Crooked hearts make crooked music, but the upright are the Lord's delight. Praise is the dress of saints in heaven, it is meet that they should fit it on below.

2. *" Praise the Lord with harp."* Men need all the help they can get to stir them up to praise. This is the lesson to be gathered from the use of musical instruments under the old dispensation. Israel was at school, and used childish things to help her to learn ; but in these days, when Jesus gives us spiritual manhood, we can make melody without strings and pipes. We who do not believe these things to be expedient in worship, lest they should mar its simplicity, do not affirm them to be unlawful, and if any George Herbert or Martin Luther can worship God better by the aid of well-tuned instruments, who shall gainsay their right ? *We* do not need them, they would hinder than help our praise, but if others are otherwise minded, are they not living in gospel liberty ? *" Sing unto him."* This is the sweetest and best of music. No instrument like the human voice. As a help to singing the instrument is alone to be tolerated, for keys and strings do not praise the Lord. *" With the psaltery and an instrument of ten strings."* The Lord must have a full octave, for all notes are his, and all music belongs to him. Where several pieces of music are mentioned, we are taught to praise God with all the powers which we possess.

3. *" Sing unto him a new song."* All songs of praise should be *" unto him."* Singing for singing's sake is nothing worth ; we must carry our tribute to the King, and not cast it to the winds. Do most worshippers mind this ? Our faculties should be exercised when we are magnifying the Lord, so as not to run in an old groove without thought ; we ought to make every hymn of praise a new song. To keep up the freshness of worship is a great thing, and in private it is indispensable.

Let us not present old worn-out praise, but put life, and soul, and heart, into every song, since we have new mercies every day, and see new beauties in the work and word of our Lord. *"Play skilfully."* It is wretched to hear God praised in a slovenly manner. He deserves the best that we have. Every Christian should endeavour to sing according to the rules of the art, so that he may keep time and tune with the congregation. The sweetest tunes and the sweetest voices, with the sweetest words, are all too little for the Lord our God; let us not offer him limping rhymes, set to harsh tunes, and growled out by discordant voices. *"With a loud noise."* Heartiness should be conspicuous in divine worship. Well-bred whispers are disreputable here. It is not that the Lord cannot hear us, but that it is natural for great exultation to express itself in the loudest manner. Men shout at the sight of their kings: shall we offer no loud hosannahs to the Son of David?

4 For the word of the LORD *is* right; and all his works *are done* in truth.

5 He loveth righteousness and judgment: the earth is full of the goodness of the LORD.

4. *"For the word of the Lord is right."* His ordinances both natural, moral, and spiritual, are right, and especially his incarnate Word, who is the Lord our righteousness. Whatever God has ordained must be good, and just, and excellent. There are no anomalies in God's universe, except what sin has made; his word of command made all things good. When we look at his word of promise, and remember its faithfulness, what reasons have we for joy and thankfulness! *"And all his works are done in truth."* His work is the outflow of his word, and it is true to it. He neither doth nor saith anything ill; in deed and speech he agrees with himself and the purest truth. There is no lie in God's word, and no sham in his works; in creation, providence, and revelation, unalloyed truth abounds. To act truth as well as to utter it is divine, let not children of God ever yield their principles in practice any more than in heart. What a God we serve! The more we know of him, the more our better natures approve his surpassing excellence; even his afflicting works are according to his truthful word.

> "Why should I complain of want or distress,
> Affliction or pain? he told me no less;
> The heirs of salvation, I know from his word,
> Through much tribulation must follow their Lord."

God writes with a pen that never blots, speaks with a tongue that never slips, acts with a hand which never fails. Bless his name.

5. *"He loveth righteousness and judgment."* The theory and the practice of right he intensely loves. He doth not only approve the true and the just, but his inmost soul delights therein. The character of God is a sea, every drop of which should become a wellhead of praise for his people. The righteousness of Jesus is peculiarly dear to the Father, and for its sake he takes pleasure in those to whom it is imputed. Sin, on the other hand, is infinitely abhorrent to the Lord, and woe unto those who die in it; if he sees no righteousness in them, he will deal righteously with them, and judgment stern and final will be the result. *"The earth is full of the goodness of the Lord."* Come hither, astronomers, geologists, naturalists, botanists, chemists, miners, yea, all of you who study the works of God, for all your truthful stories confirm this declaration. From the midge in the sunbeam to leviathan in the ocean all creatures own the bounty of the Creator. Even the pathless desert blazes with some undiscovered mercy, and the caverns of ocean conceal the treasures of love. Earth might have been as full of terror as of grace, but instead thereof it teems and overflows with kindness. He who cannot see it, and yet lives in it as the fish lives in the water, deserves to die. If earth be full of mercy, what must heaven be where goodness concentrates its beams?

6 By the word of the LORD were the heavens made; and all the host of them by the breath of his mouth.

7 He gathereth the waters of the sea together as an heap: he layeth up the depth in storehouses.

6. *"By the word of the Lord were the heavens made."* The angelic heavens, the sidereal heavens, and the firmament or terrestrial heavens, were all made to start

into existence by a word; what if we say by *the* Word, "For without him was not anything made that is made." It is interesting to note the mention of the Spirit in the next clause, "*and all the host of them by the breath of his mouth;*" the word "*breath*" is the same as is elsewhere rendered Spirit. Thus the three persons of the Godhead unite in creating all things. How easy for the Lord to make the most ponderous orbs, and the most glorious angels! A word, a breath could do it. It is as easy for God to create the universe as for a man to breathe, nay, far easier, for man breathes not independently, but borrows the breath in his nostrils from his Maker. It may be gathered from this verse that the constitution of all things is from the infinite wisdom, for his word may mean his appointment and determination. A wise and merciful Word has arranged, and a living Spirit sustains all the creation of Jehovah.

7. "*He gathereth the waters of the sea together as an heap.*" The waters were once scattered like corn strewn upon a threshing floor: they are now collected in one spot as an heap. Who else could have gathered them into one channel but their great Lord, at whose bidding the waters fled away? The miracle of the Red Sea is repeated in nature day by day, for the sea which now invades the shore under the impulse of sun and moon, would soon devour the land if bounds were not maintained by the divine decree. "*He layeth up the depth in storehouses.*" The depths of the main are God's great cellars and storerooms for the tempestuous element. Vast reservoirs of water are secreted in the bowels of the earth, from which issue our springs and wells of water. What a merciful provision for a pressing need? May not the text also refer to the clouds, and the magazines of hail, and snow, and rain, those treasuries of merciful wealth for the fields of earth? These aqueous masses are not piled away as in lumber rooms, but in storehouses for future beneficial use. Abundant tenderness is seen in the foresight of our heavenly Joseph, whose granaries are already filled against earth's time of need. These stores might have been, as once they were, the ammunition of vengeance, they are now a part of the commissariat of mercy.

8 Let all the earth fear the Lord: let all the inhabitants of the world stand in awe of him.

9 For he spake, and it was *done;* he commanded, and it stood fast.

10 The LORD bringeth the counsel of the heathen to nought: he maketh the devices of the people of none effect.

11. The counsel of the LORD standeth for ever, the thoughts of his heart to all generations.

8. "*Let all the earth fear the Lord.*" Not only Jews, but Gentiles. The Psalmist was not a man blinded by national prejudice, he did not desire to restrict the worship of Jehovah to the seed of Abraham. He looks for homage even to far-off nations. If they are not well enough instructed to be able to praise at least let them fear. There is an inferior kind of worship in the trembling which involuntarily admits the boundless power of the thundering God. A defiant blasphemer is out of place in a world covered with tokens of the divine power and Godhead: the whole earth cannot afford a spot congenial for the erection of a synagogue of Atheism, nor a man in whom it is becoming to profane the name of God. "*Let all the inhabitants of the world stand in awe of him.*" Let them forsake their idols, and reverently regard the only living God. What is here placed as a wish may also be read as a prophecy: the adoration of God will yet be universal.

9. "*For he spake, and it was done.*" Creation was the fruit of a word. Jehovah said, "Light be," and light was. The Lord's acts are sublime in their ease and instantaneousness. "What a word is this?" This was the wondering enquiry of old, and it may be ours to this day. "*He commanded, and it stood fast.*" Out of nothing creation stood forth, and was confirmed in existence. The same power which first uplifted, now makes the universe to abide; although we may not observe it, there is as great a display of sublime power in confirming as in creating. Happy is the man who has learned to lean his all upon the sure word of him who built the skies!

10. "*The Lord bringeth the counsel of the heathen to nought.*" While his own will is done, he takes care to anticipate the wilfulness of his enemies. Before they **come** to action he vanquishes them in the council-chamber; and when, well armed

with craft, they march to the assault, he frustrates their knaveries, and makes their promising plots to end in nothing. Not only the folly of the heathen, but their wisdom too, shall yield to the power of the cross of Jesus : what a comfort is this to those who have to labour where sophistry, and philosophy, falsely so called, are set in opposition to the truth as it is in Jesus. *" He maketh the devices of the people of none effect."* Their persecutions, slanders, falsehoods, are like puff-balls flung against a granite wall—they produce no result at all ; for the Lord overrules the evil, and brings good out of it. The cause of God is never in danger : infernal craft is outwitted by infinite wisdom, and Satanic malice held in check by boundless power.

11. *" The counsel of the Lord standeth for ever."* He changes not his purpose, his decree is not frustrated, his designs are accomplished. God has a predestination according to the counsel of his will, and none of the devices of his foes can thwart his decree for a moment. Men's purposes are blown to and fro like the thread of the gossamer or the down of the thistle, but the eternal purposes are firmer than the earth. *" The thoughts of his heart to all generations."* Men come and go, sons follow their sires to the grave, but the undisturbed mind of God moves on in unbroken serenity, producing ordained results with unerring certainty. No man can expect his will or plan to be carried out from age to age ; the wisdom of one period is the folly of another, but the Lord's wisdom is always wise, and his designs run on from century to century. His power to fulfil his purposes is by no means diminished by the lapse of years. He who was absolute over Pharaoh in Egypt is not one whit the less to-day the King of kings and Lord of lords ; still do his chariot wheels roll onward in imperial grandeur, none being for a moment able to resist his eternal will.

12 Blessed *is* the nation whose God *is* the LORD ; *and* the people *whom* he hath chosen for his own inheritance.

12. *" Blessed is the nation whose God is the Lord."* Israel was happy in the worship of the only true God. It was the blessedness of the chosen nation to have received a revelation from Jehovah. While others grovelled before their idols, the chosen people were elevated by a spiritual religion which introduced them to the invisible God, and led them to trust in him. All who confide in the Lord are blessed in the largest and deepest sense, and none can reverse the blessing. *" And the people whom he hath chosen for his own inheritance."* Election is at the bottom of it all. The divine choice rules the day ; none take Jehovah to be their God till he takes them to be his people. What an ennobling choice this is ! We are selected to no mean estate, and for no ignoble purpose : we are made the peculiar domain and delight of the Lord our God. Being so blessed, let us rejoice in our portion, and show the world by our lives that we serve a glorious Master.

13 The LORD looketh from heaven ; he beholdeth all the sons of men.

14 From the place of his habitation he looketh upon all the inhabitants of the earth.

15 He fashioneth their hearts alike ; he considereth all their works.

16 There is no king saved by the multitude of an host ; a mighty man is not delivered by much strength.

17 An horse *is* a vain thing for safety ; neither shall he deliver *any* by his great strength.

18 Behold, the eye of the LORD *is* upon them that fear him, upon them that hope in his mercy ;

19 To deliver their soul from death, and to keep them alive in famine.

13. *" The Lord looketh from heaven."* The Lord is represented as dwelling above and looking down below ; seeing all things, but peculiarly observing and caring for those who trust in him. It is one of our choicest privileges to be always under our Father's eye, to be never out of sight of our best Friend. *" He beholdeth all the sons of men."* All Adam's sons are as well watched as was Adam himself, their lone progenitor in the garden. Ranging from the frozen pole to the scorching equator, dwelling in hills and valleys, in huts and palaces, alike doth the divine eye regard all the members of the family of man.

14. *From the place of his habitation he looketh upon all the inhabitants of the earth."* Here the sentiment is repeated : it is worth repeating, and it needs repeating, for man is most prone to forget it. As great men sit at their windows and watch the crowd below, so doth the Lord ; he gazeth intently upon his responsible creatures, and forgets nothing of what he sees.

15. *" He fashioneth their hearts alike."* By which is meant that all hearts are equally fashioned by the Lord, kings' hearts as well as the hearts of beggars. The text does not mean that all hearts are created originally alike by God, such a statement would scarcely be true, since there is the utmost variety in the constitutions and dispositions of men. All men equally owe the possession of life to the Creator, and have therefore no reason to boast themselves. What reason has the vessel to glorify itself in presence of the potter ? *" He considereth al their works."* Not in vain doth God see men's acts : he ponders and judges them. He reads the secret design in the outward behaviour, and resolves the apparent good into its real elements. This consideration foretokens a judgment when the results of the divine thoughts will be meted out in measures of happiness or woe. Consider thy ways, O man, for God considers them !

16. *" There is no king saved by the multitude of an host."* Mortal power is a fiction, and those who trust in it are dupes. Serried ranks of armed men have failed to maintain an empire, or even to save their monarch's life when a decree from the court of heaven has gone forth for the empire's overthrow. The all-seeing God preserves the poorest of his people when they are alone and friendless, but ten thousand armed men cannot ensure safety to him whom God leaves to destruction. *" A mighty man is not delivered by much strength."* So far from guarding others, the valiant veteran is not able to deliver himself. When his time comes to die, neither the force of his arms nor the speed of his legs can save him. The weakest believer dwells safely under the shadow of Jehovah's throne, while the most mighty sinner is in peril every hour. Why do we talk so much of our armies and our heroes ? the Lord alone has strength, and let him alone have praise.

17. *" An horse is a vain thing for safety."* Military strength among the Orientals lay much in horses and scythed chariots, but the Psalmist calls them a lie, a deceitful confidence. Surely the knight upon his gallant steed may be safe, either by valour or by flight ? Not so, his horse shall bear him into danger or crush him with its fall. *" Neither shall he deliver any by his great strength."* Thus the strongest defences are less than nothing when most needed. God only is to be trusted and adored. Sennacherib with all his cavalry is not a match for one angel of the Lord, Pharaoh's horses and chariots found it vain to pursue the Lord's anointed, and so shall all the leaguered might of earth and hell find themselves utterly defeated when they rise against the Lord and his chosen.

18. *" Behold."* For this is a greater wonder than hosts and horses, a surer confidence than chariots or shields. *" The eye of the Lord is upon them that fear him."* That eye of peculiar care is their glory and defence. None can take them at unawares, for the celestial watcher foresees the designs of their enemies, and provides against them. They who fear God need not fear anything else ; let them fix their eye of faith on him, and his eye of love will always rest upon them. *" Upon them that hope in his mercy."* This one would think to be a small evidence of grace, and yet it is a valid one. Humble hope shall have its share as well as courageous faith. Say, my soul, is not this an encouragement to thee ? Dost thou not hope in the mercy of God in Christ Jesus ? Then the Father's eye is as much upon thee as upon the elder born of the family. These gentle words, like soft bread, are meant for babes in grace, who need infants' food.

19. *" To deliver their soul from death."* The Lord's hand goes with his eye ; he sovereignly preserves those whom he graciously observes. Rescues and restorations hedge about the lives of the saints ; death cannot touch them till the King signs his warrant and gives him leave, and even then his touch is not so much mortal as immortal ; he doth not so much kill us as kill our mortality. *" And to keep them alive in famine."* Gaunt famine knows its master. God has meal and oil for his Elijahs somewhere. *" Verily thou shalt be fed "* is a divine provision for the man of faith. The Preserver of men will not suffer the soul of the righteous to famish. Power in human hands is outmatched by famine, but God is good at a pinch, and proves his bounty under the most straitened circumstances. Believer, wait upon thy God in temporals. His eye is upon thee, and his hand will not long delay.

20 Our soul waiteth for the LORD : he *is* our help and our shield.

21 For our heart shall rejoice in him, because we have trusted in his holy name.

20. *" Our soul waiteth for the Lord."* Here the godly avow their reliance upon him whom the Psalm extols. To wait is a great lesson. To be quiet in expectation, patient in hope, single in confidence, is one of the bright attainments of a Christian. Our soul, our life, must hang upon God ; we are not to trust him with a few gewgaws, but with all we have and are. *" He is our help and our shield."* Our help in labour, our shield in danger. The Lord answereth all things to his people. He is their all in all. Note the three *" ours "* in the text. These holdfast words are precious. Personal possession makes the Christian man ; all else is mere talk.

21. *" For our hearts shall rejoice in him."* The duty commended and commanded in the first verse is here presented to the Lord. We, who trust, cannot but be of a glad heart, our inmost nature must triumph in our faithful God. *" Because we have trusted in his holy name."* The root of faith in due time bears the flower of rejoicing. Doubts breed sorrow, confidence creates joy.

22 Let thy mercy, O LORD, be upon us, according as we hope in thee.

Here is a large and comprehensive prayer to close with. It is an appeal for *" mercy,"* which even joyful believers need ; and it is sought for in a proportion which the Lord has sanctioned. *" According to your faith be it unto you,"* is the Master's word, and he will not fall short of the scale which he has himself selected. Yet, Master, do more than *this* when hope is faint, and bless us far above what we ask or even think.

EXPLANATORY NOTES AND QUAINT SAYINGS.

Whole Psalm.—A thanksgiving of the church triumphant in the latter ages, for her final deliverance, by the overthrow of Antichrist and his armies.—*Samuel Horsley.*

Whole Psalm.—Let us follow the holy man a moment in his meditation. His Psalm is not composed in scholastic form, in which the author confines himself to fixed rules ; and, scrupulously following a philosophical method, lays down principles, and infers consequences. However, he establishes principles, the most proper to give us sublime ideas of the Creator ; and he speaks with more precision of the works and attributes of God than the greatest philosophers have spoken of them.

How absurdly have the philosophers treated of *the origin of the world !* How few of them have reasoned conclusively on this important subject ! Our prophet solves the important question by one single principle ; and, what is more remarkable, this principle, which is nobly expressed, carries the clearest evidence with it. The principle is this : " By the word of the Lord were the heavens made ; and all the host of them by the breath of his mouth," verse 6. This is the most rational account that was ever given of the creation of the world. The world is the work of a self-efficient will, and it is this principle alone that can account for its creation. The most simple appearances in nature are sufficient to lead us to this principle. Either my will is self-efficient, or there is some other being whose will is self-efficient. What I say of myself, I say of my parents ; and what I affirm of my parents I affirm of my more remote ancestors, and of all the finite creatures from whom they derived their existence. Most certainly, either finite beings have a self-efficient will, which it is impossible to suppose, for a finite creature with a self-efficient will is a contradiction : either, I say, a finite creature has a self-efficient will, or there is a First Cause who has a self-efficient will ; and that there is such a Being is the principle of the Psalmist ; " By the word of the Lord were the heavens made ; and all the host of them by the breath of his mouth."

If philosophers have reasoned inconclusively on the origin of the world, they have spoken of *its government* with equal uncertainty. The Psalmist determined this question with great facility, by a single principle, which results from the former, and which, like the former, carries its evidence with it. "The Lord looketh from heaven ; he considereth all the works of all the inhabitants of the earth," verses 13, 14. This is the doctrine of providence. And on what is the doctrine of providence founded ? On this principle : God "fashioneth their hearts alike," verse 15. Attend a moment to the evidence of this reasoning, my brethren. The doctrine of providence expressed in these words, "God considereth the works of the inhabitants of the earth," is a necessary consequence of his principle, "God fashioneth their hearts alike ; " and this principle is a necessary consequence of that which the Psalmist had before laid down to account for the origin of the world. Yes, from the doctrine of God the Creator of men, follows that of God the inspector, the director, rewarder, and the punisher of their actions. One of the most specious objections that has ever been opposed to the doctrine of providence, is a contrast between the grandeur of God and the meanness of men. How can such an insignificant creature as man be the object of the care and attention of such a magnificent being as God ? No objection can be more specious, or, in appearance, more invincible. The distance between the meanest insect and the mightiest monarch, who treads and crushes reptiles to death without the least regard to them, is a very imperfect image of the distance between God and man. That which proves that it would be beneath the dignity of a monarch to observe the motions of ants, or worms, to interest himself in their actions, to punish, or to reward them, seems to demonstrate, that God would degrade himself were he to observe, to direct, to punish, to reward mankind, who are infinitely inferior to him. But one fact is sufficient to answer this specious objection : that is, that God has created mankind. Does God degrade himself more by governing than by creating mankind ? Who can persuade himself that a wise Being has given to intelligent creatures faculties capable of obtaining knowledge and virtue, without willing that they should endeavour to acquire knowledge and virtue ? Or who can imagine, that a wise Being, who wills that his intelligent creatures should acquire knowledge and virtue, will not punish them if they neglect those acquisitions ; and will not show by the distribution of his benefits that he approves their endeavours to obtain them ?

Unenlightened philosophers have treated of *the attributes of God* with as much abstruseness as they have written of his works. The moral attributes of God, as they are called in the schools, were mysteries which they could not unfold. These may be reduced to two classes ; attributes of *goodness*, and attributes of *justice*. Philosophers, who have admitted these, have usually taken that for granted which they ought to have proved. They collected together in their minds all perfections ; they reduced them all to one object which they denominated *a perfect being :* and supposing, without proving, that a perfect being existed, they attributed to him, without proof, everything that they considered as a perfection. The Psalmist shows by a surer way that there is a God supremely just and supremely good. It is necessary, in order to convince a rational being of the justice and goodness of God, to follow such a method as that which we follow to prove his existence. When we would prove the existence of God, we say, there are creatures, therefore there is a Creator. In like manner, when we would prove that a Creator is a just and a good being, we say, there are qualities of goodness and justice in creatures, therefore he, from whom these creatures derive their existence, is a being just and good. Now, this is the reasoning of the Psalmist in this Psalm : "The Lord loveth righteousness and judgment : the earth is full of the goodness of the Lord " (verse 5) ; that is to say, it is impossible to consider the works of the Creator, without receiving evidence of his goodness. And the works of nature which demonstrate the goodness of God, prove his justice also ; for God has created us with such dispositions, that we cannot enjoy the gifts of his goodness without obeying the laws of his righteousness. The happiness of an individual who procures a pleasure by disobeying the laws of equity, is a violent happiness, which cannot be of long duration ; and the prosperity of public bodies, when it is founded in iniquity, is an edifice which, with its basis, will be presently sunk and gone.

But what we would particularly remark is, that *the excellent principles of the Psalmist, concerning God, are not mere speculations ;* but truths from which he derives practical inferences ; and he aims to extend their influence beyond private persons, even to legislators and conquerors. One would think, considering the conduct of mankind, that the consequences, which are drawn from the doctrines of which we have been speaking, belong to none but to the dregs of the people ; that lawgivers and conquerors have a plan of morality peculiar to themselves, and are above the rules to which other men must submit. Our prophet had other notions. What are his maxims of policy ? They are all included in these words : " Blessed is the nation whose God is the Lord ; and the people whom he hath chosen for his own inheritance," verse 12. What are his military maxims ? They are all included in these words : " There is no king saved by the multitude of an host : a mighty man is not delivered by much strength. An horse is a vain thing for safety : neither shall he deliver any by his great strength," verses 16, 17. Who proposes these maxims ? A hermit, who never appeared on the theatre of the world ? or a man destitute of the talents necessary to shine there ? No : one of the wisest of kings ; one of the most bold and able generals : a man whom God has self-elected to govern his chosen people, and to command those armies which fought the most obstinate battles, and gained the most complete victories. Were I to proceed in explaining the system of the Psalmist, I might prove, that as he had a right to infer the doctrine of providence from the works of nature, and that of the moral attributes of God from the works of creation ; so from the doctrines of the moral attributes of God, of providence, and of the works of creation, he had a right to conclude, that no conquerors or lawgivers could be truly happy but those who acted agreeably to the laws of the just and good Supreme.—*James Saurin.*

Verse 1.—" *Rejoice in the Lord, O ye righteous.*" *Exult, ye righteous, in Jehovah !* The Hebrew verb, according to the etymologists, originally means to dance for joy, and is therefore a very strong expression for the liveliest exultation.— *J. A. Alexander.*

Verse 1.—" *Rejoice, O ye righteous :* " not in yourselves, for that is not safe, but " *in the Lord.*"—*Augustine.*

Verse 1.—" *Praise is comely for the upright.*" Praise is not comely for any but the godly. A profane man stuck with God's praise is like a dunghill stuck with flowers. Praise in the mouth of a sinner is like an oracle in the mouth of a fool : how uncomely is it for him to praise God, whose whole life is a dishonouring of God ? It is as indecent for a wicked man to praise God, who goes on in sinful practices, as it is for an usurer to talk of living by faith, or for the devil to quote Scripture. The godly are only fit to be choristers in God's praise ; it is called, " the garment of praise." Isaiah lxi. 3. The garment sits handsome only on a saint's back.—*Thomas Watson.*

Verse 1.—This Psalm is coupled with the foregoing one by the *catchword* with which it opens, which is a repetition of the exhortation with which the preceding ends, " *Rejoice in the Lord, ye righteous ;* " " *Shout for joy, all ye upright.*"— *Christopher Wordsworth.*

Verse 1.—He pleaseth God whom God pleaseth.—*Augustine.*

Verse 2.—" *Praise the Lord with harp : sing unto him with the psaltery and an instrument of ten strings.*" Here we have the first mention of musical instruments in the Psalms. It is to be observed that the early fathers almost with one accord protest against their use in churches ; as they are forbidden in the Eastern church to this day, where yet, by the consent of all the singing is infinitely superior to anything that can be heard in the West.—*J. M. Neale.*

Verse 2.—" *Harp ;* " " *Psaltery,*" etc. Our church does not use musical instruments, as harps and psalteries, to praise God withal, that she may not seem to Judaise.—*Thomas Aquinas.* It was only permitted to the Jews, as sacrifice was, for the heaviness and grossness of their souls. God condescended to their weakness, because they were lately drawn off from idols : but now instead of organs, we may use our own bodies to praise him withal.—*Chrysostom.* The use of singing with instrumental music was not received in the Christian churches as it was among the Jews in their infant state, but only the use of plain song.—*Justin Martyr.*

Verse 2 (*last clause*).—It is said that David praised God upon " *an instrument of ten strings ;* " and he would never have told how many strings there were, but that without all doubt he made use of them all. God hath given all of us bodies, as it were, instruments of many strings ; and can we think it music good enough to strike but one string, to call upon him with our tongues only ? No, no ; when the still sound of the heart by holy thoughts, and the shrill sound of the tongue by holy words, and the loud sound of the hands by pious works, do all join together, that is God's concert, and the only music wherewith he is affected.—*Sir Richard Baker.*

Verse 3.—" *Sing unto him.*" I. Singing is the music of *nature.* The Scriptures tell us the mountains sing (Isa. lv. 12) ; the valleys sing (Ps. lxv. 13) ; the trees of the wood sing (1 Chron. xvi. 33) ; nay, the air is the bird's music room, they chant their musical notes. II. Singing is the music of *ordinances.* Augustine reports of himself, that when he came to Milan and heard the people sing, he wept for joy in the church to hear that pleasing melody. And Beza confesses that at his first entrance into the congregation, and hearing them sing the ninety-first Psalm, he felt himself exceedingly comforted, and did retain the sound of it afterwards upon his heart. The Rabbins tell us that the Jews, after the feast of the Passover was celebrated, sang the hundred-and-eleventh and five following Psalms ; and our Saviour and his apostles sang a hymn immediately after the blessed Supper. Matt. xxvi. 30. III. Singing is the music of *saints.* 1. They have performed this duty in their greatest *numbers.* Ps. cxlix. 1, 2. 2. In their greatest *straits.* Isa. xxvi. 19. 3. In their greatest *flight.* Isa. xlii. 10, 11. 4. In their greatest *deliverances.* 5. In their greatest *plenties.* Isa. lxv. 14. In all these changes singing hath been their stated duty and delight. And indeed it is meet that the saints and servants of God should sing forth their joys and praises to the Lord Almighty : every attribute of him can set both their song and their tune. IV. Singing is the music of *angels.* Job tells us, " the morning stars sang together," chap. xxxviii. 7. Now these " morning stars," as Pineda tells us, are the angels ; to which the Chaldee paraphrase accords, naming these morning stars, *aciem angelorum,* an host of angels. Nay, when this heavenly host was sent to proclaim the birth of our dearest Jesus, they deliver their message in this raised way of duty. Luke ii. 13. They were αἰνοῦντες, delivering their messages in a laudatory singing, the whole company of angels making a musical quire. Nay, in heaven there is the angels' joyous music ; they there sing hallelujahs to the Most High, and to the Lamb who sits upon the throne. Rev. v. 11. V. Singing is the music of *heaven ;* the glorious saints and angels accent their praises this way, and make one harmony in their state of blessedness ; and this is the music of the bride-chamber. The saints who were tuning here their Psalms, are now singing their hallelujahs in a louder strain, and articulating their joys, which here they could not express to their perfect satisfaction ; here they laboured with drowsy hearts, and faltering tongues ; but in glory these impediments are removed, and nothing is left to jar their joyous celebration.—*John Wells, in " Morning Exercises."*

Verse 3.—" *A new song.*" That is to say, a *new* and recent composition on account of recent benefits ; or constantly new songs, song succeeding song as daily new material for divine praise offers itself to the attentive student of the works of God. Or *new,* that is, always fresh and full of life, and renewed as new occasions offer themselves : as Job says, " My glory was fresh in me, and my bow was renewed in my hand." Or *new, i.e.,* not common but rare and exquisite ; as the new name in Rev. ii. 17 ; the new commandment, John xiii. 34. Or this respects the gospel state, wherein is a new covenant (Heb. viii. 8), a new Jerusalem (Rev. xxi. 2), a new man (Eph. ii. 15), and all things new. 2 Cor. v. 17. *New,* on account of its matter being unknown of men : as in Rev. xiv. 3, " They sung a new song, and no man could learn that song but the hundred and forty and four thousand, which were redeemed from the earth. *New* may be used in opposition to old. The song of Moses is old, and of the Lamb is new.—*Martin Geier (1614— 1681), in " Poli Synopsis Criticorum."*

Verse 3.—" *Sing unto him a new song.*" Put off oldness : ye know the new song. A new man, a New Testament, a new song. A new song belongeth not to men that are old ; none learn that but new men, renewed through grace from oldness, and belonging now to the New Testament, which is the kingdom of heaven. —*Augustine.*

Verse 3.—" *A new song ;*" namely, sung with such fervency of affections as novelties usually bring with them ; or, always new, seeing God's graces never wax old ; or, sung by the motion of this new spirit of grace, which doth not so much look after the old benefits of the creation as after the new benefit of the redemption in Christ, which reneweth all things. Ps. xl. 3, and xcvi. 1 ; Rev. v. 9, and xiv. 3.— *John Diodati.*

Verse 3.—" *Sing unto him a new song.*" It is a melancholy proof of the decline of the church, when the exhortation to sing a new song is no longer attended to : in such a case, there is need of the greatest care to prevent the old ones falling into oblivion.—*E. W. Hengstenberg.*

Verse 3.—"*Play skilfully.*" It is not an easy matter to praise God aright; it must be done *corde, ore, opere,* with the very best of the best.—*John Trapp.*

Verse 4.—"*The word of the Lord is right.*" His word of promise given to the church. The divine revelation to all setting forth what is to be believed, hoped for, and done. The decrees of God and his penal judgments. The whole counsel and determination of God in the creation and government of the world. " *Is right,*" without defect or error. The word *right* is opposed to *tortuous ;* it means true or certain.—*John de Pineda* (1577–1637) ; *D. H. Mollerus* (1639), *and others, in Synopsis.*

Verse 4.—"*All his works are done in truth.*"

> *Truth* is in each flower
> As well as in the solemnest things of God :
> *Truth* is the voice of nature and of time—
> *Truth* is the startling monitor within us—
> Nought is without it, it comes from the stars,
> The golden sun, and every breeze that blows—
> *Truth,* it is God ! and God is everywhere !
>
> *William Thomas Bacon.*

Verse 5.—"*The earth is full of the goodness of the Lord.*" If we reflect on the prodigious number of human beings who constantly receive their food, raiment, and every pleasure they enjoy, from their mother earth, we shall be convinced of the great liberality with which nature dispenses her gifts ; and not only human beings, but an innumerable quantity of living creatures besides—inhabitants of the air, the waters, and the earth—are daily indebted to nature for their support. Those animals which are under our care are still indebted to the earth for their subsistence ; for the grass, which nature spontaneously produces, is their chief food. The whole race of fishes, except those which men feed for their amusement, subsist without any of their aid. The species of birds which is perhaps the most despised and most numerous, is the sparrow. What they require for their support is incredible, but nature takes care to feed them ; they are however but the smallest part of her children. So great is the quantity of insects, that ages may pass before even their species and classes can be known. How many and how diversified the sorts of flies that play in the air ! The blood taken from us by the gnat is very accidental food for them ; and we may suppose that where there is one gnat that lives upon it, there are millions that have never tasted human blood, or that of any other animal. On what can all these creatures subsist ? Perhaps every handful of earth contains living insects ; they are discovered in every drop of water ; their multiplying and means of support are incomprehensible. While nature is thus prolific in children, she is also fruitful in means for their subsistence ; or, rather, it is the God of nature who has poured into her bosom this inexhaustible store of riches. He provides each creature with its food and dwelling. For them he causes the grass and other herbs to grow, leaving each to select its proper food. And, however mean many creatures may appear to us, he feeds and assists them all.

O Almighty God, how manifest is thy greatness ! Thou dost what the united efforts of all mankind would fail to accomplish. Thou hast given life, and breath, and being to all creatures that live in the air, the waters, or the earth. Surely thou wilt do for thy believing people what thou dost for animals and insects ! When we are filled with doubts and fears, let us consider the ravens whom the Lord feeds when they cry. Let them and all creatures beside, which man takes no care of, teach us the art of contentment. The great Author of nature knows all our wants. Let us cast our every care on him, for he careth for us ; and may we come boldly to the throne of grace in faith and sincerity that we may obtain mercy, and find grace to help us in every time of need.—*Christopher Christian Sturm.*

Verse 5.—"*The earth is full of the goodness of the Lord.*" To hear its worthless inhabitants complain, one would think that God dispensed *evil*, not *good*. To examine the operation of his hand, everything is marked with mercy, and there is no place where his goodness does not appear. The *overflowing kindness* of God fills the earth. Even the iniquities of men are rarely a bar to his goodness : he causes his sun to rise on the evil and the good, and sends his rain upon the *just* and the *unjust.*—*Adam Clarke.*

Verse 5.—"*The goodness of the Lord.*" In discoursing on the glorious perfections of God, his *goodness* must by no means be omitted; for though all his perfections are his glory, yet this is particularly so called, for when Moses, the man of God, earnestly desired to behold a grand display of the glory of Jehovah, the Lord said, in answer to his petition, " I will make all my *goodness* pass before thee ; " thus intimating that he himself accounted his goodness to be his glory (Exod. xxxiii. 19 ; xxxiv. 7) ; and it includes that mercy, grace, longsuffering, and truth, which are afterwards mentioned. When it relieves the miserable, it is *mercy ;* when it bestows favours on the worthless, it is *grace ;* when it bears with provoking rebels, it is *longsuffering ;* when it confers promised blessings, it is *truth ;* when it supplies indigent beings, it is *bounty. The goodness of God* is a very comprehensive term ; it includes all the forms of his kindness shown to men ; whether considered as creatures, as sinners, or as believers.—*George Burder,* 1838.

Verse 5.—" *The goodness of the Lord.*" He might, if he had pleased, have made everything we tasted bitter, everything we saw loathsome, everything we touched a sting, every smell a stench, every sound a discord.—*William Paley, D.D.,* 1743—1805.

Verse 6.—" *By the word of the Lord were the heavens made ; and all the host of them by the breath of his mouth.*" That the רוח is not *spirit,* but *breath,* is evident from the words " *of his mouth* " (compare Isaiah xi. 4), and from the parallelism with " *word.*" Simple *word* is simple *breath ;* both together, they stand in contrast to that exercise of strength, that labour, that use of means and instruments without which feeble man can bring nothing to perfection. Then there are the parallel passages, " All the while my breath is in me, and the Spirit of God is in my nostrils." Job xxvii. 3. " The Spirit of God hath made me, and the breath of the Almighty hath given me life." Job. xxxiii. 4. " Thou takest away their breath, they die, and return to their dust, thou sendest forth thy *breath,* they are created." Psalm civ. 29, 30. On the other hand, however, the exposition which would interpret פיו רוח, without reference to the *Spirit of God,* cannot be a correct one. In the history of the creation, to which the verse before us, as well as verses seven and nine, generally refer, the creation is described as the work of the SPIRIT of God, and his WORD. First, the *Spirit of God* moved upon the face of waters, then God *said.* We may also suppose that the Spirit and the power of God are here represented by the *figure of* breath, because that in man is the first sign of life.—*E. W. Hengstenberg.*

Verse 6.—" *By the word of the Lord.*" May be understood of the hypostatic Word, as John teaches us. John i. 1. (*John Cocceius,* 1603—1669). This is an illustration of the old saying, that while Grotius finds Christ nowhere, Cocceius finds Christ everywhere.—*C. H. S.*

Verse 6.—Let any make a world, and he shall be a God, saith Augustine ; hence is it that the church maketh it the very first article of her Creed to believe in God the Father Almighty, maker of heaven and earth.—*John Weemse.*

Verses 6, 9.—It is all one with God to do as to say, to perform as to promise ; it is as easy, he is as willing, as able, to do the one as the other. There is no such distance betwixt God's saying and doing, as amongst men. His saying is doing. " *He spake, and it was done ; he commanded, and it stood fast.*" " *By the word of the Lord were the heavens made.*" " The worlds were framed by the word of God." Heb. xi. 3. There is omnipotency in his word, both of command and promise ; therefore called, " The word of his power." Heb. i. 3. One word of his can do more in an instant than the united powers of heaven and earth can do to eternity. This consideration removes at once the chief discouragements that hinder the lively actings of faith ; for what is it that weakens our confidence of the promises' performance, but because we look upon the accomplishment as uncertain or difficult, or future and afar off ! Now from hence faith may conclude the performance is certain, easy, and present.—*David Clarkson.*

Verse 7.—" *He gathereth the waters of the sea together as an heap,*" etc. " God called the gathering together of the waters, seas." Gen. i. 10. This unstable element must, like all other elements, be put under law, and confined within bounds, that there might be a habitable earth for man and all the creatures around him. Thus the Psalmist sings, " *He gathereth the waters of the sea together as an heap : he layeth up the depth in storehouses.*" The boundary was such as to cause his servants to wonder. They looked from the shore, as we do, and under the influence of a well-known law, the billows in their heaving swells, seemed as if they would, as if they did, touch the sky itself ; and as if they were so much higher than the shore, that they were in danger of leaving their basin and stretching over the land. Just such an impression, we, with all our science, popularly hold. The prophets thus looked as we do, and under the same kind of feeling. How wonderful, they thought, is all this ! A low barrier of sand is made Jehovah's agent for bounding the deep. " The Lord hath placed the sand for the bound of the sea by a perpetual decree, that it cannot pass it : and though the waves thereof toss themselves, yet can they not prevail ; though they roar, yet can they not pass over it." Jer. v. 22. —*John Duns, D.D., in " Science and Christian Thought,"* 1868.

Verse 7.—" *The waters of the sea.*" Of all objects that I have ever seen, there is none which affects my imagination so much as the sea or ocean. I cannot see the heavings of this prodigious bulk of waters, even in a calm, without a very pleasing astonishment ; but when it is worked up in a tempest, so that the horizon on every side is nothing but foaming billows and floating mountains, it is impossible to describe the agreeable horror that rises from such a prospect. A troubled ocean, to a man who sails upon it, is, I think, the biggest object that he can see in motion, and consequently gives his imagination one of the highest kinds of pleasure that can arise from greatness. I must confess it is impossible for me to survey this world of fluid matter without thinking on the hand that first poured it out, and made a proper channel for its reception. Such an object naturally raises in my thoughts the idea of an Almighty Being, and convinces me of his existence as much as a metaphysical demonstration. The imagination prompts the understanding, and by the greatness of the sensible object, produces in it the idea of a Being who is neither circumscribed by time nor space.—*Spectator.*

Verse 7.—" *As a heap.*" Dealing with fluids as if they were solids, with an obvious allusion to Ex. xv. 8. " *Depths,*" masses of water. The main point of the description is God's handling these vast liquid masses, as men handle solid substances of moderate dimensions, heaping the waves up, and storing them away, as men might do with stones or wheat.—*J. A. Alexander.*

Verse 7.—The vast mass of waters which had hitherto covered the entire surface of the globe, was on the third day of creation brought within narrower compass, and large tracts of the submerged earth reclaimed and rendered habitable ground. . . . . The waters were, *for the most part*, congregated together in one vast body, instead of being universally diffused over the face of the earth. This is the state of things which we now contemplate ; the various great seas and oceans constituting in fact but one body of water called in different regions by different names, as the Atlantic, Pacific, Indian, Southern, etc., oceans.—*George Bush*, on Gen. i. 9.

Verse 8.—" *Let all the earth.*" For who can doubt that God can do as he wills upon earth, since he so tamed the unconquerable nature of the sea ?—*Hugo Grotius,* 1583—1645.

Verse 8.—" *Let all the earth fear the Lord,*" etc. Let them not fear another instead of him. Doth a wild beast rage ? Fear God. Doth a serpent lie in wait ? Fear God. Doth man hate thee ? Fear God. Doth the devil fight against thee ? Fear God. For the whole creation is under him whom thou art commanded to fear.—*Augustine.*

Verse 9.—" *He spake and it was done.*" As we say in Latin, *Dictum factum,* SAID DONE, no delay having interposed.—*Hugo Grotius.*

Verse 9.—" *He spake, and it was done ;* " so that the creatures were not emanations from the divine nature, but effects of the divine will, the fruits of intelligence, and design, and counsel.—*William Binnie, D.D.*

Verse 10.—" *The Lord bringeth the counsel of the heathen to nought,*" etc. The more the Pharisees of old, and their successors the prelates of late, opposed the truth, the more it prevailed. The Reformation in Germany was much furthered by the Papists' opposition ; yea, when two kings (amongst many others), wrote against Luther, namely Henry VIII. of England, and Ludovicus of Hungary, this kingly title being entered into the controversy (making men more curious to examine the matter), stirred up a general inclination towards Luther's opinions.—*Richard Younge's Christian Library,* 1655.

Verse 11.—" *The counsel of the Lord.*" Note the contrast between the counsel of the heathen in the last verse, and the counsel of the Lord in this.—*C. H. S.*

Verse 11.—" *The thoughts.*" The same word as *devices* in the preceding verse.—
William de Burgh, D.D., in loc.

Verse 11.—The wheels in a watch or a clock move contrary one to another,
some one way, some another, yet all serve the intent of the workman, to show the
time, or to make the clock to strike. So in the world, the providence of God may
seem to run cross to his promises ; one man takes this way, another runs that way ;
good men go one way, wicked men another, yet all in conclusion accomplish the will,
and centre in the purpose of God the great Creator of all things.—*Richard Sibbes.*

Verse 11 (*last clause*).—Think not, brethren, because he said, " *The thoughts
of his heart,*" that God as it were sitteth down and thinketh what he should do,
and taketh counsel to do anything, or not to do anything. To thee, O man, belongs
such tardiness.—*Augustine.*

Verse 12.—" *Blessed—whom he hath chosen.*" A man may have his name set
down in the chronicles, yet lost ; wrought in durable marble, yet perish ; set upon
a monument equal to a Colossus, yet be ignominious ; inscribed on the hospital
gates, yet go to hell ; written in the front of his own house, yet another come to
possess it ; all these are but writings in the dust, or upon the waters, where the
characters perish so soon as they are made ; they no more prove a man happy
than the fool could prove Pontius Pilate because his name was written in the Creed.
But the true comfort is this, when a man by assurance can conclude with his own
soul that his name is written in those eternal leaves of heaven, in the book of God's
election, which shall never be wrapped up in the cloudy sheets of darkness, but
remain legible to all eternity.—*Thomas Adams.*

Verse 12.—" *The people whom he hath chosen.*" Some read it, The people which
hath chosen him for their inheritance. It cometh all to one. See Deut. xxvi.
17—19.—*John Trapp.*

Verse 12.—It is an happiness to have an interest in one greater than ourselves ;
an interest in a beggar is of no worth, because he is of no power ; but interest in
a prince all men seek, therefore it is said, " *Blessed are the people whose God is the
Lord.*"—*Joseph Symonds.*

Verse 12.—Lest it should be thought that men obtain so great a good by their
own efforts and industry, David teaches us expressly that it proceeds from the
fountain of God's gracious, electing love that we are accounted the people of God.—
John Calvin.

Verse 12.—I have sometimes compared the *great* men of the world, and the
good men of the world to the *consonants* and *vowels* in the alphabet. The *consonants*
are the most and the biggest letters ; they take up most room, and carry the
greatest bulk ; but, believe it, the *vowels* though they are the fewest and least of
all the letters, yet they are most useful ; they give the greatest sound of all ; there
is no pronunciation without vowels. O beloved, though the *great* men of the world
take up room, and make a show above others, yet they are but *consonants*, a
company of mute and dumb *consonants* for the most part ; the *good men* they are
the *vowels* that are of the greatest use and most concernment at every turn : *a good
man* to help with his prayers ; *a good man* to advise with his counsels ; *a good man*
to interpose with his authority ; this is the loss we lament, we have lost *a good
man ;* death has blotted out a *vowel ;* and I fear me there will be much silence
where he is lacking ; silence in the bed, and silence in the house, and silence in the
shop, and silence in the church, and silence in the parish ; for he was everywhere
a *vowel, a good man* in every respect.—*John Kitchin, M.A., in a Funeral Sermon,*
1660.

Verse 15.—" *He fashioneth their hearts alike.*" As an illustration of the passage
as it stands in our version, we append the following :—" Every circumstance concurs
in proving that mankind are not composed of species essentially different from
each other ; that, on the contrary, there was originally but one species, which,
after multiplying and spreading over the whole surface of the earth, has undergone
various changes from the influence of climate, food, mode of living, diseases, and
mixture of dissimilar individuals ; that at first these changes were not so conspicuous, and produced only individual varieties ; that these varieties became
afterwards more specific, because they were rendered more general, more strongly
marked, and more permanent, by the continual action of the same causes ; and
that they are transmitted from generation to generation."—*G. L. Leclerc, Comte
de Buffon,* 1707—1788.

Verse 15.—The Creator of all things *" fashioneth their hearts alike ; "* the word הֵר, which signifies together at once, intimating that the hearts of all men though separated from one another by never so vast a gulf of time or place, are as exactly alike in respect of their original inclinations, as if they had been all moulded at the same time.   The worship of a God and then some kind of religion, is necessary to us, we cannot shift it off.—*William Pinke,* 1631.

Verse 15 (*last clause*).—Two men give to the poor, one seeketh his reward in heaven, the other the praise of men.   Thou in two seest one thing, God understandeth two.   For he understandeth what is within, and knoweth what is within ; their ends he seeth, their base intentions he seeth.   *" He understandeth all their works."*—*Augustine.*

Verse 16.—*" There is no king saved by the multitude of an host."*   At the battle of Arbela, the Persian hosts numbered between five hundred thousand and a million men, but they were utterly put to the rout by Alexander's band of fifty thousand ; and the once mighty Darius was soon vanquished.   Napoleon led more than half-a-million of men into Russia—

> " Not such the numbers, nor the host so dread,
>   By northern Bren, or Scythian Timour led."

But the terrible winter left the army a mere wreck, and their leader was soon a prisoner on the lone rock of St. Helena.   All along the line of history this verse has been verified.   The strongest battalions melt like snowflakes when God is against them.—*C. H. S.*

Verse 16.—*" A mighty man ; "* or, *a giant ;*   Goliath for instance.   As the most skilful swimmers are often drowned, so here.—*John Trapp.*

Verses 16, 17 :—

> Not the chief his serried lances,
> Not his strength secures the brave :
> All in vain the war-horse prances,
> Weak his force his lord to save.
>
> > *Richard Mant.*

Verses 16, 17.—The weakness and insufficiency of all human *power,* however great, as before of all human *intellect.*—*J. J. Stewart Perowne.*

Verses 16, 17.—As a passenger in a storm, that for shelter against the weather, steppeth out of the way, betaketh him to a fair spread oak, standeth under the boughs, with his back close to the body of it, and findeth good relief thereby for the space of some time ; till at length cometh a sudden gust of wind, that teareth down a main arm of it, which falling upon the poor passenger, either maimeth or mischieveth him that resorted to it for succour.   Thus falleth it out with not a few, meeting in the world with many troubles, and with manifold vexations, they step aside out of their own way, and too, too often out of God's, to get under the wing of some great one, and gain, it may be, some aid and shelter thereby for a season ; but after awhile, that great one himself coming down headlong, and falling from his former height of favour, or honour, they are also called in question, and to fall together with him, that might otherwise have stood long enough on their own legs, if they had not trusted to such an arm of flesh, such a broken staff that deceived them.—*Thomas Gataker.*

Verse 17.—*" An horse."*   If the strength of horses be of God, or be his gift (Job xxxix. 19), then trust not in the strength of horses : use the strength of horses, but do not trust the strength of horses.   If you trust that strength which God hath given to horses, you make them your god.   How often doth God forbid trusting in the strength of horses, as knowing that we are apt to trust in anything that is strong, though but a beast.   *" An horse is a vain thing for safety : neither shall he deliver any by his great strength."*   As if God had said, you think a horse can save you, but know he is a vain thing.   And when the Psalmist saith, " A horse is a vain thing," he doth not mean it of a weak horse, but of a horse of the greatest strength imaginable ; such a horse is a vain thing to save a man, neither can he deliver any by his strength ; and therefore the Lord, when he promised great deliverances to his people, lest they should expect it by the strength of horses, saith (Hos. i. 7), " I will save them by the Lord their God, and will not save them by bow, nor by sword, nor by battle, by horses, nor by horsemen;" as if he had told them, do not look after creature strength to be saved by; a horse will be a vain thing to save you, and I can save you effectually without horses, and I will. —*Joseph Caryl.*

Verses 17—20.—Man is sensible of his want of earthly blessings, and will never cease, with excessive care, diligence, and vexation, to hunt after them, till he come to know that God will provide for him. When one hath great friends which they are known to lean upon, we say of them, such need take no care, they know such-and-such will see to them. On the contrary, come to one who knows no end of toiling and caring, ask him, Why will you thus tire yourself out? He will answer, I must needs do it, I have none but myself to trust to. So Christ followeth his disciples' carefulness to this door, their unbelief, which did not let them consider our heavenly Father cared for them. No present estate, though never so great, can free the heart from distraction, because it is subject to decay and vanishing: we shall never cast the burden of care off our own shoulders, till we learn by faith to cast it upon the Lord, whose eye is over us for good. He will never renounce carnal supports who makes not God the stay of his soul for outward things. He will trust in the abundance of his riches, wisdom, friends, or strength, that makes not God his strength. The heart of man, being aware of his inability to sustain himself if he be not underset, will seek out some prop, true or false, sound or rotten, to lean unto. They will go down to Egypt for help, and stay on horses, and trust in chariots, because they are many, and in horsemen because they are very strong, who look not to the Holy One of Israel, and seek not the Lord.—*John Ball.*

Verse 18.—"*Behold,*" etc. Hitherto he hath given a proof of God's providence towards *all men,* but now he descends to a particular proof of it, by his care over his *church,* which he wonderfully guides, defends, and protects in all dangers and assaults and that notice may be taken of it, he begins with, "*Behold!*"—*Adam Clarke.*

Verse 18.—"*The eye of the Lord is upon.*" Look upon the sun, how it casts light and heat upon the whole world in its general course, how it shineth upon the good and the bad with an equal influence; but let its beams be but concentred in a burning-glass, then it sets fire on the object only, and passeth by all others: and thus God in the creation looketh upon all his works with a general love, *erant omnia valde bona,* they pleased him very well. Oh! but when he is pleased to cast the beams of his love, and cause them to shine upon his elect through Christ, then it is that their hearts burn within them, then it is that their affections are inflamed; whereas others are but as it were a little warmed, have a little shine of common graces cast upon them.—*Richard Holdsworth,* 1651.

Verse 18.—"*Behold, the eye of the Lord is upon them that fear him, upon them that hope in his mercy.*" This is a very encouraging character. They who cannot claim the higher distinctions of religion, may surely know that they "fear God, and hope in his mercy." Some may wonder at the combination; and suppose that the qualities are incompatible with each other. But the first Christians "walked in the fear of the Lord, and in the comforts of the Holy Ghost." They may think that the fear will injure the hope, or the hope the fear. But these are even mutually helpful; and they are, not only never so beautiful, but never so influential as when they are blended. The fear promotes hope by the evidence it affords; and by keeping us from loose and careless walking, which must always affect our peace and pleasure. And hope no less befriends this fear. For never is God seen so glorious, so worthy of all our devotedness to him as when we hope in his mercy; and even the more assured we are of his regard, the more we shall enquire, Lord, what wilt thou have me to do? The more we shall tremble at the thought of offending and grieving him, the more we shall continue upon our knees, praying, "Let the words of my mouth, and the meditation of my heart, be acceptable in thy sight, O Lord, *my* Strength and *my* Redeemer." It is called "a lively hope:" and Christians know, by experience, that upon all their principles and duties it has the same influence as Spring has upon the fields and the gardens.—*William Jay.*

Verse 18.—"*Who hope in his mercy.*" When thou canst not get assurance, make as much improvement of the grounds upon which thou mayst build *hopes* of salvation. The probable grounds thou hast, thou wouldst not part with for all the world. If thy heart is not full of joy through sense of God's love, yet thine eyes are full of tears, and thy soul full of sorrow, through the sense of thy sin:

wouldst thou change thy condition with any hypocrite whatsoever, with the richest man that hath no grace? I would not have thee rest satisfied with a probability, but yet bless God for a probability of salvation. Is it nothing that one that hath deserved hell most certainly, should have a probability that he should escape it? Would not this be a little ease to the torments of the damned, if they had but a strong probability that they should be saved? but *no hope* makes it heavy. When thou art sick, thou enquirest of the physician. Sir, what do you think of me? Shall I live, or shall I die? If he reply it is not certain, but there is *good hopes*, it is probable you will live and do well; this is some support unto thee in thy sickness. —*Thomas Doolittel, M.A.* (1630—1707), *in " Morning Exercises."*

Verse 18.—The weakest believer, the least of saints, hath ground to hope. The gospel is so ordered, the covenant so methodised, God hath made such ample provision, that every one may " have good hope through grace " (1 Thess. ii. 16); and all that bear this character are allowed, encouraged, nay, commanded to hope: their hoping is as mighty a pleasure to God, as it is a comfort to themselves.—*Samuel Doolittle's " Righteous Man's Hope in Death,"* 1693.

Verses 18, 19.—During the siege of Rochelle, which was endured with unexampled bravery for nearly fifteen months, the inhabitants were reduced by famine to the misery of being obliged to have recourse to the flesh of horses, asses, mules, dogs, cats, rats, and mice; and a single peck of corn is said to have been sold for a sum equivalent to about twenty-five pounds sterling of our money in the present day. There were numerous examples of great and liberal generosity among the inhabitants. Some dispensed their charity so secretly that their names were never discovered. Among the rest, the following example is narrated:—" The Sieur de la Goute, an honorary king's advocate, had a sister, the widow of a merchant named Prosni, who, being a very religious and benevolent woman, at the time when the famine became more severe than it had before been, freely assisted the poor with her present surplus. Her sister-in-law, the wife of her brother, De la Goute, being differently inclined, reproved her for her conduct, asking her in anger, ' What she would do when her all should be expended?' Her reply was, ' My sister, *the Lord will provide for me.*' The siege was continued, and the famine increased its fearful ravages; and poor widow Prosni, who had four children, found herself in a great strait—all her store of provisions being exhausted. She applied to her sister for relief, who, in the stead of comforting, reproached her for her improvidence; tauntingly adding that, as she had done mighty well to be so reduced under all her great faith and fine words, that ' *the Lord would provide for her,*' so in good time he might provide for her.

" Wounded to the heart by these words, poor widow Prosni returned to her house in sad distress; resolving, nevertheless, to meet death patiently. On reaching her home, her children met her with gladdened hearts and joyous faces, and told her that a man, to them an entire stranger, had knocked at the door, it being late; and, on its being opened, he threw in a sack of about two bushels of wheat; and then, without saying a word, suddenly departed.

" The widow Prosni, scarcely able to believe her own eyes, with an overflowing, grateful heart towards her gracious benefactor, immediately ran to her sister-in-law as quickly as her famished condition would allow; and, upon seeing her, exclaimed aloud, ' *My sister, the Lord* HATH *provided for me;*' and, saying no more, returned home again.

" By means of this unexpected relief, conveyed to her so opportunely, she was enabled to support herself and family until the end of the siege, and she never knew to whom she was instrumentally indebted for this timely and merciful assistance." —*The Biblical Treasury, Vol. IX.*

Verse 20.—" *Our soul waiteth for the Lord.*" There is an emphasis on the word *soul* which should be attended to; for although this is a common mode of speech among the Hebrews, yet it expresses earnest affections; as if believers should say, We sincerely rely upon God with our whole heart, accounting him our shield and help.—*John Calvin.*

Verse 20.—" *Our soul.*" Not our souls, but " *our soul,*" as if they all had only one. And what is the language of God by the prophet? " I will give them one heart and one way." And thus the two disciples going to Emmaus exclaimed, upon their discovery and surprise, " Did not our heart burn within us?" And thus in the beginning of the gospel it was said, " The multitude of them that believed were of one heart, and of one soul." We have seen several drops of water on the table, by being brought to touch, running into one. If Christians were better acquainted with each other, they would easily unite.—*William Jay.*

Verse 20.—"*He is our help.*" Antigonus, king of Syria, being ready to give battle near the Isle of Andreos, sent out a squadron to watch the motions of his enemies, and to descry their strength : return was made that they had more ships, and better manned than he was. " How ? " says Antigonus, " that cannot be ; *quam multis meipsum opponis* (for how many dost thou reckon me ?)" intimating that the dignity of a general weighed down many others, especially when poised with valour and experience. And where is valour, where is experience to be found, if not in God ? He is the Lord of Hosts ; with him alone is strength and power to deliver Israel out of all her troubles. He may do it, he can do it, he will do it ; he is wise in heart and mighty in strength ; besides him there is no Saviour, no deliverer ; he is a shield to the righteous, strength to the weak, a refuge to the oppressed. He is *instar omnium* (all in all), and who is like unto him in all the world ?—*John Spencer.*

Verse 20.—There is an excellent story of a young man, that was at sea in a mighty raging tempest ; and when all the passengers were at their wits' end for fear, he only was merry ; and when he was asked the reason of his mirth, he answered, " That the pilot of the ship was his father, and he knew his father would have a care of him." The great and wise God, who is our Father, hath from all eternity decreed what shall be the issue of all wars, what the event of all troubles ; he is our pilot, he sits at the stern ; and though the ship of the church or state be in a sinking condition, yet be of good comfort, our Pilot will have a care of us. There is nothing done in the lower house of Parliament on earth, but what is first decreed in the higher house in heaven. All the lesser wheels are ordered and over-ruled by the upper. Are not five sparrows, saith Christ, sold for a farthing ? One sparrow is not worth half a farthing. And there's no man shall have half a farthing's worth of harm more than God hath decreed from all eternity.—*Edmund Calamy.*

Verse 22.—"*According as we hope in thee ;* " not according to any merits of theirs, but according to the measure of grace, of the grace of hope which God had bestowed on them, and encouraged them to exercise on him, in expectation of finding grace and mercy with him.—*John Gill.*

HINTS TO PREACHERS.

Whole Psalm.—This Psalm is *eucharistic :* the contents are :—I. *An exhortation to praise God* (1, 2, 3). II. The *arguments* to enforce the duty (4—19). III. The *confidence* of God's people in his name, their happiness, and petition. (20—22).—*Adam Clarke.*

Verse 1.—Rejoicing—the soul of praise ; the Lord—a well-spring of joy. Character—indispensable to true enjoyment.

Verse 1 (*last clause*).—Praise comely. What ? Vocal, meditative, habitual praise. Why ? It is comely as wings to an angel, we mount with it ; as flowers to a tree, it is our fruit ; as a robe to a priest, it is our office ; as long hair to a woman, it our beauty ; as a crown to a king, it is our highest honour. When ? Evermore, but chiefly amid blasphemy, persecution, sickness, poverty, death. Whom ? Not from the ungodly, hypocritical, or thoughtless. To be without praise is to miss our comeliest adornment.

Verse 2.—Instrumental music. Is it lawful ? Is it expedient ? If so, its uses, limits, and laws. A sermon to improve congregational music.

Verse 3 (*first clause*).—The duty of maintaining the freshness of our devotions. Freshness, skill, and heartiness, to be combined in our congregational psalmody.

Verse 4.—God's word and works, their rightness, and agreement, and our view of both.

Verse 4 (*first clause*).—The word doctrinal, preceptive, historical, prophetic, promissory, and experimental, always right, *i.e.*, free from error or evil.

Verse 4 (second clause).—God's work of creation, providence, and grace, always in conformity with truth. His hatred of everything like a sham.

Verses 4, 5.—A fourfold argument for praise, from the *truth*, the *faithfulness*, the *justice*, and *goodness* of God : I. " *For the word of the Lord is right.*" II. " *All his works are done in truth.*" III. " *He loveth righteousness and judgment.*" IV. " *The earth is full of his goodness.*"—*Adam Clarke.*

Verse 5.—Justice and goodness equally conspicuous in the divine action.

Verse 5 (last clause).—A matchless theme for an observant eye and an eloquent tongue.

Verse 6.—The power of the Word and the Spirit in the old and new creations.

Verse 7.—God's control of destructive and re-constructive agencies.

Verse 7.—The storehouses of the Great Husbandman.

Verse 8.—Reasons for universal worship, obstacles to it, future prospects of it, our duty in relation to it.

Verse 8 (last clause).—Awe—the soul of worship.

Verse 9.—*The irresistible word of Jehovah* in creation, in calling his people, in their comfort and deliverance, in their entrance to glory.

Verse 10.—Educated and philosophical heathen within the reach of missions.

Verses 10, 11.—The opposing counsels.

Verse 11.—The eternity, immutability, efficiency, and wisdom of the divine decrees. God's purposes, " the thoughts of his heart," hence their wisdom, and yet more their love.

Verse 12.—Two elections made by a blessed people and a gracious God, and their happy result.

The happiness of the church of God.

God's delight in his people, and their delight in him.

Verse 13.—Omniscience and its lessons.

Verses 13, 14, 15.—The doctrine of providence.

Verse 15.—God's acquaintance with men's hearts, and his estimate of their actions.

The similarity of human nature.

Verse 16, 17, 18.—The fallacy of human trust, and the security of faith in God.

Verse 18.—Hoping in the mercy of God—false and true forms distinguished.

Verses 18.—I. The eyes of God's *knowledge* are upon them. II. The eyes of his *affection* are upon them. III. The eyes of his *providence* are upon them.—*William Jay.*

Verse 19.—Life in famine, natural and spiritual, specially a famine of inward hope and legal satisfaction.

Verse 20.—" *Waiting for the Lord,*" includes : I. *Conviction*—a persuasion that the Lord is the supreme good. II. *Desire*—it is expressed by hungering and thirsting after righteousness, etc. III. *Hope.* IV. *Patience.*—God is never slack concerning his promise.—*William Jay.*

Verse 20 (first clause).—The believer's hourly position.

Verse 21.—Joy, the outflow of faith.

Verse 22.—A prayer for believers only.

Verse 22.—Measure for measure, or mercy proportioned to faith.

PSALM XXXIV.

TITLE.—A Psalm of David, when he changed his behaviour before Abimelech ; who drove him away, and he departed. *Of this transaction, which reflects no credit upon David's memory, we have a brief account in 1 Samuel xxi. Although the gratitude of the Psalmist prompted him thankfully to record the goodness of the Lord in vouchsafing an undeserved deliverance, yet he weaves none of the incidents of the escape into the narrative, but dwells only on the grand fact of his being heard in the hour of peril. We may learn from his example not to parade our sins before others, as certain vainglorious professors are wont to do who seem as proud of their sins as old Greenwich pensioners of their battles and their wounds. David played the fool with singular dexterity, but he was not so real a fool as to sing of his own exploits of folly. In the original, the title does not teach us that the Psalmist composed this poem at the time of his escape from Achish, the king or Abimelech of Gath, but that it is intended to commemorate that event, and was suggested by it. It is well to mark our mercies with well carved memorials. God deserves our best handiwork. David in view of the special peril from which he was rescued, was at great pains with this Psalm, and wrote it with considerable regularity, in almost exact accordance with the letters of the Hebrew alphabet. This is the second alphabetical Psalm, the twenty-fifth being the first.*

DIVISION.—*The Psalm is split into two great divisions at the close of verse* 10, *when the Psalmist having expressed his praise to God turns in direct address to men. The first ten verses are* A HYMN, *and the last twelve* A SERMON. *For further assistance to the reader we may subdivide thus : In verses 1 to 3, David vows to bless the Lord, and invites the praise of others ; from 4 to 7 he relates his experience, and in 8, 9, 10, exhorts the godly to constancy of faith. In verses* 11—14, *he gives direct exhortation, and follows it up by didactic teaching from verses 15 to the close.*

EXPOSITION.

I WILL bless the LORD at all times : his praise *shall* continually *be* in my mouth.

2 My soul shall make her boast in the LORD : the humble shall hear *thereof,* and be glad.

3 O magnify the Lord with me, and let us exalt his name together.

1. " *I will bless the Lord at all times.*"—He is resolved and fixed, " *I will ;* " he is personally and for himself determined, let others do as they may ; he is intelligent in head and inflamed in heart—he knows to whom the praise is due, and what is due, and for what and when. To Jehovah, and not to second causes our gratitude is to be rendered. The Lord hath by right a monopoly in his creatures' praise. Even when a mercy may remind us of our sin with regard to it, as in this case David's deliverance from the Philistine monarch was sure to do, we are not to rob God of his meed of honour because our conscience justly awards a censure to our share in the transaction. Though the hook was rusty, yet God sent the fish, and we thank him for it. " *At all times,*" in every situation, under every circumstance, before, in and after trials, in bright days of glee, and dark nights of fear. He would never have done praising, because never satisfied that he had done enough ; always feeling that he fell short of the Lord's deservings. Happy is he whose fingers are wedded to his harp. He who praises God for mercies shall never want a mercy for which to praise. To bless the Lord is never unseasonable. " *His praise shall continually be in my mouth,*" not in my heart merely, but in my mouth too. Our thankfulness is not to be a dumb thing ; it should be one of the daughters of music. Our tongue is our glory, and it ought to reveal the glory of God. What a blessed mouthful is God's praise ! How sweet, how purifying, how perfuming ! If men's mouths were always thus filled, there would be no repining against God, or slander of neighbours. If we continually rolled this dainty morsel under our tongue, the bitterness of daily affliction would be

swallowed up in joy. God deserves blessing with the heart, and extolling with the mouth—good thoughts in the closet, and good words in the world.

2. "*My soul shall make her boast in the Lord.*" Boasting is a very natural propensity, and if it were used as in this case, the more it were indulged the better. The exultation of this verse is no mere tongue bragging, "*the soul*" is in it, the boasting is meant and felt before it is expressed. What scope there is for holy boasting in Jehovah! His person, attributes, covenant, promises, works, and a thousand things besides, are all incomparable, unparalleled, matchless; we may cry them up as we please, but we shall never be convicted of vain and empty speech in so doing. Truly he who writes these words of comment has nothing of his own to boast of, but much to lament over, and yet none shall stop him of his boast in God so long as he lives. "*The humble shall hear thereof, and be glad.*" They are usually grieved to hear boastings; they turn aside from vauntings and lofty speeches, but boasting in the Lord is quite another matter; by this the most lowly are consoled and encouraged. The confident expressions of tried believers are a rich solace to their brethren of less experience. We ought to talk of the Lord's goodness on purpose that others may be confirmed in their trust in a faithful God.

3. "*O magnify the Lord with me.*" Is this request addressed to the humble? If so it is most fitting. Who can make God great but those who feel themselves to be little? He bids them help him to make the Lord's fame greater among the sons of men. Jehovah is infinite, and therefore cannot really be made greater, but his name grows in manifested glory as he is made known to his creatures, and thus he is said to be magnified. It is well when the soul feels its own inability adequately to glorify the Lord, and therefore stirs up others to the gracious work; this is good both for the man himself and for his companions. No praise can excel that which lays us prostrate under a sense of our own nothingness, while divine grace like some topless Alp rises before our eyes, and sinks us lower and lower in holy awe. "*Let us exalt his name together.*" Social, congregated worship is the outgrowth of one of the natural instincts of the new life. In heaven it is enjoyed to the full, and earth is likest heaven where it abounds.

4 I sought the LORD, and he heard me, and delivered me from all my fears.

5 They looked unto him, and were lightened: and their faces were not ashamed.

6 This poor man cried, and the LORD heard *him*, and saved him out of all his troubles.

7 The angel of the LORD encampeth round about them that fear him, and delivereth them.

4. "*I sought the Lord, and he heard me.*" It must have been in a very confused manner that David prayed, and there must have been much of self-sufficiency in his prayer, or he would not have resorted to methods of such dubious morality as pretending to be mad and behaving as a lunatic; yet his poor limping prayer had an acceptance and brought him succour: the more reason for them celebrating the abounding mercy of the Lord. We may seek God even when we have sinned. If sin could blockade the mercy-seat it would be all over with us, but the mercy is that there are gifts even for the rebellious, and an advocate for men who sin. "*And delivered me from all my fears.*" God makes a perfect work of it. He clears away both our fears and their causes, all of them without exception. Glory be to his name, prayer sweeps the field, slays all the enemies and even buries their bones. Note the egoism of this verse and of those preceding it; we need not blush to speak of ourselves when in so doing we honestly aim at glorifying God, and not at exalting ourselves. Some are foolishly squeamish upon this point, but they should remember that when modesty robs God it is most immodest.

5. "*They looked unto him, and were lightened.*" The Psalmist avows that his case was not at all peculiar, it was matched in the lives of all the faithful; they too, each one of them on looking to their Lord were brightened up, their faces began to shine, their spirits were uplifted. What a means of blessing one look at the Lord may be! There is life, light, liberty, love, everything in fact, in a look at the crucified One. Never did a sore heart look in vain to the good Physician; never a dying soul turned its darkening eye to the brazen serpent to find its virtue

gone. *"And their faces were not ashamed."* Their faces were covered with joy but not with blushes. He who trusts in God has no need to be ashamed of his confidence, time and eternity will both justify his reliance.

6. *"This poor man cried."* Here he returns to his own case. He was poor indeed, and so utterly friendless that his life was in great jeopardy; but he cried in his heart to the protector of his people and found relief. His prayer was a cry, for brevity and bitterness, for earnestness and simplicity, for artlessness and grief; it was a poor man's cry, but it was none the less powerful with heaven, for *"the Lord heard him,"* and to be heard of God is to be delivered; and so it is added the Lord *"saved him out of all his troubles."* At once and altogether David was clean rid of all his woes. The Lord sweeps our griefs away as men destroy a hive of hornets, or as the winds clear away the mists. Prayer can clear us of troubles as easily as the Lord made a riddance of the frogs and flies of Egypt when Moses entreated him. This verse is the Psalmist's own personal testimony: he being dead yet speaketh. Let the afflicted reader take heart and be of good courage.

7. *"The angel of the Lord."* The covenant angel, the Lord Jesus, at the head of all the bands of heaven, surrounds with his army the dwellings of the saints. Like hosts entrenched so are the ministering spirits encamped around the Lord's chosen, to serve and succour, to defend and console them. *"Encampeth round about them that fear him."* On every side the watch is kept by warriors of sleepless eyes, and the Captain of the host is one whose prowess none can resist. *"And delivereth them."* We little know how many providential deliverances we owe to those unseen hands which are charged to bear us up lest we dash our foot against a stone.

8 O taste and see that the Lord *is* good: blessed *is* the man *that* trusteth in him.

9 O fear the Lord, ye his saints: for *there is* no want to them that fear him.

10 The young lions do lack, and suffer hunger: but they that seek the Lord shall not want any good *thing.*

8. *"O taste and see."* Make a trial, an inward, experimental trial of the goodness of God. You cannot see except by tasting for yourself; but if you taste you shall see, for this, like Jonathan's honey, enlightens the eyes. *"That the Lord is good."* You can only know this really and personally by experience. There is the banquet with its oxen and fatlings; its fat things full of marrow, and wines on the lees well refined; but their sweetness will be all unknown to you except you make the blessings of grace your own, by a living, inward, vital participation in them. *"Blessed is the man that trusteth in him."* Faith is the soul's taste; they who test the Lord by their confidence always find him good, and they become themselves blessed. The second clause of the verse, is the argument in support of the exhortation contained in the first sentence.

9. *"O fear the Lord, ye his saints."* Pay to him humble childlike reverence, walk in his laws, have respect to his will, tremble to offend him, hasten to serve him. Fear not the wrath of men, neither be tempted to sin through the virulence of their threats; fear God and fear nothing else. *"For there is no want to them that fear him."* Jehovah will not allow his faithful servants to starve. He may not give luxuries, but the promise binds him to supply necessaries, and he will not run back from his word. Many whims and wishes may remain ungratified, but real wants the Lord will supply. The fear of the Lord or true piety is not only the duty of those who avow themselves to be saints, that is, persons set apart and consecrated for holy duties, but it is also their path of safety and comfort. Godliness hath the promise of the life which now is. If we were to die like dogs, and there were no hereafter, yet were it well for our own happiness' sake to fear the Lord. Men seek a patron and hope to prosper; he prospers surely who hath the Lord of Hosts to be his friend and defender.

10. *"The young lions do lack, and suffer hunger."* They are fierce, cunning, strong, in all the vigour of youth, and yet they sometimes howl in their ravenous hunger, and even so crafty, designing, and oppressing men, with all their sagacity and unscrupulousness, often come to want; yet simple-minded believers, who dare not act as the greedy lions of earth, are fed with food convenient for them. To trust God is better policy than the craftiest politicians can teach or practise.

"*But they that seek the Lord shall not want any good thing.*" No really good thing shall be denied to those whose first and main end in life is to seek the Lord. Men may call them fools, but the Lord will prove them wise. They shall win where the world's wiseacres lose their all, and God shall have the glory of it.

11 Come ye children, hearken unto me : I will teach you the fear of the LORD.

12 What man *is he that* desireth life, *and* loveth *many* days, that he may see good ?

13 Keep thy tongue from evil, and thy lips from speaking guile.

14 Depart from evil, and do good ; seek peace, and pursue it.

11. "*Come, ye children.*" Though a warrior and a king, the Psalmist was not ashamed to teach children. Teachers of youth belong to the true peerage ; their work is honourable, and their reward shall be glorious. Perhaps the boys and girls of Gath had made sport of David in his seeming madness, and if so, he here aims by teaching the rising race to undo the mischief which he had done aforetime. Children are the most hopeful persons to teach—wise men who wish to propagate their principles take care to win the ear of the young. "*Hearken unto me : I will teach you the fear of the Lord.*" So far as they can be taught by word of mouth, or learned by the hearing of the ear, we are to communicate the faith and fear of God, inculcating upon the rising generation the principles and practices of piety. This verse may be the address of every Sabbath School teacher to his class, of every parent to his children. It is not without instruction in the art of teaching. We should be winning and attractive to the youngsters, bidding them "come," and not repelling them with harsh terms. We must get them away, apart from toys and sports, and try to occupy their minds with better pursuits ; for we cannot well teach them while their minds are full of other things. We must drive at the main point always, and keep the fear of the Lord ever uppermost in our teachings, and in so doing we may discreetly cast our own personality into the scale by narrating our own experiences and convictions.

12. Life spent in happiness is the desire of all, and he who can give the young a receipt for leading a happy life deserves to be popular among them. Mere existence is not life ; the art of living, truly, really, and joyfully living, it is not given to all men to know. To teach men how to live and how to die, is the aim of all useful religious instruction. The rewards of virtue are the baits with which the young are to be drawn to morality. While we teach piety to God we should also dwell much upon morality towards man.

13. "*Keep thy tongue from evil.*" Guard with careful diligence that dangerous member, the tongue, lest it utter evil, for that evil will recoil upon thee, and mar the enjoyment of thy life. Men cannot spit forth poison without feeling some of the venom burning their own flesh. "*And thy lips from speaking guile.*" Deceit must be very earnestly avoided by the man who desires happiness. A crafty schemer lives like a spy in the enemy's camp, in constant fear of exposure and execution. Clean and honest conversation, by keeping the conscience at ease, promotes happiness, but lying and wicked talk stuffs our pillow with thorns, and makes life a constant whirl of fear and shame. David had tried the tortuous policy, but he here denounces it, and begs others as they would live long and well to avoid with care the doubtful devices of guile.

14. "*Depart from evil.*" Go away from it. Not merely take your hands off, but yourself off. Live not near the pest-house. Avoid the lion's lair, leave the viper's nest. Set a distance between yourself and temptation. "*And do good.*" Be practical, active, energetic, persevering in good. Positive virtue promotes negative virtue ; he who does good is sure to avoid evil. "*Seek peace.*" Not merely prefer it, but with zeal and care endeavour to promote it. Peace with God, with thine own heart, with thy fellow man, search after this as the merchantman after a precious pearl. Nothing can more effectually promote our own happiness than peace ; strife awakens passions which eat into the heart with corroding power. Anger is murder to one's own self, as well as to its objects. "*And pursue it.*" Hunt after it, chase it with eager desire. It may soon be lost, indeed, nothing is harder to retain, but do your best, and if enmity should arise let it be no fault of yours. Follow after peace when it shuns you ; be resolved not to be of a contentious spirit.

The peace which you thus promote will be returned into your own bosom, and be a perennial spring of comfort to you.

15 The eyes of the LORD *are* upon the righteous, and his ears *are open* unto their cry.

16 The face of the LORD *is* against them that do evil, to cut off the remembrance of them from the earth.

17 *The righteous* cry, and the LORD heareth, and delivereth them out of all their troubles,

18 The LORD *is* nigh unto them that are of a broken heart ; and saveth such as be of a contrite spirit.

19 Many *are* the afflictions of the righteous : but the LORD delivereth him out of them all.

20 He keepeth all his bones : not one of them is broken.

21 Evil shall slay the wicked : and they that hate the righteous shall be desolate.

22 The Lord redeemeth the soul of his servants : and none of them that trust in him shall be desolate.

15. "*The eyes of the Lord are upon the righteous.*" He observes them with approval and tender consideration ; they are so dear to him that he cannot take his eyes off them ; he watches each one of them as carefully and intently as if there were only that one creature in the universe. "*His ears are open unto their cry.*" His eyes and ears are thus both turned by the Lord towards his saints ; his whole mind is occupied about them : if slighted by all others they are not neglected by him. Their cry he hears at once, even as a mother is sure to hear her sick babe ; the cry may be broken, plaintive, unhappy, feeble, unbelieving, yet the Father's quick ear catches each note of lament or appeal, and he is not slow to answer his children's voice.

16. "*The face of the Lord is against them that do evil.*" God is not indifferent to the deeds of sinners, but he sets his face against them, as we say, being determined that they shall have no countenance and support, but shall be thwarted and defeated. He is determinately resolved that the ungodly shall not prosper ; he sets himself with all his might to overthrow them. "*To cut off the remembrance of them from the earth.*" He will stamp out their fires, their honour shall be turned into shame, their names forgotten or accursed. Utter destruction shall be the lot of all the ungodly.

17. "*The righteous cry.*" Like Israel in Egypt, they cry out under the heavy yoke of oppression, both of sin, temptation, care and grief. "*And the Lord heareth ;*" he is like the night-watchman, who no sooner hears the alarm-bell than he flies to relieve those who need him. "*And delivereth them out of all their troubles.*" No net of trouble can so hold us that the Lord cannot free us. Our afflictions may be numerous and complicated, but prayer can set us free from them all, for the Lord will show himself strong on our behalf.

18. "*The Lord is nigh unto them that are of a broken heart.*" Near in friendship to accept and console. Broken hearts think God far away, when he is really most near to them ; their eyes are holden so that they see not their best friend. Indeed, he is with them, and in them, but they know it not. They run hither and thither, seeking peace in their own works, or in experiences, or in proposals and resolutions, whereas the Lord is nigh them, and the simple act of faith will reveal him. "*And saveth such as be of a contrite spirit.*" What a blessed token for good is a repentant, mourning heart ! Just when the sinner condemns himself, the Lord graciously absolves him. If we chasten our own spirits the Lord will spare us. He never breaks with the rod of judgment those who are already sore with the rod of conviction. Salvation is linked with contrition.

19. "*Many are the afflictions of the righteous.*" Thus are they made like Jesus their covenant Head. Scripture does not flatter us like the story books with the idea that goodness will secure us from trouble ; on the contrary, we are again and again warned to expect tribulaion while we are in this body. Our afflictions come from all points of the compass, and are as many and as tormenting as the mosquitoes

of the tropics. It is the earthly portion of the elect to find thorns and briers growing in their pathway, yea, to lie down among them, finding their rest broken and disturbed by sorrow. BUT, blessed *but*, how it takes the sting out of the previous sentence! "*But the Lord delivereth him out of them all.*" Through troops of ills Jehovah shall lead his redeemed scatheless and triumphant. There is an end to the believer's affliction, and a joyful end too. None of his trials can hurt so much as a hair of his head, neither can the furnace hold him for a moment after the Lord bids him come forth of it. Hard would be the lot of the righteous if this promise, like a bundle of camphire, were not bound up in it, but this sweetens all. The same Lord who sends the afflictions will also recall them when his design is accomplished, but he will never allow the fiercest of them to rend and devour his beloved.

20. "*He keepeth all his bones: not one of them is broken.*" David had come off with kicks and cuffs, but no broken bones. No substantial injury occurs to the saints. Eternity will heal all their wounds. Their real self is safe; they may have flesh-wounds, but no part of the essential fabric of their being shall be broken. This verse may refer to frequent providential protections vouchsafed to the saints; but as good men have had broken limbs as well as others, it cannot absolutely be applied to bodily preservations; but must, it seems to me, be spiritually applied to great injuries of soul, which are for ever prevented by divine love. Not a bone of the mystical body of Christ shall be broken, even as his corporeal frame was preserved intact. Divine love watches over every believer as it did over Jesus; no fatal injury shall happen to us, we shall neither be halt nor maimed in the kingdom, but shall be presented after life's trials are over without spot or wrinkle or any such thing, being preserved in Christ Jesus, and kept by the power of God through faith unto salvation.

21. "*Evil shall slay the wicked.*" Their adversities shall be killing; they are not medicine, but poison. Ungodly men only need rope enough and they will hang themselves; their own iniquities shall be their punishment. Hell itself is but evil fully developed, torturing those in whom it dwells. Oh! happy they who have fled to Jesus to find refuge from their former sins, such, and such only will escape. "*And they that hate the righteous shall be desolate.*" They hated the best of company, and they shall have none; they shall be forsaken, despoiled, wretched, despairing. God makes the viper poison itself. What desolation of heart do the damned feel, and how richly have they deserved it!

22. "*The Lord redeemeth the soul of his servants.*"—with price and with power, with blood and with water. All providential helps are a part of the redemption by power, hence the Lord is said still to redeem. All thus ransomed belong to him who bought them—this is the law of justice and the verdict of gratitude. Joyfully will we serve him who so graciously purchases us with his blood, and delivers us by his power. "*And none of them that trust in him shall be desolate.*" Faith is the mark of the ransomed, and wherever it is seen, though in the least and meanest of the saints, it ensures eternal salvation. Believer, thou shalt never be deserted, forsaken, given up to ruin. God, even thy God is thy guardian and friend, and bliss is thine.

EXPLANATORY NOTES AND QUAINT SAYINGS.

Title.—*Abimelech* was king of Gath, the same with Achish, 1 Sam. xxi. 20: who either had two names, or this of Abimelech, as it should seem, was a common name to all the kings of the Philistines (see Gen. xx. 2; xxvi. 8); as Pharaoh was to the Egyptian kings and Cæsar to the Roman emperors: the name signifies a *father-king*, or *my father-king*, or a *royal father;* as kings should be the fathers of their country: before him *David changed his behaviour*, his taste, sense, or reason: he imitated a madman.—*John Gill.*

Whole Psalm.—(This Psalm is alphabetical). The Alphabetical Psalms, the *psalmi abcedarii*, as the Latin fathers called them, are nine in number; and I cannot help thinking it is a pity that, except in the single instance of the hundred and nine-teenth, no hint of their existence should have been suffered to appear in our authorised version. I will not take it upon me to affirm, with Ewald, that no version is faithful in which the acrostic is suppressed ; but I do think that the existence of such a remarkable style of composition ought to be indicated in one way or another, and that some useful purposes are served by its being actually reproduced in the translation. No doubt there are difficulties in the way. The Hebrew Alphabet differs widely from any of those now employed in Europe. Besides differences of a more fundamental kind, the Hebrew has only twenty-two letters for our twenty-six ; and of the twenty-two a considerable number have no fellows in ours. An exact reproduction of a Hebrew acrostic in an English version is therefore impossible.—*William Binnie, D.D.*

Whole Psalm.—Mr. Hapstone has endeavoured to imitate the alphabetical character of this Psalm in his metrical version. The letter answering to F is wanting, and the last stanza begins with the letter answering to R. One verse of his translation may suffice—

> "At all times bless Jehovah's name will I ;
> His praise shall in my mouth be constantly :
> Boast in Jehovah shall my soul henceforth ;
> Hear it, ye meek ones, and exult with mirth."

Verse 1.—" *I will bless the Lord at all times.*" Mr. Bradford, martyr, speaking of Queen Mary, at whose cruel mercy he then lay, said, If the queen be pleased to release me, I will thank her ; if she will imprison me, I will thank her ; if she will burn me, I will thank her, etc. So saith a believing soul : Let God do with me what he will, I will be thankful.—*Samuel Clarke's " Mirrour."*

Verse 1.—Should the whole frame of nature be unhinged, and all outward friends and supporters prove false and deceitful, our worldly hopes and schemes be disappointed, and possessions torn from us, and the floods of sickness, poverty and disgrace overwhelm our soul with an impetuous tide of trouble ; the sincere lover of God, finding that none of these affects his portion and the object of his panting desires, retires from them all to God his refuge and hiding place, and there feels his Saviour incomparably better, and more than equivalent to what the whole of the universe can ever offer, or rob him of ; and his tender mercies, unexhausted fulness, and great faithfulness, yield him consolation and rest ; and enable him, what time he is afraid, to put his trust in him. Thus we find the holy Psalmist expressing himself : " *I will bless the Lord at all times : his praise shall continually be in my mouth.*"—*William Dunlop.*

Verse 1.—S. Basil tells us that the praise of God, once rightly impressed as a seal on the mind, though it may not always be carried out into action, yet in real truth causes us perpetually to praise God.—*J. M. Neale's Commentary.*

Verse 2.—" *My soul shall make her boast in the Lord.*" Not like the boasting of the Pharisee, so hateful in the eyes of God, so offensive in the ears of the humble ; for *the humble can hear this boasting and be glad,* which they would never do if it were not conformable to the rules of humility. Can any boasting be greater than to say, " I can do all things " ? Yet in this boasting there is humility when I add, " In him that strengtheneth me." For though God likes not of boasting, yet he likes of this boasting, which arrogates nothing to ourselves, but ascribes all to him.—*Sir Richard Baker.*

Verses 2—6.—There is somewhat very striking and pleasing in the sudden transitions, and the change of persons, that is observable in these few verses. " *My soul shall boast ;*" " *The humble shall hear ;*" " *I sought the Lord ;*" " *They looked to him ;*" " *This poor man cried.*" There is a force and elegance in the very unconnection of the expressions, which, had they been more closely tied by the proper particles, would have been in a great measure lost. Things thus separated from each other, and yet accelerated, discover, as Longinus observes, the earnestness and the vehemency of the inward working of the mind ; and though it may seem to interrupt, or disturb the sentence, yet quickens and enforces it.—*Samuel Chandler, D.D.*

Verse 3.—Venema remarks that after the affair with Achish, we are told in 1 Samuel xxii. 1, " His brethren, and all his father's house went down to the cave Adullam unto him," and these, together with those who were in debt, and discontented with Saul's government, formed a band of four hundred men. To these his friends and comrades, he relates the story of his escape, and bids them with united hearts and voices extol the Lord.—*C. H. S.*

Verse 4.—" *I sought the Lord, and he heard me.*" God expects to hear from you before you can expect to hear from him. If you restrain prayer, it is no wonder the mercy promised is retained. Meditation is like the lawyer's studying the case in order to his pleading at the bar : when, therefore, thou hast viewed the promise, and affected thy heart with the riches of it, then fly thee to the throne of grace, and spread it before the Lord.—*William Gurnall.*

Verse 4.—" *He delivered me from all my fears.*" To have delivered me from all my troubles had been a great favour, but a far greater to deliver me from all my fears ; for where that would but have freed me from present evil, this secures me from evil to come ; that now I enjoy not only tranquility, but security, a privilege only of the godly. The wicked may be free from trouble, but can they be free from fear ? No ; God knows, though they be not in trouble like other men, yet they live in more fear than other men. Guiltiness of mind, or mind of the world, never suffers them to be secure : though they be free sometimes from the fit of an ague, yet they are never without a grudging ; and (if I may use the expression of poets) though they feel not always the whip of Tysiphone, yet they feel always her terrors ; and, seeing the Lord hath done this for me, hath delivered me from all my fears, have I not cause, just cause, to magnify him, and exalt his name ?—*Sir Richard Baker.*

Verse 5.—" *They looked unto him.*" The more we can think upon our Lord, and the less upon ourselves, the better. Looking to him, as he is seated upon the right hand of the throne of God, will keep our heads, and especially our hearts, steady when going through the deep waters of affliction. Often have I thought of this when crossing the water opposite the old place of Langholm. I found, when I looked down on the water, I got dizzy ; I therefore fixed my eyes upon a steady object on the other side, and got comfortably through.—*David Smith,* 1792—1867.

Verse 6.—" *This poor man cried.*" The reasons of *crying* are, 1. Want cannot blush. The pinching necessity of the saints is not tied to the law of modesty. Hunger cannot be ashamed. " I mourn in my complaint, and make a noise," saith David (Ps. lv. 2) ; and Hezekiah, " Like a crane or a swallow, so did I chatter. I did mourn as a dove " (Isa. xxxviii. 14). " I went mourning without the sun : I stood up, and I cried in the congregation " (Job. xxx. 28). 2. Though God hear prayer, only as prayer offered in Christ, not because very fervent ; yet fervour is a heavenly ingredient in prayer. An arrow drawn with full strength hath a speedier issue ; therefore, the prayers of the saints are expressed by *crying* in Scripture. " O my God, I cry in the daytime, but thou hearest not " (Ps. xxii. 2). " At noon, will I pray, and cry aloud " (Ps. lv. 17). " In my distress I cried to the Lord " (Ps. xviii. 6). " Unto thee have I cried, O Lord " (Ps. lxxxviii. 13). " Out of the depths have I cried " (Ps. cxxx. 1). " Out of the belly of hell cried I " (Jonah ii. 2). " Unto thee will I cry, O Lord my rock " (Ps. xxviii. 1). Yea, it goeth to somewhat more than *crying :* " I cry out of wrong, but I am not heard " (Job xix. 7). " Also when I cry and shout, he shutteth out my prayer " (Lam. iii. 8). He who may teach us all to pray, sweet Jesus, " In the days of his flesh, when he had offered up prayers and supplications with strong crying and tears " (Heb. v. 7) ; he prayed with war shouts. 3. And these prayers are so prevalent, that God answereth them : " *This poor man cried, and the Lord heard him, and saved him out of all his fears* " (Ps. xxxiv. 6). " My cry came before him, even into his ears " (Ps. xviii. 6). The *cry* addeth wings to the prayer, as a speedy post sent to court upon life and death : " Our fathers cried unto thee, and were delivered " (Ps. xxii. 5). " *The righteous cry, and the Lord heareth* " (Ps. xxxiv. 17).—*Samuel Rutherford.*

Verse 7.—" *The angel of the Lord encampeth round about them that fear him, and delivereth them.*" I will not rub the questions, whether these angels can contract themselves, and whether they can subsist in a point, and so stand together the better in so great a number, neither will I trouble myself to examine whether they are in such-and-such a place in their *substance,* or only in their *virtue* and *operation.* But this the godly man may assure himself of, that whensoever he shall want their help, in spite of doors, and locks, and bars, he may have it in a moment's warning. For there is no impediment, either for want of power because they are spirits, or from want of good will, both because it is their duty, and because they bear an affection in him ; not only rejoicing at his first conversion (Luke xv. 10), but, I dare confidently affirm, always disposed with abundance of cheerfulness to do anything for him. I cannot let pass some words I remember of Origen's to this purpose, as I have them from his interpreter. He brings in the angels speaking after this manner :—" If he (meaning the Son of God) went down, and went down into a body, and was clothed with flesh, and endured its infirmities and died for men, what do we stand still for ? Come, let's all down from heaven together."—*Zachary Bogan.*

Verse 7.—" *The angel of the Lord encampeth round about them that fear him.*" This is the first time that, in the Psalter, we read of the ministrations of angels. But many fathers rather take this passage of the " Angel of the Great Counsel," and gloriously to him it applies.—*J. M. Neale.*

Verse 7.—" *The angel of the Lord encampeth round about them that fear him,*" etc. By whom may be meant, either the uncreated Angel, the Lord Jesus Christ, the Angel of God's presence, and of the covenant, the Captain of salvation, the Leader and Commander of the people ; and whose salvation is as walls and bulwarks about them, or as an army surrounding them ; or a created angel may be intended even a single one, which is sufficient to guard a multitude of saints, since one could destroy at once such a vast number of enemies, as in 2 Kings xix. 35 ; or one may be put for more, since they are an innumerable company that are on the side of the Lord's people, and to whom they are joined ; and these may be said to encamp about them, because they are an host or army (see Gen. xxxii. 1, 2 ; Luke ii. 13) ; and are the guardians of the saints, that stand up for them and protect them, as well as minister to them.—*John Gill.*

Verse 7.—" *The angel of the Lord* " is represented in his twofold character in this pair of Psalms, as an angel of mercy, and also as an angel of judgment. Psalm xxxv. 6. This pair of Psalms (the thirty fourth and thirty-fifth), may in this respect be compared with the twelfth chapter of the Acts of the Apostles, where the angel of the Lord is displayed as encamping about St. Peter, and delivering him, and also as smiting the persecutor, Herod Agrippa.—*Christopher Wordsworth, D.D.*

Verse 7.—" *Round about.*" In illustration of this it may be observed, that according to D'Arvieux, it is the practice of the Arabs to pitch their tents in a circular form ; the prince being in the middle, and the Arabs about him, but so as to leave a respectful distance between them. And Thevenot, describing a Turkish encampment near Cairo, having particularly noticed the spaciousness, decorations, and conveniences of the Bashaw's tent, or pavilion, adds, " Round the pale of his tent, within a pistol shot, were above two hundred tents, pitched in such a manner that the doors of them all looked towards the Bashaw's tent ; and it ever is so, that they may have their eye always upon their master's lodging, and be in readiness to assist him if he be attacked."—*Richard Mant.*

Verse 8.—" *O taste and see that the Lord is good.*" Our senses help our understandings ; we cannot by the most rational discourse perceive what the sweetness of honey is ; *taste* it and you shall perceive it. " His fruit was sweet to my *taste.*" Dwell in the light of the Lord, and let thy soul be always ravished with his love. Get out the marrow and the fatness that thy portion yields thee. Let fools learn by beholding thy face how dim their blazes are to the brightness of thy day.— *Richard Alleine, in " Heaven Opened," 1665.*

Verse 8.—" *O taste and see,*" etc. It is not enough for thee to see it afar off, and not have it, as Dives did ; or to have it in thee, and not to taste it, as Samson's lion had great store of honey in him, but tasted no sweetness of it ; but thou must as well have it as see it, and as well taste it as have it. " *O taste and see,*" says he, " *how sweet the Lord is ;* " for so indeed Christ giveth his church not only *a sight* but also " *a taste* " of his sweetness. A *sight* is where he saith thus : " We will rise up early, and go into the vineyard, and see whether the vine have budded forth the small grapes, and whether the pomegranates flourish ; " there is *a sight* of the vine. A *taste* is where he says thus, " I will bring thee into the wine cellar, and cause thee to drink spiced wine, and new wine of the pomegranates ; " there is *a taste* of the wine. The church not only goes into the vineyard and *sees* the wine, but also goes into the wine cellar, and *tastes* the wine.—*Thomas Playfere.*

Verse 8.—" *Taste and see.*" There are some things, especially in the depths of the religious life, which can only be understood by being experienced, and which even then are incapable of bing adequately embodied in words. " *O taste and see that the Lord is good.*" The enjoyment must come before the illumination ; or rather the enjoyment is the illumination. There are things that must be loved before we can know them to be worthy of our love ; things to be believed before we can understand them to be worthy of belief. And even after this—after we are conscious of a distinct apprehension of some spiritual truth, we can only, perhaps, answer, if required to explain it, in the words of the philosopher to whom the question was put, " What is God ? " " I know, *if I am not asked.*"—*Thomas Binney's* " *Sermons,*" 1869.

Verse 8.—" *Taste and see.*" Be unwilling that all the good gifts of God should be swallowed without taste or maliciously forgotten, but use your palate, know them, and consider them.—*D. H. Mollerus.*

Verse 8.—Heaven and earth are replete with the goodness of God. We omit to open our mouths and eyes, on which account the Psalmist desires us to " *taste* " and " *see.*"—*Augustus F. Tholuck.*

Verse 8.—The " *taste and see* " invite, as it were, to a sumptuous feast, which has long been ready ; to a rich sight openly exposed to view. The imperatives are in reality not hortatory but persuasive.—*E. W. Hengstenberg.*

Verse 8.—All that the believer can attain of spiritual consolation in this life is but a taste.—*David Dickson.*

Verse 8 :—

> O taste the Lord, and see how sweet He is,
> The man that trusts in him lives still in bliss.
>
> *Sir John Davies,* 1569—1626.

Verses 8, 9, 10.—All these verses are beautiful representations of the fulness, suitableness, completeness, and all-sufficiency of God in Christ to answer all the wants of his people. And is there not a vast elegance in the comparison taken from the hunger and rapacity of the lion, even the impetuousness of the young lion, to that of the patience and silent waiting of the faithful believer ? A life of faith will find food in everything, because it is all founded in Christ. The young lions may, and will lack, because nothing will supply their voracious appetites but that which is carnal.—*Robert Hawker.*

Verse 10.—" *The young lions do lack, and suffer hunger.*" The old lions will have it for them, if it be to be had. " *But they that seek the Lord shall not want any good thing.*" As they would feel no evil thing within, so they shall want no good thing without. He that freely opens the upper, will never wholly close the nether springs. There shall be no silver lacking in Benjamin's sack, while Joseph has it to throw in. Grace is not such a beggarly visitant, as will not pay its own way. When the best of beings is adored, the best of blessings are enjoyed.—*William Secker.*

Verse 10.—People are apt to fancy that a wild beast's life must be happy— in a brute's sense—and that the carnivorous and graminivorous creatures which have never come under the dominion of mankind are better off than the domesticated quadrupeds which buy their quieter and safer lives at the price of ministering to the luxuries or necessities of their human lords. But the contrary is the case : the career of a flesh-eating animal must be wretched, even from the tiger's or leopard's point of view. They must often suffer pangs of long-continued hunger, and when they find and kill food they frequently have to wage desperate war for the enjoyment of their victim. The cry of almost every wild beast is so melancholy and forlorn, that it impresses the traveller with sadness more even than with fear. If the opportunity occurs for watching them in the chase, they are seen to sneak and sniff about, far less like " kings of the forest," than poor, dejected, starving wretches, desperate upon the subject of their next meal. They suffer horribly from diseases induced by foul diet and long abstinence ; and very few are found without scars in their hide—the tokens of terrible combats. If they live to old age their lot is piteous : their teeth are worn down, their claws are blunt, and in this state numbers of them perish by starvation. Not one half of the wild animals die a natural death ; and their life, so far as it can be observed, is a series of stern privations, with desperate and bloody fights among themselves.—*Clipping from " Daily Telegraph."*

Verse 10.—"*They that seek the Lord shall not want any good thing.*" There shall be no want to such, and such shall want no good thing : so that he must be such an one to whom the promise is made ; and he must also be sure that it is *good* for him which is promised. But oftentimes it is not good for a man to abound with earthly blessings ; as strong drink is not good for weak brains. Yea, if anything be wanting to a good man, he may be sure it is not good for him ; and then better that he doth want it, than that he did enjoy it ; and what wise man will complain of the want of that, which if he had, would prove more hurtful than gainful to him ? As a sword to a madman, a knife to a child, drink to them that have a fever or the dropsy. "No good thing will God withhold," etc, and therefore, not wants themselves, which to many are also good, yea, very good things, as I could reckon up many. Want sanctified is a notable means to bring to repentance, to work in us amendment of life, it stirs up prayer, it weans from the love of the world, it keeps us always prepared for the spiritual combat, discovers whether we be true believers or hypocrites, prevents greater evils of sin and punishment to come ; it makes us humble, conformable to Christ our Head, increaseth our faith, our joy, and thankfulness, our spiritual wisdom, and likewise our patience, as I have largely shown in another treatise.—*Richard Young, in the "Poor's Advocate,"* 1653.

Verse 10.—I remember as I came through the country, that there was a poor widow woman, whose husband fell at Bothwell : the bloody soldiers came to plunder her house, telling her they would take all she had. "We will leave thee nothing," said they, "either to put in thee, or on thee." "I care not," said she, "I will not want as long as God is in the heavens." That was a believer indeed.—*Alexander Peden's Sermon*, 1682.

Verse 10.—Take a survey of heaven and earth and all things therein, and whatsoever upon sure ground appears good, ask it confidently of Christ ; his love will not deny it. If it were good for you that there were no sin, no devil, no affliction, no destruction, the love of Christ would instantly abolish these. Nay, if the possession of all the kingdoms of the world were absolutely good for any saint, the love of Christ would instantly crown him monarch of them.—*David Clarkson.*

Verse 10 (*last clause*).—Part of his last afternoon was spent by Columba in transcribing the Psalms of David. Having come to that passage in the thirty-fourth Psalm, where it is said, "*They that seek the Lord shall not want any good thing,*" he said, "I have come to the end of a page, and I will stop here, for the following verse, "*Come, ye children, hearken unto me : I will teach you the fear of the Lord,*" will better suit my successor to transcribe than me. I will leave it, therefore, to Baithen." As usual, the bell was rung at midnight for prayers. Columba was the first to hasten to church. On entering it soon after, Dermid found him on his knees in prayer, but evidently dying. Raising him up in his arms, he supported his head on his bosom. The brethren now entered. When they saw Columba in this dying condition they wept aloud. Columba heard them. He opened his eyes and attempted to speak, but his voice failed. He lifted up his hands as if to bless them, immediately after which he breathed out his spirit. His countenance retained in death the expression it wore in life, so that it seemed as if he had only fallen asleep.—"*Story of Columba and his Successors,*" in the *Christian Treasury* for 1848.

Verse 11.—"*Come, ye children.*" Venema in substance remarks that David in addressing his friends in the cave, called them his sons or children, because he was about to be their teacher, and they his disciples ; and again, because they were young men in the flower of their age, and as sons, would be the builders up of his house ; and still more, because as their leader to whose discipline and command they were subject, he had a right to address them as his children.—*C. H. S.*

Verse 11.—"*Come ye children,*" etc. You know your earthly parents, ay, but labour to know your heavenly. You know the fathers of your flesh, ay, but strive to know the Father of your spirits. You are expert in may be in Horace's Odes, Virgil's Eclogues, Cicero's Orations ; oh ! but strive to get understanding in David's Psalms, Solomon's Proverbs, and the other plain books of Holy Writ. Manna was to be gathered in the morning. The orient pearl is generated of the morning dew ; *aurora musis amica*, the morning is a friend to the muses. O "*remember thy Creator,*" know him in the morning of thy childhood. When God had created the heavens and the earth, the first thing he did was to adorn the world with light, and separate it from the darkness. Happy is that child on whom the light of saving knowledge begins to dawn early. God, in the law, required the first-born, and the first-fruits, so he doth still our first days, to be offered to him. They are wisdom's words, " They that seek me early shall find me." Prov. viii. 17. Where a rabbin observeth a ב is added to the verb more than usual, which in numbering goeth for fifty. With this note, that early seeking hath not only twenty. or thirty, but fifty, nay, indeed, an hundred fold recompense attending on it.—*Nathanael Hardy.*

Verse 11.—*" Come, ye children."* David in this latter part of the Psalm under-takes to teach children ; though a man of war and anointed to be king, he did not think it below him : though now he had his head so full of cares, and his hands of business, yet he could find heart and time to give good counsel to young people from his own experience.—*Matthew Henry.*

Verse 11.—Observe I. What he expects from them, " *Hearken unto me,"* leave your play, lay by your toys, and hear what I have to say to you ; not only give me the hearing, but observe and obey me. II. What he undertakes to teach them, " *The fear of the Lord,"* inclusive of all the duties of religion. David was a famous musician, a statesman, a soldier, but he doth not say to his children, I will teach you to play upon the harp, or to handle the sword or spear, or draw the bow, or I will teach you the maxims of state policy, but I will teach you *the fear of the Lord,* which is better than all arts and sciences, better than all burnt-offerings and sacrifices. That is it which we should be solicitous both to learn ourselves, and to teach our children.—*Matthew Henry.*

Verse 11.—*" I will teach you the fear of the Lord."* I shall introduce the *translation* and *paraphrase* from my old Psalter ; and the rather because I believe there is a reference to that very improper and unholy method of teaching youth the system of heathen mythology before they are taught one sound lesson of true divinity, till at last their *minds* are *imbued* with *heathenism,*and the vicious conduct of gods, goddesses, and heroes (here very properly called tyrants), becomes the model of their own ; and they are as heathenish *without* as they are heathenish *within.*

Trans. " **Cummes sones lere me: dred of Lard I sal you lere.**

Par. " **Cummes,** with trauth and luf : **sones,** qwam I gette in haly lere : **heres** me. With eres of hert. I **sal lere you,** noght the fabyls of poetes ; na the storys of tyrauntz ; bot the dred of oure Larde, that wyl bring you til the felaghschippe of aungels ; and thar in is lyfe." I need not paraphrase this paraphrase, as it is plain enough.—*Adam Clarke.*

Verse 11.—*" The fear of the Lord."* The Master of Sentences dwells, from this verse, on the four kinds of fear : mundane, servile, initial, filial. *Mundane,* when we fear to commit sin, simply lest we should lose some worldly advantage or incur some worldly inconvenience. *Servile,* when we fear to commit sin, simply because of hell torments due to it. *Initial,* when we fear to commit it lest we should lose the happiness of heaven. *Filial,* when we fear, only and entirely because we dread to offend that God whom we love with all our hearts. " *I will teach."* Whence notice, that this fear is not a thing to be learnt all at once ; it needs careful study and a good master. S. Chrysostom compares the Psalmist's school here with the resort of heathen students to the academy ; and S. Ephraem, referring to this passage, calls the fear of God itself the school of the mind. " As if he proclaimed," says S. Lawrence Justiniani, " I will teach you, not the courses of the stars, not the nature of things, not the secrets of the heavens, but *the fear of the Lord.* The knowledge of such matters, without fear, puffs up ; but *the fear of the Lord, without any such knowledge,* can save." " Here," says Cassiodorus, " is not fear to be feared, but to be loved. Human fear is full of bitterness ; divine fear of sweetness : the one drives to slavery, the other allures to liberty ; the one dreads the prison of Gehenna, the other opens the kingdom of heaven."—*J. M. Neale.*

Verse 11.—*" The fear of the Lord."* Let this, therefore, good children, be your principal care and study ; for what shall it avail you to be cunning in Tully, Virgil, Homer, and other profane writers, if you be unskilful in God's book ? to have learned Greek and Latin, if you learn not withal the language of Canaan ? to have your speech agreeable to the rules of Priscian, of Lily, if your lives and courses be not consonant to the rules and laws of Christianity ? to have knowledge of the creatures when you are ignorant of the Creator ? to have learned that whereby you may live a while here, and neglect that whereby you may live eternally here-after ? Learn to fear God, to serve God, and then God will bless you ; for " He will bless them that fear him, both small and great." Ps. cxv. 13.—*Thomas Gataker's " David's Instructor,"* 1637.

Verse 12.—It is no great matter to live long, or always, but to live happily. That loyal prayer, " Let the king live " (in every language) imports a prosperous state.   When the Psalmist saith, " Who is the man that would see life ? " he explaineth himself presently after by " good days." *Vivere* among the Latins is sometimes as much as *valere*, to live is as much as to be well ; and upon this account it is that as, on the one hand, the Scripture calls the state of the damned an eternal death, because their life is only a continuance in misery ; so on the other hand the state of the blessed is an eternal life, because it is a perpetual abode in felicity.—*Nathanael Hardy.*

Verse 12.—The benefit of life is not in the length, but in the use of it. He sometimes lives the least that lives the longest.—*Seneca.*

Verse 13.—" *Keep thy tongue from evil,*" etc. Ficinus, after his tracts, *De sanitate tuenda, of keeping good health ;* and another, *of recovering* health ; and a third, *of prolonging life ;* because all will not do, wisely addeth a fourth, of *laying hold on eternal life ;* which cannot be done but by mortifying this earthly member, a loose and lewd tongue. " For by thy words thou shalt be justified, and by thy words thou shalt be condemned," saith the Judge himself. Matt. xii. 37. Compare Gen. xlix. 21 with Deut. xxxiii. 23, and it will appear that good words ingratiate with God and man.—*John Trapp.*

Verse 13.—" *And thy lips from speaking guile.*" Perhaps David, in warning us that we speak no guile, reflects upon his own sin in changing his behaviour. They that truly repent of what they have done amiss, will warn others to take heed of doing likewise.—*Matthew Henry.*

Verse 14.—" *Depart from evil,*" etc. This denotes that evil is near to men ; it keeps close to them, and should be declined and shunned : and it regards all sorts of evil ; evil men and their evil company ; evil things, evil words and works, and all appearance of evil ; and the fear of the Lord shows itself in a hatred of it, and a departure from it. Prov. viii. 13 ; xvi. 6.—*John Gill.*

Verse 14.—" *Depart from evil.*" The other precepts are the duty of works, and they are four, where the precepts of words were but two ; because we must be more in works than in words ; and they are all affirmative, for it is against the nature of a work to be in the negative ; for so working should be no better than idleness : the two former are general, as general as good and evil ; that if we meet with anything that is evil, our part is to *depart*, for there is no demuring upon evil.— *Sir Richard Baker.*

Verse 14.—" *Do good.*" Negative goodness is not sufficient to entitle us to heaven. There are some in the world whose religion runs all upon negatives ; they are not drunkards, they are not swearers, and for this they do bless themselves. See how the Pharisee vapours (Luke xviii. 11), " God, I thank thee that I am not as other men are, extortioners, unjust, adulterers," etc. Alas ! the not being scandalous will no more make a Christian than a cypher will make a sum. We are bid, not only to *cease from evil*, but to *do good*. It will be a poor plea at last—Lord, I kept myself from being spotted with gross sin : I did no hurt. But what good is there in thee ? It is not enough for the servant of the vineyard that he doth no hurt there, he doth not break the trees, or destroy the hedges ; if he doth not work in the vineyard he loseth his pay. It is not enough for us to say at the last day, we have done no hurt, we have lived in no gross sin ; but what good have we done in the vineyard ? Where is the grace we have gotten ? If we cannot show this, we shall lose our pay, and miss of salvation.—*Thomas Watson.*

Verse 14.—" *Seek peace, and pursue it.*" Yea, do well, and thou shalt not need to pursue it ; peace will find thee without seeking. Augustine says, *Fiat justitia, et habebis pacem*—Live righteously, and live peaceably. Quietness shall find out righteousness wheresoever he lodgeth. But she abhorreth the house of evil. Peace will not dine where grace hath not first broken her fast. Let us embrace godliness, and " the peace of God, that passeth all understanding, shall preserve our hearts and minds in Jesus Christ." Phil. iv. 7.—*Thomas Adams.*

Verse 14.—" *Seek peace and pursue it.*" The most desirable things are not the easiest to be obtained. What is more lovely to the imagination than the tranquillity of peace ? But this great blessing does not voluntarily present itself : it must be *sought*. Even when sought it often eludes the grasp : it flies away, and must be *pursued*. 1. The man of a peaceable carriage must be cautious not to give offence when needless, or, when it may innocently be spared.   2. Another part of the peaceable man's character is, not to take offence ; especially in small matters, which are hardly worth a wise man's notice.   3. If any needless offence has been either given or taken, we must endeavour to put a stop to it as soon as may be.   If a difference is already begun, stifle it in the birth, and suffer it not to proceed farther.—*Condensed from Dr. Waterland's Sermon, in J. R. Pitman's Course of Sermons on the Psalms, 1846.*

    Verse 15.—" His ears are open unto their cry." The word " open " is not in the original, but the meaning is that the ear of God is propense, and in a leaning kind of posture, towards the cries of the righteous ; the word may here be taken emphatically, as many times in Scripture it is, for some worthy, choice, and excellent strain of righteousness.   Those who are worthy and righteous indeed, the ear of God, I say, is propense, and leans and hangs towards them and their prayers, according to that of Cant. ii. 14, " Let me hear thy voice, for sweet is thy voice." There is a kind of naturalness and pleasantness between the ear of God and the prayers and petitions, and cries of such a righteous man.   John xv. 7.—*John Goodwin.*
    Verse 15.—" His ears are open unto their cry." Hebrew, " *Are to their cry*," or as St. Peter hath it, " *His ears are into their prayers* " (1 Peter iii. 12) ; to show that though their prayers are so faint and feeble that they cannot enter into the ears of the Lord of Hosts, yet that he will bow down and incline his ears *unto*, nay, *into* their prayers, their breathings.   Lam. iii. 56.—*John Trapp.*
    Verses 15—17.—" The eyes of the Lord are upon the righteous, and his ears are open unto their cry." Strangers may howl, and we take little notice what they ail—it is a venture whether we relieve them or no ; but if our children cry, being in great distress, we hasten to their help.   Our relation to God may well strengthen our hope that our desires shall be heard.   He that can cry, *Abba*, Father, may be confident of the success of his suit, and that God wilt deal with him as a son.—*George Swinnock.*

    Verse 18.—" The Lord is nigh unto them that are of a broken heart." God is nigh *unto them* (with reverence be it spoken), God takes so much complacency in the company of such, that he cannot endure to have them far from him ; he must have them always nigh to him, always under his eyes ; as for these " *broken* " ones, he will be sure not to leave them long, nor to go far from them, but will be ready at hand to set their bones, to bind up their wounds to keep them from festering.   It may be he may put them to much pain before he brings the cure to perfection, but it is to prevent future aches.   He is a foolish cruel chirurgeon, who, for fear of putting his patient to some pain, never searcheth the wound, but skins it over presently ; and a wise man will not think him unmerciful that puts him to exquisite pain, so he make a thorough cure of it.   Thus God doth by his patients sometimes, when the nature of their distemper calls for it.   But, however, he will be sure not to be out of the way when they want him most.   It is possible they may look upon themselves as forgotten by God, they may not know their Physician when he is by them, and they may take their Friend for an enemy ; they may think God far off when he is near ; but when their eyes are opened and their distemper is pretty well worn off, they will, with shame and thankfulness, acknowledge their error ; nay, they do from their souls confess, that they do not deserve the least look of kindness from God, but to be counted strangers and enemies ; but God will let them know that he loves to act like himself, that is, like a God of love, mercy, and goodness ; and that they are the persons that he hath set his heart upon ; he will have them in his bosom, never leave them nor forsake them ; and though these contrite ones many times look upon themselves as lost, yet God will save them, and they shall sing a song of thankfulness amongst his delivered ones.—*James Janeway.*
    Verse 18.—" The Lord is nigh unto them," etc.   Consider the ADVANTAGES of this broken heart ; as I. A broken heart is acceptable and well pleasing to God, " A broken and a contrite heart, O God, thou wilt not despise." Psalm li. 17. II. It makes up many defects in your service and duties, " The sacrifices of God are a broken spirit." Psalm li. 17.   III. It makes the soul a fit receptacle for God to dwell in, " For thus saith the high and lofty One that inhabiteth eternity, whose name is holy ; I dwell in the high and holy place with him also that is of a contrite and humble spirit, to revive the spirit of the humble and to revive the heart of the contrite ones." Isaiah lvii. 15.   IV. It brings God near to men, " *The Lord is nigh unto*

them that are of a broken heart, and saveth such as be of a contrite spirit." Psalm xxxiv. 18. And V. It lays you open to Christ's sweet healing, " I will bind up that which was broken, and will strengthen that which was sick." Ezek. xxxiv. 16. And, oh, who would not be broken that they may find Christ's soft hand healing them, and find the proof of that sweet word, " For I will restore health unto thee, and I will heal thee of thy wounds, saith the Lord." Jer. xxx. 17. Yea, VI. It puts you in the right road to heaven, where all your wounds and bruises will be cured ; for there is a tree (Rev. xxii. 2) the leaves whereof are for the healing of the nations ; there is no complaining there of wounds or bruises, but all are perfectly healed.—*John Spalding, in " Synaxis, Sac a, or a Collection of Sermons,* etc., 1703.

Verse 18.—" *The Lord is nigh unto them,*" etc. We are apt to overlook men, in proportion as they are humbled beneath us ; God regards them in that proportion. Vessels of honour are made of that clay which is " *broken* " into the smallest parts. George Horne.

Verse 18.—" *Broken heart* . . . . . *contrite spirit.*" Oh, this is the misery of all miseries which ministers have most cause to complain of, that men are not fitted enough for Jesus Christ, they are not lost enough in themselves for a Saviour. " In thee the fatherless findeth mercy." Hosea xiv. 3. Were we more hopeless, helpless, and fatherless, we should find more mercy from the hand of Jesus Christ. O that God would awaken and shake some sin-sleeping soul this day ! O that this doctrine thus opened might be as a thunderbolt to let some of you see the inside of yourselves ! O poor sinner, thou hast an unsupportable burden of sin and guilt lying on thy soul, ready to press thee down to hell, and yet thou feelest it not ; thou hast the wrath of God hanging over thy head by the twined thread of a short life, which it may be thou mayest not be free from one year, nay, perhaps not one month, but thou seest it not ; it thou didst but see it, then thou wouldest cry out as he did in Bosworth field, " A horse ! a horse ! a kingdom for a horse ! " So thou wouldest cry out, None but Christ ! nothing but Christ ! ten thousand worlds for Christ ! *James Nalton,* 1664.

Verse 18.—" *A contrite spirit.*" דַּכְּאֵי־רוּחַ, *dakkeey ruach,* " the beaten-out spirit." In both words the *hammer* is necessarily implied ; in breaking to pieces the ore first, and then plating out the metal when it has been separated from the ore. This will call to the reader's remembrance Jer. xxiii. 29, " Is not my word like as a fire ? saith the Lord : and like a *hammer* that breaketh the *rock* in pieces ? " The *breaking to shivers,* and *beating out* are metaphorical expressions : so are the *hammer* and the *rock.* What the large *hammer* struck on a rock by a powerful hand would do, so does the word of the Lord when struck on the sinner's heart by the power of the Holy Spirit. The *broken heart,* and the *contrite spirit,* are two essential characteristics of true repentance.—*Adam Clarke.*

Verse 19.—" *Many are the afflictions of the righteous,*" etc. Be our troubles many in number, strange in nature, heavy in measure ; yet God's mercies are more numerous, his wisdom more wondrous, his power more miraculous ; he will deliver us out of all.—*Thomas Adams.*

Verse 19.—" *Many are the afflictions of the righteous,*" etc. When David did behold his trouble, like the host of the Aramites (2 Kings vi. 16), he looked back unto God like Elisha, and spied one with him stronger than all against him. Therefore, respecting his afflictions he crieth, " *Many are the troubles of the righteous ;*" respecting the promise he sayeth, " *The Lord delivereth him out of all.*" Thus, by his own foot, David measureth the condition of the righteous, and saith, " *Many are the troubles of the righteous.* " and then, by his own cure, he showeth how they should be healed by saying, " *The Lord will deliver him out of them all.*" . . . . . The lawyer can deliver his client but from strife, the physician can deliver his patient but from sickness, the master can deliver his servant but from bondage, but the Lord delivereth us from *all.* As when Moses came to deliver the Israelites, the would not leave a hoof behind him, so when the Lord cometh to deliver the righteous he will not leave a trouble behind him. He who saith, " I put away all thine iniquities," will also say, " I put away all thine infirmities."—*Henry Smith.*

Verse 20.—" *He keepeth all his bones,*" which were very many. Perhaps (saith Abenezra here), David had been scourged by the Philistines, but his bones were not broken, nor were our Saviour's. John xix. 36.—*John Trapp.*

Verse 20.—" *All his bones.*" Muis observes, " It says not his *body,* for this he permits to be afflicted ; but it signifies that the evils of the godly are light, and scarcely penetrate to the bone ; " but Geier observes, " This is too subtle, rather the bone reminds us of the essential parts of the body, by whose injury the whole frame is endangered. It is a proverbial form of speech like that in Matt. x. 30, ' The very hairs of your head are all numbered,' expressing the remarkable defence afforded to the righteous." Genebrard, says, " The bones are put by synecdoche for all the members."—*From Poli Synopsis.*

Verse 20.—The passover lamb, of which not a bone was broken, prefigured Jesus as one, " not a bone of whose body should be broken ; " and yet, at the same time it prefigured the complete keeping and safety of Christ's body, the church ; as it is written, " *He keepeth all his bones ; not one of them is broken."—Andrew A. Bonar's Commentary on Leviticus.*

Verse 20.—Christ's bones were in themselves breakable, but could not actually be broken by all the violence in the world, because God had fore-decreed, *a bone of him shall not be broken.* So we confess God's children mortal ; but all the power of devil or man may not, must not, cannot, kill them before their conversion, according to God's election of them to life, which must be fully accomplished.—*Thomas Fuller.*

Verse 20.—Observe as a point of resemblance between this and the following Psalm, the mention of the bones here and in Psalm xxxv. 10.—*C. Wordsworth.*

Verse 21.—" *Evil."* Afflictions though in the plural, prove not ruinous to the righteous, for the Lord delivers him out of them all, whereas *evil* in *the singular* slays the wicked, to signify the difference of God's economy towards righteous and wicked men. The former is permitted to fall into many pressures, the latter is not so frequently exercised with them, yet the many that befall the one do no hurt, but work good for him, whereas the fewer that befall the wicked, or perhaps the *one singular affliction* of his life is the utter ruin of him.—*Henry Hammond.*

Verse 21 :—

> Conscience' self the culprit tortures, gnawing him with pangs unknown ;
> For that now amendment's season is for ever past and gone,
> And that late repentance findeth pardon none for all her moan.
>
> > *S. Peter Damiano*, 988—1072.

Verse 21.—" *Shall be desolate."* In the margin it is, *shall be guilty.* And this is the proper meaning of the original word, אשם. They are guilty, and liable to punishment. Thus the word is frequently rendered in our version (see Levit. iv. 13, 22) ; and generally includes in it the idea of guilt, and the punishment incurred by it.—*Samuel Chandler. D.D.*

Verse 22.—The promises of God to his church, and his threatenings of sin recorded in the living book of his word, are not antiquate ; no age shall ever superannuate them, or put them out of full force and virtue. What if good persons and good causes do suffer oppression ? The poet is a divine in that case—

> *Informes hiemes reducit*
> *Jupiter ; idem*
> *Summovet. Non si male nunc, et olim*
> *Sic erit.*

After foul weather comes fair ; though it be ill with us now, it will not be always. What if enemies of religion and moths of commonwealth do flourish and prosper, and have all things at will, let it not trouble David and Job ; both of them saw as fair a sunshine shut up in a dark cloud, and a world of foul weather following.—*Edward Marbury.*

Verse 22.—Satan cannot tempt longer than God shall give him leave ; and he will never suffer thee to be tempted above measure, but will give a good issue unto the temptation. Thou art called to fight under the banner of Christ Jesus, and in the name of the Lord thou shalt be enabled to do valiantly and overcome. If Satan continue his assaults, " God's grace is sufficient for thee." 2 Cor. xii. 9. If thy strength be clean gone, God's power shall be magnified the more in thee, and he hath brought thee low that thou mayest not trust in thyself, but in the living Lord, and that the whole praise of the victory might be ascribed unto him. If thy strength did remain, it was not to be leaned unto ; and now it is decayed and gone, there is no cause of fear for the Lord will be thy stay. In the most difficult assaults and tedious encounters, we are exhorted to " be strong in the Lord, and in the power of his might." Be of good courage, and God will grant thee an easy, a joyful victory. Satan's drift in tempting is to turmoil, dishearten, and perplex with fears, and drive into despair; and if thou take heart to rest quietly upon God's grace, and fly unto his name, thou shalt put him to flight, thou hast already got the day. Wait but awhile, and these dark mists and terrible storms shall be dispersed. By these temptations the Lord hath taught thee to see thy weakness, and the malice of Satan; to deny thine own wisdom and prize his favour, lightly to esteem all things here below, and highly to value mercy reaching to the pardon of sin, and heavenly communion, and fellowship with God. And if this bitter potion hath wrought so kindly for thy spiritual good, why shouldst thou be dismayed? Trust in the Lord, be of good courage, and he shall strengthen thee. "*The Lord redeemeth the soul of his servants : and none of them that trust in him shall be desolate.*"—*John Ball.*

HINTS TO PREACHERS.

Verse 1.—Firm resolution, serious difficulties in carrying it out, helps for its performance, excellent consequences of so doing.

Six questions.—*Who?* " I." *What?* " Will bless." *Whom?* " The Lord." *When?* " At all times." *How? Why?*

Verse 1.—Direction for making a heaven below.

Verse 2.—The commendable boaster and his gratified audience.

We may boast of the Lord, in himself, his manifestations of himself, his relationship to us, our interest in him, our expectations from him, etc.

The duty of believers to relate their experience for the benefit of others.

Verse 3.—Invitation to united praise.

Verse 3.—*Magnifying*—or making great the work of God, a noble exercise.

Verse 4.—*Confessions of a ransomed soul.* Simple, honouring to God, exclude merit, and encourage others to seek also.

Verse 4.—*Four stages,* " fears," " sought," " heard," " delivered."

Verse 5.—The power of a faith-look.

Verse 6.—I. The poor man's heritage, " troubles." II. The poor man s friend. III. The poor man's cry. IV. The poor man's salvation.

Verse 6.—The poor man's wealth.

The position of prayer in the economy of grace, or the natural history of mercy in the soul.

Verse 7.—*Castra angelorum, salvatio bonorum.*

Verse 7.—The ministry of angels.

In what sense Jesus is " The angel of the Lord."

Verse 8.—Experience the only true test of religious truth.

Verse 8.—*Taste.* The sanctified palate, the *recherché* provision, the gratified verdict, the celestial host.

Verse 9.—The blest estate of a God-fearing man.

Verse 9.—Fear expelling fear. *Similia similibus curantur.*

Verse 10.—Lions lacking, but the children satisfied. See " Spurgeon's Sermons," No. 65. I. Description of a true Christian, " seek the Lord." II. The promise set forth by a contrast. III. The promise fulfilled.

Verse 10.—What is a good thing?

Verse 11.—A royal teacher, his youthful disciples, his mode of instruction, " Come ;" his choice subject.

Verse 11.—Sunday-school work.

Verses 12, 13, 14.—How to make the best of both worlds.

Verse 13.—Sins of the tongue—their mischief, their cause, and their cure.

Verse 14 (*first clause*).—The relation between the negative and positive virtues.

Verse 14 (*second clause*).—*The royal hunt.* The game, the difficulties of the chase, the hunters, their methods, and their rewards.

Verse 15.—Our observant God. Eyes and ears both set on us.

Verse 16.—The evil man checkmated in life, and forgotten in death.

Verse 17.—*Afflictions and their threefold blessing.* I. They make us pray.

II. They bring us the Lord's hearing ear.   III. They afford room for joyful experience of deliverance.

Verse 18.—The nearness of God to broken hearts, and the certainty of their salvation.

Verse 19.—Black and white, or bane and antidote.

Special people, special trials, special deliverances, special faith as a duty.

Verse 20.—The real safety of a believer when in great perils. His soul, his spiritual life, his faith, hope, love, etc. ; his interest in Jesus, his adoption, justification, these all kept.

Verse 21.—Wickedness, its own executioner, illustrated by scriptural cases, by history, by the lost in hell. Lessons from the solemn fact.

The forlorn condition of a man of malicious spirit.

Verses 21, 22.—Who shall and who shall not be desolate.

Verse 22.—*Redemption* in its various meanings ; *faith* in its universal preservation ; *the Lord* in his unrivalled glory in the work of grace.

PSALM XXXV.

TITLE.—A Psalm of David.—*Here is all we know concerning this Psalm, but internal evidence seems to fix the date of its composition in those troublous times when Saul hunted David over hill and dale, and when those who fawned upon the cruel king, slandered the innocent object of his wrath, or it may be referred to the unquiet days of frequent insurrections in David's old age. The whole Psalm is the appeal to heaven of a bold heart and a clear conscience, irritated beyond measure by oppression and malice. Beyond a doubt David's Lord may be seen here by the spiritual eye.*

DIVISIONS.—*The most natural mode of dividing this Psalm is to note its triple character. Its complaint, prayer, and promise of praise are repeated with remarkable parallelism three times, even as our Lord in the Garden prayed three times using the same words. The first portion occupies from verse 1 to 10, the second from 11 to 18, and the last from 19 to the close : each section ending with a note of grateful song.*

EXPOSITION.

PLEAD *my cause*, O LORD, with them that strive with me : fight against them that fight against me.

2 Take hold of shield and buckler, and stand up for mine help.

3 Draw out also the spear, and stop *the way* against them that persecute me : say unto my soul, I *am* thy salvation.

4 Let them be confounded and put to shame that seek after my soul : let them be turned back and brought to confusion that devise my hurt.

5 Let them be as chaff before the wind : and let the angel of the LORD chase *them*.

6 Let their way be dark and slippery ; and let the angel of the LORD persecute them.

7 For without cause have they hid for me their net *in* a pit, *which* without cause they have digged for my soul.

8 Let destruction come upon him at unawares ; and let his net that he hath hid catch himself : into that very destruction let him fall.

9 And my soul shall be joyful in the LORD : it shall rejoice in his salvation.

10 All my bones shall say, LORD, who *is* like unto thee, which deliverest the poor from him that is too strong for him, yea, the poor and the needy from him that spoileth him ?

1. "*Plead my cause, O Lord, with them that strive with me.*" Plead against those who plead against me ; strive with my strivers ; contend with my contenders. If they urge their suit in the law-court, Lord, meet them there, and beat them at their own weapons. Every saint of God shall have this privilege : the accuser of the brethren shall be met by the Advocate of the saints. "*Fight against them that fight against me.*" If my adversaries try force as well as fraud, be a match for them ; oppose thy strength to their strength. Jesus does this for all his beloved—for them he is both intercessor and champion ; whatever aid they need they shall receive from him, and in whatever manner they are assaulted they shall be effectually defended. Let us not fail to leave our case into the Lord's hand. Vain is the help of man, but ever effectual is the interposition of heaven. What is here asked for as a boon, may be regarded as a promise, to all the saints ; in judgment they shall have a divine advocate, in warfare a divine protection.

2 "*Take hold of shield and buckler, and stand up for mine help.*" In vivid metaphor the Lord is pictured as coming forth armed for battle, and interposing himself between his servant and his enemies. The greater and lesser protections of providence may be here intended by the two defensive weapons, and by the

Lord's standing up is meant his active and zealous preservation of his servant in the perilous hour. This poetic imagery shows how the Psalmist realised the existence and power of God; and thought of him as a real and actual personage, truly working for his afflicted.

3. " *Draw out also the spear, and stop the way against them that persecute me.*" Before the enemy comes to close quarters the Lord can push them off as with a long spear. To stave off trouble is no mean act of lovingkindness. As when some valiant warrior with his lance blocks up a defile, and keeps back a host until his weaker brethren have made good their escape, so does the Lord often hold the believer's foes at bay until the good man has taken breath, or clean fled from his foes. He often gives the foes of Zion some other work to do, and so gives rest to his church. What a glorious idea is this of Jehovah blocking the way of persecutors, holding them at the pike's end, and giving time for the hunted saint to elude their pursuit! " *Say unto my soul, I am thy salvation.*" Besides holding off the enemy the Lord can also calm the mind of his servant by express assurance from his own mouth, that he is, and shall be, safe under the Almighty wing. An inward persuasion of security in God is of all things the most precious in the furnace of persecution. One word from the Lord quiets all our fears.

4. " *Let them be confounded and put to shame that seek after my soul.*" There is nothing malicious here, the slandered man simply craves for justice, and the petition is natural and justifiable. Guided by God's good spirit the Psalmist foretells the everlasting confusion of all the haters of the righteous. Shameful disappointment shall be the portion of the enemies of the gospel, nor would the most tenderhearted Christian have it otherwise : viewing sinners as men, we love them and seek their good, but regarding them as enemies of God, we cannot think of them with anything but detestation, and a loyal desire for the confusion of their devices. No loyal subject can wish well to rebels. Squeamish sentimentality may object to the strong language here used, but in their hearts all good men wish confusion to mischief-makers.

5 " *Let them be as chaff before the wind.*" They were swift enough to attack, let them be as swift to flee. Let their own fears and the alarms of their consciences unman them so that the least breeze of trouble shall carry them hither and thither. Ungodly men are worthless in character, and light in their behaviour, being destitute of solidity and fixedness ; it is but just that those who make themselves chaff should be treated as such. When this imprecation is fulfilled in graceless men, they will find it an awful thing to be for ever without rest, without peace of mind, or stay of soul, hurried from fear to fear, and from misery to misery. " *And let the angel of the Lord chase them.*" Fallen angels shall haunt them, good angels shall afflict them. To be pursued by avenging spirits will be the lot of those who delight in persecution. Observe the whole scene as the Psalmist sketches it : the furious foe is first held at bay, then turned back, then driven to headlong flight, and chased by fiery messengers from whom there is no escape, while his pathway becomes dark and dangerous, and his destruction overwhelming.

6. " *Let their way be dark and slippery.*" What terrors are gathered here! No light, no foothold, and a fierce avenger at their heels! What a doom is appointed for the enemies of God! They may rage and rave to-day, but how altered will be their plight ere long! " *And let the angel of the Lord persecute them.*" He will follow them hot-foot, as we say, never turning aside, but like a trusty pursuivant serving the writ of vengeance upon them, and arresting them in the name of unflinching justice. Woe, woe, woe, unto those who touch the people of God ; their destruction is both swift and sure.

7. In this verse the Psalmist brings forward the gravamen of his charge against the servants of the devil. " *For without cause*"—without my having injured, assailed, or provoked them ; out of their own spontaneous malice " *have they hid for me their net in a pit,*" even as men hunt for their game with cunning and deception. Innocent persons have often been ruined by traps set for them, into which they have fallen as guilelessly as beasts which stumble into concealed pits, and are taken as in a net. It is no little thing to be able to feel that the enmity which assails us is undeserved—uncaused by any wilful offence on our part. Twice does David assert in one verse that his adversaries plotted against him " *without cause.*" Net-making and pit-digging require time and labour, and both of these the wicked will expend cheerfully if they may but overthrow the people of God. Fair warfare belongs to honourable men, but the assailants of God's church prefer

mean, ungenerous schemes, and so prove their nature and their origin. We must all of us be on our guard, for gins and pitfalls are still the favourite weapons of the powers of evil.

8. "*Let destruction come upon him at unawares.*" This tremendous imprecation is frequently fulfilled. God's judgments are often sudden and signal. Death enters the persecutor's house without pausing to knock at the door. The thunderbolt of judgment leaps from its hiding-place, and in one crash the wicked are broken for ever. "*And let his net that he hath hid catch himself: into that very destruction let him fall.*" There is a *lex talionis* with God which often works most wonderfully. Men set traps and catch their own fingers. They throw up stones, and they fall upon their own heads. How often Satan outwits himself, and burns his fingers with his own coals! This will doubtless be one of the aggravations of hell, that men will torment themselves with what were once the fond devices of their rebellious minds. They curse and are cursed; they kick the pricks and tear themselves; they pour forth floods of fire, and it burns them within and without.

9. "*And my soul shall be joyful in the Lord.*" Thus rescued, David ascribes all the honour to the Judge of the right; to his own valorous arm he offers no sacrifice of boasting. He turns away from his adversaries to his God, and finds a deep unbroken joy in Jehovah, and in that joy his spirit revels. "*It shall rejoice in his salvation.*" We do not triumph in the destruction of others, but in the salvation given to us of God. Prayer heard should always suggest praise. It were well if we were more demonstrative in our holy rejoicings. We rob God by suppressing grateful emotions.

10. As if the tongue were not enough to bless God with, David makes every limb vocal—"*All my bones shall say, Lord, who is like unto thee?*" His whole anatomy he would make resonant with gratitude. Those bones which were to have been broken by my enemies shall now praise God; every one of them shall bring its tribute, ascribing unrivalled excellence to Jehovah the Saviour of his people. Even if worn to skin and bone, yet my very skeleton shall magnify the Lord, "*which deliverest the poor from him that is too strong for him, yea, the poor and the needy from him that spoileth him.*" God is the champion, the true knight-errant of all oppressed ones. Where there is so much condescension, justice, kindness, power, and compassion, the loftiest songs should be rendered. Come, dear reader, have you not been delivered from sin, Satan, and death, and will not you bless the Redeemer? You were poor and weak, but in due time Christ sought you, and set you free. O magnify the Lord to-day, and speak well of his name.

11 False witnesses did rise up; they laid to my charge *things* that I knew not.

12 They rewarded me evil for good *to* the spoiling of my soul.

13 But as for me, when they were sick, my clothing *was* sackcloth: I humbled my soul with fasting; and my prayer returned into mine own bosom.

14 I behaved myself as though *he had been* my friend *or* brother: I bowed down heavily as one that mourneth *for his* mother.

15 But in mine adversity they rejoiced, and gathered themselves together: *yea*, the abjects gathered themselves together against me, and I knew *it* not; they did tear *me*, and ceased not:

16 With hypocritical mockers in feasts, they gnashed upon me with their teeth.

17 Lord, how long wilt thou look on? rescue my soul from their destructions, my darling from the lions.

18 I will give thee thanks in the great congregation: I will praise thee among much people.

11. "*False witnesses did rise up.*" This is the old device of the ungodly, and we must not wonder if it be used against us as against our Master. To please Saul, there were always men to be found mean enough to impeach David. "*They laid to my charge things that I knew not.*" He had not even a thought of sedition; he was loyal even to excess; yet they accused him of conspiring against the Lord's

anointed. He was not only innocent, but ignorant of the fault alleged. It is well when our hands are so clean that no trace of dirt is upon them.

12. " *They rewarded me evil for good.*" This is devilish; but men have learned the lesson well of the old Destroyer, and practise it most perfectly. " *To the spoiling of my soul.*" They robbed him of comfort, and even would have taken his life had it not been for special rescues from the hand of God. The wicked would strip the righteous naked to their very soul : they know no pity. There are only such limits to human malice as God himself may see fit to place.

13 " *But as for me, when they were sick, my clothing was sackcloth.*" David had been a man of sympathy ; he had mourned when Saul was in ill health, putting on the weeds of sorrow for him as though he were a near and dear friend. His heart went into mourning for his sick master. " *I humbled my soul with fasting.*" He prayed for his enemy, and made the sick man's case his own, pleading and confessing as if his own personal sin had brought on the evil. This showed a noble spirit in David, and greatly aggravated the baseness of those who now so cruelly persecuted him. " *And my prayer returned into mine own bosom.*" Prayer is never lost : if it bless not those for whom intercession is made, it shall bless the intercessors. Clouds do not always descend in showers upon the same spot from which the vapours ascended, but they come down somewhere ; and even so do supplications in some place or other yield their showers of mercy. If our dove find no rest for the sole of her foot among our enemies, it shall fly into our bosoms and bring an olive branch of peace in its mouth. How sharp is the contrast all through this Psalm between the righteous and his enemies ! We must be earnest to keep the line of demarcation broad and clear.

14. " *I behaved myself as though he had been my friend or brother :*" I waited on him assiduously, comforted him affectionately, and sympathised with him deeply. This may refer to those days when David played on the harp, and chased away the evil spirit from Saul. " *I bowed down heavily, as one that mourneth for his mother.*" He bowed his head as mourners do. The strongest natural grief was such as he felt when they were in trouble. The mother usually wins the deepest love, and her loss is most keenly felt : such was David's grief. How few professors in these days have such bowels of compassion ; and yet under the gospel there should be far more tender love than under the law. Had we more hearty love to manhood, and care for its innumerable ills, we might be far more useful ; certainly we should be infinitely more Christ-like. " He prayeth best that loveth best."

15. " *But in mine adversity they rejoiced.*" In my halting they were delighted. My lameness was sport to them. Danger was near, and they sang songs over my expected defeat. How glad are the wicked to see a good man limp ! " Now," say they, " he will meet with his downfall." " *And gathered themselves together,*" like kites and vultures around a dying sheep. They found a common joy in my ruin, and a recreation in my sorrow, and therefore met together to keep the feast. They laid their heads together to devise, and their tongues to deceive. " *Yea, the abjects gathered themselves together against me.*" Those who deserved horsewhipping, fellows the soles of whose feet were needing the bastinado, came together to plot, and held hole and-corner meetings. Like curs around a sick lion, the mean wretches taunted and insulted one whose name had been their terror. The very cripples hobbled out to join the malicious crew. How unanimous are the powers of evil ; how heartily do men serve the devil ; and none decline his service because they are not endowed with great abilities ! " *I knew it not.*" It was all done behind my back. What a fluster the world may be in, and the cause of it all may not even know that he has given offence. " *They did tear me, and ceased not.*" It is such dainty work to tear to pieces a good man's character, that when slanderers have their hand in they are loath to leave off. A pack of dogs tearing their prey is nothing compared with a set of malicious gossips mauling the reputation of a worthy man. That lovers of the gospel are not at this time rent and torn as in the old days of Mary, is to be attributed to the providence of God rather than to the gentleness of men.

16. " *With hypocritical mockers in feasts, they gnashed upon me with their teeth.*" Like professional buffoons who grin around the banquet to make sport, so they made a business of jeering at the good man ; not, however, out of mirth, but from violent, insatiable hatred. Like cake-scoffers, or men who will jeer for a bit of bread, these hireling miscreants persecuted David in order to get a bellyful for themselves from Saul's table : having moreover an inward grudge against the son of Jesse because he was a better man than themselves.

Very forcibly might our Lord have used the words of these verses! Let us not forget to see the Despised and Rejected of men here painted to the life. Calvary and the ribald crew around the cross seem brought before our eyes.

17. " *Lord, how long wilt thou look on ?* " Why be a mere spectator? Why so neglectful of thy servant? Art thou indifferent? Carest thou not that we perish? We may thus reason with the Lord. He permits us this familiarity. There is a time for our salvation, but to our impatience it often seems to be very slow in coming; yet wisdom has ordained the hour, and nothing shall delay it. " *Rescue my soul from their destructions.* " From their many devices; their multiplied assaults, be pleased to set me free. " *My darling,* " my lovely, only, precious soul, do thou rescue " *from the lions.* " His enemies were fierce, cunning, and strong as young lions; God only could deliver him from their jaws, to God be therefore addresses himself.

18. " *I will give thee thanks in the great congregation.* " Notable deliverances must be recorded, and their fame emblazoned. All the saints should be informed of the Lord's goodness. The theme is worthy of the largest assembly; the experience of a believer is a subject fit for an assembled universe to hear of. Most men publish their griefs, good men should proclaim their mercies. " *I will praise thee among much people.* " Among friends and foes will I glorify the God of my salvation. Praise—personal praise, public praise, perpetual praise—should be the daily revenue of the King of heaven. Thus, for the second time, David's prayer ends in praise, as indeed all prayer should.

19 Let not them that are mine enemies wrongfully rejoice over me : *neither* let them wink with the eye that hate me without a cause.

20 For they speak not peace : but they devise deceitful matters against *them that are* quiet in the land.

21 Yea, they opened their mouth wide against me, *and* said, Aha, aha, our eye hath seen it.

22 *This* thou hast seen, O LORD : keep not silence : O LORD, be not far from me.

23 Stir up thyself, and awake to my judgment, *even* unto my cause, my God and my Lord.

24 Judge me, O LORD, my God, according to thy righteousness ; and let them not rejoice over me.

25 Let them not say in their hearts, Ah, so would we have it : let them not say, We have swallowed him up.

26 Let them be ashamed and brought to confusion together that rejoice at mine hurt : let them be clothed with shame and dishonour that magnify *themselves* against me.

27 Let them shout for joy, and be glad, that favour my righteous cause : yea, let them say continually, Let the LORD be magnified, which hath pleasure in the prosperity of his servant.

28 And my tongue shall speak of thy righteousness *and* of thy praise all the day long.

19. He earnestly prays that as they have no cause for their enmity, they may have no cause for triumph either in his folly, sin, or overthrow. " *Neither let them wink with the eye that hate me without a cause.* " The winking of the eye was the low-bred sign of congratulation at the ruin of their victim, and it may also have been one of their scornful gestures as they gazed upon him whom they despised. To cause hatred is the mark of the wicked, to suffer it causelessly is the lot of the righteous. God is the natural Protector of all who are wronged, and he is the enemy of all oppressors.

20. " *For they speak not peace.* " They love it not; how can they speak it? They are such troublers themselves that they cannot judge others to be peaceable. Out of the mouth comes what is in the heart. Riotous men charge others with sedition. " *They devise deceitful matters against them that are quiet in the land.* " David would fain have been an orderly citizen, but they laboured to make him a

rebel. He could do nothing aright, all his dealings were misrepresented. This is an old trick of the enemy to brand good men with S.S. on their cheeks, as sowers of sedition, though they have ever been a harmless race, like sheep among wolves. When mischief is meant, mischief is soon made. Unscrupulous partisans could even charge Jesus with seeking to overturn Cæsar, much more will they thus accuse his household. At this very hour, those who stand up for the crown rights of King Jesus are called enemies of the church, favourers of Popery, friends of Atheists, levellers, red republicans, and it were hard to say what besides. Billingsgate and Babylon are in league.

21. "*Yea, they opened their mouth wide against me.*" As if they would swallow him. Uttering great lies which needed wide mouths. They set no bounds to their infamous charges, but poured out wholesale abuse, trusting that if all did not stick, some of it would. "*And said, Aha, aha, our eye hath seen it.*" Glad to find out a fault or a misfortune, or to swear they had seen evil where there was none. Malice has but one eye ; it is blind to all virtue in its enemy. Eyes can generally see what hearts wish. A man with a mote in his eye sees a spot in the sun. How like a man is to an ass when he brays over another's misfortunes ! how like to a devil when he laughs a hyæna-laugh over a good man's slips ! Malice is folly, and when it holds a festival its tones and gestures far exceed all the freaks and mummeries of the Lord of misrule.

22. "*This thou hast seen, O Lord.*" Here is comfort. Our heavenly Father knows all our sorrow. Omniscience is the saint's candle which never goes out. A father will not long endure to see his child abused. Shall not God avenge his own elect ? "*Keep not silence.*" Rebuke thine enemies and mine, O Lord. A word will do it. Clear my character, comfort my heart. "*O Lord, be not far from me.*" Walk the furnace with me. Stand in the pillory at my side. The sweet presence of God is the divine cordial of the persecuted ; his painful absence would be their deepest misery.

23. "*Stir up thyself.*" Be upon thy mettle. Prove that thou art no indifferent witness to all this infamy. "*Awake to my judgment.*" Take the sceptre and summon the great assize ; vindicate justice, avenge oppression. Do not tarry as men do who sleep. "*Even unto my cause, my God and my Lord.*" He claims a nearness to his God, he holds him with both hands ; he leaves his case with the righteous Judge. He begs that the suit may be brought on, heard, tried, and verdict given. Well is it for a man when his conscience is so clear that he dares to make such an appeal.

24. The appeal is here repeated ; the plaintiff feels that the joy of his accusers will be shortlived as soon as impartial justice rules. The oppressors' wrong, the proud man's contumely, the fool's grimace—all, all will cease when the righteous Lord sits down upon the judgment seat.

25. "*Let them not say in their hearts, Ah, so would we have it : let them not say, We have swallowed him up.*" Disappoint them of their prey when their mouths are ready to swallow it. Saints are too dear a morsel for the powers of evil ; God will not give his sheep over to the wolfish jaws of the persecutors. Just when they are tuning their pipes to celebrate their victory, they shall be made to laugh on the other side of their mouths. They are all too sure, and too boastful ; they reckon without their host : little do they dream of the end which will be put to their scheming. Their bird shall be flown, and they themselves shall be in the trap. The prayer of this text is a promise. Even before the lips of the wicked can frame a speech of exultation, they shall be disappointed ; their heart-speech shall be forestalled, their wishes frustrated, their knavish tricks exposed.

26. Here is the eternal result of all the laborious and crafty devices of the Lord's enemies. God will make little of them, though they "*magnified themselves ;*" he will shame them for shaming his people, bring them to confusion for making confusion, pull off their fine apparel and give them a beggarly suit of dishonour, and turn all their rejoicing into weeping and wailing, and gnashing of teeth. Truly, the saints can afford to wait.

27. "*Let them shout for joy, and be glad, that favour my righteous cause.*" Even those who could not render him active aid, but in their hearts favoured him, David would have the Lord reward most abundantly. Men of tender heart set great store by the good wishes and prayers of the Lord's people. Jesus also prizes those whose hearts are with his cause. The day is coming when shouts of victory shall be raised by all who are on Christ's side, for the battle will turn, and the foes of

truth shall be routed. " *Yea, let them say continually, Let the Lord be magnified.*" He would have their gladness contributory to the divine glory; they are not to shout to David's praise, but for the honour of Jehovah. Such acclamations may fitly be continued throughout time and eternity. " *Which hath pleasure in the prosperity of his servant.*" They recognised David as the Lord's servant, and saw with pleasure the Lord's favour to him. We can have no nobler title than " servant of God," and no greater reward than for our Master to delight in our prosperity. What true prosperity may be we are not always best able to judge. We must leave that in Jesus' hand; he will not fail to rule all things for our highest good.

> " For by his saints it stands confessed.
> That what he does is always best."

28. Unceasing praise is here vowed to the just and gracious God. From morning till evening the grateful tongue would talk and sing, and glorify the Lord. O for such a resolve carried out by us all !

EXPLANATORY NOTES AND QUAINT SAYINGS.

Whole Psalm.—Bonar entitles this Psalm, " *The awful utterance of the Righteous One regarding those that hate him without cause ;* " and he makes the following remarks thereupon :—" Throughout the endless day of eternity the Lord Jesus shall himself speak the Father's ' praise,' and shall put marked emphasis on his ' righteousness '— that righteousness which shall have been exhibited, both in the doom of those who hated the offered Redeemer, and in the salvation of those who received him. There is nothing in all this wherein his own may not fully join, especially on that day when their views of justice shall be far clearer and fuller than now. On that day we shall be able to understand how Samuel could hew Agag in pieces, and the godly hosts of Israel slay utterly in Canaan man and woman and child, at God's command. We shall be able, not only fully to agree in the doom, ' Let them be confounded,' etc., but even to sing, ' Amen, Hallelujah,' over the smoke of torment. Rev. xix. 1, 2. We should in some measure now be able to use every verse of this Psalm in the spirit in which *the Judge* speaks it, we feeling ourselves his assessors in judging the world. 1 Cor. vi. 2. We shall, at all events, be able to use it on that day when what is written here shall be all accomplished."—*Andrew A. Bonar.*

Verse 1.—" *Plead my cause, O God, with them that strive with me.*" 1. Doth the world condemn thee for thy zeal in the service of God ? Reproachfully scorn thee for thy care to maintain good works ? not blush to traduce thee with imputations of preciseness, conceited singularity, pharisaical hypocrisy ? Oh but if thy conscience condemn thee not all this while, if that be rectified by the sacred word of God, if thou aim at his glory in pursuing thine own salvation, and side not with the disturbers of the church, go on, good Christian, in the practice of piety, discourage not thyself in thy laudable endeavours, but recount with comfort that the Lord is thy judge (1 Cor. iv. 4), with a *scio cui crediderim,* " I know whom I have believed." 2 Tim. i. 12. 2. Art thou wrongfully adjudged in the erroneous courts of men ? are truth and righteousness gone aside from their proper places ? Is equity neglected, and poverty overlaid ? Well, have patience awhile, cheer up thy fainting spirits, there is a God that beholdeth the innocency of thy cause, unto whom thou hast liberty to make thy last appeal: " *Plead my cause, O Lord, with them that strive with me : fight against them that fight against me.*" Or, 3. Art thou otherwise injured by the hands of malicious men ? and doth a penurious estate disable thee to sue for amends ? Doth a *Nimrod* oppress thee ? A *Laban* defraud thee ? A covetous landlord gripe thee ? Well, yet take not the matter into thine own hands by attempting unlawful courses ; presume not to be judge in thine own cause, for default of a present redress ; but often remember what the apostle taught his Thessalonians : " It is a righteous thing with God to recompense tribulation to them that trouble you."—*Isaac Craven's Sermon at Paul's Cross,* 1630.

Verse 1.—" Plead," etc. More literally, *litigate, O Lord, with them that litigate* against me, contend against them that contend with me ; *i.e.*, avenge me of mine adversaries.—*Daniel Cresswell, D.D., F.R.S., in "The Psalms of David according to the Book of Common Prayer : with Critical and Explanatory Notes,"* 1843.

Verse 2.—*" Shield and buckler."* The word rendered *" shield "* is in the Hebrew text מָגֵן, *magen*, which was a short buckler intended merely for defence. The word rendered *" buckler "* is צִנָּה *tsinnah ;* it was double the weight of the magen, and was carried by the infantry ; the magen, being lighter and more manageable, was used by the cavalry. The *tsinnah* answered to the *scutum*, and the magento the *clypeus*, among the Romans. The word *tsinnah*, means that kind of shield from the middle of which there arose a large boss, surmounted by a dagger, and which was highly useful both as a defensive and an offensive weapon in ancient warfare.—*James Anderson, note to Calvin in loc.*

Verse 3.—*" Draw out the spear, and stop the way."* The spear in the days of Saul and David was a favourite weapon. (See 1 Chron. xi.). A valiant man bravely defending a narrow pass might simply with his lance keep back a pursuing host, and give time for his friends to escape. Very remarkable were the feats of valour of this sort performed in Oriental warfare. David would have his God become his heroic defender, making his enemies pause.—*C. H. S.*

Verse 3.—*" Draw out ;"* or, as the Hebrew phrase is, *empty*, that is *unsheath* the like is of the *sword*. Exod. xv. 9 ; Levit. xxvi. 33.—*Henry Ainsworth.*

Verse 3.—*" Say unto my soul, I am thy salvation."* Observe, 1. That salvation may be made sure to a man. David would never pray for that which could not be. Nor would Peter charge us with a duty which stood not in possibility to be performed. 2 Peter 1. 10. " Make your election sure." And to stop the bawling throats of all cavilling adversaries, Paul directly proves it : " Know ye not your own selves, how that Jesus Christ is in you, except ye be reprobates ? " 2 Cor. xiii. 5. We may then know that Christ is in us. If Christ be in us, we are in Christ ; if we be in Christ, we cannot be condemned, for (Rom. viii. 1) " There is no damnation to them which are in Christ Jesus." But I leave this point that it may be sure, as granted ; and come to ourselves that we may make it sure. The Papists deny this, and teach the contrary, that salvation cannot be made sure ; much good do it them, with their sorry and heartless doctrine ! If they make that impossible to any which God hath made easy for many, " into their secret let not my soul come." Gen. xlix. 6. Observe, 2. That the best saints have desired to make their salvation sure. David that knew it, yet entreats to know it more. " I know thou favourest me " (Psalm xli. 11) ; yet here still, *dic animæ*, " Say *unto my soul, I am thy salvation."* A man can never be too sure of his going to heaven.—*Thomas Adams.*

Verse 3.—*" Say unto my soul."* God may speak with *his own voice ;* and thus he gave assurance to Abraham, " Fear not, I am thy shield, and thy exceeding great reward." Gen. xv. 1. If God speak comfort, let hell roar horror. 2. He may speak by *his works :* actual mercies to us demonstrate that we are in his favour, and shall not be condemned. " By this I know that thou favourest me, because mine enemy doth not triumph over me." 3. He may speak by *his Son.* " Come unto me, all ye that labour and are heavy laden, and I will give you rest." Matt. xi. 28. 4. He may speak by *his Scripture ;* this is God's epistle to us, and his letters patent, wherein are granted to us all the privileges of salvation. A universal *si quis ;* " Whosoever believes, and is baptised, shall be saved." 5. He may speak by *his ministers*, to whom he hath given "the ministry of reconciliation." 2 Cor. v. 19. 6. He doth speak this by *his Spirit :* he " sendeth forth the Spirit of his Son into our hearts, crying, Abba, Father." Gal. iv. 6. By all these voices God says to his elect, " *I am your salvation."* . . . . " *My."* There is no vexation to the vexation of the soul ; so no consolation to the consolation of the soul. . . . . . Let this teach us to make much of this " *My."* Luther says there is great divinity in pronouns. The assurance that God will save some is a faith incident to devils. The very reprobates may believe that there is a book of election ; but God never told them that their names were written there. The hungry beggar at the feast-house gate smells good cheer, but the master doth not say, " This is provided for thee." It is small comfort to the harbourless wretch to pass through a goodly city, and see many glorious buildings, when he cannot say, *Hæc mea domus.* I have a place here. The beauty of that excellent city

Jerusalem, built with sapphires, emeralds, chrysolites, and such precious stones, the foundation and walls whereof are perfect gold (Rev. xxi.), affords a soul no comfort, unless he can say, *Mea civitas*, I have a mansion in it. The all-sufficient merits of Christ do thee no good, unless, *tua pars et portio*, he be thy Saviour. Happy soul that can say with the Psalmist, " O Lord, thou art my portion ! " Let us all have oil in our lamps, lest if we be then to buy, beg, or borrow, we be shut out of doors like the fools, not worthy of entrance. Pray, " *Lord, say unto my soul, I am thy salvation.*" . . . . Who ? What ? To whom ? When ? WHO ? The Lord ! To the Lord David prays. He hath made a good choice, for there is salvation in none other. " Thou hast destroyed thyself, but in me is thy help." Hosea xiii. 9. The world fails, the flesh fails, the devil kills. Only the Lord saves. WHAT ? Salvation. A special good thing ; every man's desire. I will give thee a lordship, saith God to Esau. I will give thee a kingdom, saith God to Saul. I will give thee an apostleship, saith God to Judas. But, I will be thy salvation, he says to David, and to none but saints. To WHOM ? " *My salvation.*" Not others only, but " *thine.*" A man and a Christian are two creatures. He may be a man that hath reason and outward blessings ; he is only a Christian that hath faith, and part in the salvation of Christ. God is plentiful salvation, but it is not ordinary to find a *cui*—to whom. Much of heaven is lost for lack of a hand to apprehend it. WHEN ? In the present, " *I am.*" *Sum, non sufficit quod ero.* It is comfort to Israel in captivity that God says, *Ero tua redemptio,* I will redeem thee ; but the assurance that quiets the conscience is this, " *I am thy salvation.*" As God said to Abraham, " Fear not, I am with thee." Deferred hope faints the heart. Whatsoever God forbears to assure us of, oh, pray we him not to delay this, " Lord, say to our souls, *I am your salvation.*"—*Condensed from Thomas Adams.*

Verse 4.—" *Let them be confounded and put to shame.*" Here David beginneth his imprecations, which yet, saith Theodoret, he doth not utter as cursing, but as prophesying rather. If we shall at any time take upon us thus to imprecate (as we may in some cases), we must see to it, first, that our cause be good ; secondly, that we do it not out of private revenge, but merely for the glory of God ; thirdly, that we utter not a syllable this way, but by the guidance of God's good Spirit.—*John Trapp.*

Verses 4—8, 26.—How are we to account for such prayers for vengeance ? We find them chiefly in four Psalms, the seventh, thirty-fifth, sixty-ninth, and one-hundred and ninth, and the imprecations in these form a terrible climax. In the last no less than thirty anathemas have been counted. Are these the mere outbursts of passionate and unsanctified feeling, or are they the legitimate expression of a righteous indignation ? Are they to be excused as being animated by the " spirit of Elias ? " a spirit not unholy indeed, but far removed from the meekness and gentleness of Christ ; or are they the stereotyped forms in which the spirit of devotion may utter itself ? Are they Jewish only, or may they be Christian also ? An uninstructed fastidiousness, it is well known, has made many persons recoil from reading these Psalms at all. Many have found their lips falter when they have been called to join in using them in the congregation, and have either uttered them with bated breath and doubting heart, or have interpreted them in a sense widely at variance with the letter. Some have tried to reconcile them with a more enlightened conscience, by regarding such words not as the expression of a wish, but as the utterance of a prediction ; the Hebrew optative, which is distinct enough from the simple future, absolutely forbids this expedient. Others again would see in them expressions which may lawfully be used in the soul's wrestling against spiritual enemies. And finally, some would defend them as utterances of righteous zeal for God's honour, and remind us that if we do not sympathise with such zeal, it may be not because our religion is more pure, but because our hearts are colder.

Now the real source of the difficulty lies in our not observing and bearing in mind the essential difference between the Old Testament and the New. The older dispensation was in every sense a sterner one than the new. The spirit of Elias, though not an evil spirit, was not the spirit of Christ. " The Son of Man came not to destroy men's lives, but to save them." Luke ix. 56. And through him his disciples are made partakers of the same spirit. But this was not the spirit of the older economy. The Jewish nation had been trained in a sterner school. It had been steeled and hardened by the discipline which had pledged it to a war of extermination with idolaters ; and however necessary such a discipline might be, it would not tend to foster the gentler virtues ; it is conceivable how even a righteous man, under it, feeling it to be his bounden duty to root out evil wherever he saw it, and identifying, as he did, his own enemies with the enemies of Jehovah, might use language which to us appears unnecessarily vindictive. To men so trained and taught, what we call "religious toleration," was a thing not only wrong, but absolutely inconceivable.

It may be quite true that we find revenge forbidden as directly in the Old Testament as in the New, as, for instance, in Lev. xix. 18, "Thou shalt not avenge," etc., though even there there is a limitation, "against the children of thy people." And it may be no less true that we find instances of imprecation in the New; as when St. Paul says (2 Tim. iv. 14), "Alexander the coppersmith did me much evil : the Lord reward him according to his works," or when he exclaims (Acts xxiii. 3), "God will smite thee, thou whited wall ; " or, "If any man love not the Lord Jesus Christ, let him be anathema." But even these expressions are very different from the varied, deliberate, carefully-constructed, detailed anathemas of the Psalms. And our Lord's denunciations, to which Hengstenberg refers, are in no way parallel. They are not curses upon individuals, but in fact solemn utterances of the great truth, "Except ye repent, ye shall all likewise perish." But after all, whatever may be said of particular passages, the general tone which runs through the two covenants, is unquestionably different. To deny this is not to honour Moses, but to dishonour Christ. Matt. v. 43 ; xix. 8. On the other hand, we must not forget that these imprecations are not the passionate longing for personal revenge. The singer undoubtedly sees in his enemies the enemies of God and his church. They that are not with him are against God. And because the zeal of God's house even consumes him, he prays that all the doers of iniquity may be rooted out. The indignation therefore is righteous, though it may appear to us wrongly directed, or excessive in its utterance.

Once more, the very fact that a dark cloud hid God's judgment in the world to come from the view of the Old Testament saints, may be alleged in excuse of this their desire to see him take vengeance on his enemies here. How deeply the problem of God's righteousness exercised their minds, is abundantly evident from numerous places in the Psalms. They longed to see that righteousness manifested. It could be manifested, they thought, only in the evident exaltation of the righteous, and the evident destruction of the wicked here. Hence, with their eye always fixed on temporal recompense, they could even wish and pray for the destruction of the ungodly. The awful things of the world to come were to a great extent hid from their eyes. Could they have seen these, then surely their prayer would have been not, "Let the angel of the Lord persecute them," "Blot them out of thy book ; " but rather with him who hung upon the cross ; "Father, forgive them, for they know not what they do."—*J. J. Stewart Perowne.*

Verses 4, 8, 26.—David was about as devoid of vindictiveness as any public character who can well be named. His conduct in relation to Saul, from first to last displayed a singularly noble spirit, far removed from anything like the lust of vengeance ; and the meekness with which he endured the bitter reproaches of Shimei, bore witness to the same spirit after his accession to the throne.

When David's whole career is intelligently and fairly reviewed, it leaves on the mind the impression of a man possessed of as meek and placable a temper as was ever associated with so great strength of will, and such strong passions. Even in the heats of sudden resentment, he was not apt to be hurried into deeds of revenge. Such being the case, it would certainly have been a strange and unaccountable thing if he had shown himself less the master of his own spirit in poems composed in seasons of retirement and communion with God, especially since these very poems express a keen sense of the heinousness of the sin that has been laid to his charge. He can affirm regarding his implacable enemies, "As for me, when they were sick, my clothing was sackcloth : I humbled my soul with fasting ; and my prayer returned into mine own bosom. I behaved myself as though he had been my friend or brother : I bowed down heavily, as one that mourneth for his mother." Psalm xxxv. 13, 14. "O Lord, my God, if I have done this ; if there be iniquity in my hands ; if I have rewarded evil unto him that was at peace with me (yea, I have delivered him that without cause is mine enemy) : let the enemy persecute my soul, and take it ; yea, let him tread down my life upon the earth." Psalm vii. 3—5. Surely one ought to think twice before putting on the imprecations an interpretation which would make them utterly incongruous with these appeals, uttered almost in the same breath.—*William Binnie, D.D.*

Verse 5.—" *As chaff.*" Literally, " As the thistledown."—*John Morison.*

Verse 6.—" *Let their way be dark and slippery.*" A horrible way ! Darkness alone who feareth not ? A slippery way alone who avoids not ? In a dark and slippery way, how shalt thou go ? where set foot ? These two ills are the great punishments of men : darkness, ignorance ; a slippery way, luxury. " *Let their way be darkness and slipping*; *and let the angel of the Lord persecute them,*" that they be not able to stand. For anyone in a dark and slippery way, when he seeth that if he move his foot he will fall, and there is no light before his feet, haply resolving to wait until light come ; but here is the angel of the Lord persecuting them.— *Augustine.*

Verse 6.—" *Slippery.*" Margin, as in Heb., *slipperiness.* This is a circumstance which adds increased terror to the image. It is not only a *dark* road, but a road made slippery by rains ; a road where they are in danger every moment of sliding down a precipice where they will be destroyed.—*Albert Barnes.*

Verse 7.—" *They hid for me their net in a pit.*" As if David had said that they had dug a pit, and covered and hid its mouth with a net, that I might pass upon it and fall into it.—*Kimchi.*

Verse 8.—" *Let destruction come upon him at unawares.*" Or *a storm,* such as is caused in the Eastern countries by a south wind, very sudden, violent, and destructive.—*John Gill.*

Verse 8.—" *Let his net that he hath hid catch himself : into that very destruction let him fall.*" By giving Ahithophel rope enough, the Lord preserved David from perishing. Who will not admire that Goliath should be slain with his own sword, and that proud Haman should hold Mordecai's stirrup, and be the herald of his honour ? The wicked shall be undone by their own doings ; all the arrows that they shoot at the righteous shall fall upon their own pates. Maxentius built a false bridge to drown Constantine, but was drowned himself. Henry the Third of France was stabbed in the very same chamber where he had helped to contrive the cruel massacre of the French Protestants. And his brother, Charles the Ninth, who delighted in the blood of the saints, had blood given him to drink, for he was worthy. It is usual with God to take persecutors in the snares and pits that they have laid for his people, as many thousands in this nation have experienced ; and though Rome and her confederates are this day a-laying of snares and traps and a-digging of pits for the righteous, who will rather burn than bow to their Baal, yet do but wait and weep, and weep and wait a little, and you shall see that the Lord will take them in the very snares and pits that they have laid and digged for his people.—*Condensed from Thomas Brooks.*

Verse 8.—" *Let his net that he hath hid catch himself.*" Thou fool, who opposest thy counsels to those of the Most High. He who devises evil for another, falls at last into his own pit, and the most cunning finds himself caught by what he had prepared for another. But virtue without guile, erect like the lofty palm, rises with greater vigour when it is oppressed.—*Pietro Metastasio, 1698—1782.*

Verse 9.—" *And my soul shall be joyful in the Lord,*" etc. While some ascribe to fortune, and others to their own skill, the praise of their deliverance from danger, and few, if any, yield the whole praise of it to God, David here declares that he will not forget the favour which God had bestowed upon him. My soul, says he, shall rejoice, not in a deliverance of the author of which it is ignorant, but in the salvation of God. To place the matter in a still stronger light, he assigns to his very bones the office of declaring the divine glory. As if not content that his tongue should be employed in this, he applies all the members of his body to the work of setting forth the praises of God. The style of speaking which he employs is hyperbolical, but in this way he shows unfeignedly that his love to God was so strong that he desired to spend his sinews and bones in declaring the reality and truth of his devotion.—*John Calvin.*

Verse 10.—" *All my bones*," etc. These words contain the most vivid description of the highest delight which by the whole soul and body should be experienced and openly manifested. He mentions his soul (verse 9) and all his bones as about to take part in the joy, to indicate that he most heartily and with his whole body was about to rejoice, and that the joy which he would manifest would not be of an ordinary character, but of the highest order, so that each several bone should sing forth the praises of God.—*Hermon Venema,* 1697—1787.

Verse 10.—" *All my bones.*" In the Scriptures emotions are generally ascribed to the viscera, the bones are usually regarded as passive ; in this place and Psalm li. 8, and in these two places only, exulting joy is attributed to the bones. Ordinary experience shows us that the intestines have sympathy with our passionate excitements, but we have no consciousness of the bones becoming sympathetically sensitive. The expression therefore is highly poetical, and indicates that the joy intended would be far beyond ordinary and common delight ; it would be so profound that even the most callous part of the human frame would partake of it. Doubtless the poetry has a basis of truth in it, for though we may not perceive it, there is most assuredly a true and real sympathy with our mental states in every particle of bone and muscle, as well as in those tender organs which are more apparently affected.—*C. H. S. Thoughts suggested by a passage in " Biblical Psychology," by Franz Delitzsch.*

Verse 10.—" *All my bones.*" That is, whatsoever strength and vigour is in me it shall be spent in celebrating thy praises. Or, although I have nothing left me but skin and bones, so poor am I grown, yet I will not be wanting to the work.—*John Trapp.*

Verse 10.—My bones are riving through my skin, and yet all my bones are praising him. " I said, I am cast out of thy sight, but I will look again towards thy holy temple."—*Thomas Halyburton,* 1674—1711.

Verse 11.—" *They laid to my charge things that I knew not.*" You will say, Why does God permit wicked people to lay to the charge of the godly such things as they are clear of : God if he pleased could prevent it, and stop the mouths of the wicked, that they should not be able to speak against his children ? Answer—As all things work for the best to them that love God, so this works for the good of God's people. God doth permit it for the good of his people, and thus he frustrates the hopes of the wicked : they intend evil against the godly, and God disposes of it for good. As Joseph said to his brethren, " You intended evil against me, and God disposed of it for good ; " so we may say to such as falsely slander God's people, You intended evil against the people of God, but God disposes of it for good. There is a fivefold good that God brings out of it to his people. *First,* God doth by this means humble them, and brings them to examine what is amiss : so that though they be clear of that crime laid to their charge, yet they will then examine whether there be nothing else amiss betwixt God and them ; they will search their hearts, and walk more humbly, and cleave more close to the Lord. *Secondly,* God doth by this means bring them oftener upon their knees, to seek unto him, to plead their cause, and to clear their innocency. How oft did the prophet speak unto God when the wicked did falsely accuse him ; how did he make his moan at the throne of grace unto God, beseeching him to plead his cause, and to keep him close in his way, that the wicked might not rejoice at his downfall ! So when God's people see that it is that which the wicked would have, that which is their joy, to see the godly fall into such and such a sin ; then the godly will pray more earnestly with David, Lord, lead me in a right path because of my observers ; then they will be earnest with God to keep them from falling into that sin that the wicked desire they might fall into ; and this is a second good that comes of it. *Thirdly,* God doth use the reproach of the wicked as a preventing medicine against that crime which the wicked lay to their charge. The godly have unrenewed nature as well as renewed, and if God should leave them never so little to themselves, they are not their own keepers, they might fall into that sin which the wicked lay to their charge : and every godly man and woman may say when they are falsely accused, It is God's mercy that I did not fall into that sin that lay to my charge. God doth use wicked people's tongues as a warning against such a sin, that when they see how the wicked joy at a brat of their own hatching, then they consider, if the wicked thus joy without a cause, what would they do if they had just cause ? Well, by the help of God this shall be a warning to me for ever to watch against that sin : for the time to come I will pray more against that particular sin than I have done, and watch more against that sin than I have done ; through God's help they shall never have occasion to rejoice over me in that kind. Truly, I verily believe many a child of God can say by experience, I never should have prayed and watched against such a sin so much, had not God used the tongues of the wicked as preventing physic : I knew not my own heart, but that I might have fallen into such and such a sin had not God by this means hedged up my way with thorns ; and this is the third good comes of it. *Fourthly,* God doth by this means exercise the graces of his people by letting them undergo bad report as well as good report : he tries whether they will cleave close to him in all conditions, as Psalm xliv. 15—17. *Fifthly,* God doth by this means teach them how to judge of others when they are falsely accused. For the time to come they will not receive a false report against their neighbour ; they will know the truth of a thing before they believe it, and they know how to comfort others in the like condition ; and thus God disposes of it for good, and thus God makes the wicked the servant of his people in that very thing which the wicked think to wrong them most in ; for he uses the wicked as the rod and wisp, to scour off the rust of their graces and to correct their security ; and when the rod hath done its office then it is thrown into the fire : and thus you see how God disposes of the wicked's false accusations of his people for good.— *Zephaniah Smyth's Sermon, " The Malignant's Plot,"* 1647.

Verse 12.—" *They rewarded me evil for good.*" For the good David did in killing Goliath, and slaying his ten thousands of the Philistines, and thereby saving his king and country, Saul and his courtiers envied him, and sought to slay him : so our Lord Jesus Christ, for all the good he did to the Jews, by healing their bodies of diseases, and preaching the gospel to them for the benefit of their souls, was rewarded with reproaches and persecutions, and at last with the shameful death of the cross ; and in like manner are his people used, but this is an evil that shall not go unpunished ; see Prov. xvii. 13.—*John Gill.*

Verse 12.—" *To the spoiling of my soul.*" They robbed not his body of goods but his soul of consolation. They bereaved his soul (that is the word), like a widow who loses her children in whom she delighted and found succour. They were not content with injuring his estate, but they were for ruining the man himself by their undeserved malice, they attacked him in name and reputation, which were as dear to him as his sons and daughters, or even as his soul. It is evermore an injury to the soul to be attacked with slander, it puts a man into a warring attitude, endangers his peace of mind, imperils his enjoyment of quiet contemplation, and tends to interrupt his communion with God. Thus the spiritual nature is despoiled and suffers bereavement.—*C. H. S.*

Verse 13.—" *My prayer returned into, or was directed to, my bosom.*" Of the many interpretations that are given of this passage, that appears to me the most probable which derives it from the posture of the worshipper ; who standing with his head inclined downward toward his bosom, turned away his attention from all external objects, and uttered his mournful and earnest requests, as if they were directed to his own bosom. Such a posture of devotion is in use both among Jews and Mohammedans.—*Koehler in Repertor. Lit. Orient. ; and Reland de Relig. Mohammedica, quoted by Walford in loc.*

Verse 13 (*last clause*).—We may read it thus : *Let my prayer return into my bosom ;* that is, I wished no worse to them than to myself : let me receive of God such good as I prayed for them. See Psalm lxxix. 12.—*Henry Ainsworth.*

Verse 14.—" *For his mother.*" On account of the plurality of wives in an Eastern household, the sons are usually far more attached to their mother than their father. Their father they share with a numerous band of half-brothers, who are envious of them, or of whom they are jealous, but their mother is all their own, with her they are brought up in childhood ; she takes their part in youth, in the numerous battles of the harem ; and on their part when they are grown up, they love her intensely, and hence their mourning at her decease is of the bitterest kind. —*C. H. S.*

Verse 14.—" *His mother.*" Mahomet was once asked what relation had the strongest claim upon our affection and respect ; when he instantly replied, " The mother, the mother, the mother."

Verse 14 (*last clause*).—*Bewaileth his mother : mourneth at her funeral.* In this case the affections are most strong. Therefore the priests were permitted to mourn for such. Levit. xxi. 1, 2, 3.—*Henry Ainsworth.*

Verse 15.—"*But in mine adversity they rejoiced,*" etc.—Do not glory in your neighbour's ruins. The fire-fly leaps and dances in the fire, and so do many wicked men rejoice in the sufferings of others. Such as rejoice in the sufferings of others are sick of the devil's disease ; but from that disease the Lord deliver all your souls. 'Tis sad to insult over those whom God hath humbled ; 'tis high wickedness to triumph over those to whom God hath given a cup of astonishment to drink. Such as make the desolations of their neighbours to be the matter either of their secret repast, or open exultation, such may fear that the very dregs of divine wrath are reserved for them. 'Tis bad playing upon the harp because others have been put to hang their harps upon the willows. We must not pray with him in the tragedy, but it may rain calamities ; nor with Clemens' Gnostic, Give me calamities that I may glory in them. There cannot be a greater evidence of a wicked heart, than for a man to be merry because others are in misery. " He that is glad at calamities (that is, at the calamities of others) shall not be unpunished." Prov. xvii. 5. If God be God, such as congratulate our miseries instead of condoling them, shall be sure to be punished with the worst of punishments ; for such do not only sin against the law of grace, but also against the very law of nature ; the law of nature teaching men to sympathise with those that are in misery, and not to rejoice over them because of their miseries. O, sirs, do not make others' mourning your music, do not make others' tears your wine ; as you would not be made drunk at last with the wine of astonishment.—*Thomas Brooks.*

Verse 15.—"*But in mine adversity they rejoiced,*" etc. Marvellous prophecy of the cross ! second only, if indeed second, to that in the twenty-second Psalm. Still closer to the history if we take the Vulgate : *the scourges were gathered together upon me.* Even so, O Lord Jesus, the ploughers ploughed upon thy back, and made long furrows : precious furrows for us, where are sown patience for the present life, and glory in the next ; where are sown hope that maketh not ashamed, and love that many waters cannot quench. " *The very abjects.*" Even those worst of abjects, who said, " God, I thank thee that I am not as other men are ; " who had set the poor sinner before the Lord, with their " Moses in the law commanded that such should be stoned." " *Making mouths at me.*" And is it not wonderful that, well knowing the prophecy, yet the chief priests and scribes should have so fulfilled it, as that it should be written concerning them. " They that passed by mocked him, wagging their heads " ?—*Lewis de Grenada,* 1504—1588.

Verse 15.—" *In mine adversity they rejoiced.*" Now, as men often relent at seeing the misfortunes of their enemies, so that they cease to hate or persecute those who are already miserably wretched, it was an evidence of the very cruel and fierce spirit by which David's former friends were actuated against him, when, upon seeing him cast down and afflicted, they were rather by this incited furiously and insolently to assail him.—*John Calvin.*

Verse 15.—" *The abjects.*" *The very abjects* (Prayer Book Version). The Hebrew word *Nechim,* thus translated, comes from a verb signifying *to be smitten.* Hence, in the Septuagint it is rendered *scourges.* But it may also be rendered, with Jerome, *smiters,* and may mean *smitten with the tongue.* Com. Jer. xviii. 18. Another of its meanings is, according to Buxtorf, the *wry-legged, the lame ;* and so it is used in 2 Sam. iv. 4 ; ix. 3 ; whence the epithet of *Necho* was given to one of the Pharaohs who halted in his gait. Our translators seem to have understood the word in this last sense, as a term of contempt.—*Daniel Cresswell.*

Verse 15.—David, having showed how compassionate he was to his enemies in their affliction (verse 14), he presently shows (verse 15), how incompassionate, or barbarously cruel rather, his enemies were to him in his. " *Abjects*" are vile persons, men smitten in their estates and credits ; yea, often as slaves or ill servants smitten with cudgels or whips. So a learned translator renders the Psalm, *The smitten gathered against me ;* that is, vile men who deserve to be beaten and cudgelled.—*Joseph Caryl.*

Verse 16.—" *With hypocritical mockers in feasts.*" Some cannot be merry, but it must be with Scripture ; if they want a little diversion, the saints must be the subject of their discourse ! they can vent their profane jests upon the word of God; this is their pastime over their cups upon the ale-bench. How ready they are with their contumelious reflections; they have learnt their father's dialect, they are accusers of the brethren, their speech bewrays them to be Hellians. You know that in ordinary, we can tell what countryman a person is by his speech, every country having almost a peculiar idiom; so it is here, these scoffers at religion by speaking the language of hell, let us understand whence they are. They have, it may be, a little wit, which they set off with a sort of an air in rhetorical raillery, and oh, how quick and sharp when they are upon this subject! These scoffing Ishmaelites are seated in the devil's chair, somewhat above their brethren in iniquity, as most deserving the place; and there is less ground to hope that such persons will be savingly wrought upon who arrive to such a height in sin as to make a mock of it, and to sport with holiness, than of others. Persons are got a great way towards hell when they mock at what is serious, and that with delight. This the Lord will visit for in his due time; for he knows who they are that so dishonour him by reproaching them that are his.—*Oliver Heywood.*

Verse 16.—"*Hypocritical mockers in feasts.*" בְּחַנְפֵי לֹ מ. Very difficult. The word מָעוֹג, in Kings xvii. 12, the only other passage where it occurs, means "a cake." Hence לֹ מ is interpreted by Gesenius and other to mean, hangers-on at the tables of the rich (lit. "cake-mockers") whose business it was, by witticisms and buffoonery to make entertainment for the guests, and who got their dinner in return, like the Gr. ψωμοκόλακες, κνισοκόλακες, and the Mediæv. *Lat. buccellarii.* Then the words would mean, "Amongst the profanest."—*J. J. Stewart Perowne.* [Would not our word *loafers* be somewhat analogous to these cake-eaters of antiquity!]—*C. H. S.*

Verse 16.—"*Hypocritical mockers.*" David aggravates the sin of those jeering companions who made him their table-talk, and could not taste their cheer except seasoned with some salt jest quibbled out at him, with this, that they were "*hypocritical mockers;*" they did it slily, and wrapped up their scoffs, it is like in such language as might make some think, who did not well observe them, that they applauded him. There is a way of commending which some have learned to use when they mean to cast the greatest scorn upon those they hate bitterly, and these hypocritical mockers deserve the chair to be given them from all other scorners.—*William Gurnall.*

Verse 16.—"*Mockers in feasts.*" If it were known at a feast that there was any one present or absent, whom the host disliked, it was customary for the guests to "make fun of them," and use sarcastic language respecting them. These are the "*hypocritical mockers in feasts.*"—*John Gadsby.*

Verse 17.—Satan no sooner spies our wanderings, but he presently runs with a complaint to God, filing bills against us in the star-chamber of heaven, where the matter would go hard with us, but for the Great Lord Chancellor of peace, our Advocate Jesus Christ. As God keeps all our tears in a bottle, and registereth the very groans of our holy passion in a book, so Satan keeps a record of our sins, and solicits justice against us. Were God like man, subject to passions, or incensible by the suggestions of the common barrator, woe were us. But he will hear one son of truth before ten thousand fathers of lying. No matter what the plaintiff libelleth, when the judge acquitteth. We have forfeited our estates by treason, and the busy devil begs us; but there is one that steps in, and pleads a former grant, and that both by promise and purchase. "*Lord, rescue my soul from their destructions, my darling from the lions.*" Lord Jesus, challenge thine own; let not Satan enter upon by force or fraud, what thou hast bought with thine own blood.—*Thomas Adams.*

Verse 17.—"*My darling.*" In Poole's Synopsis the critics explain this name for the soul, as my only one, my solitary one, desolate, deserted, and destitute of human hope. Such is the soul under sore affliction. See Ps. xxii. 21. "*From the lions.*" Daniel in the den was literally where David was spiritually. Shut in among fierce, cruel, and angry creatures, and himself defenceless, having no weapon but prayer, no helper but the Lord. The people of God may be exposed to the lions of hell, and their roarings may grievously affright them; but the soul which is their "darling" is also God's dear one, and therefore they shall be rescued.—*C. H. S.*

Verse 19.—"*Wink with the eye.*" Showing pleasure in their eyes because of my evil.—*Francis Vatablus,* 1545.

Verse 19.—*"Wink the eye."* This was a sign which malicious persons made to each other when the object of their malice was gained, scornfully twisting their eyes together. The Hebrew word here has no sufficiently expressive substitute in English.—*Benjamin Weiss.*

Verse 21.—*"Our eye hath seen."* Eye for eyes, unless we would say that all the wicked are so conjoined, that they may seem to have but one eye, heart, head.—*John Trapp.*

Verse 21.—Yet, O ye saints, divulge not these things to wicked men; whisper them softly one to another, with fear and trembling, lest some profane wretch or other overhear you, and take that for encouragement that was only meant for caution. What is more common than for the vilest sinners to plead for their excuse, or warrant rather, the foul miscarriages of God's dearest saints? Thus the drunkard looks upon holy Noah as a pot-companion, whereby he discovers his nakedness in a worse sense than ever Cham did; and thus the unclean sensualist quotes David, and calls him in to be the patron of his debauchery. Certainly, if there be any grief that can overcast the perfect joys of the saints in heaven, it is that their names and examples should, to the great dishonour of God, be produced by wicked and sinful men, to countenance their grossest sins and wickednesses. But let such know, that God hath set up these in his church to be monuments of his mercy, to declare to humble and penitent sinners how great sins he can pardon; yet if any hereupon imbolden themselves in sin, instead of being set up as monuments of mercy, God will set them up as pillars of salt.—*Ezekiel Hopkins (Bishop).*

Verse 21.—He who rejoices in another's fall rejoices in the devil's victory.—*Ambrose, quoted in Nichol's Proverbs.*

Verses 21, 22 :—

> They gape and drawe their mouthes in scorneful wise,
> And crie, fie, fie, wee sawe it with our eyes.
> But thou their deed, (O Lord!) dost also see;
> Then bee not silent soe, nor farr from mee.
>
> *Sir John Davies.*

Verse 23.—*"My God and my Lord."* The cry of Thomas when he saw the wounds of Jesus. If he did not count our Lord to be divine, neither does David here ascribe Deity to Jehovah, for there is no difference except in the order of the words and the tongue in which they were spoken, the meaning is identical. What words they are, with their two eyes seeing Jehovah in two aspects yet as one, grasping him with two hands in the double " my " to one heart, for the word is but one, bowing before him on both knees to worship him in lowliest reverence. Well might Nouet, in his exposition of the words as used by Thomas, exclaim, " Oh, sweet word, I will say it all my life long; I will say it in the hour of death; I will say it in eternity."—*C. H. S.*

Verse 24.—*"O Lord my God."* O Jehovah my God; here is another precious word. He takes Jehovah to be his God, in opposition to those who make idols, or riches, or their own lusts their god. He claims a full possession of all that is in the great I AM. Even though he views him as a judge he lays the hand of faith upon his God, and flinches not even before the blaze of his righteousness. It is a noble word, a grand utterance of faith; he who can pronounce that word " my " from his inmost soul in such a connection may well laugh to scorn all his enemies.—*C. H. S.*

Verse 25.—*"Let them not say we have swallowed him up."* And even if they could, like Jonah's whale, they would soon be sickened of their feast. A living child of God were more easily swallowed than digested by the malice of hell.—*C. H. S.*

Verse 27.—See how the hearts of the saints have been drawn out against their persecutors. Prayers are the arms that in times of persecution the saints have still had recourse to. The Romans being in great distress were put so hard to it, that they were fain to take the weapons out of the temples of their gods to fight with their enemies, and so they overcame them: so when the people of God have been hard put to it by reason of afflictions and persecutions, the weapons that they have fled to have been prayers and tears, and with these they have overcome their persecutors.—*Thomas Brooks.*

Verse 28.—"*My tongue shall speak of thy righteousness and of thy praise all the day long.*" See now I have made a discourse something longer; ye are wearied. Who endureth to praise God all the day long? I will suggest a remedy whereby thou mayest praise God all the day long if thou wilt. Whatever thou dost, do well, and thou hast praised God. When thou singest a hymn, thou praisest God, but what doth thy tongue, unless thy heart also praise him? Hast thou ceased from singing hymns, and departed that thou mayest refresh thyself? Be not drunken, and thou hast praised God. Dost thou go away to sleep? Rise not to do evil, and thou hast praised God. Dost thou transact business? Do no wrong, and thou hast praised God. Dost thou till thy field? Raise not strife, and thou hast praised God. In the innocency of thy works prepare thyself to praise God all the day long.—*Augustine.*

HINTS TO PREACHERS.

Verse 1.—Jesus our Advocate and Champion; our friend in the courts of heaven and the battles of earth.

Verse 2.—Jesus armed as the defender of the faithful.

Verse 3.—Enemies kept at arm's length. How the Lord does this, and the blessedness of it to us

Verse 3 (last clause)—Full assurance. An assurance positive, personal, spiritual, present, divine, complete, coming by a word from God.

Verse 3 (last clause).—Heaven made sure.—*Thomas Adams' Sermon.*

Verse 4.—The everlasting confusion of the devil.

Verse 6.—The horrible pilgrimage of the ungodly.

Verse 6.—The trinity of dangers in the pathway of the wicked, their way dark with ignorance, and slippery with temptation, while behind them is the avenger.

Verse 8.—Destruction at unawares, an awful topic.

Verse 9.—Joy in God and in his salvation.

Verse 10.—A matchless God, and his matchless grace—these are the themes. An experienced heart, thoroughly quickened—this is the songster; and from this cometh matchless music.

The music of a shattered harp.

Verse 11.—The meanness, cruelty, sinfulness, and commonness of slander.

Verse 12.—How a soul may be robbed.

Verse 13.—Christian sympathy even for the froward.

Verse 13 (last clause).—Personal benefit of intercessory prayer.

Verses 13, 14.—Compassion to the sick.—*C. Simeon.*

Verse 15.—The shameful conspiracy of men against our Lord Jesus at his passion.

Verse 17.—The limit of divine endurance.

Verse 18.—The duty, blessedness, and seasonableness of public praise.

Verse 22.—Omniscience pleaded, a word sought for, presence requested, action entreated, affiance urged as a claim.

Verse 25.—The ungodly man's delight, and the righteous man's refuge.

Verse 26.—The convict dress of the wicked—"*clothed with shame,*" etc.

Verse 27 (last clause).—What is that prosperity in which the Lord hath pleasure?

Verse 28.—A blessed theme, a fitting tongue, an endless speech.

PSALM XXXVI.

TITLE.—To the Chief Musician.—*He who had the leadership of the Temple services was charged with the use of this song in public worship. What is everybody's business is never done. It was well to have one person specially to attend to the service of song in the house of the Lord. Of David the servant of the Lord. This would seem to indicate that the Psalm peculiarly befits one who esteems it an honour to be called Jehovah's servant. It is* THE SONG OF HAPPY SERVICE ; *such a one as all may join in who bear the easy yoke of Jesus. The wicked are contrasted with the righteous, and the great Lord of devout men is heartily extolled ; thus obedience to so good a Master is indirectly insisted on, and rebellion against him is plainly condemned.*

DIVISIONS.—*From 1 to 4 David describes the rebellious : in 5 to 9 he extols the various attributes of the Lord ; in 10 and 11 he addresses the Lord in prayer, and in the last verse his faith sees in vision the overthrow of all the workers of iniquity.*

EXPOSITION.

THE transgressions of the wicked saith within my heart, *that there is* no fear of God before his eyes.

2 For he flattereth himself in his own eyes, until his iniquity be found to be hateful.

3 The words of his mouth *are* iniquity and deceit : he hath left off to be wise, *and* to do good.

4 He deviseth mischief upon his bed ; he setteth himself in a way *that is* not good ; he abhorreth not evil.

1. " *The transgression of the wicked.*" His daring and wanton sin ; his breaking the bounds of law and justice. " *Saith within my heart, that there is no fear of God before his eyes.*" Men's sins have a voice to godly ears. They are the outer index of an inner evil. It is clear that men who dare to sin constantly and presumptuously cannot respect the great Judge of all. Despite the professions of unrighteous men, when we see their unhallowed actions our heart is driven to the conclusion that they have no religion whatever. Unholiness is clear evidence of ungodliness. Wickedness is the fruit of an atheistic root. This may be made clear to the candid head by cogent reasoning, but it is clear already and intuitively to the pious heart. If God be everywhere, and I fear him, how can I dare to break his laws in his very presence ? He must be a desperate traitor who will rebel in the monarch's own halls. Whatever theoretical opinions bad men may avow, they can only be classed with atheists, since they are such practically. Those eyes which have no fear of God before them now, shall have the terrors of hell before them for ever.

2. " *For.*" Here is the argument to prove the proposition laid down in the former verse. David here runs over the process of reasoning by which he had become convinced that wicked men have no proper idea of God or respect for him. God-fearing men see their sins and bewail them, where the reverse is the case we may be sure there is no fear of God. " *He flattereth himself in his own eyes.*" He counts himself a fine fellow, worthy of great respect. He quiets his conscience, and so deceives his own judgment as to reckon himself a pattern of excellence; if not for morality, yet for having sense enough not to be enslaved by rules which are bonds to others. He is the free-thinker, the man of strong mind, the hater of cant, the philosopher ; and the servants of God are, in his esteem, mean-spirited and narrow-minded. Of all flatteries this is the most absurd and dangerous. Even the silliest bird will not set traps for itself ; the most pettifogging attorney will not cheat himself. To smoothe over one's own conduct to one's conscience (which is the meaning of the Hebrew) is to smooth one's own path to hell. The descent to eternal ruin is easy enough, without making a glissade of it, as self-flatterers do. " *Until his iniquity be found to be hateful.*" At length he is found out and detested, despite his self-conceit. Rottenness smells sooner or later too strong to be concealed. There is a time when the leprosy cannot be hidden. At last the old house can no

longer be propped up, and falls about the tenant's ears : so there is a limit to a man's self-gratulation ; he is found out amid general scorn, and can no longer keep up the farce which he played so well. If this happen not in this life, the hand of death will let light in upon the covered character, and expose the sinner to shame and contempt.

The self-flattering process plainly proves the atheism of sinners, since the bare reflection that God sees them would render such self-flatteries extremely difficult, if not impossible. Belief in God, like light reveals, and then our sin and evil are perceived ; but wicked men are in the dark, for they cannot see what is so clearly within them and around them that it stares them in the face.

3. " *The words of his mouth are iniquity and deceit.*" This pair of hell dogs generally hunt together, and what one does not catch the other will ; if iniquity cannot win by oppression, deceit will gain by chicanery. When the heart is so corrupt as to flatter itself, the tongue follows suit. The open sepulchre of the throat reveals the foulness of the inner nature. God-fearing men make a conscience of their words, and if they sin through infirmity they do not invent excuses, or go about to boast of their wickedness : but because wicked men think little of evil and artful speeches, we may be clear that God rules not in their souls. The original by declaring that the words of the wicked are falsehood and deceit is peculiarly strong ; as if they were not only false in quality, but actual falseness itself. " *He hath left off to be wise, and to do good.*" From the good way he has altogether gone aside. Men who fear God proceed from strength to strength in the right path, but godless men soon forsake what little good they once knew. How could men apostatise if they had respect unto the supreme Judge ? Is it not because they grow more and more forgetful of God, that in due season they relinquish even that hypocritical reverence of him which in former days they maintained in order to flatter their souls ?

4. " *He deviseth mischief upon his bed.*" His place of rest becomes the place for plotting. His bed is a hot-bed for poisonous weeds. God-fearing men meditate upon God and his service ; but when men turn all their thoughts and inventive faculties towards evil, their godlessness is proved to a demonstration. He hath the devil for his bed-fellow who lies abed and schemes how to sin. God is far from him. " *He setteth himself in a way that is not good.*" When he gets up he resolutely and persistently pursues the mischief which he planned. The worst of ways he prefers for his walking, for he has taught his heart to love filthiness, having accustomed himself to revel in it in imagination. " *He abhorreth not evil.*" So far from having a contempt and abhorrence for evil, he even rejoices in it, and patronises it. He never hates a wrong thing because it is wrong, but he meditates on it, defends it, and practises it.

What a portrait of a graceless man these few verses afford us ! His jauntiness of conscience, his licentiousness of speech, his intentness upon wrong-doing, his deliberate and continued preference of iniquity, and withal his atheistical heart, are all photographed to the life. Lord, save us from being such.

5 Thy mercy, O LORD, *is* in the heavens ; *and* thy faithfulness *reacheth* unto the clouds.

6 Thy righteousness *is* like the great mountains ; thy judgments *are* a great deep : O LORD, thou preservest man and beast.

7 How excellent *is* thy lovingkindness, O God ! therefore the children of men put their trust under the shadow of thy wings.

8 They shall be abundantly satisfied with the fatness of thy house ; and thou shalt make them drink of the river of thy pleasures.

9 For with thee *is* the fountain of life : in thy light shall we see light.

From the baseness of the wicked the Psalmist turns his contemplation to the glory of God. Contrasts are impressive.

5. " *Thy mercy, O Lord, is in the heavens.*" Like the ethereal blue, it encompasses the whole earth, smiling upon universal nature, acting as a canopy for all the creatures of earth, surmounting the loftiest peaks of human provocations, and rising high above the mists of mortal transgression. Clear sky is evermore above, and mercy calmly smiles above the din and smoke of this poor world. Darkness and clouds are but of earth's lower atmosphere : the heavens are evermore serene.

and bright with innumerable stars. Divine mercy abides in its vastness of expanse, and matchless patience, all unaltered by the rebellions of man. When we can measure the heavens, then shall we bound the mercy of the Lord. Towards his own servants especially, in the salvation of the Lord Jesus, he has displayed grace higher than the heaven of heavens, and wider than the universe. O that the atheist could but see this, how earnestly would he long to become a servant of Jehovah! *"Thy faithfulness reacheth unto the clouds."* Far, far above all comprehension is the truth and faithfulness of God. He never fails, nor forgets, nor falters, nor forfeits his word. Afflictions are like clouds, but the divine truthfulness is all around them. While we are under the cloud we are in the region of God's faithfulness; when we mount above it we shall not need such an assurance. To every word of threat, or promise, prophecy or covenant, the Lord has exactly adhered, for he is not a man that he should lie, nor the son of man that he should repent.

6. *"Thy righteousness is like the great mountains."* Firm and unmoved, lofty and sublime. As winds and hurricanes shake not an Alp, so the righteousness of God is never in any degree affected by circumstances; he is always just. Who can bribe the Judge of all the earth, or who can, by threatening, compel him to pervert judgment? Not even to save his elect would the Lord suffer his righteousness to be set aside. No awe inspired by mountain scenery can equal that which fills the soul when it beholds the Son of God slain as a victim to vindicate the justice of the Inflexible Lawgiver. Right across the path of every unholy man who dreams of heaven stand the towering Andes of divine righteousness, which no unregenerate sinner can ever climb. Among great mountains lie slumbering avalanches, and there the young lightnings try their callow wings until the storm rushes down amain from the awful peaks; so against the great day of the Lord's wrath the Lord has laid up in the mountains of his righteousness dreadful ammunition of war with which to overwhelm his adversaries. *"Thy judgments are a great deep."* God's dealings with men are not to be fathomed by every boaster who demands to see a why for every wherefore. The Lord is not to be questioned by us as to why this and why that. He has reasons, but he does not choose to submit them to our foolish consideration. Far and wide, terrible and irresistible like the ocean are the providential dispensations of God: at one time they appear as peaceful as the unrippled sea of glass; at another tossed with tempest and whirlwind, but evermore most glorious and full of mystery. Who shall discover the springs of the sea? He who shall do this may hope to comprehend the providence of the Eternal.

> "Undiscovered sea!
> Into thy dark, unknown, mysterious caves,
> And secret haunts unfathomably deep,
> Beneath all visible retired, none went
> And came again to tell the wonders there."

Yet as the deep mirrors the sky, so the mercy of the Lord is to be seen reflected in all the arrangements of his government on earth, and over the profound depth the covenant rainbow casts its arch of comfort, for the Lord is faithful in all that he doeth.

"O Lord, thou preservest man and beast." All the myriads of creatures, rational and irrational, are fed by Jehovah's hand. The countless beasts, the innumerable birds, the inconceivable abundance of fishes, the all but infinite armies of insects, all owe their continuance in life to the unceasing outgoings of the divine power. What a view of God this presents to us! What a debased creature must he be who sees no trace of such a God, and feels no awe of him!

7. *"How excellent is thy lovingkindness, O God."* Here we enter into the Holy of Holies. Benevolence, and mercy, and justice, are everywhere, but the excellence of that mercy only those have known whose faith has lifted the veil and passed into the brighter presence of the Lord; these behold the excellency of the Lord's mercy. The word translated *excellent* may be rendered "precious;" no gem or pearl can ever equal in value a sense of the Lord's love. This is such a brilliant as angels wear. Kings' regalia are a beggarly collection of worthless pebbles when compared with the tender mercy of Jehovah. David could not estimate it, and therefore, after putting a note of admiration, he left our hearts and imagination, and, better still, our experience, to fill up the rest. He writes *how excellent!* because he cannot tell us the half of it. *"Therefore the children of men put their trust under the shadow of thy wings."* The best of reasons for the best of courses. The figure

is very beautiful. The Lord overshadows his people as a hen protects her brood, or as an eagle covers its young ; and we as the little ones run under the blessed shelter and feel at rest. To cower down under the wings of God is so sweet. Although the enemy be far too strong for us, we have no fear, for we nestle under the Lord's wing. O that more of Adam's race knew the excellency of the heavenly shelter ! It made Jesus weep to see how they refused it : our tears may well lament the same evil.

8. " *They shall be abundantly satisfied with the fatness of thy house.*" Those who learn to put their trust in God shall be received into his house, and shall share in the provision laid up therein. The dwelling-place of the Lord is not confined to any place, and hence reside where we may, we may regard our dwelling, if we be believers, as one room in the Lord's great house ; and we shall, both in providence and grace, find a soul-contenting store supplied to us as the result of living by faith in nearness to the Lord. If we regard the assembly of the saints as being peculiarly the house of God, believers shall, indeed, find in sacred worship the richest spiritual food. Happy is the soul that can drink in the sumptuous dainties of the gospel —nothing can so completely fill the soul. " *And thou shalt make them drink of the river of thy pleasures.*" As they have the fruits of Eden to feed on, so shall they have the river of Paradise to drink from. God's everlasting love bears to us a constant and ample comfort, of which grace makes us to drink by faith, and then our pleasure is of the richest kind. The Lord not only brings us to this river, but makes us drink : herein we see the condescension of divine love. Heaven will, in the fullest sense, fulfil these words ; but they who trust in the Lord enjoy the antepast even here. The happiness given to the faithful is that of God himself ; purified spirits joy with the same joy as the Lord himself. " That my joy may be in you, that your joy may be full."

9. " *For with thee is the fountain of life.*" This verse is made of simple words, but like the first chapter of John's Gospel, it is very deep. From the Lord, as from an independent self-sufficient spring, all creature life proceeds, by him it is sustained, through him alone can it be perfected. Life is in the creature, but the fountain of it is only in the Creator. Of spiritual life, this is true in the most emphatic sense ; " it is the Spirit that quickeneth," " and we are dead, and our life is hid with Christ in God." " *In thy light shall we see light.*" Light is the glory of life. Life in the dark is misery, and rather death than life. The Lord alone can give natural, intellectual, and spiritual life ; he alone can make life bright and lustrous. In spiritual things the knowledge of God sheds a light on all other subjects. We need no candle to see the sun, we see it by its own radiance, and then see everything else by the same lustre. We never see Jesus by the light of self, but self in the light of Jesus. No inward intelligence of ours leads us to receive the Spirit's light, but the rather, it often helps to quench the sacred beam ; purely and only by his own illumination, the Holy Ghost lights up the dark recesses of our heart's ungodliness. Vain are they who look to learning and human wit, one ray from the throne of God is better than the noonday splendour of created wisdom. Lord, give me the sun, and let those who will delight in the wax candles of superstition and the phosphorescence of corrupt philosophy. Faith derives both light and life from God, and hence she neither dies nor darkens.

10 O continue thy lovingkindness unto them that know thee ; and thy righteousness to the upright in heart.

11 Let not the foot of pride come against me, and let not the hand of the wicked remove me.

10. " *O continue thy lovingkindness unto them that know thee.*" We ask no more than a continuance of the past mercy. Lord, extend this grace of thine to all the days of all who have been taught to know thy faithful love, thy tenderness, thine immutability and omnipotence. As they have been taught of the Lord to know the Lord, so go on to instruct them and perfect them. This prayer is the heart of the believer asking precisely that which the heart of his God is prepared to grant. It is well when the petition is but the reflection of the promise. " *And thy righteousness to the upright in heart.*" As thou hast never failed the righteous, so abide thou in the same manner their defender and avenger. The worst thing to be feared by the man of God is to be forsaken of heaven, hence this prayer ; but the fear is groundless, hence the peace which faith brings to us. Learn from

this verse, that although a continuance of mercy is guaranteed in the covenant, we are yet to make it a matter of prayer. For this good thing will the Lord be enquired of.

11. "*Let not the foot of pride come against me.*" The general prayer is here turned into a particular and personal one for himself. Pride is the devil's sin. Good men may well be afraid of proud men, for the serpent's seed will never cease to bite the heel of the godly. Fain would proud scoffers spurn the saints or trample them under foot : against their malice prayer lifts up her voice. No foot shall come upon us, no hand shall prevail against us, while Jehovah is on our side. "*Let not the hand of the wicked remove me.*" Suffer me not to be driven about as a fugitive, nor torn from my place like an uprooted tree. Violence with both hand and foot, with means fair and means foul, strove to overthrow the Psalmist, but he resorts to his great Patron, and sings a song of triumph in anticipation of the defeat of his foes.

12 There are the workers of iniquity fallen : they are cast down, and shall not be able to rise.

12. "*There are the workers of iniquity fallen.*" Faith sees them scattered on the plain. There ! before our very eyes sin, death, and hell, lie prostrate. Behold the vanquished foes ! "*They are cast down.*" Providence and grace have dashed them from their vantage ground. Jesus has already thrown all the foes of his people upon their faces, and in due time all sinners shall find it so. "*And shall not be able to rise.*" The defeat of the ungodly and of the powers of evil is final, total, irretrievable. Glory be to God, however high the powers of darkness may carry it at this present, the time hastens on when God shall defend the right, and give to evil such a fall as shall for ever crush the hopes of hell ; while those who trust in the Lord shall eternally praise him and rejoice in his holy name.

EXPLANATORY NOTES AND QUAINT SAYINGS.

Title.—"*To the Chief Musician,*" has given rise to many conjectures. In the Septuagint the Hebrew word is translated, εἰς τὸ τέλος, *to the end ;* a meaning so utterly vague as to defy all reasonable conjecture. . . . . The meaning of the term appears to be this : the Psalms in which it occurs were given in charge by their inspired authors to the Chief Musician overseeing some specific band of music, whether harps, psalteries, or wind instruments.—*John Jebb, A.M., in " A Literal Translation of the Book of Psalms,*" 1846.

Title.—"*The servant of the Lord.*" David only uses this title here and in Psalm eighteen. In both he describes the dealings of God both with the righteous and the wicked, and it is most fit that at the very outset he should take his place with the servants of the Lord.—*C. H. S.*

Whole Psalm.—*First part.*—A character of a wicked man (verse 1). 1. He calls evil good (verse 2). 2. He continues in it. 3. He is an hypocrite (verse 3). 4. He is obstinate. 5. He is studious in wickedness (verse 4). *Second part.*—God's patience and mercy (verses 5, 6). 1. To all, even all creatures. 2. But particularly to his people, which he admires. Upon which the faithful (1) trust, (2) are satisfied (verses 7, 8). The *Third part.*—He prays that this effect may light, 1. On God's people (verse 10). 2. On himself (verse 11). 3. His acclamation upon it (verse 12). —*William Nicholson (Bishop),* 1662.

Verse 1.—In this Psalm we have a description of sin, especially as it appears in those who have openly broken God's bands. The introduction is very striking ; "*The transgression of the wicked saith within my heart, that there is no fear of God before his eyes.*" How could the "*transgression of the wicked*" speak within the *heart* of him who in the inscription of the Psalm declares himself to be *the servant* of JEHOVAH ? These words are generally understood as signifying that the outward conduct of the sinner, as often as he thought of it, naturally suggested this conclusion to his mind, that he was destitute of all fear of God. But they may perhaps admit of another meaning, equally agreeable to the literal reading ; *wickedness, saith of the wicked, within my heart*, etc. According to this view, the Psalmist meant that notwithstanding the external pretences of the wicked, and all their attempts to cover their iniquity, he was certain that they had no real sense of the presence of God, that they secretly renounced his authority. How was he assured of this ? By a comparison of their conduct with the dictates of the heart. He could not indeed look into their hearts, but he could look into his own, and *there* he found corruption, so strong, that were it not for the fear of God that was implanted within him, he would be as bad as they.—*John Jamieson.*

Verse 1.—It is not the imperfection or shortcoming in the fear of God, but the being destitute of it altogether, that proveth a wicked man : " *There is no fear of God before his eyes.*"—*David Dickson.*

Verse 1 (last clause).—" *Not having the fear of God before his eyes,*" has become inwoven into proceedings in criminal courts. When a man has no fear of God, he is prepared for any crime.

Total depravity is not too strong a term to describe human wickedness. The sinner has " *no fear of God.*" Where that is wanting, how can there be any piety ? And if there is no piety, there must be total want of right affections, and that is the very essence of depravity.—*William S. Plumer.*

Verse 1.—Durst any mock God with flourishes and formalities in religion, if they feared him ? Durst any provoke God to his face by real and open wicked-nesses, if they feared him ? Durst any sin with the judgments of God fresh bleeding before their eyes, if they feared the Lord and his wrath ? Durst they sin with heaps of precious mercy before their eyes, if they feared the Lord and his goodness ? Durst any flatter either others or themselves with hopes of impunity in their sin, if they feared the Lord and his truth ? Durst any slight their own promises, professions, protestations, oaths, or design the entangling of others by them, rather than the binding of themselves, did they fear the Lord and his faithfulness, even the Lord who keepeth covenant and promise for ever ? All these and many more transgressions of the wicked (all these ways of transgression are found among the wicked, it were well if none of them were found among those who have a name of godliness ; I say, all these transgressions of the wicked) say, " *There is no fear of God before their eyes.*"—*Joseph Caryl.*

Verse 1.—The *wicked* man has no regard to the oracles of God : he has one in his own heart, which dictates nothing but rebellion.—*Zachary Mudge.*

Verse 2.—" *For he flattereth himself in his own eyes.*" The matter which this self-flattery especially concerns is sin, as appears from the following clause. He deceives himself as to its nature and consequences, its evil and aggravations, and he continues to do so " *until his iniquity be found to be hateful ;* " till it be fully discovered, and appear in its magnitude and atrocious circumstances both to himself and others, by some awful divine judgment, such as that mentioned in the last verse of the Psalm : " *There are the workers of iniquity fallen : they are cast down, and shall not be able to rise.*" He adduces this self-deceit and continuance in it, as illustrating the truth of that judgment he had formed of the state of such a person : " *There is no fear of God before his eyes : for he flattereth himself in his own eyes.*" And surely the proof is incontrovertible. For a man under the bondage of sin would never *flatter himself in his own eyes*, were it not that God is not before them. The reason why he thinks so well of himself is, that *God is not in all his thoughts*. He hath cast off all fear about himself because he hath no fear of God.—*John Jamieson.*

Verse 2.—" *He flattereth himself.*" 1. Some flatter themselves with a secret hope, that there is no such thing as *another world*. 2. Some flatter themselves that *death* is a great way off, and that they shall hereafter have much opportunity to seek salvation. 3. Some flatter themselves that they lead *moral* and orderly lives and therefore think that they shall not be damned. 4. Some make the *advantages* under which they live an occasion of self-flattery. They flatter them-selves that they live in a place where the gospel is powerfully preached, and among a religious people, where many have been converted ; and they think it will be much easier for them to be saved on that account. 5. Some flatter themselves with their own *intentions.* They intend to give themselves liberty for a while longer, and *then* to reform. 6. There are some who flatter themselves that they *do,* and have *done*, a great deal for their salvation, and therefore hope they shall obtain it; when indeed they neither do what they ought to do, nor what they might do even in their present state of unregeneracy; nor are they in any likely way to be converted. 7. Some hope by their strivings to obtain salvation of *themselves*. They have a secret imagination that they shall, by degrees, work in themselves sorrow and repentance of sin, and love towards God and Jesus Christ. Their striving is not so much an earnest seeking to God, as a striving to do themselves that which is the work of God. 8. Some sinners flatter themselves that they are *already* converted. They sit down and rest in a false hope, persuading themselves that all their sins are pardoned; that God loves them; that they shall go to heaven when they die; and that they need trouble themselves no more. "Because thou sayest, I am rich, and increased with goods, and have need of nothing; and knowest not that thou art wretched, and miserable, and poor, and blind, and naked." Rev. iii. 17.—*Condensed from Jonathan Edwards.*

Verse 2.—"*In his own eyes.*" He had not God before his eyes in holy awe, therefore he puts himself there in unholy admiration. He who makes little of God makes much of himself. They who forget adoration fall into adulation. The eyes must see something, and if they admire not God they will flatter self.—*C. H. S.*

Verse 2.—"*Until his iniquity be found to be hateful;*" that is, until he finds by experience that it is a more dreadful thing to sin against God, and break his holy commands, than he imagined.—*Jonathan Edwards.*

Verse 2.—"*Hateful.*" Odious to himself, to others, and to God.—*Gilbert Genebrard*, 1537—1597.

Verse 3.—"*He hath left off.*" That little light he once had, he hath lost, and cast off such good practices as once in hypocrisy he performed; neither will he learn to do better.—*John Trapp.*

Verse 3 (*last clause*).—Apostacy from God is really an undoing of all the good which we have done. 'Tis a wicked repentance quite contrary to the grace of repentance; as that is a repentance from dead works, so this is a repentance from works of a better sort: "*He hath left off to be wise, and to do good.*" 'Tis a perversion to evil after a seeming conversion from it.—*Timothy Cruso.*

Verses 3, 4 :—

> Yet did he spare his sleep, and hear the clock
> Number the midnight watches, on his bed
> Devising mischief more; and early rose.
> And made most hellish meals of good men's names.
> From door to door you might have seen him speed,
> Or placed amid a group of gaping fools.
> Peace fled the neighbourhood in which he made
> His haunts; and, like a moral pestilence,
> Before his breath the healthy shoots and blooms
> Of social joy and happiness decayed.
> Fools only in his company were seen,
> And those forsaken of God, and to themselves
> Given up. The prudent shunned him and his house
> As one who had a deadly moral plague.
>
> *Robert Pollock*, 1799—1827.

Verse 4.—"*He deviseth mischief upon his bed.*" As the man that feareth God communeth with his heart upon his bed, that he may not sin, no, not in his heart; so the man that feareth not God, deviseth how he may plot and perform sin willingly.—*David Dickson.*

Verse 4.—"*Upon his bed.*" Most diligently does Ayguan follow up the scriptural expressions concerning a bed and tell us that there are six different beds of wickedness—that of luxury, that of avarice, of ambition, of greediness, of torpor, and of cruelty, and he illustrates them all by examples from Scripture.—*J. M. Neale.*

Verse 4.—"*He setteth himself in a way that is not good.*" To wait to sin is to sin deliberately, yea, to wait to sin resolvedly. That sin is exceedingly sinfully committed which we set and prepare ourselves to commit. David, describing a wicked man, saith, "*He setteth himself in a way that is not good;*" that is, in an evil way: he doth not only fall into sin (that may be the case of a good man), but he takes or chooseth an evil way, and then sets or settles himself in it, resolving not to leave it, no, nor to be beaten out of it. Sin may be said to wait for a godly man, that is, Satan waits and watches his season to tempt him unto sin; but a godly man doth not wait nor watch to sin. It is bad enough to be overtaken with sin, or with a fault (as the apostle speaks, Gal. vi. 1); but to be taken with sin, and so to wait for a season to take our fill of it, is as bad as bad can be.—*Joseph Caryl.*

Verse 4.—"*He setteth himself in a way that is not good.*" Proud sinners have strongest conceit that they go right, at least in the way of their choice. Satan blindeth them so, that they mistake both the end and the way: in their count they are running to heaven, when they are posting to hell: he serveth them kindly with fresh post-horses. Sometimes he mounteth them on drunkenness, and when they have run a stage on that beastliness, he can mount them on lechery. Again, he can refresh them with avarice; and if they be weary of that slow jade, he setteth them on lofty ambition, and to make them more spirity he can horse them on restless contention. Every one seeth not Satan's enquiry: there is no complexion or disposition, but he hath a fit horse for it, and that of itself. Every man's predominant is a beast of Satan's saddling and providing to carry men to hell. The way is one, the post-master is one, he is to be found at every stage, mounting his gallants, their horses are all of one kind though not of one colour. Happy is the man whom God dismounteth in that evil way, and more happy is he who taketh with that stay, and turneth his course to heaven.—*William Struther.*

Verse 4.—"*He abhorreth not,*" *i.e.*, is far enough from rejecting any instrument, however sinful, for attaining his purposes.—*J. J. Stewart Perowne.*

Verse 5.—"*Thy mercy, O Lord, is in the heavens.*" David considering the thoughts and deeds of impious men, and the mercy of God towards them, utters this exclamation. When men sin so impudently, who does not admire the divine longsuffering!—*Sebastian Munster,* 1489—1552.

Verses 5—7.—This Psalm doth fitly set forth unto us the estate and condition of these times, wherein wickedness increaseth: and so in the former part of the Psalm is a discovery of wickedness, verse 3. And what should we do when there is such wickedness in the earth? In the fifth verse, "*Thy mercy, O Lord, is in the heavens; and thy faithfulness reacheth unto the clouds.*" God is gathering up all goodness, mercy, and peace from man to himself; and though there is cruelty, mischief, and wickedness in the world, in the earth, yet there is mercy, truth, and faithfulness in the clouds; and it's good that wisdom, goodness, truth, and righteousness leave the world, and cleave to God, that so we may follow it; and that what goodness, mercy, truth, and faithfulness we formerly enjoyed in man, we may enjoy in God. And when wickedness increaseth, righteousness increaseth likewise: "*Thy righteousness is like the great mountains:*" when the world tears and breaks itself in pieces, then is the righteousness of God a great mountain. "*Thy judgments are a great deep;*" when the whole world is become one sea of confusion, then are the judgments of the Lord a great deep, where not only man, but beasts may rest safely. "*Thou preservest man and beast.*" And though this time is a time of growing and spreading wickedness in man, yet it is a time of sweetest admiration and love in God; and when men that sin do cry out, O woful man! they that enjoy God, cry out, O happy man! And though men that live in the earth cry out, O miserable! what times are here? men that live in heaven cry out, "*How excellent is thy lovingkindness, O God!*" The Lord makes all things naked and bare, that we only may have him to be our safety.—*William Sedgwick* (1609—1668), in "*The Excellency of the love of God,*" a sermon in a vol., entitled "*Some flashes of Lightnings of the Son of Man,*" 1648.

Verses 5—9:—

> Thy mercie Lord doth to the HEAUENS extend,
> Thy faithfullnes doth to the CLOUDES assend;
> Thy justice stedfast as a MOUNTAINE is,
> Thy JUDGEMENTS deepe as is the great Abisse;
> Thy noble mercies saue all liueinge thinges,
> The sonnes of men creepe underneath thy winges:
> With thy great plenty they are fedd at will,
> And of thy pleasure's streame they drinke their fill;
> For euen the well of life remaines with thee,
> And in thy glorious light wee light shall see.
>
> > > > > > > > > *Sir John Davies.*

Verse 6.—" *Thy righteousness is like the great mountains.*" Lit. *mountains of God*, which men have not planted, and which men cannot move.—*Christopher Wordsworth.*

Verse 6.—" *Thy judgments are a great deep.*" Men's sins are a great deep, and Satan's ways are called a depth ; but God's judgments, his ways in the wheels, are the greatest deep of all, they are unsearchable.—*William Greenhill.*

Verse 7.—" *How excellent is thy lovingkindness, O God !* " etc. The expressions here which denote the abundance of divine blessings upon the righteous man seem to be taken from the temple, from whence they were to issue. Under the covert of the temple, the wings of the cherubim, they were to be sheltered. The richness of the sacrifices, the streams of oil, wine, odours, etc., and the light of the golden candlestick, are all plainly referred to.—*Samuel Burder.*

Verse 7.—" *Therefore the children of men put their trust under the shadow of thy wings.*" The word signifies to fly, to betake one's self to a place of safety : as the chickens in danger to be seized on, fly under the wings of the hen. " Under whose wings thou art come to trust." Ruth ii. 12. The helpless bird pursued by the kite, in danger to be devoured, runs under the shadow of the dam. Thus it is with a sinner at the first working of faith, he apprehends himself pursued by wrath and judgment ; he knows if they seize on him he must perish without remedy. Oh, the sad condition of such a soul ! Oh, but he sees Christ spreading his wings ready to secure perishing sinners ; he hears him inviting in the gospel to come under his shadow ! Oh, how sweet is that voice to him (however, while senseless he rejected it) ! He hears, obeys, and runs to Christ for shelter, and so he is safe. " *How excellent is thy lovingkindness, O God ! therefore the children of men put their trust under the shadow of thy wings.*"—*David Clarkson.*

Verse 7.—" *Thy wings.*" A common figure in the Psalms, taken more immediately, in my opinion, from the wings of the cherubim overshadowing the mercy-seat which covered the ark ; but more remotely from birds, which defend their young from the solar rays by overshadowing them with their wings.—*Francis Hare (Bishop),* 1740.

Verse 7 :—

> In lonesome cell, guarded and strong I lie,
> Bound by Christ's love, his truth to testify,
> Though walls be thick, the door no hand unclose,
> God is my strength, my solace, and repose.

In a letter of Jeroninus Segerson, written in the prison at Antwerp to his wife, named Lysken, who likewise lay a prisoner there, 1551.

Verse 8.—" *They shall be abundantly satisfied with the fatness of thy house : and thou shalt make them drink of the river of thy pleasures.*" Mark, first, the excellency of the provision, " *fatness of thy house,*" the " *river of thy pleasures.*" The fattest is esteemed the fairest and the most excellent food ; therefore the saint was enjoined to offer the fat in sacrifice under the law. As God expects the best from us, so he gives the best to us. This made David, when he had feasted so curiously, to sing so cheerfully. Fatness here is the top, the cream of all spiritual delicacies. " My soul is filled as with marrow and fatness ; and my mouth shall praise thee with joyful lips." Psalm lxiii. 5. But, though God keeps so noble a house to satisfy his people's hunger, what special care doth he take to quench their thirst ! " *Thou shalt make them drink of the rivers of thy pleasures.*" Oh, he drinks to them, and they pledge him in his own cup ! Hath the child, then, any cause, when his Father keeps so rare and costly a table, to leave such dainties and go a-begging up and down the country for scraps and fragments ? Oh, how much do these disgrace their Parent's provision, and their own discretion ! But mark, reader, secondly, the plenty as well as the excellency of this provision. Here is fatness in the abstract, a " *river of pleasure ;* " and so much as that they who enjoy it shall be *satisfied,* and *abundantly* satisfied. A river is overflowing and ever flowing ; it communicates its water and yet is never empty. It is fed with springs and fountains, and therefore it is no wonder if it always be full. They that are at such a well need not complain of want ; but here are not only rivers and fatness, but of God's people it is said, " *they shall be abundantly satisfied.*" In the original it is *inebriated.* They shall have not only a sufficiency, but a redundancy of spiritual delights. The vessels of their souls shall be filled to the brim out of that river whose streams make glad the city of God. Surely, then, they who may have bread in such abundance, enough and to spare, in their Father's house, made of the kidneys of the wheat, of the finest flour, need not hanker after the world's homely fare. Our heavenly Father doth not keep so starveling a house that the world's scraps should go down with us.—*George Swinnock.*

Verse 8.—" *They shall be abundantly satisfied with the fatness of thy house.*" I once heard a father tell, that when he removed his family to a new residence where the accommodation was much more ample, the substance much more rich and varied than that to which they had previously been accustomed, his youngest son, yet a lisping infant, ran round every room and scanned every article with ecstacy, calling out in childish wonder at every new sight, " Is this ours, father ? and is this ours ? " The child did not say " yours ; " and I observed that the father while he told the story was not offended with the freedom. You could read in his glistening eye that the infant's confidence in appropriating as his own all that his father had, was an important element in his satisfaction.

Such, I suppose, will be the surprise, and joy, and appropriating confidence with which the child of our Father's family will count all his own when he is removed from the comparatively mean condition of things present, and enters the infinite of things to come. When the glories of heaven burst upon his view, he does not stand at a distance like a stranger saying, O God, these are thine. He bounds forward to touch and taste every provision which those blessed mansions contain, exclaiming as he looks in the Father's face, Father, this and this is ours ! The dear child is glad of all the Father's riches, and the Father is gladder of his dear child.—*William Arnot.*

Verse 8.—" *The fatness of thy house.*" If there is an allusion to the temple, as Hupfield thinks, " *fatness* " would = " fat sacrifices," and men would be regarded as the priests in the house, after the analogy of Jer. xxxi. 14.—*J. J. Stewart Perowne.*

Verse 8.—" *The fatness of thy house.*" Fat was regarded among the Jews, as among all other nations of antiquity, as the richest part of animals, and therefore became synonymous with *the first, the best, the prime of anything.*—*Christian D. Ginsburg, LL.D., in Kitto's Cyclopedia.*

Verse 8.—" *Of thy house.*" This is emphatic, and means that which thou hast prepared for thine own household, thine own faithful domestics. Here is intended not the good things prepared for all men, but for the household retainers of God.—*John Piscator, 1546—1626, and D. H. Mollerus.*

Verse 8.—" *Pleasures.*" *Delights,* the same word as is translated " Eden " in Genesis, only it is here in the plural number.—*Dalman Hapstone, M.A.*

Verse 8.—And, saith one of the fathers, do you ask me what heaven is ? Saith one, When I meet you there I will tell you. The world to come, say the Rabbins, is the world where all is well. I have read of one that would willingly swim through a sea of brimstone to get to heaven, for there, and only there, is perfection of happiness. What are the silks of Persia, the spices of Egypt, the gold of Ophir and the treasures of both Indies, to the glory of another world ? Augustine tells us that one day, when he was about to write something upon the eighth verse of the thirty-sixth Psalm, " *Thou shalt make them drink of the rivers of thy pleasures,*" and being almost swallowed up with the contemplation of heavenly joys, one called unto him very loud by his name ; and, enquiring who it was, he answered, I am Jerome, with whom in my lifetime thou hadst so much conference concerning doubts in Scripture, and am now best experienced to resolve thee of any doubts concerning the joys of heaven ; but only let me first ask thee this question—Art thou able to put the whole earth, and all the waters of the sea, into a little pot ? Canst thou measure the waters in thy fist, and mete out heaven with thy span, or weigh the mountains in scales, or the hills in a balance ? If not, no more is it possible that thy understanding should comprehend the least of the joys of heaven ; and certainly the least of the joys of heaven are inconceivable and unexpressible.—*Thomas Brooks.*

Verse 9.—" *For with thee is the fountain of life.*"—These are some of the most wonderful words in the Old Testament. Their fulness of meaning no commentary can ever exhaust. They are, in fact, the kernel and the anticipation of much of the profoundest teaching of S. John.—*J. J. Stewart Perowne.*

Verse 9.—" *In thy light shall we see light.*" The object and matter of our eternal happiness is called " *light.*" It will not be a dazzling and confounding light as was the brightness of Moses' face at his coming down from the mount; the people could not behold him: it will not be an astonishing light, as that in the mount at our Lord's transfiguration; the disciples fell to the ground, their weak eyes could not behold those glimpses of glory that shined through the vail of flesh. But the light in our heaven of happiness will be *a strengthening and comforting light;* it will strengthen and confirm the eyes of our understanding to behold it. Then shall we be enabled as the young eagles, to behold the Sun of Righteousness in his brightness and glory. It was said by the Lord to Moses, "None can see my face and live." Exodus xxxiii. 20. That glorious sight which Daniel saw took strength from him. Dan. x. 8. The object being without him, drew out all his spirits to behold and admire it and so weakened him; but in heaven our God, whom we shall see and know, will be within us to strengthen us; then shall we live because we see his face. It will be also a *comforting* light, like the light of the morning to the wearied watchman, who longed after it in the night-time.—*William Colvill.*

Verse 9.—" *In thy light shall we see light.*" 'Tis but a kind of dim twilight comparatively, which we enjoy here in this world. While we are hid in this prison-house we can see but little; but our Father's house above is full of light: " *Then shall the righteous shine forth as the sun,*" etc. Matt. xiii. 43. If the Day-star be risen in your hearts, live in the pleasant and cheerful expectation of perfect day. For we can ascend but a little way into the mysteries of the kingdom, as long as we are upon the footstool; and we shall know vastly and inconceivably more in the first moment after we come to heaven, than we are capable of attaining here throughout all our days.—*Timothy Cruso.*

Verse 9.—" *In thy light shall we see light.*" The light of nature is like a spark, the light of the gospel a lamp, the light of grace a star, but the light of glory the sun itself. The higher our ascent the greater our light; God dwelleth " in the light which no man can approach unto." 1 Tim. vi. 16—no man, while he carries mortality and sin about him; but when those two corrupt and uncapable qualities shall be put off, then shall we be brought to that light. We are now glad of the sun and stars over our heads, to give us light: what light and delight shall that be when these are under our feet! That light must needs go as far beyond their light as they now go beyond us. But alas! they are only able to discourse of that light, that do enjoy it, to whom that eternal day is risen; not we that live in the humble shade of mortality and natural dimness. I leave it therefore to your meditations: it is a glorious light which we do well often to consider, considering to admire, admiring to love, loving to desire, desiring to seek, and finding to enjoy for ever.—*Thomas Adams.*

Verse 9.—" *In thy light shall we see light.*" There is a great boast of light in the world, and there is some ground for it in natural things; but, as of old the world by wisdom knew not God, so of late. If ever we know God, it must be through the medium of his word. This I take to be the meaning of the passage. The term *light* in the last clause means the true knowledge of God; and, in the first, the true medium of attaining it, namely, divine revelation. The sum seems to amount to this: the word of God is the grand medium by which we can attain a true and saving knowledge of God. What the sun and stars are to the regions of matter, that revelation is to the mental region. Gen. i. 13, 17. . . .

There are many things of which you may entertain no doubt, concerning which there may be no manner of dispute; yet, make a point of seeing them in God's light. Many content themselves with seeing them in the light in which great and good men have placed them; but, although angels, they are not the true light: they all view things partially. If what they say be true, yet, if we receive it merely on their representation, our faith will stand in the wisdom of men, and not in the power of God. 1 Cor. ii. 5. That knowledge or faith which has not God's word for its ground will not stand the day of trial.—*Andrew Fuller.*

Verse 9.—In this communion of God what can we want? Why, God shall be all and in all unto us; he shall be beauty for the eye, music for the ear, honey for the taste, the full content and satisfaction of our desires, and that immediately from himself. True it is God is all in all in this world, " In him we live, and move, and have our being; " but here he works by means of secondary causes; here he gives wine to make the heart glad, and oil, etc.; but there all intervening means between God and us is removed: " *with thee is the fountain of life: in thy light shall we see light;* " not in the light of the sun, or the light of a candle; there is no need of them (Rev. xxii. 5); but "in *thy* light," the light of God himself; yea, the whole life of glory, together with all the concomitants of it, flows from him as the sole and original fountain of it. Oh, how sweet must that happiness be that is so derived!—*Edmund Pinchbeck, B.D., in " The Fountain of Life:" a Funeral Sermon,* 1652.

Verse 9.—Whatsoever can be found in the creature, even when God blesseth the use thereof to his own children, is but a drop from the ocean, is but a little water out of the well, in comparison of what a believer will see and feel to be in God reconciled through Christ, for, " *with thee is the fountain of life.*"—*David Dickson.*

Verse 10 —" *Continue thy lovingkindness.*" When God beginneth once to let out mercy to his servants, he stints not presently, but proceeds. . . . . . When Rachel had her first son, she called his name Joseph, which signifieth adding, or increase ; for she said, " The Lord shall add to me another son." Gen. xxx. 24. Now God hath begun to show kindness, he shall not only give me this, but he shall give me another son also. When the Lord hath bestowed one mercy on you, you may name it Joseph, increase, addition, for God will bestow another upon you. Abraham had many mercies from God, one after another ; and Moses, a multitude of mercies ; he converseth with God face to face ; he heareth God speak ; he hath God's presence to go along with him ; yea, he seeth all God's goodness and glory to pass before him. When mercies come forth, God will not presently shut the door of mercy again. " *Continue thy lovingkindness.*" The Hebrew is, draw forth, or draw out thy lovingkindness : a metaphor either taken from vessels of wine, which being set abroach once, yield not only one cup, but many cups ; so when God setteth abroach the wine of his mercy, he will not fill your cup once, but twice and seven times ; or, taken from a mother, who hath her breasts full of milk, draws them out for her child, not once, but often ; the child shall have the breast many times in the day, and many times in the night, so when God beginneth to show mercy to you, he will draw out his breasts of consolation, and will bestow mercy after mercy upon you ; or, from a line which is extended, for so God being in a way of mercy, will extend the line of mercy, and measure out mercy after mercy for you. —*William Greenhill.*

Verse 10.—The true mark of a godly man standeth in the conjunction of faith in God with sincere study of obedience to him, for, *He is the man that knoweth God,* and is upright in heart.—*David Dickson.*

Verse 11.—" *Foot* " . . . . . " *Hand.*" Both foot and hand are named because both used in waging war.—*Simeon de Muis.*

Verse 12.—" *There are the workers of iniquity fallen.*" This is said as if the Psalmist pointed, when he said it, to a particular place with his finger ; and the same mode of expression occurs in Psalm xiv. 5 ; or, it may be rendered, *then* (*i.e.,* when the just are satisfied with the plenteousness of thy house, being rewarded for sincerely worshipping thee in it), *shall they fall, all that work wickedness ; they shall be cast down, and shall not be able to rise,* as is the case with persons who have been thrown with violence upon the hard ground.—*Daniel Cresswell.*

HINTS TO PREACHERS.

Verse 1.—What is the fear of God ? How does it operate ? What is the effect of its absence ? What should we learn from seeing such evil results ?
Or the atheism underlying transgression.

Verse 2.—The arts, motives, assistances, results, and punishments of self-flattery, and the discovery which concludes it.

Verse 2.—Self-flatteries.—*Jonathan Edward's Sermon.*

Verse 2.—On the deceitfulness of the heart, with regard to the commission of sin.—*Two Sermons, in Jamieson's " Sermons on the Heart."*

Verse 3.—Bad words. Two out of many kinds.

Verse 3 (*second clause*).—The relation between true wisdom and practical goodness.

Verse 4.—Diligence in doing evil, a mark of deep depravity.—*W. S. Plumer.*

Verse 4.—The abuse of retirement to wicked purposes, a sure characteristic of an habitual sinner.—*N. Marshall.*

Verse 4.—The sinner on his bed, in his conduct. in his heart ; add to this, in his death, and in his doom.

Verse 4 (*second clause*).—Ways which are not good.

Verse 4 (*last clause*).—Neutrality condemned.

Verses 5, 6.—Four glorious similes of the mercy, faithfulness, and providence of God. The preacher has here a wealth of poetic imagery never surpassed.

Verse 6.—God's word and works mysterious.—*C. Simeon.*

Verse 6 (*second clause*).—God's judgments are—1. Often unfathomable—we cannot discover the foundation or cause, and spring of them. II. They are safe sailing. Ships never strike on rocks out in the great deeps. III. They conceal great treasure. IV. They work much good—the great deep, though ignorance thinks it to be all waste, a salt and barren wilderness, is one of the greatest blessings to this round world. V. They become a highway of communion with God. The sea is to-day the great highway of the world.

Verse 6 (*last clause*).—Kindness of God to the lower animals, as well as man.

Verses 7, 8.—Admiration ! Confidence ! Expectation ! Realisation !

Verse 7.—The object, reasons, nature, and experience of faith.

Verse 8 (*first clause*).—*The provisions of the Lord's house.* What they are, their excellence and abundance, and for whom provided.

Verse 8 (*second clause*).—*The heavenly Hiddekel*—Its source, its flood, the happy drinkers, how they came to drink.

Verse 9 (*first clause*).—LIFE, natural, mental, spiritual, proceeds from God, is sustained, restored, purified, and perfected by him. In him it dwells with permanency, from him it flows freely, with freshness, abundance, and purity ; to him it should be consecrated.

Verse 9 (*second clause*).—LIGHT, what it is to see it. *Divine* light, what it is ; how it is the medium by which we see other light. The experience here described, and the duty here hinted at.

Verse 10.—I. *The character of the righteous*—he knows God, and is upright in heart. II. *His privilege*—lovingkindness and righteousness. III. *His prayer,* continue, etc.

Verse 10.—The need of daily supplies of grace.

Verse 12.—A view of the overthrow of evil powers, principles, and men.

PSALM XXXVII.

TITLE.—Of David.—*There is but this word to denote the authorship; whether it was a song or a meditation we are not told. It was written by David in his old age (verse 25), and is the more valuable as the record of so varied an experience.*

SUBJECT.—*The great riddle of the prosperity of the wicked and the affliction of the righteous, which has perplexed so many, is here dealt with in the light of the future; and fretfulness and repining are most impressively forbidden. It is a Psalm in which the Lord hushes most sweetly the too common repinings of his people, and calms their minds as to his present dealings with his own chosen flock, and the wolves by whom they are surrounded. It contains eight great precepts, is twice illustrated by autobiographical statements, and abounds in remarkable contrasts.*

DIVISION.—*The Psalm can scarcely be divided into considerable sections. It resembles a chapter of the book of Proverbs, most of the verses being complete in themselves. It is an alphabetical Psalm: in somewhat broken order, the first letters of the verses follow the Hebrew alphabet. This may have been not only a poetical invention, but a help to memory. The reader is requested to read the Psalm through without comment before he turns to our exposition.*

EXPOSITION.

FRET not thyself because of evildoers, neither be thou envious against the workers of iniquity.

2 For they shall soon be cut down like the grass, and wither as the green herb.

1. The Psalm opens with the first precept. It is alas! too common for believers in their hours of adversity to think themselves harshly dealt with when they see persons utterly destitute of religion and honesty, rejoicing in abundant prosperity. Much needed is the command, *" Fret not thyself because of evildoers."* To fret is to worry, to have the heart-burn, to fume, to become vexed. Nature is very apt to kindle a fire of jealousy when it sees law-breakers riding on horses, and obedient subjects walking in the mire: it is a lesson learned only in the school of grace, when one comes to view the most paradoxical providences with the devout complacency of one who is sure that the Lord is righteous in all his acts. It seems hard to carnal judgments that the best meat should go to the dogs, while loving children pine for want of it. *" Neither be thou envious against the workers of iniquity."* The same advice under another shape. When one is poor, despised, and in deep trial, our old Adam naturally becomes envious of the rich and great; and when we are conscious that we have been more righteous than they, the devil is sure to be at hand with blasphemous reasonings. Stormy weather may curdle even the cream of humanity. Evil men instead of being envied, are to be viewed with horror and aversion; yet their loaded tables, and gilded trappings, are too apt to fascinate our poor half-opened eyes. Who envies the fat bullock the ribbons and garlands which decorate him as he is led to the shambles? Yet the case is a parallel one; for ungodly rich men are but as beasts fattened for the slaughter.

2. *" For they shall soon be cut down like the grass."* The scythe of death is sharpening. Green grows the grass, but quick comes the scythe. The destruction of the ungodly will be speedy, sudden, sure, overwhelming, irretrievable. The grass cannot resist or escape the mower. *" And wither as the green herb."* The beauty of the herb dries up at once in the heat of the sun, and so all the glory of the wicked shall disappear at the hour of death. Death kills the ungodly man like grass, and wrath withers him like hay; he dies, and his name rots. How complete an end is made of the man whose boasts had no end! Is it worth while to waste ourselves in fretting about the insect of an hour, an ephemera which in the same day is born and dies? Within believers there is a living and incorruptible

seed which liveth and abideth for ever ; why should they envy mere flesh, and the glory of it, which are but as grass, and the flower thereof ?

3 Trust in the LORD, and do good ; *so* shalt thou dwell in the land, and verily shalt be fed.

3. " *Trust in the Lord.*" Here is the second precept, and one appropriate to the occasion. Faith cures fretting. Sight is cross-eyed, and views things only as they seem, hence her envy ; faith has clearer optics to behold things as they really are, hence her peace. " *And do good.*" True faith is actively obedient. Doing good is a fine remedy for fretting. There is a joy in holy activity which drives away the rust of discontent. " *So shalt thou dwell in the land.*" In " the land " which floweth with milk and honey ; the Canaan of the covenant. Thou shalt not wander in the wilderness of murmuring, but abide in the promised land of content and rest. " We which have believed do enter into rest." Very much of our outward depends upon the inward ; where there is heaven in the heart there will be heaven in the house. " *And verily thou shalt be fed,*" or shepherded. To integrity and faith necessaries are guaranteed. The good shepherd will exercise his pastoral care over all believers. In truth they shall be fed, and fed on truth. The promise of God shall be their perpetual banquet ; they shall neither lack in spirituals nor in temporals. Some read this as an exhortation, " *Feed on truth ;*" certainly this is good cheer, and banishes for ever the hungry heart-burnings of envy.

4 Delight thyself also in the LORD ; and he shall give thee the desires of thine heart.

4. There is an ascent in this third precept. He who was first bidden not to fret, was then commanded actively to trust, and now is told with holy desire to delight in God. " *Delight thyself also in the Lord.*" Make Jehovah the joy and rejoicing of thy spirit. Bad men delight in carnal objects ; do not envy them if they are allowed to take their fill in such vain idols ; look thou to thy better delight, and fill thyself to the full with thy sublimer portion. In a certain sense imitate the wicked ; they delight in their portion—take care to delight in yours, and so far from envying you will pity them. There is no room for fretting if we remember that God is ours, but there is every incentive to sacred enjoyment of the most elevated and ecstatic kind. Every name, attribute, word, or deed of Jehovah, should be delightful to us, and in meditating thereon our soul should be as glad as is the epicure who feeds delicately with a profound relish for his dainties. " *And he shall give thee the desires of thine heart.*" A pleasant duty is here rewarded with another pleasure. Men who delight in God desire or ask for nothing but what will please God ; hence it is safe to give them *carte blanche.* Their will is subdued to God's will, and now they may have what they will. Our innermost desires are here meant, not our casual wishes ; there are many things which nature might desire which grace would never permit us to ask for ; these deep, prayerful, *asking* desires are those to which the promise is made.

5 Commit thy way unto the LORD ; trust also in him ; and he shall bring *it* to pass.

6 And he shall bring forth thy righteousness as the light, and thy judgment as the noonday.

5. " *Commit thy way unto the Lord.*" Roll the whole burden of life upon the Lord. Leave with Jehovah not thy present fretfulness merely, but all thy cares ; in fact, submit the whole tenor of thy way to him. Cast away anxiety, resign thy will, submit thy judgment, leave all with the God of all. What a medicine is this for expelling envy ! What a high attainment does this fourth precept indicate ! How blessed must he be who lives every day in obedience to it ! " *Trust also in him ; and he shall bring it to pass.*" Our destiny shall be joyfully accomplished if we confidently entrust all to our Lord. We may serenely sing—

> " Thy way, not mine, O Lord,
>   However dark it be ;
> O lead me by thine own right hand
>   Choose out the path for me.

> Smooth let it be or rough,
> It will be still the best ;
> Winding or straight, it matters not,
> It leads me to thy rest.
>
> I dare not choose my lot,
> I would not if I might ;
> But choose Thou for me, O my God.
> So shall I walk aright.
>
> Take thou my cup, and it
> With joy or sorrow fill ;
> As ever best to thee may seem,
> Choose thou my good and ill.''

The ploughman sows and harrows, and then leaves the harvest to God. What can he do else ? He cannot cover the heavens with clouds, or command the rain, or bring forth the sun or create the dew. He does well to leave the whole matter with God ; and so to all of us it is truest wisdom, having obediently trusted in God, to leave results in his hands, and expect a blessed issue.

6. " *And he shall bring forth thy righteousness as the light.*" In the matter of personal reputation we may especially be content to be quiet, and leave our vindication with the Judge of all the earth. The more we fret in this case, the worse for us. Our strength is to sit still. The Lord will clear the slandered. If we look to his honour, he will see to ours. It is wonderful how, when faith learns to endure calumny with composure, the filth does not defile her, but falls off like snow-balls from a wall of granite. Even in the worst cases, where a good name is for awhile darkened, Providence will send a clearing like the dawning light, which shall increase until the man once censured shall be universally admired. " *And thy judgment as the noonday.*" No shade of reproach shall remain. The man shall be in his meridian of splendour. The darkness of his sorrow and his ill-repute shall both flee away.

7 Rest in the LORD, and wait patiently for him : fret not thyself because of him who prospereth in his way, because of the man who bringeth wicked devices to pass.

7. " *Rest in the Lord.*" This fifth is a most divine precept, and requires much grace to carry it out. To hush the spirit, to be silent before the Lord, to wait in holy patience the time for clearing up the difficulties of Providence—this is what every gracious heart should aim at. " Aaron held his peace : " " I opened not my mouth, because thou didst it." A silent tongue in many cases not only shows a wise head, but a holy heart. " *And wait patiently for him.*" Time is nothing to him ; let it be nothing to thee. God is worth waiting for. " He never is before his time, he never is too late." In a story we wait for the end to clear up the plot ; we ought not to prejudge the great drama of life, but stay till the closing scene, and see to what a finis the whole arrives. " *Fret not thyself because of him who prospereth in his way, because of the man who bringeth wicked devices to pass.*" There is no good, but much evil, in worrying your heart about the present success of graceless plotters : be not enticed into premature judgments—they dishonour God, they weary yourself. Determine, let the wicked succeed as they may, that you will treat the matter with indifference, and never allow a question to be raised as to the righteousness and goodness of the Lord. What if wicked devices succeed and your own plans are defeated ! there is more of the love of God in your defeats than in the successes of the wicked.

8 Cease from anger, and forsake wrath : fret not thyself in any wise to do evil.

9 For evil doers shall be cut off : but those that wait upon the LORD, they shall inherit the earth.

10 For yet a little while, and the wicked *shall* not *be* : yea, thou shalt diligently consider his place, and it *shall* not *be*.

11 But the meek shall inherit the earth ; and shall delight themselves in the abundance of peace.

8. " *Cease from anger and forsake wrath.*" Especially anger against the arrangements of Providence, and jealousies of the temporary pleasures of those who are so soon to be banished from all comfort. Anger anywhere is madness, here it is aggravated insanity. Yet since anger will try to keep us company, we must resolvedly forsake it. " *Fret not thyself in any wise to do evil.*" By no reasonings and under no circumstances be led into such a course. Fretfulness lies upon the verge of great sin. Many who have indulged a murmuring disposition have at last come to sin, in order to gain their fancied rights. Beware of carping at others, study to be yourself found in the right way ; and as you would dread outward sin, tremble at inward repining.

9. " *For evil doers shall be cut off.*" Their death shall be a penal judgment ; not a gentle removal to a better state, but an execution in which the axe of justice shall be used. " *But those that wait upon the Lord* "—those who in patient faith expect their portion in another life—" *they shall inherit the earth.*" Even in this life they have the most of real enjoyment, and in the ages to come theirs shall be the glory and the triumph. Passion, according to Bunyan's parable, has his good things first, and they are soon over ; Patience has his good things last, and they last for ever.

10. " *For yet a little while, and the wicked shall not be.*" When bad men reach to greatness, the judgments of God frequently sweep them away ; their riches melt, their powers decay, their happiness turns to wretchedness ; they themselves cease any longer to be numbered with the living. The shortness of life makes us see that the glitter of the wicked great is not true gold. O wherefore, tried believer, dost thou envy one who in a little while will lie lower than the dust ? " *Yea, thou shalt diligently consider his place, and it shall not be.*" His house shall be empty, his chair of office vacant, his estate without an owner ; he shall be utterly blotted out, perhaps cut off by his own debauchery, or brought to a deathbed of penury by his own extravagance. Gone like a passing cloud—forgotten as a dream— where are his boastings and hectorings, and where the pomp which made poor mortals think the sinner blest ?

11. " *But the meek shall inherit the earth.*" Above all others they shall enjoy life. Even if they suffer, their consolations shall overtop their tribulations. By inheriting the land is meant obtaining covenant privileges and the salvation of God. Such as are truly humble shall take their lot with the rest of the heirs of grace, to whom all good things come by a sacred birthright. " *And shall delight themselves in the abundance of peace.*" Peace they love and peace they shall have. If they find not abundance of gold, abundance of peace will serve their turn far better. Others find joy in strife, and thence arises their misery in due time, but peace leads on to peace, and the more a man loves it the more shall it come to him. In the halcyon period of the latter days, when universal peace shall make glad the earth, the full prophetic meaning of words like these will be made plain.

12 The wicked plotteth against the just, and gnasheth upon him with his teeth.

13 The Lord shall laugh at him : for he seeth that his day is coming.

14 The wicked have drawn out the sword, and have bent their bow, to cast down the poor and needy, *and* to slay such as be of upright conversation.

15 Their sword shall enter into their own heart, and their bows shall be broken.

Here is the portrait of a proud oppressor armed to the teeth.

12. " *The wicked plotteth against the just.*" Why can he not let the good man alone ? Because there is enmity between the serpent's seed and the seed of the woman. Why not attack him fairly ? Why plot and scheme ? Because it is according to the serpent's nature to be very subtle. Plain sailing does not suit those who are on board of " The Apollyon." " *And gnasheth upon him with his teeth.*" The wicked show by their gestures what they would do if they could ; if they cannot gnaw they will gnash : if they may not bite they will at least bark. This is precisely what the graceless world did with " that just One," the Prince of Peace. Yet he took no vengeance upon them, but like a silent lamb received injuries in patience.

13. " *The Lord shall laugh at him.*" The godly man needs not trouble himself,

but leave well-deserved vengeance to be dealt out by the Lord, who will utterly deride the malice of the good man's enemies. Let the proud scorner gnash his teeth and foam at the mouth ; he has one to deal with who will look down upon him and his ravings with serene contempt. "*For he seeth that his day is coming.*" The evil man does not see how close his destruction is upon his heels ; he boasts of crushing others when the foot of justice is already uplifted to trample him as the mire of the streets. Sinners, in the hand of an angry God, and yet plotting against his children ! Poor souls, thus to run upon the point of Jehovah's spear.

14. "*The wicked have drawn out the sword.*" They hold their weapon out of its sheath, and watch for a time to use it. "*And have bent their bow.*" One weapon is not enough, they carry another ready for action. They carry so strong a bow that they have trodden upon it to bend it—they will lose nothing for want of force or readiness. "*To cast down the poor and needy.*" These are their game, the objects of their accursed malice. These cowards attack not their equals, but seek out those excellent ones who, from the gentleness of their spirits and the poverty of their estates, are not able to defend themselves. Note how our meek and lowly Lord was beset by cruel foes, armed with all manner of weapons to slay him. "*And to slay such as be of upright conversation.*" Nothing short of the overthrow and death of the just will content the wicked. The sincere and straightforward are hated by the crafty schemers who delight in unrighteousness. See, then, the enemies of the godly doubly armed, and learn how true were our Lord's words, " If ye were of the world, the world would love his own : but because ye are not of the world, but I have chosen you out of the world, therefore the world hateth you."

15. "*Their sword shall enter into their own heart.*" Like Haman they shall be hanged upon the gallows built by themselves for Mordecai. Hundreds of times has this been the case. Saul, who sought to slay David, fell on his own sword ; and the bow, his favourite weapon, the use of which he taught the children of Israel, was not able to deliver him on Gilboa. "*And their bows shall be broken.*" Their inventions of evil shall be rendered useless. Malice outwits itself. It drinks the poisoned cup which it mixed for another, and burns itself in the fire which it kindled for its neighbour. Why need we fret at the prosperity of the wicked when they are so industriously ruining themselves while they fancy they are injuring the saints ?

The next nine verses mainly describe the character and blessedness of the godly, and the light is brought out with a few black touches descriptive of the wicked and their doom.

16 A little that a righteous man hath *is* better than the riches of many wicked.

17 For the arms of the wicked shall be broken : but the LORD upholdeth the righteous.

18 The LORD knoweth the days of the upright : and their inheritance shall be for ever.

19 They shall not be ashamed in the evil time : and in the days of famine they shall be satisfied.

20 But the wicked shall perish, and the enemies of the LORD *shall be* as the fat of lambs : they shall consume ; into smoke shall they consume away.

21 The wicked borroweth, and payeth not again : but the righteous sheweth mercy, and giveth.

22 For *such as be* blessed of him shall inherit the earth ; and *they that be* cursed of him shall be cut off.

23 The steps of a *good* man are ordered by the LORD : and he delighteth in his way.

24 Though he fall, he shall not be utterly cast down : for the LORD upholdeth *him with* his hand.

16. "*A little that a righteous man hath is better than the riches of many wicked.*" This is a fine proverb. The little of one good man is contrasted with the riches of many wicked, and so the expression is rendered the more forcible. There is more happiness in the godly dinner of herbs than in the stalled ox of profane rioters.

In the original there is an allusion to the noise of a multitude, as if to hint at the turmoil and hurly-burly of riotous wealth, and to contrast it with the quiet of the humbler portion of the godly. We would sooner hunger with John than feast with Herod ; better feed on scant fare with the prophets in Obadiah's cave than riot with the priests of Baal. A man's happiness consists not in the heaps of gold which he has in store. Content finds *multum in parvo*, while for a wicked heart the whole world is too little.

17. " *For the arms of the wicked shall be broken.*" Their power to do mischief shall be effectually taken away, for the arms which they lifted up against God shall be crushed even to the bone. God often makes implacable men incapable men. What is a more contemptible sight than toothless malice, armless malevolence ! " *But the Lord upholdeth the righteous.*" Their cause and course shall be safe, for they are in good keeping. The sword of two edges smites the wicked and defends the just.

18. " *The Lord knoweth the days of the upright.*" His foreknowledge made him laugh at the proud, but in the case of the upright he sees a brighter future, and treats them as heirs of salvation. Ever is this our comfort, that all events are known to our God, and that nothing in our future can take him at unawares. No arrow can pierce us by accident, no dagger smite us by stealth ; neither in time nor in eternity can any unforeseen ill occur to us. Futurity shall be but a continual development of the good things which the Lord has laid up in store for us. " *And their inheritance shall be for ever.*" Their inheritance fades not away. It is entailed, so that none can deprive them of it, and preserved, so that none shall destroy it. Eternity is the peculiar attribute of the believer's portion : what they have on earth is safe enough, but what they shall have in heaven is theirs without end.

19. " *They shall not be ashamed in the evil time.*" Calamities will come, but deliverances will come also. As the righteous never reckoned upon immunity from trouble, they will not be disappointed when they are called to take their share of it, but the rather they will cast themselves anew upon their God, and prove again his faithfulness and love. God is not a friend in the sunshine only, he is a friend indeed and a friend in need. " *And in the days of famine they shall be satisfied.*" Their barrel of meal and cruse of oil shall last out the day of distress, and if ravens do not bring them bread and meat, the supply of their needs shall come in some other way, for their bread shall be given them. Our Lord stayed himself upon this when he hungered in the wilderness, and by faith he repelled the tempter ; we too may be enabled not to fret ourselves in any wise to do evil by the same consideration. If God's providence is our inheritance, we need not worry about the price of wheat. Mildew, and smut, and bent, are all in the Lord's hands. Unbelief cannot save a single ear from being blasted, but faith, if it do not preserve the crop, can do what is better, namely, preserve our joy in the Lord.

20. " *But the wicked shall perish.*" Whatever phantom light may mock their present their future is black with dark, substantial night. Judgment has been given against them, they are but reserved for execution. Let them flaunt their scarlet and fine linen, and fare sumptuously every day ; the sword of Damocles is above their heads, and if their wits were a little more awake, their mirth would turn to misery. " *The enemies of the Lord shall be as the fat of lambs.*" As the sacrificial fat was all consumed upon the altar, so shall the ungodly utterly vanish from the place of their honour and pride. How can it be otherwise ? If the stubble dares to contend with the flame, to what end can it hope to come ? " *They shall consume.*" As dry wood, as heaps of leaves, as burning coals, they shall soon be gone, and gone altogether, for " *into smoke shall they consume away.*" *Sic transit gloria mundi.* A puff is the end of all their puffing. There fuming ends in smoke. They made themselves fat, and perished in their own grease. Consumers of the good they tried to be, and consumed they shall be.

21. " *The wicked borroweth, and payeth not again.*" Partly because he will not, but mainly because he cannot. Want follows upon waste, and debt remains undischarged. Often are the wicked thus impoverished in this life. Their wanton extravagance brings them down to the usurer's door and to the bankrupt's suit. " *But the righteous sheweth mercy, and giveth.*" Mercy has given to him, and therefore he gives in mercy. He is generous and prosperous. He is not a borrower, but a giver. So far as the good man can do it, he lends an ear to the requests of need, and instead of being impoverished by what he imparts, he grows richer, and is able to do more. He does not give to encourage idleness, but in real mercy, which

supposes real need. The text suggests to us how much better it generally is to give than to lend. Generally, lending comes to giving in the end, and it is as well to anticipate the fact, and by a little liberality forestall the inevitable. If these two sentences describe the wicked and the righteous, the writer of these lines has reason to know that in and about the ciy of London the wicked are very numerous.

22. "*For such as be blessed of him shall inherit the earth.*" God's benediction is true wealth after all. True happiness, such as the covenant secures to all the chosen of heaven, lies wrapped up in the divine favour. "*And they that be cursed of him shall be cut off.*" His frown is death; nay, more, 'tis hell.

23. "*The steps of a good man are ordered by the Lord.*" All his course of life is graciously ordained, and in lovingkindness all is fixed, settled, and maintained. No reckless fate, no fickle chance rules us; our every step is the subject of divine decree. "*He delighteth in his way.*" As parents are pleased with the tottering footsteps of their babes. All that concerns a saint is interesting to his heavenly Father. God loves to view the holy strivings of a soul pressing forward to the skies. In the trials and the joys of the faithful, Jesus has fellowship with them, and delights to be their sympathising companion.

24. "*Though he fall.*" Disasters and reverses may lay him low; he may, like Job, be stripped of everything; like Joseph, be put in prison; like Jonah, be cast into the deep. "*He shall not be utterly cast down.*" He shall not be altogether prostrate. He shall be brought on his knees, but not on his face; or, if laid prone for a moment he shall be up again ere long. No saint shall fall finally or fatally. Sorrow may bring us to the earth, and death may bring us to the grave, but lower we cannot sink, and out of the lowest of all we shall arise to the highest of all. "*For the Lord upholdeth him with his hand.*" Condescendingly, with his own hand, God upholds his saints; he does not leave them to mere delegated agency, he affords personal assistance. Even in our falls the Lord gives a measure of sustaining. Where grace does not keep from going down, it shall save from keeping down. Job had double wealth at last, Joseph reigned over Egypt, Jonah was safely landed. It is not that the saints are strong, or wise, or meritorious, that therefore they rise after every fall, but because God is their helper, and therefore none can prevail against them.

25 I have been young, and *now* am old; yet have I not seen the righteous forsaken, nor his seed begging bread.

26 *He is* ever merciful, and lendeth; and his seed *is* blessed.

25. This was David's observation, "*I have been young, and now am old; yet have I not seen the righteous forsaken, nor his seed begging bread.*" It is not *my* observation just as it stands, for I have relieved the children of undoubtedly good men, who have appealed to me as common mendicants. But this does not cast a doubt upon the observation of David. He lived under a dispensation more outward, and more of this world than the present rule of personal faith. Never are the righteous forsaken; that is a rule without exception. Seldom indeed do their seed beg bread; and although it does occasionally occur, through dissipation, idleness, or some such causes on the part of their sons, yet doubtless it is so rare a thing that there are many alive who never saw it. Go into the union house and see how few are the children of godly parents; enter the gaol and see how much rarer still is the case. Poor ministers' sons often become rich. I am not old, but I have seen the families of the poor godly become rich, and have seen the Lord reward the faithfulness of the father in the success of the son, so that I have often thought that the best way to endow one's seed with wealth is to become poor for Christ's sake. In the Indian mission of the "Baptist Missionary Society," this is abundantly illustrated.

26. "*He is ever merciful, and lendeth.*" The righteous are constantly under generous impulses; they do not prosper through parsimony, but through bounty. Like the bounteous giver of all good, of whom they are the beloved sons, they delight in doing good. How stingy, covetous professors can hope for salvation is a marvel to those who read such verses as this in the Bible. "*And his seed is blessed.*" God pays back with interest in the next generation. Where the children of the righteous are not godly, there must be some reason for it in parental neglect, or *some* other guilty cause. The friend of the father is the friend of the family. The God of Abraham is the God of Isaac and of Jacob.

27 Depart from evil, and do good ; and dwell for evermore.

28 For the LORD loveth judgment, and forsaketh not his saints ; they are preserved for ever : but the seed of the wicked shall be cut off.

29 The righteous shall inherit the land, and dwell therein for ever.

Here we have the seventh precept, which takes a negative and positive form, and is the quintessence of the entire Psalm.

27. " *Depart from evil, and do good.*" We must not envy the doers of evil, but depart altogether from their spirit and example. As Lot left Sodom without casting a look behind, so must we leave sin. No truce or parley is to be held with sin, we must turn away from it without hesitation, and set ourselves practically to work in the oposite direction. He who neglects to do good will soon fall into evil. " *And dwell for evermore.*" Obtain an abiding and quiet inheritance. Shortlived are the gains and pleasures of evil, but eternal are the rewards of grace.

28. " *For the Lord loveth judgment.*" The awarding of honour to whom honour is due is God's delight, especially when the upright man has been traduced by his fellow men. It must be a divine pleasure to right wrongs, and to defeat the machinations, of the unjust. The great Arbiter of human destinies is sure to deal out righteous measure both to rich and poor, to good and evil, for such judgment is his delight. " *And forsaketh not his saints.*" This would not be right, and, therefore, shall never be done. God is as faithful to the objects of his love as he is just towards all mankind. " *They are preserved for ever.*" By covenant engagements their security is fixed, and by suretyship fulfilments that safety is accomplished ; come what may, the saints are preserved in Christ Jesus, and because he lives, they shall live also. A king will not lose his jewels, nor will Jehovah lose his people. As the manna in the golden pot, which else had melted, was preserved in the ark of the covenant beneath the mercy-seat, so shall the faithful be preserved in the covenant by the power of Jesus their propitiation. " *But the seed of the wicked shall be cut off.*" Like the house of Jeroboam and Ahab, of which not a dog was left. Honour and wealth ill-gotten seldom reach the third generation ; the curse grows ripe before many years have passed, and falls upon the evil house. Among the legacies of wicked men the surest entail is a judgment on their family.

29. " *The righteous shall inherit the land.*" As heirs with Jesus Christ, the Canaan above, which is the antitype of " the land," shall be theirs with all covenant blessing. " *And dwell therein for ever.*" Tenures differ, but none can match the holding which believers have of heaven. Paradise is theirs for ever by inheritance, and they shall live for ever to enjoy it. Who would not be a saint on such terms ? Who would fret concerning the fleeting treasures of the godless ?

30 The mouth of the righteous speaketh wisdom, and his tongue talketh of judgment.

31 The law of his God *is* in his heart ; none of his steps shall slide.

32 The wicked watcheth the righteous, and seeketh to slay him.

33 The LORD will not leave him in his hand, nor condemn him when he is judged.

30. " *The mouth of the righteous speaketh wisdom.*" Where the whole Psalm is dedicated to a description of the different fates of the just and the wicked, it was meet to give a test by which they could be known. A man's tongue is no ill index of his character. The mouth betrays the heart. Good men, as a rule, speak that which is to edifying, sound speech, religious conversation, consistent with the divine illumination which they have received. Righteousness is wisdom in action, hence all good men are practically wise men, and well may the speech be wise. " *His tongue talketh of judgment.*" He advocates justice, gives an honest verdict on things and men, and he foretells that God's judgments will come upon the wicked, as in the former days. His talk is neither foolish nor ribald, neither vapid nor profane. Our conversation is of far more consequence than some men imagine.

31. " *The law of his God is in his heart ; none of his steps shall slide.*" The best thing in the best place, producing the best results. Well might the man's talk be so admirable when his heart was so well stored. To love holiness, to have the motives and desires sanctified, to be in one's inmost nature obedient to the Lord— this is the surest method of making the whole run of our life efficient for its great

ends, and even for securing the details of it, our *steps* from any serious mistake. To keep the even tenor of one's way, in such times as these, is given only to those whose hearts are sound towards God, who can, as in the text, call God their God. Policy slips and trips, it twists and tacks, and after all is worsted in the long run, but sincerity plods on its plain pathway and reaches the goal.

32. " *The wicked watcheth the righteous, and seeketh to slay him.*" If it were not for the laws of the land, we should soon see a massacre of the righteous. Jesus was watched by his enemies, who were thirsting for his blood : his disciples must not look for favour where their Master found hatred and death.

33. " *The Lord will not leave him in his hand.*" God often appears to deliver his servants, and when he does not do so in this life as to their bodies, he gives their souls such joy and peace that they triumphantly rise beyond their tormentor's power. We may be in the enemy's hand for awhile, as Job was, but we cannot be left there. " *Nor condemn him when he is judged.*" Time shall reverse the verdict of haste, or else eternity shall clear away the condemnation of time. In due season just men will be justified. Temporary injustices are tolerated, in the order of Providence, for purposes most wise ; but the bitter shall not always be called sweet, not light for ever be traduced as darkness ; the right shall appear in due season ; the fictitious and pretentious shall be unmasked, and the real and true shall be revealed. If we have done faithfully, we may appeal from the petty sessions of society to the solemn assize of the great day.

34 Wait on the LORD, and keep his way, and he shall exalt thee to inherit the land : when the wicked are cut off, thou shalt see *it.*

35 I have seen the wicked in great power, and spreading himself like a green bay tree.

36 Yet he passed away, and, lo, he *was* not : yea, I sought him, but he could not be found.

37 Mark the perfect *man,* and behold the upright : for the end of *that* man *is* peace.

38 But the transgressors shall be destroyed together ; the end of the wicked shall be cut off.

39 But the salvation of the righteous *is* of the LORD ; *he is* their strength in the time of trouble.

40 And the LORD shall help them, and deliver them : he shall deliver them from the wicked, and save them, because they trust in him.

34. " *Wait on the Lord.*" We have here the eighth precept, and it is a lofty eminence to attain to. Tarry the Lord's leisure. Wait in obedience as a servant, in hope as an heir, in expectation as a believer. This little word " wait " is easy to say, but hard to carry out, yet faith must do it. " *And keep his way.*" Continue in the narrow path ; let no haste for riches or ease cause unholy action. Let your motto be, " On, on, on," Never flag, or dream of turning aside. " He that endureth to the end, the same shall be saved." " *And he shall exalt thee to inherit the land.*" Thou shalt have all of earthly good which is really good, and of heavenly good there shall be no stint. Exaltation shall be the lot of the excellent. " *When the wicked are cut off, thou shalt see it.*" A sight how terrible and how instructive ! What a rebuke for fretfulness ! what an incentive to gratitude ! My soul, be still, as thou foreseest the end, the awful end of the Lord's enemies.

35. A second time David turns to his diary, and this time in poetic imagery tells us of what he had observed. It were well if we too took notes of divine providences. " *I have seen the wicked in great power.*" The man was terrible to others, ruling with much authority, and carrying things with a high hand, a Cæsar in might, a Crœsus in wealth. " *And spreading himself like a green bay tree.*" Adding house to house and field to field, rising higher and higher in the state. He seemed to be ever verdant like a laurel, he grew as a tree in its own native soil, from which it had never been transplanted. No particular tree is here meant, a spreading beech or a wide expanding oak may serve us to realise the picture ; it is a thing of earth, whose roots are in the clay ; its honours are fading leaves ; and though its shadow dwarfs the plants which are condemned to pine beneath it, yet it is itself a dying thing, as the feller's axe shall prove. In the noble tree,

which claims to be king of the forest, behold the grandeur of the ungodly to-day ; wait awhile and wonder at the change, as the timber is carried away, and the very root torn from the ground.

36. " *Yet he passed away.*" Tree and man both gone, the son of man as surely as the child of the forest. What clean sweeps death makes ! " *And lo, he was not.*" To the surprise of all men the great man was gone, his estates sold, his business bankrupt, his house alienated, his name forgotten, and all in a few months ! " *Yea, I sought him, but he could not be found.*" Moved by curiosity, if we enquire for the ungodly, they have left no trace ; like birds of ill omen none desire to remember them. Some of the humblest of the godly are immortalised, their names are imperishably fragrant in the church, while of the ablest of infidels and blasphemers hardly their names are remembered beyond a few years. Men who were in everybody's mouths but yesterday are forgotten to-morrow, for only virtue is immortal.

37. " *Mark the perfect man, and behold the upright.*" After having watched with surprise the downfall of the wicked, give your attention to the sincerely godly man, and observe the blessed contrast. Good men are men of mark, and are worth our study. Upright men are marvels of grace, and worth beholding. " *For the end of that man is peace.*" The man of peace has an end of peace. Peace without end comes in the end to the man of God. His way may be rough, but it leads home. With believers it may rain in the morning, thunder at midday, and pour in torrents in the afternoon, but it must clear up ere the sun goes down. War may last till our last hour, but them we shall hear the last of it.

38. " *But the transgressors shall be destroyed together.*" A common ruin awaits those who joined in common rebellion. " *The end of the wicked shall be cut off.*" Their time shall be shortened, their happiness shall be ended, their hopes for ever blasted, their execution hastened on. Their present is shortened by their sins ; they shall not live out half their days. They have no future worth having, while the righteous count their future as their true heritage.

39. " *But the salvation of the righteous is of the Lord.*" Sound doctrine this. The very marrow of the gospel of free grace. By salvation is meant deliverance of every kind ; not only ;he salvation which finally lands us in glory, but all the minor rescues of the way these are all to be ascribed unto the Lord, and to him alone. Let him have glory from those to whom he grants salvation. " *He is their strength in the time of trouble.*" While trouble overthrows the wicked, it only drives the righteous to their strong Helper, who rejoices to uphold them.

40. " *And the Lord shall help them.*" In all future time Jehovah will stand up for his chosen. Our Great Ally will bring up his forces in the heat of the battle. " *He shall deliver them from the wicked.*" As he rescued Daniel from the lions, so will he preserve his beloved from their enemies ; they need not therefore fret, nor be discouraged. " *And save them, because they trust in him.*" Faith shall ensure the safety of the elect. It is the mark of the sheep by which they shall be separated from the goats. Not their merit, but their believing, shall distinguish them. Who would not try the walk of faith ? Whoever truly believes in God will be no longer fretful against the apparent irregularities of this present life, but will rest assured that what is mysterious is nevertheless just, and what seems hard, is, beyond a doubt ordered in mercy. So the Psalm ends with a note which is the death-knell of the unhallowed disquietude with which the Psalm commenced. Happy they who can thus sing themselves out of ill frames into gracious conditions.

EXPLANATORY NOTES AND QUAINT SAYINGS.

Whole Psalm.—The righteous are preserved in Christ with a special preservation and in a peculiar safety. In the thirty-seventh Psalm this point is excellently and at large handled, both by direct proof, and by answer to all the usual objections against their safety. That they shall be preserved is affirmed, verses 3, 17, 23, 25, 32. The objections answered are many.

Objection 1.—Wicked men flourish.

Solution.—A righteous man should never grieve at that, for " they shall soon be cut down like the grass, and wither as the green herb." Verse 2.

Object. 2.—Righteous men are in distress.

Sol.—Verse 6.—The night of their adversity will be turned into the light of prosperity ; and as surely as they can believe when it is night that it shall be day, so surely may they be persuaded when crosses are upon them, that comfort and deliverance shall come.

Object. 3.—But there are great plots laid against the righteous, and they are pursued with great malice, and their intended ruin is come almost to the very issue.

Sol.—Verses 12—15.—The Lord sees all the plots of wicked men, and laughs at their spiteful and foolish malice ; while they are busy to destroy the righteous, and hope to have a day against them, " The Lord seeth that their own day is coming upon them, even a day of destruction, a day of great judgment and eternal misery ; " their bow shall be broken, and the sword that they have drawn shall enter into their own heart.

Object. 4.—But the just have but small means.

Sol.—Verses 16, 17.—" A little that a righteous man hath is better than the riches of many wicked. For the arms of the wicked shall be broken : but the Lord upholdeth the righteous."

Object. 5.—Heavy times are like to befall them.

Sol.—Verse 19.—" They shall not be ashamed in the evil time, and in the days of famine they shall have enough."

Object. 6.—But the wicked wax fatter and fatter, and they prevail in vexing the righteous.

Sol.—Verse 20.—Indeed the wicked are fat, but it is but " the fat of lambs," their prosperity shall soon melt ; and as they be like smoke in vexing the godly, so shall they be like smoke in vanishing away.

Object. 7.—But the righteous do fall.

Sol.—Verse 24.—Though he do fall, yet he falls not finally, nor totally, for he " is not utterly cast down ; " and besides, there is an upholding providence of God in all the falls of the righteous.

Object. 8.—We see some wicked men that do not so fall into adversity, but rather are in prosperity to their dying days.

Sol.—Verse 28.—Though they do, yet " their seed shall be cut off."

Object. 9.—But some wicked men are strong yet, and in their seed spread also.

Sol.—Verses 35, 36.—Note also that these " spreading bay-trees " many times " soon pass away ; " and they and their houses are sometimes " utterly cut off."

Object. 10.—But upright men are under many and long crosses.

Sol.—Verse 37.—Yet, " his end is peace."

Object. 11.—But nobody stands for the godly when they come into question.

Sol.—Verses 39, 40.—" Their salvation is of the Lord ; " he is their strength, he will help them and deliver them, etc.

But if we would be thus delivered, observe: 1. That we must not unthankfully fret at God's providence (verse 1). 2. We must " trust in the Lord and do good " (verse 3). 3. We must " delight ourselves in the Lord," and not place our contentment on earthly things (verse 4). 4. We must " commit our ways to God " (verse 5). 5. We must get patience and humble affections (verses 7—11). 6. We must be of upright conversation (verse 14). 7. We must be merciful (verses 25, 26). 8. We must " speak righteous things," and get " the law into our hearts " (verses 30, 31). 9. We must " keep our way," and " wait on God," and not use ill means.—*Nicholas Byfield.*

Whole Psalm.—This Psalm may well be styled, The good man's cordial in bad times : a sovereign plaister for the plague of discontent : or, a choice antidote against the poison of impatience —*Nathanael Hardy, in a Funeral Sermon,* 1649.

Whole Psalm.—This Psalm very much reminds one in its construction of the sententious and pithy conciseness of the Book of Proverbs. It does not contain any prayer, nor any direct allusion to David's own circumstances of persecution or distress It is rather the utterance of sound practical wisdom and godliness from the lips of experience and age, such as we might suppose an elder of the church, or a father of a family, to let fall as he sat with his household gathered around him, and listening to his earnest and affectionate admonition.—*Barton Bouchier.*

Whole Psalm.—The present Psalm is one of the alphabetical Psalms, it is called " *Providentiæ speculum,*" by Tertullian ; " *Potio contra murmur,*" by Isidore ; " *Vestis piorum,*" by Luther.—*Christopher Wordsworth.*

Verse 1.—" Fret," or, inflame not, burn not thyself with anger or grief.—*John Diodati.*

Verse 1.—" *Neither be thou envious,*" etc. Queen Elizabeth envied the milk-maid when she was in prison ; but if she had known what a glorious reign she should have had afterwards for fourty-four years, she would not have envied her. And as little needeth a godly man, though in misery, to envy a wicked man in the ruff of all his prosperity and jollity, considering what he hath in hand, much more what he hath in hope.—*John Trapp.*

Verse 1.—Would it not be accounted folly in a man that is heir to many thousands per annum that he should envy a stage-player, clothed in the habit of a king, and yet not heir to one foot of land ? who, though he have the form, respect, and apparel of a king or nobleman, yet he is, at the same time, a very beggar, and worth nothing ? Thus, wicked men, though they are arrayed gorgeously, and fare deliciously, wanting nothing, and having more than heart can wish, yet they are but only possessors : the godly Christian is the heir. What good doth all their prosperity do them ? It does but hasten their ruin, not their reward. The ox that is the labouring ox is the longer lived than the ox that is put into the pasture ; the very putting of him there doth but hasten his slaughter ; and when God puts the wicked men into fat pastures, into places of honour and power, it is but to hasten their ruin. Let no man, therefore, fret himself because of evil doers, nor be envious at the prosperity of the wicked ; for the candle of the wicked shall be put into everlasting darkness ; they shall soon be cut off, and wither as a green herb.—*Ludovic de Carbone, quoted by John Spencer.*

Verse 2.—" *Cut down like the grass,*" with a scythe, and even at one blow.— *Thomas Wilcocks.*

Verse 2.—" *Wither.*" O bitter word, which will make the ears of them that hear it to tingle ! O sentence intolerable, which depriveth sinners of all good things, and bringeth them to all woe ! The Lord sometime accursed the fig tree, and immediately, not only the leaves, but also the body and root were wholly withered : even so, that fearful curse of the last day shall be no less effectual ; for on whomsoever it falleth it shall so scorch them, and shall so make them destitute of God's grace, that they shall never more be able to do, to speak, think, or to hope for any good thing.—*Thomas Tymme.*

Verse 2.—" *Green herb.*" We cannot gather riper fruit of patience from any tree than is found upon the low shrubs of man's short life ; for if that fretting canker of *envy at the prosperity of the wicked* have overrun thy mind, a malady from which the saints have no shelter to be freed, out of this apothecary's shop take antidote ; either thy time is short to behold it, or theirs shorter to enjoy it : " they are set in slippery places, and are suddenly destroyed," Psalm lxxiii. 18 ; " They spend their days in wealth, and in a moment go down to the grave," Job xxi. 13 ; " *They shall soon be cut down like the grass, and wither as the green herb.*"—*Edmund Layfield's Sermon, entitled* " *The Mappe of Man's Mortality and Vanity,*" 1630.

Verse 2.—Sometimes the wicked, like the green herb, wither in their spring, they fall in their rise, they perish in the beginnings of their mischievous designs ; but if they do come to a full growth, they grow but to harvest, the fit season of their cutting off.—*Robert Mossom.*

Verse 3.—Note well the double precept " *trust* " and " *do.*" This is the true order, the two must go together, the one produces, the other proves ; the promise is to both.—*C. H. S.*

Verse 3.—" *So shalt thou dwell in the land,*" etc. Thou shalt have a settlement, a quiet settlement, and a maintenance, a comfortable maintenance : " *Verily thou shalt be fed ;* " some read it, Thou shalt be fed by faith, as the just are said to live by faith, and it is good living, good feeding upon the promises. " *Verily thou shalt be fed,*" as Elijah in the famine, with what is needful for thee. God himself is a shepherd, a feeder to all those that trust in him, Psalm xxiii. 1.—*Matthew Henry.*

Verse 3.—" *So shalt thou dwell in the land,*" etc. The land of Canaan was considered as the sum of earthly, and the type of heavenly felicity : to be provided for in the Lord's land, and there to dwell under his protection, near his ordinances, and among his people, was all that the genuine Israelite could desire.—*Thomas Scott* (1747—1821) *in loc.*

Verse 3.—" *Thou shalt be fed.*" A manner of speech taken from cattle feeding securely, under the conduct and keeping of a good shepherd.—*Henry Ainsworth.*

Verse 3.—"*Thou shalt be fed.*" Fed in plenty.— *Thomas Secker* (*Archbishop*), **1768.**

Verse 3.—Fed in security.—*John Parkhurst.*

Verse 4.—Note thy part and God's part.　Do thou " *delight*," and he will " *give*."
C. H. S.

Verse 4.—How much grace and love breathes in these words, " *Delight thyself
also in the Lord !* "　*Trust* in him was recommended before, and now, this being
added also, how plain is it that your ease and rest is the thing designed !　Is it fit
to receive so much kindness with neglect ?　Again, *he delights in you :*　I speak
to such of whom this may be supposed.　And it is indefinitely said, " His delights
were with the sons of men," Prov. viii. 31.　Think what he is, and what you are ;
and at once, both wonder and yield.　And what else have you to delight in ？ what
thing will you name that shall supply the place of GOD, or be to you in the stead
of him ?　Moreover, who should delight in him but you—his friends, his sons, those
of his own house ?　Think what life and vigour it will infuse into you, and that
" the joy of the Lord will be your strength," Nehem. viii. 10.　How pleasantly
will you hold on your course, and discharge all other duties of this your present
state !　You must serve him.　Dare you think of throwing off his yoke ?　How
desirable is it then to take delight in him whom I must serve ; which only makes
that service acceptable to him, and easy to myself !　Further, this is a pleasure none
can rob you of ; a joy that cannot be taken from you.　Other objects of your delight
are vanishing daily.　Neither men nor devils can ever hinder you delighting in
God, if your hearts be so inclined.　And were you never brought to take pleasure
in any person or thing to which you had a former aversion ?　One that had wronged
you might yet possibly win you by after kindness.　Give a reason why you should
be more difficult towards the blessed God that never wronged you, and whose way
towards you hath constantly imported so much good will !

And consider that your condition on earth is such as exposes you to many
sufferings and hardships, which, by your not delighting in him, you can never be
sure to avoid (for they are things common to men), but which, by your delighting
in him, you may be easily able to endure.　Besides all this, seriously consider that
you must die.　You can make no shift to avoid that.　How easily tolerable and
pleasant will it be to think, then, of going to him with whom you have lived in a
delightful communion before !　And how dreadful to appear before him to whom
your own heart shall accuse you to have been (against all his importunities and
allurements) a disaffected stranger !—*John Howe's " Treatise of Delight in God."*

Verse 4.—We have in the former part extended the meaning of the words
" *Delight thyself in the Lord,*" beyond what they seem at first sight literally to signify ;
so as not to understand them merely as requiring that very single act of *delight*
to be immediately and directly terminated on God himself ; but to take them as
comprehending all *the sum of all holy and religious converse with God,* i.e., as it is
delightful or as it is seasoned (intermingled, and as it were besprinkled) with delight ;
and upon the same account, of all our other converse, so far as it is influenced by
religion.　And I doubt not, to such as shall attentively have considered what hath
been said, it will be thought very reasonable to take them in that latitude ; whereof
the very letter of the text (as may be alleged for futher justification hereof) is most
fitly capable.　For the particle which we read *in* the Lord, hath not that signification
alone, but signifies also *with* or *by*, or *besides*, or *before*, or *in presence of*, as if it had
been said, " Come and sit down with God, retire thyself to him, and solace thyself
in the delights which are to be found in his presence and converse, in walking with
him, and transacting thy course as before him, and in his sight."　As a man may
be said to delight himself with a friend that puts himself under his roof, and, besides
personal converse with himself, freely enjoys the pleasure of all the entertainments,
accomodations, and provisions which he is freely willing to communicate with him,
and hath the satisfaction which a sober person would take in observing the rules
and order of a well-governed house.—*John Howe.*

Verse 4.—" *He shall give thee the desires of thine heart.*"　It shall be unto thee
even as thou wilt.　It is said of Luther that he could have what he would of
Almighty God.　What may not a favourite, who hath the royalty of his prince's
care, obtain of him ?—*John Trapp.*

Verse 4.—" *The desires of thine heart.*"　All the desires of this spiritual seed
are of the nature of this seed, namely, substantial, and shall meet with substance.
All the desires of natural man, even after God, after Christ, after righteousness, shall
burn and perish with him (for they are not the truth, nor do they come from the
truth, nor can they reach to the truth ;) but all the desires of this spirit shall live
with the Spirit of God, in rest and satisfaction for ever.—*John Pennington,* 1656.

Verse 4.—The *desires* of God and the *desires* of the righteous, agree in one ; they are of one mind in their desires.—*John Bunyan.*

Verse 5.—" *Commit thy way unto the Lord,*" etc. When we bear the burden of our own affairs ourselves, and are chastised with anxiety and want of success, and with envying the ungodly who prosper better than we do, the best remedy is first to do our duty, as we are enabled in the use of the means, then cast the care of the success over on God, as the ploughman doth when he hath harrowed his land ; and let the burden of it rest on God, and let us not take it off him again, but put our mind to rest, resolved to take the harvest in good part, as he shall send it.—*David Dickson.*

Verse 5.—" *Commit thy way unto the Lord,*" is rendered by the Vulgate, *Revela viam Domino,* reveal thy way ; and by St. Ambrose, understood of revealing our sins to God. Indeed, since is it impossible to cover, why should we not discover, our sins ? Conceal not that which God knoweth already, and would have thee to make known. It is a very ill office to be the devil's secretary. Oh, break thy league with Satan by revealing his secrets, thy sins, to God.—*Nathaniel Hardy.*

Verse 5.—" *Commit thy way unto.*" Marg. and Heb., *Roll thy way upon*—as one who lays upon the shoulder of one stronger than himself a burden which he is not able to bear.—*William De Burgh, D.D., in " A Commentary on the Book of Psalms. Dublin : 1860."*

Verse 5.—Note the double again. " *Commit* " and " *trust.*"—*C. H. S.*

Verse 5.—" *He shall bring it to pass.*" When a hard piece of work is put into the hand of an apprentice for the first assay of his skill, the beholders are justly afraid of a miscarriage in his young and unexperienced hand ; but when the worker is an old master of craft, none are afraid but his cunning hand can act again what so oft it hath wrought to the contentment of all the beholders. Were our God a novice in the great art of governing the world, and of the church in the bosom thereof ; had he to this day never given any proof of his infinite wisdom, power, and goodness, in turning about the most terrible accidents to the welfare and joy of his saints ; we might indeed be amazed whenever we feel ourselves sinking in the dangers wherein the practices of our enemies oft do plunge us over head and ears ; but the Lord having given in times past so many documents of his uncontroverted skill and most certain will to bring about all human affairs, as to his own glory, so to the real good of all that love him, it would be in us an impious and unexcusable uncharitableness to suspect the end of any work which he hath begun.—*Robert Baylie's Sermon before the House of Commons.* 1643.

Verses 5, 7 :—

To God thy way commending,
  Trust him whose arm of might,
The heavenly circles bending,
  Guides every star aright :
The winds, and clouds, and lightning,
  By his sure hand are led :
And he will, dark shades brightening,
  Show thee what path to tread.

  *   *   *   *

Although to make God falter,
  The powers of hell combine,
One jot they cannot alter
  Of his all-wise design :
All projects and volition
  Of his eternal mind,
Despite all opposition,
  Their due fulfilment find.

No more, then, droop and languish,
  Thou sorrow-stricken soul ;
E'en from the depths of anguish,
  Whose billows o'er thee roll,
Thy Father's hand shall draw thee ;
  In hope and patience stay,
And joy will soon shed o'er thee
  An ever brightening ray.

All faithless murmurs leaving,
  Bid them a last good night.
No more thy vexed soul grieving,
  Because things seem not right :
Wisely his sceptre wielding,
  God sits in regal state,
No power to mortals yielding,
  Events to regulate.

Trust with a faith untiring
  In thine Omniscient King,
And thou shalt see admiring
  What he to light will bring.
Of all thy griefs, the reason
  Shall at the last appear ;
Why now denied a season,
  Will shine in letters clear.

* * * *

Then raise thine eyes to heaven,
  Thou who canst trust his frown ;
Thence shall thy meed be given.
  The chaplet and the crown :
Thy God the palm victorious
  In thy right hand shall plant.
Whilst thou, in accents glorious,
  Melodious hymns shall chant.

* * * * *

Paul Gerhard (1606—1676), *translated by Frances Elizabeth Cox, in " Hymns from the German,"* 1864.

Verse 6.—" *He shall bring forth thy righteousness as the light,*" etc. If thou shouldst be accused as a man of evil designs, let not that trouble thee neither : for though thy fame may be obscured for a time by calumnies and slanders, as the sun is by mists and clouds, yet as that scatters them all at last, so shall thy integrity appear, and shine as bright as the sun at noonday.—*Symon Patrick.*

Verse 7.—" *Rest in the Lord, and wait patiently for him.*" There are two words in the original, which express the privilege and the duty of resting on Christ : one implies such a state of acquiescence, as silences and clamours of conscience, and composes the perturbation of the spirit ; the other signifies the refreshment and repose of a weary pilgrim, when he arrives at the end of his journey, and is settled for life in a secure, commodious, plentiful habitation.—*James Hervey.*

Verse 7.—" *Rest in the Lord, and wait patiently for him.*" Take the case of one who, with a load above his strength, has been toiling some steep and broken path, when suddenly he finds it lifted off and transferred to another whose strength he knows to be more than equal to the task, and in whose sympathy he can securely trust. What would his feeling be but one of perfect rest, and calm reliance, and joyous freedom, as they went on their way together ? And such is the blessedness of rolling our care upon the Lord—in weakness we are resting on superior strength, in perplexity and doubt we are resting on superior wisdom, in all times of trial and hard service we can stay ourselves on the assurance of his perfect sympathy. The literal meaning of the word " *rest,*" is " *be silent*" towards the Lord. With the eye fixed on him let all unbelieving thoughts be stilled, such thoughts as rise and rankle in the querulous spirit when it sees only its troubles, and not God in them, when the mists of earth hide from its sight the eternal stars of heaven. Then like Jacob, it may say morosely, " All these things are against me ; " or, like Elijah, despondently, " It is enough, now, O Lord, take away my life ; " or, like Jonah, fretfully, " I do well to be angry." In regard to all such dark and unbelieving suggestions, the heart is to keep silence, to be still and know that he is God ; silent as to murmuring, but not silent as to prayer, for in that holy meditative stillness the heart turns to commune with him. What is " resting in God," but the instinctive movement and upward glance of the spirit to him ; the confiding all one's griefs and fears to him, and feeling strengthened, patient, hopeful in the act of doing so ! It implies a willingness that he should choose for us, a conviction that the ordering of all that concerns us is safer in his hands than in our own.

A few practical remarks :—1. Our " *resting patiently*" in the Lord applies only to the trials which he sends, not to the troubles which even Christians often make for themselves. There is a difference in the burdens that come in the way of duty, and those that come through our wandering into other ways. We can roll the one upon the Lord, but with the other our punishment may be to be left to bear them long, and to be bruised in bearing them. 2. The duty here enjoined is to be carried through all our life. We all admit that *patient* waiting is needed for the great trials of life, but may not acknowledge so readily that it is needed as much for little, daily, commonplace vexations. But these are as much a test of Christian principle as the other. 3. This resting in God is a criterion of a man's spiritual state. It needs a special faculty of discernment, a new sense to be opened in the soul, before our fallen nature can understand or desire it.—*James D. Burns, M.A.*

Verse 7 (*first clause*).—"*Hold thee still*" (so it may be translated). And this is the hardest precept that is given to man; insomuch that the most difficult precept of action sinks into nothing when compared with this command to inaction.—*Jerome.*

Verse 7 (*first clause*).—The Hebrew word rendered *silent* is דום, *dom*, from which the English word *dumb* appears to be derived. The silence here enjoined is opposed to murmuring or complaining.—*James Anderson, in Calvin's Commentary.*

Verse 7.—Note again the twin duties, "*rest*" and "*wait*."

Verse 7.—"*Bringeth wicked devices to pass.*" Observe the opposition between this and *God's* bringing to pass, in verse five. The ground for grief is that the ungodly appear to achieve their end, the reason for comfort is that our end shall be achieved also, and that in the best manner by God himself.—*C. H. S.*

Verse 8.—"*Forsake wrath;*" which is anger wrought up to a greater degree; and the rather to be shunned and avoided, as being very disageeable to the character of a good man. "*Fret not thyself in any wise to do evil;*" evil may be done by fretting at the prosperity of wicked men, or by imitating them, doing as they do, in hope of being prosperous as they are.—*John Gill.*

Verse 9.—"*They shall inherit the earth.*" He means that they shall live in such a manner as that the blessing of God shall follow them, even to the grave.—*John Calvin.*

Verse 10.—"*Thou shalt diligently consider his place, and it shall not be.*" To wit because he shall be grubbed up by the roots.—*Arthur Jackson.*

Verse 10.—"*His place .. shall not be.*" The very land he occupied as a home, and the title to which was unimpeachable, is no longer "*his place.*" It has passed into other hands. Nothing of all he had on earth is his. He is as poor as the most miserable object that subsisted on alms.—*William S. Plumer.*

Verse 10.—The peacock, a glorious fowl, when he beholds that comely fan and circle which he maketh of the beautiful feathers of his tail, he rejoiceth, he setteth, and beholdeth every part thereof: but when he looketh on his feet which he perceiveth to be black and foul, he by-and-by, with great misliking, vaileth his top-gallant, and seemeth to sorrow. In like manner, a great many know by experience, that when they see themselves to abound in riches and honours, they glory and are deeply conceited of themselves; they praise their fortune, and admire themselves; they make plots, and appoint much for themselves to perform in many years to come. This year, they say, we will bear this office, and the next year that: afterward we shall have the rule of such a province; then we will build a palace in such a city, whereunto we will adjoin such gardens of pleasure, and such vineyards: and thus they make a very large reckoning aforehand, who if they did but once behold their feet, if they did but think upon the shortness of their life, so transitory and unconstant; how soon would they let fall their proud feathers, forsake their arrogancy, and change their purpose, their minds, their lives, and their manners.—*Thomas Tymme.*

Verse 11.—"*The meek shall inherit the earth.*" In the meantime, they, and they only, possess the present earth, as they go toward the kingdom of heaven, by being humble, and cheerful, and content with what their good God has allotted them. They have no turbulent, repining, vexatious thoughts that they deserve better; nor are vexed when they see others possessed of more honour, or more riches, than their wise God has allotted for their share. But they possess what they have with a meek and contented quietness : such a quietness as makes their very dreams pleasing, both to God and themselves.—*Izaak Walton* (1593—1683), *in* " *The Complete Angler.*"

Verse 11.—" *The meek.*" What is thy Beloved more than any other beloved ? It is spoken to the spouse. So what is meekness more than any other virtues ? We may say, here is *synecdoche speciei*, one particular taken for the general, one virtue for all the rest. Or the effect is put for the cause ; because meekness is one of the principal and chiefest parts of holiness. But if you will give me leave to conjecture, the Holy Ghost may seem in this promise at once to show the condition of the church, and to comfort her ; and because being laid hard at on every side, she stands in need of this virtue more than any other, to fit and fashion the reward to the virtue, to cherish and exalt it in us with the promise of something beyond our expectation, even the *inheritance of the earth.* And indeed what fitter reward can there be of meekness ? What more fit and just than that they who have been made the anvil for injuries to beat on, who have been *viri perpessitii*, as Seneca speaks of Socrates, men of great sufferance, who have suffered not only their goods to be torn from them by oppression and wrong, but their reputations to be wounded with the sharp razor of detraction, and have withstood the shock of all *spectantibus similes*, with the patience of a looker on, should be raised and comforted with a promise of that which their meekness gave up to the spoil ; and that by the providence of God which loves to thwart the practice of the world, they should be made heirs even of those possessions which the hand of violence hath snatched from them.—*Anthony Farindon, B.D.*, 1596—1658.

Verse 11.—Not the hot stirring spirits who bustle for the world shall have it, but the meek, who are thrust up and down from corner to corner, and hardly suffered to remain anywhere quietly in it. This earth, which they seem most deprived of, they only shall have and enjoy. When the Lord hath made it worth the having, then none shall have it but they. " *They shall inherit the earth.*" The earth is the Lord's ; these are the children of the Lord, and they shall inherit his earth. When the Lord taketh it into his own possession and enjoyment, they shall succeed him in the possession and enjoyment of it. It is their right, and shall descend unto them by right, by inheritance. It is the Lord's right, and by the Lord shall descend to them as their right. They cannot yet have it, for the Lord hath it not yet ; but when the Lord hath it, it shall fairly descend to them. This accursed earth they shall never have, but when it is taken into the hands of the Lord, and blessed by the Lord, then it shall be theirs, then it shall be inherited by the children of blessing.—*John Pennington.*

Verse 11.—" *And shall delight themselves in the abundance of peace.*" Surely when the glory of the Lord covers the earth, and all the kingdoms of this world become the kingdoms of the Prince of Peace, and the wicked one is rooted out, we may well expect peace in rich abundance.—*W. Wilson.*

Verses 12, 13.—Note how the gesture of the wicked in *gnashing their teeth* is returned to them in the Lord's scornful *laughter* at their devices. Their plotting, too, is countermined by that winding up of all plots, which the Lord knoweth, though they are wilfully ignorant of it.—*C. H. S.*

Verse 13.—" *The Lord shall laugh at him*," etc. He seems to provide very coldly for our consolation under sorrow, for he represents God as merely *laughing.* But if God values highly our salvation, why does he not set himself to resist the fury of our enemies, and vigorously oppose them ? We know that this, as has been said in Psalm ii. 4, is a proper trial of our patience when God does not come forth at once, armed for the discomfiture of the ungodly, but connives for a time, and withholds his hand. Lest the flesh should still murmur and complain, demanding why God should only laugh at the wicked, and not rather take vengeance upon them, the reason is added, that he sees the day of their destruction at hand. " *For he seeth that his day is coming.*"—*John Calvin.*

Verse 13.—" *For he seeth that his day is coming : *" He laughs at such poor worms, who make themselves so great upon the earth, and act so loftily in their impotence seeing it must so soon be over with them.—*Berleb. Bible, quoted by E. W. Hengstenberg.*

Verse 13.—" *For he seeth that his day is coming.*" His dismal day, his death's day, which will also be his doom's day.—*John Trapp.*

Verses 14, 15.—The tongue is a "*sword*" and a "*bow*," which shooteth its arrows, even bitter words, against the humble and upright, Jesus and his disciples. But these are not the only weapons that have been drawn against them. How the malice of the Jews returned upon their own heads no one is ignorant, though few lay it to heart, and consider them as set forth for an example.—*George Horne.*

Verses 14, 15.—When the wicked are most near to do a mischief to the Lord's people, then is a mischief most near unto them.—*David Dickson.*

Verse 16.—"*A little that a righteous man hath*," etc. To wit, 1. Because the wicked do often enrich themselves by unjust means, and so have much vexation and trouble with them, and likewise thereby do treasure up wrath against the day of wrath ; whereas the righteous with a little, well gotten, have much peace of conscience, with hope of heaven hereafter. 2. Because the righteous use theirs well, and are the better for them ; whereas the wicked abuse their many ways, and are in many respects the worse for them. 3. Because the righteous enjoy what they have from hand to mouth as the gifts of God, and the pledges of his fatherly love and care over them, and so it is to them as manna from heaven, and hereby they enjoy much sweet comfort, and are fully satisfied with what they have ; whereas the wicked have none of this joy nor satisfaction by their wealth. 4. Because God by his blessing doth usually make that the righteous enjoy to be more effectual for their good than is the abundance of the wicked. A little coarse fare makes them more healthful and strong than the wicked are with all their plenty. And, 5. Because the wicked enjoyeth not his wealth long, as the righteous man doth ; and this indeed agrees best with the following words.—*Arthur Jackson.*

Verse 16.—Strangers to Christ have the use of outward mercies, but cannot be properly said to have the enjoyment ; they seem to be masters of them, but indeed they are servants to them ; possessors as to outward use, but slaves as to their inward affections ; they serve them while they seem to dispose of them ; they do not *dominari*, but *servire*—have not the command of, but are enslaved. Nor is their use truly comfortable ; they may fancy comfort, but their comfort is but a fancy ; it flows from another fountain than can be digged in earth ; true, solid comfort is the portion of those only who have the righteousness of Christ for their portion. These may look upon every temporal enjoyment as a token of everlasting love, as a pledge and earnest of eternal glory ; and both these, because they may receive them as the purchase of the blood and righteousness of Christ ; ay, here is the well-spring of comfort, the fountain of that comfort which is better than life. Oh, what comfort is it to taste the sweetness of Christ's love in every enjoyment ! When we can say, " Christ loved me, and gave himself for me, that I might enjoy these blessings," oh, how will this raise the value of every common mercy ! Christ's righteousness which was performed, the highest expression of his love, purchased this for me ! Upon this account is that of the Psalmist true, " *A little that a righteous man hath is better than the riches of many wicked.*" He that hath but food and raiment hath in this respect more than he that hath the Turkish empire, or the gold of the Indies. He hath more ground of comfort in his little than they in all.—*David Clarkson.*

Verse 16.—If thine estate were but little, yet it would be perfumed with love and that lump of sugar in thy cup would make the liquor sweet, be it never so small. As the waters which flow from the hills of some of the islands of Molucca taste of the cinnamon and cloves which grow there, so should thy gift, though it were but water, taste of the goodwill and special grace of the Giver. Thy " *little*," with the fear of the Lord, would be " *better than the riches of many wicked men.*" As a little ring with a very costly diamond in it is far more worth than many great ones without it, so thy estate, though it were but a penny, should be joined with the precious jewel of that love which is better than life, and enjoyed by special promise, and thereby be infinitely more worth than the thousands and millions of others bestowed merely from common bounty, and enjoyed only by a general providence.—*George Swinnock.*

Verse 16.—'Tis as possible for a wicked man to fill his body with air and his chest with grace, as his mind with wealth. 'Tis with them as with a ship ; it may be overladen with silver and gold, even unto sinking, and yet have compass and sides to hold ten times more. So here, a covetous wretch, though he have enough to sink him, yet he shall never have enough to satisfy him. So that the conclusion which the Psalmist delivers is most worthy to be observed : " *A little that a righteous man hath is better than the riches of many wicked ;*" he doth not say of how many, because let us think of never so many, yea, of all of them, the righteous man's little is better in very many respects than all their greatest treasures heaped together. The King of Spain although the greatest prince in Christendom by far, having his empire so far extended, that he may truly say, that the sun ever shines upon his dominions, yet gives this for his motto, *Totus non sufficit orbis,* The whole world is not sufficient. God by Solomon tells us that " In the house of the righteous is much treasure " (Prov. xv. 6), although many times there is scarce a good bed to lie, or a seat to sit on. The time will certainly come, when the richest wicked men that ever lived will see clearly that their account would have been much narrower, and consequently their condition to all eternity less miserable, if they had been so poor as to have begged their bread from door to door all their lives long. 'Tis with the blessings of this life as 'tis with perfumed gloves ; when they are richly perfumed their perfume is much more valuable than the leather of which they are made : so, not so much earthly blessings considered in themselves, as their being perfumed with the sweet love of God in Christ, is that which maketh them blessings indeed, truly deserving the name they bear. Now all the blessings of those who have made Mary's choice are all thus perfumed ; all the barley bread they eat, be it never so coarse ; all the clothes they wear, be they never so mean ; with all their other temporal blessings, they proceed from the same sweet love of God, wherewith he was moved to bestow Jesus Christ upon them for salvation. Rom. viii. 32.— *John Glascock's Sermon, entitled " Mary's Choice,"* 1659.

Verses 16, 17.—A little blest is better than a great deal curst ; a little blest is better than a world enjoyed ; a pound blest is better than a thousand curst ; a black crust blest is better than a feast curst ; the gleanings blest are better than the whole harvest curst ; a drop of mercy blest is better than a sea of mercy curst ; Lazarus' crumbs blest was better than Dives' delicates curst ; Jacob's little blest unto him was better than Esau's great estate that was curst unto him. 'Tis always better to have scraps with a blessing, than to have manna and quails with a curse ; a thin table with a blessing is always better than a full table with a snare ; a threadbare coat with a blessing is better than a purple robe curst ; a hole, a cave, a den, a barn, a chimney-corner with a blessing, is better than stately palaces with a curse ; a woollen cap blest is better than a golden crown curst ; and it may be that emperor understood as much, that said of his crown, when he looked on it with tears : " If you knew the cares that are under this crown you would never stoop to take it up." And therefore, why should not a Christian be contented with a little, seeing his little shall be blest unto him ? Isaac tills the ground and sows his seed, and God blesses him with an hundredfold ; and Cain tills the ground and sows his seed, but the earth is cursed to him and commanded not to yield to him his strength. Oh, therefore never let a Christian murmur because he hath but little, but rather let him be still a-blessing of that God that hath blest his little, and doth bless his little, and that will bless his little to him.—*Thomas Brooks.*

Verse 17.—" *For the arms of the wicked shall be broken : but he upholdeth* (or underprops) *the righteous.*" By " *the arms of the wicked,*" you are to understand their strength, their valour, their power, their wit, their wealth, their abundance, which is all the arms they have to support and bear up themselves in the world with. Now, these arms shall be broken, and when they are broken, then, even then, will God uphold the righteous, that is, God will be a continual overflowing fountain of good to his righteous ones ; so that they shall never want, though all the springs of the wicked are dried up round about them.—*Thomas Brooks.*

Verse 18.—" *The Lord knoweth the days of the upright.*" Depositeth their days, lays them up in safety for them : for such is the original idea of יֹדֵעַ.—*John Fry.*

Verse 18.—" *The Lord knoweth the days of the upright,*" and they cannot be cut short by the malice of man.—*W. Wilson.*

Verse 20.—" *As the fat of lambs.*" As the glory of fat sheep, which are at length slain.—*Targum.*

Verse 20.—" *Fat of lambs.*" As the fat of the sacrifices was consumed on the altar by the fire (which was a type of God's righteous vengeance upon sinners), till it vanished into smoke ; so the wicked will be the sacrifices to God's justice, and be destroyed by the fire of his indignation.—*Thomas Scott.*

Verse 20.—" *Into smoke shall they consume.*" "What hath pride profited us? or what hath our boasting of riches given us?" Such are the things, they shall speak who are in hell, and who have sinned. For the hope of the ungodly is like a dry thistle-down, by the wind carried away, or the thin foam spread upon the billows or as a smoke floated hither and thither by the wind, or as the remembrance of a wayfaring man for a day.—*Wouter of Stoelwijk*, 1541.

Verse 21.—" *Payeth not again;*" *i.e.*, has it not in his power, from his straitened circumstances, to repay what he has borrowed: comp. Deut. xxviii. 12. A Jew thus circumstanced became the bond-slave of his creditors: comp. 2 Kings iv. 1.—*Daniel Cresswell.*

Verse 22.—God promiseth that the seed of his people shall inherit the earth The child of such a tenant as paid his rent well, shall not be put out of his farm.—*John Glascock.*

Verse 23.—" *The steps of a good man are ordered by the Lord.*" When this Pilot undertakes to steer their course, their vessel shall never split upon the rock, run upon the sands, or spring a leak, so as to sink in the seas. To be sure he will see them safe in their harbour. He was no Christian, yet I suppose none will deny but he spake good divinity, who said, "If a man will choose God for his Friend, he shall travel securely through a wilderness that hath many beasts of prey in it; he shall pass safely through this world; for he only is safe that hath God for his guide." (Ar. Epist. xxvii.) Doth he not speak a little like David himself (Psalm xxxvii. 23). who never expected to come to glory except he were guided by his counsel? Now, if a poor heathen could say thus, and see good reason to trust God, and admire his faithfulness as he doth frequently (and so doth Seneca, justifying God's faithfulness in all his dealings with the best men in all their sufferings, and the prosperity of the wicked); what then shall the heavenly Christian say, who hath experienced so much of God's faithfulness in answering his prayers, in fulfilling his promises, and supplying all his exigencies?—*James Janeway.*

Verse 23.—" *He delighteth in his way.*" Note that in verse four, we are bidden to delight in the Lord, and here he delights in us, and as here our way is his delight, so in verse thirty-four we are to " keep *his* way." These antitheses are instructive.—*C. H. S.*

Verses 23, 24.—Strange words to us! the very " *steps* " all " *ordered,*" and that by an Almighty One, who " delights " in the goodness of the good man's way. And yet the inference so distinctly to be drawn is that the good man *may* fall, and that his God and Guide may stand by and behold and permit!

Let us add to the suggestion of these verses, one or two references which may help us to establish the principle in our hearts, that the child of God may fall and still remain the child of God; and also to explain somewhat of the reason why this is part of their lot, whether ordered, or only permitted, at all events, a step of the " right way," by which God leads them to a city of habitation." Psalm cvii. 7.

It is observed near the close of Hezekiah's good and prosperous life that, " in the business of the ambassadors of the princes of Babylon. . . . God left him *to try him,* that he might know all that was in his heart." 2 Chron. xxxii. 31. And again, in Daniel's prophecy regarding the latter days, we find (Daniel xi. 35), "And some of them of understanding shall fall, *to try them,* and *to purge,* and *to make them white.*" In the two preceding verses, we have also some valuable details regarding such falls, such as the help with which God will uphold them, the flatteries with which the world will still beset, and hinder them from rising again; the outward troubles into which their fall shall lead them, as through a furnace; the high position (instructors of many) which yet shall not save them from their needed ordeal— the time appointed—and the end in view. So here. The acknowledgment of the possibility of the good man's fall is accompanied with the precious assurance that " *he shall not be utterly cast down.*"—*Mary B. M. Duncan, in "Under the Shadow,* 1867."

Verse 24.—" *Though he fall, he shall not be utterly cast down,*" etc. Thus the Spirit comforts and answers the secret thoughts which everyone might have, saying with himself, I have, however, seen it happen, that the righteous is oppressed, and his cause is trodden in the dust by the wicked. Nay, he replies, dear child, let it be so, that he falls ; he still cannot remain lying thus and be cast away ; he must be up again, although all the world doubts of it. For God catches him by the hand, and raises him again.—*Martin Luther.*

Verse 24.—" *Though he fall,*" namely, as one that were faint-hearted, " *he shall not be cast off,*" namely, utterly, or for ever from God (2 Cor. iv. 9) ; " *for the Lord putteth under his hand,*" *i.e.*, his power and might, namely, to uphold him from utter falling away, which we should quickly do if God were not with us.—*Thomas Wilcocks.*

Verse 24.—A man pardoned, and justified by faith in Christ, though he may, and sometimes doth, fall into foul sins, yet they never prevail so far as to reverse pardon, and reduce to a state of non-justification. " *Though he fall, he shall not be utterly cast down : for the Lord upholdeth him with his hand !* " He speaks of a good man pardoned, justified ; he may fall ; but how far ? from pardon, from justification ? No, then he should utterly fall, be cast down beneath God's hand ; but the text saith, he shall not be utterly cast down ; for the Lord upholdeth him with his hand ; or, as Montanus renders the words, the Lord upholdeth his hands, and he will not let him sink into such a condition. If it were so, then sin should have dominion over him, but, Rom. vi. 14. " Sin shall not have dominion over you ; " and chap. viii. 2, justified ones are freed from the law of sin and death ; and verse 30, the predestinated, called, justified, and glorified ones, are so linked together, that there is no breaking their chain ; if they do sin, they have an " Advocate with the Father, Jesus Christ the righteous, and he is the propitiation for our sins." 1 John ii. 1, 2.—*William Greenhill.*

Verse 25.—" *I have been young, and now am old, yet have I not seen the righteous forsaken*" (he doth not say, In my experience I never saw the righteous afflicted, but, I never saw him left or forsaken in his affliction), " *and I never saw his seed begging their bread :*" he puts in that, because begging of bread, especially in the commonwealth of Israel, and in the state of the Jews, was a note of utter dereliction ! for though God had told them that they should have the poor always with them, yet he had given an express law that there should be no beggar among them ; therefore, saith he, I have not seen the righteous so forsaken, that they should be forced to live by begging. If any say, that David himself begged, he asked bread of Abimelech and of Nabal ; I answer, it is a good rule, and it resolves the case ; transitory cases, and sudden accidents, make no beggars : we must not say, David was a beggar, or begged his bread, because once he was in a strait and asked bread of Abimelech ; and in a second strait sent to Nabal : in such sudden cases, the richest man in the world may be put to ask a piece of bread. A good man may fall into such wants, but good men are rarely, if ever or at all, left in them.—*Joseph Caryl.*

Verse 25.—" *Yet have I not seen the righteous forsaken, nor his seed begging bread.*" Perhaps it will be objected that there have been many righteous men poor : but the place speaketh of a righteous charitable man, for so the following verse showeth, which saith, " He is ever merciful, and lendeth ; and his seed is blessed." And who hath seen such a one or his seed to be brought to such poverty as to beg his bread ? When our Saviour Christ had fed four thousand with seven loaves and a few fishes, all being filled, seven baskets full of fragments were gathered up ; and it is Saint Austin's note upon it, *crescit dum impenditur victus, sic eleemosyna si indigentibus erogetur,* the victuals in expending were augmented, and so is the alms which is given to the poor.—*Michael Jermin.*

Verse 25.—" *Yet have I not seen,*" etc. I believe this to be literally true in all cases. I am now grey-headed myself ; I have travelled in different countries, and have had many opportunities of seeing and conversing with religious people in all situations in life ; and I have not, to my knowledge, seen one instance to the contrary. I have seen no *righteous man forsaken,* nor any *children* of the righteous *begging their bread.* God puts honour upon all that fear him ; and thus careful is he of *them,* and of their *posterity.*—*Adam Clarke.*

Verse 25.—" *Begging bread.*" This is not meant of an occasional seeking relief in want (for so David himself desired bread of Abimelech, 1 Samuel xxi. 3, and he and his soldiers desired some supply of victuals from Nabal, ch. xxv. 8) ; but of living in a continual way of begging from door to door, which is denounced as a curse against the wicked (Psalm cix. 10), " Let his children be continually vagabonds, and beg." Nor doth it hence follow, that neither the righteous man, nor his seed, are ever brought to this sad degree of misery ; but only that it doth so rarely happen, that David in all his time had never seen it.—*Arthur Jackson*.

Verse 25.—This observation of the Psalmist will be found generally verified. We find indeed exceptions, as in the case of Eli's family. But this was the result of his defect of character as a righteous man. And we know that the promises must fail, if they neglect the means necessary to their accomplishment (see Genesis xviii. 19). But some think that this verse admits of an explanatory supplement ; and render the last clause thus, " Nor his seed (forsaken, though) begging bread."— *David Davidson, in " The Pocket Commentary, 1836."*

Verse 25.—These words must be taken as a general observation, not absolutely verified in every case ; yet the strict fact is, I apprehend, that the immediate descendants of truly pious persons are very seldom, if ever reduced to such extremities, unless by their own great imprudence, or their abandoned practices.—*William Walford*.

Verse 25.—Here he recordeth an experiment of his (such as whereof Psalm cxix. is mostly made up), and if other men's experiences agree not altogether with his, it is no wonder : kings use not to mind beggars.—*John Trapp*.

Verses 25, 26.—Many persons are solicitously perplexed how their children shall do when they are dead ; yet they consider not, how God provided for them when they were children. Is the Lord's arm shortened ? Did he take thee from thy mother's breasts ; and when thy parents forsook thee (as the Psalmist saith), became thy Father ? And cannot this experienced mercy to thee, persuade thee that he will not forsake thine ? Is not " Jesus Christ the same yesterday, and to-day, and for ever ? " " I have been young," saith David, " and now am old ; yet have I not seen the righteous forsaken," that is granted, nay, " nor his seed begging bread."

Many distrustful fathers are so carking for their posterity, that while they live they starve their bodies, and hazard their souls, to leave them rich. To such a father it is said justly, *Dives es hœredi, pauper inopsque tibi*. Like an over-kind hen he feeds his chickens, and famisheth himself. If usury, circumvention, oppression, extortion, can make them rich, they shall not be poor. Their folly is ridiculous ; they fear lest their children should be miserable, yet take the only course to make them miserable ; for they leave them not so much heirs to their goods as to their evils They do as certainly inherit their fathers' sins as their lands : " God layeth up his iniquity for his children : and his offspring shall want a morsel of bread." Job xxi. 19.

On the contrary, the good man " *is merciful, and lendeth ; and his seed is blessed*." What the worldling thinks shall make his posterity poor, God saith shall make the good man's rich. The precept gives a promise of mercy to obedience, not confined to the obedient man's self, but extended to his seed, and that even to a thousand generations, Exodus xx. 6. Trust, then, Christ with thy children ; when thy friends shall fail, usury bear no date, oppression be condemned to hell, thyself rotten to the dust, the world itself turned and burned into cinders, still " Jesus Christ is the same, yesterday, and to-day, and for ever."—*Thomas Adams*.

Verse 26.—" *He is ever merciful, and lendeth ; and his seed is blessed*." He, the good man, is " *merciful* " to *himself*, for mercy, like charity, begins at home ; he is not afraid to eat a good meal because he hath children. And he is merciful to *others* too ; for he will lend and do good to whom he can, and then his seed fares the better for it. Mark, that the more he gives and lends in doing works of mercy, the better it is for his children ; for those children are ever best provided for whose parents bear this mind—they had rather trust God with their children, than their children with riches ; and have made this their hope, that though they die, yet God lives. Did but one of those rich and wretched parents (who pinched and pined himself to make his son a gentleman, forsooth), rise from the dead, and see that proverb of Solomon fulfilled in himself, " He begetteth a son, and in his hand is nothing ; " I persuade myself, the rumination of this world afflict him in his soul as much as any one pain of sense, even in hell itself, O consider this, you that now live and see it in others ; and remember withal, that if your goods be either ill-gotten, or worse kept, it may be your children's case when you are departed, and feel it, though you see it not.—*Matthew Griffith*.

Verse 28.—" *For the Lord . . . . forsaketh not his saints ; they are preserved for ever*." How ? since they die as others do. Mark the *antithesis*, and that will explain it." " *They are preserved for ever : but the seed of the wicked shall be cut off.*" They are preserved in their posterity : children are but the parents multiplied, and the parents continued ; 'tis *nodosa æternitas ;* when the father's life is run out to the last, there is a knot tied, and the line is still continued by the child. I confess temporal blessings, such as long life, and the promise of an happy posterity, are more visible in the eye of that dispensation of the covenant ; but yet God still taketh care for the children of his people, and many promises run that way that belong to the gospel administration, and still God's service is the surest way to establish a family, as sin is the ready way to root it out. And if it doth not always fall out accordingly, yet for the most part it doth ; and we are no competent judges of God's dispensations in this kind, because we see providence by pieces, and have not the skill to set them together ; but at the day of judgment, when the whole contexture of God's dealings is laid before us, we shall clearly understand how *the children of his servants continue, and their seed is established.* Psalm cii. 28.— *Thomas Manton.*

Verse 29.—" *The righteous shall inherit the land,*" or the earth. There is clearly an emphasis in the repetition of the same promise in the same terms which ought to have been uniformly rendered throughout verses 9, 11, 22, 29, 34. And it cannot be doubted, that there is a reference to the new heavens and the new earth of Isaiah lxvi. 17 ; 2 Peter iii. 13.—*W. Wilson.*

Verse 29.—" *The righteous shall inherit the land,*" etc. Comp. Matt. v. 5. Consider well this Bible truth, of the future exclusive possession of the earth by the righteous. The millennial kingdom furnishes a fuller explanation.—*T. C. Barth.*

Verse 31.—" *The law of his God is in his heart,*" etc. The flock of sheep that's indisposed and unwilling to drive, start out of the way into every lane's end, one this way and another that ; and just so is it with an unwilling heart ; one thought starts this way, and another that, and it's a piece of skill to drive them through. But a willing heart, a heart prepared and ready to every good work, it flies quite up an end, and delights itself in the Lord.—*Richard Steele.*

Verse 31 (*first clause*).—He hath a Bible in his head, and another in his heart ; he hath a good treasure within, and there hence bringeth good things.—*John Trapp.*

Verses 32, 33.—The Jews " *watched* " that Just One daily and hourly ; they " *sought to slay him,*" and did so ; but *Jehovah left him not in their hands,* but vindicated his innocence by raising him from the dead.—*George Horne.*

Verse 34.—" *Wait on the Lord,*" etc. He that truly trusts in God will stay God's time, and use God's means, and walk in God's way, though it seem round about ; they will not neglect their souls for haste ; they know this would be to make more haste than good speed. Nor would they step out of the way, the way that is holy and righteous, though they may escape a loss, an affliction by it, though they might gain some desirable advantage by it. True faith goes leaning upon God, and therefore will " *keep his way.*" He that will not be liberal for the promoting and honouring of the gospel ; he that fears poverty or affliction more than he fears sin ; he that is more careful for the things of the world than for his soul ; he that takes indirect or suspected courses, to get, or increase, or secure his estate ; he that is not jealous or watchful, lest his cares for the world (when he is much engaged therein) should be immoderate—it is plain he doth not trust God with his estate ; and he that does not trust God for his estate, whatever he think or pretend, he does not trust God for his soul, for his salvation ; his hopes of heaven and salvation are but presumption.—*David Clarkson.*

Verse 34.—" *Wait on the Lord.*" Bind him not to a day, wake not the Beloved till he please.—*John Trapp.*

Verse 34.—" *Wait . . . . keep.*" While we are waiting let us take heed of wavering. Go not a step out of God's way, though a lion be in the way ; avoid not duty to meet with safety ; keep God's highway, the good old way (Jer. vi. 16), the way which is paved with holiness. " And an highway shall be there, and a way, and it shall be called the way of holiness." Isaiah xxxv. 8. Avoid crooked paths, take heed of turning to the left hand, lest you be set on the left hand. Sin doth cross our hopes, it barricades up our way ; a man may as well expect to find heaven in hell, as in a sinful way.—*Thomas Watson.*

Verse 35.—" *Green bay tree.*" The LXX translates כְּאֶזְרָח רַעֲנָן as if it were כְּאֶרֶז לְבָנוֹן, " Like the cedar of Lebanon ; " but אֶזְרָח רַעֲנָן according to Delitzsch, means a noble timber-tree, one that in the course of centuries of growth has acquired a gigantic trunk, and an umbrageous, dome-like crown.

Verse 35.—" *Green bay tree.*" The marginal rendering—" a tree that groweth in his own soil "—is, no doubt, the true one. The idea generally formed of this passage by the reader of the English Bible is that the tree referred to was the bay laurel (*Prunus laurocerasus*), or cherry laurel of our gardens. But this plant belongs to an entirely different family. The bay and the Portugal laurels, whose forms of growth and evergreen leaves make them highly ornamental in shrubberies, belong to a sub-family (*Drupaceæ*, Lind.) of the rose tribe (*Rosaceæ*), but the bay tree proper, which flourisheth luxuriantly in Southern Europe, is the type of the laurel family (*Lauraceæ*). Several circumstances make it unlikely that the true bay tree represents the Hebrew *esróch*. There is no evidence that it was ever so plentiful in Palestine as to be chosen by the Psalmist in an illustration in a poem for popular use. It is indeed to be met with, but that chiefly in localities on the borders of the eastern shore of the Great Sea. The chief objection to the supposition that the bay tree was referred to by the royal poet is to be found in the Psalm itself. Having mentioned it in the lines quoted above, he adds, " Yet he passed away, and, lo, he was not : yea, I sought him, but he could not be found." The idea here is not one which could be represented and illustrated by an evergreen plant, slow of growth, and yet reaching in maturity a height of above thirty feet. The words demand a quick growing tree, in a soil more than usually favourable to its growth. Thus planted, and shooting up in calm and sunshine, it would attract every eye ; but when the storm broke over it, when the strong wind swept impetuously through its branches, it would not stand. Torn up by the root, and its timber comparatively useless, like Abraham's dead, it would be buried out of sight. And thus with the wicked. He was sought and could not be found.—*John Duns, D.D., F.R.S.E., in " Biblical Natural Science."*

Verse 35.—We see no force in the observation of Dr. Duns ; in fact, if there were not other reasons for preferring the translation given in the following note by Wilson, we should see all the more reason to keep to the bay tree. It was a tree of permanence and of long-continued verdure, and so the prosperous wicked seem to be. They look as if their happiness would be eternal ; yet, for all that, those who carefully note the dealings of providence observe with holy wonder that divine justice cuts short their glory, and they perish utterly.—*C. H. S.*

" *I have seen the wicked in great power* (terrible, fierce, violent), *and spreading himself like a green bay tree* " (a tree in its native soil, vigorous, and luxuriant, that had never been transplanted). A striking figure of the ungodly man of the world, firmly rooted in earthly things—his native soil, grown proud and wanton in his prosperity, without fear or apprehension of any reverse.—*William Wilson.*

Verse 35.—" *Like a green bay tree,*" which produceth all leaves and no fruit.—*Matthew Henry.*

Verse 35.—" *I have seen the wicked,*" saith David, " *in great power, and spreading himself like a green bay-tree.*" And why like a green bay-tree ? Because in the winter, when all other trees—as the vine-tree, fig-tree, apple-tree, &c., which are more profitable trees—are withered and naked, yet the bay-tree continueth as green in the winter as the summer. So fareth it with wicked men : when the children of God, in the storms of persecutions, and afflictions, and miseries, seem withered, and, as it were, dead, yet the wicked all that time flourish, and do appear green in the eyes of the world : they wallow in worldly wealth, but it is for their destruction ; they wax fat, but it is for the day of slaughter. It was the case of Hophni and Phinehas : the Lord gave them enough and suffered them to go on and prosper in their wickedness ; but what was the reason ? Because he would destroy them.—*J. Gore's Sermon at St. Paul's, 1633.*

Verses 35, 36.—

————" To-day he puts forth
The tender leaves of hopes, to-morrow blossoms,
And bears his blushing honours thick upon him :
The third day comes a frost, a killing frost ;
And—when he thinks, good easy man, full surely
His greatness is a ripening—nips his root,
And then he falls, as I do."

William Shakspeare, in Henry VIII.

Verses 36, 37.—The hawk flies high, and is as highly prized, being set upon a perch, vervelled with the gingling bells of encouragement, and carried on his master's fist ; but being once dead and picked over the perch, is cast upon the dunghill as good for nothing. The hen scrapes in the dust, not anything rewarded when she is alive, but being dead, is brought as a choice dish to her master's table. Thus wicked men are commonly set in high places, and prosper in this life ; and good men lie grovelling with their mouths in the dust, as the very underlings of the world ; but being once dead, the one is cast into the dungeon of hell, the other advanced to the kingdom of heaven : the one is into Abraham's bosom, whilst the other is tormented with the devil and his angels.—*Thomas Westfield, D.D.*, 1644.

Verse 37.—*" Mark . . . . . and behold."* Herodotus maketh mention of a custom among the Ethiopians to set the dead bodies of their friends in glazed sepulchres, that their proportions might be obvious to the passengers. How needless soever that custom was, 'tis doubtless no more than just that the pious lineaments of their minds who die in the Lord should be presented to the living in the mirrour of art. Indeed, commendation after death is the tribute of a religious life. Good works are jewels not to be locked up in a cabinet, but to be set forth to public view. If Christ would have Mary's name remembered in the gospel until the world's end for one box of ointment poured on his head, we cannot imagine that he would have the many pious and charitable deeds of his servants to be buried in oblivion. Consult the Scriptures, and you shall scarce find any godly man laid in his grave without an epitaph of honour. View the fathers, and you shall observe it their practice to honour the death of the good by giving them their deserved praises.—*Nathanael Hardy.*

Verse 37.—*" The perfect man,"* etc.—Divines well distinguish of a double perfection, it is *absoluta* or *comparata*. That is absolutely *perfect*, to which nothing (that may be accounted truly good) is wanting ; and thus He only is *perfectus* who is *infactus ;* God, who made all things, and himself is not made, only enjoying an all-sufficient perfection, in and of himself. That is comparatively *perfect*, in which, notwithstanding some wants, there is a fulness compared with others. Thus every saint is *perfect* in comparison of the wicked among whom he liveth. In this respect it is said of Noah, *" That he was a perfect man in his generations ; "* his grace compared with the wickedness of the old world well deserving the name of perfection ; indeed every upright man is *perfect* in comparison of them who are openly bad, or but openly good ; stained with wickedness, or but painted with holiness. Thus one saint may be *perfect* if compared with another, the strong Christian in respect of the weak, whom he outstrips in grace and piety : such saints Paul means when he saith, " We speak wisdom among them that are perfect ; " that is, such as have attained to greater measures of grace than others. It was said of Benaiah, " He was more honourable than thirty, but he attained not to the first three ; " and though no saint can ever attain to the perfections of the *first three*, the blessed Trinity, yet many saints may be honourable amongst *thirty perfect* in comparison of those among whom they live.

We must further distinguish of a double perfection, it is *extrinseca* and *intrinseca.* Extrinsical perfection so called, because by imputation, is that which every believer is partaker of through the perfect righteousness of Christ, whereby all his imperfections are covered ; in this respect the author to the Hebrews tells us, " That by one offering he hath perfected for ever them that are sanctified ; " and S. Paul tells the Colossians that they were " complete in him," meaning Christ. Indeed *omnia Dei mandata tunc facta deputantur, quando id quod non fit ignoscitur :* divine commands are then in God's account fulfilled when our defects for Christ's sake are pardoned ; and the evangelical perfection of a Christian consists not *in perfectione virtutum, sed remissione vitiorum,* in the completion of our graces, but remission of our sins.

Intrinsical perfection, so called because by inhæsion, is no less rationally than usually thus distinguished, there is *perfectio partium et graduum.* He is said to be *perfect, cui nihil deest eorum quæ ad statum salutis necessaria,* who wants no graces that accompany salvation ; or he is perfect, *cui nihil deest in gradibus gratiarum et virtutum ;* who is not defective in the measures of those graces ; both these are frequently and fitly illustrated by the resemblance of a child, and a grown man ; the one whereof hath all the essential and integral parts of a man, the other a complete use and measure of those parts.—*Nathanael Hardy.*

Verse 37.—" *The end.*" All wise men affect the conclusion to be best : to ride two or three miles of fair way, and to have a hundred deep and foul ones to pass afterward is uncomfortable ; especially when the end is worse than the way. But let the beginning be troublesome, the progress somewhat more easy, and the journey's end happy, and there is fair amends. " *Mark the perfect man, and behold the upright : for the end of that man is peace.*" Mark him in the setting out, he hath many oppositions ; mark him in the journey, he is full of tribulations ; but mark in the conclusion, and the end of that man is peace.—*Thomas Adams.*

Verse 37.—" *The end of that man is peace.*" Give me leave to determine what it is to end or die in peace. To end in peace with *Euthymius*, is to end in *pace cogitationis*, in peace of mind as it is opposed to doubting. To end in peace with *Cyprian*, is to end in *pace securitatis*, in peace of security, as it is opposed to final falling. To end in peace with *Origen*, is to end in *pace conscientiæ*, in peace of conscience as it is opposed to despairing. To end in peace with old *Irenæus*, is to end in *pace mortis*, in the peace of death as it is opposed to labouring. Again, to end in peace, is to end in *pace Dei*, in the peace of God which passeth all understanding, *i.e.*, far beyond men's apprehensions. To end in peace, is to end in *pace proximi*, in peace with our neighbours, *i.e.*, when no outcries or exclamations follow us. And lastly, to end in peace, is to end in *pace sui*, in peace with ourselves, *i.e.*, when no distractions or perturbations of mind molest us.—*Richard Parre.*

Verse 37.—The text may be divided into these two parts. Here is, 1. The godly man's *property ;* and 2. The godly man's *privilege.* His property is perfection ; his privilege is peace. Here is the saint's *character* and the saint's *crown :* he is characterised by uprightness or sincerity, and crowned with peace. Here is the Christian's *way* and his *end*, his *motion*, and his *rest.* His way is holiness, his end happiness ; his motion is towards perfection and in uprightness ; his rest is peace at his journey's end.—*John Whitlock, in a Funeral Sermon entitled, " The Upright Man and his Happy End,*" 1658.

Verse 37.—Time would fail me to tell how Christians die, nor can anything save the pen of the recording angel who has stood by their bed of death and borne them to Abraham's bosom, narrate the unnumbered instances of their delightful departure from the present world, which verify the truth of the Bible. " I could never have believed," said a dying saint, " that it was so delightful a thing to die, or that it was possible to have such views of the heavenly world as I now enjoy." The memorable Melancthon, just before he died, chanted in his sleep the words, " I will not any more eat thereof until it be fulfilled in the kingdom of God." He seemed restless, and on being asked by one near him, " Whether there were anything more that he desired ? " replied, *Aliud nihil nisi cœlum*—nothing more, unless it be heaven.—*Gardiner Spring.*

Verse 37.—To die well be sure to live well ; we must not think to have Lazarus's death, and Dives's life ; like him in Plutarch that would live with Crœsus, as he said, but he would die with Socrates. No, Balaam's wishes are foolish and fruitless : if you would die well, Christians, you must have a care to live well : *qualis vita, finis ita,* if you would die quietly, you must live strictly ; if you would die comfortably, you must live comformably ; if you would die happily, you must live holily. " *Mark the perfect man, and behold the upright, for the end of that man is peace.*"—*John Kitchin, M.A.,* 1660.

Verse 38.—" *The end of the wicked shall be cut off.*" The wicked in this world do easily run up without rub or interruption, many times with acclamations and applause, all the golden steps of honours and preferments ; but upon the highest stair they find the most slippery standing, and the top of their earthly felicity is the most immediate and certain descent unto the greatest downfall. They are royally mounted here upon earth, and gallop swiftly over the fair and green plains of plenty and pleasures ; but at the end of their race they are overturned horse and man, and tumbled headlong into the pit of destruction. They fairly glide over the sea of this world with full sail, with much calmness and serenity, and richly laden ; but in the brightest sunshine, and when they least suspect it, they suddenly and without recovery, sink into the gulf of darkness and desolation.—*Robert Bolton.*

Verse 40.—" *And the Lord shall help them.*" He *shall*, he *shall*, he *shall*. Oh, the rhetoric of God ! the safety of the saints ! the certainty of the promises !—*John Trapp.*

Luther closes his Exposition of the Psalm with the words, Oh, shame on our faithlessness, mistrust, and vile unbelief, that we do not believe such rich, powerful, consolatory, declarations of God, and take up so readily with little grounds of offence, whenever we but hear the wicked speeches of the ungodly. Help, O God, that we may once attain to right faith. Amen.

HINTS TO PREACHERS.

Verse 1.—The art of tranquillity.—*W. Jones.*

Verses 1, 2.—A frequent temptation, and a double corrective—a sight of sinners in death and in hell.

Verse 2.—How and when the wicked perish.

Verse 3.—I. A combination descriptive of holy living. II. A combination descriptive of happy living.

Verse 3.—The believer portrayed. I. His object of trust. II. His mode of life. III. His place of abode. IV. His certainty of provision.

Verse 3 (last clause).—Read it in four ways. I. " Certainly fed," or the certainty of supply. II. " Fed in verity," or the sufficiency of the provision for soul and body. III. " Fed on truth," or the spirituality of the provision. IV. " Feed on truth," or the duty of choosing such provision.

Verse 4.—Explain the delight and the desire of the believer, and show the connection between them.

Verses 5, 6.—The higher life. I. Based on hearty resignation. II. Sustained by faith. III. Constantly unfolded by the Lord. IV. Consummated in meridian splendour.

Verse 6.—Sweet comfort for slandered saints. Where their character now is. Who shall reveal it. The gradual yet sure manner of the revelation, and the glorious conclusion.

Verse 7.—" *Rest in the Lord.*" What ? Where ? When ? Why ? How ?

Verse 7.—Peace, patience, self-possession.

Verse 7.—Stillness in God.—*Bishop Wilberforce.*

Verse 7.—" *Rest in the Lord.*" I. Rest in the *will* of God, for whatever he wills is for your good, your highest good. II. Rest in the *love* of God, and often meditate on the words of Jesus on this point, " Thou hast loved them as thou hast loved me." III. Rest in the *mercy* of God. IV. Rest in the *word* of God. V. Rest in the *relation* thy God fills to thee ; he is the Father. VI. Rest in the Lord as he is manifested in Jesus, thy God *in covenant.*—*James Smith.*

Verse 8.—A SERMON FOR THE FRETFUL. I. *Cease* from present anger. It is madness, it is sin ; it shuts out our prayers ; it will grow into malice ; it may lead to worse. II. *Forsake it* for the future. Repent of it, watch temper, discipline thy passion, etc. III. *Avoid* all kindred feelings of fretfulness, impatience, envy, etc., for they lead to evil.

Verse 9.—How the humble are the true lords of the land.

Verse 10.—I. Consider what the departed sinner has left. Possessions, joys, honours, aims, hopes, etc. II. Consider where he has gone. III. Consider whether you will share the same lot.

Verses 10, 11.—Terror to the wicked : comfort to believers.—*A Farindon.*

Verse 11.—The meek man's delight, or " the harvest of a quiet eye."

Verse 14.—*Upright conversation.*—I. What it excludes. The horizontal or earthly, the crooked or crafty, the slanting or sinister. II. What it includes. Motive, object, language, action. III. What it achieves. It stands like a pillar ; it supports like a column ; it ascends like a tower ; it adorns like a monument ; it illuminates like a Pharos.

Verse 15.—The self-destructive nature of evil.

Verse 16.—How to make much of a little.

Verses 16, 17.—I. The owners contrasted. II. The possessions compared. III. The preference given. IV. The reasons declared.

Verse 17 (last clause).—I. The favoured persons. II. Their evident need,

" upholding." III. Their singular blessedness, " upheld," above trial, under trial, after trial. IV. Their august Patron.

Verse 18.—The comforts derivable from a consideration of the divine knowledge. The eternity of the righteous man's possessions.

Verse 18.—I. The *persons,* " the upright." II. The *period,* " their days." These are known to God—(1) He knows them *kindly* and *graciously ;* (2) He knows their *number ;* (3) He knows the *nature* of them. III. The *portion,* " their inheritance shall be for ever."—*William Jay.*

Verse 18 (last clause).—What it is. How they come by it. How long they hold it.

Verse 19.—Good words for hard times.

Verse 21.—Monetary transactions tests of character.

Verse 22.—The divine blessing the secret of happiness. The divine displeasure the essence of misery.

Verses 23, 24.—I. The divine predestination. II. The divine delight. III. The divine support.

Verse 24.—Temporary trials. I. To be expected. II. Have their limit. III. Have their results. IV. Our secret comfort under them.

What may be. What cannot be. What shall be.

Verse 25.—Memorandum of an aged observer.

Verse 26.—The righteous man's merciful disposition, generous action, and rich reward.

Verse 26.—The benediction of the good man's family : what it is, and what it is not.

Verse 27.—Negative, positive, remunerative.

Verse 28.—I. The Lord's love of right. II. His faithfulness to the righteous. III. Their sure preservation thus doubly guaranteed. IV. The doom of the wicked thus certified.

Verse 29.—Canaan as a type of the righteous man's inheritance.

Verse 30.—*Our speech* as a test of godliness.

Verse 31.—I. The best thing. II. In the best place. III. With the best of results.

Verses 32, 33.—Our enemies ; their inveterate malice ; our safeguard and justification.

Verse 34.—I. A twofold admonition : 1. " *Wait on the Lord.*" 2. " *And keep his way ;* " wait and work, wait and walk, get grace and exercise it. II. A two-fold promise : 1. " *He shall exalt thee to inherit the land ;* " God is the source of all elevation and honour. 2. " *When the wicked are cut off, thou shalt see it ;* " and they will be cut off.—*William Jay.*

Verse 34.—Patient faith, persevering holiness, and promised exaltation.

Verse 34 (last clause).—Emotions caused in the godly by a sight of the sinner's doom.

Verse 34 (last clause).—The wicked are often cut off—1. Even *in life,* from their places, and riches, and prospects. 2. At *death* they are cut off from all their possessions and comforts. 3. In *the last day* they will be cut off from " the resurrection of life."—*William Jay.*

Verses 35, 36, 37.—Three memorable scenes. I. The imposing spectacle. II. The astounding disappearance. III. The delightful exit.

Verses 39, 40.—I. The doctrines of grace condensed. II. The experience of the gracious epitomised. III. The promises of grace summarised. IV. The grandest evidence of grace declared : " *because they trust in him.*"

PSALM XXXVIII.

TITLE.—*A Psalm of David, to bring to remembrance. David felt as if he had been forgotten of his God, and, therefore, he recounted his sorrows and cried mightily for help under them. The same title is given to Psalm lxx., where in like manner the Psalmist pours out his complaint before the Lord. It would be foolish to make a guess as to the point in David's history when this was written; it may be a commemoration of his own sickness and endurance of cruelty; it may, on the other hand, have been composed by him for the use of sick and slandered saints, without special reference to himself.*

DIVISIONS.—*The Psalm opens with a prayer, 1; continues in a long complaint, 2—8; pauses to dart an eye to heaven, 9; proceeds with a second tale of sorrow, 10—14; interjects another word of hopeful address to God, 15; a third time pours out a flood of griefs, 16—20; and then closes as it opened, with renewed petitioning, 21 and 22.*

EXPOSITION.

O LORD, rebuke me not in thy wrath: neither chasten me in thy hot displeasure.

1. "*O Lord, rebuke me not in thy wrath.*" Rebuked I must be, for I am an erring child and thou a careful Father, but throw not too much anger into the tones of thy voice; deal gently although I have sinned grievously. The anger of others I can bear, but not thine. As thy love is most sweet to my heart, so thy displeasure is most cutting to my conscience. "*Neither chasten me in thy hot displeasure.*" Chasten me if thou wilt, it is a Father's prerogative, and to endure it obediently is a child's duty; but, O turn not the rod into a sword, smite not so as to kill. True, my sins might well inflame thee, but let thy mercy and longsuffering quench the glowing coals of thy wrath. O let me not be treated as an enemy or dealt with as a rebel. Bring to remembrance thy covenant, thy fatherhood, and my feebleness, and spare thy servant.

2 For thine arrows stick fast in me, and thy hand presseth me sore.

3 *There is* no soundness in my flesh because of thine anger; neither *is* there *any* rest in my bones because of my sin.

4 For mine iniquities are gone over mine head: as an heavy burden they are too heavy for me.

5 My wounds stink *and* are corrupt because of my foolishness.

6 I am troubled; I am bowed down greatly; I go mourning all the day long.

7 For my loins are filled with a loathsome *disease:* and *there is* no soundness in my flesh.

8 I am feeble and sore broken: I have roared by reason of the disquietness of my heart.

2. "*For thine arrows stick fast in me.*" By this he means both bodily and spiritual griefs, but we may suppose, especially the latter, for these are most piercing and stick the fastest. God's law applied by the Spirit to the conviction of the soul of sin, wounds deeply and rankles long; it is an arrow not lightly to be brushed out by careless mirthfulness, or to be extracted by the flattering hand of self-righteousness. The Lord knows how to shoot so that his bolts not only strike but stick. He can make convictions sink into the innermost spirit like arrows driven in up to the head. It seems strange that the Lord should shoot at his own beloved ones, but in truth he shoots at their sins rather than them, and those who feel his sin-killing shafts in this life, shall not be slain with his hot thunderbolts in the next world. "*And thy hand presseth me sore.*" The Lord had come to close dealings with him, and pressed him down with the weight of his hand, so that he

had no rest or strength left. By these two expressions we are taught that conviction of sin is a piercing and a pressing thing, sharp and sore, smarting and crushing. Those who know by experience " the terrors of the Lord," will be best able to vouch for the accuracy of such descriptions ; they are true to the life.

3. " *There is no soundness in my flesh because of thine anger.*" Mental depression tells upon the bodily frame ; it is enough to create and foster every disease, and is in itself the most painful of all diseases. Soul sickness tells upon the entire frame ; it weakens the body, and then bodily weakness reacts upon the mind. One drop of divine anger sets the whole of our blood boiling with misery. " *Neither is there any rest in my bones because of my sin.*" Deeper still the malady penetrates, ill the bones, the more solid parts of the system, are affected. No soundness and no rest are two sad deficiencies ; yet these are both consciously gone from every awakened conscience until Jesus gives relief. God's anger is a fire that dries up the very marrow ; it searches the secret parts of the belly. A man who has pain in his bones tosses to and fro in search of rest, but he finds none ; he becomes worn out with agony, and so in many cases a sense of sin creates in the conscience a horrible unrest which cannot be exceeded in anguish except by hell itself.

4. " *For mine iniquities are gone over mine head.*" Like waves of the deep sea ; like black mire in which a man utterly sinks. Above my hopes, my strength, and my life itself, my sin rises in its terror. Unawakened sinners think their sins to be mere shallows, but when conscience is aroused they find out the depth of iniquity. " *As an heavy burden they are too heavy for me.*" It is well when sin is an intolerable load, and when the remembrance of our sins burdens us beyond endurance. This verse is the genuine cry of one who feels himself undone by his transgressions and as yet sees not the great sacrifice.

5. " *My wounds stink and are corrupt because of my foolishness.*" Apply this to the body, and it pictures a sad condition of disease ; but read it of the soul, and it is to the life. Conscience lays on stripe after stripe till the swelling becomes a wound and suppurates, and the corruption within grows offensive. What a horrible creature man appears to be to his own consciousness when his depravity and vileness are fully opened up by the law of God, applied by the Holy Spirit ! It is true there are diseases which are correctly described in this verse, when in the worst stage ; but we prefer to receive the expressions as instructively figurative, since the words " because of my foolishness " point rather at a moral than a physical malady. Some of us know what it is to stink in our own nostrils so as to loathe ourselves. Even the most filthy diseases cannot be so foul as sin. No ulcers, cancers, or putrifying sores, can match the unutterable vileness and pollution of iniquity. Our own perceptions have made us feel this. We write what we do know, and testify what we have seen ; and even now we shudder to think that so much of evil should lie festering deep within our nature.

6. " *I am troubled.*" I am wearied with distress, writhing with pain, in sore travail on account of sin revealed within me. " *I am bowed down greatly.*" I am brought very low, grievously weakened and frightfully depressed. Nothing so pulls a man down from all loftiness as a sense of sin and of divine wrath concerning it. " *I go mourning all the day long.*" The mourner's soul-sorrow knew no intermission, even when he went about such business as he wa able to attend, he went forth like a mourner who goes to the tomb, and his words and manners were like the lamentations of those who follow the corpse. The whole verse may be the more clearly understood if we picture the Oriental mourner, covered with sackcloth and ashes, bowed as in a heap, sitting amid squalor and dirt, performing contortions and writhings expressive of his grief ; such is the awakened sinner, not in outward guise, but in very deed.

7. " *For my loins are filled with a loathsome disease*"—a hot, dry, parching disorder, probably accompanied by loathsome ulcers. Spiritually, the fire burns within when the evil of the heart is laid bare. Note the emphatic words, the evil is *loathsome*, it is in the *loins*, its seat is deep and vital—the man is *filled* with it. Those who have passed through the time of conviction understand all this. " *And there is no soundness in my flesh.*" This he had said before, and thus the Holy Spirit brings humiliating truth again and again to our memories, tears away every ground of glorying, and makes us know that in us, that is, in our flesh, there dwelleth no good thing.

8. " *I am feeble.*" The original is " benumbed," or frozen, such strange incongruities and contradictions meet in a distracted mind and a sick body—it appears

to itself to be alternately parched with heat and pinched with cold. Like souls in the Popish fabled Purgatory, tossed from burning furnaces into thick ice, so tormented hearts rush from one extreme to the other, with equal torture in each. A heat of fear, a chill of horror, a flaming desire, a horrible insensibility—by these successive miseries a convinced sinner is brought to death's door. *"And sore broken."* Crushed as in a mill, pounded as in a mortar. The body of the sick man appears to be all out of joint and smashed into a palpitating pulp, and the soul of the desponding is in an equally wretched case ; as a victim crushed under the car of Juggernaut, such is a soul over whose conscience the wheels of divine wrath have forced their awful way. *"I have roared by reason of the disquietness of my heart."* Deep and hoarse is the voice of sorrow, and often inarticulate and terrible. The heart learns groanings which cannot be uttered, and the voice fails to tone and tune itself to human speech. When our prayers appear to be rather animal than spiritual, they are none the less prevalent with the pitiful Father of mercy. He hears the murmur of the heart and the roaring of the soul because of sin, and in due time he comes to relieve his afflicted.

The more closely the preceding portrait of an awakened soul is studied in the light of experience, the more will its striking accuracy appear. It cannot be a description of merely outward disorder, graphic as it might then be ; it has a depth and pathos in it which only the soul's mysterious and awful agony can fully match.

9 Lord, all my desire *is* before thee ; and my groaning is not hid from thee.

9. *"Lord, all my desire is before thee."* If unuttered, yet perceived. Blessed be God, he reads the longings of our hearts ; nothing can be hidden from him ; what we cannot tell to him he perfectly understands. The Psalmist is conscious that he has not exaggerated, and therefore appeals to heaven for a confirmation of his words. The good Physician understands the symptoms of our disease and sees the hidden evil which they reveal, hence our case is safe in his hands. *"And my groaning is not hid from thee."*

> " He takes the meaning of our tears,
>   The language of our groans."

Sorrow and anguish hide themselves from the observation of man, but God spieth them out. None more lonely than the broken-hearted sinner, yet hath he the Lord for his companion.

10 My heart panteth, my strength faileth me : as for the light of mine eyes, it also is gone from me.

11 My lovers and my friends stand aloof from my sore ; and my kinsmen stand afar off.

12 They also that seek after my life lay snares *for me :* and they that seek my hurt speak mischievous things, and imagine deceits all the day long.

13 But I, as a deaf *man,* heard not ; and *I was* as a dumb man *that* openeth not his mouth.

14 Thus I was as a man that heareth not, and in whose mouth *are* no reproofs.

10. *"My heart panteth."* Here begins another tale of woe. He was so dreadfully pained by the unkindness of friends, that his heart was in a state of perpetual palpitation. Sharp and quick were the beatings of his heart ; he was like a hunted roe, filled with distressing alarms, and ready to fly out of itself with fear. The soul seeks sympathy in sorrow, and if it finds none, its sorrowful heart-throbs are incessant. *"My strength faileth me."* What with disease and distraction, he was weakened and ready to expire. A sense of sin, and a clear perception that none can help us in our distress, are enough to bring a man to death's door, especially if there be none to speak a gentle word, and point the broken spirit to the beloved Physician. *"As for the light of mine eyes, it also is gone from me."* Sweet light departed from his bodily eye, and consolation vanished from his soul. Those who were the very light of his eyes forsook him Hope, the last lamp of night,

was ready to go out. What a plight was the poor convict in! Yet here we have some of us been ; and here should we have perished had not infinite mercy interposed. Now, as we remember the lovingkindness of the Lord, we see how good it was for us to find our own strength fail us, since it drove us to the strong for strength ; and how right it was that our light should all be quenched, that the Lord's light should be all in all to us.

11. " *My lovers and my friends stand aloof from my sore.*" Whatever affection they might pretend to, they kept out of his company, lest as a sinking vessel often draws down boats with it, they might be made to suffer through his calamities. It is very hard when those who should be the first to come to the rescue, are the first to desert us. In times of deep soul trouble even the most affectionate friends cannot enter into the sufferer's case ; let them be as anxious as they may, the sores of a tender conscience they cannot bind up. Oh, the loneliness of a soul passing under the convincing power of the Holy Ghost ! " *And my kinsmen stand afar off.*" As the women and others of our Lord's acquaintances from afar gazed on his cross, so a soul wounded for sin sees all mankind as distant spectators, and in the whole crowd finds none to aid. Often relatives hinder seekers after Jesus, oftener still they look on with unconcern, seldom enough to do they endeavour to lead the penitent to Jesus.

12. " *They also that seek after my life lay snares for me.*" Alas ! for us when in addition to inward griefs, we are beset by outward temptations. David's foes endeavoured basely to ensnare him. If fair means would not overthrow him, foul should be tried. This snaring business is a vile one, the devil's own poachers alone condescend to it ; but prayer to God will deliver us, for the craft of the entire college of tempters can be met and overcome by those who are led of the Spirit. " *They that seek my hurt speak mischievous things.*" Lies and slanders poured from them like water from the town-pump. Their tongue was for ever going, and their heart for ever inventing lies. " *And imagine deceits all the day long.*" They were never done, their forge was going from morning to night. When they could not act they talked, and when they could not talk they imagined, and schemed, and plotted. Restless is the activity of malice. Bad men never have enough of evil. They compass sea and land to injure a saint ; no labour is too severe, no cost too great if they may utterly destroy the innocent. Our comfort is, that our glorious Head knows the pertinacious malignity of our foes, and will in due season put an end to it, as he even now sets a bound about it.

13. " *But I, as a deaf man, heard not.*" Well and bravely was this done. A sacred indifference to the slanders of malevolence is true courage and wise policy. It is well to be as if we could not hear or see. Perhaps the Psalmist means that this deafness on his part was unavoidable because he had no power to answer the taunts of the cruel, but felt much of the truth of their ungenerous accusations. " *And I was as a dumb man that openeth not his mouth.*" David was bravely silent, and herein was eminently typical of our Lord Jesus, whose marvellous silence before Pilate was far more eloquent than words. To abstain from self-defence is often most difficult, and frequently most wise.

14. " *Thus I was as a man that heareth not, and in whose mouth are no reproofs.*" He repeats the fact of his silence that we may note it, admire it, and imitate it. We have an advocate, and need not therefore plead our own cause. The Lord will rebuke our foes, for vengeance belongs to him ; we may therefore wait patiently and find it our strength to sit still.

15 For in thee, O LORD, do I hope : thou wilt hear, O Lord my God.

15. David committed himself to him that judgeth righteously, and so in patience was able to possess his soul. Hope in God's intervention, and belief in the power of prayer, are two most blessed stays to the soul in time of adversity. Turning right away from the creature to the sovereign Lord of all, and to him as our own covenant God, we shall find the richest solace in waiting upon him. Reputation like a fair pearl may be cast into the mire, but in due time when the Lord makes up his jewels, the godly character shall shine with unclouded splendour. Rest then, O slandered one, and let not thy soul be tossed to and fro with anxiety.

16 For I said, *Hear me,* lest *otherwise* they should rejoice over me : when my foot slippeth, they magnify *themselves* against me.

17 For I *am* ready to halt, and my sorrow *is* continually before me.

18 For I will declare mine iniquity ; I will be sorry for my sin.

19 But mine enemies *are* lively, *and* they are strong : and they that hate me wrongfully are multiplied.

20 They also that render evil for good are mine adversaries ; because I follow *the thing that* good *is.*

16. " *For I said, hear me, lest otherwise they should rejoice over me.*" The good man was not insensible, he dreaded the sharp stings of taunting malice ; he feared lest either by his conduct or his condition, he should give occasion to the wicked to triumph. This fear his earnest desires used as an argument in prayer as well as an incentive to prayer. " *When my foot slippeth, they magnify themselves against me.*" The least flaw in a saint is sure to be noticed ; long before it comes to a fall the enemy begins to rail, the merest trip of the foot sets all the dogs of hell barking. How careful ought we to be, and how importunate in prayer for upholding grace ! We do not wish, like blind Samson, to make sport for our enemies ; let us then beware of the treacherous Delilah of sin, by whose means our eyes may soon be put out.

17. " *For I am ready to halt.*" Like one who limps, or a person with tottering footsteps, in danger of falling. How well this befits us all. " Let him that thinketh he standeth, take heed lest he fall." How small a thing will lame a Christian, how insignificant a stumbling-block may cause him to fall ! This passage refers to weakness caused by pain and sorrow ; the sufferer was ready to give up in despair ; he was so depressed in spirit that he stumbled at a straw. Some of us painfully know what it is to be like dry tinder for the sparks of sorrow ; ready to halt, ready to mourn, and sigh and cry upon any occasion, and for any cause. " *And my sorrow is continually before me.*" He did not need to look out of window to find sorrow, he felt it within, and groaned under a body of sin which was an increasing plague to him. Deep conviction continues to irritate the conscience ; it will not endure a patched-up peace ; but cries war to the knife till the enmity is slain. Until the Holy Ghost applies the precious blood of Jesus, a truly awakened sinner is covered with raw wounds which cannot be healed nor bound up, nor mollified with ointment.

18. " *For I will declare mine iniquity.*" The slander of his enemies he repudiates, but the accusations of his conscience he admits. Open confession is good for the soul. When sorrow leads to hearty and penitent acknowledgment of sin it is blessed sorrow, a thing to thank God for most devoutly. " *I will be sorry for my sin.*" My confession shall be salted with briny tears. It is well not so much to bewail our sorrows as to denounce the sins which lie at the root of them. To be sorry for sin is no atonement for it, but it is the right spirit in which to repair to Jesus, who is the reconciliation and the Saviour. A man is near to the end of his trouble when he comes to an end with his sins.

19. " *But mine enemies are lively, and they are strong.*" However weak and dying the righteous man may be, the evils which oppose him are sure to be lively enough. Neither the world, the flesh, nor the devil, are ever afflicted with debility or inertness ; this trinity of evils labours with mighty unremitting energy to over-throw us. If the devil were sick, or our lusts feeble, or Madame Bubble infirm, we might slacken prayer ; but with such lively and vigorous enemies we must not cease to cry mightily unto our God. " *And they that hate me wrongfully are multiplied.*" Here is another misery, that as we are no match for our enemies in strength, so also they outnumber us as a hundred to one. Wrong as the cause of evil is, it is a popular one. More and more the kingdom of darkness grows. Oh, misery of miseries, that we see the professed friends of Jesus forsaking him, and the enemies of his cross and his cause mustering in increasing bands !

20. " *They also that render evil for good are mine adversaries.*" Such would a wise man wish his enemies to be. Why should we seek to be beloved of such graceless souls ? It is a fine plea against our enemies when we can without injustice declare them to be like the devil, whose nature it is to render evil for good. " *Because I follow the thing that good is.*" If men hate us for this reason we may rejoice to bear it : their wrath is the unconscious homage which vice renders to virtue. This verse is not inconsistent with the writer's previous confession ; we may feel deeply guilty before God, and yet be entirely innocent of any wrong to

our fellow men. It is one thing to acknowledge the truth, quite another thing to submit to be belied. The Lord may smite me justly, and yet I may be able to say to my fellow man, " Why smitest thou me ? "

21 Forsake me not, O LORD : O my God, be not far from me.

22 Make haste to help me, O Lord my salvation.

21. " *Forsake me not, O Lord.*" Now is the time I need thee most. When sickness, slander, and sin, all beset a saint, he requires the especial aid of heaven, and he shall have it too. He is afraid of nothing while God is with him, and God is with him evermore. " *Be not far from me.*" Withhold not the light of thy near and dear love. Reveal thyself to me. Stand at my side. Let me feel that though friendless besides, I have a most gracious and all-sufficient friend in thee.

22. " *Make haste to help me.*" Delay would prove destruction. The poor pleader was far gone and ready to expire, only speedy help would serve his turn. See how sorrow quickens the importunity of prayer ! Here is one of the sweet results of affliction, it gives new life to our pleading, and drives us with eagerness to our God. " *O Lord my salvation.*" Not my Saviour only, but my salvation. He who has the Lord on his side has salvation in present possession. Faith foresees the blessed issue of all her pleas, and in this verse begins to ascribe to God the glory of the expected mercy. We shall not be left of the Lord. His grace will succour us most opportunely, and in heaven we shall see that we had not one trial too many, or one pang too severe. A sense of sin shall melt into the joy of salvation ; grief shall lead on to gratitude, and gratitude to joy unspeakable and full of glory.

EXPLANATORY NOTES AND QUAINT SAYINGS.

Title.—The first word, MIZMOR, or Psalm, is the designation of forty-four sacred poems, thirty-two of which are ascribed to David. The English reader must observe, that this word is not the same in the original Hebrew as that which forms the general title of the book of Psalms ; the latter expressing a Hymn of Praise. The word *Psalm*, however, as used both in the context and in the titles of the individual compositions, is uniformly *Mizmor* in the original ; a term which accurately defines their poetical character. To explain its proper meaning I must have recourse to the beautiful and accurate definition of Bishop Lowth. " The word *Mizmor* signifies a composition, which in a peculiar manner is cut up into sentences, short, frequent, and measured by regular intervals." . . . . He adds that *Zamar* means to cut or prune, as applied to the removing superfluous branches from trees ; and, after mentioning the secondary sense of the word, " to sing with a voice or instrument," gives it as his opinion, that *Mizmor* may be more properly referred to the primary sense of the root, so as to mean a poem cut up into short sentences, and pruned from all superfluity of words, which is the peculiar characteristic of the Hebrew poetry.—*John Jebb.*

Title.—The title that David gives this Psalm is worth your notice, *A Psalm of David to bring to remembrance.* David was on his death-bed as he thought, and he said it shall be a Psalm of remembrance, to bring sin to remembrance, to confess to God my uncleanness with Bathsheba, to bring to my remembrance the evils of my life. Whenever God brings thee under affliction, thou art then in a fit plight to confess sin to God, and call to remembrance thy sin.—*Christopher Love.*

Title.—The Psalm is " *to bring to remembrance.*" This seems to teach us that good things need to be kept alive in our memories, that we should often sit down, look back, retrace, and turn over in our meditation things that are past, lest at any time we should let any good thing sink into oblivion. Among the things which David brought to his own remembrance, the first and foremost were, (1), *his past trials and his past deliverances.* The great point, however, in David's Psalm is to bring to remembrance, (2), *the depravity of our nature.* There is, perhaps, no Psalm which more fully than this describes human nature as seen in the light which God the Holy Ghost casts upon it in the time when he convinces us of sin. I am persuaded that the description here does not tally with any known disease of the body.

It is very like leprosy, but it has about it certain features which cannot be found to meet in any leprosy described either by ancient or modern writers. The fact is, it is a spiritual leprosy, it is an inward disease which is here described, and David paints it to the very life, and he would have us to recollect this. A third thing the Psalm brings to our remembrance is, (3), *our many enemies.* David says, that his enemies laid snares for him, and sought his hurt, and spoke mischievous things, and devised and imagined deceits all the day long. " Well," says one, " how was it that David had so many enemies ? How could he make so many ? Must he not have been imprudent and rash, or perhaps morose ? " It does not appear so in his life. He rather made enemies by his being scrupulously holy. His enemies attacked him, not because he was wicked, but as he says, in this very Psalm, they were his enemies because he loved the thing which is good. The ultimate result of the religion of Christ is to make peace everywhere, but the first result is to cause strife. Further, the Psalm reminds us of, (4), *our gracious God.* Anything which drives us to God is a blessing, and anything which weans us from leaning on an arm of flesh, and especially that weans us from trying to stand alone, is a boon to us.—*C. H. S.*

Whole Psalm.—The most wonderful features in this Psalm, are the depth of misery into which the Psalmist gradually plunges in his complaints in the first part of it, the sudden grasp at the arm of mercy and omnipotence that is made in verse 8, and the extreme height of comfort and consolation that it reaches in the end.—*Benjamin Weiss.*

Verse 1.—" *O Lord, rebuke me not in thy wrath.*" But is it not an absurd request, to require God not to rebuke me in his anger ; as though I thought he would rebuke me if he were not angry ? Is it not a senseless suit to pray to God not to chasten me in his displeasure, as though he would chasten me if he were not displeasured ? The frowardest natures that are, will yet be quiet as long as they be pleased : and shall I have such a thought of the great yet gracious God, that he should be pleased and yet not be quiet ? But, O my soul, is it all one, to rebuke in his anger and to rebuke when he is angry ? He may rebuke when he is angry, and yet restrain and bridle in his anger ; but to rebuke in his anger is to let loose the reins to his anger ; and what is it to give the reins to his anger, but to make it outrun his mercy ? And then what a miserable case should I be in, to have his anger to assault me, and not his mercy ready to relieve me ? To have his indignation fall upon me when his lovingkindness were not by to take it off ! Oh, therefore, *rebuke me not in thine anger, O God,* but let thy rebuking stay for thy mercy ; chasten me not in thy displeasure, but let thy lovingkindness have the keeping of thy rod.—*Sir Richard Baker.*

Verse 1.—" *Neither chasten me in thy hot displeasure,*" etc. Both these words, which we translate to *chasten,* and *hot displeasure,* are words of a heavy and of a vehement signification. They extend both to express the eternity of God's indignation, even to the binding of the soul and body in eternal chains of darkness. For the first *jasar,* signifies in the Scriptures, *vincire,* to bind, often with ropes, often with chains ; to fetter, or manacle, or pinion men that are to be executed ; so that it imports a slavery, a bondage all the way, and a destruction at last. And so the word is used by Rehoboam, " My father chastised you with whips, but I will chastise you with scorpions." 1 Kings xii. 11. And then, the other word, *chamath,* doth not only signify " *hot displeasure,*" but that effect of *God's hot displeasure* which is intended by the prophet Esay : " Therefore hath he poured forth his fierce wrath, and the strength of battle, and it hath set him on fire round about, yet he knew it not, and it burned him, yet he laid it not to heart." These be the fearful conditions of God's hot displeasure, to be in a furnace, and not to feel it ; to be in a habit of sin, and not know what leads us into temptation ; to be burnt to ashes, and so not only without all moisture, all holy tears, but, as ashes, without any possibility that any good thing can grow in us. And yet this word, *chamath,* hath a heavier signification than this ; for it signifies poison itself, destruction itself, for so it is twice taken in one verse : " Their poison is like the poison of a serpent " (Psalm lviii. 4) ; so that this *hot displeasure* is that poison of the soul, obduration here, and that extension of that obduration, a final impenitence in this life, and an infinite impenitableness in the next, to die without any actual penitence here, and live without all possibility of future penitence for ever hereafter. David therefore foresees, that if God *rebuke in anger*, it will come to a *chastening in hot displeasure*. For what should stop him ? For, " if a man sin against the Lord, who will plead for him ? " says Eli. " Plead thou my cause," says David ; it is only the Lord that can be of counsel with him, and plead for him ; and that Lord is both the judge and angry too.—*John Donne.*

Verse 2.—" *For thine arrows stick fast in me.*" First, we shall see in what respect he calls them " *arrows :* " and therein, first, that they are *alienæ*, they are shot from others, they are not in his own power ; a man shoots not an arrow at himself ; and then that they are *veloces*, swift in coming, he cannot give them their time ; and again, they are *vix visibiles*, though they be not altogether invisible in their coming, yet there is required a quick eye, and an express diligence and watchfulness to avoid them ; so they are arrows in the hand of another, not his own ; and swift as they come, and invisible before they come. And secondly, they are many arrows : the victory lies not in escaping one or two. And thirdly, they " *stick* " in him : they find not David so good proof as to rebound back again, and imprint no sense : and they stick " *fast :* " though the blow be felt and the wound discerned, yet there is not a present cure, he cannot shake them off ; *infixæ sunt ;* and then, with all this, they stick fast *in him ;* that is, in all him ; in his body and soul ; in him, in his thoughts and actions ; in him, in his sins and in his good works too ; *infixæ mihi*, there is no part of him, no faculty in him, in which they stick not ; for (which may well be another consideration), that " *hand*," which shot them, *presses him*, follows the blow, and presses him " *sore*," that is, vehemently. But yet (which will be our conclusion), *sagittæ tuæ*, *thy arrows*, and *manus tua, thy hand*, these arrows that are shot, and this hand that presses him so sore, are the arrows, and the hand *of God ;* and therefore, first, they must have their effect, they cannot be disappointed : but yet they bring their comfort with them, because they are his, because no arrows from him, no pressing with his hand, comes without that *balsamum* of mercy to heal as fast as he wounds.—*John Donne.*

Verse 2.—" *Thine arrows stick fast.*" Though importunity be to God most pleasing always, yet to us it is then most necessary when the cheerful face of God is turned into frowns, and when there is a justly conceived fear of the continuance of his anger : and have I not just cause to fear it, having the arrows of his anger sticking so fast in me ? If he had meant to make me but a butt, at which to shoot his arrows, he would quickly, I suppose, have taken them up again ; but now that he leaves them sticking in me, what can I think, but that he means to make me his quiver ; and then I may look long enough before he come to pluck them out. They are arrows, indeed, that are feathered with swiftness, and headed with sharpness ; and to give them a force in flying, they are shot, I may say, out of his crossbow, I am sure his bow of cross : for no arrows can fly so fast, none pierce so deep, as the crosses and afflictions with which he hath surprised me : I may truly say surprised me, seeing when I thought myself most safe, and said, " I shall never be moved," even then, these arrows of his anger lighted upon me, and stick so fast in my flesh, that no arm but his that shot them is ever able to draw them forth. Oh, then, as thou hast stretched forth thine arm of anger, O God, to shoot these arrows at me, so stretch forth thine arm of mercy to draw them forth, that I may rather sing hymns than dirges unto thee ; and that thou mayest show thy power, as well in pardoning as thou hast done in condemning.—*Sir Richard Baker.*

Verse 2.—" *Thine arrows.*" Arrows are (1) swift, (2) secret, (3) sharp, (4) killing, instruments. They are instruments drawing blood and drinking blood, even unto drunkenness (Deut. xxxii. 42) ; afflictions are like arrows in all these properties. 1. Afflictions often come very speedily, with a glance as an arrow, quick as a thought. 2. Afflictions come suddenly, unexpectedly ; an arrow is upon a man afore he is aware, so are afflictions. Though Job saith, the thing he feared came upon him, he looked for this arrow before it came ; yet usually afflictions are unlooked-for guests, they thrust in upon us when we dream not of them. 3. They come with little noise ; an arrow is felt before, or, as soon as it is heard ; an arrow flies silently and secretly, stealing upon and wounding a man, unobserved and unseen. Lastly, all afflictions are sharp, and in their own nature killing and deadly. That any have good from them, is from the grace of God, not from their nature. *Joseph Caryl.*

Verse 2.—Let no one think these expressions of penitence (verses 1—4) overstrained or excessive. They are the words of the Holy Spirit of God, speaking by the mouth of the man after God's own heart. If we were as repentant as David, we should bring home to ourselves his language ; as it is, our affections are chilled, and therefore we do not enter into his words. . . . And let us observe how all the miseries are referred to their proper end. The sin is not bewailed merely on account of its ill effect on the guilty one, but on account of the despite done to God. The Psalmist's first thought is the " *anger* " of the Lord, and his " *hot displeasure.*" It is not the " arrows " that afflict him so much as that they are God's. " *Thine* arrows stick fast in me, and *thy* hand presseth me." The reason why there is no health in his flesh is because of God's displeasure. Such is true contrition, " not the sorrow of the world which worketh death, but the sorrow that worketh repentance not to be repented of."—*A Commentary on the Seven Penitential Psalms. Chiefly from Ancient Sources* [*by A. P. F.*], 1847.

Verse 2.—" *Thy hand presseth me sore.*" Not the hand of Egypt or Ashur ; then were it hand for hand, a duel of some equality : hand to hand ; here forces and stratagems might achieve the victory : but " *Thy hand.*" The weight of a man's blow is but weak, according to the force and pulse of his arm ; as the princes of Midian answered Gideon, when he bade his son try the dint of his sword upon them ; " Rise thou, and fall upon us : for as the man is, so is his strength." Judges viii. 21. But " it is a fearful thing to fall into the hands of the living God." Heb. x. 31. As Homer called the hands of Jupiter χεῖρες ἄεπτοι, hands whose praise could not be sufficiently spoken ; which some read χεῖρες ἄαπτοι, hands inaccessible, irresistible for strength : all the gods in heaven could not ward a blow of Jupiter's hand. This hand never strikes but for sin ; and where sin is mighty his blow is heavy.—*Thomas Adams.*

Verse 3.—" *Thine anger . . . . my sin.*" I, alas ! am as an anvil under two hammers ; one of thine anger, another of my sin ; both of them beating incessantly upon me ; the hammer of thine anger beating upon my flesh and making that unsound ; the hammer of my sin beating upon my bones and making them unquiet ; although indeed both beat upon both : but thine anger more upon my flesh, as being more sensible ; my sin more upon my bones, as being more obdurate. God's anger and sin are the two efficient causes of all misery ; but the procatartic * cause indeed is sin : God's anger, like the house that Samson pulled upon his own head, falls not upon us but when we pull it upon ourselves by sin.—*Sir Richard Baker.*

Verse 3.—" *My flesh . . . . my bones.*" I know by the unsoundness of my flesh that God is angry with me ; for if it were not for his anger my flesh would be sound : but what soundness can there be in it now, when God's angry hand lies beating upon it continually, and never ceaseth ? I know by the unquietness of my bones that I have sin in my bosom ; for if it were not for sin my bones would be quiet. But what quietness can be in them now, when sin lies gnawing upon them incessantly with the worm of remorse ? One would think my bones were far enough removed and closely enough hidden from sins doing them any hurt : yet see the searching nature, the venomous poison of sin, which pierceth through my flesh, and makes unquietness in my very bones. I know my flesh is guilty of many faults, by which it justly deserves unsoundness ; but what have my bones done ? for they minister no fuel to the flames of my flesh's sensuality ; and why then should they be troubled ? But are not my bones supporters of my flesh, and are they not by this at least accessory to my flesh's faults ? As accessories, then, they are subject to the same punishment the flesh itself is, which is the principal.— *Sir Richard Baker.*

Verse 3.—" *Neither is there any rest in my bones because of my sin.*" A Christian in this life is like quicksilver, which hath a principle of motion in itself, but not of rest : we are never quiet, but as the ball upon the racket, or the ship upon the waves. As long as we have sin, this is like quicksilver : a child of God is full of motion and disquiet. . . . We are here in a perpetual hurry, in a constant fluctuation ; our life is like the tide ; sometimes ebbing, sometimes flowing ; here is no rest ; and the reason is because we are out of centre. Everything is in motion till it comes at the centre ; Christ is the centre of the soul ; the needle of the compass trembles till it comes to the North Pole.—*Thomas Watson.*

Verse 3.—Learn here of beggars how to procure succour and relief. Lay open thy sores, make known thy need, discover all thy misery, make not thy case better

---

* As applied to diseases, signifies the exciting cause.

than it is. Beggars by experience find that the more miserable they appear to be, the more they are pitied, the more succoured ; and yet the mercies of the most merciful men are but as drops in comparison of the oceans of God's mercies ; and among men there are many like the priest and Levite in the parable (Luke x. 30—32). that can pass by a naked, wounded man, left half dead, and not pity him nor succour him. But God, like the merciful Samaritan, hath always compassion on such as with sense of their misery are forced to cry out and crave help. Read how Job, chap. vi. and vii ; David, Ps. xxxviii, 3, etc., Hezekiah, Isa. xxxviii. 10, etc., and other like saints, poured out their complaints before the Lord, and withal observe what mercy was showed them of the Lord, and you may have in them both good patterns how to behave yourselves in like cases, and good encouragement so to do. This is it which God expecteth of us, and whereunto he desireth to bring us, that seeing our own emptiness and insufficiency, and the impotency and disability of others to help us, we should in all humility fly to his mercy.—*William Gouge.*

Verse 4.—" *For mine iniquities are gone over mine head : as an heavy burden they are too heavy for me.*" David proceeds to a reason why his prayer must be vehement, why these miseries of his are so violent, and why God's anger is permanent, and he finds all this to be, because in his sins, all these venomous qualities, vehemence, violence, and continuance, were complicated, and enwrapped ; for he had sinned vehemently, in the rage of lust, and violently, in the effusion of blood, and permanently, in a long and senseless security. They are all contracted in this text into two kinds, which will be our two parts in handling these words : first, the *Supergressæ super,* " *Mine iniquities are gone over my head,*" there is the multiplicity, the number, the succession, and so the continuation of his sin ; and then, the *Gravatæ super,* " *My sins are as a heavy burden, too heavy for me,*" there is the greatness, the weight, the unsupportableness of his sin. St. Augustine calls these two distinctions or considerations of sin, *ignorantiam, et difficultatem ;* first that David was ignorant, that he saw not the tide, as it swelled up upon him, *abyssus abyssum,* depth called upon depth ; and all thy waters, and all thy billows are gone over me (says he in another place) ; he perceived them not coming till they were over him, he discerned not his particular sins then when he committed them, till they came to the *supergressæ super,* to that height that he was overflowed, surrounded, his iniquities were gone over his head ; and in that St. Augustine notes *ignorantiam,* his unobservance, his inconsiderations of his own case ; and then he notes *difficultatem,* the hardness of recovering, because he that is under water hath no air to see by, no air to hear by, he hath nothing to reach to, he touches not ground, to push him up, he feels no bough to pull him up, and therein that further notes *difficultatem,* the hardness of recovering. Now Moses expresses these two miseries together, in the destruction of the Egyptians, in his song, after Israel's deliverance and the Egyptians' submersion, " The depths have covered them " (there is the *supergressæ super,* their iniquities, in that punishment of their iniquities were gone over their heads), and then, they sank into the bottom like a stone (says Moses), there is the *gravatæ super,* they depressed them, suppressed them, oppressed them, they were under them, and there they must lie. The Egyptians had, David had, we have, too many sins to swim above water, and too great sins to get above water again when we are sunk.—*John Donne.*

Verse 4.—" *As an heavy burden they are too heavy for me.*" No strength is so great but it may be overburdened : though Samson went light away with the gates of Gaza, yet when a whole house fell upon him it crushed him to death. And such, alas ! am I ; I have had sin as a burden upon me ever since I was born, but bore it a long time as light as Samson did the gates of Gaza ; but now that I have pulled a whole house of sin upon me, how can I choose but be crushed to death with so great a weight ? And crushed, O my soul, thou shouldst be indeed, if God for all his anger did not take some pity on thee, and for all his displeasure did not stay his hand from further chastening thee.—*Sir Richard Baker.*

Verse 4.—It is of singular use to us, that the backslidings of the holy men of God are recorded in Holy Writ. Spots appear nowhere more disagreeable than when seen in a most beautiful face, or on the cleanest garment. And it is expedient to have a perfect knowledge of the filthiness of sin. We also learn from them to think humbly of ourselves, to depend on the grace of God, to keep a stricter eye upon ourselves, lest perhaps we fall into the same or more grievous sins. Gal. vi. 1.—*Herman Witsius, D.D.,* 1636—1708.

Verses 4, 5.—It is only when we can enter into *all* that is implied here that we begin to see our exceeding sinfulness. There is a certain feeling of sin which does not interfere with our pride and self-respect. We can have that sort of feeling, and say pretty earnestly, " *Mine iniquities are gone over mine head : as an heavy burden they are too heavy for me.*" But it is otherwise with us when we get to know ourselves better and to feel ourselves *loathsome* in our wickedness, when our folly and meanness and ingratitude oppress us, and we begin to loathe ourselves, and can enter into verse five. Our wounds, once an object of self-pity, and something in which we could claim sympathy and healing from our friends, have become "*corrupt,*" because of the meanness and folly we feel to be in us. We hide them now, for if they were seen, would not "lovers and friends stand aloof from our sore ?" Then we are silent except to God, "For in *thee,* O Lord, do I hope : *thou* wilt hear, O Lord my God," verse 15. O love of God that turns not away ! O blessed Jesus, that turned not away from the leprous man that fell upon his face and said, "If thou wilt, thou canst make me clean," but put forth thine hand and *touched* him, saying, ' I will : be thou clean,' to whom *can* we go but unto thee ! "—*Mary B. M. Duncan.*

Verse 5.—" *My wounds stink and are corrupt,*" etc. These expressions seem to be in a great measure figurative, and significant rather of the diseased state of his mind than of his body.—*William Walford.*

Verse 5.—" *My wounds stink and are corrupt.*"—I know, O Lord, I have done most foolishly, to let my sores run so long without seeking for help ; for now, " *My wounds stink and are corrupt,*" in as ill a case as Lazarus' body was when it had been four days buried ; enough to make any man despair that did not know thee as I do. For, do not I know, that *nullum tempus occurrit tibi ;* do not I know thou hast as well wisdom to remedy my foolishness as power to cure my wounds ? Could the grave hold Lazarus when thou didst but open thy mouth to call him forth ? No more can the corruption of my sores be any hindrance to their healing when thy pleasure is to have them be cured. Although, therefore, I have done my own discretion wrong to defer my care, yet I will not do thy power wrong to despair of thy cure : for, how should I despair, who know thee to be as powerful as thou art merciful ; if I may not rather say, to be as merciful as thou art powerful !—*Sir Richard Baker.*

Verse 5.—" *My wounds stink and are corrupt.*" Either they must be understood literally of the sores that were in his body (as the words in the following verse may also seem to import) which he calls *wounds,* to intimate that he looked upon them as the wheals or swelling tumours (for so the original word may signify) which the rod of God had made in his flesh, or the wounds of those arrows of which he had spoken (verse 2), "Thine arrows stick fast in me ; " or else figuratively, of any other miseries that God had brought upon him, comparing them to stinking and festering sores ; either to imply the long continuance of them, or the sharp pains and sorrows which he felt in himself by reason thereof. Yet some, I know, would have it meant of the shame which his sins had brought upon him.—*Arthur Jackson.*

Verses 5, 6.—The spiritual feeling of sin is indispensable to the feeling of salvation. A sense of the malady must ever precede, and prepare the soul for a believing reception and due apprehension of the remedy. Wherever God intends to reveal his Son with power, wherever he intends to make the gospel to be "a joyful sound," he makes the conscience feel and groan under the burden of sin. And sure am I that when a man is labouring under the burden of sin, he will be full of complaint. The Bible records hundreds of the complaints of God's people under the burden of sin. " *My wounds stink and are corrupt,*" cries one, " *because of my foolishness. I am troubled ; I am bowed down greatly ; I go mourning all the day long.*" " My soul," cries another, " is full of troubles : and my life draweth nigh unto the grave." Psalm lxxxviii. 3. "He hath led me," groans out a third, "and brought me into darkness, but not into light." Lam. iii. 2. A living man must need cry under such circumstances. He cannot carry the burden without complaining of its weight. He cannot feel the arrow sticking in his conscience without groaning under the pain. He cannot have the worm gnawing his vitals, without complaining of its venomous tooth. He cannot feel that God is incensed against him without bitterly complaining that the Lord is his enemy. Spiritual complaint then is a mark of spiritual life, and is one which God recognises as such. " I have surely heard Ephraim bemoaning himself." Jer. xxxi. 18. It shows that he has something to mourn over ; something to make him groan being burdened ; that sin has been opened up to him in its hateful malignancy; that it is a trouble and distress to his soul; that he cannot roll it like a sweet morsel under his tongue; but that it is found out by the penetrating eye, and punished by the chastening hand of God.—*J. C. Philpot*, 1842.

Verse 6.—"*I am troubled.*" I writhe with pain. This is the proper sense of the original, which means to "turn out of its proper situation, or course;" thence to be "distorted, writhed," as a person in pain. Our Bible translation, which says in the text, "*I am troubled*," adds in the margin, "wried," an obsolete word, correctly expressing the Hebrew.—*Richard Mant.*

Verse 6.—"*I go mourning all the day long.*" And now was I both a burden and a terror to myself, nor did I ever so know, as now, what it was to be weary of my life, and yet afraid to die. Oh, how gladly now would I have been anybody but myself! Anything but a man! and in any condition but mine own! for there was nothing did pass more frequently over my mind than that it was impossible for me to be forgiven my transgression, and to be saved from wrath to come.— *John Bunyan, in "Grace Abounding."*

Verse 6.—Let a man see and feel himself under the bonds of guilt, in danger of hell, under the power of his lusts, enmity against God, and God a stranger to him; let but the sense of this condition lie upon his heart, and let him go on in his jollity if he can. What a woful creature doth a man see himself now to be! He envies the happiness of the beasts that are filled, and play in their pastures. We have heard of him who when he saw a toad, stood weeping, because God had made him a *man*, so excellent a creature, and not a toad, so abominable: the goodness of God, then, it seems, as he apprehended it, made him weep; but this man meets a toad, and he weeps also, but why? because he is a *man*, who thinks his estate infinitely worse than the condition of a toad, and if it were possible to attain it, would change states with the toad, that hath no guilt of sin, fears no wrath of God, is not under power of lusts or creatures; God is no enemy to it, which is his miserable state.—*Giles Firmin*, 1617—1697.

Verse 7.—"*For my loins are filled with a loathsome disease.*" The word here used, according to Gesenius (*Lex.*), properly denotes the internal muscles of the loins near the kidneys, to which the fat adheres The word rendered "*loathsome*"— the word "*disease*" being supplied by our translators—is derived from קלה, *kalah*, a word which means to roast, to parch, as fruit, grain, etc.; and then, in the form used here, it means scorched, burned; hence, a burning or inflammation; and the whole phrase would be synonymous with *an inflammation of the kidneys*. The *word* here used does not imply that there was any eruption, or ulcer, though it would seem from verse five that this was the fact, and that the inflammation had produced this effect.—*Albert Barnes.*

Verse 7.—"*A loathsome disease.*" In many things our estimates are extravagant; but we never over-estimate the evil of sin. It is as corrupting as it is damning. It covers the soul with plague-spots, with the leprosy. Isaiah i. 5, 6.—*William S. Plumer.*

Verse 8.—"*I am feeble.*" literally, *I am benumbed*, I have become deadly cold, cold as a corpse; possibly with reference to the burning inflammation in the previous verse, as marking the alternations in the fever fit.—*J. J. Stewart Perowne.*

Verse 8.—"*I have roared by reason of the disquietness of my heart.*" Where sin is, there will never be but unquietness of heart; and an unquiet heart will always produce these miserable effects—feebleness of body, dejectedness of mind, and roaring of voice. But how can roaring stand with feebleness, which seems to require a strength of spirits? Is it not, therefore, a roaring, perhaps not so much in loudness as in an inarticulate expressing? that having done actions more like a beast than a man, I am forced to use a voice not so much of a man as of a beast? Or is it perhaps a roaring in spirit, which the heart may send forth though the body be feeble; or rather then, most, when it is most feeble; not unlike the blaze of a candle, then greatest when going out? Howsoever it be, this is certain: the heart is that unhappy plot of ground, which, receiving into it the accursed seed of sin, brings forth in the body and soul of man these miserable fruits: and how, then, can I be free from these weeds of the fruits, since I have received into me so great a measure of the seed? Oh, vile sin, that I could as well avoid thee as I can see thee, or could as easily resist thee as I deadly hate thee, I should not then complain of either feebleness of body, or dejectedness of mind, or roaring of voice ; but I should perfectly enjoy that happy quietness in all my parts, which thou, O God, didst graciously bestow as a blessed dowry on our first parents at their creation.—*Sir Richard Baker.*

Verse 8.—" *I have roared,*" etc. It is difficult for a true penitent, in the bitterness of his soul, to go over the life which he has dragged on in sinfulness, without groaning and sighing from the bottom of his heart. But happy are these groans, happy these sighs, happy these sobs, since they flow from the influence of grace, and from the breath of the Holy Spirit, who himself in an ineffable manner groans in us and with us, and who forms these groans in our hearts by penitence and love ! but as the violence of both, that is, of penitence and of love, cannot but burst the narrow limits of a penitent heart, it must make a vent for itself by the eyes and mouth. The eyes shed tears, and the mouth sends forth sighs and groans, which it can no longer restrain ; because they are driven on by the fire of divine love, and so these lamentations frame themslves into words and intelligible sentences.— *Jean Baptiste Elias Avrillon,* 1652—1729.

Verse 8.—" *The disquietness of my heart.*" David felt pains gather about his heart, and then he cried out. The heart is the mark that God principally aims at when a Christian hath turned aside from his upright course ; other outward parts he may hit and deeply wound, but this is but to make holes in the heart, where the seat of unsoundness that principally offends him is. The fire which conscience kindles, it may flash forth into the eyes, and tongue, and hands, and make a man look fearfully, speak desperately, and do bloodily, against the body ; but the heat of the fire is principally within, in the furnace, in the spirit ; 'tis but some sparkles and flashes only that you see come forth at the lower holes of the furnace, which you behold in the eyes, words, and deeds of such men.—*Nicholas Lockyer.*

Verse 9.—There are usually, if not always, pains with desires, especially in desires after the creature, because that oftentimes there is a frustration of our desires, or an elongation of the things, the things are far off, hard to come by ; our desires oftentimes are mute, they speak not ; or the things that we desire, know not our minds : but our desires after God always speak, they are open unto God, he heareth their voice. " *Lord, all my desire is before thee,*" saith David, " *and my groaning is not hid from thee.*" Therefore it must needs be sweet, when the soul lies thus open unto God. Other desires do not assure and secure a man in the things he desires ; a man may wish this and wish that and go without both ; but the soul that thus longs after God is instated in his wish, hath a present enjoyment, and certainly shall have a full enjoyment of him. " He will fulfil the desire of those that fear him : he also will hear their cry." Ps. cxlv. 19.—*Joseph Symonds.*

Verse 9.—" *My groaning is not hid from thee.*" Secret tears for secret sins are an excellent sign of a holy heart, and a healing balsam for broken spirits. God well understands the language of half words interrupted with sighs, and interprets them as the streams and breathings of a broken heart. As all our foolishness is before him to cover it, so is all our heaviness to ease it ; and therefore shall our souls praise and please him more than a bullock with young horns and hoofs upon his altar. Holy mourning keeps out carnal sorrow and produces spirit joy. It stirs up the heart of a saint to beg preventing grace which no false heart can perform without secret reserves. This inward sorrow prevents open shame. God will never give up *such* souls to be trampled on by spiritual enemies, who are already humbled by themselves. In saints' humiliation there's a door opened for secret hope, because of the precious promises that are plighted to it, and especially of preventing future sin by strengthening grace. For as the love of God is the fountain of all true repentance, so it is the attractive of more incomes of divine love to the soul.—*Samuel Lee.*

Verse 10.—" *My heart panteth.*" The verb which David here uses signifies *to travel* or *wander hither and thither*, but here it is taken for the agitation or disquietude which distress of heart engenders when we know not whit to do. According as men are disquieted in mind, so do they turn themselves on all sides ; and so their heart may be said to turn round, or to run to and fro.—*John Calvin.*

Verse 11.—" *My lovers and my friends stand aloof from my sore ; and my kinsmen stand afar off.*" So miserable am I, that I am left alone as one utterly forsaken ;

they are all pieces that recoil and fly back at the first voice of the powder. Yet it is not so much me they stand aloof from as my sore; for if it were not for my sore, I should have enough of their company easily enough; but they cannot abide sores, their eyes are too tender to endure to see them, and yet hard enough not to relieve them. Or is it they stand aloof, that is, so near as to show they are willing enough to see them; but yet so far off as to show they have no meaning to come and help them! . . . . .

" *My lovers and my friends stand aloof from my sore,*" as fearing more my sore than me; but "*my kinsmen stand afar off,*" as fearing me no less than my sore; and where my lovers and friends by standing aloof do but violate the law of a contracted friendship, my kinsmen by standing afar off violate even the law of natural affection; and is not this a grievous thing, that the law of reason, the law of friendship, the law of nature, shall all be broken rather than I shall be relieved or find assistance?—*Sir Richard Baker.*

Verse 11.—"*My lovers and my friends stand afar off.*" Deserted by false friends, but conqueror through thee, to thee I speed, who though seeming to act the part of an enemy, yet never changest thy love; but lovest for ever him whom thou once hast loved. When thou seemest afar off, thou art near. I conceive this sorrow on account of the treachery of false friends, and the cowardliness of my kinsfolk, who are to me as piercing thorns rather than sweet-smelling roses. The proof of affection is seen by deeds. I hear the *name* of kinsman and friend; I see no deed. To thee, therefore, I flee, whose word is deed; for I need thy help.— *From the Latin of A. Rivetus.*

Verse 13.—"*But I, as a deaf man, heard not; and I was as a dumb man that openeth not his mouth.*" For why should I hear when I meant not to speak? and why should I speak when I knew beforehand I should not be heard? I knew by contesting I should but provoke them, and make them more guilty that were guilty too much before. I therefore thought it better myself to be silent than to set them a roaring and make them grow outrageous. No doubt a great wisdom in David, to know that to be deaf and dumb was in this case his best course, but yet a far greater virtue that knowing it, he was able to do it. Oh, how happy should we be, if we could always do that which we know is best to be done, and if our wills were as ready to act, as our reason is able to enact; we should then decline many rocks we now run upon, we should then avoid many errors we now run into. To be deaf and dumb are indeed great inabilities and defects, when they be natural; but when they be voluntary, and I may say artificial, they are then great abilities, or rather perfections.—*Sir Richard Baker.*

Verse 13.—"*But I, as a deaf man, heard not.*" The inspired writer here compares himself to a dumb and deaf man for two reasons. In the first place, he intimates that he was so overwhelmed with the false and wicked judgments of his enemies, that he was not even permitted to open his mouth in his own defence. In the second place, he alleges before God his own patience, as a plea to induce God the more readily to have pity upon him; for such meekness and gentleness, not only with good reason, secures favour to the afflicted and the innocent, but it is also a sign of true piety.—*John Calvin.*

Verse 14.—"*Thus I was as a man that heareth not, and in whose mouth are no reproofs.*" You, who truly know yourselves; by whom silent suffering, secret grief, and hidden joy are understood; by the knowledge of your own unspoken sorrow, unexpressed, because inexpressible feelings, by the consciousness of the unrevealed depths of your own nature, the earnest, but ever unsatisfied yearnings of your spirit, learn to reverence and love those by whom you are surrounded, whose inner life can never be completely read, but whom you are sure must need sacred sympathy and tender consideration. If a secret grief is constantly gnawing my heart, making my voice falter in the song of praise, may not my brother's downcast eye and heavy heart be occasioned by a similar cause; shall I condemn him for his want of gladness? No: but remember, "the heart knoweth his own bitterness, and a stranger doth not intermeddle with his joy." The silent breathings of the spirit are not for our ears; the hot tears which in secret fall, are not for our eyes; in mercy has the veil been drawn round each heart; but by the sacred memory of our own sadness, let our voice be gentle, our look tender, our tread quiet, as we pass amongst the mourners.—*Jessie Coombs, in "Thoughts for the Inner Life,"* 1867.

Verse 15.—A man that is to go down into a deep pit, he does not throw himself headlong into it, or leap down at all adventures, but fastens a rope at top upon a cross beam or some sure place, and so lets himself down by degrees : so let thyself down into the consideration of thy sin, hanging upon Christ ; and when thou art gone so low that thou canst endure no longer, but art ready to be overcome with the horror and darkness of thy miserable estate, dwell not too long at the gates of hell, lest the devil pull thee in, but wind thyself up again by renewed acts of faith, and " fly for refuge unto the hope that is set before thee." Heb. vi. 18.—*Thomas Cole (1627—1697), in " Morning Exercises."*

Verse 17.—" *For I am ready to halt :* " to show my infirmity in my trials and afflictions ; as Jacob halted after his wrestling with God. Gen. xxxii. 31. In the Greek, *I am ready for scourges,* that is, to suffer correction and punishment for my sins : so the Chaldee saith, *for calamity.—Henry Ainsworth.*

Verse 18.—Pliny writeth of some families that had private marks on their bodies peculiar to those of that line, and every man hath, as it were, a private sin, which is most justly called his ; but if we will confess our sins aright, we must not leave out that sin ; nay, our chiefest spite must be against it, according to David's resolve : " *I will declare mine iniquity ; I will be sorry for my sin.*" . . . . David doth not only say, " *I will declare,*" but, " *I will be sorry for my sin.*" The people of God (1 Sam. vii. 6) in the day of their confession not only say, " We have sinned," but draw water, and pour it out before the Lord in token of contrition. We should, in confessing sin, have our hearts so affected, that our eyes, with Job, may " pour tears before God " (Job xvi. 20) ; that, with David, " rivers of tears, may run down our eyes " (Psalm cxix. 136) ; yea, we should wish with Jeremiah, that " our head were waters, and our eyes a fountain of tears." Jer. ix. 1. But, however, *nonne stillabit oculus noster ?* if we cannot pour out, shall we not drop a tear ? or at least, if we cannot shed a tear, let us breathe forth a sigh for our sins. It is only the heart broken with godly sorrow that sends forth a true confession.—*Nathanael Hardy.*

Verse 20.—" *They are mine enemies because I follow the thing that good is.*" It is a bold attempt to ding Satan out of his nest. If we conform us to the men of this world we find peace with them ; they will not discord with us so long as we go their way ; but to shame them by a godly life is an affront they cannot digest ; and to rebuke their sin, findeth at their hand all that Satan disappointed or corruption provoked can devise. A sleeping dog is quiet, but being stirred, turneth all in barking and biting. Not to do as they do is matter enough of anger, but a reproof is the highest degree of disgrace in their account. All that hatred which they ought to bear to Satan and his instruments, is turned upon God in his rebuking and reclaiming servants. That anger that in remorse should burn against their own sin is set against their reprovers.—*William Struther.*

Verse 22.—" *O Lord my salvation.*" Faith the suppliant is now made faith triumphant.—*Franz Delitzsch.*

HINTS TO PREACHERS.

Title.—The art of memory. Holy memorabilia. The usefulness of sacred remembrances.

Verse 1.—The rebuke of God's wrath. I. Richly deserved. II. Reasonably dreaded. III. Earnestly deprecated.—*B. Davies.*

Verse 1.—The evil consequences of sin in this world.—*J. J. Blunt.*

Verse 1.—The bitterest of bitters, " *thy wrath ;* " why deprecated ; and how escaped.

Verse 2.—God sharply chasteneth many of his children, and yet for all that he loves them never a whit the less, nor withholdeth in good time his mercy from them.—*Thomas Wilcocks.*

Verse 3 (*last clause*).—Sin causes *unrest*. He who cures it alone gives rest. Dwell on both facts.

Verse 4 (*first clause*).—Sin in its relations to us. To the *eye* pleasing. To the *heart* disappointing. In the *bones* vexing. Over the *head* overwhelming.

Verse 4.—The confession of an awakened sinner.

Verse 4 (*last clause*).—Sin. I. Heavy—"*a* burden." II. Very heavy—"*a heavy burden.*" III. Superlatively heavy—"*too heavy for me.*" IV. Not immovable, for though too heavy *for me*, yet Jesus bore it.

Verse 5.—"*Foolishness.*" The folly of sin. Everything that a man has to do with sin shows his folly. I. Dallying with sin. II. Committing it. III. Continuing in it. IV. Hiding it. V. Palliating it.—*B. Davies.*

Verse 6.—Conviction of sin. Its grief, its depth, its continuance.

Verse 6.—" *I go mourning.*" I. Unlawful reasons for mourning. II. Legitimate themes for sorrow. III. Valuable alleviations of grief.

Verse 9.—The many desires of God's children : the fact that God understands them even when unexpressed ; and the certainty that he will grant them.

Verse 9.—Omniscience, a source of consolation to the desponding.

Verse 13.—The wisdom, dignity, power and difficulty of silence.

Verse 15.—Prayer, the offspring of hope.

Hope strengthened by confidence in God's answering prayer.

Verse 17.—Mr. Ready-to-Halt. His pedigree, and infirmity ; his crutches, and his cure ; his history, and safe departure.

Verse 18.—The excellence of penitent confession.

Verse 18.—The twin children of grace—confession and contrition : their mutual revelation and reaction.

Verse 18 (*last clause*).—There is good reason for such sorrow, God is well pleased with it. It benefits the mourner.

Verse 19.—The terrible energy and industry of the powers of evil.

Verse 22.—Faith tried, faith trembling, faith crying, faith grasping, faith conquering.

PSALM XXXIX.

TITLE.—To the Chief Musician, even to Jeduthun. *Jeduthun's name, which signifies praising or celebrating, was a most appropriate one for a leader in sacred psalmody. He was one of those ordained by the King's order " for song in the house of the Lord with cymbals, psalteries, and harps" (1 Chron. xv. 6), and his children after him appear to have remained in the same hallowed service, even so late as the days of Nehemiah. To have a name and a place in Zion is no small honour, and to hold this place by a long entail of grace is an unspeakable blessing. O that our households may never lack a man to stand before the Lord God of Israel to do him service. David left this somewhat sorrowful ode in Jeduthun's hands because he thought him most fit to set it to music, or because he would distribute the sacred honour of song among all the musicians who in their turn presided in the choir. A Psalm of David. Such as his chequered life would be sure to produce ; fit effusion for a man so tempted, so strong in his passions, and yet so firm in faith.*

DIVISION.—*The Psalmist, bowed down with sickness and sorrow, is burdened with unbelieving thoughts, which he resolves to stifle, lest any evil should come from their expression, 1, 2. But silence creates an insupportable grief, which at last demands utterance, and obtains it in the prayer of verses 3 to 6, which is almost a complaint and a sigh for death, or at best, a very desponding picture of human life. From verses 7 to 13 the tone is more submissive, and the recognition of the divine hand more distinct : the cloud has evidently passed, and the mourner's heart is relieved.*

EXPOSITION.

I SAID, I will take heed to my ways, that I sin not with my tongue : I will keep my mouth with a bridle, while the wicked is before me.

2 I was dumb with silence, I held my peace, *even* from good ; and my sorrow was stirred.

1. " *I said.*" I steadily resolved and registered a determination. In his great perplexity his greatest fear was lest he should sin ; and, therefore, he cast about for the most likely method for avoiding it, and he determined to be silent. It is right excellent when a man can strengthen himself in a good course by the remembrance of a well and wisely-formed resolve. "What I have written I have written," or what I have spoken I will perform, may prove a good strengthener to a man in a fixed course of right. " *I will take heed to my ways.*" To avoid sin one had need be very circumspect, and keep one's actions as with a guard or garrison. Unguarded ways are generally unholy ones. Heedless is another word for graceless. In times of sickness or other trouble we must watch against the sins peculiar to such trials, especially against murmuring and repining. " *That I sin not with my tongue.*" Tongue sins are great sins : like sparks of fire ill-words spread, and do great damage. If believers utter hard words of God in times of depression, the ungodly will take them up and use them as a justification for their sinful courses. If a man's own children rail at him, no wonder if his enemies' mouths are full of abuse. Our tongue always wants watching, for it is restive as an ill-broken horse ; but especially must we hold it in when the sharp cuts of the Lord's rod excite it to rebel. " *I will keep my mouth with a bridle,*" or more accurately, with a muzzle. The original does not so much mean a bridle to check the tongue as a muzzle to stop it altogether. David was not quite so wise as our translation would make him ; if he had resolved to be very guarded in his speech, it would have been altogether commendable, but when he went so far as to condemn himself to entire silence, " even from good," there must have been at least a little sullenness in his soul. In trying to avoid one fault, he fell into another. To use the tongue against God is a sin of commission, but not to use it at all involves an evident sin of omission. Commendable virtues may be followed so eagerly that we may fall into vices ; to avoid Scylla we run into Charybdis. " *While the wicked is before me.*" This qualifies the silence, and almost screens it from criticism, for bad men are so sure

to misuse even our holiest speech, that it is as well not to cast any of our pearls before such swine ; but what if the Psalmist meant, " I was silent while I had the prosperity of the wicked in my thoughts," then we see the discontent and questioning of his mind, and the muzzled mouth indicates much that is not to be commended. Yet, if we blame we must also praise, for the highest wisdom suggests that when good men are bewildered with sceptical thoughts, they should not hasten to repeat them, but should fight out their inward battle upon its own battlefield. The firmest believers are exercised with unbelief, and it would be doing the devil's work with a vengeance if they were to publish abroad all their questionings and suspicions. If I have the fever myself, there is no reason why I should communicate it to my neighbours. If any on board the vessel of my soul are diseased, I will put my heart in quarantine, and allow none to go on shore in the boat of speech till I have a clean bill of health.

2. " I was dumb with silence." He was as strictly speechless as if he had been tongueless—not a word escaped him. He was as silent as the dumb. " I held my peace, even from good." Neither bad nor good escaped his lips. Perhaps he feared that if he began to talk at all, he would be sure to speak amiss, and, therefore, he totally abstained. It was an easy, safe, and effectual way of avoiding sin, if it did not involve a neglect of the duty which he owed to God to speak well of his name. Our divine Lord was silent before the wicked, but not altogether so, for before Pontius Pilate he witnessed a good confession, and asserted his kingdom. A sound course of action may be pushed to the extreme, and become a fault. " And my sorrow was stirred." Inward grief was made to work and ferment by want of vent. The pent-up floods were swollen and agitated. Utterance is the natural outlet for the heart's anguish, and silence is, therefore, both an aggravation of the evil and a barrier against its cure. In such a case the resolve to hold one's peace needs powerful backing, and even this is most likely to give way when grief rushes upon the soul. Before a flood gathering in force and foaming for outlet the strongest banks are likely to be swept away. Nature may do her best to silence the expression of discontent, but unless grace comes to her rescue, she will be sure to succumb.

3 My heart was hot within me, while I was musing the fire burned : *then* spake I with my tongue,

4 LORD, make me to know mine end, and the measure of my days, what it *is ; that* I may know how frail I *am.*

5 Behold, thou hast made my days *as* an handbreadth ; and mine age *is* as nothing before thee : verily every man at his best state *is* altogether vanity. Selah.

6 Surely every man walketh in a vain shew : surely they are disquieted in vain : he heapeth up *riches,* and knoweth not who shall gather them.

3. " My heart was hot within me." The friction of inward thoughts produced an intense mental heat. The door of his heart was shut, and with the fire of sorrow burning within, the chamber of his soul soon grew unbearable with heat. Silence is an awful thing for a sufferer, it is the surest method to produce madness. Mourner, tell your sorrow ; do it first and most fully to God, but even to pour it out before some wise and godly friend is far from being wasted breath. " While I was musing the fire burned." As he thought upon the ease of the wicked and his own daily affliction, he could not unravel the mystery of providence, and therefore he became greatly agitated. While his heart was musing it was fusing, for the subject was confusing. It became harder every moment to be quiet ; his volcanic soul was tossed with an inward ocean of fire, and heaved to and fro with a mental earthquake ; an eruption was imminent, the burning lava must pour forth in a fiery stream. " Then spake I with my tongue." The original is grandly laconic. " I spake." The muzzled tongue burst all its bonds. The gag was hurled away. Misery, like murder, will out. You can silence praise, but anguish is clamorous. Resolve or no resolve, heed or no heed, sin or no sin, the impetuous torrent forced for itself a channel and swept away every restraint.

4. " Lord." It is well that the vent of his soul was Godward and not towards man. Oh ! if my swelling heart must speak, Lord let it speak with thee ; even if there be too much of natural heat in what I say, thou wilt be more patient with

me than man, and upon thy purity it can cast no stain ; whereas if I speak to my fellows, they may harshly rebuke me or else learn evil from my petulance. " *Make me to know my end.*" Did he mean the same as Elias in his agony, " Let me die, 1 am no better than my fathers ? " Perhaps so. At any rate, he rashly and petulantly desired to know the end of his wretched life, that he might begin to reckon the days till death should put a finis to his woe. Impatience would pry between the folded leaves. As if there were no other comfort to be had, unbelief would fain hide itself in the grave and sleep itself into oblivion. David was neither the first nor the last who had spoken unadvisedly in prayer. Yet, there is a better meaning : the Psalmist would know more of the shortness of life, that he might better bear its transient ills, and herein we may safely kneel with him, uttering the same petition. That there is no end to its misery is the hell of hell ; that there is an end to life's sorrow is the hope of all who have a hope beyond the grave. God is the best teacher of the divine philosophy which looks for an expected end. They who see death through the Lord's glass, see a fair sight, which makes them forget the evil of life in foreseeing the end of life. " *And the measure of my days.*" David would fain be assured that his days would be soon over and his trials with them ; he would be taught anew that life is measured out to us by wisdom, and is not a matter of chance. As the trader measures his cloth by inches, and ells, and yards, so with scrupulous accuracy is life measured out to man. " *That I may know how frail I am,*" or when I shall cease to be. Alas ! poor human nature, dear as life is, man quarrels with God at such a rate that he would sooner cease to be than bear the Lord's appointment. Such pettishness in a saint ! Let us wait till we are in a like position, and we shall do no better. The ship on the stocks wonders that the barque springs a leak, but when it has tried the high seas, it marvels that its timbers hold together in such storms. David's case is not recorded for our imitation, but for our learning.

5. " *Behold, thou hast made my days as an handbreadth.*" Upon consideration, the Psalmist finds little room to bewail the length of life, but rather to bemoan its shortness. What changeful creatures we are ! One moment we cry to be rid of existence, and the next instant beg to have it prolonged ! A handbreadth is one of the shortest natural measures, being the breadth of four fingers ; such is the brevity of life, by divine appointment ; God has made it so, fixing the period in wisdom. The " *behold*" calls us to attention ; to some the thought of life's hastiness will bring the acutest pain, to others the most solemn earnestness. How well should those live who are to live so little ! Is my earthly pilgrimage so brief ? then let me watch every step of it, that in the little of time there may be much of grace. " *And mine age is as nothing before thee.*" So short as not to amount to an entity. Think of eternity, and an angel is as a new-born babe, the world a fresh blown bubble, the sun a spark just fallen from the fire, and man a nullity. Before the Eeternal, all the age of frail man is less than one ticking of a clock. " *Verily, every man at his best state is altogether vanity.*" · This is the surest truth, that nothing about man is either sure or true. Take man at his best, he is but a man, and man is a mere breath, unsubstantial as the wind. Man is *settled*, as the margin has it, and by divine decree it is settled that he shall not be settled. He is constant only in inconstancy. His vanity is his only verity ; his best, of which he is vain, is but vain ; and this is verily true of every man, that everything about him is every way fleeting. This is sad news for those whose treasures are beneath the moon ; those whose glorying is in themselves may well hang the flag half-mast ; but those whose best estate is settled upon them in Christ Jesus in the land of unfading flowers, may rejoice that it is no vain thing in which they trust.

6. " *Surely every man walketh in a vain shew.*" Life is but a passing pageant. This alone is sure, that nothing is sure. All around us shadows mock us ; we walk among them, and too many live for them as if the mocking images were substantial ; acting their borrowed parts with zeal fit only to be spent on realities, and lost upon the phantoms of this passing scene. Worldly men walk like travellers in a mirage, deluded, duped, deceived, soon to be filled with disappointment and despair. " *Surely they are disquieted in vain.*" Men fret, and fume, and worry, and all for mere nothing. They are shadows pursuing shadows, while death pursues them. He who toils and contrives, and wearies himself for gold, for fame, for rank, even if he wins his desire, finds at the end his labour lost ; for like the treasure of the miser's dream, it all vanishes when the man awakes in the world of reality. Read well this text, and then listen to the clamour of the market, the hum of the ex-

change, the din of the city streets, and remember that all this *noise* (for so the word means), this breach of quiet, is made about unsubstantial, fleeting vanities. Broken rest, anxious fear, over-worked brain, failing mind, lunacy, these are steps in the process of disquieting with many, and all to be rich, or, in other words, to load one's self with the thick clay; clay, too, which a man must leave so soon. "*He heapeth up riches, and knoweth not who shall gather them.*" He misses often the result of his ventures, for there are many slips between the cup and the lips. His wheat is sheaved, but an interloping robber bears it away—as often happens with the poor Eastern husbandman; or, the wheat is even stored, but the invader feasts thereon. Many work for others all unknown to them. Especially does this verse refer to those all-gathering muckrakes, who in due time are succeeded by all-scattering forks, which scatter riches as profusely as their sires gathered them parsimoniously. We know not our heirs, for our children die, and strangers fill the old ancestral halls; estates change hands, and entail, though riveted with a thousand bonds, yields to the corroding power of time. Men rise up early and sit up late to build a house, and then the stranger tramps along its passages, laughs in its chambers, and forgetful of its first builder, calls it all his own. Here is one of the evils under the sun for which no remedy can be prescribed.

7 And now, Lord, what wait I for? my hope *is* in thee.

8 Deliver me from all my transgressions: make me not the reproach of the foolish.

9 I was dumb, I opened not my mouth; because thou didst *it*.

10 Remove thy stroke away from me: I am consumed by the blow of thine hand.

11 When thou with rebukes dost correct man for iniquity, thou makest his beauty to consume away like a moth: surely every man *is* vanity. Selah.

12 Hear my prayer, O Lord, and give ear unto my cry; hold not thy peace at my tears: for I *am* a stranger with thee, *and* a sojourner, as all my fathers *were*.

13 O spare me, that I may recover strength, before I go hence, and be no more.

7. "*And now, Lord, what wait I for?*" What is there in these phantoms to enchant me? Why should I linger where the prospect is so uninviting, and the present so trying? It were worse than vanity to linger in the abodes of sorrow to gain a heritage of emptiness. The Psalmist, therefore, turns to his God, in disgust of all things else; he has thought on the world and all things in it, and is relieved by knowing that such vain things are all passing away; he has cut all cords which bound him to earth, and is ready to sound "Boot and saddle, up and away." "*My hope is in thee.*" The Lord is self-existent and true, and therefore worthy of the confidence of men; he will live when all the creatures die, and his fulness will abide when all second causes are exhausted; to him, therefore, let us direct our expectation, and on him let us rest our confidence. Away from sand to rock let all wise builders turn themselves, for if not to-day, yet surely ere long, a storm will rise before which nothing will be able to stand but that which has the lasting element of faith in God to cement it. David had but one hope, and that hope entered within the veil, hence he brought his vessel to safe anchorage, and after a little drifting all was peace.

8. "*Deliver me from all my transgressions.*" How fair a sign it is when the Psalmist no longer harps upon his sorrows, but begs freedom from his sins! What is sorrow when compared with sin! Let but the poison of sin be gone from the cup, and we need not fear its gall, for the bitter will act medicinally. None can deliver a man from his transgressions but the blessed One who is called Jesus, because he saves his people from their sins; and when he once works this great deliverance for a man from the cause, the consequences are sure to disappear too. The thorough cleansing desired is well worthy of note: to be saved from some transgressions would be of small benefit; total and perfect deliverance is needed. "*Make me not the reproach of the foolish.*" The wicked are the foolish here meant: such are always on the watch for the faults of saints, and at once make them the theme of ridicule. It is a wretched thing for a man to be suffered to make himself the butt

of unholy scorn by apostasy from the right way. Alas, how many have thus exposed themselves to well-deserved reproach! Sin and shame go together and from both David would fain be preserved.

9. *" I was dumb, I opened not my mouth ; because thou didst it."* This had been far clearer if it had been rendered, " I am silenced, I will not open my mouth." Here we have a nobler silence, purged of all sullenness, and sweetened with submission. Nature failed to muzzle the mouth, but grace achieved the work in the worthiest manner. How like in appearance may two very different things appear! silence is ever silence, but it may be sinful in one case and saintly in another. What a reason for hushing every murmuring thought is the reflection, " because thou didst it "! It is his right to do as he wills, and he always wills to do that which is wisest and kindest ; why should I then arraign his dealings ? Nay, if it be indeed the Lord, let him do what seemeth him good.

10 *" Remove thy stroke away from me."* Silence from all repining did not prevent the voice of prayer, which must never cease. In all probability the Lord would grant the Psalmist's petition, for he usually removes affliction when we are resigned to it ; if we kiss the rod, our Father always burns it. When we are still, the rod is soon still. It is quite consistent with resignation to pray for the removal of a trial. David was fully acquiescent in the divine will, and yet found it in his heart to pray for deliverance ; indeed, it was while he was rebellious that he was prayerless about his trial, and only when he became submissive did he plead for mercy. *" I am consumed by the blow of thine hand."* Good pleas may be found in our weakness and distress. It is well to show our Father the bruises which his scourge has made, for peradventure his fatherly pity will bind his hands, and move him to comfort us in his bosom. It is not to consume us, but to consume our sins, that the Lord aims at in his chastisements.

11. *" When thou with rebukes dost correct man for iniquity."* God does not trifle with his rod ; he uses it because of sin, and with a view to whip us from it ; hence he means his strokes to be felt, and felt they are. *" Thou makest his beauty to consume away like a moth."* As the moth frets the substance of the fabric, mars all its beauty, and leaves it worn out and worthless, so do the chastisements of God discover to us our folly, weakness, and nothingness, and make us feel ourselves to be as worn-out vestures, worthless and useless. Beauty must be a poor thing when a moth can consume it and a rebuke can mar it. All our desires and delights are wretched moth-eaten things when the Lord visits us in his anger. *" Surely every man is vanity."* He is as Trapp wittily says " a curious picture of nothing." He is unsubstantial as his own breath, a vapour which appeareth for a little while, and then vanisheth away. *Selah.* Well may this truth bring us to a pause, like the dead body of Amasa, which, lying in the way, stopped the hosts of Joab.

12. *" Hear my prayer, O Lord."* Drown not my pleadings with the sound of thy strokes. Thou hast heard the clamour of my sins, Lord, hear the laments of my prayers. *" And give ear unto my cry."* Here is an advance in intensity : a cry is more vehement, pathetic, and impassioned, than a prayer. The main thing was to have the Lord's ear and heart. *" Hold not thy peace at my tears."* This is a yet higher degree of importunate pleading. Who can withstand tears, which are the irresistible weapons of weakness ? How often women, children, beggars, and sinners, have betaken themselves to tears as their last resort, and therewith have won the desire of their hearts !—" This shower, blown up by tempest of the soul," falls not in vain. Tears speak more eloquently than ten thousand tongues ; they act as keys upon the wards of tender hearts, and mercy denies them nothing, if through them the weeper looks to richer drops, even to the blood of Jesus. When our sorrows pull up the sluices of our eyes, God will ere long interpose and turn our mourning into joy. Long may he be quiet as though he regarded not, but the hour of deliverance will come, and come like the morning when the dewdrops are plentiful. *" For I am a stranger with thee."* Not *to* thee, but *with* thee. Like thee, my Lord, a stranger among the sons of men, an alien from my mother's children. God made the world, sustains it, and owns it, and yet men treat him as though he were a foreign intruder ; and as they treat the Master, so do they deal with the servants. " 'Tis no surprising thing that we should be unknown." These words may also mean, " I share the hospitality of God," like a stranger entertained by a generous host. Israel was bidden to deal tenderly with the stranger, and the God of Israel has in much compassion treated us poor aliens with unbounded liberality. *" And a sojourner, as all my fathers were."* They knew

that this was not their rest; they passed through life in pilgrim guise, they used the world as travellers use an inn, and even so do I. Why should we dream of rest on earth when our fathers' sepulchres are before our eyes? If they had been immortal, their sons would have had an abiding city this side the tomb; but as the sires were mortal, so must their offspring pass away. All of our lineage, without exception, were passing pilgrims, and such are we. David uses the fleeting nature of our life as an argument for the Lord's mercy, and it is such a one as God will regard. We show pity to poor pilgrims, and so will the Lord.

13. "*O spare me.*" Put by thy rod. Turn away thine angry face. Give me breathing time. Do not kill me. "*That I may recover strength.*" Let me have sufficient cessation from pain, to be able to take repose and nourishment, and so recruit my wasted frame. He expects to die soon, but begs a little respite from sorrow, so as to be able to rally and once more enjoy life before its close. "*Before I go hence, and be no more.*" So far as this world is concerned, death is a being no more; such a state awaits us, we are hurrying onward towards it. May the short interval which divides us from it be gilded with the sunlight of our heavenly Father's love. It is sad to be an invalid from the cradle to the grave, far worse to be under the Lord's chastisements by the month together, but what are these compared with the endurance of the endless punishment threatened to those who die in their sins!

EXPLANATORY NOTES AND QUAINT SAYINGS.

Title.—"*To Jeduthun.*" A Levite of the family of Merari, and one of the great masters of the temple of music. The department superintended by Jeduthun and his colleagues in the temple service was that of the "instruments of the song of God," by which are intended the nebel or psaltery, the kinnor or harp, and the metsiltaim or cymbals. In 2 Chron, xxxv. 15, Jeduthun is called "the king's seer," which would seem to indicate that he was the medium of divine guidance to David. The name occurs in the title of Psalms xxxix., lxii., lxxvii.; where some have thought that it indicates some special kind of composition, and others some instrument of music, but without reason.—*William Lindsay Alexander, in Kitto's Cyclopædia.*

Whole Psalm.—The most beautiful of all the elegies in the Psalter.—*H. Ewald.*

Verse 1.—"*I said.*" It was to himself that he said it; and it is impossible for any other to prove a good or a wise man, without much of this kind of speech to himself. It is one of the most excellent and distinguishing faculties of a reasonable creature; much beyond vocal speech, for in that, some birds may imitate us; but neither bird nor beast has anything of this kind of language, of reflecting or discoursing with itself. It is a wonderful brutality in the greatest part of men, who are so little conversant in this kind of speech, being framed and disposed for it, and which is not only of itself excellent, but of continual use and advantage; but it is a common evil among men to go abroad, and out of themselves, which is a madness, and a true distraction. It is true, a man hath need of a well set mind, when he speaks to himself; for otherwise, he may be worse company to himself than if he were with others. But he ought to endeavour to have a better with him, to call in God to his heart to dwell with him. If thus we did, we should find how sweet this were to speak to ourselves, by now and then intermixing our speech with discourses unto God. For want of this, the most part not only lose their time in vanity, in their converse abroad with others, but do carry in heaps of that vanity to the stock which is in their own hearts, and do converse with that in secret, which is the greatest and deepest folly in the world.—*Robert Leighton.*

Verse 1.—No lesson so hard to be learned of us here, as the wise and discreet government of the tongue. David promised a singular care of this, "*I said, I will take heed,*" etc. Socrates reports of one Pambo, an honest, well meaning man, who came to his friend, desiring him to teach him one of David's Psalms, he read to him this verse. He answered : this one verse is enough, if I learn it well. Nineteen years after, he said, in all that time he had hardly learned that one verse. —*Samuel Page.*

Verse 1.—" *That I sin not with my tongue.*" Man's mouth, though it be but a little hole, will hold a world full of sin. For there is not any sin forbidden in the law or gospel which is not spoken by the tongue, as well as thought in the heart, or done in the life. Is it not then almost as difficult to rule the tongue as to rule the world ?—*Edward Reynor.*

Verse 1.—" *I will keep a muzzle on my mouth, whilst a wicked man is before me.*" —*New Translation, by Charles Carter.*

Verse 1.—" *While the wicked is before me.*" It is a vexation to be tied to hear so much impertinent babbling in the world, but profitable to discern and abhor it. A wonder that men can cast out so much wind, and the more they have to utter, the more they are prodigal of their own breath and of the patience of others, and careless of their own reckoning. If they believed to give account of every idle word, they would be more sparing of foolish speaking. I like either to be silent, or to speak that that may edify. At tables or meetings I cannot stop the mouths of others, yet may I close mine own ears, and by a heavenly soul-speech with God divert my mind from fruitless talking. Though I be among them I shall as little partake their prattling as they do my meditation.—*William Struther.*

Verse 2.—" *I was dumb with silence,*" etc. That is, for a while I did what I resolved ; I was so long wholly silent, that I seemed in a manner to be dumb, and not able to speak. " *I held my peace, even from good ;* " that is, I forbore to speak what I might well and lawfully enough have spoken, as from alleging anything that I might have said in mine own defence, from making my complaint to God, and desiring justice at his hands, and such like ; to wit, lest by degrees I should have been brought to utter anything that was evil, and whilst I intended only to speak that which was good, some unseemly word might suddenly slip from me ; or lest mine enemies should misconstrue anything I spake.—*Arthur Jackson.*

Verse 2.—" *I was dumb with silence.*"—We shall enquire what kind of *dumbness* or *silence* this of the Psalmist was, which he is commended for, and which would so well beseem us when we smart under the rod of God, and then the doctrine will be, in a great measure, evident by its own light. We shall proceed in our enquiry, 1. Negatively, to prevent mistakes. 2. Positively, and show you what it doth import.

First, negatively. 1. This dumbness doth not import any such thing, as if the prophet had been brought to that pass that he had nothing to say to God by way of prayer and supplication. He was not so dumb, but that he could *pray and cry too.* Verses 8, 10, 11. 2. Nor was he so dumb, as that he could not frame to the confession and bewailing of his sins. 3. Nor was it a dumbness of stupidity and senselessness. It doth not imply any such thing, as if by degrees he grew to that pass, he cared not for, or made no matter of his affliction, but set, as the proverb is, an hard heart against his hard hap. No, he did make his moan to God, and as he smarted, so he did lament under the sense of his afflicting hand. 4. Neither was he so dumb as not to answer God's voice in the rod that was upon him. 5. Much less was he dumb, and kept silence in any such sort as they did of whom Amos speaks (vi. 10), that in their misery they took up a resolution *to mention the name of God no more,* in whom they had gloried formerly.

Secondly, affirmatively. 1. He was dumb so as neither to complain of, nor quarrel with God's providence, nor to entertain any hard thoughts against him. Complain *to* God he did ; but *against* him he durst not. 2. He neither did nor durst quarrel, or fall out with the ways of holiness for all his sufferings, a thing we are naturally prone unto. 3. He was dumb, so as not to defend himself, or justify his own ways before God, as if they were righteous, and he had not deserved what he suffered. 4. He was dumb, so as to hearken to the voice of the rod. " I will (saith he in another place) hear what God the Lord will speak." Psalm lxxxv. 8. Now a man cannot listen to another while he will have all the talk and discourse to himself. 5. Lastly, the prophet was dumb, that is, he did acquiesce, and rest satisfied with God's dispensation ; and that not only as good, but as best.—*Condensed from a Funeral Sermon by Thomas Burroughes, B.D., entitled, " A Soveraign Remedy for all kindes of Grief," 1657.*

Verse 2.—" *I held my peace.*" A Christian being asked what fruit he had by

Christ : Is not this fruit, said he, not to be moved at your reproaches ? In cases of this nature, we must refer all to God ; *si tu tacueris, Deus loquitur ;* if thou hold thy peace, God speaks for thee ; and if God speaks for us, it is better than we can speak for ourselves. David saith, *Obmutui, quia tu fecisti.* " I held my peace, for it was thy doing."—*Christopher Sutton, B.D., 1629, in Disce Vivere.*

Verses 2—9.—An invalid who had been ordered a couple of pills, took them very absurdly, for, in place of swallowing them at once, he rolled them about in his mouth, ground them to pieces, and so tasted their full bitterness. Gotthold was present, and thus mused : The insults and calumnies of a slanderer and adversary are bitter pills, and all do not understand the art of swallowing without chewing them. To the Christian, however, they are wholesome in many ways. They remind him of his guilt, they try his meekness and patience, they show him what he needs to guard against, and at last they redound to his honour and glory in the sight of him for whose sake they were endured. In respect of the pills of slander, however, as well as the others, it is advisable not to roll them about continually in our minds, or judge of them according to the flesh, and the world's opinion. This will only increase their bitterness, spread the savour of it to the tongue, and fill the heart with proportional enmity. The true way is to *swallow, keep silence and forget.* We must inwardly devour our grief, and say, " *I will be dumb, and not open my mouth, because thou didst it.*" The best antidotes to the bitterness of slander, are the sweet promises and consolations of Scripture, of which not the least is this, " Blessed are ye, when men shall revile you, and persecute you, and shall say all manner of evil against you falsely, for my sake. Rejoice, and be exceeding glad : for great is your reward in heaven." Matt. v. 11, 12. Alas, my God ! how hard it is to swallow the pills of obloquy, to bless them that curse me, to do good to them that hate me, and to pray for them that despitefully use me ! *But, Lord, as thou wilt have it so, give it as thou wilt have it,* for it is a matter in which, without thy grace, I can do nothing !—*Christian Scriver.*

Verse 3.—" *My heart was hot within me, while I was musing the fire burned.*" They say of the loadstone (that wonder in nature), when either by carelessness in keeping it, or by some accident it loses its virtue, yet by laying it some good space of time in the filings of steel, it will again recover its virtues : when the spirit of a Christian by not looking well to it, loses of its heavenly heat and liveliness, the way of recovery is by laying it asteep in this so warming and quickening meditation. Oh, how burning and flaming may we often observe the spirit of the holy Psalmist David, in his acting of meditation ! Musing made him hot, yea, burning hot at the heart. Thus oft in the beginning of a Psalm we find his heart low and discouraged but as this musing was acted and heightened, his spirit grew hotter, and at last flies all on a flame, flies up to a very high pitch of heavenly heat. Oh, how do all the conscientious practisers of meditation, ever and anon experience these happy, heavenly heats, and heart-enlargements ! Ah, if all the saints' so glorious heart-quickenings were gathered together, what a rich chain of pearls, pearls of rare experiences, would they make up of the heart-warming efficacies of meditation.—*Nathanael Ranew.*

Verse 3.—" *I was musing.*" What a blessed (shall I say duty or) privilege is prayer ! Now meditation is a help to prayer. Gerson calls it the nurse of prayer. Meditation is like oil to the lamp ; the lamp of prayer will soon go out unless meditation cherish and support it. Meditation and prayer are like two turtles, if you separate one the other dies ; a cunning angler observes the time and season when the fish bite best, and then he throws in the angle; when the heart is warmed by meditation, now is the best season to throw in the angle of prayer, and fish for mercy. After Isaac had been in the field meditating he was fit for prayer when he came home. When the gun is full of powder it is fittest to discharge. So when the mind is full of good thoughts, a Christian is fittest by prayer to discharge ; now he sends up whole volleys of sighs and groans to heaven. Meditation hath a double benefit in it, it pours in and pours out ; first it pours good thoughts into the mind, and then it pours out those thoughts again into prayer ; meditation first furnisheth with matter to pray and then it furnisheth with a heart to pray. " *I was musing,*" saith David, and the very next words are a prayer, " *Lord, make me to know mine end.*" I muse on the works of thy hands, I stretch forth my hands to thee. The musing of his head made way for the stretching forth of his hands in prayer. When Christ was upon the Mount, then he prayed : so when the soul is upon the mount of meditation, now it is in tune for prayer. Prayer is the child of meditation : meditation leads the van, and prayer brings up the rear.—*Thomas Watson.*

Verse 3.—" *Musing.*" Meditation is prayer in bullion, prayer in the ore, soon melted and run into holy desires. The laden cloud soon drops into rain, the piece charged soon goes off when fire is put to it. A meditating soul is *in proxima potentia* to prayer. This was an ejaculatory prayer shot from his soul when in the company of the wicked.—*William Gurnall.*

Verse 3.—" *The fire burned.*" My thoughts kindled my passions.—*Matthew Pool.*

Verse 3.—" *The fire burned.*" Meditate so long till thou findest thy heart grow warm in this duty. If, when a man is cold you ask how long he should stand by the fire ? sure, till he be thoroughly warm, and made fit for his work. So, Christian, thy heart is cold ; never a day, no, not the hottest day in summer, but it freezeth there ; now stand at the fire of meditation till thou findest thy affections warmed, and thou art made fit for spiritual service. David mused till his heart waxed hot within him. I will conclude this with that excellent saying of Bernard : " Lord, I will never come away from thee without thee." Let this be a Christian's resolution, not to leave off his meditations of God till he find something of God in him ; some moving of the bowels after God ; some flamings of love, Cant. v. 4.—*Thomas Watson.*

Verse 3.—His company was bad, but his thoughts were good ; even *while the wicked was before him his heart was hot within him, while he was musing the fire burned.* His thoughts inflame his affections with holy zeal, and this *holy fire,* as by an ante-peristasis, burnt so much the hotter for the *frost* of cursed contrariety that was about it. When the careful magistrates or officers of a city break into a suspected house in the night-time, the great question is, What company have you here ? So when God breaks in upon our dark hearts, the enquiry is, What thoughts have you here ? Why do thoughts arise in your minds ? Are ye not become judges of evil thoughts ? Luke xxiv. 38 ; James ii. 4.—*Faithful Teat.*

Verse 3.—" *Then spake I with my tongue, Lord,*" etc. It is, indeed, a happy circumstance when that silence which has long been perserved is first broken before the Lord.—*John Morison.*

Verse 4.—" *Lord, make me to know mine end,*" etc. But did not David know this ? Yes, he knew it, and yet he desires to know it. It is very fit we should ask of God that he would make us to know the things that we do know ; I mean, that what we know emptily and barely, we may know spiritually and fruitfully, and if there be any measure of this knowledge, that it may increase and grow more. . . . We know we must die, and that it is no long course to the utmost period of life ; yet our hearts are little instructed by this knowledge.—*Robert Leighton.*

Verse 4.—" *Lord, make me to know mine end.*" David would know his *end,* not so much his death—the end consuming, as Christ the Lord of life—the end and perfection of all our desires ; or know it, not for vain science, but in his experience feel the reward of his patience. Though thy chastisement be sharp, it will be but short, and therein sweet ; thou shalt lie still and be quiet, thou shalt sleep and be at rest, Job iii. 13, 17, 18, 19. How few and evil soever thy days be in the world, by patience and rolling thyself upon God they will prove unto thee both long enough and good.—*Edmund Layfielde.*

Verse 4.—" *Lord, make me to know mine end,*" etc. Seeing that both sorrow and joy are both able to kill you, and your life hangeth upon so small a thread, that the least gnat in the air can choke you, as it choked a pope of Rome ; a little hair in your milk strangle you, as it did a councillor in Rome ; a stone of a raisin stop your breath, as it did the breath of Anacreon : put not the evil day far from you, which the ordinance of God hath put so near ; " Remember your Creator in time, before the days comes wherein you shall say, We have no pleasure in them ; " walk not always with your faces to the east, sometimes have an eye to the west, where the sun goeth down ; sit not ever in the prow of the ship, sometimes go to the stern ; " stand in your watch-towers," as the creature doth (Rom. viii. 19), and wait for the hour of your deliverance ; provide your armies before that dreadful king cometh to fight against you with his greater forces ; order your houses before you die, that is, dispose of your bodies and souls, and all the implements of them both ; let not your eyes be gadding after pleasure, nor your ear itching after rumours, nor your minds wandering in the fields, when death is in your houses ; your bodies are not brass, nor your strength the strength of stones, your life none inheritance, your breath no more than as the vapour and smoke of the chimney within your nostrils, or as a stranger within your gates, coming and going again, not to return any more till the day of final redemption.—*John King.*

Verse 4.—" *Lord, make me to know mine end,*" etc. 'Tis worthy your notice, that passage you read of in Scripture, 1 Sam. x. 2. Samuel, when he had anointed Saul king, and the people had chosen him, what signal doth he give him, to confirm him anointed ? It was to go to Rachel's sepulchre. Now the reason is this, that he might not be glutted with the preferments and honours he was entering upon. The emperors of Constantinople, in their inaugurations, on their coronation days, had a mason come and show them several marble stones, and ask them to choose which of those should be made ready for their grave-stones. And so we read of Joseph of Arimathea, that he had his tomb in his garden, to check the pleasures of the place.—*Christopher Love.*

Verse 4.—" *How frail I am.*" Between Walsall and Iretsy, in Cheshire, is a house built in 1636, of thick oak framework, filled in with brick. Over the window of the tap-room is still legible, cut in the oak, the following Latin inscription :—
Fleres si scires unum tua tempora mensem ; rides cum non scis si sit forsitan una dies.
The sense of which is " You would weep if you knew that your life was limited to one month, yet you laugh while you know not but it may be restricted to a day." How sad the thought, that with this silent monitor, this truthful sermon before their very eyes, numbers have revelled in soul-destructive inebriation ! And yet this is but a likeness of what we see constantly about us.—*Quoted in a Monthly Periodical.*

Verse 5.—" *My days.*" Man's life is styled *days* because it is not conferred upon us by wholesale, by months and years, but by retail of days, hours, minutes, moments, as to check our curiosity in making enquiry how long we have to live (verse 4) ; so acquainting us with the brevity thereof, we may learn to depend upon God's bounty for the *loan* of our life, employ it for his glory, and every day prepare for the Bridegroom, Christ.—*Edmund Layfielde.*

Verse 5.—" *My days an handbreath.*" That is one of the shortest measures. We need not long lines to measure our lives by : each one carries a measure about with him, his own hand ; that is the longest and fullest measure. It is not so much as a span : that might possibly have been the measure of old age in the infancy of the world, but now it is contracted to a handbreath, and that is the longest. But how many fall short of that ! Many attain not to a finger-breadth : multitudes pass from the womb to the grave ; and how many end their course within the compass of childhood !—*Robert Leighton.*

Verse 5.—" *Behold, thou hast made my days as an handbreath.*" The line wherewith our lives are measured, is made both of coarse and fine thread.   1. It is measured by itself, and considerable in its own frailty ; so the just length of it is " *an handbreadth.*"   2. Secondly, with eternity, so it is found to be as nothing : " *Mine age is as nothing before thee.*" . . . . " *An handbreath,*" and is that all ? So he saith, that exactly measureth them all, and whatsoever else was created with his own hand. A handbreath is one of the shortest kind of measures. There is an ell, a cubit, and a palm or handbreath, whereof there be two kinds, the greater and the less. The greater handbreath is the whole space betwixt the top of the thumb and the little finger, when the hand is extended, called a span, in account near twelve inches. The lesser handbreadth, in a more proper and strict signification, is the just breadth of the four fingers of the hand closed together, here chiefly intended, this interpretation best agreeing with the original, and complying most with the prophet's mind, by the unanimous consent of the choice interpreters.—*Edmund Layfielde.*

Verse 5.—" *Mine age is as nothing before thee.*"   1. David might truly have said, Mine age is short *in respect of Methuselah's ;* the days of Methuselah are said to be nine hundred sixty and nine years ; the days of David, by computation of the time when he began and how long he reigned were not much above three score and ten, so that he lived not so many tens as Methuselah did hundreds.   2. David might have said, Mine age is very short in comparison of *the age of the world.* St. Paul saith of the fashion of this Macrocosm, it passeth away (1 Cor. vii. 31) ; but the age of the microcosm, man, passeth away far swifter.   3. David might have said, Mine age in this world is exceeding little in comparison of *the duration of the other world.*   4. Finally, David might have said, Mine age is scarcely anything *before the angels,* whose duration began with this world and shall continue in the world to come, and so is coætaneous with both the worlds. But all these are far short of this comparison which he here maketh of his age *with God* which is eternal, both *a parte ante*, and *a parte post*, from everlasting to everlasting.—*Nathanael Hardy.*

Verse 5.—"*As nothing.*"   If a man be so diminutive a creature, compared with the fabric of that great world, and the world itself so little that it cannot contain the Lord, so little and light that he feels not the weight thereof upon the tip of his finger, man will well merit the name "*nothing,*" when he is placed before the Lord. The keel of man's life is laden with more vanity than verity and substance, if the searcher of the reins and heart come aboard to view it.   Ten thousand of our days will not make God one year, and a thousand of our years in his sight are but "as a day when it is past, and as a watch in the night."   As drops of rain are unto the sea, and as a gravel stone is in comparison of the sand, so are a thousand years to the days everlasting.—*Edmund Layfielde.*

Verse 5.—"*Verily every man at his best state is altogether vanity.*"   The Holy Spirit is pleased elsewhere to speak more sparingly, as it were, in favour of man ; he discovers the nakedness, but yet comes backward to cast a garment of lenity over it, that somewhat shadows the shame of it.   "Man is like to vanity (Ps. cxliv. 4) ; their days consume in vanity (Ps lxxviii. 33) ; Man is vanity" (Ps. xxxix. 11) ; but here with open mouth and unveiled terms full of emphasis, he proclaims every man to be *abstracted vanity ;* and as if that were short he adds, *he is all vanity ; mere vanity, all manner of vanity, altogether vanity :* nothing else, nothing less ; yea, somewhat more than vanity, "*lighter than vanity*" (Ps. lxii. 9) ; and "vanity of vanities." Eccl. i. 2.   And that no place of dubitation may be left, he ushers the doctrine unto our hearts with a strong asseveration ; *assuredly, in truth,* without all controversy, "*man is altogether vanity.*"—*Edmund Layfielde.*

Verse 5.—"*Verily every man at his best state is altogether vanity.*"   Bythner expounds it thus.   "*Every man at his best state is altogether vanity ;*" *hoc est omni ex parte, ita ut vanitas et miseria quæ per creaturas frustratim spargitur in uno homine aggregata videatur : sic homo evadit compendium omnium vanitatum quæ in creaturis extant :* that is, he is the sink and centre of all the vanities in the world ; he is as it were the universe of vanity.—*Quoted in William Reynold's Funeral Sermon for the Honourable Francis Pierrepont,* 1657.

Verse 5.—"Every Adam standing is all Abel."—*See Hebrew Text.*

Verse 5.—"*Selah.*"   A little word, yet of no small difficulty to explain.   Left out of the *Bible* by the *vulgar translators*, as though it were *impertinent*, where, let them consider, whether they come not within the verge of that malediction in *Revelation* xxii. 19.   The *ancient* interpreters did not much *meddle* with it, and our editions leave it *uninterpreted.*   But seeing "*whatsoever things were written aforetime were written for our learning, that we through patience and comfort of the Scriptures might have hope*" (Romans xv. 4), and till "*heaven and earth pass, one jot or one title shall in no wise pass from the law, till all be fulfilled*" (Matt. v. 18), we have sufficient warrant after the example of the learned, and encouragement to make enquiry after the mind of the Holy Spirit, in that which he hath both *commanded* to be written, and hath *commended* unto us.   Wherein, like the crystal glass, I will rather present you with the true visage of antiquity, than use any new-framed feature or painting of my own.

Selah is mentioned *seventy-four times* in the Scripture, whereof seventy-one in the book of Psalms, and thrice in the prophet Habakkuk, which is written Psalmwise ; and it is ever placed in the end of a Psalm or verse, four places only excepted, where, like the sun in the midst of the planets, it is seated to con-join the precedent words with the subsequent, and communicate splendour unto both.   There was a threefold use of it in ancient times, whereof the first concerned the music ; the second, the matter handled unto which it was affixed ; and the third, the men or congregation assembled in the temple of the Lord, which two last may still have place among us Christians, who are ingrafted into the stock Christ, from whence the Jews were cut off, but from the first we cannot properly suck such nourishment as once they did.

First of the music.   The king's choir (1 Chron. xxv. 1—6 ; Psalm lxii., Επιγραφή ; 1 Chron. xvi. 41) learned five things by it :

1st. To make a little pause, stop, or stay, when they came to *Selah*, and to meditate awhile upon the matter foregoing.

2nd. They knew by that cessation and interval that King David, as he was prophesying unto the people, and praising God upon the loud sounding cymbals, was at that instant inspired and taught some new lesson.   Wherefore, as men being in serious discourse, when they hear a sudden noise hold their peace to listen, saying, hark ! see, lo ! so David's heart being smitten by the voice of God's Spirit, the music ceased, stopped, and he checked himself as it were thus : " Speak, Lord, for thy servant heareth."

3rd. It signifieth the change and variation of the music in some strains, or of the metre, or sense, or disjunction of the rhyme, or ceasing of some one sort of music, which howsoever St. Hierome makes some scruple of. The Septuagint, as often as they meet with Selah in the Hebrew text, in their Greek version translated it, *the change of the song.*

4th. It directed them to sing the same verse over again whereunto Selah was annexed. Lastly, it was their instruction to elevate and lift up their voices, praising God with louder voices and loud sounding cymbals. " *Selah* " called upon them for louder strains of music and shrillness of voice. But seeing the Jewish harmony and sweet melody is overwhelmed in the ruins of their glorious temple, we remain unskilled in their notes, which doth obscure our annotations upon it. Let this suffice for the " music."

II. " *Selah* " concerns the *text* of Scripture itself, or the matter handled, in five branches. 1st. Some think it to be only an ornament of speech, to grace the language with a sweet emphasis ; or a non-significant word to complete the harmony, lest the verse should halt for want of a foot, but this conjecture is infirm, and many feet wide from the truth.

2nd. It is not only an adoration of speech, but signifies *an end* of that verse, matter, or Psalm, where it is found, and it is ever in the end of Psalm and verse, these four places only exempted from this rule : Psalm lv. 19 ; lvii. 3 ; Habakkuk iii. 3, 9. For as we write " finis " at the end of a book, song, or poem, so the Jews underwrite " Selah," " Salome," or " Amen," at the end or finishing of any canticle or work. And the modern Jews at this day, following the opinion of Aben-Ezra, take " Selah " to be the same with " Amen," using it at the end of their epitaphs and prayers twice or thrice indifferently ; thus : " Amen, Selah, Amen, Selah," which receives some credit from this that the particular Psalms end with " Selah " (Psalm iii. 8), and the books of Psalms with " Amen." For whereas the Psalter is divided into five books, four of them end with " Amen "—*so be it.* As you shall find : Psalm xli. 13, the end of the first book ; Psalm lxxii. 19, the end of the second book ; Psalm lxxxix. 52, the end of the third ; and Psalm cvi. 48, the conclusion of the fourth.

3rd. *Selah* is an hyperbole or illustration of the truth by way of excess in advancing and enlarging it, to make the truth and sense more clear and evident, as if we should say, " *that is wonderful !* " or, " *that is excellent !* " and sometimes by way of *aggravation* that is " *monstrous*," " *intolerable*," " *horrible !* " " *The Lord came from Teman and the holy One from Mount Paran. Selah.*" Habak. iii. 3. *Selah.* 1. God came with *great dignity, excellency,* and *ample majesty.* " Many there be that say of my soul there is no help for him in God. *Selah.*" Psalm iii. 2. *Selah,* as if he had said, *Oh, monstrous,* and *horrible blasphemy,* to excommunicate a child out of the favour of his heavenly Father ; and limit his mercy whose hand is *omnipotent* to relieve all that rely upon him.

4th. It serves to declare *the eternity of the truth* revealed in that Psalm or verse, though perhaps it only began then to be manifested to the church, or more fully at that time than in former ages. Howsoever, the people unto whom it was published, or the persons unto whom it was sent, were otherwise persuaded at the first publication of it. That it was a veritie from everlasting and shall continue for ever : instance Psalm iii. 8, " Salvation belongs unto the Lord, thy blessing is upon thy people. Selah." As if he had said, " This is a thing beyond all controversy true, that God hath ever delivered, and will for ever bless his people." This doctrine is sempeternal and durable, that the mercy of the Lord endureth for ever. Psalm cxxxvi.

5th. It did instruct them to meditate seriously upon those themes where " Selah " was engraven, as containing matter worthy of singular observation, meditation, and remembrance, as either concerning Christ, " Who is the King of glory ? The Lord of hosts, he is the King of glory. Selah." Psalm xxiv. 10. The mysteries of grace. " The Lord of hosts is with us ; the God of Jacob is our refuge. Selah." Psalm xlvi. 7. Man's duty (Psalm iv. 4 ; Psalm xxxii. 5), or frailty (Psalm ix. 20 ; xxxii. 4). That as the diamond is of greater value than other precious stones, and the sun is more glorious than the planets, so those sentences are more resplendent, than other parcels of Scripture. Which though at the first bare view, it doth not always so appear, there being other texts of Holy Writ more excellent (if it were meet to make any comparison) where Selah is not found, yet if we dive into the *occasion*, *scope*, and *nature* of the sentence, we shall more willingly accept, when we consider, that it is an usual custom of the Holy Spirit, for our singular instruction and benefit, to propound things of a low and inferior nature to our deepest meditation. Instance Psalm ix. 16. " The Lord is known by the judgment which he executeth : the wicked is snared in the work of his own hands," which is shut up with " Higgaion Selah," meditation Selah, as if he had said, here is a matter worthy of observation and eternal meditation ; the righteous should never forget this, that the wicked perish in their own counsels, and are taken in their own net. An observation worthy to be engraven in every religious person's bosom, that God will one time or other be known among the wicked by his most severe judgments executed upon them, though they would never learn by his patience and mercies to acknowledge him for their Lord. Thus far of the matter. Now it remains for a conclusion to unfold the several instructions which " Selah " afforded unto the congregation, which are these six.

1st. It served as a *note of attention and inattention of the mind* to what was sung or said, Ps. iii. v. 2—8, that wheresoever they cast an eye upon " Selah," they might conceive they heard the Lord's voice from heaven speaking. " Hear this, all ye people, give ear, all ye inhabitants of the world. Both high and low, rich and poor together." Ps. xlix. 1, 2. That as their voices were lift up in singing, so much more their hearts and affections might be elevated, that their voice and hearts being both in tune, the joint harmony might be sweet in the ears of the Lord.

2ndly. It was a note of affirmation, whereby they declared their consent and assent unto the truth delivered, as we say when we approve of another's speech ; right, just, you say truly, it is most certain. So their " Selah " was as much as true, certain, excellent. Instance, Ps. iii. 4, " I cried unto the Lord with my voice, and he heard me out of his holy hill. *Selah,*" *i.e.*, It is most certain that the Lord knows the secrets of our hearts, and is the judge of the quick and dead, and will pass most righteous sentence upon us, giving to every man according to his deeds in the flesh, whether good or evil. Ps. lii. 3. " Thou lovest evil more than good ; and lying rather than to speak righteousness. *Selah.*"—that is to say, undeniable, we all confess it, our own experience and sorrows have made us know this, that those who have not the fear of God before their eyes love to speak and do all the mischief they are able against God's people, to *hurt* them rather than *help* them, to wound their innocent reputation rather than preserve it.

3rdly. It was a devout *ejaculation* of the heart and soul unto God, wishing and desiring the *accomplishment* of what was spoken or promised. Instance, Habak. iii. 13.—" Thou wentest forth for the salvation of thy people. *Selah.*" As if he had said, Lord, I beseech thee, evermore go out so to deliver thine anointed. Ps. lv. 17—19. " Evening, and morning, and at noon, will I pray, and cry aloud : and he shall hear my voice. He hath delivered my soul in peace from the battle that was against me ; for there were many with me. God shall hear, and afflict them, even he that abideth of old. *Selah,*" *i.e.*, O Lord, *I entreat thee,* ever bow down an ear unto my humble suit, and rise up against them that rise up against me.

4thly. It denoted their *admiration* at some strange, unusual effect, whether the work of God, or wickedness of man. Ps. lvii. 3. " He shall send from heaven and save me from the reproach of him that would swallow me up. *Selah,*" *i.e.*, Oh, wonderful and admirable goodness of God, that is pleased to send sometimes his angel from heaven, always his mercy and truth, to deliver his poor perplexed servants from them that are too strong and mighty for them, Ps. liv. 3. " Strangers are risen up against me, and oppressors seek after my soul : they have not set God before them. *Selah,*" *i.e.*, Oh, *horrible impiety* and cruelty to hunt after the life of the saints, and cast the God of life and his remembrance behind their backs.

5thly. *Of humiliation and consternation of their mind*, by the consideration of God's incomprehensible majesty, and their own great frailty and misery. Instance, Ps. lxvi. 7. " He ruleth by his power for ever ; his eyes behold the nations : let not the rebellious exalt themselves. *Selah,*" *i.e.*, here is matter of humiliation before the King of all the world, Ps. lxviii. 7, 8. " O God, when thou wentest forth before thy people, when thou didst march through the wilderness. *Selah,*' *i.e.*, my very heart trembled to consider ; I am moved out of my place, to reflect upon that majesty before whom " the earth shook, the heavens also dropped at the presence of God ; even Sinai itself was moved at the presence of God, the God of Israel." Ps. xxxix. 11. "When thou with rebukes dost correct man for iniquity, thou makest his beauty to consume away like a moth : surely every man is vanity. *Selah*." As if he should say, this may humble the proudest heart in the world, and cast him down to the ground.

6thly. *It was a note of Doxology and praising of God* in a special manner, not much unlike, or the very same with this, " For thine is the kingdom, the power and the glory, for ever and ever." As for example, " All the earth shall worship thee, and shall sing unto thee, they shall sing to thy name. *Selah*," Ps. lxvi. 4. " Yea, Lord, in thee will we boast all the day long, and praise thy name for ever. *Selah*," Ps. xliv. 8. " Blessed be the Lord God, the God of Israel, who only doeth wondrous things. And blessed be his glorious name for ever : and let the whole earth be filled with his glory ; so be it, even so be it." Ps. lxxii. 18, 19.—*Edmund Layfielde.*

Verse 6.—" *Man walketh in a vain shew*." I see that we who live are nothing else but images, and a vain shadow.—*Sophocles.*

Verse 6 (first clause).—When in the Bristol election, his competitor died, Burke said, " What shadows we are, and what shadows we pursue."—*William S. Plumer.*

Verse 6.—Every carnal man walks *in a vain shew*, and yet how vain is he of his shew of vanity! He is " *disquieted in vain*," and it is only vanity which disquiets him. He labours all his life for the profit of riches, and yet in death his riches will not profit him. He that views an ox grazing in a fat pasture, concludes that he is but preparing for the day of slaughter.—*William Secker.*

Verse 6.—" *He heapeth up riches*." This is the great foolishness and disease, especially of old age, that the less way a man has to go, he makes the greater provision for it. When the hands are stiff, and fit for no other labour, they are fitted and composed for scraping together.—*Robert Leighton.*

Verse 6.—" *He heapeth up riches*." The Hebrew word rendered, " *He heapeth up*," signifies *to rake together ;* in which there is an allusion to the husbandman's collecting his corn together before he carries it to the barn. The metaphor is elegant, intimating the precariousness of human life, and the vanity of human acquisitions ; which though heaped up together like corn, by one person, may soon become the possession of another.—*Samuel Burder.*

Verse 6.—

> To-morrow, and to-morrow, and to-morrow,
> Creeps in this petty pace from day to day.
> To the last syllable of recorded time ;
> And all our yesterdays have lighted fools
> The way to dusty death. Out, out, brief candle !
> Life's but a walking shadow ; a poor player,
> That struts and frets his hour upon the stage,
> And then is heard no more ; it is a tale
> Told by an idiot, full of sound and fury,
> Signifying nothing.

> *William Shakspeare.*

Verse 6.—The plentiful showers of tears which stand in our eyes when we come from the womb, and when we draw to the tomb, are faithful witnesses of man's vanity. We bid the world " good morrow " with grief, and " good night " with a groan.—*Edmund Layfielde.*

Verse 7.—" *Lord, what wait I for ?* "

> At first her mother earth she holdeth deare,
> And doth embrace the world and worldly things ;
> She flies close by the ground and houers here
> And mounts not up with her celestiall wings.
>
> Yet vnder heauen she cannot light on ought
> That with her heauenly nature doth agree ;
> She cannot rest, she cannot fix her thought,
> She cannot in this world contented bee.
>
> Then as a bee which among weeds doth fall.
> Which seeme sweet flowers with lustre fresh and gay
> She lights on that, and this, and tasteth all,
> But pleased with none, doth rise, and soare away.

So, when the soule finds here no true content,
  And like Noah's doue, can no sure footing take,
She doth returne from whence she first was sent,
  And flies to Him, that first her wings did make.

Sir John Davies.

Verse 7.—

O loose this frame, this knot of man untie,
  That my free soul may use her wing,
Which is now pinioned with mortality,
  As an entangled, hamper'd thing.
What have I left that I should stay and groan ?
  The most of me to heaven is fled ;
My thoughts and joys are all pack'd up and gone,
  And for their old acquaintance plead.

George Herbert.

Verse 7.—" My hope is in thee." Sweet is it that our hope should rest in him who is never shaken ; should abide in him who never changeth ; should bind us to him who can hold us fast to himself, who alone is the full contentment of the soul ; should, as it were, enter into him ; since " *in* him is our being," who is love. —*E. B. Pusey, D.D.,* 1853.

Verse 8.—Make me not the reproach of the foolish." Let not their prosperity and my misery give them occasion to deride and reproach me for my serving of thee and trusting in thee to so little purpose.—*Matthew Pool.*

Verse 8.—" Make me not the reproach of the foolish." Doubt not this ; that of all the bitter agony which will be the portion of the lost soul at that, " Depart, ye cursed," not the least will be the bitter reproaches and derision of those evil spirits who have seduced him to his ruin. " For this morsel of meat to have sold thy birthright ! For the fleshly pleasures of a few days to have bartered thine eternal jewel ! For a few grains of yellow earth to have missed the city with streets of gold, and gates of several pearls ! O fool, beyond all folly ! O madman, beyond all insanity ! Truly we have need to pray with all earnestness, ' *Make me not the reproach of the foolish.' "*—*Origen, quoted by J. M. Neale.*

Verse 9.—" I was dumb, I opened not my mouth ; because thou didst it." See David's carriage here ; it was a patience not constrained, but from satisfaction of spirit : he saw love in his affliction, and that sweetened his soul.—*Joseph Symonds.*

Verse 9.—" I was dumb, I opened not my mouth ; because thou didst it." God is training up his children here. This is the true character of his dealings with them. The education of his saints is the object he has in view. It is training for the kingdom ; it is education for eternity. . . . It is the discipline of love. Every step of it is kindness. There is no wrath nor vengeance in any part of the process. The discipline of the school may be harsh and stern ; but that of the family is love, We are sure of this ; and the consolation which it affords is unutterable. Love will not wrong us. There will be no needless suffering. Were this but kept in mind there would be fewer hard thoughts of God amongst men, even when his strokes are most severe. I know not a better illustration of what the feelings of a saint should be, in the hour of bitterness, than the case of Richard Cameron's father. The aged saint was in prison " for the Word of God, and for the testimony of Jesus Christ." The bleeding head of his martyred son was brought to him by his unfeeling persecutors, and he was asked derisively if he knew it. " I know it, I know it,"— said the father, as he kissed the mangled forehead of his fair-haired son—" it is my son's, my own dear son's ! It is the Lord ! good is the will of the Lord, who cannot wrong me or mine, but who hath made goodness and mercy to follow us all our days."—*Horatius Bonar, in " The Night of Weeping,"* 1847.

Verse 9.—" Because thou didst it." This holy man had a breach made both at his body and spirit at this time ; he was sick and sad ; yet he remembers from whose hand the blow came. Thou, Lord, didst it ; thou, whom I love dearly, and so can take it kindly ; thou whom I have offended, and so take it patiently ; yea, thou, who mightest have cast me into a bed of flames, instead of my bed of sickness, and therefore I accept thy correction thankfully. Thus he catches at the blow without retorting it back upon God by any quarrelling discontented language. —*William Gurnall.*

Verse 9.—" Because thou didst it." We digest not a blow from our equals, but a blow from our king we can well digest. If the King of kings lays his hand on our backs, let us, beloved, lay our hands on our mouths. I am sure this stopped David's mouth from venting fretful speeches. " I held my tongue and said nothing." Why didst thou so, David ? " *Because thou, Lord, didst it ; "* and God gives this testimony of such an one ; that he is a prudent man that keeps silence at an evil time. Amos v. 13.—*Nicholas Estwick, B.D.,* 1644.

Verse 9.—Perkins, in his " *Salve for a Sick Man,"* gives the " last words " of many holy men, among others of Calvin :—" I held my tongue, because thou, Lord, hast done it—I mourned as a dove—Lord, thou grindest me to powder, but it sufficeth me because it is thy hand."

Verse 9.—I wondered once at providence, and called white providence black and unjust, that I should be smothered in a town where no soul will take Christ off my hand. But providence hath another lustre* with God than with my bleared eyes. I proclaim myself a blind body, who knoweth not black and white, in the uncot† course of God's providence. Suppose that Christ should set hell where heaven is and devils up in glory beside the elect angels (which yet cannot be), I would I had a heart to acquiesce in his way, without further dispute. I see that infinite wisdom is the mother of his judgments, and that his ways pass finding out. I cannot learn, but I desire to learn, to bring my thoughts, will, and lusts in under‡ Christ's feet, that he may trample upon them. But, alas ! I am still upon Christ's wrong side.—*Samuel Rutherford.*

Verse 9.—A little girl, in the providence of God, was born deaf and dumb. She was received, and instructed, at an institution established for these afflicted ones. A visitor was one day requested to examine the children thus sadly laid aside from childhood's common joys. Several questions were asked, and quickly answered by means of a slate and pencil. At length the gentleman wrote, " *Why were you born deaf and dumb ? "* A look of anguish clouded for the moment the expressive face of the little girl; but it quickly passed, as she took her slate, and wrote, " *Even so, Father ; for so it seemeth good in thy sight."*—Mrs. Rogers, in " *The Shepherd King."*

Verse 10.—" Remove thy plague away from me : " thy plague and mine ; thine by affliction, mine by passion ; thine because thou didst send it, mine because I endure it ; thine because it comes from thy justice, mine because it answers my injustice ; remit what I have done, and remove what thou hast done. But whosoever laid it on, the Lord will take off.—*Thomas Adams.*

Verse 10.—" Remove," etc. Having first prayed off his sin, he would now pray off his pain, though it less troubled him ; and for ease he repaireth to *Jehovah that healeth,* as well as woundeth. Hosea vi. 1.—*John Trapp.*

Verse 11.—" Thou makest his beauty to consume away like a moth." The meaning may be, As the moth crumbles into dust under the slightest pressure, or the gentlest touch, so man dissolves with equal ease, and vanishes into darkness, under the finger of the Almighty.—*Paxton's Illustrations of Scripture.*

Verse 11.—" Thou makest his beauty to consume away like a moth." Moths I must not omit naming. I once saw some knives, the back bone hafts of which were said to have been half-consumed by them. I also saw the remains of a hair-seated sofa which had been devoured. It is no uncommon thing to find dresses consumed in a single night. In Isaiah li. 6, " wax old " probably refers to a garment that is moth-eaten. So in Psalm vi. 7, and xxxi. 9, " *consumed* " means moth-eaten ; and again in Psalm xxxix. 11.—*John Gadsby.*

Verse 11.—" Like a moth." The moths of the East are very large and beautiful, but short lived. After a few showers these splendid insects may be seen fluttering in every breeze, but the dry weather, and their numerous enemies, soon consign them to the common lot. Thus the beauty of man consumes away like that of this gay rover, dressed in his robes of purple, and scarlet, and green.—*John Kitto.*

Verse 11.—The body of man is as a " garment " to the soul : in this garment sin hath lodged a " moth," which, by degrees, fretteth and weareth away, first, the beauty, then the strength, and, finally, the contexture of its parts. Whoever has watched the progress of a consumption, or any other lingering distemper, nay, the

---

* Shining ; appearance. † Strange. ‡ Close under.

slow and silent devastations of time alone, in the human frame, will need no farther illustration of this just and affecting similitude; but will discern at once the propriety of the reflection which follows upon it.—" *Surely every man is vanity.*" *George Horne.*

Verse 11.—" *Surely every man is vanity.*" What is greatness? Can we predicate it of man, independently of his qualities as an immortal being? or of his actions, independently of principles and motives? Then the glitter of nobility is not superior to the plumage of the peacock; nor the valour of Alexander to the fury of a tiger; nor the sensual delights of Epicurus to those of any animal that roams the forest.—*Ebenezer Porter, D.D., in Lectures on Homiletics*, 1834.

Verse 12.—" *Hear my prayer, O Lord,*" etc. Now, in this prayer of David, we find three things, which are the chief qualifications of all acceptable prayers. The first is *humility*. He humbly confesses his sins, and his own weakness and worthlessness. We are not to put on a stoical, flinty kind of spirit under our affliction, that so we may seem to shun womanish repinings and complaints, lest we run into the other evil, of *despising the hand of God*, but we are to humble our proud hearts, and break our unruly passions. . . . The second qualification of this prayer is, *fervency* and *importunity*, which appears in the elegant gradation of the words, " *Hear my prayer,*" my words; if not that, yet " *Give ear to my cry,*" which is louder; and if that prevail not, yet, " *Hold not thy peace at my tears,*" which is the loudest of all; so David, elsewhere, calls it " *the voice of my weeping.*" . . . The third qualification is *faith*, " He who comes to God must believe that he is, and that he is a rewarder of them that diligently seek him." Heb. xi. 6. And, certainly, as he that comes to God must believe this, so he that believes this, cannot but come to God; and if he be not presently answered, " he that believes makes no haste," he resolves patiently to wait for the Lord, and to go to no other.—*Condensed from Robert Leighton.*

Verse 12.—" *Hold not thy peace at my tears.*" We may, in all humility, plead our heart-breakings and weepings in sense of want of mercies which we crave, and our pantings and faintings after the same.—*Thomas Cobbett.*

Verse 12.—" *For I am a stranger with thee, and a sojourner, as all my fathers were.*" Both in thy judgment expressed (Levit. xxv. 23), and in their own opinion (Heb. xi. 13), Upon which account thou didst take a special care of them, and therefore do so to me also.—*Matthew Pool.*

Verse 12.—" *I am a stranger with thee and a sojourner.*" How settled soever their condition be, yet this is the temper of the saints upon earth—to count themselves but strangers. All men indeed are strangers and sojourners, but the saints do best discern it, and most freely acknowledge it. Wicked men have no firm dwelling upon earth, but that is against their intentions; their inward thought and desire is that they may abide for ever; they are strangers against their wills, their abode is uncertain in the world, and they cannot help it. And pray mark, there are two distinct words used in this case, *strangers* and *sojourners*. A stranger is one that hath his abode in a foreign country, that is not a native and a denizen of the place, though he liveth there, and in opposition to the natives he is called a stranger: as if a Frenchman should live in England, he is a stranger. But a *sojourner* is one that intendeth not to settle, but only passeth through a place, and is in motion travelling homeward. So the children of God in relation to a country of their own in another place, namely, heaven, they are denizens there, but strangers in the world; and they are sojourners and pilgrims in regard of their motion and journey towards their country.—*Thomas Manton.*

Verse 12.—" *A stranger.*" 1. A stranger is one that is absent from his country, and from his father's house: so are we, heaven is our country, God is there, and Christ is there. 2. A stranger in a foreign country is not known, nor valued according to his birth and breeding; so the saints walk up and down in the world like princes in disguise. 3. Strangers are liable to inconveniences, so are godly men in the world. Religion, saith Tertullian, is like a strange plant brought from a foreign country, and doth not agree with the nature of the soil, it thriveth not in the world. 4. A stranger is patient, standeth not for ill usage, and is contented with pilgrims' fare and lodging. We are now abroad, and must expect hardship. 5. A stranger is wary, that he may not give offence, and incur the hatred and displeasure of the natives. 6. A stranger is thankful for the least favour; so we must be thankfully contented with the things God hath bestowed upon us: anything in a strange country is much. 7. A stranger, that hath a journey to go, would pass over it as soon as he can, and so we, who have a journey to heaven desire to be dissolved. 8. A stranger buyeth not such things as he cannot carry with him ; he doth not buy trees, house, household stuff, but jewels and pearls, and such things as are portable. Our great care should be to get the jewels of the covenant, the graces of God's Spirit, those things that will abide with us. 9. A stranger's heart is in his country ; so is a saint's. 10. A stranger is inquisitive after the way, fearing lest he should go amiss, so is a Christian. 11. A stranger provides for his return, as a merchant, that he may return richly laden. So we must appear before God in Sion. What manner of persons ought we to be ? Let us return from our travel well provided.—*Condensed from Thomas Manton.*

Verse 13.—" *O spare me, that I may recover strength, before I go hence, and be no more.*" Man in his corrupt state is like Nebuchadnezzar, he hath a beast's heart, that craves no more than the satisfaction of his sensual appetite ; but when renewed by grace, then his understanding returns to him, by which he is enabled in praying for temporals to elevate his desires to a nobler end. Doth David pray that some farther time may be added to his temporal life ? It is not out of a fond love for this world, but to prepare himself the better for another. Is he comforted with hopes of a longer stay here ? It is not this world's carnal pleasures that kindle this joy in his holy breast, but the advantage that thereby he shall have for praising God in the land of the living. . . . . " *O spare me, that I may recover strength.*" David was not yet recovered out of that sin which had brought him exceeding low as you may perceive, ver. 10, 11. And the good man cannot think of dying with any willingness till his heart be in a holier frame : and for the peace of the gospel, serenity of conscience, and inward joy ; alas ! all unholiness is to it as poison is to the spirits which drink them up.—*William Gurnall.*

Verse 13.—" *O spare me,*" etc. Attachment to life, the feeling cherished by the Psalmist, when he thus appealed to the Sovereign of the universe, varies in its character with the occasions and the sentiments by which it is elicited and confirmed. Take one view of it, and you pronounce it *criminal;* take another, and you pronounce it *innocent;* take a third, and you pronounce it *laudable.* I. Life may inspire a *criminal* attachment, warranting our censure. The most obvious and aggravated case is that in which the attachment has its foundations in the opportunities which life affords, of procuring " the wages of unrighteousness," and " the pleasures of sin." II. Life may inspire an *innocent* attachment, awakening our sympathy . . . . . . Life is a scene in which we often descry a verdant and luxuriant spot, teeming with health, and ease, and harmony, and joy. We have beheld the husbands and the wives whose interwoven regards have, from year to year, alleviated all their afflictions, and heightened all their privileges. We have beheld the parents and the children whose fellowship has yielded them, through the shifting seasons, a daily feast. There are indulgent masters, and faithful servants ; some neighbour-hoods are undisturbed ; some Christian societies are exquisitely attractive ; here and there we have intercourse with those individuals in whom are seen the beauties of high character irradiated by the beams of general prosperity. You would pronounce no censure on a man thus happily connected, were he, when beginning to languish, as one " going the way of all the earth, to cry," " *O spare me, that I may recover strength, before I go hence, and be no more.*" III. The last view which is has been proposed to take of human life, shows that it may inspire a *laudable* attachment, at once challenging our approbation, and urging us to bring our minds under its influence. The language before us admits of being illustrated as the prayer of a *penitent*, a *saint*, and a *philanthropist.* 1. Commend him who pleads for life as a *penitent*, Was it recently that the Holy Spirit first wounded him with the arrows of conviction ? Perhaps, he doubts the source, the quality, and the result, of his powerful feelings. He knows that we may be solemnly impressed, without being converted. There are many considerations which entitle to favourable opinion those who, not having arrived at a view of their moral state, at once evident and encouraging, wish earnestly to live, till grace shall have carried them from victory to victory, and enabled them " to make " their " calling and election sure." Even they may fall from their steadfastness ; and these words, " O spare me, that I may recover my strength," may proceed from the lips of a backslider, once more blushing, trembling, and petitioning to be restored. 2. Commend him, in the next place, who pleads for life, as a *saint.* . . . The distinguished office of pleading, acting, and suffering, for the advancement of the divine honour among the profane, the sensual, the formal, and the worldly is delegated, exclusively, to " the saints which are upon the earth." Yet, surely he whose attachment to life is strongly enhanced by a commission which dooms him to the contradiction of sinners, and defers " the fulness of joy," a saint so magnanimous and devoted, puts forth the expressions of a piety which the very angels are compelled to revere. 3. Commend him, finally, who pleads for life as a *philanthropist.* I refer to the generous *patron,* a man intent on doing good. I would also refer to a fond *parent.* I would now refer to " *a preacher of righteousness,*" " a good minister of Jesus Christ."—*Outline of a sermon entitled " Attachment to Life," preached by Joseph Hughes, M.A., as a Funeral Sermon for Rev. John Owen, M.A.,* 1822.

Verse 13.—May not the very elect and faithful themselves fear the day of judgment, and be far from fetching comfort at it ? I answer, he may. First, at his first conversion and soon after, before he have gotten a full persuasion of the remission of his sins. And again, in some spiritual desertion, when the Lord seems to leave a man to himself, as he did David and others, he may fear to think of the same. And lastly, when he hath fallen into some great sin after he is a strong man in Christ, he may fear death and judgment, and be constrained to pray with Job and David, " *O spare me, that I may recover strength, before I go hence, and be no more.*"—*John Barlow's Sermon,* 1618.

HINTS TO PREACHERS.

Verses 1, 2.—" *I was dumb, etc.*" I. There is a time to be silent. He had been enabled to do this when reproached and unjustly accused by others. He did it for good ; others might attribute it to sullenness, or pride, or timidity, or conscious guilt ; but he did it for good. Breathe upon a polished mirror and it will evaporate and leave it brighter than before ; endeavour to wipe it off, and the mark will remain. II. There is a time to meditate in silence. The greater the silence without, often the greater commotion within. " *His heart was hot.*" The more he thought, the warmer he grew. The fire of pity and compassion, the fire of love, the fire of holy zeal burned within him. III. There is a time to speak. " *Then spake I.*" The time to speak is when the truth is clear and strong in the mind, and the feeling of the truth is burning in the heart. The emotions burst forth as from a volcano. Jer. xx. 8, 9. The language should always be a faithful representation of the mind and the heart.—*G. Rogers, Tutor of the Metropolitan Tabernacle College.*

Verse 2.—There is a sevenford silence. 1. A *stoical* silence. 2. A *politic* silence. 3. A *foolish* silence. 4. A *sullen* silence. 5. A *forced* silence. 6. A *despairing* silence. 7. A *prudent,* a *holy,* a *gracious* silence.—*Thomas Brooks' "Mute Christian."*

Verse 4.—" *Make me to know mine end.*" I. *What we may desire to know about our end.* Not its *date, place, circumstances,* but 1. *Its nature.* Will it be the end of saint or sinner ? 2. *Its certainty.* 3. *Its nearness.* 4. *Its issues.* 5. *Its requirements.* In the shape of attention, preparation, passport. II. *Why ask God to make us know it ?* Because *the knowledge is important, difficult to acquire, and can be effectually imparted by the Lord only.*—*W. Jackson.*

Verse 4.—David prays, I. That he may be enabled continually to keep in view the end of life : all things should be judged by their *end.* " Then understood I their end." Life may be honourable, and cheerful, and virtuous here ; but the *end !* What will it be ? II. That he may be diligent in the performance of all the duties of this life. The measure of his days, how short, how much to be done, how little time to do it in ! III. He prays that he may gain much instruction and benefit from the frailties of life. " *That I may know,*" etc. My frailties may make me more humble, more diligent, while I am able for active service ; more dependent upon divine strength, more patient and submissive to the divine will, more ripe for heaven.—*G. Rogers.*

Verse 5 (*last clause*).—Man is vanity, *i.e.,* he is mortal, he is mutable. Observe how emphatically this truth is expressed here. I. *Every* man is vanity, without exception, high and low, rich and poor. II. He is so at his *best estate ;* when he is young, and strong, and healthful, in wealth and honour, etc.   III. He is *altogether vanity,* as vain as you can imagine. IV. *Verily* he is so. V. *Selah* is annexed, as a note commanding observation.—*Matthew Henry.*

Verse 6.—The vanity of man, as mortal, is here instanced in three things, and the vanity of each shown. I. The vanity of our joys and honours : " *Surely every man walketh in a vain show.*" II. The vanity of our griefs and fears : " *Surely they are disquieted in vain.*" III. The vanity of our cares and toils : " *He heapeth up riches, and knoweth not who shall gather them.*"—*Matthew Henry.*

Verse 6.—The world's trinity consists, 1. In fruitless honours : what appears to them to be substantial honours are but " *a vain show.*" 2. In needless cares. " *They are disquieted in vain.*" Imaginary cares are substituted for real ones. 3. In useless riches ; such as yield no lasting satisfaction to themselves, or in their descent to others.—*G. Rogers.*

Verse 7.—" *What wait I for ?* " 1. *For what salvation as a sinner ?* Of works or grace—from Sinai or Calvary. 2. *For what consolation as a sufferer ?* Earthly or heavenly ? 3. *For what supply as a suppliant ?* Meagre or bountiful ? Present or future ? 4. *For what communication as a servant ?* Miraculous or ordinary ? Pleasing or unacceptable ? 5. *For what instruction as a pupil ?* Mental or spiritual ? Elating or humbling ? Ornamental or useful ? 6. *For what inheritance as a heir ?* Sublunary or celestial ?—*W. Jackson.*

Verse 7.—I. An urgent occasion. " *And now Lord,*" etc. There are seasons that should lead us specially to look up to God, and say, " *Now, Lord.*" II. A devout exclamation, " *Now, Lord, what wait I for ?*" Where is my expectation ? Where my confidence ? To whom shall I look ? I am nothing, the world is nothing, all earthly sources of confidence and consolation fail : " *What wait I for ?* " In life, in death, in a dying world, in a coming judgment, in an eternity at hand ; what is it that I need ?—*G. Rogers.*

Verse 8.—I. Prayer should be *general :* " *Deliver me from all my transgressions.*" We often need anew to say, " God be merciful to me a sinner." Afflictions should remind us of our sins. If we pray to be delivered from all transgressions, we are sure to be delivered from the one for which affliction was sent. II. Prayer should be *particular :* " *Make me not the reproach of the foolish.*" Suffer me not so to speak or show impatience in affliction as to give occasion even to the foolish to blaspheme. The thought that many watch for our halting should be a preservative from sin.— *G. Rogers.*

Verse 9.—I. The *occasion* referred to. " *I was dumb,*" etc. We are not told what the particular trial was, that each one may apply it to his own affliction, and because all are to be viewed in the same light. II. The *conduct* of the Psalmist upon that particular occasion : " *I opened not my mouth.*" 1. Not in anger and rebellion against God in murmurs or complaints. 2. Not in impatience, **or** complaining, or angry feelings against men. III. The *reason* he assigns for this conduct : " *Because thou didst it.*"—*G. Rogers.*

Verse 10.—I. *Afflictions are sent by God.* " *Thy strokes.*" They are strokes of *his* hand, not of the rod of the law, but of the shepherd's rod. Every affliction is *his* stroke. II. *Afflictions are removed by God.* " *Remove.*" He asks not for miracles, but that God in his own way, in the use of natural means, would interpose for his deliverance. We should seek his blessing upon the means employed for our deliverance both by ourselves and others. " *Cause to remove,*" etc. III. *Afflictions have their end from God.* " *I am consumed by the conflict,*" etc. God has a controversy with his people. It is a conflict between his will and their wills. The Psalmist owns himself conquered and subdued in the struggle. We should be more anxious that this end should be accomplished than that the affliction should be removed, and when this is accomplished the affliction will be removed.—*G. Rogers.*

Verse 10.—I. The *cause* of our trials : " *for iniquity.*" Oh, this trial is come to take away my comforts, my peace of mind, and the divine smile ! No, this is all the fruit to take away their sin—the dross, none of the gold—sin, nothing but sin. II. The *effect* of our trials. All that he counted desirable in this life, but is not for his real good, is " *consumed.*" His robes which are beautiful in men's esteem are moth-eaten, but the robe of righteousness upon his soul cannot decay. III. The *design* of our trials. They are not penal inflictions, but friendly *rebukes* and fatherly *corrections.* On Christ our Surety the penal consequences were laid, upon us their paternal chastisements only. IV. The *reasonableness* of our trials. " *Surely every man is vanity.*" How in a world like this could any expect to be exempt from trials ! The world is the same to the Christian as before, and his body is the same. He has a converted soul in an unconverted body, and how can he escape the external ills of life ?—*G. Rogers.*

Verse 12.—David pleads the good impressions made upon him by his affliction. I. It had set him a weeping. II. It had set him a praying. III. It had helped to wean him from the world.—*Matthew Henry.*

Verse 12 (last clause).—Am I a stranger and a sojourner with God ? Let me realise, let me exemplify the condition. I. Let me look for *the treatment* such characters commonly meet with. II. And surely if any of my own nation be near me, I shall *be intimate with them.* III. Let me *not be entangled* in the affairs of this life. IV. Let my affection be *set on things that are above,* and my conversation be always *in heaven.* V. Let me be *not impatient for home ;* but *prizing it.*—*W. Jay.*

Verse 13.—I. The *subject* of his petition—not that he may escape death and live always in this life, because he knows that he must go hence ; but 1. That he may be recovered from his afflictions ; and, 2. That he may continue longer in this life. Such a prayer is lawful when offered in submission to the will of God. II. The *reasons* for this petition. 1. That he may remove by his future life the calumnies that had been heaped upon him. 2. That he may have brighter evidences of his interest in the divine favour. 3. That he may become a blessing to others, his family and nation. 4. That he might have greater peace and comfort in death ; and, 5. That he might " have an entrance ministered more abundantly," etc.— *G. Rogers.*

PSALM XL.

TITLE.—To the Chief Musician. *Well might so exceedingly precious a Psalm be specially committed to the most skilled of the sacred musicians. The noblest music should be made tributary to a subject so incomparable. The dedication shows that the song was intended for public worship, and was not a merely personal hymn, as its being in the first person singular might lead us to suppose.* A Psalm of David. *This is conclusive as to the authorship : lifted by the Holy Spirit into the region of prophecy, David was honoured thus to write concerning a far greater than himself.*

SUBJECT.—*Jesus is evidently here, and although it might not be a violent wresting of language to see both David and his Lord, both Christ and the church, the double comment might involve itself in obscurity, and therefore we shall let the sun shine even though this should conceal the stars. Even if the New Testament were not so express upon it, we should have concluded that David spoke of our Lord in verses* 6—9, *but the apostle in Heb.* x. 5—9, *puts all conjecture out of court, and confines the meaning to Him who came into the world to do the Father's will.*

DIVISION.—*From verses* 1—3, *is a personal thanksgiving, followed by a general declaration of Jehovah's goodness to his saints,* 4, 5. *In verses* 6—10, *we have an avowal of dedication to the Lord's will ; verses* 11—17, *contain a prayer for deliverance from pressing trouble, and for the overthrow of enemies.*

EXPOSITION.

I WAITED patiently for the LORD ; and he inclined unto me, and heard my cry.

2 He brought me up also out of an horrible pit, out of the miry clay, and set my feet upon a rock, *and* established my goings.

3 And he hath put a new song in my mouth, *even* praise unto our God : many shall see *it*, and fear, and shall trust in the LORD.

1. "*I waited patiently for the Lord.*" Patient waiting upon God was a special characteristic of our Lord Jesus. Impatience never lingered in his heart, much less escaped his lips. All through his agony in the garden, his trial of cruel mockings before Herod and Pilate, and his passion on the tree, he waited in omnipotence of patience. No glance of wrath, no word of murmuring, no deed of vengeance came from God's patient Lamb ; he waited and waited on ; was patient, and patient to perfection, far excelling all others who have according to their measure glorified God in the fires. Job on the dunghill does not equal Jesus on the cross. The Christ of God wears the imperial crown among the patient. Did the Only Begotten wait, and shall we be petulant and rebellious ? "*And he inclined unto me, and heard my cry.*" Neither Jesus the head, nor any one of the members of his body, shall ever wait upon the Lord in vain. Mark the figure of inclining, as though the suppliant cried out of the lowest depression, and condescending love stooped to hear his feeble moans. What a marvel is it that our Lord should have to cry as we do, and wait as we do, and should receive the Father's help after the same process of faith and pleading as must be gone through by ourselves ! The Saviour's prayers among the midnight mountains and in Gethsemane expound this verse. The Son of David was brought very low, but he rose to victory ; and here he teaches us how to conduct our conflicts so as to succeed after the same glorious pattern of triumph. Let us arm ourselves with the same mind ; and panoplied in patience, armed with prayer, and girt with faith, let us maintain the Holy War.

2. "*He brought me up also out of an horrible pit.*" When our Lord bore in his own person the terrible curse which was due to sin, he was so cast down as to be like a prisoner in a deep, dark, fearful dungeon, amid whose horrible glooms the captive heard a noise as of rushing torrents, while overhead resounded the tramp of furious foes. Our Lord in his anguish was like a captive in the *oubliettes*, forgotten of all mankind, immured amid horror, darkness, and desolation. Yet the Lord Jehovah made him to ascend from all his abasement ; he retraced his steps from that deep hell of anguish into which he had been cast as our substitute. He who thus delivered our surety *in extremis*, will not fail to liberate us from our far

lighter griefs. *" Out of the miry clay."* The sufferer was as one who cannot find a foothold, but slips and sinks. The figure indicates not only positive misery as in the former figure, but the absence of solid comfort by which sorrow might have been rendered supportable. Once give a man good foothold, and a burden is greatly lightened, but to be loaded and to be placed on slimy, slippery clay, is to be tried doubly. Reader, with humble gratitude, adore the dear Redeemer who, for thy sake, was deprived of all consolation while surrounded with every form of misery ; remark his gratitude at being upborne amid his arduous labours and sufferings, and if thou too hast experienced the divine help, be sure to join thy Lord in this song. *" And set my feet upon a rock, and established my goings."* The Redeemer's work is done. He reposes on the firm ground of his accomplished engagements ; he can never suffer again ; for ever does he reign in glory. What a comfort to know that Jesus our Lord and Saviour stands on a sure foundation in all that he is and does for us, and his goings forth in love are not liable to be cut short by failure in years to come, for God has fixed him firmly. He is for ever and eternally able to save unto the uttermost them that come unto God by him, seeing that in the highest heavens he ever liveth to make intercession for them. Jesus is the true Joseph taken from the pit to be Lord of all. It is something more than a " sip of sweetness " to remember that if we are cast like our Lord into the lowest pit of shame and sorrow, we shall by faith rise to stand on the same elevated, sure, and everlasting rock of divine favour and faithfulness.

3. *" And he hath put a new song in my mouth, even praise unto our God."* At the passover, before his passion, our Lord sang one of the grand old Psalms of praise ; but what is the music of his heart now, in the midst of his redeemed ! What a song is that in which his glad heart for ever leads the chorus of the elect ! Not Miriam's tabour nor Moses' triumphant hymn o'er Mizraim's chivalry can for a moment rival that ever new and exulting song. Justice magnified and grace victorious ; hell subdued and heaven glorified ; death destroyed and immortality established ; sin o'erthrown and righteousness resplendent ; what a theme for a hymn in that day when our Lord drinketh the red wine new with us all in our heavenly Father's kingdom ! Even on earth, and before his great passion, he foresaw the joy which was set before him, and was sustained by the prospect. *" Our God."* The God of Jesus, the God of Israel, " my God and your God." How will *we* praise him, but, ah ! Jesus will be the chief player on our stringed instruments ; he will lead the solemn hallelujah which shall go up from the sacramental host redeemed by blood. *" Many shall see it, and fear, and shall trust in the Lord."* A multitude that no man can number shall see the griefs and triumphs of Jesus, shall tremble because of their sinful rejection of him, and then through grace shall receive faith and become trusters in Jehovah. Here is our Lord's reward. Here is the assurance which makes preachers bold and workers persevering. Reader, are you one among the many ? Note the way of salvation, a sight, a fear, a trust ! Do you know what these mean by possessing and practising them in your own soul ? Trusting in the Lord is the evidence, nay, the essence of salvation. He who is a true believer is evidently redeemed from the dominion of sin and Satan.

4 Blessed *is* that man that maketh the LORD his trust, and respecteth not the proud, nor such as turn aside to lies.

5 Many, O LORD my God, *are* thy wonderful works *which* thou hast done, and thy thoughts *which* are to us-ward : they cannot be reckoned up in order unto thee : *if* I would declare and speak *of them*, they are more than can be numbered.

4. *" Blessed."* This is an exclamation similar to that of the first Psalm, " Oh, the happiness of the man." God's blessings are emphatic, " I wot that he whom thou blessest is blessed," indeed and in very truth. *" Is that man that maketh the Lord his trust."* Faith obtaineth promises. A simple, single-eyed confidence in God is the sure mark of blessedness. A man may be as poor as Lazarus, as hated as Mordecai, as sick as Hezekiah, as lonely as Elijah, but while his hand of faith can keep its hold on God, none of his outward afflictions can prevent his being numbered among the blessed : but the wealthiest and most prosperous man who has no faith is accursed, be he who he may. *" And respecteth not the proud."* The proud expect all men to bow down and do them reverence, as if the worship of the golden calves were again set up in Israel ; but believing men are too noble to honour

mere money-bags, or cringe before bombastic dignity. The righteous pay their respect to humble goodness, rather than to inflated self-consequence. Our Lord Jesus was in this our bright example. No flattery of kings and great ones ever fell from his lips ; he gave no honour to dishonourable men. The haughty were never his favourites. "*Nor such as turn aside to lies.*" Heresies and idolatries are lies, and so are avarice, worldliness, and pleasure-seeking. Woe to those who follow such deceptions. Our Lord was ever both the truth and the lover of truth, and the father of lies had no part in him. We must never pay deference to apostates, time-servers, and false teachers ; they are an ill leaven, and the more we purge ourselves of them the better ; they are blessed whom God preserves from all error in creed and practice. Judged by this verse, many apparently happy persons must be the reverse of blessed, for anything in the shape of a purse, a fine equipage, or a wealthy establishment, commands their reverence, whether the owner be a rake or a saint, an idiot or a philosopher. Verily, were the arch-fiend of hell to start a carriage and pair, and live like a lord, he would have thousands who would court his acquaintance.

5. "*Many, O Lord my God, are thy wonderful works which thou hast done.*" Creation, providence, and redemption, teem with wonders as the sea with life. Our special attention is called by this passage to the marvels which cluster around the cross and flash from it. The accomplished redemption achieves many ends, and compasses a variety of designs ; the outgoings of the atonement are not to be reckoned up, the influences of the cross reach further than the beams of the sun. Wonders of grace beyond all enumeration take their rise from the cross ; adoption, pardon, justification, and a long chain of godlike miracles of love proceed from it. Note that our Lord here speaks of the Lord as "my God." The man Christ Jesus claimed for himself and us a covenant relationship with Jehovah. Let our interest in our God be ever to us our peculiar treasure. "*And thy thoughts which are to us-ward.*" The divine thoughts march with the divine acts, for it is not according to God's wisdom to act without deliberation and counsel. All the divine thoughts are good and gracious towards his elect. God's thoughts of love are very many, very wonderful very practical ! Muse on them, dear reader ; no sweeter subject ever occupied your mind. God's thoughts of you are many, let not yours be few in return. "*They cannot be reckoned up in order unto thee.*" Their sum is so great as to forbid alike analysis and numeration. Human minds fail to measure, or to arrange in order, the Lord's ways and thoughts ; and it must always be so, for he hath said, "As the heavens are higher than the earth, so are my ways higher than your ways, and my thoughts than your thoughts." No maze to lose oneself in like the labyrinth of love. How sweet to be outdone, overcome and overwhelmed by the astonishing grace of the Lord our God ! "*If I would declare and speak of them,*" and surely this should be the occupation of my tongue at all seasonable opportunities, "*they are more than can be numbered ;*" far beyond all human arithmetic they are multiplied ; thoughts from all eternity, thoughts of my fall, my restoration, my redemption, my conversion, my pardon, my upholding, my perfecting, my eternal reward ; the list is too long for writing, and the value of the mercies too great for estimation. Yet, if we cannot show forth all the works of the Lord, let us not make this an excuse for silence ; for our Lord, who is in this our best example, often spake of the tender thoughts of the great Father.

6 Sacrifice and offering thou didst not desire ; mine ears hast thou opened : burnt offering and sin offering hast thou not required.

7 Then said I, Lo, I come : in the volume of the book *it is* written of me.

8 I delight to do thy will, O my God : yea, thy law *is* within my heart.

9 I have preached righteousness in the great congregation : lo, I have not refrained my lips, O LORD, thou knowest.

10 I have not hid thy righteousness within my heart ; I have declared thy faithfulness and thy salvation : I have not concealed thy lovingkindness and thy truth from the great congregation.

6. Here we enter upon one of the most wonderful passages in the whole of the Old Testament, a passage in which the incarnate Son of God is seen not through a glass darkly, but as it were face to face. "*Sacrifice and offering thou didst not desire.*" In themselves considered, and for their own sakes, the Lord saw nothing

satisfactory in the various offerings of the ceremonial law. Neither the victim pouring forth its blood, nor the fine flour rising in smoke from the altar, could yield content to Jehovah's mind ; he cared not for the flesh of bulls or of goats, neither had he pleasure in corn and wine, and oil. Typically these offerings had their worth, but when Jesus, the Antitype, came into the world, they ceased to be of value, as candles are of no estimation when the sun has arisen. *" Mine ears hast thou opened."* Our Lord was quick to hear and perform his Father's will ; his ears were as if excavated down to his soul ; they were not closed up like Isaac's wells, which the Philistines filled up, but clear passages down to the fountains of his soul. The prompt obedience of our Lord is here the first idea. There is, however, no reason whatever to reject the notion that the digging of the ear here intended may refer to the boring of the ear of the servant, who refused out of love to his master to take his liberty at the year of jubilee ; his perforated ear, the token of perpetual service, is a true picture of our blessed Lord's fidelity to his Father's business, and his love to his Father's children. Jesus irrevocably gave himself up to be the servant of servants for our sake and God's glory. The Septuagint, from which Paul quoted, has translated this passage, " A body hast thou prepared me : " how this reading arose it is not easy to imagine, but since apostolical authority has sanctioned the variation, we accept it as no mistake, but as an instance of various readings equally inspired. In any case, the passage represents the Only Begotten as coming into the world equipped for service ; and in a real and material body, by actual life and death, putting aside all the shadows of the Mosaic law. *" Burnt offering and sin offering hast thou not required."* Two other forms of offering are here mentioned ; tokens of gratitude and sacrifices for sin as typically presented are set aside ; neither the general nor the private offerings are any longer demanded. What need of mere emblems when the substance itself is present ? We learn from this verse that Jehovah values far more the obedience of the heart than all the imposing performances of ritualistic worship ; and that our expiation from sin comes not to us as the result of an elaborate ceremonial, but as the effect of our great Substitute's obedience to the will of Jehovah.

7. *" Then said I."* That is to say, when it was clearly seen that man's misery could not be remedied by sacrifices and offerings. It being certain that the mere images of atonement, and the bare symbols of propitiation were of no avail, the Lord Jesus, *in propriâ persona,* intervened. O blessed " then said I." Lord, ever give us to hear and feed on such living words as these, so peculiarly and personally thine own. *" Lo, I come."* Behold, O heavens, and thou earth, and ye places under the earth ! Here is something worthy of your intensest gaze. Sit ye down and watch with earnestness, for the invisible God comes in the likeness of sinful flesh, and as an infant the Infinite hangs at a virgin's breast ! Immanuel did not send but *come ;* he came in his own personality, in all that constituted his essential self he came forth from the ivory palaces to the abodes of misery ; he came promptly at the destined hour ; he came with sacred alacrity as one freely offering himself. *" In the volume of the book it is written of me."* In the eternal decree it is thus recorded. The mystic roll of predestination which providence gradually unfolds, contained within it, to the Saviour's knowledge, a written covenant, that in the fulness of time the divine I should descend to earth to accomplish a purpose which hecatombs of bullocks and rams could not achieve. What a privilege to find our names written in the book of life, and what an honour, since the name of Jesus heads the page ! Our Lord had respect to his ancient covenant engagements, and herein he teaches us to be scrupulously just in keeping our word ; have we so promised, is it so written in the book of remembrance ? then let us never be defaulters.

8. *" I delight to do thy will, O my God."* Our blessed Lord alone could completely do the will of God. The law is too broad for such poor creatures as we are to hope to fulfil it to the uttermost : but Jesus not only did the Father's will, but found a delight therein ; from old eternity he had desired the work set before him ; in his human life he was straitened till he reached the baptism of agony in which he magnified the law, and even in Gethsemane itself he chose the Father's will, and set aside his own. Herein is the essence of obedience, namely, in the soul's cheerful devotion to God : and our Lord's obedience, which is our righteousness, is in no measure lacking in this eminent quality. Notwithstanding his measureless griefs, our Lord found delight in his work, and for " the joy that was set before him he endured the cross, despising the shame." *" Yea, thy law is within my heart."*

No outward, formal devotion was rendered by Christ; his heart was in his work, holiness was his element, the Father's will his meat and drink. We must each of us be like our Lord in this, or we shall lack the evidence of being his disciples. Where there is no heart work, no pleasure, no delight in God's law, there can be no acceptance. Let the devout reader adore the Saviour for the spontaneous and hearty manner in which he undertook the great work of our salvation.

9. "*I have preached righteousness in the great congregation.*" The purest morality and the highest holiness were preached by Jesus. Righteousness divine was his theme. Our Lord's whole life was a sermon, eloquent beyond compare, and it is heard each day by myriads. Moreover, he never shunned in his ministry to declare the whole counsel of God; God's great plan of righteousness he plainly set forth. He taught openly in the temple, and was not ashamed to be a faithful and a true witness. He was the great evangelist; the master of itinerant preachers; the head of the clan of open-air missionaries. O servants of the Lord, hide not your lights, but reveal to others what your God has revealed to you; and especially by your lives testify for holiness, be champions for the right, both in word and deed. "*Lo, I have not refrained my lips, O Lord, thou knowest.*" Never either from love of ease, or fear of men, did the Great Teacher's lips become closed. He was instant in season and out of season. The poor listened to him, and princes heard his rebuke; Publicans rejoiced at him, and Pharisees raged, but to them both he proclaimed the truth from heaven. It is well for a tried believer when he can appeal to God and call him to witness that he has not been ashamed to bear witness for him; for rest assured if we are not ashamed to confess our God he will never be ashamed to own us. Yet what a wonder is here, that the Son of God should plead just as we plead, and urge just such arguments as would befit the mouths of his diligent ministers! How truly is he "made like unto his brethren."

10. "*I have not hid thy righteousness within my heart.*" On the contrary, "Never man spake like this man." God's divine plan of making men righteous was well known to him, and he plainly taught it. What was in our great Master's heart he poured forth in holy eloquence from his lips. The doctrine of righteousness by faith he spake with great simplicity of speech. Law and gospel equally found in him a clear expositor. "*I have declared thy faithfulness and thy salvation.*" Jehovah's fidelity to his promises and his grace in saving believers were declared by the Lord Jesus on many occasions, and are blessedly blended in the gospel which he came to preach. God, faithful to his own character, law and threatenings, and yet saving sinners, is a peculiar revelation of the gospel. God faithful to the saved ones evermore is the joy of the followers of Christ Jesus. "*I have not concealed thy lovingkindness and thy truth from the great congregation.*" The tender as well as the stern attributes of God, our Lord Jesus fully unveiled. Concealment was far from the Great Apostle of our profession. Cowardice he never exhibited, hesitancy never weakened his language. He who as a child of twelve years spake in the temple among the doctors, and afterwards preached to five thousand at Gennesaret, and to the vast crowds at Jerusalem on that great day, the last day of the feast, was always ready to proclaim the name of the Lord, and could never be charged with unholy silence. He could be dumb when so the prophecy demanded and patience suggested, but otherwise, preaching was his meat and his drink, and he kept back nothing which would be profitable to his disciples. This in the day of his trouble, according to this Psalm, he used as a plea for divine aid. He had been faithful to his God, and now begs the Lord to be faithful to him. Let every dumb professor, tongue-tied by sinful shame, bethink himself how little he will be able to plead after this fashion in the day of his distress.

11 Withhold not thou thy tender mercies from me, O Lord: let thy lovingkindness and thy truth continually preserve me.

12 For innumerable evils have compassed me about: mine iniquities have taken hold upon me, so that I am not able to look up; they are more than the hairs of mine head: therefore my heart faileth me.

13 Be pleased, O Lord, to deliver me: O Lord, make haste to help me.

14 Let them be ashamed and confounded together that seek after my soul to destroy it; let them be driven backward and put to shame that wish me evil.

15 Let them be desolate for a reward of their shame that say unto me, Aha, aha.

16 Let all those that seek thee rejoice and be glad in thee : let such as love thy salvation say continually, The LORD be magnified.

17 But I *am* poor and needy ; *yet* the Lord thinketh upon me : thou *art* my help and my deliverer ; make no tarrying, O my God.

11. *" Withhold not thou thy tender mercies from me, O Lord."* Alas ! these were to be for awhile withheld from our Lord while on the accursed tree, but meanwhile in his great agony he seeks for gentle dealing ; and the coming of the angel to strengthen him was a clear answer to his prayer. He had been blessed aforetime in the desert, and now at the entrance of the valley of the shadow of death, like a true, trustful, and experienced man, he utters a holy, plaintive desire for the tenderness of heaven. He had not withheld his testimony to God's truth, now in return he begs his Father not to withhold his compassion. This verse might more correctly be read as a declaration of his confidence that help would not be refused ; but whether we view this utterance as the cry of prayer, or the avowal of faith, in either case it is instructive to us who take our suffering Lord for an example, and it proves to us how thoroughly he was made like unto his brethren. *" Let thy lovingkindness and thy truth continually preserve me."* He had preached both of these, and now he asks for an experience of them, that he might be kept in the evil day and rescued from his enemies and his afflictions. Nothing endears our Lord to us more than to hear him thus pleading with strong crying and tears to him who was able to save. O Lord Jesus, in our nights of wrestling we will remember thee.

12. *" For innumerable evils have compassed me about."* On every side he was beset with evils ; countless woes environed the great Substitute for our sins. Our sins were innumerable, and so were his griefs. There was no escape for us from our iniquities, and there was no escape for him from the woes which we deserved. From every quarter evils accumulated about the blessed One, although in his heart evil found no place. *" Mine iniquities have taken hold upon me, so that I am not able to look up."* He had no sin, but sins were laid on him, and he took them as if they were his. *"* He was made sin for us." The transfer of sin to the Saviour was real, and produced in him as man the horror which forbade him to look into the face of God, bowing him down with crushing anguish and woe intolerable. O my soul, what would thy sins have done for thee eternally if the Friend of sinners had not condescended to take them all upon himself ? Oh, blessed Scripture ! *"* The Lord hath made to meet upon him the iniquity of us all." Oh, marvellous depth of love, which could lead the perfectly immaculate to stand in the sinner's place, and bear the horror of great trembling which sin must bring upon those conscious of it. *" They are more than the hairs of mine head : therefore my heart faileth me."* The pains of the divine penalty were beyond compute, and the Saviour's soul was so burdened with them, that he was sore amazed, and very heavy even unto a sweat of blood. His strength was gone, his spirits sank, he was in an agony.

> " Came at length the dreadful night ;
> Vengeance with its iron rod
> Stood, and with collected might
> Bruised the harmless Lamb of God.
> See, my soul, thy Saviour see
> Prostrate in Gethsemane !
>
> There my God bore all my guilt,
> This through grace can be believed ;
> But the horrors which he felt
> Are too vast to be conceived.
> None can penetrate through thee,
> Doleful, dark Gethsemane !
>
> Sins against a holy God ;
> Sins against his righteous laws ;
> Sins against his love, his blood ;
> Sins against his name and cause ;
> Sins immense as is the sea—
> Hide me, O Gethsemane ! "

13. *" Be pleased, O Lord, to deliver me : O Lord, make haste to help me."* How touching ! How humble ! How plaintive ! The words thrill us as we think that after this sort our Lord and Master prayed. His petition is not so much that the cup should pass away undrained, but that he should be sustained while drinking it, and set free from its power at the first fitting moment. He seeks deliverance and help ; and he entreats that the help may not be slow in coming ; this is after the manner of our pleadings. Is it not ? Note, reader, how our Lord was heard in that he feared, for there was after Gethsemane a calm endurance which made the fight as glorious as the victory.

14. *"Let them be ashamed and confounded together that seek after my soul to destroy it."* Whether we read this as a prayer or a prophecy it matters not, for the powers of sin, and death, and hell, may well be ashamed as they see the result of their malice for ever turned against themselves. It is to the infinite confusion of Satan that his attempt to destroy the Saviour destroyed himself ; the diabolical conclave who plotted in council are now all alike put to shame, for the Lord Jesus has met them at all points, and turned all their wisdom into foolishness. *" Let them be driven backward and put to shame that wish me evil."* It is even so ; the hosts of darkness are utterly put to the rout, and made a theme for holy derision for ever and ever. How did they gloat over the thought of crushing the seed of the woman ! but the Crucified has conquered, the Nazarene has laughed them to scorn, the dying Son of Man has become the death of death and hell's destruction. For ever blessed be his name.

15. *" Let them be desolate,"* or amazed ; even as Jesus was desolate in his agony, so let his enemies be in their despair when he defeats them. The desolation caused in the hearts of evil spirits and evil men by envy, malice, chagrin, disappointment, and despair, shall be a fit recompense for their cruelty to the Lord when he was in their hands. *" For a reward of their shame that say unto me, Aha, aha."* Did the foul fiend insult over our Lord ? Behold how shame is now his reward ! Do wicked men to-day pour shame upon the name of the Redeemer ? Their desolation shall avenge him of his adversaries ! Jesus is the gentle Lamb to all who seek mercy through his blood ; but let despisers beware, for he is the Lion of the tribe of Judah, and *" who shall rouse him up ? "* The Jewish rulers exulted and scornfully said, *" Aha, aha ; "* but when the streets of Jerusalem ran like rivers deep with gore, *" and the temple was utterly consumed,"* then their house was left unto them desolate, and the blood of the last of the prophets, according to their own desire, came upon themselves and upon their children. O ungodly reader, if such a person glance over this page, beware of persecuting Christ and his people, for God will surely avenge his own elect. Your *" ahas "* will cost you dear. It is hard for you to kick against the pricks.

16. *" Let all those that seek thee, rejoice and be glad in thee."* We have done with Ebal and turn to Gerizim. Here our Lord pronounces benedictions on his people. Note who the blessed objects of his petitions are : not all men, but some men, *" I pray for them, I pray not for the world."* He pleads for seekers : the lowest in the kingdom, the babes of the family ; those who have true desires, longing prayers, and consistent endeavours after God. Let seeking souls pluck up heart when they hear of this. What riches of grace, that in his bitterest hour Jesus should remember the lambs of the flock ! And what does he entreat for them ? it is that they may be doubly glad, intensely happy, emphatically joyful, for such the repetition of terms implies. Jesus would have all seekers made happy by finding what they seek after, and by winning peace through his grief. As deep as were his sorrows, so high would he have their joys. He groaned that we might sing, and was covered with a bloody sweat that we might be anointed with the oil of gladness. *" Let such as love thy salvation say continually, The Lord be magnified."* Another result of the Redeemer's passion is the promotion of the glory of God by those who gratefully delight in his salvation. Our Lord's desire should be our directory ; we love with all our hearts his great salvation, let us then, with all our tongues proclaim the glory of God which is resplendent therein. Never let his praises cease. As the heart is warm with gladness let it incite the tongue to perpetual praise. If we cannot do what we would for the spread of the kingdom, at least let us desire and pray for it. Be it ours to make God's glory the chief end of every breath and pulse. The suffering Redeemer regarded the consecration of his people to the service of heaven as a grand result of his atoning death ; it is the joy which was set before him ; that God is glorified is the reward of the Saviour's travail.

17. *" But I am poor and needy."*—The man of sorrows closes with another appeal, based upon his affliction and poverty. *" Yet the Lord thinketh upon me."* Sweet was this solace to the holy heart of the great sufferer. The Lord's thoughts of us are a cheering subject of meditation, for they are ever kind and never cease. His disciples forsook him, and his friends forgat him, but Jesus knew that Jehovah never turned away his heart from him, and this upheld him in the hour of need. *" Thou art my help and my deliverer."* His unmoved confidence stayed itself alone on God. O that all believers would imitate more fully their great Apostle and High Priest in his firm reliance upon God, even when afflictions abounded and the light was veiled. *" Make no tarrying, O my God."* The peril was imminent, the need urgent, the suppliant could not endure delay, nor was he made to wait, for the angel came to strengthen, and the brave heart of Jesus rose up to meet the foe.

Lord Jesus, grant that in all our adversities we may possess like precious faith, and be found like thee, more than conquerors.

EXPLANATORY NOTES AND QUAINT SAYINGS.

Whole Psalm.—*David's Psalm,* or, *a Psalm of David ;* but David's name is here set first, which elsewhere commonly is last : or, *A Psalm concerning David,* that is, *Christ,* who is called *David* in the prophets : Hos. iii. 5 ; Jer. xxx. 9 ; Ezek. xxxiv. 23, and xxxii. 24. Of him this Psalm entreateth as the apostle teacheth, Heb. x. 5, 6, etc.—*Henry Ainsworth.*

Whole Psalm.—It is plain, from verses 6—8 of this Psalm, compared with Heb. x. 5, that the prophet is speaking in the person of Christ, who, 1—5, celebrateth the deliverance wrought for his mystical body, the church, by his resurrection from the grave, effecting that of his members from the guilt and dominion of sin ; for the abolition of which he declareth, 6—8, the inefficacy of the legal sacrifices, and mentioneth his own inclination to do the will of his Father, and 9, 10, to preach righteousness to the world. 11—13. He representeth himself as praying, while under his sufferings, for his own, and his people's salvation ; he foretelleth, 14, 15, the confusion and desolation of his enemies, and, 16, the joy and thankfulness of his disciples and servants ; for the speedy accomplishment of which, 17, he preferreth a petition.—*George Horne.*

Verse 1.—*" I waited patiently for the Lord : and he inclined unto me, and heard my cry."* I see that the Lord, suppose he drifteth and delayeth the effect of his servant's prayer, and granteth not his desire at the first, yet he heareth him. I shall give a certain argument, whereby thou may know that the Lord heareth thee, suppose he delay the effect of thy prayers. Continuest thou in prayer ? Hast thou this strength given thee to persevere in suiting * anything ? Thou may be assured he heareth ; for this is one sure argument that he heareth thee, for naturallie our impatience carrieth us to desperation ; our suddenness is so great, speciallie in spiritual troubles, that we cannot continue in suiting. When thou, therefore, continues in suiting, thou may be sure that this strength is furnished of God, and cometh from heaven, and if thou have strength he letteth thee see that he heareth thy prayer ; and suppose he delay the effect and force thereof, yet pray continuallie. This doctrine is so necessary for the troubled conscience, that I think it is the meetest bridle in the Scripture to refrain our impatience ; it is the meetest bit to hold us in continual exercise of patience ; for if the heart understand that the Lord hath rejected our prayer altogether, it is not possible to continue in prayer ; so when we know that the Lord heareth us, suppose he delay, let us crave patience to abide his good will.—*Robert Bruce, 1559—1631.*

Verse 1.—*" I waited for the Lord."* The infinite םֹק being placed first brings the action strongly out : *I waited.* This strong emphasis on the waiting, has the force of an *admonition ;* it suggests to the sufferer that everything depends on *waiting.*—*E. W. Hengstenberg.*

---

* Petitioning for or praying for.

Verse 1.—" *I waited patiently :*" rather *anxiously ;* the original has it, *waiting I waited ;* a Hebraism, which signifies vehement solicitude.—*Daniel Cresswell.*

Verse 1.—" *I waited.*" The Saviour endured his sufferings *waitingly,* as well as patiently and prayerfully. He "waited for the Lord." He expected help from Jehovah ; and he waited for it until it came.—*James Frame, in " Christ and his Work : an Exposition of Psalm XL."* 1869.

Verse 1.—" *Patiently.*" Our Lord's patience under suffering was an element of perfection in his work. Had he become impatient as we often do, and lost heart, his atonement would have been vitiated. Well may we rejoice that in the midst of all his temptations, and in the thickest of the battle against sin and Satan, he remained patient and willing to finish the work which his Father had given him to do. —*James Frame.*

Verse 1.—" *Heard my cry.*" Our Saviour endured his sufferings *prayerfully* as well as *patiently.*—*James Frame.*

Verse 2.—" *An horrible pit.*" Some of the pits referred to in the Bible were prisons, one such I saw at Athens, and another at Rome. To these there were no openings, except a hole at the top, which served for both door and window The bottoms of these pits were necessarily in a filthy and revolting state, and sometimes deep in mud. " *He brought me up also out of an horrible pit, out of the miry clay ;*" one of these filthy prisons being in the Psalmist's view, in Isaiah xxxviii. 17, called " the pit of corruption," or putrefaction and filth.—*John Gadsby.*

Verse 2.—" *An horrible pit ;*" or, as it is in the Hebrew, *a pit of noise ;* so called because of waters that falling into it, with great violence, make a roaring dreadful noise ; or because of the strugglings and outcries they make that are in it ; or because when anything is cast into deep pits, it will always make a great noise ; and where he stuck fast in " *miry clay,*" without a seeming possibility of getting out. And some refer this to the greatness of Christ's terrors and sufferings, and his deliverance from them both.—*Arthur Jackson.*

Verse 2.—Three things are stated in verse two. First, resurrection as the act of God, " *He brought me up,*" etc. Secondly, the justification of the name and title of the Sufferer, " *and set my feet upon a rock.*" Jesus is set up, as alive from the dead, upon the basis of accomplished truth. Thirdly, there is his ascension, " *He establisheth my goings.*" The Son of God having trodden, in gracious and self-renouncing obedience the passage to the grave, now enters finally as Man the path of life. " He is gone into heaven," says the Spirit. And again, " He ascended on high, and led captivity captive."—*Arthur Pridham in " Notes and Reflections on the Psalms,"* 1869.

Verse 3.—" *A new song.*" See Notes on Psalm xxxiii. verse 3.

Verse 3.—" *Many shall see it, and fear, and shall trust in the Lord.*" The terms *fear,* and *hope,* or *trust,* do not seem at first view to harmonise ; but David has not improperly joined them together, for no man will ever entertain the *hope* of the favour of God but he whose mind is first imbued with the *fear* of God. I understand *fear,* in general, to mean the feeling of piety which is produced in us by the knowledge of the power, equity, and mercy of God.—*John Calvin.*

Verse 3.—" *Many shall see it, and fear, and shall trust in the Lord.*" First of all they " *see.*" Their eyes are opened ; and their opened eyes see and survey *what* they are, *where* they are, *whence* they came, and *whither* they are going. . . . . . When the attention of sinners is really and decisively arrested by the propitiation of Jesus, not only are their eyes opened to their various moral relations, not only do they " see " but they " *fear* " too. They " see " and " fear." . . . . . . Conviction follows illumination. . . . . . But while the sinner only sees and fears, he is but in the initial stage of conversion, only in a state of readiness to flee from the city of destruction. He may have set out on his pilgrimage, but he has not yet reached his Father to receive the kiss of welcome and forgiveness. The consummating step has not yet been taken. He has seen indeed ; he has feared too : but he still requires to *trust,* to trust in the Lord, and banish all his fears. This is the culminating point in the great change ; and, unless this be reached, the other experiences will either die away, like an untimely blossom, or they will only be fuel to the unquenchable fire.—*James Frame.*

Verse 5.—" *Many, O Lord my God, are thy wonderful works which thou hast done,*" etc. Behold God in the magnificence and wisdom of the works which his hands have made, even this immense universe, which is full of his glory. What art and contrivance! What regularity, harmony, and proportion, are to be seen in all his productions, in the frame of our own bodies, or those that are about us! And with what beams of majestic glory do the sun, moon, and stars proclaim how august and wonderful in knowledge their Maker is! And ought not all these numberless beauties wherewith the world is stored, which the minds of inquisitive men are ready to admire, lead up our thoughts to the great Parent of all things, and inflame our amorous souls with love to him, who is infinitely brighter and fairer than them all?

Cast abroad your eyes through the nations, and meditate on the mighty acts which he hath done, and the wisdom and power of his providence, which should charm all thy affections. Behold his admirable patience, with what pity he looks down on obstinate rebels; and how he is moved with compassion when he sees his creatures polluted in their blood, and bent upon their own destruction; how long he waits to be gracious; how unwillingly he appears to give up with sinners, and execute deserved vengeance on his enemies; and then with what joy he pardons for "with him is plenteous redemption." And what can have more force than these to win thy esteem, and make a willing conquest of thy heart? so that every object about thee is an argument of love, and furnishes fuel for this sacred fire. And whether you behold God in the firmament of his power, or the sanctuary of his grace, you cannot miss to pronounce him "altogether lovely."—*William Dunlop.*

Verse 5.—" *Thy thoughts which are to us-ward, they cannot be reckoned up in order unto thee:* " *i.e.*, there is no one can digest them in order; for although that may be attempted according to the comprehension and meaning of men, yet *not before thee*, every attempt of that nature being infinitely beneath thy immeasurable glory.—*Victorinus Bythner's* " *Lyre of David;* " *translated by T. Dee: new edition, by N. L. Benmohel, 1847.*

Verse 5.—" *Us-ward.*" It is worthy of notice that while addressing his Father, as Jehovah and his God, our Saviour speaks of the members of the human family as his fellows. This is implied in the expressions "to us-ward." He regarded himself as most intimately associated with the children of men.—*James Frame.*

Verse 5.—" *They cannot be reckoned up in order unto thee.*" They are " in order " in themselves, and if they could be " reckoned up " as they are, they would be "reckoned in order." Created mind may not be able to grasp the principle of order that pervades them, but such a principle there is. And the more we study the whole series in its interrelations, the more shall we be convinced that as to time and place all the preparations for the mediatorial work of Christ, all the parts of its accomplishment, and all the divinely appointed consequents of its acceptation throughout all time into eternity, are faultlessly in order; they are precisely what and where and when they should be.—*James Frame.*

Verse 5.—" *They are more than can be numbered.*" The pulses of Providence are quicker than those of our wrists or temples. The soul of David knew right well their multiplicity, but could not multiply them aright by any skill in arithmetic; nay, the very sum or chief heads of divine kindnesses were innumerable. His " wonderful works " and " thoughts " towards him could not be reckoned up in order by him, they were *more than could be numbered.*—*Samuel Lee* (1625—1691), *in* " *The Triumph of Mercy in the Chariot of Praise.*"

Verse 5.—It is Christ's speech, of whom the Psalm is made, and that relating unto his Father's resolved purposes and contrivements from eternity, and those continued unto his sending Christ into the world to die for us, as verses 6, 7. It follows so, as although his thoughts and purposes were but one individual act at first, and never to be altered; yet they became many, through a perpetuated reiteration of them, wherein his constancy to himself is seen. . . . . . My brethren, if God have been thinking thoughts of mercy from everlasting to those that are his, what a stock and treasury do these thoughts arise to, besides those that are in his nature and disposition! This is in his actual purposes and intentions, which he hath thought, and doth think over, again and again, every moment. " *Many, O Lord my God, are thy wonderful works which thou hast done, and thy thoughts which are to us-ward,*" saith Jesus Christ; for Psalm xl. is a Psalm of Christ, and quoted by the apostle, and applied unto Christ in Heb. x., " *How many are thy thoughts to us-ward!* "—he speaks it in the name of the human nature—that is, to me and mine. " *If I would declare and speak of them, they are more than can be numbered.*" And what is the reason? Because God hath studied mercies, mercies for his children, even from everlasting. And then, "He reneweth his mercies every morning;" not that any mercies are new, but he actually thinketh over mercies again and again, and so he brings out of his treasury, mercies both new and old, and the old are always new. What a stock, my brethren, must this needs amount unto!—*Thomas Goodwin.*

Verse 6.—"*Sacrifice and offering . . . . burnt-offering and sin-offering.*" Four kinds are here specified, both by the Psalmist and apostle: namely, *sacrifice*, זֶבַח *zebhach*, θυσία; *offering*, מִנְחָה *minchah*, προσφορά; *burnt-offering*, עֹלָה *olah*, ὁλοκαύτωμα; *sin-offering*, חֲטָאָה *chataah*, περὶ ἁμαρτίας. Of all these we may say with the apostle, it was impossible that the blood of bulls and goats, etc., should take away sin.—*Adam Clarke.*

Verse 6.—"*Mine ears hast thou opened.*" The literal translation is, *mine ears hast thou digged* (or *pierced*) *through;* which may well be interpreted as meaning, "Thou hast accepted me as thy slave," in allusion to the custom (Exod. xxi. 6) of masters boring the ear of a slave, who had refused his offered freedom, in token of retaining him.—*Daniel Cresswell.*

Vere 6.—John Calvin, in treating upon the interpretation, "mine ears hast thou bored," says, "this mode of interpretation appears to be too forced and refined."

Verse 6.—"*Mine ears hast thou opened.*" If it be said that the apostle to the Hebrews read this differently, I answer, this does not appear to me. It is true, he found a different, but corrupted translation (ὠτία, ears, as the learned have observed, having been changed into σῶμα, body) in the LXX, which was the version then in use; and he was obliged to quote it as he found it, under the penalty, if he altered it, of being deemed a false quoter. He therefore took the translation as he found it, especially as it served to illustrate his argument equally well. Upon this quotation from the LXX the apostle argues, verse 9, "He (Christ) taketh away the first (namely, legal sacrifices), that he may establish the second" (namely, obedience to God's will), in offering himself a sacrifice for the sins of mankind; and thus he must have argued upon a quotation from the Hebrew text as it stands at present.—*Green, quoted in S. Burder's "Scripture Expositor."*

Verse 6.—The apostle's reading (Heb. x. 5), though it be far distant from the letter of the Hebrew, and in part from the LXX (as I suppose it to have been originally), yet is the most perspicuous interpretation of the meaning of it: *Christ's body* comprehended the *ears*, and that assumed on purpose to perform in it the utmost degree of obedience to the will of God, to be obedient even to death, and thereby to be as the priest.—*Henry Hammond.*

Verse 6.—

> Nor sacrifice thy love can win.
> Nor offerings from the stain of sin
> Obnoxious man shall clear:
> Thy hand my mortal frame prepares,
> (Thy hand, whose signature it bears,)
> And opes my willing ear.

James Merrick, M.A., 1720—1769.

Verses 6, 7.—In these words an allusion is made to a custom of the Jews *to bore the ears* of such as were to be their perpetual servants, and *to enrol their names in a book*, or make some instrument of the covenant. "Sacrifice and burnt-offering thou wouldst not have;" but because I am thy vowed servant, bored with an awl, and enrolled in thy book, "*I said, Lo, I come; I delight to do thy will, O my God.*" These words of the Psalm are alleged by S. Paul, Heb. x. But the first of them with a most strange difference. For whereas the Psalmist hath, according to the Hebrew verity, "*Sacrifice and burnt-offering thou wouldst not: mine ears thou hast bored or digged,*" אָזְנַיִם; S. Paul reads with the LXX, σῶμα κατηρτίσω μοι, "*A body thou hast prepared or fitted me.*" What equipollency can be in sense between these two? This difficulty is so much the more augmented because most interpreters make the life of the quotation to lie in those very words where the difference is, namely, That the words, "*A body thou hast prepared* me," are brought by the apostle to prove our Saviour's incarnation; whereunto the words in the Psalm itself ("*Mine ears hast thou bored, or digged, or opened*"), take them how you will, will in no wise suit. I answer, therefore, That the life of the quotation lies not in the words of difference, nor can do, because this epistle was written to the Hebrews, and so first in the Hebrew tongue, where this translation of the LXX could have no place. And if the life of the quotation lay here, I cannot see how it can possibly be reconciled. It lies therefore in the words where there is no difference, namely, That Christ was such a High Priest as came to sanctify us, not with legal offerings and sacrifices, but by his obedience in doing like a devoted servant the will of his Father. Thus, the allegation will not depend at all upon the words of difference, and so they give us liberty to reconcile them : " *Mine ears hast thou bored*," saith the Psalmist, *i.e.*, Thou hast accepted me for a perpetual servant, as masters are wont, according to the law, to *bore* such servants' *ears* as refuse to part from them. Now the LXX, according to whom the apostle's epistle readeth, thinking perhaps the meaning of this speech would be obscure to such as knew not that custom, chose rather to translate it generally σῶμα δὲ κατηρτίσω μοι, " *Thou hast fitted my body*," namely, to be thy servant in such a manner as servants' bodies are wont to be. And so the sense is all one, though not specified to the Jewish custom of boring the ear with an awl, but left indifferently appliable to the custom of any nation in marking and stigmatising their servants' bodies.—*Joseph Mede, B.D.*, 1586—1638.

Verses 6—10.—Here we have in Christ for our instruction, and in David also (his type) for our example ; 1. A firm purpose of obedience, in a *bored ear*, and a yielding heart. 2. A ready performance thereof : " *Lo, I come.*" 3. A careful observance of the word written : " *In the volume of the book it is written of me,*" verse 7. 4. A hearty delight in that observance, verse 8. 5. A public profession and communication of God's goodness to others, verses 9, 10. Now, we should labour to express Christ to the world, to walk as he walked (1 John ii. 6) : our lives should be in some sense parallel with his life, as the transcript with the original : he left us a copy to write by, saith Saint Peter, 1st Epistle ii. 21.—*John Trapp.*

Verse 7.—" *Then said I, Lo, I come.*" As his name is above every name, so this coming of his is above every coming. We sometimes call our own births, I confess, a coming into the world ; but properly, none ever came into the world but he. For, 1. He only truly can be said to come, who is before he comes ; so were not we, only he so. 2. He only strictly comes who comes willingly ; our crying and struggling at our entrance into the world, shows how unwillingly we come into it. He alone it is that sings out, " *Lo, I come.*" 3. He only properly comes who comes from some place or other. Alas ! we had none to come from but the womb of nothing. *He* only had a place to be in before he came.—*Mark Frank.*

Verse 7.—" *Then said I, Lo, I come,*" to wit, as surety, to pay the ransom, and to do thy will, O God. Every word carrieth a special emphasis as, 1. The time, " *then,*" even so soon as he perceived that his Father had prepared his body for such an end, then, without delay. This speed implieth forwardness and readiness ; he would lose no opportunity. 2. His profession in this word, " *said I ;*" he did not closely, secretly, timorously, as being ashamed thereof, but he maketh profession beforehand. 3. This note of observation, " *Lo,*" this is a kind of calling angels and men to witness, and a desire that all might know his inward intention, and the dispositon of his heart ; wherein was as great a willingness as any could have to anything. 4. An offering of himself without any enforcement or compulsion ; this he manifesteth in this word, " *I come.*" 5. That very instant set out in the present tense, " *I come ;*" he puts it not off to a future and uncertain time, but even in that moment, he saith, " *I come.*" 6. The first person twice expressed, thus, " *I said,*" " *I come.*" He sendeth not another person, nor substituteth any in his room ; but he, even he himself in his own person, cometh. All which do abundantly evidence Christ's singular readiness and willingness, as our surety, to do his Father's will, though it were by suffering, and by being made a sacrifice for our sins.—*Thomas Brooks.*

Verse 7.—" *Lo, I come,*" *i.e.*, to appear before thee ; a phrase used to indicate the coming of an inferior into the presence of a superior, or of a slave before his master, Num. xxii. 38 ; 2 Sam. xix. 20 : as in the similar expression, " Behold, here I am," generally expressive of willingness.—*J. J. Stewart Perowne.*

Verse 7.—" *Lo, I come.*" Christ's coming in the spirit is a *joyful* coming. I think this, " *Lo, I come,*" expresses, 1. *Present* joy. 2. It expresses *certain* joy : the " *Lo,*" is a note of certainty ; the thing is certain and true ; and his joy is certain ; certain, true, solid joy. 3. It expresses *communicative* joy ; designing his people shall share of his joy, " *Lo, I come !* " The joy that Christ has as Mediator is a fulness of joy, designed for his people's use, that *out of his fulness we may receive, and grace for grace*, and joy for joy; grace answering grace in Jesus, and joy answering joy in him. 4. It expresses *solemn* joy. He comes with a solemnity; " *Lo, I come!* " according to the council of a glorious Trinity. Now, when the purpose of heaven is come to the birth, and the decree breaks forth, and the fulness of time is come, he makes heaven and earth witness, as it were, to his solemn march on the errand : he says it with a loud, " *Lo !* " that all the world of men and angels may notice, " *Lo, I come!* " And, indeed, all the elect angels brake forth into joyful songs of praise at this solemnity; when he came in the flesh, they sang, " Glory to God in the highest, peace on earth, and goodwill towards man."—*Ralph Erskine*, 1685—1752.

Verse 7.—" *Lo, I come,*" or, *am come*, to wit, *into the world* (Heb. x. 5), and particularly *to Jerusalem*, to give myself a sacrifice for sin.—*Henry Ainsworth*.

Verse 7.—" *The volume of the book.*" What book is meant, whether the Scripture, or the book of life, is not certain, probably the latter.—*W. Wilson, D.D.*

Verse 7.—" *The volume of the book.*" But what volume of manuscript roll is here meant ? Plainly, the one which was already extant when the Psalmist was writing. If the Psalmist was David himself (as the title of the Psalm seems to affirm), the only parts of the Hebrew Scriptures then extant, and of course, the only part to which he could refer, must have been the Pentateuch, and perhaps the book of Joshua. Beyond any reasonable doubt, then, the κεφαλὶς βιβλίον (מְגִלַּת סֵפֶר) was the Pentateuch. . . . But I apprehend the meaning of the writer to be, that the *book of the law*, which prescribes sacrifices that were merely σκιαὶ or παραβολαὶ of the great atoning sacrifice by Christ, did itself teach, by the use of these, that something of a higher and better nature was to be looked for than Levitical rites. In a word, it pointed to the Messiah ; or, some of the contents of the *written* law had respect to him.—*Moses Stuart, M.A., in "A Commentary on the Epistle to the Hebrews,"* 1851.

Verse 7.—" *The volume of the book,*" etc. When I first considered Rom. v. 14 and other Scriptures in the New Testament which make the first Adam, and the whole story of him both before and after, and in his sinning or falling, to be the type and lively shadow of Christ, the second Adam ; likewise observing that the apostle Paul stands admiring at the greatness of this mystery or mystical type, the Christ, the second Adam should so wonderfully be shadowed forth therein, as Eph. v. 32, he cries out, " This is a great mystery," which he speaks applying and fitting some passages about Adam and Eve unto Christ and his church ; it made me more to consider an interpretation of a passage in Heb. x. 7, out of Psalm xl. 7, which I before had not only not regarded, but wholly rejected, as being too like a postil* gloss. The passage is, that " when Christ came into the world," to take our nature on him, he alleged the reason of it to be the fulfilling of a Scripture written in " the beginning of God's book," ἐν κεφαλίδι Βιβλίου, so out of the original the words may be, and are by many interpreters, translated, though our translation reads them only thus, " *In the volume of the book it is written of me.*" It is true, indeed, that in the fortieth Psalm, whence they are quoted, the words in the Hebrew may signify no more than that in God's book (the manner of writing which was anciently in rolls of parchment, folded up in a volume) Christ was everywhere written and spoken of. Yet the word κεφαλὶς, which out of the Septuagint's translation the apostle took, signifying, as all know, the beginning of a book ; and we finding such an emphasis set by the apostle in the fifth chapter of the Ephesians, upon the history of Adam in the beginning of Genesis, as containing the mystery, yea, the great mystery about Christ, it did somewhat induce, though not so fully persuade, me to think, that the Holy Ghost in those words might have some glance at the story of Adam in the first of the first book of Moses. And withal the rather because so, the words so understood do intimate a higher and further inducement to Christ to assume our nature, the scope of the speech, Heb. x., being to render the reason why he so willingly took man's nature : not only because God liked not sacrifice and burnt-offering, which came in but upon occasion of sin, and after the fall, and could not take sins away, but further, that he was prophesied of, and his assuming a body prophetically foresignified as in the fortieth Psalm, so even by Adam's story before the fall, recorded in the very beginning of Genesis, which many other Scriptures do expressly apply it unto.—*Thomas Goodwin*.

---

* A marginal note.

Verse 8.—" *I delight to do thy will, O my God.*"   The will of God to redeem sinners by the incarnation and death of Jesus Christ, was most grateful and pleasing to the very heart of Christ.   It is said, Prov. viii. 31, when he was solacing himself in the sweetest enjoyment of his Father, whilst he lay in that blessed bosom of delights, yet the very prospect of this work gave him pleasure, then his " delights were with the sons of men."   And when he was come into the world, and had endured many abuses and injuries, and was even now come to the most difficult part of the work ; yet, " how am I straitened, or pained (saith he), till it be accomplished ! " Luke xii. 50.   Two things call our thoughts to stay upon them in this point. First.—The *decency* of it— why it ought to be so.   1.—It became Christ to go about this work with cheerfulness and delight, that thereby he might give his death the nature and formality of a sacrifice.   In all sacrifices you shall find that God had still a regard, a special respect to the will of the offerer.   See Exod. xxxv. 5, 21, and Levit. i. 3.   2.—It ought to be so in view of the unity of Christ's will with the Father's.   3.—This was necessary to commend the love of Jesus Christ to us for whom he gave himself.   That he came into the world to die for us is a mercy of the first magnitude ; but that he came in love to our souls, and underwent all his sufferings with such willingness for our sakes, this heightens it above all apprehension.   4.—It was necessary to be so for the regulating of all our obedience to God, according to this pattern ; that seeing and setting this great example of obedience before us, we might never grudge nor grumble at any duty or suffering that God should call us to.   *Secondly.*—Let us consider and examine whence it came to be so pleasant and acceptable to Jesus Christ, to come into the world and die for poor sinners.   1.—That in his sufferings there would be made a glorious display and manifestation of the divine attributes.   2.—Another delightful prospect Christ had of the fruit of his sufferings, was the recovery and salvation of all the elect by his death ; and though his sufferings were exceedingly bitter, yet such fruit of them as this was exceedingly sweet.   3.—Add to this, the glory which would redound to him from his redeemed ones to all eternity, for it will be the everlasting employment of the saints in heaven to be ascribing glory, praise, and honour to the Redeemer.   Did Christ find pleasure in abasement and torment, in suffering and dying for me, and can I find no pleasure in praying, hearing, meditating, and enjoying the sweet duties of communion with him ?   Did he come so cheerfully to die for me, and do I go so deadheartedly to prayers and sacraments to enjoy fellowship with him ? Was it a pleasure to him to shed his blood, and is it none to me to apply it, and reap the benefits of it ?   O let there be no more grumblings, lazy excuses, shiftings of duty, or dead-hearted and listless performances of them, after such an example as this.   Be ready to do the will of God, be ye also ready to suffer it.   And as to sufferings for Christ, they should not be grievous to Christians that know how cheerfully Christ came from the bosom of the Father to die for them.   What have we to leave or lose, in comparison with him ?   What are our sufferings to Christ's.   Alas ! there is no compare ; there was more bitterness in one drop of his sufferings than in a sea of ours.   To conclude : your delight and readiness in the paths of obedience is the very measure of your sanctification.—*Condensed from John Flavel.*

Verse 8.—Now, saith Christ, " *I delight to do thy will, O my God ;* " it is the joy and rejoicing of my heart to be a-seeking and a-saving lost sinners.   When Christ was an hungry, he went not into a victualling house but into the temple, and taught the people most part of the day, to show how much he delighted in the salvation of sinners, etc.   Christ did so much delight, and his heart was so much set upon the conversion and salvation of the Samaritans, that he neglected his own body to save their souls, as you may clearly see in John iv.—*Thomas Brooks.*

Verse 8.—" *To do.*"   It was Jesus who was the doer of the work.   The Father willed it ; but he did not do it.   It was Jesus who did it, who wrought it out ; who brought it in ; who carried it within the veil, and laid it as an acceptable and meritorious offering at the feet of his well-pleased Father.   The work then is done ; it is finished.   We need not attempt to do it.   We cannot do it.   We cannot do that which is already done ; and we could not do it, though it were yet undone. There is much that man can do, but he cannot make a propitiation.—*James Frame.*

Verse 8.—" *Thy will.*"   The covenant between the Father and the Son, as elsewhere, so it is most clearly expressed (Heb. x. 7, from Ps. xl. 7, 8), " Lo, I come : in the volume of the book it is written of me, I delight to do thy will, O my God." And what will ?   Verse 10, " The will by which we are sanctified through the offering of the body of Jesus Christ once for all." The will of God was, that Jesus should be offered ; and to this end, that we might be sanctified and saved. It is called "The offering of the body of Jesus Christ," in answer to what was said before, "A body hast thou prepared me," or a human nature, by a synecdoche. "My will," says God the Father, "is that thou have a body, and that thy body be offered up ; and all to this end, that the children, the elect, might be sanctified." Says the Son to this, "Lo, I come to do thy will ; "—"I accept of the condition, and give up myself to the performance of thy will."—*John Owen.*

Verse 8.—" *Thy law is within my heart.*" The law of God is not to be kept in books, but in the midst of our hearts, that we may rightly understand the same, admire it, and observe it.—*Martin Geier.*

Verse 8.—" *Thy law is within my heart.*" The will of God in which Christ delighted, was (as appears by the coherence, and the quotation of Heb. x. 5) that Christ should make his soul an offering for sin, as more acceptable to God than all other burnt-offerings and sin-offerings. This law was *in his heart,* בְּתוֹךְ מֵעָי, in the midst of his bowels. He did as much delight in it as we do in following those inclinations which nature has implanted in our hearts, as we do in eating and drinking. So he expresses it (John iv. 34), " My meat is to do the will of him that sent me, and to finish his work." He was as willing to bleed and die for thee as thou art to eat when hungry. He was delighted as much to be scourged, wounded, crucified, as thou delightest in meat when most delicious.—*David Clarkson.*

Verse 8.—" *Within my heart,*" margin, *my bowels.* The intestines or viscera are here mentioned as the place of the most profound spiritual occupation.—*Franz Delitzsch.*

Verse 9.—" *I have preached righteousness,*" etc. It is Jesus who speaks, and he speaks of himself as a PREACHER. He was a preacher, and a great preacher too. He was great—1. In *genuine eloquence.* All the handmaids of the choicest rhetoric ministered to him as he spake. His mind touched the minds of his auditors on all sides. 2. He was great in *knowledge.* Many who have an astonishing command of words, and who can use their words with astonishing rhetorical adroitness, spoil their influence by their " lack of knowledge." They go blunderingly onward when they attempt to think for themselves, or to guide their hearers into fields of thought which have not been tracked by minds of the pioneer order. 3. He was great also in *goodness.* There is a greatness in goodness, and the greatness of goodness is an important element in the greatness of a preacher. 4. Jesus was great, too, in *official status.* Official status, whether in things civil, literary, or sacred, when conferred on worthy individuals, confers, in its turn, undoubted weight and moral authority. Now Jesus was the highest official in the universe. His authority extended to all other office-bearers, his office exceeded all other offices. He came from above, and was " above all." He was Lord of lords, and King of kings. 5. Another element still in the greatness of Jesus, as a preacher, consisted in the greatness of his *essential dignity.* He was God as well as man. Such was Christ as a preacher. True he was more than a preacher ; he was likewise a pattern, and a priest, and a propitiator ; and as pattern, priest, and propitiator, he stands without a peer. But he was a preacher, too, and as a preacher, he has never had, and never will have an equal.—*Condensed from James Frame.*

Verse 9.—" *The great congregation.*" The " *congregation* " here referred to was " *great* " not only in *numbers,* but " *great* " also in the necessities of its individual members, and great in *pollution.*—*James Frame.*

Verses 9, 10.—" *I have published . . . . I would not refrain . . . . I have not covered . . . I have uttered . . . I have not hid :* " words are heaped upon words to express the eager forwardness of a heart burning to show forth its gratitude. No elaborate description could so well have given us the likeness of one whose " life was a thanksgiving."—*J. J. Stewart Perowne.*

Verses 9, 10.—The true way of justification of sinners by faith is a jewel so precious and necessary for poor souls, that it should not be concealed : " *I have not hid thy righteousness within my heart.*" One sermon on this subject is not sufficient ; it is necessary to make this mystery plain, how by faith in Christ the man that flieth to him is justified from his sins, and saved according to the covenant passed between the suffering Mediator and God the faithful promiser, to justify and save by his own way. " *I have declared thy faithfulness and thy salvation.*"—*David Dickson.*

Verses 9, 10.—"*Thy.*" The adding *thy* to every one of them is emphatical; it was *thy* righteousness I had commission to declare, *thy* faithfulness I had order to proclaim, *thy* mercy I had charge to publish; *thou* wert as much interested in all that I did as I myself was. I shall be counted false and a liar, thou wilt be counted unjust and cruel, if all be not fulfilled as I have spoken. Since it was thy rule I observed, and thy glory I aimed at in declaring it, disgrace not thyself and me in refusing the petition of such a suppliant, who believes in my word which I gave out by thy authority.—*Stephen Charnock.*

Verse 10.—"*I have not hid.*" This intimates, that whoever undertook to preach the gospel of Christ would be in great temptation to hide it, and conceal it, because it must be preached with great contention, and in the face of great opposition.—*Matthew Henry.*

Verse 10.—"*I have not hid,*" etc. What God has done for us, or for the church, we should lay *to* heart; but not lock up *in* our heart.—*Carl Bernhard Moll in Lange's* "*Bibelwerk,*" 1869.

Verse 11.—"*Withhold not thou thy tender mercies from me.*" Do not hinder them from coming showering down upon me. "*Let thy lovingkindness and thy truth continually preserve me;*" or, do thou employ them in preserving me.—*John Diodati.*

Verse 12.—"*For innumerable evils have compassed me about: mine iniquities have taken hold upon me, so that I am not able to look up; they are more than the hairs of mine head.*" We lose ourselves when we speak of the sins of our lives. It may astonish any considering man to take notice how many sins he is guilty of any one day; how many sins accompany any one single act; nay, how many bewray themselves in any one religious duty. Whensoever ye do anything forbidden, you omit the duty at that time commanded; and whenever you neglect that which is enjoined, the omission is joined with the acting of something forbidden; so that the sin, whether omission or commission, is always double; nay, the apostle makes every sin tenfold. James ii. 10. That which seems one to us, according to the sense of the law, and the account of God, is multiplied by ten. He breaks every command by sinning directly against one, and so sins ten times at once; besides that swarm of sinful circumstances and aggravations which surround every act in such numbers, as atoms use to surround your body in a dusty room; you may more easily number these than those. And though some count these but fractions, incomplete sins, yet even from hence it is more difficult to take an account of their number. And, which is more for astonishment, pick out the best religious duty that ever you performed, and even in that performance you may find such a swarm of sins as cannot be numbered. In the best prayer that ever you put up to God, irreverence, lukewarmness, unbelief, spiritual pride, self-seeking, hypocrisy, distractions, etc., and many more, that an enlightened soul grieves and bewails; and yet there are many more that the pure eye of God discerns, than any man does take notice of.—*David Clarkson.*

Verse 12.—"*Mine iniquities have taken hold upon me.*" They seized him as the sinner's substitute, to deal with him as regards their own penalty, according to the sinner's desert.—*James Frame.*

Verse 13.—The remaining verses of this Psalm are almost exactly identical with Psalm LXX.

Verse 14.—"*Let them be ashamed and confounded,*" etc. Even this prayer carried benevolence in its bosom. It sought from the divine Father, such a manifestation of what was glorious and God-like as might unnerve each rebel arm, and overawe each rebel heart in the traitor's company. If each arm were for a little unnerved, if each heart were for a little unmanned, there might be time for the better principles of their nature to rise and put an arrest upon the prosecution of their wicked design. Such being the benevolent aim of the prayer, we need not wonder that it issued from the same heart that by-and-by exclaimed, " Father, forgive them, for they know not what they do;" neither need we marvel that it was answered to the very letter, and that as soon as he said to the traitor band, " I am he," they went backward and fell to the ground.—*James Frame.*

Verse 15.—" *Aha, aha.*" An exclamation which occurs three times in the Psalms ; and in each case there seems to be reference to the mockery at the Passion. See xxxv. 21 ; and lxx. 3, which appear to belong to the same time as the present Psalm.—*Christopher Wordsworth.*

Verse 16.—" *Let all those that seek thee rejoice and be glad in thee.*" As every mercy to every believer giveth a proof of God's readiness to show the like mercy to all believers, when they stand in need ; so should every mercy shown to any of the number, being known to the rest, be made the matter and occasion of magnifying the Lord.—*David Dickson.*

Verse 16.—" *Such as love thy salvation.*" To love God's salvation is to love God himself, the Saviour, or Jesus.—*Martin Geier.*

Verse 16.—" *Such as love thy salvation.*" One would think that self-love alone should make us love salvation. Ay, but they love it because it is his, " that love *thy* salvation." It is the character of a holy saint to love salvation itself ; not as his own only, but as God's, as God's that saves him.—*Thomas Goodwin.*

Verse 16.—" *Let such as love thy salvation say continually, The Lord be magnified.*" Jesus who gave us our capacity of happiness and our capacity of speaking, realised the relation which he had established between them ; and hence in praying for his friends, he prayed that in the joy and gladness of their souls they might *say,* " The Lord be magnified." He desired them to speak of their holy happiness ; and it was his wish that when they did speak of it they should speak in terms of laudation of Jehovah, for he was the source of it. He desired them to say continually, " The Lord be magnified."—*James Frame.*

Verse 17.—In Dr. Malan's memoir, the editor, one of his sons, thus writes of his brother Jocelyn, who was for some years prior to his death, the subject of intense bodily sufferings :—" One striking feature in his character was his holy fear of God, and reverence for his will. One day I was repeating a verse from the Psalms, ' *As for me, I am poor and needy, but the Lord careth for me : thou art my helper and deliverer ; O Lord, make no long tarrying.*' He said, " Mamma, I love that verse, all but the last bit, it looks like a murmur against God. He never ' tarries ' in my case."—*From " The Life, Labours, and Writings of Cæsar Malan* (1787— 1864) : *By one of his sons,*" 1689.

Verse 17.—" *Yet the Lord thinketh upon me.*" Sacred story derives from heaven the kindness of Abimelech to Abraham, of Laban and Esau to Jacob, of Ruth to Naomi, of Boaz to Ruth, and Jonathan to David. When others think of kindness to us, let us imitate David, 'tis the Lord that thinketh upon me, and forms those thoughts within their hearts. This should calm our spirits when a former friend's heart is alienated by rash admissions of false suggestions, or when any faithful Jonathan expires his spirit into the bosom of God. It should not be lost what Hobson, the late noted carrier of Cambridge, said to a young student receiving a letter of the sad tidings of his uncle's decease (who maintained him at the University), and weeping bitterly, and reciting the cause of his grief, he replied, *Who gave you that friend ?* Which saying did greatly comfort him, and was a sweet support to him afterwards in his ministry. The Everliving God is the portion of a living faith, and *he* can never want that hath *such* an ocean. He that turns the hearts of kings like rivers at his pleasure, turns all the little brooks in the world into what scorched and parched ground he pleases.—*Samuel Lee.*

Verse 17.—" *The Lord thinketh upon me.*" There are three things in *God's thinking upon us,* that are solacing and delightful. Observe the *frequency* of his thoughts. Indeed, they are incessant. You have a friend, whom you esteem and love. You wish to live in his mind. You say when you part, and when you write, " Think of me." You give him, perhaps, a token to revive his remembrance. How naturally is Selkirk, in his solitary island, made to say :

> " My friends, do they now and then send
> A wish or a *thought* after me ?
> O tell me, I yet have a friend,
> Though a friend I am never to see.
>
> Ye winds, that have made me your sport,
> Convey to this desolate shore
> Some cordial, endearing report.
> Of a land I shall visit no more."

But the dearest connexion in the world cannot be always thinking upon you. Half his time he is in a state of unconsciousness ; and how much during the other half, is he engrossed ! But there is no remission in the Lord's thoughts. . . . Observe in the next place, the *wisdom* of his thoughts. You have a dear child, absent from you, and you follow him in your mind. But you know not his present circumstances. You left him in such a place ; but where is he now ? You left him in such a condition. But what is he now ? Perhaps, while you are thinking upon his health, he is groaning under a bruised limb, or a painful disorder. Perhaps, while you are thinking of his safety, some enemy is taking advantage of his innocency. Perhaps, while you are rejoicing in his prudence, he is going to take a step that will involve him for life. But when God thinketh upon you, he is perfectly acquainted with your situation, your dangers, your wants. He knows all your walking through this great wilderness, and can afford you the seasonable succour you need. For again, observe the *efficiency* of his thoughts. You think upon another, and you are anxious to guide, or defend, or relieve him. But in how many cases can you think only ? Solicitude cannot control the disease of the body, cannot dissipate the melancholy of the mind. But with God all things are possible. He who thinks upon you is a God at hand and not afar off ; he has all events under his control ; he is the God of all grace. If, therefore, he does not immediately deliver, it is not because **he is unable to redress**, but because **he is waiting to be** gracious.—*William Jay.*

HINTS TO PREACHERS.

Verse—I. *My part*—praying and waiting. II. *God's part*—condescension and reply.

Verse 2.—I. The *depth* of God's goodness to his people. It finds them often in a horrible pit and miry clay. There is a certain spider which forms a pit in sand, and lies concealed at the bottom, in order to seize upon other insects that fall into it. Thus David's enemies tried to bring him into a pit. II. The *height* of his goodness. He brought me out, and set my feet upon a rock. That rock is Christ. Those feet are faith and hope. III. The *breadth* of his goodness established my *goings*, restored me to my former place in his love, showing me still to have been his during my low estate. He was the same to me, though I felt not the same to him. My goings refer both to the past and the future. IV. The *strength* of his goodness *esta lished* my goings, making me stand firmer after every fall.— *George Rogers.*

Verses 2, 3.—The sinner's position by nature, and his rescue by grace.

Verses 2, 3.—By one and the same act the Lord works our salvation, our enemies' confusion, and the church's edification.—*J. P. Lange's Commentary.*

Verse 3.—The new song, the singer, the teacher.

Verse 4 (last clause).—I. Find out who turn aside to lies—Atheists, Papists, self-righteous, lovers of sin. II. Show their folly in turning aside from God and truth, and in turning to fallacies which lead to death. III. Show how to be preserved from the like folly, by choosing truth, truthful persons, and above all the service of God.

Verse 5.—1. *There are works of God in his people and for his people.* There are his works of creation, of providence, and of redemption, and also his works of grace, wrought in them by his Spirit, and around them by his providence, as well as for them by his Son. II. *These are wonderful works ;* wonderful in their variety, their tenderness, their adaptation to their need, their co-operation with outward means and their power. III. *They are the result of the divine thoughts respecting us.* They come not by chance, not by men, but by the hand of God, and that hand is moved by his will, and that will by his thought respecting us. Every mercy, even the least, represents some kind thought in the mind of God respecting us. God thinks of each one of his people, and every moment. IV. They are innumerable. " *They cannot be reckoned up.*" Could we see all the mercies of God to us and his wonderful works wrought for us individually, they would be countless as the sands, and all these countless mercies represent countless thoughts in the mind and heart of God to each one of his people.—*George Rogers.*

Verse 5.—The multitude of God's thoughts, and deeds of grace, beginning in eternity, continuing for ever ; and dealing with this life, heaven, hell, sin, angels, devils, and indeed all things.

Verse 6.—Here David goes beyond himself, and speaks the language of David's Son. This was naturally suggested by God's wonderful works, and innumerable thoughts of love to man. I. *The sacrifices that were not required.* These were the sacrifices and burnt-offerings under the law. 1. When required ? From Adam to the coming of Christ. 2. When not required ? 3. Why required before ? As types of the one method of redemption. 4. Why not now required ? Because the great Antetype had come. II. *The sacrifice that was required.* This was the sacrifice offered on Calvary. 1. It was required by God by his justice, his wisdom, his faithfulness, his love, his honour, his glory. 2. It was required by man to give him salvation and confidence in that salvation. 3. It was required for the honour of the moral government of God throughout the universe. III. *The person by whom this sacrifice was offered.* "*Mine ears hast thou opened.*" This is the language of Christ, prospectively denoting—1. Knowledge of the sacrifice required. 2. Consecration of himself as a servant for that end.—*George Rogers.*

Verse 6.—"*Mine ears hast thou opened.*" Readiness to hear, fixity of purpose, perfection of obedience, entireness of consecration.

Verses 6—8.—The Lord gives an ear to hear his word, a mouth to confess it, a heart to love it, and power to keep it.

Verse 7.—I. The time of Christ's coming. "*Then said I.*" When types were exhausted, when prophecies looked for their fulfilment, when worldly wisdom had done its utmost, when the world was almost entirely united under one empire, when the time appointed by the Father had come. II. The design of his coming. "*In the volume*" was written—1. The constitution of his person. 2. His teaching. 3. The manner of his life. 4. The design of his death. 5. His resurrection and ascension. 6. The kingdom he would establish. III. The voluntariness of his coming, "*Lo, I come.*" Though sent by the Father, he came of his own accord. "*Christ Jesus came into the world.*" Men do not come into the world, they are sent into it. "*Lo, I come,*" denotes pre-existence, pre-determination, pre-operation. —*George Rogers.*

Verse 8.—"*To do thy will, O God.*" I. The will of God is seen in the fact of salvation. It has its origin in the will of God. II. The will of God is seen in the plan of salvation. All things have proceeded, are proceeding, and will proceed according to that plan. III. It is seen in the provision of salvation, in the appointment of his own Son to become the mediator, the atoning sacrifice, the law-fulfiller, the head of the church, that his plan required. IV. It is seen in the accomplishment of salvation.

Verse 9.—Referring to our Lord ; a great preacher, a great subject, a great congregation, and his great faithfulness in the work.

Verse 10 (first clause).—1. The righteousness *possessed* by God. II. The righteousness *prescribed* by God. III. The righteousness *provided* by God.— *James Frame.*

Verse 10.—I. The preacher must reveal his whole message. II. He must not conceal any part. 1. Not of the righteousness of the law or the gospel. 2. Not of the lovingkindness of grace. 3. Not of any portion of the truth. 1. To omit is to conceal. 2. To entangle with human reasonings. 3. To cover with flowers of rhetoric. 4. To give a partial representation. 5. To put one truth in the place of another. 6. To give the letter without the spirit.—*G. R.*

Verse 10.—The great sin of concealing what we know of God.

Verse 11.—Enrichment and preservation sought. The true riches are from God, gifts of his sovereignty, fruits of his mercy, marked with his tenderness. The best preservations are divine love and faithfulness.

Verse 12.—Compare this with verse 5. The number of our sins, and the number of his thoughts of love.

Verse 12 (second clause).—I. The soul arrested—"taken hold." II. The soul bewildered—"cannot look up." III. The soul's only refuge—prayer, ver. 13.

Verse 13.—I. The language of believing prayer—deliver me, help me ; looking for deliverance and help to God only. II. Of earnest prayer—make haste to help me. III. Of submissive prayer—be pleased, O Lord, if according to thy good pleasure. IV. Of consistent prayer. Help me, which implies efforts for his own deliverance, putting his own shoulder to the wheel.

Verses 11—13.—As an instance of clerical ingenuity, it may be well to mention that Canon Wordsworth has a sermon from these verses upon " The duty of making responses in public prayer."

Verse 14.—*Honi soit qui mal y pense ;* or, the reward of malignity.

Verse 16 (*last clause*).—An every-day saying. Who can use it ? What does it mean ? Why should *they* say it ? Why say it continually ?

Verse 17.—The humble " *But,*" and the believing " *Yet.*" The little " *I am,*" and the great " *Thou art.*" The fitting prayer.

Verse 17.—" *The Lord thinketh upon me.*" Admire the condescension, and then consider that this is—I. A promised blessing. II. A practical blessing—he thinks upon us to supply, protect, direct, sanctify, etc. III. A precious blessing— kind thoughts, continual, greatly good. He thinks of us as his creatures with pity, as his children with love, as his friends with pleasure. IV. A present blessing— promises, providences, visitations of grace.

Verse 17.—I. The less we think of ourselves the more God will think upon us. II. The less we put trust in ourselves the more we may trust in God for help and deliverance. III. The less delay in prayer and active efforts the sooner God will appear for us.

PSALM XLI.

TITLE.—To the Chief Musician. A Psalm of David. *This title has frequently occurred before and serves to remind us of the value of the Psalm, seeing that it was committed to no mean songster ; and also to inform us as to the author who has made his own experience the basis of a prophetic song, in which a far greater than David is set forth. How wide a range of experience David had ! What power it gave him to edify future ages ! And how full a type of our Lord did he become ! What was bitterness to him has proved to be a fountain of unfailing sweetness to many generations of the faithful.*

Jesus Christ betrayed of Judas Iscariot is evidently the great theme of this Psalm, but we think not exclusively. He is the antitype of David, and all his people are in their measure like him ; hence words suitable to the Great Representative are most applicable to those who are in him. Such as receive a vile return for long kindness to others, may read this song with much comfort, for they will see that it is alas ! too common for the best of men to be rewarded for their holy charity with cruelty and scorn ; and when they have been humbled by falling into sin, advantage has been taken of their low estate, their good deeds have been forgotten, and the vilest spite has been vented upon them.

DIVISION.—*The Psalmist in verses* 1—3, *describes the mercies which are promised to such as consider the poor, and this he uses as a preface to his own personal plea for succour : from verses* 4—9 *he states his own case, proceeds to prayer in verse* 10, *and closes with thanksgiving, verses* 11—13.

EXPOSITION.

BLESSED *is* he that considereth the poor : the LORD will deliver him in time of trouble.

2 The LORD will preserve him, and keep him alive ; *and* he shall be blessed upon the earth : and thou wilt not deliver him unto the will of his enemies.

3 The LORD will strengthen him upon the bed of languishing : thou wilt make all his bed in his sickness.

1. " *Blessed is he that considereth the poor.*" This is the third Psalm opening with a benediction, and there is a growth in it beyond the first two. To search the word of God comes first, pardoned sin is second, and now the forgiven sinner brings forth fruit unto God available for the good of others. The word used is as emphatic as in the former cases, and so is the blessing which follows it. The poor intended, are such as are poor in substance, weak in bodily strength, despised in repute, and desponding in spirit. These are mostly avoided and frequently scorned. The worldly proverb bequeathes the hindmost to one who has no mercy. The sick and the sorry are poor company, and the world deserts them as the Amalekite left his dying servant. Such as have been made partakers of divine grace receive a tenderer nature, and are not hardened against their own flesh and blood ; they undertake the cause of the down trodden, and turn their minds seriously to the promotion of their welfare. They do not toss them a penny and go on their way, but enquire into their sorrows, sift out their cause, study the best ways for their relief, and practically come to their rescue ; such as these have the mark of the divine favour plainly upon them, and are as surely the sheep of the Lord's pasture as if they wore a brand upon their foreheads. They are not said to have considered the poor years ago, but they still do so. Stale benevolence, when boasted of, argues present churlishness. First and foremost, yea, far above all others put together in tender compassion for the needy is our Lord Jesus, who so remembered our low estate, that though he was rich, for our sakes he became poor. All his attributes were charged with the task of our uplifting. He weighed our case and came in the fulness of wisdom to execute the wonderful work of mercy by which we are

redeemed from our destructions. Wretchedness excited his pity, misery moved his mercy, and thrice blessed is he both by his God and his saints for his attentive care and wise action towards us. He still considereth us ; his mercy is always in the present tense, and so let our praises be.

" *The Lord will deliver him in time of trouble.*" The compassionate lover of the poor thought of others and therefore God will think of him. God measures to us with our own bushel. Days of trouble come even to the most generous, and they have made the wisest provision for rainy days who have lent shelter to others when times were better with them. The promise is not that the generous saint shall have no trouble, but that he shall be preserved in it, and in due time brought out of it. How true was this of our Lord ! never trouble deeper nor triumph brighter than his, and glory be to his name, he secures the ultimate victory of all his blood-bought ones. Would that they all were more like him in putting on bowels of compassion to the poor. Much blessedness they miss who stint their alms. The joy of doing good, the sweet reaction of another's happiness, the approving smile of heaven upon the heart, if not upon the estate ; all these the niggardly soul knows nothing of. Selfishness bears in itself a curse, it is a cancer in the heart ; while liberality is happiness, and maketh fat the bones. In dark days we cannot rest upon the supposed merit of almsgiving, but still the music of memory brings with it no mean solace when it tells of widows and orphans whom we have succoured, and prisoners and sick folk to whom we have ministered.

2. " *The Lord will preserve him, and keep him alive.*" His noblest life shall be immortal, and even his mortal life shall be sacredly guarded by the power of Jehovah. Jesus lived on till his hour came, nor could the devices of crafty Herod take away his life till the destined hour had struck ; and even then no man took his life from him, but he laid it down of himself, to take it again. Here is the portion of all those who are made like their Lord, they bless and they shall be blessed, they preserve and shall be preserved, they watch over the lives of others and they themselves shall be precious in the sight of the Lord. The miser like the hog is of no use till he is dead—then let him die ; the righteous like the ox is of service during life—then let him live. " *And he shall be blessed upon the earth.*" Prosperity shall attend him. His cruse of oil shall not be dried up because he fed the poor prophet. He shall cut from his roll of cloth and find it longer at both ends.

> " There was a man, and some did count him mad,
> The more he gave away the more he had."

If temporal gains be not given him, spirituals shall be doubled to him. His little shall be blessed, bread and water shall be a feast to him. The liberal are and must be blessed even here ; they have a present as well as future portion. Our Lord's real blessedness of heart in the joy that was set before him is a subject worthy of earnest thought, especially as it is the picture of the blessing which all liberal saints may look for. " *And thou wilt not deliver him unto the will of his enemies.*" He helped the distressed, and now he shall find a champion in his God. What would not the good man's enemies do to him if they had him at their disposal ? Better be in a pit with vipers than be at the mercy of persecutors. This sentence sets before us a sweet negative, and yet it were not easy to have seen how it could be true of our Lord Jesus, did we not know that although he was exempted from much of blessing, being made a curse for us, yet even he was not altogether nor for ever left of God, but in due time was exalted above all his enemies.

3. " *The Lord will strengthen him upon the bed of languishing.*" The everlasting arms shall stay up his soul as friendly hands and downy pillows stay up the body of the sick. How tender and sympathising is this image ; how near it brings our God to our infirmities and sicknesses ! Whoever heard this of the old heathen Jove, or of the gods of India or China ? This is language peculiar to the God of Israel ; he it is who deigns to become nurse and attendant upon good men. If he smites with one hand he sustains with the other. Oh, it is blessed fainting when one falls upon the Lord's own bosom, and is upborne thereby ! Grace is the best of restoratives ; divine love is the noblest stimulant for a languishing patient ; it makes the soul strong as a giant, even when the aching bones are breaking through the skin. No physician like the Lord, no tonic like his promise, no wine like his love. " *Thou wilt make all his bed in his sickness.*" What, doth the Lord turn bedmaker to his sick children ? Herein is love indeed. Who would not consider the poor if such be the promised reward ? A bed soon grows hard when the body

is weary with tossing to and fro upon it, but grace gives patience, and God's smile gives peace, and the bed is made soft because the man's heart is content; the pillows are downy because the head is peaceful. Note that the Lord will make *all* his bed, from head to foot. What considerate and indefatigable kindness! Our dear and ever blessed Lord Jesus, though in all respects an inheritor of this promise, for our sakes condescended to forego the blessing, and died on a cross and not upon a bed; yet, even there, he was after awhile upheld and cheered by the Lord his God, so that he died in triumph.

We must not imagine that the benediction pronounced in these three verses belongs to all who casually give money to the poor, or leave it in their wills, or contribute to societies. Such do well, or act from mere custom, as the case may be, but they are not here alluded to. The blessing is for those whose habit it is to love their neighbour as themselves, and who for Christ's sake feed the hungry and clothe the naked. To imagine a man to be a saint who does not consider the poor as he has ability, is to conceive the fruitless fig tree to be acceptable; there will be sharp dealing with many professors on this point in the day when the King cometh in his glory.

4 I said, LORD, be merciful unto me: heal my soul; for I have sinned against thee.

5 Mine enemies speak evil of me, When shall he die, and his name perish?

6 And if he come to see *me*, he speaketh vanity: his heart gathereth iniquity to itself; *when* he goeth abroad, he telleth *it*.

7 All that hate me whisper together against me; against me do they devise my hurt.

8 An evil disease, *say they*, cleaveth fast unto him: and *now* that he lieth he shall rise up no more.

9 Yea, mine own familiar friend, in whom I trusted, which did eat of my bread, hath lifted up *his* heel against me.

Here we have a controversy between the pleader and his God. He had been a tender friend to the poor, and yet in the hour of his need the promised assistance was not forthcoming. In our Lord's case there was a dark and dreary night in which such arguments were well befitting himself and his condition.

4. "*I said*"—said it in earnest prayer—"*Lord, be merciful unto me.*" Prove now thy gracious dealings with my soul in adversity, since thou didst aforetime give me grace to act liberally in my prosperity. No appeal is made to justice; the petitioner but hints at the promised reward, but goes straightforward to lay his plea at the feet of mercy. How low was our Redeemer brought when such petitions could come from his reverend mouth, when his lips like lilies dropped such sweet smelling but bitter myrrh! "*Heal my soul.*" My time of languishing is come, now do as thou hast said, and strengthen me, especially in my soul. We ought to be far more earnest for the soul's healing than for the body's ease. We hear much of the cure of souls, but we often forget to care about it. "*For I have sinned against thee.*" Here was the root of sorrow. Sin and suffering are inevitable companions. Observe that by the Psalmist sin was felt to be mainly evil because directed against God. This is of the essence of true repentance. The immaculate Saviour could never have used such language as this unless there be here a reference to the sin which he took upon himself by imputation; and for our part we tremble to apply words so manifestly indicating personal rather than imputed sin. Applying the petition to David and other sinful believers, how strangely evangelical is the argument: heal me, not for I am innocent, but "*I have sinned.*" How contrary is this to all self-righteous pleading! How consonant with grace! How inconsistent with merit! Even the fact that the confessing penitent had remembered the poor, is but obliquely urged, but a direct appeal is made to mercy on the ground of great sin. O trembling reader, here is a divinely revealed precedent for thee, be not slow to follow it.

5. "*Mine enemies speak evil of me.*" It was their nature to do and speak evil; it was not possible that the child of God could escape them. The viper fastened on Paul's hand: the better the man the more likely, and the more venomous the slander. Evil tongues are busy tongues, and never deal in truth. Jesus was

traduced to the utmost, although no offence was in him. "*When shall he die, and his name perish?*" They could not be content till he was away. The world is not wide enough for evil men to live in while the righteous remain, yea, the bodily presence of the saints may be gone, but their memory is an offence to their foes. It was never merry England, say they, since men took to Psalm-singing. In the Master's case, they cried, "Away with such a fellow from the earth, it is not fit that he should live." If persecutors could have their way, the church should have but one neck, and that should be on the block. Thieves would fain blow out all candles. The lights of the world are not the delights of the world. Poor blind bats, they fly at the lamp, and try to dash it down; but the Lord liveth, and preserveth both the saints and their names.

6. "*And if he come to see me, he speaketh vanity.*" His visits of sympathy are visitations of mockery. When the fox calls on the sick lamb his words are soft, but he licks his lips in hope of the carcass. It is wretched work to have spies haunting one's bedchamber, calling in pretence of kindness, but with malice in their hearts. Hypocritical talk is always fulsome and sickening to honest men, but especially to the suffering saint. Our divine Lord had much of this from the false hearts that watched his words. "*His heart gathereth iniquity to itself.*" Like will to like. The bird makes its nest of feathers. Out of the sweetest flowers chemists can distil poison, and from the purest words and deeds malice can gather groundwork for calumnious report. It is perfectly marvellous how spite spins webs out of no materials whatever. Its is no small trial to have base persons around you lying in wait for every word which they may pervert into evil. The Master whom we serve was constantly subject to this affliction. "*When he goeth abroad, he telleth it.*" He makes his lies, and then vends them in open market. He is no sooner out of the house than he outs with his lie, and this against a sick man whom he called to see as a friend—a sick man to whose incoherent and random speeches pity should be showed. Ah, black-hearted wretch! A devil's cub indeed. How far abroad men will go to publish their slanders! They would fain placard the sky with their falsehoods. A little fault is made much of; a slip of the tongue is a libel, a mistake a crime, and if a word can bear two meanings the worse is always fathered upon it. Tell it in Gath, publish it in Askelon, that the daughters of the uncircumcised may triumph. It is base to strike a man when he is down, yet such is the meanness of mankind towards a Christian hero should he for awhile chance to be under a cloud.

7. "*All that hate me whisper together against me.*" The spy meets his comrades in conclave and sets them all a whispering. Why could they not speak out? Were they afraid of the sick warrior? Or were their designs so treacherous that they must needs be hatched in secresy? Mark the unanimity of the wicked— "*all.*" How heartily the dogs unite to hunt the stag! Would God we were half as united in holy labour as persecutors in their malicious projects, and were half as wise as they are crafty, for their whispering was craft as well as cowardice, the conspiracy must not be known till all is ready. "*Against me do they devise my hurt.*" They lay their heads together, and scheme and plot. So did Ahithophel and the rest of Absalom's counsellors, so also did the chief priests and Pharisees. Evil men are good at devising; they are given to meditation, they are deep thinkers, but the mark they aim at is evermore the hurt of the faithful. Snakes in the grass are never there for a good end.

8. "*An evil disease, say they, cleaveth fast unto him.*" They whisper that some curse has fallen upon him, and is riveted to him. They insinuate that a foul secret stains his character, the ghost whereof haunts his house, and never can be laid. An air of mystery is cast around this doubly dark saying, as if to show how indistinct are the mutterings of malice. Even thus was our Lord accounted "smitten of God and afflicted." His enemies conceived that God had forsaken him, and delivered him for ever into their hands. "*And now that he lieth he shall rise up no more.*" His sickness they hoped was mortal, and this was fine news for them. No more would the good man's holiness chide their sin, they would now be free from the check of his godliness. Like the friars around Wickliffe's bed, their prophesyings were more jubilant than accurate, but they were a sore scourge to the sick man. When the Lord smites his people with his rod of affliction for a small moment, their enemies expect to see them capitally executed, and prepare their *jubilates* to celebrate their funerals, but they are in too great a hurry, and have to alter their ditties and sing to another tune. Our Redeemer eminently fore-

tokened this, for out of his lying in the grave he has gloriously risen. **Vain the watch, the stone, the seal!** Rising he pours confusion on his enemies.

9. " *Yea.*" Here is the climax of the sufferer's woe, and he places before it the emphatic affirmation, as if he thought that such villany would scarcely be believed. " *Mine own familiar friend.*" " The man of my peace," so runs the original, with whom I had no differences, with whom I was in league, who had aforetime ministered to my peace and comfort. This was Ahithophel to David, and Iscariot with our Lord. Judas was an apostle, admitted to the privacy of the Great Teacher, hearing his secret thoughts, and, as it were, allowed to read his very heart. " *Et tu Brute?*" said the expiring Cæsar. The kiss of the traitor wounded our Lord's heart as much as the nail wounded his hand. " *In whom I trusted.*" Judas was the treasurer of the apostolic college. Where we place great confidence an unkind act is the more severely felt. " *Which did eat of my bread.*" Not only as a guest but as a dependant, a pensioner at my board. Judas dipped in the same dish with his Lord, and hence the more accursed was his treachery in his selling his Master for a slave's price. " *Hath lifted up his heel against me.*" Not merely turned his back on me, but left me with a heavy kick such as a vicious horse might give. Hard is it to be spurned in our need by those who formerly fed at our table. It is noteworthy that the Redeemer applied only the last words of this verse to Judas, perhaps because, knowing his duplicity, he had never made a familiar friend of him in the fullest sense, and had not placed implicit trust in him. Infernal malice so planned it that every circumstance in Jesus' death should add wormwood to it ; and the betrayal was one of the bitterest drops of gall. We are indeed, wretched when our *quondam* friend becomes our relentless foe, when confidence is betrayed, when all the rites of hospitality are perverted, and ingratitude is the only return for kindness ; yet in so deplorable a case we may cast ourselves upon the faithfulness of God, who, having delivered our Covenant Head, is in verity engaged to be the very present help of all for whom that covenant was made.

10 But thou O LORD, be merciful unto me, and raise me up, that I may requite them.

10. " *But thou, O Lord, be merciful unto me.*" How the hunted and affrighted soul turns to her God ! How she seems to take breath with a " but, thou ! " How she clings to the hope of mercy from God when every chance of pity from man is gone ! " *And raise me up.*" Recover me from my sickness, give me to regain my position. Jesus was raised up from the grave ; his descent was ended by an ascent. " *That I may requite them.*" This as it reads is a truly Old Testament sentence, and quite aside from the spirit of Christianity, yet we must remember that David was a person in magisterial office, and might without any personal revenge, desire to punish those who had insulted his authority and libelled his public character. Our great Apostle and High Priest had no personal animosities, but even he by his resurrection has requited the powers of evil, and avenged on death and hell all their base attacks upon his cause and person. Still the strained application of every sentence of this Psalm to Christ is not to our liking, and we prefer to call attention to the better spirit of the gospel beyond that of the old dispensation.

11 By this I know thou favourest me, because mine enemy doth not triumph over me.

12 And as for me, thou upholdest me in mine integrity, and settest me before thy face for ever.

13 Blessed *be* the LORD God of Israel from everlasting, and to everlasting. Amen and Amen.

11. We all are cheered by tokens for good, and the Psalmist felt it to be an auspicious omen, that after all his deep depression he was not utterly given over to his foe. " *By this I know that thou favourest me.*" Thou hast a special regard to me, I have the secret assurance of this in my heart, and, therefore, thine outward dealings do not dismay me, for I know that thou lovest me in them all. " *Because mine enemy doth not triumph over me.*" What if the believer has no triumph over his foes, he must be glad that they do not triumph over him. If we have not all

we would we should praise God for all we have. Much there is in us over which the ungodly might exult, and if God's mercy keeps the dogs' mouths closed when they might be opened, we must give him our heartiest gratitude. What a wonder it is that when the devil enters the lists with a poor, erring, bedridden, deserted, slandered saint, and has a thousand evil tongues to aid him, yet he cannot win the day, but in the end slinks off without renown.

> "The feeblest saint shall win the day
> Though death and hell obstruct his way."

12. "*And as for me*," despite them all and in the sight of them all, "*thou upholdest me in mine integrity ;* " thy power enables me to rise above the reach of slander by living in purity and righteousness. Our innocence and consistency are the result of the divine upholding. We are like those glasses without feet, which can only be upright while they are held in the hand ; we fall, and spill, and spoil all, if left to ourselves. The Lord should be praised every day if we are preserved from gross sin. When others sin they show us what we should do but for grace. "He to-day and I to-morrow," was the exclamation of a holy man, whenever he saw another falling into sin. Our integrity is comparative as well as dependant, we must therefore be humbled while we are grateful. If we are clear of the faults alleged against us by our calumniators, we have nevertheless quite enough of actual blameworthiness to render it shameful for us to boast. "*And settest me before thy face for ever.*" He rejoiced that he lived under the divine surveillance ; tended, cared for, and smiled upon by his Lord ; and yet more, that it would be so world without end. To stand before an earthly monarch is considered to be a singular honour, but what must it be to be a perpetual courtier in the palace of the King Eternal, Immortal, Invisible ?

13. The Psalm ends with a doxology. "*Blessed be the Lord,*" *i.e.*, let him be glorified. The blessing at the beginning from the mouth of God is returned from the mouth of his servant. We cannot add to the Lord's blessedness, but we can pour out our grateful wishes, and these he accepts, as we receive little presents of flowers from children who love us. Jehovah is the personal name of our God. "*God of Israel*" is his covenant title, and shows his special relation to his elect people. "*From everlasting and to everlasting.*" The strongest way of expressing endless duration. *We die*, but the glory of God goes on and on without pause. "*Amen and amen.*" So let it surely, firmly, and eternally be. Thus the people joined in the Psalm by a double shout of holy affirmation ; let us unite in it with all our hearts. This last verse may serve for the prayer of the universal church in all ages, but none can sing it so sweetly as those who have experienced as David did the faithfulness of God in times of extremity.

EXPLANATORY NOTES AND QUAINT SAYINGS.

Title.—The *Syriac* says, " It was a Psalm of David, when he appointed overseers to take care of the poor."—*Adam Clarke.*

Whole Psalm.—A prophecy of Christ and the traitor Judas.—*Eusebius of Cæsarea, quoted by J. M. Neale.*

Verse 1.—" *Blessed is he that considereth the poor.*" Interpreters are generally of opinion that the exercise of kindness and compassion, manifested in taking care of the miserable, and helping them, is here commended. Those, however, who maintain that the Psalmist here commends the considerate candour of those who judge wisely and charitably of men in adversity, form a better judgment of his meaning. Indeed, the participle, משכיל *maskil*, cannot be explained in any other way. At the same time it ought to be observed on what account it is that David declares those to be blessed who form a wise and prudent judgment concerning the afflictions by which God chastises his servants. . . . Doubtless it happened to him as it did to the holy patriarch Job, whom his friends reckoned to be one of the most wicked of men, when they saw God treating him with great severity. And certainly it is an error which is by far too common among men, to look upon those who are oppressed with afflictions as condemned and reprobate. . . . For the most part, indeed, we often speak rashly and indiscriminately concerning others, and, so to speak, plunge even into the lowest abyss those who labour under affliction. To restrain such a rash and unbridled spirit, David says, that they are blessed who do not suffer themselves, by speaking at random, to judge harshly of their neighbours ; but discerning aright the afflictions by which they are visited, mitigate by the wisdom of the spirit, the severe and unjust judgments to which we naturally are so prone.—*John Calvin.*

Verse 1.—*" Blessed is he that considereth the poor."* As Christ considered us in our state of poverty, so ought we most attentively to consider him in his ; to consider what he suffered in his own person ; to discern him suffering in his poor afflicted members ; and to extend to them the mercy which he extended to us. He, who was " blessed " of Jehovah, and " delivered in the evil day " by a glorious resurrection, will " bless " and " deliver " in like manner, such as for his sake, love and relieve their brethren.—*George Horne.*

Verse 1.—*" Blessed is he that considereth the poor."* Not the poor of the world in common, nor poor saints in particular but some single poor man ; for the word is in the singular number, and designs our Lord Jesus Christ, who, in the last verse of the preceding Psalm, is said to be *poor and needy.—John Gill.*

Verse 1.—*" Blessed is he that considereth the poor."* I call your attention to the way in which the Bible enjoins us to take up the care of the poor. It does not say in the text before us, Commiserate the poor ; for, if it said no more than this, it would leave their necessities to be provided for by the random ebullitions of an impetuous and unreflecting sympathy. It provides them with a better security than the mere feeling of compassion—a feeling which, however useful to the purpose of excitement, must be controlled and regulated. Feeling is but a faint and fluctuating security. Fancy may mislead it. The sober realities of life may disgust it. Disappointment may extinguish it. Ingratitude may embitter it. Deceit, with its counterfeit representations, may allure it to the wrong object. At all events, Time is the little circle in which it in general expatiates. It needs the impression of sensible objects to sustain it ; nor can it enter with zeal or with vivacity into the wants of the abstract and invisible soul. The Bible, then, instead of leaving the relief of the poor to the mere instinct of sympathy, makes it a subject for *consideration*—" Blessed is he that *considereth* the poor," a grave and prosaic exercise, I do allow, and which makes no figure in those high-wrought descriptions, where the exquisite tale of benevolence is made up of all the sensibilities of tenderness on the one hand, and of all the ecstacies of gratitude on the other. The Bible rescues the cause from the mischief to which a heedless or unthinking sensibility would expose it. It brings it under the cognisance of a higher faculty—a faculty of steadier operation than to be weary in well-doing, and of sturdier endurance than to give it up in disgust. It calls you to *consider* the poor. It makes the virtue of relieving them a matter of computation, as well as of sentiment, and in so doing puts you beyond the reach of the various delusions, by which you are at one time led to prefer the indulgence of pity to the substantial interest of its object ; at another, are led to retire chagrined and disappointed from the scene of duty, because you have not met with the gratitude or the honesty that you laid your account with ; at another, are led to expend all your anxieties upon the accommodation of time, and to overlook eternity. It is the office of *consideration* to save you from all these fallacies. Under its tutorage attention to the wants of the poor ripens into principle. . . . .

It must be obvious to all of you, that it is not enough that you give money, and add your name to the contributions of charity. You must give it with judgment. You must give your time and your attention. You must descend to the trouble of examination. You must rise from the repose of contemplation, and make yourself acquainted with the object of your benevolent exercises. . . . To give money is not to do all the work and labour of benevolence. You must go to the poor man's sick-bed. You must lend your hand to the work of assistance. This is true and unsophisticated goodness. It may be recorded in no earthly documents ; but, if done under the influence of Christian principle, in a word, if done unto Jesus, it is written in the book of heaven, and will give a new lustre to that crown to which his disciples look forward in time, and will wear through eternity.—*From a Sermon preached before the Society for Relief of the Destitute Sick, in St. Andrew's Church, Edinburgh, by Thomas Chalmers, D.D. and LL.D. (1780—1847).*

Verse 1.—*" Blessed is he that considereth the poor."* A Piedmontese nobleman into whose company I fell, at Turin, told me the following story : " I was weary of life, and after a day such as few have known, and none would wish to remember, was hurrying along the street to the river, when I felt a sudden check, I turned and beheld a little boy, who had caught the skirt of my cloak in his anxiety to solicit my notice. His look and manner were irresistible. No less so was the lesson he had learnt—' There are six of us, and we are dying for want of food.' ' Why should I not,' said I to myself, ' relieve this wretched family ? I have the means, and it will not delay me many minutes. But what if it does ? ' The scene of misery he conducted me to I cannot describe. I threw them my purse, and their burst of gratitude overcame me It filled my eyes, it went as a cordial to my heart. ' I will call again to-morrow,' I cried. ' Fool that I was to think of leaving a world where such pleasure was to be had, and so cheaply ! ' "—*Samuel Rogers (1763—1855) in " Italy."*

Verse 1.—*" He that considereth the poor : "*—

> An ardent spirit dwells with Christian love,
> The eagle's vigour in the pitying dove.
> 'Tis not enough that we with sorrow sigh,
> That we the wants of pleading man supply,
> That we in sympathy with sufferers feel,
> Nor hear a grief without a wish to heal :
> Not these suffice—to sickness, pain, and woe,
> The Christian spirit loves with aid to go :
> Will not be sought, waits not for want to plead,
> But seeks the duty—nay, prevents the need ;
> Her utmost aid to every ill applies,
> And plants relief for coming miseries.
>
> *George Crabbe,* 1754—1832.

Verse 1.—How foolish are they that fear to lose their wealth by giving it, and fear not to lose themselves by keeping it ! He that lays up his gold may be a good *jailer,* but he that lays it out is a good *steward.* Merchants traffic thither with a commodity where 'tis precious in regard of scarcity. We do not buy wines in England to carry them to France, spices in France to carry them to the Indies ; so for labour and work, repentance and mortification, there is none of them in heaven, there is peace and glory, and the favour of God indeed. A merchant without his commodity hath but a sorry welcome. God will ask men that arrive at heaven's gates, *ubi opera ?* Rev. xxii. 12. His reward shall be according to our works. Thou hast riches here, and here be objects that need thy riches—the poor ; in heaven there are riches enough but no poor, therefore, by faith in Christ make over to them thy moneys in this world, that by bill of exchange thou mayest receive it in the world to come ; that only you carry with you which you send before you. Do good while it is in your power ; relieve the oppressed, succour the fatherless, while your estates are your own ; when you are dead your riches belong to others. One light carried before a man is more serviceable than twenty carried after him. In your compassion to the distressed, or for pious uses, let your hands be your executors, and your eyes your overseers.—*Francis Raworth, Teacher to the Church at Shoreditch, in a Funeral Sermon,* 1656.

Verses 1, 3.—It is a blessed thing to receive when a man hath need ; but 'tis a more blessed thing to give than to receive. *" Blessed* (saith the prophet David) *is he that considereth the poor."* What ? to say, alas, poor man ! the world is hard with him, I would there were a course taken to do him good ? No, no ; but so to consider him as to give ; to give till the poor man be satisfied, to draw out one's sheaf, ay, one's very soul to the hungry. But what if troubles should come ? were it not better to keep money by one ? Money will not deliver one. It may be an occasion to endanger one, to bring one into, rather than help one out of trouble ; but if a man be a merciful man, *God will deliver him,* either by himself, or by some other man or matter. Ay, but what if *sickness* come ? Why, *" the Lord will strengthen him upon the bed of languishing ; "* and, which is a great ease and kindness ; God, as it were, himself *" will make all his bed in his sickness."* Here poor people have the advantage : such must not say, Alas, I am a poor woman, what works of mercy can I do ? for they are they who can best make the beds of sick folk, which we see is a great act of mercy in that it is said, that *the Lord himself will make their bed in their sickness.* And there are none so poor, but they may *make the beds* of the sick.— *Richard Capel.*

Verses 1, 5.—" *He that considereth.*" " *Mine enemies.*" Strigelius has observed, there is a perpetual antithesis in this Psalm between the few who have a due regard to the poor in spirit, and the many who afflict or desert them.—*W. Wilson, D.D.*

Verse 2.—" *The Lord will preserve him, and keep him alive.*" It is worthy of remark, that *benevolent persons,* who " *consider the poor,*" and especially the *sick poor ;* who search cellars, garrets, back lanes, and such abodes of misery, to find them out (even in the places where contagion keeps its seat), very seldom fall a prey to their own benevolence. The Lord, in an especial manner, keeps them *alive,* and preserves them ; while many, who endeavour to keep far from the contagion, are assailed by it, and fall victims to it. God loves the merciful man.—*Adam Clarke.*

Verse 2.—" *He shall be blessed upon the earth.*" None of the godly man's afflictions shall hinder or take away his begun blessedness, even in this world.— *David Dickson.*

Verse 3.—" *Thou wilt make all his bed in his sickness.*" Into what minuteness of exquisite and touching tenderness does the Lord condescend to enter ! One feels almost as we may suppose Peter felt when the Saviour came to him, and would have washed his feet, " Lord ! thou shalt never wash my feet ; " thou shalt never make my bed. And yet, " If I wash thee not, thou hast no part with me ; " if the Lord make not our bed in our sickness, there is no peace nor comfort there. We have had David calling on God to bow down his ear, like a loving mother listening to catch the feeblest whisper of her child ; and the image is full of the sweetest sympathy and condescension ; but here the Lord, the great God of heaven, he that said when on earth, " I am among you as one that serveth," does indeed take upon him the form, and is found in fashion as a servant, fulfilling all the loving and tender offices of an assiduous nurse.—*Barton Bouchier.*

Verse 3.—" *Thou wilt make all his bed in his sickness.*" The meaning rather is, " it is no longer a sick bed, for thou hast healed him of his disease."—*J. J. Stewart Perowne.*

Verse 3.—When a good man is ill at ease, God promiseth to make all his bed in his sickness. Pillow, bolster, head, feet, sides, all his bed. Surely that God who made him knows so well his measure and temper as to make his bed to please him. Herein his art is excellent, not fitting the bed to the person, but the person to the bed ; infusing patience into him. But, oh ! how shall God make my bed, who have no bed of mine own to make. Thou fool, he can make thy not having a bed to be a bed unto thee. When Jacob slept on the ground, who would not have had his hard lodging, therewithal to have his heavenly dream ?—*Thomas Fuller.*

Verse 3.—Sure that bed must need be soft which God will make.—*T. Watson.*

Verse 3.—We must not forget that Oriental beds needed not to be made in the same sense as our own. They were never more than mattresses or quilts thickly padded, and were turned when they became uncomfortable, and that is just the word here used.—*C. H. S.*

Verse 3.—When I visited one day, as he was dying, my beloved friend Benjamin Parsons, I said, " How are you to-day, Sir ? " He said, " My head is resting very sweetly on three pillows—infinite power, infinite love, and infinite wisdom." Preaching in the Canterbury Hall, in Brighton, I mentioned this some time since ; and many months after I was requested to call upon a poor but holy young woman, apparently dying. She said, " I felt I must see you before I died. I heard you tell the story of Benjamin Parsons and his three pillows ; and when I went through a surgical operation, and it was very cruel, I was leaning my head on pillows, and as they were taking them away I said, ' Mayn't I keep them ? ' The surgeon said, ' No, my dear, we must take them away.' ' But,' said I, ' you can't take away Benjamin Parsons' three pillows. I can lay my head on infinite power, infinite love, and infinite wisdom.' "—*Paxton Hood, in* " *Dark Sayings on a Harp,*" 1865.

Verses 3, 4.—What saith David from the very bottom of his heart, in his sickness ? Not, take away this death only. No ; but David being sick, first comforts himself with this promise, " *The Lord will strengthen him upon the bed of languishing : thou wilt make all his bed in his sickness ;* " and then adds, " *I said, Lord, be merciful unto me, and heal my soul ;* " that is, destroy my lusts, which are the diseases of my soul, Lord ; and heal my soul, and renew life and communion with thee, which is the health and strength of my soul. Do not take this sickness and death only away ; but this sin away, that hath dishonoured thee, hath separated between me and thee : " *Heal my soul, for I have sinned against thee.*"—*Thomas Goodwin.*

Verse 4.—" *I said, Lord, be merciful.*" Mercy, not justice ! The extreme of mercy for the extreme of misery. Righteousness as filthy rags ; a flesh in which dwelleth no good thing, on the one side ; on the other, it is " neither herb nor mollifying plaster that restored " to health ; " but thy word, O Lord, which healeth all things." Wisd. xvi. 12.—*Thomas Aquinas, quoted by J. M. Neale.*

Verse 4.—God is the strength of a Christian's heart, by healing and restoring him when the infused habits of grace fail, and sin grows strong and vigorous. A Christian never fails in the exercise of grace, but sin gives him a wound ; and therefore David prayed, "*Lord, heal my soul, for I have sinned.* And what David prayed for, God promiseth to his people : " I will heal their backsliding." Hosea xiv. 4. The weakness and decay of grace, brings a Christian presently to the falling sickness ; and so it did David and Ephraim ; ay, but God will be a physician to the soul in this case, and will heal their diseases ; and so he did David's falling sickness, for which he returned the tribute of praise. Psalm ciii. 3.—*Samuel Blackerby.*

Verse 4. (*last clause*).—Saul and Judas each said, " I have sinned ;" but David says, " I have sinned *against thee.*"—*William S. Plumer.*

Verse 5.—" *Mine enemies speak evil of me.*" To speak is here used in the sense of *to imprecate.*—*John Calvin.*

Verse 5.—" *His name.*" It is the *name*, the character, and privileges of a true servant of God, that calls out the hatred of ungodly men, and they would gladly extirpate him from their sight.—*W. Wilson, D.D.*

Verse 6.—" *If he come to see me, he speaketh vanity :* " many fair words, but none of them true.—*David Dickson.*

Verse 6.—I remember a pretty apologue that Bromiard tells :—A fowler, in a sharp frosty morning, having taken many little birds for which he had long watched, began to take up his nets, and nipping the birds on the head laid them down. A young thrush, espying the tears trickling down his cheeks by reason of the extreme cold, said to her mother, that certainly the man was very merciful and compassionate, who wept so bitterly over the calamity of the poor birds. But her mother told her more wisely, that she might better judge of the man's disposition by his hand than by his eye ; and if the hands do strike treacherously, he can never be admitted to friendship, who speaks fairly and weeps pitifully.—*Jeremy Taylor.*

Verse 6.—" *His heart gathereth iniquity to itself.*" 1. By adding sin to sin, in that he covers over his malice with such horrid hypocrisy. 2. By inventing or contriving all the several ways he can to ensnare me, or do me some mischief, thereby seeking to satisfy and please his corrupt lusts and affections ; 3. (which I like best), by observing all he can in me, and drawing what he can from me, and so laying all up together in his mind, as the ground of his unjust surmises and censures concerning me.—*Arthur Jackson.*

Verse 8.—" *An evil disease, say they, cleaveth fast unto him.*" An evil deed of Belial cleaveth fast to him. Grammarians maintain that the word *Belial* is compounded of לְבּ, *beli*, and יַעַל, *yaal*, which signify " *not to rise;*" the expression, " *thing of Belial* " (for so it is literally in the Hebrew), I understand in this place as meaning an extraordinary and hateful crime which as we commonly say can never be expiated, and from which there is no possibility of escape ; unless perhaps some would rather refer it to the affliction itself under which he laboured, as if his enemies had said that he was seized by some incurable malady.—*John Calvin.*

Verse 8.—" *An evil disease,*" etc. What is here meant by דְּבַר־בְּלִיַּעַל is matter of some difficulty. The ancient interpreters generally render it a *perverse*, or *mischievous*, or *wicked word ;* the Chaldee, a *perverse word ;* the Syriac, a *word of iniquity ;* the LXX. λόγον παράνομον ; the Latin, *iniquum verbum*, a *wicked word ;* the Arabic, *words contrary to the law.* And so in all probability it is set to signify a *great slander*, or *calumny*—that as " men of Belial " are *slanderous* persons, so the *speech of Belial* shall signify a *slanderous* speech. And this is said to " *cleave* " to him on whom it is fastened, it being the nature of calumnies, when strongly affixed on any, to *cleave* fast, and leave some *evil mark* behind them.—*Henry Hammond.*

Verse 9.—" *Yea, mine own familiar friend,*" etc. The sufferings of the church, like those of her Redeemer, generally begin at home : her open enemies can do her no harm, until her pretended friends have delivered her into their hands; and, unnatural as it may seem, they who have waxed fat upon her bounty, are sometimes the first to " *lift the heel* " against her.—*George Horne.*

Verse 9.—" *Mine own familiar friend.*" He who, on visiting me, continually saluted me with the kiss of love and veneration, and the usual address ; peace be to thee.—*Hermann Venema.*

Verse 9.—" *Which did eat of my bread.*" If the same sentiment prevailed among the Hebrews, which prevails at the present day among the Bedouin Arabs, of sacred regard to the person and property of one with whom they have eaten bread and salt, the language is very forcible. " *Hath lifted up his heel :* " a metaphor drawn from the horse, which attacks with its heel. This language may well have been used by our Saviour in John xiii. 18, in the way of rhetorical illustration or emphasis. —*George R. Noyes, D.D.*

Verse 9.—" *Hath lifted up his heel against me.*" In this phrase he seems to allude to a beast's kicking at his master by whom he is fed, or the custom of men's spurning at or trampling upon those that are cast down on the ground, in a way of despite and contempt.—*Arthur Jackson.*

Verse 9.—" *Hath lifted up his heel against me ;* " *i.e.,* hath spurned me, hath kicked at me, as a vicious beast of burden does ; hath insulted me in my misery.— *Daniel Cresswell.*

Verse 10.—" *That I may requite them.*" Either (1), kindness for injuries (as in Psalm xxxv. 13) : it is the mark of a good and brave man to do good to all in his power, to hurt no one, even though provoked by wrong : or, (2), punishment for wrong-doing—*that I may punish them ;* for am I not their magistrate, and the executioner of God's justice !—*Martin Geier.*

Verse 10.—" *That I may requite them.*" David was not as one of the common people, but a king appointed by God and invested with authority, and it is not from an impulse of the flesh, but in virtue of the nature of his office, that he is led to denounce against his enemies the punishment which they had merited.—*John Calvin.*

Verse 11.—" *By this I know that thou favourest me, because mine enemy doth not triumph over me :* " not because I have no enemies, or because I have no trouble which would overcome me. Therefore when he wrote down *many troubles*, he blotted it (as it were) with his pen again, as a merchant razeth his book when the debt is discharged ; and instead of *many troubles*, he putteth in, *the Lord delivereth.* Because he forgiveth all sins, he is said to deliver from all troubles, to show that we have need of no Saviour, no helper, no comforter, but him.—*Henry Smith.*

Verse 11.—" *By this I know that thou favourest me.*" In this text we see two things. 1. How David assureth himself of God's love towards him. 2. How thankful he is to God for assuring him of his love. The first he doth by two arguments ; one is taken from his enemies, they were prevented of their expectation " Therefore thou lovest me." The other is taken from his own estate, which was not one whit hurt, or impaired, but bettered by them. . . . Here the prophet speaketh of his knowledge, and telleth us that though he knew not all things, yet he knew that God loved him, and so long as he knoweth that, he careth not greatly for other matters, how the world goeth with him, etc. And, to say the truth, he need not, for he that is sure of that, is sure of all. God loveth all his creatures as a good God, and hateth nothing that he made, but he loveth his elect children with a more especial love than the rest, as a Father in Christ Jesus, and he that is sure that God doth so favour him, is sure, I say, of all. For to him whom God loveth, he will deny no good thing, no, not his own Son ; and if he gave us his Son, because he loved us, how shall he not with him give us all things else ?

When the child is persuaded that his father loveth him, he is bold to ask this and that of his father : so may we be bold to ask anything of God our heavenly

Father that is good for us, when we be sure that he loveth us. As Mary and Martha put Christ in mind but of two things ; the first was, that Christ loved their brother Lazarus ; the second was, that Lazarus was sick ; " He whom thou lovest is sick : " it was no need to tell him what he should do, for they knew he would do what might be done for him, because he loved him. So we may say to the Lord, when we are sure that he loveth us : Lord, he whom thou lovest wanteth this or that for his body or his soul. We need not then appoint him what to do, or when, or how ; for look what he seeth most convenient for us, and for his own glory, he will surely do it. Therefore whatsoever David knoweth, he will be sure to know this ; and whatsoever he is ignorant of, yet of this he will not be ignorant ; to teach us that whatsoever we seek to make sure, this must first be made sure, or else nothing is sure. Peter bids us make our election sure ; Job, when he saith, " I am sure that my Redeemer liveth," teacheth us to make our redemption sure. And here David teacheth us to make *God's favour* sure : now if we make that sure, then our election is sure, our redemption is sure, our vocation is sure, and our salvation is sure.— *William Burton*, 1602.

Verse 11.—"*Because mine enemy doth not triumph over me.*" When God doth deliver us from the hands of our enemies, or any trouble else, we may persuade ourselves thereby, he hath a favour unto us, as David did. But then it may be demanded, If God doth love his church, why doth he suffer his church to be troubled and molested with enemies ? The reason is this, because by this means his love may be made more manifest in saving and delivering them. For as a sure friend is not known but in time of need, so God's goodness and love is never so well perceived as it is in helping of us when we cannot help ourselves. As Adam's fall did serve to manifest God's justice and mercy, the one in punishing, the other in pardoning of sin, which otherwise we had never known : so the troubles of the church serve to manifest, first, our deserts by reason of our sins ; secondly, our weakness and inability to help ourselves ; and, thirdly, the lovingkindness of the Lord our God, in saving and defending, that so we might be truly thankful, and return all the praise and glory to God, and none to ourselves. So that the church of God may have enemies, and yet be still the beloved of God, as Lazarus was beloved of Christ, although he was sick ; for whom the Lord loveth he correcteth, and therefore he correcteth them because he loveth them.—*William Burton*.

Verse 11.—God preserves his own, and bringeth their foes to nought : after Passion week comes Easter.—*J. P. Lange's Commentary*.

Verse 12.—"*Integrity.*" This same integrity is like Noah's ark, wherein he was preserved, when others perished, being without it. It is like the red thread, which the spies of Joshua gave to Rahab, it was a charter whereby she claimed her life when the rest were destroyed, which had not the like. So is this integrity of small reckoning, I confess, with the men of this world, which think that there is no other heaven but earth ; but as Rahab's thread was better to her than all her goods and substance when the sword came, so this is better to God's children than all the world when death comes. If they have this within they care not, nay, they need not care what can come without. If Satan's buffeting come, this is a helmet of proof ; if Satan's darts fly out, this is a shield to quench them ; if floods of crosses come to carry us away, this is a boat to bear us up ; if all the world cast mire and filth in our faces. we are never a whit the more deformed, but still beautiful for all that, for " the king's daughter," (saith Solomon, Psalm xlv. 13), that is, the church of Christ, " is all glorious within."—*William Burton*.

Verse 12.—"*Settest me before thy face for ever ;* " or hast confirmed or established me in thy presence ; *i.e.*, either under thine eye and special care, or to minister unto thee, not only in thy temple, but as a king over thy people, or in that land where thou art peculiarly present.—*Matthew Pool*.

Verse 13.—"*Blessed be the Lord God of Israel from everlasting, and to everlasting. Amen, and Amen.*" We are here taught, 1. To give glory to God, as "*the Lord God of Israel*," a God in covenant with his people ; that has done great and kind things for them, and has more and better in reserve. 2. To give him glory as an eternal God, that has both his being and his blessedness "*from everlasting and to everlasting.*" 3. To do this with great affection and fervour of spirit, intimated in a double seal set to it, "*Amen, and Amen.*" We say Amen to it, and let all others say Amen too.—*Matthew Henry*.

Verse 13.—" *Amen and Amen.*"   As the Psalms were not written by one man, so neither do they form one book.   The Psalter is, in fact, a Pentateuch, and the lines of demarcation, which divide the five books one from another, are clear and distinct enough.   At the end of the 41st Psalm, of the 72nd, of the 89th, and of the 106th, we meet with the solemn *Amen,* single or redoubled, following on a doxology, which indicates that one book ends and that another is about to begin. A closer study of the Psalms shows that each book possesses characteristics of its own.   Jehovah, (" the Lord ") for example, is prominent as the divine name in the first book, Elohim (" God ") in the second.—*E. H. Plumptre, M.A., in " Biblical Studies,*" 1870.

There is also another observable difference between the two books.   In the first, all those Psalms which have any inscription at all are expressly assigned to David as their author, whereas in the second we find a whole series attributed to some of the Levitical singers.—*J. J. Stewart Perowne.*

How ancient this division is cannot now be clearly ascertained.   Jerome, in his epistle to Marcella, and Epiphanius speak of the Psalms as having been divided by the Hebrews into five books, but when this division was made they do not inform us.   The forms of ascriptions of praise, added at the end of each of the five books, are in the Septuagint version, from which we may conclude that this distribution had been made before that version was executed.   It was probably made by Ezra, after the return of the Jews from Babylon to their own country, and the establishment of the worship of God in the new temple, and it was perhaps made in imitation of a similar distribution of the books of Moses.   In making this division of the Hebrew Psalter, regard appears to have been paid to the subject matter of the Psalms.—*John Calvin.*

These forty-one Psalms, it has been observed, forming the first book, relate chiefly to the ministry of Christ upon earth, preparing those who were looking for the consolation of Israel, for his appearing amongst them.   Accordingly, the second book, commencing with Psalm xlii., may refer chiefly to the infant church of Christ.—*W. Wilson, D.D.*

May not the growth of the Book of Psalms be illustrated by the case of our Modern Hymn Books which in the course of years require first one appendix and then another, so as to incorporate the growing psalmody of the church ?   In this case the purely Davidic Psalms of the first division formed the nucleus to which other sacred songs were speedily added.—*C. H. S.*

HINTS TO PREACHERS.

Verse 1 (*first clause*).—The incidental blessings resulting from considering the pious poor.   1. We learn gratitude.   2. We see patience.   3. We often remark the triumphs of great grace.   4. We obtain light on Christian experience.   5. We have their prayers.   6. We feel the pleasure of beneficence.   7. We enter into communion with the lowly Saviour.

Verse 1.—The support of the Small-pox Hospitals recommended.—*Bishop Squire,* 1760.   Scores of sermons of this kind have been preached from this text.

Verse 2.—" *Blessed upon the earth.*"   What blessings of an earthly character godly character secures, and in general what it is to be blessed with regard to this life.

Verse 2 (*second clause*).—What it is to be delivered *in* trouble.   From impatience, from despair, from sinful expedients, from violent attacks, from losing fellowship with God.

Verse 3.—Strength in weakness.   Inward strength, divinely given, continuously sustained, enduring to the end, triumphant in death, glorifying to God, proving the reality of grace, winning others to the faith.

Verse 3 (*last clause*).—The heavenly bed-making.

Verse 4 (*first clause*).—A saying worth repeating : " *I said.*"   It expresses penitence, humility, earnestness, faith, importunity, fear of God, etc.

Verse 4.—" *Heal my soul.*"   1. The hereditary disease, breaking **out** in many disorders—open sin, unbelief, decline of grace, etc. II. Spiritual health struggling with it ; shown in spiritual pain, desire, prayer, effort. III. The well-proved Physician. Has healed, and will, by his word, his blood, his Spirit, etc.

Verse 4.—" *I have sinned against thee.*" This confession is personal, plain, without pretence of excuse, comprehensive and intelligent, for it reveals the very heart of sin—" against thee."

Verse 5.—What we may expect. What our enemies desire. What we may, therefore prize, *i.e.*, the power of Christian life and name. What we should do— tell the Lord all in prayer. What good will then come of the evil.

Verse 6 (first clause).—The folly and sin of frivolous visits.

Verse 6 (second and third clauses).—Like to like, or the way in which character draws its like to itself. The same subject might be treated under the title of *The Chiffonnier*, or the rag-collector. What he gathers ; where he puts it—in his " *heart ;* " what he does with it ; what he gets for it ; and what will become of him.

Verses 7—12.—On a sick bed a man discovers not only his enemies and his friends, but himself and his God, more intimately.

Verse 9.—The treachery of Judas.

Verse 11.—Deliverance from temptation a token of divine favour.

Verse 12.—This text reveals the insignia of those whom grace has distinguished. 1. Their integrity is manifest. 2. Their character is divinely sustained. 3. They dwell in the favour of God. 4. Their position is stable and continuous. 5. Their eternal future is secure.

Verse 13.—I. The object of praise—Jehovah, the covenant God. II. The nature of the praise—without beginning or end. III. Our participation in the praise—" Amen and Amen."

THE ancient rabbins saw in the Five Books of the Psalter the image of the Five Books of the Law. This way of looking on the Psalms as a second Pentateuch, the echo of the first, passed over into the Christian church, and found favour with some early fathers. It has commended itself to the acceptance of good recent expositors, like Dr. Delitzsch, who calls the Psalter " the Congregation's five-fold word to the Lord, even as the *Thora* (the Law) is the Lord's five-fold word to the Congregation." This may be mere fancy, but its existence from ancient times shows that the five-fold division attracted early notice.—*William Binnie, D.D.*

God presented Israel with the Law, a Pentateuch, and grateful Israel responded with a Psalter, a Pentateuch of praise, in acknowledgment of the divine gift.—*J. L. K.*

HERE ENDETH THE FIRST BOOK OF
THE PSALMS.

PSALM XLII.

TITLE.—To the Chief Musician, Maschil, for the sons of Korah.—*Dedicated to the Master of Music, this Psalm is worthy of his office ; he who can sing best can have nothing better to sing. It is called Maschil, or an instructive ode ; and full as it is of deep experimental expressions, it is eminently calculated to instruct those pilgrims whose road to heaven is of the same trying kind as David's was. It is always edifying to listen to the experience of a thoroughly gracious and much afflicted saint.*

That choice band of singers, the sons of Korah, are bidden to make this delightful Psalm one of their peculiars. They had been spared when their father and all his company, and all the children of his associates were swallowed up alive in their sin. (Num. xxvii. 11). They were the spared ones of sovereign grace. Preserved, we know not why, by the distinguishing favour of God, it may be surmised that after their remarkable election to mercy, they became so filled with gratitude that they addicted themselves to sacred music in order that their spared lives might be consecrated to the glory of God. At any rate, we who have been rescued as they were from going down into the pit, out of the mere good pleasure of Jehovah, can heartily join in this Psalm, and indeed all the songs which show forth the praises of our God and the pantings of our hearts after him. Although David is not mentioned as the author, this Psalm must be the offspring of his pen ; it is so Davidic, it smells of the son of Jesse, it bears the marks of his style and experience in every letter. We could sooner doubt the authorship of the second part of Pilgrim's Progress than question David's title to be the composer of this Psalm.

SUBJECT.—*It is the cry of a man far removed from the outward ordinances and worship of God, sighing for the long-loved house of his God ; and at the same time it is the voice of a spiritual believer, under depressions, longing for the renewal of the divine presence, struggling with doubts and fears, but yet holding his ground by faith in the living God. Most of the Lord's family have sailed on the sea which is here so graphically described. It is probable that David's flight from Absolom may have been the occasion for composing this Maschil.*

DIVISION.—*The structure of the song directs us to consider it in two parts which end with the same refrain ; 1—5 and then 6—11.*

EXPOSITION.

A S the hart panteth after the water brooks, so panteth my soul after thee, O God.

2 My soul thirsteth for God, for the living God : when shall I come and appear before God ?

3 My tears have been my meat day and night, while they continually say unto me, Where *is* thy God ?

4 When I remember these *things*, I pour out my soul in me : for I had gone with the multitude, I went with them to the house of God, with the voice of joy and praise, with a multitude that kept holyday.

5 Why art thou cast down, O my soul ? and *why* art thou disquieted in me ? hope thou in God : for I shall yet praise him *for* the help of his countenance.

1. "*As the hart panteth after the waterbrooks, so panteth my soul after thee, O God.*" As after a long drought the poor fainting hind longs for the streams, or rather as the hunted hart instinctively seeks after the river to lave its smoking flanks and to escape the dogs, even so my weary, persecuted soul pants after the Lord my God. Debarred from public worship, David was heartsick. Ease he did not seek, honour he did not covet, but the enjoyment of communion with God was an urgent need of his soul ; he viewed it not merely as the sweetest of all luxuries, but as an absolute necessity, like water to a stag. Like the parched traveller in

the wilderness, whose skin bottle is empty, and who finds the wells dry, he must drink or die—he must have his God or faint. His *soul*, his very self, his deepest life, was insatiable for a sense of the divine presence. As the hart brays so his soul prays. Give him his God and he is as content as the poor deer which at length slakes its thirst and is perfectly happy ; but deny him his Lord, and his heart heaves, his bosom palpitates, his whole frame is convulsed, like one who gasps for breath, or pants with long running. Dear reader, dost thou know what this is, by personally having felt the same ? It is a sweet bitterness. The next best thing to living in the light of the Lord's love is to be unhappy till we have it, and to pant hourly after it—hourly, did I say ? thirst is a perpetual appetite, and not to be forgotten, and even thus continual is the heart's longing after God. When it is as natural for us to long for God as for an animal to thirst, it is well with our souls, however painful our feelings. We may learn from this verse that the eagerness of our desires may be pleaded with God, and the more so, because there are special promises for the importunate and fervent.

2. " *My soul.*" All my nature, my inmost self. " *Thirsteth.*" Which is more than hungering ; hunger you can palliate, but thirst is awful, insatiable, clamorous, deadly. O to have the most intense craving after the highest good l this is no questionable mark of grace. " *For God.*" Not merely for the temple and the ordinances, but for fellowship with God himself. None but spiritual men can sympathise with this thirst. " *For the living God.*" Because he lives, and gives to men the living water ; therefore we, with greater eagerness, desire him. A dead God is a mere mockery ; we loathe such a monstrous deity ; but the ever-living God, the perennial fountain of life and light and love, is our soul's desire. What are gold, honour, pleasure, but dead idols ? May we never pant for these. " *When shall I come and appear before God ?* " He who loves the Lord loves also the assemblies wherein his name is adored. Vain are all pretences to religion where the outward means of grace have no attraction. David was never so much at home as in the house of the Lord ; he was not content with private worship ; he did not forsake the place where saints assemble, as the manner of some is. See how pathetically he questions as to the prospect of his again uniting in the joyous gathering l How he repeats and reiterates his desire l After his God, his Elohim (his God to be worshipped, who had entered into covenant with him), he pined even as the drooping flowers for the dew, or the moaning turtle for her mate. It were well if all our resortings to public worship were viewed as appearances before God, it would then be a sure mark of grace to delight in them. Alas, how many appear before the minister, or their fellow men, and think that enough l " To see the face of God " is the nearer translation of the Hebrew ; but the two ideas may be combined—he would see his God and be seen of him ; this is worth thirsting after l

3.—" *My tears have been my meat day and night.*" Salt meats, but healthful to the soul. When a man comes to tears, constant tears, plenteous tears, tears that fill his cup and trencher, he is in earnest indeed. As the big tears stand in the stag's eyes in her distress, so did the salt drops glitter in the eyes of David. His appetite was gone, his tears not only seasoned his meat, but became his only meat, he had no mind for other diet. Perhaps it was well for him that the heart could open the safety valves ; there is a dry grief far more terrible than showery sorrows. His tears since they were shed because God was blasphemed, were " honourable dew," drops of holy water, such as Jehovah putteth into his bottle. " *While they continually say unto me, Where is thy God ?* " Cruel taunts come naturally from coward minds. Surely they might have left the mourner alone ; he could weep no more than he did—it was a supererogation of malice to pump more tears from a heart which already overflowed. Note how incessant was their jeer, and how artfully they framed it l It cut the good man to the bone to have the faithfulness of his God impugned. They had better have thrust needles into his eyes than have darted insinuations against his God. Shimei may here be alluded to who after this fashion mocked David as he fled from Absalom. He roundly asserted that David was a bloody man, and that God was punishing him for sup-planting Saul and his house ; his wish was father to his thought. The wicked know that our worst misfortune would be to lose God's favour, hence their diabolical malice leads them to declare that such is the case. Glory be to God, they lie in their throats, for our God is in the heavens, ay, and in the furnace too, succouring his people.

Verse 4.—" *When I remember these things, I pour out my soul in me.*" When he harped upon his woes his heart melted into water and was poured out upon itself. God hidden, and foes raging, a pair of evils enough to bring down the stoutest heart ! Yet why let reflections so gloomy engross us, since the result is of no value : merely to turn the soul on itself, to empty it from itself into itself is useless, how much better to pour out the heart before the Lord ! The prisoner's treadwheel might sooner land him in the skies than mere inward questioning raise us nearer to consolation. *" For I had gone with the multitude, I went with them to the house of God."* Painful reflections were awakened by the memory of past joys ; he had mingled in the pious throng, their numbers had helped to give him exhilaration and to awaken holy delight, their company had been a charm to him as with them he ascended the hill of Zion. Gently proceeding with holy ease, in comely procession, with frequent strains of song, he and the people of Jehovah had marched in reverent ranks up to the shrine of sacrifice, the dear abode of peace and holiness. Far away from such goodly company the holy man pictures the sacred scene and dwells upon the details of the pious march. *" With the voice of joy and praise, with a multitude that kept holyday."* The festive noise is in his ears, and the solemn dance before his eyes. Perhaps he alludes to the removal of the ark and to the glorious gatherings of the tribes on that grand national holy day and holiday. How changed his present place ! For Zion, a wilderness ; for the priests in white linen, soldiers in garments of war ; for the song, the sneer of blasphemy ; for the festivity, lamentation ; for joy in the Lord, a mournful dirge over his absence.

> " I sigh to think of happier days
> When thou, O God, wast nigh,
> When every heart was tuned to praise ;
> And none more blest than I."

When in a foreign land, amid the idolatries of Popery, we have felt just the same home-sickness for the house of the Lord which is here described ; we have said " Ziona, Ziona, our holy and beautiful house, when shall I see thee again ? Thou church of the living God, my mother, my home, when shall I hear thy Psalms and holy prayers, and once again behold the Lord in the midst of his people ? " David appears to have had a peculiarly tender remembrance of *the singing* of the pilgrims, and assuredly it is the most delightful part of worship and that which comes nearest to the adoration of heaven. What a degradation to supplant the intelligent song of the whole congregation by the theatrical prettinesses of a quartette, the refined niceties of a choir, or the blowing off of wind from inanimate bellows and pipes ! We might as well pray by machinery as praise by it.

5. *" Why art thou cast down, O my soul ? "* As though he were two men, the Psalmist talks to himself. His faith reasons with his fears, his hope argues with his sorrows. These present troubles, are they to last for ever ? The rejoicings of my foes, are they more than empty talk ? My absence, from the solemn feasts, is that a perpetual exile ? Why this deep depression, this faithless fainting, this chicken-hearted melancholy ? As Trapp says, " David chideth David out of the dumps ; " and herein he is an example for all desponding ones. To search out the cause of our sorrow is often the best surgery for grief. Self-ignorance is not bliss ; in this case it is misery. The mist of ignorance magnifies the causes of our alarm ; a clearer view will make monsters dwindle into trifles. *" Why art thou disquieted within me ? "* Why is my quiet gone ? If I cannot keep a public Sabbath, yet wherefore do I deny my soul her indoor Sabbath ? Why am I agitated like a troubled sea, and why do my thoughts make a noise like a tumultuous multitude ? The causes are not enough to justify such utter yielding to despondency. Up, my heart ! What aileth thee ? Play the man, and thy castings down shall turn to liftings up, and thy disquietudes to calm. *" Hope thou in God."* If every evil be let loose from Pandora's box, yet is there hope at the bottom. This is the grace that swims, though the waves roar and be troubled. God is unchangeable, and therefore his grace is the ground for unshaken hope. If everything be dark, yet the day will come, and meanwhile hope carries stars in her eyes ; her lamps are not dependent upon oil from without, her light is fed by secret visitations of God, which sustain the spirit. *" For I shall yet praise him."* Yet will my sighs give place to songs, my mournful ditties shall be exchanged for triumphal pæans. A loss of the present sense of God's love is not a loss of that love itself ; the jewel is there, though it gleams not on our breast ; hope knows her title good when she cannot read it clear ; she expects the promised boon though present providence stands before

her with empty hands. " *For I shall yet praise him for the help of his countenance.*" Salvations come from the propitious face of God, and he will yet lift up his countenance upon us. Note well that the main hope and chief desire of David rest in the smile of God. His face is what he seeks and hopes to see, and this will recover his low spirits, this will put to scorn his laughing enemies, this will restore to him all the joys of those holy and happy days around which memory lingers. This is grand cheer. This verse, like the singing of Paul and Silas, looses chains and shakes prison walls. He who can use such heroic language in his gloomy hours will surely conquer. In the garden of hope grow the laurels for future victories, the roses of coming joy, the lilies of approaching peace.

6 O my God, my soul is cast down within me ; therefore will I remember thee from the land of Jordan, and of the Hermonites, from the hill Mizar.

7 Deep calleth unto deep at the noise of thy waterspouts ; all thy waves and thy billows are gone over me.

8 *Yet* the Lord will command his lovingkindness in the daytime, and in the night his song *shall be* with me, *and* my prayer unto the God of my life.

9 I will say unto God my rock, Why hast thou forgotten me ? why go I mourning because of the oppression of the enemy ?

10 *As* with a sword in my bones, mine enemies reproach me ; while they say daily unto me, Where *is* thy God ?

11 Why art thou cast down, O my soul ? and why art thou disquieted within me ? hope thou in God : for I shall yet praise him, *who is* the health of my countenance, and my God.

6. " *O my God, my soul is cast down within me.*" Here the song begins again upon the brass. So sweet an ending deserves that for the sake of a second hopeful close the Psalm should even begin again. Perhaps the Psalmist's dejection continued, the spasm of despondency returned ; well, then, he will down with his harp again, and try again its power upon himself, as in his younger days, he saw its influence upon Saul when the evil spirit came upon him. With God the song begins the second time more nearly than at first. The singer was also a little more tranquil. Outward expression of desire was gone ; there was no visible panting ; the sorrow was now all restrained within doors. Within or upon himself he was cast down ; and, verily, it may well be so, while our thoughts look more within than upward. If self were to furnish comfort, we should have but poor provender. There is no solid foundation for comfort in such fickle frames as our heart is subject to. It is well to tell the Lord how we feel, and the more plain the confession the better : David talks like a sick child to its mother, and we should learn to imitate him. " *Therefore will I remember thee.*" 'Tis well to fly to our God. Here is *terra firma.* Blessed downcasting which drives us to so sure a rock of refuge as thee, O Lord ! " *From the hill Mizar.*" He recalls his seasons of choice communion by the river and among the hills, and especially that dearest hour upon the little hill, where love spake her sweetest language and revealed her nearest fellowship. It is great wisdom to store up in memory our choice occasions of converse with heaven ; we may want them another day, when the Lord is slow in bringing back his banished ones, and our soul is aching with fear. " His love in times past " has been a precious cordial to many a fainting one ; like soft breath it has fanned the smoking flax into a flame, and bound up the bruised reed. Oh, never-to-be-forgotten valley of Achor, thou art a door of hope ! Fair days, now gone, ye have left a light behind you which cheers our present gloom. Or does David mean that even where he was he would bethink him of his God ; does he declare that, forgetful of time and place, he would count Jordan as sacred as Siloa, Hermon as holy as Zion, and even Mizar, that insignificant rising ground, as glorious as the mountains which are round about Jerusalem ! Oh ! it is a heavenly heart which can sing—

> " To me remains nor place nor time ;
> My country is in every clime ;
> I can be calm and free from care
> On any shore, since God is there.

"Could I be cast where thou art not,
That were indeed a dreadful lot,
But regions none remote I call,
Secure of finding God in all."

7. "*Deep calleth unto deep at the noise of thy waterspouts.*" Thy severe dealings with me seem to excite all creation to attack me ; heaven, and earth, and hell, call to each other, stirring each other up in dreadful conspiracy against my peace. As in a waterspout, the deeps above and below clasp hands, so it seemed to David that heaven and earth united to create a tempest around him. His woes were incessant and overwhelming. Billow followed billow, one sea echoed the roaring of another ; bodily pain aroused mental fear, Satanic suggestions chimed in with mistrustful forebodings, outward tribulation thundered in awful harmony with inward anguish : his soul seemed drowned as in a universal deluge of trouble, over whose waves the providence of the Lord moved as a watery pillar, in dreadful majesty inspiring the utmost terror. As for the afflicted one he was like a lonely bark around which the fury of a storm is bursting, or a mariner floating on a mast, almost every moment submerged. "*All thy waves and thy billows are gone over me.*" David thought that every trouble in the world had met in him, but he exaggerated, for *all* the breaking waves of Jehovah have passed over none but the Lord Jesus ; there are griefs to which he makes his children strangers for his love's sake. Sorrow naturally states its case forcibly ; the mercy is that the Lord after all hath not dealt with us according to our fears. Yet what a plight to be in ! Atlantic rollers sweeping in ceaseless succession over one's head, waterspouts coming nearer and nearer, and all the ocean in uproar around the weary swimmer ; most of the heirs of heaven can realise the description, for they have experienced the like. This is a deep experience unknown to babes in grace, but common enough to such as do business on great waters of affliction : to such it is some comfort to remember that the waves and billows are the Lords, "*thy* waves and *thy* billows," says David, they are all sent, and directed by him, and achieve his designs, and the child of God knowing this, is the more resigned.

8. "*Yet the Lord will command his lovingkindness in the daytime.*" Come what may there shall be "a certain secret something" to sweeten all. Lovingkindness is a noble life-belt in a rough sea. The day may darken into a strange and untimely midnight, but the love of God ordained of old to be the portion of the elect, shall be by sovereign decree meted out to them. No day shall ever dawn on an heir of grace and find him altogether forsaken of his Lord : the Lord reigneth, and as a sovereign he will with authority command mercy to be reserved for his chosen. "*And in the night.*" Both divisions of the day shall be illuminated with special love, and no stress of trial shall prevent it. Our God is God of the nights as well as the days ; none shall find his Israel unprotected, be the hour what it may. "*His song shall be with me.*" Songs of praise for blessings received shall cheer the gloom of night. No music sweeter than this. The belief that we shall yet glorify the Lord for mercy given in extremity is a delightful stay to the soul. Affliction may put out our candle, but if it cannot silence our song we will soon light the candle again. "*And my prayer unto the God of my life.*" Prayer is yoked with praise. He who is the living God, is the God of our life, from him we derive it, with him in prayer and praise we spend it, to him we devote it, in him we shall perfect it. To be assured that our sighs and songs shall both have free access to our glorious Lord is to have reason for hope in the most deplorable condition.

9. "*I will say unto God my rock, Why hast thou forgotten me.*" Faith is allowed to enquire of her God the causes of his displeasure, and she is even permitted to expostulate with him and put him in mind of his promises, and ask why apparently they are not fulfilled. If the Lord be indeed our refuge, when we find no refuge, it is time to be raising the question, "Why is this ?" Yet we must not let go our hold, the Lord must be "*my*" rock still ; we must keep to him as our alone confidence, and never forego our interest in him. "*Why go I mourning because of the oppression of the enemy ?*" He who condescends to be pleaded with by Abraham, his friend, allows us to put to him the question that we may search out the causes of his severity towards us. Surely he can have no pleasure in seeing the faces of his servants stained and squalid with their tears ; he can find no content in the harshness with which their foes assail them. He can never take pleasure in the tyranny with which Satan vexes them. Why then does he leave them to be mocked by his enemies and theirs ? How can the strong God, who is as firm and abiding

as a rock, be also as hard and unmoved as a rock towards those who trust in him ? Such enquiries humbly pressed often afford relief to the soul. To know the reason for sorrow is in part to know how to escape it, or at least to endure it. Want of attentive consideration often makes adversity appear to be more mysterious and hopeless than it really is. It is a pitiable thing for any man to have a limb amputated, but when we know that the operation was needful to save life, we are glad to hear that it has been successfully performed ; even thus as trial unfolds, the design of the Lord in sending it becomes far more easy to bear.

10. "*As with a sword in my bones, mine enemies reproach me.*" Cruel mockeries cut deeper than the flesh, they reach the soul as though a rapier were introduced between the ribs to prick the heart. If reproaches kill not, yet they are killing, the pain caused is excruciating. The tongue cuts to the bone, and its wounds are hard to cure. "*While they say daily unto me, Where is thy God ?*" This is the unkindest cut of all, reflecting as it does both upon the Lord's faithfulness and his servant's character. Such was the malice of David's foes, that having thought of the cruel question, they *said* it, said it *daily*, repeated *it to him*, and that for a length of time ; surely the continual yapping of these curs at his heel was enough to madden him, and perhaps would have done so had he not resorted to prayer and made the persecutions of his enemies a plea with his Lord.

11. "*Why art thou cast down, O my soul ? and why art thou disquieted within me ?*" In the rehearsal of his sorrow, he finds after all no sufficient ground for being disquieted. Looked in the face, his fears were not so overwhelming as they seemed when shrouded in obscurity. "*Hope thou in God.*" Let the anchor still keep its hold. God is faithful, God is love, therefore there is room and reason for hope. "*Who is the health of my countenance, and my God.*" This is the same hopeful expression as that contained in verse five, but the addition of "*and my God*" shows that the writer was growing in confidence, and was able defiantly to reply to the question, "Where is thy God ?" Here, even here, he is, ready to deliver me. I am not ashamed to own him amid your sneers and taunts, for he will rescue me out of your hands. Thus faith closes the struggle, a victor in fact by anticipation, and in heart by firm reliance. The saddest countenance shall yet be made to shine, if there be a taking of God at his word and an expectation of his salvation.

> "For yet I know I shall him praise
> Who graciously to me,
> The health is of my countenance,
> Yea, mine own God is he."

EXPLANATORY NOTES AND QUAINT SAYINGS.

Title.—"*Sons of Korah.*" Who were *the sons of Korah?* These opinions have more or less prevailed. One is that they sprang from some one of that name in the days of David. Mudge and others think that the sons of Korah were a society of musicians, founded or presided over by Korah. Others think that the sons of Korah were the surviving descendants of that miserable man who, together with two hundred and fifty of his adherents, who were princes, perished when "the earth opened her mouth and swallowed them up, together with Korah." In Numbers xxvi. 11, we read : "Notwithstanding the children of Korah died not." They had taken the warning given, and had departed from the tents of these wicked men. Numbers xvi. 24, 26. It must be admitted that the name *Korah* and the patronymic *Korahite* are found in the Scriptures in a way that creates considerable doubt respecting the particular man from whom the Korahites are named. See 1 Chron. i. 35 ; ii. 43 ; vi. 22, 54 ; ix. 19 : xxvi. 1 ; 2 Chron. xx. 19. Yet the more common belief is that they descended from him who perished for his gainsaying. This view is taken by Ainsworth with entire confidence, by Gill, and others. Korah, who perished, was a Levite. Whatever may have been their origin, it is clear *the sons of Korah* were a Levitical family of singers. Nothing, then, could be more appropriate than the dedication of a sacred song to these very people.—*William S. Plumer.*

Title.—" *Sons of Korah.*"   The *" Korah "* whose *" sons "* are here spoken of, is the Levite who headed the insurrection against Moses and Aaron in the wilderness. Numbers xvi.   We find his descendants existing as a powerful Levitical family in the time of David, at least, if they are to be identified, as is probable, with the Korahites mentioned in 1 Chron. xii. 6, who, like our own warlike bishops of former times, seem to have known how to doff the priestly vestment for the soldier's armour, and whose hand could wield the sword as well as strike the harp.   The Korahites were a part of the band who acknowledged David as their chief, at Ziklag ; warriors " whose faces," it is said, " were like the faces of lions, and who were (for speed) like gazelles upon the mountains."   According to 1 Chron. ix. 17—19, the Korahites were in David's time, keepers of the threshold of the tabernacle ; and still earlier, in the time of Moses, watchmen at the entrance of the camp of the Levites.   In 1 Chron. xxvi. 1—19, we find two branches of this family associated with that of Merari, as guardians of the doors of the Temple.   There is probably an allusion to this their office, in Psalm lxxxiv. 10.   But the Korahites were also celebrated musicians and singers ; see 1 Chron. vi. 16—33, where Heman, one of the three famous musicians of the time, is said to be a Korahite (comp. 1 Chron. xxv).   The musical reputation of the family continued in the time of Jehoshaphat (2 Chron. xx. 19), where we have the peculiar doubly plural form בְּנֵי הַקָּרְחִים, " *Sons of the Korahites.*"—*J. J. Stewart Perowne.*

Title.—" *Sons of Korah.*"   Mediæval writers remark how here, as so often, it was the will of God to raise up saints where they could have been least looked for. Who should imagine that from the posterity of him who said, " Ye take too much upon you, ye sons of Aaron," should have risen those whose sweet Psalms would be the heritage of the church of God to the end of time ?—*J. M. Neale.*

Verse 1.—" *The hart panteth after the water brooks.*"   And here we have started up, and sent leaping over the plain another of Solomon's favourites.   What elegant creatures those gazelles are, and how gracefully they bound ! . . . The sacred writers frequently mention gazelles under the various names of harts, roes, and hinds. . . . I have seen large flocks of these panting harts gather round the water-brooks in the great deserts of Central Syria, so subdued by thirst that you could approach quite near them before they fled.—*W. M. Thomson.*

Verse 1.—Little do the drunkards think that take so much pleasure in frequenting the houses of Bacchus that the godly take a great deal more, and have a great deal more joy in frequenting the houses of God.   But 'tis a thing that God promised long ago by the prophet : " Them will I bring to my holy mountain, and make them joyful in my house of prayer : their burnt offerings and their sacrifices shall be accepted upon mine altar ; for mine house shall be called an house of prayer for all people."   Isaiah lvi. 7.   And methinks, I hear the willing people of God's power, merrily calling one to another in the words of Micah iv. 2, " come, and let us go up to the mountain of the Lord, and to the house of the God of Jacob ; and he will teach us of his ways, and we will walk in his paths : for the law shall go forth of Zion, and the word of the Lord from Jerusalem."   How is a godly man ravished with " the beauty of holiness," when he is at such meetings !   How was holy Davd taken with being in the house of God at Jerusalem ! insomuch, that if he were kept from it but a little while, his soul panted for it, and longed after it, and fainted for lack of it, as a thirsty hart would do for lack of water !   " *As the hart panteth after the water brooks, so panteth my soul after thee, O God.   My soul thirsteth for God, for the living God : when shall I come and appear before God ? *"   The poor disconsolate captives preferred it to the best place in their memory.   " If I forget thee, O Jerusalem, let my right hand forget her cunning " (Psalm cxxxvii. 5) ; nay, they preferred it to their chiefest joy : " If I do not remember thee, let my tongue cleave to the roof of my mouth ; if I prefer not Jerusalem above my chief joy," verse 6. There was no place in the world that David regarded or cared to be in in comparison of it.   " A day in thy courts is better than a thousand.   I had rather be a door-keeper in the house of my God, than to dwell in the tents of wickedness " (Psalm lxxxiv. 10), insomuch, that he could find it in his heart, nay, and would choose, if he might have his desire, to spend all his days in that house.   Psalm xxvii. 4.— *Zachary Bogan.*

Verse 1.—The soul strongly desires acquaintance with God here in his ordinances. Chrysostom's very rhetorical upon the text, and tells us how that David, like a lover in absence, must express his affection* as they have their dainty sighs, and passionate complaints, their loving exclamations, and sundry discoveries of affection ; they can meet with never a tree, but in the bark of it they must engrave the name of their darling, Δεινὸς δ' ὁ ἔρως ὥσπες ὁ κιττὸς ἀυτὸν ἐκ πάσης ἀναδῆσαι προφάσεως ; 'twill twine upon every opportunity, as the Moralist speaks. And the true lovers of God, they are always thinking upon him, sighing for him, panting after him, talking of him, and (if 'twere possible) would engrave the name of the Lord Jesus upon the breasts of all the men in the world. Look upon David, now a banished man, and fled from the presence of Saul, and see how he behaves himself : not like Themistocles or Camillus, or some of those brave banished worthies. He does not complain of the ungratefulness of his country, the malice of his adversaries, and his own unhappy success. No, instead of murmuring, he falls a panting, and that only after his God. He is banished from the sanctuary, the palace of God's nearest presence, and chiefest residence ; he can't enjoy the beauty of holiness, and all other places seem to him but as the tents of Kedar. He is banished from the temple, and he thinks himself banished from his God, as it is in the following words, " *When shall I come and appear before God ?* " The whole stream of expositors run this way, that it is meant of his strong longing to visit the Temple, and those amiable courts of his God, with which his soul was so much taken.—*Nathanael Culverwel's " Panting Soul,"* 1652.

Verse 1, 2, 3, are an illustration of the frequent use of the word Elohim in the second book of Psalms. We give Fry's translation of the first three verses—

> As the hart looketh for the springs of water,
> So my soul looketh for thee, O Elohim.
>
> My soul is athirst for Elohim, for the living El :
> When shall I go and see the face of Elohim ?
>
> My tears have been my meat day and night,
> While they say to me continually, Where is thy Elohim ?

Verse 2.—" *My soul thirsteth for God,*" etc. See that your heart rest not short of Christ in any duty. Let go your hold of no duty until you find something of Christ in it ; and until you get not only an *handful*, but an *armful* (with old Simeon, Luke ii. 28) ; yea, a *heartful* of the blessed and beautiful babe of Bethlehem therein. Indeed you should have commerce with heaven, and communion with Christ in duty, which is therefore called *the presence of God*, or your appearing before him. Exodus xxiii. 17, and Psalm xlii. 2. Your duties then must be as a bridge to give you passage, or as a boat to carry you over into the bosom of Christ. Holy Mr. Bradford, Martyr, said he could not leave *confession* till he found his heart touched and broken for sin ; nor *supplication*, till his heart was affected with the beauty of the blessings desired ; nor *thanksgiving*, till his soul was quickened in return of praises ; nor *any duty*, until his heart was brought into a duty frame, and something of Christ was found therein. Accordingly Bernard speaks, *Nunquam abs te absque te recedam Domine :* I will never depart (in duty) from thee without thee, Lord. Augustine said he loved not Tully's elegant orations (as formerly) because he could not find *Christ* in them : nor doth a gracious soul love empty duties. Rhetorical flowers and flourishes, expressions without impressions in praying or preaching, are not true bread, but a tinkling cymbal to it, and it cannot be put off with the empty spoon of aëry notions, or lovely (that are not also lively) songs : if Christ talk with you in the way (of duty) your heart will burn within you. Luke xxiv. 16, 32.—*Christopher Ness's " Chrystal Mirrour,"* 1679.

Verses 2.—" *The living God.*" There are three respects especially in which our God is said to be the " *living God.*" First, *originally*, because he only hath life in himself, and of himself, and all creatures have it from him. Secondly, *operatively*, because he is the only giver of life unto man. Our life, in the threefold extent and capacity of it, whether we take it for natural, or spiritual, or eternal, flows to us from God. Thirdly, God is said to be the " *living God* " by way of *distinction*, and in opposition to all false gods.—*Thomas Horton.*

Verse 2 (last clause).—A wicked man can never say in good earnest, " *When shall I come and appear before God ?* " because he shall do so too soon, and before he would, as the devils that said Christ came " to torment them before their time." Ask a thief and a malefactor whether he would willingly appear before the judge. No, I warrant you, not he ; he had rather there were no judge at all to appear before. And so is it with worldly men in regard of God they desire rather to be hidden from him.—*Thomas Horton.*

Verse 2.—*" Come and appear before God."* When any of us have been at church, and waited in the sanctuary, let us examine what did we go thither to see ; a shadow of religion ? An outside of Christian forms ? A graceful orator ? The figures and shapes of devotion ? Surely then we might with as much wisdom, and more innocence, have gone to the wilderness " to see a reed shaken with the wind." Can we say as the Greeks at the feast (John xii. 21), " We would see Jesus ? " Or as Absalom (2 Sam. xiv. 32), " It is to little purpose I am come to Jerusalem if I may not see the King's face." To little purpose we go to church, or attend on ordinances, if we seek not, if we see not God there.—*Isaac Watts, D.D., 1674—1748.*

Verse 2.—If you attempt to put a little child off with toys and fine things, it will not be pleased long, it will cry for its mother's breast ; so, let a man come into the pulpit with pretty Latin and Greek sentences, and fine stories, these will not content a hungry soul, he must have the sincere milk of the word to feed upon. *Oliver Heywood.*

Verse 2.—*" When shall I come and appear before God ? "*—

> While I am banish'd from thy house
>   I mourn in secret, Lord ;
> " When shall I come and pay my vows,
>   And hear thy holy word ? "
>
> So while I dwell in bonds of clay,
>   Methinks my soul shall groan.
> " When shall I wing my heavenly way
>   And stand before thy throne ? "
>
> I love to see my Lord below,
>   His church displays his grace ;
> But upper worlds his glory know
>   And view him face to face.
>
> I love to worship at his feet,
>   Though sin attack me there,
> But saints exalted near his seat
>   Have no assaults to fear.
>
> I'm pleased to meet him in his court,
>   And taste his heavenly love,
> But still I think his visits short,
>   Or I too soon remove.
>
> He shines, and I am all delight,
>   He hides and all is pain ;
> When will he fix me in his sight,
>   And ne'er depart again ?

Isaac Watts, from his Sermons.

Verse 3.—*" My tears have been my meat day and night."* The Psalmist could eat nothing because of his extreme grief.—*John Gadsby.*

Verse 3.—*" They say unto me."* It is not only of me, but to me ; they spake it to his very face, as those who were ready to justify it and make it good, that God had forsaken him. Backbiting argues more baseness, but open reproach carries more boldness, and shamelessness, and impudence in it ; and this is that which David's enemies were guilty of here in this place.—*Thomas Horton.*

Verse 3.—*" Where is thy God ? "* God's children are impatient, as far as they are men, of reproaches ; but so far as they are Christian men, they are impatient of reproaches in religion ; *" Where is now thy God ? "* They were not such desperate Atheists as to think there was no God, to call in question whether there was a God or no, though, indeed, they were little better ; but they rather reproach and upbraid him with his singularity, *where* is *thy* God ? You are one of God's darlings ; you are one that thought nobody served God but you ; you are one that will go alone— *your* God ! So this is an ordinary reproach, an ordinary part for wicked men to cast at the best people, especially when they are in misery. What is become of your profession now ? What is become of your forwardness and strictness now ?

What is become of your God that you bragged so of, and thought yourselves so happy in, as if he had been nobody's God but yours? We may learn hence the disposition of wicked men. It is a character of a poisonful, cursed disposition to upbraid a man with his religion.

But what is the scope? The scope is worse than the words " *where is thy God?* " The scope is to shake his faith and his confidence in God, and this *that* is which touched him so nearly while they upbraided him. For the devil knows well enough that as long as God and the soul join together, it is in vain to trouble any man, therefore he labours to put jealousies, to accuse God to man, and man to God. He knows there is nothing in the world can stand against God. As long as we make God our confidence, all his enterprises are in vain. His scope is, therefore, to shake our affiance in God. " *Where is thy God?* " So he dealt with the head of the church, our blessed Saviour himself, when he came to tempt him. " If thou be the Son of God, command these stones to be made bread." Matt. iv. 3. He comes with an " *if,*" he laboured to shake him in his Sonship. The devil, since he was divided from God himself eternally, is become a spirit of division; he labours to divide even God the Father from his own Son; " *If thou be the Son of God?* " So he labours to sever Christians from their head Christ. " *Where is thy God?* " There was his scope, to breed division if he could, between his heart and God, that he might call God into jealousy, as if he had not regarded him: thou hast taken a great deal of pains in serving thy God; thou seest how he regards thee now; " *Where is thy God?* "—*Richard Sibbes.*

Verse 3.—How powerfully do the scoffs and reproaches of the ungodly tend to shake the faith of a mind already dejected! How peculiarly afflictive to the soul that loves God, is the dishonour cast upon him by his enemies!—*Henry March, in* " Sabbaths at Home," 1823.

Verse 3.—" *Where is thy God?* "

" Where is now thy God! " Oh, sorrow!
 Hourly thus to hear him say,
Finding thus the longed-for morrow,
 Mournful as the dark to-day.
Yet not thus my soul would languish,
 Would not thus be grieved and shamed,
But for that severer anguish,
 When I hear the Lord defamed.

" Where is now thy God! " Oh, aid me,
 Lord of mercy, to reply—
" He is HERE—though foes invade me,
 Know his outstretched arm is nigh."
Help me thus to be victorious,
 While the shield of faith I take;
Lord, appear, and make thee glorious:
 Help me for thy honour's sake.

Henry March.

Verse 4.—" *When I remember these things,*" etc. To a person in misery it is a great increase of misery to have been once happy; it was to David an occasion of new tears when he remembered his former joys. Time was, says the poor soul, when I thought of God with comfort, and when I thought of him as my own God; and to lose a God that I once enjoyed is the loss of all my losses, and of all my terrors the most terrible. Time was when I could go and pray to him, and ease myself in prayer; but now I have no boldness, no hope, no success in prayer. I cannot call him *my Father* any more. Time was when I could read the Bible and treasure up the promises, and survey the land of Canaan as my own inheritance; but now I dare not look into the Word lest I read my own condemnation there. The Sabbath was formerly to me as one of the days of heaven, but now it is also, as well as the rest, a sad and a mournful day. I formerly rejoiced in the name of Christ, " I sat under his shadow." Cant. ii. 3. I was in his eyes as one that found favour; but now my soul is like the deserts of Arabia, I am scorched with burning heat. From how great a height have I fallen! How fair was I once for heaven and for salvation, and now am like to come short of it! I once was flourishing in the courts of the Lord, and now all my fruit is blasted and withered away: " his dew lay all night upon my branches," but now I am like the mountains of Gilboa, no rain falls upon me. Had I never heard of heaven I could not have been so miserable as I now am: had I never known God, the loss of him had not been so terrible as now it is like to be. Job xxix. 2, 3.—*Timothy Rogers.*

Verse 4 (first clause).—The blessedness of even the remembrance of divine worship is so great, that it can save the soul from despair.—*J. P. Lange's Commentary.*

Verse 4.—" *I pour out my soul.*" The very soul of prayer lies in the pouring out of the soul before God.—*Thomas Brooks.*

Verse 4.—" *I had gone with the multitude, I went with them to the house of God, with the voice of joy and praise, with a multitude that kept holyday.*" The gracious God is pleased to esteem it his glory to have many beggars thronging at the beautiful gate of his temple, for spiritual and corporal alms. What an honour is it to our great Landlord that multitudes of tenants flock together to his house to pay their rent of thanks and worship for their all which they hold of him! How loud and lovely is the noise of many golden trumpets! Good Lord, what an echo do they make in heaven's ears! When many skilful musicians play in concert with well tuned and prepared instruments the music cannot but be ravishing to God himself. —*George Swinnock.*

Verse 4.—Do but consider David's tears and grief for want of, and his fervent prayers for the fruition of, public ordinances even then, when he had opportunities for private performances; and surely thou wilt esteem the ministry of the Word no mean mercy. See his sorrow when he was driven from God's sanctuary. " *When I remember these things I pour out my soul in me : for I had gone with the multitude, I went with them to the house of God.*" " *My soul is poured out;* " that is, I am overwhelmed with grief, and ever ready to die when I compare my present condition with my former happiness in the fruition of religious assemblies. There is an elegancy in the phrase " *poured out;* " the word is applied to water, or any liquid thing, and in Scripture signifieth abundance. Joel ii. 28. My life is ready to be poured out as water upon the ground, which cannot be gathered up again, when I remember my former mercies, and consider my present misery. . . . The loss of his father, mother, wives, children, lands, liberty—nay, of his very life, would not have gone so near his heart as the loss of public ordinances. As his sorrow was great for the want, so was his suit most earnest for the enjoyment of them. How many a prayer doth he put up for the liberty of the tabernacle! Psalm xliii. 3, 4, and xxvii. 4, 8. It is the one thing, the principal thing which he begs of God.—*Henry Smith.*

Verse 4.—The bias of the soul is remarkably shown by the objects of regretful recollection.—*Henry March.*

Verse 4.—" *With a multitude that kept holy day.*"

> Though private prayer be a brave design
> Yet public hath more promises, more love :
> And love's a weight to hearts, to eyes a sign.
> We all are but cold suitors ; let us move
>   Where it is warmest. Leave thy six and seven ;
>   Pray with the most : for where most pray, is heaven.
>
> *George Herbert, in " The Temple."*

Verse 5.—See also on verse 11, and Psalm xliii. verse 5.

Verse 5.—" WHY *art thou cast down, O my soul?* " Athanasius counselled his friend, that when any trouble should fall upon him, he should fall presently to the reading of this Psalm; for there was a way, he thought, of curing by the like, as well as by the *contrary :* for 'tis observed indeed that when two instruments are tuned to the same unison, if you touch the strings of the one, the strings of the other will move too, though untouched, if placed at a convenient distance. That therefore you may try the same experiments upon yourselves, do but set your affections for a tune in the same key in which these words were spoken ; if really you *feel* none, imagine some affliction laid upon you ; when you have done so, that you may be the more fully moved, place your attention at a convenient distance, look narrowly on this holy prophet, observe how he retires himself, shuts out the world, calls his sad soul to as sad a reckoning : *Quare tam tristis?* O my soul! thou that wert infused to give me life ; nay, says Philo the Jew, a spark, a beam of the divinity, thou, which shouldst be to this dark body of mine as the sun is to the earth, enlightening, quickening, cheering up my spirits ; tell me, why art *thou* clouded? why art *thou* cast down? . . . .

Think of this, ye that feel the heaviness of your soul ; think of it, ye that do not, for ye may feel it. Know there is a sorrow "that worketh repentance not to be repented of." Know again there is a sorrow " that worketh death." Remember there were tears that got sinful Mary heaven ; remember again, there were tears that got sinful Esau *nothing*. For as in martyrdom, it is not the sword, the boiling lead, or fire, not *what* we suffer, but *why*, that makes us martyrs ; so in our sorrows, it is not how deep they wound, but *why*, that justifies them. Let every one, therefore, that hath a troubled heart, ask his soul the " *Why :* " " *Why art thou cast down ?* " Is it not for thine own sins, or the sins of others ? Take either of them, thine eyes will have a large field to water. Is it for that thou hast been a child of wrath, a servant of the devil ? Is it for that thou art a candle set in the wind, blown at by several temptations ? or is it for that thou wouldst be freed from them ? " Woe is me, that I sojourn in Mesech, that I dwell in the tents of Kedar ! " Psalm cxx. 5. Art thou troubled as St. Augustine was, when he read that the way to heaven was narrow, the number small that travelled thither ? Or hast thou put on St. Bernard's resolution, who had made a compact with his soul, never to joy till he had heard his Saviour call him, " Come, ye blessed," nor never to leave sorrowing till he had escaped the bitter sentence, " Go, ye cursed " ? If any of these be the " *Why,*" the ground of thy sorrows, if such thoughts have *cast thee down ;* know, that thy Saviour hath already blessed thee, for, " Blessed are they that mourn." The angels are thy servants, they gather thy tears ; God is thy treasurer, he lays them up in his bottle ; the Holy Ghost is thy comforter, he will not leave thee. Fear not, then, to be thus " *cast down,*" fear not to be thus *disquieted within thee.—Brian Duppa (Bishop), 1588—1662, in a Sermon entitled " The Soule's Soliloquie."*

Verse 5.—" *Why art thou cast down, O my soul ?* " Why, or what may be the reason, that this text is three times used in this Psalm and in the next ? whereas you do not find two verses of the same length used in all the Book of Psalms besides, except in Psalm cvii., where is often repeated, ". O that men would praise the Lord," etc. Now, surely, the frequent mention of this text and words doth argue and note unto us the weightiness of the matter. . . . . .
Wicked men oppressed David, and the devil tempted him ; yet he chides his own heart and nothing else. David did not chide at Saul, nor chide at Absalom ; but he chides and checks his own heart. " Why art thou cast down, O my soul ? " Though the devil and wicked men, the one do tempt, the other do oppress as instruments of punishment for sin ; yet we with David are to chide our own hearts.
Consider, what though in our translations the words are translated and rendered passively, " *Why art thou cast down ?* " yet, in the original, they are rendered actively ; we read it, " *Why art thou cast down ?* " etc. ; but in the original it is read, יִמַה־תָּחֵמִי עָלַי מַה־תֶּשְׁתּוֹחֲחִי נַפְשִׁי " *Why bowest* (or *pressest*) *thou down thyself, my soul? and why tumultest thou against me ?* " As Arias Montanus, *Cur humiliasti te ? Cur deprimes te anima mea ?* So Lorinus, Prov. xii. 25. And the words so read, they do intimate thus much, that God's own people may be cast down too much for the sense of sin, and they are most active in their own down-casting. It is not God nor the devil that cast thee down ; but *Why dost thou cast thyself down ?* to create more trouble on thy self than either God doth inflict or the devil tempt thee to.—*Christopher Love, in " The Dejected Soul's Cure,"* 1657.

Verse 5.—" *Why art thou cast down, O my soul ?* " Consider but this, how much there is of God in the affliction. 1. Came it not without *God's privity ?* Why art thou troubled, then ? Thy Father knowing of it would have stopped its course if it had been best for thee. 2. Came it not *without his command ?* Why art thou troubled ? It is the cup that thy Father hath given thee, and wilt thou not drink it ? 3. Is it thy Father's will that thou shouldest suffer, and shall it be thy humour to rebel ? 4. Hath God done *no more than he might do ?* Why dost thou murmur, as if he had done thee wrong ? 5. Is it a piece of his *wise acting ?* Why dost thou exalt thy foolish will above his infinite wisdom ? 6. Is his way *a way of mercy ?* Why does thy mutinous spirit stumble at it, as a rough way ? 7. Is the thing *good* that is befallen thee ? Why dost thou quarrel as if it were evil ? 8. Is it *less than men suffer*, than his own people, yea, than his own Son hath suffered, and hast thou cause to complain ? 9. Is it but *thy merit ?* and less than that, too ; and shall the living man complain for the punishment of his sin ? 10. Is it *in measure*, ordered with care ? (1) by the physician's hand ; and (2) a little draught, and (3) proportioned to thy strength ; (4) measured out according to the proportion of strength and comfort he intends to measure thee out, to bear it withal ? Why art thou cast down ? Why art thou disquieted ? Is the end and fruit of it but to make thee white, and purify thee ? to purge thy sin past, and to prevent it for the time to come ? and dost thou find a present fruit in it ? Dost thou find that now thou art turned into a chalk-stone ; thy groves and images—those corruptions which did attend thee while thou wert in prosperity, and which would attend thee if thou hadst these good things which thou wantest, and art disquieted for ; and if those evils which thou feelest or fearest were far from thy sense and fear, would still attend thee—that those do not now stand up ? Lift up thy head, Christian ! say to thy soul, " *Why art thou cast down, O my soul ? and why art thou disquieted in me ?* " Meditate what there is of God in the cause of thy disquietments.—*John Collinge* (1623—1690) *in " A Cordial for a Fainting Soule,"* 1652.

Verse 5.—" *Why art thou disquieted ?* " more literally, *tumultuated,* a word frequently applied to the roaring and tumult and tossing of the sea. See Isaiah xvii. 12 ; Jer. v. 22 ; vi. 23 ; li. 55.—*Henry March.*

Verse 5.—" *Hope thou in God.*" I shall show what powerful influence *hope* hath on the Christian in affliction, and how. First, it stills and silenceth him under affliction. It keeps the king's peace in the heart, which else would soon be in an uproar. A hopeless soul is clamorous : one while it chargeth God, another while it reviles his instruments. It cannot long rest, and no wonder, when hope is not there. Hope hath a rare art in stilling a froward spirit, when nothing else can ; as the mother can make the crying child quiet by laying it to the breast, when the rod makes it cry worse. This way David took, and found it effectual ; when his soul was unquiet by reason of his present affliction, he lays it to the breast of the promise : " Why art thou cast down, O my soul ? and why art thou disquieted in me ? hope thou in God." And here his soul sweetly sleeps, as the child with the breast in his mouth ; and that this was his usual way, we may think by the frequent instances we find ; thrice we find him taking this course in two Psalms, xlii. and xliii. . . . . Secondly, this hope fills the afflicted soul with such inward joy and consolation, that it can laugh while tears are in the eye, sigh and sing all in a breath ; it is called " the rejoicing of hope," Heb. iii. 6. And hope never affords more joy than in affliction. It is on a watery cloud that the sun paints those curious colours in the rainbow. . . . . There are two graces, which Christ useth above any other, to fill the soul with joy—faith and hope, because these two fetch all their wine of joy without door. Faith tells the soul what Christ hath done for it, and so comforts it ; hope revives the soul with the news of what Christ will do : both draw at one tap—Christ and his promise.—*Condensed from William Gurnall.*

Verse 5.—" *Hope thou in God.*" The word which is here rendered " *hope* " denotes that *expectation* which is founded on faith in God, and which leads the soul to *wait* upon him. The idea is beautifully expressed in Psalm xxxix. 7. " And now, Lord, what wait I for ? my hope is in thee."—*Henry March.*

Verse 5.—" *I shall yet praise him for the help of his countenance.*" When it may be said, " He whom God loveth is sick," then it may be said, " This sickness is not unto death ; " and though it be to the first death, yet not to the second. Who would think when Jonah was in the sea (Jonah iii.), that he would preach at Ninevah ? Who would think when Nebuchadnezzar was in the forest (Dan. iv.), that he should reign again in Babel ? Who would think when Joseph was banished of his brethren, that his brethren should seek unto him like his servants ? Who would think when Job scraped his sores upon the dunghill, all his houses were burned, all his cattle stolen, and all his children dead, that he should be richer than ever he was ? These are the acts of mercy which make the righteous sing, " The Lord hath triumphed valiantly." Exodus 15—21.—*Henry Smith.*

Verse 5.—" *I shall yet praise him.*" David's mind is upon the *duty* more than upon the *mercy ;* upon the *duty,* as it is a matter of *grace,* more than upon the *mercy,* as it is a matter of *sense.* And, therefore, by a happy mistake, his tongue slips, as men are wont to do in such cases, and he puts one for the other ; when he should say, *I shall receive mercy from God,* he says, " *I shall give praise to him.*" —*Thomas Horton.*

Verse 5.—He is the skilful physician, who at the same time that he evacuates the disease, doth also comfort and strengthen nature ; and he the true Christian, that doth not content himself with a bare laying aside evil customs and practices, but labours to walk in the exercise of the contrary graces. Art thou discomposed with impatience, haunted with a discontented spirit under any affliction? Think it not enough to silence thy heart from quarrelling with God, but leave not till thou canst bring it sweetly to rely on God. Holy David drove it thus far; he did not only chide his soul for being disquieted, but he charges it to trust in God.— *William Gurnall.*

Verse 5.—There was one Alice Benden, who, among others, was imprisoned for religion in Canterbury Castle; but after awhile, by the bishop's order, she was let down into a deep dungeon, where none of her friends could come at her. There she was fed with an halfpenny bread, and a farthing beer a day, neither would they allow her any more for her money. Her lodging was upon a little straw, between a pair of stocks and a stone wall. This made her grievously to bewail and lament her estate, reasoning with herself, why her Lord God did in so heavy a wise afflict her, and suffered her thus to be sequestered from the sweet society of her loving prison-fellows. In this extremity of misery, and in the midst of these dolorous mournings she continued, till on a night, repeating that of the Psalmist: "*Why art thou so heavy, O my soul? and why art thou so cast down within me? Still trust in God,*" etc.; and, *God's right hand can change all this,* etc.; she received comfort in the midst of her sorrows, and so continued joyful to the time of her release.— *Samuel Clarke's " Mirrour."*

Verses 5, 11.—In case thou art at any time oppressed with sorrows, ask thy heart and soul that question which David did in the like case twice in one Psalm: "*Why art thou cast down, O my soul? and why art thou disquieted within me?*" and certainly the soul would return answer, My distress of sadness springs from my unbelief. You may know the disease by the cure, in the very next words, "*O put thy trust in God; hope thou in God: for I shall yet praise him, who is the health of my countenance, and my God.*" All sorrow of heart springs principally from our unbelief, not from the greatness of other evils; I mean, *destructive* sorrow, for godly sorrow is a friend to godly joy. It is not so much the weight of the burthen, as the soreness of the back, that troubles the poor beast: so it is not so much the weight of outward evils, as the inward soreness of a galled conscience, not purified nor healed by faith, that vexeth and troubleth the poor creature.—*Matthew Lawrence, in " The Use and Practice of Faith,"* 1657.

Verses 5, 11.—As afflictions do proceed from ourselves, they may be called troubles, or perturbations; for the best man doth sometimes cause this bad liquor to boil out of his own bowels. David, not once, but often, hath cried out, "*Why art thou cast down, O my soul? and why art thou disquieted in me?*" And show me the man that annoyeth and troubleth not himself in vain, because with patience he doth not tarry the Lord's leisure? The foolish bird, who, being in a room whose door is locked, and the casements shut, beateth herself against the wall and windows, breaking her feathers and bruising her body, whereas, would she stay till the passages were by the keeper opened, she might depart, being not at all wounded; even so falleth it out with us: for when the Lord doth shut us up, and straiten our liberty for a time, we would fain make way for ourselves, having many devices in our hearts to break through the walls of his providence; whereas, if we would stay his leisure, depend on his promise, and submit ourselves to be disposed of by his hand, we might with more ease endure this prison, and with less hurt at the last be set at liberty. For God is in one mind, and who can change him? He will bring to pass that thing that he hath decreed upon us.—*John Barlow's Sermon,* 1618.

Verses 5, 11.—If you would get assurance, spend more time in strengthening your evidences for heaven, than in questioning of them. It is the great fault of many Christians they will spend much time in questioning, and not in strengthening their comforts. They will reason themselves into unbelief, and say, Lord, why should I believe? Why should I take hold of a promise that am so unholy and so unmortified a creature? And so by this they reason themselves to such a pass that they dare not lay hold upon Christ, whereas it should be your work to reason yourselves into Christ as much as you can. Labour to strengthen your comforts, and reason thus, Why should I not believe in Christ? Thus David did. Psalm xlii. "*Why art thou troubled, O my soul, and why art thou cast down within me?*" Is not the mercy of God more than sin in the creature? Is not there free grace where there is guilt? Are not there pardoning mercies where condemnation is deserved? You should reason up your comforts rather than reason them down, and spend more time in strengthening than in questioning of them. You would count him a very unwise man that hath a lease of so much land, and he himself shall create scruples and doubts, and shall use no means to make his title good. And truly many Christians are as unwise for heaven. They have, as I may say, good bond and seal that God will bring them to heaven, and yet they will question and cavil themselves into unbelief. Beloved, this should not be, but you ought rather to strengthen your comforts than question them.—*Christopher Love.*

Verse 6.—" *O my God, my soul is cast down within me : therefore will I remember thee.*" "Because I am very low in spirit, am deeply sorrowful, *therefore* will I remember thee. I will remember how condescending thou art to thy ' poor and afflicted people ; ' how ready to receive them when deserted or cast out by men ; how kind and patient to hear their complaint when they pour out the soul before thee. I will remember thy lovingkindness to *me* in seasons past ; how thou hast looked on my distress, hast heard the voice of my supplications, hast delivered me from my trials, or helped me to bear their burden, strengthening me with strength in my soul. I will remember all that I have enjoyed of thy presence when waiting on thee in thy house, or when celebrating thy praises there in company with thy ' saints, the excellent of the earth.' I will remember what thou ART ; how meet an object for the trust of a desolate being like myself I For though I am poor, thou art rich ; though I am weak, thou art mighty ; though I am miserable, thou art happy. I will remember that thou art *my* God. That thou hast manifested thyself to my soul, that thou hast enabled me to choose thee for my portion, that I have trusted in thee, and have never been confounded. I will remember that word of promise on which thou hast caused me to hope, to which thou hast ever been faithful throughout all the past, and *will* be, as I truly believe, even unto the end." Oh, how happy, even in the midst of their unhappiness, are they, who in their trials, can thus take shelter in God I—*Henry March.*

Verse 6.—" MY *God.*" Astonishing expression I Who shall dare to say to the Creator of the ends of the earth, the Majesty in the heavens, " *My God* " ? An exile, a wanderer, an outcast ; a man forsaken, despised, reviled ; a soul cast down and disquieted : *he* shall dare. By what right ? Of covenant.—*Henry March.*

Verse 6.—" *Therefore will I remember thee from the land of Jordan, and of the Hermonites, from the hill Mizar.*" It is remarkable what course the Psalmist took to regain comfort ; he would remember three experiments of his goodness—" the land of *Jordan,*" the land " of the *Hermonites,*" and " the hill *Mizar.*" First will I remember the land *Jordan ;* that is, I will remember the great goodness of God in drying up the river Jordan, that so the tribes of Israel might pass over to the promised land : why, God that hath been good, will be good. Then, I will remember the land of the *Hermonites ;* in that land were Sihon, king of the Amorites, and Og king of Bashan, were defeated ; that you read of in Joshua xii. 1, 2. " Now these are the kings of the land, which the children of Israel smote, and possessed their land on the other side Jordan toward the rising of the sun, from the river Arnon unto Mount Hermon." *Mizar,* some think to be a little hill near Mount Sinai, where the law was given. I will remember God's goodness, in giving a law to his people. Here David would call to remembrance the goodness of God of old, to regain to him comfort and quietness in his mind.—*Christopher Love.*

Verse 6.—" *The Hermons,*" or the peaks or ridges of Hermon, the plural being used either because of the *two* peaks of the mountain (Wilson, " *Land of the Bible* "), or as I think probably, of the whole range of its snowy hights.—*J. J. Stewart Perowne.*

Verse 6.—" *The Hermons,*" *i.e.,* as some suppose, Mount Hermon, and the other mountains upon that side of the river, just as Baalim means Baal, and other idols worshipped with him ; or more probably Mount Hermon considered not as a single eminence, but a chain or range, like the Alps, the Alleghanies, etc.—*J. A. Alexander.*

Verse 6.—" *From the hill.*" He that has a rich life of past experience is thereby placed upon an eminence from which he may take a happy view of the path lying before him.—*J. P. Lange's Commentary.*

Verse 7.—" *Deep calleth unto deep at the noise of thy waterspouts.*" Here he has conjoined two awful and terrific phenomena of nature. It is a fact well ascertained by the evidence of travellers, that the falling of waterspouts is not uncommon on the coast of Judea. It should seem that they are occasioned by the congregating of great masses of cloud, whose waters concentrating to a point, pour themselves down in a tremendous column, accompanied with a roaring noise. Now, the image conceived in the mind of the Psalmist seems to be that of the rushing of this vast water-spout down into the sea, already agitated, and increasing the turbulence and disorder of its waves. An awful picture ! Especially if there be added to it the ideas of a black tempestuous sky, and the deafening roar occasioned by the tumult. What would be the situation of a vessel in the midst of such a tempest, the deluge pouring down from above, and all around her the furious ocean heaving its tremendous surges—how ungovernable, how helpless, how next to impossible that she should escape foundering except by some almost miraculous interference. Yet to such a situation does David here compare the state of his soul when submersed, as it were, under a sea of afflictions ; " all thy waves and thy billows are gone over me." How pungent must his sense of grief have been to occasion him to make use of such a comparison, so strongly expressive of the utmost danger and terror ! —*Henry March.*

Verse 7.—" *Deep calleth unto deep,*" etc. The abyss above calls on the abyss below, in the voice of the droppings of thy waterspouts.—*Targum.*

Verse 7.—" *Deep calleth unto deep.*" So let prayer unto prayer, and faith unto faith, and one grace to the exercise of another. If we cannot prevail with God it may be the first time, yet we may the second ; or if not then, the third.—*Thomas Horton.*

Verse 7.—" *Deep calleth unto deep.*" What's that ? Why, it is expressed in the verse before : " *O God,*" says he, " *my soul is cast down within me.*" " *Down,*" that is *deep* into the jaws of distrust and fear. And, Lord, my soul in this *depth* of sorrow, calls for help to thy *depth* of mercy. For though I am sinking and am going down, yet not so low but that thy mercy is yet underneath me. Do, of thy compassions, open those everlasting arms, and catch him that has no help or stay in himself. For so it is with one that is falling into a *well* or a *dungeon.*—*John Bunyan.*

Verse 7.—Here the Psalmist feels the spirit of bondage, which is wrath and fear ; and he prays for the joy of God's salvation, and to be upheld by God's free spirit, which is the Holy Spirit, the spirit of love and power. He complains of " *deep calling unto deep.*" A soul in the horrible pit hears little else but the calls of law and justice for vengeance, which are always answered again by the accusations of Satan and conscience. The storms of Sinai, like a *water-spout* at sea, threaten the earthen vessel with a deluge of wrath, which would soon drown it in destruction and perdition. These waves of real, and some imaginary, displeasure (no less terrible than real), rolling over the poor creature, are ready to send the bark to the bottom. This is the terrible way in which some fallen and backsliding souls are purged and reclaimed, and especially such as have brought public scandal upon the gospel, and church of Christ.—*William Huntington* (1744—1813) *in " Contemplations of the God of Israel."*

Verse 7.—" *Thy waterspouts,*" Dr. Boothroyd translates צִנּוֹרֶיךָ, " *thy cataracts.*" In justification of which translation, he observes that the situation of David suggested this forcible image. He saw the torrents falling from the precipices, and heard them resounding, and as if calling to one another for assistance ; so, says he, all thy waves, that is, afflictions and troubles, come upon me and overwhelm me.—*John Morison.*

Verse 7.—" *Waterspouts.*" Look at those clouds which hang like a heavy pall of sackcloth over the sea, along the western horizon. From them, on such windy days as these, are formed *waterspouts*, and I have already noticed several incipient " spouts " lengthening downward from their lower edge. These remarkable phenomena occur most frequently in spring, but I have also seen them in autumn. They are not accompanied with much rain ; and between the dark stratum above and the sea, the sky is clear and bright. Here and there fragments of black vapour, shaped like long funnels, are drawn down from the clouds towards the sea, and are seen to be in violent agitation, whirling round on themselves as they are driven along by the wind. Directly beneath them the surface of the sea is also in commotion by a whirlwind, which travels on in concert with the spout above. I have often seen the two actually unite in mid air, and rush toward the mountains, writhing, and twisting, and bending, like a huge serpent, with its head in the clouds and its tail on the deep.

They make a loud noise, of course, and appear very frightful. " *Deep calleth unto deep at the noise of thy waterspouts : all thy waves and thy billows are gone over me,*" said David, when his soul was cast down within him. But, though formidable in appearance, they do very little injury. I have never heard of more than one instance in which they proved destructive even to boats, though the sailors are extremely afraid of them. As soon as they approach the shore, they dissolve and disappear. That kind of waterspout which bursts on the mountains, generally in the dry months of summer, does immense mischief. In a few minutes the wadies along its track are swollen into furious rivers, which sweep away grain, olives, raisins, and every other produce of the farmer. I have frequently known them to carry off and drown flocks of sheep and goats, and even cows, horses, and their owners also.—*W. M. Thomson.*

Verse 7.—" *All thy waves and thy billows.*"

> Deep to deep incessant calling,
>   Tossed by furious tempests' roll,
> Endless waves and billows falling,
>   Overwhelm my fainting soul.
> Yet I see a Power presiding
>   Mid the tumult of the storm,
> Ever ruling, ever guiding,
>   Love's intentions to perform.
> Yes, mid sorrows most distressing,
>   Faith contemplates thy design,
> Humbly bowing, and confessing
>   All the waves and billows THINE.

Henry March.

Verse 7.—" *All thy waves and thy billows are gone over me.*"

> Wide o'er misfortune's surging tide
>   Billows succeeding billows spread;
> Should one, its fury spent, subside,
>   Another lifts its boisterous head.

Æschylus in " The Seven Chiefs against Thebes."

Verse 8.—" *Yet the Lord will command his lovingkindness.*" His expression is remarkable; he does not say simply that the Lord will bestow, but, "*command his lovingkindness.*" As the gift bestowed is grace—free favour to the unworthy; so the manner of bestowing it is sovereign. It is given by decree; it is a royal donative. And if *he* commands the blessing, who shall hinder its reception?— *Henry March.*

Verse 8.—'Tis all one to a godly man, *night* or *day.* For what *night* can there be to him who hath God always with him, who is a *sun* to comfort him, as well as a shield to protect him (Ps. lxxxiv. 11); and *the light of whose countenance*, if it be but very little, is more comfortable than all things else whatsoever that the *day* can bring with it. He can say, " When I sit in darkness, the Lord shall be a light unto me " (Mic. vii. 8); and " the Lord my God will enlighten my darkness." Ps. xviii. 28. To tell you the truth, I think the *night* is the merriest time that the godly man hath, and the saddest for the wicked man (who, though he make use of *darkness* to hide his sin, yet is he afraid, because of that very thing in which his safety consists). For if a man be merry in good company, he must needs be more merry when he enjoys it better, and there is less to disturb his mirth. So as it is with a godly man in the *night*, when the greatest part of his hindrances are removed, and he can " delight himself in the Almighty " without disturbance. Job. xxvii. 10. David says that the Lord would indeed " *command his loving-kindness in the daytime,*" but " *in the night* (says he) *his song shall be with me* "— " his song," as I think, not of *thanksgiving*, but of *joy and exultation*, such as God uses to give at that time. Job. xxxv. 10. In the *daytime* the soul is so taken up with base employments, so distracted with variety of sensible objects, and so busied with work for the body, that either she hath no leisure at all to do her own work (such as this joy is as much as anything), or she cannot do it so well as she would, or so well as she could *in the night*, when she hath less to do. I doubt not but the worldly and carnal man, now that I am talking so much of *night* and sleep, will be ready to say that I do but *dream*, and to answer me as the fellow did the hunter, when he bade him hear " what heavenly music his dogs made." For I know he counts the music and songs that we speak of, nothing but a frenzy, or a fancy at the least, such as mad and diseased people have in their brain, while they imagine it to be in the air. But, as Peter said of those upon whom the Holy Ghost fell, " These men are not drunk, as ye suppose; " so may I reply to such men, No such matter, the godly are not mad, as ye suppose, for their songs are not works of their own fancy, not made of their own head, but set for them by God himself, " who giveth songs in the night." Job. xxxv. 10.—*Zachary Bogan.*

Verse 8.—" *And my prayer unto the God of my life.*" Here may be seen that David's religion was a religion of prayer *after* deliverance, as well as before. The selfish who cry out in trouble will have done with their prayers, when the trouble is over. With David it was the very reverse. Deliverance from trouble would strengthen his confidence in God, embolden his addresses to him, and furnish him with new arguments. . . . . There is great *need* of prayer after deliverance ; for the time of deliverance is often a time of temptation, the soul being elated, and thrown off its guard. At such seasons much of the joy that is felt may be merely natural, as David's would probably be when rescued from that corroding care which injures the body as well as distresses the soul. There is danger of mistaking ; of supposing it to be all spiritual, and hence of imagining the soul to be in a higher state of grace than it really is, and so, of being imperceptibly drawn into a state of false security. There is then especial need of that prayer. " Hold thou me up, and I shall be safe." And with some peculiarly, who being of a sanguine constitution of mind, are in times of enjoyment, soon puffed up and brought into danger.—*Henry March.*

Verse 8 (*last clause*).—Your song and your prayer must be directed to God as " *the God of your life.*" You do not own him as God, except you own and adore him as your all sufficient good, and that " fulness which filleth all in all.". You detract from the glory of his Godhead, if you attribute not this to him ; and if, accordingly, as one that cannot live without him, you do not seek union with him, and join yourself to him, and then rejoice and solace yourself in that blessed conjunction.—*John Howe.*

Verse 9.—" *God my rock.*" David was a fugitive, with little means of defence, and continually pursued by enemies who were powerful and numerous. The country in which he wandered was mountainous, and he often sought and found shelter on the tops of precipitous rocks, or in their natural hollows or excavated caves. Thus the idea of shelter and defence being associated in his mind with that of a rock, how natural that he should apply the term to God, and when seeking him as his refuge and helper, should address him by that appellation. . . . . " *Why hast thou forgotten me ?* " Not that he supposed he was literally forgotten of God, so as to be given up and abandoned by him ; because he had still sufficient trust in his faithfulness to seek him for a refuge, and to hope in his mercy. His expression is to be regarded as the language of feeling, not of judgment. He felt, he seemed, as one forgotten by God. Those visits of love, those manifestations of favour with which he had formerly been indulged, and which then seemed to him to be so many tokens of the divine remembrance, were now withheld, now when, on account of his distress, they appeared so unspeakably more needful and desirable ; whence it was that he felt as one forgotten.—*Henry March.*

Verse 10.—" *Mine enemies.*" It is strange that *he* should have enemies, that was so harmless a man that when they were sick and distressed, he prayed for them, and put on sackcloth for them, as it is, Psalm xxxv. This compassionate, sweet-natured man, yet, notwithstanding, you see he had enemies, and enemies that would discover themselves to reproach him, and that bitterly ; in the bitterest manner, they reproach him in his religion. We may be armed by this observation against the scandal of opposition—that if we meet with enemies in the world, we should not be much offended at it ; grieve we may, but wonder ne need not. Was there ever any that did more good than our Saviour Christ ? " He went about doing good." Acts x. 38. He did never a miracle that was harmful (but only of the swine that were drowned in the sea, and that was their own fault), but he went about doing all the good he could ; yet, notwithstanding, we see what malicious opposites he had. That that is true of the head must be true in the members. Therefore we should rejoice in our conformity to Christ, if it be in a good cause, that we find enemies and opposition. The devil is not made a Christian yet, and he will never be made good, for he is *in termino,* as we say, he is in his bounds, his nature is immovable ; he is in hell in regard of his estate, though he be loose to do mischief. Now, until the devil be good, God's children shall never want enemies ; and he will never be good ; therefore, though there were good kings and good governors over all the world, yet good men shall never want enemies as long as the devil is alive, as long as he hath anything to do in the world. Enemies, therefore, we must look for, and such enemies as will not conceal their malice neither ; for that were something, if they would suffer their malice to boil and concoct in their own hearts, but that will not be, but " out of the abundance of the heart the mouth will speak."—*Richard Sibbes.*

Verse 10.—" *They say daily unto me.*" Here's their constancy and perseverance in this their carriage and language, it is *daily*, or *all the day*, כָּל־הַיּוֹם. It is not only for a fit and away, but it is their frequent and continual practice ; it's every, and it's all the day ; they begin in the morning, and they hold out still till night as unquiet persons use to do ; and they begin the week with it, and so they continue till the end ; he could never come into their company or near them, but he had such language from them.—*Thomas Horton.*

Verse 10.—" *Where is thy God ?*" David might rather have said to them, Where are your eyes ? where is your sight ? for God is not only in heaven, but in me. Though David was shut out from the sanctuary, yet David's soul was a sanctuary for God ; for God is not tied to a sanctuary made with hands. God hath two sanctuaries, he hath two heavens—the heaven of heavens and a broken spirit. God dwelt in David as in his temple. God was with David and in him ; and he was never more with him, nor never more in him than in his greatest afflictions. They wanted eyes, he wanted not God. Though sometimes God hide himself, not only from the world but from his own children, yet he is there ; howsoever their sorrow is such that it dims their sight (as we see *in* Hagar), so that they cannot see him for the present, he sometimes looks in their face, as we see in Mary's case. She could not see Christ distinctly, but thought him to be the gardener. There is a kind of concealment awhile in heavenly wisdom, yet not-withstanding, God is with his children always, and they know it by faith though not by feeling always. . . . . Therefore, it was an ignorant question of them to ask, *Where is thy God ?* It showed that they were ignorant of the passages of God's dealing with his children, as indeed none are greater atheists than your scoffers. *Where is thy God ?* as if God had been only a God of observation, to be observed outwardly in all his passages towards his children ; whereas, as I said, he is a God hiding himself ofttimes ; and he shows himself in contrary conditions most of all, most comfortably. His work is by contraries. But these carnal men were ignorant of the mysteries of religion, and the mysteries of divine providence towards God's children. Therefore, their question savours of their disposition, *Where is now thy God ?*—*Richard Sibbes.*

Verse 10.—" *Where is thy God ?*" It is the deriding question which persecutors put to the saints in the time of their trials and troubles, *Ubi Deus ?* " Where is now your God ? " But they may return a bold and confident answer, *Hic Deus*, " Our God is here," our God is nigh unto us, our God is round about us, our God is in the midst of us, our God has given us his promise " that he will never leave us nor forsake us." Heb. xiii. 5. In every trouble, in every danger, in every death, the Lord will be sure to keep us company. God will bear his children company, not only whilst they are in a delightful paradise, but also when they are in a howling wilderness. Hosea ii. 14. When a company of poor Christians were going into banishment, one standing by to see them pass along said, that it was a very sad condition that those poor people were in, to be thus hurried from the society of men, and to be made companions of the beasts of the fields. True, said another, it were a sad condition indeed, if they were carried to a place where they should not find their God ; but let them be of good cheer, for God goes along with them, and will exhibit the comforts of his presence whithersoever they go, his presence is infinite, and filleth all places. The Rabbins put *Makom*, which signifies *place*, among the names of God ; Bythner brings them in expounding that text (Esther iv. 14), thus : " Deliverance shall arise from another place," that is, from God. Now, they called God *place*, because he is in every place, filling heaven and earth with his presence.—*Thomas Brooks.*

Verse 10.—Forest-flies, small as they are, drive the noble war-horse mad ; therefore David says, " *As with a sword in my bones, mine enemies reproach me ; while they say daily unto me, Where is thy God ?*"—*Frederick William Robertson,* 1851.

Verse 11.—Imitate here the example of David, instead of yielding to a vague grief ; cite your soul ; *enquire* of it the particular cause of your sorrow : different remedies will be requisite according to the different sources of your distress ; and be careful that you trifle not with God, and your comfort, and your salvation, while you enquire of your soul, " *Why art thou cast down, O my soul ?* " Be impartial, there is another and more solemn judgment to succeed : be persevering, like the Psalmist, return, again and again to the investigation : be prayerful ; self-love, or the delusions of your heart, may otherwise deceive you. Pray then to God, to " search you, and see if there be any wicked way in you."—*Henry Kollock, D.D., in " Sermons,"* etc. 1822.

Verse 11.—" *Hope.*" Hope is like the sun, which, as we journey towards it, casts the shadow of our burden behind us.—*Samuel Smiles, LL.D.*

Verse 11.—" *God . . . . is the health of my countenance.*" The health of David's countenance was not in his countenance, but *in his God,* and this makes his faith silence his fears, and so peremptorily resolve upon it, that there is a time coming (how near soever he now lies to the grave's mouth) when he " *shall yet praise him.*" The health and life of thy grace lie both of them, not in thy grace, saith faith, but *in God,* who is *thy* God, therefore I shall yet live and praise him. I do not wonder that the weak Christian is melancholy and sad, when he sees his sickly face in any other glass than this.—*William Gurnall.*

Verse 11.—" *The health of my countenance.*" The countenance is often a true index to the mind. In the present awakening in religion, nothing is more remarkable than the sad or joyous looks of those whom God has spiritually exercised. It is easy to see who are sad, and who happy. There is nothing new in this ; the Psalmist says, " My soul is cast down within me." Therefore had he a dejected countenance ; but said he, " Send thy light and thy truth ; let them lead me ; then will I go unto God, my exceeding joy. . . . And he shall be *the health of my countenance.*" In his sorrow, the face of Jesus was marred more than any man's, and his visage more than the sons of men. The martyr Stephen was so filled with the sight of Jesus, that in the midst of his persecutors, with death in prospect, he had a face which " shone as the face of an angel." My friend, how is it with thee ? Is thy countenance sad ? or doth it shine with the joy of the Lord, telling the true tale of thy life and lot ?—*J. Denham Smith.* 1860.

Verse 11.—Hast thou seen the sun shine forth in February, and the sky blue, and the hedgerows bursting into bud, and the primrose peeping beneath the bank, and the birds singing in the bushes ? Thou hast thought that spring was already come in its beauty and sweet odours. But a few days, and the clouds returned, and the atmosphere was chilled, and the birds were mute, and snow was on the ground, and thou hast said that spring would never come. And thus sometimes the young convert finds his fears removed and the comforts of the gospel shed abroad in his heart, and praise and thanksgiving, and a new song put in his mouth. And he deems unadvisedly that his troubles are past for ever. But awhile, and his doubts return, and his comforts die away, and his light is taken from him, and his spirit is overwhelmed, and he is fain to conclude that salvation and all its blessings are not for him. But the spring, though late, shall break at last. " *Why art thou cast down, O my soul ? and why art thou disquieted within me ?* "—*H. G. Salter's " Book of Illustrations,"* 1840.

Verse 11.—His arguments and motives hereunto are impregnated with very great sense and strength ; and urged upon himself as the just rate thereof. " *Hope thou in God.*" For he is 1. " *God.*" 2. " *Thy God.*" 3. " *The health of thy countenance,*" and 4. *One whom thou shalt* (certainly and for ever) *praise as such.* And 5. Do it *yet,* as lamentable and hopeless as thy case appears at present through seeming difficulties or unlikelihoods. God and ourselves well understood, deeply considered, and skilfully urged and improved, give gracious hearts the best encouragements and supports under the severest accidents of time. And they will very strangely animate our hopes in God under our sorest troubles and dejections. David had (1) confidence in God ; and (2) reasons for it ; and (3) skill and a heart to urge them. When he reviewed himself, he saw that his soul was gracious ; and so he knew God valued it. It was bent for praising God ; and so he knew that he should have an opportunity and cause to do it, through some signal favours from him. He had an interest in God ; and he would neither lose it nor neglect it, and he had great experience of God's former mercies, and he would not forget them. And when he thinks on God, then praises must be thought on too, and everything relating to it, and all the divine perfections, within the circumference of his knowledge, must

have their fresh remembrances and powerful sense revived upon his own heart.—
Matthew Sylvester (1636—1708), *in " Morning Exercises."*

Verse 11.—The soul, when once greatly disturbed, is often not soon calmed,
on account of infirmities and remaining corruptions.—*Henry March.*

HINTS TO PREACHERS.

Verse 1.—The longing heart and the panting hart compared.

Verses 1, 2.—Those who have enjoyed the presence of God in the public ordinances
of religion will greatly desire, if deprived of them, to be favoured with them again. . . .
Prevention from attending the public ordinances of God's house may be made
the means of great benefit to the soul. I. By renewing our relish for the provisions
of the Lord's house, which so soon and so often palls. II. By making us to prize the
means of grace more highly. There is, through human degeneracy, a proneness
to value things less, however excellent in themselves, because of their being common,
or plentiful, or of easy attainment. III. By driving us more directly from God.
—*H. March.*

Verses 1—3.—The home-sickness of the soul. What awakens it in the soul?
To what is it directed, or does it point or tend? Wherewith can it be satisfied?
By the bitter, but ofttimes wholesome food of tears.—*J. P. Lange.*

Verse 2.—I. What thirsts? " my soul." II. For what? " for God." III. In
what way? " when shall I come." Or, the cause, incentives, excellences, and
privileges of spiritual thirst.

Verse 2 (*last clause*).—The true view of public worship.

Verse 2 (*last clause*).—Appearance before God here and hereafter.—*Isaac Watts,
D.D., Two Sermons.*

Verse 3.—The believer's Lent, and its salt meats. I. What causes the sorrow?
II. What will remove it? III. What benefit will come of it?

Verses 3, 10.—The carriage of David's enemies. I. The *nature* of it, and that
was " reproach." II. The *expression* of it, " They say unto me." III. The *constancy*
of it: " daily," or, all the day long. IV. The *specification* of it, in a scornful and
opprobrious queston : " Where is (now) thy God?"—*Thomas Horton.*

Verse 4.—I. It is common for the mind, in seasons of sorrow, to seek relief from
the present in recollections of the past. II. In recollections of past enjoyments,
those that relate to social worship will be peculiarly dear to the servant of God.
III. Man is a social being, hence he derives help from united worship.—*H. March.*

Verse 4.—" I pour out my soul in me." The uselessness of mistrustful
introspection.

Verse 4.—" I had gone with the multitude," etc. Company, if it be that which
is good, is a very blessed and comfortable accommodation in sundry respects. I. It
is an exercise of men's faculties, and the powers and abilities of the mind. II. It
is a fence against danger, and a preservative against sadness and various temptations.
III. An opportunity of doing more good.—*Thomas Horton.*

Verse 4.—" I had gone," etc. Sunny memories, their lessons of gratitude and
hope.

Verse 4 (*last clause*).—Not Chaucer's tales of the Canterbury pilgrims, but David's
tales of the Jerusalem pilgrims.

Verse 4.—" With the voice," etc. Congregational singing defended, extolled,
discriminated, and urged.

Verse 5.—Sorrow put to the question, or the Consolatory Catechism.

Verse 5.—The sweetness, safety, and rightness of hope *in* God. Good grip for
the anchor.

Verse 5.—The music of the future, " I shall yet praise him."

Verse 5.—" The help of his countenance," or the sustaining power of God's presence.

Verse 5.—" Why art thou cast down?" 1. The mind, even of a holy man may
be unduly cast down and disquieted. II. In cases of undue dejection and disquietude
the proper remedy is to expostulate with the soul, and to direct it to the *only true
source* of relief. III. Expostulation with the soul in times of distress, is then

productive of its proper end, when it leads to an immediate application to God. —*H. March.*

Verse 5.—An emphasis of *enquiry or examination ;* David calls himself to account for his present passion and trouble of mind. An emphasis of *reproof or objurgation ;* David chides and rebukes himself for his present distemper. " *Why art thou thus ? "* —*Thomas Horton.*

Verses 5 with 11, or *help* and *health.*

Verse 6.—" *Remember thee."* The consolation derivable from thoughts of God.

Verse 6.—" *Therefore will I remember thee."* There are two ways of understanding this ; each of them instructive and profitable. . . . I. It may be considered as an expression of *determined remembrance of God* should he ever be found in such places and conditions. Believers can suppose the worst, and yet hope for the best. II. The language may be considered as an expression of *encouragement derived from reflection.* He had been in these situations and circumstances, and had experienced in them displays of divine providence and grace.—*W. Jay.*

Verse 6.—Ebenezers many, varied, remembered, helpful.

Verse 7.—" *Deep calleth unto deep."* See Spurgeon's Sermons, No. 865.

Verse 7.—" *Deep calleth unto deep."* One evil inviting another. I. The *variety* of evils—one evil to another. II. The *conjunction* of evils—one evil with another. III. The *connexion* of evils, or dependence and mutual reference—one evil upon another.—*T. Horton.*

Verse 7.—The threefold depth which the saints and servants of God are subject to here in this life. I. The depth of *temptation.* II. The depth of *desertion.* III. The depth of *affliction and human calamities.*—*T. Horton.*

Verses 7, 8.—In seasons of affliction the servants of God will be distinguished from others by their ready perception and acknowledgment of the hand of God in their trials.—*H. March.*

Verse 8.—Daily mercy and nightly song ; the mercies of sunshine and shade.

Verse 8 (last clause).—The blessed alternation between praise and prayer.

Verse 8.—" *God of my life."* Author, sustainer, comforter, object, crown, consummation.

Verse 8.—" *The God of my life."* There is a threefold life whereof we partake, and God is the God of each unto us. First, the life of *nature ;* secondly, the life of *grace ;* thirdly, the life of *glory.*—*T. Horton.*

Verse 9.—" *God my rock."* Appellations of God, suited to circumstances.— *H. March.*

Verse 9.—" *My rock."* See Keach in his metaphors.

Verse 9.—I. *Why thou ?* II. *Why I ?* III. *Why he ?* It is a *why* to all three, To *God,* " *Why hast thou forgotten me ? "* To *David* himself, *"Why do I go mourning ? "* To *David's adversary,* whoever he was, " *Why does the enemy oppress me ? "*—*T. Horton.*

Verse 10.—The most grievous of taunts.

Verse 11.—" *My God."* I. It's a word of *interest*—" *My God,"* as in covenant with him. II. A word of *compliance*—" *My God,"* as submitting to him. III. A word of *affection*—" *My God,"* as taking delight and rejoicing in him.—*T. Horton.*

Verse 11.—A catechism, a consolation, a commendation.

Verse 11.—I. David's *experience* of God. " *He is the health,* or *help of my countenance."* II. His *relation* to God, and *interest* in him—" *And my God."*— *T. Horton.*

PSALM XLIII.

SUBJECT.—*On account of the similarity of the structure of this Psalm to that of Psalm forty-two, it has been supposed to be a fragment wrongly separated from the preceding song; but it is always dangerous to allow these theories of error in Holy Scripture, and in this instance it would be very difficult to show just cause for such an admission. Why should the Psalm have been broken? Its similarity would have secured its unity had it ever been part and parcel of the forty-second. Is it not far more likely that some in their fancied wisdom united them wrongly in the few MSS. in which they are found as one? We believe the fact is that the style of the poetry was pleasant to the writer, and therefore in after life he wrote this supplemental hymn after the same manner. As an appendix it needed no title. David complains of his enemies, and asks the privilege of communion with God as his surest deliverance from them.*

DIVISION.—*The Psalmist cries to God in prayer, verses 1—3. Promises praise in the anticipation of an answer, verse 4, and chides himself for his despondency, verse 5.*

EXPOSITION.

JUDGE me, O God, and plead my cause against an ungodly nation: O deliver me from the deceitful and unjust man.

2 For thou *art* the God of my strength: why dost thou cast me off? why go I mourning because of the oppression of the enemy?

3 O send out thy light and thy truth: let them lead me; let them bring me unto thy holy hill, and to thy tabernacles.

1. "*Judge me, O God.*" Others are unable to understand my motives, and unwilling to give me a just verdict. My heart is clear as to its intent, and therefore I bring my case before thee, content that thou wilt impartially weigh my character, and right my wrongs. If thou wilt judge, thy acceptance of my conduct will be enough for me; I can laugh at human misrepresentation if my conscience knows that thou art on my side; thou art the only one I care for; and besides, thy verdict will not sleep, but thou wilt see practical justice done to thy slandered servant. "*And plead my cause against an ungodly nation.*" One such advocate as the Lord will more than suffice to answer a nation of brawling accusers. When people are ungodly no wonder that they are unjust: those who are not true to God himself cannot be expected to deal rightly with his people. Hating the King they will not love his subjects. Popular opinion weighs with many, but divine opinion is far more weighty with the gracious few. One good word from God outweighs ten thousand railing speeches of men. He bears a brazen shield before him whose reliance in all things is upon his God; the arrows of calumny fall harmlessly from such a buckler. "*O deliver me from the deceitful and unjust man.*" Deceit and injustice are boon companions: he who fawns will not fear to slander. From two such devils none can deliver us but God. His wisdom can outwit the craft of the vilest serpent, and his power can overmatch the most raging lion. Whether this was Doeg or Ahithophel is small matter, such double distilled villains are plentiful, and the only way of dealing with them is to refer the matter to the righteous Judge of all; if we try to fight them with their own weapons, we shall suffer more serious injury from ourselves than from them. O child of God, leave these thine enemies in better hands, remembering that vengeance belongeth not to thee, but to the Lord. Turn to him in prayer, crying, "O deliver me," and ere long you shall publish abroad the remembrance of his salvation.

2. "*For.*"—Here is argument, which is the very sinew of prayer. If we reasoned more with the Lord we should have more victories in supplication. "*Thou art the God of my strength.*" All my strength belongs to thee—I will not, therefore, use it on my own behalf against my personal foes. All my strength comes from thee, I therefore seek help from thee, who art able to bestow it. All my strength is in thee, I leave therefore this task of combating my foes entirely in thy hands. Faith

which leaves such things alone is wise faith. Note the assurance of David, *" thou art,"* not I hope and trust so, but I know it is so ; we shall find confidence to be our consolation. *" Why dost thou cast me off ? "* Why am I treated as if thou didst loathe me ? Am I become an offence unto thee ? There are many reasons why the Lord might cast us off, but no reason shall prevail to make him do so. He hath not cast off his people, though he for awhile treats them as cast-offs. Learn from this question that it is well to enquire into dark providences, but we must enquire of God, not of our own fears. He who is the author of a mysterious trial can best expound it to us.

> " Blind unbelief is sure to err,
> And scan his work in vain ;
> God is his own interpreter,
> And he will make it plain."

" Why go I mourning because of the oppression of the enemy ? " Why do I wander hither and thither like a restless spirit ? Why wear I the weeds of sorrow on my body, and the lines of grief on my face ? Oppression makes a wise man mad ; why, Lord, am I called to endure so much of it for so long a time ? Here again is a useful question, addressed to the right quarter. The answer will often be because we are saints, and must be made like our Head, and because such sorrow is chastening to the spirit, and yieldeth comfortable fruit. We are not to cross-question the Lord in peevishness, but we may ask of him in humility ; God help us to observe the distinction so as not to sin through stress of sorrow.

3. *" O send out thy light and thy truth."* The joy of thy presence and the faithfulness of thy heart ; let both of these be manifest to me. Reveal my true character by thy light, and reward me according to thy truthful promise. As the sun darts forth his beams, so does the Lord send forth his favour and his faithfulness towards all his people ; and as all nature rejoices in the sunshine, even so the saints triumph in the manifestation of the love and fidelity of their God, which, like the golden sunbeam, lights up even the darkest surroundings with delightful splendour. *" Let them lead me."* Be these my star to guide me to my rest. Be these my Alpine guides to conduct me over mountains and precipices to the abodes of grace. *" Let them bring me unto thy holy hill, and to thy tabernacles."* First in thy mercy bring me to thine earthly courts, and end my weary exile, and then in due time admit me to thy celestial palace above. We seek not light to sin by, nor truth to be exalted by it, but that they may become our practical guides to the nearest communion with God : only such light and truth as are sent us from God will do this, common light is not strong enough to show the road to heaven, nor will mere moral or physical truths assist to the holy hill ; but the light of the Holy Spirit, and the truth as it is in Jesus, these are elevating, sanctifying, perfecting ; and hence their virtue in leading us to the glorious presence of God. It is beautiful to observe how David's longing to be away from the oppression of man always leads him to sigh more intensely for communion with God.

4 Then will I go unto the altar of God, unto God my exceeding joy : yea, upon the harp will I praise thee, O God my God.

5 Why art thou cast down, O my soul ? and why art thou disquieted within me ? hope in God : for I shall yet praise him, *who* is the health of my countenance, and my God.

4. *" Then will I go unto the altar of God."* If David might but be favoured with such a deliverance as would permit his return, it would not be his own house of heritage which would be his first resort, but to the altar of God his willing feet should conduct him. His whole heart would go as a sacrifice to the altar, he himself counting it his greatest happiness to be permitted to lie as a burnt offering wholly dedicated to the Lord. With what exultation should believers draw near unto Christ, who is the antitype of the altar ! clearer light should give greater intensity of desire. *" Unto God my exceeding joy."* It was not the altar as such that the Psalmist cared for, he was no believer in the heathenism of ritualism : his soul desired spiritual fellowship, fellowship with God himself in very deed. What are all the rites of worship unless the Lord be in them ; what, indeed, but empty shells and dry husks ? Note the holy rapture with which David regards his Lord ! He is not his *joy* alone, but his *exceeding* joy ; not the fountain of joy, the giver of joy, or the maintainer of joy, but that joy itself. The margin hath it, " The gladness

of my joy," *i.e.*, the soul, the essence, the very bowels of my joy. To draw near to God, who is such a joy to us, may well be the object of our hungering and thirsting. " *Yea, upon the harp will I praise thee.*" His best music for his best love. When God fills us with joy we ought ever to pour it out at his feet in praise, and all the skill and talent we have should be laid under contribution to increase the divine revenue of glory. " *O God, my God.*" How he dwells upon the name which he loves so well! He already harps on it as though his harp music had begun. What sweeter sounds can music know than these four words? To have God in possession, and to know it by faith, is the heart's heaven—a fulness of bliss lies therein.

5. " *Why art thou cast down, O my soul?* " If God be thine, why this dejection? If he uplifts thee, why art thou so near the ground? The dew of love is falling, O withering heart, revive. " *And why art thou disquieted within me?* " What cause is there to break the repose of thy heart? Wherefore indulge unreasonable sorrows, which benefit no one, fret thyself, and dishonour thy God? Why overburden thyself with foregodings? " *Hope in God,*" or " *wait for God.*" There is need of patience, but there is ground for hope. The Lord cannot but avenge his own elect. The heavenly Father will not stand by and see his children trampled on for ever; as surely as the sun is in the heavens, light must arise for the people of God, though for awhile they may walk in darkness. Why, then, should we not be encouraged, and lift up our head with comfortable hope? " *For I shall yet praise him.*" Times of complaint will soon end, and seasons of praise will begin. Come, my heart, look out of the window, borrow the telescopic glass, forecast a little, and sweeten thy chamber with sprigs of the sweet herb of hope. " *Who is the health of my countenance, and my God.*" My God will clear the furrows from my brow, and the tear marks from my cheek; therefore will I lift up my head and smile in the face of the storm. The Psalm has a blessed ending, such as we would fain imitate when death puts an end to our mortal existence.

EXPLANATORY NOTES AND QUAINT SAYINGS.

Whole Psalm.—This Psalm is evidently a continuation or supplement to the preceding. In some MSS. of Kennicott and de Rossi's, they are united, and make one Psalm.—*George Phillips, B.D.*

Verse 1.—" *Judge me, O God, and plead my cause,*" etc.—Believers may appeal to God's justice, and plead God's righteousness. I. Touching suffering wrongs of men. II. Touching sin in relation to God's wrath. I. Touching suffering wrongs of men, believers may appeal upon these three grounds: 1. The injustice that men do to believers, is as well against *God's just nature*, as against the believers' ease. So their appeals to God are agreeable to God's enmity against injustice; therefore, his enmity concurs with their appeals. Romans i. 18. 2. Justice in men is according to God's nature, as well as for the believer's welfare, and, therefore, the disposition and inclination of God's nature concurs with their prayers for deliverance. Psalm xi. 7; Luke xxiii. 6, 7. 3. Such wrong God who do wrong his people (2 Chron. xiv. 11; Zech. ii. 8; Acts ix. 4, 5); so that in deliverance God vindicates himself as well as the believers. II. Touching sin in relation to God's wrath, a true believer may plead God's justice or righteousness on these three grounds: 1. Christ our Advocate or Attorney so pleads. John xvii. 24, etc. Now, the client may plead the same as the advocate, seeing it is in relation to the same party and the same issue. 2. Christ hath satisfied God's justice, so that on Christ was laid all the sins of all believers. He was " wounded " for them. Now, God cannot in justice punish twice; therefore, seeing Christ was wounded, believers must be healed. Isaiah liii. 3. Believers have God's righteousness imputed to them (2 Cor. v.); therefore, God must deal with believers as he will deal with his own righteousness.

Useful is this doctrine two ways. I. For terror to the enemies of believers. How many prevailing cries to the justice of God are against such enemies? 1. Their own sins cry. 2. Believers' injuries cry. 3. Believers' prayers cry. 4. Christ's intercession cries over again their prayers and desires (Rev. vi. 9 compared with Rev. viii. 3). II. The second use is for comfort to believers, that as God's mercy is for them, so is his justice to deliver them, not only from *men*, but from *sin;* and in and through Christ they may humbly plead justice as against sinners, so against sin ; not only against the guilt but against the power, that seeing Christ died, sin should not live.—*Condensed from Nathanael Homes, 1652.*

Verse 1.—*" Ungodly .... deceitful .... unjust."* There are *ungodly* men who, being destitute of religious principle, will not scruple to injure us, when they can thereby gratify their passions or advance their worldly interests. There are *deceitful* men who will put on the garb of friendship, and acquire our confidence and esteem, and then treacherously cheat us out of our property, or our reputation, or our peace. There are *unjust* men, who by fraud or by violence, would rob us of our dearest rights and most valuable possessions, and not only reduce our powers and opportunities of doing good, but even diminish our means of comfortable subsistence. And there are *oppressors*, who taking advantage of our weakness or dependence, and trampling alike on the maxims of equity and humanity, may exact from us unreasonable services, impose upon us heavy burdens and cruel restraints, and ply us with insults, and harrassments, and deprivations, from which we can make no escape, and for which we can find no redress.—*Andrew Thomson, D.D., in " Lectures on Portions of the Psalms,"* 1826.

Verse 2.—*" Thou art the God of my strength."* The godly man hath from God a threefold strength, namely : natural, providential, and spiritual. I. *Natural,* Acts xvii. 28. This is twofold : of body, of mind. Of robustness, hardness, and agility of body ; of wit, invention, and valour of mind. Now, these donations of corporal and mental natural endowments are God's gifts. Psalm xviii. 43, 39. . . . II. *Providential* strength, which is threefold : 1. God's donation of strengthening mercies. (1) Corporal : wine to make glad, and bread to strengthen. Psalm civ. 15. (2) Mental, common gifts ; as Paul had a singular gift of language and single life ; Apollos of elocution, argument, power of convincing. 2. Providential strength is God's making way for his people to act and put forth their strength. Psalm lxxviii. 50. 3. Providential strength is God's concurrence with our lawful human acting. Psalm xviii. 29.

III. The third sort of power is *spiritual :* God is the godly man's spiritual power. I John ii. 14 : " I have written unto you, young men, because ye are strong," namely, with spiritual strength, for it follows, " The word of God abideth in you, and ye have overcome the wicked one." This is the main strength of a godly man ; as that text hints, namely, young men are naturally strong, but St. John takes no notice of that, but commends them for their spiritual strength. This spiritual strength is from the word of the Spirit, and from the Spirit of the word, that is, from the Spirit accompanying the word. 1. From *the word of the Spirit,* the word of God. Psalm cxix. 50 : " This is my comfort in my affliction : for thy word hath quickened me." To be " *quickened,"* i.e., enlivened, is to be full of vigour and spirit and to act mightily, and to " *comfort* " is, as the word signifies, to make strong ; for when a man is most cheerful with sobriety, he is most strong. St. John in that place fore-quoted, saith the young men to whom he wrote were strong because the word of God abode in them. For (Prov. xii. 25) " whereas sorrow in the heart of man maketh it stoop "—makes it sickly, weak, drooping—" a good word maketh it glad," cheerful, strong, vigorous. And so if the word of a wise friend, how much more the word of God, with its many strengthening promises ? Psalm xx. 2 ; cxix. 28. The word of God is the very mind and will of God, and power of God, and with the word God created the world, therefore, he that receives this word must needs receive a great deal of strength. Romans i. 16.

2. *The Spirit of the word,* the Holy Spirit that useth to accompany the word to them that receive it. By his Spirit God is in a believer (1 Cor, vi. 9 ; Eph. ii.) ; and this is the spirit of strength and power. Eph. iii. 16 ; 2 Tim. i. 7. As a powerful, active soul makes a vigorous body, so the Spirit in the soul makes the soul powerful and strong, being the soul of the soul of a believer. We read more than once or twice in the Scriptures, that when believers did any eminent act, it is said, *the Spirit of the Lord came upon them, and they did* so and so, *i.e.,* the Spirit of God in them did then put forth its power to make them act powerfully.—*Condensed from Nathanael Homes.*

Verse 3.—"*O send out thy light and thy truth.*" Possibly there may be an allusion to the Urim and Thummim, as the symbol of light and truth.—*J. J. Stewart Perowne.*

Verse 3.—"*Light and Truth.*" Delightful and all-comprehensive words. They contain all the salvation and all the desire of a believing, confiding soul. But it is only when thus combined—separated they are no longer a ground of trust and joy. For what would favour avail without faithfulness? It would be no more than the uncertain friendship of men, who smile to-day and reproach to-morrow; who make large promises, but do not perform them. Even the "*light*" which angels and glorified spirits enjoy in heaven would be insufficient to banish all fear and to fill them with satisfaction, were it not for their confidence in the "*truth*" of God. How much more, then, must this be the case with erring, sinful mortals on earth? When the humble spirit is bowed down under a sense of its utter unworthiness and innumerable weaknesses and defilements, its negligences, follies, and wanderings, what should save from despair but the confidence that he who has been merciful will also be faithful; that God is truth as well as light; that he hath said, "I will never leave thee nor forsake thee;" that he "*cannot* lie," and that, therefore, "his mercy endureth for ever"? On the other hand, *truth* without *light*, faithfulness without grace, would be only the dreadful execution of terrible but just denunciations on the transgressors of the holy law. "In the day that thou eatest thereof thou shalt surely die." Adam ate, and in that day became the subject of sin and death. This was *truth* executing judgment. But *light* arose around the darkness; beams of mercy tempered the heavy cloud. The promise of the Great Deliverer was given; then faithfulness was enlisted on the side of grace, and became engaged for its bestowment; "mercy and truth met together; righteousness and peace kissed each other." Since then, all humble and trusting souls have beheld them united, and have made their union the ground of their confidence and joy.—*Henry March.*

Verse 3.—"*Thy tabernacles.*" There were two tabernacles, one at Zion, where the ark stood, and another at Gibeon. 1 Chron. xvi. 37, 39. It is not to this fact that the Psalmist alludes, however, but to the circumstance, in all probability of the different parts of the tabernacle. There was, first the holiest of all, then the sanctuary, and then the tabernacle of the convocation. Heb. ix. 1—8.—*John Morison.*

Verse 4.—"*Then will I go unto the altar of God.*" Let us remember that the approach to God in the holy place is by means of the altar, whence eternally ascendeth the fragrance and the preciousness of the one whole, perfect burnt-offering, and where for ever and ever the divine holiness resteth and feedeth with its pure fire with infinite satisfaction, with inconceivable delight. Oh, what a holy, a divine, a wondrous place is this "*altar of God!*" That altar now means all the value and everlasting efficacy of the one offering of Christ unto God for us; and it is in the full power and blessedness thereof that we draw nigh to God. To this point, to this unspeakably blessed position, the light and the truth of God will attract the child of God. Toward this altar all the rays of the light of divine favour and grace, and of divine truth, and holiness, have from eternity converged; and from this point they shine forth toward and upon the soul and heart of the poor, far-off penitent, attracting him to that altar where he may meet his God. Let us then come to the altar of God; let us enter the cloud of holy incense that filleth the tabernacle of the Most High; let us realise how perfectly God is satisfied with that which Christ has done, with his obedience in dying to meet the claims of divine justice on the sinner, and to complete the perfect surrender of himself as our "*exceeding joy,*" even the gladness of our joy, the heart, essence, substance, and reality of our joy.—*John Offord,* 1868.

Verse 4.—"*Then will I go unto the altar of God.*" He would with cheerfulness run and offer up the sacrifices of thanksgiving to his gracious deliverer; he would take his own soul as the burnt-offering, and kindle and burn it up with the fire of a vigorous love and raised affections terminating upon God, the flames whereof should ascend to him alone. . . . . . "*Unto God my exceeding joy,*" or, as the Hebrew is more exactly translated, *unto God the gladness of his joy*—that which gave a relish to every other comfort, which was the soul and life of his pleasures, and could only make them real and lasting; it was God who raised his joy to fulness of satisfaction and contentment.—*William Dunlop.*

Verse 4.—"*Then will I go . . . . unto God.*" The expression of *going to God* implies SUBMISSION and FRIENDSHIP. I. *Submission.* I will go and pay my homage to him, as my Sovereign ; I will go and hear what he says ; I will go and receive his orders. II. *Friendship.* I will go and consult him, and converse with him as a friend ; and be thankful that, in such a troublesome and ensnaring world, I have such a friend to advise with. 1. I will go and tell him my *griefs ;* how greatly I am distressed with some particular disorder in my body, or with some disturbance in my family, or with some disappointment in my worldly circumstances, or (which is worse than all of them together) with a sad darkness in my soul. 2. I will go and tell him my *joys,* for even in this vale of tears " my heart is " sometimes " glad, and my glory rejoiceth." 3. I will go and tell him of my *sins.* He knows them, indeed, already, but he shall hear them from *me.* 4. I will go and tell him my *fears ;* how greatly I am distressed at times, when I perceive this or the other corruption so strong, which I thought had received its death wound. . . . . how I tremble when I have by my folly provoked the Lord to leave me, for fear he will never return again, etc. 5. I will go and tell him my *hopes,* for some hope I have amidst all my discouragements. . . . . I will go and tell him all this ; I will unbosom and unburthen my whole heart to him ; and if my *necessities* did not *drive* me to him, I should go to him from inclination.—*Condensed from Samuel Lavington.*

Verse 4.—" *Unto God.*" Believers are not satisfied in the use of religious duties, unless they arrive at God himself in those duties. We speak not here of that arrival at God himself which is by and after all duties, to a beatifical vision of God in glory, but we speak of that arrival at God himself which is to be had *in* duties, while we are in the exercise of duties ; namely, to attain to God's special presence in them, in an actual communion, communication and conversing with God, so that we are spiritually sensible he is with us therein. I say God's *special* presence and actual communion, to distinguish it from that ordinary habitual presence and communion of God's being with a believer at all times. John xiv. 16.—*Nathanael Homes.*

Verse 4.—" *My exceeding joy.*" The Psalmist might well call God his *exceeding* joy, for it infinitely exceeds all other joy in its nature, degree, and duration.—*Samuel Lavington.*

Verse 4.—" *My exceeding joy.*" As faith acquires more strength we come to think of God and address him in more endearing terms.—*J. P. Lange.*

Verse 4.—" *Exceeding joy.*" This can be said of no other joy. All other beauties have their boundaries, all other glories have their glooms. This is that illimitable sea, God.—*E. Paxton Hood.*

Verse 5.—" *Why art thou cast down O my soul.*" He comes to his former remedy ; he had stilled his grief once before with the same meditation and upbraiding of his own soul, and chiding himself ; but he comes to it here as a *probatum est,* as a tried remedy ; he takes up his soul very short, " *Why art thou so cast down, O my soul ? and why art thou disquieted within me ?*" You see how David's passions here are interlaced with comforts, and his comforts with passions, till at last he gets the victory of his own heart. Beloved, neither sin nor grief for sin, are stilled and quieted at the first. You have some short-spirited Christians, if all be not quiet at the first, all is lost with them ; but it is not so with a true Christian soul, with the best soul living. It was not so with David when he was in distemper ; he checks himself, the distemper was not yet stilled ; he checks himself again, then the distemper breaks out again ; he checks himself again, and all little enough to bring his soul to a holy, blessed, quiet, temper, to that blessed tranquillity and rest that the soul should be in before it can enjoy its own happiness, and enjoy sweet communion with God. As you see in physic, perhaps one purge will not carry away the peccant humour, then a second must be added ; perhaps that will not do it, then there must be a third ; so when the soul hath been once checked, perhaps it will not do, we must fall to it again, go to God again. And then it may be there will be breaking out of the grief and malady again ; we must to it again, and never give over, that is the right temper of a Christian.—*Richard Sibbes.*

Verse 5.—" *Hope in God.*" The more terrible the storm, the more necesary is the anchor. Heb. vi. 19.—*William S. Plumer.*

Verse 5.—" *Hope in God.*" The complete and perfect state of God's children here is not in *re,* but in *spe :* as Christ's kingdom is not of this world, so is not our hope. The worldling's motto is, " a bird in the hand." Give me to-day, say they, and take to-morrow whoso will. But the word of believers is, *spero meliora*—my hopes are better than my present possessions.—*Elnathan Parr*.

Verse 5.—The varied conflicts of the soul afford occasion for the exercise of the graces, and thus, through the divine wisdom and goodness, are made the means of eventual good.—*Henry March*.

HINTS TO PREACHERS.

Verse 1.—We apply to God—I. As our *Judge*: "*Judge me.*" II. As our *Advocate*: "*Plead my cause.*" III. As our *Deliverer*: "*O deliver me.*"

Verse 1.—Popular opinion outweighed by divine approbation.

Verse 1.—How the Lord pleads the cause of his people.

Verse 1.—Deceit and injustice twin vipers; their origin, their character, their folly, their end.

Verses 1, 2, 4, 5.—*Five mys:* 1. My cause—"*plead it.*" 2. My strength—"*thou art.*" 3. My joy—God is. 4. My soul—"*why disquieted.*" 5. My God.

Verse 2.—"*The God of my strength.*" From whom it is derived, to whom it is dedicated, in whom it resides, by whom it shall be perfected.

Verse 2 (first clause).—1. From thee it comes. 2. By thee it is sustained. 3. To thee it is dedicated. 4. By thee it will be perfected. 5. By thee it will be rewarded.

Verse 2 (second clause).—I. *The nature of apparent forsaking.* Painful, protracted, perplexing. II. *The cause of it.* Secret sin to be laid bare, past sin chastised, graces tried, faith ultimately strengthened, etc. II. *The best conduct under it.* Appeal to God, confess, submit, pray, trust, etc.

Verse 2 (last clause).—The two "whys." The questions themselves; the spirit in which they may be asked. The answers which may be given.

Verse 3.—"*O send out thy light and thy truth.*" I. What is truth? II. How truth is to be diffused. III. Why it should be diffused. IV. Who must be the main agent of it.—*Varied from Dr. Bogue.* 1800.

Verse 3.—The blessings desired; the guidance sought; the end longed for.

Verse 3.—Under what influence we should resort to divine worship.

Verse 4.—I. The good man's duty—expressed by *going to God.* II. His *blessedness*—expressed by *rejoicing in God.*—*Samuel Lavington.*

Verse 4 (first clause).—When? "*Then.*" Where? "*Altar of God.*" Who? "*I.*" Why? "*My exceeding joy.*"

Verse 4 (second clause).—It is God alone who can be an exceeding joy to his creatures.—*W. Dunlop's Sermons.*

Verse 4.—The joy of joy. The soul of soul joy.

Verse 4.—The great object of public worship, its bliss, and the praise resulting from attaining it.

Verse 4.—I. *The medium of joy*, the altar of God, or God in Christ Jesus. II. *The springs of joy*, or the attributes of God—mercy, justice, power, holiness, as seen in the atonement. III. *The value of joy*, as comfort, strength, etc.

Verse 4.—"*God my exceeding joy.*" A most rich and precious title.

Verse 4 (last clause).—Possession, praise, resolution.

Verse 5.—Discouragement's recovery.—*R. Sibbes's Sermons.*

Verse 5.—"*I shall yet praise him.*" I, even I; shall sooner or later, most assuredly; "*yet,*" despite troubles, foes, devils; "*praise*" with gratitude, confidence, exultation; "*him*" above all other helpers, though now afflicting me.

Verse 5.—"*Health of my countenance,*" removing that which mars it—sin, shame, fear, care, sorrow, weakness, etc.

PSALM XLIV.

Title.—To the Chief Musician for the sons of Korah, Maschil.—*The title is similar to the forty-second, and although this is no proof that it is by the same author it makes it highly probable. No other writer should be sought for to father any of the Psalms when David will suffice, and therefore we are loth to ascribe this sacred song to any but the great Psalmist, yet as we hardly know any period of his life which it would fairly describe, we feel compelled to look elsewhere. Some Israelitish patriot fallen on evil times, sings in mingled faith and sorrow, his country's ancient glory and her present griefs, her traditions of former favour and her experience of pressing ills. By Christians it can best be understood if put into the mouth of the church when persecution is peculiarly severe. The last verses remind us of Milton's famous lines on the Massacre of the Protestants among the mountains of Piedmont.*

The song before us is fitted for the voices of the saved by grace, the sons of Korah, *and is to them and to all others full of teaching, hence the title Maschil.*

Division.—*From 1—3, the Lord's mighty works for Israel are rehearsed, and in remembrance of them faith in the Lord is expressed 4—8. Then the notes of complaint are heard 9—16, the fidelity of the people to their God is avowed, 17—22, and the Lord is entreated to interpose, 23—26.*

EXPOSITION.

WE have heard with our ears, O God, our fathers have told us, *what* work thou didst in their days, in the times of old.

2 *How* thou didst drive out the heathen with thy hand, and plantedst them, *how* thou didst afflict the people, and cast them out.

3 For they got not the land in possession by their own sword, neither did their own arm save them : but thy right hand, and thine arm, and the light of thy countenance, because thou hadst a favour unto them.

1. *"We have heard with our ears, O God."* Thy mighty acts have been the subjects of common conversation ; not alone in books have we read thy famous deeds, but in the ordinary talk of the people we have heard of them. Among the godly Israelites the biography of their nation was preserved by oral tradition, with great diligence and accuracy. This mode of preserving and transmitting history has its disadvantages, but it certainly produces a more vivid impression on the mind than any other ; to hear with the ears affects us more sensitively than to read with the eyes ; we ought to note this, and seize every possible opportunity of telling abroad the gospel of our Lord Jesus *viva voce,* since this is the most telling mode of communication. The expression, " heard with our ears," may denote the pleasure with which they listened, the intensity of their interest, the personality of their hearing, and the lively remembrance they had of the romantic and soul-stirring narrative. Too many have ears but hear not ; happy are they who, having ears, have learned to hear.

"Our fathers have told us." They could not have had better informants. Schoolmasters are well enough, but godly fathers are, both by the order of nature and grace, the best instructors of their sons, nor can they delegate the sacred duty. It is to be feared that many children of professors could plead very little before God of what their fathers have told them. When fathers are tongue-tied religiously with their offspring, need they wonder if their children's hearts remain sin-tied ? Just as in all free nations men delight to gather around the hearth, and tell the deeds of valour of their sires " in the brave days of old," so the people of God under the old dispensation made their families cheerful around the table, by rehearsing the wondrous doings of the Lord their God. Religious conversation need not be dull, and indeed it could not be if, as in this case, it dealt more with facts and less with opinions. *"What work thou didst in their days, in the times of old."* They began with what their own eyes had witnessed, and then passed on to what were the traditions of their youth. Note that the main point of the history transmitted

from father to son was the work of God ; this is the core of history, and therefore no man can write history aright who is a stranger to the Lord's work. It is delightful to see the footprints of the Lord on the sea of changing events, to behold him riding on the whirlwind of war, pestilence, and famine, and above all to see his unchanging care for his chosen people. Those who are taught to see God in history have learned a good lesson from their fathers, and no son of believing parents should be left in ignorance of so holy an art. A nation tutored as Israel was in a history so marvellous as their own, always had an available argument in pleading with God for aid in trouble, since he who never changes gives in every deed of grace a pledge of mercy yet to come. The traditions of our past experience are powerful pleas for present help.

2. *" How thou didst drive out the heathen with thy hand."* The destruction of the Canaanites from the promised land is the work here brought to remembrance. A people numerous, warlike, gigantic and courageous, firmly established and strongly fortified, were driven out by a far feebler nation because the Lord was against them in the fight. It is clear from Scripture that God sent a plague (so that the land ate up the inhabitants thereof) and also a visitation of hornets against the Canaanites, and by other means dispirited them, so that the easy victories of Joshua were but the results of God's having worked beforehand against the idolatrous nation. *" And plantedst them."* The tribes of Israel were planted in the places formerly occupied by the heathen. Hivites and Jebusites were chased from their cities to make room for Ephraim and Judah. The Great Wonderworker tore up by the roots the oaks of Bashan, that he might plant instead thereof his own chosen "vineyard of red wine." *" How thou didst afflict the people."* With judgments and plagues the condemned nations were harassed, by fire and sword they were hunted to the death, till they were all expelled, and the enemies of Israel were banished far away. *" And cast them out."* This most probably refers to Israel and should be read, " caused them to increase." He who troubled his enemies smiled on his friends ; he meted out vengeance to the ungodly nations, but he reserved of his mercy for the chosen tribes. How fair is mercy when she stands by the side of justice ! Bright beams the star of grace amid the night of wrath ! It is a solemn thought that the greatness of divine love has its counterpart in the greatness of his indignation. The weight of mercy bestowed on Israel is balanced by the tremendous vengeance which swept the thousands of Amorites and Hittites down to hell with the edge of the sword. Hell is as deep as heaven is high, and the flame of Tophet is as everlasting as the blaze of the celestial glory. God's might, as shown in deeds both of mercy and justice, should be called to mind in troublous times as a stay to our fainting faith.

3 *" For they got not the land in possession by their own sword."* Behold how the Lord alone was exalted in bringing his people to the land which floweth with milk and honey ! He, in his distinguishing grace, had put a difference between Canaan and Israel, and therefore, by his own effectual power, he wrought *for* his chosen and *against* their adversaries. The tribes fought for their allotments, but their success was wholly due to the Lord who wrought with them. The warriors of Israel were not inactive, but their valour was secondary to that mysterious, divine working by which Jericho's walls fell down, and the hearts of the heathen failed them for fear. The efforts of all the men-at-arms were employed, but as these would have been futile without divine succour, all the honour is ascribed unto the Lord. The passage may be viewed as a beautiful parable of the work of salvation ; men are not saved without prayer, repentance, etc., but none of these save a man, salvation is altogether of the Lord. Canaan was not conquered without the armies of Israel, but equally true is it that it was not conquered by them ; the Lord was the conqueror, and the people were but instruments in his hands. *" Neither did their own arm save them."* They could not ascribe their memorable victories to themselves ; he who made sun and moon stand still for them was worthy of all their praise. A negative is put both upon their weapons and themselves as if to show us how ready men are to ascribe success to second causes. *" But thy right hand, and thine arm, and the light of thy countenance."* The divine *hand* actively fought for them, the divine *arm* powerfully sustained them with more than human energy, and the divine *smile* inspired them with dauntless courage. Who could not win with such triple help, though earth, death, and hell should rise in war against him ? What mattered the tallness of the sons of Anak, or the terror of their chariots of iron, they were as nothing when Jehovah arose for the avenging of Israel.

" *Because thou hadst a favour unto them.*" Here is the fountain from whence every stream of mercy flows. The Lord's delight in his people, his peculiar affection, his distinguishing regard—this is the mainspring which moves every wheel of a gracious providence. Israel was a chosen nation, hence their victories and the scattering of their foes ; believers are an elect people, hence their spiritual blessings and conquests. There was nothing in the people themselves to secure them success, the Lord's favour alone did it, and it is ever so in our case, our hope of final glory must not rest on anything in ourselves, but on the free and sovereign favour of the Lord of Hosts.

4 Thou art my King, O God : command deliverances for Jacob.

5 Through thee will we push down our enemies : through thy name will we tread them under that rise up against us.

6 For I will not trust in my bow, neither shall my sword save me.

7 But thou hast saved us from our enemies, and hast put them to shame that hated us.

8 In God we boast all the day long, and praise thy name for ever. Selah.

4. " *Thou art my King, O God.*" Knowing right well thy power and grace my heart is glad to own thee for her sovereign prince. Who among the mighty are so illustrious as thou art ? To whom, then, should I yield my homage or turn for aid ? God of my fathers in the olden time, thou art my soul's monarch and liege Lord. " *Command deliverances for Jacob.*" To whom should a people look but to their king ? he it is who, by virtue of his office, fights their battles for them. In the case of our King, how easy it is for him to scatter all our foes ! O Lord, the King of kings, with what ease canst thou rescue thy people ; a word of thine can do it, give but the command and thy persecuted people shall be free. Jacob's long life was crowded with trials and deliverances, and his descendants are here called by his name, as if to typify the similarity of their experience to that of their great forefather. He who would win the blessings of Israel must share the sorrows of Jacob. This verse contains a personal declaration and an intercessory prayer ; those can pray best who make most sure of their personal interest in God, and those who have the fullest assurance that the Lord is their God should be the foremost to plead for the rest of the tried family of the faithful.

5. " *Through thee will we push down our enemies.*" The fight was very close, bows were of no avail, and swords failed to be of service, it came to daggers drawing, and hand to hand wrestling, pushing and tugging. Jacob's God was renewing in the seed of Jacob their father's wrestling. And how fared it with faith then ? Could she stand foot to foot with her foe and hold her own ? Yea, verily, she came forth victorious from the encounter, for she is great at a close push, and overthrows all her adversaries, the Lord being her helper.

" *Through thy name will we tread them under that rise up against us.*" The Lord's name served instead of weapons, and enabled those who used it to leap on their foes and crush them with jubilant valour. In union and communion with God, saints work wonders ; if God be for us, who can be against us ? Mark well that all the conquests of these believers are said to be " through thee," " through thy name : " never let us forget this, lest going a warfare at our own charges, we fail most ignominiously. Let us not, however, fall into the equally dangerous sin of distrust, for the Lord can make the weakest of us equal to any emergency. Though to-day we are timid and defenceless as sheep, he can by his power make us strong as the firstling of his bullock, and cause us to push as with the horns of unicorns, until those who rose up against us shall be so crushed and battered as never to rise again. Those who of themselves can scarcely keep their feet, but like little babes totter and fall, are by divine assistance made to overthrow their foes, and set their feet upon their necks. Read Christian's fight with Apollyon, and see how

" The man so bravely played the man
He made the fiend to fly."

6. " *For I will not trust in my bow, neither shall my sword save me.*" Thy people Israel, under thy guidance, shouldered out the heathen, and gained their land, not by skill of weapons or prowess of arms, but by thy power alone ; therefore will we renounce for ever all reliance upon outward confidences, of which other

men make such boast, and we will cast ourselves upon the omnipotence of our God. Bows having been newly introduced by king Saul, were regarded as very formidable weapons in the early history of Israel, but they are here laid aside together with he all-conquering sword, in order that there may be room for faith in the living God. This verse, in the first person singular, may serve as the confession of faith of every believer renouncing his own righteousness and strength, and looking alone to the Lord Jesus.   O for grace to stand to this self-renunciation, for, alas! our proud nature is all too apt to fix its trust on the puffed-up and supposititious power of the creature. Arm of flesh, how dare I trust thee?   How dare I bring upon myself the curse of those who rely upon a man?

7. *" But thou hast saved us from our enemies."*   In ages past all our rescues have been due to thee, O God.   Never hast thou failed us.   Out of every danger thou hast brought us.   *" And hast put them to shame that hated us."*   With the back of thy saving hand thou hast given them a cuff which has made them hide their faces; thou hast defeated them in such a manner as to make them ashamed of themselves to be overthrown by such puny adversaries as they thought the Israelites to be. The double action of God in blessing his people and confounding his enemies is evermore to be observed; Pharaoh is drowned, while Israel passes through the sea; Amalek is smitten, while the tribes rejoice; the heathen are chased from their abodes while the sons of Jacob rest beneath their vine and fig-tree.

8. *" In God we boast all the day long."*   We have abundant reason for doing so while we recount his mighty acts.   What blessed boasting is this! it is the only sort of boasting that is bearable.   All other manna bred worms and stank except that which was laid up before the Lord, and all other boasting is loathsome save this glorying in the Lord, which is laudable and pleasing.   *" And praise thy name for ever."*   Praise should be perpetual.   If there were no new acts of love, yet ought the Lord to be praised for what he has done for his people.   High let the song be lifted up as we bring to remembrance the eternal love which chose us, predestinated us to be sons, redeemed us with a price, and then enriched us with all the fulness of God.

" Selah."—A pause comes in fitly here, when we are about to descend from the highest to the lowest key.   No longer are we to hear Miriam's timbrel, but rather Rachel's weeping.

9 But thou hast cast off, and put us to shame; and goest not forth with our armies.

10 Thou makest us to turn back from the enemy: and they which hate us spoil for themselves.

11 Thou hast given us like sheep *appointed* for meat; and has scattered us among the heathen.

12 Thou sellest thy people for nought, and dost not increase *thy wealth* by their price.

13 Thou makest us a reproach to our neighbours, a scorn and a derision to them that are round about us.

14 Thou makest us a byword among the heathen, a shaking of the head among the people.

15 My confusion *is* continually before me, and the shame of my face hath covered me,

16 For the voice of him that reproacheth and blasphemeth; by reason of the enemy and avenger.

9. *" But thou hast cast off, and put us to shame."*   Here the patriot bard begins to contrast the past glories of the nation's history with its present sadness and distress; which he does not ascribe to the death of some human champion, or to the accidents of war, but solely and alone to the withdrawal of Israel's God.   It seemed to the mourner that Jehovah had grown weary of his people and put them away in abhorrence, as men lay aside leprous garments, loathing the sight of them. To show his displeasures he had made his people to be ridiculed by the heathen, whose easy victories over their largest armies covered Israel with disgrace.   Alas! for a church and people when the Lord in the active energy of his Spirit withdraws

from them, they want no greater shame or sorrow. He will not cast away his people finally and totally, but many a church has been left to defeat and disgrace on account of sin, and therefore all churches should be exceedingly watchful lest the like should happen to themselves. Poverty and distress bring no shame on a people, but the Lord's absence takes from a church everything which can exalt and ennoble. "*And goest not forth with our armies.*" If the Lord be not the leader, of what avail are strong battalions ? Vain are the combined efforts of the most zealous workers if God's arm be not revealed. May none of us in our churches have to mourn over the ministry, the Sabbath school, the missionary work, the visiting, the street preaching, left to be carried out without the divine aid. If our great ally will not go with us our defeat is inevitable.

10. "*Thou makest us to turn back from the enemy.*" The humiliating consciousness that the Lord has left them soon makes men cowards. Flight closes the fight of those who have not the Lord in the van. "*And they which hate us spoil for themselves.*" After defeat and retreat, comes spoliation. The poor, vanquished nation paid a terrible penalty for being overcome ; plunder and murder desolated the conquered land, and the invaders loaded themselves with every precious thing which they could carry away. In spiritual experience we know what it is to be despoiled by our enemies ; doubts and fears rob us of our comforts, and terrible forebodings spoil us of our hopes ; and all because the Lord, for wise purposes, sees fit to leave us to ourselves. Alas ! for the deserted soul ; no calamity can equal the sorrow of being left of God, though it be but for a small moment.

11. "*Thou hast given us like sheep appointed for meat.*" As sheep are slaughtered for food, so were the people slain in flocks, with ease, and frequency. Not with the dignity of sacrifice, but with the cruelty of the shambles, were they put to death. God appeared to give them up like sheep allotted to the butcher, to abandon them as the hireling abandons the flock to wolves. The plaint is bitterly eloquent. "*And hast scattered us among the heathen.*" Many were carried into captivity, far off from the public worship of the temple of God, to pine as exiles among idolaters. All this is ascribed to the Lord as being allowed by him, and even appointed by his decree. It is well to trace the hand of God in our sorrows, for it is surely there.

12. "*Thou sellest thy people for nought.*" As men sell merchandise to any one who cares to have it, so the Lord seemed to hand over his people to any nation who might choose to make war upon them. Meanwhile no good result was perceptible from all the miseries of Israel ; so far as the Psalmist could discover, the Lord's name received no honour from the sorrows of his people ; they were given away to their foes as if they were so little valued as not to be worth the ordinary price of slaves, and the Lord did not care to gain by them so long as they did but suffer. The woe expressed in this line is as vinegar mingled with gall : the expression is worthy of the weeping prophet. "*And dost not increase thy wealth by their price.*" If Jehovah had been glorified by all this wretchedness it could have been borne patiently, but it was the reverse ; the Lord's name had, through the nation's calamities, been despised by the insulting heathen, who counted the overthrow of Israel to be the defeat of Jehovah himself It always lightens a believer's trouble when he can see that God's great name will be honoured thereby, but it is a grievous aggravation of misery when we appear to be tortured in vain. For our comfort let us rest satisfied that in reality the Lord is glorified, and when no revenue of glory is manifestly rendered to him, he none the less accomplishes his own secret purposes, of which the grand result will be revealed in due time. We do not suffer for nought, nor are our griefs without result.

13. "*Thou makest us a reproach to our neighbours.*" Scorn is always an intensely bitter ingredient in the cup of the oppressed. The taunts and jeers of the victors pain the vanquished almost as much as their swords and spears. It was a mystery indeed that God should suffer his royal nation, his peculiar people, to be taunted by all who dwelt near them. "*A scorn and a derision to them that are round about us*" The down-trodden people had become a common jest; "as base as Israel," cried the cruel tongue of the tyrant : so ordinary had the scorn become that the neighbouring nations, though perhaps equally oppressed, borrowed the language of the conquerors, and joined in the common mockery. To be a derision to both strong and weak, superiors, equals, and inferiors, is hard to bear. The tooth of scoffing bites to the bone. The Psalmist sets forth the brutality of the enemy in many words, in order to move the pity of the Lord, to whose just anger he traced all the sorrows of his people ; he used the very best of arguments, for the sufferings of

his chosen touch the heart of God far more readily than any other reasonings. Blessed be his name, our great Advocate above knows how to avail himself of this powerful plea, and if we are at this hour enduring reproach for truth's sake, he will urge it before the eternal throne; and shall not God avenge his own elect? A father will not long endure to see his children despitefully entreated; he may put up with it for a little, but his love will speedily arouse his anger, and then it will fare ill with the persecutor and reviler.

14 "*Thou makest us a byword among the heathen, a shaking of the head among the people.*" The lamentation is here repeated. They had sunk so low that none did them reverence, but universally and publicly they were treated as infamous and despicable. Those who reviled others dragged in Israel's name by the way as a garnish to their insults, and if perchance they saw one of the seed of Jacob in the street they used lewd gestures to annoy him. Those whose heads were emptiest wagged them at the separated people. They were the common butts of every fool's arrow. Such has been the lot of the righteous in ages past, such is their portion in a measure now, such may be yet again their heritage in the worst sense. The world knows not its nobility, it has no eye for true excellence: it found a cross for the Master, and cannot be expected to award crowns to his disciples.

15. "*My confusion is continually before me.*" The poet makes himself the representative of his nation, and declares his own constant distress of soul. He is a man of ill-blood who is unconcerned for the sorrows of the church of which he is a member, or the nation of which he is a citizen; the better the heart the greater its sympathy. "*And the shame of my face hath covered me.*" One constant blush, like a crimson mantle, covered him both before God and man, he felt before God that the divine desertion was well deserved, and before man, that he and his people were despicable indeed now that heavenly help was gone. It is well for a nation when there still exists in it men who lay to heart its sin and shame. God will have pity on his chastened ones, and it is a pledge thereof when he sends us choice ministers, men of tenderness, who make the people's case their own.

16. "*For the voice of him that reproacheth and blasphemeth.*" It seems that from mocking the people of God, the adversaries advanced to reviling God himself, they proceeded from persecution to the sin which is next of kin, namely blasphemy. "*By reason of the enemy and avenger.*" The enemy boasted of avenging the defeats of their forefathers; they took revenge for the ancient victories of Israel, by insulting over the now fallen people. Here was a sad plight for a nation to be placed in, but it was by no means a hopeless case, for the Lord who brought all this evil upon them could with equal ease release them from it. So long as Israel looked alone to her God, and not to her own arm, no foe could retain her beneath his foot; she *must* arise, for God was on her side.

17 All this is come upon us; yet have we not forgotten thee, neither have we dealt falsely in thy covenant.

18 Our heart is not turned back, neither have our steps declined from thy way;

19 Though thou hast sore broken us in the place of dragons, and covered us with the shadow of death.

20 If we have forgotten the name of our God, or stretched out our hands to a strange god;

21 Shall not God search this out? for he knoweth the secrets of the heart.

22 Yea, for thy sake are we killed all the day long; we are counted as sheep for the slaughter.

17. "*All this is come upon us; yet have we not forgotten thee.*" Here the Psalmist urges that Israel had not turned away from her allegiance to Jehovah. When in the midst of many griefs we can still cling to God in loving obedience, it must be well with us. True fidelity can endure rough usage. Those who follow God for what they get, will leave him when persecution is stirred up, but not so the sincere believer; he will not forget his God, even though the worst come to the worst. "*Neither have we dealt falsely in thy covenant.*" No idol was set up, the ordained worship was not relinquished, God was still nationally acknowledged,

and therefore the Psalmist is more earnest that the Lord should interpose. This and the succeeding verses are suitable for the lips of martyrs, indeed the entire Psalm might be called the martyr's complaint. Not for sin but for righteousness did the saints suffer, not for falsehood but for truth, not for forsaking the Lord but for following hard after him. Sufferings of such a sort may be very terrible, but they are exceedingly honourable, and the comforts of the Lord shall sustain those who are accounted worthy to suffer for Christ's sake.

18. *" Our heart is not turned back, neither have our steps declined from thy way."* Heart and life were agreed, and both were true to the Lord's way. Neither within nor without had the godly sufferers offended; they were not absolutely perfect, but they were sincerely free from all wilful transgression. It was a healthy sign for the nation that her prophet-poet could testify to her uprightness before God, both in heart and act; far oftener the case would have worn quite another colour, for the tribes were all too apt to set up other gods and forsake the rock of their salvation.

19. *" Though thou hast sore broken us in the place of dragons."* Though utterly crushed and rendered desolate and driven as it were to associate with creatures such as jackals, owls, serpents, which haunt deserted ruins, yet Israel remained faithful. To be true to a smiting God, even when the blows lay our joys in ruinous heaps, is to be such as the Lord delighteth in. Better to be broken by God than from God. Better to be in the place of dragons than of deceivers. *" And covered us with the shadow of death."* The language is very strong. The nation is described as completely enveloped in the dense darkness of despair and death, covered up as though coffined in hopelessness. Yet the claim is made that they still remained mindful of their God, and a glorious plea it is. Better death than false of faith. Those who are true to God shall never find him false to them.

20. An appeal is now made to the omniscience of God; he is himself called in to bear witness that Israel had not set up another god. *" If we have forgotten the name of our God."* This would be the first step in apostasy; men first forget the true, and then adore the false. *" Or stretched out our hands to a strange god."* Stretching out the hands was the symbol of adoration or of entreaty in prayer; this they had not offered to any of the idols of the heathen.

21. *" Shall not God search this out?"* Could such idolatry be concealed from him? Would he not with holy indignation have detected unfaithfulness to itself, even had it been hidden in the heart and unrevealed in the life? *" For he knoweth the secrets of the heart."* He is acquainted with the inner workings of the mind, and therefore this could not have escaped him. Not the heart only which is secret, but the secrets of the heart, which are secrets of the most secret thing, are as open to God as a book to a reader. The reasoning is that the Lord himself knew the people to be sincerely his followers, and therefore was not visiting them for sin; hence, then, affliction evidently came from quite another cause.

22. *" Yea,"* i.e., assuredly, certainly, *" for thy sake,"* not for our offences, but for obeying thee; the trials of these suppliants came upon them because they were loyal to their God. *" Are we killed all the day long."* Persecution never ceased to hound them to the death, they had no respite and found no door of escape; and all in God's behalf, because they would not forsake their covenant God and King. *" We are counted as sheep for the slaughter;"* as if we were only meant to be killed, and made on purpose to be victims; as if it were as easy and as innocent a thing to slay us as to slaughter sheep. In this and following verses we clearly hear the martyr's cry. From Piedmont and Smithfield, from St. Bartholomew's massacre and the dragoonades of Claverhouse, this appeal goes up to heaven, while the souls under the altar continue their solemn cry for vengeance. Not long shall the church plead in this fashion, her shame shall be recompensed, her triumph shall dawn.

23 Awake, why sleepest thou, O Lord? arise, cast *us* not off for ever.

24 Wherefore hidest thou thy face, *and* forgettest our affliction and our oppression?

25 For our soul is bowed down to the dust: our belly cleaveth unto the earth.

26 Arise for our help, and redeem us for thy mercies' sake.

23. *"Awake, why sleepest thou, O Lord?"* God sleepeth not, but the Psalmist puts it so, as if on no other theory he could explain the divine inaction. He would fain see the great Judge ending oppression and giving peace to the holy, therefore does he cry " Awake ; " he cannot understand why the reign of tyranny and the oppression of virtue are permitted, and therefore he enquires, " Why sleepest thou ? " *Arise.* This is all thou needest to do, one move of thine will save us. *"Cast us not off for ever."* Long enough hast thou deserted us ; the terrible effects of thine absence are destroying us ; end thou our calamities, and let thine anger be appeased. In persecuting times men are apt to cry, Where is the God of Israel ? At the thought of what the saints have endured from their haughty enemies, we join our voices in the great martyr cry, and sing with the bard of Paradise :—

> " Avenge, O Lord, thy slaughtered saints, whose bones
> Lie scattered on the Alpine mountains cold ;
> Even those who kept thy truth so pure of old,
> When all our fathers worshipped stocks and stones,
> Forget not : in thy book record their groans
> Who were thy sheep."

24. *"Wherefore hidest thou thy face, and forgettest our afflictions and our oppression ?"* Not petulantly, but piteously and enquiringly, we may question the Lord when his dealings are mysterious. We are permitted to order our case with arguments, and plead the right before the face of the august Majesty. Why, Lord, dost thou become oblivious of thy children's woes ? This question is far more easily asked than answered ; it is hard, indeed, in the midst of persecution to see the reason why we are left to suffer so severely.

25. *"For our soul is bowed down to the dust."* Our heart is low as low can be, as low as the dust beneath the soles of men's feet. When the heart sinks, the man is down indeed. Heart-sorrow is the very heart of sorrow. *"Our belly cleaveth unto the earth."* The man is prone upon the earth, and he is not only down, but fastened down on the earth and glued to it. It is misery, indeed, when the heart cannot escape from itself, is shut up in its own dejection, and bound with the cords of despondency. God's saints may be thus abject, they may be not only in the dust, but on the dunghill with Job and Lazarus, but their day cometh, and their tide will turn, and they shall have a brave summer after their bitter winter.

26. *"Arise for our help."* A short, but sweet and comprehensive prayer, much to the point, clear, simple, urgent, as all prayers should be. *"And redeem us for thy mercies' sake."* Here is the final plea. The favour is redemption, the plea is mercy ; and this, too, in the case of faithful sufferers who had not forgotten their God. Mercy is always a safe plea, and never will any man find a better.

> " Were I a martyr at the stake,
> I'd plead my Saviour's name,
> Intreat a pardon for his sake,
> And urge no other claim."

Here ends this memorable Psalm, but in heaven its power ends not, but brings down deliverance for the tried people of God.

EXPLANATORY NOTES AND QUAINT SAYINGS.

Whole Psalm.—On a survey of this Psalm, it would seem not to admit of a doubt that the speakers are of the race of Israel ; and yet expositors for the most part have found much difficulty in so understanding it, in this—the natural sense —so as even to be compelled to abandon it, owing to the impossibility of fixing on any period in the history of that people which would furnish an occasion for it, and verify its language. Thus, it cannot be referred to the times of the Babylonish captivity ; for to this it is objected, and with reason, first, that verses 11 and 14 represent the speakers as " scattered among the nations," and " a byword among the peoples," whereas their exile was then confined to one country ; and, secondly, that in verses 17—21 there is an assertion of faithful adherence to the worship of the true God, which he is called to witness as acquitting the sufferers of having brought the evil on themselves, while that captivity was a punishment of the nation for their apostasy, and especially for the grievous sin of idolatry. And the same objections lie to interpreting it with reference to the times of Antiochus Epiphanes and the Maccabees ; beside that, the history of the canon of Scripture is decisive against assigning so late a date to any of the Psalms. Still less can the times of David be looked to for the occasion, since, though religion was then pure, there was, on the other hand, no dispersion of the nation nor any calamity such as to warrant the lamentation, " Thou hast cast us off, and put us to shame. . . . Thou hast given us like sheep appointed for meat," etc. Whence it appeared that there was no alternative but to consider the Psalm as exclusively the language of the Christian church, and, in her primitive days, as the period at once of her greatest purity and suffering.—*William de Burgh.*

Whole Psalm.—S. Ambrose observes, that in former Psalms we have seen a prophecy of Christ's passion, resurrection, and ascension, and of the coming of the Holy Ghost, and that here we are taught that we ourselves must be ready to struggle and suffer, in order that these things may profit us. Human will must work together with divine grace.—*Christopher Wordsworth.*

Verse 1.—" *We have heard with our ears,*" *i.e.*, we have both heard and heeded it, with utmost attention and affection. It is not a *pleonasmus,* but an *emphasis* that is here used.—*John Trapp.*

Verse 1.—" *Our fathers have told us.*" Hear this, saith Basil, ye fathers that neglect to teach your children such things as may work his fear and love in them, and faith to rely upon and seek to him in all times of danger. They made their mouths, as it were, books, wherein the mighty deeds of the Lord might be read to his praise, and to the drawing of their children's hearts unto him.—*John Mayer.*

Verse 1.—" *What work thou didst.*" Why only " *work* " in the singular, when such innumerable deliverances had been wrought by him, from the passage of the Red Sea to the destruction of the hundred and eighty-five thousand in the camp of the Assyrians ? Because all these were but types of that one great work, that one stretching forth of the Lord's hand, when Satan was vanquished, death destroyed, and the kingdom of heaven opened to all believers.—*Ambrose.*

Verse 1.—" *What work thou didst.*" While the songs of other nations sing of the heroism of their ancestors, the songs of Israel celebrate the works of *God.*— *Augustus F. Tholuck.*

Verse 1.—Three necessary requirements for learning well : 1. Intention and attention in him who learns, " *we have heard with our ears.*" 2. Authority in him that teaches, " *our fathers* have told us." 3. Love between the teacher and the taught, " *our* fathers."—*Hugo (Cardinal), quoted in Neale's Commentary.*

Verses 1, 2, 4, 8.—Children are their parents' heirs ; it were unnatural for a father before he dies to bury up his treasure in the earth, where his children should not find or enjoy it ; now the mercies of God are not the least part of his treasure, nor the least of his children's inheritance, being both helps to their faith, matter for their praise, and spurs to their obedience. " *Our fathers have told us, what work thou didst in their days, how thou didst drive out the heathen,*" etc. (ver. 1, 2) ; from this they ground their confidence ; verse 4 : " *Thou art my King, O God : command deliverances for Jacob ;* " and excite their thankfulness, verse 8 : " *In God we boast all the day long, and praise thy name for ever.*" Indeed, as children are their parents' heirs, so they become in justice liable to pay their parents' debts ; now the great debt which the saint at death stands charged with, is that which he owes to God for his mercies, and, therefore it is but reason he should tie his posterity to the payment thereof. Thus mayest thou be praising God in heaven and earth at the same time.—*William Gurnall.*

Verse 2.—

> Thou with thine hand, hast driven out heathen,
> And hast planted them ;
> The nations thou hast broken down,
> But them thou hast engraffed."

The two clauses of this verse stand in regular contrast. The first has the figure of rooting out one kind of tree, and planting another, as the Canaanites were rooted out of Palestine, and Israel was planted in their stead. (Compare Psalm lxxx. 8).

The second figure is that of cutting off bad branches, and engrafting others in their place, in the same root, which is Palestine again.—*Benjamin Weiss*.

Verse 3.—" *They got not the land in possession by their own sword.*" The Lord's part in a work is best seen when man's part, and all that he as an instrument hath done, or could have done in it, is declared null ; being considered as separate from God who moved the instruments, and did work by them what he pleased.—*David Dickson*.

Verse 3.—" *Because thou hadst a favour unto them.*" Free grace was the fundamental cause of all their felicity. God loved them because he loved them. Deut. vii. 7. He chose them of his love, and then loved them for his choice.—*John Trapp*.

Verse 3.—God's love to Israel was free, unmerited, and amazing, and he gave them a land for which they did not labour, and cities which they built not, and vineyards and oliveyards which they planted not. Josh. xxiv. 13. In some cases neither sword nor bow were used, but hornets were the instruments of conquest. Josh. xxiv. 12. Since the fall of Adam all good things in the lot of any mere man are undeserved kindnesses.—*William S. Plumer*.

Verse 3 (last clause).—The prophet does not suppose any worthiness in the person of Abraham, nor imagine any desert in his posterity, on account of which God dealt so bountifully with them ; but ascribes the whole to the good pleasure of God. . . . . Nor does the Psalmist here treat of the general benevolence of God, which extends to the whole human race : but he discourses of the difference which exists between the elect and the rest of the world, and the cause of this difference is here referred to the mere good pleasure of God.—*John Calvin*.

Verse 4.—" *My king ;* " apparently with a personal application to himself, the poet individually claiming his own place in the covenant between God and his people.—*J. J. Stewart Perowne*.

Verse 4.—" *Thou art my king, O God ; command deliverances for Jacob.* " If there were no creature, no instrument in the world to help, yet would you not be at a loss in time of need, for he that is on the throne could do it alone. He can do all that ever you need, without any means or instruments. His bare word is sufficient, all-sufficient, for it, whatever it be, how great, how difficult, how impossible soever it seems. Such a power there is even in the word of the great King. There needs no more to deliver you, to deliver his people anywhere, how deep soever plunged, but only the *command* of him that sits on the throne. If the gospel, the interests of Christ, in these parts of the world, and the dear concerns of our souls, and the souls of posterity, were all as dry bones, in a more forlorn, and hopeless condition than they are, he could make all live with a word. He that is our King, that sits upon the throne, can command life into that which seems as far from living as a dry bone. While he keeps the throne, it is a senseless heart that fails through distrust of his power, even when all visible power and help fail.—*David Clarkson*.

Verse 5.—" *Through thee will we push down our enemies*": literally, "We will toss them in the air with our horn ; " a metaphor taken from an ox or bull tossing the dogs into the air which attack him.—*Adam Clarke*.

Verse 6.—" *I will not trust in my bow, neither shall my sword save me.*" By " bow " and " sword," he meaneth all manner of weapons and warlike instruments whatsoever ; and by " saving," he meaneth delivering from dangers, speaking under the person of one (because all the faithful are but one body), in the name of all the rest.—*Thomas Wilcocks*.

Verse 6.—" *I will not trust in my bow,*" etc. I will not trust in *my own* sword or bow, but in the *sword* of the Divine Warrior, and in the *bow* of the Divine Archer, whose arrows are sharp in the heart of his enemies, as described in the next (Psalm xlv. 3—5), which is connected by that imagery with this Psalm, as well as by its inner meaning.—*Christopher Wordsworth*.

Verse 6.—The less confidence we have in ourselves or in anything beside God, the more evidence have we of the sincerity of our faith in God.—*David Dickson*.

Verses 6, 7.—The two verses correspond exactly to verse 3. As there, in reference to the past, the salvation was ascribed wholly to God, so here in reference to the future.—*E. W. Hengstenberg*.

Verse 11.—" *Like sheep appointed for meat.*" This very strongly and strikingly intimates the extent of the persecution and slaughter to which they were exposed; there being no creature in the world of which such vast numbers are constantly slaughtered as of sheep for the subsistence of man. The constancy of such slaughter is also mentioned in verse 22 as illustrating the continual oppression to which the Hebrews were subject.—*Kitto's Pictorial Bible.*

Verse 11.—" *Like sheep appointed for meat,*" and not reserved for breeding or for wool.—*Arthur Jackson.*

Verse 12.—" *Thou sellest thy people for nought, and dost not increase thy wealth by their price.*" The sense is : Thou hast given thy people unto the power of their enemies without trouble, without causing the victory even to be dearly bought, as one who parts with a good for any price, which he despises and hates, desiring merely to get rid of it.—*E. W. Hengstenberg.*

Verse 12.—" *Thou sellest thy people for nought,*" etc. Referring to the siege of Jerusalem by Titus, Eusebius says : " Many were sold for a small price ; there were many to be sold, but few to buy."

Verse 12.—" *And dost not increase thy wealth by their price.*" Thou hast not advanced thy honour and service thereby ; for thy enemies do not serve thee more and better than thy people, nor yet so much.—*Matthew Pool.*

Verse 12 (*last clause*). *Takest no money for them ;* literally, *enhancest not the price of them,* as a seller usually does to the buyer.—*Daniel Cresswell.*

Verse 14. " *Thou makest us a byword ;* " literally, *for a similitude,* למשל stands here, as in the original passage (Deut. xxviii. 37), in the common signification, *similitude.* The misery of Israel is so great, that people would figuratively call a miserable man a Jew, just as liars were called Cretans ; wretched slaves, Sardians. So far are the people from being now " blessed of the Lord " in whom according to the promise, all the heathen are to be blessed.—*E. W. Hengstenberg.*

Verse 15.—" *My confusion is continually before me.*" When the visible church is visited with sad calamities, the true members thereof are partakers of the trouble, and sorrow, and shame of that condition.—*David Dickson.*

Verse 17.—Eusebius, narrating the cruelties inflicted upon the *Christians* by the Eastern tyrant, Maximinus, says : " He prevailed against all sorts of people, the Christians only excepted, who contemned death and despised his tyranny. The men endured burning, beheading, crucifying, ravenous devouring of beasts, drowning in the sea, maiming and broiling of the members, goring and digging out of the eyes, mangling of the whole body ; moreover, famine and imprisonment ; to be short, they suffered every kind of torment for the service of God rather than they would leave the worship of God, and embrace the adoration of idols. Women also, not inferior to men through the power of the word of God, put on a manly courage, whereof some suffered the torments with men, some attained unto the like masteries of virtue."—*From " The Ecclesiastical History of Eusebius Pamphilus."*

Verse 17.—" *Yet have we not forgotten thee, neither have we dealt falsely in thy covenant.*" Although we cannot excuse ourselves from many other sins for which thou hast justly punished us, yet this we must say for ourselves, that through thy grace we have kept ourselves from apostasy and idolatry, notwithstanding all the examples and provocations, rewards proposed and promised, or punishments threatened to induce us thereunto ; which we hope thou wilt graciously consider, and not suffer us to be tempted above what we are able to bear.—*Matthew Pool.*

Verse 17.—If any of you would abide by Jesus Christ in this storm, try how ye have covenanted with him, and how ye have closed the bargain with him, and upon what terms. But I trow there are many of you in this age that are like young wanton folk, that run fast together and marry, but never take any account how they will keep house, but presently go to poverty and beggary. I trow it falls out so with many of you that are professors in this generation. Ye take up your religion, and ye wot not how, and ye cannot give an account how ye came by it. I will tell you, sirs ; ye will abide no longer by Christ than till a storm blow, and then ye will quit him and deny his cause. Ye have need to take heed to this, for it will ruin your souls in the end of the day. But I shall tell you, sirs, the right way of covenanting with God. It is when Christ and the believer meet. Our Lord gives him his laws, statutes, and commands, and he charges him not to quit a hoof of them. No ; though he should be torn into a thousand pieces ; and the right covenanter says, Amen.—*Alexander Peden's Sermon*, 1682.

Verses 17—19.—Neither the persecuting hand of men, nor the chastising hand of God, relaxed ancient singular saints. Believers resemble the *moon*, which emerges from her eclipse by keeping her motion, and ceases not to shine because the dogs bark at her. Shall we cease to be professors because others will not cease to be persecutors ?—*William Secker.*

Verses 17—19.—The church having reported her great troubles, speaks it as an argument of much sincerity towards God, and strength of grace received from him : " *All this has come upon us* " (that is, all these common calamities and afflictions),." *yet have we not forgotten thee, neither have we dealt falsely in thy covenant. Our heart is not turned back, neither have our steps declined from thy way ;* " as if she had said, These afflictions have been strong temptations upon us to cause us to decline from thy ways, but through grace we have kept our ground and remained constant in thy covenant, yea, " *though thou hast sore broken us in the place of dragons, and covered us with the shadow of death.*" As many, yea, most of the saints have improved under the cross, so there have been some, who either through their present unbelief, or forgetfulness of " the exhortation which " (as the apostle saith, Heb. xii. 5), " speaketh unto them as unto children," have had their faintings or declinings under it.—*Joseph Caryl.*

Verse 18.—" *Our heart is not turned back.*" Serious piety has become a ludicrous subject with which the wanton wits of this atheistical world sport themselves ; but behold the wisdom and goodness of God, exhibiting to the world undeniable testimonies of the truth of religion as often as the sincere professors thereof are brought to the test by afflictions from the hand of God, or persecutions from the hands of men. Lo ! " here is the faith and patience of the saints ; " here is their courage, meekness, and self-denial, shining as gold in the fire. They have the real proofs of it before their eyes. Instead of casting them into hell, and convincing them by eternal fire, he is pleased to cast his own people into the fire of affliction, that they who scoff at them may be convinced at an easier and cheaper rate. It is no new thing to see the enemies of religion brought over to embrace it by the constancy and faithfulness of the saints in their trials and sufferings for it. God grant that the atheism of this present generation do not occasion a more fiery trial to the people of God in it than they have yet suffered.—*John Flavel.*

Verse 18.—" *Our heart.*" The word לֵב or Greek καρδία, that is rendered " *heart*," both in the Old and New Testament, doth signify the understanding, the mind, will, affections, conscience, the whole soul. " *Our heart is not turned back.*" Our understandings and minds are the same as they were in a summer's day, though now we be in a winter's storm ; though now we be afflicted, tossed, broken, and persecuted, yet notwithstanding, " *our heart is not turned back,*" our mind, will, affections, and conscience, our whole soul, is the same now as before.— *Thomas Brooks.*

Verse 19.—" *Though thou hast sore broken us in place of dragons,*" etc. Where men, comparable to dragons for their poison and cruelty, dwell particularly in Rome, and the Roman jurisdiction, both Pagan and Papal, the seat of Satan, the great red dragon, and of his wretched brood and offspring, the beast, to whom he has given his power ; where the saints and followers of Christ have been sorely afflicted and persecuted, and yet have held fast the name of Christ, and not denied his faith. See Rev. ii. 13, and xii. 3. The wilderness is the habitation of dragons ; and this is the name of the place where the church is said to be in the times of the Papacy, and where she is fed and preserved for a time, and times, and half-a-time. Rev. xii. 6, 14. " *And covered us with the shadow of death.*" As the former phrase denotes the cruelty of the enemies of Christ's church and people, this their dismal afflictions and forlorn state and condition ; and may have some respect to the darkness of Popery, when it was at the height, and the church of Christ was covered with it, there being very little appearances and breakings forth of gospel light anywhere.—*John Gill.*

Verse 19.—" *Dragons.*" The word rendered *dragons*—תנים, *tannim*—means either a great fish, a sea monster, a serpent, a dragon, or a crocodile. It may also mean a jackal, a fox, or a wolf. De Wette renders it here *jackals.* The *idea* in the passage is essentially the same, whichever interpretation of the word is adopted. The " *place* of dragons " would denote the place where such monsters are found, or where they had their abode : that is to say, in desolate places, wastes, deserts, old ruins, depopulated towns.—*Albert Barnes.*

Verse 20.—" *Stretched out our hands to a strange god.*" The stretching out the *hand* towards an object of devotion, or an holy place, was an ancient usage among the Jews and heathens both, and it *continues* in the East to this time, which continuance I do not remember to have seen remarked. That this attitude in prayer has *continued* among the Eastern people, appears by the following passage from Pitts, in his account of the religion and manners of the Mohammedans. Speaking of the Algerines throwing wax candles and pots of oil overboard, as a present to some marabbot (or Mohammedan saint), Pitts goes on, and says, " When this is done, they all together *hold up their hands,* begging the marabbot's blessing, and a prosperous voyage." In the same page he tells us, " the marabbots have generally a little neat room built over their graves, resembling in figure their mosques or churches, which is very nicely cleaned, and well looked after." And in the succeeding page he tells us, " Many people there are who will scarce pass by any of them without *lifting up* their hand, and saying some short prayer." In like manner, he tells us, that at quitting the *Beat,* or holy house at Mecca, to which they make devout pilgrimages, " *they hold up their hands towards the Beat,* making earnest petitions."— *Harmer's* " *Observations.*"

Verse 21.—" *Shall not God search this out ?*" etc. Are there such variety of trials appointed to examine the sincerity of men's graces ? How great a vanity, then, is hypocrisy ! and to how little purpose do men endeavour to conceal and hide it ! We say, murder will out ; and we may as confidently affirm, hypocrisy will out. When Rebekah had laid the plot to disguise her son Jacob, and by personating his brother, to get the blessing, Jacob thus objects against it : " My father peradventure will feel me, and I shall seem to him as a deceiver, and I shall bring a curse upon me and not a blessing." And if he should say, But what if my father detect the cheat ? How, then, shall I look him in the face ? How shall I escape a curse ? After the same manner every upright soul scares itself from the way of hypocrisy. If I dissemble, and pretend to be what I am not, my Father will find me out. There is no darkness nor shadow of death that can conceal the hypocrite ; but out it will come at last, let him use all the art he can to hide it. . . . . If men's works be not good, it is impossible they should be hid long. A gilded piece of brass may pass from hand to hand a little while, but the touchstone will discover the base metal ; and if that does not, the fire will.—*John Flavel.*

Verse 21.—A godly man dares not sin secretly. He knows that God sees in secret. As God cannot be deceived by our subtlety, so he cannot be excluded by our secrecy.—*Thomas Watson.*

Verse 21.—In time of persecution for religion, nothing can counterbalance the terrors and allurements of the persecutors, and make a man steadfast in the cause of God, save the fear of God, and love to God settled in the heart ; for the reason of the saints' steadfastness in this Psalm, is because God would have searched out their sin if they had done otherwise, " *for he knoweth the secrets of the heart.*"— *David Dickson.*

Verse 22.—" *Yea, for thy sake are we killed all the day long,*" etc. Leonard Schoener left, amongst other papers, the following admonition, to comfort all who were suffering for Christ's name :—

" We pray thee, O eternal God, to bow down thy gracious ear. Lord of Sabaoth, thou Lord of hosts, hear our complaint, for great affliction and persecution have prevailed. Pride has entered thine inheritance, and many supposed to be Christians, have united themselves therewith, and have thus brought in the abomination of desolation. They waste and destroy the Christian sanctuary. They have trodden the same under foot, and the abomination of desolation is worshipped as God. They have troubled thy holy city, thrown down thy holy altar, and slain her servants when they could lay their hands upon them. And now that we as a little flock are left, they have driven us into all thy lands with contempt and reproach. We are scattered as sheep having no shepherd. We have been compelled to forsake house and home. We are as night ravens which abide in the rocks ; our chambers are in holes and crags. They watch for us as fowls that fly in the air. We wander in the woods, they hunt us with dogs. They lead us away, seized and bound, as lambs that open not their mouths. They cry out against us as seditious persons and heretics. We are brought like sheep to the slaughter. Many sit oppressed, and in bonds which even decay their bodies. Some have sunk under their sufferings, and died without fault. Here is the patience of the saints in the earth. We must be tried by suffering here. The faithful have they hanged on trees, strangled, hewn in pieces, secretly and openly drowned. Not only men, but likewise women and maidens have borne witness to the truth, that Jesus Christ is the truth, the only way to eternal life. The world still rages, and rests not ; it raves as if mad. They invent lies against us. They cease not their fires and murders. They make the world too narrow for us. O Lord, how long wilt thou be silent ? How long wilt thou not judge the blood of thy saints ? Let it come up before thy throne. How precious in thine eye is the blood of thy holy ones ! Therefore have we comfort in all our need, a refuge in thee alone, and in none besides ; but neither comfort, nor rest, nor peace on this earth. But he who hopeth in thee shall never be confounded. O Lord, there is no sorrow so great that can separate us from thee ; therefore, without ceasing we call upon thee, through Christ thy Son our Lord, whom thou of thy free grace hast given us for our comfort. He hath prepared and made known to us the straight path, and the way to eternal life. Everlasting glory and triumph, honour and praise, be given unto thee, both now and to eternity, and let thy righteousness remain for ever. Let all the people bless thy holy name, through Christ the righteous Judge, who cometh to judge the whole world. Amen."— *From " A Martyrology of the Churches of Christ, commonly called Baptists. Edited by E. B. Underhill."* 1850.

Verse 22.—" For thy sake are we killed." It is mercy to us, that when God might punish us for our sins, he doth make our correction honourable, and our troubles to be for a good cause—" For thy sake," etc.—*David Dickson.*

Verse 22.—" For thy sake." This passage is cited by St. Paul, Rom. viii. 36, apparently from the LXX, an illustration of the fact that the church of God has in all ages been a persecuted church. But there is this remarkable difference between the tone of the Psalmist and the tone of the apostle : the former cannot understand the chastening, and complains that God's heavy hand has been laid without cause upon his people ; the latter can rejoice in persecutions also, and exclaim, " Nay, in all these things we are more than conquerors, through him that loved us."— *J. J. Stewart Perowne.*

Verse 22.—" Killed." The word here used is not from קָטַל, but from עָנַג, which means *to strangle :* this is the rendering given in " Lange's Biblewerk."

Verse 23.—" Awake, why sleepest thou, O Lord ? " and Psalm cxxi. 4, " Behold, *he that keepeth Israel shall neither slumber nor sleep."* If God at no time sleep, why doth the church call on him so often to awake ? If he must be awakened from sleep, why doth the Psalmist say he never sleeps ? Are not these places contradictory ?

ANSWER : It is one thing what the afflicted church cries in the heat of her sufferings, another thing what the Spirit of truth speaks for the comfort of the saints. It is ordinary for the best of saints and martyrs, during the storm, to go to God as Peter did to Christ at sea (sleeping in the stern of the ship), with such importunity in prayer as if the Lord were no more sensible of their agony than Jonah was of the mariners' misery, ready to perish in the turbulent ocean, and they cried out, What meanest thou, O sleeper ? Arise ! Saints are so familiar with God in prayer, as if they were at his bedside.

THE SOUL'S APPLICATION.—O thou never-slumbering Watchman of the house of Israel, carest not thou that we perish ? Awake, awake ! put on strength, gird thyself, O thou arm of God ! I know thou art up, but what am I the better except thou help me up ? I know thou sleepest not as man doth, but what advantage hath my soul by that, except thou show thyself, that I way know thou art waking ? Oh, it is I that am asleep ! Thou seemest to sleep only to awaken me. O that I could watch with thee one hour, as thou bidd'st me ; I should soon perceive then thy vigilancy over me for ever.—*William Streat in " The Dividing of the Hoof."* 1654.

Verse 23.—" Awake, why sleepest thou, O Lord ?" etc. The weakness of our faith is open to the temptation of supposing that God regards not the situation of his people in the world; and the Spirit, who knows our infirmities, provides a petition suited to this trial, which expresses at the same time an expectation that God will arise to claim his people as his own.—*W. Wilson.*

Verse 25.—" *For our soul is bowed down to the dust : our belly cleaveth unto the earth.*" We are as to body and soul, smitten and thrown down, glued as it were to the ground, so that we cannot raise ourselves up.—*E. W. Hengstenberg.*

Verse 25.—" *For our soul is bowed down to the dust,*" etc. The speech is metaphorical, expressing the depth of their misery, or the greatness of their sorrow and humiliation. 1. The depth of their misery, with the allusion to the case of a man overcome in battle, or mortally wounded, and tumbling in the dust, or to a man dead and laid in the earth; as, " Thou hast brought me into the dust of death." Psa. xxii. 15. Sure we are, the expression importeth the extremity of distress and danger, either as a man dead or near death. 2. The greatness of their sorrow and humiliation; and so the allusion is taken from a man prostrate and grovelling on the ground, which was their posture of humbling themselves before the Lord, or when any great calamity befell them. As when Herod Agrippa died, they put on sackcloth and lay upon the earth weeping.—*Thomas Manton.*

HINTS TO PREACHERS.

Verse 1.—The encouraging traditions of church history. The days of yore.

Verse 1.—The parents' duty, and the children's privilege.

Verse 1.—Family conversation, the most profitable subject for it.

Verse 1.—The true glory of the good old times.

Verse 2.—The contrast; or, the dealings of God with saints and sinners.

Verse 3.—Free grace exalted. I. In putting a negative upon human power. II. In manifestations of divine energy. III. In its secret source, " *Because thou hadst a favour unto them.*"

Verse 3.—I. The creature laid low. II. The Lord exalted. III. Discriminating grace revealed.

Verse 3 (last clause).—The eternal well-spring of all mercy.

Verse 4.—I. Divine royalty acknowledged. II. Royal interposition entreated. III. Divine covenant hinted at, " *Jacob ;* " or, the loyal subject seeking royal aid for the royal seed.

Verse 4.—Personal allegiance, and pleading intercession.

Verse 4.—" *My King.*" This intends—I. My Ruler. II. My Honour. III. My Leader. IV. My Defender.

Verse 4.—The deliverances of Jacob, illustrated by his eventful life.

Verse 5.—Our enemies, in what ways we push them down, by what strength, and in what spirit.

Verse 5.—Our enemies, their activity, the closeness of their approach, the certainty of their overthrow, the secret of our strength.

Verse 6.—Relinquishment of outward trusts. " *My bow* " may miss its aim, may be broken, may be snatched away. " *My sword* " may snap, or grow blunt, or slip from my hold. We may not trust in our abilities, our experience, our shrewdness, our wealth, etc.

Verse 6.—Self-renunciation—the duty of saint and sinner.

Verse 7.—Accomplished salvation. How never achieved, " *But.*" By whom wrought, " *thou.*" When performed, " *hast.*" For whom, " *us.*" To what extent, " *from our enemies.*"

Verse 7.—Salvation completed, hell confounded, Christ exalted.

Verse 8.—Praise, its continuance—how to make it continual, how to manifest it perpetually, influence of its continuance, and reasons to compel us to abide in it.

Verse 9.—A lament for the declension of the church.

Verse 9.—In what sense God casts off his people, and why.

Verse 9 (last clause).—The greatest of all calamities for our churches.

Verse 12.—The human and divine estimate of the results of persecution.

Verse 12.—In answer to this complaint. I. God's people lose nothing eventually by their privations. II. The wicked gain nothing by their triumphs. III. God loses none of his glory in his dealings with either.—*G. Rogers.*

Verse 13.—Trial of cruel mockings ; our conduct under them, comfort in them, and crown from them.

Verse 14.—Unholy proverbs or godless bywords.

Verse 15.—Confessions of a penitent.

Verse 17.—The trial, truth, and triumph of the godly.

Verse 17.—The faithful soul holding fast his integrity.

Verse 17.—What it is to be false to our covenant with God.

Verse 18 (first clause).—When we may be sure that our heart has not apostatised.

Verse 18.—I. The position of the heart in religion—it comes first. II. The position of the outer moral life in religion—it follows the heart. III. Necessity of the agreement of the two. IV. The need that both should be faithful to God.

Verse 18.—Connection between the heart and the life, both in constancy and apostasy.

Verse 18.—God's delight in the progress of the upright.—*Thomas Brooks.*

Upright hearts will hold on in the ways of God, and in the ways of well-doing, notwithstanding all afflictions, troubles, and discouragements, they meet withal.—*Thomas Brooks.*

Verse 18.—" *Thy ways.*" The ways of God are—1, *righteous* ways ; 2, *blessed* ways ; 3, *soul-refreshing* ways ; 4, *transcendent* ways—ways that transcend all other ways ; 5, *soul-strengthening* ways ; and 6, sometimes *afflicted, perplexed,* and *persecuted* ways.—*Thomas Brooks.*

Verse 21.—Can he not ? Will he not ?

Verse 21.—A question and an assertion.

Verse 22.—I. Innocence in the midst of suffering, " *sheep.*" II. Honour in the midst of shame, " *for thy sake.*"—*G. Rogers.*

Verse 23.—The cry of a church in sad circumstances. The plaint of a deserted soul.

Verse 24.—Reasons for the withdrawal of divine comfort.

Verse 25.—The great need, the great prayer, the great plea.

Verse 26.—A fit prayer for souls under conviction, for saints under trial or persecution, and for the church under oppression or decay.

PSALM XLV.

TITLE.—*The many titles of this Psalm mark its royalty, its deep and solemn import, and the delight which the writer had in it.* To the Chief Musician upon Shoshannim. *The most probable translation of this word is* upon the lilies, *and it is either a poetical title given to this noblest of songs after the Oriental manner, or it may relate to the tune to which it was set, or to the instrument which was meant to accompany it. We incline to the first theory, and if it be the true one, it is easy to see the fitness of borrowing a name for so beautiful, so pure, so choice, so matchless a poem from the golden lilies, whose bright array outshone the glory of Solomon.* For the sons of Korah. *Special singers are appointed for so divine a hymn. King Jesus deserves to be praised not with random, ranting ravings, but with the sweetest and most skilful music of the best trained choristers. The purest hearts in the spiritual temple are the most harmonious songsters in the ears of God; acceptable song is not a matter so much of tuneful voices as of sanctified affections, but in no case should we sing of Jesus with unprepared hearts.* Maschil, *an instructive ode, not an idle lay, or a romancing ballad, but a Psalm of holy teaching, didactic and doctrinal. This proves it is to be spiritually understood. Blessed are the people who know the meaning of its joyful sound.* A Song of loves. *Not a carnal, sentimental love song, but a celestial canticle of everlasting love fit for the tongues and ears of angels.*

SUBJECT.—*Some here see Solomon and Pharaoh's daughter only—they are short-sighted; others see both Solomon and Christ—they are cross-eyed; well-focussed spiritual eyes see here Jesus only, or if Solomon be present at all, it must be like those hazy shadows of passers-by which cross the face of the camera, and therefore are dimly traceable upon a photographic landscape. "The King," the God whose throne is for ever and ever, is no mere mortal and his everlasting dominion is not bounded by Lebanon and Egypt's river. This is no wedding song of earthly nuptials, but an Epithalamium for the Heavenly Bridegroom and his elect spouse.*

DIVISION.—*Verse 1 is an announcement of intention, a preface to the song; verse 3 adores the matchless beauty of Messiah; and from 3—9, he is addressed in admiring ascriptions of praise. Verses* 10, 11, 12, *are spoken to the bride. The church is further spoken of in verses 13—15, and the Psalm closes with another address to the King, foretelling his eternal fame,* 16—17.

EXPOSITION.

MY heart is inditing a good matter: I speak of the things which I have made touching the King: my tongue *is* the pen of a ready writer.

1. *" My heart."* There is no writing like that dictated by the heart. Heartless hymns are insults to heaven. *" Is inditing a good matter."* A good heart will only be content with good thoughts. Where the fountain is good good streams will flow forth. The learned tell us that the word may be read overfloweth, or as others, boileth or bubbleth up, denoting the warmth of the writer's love, the fulness of his heart, and the consequent richness and glow of his utterance, as though it were the ebullition of his inmost soul, when most full of affection. We have here no single cold expression ; the writer is not one who frigidly studies the elegancies and proprieties of poetry, his stanzas are the natrual outburst of his soul, comparable to the boiling jets of the geysers of Hecla. As the corn offered in sacrifice was parched in the pan, so is this tribute of love hot with sincere devotion. It is a sad thing when the heart is cold with a good matter, and worse when it is warm with a bad matter, but incomparably well when a warm heart and a good matter meet together. O that we may often offer to God an acceptable *minchah*, a sweet oblation fresh from the pan of hearts warmed with gratitude and admiration. *" I speak of the things which I have made touching the King."* This song has " the King " for its only subject, and for the King's honour alone was it composed, well might its writer call it a good matter. The Psalmist did not write carelessly ; he calls his poem his works, or things which he had made. We are not to offer to the Lord that which cost us nothing. Good material deserves good workmanship. We

should well digest in our heart's affections and our mind's meditations any dscourse or poem in which we speak of one so great and glorious as our Royal Lord. As our version reads it, the Psalmist wrote experimentally things which he had made his own, and personally tasted and handled concerning the King. "*My tongue is the pen of a ready writer*," not so much for rapidity, for there the tongue always has the preference, but for exactness, elaboration, deliberation, and skilfulness of expression. Seldom are the excited utterances of the mouth equal in real weight and accuracy to the *verba scripta* of a thoughtful accomplished penman ; but here the writer, though filled with enthusiasm, speaks as correctly as a practised writer ; his utterances therefore are no ephemeral sentences, but such as fall from men who sit down calmly to write for eternity. It is not always that the best of men are in such a key, and when they are they should not restrain the gush of their hallowed feelings. Such a condition of heart in a gifted mind creates that auspicious hour in which poetry pours forth her tuneful numbers to enrich the service of song in the house of the Lord.

2 Thou art fairer than the children of men : grace is poured into thy lips : therefore God hath blessed thee for ever.

2. "*Thou.*" As though the King himself had suddenly appeared before him, the Psalmist lost in admiration of his person, turns from his preface to address his Lord. A loving heart has the power to realise its object. The eyes of a true heart see more than the eyes of the head. Moreover, Jesus reveals himself when we are pouring forth our affections towards him. It is usually the case that when we are ready Christ appears. If our heart is warm it is an index that the sun is shining, and when we enjoy his heat we shall soon behold his light. "*Thou art fairer than the children of men.*" In person, but especially in mind and character, the King of saints is peerless in beauty. The Hebrew word is doubled, "Beautiful, beautiful art thou," Jesus is so emphatically lovely that words must be doubled, strained, yea, exhausted before he can be described. Among the children of men many have through grace been lovely in character, yet they have each had a flaw ; but in Jesus we behold every feature of a perfect character in harmonious proportion. He is lovely everywhere, and from every point of view, but never more so than when we view him in conjugal union with his church ; then love gives a ravishing flush of glory to his loveliness. "*Grace is poured into thy lips.*" Beauty and eloquence make a man majestic when they are united ; they both dwell in perfection in the all fair, all eloquent Lord Jesus. Grace of person and grace of speech reach their highest point in him. Grace has in the most copious manner been poured upon Christ, for it pleased the Father that in him should all fulness dwell, and now grace is in superabundance, poured forth from his lips to cheer and enrich his people. The testimony, the promises, the invitations, the consolations of our King pour forth from him in such volumes of meaning that we cannot but contrast those cataracts of grace with the speech of Moses which did but drop as the rain, and distil as the dew. Whoever in personal communion with the Wellbeloved has listened to his voice will feel that "never man spake like this man." Well did the bride say of him, "his lips are like lilies dropping sweet-smelling myrrh." One word from himself dissolved the heart of Saul of Tarsus, and turned him into an apostle, another word raised up John the Divine when fainting in the Isle of Patmos. Oftentimes a sentence from his lips has turned our own midnight into morning, our winter into spring. "*Therefore God hath blessed thee for ever.*" Calvin reads it, "*Because God hath blessed thee for ever.*" Christ is blessed, blessed of God, blessed for ever, and this is to us one great reason for his beauty, and the source of the gracious words which proceed out of his lips. The rare endowments of the man Christ Jesus are given him of the Father, that by them his people may be blessed with all spiritual blessings in union with himself. But if we take our own translation, we read that the Father has blessed the Mediator as a reward for all his gracious labours ; and right well does he deserve the recompense. Whom God blesses we should bless, and the more so because all his blessedness is communicated to us.

3 Gird thy sword upon *thy* thigh, O *most* mighty, with thy glory and thy majesty.

4 And in thy majesty ride prosperously because of truth and meekness *and* righteousness ; and thy right hand shall teach thee terrible things.

5 Thine arrows *are* sharp in the heart of the king's enemies ; *whereby* the people fall under thee.

6 Thy throne, O God, *is* for ever and ever : the sceptre of thy kingdom *is* a right sceptre.

7 Thou lovest righteousness, and hatest wickedness : therefore God, thy God, hath anointed thee with the oil of gladness above thy fellows.

8 All thy garments *smell* of myrrh, and aloes, *and* cassia, out of the ivory palaces, whereby they have made thee glad.

9 King's daughters *were* among thy honourable women : upon thy right hand did stand the queen in gold of Ophir.

3. *" Gird thy sword upon thy thigh."* Loving spirits jealous of the Redeemer's glory long to see him putting forth his power to vindicate his own most holy cause. Why should the sword of the Spirit lie still, like a weapon hung up in an armoury ; it is sharp and strong, both for cutting and piercing : O that the divine power of Jesus were put forth to use it against error. The words before us represent our great King as urged to arm himself for battle, by placing his sword where it is ready for use. Christ is the true champion of the church, others are but underlings who must borrow strength from him ; the single arm of Immanuel is the sole hope of the faithful. Our prayer should be that of this verse. There is at this moment an apparent suspension of our Lord's former power, we must by importunate prayer call him to the conflict, for like the Greeks without Achilles we are soon overcome by our enemies, and we are but dead men if Jesus be not in our midst. *" O most mighty."* A title well deserved, and not given from empty courtesy like the serenities, excellencies, and highnesses of our fellow mortals—titles, which are but sops for vain glory. Jesus is the truest of heroes. Hero worship in his case alone is commendable. He is mighty to save, mighty in love. *" With thy glory and thy majesty."* Let thy sword both win thee renown and dominion, or as it may mean, gird on with thy sword thy robes which indicate thy royal splendour. Love delights to see the Beloved arrayed as beseemeth his excellency ; she weeps as she sees him in the garments of humiliation, she rejoices to behold him in the vestments of his exaltation. Our precious Christ can never be made too much of. Heaven itself is but just good enough for him. All the pomp that angels and archangels, and thrones, and dominions, and principalities, and powers can pour at his feet is too little for him. Only his own essential glory is such as fully answers to the desire of his people, who can never enough extol him.

4. *" And in thy majesty ride prosperously."* The hero-monarch armed and apparelled is now entreated to ascend his triumphal car. Would to God that our Immanuel would come forth in the chariot of love to conquer our spiritual foes and seize by power the souls whom he has bought with blood. *" Because of truth and meekness and righteousness."* These words may be rendered, *" ride forth upon truth and meekness and righteousness "*—three noble chargers to draw the war-chariot of the gospel. In the sense of our translation it is a most potent argument to urge with our Lord that the cause of the true, the humble and the good, calls for his advocacy. Truth will be ridiculed, meekness will be oppressed, and righteousness slain, unless the God, the Man in whom these precious things are incarnated, shall arise for their vindication. Our earnest petition ought ever to be that Jesus would lay his almighty arm to the work of grace lest the good cause languish and wickedness prevail. *" And thy right hand shall teach thee terrible things."* Foreseeing the result of divine working, the Psalmist prophesies that the uplifted arm of Messiah will reveal to the King's own eyes the terrible overthrow of his foes. Jesus needs no guide but his own right hand, no teacher but his own might ; may he instruct us all in what he can perform, by achieving it speedily before our gladdened eyes.

5. *" Thine arrows."* Our King is master of all weapons : he can strike those who are near and those afar off with equal force. *" Are sharp."* Nothing that Jesus does is ill done, he uses no blunted shafts, no pointless darts. *" In the heart of the King's enemies."* Our Captain aims at men's hearts rather than their heads, and he hits them too ; point-blank are his shots, and they enter deep into the vital part of man's nature. Whether for love or vengeance, Christ never misses aim, and when his arrows stick, they cause a smart not soon forgotten, a wound which

only he can heal. Jesus' arrows of conviction are sharp in the quiver of his word, and sharp when on the bow of his ministers, but they are most known to be so when they find a way into careless hearts. They are *his* arrows, he made them, he shoots them. He makes them sharp, and he makes them enter the heart. May none of us ever fall under the darts of his judgment, for none kill so surely as they. "*Whereby the people fall under thee.*" On either side the slain of the Lord are many when Jesus leads on the war. Nations tremble and turn to him when he shoots abroad his truth. Under his power and presence, men are stricken down as though pricked in the heart. There is no standing against the Son of God when his bow of might is in his hands. Terrible will be that hour when his bow shall be made quite naked, and bolts of devouring fire shall be hurled upon his adversaries : then shall princes fall and nations perish.

6. "*Thy throne, O God, is for ever and ever.*" To whom can this be spoken but our Lord ? The Psalmist cannot restrain his adoration. His enlightened eye sees in the royal Husband of the church, God, God to be adored, God reigning, God reigning everlastingly. Blessed sight ! Blind are the eyes that cannot see God in Christ Jesus ! We never appreciate the tender condescension of our King in becoming one flesh with his church, and placing her at his right hand, until we have fully rejoiced in his essential glory and deity. What a mercy for us that our Saviour is God, for who but a God could execute the work of salvation ? What a glad thing it is that he reigns on a throne which will never pass away, for we need both sovereign grace and eternal love to secure our happiness. Could Jesus cease to reign we should cease to be blessed, and were he not God, and therefore eternal, this must be the case. No throne can endure for ever, but that on which God himself sitteth. "*The sceptre of thy kingdom is a right sceptre.*" He is the lawful monarch of all things that be. His rule is founded in right, its law is right, its result is right. Our King is no usurper and no oppressor. Even when he shall break his enemies with a rod of iron, he will do no man wrong ; his vengeance and his grace are both in conformity with justice. Hence we trust him without suspicion ; he cannot err ; no affliction is too severe, for he sends it ; no judgment too harsh, for he ordains it. O blessed hands of Jesus ! the reigning power is safe with you. All the just rejoice in the government of the King who reigns in righteousness.

7. "*Thou lovest righteousness, and hatest wickedness.*" Christ Jesus is not neutral in the great contest between right and wrong : as warmly as he loves the one he abhors the other. What qualifications for a sovereign ! what grounds of confidence for a people ! The whole of our Lord's life on earth proved the truth of these words ; his death to put away sin and bring in the reign of righteousness, sealed the fact beyond all question ; his providence by which he rules from his mediatorial throne, when rightly understood, reveals the same ; and his final assize will proclaim it before all worlds. We should imitate him both in his love and hate ; they are both needful to complete a righteous character. "*Therefore God, thy God, hath anointed thee with the oil of gladness above thy fellows.*" Jesus as Mediator owned God as his God, to whom, being found in fashion as a man, he became obedient. On account of our Lord's perfect life he is now rewarded with superior joy. Others there are to whom grace has given a sacred fellowship with him, but by their universal consent and his own merit, he is prince among them, the gladdest of all because the cause of all their gladness. At Oriental feasts oil was poured on the heads of distinguished and very welcome guests ; God himself anoints the man Christ Jesus, as he sits at the heavenly feasts, anoints him as a reward for his work, with higher and fuller joy than any else can know ; thus is the Son of man honoured and rewarded for all his pains. Observe the indisputable testimony to Messiah's Deity in verse six, and to his manhood in the present verse. Of whom could this be written but of Jesus of Nazareth ? Our Christ is our Elohim. Jesus is God with us.

8. "*All thy garments smell of myrrh, and aloes, and cassia.*" The divine anointing causes fragrance to distil from the robes of the Mighty Hero. He is delightful to every sense, to the eye most fair, to the ear most gracious, to the spiritual nostril most sweet. The excellences of Jesus are all most precious, comparable to the rarest spices ; they are most varied, and to be likened not to myrrh alone, but to all the perfumes blended in due proportion. The Father always finds a pleasure in him, in him he is well pleased ; and all regenerated spirits rejoice in him, for he is made of God unto us, " wisdom, righteousness, sanctification, and redemption." Note that not only is Jesus most sweet, but even his garments are so ; everything

that he has to do with is perfumed by his person. "*All*" his garments are thus fragrant ; not some of them, but all ; we delight as much in his purple of dominion as in the white linen of his priesthood, his mantle as our prophet is as dear to us as his seamless coat as our friend. All his dress is fragrant with all sweetness. To attempt to spiritualise each spice here mentioned would be unprofitable, the evident sense is that all sweetnesses meet in Jesus, and are poured forth wherever he is present. "*Out of the ivory palaces, whereby they have made thee glad.*" The abode of Jesus now is imperial in splendour, ivory and gold but faintly image his royal seat ; there is he made glad in the presence of the Father, and in the company of his saints. Oh, to behold him with his perfumed garments on ! The very smell of him from afar ravishes our spirit, what must it be to be on the other side of the pearl gate, within the palace of ivory, amid those halls of Zion, "conjubilant with song," where is the throne of David, and the abiding presence of the Prince ! To think of his gladness, to know that *he* is full of joy, gives gladness at this moment to our souls. We poor exiles can sing in our banishment since our King, our Well-beloved, has come to his throne.

9. "*Kings' daughters were among thy honourable women.*" Our Lord's courts lack not for courtiers, and those the fairest and noblest. Virgin souls are maids of honour to the court, the true lilies of heaven. The lowly and pure in heart are esteemed by the Lord Jesus as his most familiar friends, their place in his palace is not among the menials but near the throne. The day will come when those who are "kings' daughters" literally will count it their greatest honour to serve the church, and, meanwhile every believing sister is spiritually a King's daughter, a member of the royal family of heaven. "*Upon thy right hand,*" in the place of love, honour, and power, "*did stand the queen in gold of Ophir :*" the church shares her Lord's honour and happiness, he sets her in the place of dignity, he clothes her with the best of the best. Gold is the richest of metals, and Ophir gold the purest known. Jesus bestows nothing inferior or of secondary value upon his beloved church. In imparted and imputed righteousness the church is divinely arrayed. Happy those who are members of a church so honoured, so beloved ; unhappy those who persecute the beloved people, for as a husband will not endure that his wife should be insulted or maltreated, so neither will the heavenly Husband ; he will speedily avenge his own elect. Mark, then, the solemn pomp of the verses we have read. The King is seen with rapture, he girds himself as a warrior, robes himself as a monarch, mounts his chariot, darts his arrows, and conquers his foes. Then he ascends his throne with his sceptre in his hand, fills the palace hall with perfume brought from his secret chambers, his retinue stand around him, and, fairest of all, his bride is at his right hand, with daughters of subject princes as her attendants. Faith is no stranger to this sight, and every time she looks she adores, she loves, she rejoices, she expects.

10 Hearken, O daughter, and consider, and incline thine ear ; forget also thine own people, and thy father's house ;

11 So shall the king greatly desire thy beauty : for he *is* thy Lord ; and worship thou him.

12 And the daughter of Tyre *shall be there* with a gift ; *even* the rich among the people shall entreat thy favour.

10. "*Hearken, O daughter, and consider.*" Ever is this the great duty of the church. Faith cometh by hearing, and confirmation by consideration. No precept can be more worthy of the attention of those who are honoured to be espoused unto Christ than that which follows. "*And incline thine ear.*" Lean forward that no syllable may be unheard. The whole faculties of the mind should be bent upon receiving holy teaching. "*Forget also thine own people, and thy father's house.*" To renounce the world is not easy, but it must be done by all who are affianced to the Great King, for a divided heart he cannot endure ; it would be misery to the beloved one as well as dishonour to her Lord. Evil acquaintances, and even those who are but neutral, must be forsaken, they can confer no benefit, they must inflict injury. The house of our nativity is the house of sin—we were shapen in iniquity ; the carnal mind is enmity against God, we must come forth of the house of fallen nature, for it is built in the City of Destruction. Not that natural ties are broken by grace, but ties of the sinful nature, bonds of graceless affinity. We have much to forget as well as to learn, and the unlearning is so difficult that only diligent

hearing, and considering, and bending of the whole soul to it, can accomplish the work ; and even these would be too feeble did not divine grace assist. Yet why should we remember the Egypt from which we came out ? Are the leeks and the garlic, and the onions anything, when the iron bondage, and the slavish tasks, and the death-dealing Pharaoh of hell are remembered ? We part with folly for wisdom ; with bubbles for eternal joys ; with deceit for truth ; with misery for bliss ; with idols for the living God. O that Christians were more mindful of the divine precept here recorded ; but, alas ! wordliness abounds ; the church is defiled ; and the glory of the Great King is veiled. Only when the whole church leads the separated life will the full splendour and power of Christianity shine forth upon the world.

11. *" So shall the king greatly desire thy beauty."* Whole-hearted love is the duty and bliss of the marriage state in every case, but especially so in this lofty, mystic marriage. The church must forsake all others and cleave to Jesus only, or she will not please him nor enjoy the full manifestation of his love. What less can he ask, what less may she dare propose than to be wholly his ? Jesus sees a beauty in his church, a beauty which he delights in most when it is not marred by worldliness. He has always been most near and precious to his saints when they have cheerfully taken up his cross and followed him without the camp. His Spirit is grieved when they mingle themselves among the people and learn their ways. No great and lasting revival of religion can be granted us till the professed lovers of Jesus prove their affection by coming out from an ungodly world, being separated, and touching not the unclean thing. *"For he is thy Lord ; and worship thou him."* He has royal rights still ; his condescending grace does not lessen but rather enforce his authority. Our Saviour is also our Ruler. The husband is the head of the wife ; the love he bears her does not lessen but strengthen her obligation to obey. The church must reverence Jesus, and bow before him in prostrate adoration ; his tender union with her gives her liberty, but not license ; it frees her from all other burdens, but places his easy yoke upon her neck. Who would wish it to be otherwise ? The service of God is heaven in heaven, and perfectly carried out it is heaven upon earth. Jesus, thou art he whom thy church praises in her unceasing songs, and adores in her perpetual service. Teach us to be wholly thine. Bear with us, and work by thy Spirit in us till thy will is done by us on earth as it is in heaven.

12. *" And the daughter of Tyre shall be there with a gift."* When the church abounds in holiness, she shall know no lack of homage from the surrounding people. Her glory shall then impress and attract the heathen around, till they also unite in doing honour to the Lord. The power of missions abroad lies at home : a holy church will be a powerful church. Nor shall there be lack of treasure in her coffers when grace is in her heart ; the free gifts of a willing people shall enable the workers for God to carry on their sacred enterprises without stint. Commerce shall send in its revenue to endow, not with forced levies and imperial taxes, but with willing gifts the church of the Great King. *" Even the rich among the people shall intreat thy favour."* Not by pandering to their follies, but by testifying against their sins, shall the wealthy be won to the faith of Jesus. They shall come not to favour the church but to beg for her favour. She shall not be the hireling of the great, but as a queen shall she dispense her favours to the suppliant throng of the rich among the people. We go about to beg for Christ like beggars for alms, and many who should know better will make compromises and become reticent of unpopular truth to please the great ones of the earth ; not so will the true bride of Christ degrade herself, when her sanctification is more deep and more visible ; then will the hearts of men grow liberal, and offerings from afar, abundant and continual, shall be presented at the throne of the Pacific Prince.

13 The king's daughter *is* all glorious within : her clothing *is* of wrought gold.

14 She shall be brought unto the king in raiment of needlework : the virgins her companions that follow her shall be brought unto thee.

15 With gladness and rejoicing shall they be brought ; they shall enter into the king's palace.

13. *" The king's daughter is all glorious within."* Within her secret chambers her glory is great. Though unseen of men her Lord sees her, and commends her.

" It doth not yet appear what we shall be." Or the passage may be understood as meaning within herself—her beauty is not outward only or mainly ; the choicest of her charms are to be found in her heart, her secret character, her inward desires. Truth and wisdom in the hidden parts are what the Lord regards ; mere skin-deep beauty is nothing in his eyes. The church is of royal extraction, of imperial dignity, for she is a king's daughter ; and she has been purified and renewed in nature, for she is glorious within. Note the word *all*. The Bridegroom was said to have all his garments perfumed, and now the bride is *all* glorious within—entireness and completeness are great points. There is no mixture of ill savour in Jesus, nor shall there be alloy of unholiness in his people, his church shall be presented without spot or wrinkle, or any such thing. " *Her clothing is of wrought gold.*" Best material and best workmanship. How laboriously did our Lord work out the precious material of his righteousness into a vesture for his people ! no embroidery of golden threads can equal that master-piece of holy art. Such clothing becomes one so honoured by relationship to the Great King. The Lord looks to it that nothing shall be wanting to the glory and beauty of his bride.

14. " *She shall be brought unto the king in raiment of needlework.*" The day comes when the celestial marriage shall be openly celebrated, and these words describe the nuptial procession, wherein the queen is brought to her royal Husband attended by her handmaidens. In the latter-day glory, and in the consummation of all things, the glory of the bride, the Lamb's wife, shall be seen by all the universe with admiration. While she was within doors, and her saints hidden ones, the church was glorious ; what will be her splendour when she shall appear in the likeness of her Lord in the day of his manifestation ? The finest embroidery is but a faint image of the perfection of the church when sanctified by the Spirit. This verse tells us of the ultimate rest of the church—the King's own bosom ; of the way she comes to it, she is *brought* by the power of sovereign grace ; of the time when this is done—in the future, " *she shall be*," it does not yet appear ; of the state in which she shall come—clad in richest array, and attended by brightest spirits. " *The virgins her companions that follow her shall be brought unto thee.*" Those who love and serve the church for her Lord's sake shall share in her bliss " in that day." In one sense they are a part of the church, but for the sake of the imagery they are represented as maids of honour ; and, though the figure may seem incongruous, they are represented as brought to the King with the same loving familiarity as the bride, because the true servants of the church are of the church, and partake in all her happiness. Note that those who are admitted to everlasting communion with Christ, are pure in heart—*virgins*, pure in company—" *her companions*," pure in walk—" *that follow her.*" Let none hope to be brought into heaven at last who are not purified now.

15. " *With gladness and rejoicing shall they be brought.*" Joy becomes a marriage feast. What joy will that be which will be seen at the feasts of paradise when all the redeemed shall be brought home ! Gladness in the saints themselves, and rejoicing from the angels shall make the halls of the New Jerusalem ring again with shoutings. " *They shall enter into the King's palace.*" Their peaceful abodes shall be where Jesus the King reigns in state for ever. They shall not be shut out but shut in. Rights of free entrance into the holiest of all shall be accorded them. Brought by grace, they shall enter into glory. If there was joy in the bringing, what in the entering ? What in the abiding ? The glorified are not field labourers in the plains of heaven, but sons who dwell at home, princes of the blood, resident in the royal palace. Happy hour when we shall enjoy all this and forget the sorrows of time in the triumphs of eternity.

16 Instead of thy fathers shall be thy children, whom thou mayest make princes in all the earth.

17 I will make thy name to be remembered in all generations ; therefore shall the people praise thee for ever and ever.

16. " *Instead of thy fathers shall be thy children.*" The ancient saints who stood as fathers in the service of the Great King have all passed away ; but a spiritual seed is found to fill their places. The veterans depart, but volunteers fill up the vacant places. The line of grace never becomes extinct. As long as time shall last, the true apostolical succession will be maintained. " *Whom thou mayest make princes in all the earth.*" Servants of Christ are kings. Where a man has preached

successfully, and evangelised a tribe or nation, he gets to himself **more** than regal honours, and his name is like the name of the great men that be upon the earth. Jesus is the king-maker. Ambition of the noblest kind shall win her desire in the army of Christ; immortal crowns are distributed to his faithful soldiers. The whole earth shall yet be subdued for Christ, and honoured are they, who shall, through grace, have a share in the conquest—these shall reign with Christ at his coming.

17.—"*I will make thy name to be remembered in all generations.*" Jehovah by the prophet's mouth promises to the Prince of Peace eternal fame as well as a continuous progeny. His name is his fame, his character, his person; these are dear to his people now—they never can forget them; and it shall be so as long as men exist. Names renowned in one generation have been unknown to the next era, but the laurels of Jesus shall ever be fresh, his renown ever new. God will see to this; his providence and his grace shall make it so. The fame of Messiah is not left to human guardianship; the Eternal guarantees it, and his promise never fails. All down the ages the memories of Gethsemane and Calvary shall glow with unextinguishable light; nor shall the lapse of time, the smoke of error, or the malice of hell be able to dim the glory of the Redeemer's fame. "*Therefore shall the people praise thee for ever and ever.*" They shall confess thee to be what thou art, and shall render to thee in perpetuity the homage due. Praise is due from every heart to him who loved us, and redeemed us by his blood; this praise will never be fully paid, but will be ever a standing and growing debt. His daily benefits enlarge our obligations, let them increase the number of our songs. Age to age reveals more of his love, let every year swell the volume of the music of earth and heaven, and let thunders of song roll up in full diapason to the throne of him that liveth, and was dead, and is alive for evermore, and hath the keys of hell and of death.

> " Let him be crowned with majesty
> Who bowed his head to death,
> And be his honours sounded high
> By all things that have breath."

EXPLANATORY NOTES AND QUAINT SAYINGS.

Title.—" *Upon Shoshannim,*" or upon *lilies.* It will be remembered that lilies were an emblem of purity and loveliness, and were introduced as such in the building of Solomon's temple (see 1 Kings vii. 19, 22, 26; 2 Chron. iv. 5); and the church is compared in the Canticles to a " lily among thorns." Cant. ii. 2. The Psalms which bear this title, " upon lilies," are the present, the sixty-ninth and the eightieth (cp. Ps. lx.); and all these contain prophecies of Christ and his church. The sixtieth is a parallel to the forty-fourth, and represents her supplicating appeal to God, and Christ's victories. The sixty-ninth displays the victories gained by Christ through suffering. The eightieth is also parallel to the forty-fourth and sixtieth, a plaintive lament of the church in distress and a supplicating cry for deliverance. All these three Psalms are (if we may venture to use this expression) like the voice of the " lily among thorns." That there is, therefore, some reference here to the spiritual meaning of the word שׁשׁנים, or *lilies*, in this title, seems at least to be probable.—*Christopher Wordsworth.*

Title.—We think that *Shoshannim* signifies an instrument of six strings, or a song of rejoicing.—*Augustin Calmet,* 1672–1757.

Kitto, on the other hand, says that the word is so clearly *lilies*, that he is disinclined to go out of the way to bring in the Hebrew word for six.

Title.—" *To the chief musician upon Shoshannim.*" Some would have it that instruments whereon were many engravings of lilies, which are six-leaved flowers, are here meant. And, indeed, some interpreters, because of that derivation of the word, do thus translate it, *upon Shoshannim*, that is, *upon lilies;* and that either in reference to their wedding garlands, that were made much of lilies, or as intending by these lilies Christ and his church.—*Arthur Jackson.*

Title.—" *A song.*" The word שׁיר, *shir,* the meaning of which (*song*), is unquestioned, is prefixed to many of the Psalms, three times simply and thirteen times in connection with *Mizmor*. There is no mark of peculiarity in their composition. The meaning of the word seems to be discriminated from *Mizmor*, as signifying a thing to be sung, with reference to its poetical structure.—*John Jebb.*

Whole Psalm.—The Psalter, which sets forth so much truth respecting the person and work of Christ—truth more precious than gold and sweeter than the honeycomb—is not silent respecting the bond subsisting between him and his people, THE MYSTICAL UNION BETWEEN CHRIST AND THE CHURCH. When a prince sets his affections on a woman of lowly rank, and takes her home to be his wife, the two are so united that her debts become his, his wealth and honours become hers. Now, that there is formed between Christ and the church, between Christ and every soul that will consent to receive him, a connection, of which the most intimate of all natural relations is the analogue and type, we have already found to be not only taught in the Psalms, but to be implied in the very structure of many of them. He takes his people's sins upon him, and they receive the right to become the sons of God ; the One Spirit of God wherewith he was baptised without measure, dwells in them according to the measure of the grace that is given them. I will only add further, that this union, besides being implied in so many places, is expressly set forth in one most glorious Psalm—the Nuptial Song of Christ and the Church— which has for its peculiar theme the home-bringing of Christ's elect, that they may be joined to him in a union that shall survive the everlasting hills.—*William Binnie, D.D.*

Verse 1.—" My heart is inditing a good matter," and then, *" My tongue shall be like the pen of a ready writer."* Oh, then I shall go merrily on in his service, when I have matter prepared in my heart. And, indeed, as the mariner sees further new stars the further he sails, he loseth sight of the old ones and discovers new ; so the growing Christian, the further he sails in religion he discovers new wants, new Scriptures affect him, new trials afflict him, new business he finds with God, and forgetting those things that are behind, he reacheth after those things that are before, and so finds every day new business with the Lord his God ; and he that is busy trifles not ; the more business the less distraction.—*Richard Steele.*

Verse 1.—" My heart is inditing a good matter." רחשׁ *(rakhash), boileth* or *bubbleth up ;* denotes the language of the heart full and ready for utterance.—*Victorinus Bythner.*

Verse 1.—" My heart is inditing a good matter." Here you have the work of the Spirit of prophecy. By his operation the good " matter " is engendered in the Psalmist's bosom, and now his heart is heaving and labouring under the load. It is just beginning to throw it up, like water from a fountain, that it may flow off in the channel of the tongue. Here, therefore, you have some insight given you of the manner of the operation of the Spirit in the heart of man. The Psalmist says his heart is doing what the Spirit is doing in his heart. The heart does it, indeed, but it is the Spirit's working. The Psalmist took all the interest and pleasure in his subject that he could have done, if the Spirit had had nothing to do with it ; for when the Spirit works, he works not only by the heart, but in the heart ; he seizes upon all its affections, every fibre of it is bent to his will.—*George Harpur, in " Christ in the Psalms,"* 1862.

Verse 1.—" Good matter," the goodspell, or *gospel.—Christopher Wordsworth.*

Verse 1.—A similitude taken from the *mincah,* or *meat-offering* in the law, which was dressed in the frying-pan (Lev. vii. 9), and there boiled in oil, being made of fine flour unleavened, mingled with oil (Lev. ii. 5), and afterwards was presented to the Lord by the priest, ver. 8. Here the matter of this Psalm is as the *mincah* or oblation, which with the oil, the grace of the Spirit, was boiled and prepared in the prophet's heart, and now presented.—*Henry Ainsworth.*

Verse 1.—It is reported of Origen, saith Erasmus, that he was ever earnest, but most of all when he discoursed of Christ. Of Johannes Mollias, a Bononian, it is said, that whenever he spake of Jesus Christ, his eyes dropped, for he was fraught with a mighty fervency of God's Holy Spirit ; and like the Baptist, he was first a burning (boiling or bubbling), and then a shining light.—*John Trapp.*

Verse 1.—" Touching the king." It does not all concern the king immediately, for much of it concerns the queen, and about one-half of it is directly addressed to her. But it relates to him inasmuch as it relates to his family. Christ ever identifies himself with his people ; so that, whatever is done to them, is done to himself. Their interests are his.—*George Harpur.*

Verse 1.—" *My tongue* " shall be like the pen of one that takes minutes or writes shorthand : for I shall speak very briefly, and not in words at length, or so as to be understood in a literal sense, but in figures and emblems.—*From " Holy David and his old English Translators cleared," 1706. [Anon.]*

Verse 1.—" *The pen.*" We call the prophets the *penmen* of Scripture, whereas they were but the *pen.*—*Matthew Henry.*

Verse 2.—" *Thou art fairer than the children of men : grace is poured into thy lips.*" Thus he begins to set forth his beauty, wherein is the delightfulness of any person ; so is it with the soul when God hath made known to man his own filthiness and uncomeliness through sin, and that only by Jesus sin is taken away ; oh, how beautiful is this face, the first sight of him ! Secondly, " *Full of grace are thy lips :* " here is the second commendation ; which is, when Jesus hath opened his lips to us, from them he pours out grace into our soul, when he makes known the Father to us, and speaks peace to all that are far off and near ; when he calls, " Come unto me, all ye that labour and are heavy laden, and I will refresh you : " and all this is because God hath blessed him for ever ; we are assured he comes from God, and that he and his works are eternal, and therefore all his grace poured out upon us shall remain with us, and make us blessed for ever ; for he is the Word of God, and he speaks the mind of God, for he speaks nothing but what he hath heard from the Father ; and when he speaks to our souls with his Word, the Spirit is given, a certain testimony to our soul that we are the sons of God, and a pledge of our inheritance ; for the Spirit and the Word cannot be separated.—*Richard Coore, in " Christ set forth."*

Verse 2.—" *Thou art fairer than the children of men,*" etc. Nothing can be more beautiful than this abrupt way of discourse. The prophet sets out with a professed design to speak of the king. But as if in the moment he had so intended, the glorious *Person* of whom he was going to speak appeared to his view, he instantly leaves every other consideration to speak to him himself. And what a rapturous address he makes ! He first describes the glories, the beauties, the astonishing loveliness, of his *person.* Though to a carnal eye there was no beauty to desire him, his visage was marred more than any man's, and his form more than the sons of men, yet to an eye truly enlightened, he is the king in his beauty, fairer, as the glorious *Mediator,* the Head, the Bridegroom of his Church and people, than all the children of men. And, in the Father's view, so greatly beloved, so truly glorious, that *grace was poured into his lips.* Reader, observe the expression ; not simply grace put into his heart, for the holiness and purity of his person, but poured into his lips, that, like the honey, it might drop upon his people, and be for ever communicated to all his redeemed, in an endless perpetuity of all suited blessings here, and glory hereafter.—*Robert Hawker, D.D.*

Verse 2.—" *Thou art fairer than the children of men.*" Are you for *beauty ?* That takes with most : for this none like Christ. For beauty and comeliness he infinitely surpasses both men and angels. We read of Moses, that he was exceeding fair ; and of David, that he was ruddy, and of a beautiful countenance ; and Josephus reports of the one of them, that all that saw him were amazed at and enamoured of his beauty. Oh, but what was their beauty to Christ's ? Were their beauty, and with theirs the beauty of men and angels put together, it would all be nothing to the beauty of Christ ; not so much as the light of a farthing candle is to the light of the sun at noon-day.—*Edward Pearse in " The Best Match," 1673.*

Verse 2.—" *Thou art fairer,*" etc. Fair he was (1) in his *conception,* conceived in purity, and a fair angel brought the news. Fair (2) in his *nativity :* ὡραῖος is the word in the Septuagint, *tempustivus, in time,* that is, all things are beautiful in their time, Eccl. iii. 11. And *in the fulness of time* it was that he was born, and a fair star pointed to him. Fair (3) in his *childhood ;* he grew up in grace and favour, Luke ii. 52. The doctors were much taken with him. Fair (4) in his *manhood ;* had he not been so, says S. Jerome, had there not been something admirable in his countenance and presence, some heavenly beauty, the apostles and the whole world (as the Pharisees themselves confess) would not so suddenly have gone after him. Fair (5) in his *transfiguration,* white as the light, or as the snow, his face glittering as the sun (Matt. xvii. 2), even to the ravishing the very soul of S. Peter, that " he knew not what he said," could let his eyes dwell upon that face for ever.

and never come down the mount again. Fair (6) in his *passion*. *Nihil indecorum*, no uncomeliness, in his nakedness; his very wounds, and the bloody prints of the whips and scourges drew an *ecce* from the mouth of Pilate: "Behold the man!" the sweetness of his countenance and carriage in the midst of filth and spittle, whips and buffets. His very comeliness upon the cross, and his giving up the ghost, made the centurion cry out, he "*was the Son of God:*" there appeared so sweet a majesty, so heavenly a lustre in him through that very darkness that encompassed him. Fair (7) in his *resurrection;* so subtle a beauty, that mortal eyes, even the eyes of his own disciples, were not able to see or apprehend it, but when he veiled it from them. Fair (8) in his *ascension;* made his disciples stand gazing after him so long (as if they never could look long enough upon him), till an angel is sent from heaven to rebuke them, to look home, Acts i. 2.—*Mark Frank.*

Verse 2.—O fair sun, and fair moon, and fair stars, and fair flowers, and fair roses, and fair lilies; but O ten thousand thousand times fairer Lord Jesus! Alas! I have wronged him in making the comparison this way. O black sun and moon! but O fair Lord Jesus! O black flowers, and black lilies, and roses! but O fair, fair, ever fair, Lord Jesus! O black heaven! but O fair Christ! O black angels! but O surpassingly fair Lord Jesus!—*Samuel Rutherford.*

Verse 2.—In one Christ we may contemplate and must confess all the beauty and loveliness both of heaven and earth; the beauty of heaven is God, the beauty of earth is man; the beauty of heaven and earth together is this God-man.—*Edward Hyde, D.D.*, 1658.

Verse 2.—"*Thou.*" "I have a passion," observed Count Zinzendorf in one of his discourses to the congregation at Herrnhut, "and it is He—He only."

Verse 2.—"*Thou art fairer.*" Hebrew, Thou art *double fairer;* the Hebrew word is doubled, *ad corroborandum*, saith Kimchi.—*John Trapp.*

Verse 2.—"*Grace is poured into thy lips.*" This is said as if this grace were a gift, and not something inherent in our Lord himself. And is not this exactly what we learn from the histories of the evangelists? Before Jesus went forth to the work of his public mission, the Holy Ghost descended from heaven like a dove and lit upon him. The Spirit who imparts all its graces to the church of Christ imparted his graces to Christ himself. Not that the Son of God needed the anointing of the Spirit of God, but he suffered it to be so that he might be in all things like his brethren. If he was to be their example, he must show them wherein their great strength lay. They see in him the fruits of the Holy Ghost who is promised to themselves. All that Christ ever did as the Head and Representative of his people, he did by that very Spirit which is still resident in his church.—*George Harpur.*

Verse 2.—"*Grace is poured into thy lips.*" "*Full of grace are thy lips.*" Full of grace for the *matter*, and full of grace for the *manner*. I. For the *matter*, he delivered acceptable doctrine: "The law was given by Moses, but grace came by Jesus Christ." John i. 17. Moses had harsh and hard words in his law; "Cursed is he that continueth not in all things which are written in the book of the law to do them;" but Christ on the contrary speaks better things, the first words in his first sermon are, "Blessed are the poor in spirit: for theirs is the kingdom of heaven." Matt. v. 3. He cometh unto his people, *cum verbo gratiæ, cum osculo gratiæ*, saith Augustine: his lips are *full of grace*, that is, pouring out gracious words abundantly. Matt. xi. 28; John iii. 16; Luke iv. 18. "His lips are like lilies dropping down myrrh" (Cant. v. 13); all that heard him wondered at the gracious words which proceeded out of his mouth, Luke iv. 22. II. For the *manner*, he taught not as the scribes; he spake so sweetly that the very catch-poll officers, astonished at his words, gave this testimony, "Never man spake like this man," John vii. 46. He spake so graciously that the apostles forsook all things and followed him; at his call Andrew left his nets straightway, James and John their father without tarrying, Matthew from the receipt of custom, Zaccheus from the like worldly course, came hastily to receive him joyfully. Mark x. 28; Matt. iv. 20, 21; ix. 9; Luke xix. 6. Nay, beloved, he was so powerful an orator, that the very winds and waves obeyed his word. Mark iv. 39. It is reported in Holy Writ that all princes and people were desirous of hearing Solomon's eloquence; the Queen of Sheba wondering at the same, cried out, "Happy are these thy servants which stand continually before thee, and that hear thy wisdom," 1 Kings x. 8. Solomon is a type here, but Christ is the truth; and this showeth evidently that Christ is not a tyrant, but a mild prince, persuading obedience plausibly, not compelling his people violently ; his sayings are his *sceptre* and his sword : his piercing exhortations are, as it were, his *sharp arrows* by which his followers are subdued unto him.

To conclude this argument, his fair words (as the Scripture speaks) " are as an honeycomb, sweetness to the soul and health to the bones " (Prov. xvi. 24) : " an honeycomb," and what more toothsome ? " sweetness to the soul and health to the bones ; " and what, I pray, more wholesome ? The good man's soul is Christ's own spouse, to which he speaks a great many ways graciously ; sometimes correcting, and what stronger argument of love ? for " whom he loveth he chasteneth " (Heb. xii. 6) ; sometimes instructing, and his gospel is able to make " the man of God perfect, throughly furnished unto all good works " (2 Tim. iii. 17) ; sometimes wooing in amorous terms, as in his love-song everywhere : " my beloved," " my sister," " my spouse," " the fairest among women," " my love," " my dove," etc. ; sometimes promising, and that both the blessings of this life present (Fear thou not ; for I am with thee : be not dismayed ; for I am thy God : etc., Isaiah xli. 10), and of that life which is to come. John xvii. 21, 24. But Christ's excellent intercession every day to God the Father, appearing in the court of heaven, and as an advocate pleading for us, is yet fuller of grace ; for if Caleb easily granted his daughter's request, and bestowed on her " the springs above and the springs beneath " (Judges i. 15), how shall Almighty God (whose mercies are above all his works) deny the suits of such a Son in whom he is well pleased ?—*John Boys.*

Verse 2.—" *Grace is poured into thy lips.*" The former clause noted his inward perfections ; and this signifies his ability and readiness to communicate them to others.—*Matthew Pool.*

Verse 2 (second clause).—Never were there such words of love and sweetness spoken by any man as by him : never was there such a loving and tender heart as the heart of Jesus Christ : " *Grace was poured into his lips.*" Certainly never were there such words of love, sweetness, and tenderness spoken here upon this earth as those last words of his which were uttered a little before his sufferings, and are recorded in the 13th, 14th, 15th, 16th and 17th chapters of John. Read over all the books of love and friendship that were ever written by any of the sons of men, they do all come far short of those melting strains of love that are there expressed. So sweet and amiable was the conversation of Jesus Christ, that it is reported of the apostle Peter in the Ecclesiastical History, that after Christ's ascension he wept so abundantly, that he was always seen wiping his face from the tears ; and being asked why he wept so, he answered, He could not choose but weep as often as he thought of that most sweet conversation of Jesus Christ.—*John Row.*

Verse 3.—" *Gird thy sword upon thy thigh.*" The sword, according to ancient custom was hung in a belt put round the shoulders, and reaching down to the thigh. It was suspended on the back part of the thigh, almost to the ground, but was not girded upon it ; the horseman's sword was fixed on the saddle by a girth. When David, in spirit invites the Redeemer of the church to gird his sword upon his thigh, and the spouse says of the valiant of Israel, " every man hath his sword upon his thigh because of fear in the night " (Cant. iii. 8), they do not mean that the weapon was literally bound upon their thigh, but hung in the girdle on the back part of it ; for this was the mode in which, by the universal testimony of ancient writers, the infantry wore their swords. It is still the practice in the East to wear swords in this manner, for Chardin informs us, that " the Eastern people wear their swords hanging down at length ; and the Turks wear their swords on horseback, and on their thigh." But in his poetical invitation to the Redeemer, to gird his sword upon his thigh, David manifestly points to some special occasion of solemn and official character ; and a clear light is thrown upon his meaning by a custom to this day observed in the East. " When a Persian or an Ottoman prince *ascends the throne,*" says Mr. Morier, " he girds on his sabre. Mohammed Jaffer, for example, was proclaimed by the Khan, governor *pro tempore,* till the arrival of his brother, and was invested in this dignity by the *girding of a sword upon his thigh,* an honour which he accepted with a reluctance perhaps not wholly feigned."—" This ceremony," says Dr. Davey, giving an account of an Eastern coronation, " remained to be performed before the prince could be considered completely king—it was that of choosing a new name, and putting on the regal sword. The prince went in great state to the temple, where he presented offerings, and then, the sword having been girded on his thigh, the priest presented a pot of sandal-powder, in which the prince, who *may now be called* king, dipped his fingers."

From these anecdotes, it is evident girding a sword on the thigh is part of the ceremony of royal inauguration ; and that when the Psalmist addresses the Messiah, he refers to his receiving the honours and powers of the Lord of all.—*G. Paxton's Illustrations of Scripture.*

Verse 3.—" *Thy sword.*" The word of God is compared to such a weapon, for the apostle informs us that it is quick, or living, and powerful, and sharper than any two-edged sword, piercing even to the dividing asunder of the soul and spirit, and of the joints and marrow, and laying open the thoughts and intents of the heart. It must be observed, however, that this description of the word of God is applicable to it only when Christ girds it on, and employs it as his sword. Of what use is a sword, even though it be the sword of Goliath, while it lies still in its scabbard, or is grasped by the powerless hand of an infant ? In those circumstances it can neither conquer nor defend, however well suited it might be to do both in the hand of a warrior. It is the same with the sword of the Spirit. While it lies still in its scabbard, or is wielded only by the infantile hand of Christ's ministers, it is a powerless and useless weapon ; a weapon at which the weakest sinner can laugh, and against which he can defend himself with the utmost ease. But not so when he who is the Most Mighty girds it on. Then it becomes a weapon of tremendous power, a weapon resistless as the bolt of heaven. " Is not my word like a fire, and a hammer, saith the Lord, which breaketh the rock in pieces ? " It is indeed, for what can be more efficacious and irresistible than a weapon sharper than a two-edged sword, wielded by the arm of omnipotence ? What must his sword be whose glance is lightning ? Armed with this weapon, the Captain of our salvation cuts his way to the sinner with infinite ease, though surrounded by rocks and mountains, scatters his strongholds and refuges of lies, and with a mighty blow cleaves asunder his heart of adamant, and lays him prostrate and trembling at his feet. Since such are the effects of this weapon in the hand of Christ, it is with the utmost propriety that the Psalmist begins by requesting him *to gird it on*, and not suffer it to be inactive in its scabbard, or powerless in the feeble grasp of his ministers.—*Edward Payson.*

Verse 3.—" *O most mighty.*" Christ is almighty, and so able to make good all that he speaketh, and to make his word of precept, promise, and threatening effectual unto the errand for which it is sent.—*David Dickson.*

Verses 3, 4.—We may reflect with pleasure on the glorious cause in which Christ is engaged, and the holy war which he carries on, and in which he shall prosper. It is the cause of truth, of meekness, and righteousness. His gospel, his sword, which is the word of God, tends to rectify our errors by truth ; to control our passions by that meekness which it promotes, and to regulate our lives by the laws of righteousness which it inculcates. Let us rejoice that this sacred cause has hitherto prospered, and shall prosper.—*Job Orton, 1717–1783.*

Verse 4.—" *And in thy majesty ride prosperously,*" etc. The wheels of Christ's chariot, whereupon he rideth when he goeth to conquer and subdue new converts to his kingdom, are *majesty, truth, meekness, righteousness,* manifested in the preaching of his gospel ; *majesty,* when the stately magnificence of his person and offices is declared ; *truth,* when the certainty of all that he teacheth in Scripture is known ; *meekness,* when his grace and mercy is offered to rebels ; and *righteousness,* when justification by faith in his name is clearly set forth. Christ goeth no voyage in vain, he cometh not short of his intent and purpose, but doth the work for which he cometh, preaching the gospel ; *in his majesty, truth, meekness, and righteousness, he rideth prosperously.*—*David Dickson.*

Verse 4.—" *Ride prosperously, because of truth, and meekness, and righteousness.*" The literal translation would be, " Ride on the word of truth, and the meekness of righteousness," and so the Syriac has it. If this rendering be adopted, the meaning will then be, that the great object of Christ's gospel was to vindicate the cause of truth and righteousness in the world. Christ is said to ride on the word of truth, because the knowledge of the truth depends on the word—it is by the word that truth is made known. He is said to ride on the meekness or humility of righteousness, because meekness or humility is its distinguishing characteristic. The former relates to what man is to believe, the latter to how he is to live.—*George Harpur.*

Verse 4.—" *Thy right hand shall teach thee terrible things.*" This expression seems only used to imply, either that by his power he should be enabled to do terrible things, because teaching enables men to do what they are taught, or that by his almighty power he should experimentally see what great and terrible things should be done by him.—*Arthur Jackson.*

Verse 5.—" *Thine arrows are sharp in the heart of the king's enemies.*" In a still bolder metaphor the arrows which are discharged from the bow of Christ are the preachers of the gospel, especially the apostles and evangelists. " *His sagittis,*" says S. Jerome, " *totus orbis vulneratus et captus est.*" Paul, the apostle, was an arrow of the Lord, discharged from his bow from Jerusalem to Illyricum, and from Illyricum to Spain, flying from east to west, and subduing Christ's enemies beneath his feet.—*Christopher Wordsworth.*

Verse 5.—While beseeching the Redeemer to ride forth prosperously, and predicting his success, he seems suddenly to have seen his prayers answered and his predictions fulfilled. He saw his all-conquering Prince gird on his resistless sword, array himself in glory and majesty, ascend the chariot of his gospel, display the banner of his cross, and ride forth, as on the wings of the wind, while the tremendous voice of a herald proclaimed before him : " Prepare ye the way of the Lord," exalt the valleys, and level the hills ; make the crooked ways straight, and the rough places plain ; for, behold, the Lord God comes ; he comes with a strong hand, his reward is with him, and his work before him. From the bright and fiery cloud which enveloped his chariot, and concealed it from mortal eyes, he saw sharp arrows of conviction shot forth on every side, deeply wounding the obdurate hearts of sinners, and prostrating them in crowds around his path, while his right hand extended raised them again, and healed the wounds which his arrows had made ; and his omnipotent voice spoke peace to their despairing souls, and bade them follow in his train, and witness and share in his triumph. From the same bright cloud he saw the vengeful lightnings flashing thick and dreadful, to blast and consume everything that opposed his progress ; he saw sin, and death, and hell, with all its legions, baffled, defeated, and flying in trembling consternation before him ; he saw them overtaken, bound, and chained to his triumphant chariot wheels ; while enraptured voices were heard from heaven exclaiming, " Now is come salvation, and strength, and the kingdom of God, and the power of his Christ." Such was the scene which seems to have burst upon the ravished sight of the entranced prophet. Transported with the view, he exclaims, " *Thine arrows are sharp in the heart of the king's enemies ; whereby the people fall under thee.*"—*Edward Payson.*

Verse 5.—" *The king's enemies,*" is not simply an expression for " Thy enemies," as some think, but rather implies that Christ's kingship is the ground of their enmity ; just as in the second Psalm their cry was, " Let us break their *bands* asunder."—*George Harpur.*

Verse 6.—" *Thy throne, O God.*" The original word, is probably vocative, both in the Greek and in the Hebrew ; and is so taken by modern Unitarians, who seek their refuge by explaining away θεός.—*Henry Alford, D.D.,* on Heb. i. 8.

Verse 7.—" *Thou lovest righteousness, and hatest wickedness.*" Many a one loves righteousness, but would not be its champion ; such a love is not Christ's love. Many a one hates iniquity, not for its own sake, but for the sake of its consequences ; such a hate is not Christ's hate. To be like Christ we must love righteousness as he loved, and hate wickedness as he hated. To love and hate as he loves and hates is to be perfect as he is perfect. The perfection of this love and hate is moral perfection.—*George Harpur.*

Verse 7.—" *Therefore.*" Observe how usual it is to impute Christ's exaltation to his merits. God blessed him for ever, as in the second verse of this Psalm (if such be the sense of that verse), *because* he was fairer than the children of men, and grace was poured into his lips. And so the apostle. God highly exalted him and gave him a name above every name, *because* he had humbled himself, and become obedient unto death. And here God anointed him with the oil of gladness above his fellows, *because* he loved righteousness and hated iniquity.—*George Harpur.*

Verse 7.—" *Therefore.*" He says not, " Wherefore he anointed thee in order to thy being God, or King, or Son, or Word ; " for so he was before, and is for ever, as has been shown ; but rather, " Since thou art God and King, therefore thou wast anointed, since none but thou couldst unite man to the Holy Ghost, thou the image of the Father, in which we were made in the beginning: for thine is even the Spirit."—*Athanasius.*

Verse 7.—" *Therefore God, thy God.*" God was the God of Christ in covenant, that he might be our God in covenant; for in his transactions, whole Christ, Head and members, are to be considered (Gal. iii. 16 ; 1 Cor. xii. 12), the covenant being first transacted with the Head (who is given for a covenant to us, Isa. xlii. 6), and then with the members, with him in reference to us and for us. As God did not fail our surety, but supported him in his great conflict, when out of the depths he called unto him ; so neither will he fail us in time of need. Heb. iv. 16 ; xiii. 5, 6. —*William Troughton.*

Verse 7.—" *Therefore God, thy God, hath anointed thee with the oil of gladness above thy fellows ;* " i.e., enriched and filled thee in a singular and peculiar manner with the fulness of the Spirit, whereby thou art consecrated to thy office ; and by reason whereof thou out-shinest and excellest all the saints who are thy " *fellows,*' or co-partners in these graces. So that in these words you have two parts, namely first, *the saints' dignity ;* and, secondly, *Christ's pre-eminency.* First. *The saints' dignity,* which consists in this, that they are Christ's " *fellows.*" The Hebrew word חֲבֵרֶיךָ, is very full and copious, and is translated consorts, companions, co-partners, partakers ; or, as ours reads it, " *fellows ;* " i.e., such as are partakers with him in the anointing of the Spirit, who do in their measure receive the same Spirit, every Christian being anointed, *modo sibi proportionato,* with the same grace and dignified with the same titles. 1 John ii. 27 ; Rev. i. 6. Christ and the saints are in common one with another. Doth the Spirit of holiness dwell in him ? So he doth in them too. Is Christ King and Priest ? Why, so are they, too, by the grace of union with him. He hath made us kings and priests to God and his Father. This is the saints' dignity, to be Christ's fellows, consorts, or co-partners ; so that look whatever grace or excellency is in Christ, it is not impropriated to himself, but they do share with him ; for indeed he was filled with the fulness of the Spirit for their sakes and use. As the sun is filled with light not to shine to itself, but to others, so is Christ with grace ; and therefore some translate the text not *præ consortibus,* above thy fellows, but *propter consortes,* for thy fellows ;* making Christ the first receptacle of all grace, who first and immediately is filled from the fountain of the Godhead, but it is for his people who receive and derive from him according to their proportion. This is a great truth ; and the dignity of the saints lies chiefly in the partnership with Christ, though our translation, " *above thy fellows,*" suits best both with the importance of the word and scope of the place. Secondly. But then, whatever *dignity* is ascribed herein to the saints, there is, and still must be, a *pre-eminency* acknowledged and ascribed to Christ : if they are anointed with the spirit of grace, much more abundantly is Christ : " *God, thy God, hath anointed thee with the oil of gladness above thy fellows.*"—*John Flavel.*

Verse 7.—" *Oil of gladness.*" For sweet-smelling oils were also used to beautify the face upon occasions of feasting and mirth. Ps. xxiii. 5 ; civ. 15 ; Isa. lxi. 3. And likewise this oil of consecration and infusion of the gifts of the Holy Ghost hath been the cause and foundation of Christ's human nature's obtaining of the everlasting joys and glory. Phil. ii. 9 ; Heb. xii. 2.—*John Diodati.*

Verse 7.—Behold, O ye Arians, and acknowledge even hence the truth. The Psalmist speaks of us all as *fellows* or *partakers* of the Lord, but were he one of things which come out of nothing, and of things generate, he himself had been one of those who partake. But since he hymned him as the eternal God, saying, " *Thy throne, O God, is for ever and ever,*" and has declared that all other things partake of him, what conclusion must we draw, but that he is distinct from generated things, and he only the Father's veritable Word, Radiance, and Wisdom, which all things generate partake, being sanctified by him in Spirit ? And, therefore, he is here " *anointed,*" not that he may become God, for he was so even before ; nor that he may become king, for he had the kingdom eternally, existing as God's image, as the sacred oracle shows ; but in our behalf is this written, as before. For the Israelitish kings, upon their being anointed, then became kings, not being so before, as David, as Ezekias, as Josias, and the rest ; but the Saviour, on the contrary, being God, and ever ruling in the Father's kingdom, and being himself the dispenser of the Holy Ghost, nevertheless is here said to be anointed, that, as before, being said as man to be anointed with the Spirit, he might provide for us more, not only

---

* Rivetus.

exaltation and resurrection, but the indwelling and intimacy of the Spirit. . . . .
And when he received the Spirit, we it was who, by him were made recipients of it.
And, moreover, for this reason, not as Aaron, or David, or the rest, was he anointed
with oil, but in another way, above all his fellows, "*with the oil of gladness*," which
he himself interprets to be the Spirit, saying by the prophet, "The Spirit of the
Lord is upon me, because the Lord hath anointed me;" as also the apostle has
said, "How God anointed him with the Holy Ghost."—*Athanasius*.

Verse 8.—"*All thy garments smell of myrrh, and aloes, and cassia, out of the ivory
palaces, whereby they have made thee glad.*" Although there is considerable obscurity
overhanging these words, still the general idea of *a supereminent fulness of anointing*
is quite apparent, combined, however, with the other idea that the anointing oil
or ointment is of *the most exquisite quality*. Myrrh, and aloes, and cassia were celebrated for their peculiar fragrance, on which account they were used in compounding
the choicest unguents. Myrrh and cassia are mentioned in Ex. xxx. 23, 24, as two
of the spices of which the holy anointing oil was made up. All its ingredients were
considered sacred. The Israelites were forbidden to pour it upon man's flesh, or
to attempt any imitation of it in their own perfumes. Ivory was in early times,
as it still is, rare and costly, and it was highly esteemed as a material for household
decoration, on which the finest workmanship and the most princely expenditure
were displayed. In palaces of ivory, therefore, it was to be expected that, in
correspondence with the magnificence of their structure that the costliness of their
furniture, the ointment employed for anointing would be of the richest perfume,
and in the greatest profusion. According to our version of the Psalm, the divine
Saviour is thus represented as being anointed with oil of the very best kind, even
oil taken from the ivory palaces; and also as receiving it in no ordinary measure.
His anointing was not confined to a few ceremonial drops poured upon the head,
but so abundant is it said to have been, that *all* his garments *smelled* of myrrh, and
aloes, and cassia.

Bishop Horsley has proposed a change in the translation, by which means the
idea of abundance is connected, not with the fragrance arising from the anointing,
but with the anointing itself, which is a different and far more important thing.
"Thy garments are all myrrh, aloes, and cassia, excelling the palaces of ivory,
excelling those which delight thee." This translation, which is strictly literal as
well as poetical, is at the same time comparatively free from obscurity, and it visibly
sets forth, under the most expressive imagery, the surpassing measure of that
anointing which was conferred on our Lord above all his fellows. His garments
are supposed not merely to have been all richly perfumed, or even thoroughly
saturated with the oil of gladness, but to have consisted of the very articles which
entered into the composition of the most precious and odoriferous unguent. "*Thy
garments are all myrrh, aloes, and cassia.*" This is figurative language, but nothing
could more emphatically exhibit how truly "the Spirit rested on Jesus, and abode
with him" in all the plenitude of his heavenly gifts. That heavenly anointing
constituted, as it were, his very dress, "excelling" in the quantity or measure
of the anointing "the palaces of ivory;" because their furnitures, however highly
scented, were not made of aromatic materials. The strength of the perfumes would
evaporate, the fragrance would soon diminish; but permanent as well as plentiful
fragrance is secured to him whose "garments are all myrrh, aloes, and cassia."
It is added, in the way of parallelism, "excelling those which delight in thee,"
or those which make thee glad. To say that the persons here alluded to are the
occupiers of the ivory palaces, might perhaps be objected to as fanciful; but palaces
are the abodes of kings; and anointed kings, either literally, or typically, or
spiritually, are the fellows of the Lord's anointed One; and it does seem manifest
that, as his anointing causes joy and gladness to all the parties concerned in it,
so likewise there is an anointing of those who are honoured to be his fellows which
causes joy and gladness to him. The persons who are in the one verse spoken
of as giving delight to Christ, there is no reason to regard as any other than the
persons spoken of in the former verse as his "*fellows*." And if this is the case,
then we have a comparison drawn betwixt the one and the other in the matter of
their anointing, and to that of Christ a decided superiority is ascribed.—*David
Pitcairn, in "The Anointed Saviour,"* 1846.

Verse 8.—"*All thy garments smell of myrrh,*" etc. These things are true in
Jesus; by his garments is meant his righteousness; for it is written, He clothed

himself with righteousness and zeal. And here the translator hath put in " *smell*," which rather should have been *are*, for " *his garments are* of myrrh, and aloes and cassia," that is, truly purging, cleansing, and making sound ; for his righteousness, which is the righteousness of faith, maketh sound-hearted Christians ; whereas, man's righteousness, which is the righteousness of works, maketh filthy hypocrites. And by " *ivory palaces*," is meant the true faith and fear of God ; for ivory is solid and white, and palaces are king's houses ; and by Christ we are made kings, and our dwelling is in faith and fear of God ; and this is the gladness and joy of our Lord Jesus, that he brings many sons and daughters unto God.—*Richard Coore*, 1683.

Verse 8.—" *Out of the ivory palaces, whereby they have made thee glad.*" Commentators have been more perplexed in explaining these words than any other part of the Psalm. Not to detain you with the various expositions that have been proposed, I will give you what I conceive to be the meaning of the passage. The word rendered " *whereby*," is also the name of a region in Arabia Felix, namely, Minnæa, which, according to the geographer Strabo, " abounded in myrrh and frankincense." Now, it is singular that, according to the historian, Diodorus Siculus, " the inhabitants of Arabia Felix had sumptuous houses, adorned with *ivory* and precious stones." Putting these two things together, therefore, namely, that this region abounded in myrrh and frankincense, and that its inhabitants adorned their houses with ivory, we may, I conceive, find a clue to the Psalmist's meaning. If we substitute " Minnæa " for " whereby," the passage will run thus—

> " Myrrh, aloes, and cassia, are all thy garments,
> From ivory palaces of Minnæa they have made thee glad."

You recollect in the verse just going before, the oil with which Christ was said to be anointed, is called the oil of " *gladness*." Accordingly, he is here said to be made *glad* (it is the same word in both places in the Hebrew), by the spices of which that oil is composed. Those spices are said to have been brought out of the most spicy region of the land of spices, and it is implied that they are the best spices of that spicy region. " *Out of the ivory palaces*," says the Psalmist ; not only houses, but palaces—the mansions of the great, where the best spices would naturally be kept— out of these have come the myrrh, aloes, and cassia, that have composed the oil of gladness whereby thou art made glad. God anointed Christ, when he set him on his everlasting throne, with the oil of gladness ; and this anointing was so profuse, his garments were so overspread with it, that they seemed to be nothing but myrrh, aloes, and cassia. The spices, moreover, of which the anointing oil was composed were the best of their kind, brought, as they were, from the ivory palaces of Minnæa. Such appears to be the Psalmist's meaning ; and when thus understood, the passage becomes most beautifully expressive of the *excellency* and *unmeasured supply* of the gifts and graces of that Spirit with which Christ was anointed by his Father.— *George Harpur*.

Verse 8.—" *The ivory palaces.*" " *The ivory courts.*" Probably so called from the great quantity of ivory used in ornamenting and inlaying them ; as the emperor Nero's palace, mentioned by Suetonius, was named " aurea," or " golden," because " *lita auro*," " overlaid with gold." This method of ornamenting or inlaying rooms was very ancient among the Greeks. Homer, in the fourth book of the Odyssey, seems to mention it, as employed in Menelaus's palace at Lacedæmon ; and that the Romans sometimes ornamented their apartments in like manner, seems evident from Horace and Ovid. So in modern times, the winter apartment of the fair Fatima at Constantinople, has been described by an eye-witness as " wainscotted with inlaid work of mother-of-pearl, *ivory of different colours*, and olive wood." Ivory is likewise employed at Aleppo, as Dr. Russell informs us, in the decoration of some of the more expensive apartments.—*Richard Mant*.

Verse 8.—" *Ivory palaces.*" Either edifices (1 Kings xxii. 39 ; Cant. vii. 14), or ivory coffers, and wardrobes, whence those garments were taken, and are kept.— *Westminster Assembly's Annotations*.

Verse 8.—" *Whereby they have made thee glad.*" The best sense of the phrase— *from which they rejoice thee*—is had by making *they* refer to the *king's daughters* mentioned in the next verse.—*William S. Plumer*.

Verse 8.—Gesenius and Delitzsch consider מני an abbreviated form of the plural מנים (Ps. cv. 4), " strings," or " stringed instruments," and would render thus :— " *Thee glad out of the ivory palaces stringed instruments have made.*"—*Dalman Hapstone*. [With this rendering Ewald and Lange agree.—*J. L. K.*]

Verse 9.—*" Kings' daughters."* Albeit the Catholic church consisting of true converts or real saints be but the one and only true spouse of Christ, yet particular visible churches consisting of saints by calling, by obligation, by profession, and common estimation, their own or others, are many. The true church consisting of true converts (whose praise is of God, to whom only they are certainly known, and not of men), being but one, is compared to the *queen ;* but the particular, whose collections and consociations are known to men, being many, are compared to *ladies of honour* who serve the queen.—*David Dickson.*

Verse 9.—*" The queen."* It is written of Matilda, the empress, that she was the daughter of a king, the mother of a king, and the wife of a king.

Ortu magna, viro major, sed maxima prole,
Hic jacet Henrici filia, nupta, parens.

So David intimates in this hymn, that the church is the daughter of a King, at the 13th verse, " The king's daughter is all glorious within ; " and the mother of a king, at the 16th verse, " Instead of thy fathers shall be thy children, whom thou mayest make princes in all the earth ; " and the wife of a king, in this verse, " *Upon thy right hand did stand the queen,*" as being (I speak in the language of Canaan), spiritually the wedded and bedded wife to the king of glory.—*John Boys.*

Verse 10.—*" Forget also thine own people, and thy father's house."* Three *alls* I expect you to part with, saith Christ. 1. All your sinful lusts, all the ways of the old Adam, our father's house. Ever since Adam's apostacy, God and man have parted houses. Ever since, our father's house is a house of ill manners, a house of sin and wickedness. 2. All your worldly advantages. " If any man come unto me, and hate not his father, and mother, and wife, and children, and brethren, and sisters, yea, and his own life also, he cannot be my disciple." He that hath all these must be ready to part with all ; they are joined not disjunctively but copulatively. 3. All self, self-will, self-righteousness, self-sufficiencies, self-confidences, and self-seekings.—*Lewis Stuckley.*

Verse 10.—*" Forget also thine own people, and thy father's house."* If you see a bee leave a fair flower and stick upon another, you may conclude that she finds most honey-dew in that flower she most sticks upon : so here God's people would never leave so many fair flowers in the world's garden, had they not some other in which they find most sweetness. Christ hath his garden, into which he brings his beloved, and there she finds other manner of flowers than any the world hath, in which there is sweetness of a higher nature, even the honey-dew of the choice mercy and goodness and blessing of God himself : if God's people do leave the full breasts of the world, it is because they have found the breasts of consolation from which they have sucked other manner of sweetness than the breasts of the world can afford.—*Jeremiah Burroughs, in " Moses, his self-denyall."* 1649.

Verse 10.—*" Forget."* If thou be on the mountain, have no love to look back to Sodom. If thou be in the ark, fly not back to the world, as the raven did. If thou be set on Canaan, forget the flesh-pots of Egypt. If marching against Midian, forget stooping to the waters of Harod. Judg. vii. If on the house-top, forget that is below thee. Mark xiii. 15. If thy hand be put to the plough, forget that is behind thee. Luke ix. 62. Themistocles desired rather to learn the art of forgetfulness than of memory. Philosophy is an art of remembering, divinity includes in it an art of forgetting. The first lesson that Socrates taught his scholars was, Remember ; for he thought that knowledge was nothing else but a calling to remembrance of those things the mind knew ere it knew the body. But the first lesson that Christ teacheth his scholars is, *Forget :* " *Forget thine own people ;*" " Repent" (Matt. iv. 17) ; first, " eschew evil," 1 Peter iii. 11.—*Thomas Adams.*

Verse 11.—*" So shall the king greatly desire thy beauty."* This is a most sweet promise. For the Holy Spirit knoweth that this monster, Monk, sticks fast in our heart—that we want to be pure and without spot before God. Thus, under Popery, all my temptation was this. I used to say, " that I would willingly go to the sacrament if I were but worthy." Thus we seek, naturally, a purity in ourselves ; and we examine our whole life and want to find a purity in ourselves, that we might have no need of grace, but might be pronounced righteous upon the grounds of our own merit. . . . Thou wilt certainly never become righteous by thyself and thine own works. . . . The Holy Spirit saith, therefore, I will give thee wholesome counsel ; and if thou wilt hear me, thou shalt become a virgin all fair. For, if thou wouldst be beautiful in the sight of God, so that all thy works should please him, and he should say, " Thy prayer pleaseth me ; all that thou sayest, doest, and thinkest, pleaseth me ! " proceed thou thus : " hear, see, and incline thine ear ; " and thou shalt thus become all fair When thou hast heard, hast seen, hast forgotten all thine own righteousness, all the law, all traditions, and all that monkery, and hast believed, then art thou fair ; not in thine own beauty, but in the beauty of the King who has adorned thee with his Word ; because he has brought unto thee thereby his righteousness, his holiness, truth, and fortitude, and all the gifts of the Holy Spirit. . . The Holy Spirit uses the most exalted language. " *So shall the king greatly desire thy beauty :* " that is, thou wilt by this faith prevail upon him to do whatever thou desirest : so that, as one urged by the power of love, he will spontaneously follow thee, abide with thee, and take up his abode with thee. For wherever God has given his Word, there he does not leave his work which he has begun in thee ; but he brings upon thee first the temptations of the world, the devil, and the flesh ; that by them he may work upon thee. These are his embraces whereby he embraceth his spouse through impatiency of love. . . . The sum of the whole, therefore, is this : That our beauty does not consist in our own virtues, nor even in the gifts which we have received from God, by which we put forth virtues and do all those things which pertain unto the life of the law ; but in this—our apprehending Christ and believing in him. Then it is that we are truly beautiful : and it is this beauty alone that Christ looks upon, and upon no other.—*Martin Luther.*

Verse 11.—In this Psalm Christ is set forth in all his royalty and majesty ; yet he is said " *greatly to desire or delight in the beauty* " of his queen, that is, the graces of the saints ; and that not with an ordinary delight, but he " *greatly* desires ; " his desire is increased as her beauty is. For that is there brought in as a motive unto her to be more holy and conformed unto him, " to incline her ear, and forsake her father's house." " *So shall the king greatly desire thy beauty.*" Christ hath a beauty that pleaseth him as well as we have, though of another kind : and, therefore, ceaseth not till he hath got out every spot and wrinkle out of his spouse's face, as the apostle speaks (Eph. v. 27), " so as to present her glorious unto himself," that is, delightful and pleasing in his eye.—*Thomas Goodwin.*

Verse 12.—" *And the daughter of Tyre shall be there with a gift.*" The daughters of Tyre are the daughters of the Gentiles, the part standing for the whole. Tyre, a city bordering on this country where the prophecy was delivered, typified the nations that were to believe in Christ. Thence came that Canaanitish woman, who was at first called *a dog ;* for that ye may know that she was from thence, the gospel speaks thus (Matt. xv. 21—28), " Jesus departed into the coasts of Tyre and Sidon. And, behold, a woman of Canaan came out of the same coasts," with all the rest that is related there. She who at first, at the house of her " father," and among her " own people," was but *a dog,* who by coming to, and crying after that " King," was made beautiful by believing in him, what did she obtain to hear ? " O woman, great is thy faith." *The King has greatly desired thy beauty.—Augustine.*

Verse 12.—" *With a gift.*" Those who sold their property, came with presents to entreat the face of this " queen," and " laid what they brought at the apostles' feet." Warm then was love in the church.—*Augustine.*

Verse 12.—" *The rich.*" They are, indeed, rich in grace, whose graces are not hindered by riches, whose souls prosper when their bodies prosper, as the apostle John speaks in his third Epistle ; or, who, as 'tis prophesied in this verse, being full of worldly blessings, are yet hungry and eager in their pursuit after Christ. " *The daughter of Tyre shall be there with a gift ; even the rich among the people shall intreat thy favour,*" saith the Psalmist ; that is, either the favour of Christ himself, or the favour of the church, by reason of that spiritual excellence and inward glory which she hath received from Christ. Now, to see the rich bring their gifts, and, which is the thing chiefly aimed at here, giving up themselves to Christ, this is a rare sight, and a remarkable work of grace.—*Joseph Caryl.*

Verse 13.—" *The king's daughter is all glorious within,*" etc. When the children of God recollect their glorious and heavenly pedigree, they endeavour to excel others, both in the beautiful disposition of soul, and manner of life. " *The king's daughter,*" that is, the daughter of the heavenly Father, who is also the bride of the king's Son ; every believing soul " *is all glorious,*" adorned with a holiness not only glorious to herself, but also to the Father and the Bridegroom, and is the beginning of a heavenly glory ; and that chiefly " *within,*" not only when she appears abroad, and presents herself to the view of men, but also when she sits in the inner bed-chamber in the secret exercises of religion, in which she in private pleases the Father and the Bridegroom, who having a regard to the inward man, she above all endeavours to keep that pure and chaste. Her clothing is of " *gold ;*" in comparison of which whatever excellency natural men were even possessed of, is but a shining vanity ; nay, it was " *wrought*" gold, curiously beautified with various resemblances, which represents the perfections of God himself ; and of different colours, on account of the different yet harmoniously corresponding graces of the Holy Spirit ; or of needlework of the Phrygian embroiderers, or rather the work of the cunning workman, mentioned in Cant. vii. 1. Nor is the spouse only beautiful within, but also without ; " holding forth the word of life," Phil. ii. 16, she practises charity, glorifies Christ, edifies her neighbour, and in this manner she is brought unto the king, worthy to be presented to him. This is the only way by which we are to endeavour to obtain familiarity with him, and the sweetest intercourse of the chastest love, both on earth and in heaven.—*Hermann Witsius.* 1636—1708.

Verse 13.—" *The king's daughter is all glorious within.*" The meaning is, either, (1.) that her chief glory consisted in this, that she was admitted to such a familiar privacy with the king ; or, (2.) that when she sat in the inmost rooms of the king's palace, she was there in her greatest glory, because those rooms were most gorgeously set forth with all kinds of bravery and glorious furniture ; or, (3.) that she used to be gloriously attired, not only when she went abroad in public, but also when she stayed within, as being indeed adorned (which may be implied) only for the delight of the king, and not that others might gaze upon her ; or, (4.)—which I like best—that the inward virtues and endowments of her mind were her greatest ornament and glory.—*Arthur Jackson.*

Verse 13.—" *All glorious within.*" Saints must shine by the comeliness of Christ, as a gracious husband labours to change his spouse into his own image and likeness by kindnesses, precepts, and example, that he may take the more delight in her person ; so does our spiritual Solomon change the hue of his Egyptian queen to deem of things and persons as her Lord and husband judges, and frames her spirit to delight in doing his will and pleasure, and take the highest solace in obedience, to enjoy a heavenly freedom, mixed with amiable and joyful reverence. He roots out of her heart all changeable affections and worldly fancies, and hankering longings after the fond fashions of Shechem, and all carnal inclinations to the daughters of Canaan's lineage, and all the beggarly humours of the besotted world, and to pass by with a holy scorn all the pitiful pageantry of this perishing and fading life, and rise to a mean estimate of the baubles and trifles that enchant a carnal heart. At length she arrives to a noble and generous judgment, counting all but dung and dross that she may win Christ. As her prince of life was crucified by the world for her redemption, so she begins to be crucified to it in token of conformity to him, and at length becomes " *all glorious within.*"—*Samuel Lee, in " The Triumph of Mercy,*" 1676.

Verse 13.—·" *Within.*" The ark was pitched within with the same pitch with which it was pitched without withal ; such is the sincere man, within and without alike, inside and outside, all one. Yea, he is rather better than he shows, as the " *king's daughter,*" whose *outside* might sometimes be *sackcloth,* yet was " *all glorious within, and her inward garments of wrought gold.*" Or as the temple, outwardly nothing but wood and stone to be seen, inwardly all rich and beautiful, especially the *sanctum sanctorum* (when the veil was drawn) was all gold. The very floor, as well as the roof, was overlaid with gold. 1 Kings vi. 30.—*John Sheffield.*

Verse 13.—" *Her clothing is of wrought gold.*" Some read it *purled* works, or closures of *gold, enamelled* gold, such as precious *stones* were set in, which were exceeding *splendid* and glorious ; such were the *clothes* of service in the tabernacle, and the garments and robes of the *high priest,* which shadowed forth Christ's *righteousness.* Exod. xxviii. 11—14 ; Exod. xxxix. 1—6.—*William Troughton.*

Verse 13.—About this time, Father La Combe was called to preach on some public occasion. The new doctrine, as it was termed, was not altogether a secret. Public curiosity had become excited. He chose for his text the passage in Psalm xlv. 13, " *The king's daughter is all glorious within : her clothing is of wrought gold.*" By the king he understood *Christ ;* by the king's daughter, *the church.* His doctrine was, whatever might be true in regard to men's original depravity, that those who are truly given to Christ, and are in full harmony with him, are delivered from it: that is to say, are " *all glorious within.*" Like Christ, they love God with a love free from selfishness, with *pure* love. Like Christ, they are come to do the will of the Father. Christ is formed in them. They not only have faith in Christ, and faith in God through Christ, but, as the result of this faith, they have Christ's disposition. They are now in a situation to say of themselves individually, in the language of the apostle Paul, " I live, and yet not I, *but Christ liveth in me.*" He did not maintain that all Christians are necessarily the subjects of this advanced state of Christian experience, but endeavoured to show that this is a *possible* state ; that, however intense human depravity may be, the grace of God has power to overcome it ; that the example of Christ, the full and rich promises, and even the commands, give encouragement to effort, and confidence in ultimate victory.— *From the " Life, Religious Opinions and Experiences of Madame de la Mothe Guyon."*

Verse 14.—" *The virgins, her companions that follow her, shall be brought unto thee.*" The highest and most excellent Christian cannot say, *I* have no *need* of thee : the queen will not be without any of her true *companions.* As it is in the body *natural*, so it is in the church of Christ, or body *mystical ;* all the members being fitly joined together and compacted by that which every joint supplieth, according to the effectual working in the measure of every part, maketh *increase* of the body to the edifying of itself in *love.* Eph. iv. 16 ; Col. ii. 19.—*William Troughton.*

Verse 14.—" *The virgins her companions that follow her.*" These are members of the church, but the figure of a bridal train is employed to sustain the allegory. What a bright train the Royal Bride will have as she goes forth to meet the Bridegroom. Kings' daughters will be there, for every crowned head on earth shall one day bow at the foot of the cross. The daughter of Tyre shall be there—Tyre, the ancient emporium of the nations—to show that the merchandise of the world shall be holiness to the Lord. The kings of Sheba and Seba shall offer gifts. Jews and Gentiles will be there—representatives from all peoples, and tongues, and nations. They are " *virgins.*" They keep themselves unspotted from the world. They are weaned from its idols ; they dread its contaminations. Their first care is to preserve the whiteness of their souls by daily washing in the blood of the Lamb. . . . . They " *follow* " the royal Bride. They keep by her side in storm and sunshine. They follow her in the regeneration. They follow her in the search after her Beloved. Song iii. 2, 3. They follow her to the green pastures and the still waters. They follow her without the camp bearing his reproach. Like Ruth, they leave father and mother to follow her. Ruth i. 16. Like Caleb, they follow the Lord fully. When a crisis comes, and the question, " Who is on the Lord's side ? " involves heavy issues, and hollow-hearted professors fly away like swallows before the storm, they follow her. When persecution comes, and Christ's faithful witnesses have to prophesy clothed in sackcloth, and perhaps to pass through a baptism of blood to the crown, they follow her : like Peden, when—the bloodhounds of persecution in full chase after him, and the lone moor his home—he thought of Richard Cameron gone to glory, and sighed, " Oh, to be with Richie ! "—*Duncan Macgregor, M.A., in " The Shepherd of Israel ; or, Illustrations of the Inner Life,*" 1869.

Verse 15.—" *With gladness and rejoicing shall they be brought.*" No marriage was ever consummated with that triumphal solemnity as the marriage of Christ and believers shall be in heaven. Among the Jews the marriage house was called *bethillulah*—the house of praise ; there was joy on all hands, but not like the joy that will be in heaven when believers, the spouse of Christ, shall be brought thither. *God the Father* will rejoice to behold the blessed accomplishment and consummation of that glorious design and project of his love. *Jesus Christ the Bridegroom* will rejoice to see the travail of his soul, the blessed birth and issue of all his bitter pangs and agonies. Isaiah liii. 11. *The Holy Spirit* will rejoice to see the complement and perfection of that sanctifying design which was committed to his hand (2 Cor. v. 5) ; to see those souls, whom he once found as rough stones, now to shine as the bright polished stones of the spiritual temple. *Angels* will rejoice ; great was the joy when the foundation of this design was laid, in the incarnation of Christ (Luke ii. 13) ; great, therefore, must their joy be when the topstone is set up with shouting, crying, Grace, grace. *The saints* themselves shall rejoice unspeakably, when they shall enter into the king's palace, and be for ever with the Lord. 1 Thess. iv. 17 Indeed, there will be joy on all hands, except among the devils and damned, who shall gnash their teeth with envy, at the everlasting advancement and glory of believers.—*John Flavel.*

Verse 15.—*" They shall be brought."* Reader ! do not fail to observe the manner of expression, the church is *brought*, she doth not *come* of herself. No, she must be convinced, converted, made willing. No one can come to Christ, except the Father, who hath sent Christ, draw him. John vi. 44.—*Robert Hawker, D.D.*

Verse 15.—*" They shall enter into the king's palace."* There are two rich palaces mentioned in this Psalm : the one an ivory palace (verse 8), whereby is signified the assemblies of the saints, and ordinances of divine worship, in which the Lord manifests himself graciously. Here the presence of the Lord is sweet and amiable. Cant. i. 8 ; Psalm lxxxiv. 2. The other " palace " is mentioned in this fifteenth verse, and it is a palace of glory, a palace more bright and splendid than the finest gold, glorious mansions. John xiv. 2.—*William Troughton.*

Verse 16.—*" Instead of thy fathers shall be thy children."* O church of God, think not thyself abandoned then, because thou seest not Peter, nor seest Paul— seest not those through whom thou wast born. Out of thine own offspring has a body of " fathers " been raised up to thee.—*Augustine.*

Verse 16.—*" Thy children, whom thou mayest make princes in all the earth."* The new connexion is glorious to the King. Many were his glorious and royal ancestors down to Jesse, but now there are born to him, the Eternal King, sons as the dew from the womb of the morning (Ps. cx. 3), who shall, as princes, occupy the thrones of the world. So our Lord promised to his disciples, " Verily I say unto you, that ye which have followed me, in the regeneration when the Son of man shall sit in the throne of his glory, ye also shall sit upon twelve thrones, judging the twelve tribes of Israel." Matt. xix. 28. And Paul says, " Do ye not know that the saints shall judge the world ? " 1 Cor. vi. 2.—*Augustus F. Tholuck.*

Verse 16.—*" Princes in all the earth."* Others are but princes in their own dominion, but he will make you princes in all lands. . . . Such a kingdom you shall have, if you will come in to Christ, you shall have the liberty of kings, the abundance and plenty of kings, the power of kings, the victory of kings, and the glory of kings.—*John Preston.*

Verse 17.—*" Therefore shall the people praise thee."* Christ's espousing unto himself a church, and gathering more and more from age to age by his word and Spirit unto it, his converting souls and bringing them into the fellowship of his family, and giving unto them princely minds and affections, wherever they live, is a large matter of growing and everlasting glory unto his majesty ; for in regard of this point, and what is said before in this Psalm, he addeth as the close of all, *" Therefore shall the people praise thee."*—*David Dickson.*

Verse 17.—In the Hebrew text, which is here quoted, there is a particle added to the word *ever*, which in that case intendeth a proper everlastingness, without any period or end at all, and thereupon translated *" for ever and ever."*—*William Gouge, D.D.* on Hebrews i. 8.

Verse 17 (last clause) :—

" When morning gilds the skies,
My heart awaking cries ;
    May Jesus Christ be praised.

    *   *   *   *

When sleep her balm denies,
My silent spirit sighs ;
    May Jesus Christ be praised.

    *   *   *   *   *

In heaven's eternal bliss,
The loveliest strain is this ;
    May Jesus Christ be praised.

    *   *   *   *

To God the Word on high,
The hosts of angels cry ;
    May Jesus Christ be praised.

Let mortals, too, upraise
Their voice in hymns of praise;
   May Jesus Christ be praised.

Let earth's wide circle round,
In joyful notes resound;
   May Jesus Christ be praised.

Let air, and sea, and sky,
From depth to height reply;
   May Jesus Christ be praised.

Be this while life is mine,
My canticle divine;
   May Jesus Christ be praised.

Be this the eternal song
Through all the ages on;
   May Jesus Christ be praised."

Translated by Edward Caswall, in " Poems," 1861.

HINTS TO PREACHERS.

Verse 1.—In the preface, the prophet commends the subject he is to treat of, signifying, 1. That it is *a good matter—good,* as speaking of the Son of God, who is the *chief good.* 2. *Good for us ;* for upon the marriage of Christ to his church depends our good.—*Bishop Nicholson.*

Verse 1.—Character read by heart-writing. I. The true lover of Christ is sincere —" *my heart* " ? II. He is a man of emotion. III. A man of holy meditation. IV. A man of experience—" *things I have made.*" V. A man who bears witness for the Lord.

Verse 1.—Three things requisite for Christian teaching : I. That the matter be good ; and concerning the best of all subjects, " *touching the King.*" II. That the language be fluent like the pen, etc. 1. Partly from nature. 2. Partly from cultivation. 3. Partly from the Spirit of God. III. That the heart be absorbed in it—" *My heart is inditing.*"—*G. R.*

Verse 2.—In what respects Jesus is fairer than the best of men.

Verse 2.—Jesus—his person, his gospel, his fulness of blessing.

Verse 2.—I. We may and ought to praise Christ. Angels do, God does, Scripture does, Old Testament saints and New, so should we. It is the work of heaven begun on earth. II. For what should we praise him ? 1. For his beauty. Is wisdom beauty ? Is righteousness ? Is love ? Is meekness ? All are found in him supremely—

    " All human beauties, all divine,
    In our Redeemer meet and shine."

2. For his grace. Grace of God treasured up in him. 3. For his blessedness—of God and for ever.—*G. R.*

Verses 2—5.—In these verses the Lord Jesus is presented, I. As most amiable in himself. II. As the great favourite of heaven. III. As victorious over his enemies.—*Matthew Henry.*

Verse 3.—The captain's presence desired by the soldier. It is our honour, our delight, our safety, our strength, our victory, our reward.

Verses 3—5.—Messiah's victory predicted and desired.—*E. Payson's Sermon.*

Verse 5.—I. Arrows of judicial wrath are sharp. II. Arrows of providential goodness are sharper still. III. Arrows of subduing grace are sharpest of all. The quiver of the Almighty is full of these arrows.—*G. R.*

Verse 5.—Arrows—what they are ; whose they are ; whom they strike ; where they strike ; what they do, and what follows.

Verse 6.—The God, the king, his throne, its duration, his sceptre.   Let us worship, obey, trust, acquiesce, rejoice.

Verses 6, 7.—Empire, Eternity, Equity, Establishment, Exultation.

Verse 7.—" *Thou hatest wickedness.*"   He hated it when it assailed him in his temptation, hated it in others, denounced it, died to slay it, will come to condemn it.

Verse 7.—Christ's love and hate.

Verse 8.—Christ's garments—his offices, his two natures, his ordinances, his honours, all are full of fragrance.

Verse 8.—" *Whereby they have made thee glad.*"   We make Jesus glad by our love, our praise, our service, our gifts, our holiness, our fellowship with him.

Verse 8.—I. The odour of his garments, not of blood and battle, but of sweet perfume.   II. The splendour of his palaces—ivory for rareness, purity, durability, etc.   III. The source of his delight.   1. Himself, the sweet odour of his own graces. 2. His people, the savour of those who are saved.   3. His enemies, " even in them that perish."   4. All holy happy creatures who unite to make him glad.—*G. R.*

Verse 10.—" Christ the best husband : or, an earnest invitation to young women to come and see Christ."—*George Whitefield's* " *Sermon, Preached to a Society of Young Women, in Fetter Lane.*"

Verses 9, 10.—I. The connections of the Bridegroom are to be remembered, those of the Bride to be forgotten.

Verse 11.—" *So shall the king greatly desire thy beauty.*"   Christ delighting in the Beauty of the Righteous.—*Martin Luther.*   [*Select Works, by H. Cole.*   I. 281.]

Verses 13—15.—I. The Bride's *new name*—" The king's daughter."   She is the king's daughter for two reasons.   1. She is *born* of God ; and 2. She is *espoused* to the Son of God.   II. The Bride's *character*—" All glorious within."   1. Because *Christ reigns on the throne of her heart.*   2. Because *she is the temple of the Holy Ghost.* III. The Bride's *raiment*—" wrought gold," " needlework : " this is the *righteousness of Christ ;* in other words, 1. His *perfect obedience.*   2. His *atoning death.*   IV. The Bride's *companions*—" Virgins that follow her."   V. The Bride's *home-going*— " She shall be brought unto the king in raiment of needlework. . . . . With gladness and rejoicing shall they be brought : they shall enter into the king's palace."   1. *She shall see the king in his beauty.*   2. *There will be an open declaration of his love to her before all worlds.*—*Duncan Macgregor, M.A.*

Verse 14.—I. The presentation of the church to Christ.   1. When souls are first brought to him—" I have espoused you as," etc.   2. When they come before him at death.   3. When the perfected church is presented to him—" That he might present it," etc.   II. The manner of presentation—1. " in raiment," etc., such as he himself wrought out.   2. With all her followers.   (1.) Their purity—" virgins." (2.) Their fellowship—" companions."   (3.) Their succession—" that follow thee," from one age to another until they are complete.—*G. R.*

Verse 17.—I. Christ is the Father's delight.   " *I* will make," etc.   II. He is the church's theme—his name shall be remembered ; and III. He is heaven's glory, " Shall praise thee," etc.—*G. R.*

PSALM XLVI.

TITLE.—To the Chief Musician.—*He who could sing other Psalms so well was fitly entrusted with this noble ode. Trifles may be left to commoner songsters, but the most skilful musician in Israel must be charged with the due performance of this song, with the most harmonious voices and choicest music.* For the Sons of Korah. *One alone cannot fulfil the praise, there must be picked choristers under him, whose joyful privilege it shall be to celebrate the service of song in the house of the Lord. As to why the Sons of Korah were selected, see our remarks at the head of Psalm XLII. It may be well to add that they were a division of the Levites who took their turn in serving at the temple. All the works of holy service ought not to be monopolised by one order of talent, each company of believers should in due course enjoy the privilege. None ought to be without a share in the service of God.*

A Song upon Alamoth. *Which may denote that the music was to be pitched high for the treble or soprano voices of the Hebrew virgins. They went forth in their dances to sing the praises of David when he smote the Philistine, it was meet that they should make merry and be glad when the victories of Jehovah became their theme. We need to praise God upon virgin hearts, with souls chaste towards his fear, with lively and exalted expressions, and gladsome strains. Or the word Alamoth may refer to shrill-sounding instruments, as in 1 Chron. xv. 20, where we read that Zechariah, and Eliab, and Benaiah were to praise the Lord " with psalteries on Alamoth." We are not always, in a slovenly manner, to fall into one key, but with intelligence are to modulate our praises and make them fittingly expressive of the occasion and the joy it creates in our souls. These old musical terms cannot be interpreted with certainty, but they are still useful because they show that care and skill should be used in our sacred music.*

SUBJECT.—*Happen what may, the Lord's people are happy and secure, this is the doctrine of the Psalm, and it might, to help our memories, be called* THE SONG OF HOLY CONFIDENCE, *were it not that from the great reformer's love to this soul-stirring hymn it will probably be best remembered as* LUTHER'S PSALM.

DIVISION.—*It is divided by inspired authority into three parts, each of which ends with Selah.*

EXPOSITION.

GOD *is* our refuge and strength, a very present help in trouble.

2 Therefore will not we fear, though the earth be removed, and though the mountains be carried into the midst of the sea;

3 *Though* the waters thereof roar *and* be troubled, *though* the mountains shake with the swelling thereof. Selah.

1. *" God is our refuge and strength."* Not our armies, or our fortresses. Israel's boast is in Jehovah, the only living and true God. Others vaunt their impregnable castles, placed on inaccessible rocks and secured with gates of iron, but God is a far better refuge from distress than all these : and when the time comes to carry the war into the enemy's territories, the Lord stands his people in better stead than all the valour of legions or the boasted strength of chariot and horse. Soldiers of the cross, remember this, and count yourselves safe, and make yourselves strong in God. Forget not the personal possessive word " *our* ;" make sure each one of your portion in God, that you may say, " He is *my* refuge and strength." Neither forget the fact that God is our refuge just now, in the immediate present, as truly as when David penned the word. God alone is our all in all. All other refuges are refuges of lies, all other strength is weakness, for power belongeth unto God : but as God is all-sufficient, our defence and might are equal to all emergencies. *" A very present help in trouble,"* or *in distresses he has so been found,* he has been tried and proved by his people. He never withdraws himself from his afflicted. He is their help, truly, effectually, constantly ; he is present or near them, close at their side and ready for their succour, and this is emphasised by the word " *very* " in our version, he is more present than friend or relative can be, yea, more nearly

present than even the trouble itself. To all this comfortable truth is added the consideration that his assistance comes at the needed time. He is not as the swallows that leave us in the winter ; he is a friend in need and a friend indeed. When it is very dark with us, let brave spirits say, " Come, let us sing the forty-sixth Psalm."

> " A fortress firm, and steadfast rock,
> Is God in time of danger ;
> A shield and sword in every shock,
> From foe well-known or stranger."

2. " *Therefore.*" How fond the Psalmist is of therefores ! his poetry is no poetic rapture without reason, it is as logical as a mathematical demonstration. The next words are a necessary inference from these. " *Will not we fear.*" With God on our side, how irrational would fear be ! Where he is all power is, and all love, why therefore should we quail ? " *Though the earth be removed,*" though the basis of all visible things should be so convulsed as to be entirely changed. " *And though the mountains be carried into the midst of the sea ;* " though the firmest of created objects should fall to headlong ruin, and be submerged in utter destruction. The two phrases set forth the most terrible commotions within the range of imagination, and include the overthrow of dynasties, the destruction of nations, the ruin of families, the persecutions of the church, the reign of heresy, and whatever else may at any time try the faith of believers. Let the worst come to the worst, the child of God should never give way to mistrust ; since God remaineth faithful there can be no danger to his cause or people. When the elements shall melt with fervent heat, and the heavens and the earth shall pass away in the last general conflagration, we shall serenely behold " the wreck of matter, and the crash of worlds," for even then our refuge shall preserve us from all evil, our strength shall prepare us for all good.

3. " *Though the waters thereof roar and be troubled.*" When all things are excited to fury, and reveal their utmost power to disturb, faith smiles serenely. She is not afraid of noise, nor even of real force, she knows that the Lord stilleth the raging of the sea, and holdeth the waves in the hollow of his hand. " *Though the mountains shake with the swelling thereof.*" Alps and Andes may tremble, but faith rests on a firmer basis, and is not to be moved by swelling seas. Evil may ferment, wrath may boil, and pride may foam, but the brave heart of holy confidence trembles not. Great men who are like mountains may quake for fear in times of great calamity, but the man whose trust is in God needs never be dismayed.

" *Selah.*" In the midst of such a hurly-burly the music may well come to a pause, both to give the singers breath, and ourselves time for meditation. We are in no hurry, but can sit us down and wait while earth dissolves, and mountains rock, and oceans roar. Ours is not the headlong rashness which passes for courage, we can calmly confront the danger, and meditate upon terror, dwelling on its separate items and united forces. The pause is not an exclamation of dismay, but merely a rest in music : we do not suspend our song in alarm, but retune our harps with deliberation amidst the tumult of the storm. It were well if all of us could say, " *Selah,*" under tempestuous trials, but alas ! too often we speak in our haste, lay our trembling hands bewildered among the strings, strike the lyre with a rude crash, and mar the melody of our life-song.

4 *There is* a river, the streams whereof shall make glad the city of God, the holy *place* of the tabernacles of the Most High.

5 God *is* in the midst of her ; she shall not be moved : God shall help her, *and that* right early.

6 The heathen raged, the kingdoms were moved : he uttered his voice, the earth melted.

7 The Lord of hosts is with us ; the God of Jacob *is* our refuge. Selah.

4. " *There is a river.*" Divine grace like a smoothly flowing, fertilising, full, and never-failing river, yields refreshment and consolation to believers. This is the river of the water of life, of which the church above as well as the church below partakes evermore. It is no boisterous ocean, but a placid stream, it is not stayed in its course by earthquakes or crumbling mountains, it follows its serene course without disturbance. Happy are they who know from their own experience that

there is such a river of God. "*The streams whereof*" in their various influences, for they are many, "*shall make glad the city of God*," by assuring the citizens that Zion's Lord will unfailingly supply all their needs. The streams are not transient like Cherith, nor muddy like the Nile, nor furious like Kishon, nor treacherous like Job's deceitful brooks, neither are their waters "naught" like those of Jericho, they are clear, cool, fresh, abundant, and gladdening. The great fear of an Eastern city in time of war was lest the water supply should be cut off during a siege; if that were secured the city could hold out against attacks for an indefinite period. In this verse, Jerusalem, which represents the church of God, is described as well supplied with water, to set forth the fact, that in seasons of trial all-sufficient grace will be given to enable us to endure unto the end. The church is like a well-ordered city, surrounded with mighty walls of truth and justice, garrisoned by omnipotence, fairly built and adorned by infinite wisdom: its burgesses the saints enjoy high privileges; they trade with far-off lands, they live in the smile of the King; and as a great river is the very making and mainstay of a town, so is the broad river of everlasting love and grace their joy and bliss. The church is peculiarly the "*City of God*," of his designing, building, election, purchasing and indwelling. It is dedicated to his praise, and glorified by his presence. "*The holy place of the tabernacles of the Most High.*" This was the peculiar glory of Jerusalem, that the Lord within her walls had a place where he peculiarly revealed himself, and this is the choice privilege of the saints, concerning which we may cry with wonder, "Lord, how is it that thou wilt manifest thyself unto us, and not unto the world?" To be a temple for the Holy Ghost is the delightful portion of each saint, to be the living temple for the Lord our God is also the high honour of the church in her corporate capacity. Our God is here called by a worthy title, indicating his power, majesty, sublimity, and excellency; and it is worthy of note that under this character he dwells in the church. We have not a great God in nature, and a little God in grace; no, the church contains as clear and convincing a revelation of God as the works of nature, and even more amazing is the excellent glory which shines between the cherubim overshadowing that mercy-seat which is the centre and gathering place of the people of the living God. To have the Most High dwelling within her members, is to make the church on earth like the church in heaven.

5. "*God is in the midst of her.*" His help is therefore sure and near. Is she besieged, then he is himself besieged within her, and we may be certain that he will break forth upon his adversaries. How near is the Lord to the distresses of his saints, since he sojourns in their midst! Let us take heed that we do not grieve him; let us have such respect to him as Moses had when he felt the sand of Horeb's desert to be holy, and put off his shoes from off his feet when the Lord spake from the burning bush. "*She shall not be moved.*" How can she be moved unless her enemies move her Lord also? His presence renders all hope of capturing and demolishing the city utterly ridiculous. The Lord is in the vessel, and she cannot, therefore, be wrecked. "*God shall help her.*" Within her he will furnish rich supplies, and outside her walls he will lay her foes in heaps like the armies of Sennacherib, when the angel went forth and smote them. "*And that right early.*" As soon as the first ray of light proclaims the coming day, at the turning of the morning God's right arm shall be outstretched for his people. The Lord is up betimes. We are slow to meet him, but he is never tardy in helping us. Impatience complains of divine delays, but in very deed the Lord is not slack concerning his promise. Man's haste is often folly, but God's apparent delays are ever wise; and, when rightly viewed, are no delays at all. To-day the bands of evil may environ the church of God, and threaten her with destruction; but ere long they shall pass away like the foam on the waters, and the noise of their tumult shall be silent in the grave. The darkest hour of the night is just before the turning of the morning; and then, even then, shall the Lord appear as the great ally of his church.

6. "*The heathen raged.*" The nations were in a furious uproar, they gathered against the city of the Lord like wolves ravenous for their prey; they foamed, and roared, and swelled like a tempestuous sea. "*The kingdoms were moved.*" A general confusion seized upon society; the fierce invaders convulsed their own dominions by draining the population to urge on the war, and they desolated other territories by their devastating march to Jerusalem. Crowns fell from royal heads, ancient thrones rocked like trees driven of the tempest, powerful empires fell like pines uprooted by the blast: everything was in disorder, and dismay seized on all who knew not the Lord. "*He uttered his voice, the earth melted.*" With no other

instrumentality than a word the Lord ruled the storm. He gave forth a voice and stout hearts were dissolved, proud armies were annihilated, conquering powers were enfeebled. At first the confusion appeared to be worse confounded, when the element of divine power came into view; the very earth seemed turned to wax, the most solid and substantial of human things melted like the fat of rams upon the altar; but anon peace followed, the rage of man subsided, hearts capable of repentance relented, and the implacable were silenced. How mighty is a word from God! How mighty the Incarnate Word. O that such a word would come from the excellent glory even now to melt all hearts in love to Jesus, and to end for ever all the persecutions, wars, and rebellions of men!

7. "*The Lord of hosts is with us.*" This is the reason for all Zion's security, and for the overthrow of her foes. The Lord rules the angels, the stars, the elements, and all the hosts of heaven; and the heaven of heavens are under his sway. The armies of men though they know it not are made to subserve his will. This Generalissimo of the forces of the land, and the Lord High Admiral of the seas, is on our side—our august ally; woe unto those who fight against him, for they shall fly like smoke before the wind when he gives the word to scatter them. "*The God of Jacob is our refuge.*" Immanuel is Jehovah of Hosts, and Jacob's God is our high place of defence. When this glad verse is sung to music worthy of such a jubilate, well may the singers pause and the players wait awhile to retune their instruments; here, therefore, fitly stands that solemn, stately, peaceful note of rest, SELAH.

8 Come, behold the works of the LORD, what desolations he hath made in the earth.

9 He maketh wars to cease unto the end of the earth; he breaketh the bow, and cutteth the spear in sunder; he burneth the chariot in the fire.

10 Be still, and know that I *am* God: I will be exalted among the heathen, I will be exalted in the earth.

11 The LORD of hosts *is* with us; the God of Jacob *is* our refuge. Selah.

8. "*Come, behold the works of the Lord.*" The joyful citizens of Jerusalem are invited to go forth and view the remains of their enemies, that they may mark the prowess of Jehovah and the spoil which his right hand hath won for his people. It were well if we also carefully noted the providential dealings of our covenant God, and were quick to perceive his hand in the battles of his church. Whenever we read history it should be with this verse sounding in our ears. We should read the newspaper in the same spirit, to see how the Head of the Church rules the nations for his people's good, as Joseph governed Egypt for the sake of Israel. "*What desolations he hath made in the earth.*" The destroyers he destroys, the desolators he desolates. How forcible is the verse at this date! The ruined cities of Assyria, Babylon, Petra, Bashan, Canaan, are our instructors, and in tables of stone record the doings of the Lord. In every place where his cause and crown have been disregarded ruin has surely followed; sin has been a blight on nations, and left their palaces to lie in heaps. In the days of the writer of this Psalm, there had probably occurred some memorable interposition of God against his Israel's foes; and as he saw their overthrow, he called on his fellow citizens to come forth and attentively consider the terrible things in righteousness which had been wrought on their behalf. Dismantled castles and ruined abbeys in our own land stand as memorials of the Lord's victories over oppression and superstition. May there soon be more of such desolations.

> "Ye gloomy piles, ye tombs of living men,
> Ye sepulchres of womanhood, or worse;
> Ye refuges of lies, soon may ye fall,
> And 'mid your ruins may the owl, and bat,
> And dragon find congenial resting place."

9. "*He maketh wars to cease unto the end of the earth.*" His voice quiets the tumult of war, and calls for the silence of peace. However remote and barbarous the tribe, he awes the people into rest. He crushes the great powers till they cannot provoke strife again; he gives his people profound repose. "*He breaketh the bow,*" the sender of swift-winged death he renders useless. "*And cutteth the spear in sunder*"—the lance of the mighty man he shivers. "*He burneth the chariot in the*

fire"—the proud war-chariot with its death-dealing scythes he commits to the flames. All sorts of weapons he piles heaps on heaps, and utterly destroys them. So was it in Judea in the days of yore, so shall it be in all lands in eras yet to come. Blessed deed of the Prince of Peace ! when shall it be literally performed ? Already the spiritual foes of his people are despoiled of their power to destroy ; but when shall the universal victory of peace be celebrated, and instruments of wholesale murder be consigned to ignominious destruction ? How glorious will the ultimate victory of Jesus be in the day of his appearing, when every enemy shall lick the dust !

10. "*Be still, and know that I am God.*" Hold off your hands, ye enemies ! Sit down and wait in patience, ye believers ! Acknowledge that Jehovah is God, ye who feel the terrors of his wrath ! Adore him, and him only, ye who partake in the protections of his grace. Since none can worthily proclaim his nature, let " expressive silence muse his praise." The boasts of the ungodly and the timorous forebodings of the saints should certainly be hushed by a sight of what the Lord has done in past ages. "*I will be exalted among the heathen.*" They forget God, they worship idols, but Jehovah will yet be honoured by them. Reader, the prospects of missions are bright, bright as the promises of God. Let no man's heart fail him ; the solemn declarations of this verse must be fulfilled. "*I will be exalted in the earth,*" among all people, whatever may have been their wickedness or their degradation. Either by terror or love God will subdue all hearts to himself. The whole round earth shall yet reflect the light of his majesty. All the more because of the sin, and obstinacy, and pride of man shall God be glorified when grace reigns unto eternal life in all corners of the world.

11. "*The Lord of hosts is with us ; the God of Jacob is our refuge.*" It was meet to sing this twice over. It is a truth of which no believer wearies, it is a fact too often forgotten, it is a precious privilege which cannot be too often considered. Reader, is the Lord on thy side ? Is Emmanuel, God with us, thy Redeemer ? Is there a covenant between thee and God as between God and Jacob ? If so, thrice happy art thou. Show thy joy in holy song, and in times of trouble play the man by still making music for thy God.

SELAH. Here as before, lift up the heart. Rest in contemplation after praise. Still keep the soul in tune. It is easier to sing a hymn of praise than to continue in the spirit of praise, but let it be our aim to maintain the uprising devotion of our grateful hearts, and so end our song as if we intended it to be continued.

> SELAH bids the music rest,
> Pause in silence soft and blest ;
> SELAH bids uplift the strain,
> Harps and voices tune again ;
> SELAH ends the vocal praise,
> Still your hearts to God upraise.

EXPLANATORY NOTES AND QUAINT SAYINGS.

Title.—The LXX referring to the notion of the theme עֹלַם, *occultavit*, render it ὑπὲρ τῶν κρυφίων, *for the hidden ;* and the Latin, *pro arcanis ;* and the rest of the ancient interpreters take the same course ; the Chaldee referring it to *Coreh,* and those that were *hidden, i.e., swallowed up,* by the earth with him, whilst these *sons of Coreh* escaped ; as if the mention of the *sons of Coreh* in the title, by whom this song was to be sung, referred the whole Psalm to that story. Accordngly, verse 2, when the Hebrew reads, "*Though the earth be removed,*" the paraphrase is, " *When our fathers were changed from the earth.*"—*Henry Hammond.*

Title.—The title is peculiar, "*Upon Alamoth,*" suggesting "*a choir of virgins,*" as if this virgin-choir were selected to sing a Psalm that tells of perils and fears and alarms abounding, in order to show that even the feeble virgins may in that day sing without dread, because of "*The Mighty One*" on their side.—*Andrew A. Bonar.*

Title.—"*Upon Alamoth.*" [To be sung] *en soprano.*—*Armand de Mestral, quoted by Perowne.*

Whole Psalm.—We sing this Psalm to the praise of God, because God is with us, and powerfully and miraculously preserves and defends his church and his word, against all fanatical spirits, against the gates of hell, against the implacable hatred of the devil, and against all the assaults of the world, the flesh and sin.—*Martin Luther.*

Whole Psalm.—Luther and his companions, with all their bold readiness for danger and death in the cause of truth, had times when their feelings were akin to those of a divine singer, who said, " Why art thou cast down, O my soul ? " But in such hours the unflinching Reformer would cheerily say to his friend Melancthon, " Come, Philip, let us sing the forty-sixth Psalm ; " and they could sing it in Luther's own characteristic version :—

> A sure stronghold our God is He,
> A timely shield and weapon ;
> Our help he'll be, and set us free
> From every ill can happen.
>
> *   *   *   *   *
>
> And were the world with devils filled,
> All eager to devour us,
> Our souls to fear shall little yield,
> They cannot overpower us.

S. W. Christopher, in " Hymn Writers and their Hymns."

Verse 1.—" *God is our refuge and strength,*" etc. It begins abruptly, but nobly ; ye may trust in whom and in what ye please ; but GOD (ELOHIM) *is our refuge and strength.* " *A very present help.*" A help found to be very powerful and effectual in straits and difficulties. The words are very emphatic : עֶזְרָה בְצָרוֹת נִמְצָא מְאֹד, *ezrah betsaroth nimtsa meod,* " He is found an exceeding, or superlative, help in difficulties." Such we have found him, and therefore celebrate his praise.—*Adam Clarke.*

Verse 2.—" *Though the earth be removed.*" John Wesley preached in Hyde-park, on the occasion of the earthquake felt in London, March 8, 1750, and repeated these words. Charles Wesley composed Hymn 67, Wesley's Collection, the following lines of which illustrate this verse :—

> How happy then are we,
> Who build, O Lord, on thee !
> What can our foundation shock ?
> Though the shatter'd earth remove,
> Stands our city on a rock,
> On the rock of heavenly love.

Verses 2, 3.—The earth thrown into a state of wild confusion, the mountains hurled into the mighty deep, the sea tossed into a tempest, and the everlasting hills drifting on its foaming billows, are the vivid images by which the divine judgments on wicked and persecuting nations are described in the language of the prophets.—*John Morison.*

Verses 2, 3, 5.—Palestine was frequently subject to earthquakes, as might have been expected from its physical character and situation ; and it is a remarkable circumstance, that although all other parts of the land seem to have been occasionally the scene of those terrible convulsions, the capital was almost wholly free from them. Mount Moriah, or the hill of vision, was so called from its towering height, which made it a conspicuous object in the distance. It stands in the centre of a group of hills, which surround it in the form of an amphitheatre, and it was chiefly to this position, under the special blessing of God, that it stood firm and immovable amid the frequent earthquakes that agitated and ravaged the Holy Land.—*Paxton's Illustrations of Scripture.*

Verse 3.—" *Selah.*" See " Treasury of David," Vol. I., pp. 23, 26, 27 ; and Vol. II., pp. 224—227.

Verse 4.—" *There is a river, the streams whereof shall make glad the city of God.*" What is the *river* that makes glad the city of God ? I answer, God himself is the river, as in the following verse, " *God is in the midst of her.*" 1. God the *Father* is the river : " For my people have committed two evils ; they have forsaken me the fountain of living waters, and hewed them out cisterns, broken cisterns, that can hold no water." Jer. ii. 13. 2. God the *Son* is the river, the fountain of salvation : " In that day there shall be a fountain opened to the house of David, and to the inhabitants of Jerusalem for sin and for uncleanness." Zech. xiii. 1. 3. God the *Spirit* is the river : " He that believeth on me, as the Scripture hath said, out of his belly shall flow rivers of living water." " Whosoever drinketh of the water that I shall give him shall never thirst ; but the water that I shall give him shall be in him a well of water springing up into everlasting life." John vii. 38 ; iv. 14. What are the *streams* of this river ? Answer—the *perfections* of God, the *fulness* of Christ, the *operations* of the Spirit, and these running in the *channel* of the *covenant of promise.—Ralph Erskine.*

Verse 4.—" *There is a river,"* etc. This is that flood which Ezekiel beheld in vision, the waters that came down from the right side of the house, and rising first to the ancles—then as the prophet passed onward, to the knees—then to the loins— became afterwards a river that he could not pass over ; for the waters were risen, waters to swim in, a river that could not be passed over. Shall we see in this, with the angelic doctor, the river of grace which burst forth from Mount Calvary ? streams branching off hither and thither, the *pelagim* of the Hebrew—" to satisfy the desolate and waste ground, and to cause the bud of the tender herb to spring forth." Job xxxviii. O " fountain of gardens," " well of living waters," " streams from Lebanon," how do you, the " nether springs " of this world, bring to us something of the ever-lasting loveliness and peace of those " upper springs," by which the beautiful flock now feed and lie down, none making them afraid ! Or with S. Ambrose and S. Bernard, understand the verse of the " river of water of life, clear as crystal, proceeding from the throne of God and of the Lamb." And then the rivers of that flood shall indeed " *make glad the city of God,"* the house not made with hands, eternal in the heavens, where is the tree of life, that beareth twelve manner of fruits, and yieldeth her fruit every month ; that country and that river of which the old liturgies say, " They who rest in the bosom of Abraham are in the tabernacles of joy and rest, in the dwellings of light, in the world of pleasure, in the church of the true Jerusalem, where there is no place for affliction, nor way of sadness, where there are no wars with the flesh, and no resistance to temptation, where sin is forgotten, and past danger is only remembered as a present pleasure."—*Thomas Aquinas, Ambrose, and Bernard, in Neale's Commentary.*

Verse 4.—" *There is a river."* The river of God that flows from his throne. No enemy can cut off this stream from the church of Christ. Observe the reference to Isaiah xxxvi. 2 ; xxxvii. 25, compared with 2 Chron. xxxii. 2—4. These gently flowing, but full streams, are contrasted with the roaring waves of the sea.—*T. C. Barth.*

Verse 4.—" *There is a river,"* etc. The allusion is either to the river Kidron, which ran by Jerusalem, or to the waters of Shiloah, which by different courses and branches ran through the city of Jerusalem, and supplied the several parts of it with water, to the joy and comfort of its inhabitants. But the words are to be understood in a figurative sense, as applicable to gospel times ; and this river either designs the gospel, the streams of which are its doctrines, which are living waters, that went out from Jerusalem, and which publish glad tidings of great joy to all sensible sinners ; or the Spirit and his graces, which are compared to a well and rivers of living water, in the exercises of which the saints have much joy and peace ; or else the Lord himself, who is the place of broad rivers and streams to his people, and is both their refreshment and protection ; or rather his everlasting love to them is here intended.—*John Gill.*

Verse 4.—Compared with the waterless deserts around, Judæa and Jerusalem were well watered, and drought pressed more severely on the besiegers than the besieged. The allusion here is to the well-known rill and pool of Siloam. So in Isaiah viii. 6, the blessing of God's protection is represented by the waters of Siloah, which go softly.—*From " The Psalms Chronologically arranged. By Four Friends,"* 1867.

Verse 4.—" *The city."* The church of God is like a city, 1. Because a city is a place of *security.* 2. A place of *society :* what one wants another supplies ; they have mutual fellowship. 3. A place of *unity,* that people may therein live in peace and concord. 4. A place of *trade* and *traffic.* Here is the market of free grace : " Ho, every one that thirsteth," etc. Here is the *pearl of great price* exposed for sale. 5. A place of *freedom*, and *liberty*, freedom from the guilt of sin, wrath of God, curse of the law, present evil world, bondage to Satan, etc., etc. 6. A place of *order* and *regularity ;* it hath its constitutions and ordinances. 7. A place of *rest*, and commodious to live in, and thus it is opposed to the wilderness. 8. A place of *privileges*. 9. A place of *pomp* and *splendour ;* there is the king, the court, the throne. 10. A place of *pleasure* and *beauty*, Psalm xlviii. 2.—*Ralph Erskine*.

Verse 5.—" *God is in the midst of her.*" It is the real presence of Christ, and the supernatural power of his Spirit, which makes the church mighty to the conquest of souls. The church spreads because her " *God is in the midst of her.*" When at any time she has forgotten her dependence on the invisible intercession of her Head, and the gracious energy of his Spirit, she has found herself shorn of the locks of her great strength, and has become the laughing-stock of the Philistines. —*William Binnie, D.D.*

Verse 5.—" *God is in the midst of her.*" etc. The enemies of the church may toss her as waves but they shall not split her as rocks. She may be dipped in water as a *feather*, but shall not sink therein as *lead*. He that is a well of water within her to keep her from fainting, will also prove a wall of fire about her to preserve her from falling. *Tried* she may be, but *destroyed* she cannot be. Her foundation is the Rock of Ages, and her defence the everlasting Arms. It is only such fabrics as are bottomed upon the *sand*, that are overthrown by the *wind*. The adversaries of God's people will push at them as far as their horns will go, but when they have scoured them by persecution, as tarnished vessels, then God will throw such wisps into the fire.—*William Secker.*

Verse 5.—When the Papists were in their ruff, and Melancthon began sometimes to fear lest the infant Reformation should be stifled in the birth, Luther was wont to comfort him with these words : " *Si nos ruemus, ruet Christus una, scilicet ille regnator mundi, esto ruat, malo ego cum Christo ruere, quam cum Cæsare stare ;* that is, If we perish, Christ must fall too (he is in the midst of us), and if it must be so, be it so ; I had rather perish with Christ, that great Ruler of the world, than prosper with Cæsar.—*John Collings.*

Verse 5.—" *And that right early.*" Therefore, notice that all the great deliverances wrought in Holy Scriptures, were wrought *so early*, as to have been brought to pass in the middle of the night. So Gideon, with his pitchers and lamps against the Midianites ; so Saul, when he went forth against Nahash, the Ammonite ; so Joshua, when he went up to succour Gibeon ; so Samson, when he carried off in triumph the gates of Gaza ; so also the associate kings, under the guidance of Elisha, in their expedition against the Moabites, when they, according to God's command, filled the wilderness with ditches, and then beheld their enemies drawn to their destruction, by the reflection of the rising sun upon the water.—*Michael Ayguan.*

Verse 5.—" *Right early.*" Rather, with the margin, *when the morning appeareth.* The restoration of the Jews will be one of the first things at the season of the second advent. It will be accomplished in the very dawning of that day, " when the Sun of Righteousness will rise with healing on his wings."—*Samuel Horsley.*

Verse 7.—" *The Lord of hosts is with us.*" There be three sorts of God's special presence, all which may be justly accounted the church's privilege. First, his *glorious* presence, or his presence testified by eminent glory, and the residence thereof. Thus God is said to be in heaven differentially, so as he is not anywhere else ; and heaven is therefore called his throne or dwelling place (1 Kings viii. 39) ; as a king is nowhere so majestically as upon his throne, or in his chair of state ; and this is so great a privilege of the church as that she comes not to enjoy it, until she be triumphant in heaven, and therefore is not the presence here intended. Secondly, his *gracious* presence or his presence testified by tokens of his grace and favour toward a people, whether visible, as in the temple where he chose to place his name, and wherein above all places he would be worshipped, in which respect he is said to dwell between the cherubim (2 Sam. vi. 2) ; or spiritual tokens of his grace, as assistance and acceptance in the duties of his worship, together with enjoyment and benefit of his ordinances. Thus he is present with his church and people in times of the gospel : " Where two or three are gathered together in my name, there am I in the midst of them." Matt. xviii. 20. This kind of presence is a privilege of the church militant, that he will be with her in holy and spiritual administrations and ordinances ; yet this is not the presence principally intended here. Thirdly, the *providential* presence, or his presence testified by acts of special providence, wherein the power, wisdom, or any other of God's attributes are eminently put forth, either by way of assistance or defence for a people. Thus the Lord was present with Israel in the wilderness by the pillar of fire and of a cloud (Exod. xiii. 21) : " And the Lord went before them by day in a pillar of cloud, to lead them the way ; and by night in a pillar of fire, to give them light." And as this presence was intended for a guide, so was it also for a defence to his people against their enemies, and at which their enemies the Egyptians were troubled. Exodus xiv. 20. By this kind of presence the Lord is with his church militant, in reference to her external regiment, and more especially in her warfare, standing up for her and with her against her enemies ; and this is the church's privilege in these words, " *The Lord of hosts is with us.*"—*John Strickland, B.D. (1601—1670), in a Sermon, entitled,* " *Immanuel,*" 1644.

Verse 7.—"*The God of Jacob.*" If any shall ask me, Why then the God of Jacob more than the God of Isaac ? Though it might suffice that the Spirit of God is pleased so to speak, yet Mr. Calvin gives this reason, the covenant of grace was more solemnly made and publicly ratified with Abraham and Jacob, than it was with Isaac, and therefore when he will be looked upon as a God in covenant with his people, he holds forth himself more frequently by the name of the God of Abraham, and the God of Jacob, than of the God of Isaac ; albeit sometimes he is pleased to take upon him that style also.—*John Strickland.*

Verse 7.—"*Our refuge.*" Our refuge, or stronghold, where the church, as a ship in quiet haven, may anchor and ride safe ; or it may be a metaphor from the dens or burrows, where weaponless creatures find shelter, when they are hunted and pursued by their enemies, as Prov. xxx. 26, " *The conies are but a feeble folk, yet make they their houses in the rocks.*" They are safe in the rock if they can get thither, though never so weak in themselves. So the church, though pursued by bloody enemies, and though weak in herself, if yet she get under the wing of the God of Jacob, she may be fearless, for she is safe there. *He is our refuge.* It were to under-value God, if we should fear the creatures, when he is with us. Antigonus, when he overheard his soldiers reckoning how many their enemies were, he steps in unto them suddenly, demanding, " And how many do you reckon me for ? "—*John Strickland.*

Verse 8.—" *Come, behold the works of the Lord.*" *Venito, videto.* God looks that his works should be well observed, and especially when he hath wrought any great deliverance for his people. Of all things, he cannot abide to be forgotten. —*John Trapp.*

Verse 8.—" *What desolations he hath made in the earth.*" We are here first invited to a tragical sight. We are carried into the *camera di morte*, to see the ghastly visage of deaths and desolations all the world over ; than which nothing can be more horrible and dreadful. You are called out to see piles of dead carcasses ; to see whole basketfuls of heads, as was presented to Jehu : a woeful spectacle, but a necessary one. *See,* therefore *what desolations the Lord hath wrought in all the earth.* Desolations by wars : how many fields have been drenched with blood, and composted with carcasses ; how many millions of men have been cut off in all ages by the edge of the sword ! Desolations by famine ; wherein men have been forced to make their bodies one another's sepulchres, and mothers to devour their children of a span long. Desolations by plague and pestilence ; which have swept away, as our story tells us, eight hundred thousand in one city. Desolations by inundations of waters ; which have covered the faces of many regions, and rinsed the earth of her unclean inhabitants. Desolations by earthquakes, which have swallowed up whole cities, and those great and populous. Desolations wrought by the hand of his angels ; as in Egypt ; in the tents of the Assyrians, one hundred and eighty-five thousand in one night ; in the camp of Israel, in David's pestilence. Desolations wrought by the hand of men, in battles and massacres. Desolations by wild beasts ; as in the colonies of Ashur planted in Samaria. Desolations by the swarms of obnoxious and noisome creatures ; as in Egypt, and since in Africa : " He spoke the word, and the grasshoppers came, and caterpillars innumerable," Ps. cv. 34. Insomuch as, in the consulship of M. Fulvius Flaccus, after the bloody wars of Africa, followed infinite numbers of locusts ; which, after devouring of all herbs and fruit, were, by a sudden wind, hoised into the African Sea : infection followed upon their putrefaction, and thereupon a general mortality : in number, four-score thousand died : upon the sea-coast betwixt Carthage and Utica, above two-hundred thousand. Desolations every way, and by what variety of means soever ; yet all wrought by the divine hand : *" What desolations he hath wrought."* Whoever be the instrument, he is the Author.—*Joseph Hall (Bishop).*

Verse 8.—Doth not God make great desolations, when he makes that man that counted himself a most religious man, to confess himself not sufficient for one good thought ? As it was with Paul, does he not make wars to cease when he turns the heart of a persecutor, earnestly to seek peace with God and man, yea, with his very enemies ? Doth he not break the bow and all weapons of war asunder, and that in all the earth, when he proclaims peace to all that are far off and near, professor and profane, Jews and Gentiles ?—*Richard Coore.*

Verse 8—10.—*" Come, behold the works of the Lord."* What works ? ruining works. *" What desolations he hath made in the earth."* God made strange work in the world at that time. Those countries which before were as the garden of God, became like a desolate wilderness : who was able to bear this with patience ? Yet the Spirit of God saith in the next words, it must be patiently borne. When God lets men strive and war with one another to a common confusion, yet no man may strive with God about it ; and the reason given why no man may, is only this (which is indeed all the reason in the world), *He is God.* So it follows in the Psalm ; *" Be still, and know that I am God ; "* as if the Lord had said, Not a word, do not strive nor reply ; whatever you see, hold your peace ; know that I, being God, give no account of any of my matters.—*Joseph Caryl.*

Verse 9.—He that destroyeth all the instruments of war doth surely make peace ; and he that *maketh war to cease,* doth certainly make peace begin. Peace is made two ways ; first, by taking up the differences and reconciling the spirits of men ; secondly, by breaking the power and taking away all provisions of war from men. The Lord maketh peace by both these ways, or by either of them.—*Joseph Caryl.*

Verse 9.—*" He breaketh the bow, and cutteth the spear in sunder ; he burneth the chariot in the fire."* When the Romans had, in their way of speaking, given peace to a nation, by extirpating the greatest part of the miserable inhabitants, they collected the arms of the vanquished, and setting them on fire, reduced them to ashes. A medal, struck by Vespasian, the Roman emperor, on finishing his wars in Italy, and other parts of the world, represents the goddess of peace holding an olive branch in one hand, and with a lighted torch in the other, setting fire to a heap of armour. The custom is thus alluded to by Virgil :—

> *" O mihi præteritos referat si Jupiter annos !*
> *Qualis eram cum primam aciem Præneste sub ipsa*
> *Stravi, scutorumque incendi victor acervos."*

Æn. lib. iii. v. 1. 560.

" O that Jupiter would restore to me the years that are past ! Such as I was, when under Præneste itself, I routed the foremost rank of the enemy, and victorious set fire to heaps of armour."

The same practice, by the command of Jehovah, prevailed among the Jews ; the first instance of it occurs in the book of Joshua, xi. 6. It is also celebrated in the songs of Zion, as the attendant of peace, and the proof of its continuance : *"* He maketh wars to cease," etc.—*Paxton's Illustrations of Scripture.*

Verse 9.—*"* He burneth the chariot in the fire." By degrees the chariot came to be one of the recognised forces in war, and we find it mentioned throughout the books of Scriptures, not only in its literal sense, but as a metaphor which every one could understand. In the Psalms, for example, are several allusions to the war-chariot. *" He maketh wars to cease unto the end of the earth ; he breaketh the bow, and cutteth the spear in sunder ; he burneth the chariot in the fire."* Ps. xlvi. 9. Again : *"* At thy rebuke, O God of Jacob, both the chariot and horse are cast into a deep sleep." Ps. lxxvi. 6. And : *"* Some trust in chariots, and some in horses : but we will remember the name of the Lord our God." Ps. xx. 7. Now ; the force of these passages cannot be properly appreciated unless we realise to ourselves the dread in which the war-chariot was held by the foot soldiers. Even cavalry were much feared ; but the chariots were objects of almost superstitious fear, and the rushing sound of their wheels, the noise of the horses' hoofs, and the shaking of the ground as the " prancing horses and jumping chariots " (Nah. iii. 2), thundered along, are repeatedly mentioned.—*J. G. Wood.*

Verse 10.—*" Be still, and know that I am God."* The great works of God, wherein his sovereignty appeared, had been described in the foregoing verses. In the awful desolations that he made, and by delivering his people by terrible things, he showed his greatness and dominion. Herein he manifested his power and sovereignty, and so commands all *to be still, and know that he is God.* For, says he, *" I will be exalted among the heathen, I will be exalted in the earth."*

In the words may be observed, 1. A duty described, to be still before God, and under the dispensations of his providence; which implies that we must be still as to *words ;* not speaking against the sovereign dispensations of providence, or complaining of them ; not darkening counsel by words without knowledge, or justifying ourselves and speaking great swelling words of vanity. We must be still as to *actions* and outward behaviour, so as not to oppose God in his dispensations ; and as *to the inward frame of our hearts,* cultivating a calm and quiet submission of soul to the sovereign pleasure of God, whatever it may be.

2. We may observe the ground of this duty, namely *the divinity of God.* His being God is a sufficient reason why we should be *still* before him, in no wise murmuring, or objecting, or opposing, but calmly and humbly submitting to him.

3. How we must fulfill this duty of being still before God, namely, with a sense of his divinity, as seeing the ground of this duty, in that we *" know"* him to be God. Our submission is to be such as becomes rational creatures. God doth not require us to submit contrary to reason, but to submit as seeing the reason and ground of submission. Hence, the bare consideration *that God is God* may well be sufficient to still all objections and oppositions against the divine sovereign dispensations.—*Jonathan Edwards.*

Verse 10.—*" Be still, and know that I am God."* This text of Scripture forbids quarrelling and murmuring against God. Now let me apply as I go along. There are very few, and these very well circumstanced, that find themselves in no hazard of quarrelling with God. I think almost that if angels were on earth, they would be in hazard of it. I will assure you, there are none that have corruption, but they have need to be afraid of this. But many give way to this quarrelling, and consider not the hazard thereof. Beware of it, for it is a dreadful thing to quarrel with God : who may say unto him, " What doest thou ? " It is a good account of Aaron, that when God made fire to destroy his sons, he held his peace. Let us then, while we bear the yoke, " sit alone and keep silence, and put our mouths in the dust, if so be there may be hope." Lam. iii. 28, 29. Ye know, the murmuring of the children of Israel cost them very dear. *" Be still,"* that is, beware of murmuring against me, saith the Lord. God gives not an account of his matters to any ; because there may be many things ye cannot see through ; and therefore ye may think it better to have wanted them, and much more, for the credit of God and the church. I say, God gives not an account of his matters to any. Beware, then, of drawing rash conclusions.—*Richard Cameron's Sermon preached July 18th,* 1680, *three days before he was killed at Airsmoss.*

Verse 10.—*" Be still and know that I am God."* Faith gives the soul a view of the great God. It teacheth the soul to set his almightiness against sin's magnitude, and his infinitude against sin's multitude ; and so quencheth the temptation. The reason why the presumptuous sinner fears so little, and the despairing soul so much, is for want of knowing God as great ; therefore, to cure them both, the serious consideration of God, under this notion, is propounded : *" Be still, and know that I am God ; "* as if he had said, Know, O ye wicked, that I am God, who can avenge myself when I please upon you, and cease to provoke me by your sins to your own confusion ; and again, know, ye trembling souls, that I am God ; and therefore able to pardon the greatest sins, and cease to dishonour me by your unbelieving thoughts of me.—*William Gurnall.*

Verse 10.—*" Be still, and know that I am the Lord."* Not everyone is a fit scholar for God's school, but such as are purified according to the purification of the sanctuary. Carnal men are drowned in fleshly and worldly cares, and neither purged nor lifted up to receive the light of God, or else indisposed by prejudice or passion, that they cannot learn at all. We will never savingly know him, till our souls be free of these indispositions. Among all the elements the earth is fitted to receive seed of the sower ; if he cast it into the fire, it burneth ; if in the air, it withereth ;

if in the waters, it rotteth, the instability of that body is for producing monsters, because it closeth not straitly the seeds of fishes. Spirits of a fiery temper, or light in inconstancy, or moving as waters, are not for God's lessons, but such as in *stayed humility* do rest under his hand. If waters be mixed with clay in their substance, or their surface be troubled with wind, they can neither receive nor render any image ; such unstable spirits in the school of God, lose their time and endanger themselves.—*William Struther.*

Verse 10.—" *Be still, and know,*" etc. As you must come and *see* (verse 8), so come and *hear* what the Lord saith to those enemies of yours.—*John Trapp.*

Verse 11.—" *The Lord of hosts is with us.*" On Tuesday Mr. Wesley could with difficulty be understood, though he often attempted to speak. At last, with all the strength he had, he cried out, " The best of all is, God is with us." Again, raising his hand, and waving it in triumph, he exclaimed with thrilling effect, " The best of all is, God is with us." These words seem to express the leading feature of his whole life. God had been with him from early childhood ; his providence had guided him through all the devious wanderings of human life ; and now, when he was entering the " valley of the shadow of death," the same hand sustained him.— *From "Wesley and his Coadjutors." By Rev W. C. Larrabee, A.M. Edited by Rev. B. F. Tefft, D.D. Cincinnati. 1851."*

HINTS TO PREACHERS.

Verse 1.—The song of faith in troublous times. I. *Our refuge.* Our only, impregnable, accessible, delightful place of retreat is our God. II. *Our strength.* Our all-sufficient, unconquerable, honourable, and emboldening strength is our God. III. *Our help.* Ever near, sympathising, faithful, real, and potent is our God.

Verse 1.—" *A very present help in trouble.*" Religion never so valuable as in seasons of trouble, sickness, and death. God is present helping us to bear trouble, to improve it, and to survive it. Present by gracious communications and sweet manifestations ; present most when he seems absent, restraining, overruling, and sanctifying trouble. Trust and wait.—*James Smith.*

Verse 2.—The reasons, advantages, and glory of holy courage.

Verses 2, 3.—I. The great and many causes for fear. 1. What might come— mountains, waters, etc., persecution, pestilence, etc. 2. What must come— afflictions, death, judgment. II. The great and one cause for not fearing. Fearlessness under such circumstances should be well grounded. God himself is our refuge, and we confiding in him are fearless.—*G. Rogers.*

Verse 4.—Glad tidings in sad times ; or, the city of God in the times of trouble and confusion, watered with the river of consolation.—*Ralph Erskine.*

Verse 4.—What can this " *river* " be, but that blessed covenant to which David himself repaired in the time of trouble ? . . . . And what are " *the streams* " of this river, but the outgoings and effects of this divine constitution ? I. The blood of Jesus. II. The influences of the Holy Spirit. III. The doctrines and promises of the gospel. IV. The ordinances of religion. V. All the means of grace.— *W. Jay.*

Verse 4.—" *Make glad the city of God.*" There are four ways in which the streams of a river would gladden the citizens. I. The first regards *prospect.* II. The second regards *traffic.* III. The third regards *fertility.* IV. The fourth regards *supply.*—*W. Jay.*

Verse 4.—" *City of God.*" The church may be called " the city *of God,*" because, 1. He dwells in it (see verse 5). 2. He *founded* it and *built* it. 3. It derives all *privileges* and *immunities* from him. 4. He is the chief Ruler or Governor there. 5. It is his property. 6. He draws the *rent* of it.—*Ralph Erskine.*

Verses 4, 5.—To the church, Joy, Establishment, Deliverance.

Verse 6.—What man did and what God did.

Verse 8.—" *Behold the works of the Lord."* I. *They are worth beholding,* for they are all like himself ; well becoming his infinite power, wisdom, justice. II. *Our eyes were given us for this very purpose*—not for the beholding of vanity, not for the ensnaring or wounding of the soul ; but for the use and honour of the Creator. III. *The Lord delights to have his works beheld ;* he knows their excellency and perfection, and that the more they are seen and noted the more honour will accrue to the Maker of them. IV. *None but we can do it ;* there is great reason then that we should carefully " *behold,"* etc. V. *This shall be of great benefit to ourselves.* —*Bishop Hall.*

Verse 8.—The desolations of the Lord, the consolation of his saints. I. A declaration of what has happened. II. A promise of what shall be achieved.— *Spurgeon's Sermons, No.* 190.

Verse 9.—The Great Peacemaker, or the principles of the gospel our only hope, for the total abolition of war.

Verse 10.—" *Be still, and know that I am God."* The sole consideration that God is God, sufficient to still all objections to his sovereignty.—*Jonathan Edwards.*

Verse 10.—" *I am God."* 1. In that he is God, he is an absolutely and infinitely *perfect* being. 2. As he is God he is so *great,* that he is infinitely above all comprehension. 3. As he is God, all things are his *own.* 4. In that he is God, he is *worthy* to be sovereign over all things. 5. In that he is God, he *will* be sovereign, and *will* act as such. 6. In that he is God, he is able to *avenge* himself on those who oppose his sovereignty.—*Jonathan Edwards.*

PSALM XLVII.

TITLE.—To the chief Musician.—*Many songs were dedicated to this leader of the chorus, but he was not overloaded thereby. God's service is such delight that it cannot weary us ; and that choicest part of it, the singing of his praises, is so pleasurable that we cannot have too much of it. Doubtless, the chief musician, as he was commissioned with so many sacred songs, felt that the more the merrier.* A Psalm for the Sons of Korah. *We cannot agree with those who think that the sons of Korah were the authors of these Psalms : they have all the indication of David's authorship that one could expect to see. Our ear has grown accustomed to the ring of David's compositions, and we are morally certain that we hear it in this Psalm. Every expert would detect here the autography of the Son of Jesse, or we are greatly mistaken. The sons of Korah sang these Psalms, but we believe they did not write them. Fit singers were they whose origin reminded them of sin, whose existence was a proof of sovereign grace, and whose name has a close connection with the name of Calvary.*

SUBJECT.—*Whether the immediate subject of this Psalm be the carrying up of the ark from the house of Obededom to Mount Zion, or the celebration of some memorable victory, it wou'd be hard to decide. As even the doctors differ, who shall dogmatise ? But it is very clear that both the present sovereignty of Jehovah, and the final victories of our Lord, are here fitly hymned, while his ascension, as the prophecy of them, is sweetly gloried in.*

DIVISION.—*In so short a Psalm, there is no need of any other division than that indicated by the musical pause at the end of verse 4.*

EXPOSITION.

CLAP your hands, all ye people ; shout unto God with the voice of triumph.

1. *" O clap your hands."* The most natural and most enthusiastic tokens of exultation are to be used in view of the victories of the Lord, and his universal reign. Our joy in God may be demonstrative, and yet he will not censure it. *" All ye people."* The joy is to extend to all nations ; Israel may lead the van, but all the Gentiles are to follow in the march of triumph, for they have an equal share in that Kingdom where there is neither Greek nor Jew, but Christ is all and in all. Even now if they did but know it, it is the best hope of all nations that Jehovah ruleth over them. If they cannot all speak the same tongue, the symbolic language of the hands they can all use. All people will be ruled by the Lord in the latter days, and will exult in that rule ; were they wise they would submit to it now, and rejoice to do so ; yea, they would clap their hands in rapture at the thought. *" Shout,"* let your voices keep tune with your hands. *" Unto God,"* let him have all the honours of the day, and let them be loud, joyous, universal, and undivided. *" With the voice of triumph,"* with gladsome sounds, consonant with such splendid victories, so great a King, so excellent a rule, and such gladsome subjects. Many are human languages, and yet the nations may triumph as with one voice. Faith's view of God's government is full of transport. The prospect of the universal reign of the Prince of Peace is enough to make the tongue of the dumb sing ; what will the reality be ? Well might the poet of the seasons bid mountains and valleys raise their joyous hymn—

> " For the GREAT SHEPHERD reigns,
> And his *unsuffering* kingdom yet will come."

2 For the LORD most high *is* terrible ; *he is* a great King over all the earth.

2. *" For the Lord,"* or JEHOVAH, the self-existent and only God ; *" Most high,"* most great in power, lofty in dominion, eminent in wisdom, elevated in glory. *" Is terrible,"* none can resist his power or stand before his vengeance ; yet as these

terrors are wielded on the behalf of his subjects, they are fit reasons for rejoicing. Omnipotence, which is terrible to crush, is almighty to protect. At a grand review of the troops of a great prince, all his loyal subjects are filled with triumph, because their liege lord is so able to defend his own, and so much dreaded by his foes. "*He is a great King over all the earth.*" Not over Judea only, but even to the utmost isles his reign extends. Our God is no local deity, no petty ruler of a tribe ; in infinite majesty he rules the mightiest realms as absolute arbiter of destiny, sole monarch of all lands, King of kings and Lord of lords. Not a hamlet or an islet is excluded from his dominion. How glorious will that era be when this is seen and known of all ; when in the person of Jesus all flesh shall behold the glory of the Lord !

3 He shall subdue the people under us, and the nations under our feet.

3. "*He*," with whom is infinite power, "*shall subdue the people under us.*" The battle is not ours but the Lord's. He will take his own time, but he will certainly achieve victory for his church. Truth and righteousness shall through grace climb to the ascendant. We wage no doubtful warfare. Hearts the most rebellious, and wills the most stubborn, shall submit to all-conquering grace. All the Lord's people, whether Jews or Gentiles, may clap their hands at this, for God's victory will be theirs ; but surely apostles, prophets, ministers, and those who suffer and labour most, may take the largest share in the joy. Idolatry, infidelity, superstition we shall yet tread upon, as men tread down the stones of the street. "*And the nations under our feet.*" The church of God shall be the greatest of monarchies, her victory shall be signal and decisive. Christ shall take to himself his great power and reign, and all the tribes of men shall own at once his glory and the glory of his people in him. How changed will be the position of affairs in coming ages ! The people of God have been under the feet of men in long and cruel persecutions, and in daily contempt ; but God will reverse the position, and the best in character shall be first in honour.

4 He shall choose our inheritance for us, the excellency of Jacob whom he loved. Selah.

While as yet we see not all things put under him, we are glad to put ourselves and our fortunes at his disposal. "*He shall choose our inheritance for us.*" We feel his reign to be so gracious that we even now ask to be in the fullest degree the subjects of it. We submit our will, our choice, our desire, wholly to him. Our heritage here and hereafter we leave to him, let him do with us as seemeth him good. "*The excellency of Jacob whom he loved.*" He gave his ancient people their portion, he will give us ours, and we ask nothing better ; this is the most spiritual and real manner of clapping our hands because of his sovereignty, namely, to leave all our affairs in his hands, for then our hands are empty of all care for self, and free to be used in his honour. He was the boast and glory of Israel, he is and shall be ours. He loved his people and became their greatest glory ; he loves us, and he shall be our exceeding joy. As for the latter days, we ask nothing better than to stand in our appointed lot, for if we have but a portion in our Lord Jesus, it is enough for our largest desires. Our beauty, our boast, our best treasure, lies in having such a God to trust in, such a God to love us.

Selah. Yes, pause, ye faithful songsters. Here is abundant room for holy meditation—

> " Muse awhile, obedient thought,
> Lo, the theme's with rapture fraught ;
> See thy King, whose realm extends
> E'en to earth's remotest ends !
> Gladly shall the nations own
> Him their Lord and God alone ;
> Clap their hands with holy mirth,
> Hail him MONARCH OF THE EARTH.
> Come, my soul, before him bow,
> Gladdest of his subjects thou ;
> Leave thy portion to his choice,
> In his sovereign will rejoice,
> This thy purest, deepest bliss,
> He is thine and thou art his."

5 God is gone up with a shout, the LORD with the sound of a trumpet.

5. *" God is gone up with a shout."* Faith hears the people already shouting. The command of the first verse is here regarded as a fact. The fight is over, the conqueror ascends to his triumphal chariot, and rides up to the gates of the city which is made resplendent with the joy of his return. The words are fully applicable to the ascension of the Redeemer. We doubt not that angels and glorified spirits welcomed him with acclamations. He came not without song, shall we imagine that he returned in silence ? *" The Lord with the sound of a trumpet."* Jesus is Jehovah. The joyful strain of the trumpet betokens the splendour of his triumph. It was meet to welcome one returning from the wars with martial music. Fresh from Bozrah, with his garments all red from the winepress, he ascended, leading capitvity captive, and well might the clarion ring out the tidings of Immanuel's victorious return.

6 Sing praises to God, sing praises : sing praises unto our King, sing praises.

" Sing praises." What jubilation is here, when five times over the whole earth is called upon to sing *to God !* He is worthy, he is Creator, he is goodness itself *Sing praises,* keep on with the glad work. Never let the music pause. He never ceases to be good, let us never cease to be grateful. Strange that we should need so much urging to attend to so heavenly an exercise. *" Sing praises unto our King."* Let him have all our praise ; no one ought to have even a particle of it. Jesus shall have it all. Let his sovereignty be the fount of gladness. It is a sublime attribute, but full of bliss to the faithful. Let our homage be paid not in groans but in songs. He asks not slaves to grace his throne ; he is no despot ; singing is fit homage for a monarch so blessed and gracious. Let all hearts that own his sceptre sing and sing on for ever, for there is everlasting reason for thanksgiving while we dwell under the shadow of such a throne.

7 For God *is* the King of all the earth : sing ye praises with understanding.

7. *" For God is the King of all the earth."* The Jews of our Saviour's time resented this truth, but had their hearts been right they would have rejoiced in it. They would have kept their God to themselves, and not even have allowed the Gentile dogs to eat the crumbs from under his table. Alas ! how selfishness turns honey into wormwood. Jehovah is not the God of the Jews only, all the nations of the earth are, through the Messiah, yet to own him Lord. Meanwhile his providential throne governs all events beneath the sky. *" Sing ye praises with understanding."* Sing a didactic Psalm. Sound doctrine praises God. Even under the economy of types and ceremonies, it is clear that the Lord had regard to the spirituality of worship, and would be praised thoughtfully, intelligently, and with deep appreciation of the reason for song. It is to be feared from the slovenly way in which some make a noise in singing, that they fancy any sound will do. On the other hand, from the great attention paid by some to the mere music, we feel sadly sure that the sense has no effect upon them. Is it not a sin to be tickling men's ears with sounds when we profess to be adoring the Lord ? What has a sensuous delight in organs, anthems, etc., to do with devotion ? Do not men mistake physical effects for spiritual impulses ? Do they not often offer to God strains far more calculated for human amusement than for divine acceptance ? An understanding enlightened of the Holy Spirit is then and then only fully capable of offering worthy praise.

8 God reigneth over the heathen : God sitteth upon the throne of his holiness.

Now at this moment, over the most debased idolaters, God holds a secret rule ; here is work for faith. How we ought to long for the day when this truth shall be changed in its aspect, and the rule now unrecognised shall be delighted in ! The great truth that *God reigneth* in providence is the guarantee that in a gracious gospel sense his promise shall be fulfilled, and his kingdom shall come. *" He sitteth upon the throne of his holiness."* Unmoved he occupies an undisputed throne, whose decrees, acts, and commands are holiness itself. What other throne is like this ? Never was it stained with injustice, or defiled with sin. Neither is he who sits upon it dismayed, or in a dilemma. He sits in serenity, for he knows his own power, and sees that his purposes will not miscarry. Here is reason enough for holy song.

9 The princes of the people are gathered together, *even* the people of the God of Abraham: for the shields of the earth *belong* unto God: he is greatly exalted.

9. "*The princes of the people are gathered together.*" The prophetic eye of the Psalmist sees the willing subjects of the great King assembled to celebrate his glory. Not only the poor and the men of low estate are there, but nobles bow their willing necks to his sway. "All kings shall bow down before him." No people shall be unrepresented ; their great men shall be good men, their royal ones regenerate ones. How august will be the parliament where the Lord Jesus shall open the court, and princes shall rise up to do him honour ! "*Even the people of the God of Abraham.*" That same God, who was known only to here and there a patriarch like the father of the faithful, shall be adored by a seed as many as the stars of heaven. The covenant promise shall be fulfilled, "In thee and in thy seed shall all the nations of the earth be blessed." Shiloh shall come, and "to him shall the gathering of the people be." Babel's dispersion shall be obliterated by the gathering arm of the Great Shepherd King.

"*For the shields of the earth belong unto God.*" The insignia of pomp, the emblems of rank, the weapons of war, all must pay loyal homage to the King of all. Right honourables must honour Jesus, and majesties must own him to be far more majestic. Those who are earth's protectors, the shields of the commonwealth, derive their might from him, and are his. All principalities and powers must be subject unto Jehovah and his Christ, for "*He is greatly exalted.*" In nature, in power, in character, in glory, there is none to compare with him. Oh, glorious vision of a coming era ! Make haste, ye wheels of time ! Meanwhile, ye saints, "Be ye stedfast, unmovable, always abounding in the work of the Lord, forasmuch as ye know that your labour is not in vain in the Lord."

EXPLANATORY NOTES AND QUAINT SAYINGS.

Whole Psalm.—Some have applied this Psalm to Christ's ascension ; but it speaks of his Second Coming. The Mighty One is seated peacefully on his throne. We are referred back to Psalm xlv.—*Andrew A. Bonar.*

Verse 1.—"*O clap your hands, all ye people ; shout unto God with the voice of triumph.*" This should be done, 1. Cheerfully : "*Clap your hands,*" for this is a sign of inward joy, Nah. iii. 19. 2. Universally : "O clap your hands, *all ye people.*" 3. Vocally : "*Shout unto God with the voice of triumph.*" 4. Frequently : "*Sing praises to God, sing praises : sing praises unto our King, sing praises,*" verse 6 ; and again "*sing praises,*" verse 7. It cannot be done too frequently. 5. Knowingly and discreetly : "Sing ye praises *with understanding ;*" know the reason why ye are to praise him.—*Adam Clarke.*

Verse 1.—"*O clap your hands,*" etc. Such expressions of pious and devout affection as to some may seem indecent and imprudent, yet ought not to be hastily censured and condemned, much less ridiculed ; because if they come from an upright heart, God will accept the strength of the affection, and excuse the weakness of the expressions of it.—*Matthew Henry.*

Verse 1.—"*O clap your hands.*" The *voice of melody* is not so much to be uttered with the tongue or with the hands ; that is, it is our deeds not our words, by which God is here to be praised. Even as it was in him whose pattern we are to follow : "Jesus began both to do and to teach."—*J. M. Neale.*

Verse 1.—"*All ye people.*" Peoples, in the plural. Here it is used to call both Jews and Gentiles—all nations.—*William S. Plumer.*

Verse 1.—" Shout unto God." *Jubilate Deo : in* God, and *concerning* God, and *in honour of* God. He does not excite them to carnal joy.—*Martin Geier.*

Verse 2.—" For the Lord most high is terrible ; he is a great king over all the earth." The church celebrates the ascension of Christ, because then he was " highly exalted ; " then he became " *terrible* " to his enemies, all power in heaven and in earth being committed to him ; and then he began to display the excellent majesty of his universal kingdom, to which he was then inaugurated, being crowned " King of kings, and Lord of lords."—*George Horne.*

Verse 2.—" The Lord most high is terrible." Christ is " *terrible*," that is, fearful, or meet to be feared, not of his children only for their good, but of the wicked also for their punishment ; " *terrible* " to the devil, as being stronger than he, casting out the prince of darkness by the finger of God. Luke xi. 22 ; John xii. 31. And therefore so soon as an unclean spirit saw Jesus, he cried out, " What have we to do with thee, thou Jesus of Nazareth ? art thou come to destroy us ? " Mark i. 24 ; or as other devils, Matt. viii. 29, " Art thou come hither to torment us before the time ? " for the devils in believing tremble. " *Terrible* " to hypocrites, and other impious agents of the devil, as having his fan in his hand to make clean his floor, and to gather his wheat into his garner, but he will burn up the chaff with unquench-able fire. Matt. iii. 12. Or Christ is *excelsus in potentia, terribilis in justitia ;* high in power, and fearful in justice : high in exalting the good, and terrible in humbling the bad.—*John Boys.*

Verse 3.—" He shall subdue the people under us, and the nations under our feet." The consequence of our Lord's ascension was the going forth of the all-subduing Word, under the influence and direction of which the convinced and converted nations renounced their idols and their lusts, and bowed their willing necks to the yoke of Jesus. This is that great conquest, foreshowed by the victories of Joshua, David, and all the faithful heroes of old time, and foretold in language borrowed from their history.—*George Horne.*

Verse 3.—" He shall subdue the people under us," etc., or *he shall lead* like *sheep ;* or *bring unto the fold ;* as divers render the word, by comparing Isa. v. 17 ; Micah ii. 12. He seems to speak of such a subjugation of them, as was for the good of the people subdued, because this is matter of rejoicing to them, verse 1 ; which is true both of these people whom David subdued, who thereby had opportunities, obligations, and encouragements to own and worship the true God, which was the only way to their true and lasting happiness ; and especially of those Gentiles who were subdued to Christ by the preaching of the gospel. The Gentile converts were in some sort brought under the Jews, because they were subjected to Christ and to his apostles, and to the primitive church, which were Jews.—*Matthew Pool.*

Verse 3.—" And the nations under our feet." By this manner of speech is meant, that the Gentiles should be *scholars*, and the Jews *schoolmasters*, as it were to them ; for *to sit under the feet*, or *at the feet*, is used in Scripture for being a scholar, or learning, as Acts xxii. 3.—*Thomas Wilcocks.*

Verse 4.—" He shall choose." Futures are variously rendered ; and accordingly the vulgar Latin, Syriac, and Arabic, render this word, *He hath chosen.*—*Matthew Pool.*

Verse 4.—" He shall choose our inheritance for us." It is reported of a woman who, being sick, was asked whether she was willing to live or die ; she answered, " Which God pleases." But, said one, if God should refer it to you, which would you choose ? " Truly," replied she, " I would refer it to him again." Thus that man obtains his will of God, whose will is subjected to God. We are not to be troubled that we have no more *from* God, but we are to be troubled that we do no more *for* God. Christians, if the Lord be well pleased with your persons, should not you be well pleased with your conditions ? There is more reason that you should be pleased with them, than that he should be pleased with you. Believers should be like sheep, which change their pastures at the will of the shepherd ; or like vessels in a house, which stand to be filled or emptied at the pleasure of their owner. He that sails upon the sea of this world in his own bottom, will sink at last into a bottomless ocean. Never were any their own carvers, but they were sure to cut their own fingers.—*William Secker.*

Verse 4.—" *He shall choose our inheritance for us,*" means that he who knows what is better for us than ourselves, *hath chosen*, that is, hath appointed, and that of his own good will and mercy towards us, *our inheritance ;* not only things meet for this life as lands, and houses, and possessions, etc., but even all other things concerning the hope of a better life, to wit, a kingdom that cannot be shaken, an everlasting habitation, an inheritance which is immortal and undefiled, and fadeth not away, reserved for us in heaven.—*John Boys.*

Verse 4.—" *The excellency (or glory) of Jacob whom he loved ; "* that is, even all those excellent things that he gave and promised to Jacob, wherein he might glory and rejoice. The faithful mean, that they had as great, both abundance and assurance of God's grace and goodness, as ever Jacob had.—*Thomas Wilcocks.*

Verse 4.—It may be thou art godly and poor. 'Tis well ; but canst thou tell whether, if thou wert not poor, thou wouldst be godly ? Surely God knows us better than we ourselves do, and therefore can best fit the estate to the person. —*Giles Fletcher.*

Verse 5.—"*God is gone up with a shout, the Lord with the sound of a trumpet.*" It is worthy (as Origen suggests) that this mention of the " *shout,*" and the *voice* of the " *trumpet,*" serves to connect together past and future events in the history of the church and of the world, and carry our thoughts forward to Christ's coming to judgment.—*Christopher Wordsworth.*

Verse 5.—Thou hast great cause, O my soul, to praise him, and to rejoice before him, especially if thou considerest that Christ ascended not for himself, but also for thee : it is God in our nature that is gone up to heaven : whatever God acted on the person of Christ, that he did as in thy behalf, and he means to act the very same on thee. Christ as a public person ascended up to heaven ; thy interest is in this very ascension of Jesus Christ ; and therefore dost thou consider thy Head as soaring up ? O let every member praise his name ; let thy tongue (called thy *glory*), glory in this, and trumpet out his praise, that in respect of thy duty it may be verified : " Christ is *gone up with a shout, the Lord with the sound of a trumpet.*"—*Isaac Ambrose.*

Verse 7.—" *For God is the King of all the earth :* " as if he had said, " Our King, said I ? it is too little ; he is King *of all the earth.*"—*John Trapp.*

Verse 7.—" *Sing ye praises with understanding.*" How may we make melody in our hearts to God in singing of Psalms ? We must sing " *with understanding.*" We must not be guided by the *time*, but the *words* of the Psalm ; we must mind the matter more than the music, and consider what we sing, as well as how we sing ; the tune may affect the fancy, but it is the matter affects the heart, and that God principally eyes. The Psalmist adviseth us in this particular, and so doth the apostle (1 Cor. xiv. 15). Otherwise this sweet duty would be more the work of a chorister than of a Christian, and we should be more delighted in an anthem of the musician's making, than in a Psalm of the Spirit's making. A Lapide observes that in the text, 1 Cor. xiv. 15, the word *understanding* is *maschil*, מַשְׂכִּיל, profound judgment : we must sing *wisely*, if we will sing gratefully ; we must relish what we sing. In a word, we must sing as we must pray ; now the most rude petitioner will *understand* what he prays. 1 Cor. xiv. 15. If we do not understand what we sing, it argues carelessness of spirit, or hardness of heart ; and this makes the service impertinent. Upon this the worthy Davenant cries out, " Adieu to the bellowing of the Papists, who sing in an unknown tongue." God will not understand us in that service which we understand not ourselves. One of the first pieces of the creation was *light*, and this must break out in every duty.—*John Wells* (—1676), *in " Morning Exercises."*

Verse 7.—" *Sing ye praises with understanding,*" sing an *instructive song*. Let *sense* and *sound* go together. Let your *hearts* and *heads* go with your *voices*. *Understand* what you *sing*, and *feel* what you *understand.*—*Adam Clarke.*

Verse 7.—" *Sing ye praises with understanding ; "* because in the full light of the new dispensation, the darkness of the patriarchal ages, the seeing as through a glass of the Levitical law, are turned into the vision of full and very reality.—*Hugo Victorinus.*

Verse 7.—" *Sing ye praises with understanding.*" Mark this, thou who daily readest the Psalms, and yet dost not understand them.—*Simon de Muis.*

Verse 7.—" *With understanding.*" If they had sung " *with understanding,*" they had not adored stones. When a man sensible sang to a stone insensible, did he sing

" *with understanding* " ?   But now, brethren, we see not with our eyes whom we adore, and yet correctly we adore.   Much more is God commended to us, that with our eyes we see him not.—*Augustine.*

Verse 9.—" *The princes of the people are gathered together.*"   I note from hence, 1. That it is not impossible for great men to be good men ; for the heads of a country to be members of Christ ; and for princes as well as the people to serve the God of Abraham.   It is said by the prophet, " upon my peace came great bitterness ; " a thousand fall on the left hand, but ten thousand at the right hand " (Psalm xci. 7) : ten perish in their prosperity, for one that falleth in adversity. *Homo victus in paradiso, victor in stercore :* Adam in the garden of pleasure was over-come by the subtil serpent, whereas Job on the dunghill of misery was more than a conqueror.   Woodmen say that deer are more circumspect in fat pastures ; so the godly fear most in a rich estate : *nihil timendum video* (saith one), *timeo tamen.** It is a sweet prayer of our church in the Litany.   " Good Lord, deliver us in all time of our wealth," insinuating that our minds are not so wanton in want as in abundance : yet, as you see, such is Christ's unspeakable goodness towards all sorts of men, in preventing them even with the riches of his mercy, that not only the mean people, but also the mighty princes among the heathen are joined unto the church of the God of Abraham.—*John Boys.*

Verse 9.—" *Gathered together.*"   Christ's gathering of the saints together unto him will be at his second coming, his coming to judgment, the general and final judgment.   " Now we beseech you, brethren, by the coming of our Lord Jesus Christ, and by our gathering together unto him." 2. Thess. ii. 1.—*James Scot* (—1773), *in* " *A Collection of Sermons,*" 1774.

Verse 9.—" *The people of the God of Abraham.*"   First, touching *the God of Abraham,* it is Christ, whose day Abraham desired to see, and in seeing whereof he did so much rejoice (John viii.) ; that is, not only the day of his birth, which he saw, as we learn by the oath which he caused his servant to take (Gen. xxiv.), but also the day of his passion, which he saw long ago, and rejoiced in seeing it, when he said to his son Isaac in the mount, " The Lord will provide a sacrifice." Gen. xxii. 8.   Secondly, " *The people of the God of Abraham,*" are his children and posterity : not only they that are the seed of Abraham, coming out of his loins, and are " *the children of the flesh* " (Rom. ix. 9) ; but " *the children of the promise ;* " for if they that come out of Abraham's loins were only his children, then the Hagarins, the Turks, and Ishmaelites should be the people of God ; " *But in Isaac shall thy seed be called.*"   They that lay hold of the promise by faith, " They that are of the faith, are the children of Abraham " (Gal. iii. 7), that have the same spirit of faith that Abraham had.   As the apostle saith (Rom. ii. 28), " He is not a Jew that is one outwardly, but a Jew inwardly is the true Jew."   They that worship the Messias by believing in him with the faith of Abraham, they are Abraham's children, and *the people of Abraham's God,* which thing John Baptist affirmeth (Matt. iii.), " God can of stones raise up children to Abraham."   So the Gentiles, which worshipped stones, and therefore were " *like unto them* " (Psalm cxv.), were notwithstanding raised up to be children to Abraham.—*Lancelot Andrews.*

Verse 9.—" *The shields of the earth belong unto God.*"   There we have the *rulers* of the earth set forth by a double relation ; the one *upward,* they are *scuta Deo,* they belong to God ; the other *downward,* they are *scuta terræ,* " *the shields of the earth ;* " and both these noting two things, their *dignity* and their *duty.*   They belong to God, it is their honour that he hath sealed them : they belong to God, it is their duty to be subject to him.   They are " *shields of the earth,*" it is their honour that they are above others : they are " *the shields of the earth,*" it is their duty to protect others.—*Edward Reynolds (Bishop).*

Verse 9.—" *The shields of the earth are God's,*" is understood by many as spoken of princes.   I admit that this metaphor is of frequent occurrence in Scripture, nor does this sense seem to be unsuitable to the scope of the passage. . . . . Yet the sense will be more simple if we explain the words thus : That, as it is God alone who defends and preserves the world, the high and supreme majesty which is sufficient for so exalted and difficult a work as the preservation of the world, is justly looked upon with admiration.   The sacred writer expressly uses the word *shields* in the plural number, for, considering the various and almost innumerable dangers which

---

* Seneca.

unceasingly threaten every part of the world, the providence of God must necessarily interpose in many ways, and make use as it were, of many bucklers.—*John Calvin.*

Verse 9.—" *The shields of the earth.*" Magistrates are said to *bear the sword,* not to be swords ; and they are said *to be shields,* not to bear shields, and all this to show that protection and perservation are more essential and intrinsical to their office than destruction and punishment are.—*Joseph Caryl.*

HINTS TO PREACHERS.

Verse 1.—Unusual and enthusiastic expressions of joy when justifiable and even desirable.

Verses 1—4.—Joy the true spirit of worship. 1. Joy in God's character. 2. In his reign. 3. In the triumphs of his gospel. 4. In his favour to his saints.

Verse 2.—The terrors of the Lord viewed by faith as a subject of joy.

Verse 2 (second clause).—The universal reign of Christ as it is and is to be.

Verse 3.—The hope of victory to the church. What shall be subdued ? By whose instrumentality ? " *Us.*" By whose power ? " *He.*" When it shall be accomplished ? What is the token of it ? The ascension, verse 5.

Verse 3.—I. The final triumph of the saints. All enemies subdued under them in earth and hell, within and without. 1. Gradually. 2. Completely. II. The power by which it is accomplished.—" *He shall,*" etc. 1. Not without means. 2. Not by means only. 3. But by appointed means made potent by divine energy. —*G. R.*

Verse 4.—This comprehends time and eternity. It is a matter of fact, of holy acquiescence, of desire, of thankfulness.

Verse 4.—I. God is willing to choose our inheritance for us in time and eternity. II. His choice is better than ours—" *the excellency of Jacob.*" III. He will leave us to the consequences of our own choice. IV. He will help us in obtaining that which he chooses for us.—*G. R.*

Verse 5.—The ascension. Its publicity, solemnity, triumph, joy. Who went up. Where he went up. To what he went up. For what purpose. With what result.

Verse 6.—The importance of holy song. The repetition rebukes our slackness, and implies that earnestness, frequency, delight, and universality should characterise the praises offered.

Verse 7 (last clause).—The Psalmody of the instructed, and instruction by Psalmody ; praise should be both the fruit and the vehicle of teaching.

Verse 8 (last clause).—Divine sovereignty always connected with holiness.

Verse 8.—I. God has a throne of holiness, for which he is to be feared by all men. II. A throne of grace, for which he is to be loved by his redeemed. III. A throne of glory, for which he is to be praised by his whole creation.

Verse 9.—I. A shield is a *merciful* weapon, none more so. II. A shield is a *venturous* weapon, a kind of surety, which bears the blows and receives the injuries which were intended for another. III. A shield is a *strong* weapon, to repel the darts of wickedness and break them in pieces. IV. A shield is an *honourable* weapon, none more : taking away of shields was a sign of victory ; preserving them a sign of glory. V. Remember, a shield must ever *have an eye to guide it*—you the shields, the law the eye.—*Bishop Reynolds.*

PSALM XLVIII.

TITLE.—A Song and Psalm for the Sons of Korah.—*A song for joyfulness and a Psalm for reverence. Alas! every song is not a Psalm, for poets are not all heaven-born, and every Psalm is not a song, for in coming before God we have to utter mournful confessions as well as exulting praises. The Sons of Korah were happy in having so large a selection of song; the worship where such a variety of music was used could not become monotonous, but must have given scope for all the sacred passions of gracious souls.*

SUBJECT AND DIVISIONS.—*It would be idle dogmatically to attribute this song to any one event of Jewish history. Its author and date are unknown. It records the withdrawal of certain confederate kings from Jerusalem, their courage failing them before striking a blow. The mention of the ships of Tarshish may allow us to conjecture that the Psalm was written in connection with the overthrow of Ammon, Moab, and Edom in the reign of Jehoshaphat; and if the reader will turn to 2 Chron. xx., and note especially verses 19, 25, and 36, he will probably accept the suggestion. Verses 1, 2, 3, are in honour of the Lord and the city dedicated to his worship. From 4—8 the song records the confusion of Zion's foes, ascribing all the praise to God; 9, 10, 11 extolling Zion, and avowing Jehovah to be her God for evermore.*

EXPOSITION.

GREAT *is* the LORD, and greatly to be praised in the city of our God, *in* the mountain of his holiness.

2 Beautiful for situation, the joy of the whole earth, *is* mount Zion, *on* the sides of the north, the city of the great King.

3 God is known in her palaces for a refuge.

1. *"Great is the Lord."* How great Jehovah is essentially none can conceive; but we can all see that he is great in the deliverance of his people, great in their esteem who are delivered, and great in the hearts of those enemies whom he scatters by their own fears. Instead of the mad cry of Ephesus, "Great is Diana," we bear the reasonable, demonstrable, self-evident testimony, "Great is Jehovah." There is none great in the church but the Lord. Jesus is "the *great* Shepherd," he is "a Saviour, and a great one," our great God and Saviour, our great High Priest; his Father has divided him a portion with the great, and his name shall be great unto the ends of the earth. *"And greatly to be praised."* According to his nature should his worship be; it cannot be too constant, too laudatory, too earnest, too reverential, too sublime. There is none like the Lord, and there should be no praises like his praises. *"In the city of our God."* He is great there, and should be greatly praised there. If all the world beside renounced Jehovah's worship, the chosen people in his favoured city should continue to adore him, for in their midst and on their behalf his glorious power has been so manifestly revealed. In the church the Lord is to be extolled though all the nations rage against him. Jerusalem was the peculiar abode of the God of Israel, the seat of the theocratic government, and the centre of prescribed worship, and even thus is the church the place of divine manifestation. *"In the mountain of his holiness."* Where his holy temple, his holy priests, and his holy sacrifices might continually be seen. Zion was a mount, and as it was the most renowned part of the city, it is mentioned as a synonym for the city itself. The church of God is a mount for elevation and for conspicuousness, and it should be adorned with holiness, her sons being partakers of the holiness of God. Only by holy men can the Lord be fittingly praised, and they should be incessantly occupied with his worship.

2. *"Beautiful for situation."* Jerusalem was so naturally, she was styled the Queen of the East; the church is so spiritually, being placed near God's heart, within the mountains of his power, upon the hills of his faithfulness, in the centre of providential operations. The elevation of the church is her beauty. The more she is above the world the fairer she is. *"The joy of the whole earth is Mount Zion."* Jerusalem was the world's star; whatever light lingered on earth was borrowed from the oracles preserved by Israel. An ardent Israelite would esteem the holy

city as the eye of the nations, the most precious pearl of all lands. Certainly the church of God, though despised of men, is the true joy and hope of the world. " *On the sides of the north, the city of the great King.*" Either meaning that Jerusalem was in the northern extremity of Judah, or it may denote that part of the city which lay to the north of Mount Zion. It was the glory of Jerusalem to be God's city, the place of his regal dwelling, and it is the joy of the church that God is in her midst. The great God is the great King of the church, and for her sake he rules all the nations. The people among whom the Lord deigns to dwell are privileged above all others ; the lines have fallen unto them in pleasant places, and they have a goodly heritage. We who dwell in Great Britain in the sides of the north, have this for our chief glory, that the Lord is known in our land, and the abode of his love is among us.

3. " *God is known in her palaces for a refuge.*" We worship no unknown god. We know him as our refuge in distress, we delight in him as such, and run to him in every time of need. We know nothing else as our refuge. Though we are made kings, and our houses are palaces, yet we have no confidence in ourselves, but trust in the Lord Protector, whose well-known power is our bulwark.

4 For, lo, the kings were assembled, they passed by together.

5 They saw it, *and* so they marvelled ; they were troubled, *and* hasted away.

6 Fear took hold upon them there, *and* pain, as of a woman in travail.

7 Thou breakest the ships of Tarshish with an east wind.

8 As we have heard, so have we seen in the city of the Lord of hosts, in the city of our God : God will establish it for ever. Selah.

4. " *The kings were assembled, they passed by together.*" They came and they went. No sooner together than scattered. They came one way and fled twenty ways. Boastful the gathering hosts with their royal leaders, despairing the fugitive bands, with their astonished captains. They came like foam on the angry sea, like foam they melted away. This was so remarkable that the Psalmist puts in a note of exclamation, " *Lo !* " What ! have they so suddenly fled ! Even thus shall the haters of the church vanish from the field, Papists, Ritualists, Arians, Sceptics, they shall each have their day, and shall pass on to the limbo of forgetfulness.

5. " *They saw it, and so they marvelled.*" They came, they saw, but they did not conquer. There was no *veni, vidi, vici* for them. No sooner did they perceive that the Lord was in the Holy City, than they took to their heels. Before the Lord came to blows with them, they were faint-hearted, and beat a retreat. " *They were troubled and hasted away.*" The troublers were troubled. Their haste in coming was nothing to their hurry in going. Panic seized them, horses were not fleet enough ; they would have borrowed the wings of the wind. They fled ignominiously, like children in a fright. Glory be to God, it shall be even thus with the foes of his church ; when the Lord cometh to our help, our enemies shall be as nothing. Could they foresee their ignominious defeat, they would not advance to the attack.

6. " *Fear took hold upon them there.*" They were in Giant Despair's grip. Where they hoped to triumph, there they quivered with dismay. They did not take the city, but fear took hold on them. " *And pain, as of a woman in travail.*" They were as much overcome as a woman whose fright causes premature delivery ; or as full of pain as a poor mother in her pangs— a strong expression, commonly employed by Orientals to set forth the extremity of anguish. When the Lord arises for the help of his church, the proudest of his foes shall be as trembling women, and their dismay shall be but the beginning of eternal defeat.

7. " *Thou breakest the ships of Tarshish with an east wind.*" As easily as vessels are driven to shipwreck, dost thou overturn the most powerful adversaries ; or it may mean the strength of some nations lies in their ships, whose wooden walls are soon broken ; but our strength is in our God, and therefore, it fails not ; or there may be another meaning, though thou art our defence, yet thou takest vengeance on our inventions, and while thou dost preserve us, yet our ships, our comforts, our earthly ambitions, are taken from us that we may look alone to thee. God is seen at sea, but he is equally present on land. Speculative heresies, pretending to bring us wealth from afar, are constantly assailing the church, but the

breath of the Lord soon drives them to destruction. The church too often relies on the wisdom of men, and these human helps are soon shipwrecked ; yet the church itself is safe beneath the care of her God and King.

8. " *As we have heard, so have we seen in the city of the Lord of hosts, in the city of our God.*" Our fathers' stories are reproduced before our very eyes. We heard the promise, and we have seen the fulfilment. The records of Zion, wonderful as they are, are proved to be truthful, because present facts are in perfect harmony therewith. Note how the Lord is first spoken of as *Lord of hosts*, a name of power and sovereignty, and then as *our God*, a name of covenant relation and condescension. No wonder that since the Lord bears both titles, we find him dealing with us after the precedents of his lovingkindness, and the faithfulness of his promises. " *God will establish it for ever.*" The true church can never be disestablished. That which kings establish can last for time only, that which God establishes endures to all eternity. " *Selah.*" Here is a fit place to pause, viewing the past with admiration, and the future with confidence.

9 We have thought of thy lovingkindness, O God, in the midst of thy temple.

10 According to thy name, O God, so *is* thy praise unto the ends of the earth : thy right hand is full of righteousness.

11 Let mount Zion rejoice, let the daughters of Judah be glad, because of thy judgments.

9. " *We have thought.*" Holy men are thoughtful men ; they do not suffer God's wonders to pass before their eyes and melt into forgetfulness, but they meditate deeply upon them. " *Of thy lovingkindness, O God.*" What a delightful subject ! Devout minds never tire of so divine a theme. It is well to think of past loving-kindness in times of trial, and equally profitable to remember it in seasons of prosperity. Grateful memories sweeten sorrows and sober joys. " *In the midst of thy temple.*" Fit place for so devout a meditation. Where God is most seen he is best loved. The assembled saints constitute a living temple, and our deepest musings when so gathered together should have regard to the lovingkindness of the Lord, exhibited in the varied experiences of each of the living stones. Memories of mercy should be associated with continuance of praise. Hard by the table of shew-bread commemorating his bounty, should stand the altar of incense denoting our praise.

10. " *According to thy name, O God, so is thy praise unto the ends of the earth.*" Great fame is due to his great name. The glory of Jehovah's exploits overleaps the boundaries of earth ; angels behold with wonder, and from every star delighted intelligences proclaim his fame beyond the ends of the earth. What if men are silent, yet the woods, and seas, and mountains, with all their countless tribes, and all the unseen spirits that walk them, are full of the divine praise. As in a shell we listen to the murmurs of the sea, so in the convolutions of creation we hear the praises of God. " *Thy right hand is full of righteousness.*" Thy sceptre and thy sword, thy government and thy vengeance, are altogether just. Thy hand is never empty, but full of energy, of bounty, and of equity. Neither saint nor sinner shall find the Lord to be an empty-handed God ; he will in both cases deal out righteousness to the full : to the one, through Jesus, he will be just to forgive, to the other just to condemn.

11. " *Let mount Zion rejoice.*" As the first of the cities of Judah, and the main object of the enemies' attack, let her lead the song. " *Let the daughters of Judah be glad,*" let the smaller towns join the chorus, for they join in the common victory. Let the women, who fare worst in the havoc of war, be among the gladdest of the glad, now that the spoilers have fled. All the church, and each individual member, should rejoice in the Lord, and magnify his name. " *Because of thy judgments.*" The righteous acts of the Lord are legitimate subjects for joyful praise. However it may appear on earth, yet in heaven the eternal ruin of the wicked will be the theme of adoring song. Rev. xix. 1, 3 : " Alleluia ; salvation, and glory, and honour, and power, unto the Lord our God. For true and righteous are his judgments ; for he hath judged the great whore which did corrupt the earth with her fornication, and hath avenged the blood of his servants at her hand. And again they said, Alleluia, and her smoke rose up for ever and ever." Justice which to our poor optics now seems severe, will then be perceived to be perfectly consistent with God's name of love, and to be one of the brightest jewels of his crown.

12 Walk about Zion, and go round about her : tell the towers thereof.

13 Mark ye well her bulwarks, consider her palaces ; that ye may tell it to the generation following.

14 For this God *is* our God for ever and ever : he will be our guide *even* unto death.

12. " *Walk about Zion ;* " often beat her bounds, even as Israel marched around Jericho. With leisurely and careful inspection survey her. " *And go round about her.*" Encircle her again and again with loving perambulations. We cannot too frequently or too deeply consider the origin, privileges, history, security, and glory of the church. Some subjects deserve but a passing thought ; this is worthy of the most patient consideration. " *Tell the towers thereof.*" See if any of them have crumbled, or have been demolished. Is the church of God what she was in doctrine, in strength and in beauty ? Her foes counted her towers in envy first, and then in terror, let us count them with sacred exultation. The city of Lucerne, encircled by its ancient walls, adorned with a succession of towers, is a visible illustration of this figure ; and as we have gone around it, and paused at each picturesque tower, we have realised the loving, lingering inspection which the metaphor implies.

13. " *Mark ye well her bulwarks.*" Consider most attentively how strong are her ramparts, how safely her inhabitants are entrenched behind successive lines of defence. The security of the people of God is not a doctrine to be kept in the background, it may be safely taught, and frequently pondered ; only to base hearts will that glorious truth prove harmful ; the sons of perdition make a stumbling stone even of the Lord Jesus himself, it is little wonder, that they pervert the truth of God concerning the final perseverance of the saints. We are not to turn away from inspecting Zion's ramparts, because idlers skulk behind them. " *Consider her palaces.*" Examine with care the fair dwellings of the city. Let the royal promises which afford quiet resting places for believers be attentively inspected. See how sound are the defences, and how fair are the pleasaunces of " that ancient citie," of which you are citizens. A man should be best acquainted with his own home ; and the church is our dear and blest abode. Would to God professors were more considerate of the condition of the church ; so far from telling the towers, some of them scarcely know what or where they are ; they are too busy counting their money, and considering their ledgers. Freehold and copyhold, and leasehold, men measure to an inch, but heavenhold and gracehold are too often taken at peradventure, and neglected in sheer heedlessness. " *That ye may tell it to the generation following.*" An excellent reason for studious observation. We have received and we must transmit. We must be students that we may be teachers. The debt we owe to the past we must endeavour to repay by handing down the truth to the future.

14. " *For this God is our God for ever and ever.*" A good reason for preserving a record of all that he has wrought. Israel will not change her God so as to wish to forget, nor will the Lord change so as to make the past mere history. He will be the covenant God of his people world without end. There is no other God, we wish for no other, we would have no other even if other there were. There are some who are so ready to comfort the wicked, that for the sake of ending their punishment they weaken the force of language, and make " *for ever and ever,*" mean but a time ; nevertheless, despite their interpretations we exult in the hope of an eternity of bliss, and to us " everlasting," and " for ever and ever " mean what they say. " *He will be our guide even unto death.*" Throughout life, and to our dying couch, he will graciously conduct us, and even after death he will lead us to the living fountains of waters. We look to him for resurrection and eternal life. This consolation is clearly derivable from what has gone before ; hitherto our foes have been scattered, and our bulwarks have defied attack, for God has been in our midst, therefore all possible assaults in the future shall be equally futile.

> " The church has all her foes defied
> And laughed to scorn their rage ;
> E'en thus for aye she shall abide
> Secure from age to age."

Farewell, fear. Come hither, gratitude and faith, and sing right joyously.

EXPLANATORY NOTES AND QUAINT SAYINGS.

Title.—" *A Song and Psalm.*" Wherein both voice and instrument were used; the voice began first and the instrument after : and where the inscription is a Psalm and Song, there likely the instrument began and the voice followed.—*John Richardson.*

Whole Psalm.—According to Dr. Lightfoot, the constant and ordinary Psalm for the second day of the week was the forty-eighth.

Verse 1.—" *Great is the Lord, and greatly to be praised in the city of our God,*" etc. The prophet, being about to praise a certain edifice, commences by praising the architect, and says that in the holy city the wonderful skill and wisdom of God, who built it, is truly displayed. " *Great is the Lord, and greatly to be praised ;* " and so he is, whether we look at his essence, his power, his wisdom, his justice, or his mercy, for all are infinite, everlasting, and incomprehensible ; and thus, so much is God *greatly to be praised,* that all the angels, all men, even all his own works would not suffice thereto ; but of all things revealed, there is no one thing can give us a greater idea of his greatness, or for which we should praise and thank him more, than the establishment of his church ; and, therefore, the prophet adds, " *in the city of our God, in the mountain of his holiness ;* " that is to say, the greatness of God, and for which he deserves so much praise, is conspicuous in the foundation and construction of his church."—*Robert Bellarmine (Cardinal).*

Verse 1.—" *Great is the Lord.*" Greater, Job xxxiii. 12. Greatest of all, Psalm xcv. 3. Greatness itself, Psalm cxlv. 3. A degree he is above the superlative.—*John Trapp.*

Verse 1.—" *Mountain of his holiness.*" The religion in it holy, the people in it a holy people.—*William Nicholson.*

Verse 2.—" *Beautiful for situation, the joy of the whole earth, is mount zion, on the sides of the north, the city of the great King.*" What is there, or was there, about Zion to justify the high eulogium of David ? The situation is indeed eminently adapted to be the platform of a magnificent citadel. Rising high above the deep valley of Gihon and Hinnom, on the west and south, and the scarcely less deep one of the Cheesemongers on the east, it could only be assailed from the north-west ; and then " *on the sides of the north* " it was magnificently beautiful, and fortified by walls, towers, and bulwarks, the wonder and terror of the nations : " *For the kings were assembled, they passed by together. They saw it, and so they marvelled ; they were troubled, and hasted away.*" At the thought of it the royal Psalmist again bursts forth in triumph : " *Walk about Zion, and go round about her : tell the towers thereof. Mark ye well her bulwarks, consider her palaces ; that ye may tell it to the generation following.*" Alas ! her towers have long since fallen to the ground, her bulwarks have been overthrown, her palaces have crumbled to dust, and we who now walk about Zion can tell no other story than this to the generation following. There is another Zion, however, whose towers are still more glorious, and shall never be overthrown. " *God is known in her palaces for a refuge.*" And " *this God is our God for ever and ever.*" How often is this name synonymous with the church of the living God ! and no other spot but one can divide with it the affection of his people—no other name but one can awaken such joyful hopes in the Christian's heart. The temporal Zion is now in the dust, but the true Zion is rising and shaking herself from it, and putting on her beautiful garments to welcome her King when he comes to reign over the whole earth.—*W. M. Thomson, D.D.*

Verse 2.—When I stood that morning on the brow of Olivet, and looked down on the city crowning those battlemented heights, encircled by those deep and dark ravines, I involuntarily exclaimed, " *Beautiful for situation, the joy of the whole earth, is mount Zion, on the sides of the north, the city of the great King.*" And as I gazed, the red rays of the rising sun shed a halo round the top of the castle of David ; then they tipped with gold each tapering minaret, and gilded each dome of mosque and church, and at length, bathed in one flood of ruddy light the terraced roofs of the city, and the grass and foliage, the cupolas, pavements, and colossal walls of the Haram. No human being could be disappointed who first saw Jerusalem from Olivet.—*J. L. Porter.*

Verse 2 (*first clause*).—*Beautiful in climate*, that is, Mount Zion is situated in a fair and lovely climate. This is the view taken by Montanus and Ainsworth. Bate and Parkhurst read, "*Beautiful in extension, i.e.*, in the prospect which it extends to the eye."—*Editorial Note to Calvin in loc.*

Verse 2.—"*Beautiful for situation.*" This earth is, by sin, covered with deformity, and therefore justly might that spot of ground, which was thus beautified with holiness, be called "*the joy of the whole earth*," *i.e.*, what the whole earth had reason to rejoice in, because God would thus in very deed dwell with man upon the earth.—*Matthew Henry.*

Verse 2.—"*Beautiful for situation.*"

———————— Fair Jerusalem
The holy city, lifted high her towers,
And higher yet the glorious temple rear'd
Her pile, far off appearing like a mount
Of alabaster, topt with golden spires.

John Milton in "*Paradise Regained.*"

Verse 2.—"*On the sides of the north.*" Jerusalem, that is the upper and best part of it, was built on the north side of Mount Zion.—*Hadrian Reland*, 1676—1718.

Verse 2.—Jerusalem lay to the north of Sion, and this circumstance is mentioned as a proof of Mount Zion's greater security, for it was almost inaccessible on any other side except the north, and there it was defended by Jerusalem, which was very strong.—*Samuel Burder.*

Verse 2.—"*The great King.*" God is named the *great King* in opposition to the kings in verse 4.—*E. W. Hengstenberg.*

Verse 4.—They were many and powerful : kings and a plurality of them. They were confederate kings. "*The kings were assembled.*" Forces united are the most powerful. But all the endeavours of these confederate kings came to nothing. "*They passed by together*"—together they came, and together they vanished.—*William Nicholson.*

Verses 5, 6.—The potentates of the world saw the miracles of the apostles, the courage and constancy of the martyrs, and the daily increase of the church, notwithstanding all their persecutions ; they beheld with astonishment the rapid progress of the faith through the Roman empire ; they called upon their gods, but their gods could not help themselves ; idolatry expired at the foot of the victorious cross.—*George Horne.*

Verse 6.—"*Fear took hold upon them there, and pain, as of a woman in travail.*" Nothing is more unaccountable than panic. No man, no body of men can adequately guard against such terror. He who made the ears can easily make them to tingle. He who holds the winds in his fist, can easily make them whisper alarm, or roar dismay. This is especially to be expected when men so act as to have their own conscience against them. Job xv. 21. But God can at any time so forsake men as that they shall be unmanned, and play the fool exceedingly. Lev. xxvi. 36. Men have fought bravely several battles, and then played the coward.—*William S. Plumer.*

Verse 7.—"*Thou breakest the ships of Tarshish with an east wind.*" It is only by her Lord that the church gains "the true riches ; " when she enters into traffick with the world, she takes the means of the world for her resources ; and when she trusts in her wealth, in her political power, in earthly cunning, to make merchandise, the instruments she adopts come to nothing in her hands, and leave her helpless and poor.—*From* "*A Plain Commentary on the Book of Psalms* (*The Prayer Book Version*), *chiefly founded on the Fathers*," 1859.

Verse 7.—"*With an east wind*," which, in Judea, is a very violent and destructive wind. Kennicot renders the verse thus, "*As the east wind dasheth in pieces the ships of Tharshish ; "* founding his conjecture upon the similarity in form of two Hebrew letters, signifying the one *in*, the other *as*.—*Daniel Cresswell.*

Verse 9.—"*We have thought.*" The Hebrew דּוּם and דָּמָם and דָּמָה belong all to the same signification, of *quiet, rest, silence, patient expecting, thinking, considering*, and must be determined to any of these senses by the context. And here that of *expecting* or *patient waiting*, with *affiance* in him, and without all *distrust* or *repining* at his *delays*, seems to be most proper for it. For coming to the sanctuary to pray for mercy, 'tis most agreeable to say *we wait for it there*, as in the place where he hath promised to afford it, in return to *prayers.—Henry Hammond*.

Verses 12, 13.—In a spiritual sense *the towers* and *bulwarks* of Sion are those doctrines of the true faith, which are the strength and glory of the church, which are to be maintained in their soundness and stability against the assaults of heretical teachers, so that they may be transmitted unimpaired to following generations.— *Origen and Theodoret, quoted by Wordsworth*.

Verse 13.—" *Mark ye well her bulwarks.*" Margin as in the Hebrew, " *Set your heart to her bulwarks.*" That is, pay close attention to them ; make the investigation with care, not as one does whose heart is not in the thing, and who does it negligently. The word rendered " *bulwarks*," חֵיל, *khail*—means properly, a host or army, and then a fortification or entrenchment, especially the *ditch* or *trench*, with the low wall or breastwork which surrounds it. 2 Sam. xx. 15 ; Isaiah xxvi. 1. (Gesenius, *Lex.*)—*Albert Barnes*.

Verse 13.—" *Mark ye well :* " set your heart, mind earnestly, set your affections on.—*Henry Ainsworth*.

Verse 13.—" *Her bulwarks.*" I. The designation and constitution of Jesus Christ to be King of the church, King of Zion, is the great bulwark of Zion. II. The second bulwark of Zion is the promises of God, which are innumerable. III. The watchful providence of God over the church. IV. Another bulwark is God's special presence. God is in an especial manner present in his church. V. The last bulwark unto which all others may be reduced, is the covenant of God : " For this God is our God."—*John Owen*.

Verse 14.—" *This God is our God for ever and ever.*" What a portion then is that of the believer ! The landlord cannot say of his fields, these are mine, for ever and ever. The king cannot say of his crown, this is mine for ever and ever. These possessions shall soon change masters ; these possessors shall soon mingle with the dust, and even the graves they shall occupy may not long be theirs ; but it is the singular, the supreme happiness of every Christian to say, or to have a right to say, " This glorious God with all his divine perfections is my God, for ever and ever, and even death itself shall not separate me from his love."—*George Burder*.

Verse 14.—" *This God is our God.*" The people of God are sometime represented as so taken with this apprehenson of their peculiar relation to God, that they cannot be content to know, but they proclaim it ; nor was it enough the present age should know, but they must have it told the following generation : " Let Mount Zion rejoice," etc. Mark, " That ye may tell the generation following," " *For this is our God.*" See their ostentation of him ! This God ; *q.d.*, Behold what a God have we ! view him well, and take notice how glorious a God he is. And as they glory in the greatness of the God to whom they were related, so they do in the eternity of the relation. " This God is our God *for ever and ever.*"—*John Howe*.

Verse 14.—God is not only a satisfying portion, filling every crevice of thy soul with the light of joy and comfort ; and a sanctifying portion, elevating thy soul to its primitive and original perfection ; and a universal portion ; not health, or wealth, or friends, or honours, or liberty, or life, or house, or wife, or child, or pardon, or peace, or grace, or glory, or earth, or heaven, but all these, and infinitely more, but also he is an eternal portion. This God would be thy God " *for ever and ever.*" Oh, sweet word *ever !* thou art the crown of the saints' crown, and the glory of their glory. Their portion is so full that they desire no more ; they enjoy variety and plenty of delights above what they are able to ask or think, and want nothing but to have it fixed. May they but possess it in peace without interruption or cessation they will trample all kingdoms of the earth as dirt under their feet ; and lo ! thou art the welcome dove to bring this olive branch in thy mouth. " *This God is our God for ever and ever.*" All the arithmetical figures of days, and months, and years, and ages, are nothing to this infinite cipher *ever*, which, though it stand for nothing in the vulgar account, yet contains all our millions ; yea, our millions and millions of millions are less than drops to this ocean *ever.—George Swinnock*.

Verse 14.—Some expositors have strangely found a difficulty in the last verse, deeming such a profession of personal faith an inappropriate termination for a national song. Even Dr. Delitzsch, a wise and devout interpreter, shares in this notion; going, indeed, so far as to throw out the surmise, that some word must have been lost from the Hebrew text. To me it seems that the verse, as it stands, is admirably in harmony with the song, and is its crowning beauty. When the Lord does great things for church or nation, he means that all the faithful, however humble their station, should take courage from it, should repose in him fresh confidence, and cling to him with a firmer hope, and say, " *This God shall be our God for ever; he will guide us even unto death.*"—*William Binnie.*

Verse 14.—" *Unto death,*" or as some explain it, *at death, i.e.,* he will save us from it; others, *over death,* beyond it. But the most obvious explanation, and the one most agreeable to usage, is that which makes the phrase mean even to the end of life, or as long as we live. The idea of a future state, though not expressed, is not excluded.—*J. A. Alexander.*

Verse 14 (*last clause*).—The last clause is much misunderstood. It is not, " Our guide *unto* death," for the words are עֲלָמֻות עַל־מֻות, " shall lead us *over* death." Surely it means, " It is he who leads over *death* to *resurrection* "—over Jordan to Canaan. The עַל is used in Levit. xv. 25, for " *beyond,*" in regard to time, and is not this the sense here? " *Beyond* the time of death "? Till death is to us over? Till we have *stood upon the grave of death?* Yes; he it is who leads us on to this last victory; he swallows up death in victory, and leads us to *trample on death.* And so viewed, we easily discern the beautiful link of thought that joins this Psalm to that which follows. Such is the celebration of *The Mighty One become the glory of Jerusalem.*—*Andrew A. Bonar.*

HINTS TO PREACHERS.

[*All the suggestions under this Psalm, except those otherwise designated, are by our beloved friend, Rev. George Rogers, Tutor of The Pastor's College.*]

Verse 1.—I. *What the church is to God.* 1. His " *city:* " not a lawless rabble, but a well organised community. 2. A mountain of holiness, for the display of justifying righteousness, of sanctifying grace. II. *What God is to the church.* 1. Its inhabitant. It is *his* city, his mountain. There he is great. There was no room for the whole of God in Paradise, there is no room for him in his law, no room for him in the heaven of angels: in the church only is there room for all his perfections, for a triune Jehovah. Great everywhere, he is peculiarly great here. 2. The object of its praises. As he is greatest here, so are his praises, and through the universe on this account.

Verse 2.—I. *Was the ancient Zion beautiful for situation?* So is the New Testament church founded upon a rock, upon eternal purpose and grace. II. *Was it the joy of the whole earth?* So the New Testament church will become. III. *Was it the special joy of the tribes of Israel* that were almost entirely to the north of Jerusalem? So the church is to the saints. IV. *Was it a royal as well as holy city?* So is the church. " Yet have I set," etc.

Verse 3.—I. God is a refuge in his church. The church is a city of refuge, but the refuge is not in its church, but its God. 1. For sinners from wrath. 2. For saints from trials and fears. II. God is there known as such, known to thousands, not known as such elsewhere. " They that know thy name," etc.

Verses 4—7.—I. The opposition of worldly powers to the church. "The kings," etc. II. The manner in which they are subdued—by their own fears; conscience has persecuted those who have persecuted the church of God. They who have seized the ark of God have been glad to return it with an offering. III. The completeness of their overthrow. As a fleet of ships of Tarshish, dispersed, broken and engulfed by the east wind.

Verse 8.—I. God has ever been to his people what he now is; the same " *heard* " as " *seen.*" II. He is now what he ever has been: the same " *seen* " as " *heard.*" III. He will ever be what he now is. " Will establish it for ever."

Verse 9.—I. What are the lovingkindnesses of God? Pity to the wretched pardon to the penitent, help to the prayerful, comfort to the afflicted, etc. II. Where are they to be found ? " In the midst of," etc. 1. Here they are revealed. 2. Here they are dispensed. 3. Here they are sought. 4. Here they are enjoyed.

Verse 10.—As the name of God, so his praises are—I. Supreme. II. Unqualified. III. Universal. IV. Everlasting.

Verse 10. -" *Thy right hand,*" etc. I. The justice of omnipotence. II. Omnipotence controlled by justice. III. The omnipotence of justice.

Verse 11.—I. The subjects of his peoples' joy. Not mercies merely, but judgments. II. Reasons : 1. Because they are holy—needful to the purity of moral government. 2. Just—needful to vindicate law. 3. Good—needful for the greatest amount of good.

Verse 12.—I. What is to be understood by the preservation and protection of the church ? II. What is meant by searching into, and considering of, these causes and means of the church's preservation ? III. What are those causes and means of the church's preservation, those towers and bulwarks which will not fail ? IV. What reason is there why we should thus search into and consider these causes of the church's preservation and protection ? V. What is the testimony which we have to give concerning this matter to the ensuing generation ?—*John Owen's Sermon.*

Verse 14 *(first clause).*—This is the language of a *proprietary* in God : 1. Of an *assured* proprietary—" This God is *our* God." 2. Of a *permanent* proprietary— " *for ever and ever.*" 3. Of an *exulting* proprietary.—*W. Jay.*

Verse 14.—I. The language of discrimination. *This* God. *This* God in Christ, in the church. II. The language of Faith—*our* God. III. Of Hope—" *For ever and ever.*" IV. Of Resignation—" *He will be our guide,*" etc.

PSALM XLIX.

TITLE.—To the chief Musician. a Psalm for the sons of Korah. *This is precisely the same as on former occasions, and no remark is needed.*

DIVISION.—*The poet musician sings, to the accompaniment of his harp, the despicable character of those who trust in their wealth, and so he consoles the oppressed believer. The first four verses are a preface ; from 5 to 12 all fear of great oppressors is removed by the remembrance of their end and their folly ; 13 contains an expression of wonder at the perpetuity of folly ; 14 and 15 contrast the ungodly and the righteous in their future ; and from 16 to 20 the lesson from the whole is given in an admonitory form. Note the chorus in verses 12 and 20, and also the two Selahs.*

EXPOSITION.

HEAR this, all *ye* people ; give ear, all *ye* inhabitants of the world :
    2 Both low and high, rich and poor, together.

    3 My mouth shall speak of wisdom ; and the meditation of my heart *shall be* of understanding.

    4 I will incline mine ear to a parable : I will open my dark saying upon the harp.

In these four verses the poet-prophet calls universal humanity to listen to his didactic hymn.

1. "*Hear this, all ye people.*" All men are concerned in the subject, it is *of* them, and therefore *to* them that the Psalmist would speak. It is not a topic which men delight to consider, and therefore he who would instruct them must press them to give ear. Where, as in this case, the theme claims to be wisdom and understanding, attention is very properly demanded ; and when the style combines the sententiousness of the proverb with the sweetness of poesy, interest is readily excited. "*Give ear, all ye inhabitants of the world.*" "He that hath ears to hear let him hear." Men dwelling in all climes are equally concerned in the subject, for the laws of providence are the same in all lands. It is wise for each one to feel I am a man, and therefore everything which concerns mortals has a personal interest to me. We must all appear before the judgment-seat, and therefore we all should give earnest heed to holy admonition which may help us to prepare for that dread event. He who refuses to receive instruction by the ear, will not be able to escape receiving destruction by it when the Judge shall say, " Depart, ye cursed."

2. " *Both low and high, rich and poor, together.*" Sons of great men, and children of mean men, men of large estate, and ye who pine in poverty, ye are all bidden to hear the inspired minstrel as he touches his harp to a mournful but instructive lay. The low will be encouraged, the high will be warned, the rich will be sobered, the poor consoled, there will be a useful lesson for each if they are willing to learn it. Our preaching ought to have a voice for all classes, and all should have an ear for it. To suit our word to the rich alone is wicked sycophancy, and to aim only at pleasing the poor is to act the part of a demagogue. Truth may be so spoken as to command the ear of all, and wise men seek to learn that acceptable style. Rich and poor must soon meet together in the grave, they may well be content to meet together now. In the congregation of the dead all differences of rank will be obliterated, they ought not now to be obstructions to united instructions.

3. " *My mouth shall speak of wisdom.*" Inspired and therefore lifted beyond himself, the prophet is not praising his own attainments, but extolling the divine Spirit which spoke in him. He knew that the Spirit of truth and wisdom spoke through him. He who is not sure that his matter is good has no right to ask a hearing. "*And the meditation of my heart shall be of understanding.*" The same Spirit who made the ancient seers eloquent, also made them thoughtful. The help of the Holy Ghost was never meant to supersede the use of our own mental powers.

The Holy Spirit does not make us speak as Balaam's ass, which merely uttered sounds, but never meditated ; but he first leads us to consider and reflect, and then he gives us the tongue of fire to speak with power.

4. " *I will incline mine ear to a parable.*" He who would have others hear, begins by hearing himself. As the minstrel leans his ear to his harp, so must the preacher give his whole soul to his ministry. The truth came to the Psalmist as a parable, and he endeavoured to unriddle it for popular use ; he would not leave the truth in obscurity, but he listened to its voice till he so well understood it as to be able to interpret and translate it into the common language of the multitude. Still of necessity it would remain a problem, and a dark saying to the unenlightened many, but this would not be the songster's fault, for, saith he, " *I will open my dark saying upon the harp.*" The writer was no mystic, delighting in deep and cloudy things, yet he was not afraid of the most profound topics ; he tried to open the treasures of darkness, and to uplift pearls from the deep. To win attention he cast his proverbial philosophy into the form of song, and tuned his harp to the solemn tone of his subject. Let us gather round the minstrel of the King of kings, and hear the Psalm which erst was led by the chief musician, as the chorus of the sons of Korah lifted up their voices in the temple.

5 Wherefore should I fear in the days of evil, *when* the iniquity of my heels shall compass me about ?

6 They that trust in their wealth, and boast themselves in the multitude of their riches ;

7 None *of them* can by any means redeem his brother, nor give to God a ransom for him :

8 (For the redemption of their soul *is* precious, and it ceaseth for ever :)

9 That he should still live for ever, *and* not see corruption.

10 For he seeth *that* wise men die, likewise the fool and the brutish person perish, and leave their wealth to others.

11 Their inward thought *is, that* their houses *shall continue* for ever, *and* their dwelling places to all generations ; they call *their* lands after their own names.

12 Nevertheless man *being* in honour abideth not : he is like the beasts *that* perish.

5. " *Wherefore should I fear in the days of evil, when the iniquity of my heels shall compass me about ?* " The man of God looks calmly forward to dark times when those evils which have dogged his heels shall gain a temporary advantage over him. Iniquitous men, here called in the abstract *iniquity*, lie in wait for the righteous, as serpents that aim at the heels of travellers : the iniquity of our heels is that evil which aims to trip us up or impede us. It was an old prophecy that the serpent should wound the heel of the woman's seed, and the enemy of our souls is diligent to fulfil that premonition. In some dreary part of our road it may be that evil will wax stronger and bolder, and gaining upon us will openly assail us ; those who followed at our heels like a pack of wolves, may perhaps overtake us, and compass us about. What then ? Shall we yield to cowardice ? Shall we be a prey to their teeth ? God forbid. Nay, we will not even fear, for what are these foes ? What indeed, but mortal men who shall perish and pass away ? There can be no real ground of alarm to the faithful. Their enemies are too insignificant to be worthy of one thrill of fear. Doth not the Lord say to us, " I, even I, am he that comforteth thee : who art thou, that thou shouldest be afraid of a man that shall die, and of the son of man which shall be made as grass ? "

Scholars have given other renderings of this verse, but we prefer to keep to the authorised version when we can, and in this case we find in it precisely the same meaning which those would give to it who translate " *my heels,*" by the words, " *my supplanters.*"

6. What if the good man's foes be among the great ones of the earth ! yet he need not fear them. " *They that trust in their wealth.*" Poor fools, to be content with such a rotten confidence. When we set our rock in contrast with theirs, it would be folly to be afraid of them. Even though they are loud in their brags,

we can afford to smile. What if they glory " *and boast themselves in the multitude of their riches* " ? yet while we glory in our God we are not dismayed by their proud threatenings. Great strength, position, and estate, make wicked men very lofty in their own esteem, and tyrannical towards others ; but the heir of heaven is not overawed by their dignity, nor cowed by their haughtiness. He sees the small value of riches, and the helplessness of their owners in the hour of death, and therefore he is not so mean as to be afraid of an ephemera, a moth, a bubble.

7. " *None of them can by any means redeem his brother.*" With all their riches, the whole of them put together could not rescue a comrade from the chill grasp of death. They boast of what they will do with us, let them see to themselves. Let them weigh their gold in the scales of death, and see how much they can buy therewith from the worm and the grave. The poor are their equals in this respect ; let them love their friend ever so dearly, they cannot " *give to God a reason for him.*" A king's ransom would be of no avail, a Monte Rosa of rubies, an America of silver, a world of gold, a sun of diamonds, would all be utterly contemned. O ye boasters, think not to terrify us with your worthless wealth, go ye and intimidate death before ye threaten men in whom is immortality and life.

8. " *For the redemption of their soul is precious, and it ceaseth for ever.*" Too great is the price, the purchase is hopeless. For ever must the attempt to redeem a soul with money remain a failure. Death comes and wealth cannot bribe him ; hell follows, and no golden key can unlock its dungeons. Vain, then, are your threatenings, ye possessors of the yellow clay ; your childish toys are despised by men who estimate the value of possessions by the shekel of the sanctuary.

9. No price could secure for any man " *That he should still live for ever, and not see corruption.*" Mad are men now after gold, what would they be if it could buy the elixir of immortality ? Gold is lavished out of the bag to cheat the worm of the poor body by embalming it, or enshrining it in a coffin of lead, but it is a miserable business, a very burlesque and comedy. As for the soul, it is too subtle a thing to be detained when it hears the divine command to soar through tracks unknown. Never, therefore, will we fear, those base nibblers at our heels, whose boasted treasure proves to be so powerless to save.

10. "*For he seeth that wise men die.*" Every one sees this. The proud, persecuting rich man cannot help seeing it. He cannot shut his eyes to the fact that wiser men than he are dying, and that he also, with all his craft, must die. " *Likewise the fool and the brutish person perish.*" Folly has no immunity from death. Off goes the jester's cap, as well as the student's gown. Jollity cannot laugh off the dying hour ; death who visits the university, does not spare the tavern. Thoughtlessness and brutishness meet their end as surely as much care and wasting study. In fact, while the truly wise, so far as this world is concerned, *die*, the fool has a worse lot, for he *perishes*, is blotted out of remembrance, bewailed by none, remembered no more. " *And leave their wealth to others.*'" Not a farthing can they carry with them. Whether heirs male of their own body, lawfully begotten, inherit their estates, or they remain unclaimed, it matters not, their hoardings are no longer theirs ; friends may quarrel over their property, or strangers divide it as spoil, they cannot interfere. Ye boasters, hold ye your own, before ye dream of despoiling the sons of the living God. Keep shoes to your own feet in death's dark pilgrimage, ere ye seek to bite our heels.

11. " *Their inward thought is, that their houses shall continue for ever, and their dwelling places to all generations.*" He is very foolish who is more a fool in his inmost thought than he dare be in his speech. Such rotten fruit, rotten at the core, are worldlings. Down deep in their hearts, though they dare not say so, they fancy that earthly goods are real and enduring. Foolish dreamers ! The frequent dilapidations of their castles and manor-houses should teach them better, but still they cherish the delusion. They cannot tell the mirage from the true streams of water ; they fancy rainbows to be stable, and clouds to be the everlasting hills. " *They call their lands after their own names.*" Common enough is this practice. His grounds are made to bear the groundling's name, he might as well write it on the water. Men have even called countries by their own names, but what are they better for the idle compliment, even if men perpetuate their nomenclature ?

12. " *Nevertheless man being in honour abideth not.*" He is but a lodger for the hour, and does not stay a night : even when he dwells in marble halls his notice to quit is written out. Eminence is evermore in imminence of peril. The hero of the hour lasts but for an hour. Sceptres fall from the paralysed hands which

once grasped them, and coronets slip away from skulls when the life is departed.
" *He is like the beasts that perish.*"   He is not like the sheep which are preserved
of the Great Shepherd, but like the hunted beast which is doomed to die.   He lives
a brutish life and dies a brutish death.   Wallowing in riches, surfeited with pleasure,
he is fatted for the slaughter, and dies like the ox in the shambles.   Alas ! that so
noble a creature should use his life so unworthily, and end it so disgracefully.   So
far as this world is concerned, wherein does the death of many men differ from the
death of a dog ?   They go down—

> " To the vile dust from whence they sprung,
> Unwept, unhonour'd, and unsung."

What room is there, then, for fear to the godly when such natural brute beasts
assail them ?   Should they not in patience possess their souls ?

  We make a break here, because this stanza appears to be the refrain of the song,
and as such is repeated in the twentieth verse.

  13 This their way *is* their folly : yet their posterity approve their sayings.
Selah.

  13.   Their vain confidences are not casual aberrations from the path of wisdom
but *their way*, their usual and regular course ;   their whole life is regulated by such
principles.   Their life-path is essential *folly*.   They are fools ingrain.   From first
to last brutishness is their characteristic, grovelling stupidity the leading trait
of their conduct.   " *Yet their posterity approve their sayings.*"   Those who follow
them in descent follow them in folly, quote their worldly maxims, and accept their
mad career as the most prudent mode of life.   Why do they not see by their fathers'
failure their fathers' folly ?   No, the race transmits its weakness.   Grace is not
hereditary, but sordid worldliness goes from generation to generation.   The race
of fools never dies out.   No need of missionaries to teach men to be earthworms,
they crawl naturally to the dust.   " *Selah.*"   Well may the minstrel pause, and
bid us muse upon the deep-seated madness of the sons of Adam.   Take occasion,
reader, to reflect upon thine own.

  14 Like sheep they are laid in the grave ; death shall feed on them ;
and the upright shall have dominion over them in the morning ; and their
beauty shall consume in the grave from their dwelling.

  15 But God will redeem my soul from the power of the grave ; for he
shall receive me.   Selah.

  14.   " *Like sheep they are laid in the grave.*"   As dumb, driven cattle, they are
hurried to their doom, and are penned in within the gates of destruction.   As sheep
that go whither they are driven, and follow their leader without thought, so these
men who have chosen to make this world their all, are urged on by their passions,
till they find themselves at their journey's end, that end the depths of Hades.   Or
if we keep to our own translation, we have the idea of their dying peaceably, and
being buried in quiet, only that they may wake up to be ashamed at the last great day.
" *Death shall feed on them.*"   Death like a grim shepherd leads them on, and conducts
them to the place of their eternal pasturage, where all is barrenness and misery.
The righteous are led by the Good Shepherd, but the ungodly have death for their
shepherd, and he drives them onward to hell.   As the power of death rules them
in this world, for they have not passed from death unto life, so the terrors of death
shall devour them in the world to come.   As grim giants, in old stories, are said to
feed on men whom they entice to their caves, so death, the monster, feeds on the
flesh and blood of the mighty.   " *The upright shall have dominion over them in the
morning.*"   The poor saints were once the tail, but at the day-break they shall
be the head.   Sinners rule till night-fall ;   their honours wither in the evening,
and in the morning they find their position utterly reversed.   The sweetest reflection
to the upright is that " the morning " here intended begins an endless, changeless,
day.   What a vexation of spirit to the proud worldling, when the Judge of all the
earth holds his morning session, to see the man whom he despised, exalted high in
heaven, while he himself is cast away !   " *And their beauty shall consume in the
grave from their dwelling.*"   Whatever of glory the ungodly had shall disappear
in the tomb.   Form and comeliness shall vanish from them, the worm shall make

sad havoc of all their beauty. Even their last dwelling place, the grave, shall not be able to protect the relics committed to it ; their bodies shall dissolve, no trace shall remain of all their strong limbs and lofty heads, no vestige of remaining beauty shall be discoverable. The beauty of the righteous is not yet revealed, it waits its manifestations ; but all the beauty the wicked will ever have is in full bloom in this life ; it will wither, fade, decay, rot, and utterly pass away. Who, then, would envy or fear the proud sinner ?

15. "*But God will redeem my soul from the power of the grave.*" Forth from that temporary resting-place we shall come in due time, quickened by divine energy. Like our risen Head we cannot be holden by the bands of the grave ; redemption has emancipated us from the slavery of death. No redemption could man find in riches, but God has found it in the blood of his dear Son. Our Elder Brother has given to God a ransom, and we are the redeemed of the Lord : because of this redemption by price we shall assuredly be redeemed by power out of the hand of the last enemy. "*For he shall receive me.*" He shall take me out of the tomb, take me up to heaven. If it is not said of me as of Enoch, "He was not, for God took him," yet shall I reach the same glorious state. My spirit God will receive, and my body shall sleep in Jesus till, being raised in his image, it shall also be received into glory. How infinitely superior is such a hope to anything which our oppressors can boast ! Here is something which will bear meditation, and therefore again let us pause, at the bidding of the musician, who inserts a "*Selah.*"

16 Be not thou afraid when one is made rich, when the glory of his house is increased ;

17 For when he dieth he shall carry nothing away : his glory shall not descend after him.

18 Though while he lived he blessed his soul : and *men* will praise thee, when thou doest well to thyself.

19 He shall go to the generation of his fathers ; they shall never see light.

20 Man *that is* in honour, and understandeth not, is like the beasts *that* perish.

16. In these last verses the Psalmist becomes a preacher, and gives admonitory lessons which he has himself gathered from experience. "*Be not thou afraid when one is made rich.*" Let it not give thee any concern to see the godless prosper. Raise no questions as to divine justice ; suffer no foreboding to cloud thy mind. Temporal prosperity is too small a matter to be worth fretting about ; let the dogs have their bones, and the swine their draff. "*When the glory of his house is increased.*" Though the sinner and his family are in great esteem, and stand exceedingly high, never mind ; all things will be righted in due time. Only those whose judgment is worthless will esteem men the more because their lands are broader ; those who are highly estimated for such unreasonable reasons will find their level ere long, when truth and righteousness come to the fore.

17. "*For when he dieth he shall carry nothing away.*" He has but a leasehold of his acres, and death ends his tenure. Through the river of death man must pass naked. Not a rag of all his raiment, not a coin of all his treasure, not a jot of all his honour, can the dying worldling carry with him. Why then fret ourselves about so fleeting a prosperity ? "*His glory shall not descend after him.*" As he goes down, down, down for ever, none of his honours or possessions will follow him. Patents of nobility are invalid in the sepulchre. His worship, his honour, his lordship, and his grace, will alike find their titles ridiculous in the tomb. Hell knows no aristocracy. Your dainty and delicate sinners shall find that eternal burnings have no respect for their affectations and refinements.

18. "*Though while he lived he blessed his soul.*" He pronounced himself happy. He had his good things in this life. His chief end and aim were to bless himself. He was charmed with the adulations of flatterers. "*Men will praise thee, when thou doest well to thyself.*" The generality of men worship success, however it may be gained. The colour of the winning horse is no matter ; it is the winner, and that is enough. "Take care of Number One," is the world's proverbial philosophy, and he who gives good heed to it is "a clever fellow," "a fine man of business," "a shrewd common-sense tradesman," "a man with his head put on the right way," Get money, and you will be "respectable," "a substantial man," and your

house will be " an eminent firm in the city," or " one of our best county families."
To do good wins fame in heaven, but to do good *to yourself* is the prudent thing
among men of the world. Yet not a whisper of worldly congratulation can follow
the departing millionaire ; they say he died worth a mint of money, but what charm
has that fact to the dull cold ear of death ? The banker rots as fast as the shoe-
black, and the peer becomes as putrid as the pauper. Alas ! poor wealth, thou
art but the rainbow colouring of the bubble, the tint which yellows the morning
mist, but adds no substance to it.

19. " *He shall go to the generation of his fathers.*" Where the former generations
lie, the present shall also slumber. The sires beckon to their sons to come to the
land of forgetfulness. Mortal fathers beget not immortal children. As our ancestors
have departed, so also must we. " *They shall never see light.*" To this upper
region the dead worldling shall never return again to possess his estates, and enjoy
his dignities. Among the dead he must lie in the thick darkness, where no joy
or hope can come to him. Of all his treasures their remains not enough to furnish
him one poor candle ; the blaze of his glory is out for ever, and not a spark remains
to cheer him. How then can we look with fear or envy upon a wretch doomed
to such unhappiness ?

20. The song ends with the refrain, " *Man that is in honour, and understandeth
not, is like the beasts that perish.*" Understanding differences men from animals,
but if they will not follow the highest wisdom, and like beasts find their all in this
life, then their end shall be as mean and dishonourable as that of beasts slain in the
chase, or killed in the shambles. From the loftiest elevation of worldly honour
to the uttermost depth of death is but a step. Saddest of all is the reflection, that
though men are like beasts in all the degradation of perishing, yet not in the rest
which animal perishing secures, for, alas ! it is written, " These shall go away into
everlasting punishment."

So ends the minstrel's lay. Comforting as the theme is to the righteous, it is
full of warning to the worldly. Hear ye it, O ye rich and poor. Give ear to it,
ye nations of the earth.

EXPLANATORY NOTES AND QUAINT SAYINGS.

Whole Psalm.—Strange it is that two Psalms so near together, as this and the
forty-fifth should, and should alone imitate, or be the forerunners of, two works
of David's son ; this Ecclesiastes, the former—the Canticles.—*J. M. Neale.*

Verse 2.—In this Psalm David, as it were, summons and divides mankind. In
the first verse he summons : " *Hear this, all ye people ; give ear, all ye inhabitants
of the world.*" In the second verse he divides : " *Both low and high, rich and poor,
together.*" The word in the Hebrew for " *high* " is אִישׁ בְּנֵי, bene ish, sons of Ish,
and the word for " *low* " is אָדָם בְּנֵי bene Adam, sons of Adam. If we should translate
the text directly, according to the letter, the words must run, *sons of men and sons
of men ;* for, sons of *Adam* and sons of *Ish* are both translated *sons of men.* Yet
when they are set together in a way of opposition, the one signifieth " *low* " and the
other " *high ;* " and so our translators render it according to the sense, not sons
of men and sons of men, but " *low* " and " *high.*" Junius translates to this sense,
though in more words, as well they who are born of mean men, as they who are
born of honourable.—*Joseph Caryl.*

Verse 4.—" *I will incline mine ear to a parable,*" *i.e.,* I will diligently attend,
that I may not sing anything ungracefully ; a metaphor taken from musicians
who bring their ear close to the harp, that they may ascertain the harmony of the
sound.—*Victorinus Bythner.*

Verse 5.—" *Wherefore should I fear in the days of evil, when the iniquity of my
heels shall compass me about ?* " Those that are full of years are approaching the
nearer to their happiness. They have finished their voyage, and now are in sight
of the haven. Nature's provision is spent, her stock is exhausted, and now the

good man doth not so much descend as fall into the grave, and from thence he rises to heaven and eternal bliss. And shall he be disturbed at this? shall he be afraid to be made happy? If I mistake not, this is the meaning of the Psalmist's words. They are generally interpreted concerning *his ways* in general, but they seem to me to refer particularly to the calamity which his old age was incident to: for *" the days of evil "* are old age, and are so called by the wise man (Eccl. xii. 1); and as the *" heel "* is the extreme part of the body, so it is here applied to the last part of man's life, his declining age; and *" iniquity "* (as the word is sometimes used among the Hebrews) signifies here penal evil, and denotes the infirmities and decays of the concluding part of a man's life. So that the true meaning of the Psalmist's words, is this, I will not now in my last days be dejected with fear and trouble of mind, for I am coming towards my happiness, my declining years shall deliver me up to earth, and that shall consign me to everlasting life. This certainly is matter of joy rather than of fear. For this reason I account my last days to be the most eligible part of my whole life.—*John Edwards, D.D.* (1637—1716), *in " Theologia Reformata."*

Verse 5.—*" Wherefore should I fear in the days of evil, when the iniquity of my heels shall compass me about?"* That is, when my sins or failings in what I have done, come to my remembrance, or are chastened upon me. Every man's heel hath some iniquity: as we shall have some dirt cleaving to our heels while we walk in a dirty world, so there is some dirt, some defilement, upon all our actions, which we may call, *the iniquity of our heel.—Joseph Caryl.*

Verse 5.—*" When the iniquity of my heels shall compass me about?"* With Bishop Lowth, the celebrated Michaelis, Bishop Hare, and a host of other critics, I decidedly incline to the idea, that עֲקֵבַי, rendered *" my heels "* is to be regarded as the present participle of the verb עָקַב, *to supplant, to act deceitfully, to deceive, to hold one by the heel*, etc., etc. If this be correct then the proper translation will be:—

> Wherefore should I fear in the days of adversity,
> The iniquity of my supplanters who surround me?

The Syriac and Arabic read, as does also Dr. Kennicott:—

> Why should I fear in the evil day,
> When the iniquity of my enemies compasses me about?

John Morison.

Verses 5—9.

> Why should I fear the evil hour,
>   When ruthless foes in ambush lie,
> Who revel in their pride of power,
>   And on their hoarded wealth rely?
>
> A brother's ransom who can pay,
>   Or alter God's eternal doom?
> What hand can wrest from death his prey,
>   Its banquet from the rotting tomb?

From " The Psalter, or Psalms of David, in English verse. By a Member of the University of Cambridge." [*Benjamin Hall Kennedy, D.D.*] 1860.

Verse 6.—*" They that trust in their wealth, and boast themselves in the multitude of their riches."* Here we have the rich man trusting and boasting; surely that is very confident trusting which issues itself into boasting! That man is ascended to the highest step of faith in God, who makes his boast of God; such faith have they in fine gold who boast in it.—*Joseph Caryl.*

Verse 6.—*" They that trust in their wealth."* " THE COVETOUS MAN'S SOLILOQUY." Believe me, the times are hard and dangerous; charity is grown cold, and friends uncomfortable; an empty purse is full of sorrow, and hollow bags make a heavy heart. Poverty is a civil pestilence, which frights away both friends and kindred and leaves us to a " Lord have mercy upon us." It is a sickness very catching and infectious, and more commonly abhorred than cured. The best antidote against it is Angelica and providence, and the best cordial is *aurum potabile.* Gold-taking fasting is an approved sovereign. Debts are ill humours, and turn at last to dangerous obstructions. Lending is a mere consumption of the radical humour, which, if consumed, brings a patient to nothing. Let others trust to courtiers' promises, to friends' performances, to princes' favours; give me a toy called gold, give me a thing called money. O blessed Mammon, how extremely sweet is thy all-commanding presence to my thriving soul! In banishment thou art my dear companion; in captivity thou art my precious ransom; in trouble and vexation thou art my dainty rest; in sickness thou art my health; in grief my only joy; in all extremity my only trust. Virtue must veil to thee; nay, grace itself, not relished with thy sweetness, would even displease the righteous palates of the sons of men. Come, then, my soul, advise, contrive, project; go, compass sea and land; leave no exploit untried, no path untrod, no time unspent; afford thine eyes no sleep, thy head no rest; neglect thy ravenous belly, unclothe thy back; deceive, betray, swear, and forswear, to compass such a friend. If thou be base in birth, it will make thee honourable; if weak in power, it will make thee formidable. Are thy friends few? It will make them numerous. Is thy cause bad? It will gain thee advocates. True, wisdom is an excellent help, in case it bend this way; and learning is a genteel ornament, if not too chargeable: yet, by your leave, they are but estates for the term of life: but everlasting gold, if well advantaged, will not only bless thy days, but thy surviving children from generation to generation. Come, come, let others fill their brains with dear-bought wit, turn their pence into expenseful charity, and store their bosoms with unprofitable piety; let them lose all to save their imaginary consciences, and beggar themselves at home to be thought honest abroad: fill thou thy bags and barns, and lay up for many years, and take thy rest.—*Francis Quarles, in " The Covetous Man's Care."*

Verse 6.—The form of money agreeth well with the condition of it; for it is stamped round, because it is so apt to run from a man. Fire, thieves, waters, and infinite causes there are of consuming riches, and impoverishing their possessors, though they have even millions and mountains of gold; but suppose that contrary to their nature they stay by a man, yet cannot *he* stay by them, but must leave them in spite of his teeth, as the Psalmist saith (xlix. 17), "The rich man shall take away nothing when he dieth, neither shall his pomp follow after him." Thus death makes a violent divorce between the rich man and his goods, when it is said unto him, "Thou fool, this night shall they take away thy soul." The rich man sleeps (saith Job very elegantly), and when he openeth his eyes there is nothing. It fares with a rich man at his death, as it doth with a sleeping man when he wakes out of his dream. A man that dreams of the finding or fruition of some rich booty is wonderful glad, yet when he awaketh he findeth nothing, but seeth it was only a dream, and he is sorry; so the rich man seemed in the time of his life to have somewhat, but at the day of his death all vanisheth like the idea of a dream, and it vexeth him.—*J. D., in " The Threefold Resolutions,"* 1608.

Verse 6.—Who knocks more boldly at heaven-gate to be let in than they whom Christ will reject as workers of iniquity? Oh, what delusion is this! Caligula never made himself more ridiculous than when he would be honoured as a god, while he lived more like a devil. Before you would have others take you for Christians, for God's sake prove yourselves men and not beasts, as you do by your brutish lives. Talk not of your hopes of salvation so long as the marks of damnation are seen upon your flagitious lives. If the way to heaven were thus easy, I promise you the saints in all ages have been much overseen, to take so great pains in mortifying their lusts, in denying to satisfy their sensual appetite. To what purpose did they make so much waste of their sweat in their zealous serving God? and of their tears that they could serve him no better, if they might have gone to heaven as these men hope to do? That friar was far more sound in his judgment in this point, who, preaching at Rome one Lent, when some cardinals and many other great ones were present, began his sermon thus abruptly and ironically. Saint Peter was a fool, Saint Paul was a fool, and all the primitive Christians were fools; for they thought the way to heaven was by prayers and tears, watchings and fastings, severities of mortification, and denying the pomp and glory of this world; whereas you here in Rome spend your time in balls and masks, live in pomp, and pride, lust and luxury, and yet count yourselves good Christians, and hope to be saved; but at last you will prove the fools, and they will be found to have been the wise men.— *William Gurnall's Funeral Sermon for Lady Mary Vere,* 1671.

Verses 6—10.—David speaks of some "*that trust in their wealth, and boast themselves in the multitude of their riches."* Rich men can do great things, but here is a thing that they cannot do: "*None of them can by any means redeem his brother, nor give to God a ransom for him."* From what cannot a rich man redeem his brother? It is true of spiritual redemption; yea, that is furthest out of the rich man's reach money will not do it : "We are not redeemed with corrupt things, such as silver and gold, but with the precious blood of the Son of God." 1 Peter i. 18, 19. But the Psalmist speaks of a lower redemption, to which all the riches of man cannot reach : " None of them can by any means redeem his brother, nor give to God a ransom for him : " " for the redemption of their soul (that is, of their person from the grave), is precious, and it ceaseth for ever." And that he speaks of their redmption from the grave is more clearly expressed at the ninth verse : " That he should still live for ever, and not see corruption." Jesus Christ did not so redeem us that we should live for ever, and not see corruption. It was the privilege of Jesus Christ the Redeemer not to see corruption ; but Jesus Christ hath not redeemed us that we should not see corruption. He hath redeemed us that we should live for ever in heaven, but he hath not redeemed us from corruption, that we should live for ever on earth, or not see corruption in the grave ; for, as it is said in the tenth verse of the Psalm, we see " that wise men die, likewise the fool and the brutish person perish and leave their wealth to others ; " as if he had said, Neither the one nor the other sort of men could make this use or improvement of their wealth, to deliver themselves from going to the grave, for if they could they would have laid all out on that purchase ; but they could not do it, therefore, " they leave their wealth to others." —Joseph Caryl.

Verse 7.—" None of them can by any means redeem his brother," etc. Some animals devoted to God could be redeemed at a price, but no price could be assigned to the ransom of a soul. That such a ransom was to be provided, the faith of the church had always anticipated : " He shall redeem Israel from all his iniquities." Psalm cxxx. 8.—W. Wilson, D.D.

Verse 8.—" For the redemption of their soul is precious, and it ceaseth for ever." In this judgment tears will not prevail, prayers will not be heard, promises will not be admitted, repentance will be too late, and as for riches, honourable titles, sceptres and diadems, these will profit much less, and the inquisition shall be so curious and diligent, that not one light thought, not one idle word (not repented of in thy life past) shall be forgotten, for truth itself hath said, not in jest, but in earnest, of every idle word which men have spoken, they shall give an account in the day of judgment. Oh, how many which now sin with great delight, yea, even with greediness (as if we served a god of wood or of stone which seeth nothing nor can do nothing) will be then astonished, ashamed, and silent. Then shall the days of thy mirth be ended, and thou shalt be overwhelmed with everlasting darkness, and in stead of thy pleasures thou shalt have everlasting torments.—Thomas Tymme.

Verse 8.—" For it cost more to redeem their souls : so that he must let that alone for ever."—Prayer-book Version.

Verse 8.—" It ceaseth for ever." That is, wealth for ever comes short of the power necessary to accomplish this. It has always been insufficient ; it always will be. There is no hope that it ever will be sufficient, that by any increase in the amount, or by any change in the conditions of the bargain, property or riches can avail for this. The whole matter is perfectly hopeless as to the power of wealth in saving one human being from the grave. It must always fail in saving a man from death. The word rendered ceaseth—חדל, khadal, means to leave off, to desist, to fail. Gen. xi. 8 ; Ex. ix. 34 ; Isa. ii. 22.—Albert Barnes.

Verse 11.—" Their inward thought is, that their houses shall continue for ever." This is the interpretation of our actions, when we do not make God our portion, but trust in the abundance of our riches ; this is our " inward thought," the saying of our heart, Ye are my god. We do in effect say, Thou art my confidence, my hope, and my joy, and will stand by me when all things cease and fail, and wilt not suffer me to want, or to be wrong, as long as thou lastest : these are the secret speeches of our hearts. Christians ! many may (orator like), declaim against the vanity of the creature, and speak as basely of money as others do, and say, We know it is but a little refined earth ; but their hearts close with it, they are loth to part with it for God's sake, or upon God's declared will. As he that speaketh good words of God, is not said to trust in God ; so speaking bad words of worldly riches doth not exempt us from trusting them. There is a difference between declaiming as an orator, and acting like a Christian.—Thomas Manton.

Verse 11.—" Their inward thought." If good thoughts be thy deep thoughts, if, as we say, the best at the bottom, thy thoughts are then right, and thou art righteous ; for as the deep thoughts of worldlings are worldly thoughts, and the deep thoughts of wicked men are wicked thoughts, so the deep thoughts of good men are good thoughts. 'Tis a notable observation of the Holy Ghost's concerning worldly men, that *" their inward thought is that their houses shall continue for ever,"* etc. Why ? is there any thought that is not an *inward* thought ? No, but the meaning is, though they have some floating thoughts of their mortality, and the vanity and transitoriness of all worldly things, swimming, as it were, on the top ; yet they do not suffer such thoughts *to sink into their hearts*, or to go to the bottom ; but the thoughts that lodge there are such as his, who is said by our Saviour to have thought within himself, " Soul, thou hast much goods laid up for many years ; take thine ease, eat, drink, and be merry." Luke xii. 19. Note the phrase, " he thought within himself." There are other kinds of thoughts that sometimes knock at the door of the worldling's heart, nay, sometimes look in at his windows, as Paul's sermon began to press in upon Felix his heart, and to set him a-trembling ; but there are other *thoughts within*, which if they cannot keep good thoughts quite out, they will keep them off from making any due or deep impression upon the heart. Now, these thoughts that nestle themselves as it were at the very heart-roots, to keep others out from reaching thither, these *deep thoughts* are they which the Scriptures call the *" inward thoughts,"* according to that of the Psalmist (Psalm lxiv. 6), " The inward thought of every one of them, and the heart, is deep." —*Faithful Teat in " Right Thoughts the Righteous man's Evidence,"* 1666.

Verse 11.—*" They call their lands after their own names."* God makes fools of them, for how few have you that go beyond the third generation ? How few houses have you that the child or the grandchild can say, " This was my grandfather's, and my great grandfather's " ? How few houses have you that those that are now in them can say, " My ancestor dwelt here, and these were his lands " ? Go over a whole country, few can say so. Men when they build, together with building in the earth, they build castles in the air ; they have conceits. Now I build for my child, and for my child's child. God crosses them. Either they have no posterity, or by a thousand things that fall out in the world, it falls out otherwise. The time is short, and the fashion of this world passeth away ; that is, the buildings pass away, the owning passeth away, all things here pass away ; and, therefore, buy as if you possessed not, buy, so as we neglect not the best possession in heaven, and so possess these things, as being not possessed and commanded of them.— *Richard Sibbes.*

Verse 11.—Mr. A. was a wealthy farmer in Massachusetts, about sixty years of age, and it had been his ruling, and almost only passion in life to acquire property. His neighbour B. owned a small farm, which came too near the centre of A.'s extended domain, was quite a blot in his prospect, destroyed the regularity of his lands, and on the whole it was really necessary, in his opinion, that he should add it to his other property. B. became embarassed, and was sued ; judgments were obtained, and executions issued. A. now thought he should obtain the land, but one execution after another was arranged, and finally the debt was paid off without selling the land. When A. heard of the payment of the last execution, which put an end to his hopes of obtaining the land, he exclaimed, " Well, B. is an old man, and cannot live long, and when he dies I can buy the lot." B. was fifty-eight, A. was sixty ! Reader, do you ever expect to die ?—*K. Arvine's Cyclopædia of Moral and Religious Anecdotes.*

Verse 11.—I have purchased, saith one, such lands, and I have got so good a title to them, that certainly they will remain mine and my heirs for ever ; never considering how all things here below are subject to ebbings and flowings, to turns and vicissitudes every day.—*Joseph Caryl.*

Verse 11.—The fleeting nature of all earthly possessions is well illustrated in the life of William Beckford, and the unenduring character of gorgeous fabrics in the ruin of his famous Babel, Fonthill Abbey. Byron sang of Beckford's palace in Spain, in language most applicable to Fonthill :—

> " There, too, thou Vathek ! England's wealthiest son—
> Once formed thy Paradise, as not aware
> When wanton wealth her mightiest deeds hath done,
> Meek Peace voluptuous lures was ever wont to shun.
> Here didst thou dwell ; here schemes of pleasure plan,
> Beneath yon mountain's ever beauteous brow.

> But now, as if a thing unblest by man,
> Thy fairy dwelling is as lone as thou !
> Here giant weeds a passage scarce allow,
> To halls deserted, portals gaping wide ;
> Fresh lessons to the thinking bosom, how
> Vain are the pleasaunces on earth supplied,
> Swept into wrecks anon by Time's ungentle tide ! "
>
> *C. H. S.*

Verses 11, 12.—" *They call their* GROUNDS *after their names. But the* GROUNDLING, *in the midst of splendour, endureth not.*" In verse 11, we have אֲדָמוֹת " *grounds.*" In verse 12, it is אָדָם, " *groundling,*" with a designed iteration and play upon the word ; for want of an attention to which the passage has not been fully understood.— *John Mason Good.*

Verse 12.—" *Man being in honour abideth not.*" The rabbins read it thus : " Adam being in honour, *lodged not one night.*" The Hebrew word for *abide* signifies " to stay or lodge all night." Adam, then, it seems, did not take up one night's lodging in Paradise.—*Thomas Watson's Body of Divinity.*

Verse 13.—" *This their way is their folly : yet their posterity approve their sayings.*" Master Baxter speaks very well of this in his " Saints' Everlasting Rest," which is a very choice book. The gentry teach their children to follow pleasure, and the commonalty their children to follow profit, and young ones are ready to follow old ones. " *This their way is their folly.*" The very heathen condemn this, and yet Christians mind it not. Crates the philosopher said, that if possibly he might, he would willingly mount to the highest place of the city, and there cry aloud in this manner, " What mean you, my masters, and whither run you headlong ? carking and caring all that ever you can, to gather goods and make riches as you do, whiles in the meantime you make little or no reckoning at all of your children, unto whom you are to leave all your riches ? Do not most care more for the wealth of their children's outward man, than for the health of their inward man ? "—*J. Votier's Survey of Effectual Calling,* 1652.

Verse 13.—" *This their way is their folly.*" The folly of man seldom appears more than in being very busy about nothing, in making a great cry where there is little wool ; like that empty fellow that showed himself to Alexander—having spent much time, and taken much pains at it beforehand—and boasted that he could throw a pea through a little hole, expecting a great reward ; but the king gave him only a bushel of peas, for a recompense suitable to his diligent negligence, or his busy idleness. Things that are vain and empty are unworthy of our care and industry. The man that by hard labour and hazard of his life did climb up to the top of the steeple to set an egg on end, was deservedly the object of pity and laughter. We shall think him little better than mad that should make as great a fire for the roasting of an egg as for the roasting of an ox.—*George Swinnock.*

Verse 13.—" *Their folly : yet their posterity approve.*" Dr. Leifchild, in his *Remarkable Facts,*" records the following incident, of a person of property, who had been accustomed regularly to attend his ministry, but who had always manifested a covetous disposition : " I was sent for to offer to him the consolation of religion as he lay upon his dying bed. What was my surprise, after having conversed and prayed with him, to find that he was unwilling to take my hand, muttering that he knew that he had not done what was right in reference to the support and furtherance of religion, but intended to amend in that respect. He then requested me to say what I thought would become of him. How could I reply, but by exhorting him to repent, and relinquishing all further thoughts of a worldly nature, to betake himself to the sacrifice and mediation of the Son of God for pardon, safety, and salvation in that world which he was to all appearance soon about to enter ? He gazed at me with a look of disappointment. Upon a hint being given me to inquire into his thoughts at that moment, I questioned him very pointedly, and to my astonishment and horror, he reluctantly disclosed to me the fact that, while thus seemingly about to breathe his last, his hands were under the bed clothes grasping the keys of his cabinet and treasures, lest they should be taken from him ! Soon after, he departed this life, and there was, alas ! reason to fear that, together with his property, he had transmitted somewhat of his fatal passion to those who survived him. It was distressing to me to reflect that a hearer of mine should quit this world with his fingers stiffened in death around the keys of his treasures. How strong, how terrible, was the ruling passion in the death of this man ! "

Verse 13.—" *Selah.*"   See " Treasury of David," Vol. I., pp. 23, 26, 27;
and Vol. II., pp. 224—227.

Verse 14.—" *Like sheep they are laid in the grave ; death shall feed on them ;
and the upright shall have dominion over them in the morning ; and their beauty shall
consume in the grave from their dwelling,*" or as we put in the margin, " *The grave
being an habitation to every one of them, shall consume their beauty.*"   Some may
object, Is not this true of godly men too ? are not they thus handled by death
and the grave ? doth not death feed on them ? and doth not the grave consume
their beauty ?   I answer, Though it doth, yet it hath not to feed upon, nor consume
them, as it feeds upon and consumes wicked men.   For the Psalmist speaks here
of death as it were triumphing over the wicked, whereas the godly triumph over
death.   For, first, he saith, The wicked are *laid in the grave like sheep :* they lived
like *wolves* or *lions,* but they are laid in the grave like *sheep.*   If it be asked, Why
like sheep ?   I answer, not for the innocency of their lives, but for their impotency
in death ; as if it had been said, when once death took them in hand to lay them
in the grave, they could make no more resistance than a sheep can against a lion
or a wolf.   And when death hath thus laid them in the grave, then secondly, saith
the Psalmist, " *Death shall feed on them,*" as a lion doth upon a sheep, or any wild
beast upon his prey, which is a further degree of death's triumph over the wicked.
And, thirdly, " *Their beauty shall consume in the grave,*" that is, all their bodily
and natural beauty (and this is all the beauty which they have) shall consume
in the grave, whereas the godly have a beauty (and they count it their only beauty)
which the grave cannot consume, and that is the beauty of their graces, the beauty of
holiness, the spiritual beauty of the inner man, yea, and the spiritual beauty of
their outward holy actings shall not consume in the grave ; for, " Blessed are the
dead which die in the Lord from henceforth : Yea, saith the Spirit, that they may
rest from their labours ; and their works do follow them."   Rev. xiv. 13.—*Joseph
Caryl.*

Verse 14.—" *Death shall feed on them :* " rather, " *Death shall be their shepherd.*"
(*Sept.*)   At the end of the foregoing Psalm, the Psalmist had said in the name of
his people, that " God is our God, for ever and ever ; he will lead us as a shepherd
over death," and here he takes up the same pastoral figure, and contrasts with their
case the case of the proud and prosperous worldly men, who trust in their earthly
riches and power.   *They* will *not* be led in safety, under the pastoral care of God,
over death.   No ; *death* itself will be *their* Shepherd, and the grave will be their
sheep-fold ; where they will be laid together like asheep in a pen.   As Augustine
says, " Death is the shepherd of the infidel.   Life (*i.e.,* Christ) is the Shepherd of
the faithful."   " *In inferno sunt oves quibus pastor Mors est ; in cælo sunt oves
quibus pastor Vita est.*"   And so Keble—

> Even as a flock arrayed are they
> For the dark grave ; Death guides their way,
> Death is their Shepherd now.
> > > *Christopher Wordsworth.*

Verse 14.—"*In the morning,*" that is, saith Dathe, in the *time of judgment.*   He
thinks there is here an allusion to the usual time of holding courts of justice, which
was in the morning.   See Psalms lxxiii. 14, and ci. 8 ; and Jer. xxi. 12.—*Editorial
note to Calvin in loc.*

Verse 14.—" *Their beauty shall consume in the grave.*"   And now if we do but
consider a little of the tombs and sepulchres of princes and noblemen, whose glory
and majesty we have seen when they lived here on earth, and do behold the horrible
forms and shapes which they now have, shall we not cry out as men amazed, Is
this that glory ?   Is this that highness and excellency ?   Whither now are the
degrees of their waiting servants gone ?   Where are their ornaments and jewels ?
Where is their pomp, their delicacy and niceness ?   All these things are vanished
away like the smoke, and there is now nothing left but dust, horror, and stink.
The soul being dissolved, there lieth upon the ground not a human body, but a
dead carcase without life, without sense, without strength, and so fearful to look
upon, that the sight thereof may hardly be endured.   To be sure, it is a little better
(as touching the substance) than the body of a horse, or a dog, which lieth dead in
the fields, and all that pass by stop their noses and make haste away, that they
be not annoyed with the sight and stink thereof.   Such is man's body now become ;
yea, and though it were the body of a monarch, emperor, or a king.   Where is

that majesty, that excellency, that authority which he had aforetime when all men trembled to behold it, and might not come in presence thereof without all reverence and obeisance? what are all those things become? were they a dream or shadow? After those things the funeral is prepared, the which is all that men can carry with them, of all their riches and kingdom, and this also they should not have, if in their lifetime they did not appoint it for their dignity and honour. For the prophet David saith truly (verse 16), *" Be not thou afraid though one be made rich,* or, *if the glory of his house be increased ; for when he dieth he shall carry nothing away with him, neither shall his pomp follow him."—Thomas Tymme.*

Verse 14.—When we look to a charnel-house, and take a view of the grave, what amazing and dismal scenes present themselves! How many great and important images appear! Distracting horrors strike our imagination, and hideous sounds of diseases, destruction, and death, with all their woful and black train, terrify us. Ah! the melancholy confused heap of the ruins of mankind, what a terrible carnage is made of the human race! and what a solemn and awful theatre of mortality, covered with the disordered remains of our fellow creatures, presents itself to our minds! There lie the bones of a proud monarch, who fancied himself a little god, mingled with the ashes of his poorest subjects! Death seized him in the height of his vanity, he was just returning from a conquest, and his haughty mind was swelled with his power and greatness, when one of these fatal arrows pierced his heart, and at once finished all his perishing thoughts and contrivances, then the dream of glory vanished, and all his empire was confined to the grave. Look how pale that victorious general appears, how dead, and cold, and lifeless these arms that were once accustomed to war ; see if you can discern any difference betwixt his dust and that of the most despicable slave. Yonder, a numerous army, once fierce and resolute, whose conquests were rapid as lightning, and made all the nations to shake for fear of them, are now so weak that they lie a prey, exposed to the meanest animals, the loathsome worms, who crawl in triumph over them, and insult their decayed ruins. There a body that was so much doted on, and solicitously cared for, and the beauty and shape whereof were so foolishly admired, now noisome and rotten, nothing but vermin are now fond of it, so affecting a change hath death made upon it. Look, next to this, upon the inglorious ashes of a rich, covetous wretch, whose soul was glued to this world, and hugged itself in its treasures ; with what mighty throes and convulsions did death tear him from this earth? How did his hands cling to his gold! with what vehement desires did he fasten on his silver, all of them weak and fruitless! Look now if riches saved him in that day, if you can perceive any of his useless treasures lying beside him in the grave, or if the glory of his house have descended after him! Yonder, an ambitious statesman, his rotten bones are scarce to be discerned : how did he applaud his artful schemes! how securely did he think them laid, and flattered himself with the hopes of an established greatness! but death stepped in, blew them all up at once ; this grave is the whole result of his counsels. And lo, there, what horrid and suffocating stink ascends from these many hellish sacrifices of lust and impurity, who wasted their strength in debauch, and carried down with them nothing but the shame of beastly pleasures to the grave. But there is no end to the corpses, nor can we survey this terrible field of death's conquests.— *William Dunlop.*

Verse 15 *(last clause).*—*" For he shall take me."* This short half-verse is, as Böttcher remarks, the more weighty, from its very shortness. The same expression occurs again, lxxiii. 24, " Thou shalt take me," the original of both being Gen. v. 24, where it is used of the translation of Enoch, " He was not, for God *took* him."— *J. J. Stewart Perowne.*

Verse 17.—*" For when he dieth, he shall carry nothing away."* The form of money agrees well with the condition of it ; it is stamped round, because it is so apt to run away. Could we be rich so long as we live, yet that were uncertain enough, for life itself is but a dream, a shadow, but a dream of a shadow. (Augustine.) Rich men are but like hailstones ; they make a noise in the world, as the other rattle on the tiles of a house ; down they fall, lie still, and melt away. So that if riches could stay by a man, yet he cannot stay by them. Spite of his teeth, *he shall carry away nothing when he dies.* Life and goods are both in a vessel, both cast away at once ; yea, of the two, life hath the more likelihood of continuance. Let it fly never so fast away, riches have eagles' wings, and will outfly it. There be thieves in the highways, that will take our moneys and spare our lives. In our penal laws, there be not so many ways to forfeit our lives as our goods. Rich Job lived to see himself poor to a proverb. How many in this city reputed rich, yet have broken for thousands ! There are innumerable ways to be poor ; a fire, a thief, a false servant, suretyship, trusting of bad customers, an unfaithful factor, a pirate, an unskilful pilot, hath brought rich men to poverty. One gale of wind is able to make merchants rich or beggars. Man's life is like the banks of a river, his temporal estate is the stream : time will moulder away the banks, but the stream stays not for that, it glides away continually. Life is the tree, riches are the fruit, or rather the leaves ; the leaves will fall, the fruit is plucked, and yet the tree stands. Some write of the pine tree, that if the bark be pulled off, it lasts long ; being on, it rots. If the worldling's bark were stripped off, he might perhaps live the longer, there is great hope he would live the better,—*Thomas Adams*.

Verse 17.—" *He shall carry nothing away.*" It is with us in this world, as it was in the Jewish fields and vineyards : *pluck and eat* they might what they would while they were there ; but they might not pocket or put up ought to carry with them. Deut. xxiii. 24.—*Thomas Gataker*.

Verse 17.—" *He shall carry nothing away.*" " He hath swallowed down riches, and he shall vomit them up again : God shall cast them out of his belly." Job xx. 15.

Verse 17.—" *Descends.*" Death takes the sinner by the throat, and " hauls him down stairs to the grave." The indulgence in any sinful propensity has this downward, deathly tendency. Every lust, whether for riches or honours, for gambling, wine, or women, leads the deluded, wretched votary step by step to the chambers of death. There is no hope in the dread prospect ; trouble and anguish possess the spirit. Hast thou escaped, O my soul, from the net of the infernal fowler ? Never forget that it is as a brand *snatched* from the burning. Oh to grace how great a debtor !—*George Offor's note in " The Works of John Bunyan."*

Verse 17.—

You will carry none of your riches, fool, to the waters of Acheron.
You will be ferried over quite naked in the infernal boat.

Propertius.

Verse 18.—How foolish is it to account thyself a better man than another, only because thy dunghill is a little bigger than his ! These things are not at all to be reckoned into the value and worth of a man : they are all without thee, and concern thee no more than fine clothes do the health or strength of the body. It is wealth indeed, that makes all the noise and bustle in the world, and challengeth all the respect and honour to itself ; and the ignorant vulgar, whose eyes are dazzled with pomp and bravery, pay it with a stupid and astonished reverence. Yet know, that it is but thy silks and velvet, thy lands, or thy retinue and servants, they venerate, not thee : and if thou thinkest otherwise, thou art as justly ridiculous as that ass in the apologue that grew very gravely proud, and took state, when the people fell prostrate before him, adoring, not him, but the idol he carried.—*Ezekiel Hopkins*.

Verse 20.—" *Like the beasts that perish.*" My lords, it is no wonder at all, if men that affect beastly pleasures, and dote upon perishing honours, become " *like the beasts that perish.*" It is no miracle if he that lives like a beast dies like a beast. Take a man that hath lived like the fool in the gospel, and tell me, what hath this man done for his immortal soul more than a beast doth for its perishing soul ? Soul, soul, cease from care, eat, drink, and take thine ease : this is the constant ditty of most men in honour : they have studied clothes and victuals, titles and offices, ways of gain and pleasure. Am I not yet at highest ? They have, it may be, studied the black art of flattery and treachery ; they understand the humour of the times, the compliances and dependences of this and the other statesman, the projects of divers princes abroad, and the main design here at home. Is this all ? Why then, be it known unto you, that the men of this strain have made no better provision for their precious souls, than if they had the soul, the vanishing soul of a beast within them ; and certainly, if we were to judge of the substance of men's souls by their unworthy and sensual conversation, we might easily fall into that heresy, that dangerous dream of some who conceive that their souls are mortal. —*Francis Cheynell, in a Sermon entitled, " The Man of Honour," . . . . preached before the Lords of Parliament, 1645.*

Verse 20.—*" Like the beasts that perish."* Sin is both *formaliter* and *effective* vile. As it is so in itself, so it has made man vile. No creature so debased as man, being in this respect become viler than any creature. There is no such depravation in the nature of any creature, except in the diabolical nature. No creature ever razed God's image out of its nature, but only man. There is no aversions to the will of God, no inclination to what offends him, in any creature on earth but man. Man, then, who was once the glory of the creation, is become the vilest of all creatures, for that is vilest which is most contrary to the infinite glory, but so is our nature, " Man being in honour, abideth not," is now *" like the beasts that perish; "* nay, worse than they, if the greatest evil can make him worse. Man was made a little lower than the angels, crowned with glory, advanced to be lord and governor of all the works of his hands ; and all creatures in this world were put under his feet. Psalm viii. 5, 6. But by this natural corruption he that was but a little lower than angels is now something below the beasts. He was to have dominion, but is made baser than those over whom he rules. They were put under his feet, but now he is as low as they. This is the sad issue of natural corruption.—*David Clarkson.*

Verse 20.—*" Like the beasts."* Man is so much a beast, that he cannot know himself to be one till God teach him. And we never learn to be men till we have learned that we were beasts. . . . . It is not said he is like this or that beast, but *" he is like the beasts that perish."* Take any beast, or all beasts, the worst of beasts, he is the picture of them all, and he daily exemplifies the vilest of their qualities in his own.—*Joseph Caryl.*

HINTS TO PREACHERS.

Verse 2.—I. The common needs of rich and poor men. II. The common privileges of rich and poor saints. III. Their common service. IV. Their common heaven.

Verse 3.—The deep things of God are intended, I. To exercise our minds to understand them. II. To try our faith by believing them—" incline " implies a submissive mind. III. To excite our joy as we grasp them—" upon the harp." IV. To employ our faculties in explaining them to others.

Verse 5.—I. The effects of our sin remain, 1. In ourselves. 2. In others. II. In a time of conviction they " *compass us about :* " better to do so in this life, than to haunt us as ghosts for ever. III. When they are pardoned we have nothing to fear.—*G. R.*

Verse 7.—1. *Implied.* The soul needs redeeming. 2. *Denied.* Wealth, power, learning, none can redeem. 3. *Supplied*—a ransom by Jesus. 4. *Applied*—by the Spirit to our actual deliverance.

Verse 12 (*last clause*).—Wherein the ungodly are like beasts, and wherein different.

Verse 12.—Here is a twofold thwarting or crossing of the purposes of the ungodly worldling. I. The first is, *he shall not be that which he ever wished to be :* he shall not continue in honour. II. The other is this, *he shall be that which he never desired to be :* he shall be like the beasts that die. He shall miss of that which he sought for, and he shall have that which he looked not for.—*S. Hieron.*

Verse 14.—In proportion to the prosperity of the ungodly here, will be their misery hereafter : as sheep from the fat pasture led to the slaughter-house. II. In proportion to their luxury here, will be their corruption hereafter—" *Death shall feed on them :* " they have become well fed for death to feed on them. III. In proportion to their dignity here, will be their degradation hereafter—" *The upright shall have,*" etc. Oh, what a contrast between the rich man and Lazarus then ! IV. In proportion to their beauty here, will be their deformity hereafter. " Art, thou become like one of us ? "—*G. R.*

Verse 14.—Sheep, how far they image the wicked.

Verse 14.—" *In the morning.*" See the various Biblical prophecies of what will happen " in the morning."

Verse 15.—1. *Return* to the dust I shall. 2. *Redeem* from the dust he will. 3. *Receive* into heaven he will. 4. *Rejoice* for ever I shall.

Verse 17.—The loaded and unloaded sinner.

Verse 20.—I. Men of spiritual understanding without worldly honour are higher than the angels of God in heaven. II. Men in worldly honour without the true wisdom are worse than the beasts that perish.—*G. R.*

PSALM L.

TITLE.—*A Psalm of Asaph.—This is the first of the Psalms of Asaph, but whether it was the production of that eminent musician, or merely dedicated to him, we cannot tell. The titles of twelve Psalms bear his name, but it could not in all of them be meant to ascribe their authorship to him, for several of these Psalms are of too late a date to have been composed by the same writer as the others. There was an Asaph in David's time, who was one of David's chief musicians, and his family appear to have continued long after in their hereditary office of temple musicians. An Asaph is mentioned as a recorder or secretary in the days of Hezekiah (2 Kings xviii. 18), and another was keeper of the royal forests under Artaxerxes. That Asaph did most certainly write some of the Psalms is clear from 2 Chron. xxix. 30, where it is recorded that the Levites were commanded to " sing praises unto the Lord with the words of Da id, and of Asaph the seer," but that other Asaphic Psalms were not of his composition, but were only committed to his care as a musician, is equally certain from 1 Chron. xvi. 7, where David is said to have delivered a Psalm into the hand of Asaph and his brethren. It matters little to us whether he wrote or sang, for poet and musician are near akin, and if one composes words and another sets them to music, they rejoice together before the Lord.*

DIVISIONS.—*The Lord is represented as summoning the whole earth to hear his declaration, 1—6 ; he then declares the nature of the worship which he accepts, 7—15, accuses the ungodly of breaches of the precepts of the second table, 16—21, and closes the court with a word of threatening, 22, and a direction of grace, 23.*

EXPOSITION.

THE mighty God, *even* the LORD, hath spoken, and called the earth from the rising of the sun unto the going down thereof.

2 Out of Zion, the perfection of beauty, God hath shined.

3 Our God shall come, and shall not keep silence : a fire shall devour before him; and it shall be very tempestuous round about him.

4 He shall call to the heavens from above, and to the earth, that he may judge his people.

5 Gather my saints together unto me ; those that have made a covenant with me by sacrifice.

6 And the heavens shall declare his righteousness : for God *is* judge himself. Selah.

1. " *The mighty God, even the Lord* "—El, Elohim, Jehovah, three glorious names for the God of Israel. To render the address the more impressive, these august titles are mentioned, just as in royal decrees the names and dignities of monarchs are placed in the forefront. Here the true God is described as Almighty, as the only and perfect object of adoration and as the self-existent' One, " *Hath spoken, and called the earth from the rising of the sun until the going down thereof.*" The dominion of Jehovah extends over the whole earth, and therefore to all mankind is his decree directed. The east and the west are bidden to hear the God who makes his sun to rise on every quarter of the globe. Shall the summons of the great King be despised ? Will we dare provoke him to anger by slighting his call ?

2. " *Out of Zion, the perfection of beauty, God hath shined.*" The Lord is represented not only as speaking to the earth, but as coming forth to reveal the glory of his presence to an assembled universe. God of old dwelt in Zion among his chosen people, but here the beams of his splendour are described as shining forth upon all nations. The sun was spoken of in the first verse, but here is a far brighter sun. The majesty of God is most conspicuous among his own elect, but it is not confined to them ; the church is not a dark lantern, but a candlestick. God shines

not only in Zion, but out of her. She is made perfect in beauty by his indwelling and that beauty is seen by all observers when the Lord shines forth from her.

Observe how with trumpet voice and flaming ensign the infinite Jehovah summons the heavens and the earth to hearken to his word.

3. "*Our God shall come.*" The Psalmist speaks of himself and his brethren as standing in immediate anticipation of the appearing of the Lord upon the scene. "He comes," they say, "our covenant God is coming;" they can hear his voice from afar, and perceive the splendour of his attending train. Even thus should we wait the long-promised appearing of the Lord from heaven. "*And shall not keep silence.*" He comes to speak, to plead with his people, to accuse and judge the ungodly. He has been silent long in patience, but soon he will speak with power. What a moment of awe when the Omnipotent is expected to reveal himself! What will be the reverent joy and solemn expectation when the poetic scene of this Psalm becomes in the last great day an actual reality! "*A fire shall devour before him, and it shall be very tempestuous round about him.*" Flame and hurricane are frequently described as the attendants of the divine appearance. "Our God is a consuming fire." "At the brightness that was before him his thick clouds passed, hailstones and coals of fire." Psalm xviii. 12. "He rode upon a cherub, and did fly; yea, he did fly upon the wings of the wind." "The Lord Jesus shall be revealed from heaven with his mighty angels, in flaming fire taking vengeance on them that know not God." 2 Thes. i. 7, 8. Fire is the emblem of justice in action, and the tempest is a token of his overwhelming power. Who will not listen in solemn silence when such is the tribunal from which the judge pleads with heaven and earth?

4. "*He shall call to the heavens from above, and to the earth.*" Angels and men, the upper and the lower worlds, are called to witness the solemn scene. The whole creation shall stand in court to testify to the solmnity and the truth of the divine pleading. Both earth beneath and heaven above shall unite in condemning sin; the guilty shall have no appeal, though all are summoned that they may appeal if they dare. Both angels and men have seen the guilt of mankind and the goodness of the Lord, they shall therefore confess the justice of the divine utterance, and say "Amen" to the sentence of the supreme Judge. Alas, ye despisers! What will ye do and to whom will ye fly? "*That he may judge his people.*" Judgment begins at the house of God. The trial of the visible people of God will be a most awful ceremonial. He will throughly purge his floor. He will discern between his nominal and his real people, and that in open court, the whole universe looking on. My soul, when this actually takes place, how will it fare with thee? Canst thou endure the day of his coming?

5. "*Gather my saints together unto me.*" Go, ye swift-winged messengers, and separate the precious from the vile. Gather out the wheat of the heavenly garner. Let the long-scattered, but elect people known by my separating grace to be my sanctified ones, be now assembled in one place. All are not saints who seem to be so—a severance must be made; therefore let all who profess to be saints be gathered before my throne of judgment, and let them hear the word which will search and try the whole, that the false may be convicted and the true revealed. "*Those that have made a covenant with me by sacrifice;*" this is the grand test, and yet some have dared to imitate it. The covenant was ratified by the slaying of victims, the cutting and dividing of offerings; this the righteous have done by accepting with true faith the great propitiatory sacrifice, and this the pretenders have done in merely outward form. Let them be gathered before the throne for trial and testing, and as many as have really ratified the covenant by faith in the Lord Jesus shall be attested before all worlds as the objects of distinguishing grace while formalists shall learn that outward sacrifices are all in vain. Oh, solemn assize, how does my soul bow in awe at the prospect thereof!

6. "*And the heavens shall declare his righteousness.*" Celestial intelligences and the spirits of just men made perfect, shall magnify the infalliable judgment of the divine tribunal. Now they doubtless wonder at the hypocrisy of men; then they shall equally marvel at the exactness of the severance between the true and the false. "*For God is judge himself.*" This is the reason for the correctness of the judgment. Priests of old, and churches of later times, were readily deceived, but not so the all-discerning Lord. No deputy-judge sits on the great white throne; the injured Lord of all himself weighs the evidence and allots the vengeance or reward. The scene in the Psalm is a grand poetical conception, but it is also an inspired prophecy of that day which shall burn as an oven, when the Lord shall discern

between him that feareth him and him that feareth him not. "*Selah.*" Here we may well pause in reverent prostration, in deep searching of heart, in humble prayer and in awe-struck expectation.

7 Hear, O my people, and I will speak; O Israel, and I will testify against thee: I *am* God, *even* thy God.

8 I will not reprove thee for thy sacrifices or thy burnt offerings, *to have been* continually before me.

9 I will take no bullock out of thy house, *nor* he goats out of thy folds.

10 For every beast of the forest *is* mine, *and* the cattle upon a thousand hills.

11 I know all the fowls of the mountains: and the wild beasts of the field *are* mine.

12 If I were hungry, I would not tell thee: for the world *is* mine, and the fulness thereof.

13 Will I eat the flesh of bulls, or drink the blood of goats?

14 Offer unto God thanksgiving; and pay thy vows unto the most High:

15 And call upon me in the day of trouble: I will deliver thee, and thou shalt glorify me.

The address which follows is directed to the professed people of God. It is clearly, in the first place, meant for Israel; but is equally applicable to the visible church of God in every age. It declares the futility of external worship when spiritual faith is absent and the mere outward ceremonial is rested in.

7. "*Hear, O my people, and I will speak.*" Because Jehovah speaks, and they are avowedly his own people, they are bound to give earnest heed. "Let me speak," saith the great I AM. The heavens and earth are but listeners, the Lord is about both to testify and to judge. "*O Israel, and I will testify against thee.*" Their covenant name is mentioned to give point to the address; it was a double evil that the chosen nation should become so carnal, so unspiritual, so false, so heartless to their God. God himself, whose eyes sleep not, who is not misled by rumour, but sees for himself, enters on the scene as witness against his favoured nation. Alas! for us when God, even our fathers' God, testifies to the hypocrisy of the visible church. "*I am God, even thy God.*" He had taken them to be his peculiar people above all other nations, and they had in the most solemn manner avowed that he was their God. Hence the special reason for calling them to account. The law began with, "I am the Lord thy God, which brought thee up out of the land of Egypt," and now the session of their judgment opens with the same reminder of their singular position, privilege, and responsibility. It is not only that Jehovah is God, but *thy* God, O Israel; this it is that makes thee so amenable to his searching reproofs.

8. "*I will not reprove thee for thy sacrifice or thy burnt offerings, to have been ever before me.*" Though they had not failed in maintaining his outward worship, or even if they had, he was not about to call them to account for this: a more weighty matter was now under consideration. They thought the daily sacrifices and the abounding burnt offerings to be everything: he counted them nothing if the inner sacrifice of heart devotion had been neglected. What was greatest with them was least with God. It is even so to-day. Sacraments (so called) and sacred rites are the main concern with unconverted but religious men, but with the Most High the spiritual worship which they forget is the sole matter. Let the external be maintained by all means according to the divine command, but if the secret and spiritual be not in them, they are a vain oblation, a dead ritual, and even an abomination before the Lord.

9. "*I will take no bullock out of thy house.*" Foolishly they dreamed that bullocks with horns and hoofs could please the Lord, when indeed he sought for hearts and souls. Impiously they fancied that Jehovah needed these supplies, and that if they fed his altar with their fat beasts, he would be content. What he intended for their instruction, they made their confidence. They remembered not that "to obey is better than sacrifice, and to hearken than the fat of rams." "*Nor*

he goats out of thy folds."   He mentions these lesser victims as if to rouse their common sense to see that the great Creator could find no satisfaction in mere animal offerings. If he needed these, he would not appeal to their scanty stalls and folds ; in fact, he here refuses to take so much as one, if they brought them under the false and dishonouring view, that they were in themselves pleasing to him.   This shows that the sacrifices of the law were symbolical of higher and spiritual things, and were not pleasing to God except under their typical aspect.   The believing worshipper looking beyond the outward was accepted, the unspiritual who had no respect to their meaning was wasting his substance, and blaspheming the God of heaven.

10. *" For every beast of the forest is mine."*   How could they imagine that the Most High God, possessor of heaven and earth, had need of beasts, when all the countless hordes that find shelter in a thousand forests and wildernesses belong to him ?   *" And the cattle upon a thousand hills."*   Not alone the wild beasts, but also the tamer creatures are all his own.   Even if God cared for these things, he could supply himself.   Their cattle were not, after all, their own, but were still the great Creator's property, why then should he be beholden to them.   From Dan to Beersheba, from Nebaioth to Lebanon, there fed not a beast which was not marked with the name of the great Shepherd ; why, then, should he crave oblations of Israel ?   What a slight is here put even upon sacrifices of divine appointment when wrongly viewed as in themselves pleasing to God !   And all this to be so expressly stated under the law !   How much more is this clear under the gospel, when it is so much more plainly revealed, that " God is a Spirit, and they that worship him must worship him in spirit and in truth " ?   Ye Ritualists, ye Sacramentarians, ye modern Pharisees, what say ye to this ?

11. *" I know all the fowls of the mountains."*   All the winged creatures are under my inspection and near my hand ; what then can be the value of your pairs of turtledoves and your two young pigeons ?   The great Lord not only feeds all his creatures, but is well acquainted with each one ; how wondrous is this knowledge ! *" And the wild beasts of the field are mine."*   The whole population moving over the plain belongs to me ; why then should I seek your beeves and rams ?   In me all things live and move ; how mad are you to suppose that I desire your living things ! A spiritual God demands other life than that which is seen in animals ; he looks for spiritual sacrifice, for the love, the trust, the praise, the life of your hearts.

12. *" If I were hungry, I would not tell thee."*   Strange conception, a hungry God !   Yet if such an absurd ideal could be truth, and if the Lord hungered for meat he would not ask it of men.   He could provide for himself out of his own possessions ; he would not turn suppliant to his own creatures.   Even under the grossest idea of God, faith in outward ceremonies is ridiculous.   Do men fancy that the Lord needs banners, and music, and incense, and fine linen ?   If he did, the stars would emblazon his standard, the winds and the waves become his orchestra, ten thousand times ten thousand flowers would breathe forth perfume, the snow should be his alb, the rainbow his girdle, the clouds of light his mantle.   O fools and slow of heart, ye worship ye know not what !   *" For the world is mine, and the fulness thereof."* What can he need who is owner of all things and able to create as he wills ?   Thus overwhelmingly does the Lord pour forth his arguments upon formalists.

13. *" Will I eat the flesh of bulls, or drink the blood of goats ? "*   Are you so infatuated as to think this ?   Is the great I AM subject to corporeal wants, and are they to be thus grossly satisfied ?   Heathens thought thus of their idols, but dare ye think thus of the God who made the heavens and the earth ?   Can ye have fallen so low as to think thus of me, O Israel ?   What vivid reasoning is here !   How the fire-flashes dart into the idiot faces of trusters in outward forms !   Ye dupes of Rome, can ye read this and be unmoved ?   The expostulation is indignant ;   the questions utterly confound ;   the conclusion is inevitable ;   heart worship only can be acceptable with the true God.   It is inconceivable that outward things can gratify him, except so far as through them our faith and love express themselves.

14. *" Offer unto God thanksgiving."*   No longer look at your sacrifices as in themselves gifts pleasing to me, but present them as the tributes of your gratitude ; it is then that I will accept them, but not while your souls have no love and no thankfulness to offer me.   The sacrifices, as considered in themselves, are contemned, but the internal emotions of love consequent upon a remembrance of divine goodness, are commended as the substance, meaning, and soul of sacrifice.   Even when the legal ceremonials were not abolished, this was true, and when they came to an end, this truth was more than ever made manifest.   Not for want of bullocks on

the altar was Israel blamed, but for want of thankful adoration before the Lord. She excelled in the visible, but in the inward grace, which is the one thing needful, she sadly failed. Too many in these days are in the same condemnation. " *And pay thy vows unto the most High.*" Let the sacrifice be really presented to the God who seeth the heart, pay to him the love you promised, the service you covenanted to render, the loyalty of heart you have vowed to maintain. O for grace to do this ! O that we may be graciously enabled to love God, and live up to our profession ! To be, indeed, the servants of the Lord, the lovers of Jesus, this is our main concern. What avails our baptism, to what end our gatherings at the Lord's table, to what purpose our solemn assemblies, if we have not the fear of the Lord, and vital godliness reigning within our bosoms ?

15. " *And call upon me in the day of trouble.*" Oh, blessed verse ! Is this then true sacrifice ? Is it an offering to ask an alms of heaven ? It is even so. The King himself so regards it. For herein is faith manifested, herein is love proved, for in the hour of peril we fly to those we love. It seems a small thing to pray to God when we are distressed, yet is it a more acceptable worship than the mere heartless presentation of bullocks and he-goats. This is a voice from the throne, and how full of mercy it is ! It is very tempestuous round about Jehovah, and yet what soft drops of mercy's rain fall from the bosom of the storm ! Who would not suffer such sacrifice ? Troubled one, haste to present it now ! Who shall say that Old Testament saints did not know the gospel ? Its very spirit and essence breathe like frankincense all around this holy Psalm. " *I will deliver thee.*" The reality of thy sacrifice of prayer shall be seen in its answer. Whether the smoke of burning bulls. be sweet to me or no, certainly thy humble prayer shall be, and I will prove it so by my gracious reply to thy supplication. This promise is very large, and may refer both to temporal and eternal deliverances ; faith can turn it every way, like the sword of the cherubim. " *And thou shalt glorify me.*" Thy prayer will honour me, and thy grateful perception of my answering mercy will also glorify me. The goats and bullocks would prove a failure, but the true sacrifice never could. The calves of the stall might be a vain oblation, but not the calves of sincere lips.

Thus we see what is true ritual. Here we read inspired rubrics. Spiritual worship is the great, the essential matter ; all else without it is rather provoking than pleasing to God. As helps to the soul, outward offerings were precious, but when men went not beyond them, even their hallowed things were profaned in the view of heaven.

16 But unto the wicked God saith, What hast thou to do to declare my statutes, or *that* thou shouldest take my covenant in thy mouth ?

17 Seeing thou hatest instruction, and castest my words behind thee.

18 When thou sawest a thief. then thou consentedst with him, and hast been partaker with adulterers.

19 Thou givest thy mouth to evil, and thy tongue frameth deceit.

20 Thou sittest *and* speakest against thy brother ; thou slanderest thine own mother's son.

21 These *things* hast thou done, and I kept silence ; thou thoughtest that I was altogether *such an one* as thyself : *but* I will reprove thee, and set *them* in order before thine eyes.

Here the Lord turns to the manifestly wicked among his people ; and such there were even in the highest places of his sanctuary. If moral formalists had been rebuked, how much more these immoral pretenders to fellowship with heaven ? If the lack of heart spoiled the worship of the more decent and virtuous, how much more would violations of the law, committed with a high hand, corrupt the sacrifices of the wicked ?

16. " *But unto the wicked God saith.*" To the breakers of the second table he now addresses himself ; he had previously spoken to the neglecters of the first. " *What hast thou to do to declare my statutes ?* " You violate openly my moral law, and yet are great sticklers for my ceremonial commands ! What have you to do with them ? What interest can you have in them ? Do you dare to teach my law to others, and profane it yourselves ? What impudence, what blasphemy is

this! Even if you claim to be sons of Levi, what of that? Your wickedness disqualifies you, disinherits you, puts you out of the succession. It should silence you, and would if my people were as spiritual as I would have them, for they would refuse to hear you, and to pay you the portion of temporal things which is due to my true servants. You count up your holy days, you contend for rituals, you fight for externals, and yet the weightier matters of the law ye despise! Ye blind guides, ye strain out gnats and swallow camels; your hypocrisy is written on your foreheads and manifest to all. *"Or that thou shouldest take my covenant in thy mouth."* Ye talk of being in covenant with me, and yet trample my holiness beneath your feet as swine trample upon pearls; think ye that I can brook this? Your mouths are full of lying and slander, and yet ye mouth my words as if they were fit morsels for such as you! How horrible an evil it is, that to this day we see men explaining doctrines who despise precepts! They make grace a coverlet for sin, and even judge themselves to be sound in the faith, while they are rotten in life. We need the grace of the doctrines as much as the doctrines of grace, and without it an apostle is but a Judas, and a fair-spoken professor is an arrant enemy of the cross of Christ.

17. *"Seeing thou hatest instruction."* Profane professors are often too wise to learn, too besotted with conceit to be taught of God. What a monstrosity that men should declare those statutes which with their hearts they do not know, and which in their lives they openly disavow! Woe unto the men who hate the instruction which they take upon themselves to give. *"And castest my words behind thee."* Despising them, throwing them away as worthless, putting them out of sight as obnoxious. Many boasters of the law did this practically; and in these last days there are pickers and choosers of God's words who cannot endure the practical part of Scripture; they are disgusted at duty, they abhor responsibility, they disembowel texts of their plain meanings, they wrest the Scriptures to their own destruction. It is an ill sign when a man dares not look a Scripture in the face, and an evidence of brazen impudence when he tries to make it mean something less condemnatory of his sins, and endeavours to prove it to be less sweeping in its demands. How powerful is the argument that such men have no right to take the covenant of God into their mouths, seeing that its spirit does not regulate their lives!

18. *"When thou sawest a thief, then thou consentedst with him."* Moral honesty cannot be absent where true grace is present. Those who excuse others in trickery are guilty themselves; those who use others to do unjust actions for them are doubly so. If a man be ever so religious, if his own actions do not rebuke dishonesty, he is an accomplice with thieves. If we can acquiesce in anything which is not upright, we are not upright ourselves, and our religion is a lie. *"And hast been partaker with adulterers."* One by one the moral precepts are thus broken by the sinners in Zion. Under the cloak of piety, unclean livers conceal themselves. We may do this by smiling at unchaste jests, listening to indelicate expressions, and conniving at licentious behaviour in our presence; and if we thus act, how dare we preach, or lead public prayer, or wear the Christian name? See how the Lord lays righteousness to the plummet! How plainly all this declares that without holiness no man shall see the Lord! No amount of ceremonial or theological accuracy can cover dishonesty and fornication; these filthy things must be either purged from us by the blood of Jesus, or they will kindle a fire in God's anger which will burn even to the lowest hell.

19. *"Thou givest thy mouth to evil."* Sins against the ninth commandment are here mentioned. The man who surrenders himself to the habit of slander is a vile hypocrite if he associates himself with the people of God. A man's health is readily judged by his tongue. A foul mouth, a foul heart. Some slander almost as often as they breathe, and yet are great upholders of the church, and great sticklers for holiness. To what depths will not they go in evil, who delight in spreading it with their tongues? *"And thy tongue frameth deceit."* This is a more deliberate sort of slander, where the man dexterously elaborates false witness, and concocts methods of defamation. There is an ingenuity of calumny in some men, and, alas! even in some who are thought to be followers of the Lord Jesus. They manufacture falsehoods, weave them in their loom, hammer them on their anvil, and then retail their wares in every company. Are these accepted with God? Though they bring their wealth to the altar, and speak eloquently of truth and of salvation, have they any favour with God? We should blaspheme the holy God if we were to think so.

They are corrupt in his sight, a stench in his nostrils. He will cast all liars into hell. Let them preach, and pray, and sacrifice as they will; till they become truthful, the God of truth loathes them utterly.

20. "*Thou sittest and speakest against thy brother.*" He sits down to it, makes it his meat, studies it, resolves upon it, becomes a master of defamation, occupies the chair of calumny. His nearest friend is not safe, his dearest relative escapes not. "*Thou slanderest thine own mother's son.*" He ought to love him best, but he has an ill word for him. The son of one's own mother was to the Oriental a very tender relation; but the wretched slanderer knows no claims of kindred. He stabs his brother in the dark, and aims a blow at him who came forth of the same womb: yet he wraps himself in the robe of hypocrisy, and dreams that he is a favourite of heaven, an accepted worshipper of the Lord. Are such monsters to be met with nowadays? Alas! they pollute our churches still, and are roots of bitterness, spots in our solemn feasts, wandering stars for whom is reserved the blackness of darkness for ever. Perhaps some such may read these lines, but they will probably read them in vain; their eyes are too dim to see their own condition, their hearts are waxen gross, their ears are dull of hearing; they are given up to a strong delusion to believe a lie, that they may be damned.

21. "*These things hast thou done, and I kept silence.*" No swift judgment overthrew the sinner—longsuffering reigned; no thunder was heard in threatening, and no bolt of fire was hurled in execution. "*Thou thoughtest that I was altogether such an one as thyself.*" The inference drawn from the Lord's patience was infamous: the respited culprit thought his judge to be one of the same order as himself. He offered sacrifice, and deemed it accepted; he continued in sin, and remained unpunished, and therefore he rudely said, "Why need believe these crazy prophets? God cares not how we live so long as we pay our tithes. Little does he consider how we get the plunder, so long as we bring a bullock to his altar." What will not men imagine of the Lord? At one time they liken the glory of Israel to a calf and anon their brutish selves. "*But I will reprove thee.*" At last I will break silence and let thee know my mind. "*And set them in order before thine eyes.*" I will marshal thy sins in battle array. I will make thee see them, I will put them down item by item, classified, and arranged. Thou shalt know that if silent awhile, I was never blind or deaf. I will make thee perceive what thou hast tried to deny. I will leave the seat of mercy for the throne of judgment, and there will I let thee see how great the difference between thee and me.

22 Now consider this, ye that forget God, lest I tear *you* in pieces, and *there be* none to deliver.

22. "*Now*" or oh! it is a word of entreaty, for the Lord is loth even to let the most ungodly run on to destruction. "*Consider this;*" take these truths to heart, ye who trust in ceremonies and ye who live in vice, for both of you sin in that "*ye forget God.*" Bethink you how unaccepted you are, and turn unto the Lord. See how you have mocked the eternal, and repent of your iniquities. "*Lest I tear you in pieces,*" as a lion rends his prey, "*and there be none to deliver,*" no Saviour, no refuge, no hope. Ye reject the Mediator: beware, for ye will sorely need one in the day of wrath, and none will be near to plead for you. How terrible, how complete, how painful, how humiliating, will be the destruction of the wicked! God uses no soft words, or velvet metaphors, nor may his servants do so when they speak of the wrath to come. O reader, consider this.

23 Whoso offereth praise glorifieth me: and to him that ordereth *his* conversation *aright* will I shew the salvation of God.

23. "*Whoso offereth praise glorifieth me.*" Praise is the best sacrifice; true, hearty, gracious thanksgiving from a renewed mind. Not the lowing of bullocks bound to the altar, but the songs of redeemed men are the music which the ear of Jehovah delights in. Sacrifice your loving gratitude, and God is honoured thereby. "*And to him that ordereth his conversation aright will I shew the salvation of God.*" Holy living is a choice evidence of salvation. He who submits his whole way to divine guidance, and is careful to honour God in his life, brings an offering which the Lord accepts through his dear Son; and such a one shall be more and more instructed, and made experimentally to know the Lord's salvation. He

needs salvation, for the best ordering of the life cannot save us, but *that salvation he shall have*. Not to ceremonies, not to unpurified lips, is the blessing promised, but to grateful hearts and holy lives.

O Lord, give us to stand in the judgment with those who have worshipped thee aright and have seen thy salvation.

EXPLANATORY NOTES AND QUAINT SAYINGS.

Whole Psalm.—The exordium or beginning of this Psalm is the most grand and striking that can possibly be imagined—the speaker GOD, the audience an assembled world! We cannot compare or assimilate the scene here presented to us with any human resemblance; nor do I imagine that earth will ever behold su h a day till that hour when the trumpet of the archangel shall sound, and shall gather all the nations of the earth from the four winds, from one end of heaven to the other; when the dead, small and great, shall stand before God, and the sea shall give up the dead which are in it, and death and hell shall deliver up the dead that are in them.—*Barton Bouchier.*

Verse 1.—" *El, Elohim, Jehovah has spoken !* " So reads the Hebrew.—*An rew A. Bonar.*

Verse 1 (first clause).—Some have observed that these three names, *El, Elohim, Jehovah*, here mentioned, have three very distinct accents set to them, and which being joined to a verb singular דִּבֶּר, *hath spoken*, contains the mystery of the trinity of Persons in the unity of the divine Essence.—*John Gill.*

Verse 1.—" *And called the earth*," etc., *i.e., all the inhabitants of the earth* he has commanded to come as witnesses and spectators of the judgment.—*Simon de Muis.*

Verses 1—5.—

No more shall atheists mock his long delay;
His vengeance sleeps no more; behold the day!
Behold !—the Judge descends; his guards are nigh,
Tempests and fire attend him down the sky.
When God appears, all nature shall adore him.
While sinners tremble, saints rejoice before him.
Heaven, earth, and hell, draw near; let all things come,
To hear my justice, and the sinner's doom;
But gather first my saints (the Judge commands),
Bring them, ye angels, from their distant lands.
When Christ returns, wake every cheerful passion,
And shout, ye saints; he comes for your salvation.
Isaac Watts.

Verse 2.—*Out of Zion, the perfection of God's beauty hath shined; or, God has caused the perfection of beauty to shine out of Zion.*—*Martin Geier.*

Verse 2.—" *God hath shined.*" Like the sun in his strength, sometimes for the comfort of his people, as Psalm lxxx. 1; sometimes for the terror of evil-doers, as Psalm xciv. 1, and here. But evermore God is terrible out of his holy places. Psalm lxviii. 35, and lxxxix. 7.—*John Trapp.*

Verse 2.—" *God hath shined.*" The proper meaning of יָפַע is to scatter rays from afar, and from a lofty place, and to glitter. *It is a word of a grand sound,* says Ch. Schultens, *which is always used of a magnificent and flashing light.* . . . . It is apparently used of the splendid symbol of God's presence, as in Deut. xxxiv. 2, where he is said to *scatter beams* from Mount Paran. From which it is manifest that it may refer to the pillar of cloud and fire, the seat of the Divine Majesty conspicuous on Mount Sinai, or on the tabernacle, or the loftiest part of the temple. —*Hermann Venema.*

Verse 3.—" *Our God shall come, and shall not keep silence.*" He kept silence that he might be judged, he will not keep silence when he begins to judge. It would not have been said, " *He shall come manifestly,*" unless at first he had come concealed ; nor, " *He shall not keep silence,*" had he not at first kept silence. How did he keep silence ? Ask Isaiah : " He was brought as a lamb to the slaughter, and as a sheep before her shearers is dumb, so he openeth not his mouth." Isa. liii. 7. But he shall come manifestly, and shall not keep silence. How manifestly ? " *A fire shall go before him, and round about him a mighty tempest.*" That tempest is to carry wholly away the chaff from the floor which is now in threshing ; that fire, to consume what the tempest carries off. Now, however, he is silent ; silent in judgment, but not in precept. For if Christ is silent, what mean these gospels ? What the voices of the apostles ? the canticles of the Psalms ? the lofty utterances of the prophets ? Truly in all these Christ is not silent. Howbeit he is silent for the present in not taking vengeance, not in not warning. But he will come in surpassing brightness to take vengeance, and will be seen of all, even of those who believe not on him ; but now, forasmuch as although present he was not concealed, it behoved him to be despised : for unless he had been despised he would not have been crucified ; if not crucified he would not have shed his blood, the price with which he redeemed us. But in order that he might give a price for us, he was crucified ; that he might be crucified, he was despised ; that he might be despised, he appeared in humble guise.—*Augustine.*

Verse 3 (first clause).—The future in the first clause may be rendered *he is coming,* as if the sound of his voice and the light of his glory had preceded his actual appearance. The imagery is borrowed from the giving of the law at Sinai.—*J. A. Alexander.*

Verse 3 (first clause).—*May our God come !* * A prayer for the hastening of his advent, as in the Apocalypse, xxii. 20.—*Pool's Synopsis.*

Verse 3.—" *A fire shall devour before him.*" As he gave his law in fire, so in fire shall he require it.—*John Trapp.*

Verse 4.—" *He shall call to the heavens from above, and to the earth.*" That these dumb creatures may be as so many speaking evidences against an unworthy people, and witnesses of God's righteous dealings against them. See Deut. xxxii. 1 ; Isaiah i. 2 ; Mic. vi. 2. The Chaldee thus paraphraseth : *He will call the high angels from above ; and the just of the earth from beneath.*—*John Trapp.*

Verse 5.—" *Gather,*" etc. To whom are these words addressed ? Many suppose to the angels, as the ministers of God's will ; but it is unnecessary to make the expression more definite than it is in the Psalm.—*J. J. Stewart Perowne.*

Verse 5.—" *My saints,*" the objects of my mercy, those whom I have called and specially distinguished. The term is here descriptive of a relation, not of an intrinsic quality.—*J. A. Alexander.*

Verse 5.—" *Gather my saints together unto me.*" There is a double or two-fold gathering to Christ. There is a gathering unto Christ by faith, a gathering within the bond of the covenant, a gathering into the family of God, a gathering unto the root of Jesse, standing up for an ensign of the people. " In that day there shall be a root of Jesse, which shall stand for an ensign of the people ; to it shall the Gentiles seek : and his rest shall be glorious." Isa. xi. 10. This is the main end of the gospel, the great work of ministers, the gathering of sinners unto Christ. But then there is a gathering unto Christ at the general judgment ; and this is the gathering that is here spoken of. This gathering is consequential to the other. Christ will gather none to him at the last day but those that are gathered to him by faith here ; he will give orders to gather together unto him all these, and none but these, that have taken hold of his covenant. . . . . .

I would speak of Christ's owning and acknowledging the saints at his second coming. His owning and acknowledging them is imported in his giving these orders, " *Gather my saints together unto me.*" . . . . . Now upon this head I mention the things following :—1. Saintship will be the only mark of distinction in that day. There are many marks of distinction now ; but these will all cease, and this only will remain. 2. Saintship will then be Christ's badge of honour. Beware of mocking at saintship, or sanctity, holiness, and purity ; for it is Christ's badge of honour, the garment with which his followers are clothed, and will be the only badge of honour at the great day. 3. Christ will forget and misken none of the

---

* Version of Junius & Tremellius.

saints. Many of the saints are forgotten here, it is forgotten that such persons were in the world, but Christ will forget and misken none of them at the great day ; he will give forth a list of all his saints, and give orders to gather them all unto him. 4. He will confess, own, and acknowledge them before his Father, and his holy angels. Matt. x. 32 ; Luke xii. 8 ; Rev. iii. 5 ; They are to go to my Father's house, and they are to go thither in my name, in my right, and at my back ; and so it is necessary I should own and acknowledge them before my Father. But what need is there for his owning them before the angels ? *Ans.* They are to be the angels' companions, and so it is necessary he should own them before the angels. This will be like a testimonial for them unto the angels. Lastly. The evidences of his right to, and propriety in them, will then be made to appear. Mal. iii. 17 : " And they shall be mine, saith the Lord of hosts, in that day when I make up my jewels." It is too late for persons to become his then ; so the meaning is, they shall evidently appear to be mine.—*James Scot,* 1773.

Verse 5.—" *Gather my saints together unto me.*" Our text may be considered as the commission given by the great Judge to his angels—those ministering spirits who do his will, hearkening to the voice of his power. The language of the text is in accordance with that which was uttered by our Lord when, alluding to the coming of the Son of Man, he says, " And he shall send his angels with a great sound of a trumpet, and they shall gather together his elect from the four winds, from one end of heaven to the other." But previous to this final, this *general* gathering together of his saints to judgment, Jehovah gathers them together in various ways, in various places, and by various means, both of providence and of grace. Previous to his being seated on a throne of judgment, we behold him sitting on a throne of mercy, and we hear him saying, " *Gather my saints together unto me.*" These words lead us to notice—I. The characters described, " *My saints.*" II. The command issued, " *Gather my saints together unto me.*" I. THE CHARACTERS HERE DESCRIBED—"*My saints.*" By the term " *my saints,*" we are to understand *my holy ones*—those who have been sanctified and set apart by God. None of us possess this character by *nature.* We are born sinners, and there is no difference ; but by divine *grace* we experience a change of nature, and consequently a change of name. The title of saint is frequently given to the people of God in derision. " Such an one," says a man of the world, "is one of your saints." But, my brethren, no higher honour can be conferred upon us than to be denominated saints, if we truly deserve that character ; but in what way do we become saints ? We become saints—1. *By divine choice.* The saints are the objects of everlasting love ; their names are written in the Lamb's book of life ; and it is worthy of remark that wherever the people of God are spoken of in sacred Scripture, as the objects of that everlasting love, it is in connection with their *personal sanctification.* Observe, they are not chosen because they *are* saints, nor because it is foreseen that they *will* be so, but they are chosen *to be* saints ; sanctification is the effect and the only evidence of election. We become saints—2. *By a divine change which is the necessary consequence of this election.* An inward, spiritual, supernatural, universal change is effected in the saints by the power of the Holy Ghost. Thus they are renewed in the spirit of their minds, and made partakers of a divine nature. . . . . . Remember, then, this important truth, that Christians are called by the gospel to be saints ; that you are Christians, not so much by your *orthodoxy* as by your *holiness ;* that you are saints no further than as you are holy in all manner of conversation. 3. *The people of God furnish an evidence of being saints by their godly conduct.* " By their fruits," not by their feelings ; not by their lips, not by their general profession, but, " by their fruits shall ye know them." 4. The character of the saints is evidenced *by divine consecration.* The people of God are called holy inasmuch as they are dedicated to God. It is the duty and the privilege of saints to consecrate themselves to the service of God. Even a heathen philosopher could say, " I *lend* myself to the *world,* but I *give* myself to the *gods.*" But we possess more light and knowledge, and are therefore laid under greater obligations than was Seneca.

II. THE COMMAND ISSUED—" *Gather my saints together unto me.*" Jehovah gathers his saints to himself in various ways. 1. *He gathers them to himself in their conversion.* The commission given by Christ to his ministers is, " Go ye forth into all the world, and preach the gospel to every creature," or in other words, " *Gather my saints together unto me.*" The gospel is to be preached to *sinners* in order that they may become *saints.* 2. *Saints are gathered together by God in public worship.* . . .

3. *He gathers his saints together to himself in times of danger.* When storms appear to be gathering around them, he is desirous to screen them from the blast. He says to them, in the language of Isaiah, " Come, my people, and enter into thy chamber—the chamber of my perfections and my promises—enter into thy chamber and shut the doors about thee, and hide thyself until the calamity is overpast." 4. *God gathers his saints together in the service of his church.* Thus Christ collected his apostles together to give them their apostolic commission to go and teach all nations. At the period of the Reformation, the great Head of the church raised up Luther and Calvin, together with other eminent reformers, in order that they might light up a flame in Europe, yea, throughout the world, that the breath of popery should never be able to blow out. 5. *God gathers his saints together in death, and at the resurrection.* " Precious in the sight of the Lord is the death of his saints." This is the commission which death is habitually receiving—" Go, death, and gather such-and-such of my saints unto me." As the gardener enters the garden, and plucks the full-blown flower and the ripened fruit, so Jesus Christ enters the garden of his church and gathers his saints to himself; for he says, " Father, I will that all they whom thou hast given me may be with me, where I am, and behold my glory."—*Condensed from J. Sibree's " Sermon preached at the re-opening of Surrey Chapel, August 29th, 1830."*

Verse 5 (*second clause*).—" *Made,*" or *ratifying a covenant;* literally, *cutting,* striking, perhaps in allusion to the practice of slaying and dividing victims as a religious rite, accompanying solemn compacts. (See Genesis xv. 10—18). The same usage may be referred to in the following words, *over sacrifice, i.e.,* standing over it; or, *on sacrifice, i.e.,* founding the engagement on a previous appeal to God. There is probably allusion to the great covenant transaction recorded in Ex. xxiv. 4—8. This reference to sacrifice shows clearly that what follows was not intended to discredit or repudiate that essential symbol of the typical or ceremonial system.—*J. A. Alexander.*

Verse 5.—" *Made a covenant with me.*" Formerly soldiers used to take an oath not to flinch from their colours, but faithfully to cleave to their leaders; this they called *sacramentum militare,* a military oath; such an oath lies upon every Christian. It is so essential to the being of a saint, that they are described by this, " *Gather my saints together unto me; those that have made a covenant with me.*" We are not Christians till we have subscribed this covenant, and that without any reservation. When we take upon us the profession of Christ's name, we enlist ourselves in his muster-roll, and by it do promise that we will live and die with him in opposition to all his enemies. . . . He will not entertain us till we resign up ourselves freely to his disposal, that there may be no disputing with his commands afterwards, but, as one under his authority, go and come at his word.—*William Gurnall.*

Verse 6.—" *The heavens shall declare his righteousness.*" It is the manner of Scripture to commit the teaching of that which it desires should be most noticeable, and important to *the heavens and the earth:* for *the heavens* are seen by all, and their light discovers all things. Here it speaks of *the heavens,* not *the earth,* because these are everlasting, but not the earth.—*Geier and Muis in Pool's Synopsis.*

Verse 8.—" *I will not reprove thee for thy sacrifices;*" *i.e.,* for thy neglect of them, but for thy resting in them, sticking in the bark, bringing me the bare shell without the kernel, not referring to the right end and use, but satisfying thyself in the work done.—*John Trapp.*

Verse 8.—" *I will not reprove thee for thy sacrifices or thy burnt offerings continually before me.*" Those words " *to have been,*" which our translators supply, may be left out, and the sense remain perfect: or if those words be continued, then the negative particle *not,* is to be reassumed out of the first part of the verse, and the whole read thus, " *I will not reprove thee for thy sacrifices or thy burnt offerings not to have been continually before me.*" That is, I will not charge thee with a neglect of outward duty or worship, the inward or spiritual (of which he speaks, ver. 14), being that which is most pleasing unto me.—*Joseph Caryl.*

Verses 8, 9.—It is the very remonstrance which our Lord himself makes against the Pharisees of his days, for laying so much stress on the outward observance of their own traditions, the washing of pots and cups and other such like things; the paying of tithes of anise and mint and cummin; the ostentatious fulfilment of all ceremonious observances in the eyes of men, the exalting the shadow to the exclusion of the substance. And have we not seen the like in our own days, even to the very vestment of the minister, the obeisance of the knee, and the posture of the body ? as if the material church were all in all, and God were no Spirit, that demanded of those that worshipped him that they should worship him in spirit and in truth ; as if the gold and ornaments of the temple were far beyond the hidden man of the heart in that which is incorruptible, even the ornament of a meek and quiet spirit, which is in the sight of God of great price.—*Barton Bouchier.*

Verse 10.—"*For to me* [belongs] *every beast of the forest, the cattle in hills of a thousand.*" This last idiomatic phrase may either mean a thousand hills, or hills where the cattle rove by thousands, with probable allusion to the hilly grounds of Bashan beyond Jordan. According to etymology, the noun in the first clause means an *animal*, and that in the second *beasts* or *brutes* in general. But when placed in antithesis, the first denotes a wild beast, and the second domesticated animals or cattle. Both words were necessary to express God's sovereign propriety in the whole animal creation. Thus understood, the verse assigns a reason for the negative assertion in the one before it. Even if God could stand in need of animal oblations, for his own sake, or for their sake, he would not be under the necessity of coming to man for them, since the whole animal creation is his property and perfectly at his disposal.—*J. A. Alexander.*

Verses 11, 12.—We show our scorn of God's sufficiency, by secret thoughts of meriting from him by any religious act, as though God could be indebted to us, and obliged by us. As though our devotions could bring a blessedness to God more than he essentially hath ; when indeed " our goodness extends not to him." Ps. xvi. 2. Our services to God are rather services to ourselves, and bring a happiness to us, not to God. This secret opinion of merit (though disputed among the Papists, yet) is natural to man ; and this secret self-pleasing, when we have performed any duty, and upon that account expect some fair compensation from God, as having been profitable to him ; God intimates this : " The wild beasts of the field are mine. If I were hungry, I would not tell thee : for the world is mine, and the fulness thereof." He implies, that they wronged his infinite fulness, by thinking that he stood in need of their sacrifices and services, and that he was beholden to them for their adoration of him. All merit implies a moral or natural insufficiency in the person of whom we merit, and our doing something for him, which he could not, or at least so well do for himself. It is implied in our murmuring at God's dealing with us as a course of cross providences, wherein men think they have deserved better at the hands of God by their service, than to be cast aside and degraded by him. In our prosperity we are apt to have secret thoughts that our enjoyments were the debts God owed us, rather than gifts freely bestowed upon us. Hence it is that men are more unwilling to part with their righteousness than with their sins, and are apt to challenge salvation as a due, rather than beg it as an act of grace.—*Stephen Charnock.*

Verse 12.—"*If I were hungry,*" etc. Pagan sacrifices were considered as feasts of the gods.—*Daniel Cresswell.*

Verse 13.—"*Will I eat the flesh of bulls, or drink the blood of goats ?*" That is, did I want anything I would not tell thee ; but hast thou indeed such gross notions of men, as to imagine that I have appointed and required the blood and flesh of animals for their own sake and not with some design ? Dost thou think I am pleased with these, when they are offered without faith, love, and gratitude ? Nay, offer the sacrifice of praise, etc. Render to me a spiritual and reasonable service, performing thy engagements, and then thou wilt find me a very present help in trouble.—*B. Boothroyd.*

Verse 15.—"*Call upon me,*" etc. Prayer is like the ring which Queen Elizabeth gave to the Earl of Essex, bidding him if he were in any distress send that ring to her, and she would help him. God commandeth his people if they be in any perplexity to send this ring to him : "*Call upon me in the day of trouble : I will deliver thee,*" and thou shalt glorify me."—*George Swinnock.*

Verse 15.—"*Call upon me in the day of trouble,*" etc. Who will scrape to a keeper for a piece of venison who may have free access to the master of the game to ask and have ? Hanker not after other helpers, rely on him only, fully trusting him in the use of such means as he prescribeth and affordeth. God is jealous, will have no co-rival, nor allow thee (in this case) two strings to thy bow. He who worketh all in all must be unto thee all in all : of, through, and to whom are all things, to him be all praise for ever. Rom. xi. 36.—*George Gipps, in " A Sermon preached (before God, and from him) to the Honourable House of Commons, 1645."*

Verse 15.—*" Call upon me in the day of trouble,"* etc. The Lord hath promised his children supply of all good things, yet they must see the means of impetration ; by prayer. He feeds the young ravens when they call upon him. Ps. cxlvii. 9. He feeds the young ravens, but first they call upon him. God withholds from them that ask not, lest he should give to them that desire not. (Augustine.) David was confident that by God's power he should spring over a wall ; yet not without putting his own strength and agility to it. Those things we pray for, we must work for. (Augustine.) The carter in Isidore, when his cart was overthrown, would needs have his god Hercules come down from heaven, to help him up with it ; but whilst he forbore to set his own shoulder to it, his cart lay still. Abraham was as rich as any of our aldermen, David as valiant as any of our gentlemen, Solomon as wise as any of our deepest naturians, Susanna as fair as any of our painted pieces. Yet none of them thought that their riches, valour, policy, beauty, or excellent parts could save them ; but they stirred the sparks of grace, and bestirred themselves in pious work. And this is our means, if our meaning be to be saved.—*Thomas Adams.*

Verse 15.—*" I will deliver thee : "* properly, *I will draw thee forth with my own mighty hand,"* and plant thee in liberty and prosperity.—*Hermann Venema.*

Verse 16.—*" Unto the wicked God saith, What hast thou to do to declare my statutes ? "* etc. *" As snow in summer, and as rain in harvest, so honour is not seemly for a fool."* Is it not ? No wonder then that divine wisdom requires us ourselves to put off the old man (as snakes put off their skins) before we take on us the most honourable office of reproving sin ; a duty which above any other brings praise to God, and profit to men ; insomuch that God hath not a more honourable work that I know of to set us about. And what think you ? Are greasy scullions fit to stand before kings ? Are dirty kennel-rakers fit to be plenipotentiaries or ambassadors ? Are unclean beasts fit to be made lord-almoners, and sent to bestow the king's favours ? Are swine fit to cast pearl, and the very richest pearl of God's royal word ? No man dreams it ; consequently none can believe himself qualified or commissioned to be a reprover of sin " till he is washed, till he is sanctified, till he is justified in the name of our Lord Jesus Christ, and by the Spirit of our God." A lunatick beggar in Athens would not believe but that all the ships in the harbour were his. His mistake exceeded not theirs, who persuade themselves that this richer office is theirs, before they are " alive from the dead," and " born of the Spirit," before they are returned to God or to themselves. The Duke of Alva is said to have complained that, " his king sent him in fetters to fight for him ; " because without his pardon given him, and while he was a prisoner, he employed him in war. But the supreme King is a more merciful one, and orders our charity to begin at home ; making it our first duty to break off our sins ; and then when we have put off these our shackles, go to fight his battles.—*Daniel Burgess (1645—1712-13) in " The Golden Snuffers."*

Verse 16.—*" The wicked."* By whom are meant, not openly profane sinners ; but men under a profession of religion, and indeed who were teachers of others, as appears from the following expostulations with them : the Scribes, Pharisees, and doctors among the Jews, are designed, and so Kimchi interprets it of their wise men, who learnt and taught the law, but did not act according to it.—*John Gill.*

Verse 16.—*" What hast thou to do to declare my statutes ? "* etc. All the mediæval writers teach us, even from the Mosaic law concerning the leper, how the writer of this Psalm only put into words what those statutes expressed in fact. For so it is written : " The leper in whom the plague is, . . . he shall put a covering upon his upper lip." As they all, following Origen, say : Let them who are themselves of polluted lips, take good heed not to teach others. Or, to take it in the opposite way, see how Isaiah would not speak to his people, because he was a man of polluted lips, and he dwelt among a people of polluted lips, till they had been touched with the living coal from the altar ; and by that, as by a sacrament of the Old Testament, a sentence of absolution had been pronounced upon them.—*J. M. Neale.*

Verse 16 (*second clause*).—Emphasis is laid on the phrase, *to declare God's statutes,* which both denotes such an accurate knowledge of them as one may obtain by *numbering* them, and a diligent and public review of them. Properly speaking the word is derived from the Arabic, and signifies *to reckon in dust,* for the ancients were accustomed to calculate in *dust* finely sprinkled over tablets or the Abacus.—*Hermann Venema.*

Verse 16.—"*But unto the wicked God saith, What hast thou to do . . . to take my covenant into thy mouth?*" For whom is the covenant made but for the wicked? If men were not wicked or sinful, what needed there a covenant of grace? The covenant is for the wicked, and the covenant brings grace enough to pardon those who are most wicked; why, then, doth the Lord say to the wicked, "*What hast thou to do to take my covenant into thy mouth?*" Observe what follows, and his meaning is expounded: "*Seeing thou hatest to be reformed.*" As if God had said, Thou wicked man, who protectest thy sin, and holdest it close, refusing to return and hating to reform; what hast thou to do to meddle with my covenant? Lay off thy defiled hands. He that is resolved to hold his sin takes hold of the covenant in vain, or rather he lets it go, while he seems to hold it. Woe unto those who sue for mercy while they neglect duty.—*Joseph Caryl.*

Verse 16.—When a minister does not do what he teaches, this makes him a vile person; nay, this makes him ridiculous, like Lucian's apothecary, who had medicines in his shop to cure the cough, and told others that he had them, and yet was troubled with it himself. With what a forehead canst thou stand in a pulpit and publish the laws of God, and undertake the charge of souls, that when thine own nakedness appears, when thy tongue is of a larger size than thy hands, thy ministry is divided against itself, thy courses give thy doctrine the lie; thou sayest that men must be holy, and thy deeds do declare thy mouth's hypocrisy; thou doest more mischief than a hundred others.—*William Fenner.*

Verse 17.—"*And castest my words behind thee.*" *Thou castest away contemptuously.* with disgust and detestation, as idols are cast out of a city; or as Moses indignantly dashed to the earth the tables of the law.—*Martin Geier.*

Verse 17.—"*My words:*" apparently the ten commandments, accustomed to be called the *ten words,* by which God is often said to have made his covenant with Israel.—*Hermann Venema.*

Verse 18.—"*When thou sawest a thief, then thou consentedst with him;*" or *didst run with him.* This was literally true of the Scribes and Pharisees; they devoured widows' houses, and robbed them of their substance, under a pretext of long prayers; they consented to the deeds of Barabbas, a robber, when they preferred him to Jesus Christ; and they joined with the thieves on the cross in reviling him; and, in a spiritual sense, they stole away the word of the Lord, every man from his neighbour; took away the key of knowledge from the people, and put false glosses upon the sacred writings.—*John Gill.*

Verse 18.—"*Thou consentedst with him;*" *became his accomplice.* Συνέτρεχες αὐτῷ, LXX, *i.e.,* you helped him to carry off his booty and to make his escape.—*Samuel Horsley.*

Verse 18.—"*Thou consentedst with him.*" Or, thou runnest along with him. "*Hast been partaker with;*" namely, thou art his companion; a term taken from commerce of merchants, or from banquets made after the ancient manner, to which divers did contribute, and had their shares therein.—*John Diodati.*

Verse 18 (*last clause*).—To give entertainment to them we know to be dissolute, is to communicate with their sins.—*Thomas Adams.*

Verse 19.—"*Thou givest thy mouth to evil,*" etc. "*Thou givest.*" Heb., *thou sendest forth;* to wit, free; for the word is used of men's dismissing their wives or their servants, whom they left to their freedom. Thou hast an unbridled tongue, and castest off all restraints of God's law, and of thine own conscience, and givest thy tongue liberty to speak what thou pleasest, though it be offensive and dishonourable to God, and injurious to thy neighbour, or to thy own soul; which is justly produced as an evidence of their hypocrisy. "*To evil,*" either to sinful or mischievous speeches. "*Frameth deceit,*" *i.e.,* uttereth lies or fair words, wherewith to circumvent those who deal with them.—*Matthew Pool.*

Verse 19.—The ninth commandment is now added to the other two, as being habitually violated by the person here addressed.—*J. A. Alexander.*

Verse 20.—*" Thou sittest and speakest,"* etc. A man may both speak and do evil while he sits still and doth nothing ; an idle posture may serve the turn for such work as that.—*Joseph Caryl.*

Verse 20.—*" Thou sittest and speakest against thy brother,"* etc. When you are sitting still, and have nothing else to do, you are ever injuring your neighbour with your slanderous speech. Your table-talk is abuse of your nearest friends.—*Samuel Horsley.*

Verse 20.—*" Thine own mother's son."* To understand the force of this expression, it is necessary to bear in mind that polygamy was allowed amongst the Israelites. Those who were born to the same father were all brethren, but a yet more intimate relationship subsisted between those who had the same mother as well as the same father.—*French and Skinner.*

Verse 21.—*" These things hast thou done, and I kept silence."* Neither sleep nor slumber, nor connivance, nor neglect of anything can be incident to God. Because he doth not execute present judgment and visible destruction upon sinners, therefore blasphemy presumptuously inferreth—will God trouble himself about such petty matters ? So they imagined of their imaginary Jupiter. *Non vacat exiguis rebus adesse Jovem.* What a narrow and finite apprehension this is of God ! He that causeth and produceth every action—shall he not be present at every action ? What can we do without him, that cannot move but in him ? He that takes notice of sparrows, and numbers the seeds which the very ploughman thrusts in the ground, can any action of man escape his knowledge, or slip from his contemplation ? He may seem to wink at things, but never shuts his eyes. He doth not always manifest a reprehensive knowledge, yet he always retains an apprehensive knowledge. Though David smote not Shimei cursing, yet he heard Shimei cursing. As judges often determine to hear, but do not hear to determine ; so though God does not see to like, yet he likes to see.—*Thomas Adams.*

Verse 21.—*" Thou thoughtest that I was altogether such an one as thyself."* Such is the blindness and corruption of our nature, that we have very deformed and misshapen thoughts of him, till with the eye of faith we see his face in the glass of the word ; and therefore Mr. Perkins affirms, that all men who ever came of Adam (Christ alone excepted) are by nature atheists ; because at the same time that they acknowledge God, they deny his power, presence, and justice, and allow him to be only what pleaseth themselves. Indeed, it is natural for every man to desire to accommodate his lusts with such conception of God as may be most favourable to and suit best with them. God charges some for this : *" Thou thoughtest that I was altogether such an one as thyself."* Sinners do with God as the Ethiopians do with angels, whom they picture with black faces that they may be like themselves.—*William Gurnall.*

Verse 21.—*" Thou thoughtest that I was altogether such an one as thyself."* This men do when they plead for sins as little, as venial, as that which is below God to take notice of ; because they themselves think it so, therefore God must think it so too. Men, with a giant-like pride, would climb into the throne of the Almighty, and establish a contradiction to the will of God by making his own will, and not God's, the square and rule of his actions. This principle commenced, and took date in Paradise, when Adam would not depend upon the will of God revealed to him, but upon himself and his own will, and thereby makes himself as God.—*Stephen Charnock.*

Verse 21.—*" I will set them in order before thine eyes."* This is to be understood *more militari,* when sins shall be set in rank and file, in bloody array against thy soul ; or *more forensi,* when they shall be set in order as so many indictments for thy rebellion and treason.—*Stephen Charnock.*

Verse 21.—*" And set them in order before thine eyes : "* as if he should say, Thou thoughtest all thy sins were scattered and dispersed ; that there was not a sin to be found ; that they should never be rallied and brought together; but I assure thee I will make an army of those sins, a complete army of them, I will set them in rank and file before thine eyes ; and see how thou canst behold, much less contend with, such an host as they. Take heed therefore you do not levy war against your own souls ; that's the worst of all civil or intestine wars. If any army of divine terrors be so fearful, what will an army of black, hellish sins be ? when God shall bring whole regiments of sins against you—here a regiment of oaths, there a regiment of lies, there a third of false dealings, here a troop of filthy actions, and there a legion of unclean or profane thoughts, all at once fighting against thy life and everlasting peace.—*Joseph Caryl.*

Verse 21.—Atheists do mock at those Scriptures which tell us that we shall give account of all our deeds ; but God shall make them find the truth of it in that day of their reckoning. It is as easy for him to make their forgetful minds remember as to create the minds in them. When he applieth his register to their forgetful spirits they shall see all their forgotten sins. When the printer presseth clean paper upon his oiled irons, it receiveth the print of every letter: so when God shall stamp their minds with his register, they shall see all their former sins in a view. The hand was ever writing against Belshazzar, as he was ever sinning, though he saw it not till the cup was filled : so is it to the wicked ; their sins are numbered, and themselves weighed, and see not till they be divided by a fearful wakening.— *William Struther.*

Verse 21 (last clause).—" *God setteth his sins in order before his eyes.*" *Imprimis,* the sin of his conception. *Item,* the sins of his childhood. *Item,* of his youth. *Item,* of his man's estate, etc. Or, *Imprimis,* sins against the first table. *Item,* sins against the second ; so many of ignorance, so many of knowledge, so many of presumption, severally sorted by themselves. He committed sins confusedly, huddling them up in heaps ; but God *sets them in order,* and methodizes them to his hands.—*Thomas Fuller.*

Verse 22.—" *Now consider this, ye that forget God,*" etc. What is less than a grain of sand ? Yet when it comes to be multiplied, what is heavier than the sands of the sea ? A little sum multiplied rises high ; so a little sin unrepented of will damn us, as one leak in the ship, if it be not well looked to, will drown us. " Little sins," as the world calls them, but great sins against the majesty of God Almighty, whose majesty, against which they are committed, doth accent and enhance them, if not repented of, will damn. One would think it no great matter *to forget God,* yet it has *a heavy doom* attending on it. The non-improvement of talents, the non-exercise of grace, the world looks upon as a small thing ; yet we read of him who *hid* his talent in the earth—he had not spent it, only not trading it is sentenced.— *Thomas Watson.*

Verse 22.—" *Lest I tear you in pieces.*" This is a metaphorical expression, taken from the strength and irresistible fury of a lion, from which the interference of the shepherd can supply no protection, or defence, for his flock.—*William Walford.*

Verse 23.—" *Whoso offereth praise glorifieth me.*" Thanksgiving is a God-exalting work. Though nothing can add the least cubit to God's essential glory, yet praise exalts him in the eyes of others. Praise is a setting forth of God's honour, a lifting up of his name, a displaying the trophy of his goodness, a proclaiming his excellency, a spreading his renown, a breaking open the box of ointment, whereby the sweet savour and perfume of God's name is sent abroad into the world. " *To him that ordereth his conversation aright.*" Though the main work of religion lies within, yet " our light must so shine," that others may behold it : the foundation of sincerity is in the heart, yet its beautiful frontispiece appears in the conversation. The saints are called " jewels," because they cast a sparkling lustre in the eyes of others. An upright Christian is like Solomon's temple, gold within and without : sincerity is a holy leaven, which if it be in the *heart* will work itself into the life, and make it swell and rise as high as heaven. Phil. iii. 20.—*Thomas Watson.*

HINTS TO PREACHERS.

Verse 1.—It unspeakably concerns *all* men to know what God has spoken.— *W. S. Plumer.*

Verse 1.—I. Who has spoken? The mighty, not men or angels, but God himself. II. To whom has he spoken? To all nations—all ranks—all characters. This calls for, 1. Reverence—it is the voice of God. 2. Hope—because he condescends to speak to rebels. III. Where has he spoken ? 1. In creation. 2. In providence. 3. In his word.—*G. R.*

Verses 1—6.—I. The court called in the name of the King of kings. II. The judgment set, and the judge taking his seat ; v. 2, 3. III. The parties summoned ; v. 8. IV. The issue of this solemn trial foretold ; v. 6.—*Matthew Henry.*

Verses 1—15.—I. God's call to man. II. Man's call to God.

Verse 2.—I. The internal beauty of Zion. 1. *Positive* beauty of wisdom—holiness—love. 2. *Comparative* with the beauty of Paradise and the heaven of angels. 3. *Superlative*—all the perfections of God combined. II. Its external glory. Out of it God hath shined. 1. On this world. 2. On gracious souls. 3. On angels who desire to look, etc. 4. On the universe. "All the creatures heard I," etc.—*G. R.*

Verse 4.—1. What God will do for his people. He will judge them. 1. Deliver. 2. Defend. 3. Uphold. II. The means at his disposal for this purpose. "He shall call," etc—heaven and earth are subservient to him for the good of his church.—*G. R.*

Verse 4.—The judgment of the visible church. It will be by God himself, public, searching—with fire and wind, exact, final.

Verse 5.—The great family gathering. I. Who are gathered. II. How they are gathered. III. To whom. IV. When they are gathered.

Verse 5 (*last clause*).—I. The covenant. II. The sacrifice which ratifies it. III. How we may be said to make it.

Verse 6 (*last clause*).—Then slander will not pervert the sentence, undue severity will not embitter it, partiality will not excuse, falsehood will not deceive, justice will surely be done.

Verse 7.—Sins of God's people specially against God, and only known to God. A searching subject.

Verses 13—15.—What sacrifices are not, and what are acceptable with God.

Verse 15.—I. The occasion—"trouble." II. The command—"call upon me." III. The promise—"I will deliver thee." IV. The design—"thou shalt," etc.— *G. R.*

Verse 15.—"*Thou shalt glorify me.*" This we do by praying, and by praising when prayer is heard ; as also by confidence in his promises, submission to his chastisements, concern for his honour, attachment to his cause, affection to his people, and by continual obedience to his commands.

Verse 15.—I. A special invitation as to person and time. II. Special promise to those accepting it. III. Special duty involved when the promise is fulfilled.

Verses 16, 17.—I. The prohibition given. 1. The prohibited *things*—"declare my statutes." "Take my covenant," etc. (1.) Preaching. (2.) Teaching, as in Sunday-schools. (3.) Praying. (4.) Attending ordinances. 2. Prohibited *persons*. Wicked preachers, etc., while they continue in wickedness. II. The reason assigned ; v. 17. 1. No self-application of the truth. 2. Inward hatred of it. 3. Outward rejection.—*G. R.*

Verse 17.—I. *The fatal sign.* 1. Hating to be taught. 2. Hating what is taught. II. *What it indicates.* 1. Pride. 2. Contempt of God. 3. Indifference to truth. 4. Atheism at heart. 5. Deadness of conscience. II. *What it leads to.* See verse 22.

Verses 17, 18.—Rejection of salutary instruction leads sooner or later to open transgression. Instances, reasons, inferential warnings.

Verses 20, 21.—I. Man speaking and God silent. II. God speaking and man silent.

Verse 21.—I. God leaves men for a time to themselves. II. They judge of God on this account by themselves. III. He will in due time reveal their whole selves to themselves. "I will reprove," etc.—*G. R.*

Verses 21, 23.—Note the alternative ; a life rightly ordered now, or sins set in order hereafter.

Verse 22.—I. The accusation—"Ye that forget God," his omniscience, his power, his justice, his goodness, his mercy, his word, his great salvation. II. The admonition—"Consider this," rouse yourselves from your forgetfulness into serious reflection. III. The condemnation—"Lest," etc. 1. The awfulness. "Tear," as a lion or eagle its prey—tear body and soul. 2. Its irresistibleness—"None to deliver."—*G. R.*

Verse 23.—I. Salvation is the work of God. II. The evidence of salvation is holiness of heart and life. III. The effect of that evidence is praise. IV. The tendency of that praise is to glorify God. God is not glorified by the doubts, and fears, and murmurings of his people, but by their praise.—*G. R.*

Verse 23 (*last clause*).—The true order of life. I. That first which is first. II. That most which is most. III. That ever which is ever. IV. That all which is all.

PSALM LI.

TITLE.—To the chief Musician.—*Therefore not written for private meditation only, but for the public service of song. Suitable for the loneliness of individual penitence, this matchless Psalm is equally well adapted for an assembly of the poor in spirit.* A Psalm of David. *It is a marvel, but nevertheless a fact, that writers have been found to deny David's authorship of this Psalm, but their objections are frivolous, the Psalm is David-like all over. It would be far easier to imitate Milton, Shakespeare, or Tennyson, than David. His style is altogether* sui generis, *and it is as easily distinguishable as the touch of Rafaelle or the colouring of Rubens.* " When Nathan the prophet came unto him, after he had gone in to Bathsheba." *When the divine message had aroused his dormant conscience and made him see the greatness of his guilt he wrote this Psalm. He had forgotten his Psalmody while he was indulging his flesh, but he returned to his harp when his spiritual nature was awakened, and he poured out his song to the accompaniment of sighs and tears. The great sin of David is not to be excused, but it is well to remember that his case has an exceptional collection of specialities in it. He was a man of very strong passions, a soldier, and an Oriental monarch having despotic power; no other king of his time would have felt any compunction for having acted as he did, and hence there were not around him those restraints of custom and association which, when broken through, render the offence the more monstrous. He never hints at any form of extenuation, nor do we mention these facts in order to apologise for his sin, which was detestable to the last degree; but for the warning of others, that they may reflect that the like licentiousness in themselves at this day might have even a graver guilt in it than in the erring King of Israel. When we remember his sin, let us dwell most upon his penitence, and upon the long series of chastisements which rendered the after part of his life such a mournful history.*

DIVISIONS.—*It will be simplest to note in the first twelve verses the penitent's confessions and plea for pardon, and then in the last seven his anticipatory gratitude and the way in which he resolves to display it.*

EXPOSITION.

HAVE mercy upon me, O God, according to thy lovingkindness: according unto the multitude of thy tender mercies blot out my transgressions.

2 Wash me throughly from mine iniquity, and cleanse me from my sin.

3 For I acknowledge my transgressions: and my sin *is* ever before me.

4 Against thee, thee only, have I sinned, and done *this* evil in thy sight: that thou mightest be justified when thou speakest, *and* be clear when thou judgest.

5 Behold, I was shapen in iniquity; and in sin did my mother conceive me.

6 Behold, thou desirest truth in the inward parts: and in the hidden *part* thou shalt make me to know wisdom.

7. Purge me with hyssop, and I shall be clean: wash me, and I shall be whiter than snow.

8 Make me to hear joy and gladness, *that* the bones *which* thou hast broken may rejoice.

9 Hide thy face from my sins, and blot out all mine iniquities.

10 Create in me a clean heart, O God; and renew a right spirit within me.

11 Cast me not away from thy presence; and take not thy holy spirit from me.

12 Restore unto me the joy of thy salvation; and uphold me *with thy* free spirit.

1. "*Have mercy upon me, O God.*" He appeals at once to the mercy of God, even before he mentions his sin. The sight of mercy is good for eyes that are sore with penitential weeping. Pardon of sin must ever be an act of pure mercy, and therefore to that attribute the awakened sinner flies. "*According to thy loving-kindness.*" Act, O Lord, like thyself; give mercy like thy mercy. Show mercy such as is congruous with thy grace.

> "Great God, thy nature hath no bound:
> So let thy pardoning love be found."

What a choice word is that of our English version, a rare compound of precious things : love and kindness sweetly blended in one—"lovingkindness." "*According unto the multitude of thy tender mercies.*" Let thy most loving compassions come to me, and make thou thy pardons such as these would suggest. Reveal all thy gentlest attributes in my case, not only in their essence but in their abundance. Numberless have been thine acts of goodness, and vast is thy grace ; let me be the object of thine infinite mercy, and repeat it all in me. Make my one case an epitome of all thy tender mercies. By every deed of grace to others I feel encouraged, and I pray thee let me add another and a yet greater one, in my own person, to the long list of thy compassions. "*Blot out my transgressions.*" My revolts, my excesses, are all recorded against me ; but, Lord, erase the lines. Draw thy pen through the register. Obliterate the record, though now it seems engraven in the rock for ever : many strokes of thy mercy may be needed, to cut out the deep inscription, but then thou hast a multitude of mercies, and therefore, I beseech thee, erase my sins.

2. "*Wash me throughly.*" It is not enough to blot out the sin ; his person is defiled, and he fain would be purified. He would have God himself cleanse him, for none but he could do it effectually. The washing must be thorough, it must be repeated, therefore he cries, "Multiply to wash me." The dye is in itself immovable, and I, the sinner, have lain long in it, till the crimson is ingrained : but, Lord, wash, and wash, and wash again, till the last stain is gone, and not a trace of my defilement is left. The hypocrite is content if his garments be washed ; but the true suppliant cries, "wash *me.*" The careless soul is content with a nominal cleansing, but the truly-awakened conscience desires a real and practical washing, and that of a most complete and efficient kind. "*Wash me throughly from mine iniquity.*" It is viewed as one great pollution, polluting the entire nature, and as all his own ; as if nothing were so much his own as his sin. The one sin against Bathsheba, served to show the Psalmist the whole mountain of his iniquity, of which that foul deed was but one falling stone. He desires to be rid of the whole mass of his filthiness, which though once so little observed, had then become a hideous and haunting terror to his mind. "*And cleanse me from my sin.*" This is a more general expression ; as if the Psalmist said, "Lord, if washing will not do, try some other process ; if water avails not, let fire, let anything be tried, so that I may but be purified. Rid me of my sin by some means, by any means, by every means, only do purify me completely, and leave no guilt upon my soul." It is not the punishment he cries out against, but the sin. Many a murderer is more alarmed at the gallows than at the murder which brought him to it. The thief loves the plunder, though he fears the prison. Not so David : he is sick of sin as sin ; his loudest outcries are against the evil of his transgression, and not against the painful consequences of it. When we deal seriously with our sin, God will deal gently with us. When we hate what the Lord hates, he will soon make an end of it, to our joy and peace.

3. "*For I acknowledge my transgressions.*" Here he sees the plurality and immense number of his sins, and makes open declaration of them. He seems to say, I make a full confession of them. Not that this is my plea in seeking forgiveness, but it is a clear evidence that I need mercy, and am utterly unable to look to any other quarter for help. My pleading guilty has barred me from any appeal against the sentence of justice : O Lord, I must cast myself on thy mercy, refuse me not, I pray thee. Thou hast made me willing to confess. O follow up this work of grace with a full and free remission ! "*And my sin is ever before me.*" My sin as a whole is never out of my mind ; it continually oppresses my spirit. I lay it before thee because it is ever before me : Lord, put it away both from thee and me. To an awakened conscience, pain on account of sin is not transient and

occasional, but intense and permanent, and this is no sign of divine wrath, but rather a sure preface of abounding favour.

4. "*Against thee, thee only have I sinned.*" The virus of sin lies in its opposition to God : the Psalmist's sense of sin towards others rather tended to increase the force of his feeling of sin against God. All his wrong-doing centred, culminated, and came to a climax, at the foot of the divine throne. To injure our fellow men is sin, mainly because in so doing we violate the law of God. The penitent's heart was so filled with a sense of the wrong done to the Lord himself, that all other confession was swallowed up in a broken-hearted acknowledgment of offence against him. "*And done this evil in thy sight.*" To commit treason in the very court of the king and before his eye is impudence indeed : David felt that his sin was committed in all its filthiness while Jehovah himself looked on. None but a child of God cares for the eye of God, but where there is grace in the soul it reflects a fearful guilt upon every evil act, when we remember that the God whom we offend was present when the trespass was committed. "*That thou mightest be justified when thou speakest, and be clear when thou judgest.*" He could not present any argument against divine justice, if it proceeded at once to condemn him and punish him for his crime. His own confession, and the judge's own witness of the whole transaction, placed the transgression beyond all question or debate ; the iniquity was indisputably committed, and was unquestionably a foul wrong, and therefore the course of justice was clear and beyond all controversy.

5. "*Behold, I was shapen in iniquity.*" He is thunderstruck at the discovery of his inbred sin, and proceeds to set it forth. This was not intended to justify himself, but it rather meant to complete the confession. It is as if he said, not only have I sinned this once, but I am in my very nature a sinner. The fountain of my life is polluted as well as its streams. My birth-tendencies are out of the square of equity ; I naturally lean to forbidden things. Mine is a constitutional disease, rendering my very person obnoxious to thy wrath. "*And in sin did my mother conceive me.*" He goes back to the earliest moment of his being, not to traduce his mother, but to acknowledge the deep tap-roots of his sin. It is a wicked wresting of Scripture to deny that original sin and natural depravity are here taught. Surely men who cavil at this doctrine have need to be taught of the Holy Spirit what be the first principles of the faith. David's mother was the Lord's handmaid, he was born in chaste wedlock, of a good father, and he was himself "the man after God's own heart ;" and yet his nature was as fallen as that of any other son of Adam, and there only needed the occasion for the manifesting of that sad fact. In our shaping we were put out of shape, and when we were conceived our nature conceived sin. Alas, for poor humanity ! Those who will may cry it up, but he is most blessed who in his own soul has learned to lament its lost estate.

6. "*Behold.*" Here is the great matter of consideration. God desires not merely outward virtue, but inward purity, and the penitent's sense of sin is greatly deepened as with astonishment he discovers this truth, and how far he is from satisfying the divine demand. The second "Behold" is fitly set over against the first ; how great the gulf which yawns between them ! "*Thou desirest truth in the inward parts.*" Reality, sincerity, true holiness, heart-fidelity, these are the demands of God. He cares not for the pretence of purity, he looks to the mind, heart, and soul. Always has the Holy One of Israel estimated men by their inner nature, and not by their outward professions ; to him the inward is as visible as the outward, and he rightly judges that the essential character of an action lies in the motive of him who works it. "*And in the hidden part thou shalt make me to know wisdom.*" The penitent feels that God is teaching him truth concerning his nature, which he had not before perceived. The love of the heart, the mystery of its fall, and the way of its purification—this hidden wisdom we must all attain ; and it is a great blessing to be able to believe that the Lord will "make us to know it." No one can teach our innermost nature but the Lord, but he can instruct us to profit. The Holy Spirit can write the law on our heart, and that is the sum of practical wisdom. He can put the fear of the Lord within, and that is the beginning of wisdom. He can reveal Christ in us, and he is essential wisdom. Such poor, foolish, disarranged souls as ours, shall yet be ordered aright, and truth and wisdom shall reign within us.

7. "*Purge me with hyssop.*" Sprinkle the atoning blood upon me with the appointed means. Give me the reality which legal ceremonies symbolise. Nothing but blood can take away my blood-stains, nothing but the strongest purification

can avail to cleanse me. Let the sin-offering purge my sin. Let him who was appointed to atone, execute his sacred office on me ; for none can need it more than I. The passage may be read as the voice of faith as well as a prayer, and so it runs—" Thou wilt purge me with hyssop, *and I shall be clean.*" Foul as I am, there is such power in the divine propitiation, that my sin shall vanish quite away. Like the leper upon whom the priest has performed the cleansing rites, I shall be again admitted into the assembly of thy people and allowed to share in the privileges of the true Israel ; while in thy sight also, through Jesus my Lord, I shall be accepted. *"Wash me."* Let it not merely be in type that I am clean, but by real spiritual purification, which shall remove the pollution of my nature. Let the sanctifying as well as the pardoning process be perfected in me. Save me from the evils which my sin has created and nourished in me. *"And I shall be whiter than snow."* None but thyself can whiten me, but thou canst in grace outdo nature itself in its purest state. Snow soon gathers smoke and dust, it melts and disappears ; thou canst give me an enduring purity. Though snow is white below as well as on the surface, thou canst work the like inward purity in me, and make me so clean that only an hyperbole can set forth my immaculate condition. Lord, do this ; my faith believes thou wilt, and well she knows thou canst.

Scarcely does Holy Scripture contain a verse more full of faith than this. Considering the nature of the sin, and the deep sense the Psalmist had of it, it is a glorious faith to be able to see in the blood sufficient, nay, all-sufficient merit entirely to purge it away. Considering also the deep, natural inbred corruption which David saw and experienced within, it is a miracle of faith that he could rejoice in the hope of perfect purity in his inward parts. Yet, be it added, the faith is no more than the word warrants, than the blood of atonement encourages, than the promise of God deserves. O that some reader may take heart, even now while smarting under sin, to do the Lord the honour to rely thus confidently on the finished sacrifice of Calvary and the infinite mercy there revealed.

8. *"Make me to hear joy and gladness."* He prays about his sorrow late in the Psalm ; he began at once with his sin ; he asks to hear pardon, and then to hear joy. He seeks comfort at the right time and from the right source. His ear has become heavy with sinning, and so he prays, " Make me to hear." No voice could revive his dead joys but that which quickeneth the dead. Pardon from God would give him double joy—" joy and gladness." No stinted bliss awaits the forgiven one ; he shall not only *have* a double-blooming joy, but he shall *hear* it ; it shall sing with exultation. Some joy is felt but not heard, for it contends with fears ; but the joy of pardon has a voice louder than the voice of sin. God's voice speaking peace is the sweetest music an ear can hear. *"That the bones which thou hast broken may rejoice."* He was like a poor wretch whose bones are crushed, crushed by no ordinary means, but by omnipotence itself. He groaned under no mere flesh wounds ; his firmest and yet tenderest powers were " broken in pieces all asunder ; " his manhood had become a dislocated, mangled, quivering sensibility. Yet if he who crushed would cure, every wound would become a new mouth for song, every bone quivering before with agony would become equally sensible of intense delight. The figure is bold, and so is the supplicant. He is requesting a great thing ; he seeks joy for a sinful heart, music for crushed bones. Preposterous prayer anywhere but at the throne of God ! Preposterous there most of all but for the cross where Jehovah Jesus bore our sins in his own body on the tree. A penitent need not ask to be an hired servant, or settle down in despairing content with perpetual mourning ; he may ask for gladness and he shall have it ; for if when prodigals return the father is glad, and the neighbours and friends rejoice and are merry with music and dancing, what need can there be that the restored one himself should be wretched ?

9. *"Hide thy face from my sins."* Do not look at them ; be at pains not to see them. They thrust themselves in thy way ; but, Lord, refuse to behold them, lest if thou consider them, thine anger burn, and I die. *"Blot out all mine iniquities."* He repeats the prayer of the first verse with the enlargement of it by the word " all." All repetitions are not " vain repetitions." Souls in agony have no space to find variety of language : pain has to content itself with monotones. David's face was ashamed with looking on his sin, and no diverting thoughts could remove it from his memory ; but he prays the Lord to do with his sin what he himself cannot. If God hide not his face from our sin, he must hide it for ever from us ; and if he blot not out our sins, he must blot our names out of his book of life.

10. *"Create."* What! has sin so destroyed us, that the Creator must be called in again? What ruin then doth evil work among mankind! *"Create in me."* I, in outward fabric, still exist; but I am empty, desert, void. Come, then, and let thy power be seen in a new creation within my old fallen self. Thou didst make a man in the world at first; Lord, make a new man in me! *"A clean heart."* In the seventh verse he asked to be clean; now he seeks a heart suitable to that cleanliness; but he does not say, " Make my old heart clean; " he is too experienced in the hopelessness of the old nature. He would have the old man buried as a dead thing, and a new creation brought in to fill its place. None but God can create either a new heart or a new earth. Salvation is a marvellous display of supreme power; the work *in* us as much as that *for* us is wholly of Omnipotence. The affections must be rectified first, or all our nature will go amiss. The heart is the rudder of the soul, and till the Lord take it in hand we steer in a false and foul way. O Lord, thou who didst once make me, be pleased to new make me, and in my most secret parts renew me. *"Renew a right spirit within me."* It was there once, Lord, put it there again. The law on my heart has become like an inscription hard to read: new write it, gracious Maker. Remove the evil as I have entreated thee; but, O replace it with good, lest into my swept, empty, and garnished heart, from which the devil has gone out for awhile, seven other spirits more wicked than the first should enter and dwell. The two sentences make a complete prayer. *"Create"* what is not there at all; *" renew "* that which is there, but in a sadly feeble state.

11. *"Cast me not away from thy presence."* Throw me not away as worthless; banish me not, like Cain, from thy face and favour. Permit me to sit among those who share thy love, though I only be suffered to keep the door. I deserve to be for ever denied admission to thy courts; but, O good Lord, permit me still the privilege which is dear as life itself to me. *"Take not thy Holy Spirit from me."* Withdraw not his comforts, counsels, assistances, quickenings, else I am indeed as a dead man. Do not leave me as thou didst Saul, when neither by Urim, nor by prophet, nor by dream, thou wouldst answer him. Thy Spirit is my wisdom, leave me not to my folly; he is my strength, O desert me not to my own weakness. Drive me not away from thee, neither do thou go away from me. Keep up the union between us, which is my only hope of salvation. It will be a great wonder if so pure a Spirit deigns to stay in so base a heart as mine; but then, Lord, it is all wonder together, therefore do this, for thy mercy's sake, I earnestly entreat thee.

12. *"Restore unto me the joy of thy salvation."* Salvation he had known, and had known it as the Lord's own; he had also felt the joy which arises from being saved in the Lord, but he had lost it for awhile, and therefore he longed for its restoration. None but God can give back this joy; he can do it; we may ask it; he will do it for his own glory and our benefit. This joy comes not first, but follows pardon and purity: in such order it is safe, in any other it is vain presumption or idiotic delirium. *"And uphold me with thy free Spirit."* Conscious of weakness, mindful of having so lately fallen, he seeks to be kept on his feet by power superior to his own. That royal Spirit, whose holiness is true dignity, is able to make us walk as kings and priests, in all the uprightness of holiness; and he will do so if we seek his gracious upholding. Such influences will not enslave but emancipate us; for holiness is liberty, and the Holy Spirit is a free Spirit. In the roughest and most treacherous ways we are safe with such a keeper; in the best paths we stumble if left to ourselves. The praying for joy and upholding go well together; it is all over with joy if the foot is not kept; and, on the other hand, joy is a very upholding thing, and greatly aids holiness; meanwhile, the free, noble, loyal Spirit is at the bottom of both.

13 *Then* will I teach transgressors thy ways; and sinners shall be converted unto thee.

14 Deliver me from bloodguiltiness, O God, thou God of my salvation: *and* my tongue shall sing aloud of thy righteousness.

15 O Lord, open thou my lips; and my mouth shall shew forth thy praise.

16 For thou desirest not sacrifice; else would I give *it:* thou delightest not in burnt offering.

17 The sacrifices of God *are* a broken spirit: a broken and a contrite heart, O God, thou wilt not despise.

18 Do good in thy good pleasure unto Zion : build thou the walls of Jerusalem.

19 Then shalt thou be pleased with the sacrifices of righteousness, with burnt offering and whole burnt offering : then shall they offer bullocks upon thine altar.

13. " *Then will I teach transgressors thy ways.*" It was his fixed resolve to be a teacher of others ; and assuredly none instruct others so well as those who have been experimentally taught of God themselves. Reclaimed poachers make the best gamekeepers. Huntingdon's degree of S.S., or Sinner Saved, is more needful for a soul-winning evangelist than either M.A. or D.D. The pardoned sinner's matter will be good, for he has been taught in the school of experience, and his manner will be telling, for he will speak sympathetically, as one who has felt what he declares. The audience the Psalmist would choose is memorable— he would instruct transgressors like himself ; others might despise them, but, " a fellow feeling makes us wondrous kind." If unworthy to edify saints, he would creep in along with the sinners, and humbly tell them of divine love. The mercy of God to one is an illustration of his usual procedure, so that our own case helps us to understand his " ways." or his general modes of action : perhaps, too, David under that term refers to the preceptive part of the word of God, which, having broken, and having suffered thereby, he felt that he could vindicate and urge upon the reverence of other offenders. " *And sinners shall be converted unto thee.*" My fall shall be the restoration of others. Thou wilt bless my pathetic testimony to the recovery of many who, like myself, have turned aside unto crooked ways. Doubtless this Psalm and the whole story of David, have produced for many ages the most salutary results in the conversion of transgressors, and so evil has been overruled for good.

14. " *Deliver me from bloodguiltiness.*" He had been the means of the death of Uriah, the Hittite, a faithful and attached follower, and he now confesses that fact. Besides, his sin of adultery was a capital offence, and he puts himself down as one worthy to die the death. Honest penitents do not fetch a compass and confess their sins in an elegant periphrasis, but they come to the point, call a spade a spade, and make a clean breast of all. What other course is rational in dealing with the Omniscient ? " *O God, thou God of my salvation.*" He had not ventured to come so near before. It had been, " O God," up till now, but here he cries, " *Thou God of my salvation.*" Faith grows by the exercise of prayer. He confesses sin more plainly in this verse than before, and yet he deals with God more confidently : growing upward and downward at the same time are perfectly consistent. None but the King can remit the death penalty, it is therefore a joy to faith that God is King, and that he is the author and finisher of our salvation. " *And my tongue shall sing aloud of thy righteousness.*" One would rather have expected him to say, I will sing of thy mercy ; but David can see the divine way of justification, that righteousness of God which Paul afterwards spoke of by which the ungodly are justified, and he vows to sing, yea, and to sing lustily of that righteous way of mercy. After all, it is the righteousness of divine mercy which is its greatest wonder. Note how David would preach in the last verse, and now here he would sing. We can never do too much for the Lord to whom we owe more than all. If we could be preacher, precentor, doorkeeper, pewopener, footwasher, and all in one, all would be too little to show forth all our gratitude. A great sinner pardoned makes a great singer. Sin has a loud voice, and so should our thankfulness have. We shall not sing our own praises if we be saved, but our theme will be the Lord our righteousness, in whose merits we stand righteously accepted.

15. " *O Lord, open thou my lips.*" He is so afraid of himself that he commits his whole being to the divine care, and fears to speak till the Lord unstops his shame-silenced mouth. How marvellously the Lord can open our lips, and what divine things we poor simpletons pour forth under his inspiration ! This prayer of a penitent is a golden petition for a preacher. Lord, I offer it for myself and my brethren. But it may stand in good stead any one whose shame for sin makes him stammer in his prayers, and when it is fully answered, the tongue of the dumb begins to sing. " *And my mouth shall shew forth thy praise.*" If God opens the mouth he is sure to have the fruit of it. According to the porter at the gate is the nature of that which comes out of man's lips ; when vanity, anger, falsehood, or

lust unbar the door, the foulest villanies troop out ; but if the Holy Spirit opens the wicket, then grace, mercy, peace, and all the graces come forth in tuneful dances, like the daughters of Israel when they met David returning with the Philistine's head.

16. " *For thou desirest not sacrifice.*" This was the subject of the last Psalm. The Psalmist was so illuminated as to see far beyond the symbolic ritual; his eye of faith gazed with delight upon the actual atonement. " *Else would I give it.*" He would have been glad enough to present tens of thousands of victims if these would have met the case. Indeed, anything which the Lord prescribed he would cheerfully have rendered. We are ready to give up all we have if we may but be cleared of our sins ; and when sin is pardoned our joyful gratitude is prepared for any sacrifice. " *Thou delightest not in burnt offering.*" He knew that no form of burnt sacrifice was a satisfactory propitiation. His deep soul-need made him look from the type to the antitype, from the external rite to the inward grace.

17. " *The sacrifices of God are a broken spirit.*" All sacrifices are presented to thee in one, by the man whose broken heart presents the Saviour's merit to thee. When the heart mourns for sin, thou art better pleased than when the bullock bleeds beneath the axe. " A broken heart " is an expression implying deep sorrow, embittering the very life ; it carries in it the idea of all but killing anguish in that region which is so vital as to be the very source of life. So excellent is a spirit humbled and mourning for sin, that it is not only a sacrifice, but it has a plurality of excellencies, and is pre-eminently God's " *sacrifices.*" " *A broken and a contrite heart, O God, thou wilt not despise.*" A heart crushed is a fragrant heart. Men contemn those who are contemptible in their own eyes, but the Lord seeth not as man seeth. He despises what men esteem, and values that which they despise. Never yet has God spurned a lowly, weeping penitent, and never will he while God is love, and while Jesus is called the man who receiveth sinners. Bullocks and rams he desires not, but contrite hearts he seeks after ; yea, but one of them is better to him than all the varied offerings of the old Jewish sanctuary.

18. " *Do good in thy good pleasure unto Zion.*" Let blessings according to thy wont be poured upon thy holy hill and chosen city. Zion was David's favourite spot, whereon he had hoped to erect a temple. The ruling passion is so strong on him, that when he has discharged his conscience he must have a word for Zion. He felt he had hindered the project of honouring the Lord there as he desired, but he prayed God still to let the place of his ark be glorious, and to establish his worship and his worshipping people. " *Build thou the walls of Jerusalem.*" This had been one of David's schemes, to wall in the holy city, and he desires to see it completed ; but we believe he had a more spiritual meaning, and prayed for the prosperity of the Lord's cause and people. He had done mischief by his sin, and had, as it were, pulled down her walls ; he, therefore, implores the Lord to undo the evil. and establish his church. God can make his cause to prosper, and in answer to prayer he will do so. Without his building we labour in vain ; therefore are we the more instant and constant in prayer. There is surely no grace in us if we do not feel for the church of God, and take a lasting interest in its welfare.

19. In those days of joyful prosperity thy saints shall present in great abundance the richest and holiest thank offerings to thee, and thou shalt be pleased to accept them. A saved soul expects to see its prayers answered in a revived church, and then is assured that God will be greatly glorified. Though we bring no more sacrifices for sin, yet as priests unto God our solemn praises and votive gifts are thank offerings acceptable to God by Jesus Christ. We bring not the Lord our least things—our doves and pigeons ; but we present him with our best possessions—our bullocks. We are glad that in this present time we are able to fulfil in person the declaration of this verse : we also, forecasting the future, wait for days of the divine presence, when the church of God, with unspeakable joy, shall offer gifts upon the altar of God, which will far eclipse anything beheld, in these less enthusiastic days. Hasten it, O Lord.

EXPLANATORY NOTES AND QUAINT SAYINGS.

Title.—"*After he had gone in to Bathsheba.*" This was the devil's nest-egg that caused many sins to be laid, one to, and upon another. See the woful chain of David's lust, 2 Sam. xi. and xii.—*John Trapp.*

Title.—"*When Nathan the prophet came unto him as he* (*i.e.*, David) *had come unto Bathsheba.*" The significant repetition of the phrase *came unto,* is lost in the English and most other versions. "*As*" is not a mere particle of time, simply equivalent to *when,* but suggests the ideas of analogy, proportion, and retaliation.—*J. A. Alexander.*

Whole Psalm.—This Psalm is the brightest gem in the whole book, and contains instruction so large, and doctrine so precious, that the tongue of angels could not do justice to the full development.—*Victorinus Strigelius,* 1524—1569.

Whole Psalm.—This Psalm is often and fitly called THE SINNER'S GUIDE. In some of its versions it often helps the returning sinner. Athanasius recommends to some Christians, to whom he was writing, to repeat it when they awake at night. All evangelical churches are familiar with it. Luther says, "There is no other Psalm which is oftener sung or prayed in the church." This is the first Psalm in which we have the word *Spirit* used in application to the Holy Ghost.—*William S. Plumer.*

Whole Psalm.—I cannot doubt the prophetic bearing of this Psalm upon the nation of Israel. In the latter day they shall consider their ways: repentance and self-loathing will be the result. Blood-guiltiness heavier than that of David has to be removed from that nation. They will become the teachers of the Gentiles, when first the iniquity of their own transgression has been purged away.—*Arthur Pridham.*

Whole Psalm.—This is the most deeply affecting of all the Psalms, and I am sure the one most applicable to me. It seems to have been the effusion of a soul smarting under the sense of a recent and great transgression. My God, whether recent or not, give me to feel the enormity of my manifold offences, and remember not against me the sins of my youth. What a mine of rich matter and expression for prayer! Wash, cleanse me, O Lord, and let my sin and my sinfulness be ever before me. Let me feel it chiefly as sin against thee, that my sorrow may be of the godly sort. Give me to feel the virulence of my native corruption, purge me from it thoroughly, and put truth into my inward parts, that mine may be a real turning from sin unto the Saviour. Create me anew, O God. Withdraw not thy Spirit. Cause me to rejoice in a present salvation. Deliver me, O God, from the blood-guiltiness of having offended any of thy little ones; and so open my lips that I may speak of the wondrous things thou hast done for my soul! May I offer up spiritual sacrifices; and oh! let not any delinquencies of mine bring a scandal upon thy church; but do thou so purify and build her up, that even her external services, freed from all taint of corruption or hypocrisy, may be well-pleasing in thy sight.—*Thomas Chalmers.*

Verse 1.—"*Have mercy upon me, O God.*" I tremble and blush to mention my name, for my former familiarities with thee only make me more confounded at being recognised by thee after my guilt. I therefore say not, "Lord, remember David," as on a happier occasion; nor as propitiating thee, I used to say, to thy "servant," or, "to the son of thy handmaid." I suggest nothing that should recall my former relation to thee, and so enhance my wickedness. Ask not, then, Lord, who I am, but only forgive me who confess my sin, condemn my fault, and beseech thy pity. "*Have mercy upon me, O God.*" I dare not say *my* God, for that were presumption. I have lost thee by sin, I have alienated myself from thee by following the enemy, and therefore am unclean. I dare not approach thee, but standing afar off and lifting up my voice with great devotion and contrition of heart, I cry and say, "*Have mercy upon me, O God.*"—*From "A Commentary on the Seven Penitential Psalms, chiefly from ancient sources." By the Right Rev. A. P. Forbes, Bishop of Brechin,* 1857.

Verse 1.—"*Have mercy.*" The Hebrew word here translated *have mercy,* signifieth without cause or desert; Psalm xxxv. 19; lxix. 4; Ezekiel xiv. 23; and freely, without paying any price, Exodus xxi. 11. And it is made use of in

Lev. vi. 8, where Noah is said to have found *grace* in the eyes of the Lord, that is special favour, such as the Lord beareth to his chosen in Christ Jesus.—*Charles de Coetlogon, A.M., in "The Portraiture of the Christian Penitent,"* 1775.

Verse 1.—*"Mercy," " lovingkindness," " tender mercies."* I cannot but observe here, the gradation in the sense of the three words made use of, to express the divine compassion, and the propriety of the order in which they are placed, which would be regarded as a real excellence and beauty in any classical writer. The first, חָנַּנִי, denotes that kind of affection which is expressed by moaning over any object that we love and pity that στοργὴ, natural affection and tenderness, which even brute creatures discover to their young ones, by the several noises which they respectively make over them ; and particularly the shrill noise of the camel, by which it testifies its love to its foal. The second, חַסְדֶּךָ, denotes a strong proneness, a ready, large, and liberal disposition to goodness and compassion powerfully prompting to all instances of kindness and bounty ; flowing as freely and plentifully as milk into the breasts, or as waters from a perpetual fountain. This denotes a higher degree of goodness than the former. The third, רַחֲמֶיךָ, denotes what the Greeks express by σπλαγχνίζεσθαι ; that most tender pity which we signify by the moving of the heart and bowels, which argues the highest degree of compassion of which human nature is susceptible. And how reviving is the belief and consideration of these abundant and tender compassions of God to one in David's circumstances, whose mind laboured under the burthen of the most heinous complicated guilt, and the fear of the divine displeasure and vengeance !—*Samuel Chandler.*

Verse 1.—*"According to the multitude."* Men are greatly terrified at the multitude of their sins, but here is a comfort—our God hath multitude of mercies. If our sins be in number as the hairs of our head, God's mercies are as the stars of heaven ; and as he is an infinite God, so his mercies are infinite ; yea, so far are his mercies above our sins, as he himself is above us poor sinners. By this that the Psalmist seeketh for multitude of mercies, he would show how deeply he was wounded with his manifold sins, that one seemed a hundred. Thus it is with us, so long as we are under Satan's guiding, a thousand seem but one ; but if we betake ourselves to God's service, one will seem a thousand.—*Archibald Symson.*

Verse 1.—*"Tender mercies,"* or, according to Zanchy in his treatise upon the attributes of God, such a kind of affection as parents feel when they see their children in any extremity. 1 Kings iii. 26.—*Charles de Coetlogon.*

Verse 1.—*"Blot out my transgressions."* מְחֵה, *mecheh, wipe out.* There is reference here to an *indictment :* the Psalmist knows what it contains ; he pleads guilty, but begs that the writing may be *defaced ;* that a proper fluid may be applied to the parchment, *to discharge the ink,* that no record of it may ever appear against him : and this only the *mercy, lovingkindness, and tender compassions* of the Lord can do.—*Adam Clarke.*

Verse 1.—*"Blot out my transgressions."* What the Psalmist alludes to is not, as Mr. LeClerc imagines, *debts entered into a book,* and so blotted out of it when forgiven ; but the wiping or cleansing of a dish, so as nothing afterwards remains in it. The meaning of the petition is, that God would entirely and absolutely forgive him, so as that no part of the guilt he had contracted might remain, and the punishment of it might be wholly removed.—*Samuel Chandler.*

Verse 1.—*"Blot out,"* or, as it is used in Exod. xvii. 14, *utterly extirpate,* so as that there shall not be any remembrance of them for ever. Isaiah xliii. 25 ; xliv. 22. —*Charles de Coetlogon.*

Verse 1.—*" My transgressions."* Conscience, when it is healthy, ever speaks thus : " My *transgressions."* It was not the guilt of them that tempted you : they have theirs ; but each as a separate agent, has his own degree of guilt. Yours is your own : the violation of your own and not another's sense of duty ; solitary, awful, unshared, adhering to you alone of all the spirits of the universe.—*Frederick William Robertson.*

Verses 1, 2.—*"Transgressions" . . . " iniquity" . . . " sin."* 1. It is *transgression,* פֶּשַׁע, *pesha,* rebellion. 2. It is *iniquity,* עָוֹן, *avon,* crooked dealing. 3. It is *sin,* חַטָּאת, *chattath,* error and wandering.—*Adam Clarke.*

Verse 2.—*" Wash me."* David prays that the Lord would *wash* him ; therefore sin defiles, and he was made foul and filthy by his sin ; and to wash him much, and to rinse and bathe him, to show that sin had exceedingly defiled him and stained him both in soul and body, and made him loathsome, and therefore he desireth to be washed, and cleansed, and purged from the pollution of sin. Hence we may learn what a vile, filthy, and miserable thing sin is in the sight of God : it staineth a man's body, it staineth a man's soul, it maketh him more vile than the vilest creature that lives : no toad is so vile and loathsome in the sight of man, as a sinner, stained and defiled with sin, is in the sight of God, till he be cleansed and washed from it in the blood of Christ.—*Samuel Smith.*

Verse 2.—" *Wash me,*" etc. ﬦﬠﬤ is peculiarly applied to the washing and cleansing of garments as fullers wash and cleanse their cloths. 2 Kings xviii. 7 ; Exod. xix. 10 ; Levit. xvii. 15.—*Samuel Chandler.*

Verse 2.—" *Wash me throughly from mine iniquity."* No other washing will do it but *lava tu,* wash thou ; so foul, as it will need his washing *throughly.*—*Samuel Page, in " David's Broken Heart,"* 1646.

Verse 2.—"*Wash me throughly."* Heb. *multiply to wash me ;* by which phrase he implies the greatness of his guilt, and the insufficiency of all legal washings, and the absolute necessity of some other and better thing to wash him, even of God's grace, and the blood of Christ.—*Matthew Pool.*

Verse 2.—" *Wash me . . . cleanse me."* But why should David speak so superfluously ? use two words when one would serve ? For if we be cleansed, what matter is it whether it be by washing or no ? Yet David had great reason for using both words ; for he requires not that God would cleanse him by miracle, but by the ordinary way of cleansing, and this was washing ; he names therefore washing as the means, and cleansing as the end : he names washing as the work a-doing, and cleansing as the work done ; he names washing as considering the agent, and cleansing as applying it to the patient ; and indeed, as in the figure of the law there was not, so in the verity of the gospel there is not any ordinary means of cleansing, but only by washing ; and therefore out of Christ our Saviour's side there flowed water and blood.—*Sir Richard Baker.*

Verse 2.—" *Cleanse me from my sin."* Observe, it is from the guilt, and not from the punishment, that he thus asks deliverance. That the sword should never depart from his house ; that the sin, begun, not only secretly even in its full accomplishment, but far more secretly in the recesses of David's heart, should be punished before all Israel and before the sun ; that the child so dear to David should be made one great punishment of his offence ; these things, so far as this Psalm is concerned, might, or might not be. It is of the offence against God ; of the defiling, although it were not then so expressly declared, God's temple by impurity, that David speaks.—*Ambrose, in J. M. Neale's Commentary.*

Verse 2.—" *Sin."* The original word signifies to miss an aim, as an archer does who shoots short of his mark, beyond, or beside it. It is also used for treading aside, or tripping, in the act of walking. In a spiritual sense it denotes deviation from a rule, whether by omission or commission.—*Thomas T. Biddulph, A.M., in Lectures on the Fifty-first Psalm,* 1835.

Verse 2.—Sin is filthy to think of, filthy to speak of, filthy to hear of, filthy to do ; in a word, there is nothing in it but vileness.—*Archibald Symson.*

Verse 3.—"*For I acknowledge my transgressions,"* etc. To *acknowledge our transgressions,* there is confession ; and *to have our sin ever before us,* there is conviction and contrition. To acknowledge our transgressions, I say, is to confess our sins ; to call them to mind, to bring them back to our remembrance what we can ; to own them with shame, and to declare them with sorrow ; to reckon them up one by one, to give in a particular account of them, as far as our memory will serve, and to spread them before the Lord, as Hezekiah did Rabshakeh's letter, and in an humble sense of our own vileness to implore his goodness, that he would multiply his mercies over us, as we have multiplied our transgressions against him, in the free and full forgiveness of them all. *To have our sin ever before us,* is throughly to be convinced of it, to be continually troubled in mind about it, to be truly humbled under the sense of it, and to be possest of those dreads and terrors of conscience which may never let us rest or enjoy any quiet within our own breast till we have reconciled ourselves to a gracious God for it.—*Adam Littleton.*

Verse 3.—" *I acknowledge my transgressions : and my sin is ever before me."* There cannot be *agnitio* if there be not *cognitio peccati,* an acknowledging, unless there precede a knowledge of sin. David puts them together. If our sins be not before us, how can we set them before God ? And therefore, to the right exercise of this duty, there is required a previous examination of our hearts, inspection into our lives, that we may be enabled to see our sins. He that hath not yet asked himself that question, *Quid feci?* What have I done? can never make the confession, *sic feci*, thus and thus have I done; and in this respect I would, though not require, yet advise it as a pious and prudent practice, and that which I doubt not but many Christians have found benefit by, to keep a constant daily catalogue, as of mercies received, so of sins committed.—*Nathanael Hardy.*

Verse 3.—" *I,*" " *my,*" " *my.*" David did not think it sufficient to acknowledge that the whole human race were sinners; but as if he stood alone in the world, and was the only offender in it, he says, " I acknowledge *my* transgressions; and *my* sin is ever before me."—*Charles de Coetlogon.*

Verse 3.—" MY *sin.*" David owneth his sin, and confesseth it his own. Here is our natural wealth: what can we call our own but sin? Our food and raiment, the necessaries of life, are borrowings. We came hungry and naked into the world, we brought none of these with us, and we deserved none of them here. Our sin came with us, as David after confesseth. We have right of inheritance in sin, taking it by traduction and transmission from our parents; we have right of possession. So Job: " Thou makest me to possess the sins of my youth."—*Samuel Page.*

Verse 3.—" *My* SIN." It is sin, as sin, not its punishment here, nor hereafter, not simply any of its evil consequences; but sin, the sin against God, the daring impiety of my breaking the good and holy law of this living, loving God.—*Thomas Alexander, D.D., in " The Penitent's Prayer,"* 1861.

Verse 3.—" *Ever before me.*" Sorrow for sin exceeds sorrow for suffering, in the continuance and durableness thereof: the other, like a landflood, quickly come, quickly gone; this is a continual dropping or running river, keeping a constant stream. " *My sins,*" saith David, " *are ever before me ;* " so also is the sorrow for sin in the soul of a child of God, morning, evening, day, night, when sick, when sound, feasting, fasting, at home, abroad, ever within him. This grief begins at his conversion, continues all his life, ends only at his death.—*Thomas Fuller.*

Verse 3.—" *Before me.*" *Coram populo*, before the people; shame to him: *coram ecclesia*, before the church; grief to them: *coram inimicis*, before the enemies; joy to them: *coram Deo*, before God; anger against him: *coram Nathane*, before Nathan; a chiding. But if any hope of repentance and amendment, it is in *peccatum meum coram me, my sin before me.* Here is the distress of a sinner, he never discerneth how unhappy he is, till his sin is before him.—*Samuel Page.*

Verse 4.—" *Against thee, thee only, have I sinned, and done this evil in thy sight.*" This verse is differently expounded by different persons, and it has ever been considered, that this one little point is the greatest difficulty that is met with in the whole Psalm. Although, therefore, I leave it to others to go according to their own interpretations, yet I have a good hope that I shall be enabled to give thee true and genuine meaning of the text. This, then, I would first of all advise the reader to do—to bear in mind that which I observed at the beginning of the Psalm, that David is here speaking in the person of all the saints, and not in his own person only, nor in his own person as an adulterer. Although I do not say it might not be, that it was this fall which, as a medium, brought him under the knowledge of himself and of his whole human nature, and made him think thus: " Behold! I, so holy a king, who have with so much pious devotedness observed the law and the worship of God, have been so tempted and overcome by the inbred evil and sin of my flesh, that I have murdered an innocent man, and have for adulterous purposes taken away his wife! And is not this an evident proof that my nature is more deeply infected and corrupted by sin than ever I thought it was? I who was yesterday chaste am to-day an adulterer! I who yesterday had hands innocent of blood, am to-day a man of blood-guiltiness! " And it might be that in this way he derived the feeling sense of his entire sinfulness, from his fall into adultery and murder, and from thence drew this conclusion—that neither the tree nor the fruits of human nature were good, but that the whole was so deformed and lost by sin, that there was nothing sound left in the whole of nature. This I would have the reader bear in mind first of all, if he desire to have the pure meaning of this passage. In the next place, the grammatical construction is to be explained, which seems to be somewhat obscure. For what the translator has rendered by the *preterperfect*, ought to be the *present:* " *Against thee only do I sin;*" that is, I know that before thee I am nothing but a sinner; or, before thee I do nothing but evil continually; that is, my whole life is evil and depraved on account of sin. I cannot boast before thee of merit or of righteousness, but am evil altogether, and in thy sight this is my character—I do evil. I have sinned, I do sin, and shall sin to the end of the chapter. —*Martin Luther.*

Verse 4.—"*Against thee, thee only have I sinned.*" Is there not matter here to make us at a stand ? For, to say, "Against thee have I sinned," is most just and fit ; but to say, "*Against* THEE ONLY *I have sinned*," seems something hard. It had perhaps been a fit speech in the mouth of our first parent Adam ; he might justly have said to God, "*Against thee only have I sinned*," who never sinned against any other ; but for us to say it, who commit sins daily against our neighbours, and especially for David to say it, who had committed two notorious sins against his neighbour and faithful friend Uriah, what unfitter speech could possibly be devised ? But is it not that these actions of David were great wrongs indeed, and enormous iniquities against Uriah ; but can we properly say they were *sins* against Uriah ? For what is sin, but a transgression of God's law ? And how then can sin be committed against any but against him only whose law we transgress ? Or is it, that it may justly be said, "*Against thee only have I sinned*," because against others perhaps in a base *tenure*, yet only against God in *capite* ? Or is it, that David might justly say to God, "*Against thee only* have I sinned ; " because from others he might appeal, as being a king and having no superior ; but no appealing from God, as being King of kings and supreme Lord over all ? Or is it that we may justly say, "*Against thee, thee only, have I sinned*," seeing that Christ hath taken and still takes all our sins upon him ; and every sin we commit is as a new burthen laid upon his back, and upon his back only ? Or is it, lastly, that I may justly say, "*Against thee, thee only, have I sinned*," because in thy sight only I have done it ? For from others, I could hide it, and did conceal it ? But what can be hidden from thy All-seeing eye ? And yet if this had been the worst, that I had sinned only against thee, though this had been bad enough, and infinitely too much, yet it might perhaps have admitted reconcilement ; but to do this evil, "*in thy sight*," as if I should say, I would do it though thou stand thyself and look on, and as if in defiance ; what sin so formidable ? what sin can be thought of so unpardonable ? A sin of infirmity may admit apology ; a sin of ignorance may find out excuse ; but a sin of defiance can find no defence.—*Sir Richard Baker.*

Verse 4.—"*Against thee, thee only, have I sinned.*" There is a godly sorrow which leads a man to life ; and this sorrow is wrought in a man by the Spirit of God, and in the heart of the godly ; that he mourns for sin because it has displeased God, who is so dear and so sweet a Father to him. And suppose he had neither a heaven to lose, nor a hell to gain, yet he is sad and sorrowful in heart because he has grieved God.—*John Welch,* 1576—1622.

Verse 4.—"*Have I sinned.*" *Me, me, adsum, qui feci :* Here, here am I that did it. I whom thou tookest from following the ewes great with lambs, whose sheep-hook thou hast changed for a sceptre, whose sheep for thine own people Israel, upon whose head thou hast set a crown of pure gold. I whom thou didst lately invest in the full monarchy of thy people ; to whom thou gavest the possession of Jerusalem from the Jebusites ; I who settled peace, religion, and courts of justice in Jerusalem, that thou mightest be served and honoured, and I would fain have built thee an house there ; *Ego,* I, to whom God committed the trust of government to rule others, the trust of judgment to punish others, as king over his inheritance. I, to whom God committed the care of others' souls to guide them by his word, to direct them by good counsel, to allure them by his gracious promises, to terrify them by his threatenings, as the Lord's holy prophet. I, who both ways as king and prophet should have been an example of holiness and righteousness to all Israel. Nathan said, *Tu es homo,* thou art the man, in just accusation, and now David saith, *Ego sum homo,* I am the man, in humble confession.—*Samuel Page.*

Verse 4.—"*I have done this evil.*" We may find this in experience, that there be many who will not stick at a general speech that they be sinners, and yet will scarcely be known of one special evil to account for. If you fall with them into the several commandments, they will be ready to discover a conceit that there is scarce one that they are faulty in. In the first commandment they acknowledge no God but one ; in the second, they do not worship images ; in the third, they swear as little as any, and never but for the truth ; in the fourth they keep their church on Sundays as well as most ; in the second table, there is neither treason, nor murder, nor theft, nor whoredom, nor the like gross sin, but concerning it they are ready to protest their innocency. He that shall hear them in particular, I do not see how he shall believe them in the general, when they say they be sinners ; for when you arraign them at the several commandments they are ready to plead *not guilty* to them all. So long as men are thus without sense and apprehension of particulars, there is no hope of bringing them ever unto good. Happy is he that is pricked to the heart with the feeling of *" this evil."* The truth of repentance for that one, will bring him to a thorough repentance for his whole estate. *This one evil* throughly understood, brought David on his knees, brake his heart, melted his soul, made him cry for pardon, beg for purging, and importune the Lord for a free spirit to establish him.—*Samuel Hieron, in "David's Penitentiall Psalme opened,"* 1617.

Verse 4.—*"In thy sight."* David was so bent upon his sin, as that the majesty and presence of God did not awe him at all : this is a great aggravation of sin, and which makes it to be so much the more heinous. For a thief to steal in the very sight of the judge, is the highest piece of impudence that may be ; and thus it is for any man to offend in the sight of God and not to be moved with it.—*Thomas Horton.*

Verse 4.—*"That thou mightest be justified when thou speakest, and be clear when thou judgest."* But hath not David a defence for it here, and that a very just one ? For, in saying, "Against thee, thee only, have I sinned, *that thou mightest be justified in thy saying,"* doth he not speak as though he had sinned to do God a pleasure ? therefore sinned that God might be justified ? And what can be more said for justifying of God ? But far is it from David to have any such meaning ; his words import not a lessening but an aggravating of his sin, as spoken rather thus : Because a judge may justly be taxed of injustice if he lay a greater punishment upon an offender than the offence deserves ; therefore to clear thee, O God, from all possibility of erring in this kind, I acknowledge my sins to be so heinous, my offences so grievous, that thou canst never be unmerciful in punishing though thy punishing should be never so unmerciful. For how can a judge pass the bounds of equity where the delinquent hath passed all bounds of iniquity ? and what error can there be in thy being severe when the greatness of my fault is a justification of severity ? That thou canst not lay so heavy a doom upon me, which I have not deserved ? Thou canst not pronounce so hard a sentence against me, which I am not worthy of. If thou judge me to torture, it is but mildness ; if to die the death, it is but my due ; if to die everlastingly, I cannot say it were unjust.—*Sir Richard Baker.*

Verse 5.—*"Behold I was shapen in iniquity,"* etc. He said not, " Behold, this evil have I done," but *"Behold I was conceived in sin,"* etc. He says not, " Behold, *I,* David," a king, that have received such-and-such mercies from God, who would have given me more (as God told him), who had that entire communion with him, and graces from him, I, even I, have done this evil. No ; he keeps it in till he came to this, and then his heart could hold no longer : *"Oh, behold I was conceived in sin."* His debasement was at his *auge* here. And to whom is it he uttered this *behold ?* What, to man ? No ; his meaning is not to call on men, *q.d.,* O ye sons of men, behold ! That is but his secondary aim, arising out of his having penned it, and delivered it unto the church ; but when he uttered it, it was to God, or rather afore God, and yet not as calling on God to behold, for that needed not. David had elsewhere said, " God looked down," etc., " and beheld the sons of men," when speaking of this very corruption. He therefore knew God beheld it sufficiently ; but he utters it afore God, or, as spoken of himself between God and himself, thereby to express his own astonishment and amazement at the sight and conviction of this corruption, and at the sight of what a monster he saw himself to be in the sight of God in respect of this sin. It was a *behold* of astonishment at himself, as before the great and holy God ; and therefore it was he seconds and follows it with another *behold* made unto God : *"Behold, thou desirest truth in the inward parts."* And it is as if he had said in both, Oh, how am I in every way overwhelmed, whilst with one eye cast on myself I see how infinitely corrupt I am in the very constitution of my nature ; and with the other eye I behold and consider what an infinite holy God thou art in thy nature and being, and what an holiness it is which thou requirest. I am utterly overwhelmed in the intuition of both these, and able to behold no more, nor look up unto thee, O holy God !—*Thomas Goodwin.*

Verse 5.—*"Behold, I was shapen in iniquity,"* etc. We are not to suppose that David here reflects upon his parents as the medium of transmitting to him the elements of moral evil ; and that by the introduction of the doctrine of original sin he intended to extenuate the enormity of his own crimes. On the contrary, we are to regard him as afflicting himself by the humbling consideration that his very nature was fallen, that his transgressions flowed from a heart naturally at enmity with God; that he was not a sinner by accident, but by a depravity of purpose extending to the inmost desires and purposes of the soul; that there was "a law in his members, warring against the law of his mind, and bringing him into captivity to the law of sin and death" (Rom. vii. 23); and that he was one of a race of guilty beings, none of whom could plead an exemption from an evil heart of unbelief, ready at all times to depart from the living God. Till we see sin in the fountain of the heart, we shall never truly mourn over it in the life and conversation.—*John Morison.*

Verse 5.—"*Behold, I was shapen in iniquity.*" He is not low enough down yet, he must come lower. It is not enough for him to confess that the water is filthy at the pool; he goes back to the source, and confesses that the whole river is polluted up to its head. The source is unclean; the very spring wells forth foul waters.—*Thomas Alexander.*

Verse 5.—"*I was shapen in iniquity.*" I shall not easily be persuaded to think that parents, who are sinners themselves and too much under the influence of bad affections and passions, will be very likely to produce children without transmitting to them some of those disorders and corruptions of nature with which they themselves are infected. And if this be a difficulty, I would beg leave to observe that it is a difficulty which affects natural as well as revealed religion. Since we must take human nature as it is, and if it be really in a state of disorder and corruption, and cannot be otherwise, considering the common law of its production, the difficulty must have been as ancient as the first man that was born; and therefore can be no objection against the truth of revelation, but it must be equally so against natural religion, which must equally allow the thing, if it be in reality a fact, with revelation itself.—*Samuel Chandler.*

Verse 5.—Infants are no innocents, being born with original sin; the first sheet wherein they are wrapped is woven of sin, shame, blood, and filth. Ezek. xvi. 4, etc. They are said to sin as they were in the loins of Adam, just as Levi is said to pay tithes to Melchisedek, even in the loins of his forefather Abraham (Heb. vii. 9, 10); otherwise infants would not die, for death is the wages of sin (Rom. vi. 23); and the reign of death is procured by the reign of sin, which hath reigned over all mankind except Christ. All are sinners, infected with the guilt and filth of sin; the rot (according to the vulgar saying) overrunneth the whole flock. Hence David reflects upon original sin as the cause of all his actuals, saying, "*Behold, I was shapen in iniquity; and in sin did my mother conceive me.*" Thus man's malady begins betimes, even in our conception: this subtle serpent sowed his tares very early, so that we are all "born in sin." John ix. 34.—*Christopher Ness's "Divine Legacy,"* 1700.

Verse 5.—Notwithstanding all that Grotius and others have said to the contrary, I believe David to speak here of what is commonly called *original sin;* the propensity to evil which every man brings into the world with him, and which is the fruitful source whence all transgression proceeds.—*Adam Clarke.*

Verse 6.—"*Behold.*" Before he entereth on any of the parts of the verse he useth the particle of admiration, "*Behold;*" which he never useth but in some remarkable manner, thereby the more to raise us up to the contemplation of such great matters to be told.—*Archibald Symson.*

Verse 6.—"*Thou desirest truth in the inward parts.*" Thou lovest *truth*, not shadows or images, but realities; thou lovest truth *in the inward parts*, inside truth, a true heart, a pure conscience: he is a Christian who is one inwardly. Rom. ii. 29.—*John Ball.*

Verse 6.—"*Truth in the inward parts.*" A great French pear is called *le bon Chretien*, the good Christian, because they say it is never rotten at the core.—*George Swinnock.*

Verse 6.—"*In the hidden part thou shalt make me to know wisdom.*" Piscator, in his annotations on this Psalm, puts this sense upon it, that David should bless God for having made him to know this special wisdom in this hidden thing or matter, and had brought the knowledge thereof home, as a point of saving wisdom, to the hidden man of his heart, so as to see fully and clearly this native corruption as the cause of all sin, and on that account to cause him to lay it to heart.—*Thomas Goodwin.*

Verse 6.—" *In the hidden part thou shalt make me to know wisdom.*" It is one thing to be wise headed and wise tongued, and another to be wise hearted, and therefore in Scripture nothing more ordinary than to set forth wisdom that is true indeed by the heart. God himself is said *to be wise of heart.* Foolish creatures are like Ephraim, " a silly dove without heart." They may have *head* enough, notion enough, *flashing light,* appearing to others enough, but they are without a heart; they have not the great work there, a *new head* and an *old heart,* a *full head* and an *empty heart,* a *light and burning profession,* and a dark, dead, and cold heart; he that takes up in such a condition is a fool and an errant fool.—*John Murcot,* 1657.

Verse 6.—" *And in the hidden part thou shalt make me to know wisdom.*" Some read it, " In the hidden part thou *hadst* made me to know wisdom;" *that* thou hadst done, but I have fallen from my high state, marred thy handiwork. " By one plunge into lust I have fallen and fouled myself."—*Arthur Jackson.*

Verse 6.—The copulative particle which connects the two clauses, implies the correspondence between the revelation of the divine will on the one part and the desire and prayer of the penitent heart on the other. " *Thou desirest truth in the inward parts: and in the hidden part thou shalt make me to know wisdom.*" " What I want thou hast promised to give." Repentance and faith are the gifts of God, and the awakened mind is conscious that they are so.—*Thomas T. Biddulph.*

Verses 6—8.—The right conviction of sin comprehends its being acknowledged not only in our *works,* but also in our entire *being.*—*Augustus F. Tholuck.*

Verse 7.—" *Purge me with hyssop.*" Do I well to prescribe to God with that he shall purge me, as though I knew all God's medicines as well as himself? and which is worse, I to prescribe and he to administer? But excuse me, O my soul, it is not I that prescribe it to God, it is God that prescribes it to me; for hyssop is his own receipt, and one of the ingredients prescribed by himself to make the water of separation for curing the leprosy. . . . . I must confess I was glad at heart when I first heard hyssop spoken of; to think I should be purged so gently, and with a thing that may so easily be had, for hyssop grows in every garden; and then I thought I might go fetch it thence and purge myself, but now I perceive this is not the hyssop of which Solomon writ when he writ from the cedar to the hyssop; but this hyssop is rather the herb grace, which never grew in garden but in that of Paradise, and which none can fetch thence unless God himself deliver it. The truth is, this hyssop was sometimes a cedar; the highest of all trees became the lowest of all shrubs, only to be made this hyssop for us: for Christ indeed is the true hyssop, and his blood the juice of hyssop that only can purge away my sins.—*Sir Richard Baker.*

Verse 7.—" *Purge me with hyssop.*" תְּחַטְּאֵנִי. Properly, *expiate my sin* with hyssop. The Psalmist alludes to the purification from the leprosy (Levit. xiv. 52), or from the touch of a dead body (Num. xix. 19), both of which were to be done by the sprinkling of water and other things with hyssop.—*Samuel Chandler.*

Verse 7.—" *Hyssop.*" The *lasaf* or *asaf,* the caper plant, the bright green creeper which climbs out of the fissures of the rocks in the Sinaitic valleys, has been identified on grounds of great probability with the " hyssop " or *ezob* of Scripture; and thus explains whence came the green branches used, even in the desert, for sprinkling the water over the tents of the Israelites.—*Arthur Penrhyn Stanley, in " Sinai and Palestine."* 1864.

Verse 7.—" *Hyssop.*" Between twenty and thirty different plants have been proposed, but no one of them comes so near the above requirements as the caper plant (*Capparis spinosa*). It grows " out of the wall;" its stalks supply both bunch and rod admirably fitted for the ends indicated; and it has ever been esteemed in the East as possessing cleansing properties.—*John Duns, D.D., in " Biblical Natural Science."*

Verse 7.—" *Hyssop.*" What a pity that Solomon's botany is lost, in which he spoke of trees, from the cedar that is in Lebanon to the hyssop that springeth out of the wall! The cedar we know, but what is the " hyssop " of the royal botanist? Mr. B———, French consul of this city [Sidon], and an enthusiastic botanist, exhibited to me two varieties of hyssop; one, called *zatar* by the Arabs, having the fragrance of thyme, with a hot pungent taste, and long, slender stems. A bunch of these would answer very well for sprinkling the paschal and sacrificial blood on the lintel and posts of the doors, and over the persons and houses cleansed from the leprosy. Mr. B——, however, thinks that a very small green plant, like a moss which covers old walls in damp places, is the "hyssop" of Solomon. This I doubt. The other kind also springs out of walls, those of the gardens especially, and was much more likely to attract the attention of the royal student.—W. M. Thomson, D.D., in "The Land and the Book."

Verse 7.—The paraphrase of this verse in the Chaldee is : "Thou wilt sprinkle me like the priest, which sprinkleth the unclean with the purifying waters, with hyssop, with the ashes of an heifer, and I shall be clean."—John Morison.

Verse 7.—"I shall be whiter than snow." But how is this possible ? All the dyers upon earth cannot dye a red into white ; and how, then, is it possible that my sins which are as red as scarlet should ever be made as white as snow ? Indeed such retrogradation is no work of human art ; it must be only his doing who brought the sun ten degrees back in the dial of Ahaz : for God hath a nitre of grace that can bring not only the redness of scarlet sins, but even the blackness of deadly sins, into its native purity and whiteness again. But say it be possible, yet what need is there of so great a whiteness, as to be "whiter than snow" ? seeing snow is not as paries dealbatus, a painted wall, white without and foul within ; but it is white, intus et in cute, within and without, throughout and all over ; and what eye so curious but such a whiteness may content ? Yet such a whiteness will not serve, for I may be as white as snow and yet a leper still ; as it is said of Gehazi that "he went from Elisha a leper as white as snow ; " it must be therefore whiter than snow. And such a whiteness it is that God's washing works upon us, makes within us ; for no snow is so white in the eyes of men as a soul cleansed from sin is in the sight of God. And yet, a whiter whiteness than this too ; for being purged from sin we shall, induere stolam album, put on the white robe ; and this is a whiteness as much whiter than snow as angelical whiteness is more than elemental. —Sir Richard Baker.

Verse 7.—In the Hebrew language there are two words to express the different kinds of washing, and they are always used with the strictest propriety ; the one, to signify that kind of washing which pervades the substance of the thing washed, and cleanses it thoroughly ; and the other to express that kind of washing which only cleanses the surface of a substance which the water cannot penetrate. The former is applied to the washing of clothes ; the latter is used for washing some part of the body. By a beautiful and strong metaphor, David uses the former word in this and the second verse : "Wash me throughly from mine iniquity and cleanse me from my sin ; " "Wash me, and I shall be whiter than snow." So in Jer. iv. 14, the same word is applied to the heart.—Richard Mant.

Verse 8.—"Make me to hear joy and gladness." This is the exceeding great love of the Lord toward his children, that he hath not only provided a sure salvation for them through the remission of their sins in Christ Jesus, but also seals up in their heart the testimony thereof by his Holy Spirit of adoption, and that for their present consolation, lest they should be swallowed up of heaviness through continual temptations. Though he speak not to all his children as he did to Daniel, by an angel, "O man, greatly beloved of God," nor as he did to the blessed Virgin Mary, "Hail, Mary, freely beloved," yet doth he witness the same to the hearts of his children by an inward testimony : when they hear it they are alive ; when they want it they are but dead ; their souls refuse all other comfort whatsoever.—William Cowper.

Verse 8.—"Make me to hear joy and gladness." As a Christian is the most sorrowful man in the world, so there is none more glad than he. For the cause of his joy is greatest. In respect his misery was greatest, his delivery greatest, therefore his joy greatest. From hell and death is he freed, to life in heaven is he brought. . . . . The person from whom he seeketh this joy is God : "Make me to hear," saith he ; whereby he would teach us that this joy cometh only from God ; it is he who is the fountain of joy and all pleasure, for "all good things come from above." Natural joys proceed from a natural and fleshly fountain ; spiritual joys spring only from God : so he who seeketh those joys beneath seeketh hot water under cold ice.—Archibald Symson.

Verse 8.—"Make me to hear joy and gladness." Another reference to the expiation of the leper, whose ear was to be touched with the blood of the trespass-offering and the oil, as well as thumb and toe, to show that his faculties were now prepared for the service of God ; so David prays that his ears may be sanctified to the hearing of joy and gladness ; this an unsanctified heart can never receive. —*W. Wilson.*

Verse 8.—" *The bones which thou hast broken.*" God, in favour to his children, doth afflict them for sin ; and the very phrase of breaking his bones, though it express extremity of misery and pain, yet it hath hope in it, for broken bones by a cunning hand may be set again and return to their former use and strength ; so that a conscience distressed for sins is not out of hope ; yet upon that hope no wise man will adventure upon sin, saying, though I am wounded, yet I may be healed again ; though I am broken, I may be repaired ; for let him consider—1. Who breaks his bones—*Thou ;* he that made us our bones and put them in their several places, and tied them together with ligaments, and covered them with flesh ; he that keepeth all our bones from breaking ; it must be a great matter that must move him to break the bones of any of us. The God of all consolation, that comforteth us in all our distresses, when he cometh to distress us, this makes affliction weigh heavy. . . . . 2. The pain of the affliction exprest so feelingly in the breaking of bones, which, as is said, is the anguish of the soul for sin, and fear of the consuming fire of God's wrath, and the tempest, as Job calls it, of anger. 3. The pain of setting these bones again : for, though bones dislocated may be put in joint, and though bones broken may be set again, yet this is not done without pain and great extremity to the patient.

Repentance setteth all our broken, pained bones ; it recovereth the soul from the anguish thereof ; but he that once feeleth the smart of a true repentance, will say, the pleasures of sin, which are but for a season, are as hard a bargain as ever he made, and as dear bought ; they cost tears, which are *sanguis vulnerati cordis,* the blood of a wounded heart ; they cost sighs and groans which cannot be expressed ; they cost watching, fasting, taming of the body to bring it in subjection, even to the crucifying of the flesh with the lusts thereof. Therefore, let no man adventure his bones in hope of setting them again.—*Samuel Page.*

Verse 8.—" *That the bones which thou hast broken may rejoice.*" The displeasure which God expressed against the sins he had been guilty of, and the deep sense he had of the aggravated nature of them, filled him with those pains and agonies of mind, as that he compares them to that exquisite torture he must have felt had all his bones been crushed, for the original word דִּכִּיתָ, signifies more than broken, namely, being entirely mashed ; and he compares the joy that God's declaring himself fully reconciled to him would produce in his mind, to that inconceivable pleasure, which would arise from the instantaneous restoring and healing those bones, after they had been thus broken and crushed to pieces.—*Samuel Chandler.*

Verse 9.—" *Hide thy face from my sins.*" The verb כָּפַר properly signifies *to veil,* or hide with a veil.—*Samuel Chandler.*

Verse 9.—" *Hide thy face from my sins.*" He said in the third verse, that his sin was always in his sight ; and now he prays that God would put it out of his sight. This is a very good order. If we hold our sins in our eyes to pursue them, God will cast them behind his back to pardon them : if we remember them and repent, he will forget them and forgive : otherwise, *peccatum unde homo non avertit, advertit Deus : et si advertit, animadvertit*—the sin from which man turns not, God looks to it ; and if he look to it, sure he will punish it.—*William Cowper.*

Verse 9.—" *All mine iniquities.*" See how one sin calleth to mind many thousands, which though they lie asleep a long time, like a sleeping debt, yet we know not how soon they may be reckoned for. Make sure of a general pardon, and take heed of adding new sins to the old.—*John Trapp.*

Verse 10.—" *Create in me a clean heart, O God.*" O thou that createdst the first heaven and the first earth of nothing ! O thou that createst the *new heaven* and the *new earth* (wherein dwells righteousness), when sin had made the creature worse than nothing ! O thou that createst the *new creature,* the new man, fit to be an inhabitant of the new world, of the new Jerusalem ! O thou that hast said, " Behold, I make all things new : " *create* thou in me, even in me, " *a clean heart ; and renew a right spirit within me.*"—*Matthew Lawrence.*

Verse 10.—" *Create in me a clean heart, O God,*" etc. David prayeth the Lord *to create in him a new heart,* not to correct his old heart, but to create him a new heart : showing that his heart was like an old garment, so rotten and tattered that he could make no good of it by patching or piecing, but even must cut it off, and take a new. Therefore Paul saith, "Cast off the old man;" not pick him and wash him till he be clean, but cast him off and begin anew, as David did. Will ye know what this renewing is? It is the repairing of the image of God, until we be like Adam when he dwelt in Paradise. As there is a whole old man, so there must be a whole new man. The old man must change with the new man, wisdom for wisdom, love for love, fear for fear; his worldly wisdom for heavenly wisdom, his carnal love for spiritual love, his servile fear for Christian fear, his idle thoughts for holy thoughts, his vain words for wholesome words, his fleshly works for sanctified works. —*Henry Smith.*

Verse 10.—"*Create in me a clean heart.*" *Creating*, to speak properly, is to make of nought, and is here used improperly. The prophet speaketh according to his own feeling and present judgment of himself, as though he had lost all, and had no goodness in himself. No doubt the prophet's heart was in part clean, though not so much as he desired. These things thus opened, here cometh a question first to be answered. *Quest.* Whether David could have lost the cleanness of heart, having once had it? *Ans.* No. The gifts and calling of God, that is (as I take it), the gifts of effectual calling, are such as God never repenteth of or taketh away. Faith, hope, and charity are abiding gifts, as sure as the election of God, which is unchangeable. Indeed, the children of God, if we only considered them in themselves with their enemies, might fall away, but being founded upon the unchangeable nature of God, and immutability of his counsel, they cannot, the gates of hell shall not prevail against them, the elect cannot be deceived or plucked out of Christ's hands. Nay, certain it is that David did not actually leave his former cleanness. For sure it is, his heart smiting him (as here it did), so doing before in less matters, it was not wholly void of cleanness. And again, it could not pray for cleanness if it were not somewhat clean. This is most sure, that by grievous sins much filthiness cometh to the soul, as by a boisterous wind a tree may lose his leaves and some branches, so as that the party sinning may be brought into as great passions almost as if he had lost all, but the desire of grace is an infallible certainty of some grace of that kind. The prophet therefore desireth not a clean heart because he had it not in any sort, but because he could not so well perceive it in himself, and take such comfort in it as he had done before, and for that he desired it a great deal more than now he had it. So learned, so rich men, think themselves not learned, not rich, in respect of that which they do desire, and when the sun is up, the moon seemeth to have no light.—*George Estey, in " Certaine Godly and Learned Expositions," 1603.*

Verse 10.—"*Create in me a clean heart, O God,*" etc. This " creation " is from nothing. David uses the same word of our creation which Moses uses of " the creation of the heaven and the earth." Our creation " in Jesus Christ ' is no mere strengthening of our powers, no mere aiding of our natural weakness by the might of the grace of God, it is not a mere amendment, improvement of our moral habits; it is a creation out of nothing, of that which we had not before. There was nothing in us whereof to make it. We were decayed, corrupt, dead in trespasses and sins. What is dead becometh not alive, except by the infusion of what it had not. What is corrupt receiveth not soundness, save by passing away itself and being replaced by a new production. " The old man " passeth not into the new man, but is " put off." It is not the basis of the new life, but a hindrance to it. It must be " put off " and the new man " put on," " created in Christ Jesus."— *E. B. Pusey, D.D., 1853.*

Verse 10 (*first clause*).—He used the word *create* (Heb. *bara*), a word only used of the work of God, and showing that the change in him could be wrought only by God.—*Christopher Wordsworth.*

Verse 10.—"*A clean heart.*" The priest was required to make a strict examination of the skin of the leper before he could pronounce him clean; David prays God to make his heart clean.—*W. Wilson.*

Verse 10.—"*A right spirit.*" *A steadfast spirit, i.e.,* a mind steady in following the path of duty.—*French and Skinner.*

Verses 10—12.—Who was to do this work? Not *himself;* God alone. Therefore, he prays: " O God, create—O Lord, renew; uphold by thy Spirit."— *Adam Clarke.*

Verse 11.—"*Cast me not away from thy presence.*" David lamented before that sin had slain him, and made him like a dead man, wanting a heart or quickening spirit ; and now he fears lest, as the dead are abhorred by the living, so the Lord should cast him as a dead and abominable thing out of his presence. Whereof we learn this is one of the just punishments of sin ; it procures the casting out of a man from the face of God ; and it may let us see how dear bought are the pleasures of sin when a man to enjoy the face of the creature deprives himself of the comfortable face of the Creator ; as David here, for the carnal love of the face of Bathsheba, puts himself in danger to be cast out for ever from the presence of the Lord his God. If a man could remember this in all Satan's temptations, what it is that the deceiver offers, and what it is again that he seeks, he would be loth to buy the perishing pleasures of sin upon such a price as Satan selleth them, but would answer him as the apostle did Simon Magus. " Thy money, with thyself, go into perdition ; " thy gain, thy glory, thy pleasure, and whatever thou wouldst give me to offend the Lord my God, go with thyself into perdition, for what canst thou offer unto me comparable to that which thou wouldst steal from me ?

But how is it that he prays, " Cast me not out from thy presence " ? May a man be cast any way from it ? Saith he not himself, " What way can I flee from thy presence ? " This is soon answered by distinguishing his twofold presence—one in mercy, wherewith he refresheth and comforteth his own, and this without intermission they enjoy who are in heaven ; another, in wrath, whereby he terrifies and torments without intermission the damned in hell. As to them who are upon earth, certain it is he is displeased with many, who, because they see not his angry face, regard it not, borne out with temporal recreations of the creature, which will fail them ; and there are many, again, to whom he looks as a loving Father in Christ, and yet they see not his merciful face by reason of many interjected veils ; but to them who once have felt the sweetness of his favourable face it is death to want it.—*William Cowper.*

Verse 11.—" *Cast me not away from thy presence.*" Like the leper who is banished from society till cleansed, or as Saul was rejected from being king, because he obeyed not the word of the Lord. 1 Sam. xv. 23. David could not but feel that his transgressions would have deserved a similar rejection.—*W. Wilson.*

Verse 11.—" *Cast me not away.*" Lord, though I, alas ! have cast thee from me, yet cast me not away : hide not thy face from me, although I so often have refused to look at thee ; leave me not without help, to perish in my sins, though I have aforetime left thee.—*Fra Thomé de Jesu.*

Verse 11.—" *Take not thy Holy Spirit from me.*" The words of this verse imply that the Spirit had not altogether been taken away from him, however much his gifts had been temporarily obscured. . . . . Upon one point he had fallen into a deadly lethargy, but he was not " given over to a reprobate mind ; " and it is scarcely conceivable that the rebuke of Nathan the prophet should have operated so easily and so suddenly in arousing him had there been no latent spark of godliness still remaining. . . . . The truth on which we are now insisting is an important one, as many learned men have been inconsiderately drawn into the opinion that the elect, by falling into mortal sin, may lose the Spirit altogether, and be alienated from God. The contrary is clearly declared by Peter, who tells us that the word by which we are born again is an incorruptible seed (1 Peter i. 23) ; and John is equally explicit in informing us that the elect are preserved from falling away altogether. 1 John iii. 9. However much they may appear for a time to have been cast off by God, it is afterwards seen that grace must have been alive in their breast even during that interval when it seemed to be extinct. Nor is there any force in the objection that David speaks as if he feared that he might be deprived of the Spirit. It is natural that the saints, when they have fallen into sin, and have thus done what they could to expel the grace of God, should feel an anxiety upon this point ; but it is their duty to hold fast the truth, that grace is the incorruptible seed of God, which never can perish in any heart where it has been deposited. This is the spirit displayed by David. Reflecting upon his offence, he is agitated with fears, and yet rests in the persuasion that, being a child of God, he would not be deprived of what, indeed, he had justly forfeited.—*John Calvin.*

Verse 12.—" *Restore.*" It is no small comfort to a man that hath lost his receipt for a debt paid when he remembers that the man he deals with is a good and just man, though his discharge is not presently to be found. That God whom thou hast to deal with is very gracious ; what thou hast lost he is ready to restore (the evidence of thy grace I mean). David begged this, and obtained it. Yea, saith faith, if it were true what thou fearest, that thy grace was never true, there is mercy enough in God's heart to pardon all thy former hypocrisy if thou comest in the sincerity of thy heart ; and so faith persuades the soul by an act of adventure to cast itself upon God in Christ. Wilt not thou, saith faith, expect to find as much mercy at God's hands as thou canst look for at a man's ? It is not beyond the line of created mercy to forgive many unkindnesses, much falseness and unfaithfulness, upon an humble, sincere acknowledgment of the same. The world is not so bad but it abounds with parents who can do thus much for their children, and masters for their servants ; and is that hard for God to do which is so easy in his creature ? Thus faith vindicates God's name. And so long as we have not lost sight of God's merciful heart, our head will be kept above water, though we want the evidence of our own grace.—*William Gurnall.*

Verse 12.—" *Restore unto me the joy of thy salvation,*" etc. How can God restore that which he took not away ? For, can I charge God with the taking away the joy of his salvation from me ? O gracious God, I charge not thee with taking it, but myself with losing it; and such is the miserable condition of us poor wretches, that if thou shouldst restore no more to us than what thou takest from us, we should quickly be at a fault in our estates, and our ruin would be as sudden as inevitable. But why am I so earnest for restoring ? for what good will restoring do me ? and how shall I more keep it being restored, than I kept it before being enjoyed ? and if I so enjoy it, as still to fear to lose it, what joy can there be in such enjoying ? O therefore, not restore it only, but " *establish me with thy free spirit ;* " that as by thy restoring I may enjoy it entirely, so by thy establishing I may enjoy it securely.—*Sir Richard Baker.*

Verse 12.—" *Uphold me.*" I am tempted to think that I am now an established Christian, that I have overcome this or that lust so long that I have got into the habit of the opposite grace, so that there is no fear ; I may venture very near the temptation, nearer than other men. This is a lie of Satan. I might as well speak of gunpowder getting by habit a power of resisting fire, so as not to catch the spark. As long as powder is wet it resists the spark, but when it becomes dry it is ready to explode at the first touch. As long as the Spirit dwells in my heart, he deadens me to sin, so that if lawfully called through temptation I may reckon upon God carrying me through. But when the Spirit leaves me, I am like dry gunpowder. Oh, for a sense of this !—*Robert Murray M'Cheyne.*

Verse 12.—" *Uphold me with thy free spirit.*" A loving mother chooses a fitting place, and a fitting time, to let her little child fall ; it is learning to walk, it is getting over confident, it may come to a dangerous place, and if possessed of all this confidence, may fall and destroy itself. So she permits it to fall at such a place, and in such a way as that it may be hurt, wholesomely hurt, but not dangerously so. It has now lost its confidence, and clings all the more fondly and trustingly to the strong hand that is able to hold up all its goings. So this David, this little child of the great God, has fallen ; it is a sore fall, all his bones are broken, but it has been a precious and a profitable lesson to him ; he has no confidence any longer in himself, his trust is not now in an arm of flesh. " Uphold me with thy free spirit." —*Thomas Alexander.*

Verse 12 (last clause).—" *Let a free spirit sustain me ;* " that is, let me not be enslaved, as I have been, by my sinful passions.—*Henry Dimock, M.A., 1791.*

Verse 13.—" *Then will I teach transgressors thy ways,*" etc. We see our duty craves that when we have received mercy from God for ourselves, we should make vantage of it for the edification of others. Every talent received from God should be put to profit, but specially the talent of mercy ; as it is greatest, so the Lord requires greater fruit of it, both for his own glory and for the edification of our brethren. Seeing we are vessels of mercy, should not the scent and sweet odour of mercy go from us to others ? This duty Christ craved from Peter : " And thou, when thou art converted, confirm thy brethren." And this duty, as David here promiseth, so we may read how he did perform it : " Come unto me, all ye that fear God, and I will tell you what he hath done for my soul." The property of a Christian is, *fides per delectionem efficax,* faith worketh by love. What availeth it to pretend faith toward God, where there is no love toward thy neighbour ? and wherein can thy love be declared more than in this, to draw thy neighbour to the participation of that same merit whereunto God hath called thee ? By the law a man was bound to bring home his neighbour's wandering beast if he had met with it before ; how much more, then, to turn again his neighbour himself when he wanders from the Lord his God ? If two men walking on the way should both fall into one pit, and the one being relieved out of it should go his way and forget his neighbour, might it not justly be called a barbarous and inhuman cruelty ? We have all fallen into one and the same mire of iniquity ; since the Lord hath put out his merciful hand to draw us out of this prison of sin, shall we refuse to put out our hand to see if possibly we may draw up our brethren with us ?—*William Cowper (Bishop).*

Verse 14 (first clause).—" *Deliver me from bloods.*" The term *bloods* in Hebrew may denote any capital crime ; and in my opinion he is here to be considered as alluding to the sentence of death, to which he felt himself to be obnoxious, and from which he requests deliverance.—*John Calvin.*

Verse 14 (first clause).—The Chaldee reads, " *Deliver me from the judgment of murder.*"

Verse 14.—" *O God, thou God of my salvation.*" " *O God,*" is a good invocation, for he heareth prayers. Yet to distinguish him from all false gods he is so particular as to single him from all other : " *Thou God.*" And to magnify him, and to re-enforce his petition, he calleth him *Deum salutis,* " *the God of salvation,*" which expresseth him able to deliver him ; for it is his nature, and his love, and his glory, to be a preserver of men. And to bring home this joy and comfort into his own heart, he addeth, *salutis meæ,* " *of my salvation.*" So it is *oratio fervens,* and the apostle telleth us that such a prayer prevaileth much with God. For God may be a Saviour and a deliverer, and yet we may escape his saving hand, his right hand may skip us. We can have no comfort in the favours of God, except we can apply them at home ; rather we may " think on God and be troubled."—*Samuel Page.*

Verse 14.—" *And my tongue shall sing aloud of thy righteousness.*" Hierom, Basil, Euthymius, and other ancient doctors observe that natural corruptions and actual sins are the very rampiers which stop the free passage of song (verse 15). So David himself doth expound himself : " *Deliver me from bloodguiltiness, O God : and my tongue shall sing aloud of thy righteousness.*" His unthankfulness did cry, his adultery cry, his murder cry unto the Lord for revenge ; but alas ! himself was mute, till God in exceeding great mercy did stop the mouths of his clamorous adversaries, and gave him leave to speak.—*John Boys.*

Verse 14.—" *Aloud.*" This for God, for himself, for the church. 1. *For God,* that his honour may be proclaimed, therefore they borrowed the voice of still and loud instruments. . . . . . 2. *For himself.* Having received such a benefit, he cannot contain himself, this new wine of spiritual joy which filleth his vessel must have a vent. All passions are loud. Anger chides loud, sorrow cries loud, fear shrieks loud, and joy sings loud. So he expresseth the vehemency of his affection ; for to whom much is forgiven, they love much. 3. *For others.* Iron whetteth iron—examples of zeal and devotion affect much, and therefore solemn and public assemblies do generally tender the best service to God, because one provoketh another. —*Samuel Page.*

Verse 15.—" *O Lord, open thou my lips ; and my mouth shall shew forth thy praise.*" As man is a little world in the great, so the tongue is a great world in the little. *Nihil habet medium ; aut grande malum est, aut grande bonum.** It has no mean ; it is either a great evil, or a great good. If good (as Eunapius said of that famous rhetorician), *a walking library,* a whole university of edifying know-ledge ; but if bad (as St. James doth tell us, ch. iii. 6), " *a world of wickedness.*" No better dish for God's public service, when it is well seasoned ; again, none worse, when ill handled. So that if we desire to be doorkeepers in God's house, let us entreat God first to be a doorkeeper in our house, that he would shut the wicket of our mouth against unsavoury speeches, and open the door of our lips, " *that our mouth may shew forth his praise.*" This was David's prayer, and ought to be thy practice, wherein observe three points especially ; who, *the Lord ;* what, *open my lips ;* why, *that my mouth shall shew forth thy praise.* For the first—man of himself cannot untie the strings of his own stammering tongue, but it is God only which openeth " a door of utterance." Col. iv. 3. When we have a good thought, it is (as the school doth speak) *gratia infusa ;* when a good word, *gratia effusa ;* when a good work, *gratia diffusa.* Man is a lock, the Spirit of God has a key, " which

---

* Jerome.

openeth, and no man shutteth ; " again, " shutteth, and no man openeth."
Rev. iii. 7. He did open the heart of Lydia to conceive well, the ears of the prophet
to hear well, the eyes of Elisha's servant to see well, and here the lips of David
to speak well. Acts xvi. ; Isai. l. ; 2 Kings vi. And therefore, whereas in the
former verse he might seem too peremptory, saying, " *My tongue shall sing aloud
of thy righteousness ;* " he doth, as it were, correct himself by this latter edition
and second speech : O Lord, I find myself most unable to sing or say, but " *open
thou my lips,*" and touch thou my tongue, and then I am sure " *my mouth shall
shew forth thy praise.*"—*John Boys.*

Verse 15.—" *O Lord, open thou my lips,*" etc. Again he seems to have the
case of the leper before his mind, with the upper lip covered, and only crying unclean,
unclean ; and he prays as a spiritual leper to be enabled, with freedom and fulness,
to publish abroad the praise of his God.—*W. Wilson.*

Verse 15 (*first clause*).—He prays that *his lips may be opened ;* in other words,
that God would afford him matter of praise. The meaning usually attached to the
expression is, that God would so direct his tongue by the Spirit as to fit him for
singing his praises. But though it is true that God must supply us with words,
and that if he do not, we cannot fail to be silent in his praise, David seems rather
to intimate that his mouth must be shut until God called him to the exercise of thanksgiving by extending pardon.—*John Calvin.*

Verse 16.—" *For thou desirest not sacrifice ;* " etc. There may be another reason
why David here affirms that God would not accept of a sacrifice, nor be pleased
with a burnt-offering. No particular sacrifices were appointed by the law of Moses
to expiate the guilt of murder and adultery. The person who had perpetrated
these crimes was, according to the divine law, to be punished with death. David
therefore may be understood as declaring, that it was utterly vain for him to think
of resorting to sacrifices and burnt-offerings with a view to the expiation of his
guilt ; that his criminality was of such a character, that the ceremonial law made
no provision for his deliverance from the doom which his deeds of horror deserved ;
and that the only sacrifices which would avail were those mentioned in the succeeding
verse, " *The sacrifices of a broken heart.*"—*John Calvin.*

Verse 16.—" *Else would I give it thee.*" And good reason it is, that we who
lie daily at the beautiful gate of the temple begging alms of him, and receiving
from his open hand, who openeth his hand, and filleth with his plenty every living
thing, should not think much to return to him such offerings of our goods as his
law requireth.—*Samuel Page.*

Verses 16, 17.—And now I was thinking what were fit *to offer to God* for all his
lovingkindness he has showed me ; and I thought upon *sacrifices,* for they have
sometimes been pleasing to him, and he hath oftentimes smelt a sweet odour from
them ; but I considered that sacrifices were but shadows of things to come, and
are not now in that grace they have been ; for *old things are past, and new are now
come ;* the shadows are gone, the substances are come in place. The bullocks that
are to be sacrificed now are our hearts ; it were easier for me to give him bullocks
for sacrifice, than to give him my heart. But why should I offer him that he cares
not for ? my heart, I know, he cares for ; and if it be broken, and offered up by
penitence and contrition, it is the only sacrifice that now he delights in. But can
we think God to be so indifferent that he will accept of a broken heart ? Is a thing
that is broken good for anything ? Can we drink in a broken glass ? Or can we lean
upon a broken staff ? But though other things may be the worse for breaking,
yet a heart is never at the best till it be broken ; for till it be broken we cannot
see what is in it ; till it be broken, it cannot send forth its sweetest odour ; and
therefore, though God loves a whole heart in affection, yet he loves a broken heart
in sacrifice. And no marvel, indeed, seeing it is he himself that breaks it ; for as
nothing but goat's blood can break the adamant, so nothing but the blood of our
scape-goat, Jesus Christ, is able to break our adamantine hearts. Therefore, accept,
O God, my broken heart, which I offer thee with a whole heart ; seeing thou canst
neither except against it for being whole, which is broken in sacrifice, nor except
against it for being broken, which is whole in affection.—*Sir Richard Baker.*

Verse 17.—" *The sacrifices of God are a broken spirit: a broken and a contrite
heart,*" etc. When speaking of *thankfulness,* we might have expected him to say,
" a *joyful* heart, or a thankful heart," but instead of that he says, " a contrite heart."

For the joy of forgiveness does not banish sorrow and contrition for sin: this will still continue. And the deeper the sense of sin, and the truer the sorrow for it, the more heartfelt also will be the thankfulness for pardon and reconciliation. The tender, humble, broken heart, is therefore the best thank-offering.—*J. J. Stewart Perowne.*

Verse 17.—It may be observed that the second word, נִדְכֶּה, which we render *contrite*, denotes the being bruised and broken to pieces, as a thing is bruised in a mortar (See Numbers xi. 8), and therefore, in a moral sense, signifies such a weight of sorrow as must wholly crush the mind without some powerful and seasonable relief.—*Samuel Chandler.*

Verse 18.—"*In thy good pleasure.*" Whatever we seek must ever be sought under this restriction, "*Thy good pleasure.*" Build thou, but do it in thine own wise time, in thine own good way. Build thou the walls of separation that divide the church from the world; let them be *in* it, not *of* it; keep them from its evil. Build thou the walls that bind, that unite thy people into one city, under one polity, that they all may be one. Build thou, and raze thou; raze all the inner walls that divide thy people from thy people; hasten that day when, as there is but one Shepherd, so shall there be but one sheep-fold.—*Thomas Alexander.*

Verses 18, 19.—Some learned Jewish interpreters, while they assign the Psalm to the occasion mentioned in the title, conjecture that the 18th and 19th verses were added by some Jewish bard, in the time of the Babylonish captivity. This opinion is also held by Venema, Green, Street, French and Skinner. There does not, however, seem to be any sufficient ground for referring the poem, either in whole or in part, to that period. Neither the walls of Jerusalem, nor the buildings of Zion, as the royal palace and the magnificent structure of the temple, which we know David had already contemplated for the worship of God (2 Samuel vii. 1, etc.), were completed during his reign. This was only effected under the reign of his son Solomon. 1 Kings iii. 1.

The prayer, then, in the 18th verse might have a particular reference to the completion of these buildings, and especially to the rearing of the temple, in which sacrifices of unprecedented magnitude were to be offered. David's fears might easily suggest to him that his crimes might prevent the building of the temple, which God had promised should be erected. 2 Samuel vii. 13. "The king forgets not," observes Bishop Horne, "to ask mercy for his people as well as for himself; that so neither his own nor their sins might prevent either the building and flourishing of the earthly Jerusalem, or. what was of infinitely greater importance, the promised blessing of Messiah, who was to descend from him, ana to rear the walls of the New Jerusalem."—*James Anderson's Note to Calvin, in loc.*

HINTS TO PREACHERS.

[*The Psalm is upon its surface so full of suggestions for sermons that I have not attempted to offer any of my own, but have merely inserted a selection from Mr. G. Rogers and others.*]

Verse 1.—1. The Prayer. 1. For mercy, not justice, Mercy is the sinner's attribute—as much a part of the divine nature as justice. The possibility of sin is implied in its existence. The actual commission of sin is implied in its display. 2. For pardon, not pity merely, but forgiveness. II. The plea. 1. For the pardon of great sins on account of great mercies, and lovingkindness. 2. Many sins on account of multitude of mercies. 3. Hell-deserving sins on account of tender mercies. We who have sinned are human, he who pardons is divine.

> "Great God, thy *nature* hath no bound,
> *So* let thy pardoning love be found."

Verse 3.—I. Confession. "I acknowledge," etc. II. Humiliation, not a mere confession with the lips, but ever before me—in its guilt—defilement—consequences in this life and hereafter.

Verses 3, 4, 11, 12, 17.—I. Scripture estimate of sin. 1. Personal account-ability—" *My sin.*" 2. Estimated as hateful to God—" *Against thee,*" etc. 3. Sin estimated as separation from God. II. Spiritual restoration. First step—Sacrifice of a broken spirit. Last step—Spirit of liberty. " *Thy free spirit.*"—*F. W. Robertson.*

Verse 4.—1. The person—" *I.*" 2. The commission—" *done.*" 3. The trespass—" *evil.*" 4. The particularity—" *this.*" 5. The daring of it—" *in thy sight.*"—*Samuel Page.*

Verse 4.—" *Against thee.*" 1. Thee, an *holy* God—a God of pure eyes, and that cannot endure to behold iniquity. 2. Thee, a *just* God—who will *punish* sin. 3. Thee, an *Almighty* God. 4. Thee, a *gracious* God.—*T. Horton.*

Verse 4.—I. Self-condemnation. 1. For the greatness of sin. Not against self merely, or fellow men, but God. This includes all guilt, for all is against him. 2. Its effrontery, " in thy sight." II. Divine justification. 1. In the permission of sin. 2. In its punishment. 3. In its forgiveness. God must be justified when he justifies the ungodly.

Verse 6.—See T. Goodwin's Treatise, entitled, " An Unregenerate Man's Guiltiness before God, in respect of Sin and Punishment." Bk. ix. cap. i. ii. [Nichol's edition, Vol. X., p. 324 *et seq.*]

Verse 7.—Here is, I. Faith in the fact of an atonement for sin. " I shall be clean." II. Faith in the method of its application. " Purge me," etc. Sprinkled as the blood of sacrifices. III. Faith in its efficacy. " I shall be whiter," etc.

Verse 10.—I. The change to be effected. 1. A clean heart. 2. A right spirit. II. The power by which it is accomplished. 1. A creative power, such as created the world at first. 2. A renewing power, such as continually renews the face of the earth. III. The acquirement of these blessings. The prayer, " Create," etc.

Verse 11 (*first clause*).—I am not cast away, and would be thankful. I deserve to be cast away, and ought to be penitential. I am afraid of being cast away, and must be prayerful. " Cast me not away." 1. From thy *protecting* presence into *danger.* 2. From thy *loving* presence into *wrath.* 3. From thy *joyous* presence into *distress.* 4. From thy *affluent* presence into *destitution.* 5. From thy *gracious* presence into *despair.* Sin hurries us away from God ; grace hastens us into his embrace : the former severs, and the latter unites, God and the soul.—*W. Jackson.*

Verse 11.—I. There is often much comfort in much grief. " Cast me not," etc. A consciousness of still having the divine presence and a dread of losing it, prompts the prayer. II. There is often much faith in much fear. " Take not," etc. Faith in the spirit works within him while he fears.

Verses 12—13.—A threefold desire : 1. To be *happy*—" Restore," etc. 2. To be *consistent*—" Uphold," etc. 3. To be *useful*—" Then will I teach," etc.—*W. Jackson.*

Verse 13.—I. It is not our duty to seek the conversion of others until we are converted ourselves. II. The greater enjoyment we have in the ways of God, the more faithfully and earnestly we shall make them known to others. III. The more faithfully and earnestly we make them known to others the more they will be influenced by them.

Verse 15.—I. Confession. His lips are sealed on account—1. Of his fall—and well they might be. 2. Of natural timidity. 3. Of want of zeal. II. Petition. " Open thou," etc. Not my understanding merely and heart, but " lips." III. Resolution. Then he would speak freely in God's praise.

Verse 15.—I. When God does not open our lips we had better keep them closed. II. When he does open them we ought not to close them. III. When he opens them it is not to speak in our own praise, and seldom in praise of others, but always in his own praise. IV. We should use this prayer whenever we are about to speak in his name. " O Lord, open," etc.

Verses 16—17.—I. Men would gladly do something towards their own salvation if they could. " Thou desirest not," etc., else would I give it. II. All that they can do is not of the least avail. All the ceremonial observances of Jewish or Gentile churches could not procure pardon for the least transgression of the moral law. III. The only offering of man which God will not despise is a broken and a contrite heart. IV. All other requirement for his salvation God himself will provide.

Verse 18.—I. For whom is the prayer offered—for the church or Zion ? 1. Next to our own welfare we should seek the welfare of Zion. 2. All should seek it by prayer. II. For what is the prayer offered ? 1. The kind of good, not worldly or ecclesiastical, but spiritual. 2. The measure of good. " In thy good pleasure. Thine own love to it, and what thou hast already done for it. 3. The continuance of good. " Build," etc. Its doctrines, graces, zeal.

Verse 19.—I. When we are accepted of God our offerings are accepted. " Then," etc. II. We should then make the richest offerings in our power, our time, talents, influence, etc. 1. Holy obedience. 2. Self-sacrifices, not half offerings, but whole " burnt-offerings ; " not lambs merely, but " bullocks." 3. Zeal for divine ordinances. " Upon thine altar." III. God will take pleasure in such services. " Then shalt thou be pleased." 1. Because from his own redeemed. 2. Because given in the name of the Redeemer. With such sacrifices God is well pleased.

PSALM LII.

TITLE.—To the Chief Musician.—*Even short Psalms, if they record but one instance of the goodness of the Lord, and rebuke but briefly the pride of man, are worthy of our best minstrelsy. When we see that each Psalm is dedicated to " the chief musician," it should make us value our Psalmody, and forbid us to praise the Lord carelessly.* Maschil. *An Instructive. Even the malice of a Doeg may furnish instruction to* a David. *A Psalm of David. He was the prime object of Doeg's doggish hatred, and therefore the most fitting person to draw from the incident the lessons concealed within it.* When Doeg the Edomite came and told Saul, and saith unto him, David is come to the house of Ahimelech. *By this deceitful tale-bearing, he procured the death of all the priests at Nob : though it had been a crime to have succoured David as a rebel, they were not in their intent and knowledge guilty of the fault. David felt much the villany of this arch-enemy, and here he denounces him in vigorous terms ; it may be also that he has Saul in his eye.*

DIVISION.—*We shall follow the sacred pauses marked by the Selahs of the poet.*

EXPOSITION.

WHY boastest thou thyself in mischief, O mighty man ? the goodness of God *endureth* continually.

2 Thy tongue deviseth mischiefs ; like a sharp razor, working deceitfully.

3 Thou lovest evil more than good ; *and* lying rather than to speak righteousness. Selah.

1. " *Why boastest thou thyself in mischief, O mighty man ?* " Doeg had small matter for boasting in having procured the slaughter of a band of defenceless priests. A mighty man indeed to kill men who never touched a sword ! He ought to have been ashamed of his cowardice. He had no room for exultation ! Honourable titles are but irony where the wearer is mean and cruel. If David alluded to Saul, he meant by these words pityingly to say, " How can one by nature fitted for nobler deeds, descend to so low a level as to find a theme for boasting in a slaughter so heartless and mischievous ? " " *The goodness of God endureth continually.*" A beautiful contrast. The tyrant's fury cannot dry up the perennial stream of divine mercy. If priests be slain their Master lives. If Doeg for awhile triumphs the Lord will outlive him, and right the wrongs which he has done. This ought to modify the proud exultations of the wicked, for after all, while the Lord liveth, iniquity has little cause to exalt itself.

2. " *Thy tongue deviseth mischiefs.*" Thou speakest with an ulterior design. The information given was for Saul's assistance apparently, but in very deed in his heart the Edomite hated the priests of the God of Jacob. It is a mark of deep depravity, when the evil spoken is craftily intended to promote a yet greater evil. " *Like a sharp razor, working deceitfully.*" David represents the false tongue as being effectual for mischief, like a razor which, unawares to the person operated on, is making him bald ; so softly and deftly do Oriental barbers perform their work. Or he may mean that as with a razor a man's throat may be cut very speedily, under the pretence of shaving him, even thus keenly, basely, but effectually Doeg destroyed the band of the priests. Whetted by malice, and guided by craft, he did his cruel work with accursed thoroughness.

3. " *Thou lovest evil more than good.*" He loved not good at all. If both had been equally profitable and pleasant, he would have preferred evil. " *And lying rather than to speak righteousness.*" He was more at home at lying than at truth. He spake not the truth except by accident, but he delighted heartily in falsehood. " SELAH." Let us pause and look at the proud, blustering liar. Doeg is gone, but other dogs bark at the Lord's people. Saul's cattle-master is buried, but the devil still has his drovers, who fain would hurry the saints like sheep to the slaughter.

4 Thou lovest all devouring words, O *thou* deceitful tongue.

5 God shall likewise destroy thee for ever, he shall take thee away, and

pluck thee out of *thy* dwelling place, and root thee out of the land of the living. Selah.

4. " *Thou lovest.*" Thou hast a taste, a gusto for evil language. " *All devouring words.*" There are words that, like boa-constrictors, swallow men whole, or like lions, rend men to pieces ; these words evil minds are fond of. Their oratory is evermore furious and bloody. That which will most readily provoke the lowest passions they are sure to employ, and they think such pandering to the madness of the wicked to be eloquence of a high order. " *O thou deceitful tongue.*" Men can manage to say a great many furious things, and yet cover all over with the pretext of justice. They claim that they are jealous for the right, but the truth is they are determined to put down truth and holiness, and craftily go about it under this transparent pretence.

5. " *God shall likewise destroy thee for ever.*" Fain would the persecutor destroy the church, and therefore God shall destroy him, pull down his house, pluck up his roots, and make an end of him. " *He shall take thee away.*" God shall extinguish his coal and sweep him away like the ashes of the hearth ; he would have quenched the truth, and God shall quench him. " *And pluck thee out of thy dwelling place,*" like a plant torn from the place where it grew, or a captive dragged from his home. Ahimelech and his brother priests were cut off from their abode, and so should those be who compassed and contrived their murder. " *And root thee out of the land of the living.*" The persecutor shall be eradicated, stubbed up by the root, cut up root and branch. He sought the death of others and death shall fall upon him. He troubled the land of the living, and he shall be banished to that land where the wicked cease from troubling. Those who will not " let live " have no right to " live." God will turn the tables on malicious men, and mete to them a portion with their own measure. " SELAH." Pause again, and behold the divine justice proving itself more than a match for human sin.

6 The righteous also shall see, and fear, and shall laugh at him :

7 Lo, *this is* the man *that* made not God his strength ; but trusted in the abundance of his riches, *and* strengthened himself in his wickedness.

8 But I *am* like a green olive tree in the house of God : I trust in the mercy of God for ever and ever.

9 I will praise thee for ever, because thou hast done *it :* and I will wait on thy name ; for *it is* good before thy saints.

6. " *The righteous* "—the object of the tyrant's hatred—shall outlive his enmity, and " *also shall see,*" before his own face, the end of the ungodly oppressor. God permits Mordecai to see Haman hanging on the gallows. David had brought to him the tokens of Saul's death on Gilboa. " *And fear.*" Holy awe shall sober the mind of the good man ; he shall reverently adore the God of providence. " *And shall laugh at him.*" If not with righteous joy, yet with solemn contempt. Schemes so far-reaching all baffled, plans so deep, so politic, all thwarted. Mephistopheles outwitted, the old serpent taken in his own subtlety. This is a goodly theme for that deep-seated laughter which is more akin to solemnity than merriment.

7. " *Lo.*" Look ye here, and read the epitaph of a mighty man, who lorded it proudly during his little hour, and set his heel upon the necks of the Lord's chosen. " *This is the man that made not God his strength.*" Behold the man ! The great vainglorious man. He found a fortress, but not in God ; he gloried in his might, but not in the Almighty. Where is he now ? How has it fared with him in the hour of his need ? Behold his ruin, and be instructed. " *But trusted in the abundance of his riches, and strengthened himself in his wickedness.*" The substance he had gathered, and the mischiefs he had wrought, were his boast and glory. Wealth and wickedness are dreadful companions ; when combined they make a monster. When the devil is master of money bags, he is a devil indeed. Beelzebub and Mammon together heat the furnace seven times hotter for the child of God, but in the end they shall work out their own destruction. Wherever we see to-day a man great in sin and substance, we shall do well to anticipate his end. and view this verse as the divine *in memoriam.*

8. " *But I,*" hunted and persecuted though I am, " *am like a green olive tree.*" I am not plucked up or destroyed, but am like a flourishing olive, which out of

the rock draws oil, and amid the drought still lives and grows. "*In the house of God.*" He was one of the divine family, and could not be expelled from it; his place was near his God, and there was he safe and happy, despite all the machinations of his foes. He was bearing fruit, and would continue to do so when all his proud enemies were withered like branches lopped from the tree. "*I trust in the mercy of God for ever and ever.*" Eternal mercy is my present confidence. David knew God's mercy to be eternal and perpetual, and in that he trusted. What a rock to build on! What a fortress to fly to!

9. "*I will praise thee for ever.*" Like thy mercy shall my thankfulness be. While others boast in their riches I will boast in my God; and when their glorying is silenced for ever in the tomb, my song shall continue to proclaim the loving-kindness of Jehovah. "*Because thou hast done it.*" Thou hast vindicated the righteous, and punished the wicked. God's memorable acts of providence, both to saints and sinners, deserve and must have our gratitude. David views his prayers as already answered, the promises of God as already fulfilled, and therefore at once lifts up the sacred Psalm. "*And I will wait on thy name.*" God shall still be the Psalmist's hope; he will not in future look elsewhere. He whose name has been so gloriously made known in truth and righteousness, is justly chosen as our expectation for years to come. "*For it is good before thy saints.*" Before or among the saints David intended to wait, feeling it to be good both for him and them to look to the Lord alone, and wait for the manifestation of his character in due season. Men must not too much fluster us; our strength is to sit still. Let the mighty ones boast, we will wait on the Lord; and if their haste brings them present honour, our patience will have its turn by-and-by, and bring us the honour which excelleth.

EXPLANATORY NOTES AND QUAINT SAYINGS.

Title.—That *Maschil* means a sacred composition, is evident from the seventh verse of the 47th Psalm, where the passage which we render, "Sing ye praises with understanding," is literally, "Sing ye a *Maschil*," or song of instruction. This word occurs as a title in thirteen places; and six times is prefixed to compositions of David's. In several instances it occurs in consecutive Psalms; *i.e.*, in the 42nd (of which the 43rd is the sequel), the 44th and 45th, the 52nd, 53rd, 54th, and 55th, the 88th and 89th. A circumstance which favours the notion that the term was one peculiarly used by some particular editor or collector of a certain portion of the Psalter.—*John Jebb.*

Verse 1 (first clause).—*Why doth he glory in malice that is mighty?* that is, he, that in malice is mighty, why doth he glory? There is need that a man be mighty but in goodness, not in malice. Is it any great thing to glory in malice? To build a house doth belong to few men, any ignorant man you please can pull down. To sow wheat, to dress the crop, to wait until it ripen, and in that fruit on which one has laboured to rejoice, doth belong to few men: with one spark any man you please can burn all the crop. . . . . What art thou about to do, O mighty man, what art thou about to do, boasting thyself much? Thou art about to kill a man: this thing also a scorpion, this also a fever, this also a poisonous fungus can do. To this is thy mightiness reduced, that it be made equal to a poisonous fungus!— *Augustine.*

Verse 1.—By "*mischief*" is understood not simply what evil he had done, but the prosperity which he now enjoyed, obtained through mischief; as is clear both from the word *boasting* and from the seventh verse. . . . . Formerly he was the chief of Saul's shepherds (1 Sam. xxi. 8), but by that wicked destruction of the priests of God by Saul, and the execution of the cruel sentence, he obtained the chief place near to the king (*ibid.* xxii. 9).—*Hermann Venema.*

Verse 1.—"O mighty man." These words may be added either by way of irony, as if he had said, A great deal of valour and prowess you have shown in slaying a company of unarmed men, the priests of the Lord, yea, women and children, no way able to resist you; or else to imply the ground of his vain boasting, to wit, either his present greatness, as being a man in great place, and of great power with Saul ; or the great preferments he expected from Saul.—*Arthur Jackson.*

Verse 1.—" *The goodness of God endureth continually.*" He contrasts the *goodness* of God with the wealth and might of Doeg, and the foundation of his own confidence as widely different from that of Doeg, his own placed upon the goodness of God, enduring for ever and showing itself effectual. It is as if he had said, The *goodness* of God to which I trust, is most powerful and the same throughout all time, and in it I shall at all times most surely rejoice that *goodness* of God, since now it sustains me, so it will exalt me in its own good time ; it therefore *is*, and *will be above me*. . . . Not without emphasis does he say the goodness אֵל *of the strong God*, a contrast to Doeg the *hero*, and the ruinous foundation of his fortune.—*Hermann Venema.*

Verse 2.—" *Thy tongue deviseth mischiefs, like a sharp razor, working deceitfully.*" Thus our version. But I do not very well understand the propriety of *the tongue's devising mischief*, and devising it *like a sharp razor.* But we may easily avoid this harsh comparison by rendering the words : *Thou contrivest mischiefs with thy tongue, as with a sharp razor, O thou dealer in deceit* : *i.e.,* Thou contrivest with thy smooth and flattering tongue to wound the reputation and character of others, as though thou wast cutting their throats with a smooth razor.—*Samuel Chandler.*

Verse 2.—" *Like a sharp razor,*" that instead of shaving the hair lanceth the flesh ; or missing the beard cutteth the throat.—*John Trapp.*

Verse 2.—The smooth, adroit manner of executing a wicked device neither hides nor abates its wickedness. Murder with " *a sharp razor* " is as wicked as murder with a meat-axe or a bludgeon. A lie very ingeniously framed and rehearsed in an oily manner, is as great a sin, and in the end will be seen to be as great a folly as the most bungling attempt at deception.—*William S. Plumer.*

Verse 3.—" *Thou lovest evil more than good.*"—" *Thou hast loved evil,*" he says, " *more than good,*" not by simply preferring it, but by substituting it ; so that in the stead of good he hath done evil, and that from the inmost love of his soul, bent upon evil ; wherefore he does not say that he *admitted*, but *loved evil*, not *moral* only, but *physical*, for the destruction of his neighbours ; so *to have loved* it, that he willed nothing but *evil*, being averse to all good.—*Hermann Venema.*

Verse 4.—" *Thou lovest all devouring words, O thou deceitful tongue.*"—He was all *tongue* ; a *man of words* : and these the most deceitful and injurious.—*Adam Clarke.*

Verse 5.—" *God shall destroy thee for ever,*" etc. There are four words the Psalmist makes use of to denote the utter vengeance that awaited this deceitful and bloody wretch, all of them having a very strong meaning. The first, יִתָּצְךָ from נתץ, signifies *to pull down,* and break utterly into pieces ; as when an altar is demolished. (Judges vi. 30 ; viii. 9.) The second, יַחְתְּךָ from the root חתה, which signifies *to twist* anything, or *pluck it up by twisting it round,* as trees are sometimes twisted up. The third, יִסָּחֲךָ from נסח, which properly signifies *utterly to sweep away anything like dust or chaff ;* and the expression יִסָּחֲךָ מֵאֹהֶל means not *sweep thee away from thy tent,* but, *sweep thee away, that thou mayest be no longer a tent ;* thyself, thy family, thy fortune, shall be wholly and entirely swept away, and dissipated for ever ; to which the fourth word, שֵׁרֶשְׁ, answers, *eradicabit te,* he shall root thee out *from the land of the living.* 'Tis impossible words can express a more entire and absolute destruction.—*Samuel Chandler.*

Verse 5.—" *God shall likewise destroy thee for ever.*" Here are *quot verba tot tonotrua,* so many words, so many thunderclaps. As thou hast destroyed the Lord's priests, and their whole city, razing and harassing it ; so God will demolish and destroy thee utterly as an house pulled down to the ground, so that one stone is not left upon another (Lev. xiv. 45) ; so shall God pull down Doeg from that high preferment, which he by sycophancy hath got at court.—*John Trapp.*

Verse 5.—Wonderful is the force of the verbs in the original, which convey to us the four ideas of *laying prostrate, dissolving as by fire, sweeping away as with a besom, and totally extirpating root and branch,* as a tree is eradicated from the spot on which it grew. If a farther comment be wanted, it may be found in the history of David's enemies, and the crucifiers of the Son of David ; but the passage will be fully and finally explained by the destruction of the world of the ungodly at the last day.—*George Horne.*

Verse 5.—The poet accumulates dire and heavy words, and mingles various metaphors that he might paint the picture of this man's destruction in more lively colours. Three metaphors appear to be joined together, the first taken from a *building*, the second from a *tent*, the third from a *tree*, if attention is given to the force and common acceptation of the words.—*Hermann Venema.*

Verse 5.—" *He shall take thee away ; "* or, *seize thee*, as coals are taken with the tongs.—*J. J. Stewart Perowne.*

Verse 6.—" *The righteous also shall see,"* etc. That is, to use the apt words of Gejerus, " *This shall not be a secret judgment, or known only to a few, but common fame shall spread abroad throughout the kingdom, or city, the notable punishment of the ungodly. The righteous also shall not pass by such an event with indifference but with earnest eyes shall contemplate it,"* etc. I add, and hence shall they take joy, and turn it to their own use, to the greater fearing of God. . . . *The righteous,* upon whose destruction the ungodly man was intent, shall survive and spend their lives safe in the favour of God ; *they shall see* with attentive mind, they shall consider ; nor, as worldlings are accustomed, shall they pass it by without reflection or improvement, they shall see and *fear,* namely, God the just judge ; and instructed in his judgment by this instance, they shall be the more careful to abstain from all designs and crimes of the kind.—*Hermann Venema.*

Verse 6.—" *And shall laugh at him ; "* or *over him*—over the wicked man thus cast down—*they shall laugh.* Such exultation, to our modern sensibilities, seems shocking, because we can hardly conceive of it, apart from the gratification of personal vindictiveness. But there is such a thing as a righteous hatred, as a righteous scorn. There is such a thing as a shout of righteous joy at the downfall of the tyrant and the oppressor, at the triumph of righteousness and truth over wrong and falsehood.—*J. J. Stewart Perowne.*

Verse 7.—" *Lo, this is the man that made not God his strength."* David having showed (in verses 5, 6) the wicked man, by the righteous judgment of God rooted out of the land of the living, shows us in the next verse, the righteous man at once fearing and laughing at this sight, as also pointing at him saying, " *Lo this is the man that made not God his strength."* The words are a divine but cutting sarcasm. The original is *geber*, which signifieth a strong, valiant man : as we say in English, Lo, this is the brave and gallant man you wot of ! But who was this for a man ? He was one, saith he, that " *trusted in the abundance of his riches."* Oh ! 'tis hard to abound in riches and not to trust in them. Hence that caution (Psalm lxii. 10) : " If riches increase, set not your heart upon them." Now, what is the setting the heart upon riches but our rejoicing and trusting in them ? And because the heart of man is so easily persuaded into this sinful trust upon riches, therefore the apostle is urgent with Timothy to persuade all rich men—not only mere worldly rich men, but godly rich men—against it ; yea, he urgeth Timothy to persuade rich men against two sins, which are worse than all the poverty in the world, yet the usual attendants of riches—pride and confidence : " Charge them that are rich in this world, that they be not highminded." 1 Tim. vi. 17.—*Joseph Caryl.*

Verses 7, 8.—Perhaps some of you have been long professors, and yet come to little growth in love to God, humility, heavenly-mindedness, mortification ; and it is worth the digging to see what lies at the root of your profession, whether there be not a legal principle that hath too much influenced you. Have you not thought to carry all with God from your duties and services, and too much laid up your hopes in your own actings ? Alas ! this is as so much dead earth, which must be thrown out, and gospel principles laid in the room thereof. Try but this course, and try whether the spring of thy grace will not come on apace. David gives an account how he came to stand and flourish when some that were rich and mighty, on a sudden withered and came to nothing. " *Lo,"* saith he, " *this is the man that made not God his strength ; but trusted in the abundance of his riches."* " *But I am like a green olive tree in the house of God : I trust in the mercy of God for ever and ever."* While others trust in the riches of their own righteousness and services, and make not Christ their strength, do thou renounce all, and trust in the mercy of God in Christ, and thou shalt be like a green olive when they fade and wither.—*William Gurnall.*

Verse 8 *(first clause)* :—

> " But I an olive charged with fruit
> In fertile soil that grows."

This appears to express the meaning of the Hebrew words, which our translators render, " *like a green olive tree*," but which in reality have no reference to the colour, but to the flourishing, vigorous, and thriving state of the plant ; just as Homer gives it the epithet of " luxuriant," and " flourishing ; " and Ovid that of " ever-flourishing." The fact is, the colour of the leaves of this tree is not a bright, lively green ; but a dark, disagreeable, or yellowish one. Scheuchzen describes the leaves, as " *superne coloris atrovirentis, vel in virdi flavescentis.*" An English traveller, writing from Italy, thus expresses his disappointment about the olive tree :—" The fields, and indeed the whole face of Tuscany, are in a manner covered with olive trees ; but the olive tree does not answer the character I had conceived of it. The royal Psalmist and some of the sacred writers, speak with rapture of the ' green olive tree,' so that I expected a beautiful green ; and I confess to you, I was wretchedly disappointed to find its hue resembling that of our hedges when they are covered with dust." I have heard other travellers express the same feeling of disappointment. " The true way of solving the difficulty," as Harmer properly remarks, " is to consider the word translated ' green,' not as descriptive of colour, but of some other property ; youthfulness, vigour, prosperity, or the like."—*Richard Mant.*

Verse 8.—" *Green olive tree in the house of God.*"—Several expositors fancifully imagine that olive trees grew in certain of the courts of the Tabernacle ; but the notion must not be endured, it would have been too near an approach to the groves of the heathen to have been tolerated, at least in David's time. The text should surely be read with some discretion ; the poet does not refer to olive trees in God's house, but compares *himself in the house of God* to an olive tree. This reminds us of the passage, " Thy children like olive plants around thy table," where some whose imaginations have been more lively than their judgments, have seen a table surrounded, not with children, but with olive plants. Whoever, in the realms of common sense ever heard of olive plants round a table ? If, as Thrupp supposes, Nob was situated upon the Mount of Olives, we can, without any conjecture, see a reaon for the present reference to a flourishing olive tree.—*C. H. S.*

Verse 9.—He compares himself (1) With an *olive tree*, a tree always green, lasting long and fruitful, whose fruit is most useful and grateful : so he paints his future state as joyful, glorious, lasting, and useful and pleasing to men : plainly a reference is made to the *royal* and *prophetic* office, in both of which he represents himself as an *olive tree*, by supplying others with *oil* through his rule and instruction : (2) With *the olive* growing luxuriantly, and abounding in spreading boughs, and so spacious and large. . . . . (3) But why does he add *in the house of God ?* That he might indicate, unless I am deceived : (*a*) That he should possess a dwelling in that place where the *house of God* was, whence he was now exiled through the calumnies of Doeg and the attacks of Saul stirred up thereby : (*b*) That he should perform distinguished service to the house of God, by adorning it, and by restoring religion, now neglected, and practising it with zeal : (*c*) That he should derive from God and his favour, whose that house was, all his prosperity : (*d*) That he, like a son of God, should rejoice in familiarity with him, and should become heir to his possessions and promises.—*Hermann Venema.*

HINTS TO PREACHERS.

Verse 1.—The confidence of faith. I. *The circumstances were distressing.* 1. David was misjudged. 2. David exiled. 3. A bad man in power. 4. God's priests slain. II. *The consolation was abiding.* 1. There is a God. 2. He is good. 3. His goodness continues. 4. Good will, therefore, overcome. III. *The rejoinder was triumphant,* "Why boastest thou?" 1. The mischief did not touch the main point. 2. It would be overruled. 3. It would recoil. 4. It would expose the perpetrators to scorn.

Verse 3.—In what cases men clearly love evil more than good.

Verses 7, 8.—The worldling like an uprooted tree, the believer a vigorous, well-planted olive.

Verse 8.—The believer's character, position, confidence, and continuance.

Verse 9.—The double duty, and the double reason: the single heart and its single object.

Verse 9.—What God has done, what we will do, and why.

PSALM LIII

TITLE.—To the Chief Musician.—*If the leader of the choir is privileged to sing the jubilates of divine grace, he must not disdain to chant the misereres of human depravity. This is the second time he has had the same Psalm entrusted to him* (see Psalm xiv.), *and he must, therefore, be the more careful in singing it.* Upon Mahalath. *Here the tune is chosen for the musician, probably some mournfully solemn air ; or perhaps a musical instrument is here indicated, and the master of the choir is requested to make it the prominent instrument in the orchestra ; at any rate, this is a direction not found in the former copy of the Psalm, and seems to call for greater care. The word* "Mahalath" *appears to signify, in some forms of it,* " disease," *and truly this Psalm is* THE SONG OF MAN'S DISEASE—*the mortal, hereditary taint of sin.* Maschil. *This is a second additional note not found in Psalm* xiv., *indicating that double attention is to be given to this most instructive song.* A Psalm of David. *It is not a copy of the fourteenth Psalm, emended and revised by a foreign hand ; it is another edition by the same author, emphasised in certain parts, and re-written for another purpose.*

SUBJECT.—*The evil nature of man is here brought before our view a second time, in almost the same inspired words. All repetitions are not vain repetitions. We are slow to learn, and need line upon line. David after a long life, found men no better than they were in his youth. Holy Writ never repeats itself needlessly, there is good cause for the second copy of this Psalm ; let us read it with more profound attention than before. If our age has advanced from fourteen to fifty-three, we shall find the doctrine of this Psalm more evident than in our youth.*

[*The reader is requested to peruse Psalm XIV.,* " Treasury of David," *Vol. I.*]

EXPOSITION.

THE fool hath said in his heart, *There is* no God. Corrupt are they, and have done abominable iniquity : *there is* none that doeth good.

2 God looked down from heaven upon the children of men, to see if there were *any* that did understand, that did seek God.

3 Every one of them is gone back : they are altogether become filthy ; *there is* none that doeth good, no, not one.

4 Have the workers of iniquity no knowledge ? who eat up my people *as* they eat bread : they have not called upon God.

5 There were they in great fear, *where* no fear was : for God hath scattered the bones of him that encampeth *against* thee : thou hast put *them* to shame, because God hath despised them.

6 Oh that the salvation of Israel *were come* out of Zion ! When God bringeth back the captivity of his people, Jacob shall rejoice, *and* Israel shall be glad.

1. " *The fool hath said in his heart, There is no God.*" And this he does because he is a fool. Being a fool he speaks according to his nature ; being a great fool he meddles with a great subject, and comes to a wild conclusion. The atheist is, morally, as well as mentally, a fool, a fool in the heart as well as in the head ; a fool in morals as well as in philosophy. With the denial of God as a starting point, we may well conclude that the fool's progress is a rapid, riotous, raving, ruinous one. He who begins at impiety is ready for anything. " *No God,*" being interpreted, means no law, no order, no restraint to lust, no limit to passion. Who but a fool would be of this mind ? What a Bedlam, or rather what an Aceldama, would the world become if such lawless principles came to be universal ! He who heartily

entertains an irreligious spirit, and follows it out to its legitimate issues is a son of Belial, dangerous to the commonwealth, irrational and despicable. Every natural man, is, more or less a denier of God. Practical atheism is the religion of the race. " *Corrupt are they.*" They are rotten. It is idle to compliment them as sincere doubters, and amiable thinkers—they are putrid. There is too much dainty dealing nowadays with atheism ; it is not a harmless error, it is an offensive, putrid sin, and righteous men should look upon it in that light. All men being more or less atheistic in spirit, are also in that degree corrupt ; their heart is foul, their moral nature is decayed. " *And have done abominable iniquity.*" Bad principles soon lead to bad lives. One does not find virtue promoted by the example of your Voltaires and Tom Paines. Those who talk so abominably as to deny their Maker will act abominably when it serves their turn. It is the abounding denial and forgetfulness of God among men which is the source of the unrighteousness and crime which we see around us. If all men are not outwardly vicious it is to be accounted for by the power of other and better principles, but left to itself the " No God " spirit so universal in mankind would produce nothing but the most loathsome actions. " *There is none that doeth good.*" The one typical fool is reproduced in the whole race ; without a single exception men have forgotten the right way. This accusation twice made in the Psalm, and repeated a third time by the inspired apostle Paul, is an indictment most solemn and sweeping, but he who makes it cannot err, he knows what is in man; neither will he lay more to man's charge than he can prove.

2. " *God looked down from heaven upon the children of men.*" He did so in ages past, and he has continued his steadfast gaze from his all-surveying observatory. " *To see if there were any that did understand, that did seek God.*" Had there been one understanding man, one true lover of his God, the divine eye would have discovered him. Those pure heathens and admirable savages that men talk so much of, do not appear to have been visible to the eye of Omniscience, the fact being that they live nowhere but in the realm of fiction. The Lord did not look for great grace, but only for sincerity and right desire, but these he found not. He saw all nations, and all men in all nations, and all hearts in all men, and all motions of all hearts, but he saw neither a clear head nor a clean heart among them all. Where God's eyes see no favourable sign we may rest assured there is none.

3. " *Every one of them is gone back.*" The whole mass of manhood, all of it, is gone back. In the fourteenth Psalm it was said to turn aside, which was bad enough, but here it is described as running in a diametrically opposite direction. The life of unregenerate manhood is in direct defiance of the law of God, not merely apart from it but opposed to it. " *They are altogether become filthy.*" The whole lump is soured with an evil leaven, fouled with an all-pervading pollution, made rank with general putrefaction. Thus, in God's sight, our atheistic nature is not the pardonable thing that we think it to be. Errors as to God are not the mild diseases which some account them, they are abominable evils. Fair is the world to blind eyes, but to the all-seeing Jehovah it is otherwise. " *There is none that doeth good, no, not one.*" How could there be, when the whole mass was leavened with so evil a leaven ? This puts an end to the fictions of the innocent savage, the lone patriarch, " the Indian whose untutored mind," etc. Pope's verse—

> " Father of all, in every age,
>   In every clime adored,
> By saint, by savage, or by sage,
>   Jehovah, Jove, or Lord,"

evaporates in smoke. The fallen race of man, left to its own energy, has not produced a single lover of God or doer of holiness, nor will it ever do so. Grace must interpose or not one specimen of humanity will be found to follow after the good and true. This is God's verdict after looking down upon the race. Who shall gainsay it ?

4. " *Have the workers of iniquity no knowledge ?*" They have no wisdom, certainly, but even so common a thing as knowledge might have restrained them. Can they not see that there is a God ? that sin is an evil thing ? that persecution recoils upon a man's own head ? Are they such utter fools as not to know that they are their own enemies, and are ruining themselves ? " *Who eat up my people as they eat bread.*" Do they not see that such food will be hard to digest, and will bring on them a horrible vomit when God deals with them in justice ? Can they imagine that the Lord will allow them to devour his people with impunity ? They

must be insane indeed. "*They have not called upon God.*" They carry on their cruel enterprises against the saints, and use every means but that which is essential to success in every case, namely, the invocation of God. In this respect persecutors are rather more consistent than Pharisees who devoured widows' houses, and prayed too. The natural man, like Ishmael, loves not the spiritual seed, is very jealous of it, and would fain destroy it, because it is beloved of God ; yet the natural man does not seek after the like favour from God. The carnal mind envies those who obtain mercy, and yet it will not seek mercy itself. It plays the dog in the manger. Sinners will out of a malicious jealousy devour those who pray, but yet they will not pray themselves.

5. "*There were they in great fear, where no fear was.*" David sees the end of the ungodly and the ultimate triumph of the spiritual seed. The rebellious march in fury against the gracious, but suddenly they are seized with a causeless panic. The once fearless boasters tremble like the leaves of the aspen, frightened at their own shadows. In this sentence and this verse, this Psalm differs much from the fourteenth. It is evidently expressive of a higher state of realisation in the poet, he emphasises the truth by stronger expressions. Without cause the wicked are alarmed. He who denies God is at bottom a coward, and in his infidelity he is like the boy in the churchyard who " whistles to keep his courage up." "*For God hath scattered the bones of him that encampeth against thee.*" When the wicked see the destruction of their fellows they may well quail. Mighty were the hosts which besieged Zion, but they were defeated, and their unburied carcasses proved the prowess of the God whose being they dared to deny. "*Thou hast put them to shame, because God hath despised them.*" God's people may well look with derision upon their enemies since they are the objects of divine contempt. They scoff at us, but we may with far greater reason laugh them to scorn, because the Lord our God considers them as less than nothing and vanity.

6. "*Oh that the salvation of Israel were come out of Zion.*" Would God the final battle were well over. When will the Lord avenge his own elect ? When will the long oppression of the saints come to its close, and glory crown their heads ? The word " salvation " is in the plural, to show its greatness. "*When God bringeth back the capitivity of his people, Jacob shall rejoice, and Israel shall be glad.*" Inasmuch as the yoke has been heavy, and the bondage cruel, the liberty will be gladsome, and the triumph joyous. The second advent and the restoration of Israel are our hope and expectation.

We have attempted to throw into rhyme the last two verses of this Psalm :—

> The foes of Zion quake for fright,
>   Where no fear was they quail ;
> For well they know that sword of might
>   Which cuts through coats of mail.
>
> The Lord of old defiled their shields,
>   And all their spears he scorn'd ;
> Their bones lay scatter'd o'er the fields.
>   Unburied and unmourn'd.
>
> Let Zion's foes be filled with shame ;
>   Her sons are bless'd of God ;
> Though scoffers now despise their name,
>   The Lord shall break the rod.
>
> Oh ! would our God to Zion turn,
>   God with salvation clad ;
> Then Judah's harps should music learn.
>   And Israel be glad.

EXPLANATORY NOTES AND QUAINT SAYINGS.

Whole Psalm.—Probably the two Psalms *refer to different periods ;* the fourteenth to the earlier portion of the world, or of Jewish history ; the fifty-third to a later, perhaps a still future time. Jehovah, through Christ, is frequently said to turn to the world to see what its condition is, and always with the same result. " All flesh had corrupted its way " in the days of Noah, and, " when the Son of Man cometh " again, it is intimated that he will scarcely " find faith on the earth." The two Psalms also *apply to different persons.* The former refers to the enemies of God, who tremble when his presence is made known ; " *they are in great fear,*" because vengeance is about to be inflicted on them for their sins. Here the Supreme Being is called Jehovah. In the fifty-third Psalm the interests of God's people are principally kept in view. The ungodly are regarded as plotting against the righteous, and it is in this relation their case is considered. The fear that was just and reasonable, in the fourteenth Psalm, because it concerned the unrighteous under a sense of impending judgment, is said to be unfounded in the fifty-third, because God was in the midst of his people, " scattering the bones of their enemies," and showing himself, not as Jehovah, but as the Elohim of his redeemed children. The fourteenth Psalm contemplates judgment ; the fifty-third deliverance ; and thus, though seemingly alike, a different lesson is conveyed in each.

The Psalm, then, descriptive of the universal and continuous corruption of man's nature, very properly occupies an introductory place in a series intended to represent the enemies of Messiah, who oppose his church during his absence, and who are to attempt to resist his power when he comes again. Before entering upon an examination of the character of these opponents, this Psalm teaches that, until changed by grace, all are gone astray ; " there is none righteous, no, not one," and that for all there is but one remedy, " the Deliverer coming out of Zion, who shall turn away ungodliness from Jacob."—*R. H. Ryland, M.A., in* " *The Psalms restored to Messiah,*" 1853.

Whole Psalm.—The state of earth ought to be deeply felt by us. The world lying in wickedness should occupy much of our thoughts. The enormous guilt, the inconceivable pollution, the ineffably provoking Atheism of this fallen province of God's dominion, might be a theme for our ceaseless meditation and mourning. To impress it the more on us, therefore, the Psalm repeats what has been already sung in Psalm xiv. It is the same Psalm, with only a few words varied ; it is " line upon line, precept upon precept ; " the harp's most melancholy, most dismal notes again sounded in our ear. Not that the Lord would detain us always, or disproportionately long, amid scenes of sadness ; for elsewhere he repeats in like manner that most triumphant melody, Psalm lx. 6—12 ; cviii. 6—13 ; but it is good to return now and then to the open field on which we all were found, cast out in loathsome degradation.—*Andrew A. Bonar, in* " *Christ and his Church in the Book of Psalms,*" 1859.

Whole Psalm.—A second edition of the fourteenth Psalm, with variations more or less important, in each verse. That either of these compositions is an incorrect copy of the other is highly improbable, because two such copies of the same Psalm would not have been retained in the collection, and because the variations are too uniform, consistent, and significant, to be the work of chance or mere traditional corruption. That the changes were deliberately made by a later writer is improbable, because such a liberty would hardly have been taken with a Psalm of David, and because the later form, in that case, would either have been excluded from the Psalter or substituted for the first form, or immediately connected with it.

The only satisfactory hypothesis is, that the original author afterwards re-wrote it, with such modifications as were necessary to bring out certain points distinctly, but without any intention to supersede the use of the original composition, which therefore still retains its place in the collection. This supposition is confirmed by the titles, which ascribe both Psalms to David. . . . As a general fact, it may be stated, that the variations in the Psalm before us are such as render the expression stronger, bolder, and in one or two cases more obscure and difficult.— *J. A. Alexander* 1850,

Whole Psalm.—This Psalm is a variation of Psalm xiv. In each of these two Psalms the *name* of God occurs seven times. In Psalm xiv. it is three times *Elohim,* and four times *Jehovah ;* in the present Psalm it is seven times *Elohim.*—*Christopher Wordsworth,* 1868.

Whole Psalm.—God, in this Psalm, " speaketh twice," for this is the same almost verbatim with the fourteenth Psalm. The scope of it is to convince us of our sins, to set us a-blushing, and to set us a-trembling because of them ; there is need of " line upon line " to this purpose. God, by the Psalmist, here shows—

I. The *fact* of sin. God is a witness to it. He looks down from heaven and sees all the sinfulness of men's hearts and lives. All this is open and naked before him.

II. The *fault* of sin. It is iniquity (verses 1, 4) ; it is an unrighteous thing ; it is that in which there is no good (verses 1, 3) ; it is going back from God (verse 3).

III. The *fountain* of sin. How comes it that men are so bad ? Surely, it is because there is no fear of God before their eyes ; they say in their hearts, *there is no God* at all to call us to account, none that we need to stand in awe of. Men's bad practices flow from their bad principles.

IV. The *folly* of sin. He is a *fool* (in the account of God, whose judgment we are sure is right) who harbours such corrupt thoughts. The " workers of iniquity," whatever they pretend to, " have no knowledge ; " they may truly be said to know nothing that do not know God. Verse 4.

V. The *filthiness* of sin. Sinners are " corrupt " (verse 1) ; their nature is vitiated and spoiled ; their iniquity is " abominable ; " it is odious to the holy God, and renders them so ; whereas, otherwise he " hates nothing that he has made." What neatness soever proud sinners pretend to, it is certain that wickedness is the greatest nastiness in the world.

VI. The *fruit* of sin. See to what a degree of barbarity it brings men at last ! See their cruelty to their brethren ! They " eat them up as they eat bread." As if they had not only become beasts, but beasts of prey. See their contempt of God at the same time—they have not called upon him, but scorn to be beholden to him.

VII. The *fear and shame* that attends sin (verse 5). " There were they in great fear " who had made God their enemy ; their own guilty consciences frightened them and filled them with horror. This enables the virgin, the daughter of Zion, to put them to shame and expose them, " because God hath despised them."

VIII. The *faith* of the saints, and their hope and power touching this great evil (verse 6). There will come a Saviour, a great salvation, a salvation from sin. O that it might be hastened ! for it will bring in glorious and joyful times. There were those in the Old Testament times that looked and hoped, that prayed and waited for this redemption. Such salvations were often wrought, and all typical of the everlasting triumphs of the glorious church.—*Condensed from Matthew Henry,* 1662—1714.

Verse 1.—" *The fool hath said is his heart,*" etc. It is in his heart he says this ; this is the secret desire of every unconverted bosom. If the breast of God were within reach of men, it would be stabbed a million of times in one moment. When God was manifest in the flesh, he was altogether lovely ; he did no sin ; he went about continually doing good : and yet they took him and hung him on a tree ; they mocked him and spat upon him. And this is the way men would do with God again. Learn—1st. The fearful depravity of your heart. I venture to say there is not an unconverted man present, who has the most distant idea of the monstrous wickedness that is now within his breast. Stop till you are in hell, and it will break out unrestrained. But still let me tell you what it is—you have a heart that would kill God if you could. If the bosom of God were now within your reach, and one blow would rid the universe of God, you have a heart fit to do the deed. 2nd. The amazing love of Christ—" While we were enemies, Christ died for us."—*Robert Murray M'Cheyne,* 1813—1843.

Verse 1.—" *There is no God.*" אֵין is properly a noun, and means nonentity, or non-existence : " nothing of God," or " no such thing as God." It cannot be explained as a wish—" No God ! " *i.e.,* O that there were no God !—because אֵין in usage always includes the substantive verb, and denies the existence, or at least the presence of the person or thing to which it is prefixed. This is also clear from the use of the same word in the last clause, where its sense is unambiguous.—*J. A. Alexander on Psalm XIV.*

Verse 1.—" *There is no God.*" Thus denying the agency of Providence, for the word *Elohim*, here translated *God*, means *judge* (compare Exodus xxii. 28), and has reference not to the *essence*, but to the *providence* of the Deity.—*Daniel Cresswell*, 1776—1844.

Verse 1.—It is to be noted that Scripture saith, " The fool hath *said* in his heart," and not " *thought* in his heart ; " that is to say, he doth not so fully think it in judgment, as he hath a good will to be of that belief . for seeing that it makes not for him that there should be a God, he doth seek by all means accordingly to persuade and resolve himself, and studies to affirm, prove, and verify it to himself as some theme or position, all which labour, notwithstanding that sparkle of our creation light, whereby men acknowledge a Deity, burneth still within ; and in vain doth he strive utterly to alienate it or put it out, so that it is out of the corruption of his heart and will, and not out of the natural apprehension of his brain and conceit, that he doth set down his opinion, as the comical poet saith, " Then came my mind to be of my opinion," as if himself and his mind had been two diverse things ; there- fore, the atheist hath rather said, and held it in his heart, than thought or believed in his heart that there is no God.—*Francis Bacon* (1560—1626), *in* " *Thoughts on Holy Scripture.*"

Verse 2.—" *That did seek God.*" Although all things are full of God, yet is he to be *sought for* of godly men, by reason of the darkness which compasseth our minds through original sin. For both the flesh, and the senses, and earthly affections do hinder us from knowing of him, yea, though be be present—*Peter Martyr*, 1500—1562.

Verses 2, 3.—Their sin is described in gradation. They do *not understand*, because a true knowledge of things divine forms the basis of proper conduct towards God ; they do *not ask for God*, because they only care for him whose clear and sure insight apprehends him as their highest possession ; they are *gone aside*, because he who cares not for him is sure to get estranged from him, and to deviate from his paths ; and they are *altogether become filthy* (*i.e.*, worthless), because man's proper strength and fitness for virtue must well from the fountain of communion with God.—*Augustus F. Tholuck*, 1856.

Verse 3.—" *They are altogether become filthy.*" אֶלָּחוּ *neelachu*. They are become *sour and rancid ;* a metaphor taken from milk that has fermented and turned sour, rancid and worthless.—*Adam Clarke*, 1760—1832.

Verse 3 (*second clause*).—The word נֶאֱלָחוּ, rendered " *they are become filthy*," might be read, *they have become rotten or putrid.*—*John Morison*, 1829.

Verse 3 (*last clause*).—Evil men are not only guilty of sins of commission, having done abominable iniquity, but they are guilty of many sins of omission. In fact, they have never done one holy act. They may be moral, decent, amiable, they may belong to the church ; but " *there is none that doeth good, no not one.*"—*William S Plumer*, 1867.

Verse 4.—" *Have the workers of iniquity no knowledge ?* " Conscience is a means to curb and restrain, control and rebuke corrupt nature, and the swelling forms of it. It is not there as a native inhabitant, but as a garrison planted in a rebellious town by the great Governor of the world, to keep the rebellion of the inhabitants within compass, who else would break forth into present confusion. David, speaking of the corruption of man by nature after this question, Whether there be not some knowledge to discover their evil doings to them ? yes, says he, " *Have they no knowledge, who eat up my people as bread ?* " Yes ; and therefore (verse 5) " *They are often in fear,*" God having placed this there to overcome them with fear ; and by that to restrain them from many outrages against God's people, whom in their desires, and sometimes practice, they eat up as bread. Therefore this knowledge is put in as a bridle to corrupt nature, as a hook was put into Sennacherib's nostrils (Isa. xxxvii. 29) to rule and tame men, and overcome them with fear. If they had no knowledge they would eat up one another, and the church, as bread ; but there is their fear, says he, that is, thence it comes to pass they are kept in awe.—*Thomas Goodwin*, 1600—1679.

Verse 4.—" *Who eat up my people as they eat bread.*" *C'est, n'en font non plus de conscience, que de manger un morceau de pain.* [That is, they have no more scruple in doing this than in eating a morsel of bread.]—*French Margin.*

Verse 4.—" *My people.*" David may call the serious *his* people, because of his regard for them, and because they were his supporters and friends. They adhered to him in all his afflictions. [" Thy people shall be my people, and thy God my God." Ruth i. 16.]—*Benjamin Boothroyd*, 1836.

Verse 5.—" *There were they in great fear, where no fear was.*" There is a fond and superstitious fear, when men are afraid of their shadows, as Pisander was afraid of meeting his own soul ; and Antenor would never go forth of the doors, but either in a coach closed upon all sides, or with a target borne over his head, fearing, I guess, lest the sky should fall down upon it, according to that in the Psalm, " *They fear where no fear is.*"—*John King*, 1559—1621.

Verse 5.—" *There were they in great fear, where no fear was.*" Behold how fearful a hell a wounded conscience is ! For why is Cain afraid to be killed, seeing there is none living to perform it, but his father and mother, and perhaps some women children which the Scripture nameth not ? It is God's just judgment, that they that will not fear the Lord who is only to be feared, should stand in fear of them who are justly no cause of fear. He that lately feared not to kill his brother, is now made a terror to himself. Hereby also we may consider what is the repentance of the wicked ; they see perhaps the fault together with the punishment, but they admit the fault and lament the punishment.—*Nicholas Gibbens*, 1602.

HINTS TO PREACHERS.

[See the Hints of Psalm XIV.]

Verse 1.—The fool's inside and outside.

Verse 1.—I. The folly of atheism. He who says there is no God is a fool. 1. No reason for the assertion. 2. All reason against it. II. The seat of atheism is the heart ; it is a moral unbelief not an intellectual, the language of the will not of the understanding. III. Cause of atheism. 1. Loving evil. 2. Hating good.—*G. R.*

Verse 2.—I. God has not left the world to itself. II. He takes particular notice of all that is in it. III. The only thing he values in it is the knowledge of himself.—*G. R.*

Verse 4.—How far knowledge is and is not a restraint upon ungodliness.

Verse 4.—It is a sin not to call upon God. I. What is it to call upon God ? Three things required in it. 1. A drawing near to him. 2. A speaking to him. 1 Sam. i. 12, 13. 3. A praying to him. II. How should we call upon God ? 1. Reverently, considering (1) God's holiness and greatness ; (2) our own sin and weakness. Gen. xviii. 27. 2. Understandingly. 1 Cor. xiv. 15. (1) Of what we ask. (2) Of whom we ask it. 3. Submissively. 4. Believingly. Mark xi. 24 ; James i. 6. 5. Sincerely. James iv. 3. 6. Constantly. (1) So as to be always in a praying frame. (2) So as to take all occasions of pouring forth our souls in prayer to God. (3) So as to let no day slip without prayer. III. How it appears to be a sin not to call upon God. 1. He hath commanded it. Isa. lv. 6 ; 1 Tim. ii. 8. 2. Because praying is one of the principal parts of worship we owe to God. IV. Who are guilty of this sin ? 1. All who pray to any one else but God. 2. All who neglect either public, private, or family prayer. 3. All who pray, but not aright.—*William Beveridge* (1636—1708), *in* " *Thesaurus Theoligicus.*"

Verse 5.—I. What persecutors are to themselves—their own tormentors, full even of groundless fears. II. What they are to one another—though in concert here, their bones are scattered hereafter. III. What they are to those whom they persecute—made ashamed before them. IV. What they are to God—a contempt and derision.—*G. R.*

Verse 6.—I. There is salvation for Israel. II. That salvation is in Zion. III. Their salvation remains there when they are banished from it. IV. Their joy becomes greater when they return.—*G. R.*

PSALM LIV.

TITLE.—**To the Chief Musician on Neginoth.** *The music was to be that of stringed instruments. Variety is to be studied in our tunes, and in all other matters relating to sacred song. Monotony is often the death of congregational praise. Providence is varied, and so should our recording songs be.* **Maschil.** *We are to learn and to teach by what we sing. Edification must not be divorced from Psalmody.* **A Psalm of David.** *David's productions were as plentiful as they are profitable. His varied life was for our benefit, for from it we derive these hymns, which at this hour are as fresh and as precious as when he wrote them.* When the Ziphims came and said to Saul, Doth not David hide himself with us? *To curry favour with Saul they were guilty of gross inhospitality. What cared they what innocent blood was shed so that they earned the graceless monarch's smile! David came quietly among them, hoping for a little rest in his many flights, but they descried him in his solitary abode, and betrayed him. He turns to God in prayer, and so strong was his faith that he soon sang himself into delightful serenity.*

DIVISIONS.—*From verse 1 to 3, where the Selah makes a pause for us, the Psalmist pleads with God, and then in the rest of the song, laying aside all doubt, he chants a hymn of joyful triumph. The vigour of faith is the death of anxiety, and the birth of security.*

EXPOSITION.

SAVE me, O God, by thy name, and judge me by thy strength.

2 Hear my prayer, O God; give ear to the words of my mouth.

3 For strangers are risen up against me, and oppressors seek after my soul: they have not set God before them. Selah.

1. "*Save me, O God.*" Thou art my Saviour; all around me are my foes and their eager helpers. No shelter is permitted me. Every land rejects me and denies me rest. But thou, O God, wilt give me refuge, and deliver me from all my enemies. "*By thy name,*" by thy great and glorious nature. Employ all thine attributes for me. Let every one of the perfections which are blended in thy divine name work for me. Is not thine honour pledged for my defence? "*And judge me by thy strength.*" Render justice to me, for none else will or can. Thou canst give me efficient justice, and right my wrongs by thine omnipotence. We dare not appeal to God in a bad cause, but when we know that we can fearlessly carry our cause before his justice we may well commit it to his power.

2. "*Hear my prayer, O God.*" This has ever been the defence of saints. As long as God hath an open ear we cannot be shut up in trouble. All other weapons may be useless, but all-prayer is evermore available. No enemy can spike this gun. "*Give ear to the words of my mouth.*" Vocal prayer helps the supplicant, and we keep our minds more fully awake when we can use our tongues as well as our hearts. But what is prayer if God hear not? It is all one whether we babble nonsense or plead arguments if our God grant us not a hearing. When his case had become dangerous, David could not afford to pray out of mere custom, he must succeed in his pleadings, or become the prey of his adversary.

3. "*For strangers are risen up against me.*" Those who had no cause for ill-will had gone against him; persons to whom he could have given no offence, for they were strangers to him. They were aliens to his God also, and should these be allowed to worry and destroy him. A child may well complain to his father when strangers come in to molest him? What right have they to interfere? Let them leave off meddling and mind their own concerns. "*And oppressors seek after my soul.*" Saul, that persecuting tyrant, had stamped his own image on many more. Kings generally coin their own likeness. He led the way, and others followed seeking David's soul, his blood, his life, his very existence. Cruel and intense were they in their malice, they would utterly crush the good man; no half measures

would content them. "*They have not set God before them.*" They had no more regard for right and justice than if they knew no God, or cared for none. Had they regarded God they would not have betrayed the innocent to be hunted down like a poor harmless stag. David felt that atheism lay at the bottom of the enmity which pursued him. Good men are hated for God's sake, and this is a good plea for them to urge in prayer. "*Selah.*" As if he said, "Enough of this, let us pause." He is out of breath with indignation. A sense of wrong bids him suspend the music awhile. It may also be observed, that more pauses would, as a rule, improve our devotions : we are usually too much in a hurry : a little more holy meditation would make our words more suitable and our emotions more fervent.

4 Behold, God *is* mine helper : the Lord *is* with them that uphold my soul.

5 He shall reward evil unto mine enemies : cut them off in thy truth.

6 I will freely sacrifice unto thee : I will praise thy name, O LORD ; for *it is* good.

7 For he hath delivered me out of all trouble : and mine eye hath seen *his desire* upon mine enemies.

4. "*Behold, God is mine helper.*" He saw enemies everywhere, and now to his joy as he looks upon the band of his defenders he sees one whose aid is better than all the help of men ; he is overwhelmed with joy at recognising his divine champion, and cries, "*Behold.*" And is not this a theme for pious exultation in all time, that the great God protects us, his own people : what matters the number or violence of our foes when HE uplifts the shield of his omnipotence to guard us, and the sword of his power to aid us ? Little care we for the defiance of the foe while we have the defence of God. "*The Lord is with them that uphold my soul.*" The reigning Lord, the great Adonai is in the camp of my defenders. Here was a greater champion than any of the three mighties, or than all the valiant men who chose David for their captain. The Psalmist was very confident, he felt so thoroughly that his heart was on the Lord's side that he was sure God was on *his* side. He asked in the first verse for deliverance, and here he returns thanks for upholding : while we are seeking one mercy which we have not, we must not be unmindful of another which we have. It is a great mercy to have some friends left us, but a greater mercy still to see the Lord among them, for like so many cyphers our friends stand for nothing till the Lord sets himself as a great unit in the front of them.

5. "*He shall reward evil unto mine enemies.*" They worked for evil, and they shall have their wages. It cannot be that malice should go unavenged. It were cruelty to the good to be lenient to their persecutors. It is appointed, and so it must ever be, that those who shoot upward the arrows of malice shall find them fall upon themselves. The recoil of their own gun has often killed oppressors. "*Cut them off in thy truth.*" Not in ferocious revenge is this spoken, but as an Amen to the sure sentence of the just Judge. Let the veracity of thy threatenings be placed beyond dispute, the decree is right and just, let it be fulfilled. It is not a private desire, but the solemn utterance of a military man, a grossly injured man, a public leader destined to be a monarch, and a man well trained in the school of Moses, whose law ordains eye for eye, and tooth for tooth.

6. "*I will freely sacrifice unto thee.*" Spontaneously will I bring my free-will offerings. So certain is he of deliverance that he offers a vow by anticipation. His overflowing gratitude would load the altars of God with victims cheerfully presented. The more we receive, the more we ought to render. The spontaneousness of our gift is a great element in their acceptance ; the Lord loveth a cheerful giver. "*I will praise thy name, O Lord.*" As if no amount of sacrifice could express his joyful feelings, he resolves to be much in vocal thanksgiving. The name which he invoked in prayer (verse 1), he will now magnify in praise. Note how roundly he brings it out : "*O Jehovah.*" This is ever the grand name of the revealed God of Israel, a name which awakens the sublimest sentiments, and so nourishes the most acceptable praise. None can praise the Lord so well as those who have tried and proved the preciousness of his name in seasons of adversity. The Psalmist adds, "*for it is good,*" and surely we may read this with a double nominative, God's name is good, and so is his praise. It is of great use to our souls to be much in praise ;

we are never so holy or so happy as when our adoration of God abounds. Praise is good in itself, good to us, and good to all around us. If David's enemies are described in the third verse as not setting God before them, he here declares that he is of a different mind from them, for he resolves to have the Lord in perpetual remembrance in his sacrifices and praises.

7. " *For he hath delivered me out of all trouble.*" Up to that time deliverance had come, and for that danger also he felt that rescue was near. David lived a life of dangers and hair-breadth 'scapes, yet was he always safe. In the retrospect of his very many deliverances he feels that he must praise God, and looking upon the mercy which he had sought as though it were already received, he sang this song over it—

> " And a new song is in my mouth,
> To long loved music set,
> *Glory to thee for all the grace*
> *I have not tasted yet.*"

Out of all trouble our covenant God is pledged to bring us, and therefore even now let us uplift the note of triumph unto Jehovah, the faithful preserver of them that put their trust in him. Thus far we have proved his promise good ; he changes not, and therefore in all the unknown future he will be equally our guardian and defence, " showing himself strong in the behalf of them whose heart is perfect toward him." " *And mine eyes hath seen his desire upon mine enemies.*" He knew that yet he should look on his haughty foes, gazing down on them in triumph as now they looked on him in contempt. He desired this as a matter of justice, and not of personal pique. His righteous soul exulted because he knew that unprovoked and gratuitous malice would meet with a righteous punishment. Could we keep out of our hearts all personal enmity as fully as the Psalmist did in this Psalm, we might yet equally feel with him a sacred acquiescence and delight in that divine justice which will save the righteous and overthrow the malicious.

In closing, let us trust that if we are are friendless as this man of God, we may resort to prayer as he did, exercise the like faith, and find ourselves ere long singing the same joyous hymn of praise.

EXPLANATORY NOTES AND QUAINT SAYINGS.

Title.—From the inscription, learn, 1. Particular straits and particular deliveries should be particularly remarked : as David here remembereth the danger he wa in by the treachery of the *Ziphims.* 2. Mighty men will find readily more friends in an evil cause, than the godly do find in a good cause : as Saul has the Ziphims to offer their service to his cruelty, when David was in straits. 3. The wicked are very hearty to do an ill turn, and glad to find occasion of it. " *Doth not David,*" say they, " *hide himself with us ?* " as if this had been good and blessed news.— *David Dickson* (1583—1662), *in " A Brief Explication upon the Psalms."*

Whole Psalm.—The church has taken a clear view in appointing this as one of the Psalms in commemoration of the passion of Jesus. It is seen with greatest effect as a simple prophecy of Christ. Read thus, it is very plain and intelligible ; requiring little more than the first idea to exhibit a perfect correspondence with the life and feelings of the Messiah.—*William Hill Tucker, in " The Psalms . . . . with Notes,"* 1840.

Whole Psalm.—In the first three verses, David being sought for by his enemies, prays against them. That was his course, he always began his conflict with God, contending and wrestling with him for a blessing and assistance. He durst not lift up his hand even against the enemies of God (yet what durst not David do ?) till he had first lifted them up in humble supplication to the Lord his strength, " Who taught his hands to war, and his fingers to fight." Psalm cxliv. 1. This being done, his courage breaks out like lightning, he doubts not of slaying his thousands and ten thousands. So in the fourth and fifth verses, he becomes his own prophet, promising himself victory. For who can resist him who hath omnipotence for his second ? Or how can any enemy maintain a fight against that captain who hath beforehand defeated and broken their forces by his prayers ? assured his conquest before he put on his armour ? Then in the last verses, David concludes where he began, thankfully acknowledgeth God's goodness in his deliverance, and the dissipation of his enemies, obliging himself to a return of dutiful, affectionate service, in consideration of so great mercies recived.—*J. Dolben, in a Thanksgiving Sermon*, 1665.

Whole Psalm.—Blessed Redeemer! give me grace to eye thee, and to call to my recollection thine exercises amidst the false friends and open foes, which in the days of thy flesh surrounded thee. Lord! help me so to consider thee, who didst endure such a contradiction of sinners against thyself, that I may not be weary and faint in mind. And while the Ziphims of the present hour harass and distress me, and would deliver my soul up into the hand of the enemy: oh! for grace to be looking unto thee, and deriving strength from thee, that I may discover thy gracious hand delivering me out of all my troubles, and making me more than conqueror in thy strength, and in the power of thy might.—*Robert Hawker, D.D.*, 1753—1827.

Verse 1.—" *Save me, O God!* " As David was at this time placed beyond the reach of human assistance, he must be understood as praying to be saved by the *name and the power of God*, in an emphatical sense, or by these in contradistinction to the usual means of deliverance. Though all help must ultimately come from God, there are ordinary methods by which he generally extends it. When these fail, and every earthly stay is removed, he must then take the work into his own hands. It was in such a situation that David here fled to the saints' last asylum, and sought to be saved by a miracle of divine power.—*John Calvin.*

Verse 1.—" *Judge me by thy strength*," or power, *i.e.*, determine, decide my cause by thy mighty power. Saul, in the cause between him and David, was resolved to end it by force only, and to arbitrate in no other way than by a javelin, a sword, or his forces. The Psalmist well knew that Saul, in this respect, would be too hard for him; and therefore applies for protection and justice to one whose power he knew was infinitely superior to his adversaries, and who, he was assured, could and would defend him.—*Samuel Chandler* (1693—1766), *in "A Critical History of the Life of David."*

Verse 2 (second clause).—Let " *the words of my mouth* " with which I have defended my cause, be pleasing and acceptable to thee. For in this way can *prayers* and *words of the mouth* be correctly distinguished, unless any one should wish simply to understand by them *prayers uttered by the mouth* ; but, as I have said, the phrase is more emphatic.—*Hermann Venema*, 1697—1787.

Verse 3.—" *Strangers* : " aliens to his truth, men who from unbelief have estranged themselves from all lot and portion in his covenant—oppress and persecute.—*William Hill Tucker.*

Verse 3 (first clause).—The Chaldee interpreter reads, *proud men*, instead of " *strangers*," a reading which also is found in eight of Kennicott's Codices. So also Psalm lxxxvi. 14.—*William Walford, in " The Book of Psalms. A New Translation,"* etc., 1837.

Verse 3 (first clause).—There is a great mistake made by rendering the word זרים (*zarim*) " *strangers*." The Ziphites surely were Israelites, and not strangers. The fact is this, that word is taken from זרה (*zarah*) the primary meaning of which is " to scatter," " to disperse," also " to sift," as grain. Hence it signifies, likewise figuratively, to sift a matter, to investigate, to search out, to trace out. So here David complains of the new and dangerous enemies he had got in the Ziphites, who became Saul's spies. When he pleads, therefore, for deliverance, saying, " Save me, O God," etc., he describes the danger he was in : " *For spies have risen against me.*"—*Benjamin Weiss, in " New Translation, Exposition and Chronological Arrangement of the Psalms,"* 1858.

Verse 3.—" *Oppressors seek after my soul* ; " *i.e.*, my life at least ; my soul also they would destroy, if it lay in their power, as the Papists delivered up John Huss to the devil.—*John Trapp*, 1611—1662.

Verse 3.—" *Selah.*" See " Treasury of David," Vol. I., pp. 23, 26, 27 ; and Vol. II., pp. 224—227.

Verse 4.—" *Behold*," says he, I produce a certain fact, well-known, demonstrated by a new proof, and worthy of all attention ; for the particle *behold*, contains this breadth of meaning.—*Hermann Venema.*

Verse 4.—Christ sees with the utmost clearness, that God will be his *own* "*helper*," and of them—the disciples and believers—"*that uphold his soul.*" In the same moment, does he foresee the destruction of his enemies. He views, in thought, the armies of Titus, the fall of the Jewish nation, and the dispersion of the remnant. He beholds the avenging hand of God, stretched in fury over the destroyers.—*William Hill Tucker.*

Verse 4 (second clause).—Such as take part with the persecuted saints, God will take part with them : "*The Lord is with them that uphold my soul.*"—*David Dickson.*

Verses 4, 5.—He is assured of help to himself and to his friends, and of vengeance to his enemies. Whence learn, 1. Fervent prayer hath readily a swift answer, and sometimes wonderfully swift, even before a man have ended speech, as here David findeth in experience. "*Behold,*" saith he, "*God is my helper.*" 2. The sight of faith is very clear, and piercing through all clouds, when God holds forth the light of his Spirit unto it, it can demonstrate God present in an instant ; ready to help in greatest straits : "*Behold, God is my helper.*" 3. There is more joy in God's felt presence than grief in felt trouble ; for, "*Behold, God is mine helper,*" was more comfortable to David than his friends' unkindness, and strangers' malice was grievous.—*David Dickson.*

Verse 5.—"*Cut them off.*" He desires that God would destroy them with a *death-dealing blow*, which is the force the word צמת contains ; its primitive sense is *to be silent, to keep silence*, whence it is transferred to a stroke penetrating deeply and striking fatally, such as is called a *silent* blow, opposed to a *sounding* one, which is wont to rebound and not pierce deeply.—*Hermann Venema.*

Verse 6.—"*I will freely sacrifice unto thee.*" He would *sacrifice freely :* by which he does not allude to the circumstance, that sacrifices of thanksgiving were at the option of worshippers, but to the alacrity and cheerfulness with which he would pay his vow when he had escaped his present dangers.—*John Calvin.*

Verse 7.—"*Mine eye hath seen his desire upon mine enemies.*" Or, *mine eye hath looked upon mine enemies ;* that is, he was able to meet them without terror.—*Samuel Davidson, D.D.,* 1852.

Verse 7.—The reader will note that the words *his desire* are supplied by our translators, and are not in the original text.—*C. H. S.*

HINTS TO PREACHERS.

Verse 1.—In the deliverance of the saints the honour and power of God are concerned. I. Their failure would dishonour both. II. Their salvation glorifies both. III. Both are immutable, therefore we have a sure plea at all times.

Verse 2.—Our main concern in prayer. I. What is meant by God's hearing prayer. II. How we may know that he has done so. III. What is to be done when this is doubtful. IV. What is due to him when the hearing is given.

Verse 3.—Strange trials. I. They are not altogether strange. 1. Not so to God. 2. Not so in the history of the church. 3. Not so to the provisions of grace wherein they are anticipated. II. Wherein they are strange. 1. They reveal God anew. 2. Endear forgotten promises. 3. Train unused graces. 4. Bring new praises, etc.

Verse 3 (last clause).—The root of sin : if they remembered his authority they dared not, if they tasted his love they would not, if they were conformed to his nature they could not.

Verse 4.—A theme for wonder. 1. At his unmerited grace, that he should side with *me.* 2. At his gracious power, for who can resist him ? 3. At his practical help, for he has upheld my soul.

Verse 6.—We should sacrifice voluntarily, liberally, joyfully, continuously, with pure motive.

Verse 6.—The goodness of praising the good name.

Verse 7 (first clause).—The exclamation of the newly-pardoned penitent, the cry of the delivered saint, the song of the ripe Christian, the shout of the glorified believer.

PSALM LV.

TITLE.—To the Chief Musician on Neginoth.—*Another song to be accompanied by stringed instruments. The strain is at one time mournful, and at another softly sweet. It needed the chief musician's best care to see that the music was expressive of the sentiment.* Maschil. *It is not a mere personal hymn, there is teaching in it for us all, and where our Lord shines through David, his personal type, there is a great deep of meaning.* Of David. *The man of many conditions, much tried and much favoured, persecuted but delivered and exalted, was from experience enabled to write such precious verses in which he sets forth not only the sorrows of common pilgrims, but of the Lord of the way himself.*

SUBJECT.—*It would be idle to fix a time, and find an occasion for this Psalm with any dogmatism. It reads like a song of the time of Absalom and Ahithophel. It was after David had enjoyed peaceful worship (verse 14), when he was or had just been a dweller in a city (verses 9, 10, 11), and when he remembered his former roamings in the wilderness. Altogether it seems to us to relate to that mournful era when the King was betrayed by his trusted counsellor. The spiritual eye ever and anon sees the Son of David and Judas, and the chief priests appearing and disappearing upon the glowing canvas of the Psalm.*

DIVISIONS.—*From verses 1 to 8 the suppliant spreads his case in general before his God; in verses 9, 10, 11, he portrays his enemies; in verses 12—14, he mentions one special traitor, and cries for vengeance, or foretells it in verse 15. From verses 16 to 19 he consoles himself by prayer and faith; in verses 20 and 21 he again mentions the deceitful covenant-breaker, and closes with a cheering exhortation to the saints (verse 22), and a denunciation of destruction upon the wicked and deceitful (verse 23).*

EXPOSITION.

GIVE ear to my prayer, O God; and hide not thyself from my supplication.

2 Attend unto me, and hear me: I mourn in my complaint, and make a noise;

3 Because of the voice of the enemy, because of the oppression of the wicked: for they cast iniquity upon me, and in wrath they hate me.

4 My heart is sore pained within me: and the terrors of death are fallen upon me.

5 Fearfulness and trembling are come upon me, and horror hath overwhelmed me.

6 And I said, Oh that I had wings like a dove! *for then* would I fly away, and be at rest.

7 Lo, *then* would I wander far off, *and* remain in the wilderness. Selah.

8 I would hasten my escape from the windy storm *and* tempest.

1. "*Give ear to my prayer, O God.*" The fact is so commonly before us, otherwise we should be surprised to observe how universally and constantly the saints resort to prayer in seasons of distress. From the Great Elder Brother down to the very least of the divine family, all of them delight in prayer. They run as naturally to the mercy-seat in time of trouble as the little chickens to the hen in the hour of danger. But note well that it is never the bare act of prayer which satisfies the godly, they crave an audience with heaven, and an answer from the throne, and nothing less will content them. "*Hide not thyself from my supplication.*" Do not stop thine ear, or restrain thy hand. When a man saw his neighbour in distress, and deliberately passed him by, he was said to hide himself from him; and the Psalmist begs that the Lord would not so treat him. In that dread hour when Jesus bore our sins upon the tree, his Father did hide himself, and this was the

most dreadful part of all the Son of David's agony. Well may each of us deprecate such a calamity as that God should refuse to hear our cries.

2. " *Attend unto me, and hear me.*" This is the third time he prays the same prayer. He is in earnest, in deep and bitter earnest. If his God do not hear, he feels that all is over with him. He begs for his God to be a listener and an answerer. " *I mourn in my complaint, and make a noise.*" He gives a loose to his sorrows, permits his mind to rehearse her griefs, and to pour them out in such language as suggests itself at the time, whether it be coherent or not. What a comfort that we may be thus familiar with our God ! We may not complain *of* him, but we may complain *to* him. Our rambling thoughts when we are distracted with grief we may bring before him, and that too in utterances rather to be called " *a noise* " than language. He will attend so carefully that he will understand us, and he will often fulfil desires which we ourselves could not have expressed in intelligible words. " Groanings that cannot be uttered," are often prayers which cannot be refused. Our Lord himself used strong cryings and tears, and was heard in that he feared.

3. " *Because of the voice of the enemy.*" The enemy was vocal and voluble enough, and found a voice where his godly victim had nothing better than a " noise." Slander is seldom short of expression, it prates and prattles evermore. Neither David, nor our Lord, nor any of the saints were allowed to escape the attacks of venomous tongues, and this evil was in every case the cause of acute anguish. " *Because of the oppression of the wicked :* " the unjust pressed and oppressed the righteous ; like an intolerable burden they crushed them down, and brought them to their knees before the Lord. This is a thrice-told story, and to the end of time it will be true ; he that is born after the flesh will persecute him that is born after the Spirit. The great seed of the woman suffered from a bruised heel. " *For they cast iniquity upon me,*" they black me with their sootbags, throw the dust of their lying over me, cast the vitriol of their calumny over me. They endeavour to trip me up, and if I do not fall they say I do. " *And in wrath they hate me.*" With a hearty ill will they detested the holy man. It was no sleeping animosity, but a mortal rancour which reigned in their bosoms. The reader needs not that we show how applicable this is to our Lord.

4. " *My heart is sore pained within me.*" His spirit writhed in agony, like a poor worm ; he was mentally as much in pain as a woman in travail physically. His inmost soul was touched ; and a wounded spirit who can bear ? If this were written when David was attacked by his own favourite son, and ignominiously driven from his capital, he had reason enough for using these expressions. " *And the terrors of death are fallen upon me.*" Mortal fears seized him, he felt like one suddenly surrounded with the glooms of the shadow of death, upon whom the eternal night suddenly descends. Within and without he was afflicted, and his chief terror seemed to come from above, for he uses the expression, " Fallen upon me." He gave himself up for lost. He felt that he was as good as dead. The inmost centre of his nature was moved with dismay. Think of our Lord in the garden, with his " soul exceeding sorrowful even unto death," and you have a parallel to the griefs of the Psalmist. Perchance, dear reader, if as yet thou hast not trodden this gloomy way, thou wilt do soon ; then be sure to mark the footprints of thy Lord in this miry part of the road.

5. " *Fearfulness and trembling are come upon me.*" Like housebreakers these robbers were entering his soul. Like one who feels a fainting fit coming over him, so the oppressed suppliant was falling into a state of terror. His fear was so great as to make him tremble. He did not know what would happen next, or how soon the worst would come. The sly, mysterious whisperings of slander often cause a noble mind more fear than open antagonism ; we can be brave against an open foe, but cowardly, plotting conspiracies bewilder and distract us. " *And horror hath overwhelmed me.*" He was as one enveloped in a darkness that might be felt. As Jonah went down into the sea, so did David appear to go down into deeps of horror. He was unmanned, confounded, brought into a hideous state of suspense and mortal apprehension.

6. " *And I said, Oh that I had wings like a dove ! for then would I fly away, and be at rest.*" If he could not resist as an eagle, he would escape as a dove. Swiftly and unobserved, on strong, untiring pinions would he hie away from the abodes of slander and wickedness. His love of peace made him sigh for an escape from the scene of strife.

> "O for a lodge in some vast wilderness,
> Some boundless contiguity of shade,
> Where rumour of oppression and deceit
> Might never reach me more."

We are all too apt to utter this vain desire, for vain it is; no wings of doves or eagles could bear us away from the sorrows of a trembling heart. Inward grief knows nothing of place. Moreover, it is cowardly to shun the battle which God would have us fight. We had better face the danger, for we have no armour for our backs. He had need of a swifter conveyance than doves' pinions who would outfly slander; he may be at rest who does not fly, but commends his case to his God. Even the dove of old found no rest till she returned to her ark, and we amid all our sorrow may find rest in Jesus. We need not depart; all will be well if we trust in him.

7. "*Lo, then would I wander far off.*" Yet when David was far off, he sighed to be once more near Jerusalem; thus, in our ill estate we ever think the past to be better than the present. We shall be called to fly far enough away, and perchance we shall be loth to go; we need not indulge vain notions of premature escape from earth. "*And remain in the wilderness.*" He found it none such a dear abode when there, yet resolves now to make it his permanent abode. Had he been condemned to receive his wish he would ere long have felt like Selkirk, in the poet's verse—

> "O solitude, where are the charms
> That sages have found in thy face?
> Better dwell in the midst of alarms
> Than reign in this horrible place."

Our Lord, while free from all idle wishes, found much strength in solitude, and loved the mountain's brow at midnight, and the quiet shade of the olives of Gethsemane. It is better practically to use retirement than pathetically to sigh for it. Yet it is natural, when all men do us wrong, to wish to separate ourselves from their society; nature, however, must yield to grace, and we must endure the contradiction of sinners against ourselves, and not be weary and faint in our minds. "*Selah.*" After such a flight well may the mind rest. When we are going too fast, and giving way too freely to regrets, it is well to cry, "halt," and pause awhile till more sober thoughts return.

8. "*I would hasten my escape.*" He tried to pause but could not, like a horse which when pulled up slips on a little because of the speed at which he was going. David declares that he would not waste a moment, or stay to bid adieu to his friends, but up and away at once, for fear he should be too late, and because he could bear the clamour of his foes no longer. "*From the windy storm and tempest.*" A storm was brewing, and, like a dove, he would outfly it and reach a calmer region. Swifter than the storm-cloud would he fly, to avoid the deluge of rain, and the flash of the lightning. Alas! poor soul, no such wings are thine, as yet thou must tarry here and feel the tempest; but be of good cheer, thou shalt stretch thy wings ere long for a bolder flight, heaven shall receive thee, and there thy sorrows shall have a finis of felicity among the birds of paradise.

9 Destroy, O Lord, *and* divide their tongues: for I have seen violence and strife in the city.

10 Day and night they go about it upon the walls thereof: mischief also and sorrow *are* in the midst of it.

11 Wickedness *is* in the midst thereof: deceit and guile depart not from her streets.

9. "*Destroy, O Lord.*" Put mine enemies to the rout. Let them be devoured by the sword, since they have unsheathed it against me. How could we expect the exiled monarch to offer any other prayer than this against the rebellious bands of Absalom, and the crafty devices of Ahithophel? "*Divide their tongues.*" Make another Babel in their debates and councils of war. Set them at cross purposes. Divide the pack that the hunted one may escape. The divisions of error are the hope of truth. "*For I have seen violence and strife in the city.*" The rabble and their leaders were plotting and planning, raging and contending against their king, running wild with a thousand mad projects: anarchy had fermented among them,

and the king hoped that now it might come to pass that the very lawlessness which had exiled him would create weakness among his foes. Revolution devours its own children. They who are strong through violence, will sooner or later find that their strength is their death. Absalom and Ahithophel may raise the mob, but they cannot so easily rule it, nor so readily settle their own policy as to remain firm friends. The prayer of David was heard, the rebels were soon divided in their councils; Ahithophel went his way to be hanged with a rope, and Absalom to be hanged without one.

10. *" Day and night they go about it upon the walls thereof."* The city, the holy city had become a den of wickedness: conspirators met in the dark and talked in little knots in the streets even in broad daylight. Meanwhile the country was being roused to revolt, and the traitors without threatened to environ the city, and act in concert with the rebels within. No doubt there was a smothered fire of insurrection which Absalom kindled and fanned, which David perceived with alarm some time before he left Jerusalem; and when he quitted the city it broke out into an open flame. *" Mischief also and sorrow are in the midst of it."* Unhappy capital to be thus beset by foes, left by her monarch, and filled with all those elements of turbulence which breed evil and trouble. Unhappy king to be thus compelled to see the mischief which he could not avert laying waste the city which he loved so well. There was another King whose many tears watered the rebellious city, and who said, " O Jerusalem, Jerusalem, how often would I have gathered thy children together, even as a hen gathereth her chickens under her wings, and ye would not!"

11. *" Wickedness is in the midst thereof."* The very heart of the city was base. In her places of authority crime went hand in hand with calamity. All the wilder and more wicked elements were uppermost; the *canaille* were commanders; the scum floated uppermost; justice was at a discount; the population was utterly demoralised; prosperity had vanished and order with it. *" Deceit and guile depart not from her streets."* In all the places of concourse crafty tongues were busy persuading the people with cozening phrases. Crafty demagogues led the people by the nose. Their good king was defamed in all ways, and when they saw *him* go away, they fell to reviling the governors of their own choosing. The forum was the fortress of fraud, the congress was the convention of cunning. Alas, poor Jerusalem, to be thus the victim of sin and shame! Virtue reviled and vice regnant! Her solemn assemblies broken up, her priests fled, her king banished, and troops of reckless villains parading her streets, sunning themselves on her walls, and vomiting their blasphemies in her sacred shrines. Here was cause enough for the sorrow which so plaintively utters itself in these verses.

12 For *it was* not an enemy *that* reproached me; then I could have borne *it*: neither *was it* he that hated me *that* did magnify *himself* against me; then I would have hid myself from him:

13 But *it was* thou, a man mine equal, my guide, and mine acquaintance.

14 We took sweet counsel together, *and* walked unto the house of God in company.

12. The reader will do well to observe how accurately the Psalmist described his own Psalm when he said, " I mourn in my complaint," or rather " give loose to my thoughts," for he proceeds from one point of his sorrow to another, wandering on like one in a maze, making few pauses, and giving no distinct intimations that he is changing the subject. Now from the turbulent city his mind turns to the falsehearted councillor. *" For it was not an enemy that reproached me; then I could have borne it."* It was not an open foe, but a pretended friend; he went over to the other camp and tried to prove the reality of his treachery by calumniating his old friend. None are such real enemies as false friends. Reproaches from those who have been intimate with us, and trusted by us, cut us to the quick; and they are usually so well acquainted with our peculiar weaknesses that they know how to touch us where we are most sensitive, and to speak so as to do us most damage. The slanders of an avowed antagonist are seldom so mean and dastardly as those of a traitor, and the absence of the elements of ingratitude and treachery renders them less hard to bear. We can bear from Shimei what we cannot endure from Ahithophel. *" Neither was it he that hated me that did magnify himself against me;*

then I would have hid myself from him." We can find a hiding-place from open foes, but who can escape from treachery ? If our enemies proudly boast over us we nerve our souls for resistance, but when those who pretended to love us leer at us with contempt, whither shall we go ? Our blessed Lord had to endure at its worst the deceit and faithlessness of a favoured disciple ; let us not marvel when we are called to tread the road which is marked by his pierced feet.

13. *" But it was thou."* He sees him. The poetic fury is on him, he sees the traitor as though he stood before him in flesh and blood. He singles him out, he points his finger at him, he challenges him to his face. *" But thou."* *Et tu, Brute?* And thou, Ahithophel, art thou here ? Judas, betrayest *thou* the Son of Man ? *" A man mine equal."* Treated by me as one of my own rank, never looked upon as an inferior, but as a trusted friend. *" My guide,"* a counsellor so sage that I trusted thine advice and found it prudent to do so. *"And mine acquaintance,"* with whom I was on most intimate terms, who knew me even as I knew him by mutual disclosures of heart. No stranger occasionally conversed with, but a near and dear friend admitted to my secret fellowship. It was fiendish treason for such a one to prove falsehearted. There was no excuse for such villainy. Judas stood very much in this relation to our Lord, he was treated as an equal, trusted as treasurer, and in that capacity often consulted with. He knew the place where the Master was wont to spend his solitude, in fact, he knew all the Master's movements, and yet he betrayed him to his remorseless adversaries. How justly might the Lord have pointed at him and said, *" But thou ; "* but his gentler spirit warned the son of perdition in the mildest manner, and had not Iscariot been tenfold a child of hell he would have relinquished his detestable purpose.

14. *" We took sweet counsel together."* It was not merely the counsel which men take together in public or upon common themes, their fellowship had been tender and confidential. The traitor had been treated lovingly and trusted much. Solace, mutual and cheering, had grown out of their intimate communings. There were secrets between them of no common kind. Soul had been in converse with soul, at least on David's part. However feigned might have been the affection of the treacherous one, the betrayed friend had not dealt with him coldly, or guarded his utterance before him. Shame on the wretch who could belie such fellowship and betray such confidence ! *" And walked unto the house of God in company."* Religion had rendered their intercourse sacred, they had mingled their worship, and communed on heavenly themes. If ever any bonds ought to be held inviolable, religious connection should be. There is a measure of impiety, of a detestable sort, in the deceit which debases the union of men who make professions of godliness. Shall the very altar of God be defiled with hypocrisy ? Shall the gatherings of the temple be polluted by the presence of treachery ? All this was true of Ahithophel, and in a measure of Judas. His union with the Lord was on the score of faith, they were joined in the holiest of enterprises, he had been sent on the most gracious of errands. His co-operation with Jesus to serve his own abominable ends stamped him as the firstborn of hell. Better had it been for him had he never been born. Let all deceitful professors be warned by his doom, for like Ahithophel he went to his own place by his own hand, and retains a horrible pre-eminence in the calendar of notorious crime. Here was one source of heart-break for the Redeemer, and it is shared in by his followers. Of the serpent's brood some vipers still remain, who will sting the hand that cherished them, and sell for silver those who raised them to the position which rendered it possible for them to be so abominably treacherous.

15 Let death seize upon them, *and* let them go down quick into hell : for wickedness *is* in their dwellings, *and* among them.

15. Not thus would Jesus pray, but the rough soldier David so poured out the anguish of his spirit, under treachery and malice seldom equalled and altogether unprovoked. The soldier, as such, desires the overthrow of his foes, for this very end he fights ; and viewed as a matter of law and justice, David was right in his wish ; he was waging a just, defensive war against men utterly regardless of truth and justice. Read the words as a warrior's imprecation. *" Let death seize upon them."* Traitors such as these deserve to die, there is no living with them, earth is polluted by their tread ; if spies are shot, much more these sneaking villains. *" Let them go down quick into hell."* While in the vigour of life into *sheol* let them sink, let them suddenly exchange the enjoyment of the quick or living for the sepulchres

of the dead. There is, however, no need to read this verse as an imprecation, it is rather a confident expectation or prophecy : God would, he was sure, desolate them, and cast them out of the land of the living into the regions of the dead. "*For wickedness is in their dwellings, and among them.*" They are too bad to be spared, for their houses are dens of infamy, and their hearts fountains of mischief. They are a pest to the commonwealth, a moral plague, a spiritual pestilence, to be stamped out by the laws of men and the providence of God. Both Ahithophel and Judas soon ended their own lives ; Absalom was hanged in the oak, and the rebels perished in the wood in great numbers. There is justice in the universe, love itself demands it ; pity to rebels against God, as such, is no virtue—we pray for them as creatures, we abhor them as enemies of God. We need in these days far more to guard against the disguised iniquity which sympathises with evil, and counts punishment to be cruelty, than against the harshness of a former age. We have steered so far from Scylla that Charybdis is absorbing us.

16 As for me, I will call upon God ; and the LORD shall save me.

17 Evening, and morning, and at noon, will I pray, and cry aloud : and he shall hear my voice.

18 He hath delivered my soul in peace from the battle *that was* against me : for there were many with me.

19 God shall hear, and afflict them, even he that abideth of old. Selah. Because they have no changes, therefore they fear not God.

16. "*As for me, I will call upon God.*" The Psalmist would not endeavour to meet the plots of his adversaries by counterplots, nor imitate their incessant violence, but in direct opposition to their godless behaviour would continually resort to his God. Thus Jesus did, and it has been the wisdom of all believers to do the same. As this exemplifies the contrast of their character, so it will foretell the contrast of their end—the righteous shall ascend to their God, the wicked shall sink to ruin. "*And the Lord shall save me.*" Jehovah will fulfil my desire, and glorify himself in my deliverance. The Psalmist is quite sure. He knows that he will pray, and is equally clear that he will be heard. The covenant name is the pledge of the covenant promise.

17. "*Evening, and morning, and at noon, will I pray.*" Often, but none too often. Seasons of great need call for frequent seasons of devotion. The three periods chosen are most fitting ; to begin, continue, and end the day with God is supreme wisdom. Where time has naturally set up a boundary, there let us set up an altar-stone. The Psalmist means that he will always pray ; he will run a line of prayer right along the day and track the sun with his petitions. Day and night he saw his enemies busy (verse 10), and therefore he would meet their activity by continuous prayer. "*And cry aloud.*" He would give a tongue to his complaint ; he would be very earnest in his pleas with heaven. Some cry aloud who never say a word. It is the bell of the heart that rings loudest in heaven. Some read it, "I will muse and murmur ; " deep heart-thoughts should be attended with inarticulate but vehement utterances of grief. Blessed be God, moaning is translatable in heaven. A father's heart reads a child's heart. "*And he shall hear my voice.*" He is confident that he will prevail ; he makes no question that he would be heard, he speaks as if already he were answered. When our window is opened towards heaven, the windows of heaven are open to us. Have but a pleading heart and God will have a plenteous hand.

18. "*He hath delivered my soul in peace from the battle that was against me.*" The deliverance has come. Joab has routed the rebels. The Lord has justified the cause of his anointed. Faith sees as well as foresees ; to her foresight is sight. He is not only safe but serene, "*delivered in peace* "—peace in his inmost soul. "*For there were many with me ;*" many contending against me. Or it may be that he thankfully acknowledges that the Lord raised him up unexpected allies, fetched him succour when he most needed it, and made the friendless monarch once more the head of a great army. The Lord can soon change our condition, and he often does so when our prayers become fervent. The crisis of life is usually the secret place of wrestling. Jabbok makes Jacob a prevailing prince. He who stripped us of all friends to make us see himself in their absence, can give them back again in greater numbers that we may see him more joyfully in the fact of their presence.

19. " *God shall hear, and afflict them.*" They make a noise as well as I, and God will hear them. The voice of slander, malice, and pride, is not alone heard by those whom it grieves, it reaches to heaven, it penetrates the divine ear, it demands vengeance, and shall have it. God hears and delivers his people, he hears and destroys the wicked. Their cruel jests, their base falsehoods, their cowardly insults, their daring blasphemies are heard, and shall be repaid to them by the eternal Judge. " *Even he that abideth of old.*" He sits in eternity, enthroned judge for evermore ; all the prayers of saints and profanities of sinners are before his judgment-seat, and he will see that justice is done. " *Selah.*" The singer pauses, overwhelmed with awe in the presence of the everlasting God. " *Because they have no changes, therefore they fear not God.*" His own reverential feeling causes him to remember the daring godlessness of the wicked ; he feels that his trials have driven him to his God, and he declares that their uninterrupted prosperity was the cause of their living in such neglect of the Most High. It is a very manifest fact that long-continued ease and pleasure are sure to produce the worst influences upon graceless men : though troubles do not convert them, yet the absence of them makes their corrupt nature more readily develop itself. Stagnant water becomes putrid. Summer heat breeds noxious insects. He who is without trouble is often without God. It is a forcible proof of human depravity that man turns the mercy of God into nutriment for sin : the Lord save us from this.

20 He hath put forth his hands against such as be at peace with him : he hath broken his covenant.

21 *The words* of his mouth were smoother than butter, but war *was* in his heart : his words were softer than oil, yet *were* they drawn swords.

20. The Psalmist cannot forget the traitor's conduct, and returns again to consider it. " *He hath put forth his hands against such as be at peace with him.*" He smites those to whom he had given the hand of friendship, he breaks the bonds of alliance, he is perfidious to those who dwell at ease because of his friendly professions. " *He hath broken his covenant.*" The most solemn league he has profaned, he is regardless of oaths and promises.

21. " *The words of his mouth were smoother than butter.*" He lauded and larded the man he hoped to devour. He buttered him with flattery and then battered him with malice. Beware of a man who has too much honey on his tongue ; a trap is to be suspected where the bait is so tempting. Soft, smooth, oily words are most plentiful where truth and sincerity are most scarce. " *But war was in his heart.*" He brought forth butter in a lordly dish, but he had a tent-pin ready for the temples of his guest. When heart and lip so widely differ, the man is a monster, and those whom he assails are afflicted indeed. " *His words were softer than oil.*" Nothing could be more unctuous and fluent, there were no objectionable syllables, no jars or discords, his words were as yielding as the best juice of the olive ; " *yet were they drawn swords,*" rapiers unsheathed, weapons brandished for the fray. Ah ! base wretch, to be cajoling your victim while intending to devour him ! entrapping him as if he were but a beast of prey ; surely, such art thou thyself !

22. Cast thy burden upon the Lord, and he shall sustain thee : he shall never suffer the righteous to be moved.

22. " *Thy burden,*" or what thy God lays upon thee, lay thou it " *upon the Lord.*" His wisdom casts it on thee, it is thy wisdom to cast it on him. He cast thy lot for thee, cast thy lot on him. He gives thee thy portion of suffering, accept it with cheerful resignation, and then take it back to him by thine assured confidence. " *He shall sustain thee.*" Thy bread shall be given thee, thy waters shall be sure. Abundant nourishment shall fit thee to bear all thy labours and trials. As thy days so shall thy strength be. " *He shall never suffer the righteous to be moved.*" He may move like the boughs of a tree in the tempest, but he shall never be moved like a tree torn up by the roots. He stands firm who stands in God. Many would destroy the saints, but God has not suffered it, and never will. Like pillars, the godly stand immovable, to the glory of the Great Architect.

23 But thou, O God, shalt bring them down into the pit of destruction ; bloody and deceitful men shall not live out half their days : but I will trust in thee.

23. For the ungodly a sure, terrible, and fatal overthrow is appointed. Climb as they may, *the pit* yawns for them, God himself will cause them to descend into it, and *destruction* there shall be their portion. *"Bloody and deceitful men,"* with double iniquity of cruelty and craft upon them, *" shall not live out half their days ; "* they shall be cut off in their quarrels, or being disappointed in their artifices, vexation shall end them. They were in heart murderers of others, and they became in reality self-murderers. Doubt not that virtue lengthens life, and that vice tends to shorten it. *" But I will trust in thee."* A very wise, practical conclusion. We can have no better ground of confidence. The Lord is all, and more than all that faith can need as the foundation of peaceful dependence. Lord, increase our faith evermore.

EXPLANATORY NOTES AND QUAINT SAYINGS.

Title.—Maschil. This is often prefixed to those Psalms in which David speaks of himself as being chastened by God, inasmuch as the end of chastisement is instruction.—*Simon de Muis,* 1587—1644.

Whole Psalm.—A prayer of the Man Christ in his humiliation, despised and rejected of men, when he was made sin for his people, that they might be made the righteousness of God in him, when he was about to suffer their punishment, pay their debt, and discharge their ransom.

Utter depravity of the inhabitants of Jerusalem ; betrayment of Messiah by one of the twelve whom he had ordained to the apostolical office, and who was Messiah's constant attendant in all his ministerial circuits.

Premature and punitive death of the traitor Judas, and of others banded together to crucify the Lord of glory.—*John Noble Coleman, M.A., in " A Revision of the authorised English Versions of the Book of Psalms,"* 1863.

Verse 1.—In the first clause he uses the word אתפלל, that he might indicate that he merely sought justice from God as a Judge ; but in the second he implores the *favour of God,* that if perchance the prayer for *justice* be less becoming to himself as a sinner, God may not deny his grace.—*Hermann Venema.*

Verse 1.—*" Hide not thyself from my supplication."* A figure taken from the conduct of a king who debars an offender from seeing his face (2 Sam. xiv. 24), or from an enemy, who conceals himself from the ox, etc. ; that is, pretends not to see it, and goes away, leaving it (see Deut. xxii. 1, 3, 4 ; and Isa. lviii. 7) ; or, from a false friend, or an unkind person, who, foreseeing that he may be entreated by a miserable and needy man, will not let himself be seen, but seeks to make escape.—*Martin Geier,* 1614—1681.

Verse 2.—*" I mourn."* As one cast down with sorrow, making a doleful noise.—*Henry Ainsworth,* 1622.

Verse 2.—*" I mourn,"* etc. A mourning suppliant shall neither lose his prayers nor his tears ; for, *" I mourn,"* is brought for a reason of his hope that God shall attend and hear him.—*David Dickson.*

Verse 2.—*" I mourn in my complaint."* The literal translation of these words is, *I will suffer to wander in my thinking ; i.e.,* I will let my mind wander, or my thoughts rove as they will.—*J. A. Alexander.*

Verse 2.—*" In my complaint."* Saints have their complaints on account of their sins and corruptions, their barrenness and unfruitfulness, and the decay of vital religion in them, and because of the low estate of Zion, the declining state of the interest of Christ, and the little success of his gospel; and they mourn, in these complaints, over their own sins, and the sins of others, professors and profane, and under afflictions temporal and spiritual, both their own and the church's. Christ also in the days of his flesh, had his complaints of the perverseness and faithlessness of the generation of men among whom he lived ; of the frowardness, pride, and contentions, of his disciples ; of the reproaches, insult, and injuries of his enemies ; and of the dereliction of his God and Father; and he often mourned on account of one or other of these things, being a man of sorrows and acquainted with griefs.—*John Gill.*

Verse 2.—" *In my complaint.*" The word here employed commonly means discourse, meditation. It here occurs in the sense of *complaint*, as in Job vii. 13 ; ix. 27 ; xxi. 4 ; xxiii. 2 ; Ps. cxlii. 2 ; 1 Sam. i. 16. It is not used, however, to denote complaint in the sense of fault-finding, complaining, accusing, or the idea that we have been dealt with unjustly. This is not the meaning in this place or in the Scriptures generally. It is the language of a *troubled*, not of an *injured* spirit.—*Albert Barnes*, 1868.

Verse 2.—In confession, when the soul melts into a holy shame and sorrow for the sins he spreads before the Lord, he feels a holy smart and pain within, and doth not act a tragical part with a comical heart. Chrysostom saith, " To paint tears is worse than to paint the face." Here is true fervency, " *I mourn in my complaint and make a noise.*" There may be fire in the pan when there is none in the piece ; a loud wind but no rain with it. David made a noise with his voice, and mourned in his spirit.—*William Gurnall*, 1617—1679.

Verse 3.—" *Because of the voice of the enemy,*" there is their railing ; " *because of the oppression of the wicked,*" there is their violent robbing him of his estate ; " *they cast iniquity upon me,*" there are their slanderous traducings of him, and charging him with faults falsely ; " *in wrath they hate me,*" there is their cruel seeking to kill.—*David Dickson.*

Verse 3.—" *For they cast iniquity upon me.*" They tumble it on me, as men do stones or anything else upon their besiegers, to endamage them ; so did these sin, shame, anything, upon innocent David, to make him odious.—*John Trapp.*

Verse 4.—" *Is sore pained,*" or, *trembleth with pain.* The word usually meaneth such *pains as a woman feeleth in her travail.*—*Henry Ainsworth.*

Verse 4.—" *The terrors of death are fallen upon me.*" " *My heart,*" said the afflicted Psalmist, " *is sore pained within me ;* " and though I am repeatedly assured of my interest in the divine love and favour, yet now " *the terrors of death are fallen upon me.*" The case of David is so far from being peculiar to himself, that it portrays in the most striking colours, a state of mind to which many of the most exemplary Christians are frequently, if not constantly, subject. Many, whose hopes are placed on the right foundation, even Christ Jesus, and whose conduct is uniform and consistent, are yet harassed almost continually by the tormenting fears of death. . . . It will be an interesting and useful enquiry to examine into the real causes of a fear, which cultivates melancholy and despondency on the one hand and destroys our happiness on the other. To effect this design I shall consider, I. The various causes of the fear of death. II. The arguments calculated to remove it. There are few, indeed, so hardened in the slavery of vice, or so utterly regardless of every admonition, as to consider the awful period of dissolution without some emotions of terror and dismay. There is something so peculiarly awful in the idea of a change hitherto unknown, and of a state hitherto untried, that the most hardy veterans have owned its tremendous aspects. . . . One of the first causes of the fear of death is *conscious guilt.* The most hardened are conscious of many things which they may not readily confess ; and the most self-righteous is conscious of many crimes which he artfully studies to conceal. Whilst the Christian is looking only to his own habits and temper, he may and will be always wretched ; but if he looks to the great Surety, Christ Jesus, his gloomy prospect will soon be turned to joy. An *attachment to this world* is also a (second) cause of the fear of death. A principle of self-preservation is also a (third) cause of the fear of death. That our bodies, which are pampered by pride and nourished by indulgence, should be consigned to the silent grave, and become even the food of worms, is a humbling reflection to the boasted dignity of man. Besides, nature revolts at the idea of its own dissolution ; hence a desire of preserving life, evidently implanted in us. The devil is also (fourthly) often permitted to terrify the consciences of men, and thereby increase at least the fear of death. Unbelief is also a (fifth) cause of the fear of death. Were our faith more frequently in exercise, we should be enabled to look beyond the dreary mansions of the grave with a hope full of immortality. Our fears of death may be often caused by looking for that perfection in ourselves, which we shall never easily discover. II. Consider the arguments calculated to remove the fear of death. It may be necessary to premise that the consolations of religion belong only to real Christians ; for the wicked have just reason to dread the approach of death. But to such as are humbled under a sense of their own unworthiness, and who have fled to Christ for pardon and salvation, they have no cause to apprehend either the pain or the consequences of death; because first, the sting of death is taken away. Secondly, because death is no longer an enemy but a friend. Instead of threatening us with misery, it invites us to happiness. Thirdly, the safety of our state is founded on the oath, the purpose, and promise of God. A fourth argument calculated to remove the fear of death, is the consideration of the benefits resulting from it. The benefits which believers receive from Christ at the resurrection also, is a fifth argument calculated to remove the fear of death.—*Condensed from a Sermon by John Grove, M.A., F.A.S., 1802.*

Verses 4, 5.—In the version of the Psalter used in the Prayer-book, this verse stands with a more homely and expressive simplicity, " My heart is disquieted within me, and the fear of death is fallen upon me. Fearfulness and trembling are come upon me, and an horrible dread hath overwhelmed me." The fear of death is upon all flesh. It is no sign of manhood to be without it. To overcome it in the way of duty is courage ; to meet death with patience is faith ; but not to fear it is either a gift of special grace, or a dangerous insensibility. No doubt great saints have been able to say, " I have a desire to depart." And many have rushed to martyrdom, as to the love and bosom of their Lord ; but for the rest, the multitude of his flock, who are neither wilful sinners, nor to be numbered among the saints, the thought of death is a thought of fear. We see that, on the first feeling of their having so much as set foot in the path leading to the grave, even good men feel the " terror of death," " a horrible dread," which makes every pulse to beat with a hurried and vehement speed. Their whole nature, both in body and in soul, trembles to its very centre ; and their heart is " disquieted," " sore pained," within them. . . . .

Let us see what are the causes or reasons of this " fear of death." The fact must needs be a consciousness of personal sinfulness. A sense of unfitness to meet God, our unreadiness to die, a multitude of personal faults, evil tempers, thoughts, and inclinations ; the recollection of innumerable sins, of great omissions and lukewarmness in all religious duties, the little love or gratitude we have to God, and the great imperfection of our repentance ; all these make us tremble at the thought of going to give up our account. We feel as if it were impossible we could be saved. Shame, fear, and a " horrible dread " fall upon us.—*Henry Edward Manning, M.A., 1850.*

Verse 5.—" *Fearfulness and trembling are come upon me.*" In this pitiful condition of mind, learn, that it is not a thing inconsistent with godliness to be much moved with fear in time of danger ; natural affections are not taken away in conversion, but sanctified and moderated.—*Daniel Dickson.*

Verse 5.—" *Fearfulness.*" How natural is this description ! He is *in distress*, he *mourns, makes a noise, sobs* and *sighs*, his *heart is wounded*, he expects nothing but *death* ; this produces *fear*, this produces *tremor*, which terminates in that *deep apprehension* of *approaching* and *inevitable ruin* that *overwhelms* him with *horror*. No man ever described a wounded heart like David.—*Adam Clarke.*

Verse 6.—" *And I said, Oh that I had wings like a dove ! for then would I fly away, and be at rest.*" Wherever the Psalmist cast his eye, the inscription was vanity and vexation. A deluge of sin and misery covered the world, so that like Noah's dove he could find no rest for the sole of his foot below, therefore does he direct his course toward heaven, and say, " *Oh that I had wings like a dove ! for then would I fly away and be at rest ;* " but rest is not a denizen of this world, nothing but the heaven of heavens is at rest, and here does he fix only.—*Thomas Sharp (1630—1693), in " Divine Comforts."*

Verse 6.—" *Oh that I had wings like a dove ! for then would I fly away, and be at rest.*" King David, though for innocency not only a *dove*, but the phœnix of doves, and so a notable type of Christ, upon whom the Holy Ghost descended in the shape of a dove, yet was his whole life nothing else but *bellum sine induciis*, a perpetual persecution without intermission. Such was also the portion of Christ the Lord of David ; and such to the world's end will ever be the lot of those that are the heritage of Christ. My text imports no less ; which, taken *historically*, is the voice of David pursued by his enemies ; *prophetically*, the voice of Christ at his passion ; *mystically*, the voice of that mystical dove, the innocent soul, surrounded and environed with the snares of death ; even *generalis quædam querela* (saith Pellican), a general complaint of the malice of the wicked persecuting the righteous. For (alas that it should be ! yet so it is)—

> " *Non rete accipitri tenditur, neque milvio,*
> *Qui malè faciunt, nobis ; illis qui nil faciunt, tenditur.*"*

" The net is not pitched for ravenous birds, as are the hawk and the kite ; but for poor harmless birds, that never meditate mischief.' And

> " *Dat veniam corvis, vexat, censura columbas.*"

" The dove shall surely be shot at, when the carrion-crow shall go shot-free."†

It will then be no news unto you, that here the faithful soul, the spouse, the dove of Christ, when trouble and heaviness take hold upon her, and the floods of Belial compass her about *Tanquam avis e cave liberari cupit* (as St. Austin speaks of the cloistered monks in his time), " Desireth like a bird to be loosed out of her cage." Or, that as Jonas (by interpretation *a dove*), after three days' and three nights' imprisonment in the whale's belly, could not but long after his enlargement. So the dove-like soul of man, when not three, but many days, and months, and years, she hath been imprisoned in the body, hath a longing desire to be enlarged, and to fly unto God that made her ; and so *mourning* like a dove in devout *supplication* and *mounting* like a dove in divine *speculation*, breaks forth into these sad elegies : " Oh that I had wings ! " and " Alas, that I have not wings ! Woe is me that I am constrained to dwell with Mesech, and to have mine habitation among the tents of Kedar. Like as the hart desires the water-brook, so longeth my soul to be with thee, O God. I desire to be dissolved and to be with Christ. Who will give me wings ? " etc. Which is as if the poor distressed soul, pathetically bemoaning her forlorn estate of pilgrimage, should thus more plentifully enlarge herself. " My spouse is already ascended higher than the winds, than the clouds, than the highest heavens, and I, poor soul, as a husbandless widow, as a tutorless orphan, as a comfortless exile, am left desolate and disconsolate in this valley of tears ; none to care for me, none to comfort me, till I have regained him whom I love, and in whom I live. Nay (which worse is), this mine own familiar friend, this nearest and dearest companion of mine, *my body*, is even a burden unto me. The weight of it, and oft the sins that hang so fast on it, doth so clog and shackle me, so glue and nail me to the earth, that I cannot raise or rear up myself towards heaven. Or let him therefore descend to relieve me, being *filia, sponsa, soror*, his daughter, and spouse, and sister ; or let him give me wings wherewith I may ascend to him, under the shadow of whose wings I shall surely rest in safety." Ps. xci. 4.

" I must confess it was the very bitterness of extremity that first compelled me to love him, though of himself no less lovely than love itself. It was the sharp sauce of affliction that gave edge to mine affections, and sharpened mine appetite to that ' sweet meat that endureth to everlasting life.' But now, having had some little foretaste of him, I am even in an holy ecstacy, so ravished, so transported with a fervent desire of him and of his presence, that *ubi sum, ibi non sum ; ubi non sum, ibi animus est :* " where I am, there I am not ; and where I am not, there am I." For, *anima est ubi amat, non ubi animat :*‡ " The soul is where it loveth, not where it liveth." Now sigh I not so much for the present dangers I would decline, as because of my absent love, whom I most desire. " *Who will give me wings ? * " etc.

In the scanning of which verse, ye will observe with me,

I. The *efficient* or *author* of these wings—God. " Who will give me ? " Who ? that is, who but *God ?*

II. The *matter* of the wish—" *wings.*" " Who will give me wings ? "

III. The *form* of those wings—*dove-like.* " Who will give me wings like unto a dove ? "

IV. The *end mediate*—*flying.* " Then would I fly away."

V. The *end ultimate*—*resting.* " And be at rest."

I. " Who will give me ? " There's *Christian humility.* II. " Who will give

---

* Terence.   † Juvenal.   ‡ Erasmus.

me wings?" There's *prudent celerity.* III. "Wings like unto a dove." There's *innocent simplicity.* IV. "Then would I fly away." There's *devout sublimity.* V. "And be at rest." There's *permanent security.—John Rawlinson, in "The Dove-like Sovle. A Sermon preached before the Prince's Highnes at Whitehall,"* Feb. 19, 1618.

Verse 6.—"Oh that I had wings," etc. Some of the most astounding sermons ever delivered have been preached on this text, which was a very favourite one with the old divines. They ransacked Pliny and Aldrovandus for the most outrageous fables about doves, their eyes, their livers, their crops, and even their dung, and then went on to find emblems of Christians in every fact and fable. Griffith Williams, at considerable length, enlarges upon the fact that David did not desire wings like a grasshopper to hop from flower to flower, as those hasty souls who leap in religion but do not run with perseverance; nor like an ostrich which keeps to the earth, though it be a bird, as hypocrites do who never mount towards heavenly things; nor like an eagle, or a peacock, or a beetle, or a crow, or a kite, or a bat; and after he has shown in many ways the similarity between the godly and doves, he refers us to Hugo Cardinalis, and others, for more. We do not think it would be to edification to load these pages with such eccentricities and conceits. This one single sentence from Bishop Patrick is worth them all, "He rather wished than hoped to escape." He saw no way of escape except by some improbable or impossible means.—*C. H. S.*

Verse 6.—When the Gauls had tasted the wine of Italy, they asked where the grapes grew, and would never be quiet till they came there. Thus may you cry, "*Oh that I had wings like a dove! for then would I fly away, and be at rest.*" A believer is willing to lose the world for the enjoyment of grace; and he is willing to leave the world for the fruition of glory.—*William Secker.*

Verse 6.—"Wings like a dove." The pigeon, or dove, is one of the swiftest of birds.—*The Religious Tract Society's "Book of Psalms, with Preface and Explanatory Notes."*

Verse 6.—An old writer tells us it would have been more honourable for him to have asked for the strength of an ox to bear his trials, than for the wings of a dove to flee from them.—*William Jay,* 1769—1853.

Verse 6.—"Dove." The reference is to the turtle-dove, I suppose. Their low, sad plaint may be heard all day long at certain seasons in the olive-groves, and in the solitary and shady valleys among these mountains; I have, however, been more affected by it in the vast orchards round Damascus than anywhere else— so subdued, so very sorrowful among the trees, where the air sighs softly, and little rills roll their melting murmurs down the flowery aisles. These birds can never be tamed. Confined in a cage they droop, and like Cowper, sigh for

"A lodge in some vast wilderness—some boundless contiguity of shade;"

and no sooner are they set at liberty than they flee, as a bird, to their mountain Ps. xi. 1. David refers to their habits in this respect when his heart was sore pained within him: "*Oh that I had wings like a dove! for then would I fly away, and be at rest. Lo, then would I wander far off, and remain in the wilderness.*" And there you will meet these timid birds far away from the haunts of cruel hunters, of whose society they are peculiarly suspicious.—*W. M. Thomson, in "The Land and the Book,"* 1859.

Verse 6.—"Oh that I had wings," etc.—

> At first her mother-earth she holdeth deare,
> And doth embrace the world and worldly things;
> She flies close by the ground, and hovers here,
> And mounts not up with her celestiall wings.
>
> Yet under heaven she cannot light on ought
> That with her heavenly nature doth agree;
> She cannot rest, she cannot fix her thought,
> She cannot in this world contented be:
>
> * * * * * *
>
> Then as a bee which among weeds doth fall,
> Which seeme sweet flowers, with lustre fresh and gay;
> She lights on that, and this, and tasteth all,
> But pleas'd with none, doth rise and soare away,

So when the Soule finds here no true content ;
And, like Noah's dove, can no sure footing take,
She doth returne from whence she first was sent,
And flies to him that first her wings did make.

Sir John Davies, 1569—1626.

Verse 7.—" *Lo, then would I wander far off,*" etc. A passage in the " Octavia " of Seneca has been referred to as being parallel to this of David. It is in the answer of Octavia to the Chorus, act v., ver. 914—923.

My woes who enough can bewail ?
O what notes can my sorrows express ?
Sweet Philomel's self e'en would fail
To respond with her plaintive distress.
O had I her wings, I would fly
To where sorrows I ne'er should feel more,
Upborne on her plumes through the sky,
Regions far from mankind would explore.
In a grove where sad silence should reign,
On a spray would I seat me alone ;
In shrill lamentations complain,
And in wailings would pour forth my moan.

J. B. Clarke [From Adam Clarke, in loc.]

Verse 8.—" *I would hasten my escape from the windy storm and tempest.*" There was a windy storm and tempest without, and which is worse, a tumult and combustion within in his thoughts. A man may escape from external confusions, but how shall he fly from himself ? If he be out of the reach of all the blood-suckers on earth, and all the furies in hell, yet be dogged and haunted with his own turbulent, ungovernable cogitations, he needs no other tormentors. This holy man was thus doubly distressed, a storm abroad and an earthquake at home rendered his condition most dolorous ; but for both he hath εν μεγα ; he goes not about with the foxes of this world to relieve himself with subtle stratagems and wiles, by carnal shifts and policies, a vanity tossed to and fro by them that seek death. No, his one great refuge is to get aloft, to ascend to God.—*Thomas Sharp.*

Verse 9.—" *Destroy, Lord, and divide their tongues.*" In the first place, their tongues were truly destroyed and they themselves divided, when the testimony of the two false witnesses agreed not so together. Then, secondly, by the contradictory account of the soldiers that kept watch at the sepulchre.—*Michael Ayguan (1416), in J. M. Neale's Commentary, 1860.*

Verse 9.—" *Divide their tongues :* " *i.e.,* cause them to give conflicting opinions.— *French and Skinner, 1842.*

Verse 10.—" *Mischief also and sorrow are in the midst of it.*" The city, as Abenezra observes, was like a circle ; violence and strife were as a line round about it, and mischief and sorrow the centre of it ; and these two commonly go together : where mischief is, sorrow follows.—*John Gill.*

Verse 12.—" *Then I could have borne it.*" It is remarkable that the Lord, who endured the other unspeakable sorrows and agonies of his passion in perfect and marvellous silence, allowed his grief at this one alone to escape him, bewailing himself to his disciples that one of them should betray him, and addressing that one, when he was taken, in these words of reproach—" Judas, betrayest thou the Son of Man with a kiss ? "—*Fra Thomé de Jesu, 1582.*

Verse 12.—" *Then I would have hid myself from him.*" It is generally easy to get out of the way of an avowed enemy, but how can one be on his guard against a treacherous friend ?—*A. R. Fausset, in " A Commentary, Critical, Experimental, and Practical," 1866.*

Verse 13.—" *A man mine equal.*" The LXX here not badly, ισόψυχε (of equal soul), Jerome, *unanimus mens* (of one mind).—*Hermann Venema.*

Verse 14.—" *We took sweet counsel.*" From מתק, *to be sweet,* and the ordinary notion of סוד for *secret,* the phrase נמתיק סוד will literally be read, *we made our secret sweet.* And so it may be an elegance, to signify the pleasure of his friendship, or of communicating secrets to him.—*Henry Hammond.*

Verse 14.—The first clause speaks of private intimacy, the next of association in public acts, and especially in the great festivals and processions of the temple.—*J. J. Stewart Perowne,* 1864.

Verse 14.—" *In company.*" In the end of the verse בְּרָגֶשׁ may be rendered *with a noise :* and so the Chaldee seems to have taken it, which reads *with haste ;* and to that agree the Jewish doctors, who tell us men are to go in *haste* and with *speed* to the *synagogue,* but return thence very *leisurely.*—*Henry Hammond.*

Verse 15.—" *Let death seize upon them, and let them go down quick into hell.*" The last part and end of sinners' lives is worst with them. They have in their lives been busily trading in the world, buying and selling, and getting gain and ruffling it in the world, but meanwhile by their sins they run deep in debt with God, and for want of interest in Christ to be their surety at death (it may be on the sudden) it comes to that of the Psalmist, " *Let death seize upon them, and let them go down quick into hell.*" Death seizeth on them unawares, as a sergeant or pursevant, casts them into prison, which is expressed by their going down quick into hell (as it is said, Num. xvi. 32, 33), that Korah and his company did.—*Anthony Tuckney,* 1599—1670.

Verse 15.—" *Let death seize upon them*" by divine warrant, and let them go quick into hell ; let them be dead and buried, and damned in a moment ; for wickedness is wherever they are, it is in the midst of them. The souls of impenitent sinners go down quick, or alive, into hell ; for they have a perfect sense of their miseries, and shall therefore live still, that they may be still miserable. This prayer is a prophecy of the utter, the final, the everlasting ruin of all those who, whether secretly or openly, oppose and rebel against the Lord's Messiah.—*Matthew Henry.*

Verse 15.—" *Quick,*" that is, *alive,* like Korah, Dathan and Abiram.—*From* " *The Psalms chronologically arranged. By Four Friends,*" 1867.

Verse 15.—Throughout this series of Psalms, there appears to be a peculiar penalty attached to each class of transgressions, or, each variety of opposition against God meets a suitable end. The ungodly, that is, the irreligious and indifferent lay up for themselves an evil recompence when the wrath of God shall be revealed (Psalm liv. 5) : but an instant punishment falls upon false and treacherous professors ; as Paul denounced " anathema " against any who perverted the gospel of Christ in the churches of Galatia ; so in this Psalm, " *Let death seize upon them, and let them go down quick into hell,*" announces the awful judgment of Jehovah, as once it was shown upon Dathan and Abiram ; a punishment that will by its suddenness and notoriety at the same time expose the guilt, and make manifest the displeasure of the Almighty against it.—*R. H. Ryland, in* " *The Psalms restored to Messiah,*" 1853.

Verse 17.—" *Evening, and morning, and at noon, will I pray.*" This was the custom of the pious Hebrews. See Dan. vi. 10. The Hebrews began their day in the *evening,* and hence David mentions the *evening first.* The rabbins say, men should pray three times each day, because the day changes three times. This was observed in the primitive church ; but the times in different places were various. The old Psalter gives this a curious turn: "At *even* I sall tel his louing (*praise*) what tim Crist was on the Crosse ; and at *morn* I sall schew his louing, what tim he ros fra dede. And sua he sall here my voice at *midday,* that is sitand at the right hand of his fader, wheder he stegh (ascended) at midday."—*Adam Clarke.*

Verse 17.—" *Evening and morning,*" etc. The three principal parts of the day are mentioned, not as marking special times set apart for prayer, but as a poetical expression for " the whole day," " at all times," " without ceasing."—*J. J. Stewart Perowne.*

Verse 17.—If our poor, frail bodies need refreshment from food three times a day, who, that knows his own weakness, will say that we need not as frequent refreshment for our poor frail spirits ?—*William S. Plumer,* 1867.

Verse 17.—I can no more believe him to be frequent and spiritual in ejaculatory prayer, who neglects the season of solemn prayer, than I can believe that he keeps every day in the week a Sabbath, who neglects to keep that one which God hath appointed.—*William Gurnall,* 1617—1679.

Verse 17.—There is no limited time in the court of heaven for hearing petitions.

It is not like the court of earthly princes, for there is a free access any day of the week, any hour of the day, or the night, any minute of the hour. As the lawyer saith of the king, for having his due, *Nullum tempus occurrit regi :* so may I say of the godly, for making his prayers and granting his requests, *Nullum tempus occurrit fidelibus*, no time unseasonable, so the heart be seasoned with faith ; no *non term* in God's court of requests. He keeps continually open house for all comers and goers ; and indeed, most for comers, then goers. His eyes are always ‹ pen to behold our tears ; his ears are always open to hear our groans ; his heart also and his bowels are always open, and never shut up so fast, but they will yearn and turn within him, if our misery be never so little. For as we have not an High Priest to pray by " that cannot be touched with the feeling of our infirmities ; " so neither have we a God to pray to, that shall see us in distress, and hear us call and cry, and never be moved.—*Zachary Bogan* (1625—1659), *in " Meditations of the Mirth of a Christian Life."*

Verse 17.—*" And cry aloud."* The word here employed properly means to murmur ; to make a humming sound ; to sigh ; to growl ; to groan. Here the language means that he would give utterance to his deep feelings in appropriate tones—whether words, sighs, or groans.—*Albert Barnes.*

Verse 17.—*" And he shall hear."* And what will this loud cry obtain ? A hearing without doubt, so he assures himself, *" He shall hear me."* Not that God hears any prayers whether he will or no (as men sometimes do that upon importunity which they have no mind to) ; but he hath no will, no mind not to hear such prayers, the prayers of those who cry aloud to him.—*Joseph Caryl*, 1602—1673.

Verse 18.—*" He hath delivered my soul in peace from the battle."* In the midst of war the Lord can keep a man as safe as in the time of peace, and in extreme perils preserve him from danger. He that depends upon God in the time of trouble, albeit he had an host against him, yet hath he more with him when God is with him, than can be against him.—*David Dickson.*

Verse 18.—*" For."* The *" for "* implies the reason why God interposed to deliver him ; namely, because of the general principle that God ministers relief when his people are come to an extremity.—*A. R. Fausset.*

Verse 18.—*" There were many with me."* This is doubtful whether it be meant of *foes* or *friends*. If of *foes*, it may be resolved thus : *for with many* (with a great multitude) *they were fighters with me*. If of *friends*, it may be understood of God's *angels*, that *in a great number were with him*, pitching camp for his aid (Psalm xxxiv. 7) ; as Elisha said, " Many more are with us than with them." 2 Kings vi. 16, 17. The Chaldee explaineth it, " For in many afflictions his word was for my help."—*Henry Ainsworth.*

Verse 19.—*" Even he that abideth of old."* The deeds by which God had already showed himself from of old as the righteous King and Judge, the judgments, for example, upon the wicked in the land of Shinar (ver. 9), the company of Korah (ver. 9 and 18), the cities of the plain (ver. 15), pledge his still ready interposition. He who had already so long held the throne, must now also show himself as King and Judge ; he cannot now, at so late a period, be another.—*E. W. Hengstenberg*, 1845.

Verse 19.—*" Because they have no changes, therefore they fear not God."* That is, there is no new thing among them, no extraordinary providential turns, no judiciary changes, their prosperity keeps a settled course, and because they find all things going on in the old course of providence, therefore they go on in their old course of sinfulness, *" they fear not God ; "* intimating, that as such *changes* always should, so usually they do, awaken fear ; and that, if the Lord would but change, and toss, and tumble them about, by various troublesome dispensations, surely they would fear him.—*Joseph Caryl.*

Verse 19.—*" Because they have no changes,"* etc. Or, *" with whom also there be no changes, yet they fear not God."* If *changes* be referred to their temporal estates and welfare, as Job x. 17 (it is the same word there as here, חֲלִיפָה), " changes and war are against me ; " then, according to the first translation, *" because,"* etc., a reason is given of their perseverance in wickedness, and contempt of God ; to wit, their constant and uninterrupted world prosperity. Or, according to the second, *" With whom there are no changes, yet,"* etc. ; it is a great aggravation of their impenitency, that notwithstanding so much goodness vouchsafed unto them, they should continue so unthankful as to requite so ill, or so stupid and insensible as not to acknowledge the author. But if changes be referred, as by many, to the soul, then the meaning is—that through long use and continuance of sinning, they are, through God's just judgment, become altogether obdurate and inflexible; and therefore, no wonder if nothing work upon them to their conversion. " Can the Ethiopian change his skin ? " etc. Jer. xiii. 23. But this " changes " might also have another meaning. The Grecians used to say, στρέπται φρένες ἐσθλῶν, that the minds or hearts of good men are changeable; their meaning is, that good men are merciful. Quos quisque est major, magis est placabilis ira: et faciles motus mens generosa capit, as the Latin proverb expresses it. He may therefore say, that they show by their cruel unmercifulness, that they have no fear or sense of God at all; else they would fear him, of whose mercy themselves stood in so much need, and consider that they whom they so fiercely persecute are his creatures as well as they.—Westminster Assembly's Annotations.

Verse 19.—" They have no changes," etc. Who are they who have no changes ? Apparently those whom God is said to humble or chastise. And what is the meaning of the word " changes " as here used ? Many understand it of a moral change; " who are without change of heart or reformation." But the word never occurs in this sense. It means, properly, " a change," in the sense of succession; as of garments, of troops relieving guard, servants leaving work, and the like. Hence it would rather mean in a moral sense: " They who have no cessation in their course (by being relieved guard, for instance), who always continue, and persevere in their evil life." Calvin and others understand it of change of fortune, i.e., " who are always prosperous; " but this again is not supported by usage.—J. J. Stewart Perowne.

Verse 19.—" They fear not God." The fear required here, is to fear him as God, and as God presented in this name, Elohim; which, though it be a name primarily rooted in power and strength (for El is Deus fortis, The powerful God; and as there is no love without fear, so there is no fear without power), yet properly it signifies his judgment, and order, and providence, and dispensations and government of his creatures. It is that name which goes through all God's whole work of the creation, and disposition of all creatures in the first of Genesis: in all that he is called by no other name than this, the name God; not by Jehovah, to present an infinite majesty; nor by Adonai, to present an absolute power; nor by Tzebaoth, to present a force, or conquest: but only the name of God, his name of government. All ends in this; to fear God is to adhere to him, in his way, as he hath dispensed and notified himself to us; that is, as God is manifested in Christ, in the Scriptures, and applied to us out of those Scriptures, by the church: not to rest in nature without God, nor in God without Christ.—John Donne, 1573— 1631.

Verse 21.—" The words of his mouth were smoother than butter," etc. Of this complexion are the cant of hypocrites, the charity of bigots and fanatics, the benevolence of atheists, the professions of the world, the allurements of the flesh, and the temptations of Satan, when he thinks proper to appear in the character of an angel of light.—George Horne, 1730—1792.

Verse 21.—" Butter." The Eastern butter is by no means like the solid substance, which is known by that name in these colder climates; but is liquid and flowing, as appears from different passages in Scripture, particularly Job xxix. 6; xx. 17; and as is confirmed by the accounts of modern travellers; so that in fact it more resembles " cream," which Vitringa says is the genuine sense of the word here used.—Richard Mant, 1776—1849.

Verse 21.—To avoid all difficulties, the readiest expedient is to receive the Septuagint rendering of חָלְקוּ, διεμερίσθησαν, they were, or are divided, viz., the members of the wicked man there spoken of, they are at great distance one from the other; מַחְמָאֹת פִּיו, butter their mouth, or, their mouth is butter, וּקְרָב־לִבּוֹ and war their heart, or, their heart is war; and this seems to be the fairest rendering of it.—Henry Hammond, 1605—1660.

Verse 21.—A feigned friend is much like a crocodile who, when he smileth, poisoneth; and when he weepeth, devoureth; or the hyæna, having the voice of a man and the mind of a wolf, speaking like a friend and devouring like a fiend; or the flattering sirens that sweetly sing the sailor's wreck; or the fowler's pipe that pleasantly playeth the bird's death; or the bee, who carrieth honey in her mouth and a sting in her tail; or the box-tree, whose leaves are always green, but the seeds poison. So his countenance is friendly and his words pleasant, but his intent dangerous, and his deeds unwholesome.

> His fetch is to flatter, to catch what he can ;
> His purpose obtained, a fig for his man.

L. Wright, 1616.

Verse 21.—" *The words of his mouth were smoother than butter, but war was in his heart : his words were softer than oil, yet were they drawn swords.*" Well, when I came to the justice again, there was Mr. Foster, of Bedford, who coming out of another room, and seeing me by the light of the candle, for it was dark night when I came thither, he said unto me, " Who is there ? John Bunyan ? " with much seeming affection, as if he would have leaped in my neck and kissed me,* which made me somewhat wonder that such a man as he, with whom I had so little acquaintance, and, besides, that had ever been a close opposer of the ways of God, should carry himself so full of love to me, but afterwards when I saw what he did, it caused me to remember those sayings, " *Their tongues were softer than oil, yet were they drawn swords,*" and again, " Beware of men," etc. When I had answered him that, blessed be God, I was well, he said, " What is the occasion of your being here ? " or to that purpose. To whom I answered that I was at a meeting of people a little way off, intending to speak a word of exhortation to them ; but the justice hearing thereof (said I) was pleased to send his warrant to fetch me before him, etc.—*John Bunyan. In relation to J. B.'s imprisonment : written by himself. Offor's edit., Vol. I. p.* 52.

Verse 21 *(first clause).*—

> Smooth are his words, his voice as honey sweet,
> Yet war is in his heart, and dark deceit.

Mosschus (B.C. 250).

Verse 22.—" *Cast thy burden upon the Lord,*" etc. The remedy which the Psalm suggests, and, perhaps, the only resource in a difficulty of the kind, where the enemies of true religion are fighting under the semblance of friendship, is announced in an oracular voice from God : " Cast thy care upon Jehovah, for he will sustain thee ; he will not suffer the just one to be tossed about for ever."—*R. H. Ryland.*

Verse 22.—" *Cast thy burden upon the Lord,*" etc. The best way to ease thyself is to lay thy load upon God ; he will take it up and also carry thee. There is many a man would be willing to go of himself, if another would but carry his burden for him ; but if thou throwest thy burden upon God he will not only carry that, but will also carry thee. He cares not how much weight a Christian layeth on his back ; a true Israelite may ease himself, and best please his God at once. God delights not to see tears in thine eyes, or paleness in thy countenance ; thy groans and sighs make no music in his ears. He had rather that thou wouldst free thyself of thy burden by casting it upon him, that he might rejoice in thy joy and comfort. Now, true confidence in God, and resting upon God, will both free thee of thy burden and also bring in the strength of God to sustain and bear thee up from falling. Wouldst thou, therefore, own God as thy strength, and fetch strength from God to thy soul ? rest upon God, roll thyself upon him, and that, (1) In time of greatest weakness. (2) In time of greatest service. (3) In times of greatest trials.—*Samuel Blackerby,* 1674.

Verse 22.—" *Cast thy burden* " on him in the same way that the ship in a storm casts her burden on the anchor, which anchor holds on to its sure fixing place. And to my mind, that is the more beautiful sense of the two—a sense which once entered into, may be followed out in these glorious verses :—

> And I see the good ship riding, all in a perilous road ;
> The low reef booming on her lee ; the swell of ocean poured
> Sea after sea, from stem to stern ; the mainmast by the broad ;
> The bulwarks down ; the rudder gone ; the boats stove by the chains.
> But courage still, brave mariners, the ANCHOR yet remains :
> And he will flinch—no, never an inch—until ye pitch sky high ;
> Then he moves his head as if he said, " Fear nought ; for here am I ! "

J. M. Neale's Commentary.

Verse 23.—" *Shalt bring them down.*" Indicating a violent death, like that of the slain ox, which is said to *descend,* when it falls under the stroke. The *pit of*

---

* A right Judas.

putrefaction is meant, in which the corpse decays, nor does it here merely denote the sepulchre, but the ignominious condition of a corpse cast forth, as when it is thrown into a pit.—*Hermann Venema.*

Verse 23.—" *Bloody and deceitful men shall not live out half their days.*" A wicked man never lives out half his days ; for either he is cut off before he hath lived half the course of nature, or he is cut off before he hath lived a quarter of the course of his desires ; either he lives not half so long as he might, or not a tenth, not a hundredth part so long as he would ; and therefore let him die when he will, his death is full of terror, trouble, and confusion, because he dies out of season. He never kept time or season with God, and surely God will not keep or regard his time or season.—*Joseph Caryl.*

Verse 23.—" *Half their days.*" In the Jewish account threescore years was the age of a man, and death at any time before that was looked upon as untimely, and deemed and styled כּרת excision, of which they made thirty-six degrees ; so that *not to live out half one's days*, is in their style *to die before thirty years old.*—*Henry Hammond.*

Verse 23 (second clause).—The more sins we do commit, the more we hasten our own death ; because as the wise man saith, " The fear of the Lord prolongeth days, but the years of the wicked shall be shortened " (Prov. x. 27) ; and the prophet David saith, " *Bloody and deceitful men shall not live out half their days ;* " for sin is an epitomiser or shortener of everything : it consumes our wealth, it confines our liberty, it impeacheth our health, and it abbreviateth our life, and brings us speedily into our graves.—*Griffith Williams*, 1636.

HINTS TO PREACHERS.

Verse 1 (second clause).—I. An evil to be dreaded : " *Hide not thyself,*" etc. 1. By long delay in an urgent case. 2. In the sinner's case by refusing to hear altogether. II. Causes which may produce it. 1. In the man. 2. In the prayer itself. 3. In the manner of the prayer. III. Evils which will follow—a list which the preacher can readily think of. IV. Remedies for the evil. There is none if it should continue ; but heart-searching, repentance, importunity, pleading the name of Jesus, etc., will lead to its removal.

Verse 2.—The Great Hearer. I. What address shall we present to him ? II. What sort of attention do we desire ? III. How shall we secure it ? IV. What is the reflex duty on our part ?—To attend and hear him.

Verse 2 (second clause).—Allowable complaining. I. Not *of* God but *to* God. II. Mainly of ourselves. III. Of the world as against God and right. IV. Ever with holy grief, and not selfish vexation.

Verse 4.—The terrors of death. See Sermon by *Grove* in the Notes.

Verse 7.—Solitude. I. Its fancied benefits. II. Its sore temptations. III. Its occasional benefits. IV. Its sweet solaces.

Verse 8.—Too hasty a flight from trial. 1. Would show rebellion against God. 2. Would manifest cowardly want of faith. 3. Would involve loss of useful experience. 4. Would land us in other and worse trials. 5. Would prevent our glorifying God. 6. Would mar our conformity to Christ and fellowship with his people. 7. Would lessen the value of heaven.

Verse 9 (first clause).—The Babel of heresies. *Essential*, for truth is one. *Inevitable*, for the motives of heretics clash. *Providential*, for so they weaken each other. *Judicial*, for so they torment each other.

Verse 10 (first clause).—The activity of evil.

Verse 10 (second clause).—The diabolical twins, or cause and effect.

Verse 14.—The social companionships which grow out of religion. 1. They are on a good foundation. 2. They yield profit—" counsel." 3. They yield pleasure—" sweet." 4. They lead to enthusiasm—" walked in company." 5. They ought to be sacredly maintained. 6. But they need to be carefully watched.

Verse 16.—The contrast. I. A child of God will not wrong others as they do him. II. He will call upon God as they do not. III. God will hear him as he does not the wicked. IV. God will deal with him at last otherwise than with them.

Verse 17. 1.—David will pray fervently ; *"I will pray and cry aloud."* 2. He will pray frequently ; every day, and three times a day, evening and morning, and at noon.—*Matthew Henry.*

Verse 18.—Our battles, our almost rout, our helper, our deliverances, our praise.

Verse 19.—The eternal government of God a threat to the ungodly.

Verse 19 (second part).—Prosperity creating atheism. This involves—1. Ingratitude—they ought to be the more devout. 2. Impudence—they think themselves as God. 3. Forgetfulness—they forget that changes will come. 4. Ignorance—they know not that unbroken prosperity is often for awhile the portion of the accursed. 5. Insanity—for there is no reason in their conduct. 6. Rottenness—preparing them to be cast away for ever.

Verse 21.—The hypocrite's mouth. 1. It has many words. 2. They are only from his mouth. 3. They are very smooth. 4. They conceal rather than reveal his purpose. 5. They are cutting and killing. 6. They will kill himself.

Verse 22 (first clause).—Here we see the believer has—1. A *burden* to try him. 2. A *duty* to engage him, " Cast thy burden," etc. 3. A *promise* to encourage him, " He shall sustain," etc.—*Ebenezer Temple,* 1850.

Verse 22 (last clause).—Who are the righteous ? What is meant by their being moved ? Whose permission is needful to accomplish it ? Will he give it ? " Never." Why not ?

Verse 23 (last clause).—The grand " I will." Sum up the Psalm.—When I pray, 1—3. II. When I faint, 4—7. III. When I am sore beset, 9—11. IV. When I am betrayed, 12—14, 20, 21. V. When others perish, 15. VI. After I am delivered, 18. VII. In every condition, 22.

PSALM LVI.

TITLE.—**To the Chief Musician.** *That mighty minstrel by degrees acquired a noble repertoire of hallowed songs, and set them all to music.* Upon Jonath-elem-rechokim—*this was probably the title of the tune, as we should say Old Hundred, or Sicilian Mariners. Perhaps the title may however belong to the Psalm, and if so it is instructive, for it has been translated "the silent dove in distant places." We have here the songs of God's servant, who rejoices once more to return from banishment, and to leave those dangerous places where he was compelled to hold his peace even from good. There is such deep spiritual knowledge in this Psalm that we might say of it, "Blessed art thou David Bar-jonas, for flesh and blood hath not revealed this unto thee." When David plays the Jonah he is not like the prophet of that name; in David the love of the dove predominates, but in Jonah its moaning and complaining are most notable.* Michtam of David. *This is the second golden Psalm; we had the first in Psalm xvi., to which this Psalm has a great likeness, especially in its close, for it ends in the joyful presence. A golden mystery, the gracious secret of the life of faith is in both these Psalms most sweetly unveiled, and a pillar is set up because of God's truth.* When the Philistines took him in Gath. *He was then like a dove in strangers' hands, and on his escape he records his gratitude.*

DIVISIONS.—*In verses 1 and 2, he pours out his complaint; in verses 3 and 4 he declares his confidence in God; in verses 5 and 6 he returns to his complaining, but pleads with earnest hope in verses 7—9, and sings a grateful song from verse 10 to the close.*

EXPOSITION.

BE merciful unto me, O God : for man would swallow me up ; he fighting daily oppresseth me.

2 Mine enemies would daily swallow *me* up : for *they be* many that fight against me, O thou most High.

" *Be merciful unto me, O God.*" In my deep distress my soul turns to thee, my God. Man has no mercy on me, therefore double thy mercy to me. If thy justice has let loose my enemies, let thy mercy shorten their chain. It is sweet to see how the tender dove-like spirit of the Psalmist flies to the tenderest attribute for succour in the hour of peril. " *For man would swallow me up.*" He is but thy creature, a mere man, yet like a monster he is eager for blood, he pants, he gapes for me ; he would not merely wound me, or feed on my substance, but he would fain swallow me altogether, and so make an end of me. The open mouths of sinners when they rage against us should open our mouths in prayer. We may plead the cruelty of men as a reason for the divine interposition—a father is soon aroused when his children are shamefully entreated. " *He fighting daily oppresseth me.*" He gives me no interval—he fights daily. He is successful in his unrighteous war—he oppresses me, he crushes me, he presses me sore. David has his eye on the leader of his foes, and lays his plaint against him in the right place. If we may thus plead against man, much more against that great enemy of souls, the devil. We ask the Lord to forgive us our trespasses, which is another way of saying, " Be merciful unto me, O God," and then we say, " Lead us not into temptation, but deliver us from the evil one." The more violent the attack of Satan the stronger our plea for deliverance.

2. " *Mine enemies would daily swallow me up.*" Their appetite for blood never fails them. With them there is no truce or armistice. They are many, but one mind animates them. Nothing I can do can make them relent. Unless they can quite devour me they will never be content. The ogres of nursery tales exist in reality in the enemies of the church, who would crush the bones of the godly, and make a mouthful of them if they could. " *For they be many that fight against me.*" Sinners are gregarious creatures. Persecutors hunt in packs. These wolves of the

church seldom come down upon us singly. The number of our foes is a powerful plea for the interposition of the one Defender of the faithful, who is mightier than all their bands. These foes of the gracious are also keen-eyed, and ever on the watch, hence the margin calls them " observers." " *O thou most High.*" Thus he invokes against the lofty ones of the earth the aid of one who is higher than the highest. Some translate the words differently, and think that the writer means that his foes assailed him from the high places in which pride and power had placed them. Saul, his great foe, attacked him from his throne with all the force which his high position placed at his disposal : our comfort in such a case is near to hand, for God will help us from a higher place than our proudest foes can occupy. The greatness of God as the Most High is a fertile source of consolation to weak saints oppressed by mighty enemies.

3 What time I am afraid, I will trust in thee.

4 In God I will praise his word, in God I have put my trust ; I will not fear what flesh can do unto me.

"*What time I am afraid.*" David was no braggart, he does not claim never to be afraid, and he was no brutish Stoic free from fear because of the lack of tenderness. David's intelligence deprived him of the stupid heedlessness of ignorance, he saw the imminence of his peril, and was afraid. We are men, and therefore liable to overthrow ; we are feeble, and therefore unable to prevent it ; we are sinful men, and therefore deserving it, and for all these reasons we are afraid. But the condition of the Psalmist's mind was complex—he feared, but that fear did not fill the whole area of his mind, for he adds, " *I will trust in thee.*" It is possible, then, for fear and faith to occupy the mind at the same moment. We are strange beings, and our experience in the divine life is stranger still. We are often in a twilight, where light and darkness are both present, and it is hard to tell which predominates. It is a blessed fear which drives us to trust. Unregenerate fear drives from God, gracious fear drives to him. If I fear man I have only to trust God, and I have the best antidote. To trust when there is no cause for fear, is but the name of faith, but to be reliant upon God when occasions for alarm are abundant and pressing, is the conquering faith of God's elect. Though the verse is in the form of a resolve, it became a fact in David's life, let us make it so in ours. Whether the fear arise from without or within, from past, present, or future, from temporals, or spirituals, from men or devils, let us maintain faith, and we shall soon recover courage.

4. " *In God I will praise his word.*" Faith brings forth praise. He who can trust will soon sing. God's promise, when fulfilled, is a noble subject for praise, and even before fulfilment it should be the theme of song. It is in or through God that we are able to praise. We praise as well as pray in the Spirit. Or we may read it—in extolling the Lord one of the main points for thanksgiving is his revealed will in the Scriptures, and the fidelity with which he keeps his word of promise. " *In God I have put my trust.*" Altogether and alone should we stay ourselves on God. What was a gracious resolve in the former verse, is here asserted as already done. " *I will not fear what flesh can do unto me.*" Faith exercised, fear is banished, and holy triumph ensues, so that the soul asks, " What can flesh do unto me ? " What indeed ? He can do me no real injury ; all his malice shall be overruled for my good. Man is flesh, flesh is grass—Lord, in thy name I defy its utmost wrath. There were two verses of complaint, and here are two of confidence ; it is well to weigh out a sufficient quantity of the sweet to counteract the sour.

5 Every day they wrest my words : all their thoughts *are* against me for evil.

6 They gather themselves together, they hide themselves, they mark my steps, when they wait for my soul.

5. " *Every day they wrest my words.*" This is a common mode of warfare among the ungodly. They put our language on the rack, they extort meanings from it which it cannot be made fairly to contain. Thus our Saviour's prophecy concerning the temple of his body, and countless accusations against his servants, were founded on wilful perversions. They who do this every day become great adepts in the art. A wolf can always find in a lamb's discourse a reason for eating him. Prayers

are blasphemies if you choose to read them the wrong way upwards. "*All their thoughts are against me for evil.*" No mixture of good will tone down their malice. Whether they viewed him as a king, a Psalmist, a man, a father, a warrior, a sufferer, it was all the same, they saw through coloured glass, and could not think a generous thought towards him. Even those actions of his which were an undoubted blessing to the commonwealth, they endeavoured to undervalue. Oh, foul spring, from which never a drop of pure water can come !

6. "*They gather themselves together.*" Firebrands burn the fiercer for being pushed together. They are afraid to meet the good man till their numbers place terrible odds against him. Come out, ye cowards, man by man, and fight the old hero ! No, ye wait till ye are assembled like thieves in bands, and even then ye waylay the man. There is nothing brave about you. "*They hide themselves.*" In ambuscade they wait their opportunity. Men of malice are men of cowardice. He who dares not meet his man on the king's highway, writes himself down a villain. Constantly are the reputations of good men assailed with deep-laid schemes, and diabolical plots, in which the anonymous enemies stab in the dark. "*They mark my steps,*" as hunters mark the trail of their game, and so track them. Malicious men are frequently very sharp-sighted to detect the failings, or supposed failings, of the righteous. Spies and *mouchards* are not all in the pay of earthly governments, some of them will have wages to take in red-hot coin from one who himself is more subtle than all the beasts of the field. "*When they wait for my soul.*" Nothing less than his life would content them, only his present and eternal ruin could altogether glut them. The good man is no fool, he sees that he has enemies, and that they are many and crafty ; he sees also his own danger, and then he shows his wisdom by spreading the whole case before the Lord, and putting himself under divine protection.

7 Shall they escape by iniquity ? in *thine* anger cast down the people, O God.

8 Thou tellest my wanderings : put thou my tears into thy bottle : *are they* not in thy book ?

9 When I cry *unto thee*, then shall mine enemies turn back : this I know ; for God *is* for me.

7. "*Shall they escape by iniquity ?*" Will such wickedness as this stand them in good stead ? Can it be that this conduct shall enable them to avoid the sentence of earthly punishment ? They slander the good man to screen themselves—will this avail them ? They have cunningly managed hitherto, but will there not be an end to their games ? "*In thine anger cast down the people, O God.*" Trip them up in their tricks. Hurl them from the Tarpeian rock. A persecuted man finds a friend even in an angry God, how much more in the God of love ! When men seek to cast us down, it is but natural and not at all unlawful to pray that they may be disabled from the accomplishment of their infamous designs. What God often does we may safely ask him to do.

8. "*Thou tellest my wanderings.*" Every step which the fugitive had taken when pursued by his enemies, was not only observed but thought worthy of counting and recording. We perhaps are so confused after a long course of trouble, that we hardly know where we have or where we have not been ; but the omniscient and considerate Father of our spirits remembers all in detail, for he has counted them over as men count their gold, for even the trial of our faith is precious in his sight. "*Put thou my tears into thy bottle.*" His sorrows were so many that there would need a great wine-skin to hold them all. There is no allusion to the little complimentary lachrymatories of fashionable and fanciful Romans, it is a robuster metaphor by far ; such floods of tears had David wept that a leathern bottle would scarce hold them. He trusts that the Lord will be so considerate of his tears as to store them up as men do the juice of the vine, and he hopes that the place of storage will be a special one—"*thy* bottle," not *a* bottle. "*Are they not in thy book ?*" Yes, they are recorded there, but let not only the record but the grief itself be present to thee. Look on my griefs as real things, for these move the heart more than a mere account, however exact. How condescending is the Lord ! How exact his knowledge of us ! How generous his estimations ! How tender his regard !

9. " *When I cry unto thee, then shall mine enemies turn back.*" So soon as I pray they shall fly. So surely as I cry they shall be put to the rout.

" So swift is prayer to reach the sky,
So kind is God to me."

The machinery of prayer is not always visible, but it is most efficient. God inclines us to pray, we cry in anguish of heart, he hears, he acts, the enemy is turned back. What irresistible artillery is this which wins the battle as soon as its report is heard ! What a God is this who hearkens to the cry of his children, and in a moment delivers them from the mightiest adversaries ! " *This I know.*" This is one of the believer's certainties, his axioms, his infallible, indisputable verities. " *For God is for me.*" This we know, and we know, therefore, that none can be against us who are worth a moment's fear. " If God be for us, who can be against us ? " Who will restrain prayer when it is so potent ? Who will seek any other ally than God, who is instantly present so soon as we give the ordained signal, by which we testify both our need and our confidence ?

10 In God will I praise *his* word : in the LORD will I praise *his* word.

11 In God have I put my trust : I will not be afraid what man can do unto me.

12 Thy vows *are* upon me, O God : I will render praises unto thee.

13 For thou hast delivered my soul from death : *wilt* not *thou deliver* my feet from falling, that I way walk before God in the light of the living ?

10. " *In God will I praise his word.*" Now comes the thanksgiving. He is a wretch who, having obtained help, forgets to return a grateful acknowledgment. The least we can do is to praise him from whom we receive such distinguished favours. Does David here mean " by God's grace I will praise him ? " If so, he shows us that all our emotions towards God must be in God, produced by him and presented as such. Or does he mean, " that which in God is most the object of my praise is his word, and the faithfulness with which he keeps it ? " If so, we see how attached our hearts should be to the sure word of promise, and especially to *him* who is the WORD incarnate. The Lord is to be praised under every aspect, and in all his attributes and acts, but certain mercies more peculiarly draw out our admiration towards special portions of the great whole. That praise which is never special in its direction cannot be very thoughtful, and it is to be feared cannot be very acceptable. " *In the Lord will I praise his word.*" He delights to dwell on his praise, he therefore repeats his song. The change by which he brings in the glorious name of Jehovah is doubtless meant to indicate that under every aspect he delights in his God and in his word.

11. " *In God have I put my trust.*" This and the former verse are evidently the chorus of the Psalm. We cannot be too careful of our faith, or see too sedulously that it is grounded on the Lord alone. " *I will not be afraid what man can do unto me.*" Faith has banished fear. He views his foes in their most forcible character, calling them not *flesh*, but indicating them as *man*, yet he dreads them not ; though the whole race were his enemies he would not be afraid now that his trust is stayed on God. He is not afraid of what they threaten to do, for much of that they cannot do ; and even what is in their power, what they *can do*, he defies with holy daring. He speaks for the future, " I will not," for he is sure that the security of the present will suffice for days to come.

12. " *Thy vows are upon me, O God.*" Vows made in his trouble he does not lightly forget, nor should we. We voluntarily made them, let us cheerfully keep them. All professed Christians are men under vows, but especially those who in hours of dire distress have re-dedicated themselves unto the Lord. " *I will render praises unto thee.*" With heart, and voice, and gift, we should cheerfully extol the God of our salvation. The practice of making solemn vows in times of trouble is to be commended, when it is followed by the far less common custom of fulfilling them when the trouble is over.

13. " *For thou hast delivered my soul from death.*" His enemies were defeated in their attempts upon his life, and therefore he vowed to devote his life to God. "*Wilt not thou deliver my feet from falling ?*" One mercy is a plea for another, for indeed it may happen that the second is the necessary complement of the first.

It little boots that we live, if we are made to fall in character by the thrusts of our enemies. As lief not be, as live to be bereft of honour, and fallen prostrate before my enemies. *" That I may walk before God in the light of the living,"* enjoying the favour and presence of God, and finding the joy and brightness of life therein. Walking at liberty, in holy service, in sacred communion, in constant progress in holiness, enjoying the smile of heaven—this I seek after. Here is the loftiest reach of a good man's ambition, to dwell with God, to walk in righteousness before him, to rejoice in his presence, and in the light and glory which it yields. Thus in this short Psalm, we have climbed from the ravenous jaws of the enemy into the light of Jehovah's presence, a path which only faith can tread.

EXPLANATORY NOTES AND QUAINT SAYINGS.

Title.—The words *" Jonath-elem-rechokim "* may be rendered, *concerning the mute dove among them that are afar off,* or *in far places.*—*John Gill.*

Title.—*" Michtam."* See also Explanatory Notes on Psalm xvi., in the " Treasury of David," Vol. I., pp. 197, 198.

Verse 1.—*" Be merciful."* This is the second of the Psalms beginning with the miserere ; the fifty-first being the first of them.—*C. H. S.*

Verse 1.—*" Be merciful unto me, O God."* This is to me the one source of all my expectations, the one fountain of all promises : *Miserere mei, Deus, miserere mei.*—*Bernard,* 1091—1157.

Verse 1.—*" Be merciful."* His first wrestling in prayer is with the check of his conscience, whether for his daily sins, or in particular for casting himself in such apparent danger, as to have ventured without probable security, to seek shelter among the enemies of the people of God, whose blood he himself had shed abundantly ; for this rashness or other sins he beggeth mercy.—*David Dickson.*

Verse 1.—*" Man."* He uses the indefinite term *man* in this verse, though in the next he speaks of having many enemies, the more forcibly to express the truth, that the whole world was combined against him, that he experienced no humanity amongst men, and stood in the last necessity of divine help.—*John Calvin.*

Verse 1.—*" Would swallow me up."* *Soop me up* (as the Hebrew word soundeth) ; make but one draught of me or suck me in as a whirlpool, swallow me up as a ravenous wild beast.—*John Trapp.*

Verse 1.—*" He fighting daily."* There is no morning on which we can arise and go forth into the world, and say, " No enemy will come out against me to-day." There is no night in which we can retire from that world, and think to find safety in the solitude of our own chambers, and say, " No evil can enter here."—*Barton Bouchier, in " Manna in the Heart,"* 1855.

Verses 1, 2.—The same words are applicable to the situation and circumstances of David, pursued by his enemies ; of Christ, persecuted by the Jews ; of the church, afflicted in the world ; and of the soul, encompassed by enemies, against whom she is forced to wage perpetual war.—*George Horne.*

Verse 2.—*" O thou most High."* The Hebrew is not that rendered " *Most High* " in Ps. vii. 17 ; nor in our version is it ever rendered " *Most High* " in any other place, although found in the Hebrew Bible more than *fifty* times. There are but two other places where it is applied, as an epithet, to God ; Ps. xcii. 8 ; Mic. vi. 6. It is commonly rendered *from above, on high, high places, high ;* once *loftily,* Ps. lxxiii. 8. . . . The probable meaning is, they " fight against me from the high places of authority, both in Jerusalem and in Gath," *q.d.,* mine enemies are in power.—*William S. Plumer's " Studies in the Book of Psalms,"* 1867.

Verse 3.—*" What time I am afraid, I will trust in thee."* There is nothing like faith to help at a pinch ; faith dissolves doubts as the sun drives away the mists. And that you may not be put out, know that your time for believing always is.

There are times when some graces may be out of use, but there is no time wherein faith can be said to be so. Wherefore faith must be always in exercise. Faith is the eye, is the mouth, is the hand, and one of these is of use all the day long. Faith is to see, to receive, to work, or to eat; and a Christian should be seeing or receiving, or working, or feeding all day long. Let it rain, let it blow, let it thunder, let it lighten, a Christian must still believe. "At what time," said the good man, "I am afraid, I will trust in thee."—*John Bunyan.*

Verse 3.—"*What time I am afraid,*" etc. A divine spark may live in a smoke of doubts without a speedy rising into a flame. When grace is at the bottom of doubting, there will be reliance on Christ and lively petitions to him. Peter's faith staggers when he began to sink, but he casts a look and sends forth a cry to his Saviour, acknowledging his sufficiency; Matt. xiv. 30, "Lord, save me." Sometimes those doubtings strengthen our trust and make us take hold faster on God. Ps. lvi. 3, "What time I am afraid, I will trust in thee." This was a fear of himself or others, rather than a jealousy of God. Had he had unworthy suspicions of him, he would not have trusted him; he would not have run for remedy to the object of his fear. The waverings where faith is, are like the tossings of a ship fast at anchor (still there is a relying upon God), not like a boat carried by the waves of the sea to be dashed against a rock. If the heart stay on Christ in the midst of those doubtings, it is not an evil heart of unbelief. Such doubtings consist with the indwelling of the Spirit, who is in the heart, to perform the office of a Comforter against such fears and to expel those thick fumes of nature.—*Stephen Charnock.*

Verse 3.—"*What time I am afraid,*" etc. I know not what to do, but I'll try my old way, 'tis good for me to draw near still; I'll do so still as I use to do; I'll cast myself down upon the free grace of Christ in the promises; I'll lay the weight of my sinking spirit there, I'll renew my hold, life, expectation there; this is my old path, I'll never be turned or beaten out here. This Christian in his strength may challenge all the gates of hell. This was David's course (Ps. lxxi. 5), "Thou art my trust from my youth," etc. Thence was it that he could say, "*What time I am afraid, I will trust in thee:*" his shield and sword was always in his hand, therefore he could make use of it when fear and inward trouble offered themselves. "*Afraid!*" alas, who is not? but what course will you take then? Even what course you used to take, *i.e.*, believe; use faith always; and have it now.—*Elias Pledger (—1676), in "Morning Exercises."*

Verse 3.—"*What time,*" etc. Literally, "*What day.*" As "Man *daily* oppresseth me" (ver. 1), so "Every *day,* when I am afraid, I trust in thee."—*A. R. Fausset.*

Verse 3.—It is a good maxim with which to go into a world of danger; a good maxim to go to sea with; a good maxim in a storm; a good maxim when in danger on the land; a good maxim when we are sick; a good maxim when we think of death and the judgment—"*What time I am afraid,* I WILL TRUST IN THEE."—*Albert Barnes.*

Verse 3.—"*I will trust in thee.*" Faith and fear stand together; and so fear and love.—*John Richardson,* 1654.

Verses 3, 4.—Sometimes faith comes from prayer in triumph, and cries, *Victoria.* It gives such a being and existence to the mercy prayed for in the Christian's soul, before any likelihood of it appears to sense and reason, that the Christian can silence all his troubled thoughts with the expectation of its coming. So Hannah prayed, "and was no more sad." 1 Samuel i. 18. Yea, it will make the Christian disburse his praises for the mercy long before it is received. Thus high faith wrought in David. "*At what time I am afraid, I will trust in thee,*" and in the next words, "*In God I will praise his word;* " that is, he would praise God for his promise before there was any performance of it to him, when it had no existence but in God's faithfulness and David's faith. This holy man had such a piercing eye of faith, that he could see the promise when he was at the lowest ebb of misery, so certain and unquestionable in the power and truth of God, that he could then praise God as if the promised mercy had been actually fulfilled to him.—*William Gurnall.*

Verse 4.—"*In God I will praise his word.*" Or, praise him for his word; for the whole Scripture that was then in being.—*John Gill.*

Verse 4.—The best hold that faith can have of God, is to take him by "*his word,*" however his dispensation seems to be; this will give satisfaction at length; for "*In God I will praise his word,*" is as much as to say, albeit he withhold comfort and deliverance from me, so that I cannot find what I would, yet let me have " *his word*," and I will give him the glory of all his attributes.—*David Dickson.*

Verse 4.—" *I will not fear what flesh can do unto me.*" Fear not man, he is but flesh. Thou needest not, thou oughtest not to fear. Thou needest not. What, not such a great man ; not such a number of men, who have the keys of all the prisons at their girdle ; who can kill or save alive ? No, not these ; only look they be thy enemies for righteousness' sake. Take heed thou makest not the least child thine enemy, by offering wrong to him ; God will right the wicked even upon the saint. If he offends he shall find no shelter under God's wing for his sin. This made Jerome complain that the Christians' sin made the arms of those barbarous nations which invaded Christendom victorious : *Nostris peccatis fortes sunt barbari.* But if man's wrath find thee in God's way, and his fury take fire at thy holiness, thou needest not fear though thy life be the prey he hunts for. Flesh can only wound flesh ; he may kill thee, but not hurt thee. Why shouldest thou fear to be stripped of that which thou hast resigned already to Christ ? It is the first lesson thou learnest, if a Christian, to deny thyself, take up thy cross, and follow thy master ; so that the enemy comes too late ; thou hast no life to lose, because thou hast given it already to Christ ; nor can man take away that without God's leave ; all thou hast is insured ; and though God hath not promised thee immunity from suffering in this kind, yet he hath undertaken to bear the loss, yea, to pay thee a hundredfold, and thou shalt not stay for it till another world. Again, thou oughtest not to fear flesh. Our Saviour (Matt. x.) thrice, in the compass of six verses, commands us not to fear man : if thy heart quail at him, how wilt thou behave thyself in the list against Satan, whose little finger is heavier than man's loins ? The Romans had *arma prælusoria*, weapons rebated, or cudgels, which they were tried at before they came to the sharp. If thou canst not bear a bruise in thy flesh from man's cudgels and blunt weapons, what wilt thou do when thou shalt have Satan's sword in thy side ? God counts himself reproached when his children fear a sorry man ; therefore we are bid sanctify the Lord, not to fear their fear.—*William Gurnall.*

Verse 4.—" *I will not fear,*" etc. Eusebius tells us of a notable speech that Ignatius used when he was in his enemies' hands, not long before he was to suffer, which argued a raised spirit to a wonderful height above the world, and above himself. " I care," says he, " for nothing visible or invisible, that I might get Christ. Let fire, the cross, the letting out of beasts upon me, breaking of my bones, the tearing of my members, the grinding of my whole body, and the torments of the devils come upon me, so be it I may get Christ.—*From Jeremiah Burroughs'* " *Moses his Self-denyall,*" 1649.

Verse 4.—" *What flesh can do,*" etc. It is according to the phrase of Scripture, when it would speak contemptibly of man and show him to be the lowest creature, to call him " flesh," to set forth the weakness that man is subject to.—*John Arrowsmith,* 1600—1660.

Verse 4 (last clause).—*Fear of man*—grim idol, bloody mouthed ; many souls has he devoured and trampled down into hell ! His eyes are full of hatred to Christ's disciples. Scoffs and jeers lurk in his eye. The laugh of the scorner growls in his throat. Cast down this idol. This keeps some of you from secret prayer, from worshipping God in your family, from going to lay your case before ministers, from openly confessing Christ. You that have felt God's love and Spirit, dash this idol to pieces. " Who art thou, that thou shouldest be afraid of a man that shall die ? " " Fear not, thou worm Jacob." " What have I to do any more with idols ? "— *Robert Murray M'Cheyne,* 1813—1843.

Verse 4.—Faith groweth valiant in fight ; albeit it began like a coward, and staggered in the first conflict, yet it groweth stout, incontinent, and pulls its adversaries under foot : " *In God I have put my trust ; I will not fear what flesh can do unto me.*"—*David Dickson.*

Verse 5.—" *Every day they wrest my words ;* " or, they put my words to pain and grief, or, they painfully and grievously wrest my words. David's enemies took up what he spake, and put a new shape upon it ; and this they did so vexingly, that they are said to *"wrest"* his words : a thing is vexed when it is wrested or wrought quite out of the form it before had. The same metaphor the apostle Peter useth in reference to doctrine, speaking of the Epistles of Paul, in which " are some things hard to be understood, which they that are unlearned and unstable *wrest,*" or put upon the rack ; they painfully form his words, and represent them in a meaning which he never intended. 2 Pet. iii. 16. What is spoken may be right both in the matter and intendment of the speaker, yet another wrests, forms and fashions it in his own mould, and makes it bear a sense which the speaker never dreamed of.—*Joseph Caryl.*

Verse 5.—" Every day they wrest my words," etc. Mr. Jewel, the Bishop of Salisbury, who, according to his life, died most godly and patiently, at the point of death used the versicle of the Hymn, " Te Deum," " O Lord, in thee have I trusted, let me never be confounded," whereupon, suppressing the rest, they published, that the principal champion of the heretics, in his very last words, cried he was confounded.—*Lord Bacon's " Bible Thoughts."*

Verse 5.—" They wrest my words." Whatever Christ said in justification of himself was twisted to a meaning injurious to him. So it is still in the world, self-justification by words answers but little purpose with ungodly men.—*W. Wilson, D.D.,* 1860.

Verse 6.—" They mark my steps." Go whither I will, they are at my heels.—*William Nicholson* (1671), *in " David's Harp Strung and Tuned."*

Verse 8.—" Put thou my tears in thy bottle." Among other things in the collection of Mr. Abbott, of Cairo, he had a lachrymatory, or tear bottle, which had been found in a tomb at Thebes. This interested me very much. The custom in old times was, when a person was ill, or in great distress, for his friends to go to see him, and take with them a tear bottle. Then, as the tears rolled down the cheeks of the sufferer, they were caught in these bottles, sealed up, and preserved as a memorial of the event. This is what David referred to in Psalm lvi. 8. *" Put thou my tears into thy bottle."* But it implies much more than at first suggests itself, and much more than I can attempt to write. For instance, it is as if David had said, " Visit me, and behold my tears ; " (" O visit me with thy salvation ! ") for without such *visit* there could be no bottling of his tears. " Thou tellest my wanderings ; O visit me, and behold my anguish ; put my tears into thy bottle," for " they have been my meat day and night." Psalm xliii. 3. " Keep them before thee, by way of remembrance, and when thou seest the bottle, O think of him whose tears it contains. Are they not in thy book ? " That is, God's book of remembrance, that was written for those " who thought upon his name " (Mal. iii. 16), just as the kings of old used to keep a book of chronicles of important events. See Esther vi. 1—11.—*John Gadsby,* 1860.

[We insert this to show what has been said by others ; but we do not think there is the slightest allusion to this piece of *Roman* etiquette in this text.—*C. H. S.*]

Verse 8.—" My tear : " the singular used collectively. *" In thy bottle : "* as if one should say, take care of my tears, as of a kind of wine that is very costly, and very pleasant to thee ; or, that hereafter you may measure out to me just that quantity of joys : a metaphor from the keeper of a vineyard, who receives into his vessel the drops of the grapes pressed out by the wine-press of affliction. The word נאד (*uter**) denotes the manner in which they preserved their wine. (1 Samuel xvi. 20 ; Joshua ix. 4, 13), and milk also (Judges iv. 19).—*Martin Geier.*

Verse 8.—" Put thou my tears into thy bottle." What a sweet thought is suggested here of God's remembrance of his peoples' affliction ! It is an interesting figure of speech, of *bottling their tears.* But the sense is, they are remembered. And woe will be to the man that offends one of God's little ones on his account. What are now bottles of tears, will be poured out in the end as so many vials of wrath. But reader ! think how the tears of Jesus have been treasured up when shedding for the sins of his people.—*Robert Hawker,* 1753—1827.

Verse 8.—" Put thou my tears into thy bottle." It is the witty observation of one, that God is said in Scripture to have a bag and a bottle, a *bag* for our sins, and a *bottle* for our tears ; and that we should help to fill this, as we have that. There is an allusion here in the original that cannot be Englished.—*John Trapp.*

Verse 8.—" Are they not in thy book ? " While we remain in this vale of misery, God keeps all our tears in a bottle ; so precious is the water that is distilled from penitent eyes : and because he will be sure not to fail, he notes how many drops there be in his register. It was a precious ointment wherewith the woman in the

---

* Leather or skin bottle.

Pharisee's house (it is thought Mary Magdalene) anointed the feet of Christ ; but her *tears*, wherewith she washed them, were more worth than her spikenard.— *Abraham Wright, in " A Practical Commentary or Exposition upon the Book of Psalms,"* 1661.

Verse 9.—" *When I cry."* The cry of faith and prayer to God is more dreadful to our spiritual foes than the war-whoop of the Indian is to his surprised brother savages.—*Adam Clarke.*

Verse 9 (first clause).—It was somewhat that when David prayed he was saved from his enemies. " I will call on the Lord : so shall I be saved from mine enemies." (2 Sam. xxii. 4) ; there is the *defensive* power of prayer ; but it is more that it puts enemies to the foil. " *When I cry unto thee, then shall mine enemies turn back* " and be put to flight : there is the *offensive* power of prayer. In David's tower there was an armoury, *thalpijoth,* a place to hang swords with two edges, swords with two mouths (Cant. iv. 4) ; a defensive and an offensive edge. Both edges must be used by such as seek safety. Prayer is a sword with two edges. " Put up thy sword into his place," says Christ to Peter ; " for all they that take the sword shall perish with the sword." Matt. xxii. 52. But he that takes not this sword may happen to perish by the sword ; and the drawing of this sword may save a man from perishing by the sword. Mark that last reason that our Saviour adds why Peter should put up his sword : " Thinkest thou that I cannot now pray to my Father, and he shall presently give me more than twelve legions of angels ? " (ver. 53.) As if he had said, If it were my mind to confound these mine enemies that now set upon me, I should not need thy sword to do it. I could pray to my Father, and could presently by prayer bring such forces into the field as should rout and scatter all mine enemies ; hereby implying, that if he would, he could do his enemies more damage and mischief by his prayers against them than by the sword and all instruments of war. Prayer is *twelve legions* strong, yea, twelve legions of angels strong against enemies.—*Jeremiah Dyke* (1620), *in the Righteous Man's Tower.*

Verse 9.—" *This I know."* Faith goeth upon solid grounds, and is not a fallible conjecture, but a sure knowledge.—*David Dickson.*

Verse 10.—" *In God will I praise his word : in the Lord will I praise his word."*— The first word, *Elohim,* is a name belonging to God as a judge, the second word, *Jehovah,* is a name of mercy. I will praise God whether he deal with me in a way of justice or in a way of mercy, when he hath thunder in his voice, as well as when he hath honey under his tongue. Oh, how should we praise God, and pleasure ourselves by such a frame !—*Stephen Charnock.*

Verse 10 (first clause).—By the assistance of God I shall be enabled to praise him for the performance of his promises.—*Symon Patrick,* 1626—1707.

Verse 12.—" *Thy vows are upon me, O God."* Whoever is conversant with the Psalms of David, will find him frequently making *vows,* and careful in paying them. When these words dropt from him he was just delivered out of a pressing danger among the Philistines, with whom he took shelter from the rage of King Saul, who unweariedly pursued him ; but he soon found that the remembrance of his past achievements to their damage was still so fresh amongst them, and they so exasperated thereupon, that his life was in constant danger. In his distress he flies to God, his wonted refuge, and sends up earnest addresses to him, *vowing* if he would open a way for his deliverance out of these new straits, he would show his grateful sense of so signal a mercy, by the exactness and accuracy of his future obedience. God hears and succours him ; and he thereupon gratefully looks back, endeavours to renew the sense of his former obligation to his great Deliverer, and to stir up himself by suitable returns, and so cries out, " *Thy vows are upon me, O God ;* " as if he should say, I resolve, O Lord, not to forget what was transacted while I was under my fears. Thou hast heard my cries, and I own myself firmly bound by my *vows.* I was serious and in earnest when I made them, and I will endeavour to show that I was so by my care to perform them. " *Thy vows,"* O God, made indeed on my part, but justly to be exacted on thine, " *are upon me,"* they do in reality hold me fast, and I desire not to be released. I am sensible I deserve to be stigmatised for a perfidious wretch if I ever forget them. This temper of holy David with reference to the *vows* he made on this occasion, should be ours with reference to all the sacred *vows* we any way come under. All Christians, as such, are necessarily under *vows* to the blessed God ; and particular circumstances may make it expedient for us to come under special engagements to him. But wherever they are such as that they may justly be denominated *vows of God, i.e.,* are such as his word will warrant ; we should make holy David, as speaking in this text, our pattern, and set ourselves to imitate him, in seriously owning their binding force, and endeavouring to answer and pay them.—*Edmund Calamy, in " A Practical Discourse Concerning Vows,"* 1704.

Verse 12.—" *Thy vows are upon me, O God."* A well-composed *vow* will make thee more circumspect and wary in the general course of thy life. Such an influence it hath, as doth more directly work on one particular part, yet is not terminated to that particular only. Thus it was with David. These *" vows "* were made when he was in danger of his life, as it seemeth from verse 13 : for when God heard him, he delivered his soul from death : for this he vowed praises in particular, and he will render them. But, withal, he takes himself to be hereby engaged to a more exact and circumspect walk before God in all duties ; so he expresseth himself in the latter part of verse 13.—*Henry Hurst (1629—1696), in " The Morning Exercise at Cripplegate,"* 1661.

Verses 12, 13.—" *Thy vows are upon me, O God."* Passively, vows made to God, not by God ; or the obligations of those vows and prayers which I have made and upon which I have received answers. Sacrifices of thanksgiving were called vows, as having been vowed to God upon the want, and to be paid upon the receipt, of mercy. Lev. i. 1, " If the sacrifice that is offered be a vow." Thy vows are upon me ; the fruit of my vows, so that I stand indebted to God for the return of praise. " *Thou hast delivered."* He understands some great danger wherein he had sunk had not God stood by him, and from a greater mercy, the deliverance of his soul from death, argues for a less, the keeping his feet from falling. " *That I may walk before God in the light of the living."* By light of the living is meant life, which is called being enlightened with the " light of the living." Job. xxxiii. 30. Sometimes eternal life in heaven. John viii. 12, " He that follows me shall not walk in darkness, but shall have the light of life." " To walk before God." To walk obediently in the sight of God ; with a respect to his presence ; a walking unto all well pleasing. This is the last argument in the Psalm whereon he builds his strongest plea, as if he knew not what to urge if this should fail him ; as if he should have said, Lord, I have had experience of thy wisdom in contriving, thy power in effecting, thy mercy in bestowing deliverance upon me, thy goodness in answering my vows and prayers. " Thou hast delivered from death," a danger as great and unavoidable as death itself; O Lord, art not thou the same as thou wert ? Art not thou still as wise to design, and as gracious to confer further mercy ? Wilt thou not as certainly also deliver my feet from falling ? The one contains his experience, the other the inference or conclusion he draws from it. Mercies received are in a special manner to be remembered. Mercies received are encouragements to ask, and strong grounds to hope for the mercies we want.—*Stephen Charnock.*

Verse 13.—" *From falling,"* or, as more literally translated, from a *thrust,* or a *push,* by which one is caused to fall.—*O. Prescott Hiller.*

Verse 13 (*last clause*).—*To walk in the presence of God* is partly under his eyes, his guidance and care, partly in particular, where God is wont to be *present,* where he is *worshipped* by his people, and scatters his blessings, opposed to his present state by which he was removed from the place of his worship and presence. Conf. 1 Sam. xxvi. 19, etc. Lastly, *to walk in the light of the living* denotes in general to live amongst *those who live in the light,* or who enjoy the *light,* as it is said elsewhere, *in the land of the living*—Psalm xxvii. 13 ; Isaiah xxxviii. 11 ; liii. 8 ; Ezekiel xxxii. 32 ; Psalm cxlii. 6—opposed to the *dead* or *the region of the dead,* who dwell *in darkness.* But in particular it signifies to live in a *safe* and *prosperous* state, whose well-known emblem is *light.*—*Hermann Venema.*

Verse 13 (*last clause*).—We cannot restrict this phrase to the light of mortal life ; David's vows bound him to walk in the *light of spiritual life,* and also in the *light of eternal life,* of which by faith he was a partaker. And most commentators have applied this verse to the *light of glory* in the world to come, as the real and final object of the believer's conversation here on earth.—*W. Wilson, D.D.*

HINTS TO PREACHERS

Verses 2, 3.—I. *Fears are common to all men,* at one time or another. II. *Improper and inefficacious means* of removing fear are often resorted to. III. There is here suggested *a true and effectual method* of removing fear.—*Robert Morrison* (1782—1834), *in " A Parting Memorial."*

Verse 3.—*" What time I am afraid, I will trust in thee."* Whensoever we are afraid of any evil, we are still to put our trust in God. I. What is it to put our trust in God? 1. To keep our hearts from desponding or sinking down under any fears. 2. To comfort ourselves in God. 3. To expect deliverance from him. II. What is there in God we ought to put our trust in ? 1. In his promises. 2. In his properties. His power, wisdom, justice, mercy, all-sufficiency. III. Why should we in all our fears put our trust in God ? 1. Because there is none else can secure us from our fears. Whereas, 2. There are no fears but God can, secure us from them, either by removing the thing feared, or by subduing the fear of the thing.—*Bishop Beveridge.*

Verse 3.—I. There is fear without trust. II. There is trust without fear. III. There is fear and trust united.—*G. R.*

Verse 7.—1. From iniquity there is an escape. II. By iniquity there is no escape. The mercy of God secures the one. The justice of God prevents the other.—*G. R.*

Verse 8.—Here are—I. Manifold mercies, to reclaim from wanderings. II. Tender mercies, putting tears in a bottle. III. Covenant mercies, " Are they not," etc.—*G. R.*

Verse 9.—I. God is on the side of his people. II. He is known to be on their side. III. In answer to prayer he appears on their side. IV. When he appears enemies flee. Or—1. The fact, God is for me. II. The knowledge of that fact—" This I know." III. The use of that knowledge—" When I cry," etc. IV. The consequence of that use—" Mine enemies turn back."—*G. R.*

Verse 10.—" I will praise God *for* his word." II. *In* his word, as he is there revealed. III. *By* his word. " Thou hast put a song," etc.

Verse 12.—Here is—I. Past dedication. II. Present consecration. III. Future glorification.—*G. R.*

Verses 12, 13.—You have here—1. The commemoration of former mercies: " Thou hast delivered." 2. The confidence of future : " Wilt not thou." 3. The end of all : " To walk before God in the light of the living."—*Stephen Charnock.*

Verse 13.—I. The language of Gratitude—" Thou hast," etc. II. Of Faith—" Wilt not thou," etc. III. Of Hope—" That I may walk," etc.—*G. R.*

PSALM LVII.

TITLE.—To the Chief Musician.—*So glad a song as this becomes ere it closes, should be in the keeping of the most skilled of all the temple minstrels.* Al-taschith, *i.e.*, DESTROY NOT. *This petition is a very sententious prayer, as full as it is brief, and well worthy to be the motto for a sacred song. David had said, "destroy not," in reference to Saul, when he had him in his power and now he takes pleasure in employing the same words in supplication to God. We may infer from the spirit of the Lord's prayer, that the Lord will spare us as we spare our foes. There are four of these "Destroy not" Psalms, namely, the 57th, 58th, 59th, and 75th. In all of them there is a distinct declaration of the destruction of the wicked and the preservation of the righteous, and they all have probably a reference to the overthrow of the Jews, on account of their persecution of the great Son of David : they will endure heavy chastisement, but concerning them it is written in the divine decree, " Destroy them not." Michtam of David. For quality this Psalm is called golden, or a secret, and it well deserves the name. We may read the words and yet not know the secret joy of David, which he has locked up in this golden casket. When he fled from Saul in the cave. This is a song from the bowels of the earth, and, like Jonah's prayer from the bottom of the sea, it has a taste of the place. The poet is in the shadow of the cave at first, but he comes to the cavern's mouth at last, and sings in the sweet fresh air, with his eye on the heavens, watching joyously the clouds floating therein.*

DIVISIONS.—*We have here prayer,* 1—6, *and praise,* 7—11. *The hunted one takes a long breath of prayer, and when he is fully inspired, he breathes out his soul in jubilant song.*

EXPOSITION.

BE merciful unto me, O God, be merciful unto me : for my soul trusteth in thee : yea, in the shadow of thy wings will I make my refuge, until *these* calamities be overpast.

2 I will cry unto God most high ; unto God that performeth *all things* for me.

3 He shall send from heaven, and save me *from* the reproach of him that would swallow me up. Selah. God shall send forth his mercy and his truth.

4 My soul *is* among lions : *and* I lie *even among* them that are set on fire, *even* the sons of men, whose teeth *are* spears and arrows, and their tongue a sharp sword.

5 Be thou exalted, O God, above the heavens ; *let* thy glory *be* above all the earth.

6 They have prepared a net for my steps ; my soul is bowed down : they have digged a pit before me, into the midst whereof they are fallen *themselves*. Selah.

1. "*Be merciful unto me, O God, be merciful unto me.*" Urgent need suggests the repetition of the cry, for thus intense urgency of desire is expressed. If "he gives twice who gives quickly," so he who would receive quickly must ask twice. For mercy the Psalmist pleads at first, and he feels he cannot improve upon his plea, and therefore returns to it. God is the God of mercy, and the Father of mercies, it is most fit therefore that in distress we should seek mercy from him in whom it dwells. "*For my soul trusteth in thee.*" Faith urges her suit right well. How can the Lord be unmerciful to a trustful soul ? Our faith does not deserve mercy, but it always wins it from the sovereign grace of God when it is sincere, as in this case where *the soul* of the man believed. "With the heart man believeth unto righteousness." "*Yea, in the shadow of thy wings will I make my refuge.*" Not in the cave alone would he hide, but in the cleft of the Rock of ages. As the little birds find ample shelter beneath the parental wing, even so would the fugitive place

himself beneath the secure protection of the divine power. The emblem is delightfully familiar and suggestive. May we all experimentally know its meaning. When we cannot see the sunshine of God's face, it is blessed to cower down beneath the shadow of his wings. " *Until these calamities be overpast.*" Evil will pass away, and the eternal wings will abide over us till then. Blessed be God, our calamities are matters of time, but our safety is a matter of eternity. When we are under the divine shadow, the passing over of trouble cannot harm us ; the hawk flies across the sky, but this is no evil to the chicks when they are safely nestling beneath the hen.

2. " *I will cry.*" He is quite safe, but yet he prays, for faith is never dumb. We pray because we believe. We exercise by faith the spirit of adoption whereby we cry. He says not, I do cry, or I have cried, but I will cry, and indeed, this resolution may stand with all of us until we pass through the gates of pearl ; for while we are here below we shall still have need to cry. " *Unto God most high*"— Prayers are for God only ; the greatness and sublimity of his person and character suggest and encourage prayer : however high our enemies, our heavenly Friend is higher, for he is " *Most high,*" and he can readily send from the height of his power the succour which we need. " *Unto God that performeth all things for me.*" He has cogent reason for praying, for he sees God performing The believer waits and God works. The Lord has undertaken for us, and he will not draw back, he will go through with his covenant engagements. Our translators have very properly inserted the words, " all things," for there is a blank in the Hebrew, as if it were a *carte blanche,* and you might write therein that the Lord would finish anything and everything which he has begun. Whatsoever the Lord takes in hand he will accomplish ; hence past mercies are guarantees for the future, and admirable reasons for continuing to cry unto him.

3. " *He shall send from heaven.*" If there be no fit instruments on earth, heaven shall yield up its legions of angels for the succour of the saints. We may in times of great straits expect mercies of a remarkable kind ; like the Israelites in the wilderness, we shall have our bread hot from heaven, new every morning ; and for the overthrow of our enemies God shall open his celestial batteries, and put them to utter confusion. Wherever the battle is more fierce than ordinary, there shall come succours from headquarters, for the Commander-in-chief sees all. " *And save me from the reproach of him that would swallow me up.*" He will be in time, not only to rescue his servants from being swallowed up, but even from being reproached. Not only shall they escape the flames, but not even the smell of fire shall pass upon them. O dog of hell, I am not only delivered from thy bite, but even from thy bark. Our foes shall not have the power to sneer at us, their cruel jests and taunting gibes shall be ended by the message from heaven, which shall for ever save us. " *Selah.*" Such mercy may well make us pause to meditate and give thanks. Rest, singer, for God has given thee rest ! " *God shall send forth his mercy and his truth.*" He asked for mercy, and truth came with it. Thus evermore doth God give us more than we ask or think. His attributes, like angels on the wing, are ever ready to come to the rescue of his chosen.

4. " *My soul is among lions.*" He was a very Daniel. Howled at, hunted, wounded, but not slain. His place was in itself one of extreme peril, and yet faith made him feel himself secure, so that he could lie down. The cave may have reminded him of a lion's den, and Saul and his band shouting and yelling in their disappointment at missing him, were the lions ; yet beneath the divine shelter he felt himself safe. " *And I lie even among them that are set on fire.*" Perhaps Saul and his band kindled a fire in the cavern while they halted in it, and David was thus reminded of the fiercer fire of their hate which burned within their hearts. Like the bush in Horeb, the believer is often in the midst of flames, but n ver consumed. It is a mighty triumph of faith when we can lie down even among firebrands and find rest, because God is our defence. " *Even the sons of men, whose teeth are spears and arrows, and their tongue a sharp sword.*" Malicious men carry a whole armoury in their mouths ; they have not harmless mouths, whose teeth grind their own food as in a mill, but their jaws are as mischievous as if every tooth were a javelin or an arrow. They have no molars, all their teeth are canine, and their nature is canine, leonine, wolfish, devilish. As for that busy member the tongue, in the case of the malicious, it is a two-edged, keen, cutting, killing sword. The tongue, which is here compared to a sword, has the adjective *sharp* added to it, which is not used in reference to the teeth, which are compared to spears, as if to show

that if men were actually to tear us with their teeth, like wild beasts, they could not thereby wound us so severely as they can do with their tongues. No weapon is so terrible as a tongue sharpened on the devil's grindstone; yet even this we need not fear, for "No weapon that is formed against thee shall prosper, and every tongue that riseth against thee in judgment thou shalt condemn."

5. " Be thou exalted, O God, above the heavens." This is the chorus of the Psalm. Before he has quite concluded his prayer the good man interjects a verse of praise; and glorious praise too, seeing it comes up from the lion's den and from amid the coals of fire. Higher than the heavens is the Most High, and so high ought our praises to rise. Above even the power of cherubim and seraphim to express it, the glory of God is revealed and is to be acknowledged by us. " Let thy glory be above all the earth." As above, so below, let thy praises, O thou great Jehovah, be universally proclaimed. As the air surrounds all nature, so let thy praises gird the earth with a zone of song.

6. " They have prepared a net for my steps." The enemies of the godly spare no pains, but go about their wicked work with the coolest deliberation. As for each sort of fish, or bird, or beast, a fitting net is needed, so do the ungodly suit their net to their victim's circumstances and character with a careful craftiness of malice. Whatever David might do, and whichever way he might turn, his enemies were ready to entrap him in some way or other. " My soul is bowed down." He was held down like a bird in a trap; his enemies took care to leave him no chance of comfort. " They have digged a pit before me, into the midst whereof they are fallen themselves." He likens the designs of his persecutors to pits, which were commonly dug by hunters to entrap their prey; these were made in the usual path of the victim, and in this case David says, " before me," i.e., in my ordinary way. He rejoices because these devices had recoiled upon themselves. Saul hunted David, but David caught him more than once and might have slain him on the spot. Evil is a stream which one day flows back to its source. " Selah." We may sit down at the pit's mouth and view with wonder the just retaliations of providence.

7 My heart is fixed, O God, my heart is fixed: I will sing and give praise.
8 Awake up, my glory; awake, psaltery and harp: I myself will awake early.
9 I will praise thee, O Lord, among the people: I will sing unto thee among the nations.
10 For thy mercy is great unto the heavens, and thy truth unto the clouds.
11 Be thou exalted, O God, above the heavens: let thy glory be above all the earth.

7. " My heart is fixed." One would have thought he would have said, " My heart is fluttered;" but no, he is calm, firm, happy, resolute, established. When the central axle is secure, the whole wheel is right. If our great bower anchor holds, the ship cannot drive. " O God, my heart is fixed." I am resolved to trust thee, to serve thee, and to praise thee. Twice does he declare this to the glory of God who thus comforts the souls of his servants. Reader, it is surely well with thee, if thy once roving heart is now firmly fixed upon God and the proclamation of his glory. " I will sing and give praise." Vocally and instrumentally will I celebrate thy worship. With lip and with heart will I ascribe honour to thee. Satan shall not stop me, nor Saul, nor the Philistines. I will make Adullam ring with music, and all the caverns thereof echo with joyous song. Believer, make a firm decree that your soul in all seasons shall magnify the Lord.

> " Sing, though sense and carnal reason
>   Fain would stop the joyful song:
> Sing, and count it highest treason
>   For a saint to hold his tongue."

8. " Awake up, my glory." Let the noblest powers of my nature bestir themselves: the intellect which conceives thought, the tongue which expresses it, and the inspired imagination which beautifies it—let all be on the alert now that the hour for praise has come. " Awake, Psaltery and harp." Let all the music with which I am familiar be well attuned for the hallowed service of praise. " I myself will awake early." I will awake the dawn with my joyous notes. No sleepy verses and weary notes shall be heard from me; I will thoroughly arouse myself for this

high employ. When we are at our best we fall far short of the Lord's deserts, let us, therefore, make sure that what we bring him is our best, and, if marred with infirmity, at least let it not be deteriorated by indolence. Three times the Psalmist calls upon himself to awake. Do we need so much arousing, and for such work? Then let us not spare it, for the engagement is too honourable, too needful to be left undone or ill done for want of arousing ourselves.

9. "*I will praise thee, O Lord, among the people.*" Gentiles shall hear my praise. Here is an instance of the way in which the truly devout evangelic spirit o'erleaps the boundaries which bigotry sets up. The ordinary Jew would never wish the Gentile dogs to hear Jehovah's name, except to tremble at it ; but this grace-taught Psalmist has a missionary spirit, and would spread the praise and fame of his God. "*I will sing unto thee among the nations.*" However far off they may be, I would make them hear of thee through my glad Psalmody.

10. "*For thy mercy is great unto the heavens.*" Right up from man's lowliness to heaven's loftiness mercy reaches. Imagination fails to guess the height of heaven, and even thus the riches of mercy exceed our highest thoughts. The Psalmist, as he sits at the cave's mouth and looks up to the firmament, rejoices that God's goodness is vaster and sublimer than even the vaulted skies. "*And thy truth unto the clouds.*" Upon the cloud he sets the seal of his truth, the rainbow, which ratifies his covenant ; in the cloud he hides his rain and snow, which prove his truth by bringing to us seedtime and harvest, cold and heat. Creation is great, but the Creator greater far. Heaven cannot contain him ; above clouds and stars his goodness far exceeds.

11. "*Be thou exalted, O God, above the heavens.*" A grand chorus. Take it up, ye angels and ye spirits made perfect, and join in it, ye sons of men below, as ye say, "*Let thy glory be above all the earth.*" The prophet in the previous verse spoke of mercy "unto the heavens," but here his song flies "above the heavens ; " praise rises higher and higher, and knows no bound.

EXPLANATORY NOTES AND QUAINT SAYINGS.

Title.—This Psalm was composed, as the title notes, by David prayer-wise, when he hid himself from Saul in the cave, and is inscribed with a double title, *Al-taschith, Michtam of David.* *Al-taschith* refers to the scope, and *Michtam* to the dignity of the subject-matter. The former signifies *destroy not,* or, let there be no slaughter ; and may either refer to Saul, concerning whom he gave charge to his servants not to destroy him ; or rather it hath reference to God, to whom in this great exigence he poured out his soul in this pathetical ejaculation : *Al-taschith,* destroy not. The latter title, *Michtam,* signifies a golden ornament, and so is suited to the choice and excellent matter of the Psalm, which much more deserves such a title than Pythagoras' golden verses did.—*John Flavel* (1627—1691), *in " Divine Conduct, or the Mystery of Providence."*

Title.—A Psalm composed *when David fled from Saul in the cave,* which is referred to in Ps. cxlii., and which, because it is without any other distinction called "the cave," is probably that celebrated cave where David with his six hundred followers lay concealed when Saul entered and David cut off the skirt of his robe. The king, accompanied by three thousand followers, chased him to the loftiest alpine heights—" to the sheep-cotes," where the cattle where driven in the hottest summer months only—to hunt him in every hiding-place. There was a cave, in the darkened cool of which David and his men were hid. Such caves in Palestine and the East are frequently enlarged by human hands, and so capacious that they accommodate thousands of people. This song of complaint was written during the hours of suspense which David spent there, to wait until the calamity was overpast (ver. 2) ; in which he only gradually gains a stout heart (ver. 8). His life was really suspended by a hair if Saul or any of his attendants had espied him !—*Augustus F. Tholuck,* 1856.

Title.—" The cave." There appear good grounds for the local tradition which fixes the cave on the borders of the Dead Sea, although there is no certainty with regard to the particular cave pointed out. The cave so designated is at a point to which David was far more likely to summon his parents, whom he intended to take from Bethlehem into Moab, than to any place in the western plains. . . . . . . It is an immense natural cavern, the mouth of which can be approached only on foot along the side of the cliff. Irby and Mangles, who visited it without being aware that is was the reputed Cave of Adullam, state that it " runs in by a long winding, narrow passage, with small chambers or cavities on either side. We soon came to a large chamber with natural arches of great height ; from this last there were numerous passages, leading in all directions, occasionally joined by others at right angles, and forming a perfect labyrinth, which our guides assured us had never been perfectly explored—the people being afraid of losing themselves. The passages are generally four feet high by three feet wide, and were all on a level with each other." . . . . It seems probable that David as a native of Bethlehem, must have been well acquainted with this remarkable spot, and had probably often availed himself of its shelter, when out with his father's flocks. It would, therefore, naturally occur to him as a place of refuge when he fled from Gath.—*John Kitto* (1804—1854), *in " A Cyclopædia of Biblical Literature."*

Whole Psalm.—Mystically this hymn may be construed of Christ, who was in the days of his flesh assaulted by the tyranny both of spiritual and temporal enemies. His temporal enemies, Herod and Pontius Pilate, with the Gentiles and people of Israel, furiously raged and took counsel together against him. The chief priests and princes were, saith Hierome, like *lions*, and the people like the *whelps of lions*, all of them in a readiness to devour his soul. The rulers *laid a net for his feet* in their captious interrogatories, asking (Matt. xxii. 17), " Is it lawful to give tribute unto Cæsar, or not ? " and (John viii. 5) whether the woman taken in the very act of adultery should be stoned to death or no. The people were " *set on fire*," when as they raged against him, and *their teeth and tongues were spears and swords*, in crying, " Crucify him, crucify him." His spiritual enemies also sought *to swallow him up ;* his *soul* was *among lions* all the days of his life, at the hour of his death especially. The devil in tempting and troubling him, had *laid a snare for his feet ;* and death, in *digging a pit* for him, had thought *to devour* him. As David was in the *cave,* so Christ the Son of David was in the *grave.*—*John Boys,* 1571—1625.

Verse 1.—" *Be merciful unto me, O God,*" etc. This excellent Psalm was composed by David when there was enough to discompose the best man in the world. The repetition notes both the extremity of the danger, and the ardency of the supplicant. *Mercy ! Mercy ! Nothing but mercy,* and that exerting itself in an extraordenary way, can now save him from ruin. The arguments he pleads for obtaining mercy in this distress are very considerable. 1. He pleads his reliance upon God as an argument to move mercy. " *My soul trusteth in thee,*" etc. This his trust and dependence upon God, though it be not argumentative in respect of the dignity of the *act ;* yet it is so in respect both of the nature of the *object,* a compassionate God, who will not expose any that take shelter under his wings, and in respect of the *promise,* whereby protection is assured to them that fly to him for sanctuary. Isa. xxvi. 3. 2. He pleads former experiences of his help in past distresses, as an argument encouraging hope under the present strait (ver. 2). —*John Flavel.*

Verse 1.—" *Be merciful unto me.*" According to the weight of the burden that grieveth us, is the cry that comes upon us. How do poor condemned prisoners cry to their judges, " Have pity upon us, have pity upon us ! " David, in the day of his calamities doubles his prayer for mercy : " *Be merciful unto me, O God, be merciful unto me : for my soul trusteth in thee,*" etc. " *Until these calamities be overpast.*" It was not a single calamity, but a multitude of calamities which compassed David, and therefore he compasseth the Lord about with petitions. His spirit being up in prayer, like a bell that rings out, he strikes on both sides, " *Be merciful unto me, O God, be merciful unto me.*"—*Joseph Caryl.*

Verse 1.—" *Be merciful unto me.*" The first clause contains the prayer itself in a very forcible word חָנֵּנִי, properly, " Show thy most tender affection to me," such as animals, with a humming sound, show to their young.—*Hermann Venema.*

Verse 1.—" *For my soul trusteth in thee.*" The best reason with God, who " taketh pleasure in those that hope in his mercy." Ps. cxlvii. 11.—*Pool's Synopsis.*

Verse 1.—" *Soul.*" His *soul* trusted in God ; and this is a form of expression

the force of which is not to be overlooked ; for it implies that the trust which he
exercised proceeded from his very innermost affections—that it was of no volatile
character, but deeply and strongly rooted.   He declares the same truth in figurative
terms, when he adds his persuasion that God would cover him with the shadow of
his wings.—*John Calvin.*

Verse 1.—" *In the shadow of thy wings I will trust ;* " properly, I will seek for
protection.   The very delightful figure here employed, is taken from the chicken
lying safely hid under the mother's wings : at the same time it seems to have
reference to the wings of the cherubim, by which the mercy-seat was covered.—
Simon de Muis, 1587—1644.

Verse 1.—" *The shadow of thy wings.*"   Compare Psalm xvii. 8 ; lxi. 4 ; and
Matthew xxiii. 37 ; and the Apocalyptic imagery, describing the church fleeing
from the dragon in the wilderness ; and " to her are given the two wings of the
great eagle," and she is delivered from the dragon, who desires to *swallow her up.*
See Rev. xii. 6, 15, 16.—*Christopher Wordsworth,* 1868.

Verse 1.—" *Until these calamities be overpast.*"   He compareth his affliction and
calamity to a storm that cometh and goeth : as it is not always fair weather with
us in this life, so not always foul.   Athanasius said of Julian furiously raging against
the Lord's Anointed, " *Nubecula est, cito transibit,*" he is a little cloud ; he will
soon pass away.   Man is born to labour and dolor, to travail and trouble ; to labour
in his actions, to dolor in his passions ; and so, " Great are the troubles of the
righteous, but the Lord delivereth him out of all."   If we put our trust in him
and cast all our care upon him, he will in his good time bring it to pass, that all our
afflictions shall overpass.   He will either take them from us or us from them, and
then we shall assuredly know that the troubles of this life present are not worthy
of the glory which in the life to come shall be showed unto us.   For as the globe
of the earth, which improperly for his show of bigness we term the world, and is,
after the mathematician's account, many thousand miles in compass ; yet, being
compared unto the greatness of the starry sky's circumference, is but a centre or
little prick : so the travail and affliction in this life temporal, in respect of the joys
eternal in the world to come, bear not any proportion, but are to be reputed in
comparison a very nothing, as a dark cloud that cometh and goeth in a moment.—
John Boys.

Verses 1, 2, 3.—" *In the shadow of thy wings will I make my refuge, until these
calamities be overpast,*" etc.   As if he said, Lord, I am already in the cave and in the
hold, and in the shadow of it, but yet for all that I think not myself safe indeed,
till I have made my refuge in the shadow of thy wings : that is therefore the course I
resolve and build upon.   It was wisely done of him : and mark what course he
takes to do it, verse 2, " I will cry unto God most high," I wil by prayer put myself
under the shadow of God's wings ; and mark what success should follow, verse 3,
" He shall send from heaven, and save me from the reproach of him that would
swallow me up.   God shall send forth his mercy and his truth."   When we send
prayers up to heaven, God will send help down from heaven.   But yet David *prays*
to God, as well as *trusts* in God.   And unless we pray as well as trust, our trust will
fail us, for we must trust to God for that we pray for.—*Jeremiah Dyke,* 1620.

Verse 2.—" *Unto God that performeth all things for me.*"   God's favours already
received are a pledge that he will complete his work of love " *upon* (עלי) *me.*"   The
beginning is the earnest of the completion.   His *word* is a gurantee for the *performance* of " all things " that I need.   (Compare verse 3 ; Psalm lvi. 4 ; 1 Samuel ii. 9 ;
iii. 12 ; xxiii. 17 ; xxiv. 21 ; Psalm cxxviii. 8 ; Job x. 3, 8 ; xiv, 15 ; Philippians
i. 6 ; Isaiah xxvi. 12).—*A. R. Fausset.*

Verse 2.—" *God that performeth all things for me.*"   Heb. *that performeth* (or
perfecteth, or *finisheth,* as this word is rendered, Psalm cxxxviii. 8   *i.e.,* will
certainly perform or finish), *for,* or *towards,* or *concerning me.*   He doth not express
what he performeth, or perfecteth, or fulfilleth, but leaveth it to be understood,
as being easy to be understood.   " *He performeth* " or *perfecteth,* to wit, all that
he hath promised ; engaged himself to perform what he hath begun to do, or what
is yet to be performed ; it being usual in the Hebrew language to understand a
verbal noun after the verb.   He implies that God is not like men, who make large
promises, but either through inability, or carelessness, or unfaithfulness, do not
perform them, but will certainly be as good as his word.—*Matthew Pool,* 1624—1679.

Verse 2 (*last clause*).—The word which we translate " *performeth* " comes from a root that signifies both to *perfect* and to *desist* or *cease*. For wnen a business is performed and perfected, the agent then ceases and desists from working : he puts to the last hand when he finishes the work. To such a happy issue the Lord hath brought all his doubtful and difficult matters before ; and this gives him encouragement that he will still be gracious, and perfect that which concerneth him now, as he speaks, Psalm cxxxviii. 8, " The Lord will perfect that which concerneth me." The Septuagint renders it by τόν ἐνεργετη σουτά με, who *profiteth* or *benefiteth* me. And it is a certain truth, that all the results and issues of providence are profitable and beneficial to the saints. But the supplement in our translation well conveys the importance of the place : " who performeth *all things ;* " and it involves the most strict and proper notion of providence, which is nothing else but the performance of God's gracious purposes and promises to his people. And therefore Vatablus and Muis supply and fill up the room which the conciseness of the original leaves, with *quæ promisit :* " I will cry unto God most high ; unto God that performeth *the things which he hath promised.*" Payment is the performance of promises. Grace makes the promise, and providence the payment. Piscator fills it with *benignitatem et misericordiam suam ;* " unto God that performeth *his kindness and mercy.*" But still it supposes the mercy performed to be contained in the promise, and much more so in the providential performance of it to us.—*John Flavel.*

Verse 2 (last clause).—David even then when he fled from Saul in the cave he looks upon God as having *performed all things for him.* The word is, he hath *perfected all things ;* and it is observable that David uses the same expression of praising God here when he was in the cave, hiding himself to save his life as he did when he triumphed over his enemies.—Ps. vi. and Ps. cviii.—*Jeremiah Burroughs,* 1599—1646.

Verse 2 (last clause).—The Targum curiously paraphrases this clause : " Who ordered the spider that wrought the web, on my account, at the mouth of the cave ; " applying a later historical fact, which, however, may have had its prototype in David's history.—*Andrew A. Bonar. in " Christ and his Church in the Book of Psalms,"* 1859.

Verse 3.—" *Him that would swallow me up.*" If I were to take you to my house, and say that I had an exquisitely fat man, and wished you to join me in eating him, your indignation could be restrained by nothing. You would pronounce me to be crazy. There is not in New York a man so mean that he would not put down a man who should propose to have a banquet off from a fellow man, cutting steaks out of him, and eating them. And that is nothing but feasting on the human body, while they all will sit down, and take a man's soul, and look for the tender loins, and invite their neighbours in to partake of the little titbits. They will take a man's honour and name, and broil them over the coals of their indignation, and fill the whole room with the aroma thereof, and give their neighbour a piece, and watch him, and wink as he tastes it. You all eat men up. . . . You eat the souls, the finest elements of men. You are more than glad if you can whisper a word that is derogatory to a neighbour, or his wife, or his daughter. . . . The morsel is too exquisite to be lost. Here is the soul of a person, here is a person's hope for this world and the world to come, and you have it on your fork, and you cannot refrain from tasting it, and give it to some one else to taste. You are cannibals, eating men's honour and name and rejoicing in it—and that, too, when you do not always know that the things charged against them are true ; when in ninety-nine cases out of a hundred the probabilities are that they are not true.—*Henry Ward Beecher,* 1870.

Verse 3.—" *God shall send forth his mercy and his truth,*" viz., to save me. That is to say, God, to manifest his mercy, and vindicate the truth of his promises, will save me. The reader will observe, that mercy and truth are here poetically represented as ministers of God, standing in his presence, ready to execute his pleasure, and employed by him in the salvation of his people.—*Samuel Chandler.*

Verse 3.—" *His mercy and his truth.*" He need not send down angels, he need send but " *mercy and truth* " down, which elsewhere it is said he prepares in the heavens. Ps. lxi. 7. He prepares commissions for them, and sends them down with them for execution.—*Thomas Goodwin.*

Verse 4.—" *My soul is among lions.*" This may also be construed of the church and that both in respect of her spiritual enemies and temporal. As for her ghostly foes, the devil is a *roaring lion* (1 Pet. v. 8), and our sins are the *whelps of lions*, ready to devour us. And concerning outward enemies, the church in this world is like Daniel in the lion's den, or as "the sucking child playing upon the hole of the asp." Isa. xi. 8. She hath here no visible power or outward help to fly to for succour, all her trust is in the Lord, and "under the shadow of his wings is her refuge, till this evil is overpast." . . . . And surely, beloved, if the church had not any other enemies, but only these monstrous Antichrists of Rome, yet she might truly complain with our prophet here, "*My soul is among lions.*" Eleven popes had that name, whereof all, excepting two or three, were roaring lions in their Bulls, and ravening lions in seeking after their prey. *Leo* the tenth so pilled* and polled† the goodly nations of Germany with his impardonable pardons and merciless indulgences, as that his insupportable cruelty gave the first occasion of the Reformation of religion in that country.—*John Boys.*

Verse 4 (*first clause*).—"Mudge translates literally, 'I lie with my soul amidst lionesses.'" This agrees with the opinion of Bochart, who thinks that the animals here intended are lionesses, properly, when giving suck to their young, a time when they are peculiarly fierce and dangerous, "nor need we wonder," he observes, "that the lioness is reckoned among the fiercest lions; for the lioness equals, or even exceeds, the lion in strength and fierceness;" and this he proves from the testimonies of ancient writers.—*James Anderson's Note to Calvin in loc.*, 1846.

Verse 4.—"*And I lie even among them that are set on fire.*" The whole pith lies in the word אֶשְׁכְּבָה, *I will recline*, which denotes a tranquil and secure condition of body and mind, like a man *reclining* and sleeping, as Ps. iii. 5: "*I laid me down and slept, I awaked;*" and lived composedly; Ps. iv. 9; "*I will both lay me down in peace,*" etc.—*Hermann Venema.*

Verse 4.—The horrors of a lion's den, the burning of a fiery furnace, and the cruel onset of war, are the striking images by which David here describes the peril and wretchedness of his present condition.—*John Morison.*

Verse 6.—"*Net.*" Not having fire-arms, the ancients were much more skilful than the moderns in the use of snares, nets, and pits for capturing wild animals. A large class of Biblical figures and allusions necessarily presupposes this state of things.—*W. M. Thomson.*

Verse 7.—"*My heart is fixed, O God,*" etc. The Psalmist, knowing that it is the order and work of God, first to prepare the heart for communion, and then to incline his own ear to hear his people, and to entertain communion with them in ordinances, he doth observe this order, and follow it with a practise suitable to it in his daily addresses to God, that is thus, wheresoever he doth find his heart put into a fitted and prepared frame for communion with God, he doth not let it die again, and go out of frame by a slothful neglect of such a disposition of heart. No, but he immediately sets himself to duty, to worship God, and to the acts of his worship, in his ordinances, as he expresseth himself in Ps. lvii, 7; viz., thus— נָכוֹן לִבִּי אֱלֹהִים נָכוֹן לִבִּי, *Nachon libbi Elohim, nachon libbi* (there is the first; he finds his heart fitted and prepared for communion with God): "My heart," saith he, "is fitted or prepared" (for the word נָכוֹן, *nachon* is the passive conjugation *niphal*, signifying, he is fitted or prepared, from the root, כּוּן *chun*, he fitted or prepared, in the active; and so it is rather to be rendered prepared or fitted, then "fixed," thus: לִבִּי, *libbi*, my heart; נָכוֹן, *nachon*, is fitted or prepared), "O God, my heart is fitted or prepared" for communion with thee. Well, what follows? He presently sets himself upon that great duty and ordinance of communion with God, in the praising of his name and singing forth those praises, as in the words immediately following in the same verse, thus: "My heart is prepared, O God, my heart is prepared:" therefore, וַאֲזַמֵּרָה, *ashidah va-azamerah*, "*I will sing and give praise.*" —*William Strong, in "Communion with God,"* 1656.

Verse 7.—"*My heart is fixed, O God,*" etc. Fitness for duty lies in the orderly temper of body and mind, making a man willing to undertake, and able to finish his work with comfortable satisfaction. If either the body or mind be distempered, a man is unfit for such an undertaking; both must be in a suitable frame, like a well-tuned instrument, else there will be no melody: hence when David prepared himself for praises and worship, he tells us *his heart was ready and fixed*, and then, his *tongue*

---

* Pill=peel, to pillage, plunder, strip.   † Poll, used synonymously with peel.

was ready also (Psalm xlv. 1.), so was his hand with Psaltery and harp; all these were awakened into a suitable posture. That a man is or hath been in a fit order for service may be concluded from (1.) His alacrity to undertake a duty. (2.) His activity in the prosecution. (3.) His satisfaction afterward. Right grounds and principles in these things being still pre-supposed.—*Richard Gilpin*, (1625—1699, 1700) *in "Dæmonologia Sacra."*

Verse 7.—" *I will sing.*" It should alarm the wicked that they are contending with a people who sing and shout on the battle-field. Yea, they never sing louder than when most distressed and afflicted. Whether saints conquer or are conquered they still sing on. Blessed be God for that. Let sinners tremble at contending with men of a spirit so heavenly.—*William S. Plumer.*

Verse 7.—Sincerity makes the Christian sing, when he hath nothing to his supper, David was in none of the best case when in the cave, yet we never find him merrier: his heart makes sweeter music than ever his harp did.—*William Gurnall.*

Verses 7, 8.—That worship that is performed with a sleepy, drowsy body, is a weak worship, but the Psalmist here makes the awaking of the body to be the fruit and effect of the preparation of the heart; " *Awake up, my glory; awake, Psaltery and harp: I myself will awake early.*" Why so? My heart is prepared. The heart prepared and thereby awakened, will awake the body. To worship God therefore without a prepared heart, is to worship him with a drowsy body, because with a drowsy heart, and therefore weakly.—*John Angier, in "An Help to better Hearts, for better Times,"* 1647.

Verse 8.—" *Awake up, my glory; awake, Psaltery and harp: I myself will awake early.*" We must prevent God by early praise as well as prayer; " The God of my mercy shall prevent me," sings David; and every child of David must prevent God again with his songs. Jehoshaphat delighted God with instruments of music before his deliverance. Faith must tune an ἐπινίκιον, a psalm of victory before the triumph. Praise is the ingenious mother of future mercies; as the Virgin Mary sang at Hebron before the birth of her son at Bethlehem. Oh, heavenly contention between mercy and duty!—*Samuel Lee*, 1625—1691.

Verse 8.—" *Awake up, my glory,*" etc. We must sing *with excited grace.* Not only with grace habitual, but with excited and actual: the musical instrument delights not but when it is played upon. In this duty we must follow Paul's advice to Timothy (2 Tim. i. 6), ἀναζωπυρεῖν, stir up the grace that is in us, and cry out as David, " *Awake love, awake delight.*" Ps. lvii. 8. The clock must be wound up before it can guide our time; the bird pleaseth not in her nest, but in her notes; the chimes only make music while they are going. Let us therefore beg the Spirit to blow upon our garden, that the spices thereof may flow out, when we set upon this joyous service. God loves active grace in duty, that the soul should be ready trimmed when it presents itself to Christ in any worship.—*John Wells, in "Morning Exercises,"* 1674.

Verse 8.—" *I will awake early,*" Literally, " I will awake the dawn," a bold figure of poetry, as if the writer had said—The morning shall not awake me to praise; but in my songs I will anticipate the dawn.—*R. T. Society's Notes.*

Verse 8.—It will answer our purpose to take notice, first, of the *terms* David uses, and then, secondly, press the *exhortation.* Of the terms he uses: 1. My *glory.* That is my *soul* (say some) because the spirit of a man is the glory of a man, whereby he is dignified and raised so much above the *brutes*, as to be but a " little lower than the angels," nay, to be akin to God himself, " the Father of spirits." My *musical skill*, say others, the glory of the artist above the unskilful; and that wherein David had the glory of excelling, as Jubal had of the first invention. My *tongue*, say others; for this is also the glory of a man above dumb creatures, and the glory of a wise man above a fool. And as the tongue is the glory of a man, so the glory of the tongue is to glorify God. Praise is the glory of all other uses to which the tongue is employed; and the tongue is, in the body, that " temple of the Holy Ghost," what the silver trumpet was in the temple of Solomon; to sound the high praises of God, and express the raised affections of our souls.

2. " *Awake Psaltery and harp.*" The one for a Psalm, the other for a spiritual song or hymn; that is to say, all my musical instruments and skill I will employ in, and consecrate to the glory of him who " puts new songs into my mouth." He first teaches my fingers to fight, and then to play the *epinikion*, or song of triumph. Sound, then, my Psaltery and harp, emulous of those that are around the throne

above ; your melody can soften my cares, lay my fears, and turn my *cave* into a *choir*. As to these instruments in the worship of God, they were doubtless allowed to David, and to the church in his time. They were agreeable to the state of that church and people, who were led very much by their senses ; and whose infant and less discerning condition made it needful for the natural man to have something to fasten upon and be entertained with in the worship of God, and to sweeten and take off from the labour and burden of that service. But as the gospel worship and appointments are a more spiritual, pleasant, and reasonable service, and need them less, so in the gospel institution we find no footsteps of them ; and we know who first brought them into the church, as well as who first brought them into the world. It is not my business here to dispute this matter; and he must at any time do it but indifferently, whose inclination is against him all the while, and whose genius tempts him to wish himself solidly confuted in all he can advance. But since I find these instruments in my text, and since the sound of such texts as these is made use of to turn the public worship so frequently into concerts of music, I shall leave them with this remark : that to let them alone, especially in public worship, though one thought them tolerable, has a much better grace with it than to declare them " sorely displeasing to God, and that they filthily defile his holy house and place of prayer."

3. " *I myself will awake early.*" And without this, all the rest had been an empty sound ; there would have been no melody to the Lord, whatsoever good music he might have made to himself. He would not put God off with a sacrifice of mere air. He summons the attendance of all his powers. Himself is the offering ; and his music plays to the sacrifice, as it goes up in holy affections and spiritual joys ; and unless these accompany the song, the mere breath of an organ, or the trembling of the strings of an harp is as good devotion and less offensive to God. Consider the *nature and excellency of the duty*. Singing Psalms is a compound of several other duties. It contains prayer to a very great advantage : the stretch of the voice does humour and lead on the earnest reaching of the mind after the desired blessing. It is the very element and breath of praise ; and the apostle tells us that " teaching and admonishing one another " is performed in singing " Psalms and hymns and spiritual songs." For when we sing of *judgment*, it is awakening to sinners ; and when we sing of *mercy*, it is comforting to all. Meditation cannot have a better help. The solemn movement of the time gives room for the mind to compass the full sense of the matter, and to impress it deep ; and while the tongue is making the *pause*, the heart may make *elevation*. In short, it gives an accent to all duty ; it is the music of all other ordinances; it is adapted and suited to all circumstances ; as appears from the Psalms composed upon all occasions and subjects, doctrinal, prophetical, hortatory, and historical ; of praise and prayer, of grief and joy, in the penitential and complaining, in the triumphal and rejoicing ; as if singing of psalms could stand for everything, and, like the manna in the wilderness, gives a taste of all the other food we enjoy in the house of God.—*Benjamin Grosvenor, D.D.* (1675—1758), *in " An Exhortation to the Duty of Singing." Eastcheap Lectures,* 1810.

Verse 8.—The *Psaltery* was a stringed instrument, usually with twelve strings, and played with the fingers. The *harp* or lyre was a stringed instrument, usually consisting of ten strings. Josephus says that it was struck or played with a key. It appears, however, that it was sometimes played with the fingers.—*Albert Barnes.*

Verse 9.—" *I will praise thee, O Lord, among the people.*" The Spirit of God who indited this scripture, made his penman know that the Gentiles should have the use of his Psalms.—*David Dickson.*

Verse 9.—" *The people* "—" *the nations.*" The Hebrew church was neither called nor qualified to be a missionary society, but it never ceased to desire and hope for the conversion of the nations. This is seen in those passages in which the Psalmists betray a consciousness that they shall one day have all the world for auditors. How boldly does David exclaim, " *I will sing unto thee among the nations.*" In the same spirit, a later Psalmist summons the church to lift up her voice, so that all the nations may hear her recital of the Lord's mighty acts : " O give thanks unto the Lord ; call upon his name : make known his deeds among the people." Ps. cv. 1. The full import of this class of texts is often hidden from the English reader by the circumstance that our translators have hardly ever used the word *people* in its plural form. Twice in the Revelation they venture to write *peoples* ;

everywhere else the singular form has to do duty for both numbers ; so that in not a few passages the sense is greatly obscured to those who have no access either to the original or to other versions. In the Psalms, in particular, the mention of the Gentiles is more frequent than the English reader is made aware of. It is to be observed, moreover, that in addition to this strain of indirect prediction, the conversion of the world is articulately celebrated in many glorious Psalms. Indeed, so numerous are these, and so generally distributed over the centuries between David and Ezra, that it would seem that at no time during the long history of inspired Psalmody, did the Spirit cease to indite new songs in which the children of Zion might give utterance to their world-embracing hopes.—*William Binnie, D.D., in " The Psalms : their History, Teachings, and Use," 1870.*

Verses 10, 11.—A hard and ungrateful heart beholds even in prosperity only isolated drops of divine grace ; but a grateful one like David's, though chased by persecutors, and striking the harp in the gloom of a cave, looks upon the mercy and faithfulness of God as a mighty ocean, waving and heaving from the earth to the clouds, and from the clouds to the earth again.—*Augustus F. Tholuck.*

Verse 11.—" *Be thou exalted, O God, above the heavens,*" etc. Greater words of prayer than these never came from human lips. Heaven and earth have as they imply, a mutually interwoven history, and the blessed, glorious end of this is in the sunrise of the Divine glory over both.—*Franz Delitzsch, 1869.*

HINTS TO PREACHERS.

Verse 1 (*first clause*).—*Repetiton in prayer.* I. Its dangers. May degenerate into " vain repetitions." Carried to excess painfully suggests the idea, God is unwilling. II. Its uses. Eases the soul like tears. Manifests intense emotion. Enables those of less mental activity to join in a general supplication.—*R. A. Griffin.*

Verse 1.—Here are—I. Calamities. 1. War. 2. Pestilence. 3. Privations. 4. Sin, greatest of all. 5. Death. 6. Curse of a broken law. II. Here is a refuge from these calamities. 1. In God. 2. Specially in the mercy of God. III. There is flying to that refuge. 1. By faith ; " *My soul trusteth in thee ;*" " *Under the shadow,*" etc. 2. By prayer ; " *Be,*" etc. IV. Here is continuance both in faith and prayer ; " *until,*" etc.—*G. R.*

Verses 1, 4, 6, 7.—Note the varying condition of the same heart, at the same time. " *My soul trusteth in thee.*" " *My soul is among lions.*" " *My soul is bowed down.*" " *My heart is fixed.*"

Verse 2.—Prayer to the performing God. He performs all his promises, all my salvation, all my preservation, all needed between here and heaven. Here he reveals his omnipotence, his grace, his faithfulness, his immutability ; and we are bound to show our faith, patience, joy, and gratitude.

Verse 2.—Strange reasons. I. The Psalmist, in the depths of distress, cries to God, because he is most high in glory. Surely this thought might well paralyse him with the fear of divine inaccessibility, but the soul quickened with suffering, sees through and beyond the metaphor, rejoices in the truth, " Though the Lord be high, yet hath he respect unto the lowly." II. He cries to God for help, because God *is* performing all things for him. Why urge him then ? Prayer is the music to which " the mighty man of war " goes forth to battle.—*R. A. G.*

Verse 3.—The saint's comfort in adversity. I. All contingencies are provided for : " *He shall* (or will) *send.*" II. The highest resources are available : " *from heaven.*" III. The worst foes will be overcome in the end : " *him that would swallow me up.*" IV. By the holiest means : " *mercy and truth.*"—*R. A. G.*

Verse 3.—The celestial messengers. What they are. The certainty of their being sent. Their effectual operation. The grateful receiver.

Verse 3 (*last clause*).—The harmony of the divine attributes in salvation. Mercy founded on truth, truth vindicating mercy. Mercy without injustice, justice honoured in mercy.

Verse 4.—" My soul is among lions." How came I there? If for God's sake, then I may remember—1. So was my Lord in the wilderness. 2. The lions are chained. 3. Their howling is all they can do. 4. I shall come out of their den alive, unhurt, honoured. 5. The Lion of Judah is with me. 6. I shall soon be among the angels.

Verse 5.—I. The end which God has in view, both in heaven and earth, in a sinful and in sinless worlds—his own glory. II. Our duty to acquiesce in that end : *" Be thou,"* etc.—not self, not men, not angels—*" Be thou exalted,"* etc. In this we would acquiesce—1. Actively, by seeking that end. 2. Passively, by submission to his will.—*G. R.*

Verse 6 (first clause).—I. Who are they? 1. Those who lead us into sin. 2. Who argue from worldly philosophy. 3. Who proclaim priestly and sacramental superstition. 4. Who decoy us from the church of God. 5. Who teach Antinomian doctrine. II. How shall we escape them? 1. Keep out of their way. 2. Keep to God's way. 3. Trust daily in the Lord.

Verse 6.—" My soul is bowed down." I. *The prostration.* 1. Caused by enemies, weakness, fear, pain. 2. Deep, agonising, self-revealing. 3. Common to the Head and the members. II. *The consolation.* 1. Bowed down, but not condemned. 2. Hoping in the promise. 3. Trusting in God. 4. Expecting a blessing from the trial.

Verse 7 (first clause).—It is implied that the *" heart"* is the main thing required in all acts of devotion ; nothing is done to purpose in religion further than it is done with the heart. The heart must be *" fixed ; "* fixed *for* the duty, fitted and put in frame for it ; fixed *in* the duty by a close application ; *attending on the Lord* without distraction.—*Matthew Henry.*

Verse 7.—I. What is fixed? the heart, not the mind merely, but the will, the conscience, the affections, which draw the mind after them : *" My heart is fixed"* —found an anchorage, a resting-place, not therefore at the mercy of every gale, etc. II. The objects upon which it is fixed. 1. Upon God. 2. Upon his word. 3. Upon his salvation. 4. Upon heaven. III. The fixedness of the heart upon these objects, denotes—1. Singleness of aim. 2. Uniformity of action. 3. Perseverance to the end.—*G. R.*

Verses 7, 8, 9.—1. He that will be thankful must treasure up in his heart and memory the courtesy that is done him ; so had David done, and therefore he mentions *his heart ;* and to make it more emphatical, he names it again, *" My heart."* 2. After he remembers it, he must be affected with it, and resolve upon it ; so doth David : *" My heart is ready,"* or else, *" My heart is fixed ; "* confirmed I am in it to be thankful, and I cannot be altered. 3. 'Tis not enough that a man carry about with him a thankful heart ; he must *anunciare,* tell it abroad, and make it known publicly what God hath done for him ; yea, and do it joyfully too : *" I will,"* saith David, *" sing and give praise."* 4. He must use all means he can to make it known—*" tongue," " psaltery,"* and *" harp,"* all are little enough. Whence, by an apostrophe, David turns to these. *" Awake, my glory : "* i.e. *Tongue, awake ; lute and harp, awake ; I myself will awake.* 5. He must not do it in a sleepy manner, but with intention and earnestness of spirit : *" Awake, awake, I will awake."* 6. He must take the first opportunity to do it, and not hang off and delay it : *" I will awake early."* 7. He must do it in such a place, and such an assembly as may most redound to God's honour : *" I will praise thee, O Lord, among the people :* I will sing unto thee *among the nations."*—*William Nicholson.*

Verse 8.—" I myself will wake early." I will sleep lightly, for I am in an enemy's country ; I will ask God to arouse me ; I will set the alarum of watchfulness ; I will hear the cock of providential warning ; the light of the Sun shall arouse me ; the activities of the church, the trumpet of my foes, and the bell of duty shall combine to awaken me.

Verse 9.—Who? *" I."* What? *" Will praise."* Whom? *" Thee, O Lord."* Where? *" Among the people."* Why?

Verse 9.—Public profession. I. A necessity. II. A privilege. III. A duty. —*R. A. G.*

Verse 10.—The mercy of God reaches to the heavens—I. As a throne. God is exalted in our eyes by his mercy. II. As a ladder. By mercy we ascend from earth to heaven. III. As a rainbow. Present and past mercies argue exemption for the saints from the wrath of heaven. IV. As a mountain. Its base is on the earth though its summit is lost in clouds. The influence of the cross towers to the heaven of heavens. Who can tell the glory of the summit of this mountain, whose *base* is refulgent with glory !—*R. A. G.*

Verse 10.—The amazing greatness of mercy. It is not said merely that it is high as heaven, but great unto the heavens. It is *high* as the heavens, over-topping the greatest sin, and highest thought of man. II. It is *wide* as the far-reaching sky, compassing men of all ages, countries, classes, etc. III. It is *deep.* Everything of God is proportionate ; this, therefore, is deep in abiding foundation, and infinite wisdom.

THE
TREASURY OF DAVID

PREFACE.

THIS volume completes one half of my labour upon this priceless book, and my humble prayer is that I may be spared to conclude the other portion So uncertain is human life, and so often have men's best designs remained unfinished, that I will press on with all diligence, lest, perhaps, the lamp of life should go out ere the writer has seen by its light the word FINIS at the conclusion of the last verse.

This volume has cost more labour than any other, because upon the larger proportion of the Psalms contained in it no great writers have expatiated at length. Some six or seven of them are specially notable, and have, therefore, been expounded and preached upon on all hands, but the rest remain almost untrodden ground in sacred literature, hence the gathering of extracts has required a wider range of reading and far more laborious research. Where one author writes upon a portion of Scripture, all write, while other passages remain almost untouched. This has driven me very much more to the Latin authors, and in them to a vein of exposition very little worked in these days. The neglect of these voluminous expositors is, however, not very censurable, for as a rule the authors are rather heavy than weighty. "Art is long and life is short," hence I found myself unequal to the unaided accomplishment of my task, and I have had to call in the aid of my excellent friend Mr. Gracey, the accomplished classical tutor of "the Pastors' College," to assist me in the work of winnowing the enormous heaps of Latin comments. Huge folios, full of dreary wordspinning, yield here and there a few goodly grains, and these, I trust, will be valuable enough to my readers to repay my coadjutor and myself for our pains. For the selection of extracts I alone am responsible, for the accuracy of the translations we are jointly accountable. The reader will note that not without much expense of money, as well as toil, he has here furnished to his hand the pith of Venema, Le Blanc, Lorinus, Gerhohus, Musculus, Martin Geier, Mollerus, and Simon de Muis ; with occasional notes from Vitringa, Jansenius, Savonarola, Vatablus, Turrecremata, Marloratus, Palanterius, Theodoret, and others, as they were judged worthy of insertion. I can truly say that I have never flinched from a difficulty, or spared exertion in order to make the work as complete as it lay in my power to render it, either by my own endeavours or the help of others. My faithful amanuensis, Mr. Keys, has been spared to me, and has been a continual visitor at the British Museum. Lambeth

Palace, Dr. Williams' Museum, and Sion College; and many have been the courtesies which, despite differences of creed, I have received in his person from those who are in authority in those treasures of literature; for all which I would now record my hearty thanks.

No object has been before me but that of serving the church and glorifying God by doing this work right thoroughly. I cannot hope to be remunerated pecuniarily; if only the bare outlay be met I shall be well content, the rest is an offering to the best of Masters, whose word is meat and drink to those who study it. The enjoyment of the work is more than sufficient reward, and the hope of helping my brethren in their Biblical studies is very sweet to me.

The late increase of wages to printers, and the rise both in paper and binding, may compel an advance in the very low price charged for these volumes hitherto, but this shall not be made unless it becomes absolutely necessary to screen me from loss. As a larger sale will secure a return of my outlay, the matter is mainly in the hands of the public. Volume I. being now in the third edition, and the second edition of Volume II. being upon the press, I am led to hope that the present volume will also meet with a large and rapid sale; and if so, the old price may suffice to cover the outlay.

My venerable friend, Mr. George Rogers, has furnished me with many hints for the notes to preachers, and it is hoped that this portion of the work has been so improved that it will not be the least useful part of it. Testimonies received lead to the belief that in the two former volumes numerous students have found help in that department.

There is no need to multiply words in this preface, but it is incumbent upon me to bless the Lord for help given, help daily and hourly sought while I have been occupied in this service; and it is also on my heart to ask a favourable mention of my volumes among their friends from those who kindly appreciate them.

C. H. Spurgeon

INDEX

OF AUTHORS QUOTED OR REFERRED TO.

PSALM LVIII.

To the Chief Musician.—*Although David had his own case in his mind's eye, yet he wrote not as a private person, but as an inspired prophet, and therefore his song is presented, for public and perpetual use, to the appointed guardian of the Temple psalmody.* Al-taschith. *The wicked are here judged and condemned, but over the godly the sacred " Destroy not " is solemnly pronounced.* Michtam of David. *This is the fourth of the Psalms of the Golden Secret, and the second of the " Destroy nots." These names if they serve for nothing else may be useful to aid the memory. Men give names to their horses, jewels, and other valuables, and these names are meant not so much to describe as to distinguish them, and in some cases to set forth the owner's high esteem of his treasure ; after the same fashion the Oriental poet gave a title to the song he loved, and so aided his memory, and expressed his estimation of the strain. We are not always to look for a meaning in these superscriptions, but to treat them as we would the titles of poems, or the names of tunes.*

DIVISION.—*The ungodly enemy is accused, verses 1—5 ; judgment is sought from the judge, verses 6—8 ; and seen in prophetic vision as already executed, verses 9—11.*

EXPOSITION.

DO ye indeed speak righteousness, O congregation ? do ye judge uprightly, O ye sons of men ?

2 Yea, in heart ye work wickedness ; ye weigh the violence of your hands in the earth.

3 The wicked are estranged from the womb : they go astray as soon as they be born, speaking lies.

4 Their poison *is* like the poison of a serpent : *they are* like the deaf adder *that* stoppeth her ear ;

5 Which will not hearken to the voice of charmers, charming never so wisely.

1. " *Do ye indeed speak righteousness, O congregation ?* " The enemies of David were a numerous and united band, and because they so unanimously condemned the persecuted one, they were apt to take it for granted that their verdict was a right one. " What everybody says must be true," is a lying proverb based upon the presumption which comes of large combinations. Have we not all agreed to hound the man to the death, and who dare hint that so many great ones can be mistaken ? Yet the persecuted one lays the axe at the root by requiring his judges to answer the question whether or not they were acting according to justice. It were well if men would sometimes pause, and candidly consider this. Some of those who surrounded Saul were rather passive than active persecutors ; they held their tongues when the object of royal hate was slandered ; in the original, this first sentence appears to be addressed to them, and they are asked to justify their silence. Silence gives consent. He who refrains from defending the right is himself an accomplice in the wrong. " *Do ye judge uprightly, O ye sons of men ?* " Ye too are only men though dressed in a little brief authority. Your office for men, and your relation to men both bind you to rectitude ; but have ye remembered this ? Have ye not put aside all truth when ye have condemned the godly, and united in seeking the overthrow of the innocent ? Yet in doing this be not too sure of success, for ye are only the " sons of men," and there is a God who can and will reverse your verdicts.

2. " *Yea, in heart ye work wickedness.* " Down deep in your very souls ye hold a rehearsal of the injustice ye intend to practise, and when your opportunity arrives, ye wreak vengeance with a gusto ; your hearts are in your wicked work, and your hands are therefore ready enough. Those very men who sat as judges, and pretended to so much indignation at the faults imputed to their victim, were in their

hearts perpetrating all manner of evil. *" Ye weigh the violence of your hands in the earth."* They were deliberate sinners, cold, calculating villains. As righteous judges ponder the law, balance the evidence, and weigh the case, so the malicious dispense injustice with malice aforethought in cold blood. Note in this verse that the men described sinned with heart and hand ; privately in their heart, publicly in the earth ; they worked and they weighed—they were active, and yet deliberate. See what a generation saints have to deal with ! Such were the foes of our Lord, a generation of vipers, an evil and adulterous generation ; they sought to kill him because he was righteousness itself, yet they masked their hatred to his goodness by charging him with sin.

3. *" The wicked are estranged from the womb."* It is small wonder that some men persecute the righteous seed of the woman, since all of them are of the serpent's brood, and enmity is set between them. No sooner born than alienated from God —what a condition to be found in ! Do we so early leave the right track ? Do we at the same moment begin to be men and commence to be sinners ? *" They go astray as soon as they be born, speaking lies."* Every observer may see how very soon infants act lies. Before they can speak they practise little deceptive arts. This is especially the case in those who grow up to be adepts in slander, they begin their evil trade early, and there is no marvel that they become adepts in it. He who starts early in the morning will go far before night. To be untruthful is one of the surest proofs of a fallen state, and since falsehood is universal, so also is human depravity.

4. *" Their poison is like the poison of a serpent."* Is man also a poisonous reptile ? Yes, and his venom is even as that of a serpent. The viper has but death for the body in his fangs ; but unregenerate man carries poison under his tongue, destructive to the nobler nature. *" They are like the deaf adder that stoppeth her ear."* While speaking of serpents the Psalmist remembers that many of them have been conquered by the charmer's art, but men such as he had to deal with, no art could tame or restrain ; therefore, he likens them to a serpent less susceptible than others to the charmer's music, and says that they refused to hear reason, even as the adder shuts her ear to those incantations which fascinate other reptiles. Man, in his natural corruption, appears to have all the ill points of a serpent without its excellences. O sin, what hast thou done !

5. *" Which will not hearken to the voice of charmers, charming never so wisely."* Ungodly men are not to be won to right by arguments the most logical, or appeals the most pathetic. Try all your arts, ye preachers of the word ! Lay yourselves out to meet the prejudices and tastes of sinners, and ye shall yet have to cry, " Who hath believed our report ? " It is not in your music, but in the sinner's ear that the cause of failure lies, and it is only the power of God that can remove it.

> " You can call spirits from the vasty deep,
> But will they come when you do call for them ? "

No, we call and call, and call in vain, till the arm of the Lord is revealed. This is at once the sinner's guilt and danger. He ought to hear but will not, and because he will not hear, he cannot escape the damnation of hell.

6 Break their teeth, O God, in their mouth : break out the great teeth of the young lions, O LORD.

7 Let them melt away as waters *which* run continually : *when* he bendeth *his bow to shoot* his arrows, let them be as cut in pieces.

8 As a snail *which* melteth, let *every one of them* pass away : *like* the untimely birth of a woman, *that* they may not see the sun.

6. *" Break their teeth, O God, in their mouth."* If they have no capacity for good, at least deprive them of their ability for evil. Treat them as the snake-charmers do their serpents, extract their fangs, break their teeth. The Lord can do this, and he will. He will not suffer the malice of the wicked to triumph, he will deal them such a blow as shall disable them from mischief. *" Break out the great teeth of the young lions, O Lord."* As if one brute creature had not enough of evil in it to complete the emblem of ungodly nature, another specimen of *feræ naturæ* is fetched in. For fierce cruelty the wicked are likened to young lions, monsters in the prime of their vigour, and the fury of their lustiness ; and it is asked that

their grinders may be smashed in, broken off, or dashed out, that the creatures may henceforth be harmless. One can well understand how the banished son of Jesse, while poisoned by the venomous slander of his foes, and worried by their cruel power, should appeal to heaven for a speedy and complete riddance from his enemies.

7. *"Let them melt away as waters which run continually."* Like mountain torrents dried up by the summer heats let them disappear ; or like running streams whose waters are swiftly gone, so let them pass away ; or like water spilt which none can find again, so let them vanish out of existence. Begone, ye foul streams, the sooner ye are forgotten the better for the universe. *"When he bendeth his bow to shoot his arrows, let them be as cut in pieces."* When the Lord goes forth to war, let his judgments so tell upon these persecutors that they may be utterly cut in pieces as a mark shattered by many shafts. Or perhaps the meaning is, when the ungodly man marches to the conflict, let his arrows and his bow drop into fragments, the string cut, the bow snapped, the arrows headless, the points blunted ; so that the boastful warrior may not have wherewithal to hurt the object of his enmity. In either sense the prayer of the Psalm has often become fact, and will be again fulfilled as often as need arises.

8. *"As a snail which melteth, let every one of them pass away."* As the snail makes its own way by its slime, and so dissolves as it goes, or as its shell is often found empty, as though the inhabitant had melted away, so shall the malicious eat out their own strength while they proceed upon their malevolent designs, and shall themselves disappear. To destroy himself by envy and chagrin is the portion of the ill-disposed. *"Like the untimely birth of a woman, that they may not see the sun."* Solemn is this curse, but how surely does it fall on many graceless wretches ! They are as if they had never been. Their character is shapeless, hideous, revolting. They are fitter to be hidden away in an unknown grave than to be reckoned among men. Their life comes never to ripeness, their aims are abortive, their only achievement is to have brought misery to others, and horror to themselves. Such men as Herod, Judas, Alva, Bonner, had it not been better for them if they had never been born ? Better for the mothers who bore them ? Better for the lands they cursed ? Better for the earth in which their putrid carcasses are hidden from the sun ? Every unregenerate man is an abortion. He misses the true form of God-made manhood ; he corrupts in the darkness of sin ; he never sees or shall see the light of God in purity, in heaven.

9 Before your pots can feel the thorns, he shall take them away as with a whirlwind, both living, and in *his* wrath.

10 The righteous shall rejoice when he seeth the vengeance : he shall wash his feet in the blood of the wicked.

11 So that a man shall say, Verily *there is* a reward for the righteous : verily he is a God that judgeth in the earth.

9. *"Before your pots can feel the thorns."* So sudden is the overthrow of the wicked, so great a failure is their life, that they never see joy. Their pot is put upon the hook to prepare a feast of joy, and the fuel is placed beneath, but before the thorns are lit, before any heat can be brought to bear upon the pot, yea, even as soon as the fuel has touched the cooking vessel, a storm comes and sweeps all away ; the pot is overturned, the fuel is scattered far and wide. Perhaps the figure may suppose the thorns, which are the fuel, to be kindled, and then the flame is so rapid that before any heat can be produced the fire is out, the meat remains raw, the man is disappointed, his work is altogether a failure. *"He shall take them away as with a whirlwind."* Cook, fire, pot, meat and all, disappear at once, whirled away to destruction. *"Both living, and in his wrath."* In the very midst of the man's life, and in the fury of his rage against the righteous, the persecutor is overwhelmed with a tornado, his designs are baffled, his contrivances defeated, and himself destroyed. The passage is difficult, but this is probably its meaning, and a very terrible one it is. The malicious wretch puts on his great seething pot, he gathers his fuel, he means to play the cannibal with the godly ; but he reckons without his host, or rather without the Lord of hosts, and the unexpected tempest removes all trace of him, and his fire, and his feast, and that in a moment.

10. *"The righteous shall rejoice when he seeth the vengeance."* He will have

no hand in meting it out, neither will he rejoice in the spirit of revenge, but his righteous soul shall acquiesce in the judgments of God, and he shall rejoice to see justice triumphant. There is nothing in Scripture of that sympathy with God's enemies which modern traitors are so fond of parading as the finest species of benevolence. We shall at the last say, "Amen," to the condemnation of the wicked, and feel no disposition to question the ways of God with the impenitent. Remember how John, the loving disciple, puts it. "And after these things I heard a great voice of much people in heaven, saying, Alleluia; Salvation, and glory, and honour, and power, unto the Lord our God: for true and righteous are his judgments: for he hath judged the great whore, which did corrupt the earth with her fornication, and hath avenged the blood of his servants at her hand. And again they said, Alleluia. And her smoke rose up for ever and ever." "*He shall wash his feet in the blood of the wicked.*" He shall triumph over them, they shall be so utterly vanquished that their overthrow shall be final and fatal, and his deliverance complete and crowning. The damnation of sinners shall not mar the happiness of saints.

11. "*So that a man shall say.*" Every man however ignorant shall be compelled to say, "Verily," in very deed, assuredly, "*there is a reward for the righteous.*" If nothing else be true this is. The godly are not after all forsaken and given over to their enemies; the wicked are not to have the best of it, truth and goodness are recompensed in the long run. "*Verily he is a God that judgeth in the earth.*" All men shall be forced by the sight of the final judgment to see that there is a God, and that he is the righteous ruler of the universe. Two things will come out clearly after all—there is a God and there is a reward for the righteous. Time will remove doubts, solve difficulties, and reveal secrets; meanwhile faith's foreseeing eye discerns the truth even now, and is glad thereat.

EXPLANATORY NOTES AND QUAINT SAYINGS.

Title.—The proper meaning of the root of *Michtam* is *to engrave*, or *to stamp a metal*. It therefore, in strictness, means, *an engraving* or *sculpture*. Hence in the Septuagint, it is translated στηλογραφία, an inscription on a column. I would venture to offer a conjecture in perfect harmony with this view. It appears by the titles of four out of these six Psalms, that they were composed by David while flying and hiding from the persecutions of Saul. What, then, should hinder us from imagining that they were inscribed on the rocks and on the sides of the caves which so often formed his place of refuge? This view would accord with the strict etymological meaning of the word, and explain the rendering of the Septuagint.— *John Jebb, in " A Literal Translation of the Book of Psalms,"* 1846.

[See also Explanatory Notes on Psalms xvi. and lvi. "Treasury of David," Vol. I., pp. 192, 197—98; Vol. II., pp. 464, 468.]

Whole Psalm.—Kimchi says this Psalm was written on account of Abner, and the rest of Saul's princes, who judged David as a rebel against the government, and said it was for Saul to pursue after him to slay him; for if they had restrained him, Saul would not have pursued after him; and indeed they seem to be wicked judges who are addressed in this Psalm; *do not destroy*. Arama says, it declares the wickedness of Saul's judges.—*John Gill.*

Verse 1.—"*Are ye dumb* (when) *ye* (should) *speak righteousness,* (and) *judge equitably, sons of man?*" The first words are exceedingly obscure. One of them (אלם), not expressed in the English, and the ancient versions, means *dumbness,* as in Psalm lxi. 1, and seems to be here used as a strong expression for *entirely speechless*. In what respect they were thus dumb, is indicated by the verb which follows, but the connection can be made clear in English only by a circumlocution. The interrogation, *are ye indeed*, expresses wonder, as at something scarcely credible. Can it be so? Is it possible? are you really silent, you, whose very office is to speak for God, and against the sins of men?—*Joseph Addison Alexander.*

Verse 1.—" *O congregation,*" *O band,* or *company.* The Hebrew *ælem,* which hath the signification of *binding as a sheaf or bundle,* seemeth here to be a company that are combined or confederate.—*Henry Ainsworth.*

Verse 2.—" *In heart ye work wickedness,*" etc. The Psalmist doth not say, they had wickedness in their heart, but they did work it there : the heart is a shop within, an under-ground shop ; there they did closely contrive, forge, and hammer out their wicked purposes, and fit them into actions ; yea, *they weighed the violence of their hands in the earth.* That is an allusion to merchants, who buy and sell by weight ; they weigh their commodity to an ounce ; they do not give it out in gross, but by exact weight. Thus saith the Psalmist, *they weigh the violence of their hands ;* they do not oppress grossly, but with a kind of exactness and skill, they sit down and consider what and how much violence they may use in such a case, or how much such a person may endure, or such a season may bear. They are wiser than to do all at once, or all to one, lest they spoil all. They *" weigh "* what they do, though what they do be so bad that it will hold no weight when God comes to weigh it. Nor do they arrive at this skill presently, but after they have, as it were, served an apprenticeship at it ; and they bind themselves to the trade very early ; for as it follows at the third verse of the Psalm, " *The wicked are estranged from the womb : they go astray as soon as they be born, speaking lies,*" that is, they are estranged both by nature and by early practice ; they lose no time, they go to it young, even " as soon as they are born," as soon as they are fit for any use, or to do any thing, they are using and setting themselves to do wickedly.—*Joseph Caryl.*

Verse 2.—The word עַוְלָה, *wickedness,* properly signifies the *inclinations of scales,* when the scale weighs down to one side ; then it is transferred to respect of persons, to injustice and iniquity, especially in public tribunals and decisions, as in Psalm lxxxii. 2, *How long will ye judge* (עָוֶל) by *an unjust inclination of the scales ?*—*Hermann Venema.*

Verse 2.—The principles of the wicked are even worse than their practices, premeditated violence is doubly guilty.—*George Rogers.*

Verse 3.—" *The wicked are estranged from the womb,*" etc. How early men do sin ! How late do they repent ! *As soon as they are born* " they go astray," but if left to themselves they will not return till they die ; they will never return. Children can neither go nor speak as soon as born, but as soon as born they can " go astray " and " speak lies ; " that is, their first speaking is lying, and their first going is straying ; yea, when they cannot go naturally, they can go astray morally or metaphorically : the first step they are able to take is a step out of the way.—*Joseph Caryl.*

Verse 3.—" *They go astray as soon as they be born, speaking lies.*" Of all sins, no sin can call Satan father like to lying. All the corruption that is in us came from Satan, but yet this sin of forging and lying is from the devil more than any; tastes of the devil more than any. Hence every man is a liar (Romans iii. 4), and so every man is every sinner else ; but in a special manner every man is a liar ; for that the very first depravation of our nature came in by lying, and our nature doth taste much still of this old block to be given to lying, the devil also breathing into us a strong breath to stir us up to lying. Hence *no sooner do we speak but we lie.* As we are in body, subject to all diseases, but yet, some to one sickness rather than to another : so in the soul, all are apt enough to all sin, and some rather to one vice than to another ; but all are much inclined to lying. A liar then is as like the devil as ever he can look : as unlike to God as ever he can be.—*Richard Capel,* 1586—1656, *in " Tentations, their Nature, Danger, Cure."*

Verse 3.—The figure of the wicked going astray as soon as they are born, seems to be taken from the disposition and power of a young serpent soon after its birth. The youngest serpent can convey poison to anything which it bites ; and the suffering in all cases is great, though the bite is seldom fatal. Place a stick near the reptile whose age does not amount to many days, and he will immediately snap at it. The offspring of the tiger and of the alligator are equally fierce in their earliest habits.—*Joseph Roberts, in " Oriental Illustrations of the Sacred Scriptures,"* 1844.

Verse 4.—" *Poison.*" There is such a thing as poison ; but where to be found ? *Ubicanque fuerit, in homine quis quæreret ?* Wheresoever it is, in man who would look for it ? God made man's body of the dust ; he mingled no poison with it.

He inspireth his soul from heaven ; he breathes no poison with it. He feeds him
with bread ; he conveys no poison with it. *Unde venenum ?* Whence is the poison ?
Matt. xiii. 27—" Didst not thou, O Lord, sow good seed in thy field ? " *Unde
zizaniæ*—" From whence then hath it tares ? " Whence ? *Hoc fecit inimicus*—
" The enemy hath done this." We may perceive the devil in it. That great
serpent, the red dragon, hath poured into wicked hearts this poison. His own
poison, *malitiam*, wickedness. *Cum infundit peccatum, infundit venenum*—" When
he pours in sin he pours in poison." Sin is poison. Original pravity is called corruption ; actual poison. The violence and virulence of this venomous quality
comes not at first. *Nemo fit repente pessimus*—No man becomes worst at the first
dash. We are born corrupt, we have made ourselves poisonous. There be three
degrees, as it were so many ages, in sin. *First*—secret sin ; an ulcer lying in the
bones, but skinned over with hypocrisy. *Secondly*—open sin, bursting forth into
manifest villainy. The former is corruption, the second is eruption. *Thirdly*—
frequented and confirmed sin, and that is rank poison, envenoming soul and body.—
Thomas Adams, 1614.

Verse 4.—"*Adder.*" Heb. ןתפ, *pethen*, the Egyptian cobra (*Naja hage*), one
of the venomous *Colubrine* Snakes (*Colubridœ*). This is one of the so called hooded
snakes, with which serpent charmers chiefly deal. The Spectacled Snake proper
(*Naja tripudians*) is a closely related species. The well known Cobra di Capello
is another. They are all noted for their deadly bite. The hollow fangs communicate
with a poison gland, which being pressed in the act of biting, sends a few drops
into the puncture. The venom quickly acts on the whole system, and death soon
ensues.—*John Duns, D.D., in " Biblical Natural Science,"* 1868.

Verse 4.—" *The deaf adder.*" Certain it is, says a modern writer upon the
Psalms, that the common adder or viper here in England, the bite of which too,
by the way, is very venomous, if it is not wholly *deaf*, has the sense of hearing very
imperfectly. This is evident from the danger there is of treading upon these animals,
unless you happen to see them ; for if they do not see you, and you do not disturb
them, they never endeavour to avoid you, which when they are disturbed and do
see you, they are very solicitous of doing. Allowing, then, that there is a species
of these noxious animals, which either not having the sense of hearing at all, or
having it only in a low degree, may very well be said to be deaf ; this may help to
explain the present poetical passage of the Psalmist. He very elegantly compares
the pernicious and destructive practices of wicked men to the venom of a serpent ;
and his mentioning this species of animals, seems to have brought to his mind
another property of at least one sort of them, in which they likewise resembled
perverse and obstinate sinners, who are deaf to all advice, utterly irreclaimable,
and not to be persuaded. This the adder resembled, which is a very venomous
animal, and moreover is deaf, or very near it. And perhaps his saying that *she
stoppeth her ear*, may be no more than a poetical expression for deafness ; just as
the *mole*, which in common speech is said to be *blind*, might in a poetical phrase,
be said to shut her eyes ; as in fact she does when you expose her to the light. The
next clause, " *Which refuseth to hear*," etc., is another poetical expression for the
same thing.—*Samuel Burder, in " The Scripture Expositor,"* 1810.

Verse 4.—" *The deaf adder.*" Several of the serpent tribe are believed to be
either quite deaf, or very dull of hearing. Perhaps that which is called the *puddeyan*,
the " beaver-serpent," is more so than any other. I have frequently come close
up to these reptiles ; but they did not make any effort to move out of the way.
They lurk in the path, and the victim on whom they pounce will expire within a
few minutes after he is bitten.—*Joseph Roberts.*

Verse 4.—" *The deaf adder.*" The " adder," or " asp," is the *haje naja* or *cobra*
of Egypt, according to Cuvier. The hearing of all the serpent tribes is imperfect,
as all are destitute of a tympanic cavity, and of external openings to the ear. The
" *deaf adder* " is not a particular species. The point of the rebuke is, the *pethen*,
or " adder," here in question, *could* hear in some degree but *would* not ; just as the
unrighteous judges, or persecutors, of David could hear with their outward ears
such appeals as he makes in verses 1, 2, but would not. The charmer usually could
charm the serpent by shrill sounds, either of his voice or of the flute, the serpent's
comparative deafness rendering it the more amenable to those sounds which it
could hear. But exceptional cases occurred of a " *deaf adder* " which was *deaf*
only in the sense that it refused to hear, or to be acted on. Also Jer. viii. 17 ;
compare Eccl. x. 11.—*A. R. Fausset.*

Verse 4.—" *The deaf adder that stoppeth her ear.*" With respect to what is said of the animal's stopping its ears, it is not necessary to have recourse to the supposition of its actually doing so, which by some persons has been stated, but it is sufficient to know, that whilst some serpents are operated upon in the manner above described, others are partly or altogether insensible to the incantation.—*Richard Mant.*

Verse 4 (second clause).—This clause admits of a different construction, *like the deaf adder he stops his ear*, which some interpreters prefer, because an adder cannot stop its ears, and need not stop them if naturally deaf, whereas it is by stopping his, that the wicked man becomes like a deaf adder.—*J. A. Alexander.*

Verses 4, 5.—Experienced and skilful as the serpent-charmers are, however, they do not invariably escape with impunity. Fatal terminations to these exhibitions of the psyllic art now and then occur ; for there are still to be found *"deaf adders, which will not hearken to the voice of charmers, charming never so wisely."* . . . . Roberts mentions the instance of a man who came to a gentleman's house to exhibit tame snakes, and on being told that a cobra, or hooded snake, was in a cage in the house, was asked if he could charm it ; on his replying in the affirmative, the serpent was released from the cage, and no doubt, in a state of high irritation. The man began his incantations, and repeated his charms; but the snake darted at him, fastened upon his arm, and before night he was a corpse.—*Philip Henry Gosse, in "The Romance of Natural History,"* 1681.

Verses 4, 5.—One day, a rattlesnake entered our encampment. Among us was a Canadian who could play the flute, and who, to divert us, marched against the serpent with his new species of weapon. On the approach of his enemy, the haughty reptile curls himself into a spiral line, flattens his head, inflates his cheeks, contracts his lips, displays his envenomed fangs and his bold throat ; his tongue flows like two flames of fire ; his eyes are burning coals ; his body, swoollen with rage, rises and falls like the bellows of a forge ; his dilated skin assumes a dull and scaly appearance ; and his tail, whence proceeds the death-announcing sound, vibrates with such rapidity as to resemble a light vapour. The Canadian begins to play upon his flute—the serpent starts with surprise, and draws back his head. In proportion as he is struck with the magic notes, his eyes lose their fierceness ; the oscillations of his tail become slower, and the sounds which it makes become weaker, and gradually die away. Less perpendicular upon their spiral line, the rings of the charmed serpent are by degrees expanded, and sink one after another on the ground in concentric circles. The shades of azure, green, white, and gold recover their brightness on his quivering skin, and slightly turning his head, he remains motionless, in the attitude of attention and pleasure. At this moment the Canadian advances a few steps, producing with the flute sweet and simple notes. The serpent, inclining his variegated neck, opens a passage with the head through the high grass, and begins to creep after the musician ; stopping when he stops, and beginning to follow him again as soon as he advances forward. In this manner he was led out of the camp, attended by a great number of spectators, both savages and Europeans, who could scarcely believe their eyes which had witnessed this effect of harmony.—*François Auguste, Viscount de Chateaubriand,* 1768—1848.

Verses 4, 5.—The serpent, when she begins to feel the charmer, clappeth one ear presently to the ground, and stoppeth the other ear with her tail, although by hearkening to the charmer, as some observe, she would be provoked to spit out her poison, and renew her age.* So hot is man upon his harlot sin, that he is deaf to all that would counsel him to the contrary ; he stoppeth his ear, hardeneth his heart, stiffeneth his neck against the thunders of the law, the still voice of the gospel, the motions of the Spirit, and the convictions of his own conscience. When sin calls, they run through thick and thin for haste ; when the world commands, how readily do they hearken, how quickly do they hear, how faithfully do they obey ! but when the blessed God crieth to them, chargeth them by his unquestionable authority, beseecheth them for their own unchangeable felicity, they, like statues of men, rather than living creatures, stand still and stir not at all. Other things move swiftly to their centres ; stones fall tumbling downward, sparks fly apace upward, coneys run with speed to their burrows, rivers with violence to the ocean, and yet silly man hangs off from his Maker, that neither entreaties, nor threatenings,

---

* This is a specimen of the old-fashioned *un*-natural history. No one will be misled by it.—*C. H. S.*

nor the word, nor the works of God, nòr hope of heaven, nor fear of hell, can quicken or hasten him to his happiness. Who would imagine that a reasonable soul should act so much against sense and reason ?—*George Swinnock*, 1627—1673.

Verse 5.—"*Will not hearken.*" The Lord hath some of his elect ones whom he seeth walking in by-paths and crooked ways : the Lord giveth a commission to his servants, the ministers, and saith, Go invite and call yon soul to come to me, and say, Return, O Shulamite ; but the soul stirs not : the Lord sends and calls again : yet with the deaf adder, he hearkeneth not to the voice of the enchanter : well, saith the Lord, " If you will not come ; I will fetch you ; if fair means will not do, foul means must ; then he hisseth for the fly and the bee of affliction, and calls forth armies of trouble, and gives them commission to seize upon, and to lay siege to such a man or woman, and saith, Ply them with your cannon shot, till you make them yield, give up the keys and strike the sail ; he sends sickness to their bodies, a consumption to their estate, death to their friends, shame to their reputation, a fire to their house, and the like, and bids them prey and spoil, till they see and acknowledge the hand of the Lord lifted up.—*J. Votier's "Survey of Effectual Calling,"* 1652.

Verse 6.—"*Break their teeth,*" *destroy the fangs* of these serpents, in which *their poison is* contained. This will amount to the same meaning as above. Save me from the *adders*, the sly and poisonous slanderers : save me also from the *lions*— the tyrannical and bloodthirsty men.—*Adam Clarke.*

Verse 6.—"*Great teeth.*" מַלְתְּעוֹת, according to Michaelis and Gesenius, are the *eye-teeth*, which in lions are sharp and terrible.—*George Phillips, B.D., in " The Psalms in Hebrew : With a Commentary,"* 1846.

Verses 6—9.—David's enemies were strong and fierce as young lions : he therefore prayed that *their teeth might be broken*, even their strongest teeth, their *grinders*, with which they were ready to devour him ; that so they might be disabled from doing mischief. They overwhelmed him like an inundation : but he desired it might prove a land-flood, which is soon wasted. They were about to shoot at him : but he would have their bows, or their arrows, to be shivered to pieces, and become like straw, and do no execution, and he prayed that they might waste insensibly as the snail, which leaves its substance all along its track ; and that they might come to nothing, like an abortion. He also predicted, that their prosperous rage (which resembled the crackling of thorns under a pot), would soon be extinct, and produce no effect ; while the Lord in his wrath would hurry them into speedy destruction ; as a furious whirlwind drives a living man down a precipice, or into a dreadful pit.—*Thomas Scott*, 1747—1821.

Verse 7 (*first clause*).—Perowne renders this clause, " *Let them melt away, as water (which) runneth apace*," and says that the reference is to " water running away, and so wasted and lost."

Verse 7 (*first clause*).—In desert parts of Africa it has afforded much joy to fall in with a brook of water, especially when running in the direction of the journey, expecting it would prove a valuable companion. Perhaps before it accompanied us two miles it became invisible by sinking into the sand ; but two miles further along it would re-appear, and raise hopes of its continuance ; but after running a few hundred yards, would sink finally into the sand, no more again to rise.— *John Campbell*, 1766—1840.

Verse 8.—" *As a snail which melteth away as it goeth*," lit., " *which goeth in melting* " (or slime), the noun being in the accusative as describing the nature of the action, and the allusion being to the slimy trail which the snail leaves behind it, so that *it seems* to waste away. Evidently this is nothing more than a poetical hyperbole, and need not be explained, therefore, as a popular error or a mistake in natural history.—*J. J. Stewart Perowne, B.D., in " The Book of Psalms ; a New Translation, with Introductions and Notes,"* 1864.

Verse 8.—"*As a snail which melteth,*" etc. This is a very remarkable and not very intelligible passage. The Jewish Bible renders the passage in a way which explains the idea which evidently prevailed at the time the Psalms were composed : " As a snail let him melt as he passeth on." The ancients had an idea that the slimy track made by a snail as it crawled along was subtracted from the substance of its body, and that in consequence the farther it crept the smaller it became, until at last it wasted entirely away. The commentators on the Talmud took this view of the case. The Hebrew word, שַׁבְּלוּל *shablul*, which undoubtedly does signify a snail of some kind, is thus explained :—" The Shablul is a creeping thing ; when it comes out of its shell, saliva pours from itself until it becomes liquid, and so dies." Other explanations of this passage have been offered, but there is no doubt that the view taken by these commentators is the correct one, and that the Psalmist, when he wrote the terrible series of denunciations in which the passage occurs, had in his mind the popular belief regarding the gradual wasting away of the snail as it " passeth on." It is needless to say that no particular species of snail is mentioned, and almost as needless to state that in Palestine there are many species of snails, to any or all of which these words are equally applicable.—*J. G. Wood, in " Bible Animals,"* 1869.

Verse 8.—" *The untimely birth of a woman.*" The wicked are all, so to speak, human abortions ; they are and for ever remain defective beings, who have not accomplished the great purpose of their existence. Heaven is the one end for which man is created, and he who falls short of it does not attain the purpose of his being ; he is an eternal abortion.—*O. Prescott Hiller.*

Verse 8 (*second clause*).—David when he curseth the plots of wicked men, that though they have conceived mischief ; and though they have gone with it a long time, and are ready to bring it forth, yet saith he, " *Let them be* " (that is, let their counsels and designs be) " *like the untimely birth of a woman, that they may not see the sun :* " that is, let them be dashed and blasted, let them never bring forth their poisonous brood to the hurt and trouble of the world.—*Joseph Caryl.*

Verse 9 (*first clause*).—" *Before your cooking vessels,*" etc. It would puzzle Œdipus himself to make any tolerable sense of the English translation of this verse. It refers to the usage of travellers in the East, who when journeying through the deserts, make a hasty blaze with the thorns which they collect, some green and full of sap, others dry and withered, for the purpose of dressing their food ; in which circumstances, violent storms of wind not unfrequently arise, which sweep away their fuel and entire apparatus, before the vessels which they use become warm by the heat. An expressive and graphical image of the overwhelming ruin of wicked men !—*William Walford,* 1837.

Verse 9.—" *Before your pots feel the bramble.*" By this proverbial expression the Psalmist describes the sudden eruption of the divine wrath ; sudden and violent as the ascension of the dry bramble underneath the housewife's pot. The brightness of the flame which this furnishes, the height to which it mounts in an instant, the fury with which it seems to rage on all sides of the vessel, give force, and even sublimity to the image, though taken from one of the commonest occurrences of the lowest life—a cottager's wife boiling her pot ! The sense, then, will be : " Before your pots feel the bramble, he shall sweep them away in whirlwind and hurricane."—*Samuel Horsley,* 1733—1806.

Verse 9.—In all the book of God I do not remember any sentence so variously and differently translated as this verse. . . . This variety of translations ariseth chiefly from the original Hebrew word, סִירוֹת *siroth*, which in the Hebrew tongue signifies, first, *pots* or *caldrons*, wherein flesh is sod, as Ex. xvi. 3 ; xxxviii. 3 ; Ezek. xi. 11. Secondly, *thorns*, and pricks of thorns and briers, as Isa. xxxiv. 13 ; Hosea ii. 8. Thirdly, because the pricks of the great bramble are very sharp and hooked, this word is used to signify fish-hooks. Amos iv. 2. In all our English Bibles of the old, new and Geneva translation, and some Latin Bibles, this word is taken to signify pots or caldrons ; but the Septuagint, Hierome, vulgar Latin, Austine, Pagnine, Tremellius, and all others that I have seen, take this word in the second sense, for the sharp pricks of thorns and brambles. Here, certainly, this word signifies the sharp pricks of the great dog-bramble, where here in the Hebrew text is אָטָד *atad*, and is used (Jud. ix. 14, 15) in Jotham's parable to signify the bramble, which being made king of the trees, kindled a fire, which devoured the cedars of Lebanon. Now this bramble in the body, and every branch of it, is beset with sharp hooked pricks, some of which are green and have life and moisture in them, and though they be sharp, yet they are not so stiff and strong as to make any deep wound in a man's flesh. Others are greater, more hooked, and hardened by drying and parching with the vehement heat of the sun ; and they strike to the quick, and bold fast, or tear where they catch hold of man's skin or flesh. The first are here called, –, living or green; the others are called, ןוׁיק, dried, or parched and hardened; and the prophetical Psalmist affirmeth that " God who judgeth in the earth, will take away and destroy as with a tempestuous whirlwind, every one of them, as well the green as the dry," as Tremellius out of the original doth most truly translate the word. . . . The whole text runs thus : " Before they feel your thorns or pricks, O ye bramble, he will take away every one as with a whirlwind, as well the green as the dry." " Before they," that is, the righteous whom ye hate and persecute ; " do feel," that is, have a full sense and understanding of your thorns or pricks, that is, of the sharpness, fury, and mischief which is in the heart and hand of all and every one among you ; for every one in your band and congregation is a grievous thorn and sharp prick of the cursed bramble, sharply set and bent to do mischief in malice and fury to the people and church of God. " He that is God who judgeth in the earth " (as it is expressed in the eleventh verse, in the last words) " will take away as with a whirlwind " (that is, scatter and destroy tempestuously), " every one, as well the living and green as the dry and hardened." That is, of every sort banded together, as well the green-headed and young perse- cutors, sharp set, but not so strong to hurt, as the old and dry who are hardened in malice by long custom, and in power and policy are strong to do mischief.— *George Walker, in a Fast Sermon before the House of Commons,* 1644.

Verse 10.—" *The righteous shall rejoice when he seeth the vengeance.*" When the just man seeth the vengeance and rejoiceth, it is not of malice, but of benevolence, either hoping that the wicked may by punishment be amended, or loving God's justice above men's persons, not being displeased with the punishment of the wicked, because it proceedeth from the Lord, nor desiring that the wicked may be acquitted from penalty because they deserve in justice to be punished.—*Nicholas Gibbens.*

Verse 10.—" *The righteous shall rejoice when he seeth the vengeance.*" Not that he shall be glad of the vengeance purely as it is a hurt, or a suffering to the creature, but the righteous shall be glad when he seeth the vengeance of God, as it is a fulfilling of the threatening of God against the sin of man, and an evidence of his own holiness. Psalm lxiv. 9, 10.—*Joseph Caryl.*

Verse 10.—" *He shall wash his feet,*" etc. That is, he gets comfort and encourage- ment by seeing the Lord avenge his cause against his adversaries.—*Joseph Caryl.*

Verse 10.—" *He shall wash his feet in the blood,*" etc. As the victorious survivor of a conflict, walking over the battle-field, might be said to do.—*R. T. Society's Notes.*

Verse 10.—When angels execute God's judgments upon sinners, the saints see much in it ; they see matter of fear and praise ; of fear, in that God's power, wrath, and hatred are manifested in them against sin and sinners ; of praise, in that them- selves are delivered and justice is performed. When the wicked are taken away by a divine stroke, by the hand of justice, and God hath the glory of his justice, *the righteous rejoice at it :* but is that all ? No, " *he washeth his feet in the blood of the wicked ;* " that is, by this judgment he fears and reforms. It is a metaphor taken from the practice of those parts where they went barefoot, or with sandals and so contracted much filth, and used to wash and cleanse their feet when they came in ; so here, the godly seeing the hand of God upon the wicked, fears and judges himself for his sins, purges his conscience and affections, and stands now in awe of that God who hath stricken the wicked for those sins which he himself in part is guilty of. Waldus, a man of note in Lyons, seeing one struck dead in his presence, he washed his hand in his blood ; for presently he gave alms to the poor, instructed his family in the true knowledge of God, and exhorted all that came unto him to repentance and holiness of life.—*William Greenhill,* 1691—1677.

Verse 10.—No doubt, at the sight of Sodom, Gomorrah, Admah, and Zeboim destroyed, angels saw cause to rejoice and sing, " Hallelujah." Wickedness was swept away ; earth was lightened of a burden ; justice, the justice of God, was highly exalted ; love to his other creatures was displayed in freeing them from the neighbourhood of hellish contaminations. On the same principles (entering, however, yet deeper into the mind of the Father, and sympathising to the full in his justice), the Lord Jesus himself, and each one of his members shall cry " Hallelujah," over Antichrist's ruined hosts. Rev. xix. 3. " *The righteous shall rejoice when he seeth the vengeance : he shall wash his feet in the blood of the wicked.*" He shall be refreshed at the end of his journey (John xiii. 5 ; Luke vii. 44 ; Gen. xviii. 4), he shall wipe off all the dust of the way, and end its weariness by entering into that strange, that divine joy over sin destroyed, justice honoured, the law magnified, vengeance taken for the insult done to Godhead, the triumph of the Holy One over the unholy. It is not merely *the time when* that joy begins—it is also the occasion and cause of that day's rapturous delight.—*Andrew A. Bonar.*

Verse 10.—A broad and vital distinction is to be made between *desire for the gratification of personal vengeance,* and zeal for the vindication *of the glory of God.* "The glory of God" includes necessarily the real good of the offender and the well-being of society. Desire for *retaliation* is always wrong ; desire for *retribution* may be in the highest degree praiseworthy. For personal motives only can I desire retaliation upon the wrong-doer ; but for motives most interested and noble I may desire retribution.—*R. A. Bertram, in " The Imprecatory Psalms,"* 1867.

Verse 11.—" *So that a man shall say, Verily,*" etc. This shall be said not by *a man,* nor by any particular man, but by men in general, by man as opposed to God. The particle translated "*verily*" really means *only,* and denotes that this and nothing else is true.—*J. A. Alexander.*

Verse 11.—" *So that,*" etc. There is something worth noting from the connexion of this verse with the context, and is implied in the first word, "*so that,*" which joins this verse with the former parts of this Psalm, and shows this to be an illation from them. What ? did God so suddenly, " as with a whirlwind," overthrow those wicked judges who lorded it over his people ? did he make those "lions" melt like snails ? did he confirm the joints of his people, which were little before, trembling and smiting one against another, as if they had been so many forlorn wretches exposed and cast forth, and no eye to pity them ; as if they had been floating with Moses upon the sea in a basket of bulrushes, without any pilot to guide them, and even ready to cry out with the disciple, " Master, carest thou not that we perish ? " Did he then command a calm, and bring them to the haven where they would be ? Did he turn their howling like dragons and chattering like cranes, under the whips and saws of tyrannical taskmasters, into a song of joy and triumph ? Did he dismantle himself of that cloud wherein for a time he had so enveloped himself, that he seemed not to behold the pressures of his people ? Did he, I say, then step in to his people's rescue, by breaking their yokes as in the day of Midian, and kissing them with the kisses of his mouth ?   " *So that a man shall say, Verily there is a reward for the righteous : verily he is a God that judgeth in the earth.*" Observe : Though the passages of God's providence may seem so rugged and uncouth, as if they were destructive to his church, and likely to put out the eye of his own glory ; yet our God will so dispose of them in the close, that they shall have an advantageous tendency, to the setting forth of his honour and our good.—*John Hinckley,* 1657.

Verse 11.—Some of the judgments of God are a shallow, or a ford, over which a lamb may wade ; every child may read the meaning of them ; and " *a man* "— any ordinary man—" *may say, Verily there is a reward for the righteous : verily he is a God that judgeth in the earth.*"—*Joseph Caryl.*

Verse 11.—This judging here does not refer to the judgment to come, at the last day, when there shall be a general convention of quick and dead before the Lord's dreadful tribunal ; though so, 'tis most true *affore tempus,* that there will be a time when God will ride his circuit here in a solemn manner, " so that a man shall say, Verily there is a reward for the righteous : verily he is a God that judgeth in the earth ; " but that is not the scope of this place. 'Tis in the present tense, ο κρινων, *that now judgeth,* or *is now judging* the earth and the inhabitants thereof ; and therefore it must be understood of a judgment on this side, the judgment of the great day ; and so God judges the earth, or in the earth, three manner of ways. First, by a providential ordering and wise disposal of all the affairs of all creatures. Secondly, in relieving the oppressed and pleading the cause of the innocent. Thirdly, in overthrowing and plaguing the wicked doers.—*John Hinckley.*

HINTS TO PREACHERS.

Verse 3.—I. The natural effects of original sin are seen in early suffering and death. II. Its moral effects are seen in the early commission of actual sin. III. Early depravity is evinced in the conscious guilt of telling lies.—*G. R.*

Verse 3 (first clause).—The inner pandemonium, or the calendar of the heart's crime.

Verse 4 (first clause).—A generation of serpents.—*T. Adams's Sermon.*

Verse 4.—Sin as a poison. Poisons may be attractive in colour and taste, slow or rapid in action, painful in effect, withering, soporific or maddening. In all cases deadly.

Verse 5.—The serpent charmer. I. He charms with moral suasion, promise, threatening, etc. II. He charms wisely, earnestly, affectionately, argumentatively. III. He charms in vain ; the will is averse. Hence the need of divine grace and of the gospel.

Verse 8.—The snail-like course of ungodly men. Their sin destroys their property, health, time, influence, life.

Verse 11.—Remarkable cases of divine judgments and their results.

PSALM LIX.

To the Chief Musician.—*Strange that the painful events in David's life should end in enriching the repertoire of the national minstrelsy. Out of a sour, ungenerous soil spring up the honey-bearing flowers of Psalmody. Had he never been cruelly hunted by Saul, Israel and the church of God in after ages would have missed this song. The music of the sanctuary is in no small degree indebted to the trials of the saints. Affliction is the tuner of the harps of sanctified songsters.* Altaschith. *Another "destroy not" Psalm. Whom God preserves Satan cannot destroy. The Lord can even preserve the lives of his prophets by the very ravens that would naturally pick out their eyes. David always found a friend to help him when his case was peculiarly dangerous, and that friend was in his enemy's household; in this instance it was Michal, Saul's daughter, as on former occasions it had been Jonathan, Saul's son.* Michtam of David. *This is the Fifth of the Golden Secrets of David; God's chosen people have many such.* When Saul sent, and they watched the house to kill him. *Great efforts are made to carry the Psalms away to other authors and seasons than those assigned in the headings, it being the fashion just now to prove one's learning by disagreeing with all who have gone before. Perhaps in a few years the old titles will be as much reverenced as they are now rejected. There are spasms in these matters, and in many other things among the would-be "intellectuals" of the schools. We are not anxious to show our readiness at conjecture, and therefore are content with reading this Psalm in the light of the circumstance here mentioned; it does not seem unsuitable to any verse, and in some the words are very appropriate to the specified occasion.*

DIVISIONS.—*In verses 1 and 2 he prays, in 3 and 4 he complains of his woes, and again in verse 5 he prays. Here he inserts a Selah, and ends one portion of his song. In 6 and 7 he renews his complaint, in 8, 9, 10 declares his confidence in God, and in 11, 12, 13 lifts up his heart in prayer; closing another part of his Psalm with Selah. Then he prays again in 14, 15, and afterwards betakes himself to singing.*

EXPOSITION.

DELIVER me from mine enemies, O my God: defend me from them that rise up against me.

2 Deliver me from the workers of iniquity, and save me from bloody men.

1. "*Deliver me from mine enemies, O my God.*" They were all round the house with the warrant of authority, and a force equal to the carrying of it out. He was to be taken dead or alive, well or ill, and carried to the slaughter. No prowess could avail him to break the cordon of armed men, neither could any eloquence stay the hand of his bloody persecutor. He was taken like a bird in a net, and no friend was near to set him free. Unlike the famous starling, he did not cry, "I can't get out," but his faith uttered quite another note. Unbelief would have suggested that prayer was a waste of breath, but not so thought the good man, for he makes it his sole resort. He cries for deliverance and leaves ways and means with his God. "*Defend me from them that rise up against me.*" Saul was a king, and therefore sat in high places, and used all his authority to crush David; the persecuted one therefore beseeches the Lord to set him on high also, only in another sense. He asks to be lifted up, as into a lofty tower, beyond the reach of his adversary. Note how he sets the title "*My God,*" over against the word "*mine enemies.*" This is the right method of effectually catching and quenching the fiery darts of the enemy upon the shield of faith. God is our God, and therefore deliverance and defence are ours.

2. "*Deliver me from the workers of iniquity.*" Saul was treating him very unjustly, and besides that was pursuing a tyrannical and unrighteous course towards others, therefore David the more vehemently appeals against him. Evil men

were in the ascendant at court, and were the ready tools of the tyrant, against these also he prays. Bad men in a bad cause may be pleaded against without question. When a habitation is beset by thieves, the good man of the house rings the alarm-bell ; and in these verses we may hear it ring out loudly, " *deliver me*," " *defend me*," " *deliver me*," " *save me*." Saul had more cause to fear than David had, for the invincible weapon of prayer was being used against him, and heaven was being aroused to give him battle. " *And save me from bloody men*." As David remembers how often Saul had sought to assassinate him, he knows what he has to expect from that quarter and from the king's creatures and minions who were watching for him. David represents his enemy in his true colours before God ; the bloodthirstiness of the foe is a fit reason for the interposition of the righteous God, for the Lord abhors all those who delight in blood.

3 For, lo, they lie in wait for my soul : the mighty are gathered against me ; not *for* my transgression, nor *for* my sin, O LORD.

4 They run and prepare themselves without *my* fault : awake to help me, and behold.

3. " *For, lo, they lie in wait for my soul*." They were in ambuscade for the good man's life. He knew their design and cried to God to be rescued from it. Like wild beasts they crouched, and waited to make the fatal spring ; but their victim used effectual means to baffle them, for he laid the matter before the Lord. While the enemy lies waiting in the posture of a beast, we wait before God in the posture of prayer, for God waits to be gracious to us and terrible towards our foes. " *The mighty are gathered against me*." None of them were absent from the muster when a saint was to be murdered. They were too fond of such sport to be away. The men at arms who ought to have been fighting their country's battles, are instead thereof hunting a quiet citizen ; the gigantic monarch is spending all his strength to slay a faithful follower. " *Not for my transgressions, nor for my sin, O Lord*." He appeals to Jehovah that he had done no ill. His only fault was, that he was too valiant and too gracious, and was, besides, the chosen of the Lord, therefore the envious king could not rest till he had washed his hands in the blood of his too popular rival. We shall always find it to be a great thing to be innocent; if it does not carry our cause before an earthly tribunal, it will ever prove the best of arguments in the court of conscience, and a standing consolation when we are under persecution. Note the repetition of his declaration of integrity. David is sure of his innocence. He dares repeat the plea.

4. " *They run and prepare themselves without my fault*." They are all alive and active, they are swift to shed blood. They prepare and use their best tactics ; they besiege me in my house, and lay their ambuscades as for some notable enemy. They come up fully armed to the attack, and assail me with all the vigour and skill of a host about to storm a castle ; and all for no cause, but out of gratuitous malice. So quick are they to obey their cruel master, that they never stay to consider whether their errand is a good one or not ; they run at once, and buckle on their harness as they run. To be thus gratuitously attacked is a great grief. To a brave man the danger causes little distress of mind compared with the injustice to which he is subjected. It was a cruel and crying shame that such a hero as David should be hounded down as if he were a monster, and beset in his house like a wild beast in its den. " *Awake to help me, and behold*." When others go to sleep, keep thou watch, O God. Put forth thy might. Arouse thee from thine inaction. Only look at thy servant's sad condition and thy hand will be sure to deliver me. We see how thorough was the Psalmist's faith in the mercy of his Lord, for he is satisfied that if the Lord do but look on his case it will move his active compassion.

5 Thou therefore, O LORD God of hosts, the God of Israel, awake to visit all the heathen : be not merciful to any wicked transgressors. Selah.

5. " *Thou*," thyself, work for me personally, for the case needs thine interposition. " *Therefore*," because I am unjustly assailed, and cannot help myself. " *O Lord*," everliving, " *God of Hosts*," able to rescue me ; " *the God of Israel*," pledged by covenant to redeem thine oppressed servant ; " *awake to visit all the heathen*," arouse thy holy mind, bestow thy sacred energies, punish the heathen among thine Israel, the falsehearted who say they are Jews and are not, but do lie. And when thou art about the business, let all the nations of thine enemies, and all the heathenish

people at home and abroad know that thou art upon circuit, judging and punishing. It is the mark of a thoughtful prayer that the titles which are in it applied to God are appropriate, and are, as it were, congruous to the matter, and fitted to add force to the argument. Shall Jehovah endure to see his people oppressed? Shall the God of hosts permit his enemies to exult over his servant? Shall the faithful God of a chosen people leave his chosen to perish? The name of God is, even in a literal sense, a fortress and high tower for all his people. What a forceful petition is contained in the words, "*awake to visit!*" Actively punish, in wisdom judge, with force chastise. "*Be not merciful to any wicked transgressors.*" Be merciful to them as men, but not as transgressors; if they continue hardened in their sin, do not wink at their oppression. To wink at sin in transgressors will be to leave the righteous under their power, therefore do not pass by their offences but deal out the due reward. The Psalmist feels that the overthrow of oppression which was so needful for himself must be equally desirable for multitudes of the godly placed in like positions, and therefore he prays for the whole company of the faithful, and against the entire confraternity of traitors. "*Selah.*" With such a subject before us we may well pause. Who would not sit still and consider, when vengeance is being meted out to all the enemies of God? How wrong is that state of mind which hates to hear of the punishment of the wicked!

6 They return at evening: they make a noise like a dog, and go round about the city.

7 Behold, they belch out with their mouth: swords *are* in their lips: for who, *say they*, doth hear?

6. "*They return at evening.*" Like wild beasts that roam at night, they come forth to do mischief. If foiled in the light, they seek the more congenial darkness in which to accomplish their designs. They mean to break into the house in the dead of night. "*They make a noise like a dog, and go round about the city.*" Howling with hunger for their prey, they sneak round and round the walls, prowling with stealthy footstep, and barking in unamiable concert. David compares his foes to Eastern dogs, despised, unowned, loathsome, degraded, lean, and hungry, and he represents them as howling with disappointment, because they cannot find the food they seek. Saul's watchmen and the cruel king himself must have raved and raged fiercely when they found the image and the pillow of goats' hair in the bed instead of David. Vain were their watchings, the victim had been delivered, and that by the daughter of the man who desired his blood. Go, ye dogs, to your kennels and gnaw your bones, for this good man is not meat for your jaws.

7. "*Behold, they belch out with their mouth.*" The noisy creatures are so remarkable in their way, that attention is called to them with a *behold*. *Ecce homines*, might we not say, *Ecce canes!* Their malicious speech gushes from them as from a bubbling fountain. The wicked are voluble in slander; their vocabulary of abuse is copious, and as detestable as it is abundant. What torrents of wrathful imprecation will they pour on the godly! They need no prompters, their feelings force for themselves their own vent, and fashion their own expressions. "*Swords are in their lips.*" They speak daggers. Their words pierce like rapiers, and cleave like cutlasses. As the cushion of a lion's paw conceals his claw, so their soft ruby lips contain bloody words. "*For who, say they, doth hear?*" They are free from all restraint, they fear no God in heaven, and the government on earth is with them. When men have none to call them to account, there is no accounting for what they will do. He who neither fears God nor regards man sets out upon errands of oppression with gusto, and uses language concerning it of the most atrociously cruel sort. David must have been in a singular plight when he could hear the foul talk and hideous braggings of Saul's black guards around the house. After the style in which a Cavalier would have cursed a Puritan, or Claverhouse a Covenanter, the Saulites swore at the upstart whom the king's majesty had sent them to arrest. David called them dogs, and no doubt a pretty pack they were, a cursed cursing company of curs. When they said, "Who doth hear?" God was listening, and this David knew, and therefore took courage.

8 But thou, O LORD, shalt laugh at them; thou shalt have all the heathen in derision.

9 *Because of* his strength will I wait upon thee : for God *is* my defence.

10 The God of my mercy shall prevent me : God shall let me see *my desire* upon mine enemies.

8. " *But thou, O Lord, shalt laugh at them.*" He speaks to God as to one who is close at hand. He points to the liers in wait and speaks to God about them. They are laughing at me, and longing for my destruction, but thou hast the laugh of them seeing thou hast determined to send them away without their victim, and made fools of by Michal. The greatest, cleverest, and most malicious of the enemies of the church are only objects of ridicule to the Lord ; their attempts are utterly futile, they need give no concern to our faith. " *Thou shalt have all the heathen in derision.*" As if David had said—What are these fellows who lie in ambush ? And what is the king their master, if God be on my side ? If not only these but all the heathen nations were besetting the house, yet Jehovah would readily enough disappoint them and deliver me. In the end of all things it will be seen how utterly contemptible and despicable are all the enemies of the cause and kingdom of God. He is a brave man who sees this to-day when the enemy is in great power, and while the church is often as one shut up and besieged in his house.

9. " *Because of his strength will I wait upon thee.*" Is my persecutor strong ? Then, my God, for this very reason I will turn myself to thee, and leave my matters in thy hand. It is a wise thing to find in the greatness of our difficulties a reason for casting ourselves upon the Lord.

> " And when it seems no chance nor change
> From grief can set me free,
> Hope finds its strength in helplessness,
> And, patient, waits on thee."

" *For God is my defence,*" my high place, my fortress, the place of my resort in the time of my danger. If the foe be too strong for me to cope with him, I will retreat into my castle, where he cannot reach me.

10. " *The God of my mercy shall prevent me.*" God who is the giver and fountain of all the undeserved goodness I have received, will go before me and lead my way as I march onward. He will meet me in my time of need. Not alone shall I have to confront my foes, but he whose goodness I have long tried and proved will gently clear my way, and be my faithful protector. How frequently have we met with preventing mercy—the supply prepared before the need occurred, the refuge built before the danger arose. Far ahead into the future the foreseeing grace of heaven has projected itself, and forestalled every difficulty. " *God shall let me see my desire upon mine enemies.*" Observe that the words, " *my desire,*" are not in the original. From the Hebrew we are taught that David expected to see his enemies without fear. God will enable his servant to gaze steadily upon the foe without trepidation ; he shall be calm, and self possessed, in the hour of peril ; and ere long he shall look down on the same foes discomfited, overthrown, destroyed. When Jehovah leads the way victory follows at his heels. See God, and you need not fear to see your enemies. Thus the hunted David, besieged in his own house by traitors, looks only to God, and exults over his enemies.

11 Slay them not, lest my people forget : scatter them by thy power ; and bring them down, O Lord, our shield.

12 *For* the sin of their mouth *and* the words of their lips let them even be taken in their pride : and for cursing and lying *which* they speak.

13 Consume *them* in wrath, consume *them*, that they *may* not *be* : and let them know that God ruleth in Jacob unto the ends of the earth. Selah.

11. " *Slay them not, lest my people forget.*" It argues great faith on David's part, that even while his house was surrounded by his enemies he is yet so fully sure of their overthrow, and so completely realises it in his own mind, that he puts in a detailed petition that they may not be too soon or too fully exterminated. God's victory over the craft and cruelty of the wicked is so easy and so glorious that it seems a pity to end the conflict too soon. To sweep away the plotters all at once were to end the great drama of retribution too abruptly. Nay, let the righteous be buffeted a little longer, and let the boasting oppressor puff and brag through

his little hour, it will help to keep Israel in mind of the Lord's justice, and make the brave party who side with God's champion accustomed to divine interpositions. It were a pity for good men to be without detractors, seeing that virtue shines the brighter for the foil of slander. Enemies help to keep the Lord's servants awake. A lively, vexatious devil is less to be dreaded than a sleepy, forgetful spirit which is given to slumber. " *Scatter them by thy power.*" Blow them to and fro, like chaff in the wind. Let the foemen live as a vagabond race. Make Cains of them. Let them be living monuments of divine power, advertisements of heaven's truth. To the fullest extent let divine justice be illustrated in them. " *And bring them down.*" Like rotten fruit from a tree. From the seats of power which they disgrace, and the positions of influence which they pollute, let them be hurled into humiliation. This was a righteous wish, and if it be untempered by the gentleness of Jesus, we must remember that it is a soldier's prayer, and the wish of one who was smarting under injustice and malice of no ordinary kind. " *O Lord, our shield.*" David felt himself to be the representative of the religious party in Israel, and therefore he says " *our shield,*" speaking in the name of all those who make Jehovah their defence. We are in good company when we hide beneath the buckler of the Eternal ; meanwhile he who is the shield of his people is the scatterer of their enemies.

12. " *For the sin of their mouth and the words of their lips let them even be taken in their pride.*" Such dreadful language of atheism and insolence deserves a fit return. As they hope to take their victims, so let them be taken themselves, entangled in their own net, arrested in the midst of their boastful security. Sins of the lips are real sins, and punishable sins. Men must not think because their hatred gets no further than railing and blasphemy that therefore they shall be excused. He who takes the will for the deed, will take the word for the deed and deal with men accordingly. Wretches who are persecutors in talk, burners and stabbers with the tongue, shall have a reckoning for their would-be transgressions. Pride though it show not itself in clothes, but only in speech, is a sin ; and persecuting pride, though it pile no fagots at Smithfield, but only revile with its lips, shall have to answer for it among the unholy crew of inquisitors. " *And for cursing and lying which they speak.*" Sins, like hounds, often hunt in couples. He who is not ashamed to curse before God, will be sure to lie unto men. Every swearer is a liar. Persecution leads on to perjury. They lie and swear to it. They curse and give a lying reason for their hate. This shall not go unnoted of the Lord, but shall bring down its recompense. How often has it happened that while haughty speeches have been fresh in the mouths of the wicked they have been overtaken by avenging providence, and made to see their mischief recoil upon themselves !

13. " *Consume them in wrath.*" As if he had changed his mind and would have them brought to a speedy end, or if spared would have them exist as ruins, he cries, " *consume them,*" and he redoubles his cry, " *consume them,*" nay, he gives a triple note, " *that they may not be.*" Revilers of God whose mouths pour forth such filth as David was on this occasion obliged to hear, are not to be tolerated by a holy soul ; indignation must flame forth, and cry to God against them. When men curse the age and the place in which they live, common humanity leads the righteous to desire that they may be removed. If they could be reformed it would be infinitely better ; but if they cannot, if they must and will continue to be like mad dogs in a city, then let them cease to be. Who can desire to see such a generation perpetuated ? " *And let them know ;*" i.e., let all the nations know, " *that God ruleth in Jacob unto the ends of the earth.*" He whose government is universal fixes his headquarters among his chosen people, and there in special he punishes sin. So David would have all men see. Let even the most remote nations know that the great moral Governor has power to destroy ungodliness, and does not wink at iniquity in any, at any time, or in any place. When sin is manifestly punished it is a valuable lesson to all mankind. The overthrow of a Napoleon, is a homily for all monarchs, the death of a Tom Paine a warning to all infidels, the siege of Paris a sermon to all cities. *Selah.* Good cause there is for this rest, when a theme so wide and important is introduced. Solemn subjects ought not to be hurried over ; nor should the condition of the heart while contemplating themes so high be a matter of indifference. Reader, bethink thee. Sit thou still awhile and consider the ways of God with man.

14 And at evening let them return ; *and* let them make a noise like a dog, and go round about the city.

15 Let them wander up and down for meat, and grudge if they be not satisfied.

14. Here verse six is repeated, as if the songster defied his foes and revelled in the thought of their futile search, their malice, their disappointment, their rage, their defeated vigilance, their wasted energy. He laughs to think that all the city would know how they were deceived, and all Israel would ring with the story of the image and the goats' hair in the bed. Nothing was more a subject of Oriental merriment, than a case in which the crafty are deceived, and nothing more makes a man the object of derision than to be outwitted by a woman, as in this instance Saul and his base minions were by Michal. The warrior poet hears in fancy the howl of rage in the council of his foes when they found their victim clean escaped from their hands.

15. " *Let them wander up and down for meat.*" Like dogs that have missed the expected carcass, let them go up and down dissatisfied, snapping at one another, and too disappointed to be quiet and take the matter easily. " *And grudge if they be not satisfied.*" Let them act like those who cannot believe that they have lost their prey : like a herd of Oriental dogs, unhoused, unkennelled, let them prowl about seeking a prey which they shall never find. Thus the menial followers of Saul paraded the city in vain hope of satisfying their malice and their master. " Surely," say they, " we shall have him yet. We cannot endure to miss him. Perhaps he is in yonder corner, or concealed in such a hidingplace. We must have him. We grudge him his life. Our lust for his blood is hot, nor can we be persuaded but that we shall light upon him." See the restlessness of wicked men ; this will increase as their enmity to God increases, and in hell it will be their infinite torment. What is the state of the lost, but the condition of an ambitious camp of rebels, who have espoused a hopeless cause, and will not give it up, but are impelled by their raging passions to rave on against the cause of God, of truth, and of his people.

16 But I will sing of thy power ; yea, I will sing aloud of thy mercy in the morning : for thou hast been my defence and refuge in the day of my trouble.

17 Unto thee, O my strength, will I sing : for God *is* my defence, *and* the God of my mercy.

16. " *But I will sing of thy power.*" The wicked howl, but I sing and will sing. Their power is weakness, but thine is omnipotence ; I see them vanquished and thy power victorious, and for ever and ever will I sing of thee. " *Yea, I will sing aloud of thy mercy in the morning.*" When those lovers of darkness find their game is up, and their midnight howlings die away, then will I lift up my voice on high and praise the lovingkindness of God without fear of being disturbed. What a blessed morning will soon break for the righteous, and what a song will be theirs ! Sons of the morning, ye may sigh to-night, but joy will come on the wings of the rising sun. Tune your harps even now, for the signal to commence the eternal music will soon be given ; the morning cometh and your sun shall go no more down for ever. " *For thou hast been my defence.*" The song is for God alone, and it is one which none can sing but those who have experienced the lovingkindness of their God. Looking back upon a past all full of mercy, the saints will bless the Lord with their whole hearts, and triumph in him as the high place of their security. " *And refuge in the day of my trouble.*" The greater our present trials the louder will our future songs be, and the more intense our joyful gratitude. Had we no day of trouble, where were our season of retrospective thanksgiving ? David's besetment by Saul's bloodhounds creates an opportunity for divine interposition and so for triumphant praise.

17. " *Unto thee, O my strength, will I sing.*" What transport is here ! What a monopolising of all his emotions for the one object of praising God ! Strength has been overcome by strength ; not by the hero's own prowess, but by the might of God alone. See how the singer girds himself with the almightiness of God, and calls it all his own by faith. Sweet is the music of experience, but it is all for God ; there is not even a stray note for man, for self, or for human helpers. " *For God is my defence, and the God of my mercy.*" With full assurance he claims possession of the Infinite as his protection and security. He sees God in all, and all his own. Mercy rises before him, conspicuous and manifold, for he feels he is undeserving,

and security is with him, undisturbed and impregnable, for he knows that he is safe in divine keeping. Oh, choice song! My soul would sing it now in defiance of all the dogs of hell. Away, away, ye adversaries of my soul, the God of my mercy will keep ye all at bay—

> " Nor shall th' infernal lion rend
> Whom he designs to keep."

EXPLANATORY NOTES AND QUAINT SAYINGS.

This Psalm has in its stern contents something no doubt strange to our ears. But never let us omit to distinguish from each other the times and diverse economies, and to place ourselves, as far as possible, in sympathy with the experience of a heart which burned for nothing more than for the glorifying of God in this world. Everything that tended to obscure the theocratic relation of God to his people, called up in the soul of David the most vehement passion. The scornful oppression with which Saul and his venal satellites visited him, the man of God, could not but have, upon the eyes of all, the appearance as if Jehovah were no longer Lord in his own land, who inexorably adhered to his laws and rights. Treason, falsehood, and every kind of evil then prevailed unchecked. What wonder, that as formerly Moses in the wilderness was provoked against the stiff-necked people, so also David, whom the awful holiness of God had already made to tremble, should feel his spirit stirred against the ungodly who surrounded him, and should say, with Job, " My bowels boiled within me."—*Frederick William Krummacher, D.D., in " David, the King of Israel,"* 1867.

Verse 1.—" O my God." There are two pleas which the Psalmist makes use of ; one was, that God was *his* God, ver. 1 ; the other was the *power* and *strength* of his *enemies*. It is a blessed thing to have the covenant to fly to in all times of straits and troubles ; there is always an anchor-hold of hope there. " *My God*," is such a plea as infinitely over-balances all other things. He has engaged himself to do his people good ; and it is time for him to work when the enemy exalts himself. The church's enemies are never so near destruction as when they think they have nothing to do, but take and divide the spoil. We may plead God's promise and the enemies' power too ; both are a ground of hope to a believer in Jesus.—*John Hill (1711–1746), in " Sermons on Several Occasions."*

Verse 1.—" That rise up against me." He insists upon the strength and violence of his enemies, with the view of exciting his mind to greater fervour in the duty of prayer. These he describes as *rising up* against him, in which expression he alludes, not simply to the audacity or fierceness of their assaults, but to the eminent superiority of power which they possessed ; and yet he asks that he may be lifted up on high, as it were, above the reach of this over-swelling inundation.—*John Calvin.*

Verse 3 (*first clause*).—On the expression, " they lie in wait for my *soul*," compare 1 Sam. xix. 11, " And Michal, David's wife, told him, saying, If thou save not thy life [*soul*] to night, to-morrow thou shalt be slain ; " and Ps. vii. 2, 5.—*E. W. Hengstenberg.*

Verse 3.—" The mighty are gathered against me," is rendered by Chandler, The mighty are turned aside to lay snares against me.

Verse 3.—" The mighty are gathered against me." As if he would say, " But I am weak, be thou, however, my strength, and vindicate my innocence.—*Arnd.*

Verses 3, 4.—He pleads his own innocency, not as to God, but as to his persecutors. Note, 1. The innocency of the godly will not secure them from the malignity of the wicked. Those that are harmless like doves, yet for Christ's sake are hated of all men, as if they were noxious like serpents, and obnoxious accordingly. 2. Though our innocency will not secure us from troubles, yet it will greatly support and comfort us under our troubles. The testimony of our conscience for us, that we have behaved ourselves well toward those that have behaved themselves ill towards us, will be very much our rejoicing in the day of evil. If we are conscious to ourselves of our innocency, we may with humble confidence appeal to God, and beg of him to plead our injured cause which he will do in due time.—*Matthew Henry.*

Verse 4.—" *They run,*" as armed warriors rushing to the assault (Ps. xviii. 29). The Hebrew for " prepare themselves," (נכון) means also " they *establish* themselves ; " they make firm their footing, like forces assaulting a city. Job xxx. 14.—*A. R. Fausset.*

Verse 4.—" *They run and prepare.*" The zeal and diligence of the wicked in the cause of unrighteousness might well reprove the languor and tardiness of saints in the work of faith and labour of love. In the church of God nothing is the source of more mischief than the want of true zeal and liveliness. It is only when " many run to and fro " that " knowledge shall be increased."—*William S. Plumer.*

Verse 4.—" *Without fault.*" As it respected Saul, he was a faithful subject and an obedient son-in-law.—*Benjamin Boothroyd.*

Verse 4.—" *Awake to help me,*" literally, *Awake to meet me.* In time of temptation the Lord seems to be absent from us, and not to observe our distress—to be, as it were, as Jesus, in the storm, is described as having been " asleep in the hinder part of the ship." Mark iv. 38. But it is only an appearance ; the Lord neither slumbers nor sleeps (Ps. cxxi. 4) ; he is always ready to come to our help when we call upon him.—*O. Prescott Hiller.*

Verse 4.—" *And behold.*" The expression is one which savours at once of faith and of the infirmity of the flesh. In speaking of God, as if his eyes had been hitherto shut to the wrongs which he had suffered, and needed now for the first time to be opened for the discovery of them, he expresses himself according to the weakness of our human apprehension. On the other hand, in calling upon God *to behold* his cause, he shows his faith by virtually acknowledging that nothing was hid from his providential cognisance.—*John Calvin.*

Verse 5.—" *O Lord God of hosts, the God of Israel.*" In time of straits we should set our eyes most upon those styles of God which most serve to strengthen our faith, especially such as hold forth his power and goodwill to employ his power for us.—*David Dickson.*

Verse 5.—" *Lord God of hosts.*" YAHVEH, *Elohim, Tsebaoth ;* as in lxxx. 4, 19 ; lxxxiv. 8. Comp. 2 Sam. v. 10 ; 1 Kings xix. 10, 14 ; Ps. lxxxix. 8.—*From " The Psalms translated from the Hebrew, with Notes chiefly exegetical. By William Kay, D.D., 1871."*

Verse 5.—" *Lord God of hosts.*" Some have thought this equivalent to God of battles ; the true force of the epithet, however, is, " Sovereign of the stars, material hosts of heaven, and of the angels their inhabitants."—*A. A. Hodge, in* " *Outlines of Theology,*" 1866.

Verse 5.—1. " *God of hosts,*" and therefore *able ;* 2. " *God of Israel,*" and therefore *willing.*—*Andrew A. Bonar.*

Verse 6.—" *At evening.*" The *evening* expresses the time of calamity and want, and alludes to the wild beasts which are wont in the *evening* to go forth in quest of prey.—*Hermann Venema.*

Verse 6.—" *They make a noise like a dog.*" The noise I heard then I shall never forget. To say that if all the sheep-dogs in going to Smithfield on a market-day, had been kept on the constant bark and pitted against the yelping curs upon all the carts in London, they could have given any idea of the canine uproar that now first astonished me, would be to make the feeblest of images. The whole city rang with one vast riot. Down below me, at Tophane ; over about Stamboul ; far away at Scutari ; the whole sixty thousand dogs that are said to overrun Constantinople, appeared engaged in the most active extermination of each other, without a moment's cessation. The yelping, howling, barking, growling, and snarling, were all merged into one uniform and continuous even sound, as the noise of frogs becomes, when heard at a distance. For hours there was no lull. I went to sleep and woke again, and still, with my windows open, I heard the same tumult going on ; nor was it until daybreak that anything like tranquility was restored.—*Albert Smith, in " A Month at Constantinople,*" 1850.

Verse 6.—In bringing their secret plans to bear, they are represented as hungry dogs, prowling about the city in the darkness for prey ; ranging, each with his own object, but in one common cause. To take in the full force of this metaphor it must be remembered that in Eastern cities formerly, as at the present day, it was the custom to cast out all the refuse of food—bones, offal, etc.—into the streets, which was consumed chiefly by dogs, great numbers of which were kept, as it would seem, for that particular purpose. With this idea in mind, the metaphor has great propriety in its application to Christ's enemies.

> " Every evening they return,
> They howl like dogs,
> And surround the city.'

William Hill Tucker.

Verses 6, 7.—This is a continued metaphor, which must be well observed, of a famished and rabid dog, unable to satisfy either its hunger or thirst ; and describes men, howling formerly like dogs, pursuing, seizing all good things for themselves, and devouring ; but now destitute of all things, unable to quench their cupidity, despised, miserable, and desperate wanderers. Such did Saul and his messengers sent against David in Najoth Rama show themselves to be, and give the prelude to their coming misery.—*Hermann Venema.*

Verses 6, 7.—1. They are diligent about it: " *They return at evening.*" 2. *Mad*, and set to do it : " *They make a noise like a dog*," and threaten boldly. 3. Unwearied and obdurate in their purpose: " *They go round about the city.*" 4. Impudent, and brag what they will do to me : " *Behold, they belch out with their mouth.*" 5. And their words are bloody : " *Swords are in their lips.*"—*Adam Clarke.*

Verse 7.—" *Behold, they belch out with their mouth,*" etc. Bark like dogs, so Aben Ezra ; or, *bubble out*, as a fountain bubbles out with water ; so they cast out their wickedness in great abundance (see Jer. vi. 7) ; the phrase denotes the abundance of evil things and wicked speeches that come out of their mouths, which showed the naughtiness of their hearts ; so David's enemies blustered and threatened what they would do to him could they find him ; and Christ's enemies poured out their wicked charges of blasphemy and sedition against him in great plenty, and without proof.—*John Gill.*

Verse 8.—God seeth and smileth, he looketh and laugheth at these giants ; he sitteth in heaven far above their reach ; neither doth he much trouble himself about the matter ; no more should we, but trust in him, and know that there is a counsel in heaven, that will dash the mould of all contrary counsels upon the earth, as the stone cut out of the mountain did the four great monarchies. Dan. ii. 34. And therefore though the wicked, in the pride of his heart, doth persecute the poor ; though they belch out with their mouth, and seek to double murder the innocent, by detraction and by deadly practice, yet God both hears and jeers at their madness, and will bring all their purposes to nought with little ado ; nay, the very cruelty of his enemies will move God to make haste. The saints fare the better for the insolence and outrages of their enemies, whose ruin is thereby accelerated ; and somewhat God will do the sooner for his people, lest the enemy exalt himself. Ps. cxl. 8.—*Abraham Wright.*

Verse 8 (last clause).—In the close of the verse, mention is made of *all nations*, to intimate, that though they might equal the whole world in numbers, they would prove a mere mockery with all their influence and resources. Or the words may be read—EVEN AS *thou hast all the nations in derision.* One thing is obvious, that David ridicules the vain boasting of his enemies, who thought no undertaking too great to be accomplished by their numbers.—*John Calvin.*

Verses 8, 9 :—

> 8 But thou, Lord, laughest at them ;
> Thou deridest all the heathen.
> 9 His strength ! Toward thee will I keep watch,
> For God is my high-fort.

William Kay

Verse 9.—" *Because of his strength will I wait upon thee.*" Those seem to come nearest the meaning of the Psalmist, who construe the words as one continuous sentence, " *I will put in trust his strength with thee,*" meaning that however intemperately Saul might boast of his strength, he would rest satisfied in the assurance that there was a secret divine providence restraining his actions. We must learn to view all men as subordinated in this manner, and to conceive of their strength and their enterprises as depending upon the sovereign will of God. In my opinion, the following version is the best—" *His strength is with thee, I will wait.*" The words are parallel with those in the end of the Psalm, where there can be no doubt that the nominative case is employed, " *My strength is with thee,* I will sing."—*John Calvin.*

Verse 9 (*first clause*).—"*His strength*" is great, humanly viewed ; but to the eye of faith what is it ! LXX, τὸ κράτος μοι (= *uzzi*) ; and so most ancient versions. (The contrast is given in verses 16, 17.)—*William Kay.*

Verse 9.—"*Will I wait upon thee,*" lit., "*I will keep watch* to thee," alluding to the title, " When Saul sent, and they *watched* the house *to kill* him." David sets *watching before God,* against their *watching to kill* him.—*A. R. Fausset.*

Verse 9.—How weak soever the believer finds himself, and how powerful soever he perceives his enemy to be, it is all one to him, he hath no more to do but to put faith on work, and to wait till God works. " *Because of his* (that is, the enemy's) *strength, I will wait upon thee,*" saith he to the Lord, " *for God is my defence.*"— *David Dickson.*

Verse 10.—" *The God of my mercy shall prevent me.*" Oh, how the saints sing of the love of Christ ! Oh, how they sing that this love was not moved by worthiness, and it disdains all hire and price, but loves us because he loves us ! Deut. vii. 8. O sing of his wonderful love, and of the *prevention* of this love of Christ : " *The God of my mercy shall prevent me.*" How, 1. It preventeth thy love to him. 1 John iv. 19 : "We love God, because he first loved us." 2. It preventeth our sins, as in Paul's case. Acts ix. 3 : " And as he journeyed, he came near Damascus : and suddenly there shined round about him a light from heaven." 3. It preventeth our calamities. Psalm lxxix. 8 : " Let thy tender mercies speedily prevent us." And, 4. It prevents our endeavours : " *The God of my mercy shall prevent me.*"— *John Spalding, in* " *Synaxis Sacra,*" 1703.

Verse 10 (*first clause*).—The Psalmist was sure of mercy upon these grounds, he knew he was safe, because God was his God, and the God of his mercy : "*The God of my mercy shall prevent me.*" Some read it, *hath prevented me ;* others, *doth prevent me ;*" and others as in my text, *shall prevent me.* Each of these senses is exceedingly sweet and full. Take it in the first sense, *hath prevented me,* and it implies thus much, that the Psalmist never was in any difficulty, temptation, or fear, but God was beforehand with him ; having always the mercy ready which he stood in need of ; and had given it in due season, and that when he least expected it, and it may be was least prepared for it. Take it in the second sense, *doth prevent,* it argues the Psalmist's ground of confidence when all present appearances were gone ; as if he had said, " God is of one mind, his thoughts are thoughts of peace, and not of evil ; he may vary his providence, but his heart is the same as ever ; why should I fear, why should I not hope and rejoice ? for my God is a tried God, he is working for me even now. He prevents my fears, and he will prevent my falling." Take the words as they lie in my text, and it comes to the same thing. " God sees all my enemies' designs, and he is ready for them ; my prayer is heard, and sure I am deliverance will come, though I know not the time of it."

My design, under the Spirit's influence, is to look into my own heart and yours, and show you what wonders of providence and grace God, as *the God of our mercy,* has caused to pass before us. In discoursing on these words, I shall enquire, I. In what sense, or in what respects, God is *the God of our mercy ?* II. How, as the God of our mercy, he doth prevent us ? III. Apply, I. I am to enquire in what respects God is said to be *the God of his people's mercy,* and it seems to include in it these three things. I. That all the mercy which is in God's nature, is for his saints. It is a great word that (1 Peter v. 10), " *the God of all grace.*" God has in him all sorts of grace for his saints. He hath pardoning, quickening, strengthening, comforting, and preserving grace. His mercy is rich mercy, abundant mercy, inexhaustible mercy, sure mercy. A man's riches are his glory ; God glories in his mercy ; it is his delight, he rests in it ; and so may we, because there is an infinite inconceivable fulness of it in *him.* " With thee is the fountain of life." God distributes and parcels out this mercy, that we may conceive of it the better ; hence he is called by the apostle, " *The Father of mercies,* and the *God of all comfort.*"

2 Cor. i. 3. God is not called the author of our mercies, but the *Father* of them ; to show how freely they come from him ; they are his bowels ; he is pleased with them, as the father is with his own child ; dwell on the name, it is a sweet one, the *Father of mercies.* In my text, David grasps all this mercy, lays hold of it as his own mercy : " *The God of my mercy* shall prevent me." That is one sense. 2. It supposes, farther, that there is a portion of mercy laid by, in the purpose of God, for every saint ; a portion of mercy which he may call *his own.* This some understand to be Christ's meaning to Paul (2 Cor. xii. 9) : " My grace is sufficient for thee ; " *i.e.*, that grace which I have allotted for thee thou wilt find sufficient. I knew what thou wouldst need in my eternal counsels ; I have made provision beforehand ; I have taken care thou shouldst have enough. 3. The words suppose, farther, that God has taken it upon him as his charge, to keep this portion of his mercy for his people. Whatever it be, soul, it is trust for thee with him. Every saint may apply to God, as the God of every mercy which he needs.—*Condensed from John Hill's Sermon.*

Verse 10.—" *God shall let me see* my desire *upon mine enemies.*" The words " *my desire,*" are not in the original, and would be better omitted. The sense is —God will enable me to look down calmly upon my enemies. So Christ looked upon his murderers. So Stephen was enabled to do when they " gnashed upon him with their teeth." " All that sat in the council looking steadfastly on him, saw his face as it had been the face of an angel." Acts vi. 15.—*Christopher Wordsworth.*

Verse 11.—" *Slay them not,*" that they may be a whetstone to others' faith— as the Spartans (mentioned in Plutarch's Apothegms) refused to allow the destruction of a neighbouring city which had often called forth their armies, saying, " Destroy not the whetstone of our young men."—*Andrew A. Bonar.*

Verse 11.—" *Slay them not :* "—

" Live loathed and long
You smiling, smooth, detested parasites."

W. Shakspeare.

Verse 11.—The enemies must serve for monuments of the divine righteousness, not less in the abiding wretchedness of their race than by their own sudden destruction. Parallel to this verse, and to verses 6, 14, is the curse which David utters upon Joab, in 2 Sam. iii. 29 : " Let there not fail from the house of Joab one that hath an issue, or that is a leper, or that leaneth on a staff, or that falleth on the sword, or that *lacketh bread ;* " then the threatening of the man of God to Eli, in 1 Sam. ii. 36, where, after announcing the violent death of the evildoers themselves, corresponding to verse 13 here, it is said : " And it shall come to pass that every one that is left in thine house shall come and crouch to him [the new high priest] for a piece of silver and a morsel of bread, and shall say, Put me, I pray thee, into one of the priests' offices, that I may eat a piece of bread." Christian expositors have all along drawn attention to the fact, that the substance of our verse, as that also of verses 6, 14, has gone into fulfilment on the Jews. " They have been scattered into all lands, and must go and stand before the eyes of all Christians as a living witness, that they have crucified the true Messiah and Saviour of the world. So that if you see a Jew, think on this word." (*Arnd.*)— *E. W. Hengstenberg.*

Verse 11.—" *Slay them not ;* " namely, suddenly. " *Scatter them.*" It should seem that he hath a relation to Cain's punishment, whom God would not have killed, but would have him to be a wanderer all the days of his life for a spectacle, and an example of his judgments. Gen. iv. 12. Others translate it, *shake them ;* namely, their degree of honour and glory.—*John Diodati,* 1576—1649.

Verse 12.—" *For the sin of their mouth and the words of their lips,*" etc. Albeit the persecutors do not accomplish their purpose against the righteous ; yet their pride, their brags, their lies, their slanders, their curses against the godly, are a sufficient ditty for damnation and wrath to come upon them.—*David Dickson.*

Verse 12.—" *The word of their lips.* The phrase, *word of the lips,* is often used for empty loquacity and boasting ; the opposite of a word that is solid and founded on fact, as in 2 Kings xviii. 20. " Thou speakest, but it is only a *word of the lips.*" Prov. xiv. 23. " In all labour there is profit : but the *word of the lips* tendeth only to penury."—*Hermann Venema.*

Verse 13.—" *Consume them,*" emphatically, " *consume them in wrath, that they may not be;* " which at first sight seems contrary to his first desire, " *Slay them not;* " but it is not so, for he speaks not of their life, as if he would have them so consumed, that they should not remain alive ; but he desires only a consumption of their power, royalty, command, etc. And so these words are a farther explication of his second desire, " *Bring them down.*" He would have them so brought down and consumed in their strength, dignity, command, wealth, riches, that made them proud, that they never be able any more to oppose God, hurt his people, trample upon religion and his church ; he would have them live.—*William Nicholson.*

Verse 13.—" *Consume them.*" I hear of sad doings in Poland, of villages burnt down, of peaceable men deported to Siberia by hundreds, of women flogged ; and when I look away to that Warsaw market-place where a woman, nearly naked, is being publicly beaten, and when I see cruel Mouravieff smile as the blood jets forth from the scourged shoulders, I will not deny that I feel very much tempted to say, " Happy man, whose bullet in fair fight should empty that saddle ! " Am I bloodthirsty in this ? Am I vindictive ? Do you condemn me for this feeling ?— *R. A. Bertram.*

Verse 13.—" *That they may not be.*" By the word, וְאֵינֵמוֹ, *that they may not be,* may be understood either a vile and wretched state in general, or even total destruction. The *former* must indeed here be admitted, as is plain from the context, yet not to the exclusion of the *latter* sense ; since a miserable condition, such as in a disease, issues in destruction at length. *Not to be* is evidently by no means rarely taken for to be *nobody,* to be wretched, afflicted, despised. Comp. Jer. xxxi. 15.— *Hermann Venema.*

Verse 13.—" *Selah.*" Though God be in all his words *Yea* and *Amen,* yet in setting this seal of " *Selah* " to this doctrine, he hath testified his will that he would have all these things the better understood and the deeplier imprinted ; that if the wicked go on to persecute the godly, " *Selah,*" assuredly God will have them in derision ; " *Selah,*" assuredly God shall shiver their bones, shake their best actions, and discover their impurity ; " *Selah,*" assuredly God's hand shall be heavy upon them, and they shall not discern it to be his hand till they are consumed. " *Selah,*" assuredly, verily, amen, this is a faithful, an infallible truth ; as the Lord liveth it shall be so.—*Abraham Wright.*

Verse 14.—" *Dog.*" Is it the influence of Christianity extending its law of kindness to the lower animals, or something in the nature of northern dogs and northern men, which makes dogs among us Anglo-Saxons, and all the associations connected with them, so entirely different from what they are in the East ? Imagine the effigy of an Oriental saint reposing with its feet on a dog, like that of William the Silent, the heroic Prince of Orange, on the faithful spaniel which rescued his life in the night attack of the Spanish troops, and like so many a sculptured knight of mediæval times ! The very presence of such an image would, in Oriental eyes, be the greatest desecration an enemy could inflict on a sacred edifice. And in the Bible how exceedingly contemptuous, and how inapplicable to English dogs, are the terms employed in describing canine habits. " *They grin like a dog, and go about the city, and grudge if they be not satisfied ;* " " *Without are dogs.*" What possible resemblance is there between such a description and the grave dignity of a New-foundland ; the sagacious, acute expression of a terrier ; the wistful, almost human eyes of our house spaniels ? But here at Tyre, as in most Eastern towns, the familiar words came to us with all their true and forcible meaning. The wolfish, hungry, masterless dogs which " go about the cities (of Alexandria, for instance), gathering in packs like jackals, prowling about for offal, and grudging if they be not satisfied ; " or the famished outcasts, like our dogs at Tyre, prowling " outside " the city. To these we may apply the highly unfavourable definitions of Scripture, which every Englishman and Englishwoman must indignantly disclaim on behalf of the loyal, faithful, patient creatures who watch beside our homes like sentinels, and guard our flocks like shepherds, and welcome us with ecstatic joy when we come home again, and sometimes will even die rather than desert a master's grave.— *From " Wanderings over Bible Lands and Seas."* 1862.

Verse 14.—Those that repent of their sins when they are in trouble, *mourn like doves ;* those whose hearts are hardened when they are in trouble, *make a noise like dogs.*—*Matthew Henry.*

Verse 15.—"*Let them wander up and down,*" etc. A beggarly and indigent, and so an unsatisfied and wearisome condition, shall be their lot ; the greatest worldly plague that can fall on any—large appetites and no possessions or acquests to satisfy them.—*Henry Hammond.*

Verse 15.—"*And grudge if they be not satisfied.*" A contented man, if he has not what he would have, yet doth not grudge, doth not quarrel with providence, nor fret within himself ; but those whose God is their belly, if that be not filled and its appetites gratified, fall out both with God and themselves. It is not poverty, but discontent that makes a man unhappy.—*Matthew Henry.*

Verse 15.—The hunger of a dog is deservedly their plague, of whom a resemblance of that unclean animal's disposition hath been the sin. Reader, be it thy care to avoid such sins, and cultivate a spirit of lively devotion ; that, instead of receiving thy portion where there is weeping, wailing, and gnashing of teeth, thou mayst sing to the God of thy mercy for ever.—*Benjamin Boothroyd.*

Verse 16.—We must not pass by the contrast with the wretched condition of the wicked, which is indicated by the pronouns הֵמָּה, *they,* in verse fifteen, and וַאֲנִי *but I,* which are in exact antithesis ; also the "*evening,*" mentioned above, and the "*morning,*" now occurring, for the times of trouble and happiness, and the *dog-like noise* of the wicked, and the *singing* with joyful sound of David, to pass by other particulars, likewise give to the diverse states additional difference.—*Hermann Venema.*

Verse 16.—*Cantabo* and *exaltabo,* "*I will sing,*" and "*I will sing aloud.*" Here is *singing* only of God's *power ;* but there is *singing aloud* of his *mercy ;* as if his *mercy* were more exaltable than his power, and *that* reached the very *heavens ; this* unto the *clouds.* Ps. xxxvi. 5.—*From Humphrey Sydenham's Sermon, entitled "The Well-toned Cymball,"* 1637.

Verse 17.—"*Unto thee, O my strength, will I sing.*"—Formerly he had said that the strength of his enemy was with God, and now he asserts the same thing of his own. The expression, however, which admits of two meanings, he elegantly applies to himself in a different sense. God has the strength of the wicked in his hands, to curb and to restrain it, and to show that any power of which they boast is vain and fallacious. His own people, on the other hand, he supports and secures against the possibility of falling, by supplies of strength from himself.—*John Calvin.*

Verse 17.—"*Unto thee, O my strength.*" In opposition to *the enemy's* "*strength,*" ver. 9. "*Thy* power," or "*strength*"—the Hebrew word is the same (*ver.* 16)—is "*my* strength." There is an elegant play on similar sounds in the Hebrew for "I will *wait* upon thee," אֶשְׁמֹרָה (ver. 9), and "I will sing,"—אֲזַמֵּרָה—*A. R. Faussett.*

Verse 17 (*first clause*).—As on account of *Saul's strength* my *watching* was directed to thee ; so now, on account of *thy strength* vouchsafed to me, my *singing* of praises also shall be directed to thee alone.—*Martin Geier.*

Verse 17.—"*Strength*"—"*Mercy.*" He joins these two attributes, "*strength*" and "*mercy,*" very well ; for take away *strength* from him, and he cannot ; remove mercy, and he will not, protect ; both must go together in any one that will defend : *power,* that he can, *mercy,* that he will ; otherwise 'tis but in vain to hope for help from him. David found God to be both, and for both he extols him.—*William Nicholson.*

HINTS TO PREACHERS.

Verse 1 (*first clause*).—Deliver me from temptation, uphold me in temptation, cleanse me from the result of temptation. The world, the flesh, the devil, and chiefly sin, these are our enemies. We cannot escape them of ourselves, but the Lord by providence and grace can rescue us.

Verse 2 (*first clause*).—From being tempted by their promises, cowed by their threats, corrupted by their teaching, influenced by their example, injured by their slander, hindered in usefulness by their opposition.

Verse 3 (*first clause*).—The subtleties of Satan. Watches for places, times, states, and ways in which to assail us. Errors in doctrine, practice, spirit, set forth to entrap us. " Ye are not ignorant of his devices." Or, the diabolical ambush, discovered by watchfulness, and defeated by faith.

Verse 4.—The activity of the evil a rebuke for the good.   I. Their activity, " run."   II. Unanimity—" *they* run."   III. Their care—" prepare themselves." IV. Their readiness—" without my fault."

Verse 5.—" *O Lord God of hosts, the God of Israel.*"   This title furnishes an admirable topic.

Verse 9.—The greatness of difficulty a reason for prayer and faith.

Verse 10 (*first clause*).—The divine forwardness to bless.

Verse 11.—The continuance of our enemies a salutary ordinance of God for the prevention of an evil to which we are very liable.

Verse 13 (*last clause*).—God as the God of the church, his government as such, known in all human history.

Verse 16.—The heavenly chorister.   I. His song is sweet in contrast with the revilings of others—" but I."   II. It treats of subjects which terrify others—" thy power."   III. It grows louder on tender themes—" thy mercy."   IV. It has its choice seasons—" in the morning."   V. It is tuned by experience—" for thou hast."   VI. It is all to God's glory—" *thy* power," " *thy* mercy," " *thou* hast."

Verse 17.—I. *A doctrine*—God is his people's strength.   II. *An appropriation* —" my strength."   III. *A resolution.*   The song of gratitude for the past, faith for the present, hope for the future, of bliss for eternity.

PSALM LX.

TITLE.—*Here is a lengthy title, but it helps us much to expound the Psalm.* **To the Chief Musician upon Shushan-eduth, or the Lily of Testimony.** *The forty-fifth was on the lilies, and represented the kingly warrior in his beauty going forth to war; here we see him dividing the spoil and bearing testimony to the glory of God. Tunes have strange names apparently, but this results from the fact that we do not know what was in the composer's mind, else they might seem to be touchingly appropriate; perhaps the music or the musical instruments have more to do with this title than the Psalm itself. Yet in war-songs roses and lilies are often mentioned, and one remembers Macaulay's Song of the Huguenots, though perhaps we err in mentioning so carnal a verse—*

> "*Now by the lips of those ye love, fair gentlemen of France,*
> *Charge for the golden lillies now, upon them, with the lance.*"

Michtam of David, to teach. *David obeyed the precept to teach the children of Israel; he recorded the Lord's mighty acts that they might be rehearsed in the ears of generations to come. Golden secrets are to be told on the house-tops; these things were not done in a corner and ought not to be buried in silence. We ought gladly to learn what inspiration so beautifully teaches.* **When he strove with Aram-naharaim and with Aram-zobah.** *The combined Aramean tribes sought to overcome Israel, but were signally defeated.* **When Joab returned.** *He had been engaged in another region, and the enemies of Israel took advantage of his absence, but on his return with Abishai the fortunes of war were changed.* **And smote of Edom in the valley of salt twelve thousand.** *More than this appear to have fallen according to 1 Chron. xviii. 12, but this commemorates one memorable part of the conflict. Terrible must have been the battle, but decisive indeed were the results, and the power of the enemy was utterly broken. Well did the Lord deserve a song from his servant.*

DIVISIONS.—*Properly the song may be said to consist of three parts: the complaining verses, 1—3; the gladsome, 4—8; the prayerful, 9—12. We have divided it as the sense appeared to change.*

EXPOSITION.

O GOD, thou hast cast us off, thou hast scattered us, thou hast been displeased; O turn thyself to us again.

2 Thou hast made the earth to tremble; thou hast broken it: heal the breaches thereof, for it shaketh.

3 Thou hast showed thy people hard things: thou hast made us to drink the wine of astonishment.

1. Before the days of Saul, Israel had been brought very low; during his government it had suffered from internal strife, and his reign was closed by an overwhelming disaster at Gilboa. David found himself the possessor of a tottering throne, troubled with the double evil of faction at home, and invasion from abroad. He traced at once the evil to its true source, and began at the fountainhead. His were the politics of piety, which after all are the wisest and most profound. He knew that the displeasure of the Lord had brought calamity upon the nation, and to the removal of that displeasure he set himself by earnest prayer. "*O God, thou hast cast us off.*" Thou hast treated us as foul and offensive things, to be put away; as mean and beggarly persons, to be shunned with contempt; as useless dead boughs, to be torn away from the tree which they disfigure. To be cast off by God is the worst calamity that can befal a man or a people; but the worst form of it is when the person is not aware of it and is indifferent to it. When the divine desertion causes mourning and repentance, it will be but partial and temporary. When a cast-off soul sighs for its God it is not indeed cast off at all. "*Thou hast scattered us.*" David clearly sees the fruits of the divine anger, he traces the flight of Israel's warriors, the breaking of her power, the division in her body politic,

to the hand of God. Whoever might be the secondary agent of these disasters, he beholds the Lord's hand as the prime moving cause, and pleads with the Lord concerning the matter. Israel was like a city with a breach made in its wall, because her God was wroth with her. These first two verses, with their depressing confession, must be regarded as greatly enhancing the power of the faith which in the after verses rejoices in better days, through the Lord's gracious return unto his people. *" Thou hast been displeased."* This is the secret of our miseries. Had we pleased thee, thou wouldst have pleased us ; but as we have walked contrary to thee, thou hast walked contrary to us. *" O turn thyself to us again."* Forgive the sin and smile once more. Turn us to thee, turn thou to us. Aforetime thy face was towards thy people, be pleased to look on us again with thy favour and grace. Some read it, "Thou wilt turn to us again," and it makes but slight difference which way we take it, for a true-hearted prayer brings a blessing so soon that it is no presumption to consider it as already obtained. There was more need for God to turn to his people than for Judah's troops to be brave, or Joab and the commanders wise. God with us is better than strong battalions ; God displeased is more terrible than all the Edomites that ever marched into the valley of salt, or all the devils that ever opposed the church. If the Lord turn to us, what care we for Aram-naharaim or Aram-zobah, or death, or hell ? but if he withdraw his presence we tremble at the fall of a leaf.

2. *" Thou hast made the earth to tremble."* Things were as unsettled as though the solid earth had been made to quake ; nothing was stable ; the priests had been murdered by Saul, the worst men had been put in office, the military power had been broken by the Philistines, and the civil authority had grown despicable through insurrections and intestine contests. *" Thou hast broken it."* As the earth cracks, and opens itself in rifts during violent earthquakes, so was the kingdom rent with strife and calamity. *" Heal the breaches thereof."* As a house in time of earthquakes is shaken, and the walls begin to crack, and gape with threatening fissures, so was it with the kingdom. *" For it shaketh."* It tottered to a fall ; if not soon propped up and repaired it would surely come down in complete ruin. So far gone was Israel, that only God's interposition could preserve it from utter destruction. How often have we seen churches in this condition, and how suitable is the prayer before us, in which the extremity of the need is used, as an argument for help. The like may be said of our own personal religion, it is sometimes so tried, that like a house shaken by earthquake it is ready to come down with a crash, and none but the Lord himself can repair its breaches, and save us from utter destruction.

3. *" Thou hast showed thy people hard things."* Hardships had been heaped upon them, and the Psalmist traces these rigorous providences to their fountain-head. Nothing had happened by chance, but all had come by divine design and with a purpose, yet for all that things had gone hard with Israel. The Psalmist claims that they were still the Lord's own people, though in the first verse he had said, "thou hast cast us off." The language of complaint is usually confused, and faith in time of trouble ere long contradicts the desponding statements of the flesh. *" Thou hast made us to drink the wine of astonishment."* Our afflictions have made us like men drunken with some potent and bitter wine ; we are in amazement, confusion, delirium ; our steps reel, and we stagger as those about to fall. The great physician gives his patients potent potions to purge out their abounding and deep-seated diseases. Astonishing evils bring with them astonishing results. The grapes of the vineyard of sin produce a wine which fills the most hardened with anguish when justice compels them to quaff the cup. There is a fire-water of anguish of soul which even to the righteous makes a cup of trembling, which causes them to be exceeding sorrowful almost unto death. When grief becomes so habitual as to be our drink, and to take the place of our joys, becoming our only wine, then are we in an evil case indeed.

4 Thou has given a banner to them that fear thee, that it may be displayed because of the truth. Selah.

5 That thy beloved may be delivered ; save *with* thy right hand, and hear me.

4. Here the strain takes a turn. The Lord has called back to himself his servants, and commissioned them for his service, presenting them with a standard to be

used in his wars. " *Thou hast given a banner to them that fear thee.*" Their afflictions had led them to exhibit holy fear, and then being fitted for the Lord's favour, he gave them an ensign, which would be both a rallying point for their hosts, a proof that he had sent them to fight, and a guarantee of victory. The bravest men are usually intrusted with the banner, and it is certain that those who fear God most have less fear of man than any others. The Lord has given us the standard of the gospel, let us live to uphold it, and if needful die to defend it. Our right to contend for God, and our reason for expecting success, are found in the fact that the faith has been once committed to the saints, and that by the Lord himself. " *That it may be displayed because of the truth.*" Banners are for the breeze, the sun, the battle. Israel might well come forth boldly, for a sacred standard was borne aloft before them. To publish the gospel is a sacred duty, to be ashamed of it a deadly sin. The truth of God was involved in the triumph of David's armies, he had promised them victory; and so in the proclamation of the gospel we need feel no hesitancy, for as surely as God is true he will give success to his own word. For the truth's sake, and because the true God is on our side, let us in these modern days of warfare emulate the warriors of Israel, and unfurl our banners to the breeze with confident joy. Dark signs of present or coming ill must not dishearten us; if the Lord had meant to destroy us he would not have given us the gospel; the very fact that he has revealed himself in Christ Jesus involves the certainty of victory *Magna est veritas et prævalebit.*

" Hard things thou hast upon us laid,
And made us drink most bitter wine;
But still thy banner we've display'd,
And borne aloft thy truth divine.

" Our courage fails not, though the night
No earthly lamp avails to break,
For thou wilt soon arise in might,
And of our captors captives make."

" *Selah.*" There is so much in the fact of a banner being given to the hosts of Israel, so much of hope, of duty, of comfort, that a pause is fitly introduced. The sense justifies it, and the more joyful strain of the music necessitates it.

5. " *That thy beloved may be delivered.*" David was the Lord's beloved, his name signifies " dear, or beloved," and there was in Israel a remnant according to the election of grace, who were the beloved of the Lord; for their sakes the Lord wrought great marvels, and he had an eye to them in all his mighty acts. God's beloved are the inner seed, for whose sake he preserves the entire nation, which acts as a husk to the vital part. This is the main design of providence, " *That thy beloved may be delivered;*" if it were not for their sakes he would neither give a banner nor send victory to it. " *Save with thy right hand, and hear me.*" Save at once, before the prayer is over; the case is desperate unless there be immediate salvation. Tarry not, O Lord, till I have done pleading: save first and hear afterwards. The salvation must be a right royal and eminent one, such as only the omnipotent hand of God linked with his dexterous wisdom can achieve. Urgent distress puts men upon pressing and bold petitions such as this. We may by faith ask for and expect that our extremity will be God's opportunity: special and memorable deliverances will be wrought out when dire calamities appear to be imminent. Here is one suppliant for many, even as in the case of our Lord's intercession for his saints. He, the Lord's David, pleads for the rest of the beloved, beloved and accepted in him the Chief Beloved; he seeks salvation as though it were for himself, but his eye is ever upon all those who are one with him in the Father's love. When divine interposition is necessary for the rescue of the elect it must occur, for the first and greatest necessity of providence is the honour of God, and the salvation of his chosen. This is fixed fate, the centre of the immutable decree, the inmost thought of the unchangeable Jehovah.

6 God hath spoken in his holiness; 1 will rejoice, I will divide Shechem, and mete out the valley of Succoth.

7 Gilead *is* mine, and Manasseh *is* mine; Ephraim also *is* the strength of mine head; Judah *is* my lawgiver;

8 Moab *is* my washpot; over Edom will I cast out my shoe: Philistia, triumph thou because of me.

6. "*God hath spoken in his holiness.*" Faith is never happier than when it can fall back upon the promise of God. She sets this over against all discouraging circumstances ; let outward providences say what they will, the voice of a faithful God drowns every sound of fear. God had promised Israel victory, and David the kingdom : the holiness of God secured the fulfilment of his own covenant, and therefore the king spake confidently. The goodly land had been secured to the tribes by the promise made to Abraham, and that divine grant was an abundantly sufficient warrant for the belief that Israel's arms would be successful in battle. Believer make good use of this, and banish doubts while promises remain. "*I will rejoice,*" or "*I will triumph.*" Faith regards the promise not as fiction but fact, and therefore drinks in joy from it, and grasps victory by it. "God hath spoken ; I will rejoice ;" here is a fit motto for every soldier of the cross. "*I will divide Shechem.*" As a victor David would allot the conquered territory to those to whom God had given it by lot. Shechem was an important portion of the country which as yet had not yielded to his government ; but he saw that by Jehovah's help it would be, and indeed was all his own. Faith divides the spoil, she is sure of what God has promised, and enters at once into possession. "*And mete out the valley of Succoth.*" As the east so the west of Jordan should be allotted to the proper persons. Enemies should be expelled, and the landmarks of peaceful ownership set up. Where Jacob had pitched his tent, there his rightful heirs should till the soil. When God has spoken, his divine *shall*, our "*I will,*" becomes no idle boast, but the fit echo of the Lord's decree. Believer, up and take possession of covenant mercies, "*Divide Shechem, and mete out the valley of Succoth.*" Let not Canaanitish doubts and legalisms keep thee out of the inheritance of grace. Live up to thy privileges, take the good which God provides thee.

7. "*Gilead is mine, and Manasseh is mine.*" He claims the whole land on account of the promise. Two other great divisions of the country he mentions, evidently delighting to survey the goodly land which the Lord had given him. All things are ours, whether things present or things to come ; no mean portion belongs to the believer, and let him not think meanly of it. No enemy shall withhold from true faith what God has given her, for grace makes her mighty to wrest it from the foe. Life is mine, death is mine, for Christ is mine. "*Ephraim also is the strength of mine head.*" All the military power of the valiant tribe was at the command of David, and he praises God for it. God will bow to the accomplishment of his purposes all the valour of men : the church may cry, "the prowess of armies is mine," God will overrule all their achievements for the progress of his cause. "*Judah is my lawgiver.*" There the civil power was concentrated : the king being of that tribe sent forth his laws out of her midst. We know no lawgiver, but the King who came out of Judah. To all the claims of Rome, or Oxford, or the councils of men, we pay no attention ; we are free from all other ecclesiastical rule, but that of Christ ; but we yield joyful obedience to him : "*Judah is my lawgiver.*" Amid distractions it is a great thing to have good and sound legislation, it was a balm for Israel's wounds, it is our joy in the church of Christ.

8. Having looked at home with satisfaction, the hero-king now looks abroad with exultation. "*Moab,*" so injurious to me in former years, "*is my washpot.*" The basin into which the water falls when it is poured from an ewer upon my feet. A mere pot to hold the dirty water after my feet have been washed in it. Once she defiled Israel, according to the counsel of Balaam, the son of Beor ; but she shall be no longer able to perpetrate such baseness ; she shall be a washpot for those whom she sought to pollute. The wicked as we see in them the evil, the fruit, and the punishment of sin, shall help on the purification of the saints. This is contrary to their will, and to the nature of things, but faith finds honey in the lion, and a washpot in filthy Moab. David treats his foes as but insignificant and inconsiderable ; a whole nation he counts but as a footbath for his kingdom. "*Over Edom will I cast out my shoe.*" As a man when bathing throws his shoes on one side, so would he obtain his dominion over haughty Esau's descendants as easily as a man casts a shoe. Perhaps he would throw his shoe as nowadays men throw their glove, as a challenge to them to dare dispute his sway. He did not need draw a sword to smite his now crippled and utterly despondent adversary, for if he dared revolt he would only need to throw his slipper at him, and he would tremble. Easily are we victors when Omnipotence leads the way. The day shall come when the church shall with equal ease subdue China and Ethiopia to the sceptre of the Son of David. Every believer also may by faith triumph over all difficulties, and reign

with him who hath made us kings and priests. "They overcame through the blood of the Lamb," shall yet be said of all who rest in the power of Jesus. "*Philistia, triumph thou because of me.*" Be so subdued as to rejoice in my victories over my other foes. Or does he mean, I who smote thy champion have at length so subdued thee that thou shalt never be able to rejoice over Israel again ; but if thou must needs triumph it must be with me, and not against me ; or rather is it a taunting defiance, a piece of irony ? O proud Philistia, where are thy vaunts ? Where now thy haughty looks, and promised conquests ? Thus dare we defy the last enemy, " O death, where is thy sting ? O grave, where is thy victory ? " So utterly hopeless is the cause of hell when the Lord comes forth to the battle, that even the weakest daughter of Zion may shake her head at the enemy, and laugh him to scorn. O the glorying of faith ! There is not a grain of vainglory in it, but yet her holy boastings none can hinder. When the Lord speaks the promise, we will not be slow to rejoice and glory in it.

9 Who will bring me *into* the strong city ? who will lead me into Edom ?

10 *Wilt* not thou, O God, *which* hadst cast us off ? and *thou*, O God, *which* didst not go out with our armies ?

9. As yet the interior fortresses of Edom had not been subdued. Their invading bands had been slain in the valley of salt, and David intended to push his conquests even to Petra the city of the rock, deemed to be impregnable. "*Who will bring me into the strong city?*" It was all but inaccessible, and hence the question of David. When we have achieved great success it must be a stimulus to greater efforts, but it must not become a reason for self-confidence. We must look to the strong for strength as much at the close of a campaign as at its beginning. "*Who will lead me into Edom?*" High up among the stars stood the city of stone, but God could lead his servant up to it. No heights of grace are too elevated for us, the Lord being our leader, but we must beware of high things attempted in self-reliance. EXCELSIOR is well enough as a cry, but we must look to the highest of all for guidance. Joab could not bring David into Edom. The veterans of the valley of salt could not force the passage, yet was it to be attempted, and David looked to the Lord for help. Heathen nations are yet to be subdued. The city of the seven hills must yet hear the gospel. Who will give the church the power to accomplish this ? The answer is not far to seek.

10. "*Wilt not thou, O God, which hadst cast us off ?*" Yes, the chastising God is our only hope. He loves us still. For a small moment does he forsake, but with great mercy does he gather his people. Strong to smite, he is also strong to save. He who proved to us our need of him by showing us what poor creatures we are without him, will now reveal the glory of his help by conducting great enterprises to a noble issue. "*And thou, O God, which didst not go out with our armies ?*" The self-same God art thou, and to thee faith cleaves. Though thou slay us, we trust in thee, and look for thy merciful help.

11 Give us help from trouble ; for vain *is* the help of man.

12 Through God we shall do valiantly : for he *it is that* shall tread down our enemies.

11. "*Give us help from trouble.*" Help us to overcome the disasters of civil strife and foreign invasion ; save us from further incursions from without and division within. Do thou, O Lord, work this deliverance, "*for vain is the help of man.*" We have painfully learned the utter impotence of armies, kings, and nations without thine help. Our banners trailed in the mire have proven our weakness without thee, but yonder standard borne aloft before us shall witness to our valour now that thou hast come to our rescue. How sweetly will this verse suit the tried people of God as a frequent ejaculation. We know how true it is.

12. "*Through God we shall do valiantly.*" From God all power proceeds, and all we do well is done by divine operation ; but still we, as soldiers of the great king, are to fight, and to fight valiantly too. Divine working is not an argument for human inaction, but rather is it the best excitement for courageous effort. Helped in the past, we shall also be helped in the future, and being assured of this we resolve to play the man. "*For he it is that shall tread down our enemies.*" From him shall the might proceed, to him shall the honour be given. Like straw on the thrashing-floor beneath the feet of the oxen shall we tread upon our abject foes,

but it shall rather be *his* foot which presses them down than ours; his hand shall go out against them so as to put them down and keep them in subjection. In the case of Christians there is much encouragement for a resolve similar to that of the first clause. "*We shall do valiantly.*" We will not be ashamed of our colours, afraid of our foes, or fearful of our cause. The Lord is with us, omnipotence sustains us, and we will not hesitate, we dare not be cowards. O that our King, the true David, were come to claim the earth, for the kingdom is the Lord's, and he is the governor among the nations.

EXPLANATORY NOTES AND QUAINT SAYINGS.

Title.—There are some difficulties attendant upon the title of this Psalm, when it is compared with the contents. We naturally expect after such an inscription, joy, congratulation, and praise for victory; but the Psalmist breaks out into lamentations and bitter complaints: his strains are, however, changed, when he has proceeded as far as verse three, where he begins to feel confidence, and to employ the language of exultation and triumph. The best means of removing this discrepancy seems to be by remarking, that this Psalm was written after some of the battles of which mention is made in the title, but that the author does not restrict himself to those events without taking a wider range, so as to embrace the afflictive condition both of Israel and Judah during the latter part of Saul's life, and the former years of David's reign. In the concluding years of Saul, the Philistines obtained a superiority over him, and finally destroyed him with his army. Subsequently to these events the whole land was in a very disturbed and agitated condition, arising out of the contentions between the partisans of Saul's family, and those who were attached to David. The nations which inhabited the regions adjacent to the land of Canaan were at all times inimical to the Jews, and seized every opportunity of attacking and injuring them. But when David had succeeded in uniting the whole nation under his authority, he proceeded to avenge the injuries and insults that had been inflicted on his countrymen by the Philistines, Edomites, Moabites, and Syrians; and God was pleased to give him signal success in his undertakings. He appears, therefore, to have combined all these transactions, and made them the subject of this Psalm.—*William Walford.*

Title.—"*Shushan-eduth.*" *The lilies of the testimony*—means, that this Psalm has for its chief subject something very lovely and cheering in the law: namely, the words of promise quoted in the beginning of verse six, according to which the land of Canaan belonged to the Israelites, upon which is thus established the confidence expressed in verses 6—8, with respect to their right of property over the land, and their possession of it. This promise, not to cite many other passages which occur in the Five Books of Moses, and even so early as the patriarchs, is contained in Genesis xlix., and Deut. xxxiii. It is evident of what value and importance this promise was, and particularly the remembrance of it at this time.— *T. C. Barth's "Bible Manual,"* 1865.

Title.—The only other "*eduth*" or "*testimony*" in the Psalter, Psalm lxxx., makes mention by name of the tribes of Ephraim, Benjamin, and Manasseh, and is a witness against those tribes for forsaking the Shepherd of Israel who had brought them up out of the land of Egypt.—*Joseph Francis Thrupp, M.A., in "An Introduction to the Study and Use of the Psalms,"* 1860.

Title.—*Aram-naharaim.*—The name *Aram* corresponds to *Syria* in its widest and vaguest sense, and is joined with other names to designate particular parts of that large country. It even includes Mesopotamia, which is a term of physical rather than political geography, and denotes the space between the Tigris and Euphrates, corresponding to *Aram-Naharaim*, or *Syria of the Two Rivers*, in the verse before us. The king of this country was tributary to the king of Aram-Zobah, as appears from the account of David's second Aramean war (2 Sam. x. 16, 19).— *Joseph Addison Alexander.*

Title.—"*When he strove with Aram-naharaim and with Aram-zobah.*" An insult offered to David's ambassadors by Hanun, king of the Ammonites, led to a serious war. Hanun obtained mercenaries from Syria to reinforce his army, Joab and

Abishai his brother, David's generals, gave them battle. Joab, opposed to the Syrians, gained the first success, and the Ammonites, seeing their allies routed, took to flight into their town. But this defeat provoked a great coalition, embracing all the people between the Jordan and the Euphrates. David, however, fearlessly marched against them at the head of his army; he vanquished all his enemies, and made himself master of the small Aramæan kingdoms of Damascus, Zobah, and Hamath, and subjugated the Eastern Idumæans, who met their final defeat in the Valley of Salt.—*François Lenormant and E. Chevallier, in "A Manual of the Ancient History of the East,"* 1869.

Title.—" *Joab returned, and smote of Edom in the valley of salt twelve thousand,*" compared with 2 Sam. viii. 13, " David gat him a name when he returned from smiting of the Syrians in the valley of salt, being eighteen thousand men," and 1 Chron. xviii. 12, where this very service was performed by *Abishai.* Answer. It is one thing to attribute the victory for the honour of the king that was the cause. But the mentioning of these chief generals, by whom the service was performed, is another. David, under God, must have the honour of the work, for the increase of his name, being set for the typing out of Christ, who must have all the glory of the day, whatever conquest he gets by instruments of that service here, who likewise are typed out in David's worthies, of whom Joab and Abishai were chief. By these he obtained that great victory over Hadadezer. In returning from which Joab found his brother Abishai engaged " *in the valley of salt* " against eighteen thousand Edomites or Syrians (all one), whose valour the Almighty so looked on, as he attributes the whole slaughter to him, because first attempting it. Joab, it seems, took this in his return from the former slaughter, and fell in for the assistance of his brother Abishai (for that was their usual course : though they divided their armies, they did not divide their hearts). But if the enemies were too strong, one would help the other. 1 Chron. xix. 12. And of this eighteen thousand attributed to David and Abishai before, Joab slew twelve thousand of them; the memory of which service is here embalmed with a Psalm; first showing the extremes they were in, doubtful at first they should not get the victory. Secondly, applying it to the kingdom of Christ. Lastly, ascribing all the honour of the conquest to God; saying, through God this valiant service was done; it was he that trod down our enemies; and will do (last verse).—*William Streat, in " The Dividing of the Hoof,"* 1654.

Title.—" *The Valley of Salt."* The ridge of Usdum exhibits more distinctly its peculiar formation; *the main body of the mountain being a solid mass of rock salt.* . . . We could at first hardly believe our eyes, until we had several times approached the precipices, and broken off pieces to satisfy ourselves, both by the touch and taste. The salt, where thus exposed, is everywhere more or less furrowed by the rains. As we advanced, large lumps and masses, broken off from above, lay like rocks along the shore, or were fallen down as *débris.* The very stones beneath our feet were wholly of salt. . . . The position of this mountain, at the south end of the sea, enables us also to ascertain the place of " *The Valley of Salt* " mentioned in Scripture, where the Hebrews under David, and again under Amaziah, gained decisive victories over Edom. This valley could have been no other than the Ghôr south of the Dead Sea, adjacent to the mountain of salt ; · it separates indeed the ancient territories of Judah and Edom.—*Edward Robinson's " Biblical Researches in Palestine."*

Title.—The historic record mentions *eighteen thousand* slain, and here but *twelve thousand.* The greater of course includes the less. The discrepancy may be explained by supposing that the title contains the numbers slain by one division of the army, or that the *twelve thousand* were slain in the battle, and the residue in the flight. Or an error may have crept into the text. Every scholar admits that there is sometimes serious difficulty in settling the numbers of the Old Testament. In this place Calvin has *two and twenty thousand,* the common version *twelve thousand,* while the original is *two ten thousand,* which taken in one way would mean *twenty thousand, i.e., two tens of thousands.* Hammond refers the numbers slain to different battles, and so avoids the difficulty.—*William S. Plumer.*

Verse 1.—" *O God, thou hast cast us off."* The word here used means properly to be foul, rancid, offensive ; and then, to treat anything *as if* it were foul or rancid ; to repel, to spurn, to cast away. It is strong language, meaning that God had seemed to treat them as if they were loathsome or offensive to him.—*Albert Barnes.*

Verse 2.—"*Heal the breaches thereof; for it shaketh.*" They pray that this may be done with the utmost speed, because there was danger in delay, for the kingdom was already pressed down with a heavy calamity, and on the brink of ruin, which is signified by the word מָטָה whose origin is in a very strong and tremulous inclination to one side, properly from the application of a *lever*, and is applied to those who are leaning so far to one side that they are just on the point of falling; figuratively, therefore, it expresses a *most perilous condition*, in which one is on the edge of destruction.—*Hermann Venema.*

Verses 2.—"*Heal the breaches thereof.*" Even Israel is subject to "*breaches.*" So it was with the literal typical Israel, David's kingdom; so it may be with spiritual mystical Israel, the kingdom of Christ, the church of God upon earth. There are "*breaches*" from *without*, and "*breaches*" from *within*. I will invert the order. From *without*, by open *persecution;* from *within*, by intestine and home-bred *divisions*. Of both these the church of God in all ages hath had sufficient experience. Look we upon the *primitive* times, during the infancy of the church, however the *soundest* and entirest church that ever was, yet how was it *broken!* Broken, as by foreign persecutions, so by home-bred divisions. Both these ways was the church during the apostles' times broken, distressed by enemies from without who persecuted it.—*John Brinsley (1600—1665), in "The Healing of Israel's Breaches."*

Verse 2.—"*It shaketh.*" That is, presaging nothing but *ruin* and *downfall*, unless it be speedily underpropped, and "*the breaches thereof*" made up and "*healed.*" Thus did David look upon Israel's disease, and hereupon it was that he was so deeply affected with it, so earnestly desiring the cure of it. The reference, as interpreters conceive, is to those *home-bred divisions*, those civil wars betwixt the two houses of Saul and David, after the death of Saul; then did the "*earth,*" the land, that land of Israel (as the Chaldee explains it), *quake and tremble*, being *broken, riven* (as the word in the original signifieth): even as the earth sometimes by earthquakes is riven, and torn asunder with prodigious chasms, openings, or gapings: so was that kingdom divided in those civil commotions, the nobles and commons taking parts and siding, some with David, some with Ishbosheth.—*John Brinsley.*

Verse 3.—"*Thou hast showed thy people hard things,*" God will be sure to plough his own ground, whatsoever becometh of the waste; and to weed his own garden, though the rest of the world should be let alone to grow wild.—*John Trapp.*

Verse 3.—"*Thou hast given us to drink infatuation, or bewilderment, as men drink wine.*" So Hupfeld explains the construction, referring to Psalm lxxx. 5, "Thou hast made them feed upon weeping like bread;" 1 Kings xxii. 27, "Feed him with affliction as bread, and with affliction as water" (מֵי לַחַץ); Isaiah xxx. 20. But the apposition is capable of being explained in another way, for the second noun may in fact be a predicate further defining the first: "Thou hast given us wine to drink which is (not wine, but) bewilderment."—*J. J. Stewart Perowne.*

Verse 3.—"*The wine of astonishment.*" "*Intoxicating wine.*" Hebrew, "Wine of staggering," that is, which causeth staggering, or, in other words, intoxicating. Some render, "wine of stupor," or stupefying. Symmachus, "wine of agitation," and this sense I have adopted, which is also that of the Syriac.—*Benjamin Boothroyd.*

Verse 4.—"*Thou hast given a banner to them that fear thee.*" Perhaps the delivery of a *banner* was anciently esteemed an obligation to protect, and that the Psalmist might consider it in this light, when, upon a victory over the Syrians and Edomites, after the public affairs of Israel had been in a bad state, he says, "*Thou hast shewed thy people hard things,*" etc. "*Thou hast given a banner to them that fear thee.*" Though thou didst for a time give up thine Israel into the hands of their enemies, thou hast now given them an assurance of thy having received them under thy protection.—*Thomas Harmer (1715—1788), in "Observations on Divers Passages of Scripture."*

Verse 4.—"*Thou hast given a banner,*" etc. Thou hast given us by the recent victory, after our prostrate condition, a banner of triumph to *lift up* (so the Hebrew), because of thy faithfulness to thy promise. "*The truth*" here answers to God's "*holiness*" (ver. 6). So long as soldiers see their banner *uplifted*, they flock round it with confidence. But when it is prostrate their spirits and hopes fall. The "*banner*" is a pledge of safety, and a rallying point to those who fight under it.—*A. R. Fausset.*

Verse 4.—" *Thou hast given a banner,*" etc. The Psalmist compares the *salvation* which the Lord bestows upon his people to a highly excellent " *banner,*" which serves as a signal to one lying prostrate in his misery, to rise up, with an allusion perhaps to Numbers xxi. 8. " And the Lord said to Moses, Make thee a serpent and set it upon a *standard-pole ;* and it happened that every one who was bitten, and looked at it, lived." At any rate, that passage in which the serpent is a sympol of the healing power of God, may serve to illustrate the passage before us. Compare " *heal its breaches.*"—*E. W. Hengstenberg.*

Verse 4.—" *A banner,*" which is a sign or instrument :—1. Of union. This people, who were lately divided and under several banners, thou hast now gathered together and united under one banner ; to wit, under my government. 2. Of battle. Thou hast given us an army and power to oppose our enemies. We had our banner to set against theirs. 3. Of triumph. We have not lost our banner but gained theirs, and brought it away in triumph. Comp. Ps. xx. 5.—*Matthew Pool.*

Verse 6.—" *God hath spoken in his holiness.*" That is, by Samuel he hath promised, as he is an holy God, and true of his word, that I should be king of all Israel, and now he hath performed it. (Sam. v.) Yet Calvin speaks of it as not yet performed ; but the course of the history makes it plain that David was now king over the parts of which he here speaketh. " *I will divide Shechem,*" as subject to me, as Joshua having the land under him, divided it amongst his people : so David being king over all the parts of the land, divides to his followers such portions as belonged unto them by inheritance, from which happily some of them had been expelled in the time of Ish-bosheth his reign ; or some families in the time of those wars might be utterly wasted away, and so the king having free power to dispose of their lands, might give them amongst his men, and take part to himself.—*John Mayer.*

Verse 6.—" *God hath spoken in his holiness.*" That is, he hath given out his word from heaven, the habitation of his holiness and of his glory ; or, he hath spoken it certainly, there is nothing but holiness in his word (and that is the strength of words). David having received this word stands assured, that as Shechem and Succoth, Gilead and Manasseh, Ephraim and Judah would willingly submit to him and yield obedience : so, also, that Moab, Edom, and Philistia, who were his professed enemies, should be subdued to him. He expected to conquer and triumph over them, to put them to the basest offices, as his vassals, because God had decreed and spoken it in his holiness. God hath spoken the word, saith he, therefore it shall be done, yea, 'tis done ; and therefore David cried, *All's mine, Gilead is mine, Manasseh is mine, Moab and Edom are mine,* as soon as God had spoken the word,—*Joseph Caryl.*

Verse 6.—" *I will divide Shechem.*" It is as much as if he should say, I will not look to have my share measured out by others, but I will divide it, and measure myself, and will be the right owner and possessor thereof.—*Thomas Wilcocks.*

Verse 6.—" *I will divide Shechem,*" etc. Of *Shechem* and the *Valley of Succoth,* or *booths,* so called from Jacob's making *booths,* and *feeding his cattle* there. (See Genesis xxxiii. 17, 18.) By these are meant Samaria ; and *David's dividing* or *meting* them out, is a phrase to express his *dominion* over them, in being part of the *regal* power to *distribute* his province into cities and regions, and place judges and magistrates over them. To these the addition of *Gilead* (which contains the whole region of *Bashan,* etc., on the *other side of Jordan*), and then the mention of *Manasseh* and *Ephraim,* are designed, as by so many parts, to denote the kingdom of Israel, or the ten tribes ; and their being *his,* and " *the strength of his head,*" notes him to be the *Lord* over them, and to make use of their strength of his wars, for the defending or enlarging his dominions. And then " *Judah* (מְחֹקְקִי) *is my law-giver ;*" as it refers to Jacob's prophecy of the *sceptre and lawgiver not departing from Judah,* denoting that to be the *royal* tribe ; so by it is signified the *kingdom of Judah* (under which *Benjamin* is comprehended), that David is possessed of that also.—*Henry Hammond.*

Verse 6.—" *Succoth.*" If the preceding views are correct, we may rest in the result, that the present Sâkût represents the name and site of the ancient Succoth . . . . We passed obliquely along the northern slope of the same broad swell, where the ground was covered only by a thick crop of thistles. On our right was a region of lower ground to which we gradually descended ; full of grass, wild oats, and thistles, with an occasional thornbush. The soil was like that of an Ohio bottom. The grass, intermingled with tall daisies and the wild oats, reached to the horses' backs; while the thistles sometimes overtopped the riders' heads. All was now dry; and in some places it was difficult to make our way through the exuberant growth. At last we came to the cause of this fertility, a fine brook winding along the bottom. We crossed it, and passed up again obliquely over another like swell, covered as before only with thistles. Here was an ancient oil vat, very large and of a single stone; it was evidently brought hither, and indicates the former growth of the olive in these parts. We struck the same stream again at its source, called 'Ain el-Beida, a large and fine fountain surrounded with gardens of cucumbers, and watering an extensive tract. We were here on the edge of the higher portion of the Ghôr, where low ridges and swells project out from the foot of the western mountains, and form a rolling plain or plateau, which is well watered, arable, and very extensively cultivated for wheat. The tract further east, which we had now crossed, may be said to extend to the high bank of the lower Jordan valley. It is less elevated, is more generally level, though crossed by low swells between the water-courses, and has little tillage. The inhabitants of Tûbâs are divided into three hostile parties; and they carry their divisions into their agriculture in the Ghôr. One party sows at 'Ain el-Beida, where we now were; another around 'Ain Mak-hûz, more in the north; and the third at Ridghah, Sâkût, and further south. The people of Teyâsîr also sow on the south of Mâlih; the water of which is used for irrigation. The whole tract north of Wady Mâlih was said to be farmed from the government by one of the Sheikhs of the Jenâr family, who live at Jeba' and in its neighbourhood. By him it is again let to the different villages.—*Robinson's "Biblical Researches in Palestine."*

Verses 6, 7.—The chief and principal places where the seditious party had their residence and abode, were those which the Psalmist mentioneth in the sixth and seventh verses, namely *Shechem*, a city in the tribe of Ehpraim; *Succoth*, a city in the tribe of Gad; *Gilead* and *Manasseh*, the utmost borders of the land of Canaan, beyond Jordan. These were some of the chief places which sided with Ish-bosheth whilst he lived, as you may see, 2 Sam. ii.; and, as it seemeth, they still cleaved to the house of Saul after he was dead, not acknowledging David for their king.—*John Brinsley.*

Verse 7.—" *Gilead is mine and Manasseh is mine.*" That is to say, I will possess myself of them and rule over them; not as a *conqueror* over *slaves*, but as a lord over *subjects*, as a father over children, owning and acknowledging them as *mine*. They are my inheritance, and shall be my people, my subjects.—*John Brinsley.*

Verse 7.—" *Ephraim also is the strength of mine head.*" The strong and warlike tribe of Ephraim being to the state what the helmet is to the warriors in battle; or, perhaps the allusion is to Deut. xxxiii. 17: " His glory is like the firstling of his bullock, and his horns are like the horns of unicorns: with them he shall push the nations."—*J. J. Stewart Perowne.*

Verse 7.—" *Judah is* (or *shall be*) *my lawgiver,*" *i.e.*, all his subjects should be brought under one *Head*, one governor, who should give them laws, according to which they should be ordered or governed, which power and authority belonged to the tribe of *Judah*, according to that prophecy of Jacob (Gen. xlix. 10), to which the Psalmist here alludeth. No way, no means to bring the people unto unity, to bring them into one *body*, but by bringing them under one *head*, one *lawgiver*, by whose laws they may be regulated and governed. Now in the church, and in matters of religion, this one *Head* is *Christ*, even that " Lion of the tribe of Judah," as he is called (Rev. v. 5). He is the *Law-giver* of his church, and let him so be. This will be found one, ay, and the only means to breed an holy and religious unity, and bring home straying, wandering sheep.—*John Brinsley.*

Verse 7.—No government could stand which was not resident in Judah.—*John Calvin.*

Verse 8.—" *Moab is my washpot.*" Implying that Moab should be reduced to slavery, it being the business of a slave to present the wash-hand basin to his master. With the Greeks, πλύνειν τινά, to wash down any one, was a slang term, signifying to ridicule, abuse, or beat; hence we have the word *washpot* applied to the subject of such treatment.

" You don't appear to be in your right senses, who make a washpot of me in the presence of many men." Aristophanes.—*Thomas S. Millington*, in " *The Testimony of the Heathen to the Truths of Holy Writ,*" 1863.

Verse 8 (second clause).—When, keeping in view the idea of washing the feet, a person throws his shoes, which he has taken off, to any one to be taken away or to be cleaned—הִשְׁלִיךְ with עַל and also with אֶל, 1 Kings xix. 19, is *"to throw to any one"*—the individual to whom it belongs to perform such an office must be a slave of the lowest kind.—*E. W. Hengstenberg.*

Verse 8.—*" Over Edom will I cast out my shoe,"* which notes either contempt of them, as if he had said, I look upon them as worthy only to scrape and make clean my shoes. Or secondly, conquest over them—I will walk through Edom and subdue it.—*Joseph Caryl.*

Verse 8.—*" Over Edom will I cast out my shoe."* By extension, immission, or projection of the shoe either upon the necks of people, or over their countries, is meant nothing else but to overcome, subdue, bring under power, possess, and subject to vileness such men and such countries. The very vulgar acceptation of the word *possession,* in the grammatical sense, importeth as much; for the etymology of *possessio* is no more but *pedum positio.* This manner of speaking hath also allusion to the positive law recorded in Deuteronomy (xxv. 6—10); for the letter of the law is, that if the kinsman would not marry the brother's widow and raise up seed unto his brother; the widow loosing his shoe, and spitting in his face, he lost the claim and interest of such possessions as belonged to the woman in right of her husband. And the house of such a man was called *domus discalceati,* that is to say, " The house of him that hath his shoe loosed." The practice also of this law we find recorded in the book of Ruth, in the case of Elimelech's land, between Boaz and the kinsman, about the widow Ruth, who had her interest by right of her husband in the said land. Moreover the frequent use of this phrase meeting us very often in the book of God, makes this to be the meaning of the words, as clear as the day. This king elsewhere singing his trophies, saith, " They are fallen under my feet." " Caleb the son of Jephunneh; he shall see it, and to him will I give the land that he hath trodden upon." But the people must "not meddle with Mount Seir; for God would not give them thereof so much as a foot's breadth;" yet even the place whereon the soles of their feet should tread, from the wilderness of Lebanon and from the river Euphrates unto the utmost sea, should be theirs. Psalm xviii. 38; Deut. i. 36.; ii. 5.—*William Loe, in " A sermon before the King at Theobalds," entitled, " The King's Shoe, made and ordained to trample on, and to tread down enemies,"* 1623.

Verse 8.—*" Over Edom will I cast out my shoe."* Turnus, having slain Pallas—

" Bestrode the corpse, and pressed it with his foot."

Virgil.

Verse 8.—Of the Philistines he says, *Over Philistia it is mine to boast;* for so I would translate, and not, as is usual, *Philistia, triumph thou over me,* which does not yield a consistent meaning.—*Hermann Venema.*

Verse 8 (last clause).—Let not our adversaries triumph over our *breaches.* " Rejoice not against me, O mine enemy." Or, if they will, let them triumph: " Triumph thou, O Philistia, because of me, or, over me."—*John Brinsley.*

Verses 8—10.—Moab in the East, Edom in the South, and Philistia in the West (the North is not mentioned, because the banner of David had already been victorious there).—*Augustus F. Tholuck.*

Verse 9.—*" Who will lead me into Edom?"* The entrance of Petra is by a narrow gorge, lined by lofty precipices, formed by the channel of a rivulet. This defile is nearly two miles in length. At some places the overhanging rocks approach so near to each other that only two horsemen can proceed abreast.—*Dr. Tweedie, in " Ruined Cities of the East,"* 1859.

Verse 9.—The believer, when he promiseth to himself great things, must neither be senseless of the difficutlies of opposition which he is to meet with, nor of his own inability to overcome difficulties; but being sensible of both, most look to God for assistance and furniture to overcome; for when David considered the strength of the fenced royal cities of the enemy, he saith, " Who will bring me into the strong city? who will lead me into Edom? Wilt not thou, O God?"—*David Dickson.*

Verse 11.—*" For vain is the help of man."* As they had lately experimented in *Saul,* a king of their own choosing, but not able to save them from those proud Philistines.—*John Trapp.*

Verse 11.—So long as sight and reason find footing in matters, there is no place for faith and hope ; the abundance of human helps puts not grace to proof, but the strength of faith is in the absence of them all. A man is stronger when he goeth on his feet alone, than when he standeth by a grip in his infancy, or leaneth on a staff in his old age : the two feet of faith and hope serve us best when we are fixed on the Rock of Sion alone.—*William Struther.*

Verse 12.—" *Through God we shall do,*" etc. In war these two must be joined, and indeed in all actions : HE, *we* ; God and *man.* 1. " We shall do valiantly," for God helps not remiss, or cowardly, or negligent men. 2. And yet, that being done, the work is *his* : " He shall tread down ; " the blow and the overthrow are not to be attributed to *us*, but to *him.*—*Adam Clarke.*

HINTS TO PREACHERS.

Verse 1.—Prayer of a church in low condition. I. *Complaint.* 1. Left of God's Spirit. 2. Scattered. II. *Cause.* Something displeasing to God. Neglect or actual sin ; a subject for self-examination. III. *Cure.* The Lord's return to us and ours to him. In our version it is a prayer ; in the Septuagint an expression of faith—" Thou wilt return."

Verse 2.—The perturbation, the prayer, the plea.—*G. R.*

Verse 3.—That God does afflict his people severely, and that he has good reason for the same.

Verse 3.—" *The wine of astonishment.*" A purgative, a tonic. Astonishing sin followed by astonishing chastisements, discoveries of corruption, of the spirituality of the law, of the terror of divine wrath, and by astonishing depressions, temptations, and conflicts.

Verse 4.—The banner of the gospel. I. Why a banner ? A rallying point, meant to fight under, etc. II. By whom given. " *Thou.*" III. To whom. " *To them that fear thee.*" IV. What is to be done with it. " *To be displayed.*" V. For what cause. " *Because of the truth.*" Truth promotes truth.

Verse 5.—The deliverance of the elect needs a saving God, a mighty God (" *right hand* "), and a prayer-hearing God.

Verse 5 (*last clause*). " *Save . . . and hear.*" The remarkable order of these words—1. In the purpose of God. 2. In the first works of grace. 3. Often under trial. 4. And specially in fierce temptations, God's saving precedes man's praying.

Verse 6.—God's holy promise, ground for present joy, and for boldly taking possession of the promised good.

Verse 7.—" *Gilead is mine, and Manasseh is mine.*" How, and in what respect, this world is the Christians.

Verse 7.—" *Judah is my lawgiver.*" The believer owning no law but that which comes from Christ.

Verse 8.—" *Moab is my washpot.*" How we may make sinners subservient to our sanctification. We are warned by their sin, and punishment, etc. See " Spurgeon's Sermons," No. 983, " Moab is my washpot."

Verse 9.—The soulwinners question. I. The object of attack ; the strong city of man's heart, barricaded by depravity, ignorance, prejudice, custom, etc. II. Our main design. To penetrate, to reach the citadel for Jesus. III. Our great enquiry. Eloquence, learning, wit, none of these can force the gate, but there is One who can.

Verse 12.—Divine operation a reason for human activity.

PSALM LXI.

TITLE.—To the Chief Musician upon Neginah, a Psalm of David.—*The original indicates that both the hymns and the musical instrument were David's. He wrote the verses, and himself sang them to the stringed instrument whose sound he loved so well. We have left the Psalms entitled* Michtam, *but we shall still find much precious meaning though the golden name be wanting. We have met with the title of this Psalm before, in Psalms IV., VI., LIV., and LV., but with this difference, that in the present case the word is in the singular number : the Psalm itself is very personal, and well adapted for the private devotion of a single individual.*

SUBJECT AND DIVISION.—*This Psalm is a pearl. It is little, but precious. To many a mourner it has furnished utterance when the mind could not have devised speech for itself. It was evidently composed by David after he had come to the throne—see verse 6. The second verse leads us to believe that it was written during the Psalmist's enforced exile from the tabernacle, which was the visible abode of God : if so, the period of Absalom's rebellion has been most suitably suggested as the date of its authorship, and Delitzsch is correct in entitling it, " Prayer and thanksgiving of an expelled King on his way back to his throne."*

We might divide the verses according to the sense, but it is preferable to follow the author's own arrangement, and make a break at each SELAH.

EXPOSITION.

HEAR my cry, O God ; attend unto my prayer.

2 From the end of the earth will I cry unto thee, when my heart is overwhelmed : lead me to the rock *that* is higher than I.

3. For thou hast been a shelter for me, *and* a strong tower from the enemy.

4 I will abide in thy tabernacle for ever : I will trust in the covert of thy wings. Selah.

1. " *Hear my cry, O God.*" He was in terrible earnest ; he shouted, he lifted up his voice on high. He is not however content with the expression of his need : to give his sorrows vent is not enough for him, he wants actual audience of heaven, and manifest succour as the result. Pharisees may rest in their prayers ; true believers are eager for an answer to them : ritualists may be satisfied when they have " said or sung " their litanies and collects, but living children of God will never rest till their supplications have entered the ears of the Lord God of Sabaoth. " *Attend unto my prayer.*" Give it thy consideration, and such an answer as thy wisdom sees fit. When it comes to crying with us, we need not doubt but that it will come to attending with God. Our heavenly Father is not hardened against the cries of his own children. What a consoling thought it is that the Lord at all times hears his people's cries, and is never forgetful of their prayers ; whatever else fails to move him, praying breath is never spent in vain !

2. " *From the end of the earth will I cry unto thee.*" He was banished from the spot which was the centre of his delight, and at the same time his mind was in a depressed and melancholy condition ; both actually and figuratively he was an outcast, yet he does not therefore restrain prayer, but rather finds therein a reason for the louder and more importunate cries. To be absent from the place of divine worship was a sore sorrow to saints in the olden times ; they looked upon the tabernacle as the centre of the world, and they counted themselves to be at the fag-end of the universe when they could no longer resort to the sacred shrine ; their heart was heavy as in a strange land when they were banished from its solemnities. Yet even they knew right well that no place is unsuitable for prayer. There may be an end of the earth, but there must not be an end to devotion. On creation's verge we may call upon God, for even there he is within call. No spot

is too dreary, no condition too deplorable; whether it be the world's end or life's end, prayer is equally available. To pray in some circumstances needs resolve, and the Psalmist here expresses it, " *I will cry.*" It was a wise resolution, for had he ceased to pray he would have become the victim of despair; there is an end to a man when he makes an end to prayer. Observe that David never dreamed of seeking any other God; he did not imagine the dominion of Jehovah to be local: he was at the end of the promised land, but he knew himself to be still in the territory of the Great King; to him only does he address his petitions. " *When my heart is overwhelmed :* "—when the huge waves of trouble wash over me, and I am completely submerged, not only as to my head, but also my heart. It is hard to pray when the very heart is drowning, yet gracious men plead best at such times. Tribulation brings us to God, and brings God to us. Faith's greatest triumphs are achieved in her heaviest trials. It is all over with me, affliction is all over me; it encompasses me as a cloud, it swallows me up like a sea, it shuts me in with thick darkness, yet God is near, near enough to hear my voice, and I will call him. Is not this brave talk? Mark how our Psalmist tells the Lord, as if he knew he were hearing him, that he intended to call upon him: our prayer by reason of our distress may be like to a call upon a far-off friend, but our inmost faith has its quiet heart-whispers to the Lord as to one who is assuredly our very present help.

"*Lead me to the rock that is higher than I.*" I see thee to be my refuge, sure and strong; but alas! I am confused, and cannot find thee; I am weak, and cannot climb thee. Thou art so steadfast, guide me; thou art so high, uplift me. There is a mine of meaning in this brief prayer. Along the iron-bound coast of our northern shores, lives are lost because the rocks are inaccessible to the shipwrecked mariner. A clergyman of one of the coast villages has with immense labour cut steps up from the beach to a large chamber, which he has excavated in the chalk cliff: here many mariners have been saved; they have climbed the rock, which had else been too high for them, and they have escaped. We have heard of late, however, that the steps have been worn away by the storms, and that poor sailors have perished miserably within sight of the refuge which they could not reach, for it was too high for them: it is therefore proposed to drive in iron stanchions, and to hang up chain ladders that shipwrecked mariners may reach the chambers in the rock. The illustration is self-interpreting. Our experience leads us to understand this verse right well, for the time was with us when we were in such amazement of soul by reason of sin, that although we knew the Lord Jesus to be a sure salvation for sinners, yet we could not come at him, by reason of our many doubts and forebodings. A Saviour would have been of no use to us if the Holy Spirit had not gently led us to him, and enabled us to rest upon him. To this day we often feel that we not only want a rock, but to be led to it. With this in view we treat very leniently the half-unbelieving prayers of awakened souls; for in their bewildered state we cannot expect from them all at once a fully believing cry. A seeking soul should at once believe in Jesus, but it is legitimate for a man to ask to be led to Jesus, the Holy Spirit is able to effect such a leading, and he can do it even though the heart be on the borders of despair.

How infinitely higher than we are is the salvation of God. We are low and grovelling, but it towers like some tall cliff far above us. This is its glory, and is our delight when we have once climbed into the rock, and claimed an interest in it; but while we are as yet trembling seekers, the glory and sublimity of salvation appal us, and we feel that we are too unworthy even to be partakers of it; hence we are led to cry for grace upon grace, and to see how dependent we are for every-thing, not only for the Saviour, but for the power to believe on him.

3. " *For thou hast been a shelter for me.*" Observe how the Psalmist rings the changes on, " *Thou hast,*" and " *I will,*"—verses 3, 4, 5, and 6. Experience is the nurse of faith. From the past we gather arguments for present confidence. Many and many a time had the persecutions of Saul and the perils of battle emperilled David's life, and only by miracle had he escaped, yet was he still alive and unhurt; this he remembers, and he is full of hope. " *And a strong tower from the enemy.*" As in a fort impregnable, David had dwelt, because surrounded by omnipotence. Sweet is it beyond expression to remember the lovingkindnesses of the Lord in our former days, for he is unchangeable, and therefore will continue to guard us from all evil.

4. " *I will abide in thy tabernacle for ever.*" Let me once get back to thy courts, and nothing shall again expel me from them: even now in my banishment my

heart is there; and ever will I continue to worship thee in spirit wherever my lot may be cast. Perhaps by the word "*tabernacle*" is here meant the dwelling-place of God; and if so, the sense is, I will dwell with the Lord, enjoying his sacred hospitality, and sure protection.

> " There would I find a settled rest,
>   While others go and come;
> No more a stranger, or a guest,
>   But like a child at home."

He who communes with God is always at home. The divine omnipresence surrounds such a one consciously; his faith sees all around him the palace of the King, in which he walks with exulting security and overflowing delight. Happy are the indoor servants who go not out from his presence. Hewers of wood and drawers of water in the tents of Jehovah are more to be envied than the princes who riot in the pavilions of kings. The best of all is that our residence with God is not for a limited period of time, but for ages; yea, for ages of ages, for time and for eternity: this is our highest and most heavenly privilege, " *I will abide in thy tabernacle for ever.*"

" *I will trust in the covert of thy wings.*" Often does our sweet singer use this figure; and far better is it to repeat one apt and instructive image, than for the sake of novelty to ransack creation for poor, strained metaphors. The chicks beneath the hen how safe, how comfortable, how happy! How warm the parent's bosom! How soft the cherishing feathers! Divine condescension allows us to appropriate the picture to ourselves, and how blessedly instructive and consoling it is! O for more trust; it cannot be too implicit: such a covert invites us to the most unbroken repose. SELAH. Rest we well may when we reach this point. Even the harp may be eloquently silent when deep, profound calm completely fills the bosom, and sorrow has sobbed itself into a peaceful slumber.

5 For thou, O God, hast heard my vows: thou hast given *me* the heritage of those that fear thy name.

6 Thou wilt prolong the king's life: *and* his years as many generations.

7 He shall abide before God for ever: O prepare mercy and truth, *which* may preserve him.

8 So will I sing praise unto thy name for ever, that I may daily perform my vows.

5. " *For thou, O God, hast heard my vows.*" Proofs of divine faithfulness are to be had in remembrance, and to be mentioned to the Lord's honour. The prayer of verse 1 is certain of an answer because of the experience of verse 5, since we deal with an immutable God. " *Vows*" may rightly be joined with prayers when they are lawful, well-considered, and truly for God's glory. It is great mercy on God's part to take any notice of the vows and promises of such faithless and deceitful creatures as we are. What we promise him is his due already, and yet he deigns to accept our vows as if we were not so much his servants as his free suitors who could give or withhold at pleasure. " *Thou hast given me the heritage of those that fear thy name.*" We are made heirs, joint-heirs with all the saints, partakers of the same portion. With this we ought to be delighted. If we suffer, it is the heritage of the saints; if we are persecuted, are in poverty, or in temptation, all this is contained in the title-deeds of the heritage of the chosen. Those we are to sup with we may well be content to dine with. We have the same inheritance as the First-born himself; what better is conceivable? Saints are described as fearing the name of God; they are reverent worshippers; they stand in awe of the Lord's authority; they are afraid of offending him, they feel their own nothingness in the sight of the Infinite One. To share with such men, to be treated by God with the same favour as he metes out to them, is matter for endless thanksgiving. All the privileges of all the saints are also the privilege of each one.

6. " *Thou wilt prolong the king's life;*" or, better, " days to the days of the King thou wilt add." Death threatened, but God preserved his beloved. David, considering his many perils, enjoyed a long and prosperous reign. " *And his years as many generations.*" He lived to see generation after generation personally; in his descendants he lived as king through a very long period; his dynasty continued

for many generations ; and in Christ Jesus, his seed and son, spiritually David reigns on evermore. Thus he who began at the foot of the rock, half drowned, and almost dead, is here led to the summit, and sings as a priest abiding in the tabernacle, a king ruling with God for ever, and a prophet foretelling good things to come. (Verse 7.) See the uplifting power of faith and prayer. None so low but they may yet be set on high.

7. " *He shall abide before God for ever.*" Though this is true of David in a modified sense, we prefer to view the Lord Jesus as here intended as the lineal descendant of David, and the representative of his royal race. Jesus is enthroned before God to eternity ; here is our safety, dignity, and delight. We reign in him ; in him we are made to sit together in the heavenlies. David's personal claim to sit enthroned for ever is but a foreshadowing of the revealed privilege of all true believers. " *O prepare mercy and truth, which may preserve him.*" As men cry, " Long live the king," so we hail with acclamation our enthroned Immanuel, and cry, " Let mercy and truth preserve him." Eternal love and immutable faithfulness are the bodyguards of Jesus' throne, and they are both the providers and the preservers of all those who in him are made kings and priests unto God. We cannot keep ourselves, and nothing short of divine mercy and truth can do it ; but these both can and will, nor shall the least of the people of God be suffered to perish.

8. " *So will I sing praise unto thy name for ever.*" Because my prayer is answered, my song shall be perpetual ; because Jesus for ever sits at thy right hand, it shall be acceptable ; because I am preserved in him, it shall be grateful. David had given vocal utterance to his prayer by a cry : he will now give expression to his praise by a song : there should be a parallel between our supplications and our thanksgivings. We ought not to leap in prayer, and limp in praise. The vow to celebrate the divine name " *for ever* " is no hyperbolical piece of extravagance, but such as grace and glory shall enable us to carry out to the letter. " *That I 'may daily perform my vows.*" To God who adds days to our days we will devote all our days. We vowed perpetual praise, and we desire to render it without inter-mission. We would worship God *de die in diem*, going right on as the days roll on. We ask no vacation from this heavenly vocation ; we would make no pause in this sacred service. God daily performs his promises, let us daily perform our vows : he keeps his covenant let us not forget ours. Blessed be the name of the Lord from this time forth, even for evermore.

EXPLANATORY NOTES AND QUAINT SAYINGS.

Title.—The word *Neginah* (the singular of *Neginoth*) may be understood to be synonymous with the *kinnor* or harp : that is to say, the instrument of eight strings, probably played with a bow or plectrum.—*John Jebb.*

Verse 1.—" *Hear my cry, O God ; attend unto my prayer.*" Aquinas saith that some read the words thus, *Intende ad cantica mea*, attend unto my songs and so the words may be safely read, from the Hebrew word, רנה *ranah*, which signifies to shout or shrill out for joy—to note that the prayers of the saints are like pleasant songs and delightful ditties in the ears of God. No mirth, no music, can be so pleasing to us as the prayers of the saints are pleasing to God. Cant. ii. 14 ; Psalm cxli. 2.—*Thomas Brooks.*

Verse 1.—" *My cry.*" There is a text in Job where the " hypocrites in heart " are spoken of condemingly, because " they cry not when he bindeth them." I like to feel that no hard fortitude is required of the chastened child of God, but that it ought to feel, and may cry, under the rod, without a single rebellious thought.—*Mary B. M. Duncan.*

Verses 1, 2.—One ejaculation begetteth another. " *Hear my cry ;* " " *attend unto my prayer* " (yet no words hereof mentioned) ; and verse 2. " *From the end of the earth will I cry :* " he had thus cried, and he will therefore cry again and again. As billows of temptation ever and anon stop his mouth and interrupt him, so as he now and then doth but peep above water, and get breathing space, he will thus cry, "*Lead me*," or "*guide me*," or carry me to yonder "*rock which is higher than I.*"—*Thomas Cobbet* (1608—1686), *on Prayer.*

Verse 2.—"*From the end of the earth.*" This may be taken two ways : either *naturally*, and then it is an allusion to men that are far distant and remote from help, relief and comfort ; or, as I may say, *ecclesiastically*, with reference to the temple of God, which was "*in medio terræ,*" "in the midst and heart of the land," where God manifested and gave tokens of his gracious presence and favour : as if he had said, "I am at the end of the earth ; far from any tokens, pledges, or manifestations of the love and favour of God, as well as from outward help and assistance.—*John Owen.*

Verse 2.—"*The end of the earth.*" What place was this, "*the end of the earth,*" referring the expression to the writer of the Psalm ? We know that the centre of the affections and devotions of the pious Israelite was the "holy city, Jerusalem ; whither the tribes went up, even the tribes of the Lord, to testify unto Israel, and to give thanks unto the name of the Lord." The country of which this city was the capital, was to the Jew the world ; it was the world within the world ; the earth within the earth ; the whole globe beside was to him a waste, a place out of the world ; an extra-terrestrial territory, beyond the limits set up by the Lord Almighty. Thus in Holy Writ what is called the world, or the earth, frequently signifieth only that part thereof which was the heritage of the chosen people. . . . "*The end of the earth,*" then, as referred to the Psalmist, would signify any place of bodily absence from the temple where the Deity had taken up his special abode, or any place whence his spiritual affections were unable to reach that temple. As referred to us, the expression signifies any sensible distance from God : for as God is the centre of life, hope, love, and joy, distance from him, of whatsoever degree, is the antipodes of the soul, a region of sterility and darkness ; the Iceland of man's spirit.—*Alfred Bowen Evans*, 1852.

Verse 2.—"*I will cry unto thee.*" There is in this expression an endeavour to approach unto God ; as you do when you "*cry*" after one whom you see at a distance, and are afraid he will go farther from you. It is the great work of faith to cry out after God, at a distance, when you are afraid lest at the next turn he should be quite out of sight. Crying to the Lord supposes him to be withdrawing or departing.—*John Owen.*

Verse 2.—"*Cry.*" No matter how abrupt the prayer be, so it be the representation of our hearts. Thus David. Where doth he pray ? In banishment. When ? When his spirit "*is overwhelmed.*" How doth he pray ? He "*cried.*" Thus Hannah prayed herself into a composed state of mind. Remember, resignation is the work of the Spirit of God ; and therefore you must plead for it before you have it.—*John Singleton* (—1706), *in* "*The Morning Exercises.*"

Verse 2.—"*Cry.*" Crying is a substitute for speech ; and also the expression of earnestness.—*William Jay.*

Verse 2.—"*When my heart is overwhelmed.*" Troubles are of various kinds ; some are *provoking*, some are *gnawing*, some are *perplexing*, and some are *overwhelming ;* but whatever form they assume, they are troubles, and are part of the wear and tear of life. . . . . *Overwhelming troubles* are such as sweep over a man, just as the mighty billows of the ocean sweep over and submerge the sands. These are troubles which struggle with us, as it were, for life and death ; troubles which would leave us helpless wrecks ; troubles which enter into conflict with us in our prime, which grapple with us in our health and strength, and threaten to conquer us by sheer force, no matter how bravely we may contend. Such trouble the Psalmist knew.—*Philip Bennett Power, in* "*The 'I wills' of the Psalms,*" 1861.

Verse 2.—"*Heart.*" The heart is here represented to us as being overwhelmed, or, as it is otherwise translated, "covered over ; " it is smothered in, unable to perform its functions with proper action, unable to throw out the blood to the extremities, to give them needed vitality and power for necessary effort. When the action of the heart is paralyzed, even temporally, it will tell upon all the members, a chill there sends its cold vibration through every limb ; Satan knows this well, and so all his dealings are heart dealings, efforts to paralyze the very spring of life itself. This is precisely what we ourselves have experienced ; we have partially felt death within us, we have felt a gradual numbing of our heart ; a gradual diminution in the quickness of its beat ; a gradual closing in, and pressure of a weight upon it, and this was the "*overwhelming*" process.—*Philip Bennett Power.*

Verse 2.—"*Lead me to the rock that is higher than I.*" The *tower*, in Psalm xviii. 2, is "*an high tower,*" and the *rock* is here an *high rock*, the rock "*higher than I ;*" and yet there is a way to get into the highest towers ; by scaling ladders a man may get over the high walls of towers. This tower and rock were too high for David himself to get into, and therefore he sets to the scaling ladder. "*Lead me to the rock*, and into the tower *that is higher than I. Hear my cry, attend unto my prayer.*" So he makes prayer the scaling ladder to get upon that rock and into that tower that otherwise had been too high for him ; he gets that safety and deliverance which otherwise but by prayer unto God had been impossible to have been obtained.—*Jeremiah Dyke.*

Verse 2.—"*Lead me to the rock that is higher than I.*" The language is very remarkable. It gives us the idea of a man suffering shipwreck. The vessel in which he has been sailing has sunk. He has been plunged into the mighty ocean ; and there he is buffeting the waves, struggling for life, panting for breath, and just about to give up all for lost. Suddenly he discovers a *rock* towering above him. If he can but climb up to the top of it, and get sure footing upon it, the billows will not be able to reach him, and he will be safe. Now, the prayer in our text is the cry of that poor wretch for help. He is so spent and exhausted, that he cannot reach the rock *himself.* He shouts aloud for the friendly hand of some one stronger than himself, or for a rope that may be flung to him by those who are already safe on the rock, if by these helps he may gain it. "*Lead me to the rock,*" cries the poor perishing wretch. "O, lead me, guide me, direct me to it ; for I am so worn and spent, that I cannot reach it otherwise. I am at the point to die ; and I must sink, and be no more seen for ever, if there is none to help me." Thus he calls for some one to rescue him from the deep, and to place him on the "*rock.*" But what rock ? He knows that unless the rock be a high one, he will not be in safety, though he should be on it. "*The rock,*" he says, "must be *higher than I*, or the waves will reach me, and wash me off again." It is not a rock, the top of which just shows itself above the sea, no higher than a man's own body, that will save the life of a shipwrecked mariner. Such a rock may occasion the wreck, but it will not afford any help to the sufferers afterwards ; it is a rock to split upon for destruction, not to stand upon for safety. "*Lead me to the rock,*" or as it is in the Prayer-book version, "Set me upon the rock, that is *higher than I !* " . . . . The text having shown us the *danger of sin*, does not leave us comfortless ; it shows us the *security of the refuge.* We have before remarked, that the prayer of David, as a shipwrecked man, is, to be "led to," and set upon, a "*rock,*" that is *higher than himself.* The expression seems to imply much. The rock that is higher than *he*, must be higher than *any man ;* for David was a mighty monarch. He implies, therefore, that the refuge he seeks must be more than any "arm of flesh" can afford him ; it must be therefore *divine.*—*Condensed from a Sermon by Fountain Elwin*, 1842.

Verse 2.—It is more the image of one overtaken by the tide, as he is hastening onwards to get beyond its reach, and yet with every step he sees it rolling nearer and nearer to him ; he hears its angry roar, the loosening sand sinks beneath his tread—a few minutes more, and the waves will be around him ; despair hath "*over-whelmed his heart ;* " when in the very depths of his agony he sees a point of rock high above the waves. ".O that I could reach it and be safe ! " And then comes the cry, the agonising cry, to him that is mighty to save, "*Lead me to the rock that is higher than I.*" It is the sinner's cry to the sinner's Saviour !—*Barton Bouchier, A.M., in "Manna in the Heart ; or, Daily Comments on the Book of Psalms,*" 1855.

Verse 2.—"*Lead me to the rock.*" If we would find ourselves upon the rock, and enjoy the realisation of being so, we must be dependent upon another's hand. And that hand can do everything for us, even in our worst of times. When we are so blinded by the salt waves that dash in our eyes, so reeling in brain that we cannot perhaps think, much less make continuous efforts, there is a hand which can lead us, which can draw us out of the waters, which can set our feet upon the rock. Surely we have already experienced the power and tenderness of that hand ? and it may be that in the reader's case, the waves, as they made sure of their prey, found it supernaturally drawn forth from them, that it might be set upon a rock, immovable amid all waters, and sufficient amid all storms !—*Philip Bennett Power.*

Verse 2.—"*The rock that is higher than I.*" The rock of our salvation, then, is "higher than we." Here we have the Deity of Christ, the Rock, set forth ; in this he is "higher than we." And except as he is thus higher, as he is God, he could not be a Saviour ; for " He is a just God, as well as a Saviour." A being no higher than we, or but a little higher, as the angels (for we are but " a little lower than they "), though he might teach us, or warn us, or console us, could never save us. The prey is in the hands of the mighty, and the All-mighty alone is mightier. But a rock is not only high, but deep ; it not only erects its front above the waves, but its base is fixed in the ocean's bed. " Canst thou by searching find out God ? canst thou find out the Almighty unto perfection ? It is as high as heaven ; what canst thou do ? deeper than hell ; what canst thou know ? The measure thereof is longer than the earth, and broader than the sea." Job. xi. 7. Here we have the humanity of him who is the rock ; that humanity by which he was able to go down to the deeps, as well as ride triumphantly on the bosom of the waters—those deeps, whereof David speaking experimentally of himself, spake prophetically of him ; the depths of our fall and degradation—that humanity in which he went down into the grave, into the recesses of the intermediate state, and " preached to the spirits in prison." This is our rock, both deep and high; the rock of our salvation ; to which those whose sins have set them at " the end of the earth," desire to be brought, that they may find a place of safe standing. Let not those fear who feel the bitterness of distance from God, for they shall be brought nigh ; desolate may be the coast to which they are driven, but over against it is the Paradise of God ; clouds and darkness may gather at the base of this rock of safety, but " eternal sunshine settles on its head."—*Alfred Bowen Evans.*

Verse 2.—" *Higher.*" A hiding place must be *locus excelsissimus.* Your low houses are soon scaled. Jesus Christ is a high place ; he is as high as heaven. He is the Jacob's ladder that reacheth from earth to heaven. Gen. xxviii. 12. He is too high for men, too high for devils ; no creature can scale these high walls.— *Ralph Robinson* (1614—1655), *in " Christ All and in All."*

Verse 4.—" *I will abide in thy tabernacle.*" Some render it, *I shall dwell in thy tent* or *pavilion royal*, making it a metaphor from warfare, where those that are in the king's own tent must needs be in greatest safety. And this sense suiteth well with the following words : " *I will trust in the covert of thy wings.*"—*John Trapp.*

Verse 4.—" *Covert of thy wings.*" To a person who should penetrate the Holy of Holies in the tabernacle, the most conspicuous object would be the outspread wings above the mercy-seat : under their shelter and upon the mercy-seat David would abide in quiet confidence.—*C. H. S.*

Verse 5 (*first clause*).—About this time I began to know that there is a God who hears and answers prayer.—*John Newton, in his Journal.*

Verse 5.—" *Thou, O God, hast heard my vows :* " that is, his prayers, which are always to be put up with vows. Indeed, that prayer is a blank which hath not a vow in it. Is it a mercy thou prayest him to give ? If sincere, thou wilt vow to praise him for it, and serve him with it. Is it a sin thou prayest against ? Except thou jugglest with God, thou wilt vow as well as pray against it.—*William Gurnall.*

Verse 5.—" *The heritage.*" Eternal life is called an inheritance. Theodoret remarks : " The true inheritance is eternal life, concerning which Christ saith to the sheep on his right hand, Come, ye blessed of my Father, inherit the kingdom prepared for you before the foundation of the world. This inheritance the Lord giveth to them that fear him." In Ephesians i. 14, the Spirit is called " the earnest of our inheritance." In Colossians i. 12, the apostle exhorts them " to give thanks unto the Father, who hath made them meet to be partakers of the inheritance of the saints in light." On this verse we have the golden comment of Chrysostom, reiterated by Theophylact. He calls it an inheritance, to show that no man obtaineth the kingdom by his own good works ; for no man hath so lived as to render himself worthy of the kingdom, but all is of the grace of God. Wherefore, he saith, " When ye have done all, say that we are unprofitable servants, for we have only done what we ought to have done."—*John Casper Suicer's " Thesaurus,"* 1728.

Verse 6.—" *Thou wilt prolong the king's life,*" etc. David cannot be considered as using these words of gratulation with an exclusive reference to himself. It is true that he lived to an extreme old age, and died full of days, leaving the kingdom in a settled condition, and in the hands of his son, who succeeded him ; but he did not exceed the period of one man's life, and the greater part of it was spent in continued dangers and anxieties. There can be no doubt, therefore, that the series of years, and even ages, of which he speaks, extends prospectively to the coming of Christ, it being the very condition of the kingdom, as I have often remarked, that God maintained them as one people under one head, or when scattered, united them again. The same succession still subsists in reference to ourselves. Christ must be viewed as living in his members to the end of the world. To this Isaiah alludes, when he says, "Who shall declare his generation or age?"—words in which he predicts that the church would survive through all ages, notwithstanding the incessant danger of destruction to which it is exposed through the attacks of its enemies, and the many storms assailing it. So here David foretells the uninterrupted succession of the kingdom down to the time of Christ.—*John Calvin.*

Verse 6.—"*The king's life: and his years.*" David speaks designedly of the days of the "*king*" instead of his *own* days, as might have been expected from what had been said, for the purpose of showing that he considered the promise of eternal dominion as relating not to himself personally, but to his family—the royal family of David.—*E. W. Hengstenberg.*

Verse 7.—"*O prepare mercy.*" David having declared in his own behalf the purpose of God towards him for everlasting salvation, "*he,*" speaking of himself, "*shall abide before God for ever:*" he withal considering what he was to run through in this life, and what it might require to keep him unto the end, and so "*for ever,*" doth presently thereupon, in way of prayer, subjoin, "*O prepare mercy and truth, which may preserve me.*" As if he had said, I have yet a long journey to go, and through many hazards, and thy promise is, *I shall abide afore thee for ever.* Lord, thou hast need lay up and aforehand prepare an abundance of mercy and truth to preserve me for time to come.—*Thomas Goodwin.*

Verse 8.—They that are godly are oppressed and vexed in the church or congregation for this purpose: that when they are pressed, they should cry; and when they cry, that they should be heard; and when they are heard, that they should laud and praise God.—*Augustine.*

HINTS TO PREACHERS.

Whole Psalm.—The progressive "*I wills.*" I. I will cry. II. I will abide in thy tabernacle. III. I will trust. IV. I will sing praise.

Verse 1.—Answers to prayer to be earnestly sought. I. What hinders the answer of prayer? II. What is our duty when answers are denied? III. What encouragements we have to believe that the delay is only temporary.

Verse 2.—"*Lead me.*" I. Show me the way: reveal Jesus. II. Enable me to tread it: work faith in me. III. Uplift me where I cannot tread: do for me what is beyond me.

Verse 2.—"*Higher than I.*" Jesus greater than our highest efforts, attainments, desires, expectations, conceptions.

Verse 2.—God, the saints' rock.—*John Owen's Two Sermons.* Works. Vol. IX., pp. 237—256.

Verse 2.—The heart's cry and desire. I. A recognition of a place of safety; then, II. We have this place brought before us, as abundantly sufficient, when personal weakness has been realised. IV. The character of this refuge, and the position of a believer when availing himself of it: the place of refuge is "a rock," and the position of the believer is "upon a rock."—*P. B. Power.*

Verses 2, 3.—I. *How* would he pray? "I will *cry* unto thee." II. *Where* would he pray? "From the ends of the earth." III. *When* would he pray? "When my heart is overwhelmed." IV. *For what* would he pray? "Lead me to the rock that is higher than I." V. *Whence* does he derive his encouragement to pray? "For thou *hast been,*" etc. (verse 3).—*William Jay.*

Verse 3.—"*A shelter*" from the rain of trouble, the storm of persecution, the floods of Satanic temptation, the heat of divine wrath, the blast of death. The ark, Lot's mountain, the blood-stained door in Egypt, the city of refuge, the cave Adullam. "*A strong tower :*" lasting in itself, impregnable against foes, secure for the occupant.

Verses 4, 7.—I. My privilege, "*I will abide*" (verse 4). II. The ground of it, "*He shall abide,*" etc. (verse 7).

Verse 4 (first clause).—Where the priest has presented the sacrifice ; where the law is laid up in the ark as fulfilled ; where the light of the Spirit's candlestick shines ; where the manna abides ; where the glory is above the mercy-seat ; where no enemy can enter ; where I commune with a covenant God.

Verse 5 (second clause).—Enquire whether or no it fares with us as with the saints.

Verses 5, 8.—I. Vows heard in heaven. II. Vows to be carefully fulfilled on earth.

Verse 5 (second clause).—I. They that fear God have a "heritage." II. This heritage is "given." III. We may know that we possess it.—*William Jay.*

Verse 6.—Our King, his eternal existence, our personal joy in this, and our joy for our descendants.

PSALM LXII.

TITLE.—To the Chief Musician, to Jeduthun.—*This is the second Psalm which is dedicated to Jeduthun or Ethan, the former one being the thirty-ninth, a Psalm which is almost a twin with this in many respects, containing in the original the word translated only four times as this does six. We shall meet with two other Psalms similarly appointed for Jeduthun: namely, Psalms LXXVII. and LXXXIX. The sons of Jeduthun were porters or doorkeepers, according to 1 Chron. xvi. 42. Those who serve well make the best of singers, and those who occupy the highest posts in the choir must not be ashamed to wait at the posts of the doors of the Lord's house.*

A PSALM OF DAVID.—*Even had not the signature of the royal poet been here placed, we should have been sure from internal evidence that he alone penned these stanzas; they are truly Davidic. From the sixfold use of the word, ac or only, we have been wont to call it* THE ONLY PSALM.

DIVISION.—*The Psalmist has marked his own pauses, by inserting* SELAH *at the end of verses 4 and 8. His true and sole confidence in God laughs to scorn all its enemies. When this Psalm was composed it was not necessary for us to know, since true faith is always in season, and is usually under trial. Moreover, the sentiments here uttered are suitable to occasions which are very frequent in a believer's life, and therefore no one historic incident is needful for their explanation.*

EXPOSITION.

TRULY my soul waiteth upon God; from him *cometh* my salvation.

2 He only *is* my rock and my salvation; *he is* my defence; I shall not be greatly moved.

3 How long will ye imagine mischief against a man? ye shall be slain all of you: as a bowing wall *shall ye be, and as* a tottering fence.

4 They only consult to cast *him* down from his excellency: they delight in lies: they bless with their mouth, but they curse inwardly. Selah.

1. " *Truly*," or verily, or only. The last is probably the most prominent sense here. That faith alone is true which rests on God alone, that confidence which relies but partly on the Lord is vain confidence. If we Englished the word by our word " *verily*," as some do, we should have here a striking reminder of our blessed Lord's frequent use of that adverb. " *My soul waiteth upon God.*" My inmost self draws near in reverent obedience to God. I am no hypocrite or mere posture maker. To wait upon God, and for God, is the habitual position of faith; to wait on him truly is sincerity; to wait on him only is spiritual chastity. The original is, " only to God is my soul silence." The presence of God alone could awe his heart into quietude, submission, rest, and acquiescence; but when that was felt, not a rebellious word or thought broke the peaceful silence. The proverb that speech is silver but silence is gold, is more than true in this case. No eloquence in the world is half so full of meaning as the patient silence of a child of God. It is an eminent work of grace to bring down the will and subdue the affections to such a degree, that the whole mind lies before the Lord like the sea beneath the wind, ready to be moved by every breath of his mouth, but free from all inward and self-caused emotion, as also from all power to be moved by anything other than the divine will. We should be wax to the Lord, but adamant to every other force. " *From him cometh my salvation.*" The good man will, therefore, in patience possess his soul till deliverance comes: faith can hear the footsteps of coming salvation because she has learned to be silent. Our salvation in no measure or degree comes to us from any inferior source; let us, therefore, look alone to the true fountain, and avoid the detestable crime of ascribing to the creature what belongs alone to the Creator. If to wait on God be worship, to wait on the creature is idolatry;

if to wait on God alone be true faith, to associate an arm of flesh with him is audacious unbelief.

2. "*He only is my rock and my salvation.*" Sometimes a metaphor may be more full of meaning and more suggestive than literal speech; hence the use of the figure of a rock, the very mention of which would awaken grateful memories in the Psalmist's mind. David had often lain concealed in rocky caverns, and here he compares his God to such a secure refuge; and, indeed, declares him to be his only real protection, all-sufficient in himself and never failing. At the same time, as if to show us that what he wrote was not mere poetic sentiment, but blessed reality, the literal word "*salvation*" follows the figurative expression: that our God is our refuge is no fiction, nothing in the world is more a matter of fact. "*He is my defence*," my height, my lofty rampart, my high-fort. Here we have another and bolder image; the tried believer not only abides in God as in a cavernous rock; but dwells in him as a warrior in some bravely defiant tower or lordly castle. "*I shall not be greatly moved.*" His personal weakness might cause him to be somewhat moved; but his faith would come in to prevent any very great disturbance: not much would he be tossed about. "*Moved,*" as one says, "but not removed." Moved like a ship at anchor which swings with the tide, but is not swept away by the tempest. When a man knows assuredly that the Lord is his salvation, he cannot be very much cast down: it would need more than all the devils in hell greatly to alarm a heart which knows God to be its salvation.

3. "*How long will ye imagine mischief against a man?*" It is always best to begin with God, and then may we confront our enemies. Make all sure with heaven, then may you grapple with earth and hell. David expostulates with his insensate foes; he marvels at their dogged perseverance in malice, after so many failures and with certain defeat before them. He tells them that their design was an imaginary one, which they never could accomplish however deeply they might plot. It is a marvel that men will readily enough continue in vain and sinful courses, and yet to persevere in grace is so great a difficulty as to be an impossibility, were it not for divine assistance. The persistency of those who oppose the people of God is so strange that we may well expostulate with them and say, "How long will ye thus display your malice?" A hint is given in the text as to the cowardliness of so many pressing upon one man; but none are less likely to act a fair and manly part than those who are opposed to God's people for righteousness' sake. Satan could not enter into combat with Job in fair duel, but must needs call in the Sabeans and Chaldeans, and even then must borrow the lightning and the wind before his first attack was complete. If there were any shame in him, or in his children, they would be ashamed of the dastardly manner in which they have waged war against the seed of the woman. Ten thousand to one has not seemed to them too mean an advantage; there is not a drop of chivalrous blood in all their veins. "*Ye shall be slain all of you.*" Your edged tools will cut your own fingers. Those who take the sword shall perish with the sword. However many or fierce the bands of the wicked may be, they shall not escape the just retribution of heaven; rigorously shall the great Lawgiver exact blood from men of blood, and award death to those who seek the death of others. "*As a bowing wall shall ye be, and as a tottering fence.*" Boastful persecutors bulge and swell with pride, but they are only as a bulging wall ready to fall in a heap; they lean forward to seize their prey, but it is only as a tottering fence inclines to the earth upon which it will soon lie at length. They expect men to bow to them, and quake for fear in their presence; but men made bold by faith see nothing in them to honour, and very, very much to despise. It is never well on our part to think highly of ungodly persons; whatever their position, they are near their destruction, they totter to their fall; it will be our wisdom to keep our distance, for no one is advantaged by being near a falling wall; if it does not crush with its weight, it may stifle with its dust.

The passage is thought to be more correctly rendered as follows:—"How long will ye press on one man, that ye may crush him in a body, like a toppling wall, a sinking fence?" * We have, however, kept to our own version as yielding a good and profitable meaning. Both senses may blend in our meditations; for if David's enemies battered him as though they could throw him down like a bulging wall, he, on the other hand, foresaw that they themselves would by retributive justice be overthrown like an old, crumbling, leaning, yielding fence.

---

* So Dr. Kay, of Calcutta, translates it.

4. "*They only consult to cast him down from his excellency.*" The excellencies of the righteous are obnoxious to the wicked, and the main object of their fury. The elevation which God gives to the godly in Providence, or in repute, is also the envy of the baser sort, and they labour to pull them down to their own level. Observe the concentration of malice upon one point *only*, as here set in contrast with the sole reliance of the gracious one upon his Lord. If the wicked could but ruin the work of grace in us, they would be content ; to crush our character, to overturn our influence, is the object of their consultation. "*They delight in lies ;*" hence they hate the truth and the truthful, and by falsehood endeavour to compass their overthrow. To lie is bad enough, but to delight in it is one of the blackest marks of infamy. "*They bless with their mouth, but they curse inwardly.*" Flattery has ever been a favourite weapon with the enemies of good men ; they can curse bitterly enough when it serves their turn ; meanwhile, since it answers their purpose, they mask their wrath, and with smooth words pretend to bless those whom they would willingly tear in pieces. It was fortunate for David that he was well practised in silence, for to cozening deceivers there is no other safe reply. "*Selah.*" Here pause, and consider with astonishment the futile rancour of unholy men, and the perfect security of such as rest themselves upon the Lord.

5 My soul, wait thou only upon God ; for my expectation *is* from him.

6 He only *is* my rock and my salvation : *he is* my defence ; I shall not be moved.

7 In God *is* my salvation and my glory : the rock of my strength, *and* my refuge, *is* in God.

8 Trust in him at all times ; ye people, pour out your heart before him : God *is* a refuge for us. Selah.

"*My soul, wait thou only upon God.*" When we have already practised a virtue, it is yet needful that we bind ourselves to a continuance in it. The soul is apt to be dragged away from its anchorage, or is readily tempted to add a second confidence to the one sole and sure ground of reliance ; we must, therefore, stir ourselves up to maintain the holy position which we were at first able to assume. Be still silent, O my soul ! submit thyself completely, trust immovably, wait patiently. Let none of thy enemies' imaginings, consultings, flatteries, or maledictions cause thee to break the King's peace. Be like the sheep before her shearers, and like thy Lord, conquer by the passive resistance of victorious patience : thou canst only achieve this as thou shalt be inwardly persuaded of God's presence, and as thou waitest solely and alone on him. Unmingled faith is undismayed. Faith with a single eye sees herself secure, but if her eye be darkened by two confidences, she is blind and useless. "*For my expectation is from him.*" We expect from God because we believe in him. Expectation is the child of prayer and faith, and is owned of the Lord as an acceptable grace. We should desire nothing but what it would be right for God to give, then our expectation would be all from God ; and concerning truly good things we should not look to second causes, but to the Lord alone, and so again our expectation would be all from him. The vain expectations of worldly men come not ; they promise, but there is no performance ; our expectations are on the way, and in due season will arrive to satisfy our hopes. Happy is the man who feels that all he has, all he wants, and all he expects are to be found in his God.

6. "*He only is my rock and my salvation.*" Alone, and without other help, God is the foundation and completion of my safety. We cannot too often hear the toll of that great bell *only ;* let it ring the death-knell of all carnal reliances, and lead us to cast ourselves on the bare arm of God. "*He is my defence.*" Not my defender only, but my actual protection. I am secure, because he is faithful. "*I shall not be moved*"—not even in the least degree. See how his confidence grows. In the second verse an adverb qualified his quiet ; here, however, it is absolute ; he altogether defies the rage of his adversaries, he will not stir an inch, nor be made to fear even in the smallest degree. A living faith grows ; experience develops the spiritual muscles of the saint, and gives a manly force which our religious childhood has not yet reached.

7. "*In God is my salvation and my glory.*" Wherein should we glory but in him who saves us ? Our honour may well be left with him who secures our souls.

To find all in God, and to glory that it is so, is one of the sure marks of an enlightened soul. " *The rock of my strength, and my refuge is in God.*" He multiplies titles, for he would render much honour to the Lord, whom he had tried, and proved to be a faithful God under so many aspects. Ignorance needs but few words, but when experience brings a wealth of knowledge, we need varied expressions to serve as coffers for our treasure. God who is our rock when we flee for shelter, is also our *strong* rock when we stand firm and defy the foe ; he is to be praised under both characters. Observe how the Psalmist brands his own initials upon every name which he rejoicingly gives to his God—*my* expectation, *my* rock, *my* salvation, *my* glory, *my* strength, *my* refuge ; he is not content to know that the Lord is all these things ; he acts faith towards him, and lays claim to him under every character. What are the mines of Peru or Golconda to me if I have no inheritance in them ? It is the word *my* which puts the honey into the comb. If our experience has not yet enabled us to realise the Lord under any of these consoling titles, we must seek grace that we may yet be partakers of their sweetness. The bees in some way or other penetrate the flowers and collect their juices ; it must be hard for them to enter the closed cups and mouthless bags of some of the favourites of the garden, yet the honey-gatherers find or make a passage ; and in this they are our instructors, for into each delightful name, character, and office of our covenant God our persevering faith must find an entrance, and from each it must draw delight.

8. " *Trust in him at all times.*" Faith is an abiding duty, a perpetual privilege. We should trust when we can see, as well as when we are utterly in the dark. Adversity is a fit season for faith ; but prosperity is not less so. God at all times deserves our confidence. We at all times need to place our confidence in him. A day without trust in God is a day of wrath, even if it be a day of mirth. Lean ever, ye saints, on him, on whom the world leans. " *Ye people, pour out your heart before him.*" Ye to whom his love is revealed, reveal yourselves to him. His heart is set on you, lay bare your hearts to him. Turn the vessel of your soul upside down in his secret presence, and let your inmost thoughts, desires, sorrows, and sins be poured out like water. Hide nothing from him, for you *can* hide nothing. To the Lord unburden your soul : let him be your only father-confessor, for he only can absolve you when he has heard your confession. To keep our griefs to ourselves is to hoard up wretchedness. The stream will swell and rage if you dam it up : give it a clear course, and it leaps along and creates no alarm. Sympathy we need, and if we unload our hearts at Jesus' feet, we shall obtain a sympathy as practical as it is sincere, as consolatory as it is ennobling. The writer in the *Westminster Assembly's Annotations* well observes that it is the tendency of our wicked nature to bite on the bridle, and hide our grief in sullenness ; but the gracious soul will overcome this propensity, and utter its sorrow before the Lord. " *God is a refuge for us.*" Whatever he may be to others, his own people have a peculiar heritage in him ; " *for us* " he is undoubtedly a refuge ; here then is the best of reasons for resorting to him whenever sorrows weigh upon our bosoms. Prayer is peculiarly the duty of those to whom the Lord has specially revealed himself as their defence.

" SELAH." Precious pause ! Timely silence ! Sheep may well lie down when such pasture is before them.

9 Surely men of low degree *are* vanity, *and* men of high degree *are* a lie : to be laid in the balance, they *are* altogether *lighter* than vanity.

10 Trust not in oppression, and become not vain in robbery : if riches increase, set not your heart *upon them.*

11 God hath spoken once ; twice have I heard this ; that power *belongeth* unto God.

12 Also unto thee, O Lord, *belongeth* mercy : for thou renderest to every man according to his work.

9. " *Surely men of low degree are vanity.*" Here the word is *only* again ; men of low degree are only vanity, nothing more. They are many and enthusiastic, but they are not to be depended on ; they are mobile as the waves of the sea, ready to be driven to and fro by any and every wind ; they cry " Hosanna " to-day, and " Crucify him " to-morrow. The instability of popular applause is a proverb ;

as well build a house with smoke as find comfort in the adulation of the multitude. As the first son of Adam was called Abel or vanity, so here we are taught that all the sons of Adam are Abels: it were well if they were all so in character as well as in name; but alas! in this respect, too many of them are Cains. *"And men of high degree are a lie."* That is worse. We gain little by putting our trust in the aristocracy, they are not one whit better than the democracy; nay, they are even worse, for we expect something from them, but get nothing. May we not trust the *élite?* Surely reliance may be placed in the educated, the chivalrous, the intelligent? For this reason are they a lie; because they promise so much, and in the end, when relied upon, yield nothing but disappointment. How wretched is that poor man who puts his trust in princes. The more we rely upon God, the more shall we perceive the utter hollowness of every other confidence. *"To be laid in the balance, they are altogether lighter than vanity."* Take a true estimate of them; judge them neither by quantity nor by appearance, but by weight, and they will no longer deceive you. Calmly deliberate, quietly ponder, and your verdict will be that which inspiration here records. Vainer than vanity itself are all human confidences: the great and the mean, alike, are unworthy of our trust. A feather has some weight in the scale, vanity has none, and creature confidence has less than that: yet such is the universal infatuation, that mankind prefer an arm of flesh to the power of the invisible but almighty Creator; and even God's own children are too apt to be bitten with this madness.

10. *"Trust not in oppression, and become not vain in robbery."* Wealth ill-gotten is the trust only of fools, for the deadly pest lies in it; it is full of canker, it reeks with God's curse. To tread down the poor and silence their cries for justice, is the delight of many a braggart bully, who in his arrogance imagines that he may defy both God and man; but he is warned in these words, and it will be well for him if he takes the warning, for the Judge of all the earth will surely visit upon men the oppression of the innocent, and the robbery of the poor: both of these may be effected legally in the courts of man, but no twistings of the law, no tricks and evasions will avail with the Court of Heaven. *"If riches increase, set not your heart upon them."* If they grow in an honest, providential manner, as the result of industry or commercial success, do not make much account of the circumstance; be not unduly elated, do not fix your love upon your money-bags. To bow an immortal spirit to the constant contemplation of fading possessions is extreme folly. Shall those who call the Lord their glory, glory in yellow earth? Shall the image and superscription of Cæsar deprive them of communion with him who is the image of the invisible God? As we must not rest in men, so neither must we repose in money. Gain and fame are only so much foam of the sea. All the wealth and honour the whole world can afford would be too slender a thread to bear up the happiness of an immortal soul.

11. *"God hath spoken once."* So immutable is God that he need not speak twice, as though he had changed; so infallible, that one utterance suffices, for he cannot err; so omnipotent, that his solitary word achieves all his designs. We speak often and say nothing; God speaks once and utters eternal verities. All our speaking may yet end in sound; but he speaks, and it is done; he commands, and it stands fast. *"Twice have I heard this."* Our meditative soul should hear the echo of God's voice again and again. What he speaks once in revelation, we should be always hearing. Creation and providence are evermore echoing the voice of God; "He that hath hears to hear, let him hear." We have two ears, that we may hear attentively, and the spiritual have inner ears with which they hear indeed. He hears twice in the best sense who hears with his heart as well as his ears. *"That power belongeth unto God."* He is the source of it, and in him it actually abides. This one voice of God we ought always to hear, so as to be preserved from putting our trust in creatures in whom there can be no power, since all power is in God. What reason for faith is here! It can never be unwise to rest upon the almighty arm. Out of all troubles he can release us, under all burdens sustain us, while men must fail us at the last, and may deceive us even now. May our souls hear the thunder of Jehovah's voice as he claims all power, and henceforth may we wait only upon God!

12. *"Also unto thee, O Lord, belongeth mercy."* This tender attribute sweetens the grand thought of his power: the divine strength will not crush us, but will be used for our good; God is so full of mercy that it belongs to him, as if all the mercy in the universe came from God, and still was claimed by him as his possession.

His mercy, like his power, endureth for ever, and is ever present in him, ready to be revealed, *"For thou renderest to every man according to his work,"* This looks rather like justice than mercy; but if we understand it to mean that God graciously rewards the poor, imperfect works of his people, we see in it a clear display of mercy. May it not also mean that according to the work he allots us is the strength which he renders to us? he is not a hard master; he does not bid us make bricks without straw, but he metes out to us strength equal to our day. In either meaning we have power and mercy blended, and have a double reason for waiting only upon God. Man neither helps us nor rewards us; God will do both. In him power and grace are eternally resident; our faith should therefore patiently hope and quietly wait, for we shall surely see the salvation of God. *Deo soli gloria.* All glory be to God only.

EXPLANATORY NOTES AND QUAINT SAYINGS.

Psalms lxii. *and* lxiii. *compared.*—ONLY AND EARLY.—There is a sweet and profitable lesson taught us in Psalms lxii. and lxiii. The heart is ever prone to divide its confidence between God and the creature. This will never do. We must " wait *only* upon God." " He *only*" must be our " rock," our " salvation," and our " defence." Then we are frequently tempted to look to an arm of flesh *first*, and when that fails us, we look to God. This will never do either. He must be our *first* as well as our *only* resource. " O God, thou art my God, *early* will I seek thee." This is the way in which the heart should ever treat the blessed God. This is the lesson of Psalm lxiii. When we have learnt the blessedness of seeking God " *only*," we shall be sure to seek him " *early*."—*Charles Mackintosh, in " Things New and Old,"* 1858.

Whole Psalm.—There is in it throughout not one single word (and this is a rare occurrence), in which the prophet expresses *fear* or *dejection;* and there is also no prayer in it, although, on other occasions, when in danger, he never omits to pray. . . . . The prophet found himself remarkably well furnished in reference to that part of piety which consists in πληροφορία, the full assurance and perfection of faith; and therefore he designed to rear a monument of this his state of mind, for the purpose of stimulating the reader to the same attainment.—*Moses Amyraut,* 1596—1664.

Whole Psalm.—Athanasius says of this Psalm: " Against all attempts upon thy body, thy state, thy soul, thy fame, temptations, tribulations, machinations, defamations, say this Psalm."—*John Donne.*

Verse 1.—*"Only."* The particle may be rendered *only*, as restrictive; or, *surely*, as affirmative. Our translators have rendered it differently in different verses of this Psalm; in verse 1, " *truly*; " in verses, 2, 4, 5, 6, " *only*; " in verse 9, " *surely.*" If we render *"only,"* the meaning will be here that God exclusively is the object of trust; if " *surely*," that this truth, that God is his salvation, has come home to him with a more lively conviction, with a more blessed certainty than ever.—The first line of the verse rendered literally is, " *Only unto God my soul is silence.*"—*J. J. Stewart Perowne.*

Verse 1.—*"Truly my soul waiteth upon God,"* etc. In the use of means, for answers of prayer, for performance of promises, and for deliverance from enemies, and out of every trouble: or, *is silent*, as the Targum; not as to prayer, but as to murmuring; patiently and quietly waiting for salvation until the Lord's time come to give it; being *subject* to him, as the Septuagint, Vulgate Latin, Arabic, and Ethiopic versions; resigned to his will, and patient under his afflicting hand: it denotes a quiet, patient waiting on the Lord, and not merely bodily exercise in outward ordinances; but an inward frame of spirit, a soul-waiting on the Lord, and that in truth and reality, in opposition to mere form and show.—*John Gill.*

Verse 1.—" *Truly my soul waiteth upon God*; " or, as the Hebrew, *My soul is silent.* Indeed, waiting on God for deliverance, in an afflicted state, consists much in a holy silence. It is a great mercy, in an affliction, to have bodily senses, so as not to lie raving, but still and quiet, much more to have the heart silent and patient;

and we find the heart is as soon heated into a distemper as the head. Now what the sponge is to the cannon, when hot with often shooting, hope is to the soul in multiplied afflictions ; it cools the spirit and meekens it, so that it doth not break out into distempered thoughts or words against God. [See also verse 5].—*William Gurnall.*

Verse 1.—*"Waiteth." Waiting is nothing else but hope and trust lengthened.*—*John Trapp.*

Verse 1.—*" My soul is silent before God."* As if he had said : To me as a man God has put in subjection all his creatures ; to me as a king he has subjected the whole of Judæa, the Philistines, the Moabites, Syrians, Idumeans, Ammonites, and other tribes ; having taken me from the sheep-cotes he has adorned me with a crown and a sceptre now these thirty years, and extended my kingdom to the sea, and to the great river Euphrates ; it is not without reason, then, that I subject myself to God alone in this affliction, wherein Absalom thirsts to crush me, especially since he reveals the deliverance prepared for me, and from him alone can I expect it.—*Thomas Le Blanc* (—1669), *in Psalmorum Davidicorum Ana ysis.*

Verse 1.—*" Is silent."* The Hebrew word used is דוּמִיָּה *dumijah*, that is, silent, resting, expecting, reflecting, solicitous, and observing. For, first, we ought to be subject to God as silent disciples before a master. . . . Whatever God has allowed to happen to me, yet I will be silent before him, and from my heart admire, both enduring his strokes and receiving his teaching. . . . Secondly, we ought to be subject to God as creatures keeping quiet before their Creator. . . " Woe unto him that striveth with his Maker." Isaiah xlv. 9. Thirdly, we ought to be subject to God as clay in the hands of the potter, ready for the form into which he wishes *to fashion us.* . . " *As clay is in the potter's hand, so are ye in mine hand, O house of Israel."* Jer. xviii. 6. Fourthly, we ought to be subject to God, as a maid servant to her master, observing his wish, even in the most menial affairs. . . . Fifthly, we ought to be subject to God, as a wife to her husband (*sponsa sponso*), who in her love is solicitous and careful to do whatever may be pleasing to him. *" My beloved is mine, and I am his."* Cant. ii. 16. And, *" I am my beloved's."* Cant. vi. 3.—*Thomas Le Blanc.*

Verse 1.—After almost every quiet prayer and holy meditation in the divine presence, we have the consciousness that there was an ear which heard us, and a heart which received our sighs. The effect of a silent colloquy with God is so soothing ! There was a time when I used greatly to wonder at these words of Luther :—

> " Bear and forbear, and *silent* be,
> Tell to no man thy misery ;
> Yield not in trouble to dismay,
> God can deliver any day."

I wondered because we feel the outpouring of grief into the heart of a friend to be so sweet. At the same time, he who talks much of his troubles to *men* is apt to fall into a way of saying too little of them to *God :* while, on the other hand, he who has often experienced the blessed alleviation which flows from silent converse with the Eternal, loses much of his desire for the sympathy of his fellows. It appears to me now as if spreading out our distress *too largely* before men served only to make it broader, and to take away its *zest ;* and hence the proverb, " Talking of trouble makes it double." On the contrary, if when in distress we can contrive to maintain calm composure of mind, and to bear it always as in the sight of God, submissively waiting for succour from him, according to the words of the Psalmist, *"Truly my soul waiteth upon God : from him cometh my salvation ; "* in that case, the distress neither extends in breadth nor sinks in depth. It lies upon the surface of the heart like the morning mist, which the sun as it ascends dissipates into light clouds.—*Augustus F. Tholuck, in " Hours of Christian Devotion,"* 1870.

Verse 1.—The natural mind is ever prone to *reason,* when we ought *to believe ;* to be *at work,* when we ought to be *quiet ;* to go our own way, when we ought steadily to walk on in God's ways, however trying to nature. . . . And how does it work, when we thus anticipate God, by going our own way ? We bring, in many instances, guilt on our conscience ; but if not, we certainly weaken faith, instead of increasing it ; and each time we work thus a deliverance of our own, we find it more and more difficult to trust in God, till at last we give way entirely to our natural fallen reason, and unbelief prevails. How different if one is enabled to wait God's own time, and to look alone to him for help and deliverance ! When at last help comes, after many seasons of prayer it may be, and after much exercise of faith and patience it may be, how sweet it is, and what a present recompense does the soul at once receive for trusting in God, and waiting patiently for his deliverance ! Dear Christian reader, if you have never walked in this path of obedience before, do so now, and you will then know experimentally the sweetness of the joy which results from it.—*George Müller, in "A Narrative of some of the Lord's Dealings,"* 1856.

Verse 2.—*" I shall not be greatly moved."* Grace makes the heart move leisurely to all things except God. A mortified man is as a sea that hath no winds, that ebbs not and flows not. The mortified man sings and is not light, and weeps and is not sad, is zealous in God's cause, and yet composed in spirit ; he is not so eager on anything, but he can quit it for God. Ah ! few can act, but they over act.— *Alexander Carmichael, in " The Believer's Mortification of Sin,"* 1677.

Verse 3 :—

> " How long will ye assault a man ?
> How long will ye all crush him,
> As though he were a leaning wall—
> A fence nearly thrust down ? "

French and Skinner.

Verse 3.—*" Against a man."* That sure is but a poetical expression for *against me, i.e., David,* the speaker, against whom the neighbouring nations raised war, and his own subjects rebellions. Thus doth Christ oft speak of himself under the title of the *Son of Man,* in the third person ; and Paul (2 Cor. xii. 2), Οἶδα ἄνθρωπον, *" I knew a man,"* i.e., undoubtedly *himself.—Henry Hammond.*

Verse 3.—*" As a bowing wall shall ye be, and as a tottering fence."* Christ gave no blow, but merely asked his murderers whom they sought for ; and yet they fell flat and prostrate to the ground (John xviii.), so that the wicked persecutors of the godly are aptly and properly likened and compared to a tottering and trembling wall. For as soon as ever the blasts of God's wrath and judgment are moved and kindled against them, they are so quivering and comfortless, that they would take them to be most their friends who would soonest despatch them out of the world ; as Christ said aptly of them, they would pray the mountains to fall upon them. Luke xxiii.—*John Hooper.*

Verse 3.—*" As a bowing wall shall ye be."* In consequence of heavy rains and floods, and unsound foundations, it is very common to see walls much out of perpendicular ; and some of them so much so, that it might be thought scarcely possible for them to stand. " Poor old Rāman is very ill, I hear." " Yes, the wall is bowing." " Begone, thou low caste ! thou art a *kutte-chiover,"* that is, " a ruined wall." " By the oppression of the head-man, the people of that village are like a ruined wall."—*J. Roberts's " Oriental Illustrations."*

Verse 3.—*" A bowing wall."* A wall, when ill built, bulges out in the centre, presenting the appearance of nearly twice its actual breadth ; but, as it is hollow within, it soon falls to ruin. The wicked, in like manner, are dilated with pride and assume, in their consultations, a most formidable appearance ; but David predicts that they would be brought to unexpected and utter destruction, like a wall badly constructed, and hollow in the interior, which falls with a sudden crash, and is broken by its own weight into a thousand pieces.—*John Calvin.*

Verse 4.—*" They only consult,"* etc. Truly I am he whom if *" they shall consult to cast down from his excellency, they shall delight in a lie, they shall bless with their mouth and curse inwardly."* That is : what I have said of worldly men, boasting themselves upon a man, falling into ruin, I desire that you should know that the same fate shall never befall me who trust in God ; for otherwise does the matter stand.—*Hermann Venema.*

Verse 4.—*" Excellency."* Rather, *elevation ;* the figure of the preceding verse being followed out.—*Religious Tract Society's Notes.*

Verse 5.—*" My soul, wait thou only upon God."* They trust not God *at all* who trust him not *alone.* He that stands with one foot on a rock, and another foot upon a quicksand, will sink and perish, as certainly as he that standeth with both feet upon a quicksand. David knew this, and therefore calleth earnestly upon his soul (for his business lay most within doors) to trust only upon God. See verse 1.—*John Trapp.*

Verse 5.—"*My expectation is from him.*" As if he had said, never will he frustrate the patient waiting of his saints ; doubtless my silence shall meet with its reward ; I shall restrain myself, and not make that false haste which will only retard my deliverance.—*John Calvin.*

Verse 5.—"*My expectation is from him.*" In an account of the voyage of some of the early missionaries who left Hermannsburg for South Africa, is the following incident :—After a long calm, a brother prayed thus to the Lord for favouring wind : " Lord, thou givest them that fear thee the desires of their heart, and dost help them ; help us now, that we may no longer be becalmed upon the sea ; help us on our journey, thou who ridest on the wings of the wind." He was so joyful over this word of the Lord, that he rose up and said in his heart : " Now I have already that for which I prayed." After the prayer, one of the crew stepped over to the helmsman, and said, half mocking, half in earnest, " So we shall have wind : didn't you hear the prayer ? It doesn't look very like it ! " So he said, and half an hour after there came so strong a blast that the waves broke over the ship.—*William Fleming Stevenson, in " Praying and Working,"* 1862.

Verse 5.—He shifteth much needless labour, and provideth great contentment, who closeth himself with God alone. To deal with man alone, apart from God, is both an endless and fruitless labour. If we have counsel to ask, help or benefit to obtain, or approbation to seek, there is none end with man : for every man we must have sundry reasons and motives ; and what pleaseth one will offend twenty : as many heads, as many wits and fancies. No man can give contentment to all, or change himself into so many fashions, as he shall encounter humours ; and yet it is more easy to take sundry fashions than to be acceptable in them.—*William Struther.*

Verses 6, 7.—Twice in this Psalm hath he repeated this, in the second and in the sixth verses, "*He is my rock, and my salvation, and my defence,*" and (as it is enlarged in the seventh verse) "*my refuge and my glory.*" If my " *refuge,*" what enemy can pursue me ? If my " *defence,*" what temptation shall wound me ? If my " *rock,*" what storm shall shake me ? If my "*salvation,*" what melancholy shall deject me ? If my " *glory,*" what calumny shall defame me ?—*John Donne.*

Verses 6, 7.—How quickly the soul of the faithful returns again to the God of its confidence. He spared a moment to admonish the ungodly, but like the dove of Noah he returns to the ark. Observe how the expressions of this holy confidence are repeated, with every pleasing variety of expression, to denote the comfort of his heart. Reader, ask yourself—are such views of Christ your views of him ? Do you know him in those covenant characters ? Is Jesus your rock, your salvation, your defence ?—*Robert Hawker, D.D.*

Verse 7 (first clause).—On the shields of the Greeks, Neptune was depicted ; on the shields of the Trojans, Minerva ; because in them they put their confidence, and in their protection deemed themselves secure. . . . Now, Christ is the insignia of our shields. Often does David say, God is his protector. The Hebrew is *magen ;* that is, shield, buckler, as Ps. xviii. 2 & 30.—*Thomas Le Blanc.*

Verse 7.—There are several names of God given in this verse, that so every soul may take with him that name which may minister most comfort to him. Let him that is pursued by any particular temptation, invest God, as God is *a refuge, a sanctuary ;* let him that is buffeted with Satan, battered with his own concupiscence, receive God, as God is his *defence* and *target ;* let him that is shaked with perplexities in his understanding, or scruples in his conscience, lay hold on God, as God is his *rock* and his *anchor ;* let him that hath any diffident jealousy and suspicion of the free and full mercy of God, apprehend God, as God is his *salvation ;* and let him that walks in the ingloriousness and contempt of the world, contemplate God, as God is *glory.* Any of these notions is enough to any man ; but God is all these, and all else, that all souls can think, to every man.—*Abraham Wright.*

Verse 8.—" *Trust in him,*" etc. To trust in God is to cast our burden on the Lord, when it is too heavy for our own shoulder (Ps. lv. 22) ; to dwell " in the secret place of the Most High " when we know not where to lay our heads on earth

(Ps. xci. 1); to "look to our Maker" and to " have respect to the Holy One of Israel" (Isaiah xvii. 7) ; to lean on our Beloved (Cant. viii. 5 ; Isaiah xxxvi. 6); to stay ourselves, when sinking, on the Lord our God (Isaiah xxvi. 3). In a word, trust in God is that high act or exercise of faith whereby the soul, looking upon God and casting itself on his goodness, power, promises, faithfulness, and providence, is lifted up above carnal fears and discouragements ; above perplexing doubts and disquietments ; either for the obtaining and continuance of that which is good, or for the preventing or removing of that which is evil. . . . "*Trust in him at all times.*" This holy duty is indeed never out of season ; so much the original word for *time*, חֵע, imports. True, indeed, our Saviour saith, and saith truly, " My time," *i.e.*, my time of discovering myself to be a wonder-working God, " is not yet come." Yea, but *all time* in respect of *trust in God*, is an appointed, yea, and an *accepted* time. The wise man tells us (Eccl. iii. 1), " There is an appointed time for every purpose under heaven : " a time to kill and to heal, to plant and to pluck up, to weep and to laugh, to get and to lose, to be born and to die. In *all* these *trust in God* is not, like snow in harvest, uncomely, but seasonable, yea, necessary. There may be, indeed, a time when God will not be found, but no time wherein he must not be trusted. *Nullum tempus occurrit regi*, saith the law ; let me add, *nec fiduciæ*, and it is sound divinity. The time of trusting in God cannot be lapsed. But more expressly. There are some *special* instances and nicks of time for trust. 1. *The time of prosperity ;* when we sit under the warm beams of a meridian sun ; when we wash our steps in butter and feet in oil; when the candle of the Lord shines on our tabernacle ; when " our mountain stands strong : " now, now is the time for trust, but not in our mountain (for it is a mountain of ice and may soon dissolve), but *in our God*. Halcyon days to come are temptations to security, but to saints times for trust. . . . 2. *The time for adversity*. This also is a seasonable time for trust ; when we have no bread to eat, but that of " carefulness ;" nor wine to drink, but that of " affliction " and " astonishment ; " no, not water either, but that of our " tears." *Now* is a time, not for overgrieving, murmuring, sinking, desponding, but for *trusting*, In a tempest, then, a believer thinks it seasonable to cast anchor upward. Thus did good Jehoshaphat : " O our God ; we know not what to do : only *our eyes are unto thee.*" 2 Chron. xx. 12. Thus David : " What time I am afraid, I will trust in thee." Ps. lvi. 3. Times of trouble are proper times for trust, be the trouble either spiritual or temporal. . . . " *At all times.*" 1. *Quando :* When must we trust ? " At what time ? " At all times, *omni hora*, " every hour : " so the Syriac version. As a true friend is to love, so a sound believer is to trust, at all times. Prov. xvii. 17. 2. *Quamdiu :* The duration of this trust : " How long ? " " All the day long." Ps. xliv. 8. All our lives long : all the days of their *appointed* time must God's Jobs not only " wait," but " trust," till their change come. Yea, " for ever " (Isaiah xxvi. 4) ; nay, " for ever and ever." Ps. lii. 8.— *Thomas Lye, M.A.* (1621—1684), *in* " *The Morning Exercises at Cripplegate.*"

Verse 8.—" *Trust in him at all times ; ye people, pour out your heart before him.*" According to our love, so is our faith and trust in God ; and according to our trust, such is our freedom at the throne of grace. Trust in him, and pour out your hearts before him ; pour them out, like water, in joyful tears. For when the stone in the heart is melted by mercy, the eyes will issue like a fountain of tears. Good men have melting spirits. It is a branch of the covenant and a fruit of the effusion of the Spirit of grace. It is asserted by the learned in chemistry that no menstruums are so powerful as sulphureous and oily liquors to melt down the hardest minerals ; to be sure there is nothing like the oil of mercy, so potent a solvent for an iron heart.— *Samuel Lee.*

Verse 8.—"*At all times.*" I might mention many times in which we might trust in the Lord, but they are comprised in this little word " *all*," and a precious word it is : " Trust in him at *all* times." When you are full of fears, then you shall bring the little word " *all* " unto him, and say, I have nothing to encourage me to come to thee but that precious little word, " *all.*"—*John Berridge.*

Verse 8.—" *Pour out your heart.*" The word " *pour* " plainly signifies that the heart is full of grief, and almost afraid to empty itself before the Lord. What does he say to you ? " Come and pour out all your trouble before me." He is never weary with hearing the complaints of his people ; therefore you should go and keep nothing back ; tell him everything that hurts you, and pour " all your complaints into his merciful bosom." That is a precious word : " *Pour out your heart before him.*" Make him your counsellor and friend ; you cannot please him better than when your hearts rely wholly upon him. You may tell him, if you please, you have been so foolish as to look to this friend and the other for relief, and found none ; and you now come to him, who commands you, to " *pour out your heart before him.*"—*John Berridge.*

Verse 8.—" *Pour out your heart.*" Pour it out as water. Not as milk, whose colour remains. Not as wine, whose savour remains. Not as honey, whose taste remains. But as water, of which, when it is poured out, nothing remains. So let sin be poured out of the heart, that no colour of it may remain in external marks, no savour in our words, no taste in our affections. " I will cut off from Babylon the name, and remnant, and son, and nephew, saith the Lord." Isaiah xiv. 22. Thus Hugo. But if you fear lest there remain anything in your heart not poured forth, bring the whole heart, and cast it before the eyes of the Lord, and sacrifice it to him, that he may create a new heart in thee.—*Thomas Le Blanc.*

Verse 9.—Other doctrines, moral or civil instructions, may be delivered to us possibly, and probably, and likely, and credibly, and under the like terms and modifications, but this in our text, is assuredly, undoubtedly, undeniably, irrefragably. " *Surely men of low degree,*" etc. For howsoever when they two are compared together with one another, it may admit discourse and disputation, whether men of high degree, or of low degree, do most violate the laws of God ; that is, whether prosperity or adversity make men most obnoxious to sin ; yet, when they come to be compared, not with one another, but both with God, this asseveration, this " *surely* " reaches to both : " *Surely men of low degree are vanity,* and, as *surely men of high degree are a lie.*" And though this may seem to leave room for men of middle ranks, and fortunes, and places, that there is a mediocrity that might give an assurance, and an establishment, yet there is no such thing in this case ; for (as *surely* still) " *to be laid in the balance, they are all* " (not all of low, and all of high degree, all rich, and all poor), but all, of all conditions, " *altogether lighter than vanity.*" Now, all this doth destroy, not extinguish, not annihilate, that affection in man, of hope and trust, and confidence in anything ; but it rectifies that hope, and trust, and confidence, and directs it upon the right object. Trust not in flesh, but in spiritual things, that we neither bend our hope downward, to infernal spirits, to seek help in witches ; nor miscarry it upward, to seek it in saints or angels, but fix it in him who is nearer us than our own souls—our blessed, and gracious, and powerful God, who in this one Psalm is presented unto us by so many names of assurance and confidence : " *my expectation, my salvation, my rock, my defence, my glory, my strength, my refuge,*" and the rest. . . . "*Men of high degree are a lie.*" The Holy Ghost hath been pleased to vary the phrase here, and to call "*men of high degree*" not "*vanity,*" but "*a lie ;*" because the poor, men of low degree, in their condition promise no assistance, feed not men with hope, and therefore cannot be said *to lie ;* but in the condition of men of high degree, who are of power, there is a tacit promise, a natural and inherent assurance of protection and assistance flowing from them. For the magistrate cannot say that he never promised me justice, never promised me protection ; for in his assuming that place, he made me that promise. I cannot say that I never promised my parish my service ; for in my induction I made them that promise, and if I perform it not I am *a lie :* for so the word *chasab* (which we translate *a lie*) is frequently used in the Scriptures, for that which is defective in the duty it should perform : " Thou shalt be a spring of water " (says God in Isaiah), *cujus aquæ non mentiuntur,* " whose waters never lie ; " that is, never dry, never fail. So, then, when men of high degree do not perform the duties of their places, then they are a lie of their own making ; and when I over-magnify them in their place, flatter them, humour them, ascribe more to them, expect more from them, rely more upon them than I should, then they are a lie of my making. . . . . . "*To be laid in the balance, they are altogether lighter than vanity.*" Vanity is nothing, but there is a condition worse than nothing. Confidence in the things or persons of this world, but most of all a confidence in ourselves, will bring us at last to that state wherein we would fain be nothing, and cannot. But yet we have a "*balance*" in our text ; and all these are but put together in one balance. In the other scale there is something put too, in comparison whereof all this world is so light. God does not leave our great and noble faculty and affection of hope, and trust, and confidence without something to direct itself upon, and rectify itself in. He does not ; for, for that he proposes himself. The words immediately before the text are, God "*is a refuge ;* " and, in comparison of him, " *To be laid in the balance, they are altogether lighter than vanity.*"—*John Donne.*

Verse 9.—" *Surely men of low degree are vanity.*"

> " Who o'er the herd would wish to reign,
> Fantastic, fickle, fierce, and vain !
> Vain as the leaf upon the stream,
> And fickle as a changeful dream ;
> Fantastic as a woman's mood,
> And fierce as Frenzy's fevered blood,
> Thou many-headed monster thing,
> O, who would with to be thy king ! "
>
> *Walter Scott* (1771—1832).

Verse 9.—" *Surely men of low degree are vanity,*" etc. Or, *sons of Adam ;* of the earthly man ; of fallen Adam ; one of his immediate sons was called Hebel, *vanity ;* and it is true of all his sons, but here it designs only one sort of them ; such as are poor and low in the world ; mean men, as the phrase is rendered in Isaiah ii. 9 ; these are subject to sinful vanity ; their thoughts are vain, their affections vain, their minds vain, their conversation vain, sinful, foolish, fallacious, and inconstant.—*John Gill.*

Verse 9.—"*Men . . . are a lie.*" An active lie—they deceive others ; and a passive lie—they are deceived by others ; and they who are most actively a lie, are most usually and most deservedly a passive lie, or fed with lies.—*Joseph Caryl.*

Verse 9.—"*Lighter than vanity.*"—If there were any one among men immortal, not liable to sin, or change, whom it were impossible for any one to overcome, but who was strong as an angel, such a one might be something ; but inasmuch as every one is a man, a sinner, mortal, weak, liable to sickness and death, exposed to pain and terror, like Pharaoh, even from the most insignificant animals, and liable to so many miseries that it is impossible to count them, the conclusion must be a valid one : " Man is nothing."—*Arndt.*

Verse 10.—" *Trust not in oppression, and become not vain in robbery.*" Now this robbery and wrong is done two manner of ways—to God and to man. He that putteth his trust for salvation in any other, save in God, loses not only his salvation, but also robs God of his glory, and does God manifest wrong, as much as lieth in him ; as the wicked people amongst the Jews did, who said as long as they honoured and trusted unto the queen of heaven, all things prospered with them ; but when they hearkened to the true preachers of God's word, all things came into a worse state, and they were overwhelmed with scarcity and trouble. Hosea ii. ; Jeremiah xliv. He also that puts his trust and confidence in any learning or doctrine beside God's word, not only falls into error and loses the truth ; but also, as much as lies in him, he robs God's book of his sufficient truth and verity, and ascribes it to the book of men's decrees ; which is as much wrong to God and his book as may be thought or done. In which robbery, or rather sacrilege, no man should put his trust, as the prophet saith.—*John Hooper.*

Verse 10.—"*Become not vain in robbery.*" What ? would he have them serious in robbery ? No ; the meaning is this : do not trust in a thing of nought ; if you rob, oppress, deceive, or wrong others, you trust to a vain thing—in a thing that is not—in a thing that will never do you good : there will be no tack, no hold in anything got in such a manner. When you think to get riches by wrong dealing, or closely circumventing others, you " *become vain in robbery.*"—*Joseph Caryl.*

Verse 10.—"*If riches increase, set not your heart upon them.*" We naturally love riches, and therefore as naturally spend many thoughts, both how to get and how to keep them. If a man have riches, or an increase of riches, it is not unlawful for him to think of them (yet we should be as sparing of our thoughts that way as may be, our thoughts and the bent of our souls should always be upon God), but that which the Psalmist forbids is the settling of our hearts ; as if he had said, Let not your thoughts stay or dwell here. Riches are themselves transient things, therefore they should have but our transient thoughts. *"Set not your hearts upon them,"* for they may quickly be unsettled. Samuel bespake Saul in the same language about a worldly concernment, when he went out to seek his father's asses : " Set not thy mind on them." 1 Sam. ix. 20. 'Tis like Saul was overburdened with this thought, " What's become of, or what shall I do for, my father's asses ? "

" Be not solicitous about them," saith Samuel, " greater things are towards thee."—
Joseph Caryl.

Verse 10.—*"If riches increase, set not your heart upon them."* Consider what
is here meant by " riches." Indeed, some may imagine that it is hardly possible
to mistake the meaning of this common word. Yet, in truth, there are thousands
in this mistake ; and many of them quite innocently. A person of note hearing
a sermon preached upon this subject several years since, between surprise and
indignation, broke out aloud, " Why does he talk about riches here ? There is no
rich man at Whitehaven, but Sir James L———r." And it is true there was none
but he that had forty thousand pounds a year, and some millions in ready money.
But a man may be rich that has not a hundred a year—not even one thousand
pounds in cash. Whosoever has food to eat, and raiment to put on, with something
over, is rich. Whoever has the necessaries and conveniences of life for himself
and his family, and a little to spare for them that have not, is properly a rich man ;
unless he is a miser, a lover of money, one that hoards up what he can and ought
to give to the poor. For if so, he is a poor man still, though he has millions in the
bank ; yea, he is the poorest of men ; for

> " The beggars but a common lot deplore
> The rich poor man's emphatically poor."

. . . . O ! who can convince a rich man that he sets his
heart upon riches ? For considerably above half a century I have spoken on this
head, with all the plainness that was in my power. But with how little effect !
I doubt whether I have in all that time convinced fifty misers of covetousness.
When the lover of money was described ever so clearly, and painted in the strongest
colours, who applied it to himself ? To whom did God and all that knew him say,
" Thou art the man ? " If he speaks to any of you that are present, O do not stop
your ears ! Rather say, with Zaccheus, " Behold, Lord, the half of my goods I
give to the poor ; and if I have done any wrong to any man, I restore him fourfold." He did not mean that he had done this in time past ; but that he determined
to do so for the time to come. I charge thee before God, thou lover of money, to
" go and do likewise ! "

I have a message from God unto thee, O rich man ! whether thou wilt hear or
whether thou wilt forbear. Riches have increased with thee ; at the peril of thy
soul, " set not thine heart upon them ! " Be thankful to him that gave thee such
a talent, so much power of doing good. Yet dare not rejoice over them but with
fear and trembling. *Cave ne inhœreas,* says pious Kempis, *ne capiaris et pereas ;*
" Beware thou cleave not unto them, lest thou be entangled and perish." Do not
make them thy end, thy chief delight, thy happiness, thy god ! See that thou
expect not happiness in money, nor anything that is purchasable thereby ; in
gratifying either the desire of the flesh, the desire of the eyes, or the pride of life.—
John Wesley's Sermon "On the Danger of Increasing Riches."

Verse 10.—*"If riches increase,"* etc.—" The lust of riches," says Valerian, " stirs
with its stimulus the hearts of men, as oxen perpetually plough the soil." Hugo,
on Isaiah, says : " The more deeply riches are sown in the heart through love, the
more deeply will they pierce through grief."—*Thomas Le Blanc.*

Verse 10.—*"If riches increase"* (בוג)—*lit.,* " sprout up " *of their own accord,*
as distinguished from riches acquired by " oppression " and " robbery "—*A. R.
Fausset.*

Verse 10.—Riches have in them uncertainty and deceitfulness. Riches have
never been true to those that trusted in them, but ever have proved " a lie in their
right hand." Isaiah xliv. 20. Hence they are called " lying vanities," Jonah ii. 8 ;
and compared to a flock of birds sitting upon a man's ground, which upon the least
fright, take wing and fly away. Riches have " wings," saith Solomon ; and rather
than want they will *make* to themselves wings." Prov. xxiii. 5. Yea, though
they have not the wings so much as of a little sparrow, wherewith to fly to you ;
yet will they make to themselves the large wings of a great eagle, wherewith to
fly from you. Oh, how many have riches served as Absalom's mule served her
master, whom she lurched, and left, in his greatest need, hanging betwixt heaven
and earth, as if rejected of both ! A spark of fire may set them on flying, a thief
may steal them, a wicked servant may embezzle and purloin them, a pirate or shipwreck at sea, a robber or bad debtor at land ; yea, an hundred ways sets them
packing. They are as the apples of Sodom, that look fair yet crumble away with

the least touch—golden delusions, a mere mathematical scheme or fancy of man's brain, 1 Cor. vii. 31 ; the semblances and empty show of good without any reality or solid consistency : *nec vera, nec vestra ;* as they are slippery upon the account of verity, so they are no less in respect of prosperity and possession, for they are winged birds, especially in this, that they fly from man to man (as the birds do from tree to tree), and always from the owner of them. This is a sore deceit and cosenage, yet your heart is more deceitful, inasmuch as it will deceive you with these deceitful riches, *a quo aliquid tale est, illud est magis tale ;* they are so, because the heart is so.—*Christopher Love* (1618—1651), *in "A Chrystal Mirrour, or Christian Looking-glass,"* 1679.

Verse 10.—*" Set not your heart upon them."* The word נׁשׁ properly is *to place,* to arrange in a fixed firm order, is specially used of the foundation stones of a building being placed fitly and firmly together . . . Therefore *to set the heart* upon riches is, to fix the mind closely and firmly upon them, to give it wholly up to them with all its powers ; at the same time to be puffed up with confidence and arrogance, as Cl. Schultens observes.—*Hermann Venema.*

Verses 10—13.—Our estimate of man depends upon our estimate of God. David knows that men of low and high degree, if separated from the primal fount of every good, weigh *nothing,* and are less than nothing. Riches are nothing, especially ill-gotten ones. Man is not to get proud when riches increase. But such is the course of things, that in proportion as the gifts of God are rich, men confide more in the gifts than in the rich giver. But holy David is better instructed. Once and again he has heard the divine voice in his soul, " that power belongeth unto God only." Job xxxiii. 14. This powerful God is merciful : can then any merit attach to our poor works ? and yet the Lord rendereth to every pious man according to his imperfect pious work.—*Augustus F. Tholuck.*

Verse 11.—*"God hath spoken once ; twice have I heard this."* Nothing is able to settle our confidence in God, but the powerful impression of his own word. *"Twice have I heard this ; that power,"* etc. How did he hear this *"twice ? "* Once from the voice of *creation,* and again from the voice of *government.* Mercy was heard in government after man had sinned, not in creation : but we have heard of the power of God twice ; once we heard of it in creation, and again more gloriously in the work of redemption, wherein his power and mercy were linked together. Or, *"Twice have I heard this ; that power,"* etc. ; that is, it is a most certain and undoubted truth, that *power* is essential to the divine nature. The repetition of a thing confirms the certainty of it. *Mercy* is also essential ; but power is more apparently so, because no act of *mercy* can be exercised without *power.* Or, though God spake this but *once,* yet David heard it *twice,* or often : that is, he thoroughly weighed and considered it as God's *once* speaking. In this sense a gracious person hears that *twice* that God speaks but *once.* Or, *twice,* that is, frequently ; because what God had *once* spoken, had been often repeated and inculcated, and often cleared and confirmed to him by repeated experimental evidence of the certainty thereof ; and he had thereupon received the same more and more heartily, and had taken deeper impressions of it by repeated and inculcated thoughts. —*William Wisheart* (1657—1727), *in "Theologia ; or, Discourses of God."*

Verse 11.—*"God hath spoken once,"* etc. He made it known irrevocably and with great solemnity, so that it was not necessary to repeat it. With the Romans anything is said to be done *once,* which there is either no need to repeat, or which has no return. With the Hebrews also, and Orientals, אחת *is at one turn,* as in 1 Sam. xxvi. 8 : *"Now therefore let me smite him, I pray thee, with the spear even to the earth* AT ONE TURN, and I will not *smite him the second time.* See Schultens. So also Ps. lxxxix. 35. " ONCE *have I sworn in my holiness, I will not lie unto David."* But what is the force of *to hear twice ?* It may be taken in various ways. *To hear twice* can be regarded in the general sense of *frequently* or often. This will give the meaning :—God has but once spoken, yet I have often observed in my experience that his declaration is true.—*Hermann Venema.*

Verse 11.—*"Once ; yea twice."* This is answerable to the phrase of the Latins, *Semel atque iterum ;* and it is usual in all writers to use a certain number for an uncertain, and particularly among poets : *Felice ter et amplius, Horace.*—*John Tillotson,* 1630—1694.

Verse 11.—*"Twice have I heard,"* etc. There are several renderings and inter-pretations of these words ; but that which to me seems most intended by our rendering is, I heard what was once spoken twice at once ; that is, I heard it speedily, and I heard it believingly : as soon as ever the word came to me I received it, and I received it not only with my ear, but with my heart. That is a blessed way of hearing ; and they who hear so, at first speaking, may well be said to hear that *twice* which God speaketh once.—*Joseph Caryl.*

Verse 11.—"*Power belongeth unto God.*" Believe the mighty power of God. Consider (1). It is difficult to believe his power. But how can that be ? Is not this a piece of natural divinity, that God is almighty ? What need is there, then, to press people to believe it ? Great need ; because this is the great thing we are apt to question in cases of difficulty. Else, why do we pray with cheerfulness when we see great probability of a thing, but faint in prayer when it is otherwise ? And why do we cry out, in sad times, " Oh, we shall never see good days again ? " (2.) The firm belief of God's power is of great concern and moment in religion. Faith is never quite laid by till the soul questions the power of God. " Oh, he cannot pardon, he cannot save ! " When it cometh to this, the soul is no longer able to hold out. So that the life and vigour of faith is very much concerned in the belief of God's power. It is, indeed, one of the first steps to all religion. Therefore it is put in the front of our creed : " I believe in God, the Father ALMIGHTY ; " and he that believes that first article will the more easily believe all the rest. (3.) God is much displeased, even with his own children, when his power is questioned by them. For this God takes up Moses short : " Is the Lord's hand waxed short ? " (Numb. xi. 23) ; as if he had said : "What, Moses, dost thou think that my power is exhausted or weakened ? What an unworthy conceit is this ! " For this also Christ rebuked Martha very sharply : " Said I not unto thee, that if thou wouldest believe, thou shouldest see the glory of God ? " John xi. 40. Yea, God is so tender of the glory of his power, and he hath sharply chastened his dear children when their faith staggered in this matter ; as we see in Zacharias, who, for questioning the power of God, was immediately stricken dumb upon the place. Well, then, let it be your great care to have your faith confirmed in the belief of God's almighty power. For this end, ponder the verbal declarations made of it in the Holy Scriptures ; consider and improve the manifestations he hath given of it, both in your own and former times ; and pray much that God would strengthen and increase your faith.—*William Wisheart.*

Verses 11, 12.—Except some of the ancient versions, almost every version, translation, and commentary, says Dr. A. Clarke, have missed the sense and meaning of this verse. Of the former verse the Doctor offers the following translation : " Once hath God spoken ; these two things have I heard." But what are the two things the Psalmist had heard ? 1. כִּי עֹז לֵאלֹהִים, "*That strength is the Lord's ;* " that is, he is the origin of power. 2. וּלְךָ־אֲדֹנָי חָסֶד, "*and to thee, Lord, is mercy ;* " that is, *he is the fountain of mercy.* These, then, are the *two* grand truths that the *law,* yea, the whole *revelation* of God, declares through every page. He is the *Almighty*—he is the *Most Merciful ;* and hence the *inference,* the powerful, just, and holy God, the most merciful and compassionate Lord, *will* by-and-by *judge the world,* and *will render to man according to his works.* How this beautiful meaning, adds the Doctor, should have been unseen by almost every interpreter is hard to say ; but these verses contain one of the most instructive truths in the Bible.— *William Carpenter, in "An Explanation of Scripture Difficulties,"* 1828.

Verses 11, 12.—I confess I wonder to find so constantly in Scripture that the inspired writers put " merciful " and " mighty," " terrible " and " great," all together : you shall find it so. Neh. i. 5. " O Lord God of heaven, the great and terrible God, that keepeth covenant and mercy," etc. You have it also in Dan. ix. 4, in his solemn prayer. " O Lord," says he, " the great and dreadful God, keeping the covenant and mercy," etc. Thus mercy, and great, and terrible are constantly joined together.—*Thomas Goodwin.*

Verse 12.—"*Also unto thee, O Lord, belongeth mercy.*" Something more is necessary to invite us to a dependence on God than his bare "*power*" and ability to help us. There must be also a firm persuasion of the promptitude and readiness of his will to do what he is able ; and this we have in the other attribute of his "*mercy.*" . . . . " Unto thee," unto thee *alone,* and unto none else. The tenderest mercy amongst the creatures is none at all, being compared with the divine mercy. It belongeth "*unto thee,*" as thy prerogative and peculiar excellency. Mercy is a peculiar jewel of his crown. Or, *thine, O Lord, is mercy.* Nothing amongst the creatures deserves the name of mercy but his own. Nothing is worthy to be so called, but what is proper and peculiar to God. Or, *with thee is mercy*, as it is expressed elsewhere. Psalm cxxx. 4, 7. It is *with him;* that is, it is inseparable from his nature. He is merciful in a way peculiar to himself, " the Father of mercies." 2 Cor. i. 3.—*William Wisheart.*

Verse 12.—*"For thou renderest to every man according to his work;"* namely— judgment to the wicked, and mercy to the righteous; where the Syriac interpreter giveth the good note: *Est gratia Dei ut reddat homini secunda opera bona, quia merces bonorum operum est ex gratia:* It is mercy in God to set his love on them that keep his commandments. Exod. xx. 6.—*John Trapp.*

Verse 12.—*"Thou renderest to every man according to his work."* Learn to admire the grace of God in rewarding your works. It is much that he accepts them; and what is it, then, that he rewards them? It is much that he doth not damn you for them, seeing they are all defiled, and have something of sin cleaving to them; and what is it, then, that he crowns them? You would admire the bounty and munificence of a man that should give you a kingdom for taking up a straw at his foot, or give you a hundred thousand pounds for paying him a penny rent you owed him: how, then, should you adore the rich grace and transcendent bounty of God in so largely recompensing such mean services, in setting a crown of glory upon your heads, as the reward of those works which you can scarcely find in your hearts to call good ones! You will even blush one day to see yourselves so much honoured for what you are ashamed of, and are conscious to yourselves that you have deserved nothing by. You will wonder then to see God recompensing you for doing what was your duty to do, and what was his work in you; giving you grace, and crowning that grace; enabling you to do things acceptable to him, and then rewarding you as having done them.—*Edward Veal* (—1708), *in "The Morning Exercises."*

HINTS TO PREACHERS.

Verse 1.—I. *What* he did? " Waited upon God." Believed, was patient, was silent in resignation, was obedient. II. To whom he did it? To his God, who is true, a sovereign, gracious, etc. III. How he did it? With his soul, truly, and only. IV. What came of it? Salvation present, personal, eternal, etc.

Verse 2.—*"God a rock."* David speaks of him as high and strong, and as a rock to stand upon, a rock of defence and refuge, a rock of habitation (Psalm lxxi. 3, in Hebrew), and a rock to be praised. Ps. xcv. i. See the Concordance for many hints.

[*"Christ the Rock:"* a Sermon on 1 Cor. x. 4. By RALPH ROBINSON, in *"Christ All and In All."*]

Verse 2 (first clause).—See " SPURGEON'S *Sermons,"* No. 80, *"God alone the Salvation of His People."*

Verses 2 & 6.—*"I shall not be greatly moved."* *"I shall not be moved."* Growth in faith. How it is produced, preserved, and evidenced.

Verse 4.—Wherein lies a believer's excellency? Who would cast him down, and why, and how they seek to do it?

Verse 4.—*"They delight in lies."* Those who invent them, or spread them, or laugh at them, or readily believe them. Romanists, self-righteous persons, the presumptuous, persecutors, zealous errorists, etc.

Verse 5 (first clause).—See " SPURGEON'S *Sermons,"* No. 144, *"Waiting only upon God."*

Verse 5 (second clause).—Great expectations from a great God; because of great promises, great provisions, and great foretastes.

Verse 5 (last clause).—What we expect from God, and why and when?

Verse 8 (first clause).—How are we to live by faith on divine providence?— T. Lye's Sermon in *"Morning Exercises."*

Verse 8 (first clause).—All trust, from all saints, at all times.

Verse 8 (*first clause*).—Times when this exhortation is most needed. Times of prosperity, of desertion by friends, of calumny, of poverty, of conscious sin, of chastisement, of death.

Verse 8.—"*Pour out your hearts.*" This teacheth us to deal plainly with God in laying open our hearts before him ; and then, no doubt, we shall find ease.—*Thomas Wilcocks.*

Verse 8 (*last clause*).—The peculiar security of the peculiar people.

Verse 10.—Evils usually connected with the love of riches. Idolatry, covetousness, carking care, meanness, forgetfulness of God and spiritual truth, neglect of charity, hardness of heart, tendency to injustice, etc. Means for escaping this seductive sin.

Verse 11.—I. How God speaks. "*Once,*" plainly, powerfully, immutably, etc. II. How we should hear. "*Twice,*" continually, in heart as well as ear, observantly in practice, in spirit as well as in letter.

Verses 11 & 12.—The constant union of power and mercy in the language of Scripture.

PSALM LXIII.

Title.—A Psalm of David, when he was in the wilderness of Judah.—*This was probably written while David was fleeing from Absalom ; certainly at the time he wrote it he was king (verse 11), and hard pressed by those who sought his life. David did not leave off singing because he was in the wilderness, neither did he in slovenly idleness go on repeating Psalms intended for other occasions ; but he carefully made his worship suitable to his circumstances, and presented to his God a wilderness hymn when he was in the wilderness. There was no desert in his heart, though there was a desert around him. We too may expect to be cast into rough places ere we go hence. In such seasons, may the Eternal Comforter abide with us, and cause us to bless the Lord at all times, making even the solitary place to become a temple for Jehovah.*

The distinguishing word of this Psalm is " Early.*" When the bed is softest we are most tempted to rise at lazy hours ; but when comfort is gone, and the couch is hard, if we rise the earlier to seek the Lord, we have much for which to thank the wilderness.*

Division.—*In the first eight verses the writer expresses his holy desires after God, and his confidence in him, and then in the remaining three verses he prophesies the overthrow of all his enemies. The Psalm is peculiarly suitable for the bed of sickness, or in any constrained absence from public worship.*

EXPOSITION.

O GOD, thou *art* my God ; early will I seek thee : my soul thirsteth for thee, my flesh longeth for thee in a dry and thirsty land, where no water is ;

2 To see thy power and thy glory, so *as* I have seen thee in the sanctuary.

3 Because thy lovingkindness *is* better than life, my lips shall praise thee.

4 Thus will I bless thee while I live : I will lift up my hands in thy name.

5 My soul shall be satisfied as *with* marrow and fatness ; and my mouth shall praise *thee* with joyful lips :

6 When I remember thee upon my bed, *and* meditate on thee in the *night* watches.

7 Because thou hast been my help, therefore in the shadow of thy wings will I rejoice.

8 My soul followeth hard after thee : thy right hand upholdeth me.

1. "*O God, thou art my God ;* " or, O God, thou art my Mighty One. The last Psalm left the echo of *power* ringing in the ear, and it is here remembered. Strong affiance bids the fugitive poet confess his allegiance to the only living God ; and firm faith enables him to claim him as his own. He has no doubts about his possession of his God ; and why should other believers have any ? The straightforward, clear language of this opening sentence would be far more becoming in Christians than the timorous and doubtful expressions so usual among professors. How sweet is such language ! Is there any other word comparable to it for delights ? *Meus Deus.* Can angels say more ? "*Early will I seek thee.*" Possession breeds desire. Full assurance is no hindrance to diligence, but is the mainspring of it. How can I seek another man's God ? but it is with ardent desire that I seek after him whom I know to be my own. Observe the eagerness implied in the time mentioned ; he will not wait for noon or the cool eventide ; he is up at cockcrowing to meet his God. Communion with God is so sweet that the chill of the morning is forgotten, and the luxury of the couch is despised. The morning is the time for dew and freshness, and the Psalmist consecrates it to prayer and devout fellowship. The best of men have been betimes on their knees. The word "*early*" has not only the sense of early in the morning, but that of eagerness, immediateness.

He who truly longs for God longs for him now. Holy desires are among the most powerful influences that stir our inner nature ; hence the next sentence, *"My soul thirsteth for thee."* Thirst is an insatiable longing after that which is one of the most essential supports of life ; there is no reasoning with it, no forgetting it, no despising it, no overcoming it by stoical indifference. Thirst will be heard ; the whole man must yield to its power : even thus is it with that divine desire which the grace of God creates in regenerate men ; only God himself can satisfy the craving of a soul really aroused by the Holy Spirit. *"My flesh longeth for thee ;"* by the two words *"soul"* and *"flesh,"* he denotes the whole of his being. " The *flesh*," in the New Testament sense of it, never longs after the Lord, but rather it lusteth against the spirit ; David only refers to that sympathy which is sometimes created in our bodily frame by vehement emotions of the soul. Our corporeal nature usually tugs in the other direction, but the spirit when ardent can compel it to throw in what power it has upon the other side. When the wilderness caused David weariness, discomfort, and thirst, his flesh cried out in unison with the desire of his soul. *"In a dry and thirsty land, where no water is."* A weary place and a weary heart make the presence of God the more desirable ; if there be nothing below and nothing within to cheer, it is a thousand mercies that we may look up and find all we need. How frequently have believers traversed in their experience this *"dry and thirsty land,"* where spiritual joys are things forgotten ! and how truly can they testify that the only true necessity of that country is the near presence of their God ! The absence of outward comforts can be borne with serenity when we walk with God ; and the most lavish multiplication of them avails not when he withdraws. Only after God, therefore, let us pant. Let all desires be gathered into one. Seeking first the kingdom of God—all else shall be added unto us.

2. *"To see thy power and thy glory, so as I have seen thee in the sanctuary."* He longed not so much to see the sanctuary as to see his God ; he looked through the veil of ceremonies to the invisible One. Often had his heart been gladdened by communion with God in the outward ordinances, and for this great blessing he sighs again ; as well he might, for it is the weightiest of all earth's sorrows for a Christian man to lose the conscious presence of his covenant God. He remembers and mentions the two attributes which had most impressed themselves upon his mind when he had been rapt in adoration in the holy place ; upon these his mind had dwelt in the preceding Psalm, and the savour of that contemplation is evidently upon his heart when in the wilderness : these he desires to behold again in the place of his banishment. It is a precious thought that the divine power and glory are not confined in their manifestation to any places or localities ; they are to be heard above the roaring of the sea, seen amid the glare of the tempest, felt in the forest and the prairie, and enjoyed wherever there is a heart that longs and thirsts to behold them. Our misery is that we thirst so little for these sublime things, and so much for the mocking trifles of time and sense. We are in very truth always in a weary land, for this is not our rest ; and it is marvellous that believers do not more continuously thirst after their portion far beyond the river where they shall hunger no more, neither thirst any more ; but shall see the face of their God, and his name shall be in their foreheads. David did not thirst for water or any earthly thing, but only for spiritual manifestations. The sight of God was enough for him, but nothing short of that would content him. How great a friend is he, the very sight of whom is consolation. Oh, my soul, imitate the Psalmist, and let all thy desires ascend towards the highest good ; longing here to see God, and having no higher joy even for eternity.

3. *"Because thy lovingkindness is better than life."* A reason for that which went before, as well as for that which follows. Life is dear, but God's love is dearer. To dwell with God is better than life at its best ; life at ease, in a palace, in health, in honour, in wealth, in pleasure ; yea, a thousand lives are not equal to the eternal life which abides in Jehovah's smile. In him we truly live, and move, and have our being ; the withdrawal of the light of his countenance is as the shadow of death to us : hence we cannot but long after the Lord's gracious appearing. Life is to many men a doubtful good ; lovingkindness is an unquestioned boon : life is but transient, mercy is everlasting : life is shared in by the lowest animals, but the lovingkindness of the Lord is the peculiar portion of the chosen. *"My lips shall praise thee."* Openly, so that thy glory shall be made known, I will tell of thy goodness. Even when our heart is rather desiring than enjoying we should still continue to magnify the Most High, for his love is truly precious ; even if we do

not personally, for the time being, happen to be rejoicing in it. We ought not ot make our praises of God to depend upon our own personal and present reception of benefits; this would be mere selfishness: even publicans and sinners have a good word for those whose hands are enriching them with gifts; it is the true believer only who will bless the Lord when he takes away his gifts or hides his face.

4. "*Thus will I bless thee while I live.*" As I now bless thee so will I ever do; or rather, *so* as thou shalt reveal thy lovingkindness to me, I will in return continue to extol thee. While we live we will love. If we see no cause to rejoice in our estate, we shall always have reason for rejoicing in the Lord. If none others bless God, yet his people will; his very nature, as being the infinitely good God, is a sufficient argument for our praising him as long as we exist. "*I will lift up my hands in thy name.*" For worship the hands were uplifted, as also in joy, in thanksgiving, in labour, in confidence; in all these senses we would lift up our hands in Jehovah's name alone. No hands need hang down when God draws near in love. The name of Jesus has often made lame men leap as a hart, and it has made sad men clap their hands for joy.

5. "*My soul shall be satisfied as with marrow and fatness.*" Though unable to feast on the sacrifice at thine altar, my soul shall even here be filled with spiritual joys, and shall possess a complete, a double contentment. There is in the love of God a richness, a sumptuousness, a fulness of soul-filling joy, comparable to the richest food with which the body can be nourished. The Hebrews were more fond of fat than we are, and their highest idea of festive provision is embodied in the two words, "*marrow and fatness:*" a soul hopeful in God and full of his favour is thus represented as feeding upon the best of the best, the dainties of a royal banquet. "*And my mouth shall praise thee with joyful lips.*" More joy, more praise. When the mouth is full of mercy, it should be also full of thanksgiving. When God gives us the marrow of his love, we must present to him the marrow of our hearts. Vocal praise should be rendered to God as well as mental adoration; others see our mercies, let them also hear our thanks.

6. "*When I remember thee upon my bed.*" Lying awake, the good man betook himself to meditation, and then began to sing. He had a feast in the night, and a song in the night. He turned his bedchamber into an oratory, he consecrated his pillow, his praise anticipated the place of which it is written, "There is no night there." Perhaps the wilderness helped to keep him awake; and if so, all the ages are debtors to it for this delightful hymn. If day's cares tempt us to forget God, it is well that night's quiet should lead us to remember him. We see best in the dark if we there see God best. "*And meditate on thee in the night watches.*" Keeping up sacred worship in my heart as the priests and Levites celebrated it in the sanctuary. Perhaps David had formerly united with those "who by night stand in the house of the Lord," and now as he could not be with them in person, he remembers the hours as they pass, and unites with the choristers in spirit, blessing Jehovah as they did. It may be, moreover, that the king heard the voices of the sentries as they relieved guard, and each time he returned with renewed solemnity to his meditations upon his God. Night is congenial, in its silence and darkness, to a soul which would forget the world, and rise into a higher sphere. Absorption in the most hallowed of all themes makes watches, which else would be weary, glide away all too rapidly; it causes the lonely and hard couch to yield the most delightful repose—repose more restful than even sleep itself. We read of beds of ivory, but beds of piety are better far. Some revel in the night, but they are not a tithe so happy as those who meditate in God.

7. "*Because thou hast been my help.*" Meditation had refreshed his memory and recalled to him his past deliverances. It were well if we oftener read our own diaries, especially noting the hand of the Lord in helping us in suffering, want, labour, or dilemma. This is the grand use of memory, to furnish us with proofs of the Lord's faithfulness, and lead us onward to a growing confidence in him. "*Therefore in the shadow of thy wings will I rejoice.*" The very shade of God is sweet to a believer. Under the eagle wings of Jehovah we hide from all fear, and we do this naturally and at once, because we have aforetime tried and proved both his love and his power. We are not only safe, but happy in God; we "*rejoice*" as well as repose.

8. "*My soul followeth hard after thee,*" or is glued to thee. We follow close at the Lord's heel, because we are one with him. Who shall divide us from his love? If we cannot walk with him with equal footsteps, we will at least follow after with

all the strength he lends us, earnestly panting to reach him and abide in his fellowship. When professors follow hard after the world, they will fall into the ditch ; but none are ever too eager after communion with the Lord. *"Thy right hand upholdeth me."* Else he would not have followed the Lord with constancy, or even have longed after him. The divine power, which has so often been dwelt upon in this and the preceding Psalms, is here mentioned as the source of man's attachment to God. How strong are we when the Lord works in us by his own right hand, and how utterly helpless if he withhold his aid !

9 But those *that* seek my soul, to destroy *it*, shall go into the lower parts of the earth.

10 They shall fall by the sword : they shall be a portion for foxes.

11 But the king shall rejoice in God ; every one that sweareth by him shall glory : but the mouth of them that speak lies shall be stopped.

9. As David earnestly sought for God, so there were men of another order who as eagerly sought after his blood ; of these he speaks : *"But those that seek my soul, to destroy it."* At his life they aimed, at his honour, his best welfare ; and this they would not merely injure but utterly ruin. The devil is a destroyer, and all his seed are greedy to do the same mischief ; and as he has ruined himself by his crafty devices, so also shall they. Destroyers shall be destroyed. Those who hunt souls shall be themselves the victims. *"Shall go into the lower parts of the earth."* Into the pits which they digged for others they shall fall themselves. The slayers shall be slain, and the grave shall cover them. The hell which they in their curse invoked for others, shall shut its mouth upon them. Every blow aimed against the godly will recoil on the persecutor ; he who smites a believer drives a nail in his own coffin.

10. *"They shall fall by the sword."* So David's enemies did. They that take the sword shall perish with the sword ; bloody men shall feel their own life gushing forth from them, when their evil day shall at last come, and they shall be given up to feel in their own persons the horrors of death. *" They shall be a portion for foxes."* Too mean to be fit food for the lions, the foxes shall sniff around their corpses, and the jackals shall hold carnival over their carcasses. Unburied and unhonoured they shall be meat for the dogs of war. Frequently have malicious men met with a fate so dire as to be evidently the award of retributive justice. Although the great assize is reserved for another world, yet even here, at the common sessions of providence, justice often bears her avenging sword in the eyes of all the people.

11. *"But the king shall rejoice in God."* Usurpers shall fade, but he shall flourish ; and his prosperity shall be publicly acknowledged as the gift of God. The Lord's anointed shall not fail to offer his joyful thanksgiving : his well-established throne shall own the superior lordship of the King of kings ; his rejoicing shall be alone in God. When his subjects sing, *"Io triumphe,"* he will bid them chant, *"Te Deum."* *"Every one that sweareth by him shall glory."* His faithful followers shall have occasion for triumph : they shall never need to blush for the oath of their allegiance. Or, " swearing by *him*," may signify adherence to *God*, and worship paid to him. The heathen swore by their gods, and the Israelite called Jehovah to witness to his asseveration ; those, therefore, who owned the Lord as their God should have reason to glory when he proved himself the defender of the king's righteous cause, and the destroyer of traitors. *"But the mouth of them that speak lies shall be stopped."* And the sooner the better. If shame will not do it, nor fear, nor reason, then let them be stopped with the sexton's shovel-full of earth ; for a liar is a human devil, he is the curse of men, and accursed of God, who has comprehensively said, " all liars shall have their part in the lake which burneth with fire and brimstone." See the difference between the mouth that praises God, and the mouth that forges lies : the first shall never be stopped, but shall sing on for ever ; the second shall be made speechless at the bar of God.

O Lord, we seek thee and thy truth ; deliver us from all malice and slander, and reveal to us thine own self, for Jesus' sake. Amen.

EXPLANATORY NOTES AND QUAINT SAYINGS.

Title.—"*When he was in the wilderness of Judah.*" Even in Canaan, though a fruitful land, and the people numerous, yet there were wildernesses. . . . It will be so in the world, in the church, but not in heaven. . . . All the straits and difficulties of a wilderness must not put us out of tune for sacred songs ; but even then it is our duty and interest to keep up a cheerful communion with God. There are Psalms proper for a wilderness ; and we have reason to thank God it is the wilderness of Judah we are in, not the wilderness of Sin.—*Matthew Henry.*

Title.—"*The Wilderness of Judah*" is the whole wilderness towards the east of the tribe of Judah, bounded on the north by the tribe of Benjamin, stretching southward to the south-west end of the Dead Sea ; westward, to the Dead Sea and the Jordan ; and eastward, to the mountains of Judah.—*E. W. Hengstenberg.*

Title.—The term *"wilderness"* (מִדְבָּר, as distinguished from עֲרָבָה, a *steppe*) was given to a district which was not regularly cultivated and inhabited, but used for pasturage (from דָּבַר, to *drive*), being generally without wood and defective in water, but not entirely destitute of vegetation.—*J. P. Lange.*

Title.—Hagar saw God in the wilderness, and called a well by the name derived from that vision, *Beer-lahai-roi.* Gen. xvi. 13, 14. Moses saw God in the wilderness. Exod. iii. 1—4. Elijah saw God in the wilderness. 1 Kings xix. 4—18. David saw God in the wilderness. The Christian church will see God in the wilderness. Rev. xii. 6—14. Every devout soul which has loved to see God in his house will be refreshed by visions of God in the wilderness of solitude, sorrow, sickness, and death.—*Christopher Wordsworth.*

Whole Psalm.—This is unquestionably one of the most beautiful and touching Psalms in the whole Psalter. Donne says of it : " As the whole Book of Psalms is, *oleum effusum* (as the spouse speaks of the name of Christ), an ointment poured out upon all sorts of sores, a cerecloth that supples all bruises, a balm that searches all wounds ; so are there some certain Psalms that are imperial Psalms, that command over all our affections, and spread themselves over all occasions—catholic, universal Psalms, that apply themselves to all necessities. This is one of these ; for of those constitutions which are called apostolical, one is that the church should meet every day to sing this Psalm. And, accordingly, St. Chrysostom testifies ' That it was decreed and ordained by the primitive Fathers, that no day should pass without the public singing of this Psalm.' "—*J. J. Stewart Perowne.*

Whole Psalm.—This Psalm is aptly described by Clauss as " A precious confession of a soul thirsting after God and his grace, and finding itself quickened through inward communion with him, and which knows how to commit its outward lot also into his hand." Its lesson is, that the consciousness of communion with God in trouble is the sure pledge of deliverance. This is the peculiar fountain of consolation which is opened up to the sufferer in the Psalm. The Berleb Bible describes it as a Psalm " which proceeds from a spirit really in earnest. It was the favourite Psalm of M. Schade, the famous preacher in Berlin, which he daily prayed with such earnestness and appropriation to himself, that it was impossible to hear it without emotion."—*E. W. Hengstenberg.*

Verse 1.—"*O God, thou art my God ; early will I seek thee*" (or, I will diligently seek thee, as merchants precious stones that are of greatest value) : *"my soul thirsteth for thee."* He doth not say my soul thirsteth for water, but my soul thirsteth for *thee ;* nor he doth not say my soul thirsteth for the blood of my enemies, but my soul thirsteth for *thee ;* nor he doth not say my soul thirsteth for deliverance out of this dry and barren wilderness, but my soul thirsteth for *thee* in a dry and thirsty land, where no water is ; nor he doth not say my soul thirsteth for a crown, a kingdom, but my soul thirsteth for *thee*, my flesh longeth for *thee.* These words are a notable metaphor, taken from women with child, to note his earnest, ardent, and strong affections towards God.—*Thomas Brooks.*

Verse 1.—"*O God.*" This is a serious word ; pity it should ever be used as a by-word.—*Matthew Henry.*

Verse 1.—"*My God*" in Hebrew is the same word with which the Lord cried out upon the cross to the Father about the ninth hour : " My God, my God, why hast thou forsaken me ? " For in Hebrew this Psalm begins *Elohim, Eli.* Now, *Elohim* is *plural*, and *Eli* is singular, to express the mystery of the Trinity, the mystery of the Unity, the distinct subsistence of the (three) hypostases, and their consubstantiality.—*Psalterium Quin. Fabri stapulensis,* 1513.

Verse 1 (*first clause*).—In David we have a notable example of a sensitive, tender, self-analyzing soul, living in sustained communion with God, while deeply sensible of the claims of the civil and religious polity of Israel, and, moreover, while externally devoted to a large round of exacting public duties. And in this Psalm public misfortunes do but force him back upon the central strength of the life of his spirit. For the time his crown, his palace, his honours, the hearts of his people, the love of his child, whom he loved, as we know, with such passing tenderness, are forfeited. The Psalmist is alone with God. In his hour of desolation he looks up from the desert to heaven. *"O God,"* he cries, *"thou art my God."* In the original language he does not repeat the word which is translated *"God."* In *Elohim,* the true idea of the root is that of awe, while the adjectival form implies permanency. In *Eli,* the second word employed, the etymological idea is that of might, strength. We might paraphrase, "O thou Ever-awful One, my Strength, or my Strong-God art thou." But the second word, *Eli,* is in itself nothing less than a separate revelation of an entire aspect of the Being of God. It is, indeed, used as a proper and distinct name of God. The pronominal suffixes for the second and third persons are, as Gesenius has remarked, never once found with this name *El;* whereas *Eli,* the first person, occurs very frequently in the Psalter alone. We all of us remember it in the words actually uttered by our Lord upon the cross, and which he took from the Syriacised version of Psalm xxii. The word unveils a truth unknown beyond the precincts of revelation. It teaches us that the Almighty and Eternal gives himself in the fulness of his Being to the soul that seeks him. Heathenism, indeed, in its cultus of domestic and local deities, of its penates, of its θεοὶ ἐπιχώριοι, bore witness by these superstitions to the deep yearning of the human heart for the individualizing love of a higher power. To know the true God was to know that such a craving was satisfied. *"My God."* The word represents not a human impression, or desire, or conceit, but an aspect, a truth, a necessity of the divine nature. Man can, indeed, give himself by halves; he can bestow a little of his thought, of his heart, of his endeavour, upon his brother man. In other words, man can be imperfect in his acts as he is imperfect and finite in his nature. But when God, the Perfect Being, loves the creature of his hand, he cannot thus divide his love. He must perforce love with the whole directness, and strength, and intensity of his Being; for he is God, and therefore incapable of partial and imperfect action. He must give himself to the single soul with as absolute a completeness as if there were no other being besides it, and, on his side, man knows that this gift of himself by God is thus entire; and in no narrow spirit of ambitious egotism, but as grasping and representing the literal fact, he cries, *"My God."* Therefore does this word enter so largely into the composition of Hebrew names. Men loved to dwell upon that wondrous relation of the Creator to their personal life which is so strikingly manifested. Therefore, when God had " so loved the world, that he gave his only begotten Son, that whosoever believeth in him should not perish, but have everlasting life," we find St. Paul writing to the Galatians as if his own single soul had been redeemed by the sacrifice of Calvary : " He loved me, and gave himself for me."—*Henry Parry Liddon, in "Some Words for God : being Sermons preached before the University of Oxford,* 1863—1865."

Verse 1 (*first clause*).—There is a great deal more in it than men of the world are aware of ; to say, "*O God, thou art my God,"* in this connection and conjunction : there is more in it in regard of excellency, and there is more in it in regard of difficulty likewise. It is not an unfruitful thing to say it, and it is not an easy thing to say it neither. It confers a great deal of benefit, and requires a great deal of grace, which belongs unto it, in the truth and reality of it. The benefit of it, first, is very great ; yea, in effect all things else. To say God is ours, is to say the whole world is ours, and a great deal more ; it is to give us title to everything which may be requisite or convenient for us. Whatever we can desire or stand in need of, it is all wrapt up in this, *"Thou art my God."* But then, again, it is a matter of difficulty (as those things which are excellent are). It is a thing which is not so easily said as the world imagines it and thinks it to be. Indeed, it is easy to the mouth, but it is not easy to the heart. It is easy to have a fancy to say it, but it is not to have a faith to say it : this carries some kind of hardship with it, and it is not presently attained unto ; but the mind of man withdraws from it. There are two states and conditions in which it is very difficult to say, *"O God, thou art my God :"* the one is the state of nature and unregeneracy ; and the other is the state of desertion, and the hiding of God's face from the soul.—*Thomas Horton* (—1673).

Verse 1 (*second clause*).—The relations of God to his people are not bare and empty titles, but they carry some activity with them, both from him towards them, and from them also answerably towards him. Those whom God is a God to, he bestows special favours upon them ; and those to whom God is a God, they return special services to him. And so we shall find it to be all along in Scripture, as this David in another place : " Thou art my God, and I will praise thee : thou art my God, I wilk exalt thee." Ps. cxviii. 28. And so here : "*Thou art my God ; early will I seek thee.*" While the servants of God have claimed any interest in him, they have also entitled duty to him. The text is an expression not only of faith, but likewise of obedience, and so to be looked upon by us.—*Thomas Horton*.

Verse 1.—"*Early ;* " *in the morning*, before all things, God is to be sought, other-wise he is sought in vain : as the manna, unless collected at early dawn, dissolves.—*Simon de Muis*.

Verse 1.—"*My soul thirsteth for thee.*" Oh that Christ would come near, and stand still, and give me leave to look upon him ! for to look seemeth the poor man's privilege, since he may, for nothing and without hire, behold the sun. I should have a king's life, if I had no other thing to do than for evermore to behold and eye my fair Lord Jesus : nay, suppose I were holden out at heaven's fair entry, I should be happy for evermore, to look through a hole in the door, and see my dearest and fairest Lord's face. O great King ! why standest thou aloof ? Why remainest thou beyond the mountains ? O Well-beloved, why dost thou pain a poor soul with delays ? A long time out of thy glorious presence is two deaths and two hells to me. We must meet. I must see him, I dow* not want him. Hunger and longing for Christ hath brought on such a necessity of enjoying Christ, that, cost me what it will, I cannot but assure Christ that I will not, I dow not want him ; for I cannot master nor command Christ's love.—*Samuel Rutherford* (1600—1661).

Verse 1.—"*My flesh*," that is, my bodily sensitive appetite, which thirsts, ardently longs for consolation, which it receives from the abounding of spiritual consolation to the soul. This meaning greatly pleases me. God giveth the upper and the nether springs. Rebekah, after drawing water in her pitcher, for Eliezer, Abraham's servant, added, "*I will draw water for thy camels also, until they have done drinking*," Gen. xxiv. 19. Jacob dug a well near to Sychar, which was after-wards called Samaria, and as the woman of Samaria said, "*drank thereof himself, and his children, and his cattle*," John iv. 12. When Moses with the rod smote the rock twice, "*the water came out abundantly, and the congregation drank, and their beasts also*," Numb. xx. 11. So God satisfies with this consolation both our higher and lower nature.—*Thomas Le Blanc*.

Verse 1.—"*My flesh longeth for thee.*" The verb כָּמַהּ is used only in this place, and therefore the signification of it is rather uncertain, but it will receive light from the Arabic dialect. In Golius's Lexicon it signifies, *caligavit oculus, alteratus colore, et mente debilitatus fuit*. His eye grew dim, his colour was changed, and his mind was weakened ; and therefore, as used by the Psalmist, implies the utmost intense-ness of fervency of desire, as though it almost impaired his sight, altered the very hue of his body, and even injured his understanding ; effects sometimes of eager and unsatisfied desires.—*Samuel Chandler*.

Verse 1.—"*In a dry.*" Here we must read, כְּאֶרֶץ [Keeretz], instead of בְּאֶרֶץ [Beeretz], for it is, "*like this*," and not, "*in this*" (which has no force), even like this dry, wearied, and waterless region ; so am I for seeing thee in the sanctuary, for beholding thy power and thy glory.—*Benjamin Weiss*, in a "*New Translation of the Book of Psalms, with Critical Notes*," etc., 1858.

Weiss appears to have the authority of several MSS. for this, but he seldom errs in the direction of too little dogmatism.—*C. H. S.*

Verses 1, 2.—"*O God, thou art my God.*"—He embraceth him at first word, as we use to do friends at first meeting. "*Early will I seek thee*," says he : "*my soul thirsteth for thee, my flesh*" (that is, *myself*) "*longeth for thee in a dry and thirsty land, where no water is.*" Surely David had some extraordinary business now with God to be done for himself, as it follows (verse 2) : "*To see thy power and thy glory, so as I have seen thee in the sanctuary ;*" where God had met him, and manifested himself to him. . . . The very sight of a friend rejoiceth a man (Prov. xxxvii. 17) :

---

* Am not able to do without him.

"As iron sharpeneth iron, so doth a man the face of his friend." It alone whets up joy by a sympathy of spirits; and in answer hereunto it is characteristically to God's people called the seeking of God's face, that is, himself, for so his face is taken: "Thou shalt have no other gods before my face;" that is, thou shalt have myself, or none but myself. Personal communion with God is the end of our graces; for as reason and the intercourse of it makes men sociable one with another, so the divine nature makes us sociable with God himself: and the life we live by is but an engine, a glass to bring God down to us.—*Thomas Goodwin.*

Verse 2.—*"To see thy power,"* etc. I. It is, or should be, the desire of every Christian to see and enjoy more and more of the glory of God. II. That the accomplishment of this design is to be sought by a devout and diligent attendance upon the worship of the sanctuary. How is God's character in the sanctuary manifested to believers? 1. By the ministry of reconciliation—by the exhibition of gospel truth. 2. Believers grow in their knowledge of the divine character in the sanctuary, by observing and feeling the application of those great doctrines to the souls of men, by the power and influence of the Holy Spirit. III. The effects that result to the believer in his history and experience, from an increasing knowledge of the power and glory of God. The effects of this knowledge are great and manifold. 1. The believer, by fresh displays of the divine glory, is disenchanted from the fascination of the world. 2. Another effect of an increasing acquaintance with God, and of every view of the divine glory we obtain, is that the mind is disentangled from the embarrassments into which it is sometimes thrown by the aspect of providence. 3. By seeing the divine power and glory in the sanctuary, we shall have our strength renewed to go on our Christian course afresh. 4. A view of the divine glory crucifies our lusts, and puts the corruptions of our heart to death. 5. Fresh views of the divine power and glory nourish our humility. 6. These views of the divine glory in the sanctuary arm us for our conflict with the last enemy. Concluding remarks: 1. That it is characteristic of every good man, that he is devoutly attached to the solemnities of public worship. 2. That his object in going to the sanctuary is definite and distinct.—*John Angell James.*

Verse 2.—*"So as I have seen thee in the sanctuary."* To converse with ordinances, and not to converse with God; to have to do with ordinances, and not to have to do with God, alas! they are but dry breasts, and a miscarrying womb that will never bring forth the fruits of holiness. Ordinances without God are but like bones that have no marrow in them; they are but like shells without a kernel. Your hearing will be in vain; and your praying will be in vain; there will be no spirit-moving, no voice-answering, no heart-warnings, no soul-refreshing, no God-meetings. —*William Strong* (—1654) *in the "Saints' Communion."*

Verse 2.—God's glory is in the firmament, in all the creatures, but more especially and fully in the church. Psalm xxix. 9, "In his temple doth every one speak of his glory;" there it is most visible, affecting, and provoking of every one to speak. In the world few take notice of it, but in the temple every one sees it, and speaks of it. The world is God opened, and so glorious; the church is Christ opened, and so very glorious. This made David long to be in the sanctuary when he was in the wilderness; and why so? *"To see thy power and thy glory."* Could not David see them in the heavens, in the mountains, in the goodly cedars, and other works of God? Yes, but not as in the sanctuary; and therefore he saith, *"To see thy power and thy glory, so as I have seen thee in the sanctuary;"* there I have seen thee otherwise than ever elsewhere; there he saw the king upon his throne and in his glory.—*William Greenhill.*

Verse 3.—*"Thy lovingkindness is better than life;"* or, *"better than lives,"* as the Hebrew hath it [*chaiim*]. Divine favour is better than life; it is better than life with all its revenues, with all its appurtenances, as honours, riches, pleasures, applause, etc.; yea, it is better than many lives put together. Now you know at what a high rate men value their lives; they will bleed, sweat, vomit, purge, part with an estate, yea, with a limb, yea, limbs, to preserve their lives. As he cried out, "Give me any deformity, any torment, any misery, so you spare my life." Now, though life be so dear and precious to a man, yet a deserted soul prizes the returnings of divine favour upon him above life, yea, above many lives. Many men have been weary of their lives, as is evident in Scripture and history; but no man was ever yet found that was weary of the love and favour of God. No man sets so high a price upon the sun as he that hath long lain in a dark dungeon, etc.— *Thomas Brooks.*

Verse 3.—*"Thy lovingkindness is better than life."* The love of life is a very frequent and pernicious snare, which a sense of God's love must deliver us from being entangled by. What so desirable as life, if a man have no place in the heart of God? This is the greatest temporal blessing, and nothing can outdo it, but the favour of the God of our life; and this excels indeed. What comparison is there between the breath in our nostrils, and the favour of an eternal God? any more than there is between an everlasting light and a poor vanishing vapour. Compare Isaiah lx. 19 with James iv. 14. Who would not, therefore, hate his own life, which hangs in doubt continually before him, and of which he can have no assurance, when he knows that the living God is his certain portion? Who would not freely yield up and part with ten thousand such lives, one after another (if he had so many), rather than the wrath of God should be kindled but a little.—*Timothy Cruso* (1657—1697).

Verse 3 (*first clause*).—*God's mercy is better than lives.* What lives? Those which for themselves men have chosen. One hath chosen for himself a life of business, another a country life, another a life of usury, another a military life; one this, another that. Divers are the lives, but *better is thy life than* our *lives.* Better is that which thou givest to men amended, than that which perverse men choose? One life thou givest, which should be preferred to all our lives, whatsoever in the world we might have chosen.—*Augustine.*

Verse 3.—*"Life"* is an *impure good.* It is a good which is implicated and involved with abundance of evils. There are many crosses, and troubles, and calamities, which the life of man is subject unto; which, though it have some comfort in it, yet that comfort is much troubled and mixed; yea, but now the favour of God it is good, and nothing but good. As it is said of his blessing, it adds no sorrow with it, nor has it any inconvenience in it, nor has it any evil attendant upon it.—*Thomas Horton.*

Verse 3.—*"My lips shall praise thee."* Is it possible that any man should love another and not commend him, nor speak of him? If thou hast but a hawk or a hound that thou lovest, thou wilt commend it; and can it stand with love to Christ, yet seldom or never to speak of him nor of his love, never to commend him unto others, that they may fall in love with him also? You shall see the Spouse (Cant. v. 9, 16) when she was asked, *what her beloved was above others?* she sets him out in every part of him, and concludes with this: *"he is altogether lovely:" "because thy lovingkindness* (saith *David*) *is better than life, my lips shall praise thee, and I will bless thee while I live."* Can it stand with this life of love, to be always speaking about worldly affairs, or news at the best; both week-day and Sabbath-day, in bend and at board, in good company and in bad, at home and abroad? I tell you, it will be one main reason why you desire to live, that you may make the Lord Jesus known to your children, friends, acquaintance, that so in the ages to come his name might ring, and his memorial might be of sweet odour, from generation to generation. Ps. lxxi. 18. If before thy conversion, especially, thou hast poisoned others by thy vain and corrupt speeches, after thy conversion thou wilt seek to season the hearts of others by a gracious, sweet, and wise communication of savoury and blessed speeches; what the Lord hath taught thee thou wilt talk of it unto others, for the sake of him whom thou lovest.—*Thomas Sheppard* (1605—1649), *in "The Sound Beleever."*

Verses 3—6.—David exalts *lovingkindness* as a queen above all other, even the most precious, blessings bestowed upon him, *"because thy lovingkindness is better than* [above] *life."* Around her throne he places seven members of his body and faculties of his mind, as the seven chief angels . . . who stand before the Lord, that they may praise and admire her; these are his lips, his tongue, his hands, his will, his mouth, his memory, and his intellect. For first, he extols the lovingkindness of God with his lips (verse 3): *"My lips shall praise thee."* Secondly, with his tongue (verse 4): *"Thus will I bless thee while I live."* Thirdly, with his hands: *"I will lift up my hands in thy name."* Fourthly, with his will (verse 5): *"My soul shall be satisfied as with marrow and fatness."* Fifthly, with his mouth: *"And my mouth shall praise thee with joyful lips."* Sixthly, with his memory (verse 6): *"When I remember thee upon my bed."* Seventhly and lastly, with his intellect: *"And meditate on thee in the night watches."*—*Thomas Le Blanc.*

Verse 4.—"*Thus will I bless thee.*" There are two ways. especially in which God is blest of his creatures. The one is *objectively*, by way of representation; and the other is *significatively*, by way of publication. According to the first sense, so all the creatures bless him : " The heavens declare the glory of God ; and the firmament showeth his handiwork." Psalm xix. 1. " Sun and moon, and fire and hail, and snow and vapours." Psalm cxlviii. 3, 7, 8. All these they so bless him thus. But according to the second sense, so he is blest only by angels and men, who are therefore to do it with so much the greater intension. " All thy works shall praise thee, O Lord ; and thy saints shall bless thee. They shall speak of the glory of thy kingdom, and talk of thy power," etc. Psalm cxlv. 10, 11.—*Thomas Horton.*

Verse 4.—" *I will lift up my hands.*" The practice of lifting up the hands in prayer towards heaven, the supposed residence of the object to which prayer is addressed, was anciently used both by believers, as appears from various passages in the Old Testament ; and by the heathen, agreeably to numerous instances in the classical writers. Parkhurst, considering the " hand " to be the chief organ or instrument of man's power and operations, and properly supposing the word to be thence used very extensively by the Hebrews for power, agency, dominion, assistance, and the like, regards the lifting up of men's hands in prayer, as an emblematical acknowledging of the *power*, and imploring of the *assistance*, of their respective gods. Is it not, however, the natural and unstudied gesture of earnest supplication ?—*Richard Mant.*

Verse 5.—" *My soul shall be satisfied as with marrow and fatness.*" My soul shall be satisfied as if I had received all that is intimated by the rich pieces of the peace-offering.—*Andrew A. Bonar*, on Levit. iii. 9, 10.

Verse 5.—" *My soul shall be satisfied with fatness and fatness ;*" so the Hebrew hath it ; that is, my soul shall be topful of comfort, it shall be filled up to the brim with pleasure and delight, in the remembrance and enjoyment of God upon my bed, or upon my beds, in the plural, as the Hebrew hath it. David had many a hard bed and many a hard lodging, whilst he was in his wilderness condition. It oftentimes so fell out that he had nothing but the bare ground for his bed, and the stones for his pillows, and the hedges for his curtains, and the heavens for his canopy : yet, in this condition, God was sweeter than marrow and fatness to him ; though his bed was never so hard, yet in God he had full satisfaction and content. Jer. xxxi. 14 ; Philip. iv. 9.—*Thomas Brooks.*

Verse 5.—There is that in a gracious God and in communion with him, which gives abundant satisfaction to a soul. Psalm xxxvi. 8 ; lxv. 4. And there is that in a gracious soul, which takes abundant satisfaction in God, and in communion with him.—*Matthew Henry.*

Verse 5.—Sanctified *Knowledge*, saith, There is an infinite fulness in Christ, the fulness of a fountain. *Faith* saith, This is all for me, for he is my husband ; then *Prayer* saith, If all this be thine, I will go and fetch it for thee ; and *Thankfulness* says, I will return praise to God for it (and that's better than the receiving of mercies) : " *My soul shall be satisfied as with marrow and fatness ; and my mouth shall praise thee with joyful lips.*"—*Matthew Lawrence*, in " The Use and Practice of Faith," 1657.

Verse 5.—In the words which I have chosen as the subject of discourse, the Psalmist expresses his humble expectation of having his soul feasted in the sanctuary. I intend, *first*, to show how the Lord satisfies the souls of men as with marrow and fatness ; and, *secondly*, to point out the reason which believers have to conclude that they shall be thus satisfied in the ordinances of divine worship. I. I will endeavour, then, in the first place, to show how the Lord satisfies the souls of men as with marrow and fatness. And, in general, it may be observed, that he imparts such satisfaction by condescending to hold 'communion with them. This is the feast which our Lord promises to every sinner who opens his heart to receive him : " Behold, I stand at the door and knock : if any man hear my voice, and open the door, I will come in to him, and will sup with him, and he with me." Rev. iii. 20. This was also the banquet to which the spouse of Christ was admitted, when she said, " He brought me to the banqueting house, and his banner over me was love." S. Song ii. 4. More particularly, 1. The Lord satisfies the souls of his people as with marrow and fatness, *by feasting them with the flesh and blood of Jesus Christ*. The Son of God became incarnate, shed his blood, and fulfilled all righteousness, that he might be food for our souls. " The Word was made flesh, and dwelt among us." John i. 14. And in his incarnate person he is living bread to us, bread that gives spiritual and eternal life to our souls, and effectually prevents them from perishing. . . . 2. The Lord satisfies the souls of his people as with marrow and fatness, *by showing them his glory in the face of Christ.* By this means the Psalmist David desired and expected to have his soul feasted, as we learn from the second verse of this Psalm : " To see thy power and thy glory, so as I have seen thee in the sanctuary." . . . A saving sight of the glory of God in our Immanuel must be inexpressibly comfortable ; it is a feast to the soul, and is productive of joy unspeakable and full of glory. . . . 3. The Lord satisfies the souls of his people as with marrow and fatness, *by shedding abroad his love in their hearts.* This was another way in which David expected to have his soul feasted. He had felt the sweetness of divine love, he had tasted that the Lord was gracious ; he knew by happy experience that his lovingkindness was sweeter than all the comforts of life ; and he hoped to be blessed with further experience of his love, with such experience as would warm his heart, and afford matter of a new song of praise to God : and thus be expected to be satisfied as with marrow and fatness. He says, therefore, in the third verse of this Psalm, " Because thy lovingkindness is better than life, my lips shall praise thee." . . . 4. The Lord satisfies the souls of his people as with marrow and fatness, *when he feasts them with new-covenant promises.* He hath given us exceeding great and precious promises ; promises which are filled with all the fulness of God, and which are all in Christ, yea, and amen, to the glory of God. These promises are published to us all in the gospel, that we may embrace them by faith. But, alas ! so great is the folly of men, that they put from them these words of grace, and judge themselves unworthy of everlasting life. Such folly is natural even to the people of God as well as others. . . . . But when the rock of Israel, in a day of power, speaks these promises to them, they no longer reject, but cordially receive them in Christ, and gladly feast upon them. Then his words are found, and they eat them ; and his word is the joy and rejoicing of their hearts. . . . 5. The Lord also satisfies the souls of his people, *by filling them with the Spirit.* We are famishing while we are in a state of nature, " having not the Spirit ; " for while without the Spirit, we are also without Christ. But when the Lord puts his Spirit within us, then our starving souls begin to be feasted ; for this blessed Spirit shows us the things of Christ, and applies him to us ; by which means we are enabled to eat his flesh, and drink his blood. And after the Holy Ghost is thus given, he is never taken away. . . . It is the promise of our Redeemer, that, if a man believe on him, " out of his belly shall flow rivers of living water : " and " this spake he of the Spirit, which they that believe on him should receive." John vii. 38, 39. 6. The Lord satisfies his people as with marrow and fatness, *when he revives former experiences* of his kindness. Often he gives them, so to speak, a new feast upon an old experience. . . . II. I now proceed to point out some of the reasons which believers have to conclude that their souls shall be satisfied in the ordinances of divine worship. And, 1. They may reasonably found such a conclusion upon *the divine goodness.* 2. Believers may ground an expectation of being satisfied as with marrow and fatness, on the incarnation, the humiliation, and the death of Christ. 3. The fulness laid up in Christ is also a good foundation for such a hope. 4. Believers may also conclude from the divine promise that their souls shall be satisfied as with marrow and fatness. 5. From their being blessed with the spiritual appetite. 6. Their former experience of the Lord's satisfying them, may also encourage believers to hope that he will again satisfy them, as with marrow and fatness.—*Outline of a Sermon, by John Fraser* (1745—1818).

Verse 5 :—

> Ever full, but hungry ever,
> What they have, they still desire ;
> Never suffer surfeit's loathing,
> Nor yet famine's torments dire :
> Hungering still, they eat, and eating,
> Still the sacred food require.

Peter Damiano (988—1072).

Verses 5, 6.—David had his sweetmeats and heavenly junkets in the night, when the eyes of others were closed, and saw not the charger which was sent from above for his spiritual refreshment. His solitary meditations brought him more solace and comfort than the whole creation could afford him : " *When I remember* thee upon my bed, and meditate on thee in the night watches, my soul shall be satisfied as with marrow and fatness." Communion with God in secret is a heaven upon earth. What food can compare with the hidden manna? Some persons have excellent banquets in their closets. That bread which the saints eat in secret, how pleasant is it! Ah! what stranger can imagine the joy, the melody, which even the secret tears of the saints cause! Believers find rich mines of silver and gold in solitary places; they fetch up precious jewels out of secret holes, out of the bottom of the ocean, where are no inhabitants. Naturalists observe that those fish are sweetest which lie hid. Saints have often sweet joy and refreshment in secret; they have meat to eat, which the world knoweth not of. The fig-tree, olive, and vine would not leave their sweetness, fatness, and cheerfulness, to be kings over other trees. Judges ix. 11—13. They that know what it is to enjoy God in secret, would not leave it, or lose it, to be kings or commanders over the whole world.—George Swinnock.

Verse 6.—" When I remember thee upon my bed (and), meditate on thee in the night watches." Thus the English version connects this verse with verse 5. But the division of the strophes renders the following translation preferable, which, moreover, obviates the need of supplying " and : " " Whenever I remember thee upon my bed, I meditate on thee in the night watches." The remembrance of thee on my bed so engrosses me, that I cannot draw my mind off the thought, so as to fall into the obliviousness of sleep; I often meditate on thee through the whole night watches. So Ps. cxix. 55, 148; Ps. i. 2. The Hebrew is beds; probably alluding to the fact that in his unsettled life in exile, he seldom slept for many nights in the same bed, but through fear of adversaries slept in different places. There were three night watches : the first (Lam. ii. 19); the middle (Judg. vii. 19); the third, or morning watch (Exod. xiv. 24; 1 Sam. ii. 11). In the New Testament the Roman usage of four prevails.—A. R. Fausset.

Verse 6.—"Remember—and meditate." The meditation of anything hath more sweetness in it than bare remembrance. The memory is the chest to lay up a truth, but meditation is the palate to feed upon it. The memory is like the ark in which the manna was laid up; meditation is like Israel's eating of the manna. When David began to meditate upon God, it was sweet to him as marrow. There is as much difference between a truth remembered and a truth meditated, as between a cordial in the glass and a cordial drunk down.—John Wells (1668), in Sabbath Holiness."

Verse 6.—" Upon my bed." The bed may be looked upon as a place for the remembrance of God in it, according to a threefold notion. I. As a place of choice. In the bed, of choice, rather than anywhere else, where I am left to my liberty. David when he had a mind to remember God, he would make choice of his bed for it, as most suitable and agreeable to it. In case of excessive weariness, or weakness contracted to the body from some occasion (this is often put accidentally in Scripture,) " To commune with our hearts upon our bed," etc., the occasion of it here ; it may fall out that the bed may be the fittest place for such a duty as this. Ps. iv. 4. II. As it is a place of necessity. In my bed at least, when I cannot anywhere else, as having restraints upon me. David, when (as now it was with him) he was detained from the public ordinances, whether by sickness, or any other impediment which he could not withstand, yet he would not now wholly forget God ; he would remember him even in his bed. This is another notion in which we may take it. III. As a place of indifferency; that is, there as well as anywhere besides. I will not only remember thee when I am up, when I shall make it my business to remember thee, but even in my bed too. I will take an occasion and opportunity to remember thee there. By commending myself to thee, when I lie down to rest, and acknowledging and owning of thee when I first awake.—Thomas Horton.

Verse 6.—There were " night watches " kept in the tabernacle for praising God (Ps. cxxxiv. i,), which it is probable David, when he had liberty, joined with the Levites in ; but now he could not keep place with them, he kept time with them, and wished himself among them.—Matthew Henry.

Verse 7.—"Because thou hast been." The surest way, and the nearest way, to lay hold upon God is the consideration of that which he hath done already, which was David's way here ; because, says he, this was God's way before, therefore will I look for God in this way still. The language in which God spake to man, the Hebrew, hath no present tense. They form not their verbs, as our western languages do, in the present tense, but they begin at that which is past. God carries us in his language, in his speaking, upon that which is past, upon that which he hath done already. I cannot have better security for present nor future than God's former mercies exhibited to me.—*Abraham Wright.*

Verse 7.—"*Thou hast been my help.*" From this one word—that God hath been my help—I make account that we have both these notions; first, that God hath not left me to myself, he hath come to my succour, he hath helped me ; and then, that God hath not left out myself, he hath been my help, but he hath left something for me to do with him and by his help. My security for the future in this consideration of that which is past lies not only in this, that God hath delivered me, but in this also, that he hath delivered me by way of a help, and help always presumes an endeavour and co-operation in him that is helped. God did not elect me as a helper, nor create me, nor redeem me, nor convert me, by way of helping me ; for he alone did all, and he had no use at all for me. God infuses his first grace, the first way, merely as a giver ; entirely, all himself ; but his subsequent grace as a helper ; therefore we call them auxiliant graces, helping graces, and we always receive them when we endeavour to make use of his former grace.—*John Donne.*

Verse 7.—"*My help.*" I. In *duty*. He helps his people here. There is nothing which God requires of his people, as to be done by them, but himself helps them in the doing of it. He is not like the Egyptian task-masters, which require brick and give no straw wherewithal to make it. II. In *conflict*. He assists here also. As when the Israelite and the Egyptian strove together, Moses came in and helped the Israelite (Exod. ii. 12) ; even so does God in this case with us, when we are wrestling and struggling with Satan, who is our spiritual enemy, the Lord is here nigh to help us, which may encourage us still in our resistance and opposition : we have a mighty second to stand for us, and to take up our quarrel. III. In *affliction*. God helps his people ; namely, to bear patiently those crosses which he lays upon them. He takes part with them in their sufferings, and in all their afflictions is afflicted himself, as sometimes he expresses it. He lays no more upon them than he does help them, and enable them, to endure. 1. He helps them *from*, by way of prevention. 2. He helps them *in*, by way of support. 3. He helps them *out*, by way of rescue, and redemption, and deliverance.—*Thomas Horton.*

Verse 7.—"*My help.* Thou hast been not only my helper, but my " help," for we could never have helped ourselves, nor could any creature have been helpful to us but by him.—*Matthew Henry.*

Verse 7.—"*MY help.*" There is more encouragement in the least blessing bestowed upon ourselves than in the greatest blessing bestowed upon a stranger ; and, therefore, on every account we may safely say, that a whole library of biographical books, and those relating exclusively to righteous individuals, could not so minister to the assurance of a believer as the documents which his own memory can furnish. These, then, should often engage his study, whether he be the rich or the poor. He should do just as David did. Doubtless David was well acquainted with the histories of Noah, and of Abraham, of Jacob, of Joseph, of Moses ; and the records of these eminent servants of God were records of surprising deliverances, of divine promises made good, and human wants supplied. Nevertheless, when himself in the wilderness, David did not recur to these records for encouragement. His exclamation is : "*Because thou hast been MY help, therefore in the shadow of thy wings will I rejoice.*"—*Henry Melvill.*

Verse 7.—"*Will I rejoice.*" As a bird, sheltered in the rich foliage from the heat of he sun, sings its merry notes ; so he celebrates his songs of praise from the shadow of the wings of God.—*Augustus F. Tholuck.*

Verse 8.—"*My soul followeth hard after thee.*" This is the language of a good man in his worst frames ; for when he has lost his nearness to God, he will be uneasy till he has again obtained it, and will follow after it with all his might. It is also his language in his best frames ; for when he knows and enjoys most of God, he wants to know and enjoy more. But it may especially be considered as the language of an afflicted and seeking soul, not sinking under its burden, but earnestly breathing after deliverance, and supported by the prospect of obtaining it. Hence it follows, " *Thy right hand upholdeth me.*" . . . I. I shall consider what is implied in the soul's following hard after God, and then enquire the reason of it. I. Following hard after God supposes, 1. A previous acquaintance with him. An unknown good, be it ever so desirable in itself, cannot be the object of desire. Hence, when God shines into the heart, it is to give the light of the knowledge of the glory of God in the face of Jesus Christ, as the foundation of all gracious exercises, and especially as the source of all fervent desires after him. 2. Following hard after God is expressive of ardent and intense desires. It does not consist in cold and languid wishes, but insatiable longings after communion with God and conformity to his will. 3. It implies laborious exertion. My soul followeth, it followeth *hard after thee.* Not earth nor heaven merely is the object of pursuit, but God himself. And the desires of a truly renewed soul are not sluggish and ineffectual ; they lead him to the use of all appointed means, and to the exertion of his utmost endeavours till the object be attained. 4. Perseverance in seeking. *To follow* implies this, and to follow *hard* implies it more strongly. It is as if the Psalmist had said, " Does God retire ? I will pursue. Does he withhold the blessing ? I will wrestle with him till I obtain it. He long waited to be gracious, and I will now wait till he is so." II. We are to enquire the reason why David thus followed hard after God. 1. Guilt and distress followed hard after him. 2. His enemies also followed hard after him. Satan did so, and once and again caused him to stumble and fall. 3. He had followed hard after other things to no purpose. 4. We may add the powerful attractives of divine grace.—*Condensed from Benjamin Beddome's Sermon, " The Christian's Pursuit," in " Short Discourses,"* 1809.

Verse 8.—*"My soul followeth hard after thee."* דָּבְקָה אַחֲרֶיךָ. The primary sense of דָּבַק is *agglutinavit,* to glue together ; from thence it signifies figuratively *to associate,* to adhere to, to be united with ; and particularly to be firmly united with strong affection. " Therefore shall a man leave his father and mother, בְּאִשְׁתּוֹ וְדָבַק, and cleave to his wife ; " properly, be closely united and compacted with his wife, with the most permanent affection. Gen. ii. 24. The Psalmist, therefore, means that his soul adhered to God with the warmest affection, and longed to offer up his sacrifices of praise in his sanctuary.—*Samuel Chandler.*

Verse 8.—*"My soul followeth hard after thee."* דָּבְקָה, *adhæsit, adherescit anima mea post te :* My soul cleaves after thee, as do things which hang by another ; the root is of so great frequency in Scripture, as of enquiry amongst critics ; it importeth here the posture of David's spirit, and speaketh it close to God ; and so depending upon him, as nothing could loosen it from him ; Satan's subtlety, Saul's cruelty, his own personal loss and indemnity, are not all of them of any force or dexterity, to cut asunder or untie the Gordian knot of this unity. The cleaving of David's spirit was a glueing of the Lord's spirit : a marriage of the Lord's making is altogether incapable of the devil's breaking.

It is no wonder David's words report him so much devoted to God, seeing with the same breath they speak him supported by God : " *Thy right hand upholdeth me,"* saith he.—*Alexander Pringle, in "A Stay in Trouble ; or, the Saint's Rest in the Evil Day,"* 1657.

Verse 8.—*"My soul followeth hard after thee."* The original is נַפְשִׁי אַחֲרֶיךָ. " *My soul cleaves after thee."* As if he had said, Go, lead on, my God ! Behold, I follow as near, as close, as I can ; *e vestigio ;* I would not leave any distance, but pursue thy footsteps, step by step, leaning upon thine everlasting arms, that are underneath me, and following thy manuduction.—*John Gibbon, in " The Morning Exercises,"* 1661.

Verse 8.—The *soul's* following, and following *hard* after God—what means this ? Surely it intends much more than a languid, inert inclination ; or " the desire of the slothful which killeth him, because his hands refuse to labour." It evinces an intenseness of concern that quickens and rouses the man into life and earnestness ; that draws his very soul along with it ; that reconciles him to every needful exertion and sacrifice, however trying ; and urges him to persevere, whatever difficulties or discouragements he meets with in his course. And sometimes the distance is long, and the progress up hill, and the road rough, and the weather unfriendly, and enemies would thrust us back ; and sometimes we lose sight of him, and ask those we meet : " Saw ye him whom my soul loveth ? " and when we spy him again, he seems to advance as we advance, and when we gain upon him and get nearer, he seems to look back and frown, and tell us to retire. The exercises and feelings of Christians in the divine life will enable them to explain these allusions. Who among them all has not, like the Jews, been sometimes " discouraged because of the way ? " Who has not resembled Barak's adherents—" Faint, yet

pursuing?" Who has not frequently said, "*My soul followeth hard after thee*"?
—*William Jay.*

Verses 9, 10.—If the Psalmist's divine longing was unquenched, so also was his faith; and in the latter part of the Psalm he foretells with full assurance the final overthrow of his enemies. Nor did his denunciations fail to meet with a certain accuracy of fulfilment even in the battle by which his own deliverance was effected. The armies encountered in the wood of Ephraim, across the Jordan; there was "a great slaughter that day of tweny thousand men;" "and the wood devoured more people that day than the sword devoured." Thus David's words concerning the "*lower parts of the earth*," and the "*sword*," and the "*foxes*," had not been idly spoken: the pitfalls of the forest, and the swords of the royal pursuers, and the wild beasts that had there made their lairs, all effectually did their work; and the fate of the rebel army was shared by their leader, who, caught in the thick boughs of the oak, pierced through the heart by Joab, and cut down by his attendants, received no further funeral honours than to be cast "into a great pit in the wood," and have a "very great heap of stones" laid upon him to cover him.—*Joseph Francis Thrupp, in "An Introduction to the Study and Use of the Psalms,"* 1860.

Verse 10.—"*They shall fall.*" The word is ordinarily applied to *water*. 2 Sam. xiv. 14; Lam. iii. 49. But here, by the immediate mention of the "*sword*," it is restrained to the *effusion of blood*, and being in the third person plural, in the active sense, it is after the Hebrew idiom to be interpreted in the passive sense, *they shall pour out by the hand of the sword, i.e., they shall be poured out by the sword*, the *hand* of *the sword* being no more than the edge of the sword.—*Henry Hammond.*

Verse 10.—"*They shall be a portion for foxes.*" Beasts were given to men for their food, but here men are given to beasts for a prey. A lamentable spectacle to see the vilest of all creatures ravenously feast themselves with the flesh of the noblest, and irrespectively hale and tear in pieces the casket which whilome enclosed the richest jewel in the world. Is it not against the law of nature that men should become beasts' meat; yea, the meat of such beasts as are carrion, and not man's meat? Questionless it is, yet nature giveth her consent to this kind of punishment of unnatural crimes. For it is consonant to reason, that the law of nature should be broken in their punishment who brake it in their sin; that they who devoured men like beasts should be devoured of beasts like men, that they who with their hands offered unnatural violence to their sovereign should suffer the like by the claws and teeth of wild beasts, their slaves; that they who bear a fox in their breast in their life, should be entombed in the belly of a fox at their death.

St. Austin, expounding this whole prophecy of Christ, yieldeth a special reason of this judgment of God by which the Jews were condemned to foxes. The Jews, saith he, therefore killed Christ that they might not lose their country; but, indeed, they therefore lost their country because they killed Christ; because they refused the Lamb and chose Herod the fox before him, therefore by the just retribution of the Almighty, they were allotted to the foxes for their portion. Notwithstanding this allusion of St. Austin to foxes in special, Jansenius and other expositors extend this grant in my text to all wild beasts and fowls, which are, as it were, impatient with the fox, and have full power and liberty given them to seize upon the corpses of traitors to God and their country; but foxes bear the name because they abound in those parts where was such store of them, that Samson in a short time, with a wet finger, caught three hundred.—*Daniel Featley, D.D., in "Clavis Mystica,"* 1636.

Verse 10.—"*They shall be a portion for foxes.*" If the body of a human being were to be left on the ground, the *jackals* would certainly leave but little traces of it; and in the olden times of warfare, they must have held high revelry in the battle-fields after the armies had retired. It is to this propensity of the *jackal* that David refers—himself a man of war, who had fought on many a battle-field, and must have seen the carcasses of the slain mangled by these nocturnal prowlers.—*J. G. Wood.*

Verse 10.—What a doom is that which David pronounces upon those who seek the soul of the righteous to destroy it: "*They shall be a portion for foxes;*" by which *jackals* are meant, as I suppose. These sinister, guilty, woebegone brutes, when pressed with hunger, gather in gangs among the graves, and yell in rage, and fight like fiends over their midnight orgies ; but on the battle-field is their great carnival.　Oh ! let me never even dream that any one dear to me has *fallen by the sword*, and lies there to be torn, and gnawed at, and dragged about by these hideous howlers.—*W. M. Thomson, D.D., in " The Land and the Book," 1861.*

Verse 11.—*"Every one that sweareth by him,"* i.e., to David, that comes into his interest, and takes an oath of allegiance to him, shall glory in his success.　Or, *" that swears by him,"* i.e., by the blessed name of God, and not by any idol. Deut. vi. 15.　And then it means all good people that make a sincere and open profession of God's name : they shall glory in God ; they shall glory in David's advancement : " They that fear thee will be glad when they see me."　They that heartily espouse the cause of Christ, shall glory in its victory at last.　" If we suffer with him, we shall reign with him."—*Matthew Henry.*

HINTS TO PREACHERS.

Verse 1 (*first clause*).—While the Atheist says, " No God," and the heathen worship " gods many," the true believer says, " O God, thou art my God."　He is so, 1. By choice.　II. By covenant.　III. By confession.

Verse 1 (*second clause*).—Seeking God *" early."*　1. Early in respect of *life*. II. Early in respect of *diligence*.　III. Early in respect of *fervour*.　IV. Early in respect of *times* or *continuance.—Alexander Shanks.*

Verse 1 (*second clause*).—*Earnest seeking.*　That which is longed for will be eagerly sought.　1. The soul is *resolute.*　" I *will* seek."　2. The soul is *reasonable.* " I will *seek*."　3. The soul is *ready.*　" *Early* will I."　4. The soul is *persevering.* Let this be the resolution and action of both saved and unsaved.—*G. J. K.*

Verse 3.—I. *Love's resolution.*　" My lips shall praise thee."　1. *To praise.* This is congenial to the renewed nature.　It delights not in grumbling, reproaching, or scolding.　Praise expresses appreciation, gratitude, happiness, affection.　2. *To praise God.*　3. *To praise God practically.*　" *My lips.*"　By speaking well *to* him ; by speaking well *of* him ; of his wisdom, justice, love, grace, etc.　4. *To praise God continually.*　" As long as I live," etc.　II. *Love's reason.*　" Because thy lovingkindness."　Love must praise God because—1. It owes its existence to him. " We love him because he first loved us."　2. Because it is fostered by him.　" The love of God is shed abroad," etc.　3. Because the expressions of his love demand praise.　" Kindness " to needy, helpless, lost.　" Lovingkindness," not wounding our natures.　" Better than life ; " either the principle, pleasures, or pursuits of life.—*G. J. K.*

Verse 3.—" *Thy lovingkindness is better than life.*"　I. *Love enjoyed with life.* II. *Love compared with life.*　III. *Love preferred to life.—G. J. K.*

Verses 5, 6.—I. *The empty vessel filled.*　How ?　By meditation.　With what ? God's goodness as marrow and fatness.　To what extent ?　Satisfaction　II. *The full vessel running over.*　" My mouth shall praise thee with joyful lips."　The soul overflows with praise—joyful praise.—*G. J. K.*

Verses 5, 6.—Describe the nature of, and show the intimate connection between, (1) the believer's employments and (2) his enjoyments.—*J. S. Bruce.*

Verse 6.—I. Important duties too much neglected : " Remembering God," " Meditating on him."　II. Favourable seasons within the reach of all : " Upon my bed ; " " In the night watches."—*J. S. B.*

Verse 7.—A well-founded resolve.　I. Upon what based.　II. How expressed.— *J. S. B.*

Verse 8.—I. *The soul's pursuit after God.*　It follows, 1. In desire.　2. In action. 3. Earnestly.　4. Quickly.　5. Closely.　II. *The soul's support.*　" *Thy* right hand upholdeth me," the arm of strength.　In doing and bearing.—*G. J. K.*

Verse 8.—" A mighty hunter before the Lord."　I. The object of pursuit :

' Thee." II. The manner of pursuit : " Hard after." III. The dangers encountered.—*J. S. B.*

Verse 8 (*second clause*).—God's right hand upholds his people three ways. I. As to *sin ;* lest they should fall by it. II. As to *suffering ;* lest they should sink under it. III. As to *duty ;* lest they should decline from it.—*W. Jay.*

Verses 9, 10.—I. The enemies of the Christian. Evil spirits, evil men, evil habits, etc., etc. II. Their intent. To destroy the soul. III. Their fall. Certain, shameful, destructive. IV. Their future. Hell is reserved for them.—*G. J. K.*

Verse 11.—Three topics. I. Royal rejoicing. II. Lawful swearing. III. Evil speaking.

PSALM LXIV.

TITLE.—To the chief Musician. *The leader of the choir, for the time-being, is charged with this song. It were well if the chief musicians of all our congregations estimated their duty at its due solemnity, for it is no mean thing to be called to lead the sacred song of God's people, and the responsibility is by no means light.*

A Psalm of David.—*His life was one of conflict, and very seldom does he finish a Psalm without mentioning his enemies; in this instance his thoughts are wholly occupied with prayer against them.*

DIVISION.—*From 1—6 he describes the cruelty and craftiness of his foes, and from 7—10 he prophesies their overthrow.*

EXPOSITION.

HEAR my voice, O God, in my prayer: preserve my life from fear of the enemy.

2 Hide me from the secret counsel of the wicked; from the insurrection of the workers of iniquity:

3 Who whet their tongue like a sword, *and* bend *their bows to shoot* their arrows, *even* bitter words:

4 That they may shoot in secret at the perfect: suddenly do they shoot at him, and fear not.

5 They encourage themselves *in* an evil matter: they commune of laying snares privily; they say, Who shall see them?

6 They search out iniquities; they accomplish a diligent search: both the inward *thought* of every one *of them*, and the heart, *is* deep.

1. *"Hear my voice, O God, in my prayer."* It often helps devotion if we are able to use the voice and speak audibly; but even mental prayer has a voice with God which he will hear. We do not read that Moses had spoken with his lips at the Red Sea, and yet the Lord said to him, " Why criest thou unto me ? " Prayers which are unheard on earth may be among the best heard in heaven. It is our duty to note how constantly David turns to prayer; it is his battleaxe and weapon of war: he uses it under every pressure, whether of inward sin or outward wrath, foreign invasion or domestic rebellion. We shall act wisely if we make prayer to God our first and best trusted resource in every hour of need. *" Preserve my life from fear of the enemy."* From harm and dread of harm protect me; or it may be read as an expression of his assurance that it would be so; " from fear of the foe thou wilt preserve me." With all our sacrifices of prayer we should offer the salt of faith.

2. *"Hide me from the secret counsel of the wicked."* From their hidden snares hide me. Circumvent their counsels; let their secrets be met by thy secret providence, their counsels of malice by thy counsels of love. *" From the insurrection of the workers of iniquity."* When their secret counsels break forth into clamorous tumults, be thou still my preserver. When they think evil, let thy divine thoughts defeat them; and when they do evil, let thy powerful justice overthrow them: in both cases, let me be out of reach of their cruel hand, and even out of sight of their evil eye. It is a good thing to conquer malicious foes, but a better thing still to be screened from all conflict with them, by being hidden from the strife. The Lord knows how to give his people peace, and when he wills to make quiet, he is more than a match for all disturbers, and can defeat alike their deep-laid plots and their overt hostilities.

3. *"Who whet their tongue like a sword."* Slander has ever been the master

weapon of the good man's enemies, and great is the care of the malicious to use it effectively. As warriors grind their swords, to give them an edge which will cut deep and wound desperately, so do the unscrupulous invent falsehoods which shall be calculated to inflict pain, to stab the reputation, to kill the honour of the righteous. What is there which an evil tongue will not say? What misery will it not labour to inflict? *"And bend their bows to shoot their arrows, even bitter words."* Far off they dart their calumnies, as archers shoot their poisoned arrows. They studiously and with force prepare their speech as bended bows, and then with cool, deliberate aim, they let fly the shaft which they have dipped in bitterness. To sting, to inflict anguish, to destroy, is their one design. Insult, sarcasm, taunting defiance, nicknaming, all these were practised among Orientals as a kind of art; and if in these Western regions, with more refined manners, we are less addicted to the use of rough abuse, it is yet to be feared that the less apparent venom of the tongue inflicts none the less poignant pain. However, in all cases, let us fly to the Lord for help. David had but the one resource of prayer against the twofold weapons of the wicked, for defence against sword or arrow he used the one defence of faith in God.

4. *"That they may shoot in secret at the perfect."* They lie in ambush, with bows ready bent to aim a coward's shaft at the upright man. Sincere and upright conduct will not secure us from the assaults of slander. The devil shot at our Lord himself, and we may rest assured he has a fiery dart in reserve for us; He was absolutely perfect, we are only so in a relative sense, hence in us there is fuel for fiery darts to kindle on. Observe the meanness of malicious men; they will not accept fair combat, they shun the open field, and skulk in the bushes, lying in ambush against those who are not so acquainted with deceit as to suspect their treachery, and are too manly to imitate their despicable modes of warfare. *"Suddenly do they shoot at him, and fear not."* To secrecy they add suddenness. They give their unsuspecting victim no chance of defending himself; they pounce on him like a wild beast leaping on its prey. They lay their plans so warily that they fear no detection. We have seen in daily life the arrow of calumny wounding its victim sorely; and yet we have not been able to discover the quarter from which the weapon was shot, nor to detect the hand which forged the arrowhead, or tinged it with the poison. Is it possible for justice to invent a punishment sufficiently severe to meet the case of the dastard who defiles my good name, and remains himself in concealment? An open liar is an angel compared with this demon. Vipers and cobras are harmless and amiable creatures compared with such a reptile. The devil himself might blush at being the father so so base an offspring.

5. *"They encourage themselves in an evil matter."* Good men are frequently discouraged, and not unfrequently discourage one another, but the children of darkness are wise in their generation and keep their spirits up, and each one has a cheering word to say to his fellow villain. Anything by which they can strengthen each other's hands in their one common design they resort to; their hearts are thoroughly in their black work. *"They commune of laying snares privily."* Laying their heads together they count and recount their various devices, so as to come at some new and masterly device. They know the benefit of co-operation, and are not sparing in it they pour their experience into one common fund, they teach each other fresh methods. *"They say, Who shall see them?"* So sedulously do they mask their attacks, that they defy discovery; their pitfalls are too well hidden, and themselves too carefully concealed to be found out. So they think, but they forget the all-seeing eye, and the all-discovering hand, which are ever hard by them. Great plots are usually laid bare. As in the Gunpowder Plot, there is usually a breakdown somewhere or other; among the conspirators themselves truth finds an ally, or the stones of the field cry out against them. Let no christian be in bondage through fear of deep-laid Jesuitical schemes for surely there is no enchantment against Jacob, nor divination against Israel; the toils of the net are broken, the arrows of the bow are snapped, the devices of the wicked are foiled. Therefore, fear not, ye tremblers; for the Lord is at your right hand, and ye shall not be hurt of the enemy.

6. *"They search out iniquities."* Diligently they consider, invent, devise, and seek for wicked plans to wreak their malice. These are no common villains, but explorers in iniquity, inventors and concoctors of evil. Sad indeed it is that to ruin a good man the evil-disposed will often show as much avidity as if they were searching after treasure. The Inquisition could display instruments of torture.

revealing as much skill as the machinery of our modern exhibitions. The deep places of history, manifesting most the skill of the human mind, are those in which revenge has arranged diplomacy, and used intrigue to compass its diabolical purposes. *"They accomplish a diligent search."* Their design is perfected, consummated, and brought into working order. They cry "Eureka;" they have sought and found the sure method of vengeance. Exquisite are the refinements of malice! hell's craft furnishes inspiration to the *artistes* who fashion deceit. Earth and the places under it are ransacked for the *materiel* of war, and profound skill turns all to account. *"Both the inward thought of every one of them, and the heart, is deep."* No superficial wit is theirs; but sagacity, sharpened by practice and keen hatred. Wicked men have frequently the craft to hasten slowly, to please in order to ruin, to flatter that ere long they may devour, to bow the knee that they may ultimately crush beneath their foot. He who deals with the serpent's seed has good need of the wisdom which is from above: the generation of vipers twist and turn, wind and wriggle, yet evermore they are set upon their purpose, and go the nearest way to it when they wander round about. Alas! how dangerous is the believer's condition, and how readily may he be overcome if left to himself. This is the complaint of reason and the moan of unbelief. When faith comes in, we see that even in all this the saints are still secure, for they are all in the hands of God.

7 But God shall shoot at them *with* an arrow; suddenly shall they be wounded.

8 So they shall make their own tongue to fall upon themselves: all that see them shall flee away.

9 And all men shall fear, and shall declare the work of God; for they shall wisely consider of his doing.

10 The righteous shall be glad in the LORD, and shall trust in him; and all the upright in heart shall glory.

7. *"But God shall shoot at them with an arrow."* They shoot, and shall be shot. A greater archer than they are shall take sure aim at their hearts. One of his arrows shall be enough, for he never misses his aim. The Lord turns the tables on his adversaries, and defeats them at their own weapons. *"Suddenly shall they be wounded."* They were looking to surprise the saint, but, lo! they are taken at unawares themselves; they desired to inflict deadly wounds, and are smitten themselves with wounds which none can heal. While they were bending their bows, the great Lord had prepared his bow already, and he let slip the shaft when least they looked for such an unsparing messenger of justice. "Vengeance is mine; I will repay, saith the Lord." The righteous need not learn the arts of self-defence or of attack, their avengement is in better hands than their own.

8. *"So they shall make their own tongue to fall upon themselves."* Their slander shall recoil. Their curses shall come home to roost. Their tongue shall cut their throats. It was both sword, and bow and arrow; it shall be turned against them, and bring home to them full punishment. *"All that see them shall flee away."* Afraid, both of them and their overthrow, their former friends shall give them wide space, lest they perish with them. Who cares to go near to Herod when the worms are eating him? or to be in the same chariot with Pharaoh when the waves roar round him? Those who crowded around a powerful persecutor, and cringed at his feet, are among the first to desert him in the day of wrath. Woe unto you, ye liars! Who will desire fellowship with you in your seething lake of fire?

9. *"And all men shall fear."* They shall be filled with awe by the just judgments of God, as the Canaanites were by the overthrow of Pharaoh at the Red Sea. Those who might have been bold in sin shall be made to tremble and to stand in awe of the righteous Judge. *"And shall declare the work of God."* It shall become the subject of general conversation. So strange, so pointed, so terrible shall be the Lord's overthrow of the malicious, that it shall be spoken of in all companies. They sinned secretly, but their punishment shall be wrought before the face of the sun. *"For they shall wisely consider of his doing."* The judgments of God are frequently so clear and manifest that men cannot mis-read them, and if they have any thought at all, they must extract the true teaching from them. Some of the divine judgments are a great deep, but in the case of malicious persecutors the matter is plain enough, and the most illiterate can understand.

10. *"The righteous shall be glad in the Lord."* Admiring his justice and fully acquiescing in its displays, they shall also rejoice at the rescue of injured innocence yet, their joy shall not be selfish or sensual, but altogether in reference to the Lord. *"And shall trust in him."* Their observation of providence shall increase their faith ; since he who fulfils his threatenings will not forget his promises. *" And all the upright in heart shall glory."* The victory of the oppressed shall be the victory of all upright men ; the whole host of the elect shall rejoice in the triumph of virtue. While strangers fear, the children are glad in view of their Father's power and justice. That which alarms the evil, cheers the good. Lord God of mercy, grant to us to be preserved from all our enemies, and saved in thy Son with an everlasting salvation.

EXPLANATORY NOTES AND QUAINT SAYINGS.

Whole Psalm.—This Psalm is applied by R. Obadiah to Haman and Moredecai. The enemy is Haman, the perfect man shot at is Mordecai ; about whom Haman communed with his friends to lay snares for him, and search diligently for occasions against him and his people, which issued in his own destruction. The ancient Midrash of the Jews applies it to Daniel, when cast into the den of lions ; and Jarchi supposes that David, by a spirit of prophecy, foresaw it, and prayed for him who was of his seed ; and that everything in the Psalm beautifully falls in with that account. Daniel is the perfect man aimed at ; the enemy are the princes of Darius's court, who consulted against him, communed of laying snares for him, and gained their point, which proved their own ruin. But the Psalm literally belongs to David, by whom it was composed.—*John Gill.*

Whole Psalm.—A cry of God's elect, when persecuted for righteousness' sake, to their Deliverer and sure Avenger. The general principle stated is very clear. The Psalm will adjust itself, as an experimental utterance, to the lips of Christian faith whenever brought into contact with the evil forces of the prince of this world, so as to suffer affliction for the gospel's sake ; for it expresses the condition and the hope of one actually imperilled for the truth. How aptly a portion of this Psalm applies to the suffering Truth Himself in the days of his affliction, when, pierced in his spirit by lying words, he endured the contradiction of sinners against himself, needs not be pointed out.—*Arthur Pridham, in " Notes and Reflections on the Psalms,"* 1869.

Verse 1.—*"Preserve my life."* Hebrew, *lives ;* so called for the many faculties, operations, revolutions, and commodities of life.—*John Trapp.*

Verse 3.—*"Who whet their tongue,"* etc. The verb means, says Parkhurst, " to whet, sharpen," which is performed by *reiterated* motion or friction ; and by a beautiful metaphor it is applied to a wicked tongue. It has, however, been rendered, *" vibrate,"* as it is certain a serpent does his tongue.—*Richard Mant.*

Verse 3.—The ingenuity of man has been wonderfully tasked and exercised in two things, inventing destructive weapons of war, and devising various methods of ruining men by wicked words. The list of the former is found in military writings. But the various forms of evil speaking can hardly be catalogued. Evil speakers have arrows, sharp, barbed, dipped in poison. They have " swords, flaming, swords, two-edged swords, drawn swords, drawn in anger, with which they cut, and wound, and kill the good name of their neighbour." Sins of the tongue are commonly very cruel. When slander is secret, as it commonly is, you cannot defend yourself from its assaults. Its canons are infernal. One of them is, " If a lie will do better than the truth, tell a lie." Another is, " Heap on reproach ; some of it will stick."— *William S. Plumer.*

Verses 3, 4.—We saw in the Museum at Venice an instrument with which one of the old Italian tyrants was accustomed to shoot poisoned needles at the objects of his wanton malignity. We thought of gossips, backbiters, and secret slanderers, and wished that their mischievous devices might come to a speedy end. Their weapons of inuendo, shrug, and whisper, appear to be as insignificant as needles ;

but the venom which they instil is deadly to many a reputation.—*C. H. Spurgeon*, in " *Feathers for Arrows ; or, Illustrations for Preachers and Teachers.*"

Verses 3, 4.—David, upon sad experience, compareth a wicked, reviling tongue to three fatal weapons—a *razor*, a *sword*, and an *arrow*. To a *razor*, such a one as will take off every little hair : so a reviling tongue will not only take advantage of every gross sin committed by others, but those peccadilloes, the least infirmities which others better qualified cannot so much as discern ; secondly, to a *sword* that wounds : so the tongues of reproaching men cut deeply into the credits and reputations of their brethren, but a sword doth mischief only near hand, not afar off ; and, therefore, it is in the third place compared to an *arrow*, that can hit at a distance : and so revilers do not ill offices to those only in the parish or town where they live, but to others far remote. How much, then, doth it concern every man to walk circumspectly ; to give no just cause of reproach, not to make himself a scorn to the fools of the world ; but, if they will reproach (as certainly they will), let it be for forwardness in God's ways, and not for sin, that so the reproach may fall upon their own heads, and their scandalous language into their own throats.— *Jeremiah Burroughs.*

Verses 3, 7, 8.—The most mischievous weapons of the wicked are *words*, " even bitter words ; " but *the Word* is the chief weapon of the Holy Spirit : and as with this sword the great Captain foiled the tempter in the wilderness, so may we vanquish " the workers of iniquity " with the true Jerusalem blade.—*J. L. K.*

Verse 4.—"*That they may shoot in secret.*" The wicked are said to shoot their arrows *in secret* at the perfect ; and then " they say, Who shall see them ? " verse 5. Thus Satan lets fly a temptation so secretly, that he is hardly suspected in the thing. Sometimes he useth a wife's tongue to do his errand ; another while he gets behind the back of a husband, friend, servant, etc., and is not seen all the while he is doing his work. Who would have thought to have found a devil in Peter, tempting his Master, or suspected that Abraham should be his instrument to betray his beloved wife into the hands of a sin ? yet it was so. Nay, sometimes he is so secret, that he borrows God's bow to shoot his arrows from, and the poor Christian is abused, thinking it is God chides and is angry, when it is the devil tempts him to think so, and only counterfeits God's voice.—*William Gurnall.*

Verse 6.—" *They search out iniquities,*" etc. It is a sign that malice boils up to a great height in men's hearts, when they are so active to find matter against their neighbours. Love would rather not see or hear of others' failings ; or if it doth and must, busieth itself in healing and reforming them to the utmost of its power.— *John Milward* (—1684), *in " Morning Exercises.*"

Verse 7.—"*With an arrow suddenly.*" As was Ahab, and the rich fool (Luke xii.) : while he sat pruning himself like a bird on a bough, death fetched him off suddenly by his shaft, shot at him, and down he came tumbling. See 1 Thess. v. 3.— *John Trapp.*

Verse 8 (first clause).—

> In these cases,
> We still have judgment here, that we but teach
> Bloody instructions, which, being taught, return
> To plague the inventor : This even-handed justice
> Commends the ingredients of our poison'd chalice
> To our own lips.

William Shakspere.

Verse 8.—"*Their own tongue to fall upon themselves.*" That is, their own words shall be brought as a testimony against them, and condemn them. " The tongue is a little member " (saith the apostle James, ch. iii. 5), and therefore a light member ; yet it falls heavy, as heavy as lead. A man were better have his house fall upon him, than that, in this sense, his tongue should fall upon him. Some have been pressed to death because they would not speak, but stood mute before the judge ; but more have been pressed to death by their sinful freedom, or rather licentiousness in speaking ; this hath brought them to judgment, and cast them in judgment. . . . A strange thing that the fall of a man's tongue should oppress his body and whole estate ; yet so it is, the weight of a man's tongue falling upon him crushes him to powder.—*Joseph Caryl.*

Verse 8.—*"Their own tongue to fall upon themselves."*　The arrows of idle words, though shot out of sight, and possibly quite forgotten, will hereafter drop down upon the heads of such as drew the bow.　Words are but wind, is the common saying, but they are such wind as will either blow the soul to its haven of rest, if holy, wholesome, savoury, spiritual, and tending to edification, or else sink it into the Dead Sea, and bottomless gulf of eternal misery, if idle, prophane, frothy, and unprofitable.—*Edward Reyner* (1600—1670), *in " Rules for the Government of the Tongue."*

Verse 10.—*" The righteous shall be glad in the Lord, and shall trust in him."*　That is, if they have failed in their trust heretofore, and not given God honour by confiding in him, yet these wonderful works of God (of which he speaks in the Psalm) work this hope.—*Joseph Caryl.*

Verse 10.—*"All the upright in heart."*　The word of this text, *jashar*, signifies *rectitudinem*, and *planitiem*, it signifies a direct way ; for the devil's way was circular, compassing the earth ; but the angel's way to heaven upon Jacob's ladder was a straight, a direct way.　And then it signifies, as a direct and straight, so a plain, a smooth, an even way, a way that hath been beaten into a path before, a way that the fathers and the church have walked in before, and not a discovery made by our curiosity, or our confidence, in venturing from ourselves, or embracing from others, new doctrines and opinions.　The persons, then, whom God proposes to be partakers of his retributions, are first, *recti* (that is, both direct men, and plain men), and then, *recti corde*, this qualification, this straightness and smoothness must be in the heart ; all the upright in heart shall have it.　Upon this earth, a man cannot possibly make one step in a straight and a direct line.　The earth itself being round, every step we make upon it must necessarily be a segment, an arc of a circle.　But yet, though no piece of a circle be a straight line, yet if we take any piece, nay, if we take the whole circle, there is no corner, no angle in any place, in any entire circle.　A perfect rectitude we cannot have in any way in this world ; in every calling there are some inevitable temptations.　But, though we cannot make up one circle of a straight line (that is impossible to human frailty), yet we may pass on without angles and corners, that is, without disguises in our religion, and without the love of craft and falsehood, and circumvention, in our civil actions. A compass is a necessary thing in a ship, and the help of that compass brings the ship home safe, and yet that compass hath some variations, it doth not look directly north ; neither is that star which we call the north-pole, or by which we know the north-pole, the very pole itself ; but we call it so, and we make our uses of it, and our conclusions by it, as if it were so, because it is the nearest star to that pole. He that comes as near uprightness as infirmities admit, is an upright man, though he have some obliquities.—*John Donne.*

Verse 10.—*"All the uprigh in heart shall glory."*　The Psalm began in the first person singular, " Hear my voice, O God," but it ends by comprehending all the righteous.　He who is most anxious about his own salvation will be found to be the man of the truest and widest love to others ; while, he who talks most of unselfishness in religion is generally the most selfish.　We cannot take a more efficient method for benefiting others than by being earnestly prayerful for ourselves that we may be preserved from sin.　Our example will in itself be useful, and our godliness, by putting power into testimony, will increase the value of every rebuke, exhortation, or encouragement we may utter.　Our sin is or will be the church's sorrow, and the way to make all the upright rejoice is to be upright ourselves.—*C.H. S.*

Verse 10.—*"Shall glory."*　This retribution is expressed in the original in the word *halal ;* and *halal*, to those translators that made up our Book of Common Prayer, presented the signification of gladness, for so it is there : *"They shall be glad."*　So it did to the translators that came after, for there it is, *"They shall rejoice ; "* and to our last translators it seemed to signify glory, *"They shall glory,"* say they.　But the first translation of all into our language (which was long before any of these three), calls it *praise*, and puts it into the passive : *" All men of rightful heart shall be praised."*　And so truly *jithhalelu*, in the original, bears it, nay, requires it ; which is not of praise which they shall give to God, but of a praise that they shall receive for having served God with an upright heart ; not that they shall praise God in doing so, but that godly men shall praise them for having done so.　All this will grow naturally out of the root ; for the root of this word is *lucere, splendere*, to shine out in the eyes of men, and to create in them a holy and a reverential admiration; as it was John Baptist's praise, that he was "*A burning and a shining lamp.*" Properly it is, by a good and a holy exemplary life, to occasion others to set a right value upon holiness, and to give a due respect for holy men. . . . "*Shall glory.*" It is so far from diminishing this glory, as that it exalts our consolation that God places this retribution in the future; if they do not yet, certainly they *shall* glory, and if they do now, that glory shall not go out, still they shall, they shall for ever glory.—*John Donne.*

HINTS TO PREACHERS.

Verse 1.—I. *The preservation of life desired.* 1. The desire expressed. 2. Qualified—from violent death, from fear of, etc. II. *The preservation of life prayed for.* 1. For self-improvement. 2. For usefulness. 3. For the divine glory.—*G. R.*

Verse 2 (first clause).—Applied to Satan. I. *The danger considered.* 1. The enemy, wicked, mighty, malicious, experienced. 2. His counsel. He tempts cunningly, and with deliberation. 3. The secrecy of it. He may be exciting others against me, or sowing evil in myself. II. *The deliverance implored.* "Hide me." 1. Keep me from being tempted. 2. Keep me from evil when tempted. 3. Bring me out of it all unharmed. 4. Meanwhile, let me be in thy secret place. III. *The consolation of faith.* 1. God does preserve praying ones. 2. Our enemy is *his* enemy. 3. He has preserved us. 4. We are his own. 5. His honour is involved.

Verse 3.—"*Bitter words.*" An excellent topic in reference both to the sinner and to professed saints.

Verse 3.—*The whetting of the tongue.* Fresh faults discovered, evil motives imputed, exaggerations invented, lies forged, inuendoes suggested, old slanders furbished, and ancient hatreds rekindled.

Verse 5.—The mutual encouragements of sinners a rebuke to professors who dishearten each other.

Verse 6 (two first clauses).—The fault-hunter; his motive, his character, his pretences, and his punishment.

Verse 9.—I. *The subject for consideration*—Judgments upon the wicked. 1. As judgments. 2. As judgments from God—that work of God—his doing. II. *The consideration of the subject.* 1. They are to be considered by others. 1. They are to be considered wisely. III. *The effect of this consideration.* 1. Fear of God. 2. Praise to God; shall declare, etc.—*G. R.*

Verse 10.—I. *The persons.* 1. What they are, in distinction from others; the righteous; the justified. 2. What they are in themselves; upright in heart; not perfect, but sincere. II. *Their privilege.* 1. Amidst all their persecutions to joy in God. 2. Amidst all their dangers to trust in God.—*G. R.*

Verses 9, 10.—I. An act of God; something of his doing. II. Its effect upon men in general: "*All men shall fear, and shall declare,*" etc. III. A special duty resulting from it, incumbent on good men: "*The righteous,*" etc.—*H. Dove.*

PSALM LXV.

TITLE.—*This title is very similar to many we have before studied.* To the Chief Musician. *It is consigned to the care of the usual overseer of song. When a man does his work well, there is no use in calling in others for novelty's sake.* A Psalm and Song of David. *The Hebrew calls it a* Shur *and* Mizmor, *a combination of psalm and song, which may be best described by the term, "A Lyrical Poem." In this case the psalm may be said or sung, and be equally suitable. We have had two such Psalms before, Psalms XXX. and XLVIII., and we have now the first of a little series of four following each other. It was meet that Psalms of pleading and longing should be followed by hymns of praise.*

SUBJECT AND DIVISIONS.—*David sings of the glory of God in his church, and in the fields of nature : here is the song both of grace and providence. It may be that he intended hereby to commemorate a remarkably plentiful harvest, or to compose a harvest hymn for all ages. It appears to have been written after a violent rebellion had been quelled, verse 7, and foreign enemies had been subdued by signal victory, verse 8. It is one of the most delightful hymns in any language.*

We shall view in the first four verses the way of approach to God, then from 5 to 8 we shall see the Lord in answer to prayer performing wonders for which he is praised, and then from 9—13 we shall sing the special harvest-song.

EXPOSITION.

PRAISE waiteth for thee, O God, in Sion : and unto thee shall the vow be performed.

2 O thou that hearest prayer, unto thee shall all flesh come.

3 Iniquities prevail against me : *as for* our transgressions, thou shalt purge them away.

4 Blessed *is the man whom* thou choosest, and causest to approach *unto thee, that* he may dwell in thy courts : we shall be satisfied with the goodness of thy house, *even* of thy holy temple.

1. *"Praise waiteth for thee, O God, in Sion."* Though Babylon adores Antichrist, Zion remains faithful to her King ; to him, and to him only, she brings her perpetual oblation of worship. Those who have seen in Zion the blood of sprinkling, and know themselves to belong to the church of the firstborn, can never think of her without presenting humble praise to Zion's God ; his mercies are too numerous and precious to be forgotten. The praises of the saints wait for a signal from the divine Lord, and when he shows his face they burst forth at once. Like a company of musicians gathered to welcome and honour a prince, who wait till he makes his appearance, so do we reserve our best praises till the Lord reveals himself in the assembly of his saints ; and, indeed, till he shall descend from heaven in the day of his appearing. Praise also waits like a servant or courtier in the royal halls— gratitude is humble and obedient. Praise attends the Lord's pleasure, and continues to bless him, whether he shows tokens of present favour or no ; she is not soon wearied, but all through the night she sings on in sure hope that the morning cometh. We shall continue to wait on, tuning our harps, amid the tears of earth ; but O what harmonies will those be which we will pour forth, when the home-bringing is come, and the King shall appear in his glory. The passage may be rendered "praise is silent for thee ; " it is calm, peaceful, and ready to adore thee in quietness. Or, it may mean, our praise is but silence compared with thy deservings, O God. Or, in solemn silence we worship thee, because our praise cannot be uttered ; accept, therefore, our silence as praise. Or, we are so engrossed in thy praise, that to all other things we are dumb ; we have no tongue for anything but thee. Perhaps the poet best expressed the thought of the Psalmist when he said—

> "A sacred reverence checks our songs,
> And praise sits silent on our tongues."

Certainly, when the soul is most filled with adoring awe, she is least content with her own expressions, and feels most deeply how inadequate are all mortal songs to proclaim the divine goodness. A church, bowed into silent adoration by a profound sense of divine mercy, would certainly offer more real praise than the sweetest voices aided by pipes and strings ; yet, vocal music is not to be neglected, for this sacred hymn was meant to be sung. It is well before singing to have the soul placed in a waiting attitude, and to be humbly conscious that our best praise is but silence compared with Jehovah's glory.

"*And unto thee shall the vow be performed.*" Perhaps a special vow made during a season of drought and political danger. Nations and churches must be honest and prompt in redeeming their promises to the Lord, who cannot be mocked with impunity. So, too, must individuals. We are not to forget our vows, or to redeem them to be seen of men—*unto God* alone must they be performed, with a single eye to his acceptance. Believers are all under covenant, which they made at conversion, and have renewed upon being baptised, joining the church, and coming to the table, and some of them are under special pledges which they entered into under peculiar circumstances : these are to be piously and punctually fulfilled. We ought to be very deliberate in promising, and very punctilious in performing. A vow unkept will burn the conscience like a hot iron. Vows of service, of donation, of praise, or whatever they may be, are no trifles ; and in the day of grateful praise they should, without fail, be fulfilled to the utmost of our power.

2. "*O thou that hearest prayer.*" This is thy name, thy nature, thy glory. God not only has heard, but is now hearing prayer, and always must hear prayer, since he is an immutable being, and never changes in his attributes. What a delightful title for the God and Father of our Lord Jesus Christ ! Every right and sincere prayer is as surely heard as it is offered. Here the Psalmist brings in the personal pronoun "*thou*," and we beg the reader to notice how often "thou," "thee," and "thy," occur in this hymn ; David evidently believed in a personal God, and did not adore a mere idea or abstraction. "*Unto thee shall all flesh come.*" This shall encourage men of all nations to become suppliants to the one and only God, who proves his Deity by answering those who seek his face. Flesh they are, and therefore weak ; frail and sinful, they need to pray ; and thou art such a God as they need, for thou art touched with compassion, and dost condescend to hear the cries of poor flesh and blood. Many come to thee now in humble faith, and are filled with good, but more shall be drawn to thee by the attractiveness of thy love, and at length the whole earth shall bow at thy feet. To come to God is the life of true religion ; we come weeping in conversion, hoping in supplication, rejoicing in praise, and delighting in service. False gods must in due time lose their deluded votaries, for man when enlightened will not be longer befooled ; but each one who tries the true God is encouraged by his own success to persuade others also, and so the kingdom of God comes to men, and men come to it.

3. "*Iniquities prevail against me.*" Others accuse and slander me, and in addition my own sins rise up and would beset me to my confusion, were it not for the remembrance of the atonement which covers every one of my iniquities. Our sins would, but for grace, prevail against us in the court of divine justice, in the court of conscience, and in the battle of life. Unhappy is the man who despises these enemies, and worse still is he who counts them his friends ! He is best instructed who knows their deadly power, and flees for refuge to him who pardons iniquity. "*As for our transgressions, thou shalt purge them away.*" Thou dost cover them all, for thou hast provided a covering propitiation, a mercy-seat which wholly covers thy law. Note the word "*our*," the faith of the one penitent who speaks for himself in the first clause, here embraces all the faithful in Zion ; and he is so persuaded of the largeness of forgiving love that he leads all the saints to sing of the blessing. What a comfort that iniquities which prevail against us, do not prevail against God. They would keep us away from God, but he sweeps them away from before himself and us ; they are too strong for us, but not for our Redeemer, who is mighty, yea, and almighty to save. It is worthy of note that as the priest washed in the laver before he sacrificed, so David leads us to obtain purification from sin before we enter upon the service of song. When we have washed our robes and made them white in his blood, then shall we acceptably sing, " Worthy is the Lamb that was slain."

4. "*Blessed is the man whom thou choosest, and causest to approach unto thee.*" After cleansing comes benediction, and truly this is a very rich one. It comprehends

both election, effectual calling, access, acceptance, and sonship. First, we are chosen of God, according to the good pleasure of his will, and this alone is blessedness. Then, since we cannot and will not come to God of ourselves, he works graciously in us, and attracts us powerfully ; he subdues our unwillingness, and removes our inability by the almighty workings of his transforming grace. This also is no slight blessedness. Furthermore, we, by his divine drawings, are made nigh by the blood of his Son, and brought near by his Spirit, into intimate fellowship ; so that we have access with boldness, and are no longer as those who are afar off by wicked works : here also is unrivalled blessedness. To crown all, we do not come nigh in peril of dire destruction, as Nadab and Abihu did, but we approach as chosen and accepted ones, to become dwellers in the divine household : this is heaped-up blessedness, vast beyond conception. But dwelling in the house we are treated as sons, for the servant abideth not in the house for ever, but the son abideth ever. Behold what manner of love and blessedness the Father has bestowed upon us that we may dwell in his house, and go no more out for ever. Happy men who dwell at home with God. May both writer and reader be such men. *"That he may dwell in thy courts."* Acceptance leads to abiding : God does not make a temporary choice, or give and take ; his gifts and calling are without repentance. He who is once admitted to God's courts shall inhabit them for ever ; he shall be

" No more a stranger or a guest,
But like a child at home."

Permanence gives preciousness. Terminating blessings are but half-blessings. To dwell in the courts of the Great King is to be ennobled ; to dwell there for ever is to be emparadised : yet such is the portion of every man whom God has chosen and caused to approach unto him, though once his iniquities prevailed against him.

5 *By* terrible things in righteousness wilt thou answer us, O God of our salvation ; *who art* the confidence of all the ends of the earth, and of them that are afar off *upon* the sea :

6 Which by his strength setteth fast the mountains ; *being* girded with power :

7 Which stilleth the noise of the seas, the noise of their waves, and the tumult of the people.

8 They also that dwell in the uttermost parts are afraid at thy tokens : thou makest the outgoings of the morning and evening to rejoice.

5. *"By terrible things in righteousness wilt thou answer us, O God of our salvation."* God's memorial is that he hears prayer, and his glory is that he answers it in a manner fitted to inspire awe in the hearts of his people. The saints, in the commencement of the Psalm, offered praise in reverential silence ; and now, in the like awe-stricken spirit, they receive answers to their prayers. The direct allusion here is, no doubt, to the Lord's overthrow of the enemies of his people in ways calculated to strike terror into all beholders ; his judgments in their severe righteousness were calculated to excite fear both among friends and foes. Who would not fear a God whose blows are so crushing ? We do not always know what we are asking for when we pray ; when the answer comes, the veritable answer, it is possible that we may be terrified by it. We seek sanctification, and trial will be the reply : we ask for more faith, and more affliction is the result : we pray for the spread of the gospel, and persecution scatters us. Nevertheless, it is good to ask on, for nothing which the Lord grants in his love can do us any harm. Terrible things will turn out to be blessed things after all, when they come in answer to prayer.

See in this verse how righteousness and salvation are united, the terrible things with the gracious answers. Where but in Jesus could they be blended ? The God who saves may answer our prayers in a way which puts unbelief into a flutter ; but when faith spies the Saviour, she remembers that " things are not what they seem," and she is of good courage. He who is terrible is also our refuge from terror when we see him in the Well-beloved. *"Who art the confidence of all the ends of the earth."* The dwellers in the far-off isles trust in God ; those most remote from Zion yet confide in the ever living Jehovah. Even those who dwell in countries, frozen or torrid, where nature puts on her varied terrors, and those who see dread wonders on the deep, yet fly from the terrors of God and place their confidence in the God of terrors. His arm is strong to smite, but also strong to save. *"And of them that are afar off upon the sea."* Both elements have their elect bands of believers. If the land gave Moses elders, the sea gave Jesus apostles. Noah, when all was ocean, was as calm with God as Abraham in his tent. All men are equally dependent upon God : the seafaring man is usually most conscious of this, but in reality he is not more so than the husbandman, nor the husbandman than anyone else. There is no room for self-confidence on land or sea, since God is the only true confidence of men on earth or ocean. Faith is a plant of universal growth, it is a tree of life on shore and a plant of renown at sea ; and, blessed be God, those who exercise faith in him anywhere shall find that he is swift and strong to answer their prayers. A remembrance of this should quicken our devotions when we approach unto the Lord our God.

6. *"Which by his strength setteth fast the mountains."* He, as it were, fixed them in their sockets, and preserved them from falling by earthquake or storm. The firmest owe their stability to him. Philosophers of the forget-God school are too much engrossed with their laws of upheaval to think of the Upheaver. Their theories of volcanic action and glacier action, etc., etc., are frequently used as bolts and bars to shut the Lord out of his own world. Our poet is of another mind, and sees God's hand settling Alps and Andes on their bases, and therefore he sings in his praise. Let me for ever be just such an unphilosophic simpleton as David was, for he was nearer akin to Solomon than any of our modern theorists. *"Being girded with power."* The Lord is so himself, and he therefore casts a girdle of strength around the hills, and there they stand, braced, belted, and bulwarked with his might. The poetry is such as would naturally suggest itself to one familiar with mountain scenery ; power everywhere meets you, sublimity, massive grandeur, and stupendous force are all around you ; and God is there, the author and source of all.

Let us learn that we poor puny ones, if we wish for true establishment, must go to the strong for strength. Without him, the everlasting hills would crumble ; how much more shall all our plans, projects, and labours come to decay. Repose, O believer, where the mountains find their bases—viz., in the undiminished might of the Lord God.

7. *"Which stilleth the noise of the seas."* His soft breath smooths the sea into a glass, and the mountainous waves into ripples. God does this. Calms are of the God of peace ; it needs not that we look for a hurricane when it is said that he cometh. He walked of old in the garden in the cool of the day ; he is resting even now, for his great seventh day is not yet over, and he is always " the Lord and giver of peace." Let mariners magnify the God who rules the waves. *"The noise of their waves."* Each separate brawler amid the riot of the storm is quieted by the divine voice. *"And the tumult of the people."* Nations are as difficult to rule as the sea itself, they are as fitful, treacherous, restless, and furious ; they will not brook the bridle nor be restrained by laws. Canute had not a more perilous sea by the rising billows than many a king and emperor has had when the multitude have been set on mischief, and have grown weary of their lords. God alone is King of nations. The sea obeys him, and the yet more tumultuous nations are kept in check by him. Human society owes its preservation to the continued power of God : evil passions would secure its instant dissolution ; envy, ambition, and cruelty would create anarchy to-morrow, if God did not prevent ; whereof we have had clear proof in the various French revolutions. Glory be unto God who maintains the fabric of social order, and checks the wicked, who would fain overthrow all things. The child of God in seasons of trouble should fly at once to him who stills the seas : nothing is too hard for him.

8. *"They also that dwell in the uttermost parts are afraid at thy tokens."* Signs of God's presence are not few, nor confined to any one region. Zembla sees them as well as Zion, and Terra del Fuego as surely as the Terra Sacra. These tokens are sometimes terrible phenomena in nature—such as earthquake, pestilence, tornado, or storm ; and when these are seen, even the most barbarous people tremble before God. At other times they are dread works of providence—such as the overthrow of Sodom, and the destruction of Pharaoh. The rumour of these judgments travels to earth's utmost verge, and impresses all people with a fear and trembling at such a just and holy God. We bless God that we are not afraid but rejoice at his tokens ; with solemn awe we are glad when we behold his mighty acts. We fear,

but not with slavish fear. *"Thou makest the outgoings of the morning and evening to rejoice."* East and west are made happy by God's favour to the dwellers therein. Our rising hours are bright with hope, and our evening moments mellow with thanksgiving. Whether the sun go forth or come in we bless God and rejoice in the gates of the day. When the fair morning blushes with the rosy dawn we rejoice ; and when the calm evening smiles restfully we rejoice still. We do not believe that the dew weeps the death of the day ; we only see jewels bequeathed by the departing day for its successor to gather up from the earth. Faith, when she sees God, rounds the day with joy. She cannot fast, because the bridegroom is with her. Night and day are alike to her, for the same God made them and blessed them. She would have no rejoicing if God did not make her glad ; but, blessed be his name, he never ceases to make joy for those who find their joy in him.

9 Thou visitest the earth, and waterest it : thou greatly enrichest it with the river of God, *which* is full of water : thou preparest them corn, when thou hast so provided for it.

10 Thou waterest the ridges thereof abundantly : thou settlest the furrows thereof : thou makest it soft with showers : thou blessest the springing thereof.

11 Thou crownest the year with thy goodness ; and thy paths drop fatness.

12 They drop *upon* the pastures of the wilderness ; and the little hills rejoice on every side.

13 The pastures are clothed with flocks ; the valleys also are covered over with corn ; they shout for joy, they also sing.

9. *"Thou visitest the earth, and waterest it."* God's visits leave a blessing behind ; this is more than can be said of every visitor. When the Lord goes on visitations of mercy, he has abundance of necessary things for all his needy creatures. He is represented here as going round the earth, as a gardener surveys his garden, and as giving water to every plant that requires it, and that not in small quantities, but until the earth is drenched and soaked with a rich supply of refreshment. O Lord, in this manner visit thy church, and my poor, parched, and withering piety. Make thy grace to overflow towards my graces ; water me, for no plant of thy garden needs it more.

" My stock lies dead, and no increase
Doth my dull husbandry improve ;
O let thy graces without cease
Drop from above."

"Thou greatly enrichest it." Millions of money could not so much enrich mankind as the showers do. The soil is made rich by the rain, and then yields its riches to man ; but God is the first giver of all. How truly rich are those who are enriched with grace ; this is great riches. *"With the river of God, which is full of water.* The brooks of earth are soon dried up, and all human resources, being finite, are liable to failure ; but God's provision for the supply of rain is inexhaustible ; there is no bottom or shore to his river. The deluge poured from the clouds yesterday may be succeeded by another to-morrow, and yet the waters above the firmament shall not fail. How true is this in the realm of grace ; there " the river of God is full of water," and " of his fulness have all we received, and grace for grace." The ancients in their fables spake of Pactolus, which flowed over sands of gold ; but this river of God, which flows above and from which the rain is poured, is far more enriching ; for, after all, the wealth of men lies mainly in the harvest of their fields, without which even gold would be of no value whatever. *"Thou preparest them corn."* Corn is specially set apart to be the food of man. In its various species it is a divine provision for the nutriment of our race, and is truly called the staff of life. We hear in commerce of " prepared corn-flour," but God prepared it long before man touched it. As surely as the manna was prepared of God for the tribes, so certainly is corn made and sent by God for our daily use. What is the difference whether we gather wheat-ears or manna, and what matters it if the first comes upward to us, and the second downward ? God is as much

present beneath as above ; it is as great a marvel that food should rise out of the dust, as that it should fall from the skies. *"When thou hast so provided for it."* When all is prepared to produce corn, the Lord puts the finishing stroke, and the grain is forthcoming ; not even, when all the material is prepared, will the wheat be perfected without the continuous and perfecting operation of the Most High. Blessed be the Great Householder ; he does not suffer the harvest to fail, he supplies the teeming myriads of earth with bread enough from year to year. Even thus does he vouchsafe heavenly food to his redeemed ones : "He hath given meat unto them that fear him ; he is ever mindful of his covenant."

10. *"Thou waterest the ridges thereof abundantly : thou settlest the furrows thereof."* Ridge and furrow are drenched. The ridges beaten down and settled, and the furrows made to stand like gutters flooded to the full. *"Thou makest it soft with showers."* The drought turned the clods into iron, but the plenteous showers dissolve and loosen the soil. *"Thou blessest the springing thereof."* Vegetation enlivened by the moisture leaps into vigour, the seed germinates and sends forth its green shoot, and the smell is that of a field which the Lord has blessed. All this may furnish us with a figure of the operations of the Holy Spirit in beating down high thoughts, filling our lowly desires, softening the soul, and causing every holy thing to increase and spread.

11. *"Thou crownest the year with thy goodness."* The harvest is the plainest display of the divine bounty, and the crown of the year. The Lord himself conducts the coronation, and sets the golden coronal upon the brow of the year. Or, we may understand the expression to mean that God's love encircles the year as with a crown ; each month has its gems, each day its pearl. Unceasing kindness girdles all time with a belt of love. The providence of God in its visitations makes a complete circuit, and surrounds the year. *"And thy paths drop fatness."* The footsteps of God, when he visits the land with rain, create fertility. It was said of the Tartar hordes, that grass grew no more where their horses' feet had trodden ; so, on the contrary, it may be said that the march of Jehovah, the Fertiliser, may be traced by the abundance which he creates. For spiritual harvests we must look to him, for he alone can give " times of refreshing " and feasts of Pentecost.

12. *"They drop upon the pastures of the wilderness."* Not alone where man is found do the showers descend, but away in the lone places, where only wild animals have their haunt, there the bountiful Lord makes the refreshing rain to drop. Ten thousand oases smile while the Lord of mercy passes by. The birds of the air, the wild goats, and the fleet stags rejoice as they drink from the pools, new filled from heaven. The most lonely and solitary souls God will visit in love. *"And the little hills rejoice on every side."* On all hands the eminences are girt with gladness. Soon they languish under the effects of drought, but after a season of rain they laugh again with verdure.

13. *"The pastures are clothed with flocks."* The clothing of man first clothes the fields. Pastures appear to be quite covered with numerous flocks when the grass is abundant. *"The valleys also are covered over with corn."* The arable as well as the pasture land is rendered fruitful. God's clouds, like ravens, bring us both bread and flesh. Grazing flocks and waving crops are equally the gifts of the Preserver of men, and for both praise should be rendered. Sheep-shearing and harvest should both be holiness unto the Lord. *"They shout for joy."* The bounty of God makes the earth vocal with his praise, and in opened ears it lifts up a joyous shout. The cattle low out the divine praises, and the rustling ears of grain sing a soft sweet melody unto the Lord.

> " Ye forests bend, ye harvests wave to him ;
> Breathe your still song into the reaper's heart,
> As home he goes beneath the joyous moon.
> Bleat out afresh, ye hills ; ye mossy rocks
> Retain the sound ; the broad responsive low
> Ye valleys raise ; for the GREAT SHEPHERD reigns,
> And his *unsuffering* kingdom yet will come."

"They also sing." The voice of nature is articulate to God ; it is not only a shout, but a song. Well ordered are the sounds of animate creation as they combine with the equally well-tuned ripple of the waters, and sighings of the wind. Nature has no discords. Her airs are melodious, her chorus is full of harmony. All, all is for the Lord ; the world is a hymn to the Eternal, blessed is he who, hearing, joins in it, and makes one singer in the mighty chorus.

EXPLANATORY NOTES AND QUAINT SAYINGS.

From Psalm lxv. onwards we find ourselves in the midst of a series of Psalms which, with a varying arrangement of the words, are inscribed both מִזְמוֹ and שִׁיר (lxv.—lxviii.) The two words signify a *Psalm-song*. This series, as is universally the case, is arranged according to the community of prominent watchwords. In Psalm lxv. 2 we read : *"To thee is the vow paid ; "* and in lxvi. 13 : *"I will pay thee my vows ; "* in Psalm lxvi. 20 : *"Blessed be Elohim ; "* and in lxvii. 8 : *"Elohim shall bless us."* Besides Psalms lxvi. and lxvii. have this feature in common, that לַמְנַצֵּחַ, which occurs fifty-five times in the Psalter, is accompanied by the name of the poet in every instance, with the exception of these two anonymous Psalms. The frequently occurring *Sela* of both Psalms also indicates that they were intended to have a musical accompaniment.—*Franz Delitzsch.*

*Title.—A Psalm of Jeremiah and Ezekiel.—*The Psalm is assigned to them, not as being its authors, but because it is supposed that it was often rehearsed by them at the beginning of the return from captivity, to teach us that those things ought especially to be sung concerning that happy restoration which these prophets were wont to sing about. But this inscription is not in the Hebrew text, nor in some translations, but only in certain versions. Jeremiah was not carried away to Babylon ; see Jeremiah xxxix. 11, etc. Moreover, both he and Ezekiel died before the return.—*Pool's Synopsis.*

*Whole Psalm.—*The author of the Psalm is mentioned, but not the date of its composition ; but, from an examination of its contents, it would seem to have been intended as a song for the " day of atonement," and for the " feast of tabernacles," which followed immediately after. Num. xxix. 7, 12. The sins of the year were then " covered over," and a thorough purification of the sanctuary was made by a special service of expiation. The labours of the year were also by that time all concluded, and its fruits secured ; and Israel could look on the goodness of God towards them, through its entire extent ; and this Psalm was penned to serve as a fitting expression of their feelings. It opens with a reference to the " silence " that reigned in the sanctuary ; to the profound, unbroken, solemn stillness that reigned within it ; while, in deep abasement, the people without waited in hushed expectation the return of their high priest from the immediate presence of God. Lev. xvi. 17. It goes on to a statement of the blessedness of those who are accepted of God, and admitted to fellowship with One so unspeakably great ; and concludes with a description of the various processes by which the Almighty had fitted the earth to yield a year's supplies for his people.—*Dalman Hapstone, in "The Ancient Psalms in appropriate Metres. . . . . with Notes."* 1867.

*Whole Psalm.—*We have here a psalm of thanksgiving to be sung in the Temple during a public festivity, at which the sacrifices were to be offered which had been vowed during a long and protracted drought (verses 1, 2). To the thanksgiving, however, for a gracious rain, and the hope of an abundant harvest (verses 9—14), is added gratitude for a signal deliverance during a time of distress and commotion affecting all the nations around (verses 7, 8). Thus the Psalm becomes a song of praise to Jehovah as the God of history and the God of nature alike.—*From the "Psalms Chronologically Arranged. By Four Friends."* 1867.

*Whole Psalm.—*This is a charming psalm. Coming after the previous sad ones, it seems like the morning after the darkness of night. There is a dewy freshness about it, and from the ninth verse to the end there is a sweet succession of landscape pictures that reminds one of the loveliness of spring ; and truly it is a description, in natural figures, of that happy state of men's minds which will be the result of the " Day-Spring's visiting us from on high." Luke i. 7, 8.—*O. Prescott Hiller.*

Verse 1.—"Praise waiteth for thee, O God, in Sion." The believer sometimes seems to want words to exalt God, and stops, as it were, in the middle ; his thoughts are overmatched. Thus praise waits, or is silent for God ; it is silent to other things, and it waits to be employed about him. The soul is often put to a nonplus in crying up the grace of God, and wants words to express its greatness ; yea, to answer the elevation of the thoughts ; the heart indites a song of praise, but it cannot tune it. The Psalmist is stopped, as it were, through admiration (which is *silentium intellectus*), for when the mind can rise no higher, it falls admiring ; hence some say, God is most exalted with fewest words.—*Alexander Carmichael.*

Verse 1.—"*Praise waiteth for thee, O God.*" Mercy is not yet come, we expect it : whilst thou art preparing the mercy, we are preparing the praise.—*Edward Leigh in "Annotations on the Five Poetical Books of the Old Testament."* 1657.

Verse 1.—"*Praise waiteth on thee.*" As a servant, whose duty it is to do what thou commandest ; or, *for thee ;* is ready to be offered in thy courts for special favours. I think there is an allusion to the daily service in which God was praised. —*Benjamin Boothroyd.*

Verse 1.—"*Praise waiteth for thee, O God.*" *Te decet hymnus,* so the vulgar edition reads this place. To thee, O Lord, belong our hymns, our psalms, our praises, our cheerful acclamations, and conformable to that, we translate it, "*Praise waiteth for thee, O God.*" But if we take it according to the original, it must be *tibi silentium laus est,* Thy praise, O Lord, consists in silence. That man praises God best that says least of him ; of his mysterious essence, of his unrevealed will and secret purposes.—*Abraham Wright.*

Verse 1.—"*To thee is silence and praise.*"—*Piscator.*

Verse 1.—The Hebrew may be rendered, "*Praise is silent for thee.*" As if the holy man had said, " Lord, I quietly wait for a time to praise thee ; my soul is not in an uproar because thou stayest. I am not murmuring, but rather stringing my harp and tuning my instrument with much patience and confidence, that I may be ready to strike up when the joyful news of my deliverance come."—*William Gurnall.*

Verse 1.—"*To thee belongeth silence-praise.*" Praise without any tumult. (Alexander.) It has been said, " The most intense feeling is the most calm, being condensed by repression." And Hooker says of prayer, " The very silence which our unworthiness putteth us unto doth itself make request for us, and that in the confidence of his grace. Looking inward, we are stricken dumb ; looking upward, we speak and prevail." Horsley renders it, " Upon thee is the repose of prayer."— *Andrew A. Bonar.*

Verse 1.—*Praise is silent for thee.*" The Chaldee interpretation is, that our praise is not sufficiently worthy that we should praise God. The very praises of angels are esteemed as nothing before him. For so its rendering is : "*Before thee, O God, whose Majesty dwells in Zion, the praise of angels is regarded as silence.*" . . . . Jerome's version here is, "*To thee silence is praise, O God, in Zion.*" Atheneus says, silence is a divine thing ; and Thomas à Kempis calls silence the nutriment of devotion.—*Thomas Le Blanc.*

Verse 1.—"*To thee belong submission, praise, O God, in Sion.*" [Version of the American Bible Union.] Thou hast a claim for submission in times of sorrow, for praise in seasons of joy.—*Thomas J. Conant, in "The Psalms. . . with occasional Notes."* 1871.

Verse 1.—"*Vow.*" A vow is a voluntary and deliberate promise made unto God in an extraordinary case. " It is a religious promise made unto God in a holy manner : " so a modern writer defines it.* It is a " holy and religious promise, advisedly and freely made unto God, concerning something which to do or to omit appeareth to be grateful and well-pleasing unto him : " so Bucanus. I forbear Aquinas's definition of a vow. If these which I have given satisfy not, then view it in the words of Peter Martyr, a man of repute, and well-known to our own nation in the days of Edward VI., of ever-blessed memory : " It is a holy promise, whereby we bind ourselves to offer somewhat unto God." There is one more who defines it, and he is a man whose judgment, learning, and holiness hath perfumed his name ; it is learned Perkins, in his " Cases of Conscience." " A vow," saith he, " is a promise made unto God of things lawful and possible."—*Henry Hurst* (—1690), *in "The Morning Exercises."*

Verse 1 (*last clause*).—The reference here is to the vows or promises which the people had made in view of the manifested judgments of God, and the proofs of his goodness. Those vows they were now ready to carry out in expressions of praise.—*Albert Barnes.*

Verse 2.—"*O thou that hearest prayer,*" etc. This is one of his titles of honour, he is a God that hears prayer ; and it is as truly ascribed to him as mercy or justice.

---

* Szegedinus.

He hears all prayer, therefore, "*unto thee shall all flesh come.*" He never rejects any that deserves the name of prayer, how weak, how unworthy soever the petitioner be. "*All flesh!*" And will he (may faith say) reject mine only? Rom. x. 12, "He is rich unto all that call upon him;" Ps. lxxxvi. 5, "Thou art plenteous in mercy to all that call upon thee;" Heb. xi. 6. "A rewarder of them that diligently seek him." This must be believed as certainly as we believe that God is. As sure as God is the true God, so sure is it that none who sought him diligently departed from him without a reward. He rewards all seekers, for *indefinita in materia necessaria æquipollet universali.* And if all, why not me? You may as well donbt that he is God, as doubt that he will not reward, not hear prayer; so James i. 5, "If any of you lack wisdom, let him ask of God, that giveth to all men liberally, and upbraideth not; and it shall be given him."—*David Clarkson.*

Verse 2.—"*O thou that hearest prayer, unto thee shall all flesh come.*" What avails prayer, if it be not heard? But God's people need not lay it aside on that score. Our text bears two things with respect to that matter. 1. A comfortable title ascribed to God, with the unanimous consent of all the sons of Zion, who are all praying persons: "*O thou that hearest prayer.*" He speaks to "*God in Zion,*" or Zion's God, that is in New Testament language, to God in Christ. An absolute God thundereth on sinners from Sinai, there can be no comfortable intercourse betwixt God and them, by the law: but in Zion, from the mercy-seat, in Christ, he is the hearer of prayer; they give in their supplications, and he graciously hears them. Such faith of it they have, that praise waits there for the prayer-hearing God. 2. The effect of the savour of this title of God, spread abroad in the world: "*Unto thee shall all flesh come:*" not only Jews, but Gentiles. The poor Gentiles who have long in vain implored the aid of their idols, hearing and believing that God is the hearer of prayer, will flock to him, and present their petitions. They will throng in about his door, where by the gospel they understand beggars are so well served. They will "*come in even unto thee,*" Heb. They will come in even to thy seat, thy throne of grace, even unto thyself through the Mediator. . . . That God is the hearer of prayer, and will hear the prayers of his people, is evident from these considerations:—First. The supernatural instinct of praying that is found in all that are born of God, Gal. iv. 6. It is as natural for them to fall a praying when the grace of God has touched their hearts, as for children when they are born into the world to cry, or to desire the breasts. Zechariah xii. 10, compared with Acts ix. 11, where in the account that is given of Paul, at his conversion, it is particularly noticed, "Behold he prayeth." Hence the whole saving change on a soul comes under the character of this instinct. Jeremiah iii. 4, 19. Secondly. The intercession of Christ, Rom. viii. 34. It is a great part of the work of Christ's intercession to present the prayers of his people before his Father, Rev. viii. 4, to take their causes in hand, contained in their supplications. 1 John ii. 1. Thirdly. The promise of the covenant, whereby God's faithfulness is impawned for the hearing of prayer, as Matt. vii. 7: see also Isaiah lxv. 24. Fourthly. The many encouragements given in the Word to the people of God, to come with their cases unto the Lord by prayer. He invites them to his throne of grace with their petitions for supply of their needs. Cant. ii. 14. He sends afflictions to press them to come. Hosea v. 15. He gives them ground of hope of success, Psalm l. 15, whatever extremity their case is brought to. Isaiah xli. 17. He shows them that however long he may delay for their trial, yet praying and not fainting shall be successful at length. Luke xviii. 8. Fifthly. The gracious nature of God, with the endearing relations he stands in to his people. Exodus xxii. 27. He wants not power and ability to fulfil the holy desires of his people; he is gracious, and will withhold no good from them that they really need. He has the bowels of a father to pity them, the bowels of a mother to her sucking child. He has a most tender sympathy with them in all their afflictions, the touches on them are as on the apple of his eye; and he never refuses them a request, but for their good. Rom. viii. 28. Sixthly. The experiences which the saints of all ages have had of the answer of prayer. The faith of it brings them to God at conversion, as the text intimates; and they that believe cannot be disappointed. Lastly. The present ease and relief that prayer sometimes gives to the saints, while yet the full answer of prayer is not come. Psalm cxxxviii. 3.—*Thomas Boston* (1676—1732).

Verse 2.—"*O thou that hearest prayer.*" Observe 1. That God is called the hearer of prayers, since he hears, without distinction of persons, the prayers of every one poured forth with piety, not only of the Jews, but also of the Gentiles; as in

Acts x. 34, 35. . . . . It follows, therefore, as a necessary consequence, *that all flesh should come to him.* 2. *To come to God,* is not indeed simply tantamount to saying, *to draw near to God,* to adore, call upon, and worship him, but to come *to Zion* for the purpose of adoring God ; for it was just now said, that God must be praised in Zion, and to this the phrase, *to come to God,* must be referred. On this account also אֵל is not used, but עֲד, whose proper force is *right up to God,* or to the place of the habitation of God to render adoration to God.—*Hermann Venema.*

Verse 2.—*"To thee shall all flesh come."* To Christ *"all flesh comes,"* that is (1), every sinner and carnal man. He himself says, Matt. ix. 13, *"I came not to call the righteous, but sinners."* The Grecian priest in olden times, when approaching to receive the sacrifice, used to exclaim, *Who comes there ?* and the reply was, *Many and good.* But God receives publicans and sinners, and inviteth them to his banquet, and eateth with them ; but for the purpose of delivering them from sin. *"All flesh shall see the salvation of God."* (2.) *All flesh* may be taken for the whole flesh, the whole body ; all the senses and members of the body shall come to God that they may pay him tribute as their King.—*Thomas Le Blanc.*

Verse 2.—*"All flesh."* By *flesh* is meant man in his weakness and need.—*J. J. Stewart Perowne.*

Verse 3.—*"Iniquities prevail against me."* There are two ways in which iniquities may prevail against the Christian—the first is in the growing sense of his guilt, the second is in the power of their acting. This prevalence cannot be entire, for sin shall not have dominion over them ; but it may be occasional and partial. There are two ways, according to Scripture, in which God purges our transgressions ; and they always go together. The one is by pardoning mercy. Thus David prays " Purge me with hyssop, and I shall be clean." Thus the blood of Jesus Christ cleanseth us from all sin. The other is by sanctifying grace : " I will sprinkle clean water upon you, and ye shall be clean." And this is as much the work of God as the former. He subdues our iniquities as well as forgives them.—*William Jay.*

Verse 3.—*"Iniquities."* Literally, *Words of iniquities,* by some regarded as a pleonastic phrase for iniquities themselves. More probably, however, the phrase means the charge or accusation of iniquity.—*Joseph Addison Alexander.*

Verse 3.—The deeds of iniquity are said *to prevail against us,* in so far as they are too strong and powerful for us to deny or refute, and to subject us to a demand of those penalties which the sin merits ; hence there remains no other refuge than the clemency and grace of God, the Judge. See Psalms cxliii. 2 ; cxxx. 3, 4.—*Hermann Venema.*

Verse 3.—*"As for our transgressions, thou shalt purge them away."* In the Hebrew it is, Thou shalt hide them. It alludes to the mercy-seat, which was covered with the wings of the Cherubim ; so are the sins of the godly, when repented of, covered with the wings of mercy and favour.—*Thomas Watson.*

Verse 3.—*"Thou shalt purge them away ; "* or *"Thou coverest them."* The pronoun is emphatic, as though to express the conviction that God and God alone could do this.—*J. J. Stewart Perowne.*

Verse 3.—The holy prophets, and penmen of Scripture, have no grounds of hope for pardon of sin, save those which are common to the meanest of God's people ; for David, in his confession, cometh in by himself alone, aggravating his own sins most : *"Iniquities prevail against me,"* saith he. But in hope of pardon, he joineth with the rest of God's people, saying, " *As for our transgressions, thou shalt purge them away."*—*David Dickson.*

Verses 3, 4.—Now, soul, thou art molested with many lusts that infest thee, and obstruct thy commerce with heaven ; yea, thou hast complained to thy God, what loss thou hast suffered by them ; is it now presumption to expect relief from him, that he will rescue thee from them, that thou mayest serve him without fear, who is thy liege Lord ? You have the saints for your precedents ; who, when they have been in combat with their corruptions, yea, been foiled by them, have even then exercised their faith on God, and expected the ruin of those enemies, which, for the present, have overrun them. *"Iniquities prevail against me ; "* he means his own sins ; but see his faith ; at the same time that they prevailed over him, he beholds God destroying them, as appears in the very next words, *"As for our transgressions, thou shalt purge them away."* See here, poor Christian, who thinkest that thou shalt never get above deck, holy David has a faith, not only for himself, but also for all believers, of whose number I suppose thee one. And mark the ground he hath for this his confidence, taken from God's choosing act : *"Blessed is the man whom thou choosest, and causest to approach unto thee, that he may dwell in thy courts."* As if he had said, Surely he will not let them be under the power of sin, or in want of his gracious succour, whom he sets so near himself. This is Christ's own argument against Satan, in the behalf of his people. *"The Lord said unto Satan, the Lord rebuke thee."* Zech. iii. 2.—*William Gurnall.*

Verse 4.—*"Blessed is the man whom thou choosest."* The benedictions of the Psalter advance in spirituality and indicate a growth. The first blessed the godly reader of the word. Ps. i. 1. The second described the pardoned child. Ps. xxxii. 1. The third pronounced a blessing upon faith. Ps. xxxiv. 8 and Ps. xl. 4. The fourth commended the active and generous believer, abundant in deeds of charity (Ps. xli. 1) ; and this last, mounting to the fountain head of all benediction, blesses the elect of God.—*C. H. S.*

Verse 4.—*"The man whom thou choosest."* Christ, whom God chose, and of whom he said, " This is my beloved Son in whom I am well pleased," is, indeed, " over all, God blessed for ever ; " but in him his elect are blessed too. For his sake, not for our own, are we chosen ; in him, not in ourselves, are we received by God, being accepted in the Beloved ; and, therefore, in him are we blessed : he is our blessing. With that High Priest who has ascended into the holy place and entered within the vail, we enter into the house of God ; we learn to dwell therein ; we are filled with its spiritual joys ; we partake of its holy mysteries and sacraments of grace and love.—*From "A Plain Commentary on the Book of Psalms,"* 1859.

Verse 4.—*" We shall be satisfied with the goodness of thy house, even of thy holy temple."* We shall be so filled, that nothing can be said to be wanting, we shall have nothing to look for outside. What can be wanting, in the house of him who made everything, who is the master of everything, who will be all unto all, in whom is an inexhaustible treasure of good. Of him is said in Psalm ciii. " Who satisfieth thy mouth with good things ; " and in Psalm xvii. " I shall be satisfied, when I awake, with thy likeness."—*Robert Bellarmine* (1542—1621).

Verse 4.—*"Satisfied with the goodness of thy house."* There is an allusion here to the oblations which were devoted to God, of which, also, sacred persons partook.— *Hermann Venema.*

Verse 5.—*"By terrible things in righteousness wilt thou answer us."* The reason why he answers thus is, because what God doth for his people, take one thing with another, is still in order to the crucifying of the flesh ; and what more *terrible* than such a death ? We pray for *pleasing* things, as we imagine, but as we are flesh as well as spirit ; so the flesh hath still a part in every prayer, and what we beg is partly carnal, and upon the matter, in part, we beg we know not what. Now, the answer as it comes from God, take all together, is spiritual, which is a crucifying thing to sinful flesh ; hence comes in all the terror. . . . You pray for pardon ; that is a pleasing thing, yet rightly understood not pleasing to the flesh ; it mortifies corruption, breaks the heart, engages to a holy life : every answer from our God to us, one way or the other, first or last, shall tend that way. God useth so to give good things unto his children, as withal to give himself, and show to them his heavenly glory in what is done. . . . Now God is *terrible* to sinful flesh : so far as he appears, it dies. Jacob, therefore, whilst he conquered God in prayer, himself was overcome, signified by that touch upon his thigh put out of joint, where the chiefest stress in wrestling lies. When we are weak, then are we strong ; because as God appears, we die unto ourselves and live in him.—*William Carter, in a Fast Sermon entitled,* " Light in Darkness," 1648.

Verse 5.—God's judgments are these *terribilia,* terrible, fearful things ; and he is faithful in his covenant ; and by terrible judgments he will answer, that is, satisfy our expectation : and that is a convenient sense of these words. But the word which we translate " righteousness " here, is *tzadok,* and *tzadok* is not faithfulness, but holiness ; and these " terrible things " are reverend things ; and so Tremellius translates it, and well. *Per res reverendas, by reverend things,* things to which there belongs a reverence—" thou shalt answer us." And thus, the sense of this place will be, that the God of our salvation (that is, God working in the Christian church) calls us to holiness, to righteousness, by terrible things ; not terrible in the way and nature of revenge, but terrible, that is, stupendous, reverend, mysterious ; so that we should not make religion too homely a thing, but come always to all acts and exercises of religion with reverence, with fear, and trembling, and make a difference between religious and civil actions.—*John Donne.*

Verse 5.—God's deliverance of his church and people "*by terrible things*" is "*in righteousness.*" The meaning of the point is this : God in all the deliverances of his people by terrible things, doth therein manifest his righteosuness. He doth therein nothing but what is according to righteousness and justice. To clear this, consider that there is a double righteousness, the righteousness of his word, which is the righteousness of his faithfulness ; and the righteousness of his works, or his just acts of righteousness. And God doth manifest both these in his deliverance of his people by terrible things.—*John Bewick.* 1644.

Verse 5.—But what is the meaning when they say, "*wilt thou answer us ?*" Us, who are inhabitants of Zion, who are constituted thy people, and truly worship Thee ; *us*, moreover, in contact with enemies, who stirred up strife against us, and wished us ill ; *us*, lastly, who aim at and seek the stability of the Kingdom and Church, and every kind of felicity and safety ; with such things *wilt thou answer us*, it says, that is, for our advantage and benefit, and according to our vows, and therefore by pleading our cause, and deciding in our favour, and satisfying our desires ; and in this way rendering us happy and establishing us, and subduing and confounding our foes.—*Hermann Venema.*

Verse 5.—"*Who art the confidence of all the ends of the earth.*" How could God be the confidence of all the ends of the earth, if he does not reign and constantly work ? The stability of the mountains is ascribed not to certain physical laws, but to the power of God. The noise of the seas is stilled not by laws without a powerful agent, but by the immediate influence of the Almighty Ruler. Human laws also may be the means of restraining persecution, but they are only means ; and it is God who stilleth the tumult of the people. It is God who maketh the outgoings of the morning and evening to sing. The Scriptures, in viewing the works which God does through means, never lose sight of God himself. God visits and waters the earth : God prepares the corn. Without his own immediate power, the laws of nature could not produce their effect. How consoling and satisfactory is this view of Divine Providence, compared with that of an infidel philosophy, that forbids us to go further back than to the power of certain physical laws, which it grants, indeed, were at first established by God, but which can now perform their office without him.—*Alexander Carson.* (1776—1844).

Verse 5.—"*All the ends of the earth.*" God is *in himself potentially,* "*The confidence of all the ends of the earth.*" Hereafter he will be recognised by all to be so (Ps. xxiii. 27, 28), of which the Queen of Sheba's coming to Solomon "from the uttermost parts of the earth " is a type. Matt. xii. 42.—*A. R. Fausset.*

Verse 5.—"*And of them that are afar off upon the sea.*" We must beseech God in the words of this Psalm, that since He stands upon the shore, and beholds our perils, he would make us, who are tossed on the turbulent sea, secure for his name's sake, and enable us to hold between Scylla and Charybdis, the middle course, and escaping the danger on either hand, with a sound vessel and safe merchandise, reach the port.—*Lorinus (from Augustine).*

Verses 5—8.—The divine watering of the earth is obviously symbolical of the descent of the Holy Spirit after Christ's ascension ; and when on the great day of Pentecost the devout Jews, " out of every nation under heaven," heard the apostle speaking in their several tongues the wonderful works of God, it was a testimony that God was beginning spiritually to make "*the outgoings of the morning and evening to rejoice.*" To God "which stilleth the noise of the waves and the tumult of the people," the apostles betook themselves in prayer after their first conflict with Jewish authorities, the first conflict of the infant Christian community with the powers of this world : the language of the Psalm (ver. 5), "*O God of our salvation ; who art the confidence of all the ends of the earth, and of them that are afar off upon the sea,*" is reflected in the opening words of their prayer on that occasion (Acts iv. 24), " Lord, thou art God, which hast made heaven, and earth, and the sea, and all that in them is ; " and if, when they prayed, " the place was shaken where they were assembled together, and they were all filled with the Holy Ghost," it was no idle sign that " by terrible things in righteousness " were they being answered by the God of their salvation. These are, of course, mere illustrations of the inner harmony of Scripture ; but, as such, they may not be without their value.—*Joseph Francis Thrupp.*

Verse 6.—" *Setteth fast the mountains.*" It is by thy strength they have been raised, and by thy power they are girded about and preserved. He represents the mountains as being formed and pitched into their proper places by the mighty hand of God ; and shows that they are preserved from splitting, falling down, or mouldering away, as it were, by a girdle by which they are surrounded. The image is very fine. They were hooped about by the divine power.—*Adam Clarke.*

Verse 8.—" *Thou makest the outgoings of the morning and evening to rejoice.*" That is, thou makest men to rejoice, they are glad, they rejoice in, or at, the out-goings in the morning. And at the evening men rejoice too, for then they go to their rest, being wearied with the labour of the day. Or, we may thus expound it : Thou makest men who live at the outgoings of the morning, and at the outgoings of the evening, to rejoice. As if it had been said, Thou makest the eastern people and the western people, all people from east to west, rejoice. And that which makes all people to rejoice, naturally, is the rising of light with them in the east, and the coming of light towards them in the west.—*Joseph Caryl.*

Verse 8.—" *Thou makest the outgoings of the morning and evening to rejoice.*" How contrary soever light and darkness are to each other, and how inviolable soever the partition between them (Gen. i. 4), both are equally welcome to the world in their season ; it is hard to say which is more welcome to us, the light of the morning which befriends the business of the day, or the shadows of the evening which befriend the repose of the night. Doth the watchman wait for the morning ? so doth the hireling earnestly desire the shadow. Some understand it for the morning and evening sacrifice, which good people greatly rejoiced in, and in which God was constantly honoured. Thou makest them to sing, so the word is ; for every morning and every evening songs of praise were sung by the Levites ; it was that which the duty of every day required. And we are to look upon our daily worship alone, and with our families, to be both the most needful of our daily business, and the most delightful of our daily comforts ; and if therein we keep up our communion with God, the outgoings both of the morning and of the evening are thereby made truly to rejoice.—*Matthew Henry.*

Verse 8.—Lyranus, Dionysius Carthusianus, Cajetanus, Placidus Parmensis, (who treads in the footsteps of Cajetanus though he does not mention him,) take the first clause to refer to the wonder of all mankind at the wonderful works of God on the land and the sea ; and explain the second respecting the sacrifices which were wont to be offered in the morning and evening : that God made these acceptable to himself and delightful to those who offered them, especially after the return from captivity. In the beginning of the Psalm sacrifices are hinted at by *praise* and *vows*, as we have seen, and in the history of Esdra it is recorded, that *the morning and evening sacrifice were offered unto the Lord* by those who had returned ; and that those who approached, when they entered, and others who had made their offerings, when they departed, gave praises to God. Hence it is here said, that the outgoings of the morning and of the evening, that is to say, when they who praise God go forth from either sacrifice, God will be well pleased, he will receive delight from that praise, and it will be grateful to him.—*Lorinus.*

Verse 8.—Figuratively, " *the outgoing of the morning,*" or dawn, is the light of grace in the beginning of conversion ; " *the outgoing of the evening* " is the fine light of grace in the hour of death.—*Thomas Le Blanc.*

Verse 9.—" *Thou visitest the earth, and waterest it,*" etc. How beautiful are the words of the inspired poet, read in this month of harvest, nearly three thousand years after they were written ! For nearly three thousand years since the royal poet looked over the plains of Judea covered with the bounty of God, and broke forth into his magnificent hymn of praise, has the earth rolled on in her course, and the hand of God has blessed her, and all her children, with seed-time and harvest, with joy and abundance. The very steadfastness of the Almighty's liberality, flowing like a mighty ocean through the infinite vast of the universe, makes his creatures forget to wonder at its wonderfulness, to feel true thankfulness at its immeasurable goodness. The sun rises and sets so surely ; the seasons run on amid all their changes with such inimitable truth, that we take as a matter of course that which is amazing beyond all stretch of imagination, and good beyond the widest expansion of the noblest human heart.

The poor man, with his half-dozen children, toils, and often dies, under the vain labour of winning bread for them. God feeds his family of countless myriads swarming over the surface of all countless worlds, and none know need but through the follies of themselves, or the cruelty of their fellows. God pours his light from innumerable suns on innumerable rejoicing planets; he waters them everywhere in the fittest moment; he ripens the food of globes and of nations, and gives them fair weather to garner it. And from age to age, amid his endless creatures of endless forms and powers, in the beauty and the sunshine, and the magnificence of nature, he seems to sing throughout creation the glorious song of his own divine joy, in the immortality of his youth, in the omnipotence of his nature, in the eternity of his patience, and the abounding boundlessness of his love. What a family hangs on his sustaining arm! The life and soul of infinite ages, and of uncounted worlds! Let a moment's failure of his power, of his watchfulness, or of his will to do good, occur, and what a sweep of death and annihilation through the universe! How stars would reel, planets expire, and nations perish! But from age to age, no such catastrophe occurs, even in the midst of national crimes, and of atheism that denies the hand that made and feeds it. Life springs with a power ever new; food springs up as plentifully to sustain it, and sunshine and joy are poured over all from the invisible throne of God, as the poetry of the existence which he has given. If there come seasons of dearth, or of failure, they come but as warnings to proud and tyrannic man. The potato is smitten that a nation may not be oppressed for ever; and the harvest is diminished that the laws of man's unnatural avarice may be rent asunder. And then, again, the sun shines, the rain falls, and the earth rejoices in a renewed beauty, and in a redoubled plenty.—*William Howitt, in " The Year-Book of the Country,"* 1850.

Verse 9.—*" Thou visitest the earth."* God seems to come with the coming-in of each of the seasons. In some respects, during winter, God seems like a man travelling into a far country. Darkness, and barrenness, and coldness, suggest absence on the part of God. The spring looks like his return. The great change it involves cheerily whispers, " He is not far from any one of us." In longer days, and a warmer atmosphere, and a revived earth, God comes to us. These things are not of necessity, but of providence. There are second causes, but above all these is the First Cause, intelligent, loving, and free, God rules in all, over all, and above all. He is not displaced or supplanted by the forces and agencies which he employs, he is not absorbed by care of other worlds, he is not indifferent toward the earth. A personal superintendence and providence are not beneath his dignity, or in anywise distasteful to him. As Maker, and Life-giver, and Father, *" Thou visitest the earth, and waterest it."*—*Samuel Martin, in " Rain upon the Mown Grass, and other Sermons."* 1871.

Verse 9.—The Psalmist is here foretelling the gracious outpouring of the Holy Spirit, and the conversion of the nations of the earth to Christ.—*Origen.*

Verse 9.—The chiefs of Hebrew theology attribute four keys to God, which he never entrusted to any angel or seraph, and as the first of these they place *the key of rain.* He himself is said, in Job xxviii. 26, to give a law to the rain, and in chap. xxvi. 8, *to bind up the waters in the clouds.*—*Thomas Le Blanc.*

Verse 9.—*" With the river of God, which is full of water."* That is, the clouds figuratively described.—*Edward Leigh* (1602-3—1671).

Verse 9.—*" The river of God,"* as opposed to earthly streams. However these may fail, the divine resources are exhaustless.—*Joseph Addison Alexander.*

Verse 9.—*" The river of God."* The Chaldee paraphrase is, *From the fountain of God which is in the heavens, which is full of the rain-storms of blessing, thou wilt prepare their cornfields.*—*Lorinus.*

Verse 9.—*" Thou preparest their grain; for so dost thou prepare the earth."* [Version of Am. Bib. Un.] *" So,"* namely, with this design, and for this end. In the Hebrew, " for so dost thou prepare her: " referring to " the earth," which in Hebrew is *fem.,* while grain is *masc.* The meaning can be expressed in English only by using the word (earth) which the Hebrew pronoun represents. The English pronoun (it) would necessarily refer to " grain," and would represent neither the meaning of the Hebrew nor its form.—*Thomas J. Conant.*

Verse 9.—*" Thou preparest them corn,"* etc. Corn is the special gift of God to man. There are several interesting and instructive ideas connected with this view of it. All the other plants we use as food are unfit for this purpose in their natural condition, and require to have their nutritious qualities developed, and their natures and forms to a certain extent changed by a gradual process of cultivation. There is not a single useful plant grown in our gardens and fields, but is utterly worthless for food in its normal or wild state ; and man has been left to himself to find out, slowly and painfully, how to convert these crudities of nature into nutritious vegetables. But it is not so with corn. It has from the very beginning been an abnormal production. God gave it to Adam, we have every reason to believe, in the same perfect state of preparation for food in which we find it at the present day. It was made expressly for man, and given directly into his hands. " Behold," says the Creator, " I have given you every herb bearing seed which is upon the face of all the earth ; " that is, all the cereal plants—such as corn, wheat, barley, rice, maize, etc., whose peculiar characteristic it is to produce seed. . . . .

There is another proof that corn was created for man's use, in the fact that it has never been found in a wild state. The primitive types from which all our other esculent plants were derived are still to be found in a state of nature in this or other countries. The wild beet and cabbage still grow on our sea-shores ; the crab-apple and the sloe, the savage parents of our luscious pippins and plums, are still found among the trees of the wood ; but where are the original types of our corn plants ? Where are the wild grasses which, according to some authors, the cumulative processes of agriculture, carried on through successive ages, have developed into corn, wheat, and barley ? Much has been written, and many experiments have been tried, to determine the natural origin of these cereals, but every effort has hitherto proved in vain. Reports have again and again been circulated that corn and wheat have been found growing wild in some parts of Persia and the steppes of Tartary, apparently far from the influence of cultivation ; but when tested by botanical data, these reports have turned out, in every instance, to be unfounded. Corn has never been known as anything else than a cultivated plant.

History and observation probe that it cannot grow spontaneously. It is never, like other plants, self-sown and self-diffused. Neglected of men, it speedily disappears and becomes extinct. It does not return, as do all other cultivated varieties of plants, to a natural condition, and so become worthless as food, but utterly perishes, being constitutionally unfitted to maintain the struggle for existence with the aboriginal vegetation of the soil. All this proves that it must have been produced miraculously ; or, in other words, given by God to man directly, in the same abnormal condition in which it now appears ; for nature never could have developed or preserved it. In the mythologies of all the ancient nations it was confidently affirmed to have had a supernatural origin. The Greeks and Romans believed it to be the gift of the goddess Ceres, who taught her son, Triptolemus, to cultivate and distribute it over the earth ; and from her, the whole class of plants received the name of cereals, which they now bear. And we only express the same truth when we say to him, whom these pagans ignorantly worshipped, " *Thou preparest them corn, when thou hast so provided for it.*"

Let me bring forth one more proof of special design, enabling us to recognise the hand of God in this mercy. Corn is universally diffused. It is almost the only species of plant which is capable of growing everywhere in almost every soil, in almost any situation. In some form or other, adapted to the various modifications of climate and physical conditions, which occur in different countries, it is spread over an area of the earth's surface as extensive as the occupancy of the human race. . . . .

Rice is grown in tropical countries where periodical rains and inundations, followed by excessive heat, occur, and furnishes the chief article of diet for the largest proportion of the human race. Wheat will not thrive in hot climates, but flourishes all over the temperate zone, at various ranges of elevation, and is admirably adapted to the wants of highly civilised communities. Maize spreads over an immense geographical area in the new world, where it has been known from time immemorial, and formed a principal element of that Indian civilisation which surprised the Spaniards in Mexico and Peru. Barley is cultivated in those parts of Europe and Asia where the soil and climate are not adapted for wheat ; while oats and rye extend far into the black north, and disappear only from those desolate Arctic regions where man cannot exist in his social capacity. By these striking adaptations of different varieties of grain, containing the same essential ingredients, to different soils and climates, Providence has furnished the indispensable food for the sustenance of the human race throughout the whole habitable globe and all nations, and tribes, and tongues can rejoice together, as one great family, with the joy of harvest.—*Hugh Macmillan, in " Bible Teachings in Nature."* 1868.

Verses 9—13.—I do not know any picture of rural life that in any measure comes up to the exquisite description here brought before us, and which every one's heart at once recognises as so true to nature in all its branches. In the brief compass of five verses we have the whole scene vividly sketched, from the first preparation of the earth or soil ; the provision of the corn-seed for the sower ; the rain in its season, the former and the latter rain, watering the ridges, settling the furrows, and causing the seed to swell and to spring forth, and bud and blossom ; then the crowning of the whole year in the appointed weeks of harvest, and men's hearts rejoicing before God according to the joy in harvest, the very foot-paths dropping with fatness, and the valleys shouting and singing for joy. Our harvest-homes are times of rejoicing too, but I would that our tillers and reapers of the soil would as piously refer all to God as the Psalmist did. " *Thou* waterest the earth, *Thou* greatly enrichest it, *Thou* preparest the corn, *Thou* waterest the ridges, *Thou* settlest the furrows, *Thou* makest it soft with showers, *Thou* blessest the springing thereof, *Thou* crownest the year with thy goodness." Not one word of man, of man's skill, or of man's labour, not one thought of self. How different from him whose grounds brought forth abundantly, and whose only thought was, " I will say to my soul, Soul, thou hast much goods laid up for many years ; take thine ease, eat, drink, and be merry."—*Barton Bouchier.*

Verse 10.—The rain hath a *mollifying nature*. When the earth is like iron under our feet by long droughts or hard frosts, a few good showers supple it, and make it tender. David, speaking of the earth, saith, " *Thou makest it soft with showers.*" Jesus Christ hath a softening virtue. Sometimes the heart is hardened by the deceitfulness of sin. . . . . If Christ would but now drop a few drops from heaven, the veriest flint in the congregation would be turned into a fountain of water. . . . . The rain hath a *fructifying virtue*. All the labour of the husbandman comes to nothing if either the former or the latter rain be denied. The Psalmist sets out this virtue of the rain in verses 9—13. Want of rain brings a famine upon the earth. . . . . If Christ do not rain, there will be no fruits ; but if Christ will drop down his dew, the pastures will be green. All the labour and pains of the spiritual husbandman will come to nothing if the rain come not down from Christ ; and, if he please to pour down showers, let not the eunuch say, " I am a dry tree." Though your heart be as dry and withered as the rod of Aaron was, yet if Christ will rain upon it, it shall both bud, and blossom, and bring forth almonds. . . . . The rain hath a *recreating virtue*. It causeth a gladness and cheerfulness in the hearts of men, and it begets a kind of briskness in the sensitive creatures : the birds chirp, the beasts of the field rejoice in their kind ; yea, there is a kind of joy in the very inanimate creatures. The Psalmist speaks of this : " The pastures are clothed with flocks, the valleys also are covered over with corn ; they shout for joy, they also sing." When rain comes after a long drought, there is melody made by all creatures in this lower world. Jesus Christ hath a cheering virtue ; he doth fill the soul with joy when he comes down into the soul ; the heart that was dead, and dull, and heavy is made pleasant and joyful when these showers fall upon it. When Jesus Christ comes to the soul, he brings joy to the soul : " They joy before thee according to the joy in harvest, and as men rejoice when they divide the spoil." Isa. ix. 3.—*Ralph Robinson.*

Verse 10.—Thou art the right Master-cultivator, who cultivates the land much more and much better than the farmer does. He does nothing more to it than break up the ground, and plough, and sow, and then lets it lie. But God must be always attending to it with rain and heat, and must do everything to make it grow and prosper, while the farmer lies at home and sleeps.—*Martin Luther.*

Verse 11.—"*Thou crownest the year with thy goodness.*" Dr. William Whewell, in his Bridgewater Treatise, notes the evidence of design in the length of the year, and, although it may not perhaps be considered to be a direct comment on the text, I beg to quote it here, as it may awaken a train of thought, and make more conspicuous the goodness of God, in the revolution of the seasons. " If any change in the length of the year were to take place, the working of the botanical world would be thrown into utter disorder, the functions of plants would be entirely deranged, and the whole vegetable kingdom involved in instant decay and rapid extinction. That this would be the case, may be collected from innumerable indications. Most of our fruit trees, for example, require the year to be of its present length. If the summer and the autumn were much shorter, the fruit could not ripen ; if these seasons were much longer, the tree would put forth a fresh suit of blossoms, to be cut down by the winter. Or, if the year were twice its present length, a second crop of fruit would probably not be matured, for want, among other things, of an immediate season of rest and consolidation, such as the winter is. Our forest trees, in like manner, appear to need all the seasons of our present year for their perfection ; the spring, summer, and autumn, for the development of their leaves and consequent formation of their *proper juice*, and of wood from this ; and the winter for the hardening and solidifying the substance thus formed. . . . . . . The processes of the rising of the sap, of the formation of proper juices, of the unfolding of leaves, the opening of flowers, the fecundation of the fruit, the ripening of the seed, its proper deposition in order for the reproduction of a new plant ; all these operations require a certain portion of time, and could not be compressed into a space less than a year, or at least could not be abbreviated in any very great degree. And, on the other hand, if the winter were greatly longer than it now is, many seeds would not germinate at the return of spring. Seeds which have been kept too long, require stimulants to make them fertile. If, therefore, the duration of the seasons were much to change, the processes of vegetable life would be interrupted, deranged, distempered. What, for instance, would become of our calendar of Flora, if the year were lengthened or shortened by six months ? Some of the dates would never arrive in the one case, and the vegetable processes which mark them would be superseded ; some seasons would be without dates in the other case, and these periods would be employed in a way hurtful to the plants, and no doubt speedily destructive. We should have, not only a *year of confusion*, but, if it were repeated and continued, a year of death. . . . . The same kind of argument might be applied to the animal creation. The pairing, nesting, hatching, fledging, and flight of birds, for instance, occupy each its peculiar time of the year ; and, together with a proper period of rest, fill up the twelve months ; the transformations of most insects have a similar reference to the seasons, their progress and duration. ' In every species ' (except man's), says a writer[*] on animals, ' there is a particular period of the year in which the reproductive system exercises its energies. And the season of love and the period of gestation are so arranged that the young ones are produced at the time wherein the conditions of temperature are most suited to the commencement of life.' It is not our business here to consider the details of such provisions, beautiful and striking as they are. But the prevalence of the great law of periodicity in the vital functions of organised beings will be allowed to have a claim to be considered in its reference to astronomy, when it is seen that their periodical constitution derives its use from the periodical nature of the motions of the planets round the sun ; and that the duration of such cycles in the existence of plants and animals has a reference to the arbitrary elements of the solar system, a reference which, we maintain, is inexplicable and unintelligible, except by admitting into our conceptions an intelligent Author, alike of the organic and inorganic universe."

Verse 11.—"*Thou crownest the year with thy goodness.*" God has surrounded this year with his goodness, " compassed and enclosed it " on every side. So we translate the same word, (Ps. v. 12) " With favour wilt thou compass (or crown) him as with a shield." He has given us instances of his goodness in every thing that concerns us ; so that turn which way we will, we meet with the tokens of his favour ; every part of the year has been enriched with the blessings of heaven, and no gap has been left open for any desolating judgment to enter by.—*Matthew Henry.*

Verse 11.—"*Thou crownest the year.*" A full and *plentiful harvest* is the *crown* of the year ; and this springs from the unmerited *goodness* of God. This is the *diadem* of the earth. עטרת *ittarta*, "*Thou encirclest*," as with a diadem. A most elegant expression, to show the progress of the sun through the *twelve* signs of the zodiac, producing the seasons, and giving a sufficiency of light and heat alternately, to all places on the surface of the globe, by its north and south declination (amounting to 23° 28' at the solstices) on each side of the equator. A more beautiful image

---

could not have been chosen; and the very appearance of the *space*, termed the *zodiac* on a celestial globe, shows with what propriety the idea of a *circle* or *diadem* was conceived by this inimitable poet.—*Adam Clarke.*

Verse 11.—"*Thou crownest.*" The herbs, fruits, and flowers, produced by the earth, are here finely represented as a beautiful variegated crown, set upon her head, by the hands of the great Creator.—*Samuel Burder.*

Verse 11.—*To crown* the year of goodness, is to raise it to the highest degree and summit of prosperity, happiness and glory. *To crown,* to fill up, to make glorious and joyful : *the year of the goodness* of God is the time in which he unfolds his own highest goodness ; *one is crowned,* when the effects of this goodness are displayed on the grandest scale, and bring great glory and joy. Such was the time when he shone forth, and the clouds dropped fatness, and all parts of the earth were filled with fertility. . . . . The paths of God are the clouds, before called the *river* of God (see Ps. civ. 3), now the *paths* in which God himself seems to move, and whence, from the place of rain, from the river of God, flows fatness itself, or the copious abundance of all that is sweetest and best.—*Hermann Venema.*

Verse 11.—"*Thy paths drop fatness.*" When the conqueror journeys through the nations, his paths drop blood ; fire and vapour of smoke are in his track, and tears, and groans, and sighs attend him. But where the Lord journeys, his "*paths drop fatness.*" When the kings of old made a progress through their dominions, they caused a famine wherever they tarried ; for the greedy courtiers who swarmed in their camp devoured all things like locusts, and were as greedily ravenous as palmer-worms and caterpillars. But where the great King of kings journeys, he enriches the land ; his "*paths drop fatness.*" By a bold Hebrew metaphor the clouds are represented as the chariots of God : "He maketh the clouds his chariot ; " and as the Lord Jehovah rides upon the heavens in the greatness of his strength, and in his excellency on the sky, the rains drop down upon the lands, and so the wheel-tracks of Jehovah are marked by the fatness which makes glad the earth. Happy, happy are the people who worship such a God, whose coming is ever a coming of goodness and of grace to his creatures.—*C. H. S.*

Verse 11.—"*Paths*" here are properly such tracks as are made by chariot wheels. —*Henry Ainsworth.*

Verse 12.—"*The wilderness.*" By *desert,* or *wilderness,* the reader is not always to understand a country altogether barren and unfruitful, but such only as is rarely or never sown or cultivated ; which, though it yields no crops of corn or fruit, yet affords herbage more or less for the grazing of cattle, with fountains or rills of water, though more sparingly interspersed than in other places.—*Thomas Shaw* (1692— 1751).

Verse 13.—The phrase, "*the pastures are clothed with flocks,*" cannot be regarded as the vulgar language of poetry. It appears peculiarly beautiful and appropriate, when we consider the numerous flocks which whitened the plains of Syria and Canaan. In the eastern countries, sheep are much more prolific than with us, and they derive their name from their great fruitfulness ; bringing forth, as they are said to do, " thousands and ten thousands in their streets," Ps. cxliv. 13. They, therefore, formed no mean part of the wealth of the East.—*James Anderson, in editorial Note to Calvin in loc.*

Verse 13.—The hills, where not tilled, were bushy and green, and sprinkled with numerous flocks ; the valleys broad and covered with a rich crop of wheat ; the fields full of reapers and gleaners in the midst of the harvest, with asses and camels receiving their loads of sheaves, and feeding unmuzzled and undisturbed upon the ripe grain.—*Edward Robinson.*

Verse 13.—It may seem strange, that he should first tell us, that "*they shout for joy,*" and then add the feebler expression, that "*they sing ; *" interposing, too, the intensative particle, אף, *aph, they shout for joy,* YEA, *they also sing.* The verb, however, admits of being taken in the future tense, *they shall sing ;* and this denotes a continuation of joy, that they would rejoice, not only one year, but through the endless succession of the seasons. I may add, what is well-known, that in Hebrew the order of expression is frequently inverted in this way.—*John Calvin.*

Verse 13.—"*They also sing.*" They ardently sing : such is the real meaning of אף ; primarily " heat " or " warmth," thence " ardour, passion, anger," and thence again " the nostrils," as the supposed seat of this feeling.—*John Mason Good.*

HINTS TO PREACHERS.

Verse 1.—The fitness, place, use, and power of silence in worship.

Verse 1.—The limitations, advantages, and obligations of vows.

Verse 2 (*first clause*).—The hearing and granting of prayer is the Lord's property, his usual practice, his pleasure, his nature, and his glory.—*David Dickson.*

Verse 3.—I. *The humble confession.* Sins prevail against us. 1. *When* we are unwatchful, or go into temptation, and even after most sacred engagements. 2. *How.* Through our inbred corruption, natural constitution, suddenness of temptation, neglect of means of grace, and want of fellowship. 3. In *whom.* In the best of men: David says, "against me." Let us take home the caution. II. *The reassuring confidence.* Sin is forgiven. 1. By God: "Thou." 2. By atonement: covering all. 3. Effectually: "purge away." 4. Comprehensively: "our transgressions."

Verse 3.—I. *A cry of distress.* Mansoul besieged: "Iniquities prevail against me." II. *A shout of delight.* Mansoul relieved: "Thou shalt purge them away."—*E. G. Gange.*

Verse 4.—Nearness to God is the foundation of a creature's happiness. This doctrine appears in full evidence, while we consider the three chief ingredients of true felicity, *viz.*, the contemplation of the noblest object, to satisfy all the powers of the understanding; the love of the supreme good, to answer the utmost propensities of the will, and the sweet and everlasting sensation and assurance of the love of an Almighty Friend, who will free us from all the evils which our nature can fear, and confer upon us all the good which a wise and innocent creature can desire. Thus all the capacities of man are employed in their highest and sweetest exercises and enjoyments.—*Isaac Watts.*

Verse 4.—Election, effectual calling, access, adoption, final perseverance, satisfaction. This verse is a body of divinity in miniature.

Verse 5.—Treat the first clause experimentally, and show how prayers for our own sanctification are answered by trial; for God's glory, by our persecution; for our babes' salvation, by their death; for the good of others, by their sickness, etc., etc.

Verse 7.—The Lord, the giver, creator, and preserver of peace.

Verse 8.—Tokens of God's presence; those causing terror, and those inspiring joy.

Verse 8 (*last clause*).—The peculiar joys of morning and evening.

Verse 9.—"*The river of God.*" John Bunyan's treatise on "The Water of Life" would be suggestive on this topic.

Verse 9.—Divine visits and their consequences.

Verses 9—13.—A Harvest Sermon. I. *The general goodness of God.* Visiting the earth in rotation of seasons: "Seed time and harvest," etc. II. *The greatness of his resources:* "The river of God, which is full of water;" not like Elijah's brook, which dried up. III. *The variety of his benefactions:* "Corn;" "Water;" "Blessest the springing thereof," etc. IV. *The perpetuity of his blessings:* "Crownest the year."—*E. G. G.*

Verse 10.—Divine grace like rain. I. In itself. II. In its abundance. III. In its effects on the heart and entire nature; falling on ridge and furrow; softening, etc. IV. In its fruitful results. See the extract from Ralph Robinson *in loc.*

Verse 10 (*last clause*).—See "Spurgeon's Sermons," No. 675: "Spring in the Heart."

Verse 11.—See "Spurgeon's Sermons," No. 532: "Thanksgiving and Prayer."

Verse 12 (*first clause*).—I. *Our dwelling place:* "the wilderness." II. *Our spiritual provision:* "pastures." III. *Our heavenly refreshment:* "they drop."

Verse 12.—Causes for joy for small churches. God remembers them, stablishes and increases them, feeds them and revives them, etc.

Verse 13.—The song of nature and the ear which hears it.

PSALM LXVI.

TITLE.—To the Chief Musician.—*He had need be a man of great skill, worthily to sing such a Psalm as this : the best music in the world would be honoured by marriage with such expressions. A Song or Psalm, or a Song and Psalm. It may be either said or sung ; it is a marvellous poem if it be but read ; but set to suitable music, it must have been one of the noblest strains ever heard by the Jewish people. We do not know who is its author, but we see no reason to doubt that David wrote it. It is in the Davidic style, and has nothing in it unsuited to his times. It is true the " house " of God is mentioned, but the tabernacle was entitled to that designation as well as the temple.*

SUBJECT AND DIVISION.—*Praise is the topic, and the subjects for song are the Lord's great works, his gracious benefits, his faithful deliverances, and all his dealings with his people, brought to a close by a personal testimony to special kindness received by the prophet-bard himself. Verses 1, 2, 3, 4 are a kind of introductory hymn, calling upon all nations to praise God, and dictating to them the words of a suitable song. Verses 5, 6, 7 invite the beholder to " Come and see " the works of the Lord, pointing attention to the Red Sea, and perhaps the passage of Jordan. This suggests the similar position of the afflicted people which is described, and its joyful issue predicted, from verse 8 to verse 12. The singer then becomes personal, and confesses his own obligations to the Lord (verses 13, 14, 15) ; and, bursting forth with a vehement " Come and hear," declares with thanksgiving the special favour of the Lord to himself, verses 16—20.*

EXPOSITION.

MAKE a joyful noise unto God, all ye lands :

2 Sing forth the honour of his name : make his praise glorious.

3 Say unto God, How terrible *art thou in* thy works ! through the greatness of thy power shall thine enemies submit themselves unto thee.

4 All the earth shall worship thee, and shall sing unto thee ; they shall sing *to* thy name. Selah.

1. *" Make a joyful noise unto God."* " In Zion," where the more instructed saints were accustomed to profound meditation, the song was silent unto God, and was accepted of him : but in the great popular assemblies a joyful noise was more appropriate and natural, and it would be equally acceptable. If praise is to be wide-spread, it must be vocal ; exulting sounds stir the soul and cause a sacred contagion of thanksgiving. Composers of tunes for the congregation should see to it that their airs are cheerful ; we need not so much noise, as *joyful* noise. God is to be praised with the voice, and the heart should go therewith in holy exultation. All praise from all nations should be rendered unto the Lord. Happy the day when no shouts shall be presented to Juggernaut or Buddha, but all the earth shall adore the Creator thereof. *" All ye lands."* Ye heathen nations, ye who have not known Jehovah hitherto, with one consent let the whole earth rejoice before God. The languages of the lands are many, but their praises should be one, addressed to one only God.

2. *" Sing forth the honour of his name."* The noise is to be modulated with tune and time, and fashioned into singing, for we adore the God of order and harmony. The honour of God should be our subject, and to honour him our object when we sing. To give glory to God is but to restore to him his own. It is our glory to be able to give God glory ; and all our true glory should be ascribed unto God, for it is his glory. " All worship be to God only," should be the motto of all true believers. The name, nature, and person of God are worthy of the highest honour. *" Make his praise glorious."* Let not his praise be mean and grovelling : let it arise with grandeur and solemnity before him. The pomp of the ancient festivals is not to be imitated by us, under this dispensation of the Spirit, but we are to

throw so much of heart and holy reverence into all our worship that it shall be the best we can render. Heart worship and spiritual joy render praise more glorious than vestments, incense, and music could do.

3. "*Say unto God.*" Turn all your praises to him. Devotion, unless it be resolutely directed to the Lord, is no better than whistling to the wind. "*How terrible art thou in thy works.*" The mind is usually first arrested by those attributes which cause fear and trembling; and, even when the heart has come to love God, and rest in him, there is an increase of worship when the soul is awed by an extraordinary display of the more dreadful of the divine characteristics. Looking upon the convulsions which have shaken continents, the hurricanes which have devastated nations, the plagues which have desolated cities, and other great and amazing displays of divine working, men may well say: "How terrible art thou in thy works." Till we see God in Christ, the terrible predominates in all our apprehensions of him. "*Through the greatness of thy power shall thine enemies submit themselves unto thee;*" but, as the Hebrew clearly intimates, it will be a forced and false submission. Power brings a man to his knee, but love alone wins his heart. Pharaoh said he would let Israel go, but he lied unto God; he submitted in word but not in deed. Tens of thousands, both in earth and hell, are rendering this constrained homage to the Almighty; they only submit because they cannot do otherwise; it is not their loyalty, but his power, which keeps them subjects of his boundless dominion.

4. "*All the earth shall worship thee, and shall sing unto thee.*" All men must even now prostrate themselves before thee, but a time will come when they shall do this cheerfully: to the worship of fear shall be added the singing of love. What a change shall have taken place when singing shall displace sighing, and music shall thrust out misery! "*They shall sing to thy name.*" The nature and works of God will be the theme of earth's universal song, and he himself shall be the object of the joyful adoration of our emancipated race. Acceptable worship not only praises God as the mysterious Lord, but it is rendered fragrant by some measure of knowledge of his name or character. God would not be worshipped as an unknown God, nor have it said of his people, "Ye worship ye know not what." May the knowledge of the Lord soon cover the earth, that so the universality of intelligent worship may be possible: such a consummation was evidently expected by the writer of this Psalm; and, indeed, throughout all Old Testament writings, there are intimations of the future general spread of the worship of God. It was an instance of wilful ignorance and bigotry when the Jews raged against the preaching of the gospel to the Gentiles. Perverted Judaism may be exculsive, but the religion of Moses, and David, and Isaiah was not so.

"*Selah.*" A little pause for holy expectation is well inserted after so great a prophecy, and the uplifting of the heart is also a seasonable direction. No meditation can be more joyous than that excited by the prospect of a world reconciled to its Creator.

5 Come and see the works of God: *he is* terrible *in his* doing toward the children of men.

6 He turned the sea into dry *land :* they went through the flood on foot : there did we rejoice in him.

7 He ruleth by his power for ever ; his eyes behold the nations : let not the rebellious exalt themselves. Selah.

5. "*Come and see the works of God.*" Such glorious events, as the cleaving of the Red Sea and the overthrow of Pharaoh, are standing wonders, and throughout all time a voice sounds forth concerning them—"Come and see." Even till the close of all things, the marvellous works of God at the Red Sea will be the subject of meditation and praise; for, standing on the sea of glass mingled with fire, the triumphal armies of heaven sing the song of Moses, the servant of God, and the song of the Lamb. It has always been the favourite subject of the inspired bards, and their choice was most natural. "*He is terrible in his doing toward the children of men.*" For the defence of his church and the overthrow of her foes he deals terrific blows, and strikes the mighty with fear. O thou enemy, wherefore dost thou vaunt thyself? Speak no more so exceeding proudly, but remember the plagues which bowed the will of Pharaoh, the drowning of Egypt's chariots in the Red Sea, the

overthrow of Og and Sihon, the scattering of the Canaanites before the tribes. This same God still liveth, and is to be worshipped with trembling reverence.

6. "*He turned the sea into dry land.*" It was no slight miracle to divide a pathway through such a sea, and to make it fit for the traffic of a whole nation. He who did this can do anything, and must be God, the worthy object of adoration. The Christian's inference is that no obstacle in his journey heavenward need hinder him, for the sea could not hinder Israel, and even death itself shall be as life ; the sea shall be dry land when God's presence is felt. "*They went through the flood on foot.*" Through the river the tribes passed dry-shod, Jordan was afraid because of them.

> "What ail'd thee, O thou mighty sea ?
> Why roll'd thy waves in dread ?
> What bade thy tide, O Jordan, flee
> And bare its deepest bed ?
>
> O earth, before the Lord, the God
> Of Jacob, tremble still ;
> Who makes the waste a water'd sod,
> The flint a gushing rill."

"*There did we rejoice in him.*" We participate this day in that ancient joy. The scene is so vividly before us that it seems as if we were there personally, singing unto the Lord because he hath triumphed gloriously. Faith casts herself bodily into the past joys of the saints, and realises them for herself in much the same fashion in which she projects herself into the bliss of the future, and becomes the substance of things hoped for. It is to be remarked that Israel's joy was in her God, and there let ours be. It is not so much what he has done, as what he is, that should excite in us a sacred rejoicing. " He is my God, and I will prepare him an habitation ; my father's God, and I will exalt him."

7. "*He ruleth by his power for ever.*" He has not deceased, nor abdicated, nor suffered defeat. The prowess displayed at the Red Sea is undiminished : the divine dominion endures throughout eternity. "*His eyes behold the nations.*" Even as he looked out of the cloud upon the Egyptians and discomfited them, so does he spy out his enemies, and mark their conspiracies. His hand rules and his eye observes, his hand has not waxed weak, nor his eye dim. As so many grasshoppers he sees the people and tribes, at one glance he takes in all their ways. He oversees all and overlooks none. "*Let not the rebellious exalt themselves.*" The proudest have no cause to be proud. Could they see themselves as God sees them they would shrivel into nothing. Where rebellion reaches to a great head, and hopes most confidently for success, it is a sufficient reason for abating our fears, that the Omnipotent ruler is also an Omniscient observer. O proud rebels, remember that the Lord aims his arrows at the high-soaring eagles, and brings them down from their nests among the stars. "He hath put down the mighty from their seats, and exalted them of low degree." After a survey of the Red Sea and Jordan, rebels, if they were in their senses, would have no more stomach for the fight, but would humble themselves at the Conqueror's feet. "*Selah.*" Pause again, and take time to bow low before the throne of the Eternal.

8 O bless our God, ye people, and make the voice of his praise to be heard :
9 Which holdeth our soul in life, and suffereth not our feet to be moved.
10 For thou, O God, hast proved us : thou hast tried us, as silver is tried.
11 Thou broughtest us into the net ; thou laidst affliction upon our loins.
12 Thou hast caused men to ride over our heads ; we went through fire and through water : but thou broughtest us out into a wealthy *place.*

8. "*O bless our God, ye people.*" Ye chosen seed, peculiarly beloved, it is yours to bless your covenant God as other nations cannot. Ye should lead the strain, for he is peculiarly your God. First visited by his love, ye should be foremost in his praise. "*And make the voice of his praise to be heard.*" Whoever else may sing with bated breath, do you be sure to give full tongue and volume to the song. Compel unwilling ears to hear the praises of your covenant God. Make rocks, and hills, and earth, and sea, and heaven itself to echo with your joyful shouts.

9. "*Which holdeth our soul in life.*" At any time the preservation of life, and especially the soul's life, is a great reason for gratitude, but much more when we

are called to undergo extreme trials, which of themselves would crush our being. Blessed be God, who, having put our souls into possession of life, has been pleased to preserve that heaven-given life from the destroying power of the enemy. *" And suffereth not our feet to be moved."* This is another and precious boon. If God has enabled us not only to keep our life, but our position, we are bound to give him double praise. Living and standing is the saint's condition through divine grace. Immortal and immovable are those whom God preserves. Satan is put to shame, for instead of being able to slay the saints, as he hoped, he is not even able to trip them up. God is able to make the weakest to stand fast, and he will do so.

10. *" For thou, O God, hast proved us."* He proved his Israel with sore trials. David had his temptations. All the saints must go to the proving house; God had one Son without sin, but he never had a son without trial. Why ought we to complain if we are subjected to the rule which is common to all the family, and from which so much benefit has flowed to them? The Lord himself proves us, who then shall raise a question as to the wisdom and the love which are displayed in the operation? The day may come when, as in this case, we shall make hymns out of our griefs, and sing all the more sweetly because our mouths have been purified with bitter draughts. *" Thou hast tried us, as silver is tried."* Searching and repeated, severe and thorough, has been the test; the same result has followed as in the case of precious metal, for the dross and tin have been consumed, and the pure ore has been discovered. Since trial is sanctified to so desirable an end, ought we not to submit to it with abounding resignation.

11. *" Thou broughtest us into the net."* The people of God in the olden time were often enclosed by the power of their enemies, like fishes or birds entangled in a net; there seemed no way of escape for them. The only comfort was that God himself had brought them there, but even this was not readily available, since they knew that he had led them there in anger as a punishment for their transgressions; Israel in Egypt was much like a bird in the fowler's net. *" Thou laidst affliction upon our loins."* They were pressed even to anguish by their burdens and pains. Not on their backs alone was the load, but their loins were pressed and squeezed with the straits and weights of adversity. God's people and affliction are intimate companions. As in Egypt every Israelite was a burden-bearer, so is every believer while he is in this foreign land. As Israel cried to God by reason of their sore bondage, so also do the saints. We too often forget that God lays our afflictions upon us; if we remembered this fact, we should more patiently submit to the pressure which now pains us. The time will come when, for every ounce of present burden, we shall receive a far more exceeding and eternal weight of glory.

12. *"Thou hast caused men to ride over our heads."* They stormed, and hectored, and treated us like the mire of the street. Riding the high horse, in their arrogance, they, who were in themselves mean men, treated the Lord's people as if they were the meanest of mankind. They even turned their captives into beasts of burden, and rode upon their heads, as some read the Hebrew. Nothing is too bad for the servants of God when they fall into the hands of proud persecutors. *"We went through fire and through water."* Trials many and varied were endured by Israel in Egypt, and are still the portion of the saints. The fires of the brick-kilns and the waters of the Nile did their worst to destroy the chosen race; hard labour and child-murder were both tried by the tyrant, but Israel went through both ordeals unharmed, and ever thus the church of God has outlived, and will outlive, all the artifices and cruelties of man. Fire and water are pitiless and devouring, but a divine fiat stays their fury, and forbids these or any other agents from utterly destroying the chosen seed. Many an heir of heaven has had a dire experience of tribulation; the fire through which he has passed has been more terrible than that which chars the bones, for it has fed upon the marrow of his spirit, and burned into the core of his heart; while the waterfloods of affliction have been even more to be feared than the remorseless sea, for they have gone in even unto the soul, and carried the inner nature down into deeps horrible, and not to be imagined without trembling. Yet each saint has been more than conqueror hitherto, and, as it has been, so it shall be. The fire is not kindled which can burn the woman's seed, neither does the dragon know how to vomit a flood which shall suffice to drown it. *" But thou broughtest us out into a wealthy place."* A blessed issue to a mournful story. Canaan was indeed a broad and royal domain for the once enslaved tribes: God, who took them into Egypt, also brought them into the land which flowed

with milk and honey, and Egypt was in his purposes *en route* to Canaan. The way to heaven is *viâ* tribulation.

"The path of sorrow and that path alone,
Leads to the land where sorrow is unknown,"

How wealthy is the place of every believer, and how doubly does he feel it to be so in contrast with his former slavery : what songs shall suffice to set forth our joy and gratitude for such a glorious deliverance and such a bountiful heritage. More awaits us. The depth of our griefs bears no proportion to the height of our bliss. For our shame we shall have double, and more than double. Like Joseph we shall rise from the prison to the palace, like Mordecai we shall escape the gallows prepared by malignity, and ride the white horse and wear the royal robe appointed by benignity. Instead of the net, liberty ; instead of a burden on the loins, a crown on our heads ; instead of men riding over us, we shall rule over the nations : fire shall no more try us, for we shall stand in glory on the sea of glass mingled with fire ; and water shall not harm us, for there shall be no more sea. O the splendour of this brilliant conclusion to a gloomy history. Glory be unto him who saw in the apparent evil the true way to the real good. With patience we will endure the present gloom, for the morning cometh. Over the hills faith sees the daybreak, in whose light we shall enter into the wealthy place.

13 I will go into thy house with burnt offerings : I will pay thee my vows,

14 Which my lips have uttered, and my mouth hath spoken, when I was in trouble.

15 I will offer unto thee burnt sacrifices of fatlings, with the incense of rams ; I will offer bullocks with goats. Selah.

13. "*I will.*" The child of God is so sensible of his own personal indebtedness to grace, that he feels he must utter a song of his own. He joins in the common thanksgiving, but since the best public form must fail to meet each individual case, he makes sure that the special mercies received by him shall not be forgotten, for he records them with his own pen, and sings of them with his own lips. "*I will go into thy house with burnt offerings ;* " the usual sacrifices of godly men. Even the thankful heart dares not come to God without a victim of grateful praise ; of this as well as of every other form of worship, we may say, " the blood is the life thereof." Reader, never attempt to come before God without Jesus, the divinely promised, given, and accepted burnt offering. "*I will pay thee my vows.*" He would not appear before the Lord empty, but at the same time he would not boast of what he offered, seeing it was all due on account of former vows. After all, our largest gifts are but payments ; when we have given all, we must confess, " O Lord, of thine own have we given unto thee." We should be slow in making vows, but prompt in discharging them. When we are released from trouble, and can once more go up to the house of the Lord, we should take immediate occasion to fulfil our promises. How can we hope for help another time, if we prove faithless to covenants voluntarily entered upon in hours of need.

14. "*Which my lips have uttered,*" or vehemently declared ; blurted out, as we say in common speech. His vows had been wrung from him ; extreme distress burst open the door of his lips, and out rushed the vow like a long pent-up torrent, which had at last found a vent. What we were so eager to vow, we should be equally earnest to perform ; but, alas ! many a vow runs so fast in words that it lames itself for deeds. "*And my mouth hath spoken.*" He had made the promise public, and had no desire to go back ; an honest man is always ready to acknowledge a debt. "*When I was in trouble.*" Distress suggested the vow ; God in answer to the vow removed the distress, and now the votary desires to make good his promise. It is well for each man to remember that he was in trouble : proud spirits are apt to speak as if the road had always been smooth for them, as if no dog dare bark at their nobility, and scarce a drop of rain would venture to besprinkle their splendour ; yet these very upstarts were probably once so low in spirits and condition that they would have been glad enough of the help of those they now despise. Even great Cæsar, whose look did awe the world, must have his trouble and become weak as other men ; so that his enemy could say in bitterness, " when the fit was on him, I did mark how he did shake." Of the strong and vigorous man the nurse could tell a tale of weakness, and his wife could say of the boaster, " I did hear him groan ;

his coward lips did from their colour fly." All men have trouble, but they act not in the same manner while under it ; the profane take to swearing and the godly to praying. Both bad and good have been known to resort to vowing, but the one is a liar unto God, and the other a conscientious respecter of his word.

15. *"I will offer unto thee burnt sacrifices of fatlings."* The good man will give his best things to God. No starveling goat upon the hills will he present at the altar, but the well-fed bullocks of the luxuriant pastures shall ascend in smoke from the sacred fire. He who is miserly with God is a wretch indeed. Few devise liberal things, but those few find a rich reward in so doing. *"With the incense of rams."* The smoke of burning rams should also rise from the altar ; he would offer the strength and prime of his flocks as well as his herds. Of all we have we should give the Lord his portion, and that should be the choicest we can select. It was no waste to burn the fat upon Jehovah's altar, nor to pour the precious ointment upon Jesus's head ; neither are large gifts and bountiful offerings to the church of God any diminution to a man's estate : such money is put to good interest and placed where it cannot be stolen by thieves nor corroded by rust. *"I will offer bullocks with goats."* A perfect sacrifice, completing the circle of offerings, should show forth the intense love of his heart. We should magnify the Lord with the great and the little. None of his ordinances should be disregarded ; we must not omit either the bullocks or the goats. In these three verses we have gratitude in action, not content with words, but proving its own sincerity by deeds of obedient sacrifice.

"Selah." It is most fit that we should suspend the song while the smoke of the victims ascends the heavens : let the burnt-offerings stand for praises while we meditate upon the infinitely greater sacrifice of Calvary.

16 Come *and* hear, all ye that fear God, and I will declare what he hath done for my soul.

17 I cried unto him with my mouth, and he was extolled with my tongue.

18 If I regard iniquity in my heart, the Lord will not hear *me :*

19 *But* verily God hath heard *me ;* he hath attended to the voice of my prayer.

20 Blessed *be* God, which hath not turned away my prayer, nor his mercy from me.

16. *"Come and hear."* Before, they were bidden to come and see. Hearing is faith's seeing. Mercy comes to us by way of ear-gate. " Hear, and your soul shall live." They saw how terrible God was, but they heard how gracious he was. *"All ye that fear God."* These are a fit audience when a good man is about to relate his experience ; and it is well to select our hearers when inward soul matters are our theme. It is forbidden us to throw pearls before swine. We do not want to furnish wanton minds with subjects for their comedies, and therefore it is wise to speak of personal spiritual matters where they can be understood, and not where they will be burlesqued. All God-fearing men may hear us, but far hence ye profane. *"And I will declare what he hath done for my soul."* I will count and recount the mercies of God to me, to my soul, my best part, my most real self. Testimonies ought to be borne by all experienced Christians, in order that the younger and feebler sort may be encouraged by the recital to put their trust in the Lord. To declare man's doings is needless ; they are too trivial, and, besides, there are trumpeters enough of man's trumpery deeds ; but to declare the gracious acts of God is instructive, consoling, inspiriting, and beneficial in many respects. Let each man speak for himself, for a personal witness is the surest and most forcible ; second-hand experience is like " cauld kale het again ; " it lacks the flavour of first-hand interest. Let no mock modesty restrain the grateful believer from speaking of himself, or rather of God's dealings to himself, for it is justly due to God ; neither let him shun the individual use of the first person, which is most correct in detailing the Lord's ways of love. We must not be egotists, but we must be egotists when we bear witness for the Lord.

17. *"I cried unto him with my mouth, and he was extolled with my tongue."* It is well when prayer and praise go together, like the horses in Pharaoh's chariot. Some cry who do not sing, and some sing who do not cry : both together are best. Since the Lord's answers so frequently follow close at the heels of our petitions,

and even overtake them, it becomes us to let our grateful praises keep pace with our humble prayers. Observe that the Psalmist did both cry and speak ; the Lord hast cast the dumb devil out of his children, and those of them who are least fluent with their tongues are often the most eloquent with their hearts.

18. *"If I regard iniquity in my heart."* If, having seen it to be there, I continue to gaze upon it without aversion ; if I cherish it, have a side glance of love towards it, excuse it, and palliate it ; *"The Lord will not hear me."* How can he ? Can I desire him to connive at my sin, and accept me while I wilfully cling to any evil way ? Nothing hinders prayer like iniquity harboured in the breast ; as with Cain, so with us, sin lieth at the door, and blocks the passage. If thou listen to the devil, God will not listen to thee. If thou refusest to hear God's commands, he will surely refuse to hear thy prayers. An imperfect petition God will hear for Christ's sake, but not one which is wilfully mis-written by a traitor's hand. For God to accept our devotions, while we are delighting in sin, would be to make himself the God of hypocrites, which is a fitter name for Satan than for the Holy One of Israel.

19. *"But verily God hath heard me."* Sure sign this that the petitioner was no secret lover of sin. The answer to his prayer was a fresh assurance that his heart was sincere before the Lord. See how sure the Psalmist is that he has been heard ; it is with him no hope, surmise, or fancy, but he seals it with a *"verily."* Facts are blessed things when they reveal both God's heart as loving and our own heart as sincere. *"He hath attended to the voice of my prayer."* He gave his mind to consider my cries, interpreted them, accepted them, and replied to them ; and therein proved his grace and also my uprightness of heart. Love of sin is a plague spot, a condemning mark, a killing sign, but those prayers, which evidently live and prevail with God, most clearly arise from a heart which is free from dalliance with evil. Let the reader see to it, that his inmost soul be rid of all alliance with inquity, all toleration of secret lust, or hidden wrong.

20. *"Blessed be God."* Be his name honoured and loved. *"Which hath not turned away my prayer, nor his mercy from me."* He has neither withdrawn his love nor my liberty to pray. He has neither cast out my prayer nor me. His mercy and my cries still meet each other. The Psalm ends on its key note. Praise all through is its spirit and design. Lord enable us to enter into it. Amen.

EXPLANATORY NOTES AND QUAINT SAYINGS.

Whole Psalm.—This Psalm is said to be recited on Easter day, by the Greek church : it is described in the Greek Bible as *A Psalm of the Resurrection,* and may be understood to refer, in a prophetic sense, to the regeneration of the world, through the conversion of the Gentiles.—*Daniel Cresswell.*

Verse 1.—*"Make a joyful noise unto God, all ye lands :"* Heb., *all the earth ;* shout aloud for joy, as the people did at the return of the ark, so that the earth rang again. God shall show himself to be the God not of *Jews* only, but of *Gentiles* also ; these shall as well cry *Christ,* as those *Jesus ;* these say, *Father,* as those *Abba.* And, as there was great joy in Samaria when the gospel was there received (Acts viii. 8), so shall there be the like in all other parts of the earth.—*John Trapp.*

Verse 1.—*"All ye lands."* Where, consider, that he does not sing praises well, who desires to sing alone.—*Thomas Le Blanc.*

Verse 2.—*"Make his praise glorious."* Another meaning is, *give* or *place glory,* that is, your glory *to his praise,* be fully persuaded when you praise him that it will redound to your own glory, regard this as your own glory ; praise him in such a way that all your praises may be given to glorify God ; or, let your glory tend in this direction that he may be praised. Desire not the glory of eternal blessedness, unless for the praise of God, as the blessed spirits in that temple do nothing but say glory to God, and sing the hymn of his glory without end, " Holy, holy, holy." —*Lorinus.*

Verse 3.—"Say." Dicite, *say,* says David, delight to speak of God; *Dicite,* say something. There was more required than to think of God. Consideration, meditation, speculation, contemplation upon God and divine objects, have their place and their season; but this is more than that, and more than admiration too; for all these may come to an end in ecstacies, and in stupidities, and in useless and frivolous imaginations.—*John Donne.*

Verse 3.—"Unto God." To God, not *concerning* God, as some interpret, but *to God himself;* to his praises, and with minds raised to God, as it is in verse 4, *sing to himself;* Gejerus also correctly remarks, that the following discourse is addressed to God. Besides, it is to *our God,* as in verse 8, *"O bless our God, ye people:"* he is called God absolutely, because he alone is the true God.—*Hermann Venema.*

Verse 3.—"How terrible." Take from the Bible its awful doctrines and from providence its *terrible* acts, and the whole system, under which God has placed us, would be emasculated.—*William S. Plumer.*

Verse 3.—"Thine enemies shall submit themselves unto thee." In this, our first consideration is, that *God himself hath enemies;* and then, how should we hope to be, nay, why should we wish to be, without them. God had good, that is, glory from his enemies; and we may have good, that is, advantage in the way to glory, by the exercise of our patience, from enemies too. Those for whom God had done most, the angels, turned enemies first; vex not thou thyself, if those whom thou hast loved best hate thee deadliest. . . . . God himself hath enemies. *"Thine enemies shall submit,"* says the text, to God; there thou hast one comfort, though thou have enemies too; but the greater comfort is, that God calls thine enemies his. *Nolite tangere Christos meos* (Ps. cv. 15), says God of all holy people; you were as good touch me, as touch any of them, for, "they are the apple of mine eye" (Ps. xvii. 8). Our Saviour Christ never expostulated for himself; never said, Why scourge you me? why spit you upon me? why crucify you me? As long as their rage determined in his person, he opened not his mouth; when Saul extended the violence to the church, to his servants, then Christ came to that, "Saul, Saul, why persecutest thou me?" . . . Here is a holy league, defensive and offensive; God shall not only protect us from others, but he shall fight for us against them; our enemies are his enemies.—*Condensed from John Donne.*

Verse 3.—"Thine enemies submit themselves." Literally, *lie unto thee.* This was remarkably the case with *Pharaoh* and the *Egyptians.* They promised again and again to let the people go, when the hand of the Lord was upon them; and they as frequently falsified their word.—*Adam Clarke.*

Verse 3 (second clause).—In times of affliction every hypocrite—all tag and rag—will be ready to come in to God in an outward profession; but usually this submission to God at this time is not out of truth. Hence it is said, *"Through the greatness of thy power shall thine enemies submit themselves unto thee:"* in the original it is, *"they shall lie unto thee,"* and so it is translated by Arias Montanus, and some others, noting hereby that a forced submission to God is seldom in truth. —*Jeremiah Burroughs.*

Verse 3.—The earthquakes in New England occasioned a kind of religious panic. A writer, who was then one of the ministers of Boston, informs us, that immediately after the great earthquake, as it was called, a great number of his flock came and expressed a wish to unite themselves with the church. But, on conversing with them, he could find no evidence of improvement in their religious views or feelings, no convictions of their own sinfulness; nothing, in short, but a kind of superstitious fear, occasioned by a belief that the end of the world was at hand. All their replies proved that they had not found God, though they had seen *"the greatness of his power"* in the earthquake.—*Edward Payson, D.D.*

Verse 5.—"Come and see the works of God." An indirect censure is here passed upon that almost universal thoughtlessness which leads men to neglect the praises of God.—*John Calvin.*

Verse 5.—"Come and see." The church at all times appeals to the world. *"Come and see,"* as Jesus said to the two disciples of John the Baptist, and Philip to Nathanael. John i. 39, 46. God's marvels are to be seen by all, and *seeing* them is the first step towards *believing* in their divine author.—*A. R. Fausset.*

Verse 6.—"He turned the sea into dry land." The Psalmist refers to the passage through the Red Sea and the Jordan, not as to transactions which took place and

were concluded at a given period of time, but as happening really in every age.
God's guidance of his people is a constant drying up of the sea and of the Jordan,
and the joy over his mighty deeds is always receiving new materials.—*E. W.
Hengstenberg.*

Verse 6.—*"There did we rejoice in him;"* where those things have been done,
there have we rejoiced in him, not taking any credit to ourselves as if they were
our acts, but rejoicing and glorying in God, and have praised him, as may be seen
in Exod. xv. and Joshua iii. The prophet uses the future for the past, unless,
perhaps, he meant to insinuate that these miracles would be succeeded by much
greater ones, of which they were only the types and figures. A much greater miracle
is that men should pass over the bitter sea of this life, and cross the river of mortality,
that never ceases to run, and which swallows up and drowns so many, and still come
safe and alive to the land of eternal promise, and there rejoice in God himself, beholding him face to face; and yet this greater miracle is so accomplished by God,
that many pass through this sea as if it were dry land, and cross this river with dry
feet; that is to say, having no difficulty in despising all things temporal, be they
good or be they bad; that is to say, being neither attached to the good things, nor
fearing the evil things, of this world, that they may arrive in security at the heavenly
Jerusalem, where we will rejoice in him, not in hope, but in complete possession
for eternity.—*Robert Bellarmine.*

Verse 7.—*"His eyes behold the nations."* The radical meaning of the word צָפָה
is αὐγάζειν, *to shine,* and metonymically *to examine with a bright eye;* to inspect
with a piercing glance, and thence *to behold,* for either good or evil, as Prov. xv. 3:
"The eyes of the Lord are in every place, beholding the evil and the good." Here it
is taken in an adverse sense, and means, to watch from a watch-tower, to threaten
from a lofty place. Ps. xxxvii. 32: *"The wicked watcheth the righteous;"* and Job
xv. 22: He is waited for *"from the watch-tower for the sword;"* that is to say, *the
sword is drawn above the head of the wicked, as if it threatened him from the watch-
tower of God.* But, at the same time, there is also a reference to God's looking from
the pillar of fire, and of cloud, upon the host of Pharaoh in the Red Sea. Exod. xiv.
24.—*Hermann Venema.*

Verse 7.—*"His eyes behold the nations."* This should give check to much iniquity.
Can a man's conscience easily and delightfully swallow that which he is sensible
falls under the cognizance of God, when it is hateful to the eye of his holiness, and
renders the action odious to him? " Doth not he see my ways, and count all my
steps ? " saith Job (chap. xxxi. 4). . . . . The consideration of this attribute should
make us humble. How dejected would a person be if he were sure all the angels
in heaven, and men upon earth, did perfectly know his crimes, with all their aggravations ! But what is created knowledge to an infinite and just censuring understanding? When we consider that he knows our actions, where of there are multitudes,
and our thoughts, whereof there are millions; that he views all the blessings bestowed
upon us; all the injuries we have returned to him; that he exactly knows his own
bounty, and our ingratitude; all the idolatry, blasphemy, and secret enmity in
every man's heart against him; all tyrannical oppressions, hidden lusts, omissions
of necessary duties, violations of plain precepts, every foolish imagination, with
all the circumstances of them, and that perfectly in all their full anatomy, every
mite of unworthiness and wickedness in every circumstance . . . . should not the
consideration of this melt our hearts into humiliation before him, and make us
earnest in begging pardon and forgiveness of him.—*Stephen Charnock.*

Verse 9.—*"Which holdeth our soul in life."* As the works of creation at first,
and upholding all by his power and providence, are yoked together as works of
a like wonder, vouchsafed the creation in common, Heb. i. 2, 3; so just in the like
manner we find regeneration and perseverance joined, as the sum of all other works
in this life. Thus " begotten again," and " kept by the power of God to salvation,"
are joined by the Apostle, 1 Pet. i. 3 and 5, " Called and preserved in Christ Jesus ; "
so in Jude, verse 1. . . . . . " Blessed be God," says Peter, " who, according to his
abundant mercy, hath begotten us again." And, " O bless our God, ye people,
which holdeth our souls in life," says the Psalmist. Yea, if we do narrowly
eye the words in either, both Peter and the Psalmist do bless God for both at once.
Blessed be God for " begetting us," who are also " kept by the power of God ; "
so it follows in Peter. In the Psalmist both are comprehended in this one word:

1. " which *putteth* our souls in life " (so the margin, out of the Hebrew), that is, who puts life into your soul at the first, as he did into Adam when he made him a living soul ; 2. and then which "*holdeth*," that is, continueth our souls in that life. So the translators render it also, according to the Psalmist's scope, and " O bless the Lord," saith the Psalmist, for these and both these.—*Thomas Goodwin.*

Verse 9.—"*Which holdest our soul in life.*" It is truth, that all we have is in the hand of God ; but God keeps our life in his hand last of all, and he hath that in his hand in a special manner. Though the soul continue, *life* may not continue ; there is the soul when there is not life : life is that which is the union of soul and body. "*Thou holdest our soul in life ;* " that is, thou holdest soul and body together. So Daniel describes God to Belshazzar, Dan. v. 23, " The God in whose hand thy breath is, and whose are all thy ways, hast thou not glorified." The breath of princes is in the hand of God, and the same hand holds the breath of the meanest subject. This may be matter of comfort to us in times of danger, and times of death : when the hand of man is lifted up to take thy life remember thy life is held in the hand of God ; and, as God said to Satan (Job. ii. 6) : Afflict the body of Job, but save his life ; so God saith still to bloody wretches, who are as the limbs of Satan : The bodies of such and such are in your hands, the estates of such and such are in your hands, but save their lives.—*Joseph Caryl.*

Verse 9.—"*Putteth our soul in life.*" An elegant and emphatic expression, only to be understood by observing the exact force of the words. The *soul* is the *life*, as is well known, the word שם is *to place, to place upon, to press in,* the word מים signifies properly *joinings, fastenings together,* and hence those faculties and powers by which nature is held together and made firm.—*Hermann Venema.*

Verse 9.—"*Which holdeth our soul in life.*" He holdeth our soul in life, that it may not drop away of itself ; for being continually in our hands, it is apt to slip through our fingers.—*Matthew Henry.*

Verse 9.—"*And suffereth not our feet to be moved.*" It is a great mercy to be kept from desperate courses in the time of sad calamities, to be supported under burdens, that we sink not ; and to be prevented from denying God, or his truth, in time of persecution.—*David Dickson.*

Verse 10.—"*Thou, O God, hast proved us.*" It is not known what corn will yield, till it come to the flail ; nor what grapes, till they come to the press. Grace is hid in nature, as sweet water in rose-leaves ; the fire of affliction fetcheth it out. "*Thou hast tried us as silver.*" The wicked also are tried (Rev. iii. 10), but they prove reprobate silver (Jer. vi. 28), or at best, as alchymy gold, that will not bear the seventh fire, as Job did (ch. xxiii. 10).—*John Trapp.*

Verse 10.—"*As silver is tried.*" Convinced from the frequent use of this illustration, that there was something more than usually instructive in the processes of assaying and purifying silver, I have collected some few facts upon the subject. The hackneyed story of the refiner seeing his image in the molten silver while in the fire, has so charmed most of us, that we have not looked further ; yet, with more careful study, much could be brought out.

To assay silver requires great personal care in the operator. " The principle of assaying gold and silver is very simple theoretically, but in practice great experience is necessary to insure accuracy ; and there is no branch of business which demands more personal and undivided attention. The result is liable to the influence of so many contingencies, that no assayer who regards his reputation will delegate the principal processes to one not equally skilled with himself. Besides the result ascertainable by weight, there are allowances and compensations to be made, which are known only to an experienced assayer, and if these were disregarded, as might be the case with the mere novice, the report would be wide from the truth." * Pagnini's version reads : " Thou hast melted us by blowing upon us," and in the monuments of Egypt, artificers are seen with the blowpipe operating with small fire-places, with cheeks to confine and reflect the heat ; the worker evidently paying personal attention, which is evident also in Malachi iii. 3, " He shall sit as a refiner and purifier of silver."

To assay silver requires a skilfully-constructed furnace. The description of this furnace would only weary the reader, but it is evidently a work of art in itself. Even the trial of our faith is much more precious than that of gold which perisheth.

---

* Encycl. Britan.

He has refined us, but not with silver, he would not trust us there, the furnace of affliction is far more skilfully arranged than that.

To assay silver the heat must be nicely regulated. "During the operation, the assayer's attention should be directed to the heat of the furnace, which must be neither too hot nor too cold : if too hot, minute portions of silver will be carried off with the lead, and so vitiate the assay ; moreover, the pores of the cupel being more open, greater absorption will ensue, and there is liability to loss from that cause. One indication of an excess of heat in the furnace, is the rapid and perpendicular rising of the fumes to the ceiling of the muffle, the mode of checking and controlling which has been pointed out in the description of the improved furnace. When the fumes are observed to fall to the bottom of the muffle, the furnace is then too cold ; and, if left unaltered, it will be found that the cupellation has been imperfectly performed, and the silver will not have entirely freed itself from the base metals.*

The assayer repeats his trying processes. Usually two or more trials of the same piece are made, so that great accuracy may be secured. Seven times silver is said to be purified, and the saints through varied trials reach the promised rest.—*C. H. S.*

Verse 11.—"*Thou broughtest us into the net,*" etc. Our enemies have pursued us (like the wild beasts taken by the hunter) into most grievous straits (1 Sam. xiii. 6). h ey have used us like beasts of burden, and laid sore loads upon us, which they have fast bound upon our backs. "*Thou laidst affliction upon our loins.*" *Coarctationem in lumbis ;* we are not only hampered, as in a net, but fettered, as with chains ; as if we had been in the jailor's or hangman's hands.—*John Trapp.*

Verse 12.—"*Thou hast caused men to ride over our heads.*" The agents are *men.* Man is a sociable-living creature, and should converse with man in love and tranquility. Man should be a supporter of man ; is he become an overthrower ? He should help and keep him up ; doth he ride over him and tread him under foot ? O apostasy, not only from religion, but even from humanity ! *Quid homini inimicissimum ? Homo.*†—The greatest danger that befalls man comes whence it should least come, from man himself. *Cætera animantia,* says Pliny, *in suo genere, probe degunt,* etc. Lions fight not with lions ; serpents spend not their venom on serpents ; but man is the main suborner of mischief to his own kind. . . . .
1. *They ride.* What need they mount themselves upon beasts, that have feet malicious enough to trample on us ? They have a "foot of pride," Psalm xxxvi. 11, from which David prayed to be delivered ; a presumptuous heel, which they dare lift up against God ; and, therefore, a tyrannous toe, to spurn dejected man. They need not horses and mules, that can kick with the foot of a revengeful malice, Psalm xxxii. 9.
2. *Over us.* The way is broad enough wherein they travel, for it is the devil's road. They might well miss the poor, there is room enough besides ; they need not ride over us. It were more brave for them to justle with champions that will not give them the way. We never contend for their path ; they have it without our envy, not without our pity. Why should they ride over us ?
3. *Over our heads.* Is it not contentment enough to their pride to *ride,* to their malice to ride *over us,* but must they delight in bloodiness to ride over our *heads ?* Will not the breaking of our arms and legs, and such inferior limbs, satisfy their indignation ? Is it not enough to rack our strength, to mock our innocence, to prey on our estates, but must they thirst after our bloods and lives ? *Quo tendit sæva libido ?*—Whither will their madness run ? But we must not tie ourselves to the letter. Here is a mystical or metaphorical gradation of their cruelty. Their riding is proud ; their riding over us is malicious ; and their riding over our heads is bloody oppression.—*Thomas Adams.*

Verse 12 (first clause).—The time was when the Bonners and butchers rode over the faces of God's saints, and madefied ‡ the earth with their bloods, every drop whereof begot a new believer.—*Thomas Adams.*

Verse 12.—"*Thou hast caused men to ride over our heads.*" This verse is like that sea (Matt. viii. 24), so tempestuous at first, that the vessel was covered with waves ; but Christ's rebuke quieted all, and there followed a great calm. Here are cruel Nimrods riding over innocent heads, as they would over fallow lands ; and

---

* Encycl. Britain   † Seneca.   ‡ Madefy, to moisten, to make wet.

dangerous passages through fire and water; but the storm is soon ended, or rather the passengers are landed. *"Thou broughtest us out into a wealthy place."* So that this strain of David's music, or Psalmody, consists of two notes—one mournful, the other mirthful; the one a touch of distress, the other of redress: which directs our course to an observation of *misery* and of *mercy;* of grievous misery, of gracious mercy. There is desolation and consolation in one verse: a deep dejection, as laid under the feet of beasts; a happy deliverance, *" broughtest us out into a wealthy place."* In both these strains God hath his stroke; he is a principal in this concert. He is brought in for an *actor,* and for an *author;* an actor in the persecution, an author in the deliverance. *"Thou causest,"* etc.; *"Thou broughtest,"* etc. In the one he is a causing worker; in the other a sole working cause. In the one he is joined with company; in the other he works alone. He hath a finger in the former; his whole hand in the latter. We must begin with *misery* before we come to *mercy.* If there were no trouble, we should not know the worth of a deliverance. The passion of the saints is given, by the hearty and ponderous description, for very grievous; yet it is written in the forehead of the text, " The Lord caused it." *"Thou causedst men to ride,"* etc. Hereupon, some wicked libertine may offer to rub his filthiness upon God's purity, and to plead an authentical derivation of all his villany against the saints from the Lord's warrant: *"He caused it."* We answer, to the justification of truth itself, that God doth ordain and order every persecution that striketh his children, without any allowance to the instrument that gives the blow. God works in the same action with others, not after the same manner. In the affliction of Job were three agents—God, Satan, and the Sabeans. The devil works on his body, the Sabeans on his goods; yet Job confesseth a third party: " The Lord gives, and the Lord takes away." Here oppressors trample on the godly, and God is said to cause it. He causeth affliction for trial (so verses 10, 11: " Thou hast tried us," etc.); they work it for malice; neither can God be accused nor they excused.—*Thomas Adams.*

Verse 12.—*"Thou hast placed men over our heads."* Thus Jerome renders, although the Hebrew noun, אֱנוֹשׁ, is in the singular, the word itself denotes *an obscure, mean man,* who is mentioned with indignity, but ought to be buried in oblivion. The singular noun is taken collectively, and so also is רֹאשֵׁנוּ, with the affix. Such were the Egyptian and Babylonish idolaters, whom the Hebrew served. *To place any one over the head of another,* or, as the Hebrew word הִרְכַּבְתָּ means, *to ride,* to be superior to, to subdue to oneself and subject, and to sit upon and insult, just as the horseman rules with the rein, and spur, and whip the beast which he rides.—*Lorinus.*

Verse 12.—*"To ride over our heads."* This is an allusion to beasts of burden, and particularly to camels, whose heads the rider almost sits over, and so domineers over them as he pleases.—*Thomas Fenton, in " Annotations on the Book of Job, and the Psalms."* 1732.

Verse 12.—*"We went through fire and through water."* The children of Israel when they had escaped the Red Sea, and seen their enemies the Egyptians dead, they thought all was cocksure, and therefore sang *Epicinia,* songs of rejoicing for the victory. But what followed within a while? The Lord stirred up another enemy against them, from out their bowels, as it were, which was hunger, and this pinched them sorer, they thought, than the Egyptian. But was this the last? No; after the hunger came thirst, and this made them to murmur as much as the former; and after the thirst came fiery serpents, and fire and pestilence, and Amalekites, and Midianites, and what not? Thus hath it been with the church not only under the law, but also under Christ, as it might be easily declared unto you. Neither hath it been better with the several members thereof; they likewise have been made conformable to the body and to the Head. What a sight of temptations did Abraham endure? So Jacob, so Joseph, so the patriarchs, so the prophets? Yea, and all they that would live godly in Christ Jesus, though their sorrow in the end were turned to joy, yet they wept and lamented first. Though they were brought at the length to a wealthy place, yet they passed through fire and water first.—*Miles Smith.*—1624.

Verse 12.—*"We went through fire and through water."* There was a great variety of such perils; and not only of several, but of contrary sorts: *"We went through fire and through water,"* either of which singly and alone denotes an extremity of evils. Thus, through water (Ps. lxix. 1, 2): " Save me, O God; for the waters are come in unto my soul. I sink in deep mire, where there is no standing: I am come into deep waters, where the floods overflow me." Or, through fire (Ezek. xv. 7): " And I will set my face against them ; they shall go out from one fire, and another fire shall devour them ; and ye shall know that I am the Lord, when I set my face against them." But when through both successively, one after the other, this denotes an accumulation of miseries, or trials, indeed : as we read Isa. xliii. 2, with God's promise to his people in such conditions : " When thou passest through the waters, I will be with thee ; and through the rivers, they shall not overflow thee : when thou walkest through the fire, thou shalt not be burned ; neither shall the flame kindle upon thee." Which promise is here, you see, acknowledged by the Psalmist to have been performed : God was with the three children when they walked through the fire, in the very letter of Isaiah's speech ; and with the children of Israel when they went through the water of the Red Sea.—*Thomas Goodwin.*

Verse 12.—"*We went through fire and through water.*" In allusion, probably, to the ordeal by fire and water, which is of great antiquity.

On the question who had interred the body of Polynices :—

" All denied :
Offering, in proof of innocence, to grasp
The burning steel, to walk through fire, and take
Their solemn oath they knew not of the deed."—*Sophocles.*

From T. S. Millington's " Testimony of the heathen to the Truths of Holy Writ." 1863.
Verse 12.—"*Fire and water.*" The Jewish law required both these for purification of spoil in war, where they could be borne. Num. xxxi. 23: " Everything that may abide the fire, ye shall make it go through the fire, and it shall be clean : nevertheless it shall be purified through the water of separation." God's saints are, therefore, subject to both ordeals.—*C. H. S.*

Verse 12.—"*But thou broughtest us out into a wealthy place.*" Every word is sweetly significant, and amplifies God's mercy to us. Four especially are remarkable :—1. The deliverer ; 2. The deliverance ; 3. The delivered ; and, 4. Their felicity or blessed advancement. So there is in the deliverer, *aliquid celsitudinis,* "*Thou ;*" in the delivery, *certitudinis,* " *broughtest out,*" in the delivered, *solitudinis,* "*us ;*" in the happiness, *plenitudinis,* "*into a wealthy place.*" There is highness and lowness, sureness and fulness. The deliverer is great, the deliverance is certain, the distress grievous, the exaltation glorious. There is yet a first word, that like a key unlocks this golden gate of mercy, a *veruntamen :*—BUT. This is *vox respirationis,* a gasp that fetcheth back again the very life of comfort. "*But thou broughtest,*" etc. We were fearfully endangered into the hands of our enemies ; they rode and trode upon us, and drove us through hard perplexities. "*But thou,*" etc. If there had been a full-point or period at our misery, if those gulfs of persecution had quite swallowed us, and all our light of comfort had been thus smothered and extinguished, we might have cried, *Periit spes nostra,* yea, *periit salus nostra.*— Our hope, our help is *quite* gone. He had mocked us that would have spoken, Be of good cheer. This same *but* is like a happy oar, that turns our vessel from the rocks of despair, and lands it at the haven of comfort.—*Thomas Adams.*

Verse 12 (*second and third clause*).—1. The outlet of the trouble is happy. They are in fire and water, yet they get through them ; we went through fire and water, and did not perish in the flames or floods. Whatever the troubles of the saints are, blessed be God there is a way through them. 2. The inlet to a better state is much more happy. "*Thou broughtest us out into a wealthy place,*" into a wellwatered place ; for the word is, *like the gardens of the Lord,* and therefore fruitful.— *Matthew Henry.*

Verse 12 (*last clause*).—Thou, O God, with the temptation hast given the issue. "*Thou broughtest us out into a wealthy place.*" 1. Thou hast proved, and thou hast brought. 2. Thou laidst the trouble, and thou tookest it off ; yea, and hast made us an ample recompense, for thou hast brought us to a moist, pleasant, lovely, fertile, rich place, a happy condition, a flourishing condition of things, so that thou hast made us to forget all our trouble.—*William Nicholson, in "David's Harp strung and tuned."* 1662.

Verse 12.—"*A wealthy place.*" The hand of God led them in that fire and water of affliction through which they went ; but who led them out ? The Psalmist tells us in the next words : "*Thou broughtest us out into a wealthy place ; "* the margin saith, *"into a moist place."* They were in fire and water before. *Fire* is the extremity of heat and dryness ; *water* is the extremity of moistness and coldness. *A moist place* notes a due temperament of heat and cold, of dryness and moistness, and therefore elegantly shadows that comfortable and contentful condition into which the good hand of God had brought them, which is significantly expressed in our translation by *"a wealthy place ; "* those places flourishing most in fruitfulness, and so in wealth, which are neither over hot nor over cold, neither over dry nor over moist.—*Joseph Caryl.*

Verse 13.—You see all the parts of this song ; the whole concert or harmony of all is praising God. You see *quo loco,* in his house ; *quo modo,* with burnt-offering ; *quo animo,* paying our vows.—*Thomas Adams.*

Verse 13.—*" Burnt-offerings."* For ourselves, be we sure that the best sacrifice we can give to God is obedience ; not a dead beast, but a living soul. The Lord takes not delight in the blood of brutish creatures. It is the mind, the life, the soul, the obedience, that he requires : 1 Sam. xv. 22, " To obey is better than sacrifice." Let this be our burnt-offering, our holocaust, a sanctified body and mind given up to the Lord, Rom. xii. 1, 2. First, the heart : " My son, give me thy heart." Is not the heart enough ? No, the hand also : Isaiah i. 16, Wash the hands from blood and pollution. Is not the hand enough ? No, the foot also : " Remove thy foot from evil." Is not the foot enough ? No, the lips also : " Guard the doors of thy mouth ; " Ps. xxxiv. 13, " Refrain thy tongue from evil." Is not thy tongue enough ? No, the ear also : " Let him that hath ears to hear, hear." Is not the ear enough ? No, the eye also : " Let thine eyes be towards the Lord." Is not all this sufficient ? No, give body and spirit : 1 Cor. vi. 20, " Ye are bought with a price : therefore glorify God in your body, and in your spirit, which are God's." When the eyes abhor lustful objects, the ear slanders, the foot erring paths, the hands wrong and violence, the tongue flattery and blasphemy, the heart pride and hypocrisy ; this is thy holocaust, thy whole burnt-offering.—*Thomas Adams.*

Verses 13, 15.—In the *"burnt-offerings,"* we see his approach to the altar with the common and general sacrifice ; and next, in his *"paying vows,"* we see he has brought his *peace-offerings* with him. Again, therefore, he says at the altar : *"I will offer unto thee burnt sacrifices of fatlings "* (ver 15). This is the general offering, brought from the best of his flock and herd. Then follow the *peace-offerings :* "*With the incense* (קְטֹרֶת, *fuming smoke*) *of rams ; I will offer bullocks with goats. Selah."* Having brought his offerings, he is in no haste to depart, notwithstanding ; for his heart is full. Ere, therefore, he leaves the sanctuary, he utters the language of a soul at peace with God : verses 16—20. This, truly, is one whom *"the very God of peace "* has sanctified, and whose whole spirit, and body, and soul he will preserve blameless unto the coming of the Lord Jesus Christ. 1 Thess. v. 23.—*Andrew A. Bonar.*

Verses 13—15.—He tells what were the vows he promised in his trouble, and says he promised the richest sacrifices of cattle that could be made according to the law. These were three: rams, cows, and goats. Rams included lambs ; cows included heifers ; and goats, kids.—*Robert Bellarmine.*

Verse 14.—*"Which my lips have uttered."* Hebrew, *have opened :* that is which I have uttered, *diductis labiis,* with lips wide open. *Videmus qualiter vota nuncupari soleant,* saith Vatablus. Here we see after what sort vows used to be made, when we are under any pressing affliction ; but when once delivered, how heavily many come off in point of payment.—*John Trapp.*

Verse 14.—Express mention is made of *opened lips* to indicate that the *vows* were made with great vehemence of mind, and in a state of need and pressure ; so that his *lips* were *broken through* and widely opened. For the root, פָּצָה contains the idea of *opening* anything *with violence ;* to *break open,* as the Latin expression is, *rumpere labia.*—*Hermann Venema.*

Verse 15.—*"I will offer,"* etc. Thou shalt have the best of the herd and of the fold.—*Adam Clarke.*

Verse 15.—*"Fatlings."* For as I will not come empty into thy house, so I will not bring thee a niggardly present ; but offer sacrifices of all sorts, and the best and choicest in every kind.—*Symon Patrick.*

Verse 15.—"*Bullocks with goats.*" That is, I will liberally provide for every part of the service at the tabernacle.—*Thomas Scott.*

Verse 16.—"*Come and hear, all ye that fear God.*" One reason why the saints are so often inviting all that fear God to come unto them is, because the saints see and know the great good that they shall get by those that fear God. The children of darkness are so wise in their generation as to desire most familiarity and acquaintance with those persons whom they conceive may prove most profitable and advantageous to them, and to pretend much friendship there where is hope of most benefit. And shall not the saints, the children of light, upon the same account wish and long for the society of those that fear God, because they see what great good they shall gain by them? It is no wonder that the company of those that fear God is so much in request, since it is altogether gainful and commodious; it's no wonder they have many invitations, since they are guests by which something is still gotten; and, indeed, among all persons living, those that fear God are the most useful and enriching.—*Samuel Heskins, in "Soul Mercies Precious in the Eyes of Saints . . . . set forth in a little Treatise on Psalm lxvi. 16."* 1654.

Verse 16.—"*All ye that fear God.*" For such only will hear to good purpose; others either cannot, or care not. "*And I will declare,*" etc. Communicate unto you my soul-secrets and experiments. There is no small good to be gotten by such declarations. Bilney, perceiving Latimer to be zealous without knowledge, came to him in his study and desired him for God's sake to hear his confession. " I did so," saith Latimer, " and, to say the truth, by his confession I learned more than afore in many years. So from that time forward I began to smell the word of God, and forsake the school-doctors, and such fooleries."—*John Trapp.*

Verse 16.—"*Ye that fear God.*" Observe the invitation given to those only "*who fear God,*" because " the fear of the Lord is the beginning of wisdom ; " he loosens the feet to "*come,*" opens the ears to "*hear ;*" and therefore, he who has no fear of God will be called to no purpose, either to come or to hear.—*Robert Bellarmine.*

Verse 16.—"*I will declare.*" Consider the ends which a believer should propose in the discharge of this duty [" of communicating Christian experience "]. The principal end he should have in view when he declares his experience is the glory of that God, who hath dealt so bountifully with him. He would surely have the Lord exalted for his faithfulness and goodness to him ; he would have it published, that the name of the Lord might be great ; that sinners might know that his God is faithful to his word ; that he hath not only engaged to be " a present help in time of need," but that he hath found him in reality to be so. As he knows the enemies of God are ready enough to charge him with neglect of his people, because of the trials and afflictions they are exercised with ; so he would, in contradiction to them, declare what he hath found in his own experience, that in very faithfulness he afflicts those that are dearest to him. And with what lustre doth the glory of God shine, when his children are ready to acknowledge that he never called them out to any duty but his grace was sufficient for them ; that he never laid his hand upon them in any afflictive exercise, but he, at the same time, supplied them with all those supports which they stood in need of ? I say, for Christians thus to stand up, on proper occasions, and bear their experimental testimony to the faithfulness and goodness of God, what a tendency hath it to make the name of the Lord, who hath been their strong tower, glorious in the midst of the earth. . . . . How may we blush and be ashamed, that we have so much conversation in the world and so little about what God hath done for our souls ? It is a very bad sign upon us, in our day, that the things of God are generally postponed ; while either the affairs of state, or the circumstances of outward life, or other things, perhaps, of a more trifling nature, are the general subjects of our conversation. What! are we ashamed of the noblest, the most interesting subject ? It is but a poor sign that we have felt anything of it, if we think it unnecessary to declare it to our fellow Christians. What think you ? Suppose any two of us were cast upon a barbarous shore, where we neither understood the language, nor the customs of the inhabitants, and were treated by them with reproach and cruelty ; do you think we should not esteem it a happiness that we could unburden ourselves to each other, and communicate our griefs and troubles ? And shall we think it less so, while we are in such a world as this, in a strange land, and at a dstance from our Father's house ? Shall we neglect conversing with each other ? No ; let our conversation not only be in heaven, but about spiritual and heavenly things.—*Samuel Wilson* (1703–1750), *in " Sermons on Various Subjects."*

Verse 16.—*"I will declare."* After we are delivered from the dreadful apprehensions of the wrath of God, it is our duty to be publicly thankful. It is for the glory of our Healer to speak of the miserable wounds that once pained us ; and of that kind hand that saved us when we were brought very low. It is for the glory of our Pilot to tell of the rocks and of the sands ; the many dangers and threatening calamities that he, by his wise conduct, made us to escape : and to see us safe on the shore, may cause others that are yet afflicted, and tost with tempests, to look to him for help ; for he is able and ready to save them as well as us. We must, like soldiers, when a tedious war is over, relate our combats, our fears, our dangers, with delight ; and make known our experiences to doubting, troubled Christians, and to those that have not yet been under such long and severe trials as we have been.—*Timothy Rogers* (1660—1729), *in "A Discourse on Trouble of Mind."*

Verse 17.—This verse may be rendered thus :*"I cried unto him with my mouth, and his exaltation was under my tongue ; "* that is, I was considering and meditating how I might lift up and exalt the name of God, and make his praise glorious. Holy thoughts are said to be under the tongue when we are in a preparation to bring them forth.—*Joseph Caryl.*

Verse 17.—*"He was extolled with my tongue."* It is a proof that prayer has proceeded from unworthy motives, when the blessings which succeed it are not acknowledged with as much fervency as when they were originally implored. The ten lepers all cried for mercy, and all obtained it, but only one returned to render thanks.—*John Morison.*

Verse 17.—*"He was extolled with my tongue : "* lit. *"* an extolling (of Him was) under my tongue," implying *fulness* of praise (Psalm x. 7). A store of praise being conceived as *under the tongue,* whence a portion might be taken on all occasions. The sense is, " scarcely had I *cried* unto him when, by delivering me, he gave me abundant reason to extol him." (Psalm xxxiv. 6.)—*A. R. Fausset.*

Verse 17.—*"With my tongue."* Let the praise of God be in thy tongue, under thy tongue, and upon thy tongue, that it may shine before all men, and that they may see that thy heart is good. The fish *lucerna* has a shining tongue,* from which it takes its name ; and in the depths of the sea the light of its tongue reveals it : if thy heart has a tongue, shining with the praises of God, it will sufficiently show itself of what sort it is. Hence the old saying, " Speak, that I may see thee."—*Thomas Le Blanc.*

Verse 18.—*"If I regard iniquity in my heart, the Lord will not hear me."* The very supposition that " if he regarded iniquity in his heart, the Lord would not hear him," implies the possibility that such may be the state even of believers ; and there is abundant reason to fear that it is in this way their prayers are so often hindered, and their supplications so frequently remain unanswered. Nor is it difficult to conceive how believers may be chargeable with regarding iniquity in their heart, even amidst all the solemnity of coming into the immediate presence of God, and directly addressing him in the language of prayer and supplication.

It is possible that they may put themselves into such a situation, in a state of mind but little fitted for engaging in that holy exercise ; the world, in one form or another, may for the time have the ascendancy in their hearts ; and there may have been so much formality in their confessions, and so much indifference in their supplications, that when the exercise is over, they could not honestly declare that they really meant what they acknowledged, or seriously desired what they prayed for. A Christian, it is true, could not be contented to remain in a state like this ; and, when he is awakened from it, as he sooner or later will be, he cannot fail to look back upon it with humiliation and shame. But we fear there are seasons in which believers themselves may make a very near approach to such a state : and what then is the true interpretation of prayers offered up at such a moment ? It is in fact just saying, that there is something which, for the time, they prefer to what they are formally asking of God ; that, though the blessings which they do ask may be for a time withheld, yet they would find a compensation in the enjoyment of the

---

* A reviewer condemns us for quoting false natural history, but no intelligent reader will be misled thereby.—*Editor.*

worldly things which do at the moment engross their affections ; and that, in reality, they would not choose to have at that instant such an abundant communication of spiritual influence imparted to them, as would render these worldly objects less valuable in their estimation, and would turn the whole tide of their affections towards spiritual things. . . . .

The Christian may sometimes betake himself to prayer, to ask counsel of God in some perplexity regarding divine truth, or to seek direction in some doubtful point of duty ; but, instead of being prepared fairly to exercise his judgment, in the hope that, while doing so, the considerations that lie on the side of truth will be made to his mind clear and convincing ; he may have allowed his inclinations so to influence and bias his judgment towards the side of error, or in favour of the line of conduct which he wishes to pursue, that when he asks counsel it may only be in the hope that his previous opinion will be confirmed, and when he seeks direction it is in reality on a point about which he was previously determined. . . . .

Another case is, I fear, but too common, and in which the believer may be still more directly chargeable with regarding iniquity in his heart. It is possible that there may be in his heart or life something which he is conscious is not altogether as it should be—some earthly attachment which he cannot easily justify—or some point of conformity to the maxims and practices of the world, which he finds it difficult to reconcile with christian principle ; and yet all the struggle which these have from time to time cost him, may only have been an effort of ingenuity on his part to retain them without doing direct violence to conscience—a laborious getting up of arguments whereby to show how they may be defended, or in what way they may lawfully be gone into ; while the true and simple reason of his going into them, namely, the love of the world, is all the while kept out of view. And, as an experimental proof how weak and inconclusive all these arguments are, and at the same time how unwilling he still is to relinquish his favourite objects, he may be conscious that in confessing his sins he leaves them out of the enumeration, rather because he would willingly pass them over, than because he is convinced that they need not be there ; he may feel that he cannot and dare not make them the immediate subject of solemn and deliberate communing with God ; and, after all his multiplied and ingenious defences, he may be reconciled to them at last, only by ceasing to agitate the question whether they are lawful or not.—*Robert Gordon, D.D.* 1825.

Verse 18.—Whence is it that a man's regarding or loving sin in his heart hinders his prayers from acceptance with God ? 1. The first reason is, because in this case he cannot pray by the Spirit. All prayers that are acceptable with God are the breathings of his own Spirit within us. Rom. viii. 26. As without the intercession of Christ we cannot have our prayers accepted, so without the intercession of the Spirit we cannot pray. . . . . II. The second reason is, because as long as a man regards inquity in his heart he cannot pray in faith ; that is, he cannot build a rational confidence upon any promise that God will accept him. Now, faith always respects the promise, and promise of acceptance is made only to the upright : so long, therefore, as men cherish a love of sin in their heart, they either understand not the promises, and so they pray without understanding, or they understand them, and yet misapply them to themselves, and so they pray in presumption : in either case, they have little cause to hope for acceptance. . . . . III. The third reason is, because while we regard iniquity in our hearts we cannot pray with fervency ; which, next to sincerity, is the great qualification of prayer, to which God has annexed a promise of acceptance (Matt. xi. 12) : "The kingdom of heaven suffereth violence, and the violent take it by force." Matt. vii. 7 : Those only that seek are like to find, and those that knock to have admittance ; all which expressions denote vehemence and importunity. Now, the cause of vehemence, in our prosecution of any good, is our love of it ; for proportionable to the affection we bear to anything is the earnestness of our desires and the diligence of our pursuit after it. So long, therefore, as the love of sin possesses our hearts, our love to spiritual things is dull, heavy, inactive, and our prayers for them must needs be answerable. O the wretched fallacy that the soul will here put upon itself ! At the same time it will love its sin and pray against it ; at the same time it will entreat for grace, with a desire not to prevail : as a father confesses of himself, that before his conversion he would pray for chastity, with a secret reserve in his wishes that God would not grant his prayer. Such are the mysterious, intricate treacheries by which the love of sin will make a soul deceive and circumvent itself. How languidly and faintly will it pray for spiritual mercies ; conscience, in the meanwhile, giving the lie to every such petition ! The soul, in this case, cannot pray against sin in earnest; it fights against it, but neither with hope nor intent to conquer; as lovers, usually, in a game one against another, with a desire to lose. So, then, while we regard iniquity, how is it possible for us to regard spiritual things, the only lawful object of our prayers? and, if we regard them not, how can we be urgent with God for the giving of them? And where there is no fervency on our part, no wonder if there is no answer on God's.—*Robert South.* 1633—1716.

Verse 18.—"*If I regard iniquity in my heart, the Lord will not hear me.*" Though the subject-matter of a saint's prayer be founded on the word, yet if the end he aims at be not levelled right, this is a door at which his prayer will be stopped: "Ye ask, and receive not, because ye ask amiss, that ye may consume it upon your lusts." James iv. 3. Take, I confess, a Christian in his right temper, and he aims at the glory of God; yet, as a needle that is touched with a loadstone may be removed from its point to which nature hath espoused it, though trembling till it again recovers it; so a gracious soul may in a particular act and request vary from this end, being jogged by Satan, yea, disturbed by an enemy nearer home —his own unmortified corruption. Do you not think it possible for a saint, in distress of body and spirit, to pray for health in the one, and comfort in the other, with too selfish a respect to his own case and quiet? Yes, surely; and to pray for gifts and assistance in some eminent service, with an eye to his own credit and applause; to pray for a child with too inordinate a desire that the honour of his house may be built up in him. And this may be understood as the sense, in part, of that expression, "*If I regard iniquity in my heart, the Lord will not hear me.*" For though to desire our own health, peace, and reputation, be not an inquity, when contained within the limits that God hath set; yet, when they overflow to such a height, as to overtop the glory of God, yea, to stand but in a level with it, they are a great abomination. That which in the first or second degree is wholesome food, would be rank poison in the fourth or fifth: therefore, Christian, catechize thy-self, before thou prayest: O, my soul, what sends thee on this errand? Know but thy own mind what thou prayest for, and thou mayest soon know God's mind how thou shalt speed. Secure God his glory, and thou mayest soon know God's mind how thou shalt speed.—*William Gurnall.*

Verse 18.—"*If I regard iniquity in my heart, the Lord will not hear me.*"

1. They regard iniquity in their heart, who practise it secretly, who are under restraint from the world, but are not possessed of an habitual fear of the omniscient God, the searcher of all hearts, and from whose eyes there is no covering of thick darkness where the workers of iniquity may hide themselves. Jer. xxiii. 24.

2. They regard iniquity in the heart, who entertain and indulge the desire of sin, although in the course of providence they may be restrained from the actual commission of it. I am persuaded the instances are not rare, of men feeding upon sinful desires, even when through want of opportunity, through the fear of man, or through some partial restraint of conscience, they dare not carry them into execution.

3. They regard iniquity in their heart, who reflect upon past sins with delight, or without sincere humiliation of mind. Perhaps our real disposition, both towards sin and duty, may be as certainly discovered by the state of our minds after, as in the time of action. The strength and suddenness of temptation may betray even a good man into the commission of sin; the backwardness of heart and power of inward corruption may make duty burdensome and occasion many defects in the performance; but every real Christian remembers his past sins with unfeigned contrition of spirit, and a deep sense of unworthiness before God; and the discharge of his duty, however difficult it may have been at the time, affords him the utmost pleasure on reflection. It is otherwise with many; they can remember their sins without sorrow, they can speak of them without shame, and sometimes even with a mixture of boasting and vain glory. Did you never hear them recall their past follies, and speak of them with such relish, that it seems to be more to renew the pleasure than to regret the sin? Even supposing such persons to have forsaken the practice of some sins, if they can thus look back upon them with inward com-placency, their seeming reformation must be owing to a very different cause from renovation of heart.

4. They regard iniquity in the heart, who look upon the sins of others with approbation; or, indeed, who can behold them without grief. Sin is so abom-inable a thing, so dishonouring to God, and so destructive to the souls of men, that

no real Christian can witness it without concern. Hence it is so frequently taken notice of in Scripture, as the character of a servant of God, that he mourns for the sins of others. Ps. cxix. 136, 158.

5. In the last place, I suspect that they regard sin in the heart, who are backward to bring themselves to the trial, and who are not truly willing that God himself would search and try them. If any, therefore, are unwilling to be tried, if they are backward to self-examination, it is an evidence of a strong and powerful attachment to sin. It can proceed from nothing but from a secret dread of some disagreeable discovery, or the detection of some lust which they cannot consent to forsake. . . . . There are but too many who, though they live in the practice of sin, and regard iniquity in their hearts, do yet continue their outward attendance on the ordinances of divine institution, and at stated times lay hold of the seals of God's covenant. Shall they find any acceptance with him? No. He counts it a profane mockery; he counts it a sacrilegious usurpation. Ps. l. 16, 17. Shall they have any comfort in it? No: unless in so far as in righteous judgment he suffers them to be deceived; and they are deceived, and they are most unhappy, who lie longest under the delusion. Ps. l. 21. Shall they have any benefit by it? No: instead of appeasing his wrath, it provokes his vengeance; instead of enlightening their minds, it blinds their eyes; instead of sanctifying their nature, it hardens their hearts. See a description of those who had been long favoured with outward privileges and gloried in them. John xii. 39, 40. So that nothing is more essential to an acceptable approach to God in the duties of his worship in general, and particularly to receiving the seals of his covenant, than a thorough and universal separation from all known sin. Job. xi. 13, 14.—*John Witherspoon (1722—1749), in a Sermon entitled "The Petitions of the Insincere Unavailing."*

Verses 18, 19, 20.—Lord, I find David making a syllogism, in mood and figure, two propositions he perfected. *"If I regard iniquity in my heart, the Lord will not hear me; but verily God hath heard me; he hath attended to the voice of my prayer."* Now I expected that David should have concluded thus: "Therefore I regard not wickedness in my heart; but far otherwise he concludes: *"Blessed be God, which hath not turned away my prayer, nor his mercy from me."* Thus David hath deceived, but not wronged me. I looked that he should have clapped the crown on his own, and he puts it on God's head. I will learn this excellent logic; for I like David's better than Aristotle's syllogisms, and whatsoever the premises be, I make God's glory the conclusion.—*Thomas Fuller.*

HINTS TO PREACHERS.

Verse 3.—The terrible in God's works of nature and providence.

Verse 4.—I. *Who?* All the earth. 1. All, collectively, all classes and tribes. 2. All numerically. 3. All harmoniously. II. *What?* Shall worship and sing. 1. Humiliation; then, 2. Exultation. III. *When?* Shall, etc. Denotes 1. Futurity. 2. Certainty. God has spoken it. All things are tending towards it. —*G. R.*

Verse 5.—Here is—I. A subject for general study: the "works of God." II. For particular study: "his doing towards," etc. 1. These are most wonderful. 2. In these we are most concerned.

Verse 6.—Great difficulties, unexpectedly overcome, made the theme of joy.

Verse 6 (*last clause*).—Our share in the past deliverances of the church.

Verse 7.—Sovereignty, immutability ("for ever"), and omniscience,—the enemies of proud rebels.

Verse 8 (*last clause*).—To get a hearing for the gospel difficult, necessary, and possible. Ways and means for so doing.

Verses 8, 9. — I. Praise *to*. 1. As God. 2. As *our* God. II. Praise *for*. Preservation. 1. Of natural life. 2. Of spiritual life. III. Praise *by*, "ye people." 1. On your own account. 2. On account of others. Or, 1. Individually. 2. Unitedly.—*G. R.*

Verse 9.—Perseverance the subject of gratitude. I. The maintenance of the inner life. II. The integrity of the outward character

Verse 10.—The assaying of the saints.

Verse 10.—I. The design of the afflictions. 1. To prove them. 2. To reprove them. II. The illustration of that design. As silver, etc. III. The issue of the trial.

Verses 11, 12.—The hand of God should be acknowledged. I. In our temptations : " Thou broughtest us." II. In our bodily afflictions : " Thou laidest," etc. III. In our persecutions : " Thou hast caused," etc. IV. In our deliverances : " Thou broughtest us out," etc.—*G. R.*

Verse 12.—*Fire and water.* Varied trials. 1. Discover different evils. 2. Test all parts of manhood. 3. Educate varied graces. 4. Endear many promises. 5. Illustrate divine attributes. 6. Afford extensive knowledge. 7. Create capacity for the varied joys of heaven.

Verse 12 (*first clause*).—The rage of oppression.—*Thomas Adams' Sermon.*

Verse 12 (*last clause*).—A plentiful place, free from penury ; a pleasant place, void of sorrow ; a safe place, free from dangers and distresses.—*Daniel Wilcocks.*

Verse 12 (*last clause*).—The victory of patience, with the expiration of malice. —*Thomas Adams' Sermon.*

Verse 12 (*last clause*).—The wealth of a soul whom God has tried and delivered. Among other riches he has the wealth of experience, of strengthened graces, of confirmed faith, and of sympathy for others.

Verse 13.—God's house ; or, the place of praises.—*Thomas Adams' Sermon.*

Verses 13—15.—I. Resolutions made (verse 13). 1. What ? To offer praise. 2. Why ? For deliverance. 3. Where ? In thy house. II. Resolutions uttered (verse 14). 1. To God. 2. Before men. III. Resolutions fulfilled. 1. In public acknowledgment. 2. In heartfelt gratitude. 3. In more frequent attendance at the house of God. 4. The renewed self-dedication. 5. In increased liberality. —*G. R.*

Verse 16.—I. What has God done for the soul of every Christian ? II. Why does the Christian wish to declare what God has done for his soul ? III. Why does he wish to make this declaration to those only who fear God ? 1. Because they alone can understand such a declaration. 2. They alone will really believe him. 3. They only will listen with interest, or join with him in praising his Benefactor.—*E. Payson.*

Verse 16.—I. Religious teaching should be *simple :* " I will declare." II. *Earnest :* " Come and hear." III. *Seasonable :* " All ye that." IV. *Discriminating :* " Fear God." V. *Experimental :* " What he hath," etc.

Verse 17.—I. The two principal parts of devotion. Prayer and praise. II. Their degree. In prayer, crying. In praise, extolling. III. Their order : 1. Prayer. 2. Then praise. What is won by prayer is worn in praise.

Verses 18, 19.—I. The test admitted. II. The test applied. III. The test approved.

Verse 19.—The fact that God has heard prayer.

Verse 20.—The mercy of God. I. In permitting prayer. II. In inclining to prayer. III. In hearing prayer.

PSALM LXVII.

TITLE.—To the Chief Musician. *Who he was matters not, and who we may be is also of small consequence, so long as the Lord is glorified.* On Neginoth, or upon *stringed instruments. This is the fifth Psalm so entitled, and no doubt like the others was meant to be sung with the accompaniment of "harpers harping with their harps." No author's name is given, but he would be a bold man who should attempt to prove that David did not write it. We will be hard pushed before we will look for any other author upon whom to father these anonymous odes which lie side by side with those ascribed to David, and wear a family likeness to them.* A Psalm or Song. *Solemnity and vivacity are here united. A Psalm is a song, but all songs are not Psalms : this is both the one and the other.*

EXPOSITION.

GOD be merciful unto us, and bless us ; *and* cause his face to shine upon us. Selah.

2 That thy way may be known upon earth, thy saving health among all nations.

3 Let the people praise thee, O God ; let all the people praise thee.

4 O let the nations be glad and sing for joy : for thou shalt judge the people righteously, and govern the nations upon earth. Selah.

5 Let the people praise thee, O God ; let all the people praise thee.

6 *Then* shall the earth yield her increase ; *and* God, *even* our own God, shall bless us.

7 God shall bless us ; and all the ends of the earth shall fear him.

1. *"God be merciful unto us, and bless us ; and cause his face to shine upon us."* This is a fit refrain to the benediction of the High Priest in the name of the Lord, as recorded in Num. vi. 24, 25. " The Lord bless thee, and keep thee : the Lord make his face shine upon thee, and be gracious unto thee." It begins at the beginning with a cry for *mercy.* Forgiveness of sin is always the first link in the chain of mercies experienced by us. Mercy is a foundation attribute in our salvation. The best saints and the worst sinners may unite in this petition. It is addressed to the God of mercy, by those who feel their need of mercy, and it implies the death of all legal hopes or claims of merit. Next, the church begs for a blessing ; *"bless us "*—a very comprehensive and far-reaching prayer. When we bless God we do but little for *our* blessings are but words, but when God blesses he enriches us indeed, for his blessings are gifts and deeds. But his blessing alone is not all his people crave, they desire a personal consciousness of his favour, and pray for a smile from his face. These three petitions include all that we need here or hereafter.

This verse may be regarded as the prayer of Israel, and spiritually of the Christian church. The largest charity is shown in this Psalm, but it begins at home. The whole church, each church, and each little company, may rightly pray, " bless *us.*" It would, however, be very wrong to let our charity end where it begins, as some do ; our love must make long marches, and our prayers must have a wide sweep, we must embrace the whole world in our intercessions.

"Selah." Lift up the heart, lift up the voice. A higher key, a sweeter note is called for.

2. *"That thy way may be known upon earth."* As showers which first fall upon the hills afterwards run down in streams into the valleys, so the blessing of the Most High comes upon the world through the church. We are blessed for the sake of others as well as ourselves. God deals in a way of mercy with his saints, and then they make that way known far and wide, and the Lord's name is made famous in the earth. Ignorance of God is the great enemy of mankind, and the

testimonies of the saints, experimental and grateful, overcome this deadly foe. God has a set way and method of dealing out mercy to men, and it is the duty and privilege of a revived church to make that *way* to be everywhere known. *"Thy saving health among all nations,"* or, *thy salvation.* One likes the old words, " saving health," yet as they are not the words of the Spirit but only of our translators, they must be given up : the word is *salvation*, and nothing else. This all nations need, but many of them do not know it, desire it, or seek it ; our prayer and labour should be, that the knowledge of salvation may become as universal as the light of the sun. Despite the gloomy notions of some, we cling to the belief that the kingdom of Christ will embrace the whole habitable globe, and that all flesh shall see the salvation of God : for this glorious consummation we agonize in prayer.

3. *"Let the people praise thee, O God."* Cause them to own thy goodness and thank thee with all their hearts ; let nations do this, and do it continually, being instructed in thy gracious way. *"Let all the people praise thee."* May every man bring his music, every citizen his canticle, every peasant his praise, every prince his Psalm. All are under obligations to thee, to thank thee will benefit all, and praise from all will greatly glorify thee ; therefore, O Lord, give all men the grace to adore thy grace, the goodness to see thy goodness. What is here expressed as a prayer in our translation, may be read as a prophecy, if we follow the original Hebrew.

4. *"O let the nations be glad and sing for joy,"* or, they shall joy and triumph. When men know God's way and see his salvation, it brings to their hearts much happiness. Nothing creates gladness so speedily, surely, and abidingly as the salvation of God. Nations never will be glad till they follow the leadership of the great Shepherd ; they may shift their modes of government from monarchies to republics, and from republics to communes, but they will retain their wretchedness till they bow before the Lord of all. What a sweet word is that " to sing for joy ! " Some sing for form, others for show, some as a duty, others as an amusement, but to sing from the heart, because overflowing joy must find a vent, this is to sing indeed. Whole nations will do this when Jesus reigns over them in the power of his grace. We have heard hundreds and even thousands sing in chorus, but what will it be to hear whole nations lifting up their voices, as the noise of many waters and like great thunders. When shall the age of song begin ? When shall groans and murmurs be exchanged for holy hymns and joyful melodies ? *"For thou shalt judge the people righteously."* Wrong on the part of governors is a fruitful source of national woe, but where the Lord rules, rectitude is supreme. He doeth ill to none. His laws are righteousness itself. He rights all wrongs and releases all who are oppressed. Justice on the throne is a fit cause for national exultation. *"And govern the nations upon earth."* He will lead them as a shepherd his flock, and through his grace they shall willingly follow, then will there be peace, plenty, and prosperity. It is great condescension on God's part to become the Shepherd, of nations, and to govern them for their good: it is a fearful crime when a people who know the salvation of God, apostatize and say to the Lord " depart from us." There is some cause for trembling lest our nation should fall into this condemnation ; may God forbid.

"Selah." Before repeating the chorus, the note is again elevated, that full force may be given to the burst of song and the accompaniment of harps.

> " Strings and voices, hands and hearts,
> In the concert bear your parts ;
> All that breathe, your Lord adore,
> Praise him, Praise him, evermore ! "

5. These words are no vain repetition, but are a chorus worthy to be sung again and again. The great theme of the Psalm is the participation of the Gentiles in the worship of Jehovah ; the Psalmist is full of it, he hardly knows how to contain or express his joy.

6. *" Then shall the earth yield her increase."* Sin first laid a curse on the soil, and grace alone can remove it. Under tyrannical governments lands become unproductive ; even the land which flowed with milk and honey is almost a wilderness under Turkish rule ; but, when the principles of true religion shall have elevated mankind, and the dominion of Jesus shall be universally acknowledged, the science of tillage shall be perfected, men shall be encouraged to labour, industry shall banish penury, and the soil shall be restored to more than its highest condition of fertility.

We read that the Lord turneth "a fruitful land into barrenness," for the wickedness of them that dwell therein, and observation confirms the truth of the divine threatening; but even under the law it was promised, "the Lord God shall make thee plenteous in every work of thine hand, in the fruit of thy cattle, and in the fruit of thy land for good." There is certainly an intimate relation between moral and physical evil, and between spiritual and physical good. Alexander notes that the Hebrew is in the past tense, and he concludes that it is ungrammatical to render it in the future; but to us it seems that the prophet-bard, hearing the nations praise the Lord, speaks of the bounteous harvest as already given in consequence. On the supposition that all the people praise Jehovah, the earth has yielded her increase. The future in the English appears to be the clearest rendering of the Hebrew.

"*And God, even our own God, shall bless us.*" He will make earth's increase to be a real blessing. Men shall see in his gifts the hand of that same God whom Israel of old adored, and Israel, especially, shall rejoice in the blessing, and exult in her own God. We never love God aright till we know him to be ours, and the more we love him the more do we long to be fully assured that he is ours. What dearer name can we give to him than " mine own God." The spouse in the song has no sweeter canticle than " my beloved is mine and I am his." Every believing Jew must feel a holy joy at the thought that the nations shall all be blessed by Abraham's God; but every Gentile believer also rejoices that the whole world shall yet worship the God and Father of our Lord and Saviour Jesus Christ, who is our Father and our God.

7. "*God shall bless us.*" The prayer of the first verse is the song of the last. We have the same phrase twice, and truly the Lord's blessing is manifold; he blesses and blesses and blesses again. How many are his beatitudes! How choice his benedictions! They are the peculiar heritage of his chosen. He is the Saviour of all men, but specially of them that believe. In this verse we find a song for all future time. God shall bless us is our assured confidence; he may smite us, or strip us, or even slay us, but he must bless us. He cannot turn away from doing good to his elect. "*And all the ends of the earth shall fear him.*" The far off shall fear. The ends of the earth shall end their idolatry, and adore their God. All tribes, without exception, shall feel a sacred awe of the God of Israel. Ignorance shall be removed, insolence subdued, injustice banished, idolatry abhorred, and the Lord's love, light, life, and liberty, shall be over all, the Lord himself being King of king and Lord of lords. *Amen, and Amen.*

EXPLANATORY NOTES AND QUAINT SAYINGS.

Whole Psalm.—How admirably balanced are the parts of this missionary song! The people of God long to see all the nations participating in their privileges, " visited with God's salvation, and gladdened with the gladness of his nation " (Psalm cvi. 5). They long to hear all the nationalities giving thanks to the Lord, and hallowing his name; to see the face of the whole earth, which sin has darkened so long, smiling with the brightness of a second Eden. This is not a vapid sentiment. The desire is so expressed as to connect with it the thought of duty and responsibility. For how do they expect that the happy times are to be reached? They trust, in the first instance, to the general diffusion of the knowledge of God's way, the spreading abroad of the truth regarding the way of salvation. With a view to that, they cry for a time of quickening from the presence of the Lord, and take encouragement in this prayer from the terms of the divinely-appointed benediction. As if they had said, " Hast thou not commanded the sons of Aaron to put thy name upon us, and to say: The Lord bless thee and keep thee; the Lord cause his face to shine on thee and be gracious to thee? Remember that sure word of thine. God be gracious unto us and bless us, and cause his face to shine upon us. Let us be thus blessed, and we shall in our turn become a blessing. All the families of the earth shall, through us, become acquainted with thy salvation." Such is the church's expectation. And who shall say it is unreasonable? If the little company of a hundred and twenty disciples who met in the upper chamber at

Jerusalem, all of them persons of humble station, and unconspicuous talents, were endued with such power by the baptism of the Holy Ghost, that within three hundred years the paganism of the empire was overthrown, one need not fear to affirm that, in order to the evangelisation of the world, nothing more is required than that the churches of Christendom be baptised with a fresh effusion of the same Spirit of power.—*William Binnie.*

Whole Psalm.—There are seven stanzas; twice three two-line stanzas, having one of three lines in the middle, which forms the clasp or spangle of the septiad, a circumstance which is strikingly appropriate to the fact that the Psalm is called " the Old Testament Paternoster " in some of the old expositors.—*Franz Delitzsch.*

Verse 1.—"*God be merciful unto us, and bless us,*" etc. God forgives, then he gives; till he be merciful to pardon our sins through Christ, he cannot bless or look kindly on us sinners. All our enjoyments are but blessings in bullion, till gospel grace and pardoning mercy stamp and make them current. God cannot so much as bear any good will to us, till Christ makes peace for us : " On earth peace, good will towards men." Luke ii. xiv. And what joy can a sinner take, though it were to hear of a kingdom fallen to him, if he may not have it with God's good will.—*William Gurnall.*

Verse 1.—"*God be merciful unto us* "—Hugo attributes these words to penitents ; "*Bless us,*" to those setting out in the Christian life ; "*Cause his face to shine upon us,*" to those who have attained, or the sanctified. The first seek for pardon, the second for justifying peace, the third for edification and the grace of contemplation.— *Lorinus.*

Verses 1 and 2.—Connect the last clause of verse 1 with the first of verse 2, and observe that God made his face to shine upon Moses, and make known to him his way. " He made known his ways unto Moses, his acts unto the children of Israel," as if the common people could only see the deeds of the Lord, but his way, his plans, his secrets were revealed only to him upon whom the light of God's face had shone. —*C. H. S.*

Verse 2.—"*That thy way may be known,*" etc. The Psalmist here supposes that there *are* certain rules or principles, in accordance with which God bestows blessings on mankind ; and he prays that those rules and principles may be every-where made known upon the earth.—*Albert Barnes.*

Verse 2.—"*That thy way may be known,*" etc. By nature we know little of God, and nothing of Christ, or the way of salvation by him. The eye of the creature, therefore, must be opened to see the way of life before he can by faith get into it. God doth not use to waft souls to heaven like passengers in a ship, who are shut under the hatches, and see nothing all the way they are sailing to their port ; if so, that prayer might have been spared which the Psalmist, inspired of God, breathes forth in the behalf of the blind Gentiles : "*That thy way may be known upon earth, thy saving health among all nations.*" As faith is not a naked assent, with affiance and innitency * on Christ ; so neither is it a blind assent, without some knowledge. If, therefore, thou continuest still in thy brutish ignorance, and knowest not so much as who Christ is, and what he hath done for the salvation of poor sinners, and what thou must do to get interest in him, thou art far enough from believing. If the day be not broke in thy soul, much less is the Sun of Righteousness arisen by faith in thy soul.—*William Gurnall.*

Verse 2.—"*That thy way may be known.*" The sinful Jew, obstinate in his unbelief, shall see and hate. He shall see, and be enraged at the salvation of the Gentiles ; but let us see and *know,* that is, love. For *to know* is often put for *to love,* as in the passages—" My sheep hear my voice, and I know them : I know mine, and am known of mine ; " that is, I love my own sheep, and they love me. . . . There is here a sudden transition from the third person to the second, that in speaking of God he might not say, "*His way,*" or "*His salvation,*" but "*thy way,*" and "*Thy salvation ;* " setting forth the vehemence of an ardent suppliant, and the grace of God as he reveals himself to that suppliant while still pouring forth his prayers.— *Gerhohus* (1093—1169).

Verse 2.—"*That thy way may be known,*" etc. As light, so the participation of God's light is communicative : we must not pray for ourselves alone, but for all

---

* Innitency.—Act of leaning on.

others, that God's way may be known upon earth, and his saving health among all nations. *"Thy way;"* that is, thy will, thy word, thy works. God's will must be known on earth, that it may be done on earth, as it is in heaven. Except we know our Master's will, how shall we do it? *Ergo,* first pray with David here: *"Let the nations be glad and sing for joy: for thou shalt judge the people righteously, and govern the nations upon earth;"* and then, *"Let all the people praise thee."* God's will is revealed in his word, and his word is his way wherein we must walk, turning neither to the right hand nor to the left. Or, *"Thy way;"* that is, thy works, as David elsewhere (Ps. xxv. 10): "All the ways of the Lord are mercy and truth." Or, as others * most fitly: *"Thy way,"* that is, thy *Christ; "Thy saving health,"* that is, thy *Jesus:* for "I am the way," saith our Saviour (John xiv. 6): "No man cometh unto the Father, but by me;" wherefore, *"Let thy Son be known upon earth; thy Jesus among all nations."—John Boys.*

Verse 3.—"Let the people praise thee." Mark the sweet order of the blessed Spirit: first, mercy; then, knowledge; last of all, praising of God. We cannot see his countenance except he be merciful to us; and we cannot praise him except his way be known upon earth. His mercy breeds knowledge; his knowledge, praise.—*John Boys.*

Verse 3.—"Let the people praise thee, O God; let all the people praise thee." What then? *"Then shall the earth yield her increase; and God, even our own God, shall bless us."* We have comforts increased, the more we praise God for what we have already received. The more vapours go up, the more showers come down; as the rivers receive, so they pour out, and all run into the sea again. There is a constant circular course and recourse from the sea, unto the sea; so there is between God and us; the more we praise him, the more our blessings come down; and the more his blessings come down, the more we praise him again; so that we do not so much bless God as bless ourselves. When the springs lie low, we pour a little water into the pump, not to enrich the fountain, but to bring up more for ourselves.—*Thomas Manton.*

*Verse 3.—*This verse is exceedingly emphatic. 1. First, by an apostrophe to God, in the pronoun, Thee. As if he said: Let the people praise *thee,* not strange gods; for thou art the only true God. 2. Secondly, inasmuch as it is not said, Let *us* praise thee, O God; but let the *people* praise thee, and let *all* the people. For here is expressed the longing of the pious heart, and its fond desire that God should be praised and magnified throughout all lands and by all people of the round earth. 3. Thirdly, by the iteration, in which the same particle is repeated in this and the fifth verse no less than four times, as if the duty could not be sufficiently inculcated. It is not enough to have said it once; it is delightful to repeat it again.—*Wolfgang Musculus* (1497—1563).

Verse 4.—"For thou shalt judge the people righteously," etc. The Psalmist may here seem to contradict himself; for if mercy make men rejoice, then judgment occasioneth men to tremble. Answer is made, that all such as have known the ways of the Lord, and rejoice in the strength of his salvation, all such as have the pardon of their sins assured and sealed, fear not that dreadful assize, because they know the judge is their advocate. Or, (as Jerome,) let all nations rejoice, because God doth judge righteously, being the God of the Gentiles as well as of the Jews. Acts x. 34. Or, *let all nations rejoice,* because God doth govern all nations; that whereas theretofore they wandered in the fond imaginations of their own hearts, in wry ways, in by-ways; now they are directed by the Spirit of truth to walk in God's highway, which leads unto the celestial Jerusalem; now they shall know Christ, the way, the truth, and the life. For judging is often used for ruling. 1 Sam. vii. 15; 2 Cor. i. 10. So David doth here expound himself: "*thou shalt judge,*" that is, thou shalt "*govern the nations."—John Boys.*

Verse 4.—"Govern." Lead and guide them as the shepherd his flock.—*Benjamin Boothroyd.*

Verse 4.—"And lead (margin) *the nations."* God now *overrules* the nations in their ways, but surely they are *led* by another guide. There is a bridle in their jaws causing them to err. They are held and shaken in the sieve of vanity, until he come to whom the government pertains.—*Arthur Pridham.*

---

* Augustine; Jerome; Hilary.

Verses 5, 6.—"*Let the people praise thee, O God ; let all the people praise thee !*" What then ? "*Then shall the earth yield her increase ; and God, even our own God, shall bless us.*" Our unthankfulness is the cause of the earth's unfruitfulness. While man is blessin God *for* his mercies, He is blessing man *with* his mercies.—*William Secker, in "The Nonsuch Professor."* 1660.

Verse 6.—"*Then shall the earth yield her increase.*" An increase of wealth is but the natural result of increased piety and intelligence. There are certain qualities essential to temporal prosperity. These are industry, economy, moderation ; and such are the qualities begotten of godliness. . . . . Nor is it an unreasonable expectation that our globe should, under the reign of righteousness, yield all those temporal advantages of which it is capable. Science, favoured by piety, may greatly add to the earth's fruitfulness ; and mechanical genius may still further abbreviate human toil, and increase human comforts. The great inventions and discoveries of science, by which toil is lessened and comfort enhanced, are all the products of Christian minds. . . . . Can we, then, doubt that in the era to which we look forward, labour shall cease to be a burden ? Can we believe that the life of the labouring classes is to continue to be all but a ceaseless round of toil and vexation—every hand stretched out to procure something that is needed, or to ward off something that is feared ? Scripture predicts the mitigation of the curse ; and, in the discoveries of science and the inventions of mechanics, we see the means by which the prediction is to be accomplished. This consummation may still be in the distant future ; but if we do not grudge the oak years for its growth, the glory to be revealed is surely worthy of a process as gradual.—*William Reid, in "Things to Come Practically Considered."* 1871.

Verse 6.—"*God, even our own God, shall bless us.*" What a rapturous expression is that. "*God, even our own God, shall bless us !*" and that, "*Thy God, thy glory !*" Upon interest in God follows their interest in his glory and blessedness ; which is so much the dearer and more valuable, as it is theirs ; their glory from their God. They shall be blessed by God, their own God ; "drink waters out of their own well." How endearing a thing is propriety ! Another man's son is ingenuous, comely, personable ; this may be a matter of envy ; but mine own is so, this is a joy. I read in the life of a devout nobleman of France,* that receiving a letter from a friend in which were inserted these words : "*Deus meus et omnia,*" my God and my all, he thus returns back to him : " I know not what your intent was to put into your letter these words, ' *Deus meus et omnia*, My God and my all : ' only you invite me thereby to return the same to you, and to all creatures. ' My God and my all ; my God and my all ; my God and my all.' If, perhaps, you take this for your motto, and use it to express how full your heart is of it, think you it possible I should be silent upon such an invitation, and not express my sense thereof ? Likewise be it known unto you, therefore, that he is ' my God and my all ; ' and, if you doubt of it, I shall speak of it a hundred times over. I shall add no more, for anything else is superfluous to him that is truly penetrated with ' my God and my all ; ' I leave you, therefore, in this happy state of jubilation, and conjure you to beg for me, of God, the solid sense of these words." And do we think, " my God and my all," or, " my God and my glory," will have lost its emphasis in heaven ? or that it will be less significant among awaked souls ? These things concur, then, concerning the object ; it is most excellent, even divine, entire, permanent, and theirs : how can it but satisfy ?—*John Howe, in " The Blessedness of the Righteous."*

Verse 6.—"*Our own God.*" How unexpressible was the inward pleasure wherewith we may suppose those words to have been uttered. How delightful an appropriation ! as if it were intended to be said, the blessing itself were less significant, it could not have that savour with it, if it were not from our own God. Not only, therefore, allow, but urge your spirits thus to look towards God, that you may both delight in him as being in himself the most excellent one, and also as being yours ; for know, you are not permitted only, but obliged to eye, accept, and rejoice in him as such.—*John Howe.*

Verses 6, 7.—The promise refers directly to the visible fertility of the renewed earth at the time of Israel's recovery, but it includes a fuller reference to higher things ; for the true increase yielded by any of God's works is the revenue of praise which redounds to his holy name. Such, then, is the promise I have to bring before

---

* Monsieur de Renti.

you. In its widest sense, the lower creation is now made subject to vanity, because of man's sin ; but in the kingdom of Christ this curse will be removed, and all God's works will yield their full increase—a tribute of unmingled honour and praise to his name.

Let us consider—1. The preparation for this increase. 2. The increase itself. 3. The blessing of God, which will crown it.

I. THE PREPARATIONS FOR THIS INCREASE. What are the means ? What is the way of its accomplishment ? Whence does it proceed ? Our Psalm is full of instruction. Consider—1. *Its fountain :* the free mercy of God. The Psalm begins, "God be merciful unto us, and bless us ; and cause his face to shine upon us." Whatever the details and steps of the work of redemption, all must be traced up to this original fountain, the sovereign grace and mercy of our God. . . . . The eternal, free, unchangeable, inexhaustible mercy of our God, revealed through his dear Son Jesus Christ ; this is the fountain-head of the blessed increase here foretold. . . . . 2. *The order* in which this increase is granted may next be considered. Salvation is given to the Jew first, and then also to the Greek. The prayer of this Psalm is, "Cause his face to shine upon us ; that thy way may be known upon earth, thy saving health among all nations." It is the divine plan first to choose his people and bless them, and then to make them a blessing, as we see in Abraham, the father of the faithful. It is through his church that God blesses the world. . . . . The same principle is true in every revival of pure religion. . . . . But all this order of divine mercy has yet to be more fully seen in what is before us ; in the restoration of Israel, and its effect upon the world at large. . . . . 3. *The immediate precursor of this increase is the return of our Lord* from heaven, the coming of Christ to judge the earth and reign over all nations. The Psalm calls all nations to rejoice in this : " O let the nations be glad and sing for joy : for thou shalt judge the people righteously, and govern the nations upon earth." . . . . The world craves, and will crave more and more for righteous government. The Lord has promised to supply this natural want of the human heart, though he take vengeance on his hardened enemies. Even in the coming of the Lord to judgment, goodness will so finally triumph that the nations are to be glad and sing for joy. . . . . It is the Lord judging the people and governing the nations, and all the people praising him, that prepares directly and immediately for the promised blessedness. "*Then shall the earth yield her increase.*" . . . .

II. THE INCREASE ITSELF. This increase has many aspects. Let us view them in a climax of benefits. 1. *Natural fertility.* The first sentence of curse and barrenness, of thorns and thistles, was pronounced on Adam's fall, and renewed on Cain's murder. It seems to have been partially removed after the deluge. . . . . Even now, two-thirds of our world are ocean, incapable of increase ; half of the rest, and perhaps more, is almost desert, and of the remainder the largest part is very imperfectly tilled. There is room, even in the latter for a vast increase, when the whole earth might become like the garden of the Lord. 2. *The redemption of art.* Its activity, its talent, and discoveries are now great and wonderful ; but it is mainly turned to human self-sufficiency and vanity, and bears little fruit to God's glory and the highest benefit of man. But in the period predicted in this Psalm, every creature, when redeemed to man's use, shall be also reclaimed to God's glory. . . . . 3. *The redemption of science.* . . . . 4. *Society will yield its increase to God.* . . . . Men now live as without God in the world, full though it be of proofs of his wisdom and love. . . . . What a change when every social circle shall be a fellowship of saints, and all bent to one great purpose, the divine glory and the blessedness of each other. 5. *The soul shall yield its increase.* The earth is only the figure of the human heart, a soil ever fertile for good or evil. Thus the apostle, in his Epistle to the Hebrews, regards it : " For the earth which drinketh in the rain that cometh oft upon it, and bringeth forth herbs meet for them by whom it is dressed, receiveth blessing from God : but that which beareth thorns and briers is rejected, and is nigh unto cursing ; whose end is to be burned. But, beloved, we are persuaded better things of you, and things that accompany salvation, though we thus speak." Then the thorns and briers of a crooked and perverse generation will cease. . . . . The fruits of righteousness will abound from the human race to the glory of God. Much praise, much zeal, much reverence, much humility, will distinguish his servants. Faith, hope, and love will all be in the fullest exercise. Christ will be all and in all, and every power will be consecrated to him. This is the best increase the earth yields to God. 6. *The large number of God's true servants*, thus yielding themselves to him, is another part of this blessedness. . . . . 7. *The perpetuity of this increase* has to be added to this glory. This is according to the promise made to the Wonderful, Counsellor, the Mighty God, the Everlasting Father, the Prince of Peace.—*Condensed from Edward Bickersteth's Sermon in the "Bloomsbury Lent Lectures."* 1848.

Verses 6, 7.—Double blessings from God—temporal and spiritual; blessings peculiar to the Jews, and blessings suited to Christians. O Lord, I refuse not the temporal blessings it pleases thee to send me; I will receive them with humble gratitude as the gift of thy goodness: but I entreat from thee especially for spiritual blessings; and that thou wouldest treat me rather as a Christian than as a Jew.— *Pasquier Quesnel (1634—1719), in "Les Psaumes de David avec des Reflexions Morales."*

Verse 7.—Note, how joy in God, and fear of God, are combined. By joy the sadness and anxiety of diffidence are excluded, but by fear, contempt and false security are banished. So Ps. ii., "Serve the Lord with fear, and rejoice with trembling."—*Wolfgang Musculus.*

HINTS TO PREACHERS.

Verse 1.—I. Here is mercy in God the Father. II. Here is blessing as the fruit of that mercy in God the Son. III. Here is the experience of that blessing in the comforts of the Holy Ghost.

Verse 1.—The need of seeking a blessing for ourselves.

Verses 1, 2.—The prosperity of the church at home, the hope for missions abroad.

Verse 2.—I. The way of God towards the earth. 1. A way of mercy. 2. Of blessing. 3. Of comfort. II. The knowledge of that way. 1. By outward means. 2. By inward teaching. III. The effect of that knowledge. Salvation among all nations.

Verse 2.—What is the true health of men?

Verse 3.—Viewed, I. As the desire of every renewed heart. II. As a prayer. III. As a prophecy.

Verse 4.—I. The reign of God in the world: it is not left to itself. II. The joy of the world on that account: "Let the nations," etc. III. The reason of that joy: "He will judge righteously." 1. As faithful to his law. 2. Faithful to his promises of mercy.

Verses 5—7.—I. The prayer (verse 5). II. The promise (verse 6). 1. Of temporal good. 2. Of spiritual good. III. The prediction (verse 7).

Verses 6, 7.—See "Spurgeon's Sermons," No. 819: "The Minstrelsy of Hope."

Verse 7.—I. God to man: "shall bless us." II. Man to God: "shall fear him."

PSALM LXVIII.

TITLE.—To the Chief Musician, a Psalm *or* Song of David.—*We have already said enough upon this title when dealing with Psalms LXV. and LXVI. The present is obviously a song to be sung at the removal of the ark ; and in all probability was rehearsed when David conducted it with holy joy from the house of Obed-edom to the prepared place on Mount Zion. It is a most soul stirring hymn. The first verses were often the battle-song of the Covenanters and Ironsides ; and the whole Psalm fitly pictures the way of the Lord Jesus among his saints, and his ascent to glory. The Psalm is at once surpassingly excellent and difficult. Its darkness in some stanzas is utterly impenetrable. Well does a German critic speak of it as a Titan very hard to master. Our slender scholarship has utterly failed us, and we have had to follow a surer Guide. We trust our thoughts may not however prove unprofitable.*

DIVISION.—*With the words of the first two verses the ark is uplifted, and the procession begins to move. In verses 3—6, the godly in the assembly are exhorted to commence their joyous songs, and arguments are adduced to help their joy. Then the glorious march of Jehovah in the wilderness is sung : verses 7—10, and his victories in war are celebrated in verses 11—14. The joyous shouts are louder as Zion comes in sight, and the ark is borne up the hill : verses 15—19. On the summit of the mount the priests sing a hymn concerning the Lord's goodness and justice ; the safety of his friends, and ruin of his foes ; verses 20—23. Meanwhile the procession is described as it winds up the hill ; verses 24—27. The poet anticipates a time of wider conquest, verses 28—31 : and concludes with a noble burst of song unto Jehovah.*

EXPOSITION.

LET God arise, let his enemies be scattered : let them also that hate him flee before him.

2 As smoke is driven away, *so* drive *them* away : as wax melteth before the fire, *so* let the wicked perish at the presence of God.

1. "*Let God arise.*" In some such words Moses spake when the cloud moved onward, and the ark was carried forward. The ark would have been a poor leader if the Lord had not been present with the symbol. Before we move, we should always desire to see the Lord lead the way. The words suppose the Lord to have been passive for awhile, suffering his enemies to rage, but restraining his power. Israel beseeches him to " arise," as elsewhere to " awake," " gird on his sword," and other similar expressions. We, also, may thus importunately cry unto the Lord, that he would be pleased to make bare his arm, and plead his own cause. "*Let his enemies be scattered.*" Our glorious Captain of the vanguard clears the way readily, however many may seek to obstruct it ; he has but to arise, and they flee, he has easily over-thrown his foes in days of yore, and will do so all through the ages to come. Sin, death, and hell know the terror of his arm ; their ranks are broken at his approach. Our enemies are *his* enemies, and in this is our confidence of victory. "*Let them also that hate him flee before him.*" To hate the infinitely good God is infamous, and the worst punishment is not too severe. Hatred of God is impotent. His proudest foes can do him no injury. Alarmed beyond measure, they shall flee before it comes to blows. Long before the army of Israel can come into the fray, the haters of God shall flee before HIM who is the champion of his chosen. He comes, he sees, he conquers. How fitting a prayer is this for the commencement of a revival ! How it suggests the true mode of conducting one :—the Lord leads the way, his people follow, the enemies flee.

2. "*As smoke is driven away.*" Easily the wind chases the smoke, completely it removes it, no trace is left ; so, Lord, do thou to the foes of thy people. They fume in pride, they darken the sky with their malice, they mount higher and higher in arrogance, they defile wherever they prevail : Lord, let thy breath, thy Spirit,

thy Providence, make them to vanish for ever from the march of thy people. Philosophic scepticism is as flimsy and as foul as smoke; may the Lord deliver his Church from the reek of it. *"As wax melteth before the fire, so let the wicked perish at the presence of God."* Wax is hard by itself, but put it to the fire, how soft it is. Wicked men are haughty till they come into contact with the Lord, and then they faint for fear; their hearts melt like wax when they feel the power of his anger. Wax, also, burns and passes away; the taper is utterly consumed by the flame: so shall all the boastful power of the opposers of the gospel be as a thing of nought. Rome, like the candles on her altars, shall dissolve, and with equal certainty shall infidelity disappear. Israel saw, in the ark, God on the mercy-seat—power in connection with propitiation—and they rejoiced in the omnipotence of such a manifestation; this is even more clearly the confidence of the New Testament church, for we see Jesus, the appointed atonement, clothed with glory and majesty, and before his advance all opposition melts like snow in the sun: the pleasure of the Lord shall prosper in his hands. When he comes by his Holy Spirit, conquest is the result; but when he arises in person, his foes shall utterly perish.

3 But let the righteous be glad; let them rejoice before God: yea, let them exceedingly rejoice.

4 Sing unto God, sing praises to his name: extol him that rideth upon the heavens by his name JAH, and rejoice before him.

5 A father of the fatherless, and a judge of the widows, *is* God in his holy habitation.

6 God setteth the solitary in families: he bringeth out those which are bound with chains: but the rebellious dwell in a dry *land*.

3. *"But let the righteous be glad."* The presence of God on the throne of grace is an overflowing source of delight to the godly; and let them not fail to drink of the streams which are meant to make them glad. *"Let them rejoice before God."* The courtiers of the happy God should wear the garments of gladness, for in his presence is fulness of joy. That presence, which is the dread and death of the wicked, is the desire and delight of the saints. *"Yea, let them exceedingly rejoice."* Let them dance with all their might, as David did, for very joy. No bounds should be set to joy in the Lord. "Again, I say, rejoice," says the apostle, as if he would have us add joy to joy without measure or pause. When God is seen to shine propitious from above the mercy-seat in the person of our Immanuel, our hearts must needs leap within us with exultation, if we are indeed among those made righteous in his righteousness, and sanctified by his Spirit. Move on, O army of the living God, with shouts of abounding triumph, for Jesus leads the van.

4. *"Sing unto God, sing praises to his name."* To time and tune, with order and care, celebrate the character and deeds of God, the God of his people. Do it again and again; and let the praise, with resolution of heart, be all directed to him. Sing not for ostentation, but devotion; not to be heard of men, but of the Lord himself. Sing not to the congregation, but "unto God." *"Extol him that rideth upon the heavens by his name JAH."* Remember his most great, incomprehensible, and awful name; reflect upon his self-existence and absolute dominion, rise to the highest pitch of joyful reverence in adoring him. Heaven beholds him riding on the clouds in storm, and earth has seen him marching over its plains with majesty. The Hebrew seems to be: "Cast up a highway for him who marcheth through the wilderness," in allusion to the wanderings of the tribes in the desert. The marches of God were in the waste howling wilderness. His eternal power and Godhead were there displayed in his feeding, ruling, and protecting the vast hosts which he had brought out of Egypt. The ark brought all this to remembrance, and suggested it as a theme for song. The name JAH is an abbreviation of the name Jehovah; it is not a diminution of that name, but an intensified word, containing in it the essence of the longer, august title. It only occurs here in our version of Scripture, except in connection with other words such as Hallelu*jah*. *"And rejoice before him."* In the presence of him who marched so gloriously at the head of the elect nation, it is most fitting that all his people should display a holy delight. We ought to avoid dulness in our worship. Our songs should be weighty with solemnity, but not heavy with sadness. Angels are nearer the throne than we, but their deepest awe is consonant with the purest bliss: our sense of divine greatness

must not minister terror but gladness to our souls; we should "rejoice before him."

It should be our wish and prayer, that in this wilderness world, a highway may be prepared for the God of grace. "Prepare ye the way of the Lord, make straight in the desert a highway for our God," is the cry of gospel heralds, and we must all zealously aim at obedience thereto; for where the God of the mercy-seat comes, blessings innumerable are given to the sons of men.

5. "*A father of the fatherless, and a judge of the widows, is God in his holy habitation.*" In the wilderness the people were like an orphan nation, but God was more than a father to them. As the generation which came out of Egypt gradually died away, there were many widows and fatherless ones in the camp, but they suffered no want or wrong, for the righteous laws and the just administrators whom God had appointed, looked well to the interests of the needy. The tabernacle was the Palace of Justice; the ark was the seat of the great King. This was great cause for joy to Israel, that they were ruled by ONE who would not suffer the poor and needy to be oppressed. To this day and for ever, God is, and will be, the peculiar guardian of the defenceless. He is the President of Orphanages, the Protector of Widows. He is so glorious that he rides on the heavens, but so compassionate that he remembers the poor of the earth. How zealously ought his church to cherish those who are here marked out as Jehovah's especial charge. Does he not here in effect say, "Feed my lambs?" Blessed duty, it shall be our privilege to make this one of our life's dearest objects. The reader is warned against mis-quoting this verse; it is generally altered into "*the husband of the widow,*" but Scripture had better be left as God gave it.

6. "*God setteth the solitary in families.*" The people had been sundered and scattered over Egypt; family ties had been disregarded, and affections crushed; but when the people escaped from Pharoah they came together again, and all the fond associations of household life were restored. This was a great joy. "*He bringeth out those which are bound with chains.*" The most oppressed in Egypt were chained and imprisoned, but the divine Emancipator brought them all forth into perfect liberty. He who did this of old continues his gracious work. The solitary heart, convinced of sin and made to pine alone, is admitted into the family of the First-born; the fettered spirit is set free, and its prison broken down, when sin is forgiven; and for all this, God is to be greatly extolled, for he hath done it, and magnified the glory of his grace. "*But the rebellious dwell in a dry land.*" If any find the rule of Jehovah to be irksome, it is because their rebellious spirits kick against his power. Israel did not find the desert dry, for the smitten rock gave forth its streams; but even in Canaan itself men were consumed with famine, because they cast off their allegiance to their covenant God. Even where God is revealed on the mercy-seat, some men persist in rebellion, and such need not wonder if they find no peace, no comfort, no joy, even where all these abound. Justice is the rule of the Lord's kingdom, and hence there is no provision for the unjust to indulge their evil lustings: a perfect earth, and even heaven itself, would be a dry land to those who can only drink of the waters of sin. Of the most soul-satisfying of sacred ordinances these witless rebels cry, "what a weariness it is!" and, under the most soul-sustaining ministry, they complain of "the foolishness of preaching." When a man has a rebellious heart, he must of necessity find all around him a dry land.

7 O God, when thou wentest forth before thy people, when thou didst march through the wilderness; Selah:

8 The earth shook, the heavens also dropped at the presence of God: even Sinai itself *was moved* at the presence of God, the God of Israel.

9 Thou, O God, didst send a plentiful rain, whereby thou didst confirm thine inheritance, when it was weary.

10 Thy congregation hath dwelt therein: thou, O God, hast prepared of thy goodness for the poor.

7. "*O God, when thou wentest forth before thy people.*" What a sweetly suitable association, "thou" and "thy people;"—thou before, and thy people following! The Lord went before, and, therefore, whether the Red Sea or burning sand lay in the way, it mattered not; the pillar of cloud and fire always led them

by a right way. "*When thou didst march through the wilderness.*" He was the Commander-in-chief of Israel, from whom they received all orders, and the march was therefore *his* march. "His stately step the region drear beheld." We may speak, if we will, of the "wanderings of the children of Israel," but we must not think them purposeless strayings, they were in reality a well-arranged and well considered march.

"SELAH." This seems an odd place for a musical pause or direction, but it is better to break a sentence than spoil praise. The sense is about to be superlatively grand, and, therefore, the *selah* intimates the fact to the players and singers, that they may with suitable solemnity perform their parts. It is never untimely to remind a congregation that the worship of God should be thoughtfully and heartily presented.

8. "*The earth shook.*" Beneath the sublime tread the solid ground trembled. "*The heavens also dropped at the presence of God,*" as if they bowed before their God, the clouds descended, and "a few dark shower-drops stole abroad." "*Even Sinai itself was moved at the presence of God.*" Moses tells us, in Ex. xix., that "the whole mountain quaked greatly." That hill, so lone and high, bowed before the manifested God. "*The God of Israel.*" The one only living and true God, whom Israel worshipped, and who had chosen that nation to be his own above all the nations of the earth. This passage is so sublime, that it would be difficult to find its equal. May the reader's heart adore the God before whom the unconscious earth and sky act as if they recognised their Maker and were moved with a tremor of reverence.

9. "*Thou, O God, didst send a plentiful rain.*" The march of God was not signalized solely by displays of terror, for goodness and bounty were also made conspicuous. Such rain as never fell before dropped on the desert sand, bread from heaven and winged fowls fell all around the host ; good gifts were poured upon them, rivers leaped forth from rocks. The earth shook with fear, and in reply, the Lord, as from a cornucopia, shook out blessings upon it ; so the original may be rendered. "*Whereby thou didst confirm thine inheritance, when it was weary.*" As at the end of each stage, when they halted, weary with the march, they found such showers of good things awaiting them that they were speedily refreshed. Their foot did not swell all those forty years. When they were exhausted, God was not. When they were weary, he was not. They were his chosen heritage, and, therefore, although for their good he allowed them to be weary, yet he watchfully tended them and tenderly considered their distresses. In like manner, to this day, the elect of God in this wilderness state are apt to become tired and faint, but their ever-loving Jehovah comes in with timely succours, cheers the faint, strengthens the weak, and refreshes the hungry ; so that once again, when the silver trumpets sound, the church militant advances with bold and firm step towards "the rest which remaineth." By this faithfulness, the faith of God's people is confirmed, and their hearts stablished ; if fatigue and want made them waver, the timely supply of grace stays them again upon the eternal foundation.

10. "*Thy congregation hath dwelt therein.*" In the wilderness itself, enclosed as in a wall of fire, thy chosen church has found a home ; or, rather, girdled by the shower of free gifts which fell all around the camp, thy flock has rested. The congregation of the faithful find the Lord to be their "dwelling-place in all generations." Where there were no dwellings of men, God was the dwelling of his people. "*Thou, O God, hast prepared of thy goodness for the poor.*" Within the guarded circle there was plenty for all ; all were poor in themselves, yet there were no beggars in all the camp, for celestial fare was to be had for the gathering. We, too, still dwell within the circling protection of the Most High, and find goodness made ready for us : although poor and needy by nature, we are enriched by grace ; divine preparations in the decree, the covenant, the atonement, providence, and the Spirit's work, have made ready for us a fulness of the blessing of the Lord. Happy people, though in the wilderness, for all things are ours, in possessing the favour and presence of our God.

11 The Lord gave the word : great *was* the company of those that published *it*.

12 Kings of armies did flee apace : and she that tarried at home divided the spoil.

13 Though ye have lien among the pots, *yet shall ye be as* the wings of a dove covered with silver, and her feathers with yellow gold.

14 When the Almighty scattered kings in it, it was *white* as snow in Salmon.

11. In the next verses we do not sing of marching, but of battle and victory "*The Lord gave the word.*" The enemy was near, and the silver trumpet from the tabernacle door was God's mouth to warn the camp ; then was there hurrying to and fro, and a general telling of the news ; "*great was the company of those that published it.*" The women ran from tent to tent and roused their lords to battle. Ready as they always were to chant the victory, they were equally swift to publish the fact that the battle-note had been sounded. The ten thousand maids of Israel, like good handmaids of the Lord, aroused the sleepers, called in the wanderers, and bade the valiant men hasten to the fray. O for the like zeal in the church to-day, that, when the gospel is published, both men and women may eagerly spread the glad tidings of great joy.

12. "*Kings of armies did flee apace.*" The lords of hosts fled before the Lord of Hosts. No sooner did the ark advance than the enemy turned his back : even the princely leaders stayed not, but took to flight. The rout was complete, the retreat hurried and disorderly ;—they " did flee, did flee ; " helter skelter, pell-mell, as we say.

> " Where are the kings of mighty hosts ?
> Fled far away, fled far and wide.
> Their triumph and their trophied boasts
> The damsels in their bowers divide."

"*And she that tarried at home divided the spoil.*" The women who had published the war-cry shared the booty. The feeblest in Israel had a portion of the prey. Gallant warriors cast their spoils at the feet of the women and bade them array themselves in splendour, taking each one " a prey of divers colours, of divers colours of needlework on both sides." When the Lord gives success to his gospel, the very least of his saints are made glad and feel themselves partakers in the blessing.

13. "*Though ye have lien among the pots.*" Does he mean that the women at home, who had been meanly clad as they performed their household work, would be so gorgeously arrayed in the spoil, that they would be like doves, of silver wing and golden plumage ? Or, would he say that Israel, which had been begrimed in the brick-kilns of Egypt, should come forth lustrous and happy in triumph and liberty ? Or, did the song signify that the ark should be brought from its poor abode with Obed-edom into a fairer dwelling-place ? It is a hard passage, a nut for the learned to crack. If we knew all that was known when this ancient hymn was composed, the allusion would no doubt strike us as being beautifully appropriate, but as we do not, we will let it rest among the unriddled things. Alexander reads it, " When ye shall lie down between the borders, ye shall be like the wings," etc., which he considers to mean, " when settled in peace, the land shall enjoy prosperity ; " but this version does not seem to us any more clear than our authorised one. Of making many conjectures there is no end ; but the sense seems to be, that from the lowest condition the Lord would lift up his people into joy, liberty, wealth, and beauty. Their enemies may have called them squatters among the pots—in allusion to their Egyptian slavery ; they may have jested at them as scullions of Pharaoh's kitchen ; but the Lord would avenge them and give them beauty for blackness, glory for grime. "*Yet shall ye be as the wings of a dove covered with silver, and her feathers with yellow gold.*" The dove's wing flashes light like silver, and anon gleams with the radiance of " the pale, pure gold." The lovely, changeable colours of the dove might well image the mild, lustrous beauty of the nation, when arrayed in white holiday-attire, bedecked with their gems, jewels, and ornaments of gold. God's saints have been in worse places than among the pots, but now they soar aloft into the heavenly places in Christ Jesus.

14. "*When the Almighty scattered kings in it, it was white as snow in Salmon.*" The victory was due to the Almighty arm alone ; he scattered the haughty ones who came against his people, and he did it as easily as snow is driven from the bleak sides of Salmon. The word *white* appears to be imported into the text, and by leaving it out the sense is easy. A traveller informed the writer that on a raw and gusty day, he saw the side of what he supposed to be Mount Salmon suddenly

swept bare by a gust of wind, so that the snow was driven hither and thither into the air like the down of thistles, or the spray of the sea : thus did the Omnipotent one scatter all the potentates that defied Israel. If our authorized version must stand, the conjectures that the bleached bones of the enemy, or the royal mantles cast away in flight. whitened the battle-field, appear to be rather too far-fetched for sacred poetry. Another opinion is, that Salmon was covered with dark forests, and appeared black, but presented quite another aspect when the snow covered it, and that by this noteworthy change, from sombre shade to gleaming whiteness, the poet sets forth the change from war to peace. Whatever may be the precise meaning, it was intended to pourtray the glory and completeness of the divine triumph over the greatest foes. In this let all believers rejoice.

15 The hill of God *is as* the hill of Bashan ; an high hill *as* the hill of Bashan.

16 Why leap ye, ye high hills ? *this is* the hill *which* God desireth to dwell in ; yea, the LORD will dwell *in it* for ever.

17 The chariots of God *are* twenty thousand, *even* thousands of angels : the Lord *is* among them, *as in* Sinai, in the holy *place.*

18 Thou hast ascended on high, thou hast led captivity captive : thou hast received gifts for men ; yea, *for* the rebellious also, that the LORD God might dwell *among them.*

19 Blessed *be* the Lord, *who* daily loadeth us *with benefits, even* the God of our salvation. Selah.

15. Here the priests on the summit of the chosen hill begin to extol the Lord for his choice of Zion as his dwelling-place. *"The hill of God is as the hill of Bashan,"* or more accurately, " a hill of God is Bashan," that is to say, Bashan is an eminent mountain, far exceeding Zion in height. According to the Hebrew custom, every great or remarkable thing is thus designated. Where we talk of the Devil's Dyke, the Devil's Ditch, the Devil's Punch Bowl, etc., the more commendable idiom of the Hebrews speaks of the hill of God, the trees of the Lord, the river of God, etc. *"An high hill as the hill of Bashan,"* or rather, " a mount of peaks is Bashan." It does not appear that Zion is compared with Bashan, but contrasted with it. Zion certainly was not a high hill comparatively ; and it is here conceded that Bashan is a greater mount, but not so glorious, for the Lord in choosing Zion had exalted it above the loftier hills. The loftiness of nature is nothing before the Lord. He chooses as pleases him, and, according to the counsel of his own will, he selects Zion, and passes by the proud, uplifted peaks of Bashan ; thus doth he make the base things of this world, and things that are despised, to become monuments of his grace and sovereignty.

16. *"Why leap ye, ye high hills ? "* Why are ye moved to envy ? Envy as ye may, the Lord's choice is fixed. Lift up yourselves, and even leap from your seats, ye cannot reach the sublimity which Jehovah's presence has bestowed on the little hill of Moriah. *"This is the hill which God desireth to dwell in."* Elohim makes Zion his abode, yea, Jehovah resides there. *"Yea, the Lord will dwell in it for ever."* Spiritually the Lord abides eternally in Zion, his chosen church, and it was Zion's glory to be typical thereof. What were Carmel and Sirion, with all their height, compared to Zion, the joy of the whole earth ! God's election is a patent of nobility. They are choice men whom God has chosen, and that place is superlatively honoured which he honours with his presence.

17. *"The chariots of God are twenty thousand."* Other countries, which in the former verse were symbolically referred to as " high hills," gloried in their chariots of war ; but Zion, though far more lowly, was stronger than they, for the omnipotence of God was to her as two myriads of chariots. The Lord of Hosts could summon more forces into the field than all the petty lords who boasted in their armies : his horses of fire and chariots of fire would be more than a match for their fiery steeds and flashing cars. The original is grandly expressive, " the war-chariots of Elohim are myriads, a thousand thousands." The marginal reading of our Bibles, *"even many thousands,"* is far more correct than the rendering, *"even thousands of angels."* It is not easy to see where our venerable translators found these " angels," for they are not in the text ; however, as it is a blessing to entertain them unawares,

we are glad to meet with them in English, even though the Hebrew knows them not ; and the more so because it cannot be doubted that they constitute a right noble squadron of the myriad hosts of God. We read in Deuteronomy xxxiii. 2, of the Lord's coming " with ten thousands of saints," or holy ones, and in Heb. xii. 22, we find upon Mount Zion " an innumerable company of angels," so that our worthy translators putting the texts together, inferred the angels, and the clause is so truthfully explanatory, that we have no fault to find with it. *"The Lord is among them, as in Sinai, in the holy place,"* or, " it is a Sinai in holiness." God is in Zion as the Commander-in-chief of his countless hosts, and where he is, there is holiness. The throne of grace on Zion is as holy as the throne of justice on Sinai. The displays of his glory may not be so terrible under the new covenant as under the old ; but they are even more marvellous if seen by the spiritual eye. Sinai has no excellency of glory beyond Zion ; but the rather it pales its light of law before the noontide splendours of Zion's grace and truth. How joyful was it to a pious Hebrew to know that God was as truly with his people in the tabernacle and temple as amid the terrors of the Mount of Horeb ; but it is even more heart-cheering to us to be assured that the Lord abides in his church, and has chosen it to be his rest for ever. May we be zealous for the maintenance of holiness in the spiritual house which God condescends to occupy : let a sense of his presence consume, as with flames of fire, every false way. The presence of God is the strength of the church ; all power is ours when God is ours. Twenty thousand chariots shall bear the gospel to the ends of the earth ; and myriads of agencies shall work for its success. Providence is on our side, and it " has servants everywhere." There is no room for a shade of doubt or discouragement, but every reason for exultation and confidence.

18. *"Thou hast ascended on high."* The ark was conducted to the summit of Zion ; God himself took possession of the high places of the earth, being extolled and very high. The antitype of the ark, the Lord Jesus, has ascended into the heavens with signal marks of triumph. To do battle with our enemies, the Lord descended and left his throne ; but now the fight is finished, he returns to his glory ; high above all things is he now exalted. *"Thou hast led captivity captive."* A multitude of the sons of men are the willing captives of Messiah's power. As great conquerors of old led whole nations into captivity, so Jesus leads forth from the territory of his foe a vast company as the trophies of his mighty grace. From the gracious character of his reign it comes to pass that to be led into captivity by him is for our captivity to cease, or to be itself led captive ; a glorious result indeed. The Lord Jesus destroys his foes with their own weapons ; he puts death to death, entombs the grave, and leads captivity captive. *"Thou hast received gifts for men,"* or, received gifts among men : they have paid thee tribute, O mighty Conqueror, and shall in every age continue to do so willingly, delighting in thy reign. Paul's rendering is the gospel one : Jesus has " received gifts for men," of which he makes plentiful distribution, enriching his church with the priceless fruits of his ascension, such as apostles, evangelists, pastors, and teachers, and all their varied endowments. In him, the man who received gifts for man, we are endowed with priceless treasures, and, moved with gratitude, we return gifts to him, yea, we give him ourselves, our all. *"Yea, for the rebellious also :"* these gifts the rebels are permitted to share in ; subdued by love, they are indulged with the benefits peculiar to the chosen. The original runs, " even the rebellious," or, " even from the rebellious," of which the sense is that rebels become captives to the Lord's power, and tributaries to his throne.

> " Great King of grace, my heart subdue,
> I would be led in triumph too ;
> A willing captive to my Lord,
> To own the conquests of his word."

"That the Lord God might dwell among them." In the conquered territory, Jah Elohim would dwell as Lord of all, blessing with his condescending nearness those who were once his foes. When Canaan was conquered, and the fort of Zion carried by storm, then was there found a resting-place for the ark of God ; and so when the weapons of victorious grace have overcome the hearts of men, the Lord God, in all the glory of his name, makes them to be his living temples. Moreover, the ascension of Jesus is the reason for the descent of the Lord God, the Holy Spirit. Because Jesus dwells with God, God dwells with men. Christ on high is the reason of the Spirit below. It was expedient that the Redeemer should rise, that the Comforter should come down.

19. *"Blessed be the Lord."* At the mention of the presence of God among men the singers utter an earnest acclamation suggested by reverential love, and return blessings to him who so plentifully blesses his people. *"Who daily loadeth us with benefits."* Our version contains a great and precious truth, though probably not the doctrine intended here. God's benefits are not few nor light, they are loads; neither are they intermittent, but they come " daily ; " nor are they confined to one or two favourites, for all Israel can say, " he loadeth *us* with benefits." Delitzsch reads it, " He daily bears our burden ; " and Alexander, " Whoever lays a load upon us, the Mighty God is our salvation." If he himself burdens us with sorrow, he gives strength sufficient to sustain it ; and if others endeavour to oppress us, there is no cause for fear, for the Lord will come to the rescue of his people. Happy nation, to be subdued by a King whose yoke is easy, and who secures his people from all fear of foreign burdens which their foes might try to force upon them. *"Even the God of our salvation."* A name most full of glory to him, and consolation to us. No matter how strong the enemy, we shall be delivered out of his hands ; for God himself, as King, undertakes to save his people from all harm. What a glorious stanza this is ! It is dark only because of its excessive light. A world of meaning is condensed into a few words. His yoke is easy, and his burden is light, therefore blessed be the Saviour's name for evermore. All hail ! thou thrice blessed Prince of Peace ! All thy saved ones adore thee, and call thee blessed.

"Selah." Well may the strings need tuning, they have borne an unparalleled strain in this mighty song. Higher and yet higher, ye men of music, lift up the strain. Dance before the ark, ye maidens of Israel ; bring forth the timbrel, and sing unto the Lord who hath triumphed gloriously.

20 *He that is* our God *is* the God of salvation ; and unto God the Lord *belong* the issues from death.

21 But God shall wound the head of his enemies, *and* the hairy scalp of such an one as goeth on still in his trespasses.

22 The Lord said, I will bring again from Bashan, I will bring *my people* again from the depths of the sea :

23 That thy foot may be dipped in the blood of *thine* enemies, *and* the tongue of thy dogs in the same.

20. *"He that is our God is the God of salvation."* The Almighty who has entered into covenant with us is the source of our safety, and the author of our deliverances. As surely as he is our God he will save us. To be his is to be safe. *"And unto God the Lord belong the issues from death."* He has ways and means of rescuing his children from death : when they are at their wit's end, and see no way of escape, he can find a door of deliverance for them. The gates of the grave none can open but himself, we shall only pass into them at his bidding; while on the heavenward-side he has set open the doors for all his people, and they shall enjoy triumphant issues from death. Jesus, our God, will save his people from their sins, and from all else besides, whether in life or death.

21. *"But God shall wound the head of his enemies."* The Preserver is also the Destroyer. He smites his foes on the crown of their pride. The seed of the woman crushes the serpent's head. There is no defence against the Lord, he can in a moment smite with utter destruction the lofty crests of his haughty foes. *"And the hairy scalp of such an one as goeth on still in his trespasses."* He may glory in his outward appearance, and make his hair his pride, as Absalom did ; but the Lord's sword shall find him out, and pour out his soul. Headstrong sinners will find that providence overcomes them despite their strong heads. They who go on in sin will find judgments come on them ; and the adornment of their pride may be made the instrument of their doom. He covers the head of his servants, but he crushes the head of his foes. At the second coming of the Lord Jesus, his enemies will find his judgments to be beyond conception terrible.

22. This verse, by the insertion of the words, *"my people,"* is made to bear the meaning which the translators thought best ; but, if their interpolated word is omitted we probably get nearer to the sense. *"The Lord said, I will bring again from Bashan, I will bring again from the depths of the sea."* Though his foes should endeavour to escape, they should not be able. Amos describes the Lord as saying, " Though they dig into hell, thence shall mine hand take them ; though they climb

up to heaven, thence will I bring them down : and though they hide themselves in the top of Carmel, I will search and take them out thence ; and though they be hid from my sight in the bottom of the sea, thence will I command the serpent, and he shall bite them." As there is no resisting Israel's God, so is there no escape from him, neither the heights of Bashan nor the depths of the great sea can shelter from his eye of detection and his hand of justice. The powers of evil may flee to the utmost ends of the earth, but the Lord will arrest them, and lead them back in chains to adorn his triumph.

23. *"That thy foot may be dipped in the blood of thine enemies."* Vengeance shall be awarded to the oppressed people, and that most complete and terrible. *"And the tongue of thy dogs in the same."* So overwhelming should be the defeat of the foe that dogs should lick their blood. Here " the stern joy which warriors feel " expresses itself in language most natural to the oriental ear. To us, except in a spiritual sense, the verse sounds harshly ; but read it with an inner sense, and we also desire the utter and crushing defeat of all evil, and that wrong and sin may be the objects of profound contempt. Terrible is the God of Israel when he cometh forth as a man of war, and dreadful is even the Christ of God when he bares his arm to smite his enemies. Contemplate Rev. xix. and note the following :—" And I saw heaven opened, and behold a white horse ; and he that sat upon him was called Faithful and True, and in righteousness he doth judge and make war. His eyes were as a flame of fire, and on his head were many crowns ; and he had a name written, that no man knew, but he himself. And he was clothed with a vesture dipped in blood : and his name is called The Word of God. . . . . And I saw an angel standing in the sun ; and he cried with a loud voice, saying to all the fowls that fly in the midst of heaven, come and gather yourselves together unto the supper of the great God ; that ye may eat the flesh of kings, and the flesh of captains, and the flesh of mighty men, and the flesh of horses, and of them that sit on them, and the flesh of all men, both free and bond, both small and great. And I saw the beast, and the kings of the earth, and their armies, gathered together to make war against him that sat on the horse, and against his army. And the beast was taken, and with him the false prophet that wrought miracles before him, with which he deceived them that had received the mark of the beast, and them that worshipped his image. These both were cast alive into a lake of fire burning with brimstone. And the remnant were slain with the sword of him that sat upon the horse, which sword proceeded out of his mouth : and all the fowls were filled with their flesh."

24 They have seen thy goings, O God ; *even* the goings of my God, my King, in the sanctuary.

25 The singers went before, the players on instruments *followed* after ; among *them were* the damsels playing with timbrels.

26 Bless ye God in the congregations, *even* the Lord, from the fountain of Israel.

27 There *is* little Benjamin *with* their ruler, the princes of Judah *and* their council, the princes of Zebulun, *and* the princes of Naphtali.

24. *"They have seen thy goings, O God."* In the song the marchings of the Lord had been described ; friends and foes had seen his goings forth with the ark and his people. We suppose that the procession was now climbing the hill, and entering the enclosure where the tabernacle of the ark was pitched ; it was suitable at this moment to declare with song that the tribes had seen the glorious progress of the Lord as he led forth his people. *"Even the goings of my God, my King, in the sanctuary."* The splendid procession of the ark, which symbolised the throne of the great King, was before the eyes of men and angels as it ascended to the holy place ; and the Psalmist points to it with exultation before he proceeds to describe it. All nature and providence are, as it were, a procession attending the great Lord, in his visitations of this lower globe. Winter and summer, sun and moon, storm and calm, and all the varied glories of nature swell the pomp of the King of kings, of whose dominion there is no end.

25. *"The singers went before, the players on instruments followed after."* This was the order of the march, and God is to be worshipped evermore with due decorum. First the singers, and lastly the musicians, for the song must lead the music, and not the music drown the singing. In the midst of the vocal and instrumental band,

or all around them, were the maidens : *"among them were the damsels playing with timbrels."* Some have imagined that this order indicates the superiority of vocal to instrumental music ; but we need not go so far for arguments, when the simplicity and spirituality of the gospel already teach us that truth. The procession depicted in this sublime song was one of joy, and every means was taken to express the delight of the nation in the Lord their God.

26. *"Bless ye God in the congregations."* Let the assembled company magnify the God whose ark they followed. United praise is like the mingled perfume which Aaron made, it should all be presented unto God. He blesses us ; let him be blessed. *"Even the Lord, from the fountain of Israel."* A parallel passage to that in Deborah's song : " They that are delivered from the noise of archers in the places of drawing water, there shall they rehearse the righteous acts of the Lord." The seat of the ark would be the fountain of refreshing for all the tribes, and there they were to celebrate his praises. " Drink," says the old inscription, " drink, weary traveller ; drink and pray." We may alter one word, and read it, drink and praise. If the Lord overflows with grace, we should overflow with gratitude. Ezekiel saw an ever-growing stream flow from under the altar, and issue out from under the threshold of the sanctuary, and wherever it flowed it gave life : let as many as have quaffed this life-giving stream glorify " the fountain of Israel."

27. *"There is little Benjamin with their ruler."* The tribe was small, having been greatly reduced in numbers, but it had the honour of including Zion within its territory. " And of Benjamin he said, The beloved of the Lord shall dwell in safety by him ; and the Lord shall cover him all the day long, and he shall dwell between his shoulders." Little Benjamin had been Jacob's darling, and now the tribe is made to march first in the procession, and to dwell nearest to the holy place. *"The princes of Judah and their council."* Judah was a large and powerful tribe, not with one governor, like Benjamin, but with many princes " and their company," for so the margin has it. " From thence is the shepherd, the stone of Israel," and the tribe was a quarry of stones wherewith to build up the nations : some such truth is hinted at in the Hebrew. *"The princes of Zebulun, and the princes of Naphtali."* Israel was there, as well as Judah ; there was no schism among the people. The north sent a representative contingent as well as the south, and so the long procession set forth the hearty loyalty of all the tribes to their Lord and King. O happy day, when all believers shall be one around the ark of the Lord ; striving for nothing but the glory of the God of grace.

28 Thy God hath commanded thy strength : strengthen, O God, that which thou hast wrought for us.

29 Because of thy temple at Jerusalem shall kings bring presents unto thee.

30 Rebuke the company of spearmen, the multitude of the bulls, with the calves of the people, *till every one* submit himself with pieces of silver : scatter thou the people *that* delight in war.

31 Princes shall come out of Egypt ; Ethiopia shall soon stretch out her hands unto God.

The prophet now puts into the mouth of the assembly a song, foretelling the future conquests of Jehovah.

28. *"Thy God hath commanded thy strength."* His decree had ordained the nation strong, and his arm had made them so. As a commander-in-chief, the Lord made the valiant men pass in battle array, and bade them be strong in the day of conflict. This is a very rich though brief sentence, and, whether applied to an individual believer, or to the whole church, it is full of consolation. *"Strengthen, O God, that which thou hast wrought for us."* As all power comes from God at first, so its continual maintenance is also of him. We who have life should pray to have it " more abundantly ; " if we have strength we should seek to be still more established. We expect God to bless his own work. He has never left any work unfinished yet, and he never will. " When we were without strength, in due time Christ died for the ungodly ; " and now, being reconciled to God, we may look to him to perfect that which concerneth us, since he never forsakes the work of his own hands.

29. *"Because of thy temple at Jerusalem shall kings bring presents unto thee."* The palace of God, which towered above Jerusalem, is prophesied as becoming a

wonder to all lands, and when it grew from the tabernacle of David to the temple of Solomon, it was so. So splendid was that edifice that the queen of far-off Sheba came with her gifts ; and many neighbouring princes, overawed by the wealth and power therein displayed, came with tribute to Israel's God. The church of God, when truly spiritual, wins for her God the homage of the nations. In the latter-day glory this truth shall be far more literally and largely verified.

30. *"Rebuke the company of spearmen ; "* or, *"the beasts of the reeds,"* as the margin more correctly renders it. Speak to Egypt, let its growing power and jealousy be kept in order, by a word from thee. Israel remembers her old enemy, already plotting the mischief, which would break out under Jeroboam, and begs for a rebuking word from her Omnipotent Friend. Anti-christ also, that great red dragon, needs the effectual word of the Lord to rebuke its insolence. *"The multitude of the bulls,"* the stronger foes ; the proud, headstrong, rampant, fat, and roaring bulls, which sought to gore the chosen nation,—these also need the Lord's rebuke, and they shall have it too. All Egypt's sacred bulls could not avail against a " thus saith Jehovah." Popish bulls, and imperial edicts, have dashed against the Lord's church, but they have not prevailed against her, and they never shall. *"With the calves of the people."* The poorer and baser sort are equally set on mischief, but the divine voice can control them ; multitudes are as nothing to the Lord when he goes forth in power ; whether bulls or calves, they are but cattle for the shambles when Omnipotence displays itself. The gospel, like the ark, has nothing to fear from great or small ; it is a stone upon which every one that stumbleth shall be broken. *"Till every one submit himself with pieces of silver."* The Lord is asked to subdue the enemies of Israel, till they rendered tribute in silver ingots. Blessed is that rebuke, which does not break but bend ; for subjection to the Lord of hosts is liberty, and tribute to him enriches him that pays it. The taxation of sin is infinitely more exacting than the tribute of religion. The little finger of lust is heavier than the loins of the law. Pieces of silver given to God are replaced with pieces of gold. *"Scatter thou the people that delight in war."* So that, notwithstanding the strong expression of verse 23, God's people were peacemen, and only desired the crushing of oppressive nations, that war might not occur again. Let the battles of peace be as fierce as they will ; heap coals of fire on the heads of enemies, and slay their enmity thereby. That " they who take the sword should perish by the sword," is a just regulation for the establishment of quiet in the earth. What peace can there be, while blood-thirsty tyrants and their myrmidons are so many ? Devoutly may we offer this prayer, and, with equal devotion, we may bless God that it is sure to be answered, for " he breaketh the bow and cutteth the spear in sunder, he burneth the chariot in the fire."

31. *"Princes shall come out of Egypt."* Old foes shall be new friends. Solomon shall find a spouse in Pharaoh's house. Christ shall gather a people from the realms of sin. Great sinners shall yield themselves to the sceptre of grace, and great men shall become good men, by coming to God. *"Ethiopia shall soon stretch out her hands unto God."* Cush shall hasten to present peace offerings. Sheba's queen shall come from the far south. Candace's chamberlain shall ask of Him who was led as a lamb to the slaughter. Abyssinia shall yet be converted, and Africa become the willing seeker after grace, eagerly desiring and embracing the Christ of God. Poor Ethiopia, thy hands have been long manacled and hardened by cruel toil, but millions of thy sons have in their bondage found the liberty with which Christ made men free ; and so thy cross, like the cross of Simon of Cyrene, has been Christ's cross, and God has been thy salvation. Hasten, O Lord, this day, when both the civilization and the barbarism of the earth shall adore thee, Egypt and Ethiopia blending with glad accord in thy worship ! Here is the confidence of thy saints, even thy promise ; hasten it in thine own time, good Lord.

32 Sing unto God, ye kingdoms of the earth ; O sing praises unto the Lord ; Selah :

33 To him that rideth upon the heavens of heavens, *which were* of old ; lo, he doth send out his voice, *and that* a mighty voice.

34 Ascribe ye strength unto God : his excellency *is* over Israel, and his strength *is* in the clouds.

35 O God, *thou art* terrible out of thy holy places : the God of Israel *is* he that giveth strength and power unto *his* people. Blessed *be* God.

32. *"Sing unto God, ye kingdoms of the earth."* Glorious shall that song be in which whole empires join. Happy are men that God is one who is consistently the object of joyous worship, for not such are the demons of the heathen. So sweet a thing is song that it ought to be all the Lord's; a secular concert seems almost a sacrilege, a licentious song is treason. *"O sing praises unto the Lord."* Again and again is God to be magnified; we have too much sinning against God, but cannot have too much singing to God. *"Selah."* Well may we rest now that our contemplations have reached the millennial glory. What heart will refuse to be lifted up by such a prospect!

33. *"To him that rideth upon the heavens of heavens, which were of old."* Before, he was described in his earthly manifestations, as marching through the desert; now, in his celestial glory, as riding in the heavens of the primeval ages. Long ere this heaven and earth were made, the loftier abodes of the Deity stood fast; before men or angels were created, the splendours of the Great King were as great as now, and his triumphs as glorious. Our knowledge reaches but to a small fragment of the life of God, whose " goings forth were of old, even from everlasting." Well might the Jewish church hymn the eternal God, and well may we join therewith the adoration of the Great Firstborn :—

> " Ere sin was born, or Satan fell,
> He led the host of morning stars.
> Thy generation who can tell ?
> Or count the number of thy years ? "

"Lo, he doth send out his voice, and that a mighty voice." Was there a thunder-clap just then heard in heaven ? Or, did the poet's mind flash backward to the time when from the heaven of heavens the voice of Jehovah broke the long silence and said, " Light be," and light was. To this hour, the voice of God is power. This gospel, which utters and reveals his word, is the power of God unto salvation to every one that believeth. Our voices are fitly called to praise him whose voice spoke us into being, and gives us the effectual grace which secures our well-being.

34. *"Ascribe ye strength unto God."* When even his voice rends the rocks and uproots the cedars, what cannot his hand do ? His finger shakes the earth; who can conceive the power of his arm ? Let us never by our doubts or our daring defiances appear to deny power unto God; on the contrary, by yielding to him and trusting in him, let our hearts acknowledge his might. When we are reconciled to God, his omnipotence is an attribute of which we sing with delight. *" His excellency is over Israel."* The favoured nation is protected by his majesty; his greatness is to them goodness, his glory is their defence. *"And his strength is in the clouds."* He does not confine his power to the sons of men, but makes it like a canopy to cover the skies. Rain, snow, hail, and tempest are his artillery; he rules all nature with awe-inspiring majesty. Nothing is so high as to be above him, or too low to be beneath him; praise him, then, in the highest.

35. *"O God, thou art terrible out of thy holy places."* Thou inspirest awe and fear. Thy saints obey with fear and trembling, and thine enemies flee in dismay. From thy threefold courts, and especially from the holy of holies, thy majesty flashes forth and makes the sons of men prostrate themselves in awe. *"The God of Israel is he that giveth strength and power unto his people."* In this thou, who art Israel's God by covenant, art terrible to thy foes by making thy people strong, so that one shall chase a thousand, and two put ten thousand to flight. All the power of Israel's warriors is derived from the Lord, the fountain of all might. He is strong, and makes strong: blessed are they who draw from his resources, they shall renew their strength. While the self-sufficient faint, the All-sufficient shall sustain the feeblest believer. *"Blessed be God."* A short but sweet conclusion : Let our souls say Amen to it; and yet, again, Amen.

NEW TRANSLATION.

In order that our readers may see the Psalm at a glance in a good translation, we subjoin the version of FRANZ DELITZSCH ; *recommending our ministerial brethren to procure the volumes of his valuable Commentary on the Psalms, issued by the* Messrs. CLARK, *of Edinburgh.*

PSALM LXVIII.

HYMN OF WAR AND VICTORY IN THE STYLE OF DEBORAH.

2 LET Elohim arise, let His enemise be scattered,
And let those who hate Him flee before His face.

3 As smoke is driven away, do Thou drive them away ;
As wax melteth before the fire,
Let the wicked perish before Elohim.

4 And let the righteous rejoice, let them exult before Elohim,
And let them be glad with joy.

5 Sing unto Elohim, harp His name,
Pave a highway for Him who rideth along through the steppes ;
Jah is his name, and exult ye before Him.

6 A Father of the fatherless and an Advocate of the widows
Is Elohim in his Holy habitation.

7 Elohim maketh a household for the solitary,
He leadeth forth prisoners into prosperity ;
Yet the rebellious abide in a land of drought.

8 Elohim, when Thou wentest forth before Thy people,
When Thou didst march along in the wilderness—(*Sela.*)

9 The earth shook,
The heavens also dropped before Elohim,
Yon Sinai before Elohim, the God of Israel.

10 With plentiful rain didst Thou, Elohim, water Thine inheritance,
And when it was parched, THOU hast confirmed it.

11 Thy creatures have settled down therein,
Thou didst provide with Thy goodness for the poor, Elohim.

12 The Lord will sound forth the mandate ;
Of the women who herald victory there is a great army.

13 The kings of hosts shall flee, shall flee,
And she that tarrieth at home shall divide the spoil.

14 If ye encamp among the sheep-folds,
The dove's wings are covered with silver
And her feathers with glistening gold.

15 When the Almighty scattereth kings therein,
It becometh snow-white upon Zalmon.

16 A mountain of Elohim is the mountain of Bashan,
A mountain full of peaks is the mountain of Bashan.

17 Why look ye enviously, ye many-peaked mountains,
Upon the mountain which Elohim hath chosen, to dwell thereon ?
Yea, Jahve will dwell [there] for ever.

18 The war-chariots of Elohim are myriads, a thousand thousands,
   The Lord is among them, it is a Sinai in holiness.
19 Thou hast ascended up to the height, Thou hast led captives captive,
   Thou hast received gifts among men,
   Even from the rebellious, that Jah Elohim might dwell [there].
20 Blessed be the Lord :
   Day by day doth He bear our burden,
   He, God, is our salvation. (Sela.)
21 He, God, is to us a God for deeds of deliverance,
   And Jahve the Lord hath ways of escape for death.
22 Yea, Elohim will smite the head of His enemies,
   The hairy scalp of him who stalketh along in his trespasses.
23 The Lord hath said : Out of Bashan will I bring back,
   I will bring back out of the depths of the sea,
24 That thou mayest bathe thy foot in blood,
   That the tongue of thy dogs may have its share of the enemy.
25 They behold Thy splendid procession, Elohim,
   The splendid procession of my God, my King in holiness.
26 Before went the singers, behind the players on stringed instruments,
   In the midst of damsels striking timbrels.
27 In the choirs of the congregation bless ye Elohim,
   The Lord, ye who are out of the fountain of Israel.
28 There is Benjamin the youngest, their ruler ;
   The princes of Judah—their motley band,
   The princes of Zebulun, the princes of Naphtali.

29 Thy God hath commanded thy supreme power—
   Uphold in power, Elohim, what Thou hast wrought for us !—
30 From Thy temple above Jerusalem
   Let kings present offerings into Thee.
31 Threaten the wild beast of the reed, the troops of bulls with the calves
          of the people,
   That they may prostrate themselves with ingots of silver !—
   He hath scattered the peoples that delight in wars.
32 Magnates come out of Egypt,
   Cush—quickly do his hands stretch out unto Elohim.

33 Ye kingdoms of the earth, sing unto Elohim,
   Praising the Lord with stringed instruments—(Sela.)
34 To Him who rideth in the heaven of heavens of the primeval time—
   Lo, He made Himself heard with His voice, a mighty voice.
35 Ascribe ye might unto Elohim !

   Over Israel is His majesty,
   And His omnipotence in the heights of the heavens.
36 Terrible is Elohim out of thy sanctuaries ;
   " The God of Israel giveth might and abundant strength to the people ! "
   Blessed be Elohim !

EXPLANATORY NOTES AND QUAINT SAYINGS.

Whole Psalm.—In this Psalm we have especial reason to condemn or to admire the timidity, or the caution and delicacy of our translators, whichever it may be considered, for the manner in which they have rendered the names of the Almighty. They almost universally translate them " God " or " Lord ; " whereas, it has been observed that, almost all the remarkable titles of the Deity are employed in describing and praising the person addressed here. He is called " Elohim " in verse 2 ; " Adonai," verse 12 ; " Shaddai," verse 15 ; " Jehovah," verse 17 ; " Jah," verse 19 ; and " Al," verse 20. The Hebrew names of God have, each of them, a distinct and peculiar meaning. No one word will suffice for them all. The vague use of the terms " God " and " Lord " in our translation can never convey to the reader's mind the important ideas which the original expressions, if properly translated, would bear, and we have lost a strong additional confirmation of the deity of Messiah, by abandoning the testimony which the ascription to him of God's peculiar titles would give to this great truth.—*R. H. Ryland.*

Whole Psalm.—As lxvii. opened with a reference to the form of blessing (Numb. vi. 24-26), so this with a reference to the prayer used when the cloud-pillar summoned the camp to commence a march. *There* the presence (*panim*) of God shed saving light on his people ; here his enemies flee from it (*mippanayv*, ver. 1). . . . In the Jewish ritual the Psalm is used at Pentecost, the Anniversary of the Giving of the Law, and the Feast of Finished Harvest. . . . The remarkable character of the Psalm is indicated by the fact that there are no fewer than thirteen words in it which are not found elsewhere. The Pentecostal Gift of Tongues seems needed for its full exposition.—*William Kay.*

Whole Psalm.—By many critics esteemed the loftiest effusion of David's lyrical muse.—*William Binnie.*

Whole Psalm.—To judge from the antiquity of its language, the concise description, the thoroughly fresh, forcible, and occasional artlessly ironical expression of its poetry, we consider this poem as one of the most ancient monuments of Hebrew poetry.—*Boettcher.*

Whole Psalm.—It must be confessed that in this Psalm there are as many precipices, and as many labyrinths, as there are verses, or even words. It has not inappropriately been designated the cross of critics, the reproach of interpreters.—*Simon de Muis.*

Whole Psalm.—The beginning of this Psalm clearly intimates that the inspired Psalmist had light given him to see the march of Israel through the wilderness, the ark of the covenant moving before the people to find a resting place. The Psalmist is filled with praise, when he is enabled to see that God revealed his Fatherly love in the whole of that movement—that his eye was upon the fatherless, the widow, the solitary, and afflicted ; but David is also carried by the Spirit to the Mount of Olives, where he sees the ascending Lord ; he sees the triumphal chariots, with an innumerable company of angels, and then beholds the Lord welcomed in glory as the mighty Conqueror ; and not only so, but as having received or purchased gifts for men, even the rebellious (ver. 18), " that the Lord God might dwell among them," or *within them.* " Wherefore," the command of our Father is, " come out from among them, and be ye separate," etc. (2 Cor. vi. 17-18). The doxology of God's people is, " Blessed be the Lord, who daily loadeth us with his benefits." Our blessed Master attends day by day to all our wants, and causes his love to flow to us, because he is God our Salvation—Selah. What comfort ought this to afford under every condition ! for the Lord Jesus goes before us through the desert. He is touched with the feeling of our infirmities. The widow, the fatherless, the desolate, are all the objects of his care and love. He has gone before us to prepare our heavenly rest ; the work is finished. He now comes, day by day, to load us with blessings, and at the last will carry us safely through death into life and glory. To the Lord our Saviour belong the issues from death ; then, " Death, where is thy sting ? " etc.—*Ridley H. Herschell, in " Strength in Weakness. Meditations on some of the Psalms in time of Trial."* 1860.

Verse 1.—" *Let God arise,*" etc. The moving ark * is a type of Jesus going forth to cast down rebel foes. It is high joy to trace the Antitype's victorious march.

---

* See Numbers **x.** 35, 36.

How mightily the Lord advanced! The strength of God was in his arm. His sword was Deity. His darts were barbed with all Jehovah's might. "He had on his vesture and on his thigh a name written, King of kings, and Lord of Lords." Rev. xix. 16. His foes, indeed, strove mightily. It was no easy work to rescue souls from Satan's grasp, or to lay low the prison-house of darkness. The enemy rushed on, clad in his fiercest armour, wild in his keenest rage, wily in his deadliest crafts. He plied his every temptation, as a terrific battery. But the true Ark never quailed. The adversary licked the dust. Malignant passions maddened in opposing breasts. The kings stood up; rulers took counsel; all plots were laid; the ignominious death was planned and executed. But still the Ark moved on. The cross gave aid, not injury. The grave could not detain. Death could not vanquish. The gates of hell fly open. The mighty conqueror appears. And, as in Canaan, the ark ascended Zion's hill amid triumphant shouts, so Jesus mounts on high. The heaven of heavens receives him. The Father welcomes the all-conquering Saviour. Angelic hosts adore the glorious God-man. The Rising Prayer has full accomplishment, "Rise up, Lord, and let thine enemies be scattered, and let them that hate thee flee before thee."

And now, from glory's throne, he cheers his humble followers in their desert march. Their toils, their conflicts, and their fears are many. They ofttimes seem as a poor worm beneath the crushing feet. But they survive, they prosper, they lift up the head. As of old the ark was victory, so Jesus is victory now. Yes, every child of faith shall surely set a conquering foot upon the host of foes. Hear this, ye mad opposers, and desist. Where are the nations who resisted Israel? Where are the Pharaohs, the beleaguered kings, the Herods, the chief-priests, the Pilates? Share not their malice, lest you share their end. Read in this word your near destruction, "Rise up, Lord, and let thine enemies be scattered, and let them that hate thee flee before thee."

And, as the Rising Prayer has never failed, so, too, the Resting Prayer now teems with life. "Return, O Lord." Jesus is ready to fly back. Israel's many thousands wait, but wait not in vain. "Yet a little while, and he that shall come will come, and will not tarry," Heb. x. 37. O joyful day, triumphant sight! What ecstacy, what shouts, what glory! Salvation's Lord returns. Welcome, welcome to him!— *Henry Law, in* "'*Christ is All.*' *The Gospel of the Old Testament.*" 1858.

Verse 1.—"*Arise.*" The mercifulness of God is seen in his patience toward the wicked, implied in the word "*arise,*" for he seemeth, as it were, to *sleep* (Psalm xliv. 23), and not to mark what is done amiss. The Lord is patient, and would have none to perish, but would have all men to come to repentance. He was longer in destroying one city (*Jericho*, Joshua vi. 4), than in building the whole world; slow to wrath, and ready to forgive, desiring not the death of a sinner, but rather he should amend. He doth not arise to particular punishments, much less to the general judgment, but after long suffering and great goodness. "O Jerusalem, Jerusalem, how often would I," quoth our Lord, "have gathered thy children together, even as a hen gathereth her chickens under her wings, and ye would not." Matt. xxiii. 37.—*John Boys.*

Verse 1.—"*Let his enemies be scattered.*" You may, if you please, take the words either as a prayer, or as a *prophecy : as a prayer* that they *may ;* or as a prophecy, that they *shall be scattered.* Or, you may read it, *Surgente Domino. As soon as the Lord shall arise, his enemies shall be scattered,* and so make it a theological axiom: and so it is a proposition *æternæ veritatis,* everlastingly true, true in the first age of the world, and true in the last age of the world, and will be true to the world's end. We may make it our prayer, that they may be destroyed ; and we may prophesy, that they *shall be destroyed. Summa votorum est, non ex incerto poscentis, sed ex cognitione scientiâque sperantis,* saith Hilary. It is a prayer not proceeding from a doubting and wavering heart, as if God did at sometimes deliver his church, and at others fail and leave her to the will of her enemies ; but grounded upon certain knowledge and infallible assurance that he will "*arise, and not keep silence,*" and avenge himself of his enemy. For there is a kind of presage and prophecy in prayer : if we pray as we should, he hath promised to grant our request ; which is a fairer assurance than any prophet can give us. "*Let God arise,*" and *God will arise,* it is but the difference of a tense, and the Hebrews commonly use the one for the other. . . . .

In this prayer or prophecy, or conclusion, you may, as in a glass, behold the providence of God over his people, and the destiny and fatal destruction of wicked men. Or, you may conceive God sitting in heaven, and looking down upon the children of men, and laughing to scorn all the designs of his enemies ; his *exsurgat*, his rising, as a tempest to scatter them, and as a fire to melt them. And these two, *exsurgat* and *dissipabuntur*, the rising of God and the destruction of his enemies, divide the text, and present before our eyes two parties or sides, as it were, in main opposition. Now, though the *exsurgat* be before the *dissipabuntur*, God's rising before the scattering, yet there must be some persons to rouse God up and awake him before he will arise to destroy. We will, therefore, as the very order of nature required, consider first the persons which are noted out unto us by three several appellations, as by so many marks and brands in their forehead. They are, 1. *Enemies ;* 2. *Haters of God ;* 3. *Wicked men.* But God, *rising* in this manner, is more especially against the fact than the person, and against the person only for the fact. We must, therefore, search and inquire after that ; and we find it wrapt up and secretly lurking in the *dissipabuntur*, in their punishment ; for scattering supposeth a gathering together, as corruption doth generation. That, then, which moved God to rise is this : his *enemies*, they that *hated him*, *the wicked*, were gathered together, and consulted against God and his church, as we see it this day ; and, seeing it, are here met together to fall down before God in all humility, that he may arise and scatter them. This is *nunc opportunitatis*, the very time and appointed time *for* God to *arise.* In which phrase is implied a kind of pause and deliberation, as if God were not always up, and ready to execute judgment. And, hereby, he manifesteth—1. His patience to the wicked : he is not always up, as it were, to destroy his enemies ; 2. His justice, which cometh at length, though it come not so soon as men in misery expect ; 3. His mercy to his children : though for a while he seem to sleep, and not to hearken to the voice of their complaints, yet, at last, he rises up and helps them. Lastly, we shall take notice of the effect, or end, of this rising ; and that is the destruction of his enemies, here drawn out to our view, in four several expressions, as in so many colours :—1. *Dissipabuntur, they shall be scattered ;* 2. *Fugient, they shall fly ;* 3. *Deficient, they shall vanish like smoke ;* 4. *Liquefient, they shall be melted as wax ;* which all meet and are concentred in *peribunt, they shall perish at the presence of God.—Anthony Farindon.*

Verses 1—3.—Whether the Jewish Church fully comprehended the meaning of the predictions or not, it is absolutely certain that her members were taught, in more places than one, earnestly to pray for Christ's second advent ; and to one of these prayers I would now direct your attention, considering, I. *The Prayer of the Jewish Church for the Second Advent of Christ.* II. *The duty of the Christian Church to join in it.* The Psalmist, moved by the Spirit of God, adopts the words used by Moses in the wilderness, when the ark, in which God dwelt between the cherubim, set forward ; for we read in the 10th of Numbers, " It came to pass, when the ark set forward, that Moses said, Rise up, Lord, and let thine enemies be scattered ; and let them that hate thee flee before thee. And when it rested, he said, Return, O Lord, unto the many thousands of Israel." But the wanderings of Israel were now over, and the ark of the Lord had found a place of rest. The people of God were in the land promised to their fathers ; their enemies were subdued ; and the ark went forth no more with the armies of Israel. It is not, therefore, the removal of the ark to which the prophet alludes in his prayer. The context of the Psalm, and the expressions used, carry us on far beyond the days of David, and refer us to times still future. David prays for the return of him of whom the ark was a type, whose glorious advent he beheld by the spirit of prophecy. The words of the text contain a prayer for the second advent of the Lord Jesus Christ. Never has this prayer been yet answered in its full extent. The Lord has oft interfered in behalf of his people, or to rouse the wicked to repentance ; but these interpositions were temporary, and the world was left again to the government of his providence. God has often given tokens sufficient to show the world what he will do when the day of his wrath is come. . . . But yet the world and the church abound with wickedness, and mourn because of sin. They that hate the Lord flee not before him, but are still suffered to open their mouths in blasphemy ; nor have the wicked perished in the presence of God. . . . This rising up, for which the Psalmist prays, is connected with the restoration of Israel, the establishment of universal peace, and the conversion of all nations : ver. 22, 29, 30, 31. II. As members of the Christian Church, we continually profess our faith in the second coming of Christ ; and, it may be, that we sometimes meditate upon his glorious appearance ; but have we, like David, adopted it as one of the subjects of our addresses at the throne of grace ? . . . . Has our faith ever enabled us to take up the language of the text, and say, "*Let God arise, let his enemies be scattered : let them also that hate him flee before him*" ? This leads me, in the second place, to point out our duty to join in the Psalmist's petitions. If it were a prayer suited only to the individual case of David, no obligation could rest upon us to unite in it ; but it is a prayer for the universal church, for every one who loves the Saviour, and desires to see "the King in his beauty," for every one who mourns over the state of the world and the church. It is a prayer frequently repeated in Holy Scripture of the Old Testament taught by our Lord, now offered up by saints in the presence of God, and with which the Scriptures of the New Testament conclude. . . . .

It is remarkable that only one prayer of the departed saints has been made known to us, and that this one should be a prayer to the same effect. In the 5th Chapter of the Revelation, the Lord is pleased to give us a view of the state of those who have died as martyrs. St. John says, "I saw under the altar the souls of them that were slain for the word of God, and for the testimony which they held : and they cried with a loud voice, saying, How long, O Lord, holy and true, dost thou not judge and avenge our blood on them that dwell on the earth ?" Though removed from this scene of woe and misery, safe from all the attempts of the wicked, and in the enjoyment of God's presence, their happiness is not yet complete, and they still find subject matter for prayer and supplication. They still long for that day when the Lord shall arise to judgment, and put an end to the triumph of the wicked. With this prayer also the New Testament concludes. . . . . We cannot, therefore, doubt, but that it is our duty to join in a prayer which the Holy Ghost has dictated, which our Lord has appointed, which the saints in heaven use, and which the beloved disciple offered up. The nature of the prayer presents another argument to enforce this duty. We are bound to pray for those things which promote the honour of Christ, and the eternal happiness of his people. But never shall the honour of Christ be complete, nor his people happy, nor the righteous be glad and rejoice exceedingly, until God arise and his enemies be scattered.— *Alexander M'Caul, D.D., in "Plain Sermons on Subjects Practical and Prophetic."* 1840.

Verse 2.—"*As smoke is driven away,*" etc. The Psalmist adds a striking figure to illustrate how easily God can overthrow the machinations of our enemies, comparing them to *smoke which vanishes away when blown upon by the wind*, or *wax which melts before the fire*. We consider it utterly incredible that such a formidable array of opposition should be made to disappear in a moment. But the Spirit takes this method of chiding the fearfulness of our carnal minds, and teaching us that there is no such strength in our enemies as we suppose—that we allow the smoke of them to blind our eyes, and the solid mass of resistance which they present to deceive us into a forgetfulness of the truth, that the mountains themselves flow down at the presence of the Lord.—*John Calvin.*

Verse 2.—"*As smoke is driven away,*" etc. "Their end was bitter as the smoke," said an aged teacher. What meanest thou, O Master ? asked his young disciple. "I was thinking of the end of the unrighteousness," replied the old man, "and of how too often I, like the Psalmist, have been envious when they were in prosperity. Their lives have seemed so bright and glowing that I have thought they resembled the blaze of a cheerful fire on a winter's night. But, as I have watched them, they have suddenly vanished like the flame that fades into black and bitter smoke ; and I have ceased to envy them. Trust not, O my scholar, only to that which appears brilliant ; but watch also for its ending, lest thou be deceived."—*Hubert Bower, in "Parables and Similitudes of the Christian Life."* 1871.

Verse 3.—"*But let the righteous be glad.*" The wicked flee from the presence of God, since it inspires them with terror ; the righteous on the other hand rejoice in it, because nothing delights them more than to think that God is near them.— *John Calvin.*

Verse 4.—"*Extol him that rideth upon the heavens.*" Or, as Symmachus, Jerome, Bishop Lowth, Merrick, and others render, "Prepare the way for him who rideth through the deserts : עֲרָבוֹת *âravoth ;* i.e., who rode through the wilderness on the cherubim ; alluding to the passage of the ark.—"*Comprehensive Bible.*"

Verse 4.—"*Rideth.*" Said, perhaps, with allusion to the cherubim on which

Jehovah was borne (xviii. 10), God himself being the Leader and Captain of his people, riding as it were at their head as an earthly captain might lead his army, riding on a war-horse.—*J. J. Stewart Perowne.*

Verse 4.—*"Upon the heavens."* The ancient versions in general render the word בָּעֲרָבוֹת, *super occasus*, or *occasum.* The *desert* or *solitude* is the proper and general meaning of it, and there is no authority to render it by *the heavens*, but that of the Rabbins, which, indeed, is little or none; and of the Chaldee paraphrase which gives it עַל כּוּרְסֵיהּ יְקָרֵיהּ בַּעֲרָבוֹת, *super thronam gloriæ ejus in nono cœlo :* who sits upon the throne of his glory in the ninth heaven. The Psalmist here alludes, as I apprehend, to the passage of the Israelites through the deserts in their way to the promised land, and describes it in many of the principal circumstances of it in the following verses; and God is said to *ride*, or, *be carried through the deserts*, as the ark of his presence was carried through them, and accompanied the Israelites in all their various stages during their continuance and pilgrimage in them.—*Samuel Chandler.*

Verse 4.—God always goes at the head of his people through the deserts of suffering and need; in the deserts of trouble they find in him a true leader.— *E. W. Hengstenberg.*

Verse 4.—*"His name* JAH." JAH, as the concentration of Jehovah, is the more emphatic term *(Stier.)* It occurs for the first time in Ex. xv. 2.—*Frederic Fysh, in "A Lyrical Literal Version of the Psalms."* 1850.

Verse 5.—*"A father of the fatherless."* In a spiritual sense, the *orphans*, whose father God is, says Hilary, are those who have renounced their father the Devil, and those to whom Christ, at his departure, sent another *Comforter*, according to his promise—" I will not leave you orphans."—*Lorinus.*

Verse 5.—Does not James i. 27, refer to this verse, for we have "the *fatherless*," " the *widow*," and then the " *holiness*," of the God we serve ?—*Andrew A. Bonar.*

Verse 5.—*"God in his holy habitation."* Albeit the Lord be infinite and uncomprehended by any place, yet hath he appointed a trysting-place where his people shall find him by his own ordinance, to wit, the assembly of his saints, his holy temple shadowing forth Christ to be incarnate, who now is in heaven, now is incarnate, and sitting at the right hand of God, in whom dwells the Godhead; here, here is God to be found.—*David Dickson.*

Verse 6.—*"God setteth the solitary in families."* It may be interpreted of the fruitfulness and increase of the church with converts, under the gospel dispensation, even from among the Gentiles, who were before solitary, or were alone, without God and Christ, and aliens from the commonwealth of Israel; but, being called and converted by the ministry of the word, were brought into and placed in gospel churches, or families. . . . . Gospel churches, like families, have a master over them, who is Christ the Son and firstborn, of whom they are named; where are saints of various ages, sizes, and standing; some fathers, some young men, and some children; where are provisions suitable for them, and stewards to give them their portion of meat in due season, who are the ministers of the word; and laws and rules, by which they are directed and regulated, and everything is kept in good decorum.—*John Gill.*

Verse 8.—*"The God of Israel."* Sinai was the seat not only of God, but of the *covenant God* of the people of Israel; from which the law was proclaimed, and the covenant struck between God and his people.—*Hermann Venema.*

Verse 9.—The *"Thou"* in the Hebrew is emphatic: " Thine inheritance, even when it was wearied (*i.e.*, worn out) *thou* didst confirm ; " or, " *fortify* it." Thou who alone couldst strengthen one worn out, didst so for thy people.—*A. R. Fausset.*

Verse 9.—*"A liberal rain."* The words translated *a liberal rain*, read literally in the Hebrew *a rain of freenesses ;* and I agree with interpreters in thinking that he alludes to the blessing as having come in the exercise of free favour, and to God, as having of his own unprompted goodness provided for all the wants of his people. Some read, *a desirable rain ;* others, *a rain flowing without violence*, or *gentle ;* but neither of these renderings seems eligible. Others read, *a copious* or *plentiful rain ;* but I have already stated what appears to me to be the preferable sense.—*John Calvin.*

Verse 9.—"A gracious rain;" that is, of manna.—*Edmund Law* (1703—1787), *quoted by Richard Warner in loc.* 1828.

Verse 9.—"Rain." One fountain, says Cyril, waters thy paradise, and the rain that falls upon all the world is the same; it is white in the bloom of the hawthorn, red in the rose, purple in the hyacinth, and diverse in diverse kinds, and all in all; yet it itself is the same and of the same kind. . . . . So also the Holy Spirit, though he is one and the same and not divisible, yet to every one he divideth grace according as he wills.—*Thomas Le Blanc.*

Verse 9.—"A plentiful rain." Thy love has been as a shower! The returns, but a dew-drop, and that dew-drop stained with sin.—*James Harrington Evans.* 1785—1849.

Verse 10.—"Thy congregation." The words are choice and expressive. Addressing God, (the poet) intentionally and emphatically calls the people of Israel חַיָּתְךָ *thy combined congregation*, in contrast to former divisions and various dissensions, to signify, that the people was now welded together, formed into one society, and united at the same time, that it was well ordered, and constituted as the *society of God*, wherein his laws flourished and were wont to be observed.—*Hermann Venema.*

Verse 10.—"Thy congregation." Or, *Thy living creatures*, חַיָּתְךָ, τὰ ζῶα LXX., *animalia*, Vulgate; probably a reference to the immense number of quails which were miraculously brought to the camp of the Israelites, and, in a manner, *dwelt around it.—Note in the " Comprehensive Bible."*

Verse 10.—"Thy congregation." Or, *Thy living creatures*. That desolate place, where only wild beasts before could live, was now by those showers of manna (verse 9) enabled to sustain a multitude of other *tamer living creatures*, even of *men* and all their *flocks* and *herds.—Henry Hammond.*

*Verse 10 (first clause).—*Rather :—" As for thy food (manna and quails), they dwelt in the midst of it.—*Edmund Law.*

Verse 10 (first clause).—As to thy food, they dwelt amidst it. The ambiguity of the word חַיָּה has occasioned various renderings of this line. Parkhurst considers the radical sense of חָיָה is " to be vigorous, strong;" hence the noun denotes *force*, a body of men (2 Sam. xxiii. 13); and also that which gives strength, the means of support, or food (Judg. vi. 4 and xvii. 10); and compare Neh. ix. 6. Our translators took the term in the first sense; I take it in the second, because the connection seems to require it, and because חיה refers always to a body of men, as soldiers, as actually engaged in some kind of warfare. Hence what is called the *troop* of Philistines (2 Sam. xxiii. 13) is called the *camp* of the Philistines. 1 Chron. xi. 15. And, lastly, because the common version has no antecedent to which בָּהּ, *in it*, or *amidst it*, can refer; but this version has one in the noun *food*. I think there is then a reference not only to the manna, but to the quails, which God brought in abundance around the camp. Exod. xvi. 13; Num. xi. 31. Thus he *prepared in his goodness for the poor.—Benjamin Boothroyd.*

Verse 10.—"Thou hast prepared in thine own sweetness for the poor, O God." In *thine own sweetness*, not in his sweetness. For the needy he is, for he hath been made weak, in order that he may be made perfect: he hath acknowledged himself indigent, that he may be replenished.—*Augustine.*

Verse 11.—"The Lord gave the word: great was the company of those that published it." You shall find, when the enemies of the church are destroyed, that God hath many preachers made that do teach his praises. . . . . The words in the original are very significant, and do note two things. First, the word which you read " *company*," in the Hebrew it is " army," " great was the army of preachers." An army of preachers is a great matter; nay, it is a great matter to have seven or eight good preachers in a great army; but to have a whole army of preachers that is glorious. Secondly, it doth note out the heartiness of this preaching army, for the word נֶפֶשׁ, soul, is to be understood as in that place of Ecclesiastes; it is said there, " The words or book of the preacher," which, being in the feminine gender, doth suppose *nephesh*, and as if he should say, as Vatablus hath it: the words or book of him that hath a preaching soul or heart, or the words of a preaching soul or heart. So here where it is said, great is the army of preachers, the word being in the feminine gender, it is as if he should say, great is the army of preaching souls, whose very hearts within them shall preach of the Lord's works. Now, my brethren, it is much to have a preaching army; but if this army shall with heart and soul preach of God's praise, O that is a blessed thing. Yet thus shall it be when the enemies of God shall be destroyed. And, therefore, seeing God will not lose all those sermons of his own praises, in due time the enemies of the church shall be scattered.—*William Bridge, in " The True Soldier's Convoy."* 1640.

Verse 11.—It is owing to the word, the appointment, and power of God, that any persons are induced or enabled to preach the gospel.—*John Newton* (1725—1807), *in "Messiah."*

Verses 11, 12.—This account of Israel's victories is applicable to victories obtained by the exalted Redeemer, when the enemies of man's salvation were vanquished by the resurrection of Christ, and the heathen nations were compelled to own his power ; and this great victory was first notified by *women* to the disciples.—*From "A Practical Illustration of the Book of Psalms ; by the Author of the Family Commentary on the New Testament."* [Mrs. Thomson.] 1826.

Verses 11, 12.—The Lord did give his word at his ascension, and there were a multitude of them that published it, and by this means kings of armies were put to flight : they conquered by the word : there is not such another way to rout kings and their armies.—*William Strong.* —1654.

Verses 11—14.

> The Lord giveth the word !
> A great company of women announce the glad tidings !
> Kings with their armies flee—they flee !
> And those, who dwell within the house, divide the spoil !
> Although they lie among the hearth-stones,
> They are become like a dove's wings overlaid with silver,
> And like her pinions overlaid with yellow gold.
> When the Almighty scattereth kings,
> They glisten therein, as snow upon Salmon.

Those who dwell within the house—i.e., the women. They are thus described in allusion to their retired habits of life, in eastern countries. *Lie among the hearth-stones—i.e.*, are habitually employed in the lowest domestic offices, and whose ordinary dress, therefore, is mean and soiled. *The hearth-stones*—Hebrew rests (for boilers). *They are become*—by being decked in the spoils of the enemy.—*Glisten as snow*—Hebrew (each woman) *is snowy : therein—i.e.*, in the spoils distributed amongst them.—*French and Skinner's Translation and Notes.*

Verse 12.—*"Kings of armies did flee apace."* In the Hebrew it is, they fled, they fled ; fled is twice. Why so ? That is, they did flee very hastily, and they fled most confusedly, they fled all ways ; they fled, they fled, noting the greatness of the flight.—*William Bridge.*

Verse 12.—*"The kings of hosts shall flee."*—The " hosts " are the numerous well-equipped armies which the kings of the heathen lead forth to the battle against the people of God. The unusual expression, " kings of hosts," sounds very much like an ironically disparaging antithesis to the customary " Jahve of Hosts."—*Böttcher, quoted by Delitzsch.*

Verse 12.—*"She that tarried at home."* That is, all the noncombatants, saith Kimchi. Or, the women also (those *domi portæ*) came forth to pillage. These days of the gospel do abound with many godly matrons and holy virgins. And it is easy to observe that the New Testament affordeth more store of good women than the old.—*John Trapp.*

Verse 12.—*"Divided the spoil,"* not merely (as Hupfeld) " receives her portion of the spoil," but rather " distributes among her daughters and handmaidens, etc., the share of the spoil " which her husband has brought home.—*J. J. Stewart Perowne.*

Verse 13.—It would neither be profitable nor possible to give the reader all the conjectures with which learned men have illustrated or darkened this passage. My aim has been to give a selection, not perhaps what may be called a judicious one, but a sort of sample selection, containing specimens of interpretations. Hammond, who is a very high authority, collects what are probably the best suggestions ; we, therefore, give the substance of his long note upon this place. Solomon Jarchi and others see in the word the idea of boundaries, ways, and paths which serve as divisions of land, hence the divergence of the Septuagint into the meaning of portions and inheritances. The boundaries were usually heaps of stones, broken bricks, and rubbish, hence another meaning. But stones, bricks, etc., were often used to support pots in the open-air cookery of the orientals, hence we come to the meaning of " among the *pots.*" And, as Job on his dunghill sat among ashes, and scraped himself with a potsherd, we see that sitting among such rubbish was a conspicuous image of the most dejected and squalid condition. In the wings of a dove, Hammond sees an allusion to the golden cherubic wings which covered the ark, whereby God's presence was exhibited to his people, and their prosperity secured. His explanation of the whole is as follows :—" The Israelites that were oppressed, and long lay in a sad and black, destitute, despised condition, were now at length advanced to all prosperity, splendour, and glory (as was remarkable in their coming out from the kilns of Egypt, with the jewels and wealth of the Egyptians, and afterward more illustriously at their enjoying of Canaan). And so, under Christ's kingdom, the heathenish idolaters that were brought to the basest and most despicable condition of any creatures, worshipping wood and stone, etc., and given up to the vilest lusts, and a reprobate mind (Rom. i.), should from that detestable condition be advanced to the service of Christ, and practice of all Christian virtues, charity, meekness, etc., the greatest inward beauties in the world."—*C. H. S.*

Verse 13.—"*Though ye have lien among the pots,*" etc. That is, probably, though ye have laboured and lain down *between the brick-kilns* in Egypt,—a poor, enslaved, and oppressed people, yet ye shall gradually rise to dignity, prosperity, and splendour ; as a dove, which has been defiled with dirt, disordered, and dejected, by washing herself in a running stream, and trimming her plumage, gradually recovers the serenity of her disposition, the purity of her colour, and the richness and varied elegance of her appearance.—*W. Greenfield, in "Comp. Bible."*

Verse 13.—"*Though ye have lien among the pots ;* " or, *between two rows of stones* (understand hearth-stones), as in camps, and elsewhere also, which even to this day used to be laid and disposed to make fire between them to dress meat by, setting on or hanging over it pots and kettles, etc. Others, *between* or *among dripping-pans,* or *pots,* the sense being all one, and this—though you should be cast or thrust out into the uttermost slavery, or vilest condition (as in Egypt), all besmoked and besmutted, like cooks and scullions, yet shall God through his gracious blessing make you to shine again like a goodly flying dove, which glistereth as if it were of silver and gold.—*Theodore Haak's "Translation of the Dutch Annotations, as ordered by the Synod of Dort in* 1618." London, 1657.

Verse 13.—"*Though ye had lain among the folds."* Though ye had been treated by the Egyptians as a company of *contemptible shepherds,* and were held in abomination by them as such. See Genesis xlvi. 34.—*William Green, in "A New Translation of the Psalms, with Notes,"* etc. 1762.

Verse 13 (*first clause*).—German, "*lie a-field,*" *i.e.,* though you thus, in deep peace, lie among the sheepfolds.—*T. C. Barth.*

Verse 13.—"*Will ye lie down among the sheepfolds ?* " A sharp remonstrance. Will ye lie at ease, in the quiet of your pastoral life, as the dove with unsoiled plumage in her peaceful nest, while your brethren are in the tumult and dust of the conflict ! Compare Judges v. 16 (from which this allusion is taken) and 17.—*Thomas J. Conant.*

Verse 13.—"*Though ye have lien among the pots,*" etc. Here is one Hebrew word in the original which especially renders the Scripture intricate ; namely שְׁפַתָּיִם, *shephattajim ;* which, being a word of divers significations and translations, occasions various interpretations. It is rendered, I. *limits or bounds ;* II. *lots* or *inheritances ;* III. *pots* or *pot-ranges.* 1. Some render it *two limits,* or *two bounds* (the word being of the *dual number*) ; *viz.,* the *two limits,* bounds, or coasts of the enemies, ready to afflict, vex, and infest them on each hand. Or, two confines of the country where they fortified themselves against their enemies. This sense some later writers embrace : and it's one of the interpretations which Ainsworth gives, though not in the first place. But this version seems here very unsuitable, for that it quite destroys the elegance and fitness of the opposition between the two metaphors, representing Israel's different conditions, *before* and *under* David's Government. Some render it *two lots,* or *two inheritances.* So the LXX., ἀνὰ μέσον τῶν κλήρων ; that is, *amidst the lots,* or *between the inheritances ; inheritances,* as in Canaan, being anciently set out by *lots.* This Hierom seems to follow, turning it, *Si dormiatis inter medios cleros :* and thus he expounds it : " When thou believest the two Testaments, in both thou shalt find the Holy Ghost. And though there be a beauty, even according to the letter, to know what thou readest, the force of all the comeliness is in the sense. Therefore, the outward ornament of the words is demonstrated by the name of *silver ;* but the more secret mysteries are contained in the hidden gifts of *gold*, etc. So that, with him, the *two lots* are the *two Testaments ;* the *dove* is the Holy Ghost ; her *wings covered with silver*, the *outward letter of the Testaments*, the *feathers of yellow gold*, the *inward, spiritual, and mysterious sense.* But this is rather a witty allegorical allusion, than a judicious and solid exposition. Augustine also expounds the words much to this effect, but altogether as unsatisfactorily. The ancient Fathers are not always the best expositors. 3. But most do render the word *pots* or *pot-ranges.* Thus : " Although ye have lien among the pots (or, *between the pot-ranges ;* or, *between the two banks* or *rows*—*viz.*, of stone to hang pots on in the camp or leaguer), yet shall ye be *as the wings of a dove covered* (or *decked*) *with silver, and her feathers with yellow-greenish gold."* And they observe in the words a double metaphor : (1.) The one of Israel's lying among the pots, as scullions lie among the pots, kettles, or cauldrons in the camp or leaguer in time of war, and so are blacked, soiled, smutted, deformed ; denoting Israel's abject, low, mean, sullied, deformed, and despicable condition under afflictions and extreme distresses in time past in Egypt, the wilderness, Canaan, and in the time of the Judges.   (2.) The other of Israel's being like *the wings of a dove* (which is of very speedy flight for escape), *of bright silver and beauteous golden colour ;* representing their escape and deliverance at last out of all their blacking, smutting, and deforming afflictions, into the contrary, beauteous, prosperous, and happy state under the kingdom of David, especially of Jesus Christ the *true* David.   *Blackness* notes extreme affliction, affliction and misery ; *doves' wings*, escape ; white *silver-colour* and beauteous *golden colour*, prosperity and felicity. Thus the metaphors are elegantly opposed one to another, and very significantly set forth the several conditions of Israel ; first, as lying among the pots of deep afflictions in former times, but after as assured of deliverance, of better days, and that they should be as a *silver-winged and golden-feathered* dove, full of beauty, comeliness, prosperity, and felicity. To this effect R. David Kimchi, Pagnin, Calvin, Muis, Foord, Ainsworth, and others expound these words.—*Francis Roberts, in a Sermon entitled "The Checquer-Work of God's Providences, towards His Own People, made up of Blacks and Whites,"* etc.   1657.

   Verse 13.—*"Though ye have lien among the pots,"* etc. Miss Whately, in her work, " Ragged Life in Egypt," describing some of the sights witnessed from the flat roofs of the houses in Cairo, among other interesting objects, states :—The roofs are usually in a great state of litter, and were it not that *Hasna*, the seller of *geeleh*, gets a palm-branch, and makes a clearance once in a while, her roof would assuredly give way under the accumulation of rubbish. One thing never seemed cleared away, and that was the heaps of old broken pitchers, sherds, and pots, that in these and similar houses are piled up in some corner ; and there is a curious observation in connection with this. A little before sunset, numbers of *pigeons* suddenly emerge from behind the pitchers and other rubbish, where they have been sleeping in the heat of the day, or pecking about to find food. They dart upwards, and career through the air in large circles, their outspread wings catching the bright glow of the sun's slanting rays, so that they really resemble bright " yellow gold ; " then, as they wheel round, and are seen *against* the light, they appear as if turned into molten silver, most of them being pure white, or else very light coloured. This may seem fanciful, but the effect of *light* in these regions is difficult to describe to those who have not seen it ; and, evening after evening, we watched the circling flight of the doves, and always observed the same appearance. It was beautiful to see these birds, rising clean and unsoiled, as doves always do, from the dust and dirt in which they had been hidden, and soaring aloft in the sky till nearly out of sight among the bright sunset clouds. Thus a believer, who leaves behind him the corruptions of the world, and is rendered bright by the Sun of Righteousness shining upon his soul, rises higher and higher, nearer and nearer to the light, till, lost to the view of those who stay behind, he has passed into the unknown brightness above !—*Miss Whately, in "Ragged Life in Egypt."*

   Verse 13.—*"Silver"* and *"yellow gold."* The changing colours of the dove's plumage are here described. Mant reads it—

   " Whose wings, a silver light illumes,
      And gleams of verdant gold play o'er her burnished plumes ! "

It will illustrate the variety of the translations, if we add that of Keble :

      ' His plumes inlaid with silver sheen,
        His pinions of the pale pure gold."

Personally, I have had cause to remark the flash of the wing of a pigeon, for, in passing before my study window, that bird has often led me to imagine that some unusual light had flashed across the sky ; in every case, a mild and silvery light. As to the varying hues of the plumage of birds, Mr. Gosse, after quoting from Sonnerat's Voyage in New Guinea, says, " In reference to the brilliant metallic hues of the epimachus and other birds, the traveller takes occasion to notice the iridiscent effect which is produced by the different angle at which light falls on the feathers. The emerald green, for instance, will often fling out rays of its two constituent primary colours, at one time being blue-green, at another gold-green, while in certain lights all colour vanishes, and a velvet-black is presented to the eye." This it seems to me is a very natural and complete explanation of the poetic language here employed.—*C. H. S.*

Verse 14.—*"Salmon"* or Zalmon, properly Tsalmon, צלמון a woody hill near Shechem (Judges ix. 48). Whether it is this that is referred to in Psalm lxviii. 14, is disputed. Some interpreters take צלמו here in its etymological meaning of darkness, =צלם ; thus Luther renders the clause " so wird es helle wo es dunkel ist," *thus it be bright where it is dark*, and understands it with a Messianic reference. Ewald adopts much the same rendering. The majority, however, retain the name as a proper name, but exhibit great variety in their explanation of the passage. Hengstenberg thinks that the phrase, " it snows on Tsalmon," is equivalent to " there is brightness where there was darkness," the hill, originally dark with wood, is now white with snow. De Dieu supposes a comparison : Tsalmon is white with the bones of the slaughtered kings, as if with snow. Some suppose that there is here a mere note of time : it was winter, the snow was on Tsalmon (Herder) ; and this Hupfeld adopts, with the explanation that the statement is made derisively, with reference to those who tarried at home, deterred by the winter's snow. He considers the passage (12—14) as a fragment of an ancient song, celebrating some of the early conquests of Israel in Canaan, and deriding those, who, from indolence or fear, shrank from the enterprise. He translates thus :

> " The kings of the armies, flee, flee,
> And the housewife shares the spoil !
> Will ye lie among the shippens ?
> Pigeon feathers decked with silver.
> And their wings with yellow gold !
> As the Almighty scattered kings therein,
> It was snowing on Tsalmon."

William Lindsay Alexander, in "A Cyclopædia of Biblical Literature." 1866.

Verse 14.—The verb may be viewed as in the second person—*Thou, O God! didst make it fair and white as Mount Salmon with snow.* The reader may adopt either construction, for the meaning is the same. It is evident that David insists still upon the figure of the whiteness of silver, which he had previously introduced. The country had, as it were, been blackened or sullied by the hostile confusion into which it was thrown, and he says that it had now recovered its fair appearance, and resembled Salmon, which is well known to have been ordinarily covered with snows. Others think that Salmon is not the name of a place, but an appellative, meaning *a dark shade.* I would retain the commonly received reading. At the same time, I think that there may have been an allusion to the etymology. It comes from the word צלם, *tselem*, signifying *a shade*, and Mount Salmon had been so called on account of its blackness. This makes the comparison more striking ; for it intimates that as the snows whitened this black mountain, so the country had resumed its former beauty, and put on an aspect of joy, when God dispelled the darkness which had lain upon it during the oppression of enemies.—*John Calvin.*

Verse 14.—*"It was as white as snow in Salmon."* That is, this thine inheritance, thy peculiar people, appeared as bright and glorious in the sight of their neighbours, as the snowy head of Salmon glisters by the reflection of the sunbeams.—*Thomas Fenton.*

Verse 14.—*"White as snow in Salmon."* The expression here used seems to denote, that everything seemed so bright and cheerful to the mind of God's people, as Salmon does to their eyes, when glistening with snow. As snow is much less common, and lies a much shorter time in Judæa than in England, no wonder that it is much more admired ; accordingly, the son of Sirach speaks of it with a kind of rapture. "The eye will be astonished at the beauty of its whiteness, and the heart transported at the raining of it." Ecclus. xliii. 18 or 20.—*Samuel Burder.*

Verse 14.—"*Salmon.*" Dean Stanley conjectures that Salmon is another name for Mount Ebal; it was certainly near Shechem (see Judges ix. 48), but it is almost hopeless to expect to identify it, for Mr. Mills, the industrious author of "Nablus and the modern Samaritans," could not find any one who knew the name of Salmon, neither could he discover any traditions in reference to it, or indeed any allusions to it in Samaritan literature. The word signifies a shade, and may, perhaps, popularly be accepted as identical with the name the "Black Forest."—*C. H. S.*

Verse 15.—"*Hill of Bashan.*" The world's physical greatness must yield to the church's spiritual grandeur. The "hill of God" is here an emblem of the *world-kingdoms*, which (Psalm lxv. 6) are great only by the grace of God. A great hill reminds us of the *creative* power of God. Hence, "the hill of Elohim" (the general name of God as *the Creator*) stands in contrast to *the hill* which (verse 16) "the Lord" (Jehovah) will dwell in for ever. It lay in the north, in the region east of Jordan, or the land of Og, the kingdom of Og, the most formidable enemy whom Israel encountered on their march to Canaan. "The hill of Bashan is the high snow-summit of Anti-Lebanon, or Hermon, the extreme limit of Bashan. There was a peculiar propriety, from its position on the boundary between Judæa and the heathen world, in employing it as a symbol of the world's might (verse 22; Psalm xlii. 6; lxxxix. 12)" (*Hengstenberg*). The original name of Hermon was Sion; *i.e.*, *lofty* (Deut. iv. 48); allied in sound to Zion, which suggested the contrast here between *the world-hills* and *the Lord's hill.*—*A. R. Fausset.*

Verses 15, 16—

> "A mountain of God Mount Bashan is:
> A mountain of peaks Mount Bashan is.
> Why are ye piqued, ye peakéd mountains?
> At the mountain *which* God desires to dwell in?
> Yea, Jehovah will dwell therein for ever."

Frederic Fysh's Version.

Verse 16.—"*Why leap ye?*" As triumphing, and making a show of your natural advantages over Sion. Or, to insult over it, and compare and equalise yourselves in honour with it; poetical kind of speeches. Others translate it, *Why gaze you, as though you were ravished with admiration?*—*John Diodati.*

Verse 16.—"*This is the hill which God desireth to dwell in.*" This low, little, barren hill of Zion; and God's election maketh the difference, as it did of Aaron's rod from the rest, and doth still of the church from the rest of the world. The Lamb Christ is on Mount Zion. Rev. xiv. 1.—*John Trapp.*

Verse 17.—"*The chariots of God.*" What are these "chariots of God?" Come, we will not stand to mince the matter, look but round about thee, and thou shalt see those *innumerable* chariots and angels here spoken of; for so many *creatures* as thou seest, so many angels and chariots of God thou seest; they are all his host, they are all his chariots wherein he rides; and, whether you see it or no, "*The Lord is among them, as in Sinai, in the holy place.*" The glory of the Lord fills them all (had we but our eyes open to see it so), and they are all at his command, and there is not one creature but doth his pleasure. Oh, brethren! how glorious and blessed a thing it is, that looking round about us to behold and see, that look how many creatures *visible* and *invisible* thou seest or conceivest in thy mind to be, for thy soul now to look on them as so many fiery chariots and horsemen for its defence, protection, and preservation! And, on the other hand, "How fearful a thing it is to fall into the hands of the living God," who hath all these chariots and horsemen at his command to execute his will and vengeance on those that neglect, hate, and oppose him.—*John Everard, in "Militia Cœlestis, or the Heavenly Host."* 1653.

Verse 17.—

> "About his chariot numberless were pour'd
> Cherub, and seraph, potentates, and thrones,
> And Virtues, winged Spirits, and chariots win
> From the armoury of God, where stand of old
> Myriads."

John Milton, in "Paradise Lost."

Verse 17.—"*Twenty thousand ;* " rather, *two myriads,* רִבֹּתַיִם singular רִבּוֹ ; for רְבוֹת only here in the dual, the infinite number doubled. "*Thousands of angels,*" lit., *thousands of iteration ; i.e.,* with marg., *many thousands* (Bythner, Gesenius, etc.), שִׁנְאָן only here, from שָׁנָה, *to repeat.* The rendering *of angels* was probably suggested by the references to Sinai, next clause (see Deut. xxxiii. 2, where for *saints* read *holy ones*) ; "*chariots*" (רֶכֶב) being used collectively for those who rode in them, as often elsewhere.—*William de Burgh.*

Verse 18.—"*Thou hast ascended on high,*" etc. Some think it refers to God's goings forth on behalf of his people Israel, leading them forth to victory, taking their enemies captive, and enriching them with the spoils. Suppose it be so, we are warranted to consider it as mainly referring to Christ, for so the apostle has applied it. Ephesians iv. 8.

The apostle not only applies it to Christ, but *proves* it applicable. Thus he reasons (verses 9, 10), " Now that he ascended, what is it but that he also descended," etc. The captivity which he led captive was our spiritual enemies who had led us captive—Satan, death ; and, having obtained the victory, he proceeds to divide the spoils. *Gifts to men*—as David made presents. And hence comes our ordinances, ministers, etc. There was a glorious fulfilment immediately after his ascension, in a rich profusion of gifts and graces to his church, like David's presents. Here it is "*received ;*" in Ephesians, "*gave.*" He received that he might give ; received the spoil that he might distribute it. But, as I wish to appropriate the passage to the work allotted me, the whole of that to which I would at this time call your attention will be contained in two things :—

I. *The great blessings of the Christian ministry.*

1. Ministers are *received for,* and are *given to,* you by Christ. As men, and as sinful men, ministers are as nothing, and wish not to make anything of themselves ; but, as the gifts of Christ, it bcomes you to make much of them. (1.) If you *love* Christ, you will make much of your minister, on account of his being *his* gift—a gift designed to supply Christ's absence in a sort. He is gone (" ascended "), but he gives you his servants. By-and-by you hope to be with him, but as yet you are as sheep in the wilderness. He gives you a shepherd. (2.) If you *fear God,* you will be afraid of treating your pastor amiss, seeing he is the gift of Christ. God took it ill of Israel for despising Moses. Numbers xii. 8. He is "*my servant.*"

2. Ministers are not only given to, but *received for* you, of God the Father, as a covenant blessing, among the spiritual blessings in heavenly places in Christ. In this view, consider that Christ received nothing at his Father's hand but what cost him dear—cost him his life. Or, if the allusion be to the dividing of the spoils, suppose we say, he received them as a conqueror receives the spoils at the hand of the foe. Your minister was one of those who, like yourselves, were brands consuming in the fire. Christ took him from your enemies and gives him to you. Make much of the gift on this account. " This I received of the Amorite."

3. Consider your unworthiness of such a blessing. You are *men,* mere men, and what is more, *rebellious* men, who had joined with Satan. And must you share the spoils ? It is not usual to divide the spoils amongst rebels. . . . Men that put him to death had these gifts given to them ; and we should all have done the same. Some of you, it is likely, have been vile and abandoned characters, and yet, etc. . . . .

4. The end of it: " That the Lord God might dwell among them." " But will God, indeed, dwell with men ? " God had not dwelt with the world, nor in it, while sin bore the rule ; but Christ's mediation was for the bringing it about. " Will God, indeed, dwell with men ? " He will ; and how ? It is by the means of ordinances and ministers. A church of Christ is God's house ; and where any one builds a house, it is a token that he means to dwell there. What a blessing to a village, a country, for God to build a house in it. It is by this that we may hope for a blessing upon the means to the conversion of our children and friends, and for the edification of believers.

II. *Point out some corresponding duties as answering to these your privileges.*

1. Constant and diligent attendance at the house of God. If the house of God be God's dwelling, let it be yours, your home. If God gives you a pastor, do you thankfully receive and prize him. He hath not dealt so with every village.

2. Cheerfully contribute to his support. Christ has given you freely, and you ought to give him freely. Consider it is not a gift, but as a debt, and not as done to him, but to Christ.

3. Follow these things which màke for peace, with which the presence and blessing of God are connected.

4. Shun those things that tend to provoke the Lord to withdraw his gifts, and to cease to dwell among you.—*Andrew Fuller's Sketch of a Sermon, addressed to the Church at Moulton, on the Ordination of Mr. (since Doctor) Carey, August 1st, 1787.*

Verse 18.—But who is he of whom it is written, that *"he ascended up on high?"* I confess that the sixty-eighth Psalm, wherein these words are first written, is literally to be understood, not of any triumph for the slaughter of the host of Sennacherib, which was done in the time of king Hezekias (as the Jews do most fabulously dream), when the very title of this Psalm, that ascribeth it unto David, doth sufficiently confute this vanity ; nor yet for any of the victories of David which he obtained against his bordering enemies, the Ammonites, the Moabites, the Idumæans, and the Philistines (as some would have it) ; but of that great and glorious pomp which was then done and showed, when king David with great joy and triumph did bring the *ark* of the covenant into the hill of Sion ; and, therefore, these words, *"Thou art gone up on high,"* do signify that the ark, which formerly had lain in an *obscure* place, and was transported from one place to another, was now ascended and seated in a most *illustrious and conspicuous* place, even in the kingly palace ; and these words, *"thou hast led captivity captive,"* do signify those *enemies* which formerly had spoiled and wasted divers countries ; but now, being *vanquished* by king David, were led *captive* in this triumph (for so it was the manner of those times, as Plutarch doth excellently declare in the life of Paulus Æmilius) ; and the other words, *"thou hast received gifts for men,"* do signify those spoils that were freely offered for conditions of peace, and were triumphantly carried about in this pompous show, for the greater solemnity of the same ; and then (as the manner was among the chieftains when they triumphed, *Bellica laudatis dona dedisse viris,* to bestow warlike gifts upon worthy men), gifts were bestowed on several men, in several manner, as Sigonius sheweth. Yet I say that, *mystically,* this Psalm is an ἐπινίκιον, or a triumphal song, penned by king David upon the foresight of Jesus Christ arising from the dead, and with great joy and triumph *ascending* up into heaven, and thence sending his Holy Spirit unto his apostles and disciples ; and, having overcome all his enemies, collecting by the ministry of his preachers, his churches and chosen people together, and so guiding and defending them here in this life, until he doth receive them into eternal glory.—*Griffith Williams.* 1636.

Verse 18.—*"Thou hast led captivity captive."* The expression is emphatical. He has conquered and triumphed over all the powers which held us in captivity, so that captivity itself is taken captive. The spirit and force of it is destroyed ; and his people, when released by him, and walking in his ways, have no more to apprehend from those whose captives they were, than a conqueror has to fear from a prisoner in chains. The energy of the phrase is not unlike that of the apostle : " Death is swallowed up in victory."—*John Newton.*

Verse 18.—*"Thou hast led captivity captive,"* etc. The ancient prophecy of David is fulfilled here on the foot of mount Olivet. To take " captivity captive," signifies that Christ conquered the allied principalities and powers, the devil, sin, death, and hell ; and that he deprived them of the instruments wherewith they enslaved men. He not only silenced the cannon on the spiritual Gibraltar, but he took rock, fortification, and all. He not only silenced the horrible and destructive battlements of the powerful and compactly-united ghostly enemies, but he threw down the towers, razed the castles, and took away the keys of the dungeons. He is the Master henceforth, and for ever. He did, also, at the same time, save his people. Where, O Jesus, is the army of which thou art the Captain ? " Here ! all the names are written in pearls on the breastplate which I wear as a high-priest." He had no sooner left the grave than he began to distribute his gifts, and did so all along the road on his way to his Father's house ; and, especially after he entered the heaven of heavens, did he shower down gifts unto men, as a mighty conqueror loaded with treasures with which to enrich and adorn his followers and people. They were gifts of mercy : gifts to the rebellious ; to those who threw down their arms at his feet in penitent submission, " that the Lord God may dwell among them." The apostle shows that a portion of these gifts are gifts of ministry. Accordingly, whenever God condescends to dwell among a people and in a country, he gives that people and country his ministry. He sends them his gospel in the mouths of faithful servants. He establishes there his house ; the board and the candlestick ; and then, in his Spirit, he dwells there and blesses his heritage.— *Christmas Evans.* 1766—1838.

Verse 18.—The apostle (Eph. iv. 8) does not quote the words of the Psalm literally, but according to the sense. The phrase, *"Thou hast received gifts,"* as applied to Christ at his glorification, could only be for the purpose of distribution, and hence the apostle quotes them in this sense, *"He gave gifts to men."* This Hebrew phrase may be rendered either, " Thou hast received gifts in the human nature," or, " Thou hast received gifts for the sake of man " (see Gen. xviii. 28 ; 2 Kings xiv. 6.) The apostle uses the words in the sense of the *purpose* for which the gifts were received, and there is no contradiction between the Psalmist and the apostle. Thus, the difficulties of this quotation vanish when we examine them closely, and the Old and New Testaments are in complete harmony. Rosenmüller expounds Ps. xviii., and never mentions the name of Christ ; and the neologists in general see no Messiah in the Old Testament. To these, indeed, Eph. iv. 8, if they had any modesty, would present a formidable obstacle. Paul asserts the Psalm belongs to Christ, and they assert he is mistaken, and that he has perverted (De Wette) and destroyed its meaning. They assert that *Lamarom*, " on high," means the heights of Mount Zion, and Paul says it means heaven. Which is right ? (see the scriptural usage of the word, Ps. vii. 7 ; xviii. 16 ; xciii. 4 ; cii. 19 ; Jer. xxv. 30 ; Is. xxxvii. 23). These passages connect the word with the heavenly mansions, and justify the application of the apostle.—*William Graham, in "Lectures on St. Paul's Epistle to the Ephesians."*

Verse 18.—No sooner is Christ inaugurated in his throne, but he scatters his coin, and gives gifts. He gives gifts, or the gift of gifts, the gift of the Holy Ghost. " If thou knewest the gift of God," said Christ to the Samaritan woman (John iv. 10) : that gift was the water of life, and that water of life was the Spirit, as John, who knew best his mind, gave the interpretation, " This spake he of the Spirit." John vii. 39. O my soul, consider of this princely gift of Christ ! Such a gift was never before, but when God gave his Son. "God so loved the world, that he gave his Son ; " and Christ so loved the world, that he gave his Spirit. But, O my soul, consider especially to whom this Spirit was given ; the application of the gift is the very soul of thy meditation ; " unto us a Son is given," said the prophet (Isa. ix. 6) ; and " unto us the Holy Ghost is given," saith the apostle (Rom. v. 5) ; and yet above all consider the reasons of this gift in reference to thyself. Was it not to make thee a temple and receptacle of the Holy Ghost ? Stand a while on this ! Admire, O my soul, at the condescending, glorious, and unspeakable love of Christ in this ! It was infinite love to come down into our nature when he was incarnate ; but this is more, to come down into thy heart by his Holy Spirit : he came near to us then, but as if that were not near enough, he comes nearer now, for now he unites himself unto thy person, now he comes and dwells in thy soul by his Holy Spirit.—*Isaac Ambrose.* 1592—1674.

Verse 18.—*"Thou hast received gifts for men."* The glorious ascending of God from Mount Sinai, after the giving of the law, was a representation of his " ascending up far above all heavens, that he might fill all things," as Eph. iv. 10. And, as God then " led captivity captive " in the destruction of Pharaoh and the Egyptians who had long held his people in captivity and under cruel bondage ; so dealt the Lord Christ now in the destruction and captivity of Satan and all his powers (Col. ii. 15) ; only, whereas it is said in the Psalm that he "received the gift for men," here (Eph. iv.) it is said that " he gave gifts to men," wherein no small mystery is couched ; for, although Christ is God, and is so gloriously represented in the Psalm, yet an intimation is given that he should act what is here mentioned in a condition wherein he was capable to receive from another, as he did in this matter. Acts ii. 33. And so the phrase in the original doth more than insinuate : מַתָּנוֹת בָּאָדָם לָקַחְתָּ " Thou hast received gifts in Adam,"—in the man, or human nature. And לָקַח signifies as well to *give* as to *receive*, especially when anything is received to be given. Christ received this gift in the human nature to give it unto others. Now, to what end is this glorious theatre, as it were, prepared, and all this preparation made, all men being called to the preparation of it ? It was to set out the greatness of the gift he would bestow, and the glory of the work which he would effect ; and this was to furnish the church with ministers, and ministers with gifts for the discharge of their office and duty. And it will one day appear that there is more glory, more excellency, in giving one poor minister unto a congregation, by furnishing him with spiritual gifts for the discharge of his duty, than in the pompous instalment of a thousand popes, cardinals, or metropolitans. The worst of men, in the observance of a few outward rites and ceremonies, can do the latter ; Christ only can do the former, and that as he is ascended up on high to that purpose.—*John Owen.*

Verse 18.—As the passage which we have now been considering is applied by Paul in a more spiritual sense to Christ (Eph. iv. 8), it may be necessary to show how this agrees with the meaning and scope of the Psalmist. It may be laid down as an incontrovertible truth, that David, in reigning over God's ancient people, shadowed forth the beginning of Christ's eternal kingdom. This must appear evident to every one who remembers the promise made to him of a never-failing succession, and which received its verification in the person of Christ. As God illustrated his power in David, by exalting him with the view of delivering his people, so has he magnified his name in his only begotten Son. But let us consider more particularly how the parallel holds. Christ, before he was exalted, emptied himself of his glory, having not merely assumed the form of a servant, but humbled himself to the death of the cross. To show how exactly the figure was fulfilled, Paul notices, that what David had foretold was accomplished in the person of Christ, by his being cast down to the lowest parts of the earth in the reproach and ignominy to which he was subjected, before he ascended to the right hand of his Father. Ps. xxii. 7. That in thinking upon the ascension, we might not confine our views to the body of Christ, our attention is called to the result and fruit of it, in his subjecting heaven and earth to his government. Those who were formerly his inveterate enemies he compelled to submission and made tributary ; this being the effect of the word of the Gospel, to lead men to renounce their pride and their obstinacy, to bring down every high thought which exalteth itself, and reduce the senses and the affections of men to obedience unto Christ. As to the devils and reprobate men who are instigated to rebellion and revolt by obstinate malice, he holds them bound by secret control, and prevents them from executing intended destruction. So far the parallel is complete. Nor, when Paul speaks of Christ having *given gifts to men*, is there any real inconsistency with what is here stated, although he has altered the words, having followed the Greek version in accommodation to the unlearned reader. It was not himself that God enriched with the spoils of the enemy, but his people ; and neither did Christ seek, or need to seek, his advancement, but made his enemies tributary, that he might adorn his Church with the spoil. From the close union subsisting between the head and members, to say that God manifest in the flesh received gifts from the captives, is one and the same thing with saying that he distributed them to his Church. What is said in the close of the verse is no less applicable to Christ : that he obtained his victories that as God he might dwell among us. Although he departed, it was not that he might remove to a distance from us, but, as Paul says, " that he might fill all things." Eph. iv. 10. By his ascension to heaven, the glory of his divinity has been only more illustriously displayed ; and, though no longer present with us in the flesh, our souls receive spiritual nourishment from his body and blood, and we find, notwithstanding distance of place, that his flesh is meat indeed, and his blood drink indeed.—*John Calvin.*

Verse 18.—"*Thou hast received gifts for men.*" Heb. בָּאָדָם, *in man ;* "*in human nature,*" says Dr. Adam Clarke, " and God, manifest in human flesh, dwells among mortals." " The gifts which Jesus Christ distributes *to man* he has received *in man*, in and by virtue of his *incarnation*, and it is in consequence of his being made man that it may be said, ' the Lord God dwells among them ; ' for Jesus was called *Immanuel*, ' God with us,' in consequence of his incarnation."—*Ed. Note to Calvin in loc.*

Verse 18.—"*Yea, for the rebellious also.*" I feared, also, that this was the mark that the Lord did set on Cain, even continual fear and trembling under the heavy load of guilt that he had charged upon him for the blood of his brother Abel. Thus did I wind and twine and shrink under the burden that was upon me, which burden also did so oppress me, that I could neither stand, nor go, nor lie, either at rest or quiet. Yet that saying would sometimes come to my mind, He hath received gifts for the rebellious. Psalm lxviii. 18. " The rebellious," thought I ; why, surely, they are such as once were under subjection to their prince, even those who, after they have sworn subjection to his government, have taken up arms against him ; and this, thought I, is my very condition ; once I loved him, feared him, served him ; but now I am a rebel ; I have sold him. I have said, let him go if he will ; but yet he has gifts for rebels, and then why not for me ?—*John Bunyan, in " Grace Abounding."*

Verse 18 (*last clause*).—Thou didst not regard their former disobedience, but, even although seeing them contradicting, thou didst continue to do them good, until thou madest them *thine own abode* (οἰκητήριον).—*Theodoret.*

Verse 18 (*last clause*).—The Chaldee has, " Upon the rebellious, who become proselytes and return by repentance, the Schechinah of the glory of the Lord God dwelleth."

Verse 19.—"*Blessed be the Lord,*" etc.   Methinks the sweet singer of Israel seems to raise his note to the emulation of the choir of heaven in the melody of their *Allelujahs ;* yea, let me say, now that he sings above in that blessed consort of glorious spirits, his ditty cannot be better than this that he sang here upon earth, and wherein we are about to bear our parts at this time.   Prepare, I beseech you, both your ears for David's song, and your hearts and tongues for your own.   And first, in this angelical strain your thoughts cannot but observe the descant and the ground. The descant of gratulation, "*Blessed be the Lord,*" wherein is both applause and excitation ;   an applause given to God's goodness, and an excitation of others to give that applause.   The ground is a threefold respect.   Of what God is in himself, *God and Lord ;* of what God is and doth to us, " *which loadeth us daily with benefits ; "* of what he is both in himself and to us, " *the God of our salvation ; "* which last (like to some rich stone) is set off with a dark foil : "*To God the Lord belong the issues from death.*"   So, in the first for his own sake, in the second for our sakes, in the third for his own and ours ;   as God, as Lord, as a benefactor ;   as a Saviour and deliverer.   "*Blessed be the Lord.*"   It is not hard to observe that David's *Allelujahs* are more than his *Hosannas,* his thanks more than his suits.   Ofttimes doth he praise God when he begs nothing ;   seldom ever doth he beg that favour, for which he doth not raise up his soul to an anticipation of thanks ;   neither is this any other than the universal undersong of all his heavenly ditties, "*Blessed be the Lord.*"   *Praises* (as our former translation hath it) is too low ;   honour is more than praise ;   blessing is more than honour.   Neither is it for nothing that from this word בָּרַךְ, *to bless,* is derived בֶּרֶךְ, *the knee,* which is bowed in blessing ;   and the crier before *Joseph* proclaimed *Abrech,* calling for the honour of the knee from all beholders.   Gen. xli. 43. Every slight, trivial acknowledgment of worth is a praise ;   blessing is in a higher strain of gratitude, that carries the whole sway of the heart with it in a kind of divine rapture.   Praise is a matter of compliment ;   blessing of devotion.   The apostle's rule is, *that the less is blessed of the greater,* Abraham of the King of Salem, the prophet's charge is, that *the greater should be blessed of the less,* yea, the greatest of the least, God of man.   This agrees well ;   blessing is an act that will bear reciprocation ;   God blesseth man, and man blesseth God.   God blesseth man imperatively ;   man blesseth God optatively.   God blesseth man in the acts of mercy ; man blesseth God in the notions, in the expressions of thanks.   God blesses man when he makes him good and happy ;   man blesseth God when he confesseth how good, how gracious, how glorious he is ;   so as the blessing is wholly taken up in agnition,* in celebration :   in the one we acknowledge the bounty of God to us ; in the other we magnify him vocally, really, for that bounty.   O see, then, what high account God makes of the affections and actions of his poor, silly, earth-creeping creatures ;   that he gives us in them power to bless himself, and takes it as an honour to be blessed of us.   *David* wonders that God should so vouchsafe to bless man ; how much more must we needs wonder at the mercy of God, that will vouchsafe to be blessed by man, a worm, an atom, a nothing ?   Yet both, *James* tells us, that *with the tongue we bless God ;* and the Psalmist calls for it here as a service of dear acceptation, "*Blessed be the Lord.*"   Even we men live not (chameleon like) upon the air of thanks, nor grow the fatter for praises ;   how much less our Maker ?   O God, we know well that whatsoever men or angels do, or do not, thou canst not but be infinitely blessed in thyself ;   before ever any creature was, thou didst equally enjoy thy blessed self from all eternity :   what can this worthless, loose film of flesh either add to or detract from thine infiniteness ?   Yet thou, *that humblest thyself to behold the things that are done in heaven and earth,* humblest thyself also to accept the weak breath of our praises, that are sent up to thee from earth to heaven.   How

---

* Agnition, acknowledgment.

should this encourage the vows, the endeavours of our hearty thankfulness, to see them graciously taken ?   If men would take up with good words, with good desires, and quit our bonds for thanks, who would be a debtor ?   With the God of Mercy this cheap payment is current.   If he, then, will honour us so far as to be blessed of us, Oh let us honour him so far as to bless him.—*Joseph Hall, in "A Sermon of Public Thanksgiving for the Wonderful Mitigation of the late Mortality."* 1625.

Verse 19.—"Blessed be the Lord."   It is not a little remarkable to see the saints so burdened and overcharged with the duty of singing his praise, that, 1. They are forced to come off with an excess of praise, and offer to praise him, and even leave it, as it were, as they found it, and say no more, lest they should spill his praises ; but, as Rev. v. 12, " Worthy is the Lamb to receive glory and honour," though I be not worthy or able to give it to him.   2. That they speak broken language and half sentences in their songs, when they are deeply loaden with the deep sense of his love, as *"Blessed be the Lord, who daily loadeth us with benefits ; "* there is no more in the original but *"Blessed be the Lord, that loadeth us."*—*John Spalding, in "Synaxis Sacra."* 1703.

Verse 19.—"Who daily loadeth us with benefits."   Though some may have more than others, yet every one hath his load, as much as he can carry.   Every vessel cannot bear up with the like sail, and therefore God, to keep us from oversetting, puts on so much as will safest bring us to heaven, our desired port.—*Ezekiel Hopkins.*

Verse 19.—"Who daily loadeth us with benefits."   Such is man's self-love that no inward worth can so attract his praises as outward beneficence.   While thou makest much of thyself, every one shall speak well of thee ; how much more while thou makest much of them !   Here God hath met with us also.   Not to perplex you with scanning the variety of senses wherewith I have observed this Psalm, above all other of David's, to abound ; see here, I beseech you, a four-fold gradation of divine bounty.   First, here are *" benefits."*   The word is not expressed in the original, but necessarily implied in the sense : for there are but three loads whereof man is capable from God, favours, precepts, punishments, the other two are out of the road of gratulation.   When we might therefore have expected judgments, behold *benefits.*   And those, secondly, not sparingly hand-fulled out to us, but dealt to us by the whole load : *" loadeth with benefits."*   Whom, thirdly, doth he load but *" us "*?   Not worthy and well-deserving subjects, but *" us,"* סוֹרְדִים, *rebels.* And, lastly, this he doth, not at one dole and no more (as even churls' rare feasts use to be plentiful), but יוֹם יוֹם successively, unweariedly, perpetually.   One favour were too much, here are *" benefits ; "* a sprinkling were too much, here is a *load* ; once were too oft, here is *daily* largition.*   Cast your eyes, therefore, a little upon this threefold exaggeration of beneficence ;   the measure, *a load of benefits ;*   the subject, unworthy *" us ; "* the time, *" daily." " Who daily loadeth us with benefits."*

Where shall we begin to survey this vast load of mercies ?   Were it no more, but that he hath given us a world to live in, a life to enjoy, air to breathe in, earth to tread on, fire to warm us, water to cool and cleanse us, clothes to cover us, food to nourish us, sleep to refresh us, houses to shelter us, variety of creatures to serve and delight us ;   here were a just load.   But now, if we yet add to these, civility of breeding, dearness of friends, competency of estate, degrees of honour, honesty or dignity of vocation, favour of princes, success in employments, domestic comforts, outward peace, good reputation, preservation from dangers, rescue from evils ; the load is well mended.   If yet, ye shall come closer, and add due proportion of body, integrity of parts, perfection of senses, strength of nature, mediocrity of health, sufficiency of appetite, vigour of digestion, wholesome temper of seasons, freedom from cares ;   this course must needs heighten it yet more.   If still ye shall add to these, the order, and power, and exercise of our inward faculties, enriched with wisdom, art, learning, experience, expressed by a not un-handsome elocution, and shall now lay all these together that concern estate, body, mind ;   how can the axle-tree of the soul but crack under the load of these favours ?   But, if from what God hath done for us as men, we look to what he hath done for us as Christians ; that he hath embraced us with an everlasting love, that he hath moulded us anew, enlivened us by his Spirit, fed us by his word and sacraments, clothed us with his merits, bought us with his blood, becoming vile to make us glorious, a curse, to invest us with blessedness ;   in a word, that he hath given himself to us, his Son for us ;   *Oh the height, and depth, and breadth* of the rich mercies of our God !   Oh

---

* Largition, largess, bounty.

the boundless, topless, bottomless, load of divine benefits, whose immensity reaches from the centre of this earth, to the unlimited extent of the very empyreal heavens ! *"Oh that men would praise the Lord for his goodness, and declare the wonders that he hath done for the children of men."—Joseph Hall.*

Verse 20.—*"Our God is the God of salvation"* (that is of deliverance, of outward deliverance) ; *" and unto God the Lord belong the issues from death,"* or the goings out from death ; that is, God'hath all ways that lead out from death in his own keeping, he keepeth the key of the door that lets us out from death. When a man is in the valley of the shadow of death, where shall he issue out ? Where shall he have a passage ? Nowhere, saith man, he shall not escape. But God keepeth all the passages ; when men think they have shut us up in the jaws of death, he can open them, and deliver us. *"To him belong the issues from death ;"* it is an allusion to one that keepeth a passage or a door : and God is a faithful keeper, and a friendly keeper, who will open the door for the escape of his people, when they cry unto him.— *Joseph Caryl.*

Verse 20.—*"And unto God the Lord belong the issues from death."* Buildings stand by the benefit of their foundations that sustain them, support them ; and of their buttresses that comprehend them, embrace them ; and of their contignations * that knit and unite them. The foundation suffers them not to sink ; the buttresses suffer them not to swerve ; the contignation and knitting suffer them not to cleave. The body of our building is in the former part of this verse ; it is this ; He that is our God is the God of salvation ; *ad salutes,* of salvations, in the plural, so it is in the original ; the God that gives us spiritual and temporal salvation too. But of this building, the foundation, the buttresses, the contignation, are in this part of the verse, which constitutes our text, and in the three diverse acceptations of the words amongst our expositors, *"Unto God the Lord belong the issues of death."* For, first, the foundation of this building (that our God is the God of all salvation) is laid in this, *"That unto this God the Lord belong the issues of death ; "* that is, it is in his power to give us an issue and deliverance, even then, when we are brought to the jaws and teeth of death, and to the lips of that whirlpool, the grave ; and so, in this acceptation, this *exitus mortis,* the issue of death, is *liberatio a morte,* a deliverance from death ; and this is the most obvious and most ordinary acceptation of these words, and that upon which our translation lays hold : *"the issues from death."* And then, secondly, the buttresses that comprehend and set le this building ; that, *"He that is our God is the God of salvation,"* are thus raised ; *"Unto God the Lord belong the issues of death,"* that is, the disposition and manner of our death, what kind of issue and transmigration we shall have out of this world, whether prepared or sudden, whether violent or natural, whether in our perfect senses or shaked and disordered by sickness ; there is [no] condemnation to be argued out of that, no judgment to be made upon that ; for howsoever they die, *precious in his sight is the death of his saints,* and with him are the issues of death, the ways of our departing out of this life are in his hands ; and so in this sense of the words, this *exitus mortis,* the issue of death, is *liberatio in morte,* a deliverance in death ; not that God will deliver us from dying, but that he will have a care of us in the hour of death, of what kind soever our passage be ; and this sense and acceptation of the words, the natural frame and contexture doth well and pregnantly administer unto us. And then, lastly, the contignation and knitting of this building, that He that is our God, is the God of all salvation, consists in this, Unto this God the Lord belong the issues of death, that is, that this God the Lord, having united and knit both natures in one, and being God, having also come into this world, in our flesh, he could have no other means to save us, he could have no other issue out of this world, no return to his former glory, but by death. And so in this sense, this *exitus mortis,* the issue of death, is *liberatio per mortem,* a deliverance by death, by the death of this God our Lord, Christ Jesus ; and this, St. Augustine's acceptation of the words, and those many and great persons that have adhered to him. In all these three lines then, we shall look upon these words, first, as the God of power, the Almighty Father, rescues his servants from the jaws of death ; and then, as the God of mercy, the glorious Son rescued us by taking upon himself the issue of death ; and then (between these two), as the God of comfort, the Holy Ghost rescues us

---

* Contignation, a framing together ; from *contigno,* to join together, or lay with beams and rafters.

from all discomfort, by his blessed impressions before ; that what manner of death soever be ordained for us, yet this *exitus mortis* shall be *introitus in vitam*, our issue in death shall be an entrance into everlasting life. And these three considerations, our deliverance *a morte, in morte, per mortem*, from death, in death, and by death, will abundantly do all the offices of the foundation, of the buttresses, of the contignation of this our building, that *"He that is our God is the God of salvation,"* because *"Unto this God the Lord belong the issues of death."*—*John Donne.*

Verse 20.—*"The issues from death."* That is, the issue, or escape, from death, both in the resurrection and in the various perils of our present life.—*Thomas Le Blanc.*

Verse 20.—*"Issues from death."* The English version cannot be sustained by the Hebrew ; for ל has never the force of *from*, and, therefore, the expression, as Dr. Hammond observes, must signify the several plagues and judgments inflicted by God on impenitent enemies—such as drowning in the sea, killing by the sword, etc. ; which were the ways of punishing and destroying the Egyptians and Canaanites. Thus the two members of the verse are antithetical : the first speaks of God as a deliverer, and the second as a punisher ; and in this respect the verse corresponds with the preceding.—*George Phillips, in "The Psalms. . . . . with a Critical, Exegetical and Philological Commentary."* 1846.

Verse 21.—*"The hairy scalp."* That is, even the most fearful enemies, that with their ghastly visage, deformed with long hair, would strike a terror into the hearts of beholders.—*Edward Leigh.*

Verse 21.—*"Hairy scalp."* It was a practice among some of the ancient inhabitants of Arabia to allow the hair to grow luxuriantly on the *top of the head*, and to shave the head in other parts.—*Francis Hare.* 1740.

Verse 22.—*"I will bring the enemy."* Both the preceding and following verse prove that this is the sense, and not as many interpreters supply, *my people.* Bashan was *east* of Judæa, and the *sea* on the west ; so that the meaning is, that God would bring his enemies from every quarter to be slain by his people.—*Benjamin Boothroyd.*

Verse 23.—*"That thy foot may be dipped,"* etc. The blood of thy enemies, shed in such abundance that thy dogs shall lap and drink it, shall be the sea in which thou shalt pass, and that red without a figure. And, proportionably shall be the destructions on the enemies of Christ and Christians in the age of the Messiah.—*Henry Hammond.*

Verses 26—28.—This Psalm was sung, it is probable, on the removal of the ark into the City of David. Numb. x. It was now that the ark had rest, and the tribes assembled three times a year at Jerusalem, the place that God had chosen. The text is a lively description of their worship.

I. Offer a few remarks by way of expounding the passage. 1. Israel had their lesser congregations in ordinary every Sabbath-day, and their national ones three times a year. Their business in all was *to bless God.* 2. This business was to be carried on by *all Israel*, beginning at the fountain head, and proceeding through all its streams. God has blessed Israel ; let Israel bless God. 3. All the tribes are supposed to be present ; four are mentioned in the name of the whole, as inhabiting the confines of the land. Their union was a source of joy ; they had been divided by civil wars, but now they are met together. 4. Those tribes which are named had each something particular attending it. Little Benjamin (see Judges xxi.) had nearly been a tribe lacking in Israel, but now appears with its ruler. Judah had been at war with Benjamin : Saul was a Benjamite ; David was of Judah : yet they happily lost their antipathies in the worship of God. Zebulun and Naphtali were distant tribes ; yet they were there ! dark, too, yet there. 5. The princes and the people were all together. 6. They were supposed to be strong, but were reminded that what they had of strength was of God's commanding. Their union and success, as well as that degree of righteousness among them which exalted the nation, was of God. They are not so strong, but that they need strengthening, and are directed to pray as well as praise : *"Strengthen, O God, that which thou hast wrought for us."*

II. Apply the subject. Two things are here exemplified, namely—diligence and brotherly union ; and three things recommended, namely—united praise ; united acknowledgment that, for what they are, they are indebted to God ; and united prayer for future mercies. Each of these affords a rule for us. 1. The worship of God must be attended with *diligence*. There are the princes of Zebulun and Naphtali. They had to travel above two hundred miles three times a year, thither and back again ; that is, twelve hundred in a year, twenty-four miles a week. Those who neglect the worship of God for little difficulties show that their heart is not in it, and when they do attend cannot expect to profit : " they have snuffed at it." Those whose hearts are in it often reap great advantage. God blessed the Israelites in their journeys, as well as when there (Psalm lxxxiv. 6) : " The rain filleth the pools ; " and so the Christians. There is a peculiar promise to those that seek him *early*. 2. The worship of God must be attended to with *brotherly love*. All the tribes must go up together. It is a kind law that enjoins *social* worship ; we need each other to stimulate. " O magnify the Lord with me, and let us exalt his name together." God has made us so that we shall be greatly influenced by each other, both to good and evil. It greatly concerns us to cultivate such a spirit. To this end we must cherish an affectionate behaviour in our common intercourse—bear, forbear, and forgive ; and, whatever differences we may have, not suffer them to hinder our worship. The tribes, as we have seen, had their differences ; yet they were there. When all Israel met at Hebron to anoint David king, what should we have said if some had kept away because others went ? 3. Our business, when assembled, must be to *bless God* in our congregations ; and a pleasant work this is. Israel had reasons, and great reasons, and Christians more. Thank him for his unspeakable gift ; bless him for the means of grace, and the hopes of glory. Bless him ; he " healeth all thy diseases," etc. Psalm ciii. This is an employment that fits for heaven. The tears of a mourner in God's house were supposed to defile his altar. We may mourn for *sin ;* but a fretful spirit, discontented and unthankful, defiles God's altar still. 4. Another part of our business is to unite in acknowledging that whatever we are, we owe it to God alone ; " Thy God hath commanded thy strength." We possess a degree of strength both individually and socially. Art thou strong in faith, in hope, in zeal ? It is in him thou art strong. Are we strong as a society ? It is God that increaseth us with men like a flock ; it is he that keeps us in union, gives us success, etc. 5. Another part of our business must be to unite in prayer for future mercies. We are not so strong, either as individuals or societies, but that there is room for increase ; and this is the proper object of prayer. God has wrought a great work for us in regeneration. God has wrought much for us as a church in giving us increase, respect, and room in the earth. Pray that each may be increased ; or, in the words of the text : "*Strengthen, O God, that which thou hast wrought for us.*" Are there none who are strangers to all this ?—*Andrew Fuller.*

Verse 27.—"*Benjamin, Judah, Zebulun, Naphtali.*" The two royal tribes, 1. that of Benjamin, from which the first king sprang ; 2. that of Judah, from which the second ; and the two learned tribes, Zebulun and Naphtali. And we may note, that the kingdom of the Messiah should at length be submitted to by all the potentates and learned men in the world.—*Henry Hammond.*

Verse 27.—"*Benjamin, Judah, Zebulun, Naphtali.*" The same tribes are prominent in the New Testament, as foremost in the battle of the church against the world. Paul, the " least " of the apostles (1 Cor. xv. 8—10), was by origin Saul of Benjamin (Phil. iii. 5). Christ, " the Lion of the tribe of Judah," James and John, the brothers, the other James, Thaddeus, and Simon, were from Judah, and the other apostles were from Naphthalim and Zabulon, or Galilee (Matt. iv. 13).—*A. R. Fausset.*

Verse 27.—"*Their ruler.*" The *prince* of that tribe. The Greek version saith, *in a trance ;* taking the Hebrew רִם to be of רָם, though it be not found elsewhere in this form ; yet rare words but once used, are sundry times found in this and other Psalms. These things applied to Christ's times and after are very mystical. *Benjamin*, the least, is put here *first ;* so in the heavenly Jerusalem, the *first foundation is a jasper* (Rev. xxi. 19), which was the *last* precious stone in Aaron's breastplate, on which *Benjamin's* name was graven (Exod. xxviii. 10, 20, 21). In this tribe *Paul* excelled as a prince of God, though one of the least apostles (1 Cor. xv. 8—10), who was converted in a *trance* or *ecstacy* (Acts ix. 3, 4, etc.) ; and in ecstacies he and other apostles saw the mysteries of Christ's kingdom.—*Henry Ainsworth.*

Verse 27.—"*Their council ;* " or, *their stone*, the Messiah, that sprung from Judah, Gen. xlix. 24 ; Ps. cxviii. 22.—*John Gill.*

Verses 27, 28.—There are all the twelve tribes of Israel with their rulers present, to conduct the ark of God to the hill, in which it pleased him to dwell ; for, though all the tribes are not mentioned, these, which are named, include the whole, since Zebulun and Naphtali are the most remote, and Judah and Benjamin the nearest tribes to Zion. Benjamin was a dwindled family through the signal depopulation of that tribe, from which it never entirely recovered. Jud. xx. 43—48 ; 1 Chron. xii. 29.—*Edward Garrard Marsh, in "The Book of Psalms translated into English Verse . . . with Practical and Explanatory Notes."* 1832.

Verse 28.—*"Thy God hath commanded thy strength."* Singularly appropriate to the occasion for which they were composed are these stimulating words. The ark of God had during several years been kept in private houses. David had pitched a tent for its reception, and intended providing a better shrine, he would deposit the ark in the temporary sanctuary, and he gathers thirty thousand chosen men of Israel, and with these and with a multitude of the people he proceeds to the house in which the ark had been kept. The people *can* render the service of song, so " David and all the house of Israel played before the Lord on all manner of instruments made of firwood, even on harps, and on psalteries, and on timbrels, and on cornets, and on cymbals" (2 Sam. vi. 5). The breach of Uzzah delayed the restoration of the ark three months ; but David returned to the work, and with gladness, with burnt offerings and peace offerings, with feasting, dancing, and the sound of a trumpet, he brought in the ark of the Lord, and set it in its place in the tabernacle he had pitched for it. David *can* provide a sacred place for the ark of his God, and his " God has commanded his strength." Thirty thousand chosen men *can* attend on this occasion, and a multitude besides. Then, why should they tarry at home ? The occasion is worthy of their presence, and their " God has commanded their strength." There are sweet singers and skilful players in Israel, and why should they be silent. The occasion calls for praise, and their " God has commanded their strength." There are cattle upon the thousand hills of Canaan, and shall no sacrifice be brought ? The occasion demands oblations, and Israel's " God has commanded their strength." There is a mountain in Canaan, beautiful for situation, and rich in historic association. God's ark *can* be brought to this mountain, and if it can be, it ought to be, for Israel's God has commanded Israel's strength. There are twelve tribes in Israel which may unite in bringing up God's ark, then let none hold back, for their " God has commanded their strength." *"Thy strength"* is thy best—all that is within thee ; all that thou canst do, and be, and become ; and all that thou hast—the two mites, if these be all, and the alabaster box of spikenard, very costly, if this be thy possession. . . . By that which God is in himself, by that which God is to us, by law on the heart, and by law oral and written, by the new kingdom of his love, and by all his benefits, *"Thy God commands thy strength."* He speaks from the beginning, and from the end of time, from the midst of chaos, and from the new heavens and new earth, from Bethel and from Gethsemane, from Sinai and from Calvary, and he saith to us all, " My son, give me thine heart," consecrate to me the best and, devote to me thy strength.—*Samuel Martin.*

Verse 30.—*"Rebuke the wild beasts of the reeds."* This is our marginal version, which is the proper one. Most modern critics consider that the lion is here intended, which frequently makes its den among reeds or brush-wood. Innumerable lions wander about among the reeds and copses, on the borders of the rivers of Mesopotamia. The river Jordan was infested with them (Jer. iv. 7, and xlix. 19). Hence, the wild beasts of the reeds may signify the Syrian kings, who often contended with David.—*Benjamin Boothroyd.*

Verse 30.—The idolatrous king of Egypt is here enigmatically represented as dwelling, like the crocodile, among the reeds of the Nile ; and with him are introduced the " *bulls* " and " *calves*," who were the gods of the people of Egypt, before whom they were ever dancing in their superstitious revels. " Quell these insults upon thy majesty, nor put down only the superstition of Egypt, but all their pomp of war also, that the Gentiles may be converted unto thee, and the idols be utterly abolished."—*Edward Garrard Marsh.*

Verse 30.—When the enemies of God rise up against his church, it is time for the church to fall down to God, to implore his aid against those enemies. Holy prayers are more powerful than profane swords.—*Thomas Wall, in "A Comment on the Times."* 1657.

Verse 30.—The words contain, first, a declaration of God's enemies ; secondly, an imprecation against those enemies. The enemies are marshalled into four ranks.

1. A company of spearman, or (as some translations read it) the beast of the reeds. 2. The multitude of the bulls. 3. The calves of the people. 4. The men that delight in war. The imprecation is also twofold; the first more gentle; it is but *"rebuke* the spearmen; " and that with a limitation too—*"till they submit themselves with pieces of silver."* For they that will not, but delight in war, more severely deal with such : Scatter them ; *"Scatter the men that delight in war."* . . . The church of God never wanted enemies, never will. "There is no peace to the wicked," saith God : there shall be no peace to the godly, say the wicked. The wicked shall have no peace which God can give ; the godly shall have no peace which the wicked can take away.—*Thomas Wall.*

Verse 30.—1. Scrupulosity. 2. Envy. 3. Ignorance. 4. Ambition or pride. Upon which these four beasts in the text do act their enmity against the church : scrupulosity sets forth unto us the beast of the reeds ; envy, the bulls ; ignorance, the calves ; the pride, the men " that delight in war."—*Thomas Wall.**

Verse 31.—*"Ethiopia."* It is a matter of fact, familiar to the learned reader, that the names *"Ethiopia,"* and *"Ethiopians,"* are frequently substituted in our English version of the Old Testament, where the Hebrew preserves the proper name, " Cush." And the name, " Cush," when so applied in Scripture, belongs uniformly not to the African, but to the Asiatic, Ethiopia, or Arabia.—*Charles Forster, in "The Historical Geography of Arabia."*

Verse 33.—*"And that a mighty voice ; "* or, *a voice of strength ;* a strong and powerful voice, such as the gospel is, when accompanied with the power and Spirit of God. It is a soul-shaking and awakening voice ; it is a heart-melting and a heart-breaking one ; it is a quickening and an enlightening voice ; it quickens dead sinners, gives life unto them, and the entrance of it gives light to dark minds : it is a soul-charming and alluring one ; it draws to Christ, engages the affections to him, and fills with unspeakable delight and pleasure.—*John Gill.*

Verse 33.—*"To him that rideth upon the heavens of heavens."* He who manages the heavens, directing their course and influence. He formed every orb, ascertained its motion, proportioned its solid contents to the orbit in which it was to revolve, and to the other bodies of the same system ; and, as an able rider manages his horse, so does God the sun, moon, planets, and all the hosts of heaven.—*W. Greenfield, in Comprehensive Bible.*

Verse 33.—The praises of the church are sung to him, who, after his sufferings here below, re-ascended to take possession of his ancient throne, high above all heavens ; who, from thence, speaketh to the world by his glorious gospel, mighty and powerful, as thunder, in its effects upon the hearts of men (see Ps. xxix. throughout). The power of Christ's voice, when he was on earth, appeared by the effects which followed, when he said, " Young man, arise: " " Lazarus, come forth: " " Peace, be still ; " and it will yet further appear, when " all that are in the graves shall hear the voice of the Son of man, and come forth."—*George Horne.*

Verse 34.—*"His strength is in the clouds."* This refers to the phenomena of thunder and lightning ; for all nations have observed that the electric fluid is an irresistible agent—destroying life, tearing towers and castles to pieces, rending the strongest oaks, and cleaving the most solid rocks ; and the most enlightened nations have justly considered it as an especial manifestation of the power and sovereignty of God.—*W. Greenfield, in Comprehensive Bible.*

---

* This instance of spiritualising may act rather as a beacon than as an example. The author was an able divine, but in this sermon gives more play to his imagination than his common sense.

HINTS TO PREACHERS.

Verses 1, 2.—First. The church of God ever had, and will have, enemies and haters; for against these doth the Psalmist arm himself and the church with this prayer.

Secondly. The church's enemies are God's enemies; they that hate the church, hate God. "Thine enemies," "them that hate thee."

Thirdly. God sometimes seems to sleep or lie still, and let these enemies and haters do what they will for a season. This, also, is implied: he to whom we say, "Arise," is either asleep or lies still.

Fourthly. There is a time when God will arise.

Fifthly. God's rising time is the enemies' scattering time, his haters' flying time.

Sixthly. It is the duty of God's people to pray him up when he seems to be down, and to exalt him in their praises when he doth arise to their rescue and redemption; for these words are both a prayer and a triumph, as they are used both by Moses and David.—*Thomas Case, in a Fast Sermon, preached before the House of Commons, entitled, "God's Rising, his Enemies' Scattering."* 1644.

Verses 1—3.—Prayer for the Second Advent.—*A. M'Caul.*

Verse 4.—I. The name that inspires the song: "Jah." 1. Self-existent. 2. Immutable. 3. Eternal. II. The song inspired by that name. 1. Of exultation. 2. Of confidence. 3. Of joy.—*G. R.*

Verse 5.—The claims of widows and orphans upon the church of God, from God's relation to them and his indwelling in the church.

Verse 6.—Comparison of churches to families. See extract from *Dr. Gill.*

Verse 6.—I. Two curable evils: "solitary," "bound with chains." II. Two rich blessings: "set in families," "bringeth out." III. One monster evil, and its miserable consequences.

Verses 7, 8.—I. God has his seasons for delivering his people from their troubles: "When thou," etc. II. His deliverance is complete: "The earth shook," etc.; all things gave way before him. III. The deliverance is greater for the delay. 1. It is so in itself. 2. It is more prized: as in the case of Job, Abraham, Israel at the Red Sea, Daniel, his three companions, etc.—*G. R.*

Verses 7, 8, 9.—I. The presence of God in his church. 1. His pre-eminence: "before." 2. As covenant God of Israel. 3. As active and making active. 4. His rule within: they follow. 5. His design without: marching for war. II. The blessed consequences. 1. The most stolid shake. 2. The lofty bow. 3. Difficulties removed: "Sinai." 4. Blessings plenteous. 5. Church revived.

Verse 9.—I. God's mercy compared to a shower. 1. It is direct from heaven; not through priests. 2. It is pure and unmixed. 3. No one has a monopoly of it. 4. There is no substitute for it. 5. It is sovereignly dispensed, as to (1) time; (2) place; (3) manner; and (4) measure. 6. It works efficiently. Isaiah lv. 10. 7. Prayer can get it. II. There are seasons when these showers fall. 1. In the house of God. 2. In the means of grace. 3. In prayer. 4. In affliction. 5. When saints are weary (1) through working; (2) through sickness; (3) through non-success. 6. By the Holy Spirit refreshing the heart. III. These showers are meant to "confirm" God's people. IV. They are wanted *now.*

Verse 9.—I. The church is God's inheritance. 1. Chosen. 2. Purchased. 3. Acquired. II. Though his inheritance, at times it may be weary. III. When weary, it will be refreshed by him.—*G. R.*

Verse 10 (*second clause*).—Special goodness, for a special people, specially prepared.

Verse 10 (*second clause*).—It is spoken in reference to the "*poor*," because, I. They are the larger mass of mankind; and, whatever pride may think, in the eye of reason, policy, and revelation, by far the most important, useful, and necessary part. II. They would be more peculiarly affected by deficiency. III. To encourage those in humble and trying life to depend upon him. IV. To enforce our attention to them from the divine example.—*W. Jay.*

Verse 11.—The divinity of the gospel; the divers ways and agents for its publication.

Verses 11, 12.—I. The word given: "The Lord," etc. II. The word proclaimed: "Great," etc. III. The word obeyed: "Kings," etc. Thus it was in

Old Testament times, when to Joshua, to Gideon, to David, etc., the Lord gave the word, and it ran through the hosts, and "kings of armies," etc. Thus it was in apostolic times, when the word of reconciliation was given. Thus it is still, and will be more signally than ever hereafter.—*G. R.*

Verse 12 (*last clause*).—The church in redemption as a spouse tarrying at home ; her home duties ; the spoil of her Lord's glorious and finished work, and her dividing it.

Verse 13.—I. The contrast. 1. Instead of humiliation, exaltation. 2. Instead of pollution, purity. 3. Instead of inertness, activity. 4. Instead of deformity, beauty. II. Its application. 1. To penitence and pardon. 2. To depravity and regeneration. 3. To affliction and recovery. 4. To desertion and consolation. 5. To death and glory.—*G. R.*

Verse 14.—I. Where earth's greatest battles are fought. "Scattered," "in it," *i.e.*, in Zion. "There brake he," etc. II. By whom ? The Almighty. III. When ? In answer to his people's faith and prayer. IV. How ? 1. Without noise, gently : as the fall of snow. 2. Without human aid : as untrodden snow. 3. Without violence : "all bloodless lay the untrodden snow."—*G. R.*

Verses 15, 16.—I. The superiority of the hill of Zion. 1. In fertility, to the hill of Bashan ; to earthly pleasures. 2. In glory, to other hills ; to human heights of learning and power. II. The reason of that superiority. 1. The place of God's choice. 2. Of his delight. 3. Of his abode. 4. Of his continuance for ever.— *G. R.*

Verse 16.—I. The church the dwelling-place of God. 1. Elected of old. 2. Favoured for ever. 3. Affording rest, etc., as a home for God. 4. Receiving honour, etc., for herself. II. The church, therefore, envied by others. 1. They feel their own greatness outdone. 2. They leap with rage. 3. They are unreasonable in so doing.

Verses 17, 18.—I. The comparison between Zion and Sinai. 1. The same Lord is there : "The Lord is among," etc. 2. The same attendants : "The chariots," etc. II. The contrast. 1. God descended at Sinai, ascended from near Zion. 2. Put a yoke upon them at Sinai, leads captivity captive at Zion. 3. At Sinai demanded obedience, in Zion bestows gifts. 4. In Sinai spoke terror, in Zion receives gifts for the rebellious. 5. In Sinai appeared for a short season, in Zion dwells for ever.—*G. R.*

Verse 18.—I. Christ's *ascension*. II. His *victories*. III. The *gifts* he received for men ; and IV. The great *end* for which he bestows them.—*J. Newton.*

Verse 18.—"*That the Lord God might dwell among them.*" It is ground for devout wonder that God should dwell among men, when we contemplate his *immensity, loftiness, independence, holiness*, and *sovereignty ;* yet he does so—I. In the coming of Christ into the world. II. In the residence of his Spirit in the heart. III. In the presence of God in his churches.—*William Staughton, D.D.* 1770—1829.

Verse 19.—I. The load of benefits. II. The load of obligation. III. The load of praise due in return.

Verse 19.—I. Salvation is not to be forgotten in the midst of daily mercies. II. Daily mercies are not to be forgotten in the enjoyment of salvation.—*G. R.*

Verse 20.—Death in God's hand. I. Escapes from it. II. Entrances to it. III. The exit out of it beyond. IV. The gate which, when closed, shuts us in it for ever.

Verse 20.—I. What God has been to his people. 1. Their salvation. 2. Their portion : "Our God." II. What he will be : With them. 1. Until death. 2. In death. 3. After death.—*G. R.*

Verse 21.—The power, pride, wisdom, and very life of evil, to be conquered by God.

Verse 22.—I. Where his people may be driven. II. The certainty of their return. III. The reasons for being assured of this.

Verse 23.—*The allowable procession in the sanctuary.* The marshalled order of doctrine, the holy walk of believers, the banners of joy, the music of devotions, the shouts to the King.

Verse 24 (*last clause*).—Work for holy women in the church.

Verse 27.—I. The variety of song. 1. The royal tribe of Benjamin in the time of Saul. 2. The princely tribe of Judah, as David was prince regent in the time of Saul. 3. The literary tribe of Zebulun : "Out of Zebulun they that handle the pen of the writer." 4. The eloquent tribe : "Naphtali giveth goodly words."

II. The harmony of song. Let all unite in praising the Lord, the fountain of Israel. "Ten thousand thousand are their tongues," etc.—*G. R.*

Verses 30, 31.—I. Hindrances to the progress of divine truth. 1. Idolatry. Worship of the crocodile—"beasts of the reeds," (LXX)—of bulls and calves, as in Egypt. 2. Covetousness. 3. War. II. The means for their removal. Prayer and the divine "rebuke." "Scatter thou," etc. III. The consequences of this removal; verse 31.

Verse 35. I. Consider God's jealousy towards his people for his holiness in the three "holy places." 1. In the outer court of profession. 2. In the holy place of our priesthood. 3. In the holy of holies with his Son. II. Consider his terribleness to his foes, as inferred from those "holy places."

Verse 35.—*"Blessed be God."* A brief, but very suggestive text.

PSALM LXIX.

TITLE.—To the Chief Musician upon Shoshannim. *Thus for the second time we have a Psalm entitled "upon the lilies." In the forty-first they were golden lilies, dropping sweet-smelling myrrh, and blooming in the fair gardens which skirt the ivory palaces: in this we have the lily among thorns, the lily of the valley, fair and beautiful, blooming in the garden of Gethsemane.* A Psalm of David. *If any enquire, "of whom speaketh the Psalmist this? of himself, or of some other man?" we would reply, "of himself, and of some other man." Who that other is, we need not be long in discovering; it is the Crucified alone who can say, "in my thirst they gave me vinegar to drink." His footprints all through this sorrowful song have been pointed out by the Holy Spirit in the New Testament, and therefore we believe, and are sure, that the Son of Man is here. Yet it seems to be the intention of the Spirit, while he gives us personal types, and so shows the likeness to the firstborn which exists in the heirs of salvation, to set forth also disparities between the best of the sons of men, and the Son of God, for there are verses here which we dare not apply to our Lord; we almost shudder when we see our brethren attempting to do so, as for instance verse 5. Especially do we note the difference between David and the Son of David in the imprecations of the one against his enemies, and the prayers of the other for them. We commence our exposition of this Psalm with much trembling, for we feel that we are entering with our Great High Priest into the most holy place.*

DIVISIONS.—*This Psalm consists of two portions of 18 verses each. These again may each be sub-divided into three parts. Under the first head, from verses 1—4, the sufferer spreads his complaint before God; then he pleads that his zeal for God is the cause of his sufferings, in verses 5—12: and this encourages him to plead for help and deliverance, from verses 13—18. In the second half of the Psalm he details the injurious conduct of his adversaries, from verses 19—21; calls for their punishment, verses 22—28, and then returns to prayer, and to a joyful anticipation of divine interposition and its results, verses 29—36.*

EXPOSITION.

SAVE me, O God; for the waters are come in unto *my* soul.

2 I sink in deep mire, where *there is* no standing; I am come into deep waters, where the floods overflow me.

3 I am weary of my crying; my throat is dried: mine eyes fail while I wait for my God.

4 They that hate me without a cause are more than the hairs of mine head: they that would destroy me, *being* mine enemies wrongfully, are mighty: then I restored *that* which I took not away.

1. *"Save me, O God."* "He saved others, himself he cannot save." With strong cryings and tears he offered up prayers and supplications unto him that was able to save him from death, and was heard in that he feared (Heb. v. 7). Thus David had prayed, and here his Son and Lord utters the same cry. This is the second Psalm which begins with a "Save me, O God," and the former (Ps. liv.) is but a short summary of this more lengthened complaint. It is remarkable that such a scene of woe should be presented to us immediately after the jubilant ascension hymn of the last Psalm, but this only shows how interwoven are the glories and the sorrows of our ever-blessed Redeemer. The head which now is crowned with glory is the same which wore the thorns; he to whom we pray, " Save us, O God," is the selfsame person who cried, " Save me, O God." *"For the waters are come in unto my soul."* Sorrows, deep, abounding, deadly, had penetrated his inner nature. Bodily anguish is not his first complaint; he begins not with the gall which embittered his lips, but with the mighty griefs which broke into his heart. All the sea outside a vessel is less to be feared than that which finds its way into the hold.

A wounded spirit who can bear.   Our Lord in this verse is seen before us as a Jonah,
crying, " The waters compassed me about, even to the soul."   He was doing business
for us on the great waters, at his Father's command ; the stormy wind was lifting
up the waves thereof, and he went down to the depths till his soul was melted
because of trouble.   In all this he has sympathy with us, and is able to succour
us when we, like Peter, beginning to sink, cry to him, " Lord, save, or we perish."

2. *"I sink in deep mire."*   In water one might swim, but in mud and mire all
struggling is hopeless ; the mire sucks down its victim.   *"Where there is no standing."*
Everything gave way under the Sufferer ; he could not get foothold for support—
this is a worse fate than drowning.   Here our Lord pictures the close, clinging
nature of his heart's woes.   " He began to be sorrowful, and very heavy."   Sin
is as mire for its filthiness, and the holy soul of the Saviour must have loathed even
that connection with it which was necessary for its expiation.   His pure and sensitive
nature seemed to sink in it, for it was not his element, he was not like us born and
acclimatised to this great dismal swamp.   Here our Redeemer became another
Jeremiah, of whom it is recorded (Jer. xxxviii. 6) that his enemies cast him into a
dungeon wherein " was no water, but mire : so Jeremiah sunk in the mire."   Let
our hearts feel the emotions, both of contrition and gratitude, as we see in this
simile the deep humiliation of our Lord.   *"I am come into deep waters, where the
floods overflow me."*   The sorrow gathers even greater force ; he is as one cast into
the sea, the waters go over his head.   His sorrows were first within, then around,
and now above him.   Our Lord was no faint-hearted sentimentalist ; his were
real woes, and though he bore them heroically, yet were they terrible even to him.
His sufferings were unlike all others in degree, the waters were such as soaked into
the soul ; the mire was the mire of the abyss itself, and the floods were deep and
overflowing.   To us the promise is, " the rivers shall not overflow thee," but no
such word of consolation was vouchsafed to him.   My soul, thy Well-beloved endured
all this for thee.   Many waters could not quench his love, neither could the floods
drown it ; and, because of this, thou hast the rich benefit of that covenant assurance,
" as I have sworn that the waters of Noah should no more go over the earth ; so
have I sworn that I would not be wroth with thee, nor rebuke thee."   He stemmed
the torrent of almighty wrath, that we might for ever rest in Jehovah's love.

3. *"I am weary of my crying."*   Not of it, but by it, with it.   He had prayed
till he sweat great drops of blood, and well might physical weariness intervene.
"My throat is dried," parched, and inflamed.   Long pleading with awful fervour
had scorched his throat as with flames of fire.   Few, very few, of his saints follow
their Lord in prayer as far as this.   We are, it is to be feared, more likely to be hoarse
with talking frivolities to men than by pleading with God ; yet our sinful nature
demands more prayer than his perfect humanity might seem to need.   His prayers
should shame us into fervour.   Our Lord's supplications were salted with fire, they
were hot with agony ; and hence they weakened his system, and made him " a
weary man and full of woes."   *"Mine eyes fail while I wait for my God."*   He wanted
in his direst distress nothing more than his God ; that would be all in all to him.
Many of us know what watching and waiting mean ; and we know something of
the failing eye when hope is long deferred : but in all this Jesus bears the palm ;
no eyes ever failed as his did or for so deep a cause.   No painter can ever depict
those eyes ; their pencils fail in every feature of his all fair but' all marred countenance, but most of all do they come short when they venture to pourtray those eyes
which were fountains of tears.   He knew how both to pray and to watch, and he
would have us learn the like.   There are times when we should pray till the throat
is dry, and watch till the eyes grow dim.   Only thus can we have fellowship with
him in his sufferings.   What ! can we not watch with him one hour ?   Does the
flesh shrink back ?   O cruel flesh to be so tender of thyself, and so ungenerous
to thy Lord !

4. *"They that hate me."*   Surprising sin that men should hate the altogether
lovely one, truly is it added, *"without a cause,"* for reason there was none for this
senseless enmity.   He neither blasphemed God, nor injured man.   As Samuel
said : " Whose ox have I taken ? or whose ass have I taken ? or whom have I
defrauded ?   Whom have I oppressed ? "   Even so might Jesus enquire.   Besides,
he had not only done us no evil, but he had bestowed countless and priceless benefits.
Well might he demand, " For which of these works do ye stone me ? "   Yet from
his cradle to his cross, beginning with Herod and not ending with Judas, he had
foes without number ; and he justly said, they *"are more than the hairs of mine*

head." Both the civilians and the military, laics and clerics, doctors and drunkards, princes and people, set themselves against the Lord's anointed. " This is the heir, let us kill him that the inheritance may be ours," was the unanimous resolve of all the keepers of the Jewish vineyard ; while the Gentiles outside the walls of the garden furnished the instruments for his murder, and actually did the deed. The hosts of earth and hell, banded together, made up vast legions of antagonists, none of whom had any just ground for hating him. *"They that would destroy me, being mine enemies wrongfully, are mighty."* It was bad that they were many, but worse that they were mighty. All the ecclesiastical and military powers of his country were arrayed against him. The might of the Sanhedrim, the mob, and the Roman legions were combined in one for his utter destruction : " Away with such a fellow from this earth ; it is not fit that he should live," was the shout of his ferocious foes. David's adversaries were on the throne when he was hiding in caverns, and our Lord's enemies were the great ones of the earth ; while he, of whom the world was not worthy, was reproached of men and despised of the people. *"Then I restored that which I took not away."* Though innocent, he was treated as guilty. Though David had no share in plots against Saul, yet he was held accountable for them. In reference to our Lord, it may be truly said that he restores what he took not away ; for he gives back to the injured honour of God a recompense, and to man his lost happiness, though the insult of the one and the fall of the other were neither of them, in any sense, his doings. Usually, when the ruler sins the people suffer, but here the proverb is reversed—the sheep go astray, and their wanderings are laid at the Shepherd's door.

5 O God, thou knowest my foolishness ; and my sins are not hid from thee.

6 Let not them that wait on thee, O Lord GOD of hosts, be ashamed for my sake : let not those that seek thee be confounded for my sake, O God of Israel.

7 Because for thy sake I have borne reproach ; shame hath covered my face.

8 I am become a stranger unto my brethren, and an alien unto my mother's children.

9 For the zeal of thine house hath eaten me up ; and the reproaches of them that reproached thee are fallen upon me.

10 When I wept, *and chastened* my soul with fasting, that was to my reproach.

11 I made sackcloth also my garment ; and I became a proverb to them.

12 They that sit in the gate speak against me ; and I *was* the song of the drunkards.

5. *"O God, thou knowest my foolishness."* David might well say this, but not David's Lord ; unless it be understood as an appeal to God as to his freedom from folly which men imputed to him when they said he was mad. That which was foolishness to men was superlative wisdom before God. How often might we use these words in their natural sense, and if we were not such fools as to be blind to our own folly, this confession would be frequently on our lips. When we feel that we have been foolish we are not, therefore, to cease from prayer, but rather to be more eager and fervent in it. Fools had good need consult with the infinitely wise. *"And my sins are not hid from thee."* They cannot be hid with any fig leaves of mine ; only the covering which thou wilt bring me can conceal their nakedness and mine. It ought to render confession easy, when we are assured that all is known already. That prayer which has no confession in it may please a Pharisee's pride, but will never bring down justification. They who have never seen their sins in the light of God's omniscience are quite unable to appeal to that omniscience in proof of their piety. He who can say, *"Thou knowest my foolishness,"* is the only man who can add, " But thou knowest that I love thee."

6. *"Let not them that wait on thee, O Lord God of hosts, be ashamed for my sake."* If he were deserted, others who were walking in the same path of faith would be discouraged and disappointed. Unbelievers are ready enough to catch at anything

which may turn humble faith into ridicule, therefore, O God of all the armies of Israel, let not my case cause the enemy to blaspheme—such is the spirit of this verse. Our blessed Lord ever had a tender concern for his people, and would not have his own oppression of spirit become a source of discouragement to them. *"Let not those that seek thee be confounded for my sake, O God of Israel."* He appealed to the Lord of hosts by his power to help him, and now to the God of Israel by his covenant faithfulness to come to the rescue. If the captain of the host fail, how will it fare with the rank and file ? If David flee, what will his followers do ? If the king of believers shall find his faith unrewarded, how will the feeble ones hold on their way ? Our Lord's behaviour during his sharpest agonies is no cause of shame to us ; he wept, for he was man, but he murmured not, for he was sinless man ; he cried, " My Father, if it be possible, let this cup pass from me ; " for he was human, but he added, " Nevertheless, not as I will, but as thou wilt," for his humanity was without taint of rebellion. In the depths of tribulation no repining word escaped him, for there was no repining in his heart. The Lord of martyrs witnessed a good confession. He was strengthened in the hour of peril, and came off more than a conqueror, as we also shall do, if we hold fast our confidence even to the end.

7. *"Because for thy sake I have borne reproach."* Because he undertook to do the Father's will, and teach his truth, the people were angry ; because he declared himself to be the Son of God, the priesthood raved. They could find no real fault in him, but were forced to hatch up a lying accusation before they could commence their sham trial of him. The bottom of the quarrel was, that God was with him, and he with God, while the Scribes and Pharisees sought only their own honour. Reproach is at all times very cutting to a man of integrity, and it must have come with acute force upon one of so unsullied a chraacter as our Lord : yet see, how he turns to his God, and finds his consolation in the fact that he is enduring all for his Father's sake. The like comfort belongs to all misrepresented and persecuted saints. *"Shame hath covered my face."* Men condemned to die frequently had their faces covered as they were dragged away from the judge's seat, as was the case with the wicked Haman in Esther vii. 8 : after this fashion they first covered our Lord with a veil of opprobious accusation, and then hurried him away to be crucified. Moreover, they passed him through the trial of cruel mockings, besmeared his face with spittle, and covered it with bruises, so that Pilate's " Ecce Homo " called the world's attention to an unexampled spectacle of woe and shame. The stripping on the cross must also have suffused the Redeemer's face with a modest blush, as he hung there exposed to the cruel gaze of a ribald multitude. Ah, blessed Lord, it was our shame which thou wast made to bear ! Nothing more deserves to be reproached and despised than sin, and lo, when thou wast made sin for us thou wast called to endure abuse and scorn. Blessed be thy name, it is over now, but we owe thee more than heart can conceive for thine amazing stoop of love.

8. *"I am become a stranger unto my brethren."* The Jews his brethren in race rejected him, his family his brethren by blood were offended at him, his disciples his brethren in spirit forsook him and fled ; one of them sold him, and another denied him with oaths and cursings. Alas, my Lord, what pangs must have smitten thy loving heart to be thus forsaken by those who should have loved thee, defended thee, and, if need be, died for thee. *"And an alien unto my mother's children."* These were the nearest of relatives, the children of a father with many wives felt the tie of consanguinity but loosely, but children of the same mother owned the band of love ; yet our Lord found his nearest and dearest ones ashamed to own him. As David's brethren envied him, and spake evil of him, so our Lord's relatives by birth were jealous of him, and his best beloved followers in the hour of his agony were afraid to be known as having any connection with him. These were sharp arrows of the mighty in the soul of Jesus, the most tender of friends. May none of us ever act as if we were strangers to him ; never may we treat him as if he were an alien to us : rather let us resolve to be crucified with him, and may grace turn the resolve into fact.

9. *"For the zeal of thine house hath eaten me up."* His burning ardour, like the flame of a candle, fed on his strength and consumed it. His heart, like a sharp sword, cut through the scabbard. Some men are eaten up with lechery, others with covetousness, and a third class with pride, but the master-passion with our great leader was the glory of God, jealousy for his name, and love to the divine family. Zeal for God is so little understood by men of the world, that it always draws down

opposition upon those who are inspired with it ; they are sure to be accused of sinister motives, or of hypocrisy, or of being out of their senses. When zeal eats us up, ungodly men seek to eat us up too, and this was pre-eminently the case with our Lord, because his holy jealousy was pre-eminent. With more than a seraph's fire he glowed, and consumed himself with his fervour. *"And the reproaches of them that reproached thee have fallen upon me."* Those who habitually blasphemed God now curse me instead. I have become the butt for arrows intended for the Lord himself. Thus, the Great Mediator was, in this respect, a substitute for God as well as for man, he bore the reproaches aimed at the one, as well as the sins committed by the other.

10. *"When I wept, and chastened my soul with fasting, that was to my reproach."* Having resolved to hate him, everything he did was made a fresh reason for reviling. If he ate and drank as others, he was a man gluttonous and a wine-bibber ; if he wept himself away and wore himself out with fasting, then he had a devil and was mad. Nothing is more cruel than prejudice, its eye colours all with the medium through which it looks, and its tongue rails at all indiscriminately. Our Saviour wept much in secret for our sins, and no doubt his private soul-chastenings on our behalf were very frequent. Lone mountains and desert places saw repeated agonies, which, if they could disclose them, would astonish us indeed. The emaciation which these exercises wrought in our Lord made him appear nearly fifty years old when he was but little over thirty ; this which was to his honour was used as a matter of reproach against him.

11. *"I made sackcloth also my garment."* This David did literally, but we have no reason to believe that Jesus did. In a spiritual sense he, as one filled with grief, was always a sackcloth wearer. *"And I became a proverb to them."* He was ridiculed as " the man of sorrows," quoted as " the acquaintance of grief." He might have said, " here I and sorrow sit." This which should have won him pity only earned him new and more general scorn. To interweave one's name into a mocking proverb is the highest stretch of malice, and to insult one's acts of devotion is to add profanity to cruelty.

12. *"They that sit in the gate speak against me."* The ordinary gossips who meet at the city gates for idle talk make me their theme, the business men who there resort for trade forget their merchandise to slander me, and even the beggars who wait at men's doors for alms contribute their share of insult to the heap of infamy. *"And I was the song of the drunkard."* The ungodly know no merrier jest than that in which the name of the holy is traduced. The flavour of slander is piquante, and gives a relish to the revellers' wine. The character of the man of Nazareth was so far above the appreciation of the men of strength to mingle strong drink, it was so much out of their way and above their thoughts, that it is no wonder it seemed to them ridiculous, and therefore well adapted to create laughter over their cups. The saints are ever choice subjects for satire. Butler's Hudibras owed more of its popularity to its irreligious banter than to any intrinsic cleverness. To this day the tavern makes rare fun of the tabernacle, and the ale-bench is the seat of the scorner. What a wonder of condescension is here that he who is the adoration of angels should stoop to be the song of drunkards ! What amazing sin that he whom seraphs worship with veiled faces should be a scornful proverb among the most abandoned of men.

> " The by-word of the passing throng,
> The ruler's scoff, the drunkard's song."

13 But as for me, my prayer *is* unto thee, O LORD, *in* an acceptable time : O God, in the multitude of thy mercy hear me, in the truth of thy salvation.

14 Deliver me out of the mire, and let me not sink : let me be delivered from them that hate me, and out of the deep waters.

15 Let not the waterflood overflow me, neither let the deep swallow me up, and let not the pit shut her mouth upon me.

16 Hear me, O LORD ; for thy lovingkindness *is* good : turn unto me according to the multitude of thy tender mercies.

17 And hide not thy face from thy servant ; for I am in trouble : hear me speedily.

18 Draw nigh unto my soul, *and* redeem it : deliver me because of mine enemies.

13. *"But as for me, my prayer is unto thee, O Lord."* He turned to Jehovah in prayer as being the most natural thing for the godly to do in their distress. To whom should a child turn but to his father. He did not answer them ; like a sheep before her shearers he was dumb to them, but he opened his mouth unto the Lord his God, for he would hear and deliver. Prayer is never out of season, it stands us in good stead in every evil day. *"In an acceptable time."* It was a time of rejection with man, but of acceptance with God. Sin ruled on earth, but grace reigned in heaven. There is to each of us an accepted time, and woe be to us if we suffer it to glide away unimproved. God's time must be our time, or it will come to pass that, when time closes, we shall look in vain for space for repentance. Our Lord's prayers were well-timed, and always met with acceptance. *"O God, in the multitude of thy mercy hear me."* Even the perfect one makes his appeal to the rich mercy of God, much more should we. To misery no attribute is more sweet than mercy, and when sorrows multiply, the multitude of mercy is much prized. When enemies are more than the hairs of our head, they are yet to be numbered, but God's mercies are altogether innumerable, and let it never be forgotten that every one of them is an available and powerful argument in the hand of faith. *"In the truth of thy salvation."* Jehovah's faithfulness is a further mighty plea. His salvation is no fiction, no mockery, no changeable thing, therefore he is asked to manifest it, and make all men see his fidelity to his promise. Our Lord teaches us here the sacred art of wrestling in prayer, and ordering our cause with arguments ; and he also indicates to us that the nature of God is the great treasury of strong reasons, which shall be to us most prevalent in supplication.

14. *"Deliver me out of the mire, and let me not sink."* He turns into prayer the very words of his complaint ; and it is well, if, when we complain, we neither feel nor say anything which we should fear to utter before the Lord as a prayer. We are allowed to ask for deliverance from trouble as well as for support under it ; both petitions are here combined. How strange it seems to hear such language from the Lord of glory. *"Let me be delivered from them that hate me, and out of the deep waters."* Both from his foes, and the griefs which they caused him, he seeks a rescue. God can help us in all ways, and we may, therefore, put up a variety of requests without fear of exceeding our liberty to ask, or his ability to answer.

15. *"Let not the waterflood overflow me."* He continues to recapitulate the terms of his lament. He is willing to bear suffering, but entreats grace that it may not get the victory over him. He was heard in that he feared. *"Neither let the deep swallow me up."* As Jonah came forth again, so let me also arise from the abyss of woe : here also our Lord was heard, and so shall we be. Death itself must disgorge us. *"Let not the pit shut her mouth upon me."* When a great stone was rolled over the well, or pit, used as a dungeon, the prisoner was altogether enclosed, and forgotten like one in the oubliettes of the Bastille ; this is an apt picture of the state of a man buried alive in grief and left without remedy ; against this the great sufferer pleaded and was heard. He was baptised in agony but not drowned in it ; the grave enclosed him, but before she could close her mouth he had burst his prison. It is said that truth lies in a well, but it is assuredly an open well, for it walks abroad in power ; and so our great Substitute in the pit of woe and death was yet the Conqueror of death and hell. How appropriately may many of us use this prayer. We deserve to be swept away as with a flood, to be drowned in our sins, to be shut up in hell ; let us, then, plead the merits of our Saviour, lest these things happen unto us.

16. *"Hear me, O Lord."* Do not refuse thy suppliant Son. It is to the covenant God, the ever-living Jehovah, that he appeals with strong cryings. *"For thy loving-kindness is good."* By the greatness of thy love have pity upon thine afflicted. It is always a stay to the soul to dwell upon the pre-eminence and excellence of the Lord's mercy. It has furnished sad souls much good cheer to take to pieces that grand old Saxon word, which is here used in our version, " *lovingkindness.*" Its composition is of two most sweet and fragrant things, fitted to inspire strength into the fainting, and make desolate hearts sing for joy. *"Turn unto me according to the multitude of thy tender mercies."* If the Lord do but turn the eye of pity, and the hand of power, the mourner's spirit revives. It is the gall of bitterness to be without the comfortable smile of God ; in our Lord's case his grief culminated in " Lama

Sabachthani," and his bitterest cry was that in which he mourned an absent God. Observe how he dwells anew upon divine tenderness, and touches again that note of abundance, " The multitude of thy compassions."

17. *"And hide not thy face from thy servant."* A good servant desires the light of his master's countenance; that *servus servorum*, who was also *rex regium*, could not bear to lose the presence of his God. The more he loved his Father, the more severely he felt the hiding of his face. *"For I am in trouble."* Stay thy rough wind in the day of thine east wind; do not add sorrow upon sorrow. If ever a man needs the comforting presence of God it is when he is in distress; and, being in distress, it is a reason to be pleaded with a merciful God why he should not desert us. We may pray that our flight be not in the winter, and that God will not add spiritual desertion to all our other tribulations. *"Hear me, speedily."* The case was urgent, delay was dangerous, nay deadly. Our Lord was the perfection of patience, yet he cried urgently for speedy mercy; and therein he gives us liberty to do the same, so long as we add, " nevertheless, not as I will, but as thou wilt."

18. *"Draw nigh unto my soul."* The near approach of God is all the sufferer needs; one smile of heaven will still the rage of hell. *"And redeem it."* It shall be redemption to me if thou wilt appear to comfort me. This is a deeply spiritual prayer, and one very suitable for a deserted soul. It is in renewed communion that we shall find redemption realised. *"Deliver me because of mine enemies,"* lest they should, in their vaunting, blaspheme thy name, and boast that thou art not able to rescue those who put their trust in thee. Jesus, in condescending to use such supplications, fulfils the request of his disciples : " Lord, teach us to pray."

19 Thou hast known my reproach, and my shame, and my dishonour : mine adversaries *are* all before thee.

20 Reproach hath broken my heart; and I am full of heaviness : and I looked *for some* to take pity, but *there was* none; and for comforters, but I found none.

21 They gave me also gall for my meat; and in my thirst they gave me vinegar to drink.

Here we have a sad recapitulation of sorrows, with more especial reference to the persons concerned in their infliction.

19. *"Thou hast known my reproach, and my shame, and my dishonour."* It is no novelty or secret, it has been long continued : thou, O God, hast seen it; and for thee to see the innocent suffer is an assurance of help. Here are three words piled up to express the Redeemer's keen sense of the contempt poured upon him; and his assurance that every form of malicious despite was observed of the Lord. *"Mine adversaries are all before thee."* The whole lewd and loud company is now present to thine eye : Judas and his treachery; Herod and his cunning; Caiaphas and his counsel; Pilate and his vacillation; Jews, priests, people, rulers, all, thou seest and wilt judge.

20. *"Reproach hath broken my heart."* There is no hammer like it. Our Lord died of a broken heart, and reproach had done the deed. Intense mental suffering arises from slander; and, in the case of the sensitive nature of the immaculate Son of Man, it sufficed to lacerate the heart till it broke. " Then burst his mighty heart." *"And I am full of heaviness."* Calumny and insult bowed him to the dust; he was sick at heart. The heaviness of our Lord in the garden is expressed by many and forcible words in the four gospels, and each term goes to show that the agony was beyond measure great; he was filled with misery, like a vessel which is full to the brim. *"And I looked for some to take pity, but there was none."* " Deserted in his utmost need by those his former bounty fed." Not one to say him a kindly word, or drop a sympathetic tear. Amongst ten thousand foes there was not one who was touched by the spectacle of his misery; not one with a heart capable of humane feeling towards him. *"And for comforters, but I found none."* His dearest ones had sought their own safety, and left their Lord alone. A sick man needs comforters, and a persecuted man needs sympathy; but our blessed Surety found neither on that dark and doleful night when the powers of darkness had their hour. A spirit like that of our Lord feels acutely desertion by beloved

and trusted friends, and yearns for real sympathy. This may be seen in the story of Gethsemane :—

> " Backwards and forwards thrice he ran,
> As if he sought some help from man ;
> Or wish'd, at least, they would condole—
> 'Twas all they could—his tortur'd soul.
>
> Whate'er he sought for, there was none ;
> Our Captain fought the field alone.
> Soon as the chief to battle led,
> That moment every soldier fled."

21. *"They gave me also gall for my meat."* This was the sole refreshment cruelty had prepared for him. Others find pleasure in their food, but his taste was made to be an additional path of pain to him. *"And in my thirst they gave me vinegar to drink."* A criminal's draught was offered to our innocent Lord, a bitter portion to our dying Master. Sorry entertainment had earth for her King and Saviour. How often have our sins filled the gall-cup for our Redeemer ? While we blame the Jews, let us not excuse ourselves.

22 Let their table become a snare before them : and *that which should have been for their* welfare, *let it become* a trap.

23 Let their eyes be darkened, that they see not ; and make their loins continually to shake.

24 Pour out thine indignation upon them, and let thy wrathful anger take hold of them.

25 Let their habitation be desolate ; *and* let none dwell in their tents.

26 For they persecute *him* whom thou hast smitten ; and they talk to the grief of those whom thou hast wounded.

27 Add iniquity unto their iniquity : and let them not come into thy righteousness.

28 Let them be blotted out of the book of the living, and not be written with the righteous.

From this point David and our Lord for awhile part company, if we accept the rendering of our version. The severe spirit of the law breathes out imprecations, while the tender heart of Jesus offers prayers for his murderers. The whole of these verses, however, may be viewed as predictions, and then they certainly refer to our Lord, for we find portions of them quoted in that manner by the apostle in Rom. xi. 9, 10, and by Christ himself in Matt. xxiii. 38.

22. *"Let their table become a snare before them."* There they laid snares, and there they shall find them. From their feasts they would afford nothing but wormwood for their innocent victim, and now their banquets shall be their ruin. It is very easy for the daily provisions of mercy to become temptations to sin. As birds and beasts are taken in a trap by means of baits for the appetite, so are men snared full often by their meats and drinks. Those who despise the upper springs of grace, shall find the nether springs of worldly comfort prove their poison. The table is used, however, not alone for feeding, but for conversation, transacting business, counsel, amusement, and religious observance : to those who are the enemies of the Lord Jesus the table may, in all these respects, become a snare. This first plague is terrible, and the second is like unto it. *"And that which should have been for their welfare, let it become a trap."* This, if we follow the original closely, and the version of Paul in the Romans, is a repetition of the former phrase ; but we shall not err if we say that, to the rejectors of Christ, even those things which are calculated to work their spiritual and eternal good, become ocasions for yet greater sin. They reject Christ, and are condemned for not believing on him ; they stumble on this stone, and are broken by it. Wretched are those men, who not only have a curse upon their common blessings, but also on the spiritual opportunities of salvation.

> " Whom oils and balsams kill, what salve can cure ? "

This second plague even exceeds the first.

23. *"Let their eyes be darkened, that they see not."* They shall wander in a darkness

that may be felt. They have loved darkness rather than light, and in darkness they shall abide. Judicial blindness fell upon Israel after our Lord's death and their persecution of his apostles ; they were blinded by the light which they would not accept. Eyes which see no beauty in the Lord Jesus, but flash wrath upon him, may well grow yet more dim, till death spiritual leads to death eternal. *"And make their loins continually to shake."* Their conscience shall be so ill at ease that they shall continually quiver with fear ; their backs shall bend to the earth (so some read it) with grovelling avarice, and their strength shall be utterly paralyzed, so that they cannot walk firmly, but shall totter at every step. See the terrifying, degrading, and enfeebling influence of unbelief. See also the retaliations of justice : those who will not see shall not see ; those who would not walk in uprightness shall be unable to do so.

24. *"Pour out thine indignation upon them."* What can be too severe a penalty for those who reject the incarnate God, and refuse to obey the commands of his mercy ? They deserve to be flooded with wrath, and they shall be ; for upon all who rebel against the Saviour, Christ the Lord, " the wrath is come to the uttermost." 1 Thess. ii. 16. God's indignation is no trifle ; the anger of a holy, just, omnipotent, and infinite Being, is above all things to be dreaded ; even a drop of it consumes, but to have it poured upon us is inconceivably dreadful. O God, who knoweth the power of thine anger ?

"And let thy wrathful anger take hold of them." Grasping them, arresting them, abiding on them. If they flee, let it overtake and seize them ; let it lay them by the heels in the condemned cell, so that they cannot escape from execution. It shall indeed be so with all the finally impenitent, and it ought to be so. God is not to be insulted with impunity ; and his Son, our ever gracious Saviour, the best gift of infinite love, is not to be scorned and scoffed at for nothing. He that despised Moses' law died without mercy, but what shall be the " sorer punishment " reserved for those who have trodden under foot the Son of God ?

25. *"Let their habitation be desolate ; and let none dwell in their tents."* This may signify that their posterity shall be cut off, and the abode which they occupy shall be left a ruin ; or, as our Lord quoted it, it refers to the temple, which was left by its divine occupant and became a desolation. What occurs on a large scale to families and nations is often fulfilled in individuals, as was conspicuously the case with Judas, to whom Peter referred this prophecy, Acts i. 20, " For it is written in the book of Psalms, let his habitation be desolate, and let no man dwell therein." The fierce proclamation of Nebuchadnezzar, " that every people, nation, and language, that speak anything amiss against the God of Shadrach, Meshach, and Abed-nego, shall be cut in pieces, and their houses shall be made a dunghill," is but an anticipation of that dread hour when the enemies of the Lord shall be broken in pieces, and perish out of the land.

26. *"For they persecute him whom thou hast smitten."* They are cruel where they should be pitiful. When a stroke comes to any in the providence of God, their friends gather around them and condole, but these wretches hunt the wounded and vex the sick. Their merciless hearts invent fresh blows for him who is " smitten of God and afflicted." *"And they talk to the grief of those whom thou hast wounded."* They lay bare the wounds with their rough tongues. They lampoon the mourner, satirise his sorrows, and deride his woes. They pointed to the Saviour's wounds, they looked and stared upon him, and then they uttered shameful accusations against him. After this fashion the world still treats the members of Christ. " Report," say they, " and we will report it." If a godly man be a little down in estate, how glad they are to push him over altogether, and, meanwhile, to talk everywhere against him. God takes note of this, and will visit it upon the enemies of his children ; he may allow them to act as a rod to his saints, but he will yet avenge his own elect. " Thus saith the Lord of hosts ; I am jealous for Jerusalem, and for Zion, with a great jealousy ; and I am very sore displeased with the heathen that are at ease : for I was but a little displeased, and they helped forward the affliction."

27. *"Add iniquity unto their iniquity."* Unbelievers will add sin to sin, and so, punishment to punishment. This is the severest imprecation, or prophecy, of all. For men to be let alone to fill up the measure of their iniquity, is most equitable, but yet most awful. *"And let them not come into thy righteousness."* If they refuse it, and resist thy gospel, let them shut themselves out of it.

" He that will not when he may,
When he would he shall have nay."

Those who choose evil shall have their choice. Men who hate divine mercy shall not have it forced upon them, but (unless sovereign grace interpose) shall be left to themselves to aggravate their guilt, and ensure their doom.

28. *"Let them be blotted out of the book of the living."* Though in their conceit they wrote themselves among the people of God, and induced others to regard them under that character, they shall be unmasked and their names removed from the register. Enrolled with honour, they shall be erased with shame. Death shall obliterate all recollection of them ; they shall be held no longer in esteem, even by those who paid them homage. Judas first, and Pilate, and Herod, and Caiaphas, all in due time, were speedily wiped out of existence ; their names only remain as by-words, but among the honoured men who live after their departure they are not recorded. *"And not be written with the righteous."* This clause is parallel with the former, and shows that the inner meaning of being blotted out from the book of life is to have it made evident that the name was never written there at all. Man in his imperfect copy of God's book of life will have to make many emendations, both of insertion and erasure ; but, as before the Lord, the record is for ever fixed and unalterable. Beware, O man, of despising Christ and his people, lest thy soul should never partake in the righteousness of God, without which men are condemned already.

29 But I *am* poor and sorrowful : let thy salvation, O God, set me up on high.

30 I will praise the name of God with a song, and will magnify him with thanksgiving.

31 *This* also shall please the LORD better than an ox *or* bullock that hath horns and hoofs.

32 The humble shall see *this, and* be glad : and your heart shall live that seek God.

33 For the LORD heareth the poor, and despiseth not his prisoners.

34 Let the heaven and earth praise him, the seas, and every thing that moveth therein.

35 For God will save Zion, and will build the cities of Judah : that they may dwell there, and have it in possession.

36 The seed also of his servants shall inherit it : and they that love his name shall dwell therein.

Imprecations, prophecies, and complaints are ended, and prayer of a milder sort begins, intermingled with bursts of thankful song, and encouraging foresights of coming good.

29. *"But I am poor and sorrowful."* The Psalmist was afflicted very much, but his faith was in God. The poor in spirit and mourners are both blessed under the gospel, so that here is a double reason for the Lord to smile on his suppliant. No man was ever poorer or more sorrowful than Jesus of Nazareth, yet his cry out of the depths was heard, and he was uplifted to the highest glory. *"Let thy salvation, O God, set me up on high."* How fully has this been answered in our great Master's case, for he not only escaped his foes personally, but he has become the author of eternal salvation to all who obey him, and this continues to glorify him more and more. O ye poor and sorrowful ones, lift up your heads, for as with your Lord so shall it be with you. You are trodden down to-day as the mire of the streets, but you shall ride upon the high places of the earth ere long ; and even now ye are raised up together, and made to sit together in the heavenlies in Christ Jesus.

30. *"I will praise the name of God with a song."* He who sang after the passover, sings yet more joyously after the resurrection and ascension. He is, in very truth, "the sweet singer of Israel." He leads the eternal melodies, and all his saints join in chorus. *"And will magnify him with thanksgiving."* How sure was our Redeemer of ultimate victory, since he vows a song even while yet in the furnace. In us, also, faith foresees the happy issue of all affliction, and makes us even now begin the music of gratitude which shall go on for ever increasing in volume, world without end. What clear shining after the rain we have in this and succeeding verses. The darkness is past, and the glory light shines forth as the sun. All the honour is

rendered unto him to whom all the prayer was presented ; he alone could deliver and did deliver, and, therefore, to him only be the praise.

31. *"This also shall please the Lord better than an ox or bullock that hath horns and hoofs."* No sacrifice is so acceptable to God, who is a Spirit, as that which is spiritual. He accepted bullocks under a dim and symbolical dispensation ; but in such offerings, in themselves considered, he had no pleasure. " Will I eat the flesh of bulls, or drink the blood of goats ? " Here he puts dishonour upon mere outward offerings by speaking of the horns and hoofs, the offal of the victim. The *opus operatum*, which our ritualists think so much of, the Lord puffs at. The horning and hoofing are nothing to him, though to Jewish ritualists these were great points, and matters for critical examination ; our modern rabbis are just as precise as to the mingling of water with their wine, the baking of their wafers, the cut of their vestments, and the performance of genuflections towards the right quarter of the compass. O fools, and slow of heart to perceive all that the Lord has declared. " Offer unto God thanksgiving " is the everlasting rubric of the true directory of worship. The depths of grief into which the suppliant had been plunged gave him all the richer an experience of divine power and grace in his salvation, and so qualified him to sing more sweetly " the song of loves." Such music is ever most acceptable to the infinite Jehovah.

32. *"The humble shall see this, and be glad."* Grateful hearts are ever on the look out for recruits, and the rejoicing Psalmist discerns with joy the fact, that other oppressed and lowly men observing the Lord's dealings with his servants are encouraged to look for a like issue to their own tribulations. The standing consolation of the godly is the experience of their Lord, for as he is so are we also in this world ; yea, moreover, his triumph has secured ours, and therefore, we may on the most solid grounds rejoice in him. This gave our great leader satisfaction as he foresaw the comforts which would flow to us from his conflict and conquest. *"And your heart shall live that seek God."* A similar assurance is given in Psalm xxii., which is near akin to this. It would have been useless to seek if Jesus' victories had not cleared the way, and opened a door of hope ; but, since the Breaker has gone up before us, and the King at the head of us, our hope is a living one, our faith is living, our love is living, and our renewed nature is full of a vitality which challenges the cold hand of death to damp it.

33. *"For the Lord heareth the poor."* The examples of David and David's Lord, and tens of thousands of the saints, all go to prove this. Monarchs of the nations are deaf to the poor, but the Sovereign of the Universe has a quick ear for the needy. None can be brought lower than was the Nazarene, but see how highly he is exalted : descend into what depths we may, the prayer-hearing God can bring us up again. *"And despiseth not his prisoners."* Poor men have their liberty, but these are bound ; however, they are God's prisoners, and, therefore, prisoners of hope. The captive in the dungeon is the lowest and least esteemed of men, but the Lord seeth not as man seeth ; he visited those who are bound with chains, and proclaims a jail-delivery for his afflicted. God despises no man, and no prayer that is honest and sincere. Distinctions of rank are nothing with him ; the poor have the gospel preached to them, and the prisoners are loosed by his grace. Let all poor and needy ones hasten to seek his face, and to yield him their love.

34. *"Let the heavens and earth praise him, the seas, and every thing that moveth therein."* The doxology of a glowing heart. The writer had fathomed the deeps, and had ascended to the heights ; and, therefore, calls on the whole range of creation to bless the Lord. Our Well-Beloved here excites us all to grateful adoration : who among us will hold back ? God's love to Christ argues good to all forms of life ; the exaltation of the Head brings good to the members, and to all in the least connected with him. Inasmuch as the creation itself also is by Christ's work to be delivered from bondage, let all that have life and motion magnify the Lord. Glory be unto thee, O Lord, for the sure and all-including pledge of our Surety's triumph : we see in this the exaltation of all thy poor and sorrowful ones, and our heart is glad.

35. *"For God will save Zion, and will build the cities of Judah."* Poor, fallen Israel shall have a portion in the mercy of the Lord ; but, above all, the church, so dear to the heart of her glorious bridegroom, shall be revived and strengthened. Ancient saints so dearly loved Zion, that even in their distresses they did not forget her ; with the first gleam of light which visited them, they fell to pleading for the faithful : see notable instances of this which have passed under our eye already.

Psalms v. 11, xiv. 7, xxii. 23, li. 18. To us, in these modern times, it is the subject of cheering hope that better days are coming for the chosen people of God, and for this we would ever pray. O Zion, whatever other memories fade away, we cannot forget thee. *"That they may dwell there, and have it in possession."* Whatever captivities may occur, or desolations be caused, the land of Canaan belongs to Israel by a covenant of salt, and they will surely repossess it ; and this shall be a sign unto us, that through the atonement of the Christ of God, all the poor in spirit shall enjoy the mercies promised in the covenant of grace. The sure mercies of David shall be the heritage of all the seed.

36. *"The seed also of his servants shall inherit it."* Under this image, which, however, we dare not regard as a mere simile, but as having in itself a literal significance, we have set forth to us the enrichment of the saints, consequent upon the sorrow of their Lord. The termination of this Psalm strongly recalls in us that of the twenty-second. The *seed* lie near the Saviour's heart, and their enjoyment of all promised good is the great concern of his disinterested soul. Because they are his Father's servants, therefore he rejoices in their welfare. *"And they that love his name shall dwell therein."* He has an eye to the Father's glory, for it is to his praise that those who love him should attain, and for ever enjoy, the utmost happiness. Thus a Psalm, which began in the deep waters, ends in the city which hath foundations. How gracious is the change. Hallelujah.

EXPLANATORY NOTES AND QUAINT SAYINGS.

Title.—*"To the Chief Musician, on the lilies, of David."* *"On the lilies,"* points to the beauty of the subject treated of.—*E. W. Hengstenberg.*

Whole Psalm.—The subject of the Psalm is an ideal person, representing the whole class of religious sufferers. The only individual in whom the various traits meet is Christ. That he is not, however, the exclusive, or even the immediate subject, is clear from the confession in verse 5. There is no Psalm, except the twenty-second, more distinctly applied to him in the New Testament.—*Joseph Addison Alexander.*

Whole Psalm.—This has usually been regarded as a Messianic Psalm. No portion of the Old Testament Scriptures is more frequently quoted in the New, with the exception of Psalm xxii. When Jesus drives the buyers and sellers from the temple (John ii. 17), his disciples are reminded of the words of verse 9 (first clause). When it is said (John xv. 25) that the enemies of Jesus hated him without a cause, this is looked upon as the fulfilment of Scripture, the reference is probably to verse 4, though it may be also to xxv. 18. To him, and the reproach which he endured for the sake of God, St. Paul refers the words of this Psalm, verse 9 (second clause), " The reproaches of them that reproached thee are fallen upon me." In verse 12 we have a foreshadowing of the mockery of our Lord by the soldiers in the prætorium (Matt. xxvii. 27—30) ; in verse 21, the giving of the vinegar and the gall found their counterpart in the scenes of the crucifixion, Matt. xxvii. 34. In John xix. 28 there is an allusion, probably to verse 21 of this Psalm, and to xxii. 15. The imprecation in verse 25 is said, in Acts i. 20, to have been fulfilled in the case of Judas Iscariot, though, as the words of the Psalm are plural, the citation is evidently made with some freedom. According to Rom. xi. 9, 10, the rejection of Israel may best be described in the words of verses 22, 23.—*J. J. Stewart Perowne.*

Whole Psalm.—This Psalm follows in striking connection with the preceeding, and in contrast with the glory of his kingdom. The two have been compared to the transfiguration on the mount, where, after the manifestation of Christ in glory, there appeared also Moses and Elias, and spake of his decease which he should accomplish at Jerusalem. The clearest anticipation of future glory must not shut out the conviction, that it is through much tribulation we must enter the kingdom.— *W. Wilson.*

Whole Psalm.—Remember this is the fourth Psalm which declares at length the passion and resurrection of our Lord. Through the whole Psalm Christ speaks in person. He prays for deliverance by the Father, because he has suffered by the

Jews, without cause, many afflictions and persecutions. He supplicates on behalf of his members, that the hope of the faithful, resting on his resurrection, may not be disappointed. By the power of his prescience he declares the future events which should occur to his enemies.—*Magnus Aurelius Cassiodorus, circa* 468—560.

Whole Psalm.—In this Psalm the whole Christ speaks ; now in his own person, now crying with the voice of his members to God his father.—*Gerhohus.*

Verse 1.—"*Save me, O God.*" Let his distances be never so great, he is resolved to cry after the Lord ; and if he get but his head never so little above water, the Lord shall hear of him. One would think his discouragements such as he were past crying any more ; *the waters entered into his soul, in deep waters, the streams running over him : he sticketh fast in the mire where is no standing* (he is at the very bottom, and there fast in the mire), *he is weary of crying ;* yet, verses 6, 13 : *But, Lord, I make my prayer to thee :* and as he recovers breath, so breathes out fresh supplications to the Lord. If men or devils would be forbidding to pray, as the multitude sometimes did the poor blind man to cry after Jesus ; yet, as he, so an importunate suppliant "*will cry so much the more,* Jesus, thou Son of David, have mercy on me." Mark x. 47, 48.—*Thomas Cobbet.*

Verse 1.—"*The waters are come in unto my soul.*" What means he by *coming in unto his soul ?* Surely no other than this :—that they oppressed his spirit, and, as it were, penetrated into his conscience, raising fears and perplexities there, by reason of his sins, which at present put his faith and hope to some disorder ; so that he could not for a while see to the comfortable end of his affliction, but was as one under water, covered with his fears, as appears by what follows (verse 2) : "*I sink in deep mire, where there is no standing.*" He compares himself to one in a quagmire that can feel no ground to bear him up ; and, observe whence his trouble rose, and where the waters made their entrance (verse 5) : "*O God, thou knowest my foolishness ; and my sins are not hid from thee.*" This holy man lay under some fresh guilt, and this made him so uncomfortable under his affliction, because he saw his sin in the face of that, and tasted some displeasure from God for it in his outward trouble, which made it so bitter in the going down ; and, therefore, when once he had humbled himself by confessing his sin, and was able to see the coast clear between heaven and him, so as to believe the pardon of his sin, and hope for good news from God again, he then returns to his sweet temper, and sings in the same affliction, where before he sunk.—*William Gurnall.*

Verse 2.—"*I sink in deep mire.*" I was taking a quiet walk along the banks [of the Nile], when I came to a part so soft and miry that I was brought to a stand, as my foot sank at every step. . . . . Being brought to a stand, I hailed the reis to heave to, and take me on board. One of the men was, therefore, sent in the small boat ; but the river, near the western side, was so shallow that he could not get the boat within some distance of the bank. He, consequently, as is usual in such cases, jumped overboard that he might carry me to the boat on his back. No sooner, however, had he sprung from the boat than I heard him scream. I turned to see what was the matter, when I found him struggling in the mud. He was sinking as though in quicksand ; and the more he struggled, the faster and deeper he sank. His fellow-boatmen were not slack. They quickly saw the dilemma he was in, and two of them dashed into the water and swam to the small boat. I was almost choked with terror, and I breathed, or rather gasped, with difficulty. " Can they reach the poor fellow ? " I said to myself ; " if not, he must inevitably be swallowed up alive ! " Now they reach the boat ! Now they near him ! And now, praise the Lord, he grasps firmly hold. O that death-like grasp of the side of the boat ! But this was not until he had sunk up to his bosom ! Seeing him safe, I breathed more freely ; and I feel that now, though only relating the circumstance, the excitement has caused an increased and painful action of the heart. How I thought of poor David ! Had he really witnessed a similar scene to this literally when, speaking of the feelings of his soul, spiritually, he said : "*I sink in deep mire, where there is no standing : I am come into deep waters, where the floods overflow me* " ? O what an agonising state to be in ! and yet many of my readers, I have no doubt, who never witnessed such a scene literally, know something about it spiritually, as David did, whether he had seen it with his bodily eyes or not. Well might he, in the struggling of his soul, exclaim : "*Deliver me out of the mire, and let me not sink !* " Let me grasp firmly hold of the ark, and be pulled safely on board ! Well ! just at the right time, just before the poor fellow's arms (shall I say his arms of faith?) were disabled, swallowed up, deliverance came.—*John Gadsby, in "My Wanderings."*

Verse 2.—*"I sink,"*—*" there is no standing."* I saw indeed there was cause of rejoicing for those that held to Jesus; but as for me, I had cut myself off by my transgressions, and left myself neither foot-hold, nor hand-hold, amongst all the stays and props in the precious word of life. And truly I did now feel myself to sink into a gulf, as an house whose foundation is destroyed; I did liken myself, in this condition, unto the case of a child that was fallen into a mill-pit, who, though it could make some shift to scrabble and sprawl in the water, yet, because it could find neither hold for hand nor foot, therefore, at last, it must die in that condition.—*John Bunyan.*

Verse 2.—*"Mire."* If the abyss be only full of water, a good swimmer has still the hope of rising again to the surface.—*The Berleb. Bible.*

Verse 2.—*"Where the floods overflow me."* The plea in effect is this: Lord, I am ready to drown; if ever thou wouldst save a poor perishing servant of thine, save me: my troubles and temptations are too deep for me, I am ready to sink over head and ears in them, and therefore, Lord, reach hither thy gracious hand, and bear up my head above water, lest otherwise I miscarry. Especially if such extremities continue, the continuance of them may be pleaded.—*Thomas Cobbet.*

Verse 2.—*"The floods overflow me."* The word *flood* in these two verses is the well-known Shibboleth which the Ephraimites were unable to pronounce. Jud. xii. 6. It occurs again, Isaiah xxvii. 12, " flood of the river."—*J. J. Stewart Perowne.*

Verse 3.—*"I am weary of my crying."* The word יגע means properly, *to gape, to gasp*, then, *to become weary. . . . .* but, *to gasp in his crying*, is not so much to grow weary because of the great vehemence thereof, but while the crying lasts, and while he is in the act, to succumb under the burden of his dangerous and shameful calamity. —*Hermann Venema.*

Verse 3.—*"I am weary of my crying."* He had cried to God for the ways of man; he had cried to man of the ways of God; he had not ceased, from his first beginning to teach, till he said upon the cross, " I thirst." His eyes had grown dim, and his flesh was faint and weary with his sufferings, through the long passion of his life on earth. He had been waiting in poverty, and insult, and treachery, and scourging, and pain, until he cried, " My God, my God, why hast thou forsaken me? "—*From "A Plain Commentary."*

Verse 3.—*"I am weary of my crying,"* etc. David is like the post, who layeth by three horses as breathless; his heart, his throat, his eyes. . . . . *Objection.* But I have neither weeping one way or other, ordinary nor marred. *Answer.* Looking up to heaven, lifting up of the eyes, goeth for prayer also in God's books. " My prayer unto thee, and will look up," (Psalm v. 3). *"Mine eyes fail with looking upward"* (Psalm lxix. 3). Because, first, prayer is a pouring out of the soul to God, and faith will come out at the eye, in lieu of another door: often affections break out at the window, when the door is closed; as smoke venteth at the window, when the chimney refuseth passage. Stephen looked up to heaven (Acts vii. 55). He sent a post; a greedy, pitiful, and hungry look up to Christ, out at the window, at the nearest passage, to tell that a poor friend was coming up to him. Second. I would wish no more, if I were in hell, but to send a look up to heaven. There be many love-looks of the saints, lying up before the throne, in the bosom of Christ. The twinkling of thy eyes in prayer are not lost to Christ; else Stephen's look, David's look, should not be registered so many hundred years in Christ's written Testament.—*Samuel Rutherford, in "The Trial and Triumph of Faith."*

Verse 3.—*"Crying."* Meanwhile, we see how the saints, in the vicissitudes of affairs, even when they are innocent, are not insensible and stony; they do not despise the threatening perils; they become anxious, they cry and sigh during their temptations.—*Musculus.*

Verse 3.—*"Mine eyes fail."* O pitiable sight! that that sight should fail, by which Jesus saw the multitudes and, therefore, ascended the mount to give the precepts of the New Testament; by which, beholding Peter and Andrew, he called them; by which, looking upon the man sitting at the receipt of custom, he called and made him an evangelist; by which, gazing upon the city, he wept over it. . . . With these eyes thou didst look upon Simon, when thou didst say, *"Thou art the son of Jonas; thou shalt be called Cephas."* With these eyes thou didst gaze upon the woman who was a sinner, to whom thou didst say, *"Thy faith hath saved thee;*

go in peace."   Turn these eyes upon us, and never turn them away from our continual prayers.—*Gerhohus.*

Verse 3.—"*I wait for my God.*"   The hour is coming when our eyes must fail, and be closed ; but, even then, "*Let us wait for our God* ; " in this respect, let us die the death of the righteous person, who died for us ; " and let our last end be like his."—*George Horne.*

Verse 4.—"*Without a cause.*"   In suffering, let not the mind be disturbed ; for the injustice which is done to the innocent in his sufferings, is not laid to the charge of the sufferer, but to his who inflicts suffering. . . . It is well known what Tertullian relates of Socrates, when his wife met him after his condemnation, and addressed him with a woman's tears : "*Thou art unjustly condemned, Socrates.*"   His reply was, "*Wouldst thou have me justly ?*"—*Lorinus.*

Verse 4.—"*Then I restored that which I took not away.*"   It was the great and blessed work of our Lord Jesus here upon the earth, to restore what he took not away.   In handling this : I. Show what is it which was taken away, and from whom ?   II. Wherein it appears that Christ took it not away.   III. How he restored it ?   IV. Why he did so ?   V. Use.

I. *What is it which was taken away, and from whom ?*   1. There was glory taken from God.   Not his essential glory, nor any perfection of his being, for that cannot be taken away ; but that glory which shines forth in the moral government of his creatures, and that glory which we are bound to give him.   2. There was righteousness, holiness, and happiness taken from man also.   (1) There was a loss of righteousness to the guilty sinner ; (2) of holiness to the polluted sinner ; (3) of happiness to the miserable sinner.   II. *Wherein it appears that Christ did not take away those things from either.*   1. It is plain, as to God, he never took away any glory from him ; for he never did anything dishonourable or offensive to God. John viii. 29 ; Isaiah l. 5 ; Luke i. 35.   2. It is also clear, as to man, that he took not away any righteousness, holiness, or happiness from him.   He was not such a fountain of guilt, pollution, and misery, as the first Adam had been, but the contrary.   3. The Scripture, therefore, speaks of Christ's being cut off, but not for himself, Dan. ix. 26 ; 1 Pet. iii. 18 ; Isa. liii. 4, 5.   4. The innocency of Christ was conspicuous in his very sufferings.   Though they found no cause of death in him, yet desired they Pilate that he should be slain.   Acts xiii. 28.   III. *How did Christ restore those things which he took not away ?*   In general, by his active and passive obedience.   1. Christ's doing the will of God in such a manner as he did it, was a greater honour to God than ever had been, or could be done before.   2. Christ's suffering of the will of God, made a considerable addition to the glory of God, which had been impaired by the sin of man, Heb. v. 8 ; John xvii. 4 ; and xiii. 31.   3. Christ hath provided for the justification of the sinner by the obedience which he fulfilled, Rom. v. 8.   4. Christ communicates that grace which is necessary for our sanctification also.   5. Christ hath merited for us a present blessedness in this world.   6. Jesus Christ hath procured for us a more full and absolute blessedness in the world to come.   IV. *Why did Jesus Christ make it his work to restore what he took not away ?*   1. It was a necessary work, a work which must be done, in order to his being a Saviour.   2. It was a work impossible for any mere creature to do ; so that if Christ did not, it could not be done by any person besides him.—*Timothy Cruso's Sermon.*

Verse 4.—"*Then I restored that which I took not away.*"   Rosenmüller observes, that this seems to be a proverbial sentence, to denote an innocent man unjustly treated.   According to the law, if a man stole and killed, or sold an ox, he was to restore five oxen ; or a sheep, he was to restore four ; and if the ox or sheep was found alive, he was to restore two..   Hence, to oblige a man to restore when he had taken nothing, was the greatest injustice.   Exod. xxii. 1—5.   Ainsworth observes, that though it may be taken for all unjust criminations, whereof David and Christ were innocent, yet in special, it was verified in Christ, who, " being in the form of God, thought it no robbery to be equal with God," Phil. ii. 6 ; notwithstanding, for witnessing himself to be the Son of God, he was put to death by the Jews. John xix. 7.—*Benjamin Boothroyd.*

Verse 4.—"*I restored that which I took not away.*"   The devil took away by arrogating in heaven what was not his, when he boasted that he was like the Most High, and for this he pays a righteous penalty. . . . Adam also took away what was not his own, when, by the enticement of the devil, " You will be as gods," he sought after a likeness to God, by yielding to the deception of the woman. But the Lord Jesus thought it not robbery to be equal with God. . . . And yet his enemies said, " Let him be crucified, for he hath made himself the Son of God."—*Gerhohus.*

Verse 4.—"*I restored that which I took not away.*" What a blessed verse is here! Amidst all the opposition and contradiction of sinners against himself, Jesus manifested that character, by which Jehovah had pointed him out to the church by the prophet ; " Thou shalt raise up the foundations of many generations ; and thou shalt be called, the repairer of the breach, the restorer of paths to dwell in." Isaiah lviii. 12. But what was it Christ restored ? Nay, all that was lost. Adam by sin had done all that he could to take away God's glory, and with it his own glory and happiness. He had robbed God of his glory, God's law of its due, himself of God's image, and of God's favour. Sin had brought in death, spiritual and eternal ; and he and all his descendants stood tremblingly exposed to everlasting misery. All these and more Jesus restored. As man's Surety and man's Representative, and called to it by the authority of Jehovah, the Lord Christ restored to God his glory, and man God's image of favour ; and having destroyed sin, death, hell, and the grave, he restored to his redeemed a better paradise than our nature had lost ! Hail ! oh, thou blessed Restorer of all our long lost privileges.—*Robert Hawker.*

Verse 5.—"*Thou knowest.*" The knowledge of God is of a double use to pious men. The first is, as we observe in this place, to console the innocent : the second is, to make them circumspect, since all their thoughts, and words, and deeds are under the very eye of God.—*Musculus.*

Verse 5.—"*Thou knowest my offences,*" etc., that is to say, that I am not an offender. This verse is not a confession of sin, but a protestation of innocence. The writer maintains that he is a sufferer, not for his sins, but for his piety. See verses 7, etc.—*George R. Noyes, in "A New Translation of the Book of Psalms, with Notes," etc. 1846.*

Verse 5.—"*My sins are not hid from thee.*" The sins of those for whom Christ died, by being imputed to him, no doubt became his in the eye of the law, in such a sense as to make him answerable for them. But the Scriptures, be it observed, while they speak of him as " wounded for *our* transgressions, and bruised for *our* iniquities," and as " bearing *our* sins in his own body on the tree," as if afraid to use any forms of expression which would even seem to derogate from his immaculate purity, never speak of the sins of those for whom he died as his *own* sins.—*James Anderson's Note to Calvin in loc.*

Verse 5.—"*My sins are not hid.*" Not as the first Adam, do I, the second Adam, hide myself or my *sins*, especially in thy sight, O God; but lifted up upon the cross I suffered without the gate for *sins* in such a way, that I desire that *my sins* should be conspicuous to every creature in heaven, earth, and hell—*my sins* which, as they refer to my person, are marked with no taint, and, as they pertain to my people believing in me, are blotted out by my blood.—*Gerhohus.*

Verse 6.—"*Let not them that wait on thee, O Lord God of hosts, be ashamed for my sake,*" etc. This says, that unless the carriage and deportment of the godly man redounds to the comfort of all the rest of the godly, it in some way tends to the discredit of the godly. Since this is the case, when they slip aside, or carry not aright ; since they are all in hazard of doing so, it should be matter of affecting and afflicting exercise, lest they do so. Fellow professors are ashamed of the person that walketh not aright ; they are ashamed that ever they should have been in company or fellowship with him ; they are ashamed that ever such a person should have owned such a cause, and that ever such a thing should have befallen a professor of such a cause ; and, besides, they are weakened by him in their hopes of persevering for themselves. Again, they are in hazard of being a discredit to all the godly, because, say they, it seems the Lord has granted no peremptory promise, as to the manner of their final perseverance ; and corruption enough remains in them still, to overturn all their stock of grace, if they get not present renewed influences.—*William Guthrie, 1620—1655.*

Verse 6.—"*Ashamed for my sake.*" I pray that they may *not be confounded* by external enemies with their boundless insults and reproaches, because they seem to be the worshippers of a God crucified and dead, and are themselves like dead men, and lie rotting before his sepulchre, as if their good name were gone. Rather let my enemies who do not wish me to live be terror-stricken at my angelic countenance, and fall like the dead.—*Gerhohus*.

Verse 6.—*"For my sake."* ‏ב‎: more exactly, *"in me."* In these words the voice of the Sponsor of his people's peace is clearly audible. The prayer of the Sufferer has its answer in the declarative testimony which now forms the basis of the gospel: " He that believeth on him shall not be confounded." 1 Peter ii. 6. —*Arthur Pridham*.

Verse 6.—Because I, for their sakes, do at thy command bear that shame which they should else have done, Lord, take it off from them, because thou hast laid it upon me ; so it expressly follows, verse 7: " Because for thy sake I have borne reproach ; shame hath covered my face."—*Thomas Goodwin*.

Verse 7.—*"Shame hath covered my face."* It is a great question whether shame or death be the greater evil. There have been those who have rather chosen death, and have wiped off a dishonour with their blood. So Saul slew himself rather than he would fall into the hands of the Philistines, who would have insulted over him, and mocked him as they did Samson. So that king (Jer. xxxviii. 19) rather chose to lose his country, life, and all, than to be given to the Jews, his subjects, to be mocked of them. . . . Confusion of face is one of the greatest miseries that hell itself is set forth unto us by. There is nothing that a noble nature more abhors than shame, for honour is a spark of God's image ; and the more of God's image there is in any one, the more is shame abhorred by him, which is the debasing of it, and so the greater and more noble any one's spirit, the more he avoids it. To a base, low spirit, indeed, shame is nothing ; but to a great spirit (as to David), than to have his " glory turned into shame," as Psalm iv. 2, is nothing more grievous. And the greater glory any loseth, the greater is his shame. What must it be then to Christ, who because he was to satisfy God in point of honour debased by man's sin, therefore of all punishments besides, he suffered most of shame ; it being also (as was said) one of the greatest punishments in hell. And Christ, as he assumed other infirmities of our nature, that made him possible in other things—as to be sensible of hunger, want of sleep, bodily torments, of unkindnesses, contempt, so likewise of disgrace and shame. He took that infirmity as well as fear ; and though he had a strength to bear and despise it (as the author to the Hebrews speaks), yet none was ever more sensible of it. As the delicacy of the temper of his body made him more sensible of pains than ever any man was, so the greatness of his spirit made him more apprehensive of the evil of shame than ever any was. So likewise the infinite love and candour of his spirit towards mankind made him take in with answerable grief the unkindnesses and injuries which they heaped upon him.—*Thomas Goodwin*.

Verse 8.—*"A stranger unto my brethren."* Unless this aversion of his brethren had pained him, he would not have complained of it. It would not have pained him unless he had felt a special affection for them.—*Musculus*.

Verse 8.—In the east where polygamy prevails, the husband is a stern and unfeeling despot ; his harem a group of trembling slaves ; and the children, while they regard their common father with indifference or terror, cling to their own mother with the fondest affection, as the only part, as the only parent, in whom they feel an interest. Hence it greatly aggravated the affliction of David that he had become *"an alien unto his mother's children :"* the enmity of the other children of his father, the children of his father's other wives, gave him less concern.— *W. Greenfield, in Comprehensive Bible*.

Verse 9.—*"For the zeal of thine house hath eaten me up."* He who recollects that the Scriptures speak of a " peace which passeth understanding," and a " joy unspeakable and full of glory," will be more disposed to lament the low state of his own feeling, than to suspect the propriety of sentiments the most rational and scriptural, merely because they rise to a pitch that he has never reached. The Sacred Oracles afford no countenance to the supposition that devotional feelings are to be condemned as visionary and enthusiastic merely on account of their intenseness and elevation ; provided they be of the right kind, and spring from legitimate sources, they never teach us to suspect they can be carried too far. David danced before the Lord with all his might, and when he was reproached for degrading himself in the eyes of his people by indulging in such transports, he replied, " If this be vile, I will yet make myself more vile." That the objects which interest the heart in religion are infinitely more durable and important than all others will not be disputed; and why should it be deemed irrational to be affected by them in a degree somewhat suitable to their value?—*Robert Hall.* 1764—1831.

Verse 9.—*"The zeal of thine house hath eaten me up."* Consider the examples of the saints of old, who have taken heaven by force. David broke his sleep for meditation. Psalm cxix. 148. His violence for heaven was boiled up to zeal, Psalm cxix. 139: "My zeal hath consumed me." And Paul did *"reach forth* (ἐπεκτεινόμενος) unto those things which were before. The Greek word signifies to stretch out the neck, a metaphor taken from racers that strain every limb, and reach forward to lay hold upon the prize. We read of Anna, a prophetess (Luke ii. 37); "she departed not from the temple, but served God with fastings and prayers night and day." How industrious was Calvin in the Lord's vineyard. When his friends persuaded him for his health's sake to remit a little of his labour, saith he, "Would you have the Lord find me idle when he comes?" Luther spent three hours a day in prayer. It is said of holy Bradford, preaching, reading, and prayer, was his whole life. I rejoice, said bishop Jewel, that my body is exhausted in the labours of my holy calling. How violent were the blessed martyrs! They wore their fetters as ornaments, they snatched up torments as crowns, and embraced the flames as cheerfully as Elijah did the fiery chariot that came to fetch him to heaven. Let racks, fires, pullies, and all manner of torments come, so I may win Christ, said Ignatius. These pious souls "resisted unto blood." How should this provoke our zeal! Write after these fair copies.—*Thomas Watson.*

Verse 9.—*"The zeal of thine house hath eaten me up."* Zeal in and for true religion is a praiseworthy thing. Was *David* zealous? it may then become a royal spirit. Was *Christ* our Saviour zealous? it may become an heroical spirit. Albeit, zeal is out of grace with most men who sit still, and love to be at quiet rest; yet it is no disgrace to any generous spirit that is regenerate, to have the zeal of God's house to eat him up. It is a slander to call it folly. Was not zealous David wiser than his teachers, than his enemies, than the aged? Lukewarm men call it fury; God's Spirit names it a "live coal," that hath a most vehement flame. Why bears zeal the imputation of indiscretion, rashness, puritanism, or headiness? Was it David's rashness? It was fervency in religion. Was Christ indiscreet? The wisdom of his Father. Festus called Paul mad, with a loud voice (Acts xxvi. 24), when he spake but words of truth and soberness (verse 25). Christ's kinsmen thought that he was beside himself. Mark iii. 21. Was the judgment of such stolid men any disparagement to our Saviour's zeal? Nay, it is a commendation. To root out evil from, and to establish good in, the house of God is a good thing. Gal. iv. 18. *Thomas Wilson, in "A Sermon preached before sundry of the Honourable House of Commons," entitled, "David's Zeale for Zion."* 1641.

Verse 9.—*"Zeal," "reproaches."* Grace never rises to so great a height as it does in times of persecution. Suffering times are a Christian's harvest times. Let me instance in that grace of zeal: I remember Moulin speaking of the French Protestants, saith, "When Papists hurt us for reading the Scriptures, we burn with zeal to be reading of them; but now persecution is over, our Bibles are like old almanacks," etc. All the reproaches, frowns, threatenings, oppositions, and persecutions that a Christian meets with in a way of holiness, do but raise his zeal and courage to a greater height. Michal's scoffing at David did but inflame and raise his zeal: "If this be to be vile, I will be more vile," 2 Sam. vi. 20—22. Look, as fire in the winter burns the hotter, by an ἀντιπερίστασις, because of the coldness of the air; so in the winter of affliction and persecution, that divine fire, the zeal of a Christian, burns so much the hotter, and flames forth so much the more vehemently and strongly. In times of greatest affliction and persecution for holiness' sake, a Christian hath, first, a good captain to lead and encourage him; secondly, a righteous cause to prompt and embolden him; thirdly, a gracious God to relieve and succour him; fourthly, a glorious heaven to receive and reward him; and, certainly, these things cannot but mightily raise him and inflame him under the greatest opposition and persecution. These things will keep him from fearing, fawning, fainting, sinking, or flying in a stormy day; yea, these things will make his face like the face of an adamant, as God promised to make Ezekiel's. Ezekiel iii. 7—9, and Job xli. 24. Now an adamant is the hardest of stones, it is harder than a flint, yea, it is harder than the nether-millstone. The naturalists [Pliny] observe, that the hardness of this stone is unspeakable: the fire cannot burn it, nor so much as heat it through, nor the hammer cannot break it, nor the water cannot dissolve it, and, therefore, the Greeks call it an adamant from its untameableness ; and in all storms the adamant shrinks not, it shrinks not, it fears not, it changeth not its hue ; let the times be what they will, the adamant is still the same. In times of persecution, a good cause, a good God, and a good conscience will make a Christian like an adamant, it will make him invincible and unchangeable. When one desired to know what kind of man Basil was, there was presented to him in a dream, saith the history, a pillar of fire with this motto, *Talis est Basilius*, Basil is such a one, he is all on a-light fire for God.   Persecutions will but set a Christian all on a-light fire for God.—*Thomas Brooks.*

Verse 9.—*"Eaten me up."*   The verb means, not only " to eat up, to devour," but " to corrode or consume," by separating the parts from each other, as fire. And the radical import of the Hebrew word for *"zeal"* seems to be " to eat into, corrode, as fire."   The word says Parkhurst, is in the Hebrew Bible generally applied to the fervent or ardent affections of the human frame ; the effects of which are well known to be ever like those of fire, corroding and consuming.   And, accordingly, the poets, both ancient and modern, abound with descriptions of these ardent and consuming affections, taken from fire and its effects.—*Richard Mant.*

Verse 9.—*"Eaten me up."*   He who is zealous in his religion, or ardent in his attachments, is said to be eaten up.   " Old Muttoo has determined to leave his home for ever ; he is to walk barefoot to the Ganges for the salvation of his soul : his zeal has eaten him up."—*J. Roberts' Oriental Illustrations.*

Verse 9.—*"The reproaches of them that reproached thee are fallen upon me."*   We should, if it were possible, labour to wipe off all the reproach of Christ, and take it upon ourselves that we might rather be spit upon and contemned than Christ.   It was a brave speech of Ambrose, " he wished it would please God to turn all the adversaries from the church upon himself, and let them satisfy their thirst with his blood : " this is a true Christian heart.   And, therefore, if it be for our sakes, and we have anything in the business by which Christ is reproached, we should be willing rather to sacrifice ourselves, than that Christ should be reproached ; and as Jonah, when he knew that the tempest rose for his sake, says he, " Cast me into the sea ; " and so Nazianzen, when contention rose about him, says he, " Cast me into the sea, let me lose my place, rather than the name of Christ should suffer for me."—*Jeremiah Burroughs.*

Verse 10.—*"When I wept, and chastened my soul with fasting, that was to my reproach."*   Behold here, virtue is accounted vice ; truth, blasphemy ; wisdom, folly.   Behold, the peace-maker of the world is judged a seditious person ; the fulfiller of the law, a breaker of the law ; our Saviour, a sinner ; our God, a devil. O poor troubled heart ! wherefore dost thou weakly wail for any injury or abuse that is offered to thee ?   God handleth thee no otherwise in this world than he handled his only Son, who hath pledged thee in this bitter potion ; not only taking essay thereof, but drinking to thee a full draught.   It is not only a comfort, but a glory, to be a partner and fellow-sufferer with Christ, who delighteth also to see in us some representation of himself.   Dogs bark not at those whom they know, and with whom they are familiar ; but against strangers they usually bark ; not always for any hurt which they feel or fear, but commonly by nature or depraved custom.   How then canst thou be a stranger to the world, if it doth not molest thee ; if it detracteth not from thee ?—*Sir John Hayward* (1560—1627), *in "The Sanctuary of a Troubled Soule."*

Verse 10.—There is nothing so well meant, but it may be ill interpreted.—*Simon Patrick.*

Verses 10, 11.—That Christ was derided and scoffed at is plain, from Mark v. ; for, when he said, " The girl is not dead, but sleepeth, they laughed him to scorn ; " and when he spoke of the necessity of giving alms, " Now, the Pharisees, who were covetous, heard all these things, and they derided him."   And, in his passion, he was derided by the soldiers, by Herod, by the high priests, and many others.—*Robert Bellarmine.*

Verse 11.—*"I made sackcloth also my garment,"* etc.   Though we nowhere read that Jesus put on *sackcloth* on any occasion, yet it is not improbable that he did ; besides, the phrase may only intend that he mourned and sorrowed at certain times, as persons do when they put on sackcloth ; moreover, as the common garb of his forerunner was raiment of camel's hair, with a leathern girdle ; so it is very likely his own was very mean, suitable to his condition, who, though he was rich, for our sakes became poor. *"And I became a proverb to them;"* a by-word; so that, when they saw any person in sackcloth or in vile raiment, behold, such an one looks like Jesus of Nazareth.—*John Gill.*

Verse 11.—*"I became a proverb."* Two things are usually implied when a man is said to be a by-word. First, that he is in a very low condition: some men are so high that the tongues of the common people dare not climb over them, but where the hedge is low every man goes over. Secondly, that he is in a despised condition: to be a by-word carries a reflexion of disgrace. He that is much spoken of, in this sense, is ill spoken of; and he is quite lost in the opinion of men, who is thus found in their discourse. . . . . Hence, observe, great sufferers in many things of this world, are the common subject of discourses, and often the subject of disgrace. Such evils as few men have felt or seen, all men will be speaking of. Great sorrows, especially if they be the sorrows of great men, are turned into songs, and poetry plays its part with the saddest disasters. . . . . Holy David met with this measure from men in the day of his sorrows: *"When I wept, and chastened my soul with fasting, that was to my reproach. I made sackcloth also my garment; and I became a proverb* (or a by-word) *to them."* In the next verse he tells us in detail who did this: *"They that sit in the gate* (that is, great ones) *speak against me, and I was the song of the drunkard,"* that is, of the common sort.—*Joseph Caryl.*

Verse 12.—*"They that sit in the gate:"* i.e., as it is generally interpreted, the judges or chief persons of the state; for the gates of cities were the places of judicature. But Hilary interprets this of those who sat *to beg* at the gates of the city; which seems a more probable interpretation, better to agree with the design of the Psalmist, and to suit with the *"drunkards,"* mentioned in the next clause.—*Samuel Burder.*

Verse 12.—*"They that sit in the gate."* The magistrates at the gate. Literally, "assessors at the gate;" "judges sitting to determine causes."—*John Mason Good.*

Verse 12.—*"I was the song of the drunkards."* Holy walking is the *drunkards' song,* as David was; and so preciseness and strictness of walking is ordinarily: the world cannot bear the burning and shining conversations of some of the saints; they are so cuttingly reproved by them, that with those heathens, they curse the sun, that by its shining doth scorch them. It is no new thing; the seed of the serpent did alway persecute the seed of the woman; and he that was born after the flesh, persecuteth him that was born after the spirit; even so it is now, saith the apostle; and so it is now, may we say. Ishmael mocked Isaac, and is it not so still? Or, if it be not so bold a sin as formerly, it is because the times, not sinners' hearts, are changed; they malign them still, watch for their halting: "report, say they, and we will report it."—*John Murcot.*

Verse 12.—*"I was the song of the drunkards."* When magistrates discountenance true religion, then it becometh a matter of derision to rascals, and to every base villain without controlment, and a table-talk to every tipler. The shame of the cross is more grievous than the rest of the trouble of it: this is the fourth time that the shame of the cross is presented unto God, in these four last verses: *"I was the song of the drunkards;"* after complaining of his being reproached and being made a proverb.—*David Dickson.*

Verse 12.—There is a tavern, or profane mirth, in drinking, and roaring, and revelling, and instead of another minstrel, David must be *the song of the drunkards;* nor can the Philistines be merry unless Samson be made the fool in the play (Judges xvi. 25): "Unless they scoff and jeer the ways and servants of God" (as Mr. Greenham saith), "the fools cannot tell how to be merry;" and then the Devil is merry with them for company. But what? Not merry without abusing their host? This some must dearly pay for, when a reckoning is called for; or, they rather called to make it. Then they will be off from their merry pins, and will find that this was very far from being the "Comfort of the Holy Ghost," wherein and whereby that good Spirit and our Comforter was grieved, and holiness scoffed and laughed at.—*Anthony Tuckney* (1599—1670), *in "A Good Day Well Improved."*

Verse 13.—*"But as for me, my prayer,"* etc. The phrase is full of emphasis; *And I, my prayer to thee:* that is, such am I altogether, this is my main occupation; as it is in Psalm cix. 4: *And I, a prayer;* this was my employment, this ever my only refuge, this my present help and remedy.—*Venema.*

Verse 13.—*"An acceptable time."* All times are not alike. We will not always find admittance at the same rate, with the same ease. As he will not always be chiding, so he will not always be so pleasing neither. We may knock, and knock again, and yet stand without a while; sometimes, so long, till our knees are ready to sink under us, our eyes ready to drop out, as well as drop with expectation, and our hearts ready to break in pieces, while none heareth, or none regardeth. We should have come before, or pitched our coming at a better time. . . . . The prophet David expressly speaks of *"an acceptable time"* to make our prayers in. And, " To-day if you will hear his voice," in the Psalmist, paraphrased by the apostle, " To-day, while it is called to-day," shows there is a set day, or days, of audience with God, wherein he sets himself, as it were, with all readiness to hear and help us—an *accepted time.* And will ye, next, know what it is that makes it so ? There are but two things that do. Either God's being in a good or pleasing disposition towards us, or our being in a good and pleasing disposition towards him. Come we but to him in either of these, and we have nicked the time; we are sure to be accepted.—*Mark Frank.* 1613—1664.

Verse 13.—

> Heavier the cross, the heartier prayer:
> The bruised herbs most fragrant are.
> If sky and wind were always fair,
> The sailor would not watch the star;
> And David's Psalms had ne'er been sung
> If grief his heart had never wrung.
>
> —*From the German.*

Verse 15.—Faith in God giveth hope to be helped, and is half a deliverance before the full deliverance come; for the Psalmist is now with his head above the water, and not so afraid as when he began the Psalm.—*David Dickson.*

Verse 15.—*"The pit."* According to Dean Stanley, the word *Beer* here used is always rendered " well," except in this and three other cases. When such wells no longer yielded a full supply of water they were used as prisons, no care being taken to cleanse out the mire remaining at the bottom. The Dean also tells us in the Appendix to his " Sinai and Palestine," that " they have a broad margin of masonry round the mouth, and often a stone filling up the orifice." The rolling of this stone over the mouth of the well was the well's " shutting her mouth; " and the poor prisoner was, to all intents and purposes, buried alive.—*C. H. S.*

Verse 17.—*"Hide not thy face from thy servant; for I am in trouble."* An upright servant, albeit he be troubled for God's cause, and do miss comfort from God; yet will he not change his Master, nor despair of his favour.—*David Dickson.*

Verse 17.—*"Hide not thy face."* The proper sense of the word סְתַר gives the meaning to the phrase, *veil not thy face from thy servant.* In this there is a reference to a king, who, to prevent promiscuous approach to his chamber, spreads a veil before it, and admits to his presence only his minister of high confidence. So in Psalm xxxi. 21. The face of God is his majesty, and his gracious and favourable presence; the *servant* of God is his minister enjoying intimate access, and *to veil the face from him* is to prevent him coming into the presence of God; and, therefore, it belongs to the servant of God to be treated in a widely different manner.—*Hermann Venema.*

Verse 17.—*"Thy servant."* Hide not, he says, from thy servant; as if he should say, such as I am, I am thy servant. It belongs to the Master to take care of his servant, if in peril for his sake. In this same verse he says he is in a strait. In verse 18 he declares that he is in jeopardy of his life.—*Musculus.*

Verse 19.—*"Thou hast known my reproach,"* etc. It is a great deal of comfort that God does take notice of our reproaches; this was the comfort of the Psalmist. If a man suffer reproach, and disgrace, and trouble for his friends, while he is abroad from them; O, says he, did my friends know what I suffer, and suffer for them, it would comfort me : if it be comfort to be known, much more when they shall be accounted their own. Christ is acquainted with all the sufferings of every member; and, therefore, do not say, I am a poor creature; who takes notice of my sufferings? Heaven takes notice of your sufferings; Christ takes notice of them better than yourselves.—*Jeremiah Burroughs.*

Verse 20.—*"Reproach hath broken my heart."* Mental emotions and passions are well known by all to affect the actions of the heart, in the way of palpitation, fainting, etc. That these emotions and passions, when in overwhelming excess, occasionally, though rarely, produce laceration or rupture of the walls of the heart, is stated by most medical authorities who have written on the affections of this organ ; and our poets even allude to this effect as an established fact.

> " The grief that does not speak,
> Whispers the o'er-fraught heart, and bids it break."

But, if ever human heart was riven and ruptured by the mere amount of mental agony that was endured, it would surely, we might even argue, *a priori*, be that of our Redeemer, when, during those dark and dreadful hours on the cross, he, "being made a curse for us," "bore our griefs, and carried our sorrows," and suffered for sin the malediction of God and man, "full of anguish," and now "exceeding sorrowful even unto death." There are theological as well as medical arguments in favour of the opinion that Christ, in reality, died from a ruptured or broken heart. If the various wondrous prophecies and minute predictions in Psalms xxii. and lxix., regarding the circumstances connected with Christ's death, be justly held as literally true, such as, " They pierced my hands and my feet," " They part my garments among them, and cast lots upon my vesture," etc., why should we regard as merely metaphorical, and not as literally true, also, the declarations in the same Psalms, *"Reproach hath broken my heart," "My heart is like wax, it is melted in the midst of my bowels."—Sir James Young Simpson* (1811—1870) *in W. Stroud's "Treatise on the Physical Cause of the Death of Christ."*

Verse 20.—*"I looked for some to take pity, but there was none."* Even under ordinary circumstances we yearn for sympathy. Without it, the heart will contract and droop, and shut like a flower in an unkindly atmosphere, but it will open again amidst the sounds of frankness and the scenes of love. When we are in trouble, this want is in proportion still more pressing ; and, for the sorrowful heart to feel alone, is a grief greater than nature can sustain. A glance of sympathy seems to help it more than the gift of untold riches ; and a loving look, even from a little child who is sorry for us, or a simple word from some homely friend, will sometimes brace the spirit to new exertions, and seem almost to waken life within the grasp of death.—*Charles Stanford, in "Central Truths."* 1859.

Verse 21.—*"They gave me also gall,"* etc. Such are the comforts often administered, by the world, to an afflicted and deserted soul.—*George Horne.*

Verse 21.—*"Gall and vinegar "* are here put together to denote the most unpalatable forms of food and drink. The passion of our Lord was providentially so ordered as to furnish a remarkable coincidence with this verse. The Romans were accustomed to give sour wine, with an infusion of myrrh, to convicts on the cross, for the purpose of deadening the pain. This practice was adhered to in our Saviour's case (Mark xv. 23). Though in itself not cruel, but the contrary, it formed part of the great process of murderous persecution. On the part of the Roman soldiery it may have been an act of kindness ; but considered as an act of the unbelieving Jews, it was giving *gall and vinegar* to one already overwhelmed with anguish. And so Matthew, in accordance with his general method, represents it as a verification of this passage (Matt. xxvii. 34). He does not contradict Mark's account, before referred to, but merely intimates that the wine and myrrh thus offered were to be regarded as identical with the gall and vinegar of this prediction. And, in order to prevent the coincidence from being overlooked, our Lord, before he died, complained of thirst, and vinegar was administered.—*Joseph Addison Alexander.*

Verse 21.—*"Gall for my meat."* Since the life of sin first began in tasting, contrary to the obedience due to God, the Redeemer of sinners willed to be obedient even unto death, upon the cross, and to end his life, in fulfilment of the prophecy, with the bitter taste of gall and vinegar, that, in this manner, we, seeing the beginning of our perdition and the end of our redemption, might feel ourselves to be most sufficiently redeemed and most perfectly cured.—*Thomé de Jesu* (1582), *in "The Sufferings of Jesus."*

Verse 21.—*"Vinegar."* Commentators have frequently remarked the refreshing quality of the Eastern vinegar. I shall not repeat their observations, but rather would ask, why the Psalmist prophetically complains of the giving him *vinegar* to drink, in that *deadly thirst*, which, in another Psalm, he describes by the tongue's cleaving to the jaws, if it be so refreshing ? Its refreshing quality cannot be doubted ; but may it not be replied, that, besides the gall which he mentions, and which ought not to be forgotten, vinegar itself, refreshing as it is, was only made use of by the meanest people ? When a *royal* personage has vinegar given him in his thirst, the *refreshment of a slave*, of a *wretched prisoner*, instead of that of a *prince*, he is greatly dishonoured, and may well complain of it as a bitter insult, or represent such insults by this image.

Sweet wines, as appears from the ancient *Eastern* translators of the Septuagint, were chiefly esteemed formerly, for that which our version renders "*royal wine* in abundance, according to the state of the King," (Esth. i. 7.) they translate, " much and *sweet* wine, such as the *King himself* drank." Perhaps, it was with a view to this, that the soldiers offered our Lord *vinegar* (wine that was become very sour), in opposition to that *sweet* wine princes were wont to drink : for Luke tells us that they did this in mockery (ch. xxiii. 36.) " And the soldiers also mocked him, coming to him, and offering him vinegar." Medicated wine, to deaden their sense of pain, was wont, we are told, to be given to Jewish criminals, when about to be put to death ; but, they gave our Lord vinegar, and that in mockery—in mockery (as they did other things) of his *claim to royalty*. But the force of this does not appear, if we do not recollect the quality of the wines drank anciently by princes, which, it seems, were of the *sweet* kind.—*Thomas Harmer*.

Verse 22.—The imprecations in this verse and those following it are revolting only when considered as the expression of malignant selfishness. If uttered by God, they shock no reader's sensibilities, nor should they, when considered as the language of an ideal person, representing the whole class of righteous sufferers, and particularly him, who, though he prayed for his murderers while dying (Luke xxiii. 34), had before applied the words of this very passage to the unbelieving Jews (Matt. xxiii. 38), as Paul did afterwards (Rom. xi. 9, 10). The general doctrine of providential retribution, far from being confined to the Old Testament, is distinctly taught in many of our Saviour's parables. See Matt. xxi. 41 ; xxii. 7 ; xxiv. 51.—*Joseph Addison Alexander*.

Verse 22.—"*Let their table become a snare.*" Their *table* figuratively sets forth their prosperity, the abundance of all things. It represents peace and security, as in Psalm xxxiii. 5 ; Job xxvi. 16. It likewise describes mutual friendship, a blending of minds and plans ; the emblem and sign whereof *convivia* are accustomed to be. Psalm xli. 10 ; Dan. xi. 27.—*Hermann Venema*.

Verse 22.—"*Let their table*," etc. One said well, *Licitis perimus omnes*, etc., " Ruin usually ariseth from the use of lawful things ; " there being most danger where it is least suspected. In all our comforts, there is a forbidden fruit, which seemeth fair and tasteth sweet, but which must not be touched.—*Henry Wilkinson* (1675), *in* "*Morning Exercises.*"

Verse 22.—"*Let their table become a snare.*"—Many would have excused themselves from following Christ, in the parable of the feast : some had bought land, some had married wives, and others had bought yokes of oxen, and could not come (Luke xiv. 18—20), that is, an immoderate love of the world hindered them : their lawful enjoyments, from servants, become their idols ; they worshipped them more than God, and would not quit them to come to God. But this is recorded to their reproach ; and we may herein see the power of self upon the worldly man, and the danger that comes to him by the abuse of lawful things. What, thy wife dearer to thee than thy Saviour ! and thy land and oxen preferred to thy soul's salvation. O beware, that thy comforts prove not snares first, and then curses : to over-rate them, is to provoke him that gave them to take them away again. Come, and follow him that giveth life eternal to the soul.—*William Penn* (1644—1718), *in* "*No Cross, No Crown.*"

Verse 22.—"*Let their table become a snare.*" That is, for a recompense for their inhumanity and cruelty towards me. Michaelis shows how exactly these comminations were fulfilled in the history of the final siege of Jerusalem by the Romans. Many thousands of the Jews had assembled in the city to eat the paschal lamb, when Titus unexpectedly made an assault upon them. In this siege, the greater part of the inhabitants of Jerusalem miserably perished.—*William Walford*.

Verses 22, 23.—Observe the Divine retribution of the Jews. They gave gall and vinegar as food and drink to Christ ; and their own spiritual food and drink has become a snare to them. His eyes were blindfolded ; their eyes were darkened. His loins were scourged ; their loins were made to shake.—*Christopher Wordsworth*.

Verses 23—28.—He denounceth ten plagues, or effects of God's wrath, to come upon them for their wickedness.—*David Dickson.*

Verse 24.—*"Pour out."* Observe what is denoted by *pouring out.* First, the facility with which God is able, without any labour, to destroy his enemies, as easy is it as to incline a vial full of liquid and pour it out. Secondly, the pouring out denotes the abundance of his anger. Thirdly, that his wrath is sudden, overwhelming, and inevitable. When it drops, one must take care ; when it is poured forth, it crushes the thoughtless.—*Thomas Le Blanc.*

Verse 25.—*"Let their habitation ; "*—that is, not only the place where they dwell, but even their very offices and functions, *"be void,"* viz., by thy just taking them away from amongst men ; *"and let none,"* viz., of their seed and posterity, *"dwell in their tents,"* viz., that they have dwelt in : he meaneth, that he would have them die without heir or issue.—*Thomas Wilcocks.*

Verse 25.—*"Let none dwell in their tents."* After the temple itself was taken, or rather turned to ashes, the miserable remnant of the Jewish people begged of Titus that he would permit them to pass through the breaches of the wall with their wives and children, and go into the wilderness—a request which he indignantly refused. (*Josephus.*) So that, literally, " there was no inhabitant for their tents."—*John Mason Good.*

Verse 26.—When David's misery deserved compassion, Shimei's foul mouth loaded him with malediction. Hereof he complained : *"They persecute him whom thou hast smitten ; and they talk to the grief of those whom thou hast wounded."* The picking out of such an opportunity doubled his malicious rancour. Such words would have galled at another time, which now are ready to kill. Let an arrow fly against the wind, it will hardly stick upright ; with the wind, it pierceth deep. While thine enemy stands, he may ward thy blows ; but once fallen on his back, he is at thy mercy : and how base is that spirit which will prey on prostrate fortunes ! Little children have so much valour and justice, as to call him a coward that strikes his adversary when he is down. To insult upon those whom God hath humbled, and to draw blood of that back which is yet blue from the Maker's stripes, is even the murder of a virulent tongue. Nor will it be any rare thing at the day of judgment for cursers to be indicted of murder. They would kill if they durst ; they do kill as far as they can. I would be loth to trust his hand, that bans one with his lips. Balaam would soon have been the death of all Israel, if either tongue or sword could have effected his will.—*Thomas Adams.*

Verse 26.—*"They talk to the grief of those whom thou hast wounded."* The very talking and venting of ill speeches, to the prejudice of Christ's cause and truth, and true holiness in his saints, especially when they are under suffering and afflictions, whatsoever, is a high provocation of God's wrath.—*David Dickson.*

Verse 26.—It were to be wished, that the sorrows of the penitent, when wounded with a sense of sin, never subjected him to the scorn and contempt of those who would be thought Christians.—*George Horne.*

Verse 27.—*"Add iniquity unto their iniquity."* This is that retaliation of sin which God returns into their bosoms that foster it ; that since " they loved cursing, it shall be unto them." Psalm cix. 17. So David here (though it was not in him *precantis votum,* but *prophetantis vaticinium,* he did not desire it to be so, but he knew it would be so), *"Add iniquity unto their iniquity."* Neither doth God this by infusion of wickedness, but by subtraction of his Spirit. He is *causa deficiens, non efficiens :* as the recalling of the sun from us causeth darkness ; so the privation of grace creates the prevalence of ungodliness. It is in him not *peccatum, sed judicium,*—not sin, but judgment. When he leaves us to ourselves, it is no wonder if we fall into horrid and prodigious sins. *Peccatum est malum in se : effectum prioris mali, et causa subsequentis : est et supplicium, et causa supplicii :* Sin is evil in itself, the effect of former evil, the cause of future : it is both punishment itself, and the cause of punishment. In all the storehouse of God's plagues there is not a greater vengeance. With other punishments the body smarteth ; the soul groaneth under this. Hence, sins multiply without limits, that the plagues may be without end. Every affliction is sore that offends us ; but that is direful which offends God. Such do at once act and suffer : it is both an active and a passive sin. The punish-

ment they suffer is (in them) sin ; the sin they do is (from God) a punishment.—
Thomas Adams.

Verse 27.—*"Add iniquity unto their iniquity."* Or, as the original signifies, *perverseness,* treat their *perverseness* with *perverseness :* act, in thy judgments, as *crookedly* towards them as they dealt *crookedly* towards thee. They shall get, in the way of punishment, what they have dealt out in the way of oppression.—*Adam Clarke.*

Verse 27.—*"Add iniquity unto their iniquity."* Sin, carried far enough, becomes its own punishment. Let but a voracious glutton be bound to sit at a well-furnished table but two hours after he had filled his stomach, he would account it an intolerable penance. Let but the drunkard be forced to drink on with those that can drink him down, how is he a burden to himself, and a scorn to his fellow drunkards ! Let but a lazy sluggard be confined three days to his bed, and how weary will he be of his bed of down ! How is the idle person more weary of his idleness than another is of work !—*Samuel Annesley* (1620—1696), *in "Morning Exercises."*

Verse 28.—*"Let them be blotted out of the book of the living."* All the Israelites who came up out of Egypt were put down in a muster-roll of the living, called " the writing of the house of Israel " (Ezek. xiii. 9), and " the book of life." Those who had died were excluded when the names were written out afresh each year. They were, thereby, consigned to oblivion (Prov. x. 7). Hence, *the book of life* was used as an image for God's *book of predestination to eternal life* (Psalm cxxxix. 16 ; Exod. xxxii. 32 ; Psalm lxxxvii. 6 ; Dan. xii. 1 ; Phil. iv. 3 ; Rev. xvii. 8 ; xiii. 8 ; xxi. 27 ; Luke x. 20). The book of life, *in the human point of view,* has names written in it who have a name to live, but are dead, being in it only by external call, or in their own estimation, and in that of others. But, *in the divine point of view,* it contains only those who are elected finally to life. The former may be blotted out, as was Judas (Rev. iii. 5 ; Matt. xiii. 12 ; xxv. 29 ; vii. 23 ; Exod. xxxii. 33) ; but the latter never (Rev. xx. 12, 15 ; John x. 28, 29 ; Acts xiii. 48).—*A. R. Fausset.*

Verse 28.—*"Let them be wiped out,"* etc. This verse alludes to the ancient Jewish practice of recording the names of the inhabitants of every division, or tribe, of the people, in a volume somewhat similar to the *Dom-boc* of the Saxons. See Luke ii.1. The names of those who died were blotted or *wiped* out, and appeared no longer on the list of the living. Such a book is attributed to God in Psalm cxxxix. 16 . and the *blotting out of Moses from God's book,* in Exod. xxxii. 32, is a figurative expression, for depriving him of life.—*Richard Warner.*

Verse 28.—*"Let them be blotted out of the book of the living,"* etc. We come to the question, Whether to be written in heaven be an infallible assurance of salvation, or, whether any there registered may come to be blotted out ? The truth is, that none written in heaven can ever be lost ; yet they object against it this verse. Hence, they infer, that some names once there recorded are afterwards put out ; but this opinion casteth a double aspersion on God himself. Either it makes him ignorant of future things, as if he foresaw not the end of elect and reprobate, and so were deceived in decreeing some to be saved that shall not be saved ; or, that his decree is mutable, in excluding those upon their sins whom he hath formerly chosen. From both these weaknesses St. Paul vindicates him (2 Tim. ii. 19) : "The foundation of God standeth sure, having this seal, the Lord knoweth them that are his." First, " The Lord knows them that are his ; " this were not true if God's prescience could be deluded. Then, his " foundation stands sure ; " but that were no sure foundation, if those he hath decreed to be his should afterwards fall out not to be his. The very conclusion of truth is this, *impossibilis est deletio ;* they which are " written in heaven " can never come into hell. To clear this from the opposed doubt, among many, I will cull out three proper distinctions :—

1. One may be said to be written in heaven *simpliciter,* and *secundum quid.* He that is simply written there, *in quantum prædestinatus ad vitam,* because elected to life, can never be blotted out. He that is written after a sort may, for he is written *non secundum Dei præscientiam, sed secundum præsentem justitiam*—not according to God's former decree, but according to his present righteousness. So they are said to be blotted out, not in respect of God's knowledge, for he knows they never were written there ; but according to their present condition, apostatising from grace to sin.*

2. Some are blotted out *non secundum rei veritatem, sed hominum opinionem*—

---
* Lyra.

not according to the truth of the thing, but according to men's opinion. It is usual in the Scriptures to say a thing is done *quando innotescat fieri*, when it is declared to be done. Hypocrites have a simulation of outward sanctity, so that men in charity judge them to be written in heaven. But when those glistening stars appear to be only *ignes fatui*, foolish meteors, and fall from the firmament of the church, then we say they are blotted out. The written *ex existentia*, by a perfect being, are never lost ; but *ex apparentia*, by a dissembled appearance, may. Some God so writes, *in se ut simpliciter habituri vitam*—that they have life simply in themselves, though not of themselves. Others he so writes, *ut habeant non in se, sed in sua causa;* from which falling they are said to be obliterated.*

3. Augustine says, we must not so take it, that God first writes and then dasheth out. For if a Pilate could say, *Quod scripsi, scripsi*—" What I have written, I have written," and it shall stand ; shall God say, *Quod scripsi, expungam*—What I have written, I will wipe out, and it shall not stand ? They are written, then, *secundum spem ipsorum, qui ibi se scriptos putabant*—according to their own hope that presumed their names there ; and are blotted out *quando ipsis constet illos non ibi fuisse*—when it is manifest to themselves that their names never had any such honour of inscription. This even that Psalm strengthens whence they fetch their opposition : *"Let them be blotted out of the book of the living, and not be written with the righteous."* So that to be blotted out of that book, it is, indeed, never to be written there. To be wiped out in the end, is but a declaration that such were not written in the beginning.—*Thomas Adams.*

Verse 32.—*" Your heart shall live that seek God."* As such who are poor in spirit, and truly humbled, do live upon God's alms, and are daily at his doors for relief of their necessities, and for communion with his gracious goodness ; so shall they thrive well in this trade.—*David Dickson.*

Verse 32.—*" Your heart shall live."* The *heart*, or the *soul*, is said *to live, to be converted*, or to return, when it is refreshed and cured of its pains and griefs. In this way it could be said of Jacob, when the good tidings were brought, that his *spirit revived.* . . . . On the contrary, when Nabal heard the bad news, it is recorded that *his heart died within him, and he became as a stone.*—*Lorinus.*

Verse 33.—*"The Lord heareth the poor."* The consolation is much greater when it is said, " The Lord heareth the poor," than if it were written, He hath heard poor David.—*Musculus.*

HINTS TO PREACHERS.

Verse 1.—Our trials like waters. I. They should be kept out of the heart. II. There are, however, leaks which admit them. III. Take note when the hold is filling. IV. Use the pumps, and cry for help.

Verses 2, 3.—The sinner aware of his position, unable to hope, overwhelmed with fear, finding no comfort in prayer, unvisited with divine consolation. Direct and console him.

Verse 3.—I. Here is faith in the midst of trouble : " My God." II. Hope in the midst of disappointment : " Mine eyes fail," etc. III. Prayer in the midst of discouragement : " I am weary," etc. ; " My throat," etc.

Or, I. There is praying beyond prayer: " I am weary," etc. II. Hoping beyond hope : " Mine eyes," etc.—*G. R.*

Verse 4.—Jesus as the Restorer, the Christian imitating him in the same office ; Christianity a power which will do this for the whole race in due season.

Verse 5.—*Our foolishness.* Wherein it appears generally, how it may display itself in individuals, what it occasions, and what are the divine provisions to meet it.

Verse 5.—I. God's knowledge of sin is an inducement to repent. 1. Because it is foolish to endeavour to hide any sin from him. 2. Because it is impossible

---

* Aquinas.

to confess all our sin to him. II. It is an encouragement to hope for pardon. 1. Because, in the full knowledge of sin, he has declared himself to be merciful and ready to forgive. 2. Because he has made provision for pardon, not according to our knowledge of sin, but his own.—*G. R.*

Verses 8, 9.—I. A grievous trial. II. An honourable reason for it : for Christ's sake. III. Consoling supports under it.

Verse 9.—I. The object of zeal : " thy house ; " thy Zion ; thy Church. II. The degree of zeal : " hath eaten me up." Our Lord was consumed by his own zeal. So Paul : " And I if I be offered up," etc. III. The manifestation of zeal : " The reproaches," etc. ; of thy justice ; of thy law ; of thy moral government ; of thy lovingkindness. " Who himself bare our sins," etc.—*G. R.*

Verses 10—12.—A prophecy. I. Of the Saviour's tears : " When I wept." II. Of his fasting. III. Of reproach. IV. Of his humiliation : " I made sackcloth," etc. V. Of the perversion of his words : as, " I will destroy this temple," etc. VI. Of the opposition of the Pharisees and rulers : " They that sit in the gate," etc. VII. Of the contempt of the lowest of the people : " I was the song," etc.—*G. R.*

Verse 11.—Proverbial sayings of a scoffing character.

Verse 13.—"*An acceptable time.*" While life lasts usually, and especially when we are repentant, feel our need, are importunate, give all glory to God, have faith in his promise, and expect a gracious reply.

Verse 13.—"*Multitude of thy mercy.*" Seen in many forbearances before conversion, countless pardons, innumerable gifts, many promises, frequent visits, and abundant deliverances. Of all these who can count the thousandth part ?

Verse 13.—"*The truth of thy salvation.*" An instructive topic. Its reality, certainty, completeness, eternity, etc., all illustrate its *truth* under various aspects.

Verses 14—16.—I. The depth from which prayer may rise. II. The height to which it may ascend. Thus Jonah, when at the bottom of the sea, says, " My prayer came up," etc.—*G. R.*

Verse 15 (last clause).—A tremendous evil, our desert of it, our hope against it, our fear of it, and the reasons which secure us against it.

Verse 17.—I. Prayer : " Hide not thy face." II. Person : " Thy servant." III. Plea : " For I am in trouble." IV. Pressure : " Hear me speedily."

Verse 19.—I. God knows what his people suffer ; how much, how long, from whom, for what. II. His people should find consolation in this knowledge. 1. That trial is permitted by him. 2. That it is apportioned by him. 3. That it has its design from him. 4. That when the design is accomplished, it will be removed by him.—*G. R.*

Verse 20.—The Saviour's broken heart.
Broken hearts, such as are sentimental, caused by disappointed pride, penitence, persecution, sympathy, etc.

Verse 21.—The conduct of men to Jesus throughout his entire life, rendering to him evil for all his good, and where good would have seemed to be the inevitable return.

Verse 22.—*The table a snare.* Excess in feasting ; looseness in conversation ; want of principle in confederate councils ; superstition in religion.

Verse 23.—The judicial curse which falls on some despisers of Christ ; their understandings fail to perceive the truth ; and they tremble, because they are unable to receive strengthening comforts.

Verse 29.—I. The humiliation that precedes exaltation. 1. Deep : " I am poor and sorrowful." 2. Confessed : " I am poor," etc. II. The exaltation that follows humiliation. 1. Divine : " Thy salvation, O Lord." " Though the Lord be high," etc. 2. Complete : God does nothing by halves. 3. Pre-eminent : " Set me up on high."—*G. R.*

Verses 30, 31.—I. The effect of deliverance upon the people of God. It fills them with praise and thanksgiving. II. The effect in relation to God. He is more pleased with it than with any other offerings : " Whoso offereth praise," etc.—*G. R.*

Verse 32.—I. The joy of a good man's heart is in the experience of others. II. The life of his heart is in God.

Verse 33.—I. What the people of God are in their own esteem : " poor " and " prisoners." II. What they are in the divine esteem : not unnoticed ; not unheard ; not despised.

Verse 34.—*"The sea,"* etc. How God is, should be, and shall be praised by the sea.

Verse 35.—Salvation, edification, preservation, peace, full assurance.

Verses 35, 36.—Observe the sequence :—" Save," " build," " dwell and have," " inherit," " love and dwell."

Verse 36.—I. The sure evidence of grace : " love his name." II. The blessing given. III. The enduring character of it : " shall dwell."

Verse 36.—I. The inheritance : " Inherit it ; " we reign with Christ on earth, then in heaven. II. The title. 1. Legal : " Seed of his servants "—Abraham. Jacob, David—David's Lord and Son. 2. Moral : " They that love his name." —*G. R.*

Verse 36.—I. The covenant inheritance. II. To whom it belongs. III. The certainty of their obtaining ; and, IV. The perpetuity of their possessing it.

PSALM LXX.

TITLE.—To the Chief Musician, a Psalm of David.—*So far the title corresponds with Psalm XL., of which this is a copy with variations. David appears to have written the full-length Psalm, and also to have made this excerpt from it, and altered it to suit the occasion. It is a fit pendant to Psalm LXIX., and a suitable preface to Psalm LXXI.* To bring to remembrance. *This is the poor man's memorial. David personally pleads with God that he may not be forgotten, but David's Lord may be heard here also. Even if the Lord seems to forget us, we must not forget him. This memorial Psalm acts as a connecting link between the two Psalms of supplicatory expostulation, and makes up with them a precious triad of song.*

EXPOSITION.

[The Reader is referred for full Exposition and Notes to Psalm XL., verses 13—17, in *"Treasury of David,"* Vol. II., pp. 239—241.]

*M*AKE *haste,* O God, to deliver me ; make haste to help me, O LORD.
2 Let them be ashamed and confounded that seek after my soul : let them be turned backward, and put to confusion, that desire my hurt.
3 Let them be turned back for a reward of their shame that say, Aha, aha.
4 Let all those that seek thee rejoice and be glad in thee : and let such as love thy salvation say continually, Let God be magnified.
5 But I *am* poor and needy : make haste unto me, O God : thou *art* my help and my deliverer ; O LORD, make no tarrying.

1. This is the second Psalm which is a repetition of another, the former being Psalm liii., which was a rehearsal of Psalm xiv. The present differs from the Fortieth Psalm at the outset, for that begins with, "Be pleased," and this, in our version, more urgently with, *"Make haste ;"* or, as in the Hebrew, with an abrupt and broken cry, *"O God, to deliver me ; O Lord, to help me hasten."* It is not forbidden us, in hours of dire distress, to ask for speed on God's part in his coming to rescue us. The only other difference between this and verse 13 of Psalm xl., is the putting of *Elohim* in the beginning of the verse for *Jehovah,* but why this is done, we know not ; perhaps, the guesses of the critics are correct, but perhaps they are not. As we have the words of this Psalm twice in the letter, let them be doubly with us in spirit. It is most meet that we should day by day cry to God for deliverance and help ; our frailty and our many dangers render this a perpetual necessity.

2. Here the words, "together," and, "to destroy it," which occur in Psalm xl., are omitted : a man in haste uses no more words than are actually necessary. His enemies desired to put his faith to shame, and he eagerly entreats that they may be disappointed, and themselves covered with confusion. It shall certainly be so ; if not sooner, yet at that dread day when the wicked shall awake to shame and everlasting contempt. *"Let them be ashamed and confounded that seek after my soul : let them be turned backward, and put to confusion, that desire my hurt ;"* turned back and driven back are merely the variations of the translators. When men labour to turn others back from the right road, it is God's retaliation to drive them back from the point they are aiming at.

3. *"Let them be turned back."* This is a milder term than that used in Psalm xl., where he cries, "let them be desolate." Had growing years matured and mellowed the Psalmist's spirit ? To be "turned back," however, may come to the same thing as to be "desolate ;" disappointed malice is the nearest akin to desolation that can well be conceived. *"For a reward of their shame that say, Aha, aha."* They thought to shame the godly, but it was their shame, and shall be their shame for

ever. How fond men are of taunts, and if they are meaningless "Ahas," more like animal cries than human words, it matters nothing, so long as they are a vent for scorn and sting the victim. Rest assured, the enemies of Christ and his people shall have wages for their work ; they shall be paid in their own coin ; they loved scoffing, and they shall be filled with it—yea, they shall become a proverb and a by-word for ever.

4. Anger against enemies must not make us forget our friends, for it is better to preserve a single citizen of Zion, than to kill a thousand enemies. *"Let all those that seek thee rejoice and be glad in thee."* All true worshippers, though as yet in the humble ranks of seekers, shall have cause for joy. Even though the seeking commence in darkness, it shall bring light with it. *"And let such as love thy salvation say continually, Let God be magnified."* Those who have tasted divine grace, and are, therefore, wedded to it, are a somewhat more advanced race, and these shall not only feel joy, but shall with holy constancy and perseverance tell abroad their joy, and call upon men to glorify God. The doxology, " Let the Lord's name be magnified," is infinitely more manly and ennobling than the dog's bark of " Aha, aha."

5. *"But I am poor and needy."* Just the same plea as in the preceding Psalm, verse 29 : it seems to be a favourite argument with tried saints ; evidently our poverty is our wealth, even as our weakness is our strength. May we learn well this riddle. *"Make haste unto me, O God."* This is written instead of " yet the Lord thinketh upon me," in Psalm xl. : and there is a reason for the change, since the key note of the Psalm frequently dictates its close. Psalm xl. sings of God's thoughts, and, therefore, ends therewith ; but the peculiar note of Psalm lxx. is " Make haste," and, therefore, so it concludes. *"Thou art my help and my deliverer."* My help in trouble, my deliverer out of it. *"O Lord, make no tarrying."* Here is the name of " Jehovah " instead of " my God." We are warranted in using all the various names of God, for each has its own beauty and majesty, and we must reverence each by its holy use as well as by abstaining from taking it in vain.

I have presumed to close this recapitulatory exposition with an original hymn, suggested by the watchword of this Psalm, " MAKE HASTE."

> Make haste, O God, my soul to bless !
> My help and my deliv'rer thou ;
> Make haste, for I'm in deep distress,
> My case is urgent ; help me *now*.
>
> Make haste, O God ! make haste to save !
> For time is short, and death is nigh ;
> Make haste ere yet I'm in my grave,
> And with the lost for ever lie.
>
> Make haste, for I am poor and low ;
> And Satan mocks my prayers and tears ;
> O God, in mercy be not slow,
> But snatch me from my horrid fears.
>
> Make haste, O God, and hear my cries ;
> Then with the souls who seek thy face,
> And those who thy salvation prize,
> I'll magnify thy matchless grace.

EXPLANATORY NOTES AND QUAINT SAYINGS.

Whole Psalm.—Francke would apply the present Psalm to the state of the Christian church after the resurrection and exaltation of Christ, and would put the words in the mouths of the faithful of that time. On the same ground of transferring the language adapted to Christ in Psalm xl. to the faithful in this Psalm, we need not hesitate to take them on our lips, as the language of the church in every age. I cannot but reassert my conviction of the intentional arrangement of the Psalms in the order in which we now have them, made in all probability, partially at least, at the time they were handed over to public use. It is surely a daring conjecture made by Walford, that the repetition of this Psalm arose from some mistake of the persons by whom the Psalms were collected and arranged, after the return from the captivity in Babylon.—*W. Wilson.*

Verse 2.—*"Let them be confounded ; "* viz., among themselves, and in their own understandings : *"and put to shame ; "* viz., in the sight and presence of men before whom they think to attain great glory, in banding themselves against me.—*Thomas Wilcocks.*

Verse 3.—*"Aha, aha."* In describing his human foes, our Saviour represents them as saying to him, *"Aha, aha."* These exclamations are ebullitions of exulting insolence. They can escape from the lips of those only who are at once haughty and cruel, and insensible to the delicacies and decorums of demeanour. Doubtless, they would be the favourite expressions of the rude rabble that accompanied the traitor in his ignoble campaign against Incarnate Love, and of the rude aristocratic mob that held over the Apostle of Heaven the mockery of an ecclesiastical trial, and of the larger, more excited, and more rancorous multitude that insultingly accompanied him to the cross, and mocked him, and wagged their heads at him, and railed upon him as he meekly, but majestically, hung on the accursed tree. The prescient Saviour would, no doubt, catch in his ears the distant mutter of all the violent and ruthless exclamations with which his foes were about to rend the air ; and, amid these heartless and sneering ejaculations, he could not but feel the keen and poisoning edge of the malevolent and hilarious cry, *"Aha, aha."* O miracle of mercy ! He who deserved the hallelujahs of an intelligent universe, and the special hosannahs of all the children of men, had first to anticipate, and then to endure from the mouths of the very rebels whom he came to bless and to save, the malicious tauntings of *"Aha, aha."*—*James Frame.*

Verse 4.—*"Such as love thy salvation."* They love it for its own sake ; they love it for the sake of him who procured it by his obedience unto death ; they love it for the sake of that Holy Spirit who moved them to seek it and accept it ; and they love it for the sake of their own souls, which they cannot but love, and which, without it, would be the most miserable outcasts in the universe. No wonder that in the light of its intrinsic importance, and of its intrinsic relations, they should be " such as love God's salvation." All men are lovers as well as seekers ; for all men love. Some love money more than God's salvation ; others love pleasure, even the pleasures of sin, more than God's salvation ; and others love bustle and business more than God's salvation. But, as the stamp of the material, the temporal and the evanescent, is on all these earthly objects of men's love, the friends of Jesus elevate above them all, as the worthier object of their regard and embrace, the salvation of God.—*James Frame.*

Verse 4.—*"Let God be magnified."* Not only *"The Lord be magnified,"* but also *"alway."* Behold, when thou wast straying, and wast turned away from him ; he recalled thee : *Be the Lord magnified.* Behold, he hath inspired thee with confession of sins ; thou hast confessed, he hath given pardon : *Be the Lord magnified.* . . . . Now, thou hast begun to advance, thou hast been justified, thou hast arrived at a sort of excellence of virtue ; is it not a seemly thing that *thou* also sometime be magnified ? No ! *Let them say, Be the Lord alway magnified.* A sinner thou art, be he magnified in order that he may call ; thou confessest, be he magnified in order that he may forgive : now thou livest justly, be he magnified in order that he may direct ; thou perseverest even unto the end, be he magnified in order that he may glorify. *Be the Lord,* then, *alway magnified.* Let just men say this, let them say this that seek him. Whosoever doth not say this, doth not seek him. . . . . *Be the Lord magnified.* But, wilt thou thyself never be great ? wilt thou be nowhere ? In him was something, in me nothing ; but if in him is whatsoever I am, *be he magnified,* not I. But, what of these ? *"But I am poor and needy : "* he is rich, he abounding, he needing nothing. Behold my light, behold whence I am illumined, for I cry, " Thou shalt illumine my candle, O Lord ; my God, thou shalt illumine my darkness. The Lord doth loose men fettered, the Lord raiseth up men crushed, the Lord maketh wise the blind men, the Lord keepeth the proselytes." Psalm xviii. 28 ; Psalm cxlvi. 7. What, then, of thee ? *"But I am needy and poor."* I am like an orphan, my soul is like a widow destitute and desolate ; help I seek,

alway mine infirmity I confess. *"But I am poor and needy."* There have been
forgiven me my sins, now I have begun to follow the commandments of God ; still,
however, I am needy and poor. Why still needy and poor ? Because I see another
law in my members fighting against the law of my mind. Rom. vii. 23. Why
needy and poor ? Because, " Blessed are they that hunger and thirst after righteous-
Matt. v. 6. Still I hunger, still I thirst.—*Augustine.*

Verse 5.—*"But I am poor and needy."* He had been rich, but for our sake he
had become poor, that we, through his poverty, might be rich. Out of the fulness
of his grace he had voluntarily entered, for our sakes, into a state in which he had
experience, and most bitter experience, of the want of the means of enjoyment.
. . . . But the word here rendered *"poor"* is often, elsewhere, translated afflicted ;
in various ways he was afflicted. He was despised and rejected of men, a man of
sorrows, and the acquaintance of grief. He was reproached, and " reproach broke
his heart."—*James Frame.*

Verse 5.—*"I am poor and needy."* By this I hold to be meant the chastisements, and fiery trials that come from *God the Father ;* the temptations and bitter
assaults of that foul and fell fiend, *Satan ;* the persecutions and vexations inflicted
by the hands of unreasonable *and wicked men ;* and (but in this following *Christ*
must be exempted) the inward corruptions, disordered motions, unsettled affections,
and the original pollutions brought from the mother's womb ; with the soul and
body's inaptness and unableness with cheerfulness and constancy to run the direct
and just paths of God's commandments. Many of these made the Head, all of
these (and more, too) the members, *"poor and needy."*—*John Barlow.* 1618.

Verse 5.—*"O Lord, make no tarrying."* His prayer for himself, like his prayer
for his foes and for his friends, was answered. The Lord made no tarrying. Ere
four and twenty hours had rolled past, his rescued spirit was in Paradise, and the
crucified thief was with him. O what a change ! The morning saw him condemned
at the bar of an earthly tribunal, sentenced to death, and nailed to the bitter tree ;
before the evening shadowed the hill of Calvary, he was nestling in the bosom of
God, and had become the great centre of attraction and of admiration to all the
holy intelligences of the universe. The morning saw him led out through the gate
of the Jerusalem below, surrounded by a ribald crowd, whose hootings rung in his
ear ; but ere the night fell, he had passed through the gate of the Jerusalem above,
and his tread was upon the streets of gold, and angel anthems rose high through
the dome of heaven, and joy filled the heart of God.—*James Frame.*

Verse 5 (third clause).—*"Helper,"* in all good works ; *"Deliverer,"* from all evil
ones. *"Make no long tarrying :"* it is the cry of the individual sinner.—*Dionysius
the Carthusian (1471), quoted in Neale and Littledale's Commentary.*

HINTS TO PREACHERS.

Verse 1.—I. Occasion of his prayer. 1. Affliction. 2. Helplessness. II.
Subject of his prayer. Deliverance, help. III. Importunity of his prayer. The
time of deliverance may be in answer to prayer, as well as deliverance itself.

Verse 1.—I. Times when such urgent prayer is allowable, praiseworthy, or
faulty. II. Reasons for expecting a speedy reply. III. Consolations if delay
should occur.

Verse 2.—I. There are those who seek our soul's hurt. II. We must oppose
them, not dally or yield. III. Our best weapon is prayer to God. IV. Their
defeat is here described.

Verse 3.—I. Who are these who cry " shame " ? II. What master do they
serve ? III. What shall their wages be ?

Verse 4.—Joy for seekers, and employment for finders.

Verse 4 (last clause).—I. The character. II. The saying. III. The wish.

Verse 5.—I. Who need help ? II. Who renders help ? III. What it comes
to : " deliver." IV. What prayer it suggests.

Verse 5.—I. Confession : " I am poor and needy." II. Profession : " Thou
art my help," etc. III. Supplication : " Make haste ; " " Make no tarrying."

PSALM LXXI.

There is no title to this Psalm, and hence some conjecture that Psalm LXX. is intended to be a prelude to it, and has been broken off from it. Such imaginings have no value with us. We have already met with five Psalms without title, which are, nevertheless, as complete as those which bear them.

We have here THE PRAYER OF THE AGED BELIEVER, *who, in holy confidence of faith, strengthened by a long and remarkable experience, pleads against his enemies, and asks further blessings for himself. Anticipating a gracious reply, he promises to magnify the Lord exceedingly.*

DIVISION.—*The first four verses are faith's cry for help ; the next four are a testimony of experience. From verse 9—13, the aged saint pleads against his foes, and then rejoices in hope, verses 14—16. He returns to prayer again in verses 17 and 18, repeats the confident hopes which cheered his soul, verses 19, 20, 21 ; and then he closes with the promise of abounding in thanksgiving. Throughout, this Psalm may be regarded as the utterance of struggling, but unstaggering, faith.*

EXPOSITION.

IN thee, O LORD, do I put my trust : let me never be put to confusion.

2 Deliver me in thy righteousness, and cause me to escape : incline thine ear unto me, and save me.

3 Be thou my strong habitation, whereunto I may continually resort : thou hast given commandment to save me ; for thou *art* my rock and my fortress.

4 Deliver me, O my God, out of the hand of the wicked, out of the hand of the unrighteous and cruel man.

1. *"In thee, O Lord, do I put my trust."* Jehovah deserves our confidence ; let him have it all. Every day must we guard against every form of reliance upon an arm of flesh, and hourly hang our faith upon the ever faithful God. Not only *on* God must we rest, as a man stands on a rock, but *in* him must we trust, as a man hides in a cave. The more intimate we are with the Lord, the firmer will our trust be. God knows our faith, and yet he loves to hear us avow it ; hence, the Psalmist not only trusts in the Lord, but tells him that he is so trusting. *"Let me never be put to confusion."* So long as the world stands, stand thou by me ; yea, for ever and ever be faithful to thy servants. If thou forsake me, men will ridicule my religion, and how shall I be able to answer them ? Confusion will silence me, and thy cause will be put to shame. This verse is a good beginning for prayer ; those who commence with trust shall conclude with joy.

2. *"Deliver me in thy righteousness, and cause me to escape."* Be true, O God, to thy word. It is a righteous thing in thee to keep the promises which thou hast made unto thy servants. I have trusted thee, and thou wilt not be unrighteous to forget my faith. I am taken as in a net, but do thou liberate me from the malice of my persecutors. *"Incline thine ear unto me, and save me."* Stoop to my feebleness, and hear my faint whispers ; be gracious to my infirmities, and smile upon me : I ask salvation ; listen thou to my petitions, and save me. Like one wounded and left for dead by mine enemies, I need that thou bend over me and bind up my wounds. These mercies are asked on the plea of faith, and they cannot, therefore, be denied.

3. *"Be thou my strong habitation."* Permit me to enter into thee, and be as much at home as a man in his own house, and then suffer me to remain in thee as my settled abode. Whereas foes molest me, I need a dwelling framed and bulwarked, to sustain a siege and resist the attacks of armies ; let, then, thine omnipotence secure me, and be as a fortress unto me. Here we see a weak man, but he is in a strong habitation ; his security rests upon the tower in which he hides, and

is not placed in jeopardy through his personal feebleness. " *Whereunto I may continually resort.*" Fast shut is this castle against all adversaries, its gates they cannot burst open ; the drawbridge is up, the portcullis is down, the bars are fast in their places ; but, there is a secret door, by which friends of the great Lord can enter at all hours of the day or night, as often as ever they please. There is never an hour when it is unlawful to pray. Mercy's gates stand wide open, and shall do so, till, at the last, the Master of the house has risen up and shut to the door. Believers find their God to be their habitation, strong and accessible, and this is for them a sufficient remedy for all the ills of their mortal life. " *Thou hast given commandment to save me.*" Nature is charged to be tender with God's servants ; Providence is ordered to work their good, and the forces of the invisible world are ordained as their guardians. David charged all his troops to spare the young man Absalom, but yet he fell. God's commandment is of far higher virtue, for it compels obedience, and secures its end. Destruction cannot destroy us, famine cannot starve us ; but we laugh at both, while God's mandate shields us. No stones of the field can throw us down, while angels bear us up in their hands ; neither can the beasts of the field devour us, while David's God delivers us from their ferocity, or Daniel's God puts them in awe of us. "*For thou art my rock and my fortress.*" In God we have all the security which nature which furnishes the rock, and art which builds the fortress, could supply ; he is the complete preserver of his people. Immutability may be set forth by the rock, and omnipotence by the fortress. Happy is he who can use the personal pronoun " my "—not only once, but as many times as the many aspects of the Lord may render desirable. Is he a strong habitation ? I will call him "*my* strong habitation," and he shall be *my* rock, *my* fortress, *my* God (verse 4), *my* hope, *my* trust (verse 5), *my* praise (verse 6). All mine shall be his, all his shall be mine. This was the reason why the Psalmist was persuaded that God had commanded his salvation, namely, because he had enabled him to exercise a calm and appropriating faith.

4. "*Deliver me, O my God, out of the hand of the wicked.*" God is on the same side with us, and those who are our enemies are also his, for they are wicked ; therefore will the Lord surely rescue his own confederates, and he will not suffer the evil to triumph over the just. He who addresses such a prayer as this to heaven, does more injury to his enemies than if he had turned a battery of Armstrongs upon them. "*Out of the hand of the unrighteous and cruel man.*" Being wicked to God, they become unrighteous towards men, and cruel in their persecutions of the godly. Two hands are here mentioned : they grasp and they crush ; they strike and they would slay if God did not prevent ; had they as many hands as Briareus, the finger of God would more than match them.

5 For thou *art* my hope, O Lord GOD : *thou art* my trust from my youth.

6 By thee have I been holden up from the womb : thou art he that took me out of my mother's bowels : my praise *shall be* continually of thee.

7 I am as a wonder unto many ; but thou *art* my strong refuge.

8 Let my mouth be filled *with* thy praise *and with* thy honour all the day.

5. "*For thou art my hope, O Lord God.*" God who gives us grace to hope in him, will assuredly fulfil our hope, and, therefore, we may plead it in prayer. His name is " Jehovah, the hope of Israel " (Jer. xvii. 13) ; and, as he cannot be a false or failing hope, we may expect to see our confidence justified. "*Thou art my trust from my youth.*" David had proved his faith by notable exploits when he was a youth and ruddy ; it was to him a cheering recollection, and he felt persuaded that the God of his youth would not forsake him in his age. They are highly favoured who can like David, Samuel, Josiah, Timothy, and others say, " Thou art my trust from my youth."

6. "*By thee have I been holden up from the womb.*" Before he was able to understand the power which preserved him, he was sustained by it. God knows us before we know anything. The elect of old lay in the bosom of God before they were laid on their mothers' bosoms ; and when their infantile weakness had no feet strong enough to carry it, the Lord upheld it. We do well to reflect upon divine goodness to us in childhood, for it is full of food for gratitude. "*Thou art he that took me out of my mother's bowels.*" Even before conscious life, the care of God is over his chosen. Birth is a mystery of mercy, and God is with both mother and babe. If marriages are registered in heaven, we may be sure that births are also.

Holy women do well to bless God for his mercy to them in nature's perilous hour; but every one who is born of woman has equal cause for thankfulness. She, whose life is preserved, should render thanks, and so should he whose life is given. *"My praise shall be continually of thee."* Where goodness has been unceasingly received, praise should unceasingly be offered. God is the circle where praise should begin, continue, and endlessly revolve, since in him we live, and move, and have our being.

7. *"I am as a wonder unto many."* " To thousand eyes a mark and gaze am I." The saints are men wondered at; often their dark side is gloomy even to amazement, while their bright side is glorious even to astonishment. The believer is a riddle, an enigma puzzling the unspiritual; he is a monster warring with those delights of the flesh, which are the all in all of other men; he is a prodigy, unaccountable to the judgments of ungodly men; a wonder gazed at, feared, and, by-and-by, contemptuously derided. Few understand us, many are surprised at us. *"But thou art my strong refuge."* Here is the answer to our riddle. If we are strong, it is in God; if we are safe, our refuge shelters us; if we are calm, our soul hath found her stay in God. When faith is understood, and the grounds of her confidence seen, the believer is no longer a wonder; but the marvel is that so much unbelief remains among the sons of men.

8. *"Let my mouth be filled with thy praise and with thy honour all the day."* What a blessed mouthful! A man never grows nauseated though the flavour of it be all day in his mouth. God's bread is always in our mouths, so should his praise be. He fills us with good; let us be also filled with gratitude. This would leave no room for murmuring or backbiting; therefore, may we well join with holy David in this sacred wish.

9 Cast me not off in the time of old age; forsake me not when my strength faileth.

10 For mine enemies speak against me; and they that lay wait for my soul take counsel together.

11 Saying, God hath forsaken him: persecute and take him; for *there* is none to deliver *him*.

12 O God, be not far from me: O my God, make haste for my help.

13 Let them be confounded *and* consumed that are adversaries to my soul; let them be covered *with* reproach and dishonour that seek my hurt.

9. *"Cast me not off in the time of old age."* David was not tired of his Master, and his only fear was lest his Master should be tired of him. The Amalekite in the Bible history left his Egyptian servant to famish when he grew old and sick, but not so the Lord of saints; even to hoar hairs he bears and carries us. Alas for us, if we were abandoned by our God, as many a courtier has been by his prince! Old age robs us of personal beauty, and deprives us of strength for active service; but it does not lower us in the love and favour of God. An ungrateful country leaves its worn-out defenders to starve upon a scanty pittance, but the pensioners of heaven are satisfied with good things. *"Forsake me not when my strength faileth."* Bear with me, and endure my infirmities. To be forsaken of God is the worst of all conceivable ills, and if the believer can be but clear of that grievous fear, he is happy: no saintly heart need be under any apprehension upon this point.

10. *"For mine enemies speak against me."* Dogs howl over a dying lion. When David's arm was able to chastise his foes, they were yet impudent enough to slander him, and he fears that now they will take fresh license in the hour of his weakness. The text most probably means that his enemies had said that God would forsake him; and, therefore, he is the more earnest that the Lord's faithful dealings may give them the lie. *"And they that lay wait for my soul take counsel together."* The Psalmist had enemies, and these were most malicious; seeking his utter destruction, they were very persevering, and staid long upon the watch; to this they added cunning, for they lay in ambush to surprise him, and take him at a disadvantage: and all this they did with the utmost unanimity and deliberation, neither spoiling their design by want of prudence, nor marring its accomplishment by a lack of unity. The Lord our God is our only and all-sufficient resort from every form of persecution.

11. *"Saying, God hath forsaken him."* O bitter taunt! There is no worse arrow in all the quivers of hell. Our Lord felt this barbed shaft, and it is no marvel

if his disciples feel the same. Were this exclamation the truth, it were indeed an ill day for us ; but, glory be to God, it is a barefaced lie. *"Persecute and take him."* Let loose the dogs of persecution upon him, seize him, worry him, *"for there is none to deliver him."* Down with him, for he has no friends. It is safe to insult him, for none will come to his rescue. O cowardly boasts of a braggart foe, how do ye wound the soul of the believer ; and only when his faith cries to his Lord is he able to endure your cruelty.

12. *"O God, be not far from me."* Nearness to God is our conscious security. A child in the dark is comforted by grasping its father's hand. *"O my God, make haste for my help."* To call God ours, as having entered into covenant with us, is a mighty plea in prayer, and a great stay to our faith. The cry of " make haste " has occurred many times in this portion of the Psalms, and it was evoked by the sore pressure of affliction. Sharp sorrows soon put an end to procrastinating prayers.

13. *"Let them be confounded and consumed that are adversaries to my soul."* It will be all this to them to see thy servant preserved ; their envy and malice, when disappointed, will fill them with life-consuming bitterness. The defeat of their plans shall nonplus them, they shall be confounded as they enquire the reason for their overthrow ; the men they seek to destroy seem so weak, and their cause so contemptible, that they will be filled with amazement as they see them not only survive all opposition, but even surmount it. How confounded must Pharaoh have been when Israel multiplied, despite his endeavours to exterminate the race ; and how consumed with rage must the Scribes and Pharisees have become when they saw the gospel spreading from land to land by the very means which they used for its destruction. *"Let them be covered with reproach and dishonour that seek my hurt."* He would have their shame made visible to all eyes, by their wearing it in their blushes as a mantle. They would have made a laughing-stock of the believer, if his God had forsaken him ; therefore, let unbelief and atheism be made a public scoffing in their persons.

14 But I will hope continually, and will yet praise thee more and more.

15 My mouth shall show forth thy righteousness *and* thy salvation all the day ; for I know not the numbers thereof.

16 I will go in the strength of the Lord GOD : I will make mention of thy righteousness, *even* of thine only.

14. The holy faith of the persecuted saint comes to the front in these three verses. *"But I will hope continually."* When I cannot rejoice in what I have, I will look forward to what shall be mine, and will still rejoice. Hope will live on a bare common, and sing on a branch laden down with snow. No date and no place are unsuitable for hope. Hell alone excepted, hope is a dweller in all regions. We may always hope, for we always have grounds for it : we will always hope, for it is a never-failing consolation. *"And will yet praise thee more and more."* He was not slack in thanksgiving ; in fact, no man was ever more diligent in it ; yet he was not content with all his former praises, but vowed to become more and more a grateful worshipper. When good things are both continual and progressive with us, we are on the right tack. We ought to be misers in doing good, and our motto should be " more and more." While we do not disdain to " rest and be thankful," we cannot settle down into resting in our thankfulness. *"Superior,"* cries the eagle, as he mounts towards the sun : higher and yet higher is also our aims, as we soar aloft in duty and devotion. It is our continual hope that we shall be able more and more to magnify the Lord.

15. *"My mouth shall shew forth thy righteousness and thy salvation all the day."* We are to bear testimony as experience enables us, and not withhold from others that which we have tasted and handled. The faithfulness of God in saving us, in delivering us out of the hand of our enemies, and in fulfilling his promises, is to be everywhere proclaimed by those who have proved it in their own history. How gloriously conspicuous is righteousness in the divine plan of redemption ! It should be the theme of constant discourse. The devil rages against the substitutionary sacrifice, and errorists of every form make this the main point of their attack ; be it ours, therefore, to love the doctrine, and to spread its glad tidings on every side, and at all times. Mouths are never so usefully employed as in recounting the righteousness of God revealed in the salvation of believers in Jesus. The

preacher who should be confined to this one theme would never need seek another : it is the *medulla theologiæ*, the very pith and marrow of revealed truth. Has our reader been silent upon this choice subject ? Let us, then, press him to tell abroad what he enjoys within : he does not well who keeps such glad tidings to himself. *"For I know not the numbers thereof."* He knew the sweetness of it, the sureness, the glory, and the truth of it ; but as to the full reckoning of its plenitude, variety, and sufficiency, he felt he could not reach to the height of the great argument. Lord, where I cannot count I will believe, and when a truth surpasses numeration I will take to admiration. When David spoke of his enemies, he said they were more in number than the hairs of his head ; he had, therefore, some idea of their number, and found a figure suitable to set it out ; but, in the case of the Lord's covenant mercies, he declares, " I know not the number," and does not venture upon any sort of comparison. To creatures belong number and limit, to God and his grace there is neither. We may, therefore, continue to tell out his great salvation all day long, for the theme is utterly inexhaustible.

16. *"I will go in the strength of the Lord God."* Our translators give us a good sense, but not the sense in this place, which is on this wise, " I will come with the mighty deeds of the Lord Jehovah." He would enter into those deeds by admiring study, and then, wherever he went, he would continue to rehearse them. He should ever be a welcome guest who can tell us of the mighty acts of the Lord, and help us to put our trust in him. The authorised version may be used by us as a resolve in all our exertions and endeavours. In our own strength we must fall ; but, when we hear the voice itself saith, " Go in this thy might," we may advance without fear. Though hell itself were in the way, the believer would pursue the path of duty, crying : *"I will go in the strength of the Lord God : I will make mention of thy righteousness, even of thine only."* Man's righteousness is not fit to be mentioned—filthy rags are best hidden ; neither is there any righteousness under heaven, or in heaven, comparable to the divine. As God himself fills all space, and is, therefore, the only God, leaving no room for another, so God's righteousness, in Christ Jesus, fills the believer's soul, and he counts all other things but dross and dung " that he may win Christ, and be found in him, not having his own righteousness which is of the law, but the righteousness which is of God by faith." What would be the use of speaking upon any other righteousness to a dying man ? and all are dying men. Let those who will cry up man's natural innocence, the dignity of the race, the purity of philosophers, the loveliness of untutored savages, the power of sacraments, and the infallibility of pontiffs ; this is the true believer's immovable resolve : " I will make mention of thy righteousness, even of thine only." For ever dedicated to thee, my Lord, be this poor, unworthy tongue, whose glory it shall be to glorify thee.

17 O God, thou hast taught me from my youth : and hitherto have I declared thy wondrous works.

18 Now also when I am old and greyheaded, O God, forsake me not ; until I have shewed thy strength unto *this* generation, *and* thy power to every one *that* is to come.

17. *"O God, thou hast taught me from my youth."* It was comfortable to the Psalmist to remember that from his earliest days he had been the Lord's disciple. None are too young to be taught of God, and they make the most proficient scholars who begin betimes. *"And hitherto have I declared thy wondrous works."* He had learned to tell what he knew, he was a pupil teacher ; he continued still learning and declaring, and did not renounce his first master ; this, also, was his comfort, but it is one which those who have been seduced from the school of the gospel, into the various colleges of philosophy and scepticism, will not be able to enjoy. A sacred conservatism is much needed in these days, when men are giving up old lights for new. We mean both to learn and to teach the wonders of redeeming love, till we can discover something nobler or more soul-satisfying ; for this reason we hope that our greyheads will be found in the same road as we have trodden, even from our beardless youth.

18. *"Now also when I am old and greyheaded, O God, forsake me not."* There is something touching in the sight of hair whitened with the snows of many a winter : the old and faithful soldier receives consideration from his king, the venerable servant is beloved by his master. When our infirmities multiply, we may, with

confidence, expect enlarged privileges in the world of grace, to make up for our narrowing range in the field of nature. Nothing shall make God forsake those who have not forsaken him. Our fear is lest he should do so ; but his promise kisses that fear into silence. *"Until I have shewed thy strength unto this generation."* He desired to continue his testimony and complete it ; he had respect to the young men and little children about him, and knowing the vast importance of training them in the fear of God, he longed to make them all acquainted with the power of God to support his people, that they also might be led to walk by faith. He had leaned on the almighty arm, and could speak experimentally of its all-sufficiency, and longed to do so ere life came to a close. *"And thy power to every one that is to come."* He would leave a record for unborn ages to read. He thought the Lord's power to be so worthy of praise, that he would make the ages ring with it till time should be no more. For this cause believers live, and they should take care to labour zealously for the accomplishment of this their most proper and necessary work. Blessed are they who begin in youth to proclaim the name of the Lord, and cease not until their last hour brings their last word for their divine Master.

19 Thy righteousness also, O God, *is* very high, who hast done great things : O God, who *is* like unto thee !

20 *Thou,* which hast shewed me great and sore troubles, shalt quicken me again, and shalt bring me up again from the depths of the earth.

21 Thou shalt increase my greatness, and comfort me on every side.

19. *"Thy righteousness also, O God, is very high."* Very sublime, unsearchable, exalted, and glorious is the holy character of God, and his way of making men righteous. His plan of righteousness uplifts men from the gates of hell to the mansions of heaven. It is a high-doctrine gospel, gives a high experience, leads to high practice, and ends in high felicity. *"'Who hast done great things."* The exploits of others are mere child's play compared with thine, and are not worthy to be mentioned in the same age. Creation, providence, redemption, are all unique, and nothing can compare with them. *"O God, who is like unto thee."* As thy works are so transcendent, so art thou. Thou art without compeer, or even second, and such are thy works, and such, especially, thy plan of justifying sinners by the righteousness which thou hast provided. Adoration is a fit frame of mind for the believer. When he draws near to God, he enters into a region where everything is surpassingly sublime ; miracles of love abound on every hand, and marvels of mingled justice and grace. A traveller among the high Alps often feels overwhelmed with awe, amid their amazing sublimities ; much more is this the case when we survey the heights and depths of the mercy and holiness of the Lord. *"O God, who is like unto thee."*

20. *"Thou, which hast shewed me great and sore troubles, shall quicken me again."* Here is faith's inference from the infinite greatness of the Lord. He has been strong to smite ; he will be also strong to save. He has shown me many heavy and severe trials, and he will also show me many and precious mercies. He has almost killed me, he will speedily revive me ; and though I have been almost dead and buried, he will give me a resurrection, and *"bring me up again from the depths of the earth."* However low the Lord may permit us to sink, he will fix a limit to the descent, and in due time will bring us up again. Even when we are laid low in the tomb, the mercy is that we can go no lower, but shall retrace our steps and mount to better lands ; and all this, because the Lord is ever mighty to save. A little God would fail us, but not Jehovah the Omnipotent. It is safe to lean on him, since he bears up the pillars both of heaven and earth.

21. *"Thou shalt increase my greatness."* As a king, David grew in influence and power. God did great things for him, and by him, and this is all the greatness believers want. May we have faith in God, such as these words evince. *"And comfort me on every side."* As we were surrounded with afflictions, so shall we be environed with consolations. From above, and from all around, light shall come to dispel our former gloom ; the change shall be great, indeed, when the Lord returns to comfort us.

22 I will also praise thee with the psaltery, *even* thy truth, O my God : unto thee will I sing with the harp, O thou Holy One of Israel.

23 My lips shall greatly rejoice when I sing unto thee ; and my soul, which thou hast redeemed.

24 My tongue also shall talk of thy righteousness all the day long : for they are confounded, for they are brought unto shame, that seek my hurt.

Here is the final vow of praise.

22. "*I will also praise thee with the psaltery.*" Love so amazing calls for sweetest praise. David would give his best music, both vocal and instrumental, to the Best of Masters. His harp should not be silent, nor his voice. "*Even thy truth, O my God.*" This is ever a most enchanting attribute—viz., the truth or faithfulness of our covenant God. On this we rest, and from it we draw streams of richest consolation. His promises are sure, his love unalterable, his veracity indisputable. What saint will not praise him as he remembers this ? "*Unto thee will I sing with the harp, O thou Holy One of Israel.*" Here is a new name, and, as it were, a new song. The Holy One of Israel is at once a lofty and an endearing name, full of teaching. Let us resolve, by all means within our power, to honour him.

23. "*My lips shall greatly rejoice when I sing unto thee.*" It shall be no weariness to me to praise thee. It shall be a delightful recreation, a solace, a joy. The essence of song lies in the holy joy of the singer. "*And my soul, which thou hast redeemed.*" Soul-singing is the soul of singing, Till men are redeemed, they are like instruments out of tune ; but when once the precious blood has set them at liberty, then are they fitted to magnify the Lord who bought them. Our being bought with a price is a more than sufficient reason for our dedicating ourselves to the earnest worship of God our Saviour.

24. "*My tongue also shall talk of thy righteousness all the day long.*" I will talk to myself, and to thee, my God, and to my fellow men : my theme shall be thy way of justifying sinners, the glorious display of thy righteousness and grace in thy dear Son ; and this most fresh and never-to-be-exhausted subject shall be ever with me, from the rising of the sun to the going down of the same. Others talk of their beloveds, and they shall be made to hear of mine. I will become an incessant talker, while this matter lies on my heart, for in all company this subject will be in season. "*For they are confounded, for they are brought unto shame, that seek my hurt.*" As in many other Psalms, the concluding stanzas speak of that as an accomplished fact, which was only requested in former verses. Faith believes that she has her request, and she has it. She is the substance of things hoped for—a substance so real and tangible, that it sets the glad soul a-singing. Already sin, Satan, and the world are vanquished, and the victory is ours.

> " Sin, Satan, Death appear
>   To harass and appal :
> Yet since the gracious Lord is near,
>   Backward they go, and fall.
>
> We meet them face to face,
>   Through Jesus' conquest blest ;
> March in the triumph of his grace,
>   Right onward to our rest."

EXPLANATORY NOTES AND QUAINT SAYINGS.

Whole Psalm.—This Psalm, which has no title in the Hebrew, in the LXX. has the title, "*By David, of the sons of Jonadab, and of those who were first made prisoners.*" If any authority be allowed to this title, we must suppose that this was a Psalm written by David, which was used, as particularly adapted to the circumstances of their condition, by the Rechabites, who were descended from Jonadab (Jer. xxxv.), and the Jews, who were taken by the Chaldeans as captives to Babylon. However this may be, it seems probable that David was the author of this Psalm, and that he wrote it in his extreme age, and but a little while before he died. The line which follows the next Psalm, and closes the second book, perhaps has a reference to this fact. Some of the Fathers interpret the Psalm mystically of the church in her old age, and her trials at the end of the world.—*"Plain Commentary."*

Whole Psalm.—The Psalm, I am aware, is anonymous, and is, therefore, by many recent critics referred to some later writer ; but I am satisfied that Venema and Hengstenberg have adduced sufficient reasons for retaining the opinion of Calvin and the older expositors, that it is from David's pen, and is the plaintive song of his old age. It shows us the soul of the aged saint, darkened by the remembrance of his great transgression, and by the swarms of sorrows with which that sin filled all his later years. But he finds comfort in reverting to the happy days of his child-hood, and especially to the irrevocable trust which he was then enabled to repose in God. The thoughts and feelings expressed remind one of those which invest with such a solemn, tender interest the Second Epistle to Timothy, which embalms the dying thoughts of the great apostle. Like Paul, David takes a retrospect of the Lord's dealings with him from the beginning ; and, in effect, declares, with the dying apostle : " I am not ashamed : for I know whom I have believed, and am persuaded that he is able to keep that which I have committed unto him against that day." 2 Tim. i. 12. Only, there is this notable difference between the two, that while Paul gathered confirmation of his faith from the experience of a thirty years' walk with his Lord, David's experience stretched over more than twice so many years ; for it began with his childhood.—*William Binnie.*

Whole Psalm.—It will be asked how Christ could use such verses as verses 9 and 18, since these look forward apparently to the frailty of age. The reply to this felt difficulty is, that these expressions are used by him in sympathy with his members, and in his own case denote the state equivalent to age. *His* old age was, ere he reached three and thirty years, as John viii. 57 is supposed to imply ; for " Worn-out men live fast." Barclay seems to give the right sense in the following lines :—

> " Grown old and weak, with pain and grief,
> Before his years were half complete."

Besides, the words signify, " Forsake me not from this time onward, even were I to live to grey hairs." This is a view that conveys precious consolation to aged ones, who might be ready to say that Christ could not altogether enter into their feelings, having never experienced the failing weakness of age, the debility, the decay, the bodily infirmities so trying to the spirit. But this Psalm shows us, that in effect he did pass through that stage of our sojourning, worn out and wasted in bodily frame and feeling, by living so much in so short a time. The aged members of his church may find his sweet sympathy breathed out in Isaiah xlvi. 3, 4 ; and, here they may almost see him learning the lesson in a human way, as he bends under the weight of our frailties. For this reason, among others, this Psalm was specially prized by Robert Blair, one of our godly forefathers. He used to call it *"His Psalm."* —*Andrew A. Bonar.*

Verse 1.—*"In thee, O Lord, do I put my trust."* As if he should say : O Lord, permit not those who put their trust in thee to be confounded, and to be held up as a laughing-stock. I have placed all my hope in thee, and thou art that God who, for the sake of thy goodness and truth, hast never deserted those who hope in thee. If thou shalt suffer me to be confounded, the enemies to triumph, and my hope to be placed in thee in vain, certainly this shame shall fall upon thine own name. . . . . Let us, therefore, learn from this place to be more anxious about what may happen to the name of God through us, than to our own ; whether it be through us in doing, or in us in suffering. The prophet is fearful lest he should be confounded on account of his hope placed in God, although it was not in his own power, nor could he prevent it. . . . .

It is necessary, first, that we should be of those who place their hope in God, then it is necessary that this piety of our hearts should not be confined to ourselves only, but should be known to all those who come in contact with us, even our opponents and enemies ; else it is not possible for us to dread this kind of confusion feared by the prophet, when nobody knows that our hope is placed in God. No artist suffers confusion, if he has never shared the good opinion of his fellow men. To no sick man can it be said, Physician, heal thyself, if his reputation for medical skill has never stood high. So of those, it cannot be said, They hoped in God, let him save them if he will have them, of whom it was never remarked that they placed any hope in God. This solicitude, therefore, belongs only to those whose hope is in the Lord : upon others it cannot fall.—*Musculus.*

Verse 1.—*"In thee, O Lord, do I put my trust."* It is a good beginning, and a recommendation to our prayers, when we can declare our faith and trust to be in God alone.—*Edward Walter, in "A Help to the profitable reading of the Psalms."* 1854.

Verse 2.—*"Deliver me in thy righteousness." "Incline thine ear."* Let my deliverance be the fruit of thy promise, and of my prayer ; and so it will be much the sweeter.—*John Trapp.*

Verse 2.—*"In thy righteousness."* The *righteousness* of God is in this place that virtue by which he makes good his promises—revenges injuries and rewards piety— which is elsewhere called his *veracity.* Upon this perfection David here calls, not because he was innocent before God, but because God had bound himself to him by promises, as if he were, in the presence of the men who were persecuting him, both innocent and righteous ; and, therefore, worthy of being delivered from this last terrible calamity into which he had fallen through Absalom, since God had thus acted towards him.—*Hermann Venema.*

Verse 2.—*"Thy righteousness."* Not *mine.* He knew that he was being chastened for his sin against Uriah. He pleads no merit of his own.—*Simon de Muis.*

Verse 2.—*"Incline thine ear."* And since I am so wounded that I am not able to send up my cry to thee, the Most High, do thou *incline thine ear to me* as I lie half-dead, left by the robbers who have wounded and spoiled me.—*Gerhohus.*

Verse 3.—*"Whereunto I may continually resort."* Would he then want to repair to him always ? Our necessities, our work, our danger require it constantly. We are commanded to pray without ceasing. And if, while we acknowledge and feel the obligation, we are renewed in the spirit of our mind, we shall not lament it. Loving him, as well as depending upon him, we shall find it good to draw near to God, and delight ourselves in the Almighty ; and we shall never find him, when we want him, inaccessible. There is a way to our *"strong habitation,"* and we know the way. There is a door, and we have the key. No sentinel keeps us back ; the dwelling is our *own :* and who dares to forbid us all its accommodations and contents ? Kings, however disposed, cannot be always approachable. Owing to the multitude of their claims, and the limitation of their powers, and the importance of keeping up a sense of their dignity, they are only accessible at certain times, and with stately formalities. But the King of kings allows us to come boldly to the throne of grace ; and enjoins us in every thing, by prayer and supplication, to make our requests unto him. We cannot be too importunate, or by our continual coming weary him.— *William Jay.*

Verse 3.—*"Thou hast given commandment to save me."* Let us observe his words ; he ascribes to the word and command of God a saving virtue, which no power on earth, none in hell, nor death itself can resist. Only, he says, give the command that I may be saved, and, in a moment, I shall be wholly saved.—*Musculus.*

Verse 4.—*"The cruel man "* is literally the leavened man, leavened with hatred of truth and enmity to God ; and, therefore, a violent opposer of his people. So, in 1 Cor. v. 8, we are cautioned against the " leaven of malice and wickedness," which, in accordance with the figure, may pervade the whole natural character of an ungodly man, his faculties and affections.—*W. Wilson.*

Verse 5.—*"Thou art my hope."* Not only is our hope *in* him, but he himself is our hope. " God our Saviour, and Lord Jesus Christ," saith St. Paul, " our hope." 1 Tim. i. 1. Yea, there is a deeper, nearer depth : " The glory of the mystery of the gospel," says St. Paul, " is Christ in you, the hope of glory." Christ himself is our hope, as the only Author of it ; Christ is our hope, as the End of it ; and Christ, who is the Beginning and the End, is our hope also by the way ; for he saith, " Christ *in* you, the hope of glory." Col. i. 27. Each yearning of our hearts, each ray of hope which gleams upon us, each touch which thrills through us, each voice which whispers in our inmost hearts of the good things laid up in store for us, if we will love God, are the light of Christ enlightening us, the touch of Christ raising us to new life, the voice of Christ, " Whoso cometh to me, I will in no wise cast out ; " it is " Christ in us, the hope of glory," drawing us up by his Spirit who dwelleth in us, unto himself our hope. For our hope is not the glory of heaven, not joy, not peace, not rest from labour, not fulness of our wishes, nor sweet contentment of the whole soul, nor understanding of all mysteries and all knowledge, not only a torrent of delight ; it is " Christ our God," " the hope of glory." Nothing which God *could* create is what we hope for ; nothing which God could give us out of himself, no created glory, or bliss, or beauty, or majesty, or riches. What we hope for is our Redeeming God himself, his love, his bliss, the joy of our Lord himself who hath so loved us, to be our joy and our portion for ever.—*E. B. Pusey.*

Verse 5.—*"From my youth."* The remembering and acknowledging of God in youth will be great satisfaction in old age. O what joy will reflection upon youthful piety yield ! Even Seneca, a heathen, could say : " Youth well spent is the greatest comfort of old age." David could confidently plead with God for deliverance out of the hand of the wicked : *"For,"* saith he, *"thou art my hope, O Lord God : thou art my trust from my youth."* " Cast me not off in the time of old age ; forsake me not when my strength faileth." (verse 9 ; see also verses 17, 18). An ingenuous master will not turn off a superannuated servant. When the proconsul bade Polycarp deny Christ and swear by the emperor, he answered : " I have served Christ these eighty-six years, and he hath not once injured me, and shall I now deny him ? " Jacob could say : " God hath fed me all my life long unto this day ; he hath been kind to me all my days, and I trust he will look to me even to the end ; and shall I now turn my back on him ? " Whither can I go to mend myself for a master ? "Thou only hast the words of eternal life." He that hath been the stay of my youth, will be the staff of my age. I dare venture my soul upon his promise who hath hitherto maintained me by his providence. " In the days of my youth, the secret of God was upon my tabernacle, his candle did shine upon my head, and by his light I walked through darkness ; " and, though now " the sun, and the light, and moon and stars be darkened," in this my natural horizon, yet " the Lord is my light and my salvation, whom shall I fear ? " " Yea, though I walk through the valley of the shadow of death, I will fear no evil : for thou art with me, thy rod and thy staff they comfort me." I have abundant experience of his grace and presence. O the days of mercy I have had many years ago ! A good man said : " I got that in my youth, which I would not for all the world have to get now."—*O.iver Heywood.* 1629—1702.

Verse 6.—He did not, like most men, recognise the hand of God only when, in an extraordinary manner, it became manifest in life ; but his eye of faith regards the ordinary works of God as miracles. The translation from his mother's womb to the light of day is to him an object of praise. (Psalm xxii. 9, 10.) And, really, is not the preservation of the embryo, in its narrow confines, a miracle ? is it not a pledge, simultaneous with man's growing into being, of our after experience in life, that we have a God " who bringeth us out of death to light " ? (Psalm lxviii. 20.) Is not the reason of our finding so little to praise, to be sought in our having no eyes for his daily miracles ? The Psalmist *has* eyes for the daily miracles of the Lord ; and, therefore, his mouth is daily full of the praise of the Lord.—*Augustus F. Tholuck.*

Verse 6.—Blessed be God that ever I was born.—*Halyburton.*

Verse 6.—This verse corresponds with the preceding, except that David proceeds farther. He not only celebrates the goodness of God, which he had experienced from his childhood, but, also, those proofs of it which he had received previous to his birth. An almost similar confession is contained in Psalm xxii. 9, 10, by which is magnified the wonderful power and inestimable goodness of God in the generation of men, the way and manner of which would be altogether incredible, were it not a fact with which we are quite familiar. If we are astonished at that part of the history of the flood, in which Moses declares (Genesis viii. 13), that Noah and his household lived ten months amidst the offensive nuisance produced by so many living creatures, when he could not draw the breath of life, have we not equal reason to marvel that the infant, shut up within its mother's womb, can live in such a condition as would suffocate the strongest man in half an hour ? But we thus see how little account we make of the miracles which God works, in consequence of our familiarity with them. The Spirit, therefore, justly rebukes this ingratitude, by commending to our consideration this memorable instance of the grace of God which is exhibited in our birth and generation. When we are born into the world, although the mother do her office, and the midwife may be present with her, and many others may lend their help, yet did not God, putting, so to speak, his hand under us, receive us into his bosom, what would become of us? and what hope would there be of the continuance of our life? Yea, rather, were it not for this, our very birth would be an entrance into a thousand deaths. God, therefore, is with the highest propriety said *to take us out of our mother's bowels.* To this corresponds the concluding part of the verse, *"My praise shall be continually of thee;"* by which the Psalmist means that he had been furnished with matter for praising God without intermission.—*John Calvin.*

Verse 7.—"I am as a wonder unto many." The Hebrew word translated *"wonder"* would, perhaps, be better expressed by *portent.* It denotes anything uncommon, and wonderful, and admits a double meaning. Some interpreters are of opinion, that it is here taken in the most favourable sense, and that the Psalmist represents himself as considered, by the many, as a *prodigy of God's goodness.* But the whole tenor of the Psalm is against this meaning; which is not badly expressed by Green: "I am become a gazing-stock to the multitude."—*Alexander Geddes.* 1737—1802.

Verse 7.—"I am as a wonder unto many," etc. On several account a converted man may be an object of surprise among his contemporaries. This may arise from the circumstance of his conversion dating at a late period of his life, when his long continuance in a state of impenitence seemed to render it almost certain that he would persist in it to the last. It is, indeed, a wonder to see any human being's course entirely altered at a late period, and to observe him afterwards moving in a totally different direction, influenced by different principles. Or, to take the instance of another convert, the character he is enabled to sustain, founded upon his great change, is in such marked and continued contrast to his former habits of life as to render it difficult to recognise in the Christian of to-day the sinner of yesterday. "Is Saul also among the prophets?" Or, in yet another example, the means divinely employed to effect conversion may be, apparently, so disproportionate to the magnitude of the result, as to place the result itself under suspicion and doubt. Every godly man, like Ananias of old, may hesitate to admit into his society the persecutor or the profligate of unhappy notoriety, except upon clearly discerning that he has become a new creature in Christ Jesus, and that old evil habits have passed away. At the same time, his former ungodly associates are mortified at his renunciation of fellowship with them, and are malicious enough to promulgate false reports concerning his character and motives. "They think it strange," says the apostle, "that ye run not with them to the same excess of riot, speaking evil of you." Yet to such a convert his God is a sun and shield—a shield from the shafts of cruel slander, and a refuge to him from all storms of persecution. In all similar cases the language of the Psalmist becomes particularly appropriate: "*I am as a wonder unto many; but thou art my strong refuge."—John Leifchild.*

Verse 7.—"A wonder." The Messiah did not attract the admiring gaze of mankind. He did arrest attention; he did excite *"wonder;"* but it was not the wonder of admiration. A few, whose eyes God had opened, saw, indeed, in some measure, the real grandeur there was amid all this apparent meanness. They "beheld his glory—the glory as of the only-begotten of the Father;" a glory that bedimmed all created lustre. But the great body of those who beheld him were "astonished" at him. His external appearance, especially when contrasted with his claim to Messiahship, shocked them. The Galilean peasant—the Nazarene carpenter—the son of Joseph, claiming God for his own Father,—declaring himself the "bread of life," and "the light of the world," and asserting that the destinies of eternity hung on the reception or rejection of him and his message; all this excited a mingled emotion of amazement and indignation, scorn and horror, in the bosom of the great majority of his countrymen. He was *"a wonder,"* a prodigy unto many. A mixture of pity and contempt, disgust and wonder, seems to have stirred the stern bosom of the Roman governor, when he brought him out wearing the robe of mock royalty and the torturing crown, and exclaimed, "Behold the man." Even his friends were confounded, though their astonishment bore a different character. The closing scene, notwithstanding what appear to us very plain forewarnings, appears to have come on them like a thunderbolt. They were overwhelmed with amazement, as well as with sorrow. What blank astonishment sat on their countenances when he made the announcement, "Verily I say unto you, one of you shall betray me!" How must their amazement have risen at the successive scenes of Gethsemane, and the hall of the high priest, and the court of Pilate, till at last they saw him, in whom they trusted that he should redeem Israel, nailed to a cross like a felonious slave—execrated of man, and deserted of God! Then their amazement reached its consummation: they were " astonished at him."—*John Brown, in "The Sufferings and Glories of the Messiah."*

Verse 8.—*"Let my mouth be filled with thy praise."* Let my mouth, I say, *be so filled with thy praise,* that from the bottom of my heart, even to the lips of my mouth, the plenitude of thy grace, O God, infused into my heart, and diffused over my lips, may loyally magnify thee; so shall I not be found like that people, of whom thou dost say : " This people honour me with their lips, but their heart is far from me." Isa. xxix. 13.—*Gerhohus.*

Verse 9.—*"Cast me not off in the time of old age,"* etc. ; for now I have most need of thee. The white rose is soonest cankered ; so is the white head soonest corrupted. *Sæpe nigrum cor est, caput album.* Satan maketh a prey of old Solomon, Asa, Lot, others ; whom when young he could never so deceive. The heathens, therefore, well warn us to look well to our old age, as that which cometh not alone, but is infested with many diseases, both of body and mind. This David knew, and, therefore, prayed as here : *"Cast me not off in the time of old age ; forsake me not when my strength faileth."* He is a rare old man that can say with Caleb (Joshua xiv. 10, 14), " Behold, the Lord hath kept me alive," etc.—*John Trapp.*

Verse 9.—*"Cast me not off in the time of old age,"* etc. It is not unnatural or improper for a man who sees old age coming upon him to pray for special grace, and special strength, to enable him to meet what he cannot ward off, and what he cannot but dread ; for who can look upon the infirmities of old age, as coming upon himself, but with sad and pensive feelings ? Who would wish *to be* an old man ? Who can look upon a man tottering with years, and broken down with infirmities ; a man whose sight and hearing are gone ; a man who is alone amidst the graves of all the friends that he had in early life ; a man who is a burden to himself, and to the world ; a man who has reached the " Last scene of all that ends the strange, eventful history "—that scene of

> " Second childishness, and mere oblivion,
> Sans teeth, sans eyes, sans taste, sans everything ; "

that scene when one can say—

> " I have lived long enough ; my way of life
> Is fallen into the sear, the yellow leaf ;
> And that which should accompany old age,
> As honour, love, obedience, troops of friends,
> I must not look to have ; "

who can think of all this and not pray for special grace for himself, should he live to see those days of infirmity and weakness ? And who, in view of such infirmities, can fail to see the propriety of seeking the favour of God in early years ?—*Albert Barnes.*

Verse 9.—*"Cast me not off in the time of old age,"* etc. David, mindful of the noble actions which, through God's assistance, he had achieved in his youth, beseeches him not to desert his servant, when persecuted by a rebellious son, in his old age. The weakness and temptations peculiar to that time of life, render this a petition necessary for all to make, before we are overtaken by it. The church findeth but too much occasion to make the same, now that she is sunk in years ; when faith languisheth, charity waxeth cold, and the infirmities of a spiritual old age are coming fast upon her.—*George Horne.*

Verse 9.—*"Cast me not off."* God had cast off his predecessor, Saul, and things looked as if he now meant to cast *him* off. His people also seemed disposed, by their joining with Absalom, to cast him off : hence the force of the petition.—*Andrew Fuller.*

Verse 9.—*" Forsake me not when my strength faileth."* Neither will Christ forsake his church in the latter days of its age, when the weakness of faith becomes more prevalent.—*W. Wilson.*

Verse 9.—*" Forsake me not when my strength faileth."* June 28. This day I enter on my eighty-sixth year. I now find I grow old : (1) My sight is decayed, so that I cannot read a small print, unless in a strong light. (2) My strength is decayed, so that I walk much slower than I did some years since. (3) My memory of names, whether of persons or places, is decayed, till I stop a little to recollect them. What I should be afraid of, is, if I took thought for the morrow, that my body should weigh down my mind, and create either stubbornness, by the decrease of my understanding, or peevishness, by the increase of bodily infirmities ; But thou shalt answer for me, O Lord my God.—*John Wesley.*

Verse 11.—All kinds of distresses are obnoxious to the worst of misjudgings from malevolent minds. The sufferings of Christ produced this censorious scoff, " Let God deliver him, if he will have him." (Matt. xxvii. 43.) David's trouble easily induced his adversaries to conclude that *"God had forsaken him, and that there was none to deliver him."* But in troubles of this nature, where especially there are frightful complainings against themselves, men are more easily drawn out to be peremptory in their uncharitable judgments concerning them, because the trouble itself is somewhat rare, and apt to beget hideous impressions, and, withal the vent which the afflicted parties give by their bemoaning of their estate, in hope to ease themselves thereby, is but taken as a testimony against themselves, and the un-doubted echoes of their real feelings.—*Richard Gilpin* (1625—1700), *in "Dæmonologia Sacra ; or, a Treatise of Satan's Temptations."* [In Nichol's Series of Puritan Divines.]

Verse 13.—*"Let them be confounded,"* etc. Let them, who were so wicked that they never hoped anything good of me, *be confounded* by the evidence of the blessings which manifestly fall upon me ; and, *let them fail*, the grounds of their abuse being taken away, as a fire fails when the fagots are removed.—*Gerhohus.*

Verse 13.—*"Let them be confounded,"* etc. By the law of retaliation (*talio*), he might have said : " Be thou an adversary to their souls, and seek their hurt." Nothing of this is hinted at : his only desire is that they may be confounded and fail, that they may be covered with disgrace and shame. He seeks nothing beyond the frustration of their attempts, that they may begin to be ashamed, and have no cause for boasting that they came off victorious.—*Musculus.*

Verse 13.—Shame ariseth from utter disappointments. If hope deferred causeth shame, then much more hope destroyed. When a man sees his hopes quite cut off, so that he can no way reach the thing he looked for, shame takes hold of him strongly. —*Joseph Caryl.*

Verse 13.—*"That are adversaries to my soul."* That hated him with a diabolical hatred, as the devil hates the souls of men, and who has his name *Satan* from the word here used. All wicked men are Satans, full of enmity against God and all good men ; and such were David's enemies, spiteful and malicious, and nothing would satisfy them but his life.—*John Gill.*

Verse 14.—*"But I will hope continually."* Behold, O Lord, I have prayed to thee, and I am comforted. Hope has thus taught me. I am glad ; because in thee I have trusted, I shall never be confounded. Sorrow returned, equipped with vast array, fortified at all points with swords and spears, and with great clamour beleaguered my city. The din of his horsemen terrified me ; and, standing at the gates, he commanded silence, and thus loudly spake : " Behold the man who trusted in God ; who said, I shall not be confounded for ever ; who took hope for a consoler." And, when he observed me blushing at these words, he drew nearer, and said : " Where are the promises which were thy trust ? Where the consolation ? Where the deliverance ? What have thy tears availed thee ? What help have thy prayers brought thee from heaven ? Thou hast cried, and no one has answered ; thou has wept, and who have been moved with pity for thee ? Thou hast called upon thy God, and he has been silent. Thou hast prayed to him, and he has hidden himself from thee : there has come no voice nor sound. . . . Arise, therefore, and flee for help to man, that he may free thee from thy prison." With these words, there arose such a din of arms in the camp—such a clamour of men and sounding of trumpets—that I could hardly keep up heart ; and, unless my beloved Hope had brought me help, Sorrow would have seized and carried me off in chains to his own place. Comes Hope to me, gleaming in divine brightness, and, smiling, said : " O soldier of Christ, how is thy heart ? What is this struggle in thy mind ? " At these words, I began to blush. " Fear not," she said, " Evil shall not capture thee ; thou shalt never perish. Behold, I am with thee, to deliver thee. Dost thou not know what is written (Psalm xii.), ' The fool hath said in his heart, there is no God.' As one of the foolish women hath this Sorrow spoken ; never shall he be able to persuade thee that there is no God, or that God does not exercise a providence over all."—*Girolamo Savonarola*, 1452—1498.

Verse 14.—*"And I will always hope, and add to* (literally, *add upon,* accumulate, increase) *all thy praise."* To all thy praise which I have uttered hitherto, I will continue still to add.—*Joseph Addison Alexander.*

Verse 14.—*"I will expect continually."* But what did he *expect?* That for which he prayed in the ninth verse—the preservation of his prosperity, the presence and the help of God to the very end of life. Wherefore, he adds, *continually,* in perpetuity, in the time of old age—*usque ad mortem.*—*Hermann Venema.*

Verse 14.—As there is no end to the lovingkindness of Jehovah, there should be none to our gratitude. The hope of a Christian enableth him to be thankful, even in the dark season of affliction.—*Mrs. Thomson.*

Verse 15.—The *"righteousness"* of God, here mentioned, includes not only the rectitude of his nature, and the equity of his proceedings, but likewise that everlasting righteousness which his Son hath brought in for our justification. God's *righteousness* and *salvation* are here joined together; and, therefore, let no man think to put them asunder, or expect salvation without righteousness.—*Mrs. Thomson.*

Verse 15.—*"I know not the numbers."* David began his arithmetic, in the 14th verse, with *addition*: "I will yet praise thee more and more;" but he is fairly beaten in this first rule of sacred mathematics. His calculation fails him, the mere enumeration of the Lord's mercies overwhelms his mind: he owns his inadequacy. Reckon either by time, by place, or by value, and the salvation of God baffles all powers of estimation.—*C. H. S.*

Verse 16.—*"I will go."* The word *to go* must be here taken in the sense of going to battle against enemies. This, he says, he will do, trusting not to his own, but to the power of the Lord, his heart fired with the memory of the righteousness of God. So is it in another place: "Some trust in chariots, some in horses, but we in the name of our God."—*Musculus.*

Verse 16.—*"I will go in the strength of the Lord."* The minister goes thus by realising this strength and depending on it. In this strength he goes into the path of communion with God, into the fields of conflict, in the privacy of domestic life, and in all the walks of active life. His boast is in the *righteousness* of Christ; and he *mentions* this to God as the ground of his confidence, to himself as the spring of his comforts, to others as the hope of salvation.—*Substance of Sermon by James Sherman. The first preached by him after his settlement at Surrey Chapel. September 4th, 1836.*

Verse 16.—*"The strengths of the Lord God."* The power of God is expressed in the plural number, to show the greatness of it, which is as a garrison to the believer.—*John Gill.*

Verse 16.—*"I will go in the strength of the Lord."* The phrase, *to go in,* or, *with the strengths of God,* does not teach us that he *would go* by means of them, by their help and assistance, as many have thought, *first,* because the word is used to signify the illustrious and mighty deeds of God; *secondly,* because it denotes the *subject* of praise; but *to go with the strengths of Jehovah,* as the rendering ought to be . . . is *to go* as if girt with his former deeds of power—girt with them as if with the *material* of praise.—*Hermann Venema.*

Verse 17.—*"O God, thou hast taught me from my youth."* Whence was it that David understood "more than the ancients"? (Psalm cxix. 100.) He had a Father to teach him; God was his instructor. Many a child of God complains of ignorance and dulness; remember this, thy Father will be thy tutor; he hath promised to give "his Spirit to lead thee into all truth" (John vi. 13); and God doth not only inform the understanding, but incline the will; he doth not only teach us what we should do, but enables us to do it. (Ezekiel xxxvi. 27): "I will cause you to walk in my statutes." What a glorious privilege is this, to have the star of the word pointing us to Christ, and the loadstone of the Spirit drawing!—*Thomas Watson.*

Verse 17.—*"Thou hast taught me from my youth."* If you ask me what were the ways by which David was taught, I might ask you what they were not. . . . . . God taught him by his shepherd's crook; and by the rod and sceptre of a king he taught him. He taught him by the shouts of the multitude—"Saul hath slain his thousands and David his ten thousands ; " and he taught him just as much, if not more, by the contempt he met in the court of the Philistines. He taught him by the arrows of Jonathan, levelled in friendship ; and he taught him by the javelin of Saul levelled at his life. He taught him by the faithlessness of Abiathar, and the faithlessness of even his faithful Joab ; and he taught him by the faithfulness of Abishai, and the faithfulness of Mephibosheth ; and, let me add too, by the rebellion of Absalom, and the selfishness of Adonijah ; they were all means, by which the Lord taught his servant. And be assured, you that are under his teaching, there is nothing in your lives, but he can teach you by it : by comforts and crosses, by your wounds and your healings, by what he gives and by what he takes away. He unteaches his child, that he may teach him ; shows him his folly, that he may make him wise ; strips him of his vain confidence, that he may give him strength ; makes him know that he is nothing, that he may show him that he has all in the Lord—in Jesus his Beloved one.—*James Harrington Evans.*

Verse 17.—*"Thou hast taught me from my youth."* Youth needs a teacher that it may embrace virtue. Seneca says, *Virtue is a hard thing to youth, it needs a ruler and guide : vices are acquired without a master.* How prone he was in his boyhood and youth to vices, we may see in Psalm xxv. " Remember not the sins of my youth, nor my transgressions." Jerome, in his Epistle to Nepotianus, says : " As fire in green wood is stifled, so wisdom in youth, impeded by temptations and con- cupiscence, does not unfold its brightness, unless by hard work, and steady application and prayer, the incentives of youth are inwardly repelled. Hence it is that almost all nations have provided good and wise teachers of the young. Among the Spartans, one was chosen from the Magistrates and Senators to be παιδονόμος, rector of the boys. . . . . At Athens there were twelve men named *Sophronistae,* elected by the suffrages of all the tribes, to moderate the manners of youth. . . . . God is a teacher of his servants. Plato says, οἰδέν εἶναι θειότερον, that there is nothing more divine than the education of children. Of God the Father, or the whole Trinity, Hannah, the mother of Samuel, says, 1 Samuel ii. 3 : " The Lord is a God of knowledge ; " [*Scientiarum,* Vulg.] that is, as the Chaldee has it, he knows all things. . . . . Socrates says, that he is *the mind of the universe.* Without him, therefore, all are demented ; but with him, and through him, in a single moment they become wise. Philo, in his treatise of the sacrifice of Cain and Abel, says, Masters cannot fill the mind of their pupils as if they were pouring water into a vessel ; but when God, the fountain of wisdom, communicates knowledge to the human race, he does it without delay, in the twinkling of an eye. . . . . *His anointing shall teach you of all things.*—1 John ii. 27.—*Thomas Le Blanc.*

Verse 17.—*"From my youth."* Is it such " a crown of glory " to be found old in the ways of righteousness ? Do you then begin to be godly betimes ; that, if you live in this world you may have this crown set upon your heads when you are ancient ; for is it not better for you to be plants of God's house than weeds upon the dunghill ? Those that are wicked are but as weeds upon a dunghill, but you that are godly are as plants in God's own orchard. In the last of the Romans, verse 7, we find that *Andronicus and Junia* are commended because they were in Christ before Paul : " They were in Christ before me." It is an honourable thing to be in Christ before others ; this is honourable when you are young ; and then going on in the ways of godliness all your young time, and so in your middle age, and till you come to be old.—*Jeremiah Burroughs.*

Verse 17.—*"Wondrous works."* Observe that he calls the blessing of divine aid so often received in affliction, *wondrous works.* By this expression, he shows us, with what grievous perils he was tossed ; then how he had been snatched from them by the hand of God, contrary to the expectation of all men. Therefore, God is wonderful among his saints. To this end the adversities of the saints tend, that they may show forth in them the wonderful works of God.—*Musculus.*

Verses 17, 18.—The integrity of our hearts and ways, in former walkings after God, and service for God, may by faith in Christ, as all in our justification, be pleaded. See also Isa. xxxviii. 3 and Psalm cxix. 10. The Lord himself maketh it to himself a motive to show mercy to his people (Isa. lxiii. 8 ; Jer. ii. 2) ; only we must use this plea more rarely and sparingly, in a self-denying way, in faith in Christ's righteousness, as made ours.—*Thomas Cobbet.*

Verse 18.—*"Now also when I am old and grey-headed, O God, forsake me not."* God exalts pardoning grace to some more, and sanctifying grace to others ; he is the God of grace. Those ships that have been in long voyages at sea, three or four years out, have gone through hot climates and cold, passed the equinoctial line again and again, and have run through many a difficulty, and great storms, and yet have been kept alive at sea, as they speak, when these shall meet one another at sea near the haven, how will they congratulate ? And old disciples should do so, that God hath kept grace alive in their souls. And I would ask you how many thousand ships have you seen cast away before your eyes ? How many that have made " shipwreck of faith and a good conscience," as the apostle speaks ? This and that profession, that has run into this and that error damnable, or false opinions and teaching, though all of smaller moment ; others that have struck upon quick-sands of worldly preferments, and many split upon rocks, and yet you have been kept. This should move you to bless this your God, the God of grace, the more. Come, let me knock at your hearts ; are none of you old professors, like old hollow oaks, who stand in the woods among professors still, and keep their stand of profession still, and go to ordinances, etc. ; but the " rain they drink in," as the apostle's word is, serves to no other end but to rot them. " These are nigh unto cursing." Or, have you green fruits still growing on you, as quickly and lively affections to God and Christ, and faith and love, as at the first, and more abounding ? O bless God you are so near the haven, and lift up your hearts, your redemption draws near ; and, withal, raise your confidence, that that God of grace, who hath called you into his eternal glory, will keep you for it, and possess you of it shortly.—*Thomas Goodwin.*

Verse 18.—"*Forsake me not ; until,*" etc. Apostasy in old age is fearful. He that climbs almost to the top of a tower, then slipping back, hath the greater fall. The patient almost recovered, is more deadly sick by a relapse. There were stars struck from heaven by the dragon's tail (Rev. xii. 4) ; they had better never have perched so high. The place where the Israelites fell into that great folly with the daughters of Moab, was in the plain, within the prospect of the Holy Land ; they saw their inheritance, and yet fell short of it. So wretched is it for old men to fall near to their very entry of heaven, as old Eli in his indulgence (1 Sam. ii.) ; old Judah in his incest (Gen. xxxviii.) ; old David with Bathsheba ; old Asa trusting in the physicians more than in God (2 Chron. xvi. 12) ; and old Solomon built the high places. Some have walked like cherubs in the midst of the stones of fire, yet have been cast as profane out of God's mountain. Ez. xxviii. 14, 16. Thus the seaman passeth all the main, and suffers wreck in the haven. The corn often promiseth a plenteous harvest in the blade, and shrinks in the ear. You have trees loaden with blossoms, yet, in the season of expectation, no fruit. A comedy that holds well many scenes, and goes lamely off in the last act, finds no applause. " Remember Lot's wife " (Luke xvii. 32) : think on that pillar of salt, that it may season thee.—*Thomas Adams.*

Verse 18.—"*Until I have shewed thy strength unto this generation,*" etc. Are there better preachers of the works of God to be found than hoary parents in the circle of their children ; or grandparents in that of their grandchildren ?—*Augustus F. Tholuck.*

Verse 18.—

With years oppressed, with sorrows worn,
Dejected, harassed, sick, forlorn,
    To thee, O God, I pray ;
To thee my withered hands arise,
To thee I lift these failing eyes :
    Oh, cast me not away !

Thy mercy heard my infant prayer ;
Thy love, with all a mother's care,
    Sustained my childish days :
Thy goodness watched my ripening youth,
And formed my heart to love thy truth,
    And filled my lips with praise.

O Saviour ! has thy grace declined ?
Can years affect the Eternal Mind,
    Or time its love destroy ?
A thousand ages pass thy sight,
And all their long and weary flight
    Is gone like yesterday.

Then, e'en in age and grief, thy name
Shall still my languid heart inflame,
    And bow my faltering knee :
Oh, yet this bosom feels the fire,
This trembling hand and drooping lyre,
    Have yet a strain for thee !

Yes, broken, tuneless, still, O Lord,
This voice, transported, shall record
    Thy goodness, tried so long ;
Till, sinking slow, with calm decay,
Its feeble murmurs melt away
    Into a seraph's song.

                        Sir Robert Grant.

Verse 19.—*"O God, who is like unto thee ? "* Either for greatness or goodness, for power or for mercy, for justice, truth, and faithfulness ; for the perfections of his nature, or the works of his hands ; and to be praised, reverenced, and adored, as he is.—*John Gill.*

Verse 19.—*"Who is like unto thee !"* מִי כָמוֹךָ, *Mi camocha.* God is alone : who can resemble him ? He is eternal ; he can have none *before*, and there can be none *after ;* for, in the infinite *unity* of *trinity*, he is that eternal, unlimited, impartible, incomprehensible, and uncompounded, ineffable Being, whose *essence* is hidden from all created intelligences, and whose *counsels* cannot be fathomed by any creature that even his own hand can form. "WHO IS LIKE UNTO THEE ! " will excite the wonder, amazement, praise, and adoration of angels and men to all eternity.—*Adam Clarke.*

Verse 20.—*"Thou shalt quicken me again,"* etc. Here Jerome triumpheth over the Jews, challenging them when this was ever verified in David, for he was never dead and quickened again ; and, therefore, this must needs be expounded of him as that in Psalm xvi : *"Thou wilt not leave my soul in the grave ; "* and to *"the depths of the earth,"* here, answer those words, Ephesians iv. 9, " Now that he ascended, what is it but that he also descended first into the lower parts of the earth ? " Yet, this may also be applied to David, being figuratively understood, as a like speech of Hannah, 1 Samuel ii.—*John Mayer.*

Verse 20.—*"And thou shalt bring me up,"* etc. This is an allusion to men who are unhappily fallen into a deep pit of water. The meaning is, Thou shalt draw me out of the extreme danger into which I am plunged, and wherein I shall perish without thy help.—*Thomas Fenton.*

Verse 21.—Greatness increasing with comfort, and comfort increasing with greatness ; very rarely united.—*George Rogers.*

Verse 22.—*"With the psaltery."* . . . *"with the harp."* There was a typical signification in them ; and upon this account they are not only rejected and condemned by the whole army of Protestant divines, as for instance, by Zuinglius, Calvin, Peter Martyr, Zepperus, Parœus, Willet, Ainsworth, Ames, Calderwood, and Cotton ; who do, with one mouth, testify against them, most of them expressly affirming that they are a part of the abrogated legal pedagogy ; so that we might as well recall the incense, tapers, sacrifices, new moons, circumcision, and all the other shadows of the law into use again. But Aquinas himself also, though a Popish schoolman, pleads against them upon the same account, *quia aliquid figurabant,* and saith, the Church in his time did not use them, *ne videatur judaizare,* lest they should seem to judaize.—*Samuel Mather, on The Types.*

Verse 22.—*"Psaltery."* . . . *"harp."* Suppose singing with instruments were not typical, but only an external solemnity of worship, fitted to the solace of the outward senses of children under age, such as the Israelites were in the Old Testament (Gal. iv. 1, 2, 3) ; yet now, in the grown age of the heirs of the New Testament, such external pompous solemnities are ceased, and no external worship reserved, but such as holdeth forth simplicity and gravity ; nor is any voice now to be heard in the church of Christ, but such as is significant and edifying by signification (1 Cor. xiv. 10, 11, 26), which the voice of instruments is not.—*John Cotton, 1585—1652.*

Verse 22.—*"Holy One of Israel."* This name of God occurs in the Psalms only in two other places, lxxviii. 41 ; lxxxix. 18 ; these last two being, according to

Delitzsch, older Psalms than this. In Isaiah, this name of God occurs thirty times ; in Habakkuk once ; in Jeremiah (who may have adopted it from Isaiah) twice (l. 29 ; li. 5).—*J. J. Stewart Perowne.*

Verse 23.—*"My lips ;" "my soul."* Hypocrites praise God with the *"lips"* only ; but David joins the *soul* to the lips.—*William Nicholson.*

Verse 23.—*"Greatly."* See how the word great is repeated. Great things done, verse 19 ; great troubles shown, verse 20 ; greatness increased, verse 21 ; and great rejoicing consequent thereon, in the present verse. In a great God, doing great things, it is meet greatly to rejoice.—*C. H. S.*

HINTS TO PREACHERS.

Arguments used to induce the Lord to hear, drawn, I. From his *justice* and *equity* : "Deliver me in thy righteousness." II. From his *word* and *promise* : "Thou hast given commandment," etc. III. From his *power* : "Thou art my rock," etc. IV. From his *relation* to him : "My God, my hope." V. From the *qualities* of his *adversaries* : "They were wicked, unrighteous, and cruel." VI. From his *confidence* : "Thou art my hope." VII. From his *gracious providence* : "By thee have I been holden up," etc. VIII. From his *thankful heart* : "My praise shall be continually," etc. IX. He had *none to trust to* but God : "Thou art my refuge."—*Adam Clarke.*

Verse 1.—Faith is a present act ; faith is a personal act, faith deals only with God, faith knows what she is about, faith kills her fears by prayer.

Verse 2.—An appeal. I. To the power of God : "Deliver me." II. To the faithfulness of God : "In thy righteousness." III. To the providence of God : "Cause me to escape." IV. To the condescension of God : "Incline thine ear." V. To the mercy of God : "Save me."

Verse 2.—*Cause me to escape.* From whom ? From what ? How ? By what power ? For what end ?

Verse 3.—(First two clauses.) The believer abiding in God and continually resorting to him.

Verse 3.—(Third clause.) A command based on the divine promise, clothed with divine power, addressed to all necessary agencies, and embracing all exigencies.

Verse 4.—I. When God is for us, the wicked are against us. II. When the wicked are against us, God is for us.

Verse 5.—God the essence of hope and faith.

Verse 7 (*first clause*) may be accommodated to, I. *The Saviour.* II. *The Saint.* He is a *wonder*, in reference to (1) What he once was ; (2) What he now is ; (3) What he will hereafter be. III. *The Sinner* is " a wonder unto many : " a wonder to three worlds : to (1) angels ; (2) saints ; (3) devils and lost souls.—*Warwell Fenn.* 1830.

Verse 7.—Consider the text, with reference to *David*, to *Christ*, and to the *Christian*. I. With reference to *David*. 1. David was a wonder as a man. 2. As a king. 3. As a servant of God. II. With respect to *Christ*. 1. Christ was a wonder in his person. 2. In his life. 3. In his miracles. 4. In his teaching. 5. In his sufferings. 6. In his ascension and mediatorial glory. III. With regard to the *Christian*. 1. The Christian is a wonder to himself. 2. To the world. 3. To wicked spirits. 4. To the angels in heaven.—*John Cawood.* 1830.

Verse 8.—I. What ? filled with what ?—murmurings ? doubts ? fears ? No ! Praise. My own ?—of men ? No. *"Thy praise." "Thy* honour." II. When ? "All the day." 1. The whole day. 2. Every day ; a good preparation for heaven.

Verse 9.—There are some peculiar circumstances of old age which render this blessing—the favour and presence of God—necessary. I. Old age is a time of but little natural enjoyment, as Barzillai acknowledged. 2 Sam. xix. 35. II. It is a time of life in which the troubles of life are often known to increase. III. Old age is a time in which the troubles of life not only increase, but become less tolerable. IV. Old age is a time that ought to command respect, and does so among dutiful children and all serious Christians : but it is often known to be attended with neglect.

This is the case especially where they are poor and dependent. It has been the case where public characters have lost their youthful vivacity, and the brilliancy of their talents.—*A. Fuller.*

Verse 9.—There is, I. Fear, mixed with faith. 1. Natural to old age. 2. Suggested by the usage of the world. II. Faith, mixed with fear : " Cast me not," etc. 1. Old age is not a sin. 2. It is a crown of glory if found, etc.

Verses 11, 12.—Two great lies and two sweet prayers.

Verses 13, 14.—I. What the wicked gain by opposing the righteous : " Let them," etc., *verse 13.*—II. What the righteous gain from being opposed by them,—*verse 14 :* " But I," etc.

Verse 14.—See " Spurgeon's Sermons," No. 998 : " More and More."

Verse 15.—I. The determination avowed. 1. To recount the instances of the divine faithfulness in his deliverances. 2. To recount them publicly : " My mouth," etc. 3. Constantly : " All the day." II. The reason assigned : " For I know not," etc. " Eternity's too short to utter all thy praise." Therefore, I begin it now, and will continue it.

Verse 16.—I. The resolution : " I will go." II. The reservation : " Thy strength only—thy righteousness only."

Verse 17.—"*O God, thou hast taught me.*" None but God can teach us experimentally ; and the lessons he teaches are always useful and important. He teaches all his scholars to know themselves—their depravity, poverty, and slavery. He teaches them his law—its purity, claims and penalty. He teaches them his gospel —its fulness, freeness, and sensibility. He teaches them to know himself ; as a reconciled God, as their Father and faithful friend. His teaching is accompanied with power and authority. We may know divine teaching by its effects : it always produces humility—they sit at his feet ; dependence upon him ; abhorrence of sin ; love to God as a teacher ; obedience to the lessons taught ; thirst for further attainments ; and it brings us daily to Jesus.—*James Smith.*

Verse 18.—The peculiar testimony of pious old age, what it is based upon, to whom it should be directed, and what we may hope from it.

Verse 19.—A sermon might be instructively worked out upon " the high things of God."

Verse 20.—I. The future benefit of present trials : " Hereafter," said Æneas to his shipwrecked companions, " it will delight us to think of these things." II. The present benefit of future mercies : " Glory to thee for all the grace we have not tasted yet."

Verse 22.—A choice subject for song—" thy truth," which may mean either doctrinal truth, or the attribute of faithfulness, its manifestation in history, and in our own experience.

Verses 22, 23.—I. The soul of music : Not in the instrument, or the voice, but in the soul. " I will sing with the understanding also." " Making melody in the heart," etc. II. The music of the soul. The " soul which thou hast redeemed." Redemption is the music of souls once lost. Their only song in heaven.

Verse 24.—How to make familiar talk edifying and useful.

PSALM LXXII.

TITLE.—*A Psalm for Solomon.—The best linguists affirm that this should be rendered, of or by Solomon. There is not sufficient ground for the rendering for. It is pretty certain that the title declares Solomon to be the author of the Psalm, and yet from verse 20 it would seem that David uttered it in prayer before he died. With some diffidence we suggest that the spirit and matter of the Psalm are David's, but that he was too near his end to pen the words, or cast them into form ; Solomon, therefore, caught his dying father's song, fashioned it into goodly verse, and, without robbing his father, made the Psalm his own. It is, we conjecture, the Prayer of David, but the Psalm of Solomon. Jesus is here, beyond all doubt, in the glory of his reign, both as he now is, and as he shall be revealed in the latter-day glory.*

DIVISION.—*We shall follow the division suggested by Alexander. "A glowing description of the reign of Messiah as righteous, verses 1—7 ; universal, verses 8—11 ; beneficent, verses 12—14 ; and perpetual, verses 15—17 ; to which are added a doxology, verses 18, 19 ; and a postscript, verse 20."*

EXPOSITION.

GIVE the king thy judgments, O God, and thy righteousness unto the king's son.

2 He shall judge thy people with righteousness, and thy poor with judgment.

3 The mountains shall bring peace to the people, and the little hills, by righteousness.

4 He shall judge the poor of the people, he shall save the children of the needy, and shall break in pieces the oppressor.

5 They shall fear thee as long as the sun and moon endure, throughout all generations.

6 He shall come down like rain upon the mown grass : as showers *that* water the earth.

7 In his days shall the righteous flourish ; and abundance of peace so long as the moon endureth.

1. *"Give the king thy judgments, O God."* The right to reign was transmitted by descent from David to Solomon, but not by that means alone : Israel was a theocracy, and the kings were but the viceroys of the greater King ; hence the prayer that the new king might be enthroned by divine right, and then endowed with divine wisdom. Our glorious King in Zion hath all judgment committed unto him. He rules in the name of God over all lands. He is king " Dei Gratia " as well as by right of inheritance. *"And thy righteousness unto the king's son."* Solomon was both king and king's son ; so also is our Lord. He has power and authority in himself, and also royal dignity given him of his Father. He is the righteous king ; in a word, he is " the Lord our righteousness." We are waiting till he shall be manifested among men as the ever-righteous Judge. May the Lord hasten in his own time the long-looked-for day. Now wars and fightings are even in Israel itself, but soon the dispensation will change, and David, the type of Jesus warring with our enemies, shall be displaced by Solomon the prince of peace.

2. *"He shall judge thy people with righteousness."* Clothed with divine authority, he shall use it on the behalf of the favoured nation, for whom he shall show himself strong, that they be not misjudged, slandered, or in any way treated maliciously. His sentence shall put their accusers to silence, and award the saints their true position as the accepted of the Lord. What a consolation to feel that none can suffer wrong in Christ's kingdom : he sits upon the great white throne, unspotted by a single deed of injustice, or even mistake of judgment : reputations are safe

enough with him. *"And thy poor with judgment."* True wisdom is manifest in all the decisions of Zion's King. We do not always understand his doings, but they are always right. Partiality has been too often shown to rich and great men, but the King of the last and best of monarchies deals out even-handed justice, to the delight of the poor and despised. Here we have the poor mentioned side by side with the king. The sovereignty of God is a delightful theme to the poor in spirit ; they love to see the Lord exalted, and have no quarrel with him for exercising the prerogatives of his crown. It is the fictitious wealth which labours to conceal real poverty, which makes men cavil at the reigning Lord, but a deep sense of spiritual need prepares the heart loyally to worship the Redeemer King. On the other hand, the King has a special delight in the humbled hearts of his contrite ones, and exercises all his power and wisdom on their behalf, even as Joseph in Egypt ruled for the welfare of his brethren.

3. *"The mountains shall bring peace to the people."* Thence, aforetime, rushed the robber bands which infested the country ; but now the forts there erected are the guardians of the land, and the watchmen publish far and near the tidings that no foe is to be seen. Where Jesus is there is peace, lasting, deep, eternal. Even those things which were once our dread, lose all terror when Jesus is owned as monarch of the heart : death itself, that dark mountain, loses all its gloom. Trials and afflictions, when the Lord is with us, bring us an increase rather than a diminution of peace. *"And the little hills, by righteousness."* Seeing that the rule of the monarch was just, every little hill seemed clothed with peace. Injustice has made Palestine a desert ; if the Turk and Bedouin were gone, the land would smile again ; for even in the most literal sense, justice is the fertilizer of lands, and men are diligent to plough and raise harvests when they have the prospect of eating the fruit of their labours. In a spiritual sense, peace is given to the heart by the righteousness of Christ ; and all the powers and passions of the soul are filled with a holy calm, when the way of salvation, by a divine righteousness, is revealed. Then do we go forth with joy, and are led forth with peace ; the mountains and the hills break forth before us into singing.

4. *"He shall judge the poor of the people."* He will do them justice, yea, and blessed be his name, more than justice, for he will delight to do them good. *"He shall save the children of the needy."* Poor, helpless things, they were packhorses for others, and paupers themselves, but their King would be their protector. Happy are God's poor and needy ones ; they are safe under the wing of the Prince of Peace, for he will save them from all their enemies. *"And shall break in pieces the oppressor."* He is strong to smite the foes of his people. Oppressors have been great breakers, but their time of retribution shall come, and they shall be broken themselves. Sin, Satan, and all our enemies must be crushed by the iron rod of King Jesus. We have, therefore, no cause to fear : but abundant reason to sing—

> " All hail the power of Jesus' name !
> Let angels prostrate fall ;
> Bring forth the royal diadem,
> And crown him Lord of all."

It is much better to be poor than to be an oppressor ; for both the needy and their children find an advocate in the heavenly Solomon, who aims all his blows at haughty ones, and rests not till they are utterly destroyed.

5. *"They shall fear thee as long as the sun and moon endure."* And well they may. Such righteousness wins the cheerful homage of the poor and the godly, and strikes dismay into the souls of unrighteous oppressors ; so that all through the lands, both good and bad are filled with awe. Where Jesus reigns in power men must render obeisance of some sort. His kingdom, moreover, is no house of cards, or dynasty of days : it is as lasting as the lights of heaven ; days and nights will cease before he abdicates his throne. Neither sun nor moon as yet manifest any failure in their radiance, nor are there any signs of decrepitude in the kingdom of Jesus ; on the contrary, it is but in its youth, and is evidently the coming power, the rising sun. Would to God that fresh vigour were imparted to all its citizens to push at once the conquests of Immanuel to the uttermost ends of the earth. *"Throughout all generations"* shall the throne of the Redeemer stand. Humanity shall not wear out the religion of the Incarnate God. No infidelity shall wither it away, nor superstition smother it ; it shall rise immortal from what seemed its grave ; as the true phœnix, it shall revive from its ashes ! As long as there are

men on earth Christ shall have a throne among them. Instead of the fathers shall be the children. Each generation shall have a regeneration in its midst, let Pope and Devil do what they may. Even at this hour we have before us the tokens of his eternal power; since he ascended to his throne, eighteen hundred years ago, his dominion has not been overturned, though the mightiest of empires have gone like visions of the night. We see on the shore of time the wrecks of the Cæsars, the relics of the Moguls, and the last remnants of the Ottomans. Charlemagne, Maximilian, Napoleon, how they flit like shadows before us! They were and are not; but Jesus for ever is. As for the houses of Hohenzollern, Guelph, or Hapsburg, they have their hour; but the Son of David has all hours and ages as his own.

6. *"He shall come down like rain upon the mown grass."* Blessings upon his gentle sway! Those great conquerors who have been the scourges of mankind have fallen like the fiery hail of Sodom, transforming fruitful lands into deserts: but he with mild, benignant influence softly refreshes the weary and wounded among men, and makes them spring up into newness of life. Pastures mown with the scythe, or shorn by the teeth of cattle, present, as it were, so many bleeding stems of grass, but when the rain falls it is balm to all these wounds, and it renews the verdure and beauty of the field; fit image of the visits and benedictions of " the consolation of Israel." My soul, how well it is for thee to be brought low, and to be even as the meadows eaten bare and trodden down by cattle, for then to thee shall the Lord have respect; he shall remember thy misery, and with his own most precious love restore thee to more than thy former glory. Welcome Jesus, thou true *Bien-aimé*, the Well-beloved, thou art far more than Titus ever was—the Delight of Mankind. *"As showers that water the earth."* Each crystal drop of rain tells of heavenly mercy which forgets not the parched plains: Jesus is all grace, all that he does is love, and his presence among men is joy. We need to preach him more, for no shower can so refresh the nations. Philosophic preaching mocks men as with a dust shower, but the gospel meets the case of fallen humanity, and happiness flourishes beneath its genial power. Come down, O Lord, upon my soul, and my heart shall blossom with thy praise :—

> " He shall come down as still and light
>   As scatter'd drops on genial field ;
> And in his time who loves the right,
>   Freely shall bloom, sweet peace her harvest yield."

7. *"In his days shall the righteous flourish."* Beneath the deadly Upas of unrighteous rule no honest principles can be developed, and good men can scarcely live; but where truth and uprightness are on the throne, the best of men prosper most. A righteous king is the patron and producer of righteous subjects. None flourish under Nero but those who are monsters like himself: like will to like; and under the gentle Jesus the godly find a happy shelter. *"And abundance of peace so long as the moon endureth."* Where Jesus reigns he is known as the true Melchizedek, king both of righteousness and peace. Peace based upon right is sure to be lasting, but no other will be. Many a so-called Holy Alliance has come to the ground ere many moons have filled their horns, because craft formed the league, perjury established it, and oppression was the design of it; but when Jesus shall proclaim the great Truce of God, he will ordain perpetual peace, and men shall learn war no more. The peace which Jesus brings is not superficial or shortlived; it is abundant in its depth and duration. Let all hearts and voices welcome the King of nations; Jesus the Good, the Great, the Just, the Ever-blessed.

8 He shall have dominion also from sea to sea, and from the river unto the ends of the earth.

9 They that dwell in the wilderness shall bow before him ; and his enemies shall lick the dust.

10 The kings of Tarshish and of the isles shall bring presents : the kings of Sheba and Seba shall offer gifts.

11 Yea, all kings shall fall down before him : all nations shall serve him.

8. *"He shall have dominion also from sea to sea."* Wide spread shall be the rule of Messiah ; only the Land's End shall end his territory : to the Ultima Thule shall his sceptre be extended. From Pacific to Atlantic, and from Atlantic to Pacific,

he shall be Lord, and the oceans which surround each pole shall be beneath his sway. All other power shall be subordinate to his; no rival nor antagonist shall he know. Men speak of the Emperor of all the Russias, but Jesus shall be Ruler of all mankind. *"And from the river unto the ends of the earth."* Start where you will, by any river you choose, and Messiah's kingdom shall reach on to the utmost bounds of the round world. As Solomon's realm embraced all the land of promise, and left no unconquered margin; so shall the Son of David rule all lands given him in the better covenant, and leave no nation to pine beneath the tyranny of the prince of darkness. We are encouraged by such a passage as this to look for the Saviour's universal reign; whether before or after his personal advent we leave for the discussion of others. In this Psalm, at least, we see a personal monarch, and he is the central figure, the focus of all the glory; not his servant, but himself do we see possessing the dominion and dispensing the government. Personal pronouns referring to our great King are constantly occurring in this Psalm; *he* has dominion, kings fall down before *him,* and serve *him;* for *he* delivers, *he* spares, *he* saves, *he* lives, and daily is *he* praised.

9. *"They that dwell in the wilderness shall bow before him."* Unconquered by arms, they shall be subdued by love. Wild and lawless as they have been, they shall gladly wear his easy yoke; then shall their deserts be made glad, yea, they shall rejoice and blossom as the rose. *"And his enemies shall lick the dust."* If they will not be his friends, they shall be utterly broken and humbled. Dust shall be the serpent's meat; the seed of the serpent shall be filled therewith. Homage among Orientals is often rendered in the most abject manner, and truly no sign is too humiliating to denote the utter discomfiture and subjugation of Messiah's foes. Tongues which rail at the Redeemer deserve to lick the dust. Those who will not joyfully bow to such a prince richly merit to be hurled down and laid prostrate; the dust is too good for them, since they trampled on the blood of Christ.

10. *"The kings of Tarshish and of the isles shall bring presents."* Trade shall be made subservient to the purposes of mediatorial rule; merchant princes, both far and near, shall joyfully contribute of their wealth to his throne. Seafaring places are good centres from which to spread the gospel; and seafaring men often make earnest heralds of the cross. Tarshish of old was so far away, that to the eastern mind it was lost in its remoteness, and seemed to be upon the verge of the universe; even so far as imagination itself can travel, shall the Son of David rule; across the blue sea shall his sceptre be stretched; the white cliffs of Britain already own him, the gems of the Southern Sea glitter for him, even Iceland's heart is warm with his love, Madagascar leaps to receive him; and if there be isles of the equatorial seas whose spices have as yet not been presented to him, even there shall he receive a revenue of glory. He has made many an islet to become a Holy Isle, and hence, a true Formosa. *"The kings of Sheba and Seba shall offer gifts."* Agriculture and pasturage shall contribute their share. Foreign princes from inland regions, as yet unexplored, shall own the all-embracing monarchy of the King of kings; they shall be prompt to pay their reverential tribute. Religious offerings shall they bring, for their King is their God. Then shall Arabia Felix be happy indeed, and the Fortunate Isles be more than fortunate. Observe, that true religion leads to generous giving; we are not taxed in Christ's dominions, but we are delighted to offer freely to him. It will be a great day when kings will do this: the poor widow has long ago been before them, it is time that they followed; their subjects would be sure to imitate the royal example. This free-will offering is all Christ and his church desire; they want no forced levies and distraints, let all men give of their own free will, kings as well as commoners; alas! the rule has been for kings to give their subjects' property to the church, and a wretched church has received this robbery for a burnt offering; it shall not be thus when Jesus more openly assumes the throne.

11. *"Yea, all kings shall fall down before him."* Personally shall they pay their reverence, however mighty they may be. No matter how high their state, how ancient their dynasty, or far-off their realms, they shall willingly accept him as their Imperial Lord. *"All nations shall serve him."* The people shall be as obedient as the governors. The extent of the mediatorial rule is set forth by the two far-reaching *alls*, all kings and all nations: we see not as yet all things put under him, but since we see Jesus crowned with glory and honour in heaven, we are altogether without doubt as to his universal monarchy on earth. It is not to be imagined that an Alexander or a Cæsar shall have wider sway than the Son of God. *"Every*

knee shall bow to him, and every tongue shall confess that Jesus Christ is Lord, to the glory of God the Father." Hasten it, O Lord, in thine own time.

12 For he shall deliver the needy when he crieth ; the poor also, and *him* that hath no helper.

13 He shall spare the poor and needy, and shall save the souls of the needy.

14 He shall redeem their soul from deceit and violence : and precious shall their blood be in his sight.

12. *"For he shall deliver the needy."* Here is an excellent reason for man's submission to the Lord Christ ; it is not because they dread his overwhelming power, but because they are won over by his just and condescending rule. Who would not fear so good a Prince, who makes the needy his peculiar care, and pledges himself to be their deliverer in times of need ? *"When he crieth."* He permits them to be so needy as to be driven to cry bitterly for help, but then he hears them, and comes to their aid. A child's cry touches a father's heart, and our King is the Father of his people. If we can do no more than cry it will bring omnipotence to our aid. A cry is the native language of a spiritually needy soul ; it has done with fine phrases and long orations, and it takes to sobs and moans ; and so, indeed, it grasps the most potent of all weapons, for heaven always yields to such artillery. *"The poor also, and him that hath no helper."* The proverb says, " God helps those that help themselves ; " but it is yet more true that Jesus helps those who cannot help themselves, nor find help in others. All helpless ones are under the especial care of Zion's compassionate King ; let them hasten to put themselves in fellowship with him. Let them look to him, for he is looking for them.

13. *"He shall spare the poor and needy."* His pity shall be manifested to them ; he will not allow their trials to overwhelm them ; his rod of correction shall fall lightly ; he will be sparing of his rebukes, and not sparing in his consolations. *"And shall save the souls of the needy."* His is the dominion of souls, a spiritual and not a worldly empire ; and the needy, that is to say, the consciously unworthy and weak, shall find that he will give them his salvation. Jesus calls not the righteous, but sinners to repentance. He does not attempt the superfluous work of aiding proud Pharisees to air their vanity ; but he is careful of poor Publicans whose eyes dare not look up to heaven by reason of their sense of sin. We ought to be anxious to be among these needy ones whom the Great King so highly favours.

14. *"He shall redeem their soul from deceit and violence."* These two things are the weapons with which the poor are assailed : both law and no law are employed to fleece them. The fox and the lion are combined against Christ's lambs, but the Shepherd will defeat them, and rescue the defenceless from their teeth. A soul hunted by the temptations of Satanic craft, and the insinuations of diabolical malice, will do well to fly to the throne of Jesus for shelter. *"And precious shall their blood be in his sight."* He will not throw away his subjects in needless wars as tyrants have done, but will take every means for preserving the humblest of them. Conquerors have reckoned thousands of lives as small items ; they have reddened fields with gore, as if blood were water, and flesh but manure for harvests ; but Jesus, though he gave his own blood, is very chary of the blood of his servants, and if they must die for him as martyrs, he loves their memory, and counts their lives as his precious things.

15 And he shall live, and to him shall be given of the gold of Sheba : prayer also shall be made for him continually ; *and* daily shall he be praised.

16 There shall be an handful of corn in the earth upon the top of the mountains ; the fruit thereof shall shake like Lebanon : and *they* of the city shall flourish like grass of the earth.

17 His name shall endure for ever : his name shall be continued as long as the sun : and *men* shall be blessed in him : all nations shall call him blessed.

15. *"And he shall live."* Vive le Roi ! O King ! live for ever ! He was slain, but is risen and ever liveth. *"And to him shall be given of the gold of Sheba."* These

are coronation gifts of the richest kind, cheerfully presented at his throne. How gladly would we give him all that we have and are, and count the tribute far too small. We may rejoice that Christ's cause will not stand still for want of funds; the silver and the gold are his, and if they are not to be found at home, far-off lands shall hasten to make up the deficit. Would to God we had more faith and more generosity. *"Prayer also shall be made for him continually."* May all blessings be upon his head; all his people desire that his cause may prosper, therefore do they hourly cry, "Thy kingdom come." Prayer *for* Jesus is a very sweet idea, and one which should be for evermore lovingly carried out; for the church is Christ's body, and the truth is his sceptre; therefore we pray for him when we plead for these. The verse may, however, be read as "through him," for it is by Christ as our Mediator that prayer enters heaven and prevails. "Continue in prayer" is the standing precept of Messiah's reign, and it implies that the Lord will continue to bless. *"And daily shall he be praised."* As he will perpetually show himself to be worthy of honour, so shall he be incessantly praised:—

> " For him shall constant prayer be made,
> And praises throng to crown his head;
> His name, like sweet perfume, shall rise
> With every morning's sacrifice."

16. *"There shall be an handful of corn in the earth upon the top of the mountains."* From small beginnings great results shall spring. A mere handful in a place naturally ungenial shall produce a matchless harvest. What a blessing that there is a handful; " except the Lord of hosts had left unto us a very small remnant we should have been as Sodom, and we should have been like unto Gomorrah; " but now the faithful are a living seed, and shall multiply in the land. *"The fruit thereof shall shake like Lebanon."* The harvest shall be so great that the wind shall rustle through it, and sound like the cedars upon Lebanon:—

> " Like Lebanon, by soft winds fann'd,
> Rustles the golden harvest far and wide."

God's church is no mean thing; its beginnings are small, but its increase is of the most astonishing kind. As Lebanon is conspicuous and celebrated, so shall the church be. *"And they of the city shall flourish like grass of the earth."* Another figure. Christ's subjects shall be as plentiful as blades of grass, and shall as suddenly appear as eastern verdure after a heavy shower. We need not fear for the cause of truth in the land; it is in good hands, where the pleasure of the Lord is sure to prosper. " Fear not, little flock, it is your Father's good pleasure to give you the kingdom." When shall these words, which open up such a vista of delight, be fulfilled in the midst of the earth?

17. *"His name shall endure for ever."* In its saving power, as the rallying point of believers, and as renowned and glorified, his name shall remain for ever the same. *"His name shall be continued as long as the sun."* While time is measured out by days, Jesus shall be glorious among men. *"And men shall be blessed in him."* There shall be cause for all this honour, for he shall really and truly be a benefactor to the race. He himself shall be earth's greatest blessing; when men wish to bless others they shall bless in his name. *"All nations shall call him blessed."* The grateful nations shall echo his benedictions, and wish him happy who has made them happy. Not only shall some glorify the Lord, but all; no land shall remain in heathenism; all nations shall delight to do him honour.

18 Blessed *be* the LORD God, the God of Israel, who only doeth wondrous things.

19 And blessed *be* his glorious name for ever: and let the whole earth be filled *with* his glory: Amen, and Amen.

20 The prayers of David the son of Jesse are ended.

18, 19. As Quesnel well observes, these verses explain themselves. They call rather for profound gratitude, and emotion of heart, than for an exercise of the understanding; they are rather to be used for adoration than for exposition. It is, and ever will be, the acme of our desires, and the climax of our prayers, to behold Jesus exalted King of kings and Lord of lords. He has done great wonders such as none else can match, leaving all others so far behind, that he remains the sole and only wonder-worker ; but equal marvels yet remain, for which we look with joyful expectation. He is the Blessed God, and his name shall be blessed ; his name is glorious, and that glory shall fill the whole earth. For so bright a consummation our heart yearns daily, and we cry *"Amen, and Amen."*

20. *"The prayers of David the son of Jesse are ended."* What more could he ask ? He has climbed the summit of the mount of God ; he desires nothing more. With this upon his lip, he is content to die. He strips himself of his own royalty and becomes only the *"* son of Jesse,*"* thrice happy to subside into nothing before the crowned Messiah. Before his believing eye the reign of Jesus, like the sun, filled all around with light, and the holy soul of the man after God's own heart exulted in it, and sung his " Nunc dimittis : " *"* Lord, now lettest thou thy servant depart in peace, for mine eyes have seen thy salvation ! " We, too, will cease from all petitioning if it be granted to us to see the day of the Lord. Our blissful spirits will then have nothing further to do but for ever to praise the Lord our God.

EXPLANATORY NOTES AND QUAINT SAYINGS.

Title.—*"For Solomon."* I shall but mention a threefold analogy between Christ and Solomon. 1. In his *personal wisdom* (1 Kings iv. 29, 30) ; so Christ (Col. ii. 3) ; " In him are hid all the treasures of wisdom and knowledge." 2. In the *glorious peace and prosperity of his kingdom* : the kingdom was peacably settled in his hand. 1 Chron. xxii. 9 ; iv. 24, 25. And so he fell to the work of building the temple, as Christ doth the church ; so Christ (Isa. ix. 6) ; he is the Prince of Peace, the great Peacemaker. Eph. ii. 14. 3. In his *marriage with Pharaoh's daughter.* Some observe that the daughter of Pharaoh never seduced him : neither is there any mention made of the Egyptian idols. 1 Kings xi. 5, 7. In his other outlandish marriages he did sin ; but *this* is mentioned as by way of special exception (1 Kings xi. 1) ; for she was a *proselyte,* and so it was no sin to marry her : and the love between her and Solomon is made a type of the love between Christ and the church. So Christ hath taken us Gentiles to be spouse unto him. Psalm xlv.—*Samuel Mather* (1626—1671), *in "The Figures or Types of the Old Testament."*

Whole Psalm.—The Seventy-second Psalm contains a description of an exalted king, and of the blessings of his reign. These blessings are of such a nature as to prove that the subject of the Psalm must be a divine person. 1. His kingdom is to be everlasting. 2. Universal. 3. It secures perfect peace with God and goodwill among men. 4. All men are to be brought to submit to him through love. 5. In him all the nations of the earth are to be blessed ; *i.e.,* as we are distinctly taught in Gal. iii. 16, it is in him that all the blessings of redemption are to come upon the world. The subject of this Psalm is, therefore, the Redeemer of the world.—*Charles Hodge, in "Systematic Theology."*—1871.

Whole Psalm.—This Psalm was penned by a king, it is dedicated to a king, and is chiefly intended concerning him who is " King of kings."—*Joseph Caryl, in a Sermon entitled "David's Prayer for Solomon."*

Whole Psalm.—Two Psalms bear *Solomon's* name in their titles. One of these is the Hundred and Twenty-seventh, the other is the Seventy-second ; and here the traces of his pen are unequivocal. A mistaken interpretation of the note appended to it, " The prayers of David the Son of Jesse are ended," led most of the old commentators to attribute the Psalm to David, and to suppose that it is a prayer offered in his old age " for Solomon," as the peaceful prince who was to succeed him on the throne. However, it has long been known that the note in question refers to the whole of the preceding portion of the Psalter, much of which was written by Asaph and the sons of Korah ; and there can be no doubt that the title can only be translated, " of Solomon." So clear are the traces of Solomon's pen that Calvin, whose sagacity in this kind of criticism has never been excelled, although he thought himself obliged, by the note at the end of the Psalm, to attribute the substance of it to David, felt Solomon's touch so sensibly, that he threw out the conjecture that the prayer was the father's, but that it was afterwards thrown into the lyrical form by the son. This is not the place for detailed exposition; I will, therefore, content myself with remarking that, properly speaking, the Psalm is not "for Solomon" at all. If it refers to him and his peaceful reign, it does so only in as far as they were types of the Person and Kingdom of the Prince of Peace. The Psalm, from beginning to end, is not only capable of being applied to Christ, but great part is incapable of being fairly applied to any other.—*William Binnie.*

Whole Psalm.—This is the fourth of those Psalms which predict the two natures of Christ. This Psalm admonishes us that we believe in Christ as perfect God, and perfect Man and King.—*Psalter of Peter Lombard* (—1164).

Whole Psalm.—That under the type of Solomon (to whom it is inscribed) the Messiah is "The King" of whom this Psalm treats, we have the consent, not only of the most eminent divines of modern times, and of the Fathers of the early Christian church, but of the ancient and most distinguished Jewish expositors; of which reference, indeed, it contains the most conclusive internal evidence. And, as under a new type, so is the kingdom here presented to us in a new aspect, in marked contradistinction to its character as foreshadowed by its other great type, the Davidical: for the character of David's reign was conquest. He was "a man of war" (1 Chron. xxviii. 1—3); the appointed instrument for subjecting the enemies of God's people Israel, by whom they were put in undisturbed possession of the promised land. But the character of Solomon's reign was peace, the import of his name, succeeding to the throne after all enemies had been subdued, and governing the kingdom which David's wars had established (1 Kings ii. 12), the two types, respectively, of Christ as he is yet to be manifested at his next appearing; first revealed as David, as seen in the vision of that event (Rev. xix. 11): "I saw heaven opened, and behold a white horse; and he that sat upon him was called Faithful and True, and in righteousness *he doth judge and make war*," etc., subduing the Antichristian confederacy (verses 19—21), as before predicted in the Second Psalm, of this same confederacy: "Thou shalt break them with a rod of iron; thou shalt dash them in pieces like a potter's vessel." And then, as Solomon, taking his throne, and extending the blessings of his kingdom of peace to the ends of the earth. David in the Second Psalm; Solomon in this.—*William De Burgh.*

Whole Psalm.—The reader is reminded of James Montgomery's hymn, beginning, "Hail to the Lord's Anointed;" it is a very beautiful versification of this Psalm, and will be found in "Our Own Hymn Book," No. 353.

Verse 1.—"*Give the king thy judgments, O God.*" Right and authority to execute judgment and justice. The Father hath committed all judgment unto the Son.—*John Fry.*

Verse 1.—"*The king*" .... "*The king's son.*" I do not apprehend, with the generality of interpreters, that by "*The king,*" and "*The king's son,*" David means himself and his son, but *Solomon* only, to whom both the titles agree, as he was David's son, and anointed by him *king* during his lifetime.—*Samuel Chandler.*

Verse 1.—"*The king*" .... "*The king's son.*" We see that our Lord is here termed both מֶלֶךְ, and בֶּן־מֶלֶךְ, being king himself, and also the son of a king; both as respects his human origin, having come forth from the stock of David, and also as to his divine origin; for the Father of the universe may, of course, be properly denominated King. Agreeably to this designation, we find on the Turkish coins the inscription: *Sultan, son of Sultan.*—*George Phillips.*

Verse 2.—"*Thy judgments.*" From whom does he seek these? O God, he says, give them. Therefore is it the gift of God that kings should judge righteously and observe justice. Moreover, he does not simply say, O God, give judgments to the king, and righteousness to the king's son; but *thy* judgments and *thy* righteousness. Grant them this grace, that what is just in thy sight they may judge. The world has its own judgments and its own righteousness, but deals in such a way that true righteousness is more oppressed than approved. Not such are the judgments and righteousness of God.—*Musculus.*

Verse 3.—"*The mountains shall bring peace to the people,*" etc. Those who apply this Psalm to Solomon expound the distich thus; "That the steep mountains on the frontier, strongly garrisoned, shall secure the land from hostile invasion; and the hills, cleared of the banditti, which in the rude ages were accustomed to inhabit them, under the government of the king, intended in this Psalm, should be the peaceful seats of a useful, civilised peasantry." This sense is not ill expressed in Mr. Merrick's translation :

> " Peace, from the fort-clad mountain's brow,
> Descending, bless the plains below ;
> And justice from each rocky cell,
> Shall violence and fraud expel."

But so little of the Psalm is at all applicable to Solomon, and the greater part of it so exclusively belongs to the Messiah, that I think these mountains and hills allude to the nature of the land of Judæa ; and the general sense is, that, in the times of the great king, the inhabitants of that mountainous region shall live in a state of peace and tranquility. The thing intended is the happy condition of the natural Israel, in the latter day restored to God's favour, and to the peaceful possession of their own land. It is a great confirmation of this sense, that *"righteousness"* is mentioned as the means of the peace which shall be enjoyed.—*Samuel Horsley.*

Verse 3.—*"The mountains shall bring peace to the people."* It was, and still is, common in the East to announce good or bad news from the tops of mountains and other eminences. By this means acts of justice were speedily communicated to the remotest parts of the country. Thus, when Solomon decided the controversy between the two harlots, the decision was quickly known over all the land. See 1 Kings iii. 28.—*Alexander Geddes.*

Verse 3.—*"The mountains shall bring peace."* The reference is to the fertility of the soil, which now is shown in an extraordinary way, when mountain summits, which are either oppressed with hopeless sterility or yield at a far inferior rate to the valleys, produce all things plentifully. And by this figure he signifies that this happiness of his kingdom shall not be the portion of a few only, but shall abound in all places and to all people, of every condition and of every age. No corner of the land, he affirms, shall be destitute of this fertility.—*Mollerus.*

Verse 3.—*"The mountains shall bring peace."* You may be sure to have peace when your mountains shall bring forth peace ; when those mountains, which heretofore were mountains of prey and hills of the robbers, shall be a quiet habitation ; when peace shall not be walled up in cities, or fenced in by bulwarks, but the open fields and highways, the mountains and the hills shall yield it abundantly ; under every hedge, and under every green tree, there shall you find it ; when the cottagers and the mountaineers shall have their fill of it ; when they shall eat and be satisfied, lie down and none shall make them afraid, then the blessing is universal : and this is the work of *righteousness.*—*Joseph Caryl.*

Verse 3.—The *"mountains"* and *"hills"* are not at all named as the most unfruitful places of the land, which they really were not, in Palestine, compare Deut. xxxiii. 15 ; Psalm cxlvii. 8, " Who maketh grass to grow upon the mountains ; " Psalm lxv. 12,—nor even because what is on them can be seen everywhere, and from all sides (*Tholuck*), compare against this, Joel iv. 18, " The mountains shall drop down new wine, and the hills shall flow with milk," Isa. lv. 12,—but, as being the most prominent points and ornaments of the country, and, therefore, as representing it, well fitted to express the thought that the country shall be *everywhere* filled with peace.—*E. W. Hengstenberg.*

Verse 4.—*"The children of the needy."* The phrase, *the children of the afflicted,* is put for *the afflicted,* an idiom quite common in Hebrew ; and a similar form of expression is sometimes used by the Greeks, as when they say υἱοὺς ἰατρῶν, *the sons of physicians* for *physicians.*—*John Calvin.*

Verse 5.—

> The lofty glory of the Flavian family shall remain,
> Enduring like the sun and stars.
>
> *Martial.*—Bk. ix. Epig. 7.

Verse 6.—*"He shall come down like rain upon the mown grass,"* etc. This is spoken and promised of Christ, and serves to teach us that Christ coming to his church and people, by the gracious influences of his Holy Spirit, is most useful and refreshing to their souls, like showers of rain to the dry ground, or a meadow newly cut to make it spring again. Christless souls are like the dry ground ; without the moisture of saving grace their hearts are hard ; neither rods, mercies, nor sermons, make impression upon them. Why? They are without Christ, the fountain of grace and spiritual influences. Before the fall man's soul was like a well-watered garden, beautiful, green, and fragrant; but by his apostasy from God, in Adam our first head, the springs of grace and holiness are quite dried up in his soul; and there is no curing of this drought but by the soul's union with a new head; to wit, Christ our second Adam, who has the Spirit given him without measure for the use of all his members. Now, when we are united by faith to Christ, our Head of influences, the dry land is turned into water-springs; Christ "comes down as the rain" by his Spirit of regeneration, and brings the springs of grace into the soul. He is the first and immediate receptacle of the Holy Spirit, and all regenerating and sanctifying influences, and out of his fulness we must by faith receive them. And when at any time the springs of grace are interrupted in the soul by sin or unbelief, so as the ground turns dry, the plants wither, and the things which remain are ready to die, the soul hath need to look up to Jesus Christ to come down with new showers upon the thirsty ground and decayed plants.

1. As the rain is the free gift of God to the dry ground, it comes free and cheap to poor and rich, small and great, and costs them nothing : so Christ with his blessings is God's free gift to a dry and perishing world; for which we should be continually thankful. 2. As nothing can stop the falling of the rain; so nothing can hinder Christ's gracious influences, when he designs to awake, convince, or soften a hard heart. When those showers do fall on sinners, the most obstinate will must yield, and cry, Lord, what wilt thou have me to do? 3. As the rain is most necessary and suitable to the dry ground, and to the various plants it produceth, and also to the different parts of every plant or tree—such as the root, trunk, branches, leaves, flowers, and fruit; so Christ is absolutely necessary, and his influence most suitable to all his people's souls, and to every faculty of them—the understanding, will, memory, and affections; and to all their different graces, faith, love, repentance, etc.; to root and establish them, strengthen and confirm them, quicken and increase them, cherish and preserve them. 4. As the rain comes in divers ways and manners to the earth, sometimes with cold winds and tempests, thunders and lightnings, and at other times with calmness and warmth; so Christ comes to sinners, sometimes with sharp convictions and legal terrors, and sometimes with alluring invitations and promises. 5. O how pleasant are the effects of rain to languishing plants, to make them green and beautiful, lively and strong, fragrant and beautiful! So the effects of Christ's influences are most desirable to drooping souls, for enlightening and enlivening them, for confirming and strengthening them, for comforting and enlarging them, for appetising and satisfying them, transforming and beautifying them. A shower from Christ would soon make the church, though withered, turn green and beautiful, and to send forth a smell as of a field that the Lord hath blessed; and likewise some drops of this shower, falling down upon the languishing graces of communicants, would soon make them vigorous and lively in showing forth their Saviour's death at his table.—*John Willison.*

Verse 6.—There cannot be a more lively image of a flourishing condition than what is conveyed to us in these words. The grass which is forced by the heat of the sun, before the ground is well prepared by rains, is weak and languid, and of a faint complexion; but when clear shining succeeds the gentle showers of spring, the field puts forth its best strength, and is more beautifully arrayed than ever Solomon in all his glory.—*Thomas Sherlock.* 1678—1761.

Verse 6.—"*He shall come down,*" ירד. There is a fourfold descending of Christ which the Scripture mentions. 1. His incarnation, the manifestation of himself in the flesh. II. The abasing himself in condition; he did not only assume human flesh, but all the natural infirmities of our flesh. III. The subjecting of himself to death. IV. The distillations of his grace and spiritual blessings upon his church.— *Ralph Robinson.*

Verse 6 (first clause).—Some render this "like dew on the fleece." The mysterious fleece of Gideon, which, on being exposed to the air, is first of all filled with the dew of heaven while all the ground around it is quite dry, and which afterwards becomes dry while the earth is watered, pictures to us, according to the old divines, that the dew of Heaven's grace was poured out upon Judæa at the time when all the rest of the world remained in barrenness and ignorance of God; but that now, by a strange alteration, this same Judæa lies in dryness and forgetfulness of God, while, on the contrary, all the other nations of the earth are inundated with the dew of heavenly grace.—*Pasquier Quesnel.*

Verse 6.—*"Upon the mown grass."* The Hebrew word used here hath a double signification. It signifies a shorn fleece of wool, and it signifies a meadow newly mown. This hath occasioned divers readings. Some read it, He shall come down like the rain into a fleece of wool : so the Septuagint. They that follow this reading make it an allusion unto the dew that fell upon Gideon's fleece (Judges vi. 37—39), when all the land beside was dry, and, again, upon the rest of the land when the fleece was dry. Others read it according to our translation : *"He shall come down like rain upon the mown grass."* This seems to me more agreeable to the meaning of the Holy Ghost ; especially because of the clause following, which is added by way of explication : *"As showers that water the earth." "As the showers,"* רְבִיבִים. Rain and showers differ only as less and more ; rain signifies smaller showers, and showers signify greater rain. Deut. xxxii. 2. Rain falling in multitude of drops is called a shower. *"That water the earth."* The word זַרְזִיף *zarziph*, which is here translated *"water,"* is only used in this place in all the Bible. It signifies to water by dispersion, to water by drops. The showers are dispersed in drops all over the face of the earth, in a very regular and artificial way. " God hath divided," saith Job, " a watercourse for the overflowings of water." Job xxxviii. 25. The rain is from the cloud spouted out by drops after such a manner that every part hath its share.—*Ralph Robinson.*

Verse 6.—*"The mown grass ;"* literally, *" that which is shorn,"* whether *fleece* or *meadow.* In the former sense it occurs Jud. vi. 37, and so the older translators all take it, (Aq. ἐπὶ κουράν, LXX. and others ἐπὶ πλόκον, Jerome and Vulgate, *in vellus*,) probably with the idea that the reign of the monarch would be accompanied by signal tokens of the divine favour and blessing, like the dew upon Gideon's fleece ; in the latter sense, the word is found Amos vii. 1 ; and this is indisputably its meaning here, as the parallel shows. The *mown* meadow is particularly mentioned, because the roots of the grass would be most exposed to the summer heat after the crop had been gathered in, and the effect would be most striking in the shooting of the young green blade after the shower.—*J. J. Stewart Perowne.*

Verse 7.—*"Righteous." "Peace."* Do you ask what he is individually ? The answer is, " King of Righteousness : " a being loving righteousness, working righteousness, promoting righteousness, procuring righteousness, imparting righteousness to those whom he saves, perfectly sinless, and the enemy and abolisher of all sin. Do you ask what he is practically, and in relation to the effect of his reign ? The answer is, " King of Peace : " a sovereign whose kingdom is a shelter for all who are miserable, a covert for all who are persecuted, a resting-place for all who are weary, a home for the destitute, and a refuge for the lost.—*Charles Stanford.*

Verse 7.—*"Abundance of peace."* Literally, *"multitude* of peace ;" that is, the things which produce peace, or which indicate peace, will not be few, but numerous ; they will abound everywhere. They will be found in towns and villages, and private dwellings ; in the calm and just administration of the affairs of the State ; in abundant harvests ; in intelligence, in education, and in undisturbable industry ; in the protection extended to the rights of all.—*Albert Barnes.*

Verse 7.—*"So long as the moon endureth."* It does not necessarily follow from these words that the moon will ever cease to exist. The idea, commonly held, of the annihilation of the starry firmament is without foundation in Scripture. Such an idea has a pernicious influence on the human mind, inasmuch as it leads men to depreciate that which bears in such striking character the stamp and impress of the divine glory.—*Frederic Fysh.*

Verse 8.—*"From the river."* There are many modern interpreters who, from the mention of the *"river "*—namely, the river Euphrates—in the other clause of the verse, think that the boundaries of the land of Palestine are here to be understood, that country being described as extending from the Red Sea to the Sea of Syria, otherwise called the Sea of the Philistines, and the Great Sea ; and from the Euphrates to the Great Desert lying behind Palestine and Egypt. These are the limits of the Israelitish territory : the former, from the south to the west ; the latter, from the north to the east. (Gen. xv. 18.) But, in this passage, there can scarcely be a doubt that by the *"river "*—to wit, the Euphrates—is indicated the extreme boundary of the earth towards the east. In a highly poetical, magnificent description, such as is given in this song, of a king exalted above all others, nothing can be conceived more inappropriate than saying that the dominions of such a king should be bounded by the limits of Palestine.—*Ernest F. C. Rosenmüller (1768—1835), in "The Biblical Cabinet,"* vol. xxxii.

Verse 9.—"They that dwell in the wilderness shall bow before him," etc. This is equivalent to saying, *the wild Arabs, that the greatest conquerors could never tame,* shall bow before him, or become his vassals ; nay, his enemies, and, consequently, these Arabs among the rest, *"shall lick the dust,"* or court him with the most abject submissions.—*T. Harmer's Observations.*

Verse 9.—"His enemies shall lick the dust." Bear in mind that it was a custom with many nations that, when individuals approached their kings, they kissed the earth, and prostrated their whole body before them. This was the custom especially throughout Asia. No one was allowed to address the Persian kings, unless he prostrated himself on the ground and kissed the footsteps of the king, as Xenophon records.—*Thomas Le Blanc.*

Verses 9, 10.—"Wilderness," "Tarshish," "Sheba." The most *uncivilized,* the most *distant,* and most *opulent* nations shall pay their homage to him.—*Augustus F. Tholuck.*

Verses 9—11.—"They that dwell in the wilderness shall bow before him ; and his enemies shall lick the dust." They shall humble themselves under the mighty hand of Christ ; they shall acknowledge and receive him as their Lord ; they shall fear and reverence him as their King ; they shall veil and bow to his sceptre ; they shall put themselves, and all that is theirs, under Christ ; they shall give themselves to the exaltation and setting up of Christ. *"The kings of Tarshish and of the isles shall bring presents : the kings of Sheba and Seba shall offer gifts."* They shall consecrate their abilities to Christ's service ; they shall communicate of their substance to the maintenance of Christ's church, and minister to the preservation and increase of Christ's kingdom. *"All kings shall fall down before him : all nations shall serve him."* All shall adore and serve him as their king ; all shall exalt and honour him, as loyal subjects, their heavenly sovereign ; all persons, from the highest to the lowest, must serve the Lord Jesus, and study to make him glorious ; grace works obedience in the hearts of princes, as well as in the hearts of beggars. The sun, as well as the stars, did obeisance unto Joseph in his vision ; kings, as well as inferior persons, do obeisance unto Christ, under his kingdom and gospel.—*Alexander Grosse (—1654), in "Sweet and Soule-Perswading Inducements leading unto Christ,"* 1632.

Verse 10.—"Tarshish" was an old, celebrated, opulent, cultivated, commercial city, which carried on trade in the Mediterranean, and with the seaports of Syria, especially Tyre and Joppa, and that it most probably lay on the extreme west of that sea. Was there then, in ancient times, any city in these parts which corresponded with these clearly ascertained facts ? There was. Such was Tartessus in Spain, said to have been a Phœnician colony ; a fact which of itself would account for its intimate connection with Palestine and the Biblical narratives.

As to the exact spot where Tartessis (so written originally) lay, authorities are not agreed, as the city had ceased to exist when geography began to receive attention ; but it was not far from the Straits of Gibraltar, and near the mouth of the Guadalquivir, consequently at no great distance from the famous Granada of later days. The reader, however, must enlarge his notion beyond that of a mere city, which, how great soever, would scarcely correspond with the ideas of magnitude, affluence, and power, that the Scriptures suggest. The name, which is of Phœnician origin, seems to denote the district of south-western Spain, comprising the several colonies which Tyre planted in that country, and so being equivalent to what we might designate Phœnician Spain. We are not, however, convinced that the opposite coast of Africa was not included, so that the word would denote to an inhabitant of Palestine the extreme western parts of the world.—*J. R. Beard, in "A Cyclopædia of Biblical Literature."* 1866.

Verse 10.—"The isles," אִיִּים, only in the Psalter besides, Ps. xcvii. 1, where, and uniformly, so rendered. The word, however, denotes all habitable land as opposed to water (see Gen. x. 5, where first it occurs, with Isa. xlii. 15), and so *" maritime land,* whether the sea coast of continent or island " (Gesenius) ; especially the countries washed by the Mediterranean, and the remote coasts to the west of Palestine. So in the parallel prophecy, Isa. lx. 9, and xi. 11 ; xli. 1, 2 ; xlii. 10—12 ; xlix. 1, etc. Accordingly, *"The isles* shall wait for his law " (Isa. xlii. 4) is expounded in Matt. xii. 22—" In Him shall *the Gentiles* trust."—*William De Burgh.*

Verse 10.—*"Sheba and Seba."* There appear to have been two nations living in the same region, viz., Southern Arabia. One of these was descended from Cush, the son of Ham, and the other from Joktan, a descendant of Shem. These two peoples were often antagonistic in interests, despite the similarity of their names, but their divisions would be healed, and unitedly they would offer tribute to the Great King. It is an Arab proverb, " divided as the Sabæans," but Christ makes them one. " The Greek geographers usually couple Abyssinia with Yemen, in Arabia, and invariably represent the Abyssinians as an Arab or Sabæan race. Modern travellers, also, unanimously agree in recognising the Arab type among those Abyssinian populations which do not belong to the African stock." That the Sabæan nations were wealthy is clear from the Greek historian Agatharchides. " The Sabæans," says he, " have in their houses an incredible number of vases and utensils of all sorts, of gold and silver, beds and tripods of silver, and all the furniture of astonishing richness. Their buildings have porticoes with columns sheathed with gold, or surmounted by capitals of silver. On the friezes, ornaments, and the framework of the doors, they place plates of gold encrusted with precious stones. They spend immense sums in adorning these edifices, employing gold, silver, ivory, precious stones, and materials of the greatest value." They appear, also, to have acquired great wealth by trading, both with India and Africa, their peninsula lying between those two regions. Rich would be their gifts if Lenormant and Chevallier's description of their commerce be correct. " The principal importations from India were gold, tin, precious stones, ivory, sandal-wood, spices, pepper, cinnamon, and cotton. Besides these articles, the storehouses of southern Arabia received the products of the opposite coast of Africa, procured by the Sabæans in the active coasting trade they carried on with this not far distant land, where Mosyton (now Ras Abourgabeh) was the principal port. These were, besides the spices that gave name to that coast, ebony, ostrich feathers, and more gold and ivory. With the addition of the products of the soil of southern Arabia itself, incense, myrrh, laudanum, precious stones, such as onyx and agates, lastly, aloes from the island of Socotra, and pearls from the fisheries in the Gulf of Ormus, we shall have the list of the articles comprised in the trade of this country with Egypt, and with those Asiatic countries bordering on the Mediterranean ; and, at the same time, by considering this list, we may form an idea of how great must have been the importance and activity of such a traffic."

Poor as God's people usually are, the era will surely arrive when the richest of the rich will count it all joy to lay their treasures at Jesus' feet.—*C. H. S.*

Verse 12.—*"He shall deliver the needy when he crieth."* There needeth no mediator between him and his subjects : *he heareth the needy when they cry.* The man that hath nothing within him or without him to commend him to Christ, to assist, help, relieve, or comfort him in heaven or earth, is not despised by Christ, but delivered from that which he feareth.—*David Dickson.*

Verse 13.—*"He shall spare ;"* more correctly, *compassionate* or *comfort the poor and needy ; and shall save the souls,* or *preserve the lives of the needy.*—*William Henry Alexander, in "The Book of Praises : being the Book of Psalms . . . . with Notes Original and Selected."* 1867.

Verse 13.—*"And shall save the souls of the needy."* Scipio used to say, that he would rather save a single citizen than slay a thousand enemies. Of this mind ought all princes to be towards their subjects ; but this affection and love rose to the highest excellence and power in the breast of Christ. So ardent is his love for his own, that he suffers not one of them to perish, but leads them to full salvation and, opposing himself to both devils and tyrants who seek to destroy their souls, he constrains their fury and confounds their rage.—*Mollerus.*

Verse 14.—*"And precious shall their blood be in his sight."* The Angolani so despised their slaves that they would sometimes give as many as twenty-two for one hunting dog. . . . But Christ prefers the soul of one of his servants to the whole world, since he died that it might be made more capable of entering into eternal felicity. For breaking one goblet the Roman cast his slave into the pond to be devoured by the muræne. But the Son of God came down from heaven to earth to deliver mankind, his vile, ungrateful, faithless servants, from the pangs of the serpent, like the golden fleece, and save them as Jonah from the whale. Is not their blood precious in his sight ?—*Thomas Le Blanc.*

Verse 15.—*"And he shall live ; "* Hebrew, *"* So shall he live ; *"* i.e., the poor man. —*Charles Carter.*

Verse 15.—*"And he shall live."* There is a clear reference to the coronation of kings in the loud acclamations, *Long live the King !* and the bestowal of the customary gifts and presents, as is plain from 2 Sam. xvi. 16 ; 1 Kings i. 39 ; 1 Sam. x. 27 ; 2 Chron. xvii. 5.—*Hermann Venema.*

Verse 15.—*"He shall live."* Alexander the Great acknowledged at death that he was a frail and feeble man. " Lo ! I," said he, " am dying, whom you falsely called a god." But Christ proved that he was God when, by his own death, he overcame, and, as I may say, slew death.—*Thomas Le Blanc.*

Verse 15.—*"He shall live."* It is a great consolation to soldiers imperilled amid many forms of death, that their king *shall live.* Whence one of the chief of these warriors, consoling himself, said, " I know that my Redeemer liveth, and that at the last day I shall rise from the earth." Great is the consolation of the dying, that he for whom, or in whom, they die, *shall live* for evermore. With whom, if we die, we shall also live again, and share his riches equally with himself ; for rich indeed is our Solomon, in whom are hidden all the treasures of the wisdom and knowledge of God.—*Gerhohus.*

Verse 15.—*"Prayer also shall be made for him continually ; and daily shall he be praised."* it might have been rendered, " Prayer also shall be made *through* him continually, and daily shall he be blessed." The word is rendered " blessed," when speaking of an act of worship towards God ; and the word translated " for " is sometimes used for " through," as Joshua ii. 15,—" Through the window." If we hold the translation " for him," then it must be understood of the saints praying for the Father's accomplishment of his promises, made to the Son in the covenant of redemption, that his kingdom may come, his name be glorified, and that he may see his seed, and that the full reward may be given him for his sufferings, and so that he may receive the joy that was set before him.—*Jonathan Edwards.*

Verse 15.—*"Prayer also shall be made for him continually ; and daily shall he be praised."* In all conquered countries, *two* things marked the subjection of the people : 1. Their money was stamped with the name of the conqueror. 2. They were obliged to pray for him in their acts of public worship.—*Adam Clarke.*

Verse 16.—*"An handful of corn in the earth upon the top of the mountains."* Not only would the soil be likely to lack depth of earth, but the seed itself would be apt to be blown away by the winds of heaven, or washed down by the teeming rain to the base beneath.—*Peter Grant.* 1867.

Verse 16.—*"An handful of corn,"* etc. Upon mature consideration, I am persuaded that the proper sense of the word פַּס, or, פִּסַּת, is " a patch " or " piece ; " and that it is used here just as we use the same words in English, in such expressions as these,—" a patch of wheat, a patch of barley, a piece of corn."—*Samuel Horsley.*

Verse 16.—*"An handful of corn."* Doubtless it has been familiar to you to see corn merchants carrying small bags with them, containing just a handful of corn, which they exhibit as specimens of the store which they have for sale. Now, let me beg of every one of you to carry a small bag with this precious corn of the gospel. When you write a letter, drop in a word for Christ ; it may be a seed that will take root. . . . Speak a word for Christ wherever you go ; it may be seed productive of a great deal of fruit. Drop a tract on the counter, or in a house ; it may be a seed productive of a plenteous harvest. The most difficult place, the steepest mountain, the spot where there is the least hope of producing fruit, is to be the first place of attack ; and the more labour there is required, the more is to be given, in the distribution of the seeds.—*James Sherman.*

Verse 16.—*"Shall shake like Lebanon."* With a plentiful ear, shall yield so large and strong a stalk that, with the motion of the wind, it shall shake cedar-like.— *Joseph Hall.*

Verse 16.—*"Shall shake as Lebanon."* That is to say, shall wave backwards and forwards with the wind, like the tall cedars of Lebanon. This implies that the corn will be lofty and luxuriant.—*French and Skinner.*

Verse 16.—Neither *wave* nor *shake* conveys the full force of the Hebrew verb רָעַשׁ which suggests the additional idea of a rushing noise, like that of the wind among the cedars of Lebanon. This comparison is certainly more natural and obvious than that which some interpreters assume with the grain-crops or harvest-fields of Lebanon itself. This would be merely likening one harvest to another, nor is any such allusion ever made elsewhere to the mountain, though its circumjacent plains and valleys were productive.—*Joseph Addison Alexander*.

Verse 16.—*"Like Lebanon."* By dint of skill and labour, they have compelled a rocky soil to become fertile. Sometimes, to avail themselves of the waters, they have made a channel for them, by means of a thousand windings, on the declivities, or have arrested them in the valleys by embankments. At other times, they have propped up the earth, that was ready to roll down, by means of terraces and walls. Almost all the mountains being thus husbanded, present the appearance of a stair-case, or of an amphitheatre, each tier of which is a row of vines or mulberry-trees. I have counted, upon one declivity, as many as a hundred, or a hundred and twenty, tiers from the bottom of the valley to the top of the hill. I forgot, for the moment, that I was in Turkey.—*Volney*.

Verse 16.—*"Like Lebanon."* To understand the images taken from Mount Lebanon, it is necessary to remark that four enclosures of mountains are described, rising one upon another. The first and lowest of these is described as rich in grain and fruits. The second is barren, being covered only with thorns, rocks, and flints. The third, though higher still, is blessed with a perpetual spring; the trees are always green. There are innumerable orchards laden with fruit, and it forms, altogether, a terrestrial paradise,

> " Where fruits and blossoms blush,
> In social sweetness, on the self-same bough."

The fourth, or highest ridge of all, is the region of perpetual snow. Now, the imagery in the 72nd Psalm is evidently taken from the first of these ridges of Lebanon, where (most probably following the ancient mode of cultivating) the monks of Lebanon, for they were the chief cultivators of the terraced soil, industriously husband every particle of productive earth. In the expressive words of Burckhardt, *"Every inch of ground is cultivated,"* so that no image could have been more singularly expressive of the universal cultivation under Messiah's reign, than to say that *"His fruit shall shake like Lebanon;"* or, understanding the Psalmist to speak figuratively, what moral landscape could be painted more richly than he does, when he intimates that those barren mountains of our world, which at present yield no fruit unto God, shall be cultivated in that day so industriously and so fully, that the fruit shall wave like the terraced corn-fields, or shake like the hanging mulberry-trees on the terraced heights of Lebanon.—*Robert Murray McCheyne*. 1813—1843.

Verse 16.—*"Shall flourish like grass."* The peculiar characters of the grass, which adapt it especially for the service of man, are its apparent *humility* and *cheerfulness*. Its humility, in that it seems created only for lowest service,—appointed to be trodden on and fed upon. Its cheerfulness, in that it seems to exult under all kinds of violence and suffering. You roll it, and it is stronger next day; you mow it, and it multiplies its shoots, as if it were grateful; you tread upon it, and it only sends up richer perfume. Spring comes, and it rejoices with all the earth,—glowing with variegated flame of flowers,—waving in soft depth of fruitful strength. Winter comes, and, though it will not mock its fellow plants by growing then, it will not pine and mourn, and turn colourless and leafless as they. It is always green; and is only the brighter and gayer for the hoar-frost.—*John Ruskin*.

Verse 17.—*"His name shall be continued."* Yinnon : The Kethiv, *yanin*, would be; " shall produce fresh progeny," or " send forth new shoots."

M. Renan was far from intending to supply a commentary on this verse, when he said of the Lord Jesus, " Son culte *se rajeunira sans cesse*." Yet it would not be easy to find a more forcible illustration of the meaning of *yanin*.—*William Kay*.

Verse 17 (*second clause*).—The version and sense which Gussetius gives seems best of all : *His name shall generate, or beget children before the sun ;* that is, his name preached, as the gospel, which is his name (Acts ix. 15), shall be the means of begetting many sons and daughters openly and publicly, in the face of the sun, and wherever that is.—*John Gill*.

Verse 17.—*"All nations shall call him blessed."* It is sometimes inadvertently said that the Old Testament is narrow and exclusive, while the New Testament is broad and catholic in its spirit. This is a mistake. The Old and New Testaments are of one mind on this matter. Many are called, and few chosen. This is the common doctrine of the New as well as of the Old. They are both equally catholic in proclaiming the gospel to all. The covenant with Adam and with Noah is still valid, and sure to all who return to God ; and the call of Abram is expressly said to be a means of extending blessing to all the families of man. The New Testament does not aim at anything more than this : it merely hails the approaching accomplishment of the same gracious end.—*James G. Murphy, in "A Critical and Exegetical Commentary on the Book of Genesis."* 1863.

Verse 19.—*"Amen, and Amen."* Rabbi Jehudah the Holy, said, " He that said *Amen* in this world is worthy to say it in the world to come. David, therefore, utters *Amen* twice in this Psalm, to show that one ' Amen ' belongs to this world, the other to that which is to come. He who saith ' Amen ' devoutly, is greater than he who uttereth the prayers, for the prayers are but the letter, and the Amen is the seal. The scribe writeth the letters, the prince alone seals them."—*Neale and Littledale.*

Verse 19.—*"Amen, and Amen."* What is *"Amen"* in Matt. xvi. 28 is ἀληθῶς or " verily " in Luke ix. 27. Our Saviour hath this phrase peculiar to himself, " Amen, Amen," to give confirmation to the doctrine, and to raise our attention and faith ; or to show that not only truth is spoken, but by him who is truth itself. . . . There is no need for a rubric by the men of the Great Synagogue, or a canon, to command a man to blush, when it is only the natural passion that will command it ; so, when the heart is warm in prayer with serious and earnest affections, a double Amen doth as naturally flow from us as milk from a mother's breast to her suckling. And *Amen* comes from אמן, *aman*, which signifies " to nurse ; " as if it were, if not the mother, yet the faithful nurse, of lively devotion. Assent to repetitions is essential unto prayer, and it is not signified publicly but by one Amen. —*Thomas Woodcock (—1695) in "Morning Exercises."*

Verse 19.—*"Amen "* is a short word, but marvellously pregnant, full of sense, full of spirit. It is a word that seals all the truths of God, and seals every particular promise of God. And it is never likely to arise in the soul, unless there be first an almighty power from heaven, to seize on the powers of the soul, to subdue them, and make it say, " Amen." There is such an inward rising of the heart, and an innate rebellion against the blessed truth of God, that unless God, by his strong arm, bring the heart down, it never will nor can say, "Amen."—*Richard Sibbes.*

Verse 20.—*"The prayers of David the son of Jesse are ended."* This announcement carries with it an intimation that other Psalms besides are to follow. It would have been superfluous, if the Psalms had not been to follow which bear on their front the name of David. To this, indeed, it must point, bearing the character of an enigma, that these additional Psalms stood in other relations than those given in the first two books. We shall attain perfect clearness and certainty by perceiving that all the Psalms of David in the last two books are inserted as component parts into the later cycles. The subscription at the end of the second book must have been designed to separate the free from the bound, the scattered and serial Psalms of David from each other. Analogous in some measure is the subscription, *at an end are the speeches of Job,* in Job xxxi. 40, which is not contradicted by the fact that Job appears again speaking in chapters xl. and xlii. ; it should rather be regarded as serving to give us a right understanding of that formal conclusion.— E. W. Hengstenberg.

Verse 20.—At the conclusion of this Psalm, the Hebrew copies have, *Here end the orisons of David, the son of Jesse.* But, as several other Psalms of David follow, we must understand the note to mean either, " Here ends this book of the orisons of David," or, " Here ends the collection of hymns made by David himself ; " additions being afterwards made to it, containing other hymns of David, by Asaph and others, and, lastly, by Esdras.—*Daniel Cresswell.*

Verse 20.—*"The prayers of David the son of Jesse are ended."* So long as the fivefold division of the Psalter was neglected, this note gave nothing but perplexity to the commentators. Augustine, and his master, Ambrose of Milan, finding it standing in their Psalters, between the seventy-second and seventy-third Psalms, took it for part of the title of the latter, and tortured their ingenuity in divining its import. Calvin saw that the note is retrospective, but, not having observed its position at the end of a book, he thought it pertained exclusively to the Psalm immediately preceding, and took it to mean that that Psalm embalms the last prayers of the aged king. But he was at a loss to reconcile this with the two obvious facts, that the *title of the* Psalm ascribes it to Solomon, and that quite a different Psalm is elsewhere preserved as " the last words of David " (2 Sam. xxiii. 1). And this perplexity of the great Reformer is shared by the older commentators generally. We get rid of it at once, by simply remarking the position of the note in question. It is set down after a doxology which marks the end of the Second Book. It has no special reference, therefore, to the seventy-second Psalm. It either refers to the Second Book, or, more probably, to both the First and Second.—*William Binnie.*

Verse 20.—*"The prayers of David the son of Jesse are ended."* [Compared with] Ps. 86, title, *"A prayer of David."* How can the prayers of David be said to be ended, when more begin? Answer: The end David had in making the Psalms, prayers, and praises, is one thing; but to make a final end of praying is another. Many several opinions have been given to reconcile this. Some that here end the prayers he made for Solomon. Some that here end the prayers he made in the days of his affliction. Some that here end the praises that he made, not the prayers, turning the word *tepillahs* into *tehillahs.* Some that here end David's, the rest that follow are Asaph's. Some that this Psalm was the last, the rest *posthumes,* found after his death. Some think it is spoken as the phrase is in Job, ch. 31, last verse: " The words of Job are ended ; " and yet he had some words after this, but not so many. But the soundest resolution is this :—Here ends the prayers of David the son of Jesse; that is, here they are perfected. If any ask hereafter what or where lies the end that all these Psalms were made for ? tell them here it lies in this Psalm, and, therefore, placed in the midst of all ; as the centre in midst of a circle, all the lines meet here, and all the Psalms determine here ; for it is only a prophetical treatise of the kingdom of Christ drawn out to the life, and it is dedicated to Solomon, because here is wisdom ; other men had other ends, it may be, but the son of Jesse had no other end in the world but to set out Christ's kingdom in making of his Psalms.—*William Streat, in "The Dividing of the Hoof."* 1654.

Verse 20.—*"The son of Jesse."* It is the note of true humility and sincere love to God to abase ourselves, and acknowledge our low condition, wherein God did find us when he did let forth his love to us, that thereby we may commend the riches of God's goodness and grace unto us, appeareth here in David.—*David Dickson.*

Verse 20.—*"Are ended."* The sense is, that David, the son of Jesse, had nothing to pray for, or to wish, beyond the great things described in this Psalm. Nothing can be more animated than this conclusion. Having described the blessings of Messiah's reign, he closes the whole with his magnificent doxology :—

> Blessed be Jehovah God,
> God of Israel, alone performing wonders ;
> And blessed be his name of glory,
> And let his glory fill the whole of the earth.
> Amen, and Amen.
> Finished are the prayers of David, the son of Jesse.
> *Samuel Horsley.*

HINTS TO PREACHERS.

Whole Psalm.—I. He shall. II. They shall. Ring the changes on these, as the Psalm does.

Verse 1.—The prayer of the ancient church now fulfilled. I. Our Lord's titles. 1. King, by divine nature. 2. King's Son, in both natures. Thus we see his power innate and derived. II. Our Lord's authority: "Judgments." 1. To rule his people. 2. To rule the world for his people's benefit. 3. To judge mankind. 4. To judge devils. III. Our Lord's character. He is righteous in rewarding and punishing, righteous towards God and man. IV. Our loyal prayer. This asks for his rule over ourselves and the universe.

Verse 2.—Christ's rule in his church. I. The subjects. 1. Thy people, the elect, called, etc. 2. Thy poor, through conviction and consciousness of sin. II. The ruler. He, only, truly, constantly, etc. III. The rule—righteous, impartial, gentle, prudent, etc. Lesson. Desire this rule.

Verse 3.—Mountains of divine decree, of immutable truth, of almighty power, of eternal grace, etc. These mountains of God are securities of peace.

Verse 4.—The poor man's King, or the benefits derived by the poor from the reign of Jesus.

Verse 5.—The perpetuity of the gospel, reasons for it, things which threaten it, and lessons derived from it.

Verse 6.—The field, the shower, the result. This verse is easily enough handled in a variety of ways.

Verse 7.—I. The righteous flourish more at one season than another. II. They flourish most when Jesus is with them: "in his days," etc. III. The fruit of their growth is proportionally abundant: "and abundance," etc.—*G. Rogers.*

Verse 7.—"*Abundance of peace.*" Abundant overtures of peace, abundant redemption making peace, abundant pardon conferring peace, abundant influences of the Spirit sealing peace, abundant promises guaranteeing peace, abundant love spreading peace, etc.

Verse 8.—The universal spread of the gospel. Other theories as to the future overturned, and their evil influence exposed; while the benefit and certainty of this truth is vindicated.

Verse 9 (last clause).—The ignoble end of Christ's enemies.

Verse 10.—Christian finance; voluntary but abundant are the gifts presented to Jesus.

Verse 12.—Christ's peculiar care of the poor.

Verse 12.—I. Pitiable characters. II. Abject condition: "cry;" "no helper." III. Natural resort: "crieth." IV. Glorious interposition.

Verse 14.—The martyr's hope in life and comfort in death.—*G. Rogers.*

Verse 14 (last clause).—The martyr's blood. I. Seen of God when shed. II. Remembered by him. III. Honoured by being a benefit to the church. IV. Rewarded especially in heaven.

Verse 15.—"*Prayer shall be made for him.*" We are to pray for Jesus Christ. Owing to the interest he has in certain objects, what is done for them is done for himself; and so he esteems it. We, therefore, pray for him when we pray for his ministers, his ordinances, his gospel, his church—in a word, his *cause.* But what should we pray for on his behalf? I. The degree of its resources; that there be always a sufficiency of suitable and able instruments to carry on the work. II. The freedom of its administration; that whatever opposes or hinders its progress may be removed. III. The diffusion of its principles; that they may become general and universal. IV. The increase of its glory, as well as its extent.—*W. Jay.*

Verse 15.—Prayer for Jesus, a suggestive topic. Daily praise, a Christian duty.

Verse 15.—A living Saviour, a giving people; the connection between the two. Or, Christ in the church fills the exchequer, fosters the prayer-meeting, and sanctifies the service of song.

Verse 16.—I. A happy description of the gospel; it is "a handful of corn." II. The places where it is sown. III. The blessed effects which this gospel, when thus sown, will produce in the world.—*J. Sherman.*

Verse 16.—I. Commencement. II. Publicity. III. Growth. IV. Result.

Verse 16.—I. What? "Corn." II. How much? "A handful." III. Where?

" In the earth upon the top of the mountains." IV. Will it grow ? " The fruit," etc. V. What then ? " They of the city," etc.

Verse 17.—I. Christ glorified in the Church : " men shall be blessed," etc. II. Glorified in the world ; " all nations," etc. III. Glorified in worlds to come : " endure," " be continued," etc. IV. Glorified for ever.—*G. Rogers.*

Verses 17, 18, 19.—The Four Blesseds, their meaning and order.

Verse 18.—The clauses may be treated under the following heads. I. The object of praise. II. The subject of praise. III. The duration of praise. IV. The extent of the praise ; and, V. The echo of the praise. " Amen, and Amen."— *G. Rogers.*

Verse 18.—"*Wondrous things.*" The unparalleled works of the Lord in providence and grace.

Verse 20.—I. Prayer should be frequent : " The prayers." II. Should be individual : " of David." III. Should be early commenced : " the son of Jesse." IV. Should be continued till they are no more needed.

**HERE ENDETH THE SECOND BOOK OF
THE PSALMS.**

PSALM LXXIII.

TITLE.—A Psalm of Asaph. *This is the second Psalm ascribed to Asaph, and the first of eleven consecutive Psalms bearing the name of this eminent singer. Some writers are not sure that Asaph wrote them, but incline to the belief that David was the author, and Asaph the person to whom they were dedicated, that he might sing them when in his turn he became the chief musician. But though our own heart turns in the same direction, facts must be heard; and we find in* 2 Chron. xxix. 30, *that Hezekiah commanded the Levites to sing "the words of David and of Asaph the seer;" and, moreover, in* Nehemiah xii. 46, *David and Asaph are mentioned together, as distinct from "the chief of the singers," and, as it would seem, as joint authors of psalmody. We may, therefore, admit Asaph to be the author of some, if not all, of the twelve Psalms ascribed to him. Often a great star which seems to be but one to the eyes of ordinary observers, turns out upon closer inspection to be of a binary character; so here the Psalms of David are those of Asaph, too. The great sun of David has a satellite in the moon of Asaph. By reading our notes on Psalm Fifty, in Vol. II., the reader will glean a little more concerning this man of God.*

SUBJECT.—*Curiously enough this Seventy-third Psalm corresponds in subject with the Thirty-seventh; it will help the memory of the young to notice the reversed figures. The theme is that ancient stumbling-block of good men, which Job's friends could not get over; viz.—the present prosperity of wicked men and the sorrows of the godly. Heathen philosophers have puzzled themselves about this, while to believers it has too often been a temptation.*

DIVISIONS.—*In verse 1 the Psalmist declares his confidence in God, and, as it were, plants his foot on a rock while he recounts his inward conflict. From 2 to 14 he states his temptation; then, from 15 to 17 he is embarrassed as to how to act, but ultimately finds deliverance from his dilemma. He describes with awe the fate of the ungodly in verses 18—20, condemns his own folly and adores the grace of God, 21—24, and concludes by renewing his allegiance to his God, whom he takes afresh to be his portion and delight.*

EXPOSITION.

TRULY God *is* good to Israel, *even* to such as are of a clean heart.

1. *"Truly,"* or, more correctly, *only, "God is good to Israel."* He is only good, nothing else but good to his own covenanted ones. He cannot act unjustly or unkindly to them; his goodness to them is beyond dispute, and without mixture. *"Even to such as are of a clean heart."* These are the true Israel, not the ceremonially clean but the really so; those who are clean in the inward parts, pure in the vital mainspring of action. To such he is, and must be, goodness itself. The writer does not doubt this, but lays it down as his firm conviction. It is well to make sure of what we do know, for this will be good anchor-hold for us when we are molested by those mysterious storms which arise from things which we do not understand. Whatever may or may not be the truth about mysterious and inscrutable things, there are certainties somewhere; experience has placed some tangible facts within our grasp; let us, then, cling to these, and they will prevent our being carried away by those hurricanes of infidelity which still come from the wilderness, and, like whirlwinds, smite the four corners of our house and threaten to overthrow it. O my God, however perplexed I may be, let me never think ill of thee. If I cannot understand thee, let me never cease to believe in thee. It must be so, it cannot be otherwise, thou art good to those whom thou hast made good; and where thou hast renewed the heart thou wilt not leave it to its enemies.

2 But as for me, my feet were almost gone; my steps had well nigh slipped.

3 For I was envious at the foolish, *when* I saw the prosperity of the wicked.

4 For *there are* no bands in their death: but their strength *is* firm.

5 They *are* not in trouble *as other* men ; neither are they plagued like *other* men.

6 Therefore pride compasseth them about as a chain ; violence covereth them *as* a garment.

7 Their eyes stand out with fatness : they have more than heart could wish.

8 They are corrupt, and speak wickedly *concerning* oppression : they speak loftily.

9 They set their mouth against the heavens, and their tongue walketh through the earth.

10 Therefore his people return hither : and waters of a full *cup* are wrung out to them.

11 And they say, How doth God know ? and is there knowledge in the most High ?

12 Behold, these *are* the ungodly, who prosper in the world ; they increase *in* riches.

13 Verily I have cleansed my heart *in* vain, and washed my hands in innocency.

14 For all the day long have I been plagued, and chastened every morning.

2. Here begins the narrative of a great soul-battle, a spiritual Marathon, a hard and well-fought field, in which the half-defeated became in the end wholly victorious. *"But as for me."* He contrasts himself with his God who is ever good ; he owns his personal want of good, and then also compares himself with the clean in heart, and goes on to confess his defilement. The Lord is good to his saints, *"but as for me,"* am I one of them ? Can I expect to share his grace ? Yes, I do share it ; but I have acted an unworthy part, very unlike one who is truly pure in heart. *"My feet were almost gone."* Errors of heart and head soon affect the conduct. There is an intimate connection between the heart and the feet. Asaph could barely stand, his uprightness was going, his knees were bowing like a falling wall. When men doubt the righteousness of God, their own integrity begins to waver. *"My steps had well nigh slipped."* Asaph could make no progress in the good road, his feet ran away from under him like those of a man on a sheet of ice. He was weakened for all practical action, and in great danger of actual sin, and so of a disgraceful fall. How ought we to watch the inner man, since it has so forcible an effect upon the outward character. The confession in this case is, as it should be, very plain and explicit.

3. *"For I was envious at the foolish."* " The foolish " is the generic title of all the wicked : they are beyond all other fools, and he must be a fool who envies fools. Some read it, " the proud ; " and, indeed, these, by their ostentation, invite envy, and many a mind which is out of gear spiritually, becomes infected with that wasting disease. It is a pitiful thing that an heir of heaven should have to confess " I was envious," but worse still that he should have to put it, " I was envious at the foolish." Yet this acknowledgment is, we fear, due from most of us. *"When I saw the prosperity of the wicked."* His eye was fixed too much on one thing ; he saw their present, and forgot their future, saw their outward display, and overlooked their soul's discomfort. Who envies the bullock his fat when he recollects the shambles ? Yet some poor afflicted saint has been sorely tempted to grudge the ungodly sinner his temporary plenty. All things considered, Dives had more cause to envy Lazarus than Lazarus to be envious of Dives.

4. *"For there are no bands in their death."* This is mentioned as the chief wonder, for we usually expect that in the solemn article of death, a difference will appear, and the wicked will become evidently in trouble. The notion is still prevalent that a quiet death means a happy hereafter. The Psalmist had observed that the very reverse is true. Careless persons become case-hardened, and continue presumptuously secure, even to the last. Some are startled at the approach of judgment, but many more have received a strong delusion to believe a lie. What with the surgeon's drugs and their own infidelity, or false peace, they glide into eternity

without a struggle. We have seen godly men bound with doubts, and fettered with anxieties, which have arisen from their holy jealousy ; but the godless know nothing of such bands : they care neither for God nor devil. *"Their strength is firm."* What care they for death ? Frequently they are brazen and insolent, and can vent defiant blasphemies even on their last couch. This may occasion sorrow and surprise among saints, but certainly should not suggest envy, for, in this case, the most terrible inward conflict is infinitely to be preferred to the profoundest calm which insolent presumption can create. Let the righteous die as they may, let my last end be like theirs.

5. *"They are not in trouble as other men."* The prosperous wicked escape the killing toils which afflict the mass of mankind ; their bread comes to them without care, their wine without stint. They have no need to enquire, " Whence shall we get bread for our children, or raiment for our little ones ? " Ordinary domestic and personal troubles do not appear to molest them. *"Neither are they plagued like other men."* Fierce trials do not arise to assail them : they smart not under the divine rod. While many saints are both poor and afflicted, the prosperous sinner is neither. He is worse than other men, and yet he is better off ; he ploughs least, and yet has the most fodder. He deserves the hottest hell, and yet has the warmest nest. All this is clear to the eye of faith, which unriddles the riddle ; but to the bleared eye of sense it seems an enigma indeed. They are to have nothing hereafter, let them have what they can here ; they, after all, only possess what is of secondary value, and their possessing it is meant to teach us to set little store by transient things. If earthly good were of much value, the Lord would not give so large a measure of it to those who have least of his love.

6. *"Therefore pride compasseth them about as a chain."* They are as great in their own esteem as if they were aldermen of the New Jerusalem ; they want no other ornament than their own pomposity. No jeweller could sufficiently adorn them ; they wear their own pride as a better ornament than a gold chain. *"Violence covereth them as a garment."* In their boastful arrogance they array themselves ; they wear the livery of the devil, and are fond of it. As soon as you see them, you perceive that room must be made for them, for, regardless of the feelings and rights of others, they intend to have their way, and achieve their own ends. They brag and bully, bluster and browbeat, as if they had taken out a license to ride roughshod over all mankind.

7. *"Their eyes stand out with fatness."* In cases of obesity the eyes usually appear to be enclosed in fat, but sometimes they protrude ; in either case the countenance is changed, loses its human form, and is assimilated to that of fatted swine. The face is here the index of the man : the man has more than suffices him ; he is glutted and surfeited with wealth, and yet is one of the wicked whom God abhorreth. *"They have more than heart could wish."* Their wishes are gratified, and more ; their very greediness is exceeded ; they call for water, and the world gives them milk ; they ask for hundreds, and thousands are lavished at their feet. The heart is beyond measure gluttonous, and yet in the case of certain ungodly millionaires, who have rivalled Sardanapalus both in lust and luxury, it has seemed as if their wishes were exceeded, and their meat surpassed their appetite.

8. *"They are corrupt."* They rot above ground ; their heart and life are depraved. *"And speak wickedly concerning oppression."* The reek of the sepulchre rises through their mouths ; the nature of the soul is revealed in the speech. They choose oppression as their subject, and they not only defend it, but advocate it, glory in it, and would fain make it the general rule among all nations. " Who are the poor ? What are they made for ? What, indeed, but to toil and slave that men of education and good family may enjoy themselves ? Out on the knaves for prating about their rights ! A set of wily demagogues are stirring them up because they get a living by agitation. Work them like horses, and feed them like dogs ; and if they dare complain, send them to the prison or let them die in the workhouse." There is still too much of this wicked talk abroad, and, although the working classes have their faults, and many of them very grave and serious ones too, yet there is a race of men who habitually speak of them as if they were an inferior order of animals. God forgive the wretches who thus talk. *"They speak loftily."* Their high heads, like tall chimneys, vomit black smoke. Big talk streams from them, their language is colossal, their magniloquence ridiculous. They are Sir Oracle in every case, they speak as from the judge's bench, and expect all the world to stand in awe of them.

9. *"They set their mouth against the heavens."* Against God himself they aim their blasphemies. One would think, to hear them, that they were demi-gods themselves, and held their heads above the clouds, for they speak down upon other men as from a sublime elevation peculiar to themselves. Yet they might let God alone, for their pride will make them enemies enough without their defying him. *"And their tongue walketh through the earth."* Leisurely and habitually they traverse the whole world to find victims for their slander and abuse. Their tongue prowls in every corner far and near, and spares none. They affect to be universal censors, and are in truth perpetual vagrants. Like the serpent, they go nowhere without leaving their slime behind them ; if there were another Eden to be found, its inno-cence and beauty would not preserve it from their filthy trail. They themselves are, beyond measure, worthy of all honour, and all the rest of mankind, except a few of their parasites, are knaves, fools, hypocrites, or worse. When these men's tongues are out for a walk, they are unhappy who meet them, for they push all travellers into the kennel : it is impossible altogether to avoid them, for in both hemispheres they take their perambulations, both on land and sea they make their voyages. The city is not free from them, and the village swarms with them. They waylay men in the king's highway, but they are able to hunt across country, too. Their whip has a long lash, and reaches both high and low.

10. *" Therefore his people return hither."* God's people are driven to fly to his throne for shelter ; the doggish tongues fetch home the sheep to the Shepherd. The saints come again, and again, to their Lord, laden with complaints on account of the persecutions which they endure from these proud and graceless men. *"And waters of a full cup are wrung out to them."* Though beloved of God, they have to drain the bitter cup ; their sorrows are as full as the wicked man's prosperity. It grieves them greatly to see the enemies of God so high, and themselves so low, yet the Lord does not alter his dispensations, but continues still to chasten his children, and indulge his foes. The medicine cup is not for rebels, but for those whom Jehovah Rophi loves.

11. *"And they say, How doth God know ? "* Thus dare the ungodly speak. They flatter themselves that their oppressions and persecutions are unobserved of heaven. If there be a God, is he not too much occupied with other matters to know what is going on upon this world ? So they console themselves if judgments be threatened. Boasting of their own knowledge, they yet dare to ask, *"Is there knowledge in the most High ? "* Well were they called foolish. A God, and not know ! This is a solecism in language, a madness of thought. Such, however, is the acted insanity of the graceless theists of this age ; theists in name, because avowed infidelity is disreputable, but atheists in practice beyond all question.

I could not bring my mind to accept the rendering of many expositors by which this verse is referred to tried and perplexed saints. I am unable to conceive that such language could flow from their lips, even under the most depressing perplexities.

12. *"Behold, these are the ungodly, who prosper in the world."* Look ! See ! Consider ! Here is the standing enigma ! The crux of Providence ! The stumbling-block of faith ! Here are the unjust rewarded and indulged, and that not for a day or an hour, but in perpetuity. From their youth up these men, who deserve perdition, revel in prosperity. They deserve to be hung in chains, and chains are hung about their necks ; they are worthy to be chased from the world, and yet the world becomes all their own. Poor purblind sense cries, Behold this ! Wonder, and be amazed, and make this square with providential justice, if you can. *"They increase in riches ;"* or, strength. Both wealth and health are their dowry. No bad debts and bankruptcies weigh them down, but robbery and usury pile up their substance. Money runs to money, gold pieces fly in flocks ; the rich grow richer, the proud grow prouder. Lord, how is this ? Thy poor servants, who become yet poorer, and groan under their burdens, are made to wonder at thy mysterious ways.

13. *"Verily I have cleansed my heart in vain."* Poor Asaph ! he questions the value of holiness when its wages are paid in the coin of affliction. With no effect has he been sincere ; no advantage has come to him through his purity, for the filthy-hearted are exalted and fed on the fat of the land. Thus foolishly will the wisest of men argue, when faith is napping. Asaph was a seer, but he could not see when reason left him in the dark ; even seers must have the sunlight of revealed truth to see by, or they grope like the blind. In the presence of temporal circum-stances, the pure in heart may seem to have cleansed themselves altogether in vain,

but we must not judge after the sight of the eyes. *"And washed my hands in inno-cency."* Asaph had been as careful of his hands as of his heart ; he had guarded his outer as well as his inner life, and it was a bitter thought that all this was useless, and left him in even a worse condition than foul-handed, black-hearted worldlings. Surely the horrible character of the conclusion must have helped to render it untenable ; it could not be so while God was God. It smelt too strong of a lie to be tolerated long in the good man's soul ; hence, in a verse or two, we see his mind turning in another direction.

14. *"For all the day long have I been plagued."* He was smitten from the moment he woke to the time he went to bed. His griefs were not only continued, but renewed with every opening day, *"And chastened every morning."* This was a vivid contrast to the lot of the ungodly. There were crowns for the reprobates and crosses for the elect. Strange that the saints should sigh and the sinners sing. Rest was given to the disturbers, and yet peace was denied to the peace-makers. The downcast seer was in a muse and a maze. The affairs of mankind appeared to him to be in a fearful tangle ; how could it be permitted by a just ruler that things should be so turned upside down, and the whole course of justice dislocated.

Here is the case stated in the plainest manner, and many a Christian will herein recognise his own experience. Such knots have we also sought to untie, and have sadly worn our fingers and broken our teeth. Dear-bought has our wisdom been, but we have bought it ; and, henceforth, we cease to fret because of evil-doers, for the Lord hath showed us what their end will be.

15 If I say, I will speak thus ; behold, I should offend *against* the generation of thy children.

16 When I thought to know this, it *was* too painful for me.

17 Until I went into the sanctuary of God ; *then* understood I their end.

15. *"If I say, I will speak thus."* It is not always wise to speak one's thoughts ; if they remain within, they will only injure ourselves ; but, once uttered, their mischief may be great. From such a man as the Psalmist, the utterance which his discontent suggested would have been a heavy blow and deep discouragement to the whole brotherhood. He dared not, therefore, come to such a resolution, but paused, and would not decide to declare his feelings. It was well, for in his case second thoughts were by far the best. *"I should offend against the generation of thy children."* I should scandalise them, grieve them, and perhaps cause them to offend also. We ought to look at the consequences of our speech to all others, and especially to the church of God. Woe unto the man by whom offence cometh ! Rash, undigested, ill-considered speech, is responsible for much of the heart-burning and trouble in the churches. Would to God that, like Asaph, men would bridle their tongues. Where we have any suspicion of being wrong, it is better to be silent ; it can do no harm to be quiet, and it may do serious damage to spread abroad our hastily formed opinions. To grieve the children of God by appearing to act perfidiously and betray the truth, is a sin so heinous, that if the consciences of heresy-mongers were not seared as with a hot iron, they would not be so glib as they are to publish abroad their novelties. Expressions which convey the impression that the Lord acts unjustly or unkindly, especially if they fall from the lips of men of known character and experience, are as dangerous as firebrands among stubble ; they are used for blasphemous purposes by the ill-disposed ; and the timid and trembling are sure to be cast down thereby, and to find reason for yet deeper distress of soul.

16. *"When I thought to know this, it was too painful for me."* The thought of scandalising the family of God he could not bear, and yet his inward thoughts seethed and fermented, and caused an intolerable anguish within. To speak might have relieved one sorrow, but, as it would have created another, he forbore so dangerous a remedy ; yet this did not remove the first pangs, which grew even worse and worse, and threatened utterly to overwhelm him. A smothered grief is hard to endure. The triumph of conscience which compels us to keep the wolf hidden beneath our own garments, does not forbid its gnawing at our vitals. Suppressed fire in the bones rages more fiercely than if it could gain a vent at the mouth. Those who know Asaph's dilemma will pity him as none others can.

17. *"Until I went into the sanctuary of God."* His mind entered the eternity where God dwells as in a holy place, he left the things of sense for the things invisible,

his heart gazed within the veil, he stood where the thrice holy God stands. Thus he shifted his point of view, and apparent disorder resolved itself into harmony. The motions of the planets appear most discordant from this world which is itself a planet ; they appear as " progressive, retrograde, and standing still ; " but could we fix our observatory in the sun, which is the centre of the system, we should perceive all the planets moving in perfect circle around the head of the great solar family. *"Then understood I their end."* He had seen too little to be able to judge ; a wider view changed his judgment ; he saw with his mind's enlightened eye the future of the wicked, and his soul was in debate no longer as to the happiness of their condition. No envy gnaws now at his heart, but a holy horror both of their impending doom, and of their present guilt, fills his soul. He recoils from being dealt with in the same manner as the proud sinners, whom just now he regarded with admiration.

18 Surely thou didst set them in slippery places : thou castedst them down into destruction.

19 How are they *brought* into desolation, as in a moment ! they are utterly consumed with terrors.

20 As a dream when *one* awaketh ; *so*, O Lord, when thou awakest, thou shalt despise their image.

18. The Psalmist's sorrow had culminated, not in the fact that the ungodly prospered, but that God had arranged it so : had it happened by mere chance, he would have wondered, but could not have complained ; but how the arranger of all things could so dispense his temporal favours, was the vexatious question. Here, to meet the case, he sees that the divine hand purposely placed these men in prosperous and eminent circumstances, not with the intent to bless them but the very reverse. *"Surely thou didst set them in slippery places."* Their position was dangerous, and, therefore, God did not set his friends there but his foes alone. He chose, in infinite love, a rougher but safer standing for his own beloved. *"Thou castedst them down into destruction."* The same hand which led them up to their Tarpeian rock, hurled them down from it. They were but elevated by judicial arrangement for the fuller execution of their doom. Eternal punishment will be all the more terrible in contrast with the former prosperity of those who are ripening for it. Taken as a whole, the case of the ungodly is horrible throughout ; and their worldly joy instead of diminishing the horror, actually renders the effect the more awful, even as the vivid lightning amid the storm does not brighten but intensify the thick darkness which lowers around. The ascent to the fatal gallows of Haman was an essential ingredient in the terror of the sentence—" hang him thereon." If the wicked had not been raised so high they could not have fallen so low.

19. *"How are they brought into desolation, as in a moment !"* This is an exclamation of godly wonder at the suddenness and completeness of the sinners' overthrow. Headlong is their fall ; without warning, without escape, without hope of future restoration ! Despite their golden chains, and goodly apparel, death stays not for manners but hurries them away ; and stern justice unbribed by their wealth hurls them into destruction. *"They are utterly consumed with terrors."* They have neither root nor branch left. They cease to exist among the sons of men, and, in the other world, there is nothing left of their former glory. Like blasted trees, consumed by the lightning, they are monuments of vengeance ; like the ruins of Babylon they reveal, in the greatness of their desolation, the judgments of the Lord against all those that unduly exalt themselves. The momentary glory of the graceless is in a moment effaced, their loftiness is in an instant consumed.

20. *"As a dream when one awaketh ; so, O Lord, when thou awakest, thou shalt despise their image."* They owe their existence and prosperity to the forbearance of God, which the Psalmist compares to a sleep ; but, as a dream vanishes so soon as a man awakes, so the instant the Lord begins to exercise his justice and call men before him, the pomp and prosperity of proud transgressors shall melt away. When God awakes to judgment, they who despise him shall be despised ; they are already " such stuff as dreams are made of," but then the baseless fabric shall not leave a wreck behind. Let them flaunt their little hour, poor unsubstantial sons of dreams ; they will soon be gone ; when the day breaketh, and the Lord awakes as a mighty man out of his sleep, they will vanish away. Who cares for the wealth of dream-

land ?   Who indeed but fools ?   Lord, leave us not to the madness which covets
unsubstantial wealth, and ever teach us thine own wisdom.

21 Thus my heart was grieved, and I was pricked in my reins.

22 So foolish *was* I, and ignorant : I was as a beast before thee.

23 Nevertheless I *am* continually with thee : thou hast holden *me* by
my right hand.

24 Thou shalt guide me with thy counsel, and afterward receive me *to*
glory.

21. The holy poet here reviews his inward struggle and awards himself censure
for his folly.   His pain had been intense ; he says, "*Thus my heart was grieved.*"
It was a deep-seated sorrow, and one which penetrated his inmost being.   Alexander
reads it, " My heart is soured."   His spirit had become embittered ; he had judged
in a harsh, crabbed, surly manner.   He had become atrabilious, full of black
bile, melancholy, and choleric ; he had poisoned his own life at the fountain-head,
and made all its streams to be bitter as gall.   "*And I was pricked in my reins.*"
He was as full of pain as a man afflicted with renal disease ; he had pierced himself
through with many sorrows ; his hard thoughts were like so many calculi in his
kidneys ; he was utterly wretched and woebegone, and all through his own
reflections.   O miserable philosophy, which stretches the mind on the rack, and
breaks it on the wheel !   O blessed faith, which drives away the inquisitors, and
sets the captives free !
22. "*So foolish was I.*"   He, though a saint of God, had acted as if he had been
one of the fools whom God abhorreth.   Had he not even envied them ?—and what is
that but to aspire to be like them ?   The wisest of men have enough folly in them
to ruin them unless grace prevents.   "*And ignorant.*"   He had acted as if he knew
nothing, had babbled like an idiot, had uttered the very drivel of a witless loon.
He did not know how sufficiently to express his sense of his own fatuity.   "*I was
as a beast before thee.*"   Even in God's presence he had been brutish, and worse than
a beast.   As the grass-eating ox has but this present life, and can only estimate
things thereby, and by the sensual pleasure which they afford, even so had the
Psalmist judged happiness by this mortal life, by outward appearances, and by
fleshly enjoyments.   Thus he had, for the time, renounced the dignity of an immortal spirit, and, like a mere animal, judged after the sight of the eyes.   We
should be very loth to call an inspired man a beast, and yet, penitence made him
call himself so ; nay, he uses the plural, by way of emphasis, and as if he were worse
than any one beast.   It was but an evidence of his true wisdom that he was so
deeply conscious of his own folly.   We see how bitterly good men bewail mental
wanderings ; they make no excuses for themselves, but set their sins in the pillory,
and cast the vilest reproaches upon them.   O for grace to detest the very appearance
of evil !
23. "*Nevertheless I am continually with thee.*"   He does not give up his faith,
though he confesses his folly.   Sin may distress us, and yet we may be in communion
with God.   It is sin beloved and delighted in which separates us from the Lord,
but when we bewail it heartily, the Lord will not withdraw from us.   What a contrast
is here in this and the former verse !   He is as a beast, and yet continually with
God.   Our double nature, as it always causes conflict, so is it a continuous paradox :
the flesh allies us with the brutes, and the spirit affiliates us to God.   "*Thou hast
holden me by my right hand.*"   With love dost thou embrace me, with honour ennoble
me, with power uphold me.   He had almost fallen, and yet was always upheld.
He was a riddle to himself, as he had been a wonder unto many.   This verse contains
the two precious mercies of communion and upholding, and as they were both given
to one who confessed himself a fool, we also may hope to enjoy them.
24. "*Thou shalt guide me with thy counsel.*"   I have done with choosing my
own way, and trying to pick a path amid the jungle of reason.   He yielded not only
the point in debate, but all intention of debating, and he puts his hand into that
of the great Father, asking to be led, and agreeing to follow.   Our former mistakes
are a blessing, when they drive us to this.   The end of our own wisdom is the beginning of our being wise.   With HIM is counsel, and when we come to him, we are sure
to be led aright.   "*And afterward.*"   " Afterward ! "   Blessed word.   We can
cheerfully put up with the present, when we foresee the future.   What is around

us just now is of small consequence, compared with afterward. *"Receive me to glory."* Take me up into thy splendour of joy. Thy guidance shall conduct me to this matchless terminus. Glory shall I have, and thou thyself wilt admit me into it. As Enoch was not, for God took him, so all the saints are taken up—received up into glory.

25 Whom have I in heaven *but thee?* and *there is* none upon earth *that* I desire beside thee.

26 My flesh and my heart faileth : *but* God *is* the strength of my heart, and my portion for ever.

27 For, lo, they that are far from thee shall perish : thou hast destroyed all them that go a whoring from thee.

28 But *it is* good for me to draw near to God : I have put my trust in the Lord God, that I may declare all thy works.

25. *"Whom have I in heaven but thee?"* Thus, then, he turns away from the glitter which fascinated him to the true gold which was his real treasure. He felt that his God was better to him than all the wealth, health, honour, and peace, which he had so much envied in the worldling ; yea, He was not only better than all on earth, but more excellent than all in heaven. He bade all things else go, that he might be filled with his God. *"And there is none upon earth that I desire beside thee."* No longer should his wishes ramble, no other object should tempt them to stray ; henceforth, the Everliving One should be his all in all.

26. *"My flesh and my heart faileth."* They had failed him already, and he had almost fallen ; they would fail him in the hour of death, and, if he relied upon them, they would fail him at once. *"But God is the strength of my heart, and my portion for ever."* His God would not fail him, either as a protection or a joy. His heart would be kept up by divine love, and filled eternally with divine glory. After having been driven far out to sea, Asaph casts anchor in the old port. We shall do well to follow his example. There is nothing desirable save God ; let us, then, desire only him. All other things must pass away ; let our hearts abide in him, who alone abideth for ever.

27. *"For, lo, they that are far from thee shall perish."* We must be near God to live ; to be far off by wicked works is death. *"Thou hast destroyed all them that go a whoring from thee."* If we pretend to be the Lord's servants, we must remember that he is a jealous God, and requires spiritual chastity from all his people. Offences against conjugal vows are very offensive, and all sins against God have the same element in them, and they are visited with the direst punishments. Mere heathens, who are far from God, perish in due season ; but those who, being his professed people, act unfaithfully to their profession, shall come under active condemnation, and be crushed beneath his wrath. We read examples of this in Israel's history ; may we never create fresh instances in our own persons.

28. *"But it is good for me to draw near to God."* Had he done so at first he would not have been immersed in such affliction ; when he did so he escaped from his dilemma, and if he continued to do so he would not fall into the same evil again. The greater our nearness to God, the less we are affected by the attractions and distractions of earth. Access into the most holy place is a great privilege, and a cure for a multitude of ills. It is good for all saints, it is good for me in particular ; it is always good, and always will be good for me to approach the greatest good, the source of all good, even God himself. *"I have put my trust in the Lord God."* He dwells upon the glorious name of the Lord Jehovah, and avows it as the basis of his faith. Faith is wisdom ; it is the key of enigmas, the clue of mazes, and the pole star of pathless seas. Trust and you will know. *"That I may declare all thy works."* He who believes shall understand, and so be able to teach. Asaph hesitated to utter his evil surmisings, but he has no diffidence in publishing abroad a good matter. God's ways are the more admired the more they are known. He who is ready to believe the goodness of God shall always see fresh goodness to believe in, and he who is willing to declare the works of God shall never be silent for lack of wonders to declare.

EXPLANATORY NOTES AND QUAINT SAYINGS.

Whole Psalm.—The Seventy-third Psalm is a very striking record of the mental struggle which an eminently pious Jew underwent, when he contemplated the respective conditions of the righteous and the wicked. Fresh from the conflict, he somewhat abruptly opens the Psalm with the confident enunciation of the truth of which victory over doubt had now made him more and more intelligently sure than ever, that *"God is good to Israel, even to such as are of a clean heart."* And then he relates the most fatal shock which his faith had received, when he contrasted the prosperity of the wicked, who, though they proudly contemned God and man, prospered in the world and increased in riches, with his own lot, who, though he had cleansed his heart and washed his hands in innocency, had been " plagued all the day long and chastened every morning." The place where his doubts were removed and his tottering faith re-established, was " the sanctuary of God." God himself was the Teacher. What, then, did he teach ? By what divinely imparted considerations was the Psalmist reassured ? Whatever is the proper rendering of the fourth verse ; whether, " There are no sorrows (tending) to their death," or, " There are no sorrows *until* their death,"—their whole life to the very last is one unchequered course of happiness—that verse conveys to us the Psalmist's *mistaken* estimate of the prosperity of the wicked, before he went unto the sanctuary of God. The true estimate, at which he afterwards arrived, is found in verses 18—20. Now, admitting (what, by the way, is somewhat difficult of belief, inasmuch as the sudden and fearful temporal destruction of *all* or even the *most* prosperous cannot be made out) that the end of these men " means only and always their end *in this world*, we come to the conclusion that, in the case of the wicked, this Psalm does not plainly and undeniably teach that punishment awaits them after death ; but only that, in estimating their condition, it is necessary, in order to vindicate the justice of God, to take in their whole career, and set over against their great prosperity the sudden and fearful reverses and destruction which they not unfrequently encounter. But, in turning to the other side of the comparison, the case of the righteous, we are *not* met by the thought, that as the prosperity of the wicked is but the preparation for their ruin, the raising higher the tower that the fall may be the greater, so the adversity of the godly is but an introduction to worldly wealth and honour. That thought is not foreign to the Old Testament writers. " Evil-doers shall be cut off ; " writes one of them, " but those that wait upon the Lord, they shall inherit the earth. For yet a little while, and the wicked shall not be : yea, thou shalt diligently consider his place, and it shall not be. But the meek shall inherit the earth ; and shall delight themselves in the abundance of peace." Psalm xxxvii. 9—11. *But it is not so much as hinted at here.* The daily chastening may continue, flesh and heart may fail, but God is good to Israel notwithstanding : he is their portion, their guide, their help while they live, and he will take them to his glorious presence when they die. " Nevertheless I am continually with thee : thou hast holden me by my right hand. Thou shalt guide me with thy counsel, and afterward receive me to glory." The New Testament has nothing higher or more spiritual than this. The reference of the last clause to happiness after death is, I believe, generally acknowledged by Jewish commentators. They left it to the candour of Christian expositors to doubt or deny it.—*Thomas Thomason Perowne, in " The Essential Coherence of the Old and New Testaments."* 1858.

Whole Psalm.—In Psalm Seventy-three the soul looks *out*, and reasons on what it sees there ; namely, successful wickedness and suffering righteousness. What is the conclusion ? " I have cleansed my heart in vain." So much for looking about. In Psalm Seventy-seven the soul looks *in*, and reasons on what it finds there. What is the conclusion ? " Hath God forgotten to be gracious ? " So much for looking in. Where, then, should we look ? Look *up*, straight up, and *believe* what you see there. What will be the conclusion ? You will understand the " *end* " of man, and trace the " *way* " of God.—*From " Things New and Old, a Monthly Magazine."* 1858.

Whole Psalm.—In this Psalm, the Psalmist (Asaph) relates the great difficulty which existed in his own mind, from the consideration of the wicked. He observes (verses 2 and 3), " As for me, my feet were almost gone ; my steps had well nigh slipped. For I was envious at the foolish, when I saw the prosperity of the wicked."

In the fourth and following verses he informs us what, in the wicked, was his tempta-tion. In the first place, he observed, that they were *prosperous*, and all things went well with them. He then observed their *behaviour* in their prosperity, and the use which they made of it ; and that God, notwithstanding such abuse, *continued* their prosperity. Then he tells us by what means he was helped out of this difficulty, viz., by going into the *sanctuary* (verses 16 and 17), and proceeds to inform us what considerations they were which helped him, viz.—1. The consideration of the *miser-able end* of wicked men. However they prosper for the present, yet they come to a woeful end at last (verses 18—20). 2. The consideration of the *blessed end* of the saints. Although the saints, while they live, may be afflicted, yet they come to a happy end at last (verses 21—24). 3. The consideration that the godly have a much *better portion* than the wicked, even though they have no other portion but God ; as in verses 25, 26. Though the wicked are in prosperity, and are not in trouble as other men ; yet the godly, though in affliction, are in a state infinitely better, because they have God for their portion. They need desire nothing else ; he that hath God hath all. Thus the Psalmist professes the sense and apprehension which he had of things : " Whom have I in heaven but thee ? and there is none upon earth that I desire beside thee." In the twenty-fourth verse the Psalmist takes notice how the saints are happy in God, both when they are in this world and also when they are taken to another. They are blessed in God in this world, in that *he guides them by his counsel ;* and when he takes them out of it they are still happy, in that he *receives them to glory.* This probably led him to declare that he desired *no other portion,* either in this world or in that to come, either in heaven or upon earth.—*Jonathan Edwards.*

Verse 1.—"*Truly :* " it is but a particle ; but the smallest filings of gold are gathered up. Little pearls are of great price. And this small particle is not of small use, being rightly applied and improved. First, take it (as our translators give it us) as *a note of asseveration.* "*Truly.*" It is a word of faith, opposite to the Psalmist's sense and Satan's injections. Whatsoever sense sees or feels, whatsoever Satan insinuates and says ; yet precious faith with confidence asserts, "*Truly, verily God is good.*" He is not only good in word, but in deed also. Not only seemingly good, but certainly good. Secondly, consider it as *an adversative particle,* "*Yet,*" so our old translation. Ainsworth renders it, *yet surely ;* taking in the former and this together. And then the sense runs thus : How ill soever things go in the world, how ill soever it fares with God's church and people amongst men, *yet God is good* to Israel. Thirdly, some conceive that the word carries *admiration.* Oh, how good is God to Israel. Where expressions and apprehensions fail, there the Psalmist takes up God's providences with admiration. Oh, how wonderfully, how trans-cendently good is God to Israel !

This "*yet* " (as I conceive) hath a threefold reference to the body of the Psalm. For as interpreters observe, though these words are set in the beginning, yet they suggest the conclusion of the Psalmist's conflict. And the Psalmist seems to begin somewhat abruptly : "*Yet God is good.*" But having filled his thoughts with his former foiles and fears, and now seeing himself in a safe condition both for the present and the future, he is full of confidence and comfort ; and that which was the strongest and chiefest in his heart now breaks out first : "*Yet God is good.*" 1. *This "yet* " relates unto his sufferings, verse 14 : "*All the day long have I been plagued, and chastened every morning.*" Notwithstanding the variety and frequency of the saint's sufferings, "*yet God is good.*" Though sorrow salutes them every morning at their first awaking, and trouble attends them to bed at night, "*yet God is good.*" Though temptations many and terrible make batteries and breaches upon their spirits, "*yet God is good to Israel.*" 2. This "*yet* " reflects upon his sinnings, the frettings and wranglings of his distempered heart (verses 2, 3, and verse 21). Though sinful motions do mutiny in the soul against God's wise administrations, though there be foolish, proud quarrellings with divine providences, and inexcusable distrust of his faithful promises ; though fretfulness at others' prosperity and discontent at their own adversity, "*yet God is good.*" Israel's sinful distempers cause not the Almighty to change the course of his accustomed goodness. While corruptions are kept from breaking out into scandal, while the soul contends against them, and is humbled for them (as the Psalmist was), this conclusion must be maintained : "*yet God is good.*" 3. This "*yet* " looks back upon his misgivings. There had been distrustful despondency upon the good man's heart. For from both the premises (viz., his sufferings and sinnings) he had inferred this conclusion, verse 13, *"Verily I have cleansed my heart in vain, and washed my hands in innocency."* As if he had said, " I have kept fasts, observed Sabbaths, heard sermons, made prayers, received sacraments, given alms, avoided sins, resisted temptations, withstood lusts, appeared for Christ and his cause and servants in vain : yea, his heart had added an asseveration (*verily*) to this faithless opinion, but now he is of another mind : *"Yet God is good."* The administrations of God are not according to the sad surmises of his people's misgiving hearts. For, though they through diffidence are apt often to give up their holy labours as lost, and all their conscientious care and carriage as utterly cast away ; *"yet God is good to Israel."—Simeon Ash, in a Sermon entitled "God's Incomparable Goodness unto Israel." 1647.*

Verse 1.—David opens the Psalm abruptly, and from this we learn what is worthy of particular notice, that, before he broke forth into this language, his mind had been agitated with many doubts and conflicting suggestions. As a brave and valiant champion, he had been exercised in very painful struggles and temptations ; but, after long and arduous exertion, he at length succeeded in shaking off all perverse imaginations, and came to the conclusion that *yet* God is gracious to his servants, and the faithful guardian of their welfare. Thus these words contain a tacit contrast between the unhallowed imaginations suggested to him by Satan, and the testimony in favour of true religion with which he now strengthens himself, denouncing, as it were, the judgment of the flesh, in giving place to misgiving thoughts with respect to the providence of God. We see, then, how emphatic is this exclamation of the Psalmist. He does not ascend into the chair to dispute after the manner of the philosophers, and to deliver his discourse in a style of studied oratory ; but, as if he had escaped from hell, he proclaims with a loud voice, and with impassioned feeling, that he had obtained the victory.—*John Calvin.*

Verse 1 (first clause).—

> Yet sure the gods are good : I would think so,
> If they would give me leave !
> But virtue in distress, and vice in triumph,
> Make atheists of mankind.
>
> *Dryden.*

Verse 1.—*"God is good."* There is a beauty in the name appropriated by the Saxon nations to the Deity, unequalled except by his most reverential Hebrew appellation. They called him " GOD," which is literally, " THE GOOD." The same word thus signifying the Deity, and his most endearing quality.—*Turner.*

Verse 1.—*"God is good."* Let the devil and his instruments say what they will to the contrary, I will never believe them ; I have said it before, and I see no reason to reverse my sentence ; *"Truly God is good."* Though sometimes he may hide his face for awhile, yet he doth that in faithfulness and love ; there is kindness in his very scourges, and love bound up in his rods ; he is good to Israel : do but mark it first or last : " The true Israelite, in whom there is no guile, shall be refreshed by his Saviour." The Israelite that wrestles with tears with God, and values his love above the whole world, that will not be put off without his Father's blessing, shall have it with a witness : " He shall reap in joy though he may at present sow in tears. Even to such as are of a clean heart." The false-hearted hypocrite, indeed, that gives God only his tongue and lip, cap and knee, but reserves his heart and love for sin and the world, that hath much of compliment, but nothing of affection and reality, why let such a one never expect, while in such a state, to taste those reviving comforts that I have been treating of ; while he drives such a trade, he must not expect God's company.—*James Janeway.* 1636—1674.

Verse 1.—*"Even to such as are of a clean heart."* Purity of heart is the characteristical note of God's people. Heart-purity denominates us the Israel of God ; it makes us of Israel indeed ; but all are not Israel which are of Israel." Romans ix. 6. Purity of heart is the jewel which is hung only upon the elect. As chastity distinguisheth a virtuous woman from an harlot, so the true saint is distinguished from the hypocrite by his heart-purity. This is like the nobleman's star or garter, which is a peculiar ensign of honour, differing him from the vulgar ; when the bright star of purity shineth in a Christian's heart it doth distinguish him from the formal professor. . . . .

God *"is good"* to the pure in heart. We all desire that God should be good to us ; it is the sick man's prayer : " The Lord be good to me." But how is God good to them ? Two ways. 1. To them that are pure all things are sanctified, Titus i. 15 : " To the pure all things are pure ; " estate is sanctified, relations are sanctified ; as the temple did sanctify the gold and the altar did sanctify the offering. To the unclean nothing is clean ; their table is a snare, their temple-devotion a sin. There is a curse entailed upon a wicked man (Deut. xxviii. 16), but holiness removeth the curse, and cuts off the entail : " to the pure all things are pure." 2. The clean hearted have all things work for their good. Romans viii. 28. Mercies and afflictions shall turn to their good ; the most poisonous drugs shall be medicinal ; the most cross providence shall carry on the design of their salvation. Who, then, would not be clean in heart ?—*Thomas Watson.*

Verse 2.—*"But as for me."* Literally, it is, *And I,* which ought to be read with emphasis ; for David means that those temptations which cast an affront upon the honour of God, and overwhelm faith, not only assail the common class of men, or those who are endued only with some small measure of the fear of God, but that he himself, who ought to have profited above all others in the school of God, had experienced his own share of them. By thus setting himself forth as an example, he designed the more effectually to arouse and incite us to take great heed to ourselves.—*John Calvin.*

Verse 2.—Let such also as fear God and begin to look aside on the things of this world, know it will be hard even for them to hold out in faith and in the fear of God in time of trial. Remember the example of David, he was a man that had spent much time in travelling towards heaven ; yet, looking but a little aside upon the glittering show of this world, had very near lost his way, his feet were almost gone, his steps had well nigh slipt.—*Edward Elton.* 1620.

Verse 2.—He tells us that his *"feet were almost gone."* The word signifies *to bow,* or *bend under one.* " My steps had *well nigh slipped,"* or *poured out, kept not* within their *true bounds ;* but like water *poured out,* and not confined, runs aside. Though these expressions be metaphorical, and seemingly dark and cloudy, yet they clearly represent unto us this truth, that his *understanding* was *misguided,* his *judgment* was *corrupt,* his *affections disordered,* turbulent, and guilty of too great a passion ; and this, the consequents (verse 22 in which he acknowledges himself *ignorant, foolish,* and *brutish*) do sufficiently evidence. Our *understanding* and *judgment* may well bear the comparison to *feet,* for as the one, in our motion, *supports the body,* so the other, in human actions and all employments, *underprops the soul.* The *affections,* also, are as *paths* and *steps ;* as these of the *feet,* so these are the *prints* and expressions of the judgment and mind.—*Edward Parry, in "David Restored."* 1660.

Verse 2.—*"Almost gone."* There is to be noted that the prophet said he was *almost* gone, and not altogether. Here is the presence, providence, strength, safeguard, and keeping of man by Almighty God, marvellously set forth. That although we are tempted and brought even to the very point to perpetrate and do all mischief, yet he stays us and keeps us, that the temptation shall not overcome us.—*John Hooper.* 1495—1555.

Verses 2—14.—But the prosperity of wicked and unjust men, both in public and in private life, who, though not leading a happy life in reality, are yet thought to do so in common opinion, being praised improperly in the works of poets, and all kinds of books, may lead you—and I am not surprised at your mistake—to a belief that the gods care nothing for the affairs of men. These matters disturb you. Being led astray by foolish thoughts, and yet not being able to think ill of the gods, you have arrived at your present state of mind, so as to think that the gods do indeed exist, but that they despise and neglect human affairs.—*Plato.*

Verse 3.—*"I was envious at the foolish,"* etc. If we consider with ourselves how unlikely a thing it is to grow big with riches, and withal to enter through the eye of a needle, how unusual a thing it is to be emparadised in this life and yet enthroned in that to come, it will afford us matter of comfort if we are piously improsperous as well as of terror if we are prosperously impious. We should be taught by the precept of the prophet David *not to fret ourselves because of evildoers,* nor to be envious against the workers of iniquity ; for " The prosperity of fools shall but destroy them," saith Solomon, and " the candle of the wicked shall be put out." Prov. xxiv. 1, 2, 19, 20. Prosperity it seems is a dangerous weapon, and none but the innocent should dare to use it. The Psalmist himself, before he thought upon this, began to envy the prosperity of wicked men.—*William Crouch, in "The Enormous Sin of Covetousness detected."* 1708.

Verse 3.—*"I was envious at the foolish."* Who would envy a malefactor's going up a high ladder, and being mounted above the rest of the people, when it is only for a little, and in order to his being turned over and hanged? That is just the case of wicked men who are mounted up high in prosperity; for it is so only that they may be cast down deeper into destruction. It would be a brutish thing to envy an ox his high and sweet pasture, when he is only thereby fitted for the day of slaughter. Who would have envied the beasts of old, the garlands and ribbons with which the heathen adorned them when they went to be sacrificed? These external ornaments of health, wealth, pleasures, and preferments, wherewith wicked men are endowed, cannot make their state happy, nor change their natures for the better. Whatever appearance these things make in the eyes of the world, they are but like a noisome dunghill covered with scarlet, as vile and loathsome in God's sight as ever. How quickly is the beauty of earthly things blasted. "The triumphing of the wicked is short." Job xx. 5. They live in pleasures on the earth for awhile, but God "sets them in slippery places," from whence they soon slide into perpetual pain and anguish. They have a short time of mirth, but they shall have an eternity of mourning.—*John Willison.*

Verse 3.—*"For I was envious at the foolish."* The sneering jest of Dionysius the younger, a tyrant of Sicily, when, after having robbed the Temple of Syracuse, he had a prosperous voyage with the plunder, is well known. "See you not," says he to those who were with him, "how the gods favour the sacrilegious?" In the same way the prosperity of the wicked is taken as an encouragement to commit sin; for we are ready to imagine that, since God grants them so much of the good things of this life, they are the objects of his approbation and favour. We see how their prosperous condition wounded David to the heart, leading him almost to think that there was nothing better for him than to join himself to their company, and to follow their course of life.—*John Calvin.*

Verse 3.—*"Envious."* If you are touched with envy at *seeing the peace of the wicked,* shut your eyes, do not look at it, for envious eyes think anything vast on which they gaze. Actius Sincerus, a man of rare wit and great reputation, when in the presence of king Frederic, witnessed a discussion among physicians on what would most effectually sharpen the eyesight? The fumes of fennel, said some; the use of a glass, said others; some one thing, some another: but I, said he, replied, Envy. The doctors were astonished, and much amusement afforded to the audience at their expense. Then I continued: Does not Envy make all things seem larger and fuller? And what could be more to your purpose than that the very faculty of seeing should itself be made greater and stronger.—*Thomas Le Blanc.*

Verse 3.—*"The prosperity of the wicked."* Socrates, being asked what would be vexatious to good men, replied, "The prosperity of the bad." What would vex the bad? "The prosperity of the good."—*Thomas Le Blanc.*

Verse 3.—Diogenes, the cynic, seeing Harpalus, a vicious fellow, still thriving in the world, he was bold to say that wicked Harpalus's living long in prosperity was an argument that God had cast off his care of the world, that he cared not which end went forward. But he was a heathen. Yet, for all that, the lights of the sanctuary have burnt dim; stars of no small magnitude have twinkled; men of eminent parts, famous in their generation for religion and piety, have staggered in their judgment to see the flourishing estate of the wicked. It made Job to complain, and Jeremiah to expostulate with God; and David was even ready to sink in seeing the prosperity of ungodly men: to see the one in wealth, the other in want; the one honourable, the other despised; the one upon a throne, the other on a dunghill.—*John Donne.*

Verse 4.—*"There are no bands in their death,"* etc. That is, when they die, they die in their strength, they do not pine away with long and tedious sickness; they live in pleasure, and die with ease. They are not bound to their beds, and tied down with the cords of chronical, lingering diseases.—*Joseph Caryl.*

Verse 4.—*"There are no bands in their death,"* etc. It is not their lot to look upon frequent and bitter deaths, like the righteous, nor is there in their affliction any firmness or permanence. If at any time affliction falls upon them, they are speedily delivered from it. Moreover, whatever calamity happens to them, they have the strength and support of riches ; and, elevated by their wealth, they appear to forget their troubles.—*Cornelius Jansenius.* 1510—1576.

Verse 4.—"*There are no bands in their death.*" The Hebrew word מַרְצֻבֹּת signifieth a *band* which is *knotted* or *tied ;* and then the sense may be, they have not that which might bind them over unto a speedy and troublesome death ; hence, *Castelio* writes, *non sunt necessitates quæ eos enecent,* there are no necessities which threaten their death—such as variety of distempers, sicknesses, and diseases, those messengers of death. *Aquila,* therefore, renders the word οὐκ εἰσι δυσπαθείαι, there are no pangs or distempers ; no *sorrows* or sicknesses, saith *Ainsworth :* they are *not bound over to death or execution* by the variety of diseases, or by the power of injury of others. The prophet, by telling us "*their strength is firm,*" expounds this phrase, and lets us know that these wicked men had lives spun of *even threads,* without danger of *ravelling* or *breaking.* They had lusty bodies, strong limbs, sound vitals, without agonies or ruptures ; lived as those that had no cause to fear death ; and when they expired, it was without much antecedent pain ; they fell as ripe apples from the tree.—*Edward Parry.*

Verse 4.—By "*bands* " we may understand, any heavy burdens, which are wont to be *bound* on them upon whom they are laid ; and so, by way of analogy, and grievous pains or torturing diseases. "*Their strength is firm,*" continues vigorous till their death.—*Thomas Fenton.*

Verse 4.—"*In their death.*" It comes upon them in vigorous health, for they are strong and robust, and drag not out a sickly existence through continuous complaints. Some regard the bands of death as hindrances, as if it were said— They suddenly die, in a moment, nor are they racked with pains, as in Job xxi. 13. It is considered the highest felicity for the profane, when they have enjoyed the pleasures and the pomp of life, to descend in an instant to the grave. Even Julius Cæsar, on the day before he was slain, declared that it seemed to him to be a happy death to die suddenly and unexpectedly. Therefore, according to these interpreters, David complains that the ungodly, without the vexations of disease, pass on to death by a smooth and tranquil course ; but there is more truth in the opinion of those who, reading both clauses of the verse together, their strength is firm, and there are no bands to death, think that they are not dragged to death like captives ; for since diseases overcome our strength, they are so many messengers of death to admonish us of our frailty. They are not, therefore, in vain compared to chains with which God binds us to his yoke lest vigour and strength should incite us to be froward. "*But their strength is firm.*"—*Franciscus Vatablus.*

Verse 4.—Men may die like lambs and yet have their place for ever with the goats.—*Matthew Henry.*

Verse 5.—"*They are not in the trouble of men,*" for God has given them over to the desires of their own hearts, that they who are filthy may be filthy still : like a sick man, are they, to whom a wise physician forbids nothing, since the disease is incurable.—*Gerhohus.*

Verse 5.—"*Other men.*" Hebrew, אָדָם *Adam :* the *whole human race.*—*A. R. Fausset.*

Verse 6.—A chain of pearl doth not better become their necks, nor the richest robes adorn their backs, than sin doth, in their judgments, become and suit their souls ; they glory in their shame. Plato saith of Protagoras that he boasted, whereas he had lived sixty years, he had spent forty years in corrupting youth. They brag of that which they ought to bewail.—*George Swinnock.*

Verse 6.—"*Violence covereth them as a garment.*" They wear it, and shew it openly as their garment. See the like phrase of cursing, Ps. cix. 18, 19. But the meek, and godly, cover themselves otherwise, Eph. iv. 24 ; Col. iii. 10, 12, 14, etc. —*John Richardson.*

Verse 7.—"*Their eyes.*" " A man may be known by his look," saith the son of Sirach, Ecclus. xix. 29. The choleric, the lascivious, the melancholy, the cunning, etc., frequently bear their tempers and ruling passions strongly marked on their countenances : but more especially doth the soul of a man look forth at his "*eyes.*" —*George Horne.*

Verse 7 (first clause).—They sink others' eyes into their heads with leanness, while their own eyes *"stand out with fulness."*—*Thomas Adams.*

Verse 8.—*"They are corrupt."* Prosperity, in an irreligious heart, breeds *corruption*, which from thence is emitted by the breath in conversation, to infect and taint the minds of others.—*George Horne.*

Verse 8.—*"They speak wickedly concerning oppression."* Indeed, we see that wicked men, after having for some time got everything to prosper according to their desires, cast off all shame, and are at no pains to conceal themselves, when about to commit iniquity, but loudly proclaim their own turpitude. "What!" they will say, "is it not in my power to deprive you of all that you possess, and even to cut your throat?" Robbers, it is true, can do the same thing; but then they hide themselves for fear. These giants, or rather inhuman monsters, of whom David speaks, on the contrary not only imagine that they are exempted from subjection to any law, but, unmindful of their own weakness, foam furiously, as if there were no distinction between good and evil, between right and wrong.—*John Calvin.*

Verse 9.—*"Their tongue walketh through the earth."* This shows the boundless and unlimited disorder of the tongue. The earth carries a numerous offspring of men, who are of several habits, states, and conditions, which give occasion of variety of discourses and different kinds of language. These men spare none: *"Their tongue walketh through the earth,"* and leaves nothing unspoken of. If men be *poor*, they talk of oppressing and mastering of them; if they *oppose*, they discourse of violence and suppressing. . . . . If in this perambulation they meet with *truth*, they darken it with lies and home-made inventions; if with *innocence*, they brand it with false accusations and bitter aspersions; if with a strict government and *good laws*, then they cry, "Let us break their bands asunder, and cast away their cords from us;" if with *religion*, they term it *heresy*, or superstition; if with *patience*, they term it obstinacy and perverseness; if with the *church*, they think of nothing less than devouring it, and cry, "Let us take the houses of God in possession;" if with the thoughts of a resurrection, and of future hopes, "Let us eat and drink," cry they, "for to-morrow we shall die." Thus no corner is left unsearched by their *abusive tongue, which walks through the earth.* . . . . They may *walk over the earth*, but they will *"set their mouth against the heavens."* Here they say, stand fixed and resolute, and take that place, as a special white they would hit.—*Edward Parry.*

Verse 10.—*"Therefore his people return hither."* It seems impossible to ascertain, with any degree of precision, the meaning of this verse, or to whom it relates. Some think it intends those people who resort to the company of the wicked, because they find their temporal advantage by it; while others are of opinion that the people of God are meant, who, by continually revolving in their thoughts the subject here treated of, namely, the prosperity of the wicked, are sore grieved and forced to shed tears in abundance. Mr. Mudge translates the verse thus: *"Therefore let his (God's) people come before them, and waters in full measure would be wrung out from them;"* that is, should God's people fall into their hands, they would squeeze them to the full, they would wring out all the juice out of their bodies. He takes *waters in full measure* to have been a proverbial expression.—*Samuel Burder.*

Verse 11.—*"How doth God know?"* etc. Men may not disbelieve a Godhead; nay, they may believe there is a God, and yet question the truth of his threatenings. Those conceits that men have of God, whereby they mould and frame him in their fancies, suitable to their humours, which is a thinking that he is such a one as ourselves (Psalm l.), are streams and vapours from this pit, and the "hearts of the sons of men are desperately set within them to do evil" upon these grounds; much more when they arise so high as in some who say: *"How doth God know? and is there knowledge in the most High?"* If men give way to this, what reason can be imagined to stand before them? All the comminations of Scripture are derided as so many theological scarecrows, and undervalued as so many pitiful contrivances to keep men in awe.—*Richard Gilpin.*

Verse 11.—Ovid thus speaks in one of his verses: *"Solicitor nullos esse putare deos;"* I am tempted to think that there are no gods.

Verse 14.—"*All the day long have I been plagued,*" etc. Sickly tempers must have a medicinal diet : to be purged both at spring and fall will scarce secure some from the malignity of their distempers. The Lord knows our frame, and sees what is usually needful for every temper ; and when he afflicts most frequently, he does no more than he sees requisite.—*David Clarkson.*

Verse 14.—If a man be watchful over his own ways, and the dealings of God with him, there is seldom a day but he may find some rod of affliction upon him ; but, as through want of care and watchfulness, we lose the sight of many mercies, so we do of many afflictions. Though God doth not every day bring a man to his bed, and break his bones, yet we seldom, if at all, pass a day without some rebuke and chastening. "*I have been chastened every morning,*" saith the Psalmist. . . . . As sure, or as soon, as I rise I have a whipping, and my breakfast is bread of sorrow and the water of adversity. . . . . Our lives are full of afflictions ; and it is as great a part of a Christian's skill to know afflictions as to know mercies ; to know when God smites, as to know when he girds us ; and it is our sin to overlook afflictions as well as to overlook mercies.—*Joseph Caryl.*

Verse 14.—The way to heaven is an *afflicted way,* a perplexed, persecuted way, *crushed close* together with crosses, as was the Israelites' way in the wilderness, or that of Jonathan and his armour-bearer, that had a sharp rock on the one side and a sharp rock on the other. And, whilst they crept upon all four, flinty stones were under them, briars and thorns on either hand of them ; mountains, crags, and promontories over them ; *sic potitur cælum,* so heaven is caught by pains, by patience, by violence, affliction being our inseparable companion. "The cross way is the highway to heaven," said that martyr [Bradford] ; and another, " If there·be any way to heaven on horseback, it is by the cross." Queen Elizabeth is said to have swum to the crown through a sea of sorrows. They that will to heaven, must sail by hell-gates ; they that will have knighthood, must kneel for it ; and they that will get in at the strait gate, must crowd for it. " Strive to enter in at the strait gate," saith our Saviour ; strive and strain, even to an *agony,* as the word signifieth. Heaven is compared to a hill ; hell to a hole. To hell a man may go without a staff, as we say ; the way thereto is easy, steep, strawed with roses ; 'tis but a yielding to Satan, a passing from sin to sin, from evil purposes to evil practices, from practice to custom, etc. *Sed revocare gradum,* but to turn short again, and make straight steps to our feet, that we may force through the strait gate, *hic labor, hoc opus est, opus non pulvinaris sed pulveris ;* this is a work of great pains, a duty of no small difficulty.—*John Trapp.*

Verse 15.—"*I should offend,*" etc. That is, I do God's church a great deal of injury, which hath always been under afflictions, if I think or say, that all her piety hath been without hope, or her hope without effect. Others understand it to mean, I deceive the generation, *viz.,* I propound a false doctrine unto them, which is apt to seduce them. Others, " behold the generation," etc. ; that is to say, notwithstanding all afflictions, it is certain that thou art a Father to the Church only ; which is sufficient to make me judge well of these afflictions ; I have done ill, and confess I have erred in this my rash judgment.—*John Diodati.*

Verse 17.—By the *sanctuaries of God* some, even among the Hebrews, understand the celestial mansions in which the spirits of the just and angels dwell ; as if David had said, This was a painful thing in my sight, until I came to acknowledge in good earnest that men are not created to flourish for a short time in this world, and to luxuriate in pleasures while in it, but that there condition here is that of pilgrims, whose aspirations, during their earthly pilgrimage, should be towards heaven. I readily admit that no man can form a right judgment of the providence of God but he who elevates his mind above the earth ; but it is more simple and natural to understand the word "*sanctuary* " as denoting celestial doctrine. As the book of the law was laid up in the sanctuary, from which the oracles of heaven were to be obtained, that is to say, the declaration of the will of God ; and as this was the true way of acquiring profitable instruction, David very properly puts *entering into the sanctuaries* for *coming to the school of God,* as if his meaning were this : Until God become my schoolmaster, and until I learn by his word what otherwise my mind, when I come to consider the government of the world, cannot comprehend, I stop short all at once, and understand nothing about the subject. When, therefore,

we are here told that men are unfit for contemplating the arrangements of divine
providence, until they obtain wisdom elsewhere than from themselves, how can
we attain to wisdom but by submissively receiving what God teaches us, both by
his word and by his Holy Spirit ? David by the word *"sanctuary"* alludes to the
external manner of teaching, which God had appointed among his ancient people ;
but along with the word he comprehends the secret illumination of the Holy Spirit.—
John Calvin.

Verse 17.—The joy of a wicked man is imperfect in itself, because it is not so
as it seems to be, or it is not sincerely so. 'Tis not pure gold, but alloyed and
adulterated with sorrow. It may look well to one that is blear eyed, but it will
not pass for good to one that looks well to it. Let any one consider and weigh
it well in the balance of *the sanctuary*, whither David went to fetch the scales for
the same purpose, and he will find it too light by many grains. 'Tis not so withinside
as it is without ; no more than a mud wall that is plastered with white, or a stinking
grave covered with a glorious monument. It is ὕπουλος, looking fair and smooth,
like true joy ; as a wounded member that is healed too soon (and you know how
God by the prophet complains of the hurt of his people that was slightly healed,
Jer. vi. 14), and it looks as well as any other part of the body ; but, underneath,
there is still a sore, which festers so much more, and is the worse, for that the outside
is so well. Where pretences, and cloaks, and disguises are the fairest ; there the
knavery, and the poison, and the evil concealed are usually foulest.—*Zachary Bogan*
(1625—1659), *in "Meditations of the Mirth of a Christian Life."*

Verse 17.—*"Then understood I."* There is a famous story of providence in
Bradwardine to this purpose. A certain hermit that was much tempted, and was
utterly unsatisfied concerning the providence of God, resolved to journey from
place to place till he met with some who could satisfy him. An angel in the shape
of a man joined himself with him as he was journeying, telling him that he was
sent from God to satisfy him in his doubts of providence. The first night they
lodged at the house of a very holy man, and they spent their time in discourses
of heaven, and praises of God, and were entertained with a great deal of freedom
and joy. In the morning, when they departed, the angel took with him a great
cup of gold. The next night they came to the house of another holy man, who
made them very welcome, and exceedingly rejoiced in their society and discourse ;
the angel, notwithstanding, at his departure killed an infant in the cradle, which
was his only son, he having been for many years before childless, and, therefore,
was a very fond father of this child. The third night they came to another house,
where they had like free entertainment as before. The master of the family had
a steward whom he highly prized, and told them how happy he accounted himself
in having such a faithful servant. Next morning he sent this his steward with
them part of their way, to direct them therein. As they were going over the bridge
the angel flung the steward into the river and drowned him. The last night they
came to a very wicked man's house, where they had very untoward entertainment,
yet the angel, next morning, gave him the cup of gold. All this being done, the angel
asked the hermit whether he understood those things ? He answered, his doubts
of providence were increased, not resolved, for he could not understand why he
should deal so hardly with those holy men, who received them with so much love
and joy, and yet give such a gift to that wicked man who used them so unworthily.
The angel said, I will now expound these things unto you. The first house where
we came the master of it was a holy man ; yet, drinking in that cup every morning,
it being too large, it did somewhat unfit him for holy duties, though not so much
that others or himself did perceive it ; so I took it away, since it is better for him
to lose the cup of gold than his temperance. The master of the family where we
lay the second night was a man given much to prayer and meditation, and spent
much time in holy duties, and was very liberal to the poor all the time he was childless ; but as soon as he had a son he grew so fond of it, and spent so much time
in playing with it, that he exceedingly neglected his former holy exercise, and gave
but little to the poor, thinking he could never lay up enough for his child ; therefore
I have taken the infant to heaven, and left him to serve God better upon earth.
The steward whom I did drown had plotted to kill his master the night following ;
and as to that wicked man to whom I gave the cup of gold, he was to have nothing
in the other world, I therefore gave him something in this, which, notwithstanding,
will prove a snare to him, for he will be more intemperate ; and " let him that is
filthy be filthy still." The truth of this story I affirm not, but the moral is very

good, for it shows that God is an indulgent Father to the saints when he most afflicts them ; and that when he sets the wicked on high he sets them also in slippery places, and their prosperity is their ruin. Proverbs i. 32.—*Thomas White, in "A Treatise of the Power of Godlinesse."* 1658.

Verse 17.—*"Their end."* Providence is often mysterious and a source of perplexity to us. Walking in Hyde Park one day, I saw a piece of paper on the grass. I picked it up ; it was a part of a letter ; the beginning was wanting, the end was not there ; I could make nothing of it. Such is providence. You cannot see beginning or end, only a part. When you can see the whole, then the mystery will be unveiled.—*Thomas Jones.* 1871.

Verse 18.—*"Slippery places."* The word in the original signifies *slick*, or *smooth*, as ice or polished marble, and is from thence by a metaphor used for flattery. Hence, Abenezra renders it, *In locis adulationis posuisti eos :* thou hast set them in places of flattery.—*Edward Parry.*

Verse 18.—They are but exalted, as the shellfish by the eagle, according to the naturalists, to be thrown down on some rock and devoured. Their most glorious prosperity is but like a rainbow, which showeth itself for a little time in all its gaudy colours, and then vanisheth. The Turks, considering the unhappy end of their viziers, use this proverb, " He that is in the greatest office is but a statue of glass." Wicked men walk on glass or ice, *"thou hast set them in slippery places ; "* on a sudden their feet slip—they fall, and break their necks.—*George Swinnock.*

Verses 18, 20.—Their banqueting-house is very *slippery*, and the feast itself a mere *dream.*—*Thomas Adams.*

Verse 19.—*"They are utterly consumed with terrors."* Their destruction is not only sudden, but entire ; it is like the breaking in pieces of a potter's vessel, a sherd of which cannot be gathered up and used ; or like the casting of a millstone into the sea, which will never rise more ; and this is done *"with terrors,"* either by terrible judgments inflicted on them from without, or with terrors inwardly seizing upon their minds and consciences, as at the time of temporal calamities, or at death, and certainly at the judgment, when the awful sentence will be pronounced upon them. See Job xxvii. 20.—*John Gill.*

Verse 19.—If thou shouldst live the longest measure of time that any man hath done, and spend all that time in nothing but pleasures (which no man ever did but met with some crosses, afflictions, or sicknesses), but at the evening of this life must take up the lodging in the " everlasting burnings " and " devouring fire " (Isaiah xxx. 14) ; were those pleasures answerable to these everlasting burnings ? An English merchant that lived at Dantzic, now with God, told us this story, and it was true. A friend of his (a merchant also), upon what grounds I know not, went to a convent, and dined with some friars. His entertainment was very noble. After he had dined and seen all, the merchant fell to commending their pleasant lives : " Yea," said one of the friars to him, " we live gallantly indeed, had we anybody to go to hell for us when we die."—*Giles Firmin* (1617—1617), *in "The Real Christian, or, A Treatise of Effectual Calling."*

Verse 20.—*"As a dream when one awaketh."* The conception is rather subtle, but seems to have been shrewdly penetrated by Shakspere, who makes the Plantagenet prince (affecting, perhaps, the airs of a ruler in God's stead) say to his discarded favourite—

> " I have long dreamt of such a kind of man,
> So surfeit-swelled, so old and so profane,
> But being awake I do despise my dream."
>
> *Henry IV.*

For as it is the inertness of the sleeper's will and intellect that gives reality to the shapes and figments, the very sentiments and purposes that throng his mind ; so it seems, as it were, to be the negligence and oversight of the Moral Ruler that makes to prosper the wicked or inane life and influence. So Paul says, in reference to the polytheism of the ancient world : " and the times of this ignorance God winked at." Acts xvii. 30.—*C. B. Cayley, in "The Psalms in Metre."* 1860.

Verse 21.—*"Thus my heart was grieved,"* etc. Two similitudes are used, by which his grief and indignation or zeal are described. First, he says his heart boiled over like yeast. The passion which was stirred up in his thoughts he compares to

the yeast which inflates the whole mass, and causes it to swell or boil over. . . . .
The other simile is taken from the internal pains which *calculi* produce : *"I was
pricked in my reins."* They who have felt them are aware of the torture, and there
is no need for a long description. It signifies that his great pain was mingled with
indignation, and that this came fresh upon him as often as he looked upon the
prosperity of the ungodly.—*Mollerus.*

Verse 21.—*"Reins."* Before all the other intestines there are the kidneys (נְלָיֹה,
νεφροί), placed on both sides of the lumbar vertebræ on the hinder wall of the ab-
domen, of which the Scripture makes such frequent mention, and in the most psychi-
cally significant manner. It brings the tenderest and the most inward experience
of a manifold kind into association with them. When man is suffering most deeply
within, *he is pricked in his kidneys* ("reins"). When fretting affliction overcomes
him, his kidneys are cloven asunder (Job xvi. 13 ; compare Lam. iii. 13) ; when
he rejoices profoundly, they exult (Prov. xxiii. 16) ; when he feels himself very
penetratingly warned, they chasten him (Psalm xvi. 7) ; when he very earnestly
longs, they are consumed away with his body (Job xix. 27) ; As the omniscient and
all-penetrating knower of the most secret hidden things of man, God is frequently
called (from Psalm vii. 10 to the Apocalypse) the Trier of the hearts and reins ;
and of the ungodly it is said, that God is far from their reins (Jeremiah xii. 2), that
is, that he, being withdrawn back into himself, allows not himself to be perceived
by them.—*Franz Delitzsch.*

Verse 22.—*"So foolish was I, and ignorant,"* etc. Is not a cavilling spirit at the
Lord's dispensations bad, both in its roots and fruits ? What are the roots of it
but (1) ignorance ; (2) pride, this lifteth up (Heb. ii. 4) ; (3) impatiency, or want
of waiting on God to see the issues of matters ; so in Jonah iv. 8—11 ; (4) forgetfulness
who the Lord is, and who man is that grumbles at his Maker, Lam. iii. 39, Rom. ix. 20.
And as for the fruits, they are none of the best, but bad enough. Men are ready
to flag in duty, yea, to throw it off, ver. 13, and Mal. iii. 14 ; yea, in the way to
blaspheme God ; see Job ii. 9 ; Mal. iii. 13 ; Rev. xvi. 9.—*Thomas Crane, in " A
Prospect of Divine Providence."* 1672.

Verse 22.—*"I was as a beast before thee."* I permitted my mind to be wholly
occupied with *sensible things,* like the beasts that perish, and did not look into a
future state, nor did I consider nor submit to the wise designs of an unerring
providence.—*Adam Clarke.*

Verse 22.—*"I was as a beast before thee."* The original has in it no word of
comparison ; it ought to be rather translated, *"I was a very beast before thee,"* and
we are told that the Hebrew word being in the plural number, gives it a peculiar
emphasis, indicating some monstrous or astonishing beast. It is the word used
by Job which is interpreted " behemoth,"—" I was a very monster before thee,"
not only a beast, but one of the most brutish of all beasts, one of the most stubborn
and intractable of all beasts. I think no man can go much lower than this in humble
confession. This is a description of human nature, and of the old man in the renewed
saint, which is not to be excelled.—*C. H. S.*

Verse 22.—Among the many arguments to prove the penmen of the Scripture
inspired by the Spirit of God, this is not the last and least—that the penmen of holy
writ do record their own faults and the faults of their dearest and nearest relatives.
For instance hereof, how coarsely doth David speak of himself : *"So foolish was I,
and ignorant : I was as a beast before thee."* And do you think that the face of
St. Paul did look the more foul by being drawn with his own pencil, when he says,
" I was a murderer, a persecutor, the greatest of sinners," etc. This is not usual in the
writings of human authors, who praise themselves to the utmost of what they could,
and rather than lose a drop of applause they will lick it up with their own tongues.
Tully writes very copiously in setting forth the good service which he did the Roman
state, but not a word of his covetousness, of his affecting popular applause, of his
pride and vain glory, of his mean extraction and the like. Whereas, clean contrary,
Moses sets down the sin and punishment of his own sister, the idolatry and superstition of Aaron his brother, and his own fault in his preposterous striking the rock,
for which he was excluded the land of Canaan.—*Thomas Fuller.*

Verse 23.—*"I am continually with thee,"* as a child under the tender care of a
parent ; and as a parent, during my danger of falling in a slippery path, *"thou hast
holden me,* thy child, *by my right hand."*—*George Horne.*

Verse 23.—*"I am continually with thee."* He does not say that the Lord is continually with " his people," and holds, and guides, and receives them ; he says, " He is continually with *me* ; He holds *me* ; He will guide *me* ; He will receive *me."* The man saw, and felt, and rejoiced in his own personal interest in God's care and love. And he did this (mark), in the very midst of affliction, with " flesh and heart failing ; " and in spite too of many wrong and opposite, and sinful feelings, that had just passed away ; under a conviction of his own sinfulness and folly, and, as he calls it, even " brutishness." Oh ! it is a blessed thing, brethren, to have a faith like this.—*Charles Bradley.* 1838.

Verse 23.—*"I am still with thee."* The word translated *still* properly means *always,* and denotes that there had been no change or interruption in the previous relation of the parties. There is a perfectly analogous usage of the French *toujours.* —*Joseph Addison Alexander.*

Verse 24.—*"Thou shalt guide me."* How are we to work our way in strange lands, if left entirely to our own resources ? Hence it is, that so much is said in the Bible about guides, and that the Lord is called the guide of his people. They are in a foreign land, a land of pits and snares ; and, without a good guide, they will be sure to fall into the one, or be caught in the other. " This God is our God, for ever and ever," said the Psalmist ; and not only so, but he *condescends* to " be our guide, and will be, even unto death " (Psalm xlviii. 14). Can we have a *better* guide ? When a guide has been well recommended to us by those who have tried him, it is our wisdom to place ourselves unreservedly in his hands ; and if he says our way lies to the right, it would show our folly to say we were determined to go to the left.—*John Gadsby.*

Verse 24.—*"Guide"* . . *"receive."* After conversion, God still works with us: he doth not only give grace, but actual help in the work of obedience : " He worketh all our works in us," Isa. xxvi. 12. His actual help is necessary to direct, quicken, strengthen, protect and defend us. In our way to heaven, we need not only a rule and path, but a guide. The rule is the *law* of God ; but the guide is the *Spirit* of God.—*Thomas Manton.*

Verse 24.—*"Afterward."* After all our toil in labour and duty, after all our crosses and afflictions, after all our doubts and fears that we should never receive it ; after all the hidings of his face, and clouds and darkness that have passed over us ; and after all our battles and fightings for it, oh, then how seasonably will the reception of this reward come in : *"Thou wilt guide me with thy counsel, and afterward receive me to glory."* O blessed *afterwards ;* when all your work is done, when all your doubts and fears are over, and when all your battles are fought ; then, Oh then, ye shall receive the reward.—*John Spalding.*

Verse 24.—*"Receive me to glory."* Mendelssohn in his *Beor,* has perceived the probable allusion in this clause to the translation of Enoch. Of Enoch it is said, (Gen. v. 24.) לָקַח אֹתוֹ אֱלֹהִים, " God *took* him." Here (Psalm lxxiii. 24), the Psalmist writes, כָּבוֹד תִּקָּחֵנִי. " Thou shalt *take* me to glory, or gloriously." In another (Psalm xlix. 16) we read, פִּי יִקָּחֵנִי. " For he (God) shall *take* me." I can hardly think that the two latter expressions were written and read in their context by Jews without reference to the former.—*Thomas Thomason Perowne.*

Verse 25.—*"Whom have I in heaven but thee,"* etc. How small is the number of those who keep their affections fixed on God alone ! We see how superstition joins to him many others as rivals for our affections. While the Papists admit in word that all things depend upon God, they are, nevertheless, constantly seeking to obtain help from this and the other quarter independent of him.—*John Calvin.*

Verse 25.—It pleased David, and it pleases all the saints, more that God is their salvation, whether temporal or eternal, than that he saves them. The saints look more at God than at all that is God's. They say, *Non tua, sed te ; we desire not thine, but thee,* or nothing of thine like thee. *"Whom have I in heaven but thee ?"* saith David. What are saints ? what are angels, to a soul without God ? 'Tis true of things as well as of persons. What have we in heaven but God ? What's joy without God ? What's glory without God ? What's all the furniture and riches, all the delicacies, yea, and all the diadems of heaven, without the God of heaven ? If God should say to the saints, Here is heaven, take it amongst you, but I will withdraw myself, how would they weep over heaven itself, and make it a *Baca,* a valley of tears indeed. Heaven is not heaven unless we enjoy God. 'Tis the

presence of God which makes heaven : glory is but our nearest being unto God.
As Mephibosheth replied, when David told him, " I have said, thou and Ziba divide
the land : " " Let him take all, if he will," saith Mephibosheth, I do not so much
regard the land as I regard thy presence ; " Let him take all, forasmuch as my
lord the king is come again in peace to his own house," where I may enjoy him.
So if God should say to the saints, Take heaven amongst you, and withdraw himself,
they would even say, Nay, let the world take heaven, if they will, if we may not
have thee in heaven, heaven will be but an earth, or rather but a hell to us. That
which saints rejoice in, is that they may be in the presence of God, that they may
sit at his table, and eat bread with him ; that is, that they may be near him continually, which was Mephibosheth's privilege with David. That's the thing which
they desire and which their souls thirst after ; that's the wine they would drink.
" My soul," saith David (Psalm xlii. 2), " thirsteth for God, for the living God ;
when " (methinks the time is very long, when) " shall I come and appear before
God ? "—*Joseph Caryl.*

Verses 25, 26.—Gotthold was invited to an entertainment, and had the hope
held out that he would meet with a friend whom he loved, and in whose society he
took the greatest delight. On joining the party, however, he learned that, owing
to some unforeseen occurrence, this friend was not to be present, and felt too much
chagrined to take any share in the hilarity. The circumstance afterwards led him
into the following train of thought : The pious soul, that sincerely loves and fervently longs for the Lord Jesus, experiences what I lately did. She seeks her Beloved
in all places, objects, and events. If she find him, who is happier ? If she find
him not, who more disconsolate ? Ah ! Lord Jesus, thou best of friends, thou art
the object of my love ; my soul seeketh thee, my heart longeth after thee. What
care I for the world, with all its pleasures and pomps, its power and glory, unless
I find thee in it ? What care I for the daintiest food, the sweetest drinks, and the
merriest company, unless thou art present, and unless I can dip my morsel in thy
wounds, sweeten my draught with thy grace, and hear thy pleasant words. Verily,
my Saviour, were I even in heaven, and did not find thee there, it would seem to me
no heaven at all. Wherefore, Lord Jesus, when with tears, sighs, yearnings of heart,
and patient hope, I seek thee, hide not thyself from me, but suffer me to find thee ;
for, " Lord ! whom have I in heaven but thee ? and there is none upon earth that
I desire beside thee. My flesh and my heart faileth : but God is the strength of
my heart, and my portion for ever."—*Christian Scriver.*

Verse 26.—"*My flesh and my heart faileth ; but God is the strength of my heart,
and my portion for ever.*" In which words we may take notice of five things.
I. The order inverted. When he mentions his malady he begins with the failing of
the flesh, and then of the heart ; but when he reports the relief he begins with that
of the heart. From hence observe *that when God works a cure in man (out of love)
he begins with the heart—he cures that first.* And there may be these reasons for it.
1. Because the sin of the heart is often the procuring cause of the malady of body
and soul. 2. The body ever fares the better for the soul, but not the soul for the
body. 3. The cure of the soul is the principal cure. II. The suitableness of the
remedy to the malady. Strength of heart for failing of heart, and a blessed portion
for the failing of the flesh. Observe, *that there is a proportionate remedy and relief
in God for all maladies and afflictions whatsoever, both within and without. If your
hearts fail you, God is strength ; if your flesh fails you, or comforts fail you, God is
a portion.* III. The prophet's interest ; he calls God his portion. Observe, *that
true Israelites have an undoubted interest in God :—He is theirs.* IV. The prophet's
experience in the worst time. He finds this to be true, that when communicated
strength fails, there is a never-failing strength in God. Observe, *that Christians'
experiences of God's all-sufficiency are then fullest and highest when created comforts
fail them.* V. There is the prophet's improvement of his experience for support
and comfort against future trials and temptations. Observe, *that a saint's consideration of his experience of God's all-sufficiency in times of exigency, is enough to
bear up and to fortify his spirit against all trials and temptations for the time to come.*
Thus you may improve the text by way of observation ; but there are two principal
doctrines to be insisted on. First, that God is the rock of a saint's heart, his strength
and his portion for ever. Secondly, that divine influence and relief passeth from

God to his people when they stand in most need thereof. 1st. God is the rock of a saint's heart, strength, and portion for ever. Here are two members or branches in this doctrine. 1. That God is the rock of a saint's heart, strength. 2. That God is the portion of a saint. Branch 1. God is the rock of a saint's heart, strength. He is not only strength, and the strength of their hearts, but the rock of their strength ; so Isaiah xvii. 10. Psalm lxii. 7, ᵓᵘᵓ, the same word that is used in the text, from hence comes our English word "sure." Explication. God is the rock of our strength, both in respect of our naturals and also of our spirituals : he is the strength of nature and of grace (Psalm xxvii. 1) ; the strength of my life natural and spiritual. God is the strength of thy natural faculties—of reason and understanding, of wisdom and prudence, of will and affections. He is the strength of all thy graces, faith, patience, meekness, temperance, hope, and charity ; both as to their being and exercise. He is the strength of all thy comfort and courage, peace and happiness, salvation and glory. Psalm cxl. 7. " O God, the rock of my salvation." In three respects. 1st. He is the author and giver of all strength. Psalm xviii. 32 : " It is God that girdeth me with strength." Psalm xxiv. 11 : " He will give strength to his people." Psalm cxxxviii. 3 ; Psalm lxviii. 35. 2ndly. He is the increaser and perfecter of a saint's strength ; it is God that makes a saint strong and mighty both to do and suffer, to bear and forbear, to believe and to hope to the end ; so Hebrews xi. 34 : "Out of weakness they were made strong ; " so 1 John ii. 14. And therefore is that prayer of Peter, 1 Peter v. 10. 3rdly. He is the preserver of your strength ; your life is laid up in God. Col. iii. 3. Your strength is kept by the strength of God ; so Psalm xci. 1. God doth overshadow the strength of saints, that no breach can be made upon it. Psalm lxiii. 7. "In the shadow of thy wings will I rejoice."—Samuel Blackerby. 1673.

Verse 26.—Oh, strange logic ! Grace hath learned to deduce strong conclusions out of weak premises, and happy out of sad. If the major be, "My flesh and my heart faileth ; " and the minor, " There is no blossom in the fig-tree, nor fruit in the vine," etc. ; yet his conclusion is firm and undeniable : "The Lord is the strength of my heart, and my portion for ever ; " or, " Yet will I rejoice in the God of my salvation." And if there be more in the conclusion than in the premises, it is the better ; God comes even in the conclusion.—John Sheffield, in "The Rising Sun." 1654.

Verse 26.—"My flesh and my heart faileth." They who take the expression in a bad sense, take it to be a confession of his former sin, and to have relation to the combat mentioned in the beginning of the Psalm, between the flesh and the spirit ; as if he said, I was so surfeited with self-conceitedness that I presumed to arraign divine actions at the bar of human reason, and to judge the stick under water crooked by the eye of my sense, when, indeed, it was straight ; but now I see that flesh is no fit judge in matters of faith ; that neither my flesh nor heart can determine rightly of God's dispensations, nor hold out uprightly under Satan's temptations ; for if God had not supported me my flesh had utterly supplanted me : "My flesh and my heart faileth : but God is the strength of my heart." Flesh is sometimes taken for corrupt nature. Gal. v. 13. First, because it is propagated by the flesh (John iii. 6) ; secondly, because it is executed by the flesh (Rom. vii. 25) ; thirdly, because corruption is nourished, strengthened, and increased by the flesh. 1 John ii. 16. They who take the words in a good sense, do not make them look back so far as to the beginning of the Psalm, but only to the neighbour verse.—George Swinnock.

Verse 26.—"God is the strength of my heart, and my portion for ever." The Hebrew carrieth it, but God is the rock of my heart, i.e., a sure, strong, and immoveable foundation to build upon. Though the winds may blow, and the waves beat, when the storm of death cometh, yet I need not fear that the house of my heart will fall, for it is built on a sure foundation : God is the rock of my heart. The strongest child that God hath is not able to stand alone ; like the hop or ivy, he must have somewhat to support him, or he is presently on the ground. Of all seasons, the Christian hath most need of succour at his dying hour ; then he must take his leave of all his comforts on earth, and then he shall be sure of the sharpest conflicts from hell, and, therefore, it is impossible he should hold out without extraordinary help from heaven. But the Psalmist had armour of proof ready, wherewith to encounter his last enemy. As weak and fearful a child as he was, he durst venture a walk in the dark entry of death, having his Father by the hand : "Though I walk through the valley of the shadow of death, I will fear no evil ; for thou art with me ; thy rod and thy staff they comfort me," Psalm xxiii. Though at the troubles of my life, and my trial at death, my heart is ready to fail me, yet I have a strong cordial which will cheer me in my saddest condition : *"God is the strength of my heart."*

"And my portion." It is a metaphor taken from the ancient custom among the Jews, of dividing inheritances, whereby every one had his allotted portion ; as if he had said, God is not only my rock to defend me from those tempests which assault me, and, thereby, my freedom from evil ; but he is also my portion, to supply my necessities, and to give me the fruition of all good. Others, indeed, have their parts on this side the land of promise, but the author of all portions is the matter of my portion. My portion doth not lie in the rubbish and lumber, as theirs doth whose portion is in this lie, be they never so large ; but my portion containeth him whom the heavens, and heaven of heavens, can never contain. God is the strength of my heart, and my portion *"for ever ; "* not for a year, or an age, or a million of ages, but for eternity. Though others' portions, like roses, the fuller they blow, the sooner they shed ; they are worsted often by their pride, and wasted through their prodigality, so that at last they come to want—and surely death always rends their persons and portions asunder ; yet my portion will be ever full, without diminution. Without alteration, this God will be my God for ever and ever, my guide and aid unto death ; nay, death, which dissolveth so many bonds, and untieth such close knots, shall never part me and my portion, but give me a perfect and everlasting possession of it.—*George Swinnock.*

Verse 28.—*"It is good for me to draw near to God."* When he saith *'tis good*, his meaning is *'tis best*. This positive is superlative. It is more than good for us to draw nigh to God at all times, it is best for us to do so, and it is at our utmost peril not to do so ; " For, lo," saith the Psalmist (verse 27), " they that are far from thee shall perish : thou hast destroyed all them that go a whoring from thee." It is dangerous to be far from God, but it is more dangerous to go far from him. Every man is far off by nature, and wicked men go further off : the former *shall perish*, the latter *shall be destroyed*. He that fares best in his withdrawings from God, fares bad enough ; therefore, it is best for us to draw nigh unto God. He is the best friend at all times, and the only friend at sometimes. And may we not say that God suffers and orders evil times, and the withdrawings of the creature, for that very end, that we might draw nearer unto him ? Doth he not give up the world to a spirit of reviling and mocking that he may stir up in his people a spirit of prayer ?—*Joseph Caryl.*

Verse 28.—*"It is good ; "* that is, it puts in us a blessed quality and disposition. It makes a man to be like God himself ; and, secondly, *"it is good,"* that is, it is comfortable ; for it is the happiness of the creature to be near the Creator ; it is beneficial and helpful. *"To draw near."* How can a man but be near to God, seeing he filleth heaven and earth : " Whither shall I go from thy presence ? " Psalm cxxxix. 7. He is present always in power and providence in all places, but graciously present with some by his Spirit, supporting, comforting, strengthening the heart of a good man. As the soul is said to be *tota in toto*, in several parts by several faculties, so God, is present to all, but in a diverse manner. Now we are said to be near to God in divers degrees : *first*, when our *understanding is enlightened ; intellectus est veritatis sponsa ;* and so the young man speaking discreetly in things concerning God, is said not to be far from the kingdom of God, Mark xii. 34. *Secondly, in minding :* when God is present to our minds, so that the soul is said to be present to that which it mindeth ; contrarily it is said of the wicked, that " God is not in all their thoughts," Psalm x. 4. *Thirdly, when the will upon the discovery of the understanding comes to choose the better part, and is drawn from that choice to cleave to him,* as it was said of Jonathan's heart, " it was knit to David," 1 Sam. xviii. 1. *Fourthly,* when *our whole affections are carried to God,* loving him as the chief good. Love is the firstborn affection. That breeds desire of communion with God. Thence comes joy in him, so that the soul pants after God, " as the hart after the water springs," Psalm xli. 1. *Fifthly,* and especially, *when the soul is touched with the Spirit of God working faith,* stirring up dependence, confidence, and trust on God. Hence ariseth sweet communion. The soul is never at rest till it rests on him. Then it is afraid to break with him or to displease him ; but it groweth zealous and resolute, and hot in love, stiff in good cases ; resolute against his enemies. And yet this is not all, for God will have also the outward man, so as the whole man must present itself before God in word, in sacraments ; speak of him and to him with reverence, and yet with strength of affection mounting up in prayer, as in a fiery chariot ; hear him speak to us ; consulting with his oracles ; fetching comforts against distresses, directions against maladies. *Sixthly*, and especially, we draw near to him *when we praise him ;* for this is the work of the souls departed and of the angels in heaven, that are continually near unto him. The prophet here saith, *"It is good for me."* How came he to know this ? Why, he had found it by experience, and by it he was thoroughly convinced.—*Richard Sibbes.*

Verse 28.—*"To draw near to God."* It is not one isolated act. It is not merely turning to God, and saying, " I have come to him." The expression is *"draw."* It is not a single act ; it is the drawing, the coming, the habitual walk, going on, and on, and on, so long as we are on earth. It is, therefore, an habitual religion which must be pressed and enforced upon ts.—*Montagu Villiers.* 1855.

Verse 28.—*"To draw near to God."* To draw near to God, I. A man should make his peace with God, in and through the Mediator Jesus Christ ; for, until once that be done, a man must be said to be far from God, and there is a partition-wall standing betwixt God and him. It is the same with that advice given by Eliphaz to Job : *"Acquaint now thyself with him, and be at peace : thereby good shall come unto thee,"* Job xxii. 21. Be friends with God, and all shall be well with you. II. It is to seek more after communion and fellowship with God, and to pursue after intimacy and familiarity with him ; and to have more of his blessed company with us in our ordinary walk and conversation ; according to that word, " Blessed is the people that know the joyful sound : they shall walk, O Lord, in the light of thy countenance," Psalm lxxxix. 15. III. As it stands here in the text, it is the expression of one who hath made up his peace already, and is on good terms with God ; and doth differ a little from what the words absolutely imply ; and so we may take it thus, I. It implies the confirming or making sure our interest in God, and so it supposeth the man's peace to be made with God ; for, whoever be the author of this Psalm, it supposeth he has made his peace ; and, therefore, in the following words it is subjoined, *"I have put my trust in the Lord,"* etc. ; that is, I have trusted my soul unto God, and made my peace with him through a mediator. It is *"good,"* whatever comes, it is always *"good "* to be *"near to God,"* that way, and to be made sure in him. II. It implies to be more conformed unto the image of God, and, therefore, this nearness to him is opposed to that of being far from God. It is good, says he, to draw near to God in my duty ; when so many are far from him. III. It implies, to lay by all things in the world, and to seek fellowship and communion with God, and to be more set apart for his blessed company, and to walk with him in a dependence upon him as the great burden-bearer, as he who is to be all in all unto us. In a word, to draw near unto God, is to make our peace with him, and to secure and confirm that peace with him, and to study a conformity unto him, and to be near unto him in our walk and conversation ; in our fellowship, and whole carriage, and deportment, to be always near unto him. —*William Guthrie.*

Verse 28.—The Epicurean, says Augustine, is wont to say, *It is good for me to enjoy the pleasures of the flesh :* The Stoic is wont to say, *For me it is good to enjoy the pleasures of the mind :* The Apostle used to say (not in words, but in sense), *It is good for me to cleave to God.*—*Lorinus.*

Verse 28.—*"The Lord God."* The names *"The Lord Jehovah "* are a combination expressive of God's sovereignty, self-existence, and covenant relation to his people. —*Joseph Addison Alexander.*

HINTS TO PREACHERS.

Whole Psalm.—It containeth the godly man's *trial*, in the former part of it, and his *triumph*, in the latter part of it. We have, I. The grievous conflict between the flesh and the spirit, to the 15th verse. II. The glorious conquest of the spirit over the flesh, to the end.—*G. Swinnock.*

Whole Psalm.—I. The cause of his distemper. II. The cure of it. III. The Psalmist's carriage after it.—*G. Swinnock.*

Verse 1.—The true Israel, the great blessing, and the sureness of it : or, the proposition of the text expounded, enforced, and applied.

Verse 1 (*first clause*).—Israel's receipts from God are, I. For quantity, the greatest; II. For variety, the choicest; III. For quality, the sweetest; IV. For security, the surest; V. For duration, the most lasting.—*Simeon Ash.*

Verse 2.—I. How far a believer may fall. II. How far he shall not fall. III. What fears are and what are not allowable.

Verse 2.—A retrospect of our slips; prospect of future danger; present preparation for it.

Verse 4.—Quiet deaths: the cases of the godly and ungodly distinguished by the causes of the quiet, and the unreliableness of mere feelings shown.

Verse 5.—The bastard's portion contrasted with that of the true son.

Verse 7.—The dangers of opulence and luxury.

Verse 8.—Connection between a corrupt heart and a proud tongue.

Verse 10.—I. The believer's cup is bitter. II. It is full. III. Its contents are varied "waters." IV. It is but a "cup," measured and limited. V. It is the cup of "his people," and, consequently, works good in the highest degree.

Verse 11.—The atheist's open question; the oppressor's practical question; the careless man's secret question; and the fearful saint's fainting question. The reasons why it is ever asked, and the conclusive reasons which put the matter beyond question.

Verse 12.—This verse suggests solemn enquiries for persons who are growing rich.

Verse 14.—The frequent and even constant chastisements of the righteous; the necessity and design thereof; and the consolations connected therewith.

Verse 15.—How we may bring injury on the saints; why we should avoid so doing, and how.

Verse 17.—I. Entrance into the place of fellowship with God, its privileges, and the way thereto. II. Lessons learned in that hallowed place; the text mentions one. III. Practical influence of the fellowship, and the instruction.

Verses 17, 18.—The sinner's end; See "Spurgeon's Sermons," No. 486.

Verse 18.—"*Thou didst set them in slippery places.*" I. It implies that they were always exposed to *sudden, unexpected destruction.* As he that walks in slippery places is every moment liable to fall, he cannot foresee one moment whether he shall stand or fall the next; and when he does fall, he falls at once without warning. II. They are liable to fall *of* themselves, without being thrown down by the hand of another; as he that stands or walks on slippery ground needs nothing but his own weight to throw him down. III. There is nothing that keeps wicked men at any one moment out of hell but the mere pleasure of God.—*Jonathan Edwards.*

Verse 19.—The first sight and sense of hell by a proud and wealthy sinner, who has just died in peace.

Verses 18—20.—The end of the wicked is, I. Near: "Thou hast set," etc. It may happen at any time. II. Judicial: "Thou bringest," etc. III. Sudden: "How are they," etc. IV. Tormenting: "They are utterly consumed," etc. V. Eternal: Left to themselves; gone from the mind of God; and disregarded as a dream when one awaketh. No after act respecting them, either for deliverance or annihilation.—*G. R.*

Verse 20.—The contemptible object:—a self-righteous, or boastful, or persecuting, or cavilling, or wealthy sinner when his soul is called before God.

Verse 22.—Our folly, ignorance, and brutishness. When displayed. What effect the fact should have upon us; and how greatly it illustrates divine grace.

Verse 23.—I. God does not forsake his people when they forsake him: "Nevertheless I am continually," etc. II. God does not lose his hold on them when they lose their hold on him: "Nevertheless thou hast holden," etc.—*G. R.*

Verses 22—25. I. The Psalmist's confession concerning the flesh. II. The faithful expressions of the spirit. III. The conclusion of the whole matter. See "Spurgeon's Sermons," No. 467.

Verses 23, 24.—I. What he says of the present: "I am continually with thee." II. What he says of the past: "Thou hast holden me," etc. III. What he says of the future: "Thou shalt guide," etc.—*W. Jay.*

Verses 23, 24.—Communion, upholding, on-leading, reception to glory, four glorious privileges; especially as bestowed on one who was grieved, foolish, ignorant, and a beast. Note the contrasts.

Verse 24.—The Enoch walk, and the Enoch reception into glory.

Verse 25.—God the best portion of the Christian.—*Jonathan Edwards' Works, Vol. II., pp.* 104—7.

Verse 25.—Heaven and earth ransacked to find a joy equal to the Lord himself. Let the preacher take up various joys and show the inferiority.

Verse 26.—I. The Psalmist's complaint: "My flesh and my heart faileth." II. His comfort: "But God," etc. Or, we may take notice, I. Of the frailty of his flesh. II. Of the flourishing of his faith. Doctrine 1. That man's flesh will fail him. The highest, the holiest man's heart will not always hold out. The prophet was great and gracious, yet his flesh failed him. Doctrine 2. That it is the comfort of a Christian, in his saddest condition, that God is his portion.— *G. Swinnock.*

Verse 26.—" The Fading of the Flesh."—*Swinnock's Treatise.* [*Nichol's Puritan Series.*]

Verse 26.—Where we fail and where we cannot fail.

Verse 27.—I. The sad conditions. II. The terrible punishments. III. The implied consolations.

Verse 28.—To draw near to God is our wisdom, our honour, our safety, our peace, our riches.—*Thomas Watson's Sermon, "The Happiness of Drawing near to God."* 1669. See also, *"The Saint's Happiness," R. Sibbes's Sermon.*

Verse 28.—David's conclusion; or, the saint's resolution.—*R. Sibbes.*

Verse 28.—I. The language of prayer: " It is good," etc. II. Of faith: " I have put," etc. III. Of praise: " That I may declare."—*G. R.*

Verse 28.—See " Spurgeon's Sermons," Nos. 287—8, " Let us pray." No. 879, " An assuredly good thing."

PSALM LXXIV.

Title.—Maschil of Asaph. *An instructive Psalm by Asaph. The history of the suffering church is always edifying; when we see how the faithful trusted and wrestled with their God in times of dire distress, we are thereby taught how to behave ourselves under similar circumstances: we learn moreover, that when the fiery trial befalls us, no strange thing has happened unto us, we are following the trail of the host of God.*

Division.—*From verse 1—11 the poet pleads the sorrows of the nation, and the despite done to the assemblies of the Lord; then he urges former displays of divine power as a reason for present deliverance (verses 12—23). Whether it is a prophetic Psalm, intended for use in troubles foreseen, or whether it was written by a later Asaph, after the invasion by Sennacherib or during the Maccabean wars, it would be very hard to determine, but we see no difficulty in the first supposition.*

EXPOSITION.

O GOD, why hast thou cast *us* off for ever? *why* doth thine anger smoke against the sheep of thy pasture?

2 Remember thy congregation, *which* thou hast purchased of old; the rod of thine inheritance, *which* thou hast redeemed; this mount Zion, wherein thou hast dwelt.

3 Lift up thy feet unto the perpetual desolations; *even* all *that* the enemy hath done wickedly in the sanctuary.

4 Thine enemies roar in the midst of thy congregations; they set up their ensigns *for* signs.

5 *A man* was famous according as he had lifted up axes upon the thick trees.

6 But now they break down the carved work thereof at once with axes and hammers.

7 They have cast fire into thy sanctuary, they have defiled *by casting down* the dwelling place of thy name to the ground.

8 They said in their hearts, Let us destroy them together: they have burned up all the synagogues of God in the land.

9 We see not our signs: *there is* no more any prophet: neither *is there* among us any that knoweth how long.

10 O God, how long shall the adversary reproach? shall the enemy blaspheme thy name for ever?

11 Why withdrawest thou thy hand, even thy right hand? pluck *it* out of thy bosom.

1. *"O God, why hast thou cast us off for ever?"* To cast us off at all were hard, but when thou dost for so long a time desert thy people it is an evil beyond all endurance—the very chief of woes and abyss of misery. It is our wisdom when under chastisement to enquire, "Show me wherefore thou contendest with me?" and if the affliction be a protracted one, we should the more eagerly enquire the purport of it. Sin is usually at the bottom of all the hidings of the Lord's face; let us ask the Lord to reveal the special form of it to us, that we may repent of it, overcome it, and henceforth forsake it. When a church is in a forsaken condition it must not sit still in apathy, but turn to the hand which smiteth it, and humbly enquire the reason why. At the same time, the enquiry of the text is a faulty one for it implies two mistakes. There are two questions, which only admit of negative replies. "Hath God cast away his people?" (Roms xi. 1); and the other, "Will

the Lord cast off for ever?" (Psalm lxxvii. 7). God is never weary of his people so as to abhor them, and even when his anger is turned against them, it is but for a small moment, and with a view to their eternal good. Grief in its distraction asks strange questions and surmises impossible terrors. It is a wonder of grace that the Lord has not long ago put us away as men lay aside cast-off garments, but he hateth putting away, and will still be patient with his chosen. "*Why doth thine anger smoke against the sheep of thy pasture?*" They are thine, they are the objects of thy care, they are poor, silly, and defenceless things: pity them, forgive them, and come to their rescue. They are but sheep, do not continue to be wroth with them. It is a terrible thing when the anger of God smokes, but it is an infinite mercy that it does not break into a devouring flame. It is meet to pray the Lord to remove every sign of his wrath, for it is to those who are truly the Lord's sheep a most painful thing to be the objects of his displeasure. To vex the Holy Spirit is no mean sin, and yet how frequently are we guilty of it; hence it is no marvel that we are often under a cloud.

2. "*Remember thy congregation, which thou hast purchased of old.*" What a mighty plea is redemption. O God, canst thou see the bloodmark on thine own sheep, and yet allow grievous wolves to devour them? The church is no new purchase of the Lord; from before the world's foundation the chosen were regarded as redeemed by the Lamb slain: shall ancient love die out, and the eternal purpose become frustrate? The Lord would have his people remember the Paschal Lamb, the bloodstained lintel, and the overthrow of Egypt; and will he forget all this himself? Let us put him in remembrance, let us plead together. Can he desert his blood-bought and forsake his redeemed? Can election fail and eternal love cease to flow? Impossible. The woes of Calvary, and the covenant of which they are the seal, are the security of the saints.

"*The rod of thine inheritance, which thou hast redeemed.*" So sweet a plea deserved to be repeated and enlarged upon. The Lord's portion is his people—will he lose his inheritance? His church is his kingdom, over which he stretches the rod of sovereignty; will he allow his possessions to be torn from him? God's property in us is a fact full of comfort: his value of us, his dominion over us, his connection with us are all so many lights to cheer our darkness. No man will willingly lose his inheritance, and no prince will relinquish his dominions; therefore we believe that the King of kings will hold his own, and maintain his rights against all comers. "*This mount Zion, wherein thou hast dwelt.*" The Lord's having made Zion the especial centre of his worship, and place of his manifestation, is yet another plea for the preservation of Jerusalem. Shall the sacred temple of Jehovah be desecrated by heathen, and the throne of the Great King be defiled by his enemies? Has the Spirit of God dwelt in our hearts, and will he leave them to become a haunt for the devil? Has he sanctified us by his indwelling, and will he, after all, vacate the throne? God forbid.

It may be well to note that this Psalm was evidently written with a view to the temple upon Zion, and not to the tabernacle which was there in David's time, and was a mere tent; but the destructions here bewailed were exercised upon the carved work of a substantial structure. Those who had seen the glory of God in Solomon's peerless temple might well mourn in bitterness, when the Lord allowed his enemies to make an utter ruin of that matchless edifice.

3. "*Lift up thy feet unto the perpetual desolations.*" The ruin made had already long been an eyesore to the suppliant, and there seemed no hope of restoration. Havoc lorded it not only for a day or a year, but with perpetual power. This is another argument with God. Would Jehovah sit still and see his own land made a wilderness, his own palace a desolation? Until he should arise, and draw near, the desolation would remain; only his presence could cure the evil, therefore is he entreated to hasten with uplifted feet for the deliverance of his people. "*Even all that the enemy hath done wickedly in the sanctuary.*" Every stone in the ruined temple appealed to the Lord; on all sides were the marks of impious spoilers, the holiest places bore evidence of their malicious wickedness; would the Lord for ever permit this? Would he not hasten to overthrow the foe who defied him to his face, and profaned the throne of his glory? Faith finds pleas in the worst circumstances, she uses even the fallen stones of her desolate palaces, and assails with them the gates of heaven, casting them forth with the great engine of prayer.

4. "*Thine enemies roar in the midst of thy congregations.*" Where thy people sang like angels, these barbarians roar like beasts. When thy saints come together

for worship, these cruel men attack them with all the fury of lions. They have no respect for the most solemn gatherings, but intrude themselves and their blasphemies into our most hallowed meetings. How often in times of persecution or prevalent heresy has the church learned the meaning of such language. May the Lord spare us such misery. When hypocrites abound in the church, and pollute her worship, the case is parallel to that before us ; Lord save us from so severe a trial. *"They set up their ensigns for signs."* Idolatrous emblems used in war were set up over God's altar, as an insulting token of victory, and of contempt for the vanquished and their God. Papists, Arians, and the modern school of Neologians have, in their day, set up their ensigns for signs. Superstition, unbelief, and carnal wisdom have endeavoured to usurp the place of Christ crucified, to the grief of the church of God. The enemies without do us small damage, but those within the church cause her serious harm ; by supplanting the truth and placing error in its stead, they deceive the people, and lead multitudes to destruction. As a Jew felt a holy horror when he saw an idolatrous emblem set up in the holy place, even so do we when in a Protestant church we see the fooleries of Rome, and when from pulpits, once occupied by men of God, we hear philosophy and vain deceit.

5. *"A man was famous according as he had lifted up axes upon the thick trees."* Once men were renowned for felling the cedars and preparing them for building the temple, but now the axe finds other work, and men are as proud of destroying as their fathers were of erecting. Thus in the olden times our sires dealt sturdy blows against the forests of error, and laboured hard to lay the axe at the root of the trees ; but, alas ! their sons appear to be quite as diligent to destroy the truth and to overthrow all that their fathers built up. O for the good old times again ! O for an hour of Luther's hatchet, or Calvin's mighty axe !

6. *"But now they break down the carved work thereof at once with axes and hammers."* The invaders were as industrious to destroy as the ancient builders had been to construct. Such fair carving it was barbarous to hew in pieces, but the Vandals had no mercy and broke down all, with any weapon which came to hand. In these days men are using axes and sledge-hammers against the gospel and the church. Glorious truths, far more exquisite than the goodliest carving, are cavilled over and smashed by the blows of modern criticism. Truths which have upheld the afflicted and cheered the dying are smitten by pretentious Goths, who would be accounted learned, but know not the first principles of the truth. With sharp ridicule, and heavy blows of sophistry, they break the faith of some ; and would, if it were possible, destroy the confidence of the elect themselves. Assyrians, Babylonians, and Romans are but types of spiritual foes who labour to crush the truth and the people of God.

7. *"They have cast fire into thy sanctuary."* Axes and hammers were not sufficient for the purpose of the destroyers, they must needs try fire. Malice knows no bounds. Those who hate God are never sparing of the most cruel weapons. To this day the enmity of the human heart is quite as great as ever ; and, if providence did not restrain, the saints would still be as fuel for the flames. *"They have defiled by casting down the dwelling place of thy name to the ground."* They made a heap of the temple, and left not one stone upon another. When the Lord left Mount Zion, and the Roman gained entrance, the military fury led the soldiery to burn out and root up the memorial of the famous House of the Lord. Could the powers of darkness have their way, a like fate would befall the church of Christ. "Rase it," say they, "rase it even to the foundation thereof." Defilement to the church is destruction ; her foes would defile her till nothing of her purity, and consequently of her real self, remained. Yet, even if they could wreak their will upon the cause of Christ, they are not able to destroy it, it would survive their blows and fires ; the Lord would hold them still like dogs in a leash, and in the end frustrate all their designs.

8. *"They said in their hearts, Let us destroy them together."* It was no idle wish, their cruelty was sincere, deep-seated, a matter of their inmost heart. Extirpation was the desire of Haman, and the aim of many another tyrant ; not a remnant of the people of God would have been left if oppressors could have had their way. Pharaoh's policy to stamp out the nation has been a precedent for others, yet the Jews survive, and will ; the bush though burning has not been consumed. Even thus the church of Christ has gone through baptisms of blood and fire, but it is all the brighter for them. *"They have burned up all the synagogues of God in the land."* Here is no allusion to places called synagogues, but to assemblies ; and as no

assemblies for worship were held but in one place, the ruin of the temple was the destruction of all the holy gatherings, and so in effect all the meeting-places were destroyed. One object of persecutors has always been to put an end to all conventicles, as they have called them. Keep them from meeting and you will scatter them, so have the foemen said; but, glory be to God, saints are independent of walls, and have met on the hill side, by the moss, or in the catacombs, or in a boat at sea. Yet has the attempt been almost successful, and the hunt so hot, that the faithful have wandered in solitude, and their solemn congregations have been under such circumstances, few and far between. What sighs and cries have in such times gone up to the ears of the Lord God of Sabaoth. How happy are we that we can meet for worship in any place we choose, and none dare molest us.

9. *"We see not our signs."* Alas, poor Israel! No Urim and Thummim blazed on the High Priest's bosom, and no Shekinah shone from between the cherubim. The smoke of sacrifice and cloud of incense no more arose from the holy hill; solemn feasts were suspended, and even circumcision, the covenant sign, was forbidden by the tyrant. We, too, as believers, know what it is to lose our evidence and grope in darkness; and too often do our churches also miss the tokens of the Redeemer's presence, and their lamps remain untrimmed. Sad plaint of a people under a cloud! *"There is no more any prophet."* Prophecy was suspended. No inspiring psalm or consoling promise fell from bard or seer. It is ill with the people of God when the voice of the preacher of the gospel fails, and a famine of the word of life falls on the people. God-sent ministers are as needful to the saints as their daily bread, and it is a great sorrow when a congregation is destitute of a faithful pastor. It is to be feared, that with all the ministers now existing, there is yet a dearth of men whose hearts and tongues are touched with the celestial fire. *"Neither is there any among us that knoweth how long."* If some one could foretell an end, the evil might be borne with a degree of patience, but when none can see a termination, or foretell an escape, the misery has a hopeless appearance, and is overwhelming. Blessed be God, he has not left his church in these days to be so deplorably destitute of cheering words; let us pray that he never may. Contempt of the word is very common, and may well provoke the Lord to withdraw it from us; may his long-suffering endure the strain, and his mercy afford us still the word of life.

10. *"O God, how long shall the adversary reproach?"* Though we know not how long yet thou dost. The times and seasons are with thee. When God is reproached, there is hope for us, for it may be he will hearken and avenge his dishonoured name. Wickedness has great license allowed it, and justice lingers on the road; God has his reasons for delay, and his seasons for action, and in the end it shall be seen that he is not slack concerning his promise as some men count slackness. *"Shall the enemy blaspheme thy name for ever?"* He will do so for ever, unless thou dost give him his quietus. Wilt thou never defend thyself, and stop slanderous tongues? Wilt thou always endure the jeers of the profane? Is there to be no end to all this sacrilege and cursing? Yes, it shall all be ended, but not by-and-by. There is a time for the sinner to rage, and a time in which patience bears with him; yet it is but a time, and then, ah, then!

11. *"Why withdrawest thou thy hand, even thy right hand?"* Wherefore this inaction, this indifference for thine own honour and thy people's safety? How bold is the suppliant! Does he err? Nay, verily, we who are so chill, and distant, and listless in prayer are the erring ones. The kingdom of heaven suffereth violence, and he who learns the art shall surely prevail with God by its means. It is fit that we should enquire why the work of grace goes on so slowly, and the enemy has so much power over men: the enquiry may suggest practical reflections of unbounded value.

> " Why dost thou from the conflict stay?
> Why do thy chariot wheels delay?
> Lift up thyself, hell's kingdom shake,
> Arm of the Lord, awake, awake."

"Pluck it out of thy bosom." A bold simile, but dying men must venture for their lives. When God seems to fold his arms we must not fold ours, but rather renew our entreaties that he would again put his hand to the work. O for more agony in prayer among professing Christians, then should we see miracles of grace. We have here before us a model of pleading, a very rapture of prayer. It is humble, but very bold, eager, fervent, and effectual. The heart of God is always moved by

such entreaties. When we bring forth our strong reasons, then will he bring forth his choice mercies.

12 For God *is* my King of old, working salvation in the midst of the earth.

13 Thou didst divide the sea by thy strength : thou brakest the heads of the dragons in the waters.

14 Thou brakest the heads of leviathan in pieces, *and* gavest him *to be* meat to the people inhabiting the wilderness.

15 Thou didst cleave the fountain and the flood : thou driedst up mighty rivers.

16 The day *is* thine, the night also *is* thine : thou hast prepared the light and the sun.

17 Thou hast set all the borders of the earth : thou hast made summer and winter.

18 Remember this, *that* the enemy hath reproached, O Lord, and *that* the foolish people have blasphemed thy name.

19 O deliver not the soul of thy turtle-dove unto the multitude *of the wicked :* forget not the congregation of thy poor for ever.

20 Have respect unto the covenant : for the dark places of the earth are full of the habitations of cruelty.

21 O let not the oppressed return ashamed : let the poor and needy praise thy name.

22 Arise, O God, plead thine own cause : remember how the foolish man reproacheth thee daily.

23 Forget not the voice of thine enemies : the tumult of those that rise up against thee increaseth continually.

Having spread the sad case before the Lord, the pleader now urges another series of arguments for divine help. He reasons from the Lord's former wonders of grace, and his deeds of power, imploring a repetition of the same divine works.

12. *"For God is my King of old."* How consoling is this avowal ! Israel in holy loyalty acknowledges her King, and claims to have been his possession from of old, and thence she derives a plea for defence and deliverance. If the Lord be indeed the sole monarch of our bosoms, he will in his love put forth his strength on our behalf ; if from eternity he has claimed us as his own, he will preserve us from the insulting foe. *"Working salvation in the midst of the earth."* From the most remote period of Israel's history the Lord had worked out for her many salvations ; especially at the Red Sea, the very heart of the world was astonished by his wonders of deliverance. Now, every believer may plead at this day the ancient deeds of the Lord, the work of Calvary, the overthrow of sin, death, and hell. He who wrought out our salvation of old will not, cannot desert us now. Each past miracle of grace assures us that he who has begun to deliver will continue to redeem us from all evil. His deeds of old were public and wrought in the teeth of his foes, they were no delusions or make-believes ; and, therefore, in all our perils we look for true and manifest assistance, and we shall surely receive it.

13. *"Thou didst divide the sea by thy strength."* Infinite power split the Red Sea in twain. Israel delighted to rehearse this famous act of the Lord. *"Thou brakest the heads of the dragons in the waters."* Monsters long accustomed to the deep found themselves left high and dry. Huge things of the sea-cave and the coral grot were deprived of their vital element, and left with crushed heads upon the dry channel bed. There, too, that old dragon Pharaoh was utterly broken, and Egypt herself had the head of her power and pomp broken with an almighty blow. Even thus is that old dragon broken by him who came to bruise the serpent's head, and the sea of wrath no longer rolls before us ; we pass through it dry-shod. Our faith as to the present is revived by glad memories of the past.

14. *"Thou brakest the heads of leviathan in pieces."* It is the Lord who has done it all. The mighty dragon of Egypt was utterly slain, and his proud heads broken in pieces. Our Lord Jesus is the true Hercules, dragons with a hundred heads are crushed beneath his foot : the infernal hydra he utterly vanquishes. *" And gavest*

him to be meat to the people inhabiting the wilderness." Not only did the wild beasts feed upon the carcasses of the Egyptians, but the dwellers along the shores stripped the bodies and enriched themselves with the spoil. Israel, too, grew rich with the relics of her drowned adversaries. How often do great afflictions work our lasting good. Leviathan, who would have devoured us, is himself devoured, and out of the monster we gather sweetness. Let us not give way to fear; hydra-headed evils shall be slain, and monstrous difficulties shall be overcome, and all things shall work our lasting good.

15. *"Thou didst cleave the fountain and the flood."* Jordan was divided by Jehovah's power; the Lord is able to repeat his miracles, what he did with a sea, he can do with a river; lesser difficulties shall be removed as well as greater ones. Perhaps the fountain refers to the smitten rock, which from its cleft poured forth a perpetual stream; so the Lord opens to us springs of water in the wilderness. *"Thou driedst up mighty rivers,"* rivers which were permanent, and not like the transient torrents of the land, were dried up for awhile; the Jordan itself, being such, was laid dry for a season. Observe the repetition of the pronoun "thou;" the song is all for God, and the prayer is all directed to him. The argument is that he who wrought such wonders would be pleased to do the like now that an emergency had arisen.

16. *"The day is thine, the night also is thine."* Thou art not restricted by times and seasons. Our prosperity comes from thee, and our adversity is ordained by thee. Thou rulest in the darkness, and one glance of thine eye kindles it into day. Lord, be not slack to keep thy word, but rise for the help of thy people. *"Thou hast prepared the light and the sun."* Both light and the light-bearer are of thee. Our help, and the instrument of it, are both in thy hand. There is no limit to thy power; be pleased to display it and make thy people glad. Let thy sacred preparations of mercy ripen; say, "Let there be light," and light shall at once dispel our gloom.

17. *"Thou hast set all the borders of the earth."* Land and sea receive their boundaries from thee. Continents and islands are mapped by thy hand. Observe, again, how everything is ascribed to the divine agency by the use of the pronoun "thou;" not a word about natural laws, and original forces, but the Lord is seen as working all. It will be well when all our "ologies" are tinctured with "theology," and the Creator is seen at work amid his universe. The argument of our text is, that he who bounds the sea can restrain his foes; and he who guards the borders of the dry land can also protect his chosen. *"Thou hast made summer and winter."* Return, then, good Lord, to us the bright summer days of joy. We know that all our changes come of thee, we have already felt the rigours of thy winter, grant us now the genial glow of thy summer smile. The God of nature is the God of grace; and we may argue from the revolving seasons that sorrow is not meant to rule the year, the flowers of hope will blossom, and ruddy fruits of joy will ripen yet.

18. *"Remember this, that the enemy hath reproached, O Lord."* Against thee, the ever glorious Maker of all things, have they spoken, thine honour have they assailed, and defied even thee. This is forcible pleading indeed, and reminds us of Moses and Hezekiah in their intercessions: "What wilt thou do unto thy great name?" "It may be that the Lord thy God will hear the words of Rabshakeh, who hath reproached the living God." Jehovah is a jealous God, and will surely glorify his own name; here our hope finds foothold. *"And that the foolish people have blasphemed thy name."* The meanness of the enemy is here pleaded. Sinners are fools, and shall fools be allowed to insult the Lord and oppress his people; shall the abjects curse the Lord and defy him to his face? When error grows too bold its day is near, and its fall certain. Arrogance foreshadows ripeness of evil, and the next step is rottenness. Instead of being alarmed when bad men grow worse and more audacious, we may reasonably take heart, for the hour of their judgment is evidently near.

19. *"O deliver not the soul of thy turtle-dove unto the multitude of the wicked."* Thy poor church is weak and defenceless as a dove, but yet her adversaries cannot touch her without thy permission; do not give them leave to devour her, consign her not to the merciless fangs of her foes. She is thy dove, thy turtle, thy favoured one, do not cast her to her enemies. Be merciful, and preserve the weak. Thus may we each plead, and with good hope of prevailing, for the Lord is very pitiful and full of compassion. *"Forget not the congregation of thy poor for ever."* They look to thee for everything, for they are very poor, and they are thy poor, and there

is a company of them, collected by thyself ; do not turn thy back on them for long, do not appear strange unto them, but let their poverty plead with thee ; turn thou unto them, and visit thine afflicted. In such pleas we also can personally join when at any time we are sorely tried, and the Lord's presence is hidden from us.

20. *"Have respect unto the covenant."* Here is the master-key,—heaven's gate must open to this. God is not a man that he should lie ; his covenant he will not break, nor alter the thing that hath gone forth out of his lips. The Lord had promised to bless the seed of Abraham, and make them a blessing ; here they plead that ancient word, even as we also may plead the covenant made with the Lord Jesus for all believers. What a grand word it is ! Reader, do you know how to cry, " Have respect unto thy covenant " ? *"For the dark places of the earth are full of the habitations of cruelty."* Darkness is the fit hour for beasts of prey, and ignorance the natural dwelling-place of cruelty. All the world is in a measure dark, and hence everywhere there are cruel enemies of the Lord's people ; but in some places a sevenfold night of superstition and unbelief has settled down, and there rage against the saints reaches to madness. Has not the Lord declared that the whole earth shall be filled with his glory ? How can this be if he always permits cruelty to riot in dark places ? Surely, he must arise, and end the days of wrong, the era of oppression. This verse is a most telling missionary prayer.

21. *"O let not the oppressed return ashamed."* Though broken and crushed they come to thee with confidence ; suffer them not to be disappointed, for then they will be ashamed of their hope. *"Let the poor and needy praise thy name."* By thy speedy answer to their cries make their hearts glad, and they will render to thee their gladdest songs. It is not the way of the Lord to allow any of those who trust in him to be put to shame ; for his word is, " He shall call upon me, and I will deliver him, and he shall glorify me."

22. *"Arise, O God, plead thine own cause."* Answer thou the taunts of the profane by arguments which shall annihilate both the blasphemy and the blasphemer. God's judgments are awful replies to the defiances of his foes. When he makes empires crumble, and smites persecutors to the heart, his cause is pleaded by himself as none other could have advocated it. O that the Lord himself would come into the battle-field. Long has the fight been trembling in the balance ; one glance of his eye, one word from his lip, and the banners of victory shall be borne on the breeze. *"Remember how the foolish man reproacheth thee daily."* The Lord is begged to remember that he is himself reproached, and that by a mere man—that man a fool, and he is also reminded that these foul reproaches are incessant, and repeated with every revolving day. It is bravely done when faith can pluck pleas out of the dragon's mouth, and out of the blasphemies of fools find arguments with God.

23. *"Forget not the voice of thine enemies."* Great warrior, let the foemen's taunt provoke thee to the fray. They challenge thee ; accept thou the gage of battle, and smite them 'with thy terrible hand. If the cries of thy children are too feeble to be heard, be pleased to note the loud voices of thy foes, and silence their profanities for ever. *"The tumult of those that rise up against thee increaseth continually."* The ungodly clamour against thee and thy people, their blasphemies are loud and incessant, they defy thee, even thee, and because thou repliest not they laugh thee to scorn. They go from bad to worse, from worse to worst ; their fury swells like the thunders of an advancing tempest. What will it come to ? What infamy will next be hurled at thee and thine ? O God, wilt thou for ever bear this ? Hast thou no regard for thine honour, no respect for thy glory ?

Much of this Psalm has passed over our mind while beholding the idolatries of Rome,* and remembering her bloody persecution of the saints. O Lord, how long shall it be ere thou wilt ease thyself of those profane wretches, the priests, and cast the harlot of Babylon into the ditch of corruption ? May thy church never cease to plead with thee till judgment shall be executed, and the Lord avenged upon Antichrist.

---

* The Author visited Rome in November and December, 1871, while this portion of the Treasury of David was in progress.

EXPLANATORY NOTES AND QUAINT SAYINGS.

Whole Psalm.—There is one singularity in this Psalm which reminds one strongly of Psalm xliv.: there is not one mention of national or personal sin throughout, no allusion to the Lord's righteous dealing in their punishment, no supplication for pardon and forgiveness; and yet one can hardly doubt that the writer of the Psalm, be he who he may, must have felt as keenly as Jeremiah, Ezekiel, Daniel, or any other prophet of the captivity, the sins and iniquities which had brought all this sore evil upon them. But still, though there be expostulation, there is no complaint; though there be mourning, there is no murmuring; there is far more the cry of a smitten child, wondering why, and grieving that his father's face is so turned away from him in displeasure, and a father's hand so heavy on the child of his love. Or, as we might almost say, it is like the cry of one of those martyred ones beneath the altar, wondering at the Lord's continued endurance of his heritage thus trampled under foot of the marauder and oppressor, and exclaiming, " How long, O Lord, how long ? " And yet it is the appeal of one who was still a sufferer, still groaning under the pressure of his calamities, " Why hast thou cast *us* off for ever ? *We* see not *our* signs, there is no more any prophet among *us*."—*Barton Bouchier.*

Whole Psalm.—The peculiarity of this Psalm is marked by the very frequent use of the נצח, *"for ever : "* verses 1, 3, 10.—*E. W. Hengstenberg.*

Verse 1.—This Psalm, and particularly these words, do contain the church's sad lamentation over the deep affliction, together with her earnest expostulations with God about the cause. Two things there are that the church in these words doth plead with God. First, *The greatness of her affliction ;* secondly, *the nearness of her relation.* 1. *The greatness of her affliction.* And there were three things in her affliction that did make it lie very heavy upon her. First, the *root* of this affliction ; and that was God's *"anger : "* " Why doth thine *anger* smoke," etc. Secondly, the *height* of this affliction : God was not only angry, but he did *"smoke"* in his anger. Thirdly, the *length* of this affliction : it was so long that God did seem to cast them off *"for ever."* 2. *The nearness of her relation :* " Against the *sheep of thy pasture ; "* as if they should have said, Lord, if thou hadst done this against thine enemies, it had been no wonder ; if thou hadst poured out thy wrath against the vessels of wrath, it had not been so much. But what ! wilt thou draw out thy sword against *the sheep of thy pasture ?* It were no wonder that thou shouldst take the fat and the strong, and pour out thy judgments upon them ; but wilt thou do it to *thy sheep ?* There be several doctrines that I may raise from these words ; as, First doctrine : That God's people are his sheep. Second doctrine : That God may be sorely angry with his own people, with his own sheep. Third doctrine : That when God is angry with his people, it becomes them carefully to enquire into the cause. Fourth doctrine : That when God's people are under afflictions, they ought to take notice of, and be much affected with, his anger, from which they do proceed. Fifth doctrine : That God's people under afflictions are, or should be, more affected with his anger than with their smart. This is that which the church doth complain of, not that the church did so smart, but that God was displeased and angry ; that did most affect them. Sixth doctrine : That God's people are apt to have misgiving thoughts of God when they are in sore afflictions. God was angry with his people, and their hearts did misgive them, as if God did cast off his people. Seventh doctrine : That God may be angry with his people, so sore, and so long, that in the judgment of sense it may seem that they are for ever cast off. Eighth doctrine : That though the people of God may not murmur against his proceedings, yet they may humbly expostulate with him about the cause.—*Joseph Alleine.* 1633—1668.

Verse 1.—*"Why doth thine anger smoke,"* etc. Anger is a fire ; and in men, and other creatures enraged, a smoke seemeth to go out of their nostrils. Xenophon saith of the Thebans, when they are angry they breathe fire. This then is spoken of God, after the manner of men.—*John Trapp.*

Verse 1.—*"The sheep of thy pasture."* There is nothing more imbecile than a sheep : simple, frugal, gentle, tame, patient, prolific, timid, domesticated, stupid, useful. Therefore, while the name of *sheep* is here used, it is suggested how pressing the necessity is for divine assistance, and how well-befitting the Most High it would be to make their cause his own.—*Lorinus.*

Verse 2.—*"Remember thy congregation."* It is not without reason that they do not say, Remember *us*, but *"Remember thy congregation,"* not ours, but thine ; nor *that* because it has now begun to be thine, but *"which thou hast purchased of old, the rod of thine inheritance which thou hast redeemed :"* likewise, this Mount Zion ; not wherein we, but wherein *"thou* hast dwelt." They had nothing which they could bring before an angry God with greater confidence, than that ancient loving-kindness shown to their fathers in former days.—*Musculus.*

Verse 2.—*"The rod of thine inheritance."* שֵׁבֶט נַחֲלָה, the inheritance-rod is the staff with which the inheritance is measured ; קְנֵה הַמִּדָּה=שֵׁבֶט, the land-surveyor's rod (Ez. xl. 3) : and this is used as גּוֹרָל, *the lot,* is for *the portion,* for the *inheritance itself.*—*E. W. Hengstenberg.*

Verse 2.—*"Thine inheritance."* It signifies a nation, which through all successions God had a peculiar right and title to.—*Henry Hammond.*

Verse 2.—*"Thou hast redeemed,"* *i.e.* the purchased people, by restoring them when they had been alienated, and had fallen into the hands of others : like a *goel,* or near kinsman, who ransoms a brother hurried into captivity, and regains an *inheritance* that has been sold.—*Hermann Venema.*

Verse 3.—*"Lift up thy feet."* Or, *thy hammers,* that is, " thy strokes," to " stamp " or " beat down " the enemy " unto perpetual desolations." Thus the " feet " are used to " tread down with," Isa. xxvi. 6 ; and so the Greek taketh it here, changing the metaphor, and translating it, " thy hands," which are also instruments to strike down with. Or, *"lift up thy feet,"* that is, come quickly to see *"the perpetual desolations,"* which the enemy hath made.—*Henry Ainsworth.*

Verse 3.—*"Lift up thy feet."* Abu Walid renders it, *Tread hard upon thine enemies.* The Jewish Arab, *Shew forth thy punishment,* adding in a note that the *lifting up the feet* implies punishment, the bringing under by force being usually expressed by *treading under the feet.*—*Henry Hammond.*

Verse 3.—*"Lift up thy feet,"* etc. To these *desolations* they seek that God would *lift up his footsteps,* that is, that he would approach. In Gen. xxix. 1, there occurs the phrase, *to lift the feet ;* here the expression is much more marked—*to lift up the footsteps*—and must be taken to mean a swift, impetuous, majestic, and powerful approach : like a hero, who strikes the ground with heavy tread, and advances rapidly with far-sounding footsteps.—*Hermann Venema.*

Verse 3.—*"In the sanctuary."* Their cities had been laid waste, their provinces, their farms, their vineyards, their oliveyards. They themselves had been everywhere cut down without striking a blow in defence, and their means of life had been snatched away without resistance. Yet they speak not of these things ; not because things of this sort ought not to cause grief, nor yet because the saints are not touched with a sense of their loss ; but because those things which threatened the extinction of religion and the worship of God, overtopped the feeling of all these other misfortunes with an intolerable sorrow.—*Musculus.*

Verse 4.—*"Thine enemies roar,"* etc. The word שָׁאַג is used especially of the roar of the lion. . . . . In this place we may justly extend the application of the verb to those noisy words, whether mirthful or boastful, blasphemous against God and calamitous to his people (verse 10), breathing terror and threatenings through edicts ; or rude and senseless, as in their idolatrous worship ; or in their prayers and thoughtless songs. As in Isa. lii. 5, its meaning is *to howl.*—*Hermann Venema.*

Verse 4.—*"They set up their ensigns for signs."* The meaning is, that the enemy, having abolished the signs of the true God, of his people and religion, such as circumcision, the feasts, sacrifices, the other ordinances of religion, and other marks of liberty, substituted his own idolatrous signs, as the signs of his authority and religion.—*Hermann Venema.*

Verses 4—7.—[*The persecution under Antiochus.* B.C. 168.] Athenæus proceeded to Jerusalem, where, with the assistance of the garrison, he prohibited and suppressed every observance of the Jewish religion, forced the people to profane the Sabbath, to eat swine's flesh and other unclean food, and expressly forbade the national rite of circumcision. The Temple was dedicated to Jupiter Olympus : the statue of that deity was erected on part of the altar of burnt offerings, and sacrifice duly performed. . . . . As a last insult, the feasts of the Bacchanalia, the license of which, as they were celebrated in the later ages of Greece, shocked the severe virtue of the older Romans, were substituted for the national festival of Tabernacles. The reluctant Jews were forced to join in these riotous orgies, and to carry the ivy, the insignia of the God. So near was the Jewish nation, and the worship of Jehovah, to total extermination.—*Henry Hart Milman* (1791—1868), *in "A History of the Jews."*

[*Under Titus.*] And now the Romans, upon the flight of the seditious into the city, and upon the burning of the holy house itself, and of all the buildings lying round about it, brought their ensigns to the temple, and set them over against its eastern-gate ; and there did they offer sacrifices to them, and there did they make Titus imperator, with the greatest acclamations of joy.—*Josephus.*

Verse 5.—"*A man was famous,*" etc. It enhances the cruelty of the enemy that the temple which had been built at the cost of so much treasure, adorned with such great elegance and splendour, and finished with untiring industry and consummate skill, was not saved thereby from their barbarous hands, but was utterly overthrown. There is a simile in these verses. The enemies breaking to pieces with great violence and casting down the altars and beams of the temple, are compared to the woodman, who with axe in hand cuts down the strong trees of the wood.—*Mollerus.*

Verse 5.—"*A man was famous,*" etc. That is, very renowned were the workmen, who, by Hiram's order, cut down the rough cedars and firs in the thick Tyrian forests, for the building of thy Temple, and thereby they did an acceptable service to thee.—*Thomas Fenton.*

Verse 6.—"*The carved work thereof.*" Even barbarian invaders are wont to spare the more splendid buildings for art's sake. Demetrius, when he had taken a picture painted by Protogenes in the suburbs of Rhodes, was besought by the Rhodians to be lenient towards art, lest he should destroy the painting. He replied that he would sooner burn the statues of his father than so great a work of art. The ferocity of these enemies, therefore, outdoes the barbarity of others, for they ruthlessly cast down an edifice sculptured and polished with the greatest skill.—*Mollerus.*

Verse 6.—"*The carved work.*" פִּתּוּחִים *Pittuchim :* used in 1 Kings vi. 29, of the " carved figures of cherubim, and palm-trees, and open flowers," which were on the Temple walls.—*William Kay.*

Verse 6.—"*With axes and hammers.*" It is noted by a learned interpreter, that the words in the original rendered in our translation, "*with axes and hammers,*" are not properly Hebrew, but Syriac words, purposely to hint thereby the time when and the persons by whom this was done.—*Arthur Jackson.*

Verse 8.—"*The synagogues of God.*" It is the opinion of Spencer, Vitringa, and of the learned in general, that the institution of synagogues for worship originated in the reading of the law publicly after the collection of its volumes by Ezra, and that, consequently, there were no such places of solemn assembly previous to the Babylonish captivity. Some of the Jews themselves have expressed a conviction that this is the fact, and the Scriptures give no intimation of their existence antecedently to that time. We are aware, however, that one of the first Hebraists of the present day, the Rev. Dr. M'Caul, inclines to the opinion of an earlier origin than that generally adopted. We quote his words : " The existence of such places before the Babylonish captivity has been much disputed ; and most writers, arguing from the silence of the Old Testament, incline to the opinion that they originated in Babylon, and that after the restoration similar oratories were opened in the land of Israel ; and hence some infer that the Seventy-fourth Psalm, which says in the eighth verse, '*They have burned up all the synagogues in the land,*' was written in the post-Babylonian times. The argument from silence is, however, far from conclusive. The translation of מוֹעֲדֵי as *synagogues,* in the verse just cited, might fairly lead to a similar translation in some other passages which were confessedly written before the captivity ; and the circumstances, character, and necessities of the Israelites, the great body of whom were far removed from the temple, prove indisputably that in their towns and villages they must have had some locality where they assembled on their sabbaths, new moons, and other solemn days, for the purpose of receiving instruction in the law, and for public prayer. That locality, however different from subsequent arrangements, was the origin of the *synagogue*. How such assemblies were conducted before the captivity it is now impossible to say."—*F. A. Cox.*

Verse 8.—"*Synagogues.*" Dr. Prideaux affirms that they had no synagogue before the Babylonish captivity ; for the main service of the synagogue, says he, being the reading of the law unto the people, where there was no book of the law to be read, there certainly could be no synagogue. But how rare the book of the law was through all Judæa, before the Babylonish captivity, many texts of Scripture tell us. When Jehoshaphat sent teachers through all Judæa, to instruct the people in the law of God, they carried a book of the law with them (2 Chron. xvii. 9), which they needed not have done if there had been any copies of the law in those cities to which they went : which certainty there would have been had there been any synagogues in them. And when Hilkiah found the law in the temple (2 Kings xxii. 8), neither he nor king Josiah needed to have been so surprised at it, had books of the law been common in those times. Their behaviour on that occasion sufficiently proves they had never seen it before, which could not be the case had there then been any other copies of it to be found among the people ; and if there were no copies of the law at that time among them, there could then be most certainly no *synagogues* for them to resort to for the hearing of it read unto them. From whence he concludes there could be no *synagogues* among the Jews, till after the Babylonish captivity.—*Cruden's Concordance.*

Verse 8.—"*Synagogues.*" The assertion of those who are in favour of the Maccabæan origin of the Psalm, that these words describe the destruction of the *synagogues*, is met by the remark, that in all the copious accounts which we have of the transactions of these times, there is nothing said of any such work of destruction.—*E. W. Hengstenberg.*

Verse 8.—"*Synagogues.*" In the Old Testament we find no traces of meetings for worship in synagogues. Temporary altars, groves, and high places were used alike by the Jewish saints and sinners for the worship of God and idols. The only pre-exile instance which seems to indicate that the devout in Israel were in the habit of resorting to pious leaders for blessings and instruction on stated occasions, is to be found in 2 Kings iv. 23, where the Shunammite's husband asks, " Wherefore wilt thou go to him (Elisha) to-day ? It is neither new moon nor Sabbath." Yet 2 Kings xxii. 8, etc. ; 2 Chron. xxxiv. 14, etc., testify undoubtedly against the existence of places of worship under the monarchy. It is during the exile, whilst the temple-worship was in abeyance, that we find indubitable proof of the systematic meetings on fasts for devotion and instruction (Zech. vii. 3—5 ; viii. 19). Religious meetings were also held on Sabbaths and fasts, to instruct the exiles in the divine law, and to admonish them to obey the divine precepts (Ezra x. 1—9 ; Neh. viii. 1—3 ; ix. 1—3 ; xiii. 1—3). These meetings, held near the temple and in other localities, were the origin of the *synagogue*, and the place in which the people assembled was denominated *the house of assembly*. Hence, also, the synagogue in the temple itself. . . . . These synagogues soon became very popular, so that the Psalmist in depicting worship in the time of the Maccabees declares that the many meeting-places of God—or "*the Synagogues of God*" as the A.V. rightly renders it—have been laid waste.—*Christian D. Ginsburg, in Cyclopædia of Biblical Literature.*

Verse 8 (*second clause*).—The sense seems to be, *they* (the Chaldæan invaders) *have abolished all the solemnities in the land*. They have taken away the daily sacrifice ; they have put an end to the festivals and feasts of our holy ritual. Compare Lam. ii. 6 : " He hath violently taken away his tabernacle ; he hath destroyed his places of the assembly," (or rather, his assembly, his *moëd*). " The Lord hath caused the solemn feasts and sabbaths to be forgotten in Zion."—*Christopher Wordsworth.*

Verse 9.—"*We see not our signs.*" As if they had said, heretofore God was wont to give us signs and tokens, he would even work miracles for us, or he would send a prophet to instruct and advise us what to do ; we had those who could tell us "*how long,*" that is, how long our troubles should last, and when we should have our expected end of them ; but now we are in trouble, and no man can tell us how long, now we are left to the wide world, to shift for ourselves as well as we can ; the Lord will not advise us what to do, nor give us his mind what's best to be done, or how to proceed : thus deplorable was their condition upon the hiding of God's face from them.—*Joseph Caryl.*

Verse 9.—*"We see not our signs."* These signs, which he mourned that he did not see, were certain outward marks of God's special favour, certain testimonies of his presence, certain memorials that he was with them to bless them. And it is said that there were five things in Solomon's temple destroyed by Nebuchadnezzar, which were not in the second temple, which was erected after the Babylonish captivity. Five memorials or tokens of God's special presence were there wanting. One was the ark of the covenant; another, the fire from heaven upon the brazen altar; the third, the Shechinah, or cloud that rested upon the mercy-seat; the fourth, the Urim and Thummim which were in the breast-plate of the high-priest; and the fifth, the spirit of prophecy. For though there were the prophets, Haggai, Zechariah, and Malachi, at the time of, and shortly after, the restoration; yet the spirit of prophecy ceased with Malachi, and did not re-appear until John the Baptist, the forerunner of the Lord Jesus. . . . . The lamentation of the church here, then, was, that she saw not her signs. So now, the church of the living God, the regenerate family of Zion, have often reason to pour out the same melancholy complaint. Signs of God's favour, marks and testimonies of the work of grace upon their souls, are often so out of sight, so buried in obscurity, so enveloped in clouds of darkness, that the living family are compelled, from soul-feeling, to take up the language of lamentation here expressed, and say, *"We see not our signs."*—*J. C. Philpot.* 1802—1869.

Verse 9.—*"Our signs."* The ordinary *"signs"* of Israel being God's peculiar people are the passover (Exod. xii. 13), the Sabbath (Exod. xxxi. 13), the temple, the altar, the sacrifices; the extraordinary ones are God's miracles wrought in his people's behalf (Ps. lxxviii. 43).—*A. R. Fausset.*

Verse 9.—*"There is no more any prophet."* By us it ought to be observed what they do not say: It is not,—here is no more any giant or warlike leader who may deliver us from the adversary: but, there is no more any prophet. And yet when the prophets were with them, they were contemptible in the eyes of all, maltreated by the wicked and put to death.—*Musculus.*

Verse 10.—*"Shall the enemy blaspheme thy name for ever?"* The sinner never leaves his sin till sin first leaves him: did not death put a stop to his sin, he would never cease from sin. This may be illustrated by a similitude thus: A company of gamesters resolve to play all night, and accordingly they sit down to chess tables or some other game; their candle, accidentally or unexpectedly, goes out, or is put out, or burnt out; their candle being out, they are forced to give over their game, and go to bed in the dark; but had the candle lasted all night, they would have played all night. This is every sinner's case in regard of sin: did not death put out the candle of life, the sinner would sin still. Should the sinner live for ever, he would sin for ever; and, therefore, it is a righteous thing with God to punish him for ever in hellish torments. Every impenitent sinner would sin to the days of eternity, if he might live to the days of eternity. *"O God, how long shall the adversary reproach? shall the enemy blaspheme thy name for ever?"* For ever, and ever more; or for ever and yet—for so the Hebrew loves to exaggerate: as if the sinner, the blasphemer, would set a term of duration longer than eternity to sin in. The Psalmist implicitly saith, Lord, if thou dost but let them alone for ever, they will certainly blaspheme thy name for ever and ever. I have read of the crocodile, that he knows no *maximum quod sic*, he is always growing bigger and bigger, and never comes to a certain pitch of monstrosity so long as he lives. *Quamdiu vivit crescit.* Every habituated sinner would, if he were let alone, be such a monster, perpetually growing worse and worse.—*Thomas Brooks.*

Verse 12.—*"God is my King of old,"* etc. Let us learn from this verse how to think of our God. First, that he is our King, and therefore we ought to be encouraged to pray for his help against the ungodly, and to place ourselves in entire submission to his will and government. Secondly, that he is not a new God, but the Ancient of Days, and that whatever salvation has been wrought not only in the midst of his own people, but in the midst of the whole earth, even among those by whom he is not acknowledged, has been wrought by him. Let this meaning strike at the root of all trust in other gods, or in any creature.—*Musculus.*

Verse 13.—*"Thou didst divide the sea."* Thou, O Lord, didst make firm the flowing sea, that there might be a way for our fathers to pass over, and in those very waters through which thou didst lead thy ransomed, thou didst utterly overthrow the hosts of Egypt, who were like dragons for ferocity, as they sought to devour thy people.—*Jansenius.*

Verse 14.—*"Thou brakest the heads of leviathan,"* etc. It is spoken of Pharaoh's army which God destroyed in the Red Sea ; that is, the destruction of the Egyptians was a pledge of the accomplishment of God's promise to cast the Canaanite out of the promised land, and to give them possession of it. Many hardships they were to pass through in the wilderness, but God gave them this mercy as food, not to their bodies, but food to their faith, while they were in the wilderness : therefore, those former great and glorious promises were accomplished. So that former mercies are food that God gives unto the faith of his people to feed upon, till he hath perfectly accomplished whatever he hath promised unto his church.—*William Strong.*

Verse 14.—*"Leviathan."* The Arabic Lexicographers (quoted by Bochart) affirm that *Pharao*, in the Egyptian language, signified a crocodile. Parkhurst remarks that in Schenchzer's Physica Sacra may be seen a medal with Julius Cæsar's head on one side, and on the reverse a crocodile with this inscription : ÆGYPTO CAPTA, *Egypt taken.* M. Mariette has discovered at Karnak a monumental stele of Thothmes, on which that king says of himself,

" Fierce as the huge crocodile, I made them see the glory of my God ;
Terrible Lord of the waters, none dare even approach him."

Verse 14.—*"Leviathan"* is a name given not only to the crocodile, but to the whale and other large fishes. The Zum, or people inhabiting the wilderness, are supposed, by many sensible writers, to be the Ichthyophagi, or fish-eaters, who occupied, according to ancient authors, a part of the coast of the Red Sea. The Psalmist is here speaking of Israel's passage through its waters ; and it is a singular fact that Diodorus, who lived about two hundred years ago, mentions a tradition, prevalent amongst these very persons, to the effect that in the time of their remote forefathers an extraordinary reflux took place, the channel of the gulf becoming dry, and the green bottom appearing, whilst the whole body of water rolled away in an opposite direction. There can be little doubt that this strange people would have used for food, and various purposes, such great fish as might have been cast ashore on the termination of the miracle. Most writers give this text a figurative meaning, but that is no reason why it may not be also literally understood ; for such a mode of speaking is common in the Bible. But whether we understand it one way or the other, we have the testimony of heathens to its propriety and force. If, by the term *"Leviathan,"* we believe Egypt to be intended, and by its *"heads"* those petty states into which that country was divided, the traditions of India, and the East, inform us that such designations were well understood, and therefore beautifully applicable.—*Anon., in "Biblical and Theological Gleanings : by William O'Neill."* 1854.

Verse 14.—*"Meat to the people inhabiting the wilderness."* May not the exact meaning be that even as the sea-monsters washed upon the shore furnished food for the inhabitants of the Red Sea, even so the symbolic dragon power of Egypt when destroyed at the Red Sea became food for Israel's faith, and even furnished provision for their wilderness journey by the spoil which was cast up by the tide.—*C. H. S.*

Verse 15.—*"Flood."* God in dividing Jordan did not only divide the water that ordinarily belonged to the river, or the water which came from its fountains, but also the extraordinary additional waters by the great rains a little before harvest. So God *cleaved* both *the fountain, i.e.,* the fountain water, *and the flood.—Jonathan Edwards.*

Verse 16.—*"The day is thine, the night also is thine."*

Ah ! don't be sorrowful, darling,
And don't be sorrowful, pray—
Taking the year together, my dear,
There isn't more night than day.

* * * * *

And God is God, my darling,
Of night as well as day ;
And we feel and know that we can go,
Wherever he leads the way.

A God of the night, my darling,
  Of the night of death so grim,
The gate that leads out of life, good wife,
  Is the gate that leads to Him.

From "In the Sere and Yellow Leaf," in "The Circling Year."

Verse 16.—"*Day.*" "*Night.*" These changes are *according to a fixed law.* Day and night are the ordinances of heaven upon earth for the growth of earth's life, and, if we could trace the sunshine and the dark in every follower of God, we should see them arranged with equal wisdom. It is a more complex work, but, be sure of this, there is order in it all, and the hand that rules the world in its orbit, and that makes it fulfil its course through light and shade, is governing our lives for a higher than earthly end. One feature of the law is presented so far for our guidance. *It is a law of alternation.* It is day and night, and, let us thank God, it is also in due time night and day. Each has its time and use.—*John Ker.* 1869.

Verse 16.—"*Thou hast prepared the light.*" It is but recently that we have been able to form any conception of the power of light as an agent in the economy of the globe ; the discoveries of Actinism are among the most interesting and marvellous of natural science. The discovery that " no substance can be exposed to the sun's rays without undergoing a chemical change," has been described as scarcely less important in its effects than the discovery of the law of gravitation. A sunbeam is one of the most powerful of all the agencies of nature ; magical as it is, it breaks up the strongest chemical affinities ; it is the author of colour, and is the creator of a myriad combinations, which all tend to the harmony of the world. Nor ought we to forget the moral influence of light. We are all aware of the sensible difference produced in our moral natures by a fine day or a dark day. Light gives zest and tone to the spirits ; light gives buoyancy and joy to the soul ; light crowds the chambers of the mind with ideas ; Light is *Life :* the merest insect could not live without light ; and even blind natures receive, in those organs which are not the property of vision, the assurance of its benignant operations. Light is *Order :* and at its wand and command the separation takes place, and dark and light pair off into their separate ranks. Light is *Beauty :* whether in the refulgence of the moon ; the chill sparkle of the stars ; the unrivalled play of colours in the attenuated film of the soap-bubble, at once the toy of childhood and the tool of the sage ; the rich play of tints in the mother-of-pearl, or the rich gorgeous rays in the plumes of birds. Light is *Purity :* forms that rankle out of the glance of its clear, steady beam, contract around themselves loathsomeness and disgust, and become the seats of foulness and shame. Light is *Growth :* where it is, we know that nature pursues her work in life and in vigour ; light gives vitality to the sap ; light removes obstructions from the pathway of the growing agencies, while, in its absence, forms become stunted, gnarled, and impaired. Light is *Health :* as it darts its clear and brilliant points to and fro, it brings in its train those blessings of elasticity and energy, which give the fulness of being—which is perfect health to the expanding forms. There is a fine consistency, when Scripture makes light to contain, as it were, the seeds of all things, and when the prelude of all creation is made to be those words, " God said, Let there be light."

This, then, is the part light is made to play in the history of the world ; it is used by moral power to become the creator of moral influence. What a long series of creations elapsed before moral causes seemed to operate in the affairs of the globe ! But he, whose nature and whose name was Light, had given to light its distinct being and work ; and that creative word, "*Let there be light,*" spoke right forwards to the moral energies which were to be superinduced by its creation. Thus light, it is true, went before all things, and became the cause of moral consequences ; but then, this arose from the divine hand, whence darted its benevolent beams. *It was God* who gave it its divine commission, to divide between light and darkness ; *it was God* who made it the fountain of knowledge and of day ; *it was God* who gave to it the faculty to become, in turn, a creator, and to warm into life and beauty a myriad seeds and shapes of loveliness.—*E. Paxton Hood.*

Verse 16.—"*The light and the sun.*" I was considerably affected in my younger days by the long-standing objection, that Moses made *light* to exist before the creation of the sun ; as books then usually taught, what some still fancy, that there could not have been light without this luminary. But not choosing, on such important point, to attach my faith to any general assertion, I sought to find out if any investigator of the nature of light had perceived any distinction in its qualities or operation, which made it a fluid or matter independent of the sun. It was not easy, before the year 1791, to meet with the works of any student of nature on such a subject, as it had been little attended to ; but I at length saw the fact asserted by Henckel, a German of the old school, of some value in his day, and soon afterwards some experiments were announced in England which confirmed the supposition. It has been a favourite point of attention with me ever since ; and no truth in philosophy seems to be now more clearly ascertained than that light has a distinct existence, separate and independent of the sun. This is a striking confirmation of the Mosaic record ; for that expressly distinguishes the existence and operation of light from the solar action upon it, and from that radiation of it which is connected with his beams and presence. By Moses, an interval of three days is placed between the luminous creation, and the appearance and position of the sun and moon. Light was, therefore, operating by its own laws and agencies, without the sun, and independently of his peculiar agency, from the first day to the fourth of our terrestrial fabrication. But from the time that the sun was placed in his central position, and his rays were appointed to act on our earth, they have been always performing most beneficial operations, essential to the general course of things.—*Sharon Turner* (1768—1847), *in "The Sacred History of the World."*

Verse 17.—*"Thou hast set all the borders of the earth."* The actual distribution of sea and land over the surface of the globe is likewise of the highest importance to the present condition of organic life. If the ocean were considerably smaller, or if Asia and America were concentrated within the tropics, the tides, the oceanic currents, and the meteorological phenomenon on which the existence of the vegetable and animal kingdoms depend, would be so profoundly modified, that it is extremely doubtful whether man could have existed, and absolutely certain that he could never have risen to a high degree of civilisation. The dependence of human progress upon the existing configuration of the globe necessarily leads us to the conclusion that both must be the harmonious work of the same Almighty Power, and that a divine and immutable plan has from all eternity presided over the destinies of our planet. It is almost superfluous to point out how largely the irregular windings and undulations of the coasts, the numerous islands scattered over the face of the waters, the promontories stretching far away into the domains of the sea, and the gulfs plunging deeply into the bosom of the land, have contributed to the civilisation of the human race by multiplying its points of contact with the ocean, the great highway of nations.—*G. Hartwig, in "The Harmonies of Nature."* 1866.

Verse 17.—*"Thou hast set all the borders of the earth."* Consider the form of the earth. It is known to be globular, and in shape nearly like an orange. And why has God chosen that form ? With a view that it might be inhabited by living creatures on its whole surface. In order to this, every part of the globe must have sufficient light and heat, the wind must have a free circulation, and the water must be diffused over all its parts. The rotundity of the earth is best calculated to promote these conveniences : for this round form admits light and heat, without which there could be no life all over the globe. The revolutions of day and night, the changes in the temperature of the air, heat, cold, dryness or moisture, could not have taken place without this form. Had the earth been square, had it been conic, had it been an hexagon, or any other angular form, what must the consequence have been ? The greatest part of our earth would have been drowned, whilst the rest would have languished with drought. Some countries must have been torn in pieces by storms, while others would have been deprived of the wholesome circulation of wind. I have new reason to admire the supreme wisdom, when I reflect on the enormous mass which composes our world. Were the earth softer, or more spongy than it is, men and animals would sink into it ; were it harder and less penetrable, it would resist the toil of the labourer, and lose its capacity for producing and nourishing the multitude of plants, herbs, roots, and flowers, which now spring out of its bosom. There are regular and distinct strata found in the earth ; some of stone, others of metal and minerals. There are numerous and evident advantages which result from these in favour of mankind. Do not the strata of gravel, sunk deep in the earth, purify and in a manner filter the water, and render it sweet and fit for use ? On the surface of the earth there is a varied prospect ; there is an admirable mixture of plains and valleys, of small hills and mountains. The man must be blind indeed that does not see the wise purpose of the Great Author of nature, in thus diversifying the surface of the earth. Were the earth an even plain, how much beauty would it lose ? Besides, this variety of valley and mountain is very favourable to the health of living creatures, and were there no hills, the earth would be less peopled with men and animals. There would be fewer plants, fewer simples and trees. We should be deprived of metals and minerals : the vapours would not be condensed, nor should we have either springs or rivers. Must we not then acknowledge that the whole plan of the earth, its form, its inward and outward construction, are all regulated according to the wisest laws, which all combine towards the pleasure and happiness of mankind. O thou supreme Author of nature, thou hast done all things well ! Whichever way I turn my eyes, whether I penetrate into the interior structure of the globe thou hast appointed me to inhabit, or whether I examine its surface, I everywhere discover marks of profound wisdom and infinite goodness.—*Christopher Christian Sturm.*

Verse 17.—*"Thou hast made summer and winter." Plasmasti ea.* Now thou that hast done all this and more for mankind in general, wilt thou be wanting to thy church ?—*John Trapp.*

Verse 17.—*"Winter."* As if fatigued with so many cares, nature now rests ; this, however, is only to collect new force, again to be employed for the good of the world. But even this rest, which nature enjoys in winter, is a secret activity. A new creation is preparing in silence. The necessary dispositions are already making, that the desolate earth may again recover the children she has lost. The corn which is to serve us for food, already shoots. The fibres of plants, which are to adorn our fields and gardens, begin insensibly to open. O my beneficent Creator ! Here I find fresh cause to adore thy wisdom and power. The repose which nature takes is as worthy to enter into the plan of thy wise providence, as the activity she shows in spring and summer. Thou hast wisely combined the several revolutions of the earth, thou hast equally divided its rest and labour. It is thy will that each day should vary the scenes of nature, in that way which is most proper for the perfection of the whole. Pardon, O God, my temerity, if I have been so stupid as to blame anything in the government of the world. I am more than ever convinced that all the plans of thy providence, though they may appear extraordinary to my weak reason, are replete with wisdom and goodness.—*Christopher Christian Sturm.* 1750—1786.

Verse 19.—*"O deliver not,"* etc. How weak soever the church be, and how many and strong soever the enemy be, yet cannot they all devour the church, except the Lord should deliver his church over into their hands, against which evil the church hath ground of confidence to pray, *"O deliver not the soul of thy turtle-dove unto the multitude of the wicked ; "* for he hath given his church wings, and a hiding-place too, as the comparison importeth, if he please to give her the use thereof also.—*David Dickson.*

Verse 19.—The people of God are taught in this form of supplication how to edge and keen their prayers, and make them vigorous ; to wit, by disclaiming any ability or sufficiency in themselves ; by styling themselves a congregation of poor, silly, weak doves, no way able to encounter an army of bestial, cunning, crafty, bloody, boisterous enemies. This plea the people of God make use of : " With thee the fatherless findeth mercy," Hosea xiv. 3.—*John Langley.*

Verse 19.—*"The soul of thy turtledove."* They compare themselves to a turtledove, whose nature leads it, in whatever way it may be afflicted, not to indulge in noisy impatience, but to mourn in secret ; so the afflicted people of Israel were unable to do anything but breathe their sighs and groans to God.—*Musculus.*

Verse 19.—*"Thy turtledove."* God's people are an harmless, innocent people, altogether unable and insufficient to help themselves against their enemies, who are numerous, cruel, and barbarous. Hence they are resembled to sheep, doves ; called in the Word, fatherless, orphans, little ones, babes, poor, simple, needy. They are men bound to their good behaviour, may not harbour so much as a bad thought against any ; are called to suffer, not to do wrong. Julian did jeer at them for this ; he would strike them on the one cheek, and tell them that their Master taught them to turn the other ; his soldiers would take away their cloaks, and mind them that they must part with their coats also. Out of their own dispositions they judge of others, therefore may easily be deceived and entrapped. Thus Gedaliah, that sweet man, would not believe the relation of Johanan touching the conspiracy of the crocodile Ishmael against him ; nay, was even angry with him for his faithful dealing that way, and it cost him his life. Jer. xl. 16 ; and xli. That famous admiral of France, Jasper Coligny, though he had information and intelligence from sundry parts beyond the seas, that the court did intend to mischief him, and that there was no security in their promises and agreements, though backed with oaths, thrust himself, notwithstanding, upon the lion, and was smoothed with one paw and torn with the other : being such, they lie open to the rage of many adversaries. . . . .

One would think these turtles should rather win the love of all that come near them than incur the hatred of any, for they are quiet and peaceable persons. In the mount of the Lord there is no hurt done (Isa. xi. 9), yet, notwithstanding, they are maligned by a world of people. Because they are not like them (1 Peter iv. 4) ; because they are not of their number (John xv. 19) ; because their persons and their sacrifices are more acceptable with God than the others' (Gen. iv. 4) ; because they reprove them for their evil ways (John iii. 20) ; because they are for the most part poor and mean, have no great forecast in worldly affairs, are no deep politicians, they are such as those *pauperes Lugdunensis*, those poor men of Lyons in France, therefore are exposed to beasts and lions (Matt. i. 25) ; because they mourn for sin in themselves and others : they quarrel with the dove even because of her mournful note. They will jeer at sighing sisters, and men that hang the head like a bulrush ; yet, seeing this bulrush cannot grow without mire and mud, why should it not hang the head ?—*John Langley*.

Verse 19.—"*Thy turtledove.*" This expression may, perhaps, be further illustrated from the custom, ancient and modern, of keeping doves as favourite birds (see *Theocritus* v. 96, and *Virgil*, Eclog. iii. v. 68, 69), and from the care taken to secure them from such animals as are dangerous to them.—*James Merrick*.

Verse 19.—*Turtle Doves*, of whatever species they be, whether travellers or domesticated, are equally preserved by the inhabitants of Egypt : they do not kill, and never eat them. Wishing to know the motive of this abstinence among people who possess so little in the greater part of their actions, I learnt that it was for the honour of humanity. It is a consequence of the respect due to hospitality, which the Arabs hold in such high estimation, and of which they have communicated some shades to the people who dwell among them. They would regard it as a violation of this hospitality not to spare those birds, which come with a perfect confidence to live amongst them, and there to become skilful but useless receptors of love and tenderness. The very farmer, who sees his harvests a prey to the flights of turtle doves which alight on his fields, neither destroys nor harasses them, but suffers them to multiply in tranquillity.—*C. N. S. de M. Sonnini.* 1775—1811.

Verse 19.—"*Forget not the congregation of thy poor.*" Thy poor, by way of discrimination. There may be a greater distance between poor and poor, than there is between poor and rich. There are many " ragged regiments," " congregations of poor," whom the Lord will forget for ever ; but *his* poor shall be saved. And these poor are of two sorts ; either poor in regard of wealth and outward substance, or poor in regard of friends or outward assistance. A rich man, especially a godly rich man, may be in a poor case, destitute and forsaken, wanting patronage and protection. God saveth his poor in both notions, both those that have no friends, and those that have no estates.—*Joseph Caryl*.

Verse 20.—"*Have respect.*" The word, in the original signification of it, imports a fastening of the eyes upon some object, that a man desires to look into. Hence, by a metaphor, it is transferred to the eyes of the mind, and signifies a serious weighing and consideration of a thing. God is said to " wink at the times of ignorance," or not to regard it, Acts xvii. 30. God's people here look at God, as if he did wink at his covenant, and neither look at it, nor them in their miseries. The Psalmist desires him that he would be mindful of it for his people's deliverance.—*Francis Taylor, in "A Sermon preached before the House of Commons," entitled "God's Covenant the Churches Plea."* 1645.

Verse 20.—"*Have respect unto the covenant.*" This presseth the Lord more than the former ; this is the close grappling, as 'twere, with him in the words of Jacob : " I will not let thee go till thou hast blessed me." This is the throwing out of the greatest sheet-anchor in the tempest, for it lays hold on God's faithfulness, and truth, and fatherly goodness. If they be not in covenant with God, it may be charged upon them,—" you have violated my holy law, you have incensed my wrath against you by your perverse ways, therefore I will not help you, but give you up : " but now the souls that be in covenant with God will not be put off so (be it spoken with holy reverence), but will cry out, O Lord, though our iniquities testify against us, yet *"have respect unto thy covenant."* Yet be sure you walk uprightly before the Lord. . . . . With what face can any one say, *"Lord, have respect unto thy covenant,"* when he casts his own covenant behind his back, and cannot say with the prophet David, " I have a respect to all thy commandments " ? How canst thou say, " Deliver me not up to the many beasts without," when thou art not afraid to be delivered up to thy vile, bestial lusts and affections that are within ? Thou hypocrite, first labour the subduing of the monsters that are within thee, then a fair way will be open to have thine enemies subdued round about thee.—*John Langley.*

Verse 20.—*"Have respect unto the covenant."* Those persons and preachers who decline to think and speak of gospel mercies and free salvation as secured by *covenant,* deprive themselves and others of much of the blessed comforts of God's word. Such was not the manner of the inspired Psalmist.—*William S. Plumer.*

Verse 20.—God seems to his people to neglect his covenant, when they are oppressed by ungodly men. So Asaph complains. After an acknowledgment that God was the Shepherd of Israel, and so in covenant with his people, and accordingly had wonderfully brought them out of Egypt, and made them flourish marvellously in the land of Canaan, he attributes their misery to God's neglect. Many reasons may be given of this unkind carriage of God's people to him. As, first, because their misery blinds them ; and blind men when they are smitten suspect every man that comes near them. Secondly, self-love makes us suspect any rather than ourselves, yea, even God himself. The people should have reflected upon themselves that were nocent, but in their sorrows they reflect upon God that was innocent. We are all Adam and Eve's children. When Eve had eaten of the forbidden fruit, she tacitly lays the fault upon God : " The serpent beguiled me, and I did eat." Gen. iii. 13. Hadst thou not made a subtil serpent I had not broken thy commandment. Adam lays it openly upon God : " The woman whom thou gavest to be with me, she gave me of the tree, and I did eat." Gen. iii. 12. Hadst thou not given me such a companion to betray me, I had been innocent. So we their posterity, when trouble is upon us, suspect God's breaking covenant, rather than our own. Thus our nurses beat the stone when children stumble through their own neglect. Thirdly, in time of need we most commonly suspect such as are best able to help us. The sick man, if he be in danger of death, suspects not his ignorant neighbours, but his skilful physician. He that is oppressed in his estate, when the sentence goes against him, suspects none more than the advocate, or the judge. We know God is best able to help us ; our corruption, therefore, makes us to suspect him most, if our troubles continue. Fourthly, we most suspect those who, as we think, have most reason to help us in our miseries, and do it not. If the servant want meal or apparel, he complains not of his fellow servants but of his master, who is tied by covenant to provide for him ; if the child be wronged by the servants, he lays not the fault upon his brethren but upon his father, who by bands of nature is obliged to take care of him. So we, being in covenant with God, wonder not much if others fail us, but complain heavily if God seems to neglect us.—*Francis Taylor.*

Verse 20.—The Psalmist moves God in prayer to look to his covenant by this argument : *"For the dark places of the earth are full of the habitations of cruelty ; "* that is, of cruel men, or of men so full of cruelty, that they deserve rather to be called *cruelty* than cruel : this sort of men inhabit and fill up all those places where the light of holy truth doth not shine. Now, if they who want the light, or have no true knowledge of God among them, are hereby prepared for the acting of all manner of wickedness, how much more are they prepared for the acting of any wickedness who have thrust the light from them, and are in dark places of their own making ? The prophet Hosea shews (ch. iv. 1), that where there is no knowledge of God in a land, for want of means, there is no truth nor mercy (that is, there is none exercised) in that land, but oppression, deceit, and falsehood bear down all : how much more must it be so where there is no knowledge of God in a land, because of the contempt of means, and rebellion against the light ? What wickedness will not they do in the dark, who put out the candle that they may not see what they do.—*Joseph Caryl.*

Verse 20 (*second clause*).—This might have some literal meaning. *"The dark places of the earth,"* some have thought, may here describe in the first instance, the caves, the dens, and the woods of the land ; for there are many such (as travellers testify) in the land of Judæa, and in unsettled times they have often been the abodes of robbers and murderers, who have thence sallied forth to molest and cut off the traveller, to ravish peaceful villages, to waylay and plunder the merchant, to commit all sorts of crimes, and then to return in impunity to these their dark retreats, where they laugh at all law, human or divine ; they quaff, with horrid pleasure, the recollection of the widow's tears, and listen with inhuman joy to the echoing remembrance of the orphan's moan and the dying father's shriek. But what a land thus infested would be, is but a faint image of the heathen world. Wherever heathenism spreads itself, there are *"the dark places of the earth."* The Scripture often tells us that.—*John Hambleton.* 1839.

Verse 20.—*"The dark places."* An allusion, as some interpreters conceive, to the dens of wild beasts, wherein they hide themselves to seize upon their prey, Psalm civ. 21, 22. To these cruel men are compared. Psalm x. 8, 9. " He sitteth in the lurking places of the villages : in the secret places doth he murder the innocent. He lieth in wait secretly as a lion in his den : he lieth in wait to catch the poor." Such places oppressors and robbers choose. Others take it for an allusion to prisons and dark dungeons void of light. As the prophet, Isaiah xlii. 7, describes a prison : " To open the blind eyes, to bring out the prisoners from the prison, and them that sit in darkness out of the prison house." So trouble in Scripture is compared to darkness, and prosperity to light ; because darkness is irksome, and light comfortable : " The people that walked in darkness have seen a great light ; " and then the sorry hiding-places whither God's people went to hide themselves are here meant. Yet, could they not there be quiet, but were pursued, found out, and spoiled by their adversaries. Others take *"dark places"* for obscure and mean places, as *dark men*, in the original, are called *mean men* in our translation, Prov. xxii. 29. And then it may either signify that the meanest men did oppress God's people, or, that the poorest and meanest of God's people were not spared. Such usage have we found in our time, when the poor cottages of our foes have sent out pillagers, and no cottagers of ours have escaped spoiling in divers places.—*Francis Taylor.*

Verse 20.—*"Cruelty."* Heathenism is cruel. It is not changed in character since the days when parents made their children to pass through fire to Moloch. At this very day, for instance, infanticide prevails in China ; and the " law," says a book of authority—" the law, otherwise so rigorous, does not take the slightest cognisance of that crime, nor ever subjects those guilty of it to punishment. Every morning before it is light, waggons traverse the different quarters of the city of Pekin to receive the dead infants." Well may they go " before it is light ; " " the dark places of the earth are full of the habitations of cruelty." " The missionaries of that city obtained details, which justify belief that the number of infants (chiefly females) destroyed there is upwards of three thousand annually." Think of this same proportion, extended throughout that densely-peopled empire. Among the same people, suicide is also of frequent occurrence. What a contrast with the religion which stays the rash hand, and calls out, " Do thyself no harm ! "

We might pass to India ; and there the flames of the funeral piles, on which so many widows were annually burnt, had hardly expired, when we were shocked, only a few years since, with other proofs of the cruelty of heathenism. What painful details were those, which our government brought to light respecting the secret murderers of India ! What think you of a vast fraternity of murderers, consisting of many thousands of persons, which has existed from generation to generation, which has been ramified over the whole country from Cape Comorin to the Himalaya mountains, which has flourished alike under Hindoo, Mahometan, and British rulers, and which has every year destroyed multitudes of victims—and all this under the sanction of religion ? The murderous system, they say, has been enjoined them by the goddess Kalee, who is represented as having made a grant of half the human race to her votaries (to be murdered, that is,) according to certain prescribed forms.— *John Hambleton.*

Verse 23.—If we are compelled to close our most solemn and urgent devotions, and our most earnest supplications, without seeing one ray of light beaming upon our path, it may comfort us to remember that so the pious Psalmist closed this complaint. To hope against hope is the most blessed kind of hope.—*William S. Plumer.*

HINTS TO PREACHERS.

Verse 1.—I. The divine displeasure a fact. II. It is but in measure, and we are very liable to exaggerate it. III. Even while it lasts our relation to him is unaffected: " Sheep of thy pasture." IV. Our business is to enquire the reason of it, and act accordingly.

Verse 1 (*second clause*).—The Lord's anger with his people compared to smoke.— I. It is not a consuming fire. II. It suggests fear of the fire. III. It darkens the light of joy. IV. It blinds the eyes of faith. V. It checks the breath of life. VI. It blackens the beauty of our worldly comforts.

Verse 2.—I. The Lord's relation to his people. 1. Election. 2. Redemption. 3. Indwelling. II. The prayer arising from it : " Remember."

Verse 3.—Church mischief. I. The church has enemies. II. Wickedness in the church is their great weapon. III. This causes much desolation to weak saints, to enquirers, to peace, to prayer, to usefulness. IV. The cure for it is God's inter-position.

Verses 3, 4.—The power of prayer. I. On one side were, 1. Desolation : " per-petual," etc. 2. Desecration. 3. Declamation : " enemies roar." 4. Demon-stration : " they set up." II. On the other side is, 1. Supplication. 2. This brings God to the rescue effectually and quickly.

Verse 4.—*"Ensigns for signs."* The craft of Satan in supplanting truth with deceptive counterfeits.

Verse 5.—True fame. To build for God with labour, daring, diligence, skill, etc.

Verse 6.—Vandal work against the truth of God.

Verses 6, 7.—Things feared by a church. I. Injury to her doctrines or ordi-nances : " carved work." II. The fire of strife, division, etc. III. The defilement of sin. Either of these three will throw a church down ; let her guard and pray against them.

Verse 8.—The destruction of rural churches, the aim of our enemies : the injury they would so do, and our duty to prevent it : the means the destroyers use : bribery, oppression, etc. Our proper method for sustaining such churches.

Verse 9 (*first clause*).—I. There are such things as *"signs,"* that is, tokens and marks of God's special favour to the soul. II. There is also *"a seeing* those signs, when God, the Holy Ghost, is pleased to shine upon them. III. There is a third state, where there is *not seeing the signs,* those signs being enveloped in darkness, dimness, and obscurity.—*J. C. Philpot.*

Verse 9.—Teacheth us, that evident signs of God's wrath and displeasure, as the want of his word, the stopping of the true ministers' mouths, etc., should touch us to the quick.—*T. Wilcocks.*

Verse 10.—A prayer for revival. I. How God is reproached. II. What are the ill effects of it. III. When we may expect him to arise.

Verse 11.—I. The patience of God with man: He " withdraws his hand, even," etc., he hesitates to strike. II. The impatience of man with God : " pluck it," etc. —*G. R.*

Verse 12.—I. The sovereignty of God. II. Its antiquity. III. Our loyalty to it. IV. The practical character of his reign : " working." V. The graciousness of it : " working salvation." VI. The place of its operation : " in the midst of the earth."

Verse 14.—God's defeat of our enemies, and the benefit accruing to ourselves.

Verse 15.—The wonderful nature of gracious supplies, illustrated by the smitten rock.

Verse 16.—God present alike in all dispensations of providence.

Verses 16, 17.—I. The God of grace is the God of nature : " The day is thine," etc. II. The God of nature is the God of grace : the wisdom, the power, the faith-fulness the same. See Psalm xix.—*G. R.*

Verse 19.—The soul of the believer compared to a turtledove.

Verse 20.—The title given to heathen nations : " dark places of the earth." Not without the light of nature, or of reason, or of natural conscience, or of philosophy, as of Greece and Rome ; but without the light of revelation. II. Their condition : " full of," etc. : cruelty in their public, social, and private relationships. See Rom i. :

"without natural affection, implacable, unmerciful." III. Their part in the covenant. This is known from their part in its promises, and in prophecies : " I will give thee the heathen," etc. IV. The prayer of others on their behalf : " Have respect," etc. ; " Oh send forth thy light," etc. The conversion of the world will be in answer to the prayers of the church.—*G. R.*

Verse 22.—God pleading his own cause in providential visitations of nations and individuals, as also in remarkable conversions and awakenings.

Verse 22.—I. The glory of our cause : it is the Lord's own. II. The hope of our cause : he will plead it himself. III. The hope thus derivable from the violence of man : it will move the Lord to arise.

PSALM LXXV.

TITLE.—To the chief Musician. *Here is noble work for him, for the cry of the last Psalm is about to be heard, and the challenge of the foes of Israel taken up by God himself. Here the virgin daughter of Zion despises her foe, and laughs him to scorn. The destruction of Sennacherib's army is a notable illustration of this sacred song.* Al-taschith. *Here is another of the "destroy not" Psalms, and the title may be intended as a check upon the natural fierceness of the oppressed, or a taunt for the savage foe, who is here bitterly bidden to destroy not, because the nation is well aware that he cannot. Here, in holy faith, the sucking child plays at the hole of the asp, and the weaned child puts his hand on the cockatrice den.* A Psalm or Song of Asaph. *For reading or singing. A hymn to God and a song for his saints. Happy were the people who having found a Milton in David had an almost equal songster in Asaph; happiest of all, because these poets were not inspired by earth's Castalian fount, but drank of "the fount of every blessing."*

DIVISION.—*The people's song of gratitude and adoration begins the hymn in verse 1. In the next four verses 2—5, the Lord reveals himself as ruling the world in righteousness. Then follows a warning voice from the church to her enemies, verses 6—8, and a closing song anticipatory of the glory due to God and the utter defeat of the foe.*

EXPOSITION.

UNTO thee, O God, do we give thanks, *unto thee* do we give thanks : for *that* thy name is near thy wondrous works declare.

1. *"Unto thee, O God, do we give thanks."* Not to ourselves for we were helpless, but to Elohim who heard our cry, and replied to the taunt of our foes. Never let us neglect thanksgiving, or we may fear that another time our prayers will remain unanswered. As the smiling flowers gratefully reflect in their lovely colours the various constituents of the solar ray, so should gratitude spring up in our hearts after the smiles of God's providence. *"Unto thee do we give thanks."* We should praise God again and again. Stinted gratitude is ingratitude. For infinite goodness there should be measureless thanks. Faith promises redoubled praise for greatly needed and signal deliverances. *"For that thy name is near thy wondrous works declare."* God is at hand to answer and do wonders—adore we then the present Deity. We sing not of a hidden God, who sleeps and leaves the church to her fate, but of one who ever in our darkest days is most near, a very present help in trouble, "Near is his name." Baal is on a journey, but Jehovah dwells in his church. Glory be unto the Lord, whose perpetual deeds of grace and majesty are the sure tokens of his being with us always, even unto the end of the world.

2 When I shall receive the congregation I will judge uprightly.

3 The earth and all the inhabitants thereof are dissolved : I bear up the pillars of it. Selah.

4 I said unto the fools, Deal not foolishly : and to the wicked, Lift not up the horn.

5 Lift not up your horn on high : speak *not with* a stiff neck.

2. *"When I shall receive the congregation I will judge uprightly."* This is generally believed to be the voice of God, who will, when he accepts his people, mount his judgment seat and avenge their cause in righteousness. It is rendered by some, " I will take a set time ; " and by others, " I will seize the moment."

> " God never is before his time,
> He never is too late."

He determines the period of interposition, and when that arrives swift are his blows and sure are his deliverances. God sends no delegated judge, but sits himself upon the throne. O Lord, let thy set time come for grace. Tarry no longer, but for the truth and the throne of Jesus be thou speedily at work. Let the appointed assize come, O Jesus, and sit thou on thy throne to judge the world in equity.

3. *"The earth and all the inhabitants thereof are dissolved."* When anarchy is abroad, and tyrants are in power, everything is unloosed, dissolution threatens all things, the solid mountains of government melt as wax ; but even then the Lord upholds and sustains the right. *"I bear up the pillars of it."* Hence, there is no real cause for fear. While the pillars stand, and stand they must for God upholds them, the house will brave out the storm. In the day of the Lord's appearing a general melting will take place, but in that day our covenant God will be the sure support of our confidence.

> " How can I sink with such a prop
>   As my eternal God,
> Who bears the earth's huge pillars up,
>   And spreads the heavens abroad."

"Selah." Here may the music pause while the sublime vision passes before our view ; a world dissolved and an immutable God uplifting all his people above the terrible commotion.

4. *"I said unto the fools, Deal not foolishly."* The Lord bids the boasters boast not, and commands the mad oppressors to stay their folly. How calm is he, how quiet are his words, yet how divine the rebuke. If the wicked were not insane, they would even now hear in their consciences the still small voice bidding them cease from evil, and forbear their pride. *"And to the wicked, Lift not up the horn."* He bids the ungodly stay their haughtiness. The horn was the emblem of boastful power ; only the foolish, like wild and savage beasts, will lift it high ; but they assail heaven itself with it, as if they would gore the Almighty himself. In dignified majesty he rebukes the inane glories of the wicked, who beyond measure exalt themselves in the day of their fancied power.

5. *"Lift not up your horn on high."* For their abounding pride there is a double rebuke. A word from God soon abases the lofty. Would to God that all proud men would obey the word here given them ; for, if they do not, he will take effectual means to secure obedience, and then woe will come upon them, such as shall break their horns and roll their glory in the mire for ever. *"Speak not with a stiff neck."* Impudence before God is madness. The out-stretched neck of insolent pride is sure to provoke his axe. Those who carry their heads high shall find that they will be lifted yet higher, as Haman was upon the gallows which he had prepared for the righteous man. Silence, thou silly boaster ! Silence ! or God will answer thee. Who art thou, thou worm, that thou shouldst arrogantly object against thy Maker's laws and cavil at his truth ? Be hushed, thou vainglorious prater, or vengeance shall silence thee to thine eternal confusion.

6 For promotion *cometh* neither from the east, nor from the west, nor from the south.

7 But God *is* the judge : he putteth down one, and setteth up another.

8 For in the hand of the LORD *there is* a cup, and the wine is red ; it is full of mixture ; and he poureth out of the same : but the dregs thereof, all the wicked of the earth shall wring *them* out, *and* drink *them*.

6. *"For promotion cometh neither from the east, nor from the west, nor from the south."* There is a God, and a providence, and things happen not by chance. Though deliverance be hopeless from all points of the compass, yet God can work it for his people ; and though judgment come neither from the rising or the setting of the sun, nor from the wilderness of mountains, yet come it will, for the Lord reigneth. Men forget that all things are ordained in heaven ; they see but the human force, and the carnal passion, but the unseen Lord is more real far than these. He is at work behind and within the cloud. The foolish dream that he is not, but he is near even now, and on the way to bring in his hand that cup of spiced wine of vengeance, one draught of which shall stagger all his foes.

7. *"But God is the judge."* Even now he is actually judging. His seat is not vacant ; his authority is not abdicated ; the Lord reigneth evermore. *"He putteth down one, and setteth up another."* Empires rise and fall at his bidding. A dungeon

here, and there a throne, his will assigns. Assyria yields to Babylon, and Babylon to the Medes. Kings are but puppets in his hand ; they serve his purpose when they rise and when they fall. A certain author has issued a work called " Historic Ninepins,"* a fit name of scorn for all the great ones of the earth. God only is ; all power belongs to him ; all else is shadow, coming and going, unsubstantial, misty, dream-like.

8. *"For in the hand of the Lord there is a cup."* The punishment of the wicked is prepared, God himself holds it in readiness ; he has collected and concocted woes most dread, and in the chalice of his wrath he holds it. They scoffed his feast of love ; they shall be dragged to his table of justice, and made to drink their due deserts. *"And the wine is red."* The retribution is terrible, it is blood for blood, foaming vengeance for foaming malice. The very colour of divine wrath is terrible ; what must the taste be ? *"It is full of mixture."* Spices of anger, justice, and incensed mercy are there. Their misdeeds, their blasphemies, their persecutions have strengthened the liquor as with potent drugs :

> " Mingled, strong, and mantling high ;
> Behold the wrath divine."

Ten thousand woes are burning in the depths of that fiery cup, which to the brim is filled with indignation. *"And he poureth out of the same."* The full cup must be quaffed, the wicked cannot refuse the terrible draught, for God himself pours it out for them and into them. Vain are their cries and entreaties. They could once defy him, but that hour is over, and the time to requite them is fully come. *"But the dregs thereof, all the wicked of the earth shall wring them out, and drink them."* Even to the bitter end must wrath proceed. They must drink on and on for ever, even to the bottom where lie the lees of deep damnation ; these they must suck up, and still must they drain the cup. Oh the anguish and the heart-break of the day of wrath ! Mark well, it is for all the wicked ; all hell for all the ungodly ; the dregs for the dregs ; bitters for the bitter ; wrath for the heirs of wrath. Righteousness is conspicuous, but over all terror spreads a tenfold night, cheerless, without a star, Oh happy they who drink the cup of godly sorrow, and the cup of salvation ; these, though now despised, will then be envied by the very men who trod them under foot.

9 But I will declare for ever ; I will sing praises to the God of Jacob.

10 All the horns of the wicked also will I cut off ; *but* the horns of the righteous shall be exalted.

9. *"But I will declare for ever."* Thus will the saints occupy themselves with rehearsing Jehovah's praises, while their foes are drunken with the wrath-wine. They shall chant while the others roar in anguish. and justly so, for the former Psalm informed us that such had been the case on earth,—" thine enemies roar in the sanctuary,"—the place where the chosen praised the Lord. *"I will sing praises to the God of Jacob."* The covenant God, who delivered Jacob from a thousand afflictions, our soul shall magnify. He has kept his covenant which he made with the patriarch, and has redeemed his seed, therefore will we spread abroad his fame world without end.

10. *"All the horns of the wicked also will I cut off."* Power and liberty being restored to Israel, she begins again to execute justice, by abasing the godless who had gloried in the reign of oppression. Their power and pomp are to be smitten down. Men wore horns in those days as a part of their state, and these, both literally and figuratively, were to be lopped off ; for since God abhors the proud, his church will not tolerate them any longer. *"But the horns of the righteous shall be exalted."* In a rightly ordered society, good men are counted great men, virtue confers true rank, and grace is more esteemed than gold. Being saved from unrighteous domination, the chief among the chosen people here promises to rectify the errors which had crept into the commonwealth, and after the example of the Lord himself, to abase the haughty and elevate the humble.

This memorable ode may be sung in times of great depression, when prayer has performed her errand at the mercy-seat, and when faith is watching for speedy deliverance. It is a song of the second advent, CONCERNING THE NEARNESS OF THE JUDGE WITH THE CUP OF WRATH.

---

* Timbs.

EXPLANATORY NOTES AND QUAINT SAYINGS.

Title.—*"Al-taschith." Destroy not.* This seems to have been used by David as a maxim during the violent persecutions of Saul, as if to remind himself to forbear revenge, though it was often in his power to inflict it, upon his unnatural enemy.— *F. G. Hubbard, in "The Psalms Chronologically arranged, with Historical Introductions. New York."* [1856.]

Whole Psalm.—As these words are really a prayer, while at the same time the Psalm is thrown into the form, not of petitions, but of a thanksgiving, it ought to be considered as a thank-prayer, uttered beforehand, and containing petitions within it.—*Berleb. Bible*

Verse 1.—*"Thy name is near."* The *name of God* is said to be *near*, because it had come into public notice, and was in every mind and every tongue—opposed to what is *unknown* and *obscure*, which is said to be far remote. Compare Deut. xxx. 11.—*Hermann Venema.*

Verse 1.—The Psalmist doubles this duty in the practice of the saints ; *"Unto thee, O God, do we give thanks, we give thanks,"* we do it, we do it ; as if none else did it but they, or as if they had done nothing else.—*Joseph Caryl, in "A Sermon before the House of Commons," entitled, "The Saints' Thankfull Acclamation."*

Verse 3.—*"I bear up the pillars of it."* I prevent it from falling to pieces, as a house, supported by columns too weak to bear its weight, would do.—*Daniel Cresswell.*

Verse 3.—*"I bear up the pillars of it."* Learn to whom the glory of bearing up the world is due. God's providence is the true Atlas which supports the world, and doth shoulder up the world, whilst it treads on sin and sinners. Upon a serious view taken of providence on this wise displayed, we may say as they said of old, " The Lord, he is the God ; the Lord, he is the God," 1 Kings xviii. 39.—*Thomas Crane.*

Verse 3.—We can imagine a monarch, and especially an eastern monarch, in the plentitude of his power, and the arrogance of his pride, as he casts his haughty glance over the ensigns of his might, saying to himself, " I bear up the pillars of the earth." But one could never imagine such a thought arising in the heart, or proceeding from the lips of David or Hezekiah. I know not who of the sons of Adam, frail and feeble at their best estate, could have ever said, *"The earth and all the inhabitants thereof are dissolved : I bear up the pillars of it."* I know of none but him who said, " All power is given unto me in heaven and in earth," and who, as he said these words, ascended up into heaven to exercise that sovereignty, and repair that mighty ruin which had been wrought on earth when Satan triumphed in Paradise.—*Barton Bouchier.*

Verse 4.—*"Fools."* The ungodly are spiritual fools. If one had a child very beautiful, yet if he were a fool, the parent would have little joy in him. The Scripture hath dressed the sinner in a fool's coat : and let me tell you, better be a fool void of reason, than a fool void of grace : this is the devil's fool. Prov. xiv. 9. Is not he a fool who refuseth a rich portion ? God offers Christ and salvation, but the sinner refuseth this portion : " Israel would none of me." Ps. lxxxi. 11. Is not he a fool who preferreth an annuity before an inheritance ? Is not he a fool who tends this mortal part, and neglects his angelical part ? As if one should paint the wall of his house, and let the timber rot. Is not he a fool who will feed the devil with his soul ? As that emperor who fed his lion with a pheasant. Is not he a fool who lays a snare for himself ? Prov. i. 18. Who consults his own shame ? Hab. ii. 10. Who loves death ? Prov. viii. 36.—*Thomas Watson.*

Verse 5.—*"Horn."* The word *horn* was used in the Hebrew metaphorically to express either *honour*, as Ps. cxii. 9 ; cxxxii. 18, etc. ; or *strength*, Mic. iv. 13, " I will make thine horn iron." Deut. xxxiii. 17, etc. To humble and cast down was often represented by the figure of breaking or cutting off the horn, as here (ver. 10). Lam. ii. 3, " Cut off all the horn of Israel." To exalt the horn of any one was to bestow honour and dignity upon him ; so also, to make it bud. Ps. cxxxii. 17, lxxxix. 18 ; Ezek. xxix. 21. Here, *to lift up the horn* betokens presumption. It was also somewhat later a symbol for kingdom, Zech. i. 18, and Daniel.—*"Four Friends."*

Verse 5.—*"Speak not with a stiff neck."* Mr. Bruce has observed that the Abyssinian kings have a *horn* on their *diadem;* and that the keeping it erect, or in a projecting form, makes them appear as if they had a *stiff neck;* and refers to this passage for the antiquity of the usage, and the *appearance* also.—*Adam Clarke.*

Verse 6.—*"For promotion cometh neither from the east,"* etc. The word *"promotion "* here is used in a very expressive way ; it means the *desire of self-advancement,* הָרִים (*harim*), and would teach us that all our inward schemes, and outward plans, cannot gain for us advancement, unless based upon the fear and love of God ; we look forward to improve our circumstances, like to the ascending of a mountain, and nerve ourselves to the effort of ascent, fondly thinking that no eye watches our efforts ; but as " shame is the promotion of fools," so disappointment is often the return of rashness. . . . . From the *east* promotion doth not come ; the word *"east "* here is very expressive, מִמּוֹצָא (*mimmotza*), the rising of the sun, the outgoing of light, the dawning of the day, and the manifesting or revealing of God. We look around ; and in the early dawning of youth, with high hopes, mental energies, and perhaps superior talents, anticipate victory over our compeers, and a course of worldly success and prosperity ; but alas ! how often are all these hopes blighted and a succession of reverses humbles our spirits.

Promotion cometh not from the *" west."* The original is וּמִמַּעֲרָב (*umimmagnarab*) and it means duskiness, darkness, and the setting sun,—hence the west. When the clouds of years press upon us, and darkened shadows overtake us in various ways, such as loss of dear and early friends, the buoyancy of youth gone by, hopes softened down to personal ease, and the power of the constitution reduced ; then God often wills that promotion shall not come.

We now approach to the last point from whence promotion cometh not, that is from the *"south,"* מִדְבָּר (*midbar*) a waste place, the Arabian desert ; hence the south. In dry and solitary places like the sandy desert little advancement can be looked for ; like the human intellect, unless cultivated and improved by care and education it is barren as the desert to all holy feelings and improvement, the natural passions like *sand* choke up every patch susceptible of cultivation, and close up all the avenues to thought and devotion. A godless man is like the Arabian desert, of no profit to himself or his neighbours ; like ever-shifting sands being tossed to and fro by his own wayward passions ; heated with the suns of turbulence, self-will, and recklessness, he is a desert, a waste where God will not vouchsafe the light of his countenance for promotion. Like the disobedient Jews of old, Psalm lxxviii. 49, we may speak of this man saying, " How oft did he provoke him in the wilderness and grieve him in the desert ! " Let us then cultivate the higher part of our being, and then we may produce fruit unto holiness ; let us not wreck so noble a ship as the soul by careless steering and neglect, but trim its sails with early good instruction, and then may we arrive at the haven where we would be.

Having now illustrated the three points mentioned in our text, let us turn to the *one* (*the north*) where promotion or advancement may be looked for. Coldness is emblematical of purity, and coldness is an attribute of the north. The pure in heart shall see God. God is the northern light that gleams over the stillness of life's night. " He giveth snow like wool ; he scattereth the hoar frost like ashes ; he casteth forth his ice like morsels."

Be it ours to be humbly dependent upon God ; for whatever station he may choose to keep us in, godliness alone will prove our promotion and true riches. If our anxieties are directed towards pleasing him, then shall we prosper, and he will shew us " a pure river of water of life, clear as crystal, proceeding out of the throne of God and of the Lamb." (Rev. xxii. 1.)—*Condensed from a Sermon by Gregory Bateman, preached March 16th, 1862, on his entering upon the Vicarage of Ulrome.*

Verse 6.—*"For promotion cometh neither from the east, nor from the west, nor from the south."* Here are three of the four winds specified, and it is said, " promotion " comes from neither of them. But why is it not also said that promotion comes not from the *north?* that is the question. I answer ;—it were answer enough to say, that we ought not to put questions curiously about such things ; it should satisfy us that the Spirit of God is pleased to say it is so, and no more. Yet some tell us, the reason why it is not said promotion cometh not from the *north*, is because indeed it cometh out of the north, which, say they, is intimated in the Hebrew word for the *north*, which signifies *hidden* or *secret*. Promotion comes not from the east, nor west, nor south, but from the *north*. It comes from the north in a figure or mystery, that is, it comes from some hidden providence, or secret hand, which many take no more notice of than we do of the furthest part of the *north*. God promotes many in this world to power, and sends them great prosperity, we see not how or which way: the causes and contrivances of it are hidden close, and in the breast of God. This also is a truth; in that sense we may say, " Fair weather cometh from the *north*." Promotion is visible, but the manner of it is a secret; we see not the causes for which, nor the ways in which it cometh. It is enough to touch these niceties, and to touch them can do no hurt, while the matter arising from them hath the clear consent of, and is harmonious with other plain places of Scripture.—*Joseph Caryl.*

Verse 6.—"*Promotion ;*" or, " *lifting up.*" The word is evidently an emphatic word in the Psalm; it is the same which occurs in verses four and five, and again in verse seven and verse ten. I have, therefore, given the same rendering of it throughout. The rendering of the authorised version "*promotion*," besides losing sight of the manifestly designed repetition of the same word, is peculiarly unfortunate in conveying a wrong idea. "*Lifting up*," in its Hebrew sense, does not mean "*promotion*," as we commonly understand it, but deliverance from trouble, safety, victory. The image, in particular, of lifting up the head or the horn (the last, borrowed from wild beasts, such as buffaloes, etc., in whom the horn is the symbol of strength), denotes courage, strength, and victory over enemies.—*J. J. Stewart Perowne.*

Verse 6.—"*Nor from the south.*" " From the wilderness," the great wilderness lying in that direction. Three quarters are mentioned, the north only being omitted. This may be accounted for, supposing the Psalm to refer to Sennacherib, by the fact that the Assyrian army approached from the north; and therefore it would be natural to look in all directions but that for assistance to repel the invader.—*J. J. Stewart Perowne.*

Verses 6, 7.—" I thought to promote thee to great honour," said the king of Moab to Balaam; and yet that promotion ended in a dishonoured and a bloody death. I have often thought of many of the Lord's servants on earth, so superciliously passed by and passed over in man's catalogue of worthies, with what glad and grateful surprise they will at length receive that promotion denied on earth, when their own Master shall say to them, " Friend, come up higher ; " and then as they sit down with Abraham, and Isaac, and Jacob in the kingdom of heaven, shall they have honour of them that sit at meat with them.—*Barton Bouchier.*

Verses 6—10.—The rise and fall of nations and empires are in this Psalm ascribed to God. He exalts one and puts down another at his pleasure. In this he generally uses instrumentality, but that instrumentality is always rendered effectual by his own agency. When nations or individuals are prosperous, and glorious, and powerful, they usually ascribe all to themselves or to fortune. But it is God who has raised them to eminence. When they boast he can humble them. In these verses God is considered as the governor of the world, punishing the wicked, and pouring out judgments on his enemies. The calamities of war, pestilence, and famine, are all ministers of providence to execute wrath.—*Alexander Carson.*

Verse 7.—

> " Here he exalts neglected worms
> To sceptres and a crown ;
> Anon the following page he turns,
> And treads the monarch down."

—*Isaac Watts.*

Verse 8.—"*In the hand of the Lord there is a cup, and the wine is red* (which notes fierce wrath) ; *and it is full of mixture.*" This mixture is of judgments, plagues, and punishments; " this is the portion of their cup " (Ps. xi.). But what will the Lord do with this mixed cup? Who shall sip at the top of the cup he tells us not; but he is express whose the bottom is : "*he poureth out of the same*"—some drops are spilt here and there—"*but the dregs thereof, all the wicked of the earth shall wring them out, and drink them.*" Alas, they loathe it, their stomachs turn at it ; they have not been brought up to drink dregs ; they have had their wine well refined, and sparkling with spirits in crystal glasses ; and how can they get this down ?

They who have drunk so willingly and freely of the cup of sin, shall be forced, whether they will or no, to drink the cup of judgment. And it is not a sip or two shall serve their turns; they must drink all, dregs and all, they shall drink it to the bottom, and yet they shall never come to the bottom; they have loved long draughts, and now they shall have one long enough; there is eternity to the bottom. If a cup of affliction, which, in the effect, is a cup of salvation, be sometime, or for a time, nauseous to the godly, how deadly sick will the ungodly be, who must for ever, drink a cup of wrath and death.—*Joseph Caryl.*

Verse 8.—*"In the hand of the Lord there is a cup,"* etc. It is a *"cup:"* well, there is a cup that David thirsts for: " I will take the cup of salvation." Ps. cxvi. 13. There is *"wine"* in it: better; for wine cheers the hearts, and puts alacrity into the spirits. That wine is *"red:"* better still; so it should be; this argues the lustre and goodness of it: " Look not thou upon the wine when it is red, when it giveth his colour in the cup," Prov. xxiii. 31 : the colour adds to the pleasure. But now it is *"full of mixture:"* alas, this mixture spoils all. It is compounded, brewed, made unwholesome: this changeth the condition of the cup, of the wine, of the colour, of all. It is mixed with the wrath of God, the malice of Satan, the anguish of soul, the gall of sin, the tears of despair: it is *"red,"* that is, of a sanguine colour, the wine of blood. But yet so long as it is in the cup, they need not meddle with it: nay, but the Lord will *"pour it out;"* he shall hold their mouths to it, and make them drink it: the rankest poison in the world, the gall of dragons, and venom of asps, is pleasant and healthful to it. Yet be it but a little of the top, let them but taste it; nay, they must *"drink it off,"* to the very bottom, the sediments, dregs, lees, and all; even the very filth of vengeance. And lest any drops should be left behind, they shall *"wring them out,"* and suck them down to their confusion. The cup is all bitter, and full of sorrow, saith Augustine: the godly do often taste the top, and feel the bitterness, but then it is suddenly snatched from them; but the ungodly shall drink the very grounds, and extremest poison.—*Thomas Adams.*

Verse 8.—*"In the hand of the Lord there is a cup, and the wine is red;"* red with wrath, in the day of God's wrath. *"It is full of mixture:"* it hath no mixture of good, no sweetness at all in it, but all sorts of evil are mingled in that cup. *"And he poureth out of the same;"* upon many occasions he pours it out in the world; *"but the dregs thereof, all the wicked of the earth shall wring them out, and drink:"* they have not only the cup, but the dregs of the cup, that is, the worst of the cup; for as in a good cup, the deeper the sweeter; so in an evil cup, the deeper the worse: the dregs are the worst, the bottom is the bitterest of a bitter cup.—*Joseph Caryl.*

Verse 8.—*"A cup."* There seems to be here an allusion to the *cup of malediction,* as the Jews called that " mixed cup of wine " and frankincense, which used to be given to condemned criminals before their execution, in order to take away their senses.—*Richard Mant.*

Verse 8.—*"The wine is red,"* or " the wine *foameth,"* i.e., as it is poured into the cup from the wine-jar, as is expressed in the next member of the verse. *"Mixture,"* i.e. the aromatic herbs, etc., which were put into the wine to make it more intoxicating.—*J. J. Stewart Perowne.*

Verse 8.—*"The wine is red."* The remedy is suitable to the disease, and the punishment to the sin: *Sanguinem sitisti sanguinem vitis* (as he once says); Thou hast thirsted after blood, and blood thou shalt drink. Because men delight in blood, therefore, blood shall be poured out unto them; yea, *their own blood* shall be poured out. This is the way of God's providence, and the manner of his dealings in the world; which because it is filled with cruelty shall be therefore filled with blood.—*Thomas Horton.*

Verse 8.—*"Red."* The Hebrew word חמר rather means *turbid:* and it probably contains a further allusion to the particulars above mentioned; the wine being rendered *turbid* by stirring up the lees, and by the mixture of intoxicating drugs.—*Richard Mant.*

Verse 8.—*"Full of mixture."* There are some who think that mixture is here named because they rarely drink pure wine in those regions, since they are so warm; and because the wine is there more generous than in these colder quarters. But a different signification is intended; it is that spices are mingled with the wine.—*Francis Vatablus.* 1547.

Verse 8.—*"Mixture."* In all the afflictions of God's people there is an inter-mixture and temperament of love and favour, which shews itself in them. As, first of all, there is a mixture of *strength and patience* for the bearing of it. Secondly, there is a mixture of *comfort and goodness* as to the things themselves. God is not altogether in affliction, but he is very much in mercy with it ; and as he is pleased to exercise his servants with several troubles, so he does likewise vouchsafe them many blessings together with them, which he does comfort them withal. And then, thirdly, there is another thing also which is much observable in the afflictions of God's people, which makes this mixture complete, and that is, a mixture of *improvement and edification.—Thomas Horton.*

Verse 8.—*"The dregs."** Now, as the cup of red wine is the Christian doctrine which converts the soul, and in which the true believer spiritually luxuriates, so *"the dregs thereof"* are those merely outward, formal, and ceremonious circumstancials, which are nothing in themselves more than the dregs and leavings of the signified reality and spiritual substance. And when the text says that the wicked shall wring out the dregs of Christian doctrine, and shall drink of them, we are led to fix our attention upon the main peculiarity of Pharisaical religion. As God satisfies his people with the true spiritual refreshment of genuine Christian doctrine ; so does he leave to the unenlightened spirit, who will not seek him as he ought to do, the mere outside formalities, which belong indeed to religion necessarily, but of it form no vital part. They are but the refuse of the magnificent heaven-realising substance.—*T. D. Gregg.* 1855.

Verse 8.—*"All the wicked."* They shall *all* do it too, we may not omit that : *"all* the wicked of the earth." As there is an universality of the *judgment,* so there is universality of the sufferers ; they shall drink *all* of it, and they shall *all* of them drink it, that so no man may favour or flatter himself with hope of escape.—*Thomas Horton.*

Verse 8.—*"Shall wring them out."* Here is the necessity also of it ; it is *unavoidable; "They shall drink it,"* that is, even against their minds, whether they will or no. It is very likely that wicked men would be very loath to come to this condition : they can be content to sin, but they cannot endure to be punished for sin. . . . . This cup shall not pass from them, but they shall drink of it, even against their stomachs, where they never so much loath it. Yea, and which is more, they shall suck it up ; God will turn the cup up to them, and will make them to take it every jot ; he will not spare them one drop of it, which they shall be suffered to leave behind. . . . . The Lord himself (as I may say) will stand over them, and see them do it without any favour or indulgence.—*Thomas Horton.*

Verse 8.—When God's people have drunk the red wine in the cup, the wicked must drink the dregs : the cup passeth from place to place till all be drank off.—*William Greenhill.*

HINTS TO PREACHERS.

Verse 1.—The unceasing thanksgiving of the church, her grand cause for adoration : the nearness of her God, and the evident proof thereof in the displays of his power.

Verse 1.—I. Do we give thanks ? II. We do give thanks. III. What thanks do we give ? IV. When do we give thanks ? V. Let us give thanks again.

Verse 2.—Good resolutions commendable, how they should be made, strengthened, and performed.

Verse 3.—The Lord the stay of his people under the worst circumstances.

Verse 3.—Teacheth us that no disorder or confusion should hinder us from doing that which God requireth of us ; nay, rather, the more things are out of order the more readily should we labour to redress them.—*Thomas Wilcocks.*

Verse 4.—I. Who spoke to them ? "I." II. Who were they ? "Fools," "wicked." III. What did you say ? IV. What was the good of it ? Or, Rebuke of sin, a duty.

---

* We quote this for its singularity rather than its value. It is a notable instance of the force of party zeal. Thus the Evangelical Anglican, in his ardour against Ritualistic errors, finds aid in a passage which would not ordinarily be understood to relate to the question. Any stick is good enough to beat a dog with.

Verse 4.—The unhallowed trio :—wickedness, folly, pride.

Verse 5.—Arguments against pride in heart, appearance, and speech.

Verses 6, 7.—The changes of providence not the tricks of fortune.

Verse 7.—God acts as a judge and not arbitrarily in his providential arrangements.

Verse 8.—"*In the hand of the Lord there is a cup,*" etc.   I. As a matter of *preparation,* consider it so, and thus it is "in the hand of the Lord."   II. By way of *qualification :* it is he that tempers it ; it was "full of mixture."   III. By way of *distribution,* as giving to every one his share and portion in it.—*Thomas Horton.*

Verse 8.—The cup of wrath.   Where it is, what it is, how full it is, who brings it, who must drink it.

Verse 8.—"Full of mixture."   Wrath of God, remorse, memory of lost joy, fear of future, recriminations, despair, shame, etc., all these are ingredients of the mingled cup.

Verse 8 (last clause).—I. "The dregs" of the cup : the wrath of wrath, the gall of bitterness.   II. The dregs of the people : "all the wicked."

Verse 9.—Our life work : to declare and to sing.

PSALM LXXVI.

TITLE.—To the chief Musician on Neginoth. *The Precentor is here instructed to perform this song to the music of stringed instruments. The Master of the harpers was called upon for his most skilful minstrelsy, and truly the song is worthy of the sweetest sounds that strings can yield.* A Psalm or Song of Asaph. *The style and matter indicate the same hand as that which wrote the preceding; and it is an admirable arrangement which placed the two in juxtaposition. Faith in the 75th Psalm sung of victories to come, and here it sings of triumphs achieved. The present Psalm is a most jubilant war song, a pæan to the King of kings, the hymn of a theocratic nation to its divine ruler. We have no need to mark divisions in a song where the unity is so well preserved.*

EXPOSITION.

IN Judah *is* God known: his name *is* great in Israel.

2 In Salem also is his tabernacle, and his dwelling place in Zion.

3 There brake he the arrows of the bow, the shield, and the sword, and the battle. Selah.

4 Thou *art* more glorious *and* excellent than the mountains of prey.

5 The stouthearted are spoiled, they have slept their sleep: and none of the men of might have found their hands.

6 At thy rebuke, O God of Jacob, both the chariot and horse are cast into a dead sleep.

7 Thou, *even* thou, *art* to be feared: and who may stand in thy sight when once thou art angry?

8 Thou didst cause judgment to be heard from heaven; the earth feared, and was still.

9 When God arose to judgment, to save all the meek of the earth. Selah.

10 Surely the wrath of man shall praise thee: the remainder of wrath shalt thou restrain.

11 Vow, and pay unto the LORD your God: let all that be round about him bring presents unto him that ought to be feared.

12 He shall cut off the spirit of princes: *he is* terrible to the kings of the earth.

1. "*In Judah is God known.*" If unknown in all the world beside, he has so revealed himself to his people by his deeds of grace, that he is no unknown God to them. "*His name is great in Israel.*" To be known, in the Lord's case, is to be honoured: those who know his name admire the greatness of it. Although Judah and Israel were unhappily divided politically, yet the godly of both nations were agreed concerning Jehovah their God; and truly whatever schisms may mar the visible church, the saints always "appear as one" in magnifying the Lord their God. Dark is the outer world, but within the favoured circle Jehovah is revealed, and is the adoration of all who behold him. The world knows him not and therefore blasphemes him, but his church is full of ardour to proclaim his fame unto the ends of the earth.

2. "*In Salem also is his tabernacle.*" In the peaceful city he dwells, and the peace is perpetuated, because there his sacred tent is pitched. The church of God is the place where the Lord abides, and he is to her the Lord and giver of peace. "*And his dwelling place in Zion.*" Upon the chosen hill was the palace of Israel's Lord. It is the glory of the church that the Redeemer inhabits her by his Holy Spirit. Vain are the assaults of the enemy, for they attack not us alone, but the

Lord himself. Immanuel, God with us, finds a home among his people, who then shall work us ill ?

3. *"There brake he the arrows of the bow."* Without leaving his tranquil abode, he sent forth his word and snapped the arrows of his enemies before they could shoot them. The idea is sublime, and marks the ease, completeness, and rapidity of the divine action. *"The shield, and the sword, and the battle."* Every weapon, offensive and defensive, the Lord dashed in pieces ; death-bearing bolts and life-preserving armour were alike of no avail when the Breaker sent forth his word of power. In the spiritual conflicts of this and every age, the like will be seen ; no weapon that is formed against the church shall prosper, and every tongue that rises against her in judgment she shall condemn. *"Selah."* It is meet that we should dwell on so soul-stirring a theme, and give the Lord our grateful adoration,—hence a pause is inserted.

4. *"Thou art more glorious and excellent than the mountains of prey."* Far more is Jehovah to be extolled than all the invading powers which sought to oppress his people, though they were for power and greatness comparable to mountains. Assyria had pillaged the nations till it had become rich with mountains of spoil, this was talked of among men as glory, but the Psalmist despises such renown, and declares that the Lord was far more illustrious. What are the honours of war but brags of murder ? What the fame of conquerors but the reek of manslaughter ? But the Lord is glorious in holiness, and his terrible deeds are done in justice for the defence of the weak and the deliverance of the enslaved. Mere power may be glorious, but it is not excellent : when we behold the mighty acts of the Lord, we see a perfect blending of the two qualities.

5. *"The stouthearted are spoiled."* They came to spoil, and lo ! they are spoiled themselves. Their stouthearts are cold in death, the angel of the pestilence has dried up their life-blood, their very heart is taken from them. *"They have slept their sleep."* Their last sleep—the sleep of death. *"And none of the men of might have found their hands."* Their arms are palsied, they cannot lift a finger, for the rigor of death has stiffened them. What a scene was that when Sennacherib's host was utterly destroyed in one night. The hands which were furious to pull down Jerusalem, could not even be raised from the sod, the most valiant warriors were as weak as the palsied cripples at the temple gate, yea, their eyes they could not open, a deep sleep sealed their vision in everlasting darkness. O God, how terrible art thou ! Thus shalt thou fight for us, and in the hour of peril overthrow the enemies of thy gospel. Therefore in thee will we trust and not be afraid.

6. *"At thy rebuke."* A word accomplished all, there was no need of a single blow. *"O God of Jacob."* God of thy wrestling people, who again like their father supplant their enemy ; God of the covenant and the promise, thou hast in this gracious character fought for thine elect nation. *"Both the chariot and horse are cast into a dead sleep."* They will neither neigh nor rattle again ; still are the trampings of the horses and the crash of the cars ; the cavalry no more creates its din. The Israelites always had a special fear of horses and scythed chariots ; and, therefore, the sudden stillness of the entire force of the enemy in this department is made the theme of special rejoicing. The horses were stretched on the ground, and the chariots stood still, as if the whole camp had fallen asleep. Thus can the Lord send a judicial sleep over the enemies of the church, a premonition of the second death, and this he can do when they are in the zenith of power ; and, as they imagine, in the very act of blotting out the remembrance of his people. The world's Rabshakehs can write terrible letters, but the Lord answers not with pen and ink, but with rebukes, which bear death in every syllable.

7. *"Thou, even thou, art to be feared."* Not Sennacherib, nor Nisroch his god, but Jehovah alone, who with a silent rebuke had withered all the monarch's host.

> " Fear him, ye saints, and then ye shall
> Have nothing else to fear."

The fear of man is a snare, but the fear of God is a great virtue, and has great power for good over the human mind. God is to be feared profoundly, continually, and alone. Let all worship be to him only. *"And who may stand in thy sight when once thou art angry ?"* Who indeed ? The angels fell when their rebellion provoked his justice ; Adam lost his place in Paradise in the same manner ; Pharaoh and other proud monarchs passed away at his frown ; neither is there in earth or hell any who can abide the terror of his wrath. How blest are they who are sheltered in the atonement of Jesus, and hence have no cause to fear the righteous anger of the Judge of all the earth.

8. "*Thou didst cause judgment to be heard from heaven.*" So complete an overthrow was evidently a judgment from heaven ; those who saw it not, yet heard the the report of it, and said, " This is the finger of God." Man will not hear God's voice if he can help it, but God takes care to cause it to be heard. The echoes of that judgment executed on the haughty Assyrian are heard still, and will ring on adown all the ages, to the praise of divine justice. "*The earth feared, and was still.*" All nations trembled at the tidings, and sat in humbled awe. Repose followed the former turmoils of war, when the oppressor's power was broken, and God was reverenced for having given quiet to the peoples. How readily can Jehovah command an audience ! It may be that in the latter days he will, by some such miracles of power in the realms of grace, constrain all earth's inhabitants to attend to the gospel, and submit to the reign of his all-glorious Son. So be it, good Lord.

9. "*When God arose to judgment.*" Men were hushed when he ascended the judgment-seat and actively carried out the decrees of justice. When God is still the people are in tumult ; when he arises they are still as a stone. "*To save all the meek of the earth.*" The Ruler of men has a special eye towards the poor and despised ; he makes it his first point to right all their wrongs. " Blessed are the meek, for they shall inherit the earth." They have little enough of it now, but their avenger is strong and he will surely save them. He who saves his people is the same God who overthrew their enemies ; he is as omnipotent to save as to destroy. Glory be unto his name. "*Selah.*" Here pause, and let devout contemplations adore the God of Jacob.

10. "*Surely the wrath of man shall praise thee.*" It shall not only be overcome but rendered subservient to thy glory. Man with his breath of threatening is but blowing the trumpet of the Lord's eternal fame. Furious winds often drive vessels the more swiftly into port. The devil blows the fire and melts the iron, and then the Lord fashions it for his own purposes. Let men and devils rage as they may, they cannot do otherwise than subserve the divine purposes. "*The remainder of wrath shalt thou restrain.*" Malice is tethered and cannot break its bounds. The fire which cannot be utilised shall be damped. Some read it " thou shalt gird," as if the Lord girded on the wrath of man as a sword to be used for his own designs, and certainly men of the world are often a sword in the hand of God, to scourge others. The verse clearly teaches that even the most rampant evil is under the control of the Lord, and will in the end be overruled for his praise.

11. "*Vow, and pay unto the Lord your God.*" Well may we do so in memory of such mercies and judgments. To vow or not is a matter of choice, but to discharge our vows is our bounden duty. He who would defraud God, his own God, is a wretch indeed. He keeps his promises, let not his people fail in theirs. He is their faithful God and deserves to have a faithful people. "*Let all that be round about him bring presents unto him that ought to be feared.*" Let surrounding nations submit to the only living God, let his own people with alacrity present their offerings, and let his priests and Levites be leaders in the sacred sacrifice. He who deserves to be praised as our God does, should not have mere verbal homage, but substantial tribute. Dread Sovereign, behold I give myself to thee.

12. "*He shall cut off the spirit of princes.*" Their courage, skill, and life are in his hands, and he can remove them as a gardener cuts off a slip from a plant. None are great in his hand. Cæsars and Napoleons fall under his power as the boughs of the tree beneath the woodman's axe. "*He is terrible to the kings of the earth.*" While they are terrible to others he is terrible to them. If they oppose themselves to his people, he will make short work of them ; they shall perish before the terror of his arm, " for the Lord is a man of war, the Lord is his name." Rejoice before him all ye who adore the God of Jacob.

EXPLANATORY NOTES AND QUAINT SAYINGS.

Whole Psalm.—No Psalm has a greater right to follow Ps. lxxv. than this, which is inscribed *To the Precentor, with accompaniment of stringed instruments (vid.* iv. 1), *a Psalm by Asaph, a song.* Similar expressions (*God of Jacob,* lxxv. 10, lxxvii. 7 ; *saints, wicked of the earth,* lxxv. 9, lxxvi. 10), and the same impress throughout speak in favour of unity of authorship. In other respects too, they form a pair : Ps. lxxv. prepares the way for the divine deed of judgment as imminent, which Ps. lxxvi. celebrates as having taken place.—*Franz Delitzsch.*

Verse 1.—*"In Judah is God known."* God is truly and savingly known only in and through his Son ; God indeed is obscurely and darkly known in his *works,* as a God of power ; in his providence, as a God of authority, wisdom, and order ; in his common mercies, as a God of bounty ; and in his punishments and judgments, as a God of justice ; but in Christ opened and preached in the gospel, God is known with a clear, a comfortable, and saving knowledge, as a father of grace and singular mercy and lovingkindness. *"In Judah"* (saith the Psalmist) *"is God known : his name is great in Israel."* *"In Judah,"* in his church, where his word and ordinances are, where Christ is preached, and the mystery of man's salvation is opened, there God is known *truly* without error, *perspicuously* without obscurities, and *savingly* without uncertainties ; there he is known as a *King* in his courts, for the glory and beauty which he there manifesteth ; as a *teacher* in his school, for the wisdom and knowledge which he there dispenseth ; as a *dweller* in his house, for the holy orders he there prescribeth, and gracious rule and dominion he there erecteth and beareth in the souls of his servants ; as a *bridegroom* in the banqueting house, for the spiritual dainties he there maketh, for the clear and open manifestation of himself, and love and comforts he there ministereth to his spiritual friends and guests ; *"and his name is great in Israel ; "* his power, wisdom, truth, love, and goodness is much magnified and very glorious in their apprehensions who know him in Christ Jesus.—*Alexander Grosse.*

Verse 1.—*"His name."* By the *"name "* of God here, God himself is understood ; for in so many good effects as God uttereth himself toward his kirk, *so many names* he giveth to himself whereby he may be praised of her. As for example, when he promiseth unto his kirk freely grace and mercy, his kirk giveth him a *name,* and calleth him merciful. When he keepeth his promise, and uttereth himself a faithful God to his kirk, his kirk giveth him a *name,* and calleth him a true God. When he delivereth his kirk out of danger, and sheweth him a mighty God, and terrible against his enemies, the kirk giveth him a *name,* and calleth him a potent God, and so forth in the rest of his effects : so that by the *name* of God is understood here God himself, as God maketh himself to be known in his wonderful works.—*Robert Bruce.*

Verse 1.—*"His name is great in Israel."* Properly the great name in Israel, that is, the church, is the name of Jesus, which is great, first, by its efficacy : for it signifies Saviour. There is no other name under heaven by which we must be saved. Secondly, it is great in dignity : for it is the name that is above every name. . . . . Thirdly, it is great in the breadth of its range, Ps. viii. 1 : *"How excellent is thy name in all the earth."*—*Thomas Le Blanc.*

Verse 2.—*"In Salem also is his tabernacle."* It is not without meaning that Jerusalem has the appellation of *Salem ;* for it is thereby insinuated that the *tabernacle* of God, notwithstanding the assaults of foes, in the very heart of the tumults of war remained *in peace.* How much more now that the invaders had been overthrown, would *prosperity* be enjoyed ?—*Hermann Venema.*

Verse 2.—*"In Salem also is his tabernacle."* God the Holy Ghost is a spirit of peace, he is the comforter ; he seals up peace (2 Corinthians i. 22). This blessed dove brings the olive branch of peace in his mouth : now a peaceable disposition evidenceth something of God in a man, therefore God loves to dwell there. " In Salem is God's tabernacle : " Salem signifies peace ; God dwells in a peaceable spirit.—*Thomas Watson.*

Verse 2.—*"In Salem also is his tabernacle,"* etc. All the old versions, as well as the two English ones, have missed one especial force of this passage. There is no direct reference in words to any human habitation, but to the lair of the Lion of Judah. The word סֻכּוֹ does not only mean *his tabernacle,* but *his covert,* and is so translated in another place (Jer. xxv. 38): "He hath forsaken his covert, as the lion:" and the vaguer word מְעוֹנָתוֹ which succeeds may well be translated by "den," or some equivalent phrase.   Ps. x. 9.—*Simon De Muis.*

Verses 2, 3.—The care of Salem, or Zion, lies at the bottom of all God's powerful actings and workings among the sons of men.   Every mighty work of God throughout the world may be prefaced with these two verses.   The whole course of affairs in the world is steered by Providence in reference to the good of Salem.—*John Owen.*

Verse 3.—"*There.*"   Observe how it is said, "*There he brake,*" namely, in his temple, his habitation there.   For unto that his temple doth the coherence in the verse afore carry it, for that was last in mention, and with the greatest emphasis. In the story we read how that Sennacherib's overthrow was from Hezekiah's prayer in the temple ; for upon Sennacherib's letter, and Hezekiah's hearsay of the blasphemy, he took himself thither, went instantly into the temple, and began his prayer thus : " O thou God of Israel, that dwellest between the cherubims."   He invocates him under that style of his dwelling in the holiest, and so hearing prayers there. Thus you have it recorded both in Isaiah and in 2 Kings xxix. 15.   And how suitably, in answer hereunto, it is said here in the Psalm, that God gave forth sentence presently out of his tabernacle : yea, and that so suddenly too, as that the very execution is said to be done there, that is, from thence.   And yet again, in the eighth verse of the Psalm, it is said to be a sentence from heaven too ; "*Thou didst cause judgment*" (so called because it was the sentence of God as a judge) "*to be heard from heaven.*"   Thus Hezekiah prayed, and thus God heard ; and both as in the temple.—*Thomas Goodwin.*

Verse 3.—"*There.*"   These men, to wit the King of Asshur and his accomplices, came to cast out God out of his dwelling place ; but he stood to the defence of his own house, and showed them that he would not remove for their pleasure.—*Robert Bruce.*

Verse 4.—God was not known in Babylon, in Egypt, in other nations ; his tabernacle and dwelling place was not amongst them, therefore they were not glorious. But see what is in the 4th verse, "*Thou art more glorious and excellent than the mountains of prey;*" thou Judah, thou Israel, thou Salem, thou Zion, that hast spiritual mercies and blessings, art more glorious than they, whatever their glory be.   Have the nations abroad goodly towers ? thou hast the temple; have they stately cities ? thou hast Jerusalem, the city of God ; have they wise men ? thou hast the prophets ; have they gods of gold, silver, and stones ? thou hast the true living God, Jehovah, to be thy God ; have they human laws that are good ? thou hast divine laws that excel ; have they temporal excellencies ? thou hast spiritual ; have they the glory of the world ? thou hast the glory of heaven.—*William Greenhill.*

Verse 4.—"*The mountains of prey.*"   Why are they called the mountains *of prey ?*   There is a reference to *the lairs of the lions* in the mountains, whence they rush forth upon those who come that way, and tear them in pieces.   In the same way the dwelling place of God was represented above under the title of a tabernacle or lair.   Moreover, this is a mystic epithet of the *mountains of Judah,* by which it is hinted that the enemies who venture to approach that lair are wont to be torn in sunder : a terrible example of which had just been shown in the case of the Assyrian, there overthrown, torn, and spoiled.   Compare Isaiah xxxi. 4.—*Hermann Venema.*

Verse 5.—"*The stouthearted are spoiled.*"   There is indicated in these words that consternation of mind which deprives of judgment and power.   *The valiant are spoiled of their heart :* that is, they who at other times were wise and courageous have now *lost their heart,* and have been reduced to foolishness and stupidity.— *Hermann Venema.*

Verse 5.—"*The stouthearted are spoiled.*"   After the breaking of their weapons their spoliation is recorded, for that follows the slaughter of foes.   Nor is mention made of that without reason.   They had come to spoil, therefore are they deservedly spoiled.—*Musculus.*

Verse 5.—"*The stouthearted are spoiled.*"   Some translate it, "*They are spoiled of their stout heart.*"   The stouthearted, the strong, are spoiled.   The strong man may be spoiled by a stronger ; that's a good sense, but it is more elegantly rendered, "*they are spoiled of their stout heart ;* " that is, the Lord takes their heart out of their bosom.   Daring men, who fear nothing, are turned into *Magor-missabibs*—

fear round about ; their stout hearts are taken from them, and then they are so far from being a terror to other men, that they run from the shadow of a man ; their courage is down ; they cannot give a child a confident look, much less look dangers or enemies in the face.—*Joseph Caryl.*

Verse 5 (last clause).—The strength and power of a man is in his hands ; if they be gone, all his hope is gone. If a man's sword be taken from him, he will do what he can with his hands ; but if his hands be gone, he may go to sleep for any disturbance he will work. For men not to find their hands, is not to have that power for the execution of their designs which formerly they had.—*John Owen.*

Verse 5 (last clause).—As we say of a man that goes lamely or lazily, " he cannot find his feet ; " so of a man that acts lamely or lazily, or of a soldier that fights faintly and cowardly, "*he cannot find his hands.*"—*Joseph Caryl.*

Verses 5, 6.—

> For the Angel of Death spread his wings on the blast,
> And breathed in the face of the foe as he passed ;
> And the eyes of the sleepers waxed deadly and chill,
> And their hearts but once heaved, and for ever were still !
>
> And there lay the steed with his nostril all wide,
> But through it there rolled not the breath of his pride :
> And the foam of his gasping lay white on the turf,
> And cold as the spray of the rock-beating surf.
>
> And there lay the rider distorted and pale,
> With the dew on his brow and the rust on his mail ;
> And the tents were all silent, the banners alone,
> The lances unlifted, the trumpet unblown.
>
> —*George Gordon, Lord Byron.*

Verse 6.—"*Cast into a deep sleep.*" It is observable, that the verb here used is the same as is used in the narrative of the act of Jael, and of the death of the proud enemy of Israel, Sisera, "*cast into a deep sleep,*" by God's power, working by the hand of a woman.—*Christopher Wordsworth.*

Verse 7.—"*Thou, even thou, art to be feared.*" The emphasis in the word "*thou,*" redoubled, implies as much as if he had said, Not principalities, not powers, not hell, not death, nor anything for themselves, but thou, O Lord, alone art to be feared. Arguments and reasons to confirm it are two, here laid down in the text : the first is drawn from God's anger, who hath decreed, and accordingly executes vengeance upon all the proud. The second is drawn from his power ; not princes, not armies, not men, not angels, are able to endure the breath of his fury ; for, "*Who may stand in thy sight when once thou art angry ?*" . . . . The anger of God is a terrible, unspeakable, unsupportable, intolerable burden. Every word in the text hath a special emphasis to prove this. "*Who may stand ?*" Who ? Shall angels ? They are but like refracted beams or rays, if God should hide his face, they would cease to shine. Shall man ? His glory and pomp, like the colours in the rainbow, vanish away, when God puts forth in anger the brightness of his face. Shall devils ? If he speak the word they are tumbled down from heaven like lightning. "*Stand in thy sight.*" "*Stand.*" What ! a reed against a cedar, a thistle in Lebanon against a cedar in Lebanon ; a feather against a flame, a grasshopper against an Almighty, a head of glass against a rod of brass ? "*When once thou art angry ?*" "*Angry.*" By sending out his wrath, that it wounds like arrows ; angry, in pouring it out, that it drowns like water ; angry, in kindling of it, that it burns like fire ; a consuming fire, but you tell me such a fire may be quenched ; an unquenchable fire, but since that may cease to burn, when it lacks matter, it is in one word an everlasing fire, that never goes out. That, that's it ; such anger as is never fully shown, but in punishment of reprobates ; in no punishment, but that in hell ; in none in hell, but that eternal.—*John Cragge's "Cabinet of Spirituall Jewells."* 1657.

Verse 9.—"*God arose to judgment.*" This great judgment was wrought upon the enemies *when God rose :* it was not done when God sat ; for the whole time when he sat his enemies were aloft, stirring their time, raging in murder, oppression, and blood. . . . . He bringeth in God here after the manner of earthly judges after the custom of our judges; for first they sit down, they try, seek out, and advise, and after consideration they resolve, and after resolution they rise up, give forth judgment, and pronounce the sentence; even so the prophet bringeth in God after the same manner; sitting, and after sitting, rising and pronouncing the sentence. —*Robert Bruce.*

Verse 9.—*"To save all the meek."* We see from this passage what care God takes of the afflicted. When he is angry with the ungodly, he is angry with them chiefly because they have oppressed the poor and the innocent. Although he detests all iniquity, yet he is most indignant with that which is committed against the needy and guiltless. So in Ps. xii. " For the oppression of the poor, for the sighing of the needy, now will I arise, saith the Lord." So in this verse, when God arose to judgment, to save all the meek of the earth.—*Musculus.*

Verse 9.—Is not this the day when the Saviour comes to reign? the day when the results of things shall best be seen; the day when every saint with anointed eye shall see that events all tended to the glory of God; the day when they shall sing better far than now.

" Surely the wrath of man praiseth thee.
Thou girdest thyself with the remnant of wrath."

—*Andrew A. Bonar.*

Verse 10.—*"Surely the wrath of man shall praise thee."* Persecutions tend to correct the failings of good men, and to exercise and illustrate their several graces and virtues. By these, good men are usually made much better and more approved, while they tend to exercise our patience, to quicken our devotion, to evidence our zeal and Christian fortitude, and to show to the whole world what love we bear to the truth, and how much we are willing to undergo for the honour of God. Till they have suffered something for it, truth is too apt to grow cheap and be less prized many times, even by those that are good men in the main; whereas we are apt on the contrary, never to value it at a higher rate, or to be more zealous for it, or to make better use of it, than when it is opposed and persecuted. What more truly beneficial therefore, or tending to the divine glory, than for God, who useth to bring good out of evil, to make use also of the opposers of his truth, to rouse up his servants whom he sees growing more remiss and negligent than they should be, and to suffer such temptations to assault them, by which their drowsy minds may be spurred on into a greater love and zeal for the truth, and a deeper sense of the divine benefit in it, and, in general, excited to the more diligent performance of their duty.—*Richard Pearson.* 1684.

Verse 10.—*"The wrath of man shall praise thee."* In the Septuagint it is, The wrath of man shall *keep holy-day* to thee, shall increase a festival for thee. God many times gets up in the world on Satan's shoulders. When matters are ravelled and disordered, he can find out the right end of the thread, and how to disentangle us again; and when we have spoiled a business, he can dispose it for good, and make an advantage of those things which seem to obscure the glory of his name.—*Thomas Manton.*

Verse 10.—*"The wrath of man shall praise thee."* The wrath of wicked men against the people of God is very tributary to his praise. 1. It puts them upon many subtil devices and cunning stratagems, in frustrating of which the wisdom of God and his care of his Church is very much illustrated. 2. The wrath of wicked men impels them to many violent and forcible attempts upon the people of God to destroy them, and so gives him occasion to manifest his power in their defence. 3. It makes them sometimes fit to be his instruments in correcting his people, and so he vindicates himself from the suspicion of being a patron to sin in them that are nearest to him, and makes them that hate holiness promote it in his people, and them that intend them the greatest hurt, to do them the greatest good. 4. It administers occasion to him for the manifestation of the power of his grace in upholding the spirits of his people and the being of his church in despite of all that enemies can do against them. 5. It serves very much to adorn God's most signal undertakings for his people in the world. 6. It serves to manifest the glory of God's justice upon his people's enemies in the day when he rises up to avenge himself upon them, when he shall stand over them, lashing them with scorpions, and at every blow mind their former cruelties. Here, take that for your inhuman rage against my people at such a place, and that for your barbarous usage of them at such a time. Now see how good it is to be imprisoned, beaten, tortured, burnt, and sawn asunder. Thus the enemies themselves are often constrained to acknowledge with Adoni-Bezek the righteous hand of God upon them in the day of inquisition.—*Condensed from John Warren's Sermon before Parliament.* 1656.

Verse 10.—*"The wrath of man."* Wrath is anger accented unto the highest pitch, or blown up into a flame. *"The wrath of man,"* (in the original it is *The wrath of Adam,* or *the wrath of clay,* weak, impotent man) *"shall praise thee,"* i.e., it shall turn to the praise and glory of God through his overruling providence, though quite otherwise intended. God will bring honour to himself, and serve his own holy and wise designs out of it. . . . . This expression, *"the wrath of man,"* imports the weakness and impotence of it ; it is but the wrath of *Adam,* or of *red clay.* How contemptibly doth the Spirit of God speak of man, and of the power of man, in Scripture ? " Cease ye from man, whose breath is in his nostrils ; for wherein is he to be accounted of ? " The wrath of man, when it is lengthened out to its utmost boundaries, can only go to the length of killing the body or of the breaking the sheath of clay in which the soul lodges, and then it can do no more.—*Ebenezer Erskine.*

Verse 10.—*"Shall praise thee."* God turns the wrath of man to the praise of his adorable sovereignty. Never have the Lord's people had such awful impressions of the sovereignty of God, as when they have been in the furnace of man's wrath, then they became dumb with silence. When the Chaldean and Sabean robbers are let loose to plunder and spoil the substance of Job, he is made to view adorable sovereignty in it, saying, " The Lord gave, the Lord hath taken away : blessed be the name of the Lord." It is in such a case as this that God says to his own people, " Be still, and know that I am God ; I will be exalted among the heathen." What work of God about the church is advanced by the wrath of men ? 1. His *discovering* work ; for by the wind of man's wrath he separates between the precious and the vile, betwixt the chaff and the wheat. In the day of the church's prosperity and quiet hypocrites and true believers are mingled together, like the chaff and the wheat in the barn floor : but the Lord, like the husbandman, opens the door of his barn, and puts the wind of man's wrath through it, that the world may know which is which. O, sirs, much chaff is cast up already, both among ministers and professors ; but it is like the wind and sieve, may cast up much more yet ere all be done. 2. God's *purging* work is advanced among his own children by the wrath of men : there is much of the dross of corruption cleaves to the Lord's people while in the wilderness. Now, the Lord heats the furnace of man's wrath, and casts his people into it, that when he has tried them, he may bring them forth as gold. 3. God's *uniting* work is thereby advanced. In a time of peace and external tranquility the sheep of Christ scatter and divide among themselves ; but God lets loose the dogs upon them, and then the flock runs together ; or like pieces of metal cast into the fire, they run together in a lump. 4. God's *enlarging* work, or his work of spreading the gospel, is sometimes advanced by the wrath of man. Acts viii. 1—5. The gospel, like the chamomile, the more it is trodden upon, the more it spreads.—*Ebenezer Erskine.*

Verse 10.—*"The remainder of wrath shalt thou restrain."* *"The remainder of wrath,"* i.e., what is left behind of the wrath of men, when God has glorified himself thereby. Even after God has defeated the purposes of wicked men, and made them contribute to his glory, yet there is abundance of wrath remaining. But what becomes of that wrath that is left ? God shall *"restrain"* it. The word signifies to *gird up.* However God may see fit to slacken the bridle of his providence, and suffer wicked men to vent their wrath and enmity, as far as it shall contribute to his glory ; yet the superplus and the remainder of his wrath that is not for his glory and his people's profit, God will gird it up, that they shall not get it vented. . . . . If any wrath of man remain beyond what shall bring in a revenue of praise unto God, he will *restrain it,* and bind it up like the waters of a mill : he will suffer as much of the current of water to run upon the wheel, as serves to carry it about and grind his corn, but the remainder of the water he sets it off another way : so God will let out as much of the current of man's wrath as shall serve the ends of his glory and our good, but the remainder of the stream and current he will *restrain,* and turn another way. In Isai. xxviii. we are told that God will not be aye " threshing his corn, nor break it with the wheel of his cart, nor bruise it with his horsemen. This cometh forth from the Lord of hosts, which is wonderful in counsel, and excellent in working." All this comfort is sure and certain, there is not the least peradventure about it, that the flame of man's wrath shall praise the Lord, and the superfluous fire shall be quenched, or hemmed in ; for here we have God's parole of honour for it : "*Surely* the wrath of man shall praise thee : the remainder of wrath shalt thou restrain."—*Ebenezer Erskine.*

Verse 10.—"*The remainder of wrath shalt thou restrain,*" מֹשׂח *Chemoth* "wrath," in the plural number, seems to be put in opposition to *chamoth*, the *single wrath* of man in the former part of the verse ; to shew there is more wrath which God is to restrain, than merely that of man. There is also more pride which needs a like restraint ; namely, that of the *first Lucifer,* who sinned, and, as is thought, fell by aspiring to ascend, and to be like the Most High. There are finally, other *counsels* also, as well as other *wrath* and *pride,* besides human, which God confounds. There is a wisdom that descendeth not from above (no, nor grows on earth) but is devilish, James iii. 15. And both *wrath, pride,* and *wisdom,* of *devils* as well as *men,* shall God *restrain,* when he pleases not to turn them to his praise. Let there be hellish plots, yet our God shall confound them.—*From "A Sermon preached. . . . before the Queen. . . . . By Edward* [*Wetenhall*] *Lord Bishop of Corke and Rosse.* 1691."

Verse 10.—"*Thou shalt restrain.*" This, in the Hebrew, is expressed in one word, תַּחְגֹּר, which imports the begirding or binding of it in on every side, that it shall by no means break out, but shall be kept in, as a dog in a chain, as a lion in his den, how violent soever.—*Cornelius Burges, in "Another Sermon preached to the Honourable House of Commons. . . . November the fifth,* 1641."

Verse 11.—"*Round about him.*" A description of his people, as the twelve tribes pitched about the tabernacle, Num. ii. 2 ; and the four-and-twenty elders were round about God's throne, Rev. iv. 4. So the Chaldee expoundeth it ;—*Ye that dwell about his sanctuary.*—*Henry Ainsworth.*

Verse 12.—"*Cut off.*" He deals with princes as men deal with a vine. An axe is too strong for a cluster of grapes, or a sprig of a vine ; it easily cuts them off : so God by a judgment easily cuts off the spirit of princes ; they are not able to stand against the least judgments of God : when he puts strength into worms, or any other creatures they fall.—*William Greenhill, in a Sermon, entitled, "The Axe at the Root."*

Verse 12.—The Lord *cuts off the spirit of princes ;* the word is, *he slips off,* as one should slip off a flower between one's fingers, or as one should slip off a bunch of grapes from a vine, so soon is it done. How great uncertainty have many great ones, by their miserable experience, found in their outward glory and worldly felicity ! What a change hath a little time made in all their honours, riches, and delights ! That victorious emperor Henry the Fourth, who had fought two-and-fifty pitched battles, fell to that poverty before he died, that he was forced to petition to be a prebend in the church of Spier, to maintain him in his old age. And Procopius reports of King Gillimer, who was a potent king of the Vandals, who was so low brought, as to intreat his friend to send him a sponge, a loaf of bread, and a harp ; a sponge to dry up his tears, a loaf of bread to maintain his life, and a harp to solace himself in his misery. Philip de Comines reports of a Duke of Exeter, who though he had married Edward the Fourth's sister, yet he saw him in the Low Countries begging barefoot. Bellisarius, the chief man living in his time, having his eyes put out, was led at last in a string, crying, " give a halfpenny to Bellisarius."—*Jeremiah Burroughs.*

HINTS TO PREACHERS.

Verse 1.—Reverence for God's name proportionate to true knowledge of it.

Verse 2.—The peculiar relation of God to his church.

Verse 2 (*first clause*).—A peaceful church the tabernacle of God. The benefits peace confers, the evils of strife, the causes of dissension, and the means of promoting unity.

Verse 3.—Christian glories, or the victories vouchsafed to the church over heathenism, heresy, persecution, etc.

Verse 3.—I. Where enemies are conquered ; " There ; " not on the battle-field so much as in the house of God ; as Amalek by Moses on the Mount ; Sennacherib by Hezekiah in the Sanctuary. II. How there ? 1. By faith. 2. By prayer. "*The* weapons of our warfare," etc.—*G. R.*

Verse 4.—The Lord, our portion, compared with the treasures of empires.

Verse 4.—I. What the world is, compared with the church : " Mountains of prey." 1. Cruelty instead of love. 2. Violence instead of peace. II. What the church is, compared with the world. 1. " More glorious," because " more excellent." 2. " More excellent," because " more glorious." Both are more real and abiding.— *G. R.*

Verse 5.—"*They have slept their sleep.*" Divers kinds of deaths or sleeps for the various classes of men.

Verse 7.—The anger of God. A very suggestive subject.

Verses 8, 9.—I. The characters described : " the meek of the earth." II. The need implied. 1. To be vindicated. 2. To be saved. III. The divine interposition on their behalf : " Thou didst cause," etc. " When God arose," etc. IV. The effect of their deliverance : " The earth feared," etc.—*G. R.*

Verse 10.—I. Evil permitted for good : " The wrath," etc. II. Restrained for good : " The remainder," etc. Or, I. Ruled. II. Overruled.—*G. R.*

Verse 11.—I. To whom vows may be made. Not to man, but God. II. What vows should be thus made. 1. Of self-dedication. 2. Of self-service. 3. Of self-sacrifice. III. How kept : " Vow and pay." 1. From duty. 2. From fear of his displeasure.—*G. R.*

Verse 11.—The propriety, obligation, pleasure, and profit of presenting gifts unto the Lord.

PSALM LXXVII.

TITLE.—To the Chief Musician, to Jeduthun. *It was meet that another leader of the psalmody should take his turn. No harp should be silent in the courts of the Lord's house.* A Psalm of Asaph. *Asaph was a man of exercised mind, and often touched the minor key; he was thoughtful, contemplative, believing, but withal there was a dash of sadness about him, and this imparted a tonic flavour to his songs. To follow him with understanding, it is needful to have done business on the great waters, and weathered many an Atlantic gale.*

DIVISIONS.—*If we follow the poetical arrangement, and divide at the Selahs, we shall find the troubled man of God pleading in verses 1—3, and then we shall hear him lamenting and arguing within himself, 4—9. From verses 10—15 his meditations run Godward, and in the close he seems as in a vision to behold the wonders of the Red Sea and the wilderness. At this point, as if lost in an ecstacy, he hurriedly closes the Psalm with an abruptness, the effect of which is quite startling. The Spirit of God knows when to cease speaking, which is more than those do who, for the sake of making a methodical conclusion, prolong their words even to weariness. Perhaps this Psalm was meant to be a prelude to the next, and, if so, its sudden close is accounted for. The hymn now before us is for experienced saints only, but to them it will be of rare value as a transcript of their own inner conflicts.*

EXPOSITION.

I CRIED unto God with my voice, *even* unto God with my voice ; and he gave ear unto me.

2 In the day of my trouble I sought the Lord : my sore ran in the night, and ceased not : my soul refused to be comforted.

3 I remembered God, and was troubled : I complained, and my spirit was overwhelmed. Selah.

1. *"I cried unto God with my voice."* This Psalm has much sadness in it, but we may be sure it will end well, for it begins with prayer, and prayer never has an ill issue. Asaph did not run to man but to the Lord, and to him he went, not with studied, stately, stilted words, but with a cry, the natural, unaffected, unfeigned expression of pain. He used his voice also, for though vocal utterance is not necessary to the life of prayer, it often seems forced upon us by the energy of our desires. Sometimes the soul feels compelled to use the voice, for thus it finds a freer vent for its agony. It is a comfort to hear the alarm-bell ringing when the house is invaded by thieves. *"Even unto God with my voice."* He returned to his pleading. If once sufficed not, he cried again. He needed an answer, he expected one, he was eager to have it soon, therefore he cried again and again, and with his voice too, for the sound helped his earnestness. *"And he gave ear unto me."* Importunity prevailed. The gate opened to the steady knock. It shall be so with us in our hour of trial, the God of grace will hear us in due season.

2. *"In the day of my trouble I sought the Lord."* All day long his distress drove him to his God, so that when night came he continued still in the same search. God had hidden his face from his servant, therefore the first care of the troubled saint was to seek his Lord again. This was going to the root of the matter and removing the main impediment first. Diseases and tribulations are easily enough endured when God is found of us, but without him they crush us to the earth. *"My sore ran in the night, and ceased not."* As by day so by night his trouble was on him and his prayer continued. Some of us know what it is, both physically and spiritually, to be compelled to use these words : no respite has been afforded us by the silence of the night, our bed has been a rack to us, our body has been in torment, and our spirit in anguish. It appears that this sentence is wrongly translated, and should be, " my hand was stretched out all night ; " this shews that his prayer ceased not, but with uplifted hand he continued to seek succour of his God. *"My soul refused*

to be comforted." He refused some comforts as too weak for his case, others as untrue, others as unhallowed ; but chiefly because of distraction, he declined even those grounds of consolation which ought to have been effectual with him. As a sick man turns away even from the most nourishing food, so did he. It is impossible to comfort those who refuse to be comforted. You may bring them to the waters of the promise, but who shall make them drink if they will not do so ? Many a daughter of despondency has pushed aside the cup of gladness, and many a son of sorrow has hugged his chains. There are times when we are suspicious of good news, and are not to be persuaded into peace, though the happy truth should be as plain before us as the King's highway.

3. *"I remembered God, and was troubled."* He who is the wellspring of delight to faith became an object of dread to the Psalmist's distracted heart. The justice, holiness, power, and truth of God have all a dark side, and indeed all the attributes may be made to look black upon us if our eye be evil ; even the brightness of divine love blinds us, and fills us with a horrible suspicion that we have neither part nor lot in it. He is wretched indeed whose memories of The Ever Blessed prove distressing to him ; yet the best of men know the depth of this abyss. *"I complained, and my spirit was overwhelmed."* He mused and mused but only sank the deeper. His inward disquietudes did not fall asleep as soon as they were expressed, but rather they returned upon him, and leaped over him like raging billows of an angry sea. It was not his body alone which smarted, but his noblest nature writhed in pain, his life itself seemed crushed into the earth. It is in such a case that death is coveted as a relief, for life becomes an intolerable burden. With no spirit left in us to sustain our infirmity, our case becomes forlorn ; like a man in a tangle of briars who is stripped of his clothes, every hook of the thorns becomes a lancet, and we bleed with ten thousand wounds. Alas, my God, the writer of this exposition well knows what thy servant Asaph meant, for his soul is familiar with the way of grief. Deep glens and lonely caves of soul depressions, my spirit knows full well your awful glooms ! *"Selah."* Let the song go softly ; this is no merry dance for the swift feet of the daughters of music, pause ye awhile, and let sorrow take breath between her sighs.

4 Thou holdest mine eyes waking : I am so troubled that I cannot speak.

5 I have considered the days of old, the years of ancient times.

6 I call to remembrance my song in the night : I commune with mine own heart : and my spirit made diligent search.

7 Will the Lord cast off for ever ? and will he be favourable no more ?

8 Is his mercy clean gone for ever ? doth *his* promise fail for evermore ?

9 Hath God forgotten to be gracious ? hath he in anger shut up his tender mercies ? Selah.

4. *"Thou holdest mine eyes waking."* The fears which thy strokes excite in me forbid my eyelids to fall, my eyes continue to watch as sentinels forbidden to rest. Sleep is a great comforter, but it forsakes the sorrowful, and then their sorrow deepens and eats into the soul. If God holds the eyes waking, what anodyne shall give us rest ? How much we owe to him who giveth his beloved sleep ! *"I am so troubled that I cannot speak."* Great griefs are dumb. Deep streams brawl not among the pebbles like the shallow brooklets which live on passing showers. Words fail the man whose heart fails him. He had cried to God but he could not speak to man, what a mercy it is that if we can do the first, we need not despair though the second should be quite out of our power. Sleepless and speechless Asaph was reduced to great extremities, and yet he rallied, and even so shall we.

5. *"I have considered the days of old, the years of ancient times."* If no good was in the present, memory ransacked the past to find consolation. She fain would borrow a light from the altars of yesterday to light the gloom of to-day. It is our duty to search for comfort, and not in sullen indolence yield to despair ; in quiet contemplation topics may occur to us which will prove the means of raising our spirits, and there is scarcely any theme more likely to prove consolatory than that which deals with the days of yore, the years of the olden time, when the Lord's faithfulness was tried and proved by hosts of his people. Yet it seems that even this consideration created depression rather than delight in the good man's soul, for he contrasted his own mournful condition with all that was bright in the venerable

experiences of ancient saints, and so complained the more. Ah, sad calamity of a jaundiced mind to see nothing as it should be seen, but everything as through a veil of mist.

6. *"I call to remembrance my song in the night."* At other times his spirit had a song for the darkest hour, but now he could only recall the strain as a departed memory. Where is the harp which once thrilled sympathetically to the touch of these joyful fingers? My tongue, hast thou forgotten to praise? Hast thou no skill except in mournful ditties? Ah me, how sadly fallen am I! How lamentable that I who like the nightingale could charm the night, am now fit comrade for the hooting owl. *"I commune with mine own heart."* He did not cease from introspection, for he was resolved to find the bottom of his sorrow, and trace it to its fountain head. He made sure work of it by talking not with his mind only, but his inmost heart; it was heart work with him. He was no idler, no melancholy trifler; he was up and at it, resolutely resolved that he would not tamely die of despair, but would fight for his hope to the last moment of life. *"And my spirit made diligent search."* He ransacked his experience, his memory, his intellect, his whole nature, his entire self, either to find comfort or to discover the reason why it was denied him. That man will not die by the hand of the enemy who has enough force of soul remaining to struggle in this fashion.

7. *"Will the Lord cast off for ever?"* This was one of the matters he enquired into. He painfully knew that the Lord might leave his people for a season, but his fear was that the time might be prolonged and have no close; eagerly, therefore, he asked, will the Lord utterly and finally reject those who are his own, and suffer them to be the objects of his contemptuous reprobation, his everlasting castoffs? This he was persuaded could not be. No instance in the years of ancient times led him to fear that such could be the case. *"And will he be favourable no more?"* Favourable he had been; would that goodwill never again show itself? Was the sun set never to rise again? Would spring never follow the long and dreary winter? The questions are suggested by fear, but they are also the cure of fear. It is a blessed thing to have grace enough to look such questions in the face, for their answer is self-evident and eminently fitted to cheer the heart.

8. *"Is his mercy clean gone for ever?"* If he has no love for his elect, has he not still his mercy left? Has that dried up? Has he no pity for the sorrowful? *"Doth his promise fail for evermore?"* His word is pledged to those who plead with him; is that become of none effect? Shall it be said that from one generation to another the Lord's word has fallen to the ground; whereas aforetime he kept his covenant to all generations of them that fear him? It is a wise thing thus to put unbelief through the catechism. Each one of the questions is a dart aimed at the very heart of despair. Thus have we also in our days of darkness done battle for life itself.

9. *"Hath God forgotten to be gracious?"* Has El, the Mighty One, become great in everything but grace? Does he know how to afflict, but not how to uphold? Can he forget anything? Above all, can he forget to exercise that attribute which lies nearest to his essence, for he is love? *"Hath he in anger shut up his tender mercies?"* Are the pipes of goodness choked up so that love can no more flow through them? Do the bowels of Jehovah no longer yearn towards his own beloved children? Thus with cord after cord unbelief is smitten and driven out of the soul; it raises questions and we will meet it with questions: it makes us think and act ridiculously, and we will heap scorn upon it. The argument of this passage assumes very much the form of a *reductio ad absurdum*. Strip it naked, and mistrust is a monstrous piece of folly. *"Selah."* Here rest awhile, for the battle of questions needs a lull.

10 And I said, This *is* my infirmity: *but I will remember* the years of the right hand of the most High.

11 I will remember the works of the LORD: surely I will remember thy wonders of old.

12 I will meditate also of all thy work, and talk of thy doings.

13 Thy way, O God, *is* in the sanctuary: who *is so* great a God as *our* God?

14 Thou *art* the God that doest wonders: thou hast declared thy strength among the people.

15 Thou hast with *thine* arm redeemed thy people, the sons of Jacob and Joseph. Selah.

10. *"And I said, This is my infirmity."* He has won the day, he talks reasonably now, and surveys the field with a cooler mind. He confesses that unbelief is an infirmity, a weakness, a folly, a sin. He may also be understood to mean, " this is my appointed sorrow," I will bear it without complaint. When we perceive that our affliction is meted out by the Lord, and is the ordained portion of our cup, we become reconciled to it, and no longer rebel against the inevitable. Why should we not be content if it be the Lord's will? What he arranges it is not for us to cavil at. *"But I will remember the years of the right hand of the most High."* Here a good deal is supplied by our translators, and they make the sense to be that the Psalmist would console himself by remembering the goodness of God to himself and others of his people in times gone by : but the original seems to consist only of the words, " the years of the right hand of the most High," and to express the idea that his long continued affliction, reaching through several years, was allotted to him by the Sovereign Lord of all. 'Tis well when a consideration of the divine goodness and greatness silences all complaining, and creates a childlike acquiescence.

11. *"I will remember the works of the Lord."* Fly back, my soul, away from present turmoils, to the grandeurs of history, the sublime deeds of Jehovah, the Lord of Hosts ; for he is the same and is ready even now to defend his servants as in the days of yore. *"Surely I will remember thy wonders of old."* Whatever else may glide into oblivion, the marvellous works of the Lord in the ancient days must not be suffered to be forgotten. Memory is a fit handmaid for faith. When faith has its seven years of famine, memory like Joseph in Egypt opens her granaries.

12. *"I will meditate also of all thy work."* Sweet work to enter into Jehovah's work of grace, and there to lie down and ruminate, every thought being absorbed in the one precious subject. *"And talk of thy doings."* It is well that the overflow of the mouth should indicate the good matter which fills the heart. Meditation makes rich talking ; it is to be lamented that so much of the conversation of professors is utterly barren, because they take no time for contemplation. A meditative man should be a talker, otherwise he is a mental miser, a mill which grinds corn only for the miller. The subject of our meditation should be choice, and then our talk will be edifying ; if we meditate on folly and affect to speak wisdom, our double-mindedness will soon be known unto all men. Holy talk following upon meditation has a consoling power in it for ourselves as well as for those who listen, hence its value in the connection in which we find it in this passage.

13. *"Thy way, O God, is in the sanctuary,"* or *in holiness.* In the holy place we understand our God, and rest assured that all his ways are just and right. When we cannot trace his way, because it is " in the sea," it is a rich consolation that we can trust it, for it is in holiness. We must have fellowship with holiness if we would understand " the ways of God to man." He who would be wise must worship. The pure in heart shall see God, and pure worship is the way to the philosophy of providence. *"Who is so great a God as our God ?"* In him the good and the great are blended. He surpasses in both. None can for a moment be compared with the mighty One of Israel.

14. *"Thou art the God that doest wonders."* Thou alone art Almighty. The false gods are surrounded with the pretence of wonders, but thou really workest them. It is thy peculiar prerogative to work marvels : it is no new or strange thing with thee, it is according to thy wont and use. Herein is renewed reason for holy confidence. It would be a great wonder if we did not trust the wonder-working God. *"Thou hast declared thy strength among the people."* Not only Israel, but Egypt, Bashan, Edom, Philistia, and all the nations have seen Jehovah's power. It was no secret in the olden time and to this day it is published abroad. God's providence and grace are both full of displays of his power ; he is in the latter peculiarly conspicuous as " mighty to save." Who will not be strong in faith when there is so strong an arm to lean upon ? Shall our trust be doubtful when his power is beyond all question ? My soul see to it that these considerations banish thy mistrust.

15. *"Thou hast with thine arm redeemed thy people, the sons of Jacob and Joseph."* All Israel, the two tribes of Joseph as well as those which sprang from the other sons of Jacob, were brought out of Egypt by a display of divine power, which is here ascribed not to the hand but to the arm of the Lord, because it was the fulness of

his might. Ancient believers were in the constant habit of referring to the wonders of the Red Sea, and we also can unite with them, taking care to add the song of the Lamb to that of Moses, the servant of God. The comfort derivable from such a meditation is obvious and abundant, for he who brought up his people from the house of bondage will continue to redeem and deliver till we come into the promised rest. *"Selah."* Here we have another pause preparatory to a final burst of song.

16 The waters saw thee, O God, the waters saw thee ; they were afraid : the depths also were troubled.

17 The clouds poured out water : the skies sent out a sound : thine arrows also went abroad.

18 The voice of thy thunder *was* in the heaven : the lightnings lightened the world : the earth trembled and shook.

19 Thy way *is* in the sea, and thy path in the great waters, and thy foot-steps are not known.

20 Thou leddest thy people like a flock by the hand of Moses and Aaron.

16. *"The waters saw thee, O God, the waters saw thee ; they were afraid."* As if conscious of its Maker's presence, the sea was ready to flee from before his face. The conception is highly poetical, the Psalmist has the scene before his mind's eye, and describes it gloriously. The water saw its God, but man refuses to discern him ; it was afraid, but proud sinners are rebellious and fear not the Lord. *"The depths also were troubled."* To their heart the floods were made afraid. Quiet caves of the sea, far down in the abyss, were moved with affright ; and the lowest channels were left bare, as the water rushed away from its place, in terror of the God of Israel.

17. *"The clouds poured out water."* Obedient to the Lord, the lower region of the atmosphere yielded its aid to overthrow the Egyptian host. The cloudy chariots of heaven hurried forward to discharge their floods. *"The skies sent out a sound."* From the loftier aerial regions thundered the dread artillery of the Lord of Hosts. Peal on peal the skies sounded over the heads of the routed enemies, confusing their minds and adding to their horror. *"Thine arrows also went abroad."* Lightnings flew like bolts from the bow of God. Swiftly, hither and thither, went the red tongues of flame, on helm and shield they gleamed ; anon with blue bale-fires revealing the innermost caverns of the hungry sea which waited to swallow up the pride of Mizraim. Behold, how all the creatures wait upon their God, and show themselves strong to overthrow his enemies.

18. *"The voice of thy thunder was in the heaven,"* or *"in the whirlwind."* Rushing on with terrific swiftness and bearing all before it, the storm was as a chariot driven furiously, and a voice was heard (even thy voice, O Lord !) out of the fiery car, even as when a mighty man in battle urges forward his charger, and shouts to it aloud. All heaven resounded with the voice of the Lord. *"The lightnings lightened the world."* The entire globe shone in the blaze of Jehovah's lightnings. No need for other light amid the battle of that terrible night, every wave gleamed in the fire-flashes, and the shore was lit up with the blaze. How pale were men's faces in that hour, when all around the fire leaped from sea to shore, from crag to hill, from mountain to star till the whole universe was illuminated in honour of Jehovah's triumph. *"The earth trembled and shook."* It quaked and quaked again. Sympathetic with the sea, the solid shore forgot its quiescence and heaved in dread. How dreadful art thou, O God, when thou comest forth in thy majesty to humble thine arrogant adversaries.

19. *"Thy way is in the sea."* Far down in secret channels of the deep is thy roadway ; when thou wilt thou canst make a sea a highway for thy glorious march. *"And thy path in the great waters."* There, where the billows surge and swell, thou still dost walk ; Lord of each crested wave. *"And thy footsteps are not known."* None can follow thy tracks by foot or eye. Thou art alone in thy glory, and thy ways are hidden from mortal ken. Thy purposes thou wilt accomplish, but the means are often concealed, yea, they need no concealing, they are in themselves too vast and mysterious for human understanding. Glory be to thee, O Jehovah.

20. *"Thou leddest thy people like a flock by the hand of Moses and Aaron."* What a transition from tempest to peace, from wrath to love. Quietly as a flock Israel was guided on, by human agency which veiled the excessive glory of the divine

presence. The smiter of Egypt was the shepherd of Israel. He drove his foes before him, but went before his people. Heaven and earth fought on his side against the sons of Ham, but they were equally subservient to the interests of the sons of Jacob. Therefore, with devout joy and full of consolation, we close this Psalm; the song of one who forgot how to speak and yet learned to sing far more sweetly than his fellows.

EXPLANATORY NOTES AND QUAINT SAYINGS.

Whole Psalm.—Whenever, and by whomsoever, the Psalm may have been written, it clearly is individual, not national. It utterly destroys all the beauty, all the tenderness and depth of feeling in the opening portion, if we suppose that the people are introduced speaking in the first person. The allusions to the national history may indeed show that the season was a season of national distress, and that the sweet singer was himself bowed down by the burden of the time, and oppressed by woes which he had no power to alleviate; but it is his own sorrow, not the sorrow of others under which he sighs, and of which he has left the pathetic record.—*J. J. Stewart Perowne.*

Verse 1.—In the beginning of the Psalm, before speaking of his sorrows, he hastens to show the necessary and most efficacious remedy for allaying sorrow. He says that he did not, as many do, out of their impatience of grief or murmuring, either accuse God of cruelty or tyranny, or utter blasphemous words by which dishonour might fall upon God, or by indulging in sorrow and distrust hasten his own destruction, or fill the air with vain complainings, but fled straight to God, and to him unburdened his sorrow, and sought that he would not shut him from that grace which he bountifully offers to all. This is the only and sure sovereign remedy which most effectually heals his griefs.—*Mollerus.*

Verse 1.—"*I cried.*" To the Orientals the word פוץ presented the idea of a *crash*, as of the heavens sending out thunders and lightnings. Whence beyond other things he metaphorically says, *he cried for sorrow;* . . . shaken with a tempest of thoughts he burst out into an open and loud-sounding complaint.—*Hermann Venema.*

Verse 1.—"*Even unto God with my voice.*" The repetition here is emphatic. The idea is that it was an earnest or fervent cry.—*Albert Barnes.*

Verse 1 (last clause).—At the second knock, the door of grace flew open: *the Lord heard me.*—*John Collings.*

Verse 2.—"*In the day of my trouble I sought the Lord.*" Days of trouble must be days of prayer; in days of inward trouble, especially when God seems to have withdrawn from us, we must seek him, and seek till we find him. In the day of his trouble he did not seek for the diversions of business or recreation, to shake off his trouble that way, but he sought God, and his favour and grace. Those that are under trouble of mind, must not think to drink it away, or laugh it away, but pray it away.—*Matthew Henry.*

Verse 2.—"*My sore ran in the night.*" Hebrew: *My hand was poured out;* that is, stretched out in prayer; or wet with continual weeping. *Non fuit remissa, nec retracta in lectum.*—*John Trapp.*

Verse 2.—"*My sore ran in the night, and ceased not,*" etc.—"There is no healing of this wound, no easing of this sore, no cleansing of the conscience, no quieting of a man's spirit: till God whom the soul seeketh show himself as the Physician, the evil continueth still and groweth."—*David Dickson.*

Verse 2.—"*My soul refused to be comforted.*" God has provided suitable and sufficient comfort for his people. He sends them comforters just as their circumstances require. But they at times refuse to hear the voice of the charmer. The Lord has perhaps taken away an idol—or he withholds his sensible presence, that they may learn to live by faith—or he has blighted their worldly prospects—or he has written vanity and emptiness upon all their gourds, cisterns, and delights. They give way to passion, as did Jonah—or they sink into sullen gloom—or allow unhumbled pride to rule the spirit—or yield to extreme sorrow, as Rachel did—or fall under the power of temptation—or imbibe the notion that they have no right to comfort. This is wrong, all wrong, decidedly wrong. Look at what is left you, at what the gospel presents to you, at what heaven will be to you. But the Psalmist was recovered from this state. He was convinced that it was wrong. He was sorry for his sin. He was reformed in his spirit and conduct. He wrote this Psalm to instruct, caution, and warn us. Observe, they who are entitled to all comfort, often through their own folly, enjoy the least. The Lord's people are often their own tormentors, they put away the cup of comfort from them, and say they are unworthy of it.

> O Thou source of every blessing,
> Chase my sorrows, cheer my heart,
> Till in heaven, thy smiles possessing,
> Life, and joy, and peace impart.

> —*James Smith.*

Verse 2.—"My soul refused to be comforted." Poor I, that am but of yesterday, have known some that have been so deeply plunged in the gulf of despair, that they would throw all the spiritual cordials that have been tendered to them against the walls. They were strong in reasoning against their own souls, and resolved against everything that might be a comfort and support unto them. They have been much set against all ordinances and religious services; they have cast off holy duties themselves, and peremptorily refused to join with others in them; yea, they have, out of a sense of sin and wrath, which hath laid hard upon them, refused the necessary comforts of this life, even to the overthrow of natural life, and yet out of this horrible pit, this hell upon earth, hath God delivered their souls, and given them such manifestations of his grace and favour, that they would not exchange them for a thousand worlds. O despairing souls, you see that others, whose conditions have been as bad if not worse than yours, have obtained mercy. God hath turned their hell into a heaven; he hath remembered them in their low estate; he hath pacified their raging consciences, and quieted their distracted souls; he hath wiped all tears from their eyes; and he hath been a well-spring of life unto their hearts. Therefore be not discouraged, O despairing souls, but look up to the mercy-seat.—*Thomas Brooks.*

Verse 3.—"I remembered God, and was troubled." If our hearts or consciences condemn us, it is impossible to remember him without being troubled. It will then be painful to remember that he is our Creator and Benefactor, for the remembrance will be attended with a consciousness of base ingratitude. It will be painful to think of him as Lawgiver; for such thoughts will remind us that we have broken his law. It will be painful to think of his holiness; for if he is holy, he must hate our sins, and be angry with us as sinners:—of his justice and truth, for these perfections make it necessary that he should fulfil his threatenings and punish us for our sins. It will be painful to think of his omniscience—for this perfection makes him acquainted with our most secret offences, and renders it impossible to conceal them from his view; of his omnipresence—for the constant presence of an invisible witness must be disagreeable to those who wish to indulge their sinful propensities. It will be painful to think of his power—for it enables him to restrain or destroy, as he pleases: of his sovereignty, for sinners always hate to see themselves in the hands of a sovereign God: of his eternity and immutability—for from his possessing these perfections it follows that he will never alter the threatenings which he has denounced against sinners, and that he will always live to execute them. It will be painful to think of him as judge; for we shall feel, that as sinners, we have no reason to expect a favourable sentence from his lips. It will even be painful to think of the perfect goodness and excellence of his character; for his goodness leaves us without excuse in rebelling against him, and makes our sins appear exceeding sinful.—*Edward Payson.*

Verse 3.—"I remembered God, and was troubled." All had not been well between God and him; and whereas formerly, in his remembrance of God, his thoughts were chiefly exercised about his love and kindness, now they were wholly possessed with his own sin and unkindness. This causeth his trouble. Herein lies a share of the entanglements occasioned by sin. Saith such a soul in itself, " Foolish creature, hast thou thus requited the Lord? Is this the return that thou hast made unto him for all his love, his kindness, his consolations, mercies? Is this thy kindness for him, thy love to him ? Is this thy kindness to thy friend ? Is this thy boasting of him, that thou hadst found so much goodness and excellence in him and his love, that though all men should forsake him, thou never wouldst do so ? Are all thy promises, all thy engagements which thou madest unto God, in times of distress, upon prevailing obligations, and mighty impressions of his good Spirit upon thy soul, now come to this, that thou shouldst so foolishly forget, neglect, despise, cast him off ? Well ! now he is gone ; he is withdrawn from thee ; and what wilt thou do ? Art thou not even ashamed to desire him to return ? " They were thoughts of this nature that cut Peter to the heart upon his fall. The soul finds them cruel as death, and strong as the grave. It is bound in the chains of them, and cannot be comforted, Ps. xxxviii. 3—6.—*John Owen.*

Verse 3.—There are moments in the life of all believers when God and his ways become unintelligible to them. They get lost in profound meditation, and nothing is left them but a desponding sigh. But we know from Paul the apostle that the Holy Spirit intercedes for believers with God, when they cannot utter their sighs. Romans viii. 26.—*Augustus F. Tholuck.*

Verse 3.—"*Selah.*" In the end of this verse is put the word "*Selah.*" And it doth note unto the reader or hearer what a miserable and comfortless thing man is in trouble, if God be not present with him to help him. It is also put as a spur and prick for every Christian man and woman to remember and call upon God in the days of their troubles. For as the Jews say, wheresoever this word "*Selah*" is, it doth admonish and stir up the reader or hearer to mark what was said before it ; for it is a word always put after very notable sentences.—*John Hooper.*

Verse 4.—"*Thou holdest mine eyes waking.*" Thou art afflicted with want of sleep :—A complaint incident to distempered bodies and thoughtful minds. Oh, how wearisome a thing it is to spend the long night in tossing up and down in a restless bed, in the chase of sleep ; which the more eagerly it is followed, flies so much the farther from us ! Couldst thou obtain of thyself to forbear the desire of it, perhaps it would come alone : now that thou suest for it, like to some froward piece, it is coy and overly, and punishes thee with thy longing. Lo, he that could command a hundred and seven and twenty provinces, yet could not command rest. ' On that night his sleep departed from him,' Esth. vi. 1, neither could be forced or entreated to his bed. And the great Babylonian monarch, though he had laid some hand on sleep, yet he could not hold it ; for " his sleep brake from him," Dan. ii. 1. And, for great and wise Solomon, it would not so much as come within his view. " Neither day nor night seeth he sleep with his eyes," Eccl. viii. 16. Surely, as there is no earthly thing more comfortable to nature than bodily rest (Jer. xxxi. 26) ; so, there is nothing whose loss is more grievous and disheartening. . . . . Instead of closing thy lids to wait for sleep, lift up thy stiff eyes to him that " giveth his beloved rest," Psalm cxxvii. 2. Whatever be the means, he it is that "*holdeth mine eyes waking.*" He that made thine eyes, keeps off sleep from thy body, for the good of thy soul : let not thine eyes wake, without thy heart. The spouse of Christ can say, " I sleep, but my heart waketh," Cant. v. 2. How much more should she say, " Mine eyes wake, and my heart waketh also ! " When thou canst not sleep with thine eyes, labour to see him that is invisible : one glimpse of that sight is more worth than all the sleep that thine eyes can be capable of. Give thyself up into his hands, to be disposed of at his will. What is this sweet acquiescence but the rest of the soul ? which if thou canst find in thyself, thou shalt quietly digest the want of thy bodily sleep.—*Joseph Hall, in his "Balm of Gilead."*

Verse 4.—"*I am so troubled that I cannot speak.*" He adds that he was so cut down and lifeless that he could not speak. Little griefs, as it is often said, are uttered, great ones strike us dumb. In great troubles and affrights the spirit fails the exterior members, and flows back to its fountain ; the limbs stand motionless, the whole body trembles, the eyes remain fixed, and the tongue forgets its office. Hence it is that Niobe was represented by the poets as turned into a stone. The history of Psammenitus also, in Herodotus, is well known, how over the misfortunes of his children he sat silent and overwhelmed, but when he saw his friend's calamities he bewailed them with bitter tears.—*Mollerus.*

Verse 4.—"*I am so troubled that I cannot speak.*" Sometimes our grief is so violent that it finds no vent, it strangles us, and we are overcome. It is with us in our desertions as with a man that gets a slight hurt ; at first he walks up and down, but not looking betimes to prevent a growing mischief, the neglected wound begins to fester, or to gangrene, and brings him to greater pain and loss. So it is with us many times in our spiritual sadness; when we are first troubled, we pray and pour out our souls before the Lord; but afterwards the waters of our grief drown our cries and we are so overwhelmed, that if we might have all the world we cannot pray, or at least we can find no enlargement, no life, no pleasure in our prayers; and God himself seems to take no delight in them, and that makes us more sad, Psalm xxii. 1.—*Timothy Rogers* (1660—1729), *in "A Discourse on Trouble of Mind, and the Disease of Melancholy."*

Verse 4.—*"Troubled."* Or, *bruised:* the Hebrew word properly signifieth an astonishment caused by some great blow received.—*John Diodati.*

Verse 4.—*"I cannot speak."* Words are but the body, the garment, the outside of prayer; sighs are nearer the heart work. A dumb beggar getteth an alms at Christ's gates, even by making sighs, when his tongue cannot plead for him; and the rather, because he is dumb. *Objection.* I have not so much as a voice to utter to God; and Christ saith, "Cause me to hear thy voice" (Cant. ii. 14). *Answer.* Yea, but some other thing hath a voice beside the tongue: "The Lord has heard the voice of my weeping" (Psalm vi. 8). Tears have a tongue, and grammar, and language, that our Father knoweth. Babes have no prayer for the breast, but weeping: the mother can read hunger in weeping.—*Samuel Rutherford.*

Verse 4.—If through all thy discouragements thy condition prove worse and worse, so that thou canst not pray, but art struck dumb when thou comest into his presence, as David, then fall a-making signs when thou canst not speak; groan, sigh, sob, "chatter," as Hezekiah did; bemoan thyself for thine unworthiness, and desire Christ to speak thy requests for thee, and God to hear him for thee.— *Thomas Goodwin.*

Verse 5.—*"The days of old."* Doubtless to our first parents the darkness of the first night was somewhat strange; persons who had never seen anything but the light of the day, when the shadows of the night first did encompass them, could not be without some apprehension: yet when at the back of a number of nights they had seen the day-spring of the morning light constantly to arise; the darkness of the blackest nights was passed over without fear, and in as great security, as the light of the fairest days. To men who have always lived upon land, when first they set to sea, the winds, waves, and storms are exceeding terrible; but when they are a little beaten with the experience of tempests, their fears do change into resolution and courage. It is of no small use to remember that those things which vex most our spirit, are not new, but have already been in times before our days.— *Robert Baylie's Sermon before the House of Commons.* 1643.

Verse 6.—*"I call to remembrance my song in the night."* Either, (1) "I will now, in the present night of affliction, remember my former songs." "Though this is a time of distress, and my present circumstances are gloomy, yet I have known brighter days. He that lifted me up, has cast me down, and he can raise me up again." Sometimes this reflection, indeed, adds a poignancy to our distress, as it did to David's trouble, Ps. xlii. 4. Yet it will bear a better improvement, which he seems to make of it; verse 11, and so Job, (ii. 10.) *"Shall we receive good at the hand of God, and shall we not receive evil?"* And his case shows that after the most sweeping calamities the Lord can again give things a turn in favour of them that hope in him. Therefore, present troubles should not make us forget former comforts, especially as the former so much exceeded our deserts, and the present afflictions fall so short of our demerits. Or, (2) the text may mean, "I will remember how I have been enabled to sing in the former nights of affliction." And surely it is especially seasonable to remember supports and consolations granted under preceding distresses. Elihu complained (Job xxxv. 10), "There is none that saith, Where is God my maker, who giveth songs in the night." David comforted himself with the thought, "Though deep calleth unto deep, yet the Lord will command his loving-kindness in the daytime, and in the night his song shall be with me." Ps. xlii. 8. And the Lord promised by Isaiah (xxx. 29), "Ye shall have a song, as in the night when a holy solemnity is kept." No doubt Paul and Silas remembered their song in the night, when imprisoned at Philippi; and it afforded them encouragement under subsequent trials. And cannot many of you, my brethren, in like manner, remember the supports and consolations you have enjoyed in former difficulties, and how the Lord turned the shadow of death into morning ?   And ought you not to trust to him that hath delivered, that he will yet deliver ?   He that hath delivered in six troubles will not forsake you in seven.   The " clouds may return after the rain ; " but not a drop can fall without the leave of him, who rides on the heavens for your help, and in his excellency on the sky.   Did you not forbode at first a very different termination of the former troubles ? and did the Lord disappoint your fears, and put a new song into your mouth ; and will you not now begin to trust him, and triumph in him ?   Surely you have found that the Lord can clear the darkest skies.   " Light is sown for the righteous," and ere long you shall see an eternal day.   If such songs are given to the pilgrims of the night, how shall they sing in that world where the sun shall set no more !   There will be no night there. —*John Ryland.* 1753—1825.

Verse 6.—"*I call to remembrance :* " being glad in this scarcity of comfort, to live upon the old store, as bees do in winter.—*John Trapp.*

Verse 6.—"*My song in the night.*" The " songs of the night " is as favourite a word of the Old Testament as " glory in tribulation " is of the New, and it is one of those which prove that both Testaments have the self-same root and spirit.— *John Ker.*

Verse 6.—"*My spirit made diligent search.*" He falls upon self-examination, and searcheth his spirit, to consider why the hand of God was so against him, and why the face of God was so hid from him.   Some read it, " I digged into my spirit ; " as Ezekiel digged into the wall, to search for and find out the abomination, that made the Lord thus leave him in the dark, and hide his face from him.   He searcheth the wound of his spirit ; that was another way to cure it.   It is a notable way to cure the wounds of the soul, for the soul to search them.—*John Collings.*

Verse 6.—"*My spirit made diligent search.*" The verb חפש, *chaphas,* signifies such an investigation as a man makes who is obliged to *strip himself* in order to do it ; or, *to lift up coverings,* to search fold by fold, or in our own phrase, *to leave no stone unturned.*—*Adam Clarke.*

Verse 6.—"*My spirit made diligent search.*"   As Ahasuerus, when he could not sleep, called for the records and chronicles of his kingdom, so the doubting soul betakes himself to the records of heaven, the word of God in the Scriptures, and one while he is reading there, another while looking into his heart, if he can find there anything that answers the characters of Scripture-faith, as the face in the glass doth the face of man.   David, when he was at a loss what to think of himself, and many doubts did clog his faith, insomuch that the thinking of God increased his trouble, he did not sit down and let the ship drive, as we say, not regarding whether God loved him or no, but *communes with his own heart, and his spirit makes diligent search.*   Thus it is with every sincere soul under doubtings : he dares no more sit down contented in that unresolved condition, than one who thinks he smells fire in his house dares settle himself to sleep till he hath looked in every room and corner, and satisfied himself that all is safe, lest he should be waked with the fire about his ears in the night ; and the poor doubting soul is much more afraid, lest it should wake with hell-fire about it : whereas a soul in a state and under the power of unbelief is secure and careless.—*William Gurnall.*

Verse 6.—"*Diligent search.*" This duty requires diligence. External acts of religion are facile ; to lift up the eye to heaven, to bow the knee, to read a prayer, this requires no more labour than for a papist to tell over his beads ; but to examine a man's self, to take the heart all in pieces as a watch, and see what is defective, this is not easy. Reflective acts are hardest. The eye can see everything but itself.   It is easy to spy the faults of others, but hard to find out our own. —*Thomas Wat on.*

Verse 8.—"*Doth his promise fail for evermore ?* " Let no appearing impossibilities make you question God's accomplishment of any of his gracious words. Though you cannot see how the thing can be done, 'tis enough, if God has said that he will do it.   There can be no obstructions to promised salvation, which we need to fear. He who is the God of this salvation, and the Author of the promise, will prepare his own way for the doing of his own work, so that " every valley shall be filled, and every mountain and hill brought low." Luke iii. 5.   Though the valleys be so deep that we cannot see the bottom, and the mountains so high that we cannot see the tops of them, yet God knows how to raise the one and level the other ; Isa. lxiii. 1 : " I that speak in righteousness (or faithfulness) am mighty to save."   If anything would keep back the kingdom of Christ, it would be our infidelity; but he will come, though he should find no faith on the earth. See Rom. iii. 3. Cast not away your confidence because God defers his performances. Though providences run cross, though they move backwards and forwards, you have a sure and faithful word to rely upon. Promises, though they be for a time seemingly delayed, cannot be finally frustrated. Dare not to harbour such a thought within yourselves. The being of God may as well fail as the promise of God. That which does not come in your time, will be hastened in his time, which is always the more convenient season.—*Timothy Cruso.*

Verse 9.—*"Hath God forgotten to be gracious?"* In what pangs couldst thou be, O Asaph, that so woeful a word should fall from thee: *"Hath God forgotten to be gracious?"* Surely, the temptation went so high, that the next step had been blasphemy. Had not that good God, whom thy bold weakness questions for forgetfulness, in great mercies remembered thee, and brought thee speedily to remember thyself and him; that, which thou confessest to have been infirmity, had proved a sinful despair. I dare say for thee, that word washed thy cheeks with many a tear, and was worthy of more; for, O God, what can be so dear to thee, as the glory of thy mercy? There is none of thy blessed attributes, which thou desirest to set forth so much unto the sons of men, and so much abhorrest to be disparaged by our detraction, as thy mercy. Thou canst, O Lord, forget thy displeasure against thy people; thou canst forget our iniquities, and cast our sins out of thy remembrance, Micah vii. 18, 19; but thou canst no more forget to be gracious, than thou canst cease to be thyself. O my God, I sin against thy justice hourly, and thy mercy interposes for my remission: but, oh, keep me from sinning against thy mercy. What plea can I hope for, when I have made my advocate my enemy? —*Joseph Hall.*

Verse 9.—*"Hath God forgotten to be gracious?"* The poor child crieth after the mother. What shall I do for my mother! Oh, my mother, my mother, what shall I do for my mother! And it may be the mother stands behind the back of the child, only she hides herself, to try the affection of the child: so the poor soul cries after God, and complains, Oh, my Father! my Father; Where is my heavenly Father? Hath he forgotten to be gracious? Hath he shut up his loving-kindness in displeasure? when (all the while), God is nearer than they think for, shining upon them in "a spirit of grace and supplications," with sighs and "groans that cannot be uttered." Thus the gracious woman, Mary Magdalene, she seeks after Christ, she enquires, she cries after him, and weeps: My dear Saviour, my dear Lord and Master, he is "taken out of the sepulchre, and I know not where they have laid him!" Thus she complains to the disciples, and thus she complains to the angels, when Christ stood at her very back and overheard all: nay, when she turned her about and saw him, yet at first she did not know him; nay, when he spoke to her and she to him, yet she knew him not, but thought he had been the gardener, John xx. 15. Thus is it with many a gracious soul; though God speaks home to their hearts in his Word, and they speak to him by prayer, and they cannot say but the Spirit *"helps their infirmities;"* yet they complain for want of his presence, as if there were nothing of God in them.—*Matthew Lawrence.*

Verse 9.—*"Hath he in anger shut up his tender mercies?"* The metaphor here is taken from a *spring*, the mouth of which is closed, so that its waters can no longer run in the same channel; but, being confined, break out and take some other course. Wilt thou take thy mercy from the Israelites and give it to some other people?— *Adam Clarke.*

Verse 9.—*"Selah."* Thus was he going on with his dark and dismal apprehensions, when on a sudden he first checked himself with that word, *"Selah;"* stop there; go no further; let us hear no more of these unbelieving surmises; and he then chid himself, verse 10: "This is mine infirmity."—*Matthew Henry.*

Verse 10.—*"This is my infirmity."* Literally, this is my disease,—which appears to mean, This is my lot and I must bear it; lo! it is a partial evil, for which the equity of God's government should not be questioned. The authorised version, *"This is my infirmity,"* suggests, perhaps advisedly, another signification, viz., These thoughts are but hallucinations of my agony,—but to this gloss I should scruple to commit myself.—*C. B. Cayley.*

Verse 10.—It is the *"infirmity"* of a believer to be thinking of himself, and drawing false inferences (for all such inferences are necessarily erroneous), from what he sees or feels, as to the light in which he is beheld and estimated on the part of God. It is his *strength*, on the other hand, to remember the right hand of the Most High—to meditate upon the changeless truth and mercy of that God who has committed himself in holiness to the believing sinner's sure salvation, by causing the Son of his love to suffer in our stead the dread reality of penal death.—*Arthur Pridham.*

Verse 10.—*"Infirmity."* An *"infirmity"* is this,—some sickness or indisposition of the soul, that arises from the weakness of grace. Or an infirmity is this,—when the purpose and inclination of the heart is upright, but a man wants strength to perform that purpose; when " the spirit is willing, but the flesh is weak " (Matt. xxvi. 41); when a man can say with the apostle, " To will is present with me; but how to perform that which is good I find not," Rom. vii. 18. When the bent and inclination of the soul is right, but either through some violence of corruption or strength of temptation, a man is diverted and turned out of the way. As the needle in the seaman's compass, you know if it be right it will stand always northwards, the bent of it will be toward the North Pole, but being jogged and troubled, it may sometimes be put out of frame and order, yet the bent and inclination of it is still northward; this is an infirmity.—*James Nalton.* 1664.

Verse 10.—It is unnecessary to state all the renderings which the learned have given of this verse. It is unquestionably ambiguous, as the word חַלּוֹתִי may be derived from different roots, which have different significations. I derive it from חוּל or חָלַל which signifies to be *in pain* as a woman in labour, and as it is in the infinitive, I render it, *"the time of my sorrow or pain."* The next term, שְׁנוֹת, I derive from שָׁנָה *to change*, as the Chaldee does, Ainsworth, Hammond, and others; and I render potentially. I consider the whole as a beautiful metaphor. The author considers himself as in distress, like a woman in travail; and like her, hopes soon to have his sorrow turned to joy. He confides in God's power to effect such a change; and hence naturally recollects the past instances of God's favour to his people.— *Benjamin Boothroyd.*

Verse 10.—*"I will remember the years of the right hand of the Most High."* Not the moments, nor the hours, nor days of a few short afflictions, that his left hand hath dealt to me : but the *"years of his right hand ; "* those long, large, and boundless mercies wherewith he hath comforted me.—*Thomas Adams.*

Verse 10.—*"I will remember the years,"* etc. The words in the Hebrew text are *shenoth jemin gneljon*, which I find to be variously rendered and translated by interpreters. I shall not trouble you with them all at this present time, but only take notice of two of them, which I conceive are the principal and most comprehensive; the one is of our oldest English translation, and the other of our last and newest; the former reads the words thus : *"The right hand of the Most High can change all this."* The latter reads the words thus, as we have it now before us, *"I will remember the years,"* etc. The main ground of this variation is the different exposition of the Hebrew word *shenoth*, which may be translated either *to change*, from the *verb* in the *infinitive mood*, or else may be translated *years*, from the *noun* in the *plural number*. This hath given the occasion to this difference and variety of translation, but the sense is very good and agreeable which way soever we take it—

First, take it according to the *former* translation, as it does exhibit to us the power of God. *"The right hand of the Lord can change all this."* This was that whereby David did support himself in his present affliction; that the Lord was able *to change and alter* this his condition to him, and that *for the better. . . . .* For the second sense here before us, that's this : *"I will remember the years of the right hand of the most High ; "* where the word *"remember"* is borrowed from the next following verse, to supply the sense of this, as otherwise being not in the text. Now here the prophet David fetches a ground of comfort from God's *practice*, as before he did from his *power ;* there, from what God *could* do ; here, from what he had done already in former time, and ages, and generations.—*Thomas Horton.*

Verse 11.—*"I will remember,"* etc. *Remember* and *commemorate* as the Hebrew (by a double reading) importeth.—*John Trapp.*

Verse 11.—*"I will remember."* Faith is a considering grace : he that believes will not make haste ; no, not to think or speak of God. Faith hath a good memory, and can tell the Christian many stories of ancient mercies ; and when his present meal falls short, it can entertain the soul with a cold dish, and not complain that

God keeps a bad house. Thus David recovered himself, when he was even tumbling down the hill of temptation : *"This is my infirmity ; but I will remember the years of the right hand of the Most High. I will remember thy wonders of old."* Therefore, Christian, when thou art in the depths of affliction, and Satan tempts thee to asperse God, as if he were forgetful of thee, stop his mouth with this : No, Satan, God hath not forgot to do for me, but I have forgot what he hath done for me, or else I could not question his fatherly care at present over me. Go, Christian, play over thy own lessons, praise God for past mercies, and it will not be long before thou hast a new song put into thy mouth for a present mercy. . . . .

Sometimes a little writing is found in a man's study that helps to save his estate, for want of which he had gone to prison ; and some one experience remembered keeps the soul from despair, a prison which the devil longs to have the Christian in. " This I recall to my mind, therefore have I hope," Lam. iii. 21. David was famous for his hope, and not less eminent for his care to observe and preserve the experiences he had of God's goodness. He was able to recount the dealings of God with him ; they were so often the subject of his meditation and matter of his discourse, that he had made them familiar to him. When his hope is at a loss, he doth but exercise his memory a little, and he recovers himself presently, and chides himself for his weakness. *"I said, this is my infirmity : but I will remember the years of the right hand of the Most High."* The hound, when he hath lost the scent, hunts backward and so recovers it, and pursues his game with louder cry than ever. Thus, Christian, when thy hope is at a loss, and thou questionest thy salvation in another world, then look backward and see what God hath already done for thee. Some promises have their day of payment here, and others we must stay to receive in heaven. Now the payment which God makes of some promises here, is an earnest given to our faith that the others also shall be faithfully discharged when their date expires ; as every judgment inflicted here on the wicked is sent as a pledge of that wrath the full sum whereof God will make up in hell.—*William Gurnall.*

Verse 11.—*"The works of the Lord." . . . . "Thy wonders."* The Psalmist does not mean to draw a distinction between the *works* and the *wonders* of God ; but, rather, to state that all God's works are wonders. . . . . all, whether in providence or grace—all God's works are wonderful. If we take the individual experience of the Christian, of what is that experience made up ? Of wonders. The work of his conversion, wonderful !—arrested in a course of thoughtlessness and impiety ; graciously sought and gently compelled to be at peace with God, whose wrath he had provoked. The communication of knowledge, wonderful !—Deity and eternity gradually piled up ; the Bible taken page by page, and each page made a volume which no searching can exhaust. The assistance in warfare, wonderful !—himself a child of corruption, yet enabled to grapple with the world, the flesh, and the devil, and often to trample them under foot. The solaces in affliction, wonderful !— sorrow sanctified so as to minister to joy, and a harvest of gladness reaped from a field which has been watered with tears. The foretastes of heaven, wonderful !— angels bringing down the clusters of the land, and the spirit walking with lightsome tread the crystal river and the streets of gold. All wonderful ! Wonderful that the Spirit should strive with man ; wonderful that God should bear with his backslidings ; wonderful that God should love him notwithstanding his pollution ; wonderful that God should persist in saving him, in spite, as it were, of himself. Oh ! those amongst you who know anything, experimentally, of salvation through Christ, well know that the work is wonderful in its commencement, wonderful in its continuance, and they will need no argument to vindicate the transition from *"works"* to *"wonders."* It will be the transition of your own thoughts and your own feelings, and you will never give in the record of God's dealings with yourselves without passing, as the Psalmist passed, from mentioning to ascription. Ye may set yourselves to commemorate God's *"works,"* ye will find yourselves extolling God's *"wonders."* Ye may begin with saying, *"I will remember the works of the Lord ; "* but ye will conclude by exclaiming, *"Surely I will remember thy wonders of old."*—*Henry Melvill.*

Verse 11.—*"Thy wonders."* The word is in the singular here, and also in verse 14. So also in the next verse, *"Thy work,"* because the one great wonder, the one great work in which all others were included, is before his thoughts.—*J. J. Stewart Perowne.*

Verse 11.— *"Thy wonders."* He had before spoken to others, but here he turns to God. It is good for a soul in a hard exercise, to raise itself from thinking of God and of his works, unto speaking unto God directly : no ease or relief will be found till address be made unto himself, till we turn our face toward him and direct our speech unto him, as here the Psalmist doth, from the midst of the eleventh verse to the end of the psalm.—*David Dickson.*

Verse 13.—"*Thy way, O God, is in the sanctuary.*" The word "*sanctuary*" is to be taken either for heaven or for the temple. I am rather inclined to refer it to heaven, conceiving the meaning to be, that the ways of God rise high above the world, so that if we are truly desirous to know them, we must ascend above all heavens. Although the works of God are in part manifest to us, yet all our knowledge of them comes far short of their immeasurable height. Besides, it is to be observed, that none enjoy the least taste of his works but those who by faith rise up to heaven. And yet, the utmost point to which we can ever attain is, to contemplate with admiration and reverence the hidden wisdom and power of God, which, while they shine forth in his works, yet far surpass the limited powers of our understanding.—*John Calvin.*

Verse 13.—"*Thy way is in the sanctuary.*" That is, every one of the elect may and ought to learn in thy church the conduct and proceedings of thy providence towards those that were thine.—*John Diodati.*

Verses 13, 19.—"*In the sanctuary*" and "*In the sea.*" His "*way*" is "*in the sanctuary,*" and His "*way*" is "*in the sea.*" Now there is a great difference between these two things. First of all, God's way is in the *sanctuary,* where all is *light,* all is *clear.* There is no mistake there. There is nothing, in the least degree, that is a harass to the spirit. On the contrary, it is when the poor, troubled one enters into the sanctuary, and views things there in the light of God, that he sees the end of all else—everything that is entangled, the end of which he cannot find on the earth. But not only is God's way in the sanctuary (and when we are there, all is bright and happy); but God's way is in the "*sea.*" He walks *where we cannot always trace his footsteps.* God moves mysteriously by times, as we all know. There are ways of God which are purposely to try us. I need not say that it is not at all as if God had pleasure in our perplexities. Nor is it as if we had no sanctuary to draw near to, where we can rise above it. But, still, there is a great deal in the ways of God that must be left entirely in his own hands. The way of God is thus not only in the sanctuary, but also in the sea. And yet, what we find even in connection with his footsteps being in the sea is, " Thou leddest thy people like a flock, by the hand of Moses and Aaron." That was through the sea; afterwards, it was through the wilderness. But it had been through the sea. The beginnings of the ways of God with his people were there; because, from first to last, God must be the confidence of the saint. It may be an early lesson of his soul, but it never ceases to be the thing to learn. How happy to know that, while the sanctuary is open to us, yet God himself is nearer still—and to him we are brought now. As it is said (1 Pet. iii.), " Christ also hath once suffered for sins, the just for the unjust, to bring us to God." This is a most precious thing; because there we are in the sanctuary at once, and brought to God himself. And I am bold to say, that heaven itself would be but a small matter if it were not to God that we are brought. It is better than any freedom from trial—better than any blessing, to be in the presence of the One we belong to ; who is himself the source of all blessing and joy. That we are brought to him now is infinitely precious. There we are in the sanctuary brought to God. But, still, there are other ways of God outside the sanctuary—"*In the sea.*" And there we often find ourselves at a loss. If we are occupied with the sea itself, and with trying to scan God's footsteps there, then "*they are not known.*" But confidence in God himself is always the strength of faith. May the Lord grant us increasing simplicity and quietness in the midst of all that we pass through, for his name's sake.—*From* "*Things New and Old.*" 1865.

Verse 14.—"*The God that doest wonders.*" If he said, *Thou art the God that hast done wonders,* it would be plain that he spake only of those ancient miracles which were wrought in former days : but now that he saith, *Thou art the God that doest wonders,* he evidently refers to those wonderful works, which he is doing now, and shall not cease to do even to the end of the world.—*Gerhohus.*

Verse 15.—"*The sons of Jacob and Joseph.*" The distinction between the sons of Jacob and Joseph is not meaningless. For by the sons of Jacob or Israel the believing Jews are properly intended, those that trace their descent to him not only according to the flesh but according to faith. Of whom although *Joseph* was one, yet since he was sold by his brethren and after many sufferings among foreign tribes raised to high rank, it is highly congruous to distinguish him from the sons of *Jacob*, and he is fitly regarded as a prince of the Gentiles apart from *Jacob's* sons, who sold him.—*Gerhohus.*

Verse 15.—*"The sons of Jacob and Joseph."* Was it Joseph or was it Jacob that begat the children of Israel ? Certainly Jacob begat ; but as Joseph nourished them, they are called by his name also.—*Talmud.*

Verse 16.—*"The waters saw thee, O God,"* etc. " The waters of the Red Sea," says Bishop Horne, " are here beautifully represented as endued with sensibility ; as seeing, feeling, and being confounded, even to the lowest depths, at the presence and power of their great Creator, when he commanded them to open a way, and to form a wall on each side of it, until his people were passed over." This in fact is true poetry ; and in this attributing of life, spirit, feeling, action, and suffering to inanimate objects, there are no poets who can vie with those of the Hebrew nation. —*Richard Mant.*

Verse 16.—*"The depths also were troubled."* The *depths* are mentioned in addition to the *waters*, to show that the dominion and power of God reach not only to the surface of the waters, but penetrate to the most profound abysses, and agitate and restrain the waters from their lowest bottom.—*Mollerus.*

Verses 16—18.—The waters saw thee, but men do not see thee. The depths were troubled, but men say in their heart, There is no God. The clouds poured out water, but men pour not out cries and tears unto God. The skies send out a sound, but men say not, Where is God my Maker ? Thine arrows also went abroad, but no arrows of contrition and supplication are sent back by men in return. The voice of thy thunder was in the heaven, but men hear not the louder thunders of the law. The lightnings lightened the world, but the light of truth shines in darkness and the darkness comprehendeth it not. The earth trembled and shook, but human hearts remain unmoved.

> " My heart it shakes not at the wrath
> And terrors of a God."

—*George Rogers.*

Verses 16—19.—As soon as ever the whole Egyptian army was within it, the sea flowed to its own place, and came down with a torrent raised by storms of wind and encompassed the Egyptians. Showers of rain also came down from the sky, and dreadful thunders and lightning, with flashes of fire. Thunder-bolts also were darted upon them ; nor was there anything which used to be sent by God upon men, as indications of his wrath, which did not happen at this time ; for a dark and dismal night oppressed them. And thus did all these men perish, so that there was not one man left to be a messenger of this calamity to the rest of the Egyptians.— *Josephus.*

Verse 19.—*"Thy way is in the sea, and thy path in the great waters,"* etc. Until lately, not much was known of oceanic currents, nor of their influences on the condition of particular localities and the intercourse of man with man. They are now seen to be the *"way"* or *"path"* of the Creator *"in the great waters."* Numerous agencies tend to the production of these currents. Amongst them we may reckon the propagation of the tide wave in its progress over the globe, the duration and strength of certain winds, the variations in density which sea-water undergoes in different latitudes, and at different depths, by change of temperature, and the quantity of salt it contains, and by the hourly alterations of atmospheric pressure which take place within the tropics. The oceanic currents are nearly constant in breadth, crossing the sea in many directions. Long bands of seaweed carried by the currents shew at once their velocity, and the line of demarcation between the waters at rest and the waters in motion. Between the tropics there is a general movement of the sea from east to west, called the equatorial current, supposed to be due to the trade winds, and the progress of the tide wave. There are narrower currents carrying warm water to higher and cold water to lower latitudes.—*Edwin Sidney, in "Conversations on the Bible and Science."* 1866.

Verse 19.—*"Thy way is in the sea,"* where no man can wade, except God be before him, but where any man may walk if God take him by the hand and lead him through. —*David Dickson.*

Verse 19.—"*Thy footsteps are not known.*" He often goeth so much out of our sight, that we are unable to give an account of what he doeth, or what he is about to do. Frequently the pillar of divine providence is dark throughout, to Israelites as well as Egyptians; so that his own people understand not the riddles, till he is pleased to be his own interpreter, and to lead them into his secrets.—*Samuel Slater* (—1704), *in "The Morning Exercises."*

Verse 19.—"*Thy footsteps are not known.*" That is, they are not always known; or, they are not known in all things; yea, they are not altogether known in anything. —*Joseph Caryl.*

Verse 19.—"*Thy footsteps are not known.*" Upon some affair of great consequence, which had occurred in some providential dispensations, Luther was very importunate at the throne of grace to know the mind of God in it; and it seemed to him as if he heard God speak to his heart thus: " I am not to be traced." Referring to this incident, one adds, " If he is not to be traced, he may be trusted; " and that religion is of little value which will not enable a man to trust God where he can neither trace nor see him. But there is a time for everything beneath the sun, and the Almighty has his ' times and seasons.' It has been frequently with my hopes and desires, in regard to providence, as with my watch and the sun, which has often been ahead of true time; I have gone faster than providence, and have been forced to stand still and wait, or I have been set back painfully. That was a fine sentiment of Flavel, " Some providences, like Hebrew letters, must be read backwards."— *Quoted in " Christian Treasury,"* 1849. *Author not mentioned.*

Verse 19.—See also notes on verse 13.

Verse 20.—"*Thou leddest thy people like a flock,*" etc. From this verse the afflicted may learn many consolations. First, that the best people that be are no better able to resist temptation, than the simple sheep is able to withstand the brier that catcheth him. The next, that man is of no more ability to beware of temptations, than the poor sheep is to avoid the brier, being preserved only by the diligence of the shepherd. The third, that as the shepherd is careful of his entangled and briered sheep, so is God of his afflicted faithful. And the fourth is, that the people of Israel could take no harm of the water, because they entered the sea at God's commandment. Whereof we learn, that no danger can hurt when God doth command us to enter into it; and all dangers overcome us if we choose them ourselves, besides God's commandment; as Peter, when he went at God's commandment upon the water, took no hurt; but when he entered into the bishop's house upon his own presumption, was overcome and denied Christ. The Israelites, when they fought at God's commandment, the peril was nothing; but when they would do it of their own heads, they perished: so that we are bound to attend upon God's commandment, and then no danger shall destroy us, though it pain us. The other doctrine is in this, that God used the ministry of Moses and Aaron in the deliverance of his people, who did command them to do nothing but that the Lord did first bid. Whereof we learn that such as be ministers appointed of God, and do nothing but as God commandeth, are to be followed; as Paul saith, " Follow me, as I follow Christ."— *John Hooper.*

Verse 20.—"*Thou leddest thy people like a flock.*" Observe, the good shepherd leads his followers *like sheep:* First, with great solicitude and care, to protect them from wolves. Secondly, with consideration and kindness, for the sheep is a harmless animal. Thirdly, with a wise strictness, for sheep easily wander, and they are of all animals the most stupid.—*Thomas Le Blanc.*

Verse 20.—"*Leddest thy people.*" Our guiding must be mild and gentle, else it is not *duxisti,* but *traxisti;* drawing and driving, and no leading. *Leni spiritu non dura manu,* rather by an inward sweet influence to be led, than by an outward extreme violence to be forced forward. So did God lead his people here. Not the greatest pace, I wis, for they were a year marching that they might have posted in eleven days, as Moses saith. (Deut. i. 2.) No nor yet the nearest way neither, as Moses telleth us. (Ex. xiii. 18.) For he fetched a compass divers times, as all wise governors by his example must do, that desire rather safely to lead, than hastily to drive forward. " The Spirit of God leadeth this people," saith Isaiah (ch. lxiii. 14) " as an horse is ridden down the hill into a valley; " which must not be at a gallop, lest horse and ruler both come down one over another; but warily and easily.— *Lancelot Andrewes.*

Verse 20.—"*By the hand of Moses and Aaron.*" He says not, Moses and Aaron led the people of Israel; but, *Thou* leddest the people, and that *thy* people, by the hand of Moses and Aaron. Great was the power of these two men; nevertheless neither of them was the shepherd of the sheep, but each was a servant to the one and only true shepherd, to whom the sheep exclusively belonged. Nor yet was either the leader of the sheep, but the shepherd himself was present and led his own flock, to whom these two acted as servants. There are therefore three things to be learned from this passage. First, the sheep do not belong to the servants, but to the true shepherd. Secondly, the true shepherd is the leader of his own sheep. Thirdly, the office of Moses and Aaron was to attend to this duty, that the Lord's sheep should be properly led and pastured. So Christ himself leads the sheep, his own sheep, and for this work he employs the ministry of his servants.—*Musculus.*

Verse 20.—The Psalmist has reached the climax of his strain, he has found relief from his sorrow by forcing his thoughts into another channel, by dwelling on all God's mightiest wonders of old; but there he must end: in his present intensity of passion he cannot trust himself to draw forth in detail any mere *lessons* of comfort. There are seasons when even the holiest faith cannot bear to listen to words of reasoning; though it can still find a support whereon to rest, in the simple contemplation, in all their native grandeur, of the deeds that God hath wrought.—*Joseph Francis Thrupp.*

HINTS TO PREACHERS.

Verse 1.—The benefit of using the voice in private prayer.

Verses 1, 3, 5, 10.—Note the wise man's progress out of his soul trouble. I. I cried. II. I remembered. III. I considered. IV. I said.

Verse 2.—See "Spurgeon's Sermons," No. 853. "A Sermon for the Most Miserable of Men."

Verse 2.—I. Special prayer: "In the day," etc. II. Persevering prayer: hands lifted up to God by night as well as by day. III. Agonising prayer: "my soul refused to be comforted," until the answer came. "Being in an agony, he prayed," etc.—*G. R.*

Verse 2 (last clause).—When this is wise, and when it is censurable.

Verse 4.—I. A good man cannot rest on his bed until his soul rests on God. II. He cannot speak freely to others until God speaks peace to his soul.—*G. R.*

Verse 4.—Occupation for the sleepless, and consolation for the speechless.

Verses 5, 6.—There are four rules for obtaining comfort in affliction. I. The consideration of God's goodness to his people of old. II. Remembrance of our own past experience. III. Self-examination. IV. The diligent study of the word.—*G. R.*

Verse 6.—"*Remembrance.*" A good memory is very helpful and useful. 1. It is a great means of *knowledge*: for what signifies your reading or hearing, if you remember nothing? 2. It is a means of *faith*: 1 Cor. xv. 2. 3. It is a means of *comfort.* If a poor Christian in distress could remember God's promises they would inspire him with new life; but when they are forgotten, his spirits sink. 4. It is a means of *thankfulness.* 5. It is a means of *hope*; for "experience worketh hope" (Rom. v. 4), and the memory is the storehouse of experience. 6. It is a means of *repentance*; for, how can we repent or mourn for what we have forgotten? 7. It is a means of *usefulness.* When one spark of grace is truly kindled in the heart, it will quickly endeavour to heat others also.—*R. Steele.*

Verse 7 (first clause).—To place the question in a strong light, let us consider, I. Of whom is the question raised? "the Lord." II. What course of action is in question? "cast off for ever." III. Towards whom would the action be performed?

Verse 8.—These questions, I. Suppose a change in the immutable Jehovah in two glorious attributes. II. Are contrary to all past evidence. III. Can only arise from the flesh and Satan; and, therefore, IV. Are to be met in the power of the Spirit, with strong faith in the Eternal God.

Verse 10.—A confession applicable to many other matters. Such as, fear of death, fear of desertion, dread of public service, sensitiveness of neglect, etc.

Verse 10.—"*My infirmity.*" Different meanings of this word. These would furnish a good subject. Some infirmities are to be patiently endured, others gloried in, others taken in prayer to God for his Spirit's help, and others lamented and repented of.

Verses 10, 11, 12.—Remember, meditate, talk.

Verses 11, 12.—I. Consolation derived from the remembrance of the past. II. Consolation increased by meditation. III. Consolation strengthened by communication : " and talk," etc.—*G. R.*

Verse 12.—Themes for thought and topics for conversation. Creation, Providence, Redemption, etc.

Verses 13, 19.—"*In the sea,*" "*in the sanctuary.*" God's way incomprehensible, though undoubtedly right : in his holiness lies the answer to the enigmas.

Verse 14.—*Thaumaturgeis,* or the Great Wonder-worker.

Verse 15.—"*And Joseph.*" The honour of nourishing those who have been begotten of God by other men's labours.

Verse 15.—Redemption by power, the consequence, evidence, and necessary attendant of redemption by price.

Verse 15.—I. The redeemed : " thy people ; " " the sons of," etc. 1. In captivity though they are his people. 2. His people though they are in captivity. II. The redemption : from Egyptian bondage. III. The Redeemer : " Thou, with thine arm," etc. God by Christ, his arm : " Mine own arm brought," etc. ' To whom is the arm of the Lord revealed ? " etc.—*G. R.*

Verses 16—18.—I. The homage of nature to the God of grace. II. Its subserviency to his designs.—*G. R.*

Verse 19.—I. The ways of God to men are peculiar : " in the sea : " " thy path," etc. II. They are uniform, they lie in regular " footsteps." III. They are inscrutable : like the path of the ship upon the waters, not of the ploughshare on the land.

Verse 19.—God's way is in the sea. In things changeable, ungovernable, vast, unfathomable, terrible, overwhelming, the Lord has the ruling power.

Verse 20.—I. The subjects of divine guidance : " thy people." II. The manner of their guidance : " like a flock "—separated, united, dependent. III. The agents employed : " by the hand ; " the Great Shepherd leads by the hand of undershepherds. " May every under-shepherd keep his eye intent on Thee."—*G. R.*

Verse 20.—Church history. I. The church a flock. II. God seen as leading it on. III. Instrumentality always used.

PSALM LXXVIII.

TITLE.—*Maschil of Asaph. This is rightly entitled an instructive Psalm. It is not a mere recapitulation of important events in Israelitish history, but is intended to be viewed as a parable setting forth the conduct and experience of believers in all ages. It is a singular proof of the obtuseness of mind of many professors that they will object to sermons and expositions upon the historical parts of Scripture, as if they contained no instruction in spiritual matters : were such persons truly enlightened by the Spirit of God, they would perceive that all Scripture is profitable, and would blush at their own folly in undervaluing any portion of the inspired volume.*

DIVISION.—*The unity is well maintained throughout, but, for the sake of the reader's convenience, we may note that verses 1—8 may be viewed as a preface, setting forth the Psalmist's object in the epic which he is composing. From 9—41 the theme is Israel in the wilderness ; then intervenes an account of the Lord's preceding goodness towards his people in bringing them out of Egypt by plagues and wonders, 42—52. The history of the tribes is resumed at verse 53, and continued to verse 66, where we reach the time of the removal of the ark to Zion, and the transference of the leadership of Israel from Ephraim to Judah, which is rehearsed in song from verses 67—72.*

EXPOSITION.

GIVE ear, O my people, *to* my law : incline your ears to the words of my mouth.

2 I will open my mouth in a parable : I will utter dark sayings of old :

3 Which we have heard and known, and our fathers have told us.

4 We will not hide *them* from their children, shewing to the generation to come the praises of the LORD, and his strength, and his wonderful works that he hath done.

5 For he established a testimony in Jacob, and appointed a law in Israel, which he commanded our fathers, that they should make them known to their children :

6 That the generation to come might know *them, even* the children *which* should be born ; *who* should arise and declare *them* to their children :

7 That they might set their hope in God, and not forget the works of God, but keep his commandments :

8 And might not be as their fathers, a stubborn and rebellious generation ; a generation *that* set not their heart aright, and whose spirit was not stedfast with God.

1. "*Give ear, O my people, to my law.* The inspired bard calls on his countrymen to give heed to his patriotic teaching. We naturally expect God's chosen nation to be first in hearkening to his voice. When God gives his truth a tongue, and sends forth his messengers trained to declare his word with power, it is the least we can do to give them our ears and the earnest obedience of our hearts. Shall God speak, and his children refuse to hear ? His teaching has the force of law, let us yield both ear and heart to it. "*Incline your ears to the words of my mouth.*" Give earnest attention, bow your stiff necks, lean forward to catch every syllable. We are at this day, as readers of the sacred records, bound to study them deeply, exploring their meaning, and labouring to practise their teaching. As the officer of an army commences his drill by calling for " Attention," even so every trained soldier of Christ is called upon to give ear to his words. Men lend their ears to music, how much more then should they listen to the harmonies of the gospel ; they sit enthralled in the presence of an orator, how much rather should they yield to the eloquence of heaven.

2. "*I will open my mouth in a parable.* Analogies are not only to be imagined, but are intended by God to be traced between the story of Israel and the lives of believers. Israel was ordained to be a type ; the tribes and their marchings are living allegories traced by the hand of an all-wise providence. Unspiritual persons may sneer about fancies and mysticisms, but Paul spake well when he said " which things are an allegory," and Asaph in the present case spake to the point when he called his narrative " a parable." That such was his meaning is clear from the quotation, " All these things spake Jesus unto the multitude in parables ; and without a parable spake he not unto them : that it might be fulfilled which was spoken by the prophet, saying, I will open my mouth in parables ; I will utter things which have been kept secret from the foundation of the world."—Matthew xiii. 34, 35. "*I will utter dark sayings of old ;*"—enigmas of antiquity, riddles of yore. The mind of the poet-prophet was so full of ancient lore that he poured it forth in a copious stream of song, while beneath the gushing flood lay pearls and gems of spiritual truth, capable of enriching those who could dive into the depths and bring them up. The letter of this song is precious, but the inner sense is beyond all price. Whereas the first verse called for attention, the second justifies the demand by hinting that the outer sense conceals an inner and hidden meaning, which only the thoughtful will be able to perceive.

3. "*Which we have heard and known, and our fathers have told us.*" Tradition was of the utmost service to the people of God in the olden time, before the more sure word of prophecy had become complete and generally accessible. The receipt of truth from the lips of others laid the instructed believer under solemn obligation to pass on the truth to the next generation. Truth, endeared to us by its fond associations with godly parents and venerable friends, deserves of us our best exertions to preserve and propagate it. Our fathers told us, we heard them, and we know personally what they taught ; it remains for us in our turn to hand it on. Blessed be God we have now the less mutable testimony of written revelation, but this by no means lessens our obligation to instruct our children in divine truth by word of mouth : rather, with such a gracious help, we ought to teach them far more fully the things of God. Dr. Doddridge owed much to the Dutch tiles and his mother's explanations of the Bible narratives. The more of parental teaching the better ; ministers and Sabbath-school teachers were never meant to be substitutes for mothers' tears and fathers' prayers.

4. "*We will not hide them from their children.*" Our negligent silence shall not deprive our own and our father's offspring of the precious truth of God, it would be shameful indeed if we did so. "*Shewing to the generation to come the praises of the Lord.*" We will look forward to future generations, and endeavour to provide for their godly education. It is the duty of the church of God to maintain, in fullest vigour, every agency intended for the religious education of the young ; to them we must look for the church of the future, and as we sow towards them so shall we reap. Children are to be taught to magnify the Lord ; they ought to be well informed as to his wonderful doings in ages past, and should be made to know "*his strength, and his wonderful works that he hath done.*" The best education is education in the best things. The first lesson for a child should be concerning his mother's God. Teach him what you will, if he learn not the fear of the Lord, he will perish for lack of knowledge. Grammar is poor food for the soul if it be not flavoured with grace. Every satchel should have a Bible in it. The world may teach secular knowledge alone, 'tis all she has a heart to know, but the church must not deal so with her offspring ; she should look well to every Timothy, and see to it that from a child he knows the Holy Scriptures. Around the fire-side fathers should repeat not only the Bible records, but the deeds of the martyrs and reformers, and moreover the dealings of the Lord with themselves both in providence and grace. We dare not follow the vain and vicious traditions of the apostate church of Rome, neither would we compare the fallible record of the best human memories with the infallible written word, yet would we fain see oral tradition practised by every Christian in his family, and children taught cheerfully by word of mouth by their own mothers and fathers, as well as by the printed pages of what they too often regard as dull, dry task books. What happy hours and pleasant evenings have children had at their parents' knees as they have listened to some " sweet story of old." Reader, if you have children, mind you do not fail in this duty.

5. "*For he established a testimony in Jacob.*" The favoured nation existed for the very purpose of maintaining God's truth in the midst of surrounding idolatry.

Theirs were the oracles, they were the conservators and guardians of the truth. *"And appointed a law in Israel, which he commanded our fathers, that they should make them known to their children."* The testimony for the true God was to be transmitted from generation to generation by the careful instruction of succeeding families. We have the command for this oral transmission very frequently given in the Pentateuch, and it may suffice to quote one instance from Deut. vi. 7 : "And thou shalt teach them diligently unto thy children, and shalt talk of them when thou sittest in thine house, and when thou walkest by the way, and when thou liest down, and when thou risest up." Reader, if you are a parent, have you conscientiously discharged this duty ?

6. *"That the generation to come might know them, even the children which should be born."* As far on as our brief life allows us to arrange, we must industriously provide for the godly nurture of youth. The narratives, commands, and doctrines of the word of God are not worn out ; they are calculated to exert an influence as long as our race shall exist. *"Who should arise and declare them to their children."* The one object aimed at is transmission ; the testimony is only given that it may be passed on to succeeding generations.

7. *"That they might set their hope in God."* Faith cometh by hearing. Those who know the name of the Lord will set their hope in him, and that they may be led to do so is the main end of all spiritual teaching. *"And not forget the works of God."* Grace cures bad memories ; those who soon forget the merciful works of the Lord have need of teaching ; they require to learn the divine art of holy memory. *"But keep his commandments."* Those who forget God's works are sure to fail in their own. He who does not keep God's love in memory is not likely to remember his law. The design of teaching is practical : holiness towards God is the end we aim at, and not the filling of the head with speculative notions.

8. *"And might not be as their fathers, a stubborn and rebellious generation."* There was room for improvement. Fathers stubborn in their own way, and rebellious against God's way, are sorry examples for their children ; and it is earnestly desired that better instruction may bring forth a better race. It is common in some regions for men to count their family custom as the very best rule ; but disobedience is not to be excused because it is hereditary. The leprosy was none the less loathsome because it had been long in the family. If our fathers were rebellious we must be better than they were, or else we shall perish as they did. *"A generation that set not their heart aright."* They had no decision for righteousness and truth. In them there was no preparedness, or willingness of heart, to entertain the Saviour ; neither judgments, nor mercies could bind their affections to their God ; they were fickle as the winds, and changeful as the waves. *"And whose spirit was not stedfast with God."* The tribes in the wilderness were constant only in their inconstancy ; there was no depending upon them. It was, indeed, needful that their descendants should be warned, so that they might not blindly imitate them. How blessed would it be if each age improved upon its predecessor ; but, alas ! it is to be feared that decline is more general than progress, and too often the heirs of true saints are far more rebellious than even their fathers were in their unregeneracy. May the reading of this patriotic and divine song move many to labour after the elevation of themselves and their posterity.

9 The children of Ephraim, *being* armed, *and* carrying bows, turned back in the day of battle.

10 They kept not the covenant of God, and refused to walk in his law ;

11 And forgat his works, and his wonders that he had shewed them.

12 Marvellous things did he in the sight of their fathers, in the land of Egypt, *in* the field of Zoan.

13 He divided the sea, and caused them to pass through ; and he made the waters to stand as an heap.

14 In the daytime also he led them with a cloud, and all the night with a light of fire.

15 He clave the rocks in the wilderness, and gave *them* drink as *out of* the great depths.

16 He brought streams also out of the rock, and caused waters to run down like rivers.

17 And they sinned yet more against him by provoking the most High in the wilderness.

18 And they tempted God in their heart by asking meat for their lust.

19 Yea, they spake against God; they said, Can God furnish a table in the wilderness?

20 Behold, he smote the rock, that the waters gushed out, and the streams overflowed; can he give bread also? can he provide flesh for his people?

21 Therefore the LORD heard *this*, and was wroth: so a fire was kindled against Jacob, and anger also came up against Israel;

22 Because they believed not in God, and trusted not in his salvation:

23 Though he had commanded the clouds from above, and opened the doors of heaven,

24 And had rained down manna upon them to eat, and had given them of the corn of heaven.

25 Man did eat angels' food: he sent them meat to the full.

26 He caused an east wind to blow in the heaven; and by his power he brought in the south wind.

27 He rained flesh also upon them as dust, and feathered fowls like as the sand of the sea:

28 And he let *it* fall in the midst of their camp, round about their habitations.

29 So they did eat, and were well filled: for he gave them their own desire;

30 They were not estranged from their lust. But while their meat *was* yet in their mouths,

31 The wrath of God came upon them, and slew the fattest of them and smote down the chosen *men* of Israel.

32 For all this they sinned still, and believed not for his wondrous works.

33 Therefore their days did he consume in vanity, and their years in trouble.

34 When he slew them, then they sought him: and they returned and enquired early after God.

35 And they remembered that God *was* their rock, and the high God their redeemer.

36 Nevertheless they did flatter him with their mouth, and they lied unto him with their tongues.

37 For their heart was not right with him, neither were they stedfast in his covenant.

38 But he, *being* full of compassion, forgave *their* iniquity, and destroyed *them* not: yea, many a time turned he his anger away, and did not stir up all his wrath.

39 For he remembered that they *were but* flesh; a wind that passeth away, and cometh not again.

40 How oft did they provoke him in the wilderness, *and* grieve him in the desert!

41 Yea, they turned back and tempted God, and limited the Holy One of Israel.

9. *"The children of Ephraim, being armed, and carrying bows, turned back in the day of battle."* Well equipped and furnished with the best weapons of the times, the leading tribe failed in faith and courage and retreated before the foe. There were several particular instances of this, but probably the Psalmist refers to the general failure of Ephraim to lead the tribes to the conquest of Canaan. How often have

we also, though supplied with every gracious weapon, failed to wage successful war against our sins, we have marched onward gallantly enough till the testing hour has come, and then " in the day of battle " we have proved false to good resolutions and holy obligations. How altogether vain is unregenerate man ! Array him in the best that nature and grace can supply, he still remains a helpless coward in the holy war, so long as he lacks a loyal faith in his God.

10. *"They kept not the covenant of God."* Vows and promises were broken, idols were set up, and the living God was forsaken. They were brought out of Egypt in order to be a people separated unto the Lord, but they fell into the sins of other nations, and did not maintain a pure testimony for the one only true God. *"And refused to walk in his law."* They gave way to fornication, and idolatry, and other violations of the decalogue, and were often in a state of rebellion against the benign theocracy under which they lived. They had pledged themselves at Sinai to keep the law, and then they wilfully disobeyed it, and so became covenant-breakers.

11. *"And forgat his works, and his wonders that he had shewed them."* Had they remembered them they would have been filled with gratitude and inspired with holy awe : but the memory of God's mercies to them was as soon effaced as if written upon water. Scarcely could one generation retain the sense of the divine presence in miraculous power, the succeeding race needed a renewal of the extraordinary manifestations, and even then was not satisfied without many displays thereof. Ere we condemn them, let us repent of our own wicked forgetfulness, and confess the many occasions upon which we also have been unmindful of past favours.

12. Egypt, here called *the field of Zoan*, was the scene of marvellous things which were done in open day *in the sight of* Israel. These were extraordinary, upon a vast scale, astounding, indisputable, and such as ought to have rendered it impossible for an Israelite to be disloyal to Jehovah, Israel's God.

13. *"He divided the sea, and caused them to pass through."* A double wonder, for when the waters were divided the bottom of the sea would naturally be in a very unfit state for the passage of so vast a host as that of Israel ; it would in fact have been impassable, had not the Lord made the road for his people. Who else has ever led a nation through a sea ? Yet the Lord has done this full often for his saints in providential deliverances, making a highway for them where nothing short of an almighty arm could have done so. *"And he made the waters to stand as an heap."* He forbade a drop to fall upon his chosen, they felt no spray from the crystal walls on either hand. Fire will descend and water stand upright at the bidding of the Lord of all. The nature of creatures is not their own intrinsically, but is retained or altered at the will of him who first created them. The Lord can cause those evils which threaten to overwhelm us to suspend their ordinary action, and become innocuous to us.

14. *"In the daytime also he led them with a cloud."* He did it all. He alone. He brought them into the wilderness, and he led them through it ; it is not the Lord's manner to begin a work, and then cease from it while it is incomplete. The cloud both led and shadowed the tribes. It was by day a vast sun-screen, rendering the fierce heat of the sun and the glare of the desert sand bearable. *"And all the night with a light of fire."* So constant was the care of the Great Shepherd that all night and every night the token of his presence was with his people. That cloud which was a shade by day was as a sun by night. Even thus the grace which cools and calms our joys, soothes and solaces our sorrows. What a mercy to have a light of fire with us amid the lonely horrors of the wilderness of affliction. Our God has been all this to us, and shall we prove unfaithful to him ? We have felt him to be both shade and light, according as our changing circumstances have required.

> " He hath been our joy in woe,
> Cheer'd our heart when it was low,
> And, with warnings softly sad,
> Calm'd our heart when it was glad."

May this frequently renewed experience knit our hearts to him in firmest bonds.

15. *"He clave the rocks in the wilderness."* Moses was the instrument, but the Lord did it all. Twice he made the flint a gushing rill. What can he not do ? *"And gave them drink as out of the great depths,"*—as though it gushed from earth's innermost reservoirs. The streams were so fresh, so copious, so constant, that they seemed to well up from earth's primeval fountains, and to leap at once from " the deep which coucheth beneath." Here was a divine supply for Israel's urgent

need, and such an one as ought to have held them for ever in unwavering fidelity
to their wonder-working God.

16. The supply of water was as plenteous in quantity as it was miraculous in
origin. Torrents, not driblets came from the rocks. Streams followed the camp ;
the supply was not for an hour or a day. This was a marvel of goodness. If we
contemplate the aboundings of divine grace we shall be lost in admiration. Mighty
rivers of love have flowed for us in the wilderness. Alas, great God ! our return
has not been commensurate therewith, but far otherwise.

17. *"And they sinned yet more against him."* Outdoing former sins, going into
greater deeps of evil : the more they had the more loudly they clamoured for more,
and murmured because they had not every luxury that pampered appetites could
desire. It was bad enough to mistrust their God for necessaries, but to revolt
against him in a greedy rage for superfluities was far worse. Ever is it the nature
of the disease of sin to proceed from bad to worse : men never weary of sinning,
but rather increase their speed in the race of iniquity. In the case before us the
goodness of God was abused into a reason for greater sin. Had not the Lord been
so good they would not have been so bad. If he had wrought fewer miracles before,
they would not have been so inexcusable in their unbelief, so wanton in their idolatry.
"By provoking the most High in the wilderness." Although they were in a position
of obvious dependence upon God for everything, being in a desert where the soil
could yield them no support, yet they were graceless enough to provoke their benefactor. At one time they provoked his jealousy by their hankering after false gods,
anon they excited his wrath by their challenges of his power, their slanders against
his love, their rebellions against his will. He was all bounty of love, and they all
superfluity of naughtiness. They were favoured above all nations, and yet none
were more ill-favoured. For them the heavens dropped manna, and they returned
murmurs ; the rocks gave them rivers, and they replied with floods of wickedness.
Herein, as in a mirror, we see ourselves. Israel in the wilderness acted out, as in a
drama, all the story of man's conduct towards his God.

18. *"And they tempted God in their heart."* He was not tempted, for he cannot
be tempted by any, but they acted in a manner calculated to tempt him, and it is
always just to charge that upon men which is the obvious tendency of their conduct.
Christ cannot die again, and yet many crucify him afresh, because such would be
the legitimate result of their behaviour if its effects were not prevented by other
forces. The sinners in the wilderness would have had the Lord change his wise
proceedings to humour their whims, hence they are said to tempt him. *"By asking
meat for their lust."* Would they have God become purveyor for their greediness ?
Was there nothing for it but that he must give them whatever their diseased appetites
might crave ? The sin began in their hearts, but it soon reached their tongues.
What they at first silently wished for, they soon loudly demanded with menaces,
insinuations, and upbraidings.

19. From this verse we learn that unbelief of God is a slander against him.
" Yea, they spake against God." But how ? The answer is, *"They said, Can God
furnish a table in the wilderness ? "* To question the ability of one who is manifestly
Almighty, is to speak against him. These people were base enough to say that
although their God had given them bread and water, yet he could not properly
order or furnish a table. He could give them coarse food, but could not prepare a
feast properly arranged, so they were ungrateful enough to declare. As if the
manna was a mere make-shift, and the flowing rock-stream a temporary expedient,
they ask to have a regularly furnished table, such as they had been accustomed
to in Egypt. Alas, how have we also quarrelled with our mercies, and querulously
pined for some imaginary good, counting our actual enjoyments to be nothing
because they did not happen to be exactly conformed to our foolish fancies. They
who will not be content will speak against providence even when it daily loadeth
them with benefits.

20. *"Behold, he smote the rock, that the waters gushed out, and the streams overflowed."* They admit what he had done, and yet, with superabundant folly and
insolence, demand further proofs of his omnipotence. *"Can he give bread also ?
can he provide flesh for his people ? "* As if the manna were nothing, as if animal
food alone was true nourishment for men. If they had argued, " can he *not* give
flesh ? " the argument would have been reasonable, but they ran into insanity ;
when, having seen many marvels of omnipotence, they dared to insinuate that other
things were beyond the divine power. Yet, in this also, we have imitated their

senseless conduct. Each new difficulty has excited fresh incredulity. We are still fools and slow of heart to believe our God, and this is a fault to be bemoaned with deepest penitence. For this cause the Lord is often wroth with us and chastens us sorely ; for unbelief has in it a degree of provocation of the highest kind.

21. *"Therefore the Lord heard this, and was wroth."* He was not indifferent to what they said. He dwelt among them in the holy place, and, therefore, they insulted him to his face. He did not hear a report of it, but the language itself came into his ears. *"So a fire was kindled against Jacob."* The fire of his anger which was also attended with literal burnings. *"And anger also came up against Israel."* Whether he viewed them in the lower or higher light, as Jacob or as Israel, he was angry with them : even as mere men they ought to have believed him ; and, as chosen tribes, their wicked unbelief was without excuse. The Lord doeth well to be angry at so ungrateful, gratuitous and dastardly an insult as the questioning of his power.

22. *"Because they believed not in God, and trusted not in his salvation."* This is the master sin, the crying sin. Like Jeroboam, the son of Nebat, it sins and makes Israel to sin ; it is in itself evil and the parent of evils. It was this sin which shut Israel out of Canaan, and it shuts myriads out of heaven. God is ready to save, combining power with willingness, but rebellious man will not trust his Saviour, and therefore is condemned already. In the text it appears as if all Israel's other sins were as nothing compared with this ; this is the peculiar spot which the Lord points at, the special provocation which angered him. From this let every unbeliever learn to tremble more at his unbelief than at anything else. If he be no fornicator, or thief, or liar, let him reflect that it is quite enough to condemn him that he trusts not in God's salvation.

23. *"Though he had commanded the clouds from above."* Such a marvel ought to have rendered unbelief impossible : when clouds become granaries, seeing should be believing, and doubts should dissolve. *"And opened the doors of heaven."* The great storehouse doors were set wide open, and the corn of heaven poured out in heaps. Those who would not believe in such a case were hardened indeed ; and yet our own position is very similar, for the Lord has wrought for us great deliverances, quite as memorable and undeniable, and yet suspicions and forebodings haunt us. He might have shut the gates of hell upon us, instead of which he has opened the doors of heaven ; shall we not both believe in him and magnify him for this ?

24. *"And had rained down manna upon them to eat."* There was so much of it, the skies poured with food, the clouds burst with provender. It was fit food, proper not for looking at but for eating ; they could eat it as they gathered it. Mysterious though it was, so they that called it manna, or " what is it ? " yet it was eminently adapted for human nourishment ; and as it was both abundant and adapted, so also was it available ! They had not far to fetch it, it was nigh them, and they had only to gather it up. O Lord Jesus, thou blessed manna of heaven, how all this agrees with Thee ! We will even now feed on Thee as our spiritual meat, and will pray Thee to chase away all wicked unbelief from us. Our fathers ate manna and doubted ; we feed upon Thee and are filled with assurance. *"And had given them of the corn of heaven."* It was all a gift without money and without price. Food which dropped from above, and was of the best quality, so as to be called heavenly corn, was freely granted them. The manna was round, like coriander seed, and hence was rightly called corn ; it did not rise from the earth, but descended from the clouds, and hence the words of the verse are literally accurate. The point to be noted is that this wonder of wonders left the beholders, and the feasters, as prone as ever to mistrust their Lord.

25. *"Man did eat angels' food."* The delicacies of kings were outdone, for the dainties of angels were supplied. Bread of the mighty ones fell on feeble man. Those who are lower than the angels fared as well. It was not for the priests, or the princes, that the manna fell ; but for all the nation, for every man, woman and child in the camp : and there was sufficient for them all, for *"he sent them meat to the full."* God's banquets are never stinted ; he gives the best diet, and plenty of it. Gospel provisions deserve every praise that we can heap upon them ; they are free, full, and pre-eminent ; they are of God's preparing, sending, and bestowing. He is well fed whom God feeds ; heaven's meat is nourishing and plentiful. If we have ever fed upon Jesus we have tasted better than angels' food ; for

" Never did angels taste above
Redeeming grace and dying love."

It will be our wisdom to eat to the full of it, for God has so sent it that we are not straitened in him, but in our own bowels. Happy pilgrims who in the desert have their meat sent from the Lord's own palace above ; let them eat abundantly of the celestial banquet, and magnify the all-sufficient grace which supplies all their needs, according to His riches in glory, by Christ Jesus.

26. *"He caused an east wind to blow in the heaven."* He is Lord Paramount, above the prince of the power of the air : storms arise and tempests blow at his command. Winds sleep till God arouses them, and then, like Samuel, each one answers, " Here am I, for thou didst call me." *"And by his power he brought in the south wind."* Either these winds followed each other, and so blew the birds in the desired direction, or else they combined to form a south-east wind ; in either case they fulfilled the design of the Lord, and illustrated his supreme and universal power. If one wind will not serve, another shall ; and if need be, they shall both blow at once. We speak of *fickle* winds, but their obedience to their Lord is such that they deserve a better word. If we ourselves were half as obedient as the winds, we should be far superior to what we now are.

27. *"He rained flesh also upon them as dust."* First, he rained bread and then flesh, when he might have rained fire and brimstone. The words indicate the speed, and the abundance of the descending quails. *"And feathered fowls like as the sand of the sea ; "* there was no counting them. By a remarkable providence, if not by miracle, enormous numbers of migratory birds were caused to alight around the tents of the tribes. It was, however, a doubtful blessing, as easily acquired, and superabounding riches generally are. The Lord save us from meat which is seasoned with divine wrath.

28. *"And he let it fall in the midst of their camp."* They had no journey to make ; they had clamoured for flesh, and it almost flew into their mouths, *"round about their habitations."* This made them glad for the moment, but they knew not that mercies can be sent in anger, else had they trembled at sight of the good things which they had lusted after.

29. *"So they did eat, and were well filled."* They greedily devoured the birds, even to repletion. The Lord shewed them that he could " provide flesh for his people," even enough and to spare. He also shewed them that when lust wins its desire it is disappointed, and by the way of satiety arrives at distate. First the food satiates, then it nauseates. *"For he gave them their own desire."* They were filled with their own ways. The flesh-meat was unhealthy for them, but as they cried for it they had it, and a curse with it. O my God, deny me my most urgent prayers sooner than answer them in displeasure. Better hunger and thirst after righteousness than to be well filled with sin's dainties.

30, 31. *"They were not estranged from their lust."* Lust grows upon that which it feeds on. If sick of too much flesh, yet men grow not weary of lust, they change the object, and go on lusting still. When one sin is proved to be a bitterness, men do not desist, but pursue another iniquity. If, like Jehu, they turn from Baal, they fall to worshipping the calves of Bethel.

"But while their meat was yet in their mouths," before they could digest their coveted meat, it turned to their destruction. *"The wrath of God came upon them "* before they could swallow their first meal of flesh. Short was the pleasure, sudden was the doom. The festival ended in a funeral. *"And slew the fattest of them, and smote down the chosen men of Israel."* Perhaps these were the ringleaders in the lusting ; they are first in the punishment. God's justice has no respect of persons, the strong and the valiant fall as well as the weak and the mean. What they ate on earth they digested in hell, as many have done since. How soon they died, though they felt not the edge of the sword ! How terrible was the havoc, though not amid the din of battle ! My soul, see here the danger of gratified passions ; they are the janitors of hell. When the Lord's people hunger God loves them, Lazarus is his beloved, though he pines upon crumbs ; but when he fattens the wicked he abhors them; Dives is hated of heaven when he fares sumptuously every day. We must never dare to judge men's happiness by their tables, the heart is the place to look at. The poorest starveling believer is more to be envied than the most full-fleshed of the favourites of the world. Better be God's dog than the devil's darling.

32. *"For all this they sinned still."* Judgments moved them no more than mercies. They defied the wrath of God. Though death was in the cup of their iniquity, yet they would not put it away, but continued to quaff it as if it were a healthful

potion. How truly might these words be applied to ungodly men who have been often afflicted, laid upon a sick bed, broken in spirit, and impoverished in estate, and yet have persevered in their evil ways, unmoved by terrors, unswayed by threatenings. *"And believed not for his wondrous works."* Their unbelief was chronic and incurable. Miracles both of mercy and judgment were unavailing. They might be made to wonder, but they could not be taught to believe. Continuance in sin and in unbelief go together. Had they believed they would not have sinned, had they not have been blinded by sin they would have believed. There is a reflex action between faith and character. How can the lover of sin believe ? How, on the other hand, can the unbeliever cease from sin ? God's ways with us in providence are in themselves both convincing and converting, but unrenewed nature refuses to be either convinced or converted by them.

33. *"Therefore their days did he consume in vanity."* Apart from faith life is vanity. To wander up and down in the wilderness was a vain thing indeed, when unbelief had shut them out of the promised land. It was meet that those who would not live to answer the divine purpose by believing and obeying their God should be made to live to no purpose, and to die before their time, unsatisfied, unblest. Those who wasted their days in sin had little cause to wonder when the Lord cut short their lives, and sware that they should never enter the rest which they had despised. *"And their years in trouble."* Weary marches were their trouble, and to come to no resting place was their vanity. Innumerable graves were left all along the track of Israel, and if any ask, " Who slew all these ? " the answer must be, " They could not enter in because of unbelief." Doubtless much of the vexation and failure of many lives results from their being sapped by unbelief, and honeycombed by evil passions. None live so fruitlessly and so wretchedly as those who allow sense and sight to override faith, and their reason and appetite to domineer over their fear of God. Our days go fast enough according to the ordinary lapse of time, but the Lord can make them rust away at a bitterer rate, till we feel as if sorrow actually ate out the heart of our life, and like a canker devoured our existence. Such was the punishment of rebellious Israel, the Lord grant it may not be ours.

34. *"When he slew them, then they sought him."* Like whipped curs, they licked their Master's feet. They obeyed only so long as they felt the whip about their loins. Hard are the hearts which only death can move. While thousands died around them, the people of Israel became suddenly religious, and repaired to the tabernacle door, like sheep who run in a mass while the black dog drives them, but scatter and wander when the shepherd whistles him off. *"And they returned and enquired early after God."* They could not be too zealous, they were in hot haste to prove their loyalty to their divine King. " The devil was sick, and the devil a monk would be." Who would not be pious when the plague is abroad ? Doors, which were never so sanctified before, put on the white cross then. Even reprobates send for the minister when they lie a dying. Thus sinners pay involuntary homage to the power of right and the supremacy of God, but their hypocritical homage is of small value in the sight of the Great Judge.

35. *"And they remembered that God was their rock."* Sharp strokes awoke their sleepy memories. Reflection followed infliction. They were led to see that all their dependence must be placed upon their God ; for he alone had been their shelter, their foundation, their fountain of supply, and their unchangeable friend. What could have made them forget this ? Was it that their stomachs were so full of flesh that they had no space for ruminating upon spiritual things ? *"And the high God their redeemer."* They had forgotten this also. The high hand and outstretched arm which redeemed them out of bondage had both faded from their mental vision. Alas, poor man, how readily dost thou forget thy God ! Shame on thee, ungrateful worm, to have no sense of favours a few days after they had been received. Will nothing make thee keep in memory the mercy of thy God except the utter withdrawal of it ?

36. *"Nevertheless they did flatter him with their mouth."* Bad were they at their best. False on their knees, liars in their prayers. Mouth-worship must be very destestable to God when dissociated from the heart : other kings love flattery, but the King of kings abhors it. Since the sharpest afflictions only extort from carnal men a feigned submission to God, there is proof positive that the heart is desperately set on mischief, and that sin is ingrained in our very nature. If you beat a tiger with many stripes you cannot turn him into a sheep. The devil cannot be whipped out of human nature, though another devil, namely hypocrisy, may be whipped

into it. Piety produced by the damps of sorrow and the heats of terror is of mushroom growth ; it is rapid in its upspringing—" they enquired early after God "—but it is a mere unsubstantial fungus of unabiding excitement. *"And they lied unto him with their tongues."* Their godly speech was cant, their praise mere wind, their prayer a fraud. Their skin-deep repentance was a film too thin to conceal the deadly wound of sin. This teaches us to place small reliance upon professions of repentance made by dying men, or upon such even in others when the basis is evidently slavish fear, and nothing more. Any thief will whine out repentance if he thinks the judge will thereby be moved to let him go scot free.

37. *"For their heart was not right with him."* There was no depth in their repentance, it was not heart work. They were fickle as a weathercock, every wind turned them, their mind was not settled upon God. *"Neither were they stedfast in his covenant."* Their promises were no sooner made than broken, as if only made in mockery. Good resolutions called at their hearts as men do at inns ; they tarried awhile, and then took their leave. They were hot to-day for holiness, but cold towards it to-morrow. Variable as the hues of the dolphin, they changed from reverence to rebellion, from thankfulness to murmuring. One day they gave their gold to build a tabernacle for Jehovah, and the next they plucked off their ear-rings to make a golden calf. Surely the heart is a chameleon. Proteus had not so many changes. As in the ague we both burn and freeze so do inconstant natures in their religion.

38. *"But he, being full of compassion, forgave their iniquity, and destroyed them not."* Though they were full of flattery, he was full of mercy, and for this cause he had pity on them. Not because of their pitiful and hypocritical pretensions to penitence, but because of his own real compassion for them he overlooked their provocations. *"Yea, many a time turned he his anger away."* When he had grown angry with them he withdrew his displeasure. Even unto seventy times seven did he forgive their offences. He was slow, very slow, to anger. The sword was uplifted and flashed in mid-air, but it was sheathed again, and the nation yet lived. Though not mentioned in the text, we know from the history that a mediator interposed, the man Moses stood in the gap ; even so at this hour the Lord Jesus pleads for sinners, and averts the divine wrath. Many a barren tree is left standing because the dresser of the vineyard cries, " let it alone this year also." *"And did not stir up all his wrath."* Had he done so they must have perished in a moment. When his wrath is kindled but a little men are burned up as chaff ; but were he to let loose his indignation, the solid earth itself would melt, and hell would engulf every rebel. Who knoweth the power of thine anger, O Lord ? We see the fulness of God's compassion, but we never see all his wrath.

39. *" For he remembered that they were but flesh."* They were forgetful of God, but he was mindful of them. He knew that they were made of earthy, frail, corruptible material, and therefore he dealt leniently with them. Though in this he saw no excuse for their sin, yet he constrained it into a reason for mercy; the Lord is ever ready to discover some plea or other upon which he may have compassion. *"A wind that passeth away, and cometh not again."* Man is but a breath, gone never to return. Spirit and wind are in this alike, so far as our humanity is concerned ; they pass and cannot be recalled. What a nothing is our life. How gracious on the Lord's part to make man's insignificance an argument for staying his wrath.

40. *"How oft did they provoke him in the wilderness."* Times enough did they rebel : they were as constant in provocation as he was in his patience. In our own case, who can count his errors ? In what book could all our perverse rebellions be recorded ? The wilderness was a place of manifest dependence, where the tribes were helpless without divine supplies, yet they wounded the hand which fed them while it was in the act of feeding them. Is there no likeness between us and them ? Does it bring no tears into our eyes, while, as in a glass, we see our own selves. *"And grieve him in the desert."* Their provocations had an effect ; God was not insensible to them, he is said to have been grieved. His holiness could not find pleasure in their sin, his justice in their unjust treatment, or his truth in their falsehood. What must it be to grieve the Lord of love ! Yet we also have vexed the Holy Spirit, and he would long ago have withdrawn himself from us, were it not that he is God and not man. We are in the desert where we need our God, let us not make it a wilderness of sin by grieving him.

41. *"Yea, they turned back."* Their hearts sighed for Egypt and its fleshpots.

They turned to their old ways again and again, after they had been scourged out of them. Full of twists and turns, they never kept the straight path. *"And tempted God."* As far as in them lay they tempted him. His ways were good, and they in desiring to have them altered tempted God. Before they would believe in him they demanded signs, defying the Lord to do this and that, and acting as if he could be cajoled into being the minion of their lusts. What blasphemy was this! Yet let us not tempt Christ lest we also be destroyed by the destroyer. *"And limited the Holy One of Israel."* Doubted his power and so limited him, dictated to his wisdom and so did the same. To chalk out a path for God is arrogant impiety. The Holy One must do right, the covenant God of Israel must be true, it is profanity itself to say unto him thou shalt do this or that, or otherwise I will not worship thee. Not thus is the Eternal God to be led by a string by his impotent creature. He is the Lord and he will do as seemeth him good.

42 They remembered not his hand, *nor* the day when he delivered them from the enemy.

43 How he had wrought his signs in Egypt, and his wonders in the field of Zoan:

44 And had turned their rivers into blood; and their floods, that they could not drink.

45 He sent divers sorts of flies among them, which devoured them; and frogs, which destroyed them.

46 He gave also their increase unto the caterpiller, and their labour unto the locust.

47 He destroyed their vines with hail, and their sycomore trees with frost.

48 He gave up their cattle also to the hail, and their flocks to hot thunderbolts.

49 He cast upon them the fierceness of his anger, wrath, and indignation, and trouble, by sending evil angels *among them.*

50 He made a way to his anger; he spared not their soul from death, but gave their life over to the pestilence;

51 And smote all the firstborn in Egypt; the chief of *their* strength in the tabernacles of Ham:

52 But made his own people to go forth like sheep, and guided them in the wilderness like a flock.

53 And he led them on safely, so that they feared not: but the sea overwhelmed their enemies.

42. *"They remembered not his hand."* Yet it must have been difficult to forget it. Such displays of divine power as those which smote Egypt with astonishment, it must have needed some more than usual effort to blot from the tablets of memory. It is probably meant that they practically, rather than actually, forgot. He who forgets the natural returns of gratitude, may justly be charged with not remembering the obligation. *"Nor the day when he delivered them from the enemy."* The day itself was erased from their calendar, so far as any due result from it or return for it. Strange is the faculty of memory in its oblivions as well as its records. Sin perverts man's powers, makes them forceful only in wrong directions, and practically dead for righteous ends.

43. *"How he had wrought his signs in Egypt."* The plagues were ensigns of Jehovah's presence and proofs of his hatred of idols; these instructive acts of power were wrought in the open view of all, as signals are set up to be observed by those far and near. *"And his wonders in the field of Zoan."* In the whole land were miracles wrought, not in cities alone, but in the broad territory, in the most select and ancient regions of the proud nation. This the Israelites ought not to have forgotten, for they were the favoured people for whom these memorable deeds were wrought.

44. *"And had turned their rivers into blood."* The waters had been made the

means of the destruction of Israel's newborn infants, and now they do as it were betray the crime—they blush for it, they avenge it on the murderers. The Nile was the vitality of Egypt, its true life-blood, but at God's command it became a flowing curse ; every drop of it was a horror, poison to drink, and terror to gaze on. Sometimes he has allowed men, who were his rod, to make rivers crimson with gore, and this is a severe judgment ; but the event now before us was more mysterious, more general, more complete, and must, therefore, have been a plague of the first magnitude. *"And their floods, that they could not drink."* Lesser streams partook in the curse, reservoirs and canals felt the evil ; God does nothing by halves. All Egypt boasted of the sweet waters of their river, but they were made to loathe it more than they had ever loved it. Our mercies may soon become our miseries if the Lord shall deal with us in wrath.

45. *"He sent divers sorts of flies among them, which devoured them."* Small creatures become great tormentors. When they swarm they can sting a man till they threaten to eat him up. In this case, various orders of insects fought under the same banner ; lice and beetles, gnats and hornets, wasps and gadflies dashed forward in fierce battalions, and worried the sinners of Egypt without mercy. The tiniest plagues are the greatest. What sword or spear could fight with these innumerable bands ? Vain were the monarch's armour and robes of majesty, the little cannibals were no more lenient towards royal flesh than any other ; it had the same blood in it, and the same sin upon it. How great is that God who thus by the minute can crush the magnificent. *"And frogs, which destroyed them."* These creatures swarmed everywhere when they were alive, until the people felt ready to die at the sight ; and when the reptiles died, the heaps of their bodies made the land to stink so foully, that a pestilence was imminent. Thus not only did earth and air send forth armies of horrible life, but the water also added its legions of loathsomeness. It seemed as if the Nile was first made nauseous and then caused to leave its bed altogether, crawling and leaping in the form of frogs. Those who contend with the Almighty, little know what arrows are in his quiver ; surprising sin shall be visited with surprising punishment.

46. *"He gave also their increase unto the caterpiller, and their labour unto the locust."* Different sorts of devourers ate up every green herb and tree. What one would not eat another did. What they expected from the natural fertility of the soil, and what they looked for from their own toil, they saw devoured before their eyes by an insatiable multitude against whose depredations no defence could be found. Observe in the text that the Lord did it all—" he sent," " he gave," " he destroyed," " he gave up," etc. ; whatever the second agent may be, the direct hand of the Lord is in every national visitation.

47. *"He destroyed their vines with hail."* No more shall thy butler press the clusters into thy cup, O Pharaoh ! The young fruitbearing shoots were broken off, the vintage failed. *"And their sycomore trees with frost."* Frost was not usual, but Jehovah regards no laws of nature when men regard not his moral laws. The sycomore fig was perhaps more the fruit of the many than was the vine, therefore this judgment was meant to smite the poor, while the former fell most heavily upon the rich. Mark how the heavens obey their Lord and yield their stores of hail, and note how the fickle weather is equally subservient to the divine will.

48. *"He gave up their cattle also to the hail."* What hail it must have been to have force enough to batter down bullocks and other great beasts. God usually protects animals from such destruction, but here he withdrew his safeguards and gave them up : may the Lord never give *us* up. Some read, " shut up," and the idea of being abandoned to destructive influences is then before us in another shape. *"And their flocks to hot thunderbolts."* Fire was mingled with the hail, the fire ran along upon the ground, it smote the smaller cattle. What a storm must that have been : its effects were terrible enough upon plants, but to see the poor dumb creatures stricken must have been heart breaking. Adamantine was the heart which quailed not under such plagues as these, harder than adamant those hearts which in after years forgot all that the Lord had done, and broke off from their allegiance to him.

49. *"He cast upon them the fierceness of his anger, wrath, and indignation, and trouble."* His last arrow was the sharpest. He reserved the strong wine of his indignation to the last. Note how the Psalmist piles up the words, and well he might ; for blow followed blow, each one more staggering than its predecessor, and then the crushing stroke was reserved for the end. *"By sending evil angels among them."* Messengers of evil entered their houses at midnight, and smote the

dearest objects of their love. The angels were evil to them, though good enough in themselves ; those who to the heirs of salvation are ministers of grace, are to the heirs of wrath executioners of judgment. When God sends angels, they are sure to come, and if he bids them slay they will not spare. See how sin sets all the powers of heaven in array against man ; he has no friend left in the universe when God is his enemy.

50. *"He made a way to his anger,"* coming to the point with them by slow degrees ; assailing their outworks first by destroying their property, and then coming in upon their persons as through an open breach in the walls. He broke down all the comforts of their life, and then advanced against their life itself. Nothing could stand in his way ; he cleared a space in which to do execution upon his adversaries. *"He spared not their soul from death, but gave their life over to the pestilence."* In their soul was the origin of the sin, and he followed it to its source and smote it there. A fierce disease filled the land with countless funerals ; Jehovah dealt out myriads of blows, and multitudes of spirits failed before him.

51. *"And smote all the firstborn in Egypt."* No exceptions were made, the monarch bewailed his heir as did the menial at the mill. They smote the Lord's firstborn, even Israel, and he smites theirs. *"The chief of their strength in the taber-nacles of Ham."* Swinging his scythe over the field, death topped off the highest flowers. The tents of Ham knew each one its own peculiar sorrow, and were made to sympathise with the sorrows which had been ruthlessly inflicted upon the habitations of Israel. Thus curses come home to roost. Oppressors are repaid in their own coin, without the discount of a penny

52. *"But made his own people to go forth like sheep."* The contrast is striking, and ought never to have been forgotten by the people. The wolves were slain in heaps, the sheep were carefully gathered, and triumphantly delivered. The tables were turned, and the poor serfs became the honoured people, while their oppressors were humbled before them. Israel went out in a compact body like a flock ; they were defenceless in themselves as sheep, but they were safe under their Great Shepherd ; they left Egypt as easily as a flock leaves one pasture for another. *"And guided them in the wilderness like a flock."* Knowing nothing of the way by their own understanding or experience, they were, nevertheless, rightly directed, for the All-wise God knew every spot of the wilderness. To the sea, through the sea, and from the sea, the Lord led his chosen ; while their former taskmasters were too cowed in spirit, and broken in power, to dare to molest them.

53. *"And he led them on safely, so that they feared not."* After the first little alarm, natural enough when they found themselves pursued by their old task-masters, they plucked up courage and ventured boldly into the sea, and afterwards into the desert where no man dwelt. *"But the sea overwhelmed their enemies."* They were gone, gone for ever, never to disturb the fugitives again. That tremendous blow effectually defended the tribes for forty years from any further attempt to drive them back. Egypt found the stone too heavy and was glad to let it alone. Let the Lord be praised who thus effectually freed his elect nation.

What a grand narrative have we been considering. Well might the mightiest master of sacred song select " Israel in Egypt " as a choice theme for his genius ; and well may every believing mind linger over every item of the amazing transaction. The marvel is that the favoured nation should live as if unmindful of it all, and yet such is human nature. Alas, poor man ! Rather, alas, base heart !

We now, after a pause, follow again the chain of events, the narration of which had been interrupted by a retrospect, and we find Israel entering into the promised land, there to repeat her follies and enlarge her crimes.

54 And he brought them to the border of his sanctuary, *even to* this mountain, *which* his right hand had purchased.

55 He cast out the heathen also before them, and divided them an inheritance by line, and made the tribes of Israel to dwell in their tents.

56 Yet they tempted and provoked the most high God, and kept not his testimonies :

57 But turned back, and dealt unfaithfully like their fathers : they were turned aside like a deceitful bow.

58 For they provoked him to anger with their high places, and moved him to jealousy with their graven images.

59 When God heard *this*, he was wroth, and greatly abhorred Israel:

60 So that he forsook the tabernacle of Shiloh, the tent *which* he placed among men;

61 And delivered his strength into captivity, and his glory into the enemy's hand.

62 He gave his people over also unto the sword; and was wroth with his inheritance.

63 The fire consumed their young men; and their maidens were not given to marriage.

64 Their priests fell by the sword; and their widows made no lamentation.

65 Then the Lord awaked as one out of sleep, *and* like a mighty man that shouteth by reason of wine.

66 And he smote his enemies in the hinder parts: he put them to a perpetual reproach.

54. "*And he brought them to the border of his sanctuary.*" He conducted them to the frontier of the Holy Land, where he intended the tabernacle to become the permanent symbol of his abode among his people. He did not leave them halfway upon their journey to their heritage; his power and wisdom preserved the nation till the palm trees of Jericho were within sight on the other side of the river. "*Even to this mountain, which his right hand had purchased.*" Nor did he leave them then, but still conducted them till they were in the region round about Zion, which was to be the central seat of his worship. This the Lord had purchased in type of old by the sacrifice of Isaac, fit symbol of the greater sacrifice which was in due season to be presented there: that mountain was also redeemed by power, when the Lord's right hand enabled his valiant men to smite the Jebusites, and take the sacred hill from the insulting Canaanite. Thus shall the elect of God enjoy the sure protection of the Lord of hosts, even to the border land of death, and through the river, up to the hill of the Lord in glory. The purchased people shall safely reach the purchased inheritance.

55. "*He cast out the heathen also before them,*" or "he drove out the nations." Not only were armies routed, but whole peoples displaced. The iniquity of the Canaanites was full; their vices made them rot above ground; therefore, the land ate up its inhabitants, the hornets vexed them, the pestilence destroyed them, and the sword of the tribes completed the execution to which the justice of long provoked heaven had at length appointed them. The Lord was the true conqueror of Canaan; he cast out the nations as men cast out filth from their habitations, he uprooted them as noxious weeds are extirpated by the husbandman. "*And divided them an inheritance by line.*" He divided the land of the nations among the tribes by lot and measure, assigning Hivite, Perizzite, and Jebusite territory to Simeon, Judah, or Ephraim, as the case might be. Among those condemned nations were not only giants in stature, but also giants in crime; those monsters of iniquity had too long defiled the earth; it was time that they should no more indulge the unnatural crimes for which they were infamous; they were, therefore, doomed to forfeit life and lands by the hands of the tribes of Israel. The distribution of the forfeited country was made by divine appointment; it was no scramble, but a judicial appointment of lands which had fallen to the crown by the attainder of the former holders. "*And made the tribes of Israel to dwell in their tents.*" The favoured people entered upon a furnished house: they found the larder supplied, for they fed upon the old corn of the land, and the dwellings were already builded in which they could dwell. Thus does another race often enter into the lot of a former people, and it is sad indeed when the change which judgment decrees does not turn out to be much for the better, because the incomers inherit the evils as well as the goods of the ejected. Such a case of judicial visitation ought to have had a salutary influence upon the tribes; but, alas, they were incorrigible, and would not learn even from examples so near at home and so terribly suggestive.

56. "*Yet they tempted and provoked the most high God.*" Change of condition had not altered their manners. They left their nomadic habits, but not their

tendencies to wander from their God. Though every divine promise had been fulfilled to the letter, and the land flowing with milk and honey was actually their own, yet they tried the Lord again with unbelief, and provoked him with other sins. He is not only high and glorious, but most High, yea *the* most High, the only being who deserves to be so highly had in honour; yet, instead of honouring him, Israel grieved him with rebellion. *"And kept not his testimonies."* They were true to nothing but hereditary treachery; steadfast in nothing but in falsehood. They knew his truth and forgot it, his will and disobeyed it, his grace and perverted it to an occasion for greater transgression. Reader, dost thou need a looking-glass? See here is one which suits the present expositor well; does it not also reflect thine image?

57. *"But turned back."* Turned over the old leaf, repeated the same offences, started aside like an ill-made bow, were false and faithless to their best promises. *"And dealt unfaithfully like their fathers,"* proving themselves legitimate by manifesting the treachery of their sires. They were a new generation, but not a new nation—another race yet not another. Evil propensities are transmitted; the birth follows the progenitor; the wild ass breeds wild asses; the children of the raven fly to the carrion. Human nature does not improve, the new editions contain all the errata of the first, and sometimes fresh errors are imported. *"They were turned aside like a deceitful bow,"* which not only fails to send the arrow towards the mark in a direct line, but springs back to the archer's hurt, and perhaps sends the shaft among his friends to their serious jeopardy. Israel boasted of the bow as the national weapon, they sang the song of the bow, and hence a deceitful bow is made to be the type and symbol of their own unsteadfastness; God can make men's glory the very ensign of their shame, he draws a bar sinister across the escutcheon of traitors.

58. *"For they provoked him to anger with their high places."* This was their first error—will worship, or the worship of God, otherwise than according to his command. Many think lightly of this, but indeed it is no mean sin; and its tendencies to further offence are very powerful. The Lord would have his holy place remain as the only spot for sacrifice; and Israel, in wilful rebellion, (no doubt glossed over by the plea of great devotion,) determined to have many altars upon many hills. If they might have but one God, they insisted upon it that they would not be restricted to one sacred place of sacrifice. How much of the worship of the present day is neither more nor less than sheer will-worship! Nobody dare plead a divine appointment for a tithe of the offices, festivals, ceremonies, and observances of certain churches. Doubtless God, so far from being honoured by worship which he has not commanded, is greatly angered at it. *"And moved him to jealousy with their graven images."* This was but one more step; they manufactured symbols of the invisible God, for they lusted after something tangible and visible to which they could shew reverence. This also is the crying sin of modern times. Do we not hear and see superstition abounding. Images, pictures, crucifixes, and a host of visible things are had in religious honour, and worst of all men now-a-days worship what they eat, and call that a God which passes into their belly, and thence into baser places still. Surely the Lord is very patient, or he would visit the earth for this worst and basest of idolatry. He is a jealous God, and abhors to see himself dishonoured by any form of representation which can come from man's hands.

59. *"When God heard this, he was wroth."* The mere report of it filled him with indignation; he could not bear it, he was incensed to the uttermost, and most justly so. *"And greatly abhorred Israel."* He cast his idolatrous people from his favour, and left them to themselves, and their own devices. How could he have fellowship with idols? What concord hath Christ with Belial? Sin is in itself so offensive that it makes the sinner offensive too. Idols of any sort are highly abhorrent to God, and we must see to it that we keep ourselves from them through divine grace, for rest assured idolatry is not consistent with true grace in the heart. If Dagon sit aloft in any soul, the ark of God is not there. Where the Lord dwells no image of jealousy will be tolerated. A visible church will soon become a visible curse if idols be set up in it, and then the pruning knife will remove it as a dead branch from the vine.

Note that God did not utterly cast away his people Israel even when he greatly abhorred them, for he returned in mercy to them, so the subsequent verses tell us: so now the seed of Abraham, though for awhile under a heavy cloud, will be gathered yet again, for the covenant of salt shall not be broken. As for the spiritual seed, the Lord hath not despised nor abhorred them ; they are his peculiar treasure and lie for ever near his heart.

60. *So that he forsook the tabernacle of Shiloh, the tent which he placed among men."* His glory would no more reveal itself there, he left Shiloh to become a complete ruin. At the door of that tent shameless sin had been perpetrated, and all around it idols had been adored, and therefore the glory departed, and Ichabod was sounded as a word of dread concerning Shiloh and the tribe of Ephraim. Thus may the candlestick be removed though the candle is not quenched. Erring churches become apostate, but a true church still remains ; if Shiloh be profaned Zion is consecrated. Yet is it ever a solemn caution to all the assemblies of the saints, admonishing them to walk humbly with their God, when we read such words as those of the prophet Jeremiah in his seventh chapter, " Trust ye not in lying words, saying, The temple of the Lord, The temple of the Lord, The temple of the Lord, are these. Go ye now unto my place which was in Shiloh, where I set my name at the first, and see what I did to it for the wickedness of my people Israel." Let us take heed, lest as the ark never returned to Shiloh after its capture by the Philistines, so the gospel may be taken from us in judgment, never to be restored to the same church again.

61. *"And delivered his strength into captivity."* The ark was captured by the Philistines in battle, only because the Lord for the punishment of Israel chose to deliver it into their hands, otherwise they could have had no power at all against it. The token of the divine presence is here poetically called " his strength ; " and, indeed, the presence of the Lord is his strength among his people. It was a black day when the mercy-seat was removed, when the cherubim took flight, and Israel's palladium was carried away. *"And his glory into the enemy's hand."* The ark was the place for the revealed glory of God, and his enemies exulted greatly when they bore it away into their own cities. Nothing could more clearly have shewn the divine displeasure. It seemed to say that Jehovah would sooner dwell among his avowed adversaries than among so false a people as Israel ; he would sooner bear the insults of Philistia than the treacheries of Ephraim. This was a fearful downfall for the favoured nation, and it was followed by dire judgments of most appalling nature. When God is gone all is gone. No calamity can equal the withdrawal of the divine presence from a people. O Israel, how art thou brought low ! Who shall help thee now that thy God has left thee !

62. *"He gave his people over also unto the sword."* They fell in battle because they were no longer aided by the divine strength. Sharp was the sword, but sharper still the cause of its being unsheathed. *"And was wroth with his inheritance."* They were *his* still, and twice in this verse they are called so ; yet his regard for them did not prevent his chastising them, even with a rod of steel. Where the love is most fervent, the jealousy is most cruel. Sin cannot be tolerated in those who are a people near unto God.

63. *"The fire consumed their young men."* As fire slew Nadab and Abihu literally, so the fire of divine wrath fell on the sons of Eli, who defiled the sanctuary of the Lord, and the like fire, in the form of war, consumed the flower of the people. *"And their maidens were not given to marriage."* No nuptial hymns were sung, the bride lacked her bridegroom, the edge of the sword had cut the bands of their espousals, and left unmarried those who else had been extolled in hymns of congratulation. Thus Israel was brought very low, she could not find husbands for her maids, and therefore her state was not replenished ; no young children clustered around parental knees. The nation had failed in its solemn task of instructing the young in the fear of Jehovah, and it was a fitting judgment that the very production of a posterity should be endangered.

64. *"Their priests fell by the sword."* Hophni and Phineas were slain ; they were among the chief in sin, and, therefore, they perished with the rest. Priesthood is no shelter for transgressors ; the jewelled breastplate cannot turn aside the arrows of judgment. *"And their widows made no lamentation."* Their private griefs were swallowed up in the greater national agony, because the ark of God was taken. As the maidens had no heart for the marriage song, so the widows had no spirit, even to utter the funeral wail. The dead were buried too often and too hurriedly to allow of the usual rites of lamentation. This was the lowest depth ; from this point things will take a gracious turn.

65. *"The Lord awaked as one out of sleep."* Justly inactive he had suffered the enemy to triumph, his ark to be captured, and his people to be slain ; but now he arouses himself, his heart is full of pity for his chosen, and anger against the insulting

foe. Woe to thee, O Philistia, now shalt thou feel the weight of his right hand !
Waking and putting forth strength like a man who had taken a refreshing draught
the Lord is said to be, "*like a mighty man that shouteth by reason of wine.*" Strong and
full of energy the Lord dashed upon his foes, and made them stagger beneath his
blows. His ark from city to city went as an avenger rather than as a trophy, and
in every place the false gods fell helplessly before it.

66. "*He smote his enemies in the hinder parts.*" The emerods rendered them
ridiculous, and their numerous defeats made them yet more so. They fled but
were overtaken and wounded in the back to their eternal disgrace. "*He put them
to a perpetual reproach.*" Orientals are not very refined, and we can well believe
that the hemorrhoids were the subject of many a taunt against the Philistines, as
also were their frequent defeats by Israel until at last they were crushed under,
never to exist again as a distinct nation.

67 Moreover he refused the tabernacle of Joseph, and chose not the tribe
of Ephraim :

68 But chose the tribe of Judah, the mount Zion which he loved.

69 And he built his sanctuary like high *palaces*, like the earth which he
hath established for ever.

70 He chose David also his servant, and took him from the sheepfolds :

71 From following the ewes great with young he brought him to feed
Jacob his people, and Israel his inheritance.

72 So he fed them according to the integrity of his heart ; and guided
them by the skilfulness of his hands.

67. "*Moreover he refused the tabernacle of Joseph.*" God had honoured Ephraim,
for to that tribe belonged Joshua the great conqueror, and Gideon the great judge,
and within its borders was Shiloh the place of the ark and the sanctuary ; but now
the Lord would change all this and set up other rulers. He would no longer leave
matters to the leadership of Ephraim, since that tribe had been tried and found
wanting. "*And chose not the tribe of Ephraim.*" Sin had been found in them, folly
and instability, and therefore they were set aside as unfit to lead.

68. "*But chose the tribe of Judah.*" To give the nation another trial this tribe
was elected to supremacy. This was according to Jacob's dying prophecy. Our
Lord sprang out of Judah and he it is whom his brethren shall praise. "*The Mount
Zion which he loved.*" The tabernacle and ark were removed to Zion during the
reign of David ; no honour was left to the wayward Ephraimites. Hard by this
mountain the Father of the Faithful had offered up his only son, and there in future
days the great gatherings of his chosen seed would be, and therefore Zion is said
to be lovely unto God.

69. "*And he built his sanctuary like high palaces.*" The tabernacle was placed
on high, literally and spiritually it was as a mountain of beauty. True religion was
exalted in the land. For sanctity it was a temple, for majesty it was a palace.
"*Like the earth which he hath established for ever.*" Stability as well as stateliness
were seen in the temple, and so also in the church of God. The prophet saw both
in vision.

70. "*He chose David also his servant.*" It was an election of a sovereignly gracious
kind, and it operated practically by making the chosen man a willing servant of the
Lord. He was not chosen because he was a servant, but in order that he might be so.
David always esteemed it to be a high honour that he was both elect of God, and a
servant of God. "*And took him from the sheepfolds.*" A shepherd of sheep he had
been, and this was a fit school for a shepherd of men. Lowliness of occupation will
debar no man from such honours as the Lord's election confers, the Lord seeth not
as man seeth. He delights to bless those who are of low estate.

71. "*From following the ewes great with young he brought him to feed Jacob his
people, and Israel his inheritance.*" Exercising the care and art of those who watch
for the young lambs, David followed the ewes in their wanderings ; the tenderness
and patience thus acquired would tend to the development of characteristics most
becoming in a king. To the man thus prepared, the office and dignity which God
had appointed for him, came in due season, and he was enabled worthily to wear
them. It is wonderful how often divine wisdom so arranges the early and obscure

portion of a choice life, so as to make it a preparatory school for a more active and noble future.

72. *"So he fed them according to the integrity of his heart."* David was upright before God, and never swerved in heart from the obedient worship of Jehovah. Whatever faults he had, he was unfeignedly sincere in his allegiance to Israel's superior king; he shepherded for God with honest heart. *"And guided them by the skilfulness of his hands."* He was a sagacious ruler, and the Psalmist magnifies the Lord for having appointed him. Under David, the Jewish kingdom first rose to an honourable position among the nations, and exercised an influence over its neighbours. In closing the Psalm which has described the varying conditions of the chosen nation, we are glad to end so peacefully; with all noise of tumult or of sinful rites hushed into silence. After a long voyage over a stormy sea, the ark of the Jewish state rested on its Ararat, beneath a wise and gentle reign, to be wafted no more hither and thither by floods and gales. The Psalmist had all along intended to make this his last stanza, and we too may be content to finish all our songs of love with the reign of the Lord's anointed. Only we may eagerly enquire, when will it come? When shall we end these desert roamings, these rebellions, and chastisings, and enter into the rest of a settled kingdom, with the Lord Jesus reigning as "the Prince of the house of David?"

Thus have we ended this lengthy parable, may we in our life-parable have less of sin, and as much of grace as are displayed in Israel's history, and may we close it under the safe guidance of "that great Shepherd of the sheep." AMEN.

EXPLANATORY NOTES AND QUAINT SAYINGS.

Whole Psalm.—This Psalm appears to have been occasioned by the removal of the sanctuary from Shiloh in the tribe of Judah, and the co-incident transfer of pre-eminence in Israel from the former to the latter tribe, as clearly evinced by David's settlement as the head of the church and nation. Though this was the execution of God's purpose, the writer here shows that it also proceeded from the divine judgment on Ephraim, under whose leadership the people had manifested the same sinful and rebellious character which had distinguished their ancestors in Egypt.—*B. M. Smith, in "The Critical and Explanatory Pocket Bible."* 1867.

Verse 1.—*"Give ear, O my people, to my law: incline your ears."* Inclining the ears does not denote any ordinary sort of hearing, but such as a disciple renders to the words of his master, with submission and reverence of mind, silent and earnest, that whatever is enunciated for the purpose of instruction may be heard and properly understood, and nothing be allowed to escape. He is a hearer of a different stamp, who hears carelessly, not for the purpose of learning or imitation, but to criticise, to make merry, to indulge animosity, or to kill time.—*Musculus.*

Verse 1.—*"Incline your ears."* Lay them close to my lips, that no parcel of this sacred language fall to the ground by your default.—*John Trapp.*

Verse 1.—*"To the words of my mouth."* Was it not sufficient for the parallelism to say, *To my words?* Obviously. Why then is there any notice taken of the *mouth?* Because those who can prescribe laws to their subjects are also those who scorn to address them with their mouth. Such is the custom of kings, princes, pontiffs, both Roman and others. For the higher every one rises in dignity, the less he considers it becoming to him to speak to the people, to teach and instruct them by word of mouth. They think they owe nothing to the people, but are altogether taken up with this, that they may be looked up to as princes, and so retain a certain secular majesty of command. But, with one's own mouth to teach the ignorant, is a singular proof of love and paternal affection, such as becomes the preceptor, pastor and teacher. This Christ most constantly employed, because he was touched with paternal affection towards the lost sheep, and came as a shepherd to seek them. The manner of earthly princes he therefore rejected, and clothed himself with that paternal custom which becomes the shepherd and teacher, going about and opening his mouth in order to give instruction. See Matthew v. 1. Rightly, therefore, was the prophet not content with saying, "*Give ear, O my people, to my law :* " he adds, "*Incline your ears to the words of my mouth.*" Thus he indicates that he was about to address and instruct them with paternal affection.—*Musculus.*

Verse 2.—"*Parable.*" "*Dark sayings.*" מָשָׁל, *an authoritative weighty speech or saying.* The Hebrew term very nearly answers to the Greek, κύριαι δόξαι, *i.e.,* *authoritative sentences or maxims,* or *weighty sayings,* expressing or implying *a comparison,* as such sayings frequently do. חִידָה, *an enigma, a parable,* which penetrates the mind, and when understood makes a deep impression of what is intended or represented by it. Here חִידוֹת seems to refer to the historical facts mentioned in the subsequent part of the Psalm, considered as *enigmas* of spiritual concerns.—*John Parkhurst.*

Verse 2.—"*Parable.*" Parables are the speeches of wise men, yea, they are the extracts and spirits of wisdom. The Hebrew word signifies to rule, or have authority, because such speeches come upon us with authority, and subdue our reason by the weight of theirs.—*Joseph Caryl.*

Verse 2.—"*I will utter.*" The metaphor in this word is taken from a fountain which pours forth water abundantly. For נָבַע properly means to gush forth, or bubble up. The heart of teachers in the Church ought to be full, and ready to pour forth those streams by which the Church is watered. Their spring ought not to become exhausted, and fail in the summer.—*Mollerus.*

Verse 3.—"*Which we have heard and known.*" We have "*heard*" the *law* and "*known*" the *facts.*—*Adam Clarke.*

Verse 3.—"*Fathers.*" Those are worthy of the name of *fathers* in the church, in relation to posterity, who transmit to posterity the truth of God contained in Scripture, such as here is set down in this Psalm : and this is the only infallible sort of tradition, which delivereth to posterity what God delivered to the prophets or their predecessors by Scripture, such as is the doctrine delivered in this Psalm.— *David Dickson.*

Verse 4.—"*We will not hide them from their children,*" etc. Thou must not only praise God thyself, but endeavour to transmit the memorial of his goodness to posterity. Children are their parents' heirs ; it were unnatural for a father, before he dies, to bury up his treasure in the earth, where his children should not find or enjoy it ; now the mercies of God are not the least part of a good man's treasure, nor the least of his children's inheritance, being both helps to their faith, matter for their praise, and spurs to their obedience. " Our fathers have told us what works thou didst in their days, how thou didst drive out the heathen," etc., Psalm xliv. 1, 2 ; from this they ground their confidence, verse 4, " Thou art my King, O God ; command deliverances for Jacob," and excite their thankfulness, verse 8, " In God we boast all the day long, and praise thy name for ever." Indeed, as children are their parents' heirs, so they become in justice liable to pay their parents' debts ; now the great debt which the saint at death stands charged with, is that which he owes to God for his mercies, and, therefore, it is but reason he should tie his posterity to the payment thereof. Thus mayest thou be praising God in heaven and earth at the same time.—*William Gurnall.*

Verses 4—6.—The cloth that is dyed in the wool will keep colour best. Disciples in youth will prove angels in age. Use and experience strengthen and confirm in any art or science. The longer thy child hath been brought up in Christ's school, the more able he will be to find out Satan's wiles and fallacies, and to avoid them. The longer he hath been at the trade the more skill and delight will he have in worshipping and enjoying the blessed God. The tree when it is old stands strongly against the wind, just as it was set when it was young.

The children of Merindal so answered one another in the matters of religion, before the persecuting Bishop of Cavaillon, that a stander-by said unto the bishop, I must needs confess I have often been at the disputations of the doctors in the Sorbonne, but I never learned so much as by these children. Seven children at one time suffered martyrdom with Symphrosia, a godly matron, their mother. Such a blessing doth often accompany religious breeding ; therefore Julian the apostate, to hinder the growth and increase of Christianity, would not suffer children to be taught either human or divine learning.

Philip was glad that Alexander was born whilst Aristotle lived, that he might be instructed by Aristotle in philosophy. It is no mean mercy that thy children are born in the days of the gospel, and in a valley of vision, a land of light, where they may be instructed in Christianity. Oh, do not fail, therefore, to acquaint thy children with the nature of God, the natures and offices of Christ, their own natural sinfulness and misery, the way and means of their recovery, the end and errand for which they were sent into the world, the necessity of regeneration and a holy life, if ever they would escape eternal death! Alas! how is it possible they should ever arrive at heaven if they know not the way thither?

The inhabitants of Mitylene, sometime the lords of the seas, if any of their neighbours revolted, did inflict this punishment,—they forbade them to instruct their children, esteeming this a sufficient revenge.—(*Ælian*.) Reader, if thou art careless of this duty, I would ask thee what wrong thy children have done thee that thou shouldst revenge thyself by denying them that which is their due. I mean pious instruction.

The Jewish rabbis speak of a very strict custom and method for the instruction of their children, according to their age and capacity. At five years old they were *filii legis*, sons of the law, to read it. At thirteen they were *filii præcepti*, sons of the precept, to understand the law. At fifteen they were *Talmudistæ*, and went to deeper points of the law, even to Talmudic doubts. As thy children grow up, so do thou go on to instruct them in God's will. They are " born like the wild ass's colt," Job xi. 12—that is, unruly, foolish, and ignorant. We often call a fool an ass, but here it is a " wild ass," which is more silly and untractable than a tame one ; nay, it is a " wild ass's colt," which is most rude, unruly, and foolish. How, then, shall thy ignorant children come to know God or themselves without instruction?

Thy duty is to acquaint thy children with the works of God. Teach them his doings as well as his sayings. " Take heed to thyself, lest thou forget the things which thine eyes have seen : but teach them thy sons, and thy sons' sons," Deut. iv. 9. God's wonders should be had in everlasting remembrance. " He hath made his wonderful works to be remembered," Ps. cxi. 4. Now, one special way to do this is by writing them in our children's memories, hereby they are transmitted to posterity. This was the godly practice of the patriarchs, to instruct their children concerning the creation of the world, transgression of man, destruction of the old world, God's providence, the Messiah to be revealed, and the like. The parents' mouths were large books, in which their children did read the noble acts of the Lord. The precept is here urged [verses 2—7] upon a double ground, *partly for God's praise*, in the perpetuity of his worthy deeds : his words are of great weight, and therefore, as curious pictures or precious jewels, must in memory of him be bequeathed from father to son whilst the world continueth. If they are written on paper or parchment they may perish (and is it not a thousand pities that such excellent records should be lost?) ; but if they be written by fathers successfully on their children's hearts, no time shall blot or wear them out, Exod. xii. 26, 27. Therefore, as the rabbis observe, the night before the passover the Jews (to keep God's mercies in memory to his honour) were wont to confer with their children on this wise. The child said, Why is it called the passover? The father said, Because the angel passed over us when it slew the Egyptians, and destroyed us not. The child said, Why do we eat unleavened bread? The father answered, Because we were forced to hasten out of Egypt. The child said, Why do we eat bitter herbs? The father answered, To mind us of our afflictions in Egypt.

But the duty is also urged, *partly for their own profit*, verse 7, "*That they might set their hope in God*," etc. Acquaintance with God's favour will encourage their faith ; knowledge of his power will help them to believe his promise. Reader, obedience to this precept may tend much to thy own and thy children's profit. By teaching thy children God's actions, thou wilt fix them the faster, and they will make the greater impression, upon thy own spirit. A frequent mention of things is the best art of memory : what the mouth preacheth often the mind will ponder much. Besides, it may work for thy children's weal ; the more they be acquainted with the goodness, wisdom, power, and faithfulness of God which appear in his works, the more they will fear, love, and trust him.—*George Swinnock*.

Verse 5.—"*He established a testimony in Jacob*," etc. The meaning is, that God ordained a law, and commanded that the fathers should each one tell his children those things which he had learned from his parents. In this verse therefore we understand by "*testimony*" and "*law*," that particular law which is written in

Deut. iv. 9 in these words : " Only take heed to thyself, and keep thy soul diligently lest thou forget the things which thine eyes have seen, and lest they depart from thy heart all the days of thy life : but teach them thy sons, and thy sons' sons."— *Simon de Muis.*

Verse 5.—By the *"testimony"* and *"law"* are meant the whole contents of the Pentateuch, the direct commandments contained in it, and the deeds of the Lord, which are to be considered as indirect commandments : for all the deeds of God contain a kernel of instruction, of duty, and of warning ; " I have done this for thee, what dost thou for me ? "—*E. W. Hengstenberg.*

Verse 5.—*"To their children."* He who learns the law in his youth, resembles him that writes easily on new and pliable parchment ; but he who begins to learn it in his old age, is like a man that tries to write on old and shrivelled parchment.— *John Van den Driesche, [Drusius.]* 1550—1616.

Verses 5, 6.—Five generations appear to be mentioned : 1. " Fathers ; " 2. " Their children ; " 3. " The generation to come ; " 4. " And their children ; " 5. And their children.—*Adam Clarke.*

Verse 6.—Children should earnestly hearken to the instruction of their parents that they themselves may afterwards be able to tell the same to their sons, and so a golden chain be formed, wherewith being bound together, the whole family may seek the skies. Whilst the father draws the son, the son the grandson, the grandson his children to Christ, as the magnet of them all, that they all may be made one.— *Thomas Le Blanc.*

Verse 7.—*"Set their hope in God."* Their hope was to be set not in the law which punishes, but in grace freely given which redeems ; therefore is it added *"and not forget the works of God."*—*Johannes De Turrecremata.* 1476.

Verse 8.—*"And might not be as their fathers."* The warning is taken from an example at home. He does not say, That they might not be as the nations, which know not God : but, That they might not be *"as their fathers."* Domestic examples of vice are much more pernicious than foreign ones. Hence one says : *Sic natura jubet, velocius et citius nos corrumpunt vitiorum exempla domestica.* Let us learn from this place, that it is not safe in all things to cleave to the footsteps of our fathers. He speaks of those fathers who perished in the wilderness : of whom, see Num. xiv., Deut. i., and Ps. lxviii. 6.—*Musculus.*

Verse 8.—*"As their fathers, a stubborn and rebellious generation."* Forasmuch as this bad emulation of their ancestors is with difficulty plucked from the minds of men, because of our innate reverence for our fathers, the prophet heaps up words in the description of the crimes of their fathers. He says they were דּוֹר סֹרֵר, that is, a generation detracting from the authority of God, and continually breaking the bonds of the law, and in their petulance shaking off the yoke, as a violent and refractory horse, or an untamed bullock, enduring not the rein, or refusing to yield its neck to the yoke, but constantly drawing back and rejecting the bridle.—*Mollerus.*

Verse 8, 9.—Look carefully to the ground of the active obedience, that it be sound and sincere. The same right principles whereby the sincere soul acts for Christ, will carry him to suffer for Christ, when a call from God comes with such an errand. " The children of Ephraim, being armed, and carrying bows, turned back in the day of battle." Why ? what is the matter ? so well armed, and yet so cowardly ? This seems strange : read the preceding verse and you will cease wondering ; they are called there, *"A generation that set not their heart aright, and whose spirit was not steadfast with God."* Let the armour be what it will, yea, if soldiers were in a castle, whose foundations were rock, and walls brass ; yet if their hearts be not right to their prince, an easy storm will drive them from the walls, and a little scare open their gate, which hath not this bolt of sincerity on it to hold it fast. In our late wars we have seen that the honest hearts within thin and weak works have held the town, when no walls could defend treachery from betraying trust.—*William Gurnall.*

Verse 9.—*"The children of Ephraim, being armed,"* etc. " When ye had girded on every man his weapons of war, ye were ready to go up into the hill. And the Lord said unto me, Say unto them, Go not up, neither fight ; for I am not among you ; lest ye be smitten before your enemies. So I spake unto you ; and ye would not hear, but rebelled against the commandment of the Lord, and went presumptuously up into the hill. And the Amorites, which dwelt in that mountain, came out against you, and chased you, as bees do, and destroyed you in Seir, even unto Hormah." Deut. i. 41—44.

Verse 9.—Many persons suppose the passage to refer to the event recorded in 1 Chron. vii. 21, 22, where are mentioned the sons of Ephraim, " whom the men of Gath that were born in the land slew, because they came down to take away their cattle. And Ephraim their father mourned many days, and his brethren came to comfort him." The manner of the relation shews that the slaughter must have been great ; and this flight and defeat, and their not acknowledging their dependence upon God, it is supposed the Psalmist has in view in this place. But the objection to this interpretation is, that the event referred to in the book of Chronicles, evidently occurred at a time anterior to that of the Israelitish exodus from Egypt ; whilst the 11th verse of this Psalm speaks of these same Ephraimites being forgetful of God's doings and wonderful works which he did at the time of their exit from Egypt. It is, therefore, more probable that בְּנֵי אֶפְרַיִם may designate the Israelitish people generally, which Mendlessohn thinks to be the case. He observes that " the meaning of the noun Ephraim was that of a general term for Israel before the reigning of the house of David, because that Joshua the son of Nun, the first judge, was of this tribe ; also because the territory assigned to this tribe was in the region of Shiloh : and it is possible that because of the reputation of this tribe in those days, all those who were in high esteem were also called Ephraimites." He might have added another and stronger reason than any of the preceding for this application of the term to Israel, and it is, that Jeroboam, who may be regarded as the founder of the Israelitish monarchy, is said, in 1 Kings xi. 26, to have been a descendant of Ephraim. The war alluded to may have been one of those which were waged between the ten tribes and the people of Judah.—*George Phillips.*

Verse 10.—*"Walk in his law."* Note, we must walk in the law of God, this is that narrow and sacred way which Christ traces before us. At Athens there was ιερα ὁδος, the sacred way, by which, as Harpocratio relates, the priests of the mysteries travelled to Eleusin. At Rome also there was a way which was called *Via Sacra.* To us also there is a way to the skies, consecrated by the footsteps of the saints. It behoves us therefore not to loiter, but to be ever on the march.—*Thomas Le Blanc.*

Verse 12.—*"Zoan."* The name of a city in Egypt (Numb. xiii. 22), though it be not set down in the story in Exodus, is twice specified by the writer of this psalm, here, and verse 43, as the scene wherein the wondrous works were wrought on Pharaoh by Moses ; either because really the first and principal of the miracles were shewed Pharaoh there, this city being the seat of the king, and a most ancient city, as appears by the expression used of Hebron, in Numbers xiii. 22, where to set out the antiquity of that city, where Abraham, the tenth from Noah, dwelt, 'tis said, that " it was built seven years before Zoan in Egypt ; " or perhaps only in poetical style, as " the field " or country of Zoan, is all one with the " land of Egypt " foregoing. Thus, in other prophetic writings, when judgments are threatened, instead of " Egypt " sometimes we find " Zoan " alone, Isa. xix. 11, where " the princes of Zoan " are all one with the counsellors of Pharoah ; sometimes " the princes of Zoan," with the addition of some other city, as verse 13, " the princes of Zoan, the princes of Noph," *i.e.*, again, the counsellors of that kingdom, which as it follows, " have seduced Egypt,"—brought the whole nation to ruin. So Isa. xxx. 4, where they send to Egypt for relief, 'tis said, their " princes were at Zoan, their ambassadors at Hanes."—*Henry Hammond.*

Verse 12.—*"In the field of Zoan."* We see in this passage that it was not without reason that God most powerfully displayed his wondrous works, his virtue and his glory in the more famous cities : not that he despised the humbler and obscure, but that he might more conveniently in this way scatter abroad the knowledge and renown of his name. For this cause he desired Moses to perform his miracles in the royal city, and in its *field ;* for the same reason he afterwards fixed his dwelling-place in the most famous city of Canaan, in which he decreed also that Christ his Son should be crucified and the foundation of his heavenly kingdom laid.—*Musculus*

Verse 13.—*"He made the waters to stand as an heap."* The original word imports, those great heaps which are made use of as dykes or banks to restrain the waters.

But the Jews have not only understood these expressions literally, but have likewise taken upon them to add particular circumstances, as if the history had been so concise, that it wanted to be supplied therewith. They say, that the sea had formed, as it were, twelve roads or causeways, according to the number of the tribes of the Israelites.—*James Saurin.*

Verse 13.—"He made the waters to stand as an heap." God did not wish altogether to take the sea from the gaze of the Hebrews, but to interrupt and divide it, that like a wall it might stand firm on either side of the way. This was done, first, that the miracle might be evident, for in that sea there is no tidal rise or fall of the waters. Secondly, that the people might have greater joy at the sight of so great a miracle. Thirdly, that in their whole passage they might depend more upon the providence of God, who, in a single moment, could allow the sea to return to its bed and drown all of them. It is God's will that we should flee to him the more ardently at the aspect of present danger. Fourthly and lastly, that the people might pass over the more rapidly, since they knew not how long God wished the miracle to last.—*Thomas Le Blanc.*

Verse 14.—That there was a mystery in this *pillar of cloud and fire* is clear from Isaiah iv. 5, 6, for there never was a *literal* cloud and fire upon Mount Zion. This fiery pillar did cease when they were entered into Canaan ; Isaiah therefore intends a *spiritual* thing under those expressions. So it is represented by the Apostle as representing a gospel-mystery: 1 Cor. x. 2. It signified and shadowed forth, 1. Something of *Christ himself* ; 2. The *benefits* of Christ ; 3. The *ordinances* of Christ.

1. *Christ himself.*—Some have noted a shadow both of his *Deity* and *humanity*. There was a *fiery brightness* in the clouds, which yet was but a dark shadow of the glory of his Deity, which was often in visions so represented ; but his divine nature was veiled and over-clouded by his human, as in this shadow there was a pillar of *cloud* as well as *fire*. In Rev. x. 1, Christ is represented as *clothed with a cloud, and his feet as pillars of fire ;* expressions notably answering this ancient type and shadow. 2. It holds forth something of the *benefits* of Christ. What benefits had they from this pillar of fire and cloud ? They had three : (1) Light and direction. (2) Defence and protection. (3) Ornament and glory. All which we have in a higher manner in Christ by the gospel. 3. It figured also the *ordinances*, and his presence in and with them ; for the ordinances are the outward and visible tokens of God's presence with his people, as this fiery pillar was of old. And, therefore, when the Tabernacle was made and set up, *it rested upon the Tabernacle*, Exodus xl. 38. There be some duties are secret, which the world sees not, nor may see ; as alms-deeds and personal and secret prayer. But the *ordinances* of institution are things that ought to be practised with all the publickness that may be : they are outward and visible tokens of God's presence, particularly that great ordinance of *baptism*, as in 1 Cor. x. 2. The cloud, it seems, had a refreshing moisture in it, to shade, refresh, and cool them from the burning heat ; and they were bedewed * with it, as we are with the water of baptism ; whereby this legal cloud became a type of gospel baptism. And so you see how it represented something of *Christ himself*, and something of his *benefits*, and something of all his *ordinances* under the New Testament.—*Samuel Mather.*

Verse 14.—"All the night." We need not dwell long upon the thought of what this *"all"* was to the Israelites. In night *marchings*, and night restings, it was very precious ; whether they were in motion or at rest, it was alike needed, alike good. This light of fire, unless continuous, would have been of comparatively little worth. Were it suddenly extinguished as they marched, all Israel would have been plunged into confusion and dismay ; the quenching of the light would have changed into a disordered rabble, the marshalled host.—*Philip Bennett Power, in "Breviates : or Short Texts and their Teachings."*

Verse 15.—"The rocks." They were typical of Christ, 1 Cor. x. 4 ; who is frequently compared to one for height, strength, and duration, shade, shelter, and protection ; and is called the " Rock of Israel," the " Rock of offence to both houses of Israel," the " Rock of salvation," the " Rock of refuge," the " Rock of strength," the " Rock that is higher than " the saints, and on which the church is built, and who is " the shadow of a great rock in a weary land."—*John Gill.*

---

* Rather "*baptised*" in it, as Paul puts it in 1 Cor. x. 2.

Verse 15.—"Gave them drink as out of the great depths." As if he had formed a lake or an ocean, furnishing an inexhaustible supply.—*Albert Barnes.*

Verse 16.—"He brought streams also out of the rock," etc. " Where sin abounded, grace did much more abound." The second murmuring for water at Kadesh seems to have been a more aggravated act of rebellion than the former, and yet the water is given in greater abundance. Oh, the freeness of the sovereign grace of God !— *W. Wilson.*

Verse 17.—"And they sinned yet more against him." He does not say that they sinned only, but that they sinned against God. *"And they sinned yet more against him,"* namely, God. Against what God ? Against him who had delivered them by great and unheard of wonders out of Egypt, who had led them as free men across the Red Sea with a dry foot, who had continued to lead and to protect them with pillars of cloud and fire by day and night, and had given them to drink abundantly of water drawn from the arid rock. Against this God they had added sin to sin. Simply to sin is human, and happens to the saints even after they have received grace : but to sin against God argues a singular degree of impiety. To sin against God is to injure and dishonour him in things immediately pertaining to himself. So they sinned against God, because after so many distinguished proofs and testimonies of his care made manifest to them, they continued to think and speak evil against him. All sins indeed, of whatever class they may be, are done against God, because they are opposed to his will ; but those which are committed peculiarly against God, are certainly greater than others. Such are those wrought against his name, goodness, providence, power, truth, and worship, and against those things which specially concern him, whatever they may be. So we read of the sins of the sons of Eli, 1 Sam. ii. 24, 25 : " It is no good report that I hear : ye make the Lord's people to transgress. If one man sin against another, the judge shall judge him ; but if a man sin against the Lord, who shall intreat for him ? "—*Musculus.*

Verse 17.—They sinned yet more." Their sin was not murmuring only, sinful as that is, but *uncontrolled desire.* And for what was that desire ? It was for meat. They had grown so weary of the bread of heaven which God so mercifully provided ; and they wanted something in addition—something, too, which was not absolutely necessary to their existence. When they murmured for water at Massah, they murmured for something *needful.* Their sin *then* was in *murmuring,* instead of *praying.* But here they lusted for something *unnecessary,* and this was an aggravation of their sin. And thus the Psalmist, evidently comparing this sin with the murmuring at Massah, says, " They sinned *yet more* against him."—*George Wagner, in "The Wanderings of the Children of Israel."*

Verse 18.—"They tempted God in their heart." They tempted God, tried his patience over and over again, made as it were another experiment upon it ; and, from the expression of *"tempting him in their heart,"* it would seem as if they had made it a thing of mental calculation whether he would still bear with them.— *Thomas Chalmers (1780—1847), in "Daily Scripture Readings."*

Verse 18.—"They tempted God." We know that, although " God cannot be tempted with evil," he may justly be said to be tempted, whensoever men, by being dissatisfied with his dealings, virtually ask that he will alter those dealings, and proceed in a way more congenial with their feelings. If you reflect a little, you can hardly fail to peceive, that in a very strict sense, this and the like may be said to be a tempting of God. Suppose a man to be discontended with the appointments of Providence ; suppose him to murmur and repine at what the Almighty allots him to do or to bear : is he not to be charged with provoking God to change his purposes ? and what is this if it be not " tempting " God—a striving to induce him to swerve from his plans, though every one of those plans has been settled by infinite wisdom ? Or, again, if any one of us, notwithstanding multiplied proofs of the Divine lovingkindness, doubt or question whether God do indeed love him ; of what is he guilty, if not of tempting the Lord, seeing that he solicits God to give additional evidence, as though there were deficiency, and challenges him to fresh demonstrations of what he has already abundantly displayed ? This would be called *"tempting"* amongst men. If a child were to show by his actions that he doubted or disbelieved the affection of his parents, he would be considered as thereby striving to extort from them fresh proofs of that affection, though they had already done as much as either in justice or in wisdom they ought to have done ; this would be a clear tempting of them, and that too in the ordinary sense of the term.   In short, unbelief of every kind and degree may be said to be a tempting of God ; for not to believe on the evidence which he has seen fit to give, is to tempt him to give more than he has already given—offering our possible assent, if proof were increased, as an inducement to him to go beyond what his wisdom has prescribed. . . . You cannot distrust God, and not accuse him of a want either of power or of goodness ; you cannot repine,—no, not even in thought—without virtually telling him that his plans are not the best, nor his dispensations the wisest, which might have been appointed in respect of yourselves.   So that your fear, or your despondency, or your anxiety in circumstances of perplexity, or of peril, is nothing less than a call upon God to depart from his fixed course,—a suspicion, or rather an assertion, that he might proceed in a manner more worthy of himself, and therefore a challenge to him to alter his dealings, if he would prove that he possesses the attributes which he claims.   You may not intend thus to accuse, or provoke God, whenever you murmur ; but your murmuring does all this, and cannot fail to do it.   You cannot be dissatisfied, without virtually saying that God might order things better ; you cannot say that he might order things better, without virtually demanding that he change his course of acting, and give other proofs of his infinite perfections.   And thus you *tempt* him, tempt him even as did the Israelites in the wilderness.—*Henry Melvill.*

Verse 18.—*"Asking meat for their lust."*   God had given them meat for their hunger in the manna, wholesome, pleasant food, and in abundance ; he had given them meat for their faith, out of the heads of Leviathan which he brake in pieces, Ps. lxxiv. 14.   But all this would not serve, they must have meat *"for their lust ; "* dainties and varieties to gratify a luxurious appetite.   Nothing is more provoking to God, than our quarrelling with our allotment, and indulging the desires of the flesh.—*Matthew Henry.*

Verse 19.—It is particularly to be observed, that the sin of which the children of Israel were on this occasion guilty, was not in wishing for bread and water, but in thinking for one moment, that after the Lord had brought them out of Egypt, he would suffer them for the lack of any needful thing, to come short of Canaan. It was no sin to be hungry and thirsty ; it was a necessity of their nature.   There is nothing living that does not desire and require food : when we do not we are dead, and that they did so was no sin.   Their sin was *to doubt that God could or would support them in the wilderness, or allow those who followed his leadings to lack any good thing.*   This was their sin.   It is just the same with the Christian now.   These Israelites did not more literally require a supply of daily food for their bodies, than does the Christian for his soul.   Not to do so is a sign of death, and the living soul would soon die without it.   And so far from its being a sin, our Lord has pronounced that man blessed who hungers and thirsts after righteousness, adding the most precious promise, that all such shall be satisfied.   But it is a sin, and very great sin, should this food not be perceptibly, and to the evidence of our senses, immediately supplied, to murmur and be fearful.   It was for *the trial of their faith* that these things happened to the Israelites, as do the trials of all Christians in all ages : and it is " after we have suffered awhile " that we may expect to be established, strengthened, settled.—*Brownlow North, in "Ourselves. A Picture sketched from the History of the Children of Israel."*   [1865.]

Verses 19, 20.—After all their experience, they doubted the divine omnipotence, as if it were to be regarded as nothing, when it refused to gratify their lusts.   Unbelief is so deeply rooted in the human heart, that when God performs miracles on *earth,* unbelief doubts whether he can perform them in *heaven,* and when he does them in *heaven,* whether he can do them on *earth ?*—*Augustus F. Tholuck.*

Verse 20.—*"Can he give bread also ? "*   They should have said, " Will he serve our lusts ? " but that they were ashamed to say.—*John Trapp.*

Verse 0.—Who will say that a man is thankful to his friend for a past kindness, if he nourishes an ill opinion of him for the future ?   This was all that ungrateful Israel returned to God, for his miraculously broaching the rock to quench their thirst : " Behold, he smote the rock,"—*"Can he give bread also ? "*   This, indeed, was their trade all the time they were in the wilderness. Wherefore, God gives them their character, not by what they seemed to be while his mercies were before them ; then they could say, "God was their rock, and the High God their Redeemer ; " but by their temper and carriage in straits ; when the cloth was drawn, and the feast taken out of their sight, what opinion then had they of God ? Could they sanctify his name so far as to trust him for their dinner to-morrow who feasted them yesterday ? Truly no, as soon as they feel their hunger return, like froward children, they are crying, as if God meant to starve them. Wherefore, God rejects their praises, and owns not their hypocritical acknowledgments, but sets their ingratitude upon record ; they forgot his works, and waited not for his counsel. O how sad is this, that after God hath entertained a soul at his table with choice mercies and deliverances, these should be so ill husbanded, that not a bit of them should be left to give faith a meal, to keep the heart from fainting, when God comes not so fast to deliver as desired. He is the most thankful man that treasures up the mercies of God in his memory, and can feed his faith with what God hath done for him, so as to walk in the strength thereof in present straits.— *William Gurnall.*

Verse 23.—*"Opened the doors of heaven."* There is an allusion here to the flood as in verse 15.—*A. R. Fausset.*

Verse 23.—*"Opened the doors of heaven."* God, who has the key of the clouds, *"opened the doors of heaven,"* that is more than *opening the windows,* which yet is spoken of as a great blessing, Mal. iii. 19.—*Matthew Henry.*

Verse 23.—*"Opened the doors of heaven."* This is a metaphor taken from a granary, from which corn is brought ; and by *opening the doors* is signified, that the manna fell very plentifully. Compare Gen. vii. 11.—*Thomas Fenton.*

Verses 24, 25.—*"Manna."* The prophet celebrates this miracle, *first,* because of the unusual place whence the manna was sent. For he did not produce fruits from the earth wherewith to feed them, but rained down this food from the clouds, and from the depths of the skies. *Secondly,* because of the facility of the distribution. By the command of God alone, without any labour of men, yea, while they slept, this food was prepared. Therefore is it said, *"He gave,"* etc. *Thirdly,* he celebrates its great abundance which sufficed to supply so great a multitude. *Fourthly,* the excellence of the food. He calls it the food of the excellent or the strong, such as was not pleasant merely to the common multitude, but to the princes also, and to the heroes, for it was the food of *"the mighty ones."*—*Mollerus.*

Verse 25.—*"Man."* Rather, as Exodus xvi. 6, *"every* man." Not one of them was left without it.—*A. R. Fausset.*

Verse 25.—*"Man did eat angels' food."* 'Tis called *"angels' food,"* not because the angels do daily feed upon it, but because it was both made and ministered by the ministry of angels, and that phrase sets forth the excellency of it.—*Christopher Ness* (1621—1705), *in "The Sacred History and Mystery of the Old Testament."*

Verse 25.—*"Angels' food."* Manna is called *the bread of angels* because it was brought down by their ministry ; and it was so pleasant in taste, that if the angels had eaten bread, it might have served them.—*John Weemse.*

Verse 25.—*"Angels' food."* So their manna was called, either, 1. because it was provided and sent by the ministry of angels ; or, 2. because it seemed to come down from heaven, the dwelling-place of the angels ; or, 3. to set forth the excellency of this bread, that it was meat, as one would say, fit for angels, if angels needed meat. And so, indeed, the exceeding glory of Stephen's countenance is set forth by this, that they " saw his face as it had been the face of an angel," Acts vi. 15 ; and Paul calls an excellent tongue, " the tongue of angels," 1 Cor. xiii. 1.—*Arthur Jackson.*

Verse 25.—The more excellent the benefit is which God giveth, the greater is the ingratitude of him who doth not esteem of it and make use of it as becometh ; as we see in Israel's sin, who did not esteem of manna as they should have done. Had the Lord fed them with dust of earth, or roots of grass, or any other mean thing, they should have had no reason to complain : but when he giveth them a new food, created every morning for their sakes, sent down from heaven as fresh furniture every day, of such excellent colour, taste, smell and wholesomeness ;

what a provocation of God was it, not to be content now ; in special, when he gave them abundantly of it ? " He sent them meat to the full."—*David Dickson.*

Verse 26.—*"He caused an east wind to blow in the heaven : and by his power he brought in the south wind."* Here, on examining the geographical position of the Israelites, we see exactly how the south-east winds would bring the " *quails,"* The Israelites had just passed the Red Sea, and had began to experience a foretaste of the privations which they were to expect in the desert, through which they had to pass. Passing northwards in their usual migrations, the birds would come to the coast of the Red Sea, and there would wait until a favourable wind enabled them to cross the water. The south-east wind afforded them just the very assistance which they needed, and they would naturally take advantage of it.—*J. G. Wood, in "Bible Animals."* 1869.

Verse 27.—*"As dust."* The amazing clouds of fine dust or sand, which a violent wind raises in the deserts of the East, constitute the point of comparison.—*William Keatinge Clay.*

Verse 27.—*"Feathered fowls."* Hebrew, " fowl of wing ; " *i.e.,* flying fowls, in distinction from domestic poultry.—*Williams, in Notes to Calvin in loc.*

Verses 27, 31.—If the cemetery on Sarbut-el-Khadem be, what all the antecedent evidences combine to indicate, the workmanship of the Israelites, (a chief burial-ground of their fatal encampment at Kibroth-Hattaavah), it may most reasonably be expected that its monuments shall contain symbolic representations of the miracle of the " feathered fowls," and of the awful plague which followed it. Now Niebuhr happily enables us to meet this just expectation, by his copies of the hieroglyphics on three of those tombstones, published in the XLVth. and XLVIth. plates of his first volume, and prefaced plate XLIV. by *a plan of the cemetery itself,* which is of more value than any or all subsequent descriptions. It was discovered by the present writer (as stated in a former work, [" The Voice of Israel "] on the evidence of no less than four Sinaitic inscriptions, that the birds of the miracle, named by Moses, generically, שְׂלָו, *salu,* and by the Psalmist, still more generally, עוֹף כָּנָף, *"winged fowls,"* or more correctly " long-winged fowls," were not (as rendered by all our versions, ancient and modern) *"quails,"* but a crane-like red bird resembling a goose, named in the Arabic *nuham.* The discovery received subsequently a singular and signal corroboration from the further discovery, by Dean Stanley, and previously by Schubert, of immense flocks of these very nuhams on the reputed scene of the miracle at Kibroth-Hattaavah. With these antecedents in his mind, the reader will now turn to the three monuments copied by Niebuhr in the cemetery of Sarbut-el-Khadem. He will at once see that a crane-like bird resembling a goose, with slender body and long-legs, is the leading hieroglyphic symbol in all the three tablets. No fewer than twenty-five of these symbolic birds occur in the first, ten in the second, and fifteen in the third tablet. The goose appears occasionally, but the principal specimens have the air of the goose, but the form of the crane. In a word, they are the very species of birds seen by Dean Stanley, both at this point of Sinai, and at the first cataract of the Nile ; and which constantly occur also in Egyptian monuments : as though the very food of Egypt, after which the Israelites lusted, was sent to be at once their prey and their plague. " And the children of Israel said unto them, Would to God we had died by the hand of the Lord in the land of Egypt, *when we sat by the flesh pots."* Exod. xvi. 3.

The reader has here before him the irrefragable fact that the very birds which by every kind of evidence stand identified with the *salus,* or long-legged and long-winged fowls of the miracle, are the very birds depicted on the tombstones of Sarbut-el-Khadem, both standing, flying, and apparently even trussed and cooked. . . . The inevitable inference is . . . that these tombstones record the miracle of the " feathered fowls," and stand over the graves of the gluttons who consumed them. —*Charles Forster, in "Israel in the Wilderness."* 1865.

Mr. Forster thus deciphers by his alphabet some of the mixed legends and devices :—

" From the sea the cranes congregate to one spot ;
The archers shoot at the cranes passing over the plain.
Evil-stomached they rush after the prey—
The sepulchre their doom—their marrow corrupted by God.
The sleepy owl, emblem of death, God sends destruction among them.

* * * * * * * * *

> The mother of sepulchres—the black and white geese,
> A sudden death, greedily lusting after flesh, die the gluttons.
> The mountain top ascend the Hebrews,
> They eat, devour, consume, till nothing is left, exceeding all bounds.
> Their bodies corrupted, by gluttony they die."

Verse 29.—Note: The prophet in this Psalm institutes, as it were, a conflict between God and man. God contends with blessings, man with sins. God exerts his power for the benefit of undeserving man, v. 12, " Marvellous things did he in the sight of their fathers:" man repays the divine power with infidelity, v. 17, " And they sinned yet more against him." And farther on, in v. 19, " Can God furnish a table in the wilderness?" *Secondly*, God showers down his bounty to overwhelm ungrateful sinners with his gifts, v. 23, " He commanded the clouds from above, etc., and rained down manna upon them." These less than men (*homunciones*) oppose their gluttony to the liberality of God, and abuse the gifts conferred, v. 29, " They did eat, and were well filled." *Thirdly*, divine justice renews the conflict to scourge at once stupidity out of them, v. 30, 31, " While their meat was yet in their mouths, the wrath of God came upon them." Still obdurate they kick against the goad, v. 32, " For all this they sinned still." *Fourthly*, mercy flies down from heaven, to invite them to peace, v. 38, " But he being full of compassion." Men are but emboldened by his compassion, and the more easily relapse into sin, v. 40, " How oft did they provoke him in the wilderness?" *Fifthly*, and *lastly*, when all seems lost, love draws nigh, and performs unheard-of wonders, to touch their hardness, and to deliver them from the dangers by which they were pressed, v. 43, " How he set his signs in Egypt." To these shafts of his love sinners oppose a forgetfulness of all his benefits, v. 42, " They remembered not his hand nor the day when he delivered them from the enemy." And all this took place before they entered the land of promise. The conflict that happened between the Hebrews and God in the land of promise is related in the next section of the Psalm.—*Thomas Le Blanc.*

Verse 30.—"*They were not estranged from their lust.*" This implies, that they were still burning with their lust. If it is objected that this does not agree with the preceding sentence, where it is said, that " they did eat, and were thoroughly filled," I would answer, that if, as is well known, the minds of men are not kept within the bounds of reason and temperance, they become insatiable; and, therefore, a great abundance will not extinguish the fire of a depraved appetite.—*John Calvin.*

Verse 30.—"*They were not estranged from their lust.*" Satiated they were, but not satisfied. It is as easy to quench the fire of Etna, as the thoughts set on fire by lust.—*John Trapp.*

Verse 30.—"*They were not estranged from their lust.*" Consider that there is more real satisfaction in mortifying lusts than in making provision for them or in fulfilling them: there is more true pleasure in crossing and pinching our flesh than in gratifying it; were there any true pleasure in sin, hell would not be hell, for the more sin, the more joy. You cannot satisfy one lust if you would do your utmost, and make yourself never so absolute a slave to it; you think if you had your heart's desire you would be at rest: you much mistake; they had it.—*Alexander Carmichael.*

Verse 31.—"*The wrath of God came upon them, and slew the fattest of them.*" Two things are here worthy of notice. 1. One, Why he gave them abundance and sufficiency of quails, and afterwards punished the murmuring and unbelieving. If he had punished them before, he would have appeared to have had greater ability to destroy them, than to give them flesh. Therefore, that he might first declare his power, and so make the unbelief of the people the more plain, and show how deserving they were of punishment, he first showed he could give, because they believed he could not, and then punished them for their unbelief. . . . . 2. The other, that he destroyed the fat and the chosen men among the people, although they all are said to have murmured. Without a doubt, they were first in the crime, and therefore they are specially mentioned in the punishment.—*Musculus.*

Verse 31.—"*Slew the fattest of them.*" They were fed as sheep for the slaughter. The butcher takes the fattest first. We may suppose there were some pious and contented Israelites that did eat moderately of the quails, and were never the worse;

for it was not the meat that poisoned them, but their own lust. Let epicures and sensualists here read their doom ; they who make "*a god of their belly, their end is destruction,*" Phil. iii. 19.—*Matthew Henry.*

Verses 31—34.—The Christian has more true pleasure from the creature than the wicked, as it comes more refined to him than to the other. The unholy wretch sucks dregs and all, dregs of sin and dregs of wrath, whereas the Christian's cup is not thus spiced. *First*, dregs of sin ; the more he hath of the creature's delights given him, the more he sins with them. Oh, it is sad to think what work they make in his naughty heart ! they are but fuel for his lusts to kindle upon ; away they run with their enjoyments, as the prodigal with his bags, or like hogs in shaking time ; no sight is to be had of them, or thought of their return as long as they can get anything abroad, among the delights of the world. None so prodigiously wicked as those who are fed high with carnal pleasures. They are to the ungodly as the dung and ordure is to the swine which grows fat by lying in it ; so their hearts grow gross and fat ; their consciences more stupid and senseless in sin by them ; whereas the comforts and delights that God gives unto a holy soul by the creature, turn to spiritual nourishment to his graces, and draw these forth into exercise, as they do others' lusts. *Secondly*, dregs of wrath. The Israelites had little pleasure from their dainties, when the wrath of God fell upon them, before they could get them down their throats. The sinner's feast is no sooner served in but divine justice is preparing to send up a reckoning after it, and the fearful expectation of this cannot but spoil the taste of the other.—*William Gurnall.*

Verse 32.—"*For all this they sinned still.*" They went on sinning, "*and believed not for his wondrous works.*" That is, even his great *wonders* or miracles, did not bring them to believe. Neither *speculative atheism*, nor *atheism of heart*, nor *practical atheism* was ever cured by miracle, because they are all founded in a wicked disposition. "Men are not always in a mood to be convinced." It is not want of evidence, but the want of right dispositions that keeps men from believing God.— *William S. Plumer.*

Verse 32.—They did believe the history of his works, namely, that such things as are there recorded were done; they could not but believe that God had wrought wonders for them in Egypt, that he had drowned Pharaoh in, and brought them safe through, the Red Sea : they saw these things, their senses were witnesses, but yet they did not believe the *prophecy* or *promise* which was virtually in those works, namely, that God would do more wonders for them till he had finished and accomplished their deliverance. That history of bringing through the Red Sea had this prophecy in it—that they should be brought safe to Canaan ; but they did not believe the voice of this prophecy. When God gave them water out of the rock, this work promised that he would give them meat out of the clouds, if they needed it ; but this they believed not. Hence the same Psalm reports their unbelief, under this notion (ver. 19, 20). "They spake against God ; they said, Can God furnish a table in the wilderness ? Behold, he smote the rock, that the waters gushed out, and the streams overflowed ; can he give bread also ? can he provide flesh for his people ? " "*When the Lord heard this* (language of unbelief) he was wroth."—*Joseph Caryl.*

Verses 32, 33.—What faith can do to a prophecy of judgment, the same can unbelief to a promise of mercy ; overthrow it. The Psalmist assigns this to the unbelief of the works of God, as well as of his word. "*They believed not his wondrous works. Therefore their days did he consume in vanity, and their years in trouble :* " but are not the days of all men consumed in vanity ? Is not man at his best estate altogether vanity ? Yes, but here was a special vanity, and somewhat more penal and judicial lay upon that generation for their unbelief, than lies upon mankind as the fruit of sin in general. And what was that ? Even the evil threatened in the text [Isa. vii. 9, latter part] : they could not be established. God lets them wander forty years in a wilderness, up and down, forward and backward ; now in hope, anon in fear ; now in joy, anon in sorrow ; now in success, by-and-by in disappointment.—*Joseph Caryl.*

Verse 32.—Experience ought to strengthen faith ; but there must be present faith to use experience.—*J. N. Darby, "in Practical Reflections on the Psalms."* [1870.]

Verse 33.—"*Their days did he consume in vanity.*" He says with great significance, In vanity their days were consumed, because they were plainly deprived of their hope, and endured all their sufferings in vain. They did not attain what they had hoped for, but only their children entered the land.—*Mollerus.*

Verse 33.—"*Days*" are put in the first place, and then "*years ;*" by which it is intimated, that the duration of their life was cut short by the curse of God, and that it was quite apparent that they failed in the midst of their course.—*John Calvin.*

Verses 34—36.—There are some if they come under afflictions, or if they fall in sickness, or a fever, and God shake death over their head ; or if they be at some solemn ordinances, they will be at resolving and purposing, and readily bringing vows on themselves, of personal covenanting with God ; but as they are easily gotten, so they easily vanish : "*When he slew them, then they sought him : and they returned and enquired early after God.*" Several times our afflictions are like a gutter ; when there is a great shower we will be running over with purposes after God. "*Nevertheless they did flatter him with their mouth, and they lied unto him with their tongues. For their heart was not right with him, neither were they stedfast in his covenant :* " and yet when he slew them they sought after him, and they early enquired after him : so that indeliberate actions and covenantings with God, as they are hastily forgotten, they no less suddenly vanish ; the action ought then to be deliberate when we indenture with the Cautioner, and oblige ourselves to more watchfulness, and more tenderness, or else it will soon vanish.—*Alexander Wedderburn, in "David's Testament, opened up in Fourty Sermons."* 1701.

Verses 34—37.—In these words you see plainly that these people are very early and earnest in seeking God to take off his hand, to remove judgments that were upon them, but not that God would cure them of those sins that provoked him to draw his sword, and to make it drunk with their blood ; for, notwithstanding the sad slaughters that divine justice had made among them, they did but flatter and lie, and play the hypocrites with God ; they would fain be rid of their sufferings, but did not care to be rid of their sins. Ah ! but a gracious soul cries out, Lord, do but take away my sins, and it will satisfy me and cheer me, though thou shouldst never take off thy heavy hand. A true Nathanael sighs it out under his greatest affliction, as that good man did, *A me, me salva, Domine,*[*] deliver me, O Lord, from that evil man myself. No burden to the burden of sin. Lord ! says the believing soul ; deliver me from my inward burden, and lay upon me what outward burden thou pleasest.—*Thomas Brooks.*

Verses 34—37.—There are a sort of men that lie in the enmity of their natures, and in an unreconciled state, living in the visible church, who are not only much restrained, and bite their enmity in, but who, by means of an inferior work of the word and Spirit of God upon their hearts, are brought to seek unto God for friendship, yea, and do much for him in outward actions, and side and take part with his friends ; and yet their hearts being unchanged, the cursed enmity of their nature remaining unkilled and not taken away, they lie still in the gall of bitterness. For instance, look to these in Psalm lxxviii. 34—37. It is said that they ' sought the Lord early as their Redeemer,' whilst he was aslaying of them ; yet they did but "*flatter him with their mouths,*" etc. A flatterer, you know, differs from a friend, in that he pretendeth much kindness, yet wants inward good-will, doing it for his own ends. And so do many seek God, that yet he accounts as enemies ; for they seek him whilst they see themselves in his lurch.

Now, it is hard to discover these, because they pretend much friendship, and externally (it may be) do as many outward kindnesses as the true friends ; as flatters will abound in outward kindnesses as much as true friends, nay, often exceed them, because they may not be discovered. Now, if none of the former signs reach to them, nor touch them, then there is no better way left than to search unto the grounds of all they do, and to examine whether it proceeds from true, inward, pure, and constant good-will, yea or no, or self-respects ? As now, when we see an ape do many things that a man doth, how do we therefore distinguish those actions in the one and in the other ? Why, by the inward principles from whence they spring, by saying that they proceed from reason in the one, but not so in the other. If, therefore, it can be evinced, that all that any man seems to do for God, comes not from good-will to him, it is enough to convince them to be persons unreconciled ; for whereas all outward kindnesses and expressions of friendship proceed not from friend-like dispositions and pure good-will, but altogether from self-respects, it is

---

[*] *Augustine.*

but feigned flattery, even among men ; and when discovered once, it breeds double hatred. And there is much more reason it should do so with God, because he being a God that knows the heart, to flatter him is the greater mockery ; for that is it which chiefly provoketh men to hate such as dissemble friendship, because there is mockery joined with it. Now, that God accounteth every one that doth not turn to him out of pure good-will a flatterer is plain by these words in verses 36, 37 : "*Notwithstanding, they did but flatter him, and dealt falsely in his covenant.*" If men's hearts be not inwardly for God, and with him, as a friend would be to a friend, in their actions he esteems them against him. " Thy heart," says Peter to Simon Magus, " is not right before the Lord," Acts viii. 22, and therefore he tells him he was " still in the gall of bitterness."—*Thomas Goodwin.*

Verse 35.—"*Redeemer.*" That is, from Egyptian bondage ; for the bulk of the people did not understand the spiritual redemption which was typified by that transaction.—*Thomas Scott.*

Verse 35.—Between this and the following verse the Masorah puts this note, "*half of the book,*" *i.e.,* half of the Book of Psalms ends here.—*John Gill.*

The numbering of the verses must differ from ours, for on counting the verses as in our version, we find verse 57 to be the centre verse of the book.—*C. H. S.*

Verse 36.—"*They did flatter him,*" etc. But could they flatter God ? Man is flattered when that is ascribed to him which he hath not, or when he is applauded for what he hath, beyond the worth of it. God cannot be flattered thus : he is as much beyond flatterings as he is beyond sufferings. The Jews, then, are said to flatter God, not because they applauded him by fair speeches more than was his due, but because by fair speeches they hoped to prevent what themselves did deserve ; or they flattered God with their own promises, not with his praises. They sinned against him, and he slew them ; and when the sword found them they sought God, they creeped to him and fawned upon him, they came as with ropes about their necks, confessing they were worthy to die, yet humbly begging for life : and if God would but humbly sheathe his sword and spare them, O what manner of men they would be in all holy conversation and godliness. Thus " they flattered God with their mouth, while their hearts were not right : " they made great shews of repentance and turning to God, but they meant no such thing ; this was their flattery. Neither can the Lord be flattered any other way. And as he cannot be flattered by over-praising him, so his person cannot be unduly honoured by over-respecting him.—*Joseph Caryl.*

Verse 36.—God may be the object, self is the end, and a heavenly object is made subservient to a carnal design. Hypocrisy passes a compliment on God, and is called "*flattery*" : "*They did flatter him with their mouth,*" etc. They gave him a parcel of good words for their own preservation. . . . . An hypocrite may well be termed a religious atheist, an atheist masked with religion.—*Stephen Charnock.*

Verse 36.—"*They lied unto him with their tongues.*" The heart is the metal of the bell, the tongue is but the clapper ; when the metal of the bell is right and good (as silver) such will the sound be ; if the metal of the bell be cracked, or lead, the sound will soon discover it to a judicious ear. God can see the diseases and spots of the heart upon the tongue. As Jacob said to his mother, " If I dissemble, my father will find me out, and I shall meet with a curse instead of a blessing."—*George Swinnock.*

Verses 36—38.—There is no disputing the fact which gives accuracy to the text, that God was moved by a repentance which had not in it even the elements of godly sorrow for sin ; which could not even, by a casual observer, much less by him who searches the heart, have been mistaken for that penitence which supposes an inward and radical change, and, nevertheless, even such a repentance as this sufficed to procure a recompense at the hands of God. Though the sackcloth was on the body and not on the soul ; though it was the punishment of the sin and not the sin itself which led to this outward humiliation, God did not turn away from the forced supplication, but vouchsafed the deliverance which was sought at his hands. Yes, God, who never expresses greater abhorrence of any character than of that of the hypocrite ; God, who rejects nothing more indignantly than outward homage when it is not the index of inward prostration—God may be said to have removed the humiliation of the people as though he could not read their hearts, or as though, having read them, and noted their unsubdued rebellion, he still thought the apparent contrition deserving of some recompense. . . . .

If God would not leave the show and semblance of contrition without a recompense, will he be unmindful of real penitence ? If *"many a time turned he his anger away"* from those who *"did but flatter him with their mouths,*and lied unto him with their tongues,"* has he nothing in store for those who are humble in spirit, and who come to him with the sacrifice of a broken heart ? Oh ! the turning away of temporal wrath because idols were outwardly abandoned, this is a mighty pledge that eternal wrath will be averted if we are inwardly stricken, and flee for refuge to the Saviour. God must have eternal good in store for his friends, if even his enemies are recompensed with temporal good. Yes, as I mark the Philistines and the Ammonites oppressing the idolatrous Israelites, and then see the oppressors driven back in return even for heartless service, oh ! I learn that true penitence for sin and true faith in the sacrifice of Jesus Christ will cause all enemies to be scattered ; I return from the contemplation of the backsliding people, emancipated notwithstanding the known hollowness of their vows, I return assured that a kingdom which neither Philistine nor Ammonite can invade, shall be the portion of all who seek deliverance through Christ.—*Henry Melvill.*

Verse 37.—*"Their heart was not right with him."* God pleases them when he replenishes them with food, not their heart with his graces ; therefore they repay him with the mouth, and not with the heart. They are altogether mouth and tongue : but God is all heart and breast. They give words ; God gives milk and perfect love. Love does not reach the inner nature of many men, it sticks in the entrance.—*Thomas Le Blanc.*

Verse 37.—*"Their heart was not right with him, neither were they stedfast,"* etc. This is the ever-repeated complaint, see verses 8, 22. There is no permanence, no stability in the reformation which has been produced. Compare Hosea vi. 4.— *J. J. Stewart Perowne.*

Verse 38.—According to *B. Kiddushin* 30a, this verse is the middle one of the 5896 פסוקים, στίχοι, of the Psalter. According to *B. Maccoth* 22b, Ps. lxxviii. 38, and previously Deut. xxviii. 58, 59 ; xxix. 9, were recited when the forty strokes of the lash save one, which, according to 2 Cor. xi. 24, Paul received five times, were being counted out to the culprit.—*Franz Delitzch.*

Verse 38.—*"He, being full of compassion,"* etc. When his hand was up, and he giving the blow, he called it back again, as one that could not find it in his heart to do it ; and when he did it, *"he did not stir up all his wrath ; "* he let fall some drops of it, but would not shed the whole shower of it ; and he giveth the reason of both, for *"they are but flesh ; "* and, indeed, his primary scope is to show mercy ; and that he afflicts is but upon occasion ; and therefore he is provoked, and provoked much before he doth it. As it is natural to the bee to give honey, but it stings ; but it stings but by occasion when it is provoked ; and this we see to be true in God by experience, who suffers men, and suffers them long ; they continue in their sins, and yet he continues in his mercies, and withholds his judgments.—*John Preston* (1587—1628), *in "The Golden Sceptre held forth to the Humble."*

Verse 38.—*"Forgave "* is a very inadequate translation of the Hebrew word, which necessarily suggests the idea of expiation as the ground of pardon.—*Joseph Addison Alexander.*

Verse 38.—*"Many a time turned he his anger away."* God is provoked every day, yet is he slow to anger. Yea, sometimes when he has determined to bring evil upon a people, and has put himself into a posture of judgment, drawn out the sword, and smitten them ; though they cease not to provoke him, he ceaseth to punish them ; as a tender father in correcting a rebellious and graceless child, holds his hand sometimes, before the child begs for mercy, and of mere grace forbears : so God did with Israel. Notwithstanding their dissembling with their flattering tongues, and covenant-breaking hearts, *"He forgave their iniquity, and destroyed them not : yea, many a time turned he his anger away, and did not stir up all his wrath."* The words are, *"He multiplied to turn away his anger : "* as they multiplied to provoke it, he multiplied to turn it away ; and so at length overnumbered their sins with his mercies, that they were not destroyed.—*John Strickland, in "A Sermon preached before the House of Commons," entitled "Mercy rejoicing against Judgment."* 1645.

Verse 38.—*"He did not stir up all his wrath."* His patience is manifest in moderating his judgments when he sends them. Doth he empty his quiver of his arrows, or exhaust his magazine of thunder? No; he could roll one thunderbolt successively upon all mankind; it is as easy with him to create a perpetual motion of lightning and thunder, as of the sun and stars, and make the world as terrible by the one as it is delightful by the other. He opens not all his store; he sends out a light party to skirmish with men, and puts not in array his whole army. "*He stirs not up all his wrath;*" he doth but pinch, where he might have torn asunder; when he takes away much, he leaves enough to support us. If he had stirred up all his anger, he had taken away all, and our lives to boot. He rakes up but a few sparks, takes but one firebrand to fling upon men, when he might discharge the whole furnace upon them; he sends but a few drops out of the cloud, which he might make to break in the gross, and fall down upon our heads to overwhelm us; he abates much of what he might do.—*Stephen Charnock.*

Verse 39.—"*A wind that passeth away.*"

> The secret wheels of hurrying time do give
> So short a warning, and so fast they drive,
> That I am dead before I seem to live.
>
> And what's a life? a weary pilgrimage,
> Whose glory in one day doth fill thy stage
> With childhood, manhood, and decrepid age.
>
> And what's a life? the flourishing array
> Of the proud summer-meadow, which to-day
> Wears her green plush, and is to-morrow hay.
>
> And what's a life? a blast sustained with clothing,
> Maintained with food, retained with vile self-loathing,
> Then weary of itself, again to nothing.
>
> —*Francis Quarles.*

Verse 40.—"*How oft did they provoke,*" etc. They provoked God at least ten times (Num. xiv. 22) during the first two years of their journey through the wilderness: (1) at the Red Sea (Exod. xiv. 11, 12): (2) at the waters of Marah (Exod. xv. 24): (3) in the wilderness of sin (Exod. xvi. 2): (4) when they kept the manna until the following day (Exod. xvi. 10): (5) when the manna was collected on the Sabbath (Exod. xvi. 27): (6) in Rephidim, where there was no water (Num. xx. 2, 13): (7) at Horeb, when a molten calf was made (Exod. xxii. 1, etc.): (8) at Taberah (Num. xi. 1, 2, 3): (9) when they lusted for flesh (Num. xi. 4): (10) when they murmured at the news brought by the men, who had been sent to search the land (Num. xiv. 1, etc.).—*Daniel Cresswell.*

Verse 40.—"*How oft.*" God kept an account how oft they provoked him, though they did not, Numb. xiv. 22: " They have tempted me these ten times."—*Matthew Henry.*

Verse 41.—"*They turned back.*" As for that expression, יָשׁוּבוּ, which we translate, "*and they turned back;* that is, say some, to go back again into *Egypt,* or as others, returned back to their *old wont* of rebellion; I say, it hath no such meaning here; it is a Hebraism, and should be rendered, "*they returned and tempted,*" that is, *sæpius tentaverunt,* they *oftentimes tempted* him, or they *tempted* him *again.*—*Thomas Froysel, in "Sermons concerning Grace and Temptations."* 1678.

Verse 41.—"*Tempted God.*" This only expresses the fact that men act towards him as if he could be tempted, or in a way fitted to put him to the proof, to provoke his righteous displeasure, and make him proceed against them, as it were just for him actually to do because of their offences. It is not in the least degree opposed to the statement of James—" God cannot be tempted with evil," which is to the effect that he cannot be influenced by evil, so as to be drawn into it, turned toward it—so as to feel its power or experience its contamination. He is infinitely far removed from it, raised above it, under all its forms. He is so because of the absolute perfection of his being and blessedness.—*John Adam, in "Exposition of the Epistle of James."* 1867.

Verse 41.—"*Limited the Holy One of Israel.*" They limited either, 1. God's power, as above, verses 19, 20. Or, 2. God's will, directing and prescribing to him what to do, and when, and in what manner; and murmuring at him if he did not always grant their particular and various desires.—*Matthew Pool.*

Verse 41.—*"They limited the Holy One of Israel."* Here, then, is an awful charge, and mysterious it seems to *us* as awful. How dreadful that man, the worm, should arrogate to himself *that*, to say to him that made him, *"Thus far shalt thou go and no farther."* Amazing, I say, the charge! to contract the dimensions and operations of the Deity. Amazing insolence, to draw a boundary line, beyond which the Creator himself must not pass, to define and prescribe to the Lawgiver of nature himself the pathway of his providence! The turpitude is immense. But we know, my friends, that the crime is not uncommon; and one of the natural results of sin seems to be this,—that the sinful spirit, whether of man or of the lost archangel, unable to shake the firm foundations of the Eternal Throne, *amuses* its malignity, and seeks a temporary cessation from its withering cares, in putting up barriers on the outskirts and frontiers of the Almighty empire, vainly hoping to annoy the Possessor of the throne they cannot disturb.

Affecting words! Do they affect you as they affect me? *"They turned back and tempted God, and limited the Holy One of Israel."* Somehow, it seems no combination of words could have been so affecting. *They* limited *God.* They limited *the Almighty.* They limited *the Infinite. No!* These words have an awful and affecting surge of meaning in them; for while they describe *Him*, they also convey his relation to us. *They* limited ;—*The One ;*—the solitary, awful and self-contained Being whose essence is eternity and power; whose self-existence is declared by the amazing marvels of nature; whose life was essential being. They limited *Him*—*The One* in whose being all being was swallowed up and absorbed—*The One* before whose glance mountains and hills fled away and were not found—*The One* from everlasting, God; *high over all, blessed for evermore. The One* to whom all the nations were as the drop of a bucket, and who took up the isles as a very little thing,— Him *"they limited."*

They had known his character as *"The Holy One"* ; it was all they knew of his character; but it was surrounded with an awfulness more dread than even the solitary power and self-repose of Deity. In awful words and meanings they had heard his character proclaimed—*The Holy One.* Him they *limited. Him*, whose throne was curtained with the dreadful wings of sinless archangels, crying through the darkness of that ineffable brightness, Holy, holy, holy, Lord God Almighty! and whose holiness was asserted even by the disorders of the rolling world.

They limited him.—More personal, and therefore more wonderful, became the enormity. The generations of their race had testified for Him, the Holy One of Israel; they had beheld the marvels of his holiness and power in Egypt, in the Red Sea; they had heard of the God of Abraham, and Isaac, and Jacob; they had heard of him who had spoken to their Captain in the bush burning with fire; they beheld his pillar of fire and cloud; they knew themselves divinely selected and chosen; and him who chose *they limited!* That which should have ensured their faith became only the fountain of their criminality.—*E. Paxton Hood.*

Verse 41.—*"They limited the Holy One of Israel."* God cannot bear it with patience, that we should *limit him*, either to the time, or manner, or means of help. He complains of the Jews for this presumption, *they limited the Holy One of Israel.* It is insufferable to circumscribe an infinite wisdom and power. He will work, but when he pleases, and how he pleases, and by what instruments he pleases, and if he please, without instruments, and if he please by weak and improbable, by despised and exploded instruments.—*Joseph Caryl, in a "Sermon before the House of Commons," entitled, "The Workes of Ephesus."*

Verse 41.—*(last clause).* This was Israel's sin, and has it not often been ours? Our God is the " Holy One," and will do what is most for His glory ; he is the Holy One " *of Israel*," and will therefore consult his people's welfare. We must not limit his *wisdom*, for it is infinite ; we must not limit his *power*, for it is omnipotent ; we must not limit his *mercy*, for it is as high as heaven and deep as hell ; we must not limit him to *time*, for he will display his sovereignty : he will not be tied to walk by our rules, or be bound to keep our time ; but he will perform his word, honour our faith, and reward them that diligently seek him.—*James Smith.*

Verse 41.—*"Limited."* In the only other place where the Hebrew word occurs (Ezra ix. 4), it means to set a mark upon a person, which some apply here, in the figurative sense of stigmatising or insulting.—*Joseph Addison Alexander.*

Verse 41.—*"Limited the Holy One of Israel,"* or *signed* him ; signed him with a sign, so the Targum ; they tempted him by asking a sign of him, as Jarchi interprets it ; insisting that a miracle be wrought, by which it might be known whether the

Lord was among them or not, Exod. xvii. 7 ; with which compare Matt. xv. 1 : or they set bounds, so Kimchi, to his power and goodness, saying, this he could do, and the other he could not ; see verses 19, 20 ; and so men limit the Lord when they fix on a blessing they would have, even that, and not another ; and the measure of it, to what degree it should be bestowed on them, as well as the set time when they would have it ; whereas the blessing itself, and the degree of it, and the time of giving it, should be all left with the Lord who knows which and what of it is most convenient for us, and when is the best time to bestow it on us.—*John Gill.*

Verse 41.—*"Limited the Holy One of Israel "*—mistrust of God's power to effectuate all his grace, to do what is needed in any case for his people, and carry out his purposes for them. The moment I suppose anything cannot be for blessing, I limit God. This is a great sin—doubly, when we think of all he has done for us. The Holy Ghost ever reasons from God's revealed, infinite love to all its consequences. He reconciled ; surely he will save to the end. He did not spare his Son ; how shall he not give all things ?—*J. N. Darby.*

Verse 42.—*"They remembered not his hand,"* etc. God hates forgetfulness of his blessings. First, because he has commanded that we should not forget them, Deut. iv. 9 ; and viii. 14. Secondly, because forgetfulness is a sign of contempt. Thirdly, it is the peculiarity of singular carelessness. Fourthly, it springs from unbelief. Fifthly, it is the greatest mark of ingratitude.—*Thomas Le Blanc.*

Verse 42.—*"They remembered not his hand,"* etc. The rallying point of faith in time of trial is *the primary manifestation of grace.* To an Israelite a remembrance of the deliverance from Egypt is the test of active faith. In like manner, to the tried believer now it is the CROSS that furnishes the outlet of deliverance from the misty darkness with which Satan sometimes is permitted to envelope our conscience, when the Lord has not been kept watchfully before our face. Because Israel forgot that first deliverance, they went on frowardly in the way of evil. Because a Christian sometimes stops short of the Cross in his spiritual conflicts, he fails to defeat the enemy and remains unfruitful and unhappy, until by some special intervention of the great Restorer, he is again brought, in spirit, to that place where God first met him, and welcomed him in Jesus in the fulness of forgiveness and of peace. No intermediate experience, how truthful soever in its character, will meet his case. It is at the cross alone that we regain a thorough right-mindedness about ourselves as well as about God. If we would glorify him, we must " hold fast the *beginning* of our confidence stedfast unto the end," Heb. iii. 14.—*Arthur Pridham.*

Verse 42.—*"They remembered not his hand,"* etc. Eaten bread is soon forgotten. *Nihil citius senescit quam gratia.* Nothing so soon grows stale as a favour.—*John Trapp.*

Verse 43.—*"Zoan,"* or *San,* seems to have been one of the principal capitals, or royal abodes of the Pharaohs (Isaiah xix. 11, 13 ; xxx. 4) : and accordingly *"the field of Zoan,"* or the fine alluvial plain around the city, is described as the scene of the marvellous works which God wrought in the time of Moses.—*John Kitto.*

Verses 43—51.—Moses wrought wonders destructive, Christ wonders preservative ; he turned water into blood, Christ water into wine ; he brought flies and frogs and locusts and caterpillars, destroying the fruits of the earth, and annoying it ; Christ increased a little of these fruits, five loaves and a few fishes, by blessing them, so that he herewith fed five thousand men : Moses smote both men and cattle with hail, and thunder and lightning, that they died, Christ made some alive that were dead, and saved from death the diseased and sick ; Moses was an instrument to bring all manner of wrath and evil angels amongst them, Christ cast out devils and did all manner of good, giving sight to the blind, hearing to the deaf, speech to the dumb, limbs to the lame, and cleansing to the leper, and when the sea was tempestuous appeasing it ; Moses slew their first-born, thus causing an horrible cry in all the land of Egypt ; Christ saveth all the first-born, or by saving makes them so ; for thus they are called, Heb. xii. 23.—*John Mayer.*

Verse 44.—*"Turned their rivers into blood,"* etc. This displays also the folly of creature worship. Pharaoh adores the life-sustaining power of nature, as embodied in the majestic river before him. The God of nature transforms the running water into a river of death before his eyes. It demonstrates, in the way that was most striking to the Hebrew and the Egyptian, that the God of Israel was the true and only God of heaven and earth, and that all other objects of worship were but the creatures of God or the works of men's hands.—*James G. Murphy.*

Verse 44.—*"Turned their river into blood,"* etc. They looked upon their river not only as consecrated to a deity ; but, if we may believe some authors, as their chief national god ; and worshipped it accordingly. . . . . They must have felt the utmost astonishment and horror, when they beheld their sacred stream changed and polluted, and the divinity whom they worshipped so shamefully soiled and debased. And these appearances must have had a salutary effect upon the Israelites ; as they were hence warned not to accede to this species of idolatry ; but to have it ever in contempt, as well as abhorrence.

It is to be observed, that God might, if it had been the divine pleasure, have many different ways tainted and polluted the streams of Egypt. But he thought proper to change it to blood. Now the Egyptians, and especially their priests, were particularly nice and delicate in their outward habit and rites ; and there was nothing which they abhorred more than blood, they seldom admitted any bloody sacrifices ; and with the least stain of gore they would have thought themselves deeply polluted. Their affectation of purity was so great that they could not bear to come within contact with a foreigner, or even to handle his clothes ; but to touch a dead body was an abomination, and required to be immediately expiated. . . . On these accounts the priests were continually making ablutions. There were four stated times, twice in the day, and as often in the night, at which they were all obliged to bathe themselves. Many accidents caused them to repeat it much oftener. Hence this evil brought upon them must have been severely felt, as "there was blood throughout all the land of Egypt," Exod. vii. 21.—*Jacob Bryant* (1715—1804), *in "Observations upon the Plagues inflicted upon the Egyptians."*

Verse 44.—*"And their floods, that they could not drink."* A third calamity accompanying this plague was the impossibility of drinking the water of the Nile, a vexation the keener felt by them, because the water of the Nile, after having been purified from the slime by a kind of almond-dough is, on the one hand, most agreeable, tasteful and healthy, so that it appears to strangers almost as an artificially prepared drink—whence the Egyptian proverb originated : "the water of the Nile is as sweet as honey and sugar," and the adage, "that if Mohammed had drank of it, he would have besought God to be immortal, that he might always enjoy it ; and it is, on the other hand, the *only* drinkable water which the inhabitants can possibly use ; for, says Maillet (I. p. 20) : "The well and cistern-water in Egypt is detestable and unwholesome ; fountains are so rare, that they are a kind of prodigy in that country ; and, as to rain-water, that is out of the question, as scarcely any rain falls in Egypt."—*M. M. Kalisch, in "A Historical and Critical Commentary on the Old Testament."* 1867.

Verse 45.—*"Flies."* [Exodus viii. 13, 14. כִּנִּם or כִּנִּים]. It is a matter of difficulty precisely to determine the species or kind of animals denoted by that expression ; but so much is certain : 1. That they must be a very small kind of insects, as they are represented to arise from the grains of dust ; 2. That they are noxious both to man and beasts (ver. 13.) and in a still higher degree than the frogs. The singular, כֵּן, is used in Isaiah li. 6, where it represents something very frail, weak, and perishable. The etymology leads to the Greek root, κνάω, to *gnaw* or pinch—and this coincides with the English noun *gnats*, with which, indeed, all the qualities just mentioned perfectly agree. And the Septuagint, which is naturally of great authority in all matters concerning the natural phenomena of Egypt, its home, translates also σκνῖφες (musquito gnats) ; which Philo, likewise an Egyptian, describes thus : "It is an insect although of very small size, yet of a most troublesome nature ; for it hurts not only the surface, causing intolerable and protracted itching, but penetrates also into the interior through the ears and noses. It flies even into the eyes of those who do not guard themselves, and produces pain." All which qualities are perfectly applicable to gnats.—*M. M. Kalisch.*

Verse 45.—*"He sent divers sorts of flies."* "I will send swarms *of flies* upon thee," etc. (Exod. viii. 21.) Heb. עָרֹב, *arob, a mixture,* or *mixed swarm,* i.e. probably of flies, wasps, hornets, and other vexatious and stinging insects. It will be observed that *"flies"* in our version, being printed in italics, is not in the original. . . . . the Septuagint renders עָרֹב, *arob,* by κυνόμυιαν, *dog fly,* from its biting, an insect that fastens its teeth so deep in the flesh, and sticks so very close, that it oftentimes makes cattle run mad. . . . .

"He sent (עֲרֹב, *arob*) *divers sorts of flies among them which devoured them."* The *arob* is described as *devouring* the Egyptians, which is an act which seems inapplicable to a fly. Upon the whole we strongly incline to the opinion which has found some able supporters of late years, that the Egyptian beetle (*blatta Ægyptiaca*) is denoted in this place. The beetle, which is almost everywhere a nuisance, is particularly abundant and offensive in Egypt, and all the circumstances which the Scriptures in different places intimates concerning the *arob*, applies with much accuracy to this species. It devours everything that comes in its way, even clothes, books, and plants, and does not hesitate to inflict severe bites on men. If also we conceive that one object of these plagues was to chasten the Egyptians through their own idols, there is no creature of its class which could be more fitly employed than this insect. What precise place it filled in the religious system of that remarkable people has never, we believe, been exactly determined ; but that it occupied a conspicuous place among their sacred creatures seems to be evinced by the fact, that there is scarcely any figure which occurs more frequently in Egyptian sculpture and painting. —*George Bush.*

Verse 45.—"Flies, which devoured them." [See Exodus viii. 24.] *"The land was corrupted by reason of the swarm of flies."* Bochart understands by *land, the inhabitants,* whose blood these flies sucked, and left such a poison in it, that their bodies swelled, and many of them died. Le Clerc understands it of the flesh and other eatables, which those vermin having preyed upon, and fly-blown, bred maggots, stench and putrefaction throughout the land.—*Jameson's Critical and Practical Exposition of the Pentateuch.* 1748.

Verse 45.—"And frogs, which destroyed them." Galerius observes, that the Egyptians were punished in this plague upon all the five senses. The sight was punished, that was offended with the multitude, with the greatness, with the hideous form and colour of these frogs. Their hearing was offended with the croaking of them ; for it was but harsh music to dainty ears. Their smell was offended with the stench of them. Their taste was offended that they came into their troughs, the places of their dough, and so hindered them of the food that was provided for their nourishment. . . . . " The frogs shall come up both on thee, and upon thy people, and upon all thy servants," (Exod. viii. 4.) So that thou shalt not rid thyself of this annoyance. What ! in their meat, and drink ; and upon their bodies ! Then observe with me, beloved, God can lay judgments upon people, that shall not be more painful, and troublesome, than odious, loathsome and noisome.—*Josias Shute, in "Judgment and Mercy : or the Plague of Frogs* { *inflicted removed.*—1645.*"*

Verse 45.—"Frogs." The Egyptians suffered most keenly from the infliction. They were a singularly fastidious people, and abhorred the contact of anything that they held to be unclean. We may well realise, therefore, the effect of a visitation of frogs, which rendered their houses unclean by entering them, and themselves unclean by leaping upon them ; which deprived them of rest by getting on their beds, and of food by crawling into their ovens and upon the dough in the kneading-troughs. And, as if to make the visitation still worse, when the plague was removed, the frogs died in the places into which they had intruded, so that the Egyptians were obliged to clear their houses of the dead carcases, and to pile them up in heaps, to be dried by the sun, or eaten by birds and other scavengers of the East. As to the species of frog which thus invaded the houses of the Egyptians, there is no doubt whatever. It can be but the *green,* or *edible frog* (*Rana esculenta*), which is so well known for the delicacy of its flesh. This is believed to be the only aquatic frog of Egypt, and therefore must be the species which came out of the river into the houses. Both in Egypt and Palestine it exists in very great numbers, swarming in every marshy place, and inhabiting the pools in such numbers that the water can scarcely be seen for the frogs. Thus the multitudes of the frogs which invaded the Egyptians was no matter of wonder, the only miraculous element being that the reptiles were simultaneously directed to the houses, and their simultaneous death when the plague was taken away.—*J. G. Wood.*

Verse 45.—"Frogs." The rod is lifted up again. Behold, that Nilus, which they had before adored, was never so beneficial as it is now troublesome ; yielding them not only a dead, but a living annoyance : it never did so store them with fish as it now plagues them with frogs. Whatsoever any man makes his god, besides the true one, shall be one day his tormentor. Those loathsome creatures leave their own element to punish them which rebelliously detained Israel from their own.

No bed, no table, can be free from them : their dainty ladies cannot keep them out of their bosoms ; neither can the Egyptians sooner open their mouths than they are ready to creep into their throats, as if they would tell them, that they came on purpose to revenge the wrongs of their Maker.—*Joseph Hall.*

Verse 46.—*"Caterpiller."* חָסִיל, *chasil*, is rendered βροῦχος by the LXX, in 2 Chron. vi. 28, and by Aquila here, and also by the Vulgate in Chron. and in Isai. xxxiii. 4, and it is rendered by Jerome here, *bruchus,* " the chaffer," which everyone knows to be a great devourer of the leaves of trees. The Syriac in Joel i. 4, ii. 25, renders it צָרָצוֹרָא *tzartzooro*, which Michaelis, from the Arabic צרצר *tsartzar*, a cricket, interprets the *mole-cricket*, which, in its grub state, is also very destructive to corn, grass, and other vegetables, by cankering the roots on which it feeds.—*Editorial Note to Calvin in loc.*

Verse 46.—*"Caterpiller."* In former times, any destructive, crawling creature occurring in cultivated places was thus called ; now, by general consent, we restrict the term to the second stage of insects of the Lepidopterous order, namely, butterflies and moths. These caterpillers, by the voracity with which they attack the leaves, the fruit, and sometimes the solid wood of plants and trees, are made conspicuous even to those who are little acquainted with natural history.—*"Biblical Treasury."*

Verse 46.—*"Locust."* Their quantity is incredible to all who have not themselves witnessed their astonishing numbers ; the whole earth is covered with them for the space of several leagues. The noise they make in browsing on the trees and herbage may be heard at a great distance, and resembles that of an army plundering in secret. The Tartars themselves are a less destructive enemy than these little animals. One would imagine that fire had followed their progress. Wherever their myriads spread, the verdure of the country disappears ; trees and plants stripped of their leaves and reduced to their naked boughs and stems, cause the dreary image of winter to succeed in an instant to the rich scenery of spring. When these clouds of locusts take their flight, to surmount any obstacles, or to traverse more rapidly a desert soil, the heavens may literally be said to be obscured with them.—*F. C., Comte de Volney.*

Verse 47.—*"He destroyed their vines with hail, and their sycamore trees with frost."* The grape vine for the rich, and the sycamore fig for the poor, were cut off by the just judgment of God upon the nation.—*W. Wilson.*

Verse 47.—The sycomore (not sycamore, for this is altogether different, though, in consequence of a typographical error, often confounded with it in our Bibles) was the name of a tree, common in Egypt, Amos. vii. 14 ; Luke xix. 4. This tree resembled the mulberry in its leaves, and the fig in its fruit ; and on its produce the inferior ranks of people, for the most part, lived. The Psalmist refers to but one sort, still he clearly means every kind, of valuable tree.—*William Keatinge Clay.*

Verse 49.—*"By sending evil angels."* Evils come uncalled, but not unsent. Are they not here called *"angels"* ? they are sent ; the word *angel* means a messenger. Not things only without life, but not living creatures neither, brute, nor men, nor Satan's self can hurt unless God bid. The three days' darkness in Egypt, how came it ? " He sent darkness," saith David. Psalm cv. 28. So the hail, thunder, and lightning, the Lord sent them, saith Moses. The frogs, flies, lice, grasshoppers, and caterpillars, that infected Egypt, and the lions that slew the idolators in Samaria (2 Kings xvii.), the text saith of them all, *Dominus immisit*, the Lord sent them. And for men—" Am I come " (said Rabshakeh) " without the Lord ? " He bade me go. Yea, the devil, the arch-evil-angel, who seeks to devour, yet must be *sent* ere he can do ought. The lying spirit in the mouths of the false prophets longed to seduce Ahab ; God must first bid ; *Egredere*, go forth, and do so. The use of this is easy without my help : not to fear, doing well ; not man, fiend, any creature, can hurt you, God not sending them. But sinning, to fear everything. The weakest creature can quell the mightiest man, if God bid, go. A mouse (saith the poet) will bite a wicked man. Be it proud Herod, great Antiochus ; if God but ask the creatures, *Quem mittam*, which of you shall I send ? the worm will answer, *Ecce me*, send me ; I will devour him. And such poor, silly, despicable creatures are some of these *"evil angels "* in my text. *"He sent : "* what sent he ? *"evil angels,"* the next thing in this Scripture.

"Evil angels ? " *Par dispar*, a pair of words which seem not well matched. The latter may say to the former, *Quid mihi et tibi*, what have I to do with thee ? Angels

were the best and holiest of God's creatures. They all were good, very good, Moses
saith ; but angels κατ᾽ ἐξοχήν, excellently good. Then is *"evil"* here an evil epithet
for angels. And is never read but here, and here (some think) not well translated.
But the phrase of *"evil angels"* hath other meaning here : *evil angels, i.e.,* the angels,
i.e., the messengers of evil. It is in the Hebrew, not מַלְאָכִים, but מַלְאֲכֵי ; insomuch
that some expositors think the Psalmist means the words of Moses and Aaron ;
that they were sent from God to be the messengers of evil, *i.e.,* of all the plagues
that God would bring on Egypt. That sense I censure not, but follow not. The
Greek Fathers have another—that by the *"evil angels"* are meant the *evil spirits.*
Christ calls them angels too, the devil's angels. Augustine likes not that sense.
The most current exposition is as a Jewish writer speaks : the " evil angels " are the
ten several plagues.—*Richard Clerke.* (—1634.)

Verse 49.—*"By sending evil angels among them."* That the devil and his angels
are so very evil, that for them everlasting fire is prepared, no believer is ignorant :
but that there should be sent by means of them an infliction from the Lord God
upon certain whom he judgeth to be deserving of this punishment, seemeth to be
a hard thing to those who are little prone to consider how the perfect justice of God
doth use well even evil things. For these indeed, as far as regardeth their substance,
what other person but himself hath made ? But evil he hath not made them ;
yet he doth use them, inasmuch as he is good, conveniently and justly ; just as on
the other hand unrighteous men do use his good creatures in evil manner : God
therefore doth use evil angels not only to punish evil men, as in the case of all those
concerning whom the Psalm doth speak, as in the case of king Ahab, whom a spirit
of lying by the will of God did beguile, in order that he might fall in war ; but also
to prove and make manifest good men, as he did in the case of Job.—*Augustine.*

Verse 50.—*"He made a way to his anger."* Literally—" weighed a way : "
implying that God, in punishing the Egyptians so severely, did nothing but what
was just and equitable, when *weighed* in the balance of right. Prov. iv. 26.—*A. R.
Fausset.*

Verse 50.—*"He made a way to his anger."* As if the Psalmist had said, If there
were not *"a way"* for his anger, that is, for the execution of his anger, *he forced* his
way ; though he did not find a way, yet he *"made"* one, and fought himself through
all difficulties which seemed to oppose the destruction of his enemies. We put in
the margin, *"he weighed a path,"* he made the path as exact as if he had put it into
a balance ; the way was fitted to the largeness of his own anger, and 'twas fitted
to the dimensions of their wickedness. Thus *"he made a way to his anger,"* both
by suiting the way to his anger and by removing all impediments out of the way
of his anger. If God will work to save, who shall let it ? and if God will work to
destroy, who or what shall let it ?—*Joseph Caryl.*

Verse 51.—*"The chief of their strength in the tabernacles of Ham."* The sun of
the last day of the sojourn of Israel in Egypt had set. It was the fourth day after
the interview with Moses. Pharaoh, his princes, and the priests of his idols would
doubtless take courage from this unwonted delay. Jehovah and his ministers are
beaten at length, for now the gods of Egypt prevail against them. The triumph
would be celebrated in pomps and sacrifices, in feasts and dances. Nothing is more
likely than that the banquet halls of Pharaoh at Rameses were blazing with lamps,
and that he and his princes were pouring forth libations of wine to their gods, and
concerting schemes amid their revelry, for the perpetuation of the thraldom of
Israel. . . . . Pharaoh Sethos started from his couch that night yelling in fierce and
bitter agony, and gnawing at the sharp arrow that was rankling in his vitals, like a
wounded lion. His son, his first-born, his only son, just arrived at man's estate,
just crowned king of Egypt, and associated with his father in the cares of sovereignty
writhed before him in mortal throes, and died. His transports of grief were re-echoed,
and with no feigned voice, by the princes, the councillors, and the priests that partook
of his revelry. Each one rends his garments and clasps to his bosom the quivering
corpse of his first-born son. On that fearful night " there was a great cry throughout
all the land of Egypt," but if we have rightly read its history, the loudest, wildest
wail of remorseful anguish would arise from Pharaoh's banquet hall !—*William
Osburn, in "Israel in Egypt."* 1856.

Verse 52.—*"But made his own people to go forth like sheep."* It is not said that
they went forth like sheep ; but that he made them go forth like sheep. It is not

a description of the character of the people, but a commendation of the providence and goodness of God, by which, after the manner of a good shepherd, he led forth from Egypt his own people with all security, like sheep snatched from the midst of wolves.—*Musculus.*

Verse 53.—*"They feared not."* First, they had no cause for fear, *in their departure from Egypt.* Though they saw the Egyptians slain, yet against them not even a dog moved its tongue. 2. They were all in sound health. 3. They were enriched with the spoils of the Egyptians. 4. They went forth a great multitude. 5. They supplied themselves with arms. Secondly, *they feared not to enter the Red Sea,* for the fear started by the approach of Pharaoh was swiftly suppressed. Thirdly, *they feared not to wander in the desert* for forty years, God going before his pillar. Fourthly, *they feared not, though enemies attacked them.*—*Thomas Le Blanc.*

Verse 54.—*"He brought them to the border of his sanctuary,"* or *holiness ;* that is, to the holy land ; so called in divers respects, but especially because of his sanctuary, the place of his residence ; to which he makes all the land to be but as bounds and limits, because of the eminency of that place, the holiness whereof did, as it were, spread to all other parts of the land, as if the whole had been a sanctuary, and consecrated ground. It is therefore to the honour of the whole land, as well as of the sanctuary, that he calleth it *"the holy border,"* a *"border of his sanctuary."*—*Westminster Assembly's Annotations.*

Verse 57.—*"They were turned aside like a deceitful bow."* The eastern bow, which when at rest is in the form of a ⌒, must be *recurved,* or *turned the contrary way,* in order to be what is called *bent* and *strung.* If a person who is unskilful or weak attempt to *recurve* and string one of these bows, if he take not great heed it will spring back and regain its quiescent position, and perhaps break his arm. And sometimes I have known it, when bent, to *start aside,* and regain its quiescent position, to my no small danger, and in one or two cases to my injury. This image is frequently used in the sacred writings ; but no person has understood it, not being acquainted with the eastern *bow* ⌒, which must be *recurved* or bent the contrary way ⌐, in order to be proper for use. If not well made, they will fly back in discharging the arrow. It is said of the *bow* of Jonathan, *"it turned not back,"* 2 Samuel i. 22, אָחוֹר נָשׂוֹג לֹא, *lo nasog achor,* " did not twist itself backward." It was a good bow, one on which he could depend. Hosea, chap. vii. 16, compares the unfaithful Israelites to a *"deceitful bow ;"* one that, when bent, would suddenly start aside and recover its former position. We may find the same passage in Jer. ix. 3. And this is precisely the kind of bow mentioned by *Homer,* Odyss. xxi., which none of Penelope's suitors could bend, called καμπύλα τόξα and αγκύλο τόξα, the *crooked bow,* in the state of rest ; but τόξον παλίντονον, the *recurved bow* when prepared for use. And of his trial of *strength* and *skill* in the bending of the bow of Ulysses, none of the critics and commentators have been able to make anything, because they knew not the instrument in question. On the τόξον θησις of Homer I have written a dissertation elsewhere. The image is very correct ; these Israelites, when brought out of their natural bent, soon recoiled, and relapsed into their former state.—*Adam Clarke.*

Verse 57.—*"Starting aside like a broken bow "* (English Prayer Book) : but if a bow breaks, it will not start aside, for the elasticity which should make it start aside will be destroyed.—*Stephen Street.*

Verse 57.—*"They were turned aside like a deceitful bow."* When the bow is unbent the rift it hath may be undiscerned, but go to use it by drawing the arrow to the head, and it flies in pieces ; thus doth a false heart when put to the trial. As the ape in the fable, drest like a man, when nuts are thrown before her, cannot then dissemble her nature any longer, but shows herself an ape indeed ; a false heart betrays itself before it is aware, when a fair occasion is presented for its lust ; whereas sincerity keeps the soul pure in the face of temptation.—*William Gurnall.*

Verse 57.—The fourth thing is *the deceitful bow,* קֶשֶׁת רְמִיָּה, a slack or warping bow *arcus doli vel dolosus seu fallax* (Hebrew) will be sure to deceive the archer that shoots in it ; 'twill turn back into belly, as the archer's phrase is ; and though he level both his eye and his arrow never so directly to the mark and think confidently with himself to hit it ; yet, in the event, the arrow, through the warping of the bow, flies a quite contrary way, yea, and sometimes reflects upon the archer himself. *Non semper feriet, quodcunque minabitur arcus,* the bow smites not all it threatens, and the ill-fashioned or casting bow will turn in the shooter's hand, and send the arrow sometimes one way and sometimes another way ; yea, and sometimes it rebounds into his own sides ; or if it be a rotten bow (though otherwise fair to look upon), when an arrow is drawn to the head it breaks in the hand, and deceives the archer.   The same thing happeneth when the string of the bow is naughty, and breaks when the arrow is drawn.   This is no less than a divine Scripture allegory. Behold, such a fallacious, warping, and rotten bow is man's deceitful heart ; his purposes and promises are the arrows that he puts upon the string, the mark he aims at is repentance, to the which (in affliction especially) he looketh with an accurate and intent eye, as though he would repent indeed ; but, alas ! his heart deceives him, as being unsound in God's statutes, Psalm cxix. 80 ; and hence it is that his promises and pretences do fall at his foot, or vanish in the air as smoke. Thus a *deceiving*, as well as a *deceived* heart, turns him aside, Isaiah xliv. 20, as it did those false Israelites : oh, then, look to the secret warpings of your own heart, and seeing you are God's bow, you must be bent by him, and stand bent for him, Zech. ix. 13 ; thereby you shall be like Jonathan's bow that " never returned empty," 2 Samuel i. 22.—*Christopher Ness, in "A Chrystal Mirrour."*   1679.

Verses 57—59.—Not to be settled in the faith, is provoking to God.   To espouse the truth, and then to fall away, brings an ill report upon the gospel, which will not go unpunished.   *"They turned back, and dealt unfaithfully.   When God heard this, he was wroth, and greatly abhorred Israel."*   The apostate drops as a windfall into the devil's mouth.—*Thomas Watson.*

Verse 58.—*"High places."*   Or, altars, chapels, and such like places, to celebrate divine service in, out of the only place which was by him consecrated, and was alone acceptable unto him ; or peradventure also dedicated to idols ; and were so called, because that they chose out the choicest hills and hillocks for those purposes.— *John Diodati.*

Verse 59.—*"When God heard this."*   The Psalmist represents the noise of the ill deeds of the people ascending to the ears of the Eternal.—*Armand de Mestral, in "Commentaire sur le Livre de Psaumes."*   1856.

Verse 60.—It is a heathenish delusion and false confidence to suppose that God is bound to any place or spot, as the Trojans thought because they had the temple of Pallas in their city it could not be taken, and in the present day the manner of the Papists is to bind Christ to Rome and the chair of Peter, and then defiantly maintain " I shall never be moved " (Ps. x. 6).   For, they say, the ship of Peter may sink a little, but not altogether.   Then the only point that is deficient is this, that they are not the ship of Peter, but rather an East Indiaman with a cargo of Indian apes and such like foreign merchandize, pearls, purple, silk, brass, iron, silver, gold, incense, lead, that they may carry on simony and make merchandize of religion, and deceive the whole world (Rev. xviii. 11—24).—*Johann Andreas Cramer.*   1723—1788.

Verse 61.—*"And delivered his strength into captivity,"* etc.   He calls the ark the *strength of God*, not because the virtue of God was shut up therein, or was so bound to it that he could not, unless through it, be powerful and strong : but because his presence, whose symbol the ark was, had always revealed its virtue and might to Israel, in the perpetual defence and various deliverances of that people.   After the same manner he calls it the beauty or glory of God, because God by his own presence declared his glory among the people, and desired that it should be conspicuous by this external symbol.—*Mollerus.*

Verse 63.—*"The fire consumed their young men."*   *"Fire"* here may be regarded as an image of destructive war, as in Num. xxi. 28.   " For there is a fire gone out of Heshbon, a flame from the city of Sihon : it hath consumed Ar of Moab," etc.— *Albert Barnes.*

Verse 63 *(first clause).*—When religion is overthrown among God's people, let not the commonwealth think to stand : when God gave his glory unto the enemies' hand, " He gave his people over also unto the sword, and *the fire consumed their young men."*—*David Dickson.*

Verse 63.—*"Not given to marriage."*   *" Not praised : "* viz. they had not been honoured with nuptial songs according to the customs of those times, see Jer. vii. 34 ; xvi. 9 ; xxv. 10.   The meaning is, they had not been honourably married, because men were grown scarce by reason of the wars, Isai. iv. 1 ; Jer. xxxi. 22.   Or, they had been married without any solemnity, like poor bond-women; or privately, as in the time of public calamities.—*John Diodati.*

Verse 64.—"*Their widows made no lamentation.*" This implies the extent of the destruction, and is full of meaning to one who has been in an Oriental city, during a plague or other devastating calamity. At first the cry of wailing, which always follows a death in ordinary circumstances, is loud and frequent: but such cries do not increase, but subside, with the increase of the calamity and desolation. Death becomes a familiar object in every house; and every one, absorbed in his own losses, has little sympathy to spare for others. Hence the loudest lamentations cease to be noticed, or to draw condoling friends to the house of mourning; and therefore, as well as from the stupefaction of feeling which scenes of continued horror never fail to produce, a new death is received in silence, or only with sighs and tears. In fact, all the usual observances are suspended. The dead are carried out and buried without mourning ceremonies, and without the presence of surviving friends, by men who make it an employment to take away the dead, on the backs of mules or asses, from the homes they leave desolate. We have seen this.—*Kitto's "Pictorial Bible."* 1856.

Verse 64.—"*Their widows made no lamentation.*" The meaning is, either 1. That being overwhelmed with sorrow they could not weep; or, 2. That being in captivity amongst the Philistines they were not suffered to lament the death of their husbands; or 3. That dying with grief, they lived not to make any lamentations for them at their funerals; or 4. That they were so taken up and oppressed with their own miseries, and especially with the miseries of the church and people of God in general, that they had not leisure to bewail their husbands; of both which last we have a clear instance in the wife of Phinehas in particular, 1 Sam. iv. 19, 20, who dying, made no mention of her husband.—*Arthur Jackson.*

Verse 64.—The daughter-in-law of Eli, when she was at once travailing, and in that travail dying, to make up the full sum of God's judgment upon that wicked house, as one insensible of the death of her father, of her husband, of herself, in comparison of this loss, calls her (then unseasonable) son Ichabod, and with her last breath says, " The glory is departed from Israel, the ark is taken."—*Joseph Hall.*

Verse 65.—"*Then the Lord awaked.*" Know how to understand this and similar passages in Scripture, as to the Lord's sleeping and forgetting his people, Ps. xiii. 1; xliv. 33; lxxvii. 9. These are not to be understood as to an universal and absolute forgetting and sleep of providence; for God hath not his vacation time; he still holds the reins of government in his hand, all the world over. Neither do they infer an absolute cessation of providence in reference to that object-matter which the Lord to our apprehension seems to forget, and lies dormant; for there is a promoting-work of providence, which we see not, and are not so sensible of for the present, as hath been shewed. Besides, such forgetting and sleep of providence, as it is such, bespeaks the beauty of providence in the way of bringing things to pass. It is so far from inferring an *interregnum,* or letting fall the sceptre of government, as that it is a glorious demonstration that God orders matters, and that wisely, whilst he seems to forget, and be as one asleep. As the night, as night, falls under the providence of God as well as the day, for there are the ordinances of heaven for the night season, Jer. xxxi. 35: so the dark night, when as to matters the Lord seems to sleep, is part and parcel of his all-wise model of government. The seventy years' captivity was a long night of the church's distress; and yet thus it must be according to the ordinance of providence. Jer. xxix. 10.—*Thomas Crane.*

Verse 65.—"*Like a mighty man that shouteth by reason of wine:*" whose spirit and courage is revived and inflamed by a liberal draught of generous wine; which comparison is no more injurious to the Divine Majesty than that of a thief's coming in the night, to which Christ's second coming is compared, 1 Thess. v. 2.—*Matthew Pool.*

Verse 66.—"*He smote his enemies in the hinder parts.*" This has reference to the Philistines being smitten with hemorrhoids, or piles, whilst the ark was retained a captive by them, 1 Sam. v. 6, 12. . . . . . The Greek version, as quoted by Suidas is, *he smote his enemies on the back parts of the seat;* signifying, he says, a disease modestly expressed.—*John Gill.*

Verse 67.—The moving of the ark is not the removing of it; Shiloh has lost it, but Israel has not. God will have a church in the world, and a kingdom among men, though this or that place may have its candlestick removed ; nay, the rejection of Shiloh is the election of Sion.—*Matthew Henry.*

Verses 67, 68.—"*Refused.*" "*Chose not.*" "*Chose.*" As God's love is set out to us, as not independently pitched, but as having all the persons in his eye and having them all in view ; so by this also, that he hath not pitched it upon everybody. This is distinct from the former ; for an indefinite is not knowing whom he pitched it upon. Now, as he knew whom he pitched upon, so he hath pitched but upon some, not on every one. . . . If God would love, it was fit he should be free. It is a strange thing that you will not allow God that which kings and princes have the prerogative of, and you will allow it them. They will have favourites whom they will love, and will not love others ; and yet men will not allow God that liberty, but he must either love all mankind, or he must be cruel and unjust. The specialness of his love greateneth it, and endeareth it to us. You shall find almost all along the Bible, that when God would express his love, he doth it with a speciality to his own elect, which he illustrates by the contrary done to others. . . . And you shall find frequently in the Scripture, when he mentioneth his choice of some persons, he holdeth up likewise on purpose his refusing of others. . . . When he speaks of an election out of the tribes, he contents not himself to say he chose Judah, but he puts in the rejection, the preterition at least, of Joseph. "*He refused the tabernacle of Joseph, and chose not the tribe of Ephraim : But chose the tribe of Judah, the mount Zion which he loved.*" . . . He speaks of the times of the judges. The rejection of the ten tribes began to show itself soon ; he says, he refused the tabernacle of Ephraim, but he chose Judah. After Solomon's time, they fell to worshipping of calves (let me tell you, it is the declining of election that undoes a nation, when election grows low, and ceases in an age), till at last the ten tribes were cast off, as they are at this day ; but the tribe of Judah had election among them. . . .

Though at the first, and for a long time, both were alike his people, yet at last election began to pass a discrimination. Ephraim, or the ten tribes, had at first the advantage of Judah in spirituals ; for the ark, the token of God's presence, was committed unto their keeping at Shiloh ; the seal of God's worship and ordinances was intrusted to them, and Judah must come up thither, if they would seek the Lord. But Ephraim, for their sinning against that worship, forfeited and lost it, and should therefore have the keeping of it no longer, no, not for ever any more ; but Judah had it at Bethlehem, till at last it was fixedly seated in Sion, as " the earth is established " (ver. 69) ; and this for no other reason than that he had loved them, and out of love had chosen them (ver. 67—69). For otherwise Judah was, as well as Ephraim, alike involved in the same guilt of sin which had forfeited it, as ver. 56—60 of the Psalm plainly show. "*Yet they tempted and provoked the most high God, and kept not his testimonies,*" etc. He speaks it of the whole in those verses, and yet takes the occasion against Ephraim to remove it for ever. Thus, the first are last, and the last first ; and those whom God's presence is with for a while, upon some eminent sin God begins to withdraw from them and by degrees, as he did by that people of the ten tribes till at last he cast them off from being a people, but dealt not so with Judah, though these made a forfeiture of their temple and worship, and nation, in the captivity of Babylon, yet God restored all again to greater glory at last. The ground was that in verse 68, " *Zion which he loved.*"— *Thomas Goodwin.*

Verse 70.—"*He took him from the sheepfolds.*" The art of feeding cattle, and the art of ruling men are sisters, saith Basil.—*John Trapp.*

Verse 71.—" *From following the ewes great with young.*" A good and steady lamber is of great value to a grazier, but I would advise all graziers to attend to this operation themselves, as few servants will be found to pay that attention which is necessary, or which a master himself would do, and the slightest neglect is, in many cases, followed with the greatest disadvantage. I have attended to the practice of lambing for several years, therefore, trust I am not a novice in it, or incompetent to give a description of it. Many lambs may be lost without its being possible to charge the lamber with neglect or ignorance, though greater attention on his part might have saved many that otherwise perish. . . . . The practice of lambing is at times very intricate, and is apt to exhaust the patience of a lamber. Sheep are obstinate, and lambing presents a scene of confusion, disorder, and trouble, which it is the lamber's business to rectify, and for which he ought always to be prepared :

some of the ewes perhaps leave their lambs, or the lambs get intermixed, and the ewes which have lost their lambs run about bleating, while others want assistance These are only a few of the various occurrences which call for the immediate attention of the lamber.—*Daniel Price, in " A System of Sheep-grazing and Management."* 1809.

Verse 71.—"From following the ewes great with young." It hath been reported that a learned doctor of Oxford hung up his leathern breeches in his study for a memorial to visitors of his mean original ; the truth I avouch not, but history tells us of Agathocles who arose from a potter to be king of Sicily, and would be served in no other plate at his table but earthenware, to mind him of his former drudgery. 'Twere well if some would remember whose shoes they have cleaned, whose coals they have carried, and whose money they have borrowed, and deal gratefully with their creditors, as the good Lord Cromwell did by the Florentine merchant in the time of Henry the Eighth, when Wolsey* like a butcher forgot the king his master. 'Twas otherwise with holy David, who being in kingly dignity, graciously calls to mind his following the ewes great with young, when now feeding the sheep of Israel. His golden sceptre points at his wooden hook, and he plays the old lessons of his oaten pipe upon his Algum harp, and spreads his Bethlehem tent within his marble palace on Mount Zion.—*Samuel Lee.*

Verse 71.—"To feed Jacob his people."† Observe a good shepherd must be humble and faithful, he ought to have bread in a wallet, a dog by a string, a staff with a rod, and a tuneful horn. The bread is the word of God, the wallet is the memory of the word ; the dog is zeal, wherewith the shepherd glows for the house of God, casts out the wolves with pious barking, following preaching and unwearied prayer : the string by which the dog is held is the moderation of zeal, and discretion, whereby the zeal of the shepherd is tempered by the spirit of piety and knowledge. The staff is the consolation of pious exhortation by which the too timid are sustained and refreshed, lest they fail in the time of tribulation ; but the rod is the authority and power by which the turbulent are restrained. The tuneful horn, which sounds so sweetly, signifies the sweetness of eternal blessedness, which the faithful shepherd gently and often instils into the ears of his flock.—*Johannes Paulus Palanterius.* 1600.

Verse 72.—In spite of his transgressions, which he always bitterly repented of, and which were therefore blotted out of the Book of God, he remains to all princes and rulers of the earth as the noblest pattern. In perfect inward truth he knew and felt himself to be *"King by the grace of God."* The crown and sceptre he bore merely in trust from the King of all kings ; and to his latest breath he endeavoured with all his earnestness to be found as a genuine theocratic king, who in everything must conduct his earthly government according to the ordinances and directions of God. Therefore the Lord made all that he took in hand prosper, and nothing was clearer to the people than that the Lord was *truly with the king.*— *Frederick William Krummacher, in " David the King of Israel."* 1867.

HINTS TO PREACHERS.

Verse 1.—The duty of attending to God's word. Modes of neglecting the duty ; ways of fulfilment ; reasons for obedience ; evils of inattention.

Verse 2 (first clause).—Preach on the " Parable of the Prodigal Nation," as given in the whole Psalm.—*C. A. Davies, of Chesterfield.*

Verses 2, 3.—I. Truths are none the worse for being old : " sayings of old." " Old wood," says Lord Bacon, " is best to burn ; old books are best to read ; and old friends are best to trust." II. Truths are none the worse for being concealed under metaphors : " I will open," etc., " in a parable ; " " dark sayings." 1. They lead to more research. 2. They become eventually better known. III. Truths

---

* Foxe's Martyrology.

† This is a curious specimen of mediæval spiritualising, and is here inserted as such. It is amusing to note that a Tractarian expositor quotes the passage with evidently intense admiration.

are none the worse for being often repeated. 1. They are more tested. 2. They are better testified.—*G. R.*

Verse 3.—The connection between what we have "heard," and what we have personally "known" in religion.

Verse 4.—A good resolution, and a blessed result.—*C. D.*

Verse 4.—I. What is to be made known? "The praises of the Lord;" "his strength and his wonderful works." II. To whom are they to be made known? "To the generations to come." III. By whom? Parents—one generation to another. IV. How made known? 1. By hiding nothing. 2. By declaring everything God has done.—*G. R.*

Verse 5.—Scriptural tradition, or the heirloom of the gospel.

Verses 5—8.—Family religion. I. The fathers' knowledge the children's heritage—verses 5, 6. II. The fathers' fall the children's preservation—verses 7, 8.—*C. D.*

Verses 5—8.—I. Truth once started can never be arrested—verses 5, 6. II. Truth received binds the soul to God—verse 7. III. Truth rejected lights beacons for others—verse 8.—*C. D.*

Verse 6.—Care for the rising generation and for future posterity.

Verse 7.—Practical philosophy. I. Fix your hope wisely. II. Store the memory richly. III. So shall you guide the actions obediently.

Verses 7, 8.—On the deceitfulness of the heart, in disregarding providential dispensations in general.—*John Jamieson's "Sermons on the Heart,"* I. 430.

Verse 8.—Stubbornness not steadfastness, or the difference between a natural vice and a gracious quality.

Verse 8.—The false heart (*middle clause*), with its left hand, "Stubbornness in the wrong" (*first clause*), and its right hand, "Fickleness in the right" (*last clause*).—*C. D.*

Verse 9.—Who were they? What had they? What did they? When did they do it?

Verses 9, 67.—The backsliding of prominent believers. I. The Lord's soldiers: who they were; belonged to God's chosen people; were distinguished by grace. Gen. xlviii. 17—20. Strong by God's blessing. Deut. xxxiii. 17. Honourable place among their brethren. Favoured with the tabernacle at Shiloh—verse 60. II. Their equipment: armour defensive and offensive; like that of others who triumphed. III. Their behaviour in battle: to turn back was traitorous, cowardly, dangerous, disastrous, dishonourable. IV. Their punishment—verse 57. Deprived of their special honour. Rev. iii. 11—*C. D.*

Verses 10, 11.—The gradations of sin: neglecting, rejecting, forgetting God.—*C. D.*

Verses 12—16.—God revealed in his deeds. The wonder-working God—verses 12—16. The avenging God—verse 12. The interposing God—verse 13. The guiding God—verse 14. The Father-God—verses 14—16.—*C. D.*

Verses 12—17.—Obstinacy of unbelief. It makes head against God's majesty—verse 17; his gracious providence—verses 14—16; his interposing care—verse 13; his avenging justice—verse 12; his distinguishing grace—verses 12—16.—*C. D.*

Verses 12—17.—Prodigies cannot convert the soul. Luke xvi. 31.—*C. D.*

Verse 14.—The adaptations of God: a beautiful theme.—*C. D.*

Verse 14.—I. Direction. II. Protection. III. Refreshment.—*R. P. Buddicom.*

Verse 14.—The Lord guides his people by being, I. Their shade in prosperity, cooling and calming. II. Their light in adversity, cheering and warming.

Verses 15, 16.—Divine supplies seasonable, plentiful, of the best, marvellous.

Verse 16.—Streams from the Rock Christ Jesus. I. Their source. II. Their variety. III. Their abundance.—*B. Davies, of Greenwich.*

Verse 17.—Sin in its progress feeds upon divine mercies to aid its advance, as also every other surrounding circumstance.

Verses 17—21.—I. They tempted God's patience; verse 17. II. They tempted God's wisdom; verse 18. III. They tempted God's power; verses 19, 20. IV. They tempted God's wrath; verse 21.—*E. G. Gange, of Bristol.*

Verse 18.—"*Meat for their lust.*" In what respects temporal mercies may be so sought, and so become.

Verses 18—21.—The progress of evil. I. They are drawn away by their lust; verse 18. II. Lust having conceived bringeth forth sin: verses 19—20. III. Sin being finished bringeth forth death: verse 21. "Their carcases fell."—*C. D.*

Verse 19.—Unbelief a slander of God.

Verses 21, 22.—Evil consequences of unbelief. I. The sin itself : they doubted the ultimate certainty, completeness, and reality of God's salvation from Egypt. II. The aggravation of it : the object of it was God ; they who entertained it were God's people : The aids to faith were overlooked : " though." III. What it led them to ; inward sin—verse 18 ; outward sin—verse 19, etc. IV. What it brought upon them ; verse 21. Fiery serpents, etc.—*C. D.*

Verse 22.—Unbelief the mother of sorrows.

Verse 25.—Different kinds of food. Beasts' food, Luke xv. 16. Sinners' food, Hosea iv. 8. Formalists' food, Hosea xii. 1. Saints' food, Jer. xv. 16 ; John vi. 53—57. Angels' food. Christ's food, John iv. 34.—*C. D.*

Verses 29—31.—Dangerous prayers. When lust dictates, wrath may answer. Let grace dictate, and mercy will answer.—*C. D.*

Verses 34—37.—The hypocrite's feet, verse 34. The hypocrite's memory, verse 35. The hypocrite's tongue, verse 36. The hypocrite's heart, verse 37. Or, the hypocrite's cloak and the hypocrite's heart.—*C. D.*

Verse 36.—Flattery of God. I. A common sin. II. A hateful sin. III. A dangerous sin.—*B. D.*

Verses 38 (*last clause*) and 50 (*first clause*).—God's anger as exercised against his people and against his foes.—*C. D.*

Verses 39 and 35.—God's memory of his people and their memory of God.

Verse 42.—The day of days. I. The enemy encountered on that day. II. The conflict endured. III. The deliverance accomplished. IV. The joy experienced.— *B. D.*

Verse 45.—The power of little things when commissioned to plague us.

Verse 47 (*last clause*).—Sometimes it will not shoot. Sometimes it will. And when it does it misses the mark.

Verse 52.—I. God has a people in the world. II. He brings them away from others. III. He brings them into fellowship with himself. IV. He brings them into fellowship with each other. V. He guides them to their rest.

Verse 55.—Divine supplantings. He supplants the fallen angels in heaven. One nation of earth by another (see all history). The thoughts and affections of the heart in regeneration, &c.—Isaiah lv. 13.—*C. D.*

Verses 56, 57.—On the deceitfulness of the heart, with respect to the performance of duty.—*J. Jamieson.* 1. 326

On the deceitfulness of the heart, with respect to the omission of duty.—*J. Jamieson.* I. 353.

Verses 59—72.—I. A gloomy sunset, verses 59, 60. II. A baleful night, verses 60—64. III. A blessed sunrise, verses 65—72.—*C. D.*

Verse 69.—The builder of the church. Its sanctity. Grandeur. Comprehensiveness (like the earth, Mark xi. 17). Perpetuity.—*C. D.*

Verses 70, 71.—I. David's calling. Two questions present themselves. 1. How was David's shepherd-life an unconscious preparation for his calling ? 2. How did the divine summons, when it came, fit him for his mighty destiny ? Observe— he was sent back to his flocks. Nothing could train him more perfectly than that waiting. Two great convictions awakened in him then, that formed in him elements of strength. (1.) The belief in a divine leader (see Ps. xxiii.) (2.) The belief in a divine choice. II. Its modern lessons. 1. There is a divine plan in every life. 2. There is a divine vocation for every man. 3. There is a divine Shepherd for every man.—*E. L. Hull.*

Verses 70—72.—Scriptural promotions. I. Analogies between lower and higher service, verse 71. II. Humbler work, a preparation for higher, verses 71, 72. III. Promotion the act of the Divine will, verses 70, 71. IV. Our powers shall be equal to the position to which God promotes us.—*C. D.*

PSALM LXXIX.

TITLE AND SUBJECT.—A Psalm of Asaph. *A Psalm of complaint such as Jeremiah might have written amid the ruins of the beloved city. It evidently treats of times of invasion, oppression, and national overthrow. Asaph was a patriotic poet, and was never more at home than when he rehearsed the history of his nation. Would to God that we had national poets whose song should be of the Lord.*

DIVISION.—*From verse 1 to 4 the complaint is poured out, from 5 to 12 prayer is presented, and, in the closing verse, praise is promised.*

EXPOSITION.

O GOD, the heathen are come into thine inheritance; thy holy temple have they defiled; they have laid Jerusalem on heaps.

2 The dead bodies of thy servants have they given *to be* meat unto the fowls of the heaven, the flesh of thy saints unto the beasts of the earth.

3 Their blood have they shed like water round about Jerusalem; and *there was* none to bury *them*.

4. We are become a reproach to our neighbours, a scorn and derision to them that are round about us.

1. "*O God, the heathen are come into thine inheritance.*" It is the cry of amazement at sacrilegious intrusion; as if the poet were struck with horror. The stranger pollutes thine hallowed courts with his tread. All Canaan is thy land, but thy foes have ravaged it. "*Thy holy temple have they defiled.*" Into the inmost sanctuary they have profanely forced their way, and there behaved themselves arrogantly. Thus, the holy land, the holy house, and the holy city, were all polluted by the uncircumcised. It is an awful thing when wicked men are found in the church and numbered with her ministry. Then are the tares sown with the wheat, and the poisoned gourds cast into the pot. "*They have laid Jerusalem on heaps.*" After devouring and defiling, they have come to destroying, and have done their work with a cruel completeness. Jerusalem, the beloved city, the joy of the nation, the abode of her God, was totally wrecked. Alas! alas, for Israel! It is sad to see the foe in our own house, but worse to meet him in the house of God: they strike hardest who smite at our religion. The Psalmist piles up the agony; he was a suppliant, and he knew how to bring out the strong points of his case. We ought to order our case before the Lord with as much care as if our success depended on our pleading. Men in earthly courts use all their powers to obtain their ends, and so also should we state our case with earnestness, and bring forth our strong arguments.

2. "*The dead bodies of thy servants have they given to be meat unto the fowls of the heaven, the flesh of thy saints unto the beasts of the earth.*" The enemy cared not to bury the dead, and there was not a sufficient number of Israel left alive to perform the funeral rites; therefore, the precious relics of the departed were left to be devoured of vultures and torn by wolves. Beasts on which man could not feed fed on him. The flesh of creation's Lord became meat for carrion crows and hungry dogs. Dire are the calamities of war, yet have they happened to God's saints and servants. This might well move the heart of the poet, and he did well to appeal to the heart of God by reciting the grievous evil. Such might have been the lamentation of an early Christian as he thought of the amphitheatre and all its deeds of blood. Note in the two verses how the plea is made to turn upon God's property in the temple and the people :—we read "thine inheritance," "thy temple," "thy servants," and "thy saints." Surely the Lord will defend his own, and will not suffer rampant adversaries to despoil them.

3. *"Their blood have they shed like water round about Jerusalem."* The invaders slew men as if their blood was of no more value than so much water ; they poured it forth as lavishly as when the floods deluge the plains. The city of holy peace became a field of blood. *"And there was none to bury them."* The few who survived were afraid to engage in the task. This was a serious trial and grievous horror to the Jews, who evinced much care concerning their burials. Has it come to this, that there are none to bury the dead of thy family, O Lord ? Can none be found to grant a shovelful of earth with which to cover up the poor bodies of thy murdered saints ? What woe is here ! How glad should we be that we live in so quiet an age, when the blast of the trumpet is no more heard in our streets.

4. *"We are become a reproach to our neighbours."* Those who have escaped the common foe make a mockery of us ; they fling our disasters into our face, and ask us, " Where is your God ? " Pity should be shown to the afflicted, but in too many cases it is not so, for a hard logic argues that those who suffer more than ordinary calamities must have been extraordinary sinners. Neighbours especially are often the reverse of neighbourly ; the nearer they dwell the less they sympathise. It is most pitiable it should be so. *"A scorn and derision to them that are round about us."* To find mirth in others' miseries, and to exult over the ills of others, is worthy only of the devil and of those whose father he is. Thus the case is stated before the Lord, and it is a very deplorable one. Asaph was an excellent advocate, for he gave a telling description of calamities which were under his own eyes, and in which he sympathised, but we have a mightier Intercessor above, who never ceases to urge our suit before the eternal throne.

5 How long, LORD ? wilt thou be angry for ever ? shall thy jealousy burn like fire ?

6 Pour out thy wrath upon the heathen that have not known thee, and upon the kingdoms that have not called upon thy name.

7 For they have devoured Jacob, and laid waste his dwelling place.

8 O remember not against us former iniquities : let thy tender mercies speedily prevent us : for we are brought very low.

9 Help us, O God of our salvation, for the glory of thy name : and deliver us, and purge away our sins, for thy name's sake.

10 Wherefore should the heathen say, Where *is* their God ? let him be known among the heathen in our sight *by* the revenging of the blood of thy servants *which* is shed.

11. Let the sighing of the prisoner come before thee ; according to the greatness of thy power preserve thou those that are appointed to die ;

12 And render unto our neighbours sevenfold into their bosom their reproach, wherewith they have reproached thee, O Lord.

5. *"How long, Lord ? "* Will there be no end to these chastisements ? They are most sharp and overwhelming ; wilt thou much longer continue them ? *"Wilt thou be angry for ever ? "* Is thy mercy gone so that thou wilt for ever smite ? *"Shall thy jealousy burn like fire ? "* There was great cause for the Lord to be jealous, since idols had been set up, and Israel had gone aside from his worship, but the Psalmist begs the Lord not to consume his people utterly as with fire, but to abate their woes.

6. *"Pour out thy wrath upon the heathen that have not known thee."* If thou must smite look further afield ; spare thy children and strike thy foes. There are lands where thou art in no measure acknowledged ; be pleased to visit these first with thy judgments, and let thine erring Israel have a respite. *"And upon the kingdoms that have not called upon thy name."* Hear us the prayerful, and avenge thyself upon the prayerless. Sometimes providence appears to deal much more severely with the righteous than with the wicked, and this verse is a bold appeal founded upon such an appearance. It in effect says—Lord, if thou must empty out the vials of thy wrath, begin with those who have no measure of regard for thee, but are openly up in arms against thee ; and be pleased to spare thy people, who are thine notwithstanding all their sins.

7. *"For they have devoured Jacob."* The oppressor would quite eat up the

saints if he could. If these lions do not swallow us, it is because the Lord has sent his angel and shut the lions' mouths. *"And laid waste his dwelling place,"* or his pasture. The invader left no food for man or beast, but devoured all as the locust. The tender mercies of the wicked are cruel.

8. *"O remember not against us former iniquities."* Sins accumulate against nations. Generations lay up stores of transgressions to be visited upon their successors ; hence this urgent prayer. In Josiah's days the most earnest repentance was not able to avert the doom which former long years of idolatry had sealed against Judah. Every man has reason to ask for an act of oblivion for his past sins, and every nation should make this a continual prayer. *"Let thy tender mercies speedily prevent us : for we are brought very low."* Hasten to our rescue, for our nation is hurrying down to destruction ; our numbers are diminished and our condition is deplorable. Observe how penitent sorrow seizes upon the sweeter attributes, and draws her pleas from the "tender mercies" of God; see, too, how she pleads her own distress, and not her goodness, as a motive for the display of mercy. Let souls who are brought very low find an argument in their abject condition. What can so powerfully appeal to pity as dire affliction ? The quaint prayer-book version is touchingly expressive : " O remember not our old sins, but have mercy upon us, and that soon ; for we are come to great misery." This supplication befits a sinner's life. We have known seasons when this would have been as good a prayer for our burdened heart as any that human mind could compose.

9. *" Help us, O God of our salvation, for the glory of thy name."* This is masterly pleading. No argument has such force as this. God's glory was tarnished in the eyes of the heathen by the defeat of his people, and the profanation of his temple ; therefore, his distressed servants implore his aid, that his great name may no more be the scorn of blaspheming enemies. *"And deliver us, and purge away our sins, for thy name's sake."* Sin,—the root of the evil—is seen and confessed ; pardon of sin is sought as well as removal of chastisement, and both are asked not as matters of right, but as gifts of grace. God's name is a second time brought into the pleading. Believers will find it their wisdom to use very frequently this noble plea : it is the great gun of the battle, the mightiest weapon in the armoury of prayer.

10. *"Wherefore should the heathen say, Where is their God ? "* Why should those impious mouths be filled with food so sweet to them, but so bitter to us ? When the afflictions of God's people become the derision of sinners, and cause them to ridicule religion, we have good ground for expostulation with the Lord. *"Let him be known among the heathen in our sight by the revenging of the blood of thy servants which is shed."* Justice is desired that God may be vindicated and feared. It is but meet that those who taunted the people of God because they smarted under the Lord's rod, should be made themselves also to smart by the same hand. If any complain of the spirit of this imprecation, we think they do so needlessly ; for it is the common feeling of every patriot to desire to see his country's wrongs redressed, and of every Christian to wish a noble vengeance for the church by the overthrow of error. The destruction of Antichrist is the recompense of the blood of the martyrs, and by no means is it to be deprecated ; far rather is it one of the most glorious hopes of the latter days.

11. *"Let the sighing of the prisoner come before thee."* When thy people cannot sing, and dare not shout aloud, then let their silent sigh ascend into thine ear, and secure for them deliverance. These words are suitable for the afflicted in a great variety of conditions ; men of experience will know how to adapt them to their own position and to use them in reference to others. *"According to the greatness of thy power preserve thou those that are appointed to die."* Faith grows while it prays ; the appeal to the Lord's tender mercy is here supplemented by another addressed to the divine power, and the petitioner rises from a request for those who are brought low, to a prayer for those who are on the verge of death, set apart as victims for the slaughter. How consoling is it to desponding believers to reflect that God can preserve even those who bear the sentence of death in themselves. Men and devils may consign us to perdition, while sickness drags us to the grave, and sorrow sinks us in the dust ; but, there is One who can keep our soul alive, ay, and bring it up again from the depths of despair. A lamb shall live between the lion's jaws if the Lord wills it. Even in the charnel, life shall vanquish death if God be near.

12. *"And render unto our neighbours sevenfold into their bosom their reproach, wherewith they have reproached thee, O Lord."* They denied thine existence, mocked thy power, insulted thy worship, and destroyed thy house; up, therefore, O Lord, and make them feel to the full that thou art not to be mocked with impunity. Pour into their laps good store of shame because they dared insult the God of Israel. Recompense them fully, till they have received the perfect number of punishments. It will be so. The wish of the text will become matter of fact. The Lord will avenge his own elect though he bear long with them.

13 So we thy people and sheep of thy pasture will give thee thanks for ever: we will shew forth thy praise to all generations.

13. *"So we thy people and sheep of thy pasture will give thee thanks for ever; we will shew forth thy praise to all generations."* The gratitude of the church is lasting as well as deep. On her tablets are memorials of great deliverances, and, as long as she shall exist, her sons will rehearse them with delight. We have a history which will survive all other records, and it is bright in every line with the glory of the Lord. From the direst calamities God's glory springs, and the dark days of his people become the prelude to unusual displays of the Lord's love and power.

EXPLANATORY NOTES AND QUAINT SAYINGS.

Whole Psalm.—This Psalm is, in every respect, the pendant of Ps. lxxiv. The points of contact are not merely matters of style (cf. lxxix. 5, " how long for ever ? " with lxxiv. 1, 10 ; lxxix. 10, יְדֵעַ, with lxxiv. 5 ; lxxix. 2, the giving over to the wild beasts, with lxxiv. 19, 14 ; lxxix. 13, the conception of Israel as of a flock, in which respect Ps. lxxix. is judiciously appended to Ps. lxxviii. 70—72, with Ps. lxxiv. 1, and also with Ps. lxxiv. 19.) But the mutual relationships lie still deeper. Both Psalms have the same Asaphic stamp, both stand in the same relation to Jeremiah, and both send forth their complaints out of the same circumstances of the time, concerning a destruction of the Temple and of Jerusalem, such as only the age of the Seleucidæ (1 Macc. 1. 31, iii. 45, 2 Macc. viii. 3), together with the Chaldæan period can exhibit, and in conjunction with a defiling of the Temple and a massacre of the servants of God, of the *Chasìdìm* (1 Macc. vii. 13, 2 Macc. xiv. 6), such as the age of the Seleucidæ exclusively can exhibit. The work of the destruction of the Temple which was in progress in Ps. lxxiv., appears in Psalm lxxix. as completed, and here, as in the former Psalm, one receives the impression of the outrages, not of some war, but of some persecution : it is straightway the religion of Israel for the sake of which the sanctuaries are destroyed and the faithful are massacred.— *Franz Delitzsch.*

Verse 1.—*"Thy holy temple have they defiled."* This was not only the highest degree of the enemy's inhumanity and barbarity, ... but also a calamity to the people of God never to be sufficiently deplored. For by the overthrow of the temple the true worship of God, which had been instituted at that temple alone, appeared to be extinguished, and the knowledge of God to vanish from among mankind. No pious heart could ponder this without the greatest grief.—*Mollerus.*

Verse 1.—*"They have laid Jerusalem on heaps."* They have made Jerusalem to be nothing but *graves.* Such multitudes were cruelly slain and murdered, that Jerusalem was, as it were, but one *grave.*—*Joseph Caryl.*

Verses 1—4.—In the time of the Maccabees, Demetrius, the son of Seleucus, sent Bacchides to Jerusalem ; who slew the scribes, who came to require justice, and the Assideans, the first of the children of Israel who sought peace of them. Bacchides " took of them threescore men, and slew them in one day, according to the words which he wrote, the flesh of thy saints have they cast out, and their blood have they shed round about Jerusalem, and there was none to bury them." And in that last and most fearful destruction, when the eagles of Rome were gathered round the doomed city, and the temple of which God had said, "Let us depart hence;" when one stone was not to be left upon another, when the fire was to consume the sanctuary, and the foundations of Sion were to be ploughed up; when Jerusalem was to be filled with slain, and the sons of Judah were to be crucified round her walls in such thick multitudes that no more room was left for death; when insult, and shame, and scorn was the lot of the child of Israel, as he wandered an outcast, a fugitive in all lands; when all these bitter and deadly things came upon Jerusalem, it was a punishment for many and long-repeated crimes; it was the accomplishment of a warning which had been often sent in vain. Yea, fiercely did thy foes assault thee, O Jerusalem, but thy sins more fiercely still!—*"Plain Commentary."*

Verses 1, 4, 5.—Entering the inhabited part of the old city, and winding through some crooked, filthy lanes, I suddenly found myself on turning a sharp corner, in a spot of singular interest; the "Jews' place of Wailing." It is a small paved quadrangle; on one side are the backs of low modern houses, without door or window; on the other is the lofty wall of the Haram, of recent date above, but having below five courses of bevelled stones in a perfect state of preservation. Here the Jews are permitted to approach the sacred enclosure, and wail over the fallen temple, whose very dust is dear to them, and in whose stones they still take pleasure (Ps. cii. 14). It was Friday, and a crowd of miserable devotees had assembled— men and women of all ages and all nations, dressed in the quaint costumes of every country of Europe and Asia. Old men were there,—pale, haggard, careworn men, tottering on pilgrim staves; and little girls with white faces, and lustrous black eyes, gazing wistfully now at their parents, now at the old wall. Some were on their knees, chanting mournfully from a book of Hebrew prayers, swaying their bodies to and fro; some were prostrate on the ground, pressing forehead and lips to the earth; some were close to the wall, burying their faces in the rents and crannies of the old stones; some were kissing them, some had their arms spread out as if they would clasp them to their bosoms, some were bathing them with tears, and all the while sobbing as if their hearts would burst. It was a sad and touching spectacle. Eighteen centuries of exile and woe have not dulled their hearts' affections, or deadened their feelings of devotion. Here we see them assembled from the ends of the earth, poor, despised, down-trodden outcasts,—amid the desolations of their fatherland, beside the dishonoured ruins of their ancient sanctuary,— chanting, now in accents of deep pathos, and now of wild woe, the prophetic words of their own Psalmist,—*"O God the heathen are come into thine inheritance; thy holy temple have they defiled . . . We are become a reproach to our neighbours, a scorn and derision to them that are round about us. How long, Lord? wilt thou be angry for ever?"—J. L. Porter, in "The Giant Cities of Bashan."* 1865.

Verse 2.—*"The dead bodies of thy servants,"* etc. It is a true saying of S. Augustine, The care of our funeral, the manner of our burial, the exequial pomp, all these *magis sunt vivorum solatia quam subsidia mortuorum*, are rather comforts for the living than any way helps for the dead. To be interred profiteth not the party deceased; his body feels it not, his soul regards it not; and we know that many holy martyrs have been excluded from burial, who in a Christian scorn thereof bespake their persecutors in words of those which were slain at Pharsalia: "Thou effectest nothing by this anger; what matters it whether disease dissolve the body, or the funeral pile!" But yet there is an honesty* which belongeth to the dead body of man. Jehu commanded Jezebel to be buried; David thanked the people of Jabesh-Gilead for burying of Saul. Peter, who commanded Ananias and Sapphira, those false abdicators of their patrimony, to die, commanded to have them buried being dead. It is an axiom of charity. *Mortuo non prohibeas gratiam,* withhold not kindness from the dead. It shows our love and regard for men in our own flesh to see them buried; it manifesteth our faith and hope of the resurrection; and therefore when that body which is to rise again, and to be made glorious and immortal in heaven, shall be cast to the fowls of the air or beasts of the field, it argueth in God great indignation against sin (Jer. xxii. 19, of Jehoiakim, "He shall be buried as an ass is buried, and cast forth without the gates of Jerusalem"); in man inhuman and barbarous cruelty.—*John Dunster, in "Prodromus."* 1613.

---

* *i.e.,* a right, a proper respect.

Verses 2, 3.—[The following extract is from the writings of a godly monk who applies the language of the Psalm to the persecutions of his time. He wrote at Rome during the period of the Reformation, and was evidently a favourer of the gospel.] At this day what river is there, what brook, in this our afflicted Europe, (if it is still ours) that we have not seen flowing with the blood of Christians ? And that too shed by the swords and spears of Christians ? Wherefore there is made a great wailing in Israel ; and the princes and elders mourn ; the young men and virgins are become weak, and the beauty of the woman is changed. Why ? The holy place itself is desolate as a wilderness. Hast thou ever seen so dire a spectacle ? They have piled up in heaps the dead bodies of thy servants to be devoured by birds : the unburied remains of thy saints, I say, they have given to the beasts of the earth. What greater cruelty could ever be committed ? So great was the effusion of human blood at that time, that the rivulets, yea, rather, the rivers round the entire circuit of the city, flowed with it. And thus truly is the form of our most beautiful city laid waste, and its loveliness ; and so reduced is it, that not even the men who carry forth dead bodies for burial can be obtained, though pressed with the offer of large rewards ; so full of fear and horror were their minds : and this was all the more bitter, because "*We are become a reproach to those round about us*," and are spoken of in derision by the infidels abroad and by enemies at home. Who is so bold as to endure this and live ? How long therefore shall this most bitter disquietude last ?—*Giambattista Folengo.* 1490—1559.

Verse 2.—"*Dead bodies of thy servants have they given to be meat unto the fowls.*" With what unconcern are we accustomed to view, on all sides of us, multitudes " dead in trespasses and sins," torn in pieces, and devoured by wild passions, filthy lusts, and infernal spirits, those dogs and vultures of the moral world ! Yet, to a discerning eye, and a thinking mind, the latter is by far the more melancholy sight of the two.—*George Horne.*

Verse 2.—" *Thy servants.*" "*Thy saints.*" No temporal wrath, no calamities whatsoever can separate the Lord's children from God's love and estimation of them, nor untie the relation between God and them : for here, albeit their carcases fall, and be devoured by the fowls of heaven and beasts of the earth, yet remain they the Lord's servants and saints under these sufferings.—*David Dickson.*

Verse 4.—"*We are become a reproach.*" If God's professing people degenerate from what themselves and their fathers were, they must expect to be told of it ; and it is well if a just reproach will help to bring us to a true repentance. But it has been the lot of the gospel Israel to be made unjustly a reproach and derision ; the apostles themselves were " counted as the off-scouring of all things."—*Matthew Henry.*

Verse 4.—"*A scorn and derision to them that are round about us.*" This was more grievous to them than stripes or wounds, saith Chrysostom, because these being inflicted upon the body are divided after a sort betwixt soul and body, but scorns and reproaches do wound the soul only. *Habet quendam aculeum contumelia,* they leave a sting behind them, as Cicero observeth.—*John Trapp.*

Verse 4.—It is the height of reproach a father casts upon his child when he commands his slave to beat him. Of all outward judgments this is the sorest, to have strangers rule over us, as being made up of shame and cruelty. If once the heathen come into God's inheritance, no wonder the church complains that she is " *become a reproach to her neighbours, a shame and derision to all round about her.*"— *Abraham Wright.*

Verse 5.—"*How long, Lord ? Wilt thou be angry for ever ?* " The voice of complaint says not, How long, Lord, shall this wickedness of our enemy endure ? How long shall we see this desolation ? But, how long, O Lord ? Wilt thou be angry for ever ? We are admonished, therefore, in this passage, that we should recognise the anger of God against us in all our afflictions, lest as the nations are accustomed, we only accuse the malice of our enemies, and never think of our sins and the divine punishment. It cannot be that he who acknowledges the anger of God that is upon him, should not at the same time acknowledge his fault also, unless he wishes to attribute the iniquity to God of being angry and inflicting stripes upon the undeserving.—*Musculus.*

Verse 5.—The word "*jealousy*" signifies not mere revenge, but revenge mingled with love, for unless he loved, says Jerome, he would not be jealous, and after the manner of a husband avenge the sin of his wife.—*Lorinus.*

Verse 6.—Neglect of prayer by unbelievers is threatened with punishment. The prophet's imprecation is the same in effect with a threatening, see Jer. x. 25, and same imprecation, Ps. lxxix. 6. The prophets would not have used such an imprecation against those that call not upon God, but that their neglect of calling on his name makes them liable to his wrath and fury; and no neglect makes men liable to the wrath of God but the neglect of duty. Prayer, then, is a duty even to the heathen, the neglect of which provokes him to pour out his fury on them.—*David Clarkson.*

Verse 7.—"*They have devoured Jacob.*" Like wolves who cruelly tear and devour a flock of sheep. For the word which follows signifies not only a habitation in general, but also a sheepcot.—*Mollerus.*

Verse 8.—"*O remember not against us former iniquities.*" The prophet numbers himself with the people not only in their affliction, but also in their distress, and liability to the anger of God because of the crimes committed. He was not a partner in those enormous sins by which they had provoked the jealousy of God, and yet he exempts not himself from the people at large. Thus, in the following verse, he says, "*And purge away our sins.*" He says not, Remember not the iniquity of this people; nor, And purge away their sins: But, Remember not *our* iniquities: and Purge away *our* sins. In this way the prophets, though holy men, were wont to make themselves sharers of the people's sins, not by sinning, but by weeping and praying and imploring the mercy of God. See Isaiah lix. 12. "*Our transgressions are multiplied before thee, and our sins testify against us.*" . . . Daniel ix. 5. "*We have sinned, and have committed iniquity, and have done wickedly, and have rebelled,*" etc. 1. Let us also follow this example, that so far we may have fellowship with the whole Church, that we may be partners of those who truly love and worship God. 2. Then, that abstaining from false worship, we may not sin wickedly with the wicked. 3. That whenever we ought to weep or pray, we may mourn and confess not only our own, but also the shortcomings of the whole church corporate, as if they were common to ourselves, even if we have no part in them, and may implore for them the mercy of God.—*Musculus.*

Verse 8.—"*O remember not against us former iniquities.*" The Jews have a saying, that there is no punishment happens to Israel, but there is an ounce in it for the sin of the calf; their meaning is, that this is always remembered and visited, according to Exodus xxxii. 34; the phrase may take in all the sins of former persons, their ancestors, and of former times, from age to age, they had continued in, which had brought ruin upon them; and all their own sins of nature and of youth, all past ones to the present time.—*John Gill.*

Verse 8.—"*O remember not against us former iniquities.*" Old debts vex most; the delay of payment increases them by interest upon interest; and the return of them being unexpected, a person is least provided for them. We count old sores, breaking forth, incurable. Augustus wondered at a person sleeping quietly that was very much in debt, and sent for his pillow, saying, "surely there is some strange virtue in it, that makes him rest so secure." My brethren, if one debt unto God's law be more than the whole creation can satisfy, what do any of us mean to rest secure with so vast a burden upon our consciences and accounts? Ah! take heed thou beest not surprised and arrested with old debts. *O God, thou rememberest former iniquities against us.* God will call over, and charge thy sins upon thee, when all the sweet is gone.—*Elias Pledger (—1676), in "Morning Exercises."*

Verse 8.—"*O remember not against us former iniquities.*" The only right way to remedy a miserable condition, is to sue for the remission of sins, and for the renewed evidence of reconciliation: for before the church here do ask any thing for their outward delivery, they pray, "*O remember not against us former iniquities.*"—*David Dickson.*

Verse 8.—"*Speedily.*" Lest they come too late, for we are at our last gasp.—*John Trapp.*

Verse 8.—"*Prevent.*" God's mercy must anticipate. "*come to meet,*" man's necessity.—*J. J. Stewart Perowne.*

Verse 8.—"*We are brought very low*." Literally, "We are greatly thinned." Few of us remain.—*Adam Clarke*.

Verse 8.—"*We are brought very low*." We are very greatly exhausted (emptied out) : that is, we are utterly destitute of all things, both fortune, and strength of mind and body, just like a well or a vessel completely emptied.—*Martin Geier*.

Verse 8.—"*Very low*." Past the hopes of all human help, and therefore the glory of our deliverance will be wholly thine.—*Matthew Pool*.

Verse 9.—"*Help us, O God of our salvation, for the glory of thy name and deliver us*." "Help us" under our troubles, that we may bear them well ; "help us" out of our troubles, that the spirit may not fail. "Deliver us" from sin, and from sinking.—*Matthew Henry*.

Verse 9.—"*God of our salvation*." If human reason were to judge of the many and great blows wherewith God so often smote and wasted his people, it would call God not the Saviour of the people, but the destroyer and oppressor. But the faith of the Prophet judges far otherwise of God, and sees even in an angry and pursuing God, the salvation of his people. The gods of the nations, though they do not afflict even in temporal things, are gods not of the salvation of their worshippers but of their perdition. But our God, even when he is most severely angry, and smites, is not the God of destruction, but of salvation.—*Musculus*.

Verse 9.—"*For thy name's sake*." Twice the appeal is made "*for thy name's sake ;* " that revelation of God which he had made of himself to Moses when he passed by and proclaimed the name of Jehovah, Ex. xxiv. 6, 7. Compare Ps. xx. 1, xxiii. 3 ; xxix. 2.—*J. J. Stewart Perowne*.

Verse 9.—"*For thy name's sake*." The good which God doth unto his church, be it temporal or spiritual, is for his own sake. What I do (saith God), I do for mine holy name's sake ; there is nothing to move me but mine own name ; that is holy, great, and glorious, and I will for my name's sake do so much for my church and people. That they were preserved in Babylon, was for his holy name's sake ; that they were brought out of Babylon, was for his holy name's sake ; that they were replanted in Canaan, was for his holy name's sake ; that they had a temple, sacrifices, priests, prophets, ordinances again, was for his name's sake ; when they were near to destruction often, in former days, God wrought for his name's sake, Ezek. xx. ; so Isaiah xlviii. 8, 9. It is not for the enemies' sake that God doth preserve or deliver his people ; nor for their sakes, their prayers, tears, faith, obedience, holiness, that he doth great things for them, bestows great mercies upon them ; but it is for his own name's sake. For man's sake God cursed the earth, Gen. viii. 21 ; but it is for his name's sake that he blesseth it. The choicest mercies God's people have, are for his name's sake : they have pardon of sin for his name's sake, Ps. xxv. 11, 1 John ii. 12 ; purging of sin for his name's sake ; Ps. lxxix. 9 ; leading in the paths of righteousness for his name's sake, Ps. xxiii. 2 ; quickening of their dead and dull hearts for his name's sake, Ps. cxliii. 11. Though his people offend him, yet he forsakes them not, for his great name's sake.—*William Greenhill*.

Verse 9.—If God could not be more glorified in our peace and reconciliation, than in our death and damnation, it were a wicked thing to desire it. But God hath cleared this up to us, that he is no loser by acts of mercy. In this lies the greatest revenue of his crown, or else he would not love " mercy rather than sacrifice." God is free to choose what suits his own heart best, and most conduceth to the exalting of his great name : and he delights more in the mercy shown to one than in the blood of all the damned, that are made a sacrifice to his justice. And, indeed, he had a higher end in their damnation than their suffering ; and that was the enhancing of the glory of his mercy, in his saved ones. This is the beautiful piece God takes delight in, and the other but the shadow of it. Then thou art in a fit disposition to pray for peace, and mayest go with encouragement when thy heart is deeply affected with the honour that will accrue to God by it. It is an argument God will not deny. " This," said Abigail to David, " shall be no grief to thee nor offence of heart unto my Lord," 1 Sam. xxv. ; she meant, he should never have cause to repent that he was kept from shedding blood. Thus mayest thou plead with God, and say, O Lord, when I shall with saints and angels be praising thy pardoning grace in heaven, it will not grieve thee that thy mercy kept thee from shedding my blood, damning my soul in hell.—*William Gurnall*.

Verse 9.—When the Lord's people are brought very low, let them not look for a lifting up or relief except from God only ; therefore say they here, "*Help us, O*

Lord." Such as have laid hold on God for salvation promised in the covenant, may also look for particular deliveries out of particular troubles, as appendices of the main benefit of salvation ; therefore, "*Help us, O God of our salvation,*" say they. When men do ask anything, the granting whereof may glorify God, they may confidently expect to have it ; and in special when God may be so glorified, and his people may also be preserved and comforted : "*Help us* (say they) *for the glory of thy name : and deliver us.*" As the conscience of sin useth to step in oftener between us and mercy, so must we call oftener for remission of sin ; for earnest affection can double and treble the same petition without babbling : "*Deliver us, and purge away our sins.*" It is the glory of the Lord to forget sin, and when re-mission of sins is prayed for according to God's promise, the Lord's glory is engaged for the helping of faith to obtain it : "*Purge away our sins, for thy name's sake.*"— *David Dickson.*

Verse 11.—"*Let the sighing of the prisoner come before thee.*" The propriety of styling the sons of Adam "*prisoners,*" can scarcely fail to be discerned when we remember the restraint which the immortal spirit endures whilst it inhabits its present earthly house, or recollect the hardships to which many of our race are subjected, or, once more, the degrading slavery to which they reduce themselves by serving their own lusts and refusing to stand fast in the liberty wherewith Christ would make them free. Now, in whichever of these senses men are prisoners, it is clear that they have occasion and that they are wont to sigh, and that it is the part of the pious and faithful believer in God to bear this in mind, and, inasmuch as he has put on bowels of compassion, to say, as well for others as for himself, "*Let the sighing of the prisoner come before thee.*" Three things, then, are suggested by the first clause of the passage before us. The first is, that all who live in this world are prisoners. . . . . We would go on to remark, secondly, that these various prisoners have their respective sorrowful sighings. Thirdly, then, let it be observed, will the believer, conscious of these several sighings of the crowd of prisoners whom he sees all around him, pray to the Almighty that they may come before his everlasting presence.—*W. C. Le Breton.* (1849.)

Verse 11.—"*The sighing.*" The nature of a sigh will suggest to us some important particulars connected with the state of bondage spoken of in the text. A sigh is an *unexpressed declaration.* Although we do not speak, still we can tell a long tale of sorrow with a sigh. How often the mourner who will not tell a human being of his grief, will vent it when he is alone, with a long-drawn, an uneven sigh ! Now, I direct your attention to this, because it is a perfect picture of the spiritual condition in which some men are. They are not loud in their complaints ; they are not standing in the corners of the streets proclaiming their exceeding sinfulness ; they are not continually making their neighbours and their friends hear them preach about their vileness—a vileness which, if any one else attributed to them, would stir up all their wrath. Theirs is not the character of men in strife ; but of men bearing a heavy burden, which presses from them an evidence of what they endure. And if any of you, brethren, thus walk in sighs and sorrow before God, he takes these sighs as applications to him for relief. Your misery, if entirely pent in, would be obstinate impenitency, but if vented, even in a sigh, is a declaration of your need. Let me encourage you, brethren, not to spare these evidences of your state. There are times when you feel so dead that you cannot enter into long confessions ; when the spirit is so weary that you feel that you cannot speak. Much might at such a season be spoken by a sign. " Destroy it not," we say, " for a blessing is in it : " pour it forth, and it will reach the throne. And here it will prove to be not only *an unexpressed declaration of your state,* but also *an unexpressed wish for deliverance* therefrom. When the captive gazes through the bars of iron which night and day stand like mute sentinels before the narrow window of his cell, and when his eyes fall upon the green fields and groves beyond, he sighs, and turns away from the scene with a wish. He spake not a word, yet he wished. That sigh was a wish that he could be set free. And such sighs as these are heard by God. Your longings, your sorrows, when they are not fulfilled, your sad thoughts,—" Oh ! when shall I be delivered from the burden of my sin, and from the coldness of my heart ! "—all these wishes were your sighs, and they have been heard on high.— *Philip Bennett Power.*

Verse 11.—" *The prisoner.*" An eastern prison is still a place of great misery, chiefly from the limited supply of water to the prisoners.—*Daniel Cresswell.*

Verse 11.—*"Come before thee."*—

> Though not a human voice he hears,
> And not a human form appears
>   His solitude to share,
> He is not all alone—the eye
> Of him who hears the prisoner's sigh
>   Is even on him there.
>
> J. L. Chester,

Verse 11.—*"Preserve thou those that are appointed to die."* Ought not pious people more closely to imitate their heavenly Father in caring for those who have been condemned to die? An eminent Christian lady keeps a record of all who have been sentenced to death, so far as she hears of them, and prays for them every day till their end come. Is not such conduct in sympathy with the heart of God! —*William S. Plummer.*

Verse 12.—*"Render unto our neighbours sevenfold into their bosom,"* etc. This may seem to be contrary to common justice; because that the punishment should not exceed the fault. But here you are to know, that this hath not respect unto what the enemies of God's church have acted, but what they have deserved. And therefore when the prophet here says, *"Render unto our neighbours sevenfold,"* it is not sevenfold beyond their deserts; for one scorn that a wicked man poureth upon a child of God (and so upon God), cannot be recompensed with ten thousand reproaches poured upon wicked men. The least reproach poured upon God is an infinite wrong. And the reproach of his people is so much his, as he reckons it as his own; and will therefore render to their enemies their reproach *"sevenfold"* (and that's but equal) *"into their bosom."*—*Abraham Wright.*

Verse 12.—*"Unto our neighbours."* Because their scorn was more intolerable, and also more inexcusable than the oppression of distant enemies.—*J. J. Stewart Perowne.*

Verse 12.—*"Into their bosom."* An expression which originally seems to have had reference to the practice of carrying and holding things in the lap, or the front fold of the flowing oriental dress, has in usage the accessory sense of retribution or retaliation.—*Joseph Addison Alexander.*

HINTS TO PREACHERS.

Verse 4.—Saints the subject of derision to sinners. When justly so. When unjustly. What do they see to excite ridicule; what shall we do under the trial; how will it end?

Verse 5.—I. The cause of the anger: jealousy. II. The moderation of it. If it continued for ever, the people would perish, the promises be unfulfilled, the covenant fail, and the Lord's honour be impeached. III. The staying of it. By prayer; by pleading his name, his glory, and the blood of Jesus.

Verse 8.—A sinner's confession, petition, and plea.

Verse 9.—I. A threefold prayer. II. An encouraging title: "God of our salvation." III. A victorious plea.

Verse 9.—I. The Prayer. "Help us," etc. 1. Purge away sin. 2. Deliver us from our troubles. 3. Help us to serve thee in future. II. The Plea. 1. For thy name's sake. 2. The glory of thy name. 3. The glory of thy name as our salvation. The order in both cases is inverted.—*G. R.*

Verse 10.—The revenge for the martyrs, which it is lawful and incumbent upon us to desire.

Verse 11.—I. The prisoner. 1. Under forced bondage to sin. 2. Under the bondage of conviction. 3. In the dungeon of despair. II. The prisoner's application for relief. III. The source from which he looked for help.—*P. B. Power.*

Verse 11.—I. The degree of protection solicited : " According to the greatness of thy power." II. The protection itself : " Preserve thou." III. The objects of it : " Those that are appointed to die."—*W. C. Le Breton.*

Verse 11.—I. Mournful condition. A prisoner, sighing, appointed to die. II. Hopeful facts : a God, a God hearing sighs, a God of great power. III. Suitable prayers : " come before thee " : " preserve."

Verse 11.—*"Appointed to die,"* used as a description of deep spiritual distress. Fears of the divine decree, of having apostatised, of having sinned away the day of grace, of the sin which is unto death, etc. How these cases can be effectually met.

Verse 13.—The obligations of the Protestant church based on her martyrs' blood, her great deliverances, her nearness to God. She ought to secure gospel teaching to coming generations.

Verse 13.—I. Relation claimed : " We thy people, the sheep of," etc. II. Obligation admitted : " So we," etc., when thou hast interposed for our deliverance, we will praise thee. III. Resolution formed. 1. To give thanks for ever. 2. To transmit his praise to generations following.—*G. R.*

PSALM LXXX.

TITLE.—To the chief Musician upon Shoshannim-Eduth. *For the fourth time we have a song upon Shoshannim, or the lilies ; the former ones being Psalms* xlv., lx., *and* lxix. *Why this title is given it would be difficult to say in every case, but the delightfully poetical form of the present Psalm may well justify the charming title.* Eduth *signifies testimony. The Psalm is a testimony of the church as a "lily among thorns." Some interpreters understand the present title to refer to an instrument of six strings, and Schleusner translates the two words, " the hexachord of testimony." It may be that further research will open up to us these "dark sayings upon a harp." We shall be content to accept them as evidence that sacred song was not lightly esteemed in the days of old.* A Psalm of Asaph. *A later Asaph we should suppose, who had the unhappiness to live, like the "last minstrel," in evil times. If by the Asaph of David's day, this Psalm was written in the spirit of prophecy, for it sings of times unknown to David.*

DIVISION.—*The Psalm divides itself naturally at the refrain which occurs three times :* "Turn us again, O God," *etc. Verses* 1—3 *is an opening address to the Lord God of Israel ; from* 4—7 *is a lamentation over the national woe ; and from* 8—19 *the same complaint is repeated, the nation being represented in a beutiful allegory as a vine. It is a mournful Psalm, and its lilies are lilies of the valley.*

EXPOSITION.

GIVE ear, O Shepherd of Israel, thou that leadest Joseph like a flock ; thou that dwellest *between* the cherubims, shine forth.

2 Before Ephraim and Benjamin and Manasseh stir up thy strength, and come *and* save us.

3 Turn us again, O God, and cause thy face to shine ; and we shall be saved.

1. *"Give ear, O Shepherd of Israel."* Hear thou the bleatings of thy suffering flock. The name is full of tenderness, and hence is selected by the troubled Psalmist : broken hearts delight in names of grace. Good old Jacob delighted to think of God as the Shepherd of Israel, and this verse may refer to his dying expression : " From thence is the Shepherd, the stone of Israel." We may be quite sure that he who deigns to be a shepherd to his people will not turn a deaf ear to their complaints *"Thou that leadest Joseph like a flock."* The people are called here by the name of that renowned son who became a second father to the tribes, and kept them alive in Egypt ; possibly they were known to the Egyptians under the name of " the family of Joseph," and if so, it seems most natural to call them by that name in this place. The term may, however, refer to the ten tribes of which Manasseh was the acknowledged head. The Lord had of old in the wilderness led, guided, shepherded all the tribes ; and, therefore, the appeal is made to him. The Lord's doings in the past are strong grounds for appeal and expectation as to the present and the future. *"Thou that dwellest between the cherubims, shine forth."* The Lord's especial presence was revealed upon the mercy-seat between the cherubim, and in all our pleadings we should come to the Lord by this way : only upon the mercy-seat will God reveal his grace, and only there can we hope to commune with him. Let us ever plead the name of Jesus, who is our true mercy-seat, to whom we may come boldly, and through whom we may look for a display of the glory of the Lord on our behalf. Our greatest dread is the withdrawal of the Lord's presence, and our brightest hope is the prospect of his return. In the darkest times of Israel, the light of her Shepherd's countenance is all she needs.

2. *"Before Ephraim and Benjamin and Manasseh stir up thy strength, and come and save us."* It is wise to mention the names of the Lord's people in prayer, for

they are precious to him. Jesus bears the names of his people on his breastplate. Just as the mention of the names of his children has power with a father, so is it with the Lord. The three names were near of kin ; Ephraim and Manasseh represent Joseph, and it was meet that Benjamin, the other son of the beloved Rachel, should be mentioned in the same breath : these three tribes were wont to march together in the wilderness, following immediately behind the ark. The prayer is that the God of Israel would be mighty on behalf of his people, chasing away their foes, and saving his people. O that in these days the Lord may be pleased to remember every part of his church, and make all her tribes to see his salvation. We would not mention our own denomination only, but lift up a prayer for all the sections of the one church.

3. *"Turn us again, O God."* It is not so much said, " turn our captivity,' but turn " us." All will come right if we are right. The best turn is not that of circumstances but of character. When the Lord turns his people he will soon turn their condition. It needs the Lord himself to do this, for conversion is as divine a work as creation ; and those who have been once turned unto God, if they at any time backslide, as much need the Lord to turn them again as to turn them at the first. The word may be read, " restore us ; " verily, it is a choice mercy that " he restoreth my soul." *"And cause thy face to shine."* Be favourable to us, smile upon us. This was the high priest's blessing upon Israel : what the Lord has already given us by our High-priest and Mediator we may right confidently ask of him. *"And we shall be saved."* All that is wanted for salvation is the Lord's favour. One glance of his gracious eye would transform Tophet into Paradise. No matter how fierce the foe, or dire the captivity, the shining face of God ensures both victory and liberty. This verse is a very useful prayer. Since we too often turn aside, let us often with our lips and heart cry, " Turn us again, O God, and cause thy face to shine, and we shall be saved."

4 O Lord God of hosts, how long wilt thou be angry against the prayer of thy people ?

5 Thou feedest them with the bread of tears ; and givest them tears to drink in great measure.

6 Thou makest us a strife unto our neighbours : and our enemies laugh among themselves.

7 Turn us again, O God of hosts, and cause thy face to shine ; and we shall be saved.

4. *"O Lord God of Hosts, how long wilt thou be angry against the prayer of thy people?"* How long shall the smoke of thy wrath drown the smoking incense of our prayers? Prayer would fain enter thy holy place but thy wrath battles with it, and prevents its entrance. That God should be angry with us when sinning seems natural enough, but that he should be angry even with our prayers is a bitter grief. With many a pang may the pleader ask, " How long ? " Commander of all the hosts of thy creatures, able to save thy saints in their extremity, shall they for ever cry to thee in vain ?

5. *"Thou feedest them with the bread of tears."* Their meat is seasoned with brine distilled from weeping eyes. Their meals, which were once such pleasant seasons of social merriment, are now like funeral feasts to which each man contributes his bitter morsel. Thy people ate bread of wheat before, but now they receive from thine own hand no better diet than bread of tears. *"And givest them tears to drink in great measure."* Tears are both their food and their drink, and that without stint. They swallow tierces of tears, and swim in gulfs of grief, and all this by God's own appointment ; not because their enemies have them in their power by force of arms, but because their God refuses to interpose. Tear-bread is even more the fruit of the curse than to eat bread in the sweat of one's face, but it shall by divine love be turned into a greater blessing by ministering to our spiritual health.

6. *Thou makest us a strife unto our neighbours."* Always jealous and malicious, Edom and Moab exulted over Israel's troubles, and then fell to disputing about their share of the spoil. A neighbour's jeer is ever most cutting, especially if a man has been superior to them, and claimed to possess more grace. None are so unneighbourly as envious neighbours. *"And our enemies laugh among themselves."* They

find mirth in our misery, comedy in our tragedy, salt for their wit in the brine of our tears, amusement in our amazement. It is devilish to sport with another's griefs; but it is the constant habit of the world which lieth in the wicked one to make merry with the saints' tribulations ; the seed of the serpent follow their progenitor and rejoice in evil.

7. *"Turn us again, O God of hosts."* The prayer rises in the form of its address to God. He is here the God of Hosts. The more we approach the Lord in prayer and contemplation the higher will our ideas of him become.

8 Thou hast brought a vine out of Egypt : thou hast cast out the heathen, and planted it.

9 Thou preparedst *room* before it, and didst cause it to take deep root, and it filled the land.

10 The hills were covered with the shadow of it, and the boughs thereof *were like* the goodly cedars.

11 She sent out her boughs unto the sea, and her branches unto the river.

12 Why hast thou *then* broken down her hedges, so that all they which pass by the way do pluck her ?

13 The boar out of the wood doth waste it, and the wild beast of the field doth devour it.

14 Return, we beseech thee, O God of hosts : look down from heaven, and behold, and visit this vine ;

15 And the vineyard which thy right hand hath planted, and the branch *that* thou madest strong for thyself.

16 *It is* burned with fire, *it is* cut down : they perish at the rebuke of thy countenance.

17 Let thy hand be upon the man of thy right hand, upon the son of man *whom* thou madest strong for thyself.

18 So will not we go back from thee : quicken us, and we will call upon thy name.

19 Turn us again, O Lord God of hosts, cause thy face to shine ; and we shall be saved.

8. *"Thou hast brought a vine out of Egypt."* There it was in unfriendly soil : the waters of the Nile watered it not, but were as death to its shoots, while the inhabitants of the land despised it and trampled it down. Glorious was the right hand of the Lord when with power and great wonders he removed his pleasant plant in the teeth of those who sought its destruction. *"Thou hast cast out the heathen, and planted it."* Seven nations were digged out to make space for the vine of the Lord ; the old trees, which long had engrossed the soil were torn up root and branch ; oaks of Bashan, and palm trees of Jericho were displaced for the chosen vine. It was securely placed in its appointed position with divine prudence and wisdom. Small in appearance, very dependent, exceeding weak, and apt to trail on the ground, yet the vine of Israel was chosen of the Lord, because he knew that by incessant care, and abounding skill, he could make of it a goodly fruitbearing plant.

9. *"Thou preparedst room before it."* The weeds, brambles, and huge stones were cleared ; the Amorites, and their brethren in iniquity, were made to quit the scene, their forces were routed, their kings slain, their cities captured, and Canaan became like a plot of land made ready for a vineyard. *"And didst cause it to take deep root, and it filled the land."* Israel became settled and established as a vine well rooted, and then it began to flourish and to spread on every side. This analogy might be applied to the experience of every believer in Jesus. The Lord has planted us, we are growing downward, " rooting roots," and by his grace we are also advancing in manifest enlargement. The same is true of the church in a yet closer degree, for at this moment through the goodwill of the dresser of the vineyard her branches spread far and wide.

10. *"The hills were covered with the shadow of it."* Israel dwelt up to the mountains' summits, cultivating every foot of soil. The nation multiplied and

became so great that other lands felt its influence, or were shadowed by it. *"And the boughs thereof were like the goodly cedars."* The nation itself was so great that even its tribes were powerful and worthy to take rank among the mighty. A more correct rendering describes the cedars as covered with the vine, and we know that in many lands vines climb the trees, and cover them. What a vine must that be which ascends the cedars of God, and even overtops them! It is a noble picture of the prosperity of the Israelitish people in their best days. In Solomon's time the little land of Israel occupied a high place among the nations. There have been times when the church of God also has been eminently conspicuous, and her power has been felt far and near.

11. *"She sent out her boughs unto the sea."* Along the Mediterranean and, perhaps, across its waters, Israel's power was felt. *"And her branches unto the river."* On her eastern side she pushed her commerce even to the Euphrates. Those were brave days for Israel, and would have continued, had not sin cut them short. When the church pleases the Lord, her influence becomes immense, far beyond the proportion which her numbers or her power would lead us to expect; but, alas! when the Lord leaves her she becomes as worthless, useless, and dspised as an untended vine, which is of all plants the most valueless.

12. *"Why hast thou then broken down her hedges?"* Thou hast withdrawn protection from her after caring for her with all this care;—wherefore is this, O Lord? A vine unprotected is exposed to every form of injury: none regard it, all prey upon it: such was Israel when given over to her enemies; such has the church full often been. *"So that all they which pass by the way do pluck her."* Her cruel neighbours have a pluck at her, and marauding bands, like roaming beasts, must need pick at her. With God no enemy can harm us, without him none are so weak as to be unable to do us damage.

13. *"The boar out of the wood doth waste it."* Such creatures are famous for rending and devouring vines. Babylon, like a beast from the marshes of the Euphrates, came up and wasted Judah and Israel. Fierce peoples, comparable to wild swine of the forest, warred with the Jewish nation, until it was gored and torn like a vine destroyed by greedy hogs. *"And the wild beast of the field doth devour it."* First one foe and then another wreaked vengeance on the nation, neither did God interpose to chase them away. Ruin followed ruin; the fox devoured the young shoots which had been saved from the damage wrought by the boar. Alas, poor land. How low wast thou brought! An oak or cedar might have been crushed by such ravages, but how canst thou endure it, O weak and tender vine? See what evils follow in the train of sin, and how terrible a thing it is for a people to be forsaken of their God.

14. *"Return, we beseech thee, O God of hosts."* Turn thyself to us as well as us to thee. Thou hast gone from us because of our sins, come back to us, for we sigh and cry after thee. Or, if it be too much to ask thee to come, then do at least give us some consideration and cast an eye upon our griefs. *"Look down from heaven, and behold, and visit this vine."* Do not close thine eyes; it is thy vine, do not utterly turn away from it as though it were quite gone from thy mind. Great Husbandman, at least note the mischief which the beasts have done, for then it may be thy heart will pity, and thy hand will be outstretched to deliver.

15. *"And the vineyard which thy right hand hath planted."* Shall all thy care be lost? Thou hast done so much, wilt thou lose thy labour? With thy power and wisdom thou didst great things for thy people, wilt thou now utterly give them up, and suffer thine enemies to exult in the evil which they delight in? *"And the branch that thou madest strong for thyself."* A prayer for the leader whom the Lord had raised up, or for the Messiah whom they expected. Though the vine had been left, yet one branch had been regarded of the Lord, as if to furnish a scion for another vine; therefore, is the prayer made in this form. Let us pray the Lord, if he will not in the first place look upon his church, to look upon the Lord Jesus, and then behold her in mercy for his sake. This is the true art of prayer, to put Christ forward and cry,

> " Him and then the sinner see,
> Look through Jesus' wounds on me."

16. *"It is burned with fire."* In broken utterances the sorrowful singer utters his distress. The vineyard was like a forest which has been set on fire; the choice vines were charred and dead. *"It is cut down."* The cruel axe had hacked after

its murderous fashion, the branches were lopped, the trunk was wounded, desolation reigned supreme. *"They perish at the rebuke of thy countenance."* God's rebuke was to Israel what fire and axe would be to a vine. His favour is life, and his wrath is as messengers of death. One angry glance from Jehovah's eye is sufficient to lay all the vineyards of Ephraim desolate. O Lord, look not thus upon our churches. Rebuke us, but not in anger.

17. *"Let thy hand be upon the man of thy right hand."* Let thy power rest on thy true Benjamin, son of thy right hand ; give a commission to some chosen man by whom thou wilt deliver. Honour him, save us, and glorify thyself. There is no doubt here an outlook to the Messiah, for whom believing Jews had learned to look as the Saviour in time of trouble. *"Upon the son of man whom thou madest strong for thyself."* Send forth thy power with him whom thou shalt strengthen to accomplish thy purposes of grace. It pleases God to work for the sons of men by sons of men. " By man came death, by man came also the resurrection from the dead." Nations rise or fall largely through the instrumentality of individuals : by a Napoleon the kingdoms are scourged, and by a Wellington nations are saved from the tyrant. It is by the man Christ Jesus that fallen Israel is yet to rise, and indeed through him, who deigns to call himself the Son of Man, the world is to be delivered from the dominion of Satan and the curse of sin. O Lord, fulfil thy promise to the man of thy right hand, who participates in thy glory, and give him to see the pleasure of the Lord prospering in his hand.

18. *"So will not we go back from thee."* Under the leadership of one whom God had chosen the nation would be kept faithful, grace would work gratitude, and so cement them to their allegiance. It is in Christ that we abide faithful : because he lives we live also. There is no hope of our perseverance apart from him. *"Quicken us, and we will call upon thy name."* If the Lord gives life out of death, his praise is sure to follow. The Lord Jesus is such a leader, that in him is life, and the life is the light of men. He is our life. When he visits our souls anew we shall be revivified, and our praise shall ascend unto the name of the Triune God.

19. *"Turn us again, O Lord of hosts."* Here we have another advance in the title and the incommunicable name of Jehovah, the I AM is introduced. Faith's day grows brighter as the hours roll on ; and her prayers grow more full and mighty. *"Cause thy face to shine ; and we shall be saved."* Even we who were so destroyed. No extremity is too great for the power of God. He is able to save at the last point, and that too by simply turning his smiling face upon his afflicted. Men can do little with their arm, but God can do all things with a glance. Oh, to live for ever in the light of Jehovah's countenance.

EXPLANATORY NOTES AND QUAINT SAYINGS.

Title.—It is an Asaph-prayer again, full of pleas in Israel's behalf. It is as if they had before them Isaiah lxiii. 11, " Then he remembered the days of old." They call to his mind the days of *Joseph*, when (Gen. xlix. 24) the Lord miraculously fed them in Egypt. And then the *tabernacle days*, when (first, since the days of Eden), the Lord was known to dwell between the cherubim, on the mercy-seat. They call to his mind *wilderness times* (verse 2), when their march was gladdened by his presence, " Ephraim, Benjamin, and Manasseh " looking on the Pillar of Glory as it rose before them, the guide and partner of their way (see Num. x. 32—34) " O God, bring us back again ! Cause thy face to shine ! and all shall be well again ! " —*Andrew A. Bonar.*

Verse 1.—The prophet does not nakedly begin his prayer, but mingles therewith certain titles, by which he most aptly addresses God, and urges his cause. He does not say, O thou who sustainest and governest all things which are in heaven and in earth, who hast placed thy dwelling-place above the heaven of heavens ; but, Thou who art the Shepherd of Israel, thou that leadest Joseph like a flock, thou that dwellest between the cherubims. Those things which enhance the favour and providence of God revealed to Israel, he brings to remembrance that he might nourish and strengthen confidence in prayer. . . . Let us learn from this example to feed and fortify our confidence in praying to God, with the marks of that divine and paternal kindness revealed to us in Christ our Shepherd and propitiation.— *Musculus.*

Verse 1.—*"Give ear, O Shepherd of Israel."* It is the part of the shepherd to give ear to the bleatings and cries of the sheep, to call them to mind, that he may readily run to their help.—*Venema.*

Verse 1.—*"O Shepherd of Israel, thou that leadest Joseph like a flock."* Yon shepherd is about to lead his flock across the river; and, as our Lord says of the good shepherd, you observe that he goes before, and the sheep follow. Not all in the same manner, however. Some enter boldly, and come straight across. These are the loved ones of the flock, who keep hard by the footsteps of the shepherd, whether sauntering through green meadows, by the still waters, feeding upon the mountains, or resting at noon beneath the shadow of great rocks. And now others enter, but in doubt and alarm. Far from their guide, they miss the ford, and are carried down the river, some more, some less, and yet, one by one, they all struggle over and make good their landing. Notice those little lambs. They refuse to enter, and must be driven into the stream by the shepherd's dog, mentioned by Job in his " parable." Poor things ! how they leap and plunge, and bleat in terror ! That weak one yonder will be swept quite away, and perish in the sea. But, no ; the shepherd himself leaps into the stream, lifts it into his bosom, and bears it trembling to the shore. All safely over, how happy they appear. The lambs frisk and gambol about in high spirits, while the older ones gather round their faithful guide, and look up to him in subdued but expressive thankfulness.

Now, can you watch such a scene, and not think of that Shepherd who leadeth Joseph like a flock, and of another river which all his sheep must cross ? He, too, goes before, and, as in the case of this flock, they who keep near him fear no evil. They hear his sweet voice saying, " When thou passest through the waters, I will be with thee ; and through the rivers, they shall not overflow thee." With eye fastened on him, they scarcely see the stream, or feel its cold and threatening waves. The great majority, however, " linger, shivering on the brink, and fear to launch away." They lag behind, look down upon the dark river, and, like Peter on stormy Gennesaret, when faith failed, they begin to sink. Then they cry for help, and not in vain. The Good Shepherd hastens to their rescue, and none of all his flock can ever perish. Even the weakest lambkins are carried safely over. I once saw flocks crossing the Jordan " to Canaan's fair and happy land," and there the scene was even more striking and impressive. The river was broader, the current stronger, and the flocks larger, while the shepherds were more picturesque and Biblical. The catastrophe, too, with which many more sheep were threatened—of being swept down into that mysterious sea of death, which swallows up the Jordan itself—was more solemn and suggestive.—*W. M. Thomson, in " The Land and the Book."*

Verse 1.—*"Thou that leadest Joseph like a flock."* Thou that leadest Joseph like a flock art considered by the unbelieving to have no thoughts for our affairs ; therefore stretch forth thine hand for our assistance, that the mouth of them that speak iniquities may be shut. We seek not gold and riches, or the dignities of this world, but we long for thy light, we desire most ardently to know thee, therefore " shine forth."—*Savonarola.*

Verse 1.—*"Thou that dwellest between the cherubims."* From this phrase the following ideas may be derived :—(1) That God is a King, sitting on his throne, and surrounded by his *"ministers."* His throne is the heavens, the symbol of which is the holy of holies, his *"ministers"* are *"angels,"* and are elsewhere distinguished by that name, as Gen. iii., Ps. xviii., 11 ; (2) that God is the *"King"* of Israel, dwelling among them by the external symbol of his presence. His most illustrious ministers are depicted by the " *cherubims,"* who comprehend his heavenly as well as earthly ministers ; (3) that God is the covenant *"King"* of his people, and has fixed his dwelling-place above the *"ark of the covenant,"* an argument that he will observe the covenant and fulfil its promises, that he will guard his people, and procure for them every felicity ; (4) lastly, that God is willing to reveal to the people his *grace* and *mercy* through the covering of the ark, called the *"mercy seat,"* on which God sat.—*Venema.*

Verse 2.—*"Before Ephraim and Benjamin and Manasseh."* The three tribes of Ephraim, Manasseh, and Benjamin, the three sons of Rachel, went immediately behind the ark. Whenever the ark arose against the enemy, Moses used to exclaim " Rise up, Lord, and let thine enemies be scattered ; and let them that hate thee flee before thee." The Psalmist repeats this exclamation. " Cause thy face to shine upon us," was the blessing of Aaron ; the Psalmist prays for the renewal of that blessing.—*Augustus F. Tholuck.*

Verse 3.—*"Turn us, and cause thy face to shine."* To thyself convert us, from the earthly to the heavenly ; convert our rebellious wills to thee, and when we are converted, show thy countenance that we may know thee ; show thy power that we may fear thee ; show thy wisdom that we may reverence thee ; show thy goodness that we may love thee ; show them once, show them a second time, show them always, that through tribulation we may pass with a happy face, and be saved. When thou dost save, we shall be saved ; when thou withdrawest thy hand, we cannot be saved.—*Savonarola.*

Verse 4.—*"Lord God of hosts."* All creatures are mustered, and trained, and put into garrison, or brought forth into the field, by his command. Which way can we look beside his armies ? If upward into heaven, there is a band of soldiers, even a multitude of the heavenly host, praising God, Luke ii. 13. If to the lower heavens, there is a band of soldiers, Gen. ii. 1 ; it was *universa militia cœli*, to which those idolaters burnt incense. On the earth, not only men are marshalled to the service ; so Israel was called the " host of the living God ; " but even the brute creatures are ranged in arrays. So God did levy a band of flies against the Egyptians ; and a band of frogs that marched into their bedchambers. He hath troops of locusts, Proverbs xxx. 27, and armies of caterpillars. Not only the chariots and horsemen of heaven to defend his prophets ; but even the beast, the most indocible, and despicable creatures, wherewith to confound his enemies. If Goliath stalk forth to defy the God of Israel, he shall be confuted with a pebble. If Herod swells up to a god, God will set his vermin on him, and all the king's guard cannot save him from them. You have heard of rats that could not be beaten off till they had destroyed that covetous prelate ; and of the fly that killed Pope Adrian. God hath more ways to punish than he hath creatures. *"The Lord God of hosts "* is not properly a title of creation, but of Providence. All creatures have their existence from God as their Maker ; but so have they also their order from him as their Governor. It refers not so much to their being as to their marshalling ; not to their natural but militant estate ; not only as creatures do they owe him for their making, but as they are soldiers for their managing. Their order is warlike, and they serve under the colours of the Almighty. So that here, God would be respected, not as a creator, but as a general.

His *anger*, therefore, seems so much the more fearful, as it is presented to us under so great a title : *" the Lord God of Hosts " is angry.* They talk of Tamerlane that he could daunt his enemies with the very look of his countenance. Oh ! then what terror dwells in the countenance of an offended God ! The reprobates shall call to the rocks to hide them from the wrath of the Lamb. Rev. vi. 16. If *ira agni* doth so affright them, how terrible is *ira leonis*, the wrath of the lion ? It may justly trouble us all to hear that the Lord, *"the Lord God of Hosts,"* is *angry ;* in the sense whereof the prophet breaks forth here into this expostulation ; *"* O Lord God of hosts, how long wilt thou be angry with thy people that prayeth ? "— *Thomas Adams.*

Verse 4.—*"Angry against the prayer of thy people."* There may be infirmities enough in our very prayers to make them unacceptable. As if they be *Exanimes*, without life and soul ; when the heart knows not what the tongue utters. Or *Perfunctoriæ*, for God will have none of those prayers that come out of feigned lips. Or *Tentativæ*, for they that will *petere tentando*, tempt God in prayer, shall go without. Or *Fluctuantes*, of a wild and wandering discourse, ranging up and down, which the Apostle calls " beating the air," as huntsmen beat the bushes, and as Saul sought his father's asses. Such prayers will not stumble upon the kingdom of heaven. Or it they be *Preproperæ*, run over in haste, so some use to chop up their prayers, and think long till they have done. But they that pray in such haste shall be heard at leisure. Or *sine fiducia ;* the faithless man had as good hold his peace as pray ; he may babble, but prays not ; he prays ineffectually, and receives not. He may lift up his hands, but he does not lift up his heart. Only the prayer of the righteous availeth, and only the believer is righteous. But the formal devotion of a faithless man is not worth the crust of bread which he asks. Or *sine humilitate,* so the pharisee's prayer was not truly *supplicatio,* but *superlatio.* A presumptuous prayer profanes the name of God instead of adoring it. All, or any, of these defects may mar the success of our prayers.—*Thomas Adams.*

Verse 5.—*"In great measure."* The Hebrew *shalish* is the name of a measure, so called of *three,* as containing *a third part of the greatest measure,* four times as big as the usual cup to drink in.—*Henry Ainsworth.*

Verse 7.—*"Turn us again, O God of hosts."* See verse 3 and observe that there it was only, *"Turn us again, O God,"* here *"O God of hosts,"* and verse 19, *"O Lord God of hosts."* As the bird by much waving gathereth wind under the wing, and mounteth higher, so doth faith in prayer : *viresque acquirit eundo.*—*John Trapp.*

Verse 7.—Salvation may be certainly expected in God's order ; and if we labour to be sure of our turning to God, and living in the sense of communion with him, we need not make question of salvation, for that shall follow infallibly on the former two. *"Turn us again, O God of hosts, and cause thy face to shine ; and we shall be saved."* The last is not put up by way of prayer here, but promised to themselves, and put out of question, that it shall follow : *"Turn us, so shall we be saved,"* say they.—*David Dickson.*

Verse 8.—*"Thou hast brought a vine out of Egypt,"* etc. The blessings are here placed before us in figurative language, taken from the *vine,* and the care usually expended upon it. They are, 1. The transplanting of the vine from an unfruitful to a very rich and fertile soil. 2. Its plantation and care. 3. Its incredible fruitfulness derived hence.—*Venema.*

Verses 8—19.—Mant's version of the passage is so exquisite that we quote it in full :—

> 8 Thy hands from Egypt brought a goodly vine,
> And planted fair in fertile Palestine ;
> 9 Clear'd for its grasping roots th' unpeopled land,
> And gave it high to rise, and firm to stand.
> 10 Far o'er the eternal hills her shadow spread,
> Her tendrils wreath'd the cedar's towering head ;
> 11 And, as the centre of the land she stood,
> Her branches reach'd the sea, her boughs the eastern flood.
>
> 12 Why hast thou now her hedges rent away,
> And left her bare, the passing traveller's prey ?
> 13 The field-fed beast devours each tender shoot,
> Fierce from the wood the boar assails her root.
> 14 Return, O God ; from heaven thine eyes incline ;
> Behold, and visit this neglected vine :
> 15 Regard the plant, thou once didst love so well,
> And chief thy pleasant branch, the hope of Israel.
>
> 16 Burnt though she be and rent, her haughty foe
> The deathful terrors of thy wrath shall know.
> 17 But on the man, by thee with strength array'd,
> The Son of Man by thee for conquest made,
> 18 Thy hand shall rest ; till we thy triumph see,
> Resound thy praise, and still remember thee.
> 19 Turn us again, thou God of heav'n's high powers,
> Beam with thy radiance forth, and peace shall still be ours.

Verse 10.—*"The hills,"* etc. That the sides of hills are the most commodious places for vineyards, is sufficiently known ; as also that the vine hath props on which it climbs, and rests itself, and that these are lower or higher, according to the nature of the several soils or climates. In fertile soils, as now-a-days in Lombardy, the vines run up the *trees,* and *cover* them. And so here with respect to the luxuriant growth of this fruitful vine, it may not unfitly be said, in the poetical style, to run up to and reach the tops of the tall *"cedars,"* as Joseph is said to be "a fruitful bough, whose branches run over the wall." Gen. xlix., 22.—*Thomas Fenton.*

Verse 12.—*"Why hast thou then broken down her hedges ?"* Why hast thou done this, O Lord ? What is the advantage ? The guard of angels thou hast removed ; they used to ward off the robbers ; they used to defend it. Where, to-day, is this faithful guard ? Where are the prophets ? Where the apostles ? Where the teachers ? Where the pastors surrounding the vine ? Casting out devils, excommunicating heretics, arresting perverse men, and guarding the imperfect. What is the hedge ? The guard of angels, the defence of pastors, the sacred doctrine of preachers. Where is the hedge ? It is destroyed. Who has destroyed it ? Thou O Lord, who hast taken away the preachers, gathered the pastors into heaven, removed the angels. Why hast thou cast down her hedges ? Was it that she might fill up her iniquities, complete the measure of her wickedness, that at length she might be punished and renovated ? But what was wanting to her ? What sin was not found in her ? Behold, Lord, for her wickedness is full. And now they gather her grapes, even all who go out of the way. Not the true vine-dressers, not the true husbandmen, gather her grapes, not all good, not a few good, not partly good and partly bad, not even one good, but all who pass beyond the way, pluck her. All who keep not thy precepts, who know not the way of God, open sinners, disreputable, these are the men that are chosen to minister at the altar, to these are benefices given, these gather her grapes for themselves, not for thee. They regard not thy poor ; they feed not the hungry ; they clothe not the naked ; they help not the stranger ; they defend not the widow and orphan : they eat up the lamb of the flock, and the fatted calf from the midst of the herd. They sing to the sound of psaltery and organ, like David ; they think they have the instruments of song, arranged in choirs, praising God with the lips, but in heart they are far from God. Drinking wine in cups, perfumed with the richest odours, they suffer nothing for the grief of Joseph ; with no pity are they moved for the needy and poor. These, then, are the men who go out of thy way and gather the grapes of thy vine. But what shall I say, Lord ? For even all who transgress thy way, gather thy vintage ? Walking in thy way and seeing the hedge of thy vine broken down, they have gone out of thy way. They have not walked in a straight course, but leaving thy way, have turned their feet to thy vine, to pluck her, to gather her fruit, not the spiritual fruit, but the temporal. What is it you say ? This I say, Lord : The rich men of this world walking in the way of their sins, seeking by thy will and against thy will the riches, honours, dignities, and pleasures of this world, have turned aside from thy ways. The riches of this world they have ceased to pursue ; its honours they seek no longer ; they are turned to thy vine, to ecclesiastical dignities and riches. The hedge is broken down which repelled the unworthy, and now even they who go out of thy way have entered, and gather her grapes. What is your indictment ? This : To-day in the theatre, to-morrow in the bishop's chair. To-day at the custom-house, to-morrow a canon in the choir. To-day a soldier, to-morrow a priest. They have transgressed thy way, and turned to thy vine : not, indeed, that they might cultivate her for thee, but that they might gather her grapes for themselves.—*Savonarola.*

Verse 13.—*"The boar out of the wood doth waste it."* The very boar that laid her waste is a singular wild beast. Singular, because proud. For thus saith every proud one, It is I, it is I, and no other.—*Augustine.*

Verse 13.—*"The boar out of the wood doth waste it."* No image of a destructive enemy could be more appropriate than that which is used. We have read of the little foxes that spoil the vines, but the *wild boar* is a much more destructive enemy, breaking its way through fences, rooting up the ground, tearing down the vines themselves, and treading them under its feet. A single party of these animals will sometimes destroy an entire vineyard in a single night. We can well imagine the damage that would be done to a vineyard even by the domesticated swine, but the wild boar is infinitely more destructive. It is of very great size, often resembling a donkey rather than a boar, and is swift and active beyond conception. The wild boar is scarcely recognisable as the very near relation of the domestic species. It runs with such speed, that a high-bred horse finds some difficulty in overtaking it, while an indifferent steed would be left hopelessly behind. Even on level ground the hunter has hard work to overtake it ; and if it can get upon broken or hilly ground, no horse can catch it. The wild boar can leap to a considerable distance, and can wheel and turn when at full speed, with an agility that makes it a singularly dangerous foe. Indeed, the inhabitants of countries where the wild boar flourishes would as soon face a lion as one of these animals, the stroke of whose razor-like tusks is made with lightning swiftness, and which is sufficient to rip up a horse and cut a dog nearly asunder.—*J. G. Wood, in " Bible Animals."* 1869.

Verse 13.—"*The boar*."
> In vengeance of neglected sacrifice,
> On Œneus' fields she sent a monstrous boar,
> That levell'd harvests and whole forests tore.

—Pope's Homer's Iliad.

Verse 13.—"*The wood*." Or rather *marsh*; that is, a moist marshy piece of ground where trees and plants flourish, and which wild beasts delight in. Such is the neighbourhood of the river Jordan, thus described by Maundrell: "After having descended the outermost bank, you go about a furlong upon a level strand, before you come to the immediate bank of the river. The second bank is so beset with bushes and trees, such as tamarisks, willows, oleanders, and the like, that you can see no water till you have made your way through them. In this thicket anciently (and the same is reported of it to this day,) several sorts of wild beasts were wont to harbour themselves." . . . . In these places, according to the same author, live many wild boars. Bp. Pococke in particular observed very large herds of them on the other side of Jordan, where it flows out of the Sea of Tiberias; and several of them on the same side on which he was, lying among the reeds by the sea.—*Richard Mant.*

Verse 13.—According to the Talmud, the middle letter of the word rendered "*wood*," in this verse, is the middle letter of the Hebrew Psalter.—*Daniel Cresswell.*

Verse 14.—"*Look down from heaven, and behold*." This prayer is fit for none but the truly contrite, and those who are in heart returning. Otherwise, with what conscience could we entreat God to look down from heaven and behold our affairs? Should we not inflame his anger all the more, if besides living in sin, we dared to challenge the all holy eyes of God to behold from heaven our wickedness?—*Musculus.*

Verse 14.—"*Look down from heaven*." Thou hast gone far from us, thou hast ascended to heaven. Thou hast departed from us, look down at least upon us from heaven, if thou art not willing to descend to earth, if our sins do not merit this.—*Savonarola.*

Verse 14.—"*Visit this vine*." Still it has roots, still some branches are living. In the beginning of the world it began, and never has failed, and never will. For thou hast said, Lo, I am with you always, even unto the end of the world. It may be diminished, it can never utterly fail. This vine is the vine which thou hast planted. There is one spirit, one faith, one baptism, one God, and Lord of all, who is all in all. Visit, then, this vine, for thy visitation preserves her spirit; visit by thy grace, by thy presence, by thy Holy Spirit. Visit with thy rod, and with thy staff; for thy rod and thy staff comfort her. Visit with thy scourge that she may be chastened and purified, for the time of pruning comes. Cast out the stones, gather up the dry branches, and bind them in bundles for burning. Raise her up, cut off the superfluous shoots, make fast her supports, enrich the soil, build up the fence, and visit this vine, as now thou visitest the earth and waterest it.—*Savonarola.*

Verse 17.—"*Let thy hand be upon the man of thy right hand*," etc. Neither the church, nor any member thereof needeth any more security for their stability and perpetuation, but Christ; for now when the vineyard is burnt, and the visible church defaced, the remnant are content to rest satisfied with this, which also they take for granted, and do subscribe unto it: "*Let thy hand be upon the man of thy right hand, upon the son of man whom thou madest strong for thyself*." The consanguinity of Christ with the believer, and his humiliation in his human nature, are strong supporters of the faith and comfort of his people that do seek salvation through him; therefore do the faithful here fix themselves on this, that as he is God's Son, so he is a branch of their vineyard also; that as he is at the right hand of the Father as God, so he is "*the man of his right hand*" also; the Son of Man, or of *Adam*, partaker of flesh and blood with us, of the same stock that we are of, in all things like to us, except sin; for the *Son of Man* is the style whereby Christ styled himself in his humiliation. The perpetuity of the church, and the perseverance of the saints, is founded upon the sufficiency of Christ; and the unfeigned believer may assure himself, as of the continuance of the church, so of his own perseverance and constant communion with God through him. "*Let thy hand be upon the man of thy right hand*," etc.; "*so will not we go back from thee*."—*David Dickson.*

Verse 17.—"*The man of thy right hand*." "*The Son of Man*." These striking expressions apply in the fullest and most perfect sense to Christ. If *the Man of*

God's right hand be the man placed there, to whom can the title apply but to him? for, "to which of the angels said God at any time, Sit on my right hand?" (Heb. i. 5); and much less has he said this of any Jewish king. As to the other appellation, *The Son of Man*, it is one of Christ's most definite titles, being given to him in Scripture no less than seventy-one times; in sixty-seven instances by himself; once by Daniel, once by the martyr Stephen; and twice by the Apostle John in the Revelation. He it is, too, whom the Father has made strong for the salvation of his church, and who will yet turn away captivity from the chosen people, and restore them to a place in the church, so that henceforth they "*will not go back from God.*"—*Editorial Note to Calvin in loc.*

Verse 17.—"*The man of thy right hand.*" The man of the right hand is, I. *Most dear*, whom one holds equally dear with his own right hand, Matt. v. 29, 30. Jacob called the son of his most beloved wife, Benjamin, the son of his right hand, Gen. xxxv. 18, who was so dear to him that his life was bound up in the lad's life, chap. xliv. 30. II. *Most honoured;* a man upon whom one wishes to confer the highest honour, is placed at the right hand as Solomon placed his mother, 1 Kings ii. 19, and the spouse stands at the right hand, Ps. xlv. 10. Sitting down at the right hand is in Scripture a proof of the greatest honour. III. *Allied*, because covenants and mutual agreements are ratified by giving the right hand, 2 Kings x. 15. Jehu said to Jehonadab, *Is thy heart right?* and Jehonadab answered, *It is. If it be, give me thine hand. And he gave him his hand.* The right hand used to be given, as in Gal. ii. 9. *The man of God's right hand*, therefore, is one most dear to God, most honoured, and joined with him in covenant.—*James Alting.* 1618—1679.

Verse 17.—Though the phrase, "*man of thy right hand,*" may have an immediate reference to the King who ruled in Judah when this psalm was penned, it must ultimately and most properly intend Jesus Christ, the great antitype of all the kings of David's line. The New Testament is the best interpreter of the Old; and it assures us that this highly dignified man is the Son of God. Heb. i. 1, 3, 13. But if we would understand the genuine import of the phrase, we must attend to a custom which obtained in Judea and other eastern countries. At meals, the master of the feast placed the person whom he loved best on his right hand, as a token of love and respect; and as they sat on couches, in the intervals between the dishes, when the master leaned on his left elbow, the man at his right hand, leaning also on his, would naturally repose his head on the master's bosom, while at the same time the master laid his right hand on the favourite's shoulder or side, in testimony of his favourable regards. This custom is obviously referred to in John xxi. 20, where John is called "the disciple whom Jesus loved, who also leaned on his breast at supper." Now, since Christ is called *the man of God's right hand*, this says that he is the object of his warmest and most honourable regards. In him he is well pleased, and in token of this, he has set him in the most honourable place. He is the Son of Man, whom the Father made to stand strong for himself, *i.e.*, to support the honour and dignity of the divine character amidst a perverse and crooked generation: the consideration of the Father's right hand being upon him, or of the Father's satisfaction in him as our Surety, serves to animate and embolden our addresses to his throne, and is the keenest incitement to put in practice that resolution, "*Henceforth will we not go back from thee.*"—*Alexander Pirie.*

Verse 18.—"*So will not we,*" etc. How are we to understand the connection between this and the preceding words? It may be understood two ways. 1. *As it would oblige them to the yielding of steadfast obedience;* it would lay them under a special engagement never to revolt any more, as they had done; if God would grant this request, it would be a most eminent tie and bond upon them to the most constant and faithful service. 2. *As it would enable them to yield such obedience.* And this I conceive to be chiefly aimed at; if God would lay such help upon Christ for them, they should receive power by that means to discharge their duty to him better than ever heretofore; though they were very feeble and wavering, false and treacherous of themselves, yet here would be a successful remedy.—*Timothy Cruso.*

Verse 19.—"*Turn us again.*" How well that we can look to God when our face is set wrong, that he may turn us, and so his face shine on us, as to bring blessing and present deliverance to his people.—*J. N. Darby.*

Verse 19.—During distress God comes: and when he comes it is no more distress. —*Gaelic Proverb.*

HINTS TO PREACHERS.

Verse 1.—In what respects the Lord acted as a Shepherd to Israel, as illustrative of his dealings with his Church.

Verse 2.—Salvation expected in connection with the people of God, their prayers, labours, and daily service.

Verse 3.—The double work in salvation, (1) Turn us ; (2) Turn to us.

Verse 4.—What prayers they are which make God angry.

Verse 5.—Unpalatable provender. I. Analyse the Provision. II. Note the hand which sends it. III. Consider the healthfulness of the diet. IV. Remember the alleviating accompaniments.

Verse 7.—Conversion, communion, confidence of salvation.

Verses 8—15.—Parallel between the Church and a vine.

Verse 12.—I. The hedges of the Church. II. Their removal. III. The deplorable consequences.

Verse 13.—What are the greatest enemies of the Church ? Where do they come from ? How shall we defeat them ?

Verses 17, 18.—The power of God seen in Jesus, the cause of the perseverance of the saints.

Verse 18 (last clauses.)—The need of quickening in order to acceptable worship.

PSALM LXXXI.

TITLE —To the chief Musician upon Gittith. *Very little is known of the meaning of this title. We have given the best explanation known to us in connection with Psalm VIII. in Vol. I. of this work. If it e intended to indicate a vintage song, it speaks well for the piety of the people for whom it was written : it is to be feared that in few places even in Christian countries would holy hymns be thought suitable to be sung in connection with the wine-press. When the bells upon the horses shall be holiness unto the Lord, then shall the juice of the grape gush forth to the accompaniment of sacred song.* A Psalm of Asaph. *This poet here again dwells upon the history of his country ; his great forte seems to be rehearsing the past in admonitory psalmody. He is the poet of the history and politics of Israel. A truly national songster, at once pious and patriotic.*

DIVISIONS.—*Praise is called for to celebrate some memorable day, perhaps the passover ; whereupon the deliverance out of Egypt is described, 1—7. Then the Lord gently chides his people for their ingratitude, and pictures their happy estate had they but been obedient to his commands.*

EXPOSITION.

SING aloud unto God our strength : make a joyful noise unto the God of Jacob.

2 Take a Psalm, and bring hither the timbrel, the pleasant harp with the psaltery.

3 Blow up the trumpet in the new moon, in the time appointed, on our solemn feast day.

4 For this *was* a statute for Israel, *and* a law of the God of Jacob.

5 This he ordained in Joseph *for* a testimony, when he went out through the land of Egypt : *where* I heard a language *that* I understood not.

6 I removed his shoulder from the burden : his hands were delivered from the pots.

7 Thou calledst in trouble, and I delivered thee ; I answered thee in the secret place of thunder : I proved thee at the waters of Meribah. Selah.

1. "*Sing*" in tune and measure, so that the public praise may be in harmony ; sing with joyful notes, and sounds melodious. "*Aloud.*" For the heartiest praise is due to our good Lord. His acts of love to us speak more loudly than any of our words of gratitude can do. No dulness should ever stupify our psalmody, or half-heartedness cause it to limp along. Sing aloud, ye debtors to sovereign grace, your hearts are profoundly grateful : let your voices express your thankfulness. "*Unto God our strength.*" The Lord was the strength of his people in delivering them out of Egypt with a high hand, and also in sustaining them in the wilderness, placing them in Canaan, preserving them from their foes, and giving them victory. To whom do men give honour but to those upon whom they rely, therefore let us sing aloud unto our God, who is our strength and our song. "*Make a joyful noise unto the God of Jacob.*" The God of the nation, the God of their father Jacob, was extolled in gladsome music by the Israelitish people : let no Christian be silent, or slack in praise, for this God is our God. It is to be regretted that the niceties of modern singing frighten our congregations from joining lustily in the hymns. For our part we delight in full bursts of praise, and had rather discover the ruggedness of a want of musical training than miss the heartiness of universal congregational song. The gentility which lisps the tune in wellbred whispers, or leaves the singing altogether to the choir, is very like a mockery of worship. The gods of Greece and Rome may be worshipped well enough with classical music, but Jehovah can only be adored

with the heart, and that music is the best for his service which gives the heart most play.

2. "*Take a psalm.*" Select a sacred song, and then raise it with your hearty voices. "*And bring hither the timbrel.*" Beat on your tambourines, ye damsels, let the sound be loud and inspiriting. "Sound the trumpets, beat the drums." God is not to be served with misery but with mirthful music, sound ye then the loud timbrel, as of old ye smote it by "Egypt's dark sea." "*The pleasant harp with the psaltery.*" The timbrel for sound, must be joined by the harp for sweetness, and this by other stringed instruments for variety. Let the full compass of music be holiness unto the Lord.

3. "*Blow up the trumpet in the new moon.*" Announce the sacred month, the beginning of months, when the Lord brought his people out of the house of bondage. Clear and shrill let the summons be which calls all Israel to adore the Redeeming Lord. "*In the time appointed, on our solemn feast day.*" Obedience is to direct our worship, not whim and sentiment : God's appointment gives a solemnity to rites and times which no ceremonial pomp or hierarchical ordinance could confer. The Jews not only observed the ordained month, but that part of the month which had been divinely set apart. The Lord's people in the olden time welcomed the times appointed for worship ; let us feel the same exultation, and never speak of the Sabbath as though it could be other than "a delight" and "honourable." Those who plead this passage as authority for their man-appointed feasts and fasts must be moonstruck. We will keep such feasts as the Lord appoints, but not those which Rome or Canterbury may ordain.

4. "*For this was a statute for Israel, and a law of the God of Jacob.*" It was a precept binding upon all the tribes that a sacred season should be set apart to commemorate the Lord's mercy ; and truly it was but the Lord's due, he had a right and a claim to such special homage. When it can be proved that the observance of Christmas, Whitsuntide, and other Popish festivals was ever instituted by a divine statute, we also will attend to them, but not till then. It is as much our duty to reject the traditions of men, as to observe the ordinances of the Lord. We ask concerning every rite and rubric, "Is this a law of the God of Jacob?" and if it be not clearly so, it is of no authority with us, who walk in Christian liberty.

5. "*This he ordained in Joseph for a testimony.*" The nation is called Joseph, because in Egypt it would probably be known and spoken of as Joseph's family, and indeed Joseph was the foster-father of the people. The passover, which is probably here alluded to, was to be a standing memorial of the redemption from Egypt ; and everything about it was intended to testify to all ages, and all peoples, the glory of the Lord in the deliverance of his chosen nation. "*When he went out through the land of Egypt.*" Much of Egypt was traversed by the tribes in their exodus march, and in every place the feast which they had kept during the night of Egypt's visitation would be a testimony for the Lord, who had also himself in the midnight slaughter gone forth through the land of Egypt. The once afflicted Israelites marched over the land of bondage as victors who trample down the slain. "*Where I heard a language that I understood not.*" Surely the connection requires that we accept these words as the language of the Lord. It would be doing great violence to language if the "I" here should be referred to one person, and the "I" in the next verse to another. But how can it be imagined that the Lord should speak of a language which he understood not, seeing he knows all things, and no form of speech is incomprehensible to him ? The reply is, that the Lord here speaks as the God of Israel identifying himself with his own chosen nation, and calling that an unknown tongue to himself which was unknown to them. He had never been adored by psalm or prayer in the tongue of Egypt ; the Hebrew was the speech known in his sacred house, and the Egyptian was outlandish and foreign there. In strictest truth, and not merely in figure, might the Lord thus speak, since the wicked customs and idolatrous rites of Egypt were disapproved of by him, and in that sense were unknown. Of the wicked, Jesus shall say, "I never knew you ;" and probably in the same sense this expression should be understood, for it may be correctly rendered, "a speech I knew not I am hearing." It was among the griefs of Israel that their taskmasters spake an unknown tongue, and they were thus continually reminded that they were strangers in a strange land. The Lord had pity upon them, and emancipated them, and hence it was their bounden duty to maintain inviolate the memorial of the divine goodness. It is no small mercy to be brought out from an ungodly world and separated unto the Lord.

6. "*I removed his shoulder from the burden.*" Israel was the drudge and slave of Egypt, but God gave him liberty. It was by God alone that the nation was set free. Other peoples owe their liberties to their own efforts and courage, but Israel received its Magna Charta as a free gift of divine power. Truly may the Lord say of everyone of his freed men, " I removed his shoulder from the burden." "*His hands were delivered from the pots.*" He was no longer compelled to carry earth, and mould it, and bake it ; the earth-basket was no more imposed upon the people, nor the tale of bricks exacted, for they came out into the open country where none could exact upon them. How typical all this is of the believer's deliverance from legal bondage, when, through faith, the burden of sin glides into the Saviour's sepulchre, and the servile labours of self-righteousness come to an end for ever.

7. "*Thou calledst in trouble, and I delivered thee.*" God heard his people's cries in Egypt, and at the Red Sea : this ought to have bound them to him. Since God does not forsake us in our need, we ought never to forsake him at any time. When our hearts wander from God, our answered prayers cry " shame " upon us. "*I answered thee in the secret place of thunder.*" Out of the cloud the Lord sent forth tempest upon the foes of his chosen. That cloud was his secret pavilion, within it he hung up his weapons of war, his javelins of lightning, his trumpet of thunder ; forth from that pavilion he came and overthrew the foe that his own elect might be secure. "*I proved thee at the waters of Meribah.*" They had proved him and found him faithful, he afterwards proved them in return. Precious things are tested, therefore Israel's loyalty to her King was put to trial, and, alas, it failed lamentably. The God who was adored one day for his goodness was reviled the next, when the people for a moment felt the pangs of hunger and thirst. The story of Israel is only our own history in another shape. God has heard us, delivered us, liberated us, and too often our unbelief makes the wretched return of mistrust, murmuring, and rebellion. Great is our sin ; great is the mercy of our God : let us reflect upon both, and pause a while. "*Selah.*" Hurried reading is of little benefit ; to sit down a while and meditate is very profitable.

8 Hear, O my people, and I will testify unto thee : O Israel, if thou wilt hearken unto me ;

9 There shall no strange God be in thee ; neither shalt thou worship any strange god.

10 I *am* the LORD thy God, which brought thee out of the land of Egypt : open thy mouth wide, and I will fill it.

11 But my people would not hearken to my voice ; and Israel would none of me.

12 So I gave them up unto their own hearts' lust : *and* they walked in their own counsels.

13 Oh that my people had hearkened unto me, *and* Israel had walked in my ways !

14 I should soon have subdued their enemies, and turned my hand against their adversaries.

15 The haters of the LORD should have submitted themselves unto him : but their time should have endured for ever.

16 He should have fed them also with the finest of the wheat : and with honey out of the rock should I have satisfied thee.

8. "*Hear, O my people, and I will testify unto thee.*" What ? Are the people so insensible as to be deaf to their God ? So it would seem, for he earnestly asks a hearing. Are we not also at times quite as careless and immovable ? "*O Israel, if thou wilt hearken unto me.*" There is much in this " if." How low have they fallen who will not hearken unto God himself ! The deaf adder is not more grovelling. We are not fond of being upbraided, we had rather avoid sharp and cutting truths ; and, though the Lord himself rebuke us, we fly from his gentle reproofs.

9. "*There shall no strange god be in thee.*" No alien god is to be tolerated in Israel's tents. "*Neither shalt thou worship any strange god.*" Where false gods are, their worship is sure to follow. Man is so desperate an idolater that the image is always a strong temptation : while the nests are there the birds will be eager to

return. No other god had done anything for the Jews, and therefore they had no reason for paying homage to any other. To us the same argument will apply. We owe all to the God and Father of our Lord Jesus Christ : the world, the flesh, the devil, none of these have been of any service to us ; they are aliens, foreigners, enemies, and it is not for us to bow down before them. "Little children keep yourselves from idols," is our Lord's voice to us, and by the power of his Spirit we would cast out every false god from our hearts.

10. "*I am the Lord thy God, which brought thee out of the land of Egypt.*" Thus did Jehovah usually introduce himself to his people. The great deliverance out of Egypt was that claim upon his people's allegiance which he most usually pleaded. If ever people were morally bound to their God, certainly Israel was a thousand times pledged unto Jehovah, by his marvellous deeds on their behalf in connection with the Exodus. "*Open thy mouth wide, and I will fill it.*" Because he had brought them out of Egypt he could do great things for them. He had proved his power and his good will ; it remained only for his people to believe in him and ask large things of him. If their expectations were enlarged to the utmost degree, they could not exceed the bounty of the Lord. Little birds in the nest open their mouths widely enough, and perhaps the parent birds fail to fill them, but it will never be so with our God. His treasures of grace are inexhaustible,

> " Deep as our helpless miseries are,
> And boundless as our sins."

The Lord began with his chosen nation upon a great scale, doing great wonders for them, and offering them vast returns for their faith and love, if they would but be faithful to him. Sad, indeed, was the result of this grand experiment.

11. "*But my people would not hearken to my voice.*" His warnings were rejected, his promises forgotten, his precepts disregarded. Though the divine voice proposed nothing but good to them, and that upon an unparalleled scale of liberality, yet they turned aside. "*And Israel would none of me.*" They would not consent to his proposals, they walked in direct opposition to his commands, they hankered after the ox-god of Egypt, and their hearts were bewitched by the idols of the nations round about. The same spirit of apostacy is in all our hearts, and if we have not altogether turned aside from the Lord, it is only grace which has prevented us.

12. "*So I gave them up unto their own hearts' lust.*" No punishment is more just or more severe than this. If men will not be checked, but madly take the bit between their teeth and refuse obedience, who shall wonder if the reins are thrown upon their necks, and they are let alone to work out their own destruction. It were better to be given up to lions than to our hearts' lusts. "*And they walked in their own counsels.*" There was no doubt as to what course they would take, for man is everywhere wilful and loves his own way,—that way being at all times in direct opposition to God's way. Men deserted of restraining grace, sin with deliberation ; they consult, and debate, and consider, and then elect evil rather than good, with malice aforethought and in cool blood. It is a remarkable obduracy of rebellion when men not only run into sin through passion, but calmly " walk in their own counsels " of iniquity.

13. "*Oh that my people had hearkened unto me, and Israel had walked in my ways !* " The condescending love of God expresses itself in painful regrets for Israel's sin and punishment. Such were the laments of Jesus over Jerusalem. Certain doctrinalists find a stumbling-stone in such passages, and set themselves to explain them away, but to men in sympathy with the divine nature the words and the emotions are plain enough. A God of mercy cannot see men heaping up sorrow for themselves through their sins without feeling his compassion excited toward them.

14. "*I should soon have subdued their enemies.*" As he did in Egypt overthrow Pharaoh, so would he have baffled every enemy. "*And turned my hand against their adversaries.*" He would have smitten them once, and then have dealt them a return blow with the back of his hand. See what we lose by sin. Our enemies find the sharpest weapons against us in the armoury of our transgressions. They could never overthrow us if we did not first overthrow ourselves. Sin strips a man of his armour, and leaves him naked to his enemies. Our doubts and fears would long ago have been slain if we had been more faithful to our God. Ten thousand evils which afflict us now would have been driven far from us if we had been more jealous of holiness in our walk and conversation. We ought to consider not only

what sin takes from our present stock, but what it prevents our gaining: reflection will soon show us that sin always costs us dear. If we depart from God, our inward corruptions are sure to make a rebellion. Satan will assail us, the world will worry us, doubts will annoy us, and all through our own fault. Solomon's departure from God raised up enemies against him, and it will be so with us, but if our ways please the Lord he will make even our enemies to be at peace with us.

15. *"The haters of the Lord should have submitted themselves unto him."* Though the submission would have been false and flattering, yet the enemies of Israel would have been so humiliated that they would have hastened to make terms with the favoured tribes. Our enemies become abashed and cowardly when we, with resolution, walk carefully with the Lord. It is in God's power to keep the fiercest in check, and he will do so if we have a filial fear, a pious awe of him. *"But their time should have endured for ever."* The people would have been firmly established, and their prosperity would have been stable. Nothing confirms a state or a church like holiness. If we be firm in obedience we shall be firm in happiness. Righteousness establishes, sin ruins.

16. *"He should have fed them also with the finest of the wheat."* Famine would have been an unknown word, they would have been fed on the best of the best food, and have had abundance of it as their every day diet. *"And with honey out of the rock should I have satisfied thee."* Luxuries as well as necessaries would be forthcoming, the very rocks of the land would yield abundant and sweet supplies; the bees would store the clefts of the rocks with luscious honey, and so turn the most sterile part of the land to good account. The Lord can do great things for an obedient people. When his people walk in the light of his countenance, and maintain unsullied holiness, the joy and consolation which he yields them are beyond conception. To them the joys of heaven have begun even upon earth. They can sing in the ways of the Lord. The spring of the eternal summer has commenced with them; they are already blest, and they look for brighter things. This shows us by contrast how sad a thing it is for a child of God to sell himself into captivity to sin, and bring his soul into a state of famine by following after another god.

O Lord, for ever bind us to thyself alone, and keep us faithful unto the end.

EXPLANATORY NOTES AND QUAINT SAYINGS.

Title.—It is remarkable that as Psalm lxxx. treats of the church of God under the figure of a vine, so the present is entitled, *"upon Gittith,"* literally upon the winepress. Whether the expression was meant to refer to a musical instrument, or to some direction as to the tune, is uncertain. In our Saviour's adoption of the figure of a vineyard to represent his church, he speaks of a winepress dug in it, Matt. xxi. 33. The idea refers itself to the final result in some sense, in a way of salvation of souls, as the same figure of a winepress is used in Rev. xiv. of the final destruction of the ungodly.—*W. Wilson.*

Verse 2.—*"Timbrel."* The *toph*, English version *tabret, timbrel*, LXX. τύμπανον, once ψαλτήριον. It was what would now be called a tambourine, being played by the hand; and was specially used by women. It is thrice mentioned in the Psalms: lxxxi. 2; cxlix. 3; cl. 4.—*Joseph Francis Thrupp.*

Verse 2.—*"The Psaltery."* It is probably impossible to be sure as to what is intended by a psaltery. The Genevan version translates it *viol*, and the ancient viol was a six-stringed guitar. In the Prayer-book version, the Hebrew word is rendered *lute*, which instrument resembled the guitar, but was superior in tone. The Greek word psalterion denotes a stringed instrument played with the fingers. Cassiodorus says that the psaltery was triangular in shape, and that it was played with a bow. Aben Ezra evidently considered it to be a kind of pipe, but the mass of authorities make it a stringed instrument. It was long in use, for we read of it in David's time as made of fir-wood (2 Sam. vi. 5), and in Solomon's reign, of algum trees (2 Chr. ix. 11), and it was still in use in the days of Nebuchadnezzar.

Verse 3.—*"Blow up the trumpet,"* etc.   The Jews say this blowing of trumpets was in commemoration of Isaac's deliverance, a ram being sacrificed for him, and therefore they sounded with trumpets made of rams' horns : or in remembrance of the trumpet blown at the giving of the law ; though it rather was an emblem of the gospel and the ministry of it, by which sinners are aroused, awakened and quickened, and souls are charmed and allured, and filled with spiritual joy and gladness.—*John Gill.*

Verse 3.—*"The trumpet."*   The sound of the trumpet is very commonly employed in Scripture as an image of the voice or word of God.   The voice of God, and the voice of the trumpet on Mount Sinai, were heard together (Ex. xix. 5, 18, 19), first the trumpet-sound as the symbol, then the reality.   So also John heard the voice of the Lord as that of a trumpet (Rev. i. 10 ; iv. 1), and the sound of the trumpet is once and again spoken of as the harbinger of the Son of Man, when coming in power and great glory, to utter the almighty word which shall quicken the dead to life, and make all things new (Matthew xxiv. 31 ; 1 Cor. xv. 52 ; 1 Thess. iv. 16). The sound of the trumpet, then, was a symbol of the majestic, omnipotent voice or word of God ; but of course only in those things in which it was employed in respect to what God had to say to men.   It might be used also as from man to God, or by the people, as from one to another.   In this case, it would be a call to a greater than the usual degree of alacrity and excitement in regard to the work and service of God.   And such probably was the more peculiar design of the blowing of trumpets at the festivals generally, and especially at the festival of trumpets on the first day of the second month.—*Joseph Francis Thrupp.*

Verse 3.—*"In the new moon,"* etc.   The feast of the *new moon* was always proclaimed by sound of trumpet.   For want of astronomical knowledge, the poor Jews were put to sad shifts to know the real time of the new moon.   They generally sent persons to the top of some hill or mountain about the time which, according to their supputations, the new moon should appear.   The first who saw it was to give immediate notice to the Sanhedrim ; they closely examined the reporter as to his credibility, and whether his information agreed with their calculations.   If all was found satisfactory, the president proclaimed the new moon by shouting out, מקדש, *mikkodesh !* "It is consecrated."   This word was repeated *twice* aloud by the people ; and was then proclaimed everywhere by *blowing of horns*, or what is called the sound of *trumpets*.   Among the Hindoos some feasts are announced by the sound of the *conch*, or *sacred shell*.—*Adam Clarke.*

Verse 3.—*"In the time appointed."*   The word rendered *"the time appointed,"* signifies the *hidden* or *covered* period ; that is, the time when the moon is concealed or covered with darkness.   This day was a joyful festival, returning every month ; but the first day of the seventh moon was the most solemn of the whole ; being not only the first of the moon, but of the civil year.   This was called the feast of trumpets, as it was celebrated by the blowing of trumpets from sun-rising to sun-setting ; according to the command, "It shall be a day of the blowing of trumpets to you."

This joy was a memorial of the joy of creation, and the joy of giving the law : it also pre-indicated the blowing of the gospel-trumpet, after the dark, the covered period of the death of Christ, when the form of the church changed, and the year of the "redeemed" began ; and, finally, it prefigured the last day, when the trumpet of God shall sound, and the dead shall be raised.—*Alexander Pirie.*

Verse 5.—*"I heard a language that I understood not."*   The *"language"* that he then heard—the religious worship of idolaters,—vows offered up "to birds and fourfooted beasts, and creeping things," Rom. i. 23, and strength and mercy sought from every object in nature, *except himself*,—was a language unknown to him— "he knew it not."—*William Hill Tucker.*

Verse 6.—*"Pots,"* or *burden-baskets.*   Compare Exodus vi. 6, 7.   Rosellini gives a drawing of these baskets from a picture discovered in a tomb at Thebes.   "Of the labourers," says he, "some are employed in transporting the clay in vessels, some in intermingling it with straw ; others are taking the bricks out of the form, and placing them in rows ; still others with a piece of wood upon their backs, and ropes on each side, carry away the bricks already burned or dried.   Their dissimilarity to the Egyptians appears at the first view : their complexion, physiognomy and beard permit us not to be mistaken in supposing them to be Hebrews."—*Frederic Fysh.*

Verse 6.—*"Pots."* The bricklayer's baskets; hanging one at each end of a yoke laid across the shoulders.—*William Kay.*

Verse 7.—To *"answer in the secret place of thunder,"* refers us to the pillar of cloud and fire, the habitation of the awful Majesty of God, whence God glanced with angry eyes upon the Egyptians, filled them with consternation and overthrew them.—*Venema.*

Verse 10.—*"Open thy mouth wide, and I will fill it."* Surely this teaches us, that the greater and more valuable the blessings are which we implore from the divine beneficence, the more sure shall we be to receive them in answer to prayer. . . . . But, though men are to be blamed, that they so seldom acknowledge God in any thing, yet they are still more to be blamed, that they seek not from him the chief good. Men may, however, possibly cry to God for inferior things, and apply in vain. Even good men may ask for temporal blessings, and not receive them; because the things we suppose good, may *not* be good, or not good *for us,* or not good for us *at present.* But none shall seek God for the best of blessings in vain. If we ask *enough,* we shall have it.

While the worldling drinks in happiness, if it will bear the name, with the mouth of an insect, the Christian imbibes bliss with the mouth of an angel. His pleasures are the same in kind, with the pleasure of the infinitely happy God.—*John Ryland.*

Verse 10.—*"Open thy mouth wide, and I will fill it."* You may easily over-expect the creature, but you cannot over-expect God: " Open thy mouth wide, and I will fill it; " widen and dilate the desires and expectations of your souls, and God is able to fill every chink to the vastest capacity. This honours God, when we greaten our expectation upon him; it is a sanctifying of God in our hearts.—*Thomas Case* (1598—1682), *in "Morning Exercises."*

Verse 10.—*"Open thy mouth wide."* This implies, 1. Warmth and fervency in prayer. To open the mouth is in effect to open the heart, that it may be both engaged and enlarged. . . . We may be said to open our mouths wide when our affections are quick and lively, and there is a correspondence between the feelings of the heart and the request of the lips; or when we really pray, and not merely seem to do so. This is strongly and beautifully expressed in Psalm cxix. 131: " I opened my mouth, and panted: for I longed for thy commandments." . . . 2. It implies a holy fluency and copiousness of expression, so as to order our cause before him, and fill our mouths with arguments. When the good man gets near to God, he has much business to transact with him, many complaints to make, and many blessings to implore; and, as such seasons do not frequently occur, he is the more careful to improve them. He then pours out his whole soul, and is at no loss for words; for when the heart is full, the tongue overflows. Sorrow and distress will even make those eloquent who are naturally slow of speech. . . . . 3. Enlarged hope and expectation. We may be too irreverent in our approaches to God, and too peremptory in our application; but if the matter and manner of our prayer be right, we cannot be too confident in our expectations from him. . . . Open thy mouth wide then, O Christian; stretch out thy desires to the utter-most, grasp heaven and earth in thy boundless wishes, and believe there is enough in God to afford thee full satisfaction. Not only come, but come with boldness to the throne of grace: it is erected for sinners, even the chief of sinners. Come to it then, and wait at it, till you obtain mercy and find grace to help in time of need. Those who expect most from God are likely to receive the most. The desire of the righteous, let it be ever so extensive, shall be granted.—*Benjamin Beddome.*

Verse 10.—*"I will fill it."* Consider the import of the promise: " Open thy mouth wide, *and I will fill it."* " Ask, and ye shall receive; seek, and ye shall find." Particularly, 1. If we open our mouths to God in prayer, he will fill them more and more with suitable petitions and arguments. When we attempt to open the mouth, God will open it still wider. Thus he dealt with Abraham when he interceded for Sodom: the longer he prayed, the more submissive and yet the more importunate he became. By praying we increase our ability to pray, and find a greater facility in the duty. " To him that hath shall be given, and he shall have more abundantly," 2. God will fill the mouth with abundant thanksgivings. Many of David's Psalms begin with prayer, and end with the most animated praises.

No mercies so dispose to thankfulness as those which are received in answer to prayer ; for according to the degree of desire will be the sweetness of fruition. . . . . 3. We shall be filled with those blessings we pray for, if they are calculated to promote our real good and the glory of God. Do we desire fresh communications of grace, and manifestations of divine love ; a renewed sense of pardoning mercy, and an application of the blood of Christ ? Do we want holiness, peace, and assurance ? Do we want to hear from God, to see him, and be like him ? The promise is, " My God shall supply all your need according to his riches in glory by Christ Jesus," Phil. iv. 19. You shall have what you desire, and be satisfied : it shall be enough, and you shall think it so. " The Lord will give grace and glory : no good thing will he withhold from them that walk uprightly."—*Benjamin Beddome.*

Verse 10.—The custom is said still to exist in Persia that when the king wishes to do a visitor, an ambassador for instance, especial honour, he desires him to open his mouth wide ; and the king then crams it as full of sweetmeats as it will hold ; and sometimes even with jewels. Curious as this custom is, it is doubtless referred to in Psalm lxxxi. 10 : *"Open thy mouth wide, and I will fill it ; "* not with baubles of jewels, but with far richer treasure.—*John Gadsby.*

Verse 11.—*"My people would not hearken to my voice ; and Israel would none of me."* Know, sinner, that if at last thou missest heaven, which, God forbid ! the Lord can wash his hands over your head, and clear himself of your blood : thy damnation will be laid at thine own door : it will then appear there was no cheat in the promise, no sophistry in the gospel, but thou didst voluntarily put eternal life from thee, whatever thy lying lips uttered to the contrary : *"My people would have none of me."* So that, when the jury shall sit on thy murdered soul, to inquire how thou camest to thy miserable end, thou wilt be found guilty of thy own damnation. No one loseth God, but he that is willing to part with him.—*William Gurnall.*

Verse 11.—*"And Israel would none of me."* It is added, *"and Israel would none of me,"* more closely, *was not borne to me by a natural bent.* For this is the original force of the word אבה, as it still survives in Job. ix. where it is used of the ships borne outward by a favourable wind and tide.—*Venema.*

Verse 11.—*"Israel would none of me."* That is, would not be content alone with me, would not *take quiet contentment in me* (as the Hebrew word signifies) ; the Lord was not good enough for them, but their hearts went out from him to other things.— *Thomas Sheppard,* 1605—1649.

Verse 12.—*"So I gave them up."* The word *give up* suggests the idea of a *divorce,* whereby a husband sends away a capricious wife, and commands her to live by herself. . . . Transferred to God, it teaches us nothing else than that God withdraws his *protecting* and *guiding* hand from the people, and leaves them to themselves ; so that he ceases to chasten and defend them, but, on the other hand, suffers them *to become hardened and to perish.*—*Venema.*

Verse 12.—*"So I gave them up unto their own hearts' lusts,"* etc. A man may be given up to Satan for the destruction of the flesh, that the soul may be saved, but to be given up to sin is a thousand times worse, because that is the fruit of divine anger, in order to the damnation of the soul ; here God wounds like an enemy and like a cruel one, and we may boldly say, God never punished any man or woman with this spiritual judgment in kindness and love.—*John Shower* (1657—1715), *in* "*The Day of Grace.*"

Verse 12.—*"I gave them up unto their own hearts' lusts."* O dreadful word ! The same will the Spirit do upon our rejecting or resisting of his leading. He may long strive, but he will " not always strive," Gen. vi. 3. If the person led shall once begin to struggle with him that leads him, and shall refuse to follow his guidance, what is then to be done, but to leave him to himself ? Continued, rooted, allowed resistance to the Spirit, makes him so to cast off a person as to lead him no more. . . . Let it be your great and constant care and endeavour to get the Spirit's leading continued to you. You have it ; pray keep it. Can it be well with a Christian, when this is suspended or withdrawn from him ? How does he wander and bewilder himself, when the Spirit does not guide him ! How backward is he to good, when the Spirit does not bend and incline him thereunto ! How unable to go, when the Spirit does not uphold him ! What vile lusts and passions rule him, when the Spirit does not put forth his holy and gracious government over him ! O, it is of infinite concern to all that belong to God, to preserve and secure to themselves the Spirit's leading ! Take a good man without this, and he is like a ship without a pilot, a blind man without a guide, a poor child that has none to sustain it, the rude multitude that have none to keep them in any order. What a sad difference is there in the same person, as to what he is when the Spirit *leads* him, and as to what he is when the Spirit *leaves* him ! . . . .

OBJECTION.—" But does the Spirit at any time do this to God's people ? Does he ever suspend and withdraw his guidance from persons who once lived under it ? "

ANSWER.—Yes ; too often. It is what he usually does, when his leadings are not followed. This is a thing that grieves him ; and when he is grieved he departs, withholds, and recalls his former gracious influences, though not totally and finally ; yet for a time and in such a degree. As a guide, that is to conduct the traveller ; if this traveller shall refuse to follow him, or shall give unkind usage to him, what does the guide then do ? Why, he recedes, and leaves him to shift for himself. It is thus in the case in hand : if we comply with the Spirit, in his motions, and use him tenderly, he will hold on in his leading of us ; but if otherwise, he will concern himself no more about us. O, take heed how you carry yourselves towards him : not only upon ingenuousness, it is base to be unkind to our Guide, (" Hast thou not procured this unto thyself, in that thou hast forsaken the Lord thy God, when he led thee by the way ? " Jer. ii. 17,) but also upon the account of self-love : for " as we behave ourselves to him, so he will behave himself to us " : "*Ita nos tractat, ut a nobis trac-tatur.*"—*Thomas Jacombe* (1622—1687), *in "Morning Exercises."*

Verses 12.—"I gave them up . . . . and they walked in their own counsels." That was to give them up to a spirit of division, to a spirit of discontent, to a spirit of envy and jealousy, to a spirit of ambition, of self-seeking and emulation, and so to a spirit of distraction and confusion, and so to ruin and destruction. Such, and no better, is the issue, when God gives a people up to their own counsels ; then they soon become a very chaos, and run themselves into a ruinous heap. As good have no counsel from man, as none but man's.—*Joseph Caryl.*

Verse 12.—God calls upon Israel to hear and obey him, they will not : " But my people would not hearken to my voice ; and Israel would none of me." What was the result of their refusal ? " So I gave them up unto their own hearts' lust : and they walked in their own counsels." God doth not testify his anger for their contempt of him by sending plague, or flames, or wild beasts among them. He doth not say, Well, since they thus slight my authority, I will be avenged on them to purpose ; I will give them up to the sword, or famine, or racking diseases, or greedy devouring lions, which would have been sad and grievous ; but he executes on them a far more sad and grievous judgment, when he saith, "*So I gave them up unto their own hearts' lust : and they walked in their own counsels.*" God's leaving one soul to one lust,* is far worse than leaving him to all the lions in the world. Alas ! it will tear the soul worse than a lion can do the body, and rend it in pieces, when there is none to deliver it. God's giving them up to their own wills, that they walked in their own counsels, is in effect a giving them up to eternal wrath and woe.—*George Swinnock.*

Verse 12.—God moves everything in his ordinary providence according to their particular natures, God moves everything ordinarily according to the nature he finds it in. Had we stood in innocency, we had been moved according to that originally righteous nature ; but since our fall we are moved according to that nature introduced into us with the expulsion of the other. Our first corruption was our own act, not God's work ; we owe our creation to God, our corruption to ourselves. Now since God will govern his creature, I do not see how it can be otherwise, than according to the present nature of the creature, unless God be pleased to alter that nature. God forces no man against his nature ; he doth not force the will in conversion, but graciously and powerfully inclines it. He doth never force nor incline the will to sin, but leaves it to the corrupt habits it hath settled in itself : "*So I gave them up unto their own hearts' lust : and they walked in their own counsels ;*" counsels of their own framing, not of God's. He moves the will, which is *sponte mala*, according to its own nature and counsels. As a man flings several things out of his hand, which are of several figures, some spherical, tetragons, cylinders, conics, some round and some square, though the motion be from the agent, yet the variety of their motions is from their own figure and frame ; and if any will hold his hand upon a ball in its motion, regularly it will move

---

* " One's soul to one's lust " ?

according to its nature and figure ; and a man by casting a bowl out of his hand, is the cause of the motion, but the bad bias is the cause of its irregular motion. The power of action is from God, but the viciousness of that action from our own nature. As when a clock or watch hath some fault in any of the wheels, the man that winds it up, or putting his hand upon the wheels moves them, he is the cause of the motion, but it is the flaw in it, a deficiency of something, is the cause of its erroneous motion ; that error was not from the person that made it, or the person that winds it up, and sets it on going, but from some other cause ; yet till it be mended it will not go otherwise, so long as it is set upon motion. Our motion is from God,—Acts xvii. 28, " In him we move,"—but not the disorder of that motion. It is the fulness of a man's stomach at sea is the cause of his sickness, and not the pilot's government of the ship.

God doth not infuse the lust, or excite it, though he doth present the object about which the lust is exercised. God delivered up Christ to the Jews, he presented him to them, but never commanded them to crucify him, nor infused that malice into them, nor quickened it ; but he, seeing such a frame, withdrew his restraining grace, and left them to the conduct of their own vitiated wills. All the corruption in the world ariseth from lust in us, not from the object which God in his providence presents to us : 2 Peter i. 4, " The corruption that is in the world through lust."— *Stephen Charnock.*

Verse 13.—"*Oh that my people had hearkened unto me,*" etc. God sometimes doth not mind his children when they cry, that they may hereby take occasion to remember how oft he hath cried and they have not minded him. Doth not the Lord cry out to his people of duty, and they do not hear him ? Doth he not complain here of this neglect, not only as a dishonour, but as a grief unto him ? No marvel then if God let his people cry out of misery, and doth not hear them. The Lord shuts his ear that we might consider how we have shut our ears ; yea, he shuts his ears that he may open ours. We are moved to hear and answer the call and command of God, though we find that he doth not hear nor answer our call and cry. If the Lord should always be swift to hear us, how slow should we be in hearing him, and while we have our desires, forget most of our duties.—*Abraham Wright.*

Verse 13.—"*Oh that my people had hearkened,*" etc. God speaks as if he were comforted when he is but heard, or as if we comforted him when we hear him. God beseecheth us, and speaks entreaties to us, that his counsels and commands may be heard : "*Oh that my people had hearkened unto me.*" The Lord tells them indeed it would have proved their consolation (ver. 14) : "*I should soon have subdued their enemies, and turned my hand against their adversaries.*" Yet while he speaks so pathetically, he seems to include his own consolation in it as well as theirs. "*Oh that my people had hearkened unto me :*" it would have been good for them, and it would have given high content to myself.—*Joseph Caryl.*

Verse 13.—"*O that my people had hearkened unto me,*" etc. There is to us a deep mysteriousness in all this ; but the desire of God for our salvation, and right moral state, is here most obviously manifested ; and let us proceed on that which is obvious, not on that which is obscure.—*Thomas Chalmers.*

Verse 13.—"*Walked in my ways.*" None are found in the *ways* of God, but those who have *hearkened* to his words.—*W. Wilson.*

Verse 14.—"*Turned my hand.*" God expresseth the utter overthrow of the enemies of his people, but by the *turning of a hand :* if God do but turn his hand, they are all gone presently, soon subdued. If he do but touch the might, the pomp, the greatness, the riches and the power of all those in the world that are opposers of his church, presently they fall to the ground : a touch from the hand of God will end our wars.—*Joseph Caryl.*

Verse 16.—"*Honey out of the rock.*" The rock spiritually and mystically designs Christ, the Rock of salvation, 1 Cor. x. 4 ; the "*honey*" out of the rock, the fulness of grace in him, and the blessings of it, the sure mercies of David, and the precious promises of the everlasting covenant ; and the gospel, which is sweeter than the honey or the honey-comb ; and with these such are filled and satisfied who hearken to Christ and walk in his ways ; for, as the whole of what is here said shows what Israel lost by disobedience, it clearly suggests what such enjoy who hear and obey.— *John Gill.*

Verse 16.—*"Honey out of the rock."* God extracts honey out of the rock—the sweetest springs and pleasures from the hardness of afflictions ; from mount Calvary and the cross, the blessings that give greatest delight ; whereas the world makes from the fountains of pleasure stones and rocks of torment.—*Thomas Le Blanc.*

Verse 16.—*"Honey out of the rock."* Most travellers who have visited Palestine in summer, have had their attention directed to the abundance of honey, which the bees of the land have stored up in the hollows of trees and in crevices of the rock. In localities where the bare rocks of the desert alone break the sameness of the scene, and all around is suggestive of desolation and death, the traveller has God's care of his chosen people vividly brought to mind, as he sees the honey, which the bees had treasured up beyond his reach, trickling in shining drops down the face of the rock.— *John Duns.*

Verse 16.—When once a people, or a person are accepted of God, he spares no cost, nor thinks anything too costly for them. *"He would have fed them also with the finest of the wheat : and with honey out of the rock should I have satisfied thee."* I would not have fed thee with wheat only, that's good ; but with the finest wheat, that's the best. We put in the margin, *"with the fat of wheat "* ; they should not have the bran, but the flour, and the finest of the flour ; they should have had not only honey, but honey out of the rock, which, as naturalists observe, is the best and purest honey. Surely God cannot think any thing of this world too good for his people, who hath not thought the next world too good for them ; certainly God cannot think any of these outward enjoyments too good for his people, who hath not thought his Son too good for his people ; that's the apostle's argument, Rom. viii. 32 : " He that spared not his own Son, but delivered him up for us all, how shall he not with him also freely give us all things ? " even the best of outward good things, when he seeth it good for us.—*Joseph Caryl.*

HINTS TO PREACHERS.

Verse 1.—Congregational singing should be general, hearty, joyful. The reasons for this, and the benefits of it.

Verses 1—3.—I. Praise should be sincere. It can come from the people of God only. II. It should be constant : they should praise God at all times. III. It should be special. There should be seasons of special praise. 1. Appointed by God, as Sabbaths and solemn feasts. 2. Demanded by providence on occasion of special deliverances and special mercies. IV. It should be public : " sing aloud : " " bring hither," etc.—*G. R.*

Verse 4.—The rule of ordinances and worship ; pleas for going beyond it ; instances in various churches ; the sin and danger of such will-worship.

Verse 5.—What there is in the language of the world which is unintelligible to the sons of God.

Verse 6.—The emancipation of believers. Law-work is burdensome, servile, never completed, unrewarded, more and more irksome. Only the Lord can deliver us from this slavish toil, and he does it by grace and by power. We do well to remember the time of our liberation, exhibit gratitude for it, and live consistently with it.

Verse 7.—I. Answered prayers,—bonds of gratitude. II. Former testing times, —warning memories. III. The present a time for new answers as it is also for resh tests.

Verse 7.—Waters of Meribah. The various test-points of the believer's life.

Verses 8—10.—I. A compassionate Father, calling to his child : " O my people, and I will testify unto thee : O Israel, if thou wilt hearken unto me." II. A jealous sovereign, laying down his law : " There shall no strange god be in thee." III. An all-sufficient Friend, challenging confidence : " I am the Lord thy God : open thy mouth wide, and I will fill it."—*Richard Cecil.* 1748—1810.

Verses 8, 11, 13.—The command, the disobedience, the regret.

Verse 9.—Idolatry our besetting sin. What are likely to become our idols. The sin of permitting them so to be. The judgments we may expect. The means we should use to purge ourselves therefrom.

Verse 10.—I. Emptiness supposed in poor sinners : they have lost God. 2. A fill proposed and offered to empty sinners. This is a soul-fill ; a filling with all the fulness of God. 3. The party communicating this soul-fill to the sinner : "*I,*" more generally, "*I the Lord,*" in opposition to strange gods. 4. The sinner's duty in order to this communication : "*Open thy mouth wide.*"—*Thomas Boston.*

Verse 10.—I. The God of past mercy : "which brought thee out of Egypt." II. Expects present petitions : "Open thy mouth wide." III. Promises future good : "I will fill it."

Verse 11.—I. Who ? "Israel," the chosen, instructed and favoured people. II. What ? "would none of me," my laws, promises, calls, worship, etc. III. Of whom ? "Of ME," their God, good, kind, loving, etc.

Verses 11, 12.—I. The sin of Israel. They would not hearken. The mouth is opened in attentive hearing : "open thy mouth wide :" but my people," etc. Their sin was greatly aggravated. 1. By what God had done for them. 2. By the gods they had preferred to him. II. The punishment. 1. Its greatness : "I gave them up," etc. 2. Its justice : "They would none of me."—*G. R.*

Verse 13.—The excellent estate of an obedient believer. I. Enemies subdued II. Enjoyments perpetuated. III. Abundance possessed.

Verses 13, 14.—The sin and loss of the backslider.

Verse 14.—Spiritual enemies best combatted by an obedient life.

Verse 16.—I. Spiritual dainties. II. By whom provided. III. To whom given. IV. With what result—"satisfied."

PSALM LXXXII.

TITLE AND SUBJECT.—*A Psalm of Asaph. This poet of the temple here acts as a preacher to the court and to the magistracy. Men who do one thing well are generally equal to another ; he who writes good verse is not unlikely to be able to preach. What preaching it would have been had Milton entered the pulpit, or had Virgil been an apostle.*

Asaph's sermon before the judges is now before us. He speaks very plainly, and his song is rather characterised by strength than by sweetness. We have here a clear proof that all psalms and hymns need not be direct expressions of praise to God ; we may, according to the example of this Psalm, admonish one another in our songs. Asaph no doubt saw around him much bribery and corruption, and while David punished it with the sword, he resolved to scourge it with a prophetic Psalm. In so doing, the sweet singer was not forsaking his profession as a musician for the Lord, but rather was practically carrying it out in another department. He was praising God when he rebuked the sin which dishonoured him, and if he was not making music, he was hushing discord when he bade rulers dispense justice with impartiality.

The Psalm is a whole and needs no formal division.

EXPOSITION.

GOD standeth in the congregation of the mighty ; he judgeth among the gods.

2 How long will ye judge unjustly, and accept the persons of the wicked ? Selah.

3 Defend the poor and fatherless : do justice to the afflicted and needy.

4 Deliver the poor and needy : rid *them* out of the hand of the wicked.

5 They know not, neither will they understand ; they walk on in darkness : all the foundations of the earth are out of course.

6 I have said, Ye *are* gods ; and all of you *are* children of the most High.

7 But ye shall die like men, and fall like one of the princes.

8 Arise, O God, judge the earth : for thou shalt inherit all nations.

1. *"God standeth in the congregation of the mighty."* He is the overlooker, who, from his own point of view, sees all that is done by the great ones of the earth. When they sit in state he stands over them, ready to deal with them if they pervert judgment. Judges shall be judged, and to justices justice shall be meted out. Our village squires and country magistrates would do well to remember this. Some of them had need go to school to Asaph till they have mastered this Psalm. Their harsh decisions and strange judgments are made in the presence of him who will surely visit them for every unseemly act, for he has no respect unto the person of any, and is the champion of the poor and needy. A higher authority will criticise the decision of petty sessions, and even the judgments of our most impartial judges will be revised by the High Court of heaven. *"He judgeth among the gods."* They are gods to other men, but he is GOD to them. He lends them his name, and this is their authority for acting as judges, but they must take care that they do not misuse the power entrusted to them, for the Judge of judges is in session among them. Our puisne judges are but puny judges, and their brethren who administer common law will one day be tried by the common law. This great truth is, upon the whole, well regarded among us in these times, but it was not so in the earlier days of English history, when Jeffries, and such as he, were an insult to the name of justice. Oriental judges, even now, are frequently, if not generally, amenable to bribes, and in past ages it was very hard to find a ruler who had any notion of justice apart from his own arbitrary will. Such plain teaching as this Psalm contains was needful indeed, and he was a bold, good man who, in such uncourtly phrases, delivered his own soul.

2. "*How long will ye judge unjustly and accept the persons of the wicked ?*" It is indirectly stated that the magistrates had been unjust and corrupt. They not only excused the wicked, but even decided in their favour against the righteous. A little of this is too much, a short time too long. Some suitors could get their claims settled at once, and in their own favour, while others were wearing out their lives by waiting for an audience, or were robbed by legal process because their opponents had the judge's ear : how long were such things to be perpetrated ? Would they never remember the Great Judge, and renounce their wickedness ? This verse is so grandly stern that one is tempted to say, " Surely an Elijah is here." "*Selah.*" This gives the offenders pause for consideration and confession.

3. "*Defend the poor and fatherless.*" Cease to do evil, learn to do well. Look not to the interests of the wealthy whose hands proffer you bribes, but protect the rights of the needy, and especially uphold the claims of orphans whose property too often becomes a prey. Do not hunt down the peasant for gathering a few sticks, and allow the gentlemanly swindler to break through the meshes of the law. "*Do justice to the afflicted and needy.*" Even they can claim from you as judge no more than justice ; your pity for their circumstances must not make you hold the scales unfairly : but if you give them no more than justice, at least be sure that you give them that to the full. Suffer not the afflicted to be further afflicted by enduring injustice, and let not the needy long stand in need of an equitable hearing.

4. "*Deliver the poor and needy : rid them out of the hand of the wicked.*" Break the nets of the man-catchers, the legal toils, the bonds, the securities, with which cunning men capture and continue to hold in bondage the poor and the embarrassed. It is a brave thing when a judge can liberate a victim like a fly from the spider's web, and a horrible case when magistrate and plunderer are in league. Law has too often been an instrument for vengeance in the hand of unscrupulous men, an instrument as deadly as poison or the dagger. It is for the judge to prevent such villainy.

5. "*They know not, neither will they understand.*" A wretched plight for a nation to be in when its justices know no justice, and its judges are devoid of judgment. Neither to know his duty nor to wish to know it is rather the mark of an incorrigible criminal than of a magistrate, yet such a stigma was justly set upon the rulers of Israel. "*They walk on in darkness.*" They are as reckless as they are ignorant. Being both ignorant and wicked they yet dare to pursue a path in which knowledge and righteousness are essential : they go on without hesitation, forgetful of the responsibilities in which they are involved, and the punishment which they are incurring. "*All the foundations of the earth are out of course.*" When the dispensers of law have dispensed with justice, settlements are unsettled, society is unhinged, the whole fabric of the nation is shaken. When injustice is committed in due course of law the world is indeed out of course. When " Justices' justice " becomes a by-word it is time that justice dealt with justices. Surely it would be well that certain of " the great unpaid " should be paid off, when day after day their judgments show that they have no judgment. When peasants may be horsewhipped by farmers with impunity, and a pretty bird is thought more precious than poor men, the foundations of the earth are indeed sinking like rotten piles unable to bear up the structures built upon them. Thank God we have, as an almost invariable rule, incorruptible judges ; may it always be so. Even our lesser magistrates are, in general, most worthy men ; for which we ought to be grateful to God evermore.

6. "*I have said, ye are gods.*" The greatest honour was thus put upon them ; they were delegated gods, clothed for a while with a little of that authority by which the Lord judges among the sons of men. "*And all of you are children of the Most High.*" This was their *ex-officio* character, not their moral or spiritual relationship. There must be some government among men, and as angels are not sent to dispense it, God allows men to rule over men, and endorses their office, so far at least that the prostitution of it becomes an insult to his own prerogatives. Magistrates would have no right to condemn the guilty if God had not sanctioned the establishment of government, the administration of law, and the execution of sentences. Here the Spirit speaks most honourably of these offices, even when it censures the officers ; and thereby teaches us to render honour to whom honour is due, honour to the office even if we award censure to the office-bearer.

7. "*But ye shall die like men.*" What sarcasm it seems ! Great as the office made the men, they were still but men, and must die. To every judge this verse is a *memento mori !* He must leave the bench to stand at the bar, and on the way

must put off the ermine to put on the shroud. *"And fall like one of the princes."* Who were usually the first to die : for battle, sedition, and luxury, made greater havoc among the great than among any others. Even as princes have been cut off by sudden and violent deaths, so should the judges be who forget to do justice. Men usually respect the office of a judge, and do not conspire to slay him, as they do to kill princes and kings ; but injustice withdraws this protection, and puts the unjust magistrate in personal danger. How quickly death unrobes the great. What a leveller he is. He is no advocate for liberty, but in promoting equality and fraternity he is a masterly democrat. Great men die as common men do. As their blood is the same, so the stroke which lets out their life produces the same pains and throes. No places are too high for death's arrows : he brings down his birds from the tallest trees. It is time that all men considered this.

8. *"Arise, O God, judge the earth."* Come thou Judge of all mankind, put the bad judges to thy bar and end their corruption and baseness. Here is the world's true hope of rescue from the fangs of tyranny. *"For thou shalt inherit all nations."* The time will come when all races of men shall own their God, and accept him as their king. There is one who is " King by right divine," and he is even now on his way. The last days shall see him enthroned, and all unrighteous potentates broken like potter's vessels by his potent sceptre. The second advent is still earth's brightest hope. Come quickly, even so, come, Lord Jesus.

EXPLANATORY NOTES AND QUAINT SAYINGS.

Whole Psalm.—Asaph, who has written so much in the previous Psalms of the coming of Christ in the flesh, now speaks of his second coming to judgment.—*Josephus Maria Thomasius.* 1649—1713.

Verse 1.—*"God standeth."* He is said to *stand*, because of his immutability, his power, his abiding presence, and also because of his promptness in act, to decide for the right, and to help the poor, as he did S. Stephen. But one commentator draws a yet deeper lesson from the word *stand.* He reminds us that it is for the judge to sit, and for the litigants or accused to stand ; as it is written, " Moses sat to judge the people ; and the people stood by Moses from the morning until the evening." Exodus xviii. 13. It is then a solemn warning for judges to remember, that whatever cause is before them is God's cause, since right and wrong are at stake in it, and that by acquitting the guilty, or condemning the innocent, they pass sentence against God himself.—*Albertus Magnus, Le Blanc, and Agellius, quoted by Neale and Littledale.*

Verse 1.—*"God standeth in the congregation of the mighty,"* or, *"of God."* These words are exegetical, and help to illustrate what he had said before : *"God standeth in the congregation of God."* What is that ? Why he judgeth as supreme amongst the judges of the world. He stands not as a cipher, or a bare spectator, but he himself makes one amongst them. 1. He judgeth actively amongst them. We look upon men, and think the judgment is theirs, but it is God that exerciseth judgment amongst them. He knows the causes, directs the judges, and executes the sentence. 2. Passively, he is so in the midst of these earthly gods, that if they do unjustly he will execute justice on them, and judge the judges of the world ; for though they be great, yet there is a greater than they, to whom they must shortly give an account.—*Thomas Hall.* 1659—60.

Verse 1.—*"In the congregation."*—Rulers must understand that they are not placed over stocks and stones, nor over swine and dogs, but over the congregation of God : they must therefore be afraid of acting against God himself when they act unjustly.—*Martin Luther.*

Verse 2.—*"And accept the persons of the wicked."* The last clause exemplifies one of the most peculiar Hebrew idioms. The combination usually rendered *respect persons* in the English Bible, and applied to judicial partiality, means literally to *take* (or *take up*) *faces.* Some suppose this to mean the raising of the countenance, or causing to look up from dejection. But the highest philological authorities are now agreed that the primary idea is that of accepting one man's face or person rather than another's, the precise form of expression, though obscure, being probably derived from the practice of admitting suitors to confer with governors or rulers face to face, a privilege which can sometimes only be obtained by bribes, especially, though not exclusively, in oriental courts.—*Joseph Addison Alexander.*

Verse 3.—It is said of Francis the First, of France, that when a woman kneeled to him to beg justice, he bade her stand up ; for, said he, Woman, it is justice that I owe thee, and justice thou shalt have ; if thou beg anything of me, let it be mercy. A happy place and people surely, where justice (as it seemeth), was not extorted, but dropt as kindly as honey from the comb ; where there was no sale of offices, no exchanging of fees, no subtleties of delay, no truckling for expedition, no making snares of petty penal statutes : where Justice had scales in her hand, not to weigh gold, but equity ; where judges and magistrates were as Noah's ark to take in weary doves, and as the horns of the altar, for oppressed innocency to betake itself unto ; where lawyers, advocates, pleaders, did not call evil good, or good evil, bitter sweet, etc., where plaintiffs and accusers did not inform or persecute through malice, envy, or for advantage ; where subordinate officers durst not help potent delinquents out of the briars, nor suffer poor men, tempest-tossed in law, to languish in their business within ken of harbour for want of giving a sop to Cerberus, or sacrificing to the great Diana of expedition ; where those setting dogs, such as base, promoting informers, were not countenanced, and severly punished upon any false, unjust, or malicious information. To close up all, where the magistrate owed justice to the people, and paid it ; where the people begged for *mercy* and had it.—*William Price*, 1642.

Verses 3, 4.—The touchstone of magistrates' justice is in the causes and cases of the *poor, fatherless, afflicted and needy,* who are not able to attend long their suits of law, have no friends nor money to deal for them ; to whom, therefore, the mighty should be eyes to direct them, and a staff to their weakness, to support and help them in their right.—*David Dickson.*

Verse 5.—"*They know not, neither will they understand,*" etc. Every judge must have in him (as Baldus acutely said) two kinds of salt : the first is *sal scientiæ,* that he may know his duty ; the second is *sal conscientiæ,* that he may do his duty. Such as fail in the first, are censured here with a *nescierunt,* and *non intellexerunt ;* such as fail in the second, are branded here with an *ambulant in tenebris.*

The dangers upon the neglect of these duties are two : the one concerning the whole commonwealth, "*All the foundations of the earth are out of course ;* " the other especially touching the private persons of the judges, at the seventh verse, "*Ye shall die like men, and fall like one of the princes,*" and after death comes judgment, verse 8 : "*Arise, O God, judge the earth.*" Almighty God " standeth in the congregation of princes, and is a judge among gods" ; he sits Chief Justice in every session and assize, to mark what matters pass, and how they pass, ready to judge those righteously, who judge others unjustly, " giving wrong judgment, and accepting the persons of the wicked." Ps. lxvii. 4.* Thus I have made the way plain before you ; God infinitely rich in mercy, grant, that both I in speaking, and you in hearing, may walk therein (as the blessed Apostle phraseth it, Gal. ii. 14) " with a right foot."

"*They know not, neither will they understand.*" That is, they neither "*know*" God, who made them gods ; nor yet "*understand* " his law, which is a lantern to their feet, and a light to their paths. Or, as Placidus Parmensis upon the place,— They neither consider how they that be called "*gods,*" as commissioners and ministers of God, ought to judge others : nor yet remember how they shall be judged themselves at the last day, when " all the foundations of the world shall be moved," and God himself shall " arise to judge the earth." Or, they be so corrupt and abominable, that they will neither learn what is their office from others, nor yet understand it by themselves. Or briefly, to give that gloss (which fits best I think the text, I am sure the time), *Nescierunt quid facti, non intelexerunt quid juris ;* they were both ignorant in the matter of fact, as not searching out the cause ; and ignorant in the matter of law, sitting (as Paul said of Ananias), to give judgment according to the law, and yet commanding that which is contrary to the law. The first concerns

---

* πρὸς τὸ κριτήριον τοῦ Θεοῦ.

a good deal the jury, the second a great deal the judges ; in both are condemned, as the nurses of all confusions in a commonwealth, *ignorantia simplex*, and *affectata ;* simple ignorance, when as they be so shallow that they cannot ; affected ignorance, when as they be so deep, that they will not understand what is right and reason.— *John Boys, in " The Judges Charge,"* 1618.

Verse 6.—*"Ye are gods,"* etc. It is of course, to civil governors, especially those entrusted with the administration of justice, that the prophet addresses this stern admonition. He calls them " the gods," and " the sons of the Most High." To the people of Israel this kind of appellation would not seem over bold : for it was applied to judges in well-known texts of the Law of Moses. Thus, in the code of civil statutes delivered at Sinai, it is said, " Thou shalt not revile *the gods,* nor curse the ruler of thy people." Exod. xxii. 28. Nor is that the only instance of the kind. In two other passages of the same code (Exod. xxi. 6, and xxii. 8, 9), the word which our translators have rendered " the judges," is in the Hebrew, " the gods," or " God." Since the ordinary Hebrew word for God (Elohim) is almost always used in the plural form, it is hard to say whether it ought to be rendered in these passages in the singular or plural. The meaning is the same either way. It is a matter of indifference, for example, whether the law in Exodus xxi. 6, be rendered thus, " his (the bondman's) master shall bring him to *the gods* "; or, with the Septuagint, " his master shall bring him to the judgment-seat of God."* In either case the terms are plainly meant to imply that the Majesty of God is present in the place of judgment. As it is said of Solomon that he " sat on the throne of the LORD as King," 1 Chron. xxix. 23, so it may be said of every magistrate that he sits in God's seat. God has put upon him a portion of his own dominion and authority ; and has ordained that he is to be obeyed, not for wrath's sake only, but for conscience sake. The civil magistrate, in discharging his high function, may justly claim to govern with a divine right.

No one needs to be told that this old doctrine of the divine right of rulers has been woefully abused. Sycophantic divines have often made of it a flattering unction for the ears of princes ; teaching them that they owed no obedience to the laws ; that they were responsible to none but God for their administration ; that any attempt on the part of the people to curb their tyranny, or to depose them from their seats when milder measures failed, was rebellion against God whose Vicegerents they were. Even now, the same doctrine occasionally makes itself heard from the pulpit and the press ; and thus men attempt to subject the consciences of the people to the caprice of tyrants. Let it be carefully observed that the harp of Asaph lends no sanction to this " right divine of kings to govern wrong." If the prophet testifies that princes are gods, he includes in the honour the humblest magistrate. The elders administering justice in the gate of Bethlehem, though their town be little among the thousands of Judah, sit in God's seat as truly as King Solomon on his ivory throne in the porch of judgment at Jerusalem. The common saying that " the divine right of kings is the divine right of constables," is a rough way of expressing a Bible truth. Let this be borne in mind, and no one will allege Scripture in defence of royal claims to indefeasible and irresponsible authority, or claim for such authority the sanction of divine right.

But while care ought to be taken to guard the divine right of civil government from abuse, the right itself is not to be forgotten. The state is an ordinance of God, having, like the family, its foundation in the very constitution of human nature. The officers of the state, whether supreme or subordinate, have a divine right to administer justice in the community over which Providence has placed them. They who resort to the civil magistrate for judgment, resort to the judgment-seat of God ; just as they who resort to the Ministry of the Word resort to the Great Prophet of the Church. Unless the magistrate had received a commission from God, he could not lawfully bear the sword. To take the life of an unarmed fellow-man, without a commission from the Most High warranting the act, would be to commit murder.—*William Binnie.*

Verse 6.—In his *Lex Rex,* Rutherford argues from this Psálm that judges are not the creatures of kings, to execute their pleasure, and do not derive their power from the monarch, but are authorized by God himself as much as the king, and are therefore bound to execute justice whether the monarch desires it or no.

---

* πρὸς τὸ κριτήριον τοῦ Θεοῦ.

Verse 6.—"*I have said, ye are gods.*" Princes and judges are "*gods*" (*Elohim*), on the ground that " unto them the word of God came " (John x. 35), constituting them such. Even here, when God is about to pass sentence on them, he begins with recognizing their divinely-appointed dignity on which they presumed, as if giving them absolute power to do as they pleased, right or wrong ; forgetting that high office has its *duties* as well as its *dignities*. Sonship is closely allied to *kingship* and *judgeship*. These combined dignities, which by all others have been abused, shall be realized in all their grandest ideal by the coming King, Judge, and Son of the Most High (Ps. ii. 6, 7, 10—12.)—*A. R. Fausset.*

Verse 6.—"*I have said, ye are gods.*" As parasites in base flattery and compliance with their pride, have vainly called some of them so, and as some princes have most wickedly and blasphemously affected to be called, yea to be adored, as gods, (God will take highest vengeance upon all those who take his name upon them, or submit to it when given them), so God himself hath put his own name upon magistrates, to mind them of their duty, or for a twofold end : First, that being called gods, they should judge and rule as God doth, or with a mind like God, free from the mixture of a private or passionate spirit, and filled with a love to, and a delight in, impartial judgment and righteousness. Secondly, that being called gods, all men might learn their duty, freely to submit to them and duly honour them ; seeing any dishonour done to them reflects upon God whose name they bear.—*Joseph Caryl.*

Verse 6.—"*Gods.*" It is not *Jah* or *Jehovah*, a name of *essence*, but *Eloah* or *Elohim*, a name of *office* that is given them.—*Thomas Gataker.*

Verses 6, 7.—"*Ye are gods ;*" there he considered their pomp and dignity : "*But ye shall die like men ;* " there he minds their end, that with the change of his note they might also change countenance. He tells them their honour, but withal their lot. In power, wealth, train, titles, friends, they differ from others ; in death they differ not from others. They are cold when winter comes, withered with age, weak with sickness, and melt away with death, as the meanest : all to ashes. " All flesh is as grass, and all the glory of man as the flower," 1 Pet. i. 24 : the glory, that is, the best of it, but a flower. No great difference, the flower shows fairer, the grass stands longer, one scythe cuts down both. Beasts fat and lean, fed in one pasture, killed in one slaughter. The prince in his lofty palace, the beggar in his lowly cottage, have double difference, local and ceremonial height and lowness ; yet meet at the grave, and are mingled in ashes. We walk in this world as a man in a field of snow ; all the way appears smooth, yet cannot we be sure of any step. All are like actors on a stage, some have one part and some another, death is still busy amongst us ; here drops one of the players, we bury him with sorrow, and to our scene again : then falls another, yea all, one after another, till death be left upon the stage. Death is that damp which puts out all the dim lights of vanity. Yet man is easier to believe that all the world shall die, than to suspect himself.—*Thomas Adams.*

Verse 7.—"*Ye shall die like men,*" etc. Even you which glisten like angels, whom all the world admires, and sues and bows to, which are called honourable, mighty and gracious lords, I will tell you to what your honour shall come : first, ye shall wax old like others, then ye shall fall sick like others, then ye shall die like others, then ye shall be buried like others, then ye shall be consumed like others, then ye shall be judged like others, even like the beggars which cry at your gates : one sickens, the other sickens ; one dies, the other dies ; one rots, the other rots : look in the grave, and shew me which was Dives and which was Lazarus. This is some comfort to the poor, that once he shall be like the rich ; one day he shall be as wealthy, and as glorious as a king ; one hour of death will make all alike ; they which crowed over others, and looked down upon them like oaks, others shall walk upon them like worms, and they shall be gone as if they had never been.—*Henry Smith.*

Verse 7.—"*Ye shall die like men, and fall like one of the princes.*" The meditation of death would pull down the plumes of pride ; thou art but dust animated ; shall dust and ashes be proud ? Thou hast a grassy body, and shall shortly be mowed down : "*I have said, ye are gods ;* " but lest they should grow proud, he adds a corrective : "*ye shall die like men ;* " ye are dying gods.—*Thomas Watson.*

Verse 7.—"*And fall like one of the princes.*" Tyrants seldom go to their graves in peace. Most of the Cæsars fell by the hands of the people, *q.d.*, If you be like tyrants in sin, expect to be like them in punishment; as I cast them out of their thrones for their insolence and violence, so will I cast you out, and you shall fall like one of these tyrannical princes.—*Thomas Hall.*

Verse 7.—1. Ye shall fall from the highest pinnacle of honour and reputation. The place of magistracy, which knoweth you now, will know you no more. One of the ancients, standing by Cæsar's tomb, crieth out, *Ubi nunc pulchritudo Cæsaris? quo abiit magnificentia ejus?* Where is now the beauty; what is become of the magnificence; where are the armies now; where the honours, the triumphs, the trophies of Cæsar? All was gone when Cæsar was gone. Your honours and your worships, your power, and your places, all die with you, if not before you. 2. Ye fall from your greatest treasures and possessions. As ye brought nothing into the world, so it is certain ye shall carry nothing out of the world, 1 Tim. vi. 7. Saladin, the mighty monarch of the east, is gone, and hath carried no more along with him than ye see—*i.e.*, a shirt hung up for that purpose—said the priest that went before the bier. 3. Ye fall from all your friends and relations; when ye die, they that were near and dear to you will leave you.—*George Swinnock.*

Verse 7.—*Impressiveness* is a leading characteristic of the "death" or "fall" of "princes:" such incidents, from a variety of causes, are most striking. But can the same remark be commonly made respecting the decease of the children of poverty? Regard being had to the startling effect which the demise of the potentate is calculated to produce,—has the departure of the *peasant*, for example, in itself, the same tendency to beget solemnity and awe, so that, even under this point of view, the peasant might be justly affirmed to "*fall like one of the princes*"? Indeed, if you think of the outward circumstances attending *his* last moments; and then, immediately afterwards, of those which belong to the close of the life of the dweller in regal or stately halls, there would seem to be hardly any ground here for instituting the slightest comparison: but I would have you to associate the man, as he lies on the eve of dissolution, not with others, his superiors in rank, in a similar case, but with *himself*, when, in the full vigour of existence, he walked to and fro, and performed his own humble but laborious share of this world's business; and, as you subsequently mark how the great Destroyer has crushed all his energies, and left but a corpse behind, you will surely admit that there is as wide a difference between the individual as he *was* and as he *is*, as there can possibly be between the scenes at the death-beds, respectively, of princes and of the poor. Yes, and as *impressive* a difference too; so that you have only to allow the exhibition of the striking change to have its legitimate effect upon the mind, and then, so far as that effect will be concerned, you may declare of the rural labourer, that "*he has fallen like one of the princes;*" seeing that he has given a lesson every whit as awakening and as emphatic in its admonitions, as could the other.—*Hugh B. Moffatt,* 1861.

Verses 7, 8.—Your day is coming! The saints are raising the loud cry of verse 8, inviting Messiah, the true God, the Son of the Most High (John x. 34), the Mighty One, the Judge and Ruler, to arise and take his *inheritance*, for he is the "*heir of all things;*" and to be the true Othniel, Ehud, Shamgar, Barak, Gideon, Tola, Jair, Jephthah, Samson, and Samuel, who will *judge*, or govern and rule, a mismanaged earth. We sing this song of Zion in his ears, urging him to come quickly; and we sing it to one another in joyful hope, while the foundations of earth seem out of course, because here we find *Messiah the true Judge of a misgoverned world.*—*Andrew A. Bonar.*

Verse 8.—"*Arise, O God.*" A metaphor taken from the common gesture of judges, whose usual manner is to sit while they are hearing of cases; to arise and stand up when they come to give sentence.—*Thomas Gataker.*

HINTS TO PREACHERS.

Verse 1.—The sovereignty of God over the most powerful and exalted. How that sovereignty reveals itself, and what we may expect from it.

Verse 1.—The Lord's presence in cabinets and senates.

Verse 2.—A common sin. Regard for the persons of men often influences our judgment of their opinions, virtues, vices, and general bearing; this involves injustice to others, as well as deep injury to the flattered.

Verse 3.—A plea for orphans.

Verse 5.—I. The characters of wicked princes. 1. Ignorance: "They know not." 2. Wilful blindness: "Neither will they," etc. 3. Unrestrained perverseness: "They walk on," etc. II. The consequences to others: "All the foundations," etc. 1. Of personal security. 2. Of social comfort. 3. Of commercial prosperity. 4. Of national tranquility. 5. Of religious liberty; all are out of course.—*G. R.*

Verse 5.—(*middle clause*).—A description of the pilgrimage of presumptuous sinners.

Verse 6.—"*Ye are gods.*" The passages in the Old Testament which involve the doctrine of the divinity of Christ.—*J. P. Lange.*

Verse 8.—I. The invocation: "Arise," etc. II. The prediction: "For thou shalt," etc.—*G. R.*

PSALM LXXXIII.

TITLE.—A Song *or* Psalm of Asaph. *This is the last occasion upon which we shall meet with this eloquent writer. The patriotic poet sings again of wars and dangers imminent, but it is no godless song of a thoughtless nation entering upon war with a light heart. Asaph the seer is well aware of the serious dangers arising from the powerful confederate nations, but his soul in faith stays itself upon Jehovah, while as a poet-preacher he excites his countrymen to prayer by means of this sacred lyric. The Asaph who penned this song was in all probability the person referred to in 2 Chron. xx. 14, for the internal evidence referring the subject of the Psalm to the times of Jehoshaphat is overwhelming. The division in the camp of the confederate peoples in the wilderness of Tekoa not only broke up their league, but led to a mutual slaughter, which crippled the power of some of the nations for many years after. They thought to destroy Israel and destroyed each other.*

DIVISION.—*An appeal to God in a general manner fills the verses from* 1—4 : *and then the Psalmist enters into details of the league,* 5—8. *This leads to an earnest entreaty for the overthrow of the enemy,* 9—15, *with an expression of desire that God's glory may be promoted thereby.*

EXPOSITION.

KEEP not thou silence, O God : hold not thy peace, and be not still, O God.

2 For, lo, thine enemies make a tumult : and they that hate thee have lifted up the head.

3 They have taken crafty counsel against thy people, and consulted against thy hidden ones.

4 They have said, Come, and let us cut them off from *being* a nation ; that the name of Israel may be no more in remembrance.

1. *"Keep not thou silence, O God."* Man is clamorous, be not thou speechless. He rails and reviles, wilt not thou reply ? One word of thine can deliver thy people ; therefore, O Lord, break thy quiet and let thy voice be heard. *"Hold not thy peace, and be not still, O God."* Here the appeal is to EL, the Mighty One. He is entreated to act and speak, because his nation suffers and is in great jeopardy. Now entirely the Psalmist looks to God ; he asks not for " a leader bold and brave," or for any form of human force, but casts his burden upon the Lord, being well assured that his eternal power and Godhead could meet every difficulty of the case.

2. *"For, lo, thine enemies make a tumult."* They are by no means sparing of their words, they are like a hungry pack of dogs, all giving tongue at once. So sure are they of devouring thy people that they already shout over the feast. *"And they that hate thee have lifted up the head."* Confident of conquest, they carry themselves proudly and exalt themselves as if their anticipated victories were already obtained. These enemies of Israel were also God's enemies, and are here described as such by way of adding intensity to the argument of the intercession. The adversaries of the church are usually a noisy and a boastful crew. Their pride is a brass which always sounds, a cymbal which is ever tinkling.

3. *"They have taken crafty counsel against thy people."* Whatever we may do, our enemies use their wits and lay their heads together ; in united conclave they discourse upon the demands and plans of the campaign, using much treachery and serpentine cunning in arranging their schemes. Malice is cold-blooded enough to plot with deliberation ; and pride, though it be never wise, is often allied with craft. *"And consulted against thy hidden ones."* Hidden away from all harm are the Lord's chosen ; their enemies think not so, but hope to smite them ; they might as well attempt to destroy the angels before the throne of God.

4. *"They have said, Come, and let us cut them off from being a nation."* **Easier** said than done. Yet it shows how thorough-going are the foes of the church. Theirs was the policy of extermination. They laid the axe at the root of the matter. Rome has always loved this method of warfare, and hence she has gloated over the massacre of Bartholomew, and the murders of the Inquisition. *"That the name of Israel may be no more in remembrance."* They would blot them out of history as well as out of existence. Evil is intolerant of good. If Israel would let Edom alone yet Edom cannot be quiet, but seeks like its ancestor to kill the chosen of the Lord. Men would be glad to cast the church out of the world because it rebukes them, and is thus a standing menace to their sinful peace.

5 For they have consulted together with one consent : they are confederate against thee :

6 The tabernacles of Edom, and the Ismaelites ; of Moab, and the Hagarenes.

7 Gebal, and Ammon, and Amalek ; the Philistines with the inhabitants of Tyre ;

8 Assur also is joined with them ; they have holpen the children of Lot. Selah.

5. *"For they have consulted together with one consent."* They are hearty and unanimous in their designs. They seem to have but one heart, and that a fierce one, against the chosen people and their God. *"They are confederate against thee."* At the Lord himself they aim through the sides of his saints. They make a covenant, and ratify it with blood, resolutely banding themselves together to war with the Mighty God.

6. *"The tabernacles of Edom."* Nearest of kin, yet first in enmity. Their sire despised the birthright, and they despise the possessors of it. Leaving their rock-built mansions for the tents of war, the Edomites invaded the land of Israel. *"And the Ishmaelites."* A persecuting spirit ran in their blood, they perpetuated the old grudge between the child of the bondwoman and the son of the freewoman. *"Of Moab."* Born of incest, but yet a near kinsman, the feud of Moab against Israel was very bitter. Little could righteous Lot have dreamed that his unhallowed seed would be such unrelenting enemies of his uncle Abraham's posterity. *"And the Hagarenes"*—perhaps descendants of Hagar by a second husband. Whoever they may have been, they cast their power into the wrong scale, and with all their might sought the ruin of Israel. Children of Hagar, and all others who dwell around Mount Sinai, which is in Arabia, are of the seed which gendereth to bondage, and hence they hate the seed according to promise.

7. *"Gebal"* was probably a near neighbour of Edom, though there was a Gebal in the region of Tyre and Sidon. *"And Ammon, and Amalek."* Two other hereditary foes of Israel, fierce and remorseless as ravening wolves. In the roll of infamy let these names remain detestably immortalised. How thick they stand ! Their name is legion, for they are many. Alas, poor Israel, how art thou to stand against such a Bloody League ? Nor is this all. Here comes another tribe of ancient foemen, *"the Philistines ; "* who once blinded Samson, and captured the ark of the Lord ; and here are old allies become new enemies ; the builders of the temple conspiring to pull it down, even *"the inhabitants of Tyre."* These last were mercenaries who cared not at whose bidding they drew sword, so long as they carved something for their own advantage. True religion has had its quarrel with merchants and craftsmen, and because it has interfered with their gains, they have conspired against it.

8. *"Assur is also joined with them."* It was then a rising power, anxious for growth, and it thus early distinguished itself for evil. What a motley group they were ; a league against Israel is always attractive, and gathers whole nations within its bonds. Herod and Pilate are friends, if Jesus is to be crucified. Romanism and Ritualism make common cause against the gospel. *"They have holpen the children of Lot."* All these have come to the aid of Moab and Ammon, which two nations were among the fiercest in the conspiracy. There were ten to one against Israel, and yet she overcame all her enemies. Her name is not blotted out ; but many, nay, most of her adversaries are now a name only, their power and their excellence are alike gone.

"Selah." There was good reason for a pause when the nation was in such jeopardy : and yet it needs faith to make a pause, for unbelief is always in a hurry.

9 Do unto them as *unto* the Midianites ; as *to* Sisera, as *to* Jabin, at the brook of Kison :

10 *Which* perished at En-dor : they became *as* dung for the earth.

11 Make their nobles like Oreb, and like Zeeb : yea, all their princes as Zebah, and as Zalmunna :

12 Who said, Let us take to ourselves the houses of God in possession.

13 O my God, make them like a wheel ; as the stubble before the wind.

14 As the fire burneth a wood, and as the flame setteth the mountains on fire ;

15 So persecute them with thy tempest, and make them afraid with thy storm.

9. *"Do unto them as unto the Midianites."* Faith delights to light upon precedents, and quote them before the Lord ; in the present instance, Asaph found a very appropriate one, for the nations in both cases were very much the same, and the plight of the Israelites very similar. Yet Midian perished, and the Psalmist trusted that Israel's present foes would meet with the like overthrow from the hand of the Lord. *"As to Sisera, as to Jabin, at the brook of Kison."* The hosts were swept away by the suddenly swollen torrent, and utterly perished ; which was a second instance of divine vengeance upon confederated enemies of Israel. When God wills it, a brook can be as deadly as a sea. Kishon was as terrible to Jabin as was the Red Sea to Pharaoh. How easily can the Lord smite the enemies of his people. God of Gideon and of Barak, wilt thou not again avenge thine heritage of their bloodthirsty foes ?

10. *"Which perished at En-dor."* There was the centre of the carnage, where the heaps of the slain lay thickest. *"They became as dung for the earth,"* manuring it with man ; making the earth, like Saturn, feed on its own children. War is cruel, but in this case its avengements were most just,—those who would not give Israel a place above ground are themselves denied a hiding-place under the ground ; they counted God's people to be as dung, and they became dung themselves. Asaph would have the same fate befall other enemies of Israel ; and his prayer was a prophecy, for so it happened to them.

11. *"Make their nobles like Oreb, and like Zeeb."* Smite the great ones as well as the common ruck. Suffer not the ringleaders to escape. As Oreb fell at the rock and Zeeb at the winepress, so do thou mete out vengeance to Zion's foes wherever thou mayest overtake them. They boastfully compare themselves to ravens and wolves ; let them receive the fate which is due to such wild beasts. *"Yea, all their princes as Zebah, and as Zalmunna."* These were captured and slain by Gideon, despite their claiming to have been anointed to the kingdom. Zebah became a sacrifice, and Zalmunna was sent to those shadowy images from which his name is derived. The Psalmist seeing these four culprits hanging in history upon a lofty gallows, earnestly asks that others of a like character may, for truth and righteousness' sake, share their fate.

12. *"Who said, Let us take to ourselves the houses of God in possession."* Viewing the temple, and also the dwellings of the tribes, as all belonging to God, these greedy plunderers determined to push out the inhabitants, slay them, and become themselves landlords and tenants of the whole. These were large words and dark designs, but God could bring them all to nothing. It is in vain for men to say " Let us take," if God does not give. He who robs God's house will find that he has a property reeking with a curse ; it will plague him and his seed for ever. " Will a man rob God ? " Let him try it, and he will find it hot and heavy work.

13. *"O my God, make them like a wheel ; "* like a rolling thing which cannot rest, but is made to move with every breath. Let them have no quiet. May their minds eternally revolve and never come to peace. Blow them away like thistle down, *"as the stubble before the wind."* Scatter them, chase them, drive them to destruction. Every patriot prays thus against the enemies of his country, he would be no better than a traitor if he did not.

14. *"As the fire burneth a wood."* Long years have strewn the ground with

deep deposits of leaves ; these being dried in the sun are very apt to take fire, and when they do so the burning is terrific. The underwood and the ferns blaze, the bushes crackle, the great trees kindle and to their very tops are wrapped in fire, while the ground is all red as a furnace. In this way, O Lord, mete out destruction to thy foes, and bring all of them to an end. *"The flame setteth the mountains on fire."* Up the hill sides the hanging woods glow like a great sacrifice, and the forests on the mountain's crown smoke towards heaven. Even thus, O Lord, do thou conspicuously and terribly overthrow the enemies of thine Israel.

15. *"So persecute them with thy tempest, and make them afraid with thy storm."* The Lord will follow up his enemies, alarm them, and chase them till they are put to a hopeless rout. He did this, according to the prayer of the present Psalm, for his servant Jehoshaphat ; and in like manner will he come to the rescue of any or all of his chosen.

16 Fill their faces with shame ; that they may seek thy name, O Lord.

17 Let them be confounded and troubled for ever ; yea, let them be put to shame, and perish :

18 That *men* may know that thou, whose name alone *is* JEHOVAH, *art* the most high over all the earth.

16. *"Fill their faces with shame ; that they may seek thy name, O Lord."* Shame has often weaned men from their idols, and set them upon seeking the Lord. If this was not the happy result, in the present instance, with the Lord's enemies, yet it would be so with his people who were so prone to err. They would be humbled by his mercy, and ashamed of themselves because of his grace ; and then they would with sincerity return to the earnest worship of Jehovah their God, who had delivered them.

17. Where no good result followed, and the men remained as fierce and obstinate as ever, justice was invoked to carry out the capital sentence. *"Let them be confounded and troubled for ever ; yea, let them be put to shame, and perish."* What else could be done with them ? It was better that they perished than that Israel should be rooted up. What a terrible doom it will be to the enemies of God to be " confounded and troubled for ever,"—to see all their schemes and hopes defeated, and their bodies and souls full of anguish without end : from such a shameful perishing may our souls be delivered.

18. *"That men may know that thou, whose name alone is JEHOVAH, art the most high over all the earth."* Hearing of the Lord's marvellous deeds in defeating such a numerous confederacy, the very heathen would be compelled to acknowledge the greatness of Jehovah. We read in 2 Chron. xx. 30, that the fear of God was on all the neighbouring kingdoms when they heard that Jehovah fought against the enemies of Israel. Jehovah is essentially the Most High. He who is self-existent is infinitely above all creatures, all the earth is but his footstool. The godless race of man disregards this, and yet at times the wonderful works of the Lord compel the most unwilling to adore his majesty.

Thus has this soul-stirring lyric risen from the words of complaint to those of adoration ; let us in our worship always seek to do the same. National trouble called out the nation's poet laureate, and well did he discourse at once of her sorrows, and prayers, and hopes. Sacred literature thus owes much to sorrow and distress. How enriching is the hand of adversity !

The following attempt to versify the Psalm, and tune it to gospel purposes, is submitted with great diffidence.

O God, be thou no longer still,
Thy foes are leagued against thy law ;
Make bare thine arm on Zion's hill,
Great Captain of our Holy War.

As Amalek and Ishmael
Had war for ever with thy seed,
So all the hosts of Rome and hell
Against thy Son their armies lead.

Though they're agreed in nought beside,
Against thy truth they all unite ;
They rave against the Crucified,
And hate the gospel's growing might.

By Kishon's brook all Jabin's band
At thy rebuke were swept away;
O Lord, display thy mighty hand,
A single stroke shall win the day.

Come, rushing wind, the stubble chase!
Come, sacred fire, the forests burn!
Come, Lord, with all thy conquering grace,
Rebellious hearts to Jesus turn!

That men may know at once that thou,
Jehovah, lovest truth right well;
And that thy church shall never bow
Before the boastful gates of hell.

EXPLANATORY NOTES AND QUAINT SAYINGS.

Title.—"*A Song* or *Psalm.*" When the two words (*Shir, Mizmor,*) occur together, the meaning seems to be, *a lyric poem appointed to be sung.*—*John Jebb.*

Title.—This Psalm, according to the title, was composed by Asaph. In accordance with this, we read, in 1 Chron. xx. 14, that the Spirit of the Lord came upon Jehasiel, of the sons of Asaph, in the midst of the assembly. This Jehasiel is probably the author of the Psalm. Our Psalm is a true picture of the state of feeling which prevailed throughout the people during the danger under Jehoshaphat. According to the history of Chronicles, they praised God at that time, in the midst of their danger, with loud voice, ver. 19; and here in the title, which is an appendage to that of Ps. xlviii., the Psalm is called a *song of praise;* and it is such in reality, although it bears the form of a *prayer,*—a song of triumph sung before the victory,— no contest, no doubt, the distress is simply committed to God.

The mention of the *Amalekites* among the enemies of Israel, in ver. 7, renders it impossible to come down to times later than that of Jehoshaphat. The last remains of the Amalekites were, according to 1 Chron. iv. 43, rooted out by the Simeonites, under Hezekiah. From that time they disappear altogether from history. Ewald's assertion that Amalek stands here " only as a name of infamy applied to parties well-known at the time," is to be considered as a miserable shift. The Psalm must have been composed previous to the extension of the empire of the Assyrians over Western Asia. For the Assyrians named last, in the eighth verse, appear here in the very extraordinary character of an ally of the sons of Lot.— *E. W. Hengstenberg.*

Verse 1.—"*Keep not thou silence, O God.*" In Scripture there are three reasons why the Lord *keeps silence* when his people are in danger, and *sits still* when there is most need to give help and assistance. One is, the Lord doth it *to try their faith,* as we see clearly, Matthew viii. 24, where it is said that our Lord Christ *was asleep:* " There arose a great tempest in the sea, insomuch that the ship was covered with the waves: but he was asleep. And his disciples came to him, and awoke him, saying, Lord, save us: we perish." We read more fully in Mark iv. and Luke viii., he left them, when the ship was covered with waves, and they were rowing for their lives, their Lord was *asleep* the while, and he said to them, " Why are ye so fearful? how is it that you have no faith? And he arose, and rebuked the wind, and said unto the sea, Peace, be still. And the wind ceased, and there was a great calm." Truly, the Lord will not suffer his people to be *overwhelmed,* that is certain, but he will suffer them to come very near, that the waves *cover* them, and fear and horror shall cover their souls, and all *to try their faith.* . . . . 2. I find another reason in Isaiah lix., and that is, the Lord doth keep silence in the midst of the troubles of his people, *to try men's uprightness,* and discover who will stick to God, and his cause, and his people, out of *uprightness of heart.* For if God should always *appear* for his cause, God and his cause should have many favourites and friends; but sometimes God leaves his cause, and leaves his people, and leaves his gospel, and his ordinances to the wide world, to see who will plead for it and stick to it. . . . . 3. There is a third reason : God, as it were, *keeps silence* in the midst of the greatest troubles, that he may, as it were, *gather the wicked into one fagot, into one bundle, that they may be destroyed together.* There is a great deal of ado to *"gather the saints "* in this world ; and truly there is some ado to gather the *wicked.* So God withdraws himself from his people, yet he hath a *hook* within their hearts, he holds them up secretly by his Spirit, that they shall not leave him ; yet the world shall not see but that God hath quite *left* them, and all their ordinances and his gospel and everything ; and there the wicked *come together* and insult, whereby God may come upon them *at once,* and destroy them, as we find ten nations in the Psalm. And so in Genesis, God stirs up the nations against Abraham and his posterity, and there are ten nations that God promised to cut off before Abraham at once, the Perizzites and the Jebuzites, and the Canaanites, etc. So God *heaps them together,* and burns them like stubble. Those that burn stubble have *rakes,* and they gather it *to heaps,* and then they fire it. This is the way of *God's keeping silence* among his people, and *sitting still* in the midst of their miseries, thus God gathers their enemies in heaps as stubble, that he may burn them together.—*Gualter [Walter] Cradock, in* "Divine Drops." 1650.

Verse 1.—*"Keep not thou silence,"* etc.—The Hebrew words have great emphasis, and express the main *causes* of silence—closing the mouth, deafness of the ears, and a tranquility maintained to such an extent as to reject all disquietude. The first clause, let not thy *mouth* be closed, and thy tongue cleave to the roof of thy mouth immovably, properly denotes, from the inherent force of the word דמי whose root means to *fix* to and compact firmly, what is fastened with *lime* or daubed with plaster. . . . The second clause, *"be not thou deaf,"* properly pertains to the ears, as Mich. vii. 16, *"Their ears shall be deaf."* The third, *"be not still,"* suggests the course of the thoughts of the mind when it is brought to a state of clear tranquility, all cares and commotions being laid aside. The word שקט is properly *to settle, to settle down,* as when the disturbed dregs of liquor settle down and seek the bottom, whence it is applied to the mind when freed from a great fermentation of cares and the sediment of anxieties and bitterness, a mind serene, clear, and refined. . . .

Let us now see what the poet had in mind when he poured out these prayers, or what he wished to indicate. He hinted, that the people were reduced to these earnest entreaties, because unless God should speedily bring help to them, it might seem that Jehovah, the God of Israel, is like the false gods, a sort of deity, either mute, or deaf, or at his ease.—*Hermann Venema.*

Verse 1.—Is the Lord silent ? Then be not thou silent ; but cry unto him till he breaks the silence.—*Starke, in Lange's Bibelwerk.*

Verse 1.—The reference to *"tumult"* in the following verse gives force to the earnest appeal in this. Amidst all the tumult of gathering foes, he earnestly calls on God to break his silence, and to speak to them in wrath.—*W. Wilson.*

Verse 2.—*"For, lo."* The prayer begins with the particle *"lo,"* which has not only the force of *arousing* God, but also gives the idea of *something present,* with the view of pointing out the opportune moment for God to gird himself for the work.—*Hermann Venema.*

Verse 2.—*"Thine enemies make a tumult."* The whole world is but like an *army,* a *brigade* of men (as it were) under a *general ;* and God is the Lord of Hosts, that is, the Lord of *his armies :* now when there is a tumult in an army, they complain to the *officers,* to the *general* especially ; and he must come and suppress it. Therefore, saith he, Thou Lord of hosts, thou art general of the world ; lo, there is a *tumult* in the world, a *mutiny.*—*Walter Cradock.*

Verse 3.—*"Thy hidden ones."* This representation of God's people is worthy our notice. It may be taken two ways. First, As referring to their *safety.* We often hide only to preserve. This is the meaning of the word in the parable, with regard to the discovery of the treasure in the field ; " which, when a man hath found, he hideth it." His aim is not to conceal but to secure ; and the cause is put for the effect. Thus God's people are hidden. He hid Noah in the Ark, and the waters that drowned the world could not *find* him. When his judgments were coming over the land, " Come, my people," saith he, " enter thou into thy chambers, and shut thy doors about thee : hide thee also for a little season, until the indignation be overpast." Hence the promise, " Thou shalt hide them in the secret of thy presence from the pride of man : thou shalt keep them secretly in a pavilion from the strife of tongues." Hence the confidence expressed by David, " In the time of trouble he shall hide me in his pavilion : in the secret of his tabernacle shall he hide me ; he shall set me upon a rock." The Saviour could say, " In the shadow of his hand hath he hid me." And, " All the saints are in his hand." They are kept by the power of God, through faith, unto salvation. For he himself is their " refuge," their " hiding-place." They are his *"hidden ones."*

Secondly. As intimating their *concealment.* This is not absolute. But it holds in various respects and degrees. It is true with regard to the nature of their *spiritual life.* Our life, says the Apostle, is hid with Christ in God ; and that he refers to its invisibleness, rather than to its safety, is obvious from the words following : " When he who is our life shall *appear, we* also shall *appear* with him in glory." . . . The heart of the believer only knows his own bitterness ; and a stranger intermeddleth not with his joy. The manna on which he feeds is hidden manna. And no one knoweth the new name in the white stone given him, but the receiver. . . .

They are sometimes hidden by *persecution.* For though this does not prevent their being Christians, it hinders them from appearing as such ; especially by secluding them from their social and public assemblies. . . .. They are sometimes hidden by the obscurity of their stations. Not many of the wise, and mighty, and noble are called : but when they *are* called, they are also *exhibited.* They are like cities set on hills, which cannot be hid. A little religion in high life goes a great way, and is much talked of, because it is so often a strange thing. But God has chosen the poor of this world ; and they are often rich in faith. Yet how is their moral wealth to be known ? How few opportunities have they for religious display or exertion ! There may be the principle of benevolence, where there is no ability to give. And the Lord seeth the heart, but men can only judge from actions. Many who are great in the sight of the Lord are living in cottages and hovels ; and are scarcely known, unless to a few neighbours equally obscure.

They are sometimes hidden by their *disposition.* They are reserved, and shrink back from notice. They are timid and self-diffident. This restrains them in religious conversation, especially as it regards their own experience. This keeps them from making a profession of religion, and joining a Christian church. Joseph of Arimathæa was a disciple of Jesus ; but secretly, for fear of the Jews. And Nicodemus, from the same cause, came to Jesus by night. They had difficulties in their situations, from which others were free. They ought to have overcome them ; and so they did at last : but it was a day of small things with them at first. Others are circumstanced and tried in a similar way ; and we must be patient towards all men.

They are sometimes hidden by their *infirmities.* We would not plead for sin ; but grace may be found along with many imperfections. The possessors have what is essential to religion in them ; but not everything that is ornamental, and lovely, and of good report.

The same will also apply to *errors.* Here, again, we are far from undervaluing divine truth. It is a good thing that the heart be established with grace. But it is impossible for us to say how much ignorance, and how many mistakes, may be found, even in the Israelites indeed, in whom there is no guile.—*William Jay.*

Verse 3.—The less the world knows thee, the better for thee ; thou mayst be satisfied with this one thing—God knows them that are his : not lost, although *hidden* is the symbol of a Christian.—*Frisch, in Lange's Bibelwerk.*

Verse 4.—*"That the name of Israel may be no more in remembrance."* This desperate and dreadful scheme, and wretched design of theirs, took not effect ; but, on the contrary, the several nations hereafter mentioned, who were in this conspiracy, are no more, and have not had a name in the world for many hundreds of years ; whilst the Jews are still a people and are preserved, in order to be called and saved, as all Israel will be in the latter day, Rom. xi. 25. So Diocletian thought to have rooted the Christian name out of the world ; but in vain.—*John Gill.*

Verse 5.—*"For they have consulted together with one consent."* Margin, as in Hebrew, *heart.* There is no division in their counsels on this subject. They have one *desire*—one *purpose*—in regard to the matter. Pilate and Herod were made friends together against Christ (Luke xxiii. 12) ; and the world, divided and hostile in other matters, has been habitually united in its opposition to Christ and to a pure and spiritual religion.—*Albert Barnes.*

Verse 5.—"*They have consulted together with one consent,*" etc. To push on this unholy war, they lay their heads together, and their horns, and their hearts too. *Fas est et ab hoste doceri.* Do the enemies of the church act with one consent to destroy it ? Are the kings of the earth of one mind to give their power and honour to the beast ? And shall not the church's friends be unanimous in serving her interests ? If Herod and Pilate are made friends that they may join in crucifying Christ, sure Paul and Barnabas, Paul and Peter, will soon be made friends, that they may join in preaching Christ.—*Matthew Henry.*

Verse 5.—"*They have consulted together,*" etc. Though there may fall out a private grudge betwixt such as are wicked, yet they will all agree and unite against the saints : if two greyhounds are snarling at a bone, yet put up a hare between them, and they will leave the bone, and follow after the hare ; so, if wicked men have private differences amongst themselves, yet if the godly be near them, they will leave snarling at one another, and will pursue after the godly.—*Thomas Watson.*

Verse 5.—"*They are confederate against thee.*" " They have made a covenant," ברית יכרתו, *berith yachrithu,* " they have cut the covenant sacrifice." They have slain an animal, divided him in twain, and passed between the pieces of the victim ; and have thus bound themselves to accomplish their purpose.—*Adam Clarke.*

Verse 6.—"*The tabernacles of Edom,*" etc. The prophet having entered his suit and complaint in general, he comes to particulars, and tells God who they are that had done this. God might say, Who are these that conspire against me, and against my people, and hidden ones ? Lord, saith the prophet, I will tell thee who they are. . . . He names some *ten nations* that joined together against *one poor Israel.* It is a thing you should observe, that when the people of God are conspired against, God rests not in *general complaints,* but he will know *who* they are. As I told you, He is the Lord of Hosts, the great *general.* When there is a mutiny the general asks, what officer, or what corporal, or what sergeant, or who did begin the mutiny ? and it is a fearful thing when the poor persecuted saint shall bring thy name as a persecutor before the God of heaven. When a poor saint shall go home and say, There is a confederacy in London, a conspiracy against the saints of God ; and when a poor saint shall say, such a magistrate, such a minister, such a man in such a street, such a woman set her husband against the saints, and against thine ordinances ; it is a fearful thing. Therefore I remember a blessed woman, if it be true that is reported of her in the *Book of Martyrs,* that when the wicked abused her, and reproached her, and oppressed her, she would say no more but this, " I will go home and tell my Father : " give over, or else I will bring your names before God, and tell him : there was all, and that was enough ; for he would presently take it up. A man may better bear a pound of dirt on his *feet,* than a grain of dirt in his *eye ;* the saints are " the apple of God's eye."—*Walter Cradock.*

Verse 6.—"*Hagarenes.*" These people dwelt on the east of Gilead ; and were nearly destroyed in the days of Saul, being totally expelled from their country, 1 Chron. v. 10, but afterwards recovered some strength and consequence.—*Adam Clarke.*

Verses 6, 7, 8.—It may be observed that these were on all sides of the land of Israel ; the Edomites, Ishmaelites, and Amalekites, were on the south ; the Moabites, Ammonites, and Hagarenes, were on the east ; the Assyrians on the north ; and the Philistines, Gebalites, and Tyrians, on the west ; so that Israel was surrounded on all sides with enemies, as the Lord's people are troubled on every side, 2 Cor. iv. 8 ; and so the Gog and Magog army, of which some understand this, will encompass the camp of the saints about, and the beloved city, Rev. xx. 9.—*John Gill.*

Verses 6—8.—The enemies of Israel, as enumerated by the Psalmist, fall into four main divisions : 1st, those most nearly connected with the Israelites themselves by the ties of blood-relationship, the descendants of Esau and Ishmael ; 2ndly, the two branches of the descendants of Lot along with their respective Arabian auxiliaries, viz., the Moabites, who had engaged the assistance of the Hagarenes, and the Ammonites, who had gathered round their standard the Giblites and Amalekites ; 3rdly, the inhabitants of the coast, the Philistines and Tyrians ; 4thly, the more distant Assyrians.

Of all these the bitterest in their hostility to Israel were those who were the most nearly allied to them in blood—the Edomites. Their hostility was founded upon hatred. From their conduct to the Israelites through a long course of years it would seem as though in them were lastingly perpetuated that older hatred wherewith their forefather Esau had hated Jacob because of Isaac's blessing. And though they had once and again succeeded, according to the prophecy, in breaking Israel's yoke from off their neck, yet they never could wrest away from Israel the possession of the birthright, and with it of the promises, which their ancestors had profanely despised : from Israel, not from Edom, was the Redeemer of the world to spring, and in Israel were all the families of the earth to be blessed. The Edomites may accordingly be appropriately viewed as the types of those whom the Church of Christ has ever found her bitterest foes, the sceptics who have refused to acknowledge that redemption through a personal Redeemer, on which, as on a basis, the church is founded, whose intellectual pride is offended by the humbling doctrines of Christianity, and who hate those that hold them for their possession of blessings which *they* have wilfully neglected ; whose human learning has nevertheless all along been subservient on the whole to the edification of the church, in spite of the violence with which they have striven, and for a while, as it would sometimes appear, successfully, to gain the mastery over her by opposing her, and to exercise a temporary dominion. Dwelling themselves in tabernacles, they cannot bear that others, more blessed than they, should have the houses of God in possession : " owning themselves to be astray, and unable to find the way to the truth, they are yet most importunate and imperious that others should come away from the ancient paths, and try to join them, or at least, wander as they are wandering." In conjunction with the Edomites the Psalmist makes mention of the Ishmaelites. And these, as the descendants of the bondwoman, may fitly represent those Jewish opponents of Christianity, still, perhaps, locally, if not generally, formidable, who in their rejection of Christian doctrine have been swayed by the same feelings of intellectual pride as the sceptics of Christian descent ; who professing to hold fast to that covenant of Mount Sinai which gendereth to bondage, persecuted, so long as they were able, those born after the Spirit. . . . .

In the descendants of Lot and their Arabian auxiliaries, we have the types of a different class of foes. The historical origin of the former marks them as the appropriate representatives of the slaves of sinful lusts ; who hate the church not for the humbling tone of her doctrines, but for the standard of holiness which she exacts and for which she is continually witnessing. And experience shews how such persons are wont, in their attacks upon the church, to enlist into their service those who are more wildly, but at the same time more ignorantly, unholy than themselves ; how in order, if possible, to uproot those fences and safeguards of the law of holiness on which, having transgressed them, they hate to look, they appeal to the unbridled passions of the lawless multitude by whom the very existence of the fences had been utterly disregarded.

From the enemies of the Church who are animated by feelings of positive hatred we pass to those who act from calculation rather than passion, and whose proceedings are all directed with a view to their own earthly aggrandisement. The Philistines and Tyrians had engaged in the hostile confederacy with the hope of obtaining Israelitish captives, from whom they might reap a profit by selling them abroad as slaves. It does not appear that they regarded the Israelites in themselves with other feelings than those of mere selfish indifference.

Both nations had tendered their services to Israel in the days of Israel's prosperity ; for the Philistines had probably furnished the Cherethites and Pelethites of David's body-guard, and the Tyrians had furnished Solomon with materials and workmen for the building of the temple : both nations were now seeking to enrich themselves at Israel's expense in the days of Israel's adversity. And these then are the fitting types of all who in their varying professions of friendliness or hostility to the Church of God are actuated by the mere mercenary desire of lucre ; favouring, and even zealously favouring her interests, when they can procure a good recompense for their services ; unhesitatingly combining with her bitterest enemies to vilify and despoil her, whenever the opportunity offer of increasing their worldly substance thereby.

The last class of enemies are those of whom Assyria is the type ; the worldly potentates, whether ecclesiastical or temporal, papal or imperial, who are unscrupulously ready to employ all means for the ultimate accomplishment of their one object, that of extending and consolidating their dominion. . . . .

Such potentates seem to represent most truly that determined and resolute selfishness, which, to eyes that are not dazzled by the grandeur of its proportions or the gorgeousness in which it is arrayed, must ever appear as one of the most terrible embodiments of the enmity of the world to God. Pride of intellect and unbelief,—unholiness and lawlessness of life,—covetousness,—worldly ambition,— such are the characteristics of four important classes of those by whom God's church is threatened.—*Joseph Francis Thrupp.*

Verse 7.—*"Gebal."* 1. It is generally supposed to indicate the mountainous tract extending from the Dead Sea southward to Petra, still named *Jebâl.* But some of the best writers identify it with No. 2, as mentioned in conjunction with Tyre. 2. A place spoken of in connection with Tyre, Ezek. xxvii. 9. Most probably the residence of the Giblites, and therefore to the north of Palestine, Josh. xiii. 5. The Giblites were employed by Hiram, king of Tyre, in preparing materials for Solomon's temple, 1 Kings v. 18, margin.

The Greek name of this place was Byblus. The town is called *Jebeil,* and has a population of about six hundred. It is about seventeen miles north of Beyroot. The ancient ruins are very extensive. Immense numbers of granite columns are strewn about in the village and over the surrounding fields. These columns are mostly small, varying from one foot to two feet in diameter. Some of the stones measure nearly twenty feet in length. The citadel is the most remarkable ruin. The port is nearly choked up with sand and ruins.—*George H. Whitney's "Hand-Book of Bible Geography."* 1872.

Verse 8.—*"Assur also,"* etc. This determines the date of this Psalm to the latter times of the Jewish kingdom ; for the other nations here mentioned had molested them before, but the Assyrians not till towards the end.—*William Wall,* 1645 or 1646—1727-8.

Verse 9.—*"Do unto them as unto the Midianites."* That is, dash their heads together, make their policies to cross one another.—*Walter Cradock.*

Verse 9.—*"The brook of Kison."* The river Kishon traverses the plain [of Esdraelon] and terminates in the Bay of Acre or Akka. This is the stream regarding which it is written, after Barak and Deborah had gained their victory over Sisera, " The river of Kishon swept them away, that ancient river, the river Kishon. O my soul, thou hast trodden down strength." Although it is now no insignificant stream, yet it needs heavy rains to make it really considerable in magnitude : it is very unequal in size, and seems to be only temporary in its character. At any rate, when Robinson passed its head waters in midsummer, he found the channels all dry, and they had been so for a whole year. On the other hand, in the winter the waters are often exceedingly abundant ; particularly in the northern and southern chief tributaries ; so that, in 1799, at the time of the French invasion, many of the vanquished Turks perished in the floods which swept down from Deburieh, and which inundated the plain. It was a scene like that described in Judges v. regarding the fate of Sisera's hosts.—*Carl Ritter* (1779—1859) *in "The Comparative Geography of Palestine and the Sinaitic Peninsula."* Translated by *William L. Gage.* 1866.

Verse 10.—*"They became as dung for the earth."* The land was enriched or made fertile by their flesh, their blood, and their bones.—*Albert Barnes.*

Verse 10.—*"They became as dung for the earth."* In the year 1830, it is estimated that more than a million bushels of " human and inhuman bones " were imported from the continent of Europe into the port of Hull. The neighbourhood of Leipsic, Austerlitz, Waterloo, etc., where the principal battles were fought some fifteen or twenty years before, were swept alike of the bones of the hero, and the horse which he rode. Thus collected from every quarter, they were shipped to Hull, and thence forwarded to the Yorkshire bone-grinders, who, by steam-engines and powerful machinery, reduced them to a granulary state. In this condition they were sent chiefly to Doncaster, one of the largest agricultural markets of the country, and were there sold to the farmers to manure their lands. The oily substance gradually evolving as the bone calcines, makes better manure than almost any other substance —particularly human bones.—*K. Arvine.*

Verse 11.—The word *nobles* is placed in antithesis with the names *Oreb* and *Zeeb.* The word נדיבים *nobles,* denotes properly *liberal, munificent,* and *beneficent* men, such as princes and potentates ought to be among men, but the names *Oreb* and *Zeeb* have the very opposite signification, for the one signifies a *raven,* the other a *wolf.* When into such rapacious and truculent beasts their nobles have degenerated, as a just reward the hostile shock shall come upon them.—*Hermann Venema.*

Verse 13.—*"A wheel."* What sort of vegetable is this whose stems our muleteers are cutting up and chewing with so much relish ? It is a wild artichoke. We can amuse ourselves with it and its behaviour for a while, and may possibly extract something more valuable than the insipid juice of which our men are so fond. You observe that in growing it throws out numerous branches of equal size and length in all directions, forming a sort of sphere or globe a foot or more in diameter. When ripe and dry in autumn, these branches become rigid and light as a feather, the parent stem breaks off at the ground, and the wind carries these vegetable globes whithersoever it pleaseth. At the proper season thousands of them come scudding over the plain, rolling, leaping, bounding with vast racket, to the dismay both of the horse and his rider. Once, on the plain north of Hamath, my horse became quite unmanageable among them. They charged down upon us on the wings of the wind, which broke them from their moorings, and sent them careering over the desert in countless numbers. Our excellent native itinerant, A—— F——, had a similar encounter with them on the eastern desert, beyond the Hauran, and his horse was so terrified that he was obliged to alight and lead him. I have long suspected that this wild artichoke is the *gulgal*, which, in Psalm lxxxiii. 13, is rendered *"wheel,"* and in Isaiah xvii. 13, *"a rolling thing."* Evidently our translators knew not what to call it. The first passage reads thus : " O my God, make them like a wheel—*gulgal*—as the stubble before the wind," and the second, " Rebuke them, and they shall flee far off, and shall be chased as the chaff of the mountains before the wind, and like a rolling thing—*gulgal*—before the whirlwind." Now, from the nature of the parallelism, the *gulgal* cannot be a *"wheel,"* but something corresponding to chaff. It must also be something that does not fly like the chaff, but in a striking manner *rolls* before the wind. The signification of *gulgal* in Hebrew and its equivalent in other Shemitic dialects, requires this, and this rolling artichoke meets the case most emphatically, and especially when it rolls before the whirlwind. In the encounter referred to north of Hamath, my eyes were half blinded with the stubble and chaff which filled the air ; but it was the extraordinary behaviour of this *"rolling thing"* that riveted my attention. Hundreds of these globes, all bounding like gazelles in one direction over the desert, would suddenly wheel short round at the bidding of a counter-blast, and dash away with equal speed on their new course. An Arab proverb addresses this " rolling thing " thus : " Ho ! 'akkûb, where do you put up to-night ? " to which it answers as it flies, " Where the wind puts up." They also derive one of their many forms of cursing from this plant : " May you be whirled, like the 'akkûb, before the wind, until you are caught in the thorns, or plunged into the sea." If this is not the *"wheel"* of David, and the *"rolling thing"* of Isaiah, from which they also borrowed their imprecations upon the wicked, I have seen nothing in the country to suggest the comparison.—*W. M. Thomson, in* *"The Land and the Book."*

Verse 13.—*"Make them like a wheel."* That is, cause them to fall into such great calamities that they can find no counsel or remedy for their misfortunes, and that they may run hither and thither like a wheel or a ball, and yet see not where they ought to stop, or whither they ought to escape. Such are the minds of wicked men in calamities, wherever they turn they find no harbour wherein to rest, no certain consolation can they discover. They are tossed with perpetual disquietude ; by running hither and thither and seeking various remedies they but weary themselves the more and plunge themselves the more deeply in their woes. This must necessarily happen to those who seek to cure evil with evil. Therefore Isaiah also says, *the wicked are like the troubled sea.*—*Mollerus.*

Verse 13.—*"Like a wheel."* Mortals, like cylinders, are rolled hither and thither, oppressed with innumerable ills. *Aurea Carmina.*—*Pythagoras (?).*

Verse 13.—There is no greater evidence against error, than that it is not constant to itself, no greater argument against these pretended great spirits, than that they cannot sit, know not where to fix, are always moving, as if the Psalmist's curse had taken hold of them, as if God had made them *"like a wheel and as stubble before the wind,"* that can sit nowhere, rest at nothing, but turn about from one uncertainty to another. The Holy Spirit is a spirit that will sit still, and be at peace, continue and abide.—*Mark Frank.*

Verses 13, 14.—In imagery both obvious and vivid to every native of the gusty hills and plains of Palestine, though to us comparatively unintelligible, the Psalmist describes them as driven over the uplands of Gilead like the clouds of chaff blown from the threshing-floors ; chased away like the spherical masses of dry weeds which course over the plains of Esdraelon and Philistia—flying with the dreadful hurry and confusion of the flames, that rush and leap from tree to tree and hill to hill when the wooded mountains of a tropical country are by chance ignited.—*William Smith in "A Dictionary of the Bible."* 1863.

Verse 14.—*"Mountains on fire."* Many of the mountains in this country are covered with dense forests. The leaves which fall every autumn accumulate, sometimes for years, until we have a particularly dry summer, when, somehow or other, either by accident or design, they are always set on fire, and burn sometimes for several days. The mountains in one of the States of the neighbouring Republic are on fire at this very moment while I am now writing, and have been burning for more than a week, and we can distinctly see the red glare in the sky above them, although from their great distance, even the tops of the mountains themselves from whence the flames arise are beyond the limits of our horizon.—*From "Philip Musgrave : or Memoirs of a Church of England Missionary in the North American Colonies."* 1846.

Verse 14.—*"Fire"* has greater force on a *mountain*, where the wind is more powerful, than upon a *wood* situated in a valley—*Honorius Augustodunensis.*

Verse 14.—Humboldt saw forests on fire in South America and thus describes them. " Several parts of the vast forests which surround the mountain, had taken fire. Reddish flames, half enveloped in clouds of smoke, presented a very grand spectacle. The inhabitants set fire to the forests, to improve the pasturage, and to destroy the shrubs that choke the grass. Enormous conflagrations, too, are often caused by the carelessness of the Indians, who neglect, when they travel, to extinguish the fires by which they have dressed their food."

Verse 14.—Let us pray the divine aid to break this power and enmity of the natural man ; that it may yield unto the word of grace ; and let the wood, hay and stubble of all false doctrine perish before the brightness of the face of God.—*Edward Walter.* 1854.

Verse 18.—*"That men may know that thou, whose name alone is JEHOVAH,"* etc. Early English History informs us, that some bloodthirsty persecutors were marching on a band of Christians. The Christians, seeing them approaching, marched out towards them, and, at the top of their voices, shouted, " Hallelujah, hallelujah ! " (Praise Jehovah). The name of the Lord being presented, the rage of the persecutors abated. Josephus says, that the Great Alexander, when on his triumphal march, being met near Jerusalem by the Jewish high priest, on whose mitre was engraved the name of Jehovah, " approached by himself, and adored that name," and was disarmed of his hostile intent. There was significance and power in the glorious old name as written by the Jews. But the name of Jesus is now far more mighty in the world than was the name Jehovah in these earlier ages.—*"The Dictionary of Illustrations,"* 1872.

Verse 18.—*"JEHOVAH"* is one of the incommunicable names of God, which signifies his eternal essence. The Jews observe that in God's name *Jehovah* the Trinity is implied. *Je* signifies the present tense, *ho* the preter-perfect tense, *vah* the future. The Jews also observe that in his name Jehovah all the Hebrew letters are *literæ quiescentes*, that denote rest, implying that in God and from God is all our rest. Every gracious soul is like Noah's dove, he can find no rest nor satisfaction but in God. God alone is the godly man's ark of rest and safety. Jehovah is the incommunicable name of God, and is never attributed to any but God : *"Thou, whose name alone is JEHOVAH."*

Verse 18.—*"The most high."* His being the High and lofty One, notes forth the transcendancy and super-excellency of his divine being in itself, and that it is utterly of another kind from creatures, and indeed that it only is truly being. When the Psalmist says, *"That men may know that thou, whose name alone is JEHOVAH art the* MOST HIGH *over all the earth,"* he thereby argues his height from his name, that his name is alone Jehovah, and therefore he is most high, and in that very respect. Now Jehovah is the name of his essence, " I AM," and he is MOST HIGH in respect of such a glorious being as is proper alone unto him.—*Thomas Goodwin.*

HINTS TO PREACHERS.

Verse 1.—The long silence of God, the reasons for it, and our reasons for desiring him to end it.

Verse 3.—*"Thy hidden ones."* I. Hidden as to their new nature, which is an enigma to men. II. Hidden for protection, as precious things. III. Hidden, for solace and rest. IV. Hidden, because not yet fully revealed.

Verse 4.—The immortality of the church.

Verse 5.—The confederacies of evils against the saints.

Verses 13—15.—The instability, restlessness, and impotence of the wicked; their horror when God deals with them in justice.

Verse 16.—A prayer for the Pope and his priests.

Verse 17.—The righteous fate of persecutors, and troublers.

Verse 18.—The Golden Lesson: how taught, to whom, by whom, through whom?

PSALM LXXXIV.

TITLE AND SUBJECT.—To the chief musician upon Gittith. A Psalm for the sons of Korah. *This Psalm well deserved to be committed to the noblest of the sons of song. No music could be too sweet for its theme, or too exquisite in sound to match the beauty of its language. Sweeter than the joy of the wine press, (for that is said to be the meaning of the word rendered* upon Gittith), *is the joy of the holy assemblies of the Lord's house; not even the favoured children of grace, who are like the sons of Korah, can have a richer subject for song than Zion's sacred festivals.*

It matters little when this Psalm was written, or by whom; for our part it exhales to us a Davidic perfume, it smells of the mountain heather and the lone places of the wilderness, where King David must have often lodged during his many wars. This sacred ode is one of the choicest of the collection; it has a mild radiance about it, entitling it to be called The Pearl of Psalms. *If the twenty-third be the most popular, the one-hundred-and-third the most joyful, the one-hundred-and-nineteenth the most deeply experimental, the fifty-first the most plaintive, this is one of the most sweet of the Psalms of Peace.*

Pilgrimages to the tabernacle were a great feature of Jewish life. In our own country, pilgrimages to the shrine of Thomas of Canterbury, and our Ladye of Walsingham, were so general as to affect the entire population, cause the formation of roads, the erection and maintenance of hostelries, and the creation of a special literature; this may help us to understand the influence of pilgrimage upon the ancient Israelites. Families journeyed together, making bands which grew at each halting place; they camped in sunny glades, sang in unison along the roads, toiled together over the hill and through the slough, and, as they went along, stored up happy memories which would never be forgotten. One who was debarred the holy company of the pilgrims, and the devout worship of the congregation, would find in this Psalm fit expression for his mournful spirit.

DIVISION.—*We will make our pauses where the poet or the musician placed them, namely, at the Selahs.*

EXPOSITION.

HOW amiable *are* thy tabernacles, O LORD of hosts!

2 My soul longeth, yea, even fainteth for the courts of the LORD: my heart and my flesh crieth out for the living God.

3 Yea, the sparrow hath found an house, and the swallow a nest for herself, where she may lay her young, *even* thine altars, O LORD of hosts, my King, and my God.

4 Blessed *are* they that dwell in thy house: they will be still praising thee. Selah.

1. *"How amiable,"* or, How *lovely!* He does not tell us how lovely they were, because he could not. His expressions show us that his feelings were inexpressible. Lovely to the memory, to the mind, to the heart, to the eye, to the whole soul, are the assemblies of the saints. Earth contains no sight so refreshing to us as the gathering of believers for worship. Those are sorry saints who see nothing amiable in the services of the Lord's house. *"Are thy tabernacles."* The tabernacle had been pitched in several places, and, moreover, was divided into several courts and portions; hence, probably, the plural number is here used. It was all and altogether lovely to David. Outer court, or inner court, he loved every portion of it. Every cord and curtain was dear to him. Even when at a distance, he rejoiced to remember the sacred tent where Jehovah revealed himself, and he cried out with exultation while he pictured in fond imagination its sacred services, and solemn

rites, as he had seen them in bygone times. Because they are *thy* tabernacles, "*O Lord of hosts,*" therefore are they so dear to thy people. Thy pavilion is the centre of the camp, around which all thy creatures gather, and towards which their eyes are turned, as armies look to the tent of the king. Thou rulest all the companies of creatures with such goodness, that all their hosts rejoice in thy dwelling-place, and the bands of thy saints especially hail thee with joyful loyalty as Jehovah of hosts.

2. "*My soul longeth,*"—it pines, and faints to meet with the saints in the Lord's house. The desire was deep and insatiable—the very soul of the man was yearning for his God. "*Yea, even fainteth ;*" as though it could not long hold out, but was exhausted with delay. He had a holy lovesickness upon him, and was wasted with an inward consumption because he was debarred the worship of the Lord in the appointed place. "*For the courts of the Lord.*" To stand once again in those areas which were dedicated to holy adoration was the soul-longing of the Psalmist. True subjects love the courts of their king. "*My heart and my flesh crieth out for the living God.*" It was God himself that he pined for, the only living and true God. His whole nature entered into his longing. Even the clay-cold flesh grew warm through the intense action of his fervent spirit. Seldom, indeed, does the flesh incline in the right direction, but in the matter of Sabbath services our weary body sometimes comes to the assistance of our longing heart, for it desires the physical rest as much as the soul desires the spiritual repose. The Psalmist declared that he could not remain silent in his desires, but began to cry out for God and his house ; he wept, he sighed, he pleaded for the privilege. Some need to be whipped to church, while here is David crying for it. He needed no clatter of bells from the belfry to ring him in, he carried his bell in his own bosom : holy appetite is a better call to worship than a full chime.

3. "*Yea, the sparrow hath found an house.*" He envied the sparrows which lived around the house of God, and picked up the stray crumbs in the courts thereof ; he only wished that he, too, could frequent the solemn assemblies and bear away a little of the heavenly food. "*And the swallow a nest for herself, where she may lay her young.*" He envied also the swallows whose nests were built under the eaves of the priests' houses, who there found a place for their young, as well as for themselves. We rejoice not only in our personal religious opportunities, but in the great blessing of taking our children with us to the sanctuary. The church of God is a house for us and a nest for our little ones. "*Even thine altars, O Lord of hosts.*" To the very altars these free birds drew near, none could restrain them nor would have wished to do so, and David wished to come and go as freely as they did. Mark how he repeats the blessed name of Jehovah of Hosts ; he found in it a sweetness which helped him to bear his inward hunger. Probably David himself was with the host, and, therefore, he dwelt with emphasis upon the title which taught him that the Lord was in the tented field as well as within the holy curtains. "*My King and my God.*" Here he utters his loyalty from afar. If he may not tread the courts, yet he loves the King. If an exile, he is not a rebel. When we cannot occupy a seat in God's house, he shall have a seat in our memories and a throne in our hearts. The double " my " is very precious ; he lays hold upon his God with both his hands, as one resolved not to let him go till the favour requested be at length accorded.

4. "*Blessed are they that dwell in thy house.*" Those he esteems to be highly favoured who are constantly engaged in divine worship—the canons residentiary, yea, the pew-openers, the menials who sweep and dust. To come and go is refreshing, but to abide in the place of prayer must be heaven below. To be the guests of God, enjoying the hospitalities of heaven, set apart for holy work, screened from a noisy world, and familiar with sacred things—why this is surely the choicest heritage a son of man can possess. "*They will be still praising thee.*" So near to God, their very life must be adoration. Surely their hearts and tongues never cease from magnifying the Lord. We fear David here drew rather a picture of what should be than of what is ; for those occupied daily with the offices needful for public worship are not always among the most devout ; on the contrary, " the nearer the church the further from God." Yet in a spiritual sense this is most true, for those children of God who in spirit abide ever in his house, are also ever full of the praises of God. Communion is the mother of adoration. They fail to praise the Lord who wander far from him, but those who dwell in him are always magnifying him.

"Selah." In such an occupation as this we might be content to remain for ever. It is worth while to pause and meditate upon the prospect of dwelling with God and praising him throughout eternity.

5 Blessed *is* the man whose strength *is* in thee ; in whose heart *are* the ways *of them.*

6 *Who* passing through the valley of Baca make it a well ; the rain also filleth the pools.

7 They go from strength to strength, *every one of them* in Zion appeareth before God.

8 O Lord God of hosts, hear my prayer : give ear, O God of Jacob. Selah.

5. *"Blessed is the man whose strength is in thee."* Having spoken of the blessedness of those who reside in the house of God, he now speaks of those who are favoured to visit it at appointed seasons, going upon pilgrimage with their devout brethren : he is not, however, indiscriminate in his eulogy, but speaks only of those who heartily attend to the sacred festivals. The blessedness of sacred worship belongs not to half-hearted, listless worshippers, but to those who throw all their energies into it. Neither prayer, nor praise, nor the hearing of the word will be pleasant or profitable to persons who have left their hearts behind them. A company of pilgrims who had left their hearts at home would be no better than a caravan of carcasses, quite unfit to blend with living saints in adoring the living God. *"In whose heart are the ways of them,"* or far better, *"in whose heart are thy ways."* Those who love the ways of God are blessed. When we have God's ways in our hearts, and our heart in his ways, we are what and where we should be, and hence we shall enjoy the divine approval.

6. *"Who passing through the valley of Baca make it a well."* Traversing joyfully the road to the great assembly, the happy pilgrims found refreshment even in the dreariest part of the road. As around a well men meet and converse cheerfully, being refreshed after their journey, so even in the vale of tears, or any other dreary glen, the pilgrims to the skies find sweet solace in brotherly communion and in anticipation of the general assembly above, with its joys unspeakable. Probably there is here a local allusion, which will never now be deciphered, but the general meaning is clear enough. There are joys of pilgrimage which make men forget the discomforts of the road. *"The rain also filleth the pools."* God gives to his people the supplies they need while traversing the roads which he points out for them. Where there were no natural supplies from below, the pilgrims found an abundant compensation in waters from above, and so also shall all the sacramental host of God's elect. Ways, which otherwise would have been deserted from want of accommodation, were made into highways abundantly furnished for the travellers' wants, because the great annual pilgrimages led in that direction ; even so, Christian converse and the joy of united worship make many duties easy and delightful which else had been difficult and painful.

7. *"They go from strength to strength."* So far from being wearied they gather strength as they proceed. Each individual becomes happier, each company becomes more numerous, each holy song more sweet and full. We grow as we advance if heaven be our goal. If we spend our strength in God's ways we shall find it increase. *"Every one of them in Zion appeareth before God."* This was the end of the pilgrims' march, the centre where all met, the delight of all hearts. Not merely to be in the assembly, but to appear before God was the object of each devout Israelite. Would to God it were the sincere desire of all who in these days mingle in our religious gatherings. Unless we realise the presence of God we have done nothing ; the mere gathering together is nothing worth.

8. *"O Lord God of hosts, hear my prayer."* Give me to go up to thy house, or if I may not do so, yet let my cry be heard. Thou listenest to the united supplications of thy saints, but do not shut out my solitary petition, unworthy though I be. *"Give ear, O God of Jacob."* Though Jehovah of hosts, thou art also the covenant God of solitary pleaders like Jacob ; regard thou, then, my plaintive supplication. I wrestle here alone with thee, while the company of thy people have gone on before me to happier scenes, and I beseech thee bless me ; for I am resolved to hold thee till thou speak the word of grace into my soul. The repetition of the request

for an answer to his prayer denotes his eagerness for a blessing. What a mercy it is that if we cannot gather with the saints, we can still speak to their Master.

Selah.—A pause was needed after a cry so vehement, a prayer so earnest.

9 Behold, O God our shield, and look upon the face of thine anointed.

10 For a day in thy courts *is* better than a thousand. I had rather be a doorkeeper in the house of my God, than to dwell in the tents of wickedness.

11 For the LORD God *is* a sun and shield : the LORD will give grace and glory : no good *thing* will he withhold from them that walk uprightly.

12 O LORD of hosts, blessed *is* the man that trusteth in thee.

9. *"Behold, O God our shield, and look upon the face of thine anointed."* Here we have the nation's prayer for David ; and the believer's prayer for the Son of David. Let but the Lord look upon our Lord Jesus, and we shall be shielded from all harm ; let him behold the face of his Anointed, and we shall be able to behold his face with joy. We also are anointed by the Lord's grace, and our desire is that he will look upon us with an eye of love in Christ Jesus. Our best prayers when we are in the best place are for our glorious King, and for the enjoyment of his Father's smile.

10. *"For a day in thy courts is better than a thousand."* Of course the Psalmist means a thousand days spent elsewhere. Under the most favourable circumstances in which earth's pleasures can be enjoyed, they are not comparable by so much as one in a thousand to the delights of the service of God. To feel his love, to rejoice in the person of the anointed Saviour, to survey the promises and feel the power of the Holy Ghost in applying precious truth to the soul, is a joy which worldlings cannot understand, but which true believers are ravished with. Even a glimpse at the love of God is better than ages spent in the pleasures of sense. *"I had rather be a doorkeeper in the house of my God, than to dwell in the tents of wickedness."* The lowest station in connection with the Lord's house is better than the highest position among the godless. Only to wait at his threshold and peep within, so as to see Jesus, is bliss. To bear burdens and open doors for the Lord is more honour than to reign among the wicked. Every man has his choice, and this is ours. God's worst is better than the devil's best. God's doorstep is a happier rest than downy couches within the pavilions of royal sinners, though we might lie there for a lifetime of luxury. Note how he calls the tabernacle " the house of *my* God ; " there's where the sweetness lies : if Jehovah be our God, his house, his altars, his doorstep, all become precious to us. We know by experience that where Jesus is within, the outside of the house is better than the noblest chambers where the Son of God is not to be found.

11. *"For the Lord God is a sun and shield."* Pilgrims need both as the weather may be, for the cold would smite them were it not for the sun, and foes are apt to waylay the sacred caravan, and would haply destroy it if it were without a shield. Heavenly pilgrims are not left uncomforted or unprotected. The pilgrim nation found both sun and shield in that fiery cloudy pillar which was the symbol of Jehovah's presence, and the Christian still finds both light and shelter in the Lord his God. A sun for happy days and a shield for dangerous ones. A sun above, a shield around. A light to show the way and a shield to ward off its perils. Blessed are they who journey with such a convoy ; the sunny and the shady side of life are alike happy to them. *"The Lord will give grace and glory."* Both in due time, both as needed, both to the full, both with absolute certainty. The Lord has both grace and glory in infinite abundance ; Jesus is the fulness of both, and, as his chosen people, we shall receive both as a free gift from the God of our salvation. What more can the Lord give, or we receive, or desire. *"No good thing will he withhold from them that walk uprightly."* Grace makes us walk uprightly and this secures every covenant blessing to us. What a wide promise ! Some apparent good may be withheld, but no real good, no, not one. " All things are yours, and ye are Christ's, and Christ is God's." God has all good, there is no good apart from him, and there is no good which he either needs to keep back or will on any account refuse us, if we are but ready to receive it. We must be upright and neither lean to this or that form of evil : and this uprightness must be practical,—we must *walk* in truth and holiness, then shall we be heirs of all things, and as we come of age all things shall be in our actual possession ; and, meanwhile, according to our capacity for receiving shall be the measure of the divine bestowal. This is true, not of a favoured few, but of all the saints for evermore.

12. *"O Lord of hosts, blessed is the man that trusteth in thee."*   Here is the key of the Psalm.   The worship is that of faith, and the blessedness is peculiar to believers. No formal worshipper can enter into this secret.   A man must know the Lord by the life of real faith, or he can have no true rejoicing in the Lord's worship, his house, his Son, or his ways.   Dear reader, how fares it with thy soul?

EXPLANATORY NOTES AND QUAINT SAYINGS.

Title.—Here note, that the sons, that is, the posterity of wicked and rebellious Korah, have an honourable place in God's sacred and solemn service: for to them sundry of David's psalms are commended. . . . . Here see the verifying of God's word, for the comfort of all godly children, that the son shall not bear the iniquity of the father, Ezek. xviii. 14, 17, 20, if he sees his father's sins and turn from them.— *Thomas Pierson (1570—1633) in "David's Heart's Desire."*

Whole Psalm.—

O Lord of hosts, how lovely in mine eyes
    The tents where thou dost dwell!
For thine abode my spirit faints and sighs;
    The courts I love so well.
        My longing soul is weary
            Within thy house to be;
        This world is waste and dreary,
            A desert land to me.

The sparrow, Lord, hath found a shelter'd home,
    The swallow hath her nest;
She layeth there her young, and though she roam,
    Returneth there to rest.
        I, to thine altar flying,
            Would there for ever be;
        My heart and flesh are crying,
            O living God, for thee!

How blest are they who in thy house abide!
    Thee evermore they praise.
How strong the man whom thou alone dost guide,
    Whose heart doth keep thy ways.
        A pilgrim and a stranger,
            He leaneth on thine arm;
        And thou, in time of danger,
            Dost shield him from alarm.

From strength to strength through Baca's vale of woe,
    They pass along in prayer,
And gushing streams of living water flow,
    Dug by their faithful care;
        Thy rain is sent from heaven
            To fertilise the land,
        And wayside grace is given
            Till they in Zion stand.

Lord God of hosts, attend unto my prayer!
    O Jacob's God, give ear!
Behold, O God, our Shield, we through thy care,
    Within thy courts appear!
        Look thou upon the glory
            Of thine Anointed's face;
        In him we stand before thee,
            To witness of thy grace!

One day with thee excelleth o'er and o'er
   A thousand days apart ;
In thine abode, within thy temple-door,
   Would stand my watchful heart.
     Men tell me of the treasure
      Hid in their tents of sin ;
     I look not there for pleasure,
      Nor choose to enter in.

Own thou the Lord to be thy Sun, thy Shield—
   No good will he withhold ;
He giveth grace, and soon shall be reveal'd
   His glory, yet untold.
     His mighty name confessing,
      Walk thou at peace and free ;
     O Lord, how rich the blessing
      Of him who trusts in thee !

                                     —German Choral Music.

Verse 1.—*"How amiable are thy tabernacles."* What was there in them that appeared so amiable ? Perchance, the edifice was famed for the skill and cost bestowed on it ? But the temple of extraordinary beauty was not yet constructed. The tabernacle was lowly, more suited to pilgrims than to a great people, and little becoming the king himself. Therefore to the pious there is no need of vast or sumptuous temples to the end that they should love the house of God.—*Musculus.*

Verse 1.—*"How amiable are thy tabernacles."* What made the tabernacle of Moses lovely was not the outside, which was very mean, as the Church of God outwardly is, through persecution, affliction, and poverty ; but what was within, having many golden vessels in it, and those typical of things much more precious : moreover, here the priests were to be seen in their robes, doing their duty and service, and, at certain times, the high priest in his rich apparel ; here were seen the sacrifices slain and offered, by which the people were taught the nature of sin, the strictness of justice, and the necessity and efficacy of the sacrifice of Christ : here the Levites were heard singing their songs, and blowing their trumpets : but much more amiable are the Church of God and its ordinances in gospel times, where Christ, the great High-Priest, is seen in the glories of his person, and the fulness of his grace ; where Zion's priests, or the ministers of the gospel, stand clothed, being full fraught with salvation, and the tidings of it ; where Christ is evidently set forth, as crucified and slain, in the ministry of the word, and the administration of ordinances ; here the gospel trumpet is blown, and its joyful sound echoed forth, and songs of love and grace are sung by all believers ; besides, what makes these tabernacles still more lovely are, the presence of God here, so that they are no other than the house of God, the gate of heaven ; the provisions that are here made, and the company that is here enjoyed.—*John Gill.*

Verse 1.—*"Amiable."* The adjective is rendered by the English versions *"amiable,"* in the sense of the French *amiable*, lovely. But the usage of the Hebrew word requires it to be understood as meaning *dear, beloved*, which is exactly the idea here required by the context. The plural, *dwellings*, has reference to the subdivisions and appurtenances of the sanctuary, and is applied to the tabernacle in Ps. xlviii. 3. Compare Ps. lxviii. 35. The divine titles are as usual significant. While one suggests the covenant relation between God and the petitioner, the other makes his sovereignty the ground of a prayer for his protection.—*Joseph Addison Alexander.*

Verse 1.—*"Tabernacles."* By the name of *"tabernacles"* we are put in mind of the church's peregrination and wandering from one place unto another, until she come unto her true country. For as tabernacle and tents of war be removed hither and thither, so the Church of God in this life hath no sure and quiet abode, but often is compelled to change her seat. This pilgrimage, whereby indeed every man, as Augustine doth say, is a pilgrim in this world, doth admonish us of sin, which is the cause of this peregrination. For, because of sin we are cast with our first parents out of Paradise into the land wherein we sojourn. So that we are removed from Jerusalem, that is, from the sight and fruition of peace, into Babylon, that is, into confusion and exile, wherein we wander far and wide.—*Nicholas Heminge* [*Hemmingius*] (1513—1600), *in "The Faith of the Church Militant."*

Verses 1, 2.—When we cannot express the greatness of a thing in direct terms, we are fain to fly to wonder, and so doth David here, because he cannot express sufficiently how amiable the Tabernacles of the Lord are, he therefore falls to wondering, and helps himself with a question ; How amiable are thy Tabernacles, O Lord of Hosts ? But is not David's wondering itself wonderful, that the tabernacles of the Lord of Hosts should be so wonderfully amiable ? Is it not a wonder they should be amiable at all ? For are not his tabernacles, tents of war ? and is there anything in war that can be amiable ? If he had said : How *terrible* are thy Tabernacles, O Lord of Hosts ; his wonder had been with some congruity ; for the Lord of Hosts is terrible in all his works ; but to say, How *amiable* are thy Tabernacles, O Lord of Hosts, seems to imply a contradiction ; for though they may be amiable, as they are tabernacles, yet they must needs be terrible, as they are Tabernacles of the Lord of Hosts ; and when this terribleness hath made an abatement in their amiableness ; what place will be left for wonder, to give cause to say, How amiable are thy Tabernacles, O Lord of Hosts ? But if he had said, How terrible are thy Tabernacles, O Lord of Hosts ; though it might have been wonderful in the degree, yet it could not be wonderful in the kind : for what wonder is it, if the Tabernacles of the Lord of Hosts be terrible ? But when he saith, How amiable are thy Tabernacles, O Lord of Hosts ; this is not only wonderful in the degree, but in the kind much more. For what can be more wonderful, than that being Tabernacles of the Lord of Hosts, they should be amiable, and so amiable as to be wondered at ? But is it not, that God is in himself so amiable, that all things of His, even his terrors themselves, are amiable ; his tabernacles and his tents, his sword and his spear, his, darts and his arrows, all amiable ; terrible no doubt to his enemies, but amiable, wonderfully amiable to all that love and fear him, and great reason they should be so seeing they are all in their defence, and for their safeguard ; though they be Tabernacles of the Lord of Hosts to the wicked, yet they are Courts of the Prince of Peace to the godly, and this makes *my soul to long for the courts of the Lord.* For I desire indeed to be a courtier, yet not as I am now : God knows I am very unfit for it, but because God's Courts are such, they make any one fit, that but comes into them ; they receive not men fit, but make them fit ; and he that was before but a shrub in Baca, as soon as he comes into the Courts of the Lord is presently made a cedar in Lebanon.—*Sir Richard Baker.*

Verse 2.—"*My soul longeth, yea, even fainteth,*" etc. Every amiableness is not so great to make a longing, nor every longing so great to make a fainting ; nor every fainting so great, to make the soul to faint ; Oh, then, consider how great this amiableness is, which makes my soul not only to long, but to faint with longing ! And blame me not for fainting, as though it were my own fault for not restraining my longing ; for seeing his Tabernacles are of infinite amiableness, they must needs work in me an infinite delighting, and that delighting an infinite longing ; and what restraint can there be of that which is infinite ? No, alas, my fainting is but answerable to my longing, and my longing but answerable to the amiableness. If I had the offer made me, which was made to Christ, to enjoy all the kingdoms of the earth, but with condition to want the Courts of the Lord ; this want would bring to my soul a greater grief than that enjoying would give it contentment : for seeing his Tabernacles are so amiable, where He is Lord of Hosts, how amiable must they needs be, where he is Prince of Peace ? and Prince of Peace he is in his Courts, though in his camp he be Lord of Hosts.—*Sir Richard Baker.*

Verse 2.—"*My soul longeth, yea, even fainteth.*" The word כלה (fainteth) signifies to be consumed with longing, as the Latins say, *deperire aliquem amore* (he is dying of love), that is, he so vehemently loves, and is enflamed with so great a desire to obtain the loved object, that he wastes and pines away unless his wish is gratified. Therefore, an ardent longing is meant, which so torments and burns the mind, that flesh and marrow waste away, so long as it is not permitted to enjoy the things desired.—*Mollerus.*

Verse 2.—"*Soul . . . heart . . . flesh.*" Marking the whole man, with every faculty and affection. The verbs are also very expressive. The first, "*longeth,*" means literally, " hath grown pale," as with the intensity of the feeling ; the second, "*fainteth,*" is more exactly " faileth," or " is consumed." Job. xix. 27.—*J. J. Stewart Perowne.*

Verse 2.—"*Crieth.*" The word that is here rendered "*crieth,*" is from רנן, that signifies to shout, shrill, or cry out, as soldiers do at the beginning of a battle, when they cry out, Fall on, fall on, fall on, or when they cry out after a victory, Victory, victory, victory ! The Hebrew word notes a strong cry, or to cry as a child cries when it is sadly hungry, for now every whit of the child cries, hands cry, and face cries, and feet cry.—*Thomas Brooks.*

Verse 2.—*"Living God."* Ps. xlii. 2, " My soul thirsteth for God, for the living God," is the only other place in the Psalms where God is so named. This particular form of expression, *El Chay,* occurs but twice beside in the Bible, Josh. iii. 10 ; Hosea i. 10.—*J. J. Stewart Perowne.*

Verse 3.—*"The sparrow hath found an house,"* etc. The tender care of God, over the least of his creatures, is here most touchingly alluded to. The Psalmist, while in exile, envies them their privileges. He longs to be nestling, as it were, in the dwelling-place of God. The believer finds a perfect home and rest in God's altars ; or, rather, in the great truths which they represent. Still, his confidence in God is sweetened and strengthened by the knowledge of his minute, universal, providential care. It becomes his admiring delight. " God fails not," as one has beautifully said, " to find a house for the most *worthless*, and a nest for the most *restless* of birds." What confidence this should give us ! How we should rest ! What repose the soul finds that casts itself on the watchful, tender care of him who provides so fully for the need of all his creatures ! We know what the expression of " nest " conveys, just as well as that of " a house." Is it not a place of security, a shelter from storm, a covert to hide oneself in, from every evil, a protection from all that can harm, " a place to rest in, to nestle in, to joy in " ? But there is one thing in these highly privileged birds which strikes us forcibly in our meditations—they knew not him from whom all this kindness flowed—they knew neither his heart nor his hand. They enjoyed the rich provisions of his tender care ; he thought of everything for their need, but there was no fellowship between them and the Great Giver. From this, O my soul, thou mayest learn a useful lesson. Never rest satisfied with merely frequenting such places, or with having certain privileges there ; but rise, in spirit, and seek and find and enjoy direct communion with the living God, through Jesus Christ our Lord. The heart of David turns to God himself. " My heart and my flesh crieth out for the living God."—*Things New and Old.*

Verse 3.—*"The swallow a nest,"* etc. The confidence which these birds place in the human race is not a little extraordinary. They not only put themselves, but their offspring in the power of men. I have seen their nests in situations where they were within the reach of one's hand, and where they might have been destroyed in an instant. I have observed them under a doorway, the eaves of a low cottage, against the wall of a tool-shed, on the knocker of a door, and the rafter of a much-frequented hay-loft.—*Edward Jesse, in "Gleanings in Natural History."* 1856.

Verse 3.—*"Even thine altars."* There were two altars ; the " brazen altar," and the " golden altar ; " to those, no doubt, the Psalmist refers. Both were of shittim wood, which sets forth the holy humanity—the perfect manhood, of the Lord Jesus. Incarnation lies at the foundation of all his work for us, and of all our blessing in him. The one altar was overlaid with brass, the other with pure gold. The *overlaying* shadows forth his Godhead, but in distinct aspects. We have the same Jesus in both, but shadowed forth in different circumstances. In the one, humiliation and suffering ; in the other, exaltation and glory.—*Things New and Old.*

Verse 3.—*"Thine altars."* There is in the original a pathetical, a vehement, a broken expressing, expressed, O *thine altars.* It is true, (says David) thou art here in the wilderness, and I may see thee here, and serve thee here, but O *thine altars,* O *Lord of Hosts, my King and my God.*—*John Donne.*

Verse 3.—*"Thine altars "* is a poetical way of saying *"Thy house."* It is manifestly a special term, instead of a general. Yet it has been seriously argued, that no birds could or would ever be suffered to build their nests on the altar. Surely this sort of expression, which is hardly a figure, is common enough. *A parte potiori fit denominatio.* We say, " There goes a sail." What should we think of a man who should argue that a sail cannot go ? The altars mean the temple. There was

" no jutty frieze,
Buttress, nor coigne of vantage, but these birds
Had made their pendant bed ; "

not to mention that trees grew within the sacred enclosure, where birds might have built their nests.—*J. J. Stewart Perowne.*

Verse 3.—A custom, existing among several nations of antiquity, is deemed capable of illustrating the present passage. For birds, whose nests chanced to be built on the temples, or within the limits of them, were not allowed to be driven away, much less to be killed, but found there a secure and undisturbed abode.—*William Keatinge Clay.*

Verse 4.—*"Blessed are they that dwell in thy house,"* etc. Alas, how happens this ? There were *tabernacles* before, as belonging to a Lord ; and *courts* as belonging to a king, and *altars* as belonging to a God ; and now to be but a *house* as belonging to a private man ; and so all this great rising to end in a fall ? No, my soul, it is no fall, it is an aggregation rather of all the other ; for where his *tabernacles* did but serve to shew his power, his *courts* but to shew his majesty ; his *altars* but to shew his deity, his *house* serves to shew them all ; for in his *house* there will still be praising him, and his praise and glory is the sum of all. Or is it that to dwell in God's house is a kind of appropriating him to ourselves, seeing his tabernacles and his courts lie open to strangers, his house open to none but his servants ; and seeing in the nearness of God, and conversing with him, consists all true blessedness ; therefore " Blessed are they that dwell in his house," but how dwell in it ? Not to look in sometimes as we pass by, or to stay in it a time, as we do at an inn, but to be constant abiders in it day and night, as to which we have devoted ourselves and vowed our service.—*Sir Richard Baker.*

Verse 4.—*"Blessed are they that dwell in thy house."* What was this house more to David than another house, save that here he reckoned upon enjoying the Divine Presence ? So that here was a heart so naturalized to this presence as to affect an abode in it, and that he might lead his life with God, and dwell with him all his days ; he could not be content with giving a visit now and then. And why should this temper of spirit in the clearer light of the gospel be looked upon as an unattainable thing ? A lazy despondency, and the mean conceit that it is modest not to aim so high, starves religion, and stifles all truly noble and generous desires. Let this then be the thing designed with you, and constantly pursue and drive the design, that you may get into this disposition of spirit toward God.—*John Howe.*

Verse 4.—*"Blessed are they that dwell in thy house,"* etc. Blessed indeed, we too may exclaim, and blessed shall they be for ever. They are *dwellers*, not *visitors*, in God's house. " I will dwell in the house of the Lord for ever." This is true, blessedly true, of all who trust in Jesus now. But though God's children are all priests by birth, as were the sons of Aaron, they are not all, alas ! priests by consecration. (See Exod. xxix.) Comparatively few know their priestly place at the golden altar. Many of them are doubting as to whether their sins, root and branch, were all consumed outside the camp ; and, consequently, such are afraid to come within the court, and as for being assured of their full justification and sanctification in the risen One, they gravely doubt and fear that such blessedness can ever be their happy lot. Hence that state of soul which answers to priestly consecration at the laver, and happy worship at the golden altar, is unknown and unenjoyed. They are not priests by consecration.

Our text is plain. *"They will still be praising thee."* Doubts, fears, unsettled questions, all are gone. Such cannot exist in the holy place. All, of course, who are in Christ, must be in God's account where he is ; but all who believe in Christ, do not know and believe that they are *in him*, as being *one with him now.* When the state of our souls answers to what is symbolized by the holy place, we can only praise : " They that dwell in thy house will be still praising thee." Then we are happily near to God, and have communion with him, in the glorified Christ, through the power of the Holy Ghost.—*Things New and Old.*

Verse 4.—*"They will be still praising thee."* How appears it to be true, that they who dwell in God's house will always be praising him, seeing it is but seldom seen that servants be so forward to praise their masters ? O my soul ! it is not so much the good dispositions of the servants, as the infinite worthiness of the Master that makes them to praise him, for when they see the admirable economy of his government, when they see how sweetly he disposeth all things in weight and measure, when they find him to use them more like children than servants, what heart can be so ungrateful as not to praise him ? And seeing by dwelling in God's house, they see these things continually, therefore they that dwell in his house will always be praising him.—*Sir Richard Baker.*

Verse 4.—*"They will be still praising thee."* As having hearts full of heaven, and consciences full of comfort. There cannot but be music in the temple of the Holy Ghost.—*John Trapp.*

Verse 4.—"Still praising." It is not enough to praise him, it must be a praising him *still,* before it will make a blessedness ; and though to praise God be an easy matter, yet *to praise him still,* will be found a busy work, indeed to flesh and blood a miserable work, for if I be still praising him, what time shall I have for any pleasure ? O my soul, if thou make it not thy pleasure, thy chief, thy only pleasure to be praising him, thou art not like in haste to come to blessedness. And marvel not that David speaks thus under the law, when St. Paul under the Gospel saith as much : " Whether ye eat or drink, or whatsoever ye do, let all be done to the glory and praise of God."— *Sir Richard Baker.*

Verse 5.—"In whose heart are thy ways." That is, who love the ways that lead to thy house.—*Ernest Hawkins.*

Verse 5.—"In whose heart are the ways of them." Literally, *"The steeps are on their hearts."* The steep ascents on which the tabernacle stood. Horsley renders, *"They are bent on climbing the steep ascents."* Perhaps the מְסִלּוֹת were more properly the *raised causeways* or stairs leading up to Mount Zion, or all through the mountain country on the road to Jerusalem.—*John Fry.*

Verse 5.—"In whose heart are the ways." The natural heart is a pathless wilderness, full of cliffs and precipices. When the heart is renewed by grace, *a road is made, a highway is prepared for our God.* See Isai. xl. 3, 4.—*Frederick Fysh.*

Verse 6.—"Who passing through the valley of Baca make it a well," etc. I consider the valley here mentioned to be the same as the valley of *Bochim,* mentioned in Judges ii. 1, 5, which received its name from the *weeping* of the Jews, when they were rebuked by an angel for their disobedience to the commands of God. This valley is called הַבְּכָאִים, *Habb'caim,* in 2 Sam. v. 24, the ה of בָּכָה, *to weep* being changed into א. Josephus mentions, that the circumstance there related occurred ἐν τοῖς ἄλσεσι τοῖς καλουμένοις Κλαυθμῶσι. Antiquit. Jud. lib. vii. c. 4. הַבְּכָאִים, *Habb'caim,* is rendered in that verse by the LXX. Κλαυθμῶν, *weepings* ; and in Judges ii. 1 הַבֹּכִים, *Habbocim,* is also rendered by the LXX. Κλαυθμῶν, *weepings.* The valley mentioned in Ps. lxxxiv. 6 is called by the LXX. Κλαυθμῶν. I am inclined therefore to think, that in this place, joining to הַבְּכָא the מ of the following word, and supplying ' before it, we ought to read הַבְּכָאִים עֵין instead of הַבְּכָא מַעְיָן . . . All the ancient versionists seem to have thought, that the valley in this verse received its name from בָּכָה, *bacah, to weep.* I translate the verse, " Passing through the valley of Bochim, they will make it a fountain even of blessings ; it shall be covered with the former rain." The Psalm has been supposed to have been written by Jehoshaphat. Probably he passed through Bochim, which seems to have been an arid valley, when he marched against the Moabites and Ammonites : see 2 Chron. xx. After the victory, the army of Jehoshaphat assembled in a valley, where they blessed the Lord ; and from this circumstance it received the name of Berachah : see ver. 26. Perhaps the word בְּרָכוֹת in this verse has an allusion to that circumstance ; and perhaps the valley of Berachah was, before that glorious occasion, called the valley of Bochim.— *Richard Dixon.*

Verse 6.—Passing through the valley of weeping make him, that is, Jehovah, *a fountain.* That is, they trust, and from him look for help, who having plain paths in their mind must pass through many difficulties. Similar help is sought by those, who, suffering from a scanty supply of water, press on through a dry valley, and yet do not despair or grow weary, but have God for their fountain, from which they drink and are refreshed.—*Venema.*

Verse 6.—"The valley of Baca." Valley of tear-shrubs.—*E. W. Hengstenberg.*

Verse 6.—"Baca," signifieth a mulberry-tree, which loves to grow in dry places that be sandy and barren, 2 Sam. v. 23, 24, or 1 Chron. xiv. 14, 15. Now they whose hearts be set upon God's house and holy worship, when they go thitherward through a sandy, dry, barren valley, do make it a well,—that is, repute and count it as a well ; the word שְׁיתוּהוּ signifieth to put or set, as Gen. iii. 15 ; Ps. xxi. 6, 12, and lxxxiii. 11, 13. For thus will they say with themselves, thinking upon the comfort of God's favour to whom they go, that it shall be to them as the rain of blessings, a plentiful and liberal rain upon the ground.—*Thomas Pierson.*

Verse 6.—"Make it a well." That which seemed an impediment turns to a furtherance ; at least, no misery can be so great, no estate so barren, but a godly heart can make it a well, out of which to draw forth water of comfort ; either water to cleanse, and make it a way to repentance ; or water to cool, and make it a way to patience ; or water to moisten, and make it a way of growing in grace ; and if the well happen to be dry, and afford no water from below, *yet the rain shall fill their pools*, and supply them with water from above. If natural forces be not sufficient, there shall be supernatural graces added to assist them, that though troubles of the world seem rubs in the way to blessedness, yet in truth they are none, they hinder not arriving at the mark we aim at, they hinder us not from being made members of Sion, they hinder us not from approaching the presence of God. No, my soul, they are rather helps, for by this means *we go from strength to strength*, from strength of patience, to strength of hope ; from strength of hope, to strength of faith, to strength of vision ; and then will be accomplished that which David speaks here ; *"Blessed is the man whose strength is in God, and in whose heart his ways are."*—*Sir Richard Baker.*

Verse 6.—*"The rain."* Little as there may be of water, that little suffices on their way. It is *"a well"* to them. They find only *"pools* (which) *the early rain has* (barely) *covered "*—but are content with the supply by the way. It is as good and sufficient to them as if showers of the heavy autumnal rains had filled the well. Pilgrims forget the scanty supply at an inn, when they have abundance in view at the end. Israelites going up to the Passover made light of deficient water, for their hearts were set on reaching Jerusalem.—*Andrew A. Bonar.*

Verses 6, 7.—The most gloomy present becomes bright to them : passing through even a terrible wilderness, they turn it into a place of springs, their joyous hope and the infinite beauty of the goal, which is worth any amount of toil and trouble, afford them enlivening comfort, refreshing, strengthening in the midst of the arid steppe.

Not only does their faith bring forth water out of the sand and rocks of the desert, but God also on his part lovingly anticipates their love, and rewardingly anticipates their faithfulness : a gentle rain, like that which refreshes the sown fields in the autumn, descends from above and enwraps the valley of Baca in a fulness of blessing . . . the arid steppe becomes resplendent with a flowery festive garment (Isai. xxxv. 1—19), not to outward appearance, but to them spiritually in a manner none the less true and real. And whereas under ordinary circumstances, the strength of the traveller diminishes in proportion as he has traversed more and more of his toilsome road, with them it is the very reverse ; *"they go from strength to strength."*—*Franz Delitzsch.*

Verse 7.—*"They go from strength to strength."* Junius reads it, and so it is in the Hebrew, " They go from company to company." As they went up to Jerusalem they went in troops and companies. Possibly we translate it strength, because much of our safety consisteth in good society.—*George Swinnock.*

Verse 7.—*"Every one of them in Zion appeareth before God."* That is, every one of them answering to the character described. Others as well as they would appear in Zion before God ; but not to enjoy his presence, and receive tokens of his favour. Blessedness was now to be enjoyed, but it could only be enjoyed by those who had been previously fitted for it by character and attainment. As certainly as these had been acquired, so certainly would the blessedness be enjoyed by each and by all of them. *"Every one of them in Zion appeareth before God."* No one has perished by the way—none been devoured by wild beasts—none cut off by the wandering banditti—none become faint-hearted and turned back. The whole bands are assembled—young and old, weak and strong ; all answer to their names, and testify to the goodness of the Lord in bearing them up, and bringing through—in affording them rest, and yielding them pleasure. So shall it ever be with true spiritual pilgrims. The grace of God will always prove sufficient to preserve them, safe and blameless, to his heavenly kingdom and glory—troubles shall not overwhelm them—temptations not wholly overcome them—spiritual enemies shall not destroy them. They are kept by the power of God, through faith unto salvation, ready to be revealed in the last time. Their names are written in the Lamb's book of life, and the Lamb himself shall see to it that each of them is found in the day of account. Then shall he be able to say, " Those whom thou hast given me I have kept, and none of them is lost." " They are all here before God."—*William Makelvie.* 1863.

Verse 8.—There are two distinct thoughts of great practical value to the Christian, in this short prayer. There is the sense of *divine majesty*, and the consciousness of *divine relationship.* As *"Lord of hosts,"* he is almighty in power ; as the *"God of Jacob,"* he is infinite in mercy and goodness to his people.—*Things New and Old.*

Verse 9.—While many, alas, are satisfied with mere formalities in religion, or with the dry discussion of doctrines, high or low, as they may be called, see thou and be occupied with Christ himself. It is the knowledge of his person that gives strength and joy to the soul. At all times, under all circumstances, we can say, *"Look upon the face of thine Anointed."* We cannot always say, *Look on us ;* but we may always say, *Look on Him.* In deepest sorrow through conscious failure, or in trials and difficulties through faithfulness to his name, we can ever plead with God what Christ is. God is ever well pleased with him—ever occupied with him as risen from the dead and exalted to his own right hand in heaven ; and he would have us also to be occupied with him as the heart's exclusive object. True faith can only rest on *God's estimate* of Christ, not on inward thoughts and feelings. That which may be called the faith of the formalist, rests on the ability of his own mind to judge of these matters. He trusts in himself. This is the essential difference between faith in appearance and faith in reality.—*Things New and Old.*

Verse 9.—*"Look upon the face of thine anointed."* For I shall never come to look upon thy face, if thou vouchsafe not first to look upon mine : if thou afford me not as well the benefit of thine eyes, to look upon me, as the favour of thine ears to hear me, I shall be left only to a bare expectation, but never come to the happiness of fruition ; but when thou vouchsafest to look upon my face, that look of thine hath an influence of all true blessedness, and makes me find what a happiness it is to have the God of Jacob for my shield.—*Sir Richard Baker.*

Verse 10.—*"A day."* The least good look that a man hath from God, and the least good word that a man hears from God, and the least love letter and love token that a man receives from God, is exceedingly precious to that man that hath God for his portion. *"One day in thy courts is better than a thousand elsewhere."* He doth not say, One year in thy courts is better than a thousand elsewhere, but *One day* in thy courts is better than a thousand elsewhere ; nor doth he say, One quarter of a year in thy courts is better than a thousand elsewhere, but *"One day* in thy courts is better than a thousand elsewhere " ; nor doth he say, One month is better than a thousand elsewhere, but *"One day* in thy courts is better than a thousand elsewhere," to shew that the very least of God is exceeding precious to a gracious soul that hath God for his portion.—*Thomas Brooks.*

Verse 10.—Another sign of God's children is, to delight to be much in God's presence. Children are to be in the presence of their father ; where the King is, there is the court ; where the presence of God is, there is heaven. God is in a special manner present in his ordinances, they are the Ark of his presence. Now, if we are his children, we love to be much in holy duties. In the use of ordinances we draw near to God, we come into our Father's presence ; in prayer we have secret conference with God ; the soul while it is praying, is as it were parlying with God. In the word we hear God speaking from heaven to us ; and how doth every child of God delight to hear his Father's voice ! In the sacrament God kisseth his children with the kisses of his lips ; he gives them a smile of his face, and a privy-seal of his love : oh, it is good to draw near to God. It is sweet being in his presence : every true child of God saith, *"A day in thy courts is better than a thousand !* "—*Thomas Watson.*

Verse 10.—*"I had rather be a doorkeeper,"* etc. Some read it, " I would rather be fixed to a post in the house of my God, than live at liberty in the tents of the wicked ;" alluding to the law concerning servants, who if they would not go out free, were to have their ear bored to the door-post, Exod. xxi. 5, 6. David loved his Master, and loved his work so well, that he desired to be tied to this service for ever, to be more free to it, but never to go out free from it, preferring bonds to duty far before the greatest liberty to sin. Such a superlative delight have holy hearts in holy duties ; no satisfaction in their account comparable to that in communion with God.—*Matthew Henry.*

Verse 10.—*"I had rather be a doorkeeper."* In the sense that Christ is a Door, David may well be content to be a Door-Keeper, and though in God's house there be many mansions, yet seeing all of them are glorious, even the door-keeper's place is not without its glory. But if you think the office to be mean, consider then whose officer he is, for even a door-keeper is an officer in God's house, and God never displaceth his officers unless it be to advance them to a higher ; whereas, in the courts of princes, the greatest officers are oftentimes displaced, turned off often with disgrace.—*Sir Richard Baker.*

Verse 10.—"*I had rather be a doorkeeper in the house of my God,*" etc. Happy are those persons, whom God will use as besoms to sweep out the dust from his temple ; or who shall tug at an oar in the boat where Christ and his church are embarked.—*William Secker, in "The Nonsuch Professor."*

Verse 10.—"*Doorkeeper.*" This is a Korhite Psalm, and the descendants of Korah were, in fact, porters, and " keepers of the gates of the tabernacle, and keepers of the entry," as well as being permitted to swell the chorus of the inspired singers of Israel.—*Bossuet, quoted by Neale and Littledale.*

Verse 10.—Instead of, "*I had rather be a doorkeeper,*" the margin has, according to the Hebrew, " I would choose rather to sit at the threshold." Ainsworth's translation is : " I have chosen to sit at the threshold, in the house of my God ; " and Dr. Boothroyd's is : " Abide, or sit, at the threshold." See 2 Kings xii. 9 ; xxii. 4 ; xxv. 18 ; 1 Chron. ix. 19 ; 2 Chron. xxiii. 4 ; Esther ii. 21 ; vi. 2. In all these passages the marginal reading is *threshold.* I think the word "*door-keeper*" does not convey the proper meaning of the words, " to sit at the threshold " ; because the preference of the Psalmist was evidently given to a very *humble* position ; whereas that of a door-keeper, in Eastern estimation, is truly respectable and confidential.

The marginal reading, however, " to sit at the threshold," at once strikes on an Eastern mind as a situation of deep humility.

See the poor heathen devotee : he goes and sits near the threshold of his temple. Look at the beggar : he sits, or prostrates himself, at the threshold of the door or gate, till he shall have gained his suit.—*Joseph Roberts.*

Verse 10.—"*House.*" "*Tents.*" Observe the force of the contrasted expressions. The "*house*" is the Lord's ; the "*tents*" are of the wicked. The pleasures of sin are for a season only ; the world passeth away, and the lusts thereof.—*Arthur Pridham.*

Verse 10.—"*The tents.*" It is not any tents, or tents of any ordinary kind, that are understood, but rich, powerful, glorious, and splendid tents.—*Venema.*

Verse 11.—"*The Lord God is a sun,*" conveys a striking and impressive truth, when we think of the sun only in his obvious character as a source of light and heat. But what new energy is given to this magnificent emblem, when we learn from astronomy that he is a grand centre of attraction, and when we, in addition, take in that sublime generalization that the sun is the ultimate source of every form of power existing in the world ! The wind wafts the commerce of every nation over the mighty deep ; but the heat of the sun has rarefied that air, and set that wind in motion. The descending stream yields a power which grinds your grain, turns your spindles, works your looms, drives your forges ; but it is because the sun gathered up the vapour from the ocean, which fell upon the hills, and is finding its way back to the source whence it came. The expansive energy of steam propels your engine ; but the force with which it operates is locked up in the coal (the remains of extinct forests stored among your hills), or is derived from the wood that abounds in your forests, which now crown and beautify their summits. Both these primeval and these existing forests drew their subsistence from the sun : it is the chemical force resident in his rays which disengaged their carbon from the atmosphere, and laid it up as a source of power for future use. The animal exerts a force by muscular contraction ; he draws it from the vegetable on which he feeds ; the vegetable derives it from the sun, whose rays determine its growth. Every time you lift your arm, every time you take a step, you are drawing on the power the sun has given you. When you step into the railway carriage, it is the sun-power that hurries you along. When gentle breezes fan your languid cheek, and when the resistless tornado levels cities in its fury, they are the servants of the sun. What an emblem of Him in whom we live, and move, and have our being !—*Professor Green.*

Verse 11.—The "*sun,*" which among all inanimate creatures is the most excellent, notes all manner of excellency, provision, and prosperity; and the "*shield,*" which among all artificial creatures is the chiefest, notes all manner of protection whatsoever. Under the name of "*grace,*" all spiritual good is wrapped up ; and under the name of "*glory,*" all eternal good is wrapped up ; and under the last clause, "*No good thing will he withhold,*" is wrapped up all temporal good : all put together speaks out God to be an all-sufficient portion.—*Thomas Brooks.*

Verse 11.—"*The Lord God is a shield.*" He is a shield to our *persons :* " Touch not," said he, " mine anointed, and do my prophets no harm." " The Lord," said Moses in his name, "the Lord shall preserve thy going out and thy coming in. He shall give his angels charge over thee to keep thee in all thy ways, lest at any time thou dash thy foot against a stone." " Hast thou considered my servant Job ? " said God to Satan :—" Yes," replied Satan, " I have : thou hast set a hedge about him. Yes, brethren ; *"the Lord God is a shield."* He is a shield to our *graces.* The dislike and malice of Satan is principally levelled at us when we become subjects of divine influence " Simon, Simon," said our Saviour, " Satan hath desired to have thee, that he may sift thee as wheat, but," he adds, " I have prayed for thee, that thy faith fail not." There was a shield to the good man's faith, or he and it too had been gone. You may remember the name of Little Faith in Bunyan's Pilgrim. It appears that Hopeful was greatly surprised that the robbers had not taken his jewels from him ; but he was given to understand that *they* were not in his own keeping. Yes, Christian, HE shall be thy *"shield"* to cover thy hope when it appears to thee to be giving up the ghost. . . . Yes, and He will be a shield *to thy property.* " Hast thou not set a hedge about *all* that he hath ? " Though Job was tried a little while, his property was only put out to interest ; by and by it came back cent. per cent. ; and he gained, besides, a vast increase of knowledge and of grace.—*Matthew Wilks.* 1746—1829.

Verse 11.—Turn your thoughts to the combination ; *"the Lord God is a sun and shield."* As a sun he shows me more and more of my sinfulness ; but then as a shield, he gives me power to oppose it and assurance that I shall conquer. As a sun, he discloses so much of the enormity of guilt, that I am forced to exclaim, " Mine iniquities are like a sore burden, too heavy for me to bear ; " but then as a shield, he shows me that he has laid the load on a Surety, who bore it into a land of forgetfulness. As a sun, he makes me daily more and more sensible of the utter impossibility of my working out a righteousness of my own ; but then, as a shield, he fastens constantly my thoughts on that righteousness of his Son, which is meritoriously conveyed to all who believe on his name. As a sun, in short, he brings facts to my knowledge, (inasmuch as he brings myself and mine enemies to my knowledge,) which would make the matter of deliverance seem out of reach and hopeless if he were not at the same time a shield ; but seeing that he is both, a shield as well as a sun, the disclosures which he makes as a sun only prepare me for the blessing which he imparts as a shield. Who then shall wonder, that after announcing the character of God, the Psalmist should break into expressions of confidence and assurance ? It may be, that as the corruption of nature is brought continually before me, deeper and wider and darker, Satan will ply me with the suggestion ; " The guiltiness is too inveterate to be eradicated, and too enormous to be pardoned "; and if God were a sun, and nothing more, it might be hard to put away the suggestion as a device of the father of lies. I might then fear. I might fear God's holiness, thinking I should never be fitted for communion with Deity ; I might fear God's justice, thinking I should never find acquittal at the last dread assize. But can I fear either, when besides a sun, God is also a shield ? Can I fear God's justice, when as a shield he places sufferings to my account, which satisfy the law, even to the last penalty ? Can I fear his holiness, when he gives me interest in an obedience, which fulfils every precept ? Does not the one character, that of a shield, help me to scatter those solicitudes, which may well be excited through the operation of the other character, that of a sun ? And am I not warranted—nay, am I not living far below my privilege—if I fail in deriving from the combination of character a boldness and a confidence, not to be overborne by those suspicions, which have Satan for their author ? As a sun, God shows me myself ; as a shield, God shows me himself. The sun discloses mine own nothingness ; the shield, Divine sufficiency. The one enables me to discern that I deserve nothing but wrath, and can earn nothing but shame ; the other, that I have a title to immortality, and may lay claim to an enduring inheritance in heaven. I learn, in short, from God as *"a Sun,"* that if I have " wages," I must have eternal death ; but from God as *"a Shield,"* that if I will receive the " free gift " I may have " eternal life." Whom then shall I fear ? Myself—confessedly my worst enemy ? " The Sun " makes a man start from himself ; the " Shield " assures him that he shall be protected against himself and builded up " for a habitation of God through the Spirit." Shall I shrink from Satan and the hosts of principalities and powers ? The " Sun " shows them awful in their might, and vehement in their malice ; but the " Shield " exhibits them spoiled and led captive, when Christ died and rose again. Shall I dread death ?

Indeed the " Sun " makes death terrible, forcing me to read God's curse in the motionless limbs and mouldering features ; but then the " Shield " displays the open sepulchre, the quickened dust, the marvels of a resurrection, the mountain and the ocean and the valley yielding up the sleeping generations. Is death to be dreaded ? Take the catalogue of things, which, inasmuch as we are fallen creatures, God, as our " Sun," instructs us to fear ; and we shall find, that insomuch as we are redeemed creatures, God as our " Shield " enables us to triumph over all our fears. Who therefore shall hesitate to agree, that there results from this combination of character exactly that system of counterpoise, which we affirm to be discoverable in grace as well as in providence ? Who can fail, if indeed we have been disciplined by that twofold tuition, which informs man first that he has destroyed himself and then that God hath " laid help on One that is mighty," the former lesson humiliating, the latter encouraging, the one making way for the other, so that the scholar is emptied of every false confidence that he may be fitted to entertain the true—oh ! who, we say, can fail to gather from the combination of Divine character the inference drawn by the Psalmist ? to exclaim (that is), after recording that "the Lord God is a Sun and Shield "—" He will give grace and glory : no good thing will he withhold from them that walk uprightly " ?—*Henry Melvill.*

Verse 11.—The words of the text are as a voice from heaven, inviting me up thither, and answering all the doubts and fears of such as believe and follow the joyful sound. Am I in *darkness*, and fear I shall never find the way ? Open thine eye, O my soul ! look up to the Father of lights : *the Lord is a sun*, whose steady beams shall direct thy steps. Is there an inward veil to be removed from my mind, as well as obscurity from my path ? He is sufficient for both. God who commanded the light to shine out of darkness, can shine into the heart, to give the light of the knowledge of his glory, and lead on to it. (2 Cor. iv. 6.) He can make the day dawn, and the day star to arise in our hearts ; (2 Peter i. 19), and by *both*, guide our feet into the way of peace. (Luke i. 79.) Doth the same light that discovers my way, discover what opposition I am like to meet with ? what enemies and dangers I am to go through ? Hear, O my soul, *the Lord is a shield*. Light and strength are conjoined ; none can miscarry under his conduct, nor have any reason to be discouraged. With this he comforteth Abraham. Gen. xv. 1, "*Fear not : I am thy shield.*" Do I groan under a sense of my unmeetness for the heavenly kingdom ? Let this support my soul, "*the Lord will give grace.*" Am I altogether unworthy of so high happiness ? It springs from his own most free, unbounded love ; "*the Lord will give glory.*" Am I urged with a thousand wants that need supply, what more can be added ? "*No good thing will he withhold from them that walk uprightly.*" Nothing that is evil can be desired ; and nothing that is good shall be denied. Here, O my soul, is a fountain opened ; here thy eager thirst may be fully satisfied ; thy largest desires filled up ; and thy mind be ever at rest.—*Daniel Wilcox.*

Verse 11.—Why need a saint fear darkness, when he has such a sun to guide him ? Or dread dangers, when he has such a shield to guard him ?—*William Secker.*

Verse 11.—"*The Lord will give glory.*" " Man," says a wise author, " is the glory of this lower world ; the soul is the glory of man ; grace is the glory of the soul ; and heaven is the glory of grace." Heaven, or glory, is grace matured and brought to infinite perfection ; there we shall see his face, and have his name written in our foreheads ; and we shall reign with him for ever and ever.—*Matthew Wilks.*

Verse 11.—"*No good thing will he withhold,*" etc. But how is this true, when God oftentimes withholds riches and honours, and health of body from men, though they walk never so uprightly ; we may therefore know that honours and riches and bodily strength are none of God's good things ; they are of the number of things indifferent which God bestows promiscuously upon the just and unjust, as the rain to fall and the sun to shine. The good things of God are chiefly peace of conscience and joy in the Holy Ghost in this life ; fruition of God's presence, and vision of his blessed face in the next, and these good things God never bestows upon the wicked, never withholds from the godly, and they are all cast up in one sum where it is said, *Beati mundo corde, quoniam ipsi Deum videbunt :* " Blessed are the pure of heart (and such are only they that walk uprightly) for they shall see God." But is walking uprightly such a matter with God, that it should be so rewarded ? Is it not more pleasing to God to see us go stooping than walking upright, seeing stooping is the gait of humility, than which there is nothing to God more pleasing ? It is no doubt a hard matter to stoop and go upright both at once, yet both must be done, and both indeed are done, are done at once by every one that is godly ; but when I say they are done both at once, I mean not of the body, I know two such postures in the body both at once are impossible ; but the soul can do it, the soul can stoop and go upright both at once ; for then doth the soul walk upright before God, when it stoops in humility before God and men.—*Sir Richard Baker.*

Verse 11.—This is an immense fountain ; the Lord fill all the buckets of our hearts at the spring, and give us capacious souls, as he hath a liberal hand. —*Thomas Adams.*

HINTS TO PREACHERS.

Verse 1.—I. Why called Tabernacles ? To include (1) the holiest of all ; (2) The holy place ; (3) The court and precincts of the Tabernacle. *"Amiable"* is predicated of these. The courts amiable—the holy place more amiable—the holiest of all most amiable. II. Why called the Tabernacles of the Lord of hosts ? To denote (1) Its connection with the boundless universe ; (2) Its distinction from it. Present everywhere where God is peculiarly present here. III. Why called *amiable ?* (1) Because of the character in which God dwells here. Is condescension amiable ? Is love ? Is mercy ? Is grace ? These are displayed here. (2) Because of the purpose for which he resides here. To save sinners ; to comfort saints.

Verse 2.—I. The Object of Desire : (1) The house of the Lord ; (2) The Lord of the house ; the life of God in us and our life in him. II. The Occasion of the Desire. Exclusion from the Sanctuary. David says not, Oh how I long for my palace, my crown, my sceptre, my kingdom ; but, Oh how I long to return to the house of God ! III. The Strength of the Desire. (1) It was an inward longing, " my soul longeth," etc. ; (2) A painful longing, " yea, fainteth ; " (3) A prayerful longing, " my heart crieth out ; " (4) An entire longing, " my heart and my flesh," etc. ; Or, I. The value of God's house is known by attending it. II. It is better known by being afterwards banished from it. III. It is best known by being restored to it.

Verses 1, 2, 3.—The Titles for God in these three verses are worth dwelling upon. " Jehovah of Hosts ; " " the living God ; " " my King and my God."

Verse 3.—I. The Eloquence of Grief. David in his banishment envies the sparrows and the swallows that had built their nests by the house of God, more than Absalom who had usurped his palace and his throne. II. The Ingenuity of Prayer. Why should sparrows and swallows be nearer to thy altars than I am, O Lord of hosts, my King and my God ! " Fear not, ye are of more value than many sparrows."

Verse 4.—I. The Privilege suggested—dwelling in the house of God. Some birds fly over the house of God—some occasionally alight upon it—others build their nests and train up their young there. This was the privilege which the Psalmist desired. II. The Fact asserted. " Blessed are they that dwell," etc., who make it the spiritual home of themselves and their children. III. The Reason given. " They will be still," etc. (1) They will have much for which to praise God ; (2) They will see much to praise in God.

Verse 5.—Man is blessed, I. When his strength is in God. Strength to believe, strength to obey, strength to suffer. II. When God's ways are in him. " In whose heart," etc. When the doctrines, precepts, and promises of God are deeply engraved upon the heart.

Verse 7.—I. Trusting God in trouble brings present comfort—" Who passing," etc. II. Present comfort ensures still larger supplies—" The rain also," etc.

Verse 8.—There is, I. Progression. " They go : " (1) The people of God cannot remain stationary ; (2) They must not recede ; (3) They should always be advancing. II. Invigoration. " From strength to strength." (1) From one ordinance to another ; (2) from one duty to another ; (3) from one grace to another ; (4) from one degree of grace to another. Add faith to faith, virtue to virtue, knowledge to knowledge," etc. III. Completion. " Every one of them," etc.

Verse 8.—I. Prayer is not confined to the Sanctuary. David, in his banishment, says, " Hear my prayer." II. Help is not confined to the sanctuary. The Lord of hosts is " here," as well as in his tabernacles. See verse 1. III. Grace is not confined to the Sanctuary. Here, too, in the wilderness is the covenanting God, the God of Jacob.

Verse 9.—Observe, I. The Faith. Our shield is thine Anointed—Thine Anointed is our Shield. This is not David, because he says *our* Shield, but David's greater Son. A gleam of Gospel light through the thick clouds. II. The Prayer. "Behold, O God," etc. "Look," etc. Look upon him as our Representative, and look upon us in him. III. The Plea. (1) He has engaged to be our defence from thine anger ; (2) he has been anointed to this office by thee.

Verse 10.—Here is, I. A comparison of places. "A day in thy courts," etc. How much more a day in heaven ! What, then, must an eternity in heaven be ! II. A comparison of Persons. "I would rather be a doorkeeper," etc. Better be the least in the Church than the greatest in the world. If " better reign in hell than serve in heaven " was Satan's first thought after he fell, it was the first thought only.

Verse 11.—I. What God is to his people. "A sun and shield." (1) The source of all good ; (2) a defence from all evil. II. What he gives. (1) Grace here ; (2) glory hereafter. III. What he withholds. All that is not good. If he withholds health or wealth, or his own smiles from us, it is because they are not good for us at that particular time.

Verse 12.—I. The one thing that makes man blessed. Trust in God. "Blessed," etc. (1) For all things ; (2) at all times ; (3) in all circumstances. II. The Blessing contained in that one thing. God himself becomes ours ; (1) his mercy for our pardon ; (2) his power for our protection ; (3) his wisdom for our guidance ; (4) his faithfulness for our preservation ; (5) his all-sufficiency for our supply. III. The certainty of the blessing. (1) From David's own experience ; (2) from his solemn appeal to God respecting it. "O Lord God of hosts," etc.

[*All the above are by Rev. George Rogers.*]

Verse 5.—The preciousness of intensity and enthusiasm in religious belief, worship, and life.

Verses 5, 6, 7.—The blessed people are described, 1. By their earnest desire and resolution to take this journey, though they dwelt far off from the tabernacle, ver. 5. 2. By their painful passage, yet some refreshments by the way, ver. 6. 3. By their constant progress, till they came to the place they aimed at, ver. 7.— *T. Manton.*

Verse 6.—As the valley of weeping symbolizes dejection, so a " well " symbolizes ever-flowing salvation and comfort (compare John iv. 14 ; also Isa. xii. 3).

Verse 6.—I. "*The valley of Baca.*" Of this valley we may observe, 1. It is much frequented. 2. Unpleasant to flesh and blood. 3. Very healthful. 4. Very safe. 5. Very profitable. II. The toilsome effort : " make it a well." 1. Comfort may be obtained in the deepest trouble. 2. Comfort must be obtained by exertion. 3. Comfort obtained by one is of use to others, as a well may be. III. The heavenly supply. "The rain also filleth the pools." All is from God ; effort is of no avail without him.

Verse 8.—Pleas for answers to prayer in the titles here used. I. He is JEHOVAH, the living, all-wise, all-powerful, faithful, gracious, and immutable God. II. He is God of hosts, having abundant agencies under his control ; he can send angels, restrain devils, actuate good men, overrule bad men, and govern all other agents. III. He is the God of Jacob, of chosen Jacob, as seen in Jacob's dream ; God of Jacob in his banishment, in his wrestling (and so a God overcome by prayer), God pardoning Jacob's sins, God preserving Jacob and his seed after him.

Verse 9.—I. What god is to us. II. What we would have him look at. III. Where we would be : hidden behind the shield—seen in the person of Christ.

Verse 10.—I. Days in God's courts. Days of hearing, of repenting, of believing, of adoration, of communion, of revival, etc. II. Their preciousness. Better than a thousand days of victory, of pleasure, of money-making, of harvest, of discussion, of travelling amid beauties of nature. III. Reasons for this preciousness. They are more pleasurable, more profitable now, and more preparatory for the future and for heaven. The employment, the society, the enjoyment, the result, etc., are all better.

Verse 12.—The blessedness of the life of faith over that of carnal enjoyment, religious feeling, self-confidence, living upon marks and evidences, trusting in man, etc.

PSALM LXXXV.

TITLE.—To the Chief Musician, A Psalm for the Sons of Korah. *There is no need to repeat our observations upon a title which is of so frequent occurrence ; the reader is referred to notes placed in the headings of preceding Psalms. Yet it may not be out of place to quote the forty-sixth verse of Nehemiah XII.—"In the days of David and Asaph of old there were chief of the singers, and songs of praise and thanksgiving unto God."*

SUBJECT AND OCCASION.—*It is the prayer of a patriot for his afflicted country, in which he pleads the Lord's former mercies, and by faith foresees brighter days. We believe that David wrote it, but many question that assertion. Certain interpreters appear to grudge the Psalmist David the authorship of any of the Psalms, and refer the sacred songs by wholesale to the times of Hezekiah, Josiah, the Captivity, and the Maccabees. It is remarkable that, as a rule, the more sceptical a writer is, the more resolute is he to have done with David ; while the purely evangelic annotators are for the most part content to leave the royal poet in the chair of authorship. The charms of a new theory also operate greatly upon writers who would have nothing at all to say if they did not invent a novel hypothesis, and twist the language of the Psalm in order to justify it. The present Psalm has of course been referred to the Captivity, the critics could not resist the temptation to do that, though, for our part, we see no need to do so : it is true a captivity is mentioned in the first verse, but that does not necessitate the nation's having been carried away into exile, since Job's captivity was turned, and yet he had never left his native land : moreover, the text speaks of the captivity of Jacob as brought back, but, had it referred to the Babylonian emigration, it would have spoken of Judah ; for Jacob or Israel, as such, did not return. The first verse in speaking of "the land" proves that the author was not an exile. Our own belief is that David penned this national hymn when the land was oppressed by the Philistines, and in the spirit of prophecy he foretold the peaceful years of his own reign and the repose of the rule of Solomon, the Psalm having all along an inner sense of which Jesus and his salvation are the key. The presence of Jesus the Saviour reconciles earth and heaven, and secures to us the golden age, the balmy days of universal peace.*

DIVISIONS.—*In the first four verses the poet sings of the Lord's former mercies and begs him to remember his people ; from 5 to 7 he pleads the cause of afflicted Israel ; and then, having listened to the sacred oracle in verse 8, he publishes joyfully the tidings of future good, 9—13.*

EXPOSITION.

LORD, thou hast been favourable unto thy land : thou hast brought back the captivity of Jacob.

2 Thou hast forgiven the iniquity of thy people, thou hast covered all their sin. Selah.

3 Thou hast taken away all thy wrath : thou hast turned *thyself* from the fierceness of thine anger.

4 Turn us, O God of our salvation, and cause thine anger toward us to cease.

1. "LORD, *thou hast been favourable unto thy land.*" The self-existent, all-sufficient JEHOVAH is addressed : by that name he revealed himself to Moses when his people were in bondage, by that name he is here pleaded with. It is wise to dwell upon that view of the divine character which arouses the sweetest memories of his love. Sweeter still is that dear name of "Our Father," with which Christians have learned to commence their prayers. The Psalmist speaks of Canaan as the Lord's land, for he chose it for his people, conveyed it to them by covenant, conquered it by his power, and dwelt in it in mercy ; it was meet therefore that he should smile upon a land so peculiarly his own. It is most wise to plead the

Lord's union of interest with ourselves, to lash our little boat as it were close to his great barque, and experience a sacred community in the tossings of the storm. It is *our* land that is devastated, but O Jehovah, it is also *thy* land. The Psalmist dwells upon the Lord's favour to the chosen land, which he had shewed in a thousand ways. God's past doings are prophetic of what he will do : hence the encouraging argument—" Thou hast been favourable unto thy land," therefore deal graciously with it again. Many a time had foes been baffled, pestilence stayed, famine averted, and deliverance vouchsafed, because of the Lord's favour ; that same favourable regard is therefore again invoked. With an immutable God this is powerful reasoning ; it is because he changes not that we are not consumed, and know we never shall be if he has once been favourable to us. From this example of prayer let us learn how to order our cause before God.

It is clear that Israel was not in exile, or the prayer before us would not have referred to *the land* but to the nation.

"Thou hast brought back the captivity of Jacob." When down-trodden and oppressed through their sins, the Ever-merciful One had looked upon them, changed their sad condition, chased away the invaders, and given to his people rest : this he had done not once, nor twice, but times without number. Many a time have we also been brought into soul-captivity by our backslidings, but we have not been left therein ; the God who brought Jacob back from Padan-aram to his father's house, has restored us to the enjoyment of holy fellowship ;—will he not do the like again ? Let us appeal to him with Jacob-like wrestlings, beseeching him to be favourable, or sovereignly gracious to us notwithstanding all our provocations of his love. Let declining churches remember their former history, and with holy confidence plead with the Lord to turn their captivity yet again.

2. *"Thou hast forgiven the iniquity of thy people."* Often and often had he done this, pausing to pardon even when his sword was bared to punish. Who is a pardoning God like thee, O Jehovah ? Who is so slow to anger, so ready to forgive ? Every believer in Jesus enjoys the blessing of pardoned sin, and he should regard this priceless boon as the pledge of all other needed mercies. He should plead it with God—" Lord hast thou pardoned me, and wilt thou let me perish for lack of grace, or fall into thine enemies' hands for want of help. Thou wilt not thus leave thy work unfinished." *"Thou hast covered all their sin."* All of it, every spot, and wrinkle, the veil of love has covered all. Sin has been divinely put out of sight. Hiding it beneath the propitiatory, covering it with the sea of the atonement, blotting it out, making it to cease to be, the Lord has put it so completely away that even his omniscient eye sees it no more. What a miracle is this ! To cover up the sun would be easy work compared with the covering up of sin. Not without a covering atonement is sin removed, but by means of the great sacrifice of our Lord Jesus, it is most effectually put away by one act, for ever. What a covering does his blood afford !

3. *"Thou hast taken away all thy wrath."* Having removed the sin, the anger is removed also. How often did the longsuffering of God take away from Israel the punishments which had been justly laid upon them ! How often also has the Lord's chastising hand been removed from us when our waywardness called for heavier strokes ! *"Thou hast turned thyself from the fierceness of thine anger."* Even when judgments had been most severe, the Lord had in mercy stayed his hand. In mid volley he had restrained his thunder. When ready to destroy, he had averted his face from his purpose of judgment and allowed mercy to interpose. The book of Judges is full of illustrations of this, and the Psalmist does well to quote them while he intercedes. Is not our experience equally studded with instances in which judgment has been stayed and tenderness has ruled ? What a difference between the fierce anger which is feared and deprecated here, and the speaking of peace which is foretold in verse 8. There are many changes in Christian experience, and therefore we must not despair when we are undergoing the drearier portion of the spiritual life, for soon, very soon, it may be transformed into gladness.

" The Lord can clear the darkest skies,
Can give us day for night,
Make drops of sacred sorrow rise
To rivers of delight."

4. *"Turn us, O God of our salvation."* This was the main business. Could the erring tribes be rendered penitent all would be well. It is not that God needs

turning from his anger so much as that we need turning from our sin ; here is the hinge of the whole matter. Our trials frequently arise out of our sins, they will not go till the sins go. We need to be turned from our sins, but only God can turn us : God the Saviour must put his hand to the work ; it is indeed a main part of our salvation. Conversion is the dawn of salvation. To turn a heart to God is as difficult as to make the world revolve upon its axis. Yet when a man learns to pray for conversion there is hope for him, he who turns to prayer is beginning to turn from sin. It is a very blessed sight to see a whole people turn unto their God ; may the Lord so send forth his converting grace on our land that we may live to see the people flocking to the loving worship of God as the doves to their cotes. *"And cause thine anger toward us to cease."* Make an end of it. Let it no longer burn. When sinners cease to rebel, the Lord ceases to be angry with them ; when they return to him he returns to them ; yea, he is first in the reconciliation and turns them when otherwise they would never turn of themselves. May all those who are now enduring the hidings of Jehovah's face seek with deep earnestness to be turned anew unto the Lord, for so shall all their despondencies come to an end.

Thus the sweet singer asks for his nation priceless blessings, and quotes the best of arguments. Because the God of Israel has been so rich in favour in bygone years, therefore he is entreated to reform and restore his backsliding nation.

5 Wilt thou be angry with us for ever ? wilt thou draw out thine anger to all generations ?

6 Wilt thou not revive us again : that thy people may rejoice in thee ?

7 Shew us thy mercy, O LORD, and grant us thy salvation.

5. *"Wilt thou be angry with us for ever ?"* See how the Psalmist makes bold to plead. We are in time as yet and not in eternity, and does not time come to an end, and therefore thy wrath ! Wilt thou be angry always as if it were eternity ? Is there no boundary to thine indignation ? Will thy wrath never have done ? And if for ever angry, yet wilt thou be angry *"with us,"* thy favoured people, the seed of Abraham, thy friend ? That our enemies should be always wroth is natural but wilt *thou,* our God, be always incensed against us ? Every word is an argument. Men in distress never waste words. *"Wilt thou draw out thine anger to all generations ?"* Shall sons suffer for their fathers' faults, and punishment become an entailed inheritance ? O merciful God, hast thou a mind to spin out thine anger, and make it as long as the ages ? Cease thou, as thou hast ceased aforetime, and let grace reign as it has done in days of yore. When we are under spiritual desertion we may beg in the like manner that the days of tribulation may be shortened, lest our spirit should utterly fail beneath the trial.

6. *"Wilt thou not revive us again ?"* Hope here grows almost confident. She feels sure that the Lord will return in all his power to save. We are dead or dying, faint and feeble, God alone can revive us, he has in other times refreshed his people, he is still the same, he will repeat his love. Will he not ? Why should he not ? We appeal to him—" Wilt thou not ? " *"That thy people may rejoice in thee."* Thou lovest to see thy children happy with that best of happiness which centres in thyself, therefore revive us, for revival will bring us the utmost joy. The words before us teach us that gratitude has an eye to the giver, even beyond the gift— " thy people may rejoice *in thee."* Those who were revived would rejoice not only in the new life but in the Lord who was the author of it. Joy in the Lord is the ripest fruit of grace, all revivals and renewals lead up to it. By our possession of it we may estimate our spiritual condition, it is a sure gauge of inward prosperity. A genuine revival without joy in the Lord is as impossible as spring without flowers, or daydawn without light. If, either in our own souls or in the hearts of others, we see declension, it becomes us to be much in the use of this prayer, and if on the other hand we are enjoying visitations of the Spirit and bedewings of grace, let us abound in holy joy and make it our constant delight to joy in God.

7. *"Shew us thy mercy, O LORD."* Reveal it to our poor half-blinded eyes. We cannot see it or believe it by reason of our long woes, but thou canst make it plain to us. Others have beheld it, Lord shew it to us. We have seen thine anger, Lord let us see thy mercy. Thy prophets have told us of it, but, O Lord, do thou thyself display it in this our hour of need. *"And grant us thy salvation."* This includes deliverance from the sin as well as the chastisement, it reaches from the

depth of their misery to the height of divine love. God's salvation is perfect in kind, comprehensive in extent, and eminent in degree ; grant us this, O Lord, and we have all.

8 I will hear what God the LORD will speak : for he will speak peace unto his people, and to his saints : but let them not turn again to folly.

9 Surely his salvation *is* nigh them that fear him ; that glory may dwell in our land.

10 Mercy and truth are met together ; righteousness and peace have kissed *each other*.

11 Truth shall spring out of the earth ; and righteousness shall look down from heaven.

12 Yea, the LORD shall give *that which is* good ; and our land shall yield her increase.

13 Righteousness shall go before him ; and shall set *us* in the way of his steps.

Having offered earnest intercession for the afflicted but penitent nation, the sacred poet in the true spirit of faith awaits a response from the sacred oracle. He pauses in joyful confidence, and then in ecstatic triumph he gives utterance to his hopes in the richest form of song.

8. "*I will hear what God the* LORD *will speak.*" When we believe that God hears us, it is but natural that we should be eager to hear him. Only from him can come the word which can speak peace to troubled spirits ; the voices of men are feeble in such a case, a plaister far too narrow for the sore ; but God's voice is power, he speaks and it is done, and hence when we hear him our distress is ended. Happy is the suppliant who has grace to lie patiently at the Lord's door, and wait until his love shall act according to its old wont and chase all sorrow far away. "*For he will speak peace unto his people, and to his saints.*" Even though for a while his voice is stern with merited rebuke, he will not always chide, the Great Father will reassume his natural tone of gentleness and pity. The speaking of peace is the peculiar prerogative of the Lord Jehovah, and deep, lasting, ay, eternal, is the peace he thus creates. Yet not to all does the divine word bring peace, but only to his own people, whom he means to make saints, and those whom he has already made so. "*But let them not turn again to folly.*" For if they do so, his rod will fall upon them again, and their peace will be invaded. Those who would enjoy communion with God must be jealous of themselves, and avoid all that would grieve the Holy Spirit ; not only the grosser sins, but even the follies of life must be guarded against by those who are favoured with the delights of conscious fellowship. We serve a jealous God, and must needs therefore be incessantly vigilant against evil. Backsliders should study this verse with the utmost care, it will console them and yet warn them, draw them back to their allegiance, and at the same time inspire them with a wholesome fear of going further astray. To turn again to folly is worse than being foolish for once ; it argues wilfulness and obstinacy, and it involves the soul in sevenfold sin. There is no fool like the man who will be a fool cost him what it may.

9. "*Surely his salvation is nigh them that fear him.*" Faith knows that a saving God is always near at hand, but *only* (for such is the true rendering) to those who fear the Lord, and worship him with holy awe. In the gospel dispensation this truth is conspicuously illustrated. If to seeking sinners salvation is nigh, it is assuredly very nigh to those who have once enjoyed it, and have lost its present enjoyment by their folly ; they have but to turn unto the Lord and they shall enjoy it again. We have not to go about by a long round of personal mortifications or spiritual preparations, we may come to the Lord, through Jesus Christ, just as we did at the first, and he will again receive us unto his loving embrace. Whether it be a nation under adversity, or a single individual under chastisement, the sweet truth before us is rich with encouragement to repentance, and renewed holiness.

"*That glory may dwell in our land.*" The object of the return of grace will be a permanent establishment of a better state of things, so that gloriously devout worship shall be rendered to God continuously, and a glorious measure of prosperity shall be enjoyed in consequence. Israel was glorious whenever she was faithful—

her dishonour always followed her disloyalty ; believers also live glorious lives when they walk obediently, and they only lose the true glory of their religion when they fall from their stedfastness.

In these two verses we have, beneath the veil of the letter, an intimation of the coming of THE WORD OF GOD to the nations in times of deep apostasy and trouble, when faithful hearts would be looking and longing for the promise which had so long tarried. By his coming, salvation is brought near, and glory, even the glory of the presence of the Lord, tabernacles among men. Of this the succeeding verses speak without obscurity.

10. "Mercy and truth are met together." In answer to prayer, the exulting Psalmist sees the attributes of God confederating to bless the once afflicted nation. Mercy comes hand-in-hand with Truth to fulfil the faithful promise of their gracious God ; the people recognise at once the grace and the veracity of Jehovah, he is to them neither a tyrant nor a deceiver. "Righteousness and peace have kissed each other." The Lord whose just severity inflicted the smart, now in pity sends peace to bind up the wound. The people being now made willing to forsake their sins, and to follow after righteousness, find peace granted to them at once. " The war-drum throbbed no longer, and the battle-flags were furled ; " for idolatry was forsaken, and Jehovah was adored.

This appears to be the immediate and primary meaning of these verses ; but the inner sense is Christ Jesus, the reconciling Word. In him, the attributes of God unite in glad unanimity in the salvation of guilty men, they meet and embrace in such a manner as else were inconceivable either to our just fears or to our enlightened hopes. God is as true as if he had fulfilled every letter of his threatenings, as righteous as if he had never spoken peace to a sinner's conscience ; his love in undiminished, splendour shines forth, but no other of his ever-blessed characteristics is eclipsed thereby. It is the custom of modern thinkers (?) to make sport of this representation of the result of our Lord's substitutionary atonement, but had they ever been themselves made to feel the weight of sin upon a spiritually awakened conscience, they would cease from their vain ridicule. Their doctrine of atonement has well been described by Dr. Duncan as the admission " that the Lord Jesus Christ did something or other, which somehow or other, was in some way or other connected with man's salvation." This is their substitute for substitution. Our facts are infinitely superior to their dreams, and yet they sneer. It is but natural that natural men should do so. We cannot expect animals to set much store by the discoveries of science, neither can we hope to see unspiritual men rightly estimate the solution of spiritual problems—they are far above and out of their sight. Meanwhile it remains for those who rejoice in the great reconciliation to continue both to wonder and adore.

11. "Truth shall spring out of the earth." Promises which lie unfulfilled, like buried seeds, shall spring up and yield harvests of joy ; and men renewed by grace shall learn to be true to one another and their God, and abhor the falsehood which they loved before. "And righteousness shall look down from heaven," as if it threw up the windows and leaned out to gaze upon a penitent people, whom it could not have looked upon before without an indignation which would have been fatal to them. This is a delicious scene. Earth yielding flowers of truth, and heaven shining with stars of holiness ; the spheres echoing to each other, or being mirrors of each other's beauties. " Earth carpeted with truth and canopied with righteousness," shall be a nether heaven. When God looks down in grace, man sends his heart upward in obedience.

The person of our adorable Lord Jesus Christ explains this verse most sweetly. In Him truth is found in our humanity, and his deity brings divine righteousness among us. His Spirit's work even now creates a hallowed harmony between his church below, and the sovereign righteousness above ; and in the latter day, earth shall be universally adorned with every precious virtue, and heaven shall hold intimate intercourse with it. There is a world of meaning in these verses, only needing meditation to draw it out. Reader, " the well is deep," but if thou hast the Spirit, it cannot be said, that " thou hast nothing to draw with."

12. "Yea, the Lord shall give that which is good." Being himself pure goodness, he will readily return from his wrath, and deal out good things to his repenting people. Our evil brings evil upon us, but when we are brought back to follow that which is good, the Lord abundantly enriches us with good things. Material good will always be bestowed where it can be enjoyed in consistency with spiritual good.

"And our land shall yield her increase." The curse of barrenness will fly with the curse of sin. When the people yielded what was due to God, the soil would recompense their husbandry. See at this day what sin has done for Palestine, making her gardens a wilderness ; her wastes are the scars of her iniquities : nothing but repentance and divine forgiveness will reclaim her desolations. The whole world also shall be bright with the same blessing in the days yet to come,—

> " Freed from the curse, the grateful garden gives
>   Its fruits in goodly revenue. Nor frost,
> Nor blight, nor mildew fall, nor cankerworm,
> Nor caterpillar, mar one ripening hope.
> The clouds drop fatness. The very elements
> Are subject to the prayerful will of those
> Whose pleasure is in unison with God's."

13. *"Righteousness shall go before him ; and shall set us in the way of his steps."* God's march of right will leave a track wherein his people will joyfully follow. He who smote in justice will also bless in justice, and in both will make his righteousness manifest, so as to affect the hearts and lives of all his people. Such are the blessings of our Lord's first advent, and such shall be yet more conspicuously the result of his second coming. Even so, come Lord Jesus. Amen.

EXPLANATORY NOTES AND QUAINT SAYINGS.

Whole Psalm.—This beautiful Psalm, like some others, has come down to us without name or date ; the production of some unknown poetic genius, touched, purified, and exalted by the fire of celestial inspiration ; a precious relic of that golden age, when the Hebrew music was instinct with a spirit such as never breathed on Greece or Rome. It is interesting to reflect on the anonymous origin of some of the Psalms : to remember how largely the church of God is indebted to some nameless worthies who wrote for us hymns and spiritual songs, full of richer strains than were ever poured forth by the most illustrious of pagan name. These holy men are passed away, they have left no record of their history ; but they have bequeathed legacies of rich, varied, and inspired sentiments, which will render the church debtors to them to the end of time.—*John Stoughton.* 1852.

Whole Psalm.—This Psalm may be thus divided : verses 1, 2, 3, express the thanks of the people for their return from captivity ; verses 4, 5, 6, their prayer for their own *reformation ;* in verse 7, they pray for the coming of the *Messiah ;* verse 8 contains the *words* of the *High-priest,* with *God's gracious answer ;* which answer is followed by the grateful acclamations *of the people,* to the end of the Psalm.

To prepare for this interpretation, let us observe, how very strangely the words are expressed at present—"*I will hear what God the Lord will say :* FOR *he shall speak peace unto his people.*" But surely, God could not be consulted, *because* it was unnecessary ; nor could the High-priest possibly say, that he would ask of God, *because* he knew what God would answer ; especially, as we have now *a question to God* proposed, and yet no *answer from God* given at all. Under these difficulties we are happily relieved ; since it appears, on satisfactory authorities, that, instead of the particle rendered *"for,"* the word here originally signified *in* or *by me,* which slight variation removes the obscurity, and restores that very light which has long been wanted.

The *people* having prayed for the speedy arrival of their great *salvation ;* the *High-priest* says, (as it should be here expressed), "*I will hear what the Almighty sayeth.—Jehovah* BY ME *sayeth,* PEACE *unto his people, even unto his saints : but let them not turn again to folly.*" Whereupon, as the Jews understood *peace* to comprehend *every* blessing, and of course *their greatest* blessing, they at once acknowledged the *certainty* of this salvation, the *glory* of their land—they proclaim it as *nigh* at hand—and then, in rapture truly prophetical, they see this glory as actually arrived, as already *dwelling* in Judea—they behold God in fulfilling most strictly what he had promised most graciously—they see therefore the *mercy* of God, and the *truth* of God met together—they see that scheme perfected, in which the *righteousness* (*i.e.*, the justice) of God harmonizes with the *peace* (*i.e.* the happiness) of man ; so that righteousness and peace *salute* each other with the tenderest affection.   In short, they see TRUTH *flourishing out of the earth ; i.e.* they see *him*, who is *the way, the truth,* and *the life,* born here *on earth ;* and they even see the *righteousness,* or justice of God, looking down from *heaven,* as being well pleased.

Verse the 12th is at present translated so unhappily, that it is quite despoiled of all its genuine glory. For, could the prophet, after all the rapturous things said before, coldly say here, that God *would give what was good*—and that *Judea* should have *a plentiful harvest ?* No ; consistency and good sense forbid it ; and truth confirms their protest against it.   The words here express the reasons of all the preceding energies, and properly signify—*Yea, Jehovah granteth* THE BLESSING ; *and our land granteth* HER OFFSPRING. And what can be *the blessing*—what, amidst these sublime images, can be *Judea's offspring*—but HE, and HE only, who was *the blessing of all lands* in general, and *the glory of Judea* in particular ? And what says the verse following ? *"Righteousness goeth before* HIM—certainly, not before *the fruits of the earth*—but certainly before that illustrious person, even the MESSIAH " —*"Righteousness goeth before* HIM, *and directeth his goings in the way."*

As to the word rendered *the blessing,* and applied to the redemption ; the same word is so used by Jeremiah, thus : " Behold, the days come, that I will perform *that good thing* (the blessing) which I have promised . . . at that time will I cause to grow up unto David the Branch of righteousness " (ch. xxxiii. 14, 15).   And as to the Messiah being here described, partly as springing up from the earth ; so says Isaiah : " In that day shall the branch of the Lord be beautiful and glorious ; and *the fruits of the earth* shall be excellent and comely." But this evangelical prophet, in another place, has the very same complication of images with that found in the Psalm before us. For Isaiah also has *the heavens,* with their *righteousness ;* and *the earth,* with *its salvation :* " Drop down, ye *heavens* from above, and let the skies pour down righteousness ; let *the earth* open, and let *them* bring forth salvation." But, " let *them* bring forth "—who, or what can be here meant by *them,* but *the heavens* and the *earth ?*   It is heaven and earth which are here represented as *bringing forth,* and introducing the Saviour of the world. For what else can be here meant as *brought forth* by *them ?* What, but HE alone ; who, deriving his *divine* nature from heaven, and his *human* from the earth, was (what no other being ever was) both GOD and MAN.—*Benjamin Kennicott.*

Verse 1.—*"Thy land."* The land of Jehovah the poet calls it, in order to point out the close relation of God to it, and to the people thereof, and so confirm the *favour* of God towards it. For this land God has chosen as the dwelling-place of his people, true religion, and his own presence ; this also in his own time He himself had trodden in the person of his Son, and in it He first gathered and founded his Church.—*Venema.*

Verse 1.—*"The captivity of Jacob."* All true believers are the sons of Jacob, and the seed of Abraham ; as well the believing Gentiles, who are the sons of Jacob according to the Spirit, as the believing Jews the sons of Jacob according to the flesh ; and the Church of these true Jacobins and Israelites is the land of the Lord, and the *captivity* here mentioned is bondage under sin. In this captivity Satan is the gaoler, the flesh is our prison, ungodly lusts are the manacles, a bad conscience the tormentor, all of them against us ; only Christ is *Emmanuel,* God with us ; he turneth away the captivity of Jacob in forgiving all his offences, and in covering all his sins.—*Abraham Wright.*

Verse 2.—*"Thou hast forgiven the iniquity."* נָשָׂאתָ עָוֹן, *nasatha avon, Thou hast borne,* or *carried away, the iniquity.* An allusion to the ceremony of the scape-goat.—*Adam Clarke.*

Verse 2.—*"Thou hast covered all their sin."* When God is said *to cover sin,* he does so not as one would cover a sore with a plaster, thereby merely hiding it only ; but he covers it with a plaster that effectually cures and removes it altogether.—*Bellarmine.*

Verse 2.—*"Selah."* Rabbi Kimchi regards it as a sign to elevate the voice. The authors of the Septuagint translation appear to have regarded it as a musical or rythmical note. Herder regarded it as indicating a change of note ; Mathewson as a musical note, equivalent, perhaps, to the word *repeat.* According to Luther and others, it means *silence*. Gesenius explains it to mean, " Let the instruments play and the singers stop." Wocher regards it as equivalent to *sursum corda*—up, my soul ! Sommer, after examining all the seventy-four passages in which the word occurs recognises in every case " an actual appeal or summons to Jehovah." They are calls for aid and prayers to be heard, expressed either with entire directness, or if not in the imperative, " Hear, Jehovah ! " or Awake, Jehovah ! and the like, still earnest addresses to God that he would remember and hear, etc. The word itself he regards as indicating a blast of the trumpets by the priests. Selah, itself, he thinks an abridged expression, used for Higgaion Selah—Higgaion indicating the sound of the stringed instruments, and Selah a vigorous blast of trumpets.—*From the "Bibliotheca Sacra," quoted by Plumer.*

Verse 3.—"*Thou hast taken away all thy wrath.*" Or *gathered* it ; sin occasions wrath, and the people of God are as deserving of it as others ; but the Lord has gathered it up, and poured it forth upon his Son, and their Surety ; hence nothing of this kind shall ever fall upon them, either here or hereafter ; and it is taken away from them, so as to have no sense, apprehension, or conscience of it, which before the law had wrought in them, when pardon is applied unto them, which is what is here meant.—*John Gill.*

Verse 3.—"*Thou hast turned thyself.*" Here are six *hasts* drawing in the next *turn*, verse 4. God hath, and therefore God will, is a strong medium of hope, if not a demonstration of Scripture-logic. See 2 Cor. i. 10.—*John Trapp.*

Verse 4.—"*Cause thine anger toward us to cease.*" The phrase, *break thine indignation towards us*, (that is, wherewith thou art angry with us, in order that it may cease of itself,) comprehends the abolition of the signs and the effects of anger. The word פור, for this is the root to be taken, properly denotes a *breaking* by means of *notches* and *gaps*, as when the *edge* of anything is broken by many notches and gaps, and it is made utterly worn and useless. *Indignation*, so long as it is vigorous and spreads its effects, has an *edge*, which smites and pierces ; but it is considered blunt and broken, when it ceases to exert itself, and produces evils no longer ; this they affirm of the *anger* of God.—*Venema.*

Verse 6.—"*Wilt thou not revive us again ?*" The Hebrew is, *Wilt thou not return and revive us ?* We translate the verb *return* by the adverb *again :* "*Wilt thou not revive us again ?*" Thou hast given us many *revives :* when we were as *dead men*, and like carcases rotting in the grave, thou didst revive us, wilt thou not revive us once more, and act over those powerfully merciful works and strong salvations once more, or again ?—*Joseph Caryl.*

Verse 6.—"*That thy people may rejoice in thee.*" Bernard in his 15th Sermon on Canticles says, Jesus is honey in the mouth, melody in the ear, joy in the heart. Is any among us sad ? Let Jesus enter the heart, and thence spring to the countenance, and behold, before the rising brightness of his name, every cloud is scattered, serenity returns. Origen in his 10th Hom. on Genesis, has the remark, Abraham rejoiced not in present things, neither in the riches of the words, nor deeds of time. But do you wish to hear, whence he drew his joy ? Listen to the Lord speaking to the Jews, John viii. 56 : " Your father, Abraham rejoiced to see my day : and he saw it, and was glad : " hope heaped up his joys.—*Le Blanc.*

Verse 6.—"*That thy people may rejoice in thee.*" When God changeth the cheer of his people, their joy should not be in the gift, but in the Giver.—*David Dickson.*

Verse 6.—It is the most natural thing, the most delightful thing, for the people of God to rejoice in God. God is the fountain of joy, and whom should he fill with it but his people ? And whom should his people breathe it into again but him ? This posture God delights to have them in ; this posture they delight to be in ; but this cannot be in that estate of death and captivity wherein God for a long season shutteth them up. " The living, the living shall praise thee," but alas, the dead cannot.—*John Pennington, 1656.*

Verse 6.—Truly sin kills. Men are dead in trespasses and sins, dead in law, dead in their affections, dead in a loss of comfortable communion with God. Probably the greatest practical heresy of each age is a low idea of our undone condition under the guilt and dominion of sin. While this prevails we shall be slow to cry for *reviving* or *quickening*. What sinners and churches need is quickening by the Holy Ghost.—*William S. Plumer.*

Verses 6—7.—*"Wilt thou not revive us,"* by the first and spiritual resurrection, and so thy people, quickened from a life of sin to a life of grace, will rejoice in thee, not in themselves, presuming nothing on their own power. And in order that these things may be fulfilled in us, *"Shew us, O Lord, thy mercy,"* that is, Christ, through whom thou hast pitied the human race, shew him to us after this exile that we may see him face to face.—*Richardus Hampolus.*

Verse 7.—*"Thy mercy."* It is not merely of the Lord's mercies that we are not consumed, but all is mercy, from first to last,—mercy that met us by the way,—mercy that looked upon us in our misery,—mercy that washed us from our sins in his own blood,—mercy that covered our nakedness and clad us in his own robe of righteousness,—mercy that led and guided us by the way,—and mercy that will never leave nor forsake us till mercy has wrought its perfect work in the eternal salvation of our souls through Jesus Christ.—*Barton Bouchier.*

Verse 8.—*"I will hear,"* etc. The true attitude for a sinner to take in the presence of divine revelation, is that of a *listener.* To enter the place of a *doer* before you have occupied that of a *listener,* is to reverse God's order, and throw everything into confusion. Adam tried this plan, and found it a failure. He tried " works." He " sewed fig leaves together," but it was no use. He could not even satisfy his own conscience, or remove his guilty fear. He had to listen to the voice of God—to hearken to divine revelation.—*"Things New and Old."* 1859.

Verse 8.—*"I will hear,"* etc. The eye as a mere organ of sense must give place to the ear. Therefore it is wittily observed, that our Saviour commanding the abscession of the offending hand, foot, and eye, (Mark ix. 43—47), yet never spake of the ear. If thy hand, thy foot, or thine eye, cause thee to offend, deprive thyself of them ; but part not with thine ear, for that is an organ to derive unto thy soul's salvation. As Christ says there, a man may enter into heaven, lamed in his feet, as Mephibosheth, blind in his sight, as Barzillai, maimed in his hand, as the dry-handed man in the gospel ; but if there be not an ear to hear of the way, there will be no foot to enter into heaven. If God be not first in the ear, he is neither sanctifiedly in the mouth, nor comfortably in the heart. The Jews had eyes to see Christ's miracles, but because they had no ears to hear his wisdom, therefore they had no feet to enter into his kingdom. The way into the house is by the door, not by the window : the eye is but the window of the heart, the ear is the door. Now Christ stands knocking at the door, not at the window. Rev. iii. 20. And he will not come in at the window, but at the door : " He that entereth in by the door is the shepherd of the sheep." John x. 2. He comes now in by his oracles, not by his miracles. " To him the porter openeth ; and the sheep hear his voice," ver. 3. The way to open and let him in is by the door ; to hear his voice. There was a man in the gospel blind and deaf : blind eyes is ill ; but deaf ears, worse. It is bad to have the eyes seeled,* but worse to have the ears sealed up. Open your ears therefore to this heavenly voice. Bernard hath this description of a good ear : Which willingly hears what is taught, wisely understands what it heareth, and obediently practises what it understandeth. O give me such an ear, and I will hang on it jewels of gold, ornaments of praise.—*Thomas Adams.*

Verse 8.—*"I will hear,"* etc. My text carries in it a poetical allusion to the consulting of the cloud of glory, which was between the cherubims, and to the receiving answer from it, upon all critical occasions. David turned his thoughts from all the other views he might have, to this, *"I will hear what God the Lord will speak"* ; that so he might depend wholly on the assurances that he should receive of God's favour, upon the repentance and prayers of the people ; and in consideration of God's covenant with them, he knew the answer would be *"peace ;"* which being the form of salutation in those ages, among friends, imported an entire reconciliation. So that by *speaking peace* is to be understood an assurance of God's love and favour *"to his people, and to his saints :"* that is, to the people that was *sanctified,* and dedicated to the service of God by so many federal rites.—*Gilbert Burnet,* 1643—1714-5.

Verse 8.—*"I will hear what God the Lord will speak."* Carnal men speak peace to themselves on account of some supposed goodness in themselves. And unsound professors steal peace from God's promises, such as Isa. lv. 7 ; Hosea xiv. 4. But

---

* *Seel,* to close up : a term in falconry.

an upright heart will not be satisfied without hearing God speak peace to his heart by his Spirit. And for this he will pray, and wait, and hearken, and when God speaks peace, there comes such sweetness with it, and such discovery of his love, as lays a powerful influence on the soul not to turn again to folly. This peace is an humbling, melting peace, which brings humiliation to the soul as well as joy ; but this never happens when men speak peace to themselves.—*John Berridge*, 1716—1793.

Verse 8.—"*I will hear what God the* LORD *will speak*," etc. His prayer being finished, and he having spoke, he now stands and listens, as you use to do when you expect an echo, what echo he should have, what answer would be returned from heaven, whether his prayer had already come : "*I will hear what the Lord will speak ;*" or, as some read it, "*I will hear what the Lord doth speak :*" for sometimes there is a present echo, a speedy answer returned to a man's heart, even ere the prayer is half finished. "*He will speak peace.*" When the child of God wants peace, he can have no peace till God speak it. . . . . Let God's people be in never so great distress, yet it is an easy thing for God to give peace to them. Mark the expression here used : it is but *speaking* peace, that is, it is as easy for him to give peace as it is for you to speak a word ; it is no more to him. Then our comfort is, that as he only must do it, so he easily can do it, even with a word.—*Thomas Goodwin.*

Verse 8.—"*He will speak peace unto his people, and to his saints*," etc. The voice of the Lord is comfortable, and his words are sweet to those that fear him. It is a plain sign that all is not well with us, when the voice of God doth cast us into fear, when we are afraid to hear the word preached, when just reproofs of our sins are unwelcome to us, and anger us, and make us think the less of our minister that chideth and threateneth us.

A good life and a well-governed conversation doth not fear the voice of God ; the word of God is the light which God hath set up in his church, to guide her feet in the ways of peace. They that do evil hate the light, and will not come near it, lest their works should be reproved ; the children of the light resort to it, and call upon God : " Search my reins and my heart, and see if there be any way of wickedness in me."—*Edward Marbury.*

Verse 8.—"*To his people and to his saints.*" He will give *prosperity* to *the people* in general ; and to *his saints*—his followers, in particular.—*Adam Clarke.*

Verse 8.—"*To his saints.*" It is remarkable that we have the suffrage of a celebrated Jewish writer, Kimchi, to understand the word rendered "*saints*" in this place, of the godly among the Gentiles, as distinguished from the Lord's people, the Jews.—*John Fry.*

Verse 8.—"*He will speak peace unto his people, and to his saints : but let them not return again to folly.*" This imports that if his *saints* turn again to folly, which by woeful experience we find too frequently done, God may *change his voice*, and turn his peace, formerly spoken, into a warlike defiance to their conscience.—*Thomas Fuller.*

Verse 8.—"*But let them not turn again to folly.*" If God did not in the end speak peace, they would indeed return to folly. For his end of speaking peace is, that they might not return to folly : Ps. cxxv. 3, " The rod of the wicked shall not always be upon the righteous, lest they put forth their hand to iniquity ; " therefore, at the last verse, " peace shall be upon Israel " . . . . .

As it is a rule in physic still to maintain nature, and therefore when that shall be in hazard to be destroyed, they leave giving purging physic, and give cordials ; so doth God with his people : though with purging physic he often brings their spirits very weak and low, yet he will uphold and maintain their spirits, so as they shall not fail and be extinguished, but then he will give cordials to raise them up again.—*Thomas Goodwin.*

Verse 8.—It is hard to know, in spiritual exercises, whether it be more difficult to attain some good frame, or to keep and maintain it when it is attained ; whether more seriousness is required for making peace with God, or for keeping of it when made ; whether more diligence should be in preparing for a communion, or more watchfulness after it : sure both are required ; and it was our blessed Lord's word, Matt. xxvi. 41, after the first celebration of his supper, " Watch and pray, that ye enter not into temptation." Here that saying holds eminently : "*Non minor est virtus, quam quærere, parta tueri :* no less virtue and valour is requisite to maintain, than to make a purchase or conquest. In the words there are, 1. A great mercy promised from the Lord to his people, viz., "*He will speak peace to them.*" 2. A special caveat and advertisement given them, pointing at their hazard : *"But let them not turn again to folly : "* that is, let not his people and saints to whom he hath spoken peace, return to sin ; let them beware of bourding* and dallying with God's mercy, and of turning his grace into wantonness, of cooling in their affections to him, of slipping back to their old way, and of embracing their old lovers and idols ; for that is folly, even in folio, to speak so.—*James Durham, in "The Unsearchable Riches of Christ."*

Verse 9.—*"That glory may dwell in our land."* What land the true church of Christ, the saints and they that fear God, do dwell in ; there doth *glory* dwell : there God, there Christ by his Spirit bringing righteousness and salvation to such a society, is glorious ; and for his presence the people are glorious ; and the land glorious above all other lands whatsoever.—*David Dickson.*

Verse 10.—*"Mercy and truth ; righteousness and peace."* Note, four virtues stand out prominently in the incarnation ; namely, mercy, truth, righteousness and peace, or love producing peace. These were like four steps of the throne of Christ, or four princes standing near and accompanying Him. 1. On the right hand, is mercy presenting the olive. 2. On the left, truth holding the white lily. 3. Before Him walks justice bearing the balance. 4. Peace follows Him, having a cornucopiæ full of flowers, and scattering the flowers around.—*Le Blanc.*

Verse 10.—*"Mercy and truth ; righteousness and peace."* These four divine attributes parted at the fall of Adam, and met again at the birth of Christ. Mercy was ever inclined to save man, and Peace could *not* be his enemy ; but Truth exacted the performance of God's threat,—" The soul that sinneth, it shall die ; " and Righteousness could not but give to every one his due, Jehovah must be true in all his ways, and righteous in all his works. Now, there is no religion upon earth, except the Christian, which can satisfy the demands of all these claimants, and restore an union between them ; which can show how God's word can be true, and his work just, and the sinner, notwithstanding, find mercy, and obtain peace.—*George Horne.*

Verse 10.—This is a remarkable text, and much has been said on it ; but there is a beauty in it which, I think, has not been noticed. *Mercy* and *peace* are on one side ; *truth* and *righteousness* on the other. *Truth* requires *righteousness ; mercy* calls for *peace.* They meet together on the way ; one going to make inquisition for sin, the other to plead for reconciliation. Having met, their differences on certain considerations, not here particularly mentioned, are adjusted ; and their mutual claims are blended together in one common interest ; on which *peace* and *righteousness* immediately embrace. Thus, *righteousness* is given to *truth,* and *peace* is given to *mercy.* Now, *where* did these meet ? In Christ Jesus. *When* were they reconciled ? When he poured out his life on Calvary.—*Adam Clarke.*

Verse 10.—*"Mercy and truth are met together."* 1. They meet together *in God ;* " all the paths of the Lord are mercy and truth," Ps. xxv. 9 ; *mercy* in making, and *truth* in keeping his promise to his people. Paul saith, Jesus Christ was a minister of the circumcision for the *truth* of God, to confirm the promises made unto the fathers, and that the Gentiles might glorify God for his *mercy.* Rom. xv. 8. God promised his Son unto the Jews ; and he gave him in the fulness of time to be both a light to the Gentiles, and glory of his people Israel ; herein shewing his *mercy* more principally to the Gentiles, his *truth* unto the Jews, and so his mercy and truth embraced each other, so that he made both people but one, to wit, one flock, in one sheepfold, under one shepherd.

If we take *truth and righteousness* for God's justice in punishing, *mercy and peace* for his graciousness in pardoning ; yet they meet together in all his ways, unto such as keep his covenant and his testimonies. For as the mercies of the wicked are full of cruelty, so the very judgments of God upon his servants are full of mercy. In his wrath he remembers pity ; punishing a little, that he may pardon a great deal ; destroying the flesh only, to save the spirit, 1 Cor. v. 5. *Misericordiæ est aliquando subtrahere misericordiam.* It was good for Joseph that he was a captive ; good for Naaman that he was a leper ; good for Bartimæus that he was blind, and for David that he was in trouble. Bradford thanked God more of his prison, than of any parlour or pleasure. All things are for the best unto the faithful, and so

---

* *Bourding*=jesting.

God's "*mercy and truth are met together; righteousness and peace have kissed each other*," his mercy being just, and his justice being merciful ; but God in giving his only Son into the world, more abundantly shewed his *mercy and justice kissing one another.* His *justice* that every soul that sins should die ; but his *mercy* desires not the death of a sinner.   Ezekiel xxxiii. 11 . . . . . .

2. Righteousness and peace meet together *in man ;* so Augustine expounds it : an unjust man is full of quarrels, like Ishmael, " every man's hand is against him, and his hand against every man " ; but he who is righteous, and giveth every man his due, shall have peace, so much as is possible with all men, especially with his own self and soul.   Righteousness and peace are so near, so dear, that thou canst not have the one without the other.

3. Righteousness and peace meet *in Christ,* God's man ; for by these two, some divines understand the Old Testament and the New.   The Law doth exact *justice,* requiring of a malefactor " eye for eye, tooth for tooth, hand for hand, foot for foot ; " but the Gospel is full of *mercy* and *peace,* saying unto the sinner, who truly repenteth him of his sins, and unfeignedly believes the word of promise, " Son, be of good comfort, thy sins are forgiven thee ; " " Daughter, be of good cheer, thy faith hath made thee whole ; " " Go thy way, thy belief hath saved thee ; " " Behold, thou art now made whole, sin no more."   These two testaments meet together in Christ, as in their proper centre, they "*kissed each other* " on this [Christmas] day, because the gospel performed what the law promised.—*John Boys.*

Verse 10.—When our Lord spake that parable of the prodigal son, and represented the Father as seeing his child afar off in his misery, and how he had compassion on him, and ran and fell on his neck and kissed him, one cannot but feel what a touching and tender illustration he has given of this most exquisite passage of his own word : " Mercy and truth are met together ; righteousness and peace have kissed each other."—*Barton Bouchier.*

Verses 10, 11.—Mercy and Peace, if they had met, or Truth and Righteousness, either of the two, it had not been strange.   But for these that seem to be in opposition to do it, that makes this meeting marvellous in our eyes.

Will you stay a little and take a view of the parties ?   Four they are.   These four, 1. Mercy, and 2. Truth, 3. Righteousness, and 4. Peace.   Which quaternion at the first sight divides itself into two and two.   Mercy and Peace, they two pair well ;   they be *collectaneæ,* as Bernard saith of them in one place, ' bed-fellows,' sleep together ; *collactaneæ,* as in another place, ' sucked one milk, one breast ' both.   And as these two, so the other two, Truth and Righteousness seem to be of one complexion and disposition, and commonly take part together.   Of these Mercy seems to favour us ;   and Peace no enemy to us or to any (seeing we must speak of them as of persons) ;   mild and gentle persons both.   For Righteousness I know not well what to say : *gestat gladium,* (bears the sword), and I fear *non frustra* (not in vain).   Nor of Truth, who is *vera* and *severa,* ' severe ' too otherwhile.   These I doubt are not like affected.   The reason of my doubt.   One of them, Righteousness, it is told here for great news, that she but " looked down hitherwards from heaven." Before then she would not have done that.   A great sign it is of heart-burning, when one will not do so much as look at another—not endure his sight.   We cannot promise ourselves much of her.   No, nor of Truth.   One was so bold in a place to say, *omnis homo mendax* (Rom. iii. 4), and feared no challenge for it.   By that it seems all stands not well with her neither.   So then two for us, two against us.

For their order.   Mercy is first, and Peace last.   With both ends we shall do well enough.   God sends us to do but so with the midst !   Yet this is not amiss that they which favour us less are in the midst ;   hemmed in on both sides, closed about with those that wish us well ;   and they between us and them.   On the one side, Mercy before ;   on the other, Peace behind another ;   that in this double meeting Mercy sorts not herself, goes not to Righteousness ;   nor Righteousness to her, but to Peace.   A kind of cross meeting, as it were, there is—the better hope of accord. Mercy and Righteousness have no symbolizing quality at all, no hope of them ; but Truth with Mercy hath.   There is truth as well in the promise of Mercy as in the threat of justice.—*Lancelot Andrewes.*

Verse 11.—"*Truth shall spring.*"   The literal sense is, that the promises which for a long time are not fulfilled, and seem like seeds or roots hidden and concealed under ground, when they shall be fulfilled, shall be considered to spring up, to grow, etc.—*Lorinus.*

Verse 11.—"*Spring.*" The Metaphor is taken from flowers and trees. In the Greek the expression is ἀνεῖλε, that is, *has sprung* like the morning, for ἀνατέλλω and ἀνατολή are properly said of the rising of the sun and moon.—*Le Blanc.*

Verse 11.—"*Shall look down.*" This *looking down*, השׁקיף rendered generally παρακύπτω in the Greek, implies such a look as in 1 Pet. i. 12, angels give into the things of salvation, and such a look as the disciples gave into the sepulchre. It is really the *Righteous One* who is resting over them in complacent love, not as in Psa. xiv. 2, and liii. 2, but fulfilling Ps. cii. 19, 20.—*Andrew A. Bonar.*

Verse 12.—It has sometimes been objected that the Christian doctrine of a Millennium cannot be true, for the earth could not support the teeming millions that would naturally be found upon it, if wars and vices should cease to waste its population. But omitting other and pertinent answers that have been given, we find one here that covers the whole ground, *the earth shall yield her increase.* Now and then the season is unusually propitious, and we have a specimen of what God can do when he chooses. He can without any miracle make it many times more fruitful than it has ever been.—*William S. Plumer.*

Verse 13.—"*Righteousness shall go before him,*" etc. The meaning of this difficult verse may probably be as follows :—Righteousness shall go before Him (Jehovah), and shall make his footsteps a pathway for his servants to walk in.—*Ernest Hawkins.*

Verse 13.—"*Shall set us in the way of his steps.*" It is reported in the Bohemian History, that St. Wenceslaus, their king, one winter night going to his devotions, in a remote church, barefooted in the snow and sharpness of unequal and pointed ice, his servant Podavivus who waited upon his master's piety, and endeavoured to imitate his affections, began to faint through the violence of the snow and cold ; till the king commanded him to follow him, and set his feet in the same footsteps, which his feet should mark for him : the servant did so, and either fancied a cure, or found one ; for he followed his prince, helped forward with shame and zeal to his imitation, and by the forming footsteps for him in the snow. In the same manner does the blessed Jesus ; for, since our way is troublesome, obscure, full of objection and danger, apt to be mistaken, and to affright our industry, he commands us to mark his footsteps, to tread where his feet have stood, and not only invites us forward by the argument of his example, but he hath trodden down much of the difficulty, and made the way easier and fit for our feet. For he knows our infirmities, and himself hath felt their experience in all things but in the neighbourhood of sin ; and therefore he hath proportioned a way and a path to our strength and capacities, and, like Jacob, hath marched softly and in evenness with the children and the cattle, to entertain us by the comforts of his company, and the influence of a perpetual guide.—*Jeremy Taylor.*

Verse 13 (last clause).—The sinner who feels his need of salvation, is *set—in the way of his steps ;* as Bartimæus sat by the way-side begging, by which way Jesus walked ; and when he came where he was, heard his prayer, and restored him his sight.—*Adam Clarke.*

HINTS TO PREACHERS.

Verse 1.—There is, I. Captivity. 1. Of the people of God. 2. Although they are the people of God. 3. Because they are the people of God. "You only have I known," etc. II. Restoration from Captivity : "Thou hast brought back," etc. 1. The fact. 2. The Author : "Thou : by thine own power ; in thine own manner ; at thine own time. III. The cause of the Restoration ; the favour of God : "Thou hast been favourable." 1. On account of favour past. "Thou hast." 2. On account of favour in reserve.

Verse 2.—I. The subjects of forgiveness : "Thy people." 1. By choice. 2. By redemption. 3 By effectual calling. II. The time of forgiveness : "Thou hast forgiven," etc. III. The method of forgiveness. 1. Forgiven. Heb. borne, same word as in Lev. xvi. 22 : "The goat shall bear upon him all their iniquities." 2. Covered ; as the mercy seat covered the law that had been broken. IV. The extent of forgiveness : "*all* their sin."

Verse 3.—I. The language of penitence. It is implied here that the wrath was, 1. Great : 2. Just : *"thy* wrath." II. The language of faith. 1. In the grace of pardon : " Thou hast turned away wrath." We could not, by anything we could do or suffer. 2. In the method of pardon : " Turned away." Turned it from us to our Surety. III. The language of praise : " Thou hast—thou hast."

Verse 4.—I. In what salvation consists. 1. In the removal of God's enmity from us. 2. In the removal of our enmity to him. II. By whom it is accomplished. By the God of salvation. 1. He causes his anger toward us to cease, and 2. Our anger toward him. III. How is it obtained ? By prayer : " Turn us," etc.

Verse 6.—I. Revivals imply decline. 1. That there is grace to be revived. 2. That this grace has declined. II. Revivals are from God : " Wilt not thou," etc. : they cannot be got up by men. III. Revivals are frequently needed : " Wilt not thou revive us *again.*" IV. Revivals are in answer to prayer : " Wilt thou not," etc. V. Revivals are occasions for great joy. 1. *To* the saints. 2. *In* God.

Verse 7.—I. Salvation is God's work : " Thy salvation." 1. The plan is his. 2. The provision is his. 3. The condition is his. 4. The application is his. 5. The consummation is his. II. Salvation is God's gift. 1. Of his mercy : " Show us thy mercy." 2. Of his grace : " Grant us," etc. III. Salvation is God's answer to prayer. 1. It is the first object of prayer. 2. It includes every other.

Verse 8.—I. We should look for an answer to prayer. Having spoken to God, we should hear what he has to say to us in reply. 1. In his word. 2. In his providence. 3. By his Spirit in our own souls. II. We should look for an answer of peace : " He will speak peace." III. We should avoid whatever might deprive us of that peace : " But let them not turn," etc.

Verse 10.—I. The attributes displayed in man's salvation. 1. Mercy in the promise. 2. Truth in its fulfilment. 3. Righteousness in the manner of its fulfilment. 4. Peace in its results. II. These attributes harmonized in man's salvation. 1. How ? " Met together—kissed each other." 2. Why ? Each on its own account. All on each others' account. 3. Where ? Met and kissed, (1.) In the covenant. (2.) At the incarnation. (3.) At the cross. (4.) At the conversion of every sinner. (5.) At the completion of the saints in heaven.

Verse 12.—I. All spiritual good is from God : " The Lord will give," etc. 1. Is repentance a good thing ? The Lord will give repentance. 2. Is pardon ? " The Lord," etc. 3. Is faith ? 4. Is justification ? 5. Is regeneration ? 6. Is growth in grace ? 7. Is preservation unto the end ? 8. Is eternal glory ? " The Lord will give," etc. II. All temporal good is from God. " Our land," etc. 1. In a lawful manner *our* land. 2. In the use of appointed means : " Shall yield her increase," etc. 3. In dependance upon the divine blessing. " Who giveth fruitful seasons," etc. Spiritual good is not less given in the use of appointed means.

Verse 13.—I. The righteousness by which we are justified long precedes our justification : this righteousness is " gone before," etc. II. Our justification by that righteousness precedes our sanctification. III. The righteousness of sanctification invariably follows that of justification.

[*All the above are by the Rev. Geo. Rogers.*]

Verse 8.—*Thomas Goodwin* has three sermons upon this verse, (*First clause*), entitled The Return of Prayers. (*Second clause*).—Tidings of Peace. (*Last clause*).— The Folly of Relapsing after Peace spoken.

Verse 8 (*last clause*).—They should not turn again to folly, I. Because it will be a greater aggravation in sinning. It is made the aggravation of Solomon's sin (1 Kings xi. 9), that " God had appeared to him twice." II. The second reason is intimated in the word *"folly :* " as if the Lord should have said, Set aside the unkindness and wrong you do to me, yet therein you befool yourselves ; you will have the worst of it.—*T.* Goodwin.

Verse 6.—Joy in the Lord the best evidence of revived piety.

Verse 12.—The fertility of our spheres of labour the gift of God.

Verse 10.—The Pulpit, vol. XXVIII, 1836, contains a sermon by R. W. Sibthorpe, in which the preacher, I. Considers the harmony of the divine perfections in *the redemption of a sinner.* II. The wisdom of the divine dealings in *the calling and guidance of the believer* ; so that mercy, truth, etc., each becomes in turn conspicuous in our experience. III. The completeness of the divine image *in the sanctified soul* so that the perfected saint abounds in mercy and truth, is filled with peace, and is conformed to his righteous Lord.

PSALM LXXXVI.

TITLE.—A Prayer of David. *We have here one of the five Psalms entitled* Tephillahs *or prayers. This Psalm consists of praise as well as prayer, but it is in all parts so directly addressed to God that it is most fitly called "a prayer." A prayer is none the less but all the more a prayer because veins of praise run through it. This Psalm would seem to ha e been specially known as David's prayer ; even as the ninetieth is " the prayer of Moses." David composed it, and no doubt often expressed himself in similar language ; both the matter and the wording are suitable to his varied circumstances and expressive of the different characteristics of his mind. In many respects it resembles Psalm XVII., which bears the same title, but in other aspects it is very different ; the prayers of a good man have a family likeness, but they vary as much as they agree. We may learn from the present Psalm that the great saints of old were accustomed to pray very much in the same fashion as we do ; believers in all ages are of one genus. The name of God occurs very frequently in this Psalm, sometimes it is Jehovah, but more commonly Adonai, which it is believed by many learned scholars was written by the Jewish transcribers instead of the sublimer title, because their superstitious dread led them to do so : we, labouring under no such tormenting fear, rejoice in Jehovah, our God. It is singular that those who were so afraid of their God, that they dared not write his name, had yet so little godly fear, that they dared to alter his word.*

DIVISION.—*The Psalm is irregular in its construction but may be divided into three portions, each ending with a note of gratitude or of confidence : we shall therefore read from 1 to 7, and then, after another pause at the end of verse 13, we will continue to the end.*

EXPOSITION.

BOW down thine ear, O LORD, hear me : for I *am* poor and needy.

2 Preserve my soul ; for I *am* holy : O thou my God, save thy servant that trusteth in thee.

3 Be merciful unto me, O Lord : for I cry unto thee daily.

4 Rejoice the soul of thy servant : for unto thee, O Lord, do I lift up my soul.

5 For thou, Lord, *art* good, and ready to forgive ; and plenteous in mercy unto all them that call upon thee.

6 Give ear, O LORD, unto my prayer ; and attend to the voice of my supplications.

7 In the day of my trouble I will call upon thee : for thou wilt answer me.

1. *"Bow down thine ear, O LORD, hear me."* In condescension to my littleness, and in pity to my weakness, " bow down thine ear, O LORD." When our prayers are lowly by reason of our humility, or feeble by reason of our sickness, or without wing by reason of our despondency, the Lord will bow down to them, the infinitely exalted Jehovah will have respect unto them. Faith, when she has the loftiest name of God on her tongue, and calls him Jehovah, yet dares to ask from him the most tender and condescending acts of love. Great as he is he loves his children to be bold with him. *"For I am poor and needy "*—doubly a son of poverty, because, first, poor and without supply for my needs, and next, needy, and so full of wants though unable to supply them. Our distress is a forcible reason for our being heard by the Lord God, merciful, and gracious, for misery is ever the master argument with mercy. Such reasoning as this would never be adopted by a proud man, and when we hear it repeated in the public congregation by those great ones of the earth who count the peasantry to be little better than the earth they tread upon, it sounds like a mockery of the Most High. Of all despicable sinners those are the worst who use the language of spiritual poverty while they think themselves to be rich and increased in goods.

2. *"Preserve my soul."* Let my life be safe from my enemies, and my spiritual nature be secure from their temptations. He feels himself unsafe except he be covered by the divine protection. *"For I am holy."* I am set apart for holy uses, therefore do not let thine enemies commit a sacrilege by injuring or defiling me : I am clear of the crimes laid to my charge, and in that sense innocent ; therefore, I beseech thee, do not allow me to suffer from unjust charges : and I am inoffensive, meek, and gentle towards others, therefore deal mercifully with me as I have dealt with my fellow men. Any of these renderings may explain the text, perhaps all together will expound it best. It is not self-righteous in good men to plead their innocence as a reason for escaping from the results of sins wrongfully ascribed to them ; penitents do not bedaub themselves with mire for the love of it, or make themselves out to be worse than they are out of compliment to heaven. No, the humblest saint is not a fool, and he is as well aware of the matters wherein he is clear as of those wherein he must cry *"peccavi."* To plead guilty to offences we have never committed is as great a lie as the denial of our real faults. *"O thou my God, save thy servant that trusteth in thee."* Lest any man should suppose that David trusted in his own holiness he immediately declared his trust in the Lord, and begged to be saved as one who was not holy in the sense of being perfect, but was even yet in need of the very elements of salvation. How sweet is that title, " my God," when joined to the other, " servant ; " and how sweet is the hope that on this ground we shall be saved ; seeing that our God is not like the Amalekitish master who left his poor sick servant to perish. Note how David's poor *I am* (or rather the *I* repeated without the *am*) appeals to the great I AM with that sacred boldness engendered by the necessity which breaks through stone walls, aided by the faith which removes mountains.

3. *"Be merciful unto me, O Lord."* The best of men need mercy, and appeal to mercy, yea to nothing else but mercy ; they need it for themselves, and crave it eagerly of their God as a personal requisite. *"For I cry unto thee daily."* Is there not a promise that importunity shall prevail ? May we not, then, plead our importunity as an argument with God. He who prays every day, and all the day, for so the word may mean, may rest assured that the Lord will hear him in the day of his need. If we cried sometimes to man, or other false confidences, we might expect to be referred to them in the hour of our calamity, but if in all former time we have looked to the Lord alone, we may be sure that he will not desert us now. See how David pleaded, first that he was poor and needy, next that he was the Lord's set-apart one, then that he was God's servant and had learned to trust in the Lord, and lastly that he had been taught to pray daily ; surely these are such holy pleadings as any tried believer may employ when wrestling with a prayer-hearing God, and with such weapons the most trembling suppliant may hope to win the day.

4. *"Rejoice the soul of thy servant."* Make my heart glad, O my Master, for I count it my honour to call myself again and again thy servant, and I reckon thy favour to be all the wages I could desire. I look for all my happiness in thee only, and therefore *"unto thee, O Lord, do I lift up my soul."* As the heliotrope looks to the sun for its smile, so turn I my heart to thee. Thou art as the brazen serpent to my sick nature, and I lift up my soul's eye to thee that I may live. I know that the nearer I am to thee the greater is my joy, therefore be pleased to draw me nearer while I am labouring to draw near. It is not easy to lift a soul at all ; it needs a strong shoulder at the wheel when a heart sticks in the miry clay of despondency : it is less easy to lift a soul up to the Lord, for the height is great as well as the weight oppressive ; but the Lord will take the will for the deed, and come in with a hand of almighty grace to raise his poor servant out of the earth and up to heaven.

5. *"For thou, Lord, art good, and ready to forgive."* Good at giving and forgiving; supplying us with *his* good, and removing *our* evil. Here was the great reason why the Psalmist looked to the Lord alone for his joy, because every joy-creating attribute is to be found in perfection in Jehovah alone. Some men who would be considered good are so self-exaltingly indignant at the injuries done them by others, that they cannot forgive ; but we may rest assured that the better a being is, the more willing he is to forgive, and the best and highest of all is ever ready to blot out the transgressions of his creatures. *"And plenteous in mercy unto all them that call upon thee."* God does not dispense his mercy from a slender store which perchance may be so impoverished as to give out altogether, but out of a cornucopia he pours forth the infinite riches of his mercy : his goodness flows forth in abounding streams

towards those who pray and in adoring worship make mention of his name. David seems to have stood in the cleft of the rock with Moses, and to have heard the name of the Lord proclaimed even as the great lawgiver did, for in two places in this Psalm he almost quotes *verbatim* the passage in Exodus xxxiv. 6—"The Lord God, merciful and gracious, longsuffering, and abundant in goodness and truth."

6. *"Give ear, O Lord, unto my prayer."* Even the glory which his spirit had beheld did not withdraw him from his prayer, but rather urged him to be more fervent in it ; hence he implores the Lord to hear his requests. *"Attend to the voice of my supplications."* Here are repetitions, but not vain repetitions. When a child cries it repeats the same note, but it is equally in earnest every time, and so was it with the suppliant here. Note the expression, " the voice of my supplications," as if they were not all voice but were partly made up of inarticulate noise, yet amid much that was superfluous there really was a distinct voice, an inner meaning, a living sense which was the heart's intention. This he would have the Lord sift out from the chaff, and hear amid the mingled din. May our prayers never be voiceless ; may the soul's intent always give them a live core of meaning.

7. *"In the day of my trouble I will call upon thee : for thou wilt answer me."* A pious resolve backed by a judicious reason. It is useless to cry to those who cannot or will not hear ; once convince men that prayer has no effect upon God, and they will have no more of it. In these busy days, and especially in troublous times, men cannot afford to waste time in entreaties which must be unavailing. Our experience confirms us in the belief that Jehovah the living God really does aid those who call upon him, and therefore we pray and mean to pray, not because we are so fascinated by prayer that for its own sake we would continue in it if it proved to be mere folly and superstition, as vain philosophers assert ; but because we really, indeed, and of a truth, find it to be a practical and effectual means of obtaining help from God in the hour of need. There can be no reason for praying if there be no expectation of the Lord's answering. Who would make a conscience of pleading with the winds, or find a solace in supplicating the waves ? The mercy seat is a mockery if there be no hearing nor answering. David, as the following verses show, believed the Lord to be a living and potent God, and indeed to be " God alone," and it was on that account that he resolved in every hour of trouble to call upon him.

8 Among the gods *there is* none like unto thee, O Lord ; neither *are there any works* like unto thy works.

9 All nations whom thou hast made shall come and worship before thee, O Lord ; and shall glorify thy name.

10 For thou *art* great, and doest wondrous things : thou *art* God alone.

11 Teach me thy way, O Lord ; I will walk in thy truth : unite my heart to fear thy name.

12 I will praise thee, O Lord my God, with all my heart : and I will glorify thy name for evermore.

13 For great *is* thy mercy toward me : and thou hast delivered my soul from the lowest hell.

8. *"Among the gods there is none like unto thee, O Lord."* There are gods by delegated office, such as kings and magistrates, but they are as nothing in the presence of Jehovah ; there are also gods by the nomination of superstition, but these are vanity itself, and cannot be compared with the living and true God. Even if the heathen idols were gods, none of them in power or even in character, could be likened unto the self-existent, all-creating God of Israel. If every imaginary deity could start into actual existence, and become really divine, yet would we choose Jehovah to be our God, and reject all others. *"Neither are there any works like unto thy works."* What have the false gods ever made or unmade ? What miracles have they wrought ? When did they divide a sea, or march through a wilderness scattering bread from the skies ? O Jehovah, in thy person and in thy works, thou art as far above all gods as the heavens are above the nethermost abyss.

9. *"All nations whom thou hast made,"* and these include all mankind, since they all come of the first Adam—thy creature, and their lives are all distinct creations of thine omnipotence. All these *"shall come"* with penitent hearts, in thine own way, to thine own self, *"and worship before thee, O Lord."* Because thou art thus

above all gods, the people who have been so long deceived shall at last discover thy greatness, and shall render thee the worship which is thy due : thou hast created them all, and unto thee shall they all yield homage.   This was David's reason for resorting to the Lord in trouble, for he felt that one day all men would acknowledge the Lord to be the only God.   It makes us content to be in the minority to-day, when we are sure that the majority will be with us to-morrow, ay, and that the truth will one day be carried unanimously and heartily.   David was not a believer in the theory that the world will grow worse and worse, and that the dispensation will wind up with general darkness, and idolatry.   Earth's sun is to go down amid tenfold night if some of our prophetic brethren are to be believed.   Not so do we expect, but we look for a day when the dwellers in all lands shall learn righteousness, shall trust in the Saviour, shall worship thee alone, O God, *"and shall glorify thy name."*   The modern notion has greatly damped the zeal of the church for missions, and the sooner it is shown to be unscriptural the better for the cause of God.   It neither consorts with prophecy, honours God, nor inspires the church with ardour. Far hence be it driven.

10. *"For thou art great."*   He had before said, "thou art good;" it is a grand thing when greatness and goodness are united ; it is only in the Divine Being that either of them exists absolutely, and essentially.   Happy is it for us that they both exist in the Lord to an equal degree.   To be great and not good might lead to tyranny in the King, and for him to be good and not great might involve countless calamities upon his subjects from foreign foes, so that either alternative would be terrible ; let the two be blended, and we have a monarch in whom the nation may rest and rejoice.   *"And doest wondrous things."*   Being good, he is said to be ready to forgive ; being great, he works wonders : we may blend the two, for there is no wonder so wonderful as the pardon of our transgressions.   All that God does or makes has wonder in it ; he breathes, and the wind is mystery ; he speaks, and the thunder astounds us ; even the commonest daisy is a marvel, and a pebble enshrines wisdom. Only to fools is anything which God has made uninteresting : the world is a world of wonders.   Note that the verb *doest* is in the present, the Lord is doing wondrous things, they are transpiring before our eyes.   Where are they ?   Look upon the bursting buds of spring or the maturing fruits of autumn, gaze on the sky or skim the sea, mark the results of providence and the victories of grace, everywhere at all times the great *Thaumaturge* stretches forth his rod of power.   *"Thou art God alone."*   Alone wast thou God before thy creatures were ; alone in godhead still art thou now that thou hast given life to throngs of beings ; alone for ever shalt thou be, for none can ever rival thee.   True religion makes no compromises, it does not admit Baal or Dagon to be a god ; it is exclusive and monopolizing, claiming for Jehovah nothing less than all.   The vaunted liberality of certain professors of modern thought is not to be cultivated by believers in the truth.   "Philosophic breadth" aims at building a Pantheon, and piles a Pandemonium ; it is not for us to be helpers in such an evil work.   Benevolently intolerant, we would, for the good of mankind, as well as for the glory of God, undeceive mankind as to the value of their compromises,—they are mere treason to truth.   Our God is not to be worshipped as one among many good and true beings, but as God alone ; and his gospel is not to be preached as one of several saving systems, but as the one sole way of salvation.   Lies can face each other beneath one common dome ; but in the temple of truth the worship is one and indivisible.

11. *"Teach me thy way, O LORD."*   Instruct me thus at all times, let me live in thy school ; but teach me now especially since I am in trouble and perplexity. Be pleased to shew me the way which thy wisdom and mercy have prepared for my escape ; behold I lay aside all wilfulness, and only desire to be informed as to thy holy and gracious mind.   Not *my* way give me, but *thy* way teach me, I would follow thee and not be wilful.   *"I will walk in thy truth."*   When taught I will practise what I know, truth shall not be a mere doctrine or sentiment to me, but a matter of daily life.   The true servant of God regulates his walk by his master's will, and hence he never walks deceitfully, for God's way is ever truth.   Providence has a way for us, and it is our wisdom to keep in it.   We must not be as the bullock which needs to be driven and urged forward because it likes not the road, but be as men who voluntarily go where their trusted friend and helper appoints their path.

"Unite my heart to fear thy name."   Having taught me one way, give me one heart to walk therein, for too often I feel a heart and a heart, two natures contending,

two principles struggling for sovereignty. Our minds are apt to be divided between a variety of objects, like trickling streamlets which waste their force in a hundred runnels ; our great desire should be to have all our life-floods poured into one channel and to have that channel directed towards the Lord alone. A man of divided heart is weak, the man of one object is *the* man. God who created the bands of our nature can draw them together, tighten, strengthen, and fasten them, and so braced and inwardly knit by his uniting grace, we shall be powerful for good, but not otherwise. To fear God is both the beginning, the growth, and the maturity of wisdom, therefore should we be undividedly given up to it, heart, and soul.

12. "*I will praise thee, O Lord my God, with all my heart.*" When my heart is one, I will give thee all of it. Praise should never be rendered with less than all our heart, and soul, and strength, or it will be both unreal and unacceptable. This is the second time in the Psalm that David calls the Lord " my God," the first time he was in an agony of prayer (verse 2), and now he is in an ecstacy of praise. If anything can make a man pray and praise, it is the knowledge that the Lord is his God. "*And I will glorify thy name for evermore ;* " into eternity gratitude will prolong its praise. God has never done blessing us, let us never have done blessing him. As he ever gives us grace, let us ever render to him the glory of it.

13. "*For great is thy mercy toward me.*" Personal experience is ever the master singer. Whatever thou art to others, to me thy mercy is most notable. The Psalmist claims to sing among the loudest, because his debt to divine mercy is among the greatest. "*And thou hast delivered my soul from the lowest hell.*" From the direst death and the deepest dishonour David had been kept by God, for his enemies would have done more than send him to hell had they been able. His sense of sin also made him feel as if the most overwhelming destruction would have been his portion had not grace prevented, therefore does he speak of deliverance from the nethermost abode of lost spirits. There are some alive now who can use this language unfeignedly, and he who pens these lines most humbly confesses that he is one. Left to myself to indulge my passions, to rush onward with my natural vehemence, and defy the Lord with recklessness of levity, what a candidate for the lowest abyss should I have made myself by this time. For me, there was but one alternative, great mercy, or the lowest hell. With my whole heart do I sing, " Great is thy mercy towards me, and thou hast delivered my soul from the lowest hell."

The Psalmist here again touches a bold and joyful note, but soon he exchanges it for the mournful string.

14 O God, the proud are risen against me, and the assemblies of violent *men* have sought after my soul ; and have not set thee before them.

15 But thou, O Lord, *art* a God full of compassion, and gracious, long-suffering, and plenteous in mercy and truth.

16 O turn unto me, and have mercy upon me ; give thy strength unto thy servant, and save the son of thine handmaid.

17 Shew me a token for good ; that they which hate me may see *it*, and be ashamed : because thou, LORD, hast holpen me, and comforted me.

14. "*O God, the proud are risen against me.*" They could not let God's poor servant alone, his walk with God was as smoke to their eyes, and therefore they determined to destroy him. None hate good men so fiercely as do the high-minded and domineering. "*And the assemblies of violent men have sought after my soul.*" Unitedly oppressors sought the good man's life ; they hunted in packs, with keen scent, and eager foot. In persecuting times many a saint has used these words in reference to Papal bishops and inquisitors. "*And have not set thee before them.*" They would not have molested the servant if they had cared one whit for the master. Those who fear not God are not afraid to commit violent and cruel acts. An atheist is a misanthrope. Irreligion is akin to inhumanity.

15. "*But thou, O Lord.*" What a contrast ! We get away from the hectorings and blusterings of proud but puny men to the glory and goodness of the Lord. We turn from the boisterous foam of chafing waves to the sea of glass mingled with fire, calm and serene. "*Art a God full of compassion, and gracious, longsuffering, and plenteous in mercy and truth.*" A truly glorious doxology, in which there is not one redundant word. As we have before observed, it is mainly transcribed from Exodus xxxiv. 6. Here is compassion for the weak and sorrowing, grace for

the undeserving, longsuffering for the provoking, mercy for the guilty, and truth for the tried. God's love assumes many forms, and is lovely in them all. Into whatsoever state we may be cast, there is a peculiar hue in the light of love which will harmonize with our condition; love is one and yet sevenfold, its white ray contains the chromatic scale. Are we sorrowful? We find the Lord full of compassion. Are we contending with temptation? His grace comes to our aid. Do we err? He is patient with us. Have we sinned? He is plenteous in mercy. Are we resting on his promise? He will fulfil it with abundant truth.

16. *"O turn unto me."* As though the face of God had been before averted in anger, the suppliant pleads for a return of conscious favour. One turn of God's face will turn all our darkness into day. *"And have mercy upon me,"* that is all he asks, for he is lowly in heart; that is all he wants, for mercy answereth all a sinner's needs. *"Give thy strength unto thy servant."* Gird me with it that I may serve thee, guard me with it that I may not be overcome. When the Lord gives us his own strength we are sufficient for all emergencies, and have no cause to fear any adversaries. *"And save the son of thine handmaid."* He meant that he was a home-born servant of God. As the sons of slaves were their master's property by their birth, so he gloried in being the son of a woman who herself belonged to the Lord. What others might think a degrading illustration he uses with delight, to show how intensely he loved the Lord's service; and also as a reason why the Lord should interpose to rescue him, seeing that he was no newly-purchased servant, but had been in the house from his very birth.

17. *"Shew me a token for good."* Let me be assured of thy mercy by being delivered out of trouble. *"That they which hate me may see it, and be ashamed."*

> " Some token of thy favour show,
>   Some sign which all my foes may see;
> And fill'd with blank confusion know,
>   My comfort and my help in thee."

What bodes good to me shall make them quail and blush. Disappointed and defeated, the foes of the good man would feel ashamed of what they had designed. *"Because thou, Lord, hast holpen me, and comforted me."* God doth nothing by halves, those whom he helps he also consoles, and so makes them not merely safe but joyful. This makes the foes of the righteous exceedingly displeased, but it brings to the Lord double honour. Lord, deal thou thus with us evermore, so will we glorify thee, world without end. Amen.

EXPLANATORY NOTES AND QUAINT SAYINGS.

Title.—The prophet David has penned two Psalms which he has eminently appropriated to himself as his own: the one is styled *David's prayer*, though many other Psalms are prayers—it is Psalm lxxxvi.; the other *David's praise.* Ps. cxlv. The first his *tephilla*, the latter his *tehilla;* in each of these he makes a solemn rehearsal of the very words of Moses, in Exodus xxxiv. 6, 7. In Psalm lxxxvi. he brings them in as they were a support unto his faith in his distresses from sins and miseries, to which use he puts them, ver. 3, 4, 6, and 7. And again, ver. 16, 17, he makes a plea of these words by way of prayer. In Psalm cxlv., he brings them in as they are an *elogium* or celebration of the glorious nature and excellencies of God, to excite the sons of men to love and praise him.—*Thomas Goodwin.*

Title.—This Psalm was published under the title of *"A Prayer of David "*; not as if David sung all his prayers, but into some of his songs he inserted prayers; for a Psalm will admit the expression of any pious and devout affections. But it is observable how very plain the language of this Psalm is, and how little there is in it of poetical flights or figures, in comparison with some other Psalms; for the flourishes of wit are not the proper ornaments of prayer.—*Matthew Henry.*

Title.—There was much, very much, of God's peculiar character, his glorious name, brought to view in the close of the last Psalm. This may account for its being followed by another, "*A Prayer of David,*" almost equally full of the character of Jehovah. The key-note of this Psalm is Jehovah's name.—*Andrew A. Bonar.*

Whole Psalm.—Christ prays throughout the whole of this Psalm. All the words are spoken exclusively by Christ, who is both God and man.—*Psalt. Cassiodori,* 1491.

Whole Psalm.—In this Psalm Christ the Son of God and Son of Man, one God with the Father, one man with men, to whom we pray as God ; prays in the form of a servant. For he prays for us, and he prays in us, and he is prayed to by us. He prays for us as our Priest. He prays in us as our Head. He is prayed to by us as our God.—*Psalt. Pet. Lombard.* 1474.

Verse 1.—"*Bow down thine ear, O Lord.*" As the careful physician doth to his feeble patient : so Basil glosseth here.—*John Trapp.*

Verses 1—4.—"*Poor,*" "*holy,*" "*trusteth,*" "*I cry.*" The petitioner is first described as *poor,* then *holy,* next *trusting,* after that *crying,* finally, *lifted up* to God. And each epithet has its fitting verb ; *bow down* to the poor, *preserve* the holy, *save* the trusting, *be merciful* to him who cries, *rejoice* the lifted-up. It is the whole gamut of love from the Incarnation to the Ascension ; it tells us that Christ's humiliation will be our glory and joy.—*Neale and Littledale's Commentary.*

Verse 2.—"*Holy.*" The word has been variously translated :—*Godly,* De Muis, Ainsworth and others ; *charitable,* or *beneficent,* Piscator ; *merciful* or *tenderhearted,* Mariana ; *diligently* or *earnestly compassionate,* Vatablus ; *meek,* Calvin ; *a beloved one,* Version of American Bible Union ; *one whom thou lovest,* Perowne ; *a devoted or dedicated man,* Weiss.

Verse 2.—"*For I am Holy.*" Some have objected to David's pleading his own good character ; but if he did not go beyond the truth, and the occasion called for it, there was nothing wrong in his so doing. Job, David, Peter, John and Paul all did it, Job xxvii. 5 ; Ps. cxvi. 16 ; John xxi. 15—17 ; Rev. i. 10 ; 1 Cor. ix. 1. Nor is it presumptuous to ask God to show mercy to us for we show it to others ; or to forgive us for we forgive others, Matt. v. 7 ; vi. 14, 15.—*William S. Plumer.*

Verse 2.—"*I am holy . . . thy servant which trusteth in thee.*" They that are holy, yet must not trust in themselves, or in their own righteousness, but only in God and his grace.—*Matthew Henry.*

Verse 2.—"*Save thy servant that trusteth in thee.*" When God saves his servant, he saves what belongs to himself ; and, when he saves him that trusts in him, he shows himself to be just and faithful, in carrying out what he promised.—*Bellarmine.*

Verses 2—5.—The aspirations after holiness which are found in this Psalm, coupled with its earnest invocation of mercy from the God with whom there is forgiveness, render it peculiarly applicable to those whose daily access is to a throne of needed grace. Christians know that while their *standing* is the blameless perfection of the Lord their righteousness, they are in many things offenders still. Nor do we ever fully prove the preciousness of Jesus as our portion, except we are drawn to him by that Spirit which reveals to us a nakedness and poverty within ourselves, which his blessed fulness can alone redress.

There is a consciousness of personal sanctification through faith (verse 2) associated with an acutely sensitive perception of intrinsic worthlessness, such as only finds relief in the remembrance of unaltered grace (verse 5), which, to the exercised spirit of one really growing in the knowledge of God, will address itself with an especial acceptance.—*Arthur Pridham.*

Verse 3.—"*Be merciful unto me.*" Lest any should by the former words, ("*I am holy,*") suspect him to be a merit-monger, he beggeth mercy with instancy and constancy of request.—*John Trapp.*

Verse 3.—"*I cry unto thee daily.*" A great difference between saints and sinners in prayer is that sinners who pray at all, pray only when they are in *trouble,* whereas saints *cry daily* unto God. Compare Job xxvii. 10.—*William S. Plumer.*

Verse 4.—"*Rejoice the soul of thy servant,*" etc. As I have not found rest in anything created, I have raised up my soul on the wings of thought and desire to thee my Creator. Love bears one's soul up ; and it has been truly said, that the soul is more where it loves, than where it actually is. Thought and desire are the wings of love ; for he that loves is borne on to, and abides in, what he loves, by thinking constantly on, and longing for, the object of his love. Whoever truly, and from his heart, loves God, by thinking on him and longing for him, lifts up his soul to God ; while, on the contrary, whoever loves the earth, by thinking on and coveting the things of the earth, lets his soul down to its level.—*Bellarmine*.

Verse 4.—"*Unto thee, O Lord, do I lift my soul.*" If thou hadst corn in thy rooms below, thou wouldst take it up higher, lest it should grow rotten. Wouldest thou remove thy corn, and dost thou suffer thy heart to rot on the earth ? Thou wouldest take thy corn up higher : lift up thy heart to heaven. And how can I, dost thou say ? What ropes are needed ? What machines ? What ladders ? Thy affections are the steps ; thy will the way. By loving thou mountest, by neglect thou descendest. Standing on the earth thou art in heaven, if thou lovest God. For the heart is not so raised as the body is raised : the body to be lifted up changes its place : the heart to be lifted up changes its will.—*Augustine*.

Verse 4.—"*Unto thee, O Lord, do I lift up my soul*," intimates that he had brought himself to the Lord as a living sacrifice, even as the *heave-offering* in the tabernacle— to show that it belonged to God and to his altar, and, that man had no part in it— was lifted up by the hands of the priests.—*Benjamin Weiss*.

Verse 4.—"*I lift up my soul.*" It denotes the devotion, fervency, heartiness, and sincerity of his prayer ; the doing of it with a true heart, the lifting up of the heart with the hands unto God, Lam. iii. 41 ; or by way of offering unto the Lord, not the body only, but the soul or heart also ; or as a deposition committed into his hands.—*John Gill*.

Verse 4.—"*Lord.*" Here, and in all the verses in this psalm where אֲדֹנָי, *Adonai*, occurs, many MSS. read יְהֹוִה, *Yehovah*. The Jews, out of reverence to the incommunicable name Jehovah pronounce אֲדֹנָי where יְהֹוִה is in the text. It is, therefore, not improbable that יְהֹוִה is the true reading in all these places.—*Note to Calvin in loc.*

Verse 5.—"*For thou, Lord, art good,*" and whither should beggars go but to the door of the good house-keeper ?—*Matthew Henry*.

Verse 5.—"*Ready to forgive.*" The mercy of God is a ready mercy, and his pardons are ready for his people ; his pardons and mercies are not to seek, he hath them at hand, he is "*good and ready to forgive.*" Whereas most men, though they will forgive, yet they are not *ready* to forgive, they are hardly brought to it, though they do it at last. But God is "*ready to forgive*" ; he hath, as it were, pardons ready drawn (as a man who would be ready to do a business, he will have such writings as concern the passing of it ready) ; there is nothing to do but to put in the date and the name ; yea indeed, the date and the name are put in from all eternity. Thus the Scripture speaks to show how forward God is to do good ; he needs not set his heart to it ; his heart is ever in the exactest fitness.—*Joseph Caryl*.

Verse 5.—"*Plenteous in mercy.*" It is a thing marvellously satisfactory and pleasing to the heart of a man to be still taking from a great heap ; and upon this ground are those proverbial sayings, There is no fishing like to a fishing in the sea, no service like the service of a king : because in one there is the greatest plenty and abundance of that kind of pleasure that fishers look after ; and for them that serve, and must live by their service, there is none like that of princes, because they have abundance of reward and opportunity whereby to recompense the services of those that do wait and attend upon them. . . .

And upon the same ground is it that the Scriptures, in several places, do not only assert and testify that God is merciful and gracious, but abundant in mercy and full of grace ; and not simply that there is redemption in him, but *plenteousness* of redemption : Ps. ciii. 8, cxxx. 7 ; Isai. lv. 7 ; "Let the wicked forsake his way," etc. ; "Let him return unto the Lord and he will have mercy ; and unto our God, for he will abundantly pardon." The commodity which we stand in need of is mercy and the pardon of our sins, in case we have been unholy and ungodly creatures ; this commodity is abundantly in God. There it is treasured up as waters are in the store-house of the sea ; there is no end of the treasures of his grace, mercy, pardon, and compassion. There is no man, being in want, but had ten times rather go to a rich man's door to be relieved, than to the door of a poor man, if he knoweth the rich man to be as liberal and bountifully disposed as the poor man can be.—*John Goodwin*.

Verse 6.—"*Supplications.*" תַּחֲנוּנֹתָי, *deprecations*. The Psalmist forms a peculiar Hebrew word, feminine plural, not found elsewhere, to convey more impressively the idea of suppliant weakness.—*A. R. Fausset*.

Verses 8—10.—There are two kinds of doubt which are wont in the hour of temptation to assail the soul ; the doubt as to God's *willingness*, and the doubt as to God's *power* to succour. The first of these the Psalmist has already put from him ; he now shows that he has overcome the second. God is able as well as willing to help, and every being on the face of the earth who receives help, receives it from the hand of Him who is the only God, and who shall one day be recognized (so speaks the strong prophetic hope within him, ver. 9) as the only God.—*J. J. S. Perowne.*

Verses 9, 10.—"*All nations shall worship before thee*," because as *King of Nations*, thou art great, thy sovereignty absolute and incontestable, thy Majesty terrible and unsupportable, thy power universal and irresistible, thy riches vast and inexhaustible, thy dominion boundless and unquestionable ; and for the proof of this, "*thou doest wondrous things*," which all nations admire, and from whence they might easily infer that "*thou art God alone ;* " not only none like thee, but none beside thee.—*Matthew Henry.*

Verse 11.—"*Teach me thy way :* " "*I will walk in thy truth : unite my heart.*" Here is the " Via, Veritas, Vita " of the Gospel (John xiv. 6). " Via tua, Veritas tua, Vita tua, Christus." Christ is our Way, Truth, and Life, because he is Man united to God, and is one substance with the Father.—*Christopher Wordsworth.*

Verse 11.—"*Teach me.*" There is no point on which the world is more dark than that of its own ignorance—we might truly say, " it is ignorant of its ignorance " —it knows enough when it learns by rote a few first principles of religion ; it comforts itself that it is not atheistical because it believes that there is a God ; but as to knowing his ways, laws, mind, or any such things, with them it has nothing at all to do. The people of the world do not care for enlightenment ; they feel no pressing need for it ; in all probability they have an instinctive feeling that if enlightened they would know a little more than they wish to know, that their newly-acquired knowledge would interfere with their old habits and ways, and this is one reason why all spiritual teaching which goes beneath the surface is distasteful to the majority of men. They cannot bear to be brought into contact with God, in anything but a general way ; the particulars of his character may not agree over well with the particulars of their lives !

It is the fashion in the present day to talk of man's enlightenment, and to represent human nature as upheaving under its load, as straining towards a knowledge of truth ; such is not in reality the case, and whenever there is an effort in the mind untaught of the Spirit, it is directed towards God as the great *moral* and not as the great *spiritual* Being. A man untaught of the Holy Ghost may long to know a *moral*, he can never desire to know a *spiritual* Being.—*John Hyatt*, 1767–1826.

Verse 11.—"*Teach.*" The common version of the verb here is too vague, as it fails to bring out the peculiar suitableness of the term to express the kind of teaching here specifically meant. The original meaning of the Hebrew word is *to point out* or *mark* the way.—*J. A. Alexander.*

Verse 11.—"*I will walk in thy truth.*" Conform to Scripture. Let us lead Scripture lives. Oh that the Bible might be seen to be printed in our lives ! Do what the Word commands. Obedience is an excellent way of commenting upon the Bible.

Let the Word be the sun-dial by which you set your life. What are we the better for having the Scriptures, if we do not direct all our speeches and actions according to it ? What is a carpenter better for his rule about him, if he sticks it at his back, and never makes use of it for measuring and squaring ? So, what are we the better for the rule of the Word, if we do not make use of it, and regulate our lives by it ?—*Thomas Watson.*

Verse 11.—"*I will walk in thy truth.*" *Walking*, in the Scripture, takes in the whole of our conversation or conduct : and to walk *in* anything, intends a fulness of it. For a man to *walk in* pride, is something more than to be proud : it says, that pride is his way, his element ; that he is wholly under the influence of it.—*William Jay.*

Verse 11.—"*Unite my heart to fear thy name.*" The *end* which he desired to secure was that he might truly fear God, or properly reverence and honour him ; the *means* which he saw to be necessary for this was that his "*heart*" might be "*united*" in this one great object ; that is, that his heart might be single in its views and purposes; that there might be no distracting purposes; that one great aim might be always before him. The *word* rendered *unite*—יַחַד, *yáhhad*—occurs as a verb only in three places. In Gen. xlix. 6 it is rendered *united:* "Unto their assembly, mine honour, be not thou *united*." In Isa. xiv. 20 it is translated *joined:* "Thou shalt not be *joined* unto them." The *adverb*—יַחַד, *ya-hhad*—occurs often, and is rendered *together*, Gen. xiii. 6; xxii. 6, 8, 19; xxxvi. 7; *et sæpe*. The *idea* is that of union, or conjunction; of being together; of constituting *one;* and this is accomplished in the heart when there is one great ruling object before the mind which nothing is allowed to interfere with. It may be added, that there is no more appropriate prayer which a man can offer than that his heart *may* have such unity of purpose, and that nothing may be allowed to interfere with that one supreme purpose.—*Albert Barnes.*

Verse 11.—"*Unite my heart,*" etc. Sincerity drives but one design, and that is to please and enjoy God; and what can more establish and fix the soul in the hour of temptation than this? The reason why the hypocrite is unstable in all his ways, is given us by the apostle: he is "a double-minded man," a man of two souls in one body; as a profane wretch once boasted, that he had one soul for God, and another for any thing. But all the designs of a gracious heart are united in one; and so the entire stream of his affections runs strong.

It is base by-ends and self-interests, that, like a great many ditches cut out of the bank of a river, draw away the stream out of its proper channel, and make its waters fail. But if the heart be *united* for God, then we may say of such a Christian, as was said of a young Roman, "What he does is done with all his might." A man of only one design, puts out all his strength to carry it; nothing can stand before him.

Sincerity brings a man's will into subjection to the will of God; and this being done, the greatest danger and difficulty is over with such a man. This is that holy oil which makes the wheels of the soul run nimbly, even in the difficult paths of obedience.—*John Flavel.*

Verse 11.—"*Unite my heart.*"

> Give me thine heart but as I gave it thee:
>   Or give it me at least as I
>   Have given mine
>   To purchase thine.
> I halv'd it not when I did die;
> But gave myself wholly to set thee free.
>
> The heart I gave thee was a living heart;
>   And when thy heart by sin was slain,
>   I laid down mine
>   To ransom thine,
> That thy dead heart might live again,
> And live entirely perfect, not in part.
>
> But whilst thine heart's divided, it is dead;
>   Dead unto me, unless it live
>   To me alone,
>   It is all one
> To keep all, and a part to give:
> For what's a body worth without an head!
>
> Yet, this is worse, that what thou keep'st from me
>   Thou dost bestow upon my foes;
>   And those not mine
>   Alone, but thine;
> The proper causes of thy woes,
> From whom I gave my life to set thee free.
>
> Have I betroth'd thee to myself, and shall
>   The devil, and the world, intrude
>   Upon my right,
>   E'en in my sight?
> Think not thou canst me so delude:
> I will have none, unless I may have all.

I made it all, I gave it all to thee,
I gave all that I had for it :
If I must lose,
I'd rather choose
Mine interest in all to quit :
Or keep it whole, or give it whole to me.
—*Francis Quarles, in "The School of the Heart."*

Verse 11.—*"Unite my heart to fear thy name."*

In knotts, to be loosed never,
Knitt my heart to thee for ever,
That I to thy name may beare
Fearful love and loving feare.
—*Francis Davison.*

Verse 12.—*"I will praise thee, O Lord my God, with all my heart : and I will glorify thy name."* We glorify God by praising him. Doxology, or praise, is a God-exalting work. Ps. l. 23. *"Whoso offereth praise glorifieth me."* The Hebrew word, *Bara*, to create, and *Barak*, to praise, are little different, because the end of creation is to praise God. Though nothing can add to God's essential glory, yet praise exalts him in the eyes of others. When we praise God, we spread his fame and renown, we display the trophies of his excellency. In this manner the angels glorify him ; they are the choristers of heaven, and do trumpet forth his praise. Praising God is one of the highest and purest acts of religion. In prayer we act like men ; in praise we act like angels. Believers are called "temples of God," 1 Cor. iii. 16. When our tongues praise, then the organs of God's spiritual temple are sounding. How sad it is that God hath no more glory from us in this way ! Many are full of murmuring and discontent, but seldom bring glory to God, by giving him the praise due to his name. We read of the saints having harps in their hands, the emblems of praise. Many have tears in their eyes and complaints in their mouths, but few have harps in their hands, blessing and glorifying God. Let us honour God this way. Praise is the quit-rent we pay to God : while God renews our lease, we must renew our rent.—*Thomas Watson.*

Verse 12.—*"I will praise thee, O Lord,"* etc. Such a soul as David was is enlarged to talk high of God : *"I will praise thee, O Lord my God, with all my heart : and I will glorify thy name for evermore."* Alas ! poor creature, how canst thou praise him *"for evermore"* ? A soul fired with desire to praise God, burns after both more perfect things and more lasting than it is able to perform. "To will is present with it," etc. See but the reachings and longings of such a soul, how it swells in desires to glorify God !—*Thomas Goodwin.*

Verse 12.—*"With all my heart."* When my *heart* is *united* to fear thy name, then shall I praise thee with my whole heart.—*Adam Clarke.*

Verse 13.—*"Hell"* is put metaphorically for great and extreme dangers, or miseries which seem irrecoverable and remediless ; these are figuratively called *hell*, because hell, properly taken, is a place from whence there is no recovery. There's no release from the chains of darkness : all changes are on earth ; heaven and hell know none. When David praises the Lord *for delivering his soul from the lowest hell*, he meaneth an estate on earth of the lowest and deepest danger imaginable : mercy helped him at the worst. To be as low as hell, is to be at the lowest.—*Joseph Caryl.*

Verse 13.—*"The lowest hell."* According to Jewish traditions, there are seven different regions, in the abode of departed souls.—*Daniel Cresswell.*

Verse 13.—*"Thou hast delivered my soul from the lowest hell."* Some one having a troublesome cause was to be sent to prison : another comes and defends him ; what does he say when he thanks him ? Thou hast delivered my soul out of prison. A debtor was to be tortured : his debt is paid ; he is said to be delivered from being tortured. They were not in all these evils ; but because they were in such due course towards them, that unless aid had been brought, they would have been in them, they rightly say that they are delivered from thence, whither they were not suffered by their deliverers to be taken.—*Augustine.*

Verses 13, 16.—There is no stronger argument of God's infallible readiness to grant our requests, than the experience of his former concessions. So David reasons, " The Lord that delivered me out of the paw of the lion, and out of the paw of the bear, he will deliver me out of the hand of this Philistine," 1 Sam. xvii. 37. This is the argument *a priori*, the voice of a strong faith, that persuades the conscience God will be gracious to him, because he hath been gracious. The prophet thus often comforted his soul : " Thou hast enlarged me when I was in distress ; " therefore, " have mercy upon me, and hear my prayer," Ps. iv. 1. So, " Thou hast delivered my soul from the lowest hell ; " therefore, *"O turn unto me, and have mercy upon me."* Let the justiciaries deduce arguments from their own present merits, my soul from God's former mercies. Thou, O Lord, madest me good, restoredst me when I was evil ; therefore have mercy upon me, miserable sinner, and give me thy salvation. Thus Paul grounded his assurance : because the Lord had stood with him, and delivered him out of the lion's mouth ; therefore the Lord shall deliver me still, from every evil work, and preserve me unto his heavenly kingdom, 2 Tim. iv. 17, 18.—*Thomas Adams.*

Verse 15.—"*Thou, O Lord,* Adonai, *art a God ;* El, the strong God, *full of compassion ;* " the same words as Moses useth. Instead of *Jehovah, Adonai* is used, " O Lord ; " but then *El,* strong God, is the same word.

The meaning is, let all the strength and power thou the strong God hast in thee be for my advantage. Now, is it not a bold request to say, Lord, wilt thou give me all thy strength to help me ? A very bold request indeed ; but his mercy moves him to grant it. Thus then petition him : Thou art a God merciful and gracious, give thy strength to me ! Thou, O God, givest all thy attributes up to thy children, to serve their advantage, as well as to serve thy own glory ; give me thy strength !—*Thomas Goodwin.*

Verse 15.—"*Full of compassion."* The original word *Rachum* is very emphatical ; it signifies such tenderness as parents have toward their children when their bowels yearn within them.—"*Critical and Practical Exposition of the Pentateuch."* 1748.

Verse 16.—"*Save the son of thine handmaid."* Deliver me, who am as completely thy property, as the offspring of a female slave born in her master's house, and which belongs of right to him. Gen. xiv. 14 ; Jer. ii. 14.—*William Keatinge Clay.*

Verse 17.—"*Shew me a token for good."* These words do not, as some think, necessarily imply David's asking for some specific or miraculous token : he regards deliverance itself as a token. We ask whether it be not true, that in the same measure as we recognise the mysteriously governing influence of God in every-day events, we regard those things as signs and miracles, which to others appear common-place.?—*Augustus F. Tholuck.*

Verse 17.—Perhaps, the "*token for good* " means that spiritual joy which he asked for in the beginning of the Psalm, when he said, "*Rejoice the soul of thy servant ;* " for such joy to a holy soul in tribulation is the clearest sign of the grace of God, and on the sight of it all manner of persecutors are confounded ; and then the meaning would be, "*shew me a token for good ;* " give me the grace of that spiritual joy that will appear exteriorly in my countenance, "*that they which hate me may see* " such calmness and tranquility of soul, "*and be confounded* " ; for thou, O Lord, hast helped me in the struggle, consoled me in my sorrow, and hast already converted my sadness into interior joy and gladness.—*Robert Bellarmine.*

Verse 17.—"*Shew me a token for good,"* may be rendered " make me a sign for good." Weiss paraphrases it, " make of me such a sign or monument of good that all my enemies may be arrested by it, and be daunted at injuring a man so assisted by the Lord."

Verse 17.—"*Hast holpen me,"* in struggle ; "*and comforted me,"* in sorrow.—*Augustine.*

HINTS TO PREACHERS.

Verse 1.—I. A singular request—that the Lord should bow his ear. II. A singular plea—" I am poor and needy." III. The singular grace of God will answer the request, because singular grace has made the petitioner feel his need.

Verse 2.—I. The blessing sought is present, spiritual, complete and final preservation. II. Our reasons for expecting it are—1. Our belonging to God—" I am holy." 2. God's belonging to us—" my God." 3. Our faith, which has the promises. 4. Our fruits, which prove our faith—" thy servant."

Verse 3.—Importunity. 1. When she pleads—" daily." 2. How she pleads—" I cry." 3. To whom she pleads—" unto thee." 4. For what she pleads—" be merciful."

Verse 3.—" I will cry daily " for pardoning, sanctifying, assisting, preserving, providing and guiding mercy.—*William Jay.*

Verse 4.—I. The believer's joy is from God—" Rejoice," etc. II. The believer's joy is in God—" unto thee," etc.—*G. R.*

Verse 4.—The great lift. I. The heavy weight—" my soul." II. The weak worker — " I lift." III. The great height — " unto thee." IV. The appointed machinery—means of grace ; and, V. The expected aid—" Rejoice," etc.

Verse 5.—Encouraging thoughts of God. 1. He has goodness in his essence. 2. He has forgiveness in readiness. 3. He has mercy in action, flowing forth from him plenteously. 4. His very discrimination is gracious—" all them that call upon him."

Verse 6.—The praying man desires above all things an answer. Objections to such an expectation. Grounds for continuing to expect, and duties incumbent upon those who realise such expectations.

Verse 6.—" The voice of supplication." It is the voice of weakness, of penitence, of faith, of hope, of the new nature, of knowledge, etc.

Verse 7.—1. Help needed. 2. Help sought. 3. Help found.—*G. R.*

Verse 7.—I. A time to be expected—" day of my trouble." II. A resolve to be practised—" I will call upon thee." III. A result to be experienced—" thou wilt answer me."

Verse 7.—Prayer is the design of trouble, the evidence that it is sanctified, its solace, and the medium of deliverance from it.—*William Jay.*

Verse 8.—I. God is one ; the only God : characters of false gods inferior far. II. His works are unique. Nature, providence, grace, all peculiar in many respects. A good theme for a thoughtful preacher.

Verse 9.—The certain conversion of the world as opposed to modern theories.

Verse 10.—I. God is " great," therefore great things may be expected of him. II. He is unsearchable, therefore " wondrous things " may be expected of him. III. He is irresistible, therefore impossibilities to others may be expected of him : " Thou art God alone."—*G. R.*

Verse 11.—In the disposition of mind which is expressed in these words, the believer stands opposed to four descriptions of character. I. The ignorant and thoughtless sinner, who neither regards his way nor his end. II. The Antinomian, who is zealous for doctrines, and averse from the practice of religion. III. The Pharisee, who disregards religious sentiment, and makes practice all in all. IV. The hypocrite, who appears to be divided between religion and the world.—*John Hyatt*, 1811.

Verse 11.—The Christian as a scholar, a man of action, and a man of devotion.

Verse 11.—Holiness taught, truth practised, God adored ; and thus the life perfected.

Verse 11 (middle clause).—We should walk in the belief of the truth, its practice, enjoyment, and profession.—*William Jay.*

Verse 11 (third clause).—The necessity, benefit, and reasonableness of wholeheartedness in religion.

Verse 12.—The art of praising God by heart.

Verse 13.—I. Where I might have been—" the lowest hell." II. What thou hast done for me—" hast delivered." III. What thou art doing—" great is thy mercy."

Verse 13 (first clause).—God's mercy *great* in election, redemption, calling, pardon, upholding, etc. It *is* so, at this very moment, in supplying my needs, preserving from danger, consoling in sorrow, etc. Great is thy mercy *towards me*—so great a sinner, with such needs, so provoking, so full of doubts, etc.

Verses 13, 14, 15.—The three verses describe salvation, consequent persecution, and all-sufficient consolation.

Verse 15.—The shades of the light of love. Compassion upon suffering, grace towards unworthiness, long-suffering to provocation, mercy towards sin, truth towards the promise.

Verse 16.—I. My pedigree—" son of thine handmaid." II. My occupation—" thy servant." III. My character—needing " mercy." IV. My request—" turn unto me."

Verse 16.—In what respects a servant of God may be girt with divine power.

Verse 17.—What inward feelings and outward providences are " tokens for good."

PSALM LXXXVII.

TITLE.—A Psalm or Song for the sons of Korah. *A sacred hymn and a national lyric. A theocracy blends the religious and the patriotic ideas in one; and in proportion as nations become Christianized, their popular songs will become deeply imbued with pious sentiments. Judged by this standard, our own land is far in arrears. This "Psalm or song" was either composed by the sons of Korah, or dedicated to them: as they kept the doors of the house of the Lord, they could use this beautiful composition as a Psalm within the doors, and as a song outside.*

SUBJECT AND DIVISION.—*The song is in honour of Zion, or Jerusalem, and it treats of God's favour to that city among the mountains, the prophecies which made it illustrious, and the honour of being a native of it. Many conceive that it was written at the founding of David's city of Zion, but does not the mention of Babylon imply a later date? It would seem to have been written after Jerusalem and the Temple had been built, and had enjoyed a history, of which glorious things could be spoken. Among other marvels of God's love in its later history, it had been untouched by Sennacherib when other cities of Israel and Judah had fallen victims to his cruelty. It was in Hezekiah's reign that Babylon became prominent, when the ambassadors came to congratulate the king concerning his recovery, at that time also Tyre would be more famous than at any period in David's day. But as we have no information, and the point is not important, we may leave it, and proceed to meditate upon the Psalm itself. We have no need to divide so brief a song.*

EXPOSITION.

HIS foundation *is* in the holy mountains.

2 The LORD loveth the gates of Zion more than all the dwellings of Jacob.

3 Glorious things are spoken of thee, O city of God. Selah.

4 I will make mention of Rahab and Babylon to them that know me: behold Philistia, and Tyre, with Ethiopia; this *man* was born there.

5 And of Zion it shall be said, This and that man was born in her: and the highest himself shall establish her.

6 The LORD shall count, when he writeth up the people, *that* this *man* was born there. Selah.

7 As well the singers as the players on instruments *shall be there*: all my springs *are* in thee.

1. *"His foundation is in the holy mountains."* The Psalm begins abruptly, the poet's heart was full, and it gained vent on a sudden.

> " God's foundation stands for ever
> On the holy mountain towers;
> Sion's gates Jehovah favours
> More than Jacob's thousand bowers."

Sudden passion is evil, but bursts of holy joy are most precious. God has chosen to found his earthly temple upon the mountains; he might have selected other spots, but it was his pleasure to have his chosen abode upon Zion. His election made the mountains holy, they were by his determination ordained and set apart for the Lord's use.

The foundation of the church, which is the mystical Jerusalem, is laid in the eternal, immutable, and invincible decrees of Jehovah. He wills that the church shall be, he settles all arrangements for her calling, salvation, maintenance and perfection, and all his attributes, like the mountains round about Jerusalem, lend their strength for her support. Not on the sand of carnal policy, nor in the morass of human kingdoms, has the Lord founded his church, but on his own power and godhead, which are pledged for the establishment of his beloved church, which is to him the chief of all his works. What a theme for meditation is the founding of the church of God in the ancient covenant engagements of eternity; the abrupt character of this first verse indicates long consideration on the part of the writer, leading up to his bursting forth in wonder and adoration. Well might such a theme cause his heart to glow. Rome stands on her seven hills and has never lacked a poet's tongue to sing her glories, but more glorious far art thou, O Ziona, among the eternal mountains of God: while pen can write or mouth can speak, thy praises shall never lie buried in inglorious silence.

2. *"The Lord loveth the gates of Zion more than all the dwellings of Jacob."* The gates are put for the city itself. The love of God is greatest to his own elect nation, descended from his servant Jacob, yet the central seat of his worship is dearer still; no other supposable comparison could have so fully displayed the favour which Jehovah bore to Jerusalem,—he loves Jacob best and Zion better than the best. At this hour the mystical teaching of these words is plain. God delights in the prayers and praises of Christian families and individuals, but he has a special eye to the assemblies of the faithful, and he has a special delight in their devotions in their church capacity. The great festivals, when the crowds surrounded the temple gates, were fair in the Lord's eyes, and even such is the general assembly and church of the first-born, whose names are written in heaven. This should lead each separate believer to identify himself with the church of God; where the Lord reveals his love the most, there should each believer most delight to be found. Our own dwellings are very dear to us, but we must not prefer them to the assemblies of the saints; we must say of the church—

> " Here my best friends, my kindred dwell:
> Here God, my Saviour reigns."

3. *"Glorious things are spoken of thee, O city of God."* This is true of Jerusalem. Her history, which is the story of the nation of which she is the capital, is full of glorious incidents, and her use and end as the abode of the true God, and of his worship, was pre-eminently glorious. Glorious things were taught in her streets, and seen in her temples. Glorious things were foretold of her, and she was the type of the most glorious things of all. This is yet more true of the church: she is founded in grace, but her pinnacles glow with glory. Men may glory in her without being braggarts, she has a lustre about her brow which none can rival. Whatever glorious things the saints may say of the church in their eulogies, they cannot exceed what prophets have foretold, what angels have sung, or what God himself has declared. Happy are the tongues which learn to occupy themselves with so excellent a subject, may they be found around our fire-sides, in our market-places, and in all the spots where men most congregate. Never let thy praises cease, O thou bride of Christ, thou fairest among women, thou in whom the Lord himself hath placed his delight, calling thee by that pearl of names, Hephzibah, —" for my delight is in her." Since the Lord has chosen thee, and deigns to dwell in thee, O thou city of beauty, none can rival thee, thou art the eye of the world, the pearl, the queen of all the cities of the universe; the true " eternal city," the metropolitan, the mother of us all. The years to come shall unveil thy beauties to the astonished eyes of all peoples, and the day of thy splendour shall come to its sevenfold noon.

"Selah." With the prospect before him of a world converted, and the most implacable foes transformed into friends, it was meet that the Psalmist should pause. How could he sing the glories of new-born Tyre and Ethiopia, received with open arms into union with Zion, until he had taken breath and prepared both voice and heart for so divine a song.

4. *"I will make mention of Rahab and Babylon to them that know me."* This shall be a glorious subject to speak of concerning Zion, that her old foes are new-born and have become her friends, worshipping in the temple of her God. Rahab or Egypt which oppressed Israel shall become a sister nation, and Babylon in which the tribes endured their second great captivity, shall become a fellow-worshipper; then shall there be mention made in familiar talk of the old enmities forgotten and the new friendships formed. Some consider that these are the words of God himself, and should be rendered " I will mention Rahab and Babylon as knowing

me : " but we feel content with our common version, and attribute the words to the Psalmist himself, who anticipates the conversion of the two great rival nations and speaks of it with exultation. *"Behold Philistia, and Tyre, with Ethiopia."* These also are to bow before the Lord. Philistia shall renounce her ancient hate, Tyre shall not be swallowed up by thoughts of her commerce, and distant Ethiopia shall not be too far off to receive the salvation of the Lord. *"This man was born there."* The word *man* is inserted by the translators to the marring of the sense, which is clear enough when the superfluous word is dropped,—" Philistia, and Tyre, with Ethiopia ; this was born there "—i.e., this nation has been born into Zion, regenerated into the church of God. Of the new births of nations we will make mention, for it is at once a great blessing and a great wonder. It is a glorious thing indeed when whole nations are born unto God.

> " Mark ye well Philistia's legions,
>   Lo, to seek the Lord they come ;
> And within the sacred regions
>   Tyre and Cush have found a home."

Many understand the sense of these verses to be that all men are proud of their native country, and so also is the citizen of Zion, so that while of one it is said, " he was born in Egypt " and of another, " he came from Ethiopia," it would be equally to the honour of others that they were home-born sons of the city of God. The passage is not so clear that any one should become dogmatical as to its meaning, but we prefer the interpretation given above.

5. *"And of Zion, it shall be said, This and that man was born in her."* Not as nations only, but one by one, as individuals, the citizens of the New Jerusalem shall be counted, and their names publicly declared. Man by man will the Lord reckon them, for they are each one precious in his sight ; the individual shall not be lost in the mass, but each one shall be of high account. What a patent of nobility is it, for a man to have it certified that he was born in Zion ; the twice born are a royal priesthood, the true aristocracy, the imperial race of men. The original, by using the noblest word for man, intimates that many remarkable men will be born in the church, and indeed every man who is renewed in the image of Christ is an eminent personage, while there are some, who, even to the dim eyes of the world, shine forth with a lustre of character which cannot but be admitted to be unusual and admirable. The church has illustrious names of prophets, apostles, martyrs, confessors, reformers, missionaries and the like, which bear comparison with the grandest names honoured by the world, nay, in many respects far excel them. Zion has no reason to be ashamed of her sons, nor her sons of her. " Wisdom is justified of her children." *"And the highest himself shall establish her "*—the only establishment worth having. When the numbers of the faithful are increased by the new birth, the Lord proves himself to be the upbuilder of the church. The Lord alone deserves to wear the title of Defender of the Faith ; he is the sole and sufficient Patron and Protector of the true church. There is no fear for the Lord's heritage, his own arm is sufficient to maintain his rights. The Highest is higher than all those who are against us, and the good old cause shall triumph over all.

6. *"The Lord shall count, when he writeth up the people, that this man was born there."* At the great census which the Lord himself shall take, he will number the nations without exception and make an exact registry of them, whether they were by their natural descent Babylonians or Tyrians, or other far-off heathen. May it be our happy lot to be numbered with the Lord's chosen both in life and death, in the church-roll below, and in the church-roll above. Jehovah's census of his chosen will differ much from ours ; he will count many whom we should have disowned, and he will leave out many whom we should have reckoned. His registration is infallible. Let us pray then for that adoption and regeneration which will secure us a place among the heaven-born. It was thought to be a great honour to have one's name written in the golden book of the Republic of Venice, kings and princes paid dearly for the honour, but the book of life confers far rarer dignity upon all whose names are recorded therein.

7. In vision the Psalmist sees the citizens of Zion rejoicing at some sacred festival, and marching in triumphant procession with vocal and instrumental music ; —*"As well the singers as the players on instruments shall be there."* Where God is there must be joy, and where the church is increased by numerous conversions

the joy becomes exuberant and finds out ways of displaying itself. Singers and dancers, Psalmists and pipers, united their efforts and made a joyful procession to the temple, inspired not by Bacchus, or by the Castalian fount, but by draughts from the sacred source of all good, of which they each one sing *"All my springs are in thee."* Did the poet mean that henceforth he would find all his joys in Zion, or that to the Lord he would look for all inspiration, comfort, strength, joy, life and everything. The last is the truest doctrine. Churches have not such all-sufficiency within them that we can afford to look to them for all, but the Lord who founded the church is the eternal source of all our supplies, and looking to him we shall never flag or fail. How truly does all our experience lead us to look to the Lord by faith, and say " all my fresh springs are in thee." The springs of my faith and all my graces ; the springs of my life and all my pleasures ; the springs of my activity and all its right doings ; the springs of my hope, and all its heavenly anticipations, all lie in thee, my Lord. Without thy Spirit I should be as a dry well, a mocking cistern, destitute of power to bless myself or others. O Lord, I am assured that I belong to the regenerate whose life is in thee, for I feel that I cannot live without thee ; therefore, with all thy joyful people will I sing thy praises.

> " With joy shall sing the choral train,
> The minstrels breathe the answering strain :
> ' O Zion, Zion, fair, I see
> The fountains of my bliss in thee.' "

EXPLANATORY NOTES AND QUAINT SAYINGS.

Title.—*"A Psalm or Song for the Sons of Korah."* The title prefixed is " A Psalm to be sung by the sons of Korah," i.e. of fallen man. Korah signifies the state in which trees are during winter, when stript of their verdure and fruit. In the same sense it is used for the bald head, when age or sickness has deprived it of its glory and left it without hair. This is a lively description of fallen man. He has lost his pristine beauty and fruitfulness. When he left God and turned to his own ways, he became like the trees of the field in winter, from which the genial warmth of the sun is withdrawn, or like the head, which by the abating of the natural heat and vigour is left naked and bald. But being brought to a right sense of this, and finding himself stript of all the glory which the first Adam had in paradise, he has been led to seek the restoration of his nature, and has obtained of the second Adam, the Lord from heaven, a much better state than he had lost. Every such person is entitled to sing this sacred hymn, and he is called upon to do it. The name of the person whom he is to celebrate is not mentioned at first, but is soon discovered by the character given of him.—*William Romaine.*

Whole Psalm.—Bishop Bruno entitles this Psalm, " The voice of prophecy concerning the heavenly Jerusalem," that is, the Church of Christ.

Verse 1.—*"His foundation is in the holy mountains."* The foundation that God has given his city is in " the holy mountains." What are these holy mountains ? What can they be but the eternal purpose of Jehovah—the purpose out of which the being of the Church and the whole dispensation of Divine love have sprung ? What but those attributes of mercy, justice, holiness, and sovereignty, from the ineffable embrace and holy co-operation of which it comes to pass that his chosen people are redeemed ? What but the promise of life that was given in Christ to the elect before the world began ? What but the everlasting covenant, " ordered in all things and sure " from which grace and salvation proceed ? What but these things, and Christ himself, the Rock of Ages, on which rock we know that the Church is so firmly founded, that the gates of hell cannot prevail against her ? Yes, these are the holy mountains, whereon the city of God is built, and in which its deep and strong foundations are laid. The sure decree, the divine perfections, the promise of him that cannot lie, the oath and covenant of God, and the incarnate Son himself, are the holy mountains, the perpetual hills, whose summits are gloriously crowned by the city of the Great King. There the city sits securely, beautiful for situation, the joy of the whole earth.—*Andrew Gray*.

Verse 1.—*"Mountains."* The situation of Jerusalem is in several respects singular amongst the cities of Palestine. Its elevation is remarkable, occasioned, not from its being on the summit of one of the numerous hills of Judæa, like most of the towns and villages, but because it is on the edge of one of the highest table-lands of the country. Hebron, indeed, is higher still, by some hundred feet; and from the south, accordingly, the approach to Jerusalem is by a slight descent. But from every other side, the ascent is perpetual; and, to the traveller approaching Jerusalem from the west or east, it must always have presented the appearance, beyond any other capital of the then known world—we may add, beyond any important city that has ever existed on the earth—of a mountain city; breathing, as compared with the sultry plains of the Jordan or of the coast, a mountain air; enthroned, as compared with Jericho or Damascus, Gaza or Tyre, on a mountain fastness. In this respect it concentrated in itself the character of the whole country of which it was to be the capital—the " mountain throne," the " mountain sanctuary," of God. " The ' mount ' of God is as the ' mount ' of Bashan; an high mount as the mount of Bashan. Why leap ye so, ye high ' mountains '? this is the ' mountain ' which God desireth to dwell in ". . . . It was emphatically the lair of the lion of Judah, of " Ariel," the Lion of God. " In Judah is God known; his name is great in Israel. In Salem is his ' leafy covert,' and his ' rocky den ' in Zion. . . . Thou art more glorious and excellent than the ' mountains of the robbers.' " And this wild and fastness-like character of Jerusalem was concentrated yet again in the fortress, the " stronghold " of Zion. That point, the highest in the city, the height which most readily catches the eye from every quarter, is emphatically the " hill fort," the " rocky hold " of Jerusalem—the refuge where first the Jebusite, and then the Lion of God, stood at bay against the hunters.—*Arthur Penrhyn Stanley*.

Verses 1, 2.—If we suppose the Psalm to have been composed in the days of Hezekiah, it will appear quite intelligible that the Psalmist should break out so suddenly at the beginning with praise of the *security* of Zion : he merely lends his mouth in this case to the full heart of the people; *"The Lord loveth the gates of Zion more than all the dwellings of Jacob,"* is seen in its true light, for this pre-ference for Sion was at that time *verified*—its gates remained closed upon the enemies, while all the rest of the country was subject to their sway.—*E. W. Hengstenberg*.

Verse 2.—*"The Lord loveth the gates,"* etc. The gates of a walled city give access to it and power over it, and therefore are naturally here put for the whole. The Hebrew participle (*loving*) implies constant and habitual attachment.—*J. A. Alexander*.

Verse 2.—*"The Lord loveth the gates of Zion."* Because of the going out and coming in of the people of God. Thus indeed the disposition of lovers is shown, that they are filled with a remarkable affection of love towards those places through which those whom they love frequently pass, as doors and gates, and those ways which they daily traverse. What other reason could God have for loving the gates of Zion ?—*Musculus*.

Verse 2.—*"The gates of Zion "* are the doctrines of the Gospel, *"the tabernacles of Jacob "* are the teachings of the law, the law was accomplished in the gospel; therefore it is said that " the Lord loveth the gates of Zion more than all the dwellings of Jacob."—*"Plain Commentary,"* 1859.

Verse 2.—*"The Lord loveth the gates of Zion more,"* etc. No doubt the prayers which the faithful put up to heaven from under their private roofs were very acceptable unto him; but if a saint's single voice in prayer be so sweet to God's ear, much more the church choir, his saints' prayers in concert together. A father is glad to see any one of his children, and makes him welcome when he visits him, but much more when they come together; the greatest feast is when they all meet at his house. The public praises of the church are the emblem of heaven itself, where all the angels make but one concert.—*William Gurnall*.

Verse 2.—*"The Lord loveth the gates of Zion more than all,"* etc. It is here assumed that the Lord loves the dwellings of Jacob—he loves those that are true Israelites. These are succeeded by the name *Christian*, for the Christian Church is now become the true Israel of God. He loves his saints on account of that image of himself which they bear; he loves them on account of those graces which are infused into them when they are renewed by the spirit; he loves them on account of the relation they stand in to him as his people, and as his church, who are qualified for the duties of the relation by that love of their Father, that reliance upon his care, that delight in his person, that enjoyment in his service, which belongs to dutiful and affectionate children. He loves them because they imitate his perfections in some humble measure—because they receive the word of his mouth —because they are ready to obey every call of his providence, setting themselves in the paths of his testimony wherever he may direct—because they yield themselves to God, as those that are alive from the dead, and their bodies as instruments of righteousness, no longer walking after the deeds of the flesh, but after the will of God. He takes a delight in them; the Lord delighteth in the righteous; he knoweth their way; he loves, approves, and confirms them. The most common occupations of life—the honest industry of the servants of God, is looked upon by him with approbation. By these they show forth their Father, and the praises of him who called them from darkness to light. The most ordinary duties of our calling become sacrifices to God, and religious duties, when performed in the spirit, and directed to the great end of glorifying God. He looks with peculiar complacency on the dwellings of his people on account of those domestic devotional acknowledgments of his majesty which are there maintained, when the head walks before his family as a priest to offer praise and thanksgiving; this attracts peculiar approbation and delight. He loves to see his people training up their children in the nurture and admonition of the Lord, and their children walking after them in the paths of that obedience which he has enjoined. He delights to see the course of purity which runs in Christian families. He loves to see the progress which the younger parts of religious families make in piety, while they grow in grace, and in favour with God and man. He looks down with peculiar delight on such circles as these: there he deigns his presence, and bestows peculiar blessings. However obscure the dwellings of Jacob may be, to him they are open and manifest at all times; and whether in cottages or in palaces, his eye rests there with complacency; and he says of such places, "Here will I dwell for ever and ever." Prayer and devotion sanctify every family, and diffuse a spirit of piety through all the avocations of life, so that we need not retire from the world, but are rather called to show forth the virtues of the Christian life in it.

But it is said, that, although "he loves the dwellings of Jacob," yet "he loves the gates of Zion more than all the dwellings of Jacob"—that nothing in the dwellings of Jacob so much attracts his attention as the people of God connected together in a spiritual capacity. I. In the first place, the Divine Being regards with peculiar complacency the worship of his saints on its own account. II. On account of that union of mind and consent of heart, evinced in the assembling of God's people together, and constituting themselves into a church. III. Because of the testimony which the church bears toward the truth. IV. Upon account of that deference to his authority, which is evinced by maintaining and keeping up the practice of those institutes which rest entirely on that authority. V. By making the assembly of the saints the grand means of conversion. VI. That peculiar presence of God is generally vouchsafed to his saints, and made manifest to them, although it be hidden from the world, which induces the conviction that God is present of a truth. VII. The Divine Being shows his preference of the gates of Zion to the dwellings of Jacob, by continually maintaining in operation those gifts which are for the edification of the saints, and without which the union of the saints would be with difficulty maintained. VIII. The Divine Being shews his preference to Zion by that marvellous protection which is afforded to the interest of the church of God; whereby, though weak, and frequently reduced to a handful of disciples, yet they have been protected, and their society on earth continued.— *Robert Hall.*

Verse 2.—Some absent themselves from public worship, under pretence that they can serve the Lord at home as well in private. How many are apt to say, they see not but their time may be as well spent at home, in praying, reading some good book, or discoursing on some profitable subject, as in the use of ordinances in public assemblies! They see not but private prayer may be as good to them as public, or private reading and opening the Scripture as profitable as public preaching; they say of their private duties, as Naaman of the waters of Damascus, 2 Kings v. 12: May I not serve the Lord as acceptably, with as much advantage, in private exercises of religion ? May I not wash in these and be clean ? They see not the great blessings God has annexed to public worship more than to private. Oh, but if it be thus, if one be as good as the other, what means the Lord to prefer one before the other ? To what purpose did the Lord choose the gates of Zion, to place his name there, if he might have been worshipped as well in the dwellings of Jacob ? How do men of this conceit run counter to the Lord ? He prefers the gates of Zion, not only before one or some, but before all the dwellings of Jacob ; and they prefer one such dwelling before the gates of Zion.—*David Clarkson.*

Verse 3.—*"Glorious things are spoken"* of the people of God. Take the church for a visible congregation, a mixed congregation ; glorious things are spoken of that. It is the house of God. Take it as visible, " the vessels of honour and dis-honour," 2 Tim. ii. 20, and the field, the " tares and the wheat," Matt. xiii. 1. etc., it is God's field. Though we take the church as visible, it hath a glorious name for the good that is in it, especially for the wheat. But take the church of God for the company of his children that are gathered by the means of grace, dwelling in the visible church, enjoying the ordinances : so they are the house and temple of Christ, " the temple of the Holy Ghost, the body of Christ, the spouse of Christ." They are God's delight, they are spiritual kings and priests, etc. The most glorious things that can be, all other excellencies in the world, are but titular things, mere shadows of things. There is some little reality in earthly things, but it is nothing in comparison, it is scarce worth the name of reality, but Solomon calls them " vanity of vanities." In comparison of the excellencies of the church all is nothing. I might be large in these particulars. It is enough to give you the generals of the delights and excellencies of God's house, " the beauty of the Lord."—*Richard Sibbes.*

Verse 3.—*"The glories of the wilderness are in thee."* The Shechinah, which appeared upon Sinai, and marshalled the army of the Israelites upon their journey through the wilderness, has now fixed its residence in thee, O city of God. Compare Ps. lxviii. 17.—*Samuel Horsley.*

Verse 4.—*"I will make mention,"* etc. As if he had said, I do not deny the due praises which belong to other places and countries, but rather am wont to make honorable mention of them among my acquaintance ; and to allow that *"this man,"* that is, some one notable person, though comparatively of no great value, was born in them.—*Thomas Fenton.*

Verse 4.—*"Rahab,"* a poetical name of *Egypt.* The same word signifies " fierce-ness, insolence, pride " ; if Hebrew when applied to Egypt, it would indicate the national character of the inhabitants.—*Smith's Dictionary of the Bible.*

Verse 4.—It should comfort the church that God is able to make her chiefest enemies to become converts, and that he hath done it sundry times, and will yet do it more ; and that he can take order with those enemies which shall not be converted, as he did with *Rahab* and *Babylon ;* for, *"I will make mention of Rahab and Babylon to them that know me,"* signifieth a mention-making of them ; *viz.* to the edification of the church's children, both concerning what God had done in those nations in justice ; and what he would do to them in mercy, or unto other enemies like unto them.—*David Dickson.*

Verse 4.—*"Rahab,"* *"Babylon,"* *"Philistia,"* *"Tyre,"* *"Ethiopia."* This is the glory of the Church, that into her the fulness of the nations shall enter,—the proud from Egypt, who for her haughtiness is called Rahab,—the worldly from Babylon, the city of confusion,—the wrathful from Philistia, so long the enemies of Israel,—the covetous from Tyre, the rich city of the traders,—and the slaves of ignorance from Cush, and from the land of Ham,—all these shall learn the love of Christ and confess his truth, and shall enter into that all-glorious city, and be admitted and acknowledged as citizens of the celestial Sion.—*"Plain Commentary."*

Verse 4.—By this testimony of the nations here mentioned, we may understand the testimony of the Gentile Christians in general, though, perhaps, a special reference is had to that extraordinary scene which took place at Jerusalem on the day of Pentecost : " And there were dwelling at Jerusalem Jews, devout men, out of every nation under heaven. Now when this was noised abroad, the multitude came together, and were confounded, because that every man heard them speak in his own language. And they were all amazed and marvelled, saying one to another, Behold, are not all these which speak Galilæans ? And how hear we every man in our own tongue, wherein we were born ? " Acts ii. 5—8.

The reader will find that there is a remarkable agreement between the nations specified in the book of the Acts, and the nations pointed out in the Psalm before us. Rahab, that is, Egypt, is first mentioned ; and in the Acts we find enumerated, " Egypt and the parts of Libya about Cyrene ; " next Babylon is in the record ; and the " Parthians, Medes, and Elamites, and the dwellers in Mesopotamia," were inhabitants of what once was the Babylonian empire : Philistia is also mentioned ; and " dwellers in Judea " are spoken of in the Acts—" dwellers in Judea " speaking a different language from what was common at Jerusalem. Who could these be, so probably, as the inhabitants of the ancient Philistia, which was in the precincts of the allotment of Judah ? Here, too, perhaps, on account of its port of Joppa, was a grand resort of " Cretes and Arabians," and " strangers of Rome."

The Grecian settlements of Asia Minor are the only ones specified in the Acts of the Apostles, which we have not noticed in the Psalm—" Cappadocia, Pontus, Asia, Phrygia, and Pamphylia : " but what could so probably indicate these countries, and all who spoke the dialects of the Grecian tongue, as the great mart of Tyre, in frequenting which, the Jews would have the most frequent opportunity of intercourse with these nations ?—*John Fry.*

Verse 4.—"Born in her." The Missionary Society set forth in the Prophets, by our Lord and by his apostles, is, the Church ; and so, whereas our natural state, after Adam's fall, was alienation from God, and disunion among ourselves, would He restore " glory to God in the highest and on the earth peace, good-will towards men," by binding us up in one holy fellowship, and making the continuance of his blessings dependent upon that unity, which he imparted and preserves. To adduce the whole proof for this, would be to go through the whole Old Testament ; for the Old Testament is direct prophecy and type, is one large prophecy of the Redeemer and his Kingdom or Church. No sooner had disunion multiplied with the multiplying of men, but in the second generation from Adam, he formed union through a Church, and " Men began to call upon the name of the Lord " (Gen. iv. 26), *i.e.,* they began to unite in worshipping the Lord, and amid the growing corruption, religion was no longer entrusted to the insulated care of single families, but concentrated in a church. And when, after the flood, one righteous man was called out of the fast-corrupting world, unity was preserved, in that one only was called, but in that one a church was founded ; for this was the reason assigned by God himself : " All the nations of the earth shall be blessed in him. For I know him, that he will command his children and his household after him, and they shall keep the way of the Lord," (Gen. xviii. 18. 19). " God called Abraham *alone,* and blessed him, and increased him " (Isai. li. 2), and formed the Jewish Church out of him, that however it might spread, it might be bound in one by its origin of one ; and he gave it also outward marks and signs between him and it, which by severing it from others, might keep it one in itself. The temporal people had their union through a temporal birth of one, and outward signs ; the Christian Church has its unity by a spiritual birth and inward graces, through the power deposited in her to give spiritual birth, so that through one mother, we are all born of one Father, God, and amongst ourselves are brethren, by being members of One, our ever-blessed Lord.

The unity of the Christian Church and her office of gathering all nations unto the Lord, are set forth, in many ways, in prophecy. Thus, in our Psalm, Zion is set forth as the special object of God's love, as having (in language which anticipates the Gospel) been " founded " by him " on the holy mountains," as the " city of God," whereof " glorious things are spoken." And what are these ? That she should be the spiritual birthplace of all nations. It is not merely said, as in other places, that they should " come to her," should " flow into her," but that they should be " born in her." " Of Zion it shall be said, This and that man (*i.e.* all, one by one) was born in her ; " and whence ? all the nations of the earth, Rahab or Egypt, Babylon, Tyre, Ethiopia, Philistia, the most learned, the most powerful, the wealthiest, the furthest, and her nearest, oldest and bitterest enemy Philistia, all, being already born after the flesh, as Egyptians, Babylonians, Ethiopians, Tyrians, Philistines, should be " born in her," and by being " born there," should become children of God, citizens of the heavenly Jerusalem, written by God in the roll of his book. "The Lord shall count, when he writeth up the people, that this man was born there;" he shall account them as his, being re-born in his Church.

In like manner, with regard to every prophecy, whereat men's hearts beat, as an encouragement to Missionary labours. Throughout, it is the Lord and Saviour of the Church, or the Church itself, filled with his Spirit, and restored and enlarged, and widening herself by his favour, and gathering his people into herself, his fold. —*E. B. Pusey, in a Sermon entitled "The Church the converter of the Heathen."* 1838.

Verses 4—6. It is made the honour and dignity of Sion, that is, of the true Church of God, to have such and such born in it : *"this and that man* was born in *her."* There are two things signified in this expression, as branches of their honour ; the one is the *quality* of the persons ; and the other is the *number* of them. For the *quality* of them, *"this ;"* for the *number* of them, *"this and that."* To have both of these born in Sion, persons of *note and eminency,* and a *multitude and plurality* of such persons ; this is a part of that dignity and renown which belongs unto it. . . . .

And so for the noun, *"man ;"* the Hebrew word אִישׁ which is here used for a man, except qualified by some other word as joined with it, signifies a man of *worth,* not a common or ordinary person. The Church brings forth as these, אַנְשֵׁי שֵׁם, men of renown, famous and eminent men, and that in all kinds of perfections, whether natural, or civil, or spiritual ; men of parts, or men of power, or men of piety. There are those in all these excellencies which have been and still are born in her.

First, take it for *natural* or *acquired* abilities ; men of parts, and knowledge, and wisdom, and improved understandings ; the church is not without these : *"this man,"* i.e., this *learned* man, or this *wise* man was born in Sion. All are not idiots who are Christians ; no, but there are some of very rare and admirable accomplishments in all kinds and pieces of learning and secular knowledge, which are graciously qualified. There's Paul with his parchments, and Peter with his fisher's net. So also secondly, take it for civil or secular qualifications ; men of dignity, and power, and estate : *"this man,"* i.e., this *honourable* man, אִישׁ פָּנִים, eminent in countenance, as he is called, Isaiah iii. 2, *he* is likewise born in Sion ; the mighty man, and the man of war. The Syriac interpreter was so far sensible of this, as that he expresses it in the very text ; and therefore instead of saying, *"This* man was born there,"* he says, *" A potent man* was born there, ' and *he* has established it ; ' "* whereby (as I conceive), he takes in the word *"highest,"* which follows afterwards in the verse, and refers it here to this place . . . . . . And again, the Chaldee paraphrast in the text, *"This King* was born there,"* understanding thereby Solomon, as most conceive and apprehend it.

Thirdly, take it for *spirituals,* and for these accomplishments especially ; *"This man,"* i.e., this *godly* man ; this is that which is most proper and essential to Sion, and to the being born in it ; yea, it is that which *makes Sion* itself, in the sense we now take it. It is the highest perfection of it, and the greatest commendation to it of any thing else. This is the great honour of the church, that it forms men to such qualities and dispositions as those are, which no other place does beside. . . . . As for other places, they may perhaps now and then reach to some *other principles,* and those likewise very glorious in the eyes of the *world*—morality, and civility, and ingenuity, and smoothness of behaviour. The school of nature and common reason may sometimes come up to these, and that in a very great measure ; yea, but now go a little higher, to brokenness of heart, to self-denial, to love of enemies, to closing with Christ, the frame and spirit of the gospel ; this is to be found nowhere but only *in Sion.* And here it is : *"This man* was born *there."*

"Behold Philistia, and Tyre, with Ethiopia ; this man was born there." Here's the excellency of the ordinances, and that power and energy which is stirring in the Church of Christ ; that it is able to work such a miraculous alteration *as this ;* to bring men from darkness to light, from Satan to God, from a state of sin and corruption and unregeneracy, to a state of grace and holiness and regeneration ; yea, from the lowest degree of the one to the highest degree of the other. That *Philistia* should turn into *Palestina, Tyre* into *Jerusalem, Ethiopia* into *Judea ;* here's the wonder of all ; the reconciling of these two opposite terms thus both together. That " princes should come out of *Egypt,"* and that *Ethiopia* should stretch out her hands to God, as it is in Ps. lxviii. 31 ; that the blackamoor should change his skin, and that the leopard should change his spots ; and that this Ethiopian should become this Christian ; that he which was born *there,* should be

born *here.*"—*Thomas Horton, in " Zion's Birth-Register unfolded in a Sermon to the native citizens of London."* 1656.

Verses 4—6.—Foreign nations are here described not as captives or tributaries, not even as doing voluntary homage to the greatness and glory of Zion, but as actually incorporated and enrolled, by a new birth, among her sons.   Even the worst enemies of their race, the tyrants and oppressors of the Jews, Egypt and Babylon, are threatened with no curse, no shout of joy is raised at the prospect of their overthrow, but the privileges of citizenship are extended to them, and they are welcomed as brothers.   Nay more, God himself receives each one as a child newly-born into his family, acknowledges each as his son, and enrols him with his own hand on the sacred register of his children.   It is the mode of anticipating a future union and brotherhood of all the nations of the earth, not by conquest, but by incorporation into one state, and by a birth-right so acquired, which is so remarkable.   In some of the prophets, more especially in Isaiah, we observe the same liberal, conciliatory, comprehensive language towards foreign states, as Tyre and Ethiopia, and still more strikingly toward Egypt and Assyria (chap. xix. 22—25).   But the Psalm stands alone amongst the writings of the Old Testament, in representing this union of nations as a new birth unto the city of God . . . . It it is the first announcement of that great amity of nations, or rather of that universal common citizenship of which heathen philosophers dreamt, which was " in the mind of Socrates when he called himself a citizen of the world," which had become a common-place of Stoic philosophy, which Judaism tried finally to realize by the admission of proselytes, through baptism, into the Jewish community ; which Rome accomplished, so far as the external semblance went, first by subduing the nations, and then by admitting them to the rights of Roman citizenship.   But the true fulfilment of this hope is to be found only in that kingdom which Christ has set up.   He has gathered into his commonwealth all the kingdoms of the earth.   He has made men one, members of the same family, by teaching them to feel that they are all children of the same Father.   He has made it evident that the hope of the Jewish singer is no false hope ; that there is a Father in heaven who cares for all, whatever name they bear.   Thus the Psalm has received a better and higher fulfilment than that which lies on the surface of its words.   It was fulfilled in Christ.—*J. J. Stewart Perowne.*

Verses 4—7.—The main thought is that contained in ver. 4—7, the glorifying of Sion by the reception of the heathen into the number of its citizens ; and a well-defined form and arrangement of this thought forms the proper kernel of the Psalm, viz.. " Sion, the *birth-place* of the nations," which occurs in every one of the three verses (4—6), which are bounded by a Selah behind and before.—*E. W. Hengstenberg.*

Verse 5.—"*This man.*"   The word rendered *"Man "* is generally used for a person of eminence ; and the clause " this and that man," is simply, " a Man and a Man," which some think is used as a peculiar superlative, and means, *the most eminent of men,* even the Lord Jesus Christ, and they suppose, that He, in his divine nature, is *"the Highest "* who *"shall establish the church."*   No doubt he is the glory of the church, and of his people Israel : but his crucifixion was the deepest disgrace imaginable to Jersusalem itself.—*Thomas Scott.*

Verse 5.—"*This man.*"   It is well to observe that the word for *"man,"* used here, is not אָדָם *adam,* the common name for man, but אִישׁ *ish,* which is usually employed when a name is introduced to be designated with distinction and honour. There are in Hebrew, in fact, three words to designate man, with varied signification —אָדָם *adam,* the common name ; אִישׁ *ish,* the name of excellency and honour ; and אֱנוֹשׁ *enosh,* man in his weak and inferior character, as liable to misfortune, misery, and death.   The illustrative discrimination with which these words are respectively employed gives to many passages of the Hebrew Scripture a force and significance which cannot be perserved in translation into a language which has but one word to represent all these meanings—or indeed has no word for man but the one answering to *Adam,* unless indeed our " male," in a sense of dignity and strength, answers in some measure to *ish.*—*John Kitto, in " The Pictorial Bible."*

Verse 6.—The Lord will "*count* " (יִסְפֹּר), *record it in a book,* when "*he writes up the people* " (בִּכְתוֹב עַמִּים), *registers the several nations* of the earth ; that *"this man was born in "* Sion.   The Psalmist here describes the peculiar regard of God to the inhabitants of *Jerusalem,* and figuratively represents him, as keeping a register of all the nations of the earth, and marking, as it were, in that register, every one that was a citizen of *Jerusalem*, as thereby entitled to his distinguishing favour and protection.—*Samuel Chandler.*

Verse 6.—*"This man was born there."* When events shall be traced to their principles at the last day, many a scene will come forth into prominence, which now is of little regard. Humble churches will then prove to have been the birthplace, and stately palaces the graves of many an immortal soul, while every saved soul will ascribe its springs of glory to its Redeemer, through the instrumentality of that church, which he has ordained.—*Edward Garrard Marsh.*

6.—*"Selah."* The Hebrew text addeth *"Selah,"* which St. Jerome translateth *semper* (always). For the Church, as a bride glorious in her husband, shall evermore be preached of ; glorious things shall be spoken of her, and in her shall be continually sung the ineffable glory of the everlasting grace of God in Christ our Lord. And so the Jews for the most part interpret the word *"Selah"* by *"everlasting."* This is evident in their epitaphs, even as the Jewish epitaph is in Hebrew at Basle— " His soul continues in Paradise, Amen, Amen, Amen, for ever and ever."—*Urbanus Regius* [? *Le Roi*] (—1541) *in "The Solace of Sion."*

7.—*"The singers ; " "the players on instruments."* Song and music were prominent features of Divine worship in David's time. This is evident from the large number of two hundred and eighty-eight Levites who were expressly appointed for singing and the performance of music. Not less than two hundred and fifty-five singing men and singing women returned from the exile . . . The chief instruments used by the Levites were, according to the records of the Books of Chronicles, cymbals, harps and lutes : according to Psalm v. (title), we should add the flute, which is frequently noticed on Egyptian monuments.—*Augustus F. Tholuck.*

Verse 7.—*(First clause). For all its inhabitants are expert musicians ;* lit. *sing like flute-players.* The Hebrews seem to have surpassed all nations in the skill of poetry and music ; and every citizen could sing and dance. This pre-eminence the Psalmist seems to hint at.—*Alexander Geddes.*

Verse 7.—*"All my springs are in thee."* The original word עין, which we render *"springs,"* is used in a figurative sense, to denote *any one's posterity.* Thus Proverbs v. 16, " Let thy fountains be dispersed abroad " ; *i.e.,* thy posterity be exceeding numerous. And thus in the place before us : the inhabitants of Jerusalem should triumph and sing, *"All my springs,"* or fountains, all my friends, my family, my children, are in thee, are thy citizens, enjoy the glorious privileges thou art favoured with, are all inserted in God's register, and entitled to his protection and favour. Thus there is a harmony and connection between all the parts of this ode, which I think is very intelligible and poetical.—*Samuel Chandler.*

Verse 7.—*"All my springs are in thee."* Whatever conduit pipe be used, Christ is the fountain and foundation of every drop of comfort ; Christ is the God of all true consolation. It is not in the power of all the angels of heaven to give any soul one drop of comfort, nor can all on earth give you one dram of comfort. They can speak the words of comfort, but they cannot cause the soul to receive comfort. God comforts by them, 2 Cor. vii. 6. Titus was but an instrument. Comforting is called frequently in Scripture the speaking to the heart, Hos. ii. 14. Who is able to speak to the heart but he who is the Lord and commander of the heart ? God hath put all the oil of spiritual joy into the hands of Christ, Isa. lxi. 3, and none but he can give it out. He that wants comfort must go to Christ, he that hath received any true comfort must ascribe it to Christ. *"All my springs,"* saith the Church, " are in thee."—*Ralph Robinson.*

Verse 7.—The silver springs of grace, and the golden springs of glory are in him.— *Thomas Watson.*

Verse 7.—*"Springs."* The meaning of this verse is obscure, partly from its abrupt brevity, and partly from the ambiguity of one word. The word *"springs "* is, beyond all controversy, to be here taken metaphorically ; but interpreters are not agreed as to the explanation of the metaphor. Some understand it as denoting *hopes,* some *affections,* and others *thoughts.* Did the idiom of the language admit, I would willingly subscribe to the opinion of those who translate it *melodies* or *songs.* But as this might be considered unsupported by the usage of the Hebrew term, I am rather inclined to adopt, as most suitable to the subject in hand, the opinion that *lookings* is the proper translation, the root of the word signifying *an eye.* It is as if the Psalmist had said, I will always be earnestly looking, as it were, with fixed eyes upon thee.—*John Calvin.*

Verse 7.—"*My springs.*"

> Whether songs or melodies
> In Thee are all my well-springs.

This passage is given obscurely in most of the versions; it is here rendered strictly, and, as the author hopes, perspicuously. As the Greeks had their Pierian springs, their fountain of Aganippe dedicated to the Muses, Jerusalem had, in like manner, her sacred springs, her fountains of inspiration, in a much higher degree. It is to these the holy bard alludes in the passages before us, as Milton does in the following, who has perhaps copied from the present in his address to the "Heavenly Muse":

> "Or if Zion's hill
> Delight thee more, or *Siloa's fount that flowed*
> *Hard by the oracle of God,* I thence
> Invoke thine aid to my adventurous song.
>   —*John Mason Good.*

Verse 7.—"*All my springs.*" Fitly may we here quote the delightful hymn of Robert Robinson which has puzzled so many, but which has in it a fine classical allusion to Hippocrene and Mount Parnassus.

> "Come, thou fount of every blessing,
>   Tune my heart to sing Thy grace,
> Streams of mercy, never ceasing,
>   Call for songs of loudest praise.
> Teach me some melodious sonnet,
>   Sung by flaming tongues above:
> Praise the mount—oh fix me on it,
>   Mount of God's unchanging love."
>   —*C. H. S.*

HINTS TO PREACHERS.

Verses 2, 3.—I. The foundation of Zion. 1. It is but one: "foundation." 2. It is the Lord's: "his." 3. It is in conformity with holiness: "holy mountains." 4. It consists of eternal purposes. 5. It is built up on immutable principles. 6. It is situated in a glorious position. II. The favour enjoyed by Zion. 1. God "loves the dwellings of Jacob." He led, fed, guarded, lighted, visited them. 2. He loves Zion "better"; and gives all those blessings in a richer form. 3. There are more to love. 4. Their occupations are more spiritual. 5. Their songs and worship are more enthusiastic. 6. Their testimony is more powerful. 7. Their knowledge of truth is more clear. 8. Their fellowship is on a scale more heavenly. Let us be in the Church, and love her. III. The fame of Zion. "Glorious things are spoken," 1. *of* her in history; 2. *in* her by ministry; 3. *for* her by Jesus; 4. *about* her in prophecy. Here is a fruitful theme.

Verse 3.—The idea of the text presents the Church as "the city of God"; let us touch upon some of the "glorious things" that are spoken of it. I. There are glorious things with respect to the *erection* of the city. 1. There is the plan of its erection. There was never a plan so faultless, so complete, so wonderful for its beauty and grandeur. The gates, the walls, the buildings, the streets, the monuments, the fountains, the gardens, unite to proclaim it a masterpiece of skill. The Architect was he who built the skies. 2. There is the *site* where the city is erected. See verse 1. 3. There is the *date* of the city's erection. A halo and a glory attach, in a case like this, to great antiquity. Now it is long since the city was built. It was standing in the days of Paul. "Ye are come unto the city of the living God." Heb. xii. 22. David was well acquainted with it. Ps. xlvi. 4. It was standing before the flood. Noah, Enoch, Abel, dwelt in it. It is almost as old as the creation. II. There are glorious things to tell of the *defences* of the city. It has been besieged ever since it was a city at all, and it is not taken to this hour. " We have a strong city," etc. III. There are glorious things in connexion with the *stores* and *supplies* on which the city depends ; 1, their excellence ; 2, their abundance ; 3, their source. IV. There are glorious things respecting the *King* of the city ; his name, person, character, etc. V. There are glorious things in connexion with the *citizens* of the city.—*Andrew Gray*, 1805—1861.

Verse 3.—I. Observe, that a city is not like a flower, a tree, or a plant—something that grows out of the earth, and is nourished from the earth, and dependent wholly on its juices. It is an artificial thing, constructed by wisdom and raised by power, as it was designed by genius and forethought. II. A city upon earth is surrounded generally by walls. III. Jerusalem (the must celebrated of cities, from which this figure is obviously drawn) was built upon the brow of a hill, an extremely conspicuous and beautiful object. IV. In a city there are various buildings, and structures of various shapes, materials and value : illustrate by the different denominations, etc. V. A city has municipal laws. VI. It has also trade, traffic, etc. VII. The figure, as applied to the Church of Christ, involves the idea of safety or security, honour, etc. VIII. There is also the idea of fewness.—*John Cumming*, 1843.

Verse 3.—The things " spoken " of the city of God. I. It shall be the permanent and the peculiar residence of God. II. It shall be the scene of delightful privileges and blessings. III. It shall be invested with absolute and inviolable security. IV. It shall possess renown and empire throughout the whole world. V. Its institutions and existence shall be perfected in the celestial state.—*James Parsons*, 1839.

Verse 4 (last clause).—I. Behold what the " man " was : a native of " Philistia," a heathen, and an enemy to God. II. Behold what happened to him : he " was born there," *i.e.*, new born in Zion. III. Behold what he became—he became by his new birth a freeman and burgess of Zion, etc.

Verses 4, 5.—I. What is not the most honourable birth-place—not Rahab nor Egypt, nor Babylon, nor any earthly palace or kingdom. II. What is ? " Of Zion," etc. 1. Because it is a nobler birth ; a being born again of the Spirit of God. 2. Because it is a nobler place ; the residence of the Highest, and established for ever. Because it brings nobler rank and privileges.—*G. R.*

Verses 4—7.—I. Zion shall produce many good and great men. II. Zion's interest shall be established by divine power. III. Zion's sons shall be registered with honour. IV. Zion's songs shall be sung with joy and triumph.—*Matthew Henry*.

Verses 4—7.—I. The excellence of the church is here stated. II. Her enlargement is here promised.—*J. Scholefield*, 1825.

Verse 5.—The renowned men of the church of God. 1. Great warriors, who have fought with temptation. 2. Great poets, whose lives were Psalms. 3. Great heroes, who have lived and died for Jesus. 4. Great kings who have ruled themselves, etc. Apostles, martyrs, confessors, reformers, men renowned for virtues such as only grace can produce.

Verse 5.—"*This and that man.*" The individuality of true religion. 1. Each soul sins for itself. 2. Rejects or accepts the Saviour for itself. 3. Must be judged, and 4. Saved or lost individually. The consequent need of personal piety ; the temptations to neglect it ; and the habits which promote it.

Verse 5 (last clause).—The Established Church of God—her Head, her protection her power, etc.

Verse 6.—I. " The Lord " will make the Census. II. He will " count " whether a man be rightly there or no. III. Every man truly born in Zion shall be admitted on the register.

Verse 6.—I. The time referred to. " When he writeth up," etc. ; when all the true Israel is saved. II. The account to be taken : " When he writeth up," etc., *i.e.*, revises and re-enters the names in the Lamb's Book of Life. Compares the called with the chosen. III. The test to be applied. 1. Their being in Zion, or having the means of grace. 2. Their being born there. IV. The completion of their number : " The Lord shall count." An exact number of stones in a perfect building and of members in a perfect body. So in Christ's Church. All make one bride. V. The notice taken of each one : " This man was born there." Men fell as a whole ; they are saved individually.—*G. R.*

Verse 7.—I. In God our joy. II. From God our supplies. III. To God our praise.

Verse 7 (*last clause*).—All the springs within me, all the springs which flow for me, are in my God. There are " upper and nether springs," springs " shut up," " valley " springs (Ps. civ. 10), rock springs, etc. ; but all these flow from the Lord.